HANDBOOK OF COMPUTER NETWORKS

HANDBOOK OF COMPUTER NETWORKS

Distributed Networks, Network Planning, Control, Management, and New Trends and Applications

Volume 3

Hossein Bidgoli
Editor-in-Chief
California State University
Bakersfield, California

BICENTENNIAL 1807 WILEY 2007 BICENTENNIAL

John Wiley & Sons, Inc.

This book is printed on acid-free paper. ♾

Published by John Wiley & Sons, Inc., Hoboken, New Jersey
Published simultaneously in Canada

For general information on our other products and services or for technical support, please contact our Customer Care Department within the United States at (800) 762-2974, outside the United States at (317) 572-3993 or fax (317) 572-4002.

Wiley also publishes its books in a variety of electronic formats. Some content that appears in print may not be available in electronic books. For more information about Wiley products, visit our web site at www.wiley.com.

Library of Congress Cataloging-in-Publication Data:

Handbook of computer networks / edited by Hossein Bidgoli.
3 v. cm.
ISBN 978-0-471-78458-6 (cloth vol 1 : alk. paper)
ISBN 978-0-471-78459-3 (cloth vol 2 : alk. paper)
ISBN 978-0-471-78460-9 (cloth vol 3 : alk. paper)
ISBN 978-0-471-78461-6 (cloth set : alk. paper)
1. Computer networks Handbooks, manuals, etc. I. Bidgoli, Hossein.
TK5105.5.H32 2008
004.6–dc22
2007012619

Printed in the United States of America

10 9 8 7 6 5 4 3 2 1

To so many fine memories of my mother Ashraf, my father Mohammad, and my brother Mohsen, for their uncompromising belief in the power of education.

About the Editor-in-Chief

Hossein Bidgoli, Ph.D., is professor of Management Information Systems at California State University. Dr. Bidgoli helped set up the first PC lab in the United States. He is the author of 43 textbooks, 27 manuals, and over five dozen technical articles and papers on various aspects of computer applications, information systems and network security, e-commerce, and decision support systems published and presented throughout the world. Dr. Bidgoli also serves as the editor-in-chief of *The Internet Encyclopedia, The Handbook of Information Security,* and *The Encyclopedia of Information Systems.*

The Encyclopedia of Information Systems was the recipient of one of the Library Journal's Best Reference Sources for 2002 and *The Internet Encyclopedia* was recipient of one of the PSP Awards (Professional and Scholarly Publishing), 2004. Dr. Bidgoli was selected as the California State University, Bakersfield's 2001–2002 Professor of the Year.

Editorial Board

Contents

Part 3: Digital and Optical Networks

Volume II: LANs, MANs, WANs, The Internet, and Global, Cellular, and Wireless Networks

Part 1: LANs, MANs, and WANs

Part 2: The Internet, Global Networks, and VoIP

Part 3: Cellular and Wireless Networks

Volume III: Distributed Networks, Network Planning, Control, Management, and New Trends and Applications

Part 1: Distributed Networks

Contributors

Tarek F. Abdelzhaer
University of Illinois, Urbana-Champaign
Mo Adda
University of Portsmouth, United Kingdom
Kemal Akkaya
Southern Illinois University, Carbondale
Fatih Alagöz
Bogazici University, Turkey
Omar Al-Bayari
Al-Balqa' Applied University, Jordan
Ala Al-Fuqaha
Western Michigan University, Kalamazoo
Jamal N. Al-Karaki
The Hashemite University, Jordan
Nirwan Ansari
New Jersey Institute of Technology
Ismail Ari
Hewlett-Packard Laboratories, Palo Alto, CA
Manuel Arriaga
New York University
Vijay Atluri
Rutgers University
Mark Baker
University of Reading, United Kingdom
Mario Baldi
Politecnico di Torino, Italy
Xiaoyi Bao
University of Ottawa, Canada
Valmir C. Barbosa
Universidade Federal do Rio de Janeiro, Brazil
Elyes Ben Ali Bdira
University of Sharjah, UAE
Keren Bergman
Columbia University
Larry A. Bergman
Jet Propulsion Laboratory (JPL), California Institute of Technology
Bhagyavati
DeSales University
Qi Bi
Bell Laboratory, Alcatel-Lucent Technologies Inc.
Hossein Bidgoli
California State University, Bakersfield
David Blockus
Independent Consultant
Fernando Boavida
University of Coimbra, Portugal
Benjamin Bock
Secure Business Austria
Noureddine Boudriga
University of the 7th of November, Tunisia
Nicholas David Bowman
Michigan State University
Thomas C. Bressoud
Denison University
Linda Bruenjes
Lasell College
Stephen F. Bush
GE Global Research
Werner Bux
IBM Corporation, Switzerland
Rajkumar Buyya
The University of Melbourne, Australia
John Cameron
University of Ottawa, Canada
Lillian N. Cassel
Villanova University
Tom S. Chan
Southern NH University
Kavitha Chandra
University of Massachusetts, Lowell
Hsiao-Hwa Chen
National Sun Yat-Sen University, Taiwan
Liang Chen
University of Ottawa, Canada
Thomas M.Chen
Southern Methodist University
Zhuojun Joyce Chen
University of Northern Iowa
Jau Ming Chew
University of Portsmouth, United Kingdom
Jaehak Chung
Inha University, Republic of Korea
Song Ci
University of Nebraska, Lincoln
Tim Collins
University of Birmingham, United Kingdom
Marco Conti
Institute of Informatics and Telematics (IIT), Italian National Research Council (CNR), Italy
David Coquil
University of Passau, Germany
Luís Cordeiro
University of Coimbra, Portugal
Marco Cremonini
University of Milan, Italy
Marilia Curado
University of Coimbra, Portugal
Leslie L. Daigle
Cisco Systems, Herndon, Virginia
Pragati Dalal
Canisius College
Marcos Dias de Assunção
The University of Melbourne, Australia
Serge Demidenko
Massey University, New Zealand, and Monash University, Malaysia
Hans-Peter Dommel
Santa Clara University

Kais Dridi
Université de Moncton, Canada
Arjan Durresi
Louisiana State University
Akihiro Enomoto
University of California, Irvine
Patrick J. Fahy
Athabasca University, Canada
Guangbin Fan
Intel Corporation
Farid Farahmand
Central Connecticut State University
Clayton Ferner
University of North Carolina at Wilmington
Daniel R. Fesenmaier
Temple University
Frank H.P. Fitzek
Aalborg University, Denmark
Sara Foresti
University of Milan, Italy
Dario Forte
University of Milano, Crema, Italy
Immanuel Freedman
Independent Consultant, Harleysville, Pennsylvania
Keita Fujii
University of California, Irvine
Muneo Fukaishi
NEC Corporation, Japan
Bruce Garrison
University of Miami
Z. Ghassemlooy
Northumbria University, United Kingdom
Filippo Giannetti
University of Pisa, Italy
William R. Gillis
WSU Center to Bridge the Digital Divide
James E. Goldman
Purdue University
Ulrike Gretzel
Texas A&M University
Qijun Gu
Texas State University
Xiaoyuan Gu
Technical University of Braunschweig, Germany
Mohsen Guizani
Western Michigan University
Sghaier Guizani
University of Quebec, Canada
Hong Guo
LLRC, Ontario Public Service, Canada
Mohamed A. Haleem
Stevens Institute of Technology
Habib Hamam
Universite de Moncton, Canada
Mohamed Hamdi
University of 7th of November, Carthage, Tunisia
Jon Hamkins
Jet Propulsion Laboratory, Pasadena, California
Omar M. Hammouri
University of Mississippi
Raymond A. Hansen
Purdue University
Shinsuke Hara
Osaka City University, Japan
David Harley
Small Blue-Green World, United Kingdom
Muhannad Harrim
Western Michigan University, Kalamazoo
Robert W. Heath
The University of Texas, Austin
Hamid Hemmati
Jet Propulsion Laboratory, California Institute of Technology
Murad Hizlan
Cleveland State University
Chengdu Haung
University of Illinois, Urbana-Champaign
Yuheng Huang
Qualcomm Inc.
James M. Hudson
PayPal, an eBay, Inc. Company
Gurdeep Singh Hura
University of Maryland, Eastern Shore
Hassan Ibrahim
The University of Maryland, College Park
François Ingelrest
IRCICA/LIFL University, France
Tariq Jadoon
Lahore University of Management Sciences (LUMS), Pakistan
Raj Jain
Washington University, St. Louis
Sushil Jajodia
George Mason University
Abbas Jamalipour
University of Sydney, Australia
Krishna Jayakar
Penn State University
Bandula Jayatilaka
Binghamton University, SUNY
Tao Jiang
University of Michigan, Dearborn
Stefan Joe-Yen
Northrup Grumman Corporation
Ari Juels
RSA Laboratories
Stella Kafetzoglou
National Technical University of Athens, Greece
Joonhyuk Kang
Information and Communications University (ICU), South Korea
Heather Kanuka
Athabasca University, Canada
Katz Marcos
Aalborg University, Denmark
Rick Kazman
University of Hawaii, Manoa
Azhar M. Khayrattee
Florida Institute of Technology
Yassine Khlifi
Carthage University, Tunisia
Chang-Su Kim
Korea University, Seoul

Nancy J. King
Oregon State University
David Klappholz
Stevens Institute of Technology
Markus Klemen
Vienna University of Technology, Austria
Harald Kosch
University of Passau, Germany
Jim Krause
Indiana University, Bloomington
Prashant Krishnamurthy
University of Pittsburgh
Peter Kroon
LSI, Pennsylvania
C.C. Jay Kuo
University of Southern California
Stan Kurkovsky
Central Connecticut State University
Yu-Kwong Kwok
The University of Hong Kong, Hong Kong
Amor Lazzez
CN&S Research Lab., University of the 7th of November at Carthage, Tunisia
Allen H. Levesque
Worcester Polytechnic Institute
Matthew Liotine
University of Illinois, Chicago
Natalia M. Litchinitser
University of Michigan, Ann Arbor
Jingxuan Liu
Frostburg State University
Mei-Ling L. Liu
Cal Poly San Luis Obispo
Peng Liu
Penn State University
Qingchong John Liu
Oakland University
Xiang Liu
Bell Laboratories, Lucent Technologies
Zhu Liu
AT&T Laboratories, Middletown, NJ
Asim Loan
University of Management and Technology, Lahore, Pakistan
David G. Loomis
Illinois State University, Normal
Robert D. Love
LAN Connect Consultants
Albert Lozano-Nieto
Pennsylvania State University
Ying Lu
University of Nebraska, Lincoln
Xuming Lu
University at Buffalo, SUNY
Michele Luglio
University of Rome Tor Vergata, Italy
Marco Luise
University of Pisa, Italy
Yuanqiu Luo
New Jersey Institute of Technology
Aarne Mämmelä
VTT Technical Research Centre of Finland
Konstantinos Markantonakis
Royal Holloway, University of London, United Kingdom
Manish Marwah
University of Colorado, Boulder
Mustafa M. Matalgah
University of Mississippi
Prabhaker Mateti
Wright State University
Emilio Matricciani
Dipartimento di Elettronica e Informazione Politecnico di Milano, Italy
Ketan Mayer-Patel
The University of North Carolina at Chapel Hill
Keith Mayes
Royal Holloway, University of London, United Kingdom
Cavan McCarthy
Louisiana State University
Patrick McDaniel
Pennsylvania State University
Daniel McFarland
Rowan University
Matthew K. McGowan
Bradley University
Amel Meddeb
University of the 7th of November at Carthage, Tunisia
Alfred Mertins
University of Lübeck, Germany
M. Farooque Mesiya
Rensselaer Polytechnic Institute
Marcus Messner
Virginia Commonwealth University
Mark Michael
Research in Motion Limited, Canada
Brent A. Miller
IBM Corporation
Milos Milosevic
Schlumberger Wireline Acquisition and Control Systems
Mário Minami
University of São Paulo, Brazil
Shivakant Mishra
University of Colorado, Boulder
Jelena Mišić
University of Manitoba, Canada
Vojislav B. Mišić
University of Manitoba, Canada
Shaheed N. Mohammed
Marist College
Edmundo Monteiro
University of Coimbra, Portugal
Michael Moore
University of California, Irvine
Syed H. Murshid
Florida Institute of Technology
Arun Srinivasa Murthy
Villanova University
B. Muthukumaran
Gemini Communication Limited, India
Tadashi Nakano
University of California, Irvine

Keivan Navaie
Tarbiat Modares University, Iran
Amiya Nayak
University of Ottawa, Canada
Thomas Neubauer
Vienna University of Technology, Austria
Darren B. Nicholson
Rowan University
Jennifer Nicholson
Rowan University
Richard Nieporent
Johns Hopkins University
Peng Ning
North Carolina State University
Paul W. Nutter
University of Manchester, United Kingdom
Mohammad S. Obaidat
Monmouth University
S. Obeidat
Arizona State University
Yoram Ofek
University of Trento, Italy
Yutaka Okaie
University of California, Irvine
Hong Ong
Oak Ridge National Laboratory, Tennessee
Priscilla Oppenheimer
Southern Oregon University
Raymond R. Panko
University of Hawaii, Manoa
G.I. Papadimitriou
Aristotle University, Thessaloniki, Greece
Symeon Papavassiliou
National Technical University of Athens, Greece
C. Papazoglou
Aristotle University, Thessaloniki, Greece
Stefano Paraboschi
University of Bergamo, Italy
Amanda Peart
University of Portsmouth, United Kingdom
Kenneth Pedrotti
University of California, Santa Cruz
Stephan Pfletschinger
Centre Tecnològic de Telecomunicacions de Catalunya (CTTC), Barcelona, Spain
Ronnie J. Phillips
Colorado State University
Thomas L. Pigg
Jackson State Community College
Martin Placek
The University of Melbourne, Australia
A.S. Pomportsis
Aristotle University, Greece
Dan Port
University of Hawaii, Manoa
G.N. Prezerakos
Technological Education Institute of Piraeus, Greece
Eddie Rabinovitch
ECI Technology
Miguel Arjona Ramírez
University of São Paulo, Brazil
Jeremy L. Rasmussen
Sypris Electronics
Indrajit Ray
Colorado State University
Mustapha Razzak
Université de Moncton, Canada
David R. Reavis
Texas A&M University, Texarkana
Slim Rekhis
CNAS Research Lab., University of Carthage, Tunisia
Jian Ren
Michigan State University, East Lansing
Vladimir V. Riabov
Rivier College
James A. Ritcey
University of Washington
Emilia Rosti
Università degli Studi di Milano, Italy
Liam Rourke
Nanyang Technological University, Singapore
Balqies Sadoun
Al-Balqa' Applied University, Jordan
Antonio Saitto
Telespazio, Italy
Hamidreza Saligheh
Harvard University
Atul A. Salvekar
Intel Corporation
Pierangela Samarati
University of Milan, Italy
Nabil J. Sarhan
Wayne State University
Damien Sauveron
University of Limoges, France
Michel Savoie
Communications Research Center (CRC), Canada
Mark Schaefer
OnStar Corporation
Chadwick Sessions
Northrup Grumman Corporation
Mark Shacklette
The University of Chicago
William A. Shay
University of Wisconsin, Green Bay
John Lucas Sherry
Michigan State University
Carolyn Siccama
University of Massachusetts, Lowell
Douglas C. Sicker
University of Colorado, Boulder
Farhan Siddiqui
Wayne State University
David Simplot-Ryl
Université de Lille, France
Robert Slade
Independent Consultant, Canada
Robert Slagter
Telematica Instituut, The Netherlands
Benjamin A. Small
Columbia University
Anthony H. Smith
Purdue University
Min Song
Old Dominion University

Hideyuki Sotobayashi
National Institute of Information and Communications Technology, Japan
Lee Sproull
New York University
William Stallings
Independent Consultant
Mark Stamp
San Jose State University
Charles Steinfield
Michigan State University
Ivan Stojmenovic
University of Birmingham, UK and University of Ottawa, Canada
Norman C. Strole
IBM Corporation
Koduvayur P. Subbalakshmi
Stevens Institute of Technology
Tatsuya Suda
University of California, Irvine
Anthony Sulistio
The University of Melbourne, Australia
Wayne C. Summers
Columbus State University
Vahid Tarokh
Harvard University
Colleen Taugher
WSU Center to Bridge the Digital Divide
Marvi Teixeira
Polytechnic University of Puerto Rico
Vassilis Tsaoussidis
Democritos University of Thrace, Xanthi, Greece
Michael Tunstall
University College Cork, Ireland
Okechukwu C. Ugweje
University of Akron
Zartash Afzal Uzmi
Lahore University of Management Sciences (LUMS), Pakistan
Shahrokh Valaee
University of Toronto, Canada
I.S. Venieris
National Technical University of Athens, Greece
Srikumar Venugopal
The University of Melbourne, Australia
Sabrina De Capitani di Vimercati
University of Milan, Italy
Linda Volonino
Canisius College
Mohamed El-Wakil
Western Michigan University, Kalamazoo
Youcheng Wang
University of Central Florida
James. L. Wayman
San Jose State University
Troy Weingart
University of Colorado, Boulder
Edgar R. Weippl
Vienna University of Technology, Austria
Stephen A. Weis
Google
Risto Wichman
Helsinki University of Technology, Finland
Barry Wilkinson
University of North Carolina, at Charlotte
Tin Win
Monash University, Malaysia
Raymond F. Wisman
Indiana University Southeast
Paul L. Witt
Texas Christian University
Albert K.S. Wong
Hong Kong University of Science and Technology, Hong Kong
Michael Workman
Florida Institute of Technology
Jing Wu
Communications Research Centre (CRC), Canada
Geoffrey G. Xie
Naval Postgraduate School
Jiang Xie
University of North Carolina, Charlotte
Xu Yan
Hong Kong University of Science and Technology, Hong Kong
Wei Ye
University of Southern California
Chee Shin Yeo
The University of Melbourne, Australia
Si Yin
New Jersey Institute of Technology
Jia Yu
The University of Melbourne, Australia
Viktor Zaharov
Polytechnic University of Puerto Rico
Faouzi Zarai
University of the 7th of November, Tunisia
S. Zeadally
University of the District of Columbia
Jingyuan Zhang
University of Alabama
Nan Zhang
Hong Kong University of Science and Technology, Hong Kong
Qinqing Zhang
Bell Laboratory, Alcatel-Lucent Technologies Inc.
Qiong (Jo) Zhang
Arizona State University, West Campus
Jiying Zhao
University of Ottawa, Canada
Mingshan Zhao
Dalian University of Technology, People's Republic of China
Wen-De Zhong
Nanyang Technological University, Singapore
Chi Zhou
Illinois Institute of Technology
Jin Zhu
University of Northern Iowa
Junaid Ahmed Zubairi
State University of New York, Fredonia

Preface

The Handbook of Computer Networks is the first comprehensive examination of the core topics in the computer network field. *The Handbook of Computer Networks,* a 3-volume reference work, with 202 chapters, 3400+ pages, is a comprehensive coverage of the computer network field with coverage of the core topics.

The primary audience is the libraries of 2-year and 4-year colleges and universities with Computer Science, Computer Engineering, Network Engineering, Telecommunications, Data Communications, MIS, CIS, IT, IS, Data Processing, and Business departments, public and private libraries and corporate libraries throughout the world, and educators and practitioners in the networking and telecommunications fields.

The secondary audience is a variety of professionals and a diverse group of academic and professional courses for the individual volumes.

Among industries expected to become increasingly dependent upon the computer networks and telecommunications and active in understanding the many issues surrounding this important and fast-growing field are: government agencies, military, education, libraries, health, medical, law enforcement, accounting firms, law firms, justice, manufacturing, financial services, insurance, communications, transportation, aerospace, energy, biotechnology, retail, and utilities.

Each volume incorporates state-of-the-art core information and computer networks and telecommunications topics, practical applications, and coverage of the emerging issues in the computer networks field.

This definitive 3-volume *Handbook* offers coverage of both established and cutting-edge theories and developments in the computer networks and telecommunications fields. The *Handbook* contains chapters from global experts in academia and industry. The *Handbook* offers the following unique features:

1. Each chapter follows a unique format including Title and Author, Outline, Introduction, Body, Conclusion, Glossary, Cross-References, and References. This unique format assists the readers to pick and choose various sections of a chapter. It also creates consistency throughout the entire series.
2. The *Handbook* has been written by more than 270 experts and reviewed by more than 1000 academics and practitioners chosen from around the world. These diverse collections of expertise have created the most definitive coverage of established and cutting-edge theories and applications of this fast-growing field.
3. Each chapter has been rigorously peer reviewed. This review process assures the accuracy and completeness of each topic.
4. Each chapter provides extensive online and off-line references for additional reading. This will enable the readers to go further with their understanding of a given topic.
5. More than 1000 illustrations and tables throughout the series highlight complex topics and assist further understanding.
6. Each chapter provides extensive cross-references. This helps the readers to read other chapters related to a particular topic, providing a one-stop knowledge base for a given topic.
7. More than 2500 glossary items define new terms and buzzwords throughout the series, assisting in understanding of concepts and applications.
8. The *Handbook* includes a complete table of contents and index sections for easy access to various parts of the series.
9. The series emphasizes both technical as well as managerial issues. This approach provides researchers, educators, students, and practitioners with a balanced understanding and the necessary background to deal with problems related to understanding computer networks and telecommunications issues and to be able to design a sound computer and telecommunications system.
10. The series has been developed based on the current core course materials in several leading universities around the world and current practices in leading computer, telecommunications, and networking corporations. This format should appeal to a diverse group of educators and researchers in the networking and telecommunications fields.

We chose to concentrate on fields and supporting technologies that have widespread applications in academic and business worlds. To develop this *Handbook,* we carefully reviewed current academic research in the networking field in leading universities and research institutions around the world.

Computer networks and telecommunications, network security, management information systems, network design and management, computer information systems (CIS), and electronic commerce curriculums, recommended by the Association of Information Technology Professionals (AITP) and the Association for Computing Management (ACM) were carefully investigated. We also researched the current practices in the networking field carried out by leading networking and telecommunications corporations. Our work assisted us in defining the boundaries and contents of this project. Its chapters address technical as well as managerial issues in the networking and telecommunications fields.

TOPIC CATEGORIES

Based on our research, we identified nine major topic areas for the Handbook:

- Key Concepts
- Hardware, Media, and Data Transmission
- Digital and Optical Networks
- LANs, MANs, and WANs
- The Internet, Global Networks, and VoIP
- Cellular and Wireless Networks
- Distributed Networks
- Network Planning, Control, and Management
- Computer Network Popular Applications and Future Directions

Although these nine categories are interrelated, each addresses one major dimension of the computer networks and telecommunications fields. The chapters in each category are also interrelated and complementary, enabling readers to compare, contrast, and draw conclusions that might not otherwise be possible.

Though the entries have been arranged logically, the light they shed knows no bounds. The *Handbook* provides unmatched coverage of fundamental topics and issues for successful design and implementation of a computer network and telecommunications systems. Its chapters can serve as material for a wide spectrum of courses such as:

Grid Computing
Distributed Intelligent Networks
Multimedia Networking
Peer-to-Peer Networks
Cluster Computing
Voice over IP
Storage Area Networks
Network Backup and Recovery Systems
Digital Networks
Optical Networks
Cellular Networks
Wireless Networks
Telecommunications Systems
Computer Network Management

Successful design and implementation of a sound computer network and telecommunications systems requires a thorough knowledge of several technologies, theories, and supporting disciplines. Networking researchers and practitioners have had to consult many resources to find answers. Some of these sources concentrate on technologies and infrastructures, some on applications and implementation issues, and some on managerial concerns. This *Handbook* provides all of this relevant information in a comprehensive three-volume set with a lively format.

Each volume incorporates core networking and telecommunications topics, practical applications, and coverage of the emerging issues in the networking and telecommunications fields. Written by scholars and practitioners from around the world, the chapters fall into nine major subject areas:

Key Concepts

Chapters in this group examine a broad range of topics. Fundamental theories, concepts, technologies, and applications related to computer networks, data communications, and telecommunications are discussed. These chapters explain the OSI reference model and then discuss various types of compression techniques including data, image, video, speech, and audio compression. This part concludes with a discussion of multimedia streaming and high definition television (HDTV) as their applications are on the rise. The chapters in this part provide a solid foundation for the rest of the Handbook.

Hardware, Media, and Data Transmission

Chapters in this group concentrate on the important types of hardware used in network and telecommunications environments and then examine popular media used in data communications including wired and wireless media. The chapters in this part explain different types of modulation techniques for both digital and optical networks and conclude with coverage of various types of multiplexing techniques that are being used to improve the efficiency and effectiveness of commutations media.

Digital and Optical Networks

Chapters in this group discuss important digital and optical technologies that are being used in modern communication and computer networks. Different optical switching techniques, optical devices, optical memories, SONET, and SDH networks are explained.

LANs, MANs, and WANs

This group of chapters examines major types of computer reworks including local, metropolitan, and wide area networks. Popular types of operating systems used in a LAN environment are discussed, including Windows and Linux. The chapters also examine various types of switching techniques including packet, circuit, and message switching. The chapters discuss broadband network applications and technologies and conclude with a discussion of multimedia networking.

The Internet, Global Networks, and VoIP

Chapters in this group explore a broad range of topics. They review the Internet fundamentals, history, domain name systems, and Internet2. The architecture and functions of the Internet and important protocols including TCP/IP, SMPT, and IP multicast are discussed. The chapters in this group also explain the network and end-system quality of service and then discuss VoIP and its various components, protocols, and applications.

Cellular and Wireless Networks

Chapters in this group explain cellular and wireless networks. Major standards, protocols, and applications in the cellar environment are discussed. This includes a detailed coverage of GSM, GPRS, UMTS, CDMA, and TDMA. The chapters in this group explore satellite communications principles, technologies, protocols, and applications in detail. The chapters conclude with coverage of wireless wide area networks and wireless broadband access.

Distributed Networks

The chapters in this group investigate distributed networks, their fundamentals, architectures, and applications. Grid computing, cluster computing, and peer-to-peer networks are discussed in detailed. These chapters also explore storage area networks, fiber channels, and fault tolerant systems. This part concludes with a discussion of distributed algorithms and distributed databases.

Network Planning, Control, and Management

The chapters in this group discuss theories, methodologies, and technologies that enhance successful network planning, control, and management. After discussion of network capacity planning and network modeling, the chapters concentrate on the identification of threats and vulnerabilities in a network environment. The chapters then present a number of tools and technologies that if properly utilized could significantly improve the integrity of data resources and computer networks by keeping hackers and crackers at bay. This part concludes with a discussion of business continuity planning, e-mail, and Internet use policies, and computer network management.

Computer Network Popular Applications and Future Directions

Chapters in this group present several popular applications of computer networks and telecommunications systems. These applications could not have been successfully utilized without a sound computer network and telecommunications system. Some of these applications include conferencing, banking, electronic commerce, travel and tourism, and Web-based training and education. This part concludes with a discussion of future trends in computer networking including biologically inspired networking, active networks, and molecular communication.

Specialists have written the *Handbook* for experienced and not so experienced readers. It is to these contributors that I am especially grateful. This remarkable collection of scholars and practitioners have distilled their knowledge into a fascinating and enlightening one-stop knowledge base in computer networks and telecommunications that "talks" to readers. This has been a massive effort, but one of the most rewarding experiences I have ever had. So many people have played a role that it is difficult to know where to begin.

I should like to thank the members of the editorial board for participating in the project and for their expert advice on help with the selection of topics, recommendations for authors, and reviewing the materials. Many thanks to more than 1000 reviewers who devoted their time by providing advice to me and the authors for improving the coverage, accuracy, and comprehensiveness of these materials.

I thank my senior editor Matt Holt, who initiated the idea of the *Handbook*. Through a dozen drafts and many reviews, the project got off the ground and then was managed flawlessly by Matt and his professional team. Matt and his team made many recommendations for keeping the project focused and maintaining its lively coverage.

Jessica Campilango, our editorial coordinator, assisted our authors and me during the many phases of its development. I am grateful for all her support. When it came to the production phase, the superb Wiley production team took over. Particularly I want to thank Deborah Schindlar and Miriam Palmer-Sherman, our production editors. I am grateful for all their hard work. I also want to thank Lynn Lustberg, our project manager from ICC Macmillan Inc. Her thoroughness made it easier to complete the project. I am grateful to all her efforts. I thank Kim Dayman and Christine Kim, our marketing team, for their impressive marketing campaign launched on behalf of the *Handbook*.

Last, but not least, I want to thank my wonderful wife, Nooshin, and my two children, Mohsen and Morvareed, for being so patient during this venture. They provided a pleasant environment that expedited the completion of this project. Mohsen and Morvareed assisted me in sending out thousands of e-mail messages to our authors and reviewers. Nooshin was a great help in designing and maintaining the authors' and reviewers' databases. Their efforts are greatly appreciated. Also, my two sisters, Azam and Akram, provided moral support throughout my life. To this family, any expression of thanks is insufficient.

Hossein Bidgoli
California State University, Bakersfield

Guide to The Handbook of Computer Networks

The Handbook of Computer Networks is a comprehensive coverage of the relatively new and very important field of computer networks and telecommunications systems. This reference work consists of three separate volumes and 202 different chapters on various aspects of this field. Each chapter in the Handbook provides a comprehensive overview of the selected topic, intended to inform a broad spectrum of readers, ranging from computer network professionals and academicians to students to the general business community.

In order that you, the reader, will derive the greatest possible benefit from *The Handbook of Computer Networks*, we have provided this Guide. It explains how the information within it can be located.

Organization

The Handbook of Computer Networks is organized to provide the maximum ease of use for its readers. All of the chapters are arranged logically in these three volumes. Individual volumes could be used independently. However, the greatest benefit is derived if all three volumes are investigated.

Table of Contents

A complete table of contents of the entire Handbook appears at the front of each volume. This list of chapter titles represents topics that have been carefully selected by the editor-in-chief, Dr. Hossein Bidgoli, and his colleagues on the Editorial Board.

Index

A Subject Index for each individual volume is located at the end of each volume. This index is the most convenient way to locate a desired topic within the Handbook. The subjects in the index are listed alphabetically and indicate the page number where information on this topic can be found.

Chapters

The author's name and affiliation are displayed at the beginning of the chapter. All chapters in the Handbook are organized according to a standard format as follow:

Title and Author
Outline
Introduction
Body
Conclusion
Glossary
Cross References
References

Outline

Each chapter begins with an outline indicating the content of the chapter to come. This outline provides a brief overview of the chapter, so that the reader can get a sense of what is contained there without having to leaf through the pages. It also serves to highlight important subtopics that will be discussed within the chapter. For example, the chapter "The Internet Fundamentals" includes sections for Information Superhighway and the World Wide Web, Domain Name Systems, Navigational Tools, Search Engines, and Directories.

The Outline is intended as an overview and thus it lists only the major headings of the chapter. In addition, second-level and third-level headings will be found within the chapter.

Introduction

The text of each chapter begins with an introductory section that defines the topic under discussion and summarizes the content of the chapter. By reading this section the readers get a general idea regarding a specific chapter.

Body

The body of each chapter discusses the items that were listed in the outline section of each chapter.

Conclusion

The conclusion section provides a summary of the materials discussed in a particular chapter. This section leaves the readers with the most important issues and concepts discussed in a particular chapter.

Glossary

The glossary contains terms that are important to an understanding of the chapter and that may be unfamiliar to the reader. Each term is defined in the context of the particular chapter in which it is used. Thus, the same term may be defined in two or more chapters with the detail of the definition varying slightly from one chapter to another. The Handbook includes approximately 2700 glossary terms. For example, the chapter "The Internet Fundamentals" includes the following glossary entries:

Extranet A secure network that uses the Internet and Web technology to connect two or more intranets of trusted business partners, enabling business-to-business, business-to-consumer, consumer-to-consumer, and consumer-to-business communications.

Intranet A network within the organization that uses Web technologies (TCP/IP, HTTP, FTP, SMTP, HTML, XML, and its variations) for collecting, storing, and disseminating useful information throughout the organization.

Cross References

All the chapters in the Handbook have cross references to other chapters. These appear at the end of the chapter, following the chapter text and preceding the References. The cross references indicate related chapters that can be consulted for further information on the same topic. The Handbook contains more than 2000 cross references in all. For example, the chapter "The Internet Fundamentals" has the following cross references:

Electronic Commerce, Electronic Data Interchange (EDI), Electronic Payment Systems, History of the Internet, Internet2, Internet Domain Name System, Information Retrieval on the Internet.

References

The References appears as the last element in a chapter. It lists recent secondary sources to aid the reader in locating more detailed or technical information. Review articles and research papers that are important to an understanding of the topic are also listed. The References in this Handbook are for the benefit of the reader, to provide references for further research on the given topic. Thus, they typically consist of a dozen to two dozen entries. They are not intended to represent a complete listing of all materials consulted by the author in preparing the chapter.

PART 1

Distributed Networks

Client/Server Computing Basics

Daniel McFarland and Darren B. Nicholson, *Rowan University*

INTRODUCTION

The name of an information system often describes the utility it provides. One can deduce that a transaction-processing system processes transactions, a decision-support system supports decisions, and an executive information system supports executives. However, client/server computing is not. Rather than describing an information system's utility, client/server is used more broadly to describe a system's architectural configuration. Moreover, the term client/server computing also incorporates a broad range of technologies and addresses a variety of business situations.

Client/server computing is a form of cooperative processing. Specifically, a client/server system includes at least two software processes working together to provide application functionality. At the most basic level, a client's software process requests services from a server's software process. For example, any time a user requests a Web page from a Web server (e.g., using the Internet to access a Web site), she/he is using client/server computing. That is, a client's application (e.g., a Web browser) is supported by a server's application (e.g., a Web server). In addition to Web pages, a client may also request from different servers a myriad organizational resources and services, such as e-mail, databases, printers, and files.

Client/server computing involves the coordination of assorted computing/networking devices and the coordination of various software processes. That is, the former (the client/server system architecture) describes the physical configuration of the computing and networking devices whereas the latter (the client/server software architecture) describes the partitioning of an application into multiple software processes.

The system architecture focuses on the physical architecture of the system. In this context, clients and servers are seen as computers rather than as software processes. In the most general sense, client/server system architectures include a client system (typically, a personal computer) that is connected to a server system (typically, a personal or midrange computer) using a network (e.g., a local area network). Each computer provides processing and memory resources to the client/server application. The system architectural perspective views a client/server application as a network of computers sharing resources to solve a problem.

The client/server software architecture describes the partitioning of an application into software processes. In this context, clients and servers are seen as software processes rather than as computers. These processes may reside on the same computer or they may be distributed across a network of computers. The software architectural perspective views a client/server application as a set of programming modules sharing resources to solve a problem.

This chapter focuses on the client/server software architectural perspective; consequently, a client shall refer to a software process that requests services from other software processes and a server shall refer to a software process that provides services to other software processes. In this context, it is important to distinguish client/server computing from peer-to-peer computing. Specifically, client/server computing is predominantly asymmetric whereas peer-to-peer computing is more symmetric in orientation. That is, in client/server computing, application processes are typically designed to satisfy specialized functions whereas in peer-to-peer computing each computer requests and provides a variety of less sophisticated functions. In this chapter, we concentrate on the former—client/server computing.

The structural motivations of client/server computing include providing flexible, interoperable, and scalable programmatic solutions. Flexibility describes the extent to which a process can be modified for use by other applications. Client/server flexibility is sustained through detailed documentation and well-structured, well-defined process functionality. Interoperability is the extent to which two or more processes are able to exchange and share information. In that a client/server application is physically partitioned into a set of two or more processes, all client/server applications must provide highly interoperable solutions. Scalability is a measure of the extent to which an application can handle increased workload/throughput typically associated with adding extra computing resources or computing burden.

The practical motivations of client/server computing include: striving to share computing and information resources, exploring the usage of lower-cost technologies, centralizing administration, and leveraging the relative strengths of desktop and back-office computing resources. For example, bug fixes and application enhancements can be made without having to deploy the revision to potentially thousands of client machines. In addition, since a server process typically provides services to many client processes, a client/server application can therefore provide unprecedented sharing of both computing and information resources. Moreover, a client's process is typically executed on a local desktop computer while a server's process is often executed on a back-office computer, thereby distributing the overall processing load. Furthermore, the increased utilization of less expensive desktop computers to provide such things as presentation services off-loads the computing burden from the more expensive back-office computers. Lastly, placing the data-centric processes on back-office computers provides improved systems management, data management, and administrative capabilities.

Client/server computing, however, has several notable disadvantages. For example, the initial design, development, and implementation can be quite costly. That is, client/server solutions often require additional physical (e.g., cables, hubs, routers) and software-based resources (e.g., network operating system). Moreover, client/server solutions can be quite complicated in that they use multiple, heterogeneous resources. As a result, an increase in potential points of failure emerges, as does the complexity of communications. These characteristics increase the system maintenance and support burden. However, in full consideration of the aforementioned advantages and disadvantages, the total-life-cycle cost of a client/server solution is thought to be significantly lower than comparable, traditional applications (e.g., client-based and server-based architectures).

This chapter begins with a review of three common client/server classification methods, namely the three-layered, the tier-based, and server functionality schemes. The subsequent section describes three broad categories of enabling technologies. These include middleware, component-based middleware solutions, and networking technologies. Next, since the Internet is the world's largest client/server environment, we briefly introduce the basic foundations of the Internet (e.g., Networking access, networking core, and networking edge) and the underpinnings for interoperability (e.g., the Internet protocol stack). The final section of this chapter reviews intranets, extranets, and the Internet, three popular client/server environments.

CLIENT/SERVER SOFTWARE CLASSIFICATIONS

A client/server classification provides information about a particular system architectural configuration. Three client/server classifications are reviewed below. The first classification, the three-layer architecture, describes the computational role of the client process—that is, how an application distributes its presentation, application processing, and data services. The second classification, the tier-based architecture, describes the number of separate processes of a client/server application. That is, it classifies a client/server application based on the number of constituent processes. The final classification, server functionality, describes the primary functional role of server processes.

Three-Layer Client/Server Classification

Client/server computing divides an application into two or more separate processes. The three-layered architecture describes the computational role of both the client and server processes (it is important to note that the three-layered architecture is synonymous with the presentation-application-data, or PAD, architecture, however, the latter term has fallen out of favor and has subsequently been replaced by the former). In particular, the three-layered architecture defines the computational requirements of an application in terms of presentation services, application services, and data services. The presentation services layer details the interaction between the user and the application. The application services layer includes the embedded programming and business logic. The data services layer describes the connectivity to organizational resources such as data, printers, and e-mail (Goldman, Rawles, and Mariga 1999). Each of these services—presentation, application, and data—is discussed next.

Presentation Services

Presentation services describe the relationship between an application and the external environment. At the most basic level, these interactions involve user input and application output. A user's input represents the portion of her or his knowledge submitted to an application. Input provides data and system operating parameters (a.k.a., user instructions to the system on what is being requested). The purpose of application output is to provide new knowledge in the form of printed reports, audio signals, screen displays, and data. In many cases, a client/server application receives input from and provides output to multiple sources, such as other users, other software processes, and/or other applications.

Presentation services can also influence the degree to which a person will use, as well as how they will use, an application. That is, a complex, synergistic relationship exists among the user, the business problem/context, and the application (Dix, Finlay, Abowd, and Beale 1998). Several areas of study are dedicated to investigating how people and technology interact; these include, but are not limited to, cybernetics, human-computer interaction, ergonomics, human factors analysis, technology acceptance and adoption, and industrial engineering.

Application Services

Application services describe how input is transformed into output. The application services layer represents the procedural knowledge (i.e., business logic) embedded in the application. These include statistical, mathematical, graphical, and/or data transformational services.

Data Services

Data services provide access to organizational resources including information-based resources (e.g., databases), hardware-based resources (e.g., printers), and communication-based resources (e.g., e-mail). The data services layer provides utility to the application services layer and/or the presentation services layer.

In general, the three-layered architecture classifies client/server applications based on the distribution of computational services between the client process and the server process. As seen in Table 1, the three-layered architectural framework includes five client/server classification levels. Each level is defined by the client-side functionality—that is, the extent to which it meaningfully participates in presentation, application, and data services.

In the first level, distributed presentation, the client shares the presentation processing with the server and the server handles all application and data services. In the second level, local presentation, the client handles the presentation services and the server handles the application and data services. In the third level, distributed application logic, the client addresses the presentation services and a portion of the application services; the server handles the data services and shares the application services with the client. In the fourth level, local application logic, the client handles the presentation and application services and the server handles the data services. In the last level, distributed data services, the client handles all presentation and application services and the data services are shared by the client and the server. Conceptually, as an application moves along the above continuum—from a distributed presentation to a distributed data service—it is also moving from a thin to a thick client.

Tier-Based Client/Server Classification

Client/server computing partitions an application into two or more separate processes. The client/server tier-based classification method views each software process as a computational component/layer/tier within the overall application. Three tier-based classifications will be discussed in detail below (e.g., two-, three-, and *n*-tier); however, before doing so, it is best to first review their predecessors, namely, host-based and client-based computing.

With host-based computing, the server performs all services (Figure 1). That is, the server (usually a mainframe in this context) is responsible for the presentation, application, and data (access and storage) processes while the client (usually a terminal in this context) merely accepts input from and displays output to the user. Compared to tier-based computing, host-based computing encountered two fundamental problems. First, the server had to process all user requests, which, in many cases, created a bottleneck for the network. Second, in order to remedy the first limitation, organizations were required to make expensive (e.g., in excess of $100,000) and bulky upgrades to their mainframes (IBM 2006).

As desktop computation power increased and as cost decreased, organizations began to shift away from host-based to client-based computing. In a client-based architecture, the client is responsible for the presentation, application, and data processing while the server is responsible for data storage (Figure 2) (e.g., file server). Like host-based computing, client-based computing experienced several key limitations. First, the network emerged as a bottleneck. For example, in client-based

Table 1: Three-Layered Architectural Framework of Client/Server Applications

	Thin Client/Server ←→ Application			Thick Client/Server Application	
Computational Service	Distributed presentation	Local presentation	Distributed application logic	Local application logic	Distributed data services
Presentation services	Shared	Client	Client	Client	Client
Application services	Server	Server	Shared	Client	Client
Data services	Server	Server	Server	Server	Shared

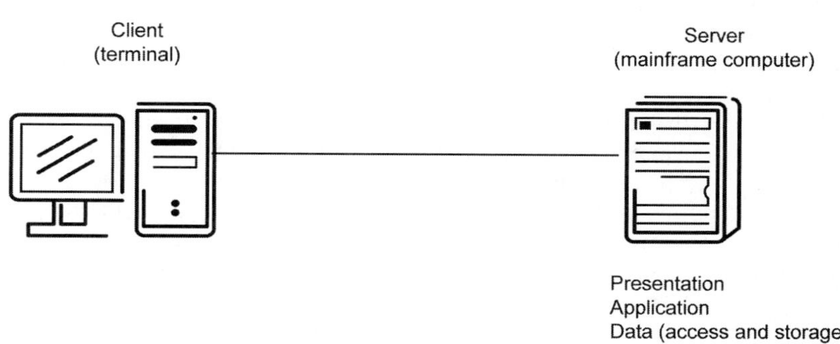

Figure 1: Host-based architecture

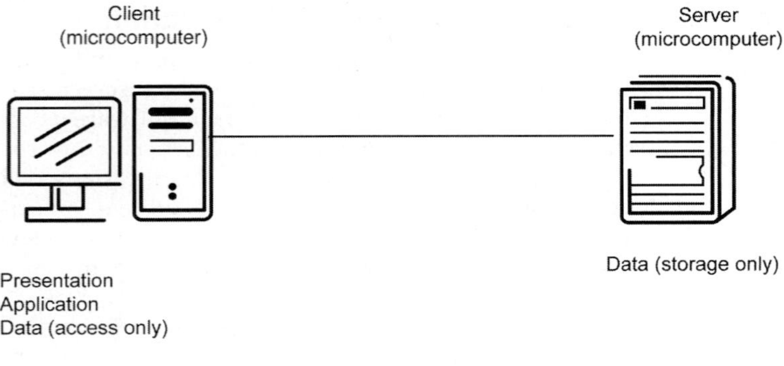

Figure 2: Client-based architecture

Figure 3: Two-tier client/server architecture

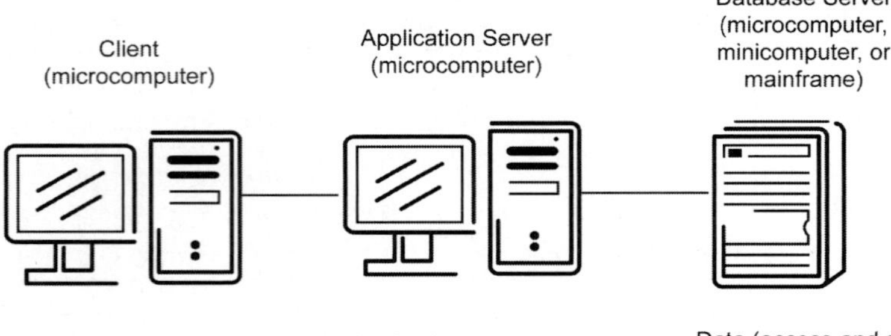

Figure 4: Three-tier client/server architecture

computing the database was often copied and transferred over the network in its entirety to the client before it could be queried. This resulted in the network circuit being overloaded (i.e., even if an application needed only a single record, all records had to be sent from the server to the client). Second, because the client performed nearly all the processing, it became a bottleneck as well. Lastly, data synchronization and sharing are problematic in client-based computing. To address these limitations, tier-based computing emerged.

A two-tier system is the simplest and oldest client/server architecture (Figure 3). In a two-tier system, a client interacts and communicates directly with a server. This architecture often strives to provide reusable, robust links to organizational resources, such as printers and data. In general, a two-tier system leaves most, if not all, the application processing to the client. As seen in Figure 3, the presentation and application processes reside on the client whereas the data access and data storage reside on the server. Compared to a purely host-based or client-based architecture, tiered-based architectures provide two primary advantages. First, tier-based computing shares the computation burden among several machines. Second, the data access and data storage processes reside in a single location (unlike client-based solutions, which duplicate and transmit the database), thereby reducing the excessive demands placed on the network circuit.

In a three-tier system (Figure 4), a client communicates to a server through an intermediary process. This intermediary process provides functionality as well as connectivity. Middle-tier functionality may include message queuing, application execution, and database staging. The middle tier also provides encapsulation for the data source and abstraction for the presentation services. As a result, changes to the data structure and/or user interface are less disruptive and more transparent. Furthermore, data encapsulation improves connectivity with legacy and/or mainframe systems. As a result, a three-tier system may support a large number of concurrent users and is able to handle very complex processing (Carnegie

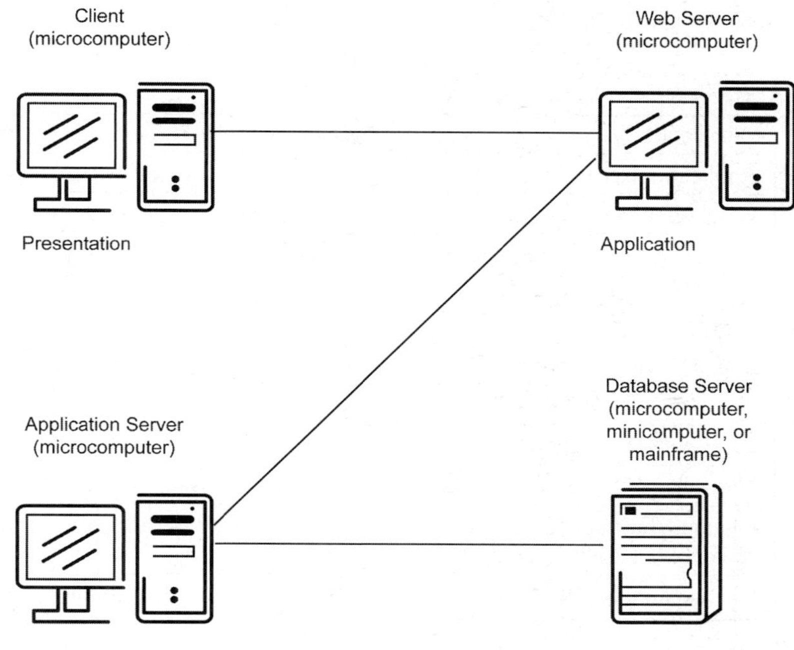

Figure 5: *n*-Tier client/server architecture

Mellon Software Engineering Institute, *Client/server software architectures*, 1997).

The *n*-tier client/server architecture (Figure 5) is a natural extension of the three-tier architecture. An *n*-tier system has an undetermined number of intermediary processes and server processes. A client process might call on a middle-tier process, which in turn might call on another middle-tier process. In combining narrowly focused processes together, the *n*-tier architecture is used to provide both application flexibility and software reusability.

In the next section, server functionality is discussed.

Server Functionality Classification

Many client/server applications strive to reuse functionality among many applications. Because a server process often embeds and hides complicated implementation details, reusing a process significantly reduces system development time and effort. Furthermore, reusing successful, robust server processes improves overall system reliability (Weiss 2001).

To promote reusability the descriptive name of a server process often describes the functionality of the process. The following list describes a few server types. Table 2 provides a summary of the servers listed below.

Web Server

A Web server creates a standardized way for objects to communicate with each other over the Internet. A Web server provides session connectivity to clients running Web browsers (e.g., Internet Explorer, Netscape, Firefox, etc.). Early Web servers fetched files for clients without processing or interpreting the content. However, technologies such as Common Gateway Interface (CGI), Active Server Pages (ASP and ASPX), Java Server Pages (JSP), Java Servlets, eXtensible Markup Language (XML), and XML-based Web services have dramatically expanded the processing and interactive capabilities of Web servers.

Application Server

Application servers provide interactive and processing functionality to clients. An application server may perform programming logic, store and process information, and/or manage user interactivity. Centralizing programming logic allows developers to reuse existing, proven application functionality as well as to simplify software version control, bug fixing, and software deployment.

Wireless Server

A wireless server provides network and Internet connectivity for wireless devices. Two popular wireless servers are wireless enablers and wireless gateways. A wireless enabling server stores information specifically designed for wireless devices, such as wireless markup language (WML). WML is a wireless-friendly version of hypertext markup language (HTML). A wireless client accessing a wireless enabling server would be provided with a WML file rather than an HTML file. Unlike a wireless enabler, a wireless gateway typically does not store content. It accepts requests from wireless and traditional devices and routes each request to an appropriate server based on the request and device type. Some wireless gateway servers also translate wireless and traditionally formatted messages to and from WML and HTML. These translations allow wireless devices to access both traditional and wireless content.

Transaction-Processing (TP) Monitoring Server

A transaction-processing (TP) monitoring server introduces performance efficiencies when serving a large

Table 2: Functional Descriptions for Several Server Types

Server Type	Functional Description
Web server	Connectivity and interactivity to clients running Web browsers
Application server	Interactivity and processing functionality
Wireless server	Wireless content–locating services and/or wireless-friendly content
Transaction-processing (TP) server	User responsiveness, processing prioritization, scheduling, and balancing
Message server	Message routing and delivery
E-mail server	Electronic-mail storage, routing, and delivery
Fax server	Fax storage, routing, and delivery
Proxy server	Intermediary content and processing functionality
Firewall	Access restriction based on a predetermined set of security criteria
Dynamic host configuration protocol (DHCP) server	Dynamic reuse of network addresses
File transfer protocol (FTP) server	File transfer capabilities

number of users. These servers accept client requests, merge requests together by type, and then transmit the resulting consolidated messages to appropriate servers. In sum, a TP can be used to monitor, prioritize, schedule, process, balance, and/or rollback service requests.

Message Server

A message server accepts and routes messages. A message is a service request that is packaged with destination information. An e-mail request is a message; it has embedded intelligence regarding the specific message destination. Thus, an e-mail server is a message server.

E-mail Server

An e-mail server accepts, routes, stores, and delivers electronic mail (e-mail) messages; it handles incoming and outgoing e-mail messages. Several e-mail standards exist, such as the Internet e-mail standards (SMTP—Simple Mail Transfer Protocol; IMAP—Internet Message Access Protocol; POP-3—Post Office Protocol), X.400, and Microsoft's Messaging Application Programming Interface (MAPI).

Fax Server

A fax server is similar to an e-mail server. It accepts, routes, stores, and delivers faxes; it handles incoming and outgoing faxes. Most fax servers provide additional features such as a direct-to-print option (i.e., allowing a fax to be sent to a printer rather than an electronic inbox).

Proxy Server

A proxy server is an intermediary process. It intercepts client requests and attempts to satisfy each request itself. If a request cannot be satisfied, the proxy server routes the request to an appropriate server.

A proxy server can be used to control and manage Internet usage. For example, by channeling all client requests through an organization's proxy server, a firm can monitor and/or limit Internet usage. A proxy server can also optimize Internet usage by using a local cache of Web pages. In addition, it reduces security threats by limiting Internet access to a single machine. A proxy server that filters Internet requests and/or logs Internet usage is acting as a firewall.

Firewall

A firewall reduces the risks associated with unauthorized access to a network and inappropriate use of networking resources. All requests entering and potentially leaving (depending on the configuration) a network must pass through a firewall. The firewall rejects requests that fail to satisfy the predetermined security criteria. Moreover, a firewall can also record user requests and network activities. In general, firewalls are configured based on organizational security and auditing concerns.

Dynamic Host Configuration Protocol (DHCP) Server

Like a postal address for a brick-and-mortar building, each computer on a network must possess a unique address (e.g., an IP address). Traditionally, these addresses were fixed, meaning: (1) each computer required individual configuration, (2) potential conflicts were inevitable, and (3) organizations were required to manage large blocks of addresses.

A dynamic host configuration protocol (DHCP) server dynamically assigns Internet addresses (IP addresses) to computers on the network. This permits an organization to standardize computer configurations, to reduce network address contention, and to continually recycle a smaller number of network addresses.

File Transfer Protocol (FTP) Server

A file transfer protocol (FTP) server facilitates the transfer of files from one computer to another via a network. An FTP server accepts file uploads (i.e., copying files to a server) and file downloads (i.e., copying files from a server). Many FTP servers provide unrestricted access; however, others restrict access to authorized users only.

ENABLING TECHNOLOGIES

Enabling technologies allow heterogeneous software processes, computing devices, and networking devices to interoperate. Enabling technologies include technical standards, organizing frameworks, and product implementations. Three enabling technologies are discussed: middleware, component-based middleware, and networking technologies.

Middleware

Middleware is a primary enabler of client/server computing. Middleware acts like glue, holding together the separate software processes. Middleware products simplify the design, development, and implementation of complex applications by hiding the location of servers, networking protocol details, and operating system differences (Carnegie Mellon Software Engineering Institute, *Middleware*, 1997). Middleware is broadly defined; it may be a type of program-to-program interface, a set of standards, or a product. Table 3 provides a summary of the middleware categories listed below, namely transactional, message-oriented, and procedural.

Transactional Middleware

Transactional middleware supports the function of transaction processing. In particular, transactional middleware strives to provide responsiveness and data integrity while supporting a large number of users. It often includes load-balancing, replication, and/or two-phase commits. The Customer Information Control System (CICS) from IBM is a transactional middleware product. CICS is commonly used on IBM mainframes and on several other IBM-platforms, including OS/2, AS/400, and RS/6000. The distributed transaction processing (DTP) protocol from the Open Group is another transactional middleware standard. Many relational and object-oriented database-management systems support DTP. BEA Tuxedo, from BEA Systems, is another popular transactional middleware product.

Table 3: Middleware Categories and Implementation Examples

Middleware Category	Implementation Examples
Transactional middleware	CICS—IBM DTP—Open Group BEA Tuxedo—BEA Systems
Message-oriented-middleware	WebSphere MQ—IBM JMS—Sun Microsystems MSMQ—Microsoft
Procedural middleware	ONC RPC—IETF DCE RPC—Open Group

Message-Oriented Middleware

Message-oriented middleware (MOM) supports client/server processes using asynchronous, peer-to-peer messages. A MOM does not require continuous, active communication between the client and the server. That is, after a client sends a message, it does not wait for a response. If a server is busy or unavailable, any received message waits in a queue until it is reconciled/satisfied. A MOM solution is well suited for event-driven and object-oriented applications. However, many MOM implementations are proprietary. As a result, they tend to be inflexible and difficult to maintain, and they lack interoperability and portability (Carnegie Mellon Software Engineering Institute, *Message-oriented middleware*, 1997). MOM middleware products include WebSphere MQ (formerly MQSeries) from IBM, Microsoft Message Queue (MSMQ) from Microsoft, and Java Message Service (JMS) from Sun Microsystems. WebSphere MQ is a mature product supporting over 35 platforms (www.ibm.com). MSMQ is also a mature product extended to Microsoft's .NET environment (representing Microsoft's shift toward ubiquitous connectivity between information, people, applications, and devices—see www.microsoft.com/net). JMS is a Java application programming interface (API) included in the Java 2 Platform, Enterprise Edition (J2EE). JMS is one of the many standards included in J2EE, which is a platform for developing distributed applications using the Java programming language. J2EE specifies many services, including asynchronous communications using JMS, naming services using Java Naming, which is the Directory Interface (JNDI), transaction services using Java Transaction API (JTA), and database access services using Java Database Connectivity (JDBC). J2EE implementations are developed and provided by a variety of vendors (Sun, *Java 2 platform, enterprise edition (J2EE)*, n.d.; Alur, Crupi, and Malks 2001).

Procedural Middleware

A remote procedure call (RPC) supports synchronous, call/wait process-to-process communications. When using an RPC, a client requests a service then waits for a response. As a result, an RPC requires continuous, active participation from the client and the server. Each RPC request is a synchronous interaction between exactly one client and one server (Carnegie Mellon Software Engineering Institute, *Remote procedure call*, 1997). Open Network Computing Remote Procedure Call (ONC RPC), developed by Sun Microsystems and now supported by the Internet Engineering Task Force (IETF), was one of the first RPC protocols and is widely deployed to a variety of platforms. The Distributed Computing Environment (DCE), developed and maintained by the Open Group (formerly known as the Open Systems Foundation), is a set of integrated services supporting the development of distributed computing environments. DCE provides distributed services and data-sharing services, including RPC, directory services (i.e., the ability to identify and locate system resources), time services, security services, and thread services (i.e., the ability to build concurrent applications). DCE data-sharing services include diskless support and distributed file system services (Open Group 1996). DCE RPC is the protocol used by several object- and component-based middleware solutions, such as Microsoft's Distributed COM (DCOM) and COM+ and is also an optional protocol in the Object Management Group's Common Object Request Broker Architecture (CORBA).

Component-Based Middleware

Component software strives to improve software development productivity through the reuse of self-describing, self-contained software modules called "components." Each component provides specific functionality. An application discovers and calls on components at run-time.

Component software exists within a component model, which defines the way components are constructed and the environment in which a component will run. The component model consists of an interface definition language (IDL), a component environment, services, utilities, and specifications. An IDL defines how a component interacts with other components to form applications (see www.omg.org for CORBA's IDL). The components exist within a component environment—a computing environment providing the ability to locate, and communicate with, components. Several popular component models—both mature and emergent in nature—are presented in this section, including Object Management Group's CORBA, Microsoft's Component Object Model (COM), Sun Microsystems' Enterprise Java Beans (EJB), and Web Services. However, before each is presented, two brief comments regarding CORBA and Web Services, as they relate to COM and EJB, are presented.

First, relative to COM, COM+, and EJB, CORBA is a lower-level architecture; however, because it is regaining popularity as a viable interoperability solution (e.g., between JAVA and .NET), as well as being embraced by other popular computing platforms (e.g., Linux), it is included in the current context (e.g., Donner 2004; Harmon 2004). Second, Web Services, although not a traditional, component-based middleware architecture per se, is nonetheless discussed in the current context in terms of an emerging, higher-level solution to the challenges of heterogeneity in distributed, component-based computing environments.

Common Object Request Broker Architecture (CORBA)

CORBA is an open, vendor-independent, mature architecture describing object-oriented process interactions over a network. CORBA, supported by the Object Management Group (OMG), uses a standard communication protocol IIOP (Internet Inter-ORB protocol). IIOP allows a CORBA process running on one computer to interact with a CORBA process running on another computer without regard to network, vendor, programming language, or platform heterogeneity. CORBA supports a variety of services, including asynchronous and synchronous, stateless and persistent, and flat and nested transactions (OMG, n.d.).

Component Object Model (COM)

Microsoft's COM is a way for multivendor software components to communicate with each other. It provides a software architecture that allows applications to be built from binary components supplied by different software vendors. COM provides the foundation for many technologies, including object linking and embedding (OLE), ActiveX, and Microsoft Transaction Server (MTS). Distributed COM extends COM by allowing remote component interactions. COM+ further expands COM by encapsulating DCOM, MTS, and a host of other services, including a dynamic load-balancing service, an in-memory database, a publish-and-subscribe events service, and a queued-components service. COM components require the COM application server, available on the Windows operating system platforms (Microsoft 1998).

Within Microsoft's .NET (pronounced "dot net") environment, material modifications to both COM and COM+ have taken place. The runtime environment known as COM+ has been absorbed into the .NET Enterprise Services space (see www.microsoft.com/net).

Enterprise Java Beans

Similar to CORBA, Sun Microsystems' Enterprise Java Beans (EJB) is a specification. An EJB must be programmed using Java and must be hosted on a J2EE application server. EJBs interact with each other using Java Remote Method Invocation (RMI). RMI is a set of APIs used to create distributed applications using Java; it is also an implementation that operates in a homogeneous environment using a Java virtual machine (JVM). RMI allows Java objects to communicate remotely with other Java objects (the Microsoft platform parallel is .NET Remoting—see http://msdn.microsoft.com). Alternatively, an EJB built with an implementation based on the EJB 2.0 specification, or higher, may communicate using the message-oriented-middleware, JMS (Marinescu and Roman 2002).

An EJB system consists of three parts, the EJB component, the EJB container, and the EJB object. An EJB component exists within an EJB container running on an EJB server. The EJB object provides access to the EJB components. An EJB component is a software module that provides specific functionality; it may be discovered and manipulated dynamically at run-time. The EJB container provides the execution environment for the EJB components; it handles the communication and interface details. An EJB container may support more than one EJB component. Whereas an EJB component runs on a server, an EJB object runs on a client. An EJB object remotely controls the EJB component (Sun, *Java remote method invocation*, n.d.).

Web Services

Although not traditional middleware per se, Web services represent a critical paradigm shift in middleware:

service-based computing. Web services represent the first successful cross-platform component architecture outside traditional component-based models. Consequently, Web services have been included in this section. According to Microsoft, Web services represent a "self-describing software module, semantically encapsulating discrete functionality, wrapped in and accessible via standard Internet communication protocols like XML and SOAP" (Microsoft 2005). What that amounts to is a platform-independent module that builds on existing Internet standards, primarily XML, to provide, validate, and interpret data. Web services also conveniently leverage the HyperText Transfer Protocol (HTTP) to provide synchronous communications as well as the Simple Mail Transfer Protocol (SMTP) to provide asynchronous communications (e.g., e-mail).

Web services provide Internet-accessible, building-block functionality to developers; they allow for incremental development and deployment. Web services support new-application development and promise to provide access to existing applications. By wrapping traditional processes in Web service protocols, an existing computing infrastructure can improve interoperability and utilization without having to reprogram existing applications. Furthermore, an existing application may enhance functionality by integrating with new Web services.

Web services are distinctive in several ways. Whereas a traditional process is designed to provide functionality to a particular application, a Web service strives to provide global access to a very well defined, packaged process designed to provide specific functionality. A Web service is not duplicated or moved; it is simply called on as required at run-time by applications. Ultimately, online providers will provide access to Web services that can be called on on an as-needed basis. Furthermore, unlike other distributed application environments, such as CORBA, J2EE, and COM+, Web services do not dictate the underlying communications framework (Singh, Stearns, Johnson, et al. 2002), rather they act as a separate and distinct bridge that uses standard Internet protocols such as HTTP, XLM, and TCP/IP.

Open, standardized interfaces are the heart of Web services. Standards define how a Web service communicates, how it exchanges data, and how it is located. The Simple Object Access Protocol (SOAP) is an XML-based protocol for exchanging information in a distributed environment. SOAP is platform-independent and consists of an envelope, a set of encoding rules, and a convention describing procedure calls. A SOAP envelope describes the contents of the message and how the message should be processed. The encoding rules describe the application-specific data types. The conventions describe remote procedure calls and responses. Other standards include the Web Services Description Language (WSDL) and the Universal Description, Discovery, and Integration (UDDI). WSDL defines the Web service interfaces, while UDDI allows developers to list/post new Web services as well as locate existing Web services (UDDI 2002).

In the next section, networking in the context of an enabling client/server technology is reviewed.

Networking

The Internet consists of host computers, client computers, routers, applications, protocols, and other hardware and software. As an organizing framework, these technologies may be categorized using three broadly defined functional areas, namely, network access, network core, and network edge (Table 4).

Network access describes how devices connect to the Internet. The network core describes the intercommunications among the computing and networking devices. The network edge describes those objects using the Internet such as clients, servers, and applications (Kurose and Ross 2001; Peterson and Davie 1999).

Network Access

An Internet access provider (IAP) provides Internet access. The structure of an IAP is roughly hierarchical. At the lowest level, a local Internet service provider (ISP) provides connectivity for residential customers and small businesses. The local ISP connects to a regional ISP. The regional ISP connects to a national/international backbone provider (NBP). The various NBPs interconnect using private connections and/or public network access points (NAPs) to form the backbone of the Internet.

To communicate with an IAP (or ISP), a connection must be established and maintained. Several connection alternatives exist, including dial-up, integrated services digital network (ISDN), asymmetric digital subscriber line (ADSL), hybrid fiber coax (HFC, via a cable modem), T-services (e.g., T1, T3, etc.), SONET (e.g., OC1, OC3, etc.), and wireless (e.g., radio, cellular, satellite, and microwave).

The Network Core

The network core describes how networking devices interconnect with each other. The backbone of the Internet is an extremely large mesh. Data are sent through this mesh using either circuit-switching or packet-switching channels. A circuit-switching network establishes and maintains a circuit (i.e., a specific network path) for the entire duration of an interaction. A circuit-switching network knows where to look for messages, and the data are

Table 4: Internet Networking Categories and Components

Internet Networking Category	Components
Network access	Internet access providers Internet connectivity: dial-up, ISDN, ADSL, HFC, wireless, T1/T3
Network core	Routers and bridges Data routing: circuit-switching, packet-switching
Network edge	Computers, users, applications Internet protocol stack

received in the order in which they are sent. A packet-switching network divides each transmission into a series of individually addressed packets. Since each packet is addressed and ordered, the network path need not be determined and packets may be sent using whatever data rate may exist at the time the message is transmitted. As a result, each packet might take a different path through the network at different transmission rates. The receiver of the message is responsible for unpackaging and resequencing the packets.

The Network Edge

The network edge consists of objects using the Internet, such as clients, servers, and applications. For one object to communicate with another object, the two must adhere to the same networking protocol. A protocol is an agreed-on set of rules governing a data transmission. The Internet supports a variety of protocols. Some protocols are competing, meaning they serve the same purpose; others are complementary, meaning they serve different purposes.

In the next section, a review of the Internet protocol stack (i.e., the foundation for interoperability) is presented.

Internet Protocol Stack

An Internet protocol stack is a framework used to organize and describe networking protocols. Each layer in a protocol stack serves a particular networking need, or needs, and describes how a given layer must communicate with adjacent layers. Furthermore, the lower layers of the stack provide a foundation for the upper layers (Kurose and Ross 2001; Peterson and Davie 1999). As seen in Table 5, the Internet protocol stack is a variation of the widely accepted OSI model. The Internet protocol stack has the following five layers: physical, data link, network, transport, and application. The application layer of the Internet protocol stack envelops the application, presentation, and session layers of the OSI model. A description of each layer of the Internet protocol stack follows.

Physical Layer. The physical layer of the Internet protocol stack describes the physical characteristics of the networking media. Media can be broadly categorized as guided or unguided. Guided media include copper wire and fiber optics. Unguided media include radio, microwave, and satellite. The media type influences bandwidth, security, interference, expandability, contention, and costs. Examples of physical layer protocols include Ethernet (IEEE 802.3), Token Passing (IEEE 802.5), Wireless (IEEE 802.11), transmission convergence sublayer (TCS) and physical medium–dependent (PMD) for asynchronous transfer mode (ATM), and transmission frame structures for T-carriers.

Data-Link Layer. The data-link layer of the Internet protocol stack describes how devices share the physical media. These protocols define host-host connections, host-router connections, and router-router connections. The primary role of data-link-layer protocols is to define flow control (i.e., how to share the media), error detection, and error correction. Data-link layer protocols include the point-to-point protocol (PPP) and the serial-line Internet protocol (SLIP), which allow clients to establish Internet connections with Web servers. Ethernet and ATM are also popular data link layer protocols.

Network Layer. The network layer of the Internet protocol stack defines host and application addressing. The Internet protocol (IP) assigns a unique number, called the IP address, to devices connected to the Internet. The IP address uniquely identifies every computer connected to the Internet.

Transport Layer. The transport layer of the Internet protocol stack defines how information is shared among applications. The Internet transport protocols include transmission control protocol (TCP) and, under certain instances, user datagram protocol (UDP).

TCP is a connection-oriented protocol. A TCP-based application establishes and maintains a connection for

Table 5: Comparison of the OSI Model and the Internet Protocol Stack

OSI Model	Internet Protocol Stack	Layer Description	Protocols
Application	Application	Specifies how applications and processes will communicate with each other	HTTP, FTP, SMTP, MIME, DNS, NFS. Middleware products: RPC, MOM, CORBA/IIOP, CICS, DTP
Presentation			
Session			
Transport	Transport	Specifies how information is transmitted	TCP, UDP SPX
Network	Network	Specifies host and application addressing	IP IPX
Data Link	Data Link	Specifies how the media are shared	PPP, SLIP, ATM, Ethernet
Physical	Physical	Specifies the physical characteristics of the media	IEEE802.3, IEEE802.5, IEEE802.11, Token Passing, TCS, PDM

the entire duration of each transaction. This connection provides reliability and congestion control. Applications using TCP include e-mail, file transfers, and Web browsing.

UDP is a connectionless protocol. A UDP-based application communicates by sending individual datagram packets. Datagrams support applications requiring large bandwidth and those tolerating some degree of data loss. Applications using UDP include telephony, streaming video, and interactive games.

Application Layer. The application layer of the Internet protocol stack defines application-application communications. For example, the HTTP protocol allows Web clients to locate, request, and subsequently interpret Web-based objects (e.g., HTML, VBScript, Jscript, Java Applets, JPG files, etc.). Application layer protocols abound; however, salient applications are briefly reviewed next.

SMTP allows user agents (e.g., Microsoft Outlook, Eudora, etc.) to send, receive, and store e-mail messages. Multipurpose Internet mail extensions (MIME) supports e-mail attachments. Post office protocol (POP3) and Internet message access protocol (IMAP) allow clients to download e-mail messages from e-mail servers. FTP allows file transfers between computers. The domain name system (DNS) resolves IP addresses and universal resource locator (URL) names. Telnet allows for remote terminal access over the Internet. The network file system (NFS) protocol allows for remote storage of files.

Networking Security Vulnerabilities

Networks suffer from many security vulnerabilities, including accessibility or altering of programs or data; intercepting, creating, or modifying data in transit; and blocking traffic. These attacks may involve social engineering, performing reconnaissance, launching denial of service attacks, impersonating users, or spoofing systems. A social engineering attack strives to manipulate or trick users and/or support staff into divulging sensitive information. These attacks may be direct, such as asking for a password reset, or they may be indirect, in which an adversary may infer or derive sensitive information from the responses of several "individually nonsensitive" questions. Reconnaissance is an information-finding activity. Adversaries may engage in reconnaissance activities ranging from searching through physical and virtual recycle bins to analyzing design diagrams and configuration information. A port scan is a common reconnaissance activity. A port is a virtual communications channel used by specific applications. A port scan is a program that systematically searches hosts to determine available ports and what applications are using them. A denial of service attack inundates a server with requests in order to overwhelm and significantly reduce the performance of the system. Impersonation is when a party assumes the identity of another person or process or host. Spoofing occurs when an adversary acts on behalf of another party. Spoofing includes masquerading and session hijacking. Masquerading involves pretending to be someone else. Session hijacking involves intercepting a connection that has been established by another party. For an in-depth review of these and other network vulnerabilities, see the chapters on Social Engineering, Intrusion Detection Systems, Network Attacks, Worms and Viruses, and Denial of Service.

In the next section, three popular client/server environments are reviewed.

CLIENT/SERVER ENVIRONMENTS

The Internet is exemplary when it comes to client/server environments. In this section we discuss the Internet as well as proprietary-based Internet environments—intranets and extranets.

Internet

The Internet is a network of networks. Hundreds of millions of computers, users, and applications use the Internet. The Internet uses a variety of protocols, including TCP/IP, HTTP, and FTP. The Internet supports Web browsing, online chat, multi-user gaming, e-mail delivery, fax delivery, and telephony, to name just a few.

As previously mentioned, the Internet typifies client/server computing. That is, resources, service, and processes are distributed, and thus shared, among and between multiple devices/users. However, when these resources are limited to a set, or possibly sets, of prespecified users (e.g., customers, employees, supply chain partners, vendors), two new internetworking environments emerge, namely intranets and the extranets.

Intranet

An intranet is a private network using the same technologies and protocols as the Internet. Since the foundation, protocols, and toolsets are the same, an intranet looks, feels, and behaves like the Internet. The difference between an intranet and the Internet is in both scope and access. That is, an intranet user is limited to visiting only those Web sites owned and maintained by the organization hosting the intranet, whereas an Internet user may visit any publicly accessible Web site. Since intranets are private, individuals outside the organization are unable to access intranet-based resources—that is, without specific organizational permission and technology (e.g., a virtual private network). As a result, organizations may publish internal and/or confidential information such as organizational directories, company policies, promotion procedures, and benefits information. The primary means of separating an intranet from the nonsecure, public Internet is a firewall.

Extranet

An extranet is an intranet that provides limited connectivity via the public Internet. Specifically, an extranet allows authorized Internet users to access a portion of a company's intranet. External access to a company's intranet is granted through a firewall and is typically facilitated via a virtual private network (VPN). That is, an Internet visitor either submits a username and password to the firewall or to an organization-provided VPN server.

If authenticated, the visitor is permitted limited access to the company's intranet.

Extranets are designed to interconnect suppliers, customers, and other business partners. The exposure of the extranet is based on the relationships a company has with its partners and the sensitivity of the content stored on the company's intranet. In the most relaxed scenario, individuals gain access to common business materials by completing a brief survey. In more restrictive scenarios, an organization may sign a contract detailing acceptable use of intranet resources or may required users to pay subscription fees. Extranets are also commonly used to support field personnel and employees working from Internet-based locations outside an organization's firewall.

CONCLUSION

Client/server computing is so broadly defined, that the name says little about a particular system. A client/server application may provide national security services to a government or it may provide publicly available editorials and commentaries. In addition, client/server computing encompasses several architectural interpretations. The client/server system architecture describes the physical configuration or topology of computing and networking devices. In this context, clients and servers are seen as computers. The client/server software architecture, however, describes the configuration of software processes. In this latter context, clients and servers are seen as software processes. Furthermore, client/server computing uses an enormous array of heterogeneous technologies, protocols, platforms, and development environments. Whereas some client/server applications are relatively simple, involving only a few technologies, others are extremely complex, involving a large variety of technologies.

Common to all client/server systems is the partitioning of an application into separate processes and the utilization of a communications mechanism (almost always a computer network). Two general categories of processes exist, those that request services (i.e., clients) and those that provide services (i.e., servers). A client process works together with a server process to provide application functionality.

A client/server classification provides information that describes a particular system. A classification may describe the computational role of the processes, the physical partitioning of an application into tiers, or the functional role of the processes. Although these classification methods help describe systems, they also serve to highlight the variety and complexity among client/server applications. The computational and functional role of the processes varies from system to system. Furthermore, a client may interconnect with many servers and a server may interconnect with many clients.

Enabling technologies strive to provide seamless integration of hardware and software in complex environments. Specifically, middleware governs the interactions among the constituent software processes. Component-based middleware provides the ability to create applications using existing, self-contained software modules while various networking technologies bridge the gaps among computing and networking devices.

Early distributed computing consisted of vendor- and platform-specific implementations. However, the trend in client/server computing is to provide standardized connectivity solutions. Web services represent one of the most promising new client/server developments. Web services strive to leverage the communication infrastructure of the Internet to deploy client/server applications. Although it is too early to know whether Web services will fulfill their potential, they promise to change the way application programs are developed and deployed. As the excitement, investment, and standardization in such technologies continue to grow, so too will the global impact of client/server computing.

GLOSSARY

Client Process: A software program that requests services from one or more server processes.

Client System: A computer that supports a client process and requests services from one or more server systems.

Client/Server Software Architecture: The logical and physical partitioning of an application into software processes.

Client/Server System Architecture: The architectural configuration of computing and networking devices supporting a client/server application.

Client/Server Tier: A well-defined, separate process representing a portion of a client/server application.

Component: A self-contained, self-describing software module that provides specific functionality, in which several can be combined to build larger applications.

Component Environment: A computing environment providing the ability to locate and communicate with components.

Component Model: The way components are constructed and the environment in which a component will run, consisting of an interface definition language, a component environment, services, utilities, and specifications.

Enabling Technology: Technology that provides a client/server application with the ability to locate, communicate with, and/or integrate the constituent processes.

Extranet: An Intranet that provides limited access to/from the Internet using firewall technology.

Interface Definition Language (IDL): Defines how a program may communicate with a component.

Internet: A global network of networks supporting hundreds of millions of computers, networking devices, applications, and users.

Internet Protocol Stack: A subset of the OSI model; a framework that organizes and describes Internet networking protocols.

Intranet: A private network based on Internet protocols and technologies.

LAN (Local Area Network): A computer network that is located within a small geographical area, such as an office or small building.

Middleware: The software governing the interaction among the client and server processes.

***n*-tier system:** An application that is partitioned into an unspecified number of separate processes that work together to provide system functionality.

Network: A series of points connected by communication circuits. See LAN.

OSI Model: A general framework that organizes and describes networking protocols.

PAD Architecture: Defines an application in terms of the following three computational services: presentation services, application services, and data services.

Process: An executing program.

Server Process: A software program that provides services to one or more client processes.

Server System: A computer that supports a server process and provides services to one or more client systems.

Three-Tier: An application that is partitioned into three separate processes that work together to provide system functionality.

Two-Tier: An application that is partitioned into two separate processes that work together to provide system functionality.

CROSS REFERENCES

See *Groupware; Network Middleware; The Internet Fundamentals.*

REFERENCES

Alur, D., J. Crupi, and D. Malks. 2001. *Core J2EE patterns.* Upper Saddle River, NJ: Prentice-Hall.

Carnegie Mellon Software Engineering Institute. 1997. *Software technology review: Middleware.* www.sei.cmu.edu/str/descriptions/middleware_body.html (accessed November 14, 2005).

Carnegie Mellon Software Engineering Institute. 1997. *Software technology review: Message-oriented middleware.* www.sei.cmu.edu/str/descriptions/momt_body.html (accessed November 14, 2005).

Carnegie Mellon Software Engineering Institute. 1997. *Software technology review: Remote procedure call.* www.sei.cmu.edu/str/descriptions/rpc_body.html (accessed November 14, 2005).

Carnegie Mellon Software Engineering Institute. 1997. *Client/server software architectures—An overview.* www.sei.cmu.edu/str/descriptions/clientserver_body.html (accessed November 14, 2005).

Dix, A., J. Finlay, G. Abowd, and R. Beale. 1998. *Human-computer interaction.* 2nd ed. Upper Saddle River, NJ: Prentice Hall.

Donner, C. 2004. *Java and .Net interoperability using CORBA.* http://www.donners.com/christian/portfolio/attachments/javaworld042004.pdf (accessed September 12, 2006).

Goldman, J. E., P. T. Rawles, and J. R. Mariga. 1999. *Client/server information systems: A business-oriented approach.* New York: Wiley.

Harmon, T. 2004. Corba is dead! www.linux-mag.com/2004-03/corba_01.html (accessed September 12, 2006).

IBM z9 Business Class Mainframe. 2006. IBM unveils breakthrough business class mainframe—Target growth of SOA transactions and data. www-03.ibm.com/press/us/en/pressrelease/19577.wss (accessed April 26, 2006).

Kurose, J. F., and K. W. Ross. 2001. *Computer networking: A top-down approach featuring the Internet.* New York: Addison Wesley.

Marinescu, F., and E. Roman. 2002. *EJB design patterns: Advanced patterns, processes, and idioms.* New York: Wiley.

Microsoft COM Technologies. 1998. www.microsoft.com/com/tech/dcom.asp (accessed September 11, 2005).

Microsoft. 2005. *.NET: Driving business value with the Microsoft platform.* www.microsoft.com/net/basics.mspx (accessed April 26, 2006).

OMG. (n.d.). CORBA. www.corba.org (accessed September 12, 2005).

Open Group. 1996. What is distributed computing and DCE? www.osf.org/dce (accessed September 11, 2005).

Peterson, L. L., and B. S. Davie. 1999. *Computer networks: A systems approach.* 2nd ed. San Francisco: Morgan Kaufmann.

Singh, I., B. Stearns, M. Johnson, et al. 2002. D*esigning enterprise applications with the J2EETM platform,* 2nd ed. Boston: Addison Wesley.

Sun. (n.d.). *Java 2 platform, enterprise edition (J2EE).* http://java.sun.com/j2ee (accessed November 20, 2005).

Sun. (n.d.). *Java remote method invocation (RMI).* http://java.sun.com/j2se/1.4.1/docs/guide/rmi (accessed November 10, 2005).

UDDI 2002. *Using WSDL in a UDDI registry,* version 1.07. www.uddi.org/bestpractices.html (accessed November 20, 2005).

Weiss, A. 2001, January 29. *The truth about servers.* www.serverwatch.com/tutorials/article.php/1354991 (accessed November 26, 2005).

Groupware

Robert Slagter, *Telematica Instituut, The Netherlands*

INTRODUCTION

Groupware applications denote any type of software application designed to support groups of people in communication and collaboration on shared information objects (Ellis et al. 1991; ter Hofte 1998). The fundamental property of groupware is its ability to mediate the results of some user interactions to other people. Well-known types of groupware include e-mail, videoconferencing, work-flow, chat, and collaborative editing systems.

Contrary to optimistic predictions in the 1970s and 1980s, groupware applications, especially videoconferencing systems, have not reached their anticipated potential. For instance, Snyder (1971) predicted that by the end of the 1970s a full 85 percent of all meetings would be electronically mediated. Obviously, this has not been the case. On the other hand, some types of computer-supported cooperation have become highly successful, such as e-mail and instant messaging (ter Hofte, Mulder, Grootveld, and Slagter 2002). Understanding in what situations groupware is an effective and efficient means to support collaboration (and thus understanding its potential) remains an important research question even today.

GROUPWARE FUNCTIONALITY

Although there is a lot of diversity in groupware applications, some typical functionality is provided by many different applications. This section provides a list that, while not being exhaustive, represents a wide range of important functionality.

- *E-mail:* Primarily text-based, asynchronous electronic form of person-to-person or person-to-group communication. The term e-mail is applied both for communication via the simple mail transfer protocol (SMTP) as well as the generic groupware functionality to send electronic messages to other people. As central servers are used to store e-mail messages, the collaborating people do not have to be online at the same moment to exchange e-mail messages.
- *Instant messaging:* Sometimes referred to as chat, instant messaging is primarily about text-based communication between a specific group of people who are online at the same moment. Such same-time collaboration is denoted as synchronous collaboration. Instant messaging is usually combined with presence awareness information about a list of contacts, sometimes denoted as buddies. This presence awareness information indicates which of your contacts are currently available for communication.
- *Discussion forum:* Primarily text-based communication via threaded discussions. A discussion forum supports asynchronous collaboration, meaning the collaborating people do not have to be online at the same moment. In contrast to e-mail, discussion forum messages are centrally stored, not sent to one or more people. The centrally stored messages can be accessed by multiple people, and typically people can react by messages as well. People who join a forum can also typically read and participate in previously started discussion. In a forum, messages and associated reactions are grouped in so-called threads.
- *Newsgroup:* A newsgroup is a specific type of discussion forum, typically part of the Usenet hierarchy, a distributed Internet discussion system.
- *Videoconferencing:* Refers to functionality that allows two or more locations to synchronously interact via two-way video and audio connections. Video conferencing systems may be room-based, allowing for groups to interact, or desktop-based, which is more focused on individuals.
- *Audioconferencing:* Refers to functionality that allows two or more locations to synchronously interact via two-way audio connections. Although audio conferencing primarily takes place via normal telephones and cell phones, there are also software tools that use the internet protocol (IP) for voice communication. The latter applications are typically referred to as voice over-IP (VoIP) applications.

- *Network games:* Refers to collaboration functionality primarily aimed at entertainment or enjoyment, although it may also serve as exercise or perform an educational, simulation or psychological role.
- *Group calendar:* Refers to functionality that allows groups of people to coordinate their actions by sharing calendar information. In a basic setting, people can view whether another person is free or busy at a specific time, but in more advanced cases they can have a detailed look at the appointments in other people's schedules. Group calendars are typically used within the context of one organization, given the sensitivity of the shared information. Group calendars require up-to-date information and a critical mass of users, before they become effective to coordinate actions.
- *Shared whiteboard:* Refers to functionality to create, edit, and share drawings, based on the white board metaphor. Shared white boards can be used for synchronous as well as asynchronous forms of collaboration.
- *Application sharing:* Functionality that allows you to synchronously collaborate using applications that were not designed to be used in a collaborative way. Application-sharing functionality typically allows one of the participants to provide input to a shared application, while the application output is distributed to all collaborating people. Typically, some coordination policy is in place to decide who is in control of the shared application. There are two main versions of application sharing: window sharing and screen sharing. In window sharing, one specific application is shared, while in screen sharing, all collaborating people see exactly what is on the presenter's screen.
- *Group decision support system:* Abbreviated GDSS, this functionality refers to a suite of collaborative functionality to facilitate group decision processes. A GDSS can be used by colocated teams as well as by geographically dispersed teams, but typically it focuses on synchronous forms of collaboration. A GDSS usually includes brainstorming tools—tools to prioritize or cluster ideas and voting tools.
- *Workflow management:* Functionality to support (asynchronous) work processes. Workflow management systems allow users to define how tasks are structured and who performs them, when, and in what order. The collaborating users are informed of any tasks they are supposed to perform and the deadline. A workflow management system keeps track of the progress and typically updates the task owner about the status of the process and any deviations in relation to the planning.
- *Shared workspace:* Refers to a suite of functionality to collaborate synchronously, but mostly asynchronously. Typical functionality includes file sharing and version control, notifications of changes to the workspace and access control to restrict who can view, edit, or delete content. Advanced shared workspaces integrate much of the above-mentioned functionality.
- *Wiki:* A Wiki is a type of Web site that allows users to easily add and edit content and is especially suited for asynchronous collaborative writing. Wikis typically reside on a central server and are served by a Wiki engine.

CLASSIFYING GROUPWARE APPLICATIONS

Historically, groupware applications have been classified based on the time-place matrix described by Johansen (1988). This matrix classifies groupware applications along two axes: whether the cooperating people work at the same time (synchronously) or at different times (asynchronously) and whether the people work at the same physical location or at different places. Table 1 represents this matrix with some example groupware applications positioned in it.

However, this time-place matrix is very rigid, and does not, for instance, allow for applications that support the transition between more synchronous and more asynchronous forms of cooperation, such as shared workspaces or applications to record and replay (virtual) meetings. Grudin ("Computer-supported cooperative work," 1994) extended this matrix to include the factor of "predictability": he argues that although people may not be working at the same time, there is an important difference between being able to predict when another person is likely to work and not being able to predict this. Similarly he has added a row to the matrix to distinguish whether it is possible to predict the place where the other people will be. The resulting matrix is shown in Table 2.

Given the focus of this handbook, most of the examples and design issues are about groupware applications that do not require cooperating people to work together at the same place.

Table 1: The Time-Place Matrix by Johansen

	Same time (synchronous)	**Different time (asynchronous)**
Same place (local)	Group decision support systems	Electronic project rooms
Different place (remote)	Videoconferencing, text-based chat, shared workspaces	E-mail, group scheduling, shared workspaces

Table 2: The Time-Place Matrix by Grudin

	Same time (synchronous)	Different time, but predictable (asynchronous)	Different time, unpredictable (asynchronous)
Same place (local)	Meeting facilitation	Work shifts	Team rooms
Different place, but predictable (remote)	Tele-, video-, desktop-conferencing	Electronic mail	Collaborative writing
Different place, unpredictable (remote)	Interactive multicast seminars	Computer bulletin boards	Workflow

Synchronous and Asynchronous Collaboration

Although the matrix by Johansen may be rigid, the distinction between synchronous and asynchronous (and any forms in between) is helpful in itself. Distinguishing different forms of collaboration and being able to select suitable groupware functionalities to support them is helpful when designing groupware support for a specific setting.

Table 3 illustrates that this is no dichotomy. In real-life settings, the situation may be even more blurred: whereas e-mail was designed as a tool to support asynchronous collaboration, sometimes messages and replies follow each other at such a rapid pace that it becomes a tool for synchronous collaboration.

Groupware applications designed for synchronous collaboration frequently apply the *conference* concept, denoted as a period of interaction by a group of cooperating people, supported by groupware functionality. During such a conference, a set of rules may apply to regulate access to groupware functions. A conference has a beginning and an end and is characterized by an explicit or implicit objective (e.g., a peer-review session, a project progress meeting, a design session). In literature, such conferences are sometimes referred to as *sessions*. Functionality to manage conferences is therefore sometimes denoted as session management.

Peer-to-Peer and Client/Server Groupware

The terms *peer-to-peer* and *client/server* refer to the architectural model on which the groupware design is based (Figure 1). In the peer-to-peer groupware model, the different collaborating people each use a groupware application

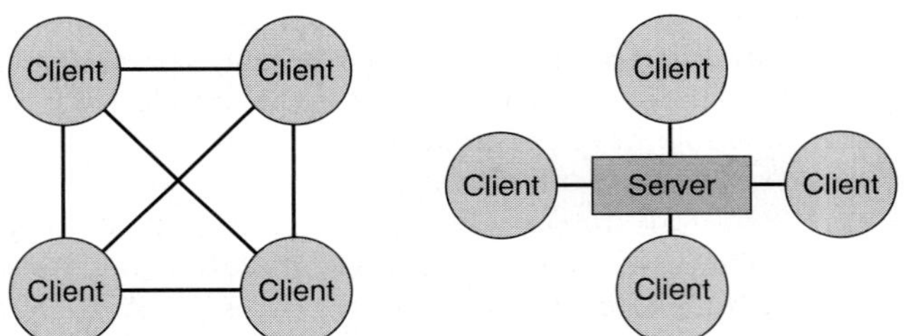

Figure 1: Peer-to-peer versus client/server architecture

Table 3: Groupware Functionality to Support Synchronous and Asynchronous Collaboration

Groupware functionality	Typically used to support synchronous collaboration	Typically used to support asynchronous collaboration
E-mail		X
Instant messaging	X	
Discussion forum		X
Newsgroup		X
Video conferencing	X	
Audio conferencing	X	
Group calendar		X
Shared white board	X	X
GDSS	X	X
Workflow management		X
Shared workspace	X	X
Collaborative software development	X	X
Wiki		X

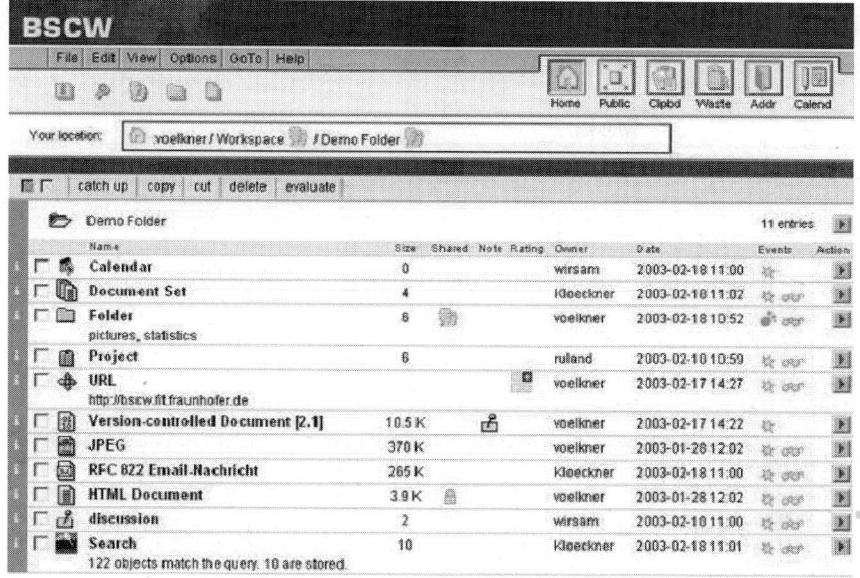

Figure 2: Example screenshot of BSCW

(client) that connects directly with the groupware application of the other people. In the client/server groupware model, the groupware applications (clients) all connect to a central server, which relays messages and can provide shared services.

The differences between the two architectural models also have implications when using applications based on these models: peer-to-peer groupware applications provide users with more control over their data and avoid dependency on a third (economic) party to host a server. The peer-to-peer model is in line with current Internet trends, whereby the computing power and storage capabilities of network peripheral hosts are used. This is in contrast with the client/server model, in which much of the intelligence is allocated to a central, high-performance host.

However, the client/server model also has some clear advantages: centralizing functionality in a server allows for "thin clients" with a small footprint. This enables people, for instance, to access groupware functionality from their PDA or smart phone. In addition, a central server can act as a meeting point and to set up connections with other participants behind a firewall. And, obviously, a central server allows you to create shared workspaces that can be accessed asynchronously.

EXAMPLES OF GROUPWARE APPLICATIONS

Many groupware applications have emerged, both in academia and in industry, each providing particular support for cooperating people. Typically, groupware applications are designed to support a particular work situation or a particular range of cooperative work situations. Well-known examples of groupware applications include e-mail, audio- and videoconferencing applications, instant messaging applications, and applications to work together using shared virtual workspaces. This section introduces some well-known groupware applications, illustrating the diversity in current groupware applications.

BSCW

BSCW (Basic Support for Cooperative Work) (BSCW 2006) is a Web-based environment for collaboration (Figure 2). It started as a Web-based application to share files, but gradually turned into a shared virtual workspace that supports document sharing, online discussions and shows, as an example, participant status information such as who has viewed, edited, or downloaded a file. BSCW offers a fixed set of collaboration tools and depends on external tools for synchronous communication between workspace participants. The BSCW environment provides services to invite people to a shared virtual workspace, assign roles to people, and specify the rights associated with each role.

Lotus Notes

Lotus Notes (Lotus Notes 2006), shown in Figure 3, is an integrated cooperative environment that combines messaging, shared databases, calendaring, and scheduling functions with a platform to create collaborative applications. These collaborative applications are founded on replicated, shared databases that users can access and update through forms. Lotus Notes provides advanced security and role-based access control, related to workflow facilities. The Notes platform provides developers with integrated tools to create tailor-made cooperative applications, based on the specific requirements of a company. Lotus Notes' databases and forms can be accessed via the Notes client, or be turned into Web applications using Lotus Domino (Lotus Domino 2006). In addition, Lotus Web Conferencing and Lotus Instant Messaging (previously known in their combined form as Lotus Sametime) provide awareness services to discover which contacts are currently online, and to start communication using text-based messages, audio, video, or application sharing. Although Lotus Notes offers a highly flexible environment, it requires programming skills to create and adapt cooperative applications.

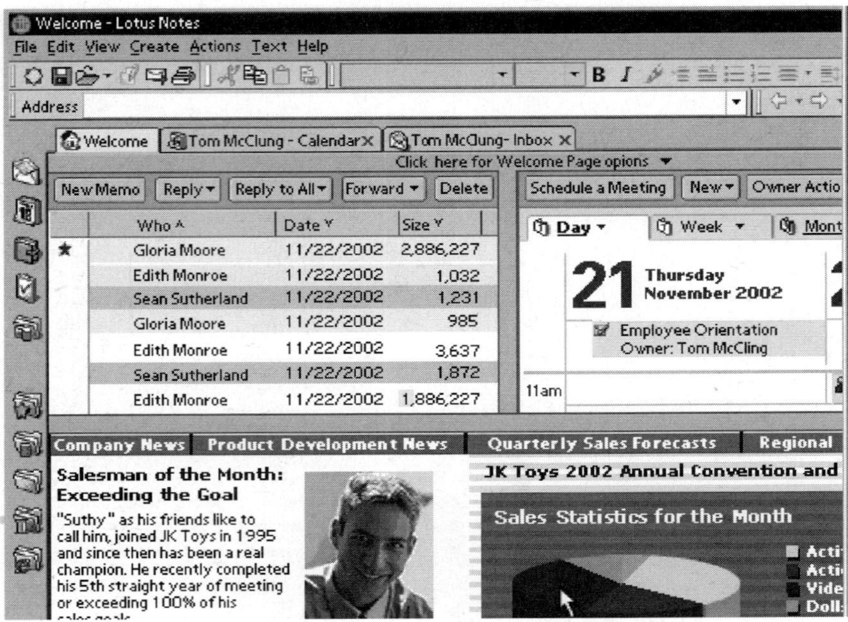

Figure 3: Example screenshot of Lotus Notes

MediaWiki

MediaWiki is an example of a Wiki engine, software that allows people to easily create, edit, and share content on Web sites and is especially suited for collaborative writing (MediaWiki 2006). MediaWiki is free server-based software. The fact that a Wiki allows people to easily and quickly change content on Web sites makes it especially suitable to support creative team processes. A good example to illustrate the possibilities of Wikis is Wikipedia, an online encyclopedia written collaboratively by volunteers using the MediaWiki engine, allowing most articles to be changed by anyone with access to a Web browser (Wikipedia 2006).

Groove

The Groove Workspace by Groove Networks, Inc. (Groove Networks 2006) is a peer-to-peer groupware application that enables people to cooperate using shared virtual workspaces. In addition, it provides synchronous communication via text-based chat and audio conferencing. Groove workspaces provide a cooperation environment in which people can exchange information and collaborate using an extensible set of tools, including a shared schedule, a collaborative editor, a file-sharing tool, and a shared presentation viewer. The Groove application, shown in Figure 4, provides services to see which of your contacts are online or active in the workspace, to invite (and uninvite) people to a workspace, and to assign roles to people and specify the rights associated with a role. In addition, the Groove Workspace application makes use of a groupware infrastructure that provides some value-added services, such as security, firewall transparency, and workspace synchronization after a participant has been offline. To do so, the infrastructure applies central servers, in contrast to the overall peer-to-peer philosophy.

GroupSystems

GroupSystems is an example of a group decision support system (GDSS) that allows workgroups to collaborate either face-to-face or remotely over the Internet (GroupSystems 2006). The software supports group processes by offering a wide range of functionalities to generate ideas, distill, clarify, organize, evaluate, and build consensus. Typically, organizations use a GDSS to increase the efficiency of group processes such as brainstorming, strategic planning, focus groups, requirements gathering, and idea management. An additional benefit is that the software helps in capturing intermediate results and documenting the process.

Skype

Skype (Skype 2006) is a *voice over-IP (VoIP)* application, meaning that it allows you to communicate by voice over the Internet. In addition, the application offers instant messaging functionality and presence awareness, indicating which of your friends who also use Skype are currently available for communication. Apart from supporting computer-to-computer calls, Skype offers value-added services for computer-to-phone calling (SkypeOut) and phone-to-computer calling (SkypeIn). Skype users can activate voicemail functionality, which allows people to leave voice messages when they cannot reach someone.

Windows Messenger

Microsoft Windows Messenger (as well as the related product MSN Messenger) (Microsoft 2006) is an instant messaging application that allows people to communicate in a synchronous manner using text messages. The application, shown in Figure 5, shows the presence status of a list of contacts, providing clues as to whether they are

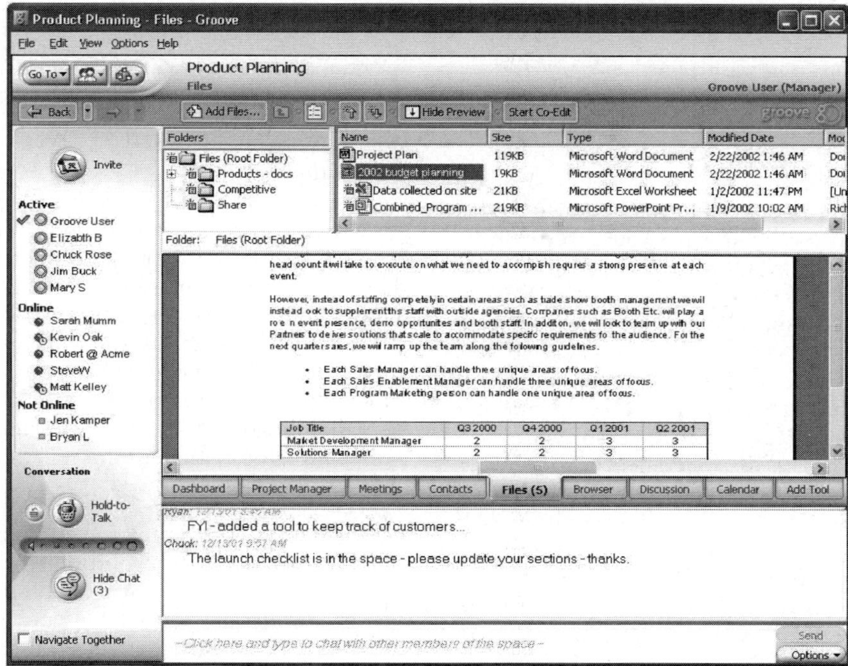

Figure 4: Example screenshot of a Groove workspace

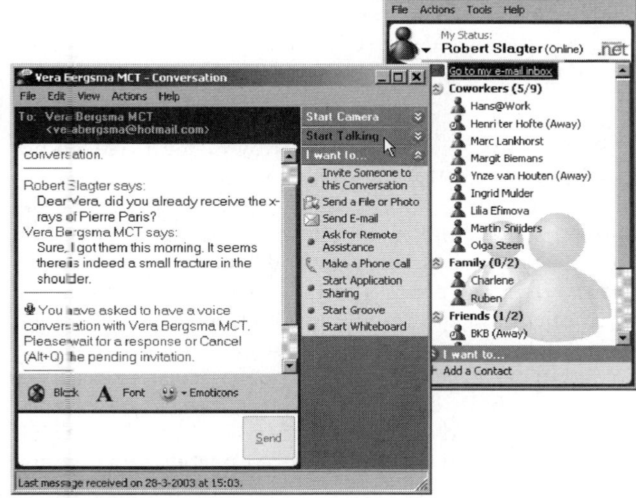

Figure 5: Examples screenshots of Windows Messenger

available for communication. The Messenger application includes facilities for voice and video communication, file sharing, and the option to collaborate using application sharing. The application also provides services to invite additional people to an online conference. The Messenger application relies on external tools for asynchronous forms of communication. The application does not provide support for access control or workflow management.

DESIGNING GROUPWARE

Groupware Design Issues

Although the biggest challenge in designing a groupware application is deciding what functionality to provide to the users and how to present that functionality, there are some other issues that groupware designers frequently face. In this section we address some of the technical groupware design issues. Many researchers focus mainly on these technical aspects; however, especially in groupware design, the "soft side" is also important. At the end of this chapter we will elaborate on a few of the social and usability groupware design issues.

All groupware applications in the "different place" side of Table 1 are distributed applications that use computer networks for communication. Especially applications in this category that include audio- and videoconferencing have strict requirements regarding network properties such as bandwidth, latency, and jitter. Associated with this, aligning video images and the corresponding audio is a frequently recurring design issue in groupware, known as the lip-synch problem.

When designing distributed groupware, one also has to consider the physical distribution of functionality: what functions are centralized on a server and what is placed locally, i.e., in the groupware clients that people use? Central servers may provide a higher reliability and more computing power, but locally placed functionality avoids network delays. In addition, in distributed groupware, different people may perform actions on the same shared object at almost the same time, whereas network delays are unpredictable. As a consequence, it is difficult to keep the different versions of locally stored replicas of a shared object consistent (e.g., Mauve 2000). To reduce the chance of inconsistencies, objects may be locked by a user. Even providing the "undo" function in this case is not trivial: What do you undo? Your own last action? Or the last action that was performed by any participant? And, what if you wish to undo your action, but somebody else already performed another action on the shared object?

Typically, methods based on operational transformations are applied to address these design issues, with the aim of preserving the intentions of all users.

Another groupware design issue is interoperability (compatibility); both the interoperability of groupware applications of different people (to make sure that people can use groupware from different vendors and still collaborate) and the interoperability of the parts of one groupware application (to make sure you can integrate functionality from different vendors in one groupware application). The latter integration of functionality is often practical from a user perspective, as different tool vendors are good at different aspects: for instance, one vendor may be good at making a groupware environment but not good at making shared CAD software, while another vendor is good only at making shared CAD software.

Deciding on the parts to distinguish in a groupware system, the responsibilities of these parts in terms of the services they provide, as well as their interfaces is an important design challenge. Various groupware reference architectures (as described later in this chapter) have been created to address this issue, but there is no accepted standard yet. Even the way the parts of a groupware system are described has changed; traditionally, the parts were described in terms of software artifacts, although more recently designers describe systems in terms of their behavior: the services a part provides to the groupware users.

Groupware Design Approaches

There are only a few design processes specific for groupware. Dewan (2001) proposed a development process for the design and the evaluation of groupware. He focused on the development of research groupware prototypes and their evaluation using self-studies, lab studies, and field studies. His approach concentrates mainly on the aspect of software design. To complement this, other researchers have added aspects regarding the explicit role of users in the design process, and described approaches on how to deal with typical groupware design processes, in which requirements are shaped as part of the process, for instance based on short iterations in which prototypes are developed and tested.

In groupware design, methods in which users participate in the design process, or are even involved as designers, have become quite prominent (e.g., Grudin, "Groupware and social dynamics," 1994; Slagter, Biemans, and ter Hofte 2001, Teege 2000). Since so-called agile software development approaches and the short development iterations they advocate are in line with the requirements of typical groupware design processes, such methods have also become prominent; for example, all of the approaches mentioned in this section can be classified as agile approaches.

Some methods also stress the importance of adaptability to suit changes in the way people collaborate. When collaborating users can perform these adaptations themselves, a system is said to be tailorable. The issue of designing tailorable groupware will be discussed separately later on in this chapter. Tailoring, as well as end user involvement, has been identified as an important factor in groupware development processes. Extended STEPS (Wulf and Rohde 1995), OTD (Wulf and Rohde 1995; Wulf et al. 1999), SER (Fischer et al. 2001), and OSDP (Schuemmer 2005; Schuemmer, Lukosch, and Slagter 2006) are design approaches that represent the state of the art in this area.

Extended STEPS

Extended STEPS is an iterative participatory development approach initially proposed by Floyd, Reisin, and Schmidt (1989) and adapted to the context of tailorable collaborative applications by Wulf and Rohde (1995). Extended STEPS combines evolutionary and participative software development with tailoring in use. The authors state that since tailoring can be performed by users, local experts, or support staff, the implementation time for small changes may be reduced significantly, which often appears to be critical to the success of an application.

OTD

The integrated organization and technology development (OTD) process is an evolutionary approach to appropriate group processes and technology to support the processes during system use (Wulf and Rohde 1995; Wulf et al. 1999). OTD is characterized by a parallel development of workplace and organizational and technical systems, the management of (existing) conflicts by discursive means and negotiation and design-time participation of prospective end users. As such, OTD includes organization development, evolutionary models of software development, work psychological analysis, qualification for participation, and tailoring in use.

SER

SER (seeding, evolutionary growth, and reseeding) (Fischer et al. 2001) is a groupware design approach focused around the notion that groupware should be designed as *seeds* that are able to evolve. SER advises a process in which developers and end users collaborate intensively, via a process of informed participation. The core concern of informed participation is to understand how collaborative design processes can be based on participation of the people affected by the decisions reached, the artifacts built, and the technology designed. Informed participation (and its conceptual embedding into the SER model) represents a framework for participatory design that is concerned with:

- The collaborative interactions that take place during the use and evolution of a system rather than just the original design and development of the system.
- Sustaining the usefulness and usability of technology in use over extended periods.

OSDP

The Oregon Software Development Process (OSDP) (Schuemmer 2005; Schuemmer et al. 2006) is based on a series of good practices, formulated as requirements for a groupware-design-process model. To meet these good practices, OSDP distinguishes four main principles:

- Fostering end-user participation
- Pattern-oriented transfer and capturing of design knowledge

- Piecemeal growth via short design and development iterations
- Frequent diagnosis and reflection on working practices and how the application supports the collaboration

An essential part of this development process is the use of patterns. These patterns are used not only as a means to capture and represent design knowledge, but also as a means of communication between end users, designers, and other stakeholders.

Given these different types of use, OSDP distinguishes two types of patterns:

- Low-level patterns targeted at software developers
- High-level patterns targeted at end users

Low-level patterns deal, for example, with class structures, control flow, or network communication.

High-level patterns focus on the system behavior, as it is perceived by end users, and empower end users to tailor their groupware application to meet new or changing requirements. In the extreme, high-level patterns describe how end users can select and compose off-the-shelf components to combine the groupware functionality they need. In that case, end users no longer need the assistance of developers or system administrators in implementing a pattern.

Groupware Architectures

Groupware architectures describe, on a high level of abstraction, the parts of a groupware system (typically in terms of functional building blocks), the relations between these building blocks and the principles surrounding why the decomposition is chosen as it is. In short, a groupware architecture describes the structure of a groupware application and a vision. This section discusses a selection of groupware architectures, to illustrate various decompositions.

CoMeCo

The CoMeCo Groupware Service Architecture by ter Hofte (1998) is a groupware reference model that decomposes groupware services into so-called grouplet service classes. The Groupware Service Architecture is named after the three grouplet service classes it distinguishes:

- *Conference management grouplet services:* These grouplet services provide users with the functionality to manage a set of online conferences, change conference membership, and, for instance, change the set of active media in the conference.
- *Medium grouplet services:* These grouplet services provide users all of the services required to support the interaction related to a single medium. In the CoMeCo Groupware Service Architecture, a medium may be a shared artifact, such as a shared whiteboard, a document, etc. It may also be a communication channel, such as an audioconferencing connection.
- *Coordination grouplet services:* These grouplet services may be applied to active media in a conference. When applied, they provide a coordination policy that specifies which conference members may or must perform which medium actions at which moment.

As illustrated in Figure 6, CoMeCo defines a conference as a collection of members, media, coordination policies, and subconferences. Media can, for instance, be shared virtual workspaces for indirect communication or conversation channels for direct communication. The CoMeCo Groupware Service Architecture has been implemented in a number of prototypes, including CoCoDoc and Media-Builder. The latter has been professionalized by Lucent Technologies into an application for high-quality audio- and videoconferencing and application sharing. CoMeCo does not specify the actions and interactions that take place as part of units of groupware behavior, nor does it describe the causal relations between units of groupware behavior.

Dewan's Generic Collaborative Architecture

Dewan (1998) has developed a generic collaborative architecture that can be considered a reference model for the internal structure of groupware applications. His architecture describes how collaborative applications can be designed using functional layers. Such functional layers can be shared (i.e., centralized) or replicated. The bottommost layers of the architecture, as depicted in Figure 7, are the workstation layers managing the screen and input devices attached to a workstation. The workstation layers are usually replicated to allow collaborators to use different workstations. The topmost layer in the architecture represents the semantic layer. Unlike the objects in the other layers, the objects in the semantic layer are themselves not an interactor for another object.

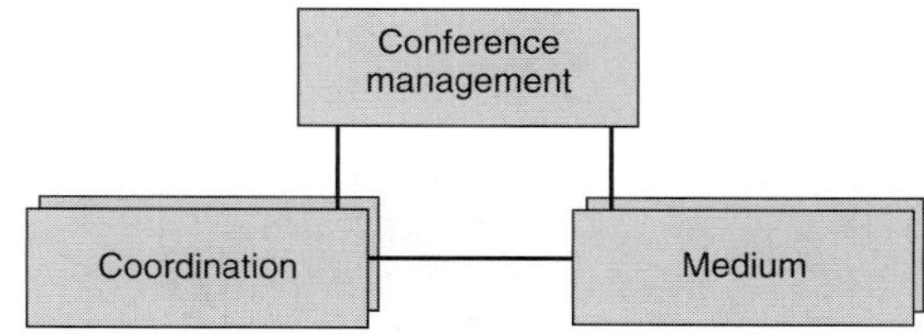

Figure 6: CoMeCo groupware service architecture

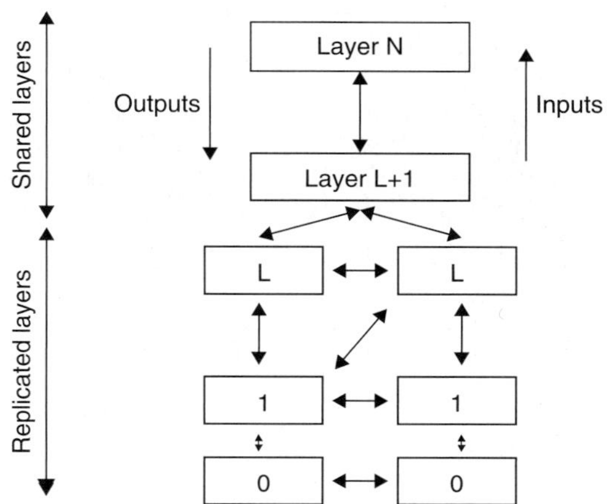

Figure 7: Dewan's generic collaborative architecture

Design choices regarding the sharing or replication of functional layers influence performance, ease of adaptation, and other properties desired by users and programmers of the application. Specifically, these design choices influence the following aspects of a collaborative application (Dewan 1998):

- *Single-user architecture:* What is the architecture for implementing single-user semantics?
- *Concurrency:* What components of the application can execute concurrently?
- *Distribution:* Which of these components can execute on separate hosts?
- *Versioning/Replication:* Which of these components are replicated?
- *Collaboration awareness:* Which of these components are collaboration-aware—that is, implement collaboration semantics?

Clover Architecture

Similar to Dewan's generic collaborative architecture, the Clover architecture for groupware defines several functional layers to implement groupware. As an extension, the Clover design model specifies at each layer a partitioning into production, communication, and coordination functions (Laurillau and Nigay 2002), as illustrated in Figure 8.

These production, communication, and co-ordination functions have been adopted from the PAC architectural model (Calvary, Coutaz, and Nigay 1997). In the Clover design model, *production functions* denote the functions needed to access and adapt a set of shared information objects (in Clover, denoted as a *caddy*). The *communication functions* allow for direct communication between the users of Clover. Finally, the *coordination functions* in Clover encompass functions to join and leave sessions, to create, join, or leave a working group, and to enter personal preferences. Note that these coordination functions correspond to conference management services identified in the CoMeCo Groupware Service Architecture, not to the coordination functions identified in that model. The combined Clover production functions and communication functions correspond to the CoMeCo communication functions.

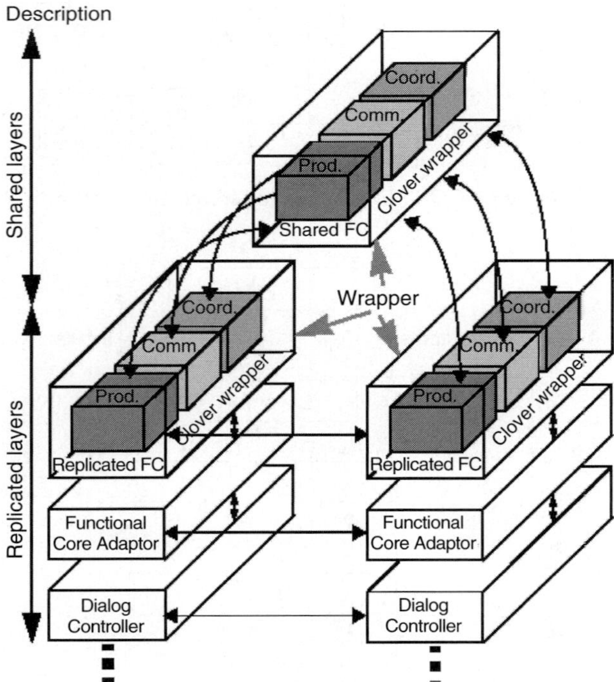

Figure 8: Clover architecture (FC = functional core)

CooPS

The CooPS groupware architecture (Slagter 2004) describes a structuring of synchronous collaborative services. The central principle of the architecture is that groupware applications should be designed in such a way that collaborating end users can select and compose the groupware behavior that matches their specific setting. The architecture provides a structuring of groupware services (i.e., groupware behavior toward collaborating people) on two levels of abstraction: it describes high-level types of units to construct groupware services behavior as well as the more fine-grained atoms to construct them. The first types, in CooPS denoted as groupware service modules (GSMs), are coarse-grained functional building blocks that group functionalities that are typically used together. These building blocks can be selected and composed by collaborating end users to tailor the groupware behavior to their needs and personal preferences. The CooPS groupware architecture distinguishes:

- Awareness building blocks, that support people in the process of launching collaboration (conference-listing GSMs and people-listing GSMs)
- A conference-management building block that provides all services related to started and stopping the conference, group management, and management of which coordination policy applies
- The coordination building block contains all services to actually specify the details of the coordination policy, such as a workflow, and to enforce it
- A communication/collaboration building block contains all services related to one collaboration function (e.g., audioconferencing, instant messaging, sharing computer-aided design drawings). A typical groupware composition includes multiple communication/collaboration building blocks.

Figure 9 illustrates the five main types of GSMs distinguished in the CooPS groupware architecture, which together provide collaborative services to end users.

The figure also illustrates that when zooming in on one individual GSM type, even smaller parts can be distinguished. In CooPS, these atoms are denoted as groupware service module elements (GSMEs). GSMEs are defined to provide one basic groupware service, and form the typical units of design and composition as used by developers.

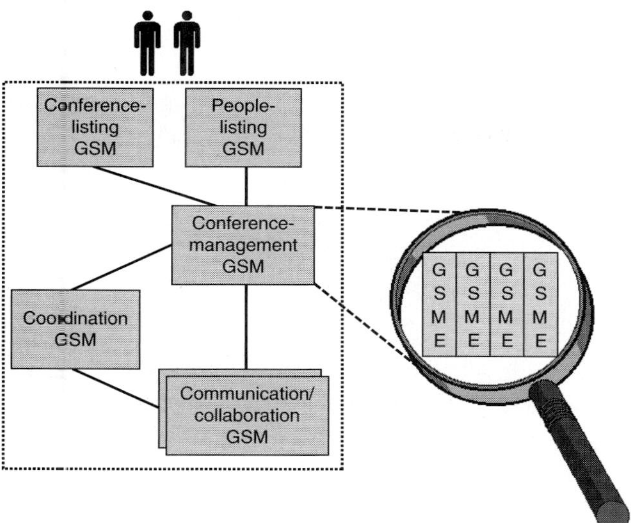

Figure 9: The CooPS groupware architecture (and zooming in on one GSM)

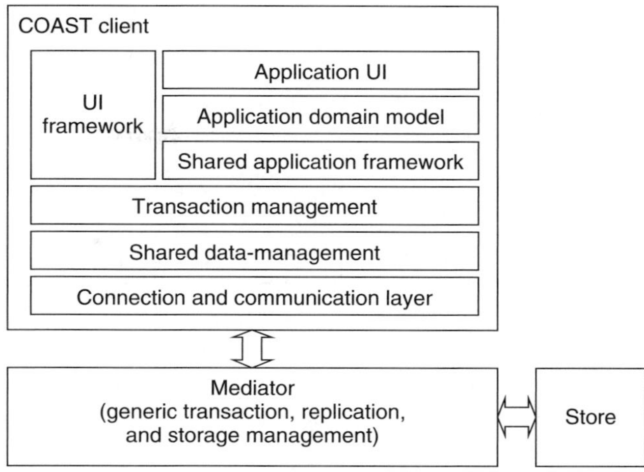

Figure 10: COAST architecture (UI = user interface)

Component Groupware Platforms and Toolkits

One possible way of creating adaptable groupware is to design these applications out of individual modules that provide a selection of groupware behavior. In that case, the behavior of an application is determined by the set of modules of which it is composed. A groupware application that is composed of such functional modules is denoted as *component groupware*. The following sections introduce various component groupware platforms and toolkits from industry and academia.

COAST

COAST (COoperative Application Systems Toolkit) is a toolkit that offers developers an architecture for cooperative applications and corresponding classes that can be used to implement such applications (Schuckmann, Kirchner, Schuemmer, and Haake 1996). The implementation of the toolkit does not require any specific platform (such as an operating system, user interface management system, or communication channel). User requirements are reflected in the following features:

- A replication mechanism combined with a fully optimistic concurrency control, which enables immediate processing of user actions independent of network latency
- A synchronization mechanism for replicated objects, ensuring fast propagation of other users' actions
- Dynamic sessions, supporting the flexible coupling of shared objects and users

The COAST groupware architecture, as depicted in Figure 10, defines a layered structure of groupware functions. End users can make use of the groupware functions through the user interface (UI) framework and the application user interface. The application user interface layer makes use of an application domain model, which in turn relies on a shared application framework. The clients of the various cooperating participants in a conference communicate through centralized mediator components, which provide generic mechanisms to transport information, for replication, and to persistently store information.

EVOLVE

The EVOLVE tailoring platform by Stiemerling (2000) applies an implementation architecture for distributed component-based tailorability for computer supported cooperative work (CSCW) applications. This architecture defines an extension of JavaBeans, called FlexiBeans. FlexiBeans solves some important issues that arise when using JavaBeans for groupware (e.g. the fact that JavaBeans has no mechanism to share remote objects as interaction primitives. The EVOLVE platform is based on a client/server architecture: the central server maintains, for example, the repository with components, keeps descriptions of the hierarchical component architectures of the applications, and manages the user accounts.

The EVOLVE architecture, depicted in Figure 11, defines both the client and the server side of a client/server groupware application. On the server side, the run-time control structures contain structural representations, denoted by a *C*, that define what components are combined in what manner into a groupware application. Such component structures can have proxy objects, denoted by a *P*, that reside either on the server or on the various clients. Each component structure can be instantiated several times, resulting in an equivalent proxy structure for each instance structure. During tailoring, the *C* structures are manipulated. All changes are directly broadcast to all instances (i.e., all *P* structures), which apply them to the running groupware application.

DISCIPLE

The DISCIPLE (DIstributed System for Collaborative Information Processing and LEarning) framework enables sharing of arbitrary JavaBeans applications in real-time synchronous group work (Marsic 1999). DISCIPLE uses a generic collaboration bus providing a plug-and-play environment that enables collaboration with applications that may or may not be collaboration aware. The framework

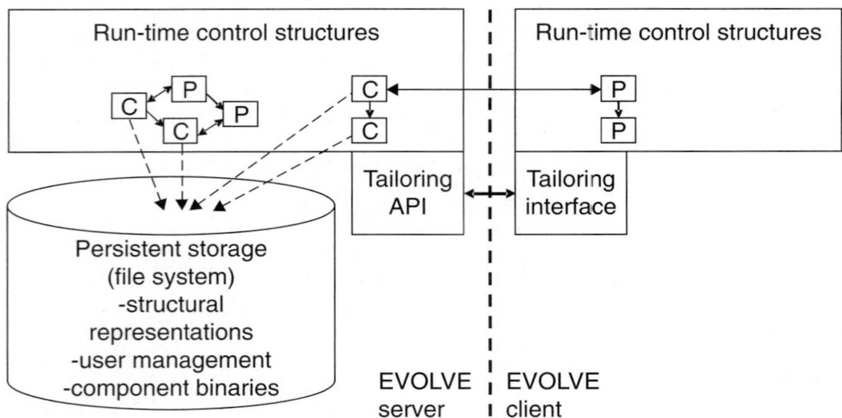

Figure 11: EVOLVE architecture (API = application programming interface)

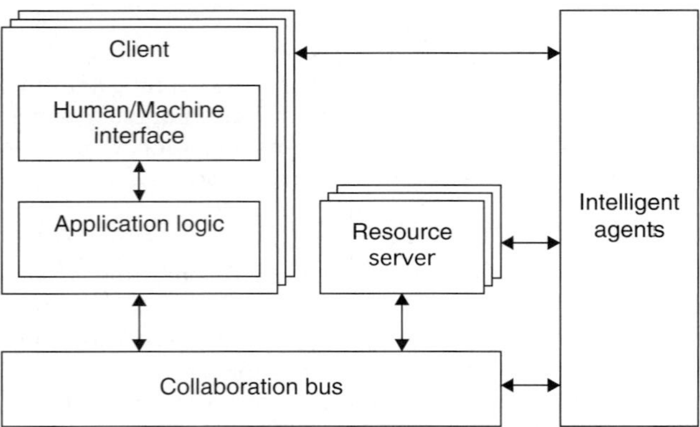

Figure 12: DISCIPLE architecture

defines a client/server architecture, as depicted in Figure 12, which aims to offer both a toolkit for development of special-purpose collaboration-aware applications and a framework for sharing existing single-user (collaboration transparent) applications. The framework is designed according to a layered architecture that describes, for example, at the client side, a multimodal human/machine interface layer on top of a layer with application logic. The latter layer makes use of the collaboration bus layer, which is the lowest layer. Spanning all layers is the intelligent agents plane, which provides separate knowledge mechanisms. DISCIPLE uses a hybrid form of a toolkit and a platform approach, specific for a component groupware architecture.

Groove

The Groove Workspace by Groove Networks, Inc., is a commercial initiative for component-based peer-to-peer groupware. The peer-to-peer approach minimizes the need for central servers and allocates as much functionality as possible to the systems of the groupware service users. In Groove, each participant in a conference has his or her own replica of the shared virtual workspace. This approach allows the users to fully control the application, while minimizing the dependency on other (economic) parties.

The Groove platform consists of a series of user interface components and a framework. The user interface components are connected by means of the framework, which provides basic functions. Such basic functions include security, firewall transparency, account and user ID management, and a basic service to synchronize the state of a workspace (described in XML) with the people with whom you are cooperating. The Groove architecture is shown in Figure 13.

Groove users manage and navigate workspaces through a so-called *transceiver*. Groove workspaces contain facilities for instant messaging and may contain multiple Groove tools.

The Groove platform comes with a set of reusable groupware tools that provide frequently needed groupware functions. More information on the Groove Workspace can be found at www.groove.net/products.

GroupKit

GroupKit is an academic groupware toolkit to support developers in creating applications for synchronous, distributed computer-based conferencing (Roseman and Greenberg 1996). GroupKit reduces the implementation complexity through some key features. The run-time infrastructure automatically manages the creation, interconnection, and communication of the distributed processes that comprise conference sessions. A set of programming abstractions allow developers to control the behavior of distributed processes, to take action on state changes, and to share relevant data.

GroupKit uses an architecture in which session management, conference applications and a central registrar are decoupled, as shown in Figure 14. All end users have a replica of the session manager and the used conference applications, while the registrar resides at a central server. GroupKit, created in Tcl/Tk, offers abstractions for multicast remote procedure calls, an event mechanism, and reading and setting environment variables. Furthermore, GroupKit offers a number of multi-user groupware widgets, which can be used by programmers in conference applications to satisfy some user-centered design requirements.

JViews

JViews is a toolkit for constructing view and repository components for multi-view systems (Grundy, Mugridge,

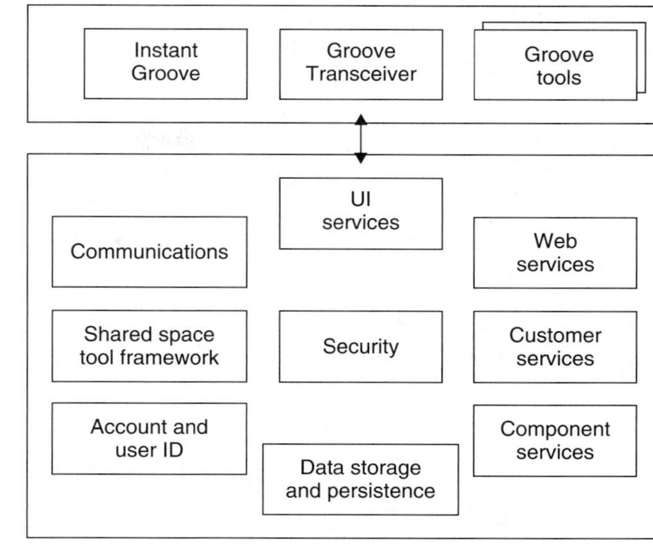

Figure 13: Groove architecture (UI = user interface)

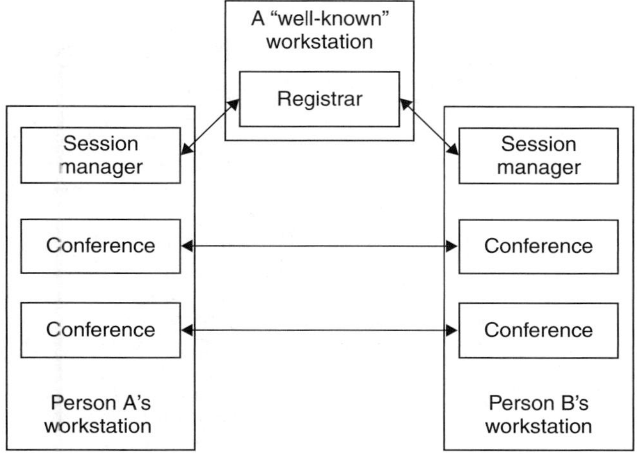

Figure 14: GroupKit architecture

and Hosking 1997; Grundy, Mugridge, Hosking, and Apperley 1998; Grundy and Hosking 2002). A multi-view system permits different, possibly overlapping, views on shared information. These different views may correspond to different end users. Consistency between the different views is maintained by automatically propagating changes to a shared repository and then to all affected views, according to the Model-View-Controller design pattern (logically only one model exists, which is associated with multiple views). JViews includes abstractions for view and repository components. The repository component corresponds to the model component in the Model-View-Controller design pattern (logically, that is; in fact, each user may have an instance of the model). Furthermore, JViews defines intercomponent relationships. The intercomponent relationships are used for data structures, to aggregate components, and to maintain intercomponent and intracomponent consistency.

The JViews groupware architecture, as depicted in Figure 15, defines a groupware client as being composed of three types of components with different responsibilities: collaboration clients (handling shared cursors, editing, and versioning of shared information objects), coordination components (handling, for instance, locking) and communication components for direct communication between conference participants.

GROUPWARE TAILORABILITY

As frequently stated in groupware design literature, in groupware one size does not fit all: the behavior provided by a groupware application has to match the requirements of the cooperative setting, in particular the task the people perform together. Moreover, the way people collaborate is likely to change over time, which requires a certain dynamic in groupware support for these processes (Bardram 1998; Bentley and Dourish 1995; Fischer et al. 2001; Kahler, Mørch, Stiemerling, and Wulf 2000; Stiemerling 2000; Slagter 2004; Koch and Teege, 1999; Zigurs, Buckland, Connolly, and Wilson 1999)

However, one cannot predict exactly how people will cooperate, and what changes may occur in the course of that cooperation. By investigating the dynamics of real life cooperation, it is possible to identify types of changes that are likely to occur. Based on this, one can derive which aspects of a groupware design have to be flexible in order to accommodate these changes (Bock and Marca 1995).

To achieve a proper match between the task and the technological support, typically denoted as the *task-technology fit*, it is possible to design an *adaptive* application: an application that adapts its own behavior based on the observations it makes regarding the way it is used. An alternative is that of *adaptable* applications. In the case of an adaptable application a human being performs the adaptation. To achieve a task-technology fit in an adaptable system, two means can be distinguished:

1. A good initial selection of groupware behavior by external experts, based on the characteristics of the collaboration "as is" and "to be." This includes the characteristics of the collaborating people, the tasks they perform together, and the context in which the collaboration takes place (e.g., in the office, on the road, or at home).

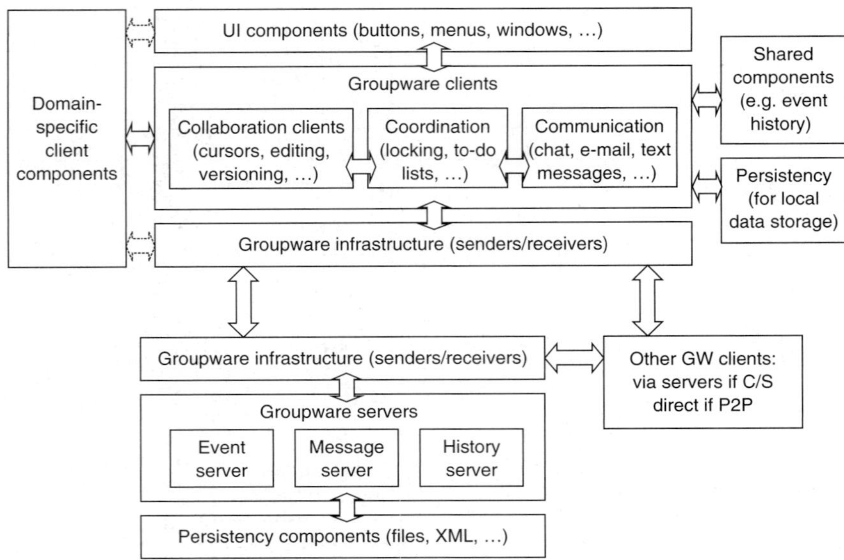

Figure 15: JViews architecture (UI = user interface; GW = groupware; C/S = client/server; P2P = peer-to-peer)

2. Allowing the collaborating people *themselves* to adapt the behavior of their groupware applications. Such adaptations by end users in the context of system use are denoted as *tailoring*.

Tailoring is defined as the activity of adapting a computer application within the context of its use (Mørch 1997). As such, tailoring is performed by end users, not by programmers.

Tailorability denotes the capacity of a computer application to be tailored. In both situations described above, people select, adjust, and combine the groupware behavior elements that suit their needs. However, the people who perform these operations differ in the two situations described above. In the first one, experts do the adaptations, while in the second one, the end users perform the adaptations. In the latter situation, one cannot assume an expert will be available to assist the end user. So, it is important to select a mechanism to adapt the behavior of groupware applications that is appropriate for experts as well as end users.

As indicated in Figure 16, tailoring is conceptually located between system use and programming: just like programming, it is applied to adapt the behavior of a system. However, the possibilities for adaptations are more limited than when programming. Tailoring is performed in the context of system use, but it is not the primary reason why people use the system: it is only a means, not the objective.

Tailoring is related to *appropriation*, which can be described as a collaborative effort of end users, who perform "appropriation activities" to make sense of the software in their work context. Besides activities to configure the software to fit into the technological, organizational, and individual work context of the users ("tailoring"), there is a larger area of technology-related communication, demonstration, and negotiation activities aimed at establishing a shared understanding of how a software artifact works and what it can contribute to the shared work context. The mutual shaping of the technology and

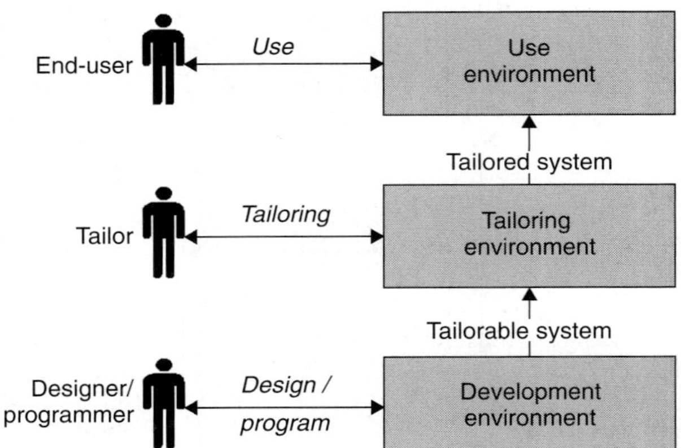

Figure 16: The relation between programming, tailoring, and use (Biemans and ter Hofte 1999)

organizational contexts resembles an ongoing design process that end users perform largely with no involvement of professional developers (Pipek 2005).

Apart from dynamic requirements, diversity is another driving factor for tailorability. Today, completely custom-built systems are the exception, because it is much more economical to tailor off-the-shelf products to an organization's specific requirements (Stiemerling 2000). On a smaller scale, the different users in an organization may have different requirements for their technological support, given their specific tasks and personal preferences. From the vendor's perspective, a tailorable software system promises to reach a larger market segment than a rigid one.

A third reason for tailoring frequently mentioned in CSCW literature results from the so-called *critical mass* problem (Markus 1990; Koch and Teege 1999): some groupware applications can be successful only when many people use the application. This has been found in e-mail, synchronous communication, and calendaring applications (Palen 1998). So, the acceptance of the software by all members of the group, rather than only by some individuals, is crucial to its success. This is, however, not always easy to achieve, since group members usually have different preferences (such as for a specific text editor), different experiences, and often heterogeneous skills and education (Koch and Teege 1999). Tailoring can help to overcome these differences, as individual group members can adapt the application according to their individual needs and preferences (Oppermann and Simm 1994), while still being able to cooperate.

THE SOFT SIDE OF GROUPWARE

The research field of CSCW, which includes the research into designing groupware, acknowledges that the success of CSCW depends on much more than a good technical design. For instance, insight in the nature of collaboration processes and human-computer interaction are essential as well. This section describes some of these aspects, which are sometimes referred to as "the soft side of groupware."

Adoption and Acceptance

Robert Metcalf's law states that the "value" or "power" of a network increases in proportion to the square of the number of nodes on the network. Applying this law to groupware, we state that the value of a groupware application increases in proportion to the square of the number of people who use it. Actually, many groupware systems require a critical mass of users before this value reaches the point at which the benefits outweigh the costs. For instance, having a videophone is useless if you are the only one who has it. Two of the most common reasons for failing to achieve critical mass are lack of interoperability and the lack of appropriate individual benefit (Brinck 2006).

Interoperability

In the early 1990s, AT&T and MCI both introduced videophones commercially, but their two systems could not communicate with each other. This lack of interoperability (compatibility) meant that anyone who wanted to buy a videophone had to make sure that everyone they wanted to talk to would buy the same system. Although some de facto standards have emerged, interoperability is essential to allow collaboration with people who use a groupware system by a different vendor. Important standards in the field of groupware are the simple mail transfer protocol (SMTP) for e-mail, the instant messaging and presence protocol (IMPP) for instant messaging, and the session initiation protocol (SIP) and session description protocol (SDP) as well as the ITU-T H.323 standard for audio- and videoconferencing.

Perceived benefit

Even when everyone in the group may benefit, if the choice is made by individuals, the system may not succeed. One example is office calendar systems: if everyone enters all their appointments, then everyone has the benefit of being able to safely schedule around other people's appointments. However, if it is not easy to enter your appointments, then it may be perceived by users as more beneficial not to enter their own appointments, while viewing other people's appointments (Brinck 2006).

This disparity of individual and group benefit is discussed in game theory as the prisoner's dilemma, or the commons problem. To solve this problem, some groups can apply social pressure to enforce groupware use (as in having the boss insist that it be used), but otherwise it is a problem for the groupware designer, who must find a way to make sure the application is perceived as useful for individuals even outside the context of adoption by the full group (Brinck 2006). Although theoretical models can estimate individual and organizational benefits, individuals may not care about the potential benefit of a system; they are likely to use simple heuristics based on usability and perceived benefit to decide whether they will use it.

Trust and Privacy

Over the past few years many researchers have investigated the role of trust in e-business and collaboration in general. These studies confirm that trust is an important requirement for effective and efficient collaboration (Bandow 1998; Daft and Lengel 1986). There are some interesting differences between building trust relations in more traditional settings and in computer-mediated communication. In mediated communication, some of the more subtle signals present in face-to-face communications are missing, as described in media richness theory (Handy 1995). The loss of such information is often considered to increase uncertainty, resulting in lower trust (Shneiderman 2000; Riegelsberger, Sasse, and McCarthy 2005).

However, this view has to be balanced with the fact that technology also offers options to supply information that would otherwise not be easily available (Whittaker 1996). A well-known example is reputation information. Web sites where people exchange goods can, for instance, collect feedback information about people who provide goods from the people who buy it. The aggregate of this information, presented as the reputation of the provider, is available to future buyers. However, gathering reputation feedback poses a challenge, as current buyers derive no direct personal benefit from sharing this information, while at the same time it typically requires an investment from them, for instance by filling in a feedback form.

Related to trust is the issue of privacy. When people use groupware, they frequently need to provide some information about themselves to facilitate the collaboration. For instance, while a shared schedule can be very helpful to coordinate the scheduling of a meeting, it also reveals much information about the people who have entered their appointments in the schedule.

One way to deal with the issue of privacy is to give users as much control as possible over what information is shared with whom and what remains private. Many groupware designs apply the principle of reciprocity: if a user wants information about another user, then they must provide the equivalent information about themselves. For instance, many instant messaging applications only allow you to see the status of someone else if you have granted that person the right to see your status.

Awareness

In addition to explicit communication, such as sending a message or speaking to someone, many group work situations benefit from implicit communication, such as indirect gestures, information about people's environment (whether their office door is open or closed), or biographical information about people in a conversation (what their job position is and what they had for lunch). Such information, referred to as "awareness information," helps people to establish common ground, to coordinate their activities, and to avoid surprises (Brinck 2006). One of the main research questions when designing groupware is to convey the right and the proper amount of awareness information: What information does one need about others for effective collaboration? It may, for instance, be helpful if I know when the others are available for communication, what they are currently doing, or where they are.

Awareness information can take many forms. In e-mail, information about the time and date of the message or the signature added by the sender provides context for making sense of the message. Instant messaging tools typically provide awareness about whether your contacts are available for communication. Some synchronous, text-based collaboration systems even provide awareness information of another person in typing a message, to subtly coordinate the actions of participants.

Obviously, awareness can be at odds with privacy concerns and, as the last section indicated, it is important to give users control over how much information about themselves is made available to others (Brinck 2006).

CONCLUSION

This chapter characterizes some existing applications for computer-mediated communication, denoted as groupware, and focuses on the design of such groupware applications. The examples of groupware functionality and existing groupware applications illustrate the diversity of the groupware landscape. After depicting this landscape, we have introduced some groupware design approaches. More than generic software design approaches, these approaches focus on the fact that typical groupware design processes are *learning processes*, not just for the prospective users, but also for the designers, who have to build a deep understanding of the collaborative setting to support.

Many collaborative settings turn out to be dynamic: the collaborating people themselves may change, the tasks they perform together may change, or the context in which they perform these tasks may change. These dynamics require flexible groupware solutions, as reflected by the fact that many recent groupware design approaches aim for adaptable groupware application. In fact, some groupware systems are designed according to an architecture that does not just allow developers to adapt the provided functionality, but even allows end users to perform such adaptations. The section on groupware tailorability goes more deeply into such adaptations by end users.

Finally, groupware design processes have a social-technical design: properly supporting collaboration requires not just appropriate technical facilities, but also requires insight in the social aspects around collaboration, such as acceptance, trust, privacy and awareness. From our experience we know that successful introduction of groupware in a work setting frequently also requires some organizational changes, and at least a deep awareness of the way people collaborate. That brings us to the primary rule of designing groupware: focus on the collaborating people, their working practices, and the services they require from the groupware application to support them in their collaboration.

GLOSSARY

Asynchronous Collaboration: A situation in which the collaborating people do not necessarily work at the same time.

Client/Server Groupware: Groupware applications that make use of a central server, typically as a virtual meeting place, for high availability or for advanced computing and storage capabilities.

Computer Supported Cooperative Work (CSCW): The field of research that investigates the social and technical aspects of computer supported human collaboration in professional settings.

Groupware: Any type of software application designed to support groups of people in communication and collaboration on shared information objects.

Groupware Reference Model: A model that prescribes the parts of a groupware system, the responsibilities of these parts and the way they interact. Groupware reference models act as standards and aim to increase interoperability.

Interoperability: When designing a groupware application out of different parts, one can distinguish two forms of interoperability: interoperability between the parts that form one groupware application (within an application), and interoperability between the groupware applications of different participants. In both cases, interoperability denotes the capacity to (technically) integrate parts or systems from different sources (such as different vendors) into a well-functioning composition. In the case of interoperability between groupware applications, this means that people can work together, even if they use groupware applications from different vendors.

Peer-to-Peer Groupware: Groupware applications that avoid reliance on central servers, but instead use the computing power and storage capabilities of the computers of the collaborating people themselves.

Social-Technical Design: Design processes that focus not only on creating appropriate technical facilities, but also on obtaining insight into and designing for the social aspects around collaboration, such as acceptance, trust, privacy, and awareness.

Synchronous Collaboration: A situation in which the collaborating people work together at the same time.

Tailorability: The ability of a system to be adapted by end users while they are using the system. In the context of this chapter, adaptations may range from changing the layout of the groupware user interface to selecting functionality to collaborate.

Voice over IP (VoIP): A class of collaboration functionality (both in hardware and software) in which the Internet protocol (IP) is used for transmitting audio between collaborating people.

CROSS REFERENCES

See *Client/Server Computing Basics; Network Middleware; Peer-to-Peer Network Architecture.*

REFERENCES

Bandow, D. 1998. Working with the Borg: Trust, systems development and dispersed work groups. In *Proceedings of the Conference on Computer Personnel Research 1998*, 163–9. New York: ACM Press.

Bardram, J. E. 1998. Designing for the dynamics of cooperative work activities. In *Proceedings of the ACM 1996 conference on computer supported cooperative work (CSCW '98)*, 89–98. New York: ACM Press.

Bentley, R., and P. Dourish. 1995. Medium versus mechanism: Supporting collaboration through customisation. In *Proceedings of the fourth European conference on computer supported cooperative work—ECSCW '95*, edited by H. Marmolin, Y. Sundblad, and K. Schmidt, 133–48. Dordrecht, The Netherlands: Kluwer.

Biemans, M. C. M., and G. H. ter Hofte. 1999. *Tailorability: The state of the art* (report no. TI/RS/99020). Enschede, The Netherlands: Telematica Instituut.

Bock, G. E., and D. A. Marca. 1995. *Designing groupware*. New York: McGraw-Hill.

Brinck, T. 2006. *Groupware: Design issues*. www.usabilityfirst.com/groupware/design-issues.txl (accessed April 11, 2007).

BSCW. 2006. *BCSW 4.3*. www.bscw.de/index_en.html (accessed April 11, 2007).

Calvary, G., J. Coutaz, and L. Nigay. 1997. From single-user architectural design to PAC: a generic software architecture model for CSCW. In *Proceedings of the SIGCHI conference on human factors in computing systems*, pp. 242–9. Atlanta: ACM Press.

Daft, R. L., and R. H. Lengel. 1986. Organisational information requirements, media richness and structural design. *Marketing Science*, 32:554–71.

Dewan, P. 1998. Architectures for collaborative applications. In *Computer supported cooperative work (CSCW)*. 7th ed. Edited by M. Beaudouin-Lafon, 169–94. New York: Wiley.

Dewan, P. 2001. An integrated approach to designing and evaluating collaborative applications and infrastructures. *Computer Supported Cooperative Work: The Journal of Collaborative Computing* 10:75–111.

Ellis, C. A., S. J. Gibbs, and G. L. Rein. 1991. Groupware: Some issues and experiences. *Communications of the ACM* 34:38–58.

Fischer, G., J. Grudin, J. McCall, J. Ostwald, D. Redmiles, B. Reeves, et al. 2001. Seeding, evolutionary growth and reseeding: The incremental development of collaborative design environments. In *Co-ordination theory and collaboration technology*, edited by G. M. Olsen, T. W. Malone, and J. Smith, 447–2. Mahwah, NJ: Lawrence Erlbaum.

Floyd, C., Reisin, F., and Schmidt, G. 1989. Steps to software development with users. In *ESEC '89: Proceedings of the 2nd European Software Engineering Conference*, 48–64. New York: Springer-Verlag.

Groove Networks 2006. *Groove*. www.groove.net/home/index.cfm (accessed April 11, 2007).

GroupSystems 2006. *GroupSystems*. www.groupsystems.com (accessed April 11, 2007).

Grudin, J. 1994. Computer-supported cooperative work: History and focus. *IEEE Computer* 27: 19–26.

Grudin, J. 1994. Groupware and social dynamics: Eight challenges for developers. *Communications of the ACM* 37:92–105.

Grundy, J. C., and J. G. Hosking. 2002. Engineering plug-in software components to support collaborative work. *Software—Practice and Experience (SPE)* 32:983–1013.

Grundy, J. C., W. B. Mugridge, and J. G. Hosking. 1997. A Java-based componentware toolkit for constructing multi-view editing systems. In *Proceedings of the 2nd Component Users' Conference (CUC '97)*. Munich, Germany: SIGS Books.

Grundy, J. C., W. B. Mugridge, J. G. Hosking, and M. D. Apperley. 1998. Tool integration, collaboration and user interaction issues in component-based software architectures. In *Proceedings of TOOLS Pacific '98*, edited by C. Mingins and B. Meyer, 289–301. Melbourne, Australia: IEEE CS Press.

Handy, C. 1995. Trust and the virtual organization. *Harvard Business Review* 73:40–50.

Johansen, R. 1988. Current user approaches to groupware. In *Groupware: Computer support for business teams*, edited by R. Johansen, 12–44. New York: Free Press.

Kahler, H., A. I. Mørch, O. Stiemerling, and V. Wulf. 2000. Introduction to special issue "Tailorable Systems and Cooperative Work." *Computer Supported Cooperative Work: The Journal of Collaborative Computing* 9:1–4.

Koch, M., and G. Teege. 1999. Support for tailoring CSCW systems: Adaptation by composition. In *Proceedings of the 7th Euromicro workshop on parallel and distributed processing*, 146–52. Funchal, Portugal: IEEE Press.

Laurillau, Y., and L. Nigay. 2002. Clover architecture for groupware. In *Proceedings of the 2002 ACM conference on Computer supported cooperative work*, 236–46. New York: ACM Press.

Lotus Domino. 2006. *Lotus Domino*. www.lotus.com/domino (accessed April 11, 2007).

Lotus Notes. 2006. *Lotus Notes*. www.lotus.com/notes (accessed April 11, 2007).

Markus, M. L. 1990. Toward a "critical mass" theory of interactive media. In *Organizations and communication technology*, edited by J. Fulk and C. W. Steinfield, 194–218. Newbury Park, CA: Sage.

Marsic, I. 1999. DISCIPLE: A framework for multimodal collaboration in heterogeneous environments. *ACM Computing Surveys* 31.

Mauve, M. 2000. Consistency in replicated continuous interactive media, In *Proceedings of the 2000 ACM Conference on Computer Supported Cooperative Work (CSCW)* (pp. 181–190). New York: ACM Press.

MediaWiki. 2006. *MediaWiki*. www.mediawiki.org (accessed April 11, 2007).

Microsoft 2006. *Windows Messenger*. http://messenger.msn.com (accessed April 11, 2007).

Mørch, A. I. 1997. Three levels of end-user tailoring: Customization, integration, and extension. In *Computers and design in context*, edited by M. Kyng and L. Mathiassen, 51–76. Cambridge, MA: MIT Press.

Oppermann, R., and H. Simm. 1994. Adaptability: User-initiated individualisation. In *Adaptive user support, Ergonomic design of manually and automatically adaptable software*, edited by R. Oppermann. Mahwah, NJ: Lawrence Erlbaum.

Palen, L. A. 1998. *Calendars on the new frontier: Challenges of groupware technology*. Irvine, CA: Information and Computer Science, University of California.

Pipek, V. 2005. *From tailoring to appropriation support: Negotiating groupware usage*. Oulu, Finland: University of Oulu.

Riegelsberger, J., M. A. Sasse, and J. D. McCarthy. 2005. The mechanisms of trust: A framework for research and design. *International Journal of Human-Computer Studies* 62:381–442.

Roseman, M., and S. Greenberg. 1996. Building real time groupware with GroupKit, a groupware toolkit. *Transactions on Computer Human Interaction (TOCHI)* 3:66–106.

Schuckmann, C., L. Kirchner, J. Schuemmer, and J. M. Haake. 1996. Designing object-oriented synchronous groupware with COAST. In *Proceedings of the 1996 ACM conference on computer supported cooperative work*, edited by M. Ackerman, 30–8. New York: ACM Press.

Schuemmer, T. 2005. *A pattern approach for end-user centred groupware development*. Lohmar, Germany: EUL Verlag.

Schuemmer, T., Lukosch, S., and Slagter, R. J. 2006. Using patterns to empower end-users—The Oregon software development process for groupware. *International Journal of Cooperative Information Systems* 15(2):259–88.

Shneiderman, B. 2000. Designing trust into online experiences. *Communications of the ACM* 43:57–9.

Skype 2006. *Skype*. www.skype.com (accessed April 11, 2007).

Slagter, R. J. 2004. *Dynamic groupware services: Modular design of tailorable groupware*. Enschede, The Netherlands: Telematica Instituut.

Slagter, R. J., M. C. M. Biemans, and G. H. ter Hofte. 2001. Evolution in use of groupware: Facilitating tailoring to the extreme. In *Proceedings of the 7th International Workshop on Groupware*, edited by M.R.S. Borges, J. M. Haake, and H. U. Hoppe, 68–73. Los Alamitos, CA: IEEE Computer Society.

Snyder, F. W. 1971. *Travel patterns: Implication for new communication facilities*. Bell Laboratories Memorandum.

Stiemerling, O. 2000. *Component-based tailorability*. Bonn, Germany: University of Bonn.

Teege, G. 2000. Users as composers: Parts and features as a basis for tailorability in CSCW systems. *Computer Supported Cooperative Work: The Journal of Collaborative Computing*, 9:101–122.

ter Hofte, G. H. 1998. *Working apart together: Foundations for component groupware*. Enschede, The Netherlands: Telematica Instituut.

ter Hofte, G. H., I. J. Mulder, M. Grootveld, and R. J. Slagter. 2002. Exploring a design space for place-based presence. In *Proceedings of the 4th International Conference on Collaborative Virtual Environments (CVE 2002)*, edited by C. Greenhalgh, E. Churchill, and W. Broll, 151–2. Bonn, Germany: ACM Press.

Whittaker, S. 1996. Talking to strangers: An evaluation of the factors affecting electronic collaboration. In *Proceedings of the ACM conference on CSCW 1996*, 409–18. New York: ACM Press.

Wikipedia 2006. *Wikipedia*. http://en.wikipedia.org/wiki/Wikipedia (accessed April 11, 2007).

Wulf, V., M. Krings, O. Stiemerling, G. Iacucci, P. Fuchs-Fronhofen, J. Hinrichs, et al. 1999. Improving inter-organizational processes with integrated organization and technology development. *Journal of Universal Computer Science* 5:229–365.

Wulf, V., and M. Rohde. 1995. Towards an integrated organization and technology development. In DIS '95: *Proceedings of the Conference on Designing Interactive Systems*, 55–64. New York: ACM Press.

Zigurs, I., B. K. Buckland, J. R. Connolly, and E. V. Wilson. 1999. A test of task-technology fit theory for group support systems. *ACM SIGMIS Database* 30:34–50.

Network Middleware

Linda Volonino and Pragati Dalal, *Canisius College*

INTRODUCTION

What Is Network Middleware?

Middleware refers to a broad range of software that enables communication or data exchange between network-based applications across networks. Specifically, network middleware enables data exchange by translating data requests and responses between clients and servers. This type of software is often described as "glue" because it connects or integrates business-critical software applications to other applications. By performing some of the tasks that an application would have performed, middleware eliminates the need for an application that is shared by multiple clients to function differently for each different type of client.

Before going in-depth on the technology let's see the difference between a *process* and a *service*. Any software application that runs on a computer is termed a "process." For example, Figure 1 shows the Windows Task Manager screen of WINWORD.EXE, a process that indicates that Microsoft Word is being used by the user. These applications are also known as "tasks."

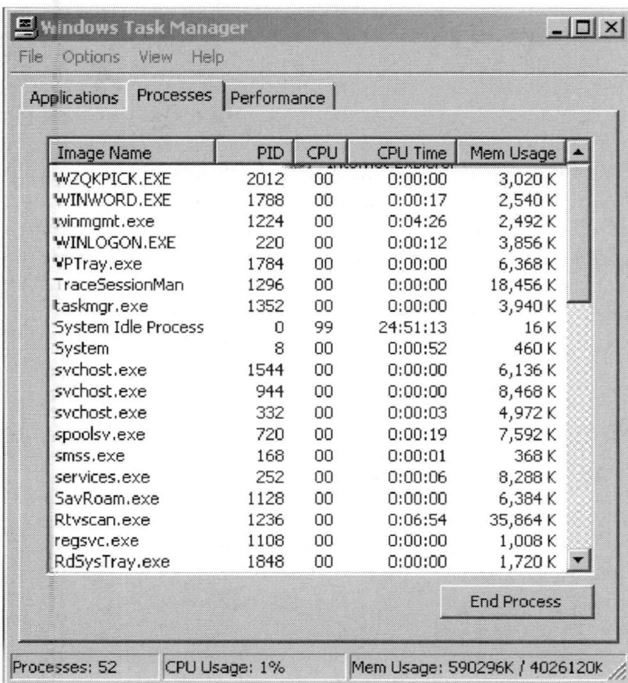

Figure 1: WINWORD.EXE

Software applications that do not require manual intervention are termed "services." They are started when the computer starts. Figure 2 shows such services.

The DHCP Client is a service that allows the client computer to communicate with the Domain controller and is responsible for obtaining an Internet protocol (IP) address from it when the user logs into the network.

These services run in the background without interfering with the user's interaction with the computer. They are different from XML Web services, which use standard protocols like HTTP and simple object access protocol (SOAP) to communicate.

Middleware Architecture and Services

Middleware typically runs as a separate service and on a separate server from the network operating system, but it may run on the same server. In a simple description of how it functions, middleware sits between two or more applications:

1. to accept requests for access to information or network services
2. to reformat those requests in such a way that the application (on the server) can interpret it
3. to send responses to those requests

For example, when a user requests information from a Web site's database, middleware provides the services for that exchange to occur. As such, it is also considered to be the "plumbing" or utility layer in networks. By promoting standardization and interoperability, middleware makes advanced network applications easier to use. Middleware provides security, identity, and the ability to access information regardless of location—in addition to authentication, authorization, directories, and encryption.

Figure 3 shows a generic middleware infrastructure. This diagram shows middleware acting as an integrator of applications and data and as a provider of secure connectivity and interoperability.

Because it is a general term for any programming that serves to "glue together" or mediate between two separate

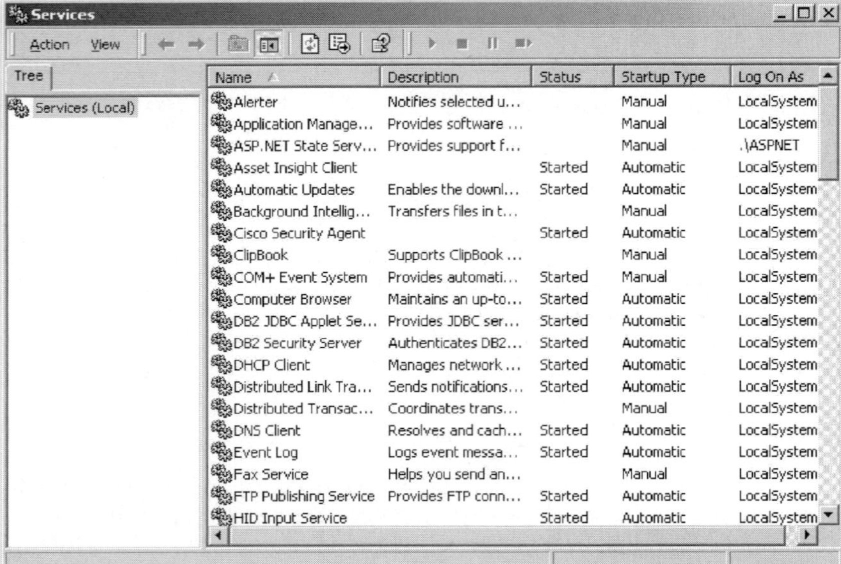

Figure 2: Windows

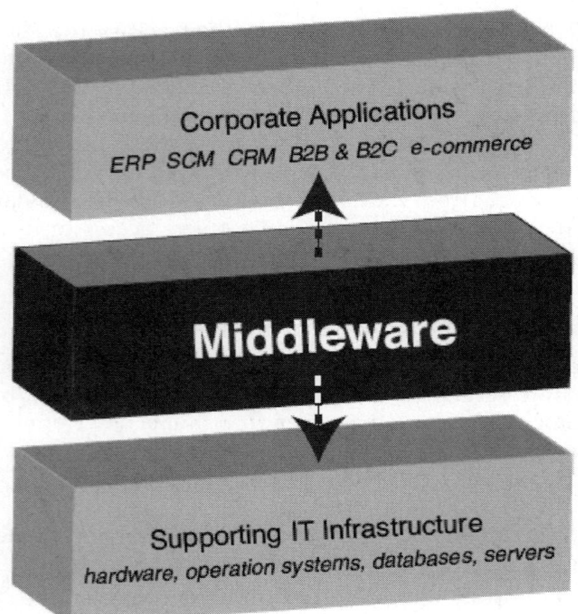

Figure 3: Generic architecture of middleware operating between the supporting information technology (IT) infrastructure and corporate applications (B2B = business-to-business (B2B); B2C = business-to-consumer; CRM = customer relationship management; ERP = enterprise resource planning; SCM = supply chain management)

and typically already existing programs, the term *middleware* is used to refer to either software or infrastructure. As software, it is the layer between a network and the applications that use it. In addition, middleware is an infrastructure that manages security, access, and information exchange on behalf of applications to make it easier and more secure for people to communicate and collaborate. It can be used to find people or objects (e.g., directory services).

Core and Industry-Specific Middleware Solutions

Business operations—especially enterprise resource planning (ERP), supply chain management (SCM), customer relationship management (CRM), and business-to-business (B2B) and business-to-consumer (B2C) electronic commerce (e-commerce)—depend on secured data transfers between today's networked-based applications.

Middleware programs are also used to provide messaging services so that different applications can communicate. This systematic tying together of disparate applications is known as enterprise application integration (EAI). A common middleware application is to enable programs written for access to a specific database to access other databases.

For end users, middleware makes sharing of network resources transparent and much easier. Moreover, it increases security by protecting against unauthorized or inappropriate use. The problem of security in a distributed environment is too difficult to be solved thoroughly by each individual application. Without middleware, applications would have to provide these services themselves, which could result in competing and incompatible standards—and increase the risk of unauthorized access. Therefore, having the middleware assume this responsibility leads to more robust and consistent solutions. This is done primarily through single sign-on (SSO) technologies. SSO makes it possible for users to enter their credentials only once and to remain authorized within the network until they log off. A widely used SSO technology is Kerberos. SSO and Kerberos are discussed in detail in the following sections.

For company networks or e-commerce operations, middleware plays a pivotal role in connecting enterprise information technology (IT) environments to the Internet. Secure connections are achieved using middleware to control access; that is, only allowing authenticated users, applications, or network end points to connect to an organization's services, applications, and data.

Some of the widely used middleware applications are distributed computing environment, common object request broker architecture (CORBA), and Microsoft's COM/DCOM. A new architecture known as service-oriented architecture (SOA) has become popular. SOA middleware is often deployed as a suite that includes an application server, repository/registry, security, and management tools. SOA is essentially a Web services–based IT infrastructure based around business processes and services instead of siloed, stand-alone applications.

Understanding the Concepts of Middleware

In today's distributed application environment it has become very important for one or more machines in the network to interact with one another, providing information/data needed by the processes running on the machines. To reach this requirement software programs are designed and developed that provide a mechanism to provide these services, these software programs are termed "middleware."

All applications are migrating from the mainframe days to a more distributed, or client/server, environment, Middleware has proved to be a very important piece in the framework to provide communication in a heterogeneous environment. Middleware can act as an abstraction for programming or as infrastructure. These roles are discussed further in detail later.

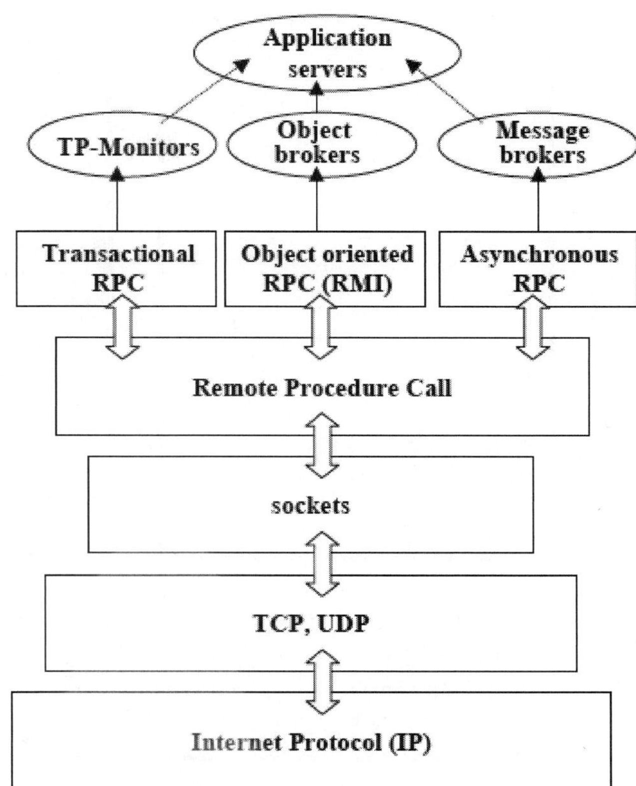

Figure 4: Structure of middleware (RMI = remote method invocation; RPC = remote procedure call; TCP = transmission control protocol; TP = transaction processing; UDP = user datagram protocol)

MIDDLEWARE PROCESSES

As just mentioned, middleware can either act as an abstract program or as an infrastructure. Let's see what this means.

Abstractions in Programming

Programming languages and software systems continuously evolve with levels of abstraction. The abstraction level can be between the platform and the hardware it is running on. Or the abstraction can isolate certain tasks that may be difficult, leaving it for the intermediates to handle. The intermediates can be compilers, load balancers, data allocations, etc. Because of these levels of abstraction, the numbers of errors are reduced during the development of software systems, resulting in huge cost savings in the maintenance of these systems. To aid in the development of these complex and distributed applications, middleware provides a set of abstractions. To understand how middleware platform functions, you must understand the programming model of the middleware. Looking at the programming model, you can determine its limitations, its usability, and its performance in a demanding environment. This understanding and insight will also give you foresight on the evolution of the platform when new technologies are developed and existing technologies are evolved. Figure 4 shows the structure of middleware.

Even though the important part of middleware is programming in abstraction, this is not the only important factor. If the implementation and the supporting system underneath the middleware are not good, the benefit of good abstraction is lost. A few good examples of this implementation are Java and the Internet itself. Java is a programming language used to develop software; it keeps the complexity of the underlying system specifications away from the coders. The only interface that a coder interacts with is the Java Virtual Machine (JVM), which is independent of the computer being used. Microsoft has come out with the .NET Framework that also offers these features. With this framework the deployment of code on different environments is easier because it helps standardize the abstractions needed in middleware.

The Internet is a network that needs enhanced abstraction. This enhancement is achieved with the simple object access protocol (SOAP), which is a part of Web services. SOAP is basically a remote procedure call (RPC) wrapped within XML and passed to the HTML page, which is easily transported across the internet. These features and middleware's role as an infrastructure are illustrated Figure 5.

Middleware's Role As Infrastructure

In the prior section, we discussed the middleware's role as an abstraction model in a programming world. As the level of abstraction in the programming area increases, the infrastructure that supports abstractions should grow as well. Each new functionality implemented increases the number of software, which proportionally affects the infrastructure in both size and the depth of complexity.

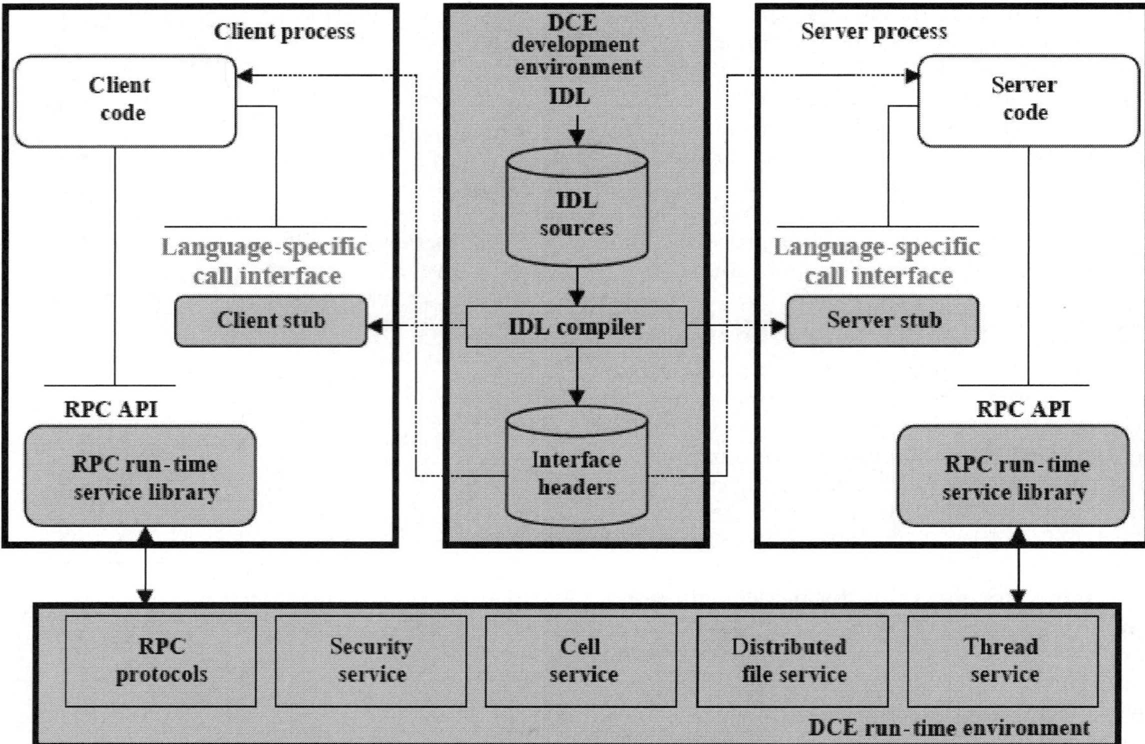

Figure 5: Middleware as an infrastructure (API = application programming interface; DCE = distributed computing environment; IDL = interface definition language)

Additional software layers require additional layers of abstraction. Another feature of the infrastructure is supporting the implementation of new functionality that will reduce the cost and increase the ease of developing, monitoring, and maintenance. It also handles attributes that are not functional, and hence are left out by models related to data, programming, and coding languages such as efficiency, managing available resources, backup and recovery, etc. The main intent of this infrastructure is to provide a robust platform to develop and run complex distributed systems. Because of this direction, software applications are purchased by single vendors to reduce the complexity and to interact with each other with minimal flaws. The goal is to integrate various platforms and to bring flexibility in configuration.

To summarize, middleware exposes a collection of functional APIs (application programming interfaces) in addition to the ones provided by the operating system and services running on a network. This architecture allows the complex application to perform the following:

- Locate and interact with other applications and services over the network.
- Act independently of the platform and network services
- Remain scalable to ever-evolving software applications without losing functionality

There are different types of middleware available, as described below.

Remote Procedure Call

The remote procedure call (RPC) (Figure 6) allows the application logic to be distributed over the network. The application logic on systems located remotely can be called as if it were located on the local system. RPC can help a programmer in implementing infrastructure for all distributed systems, which would not normally be expected of the programmer. It hides the complexity for distributed procedure calls and supplies interface definition language (IDL) to inform the services. RPC is responsible for creating code required for procedural calls remotely and other aspects of communications.

IDL is limited because RPC is a point-to-point protocol, and hence only two entities can interact at a given time. If more entities are involved, then RPC will consider each call among them as independent of each other even though that is not the situation. There may also be partial failures in the system, and recovering from these can be a complex process. For example, if someone placed an order online for an item, but the inventory was not updated, or someone paid for an order, but nothing was done to reflect this activity, then recovery from these errors would be not be easy. Attempts to avoid such errors through RPC creates an unmanageable situation.

Transactional RPC

To overcome the limitation of basic RPC, there is transactional RPC, which has a concept similar to that of RPC but also has transactional capability (Figure 7). This

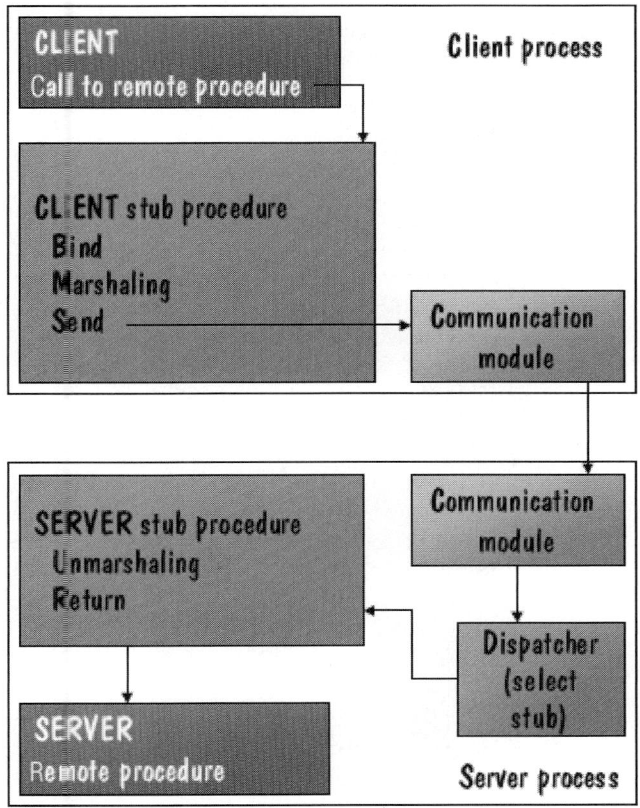

Figure 6: Remote Procedure Call

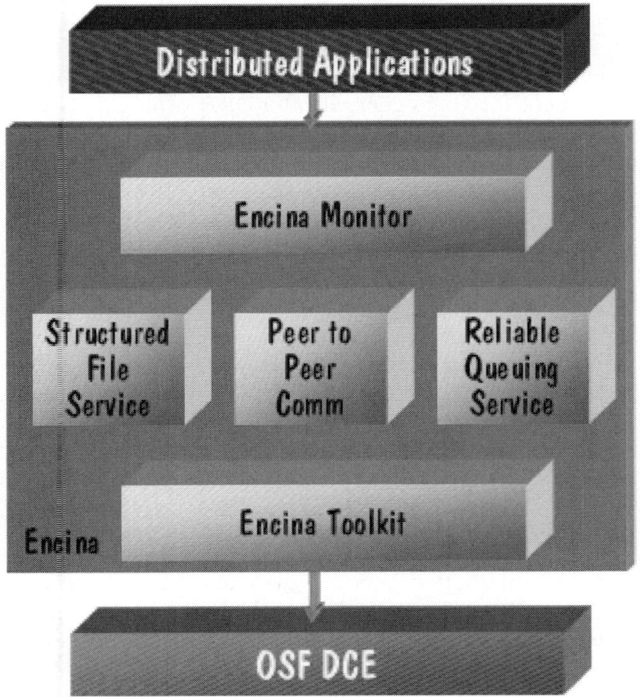

Figure 7: Transactional RPC (OSF = Open Software Foundation)

transactional feature is possible by introducing additional services or run-time supports and language constructs, hence bringing many RPC calls into a unit that maintains atomicity in a database. *Atomicity* means that changes to a database follow an *all-or-nothing* rule. Each transaction is atomic if when one part of the transaction fails, the entire transaction fails. It is critical that the database-management system maintain the atomic nature of transactions regardless of a hardware or software failure.

To make end-to-end transactions with a database it exposes interfaces that use the XA standard, which implements two-phase commit. With this connection type, resources that reside in resource managers that are connected to the region can be recovered. This is possible only with resource managers that support the XA interface.

Systems based on an RPC that supports transaction are TP (transaction processing) monitors, which are explained below.

Transaction Processing Monitors

Transaction processing (TP) technology provides the means to develop an efficient and reliable distributed client/server environment that can run transactional applications. It handles the execution of business logic and rules, updates databases, and keeps transaction systems under control. This technology was created 25 years ago by Atlantic Power and Light for their online support system, which shared information resources and system services with operating systems. This technology is used to manage data, access to the network, security, and processing orders. This is a good alternative in terms of cost as compared with upgrading database systems or system resources. Through application services, the TP monitor acts on various requests made by clients, hence the performance of the system is improved. By transferring transaction logic from the client side, the number of client upgrades is reduced. Because this technology is not dependent on the database architecture, it encourages the business model to be flexible and robust, increasing reusability.

Object Request Broker

Object request broker (ORB) middleware technology enables objects to communicate and exchange data. Since ORB technology allows developers to create applications by consuming different objects created by different vendors, as they talk to each other through ORB, it promotes interoperability in a distributed system. The ORB creates an illusion that the object consumed by the client resides on the local system when it actually may be residing on a remote system or another process. Hence, ORB provides the capability for the object to communicate across the system and across platforms. The ORB concept can be implemented in many ways, like compiled within the clients, as a separate process, or it can be included in the system's operating kernel. There are major technologies based on the ORB concept—Common Object Request Broker Architecture (CORBA), Component Object Model (COM) by Microsoft, and remote method invocation (RMI).

CORBA

The Object Management Group (OMG) came out with a standard, which acts as a base for systems based on

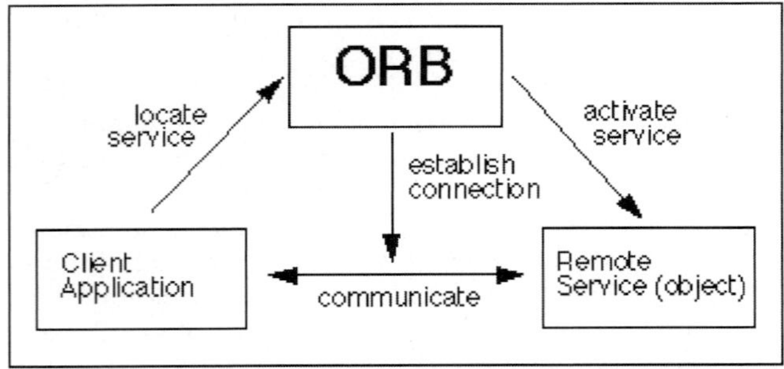

Figure 8: ORB. Source: http://www.sei.cmu.edu/str/descriptions/orb.html

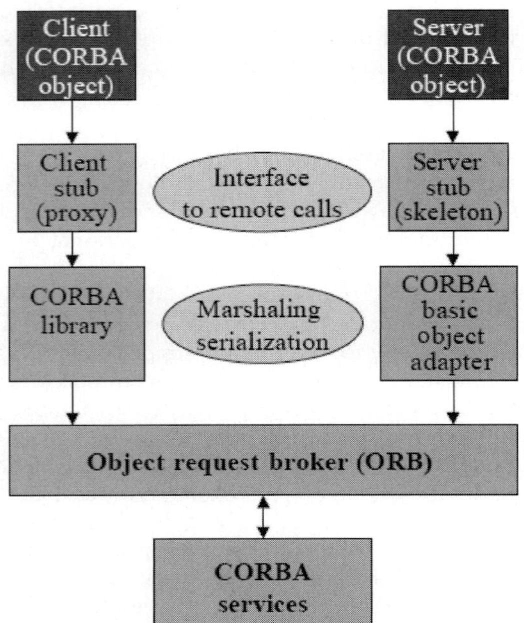

Figure 9: CORBA. Source: http://www.iks.inf.ethz.ch/education/ws03/eai/Lecture-2.pdf

components, that is, CORBA (Figure 9). Vendors use this architecture to develop ORB-based products, which provides the benefits of ORB, such as interoperability across various developing tools and operating systems. In 1988, OMG was created with more than six hundred companies from various spectrums of IT.

CORBA plays a significant role in object management architecture (OMA) that outlines various services needed to develop distributed systems. There is one important distinction between CORBA and OMA—the services that one expects to find in CORBA are actually defined in OMA. Figure 10 shows OMA.

Developing a distributed system is equivalent to using RPC. In this case, the definition of the services to be contacted is exposed by the server using IDL. The IDL compiler compiles the definition to produce a stub on the client side and a skeleton on the server side. A repository is maintained that contains information about the method signatures that can be called by the services. All the communication between the client and the server is done through stub and skeleton, hence removing the

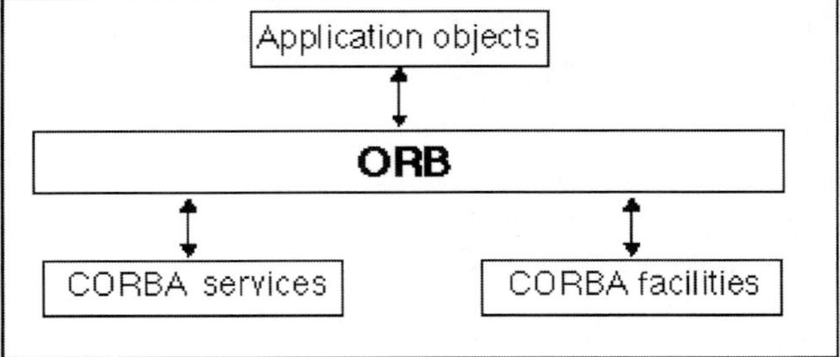

Figure 10: OMA. Source: http://www.sei.cmu.edu/str/descriptions/corba.html

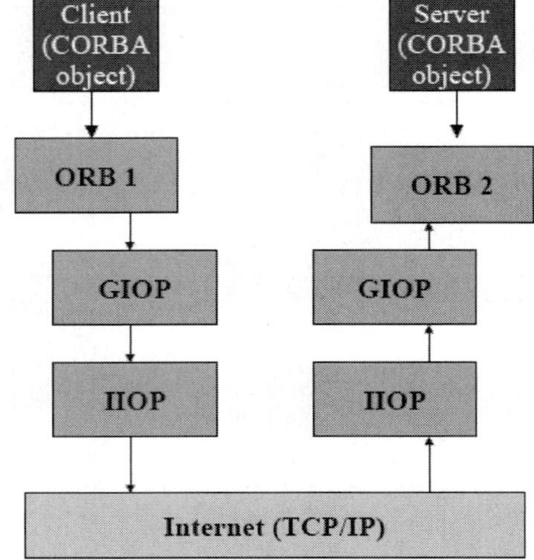

Figure 11: CORBA/Client/Server talk on Internet. Source: http://www.iks.inf.ethz.ch/education/ws03/eai/Lecture-2.pdf

dependency of client and server on developing language and the operating system. To ensure that ORB is a universal component architecture, there needs to be ways in which ORBs can talk to each other. CORBA provides a protocol for this—general inter-ORB protocol (GIOP) which defines how the ORBs send and receive calls with each other. Another protocol that converts the GIOP messages into TCP/IP is Internet inter-ORB protocol (IIOP), shown in Figure 11. All these protocols have been superseded by Web services.

Message-Oriented Middleware

Message-oriented middleware (MOM) is client/server architecture that uses synchronous communication between components, which is called as request/response model. In this model, the client component sends a request and waits for a response from the server component. This is similar to RPC, discussed earlier. Figure 12 shows typical client/server calls.

There are some disadvantages in this type of architecture. For interaction between the client component and the server component to be synchronous both need to be available. The client sends in a request and the server component works on it and then responds back to the client with the results. The client has to wait for the server to respond, as shown in Figure 13, which is referred to as *idle time*.

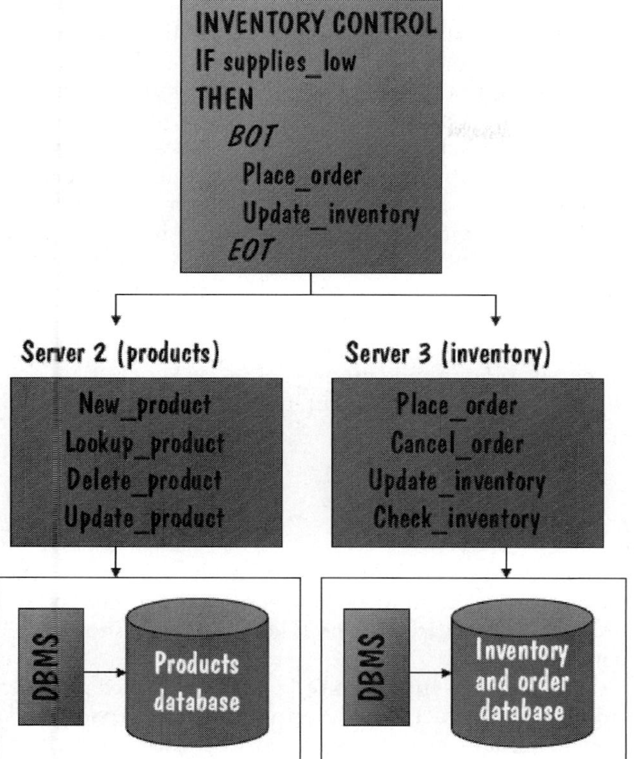

Figure 12: MOM architecture (DBMS = database-management system) (Courtesy of the Swiss Federal Institute of Technology, www.iks.inf.ethz.ch/education/ws03/eai/Lecture-5.pdf)

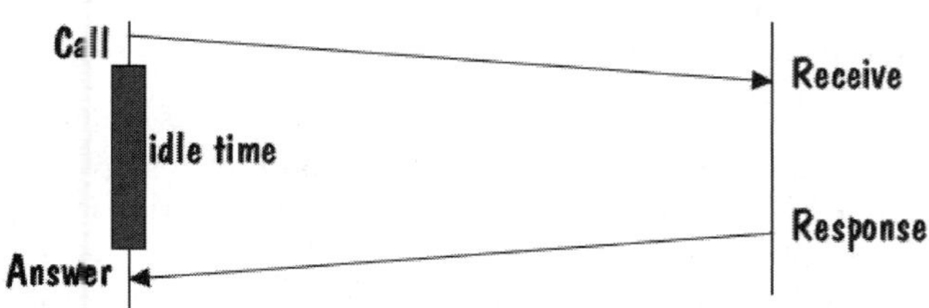

Figure 13: Idle time (Courtesy of Swiss Federal Institute of Technology, www.iks.inf.ethz.ch/education/ws03/eai/Lecture-5.pdf)

During a client call when the server is not available, CORBA or DCOM will instantiate it, which creates overhead. This connection creates a high risk of failure, and makes it difficult to recognize and react to failures. This architecture is more a one-to-one environment, and is not practical in distributed environments. Maintenance of these sessions is expensive and uses up a lot of the CPU's time. There is a fixed number of sessions available at one particular time, thus limiting the number of simultaneous connections. Connection pooling was introduced to overcome this limitation. The risk with synchronous communication is that if either the client or the server component fails, then the context is missing and resynchronization becomes difficult. Determining the time at which the failure took place will be difficult, and if there was a chain of activities then it will be difficult to find the exact location of the failure.

There are two solutions to overcome the limitations of the client/server model discussed above:

- **Improving Support**—Middleware for the client/server model provides mechanisms to handle problems due to synchronous calls, such as transactional RPC, load balancing, and replication of service; this will ensure that the service on the other system is available for the client if the current server is going down for maintenance.
- **Asynchronous Communication**—In this approach, the client component will send a message, and it will be stored until the server component accesses it. There are two ways of handling this—asynchronous RPC and queues.
  - **Asynchronous RPC**—In this case, the client component sends a request to the server component and the control returns to client. The client component has to make a second request to access results from the server component. Figure 14 shows this mechanism.
  - **Queues**—In this case, the client interact with server using messages. These messages are persistent by putting them in queues, making the system flexible (Figure 15).

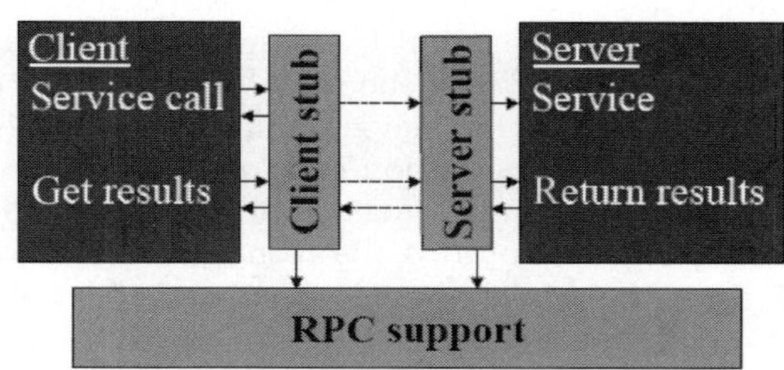

Figure 14: Asynchronous RPC (Courtesy of Swiss Federal Institute of Technology, www.iks.inf.ethz.ch/education/ws03/eai/Lecture-5.pdf)

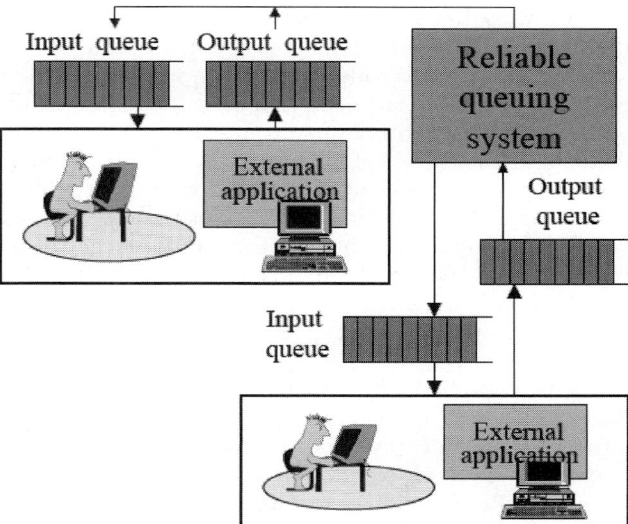

Figure 15: Queues (Courtesy of Swiss Federal Institute of Technology, www.iks.inf.ethz.ch/education/ws03/eai/Lecture-5.pdf)

Since the queues persist, the messages stored in them are available any time the application(s) start listening to the queues, which makes this a very good choice for a distributed and complex environment.

To facilitate distributed components in communicating with each other using messages and queues, a middleware has been developed called message-oriented middleware (MOM). This architecture moves the standard client/server to a more peer-to-peer communication between components. This allows the client component to send messages to components residing on the server in a distributed environment. In return, the server component sends a response message that contains detail about the execution result. This type of message communication between the distributed components is handled by queues. The messages sent by clients are placed in the queues and remain there until the server components start listening to the queues. Using the queue as a mechanism of communication makes delivery of messages asynchronous, which is the strength of MOM. The queues provide fault tolerance along with overall flexibility. The queues also provide a bridge between heterogeneous environments.

By using queues, the problems faced in the client/server model have been solved. Now that the message is persistent, if the node goes down the message will remain in the queue and is not lost. When the node comes back online, the application listening to the queue will check for messages. The queue can also serve more than one application, hence achieving multiplexing. With the use of queues, the application can merge the following into one transaction: retrieving and processing data from the queue, and then putting the response back into the queue. If anything fails, the queue ensures that consistency is maintained in any scenario.

Because of this asynchronous behavior, the clients can perform other functions until they receive a response from the server. This independence between client and server components creates more scalable architectures or applications. Another MOM strength is that it can provide the same message to a group of client components. The benefit in a workflow environment is that any client knows the status of the task and can take action accordingly.

Although MOM provides features for a real distributed environment, there are disadvantages. It becomes difficult to provide synchronous calls, making it necessary to do them manually. Scalability is provided by MOM, but it becomes complicated because MOM does not have transparent accessibility. Because clients use queues to talk to remote components, their availability for local calls is reduced. Both client and remote components have queue details hard-coded into them, which make them less flexible and less manageable.

Service-Oriented Architecture

Service-oriented architecture (SOA) has gained popularity recently, but this idea has been around since the mid-1980s. Because of limitations or nonavailability of standard APIs or middleware, this concept did not become popular. CORBA and the distributed computing environment were early attempts to bring this concept into use, but there were no significant applications to show the potential of this concept. With the introduction of Web services, the concept of SOA was given a boost, since the underlying architecture of Web Service unites with the concept perfectly.

Since both SOA and Web services architecture expose the services as an XML-based interface, it makes them in sync with each other. The only way these two differ is how they are implemented. Many of times Web services are implemented as point-to-point, which means that the Web Service cannot be discovered, since it is not public. In the case of SOA, universal description, discovery, and integration (UDDI) contains key information about the Web Service interface and methods to contact it. Because of this, it is easy to discover the Web Service to be consumed by other applications.

Any SOA architecture will include the following

- Service provider
- Service consumer
- Messaging infrastructure

What needs to be implemented in the SOA is the service consumer, the contract between the consumer and the provider of the service. The following figure shows SOA concepts in play.

It can be seen from Figure 16 that the service provider supplies a contract and description of the service to be used. The data model associated with the service is referred to by the service description. The service description can be published using any of the many available methods, such as pull or push. Once the service is discovered it does not mean it accepted the contract or will be called; it merely gives information about the interfaces provided by the service.

There are various advantages that businesses are looking at in SOA. Some are listed below:

- Cost Effectiveness. Since the financial budgets are limited SOA helps in reusing already developed services hence saves time and money for new applications.
- Providing flexibility to adapt ever changing technologies quickly.
- Extending the functionality of the application beyond firewall without compromising on infrastructure security.

MIDDLEWARE SERVICES

Before a subject can be authenticated, it has to be tagged with an identifier—a unique way of naming something. A social security number or personal e-mail address is an identifier because each uniquely names an individual—that is, unless two or more people share an e-mail account. In middleware, identifiers can name anything, including abstract concepts such as certain applications or a certain security clearance. The entity named by the identifier is known as its subject.

The key middleware defense services providing access control are authentication, authorization, directories, application programming interfaces (APIs), and abstraction.

We have seen above how abstraction services in middleware provide defense mechanisms. Below, we will briefly address the others defenses.

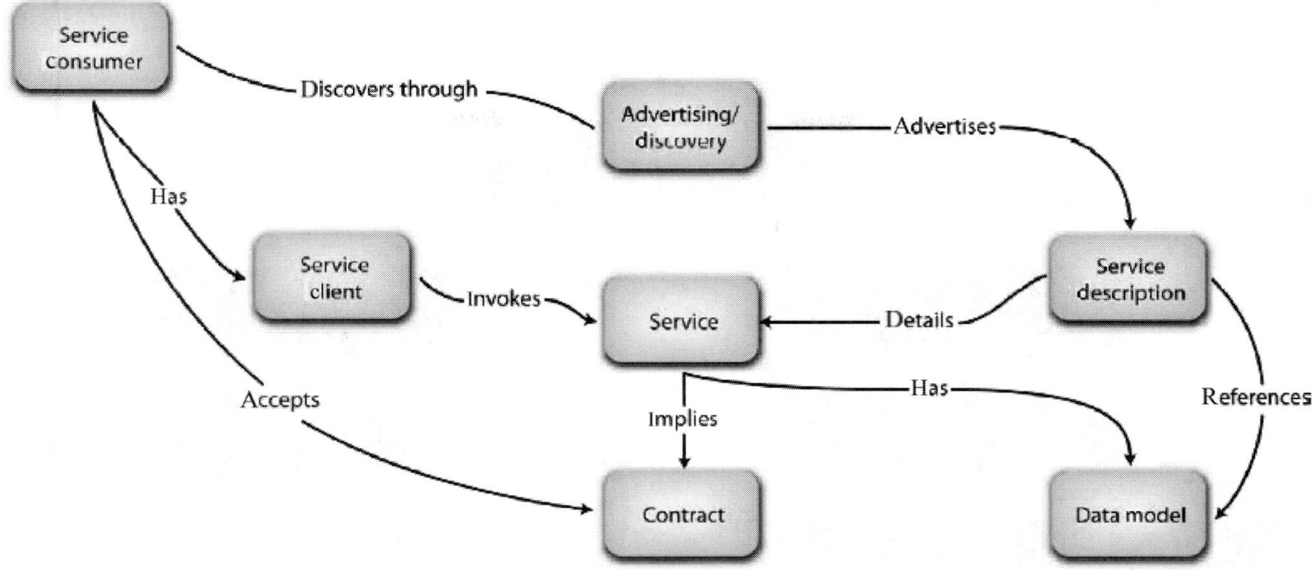

Figure 16: SOA CONCEPTS
(Courtesy of Adobe, www.adobe.com/enterprise/pdfs/Services_Oriented_Architecture_from_ Adobe.pdf)

Authentication

Authentication is the process of providing a private piece of information or physical token to establish whether a subject is who or what its identifier (e.g., username) claims it is. During authentication, a user or object proves it is the subject of an identifier. This service is generally performed by the middleware layer so that applications above it do not need to have their own authentication mechanism.

Identity is authenticated by the presentation of digital credentials. As explained previously, a user must present credentials to a network to gain access to it. In the case of people, the most common credentials used for confirming identity include:

- Something the subject knows, such as a password
- Something the subject has, such as a USB token, digital ID (certified public/private key), smartcards, or challenge-response mechanisms
- Something the subject is, such as photo identification, fingerprints, or biometrics.

As such, authentication is the validation of a user's electronic identity based on proof provided by that user, typically a unique user id/password pair. If a user cannot be authenticated, then he or she would not be granted access to nonpublic network services.

Authentication is most frequently done by asking a user to enter a username and password. Although there are more secure approaches, passwords are often transmitted through open communication channels. The quality of the authentication depends on the guarantee that can be given that the authentication process was not fraudulent or compromised by a hacker attack, such as correctly guessing a password.

The primary issues to be considered about any authentication system pertain to how secure or strong the authentication process is. The security of any authentication process depends on several variables, primarily the number of factors used to authenticate a subject. Single-factor authentication, such as using only a password, is much less secure than using a USB token activated by a password, which would be a two-factor authentication.

Figure 17 illustrates and describes the steps involved in authentication in a distributed environment, such as secure Web pages. Several of the concepts illustrated in this figure, e.g., Kerberos, are described in subsequent sections.

Steps

1. User's browser requests the secure page from the local Web server. (Go to step 2.)
2. Local Web server checks: Does user's browser have a cookie? (Go to either step 2A or 2B.)
   - A. Yes. (Go to 2Ai.)
     - i. Cookie is present. Local Web server contacts application for service (AFS) server. (Go to step 2Aii.)
     - ii. Does the cookie content correlate with the AFS file? (Go to step 2Aiia or 2Aiib.)
       - a. Yes.
         - The cookie is valid.
         - The local Web server displays the secure page.
       - b. No.
         - The cookie is invalid. Need a different cookie. (Go to step 2Bii.)
   - B. No. (Go to step 2Bi.)
     - i. Cookie is not present. (Go to step 2Bii.)
     - ii. Local Web server passes the user's browser to the secure Web server. (Go to step 2Biii.)

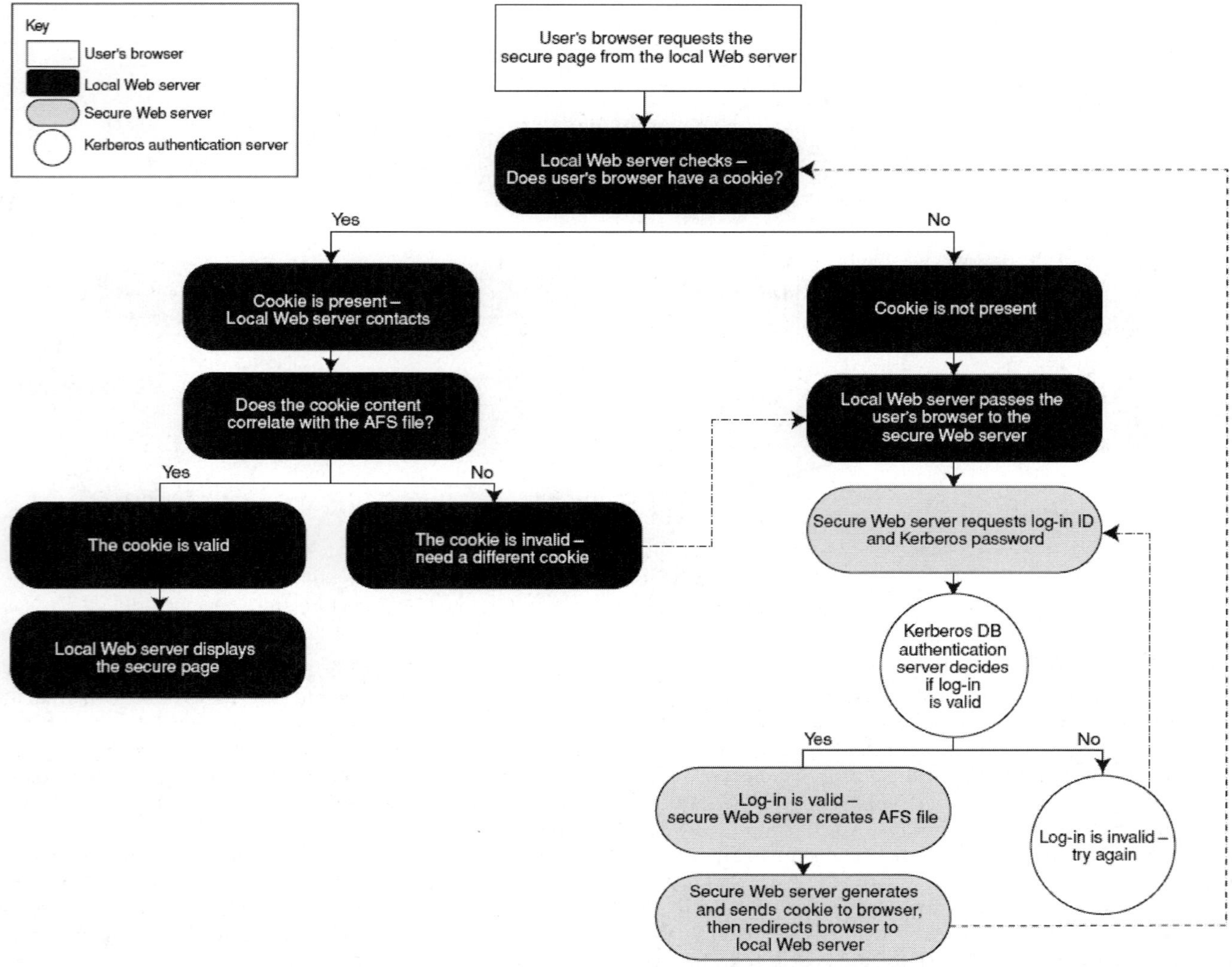

Figure 17: Distributed authentication steps for Web server access Flowchart model of distributed authentication for secure Web pages. *Source:* http://distauth.ucdavis.edu/docs/dachart.html. (AFS = application for service; DB = database)

iii. Secure Web server requests login ID and Kerberos password. (Go to step 2Biv.)

iv. Kerberos database (DB) authentication server decides whether log-in is valid. (Go to step 2Biva or 2Bivb.)

a. Yes.

- Log-in is valid. Secure Web server creates AFS file.
- Secure Web server generates and sends cookie to browser, then redirects browser to local Web server. (Go to step 2.)
- Local web server displays the secure page.

b. No.

- Log-in is invalid. Try again. (Go to step 2Biii.)

Authorization and Directories

Once authentication has been performed, more credentials or attributes are needed for a subject before that subject can be given access permissions. Authorization is a process of determining whether to allow a subject access to a specific resource or service or another subject. It is also the process of assigning authenticated subjects the rights to carry out specific operations.

Having only one valid identifier does not provide enough information about a subject. Although an authenticated identity may be sufficient for some purposes, it is often important to acquire more information, such as preferences, e-mail aliases, electronic credentials, etc. Identifiers become far more powerful when they are combined with a technology known as directories. Along with its many other uses, a directory links an identifier with other attributes about a common subject.

A directory stores and regulates permissions, such as viewing files. Directories are, in effect, databases composed of many sets of information with a similar format. A set of information is generally called an "entry," and a piece of information within an entity is called an "attribute." A primary function of a directory is to look up a given attribute from a given entry, such as a user's read or write privileges for a specific object (e.g., payroll file). Because directories make information available, access to them must also be adequately protected. Access controls can be set to regulate who can read or update specific directory fields.

The two major technical components of a middleware implementation are client software and enterprise middleware servers that provide authentication and directories. The client side does not require much work because most middleware functions can be performed by existing programs, such as Web browsers and e-mail clients. In contrast, the server side needs to perform many new services. The middleware system must provide an effective and secure layer for communication between client and server. The major client-side technological challenge is establishing the authentication system. Although these systems can be built around passwords, public keys, smart cards, or other schemes, these must be available on every machine that a user will want to use to authenticate to the middleware server.

Application Programming Interfaces

Application programming interfaces (APIs) exist for (almost) all middleware products and establish the interface with which clients (applications) request services of the servers. In other words, APIs are part of all types of middleware, not a separate type. APIs provide for data sharing across different platforms. Specifically, an API is a set of standards and protocols by which a software application can be accessed by other software, or is used for communication between application programs. APIs enable the exchange of messages or data between two or more software applications. The API must exist before a program can be called by an external program and before it can send a response to an external program.

There are several types of APIs that enable data sharing between different software applications on single or distributed platforms. Those APIs include:

1. *Remote procedure calls* (RPCs): These are protocols that provide high-level communications. An RPC implements a logical client-to-server communications system specifically for network applications.
2. *Standard query language* (SQL): SQL is an American National Standards Institute (ANSI) standard computer language for accessing and manipulating databases.
3. *File transfer*: Transporting or sharing files between remote machines.
4. *Message delivery*: Reliable message delivery ensures that Web services architecture, protocols, and interfaces deliver secure, interoperable, transactional, and robust solutions (IBM 2003).

GLOSSARY

Access: Refers to the tasks carried out on an object, such as read, write, modify, delete, etc.

Access Control: Only authorized (or intended) users can gain access to a network or application. Users have only the level of access, or least privilege, needed to accomplish authorized tasks.

API: A set of standards and protocols by which a software application can be accessed by other software, or for communication between application programs.

Application Communication Middleware: Middleware used to communicate between applications, software services, and components.

Application Communication Middleware Architecture: Facilitates and simplifies the communication between diverse, distributed applications.

Authentication: The process of providing a private piece of information or token to establish whether a subject is who or what its identifier (e.g., username) claims it is.

Authorization: The process of determining whether to allow a subject access to a specific resource service or another subject.

Availability: User access to data files or applications that are stored on networked computers. Information and systems are protected against disruption.

Certificate Authority (CA): An entity that issues digital certificates and vouches for the binding between the data items in a certificate.

CIA Triad: Refers to confidentiality, integrity, and availability of information and computing resources.

Cipher Text: Text that is unreadable by humans, such as encrypted text.

Common Object Request Broker Architecture (CORBA): An architecture for creating, distributing, and managing distributed program objects in a network.

Confidentiality: Sensitive information is protected against disclosure.

Distributed Component Object Model (DCOM): Microsoft's proprietary distributed object architecture, which it developed instead of adhering to CORBA.

Encryption: The process of changing a message (plaintext) into meaningless data (cipher text).

Enterprise Application Integration: The systematic tying together of disparate enterprise applications.

Integrity: Information and systems are protected against unauthorized modification.

Kerberos: A ticket-based authentication protocol based on symmetric key cryptography.

Kerberos ticket: A certificate issued by an authentication server, encrypted using the server key.

Message-Oriented Middleware (MOM): Application communication middleware that sends messages between software components. Applications using MOM can be deployed on multiple platforms using multiple programming languages.

Middleware: Software and APIs that act as intermediaries among application programs and services, such as gateway software between LAN-based database servers and mainframe databases. This software layer provides application, component, and data access communication.

Object: The data, service, or application that is being accessed by a subject.

Object Request Broker (ORB): In a network of clients/servers on different computers, a client program (an object) can request services from a server program or object without having to understand where the server is in a distributed network or what the interface to the server program looks like.

Open: Unprotected, such as an open network.

Packet: A collection of data transmitted as a bundle across a network connection.

Packet Switching: The process of routing and transferring packets of data via a network.

Plaintext: A message in human-readable form.

Platform: A combination of computer hardware and operating system software.

Portability: The capability to move software across different platforms.

Principal: Either a subject or an object whose identity can be verified (e.g., a workstation user or a network server)

Private key: The key that a communicating party holds privately and uses for decryption or completion of a key exchange.

Protocol: A set of rules for communication, or rules for managing the network, transferring data, and synchronizing the states of network components. Protocols enable independent technology components to communicate with each other.

Public Key: The key that a communicating party sends publicly.

Server: A computer that provides shared services to computer workstations over a network, e.g., file server, print server, mail server. In TCP/IP, a server accepts and responds to the requests of a remote system, called a "client."

Single Sign-on (SSO) Technology: This technology makes it possible for users to enter their credentials only once and to remain authorized within the network until they log off.

Subject: A person (user) or application that requests access to data, a service, application, etc.

Web Services Security (WS-Security): Provides a mechanism for associating security tokens with messages, thus improving protection through message integrity, message confidentiality, and single message authentication.

CROSS REFERENCES

See *Authentication; Virtual Private Networks; Web Services.*

REFERENCES

Franklin, C. 2004. GNOME attack puts penguin on guard. *Network Computing*, April 15, p. 23.

IBM. 2003. Reliable message delivery in a Web services world: A proposed architecture and roadmap. accessed April 17, 2007, from http://www.128.ibm.com/developerworks/webservices/library/specification/ws-rmdev/

SOA

http://searchwebservices.techtarget.com/tip/1,289483,sid26_gci899457,00.html.

http://www.adobe.com/enterprise/pdfs/Services_Oriented_Architecture_from_Adobe.pdf.

http://www.iks.inf.ethz.ch/education/ws03/eai/Lecture-2.pdf.

FURTHER READING

The importance of middleware is increasing. Middleware applications are ever-evolving layers of network and data services. These services reside between the network and more traditional applications. Their role is to manage security, access and information exchange, and the sharing of distributed resources, such as computers, data, and networks. Despite its security features, middleware has become the target of attack. A case in point—Intruders penetrated servers hosting GNOME, an open-source project offering interfaces and development tools to Linux users. This attack has demonstrated that intruders depend not only on vulnerabilities within operating systems, but also increasingly on applications, databases, Web servers, and middleware (Franklin 2004).

For information on the most widely publicized middleware initiatives, review the following:

- Open Software Foundation's Distributed Computing Environment (DCE). www.sei.cmu.edu/str/descriptions/dce.html (accessed April 17, 2007).
- Object Management Group's Common Object Request Broker Architecture (CORBA). www.sei.cmu.edu/str/descriptions/corba.html (accessed April 17, 2007).
- Microsoft's COM/DCOM (Component Object Model/Distributed COM). www.sei.cmu.edu/str/descriptions/com.html (accessed April 17, 2007).
- Cookie Eaters (MIT). http://pdos.lcs.mit.edu/cookies (accessed April 17, 2007).
- Gettes, M. R. 2000. A recipe for configuring and operating LDAP directories. http://middleware.internet2.edu/dir/docs/ldap-recipe.htm (accessed April 17, 2007).
- Kerberos Papers and Documentation. www.kerberos.isi.edu (accessed April 17, 2007).
- Kornievskaia, O., Honeyman, P. Doster, B., and Coffman, K. 2001. Kerberized credential translation: A solution to Web access control. http://www.usenix.org/events/sec01/full_papers/kornievskaia/kornievskaia_html/ (accessed April 17, 2007).
- Middleware. www.sei.cmu.edu/str/descriptions/middleware.html (accessed April 17, 2007).
- NSF Middleware Initiative. www.nsf-middleware.org (accessed April 17, 2007)
- Object request broker (ORB). www.sei.cmu.edu/str/descriptions/orb.html (accessed April 17, 2007).
- Open Group Messaging Forum. www.opengroup.org/messaging (accessed April 17, 2007).
- Remote Procedure Calls. www.cs.cf.ac.uk/Dave/C/node33.html (accessed April 17, 2007).
- Securities Industry Middleware Council (SIMC), Inc. www.simc-inc.org (accessed April 17, 2007).
- SSH Communications Security. www.ssh.com.
- TLS. accessed April 17, 2007, from www.fact-index.com/t/tr/transport_layer_security.html (accessed April 17, 2007).

Grid Computing Fundamentals

Mark Baker, *University of Reading, UK*

INTRODUCTION

The Grid concepts provide a distributed infrastructure for dynamic resource sharing and problem solving across multiple institutional boundaries. It effectively provides a virtualized wide-area distributed system that associates the underlying resources with abstract service interfaces. The Grid concepts and ideas have moved from the world of joining high-performance computing (HPC) systems together to generalized systems based on a service-oriented architecture that can provide infrastructure for a range of applications. At one end of the application spectrum are simple applications that use a client/server paradigm; but these can grow increasingly complex, for example where a workflow system may need to use a sophisticated pipeline of services to fulfil its needs. The infrastructure can support HPC for computationally or date intensive grand challenge applications, or it can provide high-throughput systems that need to spawn hundreds of thousands of tasks in parameter sweeps. The Grid infrastructure is now increasingly being used for new applications too, such as sensor networks, which may contain tens of thousands of sensors.

The aim of this chapter is to provide a brief history of the derivation of Grid concepts and a chronology of the Grid from its early days, when it was used to link HPC facilities in the United States, through today, where it provides a Web Services–based infrastructure for an increasing number of distributed applications. For clarity of understanding, this chapter also includes a definition of what is generally accepted to be a Grid and a discussion of what motivated developers to move away from the earlier procedural interfaces to the service-oriented architectures that are now being advocated. The second half of this chapter includes an extensive, but brief, overview of the nine currently available instantiations of Grid infrastructure that are based on either just Web Services, or the Web Services Resource Framework (WSRF).

A DEFINITION OF THE GRID

Currently, there appears to be some confusion about exactly what constitutes a Grid and what are its pertinent features. The reason for this confusion is caused by excessive use and overloading of the term *Grid*, so that today everything from SETI@home to a LAN-based cluster are referred to as a Grid. Foster and Kesselman (1998) provided an initial definition: “A computational Grid is a hardware and software infrastructure that provides dependable, consistent, pervasive, and inexpensive access to high-end computational capabilities.” This particular definition stems from the earlier roots of the Grid when it was focused on connecting together high-performance facilities at various U.S. laboratories and universities.

Since this early definition, there have been a number of additional attempts to define a Grid succinctly. In 2001, Foster, Kesselman, and Tuecke refined their definition of a Grid to “coordinated resource sharing and problem solving in dynamic, multi-institutional virtual organizations.” This latest definition is the one most commonly used today to abstractly define a Grid today.

Foster (2002) has also produced a checklist that can be used to help understand exactly what can be identified as a Grid system. He suggested that the checklist should have three parts to it. The first part to check off is that there is coordinated resource sharing with no centralized point of control and that the users reside within different administrative domains. If this is not true, it is probably not a Grid system. The second part to check off is the use of standard, open, general-purpose protocols and interfaces. If this is not the case, it is unlikely that system components will be able to communicate or interoperate, and it is likely that we are dealing with an application-specific system, and not the Grid. The final part to check off is that of delivering nontrivial qualities of service. Here we are considering how the components that make up a Grid can be used in a coordinated way to deliver combined services, which are appreciably greater than the sum of the individual components. These services may be associated with throughput, response time, mean time between failure, security, or many other nonfunctional facets.

Overall, the Grid is about resource sharing; this includes computers, storage, sensors, and networks. Sharing is obviously always conditional and based on factors such as trust, resource-based policies, negotiation, and how payment should be considered. The Grid also includes co-ordinated problem solving, which is beyond a simple client/server paradigm, in which we may be interested in combinations of distributed data analysis, computation, and collaboration. The Grid also involves dynamic, multi-institutional virtual organizations (VOs), where these new communities overlay classical organizational structures, and these organizations may be large or small, static or dynamic. The European-funded Enabling Grids for E-sciencE (EGEE) project, which aims to build on recent advances in Grid technologies to develop a service-oriented infrastructure, is a good example of where VOs are being used in practice.

The following items cannot be considered a Grid: A PC cluster, a network-attached storage device, a desktop PC, a scientific instrument, a network. Each might be an important component of a Grid, but by itself, it does not constitute a Grid. In addition, systems like SETI@ home, distributed.net, and folding@home are wide-area distributed systems, but not part of the Grid.

THE EVOLUTION OF THE GRID

Introduction

The early Grid efforts started as projects to link supercomputing sites; this was known, at the time as "metacomputing." The origin of the term is believed to have been the CASA project (Gigabit Testbed Initiative 1996), one of several U.S. Gigabit testbeds around in 1989. Larry Smarr, the former Director of the National Center for Supercomputing Applications, is generally accredited with popularizing the term thereafter (Catlett and Smarr, 1992). The original metacomputing or Grid environments emerged in the early to mid-1990s. Typically, the objective of these early projects was to provide computational resources to a range of high-performance applications.

Two projects (Baker and Fox, 1999) in the vanguard of this type of technology were FAFNER and I-WAY. FAFNER was a Web-based system that aimed to address the RSA (Rivest, Shamir, and Adleman) Factoring Challenge, which was capable of executing on any workstation with more than 4 Mbytes of memory. Whereas, I-WAY provided a means of unifying the resources of large U.S. supercomputing centers via specialized software. These projects differed in many ways, but were in the forefront of projects of their type, and both had to overcome a number of obstacles, including communications, resource management, and the manipulation of remote data, to be able to work efficiently and effectively.

FAFNER

The effectiveness of public key cryptosystems depends on the intractability, both computational and theoretical, of solving certain mathematical problems, for example integer factorization. Public and private keys in such systems are mathematically related, so their private key can only decrypt a message encrypted with a recipient's public key. To find a private key from a user's public key is computationally very time consuming to solve, but usually faster than trying all possible keys by brute force.

The use of this type of cryptographic technology has led to integer factorization becoming an active research area. To keep abreast of the state-of-the-art in factoring, RSA Data Security initiated the RSA Factoring Challenge in March 1991. The Factoring Challenge offers a testbed for factoring implementations and provides one of the largest collections of factoring results from many different experts worldwide.

Because factoring is computationally expensive, parallel factoring algorithms have been developed. With these parallel algorithms, factoring can be distributed over a network of computational resources; the algorithms are typically trivially parallel and require no communications after the initial set-up. This type of set-up means that it is possible that many contributors can provide a small part of a larger factoring effort. Early efforts relied on e-mail to distribute and receive factoring code and information.

In 1995, a consortium led by Bellcore Labs., Syracuse University, and Co-Operating Systems started a project of factoring via the Web, known as FAFNER. This project was set up to factor RSA130 using a new numerical technique called the Number Field Sieve (NFS) factoring method using computational Web servers. The consortium produced a Web-based system that interfaced to the NFS executable program.

With this system, a contributor used a Web form to invoke server-side common gateway interface (CGI) scripts written in Perl. Contributors downloaded and built a sieving software daemon, which became their Web client using HTTP GET/POST to get and send the resulting relations from and to a CGI script on the originating Web server. Three factors combined to make this approach succeed (Baker and Fox 1999):

1. The NFS implementation allowed even a workstation with only 4 Mbytes to perform useful work using a small bounds and sieve algorithm.
2. FAFNER supported anonymous registration—users could contribute their hardware resources to the sieving effort without revealing their identity to anyone other than the local server administrator.
3. A consortium of sites was recruited to run the CGI script package locally, forming a hierarchical network

of RSA130 Web servers, which reduced the potential administration bottleneck and allowed sieving to proceed around the clock with minimal human intervention.

The FAFNER project won an award in the TeraFlop challenge at Super Computing 95 (SC95) in San Diego. It paved the way for a wave of Web-based metacomputing projects.

I-WAY

The Information Wide Area Year (I-WAY) project (Foster, Geisler, Nickless, Smith, and Tuecke 1998) was an experimental network linking high-performance computers and visualization systems together. The I-WAY project was conceived in early 1995 to integrate existing high-bandwidth networks with telephone systems. The virtual environments, datasets, and computers used resided at seventeen different U.S. sites and were connected by ten networks of varying bandwidths and protocols, using different routing and switching technologies.

The project used an Asynchronous Transfer Mode (ATM) network, which at the time was an emerging standard that provided the wide-area backbone for various experimental networking activities at SC95. The network supported both ATM and TCP/IP over ATM.

To standardize the I-WAY software interface and management, each site installed a point-of-presence (I-POP) server to act as their gateway to the I-WAY. The I-POP servers were UNIX workstations configured uniformly with a standard software environment called I-Soft. The I-POP server provided uniform authentication, resource reservation, process creation, and communication functions across I-WAY resources. Each I-POP server was accessible via the Internet and operated within its site's firewall. It also had an ATM interface that allowed monitoring and potential management of the site's ATM switch.

The project included a resource scheduler known as the computational resource broker (CRB), which consisted of user-to-CRB and CRB-to-local scheduler protocols. The CRB implementation was set up in terms of a single central scheduler and multiple local scheduler daemons—one per I-POP server. The central scheduler maintained queues of jobs and tables representing the state of local machines, allocating jobs to machines and maintaining state information on the AFS file system.

Security was a major feature of the project, and emphasis was put on providing a uniform authentication environment. Authentication to I-POPs was handled by using a telnet client modified to use Kerberos. In addition, the CRB acted as an authentication proxy, performing subsequent authentication to resources on a user's behalf.

To support user-level tools, a low-level communications library, Nexus was adapted to execute in the I-WAY environment. Nexus supported automatic configuration mechanisms that enabled it to choose the appropriate configuration depending on the technology being used—for example, communications via TCP/IP or AAL5 (the ATM adaptation layer for framed traffic) when using the Internet or ATM. The MPICH library (a portable implementation of the Message Passing Interface (MPI) message passing standard) and CAVEcomm (networking for the CAVE virtual reality system) were also extended to use Nexus.

The I-WAY project was application-driven and defined several types of applications, including distributed supercomputing, access to remote resources, and virtual reality. The I-WAY project was demonstrated at SC95 in San Diego. The I-POP servers were shown to simplify the configuration, use, and management of this type of wide area testbed. I-Soft, the software that was used by the I-Way project was a success in terms that most applications ran, most of the time. More importantly, the experiences and software developed as part of the project fed into the Globus project, which is discussed below.

A Summary of Early Experiences

Both FAFNER and I-WAY were environments that attempted to integrate resources from opposite ends of the computing spectrum. FAFNER was a system that worked on any platform with a Web server, whereas I-WAY unified the resources at multiple supercomputing centers.

The two projects also differed in the types of applications that could utilize their environments. FAFNER was tailored to a particular factoring application that was in itself trivially parallel and was not dependent on a fast interconnect. I-WAY, on the other hand, was designed to cope with a range of diverse high-performance applications that typically needed a fast interconnect and powerful resources. Both projects, in their way, lacked scalability. For example, FAFNER was dependent on a lot of human intervention to distribute and collect sieving results, and I-WAY was limited by the design of components that made up I-POP and I-Soft.

FAFNER lacked a number of features that would now be considered obvious. For example, every client had to compile, link, and run a FAFNER daemon in order to contribute to the factoring exercise. FAFNER was really a means of task farming a large number of fine-grained computations. Individual tasks were unable to communicate with one another or with their parent Web server. Likewise, I-WAY had a number of features that would today seem inappropriate. The installation of an I-POP platform made it easier to set up I-WAY services in a uniform manner, but it meant that each site needed to be individually set up to participate. In addition, the I-POP platform and server created one, of many, single points of failure in the design of the I-WAY. Even though this was not reported to be a problem, the failure of an I-POP would mean that a site would drop out of the I-WAY environment.

Notwithstanding the aforementioned features, both FAFNER and I-WAY were both innovative and successful. Each project was in the vanguard of metacomputing and helped pave the way for many subsequent projects. FAFNER was the forerunner of the likes of SETI@home and Distributed.Net, and I-WAY for Globus and Legion.

GRID CONCEPTS AND COMPONENTS

Introduction

A Grid infrastructure will consist of all manner of networked resources, ranging from computers and mass storage devices to databases and special scientific instruments. The core features provided by the fabric of the Grid are:

- Some sort of administrative hierarchy and integration needs to exist to allow a Grid environment to be divided up to cope with a potentially global extent. This component will allow administrative information flow between groups, centers and organizations, so administrative boundaries are hidden, allowing individuals and resources to join, utilize, and leave what are now known as virtual organizations (Wikipedia, 2007).
- Communication services are required to provide Grid applications with a range of transport protocols, ranging from reliable point-to-point to unreliable multicast. The communications infrastructure needs to support protocols that are used for bulk-data transport, streaming data, group communications, and those used by distributed objects.
- A Grid is a dynamic environment in which the location and type of services available are constantly changing. The resources and services must be accessible to any process in the system, without regard to the relative location of the resource or user. It is necessary to provide a rich information environment in which services, resources, and users can publish, search for, and find the end points of interest. Information services provide the mechanisms for registering and obtaining information about the structure, resources, services, status, and nature of the environment.
- Any distributed system needs a range of security services to provide authorization, authentication, confidentiality, and integrity. Security within a Grid environment is a complex issue requiring diverse resources autonomously administered to interact in a manner that does not impact the usability of the resources or introduce security holes/gaps in individual systems or environments as a whole.
- The management of processor time, memory, network, storage, and other components in a distributed system is clearly important. The overall aim is the efficient and effective scheduling of the applications that need to utilize the available resources in the distributed environment. It is important in a Grid that a resource management and scheduling service can interact with the systems that may be installed locally, such as Condor, Load Sharing Facility or Sun's Grid Engine.

These core feature or components are provided, in some manner, by each instantiation of Grid middleware. These components are discussed further in the section on Grid Instantiations below.

The Open Grid Services Architecture

Many changes have occurred since Grid software first appeared, not the least of these has been the increasing involvement of commerce and industry as the Grid's potential has started to be realized. The effect of commercial involvement has driven the evolution of the software that supports Grid environments away from its academic/research roots toward industrial quality. This interaction has had an impact on the architecture of the Grid's infrastructure, as well as the associated protocols and standards. The most profound change has been the adoption of Web Services to underpin the infrastructure that supports the Grid.

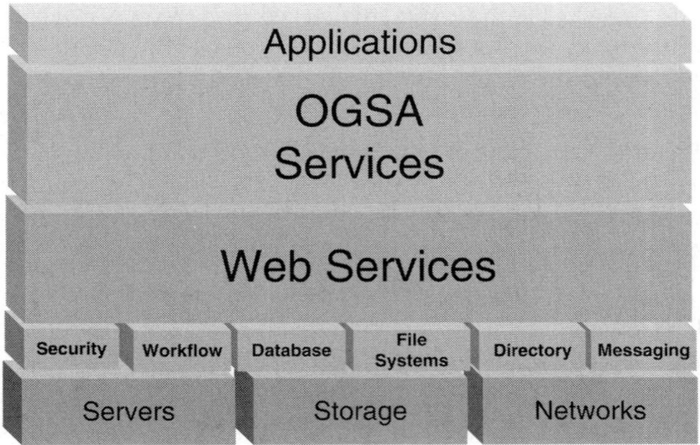

Figure 1: The Open Grid Services Architecture

In June 2002 (Foster, Kesselman, Nick, and Tuecke 2002), the Open Grid Services Architecture (OGSA), developed by the Global Grid Forum's (GGF's) OGSA Working Group OGSA v1.0 (Foster et al. 2004), emerged as a draft specification that aimed to define a common, standard, and open architecture (Figure 1) for Grid-based applications.

OGSA can be seen as the blueprint for the Grid's architecture. OGSA aims to standardize almost all the services that a Grid application may use by defining service interfaces and identifying the protocols for invoking these services. It defines a set of fundamental services—for example, job and resource management services, communications, and security. The interfaces, semantics, and interactions of these services are being standardized by the GGF working groups. OGSA specifies a service-oriented architecture (SOA) for the Grid as a set of distributed computing patterns that are realized using Web Services.

In March 2004, OGSA was declared the Open Grid Forum's (OGF) flagship architecture. Instantiations of OGSA itself depend on emerging specifications and implementations. OGSA plays the coordinating role for the efforts of working groups within the OGF and the other organizations that are participating in developing standards for the Grid. It identifies the requirements for e-Business and e-Science applications in a Grid environment, while the technical details are left to the various working groups.

OGSA extends Web services by introducing a number of interfaces and conventions. Key to OGSA are its services, which are Web Services with improved characteristics due to:

- The dynamic and potentially transient nature of a Grid environment, where service instances may come and go as tasks are dispatched, as resources are configured and provisioned, or as the system's state changes. Consequently, services need interfaces to manage their creation, destruction, and life cycle management.
- Coping with the dynamic and transient nature means that service state is needed, which comes in the form of attributes and associated data. For this purpose, Web services were extended to support state data associated with Grid-based services.
- Providing clients with the ability to register their interest in services so that when there is a change in that service, clients are notified.

The first instantiation of OGSA was the Open Grid Services Infrastructure specification version 1.0 (OGSI), released in July 2003 (Tuecke et al. 2003). OGSI defined a set of principles and extensions on the use of the Web Services Definition Language (WSDL) and XML Schema to enable stateful Web Services.

OGSI introduced the term *Grid service*, which was an enhanced Web service that implemented the GridService portType. This term is now deprecated (OGSA Glossary). In OGSI, a Grid service was created to manage each new piece of state and provided a standard set of mechanisms for managing the state of a service. Several problems were identified with OGSI, some were political and others technical (Tuecke et al. 2003; Czajkowski et al. 2004), these are described next:

- It was thought that the OGSI specification was too large and contained too much for one specification.
- OGSI did not work well with current Web Services tooling. OGSI was not a pure subset of Web services and required a modification to the standard WSDL, called the Grid-WSDL (or GWSDL). This meant that commercial and noncommercial WSDL tools would need to be extended to parse and process the WSDL for these Grid services.
- OGSI was seen as too object-oriented, even though many other Web services systems have object-oriented implementations. OGSI used concepts from object-oriented programming, such as statefulness and the factory model, which was used to create Grid service instances, thus supporting transient, potentially short-lived services.

The Motivation behind WSRF

The original Grid systems, such as the Globus Toolkit versions 1 and 2, focused on the sharing of physical resources via procedural software frameworks. These systems, however, did not fit the emerging needs of the distributed computing community. It was argued that enterprise information technology (IT) infrastructures and multi-organizational Grid systems are concerned with the creation, management, and application of dynamic ensembles of resources and services (Czajkowski et al. 2004). It was believed that a service-oriented view of architecture was more fitting for the long-term viability of the software needed to bind together distributed Grid and IT infrastructures. The goal of Service-Oriented Architectures (SOA) is to lessen the problems of heterogeneity, interoperability, and ever-changing system requirements. A SOA provides a platform for building application and other services, which are loosely coupled, location-transparent, and protocol-independent.

In software terms, a service is generally implemented as a coarse-grained, discoverable entity that exists as a single instance and interacts with applications and other services through a loosely coupled, message-based communication model. An important aspect of the Grid was the need to provide stateful resources. Historically, Grid systems provided their clients with access to some view of their internal state. Grid systems would typically allow a client to access stateful data, which may refer to CPU use, memory consumption, or job reservation information.

With Web Services, an operation's execution is available at an end point address. A service is defined in terms of the operations it implements, and an operation is defined in terms of a message exchange, such as SOAP or WSDL. The lifecycle of a Web service is described in terms of its deployment and can be found via a discovery process. HTTP is stateless, so when Web services came along, they also remained stateless. The only way to introduce state (or security for that matter) was to insert, piggy-back style, a token or other identifier into the message envelopes.

WSRF provides a set of operations that Web Services may implement to become stateful. A client can communicate with a resource, allowing data to be stored and retrieved. Foster et al. (OGSI to WSRF. 2004) have produced a technical document (Czajkowski et al. 2004) discussing the differences between OGSI and WSRF. WSRF has a standard approach to extend Web Services. It is based on a set of different standard/recommended WS-* specifications:

- WS-Resource
- WS-ResourceProperties (WSRF-RP)
- WS-ResourceLifetime (WSRF-RL)
- WS-ServiceGroup (WSRF-SG)
- WS-BaseFaults (WSRF-BF)
- WS-Addressing
- WS-Notification

WSRF is itself extendable through other WS-* specifications like WS-Policy, WS-Security, WS-Transaction, and WS-Coordination.

WSRF Specifications

WS-ResourceProperties (WS-RP)

A WS-Resource has zero or more properties expressible in XML, representing a view on the WS-Resource's state. Without WSRF, clients of a Web service can access and manipulate its state using an application-specific interface. The properties of a WS-Resource are modeled as XML elements in the resource properties document. To allow the generic use of resource properties, WSRF defines a number of standard operations that a WS-Resource may support. The operation GetResourceProperty is mandatory, whereas all the other operations are optional. WS-ResourceProperties optionally uses WS-Notification to allow clients to request notification of changes made to the values of one or more resource properties.

WS-ResourceLifetime (WS-RL)

The WS-ResourceLifetime specification standardizes the means by which a WS-Resource can be monitored, manipulated, and destroyed. The specification does not detail the means by which a resource is created, but can specify that it should be immediately destroyed, its termination time, or changes to the termination time. WS-ResourceLifetime does not mandate that the resource be destroyed immediately after the scheduled destruction time; however, the client must not assume that the resource will be available after that time.

WS-ServiceGroup (WS-SG)

The WS-ServiceGroup specification defines a means of representing and managing heterogeneous, by-reference, collections of Web services. This specification can be used to organize collections of WS-Resources—for example, to aggregate and build services that can perform collective operations on a set of WS-Resources. The WS-ServiceGroup specification can express group membership rules, constraints, and classifications using the resource property model from WS-ResourceProperties. Groups can be defined as a collection of members that meet some constraints as expressed through resource properties.

A service group is a WS-Resource, and the members of the group are modeled as Entry properties in the resource property document, together with various membership constraints that a group can impose. In addition, the member entries (not the member services) are also WS-Resources (referenced from the Entry properties), which may use WS-ResourceLifetime methods for scheduling the removal of a member service from the group (or removing it immediately).

To add members to a group, WS-ServiceGroup defines a single operation called Add, which is used by specifying the member service reference and the initial termination time for the membership. WS-ServiceGroup also provides an optional means to notify a service group about a modification using WS-Notification.

WS-BaseFaults (WS-BF)

WS-BaseFaults defines an XML Schema for base faults, which are defined in the XML Base Faults namespace, along with rules for how this base fault type is used and extended by Web services.

WS-Addressing (WSA)

WS-Addressing provides a mechanism to place the target, source, and other important address information directly within a Web Services message. In short, WS-Addressing decouples address information from any specific transport protocol. WS-Addressing provides a mechanism called an end-point reference for addressing entities managed by a service. The end-point reference provides a standard XML element that allows a structured approach to encoding fine-grained addressing. The combination of fine-grained addressing coupled with the transport-neutral encoding of the message source and destination means that Web Services' messages can be sent across a range of transports and through intermediaries. WS-Addressing also lets a sender indicate where a response should go in a transport-independent manner.

WS-Notification

WS-Notification is a family of documents including three specifications: WS-BaseNotification, WS-BrokeredNotification, and WS-Topics.

WS-BaseNotification defines the Web services interfaces for NotificationProducers and NotificationConsumers. The specification includes the standard message exchanges to be implemented by service providers that wish to act in these roles, along with operational requirements expected of them.

WS-BrokeredNotification defines the Web services interface for the NotificationBroker, which is an intermediary that, among other things, allows the publication of messages from entities that are not themselves service providers. The specification includes standard message exchanges to be implemented by NotificationBroker service providers along with operational requirements expected of service providers and requestors that participate in brokered notifications.

WS-Topics defines a mechanism to organize and categorize items of interest for subscription known as "topics." These are used in conjunction with the notification mechanisms defined in WS-BaseNotification. WS-Topics defines three topic expression dialects that can be used as subscription expressions in subscribe request messages and other parts of the WS-Notification system. It further specifies an XML model for describing metadata associated with topics.

GRID INSTANTIATIONS

Since the mid-1990s, a number of international groups have been developing software to address the concepts of a Grid environment. Today, there is an increasing number of instantiations of Grid software that conform to OGSA and implement the WSRF specifications. This section briefly describes some of the more popular systems in terms of their layout/architecture and the services that they use.

The Globus Toolkit 4 (GT4)

The Globus Toolkit is developed by the Globus Alliance. It includes a number of services, most of which are implemented on top of WSRF, although some are not.

The Globus Toolkit 4 software components are shown (Figure 2.) These components are divided into five categories: Security, Data Management, Execution Management,

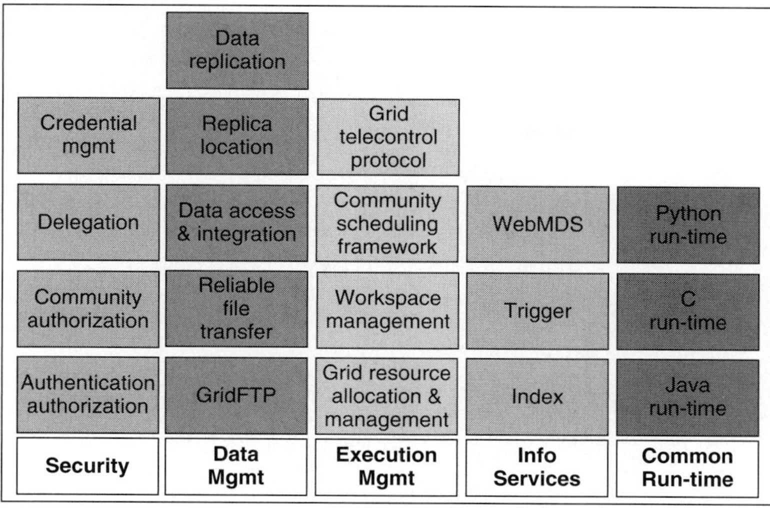

Figure 2: The Globus Toolkit Version 4 (Foster 2005)

Information Services, and the Common Run-time. Note that even though GT4 focuses on Web services, the toolkit also includes components that are based on earlier services. For example, the GridFTP component uses a non-WS protocol, which started as one used by the Globus toolkit, but later became a GGF specification.

GT4 includes the following components (shown via a layered view in Figure 2):

- The common run-time components provide a set of libraries and tools, which are needed to build all Globus services.
- The security components are based on the Grid Security Infrastructure (GSI), which allows secure authentication and communication over an open network.
- The data management components allow the management of large sets of data in a Globus-based virtual organization.
- The information services, more commonly known as the monitoring and discovery service (MDS), includes a set of components to discover and monitor resources in a virtual organization.
- The execution management components deal with the initiation, monitoring, management, scheduling, and coordination of executable programs.

UNICORE

The Uniform Interface to Computing Resources project started in August 1997. The aim of the project was to seamlessly and securely join together a number of German supercomputing centers virtually without changing their existing procedures. The UNICORE consortium consisted of developers, centers, users, and vendors. The initial UNICORE system had a security architecture based on X.509 certificates, a graphical user interface (GUI) based on Java Applets and a Web browser, and a central job scheduler that used Codine from Genias (now Sun's Grid Engine).

UNICORE Plus started in January 2000, with two years of funding support. The goal of this project was to continue the development of UNICORE with the aim of producing a Grid infrastructure together with a Web portal. It also included hardening and maturing the system for production, the integration of new functions and more components, and the deployment of further participating sites. The Grid Interoperability Project (GRIP) was a two-year project started in 2001 funded by the European Union to realize the interoperability of Globus and UNICORE and to work toward standards for interoperability in the Global Grid Forum.

The UniGrids project, which started in July 2004 aims to develop a Grid services' infrastructure based on the OGSA. This will transform UNICORE into a system with interfaces that are compliant with the WSRF and that can interoperate with other WSRF-compliant systems. The UNICORE architecture of 2003 is shown in Figure 3; it basically consists of a user tier and a server tier.

User Tier

The UNICORE Client provides a GUI to underlying services. The client communicates with the server by sending and receiving abstract job objects (AJOs) and file data via the UNICORE Protocol Layer (UPL), which uses the Secure Sockets Layer (SSL) protocol. The AJO contains platform- and site-independent descriptions of computational and data-related tasks, resource information, and workflow specifications, along with user and security information. AJOs are sent to the UNICORE Gateway in the form of serialized and signed Java objects, followed by an optional stream of bytes if file data is to be transferred.

Server Tier

The server tier contains the Gateway and the network job supervisor (NJS). The Gateway controls the access to a UNICORE Site (Usite) and acts as the secure entry point accepting and authenticating UPL requests. A Usite

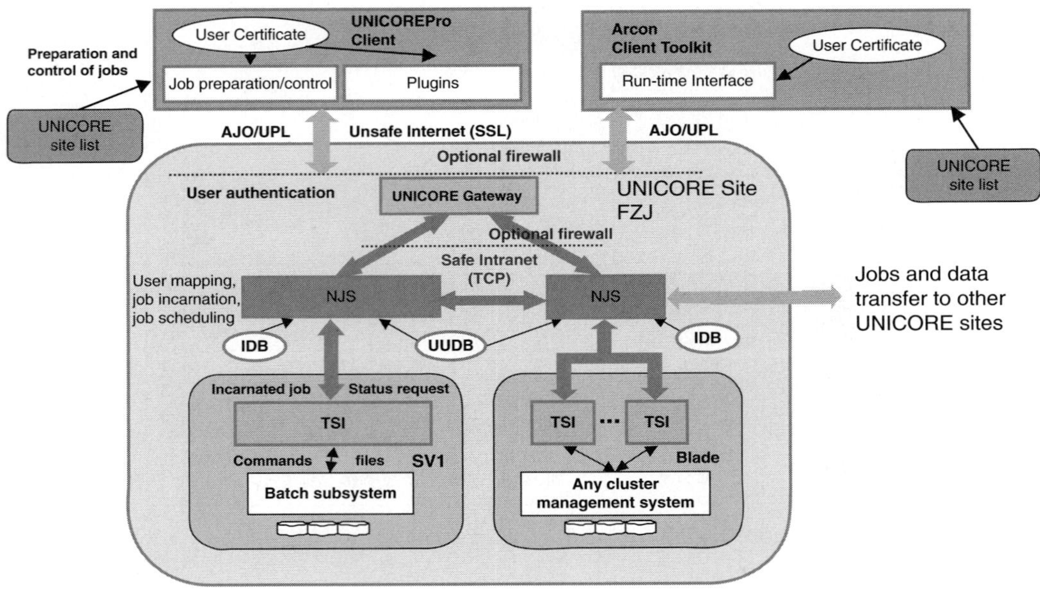

Figure 3: The UNICORE Architecture circa 2003 (Courtesy of Fujitsu Laboratories of Europe) (FZJ = http://www.fz-juelich.de/; IDB = incarnation database; NJS = network job supervisor; SV1 = Fujitsu System; TSI = target system interface; UUDB = UNICORE user database)

identifies the participating organization to the Grid with a symbolic name that resolves into the URL of the Gateway. The Gateway forwards incoming requests to the underlying NJS of a virtual site (Vsite) for further processing. The NJS represents resources with a uniform mapping scheme. Each Gateway also contains a target system interface (TSI) that implements the interface to the underlying computational resources. NJS is a stateless daemon running on the target system and interfacing with the local resource manager realized either by a batch system such as Condor or PBS or a Grid resource manager like the Globus Resource Allocation Manager (GRAM).

gLite

EGEE is a project funded by the European Sixth Framework Programme. It is building on emerging Grid technologies and earlier projects, such as the European Union (EU) DataGrid. The project joins together more than 70 institutions in 27 European countries and aims to construct a multi-science Grid infrastructure for Europe. In particular, the project will:

- Provide a secure, reliable, and robust Grid infrastructure.
- Reengineer to a so called lightweight middleware solution, gLite, specifically intended to be used by many different scientific disciplines.
- Attempt to attract, engage, and support users from science and industry, and provide them with technical support and training.

The EGEE project was started by using the existing LHC (Large Hadron Collider) Computing Grid project as its springboard. LCG aimed to provide computing resources for the analysis of data coming from the LHC at CERN, Geneva.

EGEE began work using the LCG-2 middleware, provided by the LCG project, which was based on the middleware from the EU DataGrid project. In parallel, it has produced the gLite middleware, reengineered using components from a number of sources to produce middleware that provides a full range of basic Grid services. In February 2006, gLite was at version 1.5, and consisted of some 220 packages arranged in thirty-four logical deployment modules. The core gLite components are shown in Figure 4.

Site services include a computing element (CE), which is a gateway to local computing resources, where there is a local resource management system (LRMS). Also, there are worker nodes (WN) and storage elements that are gateways to local storage, which can be disk- or tape-based. Finally, the site service includes a user interface (UI) that gives a user an access point to the Grid.

There are a number of Grid/VO-wide services, these include:

- Security services, including the Virtual Organization Membership Service (VOMS) and the MyProxy Server.
- An information system, called R-GMA, which is a relational version of the Grid Monitoring Architecture system. R-GMA provides a distributed database that aggregates service information from multiple Grid sites. It is used by workload management system (WMS) to collect information on sites and their resources.
- A job management system, which includes a WMS as well as a logging and bookkeeping service. WMS is used to find the best location for a job; it matches

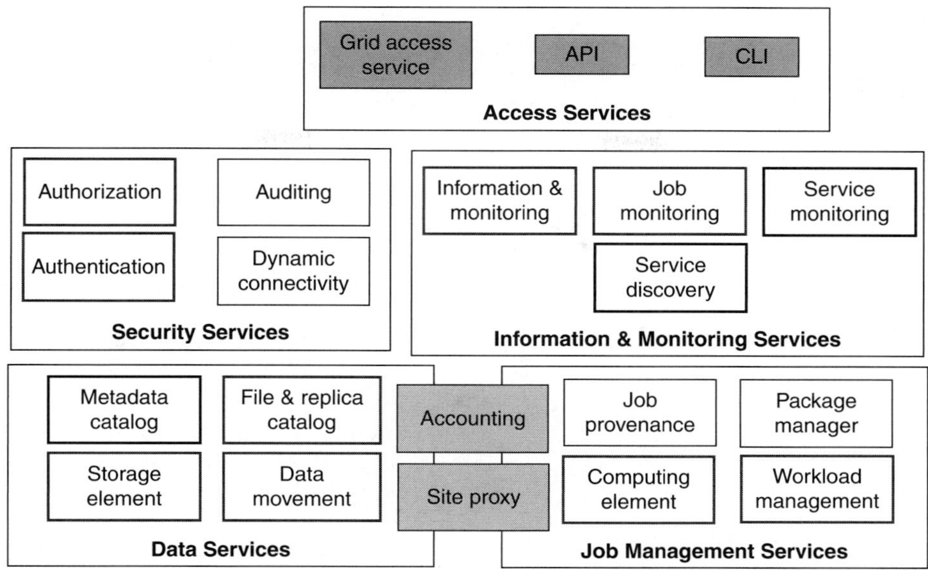

Figure 4: gLite Components

requirements with the available resources. WMS finds CEs from the R-GMA, and schedules jobs using a lazy scheduling algorithm. Logging and bookkeeping services help keep track of a job's status and resource use.

- The data management system includes various catalogues (file, replicas, and metadata) and a file transfer and placement service. This system provides services and protocols to interact with storage elements.

WSRF::Lite

WSRF::Lite is a Perl implementation of the WSRF specification developed at the University of Manchester. Like its predecessor, OGSI::Lite, it uses SOAP::Lite as its Web services tool kit. The architecture of WSRF::Lite is shown in Figure 5. Development of WSRF::Lite is being supported by the Managed Programme of the Open Middleware Infrastructure Institute (OMII) through the

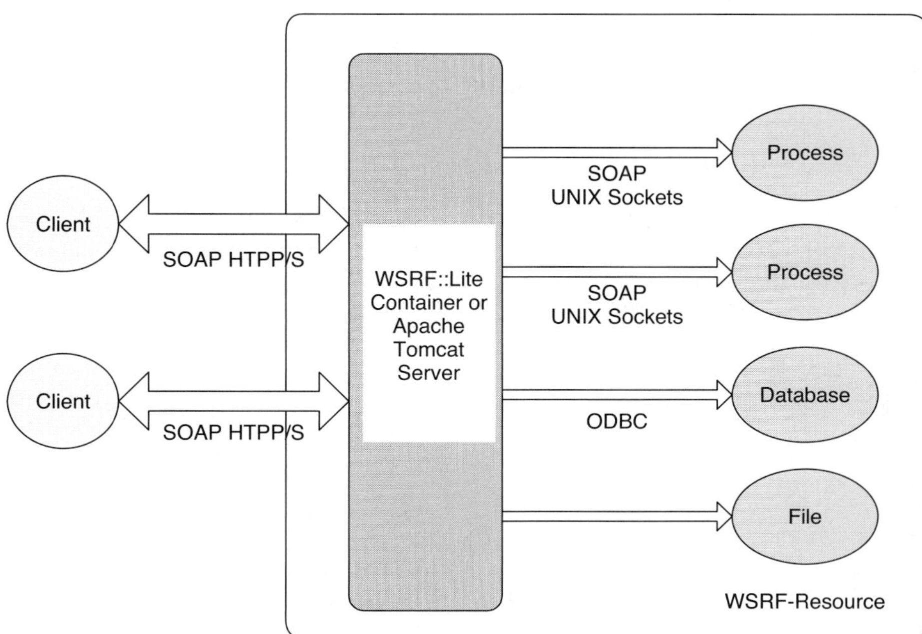

WSRF::Lite WS-Resources cabe hosted using the WSRF::Lite container or the Apache Tomcat Server. The state of the WS-Resource can be stored in system memory, in a file or a database.

Figure 5: The WSRF::Lite Architecture

project Robust Application Hosting under WSRF::Lite (RAHWL). WSRF::Lite is released as open source under a dual license scheme (the Perl Artistic License and the OMII modified Berkeley Software Distribution (BSD) license).

WSRF::Lite provides support for the following Web Services specifications:

- WS-Addressing
- WS-ResourceProperties
- WS-ResourceLifetimes
- WS-BaseFaults
- WS-ServiceGroups
- WS-Security

Apache WSRF

In November 2004, Hewlett-Packard (HP) contributed with Java implementations of early drafts of WSRF, WS-Notification (WSN), and WS-DistributedManagement (WSDM) to the Apache Software Foundation. At the same time, the Globus Alliance contributed the WSRF and WSN implementations that it had developed as the foundation for the next generation of the Globus Toolkit for building Grid middleware and applications. For WSRF and WSN, HP and Globus agreed to combine their implementations. To host the donated code and the ongoing development efforts, three new subprojects—Apollo, Hermes, and Muse—were formed within the Apache incubator, a staging area for new projects. The Apache Platform is shown in Figure 6:

- Apollo implements the WSRF specifications.
- Hermes extends Apollo to implement the WSN specifications.
- Muse extends both Apollo and Hermes to implement the WSDM MUWS (management using Web Services) specification.

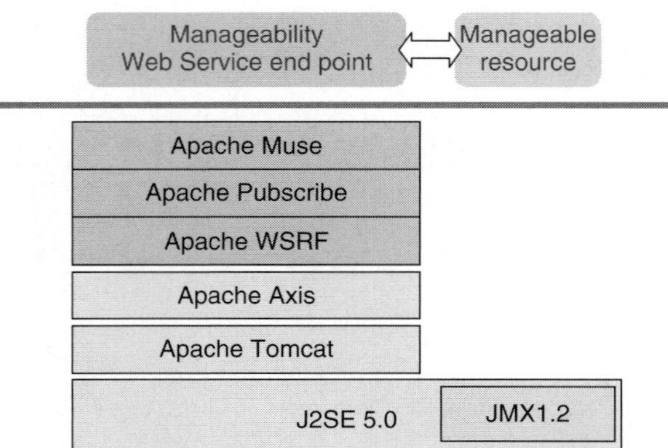

Figure 6: The Apache Platform (JMX 1.2 = Java Management Extensions (JMX); J2SE 5.0 = Java Platform, Standard Edition (Java SE) version 5)

Due to trademark concerns, Apollo was renamed WSRF, and Hermes Pubscribe. On June 3, 2005, all Apache WSRF, Pubscribe, and Muse projects officially left incubation.

Apache WSRF had a number of design goals:

1. No assumptions are made about the nature of the entity, or entities, being exposed as a WS-Resource. For example, a WS-Resource could be anything from a Java Bean, to a scheduler that is accessed via some proprietary application programming interface (API). The Apache platform provides the hooks for connecting the WS-Resource's operations and properties to the actual entity being exposed as a WS-Resource.
2. Writing and deploying WSRF services should be relatively effortless. For this purpose, the Apache platform provides implementations of all specification-defined operations and a code generator that, given a WSDL document, generates all of the Java classes and configuration files necessary to expose (via the platform) all services found in the WSDL.
3. Services built with Apache WSRF are deployable on any Java-based SOAP platform. Although Apache Axis is bundled with the WSRF distribution, it is not a requirement.

Apache WSRF consists of three parts:

1. A resource invocation framework
2. APIs for the specifications that WSRF consists of (see the section on WSRF Specifications)
3. Implementations of the operations defined by the WS-ResourceProperties and WS-ResourceLifetime specifications.

Note: The APIs and operation implementations of the WS-ServiceGroup specification are not currently provided.

WSRF.NET

WSRF.NET (WSRF.NET; Humphrey et al. 2004) is a toolkit that is implemented on top of the Microsoft .NET framework for developing and deploying WSRF-compliant Web services. WSRF.NET's development was motivated by the need to provide a familiar .NET abstraction for the Grid, to seamlessly interact with the Linux/UNIX platforms supported by the Globus Toolkit, and finally an implementation of WSRF on the .NET platform in order to undertake a full study of its capabilities. In WSRF.NET, the authors of a service annotate their Web Services code with metadata via .NET attributes. WSRF.NET tools process this information to convert the original Web service into a WSRF-compliant service. The WSRF.NET System Architecture is shown in Figure 7.

WSRF.NET services are actually ASP.NET-based Web services, which are the "normal" Web Services exposed via Internet Information Services (IIS) on a Microsoft Windows system.

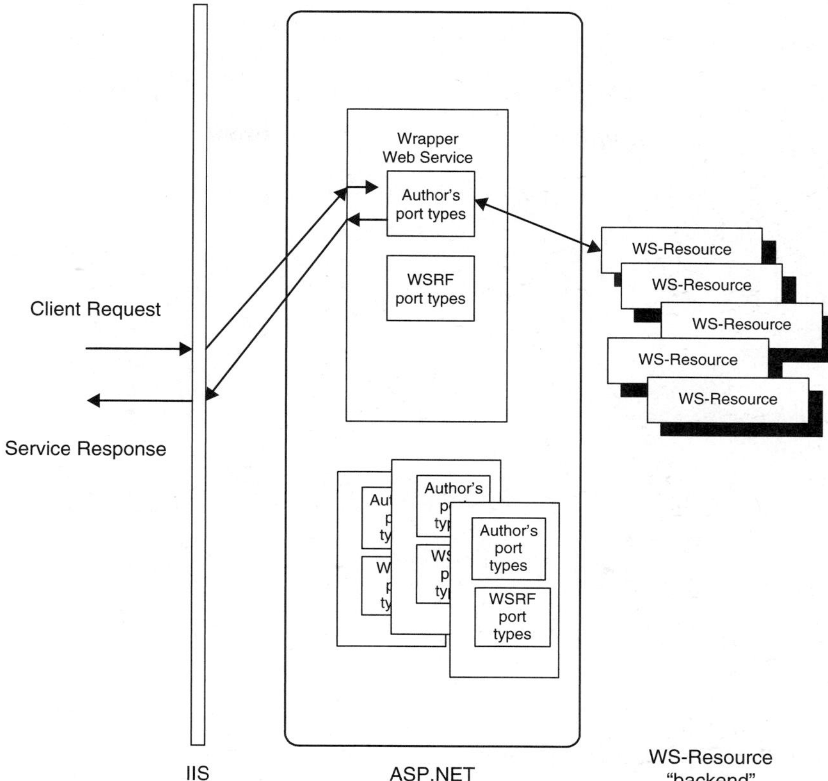

Figure 7: WSRF.NET System Architecture

The WSRF.NET tools generate a "wrapper" Web service from that written by the author of a service. This service is then executed as part of an ASP.NET worker process, which hosts the service. The IIS dispatches HTTP requests to the service, which internally invokes either a method on a port type provided by the service's author or a port type defined by WSRF. Before the method is invoked, the wrapper service uses the value of the EndpointReference in the header of the invocation SOAP message to interact with a particular WS-Resource and retrieve state values. These values are then made available to the invoked method and on completion; any changes to these values are saved. Finally, the method result will be serialized and returned to the client by ASP.NET/IIS. A number of WSRF.NET services have been developed and deployed at the University of Virginia; these include job execution, a file system, node information, and a scheduler.

CROWN

The China Research and Development Environment Over a Wide-Area Network is a Web services–based toolkit that allows the deployment of services on remote resources where there are CROWN services. CROWN 2.0 is developed by a research group at Beijing University and was released in September 2005. CROWN is a service-oriented Grid middleware suite and a testbed for China e-Science users. The CROWN architecture is shown in Figure 8. CROWN consists of the following components:

- Node Server is an extension of a Globus Toolkit 3.9.5 service container, which provides host/remote service deployment as well as dynamic resource information collection and reporting.
- Service Remote Deployment is used for remote service management, quick deployment, and load-balancing purposes.
- Resource Locating and Descripting Service (RLDS) is a distributed Grid information service architecture. It is used for collecting of information about resources (hosts) and services.
- S-Club is an overlay based RLDS management mechanism. It uses shortcuts to link all the RLDS services into an overlay network. Each club serves for a certain type of service, while each Grid Information System (GIS) may join one or more clubs.
- CROWN Designer is an Eclipse Plug-in for service development. It supports WSRF/WS-I Service development and deployment. Note that Java Development Tools (JDT) and the Plug-in Development Environment (PDE) are part of the Eclipse development environment.

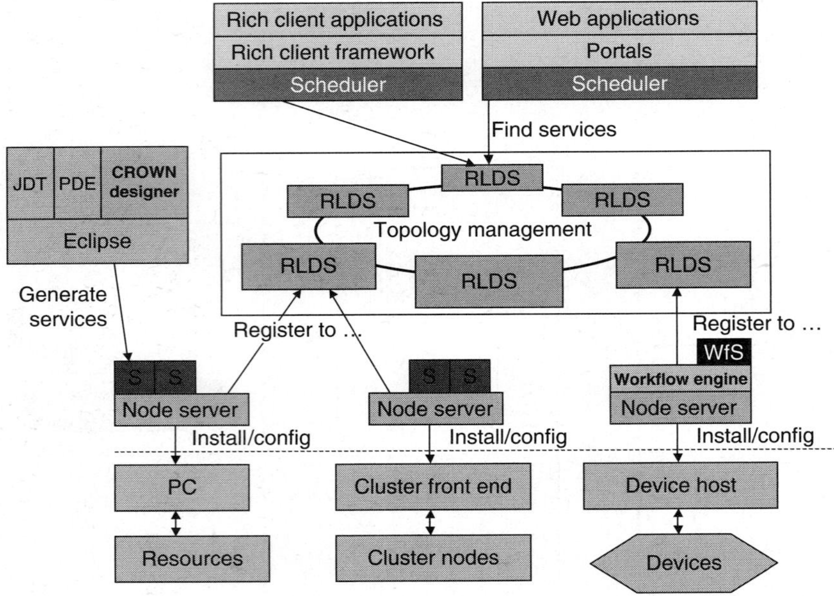

Figure 8: The Crown Architecture (Courtesy of the CROWN Project) (WfS = Work Flow System)

- CROWN Workflow is a BPEL4WS-based (WSBPEL) modeling tool and execution engine, which includes a graphical tool that supports process monitoring and control.
- CROWN Portal is a Java Server Pages (JSP)-based Web Interface, which provides application integration and user job submission.

OMII

The Open Middleware Infrastructure Institute (OMII) was established in January 2004, initially for three years with £6.5 million budget. Its purpose is to take on existing e-science Grid middleware and produce high-quality, reusable software. The OMII software architecture, shown in Figure 9, currently consists of client and server software, plus a number of integrated services and sample applications.

The OMII_2 Server Stack

The OMII_2 Server Stack consists of a Web services container based on Apache Tomcat and Axis, with specialized extensions to this container that provide secure message handling between clients and services. The services that are integrated with the server include:

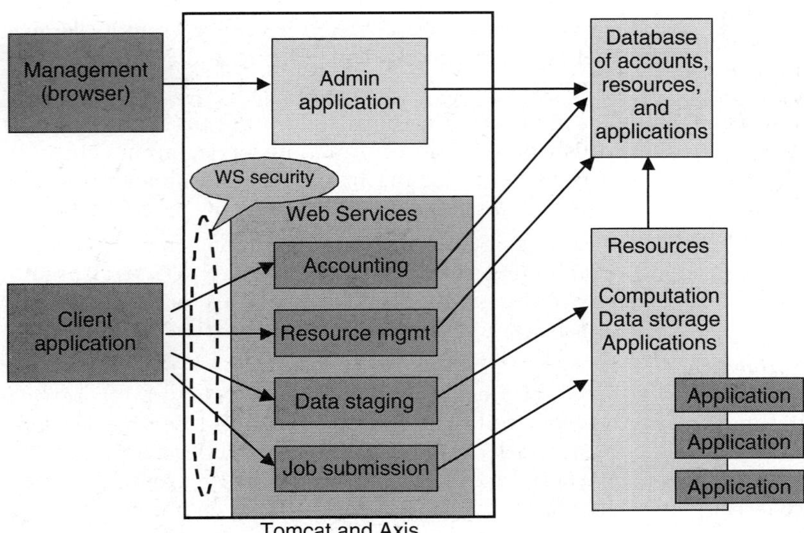

Figure 9: The OMII Architecture (WS = Web Services)

- Accounts: Which provides account creation and management, and sets up the access permissions for each individual client.
- Resource Allocation: This allows clients to request and be allocated computational and data resources.
- Job: This allows a client to submit a job to the server and manages the job requirements.
- Data: The Data Service allows remote users to upload and download data files to the service provider.

The OMII Grid middleware also includes software from the managed program:

- GridSAM is an open-source Web Service for submitting and monitoring jobs managed by a variety of distributed resource managers (DRMs). The core function of GridSAM is to translate the submission instructions specified in a Job Submission Description Language (JSDL) document to a set of resource specific actions to stage, launch, and monitor a job.
- Grimoires is a registry that hosts the description of services and workflows, which a scientist can use to form complex scientific experiments. The Grimoires registry is an implementation and extension of the business logic of UDDI, the de facto standard for publishing and discovering Web Services. The extensions include:
  - The registration of executable activities, such as workflows, are included in the registry along with service registrations,
  - Third-party attachment of executable activities' metadata is supported, which allows publishers and third-party users to publish information about services, such as semantic descriptions, functionality, and service reliability.

OMII_2 Client Overview

The OMII_2 Client includes interfaces to OMII_2 integrated services—the means to set up accounts with service providers; and the ability to request resources from remote service providers and accept offered services, specify and submit jobs, and upload data to the remote service provider—as well as interfaces to OMII sample applications.

PyGridWare

PyGridWare is an implementation of the WSRF and Web Service Notification (WSN) family of specifications. It is compatible with the Java WS Core of GT4. PyGridWare provides APIs and tools for building WS-Resources, its Python bindings can be generated from WSDL, and it incorporates transport layer and message-based security. The architecture of PyGridWare is shown in Figure 10. PyGridWare is based on standard Python software, ZSI (Salz 2007) for SOAP handling, 4Suite and PyXML for XML, and Twisted for the hosting environment and event handling.

PyGridWare provides a relatively lightweight standalone container that allows automatic service start-up on the container's start-up—this is in comparison with the Apache Tomcat container, which can be considered relatively heavyweight. There is a basic API for resource persistence and the recovery notification infrastructure. There is a subscription manager/notification producer, as well as a lightweight notification consumer. PyGridWare has a security infrastructure that provides pluggable handlers for WS-Security and secure conversation services. PyGridWare also has support for wrapping legacy codes and command line applications as Grid Services.

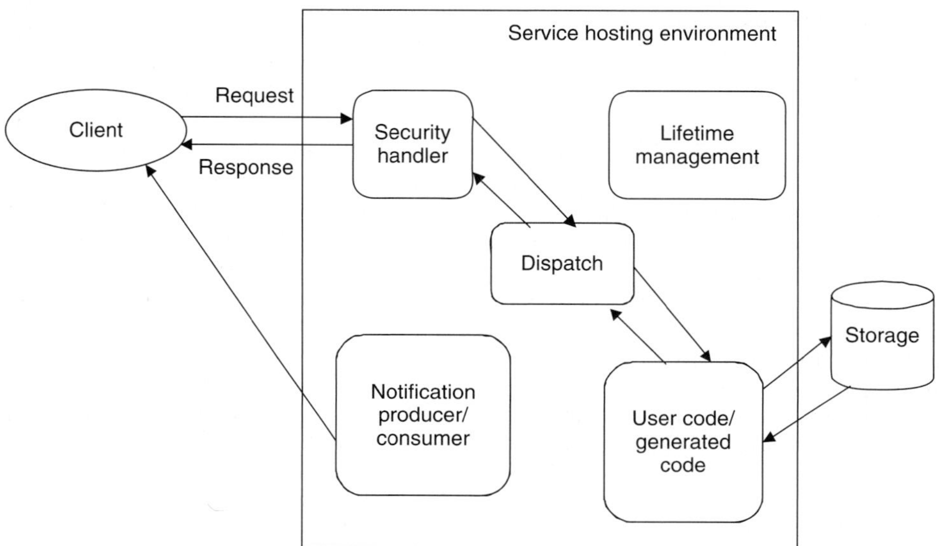

Figure 10: The PyGridWare Architecture

Summary of Grid Instantiation Services and Features

Table 1 summarizes the key features and components of all the system instantiations outlined in this section. It should be noted that, apart from gLite and OMII, all the systems follow OGSA and WSRF. Even though this is the case, there is currently no guarantee that these systems may be interoperable, as the underlying WS specifications have not yet been standardized and are still under development.

SUMMARY

This chapter first defined what can be considered a Grid system; namely, enabling-coordinated resource sharing and problem solving in dynamic, multi-institutional virtual organizations. The chapter then briefly gave a recap of the evolution of the Grid, from its origins in the mid-1990s until today. Here the forerunners of the current Grid instantiations were outlined. This was followed by a description of how the various communities working in the field of distributed systems, both commercial and academic, started to converge on a service-oriented architecture with the emergence of Web services–based technologies.

The chapter then detailed the appearance of the Open Grid Services Architecture (OGSA), and the initial instantiation of this architecture, known as the Open Grid Service Infrastructure (OGSI), and noted how this failed for a number of technical and political reasons. This was then followed by a discussion of the Web Services Resource Framework (WSRF), and the various emerging Web Services specifications then followed. The key services offered by a WSRF instantiation were then briefly discussed, including security, informational, data management, scheduling, and administrative services. The chapter then outlined the architecture of various current instantiations of Grid middleware, primarily those based on WSRF, but also some just based on Web services. This section included a table that summarized the key features of the aforementioned Grid instantiations.

CONCLUSION

The Grid concepts and infrastructure has evolved from its early days of fulfilling the requirements of integrating high-performance computing centers in the United States through to today's vision of providing an Internet-wide virtual environment in which dynamic services represent underlying resources, which can be used by a wide range of applications.

The Grid provides a dynamic wide area environment that supports distributed applications. This is not new, as there have been a number of previous systems that have attempted to provide similar environments, the most notable ones being the OSF's Distributed Computing Environment (DCE) and CORBA from the Object Management Group (OMG). Both of these systems are still being used, but neither has been widely taken up and adopted by academia, industry, and business. The reasons for this are outside the scope of this chapter, but can be assumed to be both technical and political. The important fact is that experiences from using these and other Internet-based distributed environments have fed into the Grid architecture and the instantiations that use WSRF. For example, the competing specifications for Web services–based events—WS-Eventing (Box et al. 2004) and WS-Notification (Graham and Murray; Chappell and Liu) both have features from earlier systems, such as CORBA's notification service (CORBA Notification).

Not only has the convergence of the architecture and standards used driven the emergence of the Grid concepts, in addition the speed and cost of the underlying hardware infrastructure has enabled its realization between resources that are not just hosted by high-performance computing centers, but also between smaller entities and business. This latter aspect has effectively lowered the barrier for entry into the Grid community, which has meant that not only has a wider user base become able to use these technologies, but also the number and type of resources that have become part of the hardware fabric has become increasingly diverse, ranging from traditional ones to sensor networks and other mobile devices.

Even though some may try to sell the Grid as a panacea for all applications, it is becoming clear that a variety of loosely coupled distributed applications are the most suitable for today's systems. These applications include:

- Parameter Sweeps (Condor; Nimrod; NetSolve) are applications that consist of large sets of independent tasks and arise in many fields of science and engineering. Due to their flexible task synchronization requirements, these applications are suited to large-scale distributed platforms, such as the Grid.
- Relational databases are important components associated with many distributed applications. Middleware offerings, such as OGSA-DAI, that can be used to assist with access and integration of data from separate sources via the Grid are increasingly important. Equally, software such as OGSA-DQP that should enable effective and efficient query processing across these distributed databases is being adopted too.
- Another area that has received attention is coupled simulations; these are large-scale applications that are executed on distinct resources, such as a cluster, and the output of one application becomes the input of another. Research areas, such as meteorology and oceanography (Joint Centre for Hydro-Meteorological Research) are developing these types of Grid application.
- Sharing potentially expensive resources is another popular area in which Grid technologies are being applied. The resources may be computational ones, or those used for data storage. Alternatively, the resource may be something akin to the equipment hosted by the Network for Earthquake Engineering Simulation (NEESGrid) project (large shake tables, centrifuges, and tsunami wave tanks), which is a U.S. national collaboratory for earthquake engineers.

Table 1: Summary of Features

	Name	GT 4	UNICORE	gLite	WSRF-Lite	Apache WSRF	WSRF.NET	Crown	OMII	PyGrid Ware
Systems Details	Version	4.01	5.6	1.5	0.6	1.1	3.01	2.0	2.3.3	Alpha
	Architecture	OGSA	OGSA	SOA	OGSA	OGSA	OGSA	OGSA	SOA	OGSA
	Instantiation	WSRF	WSRF	WS	WSRF	WSRF	WSRF	WSRF	WS	WSRF
	Hosting	Apache Tomcat	UNICORE Daemons	Apache Tomcat	Perl Container	Apache Tomcat	Microsoft IIS	Apache Tomcat	Apache Tomcat	Twisted Tomcat
	Languages	Java/C	Java	Java/C/ C++/Python	Perl	Java	C#/C++/VB	Java	Java	Python
	Web Services	Axis	Axis	Axis	SOAP::Lite	Axis	ASP.NET	Axis	Axis	ZSI
Core Services	Comms	GridFTP	UPL	FTS	None	None	None	GridFTP	WS-Reliable Messaging	None
	Scheduling	GRAM	TSI	WMS	None	None	None	CROWN Portal Schedular	GridSAM	None
	Security	GSI/WS-Security	PKI/SSL	VOMS/GSI	SSL/WS-Security	Apache WSS4J	WS-Security	WS-Security	Apache WSS4J	pyOpenS SLM2Crypto
	Information Service	MDS	Incarnation Database	R-GMA	None	None	None	RLDS	Grimores	None
	Other Dependency	GT 2.4		GT 2.4			Web Services extensions	GT 3.9.5		

- A Grid workflow is an automation of a process in which documents, information, or data pass from one service to another for processing, according to a set of procedural rules. A workflow can be composed of other workflow elements and used for building higher-level composite services. There are now many Grid-based workflow systems being used in business and academia (Yu, J., and R. Buyya 2005).
- Distributed data analysis is another area, similar in concept to parameter sweeps, but one in which the data are distributed and analyzed at remote end points. The classic example of this is the Grid infrastructure being set up for the Large Hadron Collider (LHC) Computing Project (LCG)at CERN.

It is clear that the drive for reliable middleware for wide-area distributed computing is now being met by instantiations of WSRF, based on standard Web Services technologies along with a suite of specifications that standardize a number of underlying core services and their attributes. Grid middleware based on a service-oriented architecture is now being increasingly taken up in science, engineering, business, and industry, and being used to provide an infrastructure to support a wide-range of diverse distributed applications.

GLOSSARY

CROWN (China Research and Development environment Over Wide-Area Network) Grid: Middleware being produced by a number of institutions in China.

EGEE: Enabling Grids for E-sciencE.

gLite: Middleware being produced by the EGEE project.

GSI: Grid Security Infrastructure.

JSDL: Job Submission Description Language.

MDS (Monitoring & Discovery System): A component provided in the Globus Toolkit that provides information about the available resources and their status.

OASIS: Organization for the Advancement of Structured Information Standards.

OGF (Open Grid Forum; formerly known as the Global Grid Forum [GGF]): A body that is attempting to standardize and document the processes and protocols that are, or will be, required to construct Grids.

OGSA (Open Grid Services Architecture): describes an abstract architecture for a service-oriented grid environment.

OGSA-DAI (Open Grid Services Architecture—Data Access and Integration): Grid services that allows data access to resources such as databases and files using Web Services.

OMII: Open Middleware Infrastructure Institute.

SOA: Service-oriented architecture.

SOAP: Simple object access protocol. Provides a standard, extensible, composable framework for packaging and exchanging XML messages between a service provider and a service requester.

UDDI (Universal Description, Discovery, and Integration): A platform-independent XML-based registry for publishing information about service provider and their services.

UNICORE (Uniform Interface to Computing Resources): A Grid middleware.

Virtual Organization (VO): Consists a set of individuals and/or institutions having direct access to computers, software, data, and other resources for collaborative problem solving or other purposes.

WSDL (Web Services Description Language): An XML-based language for describing Web Services.

Web Services Resource Framework (WSRF): A set specifications dealing with the association of Web Services with stateful resources.

CROSS REFERENCES

See *Cluster Computing Fundamentals; Grid Computing Implementation; Next Generation Cluster Networks; Utility Computing on Global Grids*.

REFERENCES

4Suite. http://4suite.org (accessed April 14, 2007).

Apache WSRF. http://ws.apache.org/wsrf (accessed April 14, 2007).

Baker, M. A., and G. C. Fox. 1999. Metacomputing: Harnessing informal supercomputers, High Performance Cluster Computing. Englewood Cliffs, NJ: Prentice Hall.

Box, D., L. F. Cabrera, C. Critchley, F. Curbera, D. Ferguson, A. Geller, S. Graham, D. Hull, G. Kakivaya, A. Lewis, B. Lovering, M. Mihic, P. Niblett, D. Orchard, J. Saiyed, S. Samdarshi, J. Schlimmer, I. Sedukhin, J. Shewchuk, B. Smith, S. Weerawarana, and D. Wortendyke. 2004. Web services eventing (WS-Eventing). http://ftpna2.bea.com/pub/downloads/WS-Eventing.pdf (accessed April 14, 2007).

Catlett, C., and L. Smarr. 1992. Metacomputing. *Communications of the ACM*, 35(6): 44–52.

Chappell, D., and L. Liu. Web Services Brokered Notification (v1.2). http://docs.oasis-open.org/wsn/2004/06/wsn-WSBrokeredNotification-1.2-draft-01.pdf (accessed April 14, 2007).

Condor. http://www.cs.wisc.edu/condor (accessed April 14, 2007).

CORBA Notification. http://www.omg.org/technology/documents/formal/notification_service.htm (accessed April 14, 2007).

CORBA. http://www.corba.org (accessed April 14, 2007).

CROWN. http://www.crown.org.cn/en (accessed April 14, 2007).

Czajkowski, K., D. Ferguson, I. Foster, J. Frey, S. Graham, T. Maguire, D. Snelling, and S. Tuecke. 2004. From Open Grid Services Infrastructure to WS-Resource Framework: Refactoring and Evolution, version 1.1. http://globus.org/wsrf/specs/ogsi_to_wsrf_1.0.pdf (accessed April 14, 2007).

DCE. http://www.opengroup.org/dce (accessed April 14, 2007).

distributed.net. www.distributed.net (accessed April 14, 2007).

Eclipse IDE. http://www.eclipse.org (accessed April 14, 2007).

EGEE. http://public.eu-egee.org (accessed April 14, 2007).

FAFNER. www.npac.syr.edu/factoring.html (accessed April 14, 2007).

folding@home. from http://folding.stanford.edu (accessed April 14, 2007).

Foster I. 2002. Three point checklist. www.Gridtoday.com/02/0722/100136.html (accessed April 14, 2007).

Foster, I. 2005. Globus toolkit version 4: Software for service-oriented systems. *Lecture Notes in Computer Science*, 3779:2–13.

Foster, I., and C. Kesselman, eds. 1998. The Grid: Blueprint for a new computing infrastructure. San Francisco: Morgan Kaufmann.

Foster, I., C. Kesselman, and S. Tuecke. 2001. The anatomy of the Grid: Enabling scalable virtual organizations. *International Journal of Supercomputer Applications*, 15(3): pp 200–222.

Foster, I., C. Kesselman, J. Nick, and S. Tuecke. 2002. The physiology of the Grid: An open grid services architecture for distributed systems integration. www.Gridforum.org/ogsi-wg/drafts/ogsa_draft2.9_2002-06-22.pdf (accessed April 14, 2007).

Foster, I., D. Berry, A. Djaoui, A. Grimshaw, B. Horn, H. Kishimoto, F. Maciel, A. Savva, F. Siebenlist, R. Subramaniam, J. Treadwell, and J. Von Reich. 2004. The Open Grid Services Architecture, Version 1.0. http://www.ggf.org/documents/Drafts/draft-ggf-ogsa-spec.pdf (accessed April 14, 2007).

Foster, I., J. Geisler, W. Nickless, W. Smith, and S. Tuecke. 1998. Software infrastructure for the I-WAY metacomputing experiment. *Concurrency: Practice and Experience*, 10(7): 567–581.

Gigabit Testbed Initiative Final Report. 1996. www.cnri.reston.va.us/gigafr (accessed May 7, 2007).

Globus Alliance WSRF. http://www.globus.org/wsrf (accessed April 14, 2007).

Globus. http://globus.org (accessed April 14, 2007).

GridSAM. http://Gridsam.sourceforge.net (accessed April 14 2007).

Grimoires. http://twiki.grimoires.org/bin/view/Grimoires/WebHome (accessed April 14, 2007).

GRIP. http://www.fz-juelich.de/zam/cooperations/grip (accessed April 14, 2007).

GSI. http://forge.Gridforum.org/projects/gsi-wg (accessed April 14, 2007).

Humphrey, M., G. Wasson, M. Morgan, and N. Beekwilder. 2004. An early evaluation of WSRF and WS-Notification via WSRF.NET. Grid Computing Workshop (associated with Supercomputing 2004), November 8, 2004, Pittsburgh.

I-WAY. www.globus.org/alliance/publications/papers/iway_overview.pdf (accessed April 14, 2007).

Job Submission Description Language (JSDL) Working Group. https://forge.Gridforum.org/projects/jsdl-wg (accessed June 20, 2007).

Joint Centre for Hydro-Meteorological Research. http://www.jchmr.org (accessed April 14, 2007).

LCG. http://lcg.web.cern.ch/LCG (accessed April 14, 2007).

Legion. www.cs.virginia.edu/~legion (accessed April 14, 2007).

LHC. http://lhc.web.cern.ch/lhc (accessed April 14, 2007).

LSF. www.platform.com (accessed April 14, 2007).

NEESGrid. http://www.neesGrid.org (accessed April 14, 2007).

NetSolve. http://icl.cs.utk.edu/netsolve (accessed April 14, 2007).

Nimrod. http://www.csse.monash.edu.au/~davida/nimrod.html (accessed April 14, 2007).

OGSA Glossary. http://www.Gridforum.org/Public_Comment_Docs/Documents/draft-ggf-ogsa-glossary-v6.pdf (accessed April 14, 2007).

OGSA-DAI. http://www.ogsadai.org.uk (accessed April 14, 2007).

OGSA-DQP. http://www.ogsadai.org.uk/about/ogsa-dqp (accessed April 14, 2007).

OMII. http://www.omii.ac.uk (accessed June 20, 2007).

pyGridWare. http://dsd.lbl.gov/gtg/projects/pyGridWare (accessed April 14, 2007).

pyXML. http://sourceforge.net/projects/pyxml (accessed April 14, 2007).

RAHWL. http://ccs.chem.ucl.ac.uk/projects/omii.shtml (accessed April 14, 2007).

RSA. 1991. www.rsa.com (accessed April 14, 2007).

Salz, R. 2007. ZSI: The Zolera Soap Infrastructure Developer's Guide. http://pywebsvcs.sourceforge.net/zsi.html (accessed April 14, 2007).

SETI@home. http://setiathome.berkeley.edu (accessed April 14, 2007).

SGE. http://Gridengine.sunsource.net (accessed April 14, 2007).

SOAP::Lite. http://soaplite.com (accessed April 14, 2007).

Tuecke, S., K. Czajkowski, I. Foster, J. Frey, S. Graham, C. Kesselman, T. Maquire, T. Sandholm, D. Snelling, and P. Vanderbilt. 2003. Open Grid Services Infrastructure (OGSI) Version 1.0, Global Grid Forum, GFD-R-P.15. http://www.ggf.org/documents/GWD-R/GFD-R.015.pdf (accessed April 14, 2007).

Twisted. http://twistedmatrix.com/products/twisted (accessed April 14, 2007).

UNICORE Plus. http://www.fz-juelich.de/unicoreplus (accessed April 14, 2007).

UNICORE. http://www.unicore.org (accessed April 14, 2007).

UniGrids. http://www.uniGrids.org (accessed April 14, 2007).

Virtual Organization. 2007. http://en.wikipedia.org/wiki/Grid_computing#Virtual_organization (accessed April 13, 2007).

Web Services Activity. www.w3.org/2002/ws (accessed April 14, 2007).

WSA. http://www.w3.org/Submission/ws-addressing/ (accessed April 14, 2007).

WS-BaseNotification. March 2004. ftp://www6.software.ibm.com/software/developer/library/ws-notification/WS-BaseN.pdf

WS-BF. http://docs.oasis-open.org/wsrf/wsrf-ws_base_faults-1.2-spec-pr-01.pdf (accessed April 14, 2007).

WS-BrokeredNotification. March 2004. ftp://www6.software.ibm.com/software/developer/library/ws-notification/WS-BrokeredN.pdf

WSBPEL. http://www-128.ibm.com/developerworks/library/specification/ws-bpel (accessed April 14, 2007).

WSRF.NET. http://www.ws-rf.net (accessed April 14, 2007).

WSRF::Lite. from http://www.sve.man.ac.uk/Research/AtoZ/ILCT (accessed April 14, 2007).

WSRF-SG. http://docs.oasis-open.org/wsrf/2004/06/wsrf-WS-ServiceGroup-1.2-draft-02.pdf (accessed April 14, 2007).

WS-RL. http://docs.oasis-open.org/wsrf/2004/06/wsrf-WS-ResourceLifetime-1.2-draft-03.pdf (accessed April 14, 2007).

WS-RP. http://docs.oasis-open.org/wsrf/2004/06/wsrf-WS-ResourceProperties-1.2-draft-06.pdf (accessed April 14, 2007).

WS-Topics.March 2004. ftp://www6.software.ibm.com/software/developer/library/ws-notification/WS-Topics.pdf

Yu, J., and R. Buyya. 2005. A taxonomy of workflow management systems for grid computing. *Journal of Grid Computing*, 3(3–4):171–200.

Grid Computing Implementation

Barry Wilkinson, *University of North Carolina at Charlotte*
Clayton Ferner, *University of North Carolina at Wilmington*

INTRODUCTION

This chapter addresses Grid computing implementation that was introduced in Chapter 139. Grid computing allows people to use geographically distributed, networked computers and resources collectively to achieve high-performance computing and resource sharing. The implementation of grids has been evolving since the mid-1990s. Early Grid computing work in the early to mid-1990s focused on customized solutions—that is, projects developed in-house software to achieve the interconnections and Grid computing faculties. The early experiences provided the impetus for later standardized work. One of the most important technical aspects of Grid computing is the use of standard Internet protocols and open standards. The use of standardized technologies is critical to the wide adoption of Grid computing. It has now been recognized that XML and Web services provide a very flexible standard way of implementing Grid computing components. We will begin by briefly outlining Web services, XML, and Web Services Description Language (WSDL). With that basis, we can then describe the components of a Grid computing infrastructure.

GRID COMPUTING INFRASTRUCTURE

Web Services

Web services are software components designed to provide specific operations ("services") that are accessible using standard Internet technology. They are usually addressed by a uniform resource locator (URL). A URL is a string of characters that is used to identify a resource on the World Wide Web. URLs conform to a defined syntax and include the protocol used to access the resource. For example www.cs.uncc.edu is the URL of the main computer science page at UNC-C, to be accessed by hypertext transfer protocol (HTTP). Web services are designed to be accessed over a network by other programs. The Web service itself may be located anywhere that can be reached on the Internet. A Web service can be used as a front end to an application to allow the application to be accessed remotely through the Web service.

Web services build on previous distributed computing concepts. An early form of distributed computing was the remote procedure call (RPC) introduced in the 1980s. This model allows a local program to execute a procedure on a remote computer and then get back results from that procedure. Later forms of distributed computing introduced distributed objects, for example CORBA (Common Object Request Broker Architecture) and Java RMI (remote method invocation). A fundamental requirement of all forms of RPCs is the need for the calling programs to know details of accessing the remote procedure. Procedures have input and output parameters with specific meanings and types. The specific calling details need to be known by the calling program. These details can be described using an interface description language (IDL). Web services use an XML-based IDL, which provides a very flexible and elegant solution, as we shall see.

RPCs introduced an important concept, that of a client-server model with a service registry, which is retained for Web services. In a client/server model, the client accesses the server for a particular operation. The server responds accordingly. For this to happen, the client needs to identify the location of the required service and know how to communicate with the service to get it to provide the actions required. You can achieve these two things by using a service registry, which is usually a third party, in a structure now known as a service-oriented architecture (SOA), as shown in Figure 1. The sequence of events then is as follows: First, the server (service provider) "publishes" its service(s) in a service registry. Second, the client (service requestor) can ask the service registry to locate the service. Third, the client (service requestor) binds with the service provider to invoke the service. An interface description language (IDL) can be used to describe the service interface.

Key aspects of using Web services in a client-registry-service model is the use of XML and Internet protocols to make the arrangement completely platform-independent and nonproprietary. Let us first consider XML and then the XML language used to describe the Web service functionality, called WSDL. Then we will discuss the

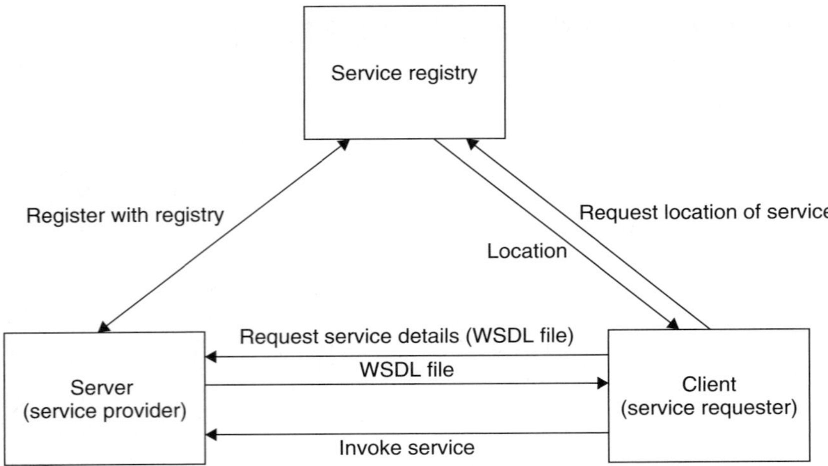

Figure 1: Service-oriented architecture

packaging communication protocols used to transmit the XML documents, known as SOAP.

XML (Extensible Mark-up Language)

Mark-up languages provide a way of describing information in a document such that the information can be recognized and extracted. The Standard Generalized Mark-Up Language (SGML) is a specification for a mark-up language ratified in 1986. A key aspect of SGML is using pairs of named tags that surround information (the body), a begin tag `<tag_name>` and a matching end tag `</tag_name>`, where `tag_name` is the name of the tag. Tags can be nested.

Hypertext Markup Language (HTML) is a subsequent mark-up language using a similar approach but specifically designed for Web pages. "Hypertext" refers to the text's ability to link to other documents. "Markup" refers to providing information that tells the browser how to display the page and other things. The meanings of tags in HTML are predefined—for example, `<B>` to start bold text and `</B>` to end bold text. Certain tags in HTML do not necessarily require end tags, such as `<P>` alone, which indicates the start of a new paragraph. Many tags can have attributes that specify something about the information between tag pair. For example, `<FONT FACE=Times COLOR=red>` specifies that the text in the body will be red and in Times font. The concept of attributes is very important and is used extensively in XML.

XML is very important standard mark-up language; it is a "simplified" SGML, ratified in 1998. XML was developed to represent textual information in a structured manner that could be read and interpreted by a computer. XML is a foundation for Web services, and Web services now form the basis of Grid computing. Two key aspects of XML are:

- Names of tags and attributes are not predefined as they are in HTML. Tags can be defined broadly at will but must be defined somewhere and associated with the document that is using the named tags.
- Tags are always used in pairs delineating information to make it easy to process. (There is an exception to this rule when the body between the tags is empty, in which case the opening and closing tags may be combined into a single tag of the form `<tagName/>`.)

Tag names and meanings can be created to suit the application and become a specific XML language. As such, an infinite number of XML languages could be invented, and many have already been.

Namespace Mechanism

If XML documents are combined, there is the problem of ambiguity if different documents use the same tag names for different purposes. The namespace mechanism provides a way of distinguishing tags with the same name, and is used widely within XML documents. With the namespace mechanism, tag names are given an additional namespace identifier to qualify it. The fully qualified name is given by namespace identifier plus the name used in the document. The namespace identifier used is a uniform resource identifier (URI). A URI is a string of characters used to identify a resource. An extension of URIs to cover international language symbols is called an international resource identifier (IRI). Typically, a namespace uses a URL. (URLs are a subset of URIs and include the protocol used to access the resource.) Even though the namespace may be a URL, the URL is only used as a means of distinguishing tag names and solve any ambiguity. The URL does not need to exist. However, typically one would place a read-me document at the location if a URL is used. This practice has been formalized into providing a Resource Directory Description Language (RDDL) document.

Rather than simply concatenate the namespace identifier with the local name throughout the document, the names in the document are given a prefix separated from the name with a colon. The association of namespace identifier and prefix is done using the `xmls` attribute in the root element, in which the qualifying name is the attribute's value. There can be more than one namespace attribute, each associated with a different prefix, and there will also be a default namespace defined for names without a prefix.

Schemas

So far, we have not said which tags are legal in a document and how the tags are associated with a particular meaning and use. One way to define which tags are legal in a particular XML document is to describe them within the document in the document type definitions (DTD). However, this approach has serious limitations in terms of system integration and flexibility and is not currently used for Web services. In fact, they are not allowed in SOAP messages (the messaging protocol used for XML documents; see below). An alternative and much more powerful approach is to define legal tags in another XML document, called a "schema," and associate that schema document with the content XML document, either explicitly or by common agreement between the parties. XML schemas, also expressed in XML, provide a flexible way of handling legal element names and have the notation of data types. This approach also leads to different XML languages, each with its own schema. Once a schema exists for a particular XML language, it can be associated with XML documents, or *instances* of possible documents using the schema.

Since a schema is also an XML language, there should also be a schema for schemas. The schema for the XML schema is predefined and specified in the XSD (XML schema definition) language. More details on XML schemas can be found at the W3C website (W3C Architecture Domain XML Schema, n.d.).

SOAP

SOAP is a communication protocol for passing XML documents, standardized by the W3C organization (World Wide Web Consortium). Originally, SOAP stood for simple object access protocol. However, the spelled-out version has since been dropped because this name was not accurate; specifically the protocol does not involve object access. The draft W3C specification (Gudgin et al. 2003) describes SOAP as follows:

> SOAP Version 1.2 (SOAP) is a lightweight protocol intended for exchanging structured information in a decentralized, distributed environment. It uses XML technologies to define an extensible messaging framework providing a message construct that can be exchanged over a variety of underlying protocols. The framework has been designed to be independent of any particular programming model and other implementation specific semantics.

SOAP provides mechanisms for defining the communication unit (a SOAP message), the data representation, error handling, and other features. SOAP messages are transported using standard Internet protocols, most likely HTTP.

Web Service Definition Language

In the Web services approach, there needs to be a way of generally and formally describing a service, what it does, how it is accessed, etc. in an IDL. The World Wide Web Consortium (W3C) has published an XML standard for describing Web services called Web Service Description Language (WSDL). WSDL version 1.1 was introduced in 2001. WSDL version 2 was introduced in 2004 and made a number of clarifying changes.

A WSDL document describes three fundamental properties of a service:

- What it is—operations (methods) it provides
- How it is accessed—data format, protocols
- Where it is located—protocol specific network address

The abstract definition of the operations is contained in the element called `interface` (called a portType in WSDL version 1.1). This element contains elements called `operation` that specify the types of message sent and received (`input` and `output` elements). These operation elements loosely correspond to a method prototype. The messages are further defined in terms of data types being passed in the type element. The `binding` element describes how to access the service—that is, how the elements in abstract interfaces are converted in actual data representations and protocols (e.g. SOAP over HTTP). In WSDL version 2, the `service` element described where to find the service. The `service` element contains the `endpoint` element, which provides the name of the end point and physical address (URL). (The `service` element was defined differently in WSDL version 1.1. The `port` elements describe the location of a service and the `service` element defined a named collection of ports.) More information on WSDL version 2 is given by Booth and Liu (2005).

Putting It Together

The basic parts of a service-oriented architecture are the service provider (server), service requestor (client), and service registry. Web services can use a UDDI (Universal Description, Discovery and Integration) registry, which itself is a Web service. UDDI is a discovery mechanism for Web services and provides a specification for modeling information targeted primarily toward business applications of Web services. For Grid computing applications, other ways of forming service information for discovery are available including using WS-Inspection Language (WSIL) (IBM 2001). After a registry is populated with Web service entries, the client can access the registry to find out whether the desired Web service exists in the registry and if so where it is located. The registry responds with the identification of the server capable of satisfying the needs of the client. Then, the client can access the server for the Web service interface. The server responds with a WSDL document describing the service and how to access it. The client can then send the Web service a request for an operation. The result of the operation is returned in a message from the Web service. All messages in this architecture are SOAP messages. It would be feasible for the registry to return the WDSL interface document and then with this in hand, the client could make a request immediately to the Web service without asking for its WSDL interface document.

Note that the registry itself has to be known both to the client and the service provider. Of course, a registry is

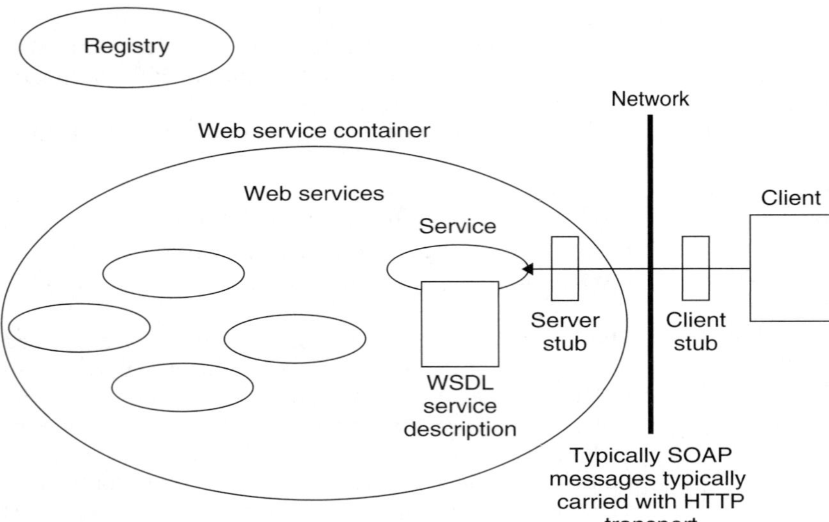

Figure 2: Web services environment

unnecessary if the client knows about the Web service already and the location of the Web service never changes. However, in a dynamic and distributed Grid computing environment, a registry or information service is necessary. Now let us look at how to implement a Web service and client. Web services are generally "hosted" in a Web service container—that is, a software environment that provides the communication mechanisms to and from the Web services. Web services are deployed within such an environment. There are several possible environments that are designed for Web services, notably, Apache Axis (Apache eXtensible Interaction System), IBM Websphere, and Microsoft .NET. The J2EE (Java 2 Enterprise Edition) server container is also a candidate for hosting Web services especially in enterprise (business) applications. Apache Axis requires an application server. It can be installed on top of a servlet engine such as Apache Jakarta Tomcat. However, it could be installed on top of a fully fledged J2EE server.

For the implementation, it is convenient to connect the service code to the client through two Java classes that act as intermediaries, one at the client end called a "client stub" (also called a "client proxy") and one at the service end called a "server stub" (also called a "skeleton"). These stubs provide a structured way to handle the messaging and different client and server implementations. Interaction is between the client and its stub, between the client stub and the server stub, and between the server and its server stub. The interaction between the stubs is across the network using SOAP messages. The client stub is responsible for taking a request from the client and converting the request into a form suitable for transmission, which is called "marshaling." The client stub is also responsible for receiving responses on the network and converting to a suitable form for the client. The server stub is responsible for receiving a SOAP request from the client stub and converting it into a suitable form for the service, called "unmarshaling." The server stub also converts the response from the service into a SOAP message for the client stub. The resulting Web service environment is shown in Figure 2.

Web services deployment descriptor (WSDD) is an XML language used to specify how to deploy a Web service. More details of Web services and their deployment can be found in Graham et al. (2005).

Grid Computing Standards

Early Grid Computing Standards

Although Web services are very attractive as a basis for creating a grid infrastructure, Grid computing requires some way of representing state—that is, values that persist from one invocation of the service to the next. Pure Web services do not have state. Another feature needed in Grid computing is the ability to make a service transient—that is, to be able to create and destroy a service. Typically, transient services are created by specific clients and do not outlive their clients. Web services are usually thought of as nontransient and do not have the concept of service creation and destruction. Hence, some changes are needed to the Web services approach if it is to be adapted to Grid computing.

The Global Grid Forum (GGF), in developing standards for Grid computing, focused on using Web services and originally developed two interrelated standards called Open Grid Services Architecture (OGSA) and Open Grid Services Infrastructure (OGSI). The term *Grid service* was introduced as the extended Web service that conforms to the OGSI standard. OGSA defines standard mechanisms for creating, naming, and discovering Grid services and deals with architectural issues to make interoperable grid services. OGSA is described in the seminal paper "The Physiology of the Grid: An Open Grid Services Architecture for Distributed Systems Integration" by Foster, Kesselman, Nick, and Tuecke (2002). OGSI specifies the way that clients interact with grid services (that is, service invocation, management of data, security mechanism, etc.). These standards appeared in the early 2000s and were implemented in the Globus Toolkit version 3 in 2003. In OGSI, the Web service model was extended to enable state to be implemented. An extension of WSDL was invented called Grid Web Service Description Language (GWSDL) to support the extra features in Grid services not present in Web services. However, OGSI had a very short life. The Grid community at large did not embrace OGSI, which was seen by many as too complex. The push was made to align OGSA more closely with Web services so that existing Web service tools could be used. This led to the Web Services Resource Framework, which is discussed below.

Web Services Resource Framework

Web Services Resource Framework (WSRF) presents a way of representing state while still using the basic WSDL for both Web services applications in general and Grid computing in particular. Instead of modifying the WSDL to handle state, the state is embodied in a separate resource. Then, the Web service acts as a front end to that resource as illustrated in Figure 3. The resource still needs to be described in the WSDL file, which is achieved in a resources properties section of the WSDL file. The combination of a Web service and resource in this framework is called a WS-Resource. The resource in this description can mean anything that has state and requires access, such as a database, or variables of a Web service that need to be retained between accesses.

The WSRF specification calls for a set of six Web services specifications:

- WS-ResourceProperties
- WS-ResourceLifetime
- WS-Notification
- WS-RenewableReferences
- WS-ServiceGroup
- WS-BaseFaults

WS-ResourceProperties describes how resources are defined and accessed. Other aspects of WSRF deal with using multiple resources, resource lifetime, and how to obtain notification of changes (WS-Notification).

Web services are traditionally addressed simply by a URL, but this does not provide much functionality. A specification called WS-Addressing has been introduced to provide more than just the URL, and it is particularly relevant to WSRF, as it provides a way of specifying resources as well as the Web service. WS-Addressing introduced a construct called an end-point reference (EPR). An end point is the destination where the service can be accessed. An end-point reference is a structure that provides the end point address as a URI (more recently as an IRI). The structure also provides other, optional information, consisting of reference parameters and metadata. The metadata include information about the behavior, capabilities, and policies of the end point.

According to the W3C document "Web Service Addressing 1.0 Core" (Gudgin and Hadley 2005), the reference parameters are "namespace qualified element information items that are required to properly interact with the endpoint." For WSRF, the reference parameter feature is used to convey the identity of the resource. (WS-Addressing originally included a parameter named "reference properties" that was used.) The end-point reference is then called "WS-Resource-qualified" (Czajkowski et al. 2004). The resource identity can simply be an assigned number or a character string. It is called a "key" by Ananthakrishnan et al. (2005). The end-point reference typically would be returned when the WS-Resource is created and can be used to identify it for access and destruction.

Software Components for Grid Computing

The Globus project (Foster 2005; The Globus Toolkit 2006) provides reference implementations for Grid computing standards and is a de facto standard itself. The approach taken by Globus is to provide a toolkit of component parts, which can be used separately or, more likely, collectively for creating a grid infrastructure. The Globus Toolkit has gone through four versions from the late 1990s to 2005. Many of the ideas embodied in Globus were present from version 1 of Globus, including job submission and security mechanisms. Globus version 2 describes the basic structural components within a grid security environment as three pillars:

- Resource Management
- Data Management
- Information Services

This division of parts essentially remains in the current release. The principal task of the resource management

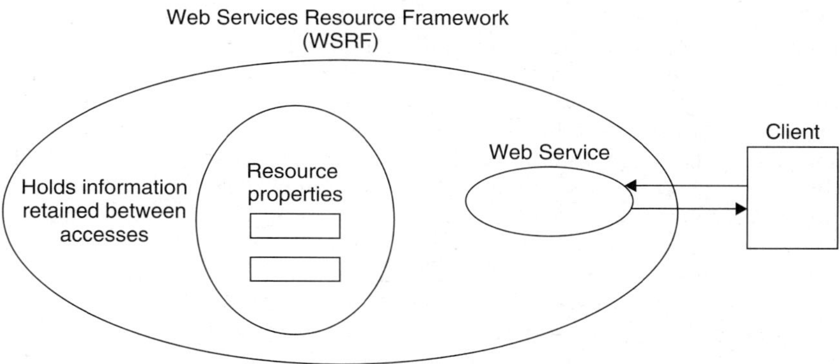

Figure 3: Web Services Resource Framework

component, GRAM (Grid Resource Allocation Manager), is to submit jobs. These jobs are submitted to local resources via a local scheduler. GRAM provides an interface to local schedulers such as load sharing facility (LSF) (Platform 2006), Portable Batch System (PBS) (Altair Grid Technologies 2006), Sun Grid Engine (SGE) (Sun N1 Grid Engine 6 2006), and Condor (Thain, Tannenbaum, and Livny 2003), which then pass the job onto the computer resources. Jobs often need data files, and the data management component provides the ability to transfer files to the required places. The key component is the grid version of FTP called GridFTP. Grid Information Services (GIS), as the name suggests, provide information about the grid infrastructure. The information directory service in Globus version 2 is called Metacomputing Directory Service (MDS), which enables Lightweight Directory Access Protocol (LDAP)–based information structures to be constructed. Globus version 2 Grid Resource Information Service (GRIS) provided information on the computational resources (configuration, capabilities, status). The Grid Index Information Service (GIIS) was also provided for pulling together information.

Globus version 3 retains the basic components of version 2 but is implemented using OGSA/OGSI standards. Globus version 4, introduced in 2005, builds on previous versions and implements the components using the WSRF standard. Note, however, that versions are not backward-compatible, as the standards they followed are not compatible; although some pre-Web-services components remain in later Web-service versions. Also note that even in the WSRF Globus version 4, for efficiency reasons, that some functionalities are not Web services. For example, GridFTP is not a Web service, although there is a Web-service front-end available (reliable file transfer [RFT] service, see below). A common feature of all versions (1, 2, 3, and 4) is the use of the public key infrastructure (PKI) for security. Security is considered in detail in the following section.

GRID SECURITY

Basic Security Concepts

It is clearly necessary in the distributed structure of a Grid infrastructure to secure communication and secure access to resources to stop unauthorized access and tampering. Security is also required in important transactions on the Internet, and hence similar mechanisms that are used there can be used in Grid computing, following the strategy that standard Internet protocols should be used for widespread adoption of Grid computing. There are some special additional security requirements for Grid computing. First, secure communication is needed not only between users but also between users and resources, such as computers, and between the resources themselves. Second, specifically related to communication between resources themselves, it is necessary to delegate the user's authority to programs to act on the user's behalf, including at remote sites, while preferably requiring the user to sign on only once (single sign-on). Before developing the full solution to these factors, let us first consider general security concepts.

Two critically important security concepts are:

- *Authentication*—The process of deciding whether a particular identity is who he, she, or it says he, she, or it is (applies to humans and systems)
- *Authorization*—The process of deciding whether a particular identity can access a particular resource, including whether the specific type of access is allowed. This latter aspect is commonly called Access control.

The traditional way to authenticate users is for each to have a username and password. Users who wish to be authenticated enter their username and password, which are sent to a server through the network. Upon receipt, the server validates the username and password and responds accordingly. There are two aspects to make such password-based authentication workable:

- Information needs to be sent in a form that is unintelligible except to the parties involved, otherwise the username and password could be stolen.
- The identity of the sender has to be proved in some fashion.

The term *data confidentiality* is used to describe the protection of the information exchange from eavesdroppers, and this is done by scrambling the binary patterns in a process called "encryption." There are many algorithms that could be used to encrypt data. Usually, the algorithm is not kept secret. Instead a number used in the algorithm is kept secret. This number is called a "key." To make it difficult to discover the key, the key chosen is a very large number, typically 128 bits or more. In secret key cryptography or symmetric key cryptography, the same key is used to encrypt the data as to decrypt it. In that case, both the sender and the receiver need to know the key, but the key has to be kept secret from everyone else.

It is possible to devise an algorithm that uses two keys, one to encrypt the data and one to decrypt it. This is known as "asymmetric key cryptography." In this form of cryptography, one key, called the "public key," is made known to everyone, while the other key, called the "private key," is known only to the owner. Data encrypted with the receiver's public key can be decrypted only by the receiver using his or her private key. Asymmetric key cryptography is also called "public key cryptography" because of the use of one key being made publicly available. In asymmetric cryptography, there is no known practical way of discovering one key from the other key. However, it is slower to encrypt/decrypt data using public key cryptography than using secret key cryptography. In addition, if you were to encrypt data using a receiver's public key, the receiver cannot be sure of the identity of the sender, as everyone has access to the public key. So mechanisms need to be in place to confirm identities.

Data integrity is the name given to ensuring that data were not modified in transit (either intentionally or by accident). Data confidentiality—that is, protecting the data from eavesdroppers—is obtained by encrypting the data. To achieve data integrity, a binary pattern called a "digest" is attached to the data, computed from the data using a hash function. The digest is different

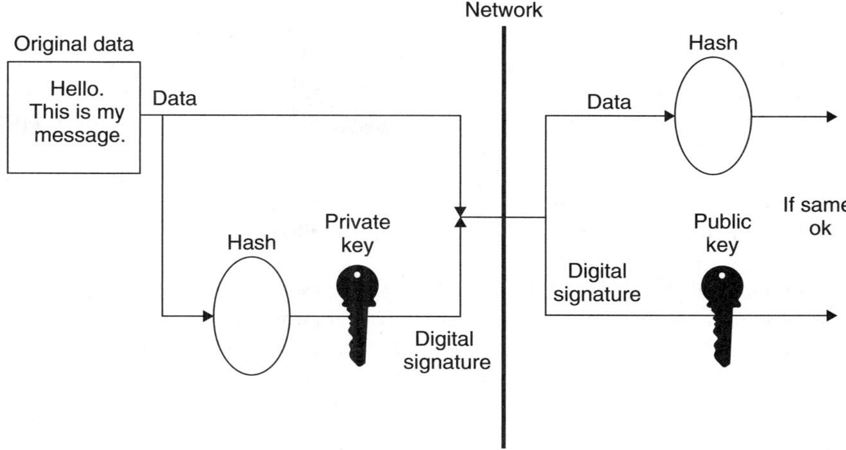

Figure 4: Checking digital signatures

if the data have been altered in transit. To achieve both data integrity and authentication, the digest is encrypted with the sender's private key to create a digital signature, which is attached to the data instead of the digest itself. The receiver can check the digital signature by decrypting the signature (with the sender's public key) and comparing the result with the digest created separately from the received data, as illustrated in Figure 4. Note that if data can be decrypted with the sender's public key, it can only have been encrypted with the sender's private key and hence by the sender.

However, digital signatures alone are not sufficient to ensure that the data are truly from the sender. It is possible that the public key is a fake—i.e. from an attacker instead of from the trusted sender. To cover this possibility, users are issued certificates, which are digital documents listing the user's specific public key. A trusted third party called a "certificate authority" (CA) certifies that the public key does in fact belong to the user named on the certificate.

Certificates are comparable to driver's licenses and passports as a form of identity. The most widely used certificate format is the X.509. Version 1 of this format was defined in 1988 by International Telecommunications Union (ITU). Versions 2 and 3 added some fields. Information provided in the certificate includes the name and digital signature of the issuer (certificate authority), algorithm used for signature, name of the subject (user), subject's public key, public key algorithm used, and validity period. Names have to be unique and recognizable. To this end, the X.500 distinguished name format is used. The X.500 naming format is a hierarchical list of attributes that is intended to make the name globally unique. An example of a distinguished name is: `/C=us/O=University of North Carolina at Charlotte/OU=Computer Science/CN=Barry Wilkinson`, where `C` indicates country, `O` the organization, `OU` the organizational unit, and `CN` the common name. Another possible attribute is `/L` for location. How names are constructed must be agreed on by all parties and is part of written certificate policies. There are obviously many possibilities, even within the constraints of the X.500 distinguished name format, from highly hierarchical to almost flat.

To obtain a signed certificate for themselves, users first contact a certificate authority. Generally, the user generates his or her own public/private key pair and sends the public key to the certificate authority, keeping the private key in a very secure place. The certificate authority returns a signed certificate. The certificate authority has to be given some means of proving the identity of the user, which may require some off-line procedure in which humans communicate—i.e. the user communicates with the manager of the certificate authority. Once the user has a signed certificate, the certificate can be sent with the data to other parties. Alternatively, the data can be sent without the sender's certificate and the receiver retrieves the sender's certificate from a public place. Either way, the receiver of a user certificate can verify the certificate by verifying the CA's signature. Then, it can trust the sender's public key contained in the certificate. It is necessary for the receiver to have the certificate authority's public key, which is obtained from the certificate authority's own certificate. (The certificate authority signs its own certificate.) This process works if one can trust the certificate authority and its public key.

There are several protocols that use the above PKI, the most notable being SSL (secure sockets layer), which can be added on top of protocols such as HTTP and FTP. The SSL protocol involves exchanging a sequence of messages that includes randomly generated numbers, and provides for mutual authentication, although in many Web applications the user is not authenticated, only the server. Commercial certificate authorities exist, such as Verisign and Entrust Technologies. Web browsers have built-in recognition for such trusted certificate authorities to allow SSL and other secure connections.

Certificates have a valid time period specified on the certificate defined by "not before" and "not after" parameters. Typically, the validity period set is quite long, say one year or five years. It is critically important to maintain the private key very securely, usually on your local computer encrypted using a password. The private key will be used to encrypt data that are to be decrypted with your public key and to decrypt data that was encrypted with your public key.

At the beginning of this section, we differentiated between authentication (the process of deciding whether a particular identity is who he says he is), and authorization (the process of deciding whether a particular identity can access a particular resource). A simple authorization mechanism is the access control list found in UNIX/Linux based systems and also in Windows systems. An access control list is a table listing the users and groups of users allowed to access particular resources and what type of access is allowed. In a UNIX/Linux-based system, for example, access to files and directories are controlled by an access control list. The access control list concept can be carried over to Grid computing systems, although the distributed nature and different administrative domains of resources of a grid make it desirable to have further mechanisms, which we shall discuss in the next section.

Grid Security Infrastructure

Grid Security Infrastructure (GSI) is the Grid computing security that is implemented in Globus; it is a GGF standard. GSI uses PKI and the SSL protocol for mutual authentication. More recently, WS-Security can be used, which is an extension to SOAP messaging for security. Grid computing projects usually form their own certificate authorities. The Globus Toolkit provides an implementation of a certificate authority called "simpleCA" that can be used for small projects. We shall discuss CAs for larger projects later. First let us consider additional security features required for Grid computing.

Delegation

Delegation is the process of giving authority to another identity (usually a computer or process) to act on one's behalf. Implicit in delegation is the concept of single sign-on, which enables users and its agents to acquire additional resources without repeated authentication. Usually, the user's private key is password-protected (encrypted with a password) and each time a user has to access the private key to perform a security-related operation, the user would need to type in the password. Single sign-on avoids this practice. Delegation is achieved by the use of additional certificates called "proxy certificates" (loosely called "proxies"). Proxy certificates are signed by the user (or the proxy entities themselves in a chain of trust) rather than by the certificate authority. Proxy certificates are created with new public and private keys and the user's name with the attribute `/CN=proxy` added to the name. The private key of the proxy is not password-protected, only file-system-protected in the user's file system. (If it were password-protected, it would defeat the purpose of reducing the need for typing passwords). To combat this insecurity, the validity period of proxy certificates is set to be short, say 12 hours, and, of course, not past the validity of the original user certificate from which it is based.

Suppose the user wants to delegate his authority to a third party to act on his behalf. This third party requires a proxy certificate signed by the user and she makes a request to the user for a signed proxy certificate, just as the user asked a certificate authority for a certificate for himself. Acting as his own proxy certificate authority, the user returns a proxy certificate signed by himself. The user also sends her own certificate. The third party requires the user's certificate to be able to validate to the proxy certificate, just as the CA's certificate is required to validate the certificate. As described by Ferreira et al. (2004), both the certificate and the proxy certificate are checked for the user's name (the proxy with the added proxy attribute). Once all validation is done, the third party can issue requests to others on the user's behalf, using the proxy's private key to encrypt messages.

The delegation process can also be chained—that is, the third party having the proxy can generate a proxy to another party using the same procedure as described for the user giving its proxy. In that case, the proxy issuing its proxy certificate signs it. Proxy certificates are part of the Globus GSI and are proposed as a standard (GT 4.0 Security: Key Concepts, n.d.). Proxies are used for delegation locally as well as remotely. Creating a proxy is one of the first actions a user must do when using Globus with the command `grid-proxy-init`.

Credential Management

A certificate and corresponding private key are collectively called the "credentials" (i.e. user credentials, proxy credentials, host credentials, etc.). However, the private key is available only to the owner, and the word *credentials* is used quite loosely as not including the private key, which should not be transferred under any circumstances. It is convenient to have a central credential repository to store proxy credentials, which then can be accessed as required rather than having to maintain the credentials in several places. Globus version 4 provides a proxy credential repository called MyProxy (MyProxy Credential Management Service 2006). MyProxy is accessed by other components to store, retrieve, and renew proxy credentials. These components include grid portals and job managers, as described later.

Authorization

To connect to a remote site, you need permission (authorization) and an account. The simplest authorization mechanism is a form of access control list called a "grid-map file." The grid-map file is a file maintained at the site and holds list of user's distinguished name (as given on their certificates) and their corresponding local account name. An entry might be: `"C=us/O=University of North Carolina at Charlotte/OU=Computer Science/CN=Barry Wilkinson" abw` where `abw` is the local username. The user's local access rights apply. It is allowable to map more than one user to a single local account if desired—i.e., to have a group working with a single account.

The grid-map file approach, although straightforward and implemented in GT 4.0, does not scale well. It requires each resource in the grid to maintain a separate grid-map file containing entries for all those expected to use the site. For a system with more than two or three sites, this becomes unmanageable.

Large-Scale Grid Computing Security Infrastructure

There are many issues in creating a large-scale Grid computing infrastructure. In the previous section, we saw that the traditional access control list, although feasible for a small system, is unworkable for a large system. Grid computing is all about large-scale geographically distributed infrastructures. Many of the problems for large-scale structures are still open research problems with many potential solutions being suggested. Building a large-scale grid system around the basic tools of GSI will require additional scalable tools.

Authentication

Rather than have a single certificate authority, one might choose to use multiple certificate authorities, perhaps one at each major site in the Grid. This was done for an undergraduate Grid computing course taught across North Carolina (Wilkinson and Ferner 2005). Each user receives a certificate issued by one of the certificate authorities. When the certificate is submitted to another site for authentication, it is necessary for that site to trust the issuing certificate authority as illustrated in Figure 5. Globus provides for the configuration of trusting multiple certificate authorities. The certificate of the certificate authority and a configuration file defining the distinguished names of the certificates signed by the certificate authority are simply loaded in the trusted certificate directory of Globus. Each Globus installation would need these two files for each certificate authority to be trusted. It is clear that this approach is not scalable or flexible for a grid that might grow or change in configuration. However, maintaining a list of trusted certificate authorities is the way a Web browser handles trusted certificate authorities.

PKI trust can be chained. Suppose A receives B's certificate for validation, and B's certificate is signed by a certificate authority C, whom A does not immediately trust. If A is also given C's certificate, which is signed by certificate authority D, whom A does trust, then A can obtain the public key of B's certificate authority and trust it. One could construct a hierarchical, tree-like certificate authority structure, with a single root certificate authority that everyone trusts. This root certificate authority signs certificates of certificate authorities below it, which themselves can sign certificates of certificate authorities below and so on until a certificate authority is reached that signs users' certificates. If A wishes to accept B's certificate, it needs to work back from B's certificate to the root certificate authority that it trusts. A certification path is established that has to be navigated. A single-root certificate authority has the disadvantage that if the root is compromised, the whole system is compromised. However, the tree structure may be convenient in some organizations having a similar physical hierarchical structure.

There are other certificate authority configurations using the feature that certificate authorities can be cross-certified. Here, a pair of certificate authorities sign each other's certificates. Usually, a user trusts the certificate authority that signs its own certificate. If a group of certificate authorities are cross-certified in pairs and there is a path between the certificate authority of A and the certificate authority of B, one can establish trust between A and B. This avoids the single trust point of a tree structure and also enables arbitrary PKIs to be formed.

If more than one PKI already exists, either a tree or some arbitrary network, a *bridge certificate authority* may be attractive, which forms a trust between one certificate authority in one PKI and one certificate authority in another PKI. Each such certificate authority is cross-certificated with the bridge. The advantages of a bridge configuration is that it reduces the number of cross certificates from $O(N^2)$ to $O(N)$, where N is the number of CAs in the configuration, and the whole configuration is not compromised if a single CA is compromised. An example of a grid using bridge cross-certification is the SURA-Grid (SURA NMI Testbed Grid PKI Bridge Certification Authority, n.d.).

Authorization

Scalable authorization structures are also needed in larger grids. The Communication Authorization Service (CAS) is a component, available in Globus versions 3 and 4, designed to handle the authorization of many distributed users and many resources. CAS maintains information on what rights the grid community grants to users.

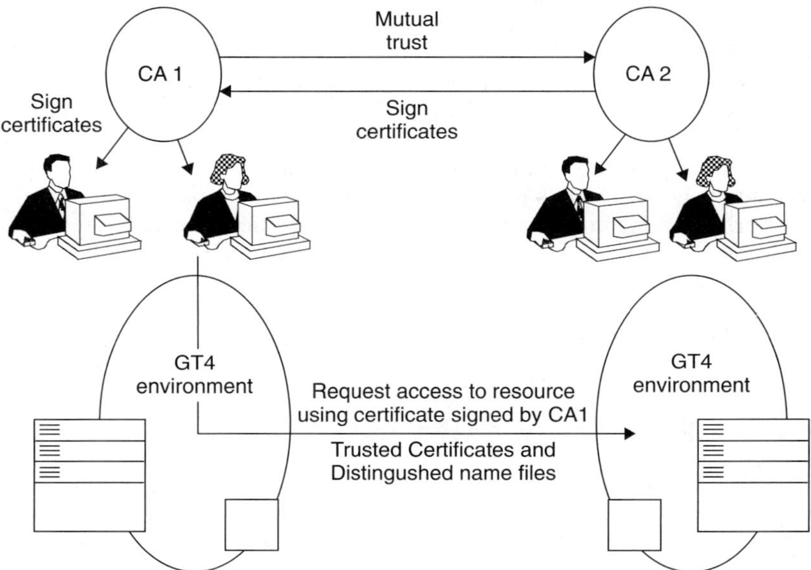

Figure 5: Certificate authorities with mutual trust

The user first asks CAS for permission to use a resource. CAS gives the user proxy credentials with specific rights—that is, a policy statement signed by CAS. The user then presents these credentials to the resource. The resource trusts credentials signed by CAS and accepts the request if the policy statement contained in the credentials authorizes the user for the specific request.

VOMS (Virtual Organization Membership Service) is another system for granting authorization to access resources in a virtual organization. In the VOMS system, the user is assigned membership of groups with roles and capabilities. This information is contained in the proxy certificates returned to the user. Interestingly, this project started by facing the difficulties of using grid-map files but does provide an automatic way of creating grid-map files. Another system that can create grid-map files locally is GUMS (Grid User Management System 2006). In GUMS, the grid-map file can be created statically or dynamically to jobs by the GUMS server.

Organizations will already have a local security system in place for their networks and computers, with which a grid security system may have to interface. One such system, created by MIT, is Kerberos, which provides a network authentication protocol. Kerberos uses tickets, which are electronic credentials used to verify your identity and provide specific access rights. Users first receive a ticket-granting ticket encrypted with their password. If they can decrypt this ticket, they have proved their identity and can obtain additional tickets for specific access rights. Kerberos has the single sign-on feature. For more information, see the Kerberos documentation (Kerberos: The Network Authentication Protocol, n.d.) The KX.509 project (KX.509: X.509 Certificates via Kerberos 2005) provides a means of creating X.509 certificates that are Kerberos-authenticated. These certificates are issued by a Kerberos-authenticated server (KCA). PKINIT is an Internet Engineering Task Force (IETF) Internet draft for authentication in Kerberos that allows a Kerberos ticket to be obtained using GSI credentials rather than a Kerberos password.

SAML (Security Assertions Markup Language) is an Organization for the Advancement of Structured Information Standards (OASIS) standard XML language for communicating user authentication and authorization information. SAML provides assertions that contain statements. These statements are grouped into authentication statements that indicate that the user has been authenticated, attribute statements used for making access control decisions, and authorization decision statements. SAML is a language for use in single sign-on authentication and authorization systems but is not an implementation. An example of a system using SAML is Shibboleth. Detailed information on SAML is given by Hughes and Maler (2005). More information on Shibboleth can be found at Shibboleth Project Web site (Shibboleth Project, n.d.).

RESOURCE MANAGEMENT

Data Management

One of the most challenging issues that has come up in recent years is the management of the large amounts of data being collected by scientists. The challenges of managing large volumes of data are where to store it, how to classify it, what metadata does it need, how to transfer it, where to find data of interest, how to deal with replication, how to deal with distribution, etc. There are several tools included with the Globus Toolkit that can assist with dealing with data in particular for transferring files.

One component is GridFTP (Allcock et al. 2005). GridFTP is actually a protocol, although the Globus Toolkit has an implementation of GridFTP. The protocol builds on the FTP protocol. The extension includes security, reliability, striping, third-party transfers, partial file access, and parallel transfers. GSI security is used, which is PKI-based. Reliability is achieved by having the receiving server periodically send restart markers to the sending server. These markers indicate which bytes have been received so far. This allows the sending server to restart the transfer as necessary. Striping is when either the sending side, receiving side, or both are clusters sharing a parallel file system. Striping allows for each node in the cluster to send part of the file in parallel. GridFTP also supports parallel data transfer through the use of multiple TCP streams between pairs of hosts.

Third-party transfers are a very useful feature, in which a user can initiate from one machine a file transfer that takes place between two other machines. For example, a scientist may want to run a program on a supercomputer with data that currently resides in a data store on another server, but the scientist is currently using a laptop for access. Third-party transfer will allow the scientist to stage the file on the supercomputer without the need to transfer it to the local laptop, which may be impractical or even infeasible if the file is large. Partial file access allows one to transfer only part of a file by providing an offset and total number of bytes desired. This is useful for file caching.

The GridFTP protocol is a low-level file transport protocol. It has very nice and useful features, but should be viewed as a tool on which higher-level tools should be developed. Reliable file transfer (RFT) (Chervenak et al., 2004) is a WSRF-compliant Web service for the transfer of files. Since it makes use of GridFTP, many of the features of GridFTP are available through RFT, such as GSI security, reliability, third-party transfers, and parallel streams. RFT also allows for file deletion and third-party file and directory transfers. RFT extends the reliability of GridFTP by using a PostgresSQL database to store restart markers. These restart markers are used as checkpoints and will allow RFT to continue the file transfer after server, network, container, or file system failures. The RFT Resource is implemented as a PersistentResource, which allows RFT to restart file transfers even after the Web services container is restarted. RFT is a very useful Web service for data management. Its primary contribution is its reliability. Although it is still fairly low-level, most higher-level tools should make use of RFT to take advantage of the security and reliability.

Once a file is transferred between hosts (either FTP, SFTP, GridFTP, or RFT) then there is an automatic duplication of that file. Often, the new copy is a temporary file and will be destroyed in short order. Other times, the file persists. One might view this as wasted space. However, duplication can also be useful. If a scientist transfers a file from a data store to a supercomputer and another scientist needs the same file for another computation on the same machine, then the file would not need to be transferred twice. More likely, there may be a copy of a desired file on a file system that is more local than the file's source. Transferring the file from the local file system will likely be faster.

Replica location service (RLS) (Cai, Chervenak, and Frank 2004) attempts to make these scenarios possible by creating a distributed registry of file replicas. RLS introduces the terms *logical file name*, which is a unique identifier associated with the file contents, and *physical file name*, which refers to an actual file on an actual file system. An RLS deployment consists of at least one local replica catalog (LRC), which stores the logical to physical file name mappings. Clients can query this catalog as well as publish newly created files.

The RLS registry may be distributed, which allows for scalability as well as reliability against a single server crash. For a distributed configuration, RLS uses one or more replica location index (RLI) nodes, which collect logical to physical file name mappings from one or more LRCs. Figure 6 shows such a configuration. When a client queries the RLI, the RLI provides it with a list of LRCs where it believes the desired mappings exist. The client would then need to query those LRCs for the physical locations of the desire file replica. Mappings are sent from the LRCs to the RLIs using a soft-state update protocol. This allows for the mappings to be transferred only periodically. Since the mappings have timeouts associated with them, a RLI that is brought back online after a failure will have its mapping restored.

The data replication service (DRS) (Chervenak et al. 2005) is a WSRF-compliant Web service built on top of RFT and RLS. It attempts to make sure that a set of files is available on a particular file system. It will query RLS to find the desired files. Then it will use RFT to carry out the transfer. After the files have been transferred, DRS will register the duplicates with RLS. DRS is a very powerful tool that provides a nice abstraction of data management to the user. There does not seem to be much use of this level of abstraction in Grid applications yet. However, tools like DRS will be necessary components as the Grid resources and number of users grow.

Job Schedulers and Resource Managers

The Globus Toolkit does not have schedulers built in (with the exception of a "fork" scheduler, which is hardly a scheduler). Schedulers are provided by third-party vendors. There are two levels of scheduling in the Globus environment: local scheduling, which Globus uses to carry out the execution of a job on a local resource, and metascheduling, which is a higher level than the grid middleware.

The basic scheduling mechanism that ships with Globus as the default scheduler is Fork. Fork simply forks a new process in which to run the job. Fork does not provide many features other than the ability to start a job and monitor its status. It is meant only as a tool to allow a server with Globus to function out of the box. Users desiring more functionality should use one of the many other third-party schedulers that provide a much richer set of features.

There are many scheduling packages available, and most of them provide similar functionality. A few of the more popular or well-known scheduling systems are Portable Batch System (PBS) (Altair Grid Technologies 2006), Sun Grid Engine (SGE) (Sun N1 Grid Engine 6 2006), Platform Load Sharing Facility (LSF) (Platform 2006), Maui, and Torque, all of which provide the basics mechanics of scheduling and executing batch jobs on a variety of execution servers. They have similar functionality, such as allowing the user to specify scheduling algorithms, job priority, job interdependency, and automatic file staging.

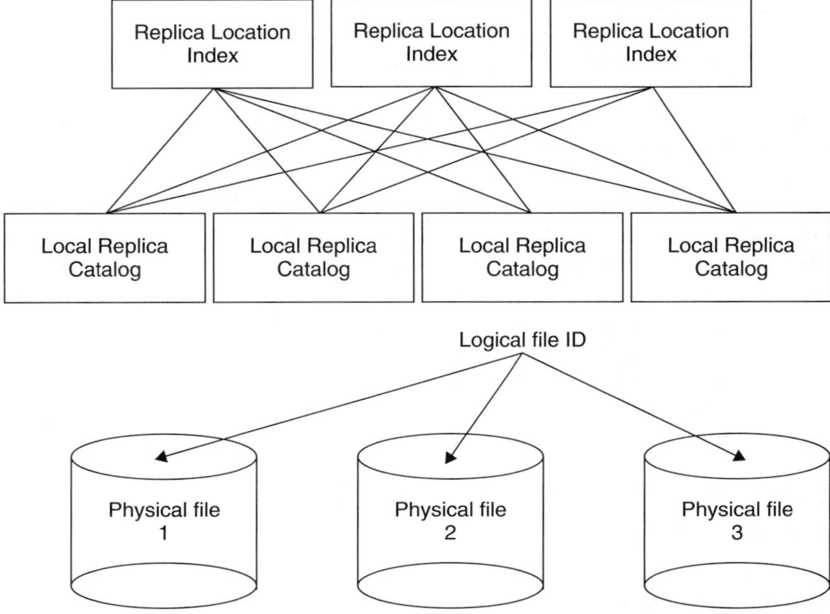

Figure 6: Replica location service configuration

The first implementation of PBS is the OpenPBS by NASA. The PBSPro (by Altair) provides some additional features such as a graphical user interface (GUI), security and access control lists, job accounting, desktop idle-cycle harvesting, automatic load-leveling, username mapping, and parallel job support by supporting libraries such as the Message Passing Interface (MPI), Parallel Virtual Machine (PVM), and High Performance Fortran (HPF). SGE also provides a GUI, checkpointing, and support for parallel jobs.

Condor (Thain, Tannenbaum, and Livny 2003) is a scheduler that is designed to allow users to make use of idle machines. One of the benefits of Condor is that the source code of the job does not need to be modified. However, if the source code can be recompiled and linked with the Condor libraries, then the job can have the benefit of being checkpointed. Checkpointing allows a job to be restarted in mid-execution. The purpose of this is to allow a job to recover after a server failure. Condor also intercepts the system calls of the job and executes them on the local machine (where the job was submitted). What this accomplishes is to allow data to reside on a separate machine, which is less intrusive on the remote machine. Furthermore, the user does not need to have an account on the remote machine.

Nimrod (Abramson et al. 1995) is a tool that controls the distributed execution of parameter-sweep applications. In parameter-sweep applications, the same program will be executed many times on a slightly difference set of input parameters each time. These types of applications are very well suited for distributed computing, as each execution can be run independently. Nimrod is a tool that makes it easy to set up and control the execution of parameter-sweep applications.

Metaschedulers

Metaschedulers are systems that are designed to work at a very high level, on top of existing grid and scheduling middleware, scheduling jobs between sites. Since grids often include systems with heterogeneous resources, they will also likely have a variety of local schedulers. Currently available metaschedulers include Community Scheduler Framework (CSF 2005), Nimrod/G (Buyya, Abramson, and Giddy 2001), and Condor-G (Thain, Tannenbaum, and Livny 2003). These metaschedulers provide similar functionality, such as the ability to submit jobs, define scheduling policies, and make reservations for resources. The resources themselves may use different local schedulers, such as Fork, PBS, LSF, SGE, Nimrod, or Condor. Metaschedulers make use of the Globus Toolkit and can take advantage of the many features provided through the toolkit, such as authentication through GSI, resource discovery through GDS (grid data service), job execution and scheduling through GRAM, and data management through RLS and DRS.

USER INTERFACE AND WORKFLOW MANAGEMENT

Most examples of Grids use a batch-mode processing model. Unfortunately, this has been the mode of operation since the beginning of the computer age. For Grids to gain widespread acceptance and use, they will eventually need to become as easy to use as, say, the World Wide Web. As the World Wide Web and the browser propelled the use of the Internet by scientists and the general population and make the Internet a household name, a similar user-friendly environment will be necessary to propel the use of grids by the general population. There are two main thrusts in the area of graphical and intuitive user interfaces for grids: portals and workflow editors, which are discussed below.

Portals

Grid portals are browser-based dynamic content environments that provide a single sign-on interface to grids. Portals are similar to servlets, in that they are Java-based components that generate dynamic content, usually in the form of HTML, extensible HTML (XHTML), or wireless markup language (WML), which is displayed in a browser. Portals are made up of Java Web-based components called "portlets," which generate the content and are managed in a portal container. Portals also use the client/server relationship as with servlets.

Of course, the purpose of portals is to provide an interface to grids. Although the architecture of portals is similar to servlets, there are a number of differences, which necessitates a separate designation for portals. The most salient of these differences include: portlets only need to generate content fragments as opposed to complete documents, portlets are not associated with a URL, there can be many instances of a portlet within a portal page, portlets can maintain persistent data, and portlets have access to and require access to the user's profile data.

The JSR 168 Portlet Specification (JSR-000168 Portlet Specification 2003) defines a standard Java API for creating portlets. This is an important specification that will ensure the interoperability of portal containers produced by different vendors. Two well-known portal toolkits that will help users created portals that are JSR 168–compliant are open grid computing environments (OGCEs) (Gannon et al. 2003) and GridSphere (Novotny, Russell, and Wehrens 2004).

Workflow Editors

Workflow editors are another form of graphical user interfaces to Grids. Whereas portals allow the user to start, monitor, terminate, etc. a Grid application, workflow editors also allow users to run several interdependent applications and describe dependencies between the applications, coordinating the inputs and outputs of various Grid applications.

OGSA-DAI (Antonioletti, Atkinson, Baxter, et al. 2004; Antonioletti, Atkinson, Borley, et al. 2004) is an initiative to create middleware that makes accessing and integrating databases much easier. OGSA-DAI provides the mechanism through Web services to access a variety of database types, including relational databases, XML files, and flat files. The data that are extracted from databases can be transformed using extensible stylesheet language transformation (XSLT) or compressed using ZIP or GZIP, then delivered to a variety of sinks. The sinks can be other OGSA-DAI services, URLs, FTP servers, GridFTP services, or simply files. Although OGSA-DAI comes with a GUI, it is intended to be middleware. OGSA-DAI is a very powerful tool that can be very helpful in building other tools, especially workflow editors.

GridNexus (Brown et al. 2006) is a workflow editor, which uses Ptolemy (Lee 2003) as its GUI to develop workflows that are described in an XML scripting language called JXPL. The GUI allows users to create actors, or modules that can function as generic clients to Web services and grid services. GridNexus also has an actor that functions as a generic client to GRAM for the submission of a batch job.

Figure 7 shows a workflow in GridNexus that uses a Web service and a grid service. The actors are configured by providing the WSDL of the Web service or `AddressingLocator` class of the grid service. Once the actor is configured, its input and output ports are created to match the inputs and outputs of the service. The user is then able to call these services simply by providing input to one of the ports.

Although the functionality of this workflow is very simple, it demonstrates how the output of one actor becomes the input of another. Given that these actors represent calls to remote services, chaining together these services without the use of a workflow editor is a rather tedious process. Consider the workflow shown in Figure 8. This workflow implements a computational chemistry application in which a user wishes to use a local molecule file as input, convert it to an intermediate format, manipulate it using an interactive program, manipulate it again using a local program, run it through a Grid service that performs analysis, then save the result of that to the local machine. The steps necessary to perform this work without the use of a workflow editor is very tedious and prone to error.

The GRAM client (GridExec actor) allows the user to run a job on a remote machine. The user can also perform file staging with this actor. If the file staging is not a viable option, then there are also actors to perform these

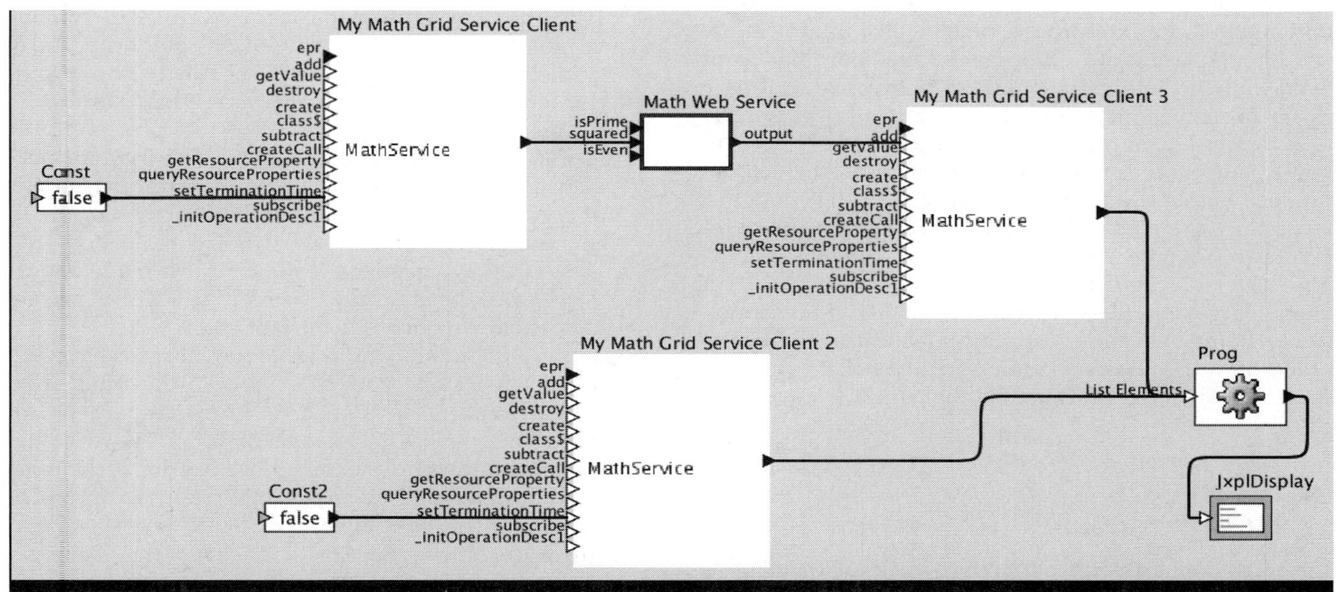

Figure 7: Simple GridNexus workflow

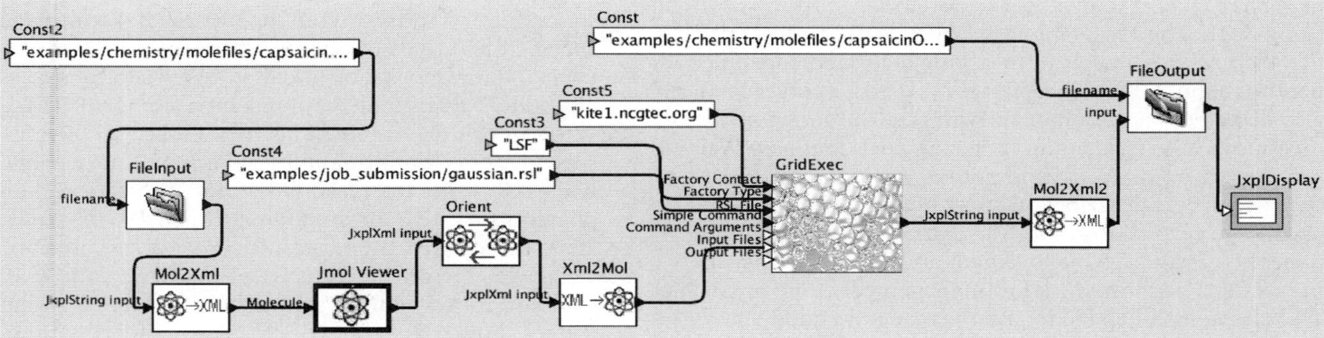

Figure 8: Chemistry application using GridNexus

functions through the use of GridFTP or SFTP (SSH file transfer protocol). GridNexus also has a set of actors to interface with OGSA-DAI.

Kepler (Altintas et al. 2005) is another workflow editor that is based on Ptolemy. One significant difference between Kepler and GridNexus is that Kepler is an extension of the Ptolemy system, whereas GridNexus uses Ptolemy to produce scripts in JXPL, and the JXPL interpreter provides the functionality. The Kepler approach has the advantage of leveraging the functionality of the already mature Ptolemy implementation. The GridNexus approach requires an additional language and corresponding interpreter. However, the advantage of using a separate language is that it separates the execution from the GUI, allowing various parts of the workflow execution to migrate to other processors.

Kepler has another component that provides a useful advantage. The library GriddleS provides a rich set of interprocess communication facilities. The GriddleS library traps input/output system calls and redirects them to services that can perform the desired operation on a local file, remote file, replicated file, or shared buffer. Access to remote files is available through GridFTP, SRB (storage resource broker), or SCP (secure copy). The shared buffer option allows for interprocess pipelined communication.

Although workflow editors make the coordination of tasks and the inputs and outputs between those tasks easier to manage, it is a challenge to adapt legacy code to a workflow actor. There are no standards with respect to how existing applications expect input or how they should produce output. Some applications expect their input to be on the command line, in input files, from standard input, or in specially named files. Furthermore, file systems may have substantially different configurations. For example, large data files may need to be placed on scratch files systems with large capacity but local to individual processors of a cluster. Dealing with the differences of these file systems is a formidable challenge for a workflow editor.

CONCLUSION

This chapter has described the components of a grid infrastructure, starting with Web services, which is an underlying technology used in grid software such as Globus. Web service technology is an attractive technology because of its language- and machine-neutral interface. Web services use XML. The SOAP protocol is used to carry information using XML. The XML language WSDL is used to describe the Web service interface in a language- and machine-neutral manner. The concept of a Web service container is also described in this chapter. With that introduction, we then move onto Grid computing standards and how Web services are used in Grid computing, in particular WSRF. Grid security is described in some detail, including ways to arrange certificate authorities. Then, we describe components for resource management and schedulers. The final section describes workflow management components. This chapter is intended to give the reader an understanding of the various fundamental components needed to create a Grid computing infrastructure.

GLOSSARY

Credentials: A certificate and corresponding private key collectively. There can be user credentials, proxy credentials, host credentials, etc. However, the private key is available only to the owner, and the word *credentials* can be used quite loosely to not include the private key.

Globus: A project that provided reference implementations for Grid computing standards. Provides a toolkit of component parts, which can be used separately or, more likely, collectively for creating a Grid infrastructure.

Grid-Map File: A form of access control list for authorization. The grid-map file is a file maintained at the site that holds the list of users' distinguished names (as given on their certificates) and their corresponding local account names.

Grid Portals: Browser-based dynamic-content environments that provide a single sign-on interface to grids.

Open Grid Services Architecture (OGSA): Defines standard mechanisms for creating, naming, and discovering services in a grid computing environment. Deals with architectural issues to make interoperable grid services.

Proxy Certificates: Certificates used in Grid computing to allow delegation of the user's authority. Proxy certificates are signed by the user (or the proxy entities themselves in a chain of trust) rather than by the certificate authority.

Public Key Infrastructure (PKI): A security arrangement that uses public key cryptography. In this form of cryptography, two keys (numbers) are used, one to encrypt the data and another (the key) to decrypt the data. One key, called the "public key," is made known to everyone, whereas the other key, called the "private key," is known only to the owner.

SOAP: A communication protocol for passing XML documents, standardized by the W3C organization (World Wide Web Consortium). Originally, SOAP stood for simple object access protocol. However, the spelled-out version has since been dropped because this name was not accurate; specifically the protocol does not involve object access.

Uniform Resource Locator (URL): A string of characters used to identify a resource on the World Wide Web; it includes the protocol used to access the resource. For example, www.cs.uncc.edu is the URL of the main computer science page at UNC-C, to be accessed by hypertext transfer protocol (HTTP).

Web Service: A software component designed to provide specific operations ("services") that are accessible using standard Internet technology. A Web service is usually addressed by a uniform resource locator (URL).

Web Services Resource Framework (WSRF): A set of specifications that present a way of representing state while still using the basic WSDL for Web services applications. Instead of modifying the WSDL to handle state, the state is embodied in a separate resource.

Web Service Definition Language (WSDL): An XML standard for formally describing a Web service—what it does, how it is accessed, etc. The standard is published by the World Wide Web Consortium (W3C).

Workflow Editor: A graphical user interface to grids that allow the user to run several interdependent applications and describe dependencies between the applications, coordinating the inputs and outputs of various grid applications.

WS-Resource: The combination of a Web service and resource in the Web Services Resource Framework (WSRF).

XML (Extensible Mark-up Language): A standard mark-up language developed to represent textual information in a structured manner that could be read and interpreted by a computer. XML is a foundation for Web services, and Web services now forms the basis of Grid computing.

CROSS REFERENCES

See *Cluster Computing Fundamentals; Grid Computing Fundamentals; Next Generation Cluster Networks; Utility Computing on Global Grids.*

REFERENCES

Abramson D., R. Sosic, J. Giddy, and B. Hall. 1995. Nimrod: A tool for performing parametised simulations using distributed workstations. *The 4th IEEE Symposium on High Performance Distributed Computing.* http://www.csse.monash.edu.au/%7Edavida/papers/nimrod.pdf (accessed April 21, 2007).

Allcock, W., J. Bresnahan, R. Kettimuthu, M. Link, C. Dumitrescu, I. Raicu, et al. 2005. The Globus Striped GridFTP Framework and Server. *Proceedings of Super Computing 2005 (SC05)*, Seattle.

Altair Grid Technologies. 2006. Portable Batch System Home Page. www.openpbs.org (accessed January 20, 2006).

Altintas, I., A. Birnbaum, K. Baldridge, W. Sudholt, M. Miller, C. Amoreira, et al. 2005. A framework for the design and reuse of Grid workflows. *International Workshop on Scientific Applications on Grid Computing (SAG'04), Lecture Notes in Computer Science* 3458.

Ananthakrishnan, R., C. Bacon, L. Childers, J. Gawor, J. Insley, and B. Clifford 2005. *How to build a service using GT4.* http://www-unix.mcs.anl.gov/~childers/tutorials/BAS/SDSC/GT4BuildAServiceV15.pdf (accessed December 29, 2005).

Antonioletti, M., M. P. Atkinson, R. Baxter, A. Borley, N. P. Chue Hong, B. Collins, B., et al. 2004. OGSA-DAI status report and future directions. *Proceedings of the UK e-Science All Hands Meeting.* Nottingham, United Kingdom.

Antonioletti, M., M. P. Atkinson, A. Borley, N. P. Chue Hong, B. Collins, J. Davies, et al. 2004. OGSA-DAI usage scenarios and behaviour: Determining good practice. *Proceedings of the UK e-Science All Hands Meeting.*

Booth, D., & C. K. Liu (2005). *Web Services Description Language (WSDL) version 2.0 part 0: Primer.* www.w3.org/2002/ws/desc/wsdl20-primer(accessed January 4, 2006).

Brown, J., Ferner, C., Hudson, T., Stapleton, A., Vetter, R., Carland, T., et al. (2006). GridNexus: A Grid Services Scientific Workflow System. *International Journal of Computer & Information Science* 6(2):72–82.

Buyya, R., D. Abramson, and J. Giddy. 2001. Nimrod-G resource broker for service-oriented grid computing. *IEEE Distributed Systems Online*, 2(7).

Cai, M., A. Chervenak, and M. Frank. 2004. A peer-to-peer replica location service based on a distributed hash table. *Proceedings of the SC2004 Conference*, Pittsburgh.

Chervenak, A. L., N. Palavalli, S. Bharathi, C. Kesselman, and R. Schwartzkopf. 2004. Performance and scalability of a replica location service. *Proceedings of the International IEEE Symposium on High Performance Distributed Computing*, HPDC-13.

Chervenak, A., R. Schuler, C. Kesselman, S. Koranda, and B. Moe. 2005. Wide area data replication for scientific collaborations. *Proceedings of 6th IEEE/ACM International Workshop on Grid Computing (Grid2005)*, Cardiff, Wales.

CSF: Community Scheduler Framework. 2005. www.globus.org/toolkit/docs/4.0/contributions/csf/CSF_Release_Notes.html (accessed January 20, 2006).

Czajkowski, K., D. F. Ferguson, I. Foster, J. Frey, S. Graham, I. Sedukhin, et al. 2004. The WS-Resource Framework, version 1.0, 03/05/2004. www.globus.org/wsrf/specs/ws-wsrf.pdf#search='WSResource%20Framework%2003%2F05%2F2004 (accessed December 29, 2005).

Ferreira, L., V. Berstis, J. Armstrong, M. Kendzierski, A. Neukoetter, M. Takagi, M., et al. 2004. *Introduction to Grid Computing with Globus.* IBM RedBooks. www.redbooks.ibm.com/abstracts/sg246895.html (accessed December 28, 2005).

Foster, I. (2005). Globus Toolkit version 4: Software for service-oriented systems. IFIP International Conference on Network and Parallel Computing. *Lecture Notes in Computer Science*, 3779:2–13.

Foster, I., C. Kesselman, J. M. Nick, and S. Tuecke. 2002. The physiology of the Grid: An Open Grid Services Architecture for Distributed Systems Integration. Global Grid Forum. Also reprinted as "Chapter 8: The Physiology of the Grid" in eds. 2003. *Grid computing: Making the global infrastructure a reality*, edited by F. Berman, G. Fox, and T. Hey, 217–49. Chichester, England: Wiley.

Gannon, D., G. Fox, M. Pierce, B. Plale, G. von Laszewski, C. Severance, et al. 2003. Grid portals: A scientist's accesspointforgridservices(draft1)September19,2003. http://www.extreme.indiana.edu/groc/ggf-portals-draft.pdf (accessed May 11, 2007).

The Globus Toolkit. 2006. www.globus.org/toolkit (accessed May 25, 2006).

Graham, S., D. Davis, S. Simeonov, G. Daniels, P. Brittenham, Y. Nakamura, et al. 2005. *Building Web services with Java: Making sense of XML, SOAP, WSDL, and UDDI.* 2nd ed. Indianapolis: SAMS.

Grid User Management System. 2006. http://grid.racf.bnl.gov/GUMS (accessed January 2, 2006).

GT 4.0 Security: Key Concepts. n.d. www.globus.org/toolkit/docs/4.0/security/key-index.html (accessed December 29, 2005).

Gudgin, M., M. Hadley, and T. Rogers. (2006). Web services addressing 1.0 – W3C recommendation May 2006.

http://www.w3.org/TR/ws-addr-core/ (accessed May 11, 2007).

Gudgin, M., Hadley, M., Mendelsohn, N., Moreau, J-J., & Nielsen, H. F., eds. 2003. SOAP Version 1.2 Part 1: messaging framework W3C recommendation 24 June 2003. www.w3.org/TR/2003/REC-soap12-part1-20030624/#intro (accessed December 29, 2005).

Hughes, J., and E. Maler, eds. 2005. Security Assertion Markup Language (SAML) 2.0 Technical Overview. http://xml.coverpages.org/SAML-TechOverview20v03-11511.pdf (accessed May 25, 2006).

IBM. 2001. Web Service Inspection Language. http://www-128.ibm.com/developerworks/library/specification/ws-wsilspec (accessed May 25, 2006).

JSR-000168 Portlet Specification, Final Release. 2003. www.jcp.org/aboutJava/communityprocess/final/jsr168 (accessed January 20, 2006).

Kerberos: The Network Authentication Protocol. n.d. http://Web.mit.edu/kerberos (accessed January 2, 2006).

KX.509: X.509 Certificates via Kerberos. 2005. http://kx509.org (accessed January 2, 2006).

Lee, E. 2003. Overview of the Ptolemy Project Technical Memorandum UCB/ERL M03/25. University of California, Berkeley, CA, 94720. http://ptolemy.eecs.berkeley.edu (accessed January 20, 2006).

MyProxy Credential Management Service. 2006. http://grid.ncsa.uiuc.edu/myproxy (accessed May 25, 2006).

Novotny, J., M. Russell, and O. Wehrens. 2004. GridSphere: An advanced portal framework. *30th EUROMICRO Conference (EUROMICRO'04)*, Rennes, France.

Platform. 2006. Platform LSF Family of Products Home Page. www.platform.com (accessed January 20, 2006).

Shibboleth Project. n.d. http://shibboleth.internet2.edu (accessed January 2, 2006).

Sun N1 Grid Engine 6. 2006. www.sun.com/software/gridware/index.xml (accessed January 20, 2006).

SURAgrid User Management and PKI Bridge Certification Authority. n.d. Available at https://www.pki.Virginia.edu/nmi-bridge (accessed May 11, 2007).

Thain, D., T. Tannenbaum, and M. Livny. 2003. Condor and the Grid. In *Grid computing: Making the global infrastructure a reality*, edited by F. Berman, A. J. K. Hey, and G. Fox 299–335. Chichester, England: Wiley.

W3C Architecture Domain XML Schema. n.d. www.w3.org/XML/Schema. (accessed January 4, 2006).

Wilkinson, B., and C. Ferner. 2005. *Grid Computing Fall 2005 Course Home Page*. www.cs.uncc.edu/~abw/ITCS4010F05/index.html (accessed December 28, 2005).

Cluster Computing Fundamentals

Hong Ong, *Oak Ridge National Laboratory, Oak Ridge, Tennessee*
Mark Baker, *The University of Reading, Reading, UK*

INTRODUCTION

Many computationally intensive applications in science, engineering, and business cannot be solved in a reasonable length of time on any single-processor machine. Parallel processing is an approach that might be considered instead—that is by dividing a large and complex computational problem into subtasks and distributing these subtasks across several processors. Each processor works on the assigned subtask concurrently. The total execution time can therefore be reduced to an acceptable level.

Parallel processing is traditionally performed on supercomputers that may have hundreds or thousands of processors as well as a large capacity for data storage. Prior to the late 1980s, the development of supercomputers was typically accomplished with custom-designed systems consisting of proprietary hardware and software. Companies such as IBM, Amdahl, Thinking Machines, and Cray developed sophisticated systems that took years to bring to market and cost tens of millions of dollars. Applications that executed on supercomputers were normally written using proprietary programming libraries and were generally not portable to other platforms. Furthermore, supercomputers are generally difficult to gain access to, and may not represent the most cost-effective solution for certain types of problem.

The concept of "connecting a collection of distinct computers together with a network" or simply a "commodity cluster" as a unique platform for parallel processing began in the late 1980s. The primary driving force was the rapid advances of commodity off-the-shelf (COTS) hardware, and the shortening of the design cycle for these components made the design of custom hardware costly in comparison. That is, by the time a company designed and developed a supercomputer, the processor speed and its capability was outpaced by commodity components. In addition to the rapid increase in COTS hardware capability that led to increased cluster performance, software capability and portability increased rapidly during the 1990s. A number of software systems that were originally built as academic projects led to the development of standard portable languages and new standard communication protocols for cluster computing.

This chapter provides a review of cluster-based systems, the various architectures, and the hardware and software components that have led to the growth in deployment, and it presents conclusions on the likely future of cluster-based computing. The aim of this chapter is to provide a high-level overview of clusters and the associated technologies and components. The chapter does not, however, present details of various cluster products and applications.

CLUSTER COMPUTING

Earning the nickname "a poor man's supercomputer," the capability of clusters increased rapidly during the 1990s. To illustrate this rapid increase, the Wiglaf Beowulf cluster, composed of 16 Intel 80486 100-MHz processors and dual 10 megabits per second (Mbps) Ethernet networks, delivered a sustained rate of 19 mega floating-point operations per second (MFLOP/s) on the N-body problem in 1995. By the end of 1996, clusters were reported to reach a sustained performance of 1 GFLOP/s (The Beowulf Project 2004). In 1997, NASA researchers at Goddard Space Flight Center further demonstrated a sustained computational rate of 10.1 GFLOP/s, using a cluster composed of 199 200-MHz Pentium Pro processors interconnected with Fast Ethernet (Merkey 2004). In 1998, a four-node Sun Enterprise cluster achieved a world record of 1 terabyte Transaction Processing Performance Council (TPC) (*Sun and Informix set new data warehousing record*, 1998) benchmark result, outperforming existing results set by proprietary solutions with significantly less hardware. In 1999, Oracle and Compaq announced a TPC-C world record (*Compaq sets Windows/NT performance record,* 2000) for Windows NT on a six-node cluster of Compaq ProLiant 6500 servers running the Oracle8 database. A cluster using the Hewlett-Packard Alpha family of processors was reported in 2000 to achieve a sustained performance level of 507 GFLOP/s. This was fast enough to earn the rank of thirty-first on the list of the world's 500 most powerful computers (*The Top500 Supercomputer sites*, 1993).

Clusters have continued to achieve significant ranking in the Top 500 Supercomputer list since 2000. In 2002, the top five supercomputers included Earth Simulator (35.86 TFLOP/s, 5120 processors), the ASCI Q systems (7.72 TFLOP/s, 4096 processors), the ASCI White (7.23 TFLOP/s, 8192 processors), and the MCR Linux Cluster (5.69 TFLOP/s, 2304 Xeon 2.4 GHz processors). Indeed, 72% of the top 500 machines listed in November 2005 are based on clusters that number between 400 and 8000 processors, connected by high-speed networks such as Gigabit Ethernet, Myrinet, or InfiniBand technology.

Cluster technologies have evolved from purely research efforts and demonstrators into a widely adopted solution for technical computing, meeting the needs of high-performance, high availability, and production-quality environments. In addition to hardware advances, cluster deployment and management tools and fast communication libraries have continuously evolved throughout the past decade. Cluster tools such as OSCAR (2000) and ROCKS (2000), using freely distributed open source Linux operating system, scheduling software, and tools, greatly eases the deployment and administration processes. Communication libraries such as the Message Passing Interface (MPI 1993) and Parallel Virtual Machine (PVM 1990) have become the leading message-passing systems for parallel applications. The development of new algorithms that are latency-tolerant has also allowed complicated applications to be executed effectively in cluster environments. Consequently, clusters have found a much wider range of application than was originally envisaged.

The success of cluster computing is the result of many concurrent threads of research and development. For instance, the Institute of Electrical & Electronics Engineers (IEEE) Technical Committee on Scalable Computing (TCSC), (IEEE Task Force on Cluster Computing 1999), previously known as the IEEE Computer Society Task Force on Cluster Computing (TFCC) (IEEE Technical Committee on Supercomputing Application 2004), which was founded in December 1998, continues to promote cluster computing as a collaborative effort between industry and academics. Today, numerous businesses, universities, and government organizations rely on clusters to perform their mission-critical computations.

The remainder of this chapter describes the various cluster architectures, surveys cluster hardware and software components, and presents conclusions on the likely future of cluster computing.

CLUSTER ARCHITECTURES

The TCSC has defined a cluster as a type of parallel or distributed system that consists of a collection of interconnected whole computers used as a single, unified computing resource, where "whole computer" is meant to indicate a normal, whole computer system that can be used on its own: processor(s), memory, input/output (I/O), operating system (OS), software subsystems, and applications (*IEEF TFCC Newsletter* 1999) Despite the success of cluster computing, the term *cluster* is still being misused today. *Cluster* means different things to different people, primarily because of their assumption of the underlying system architectures. Dongarra et al. (2005) clarified the term *cluster* and asserted that it should not be used casually to imply all parallel computer architectures, but rather it should be used to refer to "a specific class of such system."

To comprehend the basics concept of cluster computing, we describe a generic architecture through which nodes can be connected to provide aggregated processing and storage resources. In general, a generic cluster architecture is composed of three major components (see Figure 1): the computing nodes, the dedicated interconnection network, and a suite of cluster-aware software. Each node can be a single or multi-processor computer, such as PC, workstation, or symmetric multi-processor (SMP) server, equipped with its own memory, I/O devices, and operating system. The nodes are interconnected by a local area network (LAN). Various network topologies can be realized to speed up data exchange between applications, which are running on different nodes. The speed of network interconnects is normally characterized by two parameters: bandwidth and latency. Bandwidth indicates the amount of data that can be transferred through

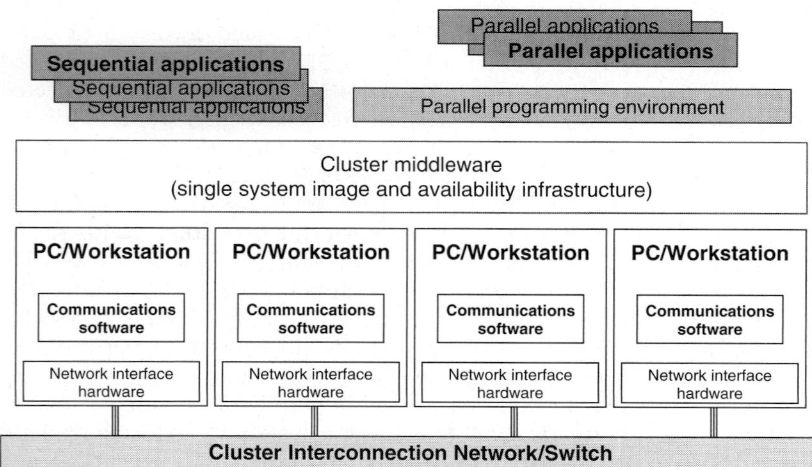

Figure 1: A generic cluster architecture

a particular network connection within a given time unit; latency is the time it takes for a networking device to process a data frame. The optimal choice of the network technology as well as its topology is generally dictated by the application's demand of speed and volume of data exchanged.

On each computing node, various operating systems, such as Linux, Solaris, and Windows, can be used to provide system services and to manage local resources. In addition, a set of software components is installed on each node. In general, this set of software can be categorized into resource management and application programming tools. Resource management tools, shown as cluster middleware in Figure 1, provide system configuration (including tools for initial installation and configuration), administration, scheduling, and allocation of both hardware and software resources as applied to user workloads. Programming tools, such as compilers, language, libraries, and debuggers, provide an environment for users to develop their parallel and distributed applications. We will describe some cluster hardware and software components in more detail in the section on Cluster Components and Technologies.

In general, a cluster's architecture is normally configured for a particular application type. The terms such as *Beowulf, Constellation, Super-cluster*, and *Meta-cluster* are commonly found in the literature to indicate a particular configuration of a cluster. In the following sections, we will describe three popular cluster configurations: high availability, high performance, and high throughput. It is worth noting that a hybrid of these configurations is used in some cases to promote a highly reliable system, characterized by high performance and balanced workloads.

High Availability

High-availability (HA) clusters are those that continue to perform critical tasks in the presence of system failures. Commodity clusters are ideal for implementing HA systems, as commodity products are easily replicated. By the late 1990s, virtually all major hardware and software vendors offered HA products based on clusters. Many applications—Web servers, e-commerce servers, and database applications, in particular—can benefit from systems that offer high availability, since these can prevent the loss of data and services in the event of a failure.

High availability depends on more than a redundant set of hardware that can take over tasks if a hardware component fails. For systems to be highly available there must be a coordinated set of software utilities that can detect failure, ensure data correctness, and manage the redistribution of tasks if necessary. Freely distributed software projects are available today for enabling HA clusters.

The High Availability Linux project (1999) (HA-Linux) began with the goal of developing extensions to Linux cluster software that will provide reliability, availability, and serviceability. The project is far-reaching in its goals to provide high availability. For example, resources in HA-Linux are anything that can move from one machine to another. Resources include file systems, processes, Internet protocol (IP) addresses, and other items, and the goal is for these to be able to be quickly migrated across a cluster in the event that a failure is detected.

The other software project that focuses on high-availability is the High Availability OSCAR Project (2002) (HA-OSCAR). HA-OSCAR is based on OSCAR, a software package designed to simplify cluster installation (see the section on Cluster Management Tools, below). HA-OSCAR introduces several enhancements and new features, mainly in the areas of availability, scalability, and security. The features included in the initial release are head node redundancy and self-recovery for hardware, service, and application outages.

High Performance

High-performance computing (HPC) clusters are optimized for workloads, which require jobs or processes running on the separate cluster nodes to communicate actively during a computation. These include computations for which intermediate results from one node's calculations will affect future calculations on other nodes. The advantage of using a HPC cluster is to reduce the total turnaround times on compute-intensive problems or when a problem is just too large to run on a single system.

One of the more popular HPC implementations is a cluster with nodes running Linux as the OS and free software to support parallelism. This configuration is often referred to as a "Beowulf cluster." Such clusters commonly run custom programs, which have been designed to exploit the parallelism available on HPC clusters. Many such programs use libraries such as MPI, which are specially designed for scientific applications executing on HPC systems.

Load Balancing

A load-balancing system allows the sharing of the processing load as evenly as possible across a cluster of computing nodes. The differentiating factor in this case is the lack of a single parallel program that runs across these nodes. Each node, in most cases, is an independent system running separate software. However, there is a common relationship between the nodes either in the form of direct communications between the nodes or through a central load-balancing server that controls each node's load. Although load-balancing systems are implemented primarily to improve response time, they commonly include high-availability features as well.

As an example, network service load balancing is a process of examining the incoming requests to a cluster and distributing the requests to each of the nodes for processing as appropriate. Often a network server takes in too many service requests to be able to process them quickly enough, and thus the requests need to be sent to the corresponding applications on other nodes. This can be optimized according to the different resources available on each node or the particular environment of the network. This type of load sharing is best for network applications such as Web or file transfer protocol (FTP) servers.

In general, load-balancing clusters can provide both high availability and scalability for important computer applications, such as those in the business, medical, and scientific arenas. However, the difficulty in accurately scheduling loads across processes should not be underestimated. Many approaches try to equalize the number of processes on the nodes or equalize their task queue lengths. Load balancing becomes more complicated if the system consists of heterogeneous nodes—for example, faster and slower processors, different amounts of memory, and different numbers of CPUs per node (SMP or multi-core). Similarly, most real applications and tasks in the system are heterogeneous. They consume different amounts of resources—i.e., they execute for short or long times and use different percentages of the CPU time. In addition, the arrival of tasks is not coordinated or planned, so load balancing has to cope with changing, unpredictable load profiles. Another complication is that parallel applications are not just sets of independent tasks, but tasks that can have dependencies on each other for proper execution. Other effects, like the overhead associated with context switching or paging delays can severely influence a system's performance. Consequently, load balancing should be adaptive—i.e., it should identify the currently important performance factors, create estimations by profiling the system behavior, and find the trade-off between load-balancing overhead and improvement in the current load situation. With all these factors to take into account, constructing an efficient load-balancing cluster is far from a trivial exercise

The use of clusters for load balancing is, however, a very attractive prospect. There are many commercial load-balancing systems available, including, the Moab Cluster Suite (2001) and the Maui Cluster Scheduler (2000). The Linux Virtual Server (1998) is another project that provides one of the commonly used free software packages for the Linux OS. The large-scale parallel nature of clusters offers a perfect setting for the distribution of work across their nodes. The disadvantage is that to get efficient sharing of the load, a lot of work has to be done to organize processes scheduling.

CLUSTER COMPONENTS AND TECHNOLOGIES

The continuous improvements of computer and network performance as well as the availability of standardized application programming interfaces (APIs) have allowed cluster computing to redefine the concept of high-performance computing and highly available systems. This section describes some of these hardware and software advances.

Hardware Components

Cluster Nodes

Each computing node of a cluster can be a single or multiple microprocessors or a multi-core system, equipped with its own memory, storage, and I/O devices.

Processors. Today's single microprocessor is almost as powerful as many of yesterday's supercomputers. Intel processors are the most commonly used in PC-based systems. Intel microprocessors offer excellent price for performance because of the economy produced by the high-volume sales. However, as these (and other) microprocessors continue to become more complex, it is becoming harder for modern compilers to be able to generate efficient code. Other popular processors include AMD (2007), IBM Power 5 (1990), and Sun Ultra-SPARC (2005).

Multi-core processors are the next wave of microprocessors. A multi-core microprocessor combines two or more independent processors into a single package, often a single integrated circuit (IC). For example, a dual-core device contains only two independent microprocessors. In general, multi-core microprocessors allow a computing device to exhibit some form of thread-level parallelism (TLP) without including multiple microprocessors in separate physical packages. This form of TLP is often known as chip-level multiprocessing, or CMP. Some examples of multicore processors are Intel's dual-core Xeon processors, code-named Paxville and Dempsey (Intel Dual-Core Server Processors 2005), and AMD's dual-core Opteron, which was released in April 2005 (AMD Multi-Core Products 2005).

Memory. Originally, the memory installed in a PC was 640 KB, usually "hardwired" onto the motherboard. Typically, a PC today will be delivered with between 512 MB and 1 GB installed in slots, with each slot holding a dual in-line memory module (DIMM). The main difference between the traditional single in-line memory modules (SIMMs) and DIMMs is that SIMMs have a 32-bit data path, while DIMMs have a 64-bit data path. Computer systems can use various types of memory, including synchronous dynamic random access memory (SDRAM), double data rate (DDR) SDRAM, and Rambus DRAM (RDRAM).

Access to DRAM is slow compared with the speed of the processor. Typically, it takes up to two orders of magnitude more time than a single processor clock cycle. Caches are used to keep recently used blocks of data for very fast access if the CPU references a word from that block again. However, the fast memory used for a cache is relatively expensive, and cache control circuitry becomes more complex as the size of the cache grows. These limitations generally restrict the total size of a cache to between 8 KB and 2 MB.

System Bus. The initial PC bus (Advanced Technology [AT]), or now known as Industry Standard Architecture [ISA]) bus [Industry SA Bus 2001]) was clocked at 5 MHz and was 8 bits wide. When first introduced, its abilities were well matched to the overall system. PCs are modular, and until recently, only the processor and memory were located on the motherboard. Other components were typically found on daughter cards, connected via the system bus. The performance of PCs has increased by several orders of magnitude since the introduction of the ISA bus. Consequently, the ISA bus became a bottleneck, limiting system capabilities.

The ISA bus was extended to be 16 bits wide and clocked in excess of 13 MHz. This, however, was not sufficient to meet the demands of contemporary CPUs, disk interfaces, and other peripherals. A group of PC manufacturers introduced the Video Electronics Standards Association (VESA) local bus (2001), a 32-bit bus that matched the system's clock speed. The VESA bus has now largely been superseded by the Intel-created PCI-bus (Peripheral

Component Interconnect [PCI] Local Bus 1993) that allows data transfer at 133 MB/s and is used inside Pentium-based PCs. PCI has been adopted for use in non–Intel-based platforms, such as the Digital AlphaServer range. The move toward a 64-bit bus was necessary to exploit the full power of Pentium processors and to make the memory architecture similar to that of a general-purpose UNIX workstation. This has further blurred the distinction between PCs and the UNIX workstation, as the I/O subsystem of a workstation is often built from commodity interfaces and interconnects.

The PCI Express (PCIe), introduced in 2004, is becoming the new backplane standard in personal computers. One driving force is that most of the new graphics cards from both ATI Technologies (2007) and NVIDIA (1995) use PCIe. In particular, NVIDIA uses the high-speed data transfer of PCIe for its newly developed scalable link interface (SLI) technology, which allows two graphics cards of the exact same chipset and model number to be run at the same time, allowing increased performance. ATI Technologies has also developed a multi-core graphic-processing unit (GPU) system based on PCIe called Crossfire (ATI Crossfire 2006).

Storage. The two disk interfaces found in personal computers are ATA (Advanced Technology Attachment) (ATA-ATAPI 2006) and SCSI (Small Computer System Interface) (SCSI Trade Association 2003) for connecting storage devices such as hard disks and CD-ROM drives.

ATA is more commonly known as IDE (integrated device electronics) or enhanced IDE (EIDE). With the introduction of serial ATA (SATA or S-ATA) in 2003, ATA was retrospectively renamed parallel ATA (PATA) to distinguish it from serial ATA. SATA is a computer bus technology primarily designed for the transfer of data to and from a hard disk. The first-generation SATA interfaces, also known as SATA/150, run at 1.5 GHz. SATA uses 8 B/10 B encoding at the physical layer. This encoding scheme has an efficiency of 80%, resulting in an actual data transfer rate of 1.2 GB per second (Gbps), or 150 MB/s. SATA-II interfaces were introduced in 2004 with clock rates reaching 3.0 GHz. SATA-II can deliver a maximum throughput of 300 MB/s and is both forward- and backward-compatible with SATA. This enables SATA hardware to interface with SATA II ports and vice versa. However, some systems, which do not support SATA speed autonegotiation, may have to manually limit their drive's speed to 150 MB/s with the use of a jumper for a 300 MB/s drive

The other disk interface is small computer serial interface (SCSI). SCSI is most commonly used for connecting a wide range of other devices, including scanners, printers, CD recorders, and DVD drives. In fact, the entire SCSI standard promotes device independence, which means that theoretically SCSI can be used with any type of computer hardware. There are three SCSI standards, SCSI-1, SCSI-2, and SCSI-3.

SCSI-1 features an 8-bit parallel bus (with parity), running asynchronously at 3.5 MB/s or 5 MB/s in synchronous mode. SCSI-2 standard has two variants: fast SCSI and wide SCSI. Fast SCSI doubled the maximum transfer rate to 10 MB/s and wide SCSI doubled the bus width to 16 bits, which enables the transfer rate of 20 MB/s. However, these improvements came at the minor cost of a reduced maximum cable length to 3 ms. SCSI-2 also specified a 32-bit version of wide SCSI, which used two 16-bit cables per bus; this was largely ignored by SCSI device makers because it was expensive and unnecessary, and it was officially retired in SCSI-3. SCSI-3 also has two variants: ultra SCSI and ultra wide SCSI interface. Ultra SCSI is capable of a peak transfer rate of about 20 MB/s in asynchronous and ultra wide SCSI is capable of 40 MB/s. A SCSI interface may contain up to sixteen devices. For similar sizes, SCSI disks tend to outperform ATA drives; however, ATA has a significant price advantage.

Cluster Interconnect

Cluster nodes are interconnected by a network that is based on local area network (LAN) or system area network (SAN) technologies. Generally, the nodes and the interconnection network are based on one of the following technologies using Ethernet, Fast Ethernet, Gigabit Ethernet, Myrinet, scalable coherent interface (SCI), Quadrics Network (QsNet), InfiniBand communication fabric, ATM, and Fibre Channel, which are discussed below.

Ethernet. Ethernet (Spurgeon 2000; TechFest Ethernet Technical Summary 1999) has been, and continues to be, the most widely used technology for local area networking. Standard Ethernet transmits at 10 Mbps and has a large installation base. However, this bandwidth is no longer sufficient for use in environments in which users are transferring large quantities of data. Standard Ethernet cannot be used seriously as the basis for cluster computing since its bandwidth and latency are not balanced compared with the computational power of the computers now available.

Fast Ethernet. An improved version of Ethernet, commonly known as Fast Ethernet (TechFest Ethernet Technical Summary 1999), provides 100 Mbps bandwidth and is designed to provide an upgrade path for existing Ethernet installations. Both standard and Fast Ethernet are based on the concept of a collision domain. Within a collision domain, the communication channel is shared so that only one node can send at a time. If another node tries to send at the same time, then a collision occurs, both messages are garbled, and both nodes retry their communication after a random waiting period. With a shared Ethernet or Fast Ethernet hub, all nodes share the same collision domain and only one node on the network can send at a time. With a switched hub, each node may be on a different collision domain, depending on the manufacturer's specifications. In this case, two nodes can send at the same time as long as they are not both sending to the same receiver. In general, all switched networks, not just Ethernet networks, have this capability. For cluster computing, switches are preferred, since the ability for more than one node to send at the same time can greatly improve overall performance.

Gigabit Ethernet. Gigabit Ethernet (TechFest Ethernet Technical Summary 1999; Baker and Scott 2000) products, except for the lowest-end hubs, are based on high-speed point-to-point switches in which each node is in its own separate collision domain. Gigabit Ethernet transmits signals at 1 Gbps. However, because of the encoding required at high speeds, Gigabit Ethernet has an effective user data rate of approximately 800 Mbps. Gigabit Ethernet products may have additional distance and wiring constraints over Fast Ethernet products because of the physical nature of sending high-speed signals. Currently, because of the speed of the processor, a single computer with a 32-bit bus can transmit data onto a network faster than Ethernet bandwidth, but somewhat slower than Fast Ethernet bandwidth.

10-Gigabit Ethernet. 10 Gigabit Ethernet (IEEE P802.3ae 10Gb/s Ethernet Task Force 2003) is the next generation in the Ethernet series. Consequently, 10-Gigabit Ethernet inherits all the advantages and disadvantages of previous Ethernet implementations. The primary advantages include interoperability with previous Ethernet generations, wide portability, and a ubiquitous interface (TCP/IP). The primary disadvantages have always been its relatively high latency and CPU load, as well as its expensive switches.

Standard and Fast Ethernet products are affordable and provide adequate capacity and latency for many cluster-computing applications. Most new computers today come with a built-in Fast and Gigabit Ethernet adapter. Gigabit Ethernet products generally cost less than other gigabit networking products, such as Myrinet and InfiniBand. Some Gigabit Ethernet switches are now offering 10-gigabit uplink ports essentially at the cost of installing the optics that is making it somewhat more practical to trunk multiple Gigabit Ethernet switches together.

Myrinet. Myrinet was one of the first interconnect technologies designed for cluster computing. Myrinet is a 1.28-Gbps full duplex network supplied by Myricom (Boden et al. 1995; Myricom 1994). It was used in the Berkeley Network of Workstations (NOW) (Anderson, Culler, and Patterson 1995) cluster and many other academic clusters. Myrinet uses low-latency cut-through routing switches, which simplify network setup and offer fault tolerance by automatically mapping the network configuration. Myrinet has a programmable on-board processor that allows for experimentation with communication protocols. Myrinet offers a native implementation of virtual interface architecture (VIA), as well as supporting the Message Passing Interface Chameleon (MPICH) implementation of MPI directly. There are Myrinet drivers for many operating systems, including Linux, Solaris, and Windows.

Myrinet is expensive as compared with Ethernet products. However, Myrinet is designed to be scalable, and its low latency, high bandwidth, and programmability make it competitive for cluster computing. Currently, Myrinet hardware uses a 2-Gbps link speed with PCI-X based network interface cards (NICs) providing one or two optical links. The dual-port NIC virtualizes the two ports to provide an effective 4-Gbps channel. The downside to the two-port NIC is cost—both the cost of the NIC and the extra switch port it requires.

Myricom announced its Myri-10G in mid-2005 (*Myricom Rolls Out 10-Gigabit Solutions* 2005). Myri-10G essentially extends Myrinet's architectural and performance advantages to 10-Gigabit speeds while also providing full interoperability with 10-Gigabit Ethernet.

Scalable Coherent Interface. Scalable coherent interface (SCI) (Gustavson 1992) was also one of the first interconnection technologies to be developed as a standard specifically for the purposes of cluster computing. The IEEE 1596 standard for SCI was published in 1992 and specifies the physical and data-link layers of the network as well as higher layers for distributed shared memory across a network. Since the layers are independent, it has been possible for many commercial products to be developed using the lower layers of SCI only. At the physical and data-link layers, SCI is a point-to-point architecture with small packet sizes. The standard defines 1-Gbps serial fiber-optic links and 1-Gbps parallel copper links. Dolphin Interconnect Solutions (1999) currently produces SCI adapter cards for the Sun SPARC SBus and PCI-based systems. At higher layers, SCI defines a directory-based cache-coherence scheme. Whenever a load or store occurs at a remote location that results in a cache miss, the cache controller accesses remote memory and data via SCI. The data are fetched to the cache with a delay on the order of a few microseconds, and then the processor continues execution. Message passing is also supported by a compatible subset of the SCI that does not invoke SCI cache-coherency protocols. Although SCI supports distributed shared memory, which programmers find appealing, the cost of a remote access is hidden to programmers so that optimization of applications is difficult. In addition, its scalability is constrained by the current generation of switches, and its components are expensive.

Quadrics. The Quadrics QSNET network (Petrini et al. 2002; Quadrics 1996) has been known mostly as a premium interconnect choice on high-end systems such as the Compaq AlphaServer SC. On systems such as the SC, the nodes tend to be larger SMPs with a higher per-node cost than the typical cluster. Consequently, the premium cost of Quadrics has posed less of a problem. Indeed some systems are configured with dual Quadrics NICs to further increase performance and to get around the performance limitation of a single PCI slot.

The QSNET system consists of intelligent NICs with an on-board I/O processor connected via copper cables (up to 10 m) to eight port switch chips arranged in a fat tree. Quadrics has released an updated version of their interconnect called QSNet II based on ELAN4 ASICs. Along with the new NICs, Quadrics has introduced new smaller switches, which has brought down the entry point substantially. In addition, the limit on the total port count has been increased to 4096 from the original 1024.

InfiniBand. InfiniBand (InfiniBand Trade Association 1999; Intel 2007) has received a great deal of attention over the past few years. InfiniBand was designed by an industry consortium to provide high-bandwidth communications for a wide range of purposes, which range from a low-level system bus to a general-purpose interconnect to be used for storage as well as internode communications.

The basic InfiniBand link speed is 2.5 Gbps (known as a 1X link). However, the links are designed to be bonded into higher bandwidth connections with four-link channels (a 4X link) providing 10 Gbps and twelve-link channels (12X links) providing 30 Gbps. Current InfiniBand implementations are available as PCI-X-based NICs and 8- or 24-port switch chips using 4X (10 Gbps) links. The switch chips can be configured for other link speeds as well including 12X links. This makes switch aggregation somewhat easier, since you can configure a switch with twelve 4X links to connect to nodes and four 12X links to connect to other switches.

Current InfiniBand pricing is enjoying the benefits of aggressive venture capital funding while the various vendors attempt to define their market. Thus, there are a variety of vendors competing with slightly different NICs and switches, even though the core silicon in most current implementations is from Mellanox (1999).

ATM. ATM, or asynchronous transfer mode (The ATM Forum 2000), is an international network standard that grew out of the needs of the telecommunications industry. ATM is designed around the concept of cells, or small, fixed-sized packets. ATM is a switch-based technology that uses the idea of virtual circuits to deliver a connection-oriented service. ATM offers several classes of data delivery. Some classes are designed for voice and video communication, which require real-time guarantees on data delivery rates. Because of the recent consolidation of many telecommunications industry and Internet services, ATM is increasingly being used as a backbone technology in many organizations. Although ATM products offer high bandwidth, in comparison to other similar technologies, it is relatively expensive.

Fibre Channel. Fibre Channel (Fibre Channel Industry Association 2004; Meggyesi 1994) is a set of standards that defines a high-performance data transport connection technology that can transport many kinds of data at speeds up to 1 Gbps through copper wire or fiber-optic cables. The Fibre Channel standard is defined in layers, beginning at the physical layer. Like the SCI standard, the standard layers are independent, enabling many companies to produce networking and cluster products based on the lower layers only. Fibre Channel is flexible, and mapping protocols have been defined that enable higher-level protocols, such as SCSI, IP, ATM, and high-performance parallel interface (HIPPI), to be used over Fibre Channel connections. Currently, the most frequent use of Fibre Channel in clusters is for data storage devices. The high-performance network capacity of Fibre Channel can be combined with SCSI and other I/O bridges to create a network of storage devices, separate from the primary cluster interconnect. A network of this type is sometimes called a storage area network (SAN), and is an important subsystem of many commercial clusters. As Fibre Channel matures it may become more widely used as a general-purpose cluster interconnection technology.

Software Components

Operating Systems

In a cluster used for parallel computing, each node is a computer that runs its own copy of the operating system. The operating system has two main functions: first, it makes the computer hardware easier to use. It creates a virtual machine that differs markedly from the real machine and hides these intricacies from the user. Second, it enables the system resources to be shared among many users.

The two most popular operating systems for PCs are Windows and UNIX—generally in the form of Linux. Unlike some earlier operating systems for PCs (e.g., DOS), Windows and Linux are both multi-tasking operating systems. A multi-tasking operating system allows multiple tasks to execute on a single-CPU machine at the same time. The tasks take turns using the CPU for a very short time period (called a quantum), often in a round-robin fashion. An advantage of this approach is that whenever a task needs to perform I/O or wait for an event to occur that does not require the use of the CPU, another task can be executing. For example, a user can edit a document while another document is printing in the background or while the compilation of a large program occurs. This capability can also be used to allow computation and communication to overlap in large parallel programs, so that the performance of a cluster is improved.

Linux. Linux (1994) is a UNIX-like operating system initially developed by Linus Torvalds, a Finnish undergraduate student in 1991–92. The original releases of Linux relied heavily on the Minix operating system. However, the efforts of a number of collaborating programmers have resulted in the development and implementation of a robust and reliable, portable operating system interface POSIX-compliant operating system.

Linux provides the features typically found in most UNIX implementations, such as preemptive multi-tasking, demand paged virtual memory, and multi-user and multiprocessor support. Although Linux was initially developed by a single author, a large number of authors are now involved in its continuing development. Linux quality control is maintained by allowing kernel releases only from a single point. In addition, its availability via the Internet helps in getting fast feedback about bugs and other problems. The following are some advantages of using Linux:

- Linux runs on cheap x86 and Pentium-based platforms, yet offers the power and flexibility of UNIX.
- Linux is readily available on the Internet and can be downloaded without cost.
- It is relatively easy to fix bugs and improve system performance. Users can develop or optimize peripheral drivers that can easily be distributed to other users.

To provide a UNIX-like environment, a Linux distribution combines the Linux kernel with a set of software that is freely available, including GNU system/application software (GNU Operating System 1996) and X.org (Xfree86 Project 1992; X.Org Foundation 2004), a public domain X-server. Table 1 lists some of the most popular Linux distribution companies and groups.

Unfortunately, there is no definite answer to which distribution is more suitable or "better" for building a Linux cluster. Indeed, several well-written books on this topic have been published (Spector 2000; Gropp, Lusk, and

Table 1: Linux Distributions

Linux Distribution	URL
Ubuntu	www.ubuntu.com
Mandriva Linux	www.mandrivalinux.com
SUSE	www.novell.com/linux
Fedora Core	www.fedoraproject.org
Debian GNU/Linux	www.debian.org
Knoppix	www.knoppix.com
Mepis	www.mepis.com
Gentoo Linux	www.gentoo.org
Slackware	www.slackware.com
Xandros	www.xandros.com

Sterling 2003; Sloan 2004). Generally, the choice comes down to three factors: technical support, ease of use, and licensing.

Microsoft Windows Server 2003. Microsoft Windows (2000) is a dominant operating system in the PC marketplace. Windows Server 2003, Compute Cluster Edition (Microsoft Windows Server System. 2007; Windows Compute Cluster Server 2003), released in early 2006, is designed for high-performance computing clusters. Windows Server 2003 is the successor of Windows 2000 Server that incorporates compatibility and other features from Windows XP. Windows Server 2003 includes compatibility modes to allow older applications to run with greater stability.

Cluster Management Tools

Cluster management is about monitoring and administering all the nodes in a cluster. It covers a wide range of functionality, such as resource monitoring, membership management, reliable group communication, and full-featured administration interfaces. As such, it is impossible to cover all aspects in this section of the chapter. The following areas form the basis of the management of cluster resources.

- System Installation and Configuration—The software addresses the means of assembling, installing, and configuring the necessary hardware and software components that make up the complete system. The challenge of implementing and maintaining common software images across nodes, especially for systems made up hundreds of nodes requires sophisticated, effective, and easy-to-use tools. Examples are Scyld (1998), ROCKS (2000), and OSCAR (Open Source Cluster Application Resources 2000).
- Job Scheduler and Management—The placement of applications onto the distributed resources of commodity clusters requires tools to allocate the software components to the nodes and to schedule the timing of their operation. Task allocation can be performed at different levels of granularity, including jobs, transaction, processes, or tasks. Examples are such as OpenPBS (1995) and Maui Scheduler (2000).

Communication Protocols

Clusters originally used the same transmission control protocol/Internet protocol (TCP/IP) that has traditionally been used in local and wide area networks. However, these protocols were designed in the 1960s for networks that had comparatively low bandwidth and high error rates as compared with the newer, high-speed networks used to interconnect modern clusters. Consequently, the traditional protocols have high overhead and low-bandwidth compared with the transmission time on high-speed networks. The performance of the cluster is dependent on the availability of efficient communications, both for exchanging data between processes that execute on different processors, and for exchanging control and synchronization information. A number of academic projects in the mid-1990s addressed this issue. The influence of these academic projects prompted Compaq, Intel, and Microsoft (1997) to organize a consortium to promote the development of a standard for low-overhead communication within a cluster. Version 1.0 of the VIA (virtual interface architecture) standard was published by the consortium on December 16, 1997. By 1999, major commercial vendors of database applications, including Oracle and IBM, were modifying their applications to execute in a cluster environment using the virtual interface architecture.

The standard TCP/IP protocols and the de facto standard Berkeley Software Distribution (BSD) sockets API for TCP and user datagram protocol (UDP) were the first messaging libraries used for clusters. However, these protocols are typically implemented using operating system services. To send a message, a user application constructs the message in user memory, and then makes an operating system request to copy the message into a system buffer. An interrupt is required for this operating system intervention before the message can be sent out by network hardware. When a message is received by network hardware, the network copies the message to system memory, and an interrupt is used to copy the message to user memory, and to notify the receiving process that the message has arrived. This operating system overhead is a significant portion of the total time to send a message. As networks became faster during the 1990s, the overhead of operating system services became significantly larger than the actual hardware transmission time for messages. The goal of the low-latency messaging systems that were developed during the 1990s was to avoid operating system intervention while at the same time providing user-level messaging services across high-speed networks.

Low-overhead messaging systems developed during the 1990s include Active Messages (von Eicken 1993), Fast Messages (Culler et al. 1996), the VMMC (Virtual Memory-Mapped Communication) system (Blumrich et al. 1995), and U-net (Basu, Welsh, and von Eicken. 1997), among others. By 1997, research on low-latency protocols had progressed sufficiently for a standards process to be initiated, and the Virtual Interface Architecture design document was formulated and published as a standard low-latency networking architecture in less than a year.

Active Messages, which was later extended to Generic Active Messages (GAM), is a low-latency communication messaging library for the Berkeley NOW system. Short messages in Active Messages are based on the concept of a request-reply protocol. The sending user-level application constructs a message in user memory. To transfer the data, the receiving process allocates a receive buffer, also in user memory on the receiving side, and sends a request to the sender. The sender replies by copying the message from the user buffer on the sending side directly to the network. Network hardware transfers the message to the receiver, and then the message is transferred from the network to the receive buffer in user memory. This process requires that memory on both the sending and receiving sides be pinned to an address in physical memory. However, once the memory buffers are established, no operating system intervention is required for a message to be sent. This protocol is also called a "zero-copy" protocol, since no copies from user memory to kernel memory are used. In GAM, a copy sometimes occurs on the receiving side so that buffers can be reused more efficiently, in which case the protocol is referred to as a "one-copy" protocol. Fast Messages is a protocol similar to Active Messages, but extends Active Messages by imposing stronger guarantees on the underlying communication. In particular, Fast Messages guarantees that all messages arrive reliably and in order, even if the underlying network hardware delivers messages out of order.

The VMMC system, later extended to VMMC-2, is the enabling low-latency protocol for the Princeton Scalable High-Performance Really Inexpensive Multi-Processor (SHRIMP) system. One goal of VMMC is to view messaging as reads and writes into the user-level virtual memory system. VMMC works by mapping a page of user virtual memory to physical memory, and in addition makes a correspondence between pages on the sending and receiving sides. VMMC also uses specially designed hardware that allows the network interface to snoop writes to memory on the local host and have these writes automatically updated on remote host memory. Various optimizations of these writes have been developed that help to minimize the total number of writes, network traffic, and overall application performance. VMMC is an example of a class of systems known as distributed shared-memory systems. In these systems memory is physically distributed among the nodes in a system, but processes in an application may view "shared" locations as identical and perform reads and writes to the shared locations.

The U-net network interface architecture strongly influenced the design of the VIA. In addition to providing zero-copy messaging when possible, U-net, and VIA add the concept of a virtual network interface for each connection in a user application. Just as an application has a virtual memory address space that is mapped to real physical memory on demand, each communication end point of the application is viewed as a virtual network interface mapped to a real set of network buffers and queues on demand. The advantage of this architecture is that once the mapping is defined, each active interface has direct access to the network without operating system intervention. The result is that communication can occur with very low latency.

The VIA is a standard that combines many of the best features of various academic projects, and will strongly influence the evolution of cluster computing. Although VIA can be used directly for application programming, it is considered by many systems designers to be at too low a level for application programming. With VIA, the application must be responsible for allocating some portion of physical memory and using it effectively. It is expected that most operating system and middleware vendors will provide an interface to VIA that is suitable for application programming. Generally, the interface to VIA that is suitable for application programming comes in the form of a message-passing interface for scientific or parallel programming.

APPLICATION DEVELOPMENT

To develop accurate and efficient high-performance applications, it is essential to have some form of easy-to-use parallel debugger and performance profiling tools. Most vendors of cluster systems provide some form of debugger and performance analyzer for their platform. Ideally, these tools should be able to work in a heterogeneous environment. Thus, it is possible to develop and debug a parallel application on an inexpensive cluster, and then perform production runs on a dedicated cluster-based HPC platform.

Parallel Programming Support

The programming paradigm for cluster computing falls primarily into two categories: message passing and distributed shared memory. Although distributed shared memory is claimed by some to be an easier programming paradigm, as the programmer has a global view of all the memory in the cluster, early standardization efforts, have instead focused on message-passing systems. Some of the most popular languages that were developed during the late 1980s and early 1990s included Express, NX, PVM (Parallel Virtual Machine, 1990), P4, and Chimp. In reaction to the wide variety of nonstandard message-passing systems around this time, the MPI Forum (1993) was formed as a consortium of about 60 people from universities, government laboratories, and industry in 1992. MPI version 1.0 was approved as a de jure standard interface for message-passing parallel applications in May 1994. The Forum continued to meet, and in April 1997, the MPI-2 standard was published. MPI-2 includes additional support for dynamic process management, one-sided communication, and parallel I/O. Many implementations of MPI-1 have been developed. Some implementations, such as MPICH, are freely available. Others are commercial products optimized for a particular manufacturer's system, such as the Sun HPC MPI. Generally, each MPI implementation is built over faster and less functional low-level interfaces, such as Active Message, BSD Sockets, or the SGI/Cray SHMEM interface. The PVM system is a research-and-development project of the Oak Ridge National Laboratory and the University of Tennessee at Knoxville.

Since much of early cluster computing was performed by application programmers who had previously programmed on supercomputers, early efforts focused on developing message-passing libraries for application programs comparable to those found on supercomputers. Early message-passing libraries all had support for at least the creation of processes, as well as sending and receiving messages between the processes.

To write parallel programs for a cluster, scientific programmers generally write applications in a high-level language such as C or FORTRAN, and include, by linking, a message-passing library. The program is written as source code, compiled, and linked, and the programmer starts the program by executing a script file that runs the application on a set of named computers. Usually the computers are identified by IP addresses or names. A background demon manages the creation of remote processes. Generally, applications are based on the SPMD (single program multiple data) programming model. Each process is a copy of the same executable code, and program behavior depends on the identifier of the process. Processes exchange data by sending and receiving messages.

The first version of the MPI standard does not specify how standard input and output are to be implemented. Typically, an application programmer initiates a parallel application from a console. If a process in the application prints to standard output, then a background demon directs the output to this console. Output from different processes will be interleaved on the console and arrive in a nondeterministic order. This problem can be overcome if the application programmer specifies that only one process write to standard output. Standard input to an application is usually performed only by root (the process running on the console), or is retrieved from the local disk of the computer that the process is executing.

The first release of the MPI standard specifies support for collective operations, and nonblocking sends and receives. Collective operations in MPI are those that have either more than one sender or more than one receiver. MPI-1 supports broadcast, scatter (of array elements from root to other processes), gather (of array elements from other processes to root), reduce (gather with a combining operation, such as the summation of array elements from other processes to root), and variations of these, such as all to all, all reduce, and all gather. MPI also implements a barrier synchronization, which allows all processes to come to a common point in a program before proceeding. MPI collective calls provide a more convenient interface for the application programmer and are often implemented using special, efficient, algorithms.

MPI-1 specifies standards for nonblocking sends and receives. These are usually a two-step operation in which the process first initiates the send (receive) call, and then uses a second call to ensure that the buffer is safe to be reused or that the data have arrived. These nonblocking calls can be used by programmers to facilitate the overlapping of communication and computation.

The second release of the MPI standard, MPI-2 specifies additional standards for one-way communications, similar to the writes to shared, distributed memory locations that were developed in VMMC and other academic systems. MPI-2 also specifies a standard way to create MPI processes, support for heterogeneous platforms, extended collective operations, I/O operations, and multi-threading on individual computers.

Debuggers

There are a limited number of parallel debuggers available for a cross-platform, heterogeneous, development environment. For this reason an effort was begun in 1996 to define a cross-platform parallel debugging standard that specified the features and interface users wanted. The High Performance Debugging Forum (HPDF) was formed as a Parallel Tools Consortium (PTools) project (1993). The HPDF members include vendors, academics and government researchers, as well as HPC users. The forum meets at regular intervals, and its efforts have culminated in the HPD version 1 (High Performance Debugging Forum 2000) specification. This standard defines the functionality, semantics, and syntax for a command-line parallel debugger. The development of cross-platform parallel debuggers is an area of active research. Ideally, a parallel debugger should be capable of at least:

- Managing multiple processes and threads within a process
- Displaying each process in its own user window
- Displaying source code, stack trace, and frame for one or more processes
- Diving into objects, subroutines, and functions
- Setting both source-level and machine-level breakpoints
- Sharing breakpoints between groups of processes
- Defining watch and evaluation points
- Displaying arrays and array slices
- The manipulation of code variables and constants

Performance Analysis Tools

Performance analysis tools exist to help programmers understand the run-time characteristics of their applications. In particular, tools help to analyze and locate parts of an application that exhibit poor performance and produce program bottlenecks. Such tools are useful for understanding the behavior of normal sequential applications and can be enormously helpful when trying to analyze the performance characteristics of parallel applications, which are typically more complex.

To create performance information, most tools produce performance data during program execution and then provide a tool to do a postmortem analysis and display of the performance information. Some tools do both steps in an integrated manner, and a few tools have the capability for run-time analysis, either in addition to or instead of postmortem analysis. Most performance monitoring tools consist of some or all of the following components:

- A means of inserting instrumentation calls to the performance monitoring routines into the user's application
- A run-time performance library that consists of a set of monitoring routines that measure and record various aspects of program performance
- A set of tools that process and display the performance data

In summary, a tool for postmortem performance analysis works by:

- Adding instrumentation calls into the source code
- Compiling and linking the application with a performance-analysis run-time library
- Running the application to generate a trace file
- Processing and viewing the trace file

A particular issue with performance-monitoring tools is the intrusiveness of the tracing calls and their impact on the application's performance. It is important that instrumentation does not affect the performance characteristics of the application and thus provide a false view of its performance behavior. A lesser, but still important, secondary issue is the format of the trace file. The file format is important for two reasons. First, it must contain detailed and useful execution information but not be huge, and second, it should conform to some "standard" format so that it is possible to use various GUI interfaces to visualize the performance data. The development of standard, nonintrusive performance tools is an area of active research.

ADVANCED TOPICS

Emerging Trends

A number of hardware trends are having an impact on cluster computing. Two of these trends are in the design and manufacture of microprocessors. One basic advance is the reduction in the size of features, which has allowed circuits to either become faster or consume less power. A second basic advance is the growth in the size of the die that can be manufactured. These factors mean that each year the average number of transistors on a chip is growing by about 40% and the clock frequency is increasing by about 30%.

Memory components are experiencing similar growth, but there is an increasing divergence between the capacity and the speed of memory. For example, the capacity of memory components increased by a factor of more than 1000 between 1990 and 2005, but speed has only doubled. Consequently, the increase in memory speed is not matching that of microprocessors. Therefore, access to data in memory is becoming a significant bottleneck. One method of overcoming this bottleneck is to configure the DRAM in banks and transfer data from these banks in parallel. In addition, multi-level memory hierarchies organized as caches make memory access more effective, but their design is complicated. This access bottleneck also applies to disk access, and consequently, to the virtual memory system of a computer.

A number of high-performance networks have been used successfully as cluster interconnects, including Fast Ethernet, Gigabit Ethernet, SCI, Myrinet, Giganet, InfiniBand, Fibre Channel, and others. Since no network has emerged as a clear winner, competition is high, and this will continue to impact price and performance. For some applications, particularly those for which the amount of data exceeds the size of physical memory, it is possible to use messaging across a high-performance network to obtain data faster than data can be obtained from a processor's own memory. These high-performance networks make cluster computing an attractive architectural alternative to the memory bottleneck of a single processor system.

Clusters dedicated to high-performance applications will continue to evolve as new and more powerful computers and network technologies become available in the marketplace. It is likely that individual cluster nodes will be composed of multiple processors. Currently multi-core–processors PCs and workstations are becoming common. Software that allows SMP nodes to be used efficiently and effectively by parallel applications will be further developed or enhanced and added to the operating system kernel in the near future. It is likely that there will be widespread use of 10-Gigabit Ethernet, as this technology will provide a low-risk solution for moving from standard or switched Ethernet. The price for using this technology will be higher communication latencies. In situations in which it is necessary for an application to attain very low latencies, network technologies that bypass the operating system kernel, thus avoiding the need for expensive system calls, will be used. This can be achieved using intelligent network interface cards or, alternatively, using on-chip network interfaces such as those on Digital Equipment Corporation's DEC Alpha 21364.

Field programmable gate array (FPGA) is another possibility to speed up computation and communication. For instance, some of the message-passing protocol can be implemented on the card, which improves acknowledgment latency and offloads some work from the processors. Furthermore, the FPGA can be configured to improve computational performance and not interact directly with network.

The two most popular operating systems for clusters are Linux and Windows. Linux has become popular because it is freely available as well as because of its increasing stability and its performance, which is superior to that of Windows. There are currently more than seven million Linux users worldwide, and its future development is being supported by many companies, such as IBM and Compaq. Linux is also available for SMP systems that have two or more processors per node. Windows XP has a large installed user base, and is gradually replacing the huge existing Windows 95/98 user base. A new version of Windows, Windows Compute Cluster Server 2003, implements the MPI Interface (MS-MPI), which is fully compatible with the reference MPICH2. Furthermore, the integration with Active Directory enables role-based security for administration and users, and the use of Microsoft Management Console provides a familiar administrative and scheduling interface, which can support the use of standard communication technologies. The ability to provide a rich set of development tools and utilities as well as the provision of robust and reliable services will determine the choice of the operating system used on future clusters. UNIX-based operating systems are likely to be most popular, but the steady improvement and acceptance of Windows will mean that it will not be far behind.

Next-Generation Cluster Computing

As computer networks become cheaper and faster, a new computing paradigm has emerged, know as the Grid (Foster, Kesselman, and Tuecke 2001). The Grid is a large system of computer-based resources that performs tasks and provides users with a point of access, commonly based on a Web interface, to widely distributed resources.

One view of the Grid is as a single computational resource. Resource management software accepts jobs submitted by users and schedules them for execution on appropriate systems in the Grid, based on site policies. Users can submit thousands of jobs at a time without being concerned about where they run. The Grid may scale from single systems to supercomputer-class computer farms that use thousands of processors. Depending on the type of applications, the interconnection between the Grid resources can be performed using dedicated high-speed networks or the Internet. By providing scalable, secure, high-performance mechanisms for discovering and negotiating access to remote resources, the Grid promises to make it possible for scientific collaborators to share resources on an unprecedented scale and for geographically distributed groups to work together in ways that were previously impossible. Several examples of new applications that benefit from using Grid technologies are:

1. A coupling of advanced scientific instrumentation or desktop computers with remote supercomputers
2. Collaborative design of complex systems via high-bandwidth access to shared resources
3. Ultra-large virtual supercomputers constructed to solve problems too large to fit on any single computer
4. Rapid, large-scale parametric studies, e.g. Monte-Carlo simulations, in which a single program is run many times in order to explore a multidimensional parameter space

The Grid technologies are currently under intensive development. Major Grid projects include the Open Science Grid (2004), TeraGrid (2000), iVDGL (International Virtual Data Grid Laboratory 2001), and the EGEE (Enabling Grid for E-sciencE 2006) project. Grid tools are available for developers today. The Globus Toolkit (2002) represents one such example and includes a set of services and software libraries to support grids and its applications.

CONCLUSION

Our need for computational resources in all fields of science, engineering, and commerce far outstrips our ability to fulfill these needs. The use of COTS-based clusters is perhaps one of most promising means by which we can bridge the gap between our needs and the available resources.

A major hurdle for cluster computing is that of education. Because of the parallel and distributed nature of clusters, computer science and other students must be trained in programming techniques that do not ordinarily arise on single-CPU or client/server-based systems; writing correct and efficient programs is more difficult in a cluster environment. Similarly, the architectural issues that arise in building clusters are more complex. The standard undergraduate curriculums in computer science and computer engineering only partially cover these topics. These curriculums need to be expanded to meet the needs of industry as cluster computing becomes more common.

The use of a COTS-based cluster has a number of advantages, including:

- An unmatched price/performance ratio as compared with dedicated parallel supercomputers
- The ability to incrementally grow a system and thus take advantage of yearly funding patterns as well as being able to incorporate the latest technologies
- The provision of a multi-purpose system: one that is, for example, used for secretarial purposes during the day and as a commodity supercomputer at night

These and other factors will continue to fuel the evolution of cluster computing.

GLOSSARY

AMD: Advanced Micro Devices.

ATM: Asynchronous transfer mode, a network and protocol for wide area network.

Bandwidth: The amount of data that can be transmitted in a fixed amount of time, usually expressed in bits per second (bps) or bytes per second.

Beowulf-CLASS System: Commodity cluster using personal computers to achieve excellent cost performance, which was initially developed by the Beowulf project, led by Donald Becker and Thomas Sterling, at the NASA Goddard Space Flight Center.

COTS: Commodity Off-The-Shelf.

DIMM: Dual in-line memory module, a small circuit board that has a 64-bit path to memory chips.

Ethernet: The first widely used and truly ubiquitous local area network operating at 10 Mbps.

Fast Ethernet: A cost-effective local area network based on the original Ethernet protocol, providing 100 Mbps.

FTP: File transfer protocol.

Gbps: 1 billion bits per second data transfer rate of bandwidth.

Gigabit Ethernet: A LAN that is the successor of Fast Ethernet, providing a peak bandwidth of 1 Gbps.

GNU: A project that promotes open source and free software tools.

InfiniBand: An input/output architecture for the transmission of data between processors and I/O devices.

LAN: Local area networks used to connect local sites.

Latency: The amount of time it takes a network packet to travel from source to destination.

Local bus: A data bus that connects directly, or almost directly, to the microprocessor.

Mbps: 1 million bits per second data transfer rate or bandwidth.

Message Passing: An approach to parallelism based on communicating data between processes running on separate computers.

MPI: Message passing interface, a community derived logical standard for the transfer of program messages between separate concurrent processes.

NIC: Network interface controller, a hardware component that enables the computer to connect to a network, usually designed for a particular type of network, protocol, and media.

PC: Personal computer.

PCI: Peripheral component interconnect, a local bus standard for PCs and workstation to support I/O controllers, including NICs.

PVM: Parallel virtual machine, a library of functions supporting an advanced message-passing semantics.

RAM: Random access memory.

SAN: System area network, a network optimized for use as a dedicated communication medium within a commodity cluster.

SCI: Scalable coherent interconnect.

SIMM: Single in-line memory module, a small circuit board that has a 32-bit path to memory chips.

SMP: Symmetric multi-processing, a multi-processing architecture in which multiple CPUs, residing in one cabinet, share the same memory.

SPMD: Single program multiple data, a programming model designed for multiprocessors system, in which parallel programs run the same subroutine but operate on different data.

TCP: Transmission control protocol.

VIA: Virtual interface architecture.

WAN: Wide area networks used to connect distant sites.

CROSS REFERENCES

See *Grid Computing Fundamentals; Grid Computing Implementation; Next Generation Cluster Networks; Utility Computing on Global Grids.*

REFERENCES

AMD Multi-Core Products. 2007. http://multicore.amd.com/en/Products (accessed May 10, 2007).

AMD: Advanced Micro Devices. 2007. www.amd.com (accessed May 10, 2007).

Anderson, T., D. Culler, and D. Patterson. 1995. A case for network of workstations. *IEEE Micro* 15(1):54–64.

ATA-ATAPI. 2006. www.ata-atapi.com (accessed May 10, 2007).

ATI Crossfire. 2006. www.ati.com/technology/crossfire (accessed May 10, 2007).

ATI Technologies. 2007. www.ati.com (accessed May 10, 2007).

ATM Forum. 2000. www.mfaforum.org (accessed May 10, 2007).

Baker, M. A., and S. L. Scott. 2000. Gigabit Ethernet performance under NT and Linux. Presented at the International Parallel and Distributed Processing Symposium 2000, Cancun, Mexico, May 2000.

Basu, A., M. Welsh, and T. von Eicken. Incorporating memory management into user-level network interfaces. *Hot Interconnects* 5.. Also available as Department of Computer Science, Cornell University, Technical Report, TR97–1620. http://www2.cs.cornell.edu/U-Net/papers.html.

Beowulf Project. 2004. www.beowulf.org (accessed May 10, 2007).

Blumrich, M. A., C. Dubnicki, E. W. Felten, K. Li, and M. R. Mesarina, 1995. Virtual memory mapped network interfaces. *IEEE Micro* 15(1):21–28.

Boden, N., D. Cohen, R. Felderman, A. Kulawik, C. Seitz, J. Seizovic, and W.-K. Su. 1995. Myrinet—A gigabit-per-second local area network. *IEEE Micro* 15(1): 29–36.

Compaq Corporation, Intel Corporation, and Microsoft Corporation. 1997. Virtual Interface Architecture Specification, version 1.0. www.viarch.org (accessed May 10, 2007).

Culler, D., L. T. Liu, R. Martin, and C. Yoshikawa. 1996. LogP performance assessment of fast network interfaces. *IEEE Micro* 12(4):404–415.

Dolphin Interconnect Solutions. 1999. www.dolphinics.com (accessed May 10, 2007).

Dongarra, J. T, Sterling, H, Simon, and E, Strohmaier. 2005. High-performance computing: Clusters, constellations, MPPs, and future directions. *Computing in Science and Engineering* 7(2):51–9.

Enabling Grid for E-sciencE (EGEE). 2006. http://public.eu-egee.org (accessed May 10, 2007).

Fibre Channel Industry Association (FCIA). 2004. www.fibrechannel.org (accessed May 10, 2007).

Foster, I., C. Kesselman, and S. Tuecke. 2001. The anatomy of the Grid. *International Journal of Supercomputer Applications* 15(3).

Globus Toolkit. 2002. www.globus.org (accessed May 10, 2007).

GNU Operating System. 1996. www.gnu.org (accessed May 10, 2007).

Gropp, W., E. Lusk, and T. Sterling. 2003. *Beowulf cluster computing with Linux*. 2nd ed. Cambridge, MA: MIT Press.

Gustavson, D. B. 1992. The scalable coherent interface and related standards projects. *IEEE Micro* 12(1):10–22.

High Availability Linux Project. 1999. www.linux-ha.org (accessed May 10, 2007).

High Availability OSCAR Project. 2002. http://xcr.cenit.latech.edu/ha-oscar (accessed May 10, 2007).

High Performance Debugging Forum. 2000. www.ptools.org/hpdf (accessed May 10, 2007).

IBM Power Architecture. 1990. http://www-03.ibm.com/chips/power (accessed May 10, 2007).

IEEE P802.3ae 10Gb/s Ethernet Task Force. 2003. http://grouper.ieee.org/groups/802/3/ae (accessed May 10, 2007).

IEEE Task Force on Cluster Computing. 1999. www.ieeetfcc.org (accessed May 10, 2007).

IEEE Technical Committee on Supercomputing Application (TCSA). 2004. www.ieeetcsc.org (accessed May 10, 2007).

IEEE TFCC Newsletter. 1999. www.eg.bucknell.edu/~hyde/tfcc/vol1no1-dialog.html (accessed May 10, 2007).

Industry SA Bus. 2001. www.pcguide.com/ref/mbsys/buses/types/older.htm (accessed May 10, 2007).

InfiniBand Trade Association. 1999. www.infinibandta.org (accessed May 10, 2007).

Intel Dual-Core Server Processors. 2005. www.intel.com/business/bss/products/server/dual-core.htm (accessed May 10, 2007).

Intel. 2007. Overview of InfiniBand Architecture, www.intel.com/technology/infiniband/index.htm (accessed May 10, 2007).

International Virtual Data Grid Laboratory (iVDGL). 2001.www.ivdgl.org (accessed May 10, 2007).

Linux Homepage. 1994. www.linux.org (accessed May 10, 2007).

Linux Virtual Server Project. 1998. www.linuxvirtualserver.org (accessed May 10, 2007).

MauiClusterSchedulerProject.2000.http://mauischeduler.sourceforge.net (accessed May 10, 2007).

Meggyesi, Z. 1994. Fibre channel overview. http://hsi.web.cern.ch/HSI/fcs/spec/overview.htm (accessed April 15, 2007).

Mellanox. 1999. www.mellanox.com (accessed May 10, 2007).

Merkey, P. 2004. Beowulf history, www.beowulf.org/overview/history.html (accessed April 15, 2007).

Microsoft Windows 2000. 2000. www.microsoft.com/windows2000 (accessed May 10, 2007).

Microsoft Windows Home. 2007. www.microsoft.com/windows (accessed May 10, 2007).

Microsoft Windows Server System. 2007. www.microsoft.com/windowsserversystem (accessed May 10, 2007).

Moab Cluster Suite. 2001. www.clusterresources.com (accessed May 10, 2007).

MPI Forum. 1993. www.mpi-forum.org (accessed May 10, 2007).

MPI Forum. 1993. www.mpi-forum.org/docs/docs.html (accessed May 10, 2007).

Myricom Rolls Out 10-Gigabit Solutions for IBM Blade Center H. 2006. www.myri.com/news/060208 (accessed May 10, 2007).

Myricom. 1994. www.myri.com (accessed May 10, 2007).

NVIDIA. 1995. www.nvidia.com (accessed May 10, 2007).

Open Science Grid. 2004. www.opensciencegrid.org (accessed May 10, 2007).

Open Source Cluster Application Resources (OSCAR). 2000. http://oscar.openclustergroup.org (accessed May 12, 2007).

OpenPBS Project. 1995. www.openpbs.org (accessed May 12, 2007).

Parallel Tools Consortium Projects. 1993. www.ptools.org/projects (accessed May 10, 2007).

Peripheral Component Interconnect (PCI) Local Bus. 1993. www.pcisig.com/specifications (accessed May 12, 2007).

Petrini, F., W. Feng, A. Hoisie, S. Coll, and E. Frachtenberg. 2002. The Quadrics Network (QsNet): High-performance clustering technology. *IEEE Micro* 22(1):46–57.

ProLiant sets TPC-C record for Windows NT, Compaq Inform. 1999. www.europe.digital.com/inform/issues/issue24/24ss1803.htm (accessed May 10, 2007).

PVM project. 1990. www.epm.ornl.gov/pvm (accessed May 12, 2007).

Quadrics. 1996. www.quadrics.com (accessed May 12, 2007).

ROCKS. 2000. www.rocksclusters.org (accessed May 12, 2007).

SCSI Trade Association. 2003. www.scsita.org (accessed May 12, 2007).

Scyld Beowulf Home. 1998. www.scyld.com (accessed May 12, 2007).

Sloan, J. D. 2004. High performance Linux clusters with OSCAR, Rocks, OpenMosix, and MPI. Cambridge, MA: O'Reilly.

Spector, D. H. M. 2000. *Building Linux clusters*. Sebastopol, CA: O'Reilly.

Spurgeon, C. E. 2000. Ethernet: The definitive guide. Cambridge, MA: O'Reilly.

Sun and Informix set new data warehousing record for one-terabyte TPC-D benchmark. 1998. www.sun.com/smi/Press/sunflash/1998–02/sunflash.980225.3.xml (accessed April 15, 2007).

Sun UltraSPARC Processors. 2005. www.sun.com/processors (accessed May 12, 2007).

TechFest Ethernet Technical Summary. 1999. www.techfest.com/networking/lan/ethernet.htm (accessed May 12, 2007).

TeraGrid. 2000. www.teragrid.org (accessed May 10, 2007).

Top500 Supercomputer sites. 1993. www.top500.org (accessed May 12, 2007).

Video Electronics Standards Association (VESA) Local Bus. 2001. www.pcguide.com/ref/mbsys/buses/types/older_VLB.htm (accessed May 12, 2007).

von Eicken, T. 1993. Active Messages: an efficient communication architecture for multiprocessors. Ph.D. Thesis. University of California at Berkeley.

Windows Compute Cluster Server. 2003. www.microsoft.com/windowsserver2003/ccs (accessed May 12, 2007).

X.Org Foundation. 2004. www.x.org (accessed May 12, 2007).

Xfree86 Project. 1992. www.xfree86.org (accessed May 12, 2007).

Next-Generation Cluster Networks

Keren Bergman and Benjamin A. Small, *Columbia University*
Larry A. Bergman, *Jet Propulsion Laboratory, California Institute of Technology*

INTRODUCTION

Since nearly the beginning of the modern era of digital electronic computers, there has been interest in ganging together multiple processors to achieve higher computational capacities than a single prevailing processor could provide. Although there is a wide range of system and algorithmic challenges to overcome to effectively parallelize an application, it has long been recognized that a high-speed communications network that can enable processors to efficiently exchange data and control information is critical. Ideally, such a network should offer seamless transparency between the primary memory systems of the processors, or more directly, their speed (bandwidth) and latency (temporal delay) should be commensurate with the high-speed memory system. The ultimate goal for efficient communications would be for a parallel processor machine to stay continuously busy performing useful work, without waiting for data or control to transfer between processors. This has given way to one basic measure of efficiency (N_{eff}) for such machines (Fox 1984):

$$N_{eff} = T_{pe}/(T_{pe} + T_{com}) \times 100,$$

where T_{pe} is the time that the processor element spends doing useful work and T_{com} is the time that the processor must wait for communications, control, and other system functions to complete before it can resume.

From this simple relationship, one can assess the overhead for an application algorithm on a given multiprocessor architecture. For example, for applications in which infrequent communication occurs between long stretches of computation, the so-called embarrassingly parallel applications, a much lower performance network can be used with virtually no degradation in overall performance, and at a lower cost as well. Conversely, for fine-grained applications, in which many messages must be exchanged after a given computation, higher-bandwidth, lower-latency networks are required. From this application- or algorithm-centric point, system communication needs can be generalized as flops per byte. The higher the number, the more infrequent the communications, generally implying that a lower-performance network can be used.

With gigahertz-class processors, many gigabytes per second (GB/s) with latencies of a few nanoseconds (ns) would be needed. Furthermore, other fundamental limits of physics begin to enter the picture, especially with regard to latency. At some point, the speed of light represents a fundamental limit that cannot be overcome because of the finite distances between components for even the densest of packaging schemes. For this reason plus a host of others, in recent years much interest has focused on novel computer architectural methods for mitigating these problems—e.g., keeping processors busy while waiting for other system functions to complete, whether they be communications, the operating system, or other system functions (see van der Steen, 2006, for an overview of modern supercomputer architecture and system elements). In many cases, new processor and system designs are required to fully realize these latency-hiding methods, and will continue to be the subject of research.

Although it would certainly be interesting to review all of the parallel computers and their interconnect systems that have been developed since the Illiac IV in the 1960s, but without losing too much context, one could cut to the chase and begin with the Beowulf commodity PC cluster developed in 1994 by Thomas Sterling (Sterling et al. 1999; Sterling 2001), then at Goddard Space Flight Center (Ridge et al. 1997). Although commodity microprocessors had been incorporated into parallel clusters almost ten years earlier (Seitz 1985), this is the first instance in which commodity motherboards and network components combined with open source software (mostly Linux) had also been used to maximize the performance/price ratio. There were functionally similar concepts being developed elsewhere at about the same time, such as the Berkeley Network of Workstations (NOW) or Apollo Workstation clusters, which used single-vendor-computer platforms with proprietary operating systems and networks. Today, Beowulf clusters have been commercialized or packaged by many vendors, both from well-known names as well as start-ups. Most, in fact, use the same basic components, but add value in terms of integration, support, and management tools. Today, more than 70% of the machines listed on the world's top 500 supercomputers (see www.top500.org) are clusters, and if one includes proprietary networks as well, the figure approaches 100%. Approximately 50% of the top 500 supercomputers use Gigabit Ethernet (Kaplan 2001) as the primary interconnect, followed by approximately 11% for Myrinet and 7% for Infiniband. More details of the current state of the art of cluster computer network technology can be found in *Cluster Computing Fundamentals* and additional references (Apon 2001; Bode 2004).

This chapter will first review the salient performance metrics by which cluster computer networks can be compared, and then briefly review the general classes of the networks that have emerged in recent years, both from an architec-tural viewpoint as well as from a protocols perspective. Next, a few case studies will be examined among the more common networks in use today. And finally, some future directions that show promise to meet the needs of the next generation of high-performance computer systems and architectures will be explored.

INTERCONNECTION NETWORKS

In contemporary multiprocessor high-performance computing systems (HPCs), the processor–memory interconnect is often the single most constraining bottleneck in overall system performance (Dally and Towles 2004). This problem originates from the limitations of electronic hardware to provide sufficient bandwidth and low latency over the physical size of the computing system. Alternative interconnection technologies have been proposed as a means of eliminating the severity of this bottleneck. Perhaps the most promising of these alternative technologies are those that leverage optical signal transmission on networks composed of photonic devices and fiberoptic components (Special Issue on Optical Interconnections 2004).

Whereas electronic transmission is limited by signal degradation and losses that rise with frequency, optical transmission degradation is functionally independent of frequency and suffers only minimal degradation over long distances. This well-known advantage of optical transmission has led to the wide use of fiber optics in nearly all long distance telecommunication systems (Agrawal 2002). HPC systems are typically very large and highly distributed, with diameters spanning tens to hundreds of meters, so the capability of covering such distances with high bandwidth and low latency while consuming minimal power represent some of the significant advantages for optical interconnects. For transmitting high data rates over long distances, optical fiber is far better suited than copper. Furthermore, because of the multiple-wavelength nature of light, conventional optical fiber is capable of transmitting more multiple-terabits per second (Tbps) in a wavelength-parallel or wavelength-division multiplexed (WDM) manner (Agrawal 2002), surpassing electronics by many orders of magnitude. A third benefit of optical signal transmission is its immunity to electromagnetic cross talk and interference; this advantage is particularly useful in high-noise digital computing systems. Last, and perhaps most critical, is the clear power-dissipation advantage of optical interconnects. This key advantage of optical interconnection networks is based on a property of the photonic medium, known as bit-rate transparency. Unlike electronic routers, which switch with every bit of the transmitted data while dissipating dynamic power that scales with the bit rate, photonic switches switch on and off at the message rate, and their energy dissipation does not depend on the bit rate. This property facilitates the transmission of very-high-bandwidth messages while avoiding the increasingly high power costs typically associated with performing such communication with equivalent electronic networks (Miller 2000).

Although it is all but certain that future generations of multiprocessor HPC systems will eventually leverage these optical technologies, photonic and optoelectronic devices are unfortunately not yet as mature and developed as comparable electronic components. Although some photonic interconnects are used in the backplanes of commercial HPC systems, advanced optical interconnection networks are still primarily an area of research. The performance of these devices is not yet as stable and robust as comparable electronic components, and the current pricing can pose a significant deterrence to large-scale commercialization. Although the importance of these weaknesses cannot be overlooked, ongoing research and development are rapidly improving optical and photonic technologies, and many experts are optimistic about their progress. Part of this optimism stems from the recent progress in integrated photonic devices fabrication in Complementary Metal Oxide Semiconductor (CMOS) compatible platforms [this is discussed further in Case Study 5].

In order to fully use the immense bandwidth and other benefits of optical signal transmission, network architectures must be designed in a way that specifically addresses the unique properties of optical technologies. That is, conventional canonical topologies that have been very successfully implemented with electronic components cannot simply be mapped into the photonic implementations. The single biggest architectural difference between electronic and optical media is that practical optical buffers are not available and are physically challenging to implement; RAM structures are nearly impossible to implement for optically transmitted signals. Also, it can be very challenging to execute significant data processing entirely within the optical domain (Blumenthal 2001; Luijten et al. 2005; Shacham, Small, Liboiron-Ladouceur, and Bergman 2005; Small, Kato, and Bergman 2005).

Fully assimilating the unique characteristics of optical technologies into interconnection network design presents novel challenges. Traditional network design principles, which are based on electronic implementations, rarely can be applied to the new technology. Instead, new paradigms for interconnect design must be adopted to accommodate the optical signal transmission. These paradigms should consider the multiple-wavelength nature of light, the lack of optical buffering and processing technologies, and the problems and costs inherent in converting signals between optical and electronic domains. A few ideas have been developed to address the future needs of optical telecommunications networks, particularly ones based on the schemes of optical packet switching (OPS) and optical burst switching (OBS), and some of these principles are beneficial to the case of photonic HPC interconnects as well (Blumenthal et al., 1992; Qiao and Yoo 1999; Hemenway et al. 2004; Barker et al. 2005; Shacham, Small, Liboiron-Ladouceur and Bergman 2005). However, the design space remains largely unexplored and is an active area of research. The challenge is to find the optimally cost-effective combination of electronics and optics to achieve the best system level performance.

Here we present principles for photonic interconnection network design that address the aforementioned challenges. The discussion is extended into possible future developments of optical interconnection network architectures intended for monolithic integration, with applications to interchip and intrachip interconnects.

The implementation of low-latency, high-capacity switching interconnection systems has benefits to numerous applications within modern data processing and communications. Leveraging the ubiquity of conventional fiber-optic components allows for a realistic network implementation that is modular, scalable, and robust. By allowing high-volume multiple-wavelength optical packets to traverse a network with minimal processing and routing logic, a complete system can be constructed for experimentation and characterization. By establishing the attractiveness of contemporary fiber-optic technology and its general flexibility, the strategies and merits of the presented architectural paradigm are elucidated.

OPTICAL INTERCONNECTION NETWORKS: TECHNOLOGIES, ARCHITECTURES, AND SYSTEMS

Design Considerations

The photonic interconnection architectural paradigm presented here is intended to have extraordinarily high capacity while exhibiting very low routing latencies. The targeted data rates are on the order of hundreds of gigabits/sec (Gbps) from each network terminal. This surpasses the current electrical interconnection technologies by almost a full two orders of magnitude (see www.top500.org; Flich et al. 2002; Petrini et al. 2002; Hurwitz and Feng 2004; Liu et al. 2005). Latencies are expected to be less than 1 μs for typical packet traffic configurations, and the interconnection networks are intended to be scalable beyond 10,000 input and output terminals. These performance specifications are in line with the needs for next-generation high-performance computing applications. In order for the system to have a reasonable uptime, the system error rate must be better than about 10^{-22} or about three errors per year for a 10,000-terminal 100-Gbps network, which implies that physical errors must certainly stay below 10^{-12} per channel, while using forward error correction (FEC) coding and other appropriate error-correcting techniques.

Using current fiber-optic communication technologies, bit rates of 10 Gbps (i.e., OC-192 or STM-64) per wavelength channel are typical. Because it is often convenient to have packet capacities on the order of 1000 bits over ten or more parallel wavelengths, packet lengths are typically tens of nanoseconds in duration, with packet rates near 100 MHz. The carrier frequencies of the channels within the optically encoded packets are set by the International Telecommunications Union (ITU) to span a range of 190.1 THz to 196.1 THz, or 1528.8 nm to 1577.0 nm, over what is called the "C-band" of the electromagnetic spectrum. The wavelengths are generally spaced by 100 GHz (0.8 nm) by the wavelength division multiplexing (WDM) standard; the dense WDM standard specifies 50-GHz (0.4-nm) spacing. These wavelengths can be transmitted over commercially available single-mode optical fiber with attenuations of just 0.3 dB/km. The chromatic dispersion (i.e., the rate at which longer wavelengths travel faster than shorter ones) is typically 18 ps/nm/km or less (Agrawal 2002).

To summarize the metrics and scales to be used in the discussion of interconnection networks: 10-channel data rates can exceed 100 Gbps with packet rates of 10 MHz or more, latencies are generally measured in hundreds of nanoseconds, and distance scales on tens of meters. The information is encoded optically according to the C-band WDM specifications, which contains sixty-one channels over the 48-nm span. The devices used often benefit from the technological advances encouraged by long-haul fiber optics while avoiding many of their physical shortcomings. The resulting networks are room-sized and suitable for numerous applications within high-performance data processing and communications.

Enabling Photonic Technologies

The advantages of fiber optic technologies have long been clear to network designers. Electronic signals suffer from numerous wave transmission difficulties, including reflections, Ohmic loading, and electromagnetic interference, all of which result in limitations to transmission distance and bandwidth and lead to excessive power consumption (Miller 2000). Optical waves can be transmitted with high data rates over monumental distances with very little power consumption. For these reasons alone, network architectures that incorporate photonic and fiberoptic elements could potentially offer significant benefits. Network designers generally relegate fiber optics to a transmission medium; however, interest has gradually emerged in performing switching and routing functions with optical signals instead of electrical ones. Although this sort of processing is obviously very well suited for contemporary microelectronic technology, the costs of converting signals between the electrical and optical domains can be quite prohibitive in terms of financial expense, latency, and power. Using photonic devices for switching functions within an interconnection network is therefore worth considering.

Beginning in the 1980s, when the data rates for fiber-optic communications were significantly slower than they are today, a few ideas about the structure of a scalable photonic switching network began to emerge. Many of these architectures incorporate a device that was relatively new to that decade, the semiconductor optical amplifier (SOA), also called the semiconductor laser amplifier. The SOA is a device capable of amplifying optical signals over a wide optical bandwidth with significantly less latency and less power than the popular erbium-doped fiber amplifier (EDFA) and Raman amplifier. Furthermore, SOAs require a relatively small amount of electrical power to turn on, and the necessary current can be provided relatively quickly. This results in a switchable wideband photonic device that is controlled electrically with low latency and minimal rise time (Blumenthal et al. 1992; Fortenberry, Cai, and Tucker 1994; Krishnamoorthy et al. 1999; Wonglumsom et al. 1999; Meagher et al. 2000; Armstrong, Andonovic, and Kelly 2004; Lin et al. 2006).

The first presentation of an SOA-based optical packet switching (OPS) node occurred in the late 1980s (Evankow and Thompson 1988), and during the early 1990s the idea gained minor attention and experienced small conceptual advances (Blumenthal et al. 1992; Fortenberry et al. 1994). This design is a simple Y-junction with two SOAs, one on each branch, and most of the designs require the SOAs to provide gain to compensate for the losses of the Y-junction and perhaps other passive optical taps and splitters in the former part of the node (Figure 1). The control and routing mechanism in these designs is either entirely electrical or based on a conventional time-division multiplexed (TDM) header.

Because this simplistic approach does not benefit from the multiple-wavelength nature of optical signals, other ideas that capitalize on wavelength parallelism began to ascend to the forefront of OPS research. These switching network designs often use the parallel transmission of multiple wavelengths as a mechanism for contention resolution or for destination addressing. Beginning in the mid-1990s, numerous unique switching node designs and architectures (e.g., Krishnamoorthy et al. 1999; Wonglumsom et al. 1999; Meagher et al. 2000) for OPS were developed and presented in the literature, many of which are based on a standard library of photonic devices, including SOAs, wavelength-tunable lasers, optical filters, arrayed waveguides (AWGs), and lithium niobate ($LiNbO_3$) switches. Summaries and comparisons of these architectures have also been published (Papadimitriou, Papazoglou, and Pomportsis 2003). Unfortunately, a shortcoming of many of these architectures is the degree of complexity required of the optical components for addressing ("label processing") at other logical functionality.

Some of the designs mentioned above use different switching methods as well. In many of the AWG-based designs, the network is better classified as a circuit switch; that is, a designated pathway between an input terminal and an output terminal is established, and communications occur on that pathway. This approach differs markedly from packet switching, in which discrete "flits" of information are routed independently, not based on the state of the underlying switching fabric. These AWG-based approaches generally rely on the wavelength of the packet itself as the means of encoding the destination address; although wavelength bands can also be used, this wavelength addressing scheme makes it impossible for terminals to service packets that are simultaneously encoded over the entire wavelength span, minimizing network bandwidth.

Although many of these architectures are meant to be implemented as routers within telecommunications networks, and therefore may have to adhere to established protocols, the packet structures are fundamentally optically encoded forms of a conventional electronic sequential header–payload packet. This structure fails to capitalize on the unique modulation schemes available to the optical domain, most especially multiple-wavelength encoding. Even though the wavelength dimension can be leveraged for contention resolution and for destination address quite effectively, one of the principal concerns for high-performance interconnection networks to be used in the applications mentioned above is high payload capacity. Clearly, multiple-wavelength data encoding over the C-band has the potential to yield the largest net transmission bandwidth.

Specialized devices that produce multiple-wavelength optical signals based on electrical inputs and the reverse are currently produced commercially, with results reported for as much as 10 wavelengths × 40 Gbps (see www.infinera.com). These transmitters and receivers represent the interface between the electrical signals that originate from the cluster nodes and the optical signals that are transmitted or perhaps even switched throughout an optical network. By leveraging the high-density integration

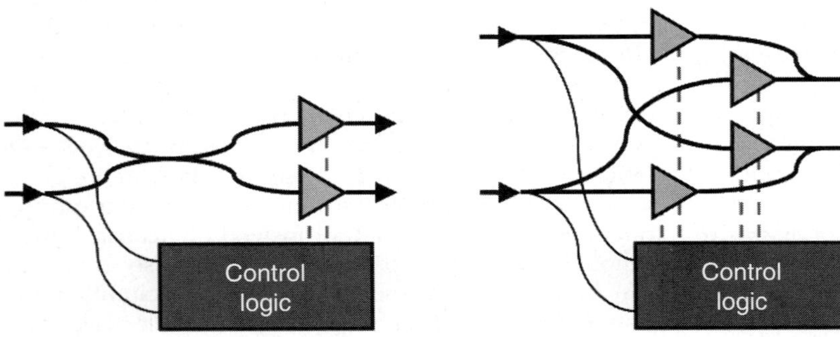

Figure 1: Schematic of simple wideband single-packet (left) and nonblocking (right) 2 × 2 switching nodes based on photonic switching elements (e.g., SOAs)

available to monolithic designs, these transmitters and receivers can easily accommodate ten high-speed electrical signals and the necessary optical/electronic (O/E) or electronic/optical (E/O) conversions. One of the companies that produces these integrated multiple-wavelength transmission devices successfully is Infinera, in Sunnyvale, California (see www.infinera.com). Their technology is based on a III-V semiconductor substrate that can support lasers, high-speed modulators, and high-speed photodetectors.

Another interesting company is Luxtera, in Carlsbad, California (see www.luxtera.com), which has taken a different approach. They used a silicon substrate as a workbench for a host of photonic devices, including modulators, which can more easily be integrated with conventional CMOS electronic devices. This allows for electrical signal processing and management to be contained on the same chip as the photonic devices. Although silicon is less amenable to optical devices in general, this "CMOS Photonics™" paradigm, as they call it, certainly has great potential in making the transition between the electrical and optical domains more seamless and flexible.

Regardless of the technology, then, the multiple-wavelength packet structure is a defining distinction between historical architectural designs and the paradigm presented here. Another distinction is the simplicity of the control mechanism that has been used in an effort to reduce routing latency.

Architecture Design

Optical networks should capitalize on the advantages of photonic technology while acknowledging its current shortcomings. The single most important advantage of optical signal encoding is the enormous bandwidth it can support, both because of the high-modulation bandwidth available to a signal channel (i.e., carrier frequency or carrier wavelength) and because of the large number of wavelength channels that can be transmitted simultaneously. With a total of 6 THz of bandwidth available for optical transmission over the C-band, efficient coding techniques can certainly support transmission capacities of more than 1 Tbps (Agrawal, 2002).

However, the strong disadvantage of optical information systems is the inability to perform arithmetic operations with agility and robustness near that of CMOS and other electrical logic families. Indeed attempts have been made to implement simple logical functions with photonic and fiber-optic technologies, but by and large, these are not yet stable nor integratable enough for arithmetic computations of even minor complexity (Agrawal 2002). Similar to this essential absence of optical logic devices is the difficulty of implementing RAM and buffers with photonic and fiberoptic technologies. These two shortcomings are important to keep in mind in the design of optical interconnection network architectures.

To summarize, an ideal design for such a network should capitalize on the gargantuan bandwidth available to fiberoptic technologies while minimizing the burden of computation and buffering on the photonic network components. Indeed, it is even beneficial to distinguish between the path and devices through which the high-bandwidth payload travels and the path and components that carry the routing information and execute the routing decision. That is, an ideal optical interconnection network design leaves the transmission capacity to the optical domain and relies on better-suited electronic technologies for routing and decision mechanisms.

In addition, in order to address general networking concerns such as scalability and modularity, multiple-stage distributed topologies are often used in interconnection networks, independent of the transmission medium (Dally and Towles 2004). For a large number of network input and output terminals, it is important that the number of switching nodes required to implement a complete topology scales efficiently. Further, it can be beneficial for a given implementation to comprise nearly identical switching nodes that need only to be configured with their position within the interconnection network, as is common for various multiple-stage topologies. For a large number of input and output terminals, it is also important for the control and routing mechanism to scale efficiently. Whereas centralized arbitration algorithms can become computationally burdensome for large numbers of network terminals at fast packet-injection rates, a distributed control scheme that delegates routing to each individual switching node can simplify the routing mechanism (Dally and Towles 2004).

In order to further simplify routing and architectural organization, packet switching is a method by which multiple input terminals can freely communicate with multiple output terminals. Designated transmission lines between every input and every output is clearly a wasteful use of resources. Moreover, because the optical switching nodes would likely subtend only hundreds of bit periods of latency, the model of circuit switching may not be fitting either. As an example, consider packets with 10 Gbps (OC-192) payloads: one hundred of these bits requires 10 ns, or 2.0 m in standard single-mode optical fiber (e.g., SMF-28). Given the current degree of integration of contemporary fiber-optic components, it is unlikely for a complete network to fit within just 2 m. Besides, there may be well more than a 2-m displacement between client terminals in the applications mentioned above. Therefore, a packet-switching perspective is perhaps most appropriate for this kind of network design. A packet-switching network based on distributed switching nodes in a multiple-stage topological configuration may therefore define an ideal architectural design space.

These topological specifications, along with the aforementioned delegation of capacity and functionality, yield an interesting switching-node design. The basic SOA-based Y-junction structure, which is almost two decades old, is still the fundamental structure of the payload optical pathways. In the design of an optical switch element, ultra-high bandwidth packets are achieved by using multiple wavelengths for packet payload encoding. Because the SOA switching elements are capable of amplifying signals over almost the full span of the C-band, the potential packet payload capacity is maximized. A whole two-dimensional matrix of payload data can be encoded in both the time dimension and the wavelength dimension by leveraging this approach.

Additional wavelengths can be designated for the packet header, which contains the necessary routing information. In order to simplify detection of the header bits and to facilitate the routing, each of the header bits may be encoded on a distinct wavelength. Thus, an n-bit header requires an additional n wavelengths more than those designated for the packet payload. However, having only one bit of information to decode on each wavelength for the entire duration of the packet dramatically simplifies header detection. One function that is simpler with photonic devices than with electronic devices is channel demultiplexing. Because of the wavelength nature of light, isolating one of these header wavelengths simply requires an optical filter. For a two-way switching node, two header bits are sufficient to establish all possible switching states. The control plane of the switching nodes is therefore driven by two simple optical filters and two low-speed optical receivers. After the optically encoded header bits have been decoded into electrical signals, all switching-node routing logic can use electronic logic devices with relative simplicity. Then the routing decision is executed by enabling one of the two SOA switching elements (Small, Shacham, and Bergman 2005). The routing for each node is entirely contained within that node, resulting in a distributed switching architecture.

Moreover, the packets should traverse the node structure in a manner that is almost perfectly transparent: optical power is preserved and very little signal distortion is introduced. In the implementations, great effort is taken to ensure that the signal exiting the switching node is almost identical to the one that entered. The losses introduced by the Y-junction and other passive optical components are exactly matched by the gain introduced by the SOA. The SOA is also operated in a regime in which very few nonlinearities occur in order to best preserve signal integrity. This structure allows for many switching nodes to be cascaded in a modular way that is almost independent of the path through the network and the number of nodes traversed. The packets fly through the system without significant degradation, traveling from one node to the next.

In order to best serve this switching-node design, the network must follow a bufferless topology. Clearly, the simple switching-node design that has been developed above lacks buffering and store-and-forward capabilities. The optical packets traverse the Y-junction at exactly the speed of light in fiber, and there is no means of halting the packet flow or even slowing it down. These restrictions are easily serviced by the architectural implementation of deflection routing or, similarly, hot-potato routing (Dally and Towles 2004).

In summary, optical interconnection network topologies, along with the switching-node designs and optical packet formats, are designed to leverage the unique benefits of fiberoptic and photonic technologies while avoiding their shortcomings. Buffering and packet storage are not required; this is avoided by deflection routing. Logical computations executed in optical media are not required; instead, digital electronic devices compute the switching-node routing decision. Moreover, the packet payload is encoded optically as a high-bandwidth multiple-wavelength structure that transparently propagates the network as a unit, staying in the optical domain throughout the entire network. Only the low-bandwidth headers are converted to the electronic domain, allowing packets to fly through the network uninhibited, with time-of-flight latencies approaching speed-of-light limitations. Using a water-flow (fire-hose) metaphor, the high-bandwidth optical packet can flow through the switching fabric, with the switching nodes as nearly transparent valves that direct the flow of this unstoppable deluge; the headers serve only to temporarily set the state of the branches. The benefits of fiber optics are complemented, not hindered, by electronics in a cooperative arrangement that maximizes the throughput of the interconnection network and minimizes transmission latencies.

Metrics

The performance of networks can be quantified by a few key metrics. Latency describes the duration required for a packet to enter the input interface (including possible input buffering) and then exit completely from the output interface; network latency includes processing times as well as the traversal "time of flight" or routing latency. The quantity of packets or information that are successfully routed by the network in a single time slot (or specified unit of time) is the throughput or bandwidth; an accurate measure of this is the bisectional bandwidth, which is defined in more detail below. Also important is the acceptance rate—of the offered load, or total quantity of packets that are presented to the network in a particular timeslot, generally some packets are rejected and must wait to be routed by the network, or be routed at a later time. When the offered load becomes so high that the acceptance rate begins to diminish, the network is said to be saturated.

Although latency, throughput, and acceptance rate are the most important measures, a few other network properties can be of interest to network designers as well. These include the more abstract attributes such as scalability, expandability, and simplicity, as well as reliability or robustness, recoverability, and reparability. And for network architectures to actually be implemented, designers must also consider financial cost or price and electrical power consumption. A complete view of network design must be concerned with both the performance metrics and these engineering and implementation considerations.

The bisectional bandwidth measures the total throughput flowing from one half of the network to the other. That is, if we imagine cutting the network geometrically in half, bisecting it between input terminals and output terminals, the throughput that traverses this boundary represents a much more meaningful measure of the aggregate network bandwidth; this is the bisectional bandwidth. Because, in general, packets cross this boundary only once, packets are counted correctly, and because the boundary crosses the entire network, the bisectional bandwidth accounts for any localized congestion or irregularities.

Even before a network reaches saturation, there are instances when not all packets are accepted into the network for routing and delivery. That is, not all of the packets offered into the network—the offered load—are immediately accepted into the network for routing.

Thus, the acceptance rate quantifies the fraction of the packet traffic that actually enters the network for routing compared with the offered load. Packets that are rejected may be buffered in one of the stages discussed above; in rare cases, packets may simply be discarded, although this option can have grave repercussions for overall system performance. All of the processing of the network interface modules counts against the latency of the network, although the routing latency can be used to describe the amount of time required between the network interface modules, discounting buffering and processing.

The key metrics for next-generation high-bandwidth interconnection networks, such as those described in this chapter, are throughput (bandwidth), latency, and acceptance rate. It is important to consider how design decisions affect each of these. The case studies provided below represent different approaches to reaching an optimal region of this design space.

CASE STUDIES

In this section, we examine a few of the emerging very-high-speed interconnection networks capable of supporting at least 100 Gbps per port, and petabits/sec to exabits/sec bisection bandwidth. These are meant to be representative of some of the key research work of the field. Most of this is experimental, but it is indicative of future trends in the field and the impending challenges. The proposed 100-Gbps Ethernet standard, which channelizes 10-Gbps Ethernet over as many WDM channels or stripes, is probably the nearest term of these, but relying on traditional electronic switching, does not offer a very elegant switching mechanism and can be expensive to implement in large-scale architectures. Other more specific optical solutions that are described include ShuffleNet, Data Vortex, and OSMOSIS. Finally, as very-large-scale integrations tip past the billion-transistor-per-chip level, many systems will rely on large arrays of multicore processor chips in which the on-chip internal bus must act as an extension of the larger global interconnection network. In fact, with clock speeds in the multiple-gigahertz range, on-chip latencies will pose similar problems that chip-to-chip network designers faced a decade earlier. Early on-chip network concepts that address these challenges include SPINet as well as possible successors to several on-chip buses for the current vintage of multicore processor chips. Common traits of these networks are low latency that can support fine-grained messages efficiently, very high speeds per port (>100 Gbps), dual E/O implementation approaches that enhance scalability to very large systems of thousands to millions of processor elements.

Case Study 1: 100-Gigabit Ethernet

By far the most popular and least expensive network interconnection technology for clusters, especially low-cost commodity clusters, is Ethernet. The original concept for Ethernet was invented (and patented) by Bob Metcalfe at Xerox PARC in 1973, but it was not commercialized until the late 1970s, when Xerox, Intel, and Digital Equipment Corporation (DEC) joined forces to propose a standard (called DIX) that specified the carrier sense multiple access/collision detection (CSMA/CD) protocol at 10 Mbps over a coax. In 1983, the first IEEE 802.3 standard appeared that was basically backward-compatible with the DIX standard. Over the next two decades, the standard was enhanced numerous times to support other forms of media and increased speed. Most notable, the modern-day 100 Mb/s (or Fast) 100BaseT standard (802.3u) appeared in 1995, followed by 1000BaseT standard (802.3z), and 10-Gigabit (802.3ae) standard by 2002. And there is advance planning underway for 100-Gigabit Ethernet, although that is not likely to appear any earlier than 2010 (more on this below).

One of the real advantages of Ethernet is that high-volume commodity pricing has made network interface controller (NIC) adapters so cheap that 10/100/1000 Mbit/s host adapters are placed on nearly every processor motherboard built today. With a price point that is typically under 1% of the motherboard cost, some motherboards actually incorporate multiple interfaces for applications such as servers, peripheral input/output (I/O) farms, routers, network attached storage, and to no surprise, cluster computer compute nodes.

With such versatility and widespread adoption, Ethernets have found several niches in Beowulf PC clusters. First, in very-low-cost systems, they of course serve as the primary interconnection network for interprocessor communications. In higher-end clusters, where an ultra-high-performance network such as Infiniband (Shanley 2002; Liu 2005), Myrinet (Flich 2002), or QsNet (Petrini 2002) is used for the primary interprocessor communications, Ethernet is often used to support secondary functions, such as system administration, control, external I/O, maintenance, and of course, backup to the primary network.

Over the span of almost 30 years, Ethernet has progressed from the original 10 Mbps standard of the late 1970s, through 100 Mbps, 1 Gbps, and now 10 Gbps standards. Although Gigabit Ethernet is backward-compatible with Fast (100 Mbps) Ethernet, a number of changes were made to the physical layer, and a large part of the data exchange protocols to improve performance and support high bandwidth media. Data rates in the 400-to-700-Mbps range are typical with TCP/IP using jumbo frames (9000 bytes), and slightly better results are possible with user datagram protocol (UDP). Unfortunately, the latency remains high in the few-hundred-microsecond range, primarily because of the TCP/IPoverhead. The cost of Gigabit Ethernet switch equipment is non-negligible in figuring the overall system cost, but is expected to continue to fall as the commercial market volumes increase.

Although the standard for 10-Gigabit Ethernet has been in place since 2002, its market penetration has been gradual because of the high cost and low volumes, much of this because the earlier Gigabit Ethernet still satisfies much of the commercial and consumer need.

Early trials of a possible 100-Gigabit Ethernet standard have already been successfully attempted (GRID Today 2006) by aggregating 10 × 10-Gbps Ethernet channels over as many WDM channels of an optical fiber. Channel-bonding schemes are introduced to guarantee that frames arrive in order at the destination. A prototype of this system was developed and demonstrated that relies on a single-chip 100-Gigabit Ethernet network interface that implements a lane-alignment and packet-resequencing scheme to bond ten parallel 10-Gbps channels into one logical flow while maintaining packet ordering at the receiver. This eliminates the need for high-speed serial/parallel multiplexers and clock recovery methods and the resulting performance issues (such as increased logic complexity and signal delay) that can arise with the use of the existing link aggregation techniques for combining multiple data channels. Services that combine multiple wavelengths to offer a single service are referred to as "super-lambda services." To date though, such a system would be cost-effective only as a wide area network. However, with appropriate refinements and increased volumes of the switch and NIC chip technology and optoelectronics, it is possible that such a system could become cost-effective as a system interconnect. However, based on the somewhat slower adoption of 10-Gigabit Ethernet, this might evolve as a somewhat slower rate over the next decade.

Case Study 2: Optical ShuffleNet

All OPS networks, both long haul and computer system interconnects, have been investigated since the late 1980s, when the National Science Foundation (NSF) and Defense Advanced Research Projects Agency (DARPA) began some investments in this area. Although most of the attention at the time was focused on long haul and wide area network systems, there were a few early investigations that focused on interconnects for parallel computer systems that were just beginning to become a dominant force in the high-performance-computing industry. One of these was ShuffleNet (Hluchyj and Karol 1991; Feehrer, Sauer, and Ramfelt 1994), in which optical packets are launched into a fiber-optic omega network of 2×2 optical switches (Figure 2). The method uses deflection routing to detect packet address header information on the fly, and then correctly throw 2×2 $LiNbO_3$ switches to the correct position for the optical packet to reach its next point in the network. The data payload of the packet never needs to be decoded electronically, thus reducing latency of the switch point and more importantly, overall system complexity. Also, in principle, the bandwidth of the packets can be much higher than normal since electronic regeneration is not required at each 2×2 switch. If two packets arrive at the 2×2 switch at the same time and both packets are vying for the same outbound port, then one packet is intentionally deflected on a nonoptimal outbound port, which may cause the packet to take a longer path, and incur more latency, on its way to its destination. This elegant form of congestion arbitration uses the network itself as a memory buffer to store packets on the fly when the same resources are being contented for.

The ShuffleNet scheme can be implemented using TDM or WDM or both technologies. One disadvantage of the scheme is the topology, in which the number of links and 2×2 switches required scales as $N \log N$ as the number of processors (or network ports) increases. More efficient use of network fabric while sacrificing very little in terms of network bisection bandwidth and network saturation characteristics can be found in the Data Vortex, which is discussed in the next section. Another significant disadvantage is that deflected packets must traverse the entire network again and again until they reach the correct output port, which can potentially lead to severe congestion.

Case Study 3: Data Vortex

The Data Vortex topology was designed specifically for implementation as an OPS network and developed primarily at Columbia University beginning in 2002. The Data Vortex architecture requires no routing buffers and can be constructed from simple single-packet 2×2 switching nodes. The multiple-stage construction of the architecture allows for a node-element building block, which must be modified only slightly depending on its

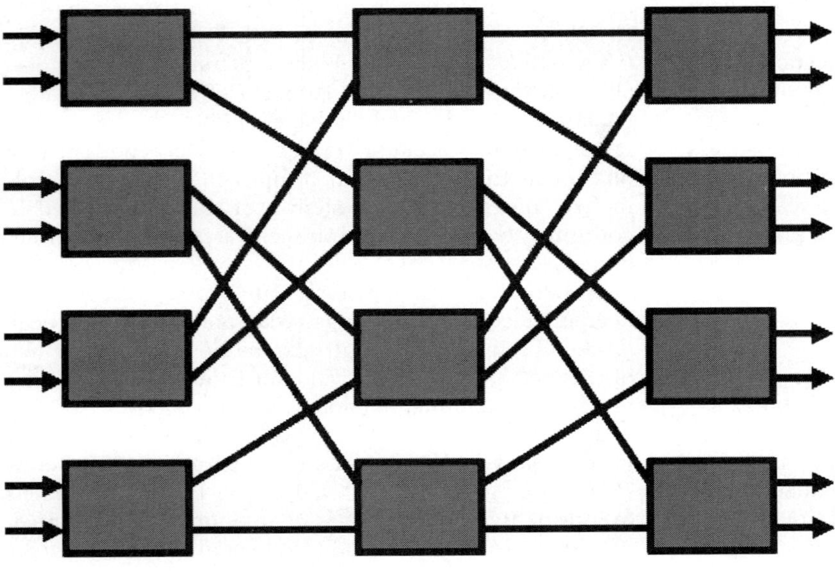

Figure 2: Illustration of an 8×8 ShuffleNet (omega) topology, composed of nonblocking 2×2 switching nodes

location with the topology. Because of this high degree of modularity, the implementation of a complete network is not an unsurpassable prospect, and it has been demonstrated, yielding a fully implemented terabit-capacity switch (Shacham, Small, Liboiron-Ladouceur, and Bergman 2005; Hawkins and Small 2007).

This project also developed a new architectural paradigm, which was used in designing the Data Vortex network. First, in order to unleash the bandwidth potential of optical transmission, multiple-wavelength (or wavelength-parallel) encoding is used for the packet payload. Each wavelength can be modulated at a high data rate (10 Gbps or higher) itself, and multiple wavelengths (sixteen or more) are transmitted in parallel throughout the network. Second, the multiple-stage (or multistage) interconnection network (MIN) contains many switching nodes between the input and output terminals, as in the ShuffleNet, and each of these switching nodes is made to be "transparent." This means that the switching nodes allow the optical information to pass through with nearly no physical change to the encoded information; power levels are preserved (or amplified following attenuations), and no signal processing is done. Thus, switching nodes can be cascaded in any sequence and at almost any length (Small, Shacham, and Bergman 2005). Third, header information is transmitted with 1 bit per wavelength to simplify decoding and minimize the latency of the routing logic. These three architectural features are independent of the topology and can be used for a variety of optical network architectures. The focus of this case study, however, is on the specifics of the Data Vortex architecture.

The Data Vortex architecture is designed for scalability to large port counts with potentially thousands of communicating terminals and thus uses a distributed routing scheme rather than central arbitration (Hawkins et al. 2007). In order to best accommodate scalability and address the problem of the absence of reliable dynamic photonic buffers, the conventional butterfly network topology is modified to contain integrated deflection routing pathways. The primary consideration in the organization of the architecture is enabling the optical packets to approach speed-of-light time-of-flight latencies. The switching nodes are therefore designed to be as simple as possible and to contain as little routing logic as possible, so that the packets do not have to be delayed while routing decisions are made. These design considerations naturally result in a very modular architecture, and one that is scalable and self-similar in such a way that a small-system implementation can help predict the performance of larger networks.

The Data Vortex topology integrates internalized buffering with banyan-style bitwise routing to result in a bufferless network, ideal for implementation with fiber-optic components. The structure can be visualized as a set of concentric cylinders or routing stages that are cyclic subgroups that allow for deflections without loss of routing progress. Moreover, the hierarchical multiple-stage structure is easily scaled to larger network sizes while uniformly maintaining fundamental architectural concepts (Hawkins et al. 2007).

This implementation of the Data Vortex architecture is meant as a demonstration of its viability and as a testbed for system analyses. The smallest-size Data Vortex topology of interest (i.e., one that demonstrates features common to larger systems) is a 12×12 network, which contains 3 cylinders of height 4 and 3 angles, viz. $(C,H,A) = (3,4,3)$. These parameters indicate that a 4×4 banyan structure is augmented with an internal deflection buffering dimension of 3. The entire system is comprised of thirty-six single-packet 2×2 switching nodes (Figure 3).

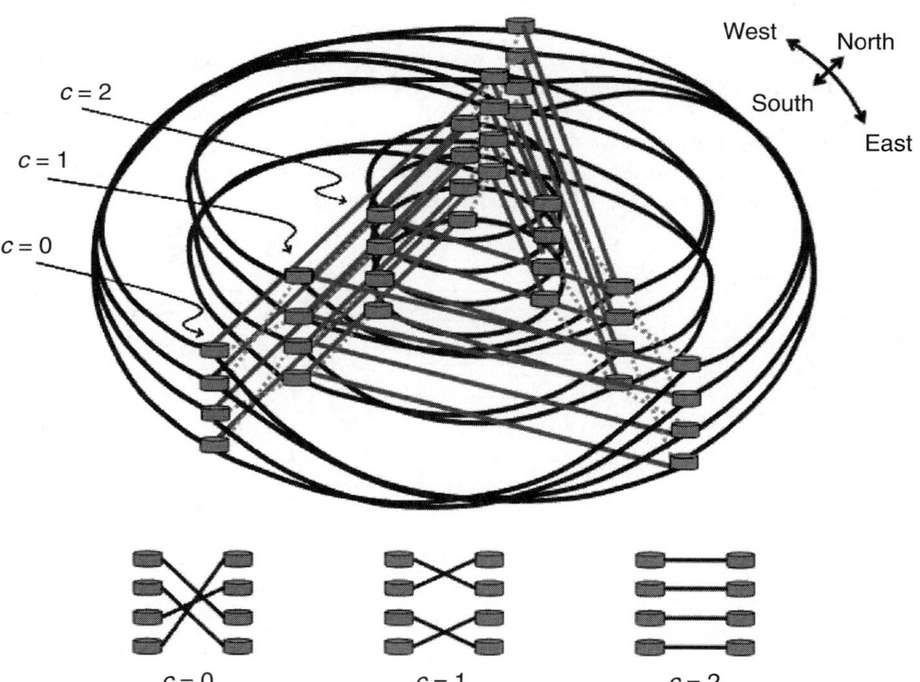

Figure 3: Three-dimensional illustration of the Data Vortex topology

The switching nodes are interconnected using a set of ingression fibers, which connect nodes of the same height in adjacent cylinders, and deflection fibers, which connect nodes of different heights within the same cylinder. The ingression fibers are of the same length throughout the entire system, as must be the deflection fibers. The deflection fibers' height-crossing patterns direct packets through different height levels at each hop to enable banyan routing (e.g., butterfly, omega) to a desired height, and assist in balancing the load throughout the system, mitigating local congestion (Hawkins et al. 2007; Hawkins and Small 2007; Hawkins and Wills 2006).

Because a complete deflection routing scheme is implemented, acceptance rates of nearly 100% can easily be achieved for the Data Vortex architecture (Yang and Bergman 2002). Although this requires a small degree of overprovisioning, the result is well worth it: the implemented Data Vortex system is in practice able to accept more than 160 Gbps (16 wavelengths at 10 Gbps) of traffic to each of its twelve input ports at every clock cycle. Because wideband SOAs are used as the only switching element, the network can potentially support packets composed of wavelengths that span the entire C-band. Not only has successful routing been demonstrated on the implemented system, but various physical measurements and characterizations have been performed as well (Small, Liboiron-Ladouceur, et al. 2005; Small et al. 2006; Small, Shacham, Athikulwongse, Hawkins, Bergman, and Wills 2004), which attest to the robustness and scalability of the architecture.

Case Study 4: OSMOSIS

In the OSMOSIS project, a hybrid electro-optical approach using electronics for buffering and scheduling, and optics for transmission and switching, is adopted. This system uses components and technologies currently available, and demonstrates that this hybrid approach easily allows for the implementation of a high-performance system (Hemenway et al. 2004). This project was a collaborative effort between IBM Research and Corning in the early 2000s.

For the OSMOSIS network, an SOA-based 64 × 64 crossbar switching fabric has been constructed and a high-speed scheduling algorithm has been developed to maximize its utilization (Figure 4). SOAs are used as the cross-points in the switching fabric, and 40-Gbps peak bandwidth per port is demonstrated. Internal paths are wavelength-multiplexed in the switching fabric to reduce the number of SOAs and the total cost. However, the wavelength-based routing used in the second stage of the crossbar restricts packets to single-wavelength transmission. High-throughput figures must therefore be the result of high modulation rates.

The simple and predictable structure of the optical pathways results in packets being routed with a fixed and known latency, unlike the Data Vortex architecture, in which deflections can result in variable packet latencies. In order to successfully manage the 64 × 64 crossbar, a central arbiter must schedule each pathway assignment between the requested input and output ports. By leveraging an electronic application-specific integrated circuit (ASIC) to execute the routing computations, the high-bandwidth packet transmission of the optical domain can be made very simple. This hybrid approach is what allows the OSMOSIS switch to deliver such high-bandwidth figures with very high packet acceptance and minimal propagation latency.

Although being the closest to actual implementation and possible commercialization, having shown a running prototype, the OSMOSIS architecture may not be the choice sought for very-large-scale systems. A scheduled crossbar requires additional communication lines, limits scalability, and is often accompanied by a notable queuing delay. In the suggested fat-tree architecture, packets can experience this delay several times, resulting in a latency penalty.

Measurements and performance evaluations have been performed on the implemented prototype system (Hemenway et al. 2004). Because the structure of the optical pathways is so simple, the network provides a large degree of physical flexibility. However, the central arbitration unit can become a system bottleneck if the routing algorithm becomes saturated. There has, therefore, been a significant effort to optimize the crossbar-arbitration algorithm and minimize overhead. The OSMOSIS architecture represents a truly unique hybridized approach to optical interconnection, leaving the high-bandwidth transmission to the optical domain, and using high-speed electronics for the routing and decision making.

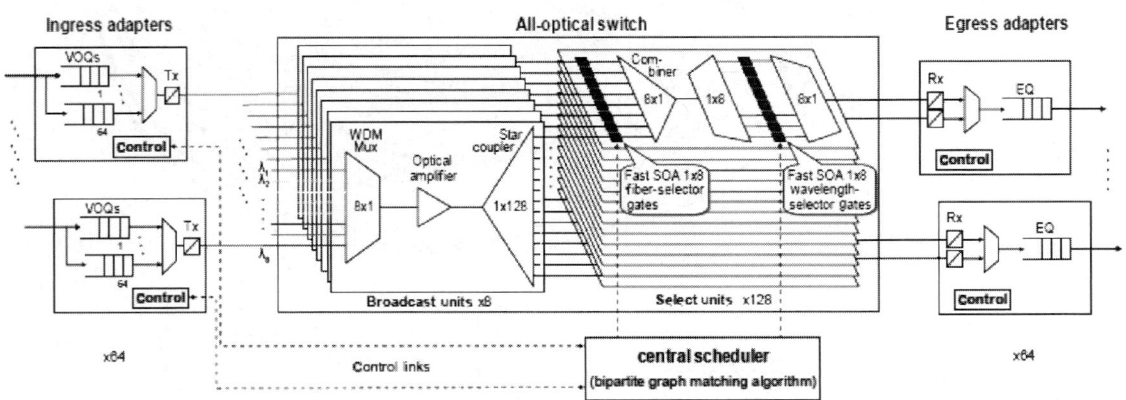

Figure 4: Schematic of the OSMOSIS (64 × 64 broadcast-and-select) architecture. (Source: Hemenway, 2004)

Case Study 5: OPSNET

Recent collaborations between a research group at Cambridge University and Intel Research has resulted in a router architecture that is similar to both the OSMOSIS and Data Vortex projects. As with those architectures, SOAs are used as the primary switching element. The OPSNET network topology of this router is a simple arbitrated crossbar structure, although it can accommodate multiple-wavelength (wavelength-striped) packets as well (Figure 5; Lin et al. 2006).

In a more advanced implementation, two crossbars are cascaded in order to deliver higher port counts. In addition to providing the routing functionality, field programmable gate array (FPGA) controllers are also programmed to equalize packet power and optimize the physical-layer properties of the routed packets.

The first-stage switch fabric is configured as a broadcast and select 4 × 4-switch-using fused fiber couplers and commercially sourced low-polarization sensitivity semiconductor optical amplifiers. No power equalization is performed in the first-stage switch, with power levels being deliberately mismatched at the input to the second-stage switch. The arbiter is implemented in a fairly sophisticated FPGA and is configured to route the WDM packets cyclically from the three hosts to the input of the second-stage fabric.

The second switch fabric is similarly equipped to implement the required paths of a 4 × 4 broadcast and select switch. Unused paths are terminated with attenuators as shown by the open boxes. The amplifiers are instead illustrated by filled boxes in Figure 5. Optical isolators are placed after each SOA. The second-stage SOA switch routes the packets from the first stage to the test port and implements the digital controller for power equalization. The input power is tapped with a 10:90 coupler, filtered, sampled, and digitized with 12-bit resolution to update the look-up table in the controller.

The control plane is implemented with partitioned FPGA. Low-line-rate 1-Gbps O-band transceivers are set to ensure time-slot synchronization between the hosts and the central arbiter. The control and data channels are transmitted on the same fiber using low-loss broadband-wavelength multiplexers. To avoid delaying the packets, the power-equalization settings for each time slot are defined ahead of payload arrival at the switch. Control information specifying the implemented paths between hosts is therefore transmitted ahead of the packets to avoid the need for delay at the optical layer. To ensure scalability, component-specific data are abstracted from the higher networking layers using a multilayered control plane.

This prototype network demonstrates that electronics can be used for physical-layer control as well as routing within high-bandwidth optical interconnection networks. This is another example of an architecture in which the optical medium and photonic devices are used as the means of conveying extremely-high-bandwidth packets, and conventional high-speed electronics are used for setting up the photonic pathways and managing the optical packets.

Case Study 6: Chip-to-Chip SPINet

The main impediment to the construction of photonic interconnection networks lies in the high cost and large footprints associated with using discrete optical elements such as lasers, modulators, switches, and passive optics. Photonic integration, the fabrication of circuits implementing many photonic functions in a single package, is promising to eliminate these final barriers (Williams 2006). When photonic integration is harnessed to construct interconnection networks, however, buffering becomes very difficult. The optical packet occupies a fixed length of a waveguiding medium, which is the product of the speed of light in the medium and the duration of the packet. A typical 100-ns packet will occupy 20 m of silica fiber or 6 m of a semiconductor waveguide. Consequently, buffering optical packets within a photonic integrated circuit (PIC) is not currently practical, and interconnection networks based on photonic integration should be truly bufferless, using other means of contention resolution.

The SPINet (Scalable Photonic Integrated Network) architecture is designed to be implemented using photonic integration technology (Shacham et al., A scalable,

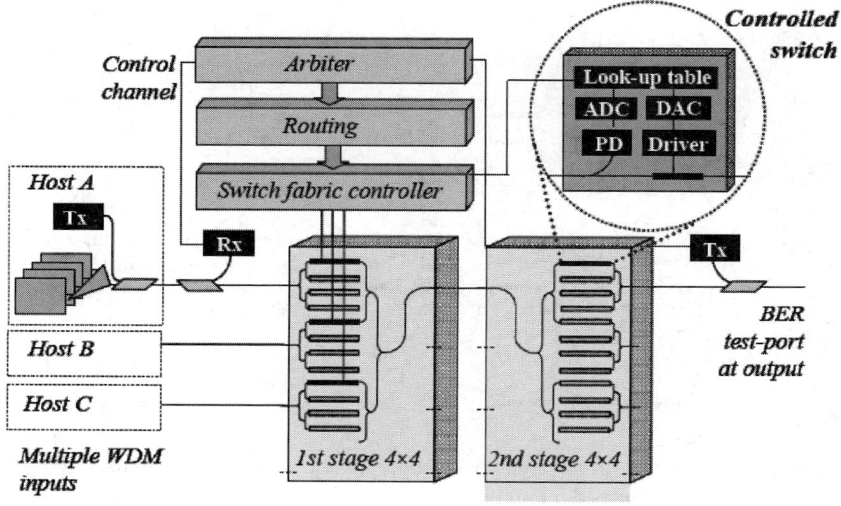

Figure 5: Schematic of the OPSNET architecture, with two cascaded 4 × 4 stages. © OSA 2007, *J. Opt. Netw.*

self-routed, 2005). Based on an indirect MIN topology, SPINet exploits WDM to simplify the network design and to provide very high bandwidths. SPINet does not use buffering, and resolves contention by dropping contending messages. A novel physical layer acknowledgment protocol provides immediate feedback notifying the terminals whether their messages are accepted and facilitates retransmissions when necessary, in a manner resembling traditional multiple-access media. In this section we describe SPINet's concepts, its design parameters, and its performance under various scenarios.

A SPINet network is a transparent optical MIN, comprised of 2 × 2 SOA-based bufferless photonic switching nodes. Topologically, it is very similar to the ShuffleNet described above, although the physical scale of a SPINet network is much smaller, and some of the particulars of contention resolution differ. The network can be of any indirect binary topology, in which 2 × 2 switching nodes are used. In the original implementation an Omega topology was chosen because of its simple stage-interconnection pattern. An $N_T{}'N_T$ Omega network consists of $N_S = log_2N_T$ identical stages. Each stage consists of a perfect-shuffle interconnection followed by N_T / 2 switching elements, as shown in Figure 6, where $N_T = 8$. The switching nodes are nonblocking, so data from both input ports may be received and routed simultaneously.

The entire network is envisioned to be integrated on a PIC, and its terminals are physically located on the computing nodes of the HPC system and are connected to the PIC by optical fibers. The terminals are assumed to be synchronized, the network is slotted and synchronous, and messages have a fixed duration. The minimal slot duration is determined by the round-trip propagation time of the optical signal from the terminals to the PIC. A slot time of 100 ns can, therefore, accommodate a nearly 20-m propagation path and a distance of 10 m between the terminals and the PIC.

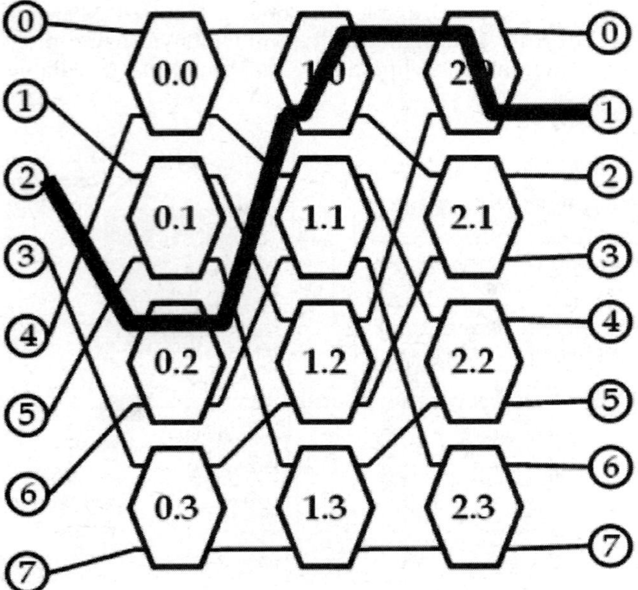

Figure 6: An 8 × 8 omega network schematic of a SPINet design wih an end-to-end lightpath

At the beginning of each slot, any terminal may start transmitting a message, without a prior request or grant. The messages propagate in the fibers to the input modules on the PIC and are transparently forwarded to the switching nodes of the first stage. At every routing stage when the leading edges of the messages are received from one or both input ports, a routing decision is made and the messages continue to propagate to their requested output ports. In the case of output-port contention in a switching node, one of the contending messages is dropped. The choice of which message to drop can be random, alternating, or priority-based. Since the propagation delay through every stage is identical, all the leading edges of the transmitted messages reach all the nodes of each stage at the same time.

Using the ultra-low-latency propagation through the PIC, SPINet eliminates the need for central scheduling using the distributed computing power of the switching nodes to produce an I/O match at every slot. This process of implicit arbitration enables scalability to large port counts without burdening a central arbiter with computing complex maximal matches. Because blocking topologies are used, to reduce hardware complexity, the network's utilization is lower than that of a traditional maximum-matched nonblocking network (e.g., switching fabrics of high-performance Internet router). In subsequent sections, techniques that exploit the properties of integrated photonics to increase utilization by adding a small number of stages are investigated.

The packet structure used for the SPINnet network is almost identical to the one described for the Data Vortex architecture, above. Multiple-wavelength packets can be used, since the switching elements have a very wide optical bandwidth. Certain wavelengths can be designated for use by the payload and modulated at high data rates, whereas other wavelengths are reserved for header and routing information.

The wavelength parallel structure also facilitates a low-cost solution for E/O conversion: the replacement of prohibitively expensive high-speed serial modulators and receivers with a set of lower-speed devices to attain the same bandwidth. These devices can be, for example, low-cost directly modulated 2.5-Gbps vertical-cavity surface-emitting lasers (VCSELs) or even on-chip silicon modulators/receivers. The achievable low-cost bandwidth and the network's inherent wide switching band and bit-rate transparency suggest a bandwidth-time trading: for a given required peak bandwidth, an $\times S$ speedup is used in the wavelength domain, while the packet rate (the load offered to the network) is reduced by a $1/S$ factor. For example, for a port designed to provide a peak bandwidth of 40 Gbps, eight wavelengths are modulated at 10 Gbps each, and a new packet is generated once every two slots, on average. This ×2 speedup lowers the load offered to the network, thus leading to reduced queuing latency.

Case Study 7: Multicore Networks-on-Chip

A major design paradigm shift is currently impacting high-performance microprocessors as critical technologies are simultaneously converging on fundamental performance limits. Accelerated local processing frequencies have clearly reached a point of diminishing returns: further increases in speed lead to tighter bounds on the logic coherently accessed on-chip, and the associated power dissipation is exacerbated in an exponential fashion. Evidence of this trend is unmistakable, as practically every commercial manufacturer of high-performance processors is currently introducing products based on multicore architectures: AMD's Opteron, Intel's Montecito, Sun's Niagara, and IBM's Cell and Power5. Clearly, within the next few years, performance gains will come from increases in the number of processor cores per chip, leading to the emergence of a key bottleneck: the global intrachip communications infrastructure. Perhaps the most daunting challenge to future systems is to realize the enormous bandwidth capacities and stringent latency requirements when interconnecting a large number of processing cores in a power-efficient fashion.

Low-latency, high-data-rate, on-chip interconnection networks have therefore become a key to relieving one of the main bottlenecks to chip-level multiprocessing (CMP) system performance. Significant research activity has focused on intrachip global communication using packet-switched micronetworks. These so-called networks-on-chip (NoCs) are made of carefully engineered links and represent a shared medium that is highly scalable and can provide enough bandwidth to replace many traditional bus-based and/or point-to-point links. However, with a fixed upper limit to the total chip-power dissipation, and the communications infrastructure emerging as a major power consumer, performance-per-watt is becoming the most critical design metric for the scaling of NoCs and CMPs. It is not clear how electronic NoCs will continue to satisfy future communication bandwidths and latency requirements within the power dissipation budget.

Photonic interconnection networks offer a potentially disruptive technology solution because of their fundamentally low power dissipation compared with equivalent electronic interconnects that remain independent of capacity while providing ultra-high throughputs and minimal-access latencies. One of the main drivers for considering photonic NoCs is the expected reduction in power expended on intrachip communications. The key power saving rises from the fact that once a photonic path is established, the data are transmitted end to end without the need for repeating, regeneration, or buffering. In electronic NoCs, on the other hand, messages are buffered, regenerated, and then transmitted on the inter-router links several times en route to their destination.

The building blocks are nanoscale PICs that use optical microcavities, particularly those based on ring resonator structures shaped from photonic waveguides, which can easily be fabricated on conventional silicon and silicon-on-insulator (SOI) substrates. High-speed optical modulators, capable of performing switching operations, have been realized using the free carrier plasma dispersion effect in these ring resonator structures or in Mach-Zehnder geometries. SiGe-based photodetectors and optical receivers are the final component necessary for making an entire self-contained PIC, and a few designs for these have been suggested recently (Special Issue on Nanoscale Integrated Photonics, 2007).

In fact, IBM and Intel, as well as other companies, have launched serious research efforts in this area, and have been developing a host of the optoelectronic and photonic devices that would be required to assemble a complete NoC. These foundries are interested in enhancing the performance of their already planned multicore CPU architectures. The most recent advances of each of these corporations are typically announced publicly and with fanfare (see www.intel.com/go/sp and www.research.ibm.com/photonics).

The proposed novel architecture of the hybrid photonic-electronic on-chip network is based on a two-layer structure: (1) a photonic interconnection network, comprised of silicon broadband photonic switches interconnected by waveguides, is used to transmit high-bandwidth messages; and (2) an electronic control network, mimicking the topology of the photonic network, in which each electronic router controls a photonic switch. The main advantage of this approach relies on a property of the photonic medium, known as bit-rate transparency. Unlike electronic routers, which switch with every bit of the transmitted data while dissipating dynamic power scaling with the bit rate, photonic switches switch on and off at the message rate, and their energy dissipation does not depend on the bit rate. This property facilitates the transmission of very-high-bandwidth messages while avoiding the power cost that is typically associated with them in traditional electronic networks.

The architecture leveraged for these nanoscale PICs relies on a similar hybrid approach to network design as is leveraged for the macroscale case studies given above. High-bandwidth optical packets are routed through photonic devices entirely within the optical domain; only the routing and arbitration is controlled by high-speed electronics.

COMPARISON OF BASIC APPROACHES

All of the optics-based case studies discussed above are united by one fundamental design principle: optics and photonics are used for transmitting the payload information across the network, and conventional electronics are used as the means of controlling the network flow. It is universally recognized that the potential bandwidth available for optical transmission vastly surpasses that of any contemporary electronic system, and will be necessary after 100-Gigabit Ethernet no longer meets the bandwidth demands of cluster computing systems. Somehow leveraging the 6 THz of bandwidth available within the C-band of the optical spectrum is a feature common to the architectures discussed above. Although devices for all-optical network control are currently being researched, these design approaches recognize that the technology is still far from being robust and able to be commercialized. On the other hand, these networks allow for payloads to be sent across the whole network in the optical domain from beginning to end; it is not necessary to convert between optics and electronics once signals enter the network.

It seems that a dominant trend for the next generation of cluster interconnection networks is toward lightwave systems, which rely on conventional electronics for routing management and arbitration. This design approach is clever in that it allows the two technological media (viz. electronics and optics) to do what each is best at: nothing to date can beat the sheer computational flexibility and simplicity of CMOS electronics, and optical signal encoding is the ideal high-bandwidth low-power method of transmitting information.

Although the architectures discussed above share this common design principle, they differ in many significant ways as well. Many of the approaches, such as ShuffleNet, OSMOSIS, OPSNET, and SPINet, topologically resemble more familiar networks, although the details of their implementation are specific to optics. In one case, the Data Vortex, an entirely new topological scheme was developed to fit the underlying optical transmission medium. Some of these network architectures, such as OSMOSIS and OPSNET, rely on centralized arbiters for managing packet routing and network flow control; whereas the ShuffleNet, Data Vortex, SPINet architectures are composed of discrete switching nodes that execute routing decisions individually, resulting in a distributed network control mechanism.

For all network topologies, optoelectronic devices are required for switching the optical signals based on electronic inputs, serving as the interface between the optical signal plane and the control plane. Many of the architectures described above rely on SOAs because they can deliver gain while maintaining very short propagation latencies and fast switching times. The ShuffleNet, mostly developed before SOAs were commercially available, instead leverages $LiNbO_3$ switches, which introduce signal loss. In either case, the discrete optoelectronic switching devices play a central role in the network: hundreds or thousands of them must be assembled and connected for the completed system. The benefit of monolithically integrated systems, such as SPINet or NoCs, is that the switching devices can be formed on the substrate in a way that is more elegant than the bulk-scale devices.

Despite some of the apparent differences between the projects discussed above, they all seek to optimize and improve upon already existing technology and maximize network throughput and transmission bandwidth. By alleviating the key interconnect bottleneck in cluster and multiprocessor interconnection networks, the ultimate computing power of these systems can truly be unleashed.

PROSPECTS FOR REALIZATION (BARRIERS, TECHNOLOGY, OR ECONOMIC)

As discussed above, a key element of the proposed next-generation optical network architectures is the optoelectronic switching elements. Although they have improved vastly, in both performance and price, over the past decade, they still have a way to go before being competitive with gigahertz-scale microelectronics. But like any emerging technology, improvements will come rapidly once there is appreciable economic incentive (Miller 2000). As the interconnect bottleneck in HPC systems becomes more and more detrimental to system performance, these next-generation technologies will become more attractive. The good news is that the technology for these solutions already exists, and designs have already been developed. In this way, cluster interconnect architectures are ahead of their time.

Monolithically integrated technologies are making significant advances as well. Demonstrations of fully functional components and subsystems have illustrated the feasibility of PICs for interconnection networks (Special Issue on Nanoscale Integrated Photonics, 2007). These on-chip interconnects have the potential to service multicore platforms and improve the performance of CPU chips themselves.

All of these next-generation architectures are exciting prospects. Because of the forthcoming severity of the supercomputer interconnect problem, these systems have valuable contributions to make to the advance of supercomputing power. By making the most of advancing technologies, these technologies show great promise in being part of the next generation of cluster computing.

CONCLUSION AND AREAS TO WATCH

What are the emerging trends? Moore's law is showing signs of slowing, at least in terms of processor clock speed. However, the Silicon Industry Association (SIA) roadmap is showing continued decrease in feature size through 2015 (see www.public.itrs.net), meaning that chip density will continue to increase. In turn, this will enable larger multicore processor chips, larger memory systems, higher levels of integration (fewer chips per motherboard), and wider data buses and greater precision logic (64-bit is hitting stride). All of these will apply back pressure for network speeds to increase, at least to the compute node (where multiple processors may reside). As Intel and AMD are now investigating moving the graphics engine onto the processor chip, doing the same for network host adaptor(s) would make sense to some, but many packaging challenges remain. But there are other downsides, in that network architecture and speed advances would have to be now in lockstep with processor advances—probably not very desirable. In terms of the network components, 100-Gigabit Ethernet is beginning to be explored by standards groups, and if it reaches convergence, products likely would not appear any sooner than 2010. Undoubtedly, other vendors will also explore product feasibility in this range. However, increased packaging density combined with higher speed and larger parallel data paths may possibly forge new directions in networking. For example, three-dimensional chip packaging may make it attractive to reexplore two-dimensional optical interconnects, which when combined with WDM, would enable tens of terabits to be coupled into one chip stack.

As speeds climb past 100 Gbps per port and to very wide data paths, other all-optic network concepts may become more viable, with speeds approaching ~1 terabits/sec (Tbps) per port. Examples include the ShuffleNet (Feehrer, Sauer, and Ramfelt 1994), which scales to very large systems using 2×2 optical switch building blocks, and the Data Vortex (Shacham, Small, Liboiron-Ladouceur, and Bergman 2005), which uses WDM for increased parallelism. One attribute of many of these networks is that the optical media topology and the routing protocol are designed as one unified system, minimizing or eliminating the need for fast-switching electronics at each network-switching note. Although many of these concepts have been proven in the laboratory, none (as yet) have reached commercial viability. But this could change in the years ahead, and certainly if and when it happens, it would represent a major paradigm shift.

GLOSSARY

Beowulf-Class System: Commodity cluster using personal computers to achieve excellent price and performance initially developed by the Beowulf Project at Goddard Space Flight Center.
CMP: Chip Level Multi-Processing
COTS: Commodity off-the-shelf
CRC: Cyclic redundancy checksum
CSMA/CD: Carrier sense multiple access/collision detection
DARPA: Defense Advanced Research Projects Agency
E/O: Electronic/optical
FEC: Forward Error Correction
GB: Gigabyte
GB/s: Gigabytes/sec
Gbps: Gigabits/sec
HPCS: High-performance computing systems
I/O: Input/output
IP: Internet protocol
ITU: International Telecommunications Union
MB: Megabyte
Mbps: Megabits/sec
Myricom: Vendor, distributor, and developer of the Myrinet network for commodity clusters
NIC: Network interface controller
NOW: Network of Workstations
ns: Nanosecond
NSF: National Science Foundation
O/E: Optical/electronic
OPS: Optical packet switching
PC: Personal computer
PCI: Peripheral component interface
PCI-X: PCI Extended
PIC: Photonic integrated circuit
Quadrics: Commercial vendor of networking hardware and software for QsNet
SIA: Silicon Industry Association
SOA: Semiconductor optical amplifier
TCP: Transmission control protocol
Tbps: Terabits/sec
μs: Microsecond
VIA: Virtual interface architecture
WDM: Wavelength division multiplex

CROSS REFERENCES

See *Cluster Computing Fundamentals; Grid Computing Fundamentals; Grid Computing Implementation; Utility Computing on Global Grids.*

REFERENCES

Agrawal, G. P. 2002. *Fiber-optic communication systems*. 3rd ed. New York: Wiley.

Apon, A., and M.A. Baker. 2001. Network Technologies, "A White Paper on Cluster Computing," *International Journal of High Performance Computing*, Sage Science Press, 15 (2).

Armstrong, I., Andonovic, I., and Kelly, A. 2004. Semiconductor optical amplifiers: Performance and applications in optical packet switching. *Journal of Optical Networking* 3:882–897.

Barker, K. J., Benner, A., Hoare, R., Hoisie, A., Jones, A. K., Kerbyson, D. K., Li, D., Melhem, R., Rajamony, R., Schenfeld, E., Shao, S., Stunkel, C., and Walker, P. 2005. On the feasibility of optical circuit switching for high performance computing systems. Supercomputing 2005: Proceedings of the ACM/IEEE, SC 2005 Conference, Nov 12–18, 2005, Seattle, WA. ISBN: 1-59593-061-2, 16 pg, Digital Object Identifier: 10.1109/SC.2005.48

Blumenthal, D. J. 2001. Routing packets with light. *Scientific American* 284:82–85.

Blumenthal, D. J., K. Y. Chen, J. Ma, R. J., Feuerstein, and J. R., Sauer. 1992. Demonstration of a deflection routing 2 × 2 photonic switch for computer interconnects. *IEEE Photonics Technology Letters* 4:169–73.

Bode, B. M., J. J. Hill, and T. R. Benjegerdes. 2004. Cluster interconnect overview. USENIX'04, Extreme Linux SIG Session, Boston, June 27–July 2, 2004. www.usenix.org/events/usenix04/tech/sigs/bode.html pp. 217–223 (accessed May 21, 2007).

Dally, W. J., and B. Towles. B. 2004. *Principles and practices of interconnection networks*. San Francisco: Morgan Kaufmann.

Evankow, J. D., and R. A. Thompson. 1988. Photonic switching modules designed with laser diode amplifiers. *IEEE Journal on Selected Areas in Communications* 6:1087–95.

Feehrer, J., J. Sauer, and L. Ramfelt. 1994. Design and implementation of a prototype optical deflection network. *Proceedings of the (ACM)_Conference on Communications Architectures, Protocols and Applications*. SIGCOMM '94, No. 8, 1994, London, England, UK. Copyright 1994 ACM 0-89791-682-4/94/0008, 191–200.

Flich, J., P. Lopez, M. P., Malumbres, and J. Duato. 2002. Boosting the performance of Myrinet networks. *IEEE Transactions on Parallel and Distributed Systems* 13:1166–82.

Fortenberry, R. M., Y. Cai, and R. S., Tucker. 1994. Demonstration of photonic packet-switched ring network with optically transparent nodes. *IEEE Photonics Technology Letters* 6:1139–41.

Fox, G. C. 1984. Concurrent processing for scientific calculations. *Proceedings of the COMPCON '84 28th IEEE Computer Society International Conference*. San Francisco, CA, USA, Feb 27–Mar 1, 1984, 70–73, ISBN: 0-8186-0525-1.

GRID Today, 2006. 100 Gigabit Ethernet Demonstrated at SC06. Nov 20, 2006. http://www.gridtoday.com/grid/1099207.html (accessed May 21, 2007).

Hawkins, C., Small, B. A., Wills, D. S., and Bergman, K. 2007. The data vortex, an all optical path multicomputer interconnection network. *IEEE Transactions on Parallel and Distributed Systems* 18(3): 409–420, March 2007.

Hawkins, C., and D. S. Wills. 2006. Impact of number of angles on the performance of the data vortex optical interconnection network. IEEE/OSA *Journal of Lightwave Technology* (*JLT*) 24(9).

Hemenway, R., R. R. Grzybowski, C. Minkenberg, and R. Luijten. 2004. Optical-packet-switched interconnect for supercomputer applications. *Journal of Optical Networking* 3:900–13.

Hluchyj, M. G., and M. J. Karol, M. J. 1991. ShuffleNet: an application of generalized perfect shuffles to multihop lightwave networks. *Journal of Lightwave Technology* 9:1386–97.

Hurwitz, J., and W.-C. Feng. 2004. End-to-end performance of 10-gigabit Ethernet on commodity systems. *IEEE Micro* 24:10–22.

Intel/UCSB Silicon Hybrid Laser. www.intel.com/research/platform/sp (accessed May 21, 2007).

Kaplan, H., and R. Noseworthy. 2001. The ethernet evolution from 10 Meg to 10 Gig—How it all works! NetWorld 2001. Atlanta. Also available at www.iol.unh.edu/services/testing/ethernet/training/The%20Ethernets%20new%20handout.pdf.

Krishnamoorthy, A. V., J. E. Ford, F. E. Kiamilev, R. G. Rozier, S. Hunsche, K. W. Goossen, B. Tseng, J. A. Walker, J. E. Cunningham, W. Y. Jan, and M. C. Nuss. 1999. The AMOEBA switch: an optoelectronic switch for multiprocessor networking using dense-WDM. *IEEE Journal of Selected Topics in Quantum Electronics* 5:261–75.

Lin, T., K. A. Williams, R. V. Penty, I. H. White, M. Glick, and D. McAuley. 2006. Performance and scalability of a single-stage SOA switch for 10 × 10 Gb/s wavelength striped packet routing. *IEEE Photonics Technology Letters* 18:691–3.

Liu, J., A. Mamidala, V. Vishnu, and D. K. Panda. 2005. Evaluating InfiniBand performance with PCI Express. *IEEE Micro* 25:20–9.

Luijten, R., C. Minkenberg, R. Hemenway, M. Sauer, and R. Grzybowski. 2005. Viable opto-electronic HPC interconnect fabrics. *Proceedings of the ACM/IEEE Supercomputing Conference*. Supercomputing 2005: Proceedings of the ACM/IEEE SC 2005 Conference, Nov 12–18, 2005, 1–2, Digital Object Identifier: 10.1109/SC.20005.78.

Meagher, B., G.-K. Chang, G. Ellinas, Y. M. Lin, W. Xin, T. F. Chen, X. Yang, A. Chowdhury, J. Young, S. J. Yoo, C. Lee, M. Z. Iqbal, T. Robe, H. Dai, Y. J. Chen, and W. I. Way. 2000. Design and implementation of ultra-low latency optical label switching for packet-switched WDM networks. *Journal of Lightwave Technology* 18:1978–87.

Miller, D. A. B. 2000. Rationale and challenges for optical interconnects to electronic chips. *Proceedings of the IEEE*, 88:728–49.

Papadimitriou, G. I., C. Papazoglou, and A. S. Pomportsis. 2003. Optical switching: Switch fabrics, techniques, and architectures. *Journal of Lightwave Technology* 21:384–405.

Petrini, F., W.-C. Feng, A. Hoisie, A. Coll, and E. Frachtenberg. 2002. The Quadrics network: high-performance clustering technology. *IEEE Micro* 22: 46–57.

Qiao, C., and M. Yoo. 1999. Optical burst switching (OBS): A new paradigm for an optical internet. *Journal of High Speed Networks* 8:69–84.

Ridge, D., D. Becker, P. Merkey, and T. Sterling. 1997. Beowulf: harnessing the power of parallelism in a pile-of-PCs. *IEEE Proceedings of the 1997 Aerospace Conference* 2:79–91.

Seitz, C. L. 1985. The cosmic cube. *Communications of the ACM* 28:22–33.

Shacham, A., B. G. Lee, and K. Bergman. 2005. A scalable, self-routed, terabit capacity, photonic interconnection network. *IEEE 13th Annual Symposium on High Performance Interconnects*. Aug 17–19, 2005, 147–150, ISSN: 1550-4794, ISBN: 0-7695-24494, INSPEC Accession Number: 8680956.

Shacham, A., B. A. Small, O. Liboiron-Ladouceur, and K. Bergman. K. 2005. A fully implemented 12 × 12 data vortex optical packet switching interconnection network. *Journal of Lightwave Technology* 23:3066–75.

Shacham, A., B. G. Lee, and K. Bergman. 2005. A wide-band, non-blocking, 2 × 2 switching node for a SPINet network. IEEE Photonics Technology Letters, 17, 2742–2744.

Shanley, T. 2002. Infiniband network architecture. Reading, MA: Addison-Wesley.

Silicon Industry Association. 2007. SIA roadmap. www.sia-online.org/iss_technology.cfm (accessed May 21, 2007).

Small, B. A., T. Kato, and K. Bergman. 2005. Dynamic power considerations in a complete 12 × 12 optical packet switching fabric. *IEEE Photonics Technology Letters* 17:2472–4.

Small, B. A., B. G. Lee, and K. Bergman. K. 2006. Flexibility of optical packet format in a complete 12 × 12 Data Vortex network. *IEEE Photonics Technology Letters* 18:1693–5.

Small, B. A., A. Shacham, and K. Bergman. 2005. Ultra-low latency optical packet switching node. *IEEE Photonics Technology Letters* 17:1564–6.

Small, B. A., A. Shacham, K, Athikulwongse, C. Hawkins, K, Bergman, and D.S. Wills. 2004. Emulation of realistic network traffic patterns on an eight-node data vortex interconnection network subsystem. *IEEE Journal of Optical Networking* 3(11):802–9.

Special Issue on Nanoscale Integrated Photonics for Optical Networks. 2007. *Journal of Lightwave Technology* 6.

Special Issue on Optical Interconnections. 2004. *Journal of Lightwave Technology* 22(9).

Sterling, T. 2001. Beowulf cluster computing with Linux. Cambridge, MA: MIT Press.

Sterling, T. L., J. Salmon, D.J. Becker, and D. F., Savarese. 1999. How to build a Beowulf: a guide to the implementation and application of PC clusters. Cambridge, MA: MIT Press.

van der Steen, A. J. 2006 May. Overview of recent supercomputers. NCF/Utrecht University. www.phys.uu.nl/%7Esteen/web06/overview.html (accessed May 21, 2007).

Verstoep, K., R. A. F. Bhoedjang, T. Ruhl, H. E. Bal, and R. F. H. Hofman. 2004. Cluster communication proto-9cols for parallel-programming systems. *ACM Transactions on Computer Systems* 22(3):281–325. Also available at www.cs.vu.nl/pub/das/lfc/tocs2004.pdf.

Williams, K. 2006. High speed integrated photonics in interconnection networks. *IEEE LEOS Newsletter* 20(6):1216.

Wonglumsom, D., I. M., White, S. M., Gemelos, K. Shrikhande, and L. G., Kazovsky. 1999. HORNET: A packet-switched WDM network: optical packet transmission and recovery. *IEEE Photonics Technology Letters* 11:1692–4.

Yang, Q., and K. Bergman. 2002. Performances of the data vortex switch architecture under non-uniform and bursty traffic. *IEEE/OSA Journal of Lightwave Technology* 20(8):1242–7.

FURTHER READING

Sterling, T. 2001. Beowulf cluster computing with Linux. Cambridge, MA: MIT Press.

van der Steen, A. J. 2006 May. Overview of recent supercomputers. NCF/Utrecht University. www.phys.uu.nl/%7Esteen/web06/overview.html (accessed May 21, 2007).

Utility Computing on Global Grids

Chee Shin Yeo, Rajkumar Buyya, Marcos Dias de Assunção, Jia Yu, Anthony Sulistio, Srikumar Venugopal, and Martin Placek,
The University of Melbourne, Melbourne, Australia

INTRODUCTION

The growing popularity of the Internet and the availability of powerful computers and high-speed networks as low-cost commodity components are changing the way we do computing. These technological developments have led to the possibility of using networks of computers as a single, unified computing resource, known as "cluster computing" (Buyya 1999; Pfister 1998). Clusters appear in various forms: high-performance clusters, high-availability clusters, dedicated clusters, nondedicated clusters, and so on. In addition, computer scientists in the mid-1990s, inspired by the electrical power grid's pervasiveness and reliability, began exploring the design and development of a new infrastructure, computational power grids, for sharing computational resources such as clusters distributed across different organizations (Foster and Kesselman 2003).

In the business world, cluster architecture–based large-scale computing systems, called "data centers," offering high-performance and high-availability hosting services are widely used. The reliable and low-cost availability of data center services has encouraged many businesses to outsource their computing needs; thus heralding a new utility computing model.

Utility computing is envisioned to be the next generation of information technology (IT) evolution that depicts how computing needs of users can be fulfilled in the future IT industry (Rappa 2004). Its analogy is derived from the real world, where service providers maintain and supply utility services, such as electrical power, gas, and water to consumers. Consumers in turn pay service providers based on their rates of use of these services. Therefore, the underlying design of utility computing is based on a service-provision model, in which users (consumers) pay providers for using computing power only when they need it.

These developments are the realization of the vision of Leonard Kleinrock, one of the chief scientists of the original Advanced Research Projects Agency Network (ARPANET) project, which seeded the Internet, who said in 1969 (Kleinrock 2005): "As of now, computer networks are still in their infancy, but as they grow up and become sophisticated, we will probably see the spread of *'computer utilities'* which, like present electric and telephone utilities, will service individual homes and offices across the country."

Benefits of Utility Computing

The utility computing model offers a number of benefits to both service providers and users. From the provider's perspective, actual hardware and software components are not set up or configured to satisfy a single solution or user, as in the case of traditional computing. Instead, virtualized resources are created and assigned dynamically to various users when needed. Providers can thus reallocate resources easily and quickly to users that have the highest demands. In turn, this efficient use of resources minimizes operational costs for providers, since they are now able to serve a larger community of users without letting unused resources get wasted. Utility computing also enables providers to achieve a better return on investment (ROI), such as total cost of ownership (TCO), since shorter times are now required to derive positive returns and incremental profits can be earned with the gradual expansion of infrastructure that grows with user demands.

For users, the most prominent advantage of utility computing is the reduction of IT-related operational costs and complexities. Users no longer need to invest heavily or encounter difficulties in building and maintaining IT infrastructures. Computing expenditures can now be modeled as a variable cost depending on the usage patterns of users, instead of as a static cost of purchasing technology and employing staff to manage operations. Users neither need to be concerned about possible over- or underutilization of their own self-managed IT infrastructures during peak or nonpeak usage periods nor worry about being confined to any single vendor's proprietary technologies. With utility computing, users can obtain appropriate amounts of computing power from providers dynamically, based on their specific service needs and requirements. This is particularly useful for users who experience rapidly increasing or unpredictable computing needs. Such an outsourcing model thus provides increased flexibility and ease for users to adapt to their changing business needs and environments (Ross and Westerman 2004).

In today's highly competitive and rapidly changing market environment, business organizations aim to be more adaptive in their business and IT strategies, in order to stay ahead of other competitors (Figure 1). An adaptive organization requires enhanced IT processes and better resource utilization in order to deliver faster response, higher productivity, and lower costs (Figure 2). Therefore, there seems to be a potential to use utility computing models for business organizations to be more adaptive and competitive.

Potential of Grids as Utility Computing Environments

The aim of *Grid computing* is to enable coordinated resource sharing and problem solving in dynamic, multi-institutional virtual organizations (Foster, Kesselman, and Tuecke 2001). An infinite number of computing devices, ranging from high-performance systems such as supercomputers and clusters, to specialized systems such as visualization devices, storage systems, and scientific instruments, are logically coupled together in a *Grid* and presented as a single unified resource (Buyya, Cortes, and Jin 2001) to the user. Figure 3 shows that a Grid user can easily use these globally distributed Grid resources by interacting with a Grid resource broker. Basically, a Grid user perceives the Grid as a single huge virtual computer that provides immense computing capabilities, identical to an Internet user who views the World Wide Web as a unified source of content.

A diverse range of applications are currently or soon to be used on Grids, some of which include aircraft engine diagnostics, earthquake engineering, virtual observatory, bioinformatics, drug discovery, digital image analysis, high-energy physics, astrophysics, and multiplayer gaming

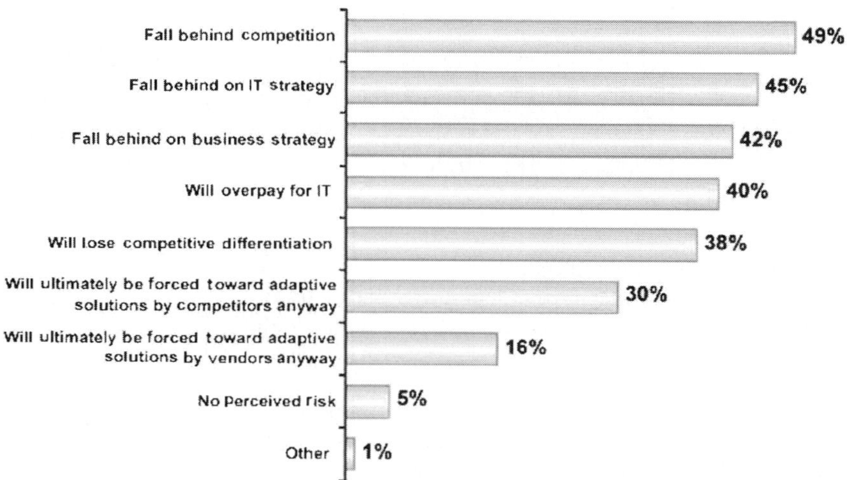

Figure 1: Risks of not becoming an adaptive organization (*Source:* META Group 2004)

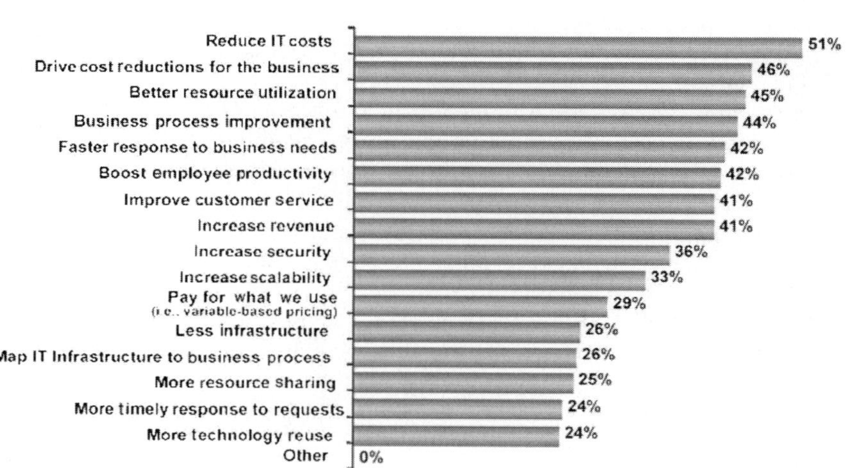

Figure 2: Goals of using adaptive solutions (*Source:* META Group 2004)

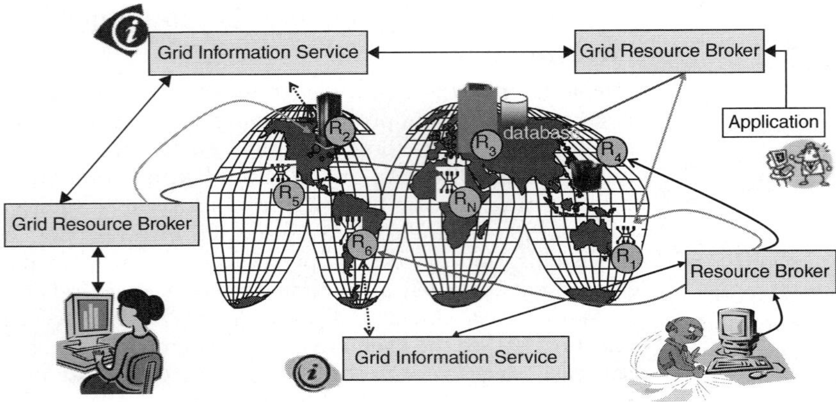

Figure 3: A generic view of a global Grid

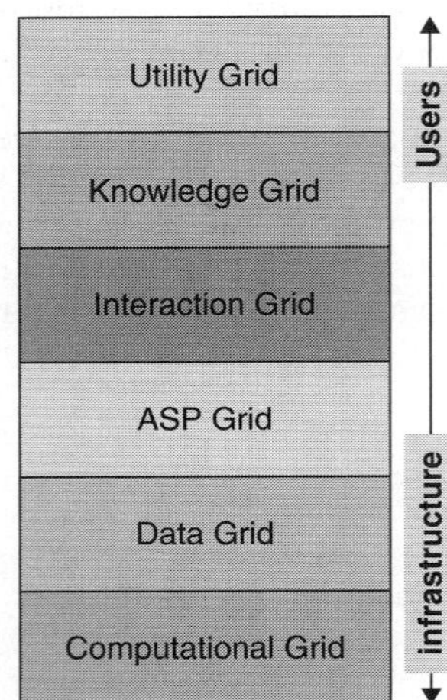

Figure 4: Types of Grids and their focus

(Foster and Kesselman 2003). Grids can be primarily classified into the following types, depending on the nature of their emphasis (Krauter, Buyya, and Maheswaran 2002), as depicted in Figure 4:

- *Computational Grid:* Aggregates the computational power of globally distributed computers, e.g., TeraGrid (Reed 2003) and ChinaGrid (Jin 2004).
- *Data Grid:* Emphasizes on a global-scale management of data to provide data access, integration, and processing through distributed data repositories, e.g., LHC Computing Grid (Lamanna 2004) and GriPhyN (Deelman et al. 2002).
- *Application Service Provisioning (ASP) Grid:* Focuses on providing access to remote applications, modules, and libraries hosted on data centers or Computational Grids, e.g., NetSolve (Agrawal et al. 2003).
- *Interaction Grid:* Focuses on interaction and collaborative visualization between participants, e.g., Access Grid (Childers et al. 2000).
- *Knowledge Grid:* Aims toward knowledge acquisition, processing, management, and providing business analytics services driven by integrated data mining services, e.g., Italian KnowledgeGrid (Cannataro and Talia 2003) and Data Mining Grid (Cannataro, Talia, and Trunfio 2002).
- *Utility Grid:* Focuses on providing all the Grid services, including compute power, data, and services to end users as IT utilities on a subscription basis and the infrastructure necessary for negotiation of required quality of service (QoS), establishment and management of contracts, and allocation of resources to meet competing demands from multiple users and applications, e.g., Gridbus (Buyya and Venugopal 2004) and Utility Data Center (Graupner, Pruyne, and Singhal 2003).

These various types of Grids follow a layered design, with the Computational Grid as the bottommost layer and the Utility Grid as the topmost. A Grid on a higher layer uses the services of Grids that operate at lower layers in the design. For example, a Data Grid uses the services of Computational Grid for data processing and hence builds on it. In addition, lower-layer Grids focus heavily on infrastructural aspects, whereas higher-layer ones focus on users and QoS delivery. Accordingly, Grids are proposed as the emerging cyber infrastructure to power utility computing applications.

Grids offer a number of benefits such as:

- Transparent and instantaneous access to geographically distributed and heterogeneous resources
- Improved productivity with reduced processing time
- Provision of extra resources to solve problems that were previously unsolvable because of the lack of resources
- A more resilient infrastructure with on-demand aggregation of resources at multiple sites to meet unforeseen resource demand
- Seamless computing power achieved by exploiting underused or unused resources that are otherwise wasted
- Maximum utilization of computing facilities to justify IT capital investments
- Coordinated resource sharing and problem solving through virtual organizations (Foster, Kesselman, and Tuecke 2001) that facilitates collaboration across physically dispersed departments and organizations
- Service Level Agreement (SLA)–based resource allocation to meet QoS requirements
- Reduced administration effort with integration of resources as compared with managing multiple standalone systems

Layered Grid Architecture

The components that are necessary to form a Grid are shown in Figure 5. The layered Grid architecture organizes various grid capabilities and components such that high-level services are built using lower-level services. Grid economy (Buyya, Abramson, and Venugopal 2005) is essential for achieving adaptive management and utility-based resource allocation and thus influences various layers of the architecture:

- *Grid fabric software layer:* Provides resource management and execution environment at local Grid resources. These local Grid resources can be computers (e.g., desktops, servers, or clusters) running a variety of operating systems (e.g., UNIX or Windows), storage devices, and special devices such as a radio telescope or heat sensor. As these resources are administered by different local resource managers and monitoring mechanisms, there needs to be Grid middleware that can interact with them.
- *Core Grid middleware layer:* Provides Grid infrastructure and essential services, which consists of information services, storage access, trading, accounting, payment, and security. As a Grid environment is a highly dynamic one in which the location and availability of services are constantly changing, information services provide the means for registering and obtaining information about Grid resources, services, and status. Resource trading based on the computational economy approach is suitable given the complex and decentralized manner of Grids. This approach provides incentives for both resource providers and users to be part of the Grid community, and allows them to develop strategies to maximize their objectives. Security services are also critical to address the confidentiality, integrity, authentication, and accountability issues for accessing resources across diverse systems that are autonomously administered.
- *User-level middleware layer:* Provides programming frameworks and policies for various types of applications, and resource brokers to select appropriate and specific resources for different applications. The Grid programming environment and tools should support common programming languages (e.g. C, C++, FORTRAN, and Java), a variety of programming paradigms (e.g., message passing [Gropp, Lusk, and Skjellum 1999] and distributed shared memory (DSM) [Nitzberg and Lo 1991]), and a suite of numerical and commonly used libraries. Resource management and scheduling should be transparent to the users such that processor time, memory, network, storage, and other resources in Grids can be used and managed effectively and efficiently using middleware such as resource brokers.
- *Grid applications layer*: Enables end users to use Grid services. Grid applications thus need to focus on usability issues so that end users can find them intuitive and easy to use. They should also be able to function on a variety of platforms and operating systems so that users can easily access them. Therefore, an increasing number of Web portals are being built, since they allow users to ubiquitously access any resource from anywhere over any platform at any time.

The design aims and benefits of Grids are analogous to those of utility computing, thus highlighting the potential and suitability of Grids to be used as utility computing environments. The current trend of implementing Grids based on open-standard service-based architectures to improve interoperability is a step toward supporting utility computing (Joseph and Fellenstein 2004). Even though most existing Grid applications are scientific research and collaboration projects, the number of Grid applications in business and industry-related projects is also gradually increasing. It is thus envisioned that the realization of utility computing through Grids will follow a similar course as that of the World Wide Web, which was first initiated as a scientific project but was later widely adopted by businesses and industries.

Challenges of Realizing Utility Computing Models

There are several challenges that need to be addressed in order to realize utility computing. One is that both

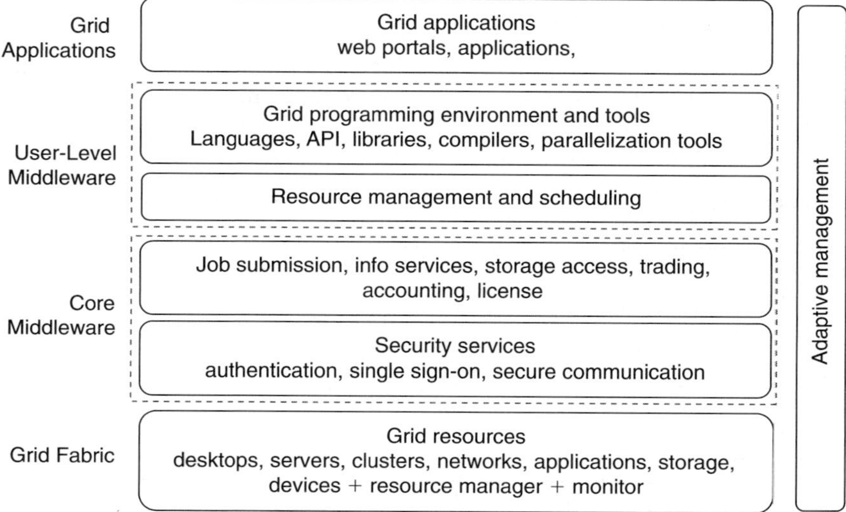

Figure 5: A layered Grid architecture (API = application programming interface)

providers and users need to redraft and reorganize their current IT-related procedures and operations to include utility computing (Ross and Westerman 2004). New IT policies need to be negotiated and agreed upon between providers and users; compared this with the previous situation, in which providers and users owned and controlled their stand-alone policies. Providers must also understand specific service needs and requirements of users in order to design suitable policies for them. Open standards need to be established to facilitate successful adoption of utility computing so that users and producers experience fewer difficulties and complexities in integrating technologies and working together, thus reducing associated costs. Table 1 lists some of the major computing standards organizations and the activities in which they are engaged.

With the changing demand of service needs from users, providers must be able to fulfill the dynamic fluctuation of peak and nonpeak service demands. Service contracts known as Service Level Agreements (SLAs) are used by providers to assure users of their level of service quality. If the expected level of service quality is not met, providers will then be liable for compensation and may incur heavy losses. Therefore, providers seek to maximize customer satisfaction by meeting service needs and minimize the risk of SLA violations (Buco et al. 2004). Improved service-oriented policies and autonomic controls (Kephart and Chess 2003; Murch 2004) are essential for achieving this.

Other than managing the technological aspects of delivering computing services, providers also need to consider the financial aspects of service delivery. Financial risk management for utility computing (Kenyon and Cheliotis 2005) is comprised of two factors: delivery risk and pricing risk. Delivery-risk factors examine the risks concerned with each possible scenario in which a service can be delivered. Pricing-risk factors study the risks involved with pricing the service with respect to the availability of resources. Given shorter contract durations, lower switching costs, and uncertain customer demands in utility computing environments, it is important to have dynamic and flexible pricing schemes to potentially maximize profits and minimize losses for providers (Paleologo 2004).

There are also potential nontechnical obstacles to the successful adoption of utility computing, such as cultural and people-related issues that will require organizations to change their current stance and perceptions (Platform Computing 2003). The most worrying issues being perceived are loss of control or access to resources, risks associated with enterprise-wide deployment, loss or reduction of budget dollars, and reduced priority of projects. Thus, overcoming these nontechnical obstacles is

Table 1: Some Major Standards Organizations

Organization	Web Site	Standard Activities
Open Grid Forum (OGF)	www.ogf.org	Grid computing, distributed computing, and peer-to-peer networking
World Wide Web Consortium (W3C)	www.w3c.org	World Wide Web (WWW), extensible markup language (XML), Web services, semantic Web, mobile Web, and voice browser
Organization for the Advancement of Structured Information Standards (OASIS)	www.oasis-open.org	Electronic commerce, systems management and Web services extensions, Business Process Execution Language for Web Services (BPEL4WS), and portals
Web Services Interoperability Organization (WS-I)	www.ws-i.org	Interoperable solutions, profiles, best practices, and verification tools
Distributed Management Task Force (DMTF)	www.dmtf.org	Systems management
Internet Engineering Task Force (IETF)	www.ietf.org	Network standards
European Computer Manufacturers Organization (ECMA)	www.ecma-international.org	Language standards (C++, C#)
International Organization for Standardization (ISO)	www.iso.org	Language standards (C++, C#)
Object Management Group (OMG)	www.omg.org	Model-driven architecture (MDA), unified modeling language (UML), common object resource broker architecture (CORBA), and real-time system modeling
Java Community Process (JCP)	www.jcp.org	Java standards

Source: Joseph, Ernest, and Fellenstein 2004

extremely critical and requires the dissemination of correct information to all levels of management with-in organizations to prevent the formation of misperceptions.

UTILITY GRIDS

This chapter focuses on the use of Grid technologies to achieve utility computing. An overview of how Grids can support utility computing is first presented through the architecture of Utility Grids. Then, utility-based resource allocation is described in detail at each level of the architecture. Finally, some industrial solutions for utility computing are discussed.

A reference service-oriented architecture for Utility Grids is shown in Figure 6. The key players in a Utility Grid are the Grid user, Grid resource broker, Grid middleware services, and Grid service providers (GSPs).

Grid users want to make use of Utility Grids to complete their applications. Refactoring existing applications is thus essential to ensure that these applications are Grid-enabled to run on Utility Grids (Kra 2004). The Grid user also needs to express the service requirements to be fulfilled by GSPs. Varying QoS parameters, such as deadline for the application to be completed and budget to be paid upon completion, are defined by different Grid users, thus resulting in dynamic fluctuation of peak and nonpeak service demands. The Grid resource broker then discovers appropriate Grid middleware services based on these service demand patterns and QoS requirements, and dynamically schedules applications on them at runtime, depending on their availability, capability, and costs. A GSP needs tools and mechanisms that support pricing specifications and schemes so they can attract users and improve resource utilization. They also require protocols that support service publication and negotiation, accounting, and payment.

The Grid resource broker comprises the following components:

- *Job control agent:* Ensures persistency of jobs by coordinating with schedule advisor for schedule generation, handling actual creation of jobs, maintaining job status, and interacting with users, schedule advisor, and deployment agent.
- *Grid explorer:* Interacts with Grid information service to discover and identify resources and their current status.
- *Schedule advisor:* Discovers Grid resources using the Grid explorer, and selects suitable Grid resources and assigns jobs to them (schedule generation) to meet users' requirements.
- *Trade manager:* Accesses market directory services for service negotiation and trading with GSPs based on resource selection algorithm of schedule advisor.
- *Deployment agent:* Activates task execution on the selected resource according to schedule advisor's instruction and periodically updates the status of task execution to job control agent.

Traditional core Grid middleware focuses on providing infrastructure services for secure and uniform access to distributed resources. Supported features include security, single sign-on, remote process management, storage access, data management, and information services. An example of such middleware is the Globus Toolkit (Foster and Kesselman 1997) which is a widely adopted Grid technology in the Grid community. Utility Grids require additional service-driven Grid middleware infrastructure that includes:

- *Grid market directory:* Allows GSPs to publish their services so as to inform and attract users.

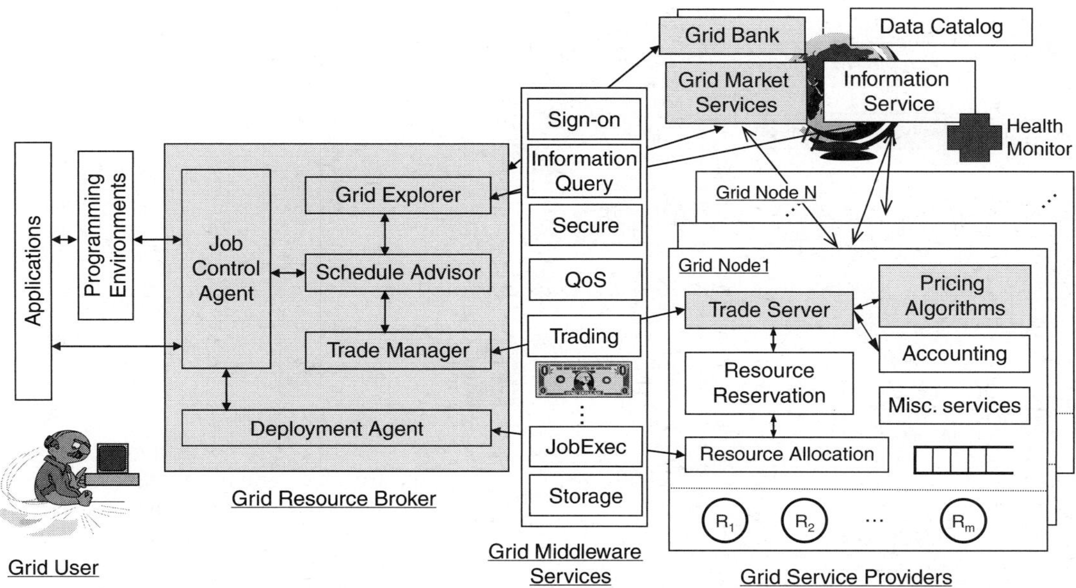

Figure 6: A reference service-oriented architecture for Utility Grids (R = resource)

- *Trade server:* Negotiates with Grid resource broker based on pricing algorithms set by the GSP and sells access to resources by recording resource usage details and billing the users based on the agreed pricing policy.
- *Pricing algorithms:* Specifies prices to be charged to users based on the GSP's objectives, such as maximizing profit or resource utilization at varying times and for different users.
- *Accounting and charging:* Records resource usage and bills the users based on the agreed terms negotiated between Grid resource broker and trade server.

Figure 7 shows how services are assembled on demand in a Utility Grid. The application code is the legacy application to be run on the Utility Grid. Users first compose their application as a distributed application such as a parameter sweep using visual application composer tools (step 1). The parameter-sweep model creates multiple independent jobs, each with a different parameter. This model is well suited for Grid computing environments wherein challenges such as load volatility, high network latencies, and high probability of individual node failures make it difficult to adopt a programming approach that favors tightly coupled systems. Accordingly, a parameter-sweep application has been termed as a "killer application" for the Grid (Abramson, Giddy, and Kotler 2000).

Visual tools allow rapid composition of applications for Grids by hiding the associated complexity from the user. The user's analysis and QoS requirements are submitted to the Grid resource broker (step 2). The Grid resource broker first discovers suitable Grid services based on user-defined characteristics, including price, through the Grid information service and the Grid market directory (steps 3 and 4). The broker then identifies the list of data sources or replicas through a data catalog and selects the optimal ones (step 5). The broker also identifies the list of GSPs that provide the required application services using the application service provider (ASP) catalog (step 6). The broker checks that the user has the necessary credit or authorized share to use the requested Grid services (step 7). The broker scheduler assigns and deploys jobs to Grid services that meet user QoS requirements (step 8). The broker agent on the Grid resource at the GSP then executes the job and returns the results (step 9). The broker consolidates the results before passing them back to the user (step 10). The metering system charges the user by passing the resource-usage information to the accounting service (step 11). The accounting service reports remaining resource share allocation and credit available to the user (step 12).

Layered Grid Architecture Realization

To enable Utility Grids, the Gridbus project (Buyya and Venugopal 2004) has offered open-source Grid middleware for various layers (as highlighted in Figure 8) that include:

- *Grid fabric software layer:* Libra, a utility-driven cluster scheduler that considers and enforces SLAs for jobs submitted into the cluster.
- *Core Grid middleware layer:* Alchemi, which is a .NET-based desktop Grid framework; Grid Market Directory, which is a directory publishing available Grid services; Grid Bank, which provides accounting, authentication, and payment facilities; and GridSim, which is an event-driven simulator that models Grid environments.
- *User-level middleware layer:* Gridbus broker, which selects suitable Grid services and schedules applications to run on them; Grid workflow engine, which provides workflow execution and monitoring on Grids; and Visual Parametric Modeler, which provides a graphical environment to parameterize applications.
- *Grid application layer:* Web portals such as Gridscape, which provides interactive and dynamic Web-based Grid monitoring portals, and G-Monitor, which manages execution of applications on Grids using brokers.

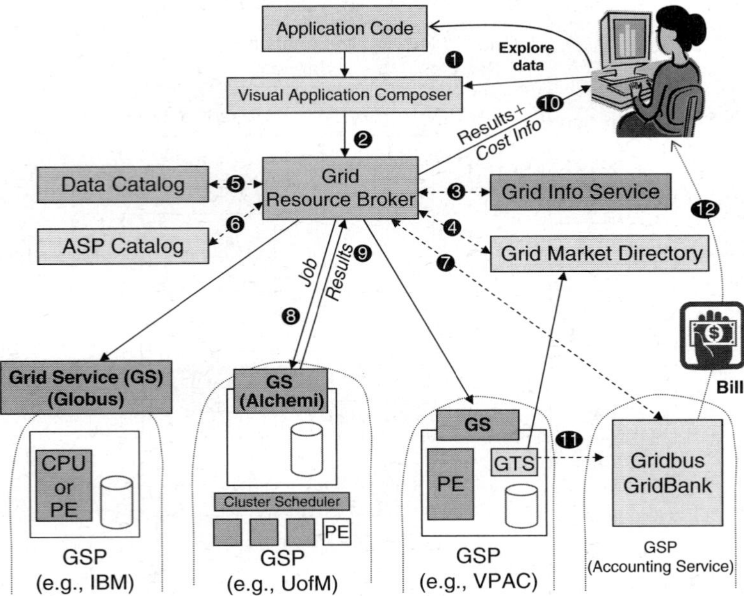

Figure 7: On-demand assembly of services in a Utility Grid (ASP = application service provider; GSP = Grid service provider; GTS = Grid trading service; PE = processing element; UofM = University of Melbourne; VPAC = Victorian partnership for advanced computing)

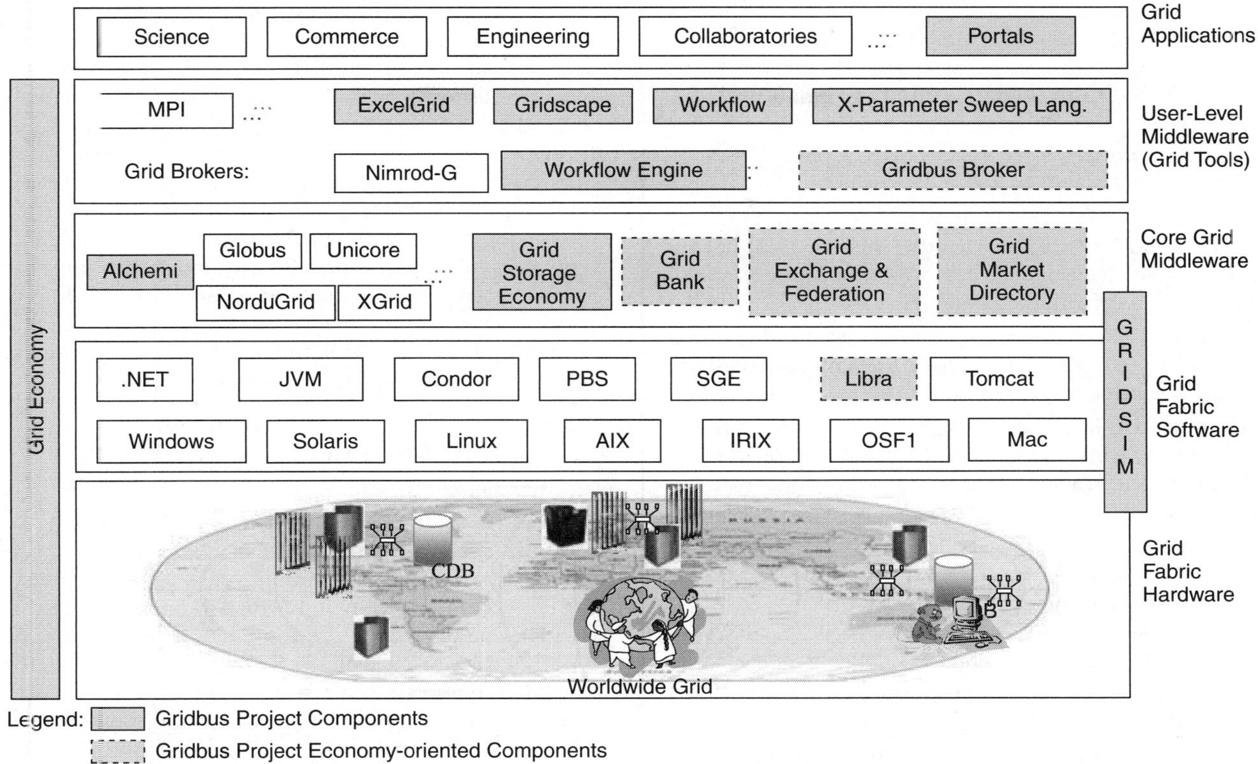

Figure 8: Realizing Utility Grids: Gridbus and complementary technologies (JVM = Java Virtual Machine; PBS = Portable Batch System; SGE = Sun Grid Engine)

UTILITY-BASED RESOURCE ALLOCATION AT VARIOUS LEVELS

Utility-based resource allocation is essential at various levels of the Utility Grid in order to realize the utility computing model. This section examines the challenges involved in clusters, distributed storage, Computational Grid brokering, Data Grids, workflow scheduling, advanced reservation, and cooperative virtual organizations.

Clusters

A *cluster* is a type of parallel or distributed computer system, which consists of a collection of interconnected stand-alone computers working together as a single integrated computing resource (Buyya 1999; Pfister 1998). Clustering these stand-alone computers together has resulted in high-performance, high-availability, and high-throughput processing on a network of computers at a much lower cost than traditional supercomputing systems thus resulting in *cluster computing* being a more viable choice as a supercomputing solution. As clusters are extensively used in data centers, which promise to provide managed computing, storage, and application services at low cost, the costs of ownership and maintenance need to be reduced. But, clusters are heavily focused on increasing peak performance using tens of thousands of power-hungry components, which is leading to intolerable operating cost and failure rates (Ge, Feng, and Cameron 2005). Thus, power-aware clusters have been built to reduce power consumption by leveraging DVS (dynamic voltage scaling) techniques and using distributed performance-directed DVS scheduling strategies. Such clusters are able to gain similar performance, yet reduce the amount of power consumption.

Currently, service-oriented Grid technologies are used to enable utility computing environments in which the majority of Grid resources are clusters. Grid schedulers such as brokers and workflow engines can then discover suitable Grid resources and submit jobs to them on behalf of the users. If the chosen Grid resource is a cluster, these Grid schedulers then interact with the cluster resource management system (RMS) to monitor the completion of submitted jobs. The cluster RMS is a middleware that provides a uniform interface to manage resources, queue jobs, schedule jobs, and execute jobs on multiple compute nodes within the cluster. With a utility model, users can specify different levels of service needed to complete their jobs. Thus, providers and users have to negotiate and agree on SLAs that serve as contracts outlining the expected level of service performance. Providers can then be liable to compensate users for any service underperformance. So, the cluster RMS must be able to enable utility-driven cluster computing by supporting SLA-based resource allocation that can meet competing user demands and enforce their service needs.

Existing cluster RMSs need to be enhanced or extended to adopt utility-driven resource allocation rather than the current system-centric resource allocation that maximizes resource throughput and utilization of the cluster. System-centric approaches assume that all job requests are equally important and thus neglect the actual levels of service required by different users. The cluster RMS should have the following components:

- *Request examiner:* Interprets the QoS parameters defined in the SLA.
- *Admission control:* Determines whether a new job request should be accepted or not. This ensures that the cluster is not overloaded with too many requests such that service performance deteriorates.
- *SLA based scheduler:* New service-oriented policies need to be incorporated to allocate resources efficiently based on service requirements.
- *Job monitor:* New measurement metrics need to be used to keep track of whether the execution progress of jobs meets the service criteria.
- *Accounting:* Maintains the actual usage of resources so that usage charges can be computed. Usage information can also be used to make better resource-allocation decisions.
- *Pricing:* Formulate charges for meeting service requests. For example, requests can be charged based on submission time (peak/off-peak), pricing rates (fixed/variant), or availability of resources (supply/demand).
- *Job control:* Enforces resource assignment for executing requests to fulfill specified service needs.

The key design factors and issues for a utility-driven cluster RMS can be addressed from five perspectives (Yeo and Buyya 2006):

- *Market model:* Considers market concepts present in real-world human economies to be applied for service-oriented resource allocation in clusters to deliver utility.
- *Resource model:* Addresses architectural framework and operating environments of clusters that need to be conformed.
- *Job model:* Examines attributes of jobs to ensure that various job types with distinct requirements can be fulfilled successfully.
- *Resource allocation model:* Analyzes factors that can influence the resource-assignment outcome.
- *Evaluation model:* Assesses the effectiveness and efficiency of the cluster RMS in satisfying the utility model.

There is therefore growing research interest in formulating effective service-oriented resource allocation policies to satisfy the utility model. Computation-at-risk (CaR) (Kleban and Clearwater 2004) determines the risk of completing jobs later than expected based on either the makespan (response time) or the expansion factor (slowdown) of all jobs in the cluster. Cluster-On-Demand (Irwin, Grit, and Chase 2004) reveals the significance of balancing the reward against the risk of accepting and executing jobs, particularly in the case of unbounded penalty. A QoS-based scheme for parallel job scheduling (QoPS) (Islam et al. 2004) incorporates an admission control to guarantee the deadline of every accepted job by accepting a new job only if its deadline can be guaranteed without violating the deadlines of already accepted jobs. LibraSLA (Yeo and Buyya 2005) accepts jobs with hard deadlines only if they can be met, and accepts jobs with soft deadlines depending on their penalties incurred for delays. Another work (Popovici and Wilkes 2005) addresses the difficulties encountered by service providers when they rent resources from resource providers to run jobs accepted from clients. These include difficulties such as which jobs to accept, when to run them, and which resources to rent to run them. It analyzes the likely impact on these difficulties in several scenarios, including changing workload, user impatience, resource availability, resource pricing, and resource uncertainty.

Distributed Storage

Storage plays a fundamental role in computing as it is present in many key components, from registers and random access memory (RAM) to hard disk drives and optical disk drives. Combining storage with networking has created a platform for distributed storage systems (DSSs). The wide proliferation of the Internet has created a global network—a platform with innovative possibilities such as offering access to storage as a utility. DSSs functioning in a global environment support sharing of storage across geographic, institutional, and administrative boundaries. The network speed (bandwidth and latency) and usage load impact the speed of remote storage access; however, they can be overcome through smart access management techniques such as demand prediction, preloading, and caching. The key benefits of such DSS are that it: (1) enables aggregation of storage resources from different sources to create mass storage systems at lower cost, (2) enhances reliability of storage through replication, (3) supports disaster management and recovery through replication of content across multiple sites, (4) provides the ability to offer access to storage as utility services, which in turn reduces the cost of ownership and management of storage systems for end users, and (5) allows organizations to barter or harness each other's storage systems for transparent sharing and preservation of digital assets such as e-books, e-music, e-journals, and scientific experimental data.

Some prominent examples of DSS are Parallel Virtual File System (PVFS) (Ligon and Ross 2001), General Parallel File System (GPFS) (Barkes et al. 1998), and Google File System (GFS) (Ghemawat, Gobioff, and Leung 2003). A key challenge in DSS is ensuring that storage services are shared fairly among users and that providers are offered incentives for making storage services available. One way to achieve this is applying economic principles. Examples of DSSs that apply economic principles to manage various aspects of operational behavior include: Mungi, which manages storage quota; Mojo Nation, which instills cooperative behavior; Stanford Archival Repository (SAR), which encourages the sharing of storage services and exchanges; and OceanStore, which provides utility storage. SAR (Cooper and Garcia-Molina 2002) is the Stanford Archival Repository, a bartering storage system for preserving information. Institutions that have common requirements and storage infrastructure can use the framework to barter with each other for storage services. For example, libraries may use this framework to replicate their archives among one another for the purpose of preservation. OceanStore (Kubiatowicz et al. 2000) is a globally scalable storage utility, providing paying users with a durable, highly available storage service by utilizing nontrusted infrastructure. Mungi (Heiser et al. 1998) is a single-address-space operating system (SASOS), which uses economic principles to manage storage quota. Mojo Nation (Wilcox-O'Hearn 2002) uses digital currency, *Mojo,* to encourage users to share resources on its network. Users that contribute services are rewarded with *Mojo,* which can then be traded for services. Storage Exchange (Placek and Buyya 2006) applies a double auction (DA) market model, allowing storage services to be traded in a global environment.

Treating storage as a tradable commodity provides incentives for users to participate in the federating and sharing of their distributed storage services. However, there are still some challenges that need to be overcome before storage utility can be fully realized:

- *Federate:* A plethora of heterogeneous storage systems exist; creating a homogenous interface is a key step in federating storage.
- *Share:* Ensuring that distributed storage resource is shared fairly among users and that no single user can deny access to others, accidentally or otherwise.
- *Security:* Operating on nontrusted infrastructure requires the use of cryptographic mechanisms in order to enforce authentication and prevent malicious behavior.
- *Reliability:* Storage medium and network failures are common in a global storage infrastructure, and therefore mechanisms of remote replicas and erasure codes need to be used to ensure that persistent reliable access to stored data is achieved.

Although the challenges are many, the weight of incentives and future from realizing a globally distributed storage utility ensure the continuing research and development in this area:

- *Monetary gain:* Institutions providing storage services (providers) are able to better use existing storage infrastructure in exchange for monetary gain. Institutions consuming these storage services (consumers) have the ability to negotiate for storage services as they require them, without needing to incur the costs associated with purchasing and maintaining storage hardware.
- *Common objectives:* There may be institutions that wish to exchange storage services between themselves because of a mutual goal such as preservation of information (Cooper and Garcia-Molina 2002).
- *Spikes in storage requirements:* Research institutions may require temporary access to mass storage (Vazhkudai et al. 2005), such as needing access to additional storage to temporarily store data generated from experiments that are carried out infrequently. In exchange, institutions may provide access to their storage services for use by others when they are not being used.
- *Donate:* Institutions may wish to donate storage services, particularly if these services are going to a noble cause.
- *Autonomic storage:* Development of a framework to support future autonomic storage systems will allow agents to broker storage on an as-needed basis.

Computational Grid Brokering

A Computational Grid broker acts as an agent for the user in Computational Grids by performing various tasks such as resource discovery, job scheduling, and job monitoring. To determine which resources to select, the broker needs to take into account various attributes from both the user perspective, such as resource requirements of the application, and the resource perspective, such as resource architecture and configuration, resource status (available memory, disk storage, and processing power), resource availability, network bandwidth, resource workload, and historical performance.

However, the Computational Grid broker needs to consider additional service-driven attributes such as QoS requirements specified by users in order to support the utility model. For example, users may specify a deadline for the completion of their application. The user may also state the maximum price to be paid for the completion. With the user's request of deadline and price for an application, the broker tries to locate the most suitable resources. Thus, during resource discovery, the broker also needs to know the costs of resources that can be obtained from a Grid market directory service and are set by GSPs. The broker must be able to negotiate with GSPs to establish an agreed price for the user, before selecting the most suitable resources with the best price based on the provided QoS. For instance, a more relaxed deadline should be able to obtain cheaper access to resources and vice versa. So, different users often have varying prices based on their specific needs. To locate the most suitable resources, we need new scheduling algorithms that take into consideration the application processing requirements, Grid resource dynamics, users' QoS requirements, such as the deadline and budget, and their optimization preferences.

The Nimrod-G resource broker (Abramson, Buyya, and Giddy 2002) and Gridbus Grid service broker (Venugopal, Buyya, and Winton 2006) are examples of service-oriented Computational Grid brokers for parameter-sweep applications. Both brokers schedule jobs based on economic principles (through the budget that the user is willing to pay) and a user-defined QoS requirement (the deadline within which the user requires the application to be completed). Nimrod-G implements four adaptive algorithms for scheduling compute-intensive parameter sweep applications:

- *Cost optimization:* Execution time is within the specified deadline and execution cost is the cheapest.
- *Time optimization:* Execution time is the shortest and execution cost is within the specified budget.
- *Cost-time optimization:* Similar to cost optimization, but if there are multiple resources with the same cost,

it applies time optimization so that execution time is the shortest with the same cost.

- *Conservative time optimization:* Similar to cost-time optimization, but ensures that each unprocessed job in the parameter-sweep application has a minimum budget per job.

The Gridbus broker extends cost and time optimization to schedule distributed data-intensive applications that require access to and processing of large datasets stored in distributed repositories.

Data Grids

Data comprise one of the most important entities within any IT infrastructure. Therefore, any utility computing platform must be able to provide secure, reliable, and efficient management of enterprise data and must be able to abstract the mechanisms involved. One of the key factors in the adoption of Grids as a utility computing platform is the creation of an infrastructure for storing, processing, cataloging, and sharing the ever-expanding volumes of data that are being produced by large enterprises such as scientific and commercial collaborations. This infrastructure, commonly known as "Data Grids," provides services that allow users to discover, transfer, and maintain large repositories of data. At the very minimum, a Data Grid provides a high-performance and reliable data-transfer mechanism and a data-replica-management infrastructure. Data-manipulation operations in a Data Grid are mediated through a security layer that, in addition to the facilities provided by the general Grid security services, also provides specific operations such as managing access permissions and encrypted data transfers.

In recent years, the Grid community has adopted the Open Grid Service Architecture (OGSA) (Foster et al. 2002) which leverages Web service technologies such as XML and SOAP to create Grid services that follow standard platform-independent mechanisms for representation, invocation, and data exchange. A subgroup of OGSA deals with providing basic interfaces, called "data services," that describe data and the mechanisms to access it. Data services virtualize the same data by providing multiple views that are differentiated by attributes and operations. They also enable different data sources, such as legacy databases, data repositories, and even spreadsheets to be treated in the same manner via standard mechanisms (Antonioletti et al. 2004).

Virtualization of data creates many possibilities for its consumption, enabled by the coupling of Grid services to enable applications such as data-intensive workflows. Already, projects such as Virtual Data Grid (VDG) (Foster et al. 2003) represent data not in terms of physical storage but as results of computational procedures. This has at least two possibilities for users: the ability to determine the provenance of data (i.e. determine how it was produced and if it is valid) and the ability to reuse the data products in future experiments in which the same procedures with the same inputs are involved. Pegasus (Deelman et al. 2003) is a workflow management system from the GriPhyN project that uses the VDG to reduce workflows by substituting previously generated data whenever possible. A similar procedure is followed by Storage Resource Broker (SRB) (Moore, Rajasekar, and Wan 2005), which uses stored procedures in its SRB Matrix to reduce dataflow graphs. Therefore, data virtualization isolates the users from the physical Data Grid environment.

Data virtualization is an important technology for creating an information-rich utility computing environment that is able to provide its users with the following abilities:

- Seamlessly discover and use available data services
- Plan ahead for future requirements and take preemptive action
- Create dynamic applications by combining services

In such an environment, QoS parameters associated with a data service play an important role in data service discovery. Such parameters include the amount of data, permissions associated with access and modification, available bandwidth to storage locations, and relevance. Relevance of data can be determined from the provenance data that describes the procedures used for producing the data. Planning, scheduling, and reserving resources in advance is conducted by resource brokers that take QoS parameters into account while selecting data sources and storage locations.

Workflow Scheduling

With the advent of Grid and application technologies, scientists and engineers are building more and more complex applications to manage and process large data sets, and execute scientific experiments on distributed resources. Such application scenarios require means for composing and executing complex workflows. Workflows are concerned with the automation of procedures whereby files and data are passed between participants according to a defined set of rules to achieve an overall goal (Hollinsworth 1995). A workflow management system defines, manages, and executes workflows automatically on computing resources. Imposing the workflow paradigm for application composition on Grids offers several advantages (Spooner et al. 2005), such as:

- Ability to build dynamic applications which orchestrate distributed resources
- Utilization of resources that are located in a particular domain to increase throughput or reduce execution costs
- Execution spanning multiple administrative domains to obtain specific processing capabilities
- Integration of multiple teams involved in managing different parts of the experiment workflow, thus promoting interorganizational collaborations

QoS support in workflow management is required by many workflow applications. For example, a workflow application for planning maxillofacial surgery (Berti et al. 2003) needs results to be delivered before a certain time. However, QoS requirements cannot be guaranteed in a conventional Grid where resources provide only best effort services. Therefore, there is a need to have Utility

Grids that allow users to negotiate with service providers on a certain service agreement with the requested QoS.

In general, scheduling workflows on Utility Grids is guided by users' QoS expectations. Workflow management systems are required to allow the user to specify their requirements, along with the descriptions of tasks and their dependencies using the workflow specification. In general, QoS constraints express the preferences of users and are essential for efficient resource allocation. QoS constraints can be classified into five dimensions (Yu and Buyya 2005): time, cost, fidelity, reliability, and security. *Time* is a basic measure of performance. For workflow systems, it refers to the total time required to execute a workflow. *Cost* represents the cost associated with the execution of workflows, including the cost of managing workflow systems and usage charge of Grid resources for processing workflow tasks. *Fidelity* refers to the measurement related to the quality of the output of workflow execution. *Reliability* is related to the number of failures for execution of workflows. *Security* refers to confidentiality of the execution of workflow tasks and trustworthiness of resources.

Several new issues arise from scheduling QoS-constrained workflows on Utility Grids:

- In general, users would like to specify a QoS constraint for the entire workflow. It is required that the scheduler determine a QoS constraint for each task in the workflow, such that the global QoS is satisfied.
- The scheduler is required to be adaptive to evaluate a proposed SLA and negotiate with a service provider for one task with respect to its current accepted set of SLAs and expected return of unscheduled tasks.
- The description language and monitoring mechanism for QoS-based workflows will be more complex as compared with traditional workflow scheduling.

To date, several efforts have been made toward QoS-aware workflow management. Web Services Agreement (WS-Agreement) (Andrieux et al. 2004) allows a resource provider and a consumer to create an agreement on the expected service qualities between them. Grid Quality of Service Management (G-QoSm) (Al-Ali et al. 2004) provides Grid services in which workflow schedulers can negotiate and reserve services based on certain quality levels. The Vienna Grid Environment (VGE) (Benkner et al. 2004) develops a dynamic negotiation model that facilitates workflow schedulers to negotiate various QoS constraints with multiple service providers. It also extends the Business Process Execution Language (BPEL) (Brandic et al. 2005) to support QoS constraint expression. A QoS-based heuristic for scheduling workflow applications can be found in Menascé and Casalicchio (2004). The heuristic attempts to assign the task into least expensive computing resources based on assigned time constraint for the local task. A cost-based scheduling algorithm (Yu, Buyya, and Tham 2005) minimizes the cost, while meeting the deadline of the workflow by distributing the deadline for the entire workflow into sub-deadlines for each task. More recently, budget-constrained workflow scheduling has been developed by Yu and Buyya (2006). It uses genetic algorithms to optimize workflow execution time while meeting the user's budget.

However, supporting QoS in the scheduling of workflow applications is still at a very preliminary stage. There is a need for many advanced capabilities in workflow systems and resource allocation such as support of cyclic and conditional checking of workflow structure, adaptive scheduling based on dynamic negotiation models, and advanced SLA monitoring and renegotiation.

Advanced Reservation

In existing Grid systems, incoming jobs to resources are scheduled via either space-shared or time-shared mode. The space-shared mode runs jobs based on their submission times; similar to first-come, first-served (FCFS), whereas the time-shared mode allows multiple executions of jobs; hence, it behaves like a round-robin approach. With a Utility Grid, jobs can be prioritized based on users' QoSs by a resource scheduler. However, a Utility Grid is not necessarily able to handle high-priority jobs or guarantee reliable service. Therefore, *advance reservation* needs to be introduced in a Utility Grid system to secure resources prior to their execution.

Advanced reservation (AR) is a process of requesting resources for use at a specific time in the future (Smith, Foster, and Taylor 2000). Common resources that can be reserved or requested are processors, memory, disk space, and network bandwidth, or a combination of any of these. The main advantage of AR is that it guarantees the availability of resources to users and applications at specific times in the future. Hence, from the user's perspective:

- Jobs can be executed straight away at a specified time rather than being held up in a queue by other jobs. This is a highly desirable approach for executing workflow applications that have one or more dependencies.
- Dropouts in a network transfer, which is not an option in multimedia streaming applications such as videoconferencing, can be avoided.

Combining utility computing with AR allows resource providers to specify criteria and requirements of usage. In addition, resource providers can match and satisfy a user's QoS. Utility computing applies to different stages of AR (Sulistio and Buyya 2004) as follows:

- *Requesting a new reservation slot:* A user asks a resource about the availability of a reservation slot by giving details such as start time, duration, and number of processors. A resource can then either accept the request or reject it if the slot is already booked. Both the user and resource can continue negotiating until they reach an agreement—i.e. to accept or not to accept.
- *Modifying an existing reservation slot:* A user or a resource can request to modify an existing reservation slot. Modification is used as a way to shorten or extend the duration of a reservation. If a user's jobs are running longer than expected, extending the duration is needed to prevent the jobs from being preempted by a resource. A user can request to shorten a reservation if jobs have finished, in order to save some costs.

- *Canceling an existing reservation slot:* A user or a resource can request to cancel an existing reservation slot. However, this can be done only when both parties have agreed beforehand. Canceling a reservation before it starts can easily be agreed to by a resource. However, some resource providers may not allow the cancellation of a reservation once it has started.

Cooperative Virtual Organizations

The concept of the virtual organization (VO) is crucial to the Grid. In current Grid collaborations, physical organizations engage in projects and alliances such as joint ventures that require shared access to compute and data resources provided by their members. The model adopted for such endeavors is that of a VO, in which resource providers and users are organized in a structure that may comprise several physical organizations. VOs may vary in several ways, such as scope, dynamism, and purpose, even though they pose similar challenges regarding their formation, operation, and dissolution (Patel et al. 2005).

Over the years, applications and compute and data resources have been virtualized to enable the utility model for business processes. With regard to the creation of a VO, it may be assumed that a VO is formed because of the need from a business process or some project. Despite the virtualization provided by Grid technologies, organizations may have difficulties in expressing their needs and requirements to their potential partners. Additional challenges are the selection of partners and the establishment of trust at a level that allows the automated creation of VOs (Dimitrakos, Golby, and Kearney 2004). However, to enable the utility model in VOs, issues regarding the responsive or even the automated creation of VOs need to be tackled.

The operational phase of a VO is also a complex task. Resource sharing in VOs is conditional and rule-driven. Also, the relationship in some VOs is peer-to-peer. To complicate matters further, the collection of participating entities is dynamic (Joseph, Ernest, and Fellenstein 2004). This scenario complicates tasks such as the negotiation of SLAs among the participants of the VO or between the participants and the VO itself. Furthermore, the reconciliation, management, and enforcement of resource usage control policies in the VO poses several challenges as presented in Dumitrescu, Wilde, and Foster (2005). For example, a simple model for providing resources as utilities in VOs requires the presence of a trusted VO manager. Resource providers are committed to deliver services to the VO according to contracts established with the VO manager. The manager is therefore responsible for assigning quotas of these resources to VO groups and users based on some VO policy. Users are allowed to use services according to these quotas and the VO policy. However, in this context, the delivery of compute and data resources in a utility-model to VO users and groups makes tasks such as enforcement of policies in a VO level and accounting difficult.

A simple model in a VO that follows a peer-to-peer sharing approach is of best effort, in which "you give what you can and get what others can offer." A more elaborate model, in which a VO manager does not exist, allows the delivery of services following a "you get what you give" approach (Wasson and Humphrey 2003). Other approaches require multilateral agreements among the members of the VO and give rise to challenges in the enforcement of resource usage policies, as described before.

Current works have not focused on aspects related to the dissolution of VOs, since this problem involves issues that are more legal and social rather than technical. Hence, the delivery of compute resources as a utility in VOs requires the investigation and solving of these problems related to various aspects of a VO. Automation and responsiveness are also required in every stage of the life cycle of a VO.

INDUSTRIAL SOLUTIONS FOR UTILITY COMPUTING

Various commercial vendors have launched industrial solutions to support utility computing. Competing marketing terms are used by different vendors even though they share the same vision of providing utility computing. This section discusses four major industrial solutions, as listed in Table 2: HP's Adaptive Enterprise, IBM's E-Business On Demand, Oracle's On Demand, and Sun Microsystems's Sun Grid. All four solutions use Grids as the core enabling technology.

HP Adaptive Enterprise

The vision of HP's Adaptive Enterprise (HP 2005) is to synchronize the business and IT processes in an enterprise in order to allow it to benefit from changes in market demands. IT processes are coordinated through the Adaptive Enterprise architecture, which comprises two dimensions: IT management and IT service capabilities. The IT management dimension involves:

- *IT business management:* Long-term IT strategies such as asset management, customer and supplier relationship management, and project portfolio management need to be developed.
- *Service delivery management:* Various operational aspects of service delivery such as availability, cost, capacity, performance, security, and quality need to be considered.
- *Service delivery:* IT services need to be provided to users by highly automated systems.

The IT service capabilities dimension that is addressed under both service delivery management and service delivery in the IT management dimension consists of:

- *Business services:* Represent top-level services related to business processes such as the composition of workflows.
- *Information services:* Consolidate and manipulate information for business services that are independent from application services.
- *Application services:* Automate and handle the processing of applications.

Table 2: Some Major Industrial Solutions for Utility Computing

Vendor	Solution and Web Site	Brief Description	Core Enabling Technology and Web Site
HP	Adaptive Enterprise www.hp.com/go/adaptive	Simplifies, standardizes, modularizes, and integrates business processes and applications with IT infrastructures to adapt effectively in a changing business environment.	Grids www.hp.com/go/grid
IBM	E-Business On Demand www.ibm.com/ondemand	Performs on-demand business processes that include research and development, engineering and product design, business analytics, and enterprise optimization.	Grids www.ibm.com/grid
Oracle	On Demand www.oracle.com/ondemand	Standardizes and consolidates servers and storage resources to automate IT process management.	Grids www.oracle.com/grid
Sun Microsystems	Sun Grid www.sun.com/service/sungrid	Offers computing power pay-as-you-go service utility by charging users $1 for every hour of processing.	Grids www.sun.com/software/grid

- *Infrastructure services:* Create a common infrastructure platform to host the application, information, and business services.

The Adaptive Enterprise architecture also defines four design principles that are to be realized for an enterprise to become more adaptive:

- *Simplification:* Complex IT environments can be streamlined through application integration, process automation, and resource virtualization to facilitate easier management and faster response.
- *Standardization:* Standardized architectures and processes enable easier incorporation of new technologies, improves collaboration, and saves cost.
- *Modularity:* Smaller reusable components can be deployed faster and more easily, increasing resource sharing and reducing cost.
- *Integration:* Dynamic linking of business processes, applications, and infrastructure components enhance agility and cost efficiency.

Grid technologies enable the successful implementation of the Adaptive Enterprise architecture to link IT infrastructure dynamically to business processes by fulfilling the following design rules:

- *Service-oriented architecture (SOA):* Grid services are defined based on OGSA (Foster et al. 2002), an open standard that leverages Web services to allow large-scale collaboration across the Internet.
- *Virtualization:* Grids harness a large pool of resources that can be shared across applications and processes to meet business demands.
- *Model-based automation:* Grid technologies integrate standalone resources and automate services, thus simplifying the process of deployment, management, and maintenance.

HP customizes the Globus Toolkit (Foster and Kesselman 1997) as the Grid infrastructure for its platforms. The Grid solutions offered by HP and its partners are listed in Table 3.

Table 3: HP and Its Partners' Grid Solutions

HP Solutions and Web Site	HP Partner Solutions and Web Site
• Management Solutions: *OpenView* www.hp.com/go/openview • Server Solutions: *BladeSystem* www.hp.com/go/bladesystem • Storage Solutions: *Storage Works Grid* www.hp.com/go/storageworksgrid	*Infrastructure:* • Application Infrastructure: *DataSynapse* www.datasynapse.com • Grid Infrastructure: *United Devices* www.ud.com • Resource Management: *Axceleon* www.axceleon.com • Workload Management: *PBS Pro* www.altair.com • Workload Management: *Platform* www.platform.com

IBM E-Business On Demand

IBM's *E-business On Demand* (IBM 2003) aims to improve the competitiveness and responsiveness of businesses through continuous innovation in products and services. To achieve this aim, E-Business On Demand optimizes the following business processes:

- *Research and development:* New innovative products and services need to be researched and developed quickly to make an impact in the highly competitive market.
- *Engineering and product design:* Products and services need to be well-engineered and designed to meet customers' requirements.
- *Business analytics:* Swift and accurate business decisions need to be made based on market performance data in order to remain a market leader.
- *Enterprise optimization:* Stand-alone resources at various global branches need to be integrated so that workload can be distributed evenly and resources used fully to satisfy demand.

E-business On Demand targets numerous industries, including:

- *Automotive and aerospace:* Collaborative design and data-intensive testing
- *Financial services:* Complex scenario simulation and decision-making
- *Government:* Coordinated operation across civil and military divisions and agencies
- *Higher education:* Advanced compute and data-intensive research
- *Life sciences:* Biological and chemical information analysis and decoding

IBM applies four core enabling technologies for E-Business On Demand: Grid computing, autonomic computing, open standards, and integration technologies. Grid technologies acts as the key component to provide the flexibility and efficiency required for various E-Business On Demand environments:

- *Research and development:* Highly compute- and data-intensive research problems can be solved with lower cost and shorter time by harnessing extra computational and data resources in a Grid.
- *Engineering and product design:* Industry partners are able to collaborate by sharing resources and coordinating engineering and design processes through VOs and open standards–based Grid architecture.
- *Business analytics:* Heavy data analysis and processing can be sped up with extra computational and data resources so that results are derived in time for decision-making.
- *Enterprise optimization:* Virtualization and replication using Grid technologies ensures that underutilized resources are not wasted, but are instead used for backup and recovery purposes.

The core component that IBM deploys for its Grid infrastructure is called the IBM Grid Toolbox, which is an enhanced version of the Globus Toolkit (Foster and Kesselman 1997). Table 4 lists Grid solutions that are available by IBM and its partners. IBM provides a general integrated Grid solution offering, called "Grid and Grow," for interested customers to easily deploy and sample Grid technologies. In addition, it has created customized Grid offerings for specific industries and applications to drive E-business On Demand.

Table 4: IBM and Its Partners' Grid Solutions

IBM Solutions and Web Site	IBM Partner Solutions and Web Site
• Application Server: *Websphere* www.ibm.com/websphere • Resource Provisioning: *Tivoli* www.ibm.com/tivoli • System Server: *eServer* www.ibm.com/servers	*Infrastructure:* • Application Infrastructure: *DataSynapse* www.datasynapse.com • Grid Infrastructure: *United Devices* www.ud.com • Grid Infrastructure: *Univa* www.univa.com • Workload Management: *PBS Pro* www.altair.com • Workload Management: *Platform* www.platform.com *Application:* • Document Production: *Sefas* www.sefas.com • Grid Deployment: *SAS* www.sas.com/grid • Risk Management: *Fortent* www.fortent.com

Oracle On Demand

Oracle's On Demand aims to enable customers to focus on more strategic business objectives by improving their IT performance and maximize the return on investment in four areas:

- *Quality:* A comprehensive and configurable set of services specifically designed to improve IT performance will be continuously delivered.
- *Cost:* IT expenses are more easily predicted and lower, as there is no need to spend on additional unexpected repairs and upgrades.
- *Agility:* The offered service is flexible and can be tailored to satisfy changing complexities, environments, and business needs.
- *Risk:* Service level commitments guarantee problem resolution, enhancements, and expansions to maximize accountability.

Oracle's On Demand is implemented using Grid solutions through three basic steps:

- *Consolidation:* Hardware, applications, and information can be shared across multiple data centers.
- *Standardization*: Using common infrastructure, application, and information services bridges the gap between various servers, storages, and operating systems.
- *Automation*: Less system administration work is required, as multiple resources can be managed concurrently and more easily.

Table 5 shows the Grid solutions from Oracle and its partners. Oracle Database 10g is the first database designed for Grid computing and offers data-provisioning capabilities, such as detaching part of a database and attaching it to another database without unloading and reloading.

Sun Microsystems Sun Grid

Sun Microsystems's Sun Grid aims to provide affordable commodity-based computing power pay-as-you-go service. Sun Grid currently supports three types of compute utility service (see Table 6 for comparison):

- *Compute utility:* A standard offering that provides instant deployment for anyone with Internet access at $1 per hour of processing.
- *Commercial utility:* A single-tenant standard offering in a multitenant hosting center that targets medium and large enterprises.
- *Variable cost infrastructure:* A customized modular offering and single-tenant utility model for large enterprises and system integrators.

The Sun Grid compute utility (Sun Microsystems 2006 January) provides a golden opportunity for non-IT users to make use of utility computing by providing a simple and easy to use Web interface that hides the complex Grid technologies involved. Given this assumption of a simple utility computing environment, the Sun Grid compute utility has several limitations:

- Submitted applications must be able to execute on the Solaris 10 operating system.
- Submitted applications must be self-contained and scripted to work with Sun N1 Grid Engine (Gentzsch 2001) software without requiring interactive access.
- Submitted applications have to be implemented using standard object libraries included with Solaris 10 Operating system or user libraries packaged with the executable file.
- The application can obtain finer control over compute resources through the interfaces provided by the Sun N1 Grid Engine software.
- The total maximum size of applications and data must be less than 10 GB.

Table 5: Oracle and Its Partners' Grid Solutions

Oracle Solutions and Web Site	Oracle Partner Solutions and Web Site
• Data Provisioning: *Oracle Database 10g* www.oracle.com/database • Management Solutions: *Oracle Fusion Middleware* www.oracle.com/middleware • Resource Provisioning: *Oracle Enterprise Manager 10g* www.oracle.com/technology/products/oem	*Infrastructure:* • Grid Infrastructure: *Apple* www.apple.com • Grid Infrastructure: *Egenera* www.egenera.com • Grid Infrastructure: *HP* www.hp.com • Grid Infrastructure: *Network Appliance* www.netapp.com *Application:* • Database Management: *GridApp* www.gridapp.com • Database Management: *Grid-Tools* www.grid-tools.com • Enterprise Automation: ORSYP www.orsyp.com

Table 6: Comparison of Sun Grid Compute Utility Services

Comparison	Sun Grid Compute Utility Services		
	Compute Utility	**Commercial Utility**	**Variable Cost Infrastructure**
Access	Portal	Dedicated	Customer or system integrator hosted
Availability	Instantaneous	Short notice	Longer-term contract
Scheduling	No reservation	Time-based reservation	Dedicated or time-based reservation
Pricing	All-inclusive $1/CPU-hour	Negotiated $/CPU-hour	Negotiated
Business terms	Standard	Service level	Capacity provisioning
Technology	Solaris 10 × 64	Solaris 10 × 64 or Redhat Linux	Menu of options
Storage	10-GB standard	Customer defined	Menu of options

- Applications and data can be uploaded only through the Web interface and may be packaged into compressed ZIP files of less than 100 MB each.

Grid technologies are used for the Sun Grid compute utility with the following compute node configuration:

- 8 GB of memory
- Solaris 10 operating system
- Sun N1 Grid Engine 6 software for resource management of compute nodes
- Grid network infrastructure built on Gigabit Ethernet
- Web-based portal for users to submit jobs and upload data
- 10 GB of storage space for each user

Industries that are targeted by the Sun Grid compute utility consist of:

- *Energy:* Reservoir simulations and seismic processing
- *Entertainment/Media:* Digital content creation, animation, rendering, and digital asset management
- *Financial services:* Risk analysis and Monte Carlo simulations
- *Government education:* Weather analysis and image processing
- *Health sciences:* Medical imaging, bioinformatics, and drug development simulations
- *Manufacturing:* Electronic design automation, mechanical computer-aided design, computational fluid dynamics, crash-test simulations, and aerodynamic modeling

Sun Microsystems, Gridwise Tech, and the Globus project have been collaborating in the joint development of interfaces between Sun Grid solutions and the Globus Toolkit (Gridwise Tech 2006). Table 7 shows Grid solutions that are developed by Sun Microsystems and its partners.

Table 7: Sun Microsystems and Its Partners' Grid Solutions

Sun Microsystems Solutions and Web Site	Sun Microsystems Partner Solutions and Web Site
• Resource Management: *N1* www.sun.com/software/n1gridsystem	*Infrastructure:* • Application Server: *GigaSpaces* www.gigaspaces.com • Autonomic Processing: *Paremus* www.paremus.com • Workload Management: *Platform* www.platform.com *Service Management:* • Collaborative Solutions: *SAP* www.sap.com • Database Solutions: *Oracle* www.oracle.com • Service-Oriented Solutions: *BEA* www.bea.com *Software As a Service:* • Pricing and Risk Solutions: *CDO2* www.cdo2.com

CONCLUSION

In this chapter, the utility computing model and its vision of being the next generation of the IT evolution is introduced. The utility computing model is significantly different from traditional IT models, and thus requires organizations to amend their existing IT procedures and operations toward this outsourcing model so as to save costs and improve quality. There is also increasing emphasis on adopting Grid computing technologies to enable utility computing environments.

This chapter has focused on the potential of Grids as utility computing environments. A reference service-oriented architecture of Utility Grids has been discussed, along with how services are assembled on demand in the Utility Grid. The challenges involved in utility-based resource allocation at various levels of the Utility Grid are then examined in detail. With commercial vendors rapidly launching utility computing solutions, industrial solutions by four pioneer vendors (HP, IBM, Oracle, and Sun Microsystems) and their realization through Grid technologies are also presented.

For recent advances in Grid computing technologies and applications, readers are recommended to browse the proceedings of CCGrid (International Symposium on Cluster Computing and the Grid (CCGrid) 2001), Grid (International Conference on Grid Computing (Grid) 2000), and e-Science (International Conference on e-Science and Grid Computing (e-Science) 2005) conference series organized by the IEEE Technical Committee on Scalable Computing (TCSC) (2005).

ACKNOWLEDGEMENT

The authors thank Hussein Gibbins and the anonymous reviewers for their comments. This work is partially supported through the Australian Research Council (ARC) Discovery Project grant.

GLOSSARY

Adaptive Enterprise: An organization that is able to adjust and benefit according to the changes in its operating environment.

Grid Computing: A model allowing organizations to access a large quantity of remotely distributed computing resources on demand.

Market-Based Resource Allocation: Assignment of resources based on market supply and demand from providers and users.

Middleware: Software designed to interface and link separate software and/or hardware.

On Demand Computing: Computing services that can be accessed when required by the user.

Service Level Agreement (SLA): A contract agreed upon between a service provider and a user that formally specifies service quality that the provider is required to provide.

Service-Oriented Architecture (SOA): An architectural framework for the definition of services that are able to fulfill the requirements of users.

Utility Computing: A model whereby service providers offer computing resources to users only when the users need them and charges the users based on usage.

Virtual Organization (VO): A temporary arrangement formed across physically dispersed departments and organizations with a common objective to facilitate collaboration and coordination.

CROSS REFERENCES

See *Cluster Computing Fundamentals; Grid Computing Fundamentals; Grid Computing Implementation; Next Generation Cluster Networks.*

REFERENCES

Abramson, D., J. Giddy, and L. Kotler. 2000. High performance parametric modeling with Nimrod/G: Killer application for the global grid? *Proceedings of the 14th International Parallel and Distributed Processing Symposium (IPDPS 2000), Cancun, Mexico, May 2000*, 520–8. Los Alamitos, CA: IEEE Computer Society Press.

Abramson, D., R. Buyya, and J. Giddy. 2002. A computational economy for grid computing and its implementation in the Nimrod-G resource broker. *Future Generation Computer Systems* 18(8):1061–74.

Agrawal, S., J. Dongarra, K. Seymour, and S. Vadhiyar. 2003. NetSolve: Past, present, and future—A look at a grid enabled server. In *Grid Computing: Making the Global Infrastructure a Reality,* edited by F. Berman, G. Fox, A. J. G. Hey, 613–22. New York: Wiley.

Al-Ali, R. J., K. Amin, G. von Laszewski, O. F. Rana, D. W. Walker, M. Hategan, and N. Zaluzec. 2004. Analysis and provision of QoS for distributed grid applications. *Journal of Grid Computing* 2(2):163–82.

Andrieux, A., K. Czajkowski, A. Dan, K. Keahey, H. Ludwig, J. Pruyne, J. Rofrano, S. Tuecke, and M. Xu. 2004 May. Web Services Agreement Specification (WS-Agreement), version 1.1, draft 18. GGF GRAAP Working Group. Lemont, IL: Open Grid Forum.

Antonioletti, M., S. Hastings, A. Krause, S. Langella, S. Laws, S. Malaika, and N. W. Paton. 2004 September. Web services data access and integration—The XML realization (WS-DAIX). GGF DAIS Working Group. Lemont, IL: Open Grid Forum.

Barkes, J., M. R. Barrios, F. Cougard, P. G. Crumley, D. Marin, H. Reddy, and T. Thitayanun. 1998. GPFS: A parallel file system. *IBM Redbook* SG24-5165-00.

Benkner, S., I. Brandic, G. Engelbrecht, and R. Schmidt. 2004. VGE—A service-oriented grid environment for on-demand supercomputing. *Proceedings of the 5th International Workshop on Grid Computing (Grid 2004), Pittsburgh, PA, November 2004*, 11–8. Los Alamitos, CA: IEEE Computer Society Press.

Berti, G., S. Benkner, J. W. Fenner, J. Fingberg, G. Lonsdale, S. E. Middleton, and M. Surridge. 2003. Medical simulation services via the grid. *Proceedings of the 1st HealthGRID Conference (HealthGRID 2003), Lyon, France, January 2003.*

Brandic, I., S. Benkner, G. Engelbrecht, and R. Schmidt. 2005. QoS support for time-critical grid workflow applications. *Proceedings of the 1st International Conference on e-Science and Grid Computing (e-Science 2005), Melbourne, Australia, December 2005*, 108–15. Los Alamitos, CA: IEEE Computer Society Press.

Buco, M. J., R. N. Chang, L. Z. Luan, C. Ward, J. L. Wolf, and P. S. Yu. 2004. Utility computing SLA management based upon business objectives. *IBM Systems Journal* 43 (1):159–78.

Buyya, R. ed. 1999. *High performance cluster computing: Architectures and systems*. Volume 1. Upper Saddle River, NJ: Prentice Hall.

Buyya, R., and S. Venugopal. 2004. The Gridbus Toolkit for service oriented grid and utility computing: An overview and status report. *Proceedings of the 1st IEEE International Workshop on Grid Economics and Business Models (GECON 2004), Seoul, Korea, April 2004*, 19–36. Piscataway, NJ: IEEE Press.

Buyya, R., D. Abramson, and S. Venugopal. 2005. The grid economy. *Proceedings of the IEEE* 93 (3):698–714.

Buyya, R., T. Cortes, and H. Jin. 2001. Single system image. *The International Journal of High Performance Computing Applications* 15 (2):124–35.

Cannataro, M., and D. Talia. 2003. The knowledge grid. *Communications of the ACM* 46 (1):89–93.

Cannataro, M., D. Talia, and P. Trunfio. 2002. Distributed data mining on the grid. *Future Generation Computer Systems* 18 (8):1101–12.

Childers, L., T. Disz, R. Olson, M. E. Papka, R. Stevens, and T. Udeshi. 2000. Access Grid: Immersive group-to-group collaborative visualization. *Proceedings of the 4th International Immersive Projection Technology Workshop (IPT 2000), Ames, IA, June 2000*. citeseer.ist.psu.edu/childers00access.html (accessed November 2006).

Cooper, B. F., and H. Garcia-Molina. 2002. Peer-to-peer data trading to preserve information. *ACM Transactions on Information Systems* 20 (2):133–70.

Deelman, E., C. Kesselman, G. Mehta, L. Meshkat, L. Pearlman, K. Blackburn, P. Ehrens, A. Lazzarini, R. Williams, and S. Koranda. 2002. GriPhyN and LIGO, building a virtual data grid for gravitational wave scientists. *Proceedings of the 11th International Symposium on High Performance Distributed Computing (HPDC11), Edinburgh, Scotland, July 2002*, 225–34. Los Alamitos, CA: IEEE Computer Society Press.

Deelman, E., J. Blythe, Y. Gil, and C. Kesselman. 2003. Workflow management in GriPhyN. In *Grid Resource Management: State of the Art and Future Trends*, edited by J. Nabrzyski, J. M. Schopf, and J. Weglarz, 99–117. Boston, MA: Kluwer.

Dimitrakos, T., D. Golby, and P. Kearney. 2004. Towards a trust and contract management framework for dynamic virtual organizations. *Proceedings of eChallenges 2004, Vienna, Austria, October 2004*. In *eAdoption and the knowledge economy: Issues, applications, case studies*. Amsterdam, the Netherlands: IOS Press.

Dumitrescu, C. L., M. Wilde, and I. Foster. 2005. A model for usage policy-based resource allocation in grids. *Proceedings of the 6th International Workshop on Policies for Distributed Systems and Networks (POLICY 2005), Stockholm, Sweden, June 2005*, 191–200. Los Alamitos, CA: IEEE Computer Society Press.

Foster, I., and C. Kesselman, eds. 2003. *The Grid 2: Blueprint for a new computing infrastructure*. San Francisco, CA: Morgan Kaufmann.

Foster, I., and C. Kesselman. 1997. Globus: A metacomputing infrastructure toolkit. *The International Journal of High Performance Computing Applications* 11 (2): 115–28.

Foster, I., C. Kesselman, and S. Tuecke. 2001. The anatomy of the grid: Enabling scalable virtual organizations. *The International Journal of High Performance Computing Applications* 15 (3):200–22.

Foster, I., C. Kesselman, J. M. Nick, and S. Tuecke. 2002 June. The physiology of the grid: An open grid services architecture for distributed systems integration. GGF OGSI Working Group. Lemont, IL: Open Grid Forum.

Foster, I., J. Vöckler, M. Wilde, and Y. Zhao 2003. The virtual data grid: A new model and architecture for data-intensive collaboration. *Proceedings of the 1st Conference on Innovative Data Systems Research (CIDR 2003), Asilomar, CA, January 2003*. www.cidrdb.org (accessed November 2006).

Ge, R., X. Feng, and K. W. Cameron. 2005. Performance-constrained distributed DVS scheduling for scientific applications on power-aware clusters. *Proceedings of the 2005 ACM/IEEE Supercomputing Conference (SC 2005), Seattle, WA, November 2005*. New York: ACM Press.

Gentzsch, W. 2001. Sun Grid Engine: Towards creating a compute power grid. *Proceedings of the 1st International Symposium on Cluster Computing and the Grid (CCGrid 2001), Brisbane, Australia, May 2001*, 35–36. Los Alamitos, CA: IEEE Computer Society Press.

Ghemawat, S., H. Gobioff, and S.-T. Leung. 2003. The Google file system. *Proceedings of the 19th ACM Symposium on Operating Systems Principles (SOSP 2003), Bolton Landing, NY, October 2003*, 29–43. New York: ACM Press.

Graupner, S., J. Pruyne, and S. Singhal. 2003. *Making the utility data center a power station for the enterprise grid.* Palo Alto, CA: HP Labs. www.hpl.hp.com/techreports/2003 (accessed November 2006).

Gridwise Tech. 2006. *Grid Engine-Globus Toolkit adapter*, www.gridwisetech.com/ge-gt (accessed November 2006).

Gropp, W., E. Lusk, and A. Skjellum. 1999. *Using MPI: Portable parallel programming with the message passing interface*. 2nd ed. Cambridge, MA: MIT Press.

Heiser, G., K. Elphinstone, J. Vochteloo, S. Russell, and J. Liedtke. 1998. The Mungi single-address-space operating system. *Software Practice and Experience* 28 (9):901–28.

Hollinsworth, D. 1995. The workflow reference model. Document Number TC00-1003. Hingham, MA: The Workflow Management Coalition.

HP. 2005. Adaptive Enterprise: Business and IT synchronized to capitalize on change. HP White Paper 4AA0-0760ENW.

IBM. 2003. Unleash the power of e-business on demand. IBM White Paper G522-2580-00.

IEEE Technical Committee on Scalable Computing (TCSC). 2005. www.ieeetcsc.org (accessed November 2006).

International Conference on e-Science and Grid Computing (e-Science). 2005. www.escience-meeting.org (accessed November 2006).

International Conference on Grid Computing (Grid). 2000. www.gridcomputing.org (accessed November 2006).

International Symposium on Cluster Computing and the Grid (CCGrid). 2001. www.buyya.com/ccgrid (accessed November 2006).

Irwin, D. E., L. E. Grit, and J. S. Chase. 2004. Balancing risk and reward in a market-based task service. *Proceedings of the 13th International Symposium on High Performance Distributed Computing (HPDC13), Honolulu, HI, June 2004*, 160–9. Los Alamitos, CA: IEEE Computer Society Press.

Islam, M., P. Balaji, P. Sadayappan, and D. K. Panda. 2004. Towards provision of quality of service guarantees in job scheduling. *Proceedings of the 6th International Conference on Cluster Computing (Cluster 2004), San Diego, CA, September 2004*, 245–54. Los Alamitos, CA: IEEE Computer Society Press.

Jin, H. 2004. ChinaGrid: Making grid computing a reality. *Proceedings of the 7th International Conference of Asian Digital Libraries (ICADL 2004)*, 13–24. Heidelberg, Germany: Springer Lecture Notes in Computer Science, 3334.

Joseph, J., and C. Fellenstein. 2004. *Grid computing*. Upper Saddle River, NJ: Prentice Hall.

Joseph, J., M. Ernest, and C. Fellenstein. 2004. Evolution of grid computing architecture and grid adoption models. *IBM Systems Journal* 43 (4):624–45.

Kenyon, C., and G. Cheliotis. 2005. Elements of financial risk management for grid and utility computing. In *handbook of integrated risk management for E-business: Measuring, modeling, and managing risk*, edited by A. Labbi, 169–91. Fort Lauderdale, FL: J. Ross Publishing.

Kephart, J. O., and D. M. Chess. 2003. The vision of autonomic computing. *Computer* 36 (1):41–50.

Kleban, S. D., and S. H. Clearwater. 2004. Computation-at-risk: Assessing job portfolio management risk on clusters. *Proceedings of the 18th International Parallel and Distributed Processing Symposium (IPDPS 2004), Santa Fe, NM, April 2004*. Los Alamitos, CA: IEEE Computer Society Press.

Kleinrock, L. 2005. A vision for the Internet. *ST Journal of Research* 2 (1):4–5.

Kra, D. 2004. *Six strategies for grid application enablement*. IBM Developer Works. www.ibm.com/developerworks /grid/library/gr-enable (accessed November 2006).

Krauter, K., R. Buyya, and M. Maheswaran. 2002. A taxonomy and survey of grid resource management systems for distributed computing. *Software: Practice and Experience* 32 (2):135–64.

Kubiatowicz, J., D. Bindel, Y. Chen, S. Czerwinski, P. Eaton, D. Geels, R. Gummadi, S. Rhea, H. Weatherspoon, W. Weimer, C. Wells, and B. Zhao. 2000. OceanStore: An architecture for global-scale persistent storage *Proceedings of the 9th International Conference on Architectural Support for Programming Languages and Operating Systems (ASPLOS 2000), Cambridge, MA, November 2000*, 190–201. New York: ACM Press.

Lamanna, M. 2004. The LHC computing grid project at CERN. *Nuclear Instruments and Methods in Physics Research Section A: Accelerators, Spectrometers, Detectors and Associated Equipment* 534(1–2):1–6.

Ligon, W. B. III, and R. Ross. 2001. PVFS: A parallel file system for Linux clusters. In *Beowulf cluster computing with Linux*, edited by T. Sterling, 391–430. Cambridge, MA: MIT Press.

Menascé, D. A., and E. Casalicchio. 2004. A framework for resource allocation in grid computing. *Proceedings of the 12th Annual International Symposium on Modeling, Analysis, and Simulation of Computer and Telecommunications Systems (MASCOTS 2004), Volendam, the Netherlands, October 2004*, 259–67. Los Alamitos, CA: IEEE Computer Society Press.

META Group. 2004 May. The adaptive organization: An examination of on demand computing. META Group Multiclient Study.

Moore, R. W., A. Rajasekar, and M. Wan. 2005. Data grids, digital libraries and persistent archives: An integrated approach to sharing, publishing, and archiving data. *Proceedings of the IEEE* 93 (3):578–88.

Murch, R. 2004. *Autonomic computing*. Upper Saddle River, NJ: Prentice Hall.

Nitzberg, B., and V. Lo. 1991. Distributed shared memory: A survey of issues and algorithms. *Computer* 24 (8)52–60.

Paleologo, G. A. 2004. Price-at-risk: A methodology for pricing utility computing services. *IBM Systems Journal* 43 (1):20–31.

Patel, J., W. T. L. Teacy, N. R. Jennings, M. Luck, S. Chalmers, N. Oren, T. J. Norman, A. Preece, P. M. D. Gray, G. Shercliff, P. J. Stockreisser, J. Shao, W. A. Gray, N. J. Fiddian, and S. Thompson. 2005. Agent-based virtual organisations for the grid, *International Journal of Multi-Agent and Grid Systems* 1 (4):237–49.

Pfister, G. F. 1998. *In search of clusters*. 2nd ed. Upper Saddle River, NJ: Prentice Hall.

Placek, M., and R. Buyya. 2006. Storage exchange: A global trading platform for storage services. *Proceedings of the 12th International European Conference on Parallel Computing (Euro-Par 2006)*, 425–36. Heidelberg, Germany: Springer Lecture Notes in Computer Science, 4128.

Platform Computing. 2003. *The politics of grid*. www2.platform.com/adoption/politics (accessed November 2006).

Popovici, F. I., and J. Wilkes. 2005. Profitable services in an uncertain world. *Proceedings of the 18th Conference on Supercomputing (SC 2005), Seattle, WA, November 2005*. New York: ACM Press.

Rappa, M. A. 2004. The utility business model and the future of computing services. *IBM Systems Journal* 43 (1):32–42.

Reed, D. A. 2003. Grids, the TeraGrid, and beyond. *Computer* 36 (1):62–8.

Ross, J. W., and G. Westerman. 2004. Preparing for utility computing: The role of IT architecture and relationship management. *IBM Systems Journal* 43 (1):5–19.

Smith, W., I. Foster, and V. Taylor. 2000. Scheduling with advanced reservations. *Proceedings of the 14th International Parallel and Distributed Processing Symposium (IPDPS 2000), Cancun, Mexico, May 2000*, 127–32. Los Alamitos, CA: IEEE Computer Society Press.

Spooner, D. P., J. Cao, S. A. Jarvis, L. He, and G. R. Nudd. 2005. Performance-aware workflow management for grid computing. *The Computer Journal* 48 (3): 347–57.

Sulistio, A., and R. Buyya. 2004. A grid simulation infrastructure supporting advance reservation. *Proceedings of the 16th International Conference on Parallel and Distributed Computing and Systems (PDCS 2004), Cambridge, MA, November 2004*, 1–7. Calgary, Alberta, Canada: ACTA Press.

Sun Microsystems. 2006 January. Sun Grid compute utility reference guide. Part No. 819-5131-10.

Vazhkudai, S. S., X. Ma, V. W. Freeh, J. W. Strickland, N. Tammineedi, and S. L. Scott. 2005. FreeLoader: Scavenging desktop storage resources for scientific data. *Proceedings of the 18th Supercomputing Conference (SC 2005), Seattle, WA, November 2005*. New York: ACM Press.

Venugopal, S., R. Buyya, and L. Winton. 2006. A grid service broker for scheduling e-science applications on global data grids. *Concurrency and Computation: Practice and Experience* 18 (6):685–99.

Wasson, G., and M. Humphrey. 2003. Policy and enforcement in virtual organizations. *Proceedings of the 4th International Workshop on Grid Computing (Grid 2003), Phoenix, AZ, November 2003*, 125–32. Los Alamitos, CA: IEEE Computer Society Press.

Wilcox-O'Hearn, B. 2002. Experiences deploying a large-scale emergent network. *Proceedings of the 1st International Workshop on Peer-to-Peer Systems (IPTPS 2002)*, 104–10. Heidelberg, Germany: Springer Lecture Notes in Computer Science, 2429.

Yeo, C. S., and R. Buyya. 2005. Service level agreement based allocation of cluster resources: Handling penalty to enhance utility. *Proceedings of the 7th International Conference on Cluster Computing (Cluster 2005), Boston, MA, September 2005*. Los Alamitos, CA: IEEE Computer Society Press.

Yeo, C. S., and R. Buyya. 2006. A taxonomy of market-based resource management systems for utility-driven cluster computing. *Software: Practice and Experience* 36 (13):1381–419.

Yu, J., and R. Buyya. 2005. A taxonomy of workflow management systems for grid computing. *Journal of Grid Computing* 3(3–4):171–200.

Yu, J., and R. Buyya. 2006. A budget constrained scheduling of workflow applications on utility grids using genetic algorithms. *Workshop on Workflows in Support of Large-Scale Science (WORKS), Proceedings of the 15th International Symposium on High Performance Distributed Computing (HPDC 2006), Paris, France, June 2006*. Los Alamitos, CA: IEEE Computer Society Press.

Yu, J., R. Buyya, and C. K. Tham. 2005. Cost-based scheduling of scientific workflow applications on utility grids. *Proceedings of the 1st International Conference on e-Science and Grid Computing (e-Science 2005), Melbourne, Australia, December 2005*, 140–7. Los Alamitos, CA: IEEE Computer Society Press.

Peer-to-Peer Network Architecture

Jing Wu and Michel Savoie, *Communications Research Center (CRC), Canada*

INTRODUCTION

The emergence of file-sharing systems such as Napster and Gnutella make the term *peer-to-peer* (P2P) popular. The benefits and challenges of such network architectures are realized by network operators and users. Their cost-effective resource aggregation capability, together with many other benefits, has motivated many new developments and products. Today, file sharing, content distribution, distributed computing, instant messaging, Internet telephony and videoconferencing, and ad hoc networking are all taking advantage of P2P network architectures. This chapter summarizes the network architectures that use the P2P concept.

We start with a discussion of what a P2P network is in the section on Definitions. Collections of the existing definitions of a P2P network are listed. Although there is no single concise definition of a P2P network, these definitions give us an informal description of a P2P network. Such an open mind is favorable, since new technologies can be accommodated as they are introduced.

An analysis of the benefits and limitations of P2P networks is given in the section on Benefits and Limitations of P2P Networks. Compared to centralized networks, P2P networks benefit from cost sharing and reduction, scalability, resource aggregation and interoperability, robustness improvement, increased autonomy, anonymity and privacy, enhanced dynamics, ad hoc communication, and collaboration. However, P2P networks are limited by their manageability, security, and service guarantee capability. It has been observed that P2P networks have limited methods to prevent cheating and selfish behaviors.

To present a general framework, we use a conceptual layered architecture to illustrate key building blocks in a P2P network in the section on PSP Network Architecture. The abstract reference P2P network architecture consists of three layers: the base overlay layer, the middleware layer, and the application layer. The base overlay layer provides peer discovery, overlay network construction, and application-level multicast. The middleware layer offers distributed search, publish and subscribe, security, distributed indexing, distributed directory, metadata, and scheduling. The application layer includes distributed communication and collaboration, file sharing, content distribution, distributed storage, and massively parallel computing. P2P network implementations use very diversified architectures. Some P2P networks are developed as single applications, possibly using proprietary implementations. Some P2P networks provide software modules that can be used to compose other applications. The three-layer reference P2P network architecture captures the major functional characteristics of P2P networks. However, it does not imply that a P2P network has to strictly follow the reference architecture.

This chapter focuses on the architectural aspects; Chapter 145 is about P2P network applications. Although ad hoc networking extensively uses P2P network architecture, we do not cover ad hoc networking in this chapter, since other chapters discuss this concept.

DEFINITIONS

The term *client* refers to a process using a service. In the context of networks, a client refers to a communication process receiving information from others or getting connected to others by the means of transit services. A client process initiates service requests to others. But a pure client process is not able to serve requests from others, unless each participating device supports linked client and server processes. In contrast to a client process, a *server* refers to a process offering services. In networks, a server process hosts information for client processes to search, download, and so on.

The term *peer* means "equal," which can be informally interpreted as a process with capability similar to the other processes with which process communicates. In the context of P2P networks, a peer process acts as a client process and at the same time as a server process for the same function. For example, a process that downloads files from others and meanwhile the process hosts shared files for others to download is a peer process in file downloading/uploading. There is no distinction between these processes in terms of which is providing or using services. Peer processes communicate with each other in a symmetric pattern. Note that the function that a peer process requests and offers must be the same within the context of a given application. A peer process can be

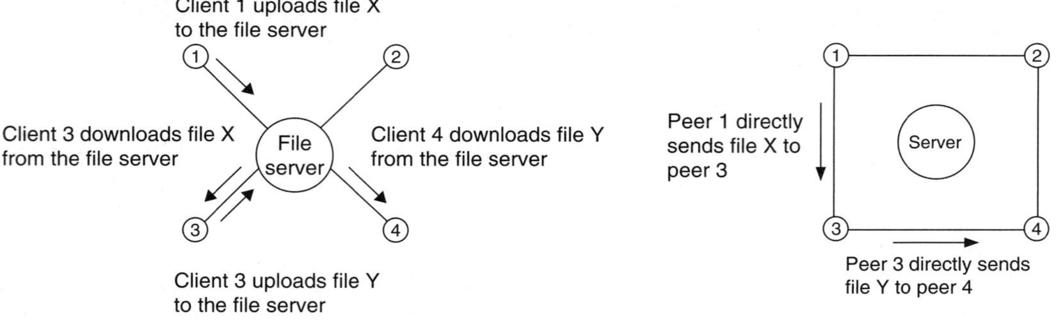

(A) The client/server model for a file uploading/downloading application

(B) The P2P model for a file transfer application

Figure 1: P2P and client/server models

instantiated variously as process, device (e.g., a network-connected computer or physical communication node), human being, etc.

Figure 1 illustrates the P2P and client/server models. In the client/server model, the server is involved in every file-uploading or downloading action. In the P2P model, peers bypass the server to transfer files among themselves. The dedicated server may still be present for some other functions, but it is unnecessary for every file to go through the server. The two models can coexist. Adding some server functions to the client and making it a peer do not eliminate the possibility of having dedicated servers for some functions.

There are several definitions of a P2P network. However, there is no well-accepted agreement about what is and what is not a P2P network. Collectively, these definitions of a P2P network give us an informal description of a P2P network, rather than a concise definition. Since P2P networks are rapidly evolving, it is healthy and desirable not to be restricted by a rigid definition, so that new technologies can be accommodated as they are introduced.

- A P2P network is the sharing of computing resources and services by direct exchange between systems (Milojicic et al. 2003).
- In a P2P network, computers at the edge provide power and those in the middle of the network are only for coordination (Milojicic et al. 2003).
- "P2P is a class of applications that takes advantage of resources—storage, cycles, content, human presence—available at the edges of the Internet. Because accessing these decentralized resources means operations in an environment of unstable connectivity and unpredictable IP addresses, P2P nodes must operate outside the DNS system and have significant or total autonomy from central servers" (Shirky 2000).
- A P2P network may be defined as an application layer overlay network in which all entities are equal and all contribute some of their resources, thus giving rise to a network in which each entity (peer) is both a content requestor and a content provider (Schollmeier 2001).
- "Peer-to-peer systems are distributed systems consisting of interconnected nodes able to self-organize into network topologies with the purpose of sharing resources such as content, CPU cycles, storage and bandwidth, capable of adapting to failures and accommodating transient populations of nodes while maintaining acceptable connectivity and performance, without requiring the intermediation or support of a global centralized server or authority" (Androutsellis-Theotokis and Spinellis 2004).
- "A P2P system is one that has these five key characteristics: i) the network facilitates real-time transmission of data or messages between the peers; ii) peers can function as both clients and servers; iii) the primary content of the network is provided by the peers; iv) the network gives control and autonomy to the peers; and v) the network accommodates peers that are not always connected and that might not have permanent Internet Protocol (IP) addresses" (Miller 2001).
- A P2P network allows every computer in the network to act as a server to every other user on the network. A P2P network supports P2P applications in which computers share resources via direct exchanges between the participating computers (Barkai 2001).

Three criteria have generally been used to identify a P2P network: it should be self-organizing, have a symmetric connection, and have decentralized control (Roussopoulos et al. 2004; Milojicic et al. 2003). Peers organize themselves into a network in a collaborative manner. Peers are considered equals by requesting and offering similar services to each other. Peers communicate in a symmetric pattern, not being confined to either client or server roles. Peers share resources, while peers determine their level of participation and their actions autonomously. Generally, there is no central controller that dictates the behaviors of individual peers.

BENEFITS AND LIMITATIONS OF P2P NETWORKS

Benefits of P2P Networks

Cost Sharing and Reduction

The most significant benefit of a P2P network is cost sharing. To build a P2P network, no entity needs to commit a large amount of resources or bear major network cost. The cost of the network infrastructure is naturally shared by participants. In a pure P2P network, every participant offers similar services to peers by contributing resources and sharing network cost. The network cost is spread to every participant, although the contribution of a participant may not be in proportion to the service that the participant receives from peers. In a hybrid P2P network, some nodes may be statically configured or dynamically assigned as supernodes offering additional services beyond that of ordinary participants. Such supernodes are mainly for bootstrapping, coordination, authentication, and so on. The major resource-consuming operations are still accomplished in a P2P manner. A well-designed P2P network should not overload the supernodes, and therefore the supernodes should not be a major cost.

A P2P network has a low entry cost for individual peers. In a centralized network, servers and the initial network infrastructure that a service provider builds bear a large percentage of the total cost, especially the initial capital expense; when such costs become too large, a P2P network helps spread the cost over all peers (Milojicic et al. 2003). This is important when no single entity has sufficient budget to build an initial centralized network, or when there is no clear business case for offering a service. In such a situation, a group of initial peers can build a P2P network by contributing their idle resources in trade for each other's additional services. A few P2P networks have evolved to millions of peers.

A fair cost sharing has always been an issue in P2P networks. Ideally, a peer trades idle resources for other resources that the peer requires to accomplish a task. Over time, the resources consumed by a peer should be in balance with the resources contributed by a peer. In reality, the lack of measurement of resource consumption and contribution may damage the faith of using a P2P network. In the extreme case, if a peer only enjoys "free services" offered by peers and does not contribute new services, then the "freerider" becomes a pure client of the network.

The cost reduction by a P2P network is a direct result of aggregating largely idle resources. A P2P network can offer services at a fraction of the cost of dedicated resources. A P2P network has a low entry cost for individual peers, although it may have a larger total cost (Roussopoulos et al. 2004). A P2P network offers an attractive alternative to a centralized network, when the initial budget is insufficient to build a service provider infrastructure using central servers.

Scalability

Different measurements of the scalability of a network or an application have been used. In Verma (2004), the scalability of an application was measured by the maximal user-level interactions that the application can support and still maintain reasonable performance. For example, the scalability of a Web server was measured by the number of user requests that it can support per second. The scalability of a directory server was measured by the maximal number of records that it can store and the maximal number of look-up operations that can be conducted within a given response time. In Mouftah and Ho (2002), scalability was measured by the size of a network to accommodate a static traffic demand pattern.

A P2P network is scalable as long as an increase in the number of nodes also leads to a proportional increase in performance of the network. In a well-designed P2P network, the total network capacity can be smoothly increased as more peers join the network. The scalability of a P2P network is limited by a number of factors: the amount of centralized operations (e.g., synchronization and coordination) that needs to be performed, the amount of state that needs to be maintained, the inherent parallelism that an application exhibits, and the programming model that is adopted (Milojicic et al. 2003). A P2P network requires communication among peers to perform various tasks and thus has an overhead. For example, some file-sharing P2P networks rely on a central or distributed index or directory to locate the host computers of a given file. The search process is an overhead for the file downloading. If the overhead is not well controlled, the potential scalability of a P2P network may not be achieved. Both client/server and P2P networks have developed techniques to achieve excellent scalability (Verma 2004). For example, popular Web sites use scalable Web servers to handle millions of requests each day. Some P2P file-sharing networks support millions of file transfers each day. The difference is that a centralized network uses dedicated servers, whereas a P2P network uses existing idle resources in each user to achieve a scalable solution.

Resource Aggregation and Interoperability

A P2P network can use spare capacity distributed in existing systems. The resources can be storage capacity, computational power, communication bandwidth, information, and files. A P2P network uses end users' resources—i.e., the resource contributors are end users of the services. The end users pool their idle resources together to create new services, which would not be possible by acting alone. For example, enterprise file-sharing and collaborative software may be able to improve the way organizations share important documents, and organize the interactions of creating and editing documents (Dougherty 2001).

To aggregate diverse resources, interoperability is essential. *Interoperability* refers to the ability of any entity (device or application) to speak to, exchange data with, and be understood by any other entity (Schoder, Fischbach, and Schmitt 2004). The resources provided by peers typically have different attributes. P2P networks have been successfully implemented using heterogeneous resources, being independent of specific devices.

Improved Robustness

P2P networks are designed to cope with system and network failures, disconnections, and unreliable resources. Treating failures as normal is one of the fundamental design principles for P2P networks. Partial failures or disconnections of peers do not stop the function of an entire P2P network. In a robust P2P network, no single part of the network is essential to the operation of the entire network. Thus, even when a few peers are disconnected or defunct, the network remains functional.

Three terms are used to describe system robustness: reliability, availability, and survivability. In the strict sense, *reliability* is defined as the probability that a system successfully performs its designated functions at the designated performance level under stated conditions for a specified period of time. Reliability is about a failure-free operational period. In contrast, *availability* is the probability that a system is able to perform (i.e., not failed, not undergoing repair) its designated functions at the stated performance level. Availability is about how much time a system can be used. Availability can be measured as the total uptime out of the measured time. All corrective and preventive actions account for maintenance downtime instead of only failures. When a system has a long uptime, it is highly available. But this does not necessarily mean the system is highly reliable. An example is when the downtime of a system is very low, but the short system maintenance or failures happen very frequently. *Survivability* is a qualitative measurement. A system is considered to be survivable if it can maintain service continuity to the end users during the occurrence of any failure by using real-time protection mechanisms (Mouftah and Ho 2002).

A well-designed P2P network is very robust, thanks to its highly redundant resources, while maintaining low cost by not pursuing high reliability (in the strict sense). Individual building blocks in a P2P network are unreliable; they are up and down frequently. A P2P network's robustness may not be protected by any real-time mechanisms. Therefore, from an end user's perspective, a P2P network may not be highly reliable. However, restoration mechanisms improve the network availability. The restoration may need an end user's intervention or it may be conducted automatically. Although for P2P networks, availability is difficult to guarantee and high fault-tolerance is expensive, P2P networks enjoy massive availability of similar resources. For non-critical applications, P2P networks are a good compromise between availability and economics. For critical missions, application-layer recovery and restoration should be used to improve the availability.

Increased Autonomy

One of the design principles of a P2P network is that each peer autonomously determines when it joins or leaves a P2P network. Ideally, a P2P network should require no centralized management, oversight, or control. No central authority should force a peer to join a P2P network or cut off a peer's access to a P2P network. Each peer should be responsible for its own actions. Based on personal judgment and preference, the peer should decide the time to join or leave a P2P network, the resources it contributes to a P2P network, and the services it uses. Although a peer may have incentives to join a P2P network—e.g., contributing certain resources in exchange for certain services—the peer's participation should be voluntary. In reality, a P2P network may not achieve complete autonomy, and may still use centralized management for certain functions.

In a P2P network, each peer has two sets of policies that regulate how others use its resources and how it uses others' resources. The policies on using its own resources are mainly for safe sharing and protection purposes. The policies on using others' resources are mainly for preference, discretion, and performance reasons. The policies include many aspects, such as when and to what extent a peer makes its resources available to other peers. The policies also depend on the characteristics of the resources and applications. For example, when a peer shares its CPU cycles, the peer may specify when others can use them, what percentage of the CPU cycles can be used by others, and which computational applications can use them.

Since each peer automatically sets up its own policies and cannot directly view or change others' policies, it is possible that different peers' policies may conflict with each other or may not respect the community's values. For example, in a file-sharing P2P network, a particular peer could have a policy specifying a preferred peer list, with which the file searching starts. If the peers at the top of the preferred peer list have a policy specifying not responding to the requests from this peer, then the performance that this peer perceives is negatively impacted. It would be advantageous if a peer's policies can be adjusted based on its past experience—e.g., removing nonresponding preferred peers after a certain number of failed trials. Real-time monitoring of resource usage and historical performance information are helpful for setting up policies.

In a P2P network, applications can be composed using components or modules distributed among different administrative domains. A centralized network is not a preferred architecture when the servers needed to host an application belong to different administrative domains. By using a P2P network, each administrative domain's autonomy is fully respected. A collaborative platform for multi-domain applications can be formed in a P2P network.

Anonymity and Privacy

A peer may prefer to be anonymous when participating in a P2P network, and may prefer to keep its communications with others private. The peer may want to protect its identity from being known to third parties, or even to its communicating partners. The peer may not want its communication activities to be monitored by third parties. In a centralized network, a server is typically able to identify a client (at least by the client's IP address), and the time and frequency of access by the client. In a P2P network, a peer may not want anyone, including a service provider, to know about its involvement—i.e., the peer may prefer to be anonymous. Three types of anonymity apply to a pair of communicating parties: sender anonymity, receiver anonymity and mutual anonymity (Pfitzmann and Waidner 1987). The spectrum of anonymity was identified in Reiter and Rubin (1998), ranging from complete anonymity (i.e., no third-party can perceive the existence of the communication) to no anonymity at all (i.e., a third-party can prove the existence of the communication, and identify the sender and receiver). Several interesting points exist in between, as shown in Figure 2.

Six techniques for improving a P2P network anonymity and privacy are summarized (Minami, Kamei, and Saito 2004): multicasting, faking a sender's address, faking identity, secret paths, intractable aliases, and nonvoluntary placement. Multicasting offers receiver anonymity. Faking a sender's address offers sender anonymity. Faking a sender's identity in the intermediate entities offers sender anonymity to the degree of possible innocence.

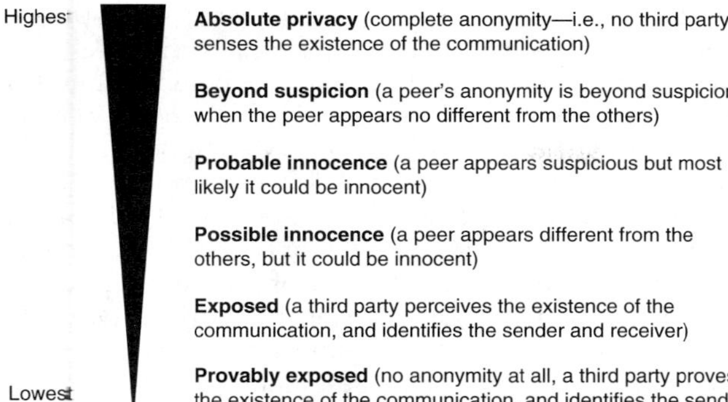

Figure 2: Degree of anonymity

A sender may protect his anonymity by using secret paths to a constantly changing middle party for store/forward. A receiver may protect her anonymity by using intractable aliases. A sender's anonymity can be protected by placement of the information in third parties without letting the third parties know it.

Privacy is information about identifiable peers. In P2P networks, privacy includes identity of peers, content, interests, location, etc. Privacy preservation in a P2P network tries to hide the association between the identity of a peer and the data that the peer is interested in. The platform for privacy preferences helps Web sites to express privacy policies while letting users automate users' acceptance or rejection decisions (Myles, Friday, and Davies 2003). Although such a platform is designed for Web sites, it can be tailored and applied to P2P networks. Such a platform does not attempt to enforce or ensure privacy through technology. Instead, social and legal pressures are relied on to compel organizations to comply with privacy policies.

Enhanced Dynamics

A P2P network offers a highly dynamic environment, where resources and peers enter and leave the network continuously. Compared to a centralized network that requires relatively stable servers, a P2P network is a natural fit for a highly dynamic environment. In traditional distributed networks, a node's disconnection is considered to be an exceptional event. However, a P2P network treats such an event as normal. A P2P network is built on a potentially large number of distributed resources that are contributed by autonomously operating peers. Thus, the inherent dynamics must be addressed by P2P network architectures. Each peer may participate in a P2P network temporarily, and leave the network without notifications to others.

P2P networks use special techniques to handle the transient nature of peers. Replication of critical resources is a widely used technique to deal with the dynamics of a P2P network. For example, files may be replicated in different peers to alleviate the impact of a peer's disconnection. To resolve the inconsistency in a reconnected peer, in Groove (www.groove.net) P2P networks, special nodes (called "relays") are used to temporarily store updates or communications, before the peer is reconnected. In Magi (www.endeavors.com) P2P networks, messages may be queued at the sender until the receiver is presented. Techniques have been developed to deal with the dynamics of servers in a P2P network. For example, central servers can be bypassed during the communication between a sender and a receiver as soon as the sender and receiver are linked together. Therefore, even though central servers may be used in a P2P network, their use is a one-time action and is not restricted to any particular server among many redundant servers.

Ad hoc Communication and Collaboration

A P2P network can be formed in an ad hoc mode, by preconfiguration, or in a hybrid manner by combining both. The ad hoc communication in P2P networks is more of membership, rather than of the infrastructure. Peers participate in a P2P network in an ad hoc mode, joining and leaving the network as they want. Peers' participation is based on their own locations, interests, resource status, and other personal circumstances. A peer's participation in a P2P network has no long-term commitment and may be for a particular occasion only.

Self-organization techniques are used to manage a P2P network without a preexisting infrastructure. The highly dynamic peer joining and leaving in a P2P network increase the probability of failures, disconnections, and out-of-service events. Self-maintenance and self-repair of the network are required. Many P2P networks have no or little predefined configuration. Even the predefined configurations that are used in some P2P networks may change during the operation of the P2P networks. Adaptation is the key to deal with changes. It would be costly to have dedicated servers and/or network operators for managing a fluctuating P2P network. Thus, distributing management among peers is an efficient solution (Minami, Kamei, and Saito 2004).

Limitations of P2P Networks

Manageability

The deployment of a P2P network potentially running on different platforms is challenging. The deployment of a P2P network has a higher risk of running into undiscovered bugs in the infrastructure than in a centralized network. Debugging distributed software requires covering complicated interaction scenarios among many components. Compared to widely available development and testing tools for a centralized network, there are only a few development tools for P2P networks.

The maintenance of an operating P2P network is also difficult. Maintenance of a P2P network includes tasks such as ensuring the continuity of its operation, restarting it if necessary, making backup copies of the generated data, upgrading software, fixing software bugs, and educating users about the network operations and functions (Verma 2004). In a centralized network, by using a standard client software (e.g., a Web browser) or interface, there are few maintenance tasks for a client. Since servers are centralized and likely under the same administration, the maintenance of servers can be well planned and be conducted in a coordinated manner. Although a P2P network uses self-organization and self-maintenance techniques to ease the difficulties of its maintenance, the manageability of a P2P network is not comparable to that of a centralized network. For example, upgrading the software of a P2P network is conducted on a voluntary basis and cannot be easily enforced. Another interesting example is that stopping a P2P network (as the last management task in its maintenance) cannot be easily accomplished due to its decentralization.

It is difficult to enforce standards in a P2P network. The operation of a P2P network needs certain common understanding and guidelines among peers. This common understanding covers technical aspects, as well as nontechnical aspects, such as social, moral, and ethical aspects. The recognition, adoption, and implementation of this common understanding are up to individual peers on a voluntary basis, as opposed to on a regulatory basis. The common understanding is in the form of recommendations, instead of standards.

The decentralized management in a P2P network results in no clear business model for a P2P network. To translate the operation of a P2P network into revenue flows, the P2P network needs management functions such as auditing, usage logging, authentication, authorization, and so on. These management requirements, to a certain extent, are contradictory to some benefits and design goals of a P2P network—e.g., anonymity and privacy. Until a successful business model of P2P networks is developed, P2P networks will operate mainly on a voluntary and amateur basis in the Internet, with virtually no technical support, or within an enterprise network where there are few requirements for a business model.

Security

A P2P network has very limited approaches to provide security against hackers, attacks, viruses, and other malicious damage. In general, the security of a centralized network can be managed much more readily than the security of a P2P network. A P2P network must apply security modules and mechanisms to many peers as opposed to a limited number of servers in a centralized network. The increased number of entities that need to be protected and the nature of multiple administration domains make the security in a P2P network even harder to solve.

Many security-management techniques rely on the proof of a party's identity. In these techniques, only after the identities of users, servers, or service providers are recognized and authenticated can further security management take actions such as granting a user access to certain information on a server, trusting the files downloaded from an accountable server, and exchanging encryption keys. However, in a P2P network, a receiver or a sender or both may want to be anonymous by hiding its identity. In addition, a peer may host files not created by the peer itself. The peer may not be aware of the contents and potential risk associated with the files. All these factors make verifying identity and contents very difficult in a P2P network.

Service Guarantee

The dynamic and transient nature of a P2P network makes it very difficult to guarantee the quality of service. In a P2P network, there is no service agreement or contract in place to formally specify each party's responsibilities and commitments. Peers interact with largely unknown and changing partners and the potential number of partners is large and varying. Although informal community common understanding may be in place, the enforcement of such common rules is not ensured.

The robustness of a P2P network is based on the assumption of a large number of available redundant resources. Again, the availability of any resource is not guaranteed and is highly dependent on the type of resources, the time of use, and many other factors. The failure recovery may not be an automatic process and may require frequent human interventions. Thus, a peer's perspective and tolerance in a P2P network are dramatically different from those in a centralized network. An entire P2P network is fault-tolerant, which means that at least part of the network is operating in the event of partial failures. But, for an individual peer, ongoing communication may or may not be fault-tolerant, depending on the design of the network. So far, P2P networks are not used for critical missions that require stringent service guarantees.

Cheating and Selfish Behaviors

Selfish behaviors have been well observed in P2P networks. P2P networks operate based on the cooperation and contribution of individual peers. When there is little incentive for a peer to obey the rules, a peer may cheat and demonstrate selfish behaviors to maximize the peer's own utility of the network. For example, it has been shown that approximately 26% of Gnutella peers share no data; these peers participate in the P2P network only to download data and not to share (Saroiu, Gummadi, and Gribble 2002). In Napster (www.napster.com), they observed that on average 60 to 80% of peers contributed 80 to 100% of the shared files, implying that 20 to 40% of peers contributed few or no files. The peers who attempt to benefit from the resources of other peers and not offering resources in exchange are called "freeriders" of P2P networks. It has been documented that in 2000, approximately 70% of Gnutella (www.gnutella.com) peers provided no files and the top 1% of Gnutella peers contributed about 37% of the total files that were available in Gnutella (Feldman and Chuang 2005). In 2005, freeriders increased to 85% of all Gnutella peers.

Cheating behaviors in P2P networks usually appear as intentionally false reporting or configuration of system parameters. The vast majority of peers participate in P2P networks using third-party-produced software. Since typically there are system parameters representing a peer's capability or participation, the peer may cheat by manipulating these system parameters. For example, it has been reported that about 22% of Napster peers specified their bandwidth as "unknown." These peers either were unaware of their connection bandwidths or intentionally hid their true bandwidth (Saroiu, Gummadi, and Gribble 2002). Since knowing a peer's connection speed is more valuable to others than to the peer, a peer that reports high bandwidth is more likely to provide downloads to other peers, consuming network resources. It is advantageous to peers to falsely report their Internet connection speeds.

Incentive mechanisms are developed to counterattack the cheating and selfish behaviors in P2P networks (Feldman and Chuang 2005). Peers may offer resources in exchange for receiving other resources, under threat of retaliation, or out of generosity. Reputation mechanisms are useful in stimulating cooperative behaviors and providing accountability (Androutsellis-Theotokis and Spinellis 2004).

P2P NETWORK ARCHITECTURES

For most P2P applications, there are common requirements (technological and architectural), characteristics, and implications. Such a commonality is outlined in this section.

An abstract reference P2P network architecture consists of three layers: the base overlay layer, the middleware layer, and the application layer (Verma 2004). The layered architecture is shown in Figure 3. P2P networks have very diversified architectures. Some P2P networks are developed as single applications, possibly using proprietary implementations. Some P2P networks provide software modules that can be used to compose other applications. The three-layer reference P2P network architecture captures the major functional characteristics of P2P networks. However, it does not imply that a P2P network has to strictly follow the reference architecture.

Base Overlay Layer

The base overlay layer is responsible for ensuring that a peer is aware of the existence of other peers in a P2P network and is able to communicate with any other peers. The base overlay layer is the foundation of a P2P network, which must be implemented in any P2P network architecture. This layer provides functions to discover other peers and then to create communication channels between them. The key functions in this layer include peer discovery, overlay network construction, and application-level multicast (Verma 2004).

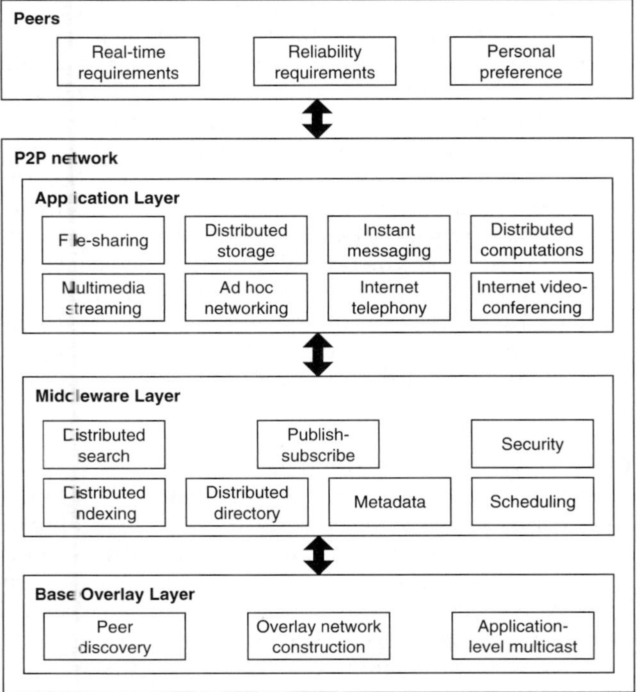

Figure 3: An abstract reference P2P network architecture

Peer Discovery

The peer discovery enables a peer to be aware of the existence of all other peers in the same P2P network. Alternatively, a peer may discover a few other peers and with the help of these peers get to know more peers. Peer discovery needs to find out the identities of other peers—e.g., the IP addresses of other peers. A peer needs to discover the other peers' port number if the P2P network does not use a fixed port. Once the minimal set of properties to facilitate communication between peers is discovered, other properties about the peers can be obtained by communicating with the peers.

Static peer discovery can be used for a relatively static P2P network with a moderate number of peers. In static peer discovery, each peer is configured with a list of the IP address and/or the port number of all other peers in the network. A peer checks the availability of other peers at the start-up and periodically during its operation. Static peer discovery does not scale well and does not apply to very dynamic P2P networks.

Some P2P networks use a centralized index server to facilitate the discovery process—e.g., Napster (Sunaga et al. 2004). Although server-assisted discovery does not meet the principles of a P2P network, content exchange is performed on a P2P basis. Therefore, Napster is considered a hybrid P2P network. The discovery process in Napster includes steps 2 and 3 shown in Figure 4 (Loo 2003). It should be noted that in the Napster P2P network, the discovery process and the distributed search process are combined. When a peer discovers its peers, the peer searches for a target file at the same time. Generally, in a server-assisted peer discovery, since a peer does not need to know all the existing peers in the network, having some out-of-date registrations in the index server is not a significant problem. The drawback of an index server is that there is a single point of failure, which makes it vulnerable to attacks and shutdowns.

A peer in the Gnutella P2P network uses a discovery request and reply mechanism to discover new peers. Discovery of new peers on the network is critical for a system with a highly dynamic topology. A disconnected peer must have offline knowledge of at least one connected peer in order to connect to the Gnutella P2P network. The address of an existing connected peer can either be learned by searching available posted peers on the Internet or be set to a well-known peer such as gnutellahosts.com: 6346, which is almost always connected to the network. Once connected to the network, a peer is always actively involved in peer discovery. The Gnutella discovery request and reply mechanism is implemented by the Ping and Pong messages. A Ping message is a request for discovery of peers. A Pong message is used to send the discovered address of a peer to the requestor. The Gnutella discovery process is shown in Figure 5. All Gnutella messages

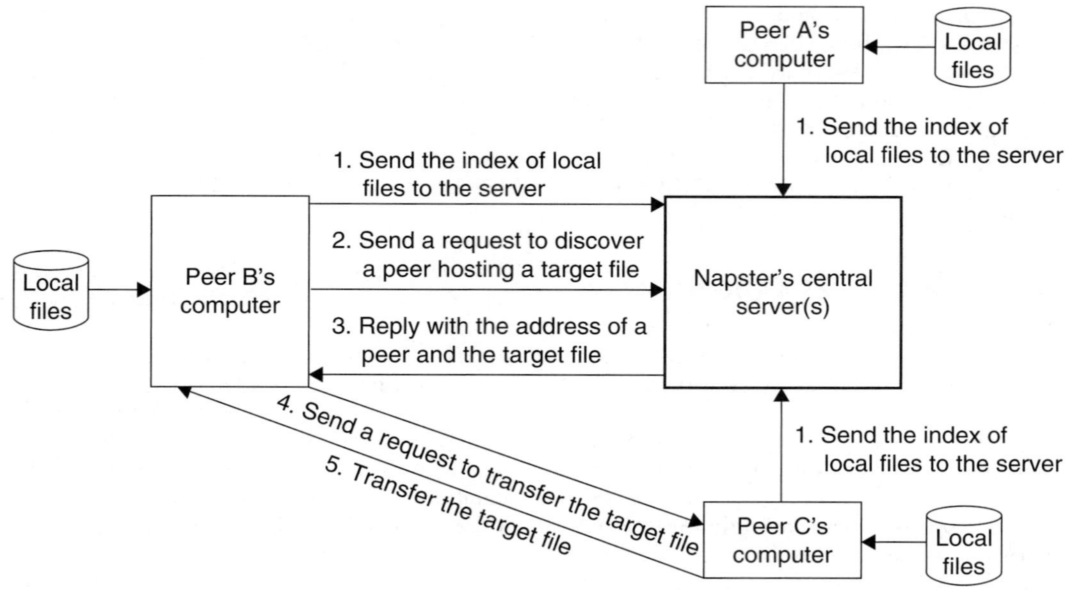

Figure 4: Operations of the Napster P2P network. The discovery process includes steps 2 and 3.

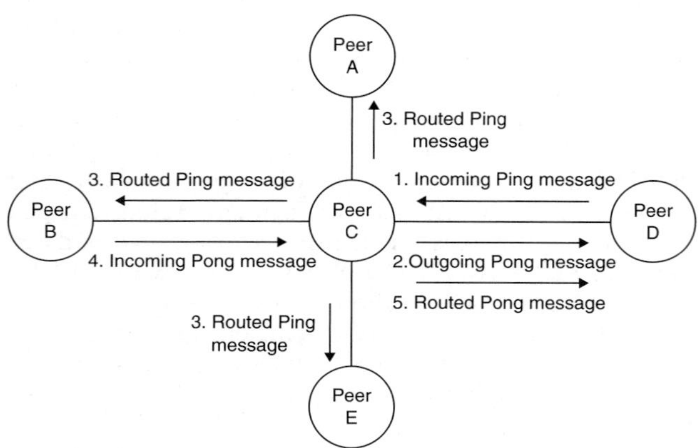

Figure 5: Gnutella discovery process

have a Time-To-Live (TTL) field that limits the message propagation range. A message ID field is used to uniquely identify each message so that a peer does not forward the same message more than once.

A gossip protocol randomly selects the peers to which a given message is forwarded (Portmann and Seneviratne 2002). Compared to the flooding technique, in which a message is forwarded to all peers except to the peer from which it was received, the gossip protocol is more scalable. Two additional parameters are specified: (1) the number of peers to which a message is forwarded, and (2) the times that a given peer forwards the same message. Since not all possible peers are forwarded to the first time, a peer needs to forward the same message more than once to find the remaining peers that the message has not been previously forwarded to.

In JXTA version 1.0, a peer announces its presence to the existing member peers by broadcasting within the local area network (LAN), and Rendezvous Points (RPs) are used to relay announcements and discovery requests (i.e., queries) beyond the LAN boundary. Figure 6 shows the basic peer discovery mechanism in JXTA version 1.0. Additional peer discovery mechanisms include discovery through invitation and cascaded discovery. A peer may be invited to know another peer by receiving the remote peer's IP address. In a cascaded discovery, after the first peer discovers the second peer, the first peer may view the peers that have already been discovered by the second peer.

JXTA version 2.0 organizes RPs into a loosely coupled network (Traversat et al. 2003). A hierarchical discovery is used, in which RPs form the higher tier. Each RP maintains its own rendezvous peer view (i.e., an ordered list of other known RPs). When a peer joins the network, the peer uses a hash function to map its name, possibly together with other attributes to an RP. Then the obtained RP and its surrounding neighbors keep the index to this new peer. RPs relay peer discovery requests to the proper RP. If the proper RP is unavailable, a limited-range random walker approach is used to find redundant RPs. JXTA peer discovery can be used in highly dynamic environments, since JXTA does not require all peers maintain a consistent view of peers that are present in the network.

Overlay Network Construction

A P2P network constructs an overlay network on top of the existing network infrastructure. In a practical-scale P2P network, it is difficult to create a direct virtual link between every pair of peers. Therefore, a multiple-hop overlay network topology needs to be formed to carry control messages. A peer sends messages to a few neighbors in the overlay network and relies on those neighbors to forward them to other peers. The data traffic may need to be carried over the same overlay network as well. Alternatively,

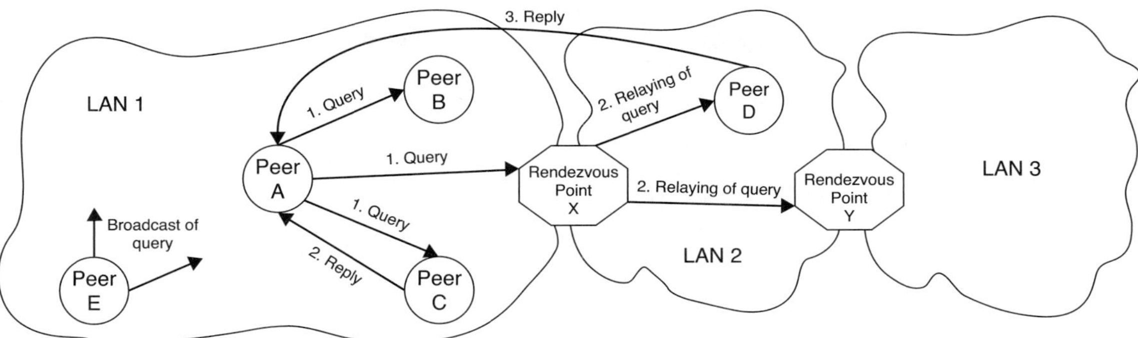

Figure 6: JXTA discovery mechanism

a virtual link may be dynamically created between the pair of peers that need to transfer data traffic. The overlay network construction consists of two key technologies: virtual link creation and virtual topology control.

A virtual link is created to connect a pair of peers, making them direct neighbors in the overlay network. A virtual link in the overlay network is a logical connection on top of the basic transport layer. If no interfering devices exist on the physical path between the two peers that want to create a virtual link, the two peers need only to know each other's IP address and transport layer port number. Then, one peer initiates a connection request to the other peer who is waiting for incoming requests. A transport layer connection can be easily created. However, firewalls, network address translators (NATs), proxies, or other interfering devices may exist on the physical path. Most firewalls allow outbound connections, so that internal users can access the external Internet, at least for selected protocols such as the Web browsing protocol hypertext transfer protocol (HTTP). But internal users may not be allowed to listen to any incoming connection request. NATs are used for a number of users to share IP addresses. The users are configured to use the NAT as their gateway. At the NAT, TCP connections are modified to use one of the small number of NAT external IP addresses. Different TCP port numbers allow the NAT to dispatch return packets to correct users. From outside, the users behind a NAT appear to have the same IP address. HTTP proxies have the same effect. Creating a virtual link across such interfering devices needs special techniques. One such technique is tunneling through firewalls using the HTTP protocol. When two peers are behind two different firewalls, they need the help of an intermediary party outside of both firewalls to create tunnels across those firewalls. The intermediary party listens for incoming requests, usually by running a Web server on the Internet that both peers can access. The peers then exchange their messages through the intermediary party.

The virtual topology of an overlay network has a profound impact on the performance of the overlay network. Ideally, the diameter of the topology should be controlled under a certain bound, so that the largest distance (either by hop counts or by communication latency) between two peers is acceptable. In addition, each peer connects to a number of other peers, providing sufficient fault tolerance and not being overloaded by the interactions with too many neighbors.

Different overlay network topologies have been developed, which can be categorized as unstructured and structured overlay networks. In an unstructured overlay network topology, peers are added in an ad hoc manner, resulting in a random and nondeterministic topology. For example, each peer randomly connects to a few of the already-connected peers. A random overlay network works very well, when all the peers in a P2P network are roughly equivalent in terms of their connectivity and processing power. A hierarchical topology can be used for the overlay network, in which peers have very diversified connectivity and processing power. An example is a two-tier hierarchy in which core peers (also known as supernodes) are suitable for forwarding messages and edge peers are not. The core peers form a mesh topology and the edge peers connect to the core peers.

A structured overlay network topology is created based on specific rules. Therefore, the overlay topology is tightly controlled. Peers together with their content or shared files are placed at precisely specified locations in the overlay network. A structured overlay network essentially provides a mapping between peers and their physical location in the form of a distributed routing table. To define the mapping rules, many attributes can be used, such as the identifiers of the shared files that a peer hosts, etc. Each peer has a list of its direct neighbor peers in the overlay network—i.e., a distributed hash table (DHT).

To create an overlay network based on a DHT, four techniques are used:

1. Generating unique numeric keys for data, and giving unique identifiers to peers.
2. Storing keys in peers. Each key is stored in one or more peers whose identifiers are "close" to the key.
3. Building routing tables adaptively. Each peer maintains information (e.g., the IP address) of a small number of other peers in routing tables. As peers join, leave, or fail, the routing tables need to be updated.
4. Forwarding a look-up for a key to an appropriate peer. A look-up for a key yields the network location of a peer that currently is responsible for the given key. Any peer that receives a query for the key must be able to forward the query to a peer whose identifier is "closer" to the key. Eventually, the query arrives at the peer that holds the key (Figure 7).

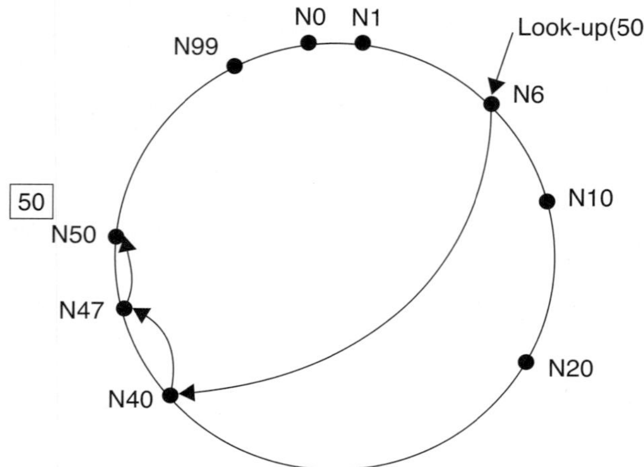

Figure 7: A look-up forwarding process in an overlay network based on a DHT. The numeric portion (s) of a peer's identifier happens to be the same as the key (k) that is held by the peer. The distance between a peer's identifier and a key is defined as $(k - s + S)$ *mod* S, where S is the total number of peers

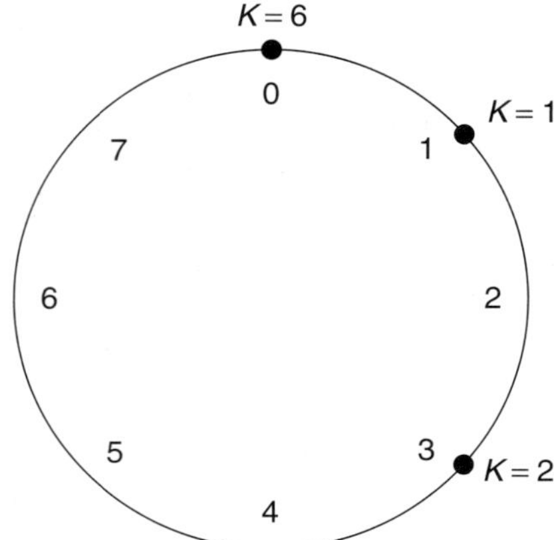

Figure 8: An example of three peers with identifiers 0, 1, and 3. Three keys—1, 2, and 6—are assigned to peers

A simple distributed file storage application based on a DHT can be built. Each file has a unique name, which can be converted into a numeric key using a hash function such as SHA-1 (secure hash algorithm 1). Then, the file is stored in the peers that are responsible for the key. A peer's file retrieval starts from a calculation of the key for the file. After that, the peer looks up for the key. If the peer does not host the file, the look-up is forwarded to an appropriate peer. The lookup forwarding continues until the peer that hosts the file is found.

Different overlay network topologies are used in different P2P networks—e.g., Chord (Stoica et al. 2001), Content Addressable Network (CAN) (Ratnasamy, Francis, et al. 2001), Pastry (Rowstron and Druschel 2001), Tapestry (Zhao et al. 2004), etc. Different overlay network topologies have different insertion overheads, measured by the number of messages for insertion when a peer joins a P2P network, different size of pointers to encode all peers and contents, and different maximum path lengths between two peers (Hildrum et al. 2002).

Chord defines a protocol to create overlay networks using a DHT (Stoica et al. 2001). It specifies how to find the locations of keys, how new peer nodes join the overlay network, and how to recover from failures or departures of peers. Each peer and key is assigned an m-bit numeric identifier. A peer's identifier can be derived by hashing the peer's IP address, while a key is generated by hashing the content, such as a filename, that is to be associated with the key. The identifier length m must be large enough so that it is very unlikely two peers (or two keys) are hashed to the same identifier. Identifiers are ordered in an "identifier circle" modulo 2^m. Key k is assigned to the first peer whose identifier is equal to or immediately after k on the identifier circle. Such a peer is called the successor of key k. Figure 8 shows the allocation of three keys to peer nodes in an overlay network.

To speed up the look-up process, Chord maintains additional routing information at each peer in the form of a "finger table." In the finger table of peer n, entry i ($1 \leq i \leq m$) points to the success of $n + 2i$. In this way, a finger table contains the IP addresses of peers halfway around the identifier circle from the peer, a quarter of the way, an eighth of the way, and so forth (Figure 9). A peer forwards a query for key k to the peer in the finger table with the highest identifier not exceeding k. Such look-up forwarding ensures that the look-up request can be forwarded at least halfway around the remaining identifier circle.

Chord provides a totally decentralized overlay network structure, in which no peer is more important than others. The storage of keys and processing of look-up requests are naturally balanced among peers. Chord can be used in very-large-scale overlay networks. In an N-peer overlay network, each peer maintains information about only a limited number of peers (i.e., $O(logN)$ peers). Each look-up request can be processed after no more than $O(logN)$ forwarding. A simple stabilization protocol is used to update the successor list and finger tables when peers join, leave, or fail.

Pastry is a mechanism to create tree-based, self-organizing overlay networks in the Internet (Rowstron and Druschel 2001; Castro et al. 2003). In Pastry, each peer node and key is assigned a numeric identifier with base 2^b, where b is a configuration parameter with a typical value of 4. A peer's routing table is organized into $\lceil \log_{2^b} N \rceil$ rows with $2^b - 1$ entries in each row, where N is the total number of peers. In row n of the routing table, each entry refers to a node whose peer identifier matches the present peer's identifier in the first n digits, but whose $(n + 1)$th digit is different from the present peer's identifier. In addition, each peer also maintains a leaf set—i.e., l number of peers among which half are closest larger identifiers and half are closest smaller identifiers compared to the present peer's identifier. l is an even integer parameter with a typical value of 16. The IP addresses of all peers in the routing table and leaf set are maintained. A look-up for a given key at the present peer starts from the present peer's leaf set. If the key is covered by the range of the leaf set, then the look-up is forwarded to the node in the leaf set whose identifier is closest to the key (possibly the present peer itself). If the key is not covered by the range of the leaf set, the look-up is forwarded to a peer that shares a common prefix with the key by at least one more digit. If no such closer peer

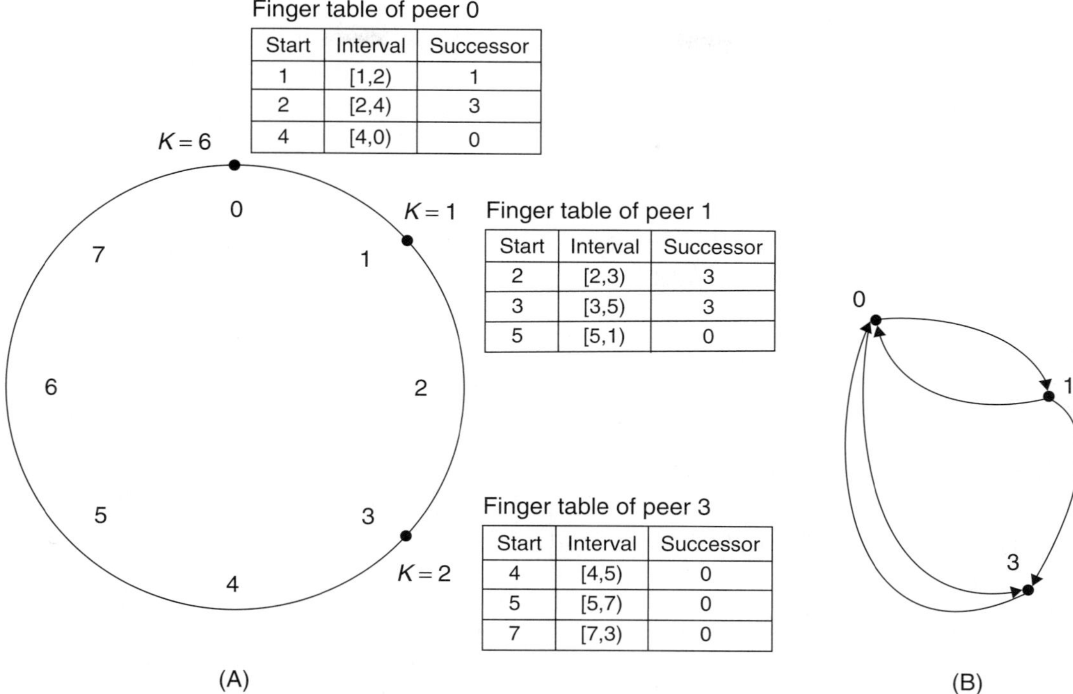

Finger table of peer 0

Start	Interval	Successor
1	[1,2)	1
2	[2,4)	3
4	[4,0)	0

Finger table of peer 1

Start	Interval	Successor
2	[2,3)	3
3	[3,5)	3
5	[5,1)	0

Finger table of peer 3

Start	Interval	Successor
4	[4,5)	0
5	[5,7)	0
7	[7,3)	0

Figure 9: Finger tables and the resultant overlay topology of an overlay network with peer nodes 0, 1, and 3. (A) Finger tables, where finger[k].start = $(n + 2^{k-1}) \bmod 2^m$, $1 \le k \le m$; interval = finger [k].start, finger[$k + 1$].start); successor(k) is the next peer node on the identifier circle and successor(k) $\ge$ finger[k].start. (B) The resultant overlay topology

exists, the look-up is forwarded to a peer that shares a prefix with the key at least as long as the present peer, but is numerically closer to the key than the present peer's identifier. Figure 10 shows the look-up-forwarding process in Pastry.

Pastry can efficiently handle look-ups and status updates in large-scale overlay networks. On average, a look-up from any peer can reach a target peer within $\lceil \log_{2^b} N \rceil$ steps. Even when multiple peers fail, a look-up can succeed unless $l/2$ or more peers with adjacent identifiers fail simultaneously. Each peer maintains only $(2^b - 1)^* \lceil \log_{2^b} N \rceil + l$ other peer's IP addresses. After a peer failure or the arrival of a new peer, the relevant routing tables can be updated by exchanging $O(\log_{2^b} N)$ messages.

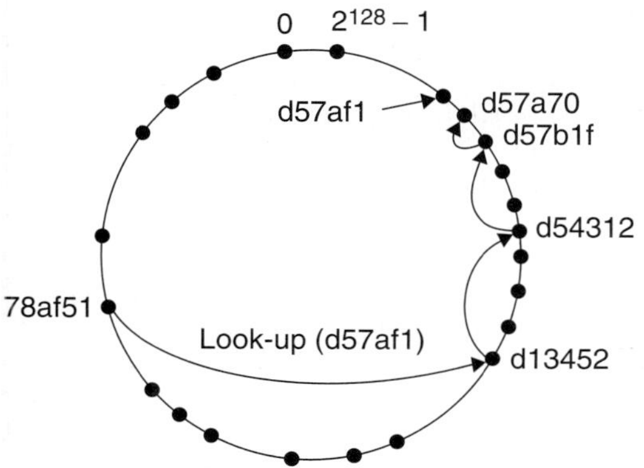

Figure 10: Forwarding a look-up from peer 78af51 for key d57af1 in Pastry. The dots indicate live peers in Pastry's namespace

CAN routes messages in a d-dimensional space, where each peer maintains a routing table with $O(d)$ entries (Ratnasamy, Francis, et al. 2001). On average, any peer can be reached in $(d/4)(N^{1/d})$ routing hops. The entries in a peer's routing table link to the peer's neighbours in the d-dimension space. When inserting a file into CAN, a set of keys are generated and mapped into diverse peers. In CAN, routing tables do not grow with the network size N. Only the number of routing hops grows (faster than $O(\log N)$, which is typical in other structured overlay networks).

Structured overlay networks (e.g., Chord, Pastry, CAN, etc.) are designed to support exact-match look-ups. The exact identifier (i.e., key) of a group of data must be known. Data are spread into peers with no consideration of data correlation. A comparison of different overlay networks is given in Milojicic et al. (2003), with respect to their models, parameters, hops to locate data, routing state, messages for a peer to join or leave, and reliability.

Application-Level Multicast

Multicast is the transmission of data to a group of receivers identified by a single destination address. In contrast, unicast is the transmission of data to a single receiver, and broadcast is the transmission of data to all possible receivers. The objective of multicast is to reduce the total amount of data traffic. Although IP layer multicast is available in some IP networks, few P2P networks use IP layer multicast for two reasons: (1) IP multicast cannot be used in conjunction with TCP, which is the transport layer protocol of choice in many P2P networks, and (2) IP multicast is not supported in every IP network. The key functions

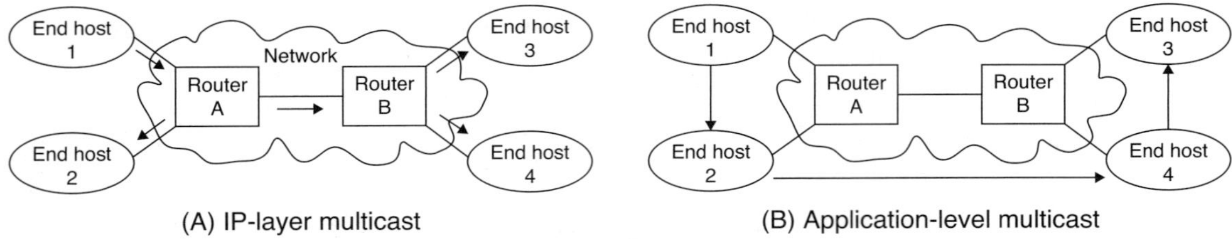

Figure 11: IP-layer multicast versus application-level multicast

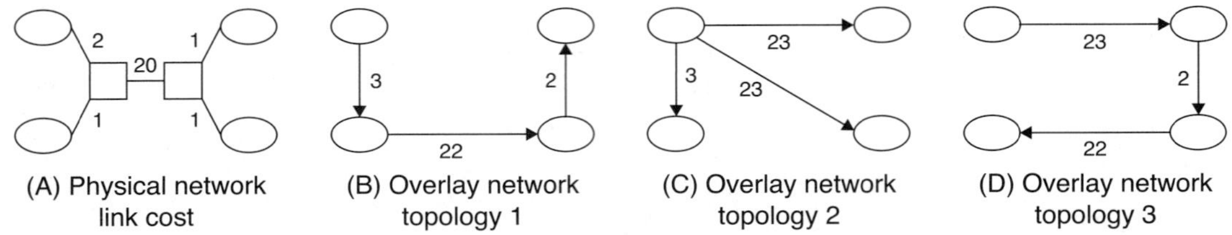

Figure 12: Different overlay network topologies lead to different total cost of the application-level multicast

to support multicast include group addressing mechanism, group maintenance, message-forwarding scheme, and multicast routing scheme. A group addressing mechanism provides a name or address as an alias for the members of a multicast group. Group maintenance supports members dynamically joining and leaving a group. When a message from a sender is forwarded to other group members, the message-forwarding scheme eliminates duplicate messages and avoids forwarding loops. The message-forwarding routes from a sender to all receivers in a multicast group is determined by a multicast routing scheme.

Application-level multicast offers a peer the capability of sending requests or announcements to a group of other peers in the same P2P network. Application-level multicast is the organization of peers in a point-to-multipoint (multicast) configuration—i.e., a delivery tree (Wierzbicki, Szezepaniak, and Buszka 2003). Application-level multicast in a P2P network can be achieved by broadcasting to a tailored overlay network, using a broadcast and filter approach to receive messages, or applying full-fledged multicast routing to an overlay network. Unlike IP layer multicast, in which data packets are replicated at routers inside the network, in application-level multicast, data packets are replicated at end hosts. Figure 11 illustrates the difference between IP-layer multicast and application-level multicast. The application-level multicast in Figure 11 does not rely on the IP-layer multicast function and is implemented on top of point-to-point IP packet delivery. However, application-level multicast incurs larger end-to-end delays than does IP multicast. Application-level multicast in a P2P network is provided over a reconfigurable overlay network topology. Thus, the integration of a multicast tree formation and an overlay network topology design may result in flexible networks and desirable performance. For example, an overlay network may be created by including only all the peers in a multicast group. The peers that want to join a multicast group can be added into the overlay network. Similarly, the peers that leave a multicast group can be withdrawn from the overlay network. By using the flooding-based broadcast mechanism solely at end hosts, application-level multicast can be achieved without changing the network infrastructure or relying on IP-layer multicast.

To optimize the performance of an overlay network, traffic patterns and the underlying physical network topology need to be considered. Figure 12 shows that different overlay network topology leads to different total costs of the application-level multicast. Some overlay network topologies do not consider the proximity to the underlying physical network, so concentration and congestion points may be formed in the physical network. For example, in the overlay network topology 2 and 3, traffic is concentrated on the costly link between the two routers. In a CAN implementation, a peer may measure its network delay to a set of landmark nodes, so that the relative position of the peer in the Internet is estimated. Such information can be used to optimize the overlay network topology. Some overlay networks (e.g., Tapestry and Pastry) choose physically nearby peers as neighbors. A performance analysis of structured overlay networks can be found in Hildrum et al. (2002).

Scribe is an application-level multicast mechanism built on top of Pastry (Castro, Druschel, Kermarrec, and Rowstron 2002). Any peer node may create a multicast group; other peers can then join the group to receive multicast messages, or send multicast messages to all members of the group when the sending peers have appropriate credentials. Each group has a unique identifier that consists of the hash of the group's textual name and its creator's name. Scribe elects the Pastry peer node whose identifier is numerically closest to the group identifier as the topic rendezvous point and root of the multicast tree. Each Scribe multicast member is connected to the root via Pastry connections. The peer nodes that are in the middle of Pastry connections from the root peer to members are called "forwarders," which may or may not be members of the group. Each forwarder maintains a children table for a group. When a peer joins or leaves a multicast group, at each peer along the route to the root, the children table is updated. In the basic Scribe mechanism, multicast messages are delivered in a best-effort manner, with no guarantee on delivery success and order. Additional guarantees can be built.

Narada uses a two-step approach to construct an application-level multicast (Chu et al. 2002). In the first step, a rich connectivity mesh is created for all group members. The path between any pair of members should have quality comparable to that of the underlying unicast path in terms of delay and bandwidth. To control the overhead of running routing algorithms on the mesh, each member should have only a limited number of neighbors in the mesh—not all members are neighbors to each other. However, Narada assumes that every member maintains a list of all other members in the group. Thus, Narada applies only to medium-sized groups. In the second step, Narada constructs spanning trees over the mesh topology obtained in the first step. Narada has advantages for several highly overlapped multicast groups. The overall group maintenance is reduced compared to maintaining individual multicast overlays.

Application-level multicast in CAN uses the routing tables maintained by CAN to flood messages to all peer nodes in a CAN overlay (Ratnasamy, Handley, et al. 2001). Therefore, no multicast tree is needed, and multicast traffic is not restricted to flow through a single multicast tree. When a peer joins a multicast group, the peer looks up a contact peer for the group in a global CAN overlay. Then the peer uses the contact peer to join the group's overlay. Only group members are involved in forwarding multicast messages in the CAN. The contact peer for the group is a performance bottleneck, since all members' join requests are handled by the contact peer.

In JXTA, application-level multicast is implemented the same way as JXTA peer discovery (Gong 2001; Traversat et al. 2003). Actually, JXTA multicasts a peer's announcement for the peer's presence and also multicasts a peer's request for discovery of other peers. Rendezvous points are used to facilitate multicast across the LAN multicast boundary.

The performance of the application-level multicast can be improved by adaptively changing the position of a peer in a multicast tree (Jannotti et al. 2000). Initially, a peer connects to the source peer itself. The source peer becomes the parent of the receiving peer in the multicast tree. Then, an iterative self-organization procedure is performed, in which the receiving peer tries to locate itself further away from the source peer. The bandwidth between the receiving peer and the current parent is measured on a direct virtual link and on indirect virtual links through each of the parent's children. If the bandwidth to the source peer does not decrease significantly, one of the children is chosen to replace the parent. The procedure stops when no suitable replacement for the parent is found from all current children. The peer periodically evaluates its position in the multicast tree by measuring the bandwidth through other children of its parent, directly through its parent, and directly through its grandparent. The peer moves down or up in the multicast tree according to the measurements. In addition, the peer keeps a list of its ancestors, which is used for reconnection if its parent goes offline.

Middleware Layer

The middleware layer of a P2P network is the system software modules that reside between P2P applications and the underlying overlay network, providing reusable services that can be composed, configured, and deployed to create P2P applications rapidly and robustly (Blair, Campbell, and Schmidt 2004).

Distributed Search

Functionally, a distributed search includes several logical steps: from keywords to names, then to addresses, and finally to the paths to target destinations (Mischke and Stiller 2004). A peer specifies the keywords that describe the desired partner peers, contents, and resources. A keyword search returns the names or identifiers that satisfy the keyword description. Such names and identifiers must be unique in the network and can be in the format of a uniform resource locator/identifier (URL/URI), filenames in a networked file system, etc. In the look-up step, the unique names are mapped into addresses in the network—e.g., IP addresses. Finally, routing is the process of finding paths and forwarding search messages to the target destinations. To optimize the efficiency of distributed search, three shortcut techniques are used, as shown in Figure 13: keyword routing (i.e., semantic routing or content routing that takes advantage of P2P overlay network topology), keyword look-up, and name routing. These shortcuts combine two or more logical steps into one action.

Index mechanisms are at the heart of P2P distributed searches. An index is a collection of pointers to places where data can be found. Index mechanisms play an

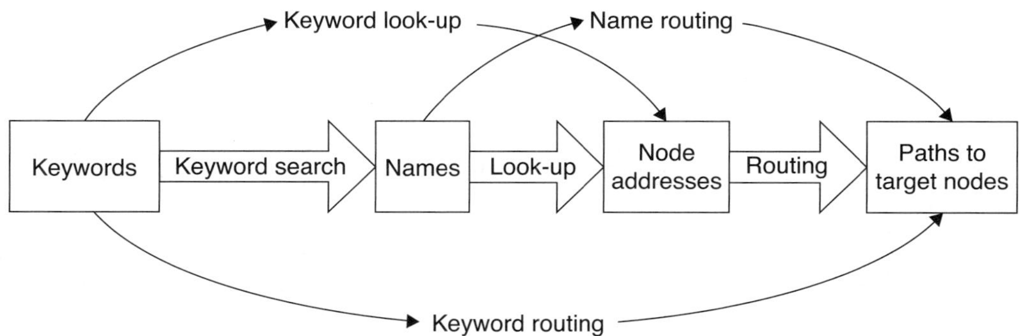

Figure 13: Logical steps in a distributed search (Mischke and Stiller 2004)

important role in keyword searches, look-ups, and routing. The search/index links model is useful in understanding the relation and difference of P2P search and index (Cooper and Garcia-Molina 2005). Peers in P2P search and index networks form a partially connected overlay. In the search/index links model, there are two types of information links in this overlay network: search links and index links. Search links are used to forward queries between peers. Index links are used to send copies of content indexes between peers.

A P2P search process is an organized query-forwarding process. When a peer receives a query for given data, the peer attempts to answer the query as best it can. If this peer cannot answer the query, the query is forwarded to other peers, which also attempt to answer the query. Whenever a peer finds data matching the query, the location of the matching data is returned to the peer that initiated the search. The representation of the location of the matching data can be a peer node name, a peer node address, or a path to a peer node.

A P2P index assists the search process. A P2P index is an organized indexing information relay process. A peer may choose to send indexing information to a neighbor peer to improve the efficiency of P2P search. For example, assuming peer Y has received peer X's indexing information, when peer Y receives a query, peer Y can process the query based on both peer Y's own index and peer X's index copy. In this way, peer Y does not need to forward the query to peer X.

As an example, the search/index links model can be used to describe the operation of the Kazaa P2P search network (shown in Figure 14). The three peers in the middle of the figure represent supernodes in Kazaa. Other peers send their indexes to supernodes over index links. Queries are forwarded to supernodes over search links. Queries are processed at the supernodes and then forwarded to other supernodes if necessary. Since ordinary peers (i.e., non-supernodes) only handle the search or index that belongs to themselves, there are neither search links nor index links pointing to ordinary peers.

Fundamentally, a P2P search requires a series of mappings, from the keyword space to the name space, then to the address space, eventually to the space of paths to peer nodes (Mischke and Stiller 2004). The mapping process in a P2P search can be classified based on a tree structure, such as that shown in Figure 15. Further information on distributed index and directory is provided in the section on Other Middleware.

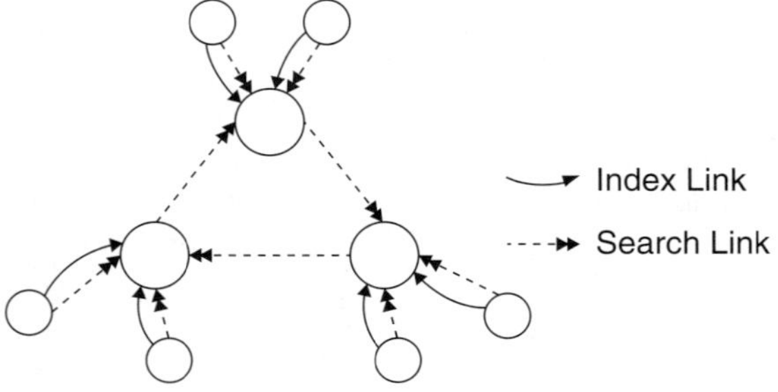

Figure 14: A representation of the Kazaa P2P search network using the search/index links model

Publish and Subscribe

Publish-subscribe is a middleware that supports sharing information among peers in a controlled manner. It provides the infrastructure on which the information-dissemination applications can be built. Publishers of information send messages (or events) to the publish-subscribe. Each message is associated with one or more subjects. In addition, each message may have a variety of attributes. Subscribers specify the subjects of the messages that they wish to receive. Subscribers may further specify under which conditions they are willing to receive the messages. Such conditions can be expressed in the format of equality tests and/or range values of the message attributes. Based on the flexibility and expressive power offered to subscribers to specify their interests, publish-subscribe can be categorized as subject-based (or topic-based) and content-based (or property-based). The content-based publish-subscribe may use brokers to match messages to interested subscribers. According to the decoupling of the communications between publishers and subscribers, publish-subscribe can be categorized along three dimensions: space, time, and synchronization decoupling (Eugster et al. 2003).

Although centralized publish-subscribe offers high throughput and reliability by using dedicated preconfigured servers, dynamically self-configured publish-subscribe is more attractive to large-scale P2P networks. The benefits and limitations of P2P networks that were discussed above generally apply to P2P publish-subscribe. In the P2P publish-subscribe, message producing, subscription, matching, and forwarding are distributed to peers.

P2P publish-subscribe can be implemented in two ways: broadcasting to all subscribers, or routing messages to subscriber groups possibly through brokers. In the first category, all messages are broadcast to all subscribers, regardless of subscribers' interests. Then, it is up to each subscriber to filter out the messages that are not of interest (Segall and Arnold 1997). Broadcasting to all subscribers is not efficient in a large P2P publish-subscribe. In the second category, a routing path for each message is created.

For subject-based publish-subscribe, application-level multicast is a readily available technique that can be used to send messages belonging to a specific subject to the subscribers along a multicast tree. Each subject needs a separate application-level multicast overlay. When a subscriber signs up for a subject, the subscriber joins the corresponding application-level multicast overlay. The publisher for a subject either becomes the root or sends messages to a proxy peer at the root of the corresponding application-level multicast tree (Castro, Druschel, Kermarrec, and Rowstron 2002; Zhuang et al. 2001). For content-based publish-subscribe, the key issues are the semantic expressiveness of content matching and the scalability of the matching mechanism. Brokers match the messages and identify the set of subscribers for the arrival messages. A peer node can be a publisher, a subscriber and a broker at the same time for different contents.

In content-based publish-subscribe, brokers are generally used to match and deliver messages. Siena and Gryphon allocate the responsibility of matching messages to a set

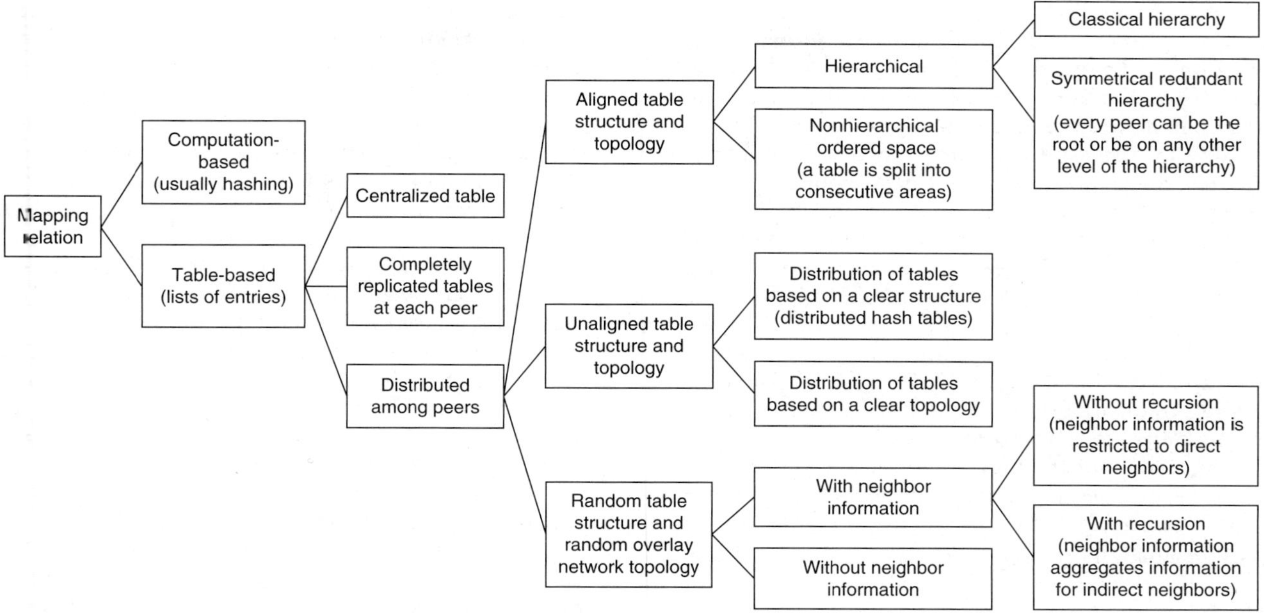

Figure 15: Classification of the mapping processes in a P2P search

of distributed broker servers (Carzaniga, Rosenblum, and Wolf 2001; Banavear et al. 1999). Messages follow a multicast tree to reach all matching subscribers. However, the self-organization capability of P2P networks is unavailable in Siena and Gryphon. Therefore, the broker servers require human intervention for set-up and management. In addition, Gryphon assumes that static subscription tables are maintained in all broker servers. Although messages are delivered only to related broker servers and eventually subscribers, subscription requests are flooded to all broker servers.

The event-distribution network (EDN) is a content-based publish-subscribe, built on top of a self-configuring overlay network of brokers (Wang et al. 2002). EDN partitions the content space into a set of disjoined partitions, and each partition is assigned to a broker. This approach minimizes message traffic by forwarding each message to only a single broker. However, subscriptions may need to be replicated to brokers. For equality tests, the attribute identifiers and values are hashed to generate a key to locate the broker managing the content partition. EDN also partitions subscription filters and assigns the partitions to different brokers. However, messages may need to be forwarded to multiple brokers. EDN is limited to a fixed set of subscriptions, and its applicability to high-dimensional content space is unclear.

A content-based publish-subscribe can be built on top of a DHT (Tam, Azimi, and Jacobsen 2003). The set of attributes and their values are hashed to decide the brokers managing the subscriptions (shown in Figure 16). The content space is partitioned by hashing a set of selected attributes and their values into brokers, similar to EDN. For the range values of an attribute, labels are used to represent intervals, and labels are also hashed to locate brokers. The fault tolerance is provided by the underlying DHT. Since brokers match messages and subscriptions based on keys hashed from selected attributes and labels, false matches are possible and should be filtered out by subscribers themselves. In addition, subscribers may receive duplicate messages, because one single subscription may be hashed into multiple keys. The subscriptions and messages are limited by the preselected attribute sets (i.e., templates).

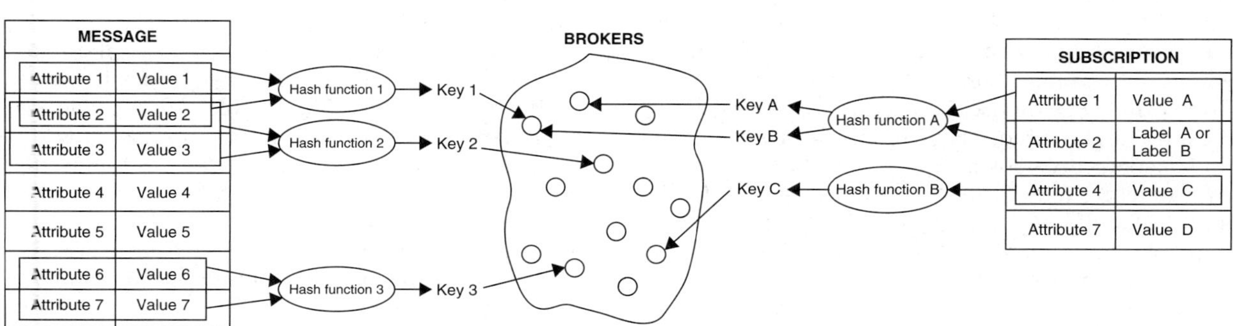

Figure 16: Hash messages and subscriptions to different brokers

Meghdoot uses CAN to build a content-based publish-subscribe (Gupta et al. 2004). Meghdoot imposes no restrictions on subscriptions or messages—i.e., no template is used. A subscription defines a rectangular region in the content space bounded by the minimal and maximal value specified. If the content space has D number of attributes, then a $2D$-dimension CAN is constructed from the minimal and maximal values of the D-dimension rectangles. A subscription is projected to a point in the $2D$-dimension CAN. A message is then mapped to a $2D$ space rectangle in which all relevant subscription points are covered.

A matching tree structure is used to organize subscriptions into hierarchical groups (C. Zhang et al. 2005). The matching tree supports multiple attribute types and allows customization of new attributes and filtering types. Messages can enter the publish-subscribe from any broker. A decentralized tree navigation algorithm is used to forward messages to tree fragments that may contain matching subscriptions.

Security

Security middleware for P2P networks is used to provide availability, privacy, confidentiality, integrity, and authentication. The attacks in P2P networks can be classified as attacks on services and attacks on data. Security middleware for P2P networks shares common security features of distributed systems, such as trust chains between peers and shared objects, session key exchange schemes, encryption, digital digests, and signatures. In addition, because of the open and autonomous nature of P2P networks, peers must be considered untrusted parties before authentications. Therefore, no assumptions can be made regarding a peer's behaviors.

In a P2P network, access keys for shared data may carry integrity verification information. When a peer inserts data into a P2P network, a cryptographic hash of the data is calculated and used to produce the data's unique access key. Since the hash function is known to all peers, when other peers retrieve the data using the unique access key, the data integrity can be verified by calculating a hash value of the retrieved data and comparing the hash value to the access key (Castro, Druschel, Ganesh, Rowstron, and Wallach 2002b).

Since P2P networks may rely on peers to forward requests and replies, a secure routing mechanism is used to prevent malicious peers from attempting to corrupt, delete, deny access to, or supply false copies of the requested data in P2P overlay networks (Castro, Druschel, Ganesh, Rowstron, and Wallach 2002). The secure routing mechanism consists of: (1) secure peer identifier assignment, (2) secure routing table maintenance, and (3) secure message forwarding. Secure peer identifier assignment uses a set of central and trusted certification authorities to prevent attackers from choosing identifiers. Without such a scheme, attackers may control all replicas of a given file or control all traffic to and from a victim peer. Secure routing-table maintenance ensures that faulty peers in routing tables do not exceed a certain percentage of total faulty peers in the entire P2P overlay network. Additional constrained routing tables are used when standard routing tables are compromised by attacks. Secure message forwarding, from time to time, tests the routes used to forward messages. If a route fails, redundant routing is used. It has been realized that the techniques for secure routing introduce significant overhead.

The high redundancy and distribution of P2P networks can be used for security purposes. A technique for sharing secrets among peers is to encrypt data with a symmetric key K, then split K into l shares (Waldman, Rubin, and Cranor 2000). An algorithm is available to guarantee that any r of the l shares can reproduce K, but K cannot be reproduced by any $(r - 1)$ shares (Shamir 1979). The algorithm is based on polynomial interpolation: given r points in the two dimensional plane $(x_1, y_1), \ldots, (x_i, y_i)$ with distinct x_i's, there is one and only one polynomial $q(x)$ of degree $(r - 1)$ such that $q(x_i) = y_i$ for all i. But, the polynomial $q(x)$ cannot be reconstructed by using only $(r - 1)$ or fewer points. In the proposed mechanism, a peer hosts all of the encrypted data and one of the l shares. When a peer tries to retrieve the data, the peer randomly chooses r other peers that host the shares, and downloads the r shares. From one of the r peers, the encrypted data are downloaded. The encryption key is reconstructed by using the r shares. Then the encrypted data are decrypted using the reconstructed key. If any of the r shares or the encrypted data are altered, the decryption detects the alteration and consequently fails. It is the retrieving peer's responsibility to redownload the encrypted data from other peers or to choose different combinations of shares.

Providing security and anonymity at the same time is a challenge. A peer may prefer to anonymously publish, store, or request certain data. The secret sharing mechanism based on the distributed storage of a split encryption key, which is described in the previous paragraph, offers publisher anonymity (Waldman, Rubin, and Cranor 2000). Anonymous cryptographic relays are used to allow peers, which act as publishers, forwarders, storers, and requesters, to communicate anonymously (Serjantov, 2002). Through anonymous connections, encrypted blocks of data are sent from a publisher to selected forwarders and then from the forwarders to storers. Once all the blocks are stored, the publisher destroys the original data and blocks in itself. The publisher announces the data description and a list of forwarders. A requester for the data contacts the forwarders and then the storers. The requester repeats the process until all blocks are downloaded. In this way, the publisher's anonymity is protected.

Freenet provides an anonymous method for storing and retrieving information (Milojicic et al. 2003). Each file in the Freenet system is identified by a key generated using a hash function. Usually a short text description of the file is hashed to generate a key pair. The public key becomes the file identifier. The private key is used to sign the file for integrity check. The file's key is made available to users by Web sites or other mechanisms. Freenet participants pass and forward messages to find the location of an existing file or the proper location to store a new file. The keys are used to assist in the routing of these messages. Freenet is completely decentralized. When a user joins the Freenet, the user must use other methods to find at least one peer.

In P2P networks, reputation mechanisms are useful in stimulating cooperative behaviors and providing accountability (Androutsellis-Theotokis and Spinellis 2004). Since strict measurement of individual peers' operation, performance, and availability may be difficult to apply in P2P networks, reputation is an alternative indicator. Reputation information is locally generated based on interactions between peers and is spread throughout the network to produce a global peer reputation rating. For example, global reputation values are computed from local reputation values assigned to a peer by other peers, weighted by the global reputation of the assigning peers. Another approach uses reputation computation agents, which are partially centralized. Then, the reputation values are encrypted and stored in such agents.

Other Middleware

Many generic functions in P2P networks can also be provided by middleware—e.g., distributed indexing, distributed directory, metadata, and scheduling. Distributed indexing can be used by applications such as a distributed storage application or a distributed file system. Distributed indexing middleware may use hash tables to map keywords of arbitrary length into a fixed-length hash value. Then the hash values are used to locate the entries corresponding to the keywords. A distributed directory middleware provides a name look-up service. A peer can look up the properties of an entity by specifying its name. Metadata middleware is used to describe the content stored in peers and may be queried to determine the location of desired information. Scheduling middleware is used in distributed computing or content-distribution applications. Computational tasks or contents are split into pieces and scheduled across peers.

Index middleware is used to store information about the location of data. In P2P networks, indexes need to be updated frequently, since peers join and leave the network constantly. Furthermore, the scalability of an index is critical, since an index may potentially be used for an Internet-scale network. A P2P index can be local, centralized, or distributed (Risson and Moors 2006). In a local index, a peer only maintains references to the peer's own data, and maintains no references to the data in other peers. Gnutella uses local indexes for each peer. Searches for data are flooded in the network. Actually, a search for data is equivalent to a search for the peers that host the data. The details of searches in Gnutella are described in the section on Peer Discovery. In a centralized index, a single server keeps references to data at all peers. Napster uses a centralized index. A centralized index is vulnerable to a single point of failure (or shutdown). The scalability issue of one single server for the entire network can be solved by linking multiple central servers. In a distributed index, pointers (direct or indirect) to data are stored in several peer indexes. The distribution of the indexes relies on the overlay networks. In a structured P2P overlay network, a peer maintains the index for the data assigned to the peer by the hash function. When searching for data, the hash value of the data is computed first. By using the hash value, the search is routed through the P2P overlay network to the peer that stores the data. When using unstructured P2P overlay networks for a distributed index, a peer may have one index summarizing the information of all peers on the path starting from this peer and within a predefined distance. Such an index can also be arranged for each of the peer's links, summarizing the information of all peers on the path starting from a link and within a predefined distance.

Distributed directory provides a name look-up service. A peer can look up the properties (including location) of an entity by specifying its name. Together with distributed index, distributed directory assists the P2P search process. The mapping process in distributed directory generally uses distributed tables as shown in Figure 15.

Metadata middleware is used to provide interoperability for different data formats. Based on the schemes to represent data, P2P networks can be classified as three types: hash key–based, fixed schema or keyword-based, and schema-based. The former two types provide only domain-specific data formats. The last type intends to provide a unified scheme to represent data, which can be understood beyond specific domains. Metadata are machine-understandable structured information about Web resources, data, or other information resources. XML schemas are the standard metadata proposed by the World Wide Web Consortium (W3C). XML schemas express shared vocabularies and enable machines to carry out rules made by people. XML schema is a tool to define the structure, content and semantics of XML documents. The resource description framework (RDF) is based on attribute-value pairs to represent information on the Web. The Edutella project specifies and implements an RDF-based metadata infrastructure for P2P networks (Nejdl et al. 2002). Metadata operations are organized as: (1) query service—standardized query and retrieval of RDF metadata, (2) replication service—providing data persistence/availability and workload balancing to maintain data integrity and consistency, (3) mapping service—translating between different metadata vocabularies to enable interoperability between different peers, (4) mediation service—solving conflicting and overlapping information from different metadata sources, and (5) annotation service.

Scheduling middleware coordinates the execution time of the subtasks that are distributed to multiple peers. Computational subtasks are distributed and scheduled to peers in computational P2P networks. For content-distribution P2P networks, the subtasks can be at the stream or packet level. Pixie uses a scheduling middle-ware to coordinate multimedia streams (Rollins and Almeroth 2002). When a peer joins a P2P network and retrieves a content-distribution stream, the peer browses the schedule and chooses a scheduled distribution stream. Alternatively, the peer may request a new distribution stream to be scheduled. When a scheduled distribution stream starts, the source peer distributes the stream to all subscribed peers. Large-scale P2P live media streaming requires stringent playback quality, network scalability, and robustness to the high churn rate of peers and fluctuation of network conditions. Packet-level scheduling middleware is critical to meet such requirements (Zhang, Zhao, Tang, Luo, and Yang, 2005). GridMedia uses the scheduling middleware to fetch absent packets from a peer's neighbors and deliver packets requested by the neighbors. Each sending peer records the largest sequence number of the packets that are pushed to each neighbor. When a just-received packet is far behind the packets that have been pushed to a neighbor, the new arrival packet is not relayed to the neighbor. Each receiving peer records the largest sequence number of the packets that are pushed from each neighbor. When a missing packet's sequence number falls behind the largest sequence number of the packets that are received from a neighbor by a threshold, the missing packet will be pulled from that neighbor. To cope with peer and network failures, when no packets have been pushed from a neighbor for a time-out period, all the packets that should have been pushed by this neighbor will be pulled from other neighbors.

Application Layer

P2P network applications can be classified into three categories: parallel computing, content and file management, and collaborative applications (Milojicic et al. 2003). Computationally intensive applications can be split into smaller pieces, which are executed in parallel over a large number of independent peers. In many cases, the same task is performed on each peer using different sets of parameters. P2P networks for content and file management use spare storage space and bandwidth. Different content- and file-management applications use different replication and search techniques. P2P file sharing and multimedia streaming are popular applications. Collaborative P2P networks allow peers to collaborate in real time, not relying on a centralized server to collect and forward information. Instant messaging, interactive gaming, Internet telephony and videoconferencing, and mobile ad hoc networking are examples of collaborative applications. More detailed discussions on P2P network applications are given in Chapter 145.

CONCLUSION

P2P networks are evolving technologies. Many exciting applications have been developed over the past few years. P2P networks have demonstrated their potential in many challenging environments and applications. The P2P network architecture will never completely replace other network architectures, such as the client/server architecture, but for particular applications, the P2P network architecture complements other network architectures.

The layered architecture of P2P networks abstracts the relations of different functions. However, different implementations of P2P networks may make design choices to use more efficient architectures. The reference P2P network architecture consists of three layers: the base overlay layer, the middleware layer, and the application layer. The base overlay layer provides peer discovery, overlay network construction, and application-level multicast. With the base overlay layer, P2P networks can be formed on top of existing physical networks by directly interacting between end users. The middleware layer offers distributed search, publish and subscribe, security, distributed indexing, distributed directory, metadata, and scheduling. The middleware layer provides some common functions that can be reused in different P2P networks. Although we are still a long way from providing interoperability between different P2P network implementations, building common middleware is an effort in that direction.

Because P2P networks are evolving very quickly in very diversified directions, this chapter is by no means complete. As many people working in the area of P2P networks have pointed out, a P2P network is more of a mindset, rather than a specific technology.

GLOSSARY

Anonymity: A peer's anonymous participation in a P2P network, and preference of keeping its communication with others private. The peer may want to protect its identity from being known to third parties, or even to its communicating partners. The peer may not want its communication activities to be monitored by third parties.

Application Level Multicast: A function through which a peer is capable of sending requests or announcements to a group of other peers in the same P2P network. Application-level multicast is the organization of peers in a point-to-multipoint (multicast) configuration—i.e., a delivery tree.

Autonomy: Each peer's autonomous decisions regarding when it joins or leaves a P2P network. No central authority should force a peer to join a P2P network or cut off a peer's access to a P2P network. Each peer should be responsible for its own actions. Based on personal judgment and preference, the peer should decide the time to join or leave a P2P network, the resources it contributes to a P2P network, and the services it uses.

Client: A process using a service. In the context of networks, a client refers to a communication process receiving information from others or getting connected to others by the means of transit services. A client process initiates service requests to others.

Hash Function: A method of transforming data into a number. Hash functions provide a way of creating a small digital "fingerprint" from any kind of data. The function abstracts and mixes (i.e., substitutes or transposes) the data to create the fingerprint (i.e., a hash value).

Metadata: A structured description of an object or collection of objects. Metadata are information about a particular dataset, which may describe, for example, how, when, and by whom it was received, created, accessed, and/or modified and how it is formatted.

Middleware: Software that mediates between an applications program and a network. In P2P networks, middleware refers to the system software modules that reside between P2P applications and the underlying overlay network, providing reusable services that can be composed, configured, and deployed to create P2P applications rapidly and robustly.

Overlay Network: A virtual network built on top of another network. Nodes in an overlay network are connected by virtual or logical links, each of which corresponds to a path, perhaps through many physical links, in the underlying network. P2P networks are overlay networks because they run on top of the Internet.

Overlay networks can be classified as structured or unstructured.

Peer: An equal, which can be informally interpreted as a process with capability similar to the other processes with which this process communicates. In the context of peer-to-peer networks, a "peer" process acts as a client process and at the same time as a server process for the same function.

Peer Discovery: The process through which a peer knows the existence of other peers in the same P2P network. A peer may discover a few other peers and with the help of these peers get to know more peers. Peer discovery needs to find out the identities of other peers—e.g., the IP addresses of other peers. A peer needs to discover the other peers' port number if the P2P network does not use a fixed port.

Peer-to-Peer (P2P) Network: A network in which resources and files are shared without centralized management. P2P networks are identified using three criteria: self-organizing, symmetric connection, and decentralized control. Peers organize themselves into a network in a collaborative manner. Peers are considered equals by requesting and offering similar services to each other. Peers communicate in a symmetric pattern, not being confined to either client or server roles. Peers share resources, while peers determine their level of participation and their actions autonomously. Generally, there is no central controller that dictates the behaviors of individual peers.

Publish and Subscribe: Middleware that supports sharing information among peers in a controlled manner. It provides the infrastructure on which the information-dissemination applications can be built. Publishers of information send messages (or events) to the publish-subscribe. Each message is associated with one or more subjects. In addition, each message may have a variety of attributes. Subscribers specify the subjects of the messages that they wish to receive. Subscribers may further specify under which conditions the subscribers are willing to receive the messages.

Rendezvous Point: A device that connects to more than one network, and is used to relay announcements, discovery requests, and queries beyond the broadcast boundary of a network.

Scalability: The ability to scale to support larger or smaller volumes of data and more or fewer users. It also refers to the ability to increase or decrease size or capability in cost-effective increments.

Server: A process offering services. In networks, a server process hosts information for client processes to search, download, and so on.

Structured Overlay Network: A type of overlay network, created based on specific rules. Peers together with their content or shared files are placed at precisely specified locations in the structured overlay networks.

Unstructured Overlay Network: A type of overlay network in which peers are added in an ad hoc manner, resulting in a random and nondeterministic topology.

CROSS REFERENCES

See *Incentive Issues in Peer-to-Peer Systems; Peer-to-Peer Network Applications.*

REFERENCES

Androutsellis-Theotokis, S., and D. Spinellis. 2004. A survey of peer-to-peer content distribution technologies. *ACM Computing Surveys* 36(4):335–371.

Banavear, G., T. Chandra, B. Mukherjee, J. Nagarajarao, R. E. Strom, and D. C. Sturman. 1999. An efficient multicast protocol for content-based publish-subscribe systems. *Proceedings of the 19th International Conference on Distributed Computing Systems (ICDCS), May 31 – June 4, 1999, Austin, TX*, 262–72.

Barkai, D. 2001. *Peer-to-peer computing: Technologies for sharing and collaborating on the Net*. Hillsboro, OR: Intel Press.

Blair, G., A. T. Campbell, and D. C. Schmidt. 2004. Middleware technologies for future communication networks. *IEEE Network* 18(1):4–5.

Carzaniga, A., D. S. Rosenblum, and A. L. Wolf. 2001. Design and evaluation of a wide-area event notification service. *ACM Transactions on Computer Systems*, 19 (3):332–83.

Castro, M., P. Druschel, A. Ganesh, A. Rowstron, and D. S. Wallach. 2002. Secure routing for structured peer-to-peer overlay networks. *Proceedings of the 5th USENIX Symposium on Operating Systems Design and Implementation (OSDI 2002), Boston, MA* Berkeley, CA: USENIX Association.

Castro, M., P. Druschel, Y. C. Hu, and A. Rowstron. 2003. Proximity neighbor selection in tree-based structured peer-to-peer overlay. Technical Report MSR-TR-2003-52, 2003. http://research.microsoft.com/%7Eantr/PAST/location-msrtr-2003-52.pdf (accessed April 26, 2007).

Castro, M., P. Druschel, A. Kermarrec, and A. Rowstron. 2002. Scribe: A large-scale and decentralized application-level multicast infrastructure. *IEEE Journal on Selected Areas in Communications* 20(8):1489–99.

Chu, Y., S. G. Rao, S. Seshan, and H. Zhang. 2002. A case for end system multicast. *IEEE Journal on Selected Areas in Communications* 20(8):1456–71.

Cooper, B. F., and H. Garcia-Molina. 2005. Ad hoc, self-supervising peer-to-peer search networks. *ACM Transactions on Information Systems* 23(2):169–200.

Dougherty, D. 2001. All the pieces of PIE. In *2001 P2P networking overview: The emergent P2P platform of presence, identity, and edge resource*, edited by C. Shirky, K. Truelove, R. Dornfest and L. Gonze. Sebastopol, CA: O'Reilly Research.

Eugster, P. T. H., P. A. Felber, R. Guerraoui, and A. Kermarrec. 2003. The many faces of publish/subscribe. *ACM Computing Surveys* 35(2):114–31.

Feldman, M., and J. Chuang. 2005. Overcoming free-riding behavior in peer-to-peer systems. *ACM SIGecom Exchanges* (5):41–50.

Gong, L. 2001. JXTA: A network programming environment. *IEEE Internet Computing* 5(3):88–95.

Gupta, A., O. D. Sahin, D. Agrawal, and A. E. Abbadi. 2004. *Meghdoot: Content-based publish/subscribe over P2P networks. Proceeding Hans-Arno Jacobsen (Ed.): Middleware 2004, ACM/IFIP/USENIX International Middleware Conference, Toronto, Canada, October 18–20, 2004, Proceedings. Springer 2004, ISBN 3-540-23428-4 of Middleware 2004*. Heidelberg, Germany: Springer verlag Lecture Notes in Computer Science 3231: 254.

Hildrum, K., J. Kubiatowicz, S. Rao, and B. Zhao. 2002. Distributed object location in a dynamic network. *Proceedings of the 14TH ACM Symposium on Parallel Algorithms and Architectures (SPAA 2002), Winnipeg, Canada*, pp. 41–52. New York: ACM Press.

Jannotti, J., D. K. Gifford, K. L. Johnson, M. F. Kaashoek, and J. W. O'Toole, Jr. 2000. Overcast: Reliable multicasting with an overlay network. *Proceedings of the 4th Symposium on Operating System Design & Implementation (OSDI 2000), San Diego, CA*, 197–212. Berkeley, CA: USENIX Association.

Loo, A. W. 2003. The future of peer-to-peer computing. *Communications of the ACM*. 46(9):57–61.

Miller, M. 2001. *Discovering P2P*. San Francisco, CA: SYBEX.

Milojicic, D. S., V. Kalogeraki, R. Lukose, K. Nagaraja, J. Pruyne, B. Richard, S. Rollins, and Z. Xu. 2003. Peer-to-peer computing. Technical Report HPL-2002-57R1. HP Laboratories. http://www.hpl.hp.com/techreports/2002/HPL-2002-57R1.html

Minami, H., S. Kamei, and H. Saito. 2004. Peer selection for parallel downloading in peer-to-peer file-sharing systems. *Proceedings of the 19th World Telecommunication Congress incorporationg the International Switching Symposium (WTC/ISS 2004). Seoul, Korea*. Piscataway, NJ: IEEE Press.

Mischke, J., and B. Stiller. 2004. A methodology for the design of distributed search in P2P middleware. *IEEE Network* 18(1):30–7.

Mouftah, H., and P. Ho. 2002. *Opticals networks: Architecture and survivability*. Boston: Kluwer.

Myles, G., A. Friday, and N. Davies. 2003. Preserving privacy in environments with location-based applications. *IEEE Pervasive Computing* 2(1):56–64.

Nejdl, W., B. Wolf, C. Qu, S. Decker, M. Sintek, A. Naeve, M. Nilsson, M. Palmér, and T. Risch. 2002. EDUTELLA: A P2P networking infrastructure based on RDF. *Proceedings of the 11th International Conference on World Wide web (WWW 2002), Honolulu, HI*, 604–15. New York: ACM Press.

Pfitzmann, A., and M. Waidner. 1987. Networks without user observability. *Computers and Security* 2(6): 158–66.

Portmann, M., and A. Seneviratne. 2002. The cost of application-layer broadcast in a fully decentralized peer-to-peer network. *Proceedings of the 7th International Symposium on Computers and Communications (ISCC 2002), July 2002, Taormina–Giardini Naxos, Italy*. 941–46. Piscataway, NJ: IEEE Press.

Ratnasamy, S., P. Francis, M. Handley, R. Karp, and S. Shenker. 2001. A scalable content-addressable network. *Proceedings of the ACM 2001 Conference on Applications, Technologies, Architectures, and Protocols for computer Communications (SIGCOMM 2001), August 2001, San Diego, CA* 161–72. New York: ACM Press.

Ratnasamy, S., M. Handley, R. Karp, and S. Shenker. 2001. Application-level multicast using content-addressable networks. *Proceedings of the 3rd International Workshop on Networked Group Communication London*, November 2001, 14–29. Heidelberg, Germany: Springer Verlag Lecture Notes in Computer Science, 2233.

Reiter, M. K., and A. D. Rubin. 1998. Crowds: Anonymity for web transactions. *ACM Transaction on Information and System Security* 1(1):66–92.

Risson, J., and T. Moors. 2006. Survey of research towards robust peer-to-peer networks: Search methods. *Computer Networks* 50(17):3485–521.

Rollins, S., and K. C. Almeroth. 2002. Pixie: A jukebox architecture to support efficient peer content exchange. *Proceeding of the 10th ACM International Conference on Multimedia (Multimedia 2002), December 1–6, 2002, Juan-les-Pins, France* 179–88. New York: ACM Press.

Roussopoulos, M., M. Baker, D. S. H. Rosenthal, T. J. Giuli, P. Maniatis, and J. Mogul. 2004. 2 P2P or not 2 P2P? In, *peer-to-peer systems III: Revised Selected Papers from the Third International Workshop on Peer-to-Peer Systems (IPTPS 2004), La Jolla, CA, February 2004*, 33–43. Heidelberg, Germany: Springer Verlag Lecture Notes in Computer Science, 3279.

Rowstron, A., and P. Druschel. 2001. Pastry: Scalable, distributed object location and routing for large scale peer-to-peer systems. *Proceedings of the 18th IFIP/ACM International Conference on Distributed Systems Platforms (Middleware), Heidelberg, Germany*. November 2001, 329–50. London: Springer Verlag Lecture Notes in Computer Science, 2218.

Saroiu, S., P. K. Gummadi, and S. D. Gribble. 2002. A measurement study of peer-to-peer file sharing systems. *Proceedings of the SPIE/ACM Conference on Multimedia Computing and Networking (MMCN 2002), San Jose, CA, January 2002*, 156–70. Bellingham, WA: SPIE. Proceedings of the WPIE, 4673.

Schoder, D., K. Fischbach, and C. Schmitt. 2004. Core concepts in peer-to-peer networking. In *peer-to-peer computing: The evolution of a disruptive technology*, edited by R. Subramanian and B. D. Goodman, 1–27. Hershey, PA: Idea Group Publishing.

Schollmeier, R. 2001. A definition of peer-to-peer networking for the classification of peer-to-peer architectures and applications. 2001. *Proceedings of the 1st IEEE International Conference on Peer-to-Peer Computing, LinKöping, Sweden*, 101–2.

Segall, B., and D. Arnold. 1997. Elvin has left the building: A publish/subscribe notification service with quenching. *Proceedings of the 1997 Australian UNIX and Open Systems Users Group Conference* Berkeley, CA: USENIX Association.

Serjantov, A. 2002. Anonymizing censorship resistant systems. *Proceedings of the 1st International Workshop on Peer-to-Peer Systems (IPTPS 2002), Cambridge, MA* New York: Springer Verlag Lecture Notes in Computer Science, 2429.

Shamir, A. 1979. How to share a *Communications of the ACM* 22(11):612–3.

Shirky, C. 2000. *What is P2P … and what isn't*. O'Reilly network. (www.openp2p.com/pub/a/p2p/2000/11/24/shirky1-whatisp2p.html (accessed April 26, 2007).

Stoica, I., R. Morris, D. Karger, M. F. Kaashoek, and H. Balakrishnan. 2001. Chord: A scalable peer-to-peer lookup service for internet applications. *Proceedings of the ACM 2001 Conference on Applications, Technologies, Architectures, and Protocols for Computer Communications (SIGCOMM 2001), August 2001, San Diego, CA*, 149–60. New York: ACM Press.

Sunaga, H., T. Hoshiai, S. Kamei, and S. Kimura. 2004. Technical trends in P2P-based communications. *IEICE Transaction on Communications* E87-B (10):2831–45.

Tam, D., R. Azimi, and H. Jacobsen. 2003. Building content-based publish/subscribe systems with distributed hash tables. *Proceedings of International Workshop on Databases, Information Systems and Peer-to-Peer Computing, Berlin, Germany*. September 2003. New York: Springer Verlag Lecture Notes in Computer Science, 2944.

Traversat, B., A. Arora, M. Abdelaziz, M. Duigou, C. Haywood, J. Hugly, E. Pouyoul, and B. Yeager. 2003. Project JXTA 2.0 super-peer virtual network. May 25, 2003, JXTA White Paper. www.jxta.org/project/www/docs/JXTA2.0protocols1.pdf (accessed April 26, 2007).

Verma, D. C. 2004. *Legitimate applications of peer-to-peer networks*. New York: Wiley.

Waldman, M., A. D. Rubin, and L. F. Cranor. 2000. Publics A robust, tamper-evident, censorship-resistant web publishing system. *Proceedings of the 9th USENIX Security Symposium. Denver, CO*, August 2000. 59–72. Berkeley, CA: USENIX Association.

Wang, Y. M., L. Qiu, D. Achlioptas, G. Das, P. Larson, and H. J. Wang. 2002. Subscription partitioning and routing in content-based publish/Subscription Networks. *Proceedings of the 16th International Symposium on Distributed Computing* Washington, DC: IEEE Computer Society Press.

Wierzbicki, A., R. Szezepaniak, and M. Buszka. 2003. Application layer multicast for efficient peer-to-peer applications. *Proceedings of the 3rd IEEE Workshop on Internet Applications (WIAPP 2003), San Jose, CA*, 126–30. Washington, DC: IEEE Computer Society Press.

Zhang, C., A. Krishnamurthy, R. Y. Wang, and J. P. Singh. 2005. Combining flexibility and scalability in a peer-to-peer publish/subscribe system. Proceedings of Middleware 2005. Lecture Notes in Computer Science 3790, p. 102.

Zhang, M., L. Zhao, Y. Tang, J. Luo, and S. Yang. 2005. Large-scale live media steaming over peer-to-peer networks through global Internet. *Proceedings of the ACM Workshop on Advances in Peer-to-Peer Multimedia Streaming (P2PMMS 2005), NOVEMBER 11, 2005, Singapore*, 21–8. New York: ACM Press.

Zhao, B. Y., L. Huang, J. Stribling, S. C. Rhea, A. D. Joseph, and J. Kubiatowicz. 2004. Tapestry: A resilient global-scale overlay for service deployment. *IEEE Journal on Selected Areas in Communications* 22(1):41–53.

Zhuang, S. Q., B. Y. Zhao, A. D. Joseph, R. Katz, and J. Kubiatowicz. 2001. Bayeux: An architecture for scalable and fault-tolerant wide area data dissemination. *Proceedings of International Workshop on Network and OS Support for Digital Audio and Video*. New York: ACM Press.

Peer-to-Peer Network Applications

Stan Kurkovsky, *Central Connecticut State University*

INTRODUCTION

The term *peer-to-peer* appeared at the forefront of the public awareness around 1999, when the first version of Napster was released by Shawn Fanning. Since then, this term has been associated with illegal file sharing, copyright infringement, and lawsuits. Despite such a reputation, peer-to-peer (P2P) systems can be and are used in a very diverse range of application domains—to build virtual communities, to create reliable storage systems, and to solve large computational problems, to name a few.

Peer-to-peer systems are built around the concept of a "peer"—an individual computer providing its computational power, storage space, and bandwidth, and equipped with the corresponding software enabling it to join the P2P network. In a pure P2P system, there are no clients or servers—only peer computer nodes that do not require a centralized server to communicate with each other. Such P2P systems increase their performance, speed, and capacity as the number of peers increases. In contrast, in a typical client/server system with a fixed number of servers, adding more clients may result in a degraded system performance. The very concept of peer-to-peer eliminates a single point of failure because removing one or more peers from the network should not result in a diminished overall system performance caused by the replication of data stored among multiple peers and the redundancy of the network communication paths.

This chapter briefly surveys historical roots of P2P systems, from their origins to current and future developments, followed by a discussion of different application domains in which P2P systems are used today, in particular communication and collaboration, file sharing, distributed storage, and massively parallel computations. The chapter includes discussion of a wide variety of sample P2P network applications, illustrating their use in different application domains.

WHAT IS PEER-TO-PEER?

An examination of the current state of the art in peer-to-peer network applications requires establishing a criterion that would determine what a P2P system is. However, there is no clear consensus in the literature about a single definition of what "peer-to-peer" is. In the strictest sense, a pure P2P system is a distributed system in which nodes have completely equivalent functionality and range of tasks they can perform. This definition implies that each peer in the network acts both as a client and as a server in communication among the peers and that there is no central server responsible for managing the P2P network. Many existing P2P systems, however, do not fall into the category of a pure peer-to-peer system because most of them have one or more centralized servers, "supernodes" (in FastTrack network used by Kazaa, Grokster, and iMesh applications), or "ultrapeers" (in Gnutella network used by a wide range of P2P file-sharing applications) that are used for managing communication among the peers. A widely accepted but much broader definition of P2P systems (Shirky 2000) describes them as "a class of applications that takes advantage of resources—storage, cycles, content, human presence—available at the edges of the Internet." Although this definition includes the true P2P systems mentioned above, it also covers many systems that rely on a central server, such as file-sharing systems (e.g., FastTrack and Overnet), a range of instant messaging systems, massively parallel computing systems (e.g., SETI@Home and Folding@Home), and Grid computing applications. This definition focuses not so much on the internal technical aspects of the system's architecture, but rather on an external perception of a system that provides for a direct communication among peers.

To address the full range of P2P network applications, it is important to mention two characteristics of a distributed system that qualify it as a peer-to-peer system. First, a P2P system must enable peer computers to share their resources with possible assistance from some kind of a centralized authority. Peers actively participate in the overall functioning of the network by performing tasks that are intrinsic to the operation of a P2P system, such as storing and locating content, routing communication messages, and locating, querying, and responding to requests from other peers, etc. Central server(s), if any, usually have a secondary role in the P2P system operation, such as assisting peers to join the network and helping them locate and establish a connection with other peers. However, central servers play a much more prominent role in some P2P network applications, in particular, in massively parallel computing systems described later in this chapter.

Second, P2P systems must be able to function effectively in conditions of varying network connectivity and constantly changing population of peers. A P2P system must be fault-tolerant and self-organizing by design, which requires having a network topology that will be adaptive to transient nodes and network connection failures (Androutsellis-Theotokis and Spinellis 2004).

HISTORICAL ROOTS OF P2P APPLICATIONS

Although the term *peer-to-peer* may be relatively new, the Internet itself was essentially conceived around the very same concept. In the 1960s, the main objective of ARPANET, the precursor to the Internet of today, was to effectively share computational resources scattered around the country. The underlying challenge was to enable communication among computers situated in the existing and future heterogeneous networks by introducing a sort of unified communication infrastructure among peer computers with equal rights (Minar and Hedlund 2001). Despite the fact that the early Internet was designed as a network of equal peers, the two original "killer apps" of the Internet, file transfer protocol (FTP) and Telnet, followed client/server architecture: a Telnet client could log on to a server computer, while an FTP client could upload files to or download files from a server. Despite this, the overall communication patterns in the early Internet were symmetric, and any peer could act as a client and as a server. Furthermore, many network applications and services built years ago were based on the fundamental principles of P2P architecture; such examples including Usenet newsgroup server network, domain name system (DNS), and border gateway protocol (BGP) interdomain routing.

Usenet Server Network

Originally conceived in 1979—a decade prior to the World Wide Web, Usenet is a long-surviving fixture on the Internet scene that was designed to facilitate a discussion-based message exchange between users. The early version of Usenet was designed as a "poor man's ARPANET" and built on top of UUCP (Unix to Unix copy protocol), which uses different types of physical and link-layer connections between two computers. In 1985, the network news transfer protocol (NNTP) was introduced to transmit Usenet traffic over TCP/IP. Although almost all of today's Usenet traffic is transported over the Internet, most Usenet messages (called "articles") still carry some UUCP-specific headers. The content of Usenet articles had evolved as well. Originally designed to carry exclusively text articles, the vast majority of the volume in Usenet traffic today is composed of binary files—images, MP3 files, videos, and software applications. Usenet articles are organized into newsgroups logically separated into hierarchically organized topics. For example, microsoft.public.xbox and microsoft.public.xbox.halo are two newsgroups within the microsoft.public hierarchy dedicated to Xbox and its Halo game, respectively. Figure 1 and Figure 2 show a part of the microsoft.public.xbox.* hierarchy displayed using the Xnews newsgroup reader and Google Groups. Usenet newsgroups are maintained and distributed over a network of NNTP servers. An NNTP server can join the Usenet network by establishing a connection with at least one other NNTP server, referred to as a newsfeed. The administrators of an NNTP server have control over which newsgroups their server carries and may decide how long different types of articles are to be retained. Today, newsgroups are flooded with sexually oriented and illegal content and therefore, some servers do not carry all of

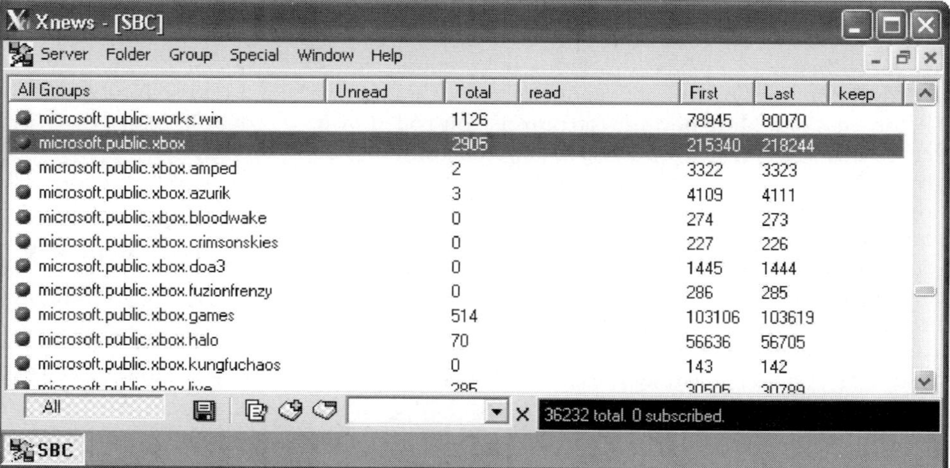

Figure 1: Xnews, a newsgroup reader software, displays a partial list of the microsoft.public.xbox newsgroup hierarchy.

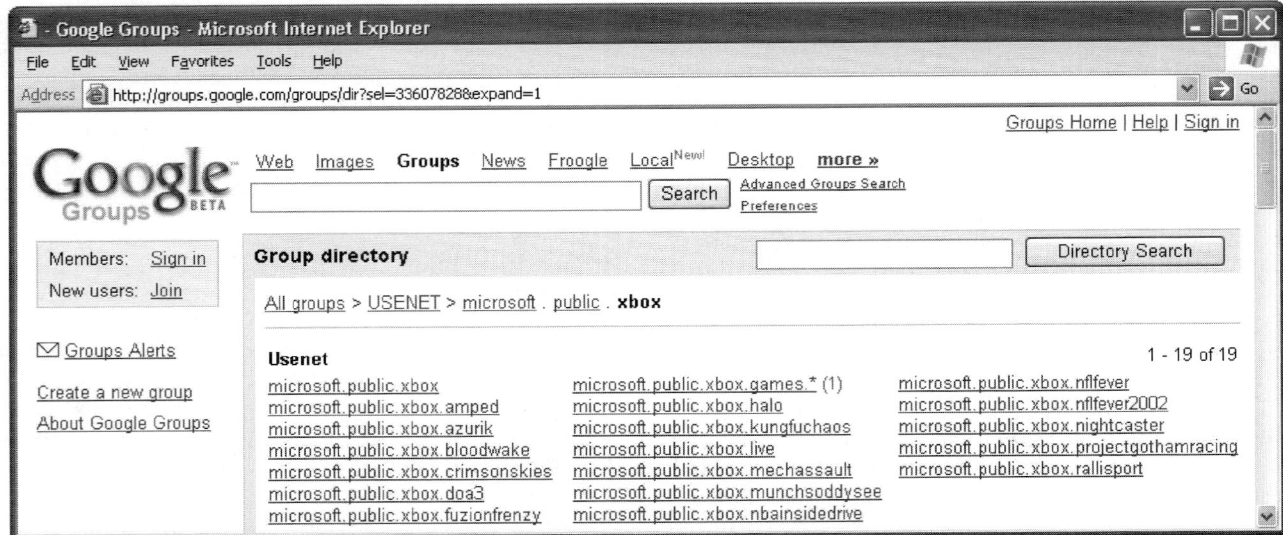

Figure 2: Google Groups can be used to access current and archived articles from virtually all Usenet newsgroups.

the available newsgroups. The alt.binaries.* newsgroup hierarchy carries almost exclusively this type of content; according to some sources, it is accountable for over 99% of all Usenet traffic volume.

A user can subscribe to a newsgroup carried by a given NNTP server, for example news.snet.sbcglobal.net. When the user posts an article to a newsgroup, initially it is available only on that server. However, during the communication with its newsfeed(s), the new article propagates to other servers and eventually reaches all NNTP servers that are subscribed to the newsgroup to which that article was posted. Many modern P2P network applications function using a similar principle: a content item is copied from one peer to another peer that is interested in receiving it. In a typical P2P system, however, a given content item is not copied by all peers, but only by those peers that request that item. The principle of content replication in Usenet may seem inefficient given the existing network bandwidth capabilities, but it is inherited from the days when network connectivity was slow and not constantly available.

Usenet is completely decentralized both from the technical and from the organizational point of view. There is no central or coordinating server in the NNTP server network—instead, all NNTP servers have equal rights and differ mainly in the list of newsgroups they carry. The process of adding new newsgroups is controlled by a democratic voting process in a special news.admin newsgroup. Newsgroups in the alt.* hierarchy are an exception because they can be created by anybody at any time. Each NNTP server implements its own set of policies, yet the Usenet network as a whole functions through the cooperation of the entire community. Most existing P2P systems are either completely or partially decentralized using the same technical and organizational principles. A true P2P system operates without the need for a centralized server; most existing content-sharing P2P systems allow its users decide which content items are available to other peers on the network. There are, however, some exceptions to these principles. For example, Freenet, a decentralized P2P data storage system aimed at fighting censorship (discussed later in this chapter), is designed to disallow any control over the content stored on the individual peer computers.

Domain Name System

Domain name system (DNS) is a vital component of the Internet because it provides functionality for associating hard-to-remember numeric IP addresses (such as 208.215.179.146) with easy-to-remember domain names (such as www.wiley.com). DNS was originally introduced in 1983 to support several thousand hosts, and it scaled extremely well to supporting hundreds of millions of hosts that exist today on the Internet. For a full description of DNS functionality, refer to Chapter 81 of this book. DNS has many features inherent to P2P systems. As DNS requests are propagated from one DNS host to the other, each host may act both as a client and as a server, which very closely resembles the peer concept in a P2P system. Caching replies to queries at each host helps the efficient scaling of DNS network. Any DNS host can query any other DNS host as may be necessary to resolve a given query, just like in P2P applications when a given peer can establish a connection with any other peer. Results of DNS queries are cached in each DNS host through which these result pass—P2P file sharing and distributed storage applications often use a similar method for replicating data.

P2P NETWORK APPLICATIONS FOR COMMUNICATION AND COLLABORATION

P2P systems are widely used for enabling direct and usually real-time communication and collaboration among peers. Early implementations of such systems include chat and instant messaging (IM) applications (ICQ [I seek

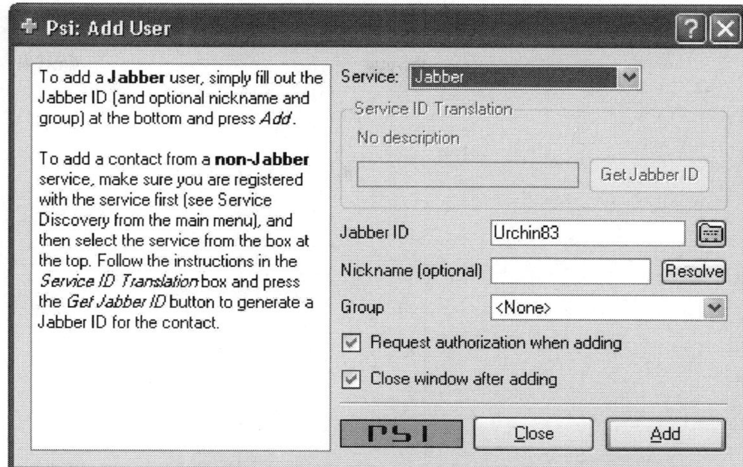

Figure 3: Psi is a Jabber-based IM client.

you] and a wide range of other systems developed by AOL, Yahoo, and MSN that copied the concept). These communication systems may be viewed as brokered P2P systems that are facilitated by one or more central servers used for managing an addressing system and for providing a unique identification for each peer. Other P2P communication and collaboration network applications that go far beyond basic instant messaging include Jabber, Skype, and Groove, which are discussed below.

Jabber

The Jabber project started in 1998 as a platform to enable interoperability among many incompatible IM applications and protocols (Miller 2001). With a first major release of software to the public in 2000, this project resulted in the development of XML-based open source extensible messaging and presence protocol (XMPP) used for instant messaging and managing presence information (which conveys a user's availability and willingness to engage in online communication). Today, according to Jabber Software Foundation (Jabber 2006), the Jabber platform and XMPP is used by over ten million people throughout the world.

The Jabber platform is decentralized and does not require a single central server, although a server is required to create an XMPP-based network. Jabber Software Foundation runs a public server at Jabber.org, and there are a large number of regional Jabber networks in many countries, each with its own server(s). In fact, any individual or a company can run a Jabber server to create his or her own public or private Jabber networks. An attractive feature of the Jabber platform is that all these networks are interoperable—that is, peers connected to different Jabber servers can still communicate with one another. In contrast, traditional IM platforms, such as MSN Messenger or AOL Instant Messenger are built around a central server and are not interoperable. Jabber allows its users not only to communicate with other peers on Jabber networks, but also with those connected to other popular IM systems through a number of specialized server-based gateways, as if they were also on a Jabber network. The Jabber Web site provides a very long list of XMPP-based clients available for various operating systems that enable users to connect to Jabber platform; Figure 3 shows Psi, free Jabber-enabled IM client software.

A combination of the voice over IP (VoIP) and IM systems, Google Talk was introduced in August 2005. Google Talk uses XMPP to implement its IM functionality, but currently it does not support server-to-server communication. This implies that any Jabber client can connect to the Google Talk server, but it becomes limited to communication only with Jabber clients that are also connected to the same server, since Google Talk requires a special account based on a g-mail address. Google plans to eventually make Google Talk interoperable with other Jabber networks.

Skype

First released to the public in August 2003, Skype (2006) is a proprietary P2P VoIP network founded by Niklas Zennström and Janus Friis, the creators of Kazaa. Unlike many other VoIP systems, Skype usually works well over different types of network connections, including network address translation (NAT) and firewalls, which makes it especially attractive to home users. Calls within the Skype network are free; paid services include calling regular telephone numbers for a relatively low per-minute fee, and receiving calls from regular phones and using voicemail on a subscription basis. To join the Skype network, the user needs to download free Skype software, which is currently implemented for Windows, Mac OS X, Pocket PC, and Linux. A Windows-based Skype client is shown in Figure 4.

The Skype network uses P2P architecture by routing all calls through other Skype peers as well as distributing its user directory among the peers on the network. Skype peers connected without NAT usually see an increase in usage of their processor and network bandwidth as they are being used to route calls of other Skype users. In fact, in September 2005, Skype usage was essentially banned

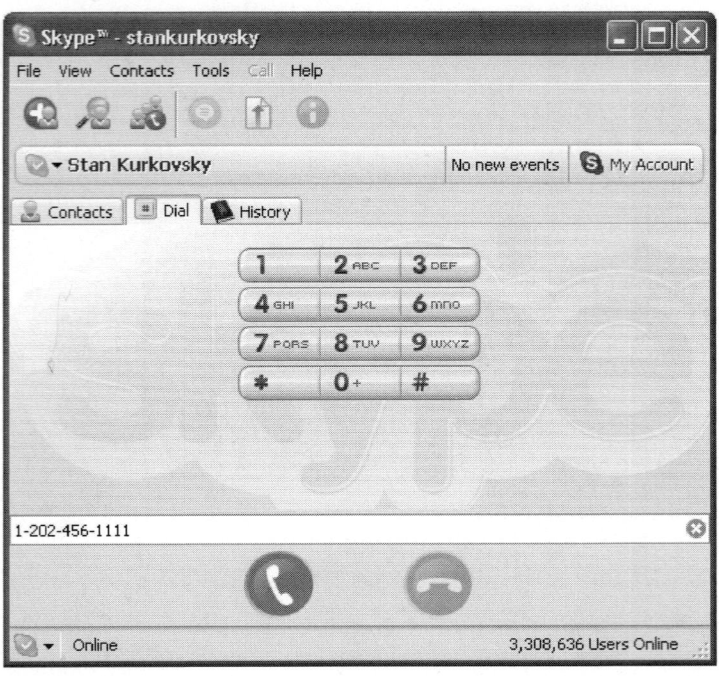

Figure 4: Skype is a P2P VoIP network application.

in French public universities and research institutions, possibly due to excessive usage of the bandwidth capacities that are widely available at such organizations.

Skype code and protocols are closed source, and the company indicated that it has no plans of making them public. Skype effectively uses strong encryption to secure all aspects of its traffic, including session establishment and call data streams, all user log-ins are certified by a public key server, and its built-in file transfer capabilities are open to common antivirus tools.

The quality of voice calls made with Skype varies from excellent (better than traditional telephony) to almost unusable. Usual drawbacks include a time lag of about 0.5 second but sometimes up to 2 seconds due to low bandwidth and/or excessive P2P routing, and dropped calls.

Skype P2P architecture has proven to be able to scale up easily—Skype indicates that as of January 2006 their software has been downloaded over 230 million times, there are over 60 million users (about a half of them in Europe, a quarter in Asia, and about 10 percent in North America, according to statistics from Skype Journal (Skypejournal 2006), and there are over three million users concurrently using Skype network.

In September 2005, eBay acquired Skype for over $2 billion. Many believe that such an astronomical amount is justified because this acquisition enables eBay to tap into the Skype user base, whose majority resides outside the current geographic pool of eBay's users, who are located mostly in North America. In late 2005, Skype 2.0 was released with a capability to make video calls to other Skype users as a major new feature.

Groove

Groove Networks was founded in 1997 by Ray Ozzie, the creator of Lotus Notes (Groove 2006). The company's product, Groove (currently marketed as Groove Virtual Office) is a P2P groupware system; using this system, a team of collaborators (peers) may form ad hoc shared workspaces used to exchange messages, documents, applications, and relevant data—all related to a group project, as shown in Figure 5. Groove allows its peers to collaborate equally well regardless of the type or characteristics of their network connection: they can be behind a firewall or NAT; they can be on a corporate LAN, broadband connection, or dialup; and they can be always on or have an intermittent network connection.

Groove supports two key features that enable collaboration—security and synchronization. In effect, shared spaces created in Groove are instant virtual private networks. Groove requires each peer to have an account residing on a local computer. Groove's underlying philosophy stresses the idea that a peer can access their shared collaboration spaces from different computing or communication devices; therefore many identities may be associated with one peer account. At the same time, a single peer may have multiple identities that can be used in different shared workspaces. All messages exchanged by peers are authenticated and encrypted and usually do not contain entire documents. Groove uses "delta messages" representing incremental changes in a document, shared workspace, or its parameters—for example, a delta message could contain an individual keystroke. One of the objectives of Groove is to eliminate the human factor in enforcing strong security, since the vast majority of security failures are caused by a human oversight or error. Therefore, Groove provides strong security by default, offering very few security-related configuration options to its peers.

Groove's shared workspaces can be created by individual peers as well as by those working in the organizational frameworks of an enterprise. To support this, Groove offers a fully decentralized P2P communication mode and also provides means of incorporating enterprise-level

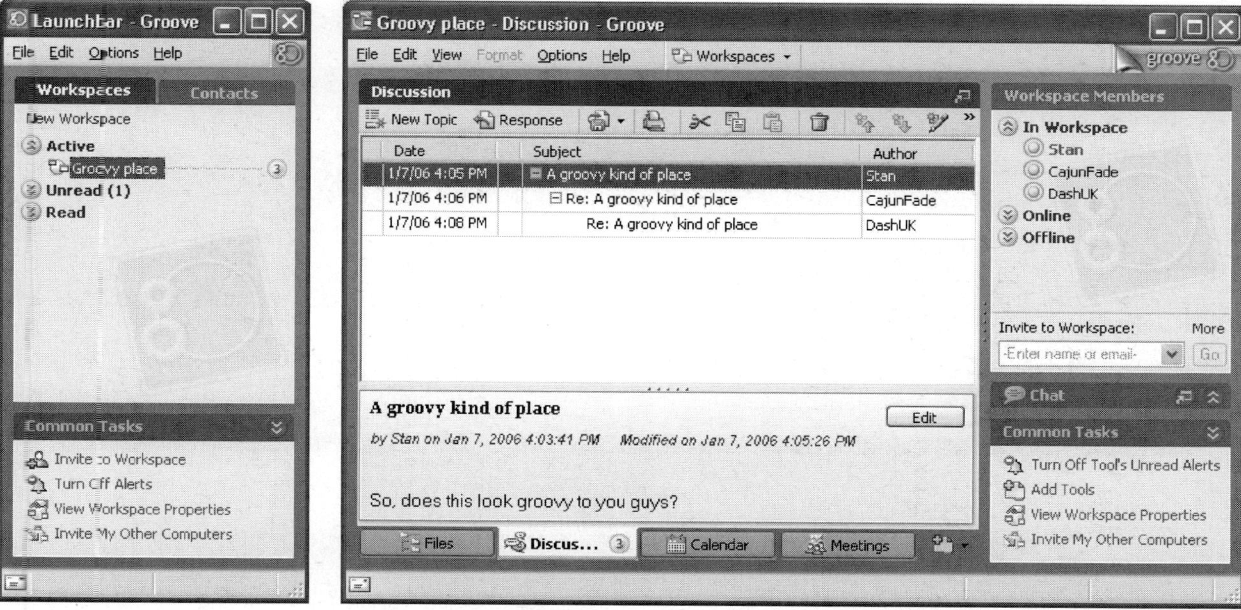

Figure 5: Groove Virtual Office is used to create a shared workspace containing files, discussions, group calendars, etc.

servers into its infrastructure (Groove 2005). In an enterprise environment, a range of servers is used by Groove: Enterprise Relay Server, supporting communication between Groove peers when a direct P2P communication cannot be established; Enterprise Data Bridge, providing integration between different workspaces and external systems' and Enterprise Management Server, supporting centralized control over licenses, security policies, and other administrative activities. Even if one or more of the central servers fail or if they do not exist at all, peers on a Groove network can still communicate and execute complex group tasks.

In March 2005 Groove Networks was acquired by Microsoft, and Ray Ozzie became one of Microsoft's three Chief Technical Officers.

P2P NETWORK APPLICATIONS FOR FILE SHARING

File-sharing applications brought P2P technology into the focus of public attention. The basic principle of file sharing is to copy a file from one computer to another using a direct network connection between the two computers. Gradually, P2P network applications took this concept to an entirely new level, from using Napster servers to help find computers with the right files to using swarm downloads in BitTorrent and ED2K (eDonkey2000) networks.

Despite frequent and numerous claims by the record industry that file sharing over P2P networks is the main cause of the decline in music sales, current research indicates that the real economic impact of file sharing is moderate at best (Oberholzer-Gee and Strumpf 2005). Although many sources disagree on the percentage figure, it remains a clear consensus that the vast majority of media distributed over P2P file sharing networks is copied illegally. However, there is a growing number of legal uses of P2P file sharing networks: large volumes of open source software are distributed as compact disk (CD) images; unsigned music bands use P2P networks to publish their music; some gaming software publishers distribute updates to their products; and Peter Jackson's video documentaries on the making of "King Kong" were officially distributed via BitTorrent.

Napster

The original Napster was released by Shawn Fanning in June 1999. Specializing exclusively in MP3 music files, this service provided an easy method of locating computers with MP3 music files to those people who wanted to download them, as shown in Figure 6. Napster used only filenames to identify the content of each file, which often led to misrepresentation of the content being downloaded. At the time when Napster became vastly popular, the only ways to obtain an MP3 file was either to copy it from someone else or to rip it from a CD yourself; therefore, all file sharing activities conducted using Napster were considered illegal by major music recording companies, since no royalties were paid. Nevertheless, the use of Napster proliferated, reaching 50 million of registered users in January 2001 (Miller 2001), as users found many justifications for using the service. Many people wanted to have just one or two songs from otherwise worthless albums; others praised the service for allowing them to download songs that were difficult to obtain, such as old records and bootleg concert recordings.

Napster software allowed users to share their MP3 files with other Napster peers while providing capabilities to search for and download MP3 files from these peers. Napster servers maintained information about all peers connected to the network at any given moment and about the files these peers were sharing. To download a file, a Napster peer had to search the server for a

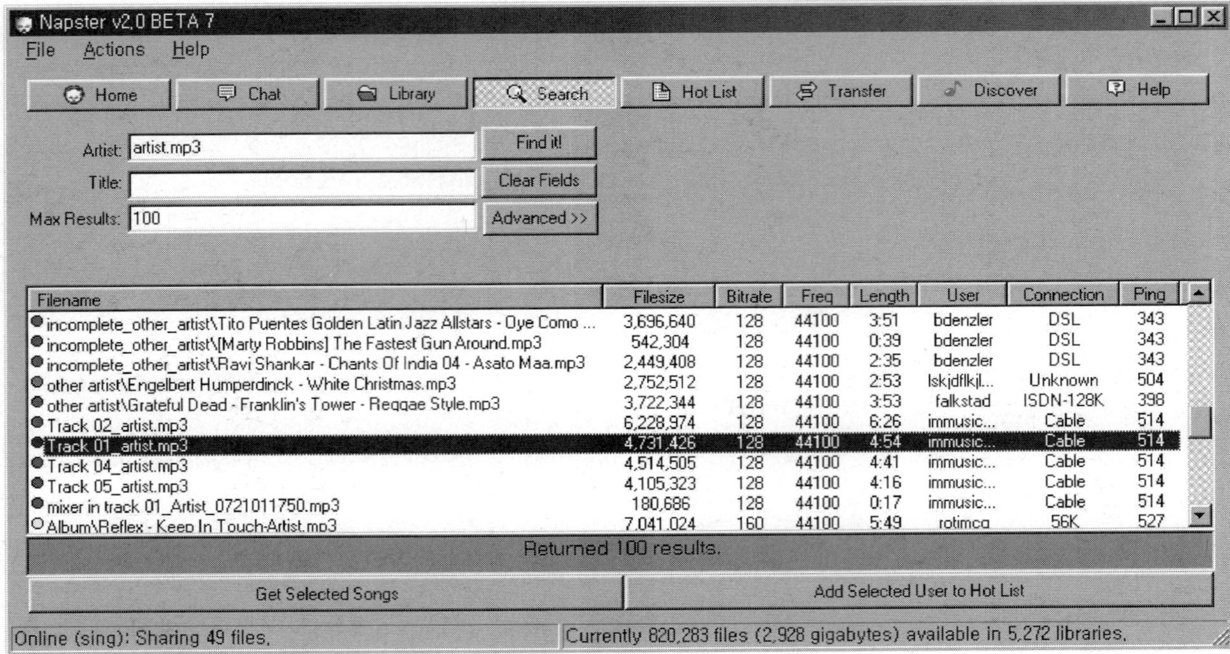

Figure 6: Napster was used to help locate computers with MP3 files available for download.

given artist and/or title (as represented by the name of the shared file) and then select a single peer that had this file from the list of results returned by the server. Once the peer with the needed MP3 file was identified, the two Napster peers established a direct connection and the file was copied. In fact, Napster architecture is very similar to that of most IM networks, which have central servers that maintain a list of active peers and help establish a direct connection between the peers.

Strong reliance on a central server made the Napster network not only technically vulnerable by creating a single point of failure, but it also enabled major copyright holders to mount a successful legal attack again Napster. Since Napster servers maintained a complete list of songs being traded, it was easy to prove in court that Napster as a company was aware of the copyright infringement. Despite numerous offers of settlement, Napster network was completely shut down in July 2001 to comply with court orders. Eventually, the Napster brand was acquired by Roxio Inc. at bankruptcy auction, which later launched a subscription-based music service, Napster 2.0.

Despite its flaws, Napster helped spark a widespread interest in and awareness of P2P network technology. It also helped create a new market for music services, which is currently dominated by Apple's iTunes. Most importantly, Napster's demise did not leave a void; instead it was quickly filled with other more advanced P2P systems used not only for file sharing, but also for many other purposes described later in this chapter.

Kazaa

Kazaa (Kazaa 2006) and its FastTrack protocol were introduced by Niklas Zennström and Janus Friis in March 2001, several months before the complete shutdown of the Napster network. Similar to Napster, Kazaa Media Desktop (shown in Figure 7) and other FastTrack clients allowed users to join a P2P network to share files. Unlike Napster, the FastTrack protocol does not make any limitations on the types of shared files, allows downloading from multiple sources, and does not use a central server. The FastTrack protocol is proprietary and uses encryption for some parts of its functionality; however, some successful attempts have been made to reverse-engineer the unencrypted part of the FastTrack protocol.

If a powerful computer runs Kazaa or another FastTrack peer on a high-bandwidth connection, it usually automatically becomes a supernode on the FastTrack network. Each FastTrack peer has an updatable list of known supernodes, one of which is contacted when the client starts. Upon a successful contact, the client updates its list of currently active supernodes. The peer picks one of the supernodes as "upstream," through which all future search requests will be routed; it then uploads a list of shared files to its upstream. To facilitate downloading from multiple peers, unlike Napster, FastTrack does not use filenames to distinguish between different files. Instead, FastTrack uses the UUHash, a very fast, but unreliable hashing algorithm. UUHash uses a relatively small percentage of the file to produce its hash value, which allowed the Recording Industry Association of America (RIAA) and others to distribute fake and corrupt files on this P2P network (Oberholzer-Gee and Strumpf 2005). The most famous incident occurred in April 2003, when a number of full-length MP3 files with songs from the "American Life" album by Madonna appeared on the FastTrack network. These files started with less than a minute of the actual song material and then contained a recording of

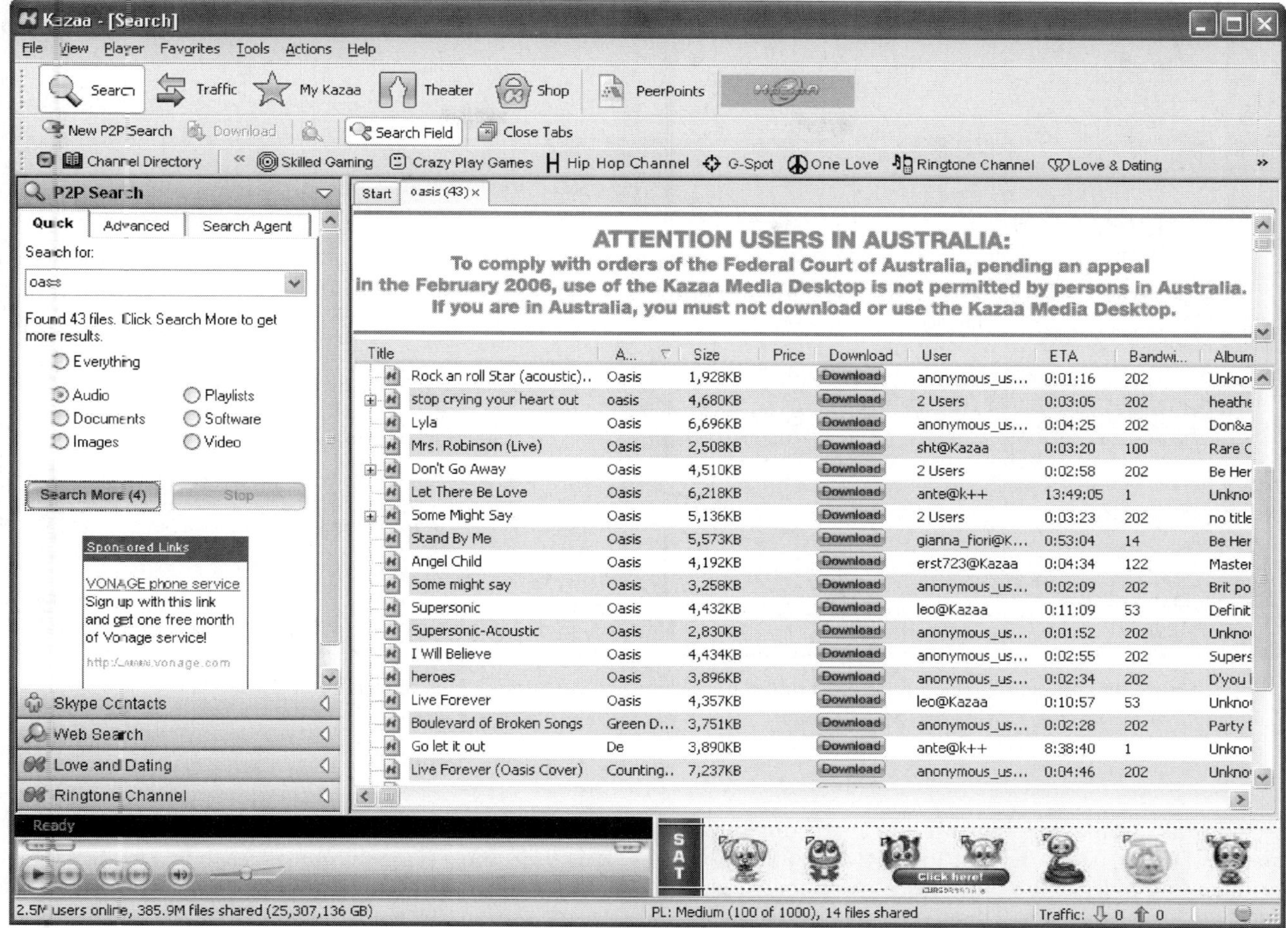

Figure 7: Kazaa allows users to search the network for various media files.

Madonna asking the listener "What the [expletive] do you think you are doing?"

Soon after the release of Kazaa Media Desktop, its distributor company was sued in the Dutch court. As a result, Kazaa was sold to a complex network of offshore companies in the South Pacific, primarily to Sharman Networks, based in Australia. Subsequently, Kazaa and manufacturers of other FastTrack-based software (Grokster) were sued by the RIAA, the MPAA (Motion Picture Association of America), the Australian Record Industry Association (ARIA), and MGM Studios. As a result of a long sequence of court rulings and appeals, many manufacturers of FastTrack applications have either closed, stopped distributing their software, or announced plans to establish new services that are free of copyright infringements. According to the Web site Slyck.com (Slyck 2006), the FastTrack network has been steadily losing ground since its peak in 2003, because of constant legal battles, including RIAA lawsuits against P2P users allegedly downloading copyrighted material, and simply because some FastTrack software plagues host computers with scores of malware. As of January 2006, Slyck.com data indicate that FastTrack has 1.9 million concurrent users on average.

Gnutella

Gnutella (Kan 2001) was developed by Justin Frankel and Tom Pepper, cofounders of Nullsoft and creators of the Winamp media player; it was released in March 2000, several months after Nullsoft was acquired by AOL. Gnutella client software was available on the AOL Web site for only one day, after which AOL removed the software from the Web site and prohibited Nullsoft from developing the project any further. Thus, the original Gnutella source code was never released, although its developers planned to do so. However, many copies of Gnutella software were downloaded; soon, the Gnutella protocol was reverse-engineered and made publicly available. Today, Gnutella is an evolving open protocol for P2P file sharing with a large number of existing peer software for Gnutella servents (*server* and *client*). Limewire, shown in Figure 8, is one of the most popular file-sharing applications using Gnutella.

Unlike the FastTrack protocol, which requires at least one supernode to form a network, Gnutella was originally designed as a protocol to build fully decentralized P2P file sharing networks of equal peers. In order to improve its scalability as the popularity of the protocol grew, Gnutella was later modified to include supernodes

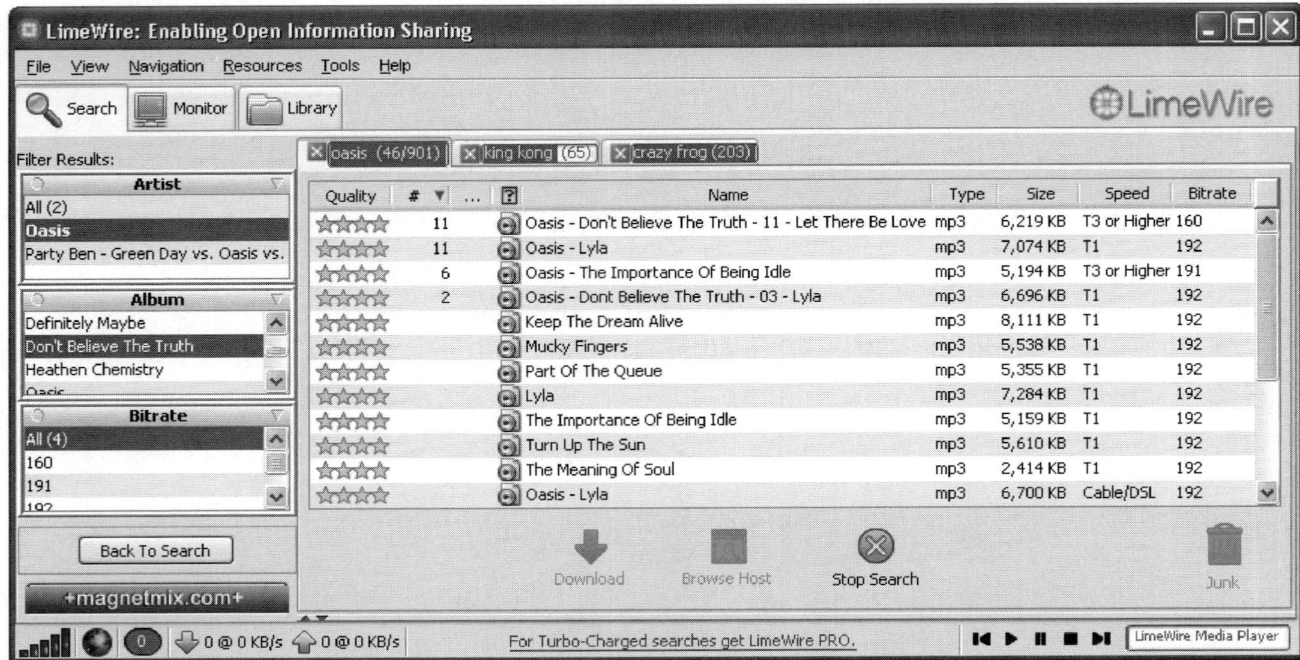

Figure 8: Limewire is one of the most popular P2P file-sharing applications based on the Gnutella protocol.

referred to as ultrapeers responsible for managing search requests of other peers. To join the network, a Gnutella peer must find at least one other peer (neighbor) already connected to the network. There are many ways of finding such neighbors: some Gnutella software comes with a list of possibly working peers, there are Web sites with such lists, and finally, Internet relay chat (IRC) channels or word of mouth can be used to obtain the IP address of a working Gnutella peer. Once connected, a new Gnutella peer receives a list of other working nodes from its new neighbor, and in this fashion it can form a "neighborhood" of a certain number of peers it is connected to, up to a certain user-specified limit.

In the original Gnutella protocol, when a peer sends a search query, it floods the network with the search request: the peer sends the query to its neighbors; each neighbor passes it on to its neighbors, unless it can provide the specified file. If the peer with the sought file is not behind a firewall, it contacts the sender of the search request directly, and they negotiate the file transfer. Otherwise, the response is sent back along the route of the original request. If the requestor peer finds more than one peer with the sought file, it can download the file simultaneously from multiple peers, which increases the download speed.

In newer versions of the Gnutella protocol, search requests are routed among ultrapeers. However, searching the Gnutella network is not always fast or reliable. Since many Gnutella peers reside behind firewalls and/or have network connections with limited bandwidth (e.g., uplink bandwidth of most residential asymmetric digital subscriber line (ADSL) connections is several times less than the downlink bandwidth), and because many peers do not stay connected to Gnutella network for a long time, most search requests reach far less than half of the network. At the same time, because of complete decentralization, the Gnutella network is extremely difficult to shut down—it will continue to exist as long as there are at least two peers. Slyck.com statistics (Slyck 2006) indicate that the population of the Gnutella network has been steadily growing, and it reached, on average, over 2.2 million daily users in January 2006.

eDonkey

The eDonkey2000 (ED2K) protocol was originally designed for the eDonkey2000 P2P file-sharing application developed and distributed by a New York–based company, MetaMachine. eDonkey2000 is a closed source software, and as of September 2005 it is no longer supported. Upon receiving a cease-and-desist letter from the RIAA, Sam Yagan, CEO of MetaMachine, said in his testimony at the U.S. Senate Judiciary Hearing on the future of P2P that MetaMachine is "in the process of complying with [RIAA's] request" and that his company intends to "convert eDonkey's user base to an online content retailer operating in a closed P2P environment." However, following these events, there was no change in the dynamics of the ED2K network population reported by Slyck.com—ED2K remains the most popular and steadily growing P2P file-sharing network, with a current average population of over 3.3 million concurrent users, as of January 2006 (Slyck 2006). One of the major reasons for the ever-growing popularity of ED2K network is the versatility of the open source protocol, allowing its peers to download multiple files from multiple peers simultaneously, and wide

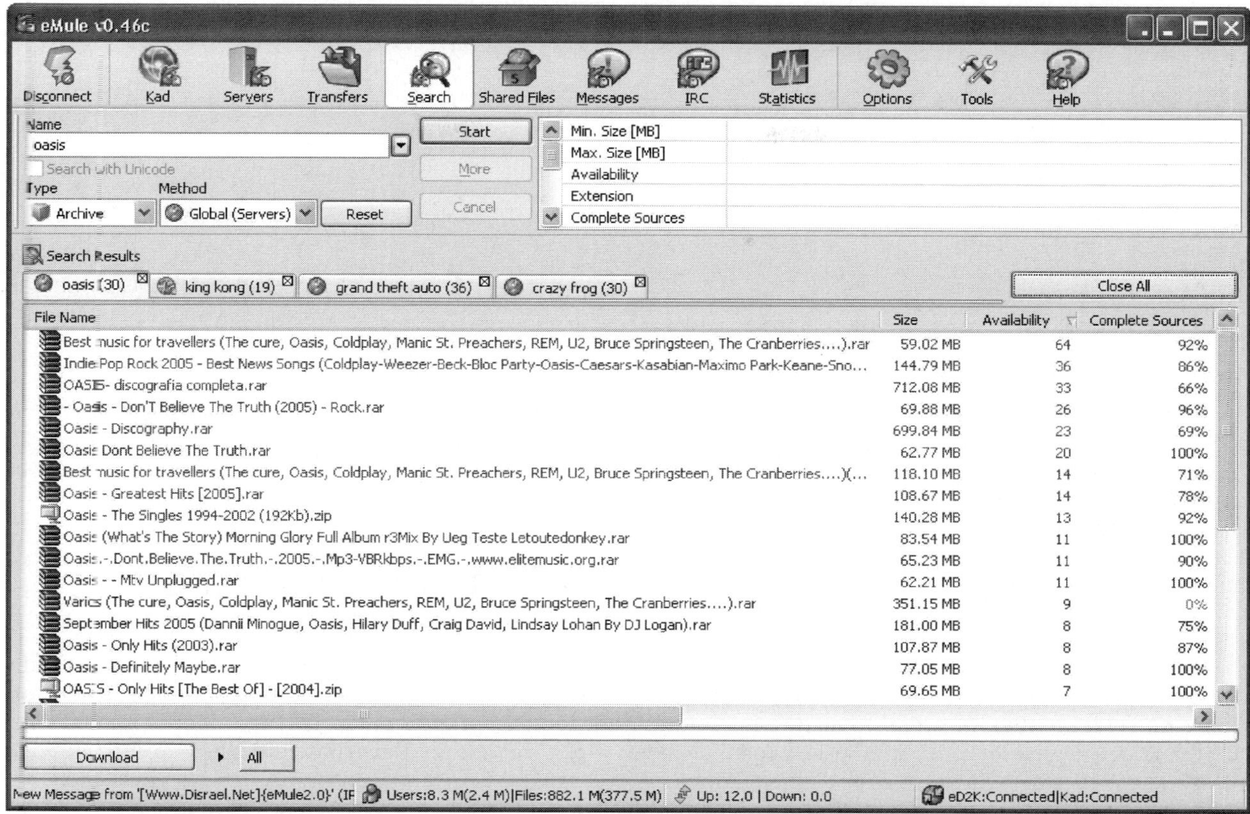

Figure 9: eMule is the most popular software used to access ED2K file-sharing network.

availability of alternatives to eDonkey2000 also supporting the ED2K protocol; eMule, shown in Figure 9, is one of the more popular ED2K applications (eMule 2006).

The ED2K protocol is well suited for fast downloads of large files, such as full-length movies, software, games, and CD images. Files greater than 9.8 Mb are split into chunks, which can be shared with other peers before the entire file is downloaded. By doing this, ED2K forces the peer downloading the file to share it with others, which greatly enhances the availability of files in this network. Each ED2K peer maintains a queue of other peers wishing to download a chunk of a given file. To speed up the distributing of files across the network, each peer usually gets to download the chunk that the fewest other peers have. ED2K clients also have built-in mechanisms that help reward peers with high upload/download ratios, as they are given higher priority in the queue. Each file in the ED2K network is identified by an MD4 hash checksum computed for each chunk individually and then hashed once again to obtain the checksum for the entire file.

To join the network, an ED2K peer needs a server, which facilitates all network requests of a peer. At any given moment, an ED2K peer can find hundreds of running servers supported by volunteers. ED2K servers maintain a list of currently connected clients and checksums of the files they share; they also route search requests among each other. To overcome the dependency on the server, MetaMachine developed an alternative protocol—Overnet—that routes search requests among peers; the open source community of eMule developers created a similar but incompatible protocol called Kademlia (usually referred to as Kad). It has been a trend to integrate at least two or more of the above protocols in a single client. For example, the latest available version of eDonkey2000 also supports BitTorrent (discussed later in this chapter) and allows a synchronized downloading of a file using BitTorrent, ED2K, and Overnet networks simultaneously. Together with the user-supported rating system, this helps eliminate fake and mislabeled files, which have become a significant problem for other P2P file-sharing networks, such as FastTrack.

According to data from Slyck.com (Slyck 2006), as of January 2006, among all P2P file sharing networks, ED2K was the most popular network, with over 3.5 million of concurrent users, on average.

BitTorrent

The concept of BitTorrent was developed by Bram Cohen, who released its first version in 2002. BitTorrent is an open protocol for a P2P file-sharing network; the same name is also used by the software, shown in Figure 10, developed by the protocol's inventor (BitTorrent 2006).

The overall functionality of BitTorrent protocol is similar to that of ED2K. Compared to ED2K, there are fewer files available to download on the BitTorrent network, but the download speeds are usually higher. However, unlike other P2P file-sharing networks, including ED2K, in which peers typically download multiple files at the same time, BitTorrent has been designed specifically to

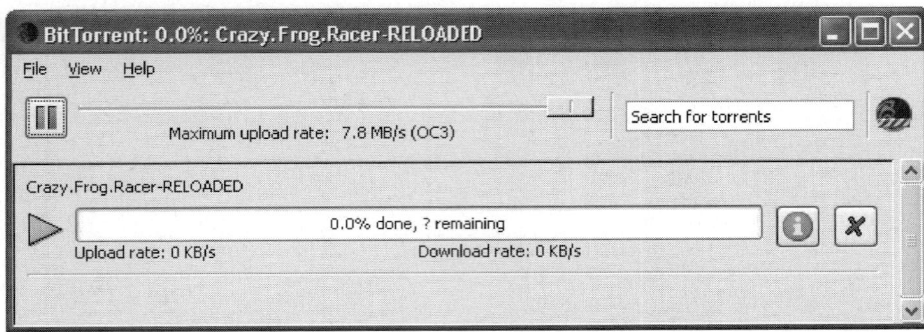

Figure 10: BitTorrent software is used to download one file at a time.

download a single file from multiple peers at the same time. Similar to ED2K, files distributed in the BitTorrent network are downloaded in small segments (usually about 256 kB). A peer (referred to as seeder) that wishes to start distributing a file (a torrent) must create a special .torrent file that contains information about the shared file (its name, size, hash value of every segment) and the address of a tracker server responsible for coordinating the swarm (an ad hoc network of seeders and peers sharing the same torrent). The tracker server usually does not reside on the same computer as the seeder and is responsible only for updating the information about which torrent segments are available from which peers. Just like in the ED2K network, peers who have not completed downloading a torrent are forced to share the downloaded segments with other peers. Peers that complete the downloading of a torrent may opt to become seeders of that file. If all seeder peers of a given torrent are no longer online, even if there are peers that have its complete copy, new peers will not be able to start downloading that file. However, all peers that start downloading the torrent will eventually complete it, as long as there is at least one distributed copy of that file.

Unlike most P2P peer software, Cohen's BitTorrent peer program does not have a built-in search feature. To start downloading a file, a user of the BitTorrent network needs to locate a .torrent file. These are usually listed on specialized Web sites providing a search capability, sent by e-mail, or posted in corresponding Usenet newsgroups.

BitTorrent facilitates distribution of large amounts of data among a large number of peers in a relatively short time. Because of its features, among all P2P file-sharing networks, BitTorrent has been the most popular with pirates to distribute copyrighted material such as recent Hollywood movies. BitTorrent proponents argue that the network is not well suited for illegal file downloads: there are no good search facilities, seeder hosts of illegal files can be easily identified, and there are many ways that BitTorrent can be used for legal purposes—e.g. for distribution of large volumes of open source software. In fact, many BitTorrent search Web sites have been shut down under the threat of lawsuits or voluntarily. Despite a strong official antipiracy stance by Bram Cohen, in May 2005 he released a new version of BitTorrent that eliminates the need for tracker servers (thus making it much easier to distribute files) and updated the BitTorrent Web site to add a search feature that makes it much easier to locate both legal and illegal files.

Although it is more difficult to gauge the population of concurrent users of BitTorrent (Pouwelse et al. 2005), it is estimated that their numbers reached over 2 million in early 2006.

P2P NETWORK APPLICATIONS FOR DISTRIBUTED STORAGE

With the falling costs and growing capacity of hard drives, the primary concern of P2P network applications for distributed storage is not to gain additional space, but instead to store data in a distributed fashion to secure it against local failures and censorship. In the past, censorship-resistant P2P systems such as Freenet and Free Haven received a lot of publicity. According to the Web site of the Free Haven project, since 2002 it has been put on the back burner until some major implementation issues are resolved. Freenet is discussed below; this system is actively used by a relatively large community, although there is a controversy regarding the kinds of data available through this system. OceanStore, an academic project for reliable distributed document storage is also presented.

Freenet

The idea of what would eventually become Freenet was originally described by Ian Clarke in a paper written in 1999 and published a year later (Clarke et al. 2000). Clarke and a number of volunteers released the first version of this open source system in March 2000 (Freenet 2006). Since censorship may manifest itself by removing objectionable documents or punishing those who read, write, or distribute them, the primary objective of Freenet is to provide a censorship-resistant avenue for communication in an anonymous environment.

Freenet is a true P2P system, which has no central servers; therefore, it cannot be controlled by any individual entity. Peers in the Freenet network are responsible for secure storage of documents as well as processing and routing of document search queries from other peers. Each document available through Freenet is identified by a hash key, which is used in the key-based routing algorithm used by Freenet to locate documents. If the document exists, this algorithm finds the peer hosting the document that is the closest to the peer requesting the document. The distance between peers is measured in the number of peers that the request has to traverse.

Each peer on the Freenet network forms a small list of trusted neighbor peers. Each neighbor in the list is also assigned certain metrics that indicate the neighbor's past performance in retrieving documents based on different keys. Unlike Gnutella's network-flooding search algorithm, these metrics are used by Freenet peers to choose the neighbor through which a document search request is routed. A mechanism is in place to choose alternative neighbors to avoid loops in the search path. Each request also has a "hops to live" value that determines the maximum number of peers it can traverse before being terminated. A peer receiving a search request from its neighbor checks whether it has the sought document, and if so, it returns the document to that neighbor, which, in turn, forwards it to its original destination along the path of the request. To support anonymity, Freenet peers are not aware whether their neighbor requesting a document is the original requester or whether it has simply passed the request along. Peers may retain a copy of documents that pass through them, which makes the network more resistant to censorship, as it makes it impossible to trace the origin of the document.

Freenet uses the same routing algorithm to insert new documents into its distributed data store. First, a search request is made for a document that does not exist yet. When the request fails, a new document is propagated along the same path as that search request, which ensures that the document is stored in the same peers that future search requests for that document will traverse.

The request routing algorithm and architecture of Freenet results in a situation in which popular documents are stored at more peers located closer to where requests for these documents are made. This makes it virtually impossible to remove a popular document from the network. Since all documents stored at Freenet peers are encrypted, users of the Freenet may not know what documents they are hosting on their computers. Freenet can be accessed using its Web-based interface, as shown in Figure 11.

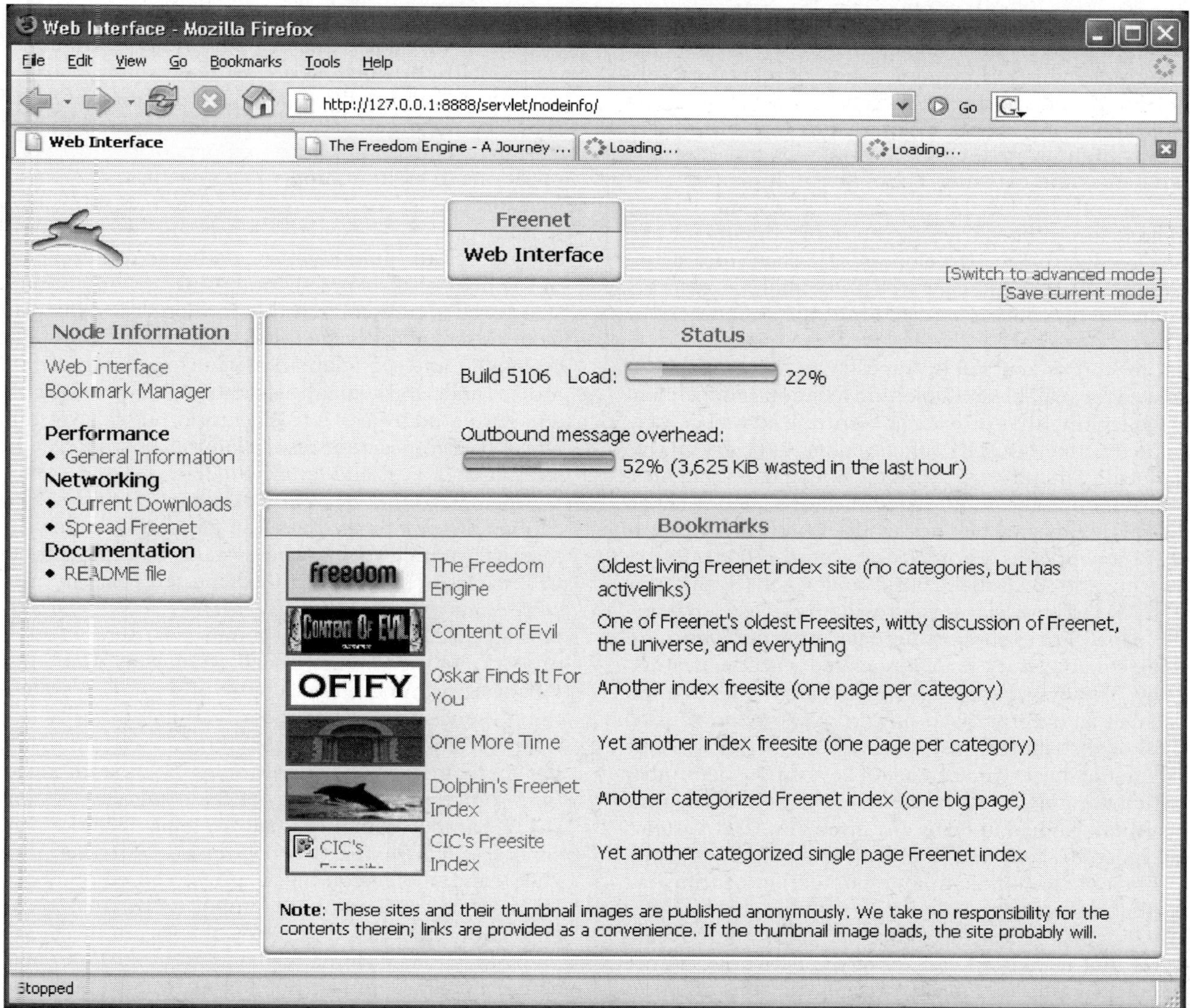

Figure 11: Web-based interface to Freenet is provided by a background service running on the peer computer.

There is no easy way to determine what content is being actually stored on Freenet, since the network is designed to make such identification extremely difficult. Some estimates indicate that the majority of text information on Freenet is drug-related and the majority of all images are pornographic. Proponents of Freenet say that in order to maintain a true freedom of speech, one needs to be tolerable to the views of others, however questionable or unpleasant they may be.

OceanStore

OceanStore is an academic project led by John Kubiatowicz from UC Berkeley (Kubiatowicz 2003); as of January 2006 it was still largely under development, although a functioning prototype was available (OceanStore 2006). As with many P2P network applications for distributed storage, the main idea behind OceanStore is to replace storage on local hard disks with secure and redundant storage distributed across multiple computers spanning the entire Internet.

The objective of OceanStore is to provide highly available, consistent, and durable data storage utility built on top of an unreliable infrastructure of untrusted peers. OceanStore implements its objectives by replicating data over multiple storage locations, using decentralized object location and routing algorithms, and using strong cryptography. Documents inserted into OceanStore are split into multiple redundant segments, which are dispersed across the network. There are multiple copies of each segment stored in the network; even if some of these segments cannot be retrieved, the entire document can still be reconstructed. Developers of OceanStore claim that their system can scale well into millions of peers and that the documents inserted into the system will be kept there forever.

OceanStore is enabled by Tapestry, a P2P overlay network used for scalable, reliable, and location-independent message routing that provides decentralized object location and routing (DOLR) functionality. Tapestry makes use of locality in message routing while maximizing message throughput and minimizing message latency (Zhao et al. 2004). Tapestry belongs to the same class of overlay P2P networks as Chord (Stoica et al. 2001), Pastry (Rowstron and Druschel 2001), and CAN (Ratnasamy et al. 2001). These systems provide key-based routing (KBR) capabilities, supporting deterministic routing of messages to a network node associated with the destination key. These systems also support higher-level interfaces, such as decentralized object location and routing (DOLR) or distributed hash tables (DHT). DHT systems distribute the ownership of a set of keys among a number of participating nodes; they can efficiently route requests to the unique node that owns any given key. DHT systems are designed to scale well as the numbers of nodes grows and to be able to handle a large population of transient nodes that are prone to failures.

A distinguishing feature of Tapestry (and thus of OceanStore) is that it takes into account the network distance when constructing its routing overlay and thus attempts to minimize the physical span of a given overlay hop. Tapestry achieves this by constructing and maintaining locally optimal routing tables. Unlike other DHT systems, Tapestry allows its applications to place content objects according to the application's needs. Tapestry makes location pointers available through its P2P network to enable efficient routing to the content objects with a minimal network stretch; as a result, queries for nearby objects are typically satisfied in the amount of time proportional to the physical network distance between the query source and the closest replica of the content object.

P2P NETWORK APPLICATIONS FOR MASSIVELY PARALLEL COMPUTING

The P2P approach is similar to grid computing architectures in that both use distributed processing by means of pooling together geographically dispersed and heterogeneous computing resources. Computational grids are primarily concerned with a coordinated distribution of computationally intensive tasks over a persistent and standardized service infrastructure. Designers of grid computing systems are also concerned with issues of scalability and fault tolerance, which will inevitably arise as computational grids grow to use an even larger number of processing nodes. Existing P2P systems are also concerned with the same issues, but their main focus lies in dealing with instability of a large population of transient peers. As mentioned earlier in this chapter, there is a growing trend among the developers of P2P network applications to build interoperable systems that share common protocols. As P2P systems continue to evolve and mature, one could expect a convergence of P2P and Grid approaches to build sophisticated network applications in the area of distributed computing, collaboration, and structured secure content distribution. These new architectures will address the issues of recovery from failures, scalability, and self-adaptation while operating in a standardized and persistent infrastructure. Today, however, "grid computing addresses infrastructure, but not yet failure, while peer-to-peer addresses failure, but not yet infrastructure" (Foster and Iamnitchi 2003).

One category of currently existing P2P network applications is sometimes classified as computational grids. Massively parallel computing systems make use of unused CPU cycles of geographically dispersed peers in order to solve a large computationally intensive task. A large computing task is broken down into relatively small units of work, which are distributed among the peers of such P2P systems. A common feature of these P2P systems is the presence of a central coordinating authority (a central server) responsible for breaking down and distributing the computational task among peers and collecting (and sometimes processing) of the results. Existing massively parallel computational systems include systems such as SETI@home (Korpela et al. 2001; SetiAtHome 2006) and the upcoming Stardust@home (StardustAtHome 2006) projects, both supported by the Space Science Laboratory at UC Berkeley; the currently terminated project Genome@Home (GenomeAtHome 2006) and the active Folding@Home (Folding-At-Home 2006; Larson et al. 2003) project, both supported by Vijay Pande of Stanford University, as well as other projects. Since many

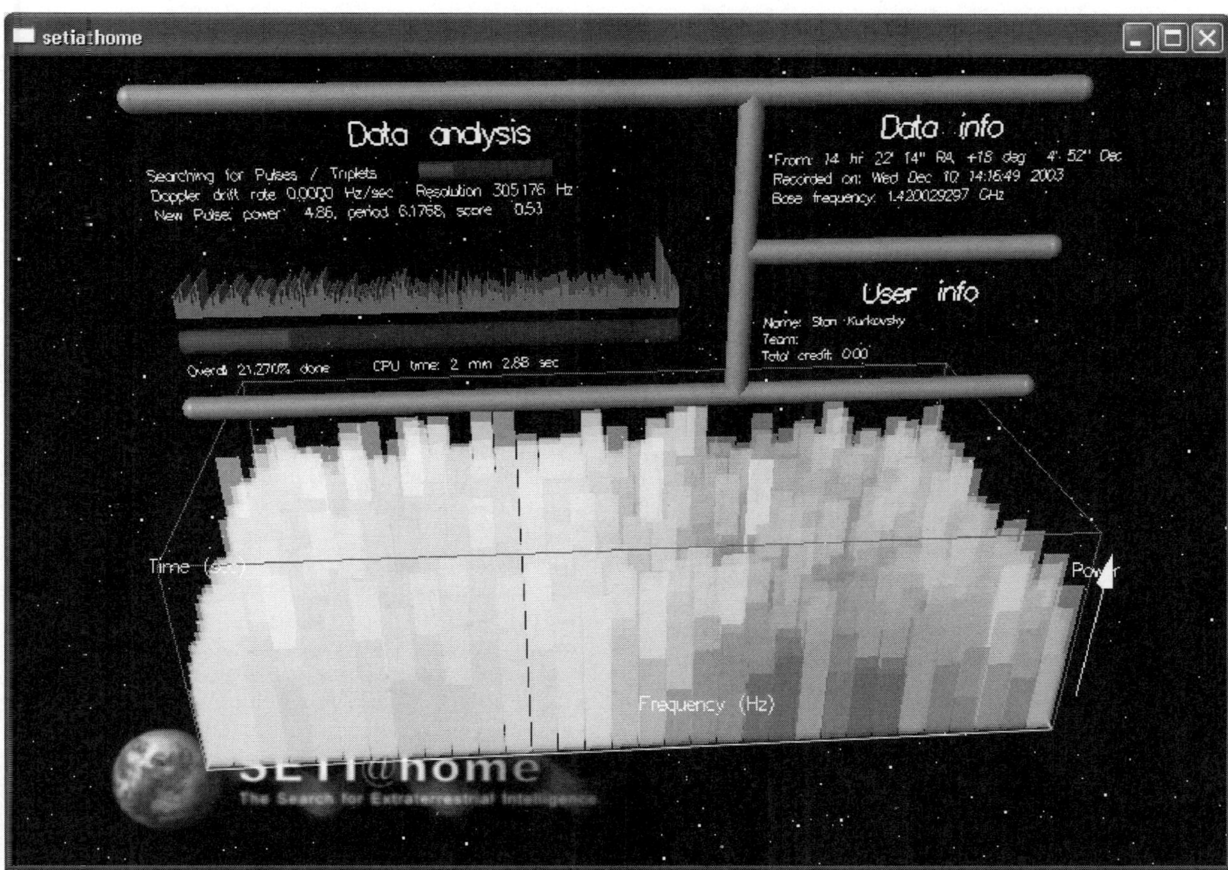

Figure 12: BOINC-based software is used by SETI@Home project on a peer computer.

of the P2P network applications for massively parallel computations share the same architectural principles and feature one sample system, only SETI@Home is discussed below.

SETI@Home

SETI@Home was launched in May 1999. The main objective of SETI@Home (Search for Extraterrestrial Intelligence) is to analyze the radio-frequency data received from the Arecibo radio telescope in order to find evidence of intelligent radio transmissions from outer space. SETI@Home is said to be the largest distributed computing project, counting over five million participants throughout the world.

Over 25 GB of data per day from the Arecibo telescope is recorded on high-capacity tapes and shipped to Berkeley, where it is divided by time and frequency into 0.25-MB chunks of data distributed to individual peers of the SETI@Home network. Each peer runs a software client based on the BOINC (Berkeley Open Infrastructure for Network Computing) platform, as shown in Figure 12 (Anderson 2004). Data received from the central servers of SETI@Home are processed by peers that perform a variety of mathematical tests, mostly based on discrete Fourier transforms; upon completion of the analysis, the results are sent back to the central server. SETI@Home peers are run exclusively by volunteers, who often set up teams altruistically competing against each other for the highest amount of work performed. SETI@Home peer software can run either as a screensaver or as a background task and is available for all major operating systems. According to the statistics provided by Boincstats.com (Boincstats 2006), as of January 2006, SETI@Home has the ability to compute over 200 TeraFLOPS while the combined computational power of all projects supported by the BOINC platform reaches over 300 TeraFLOPS.

CONCLUSION

P2P network applications have received a lot of media coverage and public attention in the recent years, primarily because of the legal implications of sharing copyrighted material. The concept of peer-to-peer architectures, however, had been used long before that; in fact, the earliest uses of P2P principles could be traced to the very roots of the Internet. Today, P2P network applications are successfully used in many areas, including file sharing, desktop collaboration, data storage, and distributed computing. Some view peer-to-peer as a disruptive technology, but it received such a label primarily because of the legal problems caused by P2P file-sharing applications. Although content traded on such networks remains largely pirated, they created a large and lively niche for legal media services providing consumers with a wide range of choices to purchase digital music and video content. Today, distributed computing systems based on P2P technologies reach computing capacities that are comparable to that of the fastest supercomputers in the world (Top500 2006). According to the estimates of CacheLogic (CacheLogic 2006), 60 to 80% of the consumer ISP network traffic is caused by P2P network applications. P2P technology has been successfully applied in VoIP applications, instant messaging, and other consumer and business-oriented areas, not to mention a large number of academic projects exploring innovative uses of P2P architectures. Today, it is becoming obvious that peer-to-peer technology is here to stay.

GLOSSARY

Client/Server: An architecture for network applications that separates the client (e.g., user interface) from the server (e.g., database).

Extensible Messaging and Presence Protocol (XMPP): An XML streaming protocol, approved by the Internet Engineering Task Force for use in instant messaging and presence information.

File Sharing: A practice of making a file available for others to download.

Groupware: Software used to integrate the work on a single project by several individuals working at different computers.

Instant Messaging (IM): The process of instant communication between two or more people.

Malware: Derived from malicious software, which is designed to damage or cause harm to the computer or its user; refers to computer viruses, worms, Trojan horses, adware, spyware, etc.

Network Address Translation (NAT): Enables multiple hosts on a private network to access the Internet using a single public IP address.

Peer: A node in a peer-to-peer computer network acting both as a client and a server.

Replication: Provision of redundant service (e.g., storage) to improve a system's reliability and fault tolerance.

Single Point of Failure: In system design, refers to a part of the system, which, if it fails, will cause a significant interruption in the service provided by the system.

CROSS REFERENCES

See *Incentive Issues in Peer-to-Peer Systems*; *Peer-to-Peer Network Architecture*.

REFERENCES

Anderson, D. 2004. BOINC: A system for public-resource computing and storage. In *Proceedings of 5th IEEE/ACM International Workshop on Grid Computing, Pittsburgh*. Los Alamitos, CA: IEEE Computer Society.

Androutsellis-Theotokis, S., and D. Spinellis. 2004. A survey of peer-to-peer content distribution technologies. *ACM Computing Surveys*, 36(4):335–371.

BitTorrent. 2006. BitTorrent Web site. www.bittorrent.com (accessed April 21, 2007).

Boincstats. 2006. BOINC Statistics Web site. www.boincstats.com (accessed April 21, 2007).

Cachelogic. 2006. CacheLogic Web site. www.cachelogic.com (accessed April 21, 2007).

Clarke, I., O. Sandberg, B. Wiley, and T. Hong, T. 2000. Freenet: A distributed anonymous information storage and retrieval system. In *Proceedings of the ICSI Workshop on Design Issues in Anonymity and Unobservability, Berkeley, CA. Berlin: Springer Verlag.*

eMule. 2006. eMule Web site. www.emule-project.net (accessed April 21, 2007).

FoldingAtHome. 2006. Folding@Home project Web site. http://folding.stanford.edu (accessed April 21, 2007).

Foster, I., and A. Iamnitchi. 2003. On death, taxes, and the convergence of peer-to-peer and grid computing. In *Proceedings of the 2nd International Workshop on Peer-to-Peer Systems (IPTPS'03). Berkley, CA. Berlin: Springer Verlag.*

Freenet. 2006. The Free Network Project Web site. http://freenetproject.org (accessed April 21, 2007).

GenomeAtHome. 2006. Genome@Home project Web site. http://genomeathome.stanford.edu (accessed April 21, 2007).

Groove. 2005. Groove Architecture white paper. www.groove.net/pdf/gaag/gaag-architecture.pdf (accessed April 21, 2007).

Groove. 2006. Groove Virtual Office Web site. www.groove.net (accessed April 21, 2007).

Jabber. 2006. Jabber Software Foundation Web site. www.jabber.org (accessed April 21, 2007).

Kan, G. 2001. Gnutella. In *Peer-to-peer: Harnessing the power of disruptive technologies*, edited by A. Oram, 94–122. Sebastopol, CA: O'Reilly.

Kazaa. 2006. Kazaa Web site. www.kazaa.com (accessed April 21, 2007).

Korpela, E., D. Werthimer, D. Anderson, J. Cobb, and M. Lebofsky. 2001. SETI@Home—Massively distributed computing for SETI. *Computing in Science & Engineering Journal*, January:78–83.

Kubiatowicz, J. 2003. Extracting guarantees from chaos. *Communications of the ACM* 46(2):33–8.

Larson, S., C. Snow, and V. Pande. 2003. Folding@Home and Genome@Home: Using distributed computing to tackle previously intractable problems in computational biology. In *Modern methods in computational biology*, Norwich, UK: Horizon Scientific Press.

Miller, J. 2001. Jabber. Conversational technologies. In *Peer-to-Peer: Harnessing the Power of Disruptive Technologies*, edited by A. Oram, 77–93. Sebastopol, CA: O'Reilly.

Minar, N., and M. Hedlund. 2001. A network of peers: Peer-to-peer models through the history of the Internet. In *Peer-to-peer: Harnessing the power of disruptive technologies*, edited by A. Oram, 77–93. Sebastopol, CA: O'Reilly.

Oberholzer-Gee, F., and K. Strumpf. 2005. The effect of file sharing on record Sales: An empirical analysis. www.unc.edu/~cigar/papers/FileSharing_June2005_final.pdf (accessed April 21, 2007).

OceanStore. 2006. OceanStore project Web site. http://oceanstore.cs.berkeley.edu (accessed April 21, 2007).

Pouwelse, J., P. Garbacki, D. Epema, and H. Sips.2005. The BitTorrent P2P file-sharing system: Measurements and analysis. In *Proceedings of the 4th International Workshop on Peer-to-Peer Systems, Ithaca, NY*. Berlin: Springer Verlag.

Ratnasamy, S., P. Francis, M. Handley, R. Karp, and S. Schenker. 2001. A scalable content-addressable network. In *Proceedings of SIGCOMM, San Diego, CA*, 61–172. New York: ACM Press.

Rowstron, A., and P. Druschel. 2001. Pastry: Scalable, distributed object location and routing for large-scale peer-to-peer systems. In *Proceedings of the 8th IFIP/ACM International Conference on Distributed Systems Platforms, Heidelberg, Germany*, 329–50. New York: ACM Press.

SetiAtHome 2006. SETI@Home project Web site. http://setiathome.ssl.berkeley.edu (accessed April 21, 2007).

Shirky, C. 2000. *What is p2p... and what isn't?* www.openp2p.com/pub/a/p2p/2000/11/24/shirky1-whatisp2p.html (accessed April 21, 2007).

Skype. 2006 Skype Web site. www.skype.com (accessed April 21, 2007).

Skypejournal. 2006. Skype Journal statistics. www.skypejournal.com/blog/archives/stats (accessed April 21, 2007).

Slyck. 2006. P2P file sharing networks statistics. http://slyck.com/stats.php (accessed May 25, 2006).

StardustAtHome. 2006. Stardust@Home project Web site. http://stardustathome.ssl.berkeley.edu (accessed April 21, 2007).

Stoica, I., R. Morris, D. Karger, M. Kaashoek, and H. Balakrishnan. 2001. Chord: A scalable peer-to-peer lookup service for internet applications. In *Proceedings of SIGCOMM, San Diego, CA*. 149–60. New York: ACM Press.

Top500. 2006. Top 500 Supercomputer Sites Web site. www.top500.org (accessed April 21, 2007).

Zhao, B., L. Huang, J. Stribling, S. Rhea, A. Joseph, and K. Kubiatowicz. 2004. Tapestry: A Resilient global-scale overlay for service deployment. *IEEE Journal on Selected Areas in Communications* 22(1):41–53.

FURTHER READING

Miller, M. 2001. Discovering P2P. Indianapolis: Sybex.

Leuf, B. 2002. Peer to peer: Collaboration and sharing over the Internet. Reading, MA: Addison-Wesley.

Oram, A., ed. 2001. *Peer-to-peer: Harnessing the power of disruptive technologies*. Sebastopol, CA: O'Reilly.

Steinmetz, R., and K. Wehrle, eds. 2005. Peer-to-peer systems and applications. New York: Springer Lecture Notes in Computer Science.

Subramanian, R., and B. Goodman. eds. 2005. Peer to peer computing: The evolution of a disruptive technology. Hershey, PA: Idea Group Publishing.

Wang, W. 2004. Steal this file sharing book. San Francisco: No Starch Press.

Incentive Issues in Peer-to-Peer Systems

Yu-Kwong Kwok, *The University of Hong Kong, Hong Kong*

INTRODUCTION

Modern computing technologies have decentralized data-processing power in an unprecedented manner. An important implication is that user machines, be it a desktop computer or a handheld PDA (personal digital assistant), have data-processing power, in terms of instruction pro-cessing rate, amount of storage, and reliability, that was inconceivable merely a decade or two ago. Indeed, computing now occurs largely at the "edge" of networks. Network infrastructure systems have also made tremendous strides thanks to ever-improving communications technologies. Advancements in computing and communication, coupled together, enable a recent trend in a new form of distributed processing—peer-to-peer (P2P) computing (Roussopolos et al. 2004).

As its name implies, P2P computing involves users (or their machines) on equal footing—there is no designated server or client, at least in a persistent sense. Every participating user can be a server and a client, depending on context. Some people have referred to this as a "democratic computing environment" (Androutselli-Theotokis and Spinellis 2004) because users are free from centralized authorities' control. This new paradigm of distributed computing has spawned many high-profile applications, most notably in file-sharing, such as: BitTorrent (Cohen 2003), Freenet (Clarke et al. 2000), Gnutella (http://gnutella.wego.com), and, of course, Napster (www.napster.com).

The highly flexible features of P2P computing, such as a dynamic population (users come and go asynchronously at will), dynamic topologies (it is impractical, if not impossible, to enforce a fixed communication structure), and anonymity, come at a significant cost—autonomy, by its very nature, is not always in harmony with tight cooperation. Consequently, inefficient cooperation or lack of cooperation could lead to undesirable effects in P2P computing. Among them, the most critical one is "free-riding" (Feldman and Chuang 2005) behavior. Loosely speaking, free-riding occurs when some users do not follow the presumed altruistic cooperation rules, such as sharing files voluntarily, sharing bandwidth voluntarily, or sharing energy voluntarily, so as to benefit the whole community.

Such altruistic sharing actions, presumably, would bring indirect and intangible (and even remote) returns to the users. For instance, if everyone shares files voluntarily, every user would eventually benefit from the high availability of a large and diverse set of selections. Unfortunately, there are some users that do not believe or buy in to such utopia-like concepts and would, then, "rationally" choose to just enjoy the benefits derived from the community, but not contribute their own resources.

To deter or avoid free-riding behaviors, the P2P community has to provide some incentives—returns for resource expenditure that are, more often than not, tangible and immediate. Such incentives would then motivate an otherwise selfish user to rationally choose to cooperate because such cooperation would bring tangible and immediate benefits. To mention an analogy, in human society, getting pay for our work is a tangible and immediate incentive to motivate us to devote our energy, which could otherwise be spent on other activities. Indeed, it is important for the incentive to be tangible so that a user can perform a cost-benefit analysis—if benefit outweighs cost, the user would then take a cooperative action (Krishnana, Smith, and Telang 2003). It is also important for the incentive to be immediate (though this is a relative concept) because any resource is associated with an opportunity cost in that if immediate return cannot be obtained from a cooperative action, then the user might want to save the effort for some other private tasks.

To provide incentives in a P2P computing system, there are basically five different classes of techniques.

1. **Payment-Based Mechanisms:** Users taking cooperative actions (e.g., sharing their files voluntarily) would obtain payments in return. The payment may be real monetary units (in cash) or virtual (i.e., tokens that can be redeemed for other services). Thus, two important components are needed: (1) currency and (2) accounting and clearing mechanisms. Obviously, if the currency is in the form of real cash, there is a need for a centralized authority, in the form of an electronic bank, that is external to the P2P system. If the currency is in the form of virtual tokens, then it might be possible to have a peer-to-peer clearing mechanism. In both cases, the major objective is to avoid fraud at the expense of significant overhead. Proper pricing of cooperative actions is also important—overpriced actions would make the system economically inefficient while underpriced actions would not be able to entice cooperation.

2. **Auction-Based Mechanisms:** In some situations, in order to come up with optimal pricing, auctioning is an effective mechanism. In simple terms, auction involves bidding from the participating users so that the user with the highest bid gets the opportunity to serve (or to be served, depending on context). An important issue in auction-based systems is the valuation problem—at how much should a user set the bid? If every user sets a bid higher than its true cost in providing a service, then the recipient of the service would pay more than the service deserves. On the other hand, if the bids are too low, the service providers may suffer. Fortunately, in some form of auctions, proper mechanisms can be constructed to induce bidders to bid at their true costs.
3. **Exchange-Based Mechanisms:** Compared to payment-based and auction-based systems, exchange (or barter)-based techniques manifest as a purer P2P interaction. Specifically, in an exchange-based environment, a pair of users (or, sometimes, a circular list of users) serve each other in a rendezvous manner. That is, service is exchanged in a synchronous and stateless transaction. For example, a pair of users meet each other and exchange files. After the transaction, the two users can forget about each other in the sense that any future transaction between them is unaffected by the current transaction. This has an important advantage—very little overhead is involved. Most importantly, peers can interact with each other without the need for intervention or mediation by a centralized external entity (e.g., a bank). Furthermore, free-riding is impractical. Of course, the downside is that service discovery and peer selection (according to price and/or quality of service) could be difficult.
4. **Reciprocity-Based Mechanisms:** Whereas pure barter-based interactions are stateless, reciprocity generally refers to stateful and history-based interactions. Specifically, a peer A may serve another peer B at time t_1 and does not get an immediate return. However, the transaction is recorded in some history database (centralized in some external entity or distributed in both A and B). At a later time $t_2 > t_1$, peer B serves peer A, possibly because peer B selects peer A as the client because of the earlier favor from A. That is, because peer A has served peer B before, peer B would give a higher preference to serve peer A. A critical problem is how to tackle a special form of free-riding behavior, namely the "whitewashing" action (i.e., a user leaves the system and rejoins with a different identity), which enables the free-rider to forget about his or her obligations.
5. **Reputation-Based Mechanisms:** A reputation-based mechanism is a generalized form of reciprocity. Specifically, while a reciprocity record is induced by a pair of peers (or a circular list of more than two peers), a reputation system records a score for each peer based on the assessments made by many peers. Each service provider (or consumer, depending on the application) can then consult the reputation system in order to judge whether it is worthwhile or safe to provide service to a particular client. Reputation-based mechanisms are by nature globally accessible, and thus, peer selection can be done easily. However, the reputation scores must be securely stored and computed, or otherwise, the scores cannot truly reflect the quality of peers. In some electronic marketplaces, such as eBay, the reputation scores are centrally administered. But such an arrangement would again need an external entity and some significant overhead. On the other hand, storing the scores in a distributed manner at the peer level would induce problems of fraud. Finally, similar to reciprocity-based mechanisms, whitewashing is a low-cost technique employed by selfish users to avoid being identified as a low-quality users, which would be excluded from the system.

The different techniques mentioned above are suitable for different applications. Generally speaking, there are two mainstream applications in P2P environments: sharing of discrete data and sharing of continuous data. Examples of the former include file-sharing systems (e.g., Napster) and data-sharing systems (e.g., sharing of financial or weather reports). A notable example of the latter is P2P video streaming. Indeed, there is an important difference between file-sharing and media-streaming systems. In the former, a user needs to wait until a file (or a discrete unit of shared information) is completely received before it can be consumed or used. Thus, there could be a significant delay between a service request and judgment of service quality. In an extreme case, a user may not discover that a shared file is indeed the one requested or just a garbage file until the file has been downloaded. By contrast, in a media-streaming application, a user would quickly discover whether the received information is good enough. The quality of service (QoS) metric used is also different in these two different applications. In a file-sharing application, the most important metrics are downloading time and the integrity of the received files. In a media-streaming application, the more crucial performance parameters are the various playback quality metrics such as jitter, frame-rate, and resolution. Furthermore, the incentive techniques surveyed in this chapter subsume the underlying P2P network topology. Specifically, in most proposed systems, the communication message-exchange mechanism is not explicitly modeled.

Currently, the majority of P2P systems are implemented over the Internet. However, wireless P2P systems are also proliferating. Although most of the incentive techniques designed for a wired environment could be applicable in a wireless system, the wireless connectivity is by itself an important bootstrap sharing problem. Indeed, on the Internet, users seldom pay attention to the connectivity issue because a user can be reached (or can reach) any other Internet user without noticeable effort. The only concern about communication is the uploading or downloading bandwidth consumption. In a wireless environment, however, the mere action of sending a request message from a client peer to a server peer would probably need several intermediate peers to help in the message forwarding because the server and client peers may be out of each other's transmission range. Consequently, incentives have to be provided to encourage such forwarding actions.

In this chapter, we survey state-of-the-art solutions proposed for tackling the incentive issues in various P2P resource-sharing systems. We describe approaches designed for providing incentives in Internet-based P2P networks. We discuss both file-sharing and media-streaming applications. We describe solutions suggested for wireless P2P systems and then provide some of our interpretations and suggestions. At the end of the chapter, we summarize and provide some remarks.

INCENTIVE ISSUES IN P2P SYSTEMS ON THE INTERNET

File-Sharing Systems

In a file-sharing system, users would like to retrieve files from other users, and would expect other users to do the same from them. Thus, each user would need to expend two different forms of resource:

- Storage: Each user has to set aside some storage space to keep files that may be needed by other users, even though such files may not be useful to the user itself.
- Bandwidth: Each user has to devote some of its outbound bandwidth for uploading requested files to other users.

Users usually perform file selection (and hence, peer selection) with the help of some directory system, which may or may not be fully distributed. For example, in Napster (www.napster.com), the directory is centralized.

Using such a sharing model, the most obvious form of free-riding behavior is that a selfish user just keeps on retrieving files from others but refuses to share its collections (and thus, has no need to expend any outbound bandwidth for file uploading). Interestingly enough, in an empirical study using the Maze file-sharing system (http://maze.pku.edu.cn), Yang et al. (2005) found that the more direct indicator of free-riding behaviors is the online time of a user. Specifically, the online time of a selfish user in a P2P file-sharing network is on average only one-third that of a cooperative peer.

In this section, we first briefly overview a contemporary file-sharing system called BitTorrent (Cohen 2003). We then survey techniques suggested for various other P2P file-sharing networks.

BitTorrent

BitTorrent (Cohen 2003) is by far one of the most successful P2P file-sharing systems. A key feature in BitTorrent is that each shared file is divided into 256-kB pieces, which are usually stored in multiple different peers. Thus, for any peer in need of a shared file, parallel downloading can take place in that the requesting peer can use multiple TCP connections to obtain different pieces of the file from several distinct peers. This feature is highly effective because the uploading burden is shared among multiple peers and the network can scale to a large size. Closely related to this parallel downloading mechanism is the incentive component used in BitTorrent. Specifically, each uploading peer selects up to four requesting peers in making uploading connections. The selection priority is based on descending order of downloading rates from the requesting peers. That is, the uploading peer selects four requesting peers that have the highest downloading rates. Here, downloading rate refers to the data rate that is used by a requesting peer in sending out pieces of some other file. Thus, the rationale of this scheme is to provide incentive for each participating peer to increase the data rate used in sending out file data (i.e., uploading, or, in BitTorrent's term, *unchoking*). There are other related mechanisms (e.g., optimistic unchoking), which are described in detail in Cohen (2003) and Qiu and Srikant (2004).

Qiu and Srikant (2004) performed an in-depth analysis of BitTorrent's incentive mechanism. By using an intricate and accurate model, it is shown that a Nash equilibrium exists in the upload/download game in BitTorrent. At the equilibrium, each peer sets its uploading data rate to be its physical maximum uploading rate (i.e., each peer is fully cooperative). On the other hand, because of the usage of the optimistic unchoking mechanism (a fifth requesting peer is randomly selected in the uploading process, for details, see Cohen [2003] and Qiu and Srikant [2004]), a free-rider can potentially achieve 20% of the possible maximum downloading rate. This theoretical result conforms nicely with the simulation findings by Jun and Ahamad (2005), who observed that in BitTorrent, free-riders are not penalized adequately and contributors are not rewarded sufficiently.

Hierarchical P2P Systems

In some situations, the P2P network may be structured in a hierarchical manner so that some specialized machines (called "superpeers") can take up a more important role for handling resource management tasks such as request forwarding and routing, directory listing, etc.

Singh et al. (2003) proposed a superpeer-based scheme. Specifically, they studied the impacts of superpeers in a P2P file-sharing network. Simply put, a superpeer is a special network node that serves as a hub to provide file indexing service to other nodes. The problem is the lack of incentive for a participating node to act as a superpeer, because any node can simply join an existing superpeer to obtain good performance. Singh et al. observed that some entities external to the P2P system, such as an Internet service provider (ISP) or a content publisher, have business-driven incentives for designating some nodes to act as superpeers, and for enhancing the capabilities of superpeers. Specifically, a superpeer can cache meta data only, instead of the files themselves. As such, the cost of acting as a superpeer is lower. Furthermore, with properly designed meta data, a superpeer can support value-added search commands (e.g., a topic-based search of files).

With such facilities incorporated in each superpeer, a hierarchical P2P file-sharing network is then much more efficient that a flat P2P system, which relies on request-flooding. Consequently, all nodes in the system have the incentive in maintaining such a P2P file-sharing system. Simulation results also indicate that the proposed superpeer scheme is effective.

Payment-Based Systems

Hausheer et al. (2003) suggested a token-based accounting system that is generic and can support different pricing schemes for charging peers in file sharing. The proposed system is depicted in Figure 1. The system mandates that each user has a permanent ID authenticated by

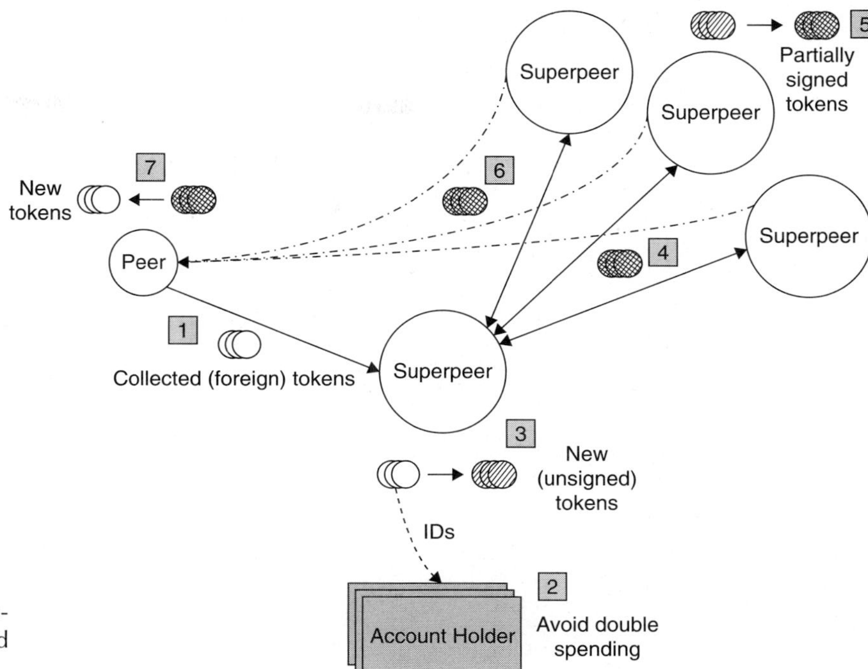

Figure 1: A superpeer-based token accounting system for P2P file sharing (based on Hausheer et al. 2003)

a certification authority. Each peer has a token account keeping track of the current amount of tokens, which are classified as local and foreign. A peer can spend its local tokens for accessing remote files. The file owner treats such tokens as foreign tokens, which cannot be spent but need to be exchanged with superpeers for new local tokens. Each token has a unique ID so that it cannot be spent multiple times.

At the beginning of each file-sharing transaction, the file consumer tells the file owner which tokens it intends to spend. The file owner then checks against file consumer's account kept at the file owner's machine. If the tokens specified are valid (i.e., they have not been spent before), then the file consumer can send the tokens in an unsigned manner to the file owner. Upon receipt of these unsigned tokens, the file owner provides the requested files to the file consumer. When the files are successfully received, the file consumer sends the signed version of the tokens to the file owner. In this manner, Hausheer et al. argued that there is no incentive for the peers to cheat.

Yang and Garcia-Molina (2003) proposed the PPay micropayment system, in which each peer can buy a coin from a broker. The peer then becomes the "owner" of the coin and can send it to some other peer. An important feature is that even after the coin is spent, the original owner still has the responsibility to check the subsequent use of the coin. For example, suppose A is the owner of a coin that is sent to B. If B wants to send the coin in turn to C, the original owner A needs to check whether such a transaction is valid (e.g., to avoid double spending of the same coin). If A is offline (e.g., temporarily departed the P2P system), then the broker is responsible for performing such checking.

Although the PPay system described above is a useful tool for supporting P2P sharing, Jia et al. (2005) observed that PPay can be further improved. Specifically, they proposed a new micropayment system, called CPay (an improved version of PPay), which has one significant new feature–the broker judiciously selects the most appropriate peer to be the owner of a coin. Specifically, the owner of a coin should be one that is expected to stay in the system for a long time. Thus, the broker's potential burden of checking coin owners' transactions can be considerably reduced.

Figueiredo, Shapiro and Towsley (2005) also considered a payment-based system to entice cooperation among peers. Specifically, each peer requiring message-forwarding services from other peers needs to pay real money to these peers. Thus, as a peer stays in the P2P network and provides forwarding service to other peers, it can gain money. Indeed, such a monetary gain represents an incentive to enhance the availability of a peer in the network.

Saito (2003) proposed an Internet-based electronic currency called *i*-WAT, which can be used by users in a P2P system for "purchasing" services. Each *i*-WAT message is an electronic ticket signed using OpenPGP. Saito, Morino, and Murai (2005) then extended the *i*-WAT system by adding a new feature called "multiplication over time," which means that a requesting peer's debt (in terms of *i*-WAT units) increases over time. This feature then encourages service-providing peers to stay in the system for a longer time so as to defer the redemption of *i*-WAT tickets, thereby increasing the gains from the requesting peers.

Cost of Sharing

Varian (2003) reported a simple but insightful analytical study on disincentives in P2P sharing. Table 1 lists the notation used in Varian's analysis.

In Varian's model, a single item (e.g., a single music file) is considered and the system is homogeneous in that all peers have the same valuation on the item. There is an external central authority (e.g., the original producer of the music) that has the incentive to discourage sharing

Table 1: Notation Used in Varian's Analysis on Disincentives for P2P Sharing

Symbol	Definition
p	Unit price
v	Value of the item as perceived by each peer
n	Number of peers in the system
D	Total cost of producing all the items
$d = \frac{D}{n}$	Average development cost
k	Number of peers in each group that share an item
t	Sharing cost incurred by each member of a group
c	Cost imposed by the central authority to those peers who participate in sharing
π	Profit derived by the central authority

among peers in the system. The issue is then how the central authority can introduce proper disincentives into the system. First, observe that for viability in producing the item, we have:

$$v - \frac{p}{k} - t - c \geq 0 \tag{1}$$

$$p\frac{n}{k} \geq D \tag{2}$$

Specifically, the above equations are to ensure that value is no smaller than the cost.

The equilibrium (where the item is just viable to be produced) price and profit are then given by:

$$p = (v - t - c)\,k \tag{3}$$

$$\pi = (v - t - c)\,kn - D \tag{4}$$

We can see that profit is, counterintuitively, decreasing in c. An interpretation is that c is not large enough to discourage sharing and price has to be cut for compensation. As an analogy, consider that c represents some copy protection mechanism, which merely brings inconvenience to customers but cannot discourage sharing. To compensate for the inconvenience, the price has to be reduced.

On the other hand, for a given value of c, suppose the price is set in such a way that it is marginally unattractive to share. That is, we have:

$$\frac{p}{k} + t + c \geq p \tag{5}$$

This in turn implies that:

$$p = \frac{k}{k-1}(t + c) \tag{6}$$

Now, as the maximum practical value of p is v, we have:

$$c = v - \frac{k-1}{k}t \tag{7}$$

Yu and Singh (2003) also investigated the issue of proper pricing in the presence of free-riders in a P2P system. A referral-based system is considered, in that each peer can either answer a remote query directly (e.g., serving a requested file) or reply with a referral (e.g., pointing to a different peer who may be able to serve the requested file). A requester (i.e., file consumer) needs to pay for both a referral and a direct answer. Each peer keeps track of reserve prices of potential referrals and direct answers from any other peer. These reserve prices are updated dynamically based on transaction experiences in that a satisfactory transaction leads to an increase in the reserve prices while an unsatisfactory one leads to a decrease. From a seller's point of view, these prices are also exponentially decreased as time goes by. Under this model, simulation results indicate that a free-rider will quickly deplete its budget. On the other hand, the price of a direct answer is found to be much higher than that of a referral.

Courcoubetis and Weber (2006) have reported an in-depth analysis of the cost of sharing in a P2P system. In their study, a P2P sharing system is modeled as a community with an excludable public good. Furthermore, the public good is assumed to be nonrivalrous, meaning that a user's consumption of the public good does not decrease the value of the good. Such a model is suitable for a P2P file-sharing network, where the excludable public good is the availability of shared files. The model is also considered as suitable for a P2P wireless LAN environment, in which the excludable public good is the common wireless channel. With their detailed modeling and analysis, an important conclusion is derived: each peer only needs to pay a fixed contribution, in terms of service provisioning (e.g., a certain fixed number of distinct files to be shared by other peers), in order to make the system viable. Such a fixed contribution is to be computed by some external administrative authority (called a "social planner") by using the statistical distribution of the peers' valuations of the public good.

Reciprocity- and Reputation-Based Systems

Feldman, Lai et al. (2004) suggested an integrated incentive mechanism for effectively deterring (or penalizing) free-riders using a reciprocity-based approach.

Specifically, the proposed integrated mechanism has three core components: discriminating server selection, maximum-flow-based subjective reputation computation, andadaptive-stranger policies.

In the discriminating server selection component, each peer is assumed to have a private history of transactions with other peers. Thus, when a file-sharing request is initiated, the peer can select a server (i.e., a file owner) from the private history. However, in any practical P2P sharing network, we can expect a high turnover rate of participation. That is, a peer may be present in the system for only a short time. Thus, when a request needs to be served, such a departed peer would not be able to help if it is selected. To mitigate this problem, a shared history is to be implemented. That is, each peer is able to select a server from a list of global transactions (i.e., not just restricted to those involving the current requesting peer). A practical method of implementing shared history is to use a distributed hash table (DHT)–based overlay networking storage system (Stoica et al. 2001). Specifically, a DHT is an effective data structure to support fast look-up of data locations.

A problem in turn induced by the shared-history facility is that collusion among noncooperative users may take place. Specifically, the noncooperative users may give each other a high reputation value (e.g., possibly by reporting bogus prior transaction records). To tackle this problem, Feldman, Lai et al. (2004) suggested a graph theoretic technique. To illustrate, consider the reputation graph shown in Figure 2. Here, each node in the graph represents a peer (C denotes a colluder) and each directed edge represents the perceived reputation value (i.e., the reputation value of the node incident by the edge as perceived by the node originating the edge). We can see that the colluders give each other a high reputation value. On the other hand, a contributing peer (e.g., the top node) gives a reputation value of 0 to each colluder because the contributing peer does not have any prior successful transaction carried out with a colluder. With this graph, we can apply the maximum-flow algorithm to compute the reputation value of a destination peer as perceived by a source peer. For instance, peer B's (the destination) perceived reputation value with respect to peer A (the source) is 0 despite many colluders giving a high reputation value to B.

Finally, an adaptive-stranger policy is proposed to deal with whitewashing. Instead of always penalizing a new user (which would discourage expansion of the P2P network), the proposed policy requires that each existing peer, before deciding whether to do a sharing transaction with a new user, computes a ratio of amount of services provided to amount of services consumed by a new user. If this ratio is great than or equal to 1, then the existing peer will work with the new user. On the other hand, if the ratio is smaller than 1, then the ratio is treated as a probability of working with this new user.

Sun and Garcia-Molina (2004) suggested an incentive system called Selfish Link-based InCentive (SLIC), which is based on pairwise reputation values. Specifically, any peer u maintains a reputation value $W(u, v)$ for each of its neighbor peer v, where the reputation value is normalized such that $0 \leq W(u, v) \leq 1$. Here, "neighbor" means a peer v currently having a logical connection with u and thus, such a peer v can potentially request service from u. With these reputation values, the peer u can then allocate the uploading bandwidth to any requesting neighbor peer v with a value of $W(u, v)/\Sigma_i W(u, i)$. The reputation value $W(u, v)$ is updated periodically based on an exponential averaging method.

Under this model, Sun and Garcia-Molina observed that each peer has the incentive to do some or all of the following, in order to increase its reputation values as perceived by other peers (and hence, enjoy a better quality of service):

- Share out more file data.
- Connect to more peers (to increase the opportunities for serving others).
- Increase its total uploading capacity.

Penalty-Based Approaches

Feldman, Papadimitriou et al. (2004) also investigated disincentive mechanisms that can discourage free-riding. Specifically, they considered various possible penalty schemes in deterring free-riders. A simple model is used. At the core of the model, each user i in the P2P sharing network is characterized by a positive real-valued *type* variable, denoted as t_i. Another key feature of the model is that the cost of contributing is equal to the reciprocal of the current percentage of contributors, which is denoted as x. Thus, for any rational user with type t_i, the user will choose to contribute if $1/x < t_i$ and free-ride if $1/x \geq t_i$.

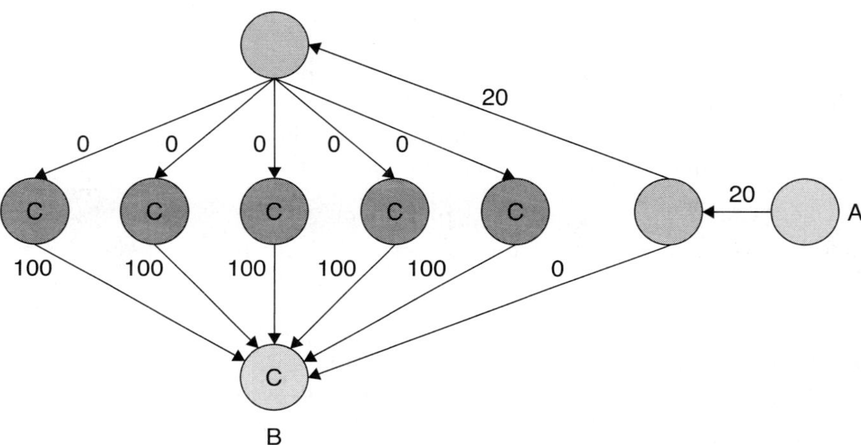

Figure 2: A graph depicting the perceived reputation values among peers (C denotes a colluder) (based on Feldman, Lai et al. 2004)

Furthermore, the benefit each user derived from the P2P network is assumed to be of the form αx^{β}, where $\beta \leq 1$ and $\alpha > 0$. With this benefit function, the system performance is defined as the difference between the average benefit and the average contribution cost. Specifically, system performance is equal to: $\alpha x^{\beta} - 1$.

Even with the simplistic model described above, Feldman et al. provided several interesting conclusions. First, they found that excluding low-type users can improve system performance only if the average type is low and α is large enough. Unfortunately, exclusion is impractical because a user's type is private and thus, cannot be determined accurately by other peers. It is then assumed that free-riding behaviors are observable (i.e., free-riders can be identified). Such free-riders are then subject to a reduction in quality of service. Quantitatively, the benefit received by a free rider is reduced by a factor of $(1 - p)$, where $0 < p \leq 1$. A simple implementation of this penalty is to exclude a free-rider with a probability of p. The second interesting conclusion is that the penalty mechanism is effective in deterring free-riders when the penalty is higher than the contribution cost. In quantitative terms, the condition is that $p > 1/\alpha$. Finally, another interesting conclusion is that for a sufficiently heavy penalty, no social cost is incurred because every user will contribute (i.e., choose not to be a free-rider) so that optimal system performance is achieved. In particular, to deal with the whitewashing problem, the analysis suggests that every new user is imposed a fixed penalty. Essentially, this is similar to the case in the eBay system, where every new user has a zero reputation and thus, will less likely be selected by other users in commercial transactions. However, this is in sharp contrast to the adaptive-stranger policies suggested also by Feldman, Papadimitriou et al. (2004).

Game Theoretic Modeling

Ranganathan et al. (2003) proposed and evaluated three schemes induced by the Multi-Person Prisoner's Dilemma (MPD) (Osborne 2004; Schelling 1978). The basic Prisoner's Dilemma game models the situation in which two competitors are both better off when they cooperate than when they do not. However, without communication, the unfortunate stable state is that both competitors would choose not to cooperate. An MPD is a generalization of the basic PD. Specifically, the key features of the MPD framework can be briefly summarized as follows:

- The MPD game is symmetric in that each of n players has the same actions, payoffs, and preferences.
- Any player's payoff is higher if other players choose some particular actions (e.g., "quiet" instead of "fink").

The MPD framework is used for modeling P2P file sharing as follows. There are n users in the system, each of which has a distinct file that can be either shared or kept only to the owner. The system is homogeneous in that all files have the same size and same degree of popularity. Now, the potential benefit gained by each user is the access of other users' files. The cost involved is the bandwidth used for serving other users' requests. With this simple model, it can be shown that the system has a unique Nash equilibrium in which no user wants to share. Obviously, this equilibrium is suboptimal (both at the individual level and at a systemwide level) in that each user could obtain a higher payoff (i.e., a higher value of net benefit) if all users choose to share their files.

Motivated by the MPD modeling, Ranganathan et al. proposed three incentive schemes:

- **Token Exchange**: This is a payment-based scheme because each file consumer has to give a token to the file owner in the sharing process. Each user is given the same number of tokens initially and each file has the same fixed price.
- **Peer-Approved**: This is a reputation-based scheme in that each user is associated with a rating that is computed using metrics such as the number of requests successfully served by the user. A user can download files from any owner who has a lower or the same rating. Thus, to gain access to more files in the system, a user has to actively provide service to other users so as to increase the rating.
- **Service Quality**: This is also a reputations-based scheme similar to peer-approved. The major difference is that a file owner provides differentiated service qualities to users with different ratings.

Theoretical analysis (Ranganathan et al. 2003) indicates that the peer-approved policy with a logarithmic benefit function (in terms of number of accessible files) can lead to the optimal equilibrium, in which every user contributes fully to the system. Simulation results also suggest that the peer-approved system generates performance (in terms of total number of files shared) comparable to that of token-exchange system, which entails a higher difficulty in practical implementation because it requires a payment system.

Becker and Clement (2004) also suggested an interesting analysis of the sharing behaviors using variants of the classical two player Prisoner's Dilemma. Specifically, the P2P file-sharing process is divided into three stages: introduction, growth, and settlement. In the introduction stage, the P2P network usually consists of just a few altruistic users who are eager to make the network viable. Thus, sharing of files is a trusted social norm. The payoffs of the two possible actions (supply files or not supply files) are depicted in Figure 3. Here, we have the payoffs ranking as: $R > T > S > P$ (*Note*: T = temptation, R = reward, S = sucker, P = punishment). Consequently, the Nash equilibrium profile is: (Supply, Supply). Notice that the payoffs ranking in the original Prisoner's Dilemma is: $T > R > P > S$, and as such, the Nash equilibrium is the action profile in the lower right corner of the table.

Player 2 / Player 1	Supply g_2^1	No Supply g_2^2
Supply g_1^1	R (Player 1), R (Player 2)	S (Player 1), T (Player 2)
No Supply g_1^2	T (Player 1), S (Player 2)	P (Player 1), P (Player 2)

Figure 3: Payoff table in the introduction stage (based on Becker and Clement 2004) (g = strategy)

Player 1 \ Player 2	Supply g_2^1	No Supply g_2^2
Supply g_1^1	R, R	S, T
No Supply g_1^2	T, S	P, P

Figure 4: Payoff table in the settlement stage (based on Becker and Clement 2004)

In the growth stage, we can expect that more and more noncooperative users join the network. For these users, the payoff ranking becomes: $T > R > P > S$, which is the same as the original Prisoner's Dilemma. Thus, the Nash equilibrium for such users occurs at the profile: (No Supply, No Supply). As the P2P network progresses to the mature stage (i.e., the size of the network becomes stabilized), we can expect that a majority of users are neither fully altruistic nor fully noncooperative. For these users, the payoff ranking is: $R > T > P > S$. As a result, the payoff matrix is as depicted in Figure 4. As can be seen, there are two equally probable Nash equilibria: (Supply, Supply) and (No Supply, No Supply). Consequently, whether the P2P network is viable or efficient depends on the relative proportions of users in these two equilibria. Results obtained in empirical studies (Becker and Clement 2004) using real P2P networks conform quite well to the simple analysis described above.

Ma et al. (*A Game Theoretic Approach*, 2004; *An Incentive Mechanism*, 2004) suggested an analytically sound incentive mechanism based on a fair bandwidth allocation algorithm. Indeed, the key idea is to model the P2P sharing as a bandwidth allocation problem. Specifically, the model is shown in Figure 5. Here, multiple file-requesting peers compete for uploading bandwidth of a source peer. Each requesting peer i sends a bidding message b_i to the source peer N_s. The source peer then divides its total uploading bandwidth W_s into portions of x_i for the peers. However, because of network problems such as congestion, each peer i may receive an actual uploading bandwidth of x'_i which is smaller than x_i.

Each bidding message b_i is the requested amount of bandwidth. Thus, we have $x_i \leq b_i$. To achieve a fair allocation, the source peer uses the contribution level C_i of each competing peer i to determine an appropriate value

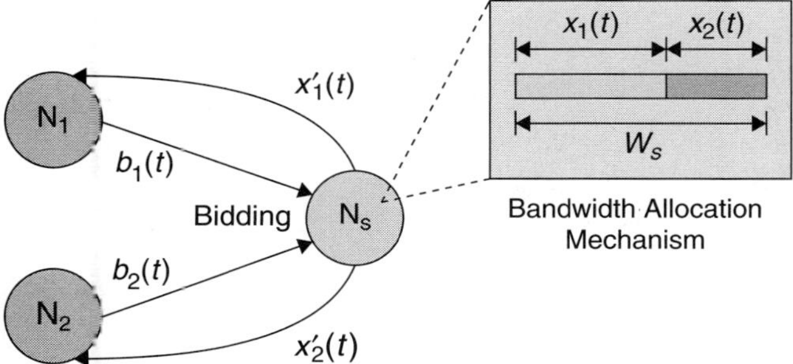

Figure 5: Two file-requesting peers (N_1 and N_2) compete for uploading bandwidth of a source peer (N_s) (based on Ma et al., *A Game Theoretic Approach*, 2004)

of x_i. Ma et al. (*A Game Theoretic Approach*, 2004; *An Incentive Mechanism*, 2004) described several allocation algorithms with different complexities and considerations: simplistic equal sharing, maximum-minimum fair allocation, incentive-based maximum-minimum fair allocation, utility based maximum-minimum fair allocation, and incentive with utility-based maximum-minimum fair allocation. The last algorithm is the most comprehensive and effective. It works by solving the following optimization problem:

$$\max \sum_{i=1}^{N} C_i \log\left(\frac{x_i}{b_i} + 1\right) \tag{8}$$

where:

$$\sum_{i=1}^{N} x_i \leq W_s \tag{9}$$

Here, the logarithmic function represents the utility as perceived by each peer i.

The above optimization problem can be solved by a progressive filling algorithm that prioritizes competing peers in descending order of the marginal utility $C_i/(b_i + x_i)$.

Given values of b_i and C_i, the source peer can compute the allocations in a deterministic manner. However, from the perspective of a requesting peer, a problem remains as to how it should set its bidding value b_i. Using a game theoretic analysis, it is shown that the action profile in which:

$$b_i = \frac{W_s C_i}{\sum_{j=1}^{N} C_j} \forall i$$

is a Nash equilibrium. Furthermore, provided that all cooperative peers use their respective strategies as specified in the Nash equilibrium action profile, collusion among noncooperative peers can be eliminated. Notice that each requesting peer i needs to know the values of W_S and $\sum_{j=1}^{N} C_j$ in order to determine its own bid b_i. In a practical situation, these two values can be supplied by the source peer to every requesting peer.

Auction-Based Approaches

Gupta and Somani (2004) proposed an auction-based pricing mechanism for P2P file object look-up services. In their model, each resource (e.g., a file object) is stored in a single node. However, the indices for such a file object are replicated at multiple nodes in the network and these nodes are called "terminal nodes." When a peer initiates a look-up request for a certain file object, the request is sent through multiple paths toward the terminal nodes, as shown in Figure 6. The problem here is that the intermediate nodes need some incentives in order to participate in the request forwarding process.

Gupta and Somani (2004) suggested a novel solution to the incentive problem. Specifically, the initiating peer attaches a price in the request message it sends to the first layer of nodes in the request chains. Each intermediate node on the request chains then updates the price by adding its own "forwarding cost." The terminal nodes do the

Figure 6: The request-forwarding process (based on Gupta and Somani 2004)

same updating before sending the request messages to the data source. Upon receiving all the request messages, the data source then performs a second price sealed bid auction (also referred to as Vickrey auction) (Osborne 2004) to select the highest bid among the terminal nodes. The selected terminal node then needs to pay the price equal to the value of the second-highest bid. With this auction-based approach, all the intermediate nodes on the request chains have the incentive to participate in the forwarding process because they might eventually get paid by the requester should their respective request chain wins the auction.

For example, consider the look-up process shown in Figure 7. We can see that the request chain terminated by node T1 wins the auction process and the payoff to the data source node B is 60. The only intermediate node (node 1) then also gets a payoff. Gupta and Somani (2004) also showed that a truthful valuation in is the optimal strategy for each intermediate node. Furthermore, based on the requirement that every message cannot be repudiated, it is also shown that the proposed mechanism can handle various potential threats such as malicious auctioneer, collusion between data source and a terminal node, forwarding of bogus request message, etc.

Wongrujira and Seneviratne (2005) proposed a similar auction-based charging scheme for forwarding nodes on a path from a requesting peer to a data source. However, they pointed out an important observation that some potential malicious peers could try to reduce the profits of other truthful peers by dropping the price messages. To mitigate this problem, a reputation system is introduced in that every peer maintains a history of interactions with other peers. The reputation value of a peer is increased every time a message is forwarded by such a peer. On the other hand, if an expected message exhibits a timeout, the responsible peer's reputation value is decreased.

Wang and Li (2005) also considered a similar problem in which a peer needs to decide how much to charge for forwarding data. Instead of using an auction, a comprehensive utility function is used. The utility function captures many realistic factors: the quantitative benefits of forwarding data, the loss in delivering such data, the cost and the benefit to the whole community. With this utility function, an upstream peer has the incentive to contribute its forwarding bandwidth while a downstream peer is guided toward spending the upstream bandwidth economically. Furthermore, a reinforcement learning component is incorporated so that each peer can dynamically adjust the parameters in its utility function so as to optimally respond to the current market situations.

Sanghavi and Hajek (2005) observed that in a typical auction-based pricing mechanism as described above, there is a heavy communication burden on the peers. Indeed, the entire set of user preferences has to be communicated from a peer to the auctioneer. Sanghavi and Hajek then analytically derived a class of alternative information mechanisms that can significantly reduce the communication overhead. Specifically, each peer's bid is only a single real number in each case, instead of an entire real-valued function.

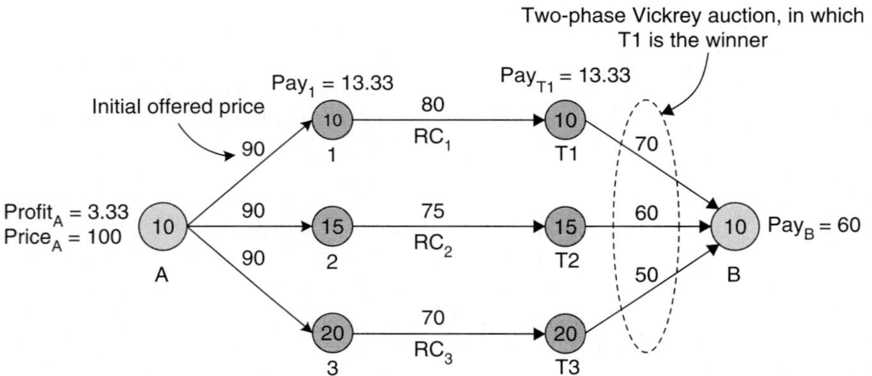

Figure 7: An example of the auction process in request forwarding (based on Gupta and Somani 2004)

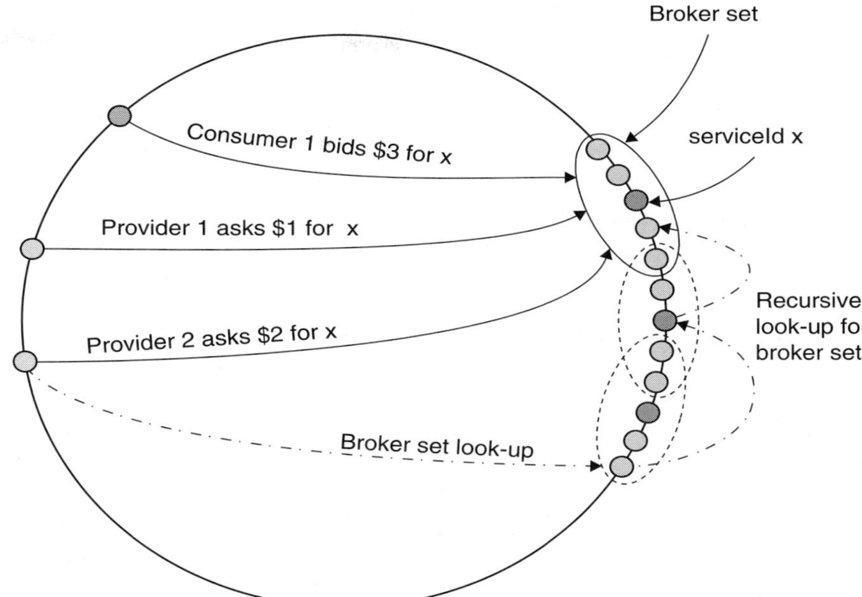

Figure 8: An example of fully decentralized auction (based on Hausheer and Stiller 2005)

Hausheer and Stiller (2005) studied a completely decentralized auction approach for electronic P2P pricing of goods in a system called PeerMart (which is built on top of Pastry (Rowstron and Druschel 2001)). The key idea is the use of a broker set, which comprises other peers in the electronic marketplace. Specifically, a broker set consists of peers' whose IDs are closest to the ID of the good in the auction. Each of these peers then potentially acts as the auctioneer in the selling process. The advantage of the broker-set-based method is that in case a particular peer in the set is faulty (or even malicious in the sense that it does not respond to auction requests), another member in the set can take up the role of auctioneer. An example is shown in Figure 8.

Exchange-Based Systems

Motivated by the fact that any payment/credit-based system entails a significant transaction and accounting overhead, Anagnostakis and Greenwald (2004) proposed an exchange-based P2P file-sharing system. The fundamental premises is that any peer gives priority to exchange transfers. That is, in simple terms, any peer is willing to send a file to a peer that is able to return a desired file. However, based on this idea, it is incorrect to consider two way exchanges only. Indeed, a "ring" of exchange involving two or more peers, as shown in Figure 9, is also a proper P2P file transfer.

In the exchange-based P2P file-sharing system, each peer maintains a data structure called incoming request queue (IRQ). Now, a crucial problem is how each peer can determine whether an incoming request should be entertained—i.e., whether such a request comes from some peer on a ring of exchange requests. It is obviously computationally formidable to determine all the potential multi peer cycles. Fortunately, Anagnostakis and Greenwald (2004) argue that based on simulation results, in practice a peer only needs to check for cycles with up to five peers.

Each peer uses a data structure called a "request tree" to check for potential request cycles. For example, as we can see in Figure 10, a peer A decides to entertain a request for file object o_2 because A finds that peer P_9 possesses an object that is needed by A. Based on this checking mechanism, the incoming requests are prioritized. Simulation

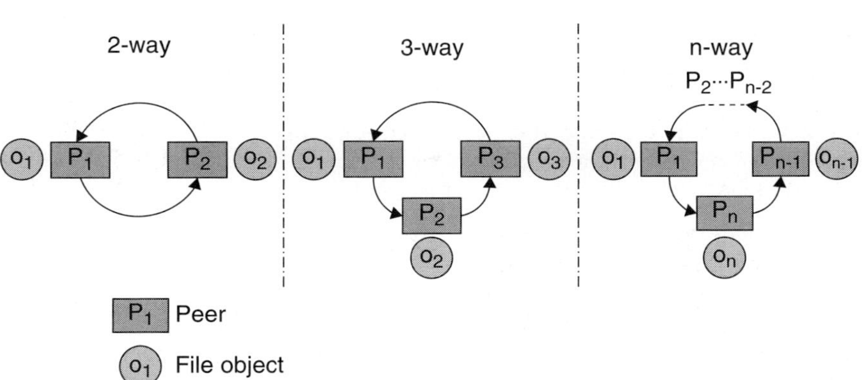

Figure 9: Different feasible forms of exchanges (based on Becker and Clement 2004)

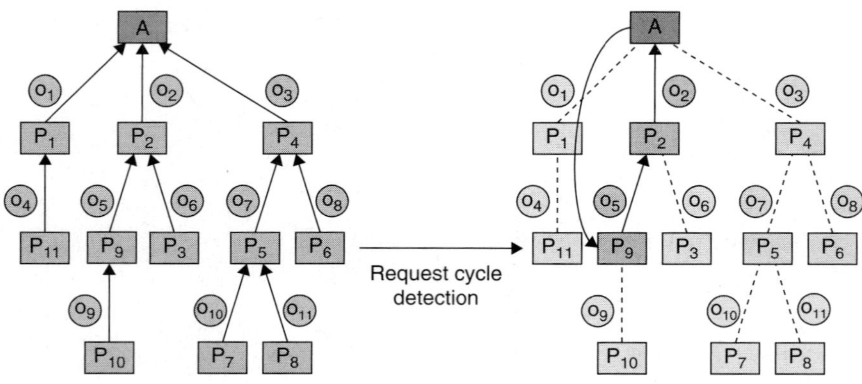

Figure 10: Request cycle detection using the request tree data structure maintained at each peer (based on Becker and Clement 2004)

Table 2: A Qualitative Comparison of Different Incentive Approaches for P2P File Sharing

	Payment	Auction	Exchange	Reciprocity	Reputation
Example	Hausheer et al. (2003)	Gupta and Somani (2004)	Anagnostakis and Greenwald (2004)	BitTorrent	Sun and Garcia-Molina (2004)
Practical Implementation	Complex	Complex	Easy	Easy	Easy
Security Requirement	High	High	Low	Low	Medium
Centralized Authority Required	Yes	Yes	No	No	Yes/No
Scalability	Medium	Low	High	High	High

results indicate that the proposed exchange-based mechanisms are effective in terms of file object download time.

Table 2 gives a qualitative comparison of different incentive approaches proposed for P2P file-sharing systems. In general, systems that involve payment would be more difficult to implement because it is not trivial to design a global "currency" for use in such systems. Furthermore, security requirement would be high because the payment could be forged by malicious peers. On the other hand, exchange-based or reciprocity-based systems are easier to implement and hence, are more scalable. The major crux is that there is much less state information to be kept by each peer. More important, the accuracy of such state information (e.g., reputation) does not need to be absolutely very high. Thus, we expect that future P2P file sharing would still be based on similar approaches.

Media-Streaming Systems

In this section, we describe several interesting techniques for providing incentives in a P2P media-streaming environment. Broadly speaking, there are two different structures used in P2P media streaming: asynchronous layered streaming and synchronous multicast streaming.

Layered Many-to-One Streaming

Xu et al. (2002) proposed a fully distributed differentiated admission control protocol called DAC_{p2p}. In this model, each requesting peer needs multiple supplying peers to send different layers of media data. That is, from a topological perspective, each streaming session involves one single recipient and multiple sources, structured as a two-level inverted tree. Of course, each supplying peer may also be a recipient of another logically different streaming session. With this streaming model, each requesting peer needs to actively contact several supplying peers in order to start a session.

This streaming model is based on a practical observation that peer requests are asynchronous and each peer's communication capability is different (i.e., heterogeneous streaming capabilities), as illustrated in Figure 11, where peers with different communication supports (e.g., DSL, dial-up, etc.) initiate streaming requests at different times.

A layer-encoded media-streaming process is assumed, as shown in Figure 12. As can be seen, each peer performs buffered playback so that the received media data are kept in a buffer and thus, can be used for streaming to other later-coming peers. For example, H_1 initiates a streaming session first and thus, it is served solely by the server. Peer H_2 starts its session next and so it can request H_1, which has buffered some media data, together with the server to send it the required data. Similarly, H_3 can stream from H_1 and H_2 without the server as it starts its session just in time to use the buffered data from the two earlier peers. On the other hand, H_4, which starts too late, cannot stream from H_1 and H_2. Instead, it receives media data from H_3 and the server.

Each potential supplying peer has only a limited capacity; thus, an admission control mechanism is needed. Peers in the system are classified into N classes according

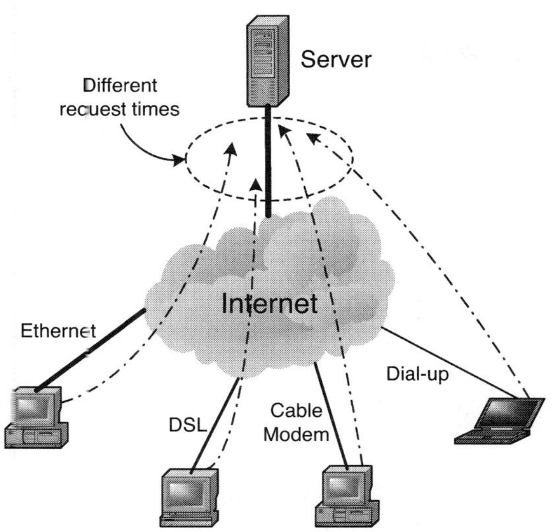

Figure 11: Asynchrony and heterogeneity of media streaming peers (based on Cui and Nahrstedt 2003)

to the different levels of uploading bandwidth available at the peers. Each potential supplying peer P_S maintains an admission probability vector: (*Pr*[1], *Pr*[2],...,*Pr*[N]). Here, a smaller index represents a class with a larger uploading bandwidth. Suppose P_S is itself a class-k peer. Then its probability vector is initialized as follows:

- For $1 \leq i \leq k, Pr[i] = 1.0$
- For $k < i \leq N, Pr[i] = \frac{1}{2^{ik}}$

Thus, P_S always grants media-streaming requests from a higher-class peer (i.e., one that has a larger uploading bandwidth) Notice that this is similar in spirit to the incentive approach used in BitTorrent (Cohen 2003). For requests from lower-class peers, P_S may serve them as governed by the respective probabilities *Pr[i]* in the vector. If P_S has not served any request during a certain period of time, then the admission probabilities of lower-class peers will be increased.

Similar to the case in BitTorrent, each peer has the incentive to report a higher uploading bandwidth because doing so will increase its probability of admission when it needs to initiate a media-streaming session. Xue et al. (2004) extended the DAC_{p2p} to a wireless environment. The key idea in the extension is to exploit the spatial distribution of mobile devices to form clusters. Users in a cluster interact using the DAC mechanism.

Habib and Chuang (2006) also explored a similar idea in providing differentiated peer selection to participating peers. Specifically, a peer has only a limited set of choices (with possibly low media quality) if it behaves selfishly in the system. The degree of selfishness is reflected by a score known to other peers. The score is increased if the peer contributes to other peers, and is decreased if it refuses the requests of other peers. Based on a practical emulation study using the PROMISE (Hefeeda et al. 2003) streaming system implemented on top of PlanetLab (www.planet-lab.org) Habib and Chuang (2006) found that the proposed incentive scheme is effective in enhancing the performance of the system.

Multicast One-to-Many Streaming

Ngan, Wallach, and Druschel (2004) considered an application-level multicast system for video streaming. The system is based on SplitStream (Castro et al. 2003) which in turn is built on top of Pastry (Rowstron and Druschel 2001). The multicast system considered critically relies on a payment-based scheme. Specifically, there are five components:

- **Debt Maintenance:** When peer *A* forwards video-streaming data to a downstream peer *B*, *B* owes *A* a unit of debt.
- **Periodic Tree Reconstruction:** The multicast tree is reconstructed periodically in order to avoid prolonged unfair connections among peers. An unfair connection is one between a well-behaved peer and a selfish peer.
- **Parental Availability:** Any new peer can obtain location and addressing information about any potential parent peers in the multicast tree. Thus, the new peer can identify a potential selfish parent if the latter consistently refuses connection.
- **Reciprocal Requests:** In the system, any two well-behaved peers are expected to have an equal chance of being parent or child in any given multicast tree.
- **Ancestor Rating:** This is a generalization of the Debt Maintenance component. Here, debts are also accounted for all ancestors of a peer. Specifically, all nodes on a path in forwarding data from the source to a peer are credited or debited in cases in which expected data are successfully received or not, respectively.

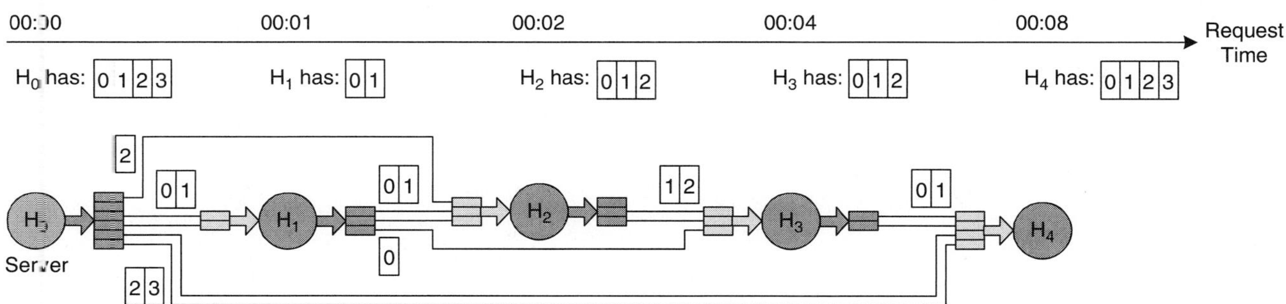

Figure 12: Layered streaming with buffering for serving asychronous requests (based on Cui and Nahrstedt 2003)

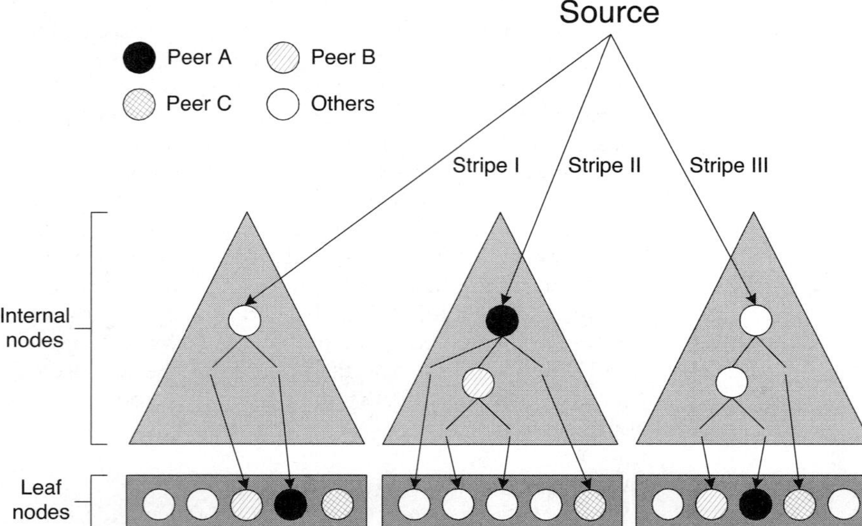

Figure 13: Layered video streaming using multiple multicast trees (based on Chu and Zhang 2004)

Simulation results indicate that a selfish free-rider is effectively penalized in terms of the amount of video-streaming data received.

Chu and Zhang (2004) also considered a multicast-based streaming environment. The streaming process is synchronous and is supported by a multiple description codec (MDC), in which a server provides several different stripes of video with different quality. A key feature in this streaming environment is that during each streaming session, multiple multicast trees are used, each of which is for sending different stripes of video. This is illustrated in Figure 13. With such a streaming structure, a peer can logically join different trees simultaneously at a different position in each tree. Specifically, when a peer joins a certain multicast tree at a higher level (e.g., peer A in the tree for stripe II), it needs to provide a larger uploading bandwidth to serve the lower-level peers in the same tree. On the other hand, a peer can also join a tree as a leaf so that it becomes a pure recipient in the tree.

With this model, Chu and Zhang (2004) then studied the effects of different degrees of altruism. They used a parameter $K = f/r$, where f is the total uploading bandwidth provided by a peer and r is its total downloading bandwidth. Thus, a larger value of K indicates a higher degree of altruism for the peer. Similar to many other P2P sharing systems described above in this chapter, a peer with a higher value of K can enjoy a better performance (in terms of media quality in the streaming application). Simulation results indicate that a small average value of K (e.g., 1.5) can already improve the overall performance of the whole system.

Shrivastava and Banerjee (2005) demonstrated that streaming based on a multicast structure could be a result of natural selection. The key idea is depicted in Figure 14. The left part of the figure illustrates a situation in which multiple peers are sharing the capacity of a single server. As a result, each peer can enjoy only a small downloading data rate. However, when peers are organized as a multicast tree, based on strategic *natural selection* (detailed below), each peer can enjoy a much larger downloading rate.

The natural selection process is illustrated in Figure 15. Here, initially the root is the only source in the system and thus, peer A selects the root as the source, enjoying

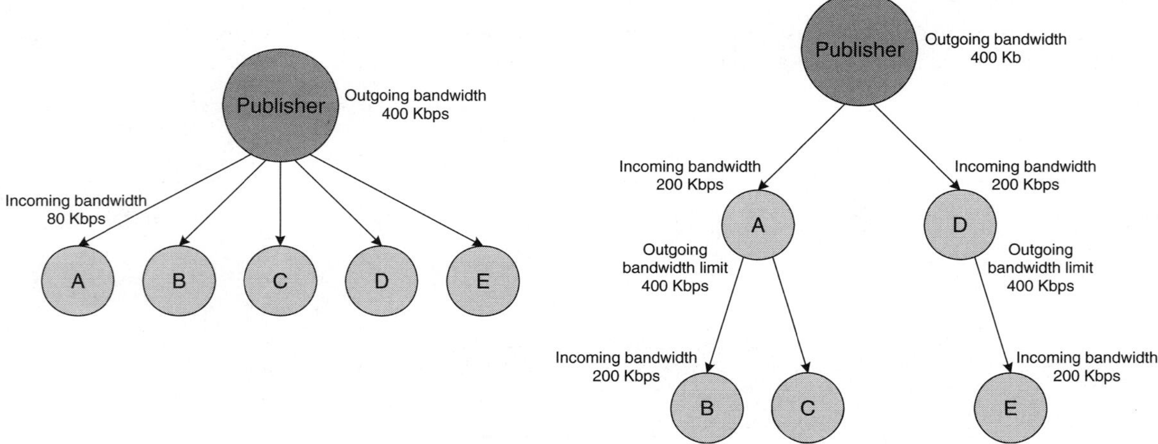

Figure 14: A multicast streaming structure is better off for every peer (based on Shrivastava and Banerjee 2005)

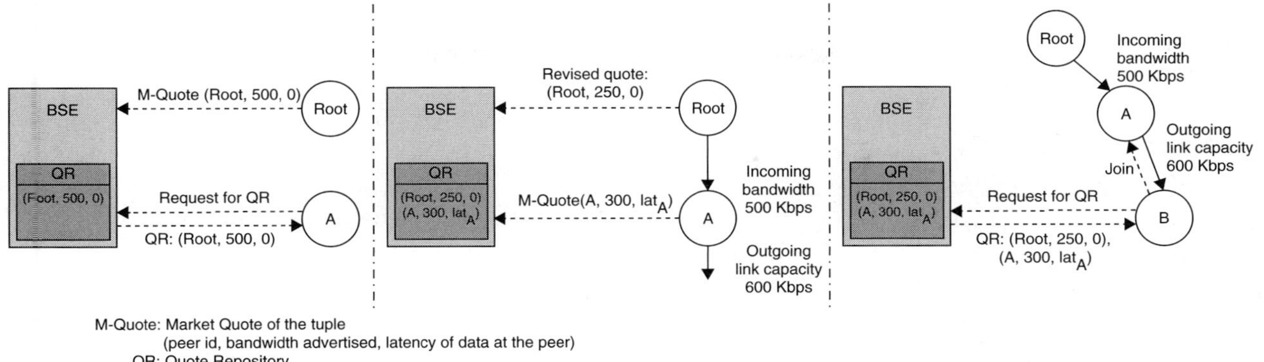

Figure 15: An illustration of the strategic natural selection process in connecting streaming sources and destinations (BSE is the bootstrap entity providing service information) (based on Shrivastava and Banerjee 2005)

a downloading rate of 500 Kbps. Now, when a new peer B joins the system, peer A has basically two choices: (1) serve peer B; or (2) do not serve peer B. To implement the second choice, which seems to be a more favorable one, peer A can declare to the bootstrap entity (BSE) that its uploading rate is 0 or a value smaller than 250 Kbps (which is half the capacity of the root). However, in doing so, peer B has no choice, but naturally selects the root to be its streaming source. In that case, peers A and B will share the root's uploading capacity and thus, each obtains only a 250 Kbps data rate. On the other hand, in anticipation of such an actually unfavorable outcome, peer A should instead strategically declare its uploading bandwidth to be 300 Kbps, which is slightly higher than the capacity declared by the root. Consequently, peer A can continue to enjoy a high downloading rate from the root, at the expense of its uploading of data to peer B at a rate of 300 Kbps.

Ye and Makedon (2004) proposed a useful detection and penalty scheme to tackle the existence of selfish peers in a multicast streaming session. They observed that a selfish peer may lie to other peers in that it claims its uploading bandwidth is large so that it can enjoy a higher probability of being admitted into a streaming session or enjoy a higher quality of media data. The key of the detection mechanism is that a downstream peer in a multicast tree returns a "streaming certificate" back to its parent peer. For example, as shown in Figure 16, peers P_4, P_5, and P_6, send streaming certificates **SCert**(P_i, P_3) to the parent peer P_3 ($i = 4, 5, 6$). The certificates are sent periodically and are time-stamped with authentication. Thus, a higher-level peer (e.g., P_1) can periodically check whether its children peers (i.e., P_2 and P_3) are selfish by asking for certificates they have received (if any) from their own children peers. If a peer cannot produce such a certificate, the higher-level peer can then remove such a potentially selfish peer from the tree. The removal process is manifested as a termination of media-data transmission.

Jun et al. (2005) explored a similar idea in their proposed Trust-Aware Multicast (TAM) protocol. Targeted for detecting and deterring uncooperative peers, which can modify, fabricate, replay, block, and delay data, the TAM protocol is based on a message structure that contains four fields: sequence number, timeout period, data payload, and cryptographic signature. The sequence number is used for detecting duplicated or missing data. The timeout period is used for detecting delayed data. Thus, a selfish (or even malicious) peer can be identified by its children peers in the multicast tree. Different from the approach suggested by Ye and Makedon (2004), the children peers are responsible for reporting such suspicious selfish peers to the root (or the server) in the tree. Jun et al.'s scheme is also more flexible in that even upon receiving such "negative reports," the root may not discard such suspected selfish peers immediately. Instead, the root keeps track of a trust metric for each peer in the tree. A negative report only decreases the trust value. Only when the trust value

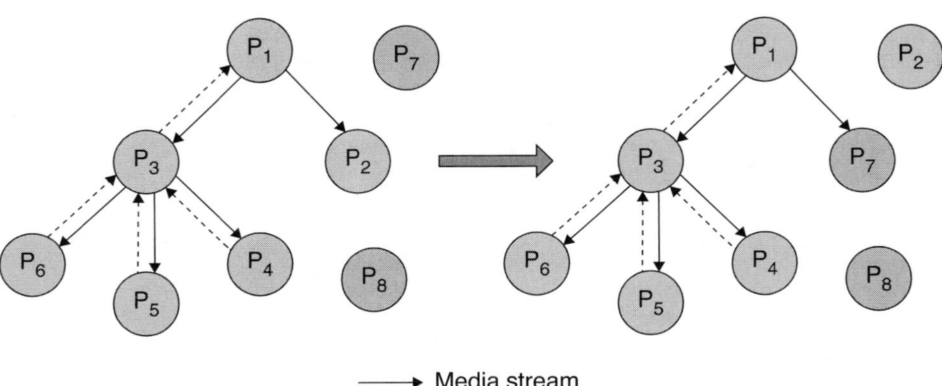

Figure 16: Detection and removal of a selfish peer from the streaming multicast tree (based on Ye and Makedon 2004)

falls below some threshold is the suspected selfish peer discarded from the tree and the peers under its sub tree are relocated.

INCENTIVE ISSUES IN WIRELESS P2P SYSTEMS

Wireless P2P systems (Hsieh and Sivakumar 2004) are proliferating in recent years. Thanks to the widely available hot-spot wireless environments, users' handheld devices can work with each other in an ad hoc and impromptu manner. As will be evident in this section, many techniques designed for wired environments are also applied in a wireless system in a similar manner. Nevertheless, there is a unique challenge in a wireless environment, namely the connectivity issue. Furthermore, there is also one more dimension of cost incurred in each wireless P2P user—the energy expenditure, which is of prime concern to the user as wireless devices are largely powered by batteries.

Routing and Data Forwarding

In a wireless P2P system, the connectivity among peers is itself a boot-strap sharing problem. Indeed, if wireless users are unwilling to cooperate in performing routing and data forwarding, the wireless network can become partitioned so that service providers cannot be reached by potential service consumers. In view of this critical challenge, there has been a plethora of important research results related to incentive issues for ad hoc routing and data forwarding. In the following, we briefly cover several interesting techniques that are based on payment mechanisms, auction mechanisms, reputation systems, and game theoretic modeling.

Ileri, Mau, and Mandayam (2005) proposed a payment-based scheme for enticing devices to cooperate in forwarding data for other devices in the network. The payment is not in monetary terms but in terms of bits per Joule. Specifically, the utility of a user i in the network is defined as:

$$u_i(p_i) = \frac{T_i(p_i)}{p_i} \tag{10}$$

where u_i is the utility p_i is the transmit power, and T_i is the throughput. That is, the utility is equal to the average amount of data received per unit energy expended, also in bit per Joule.

The payment system also involves an access point in the wireless network. Specifically, the access point also tries to maximize its revenue by using two parameters, μ and λ, judiciously. Here, λ is the unit price of service provided by the access point to any device in the network. On the other hand, μ is the unit reimbursement the access point provides to any device that has helped forward other devices' traffic. The access point's revenue is therefore given by:

$$p = \sum_{\text{all users } i} \lambda T_{in_i} - \sum_{\text{all forwarders } j} \mu T_{ja}^{eff-for} \tag{11}$$

where T_{in_i} is the service provided by the access point to user i and $T_{ja}^{eff-for}$ is the service forwarded by a forwarder j to the access point. The situation is as shown in Figure 17.

Simulation results indicate that the proposed service reimbursement scheme generally improves the network aggregate utility.

Salem et al. (2006) also considered a payment-based scheme for encouraging cooperation. However, their scheme involves real monetary costs and a payment-clearance infrastructure (e.g., a billing account for each user). The charging and rewarding scheme is similar to that we described above—a forwarder will get reimbursed and a normal user using network service will get charged.

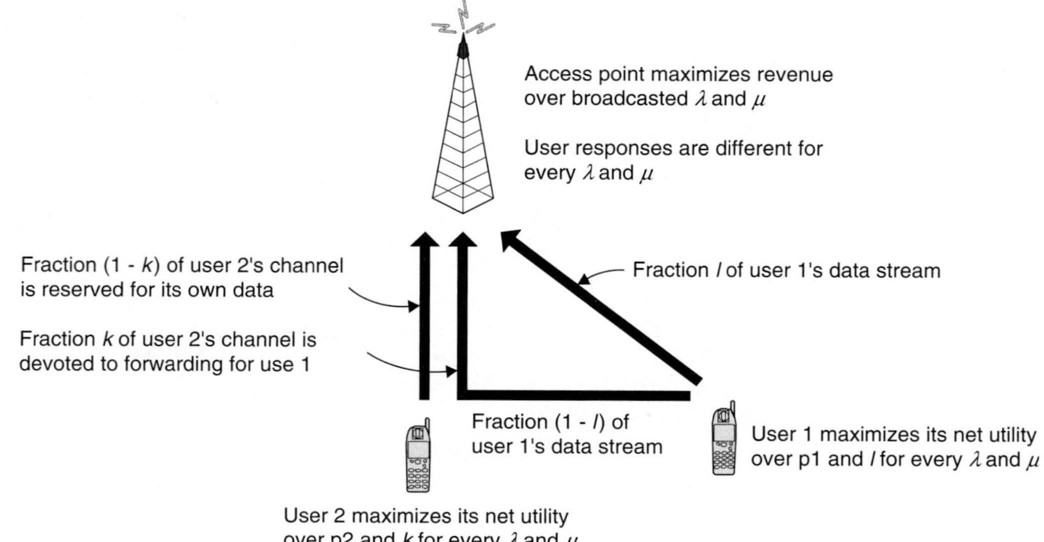

Figure 17: Charging of network service and reimbursement of data forwarding (based on Ileri et al. 2005)

Table 3: A Qualitative Comparison of Various Wireless Ad Hoc Data Forwarding Approaches

Proposed Approach	Incentive Scheme	Implementation Difficulty	Security Required	Major Drawback
Ileri et al. (2005)	Payment	Low	High	Energy-based currency
Salem et al. (2006)	Payment	High	High	Real money
Marbach and Qiu (2005)	Payment	High	High	Unlimited budget
Wang and Li (2005)	Auction	High	High	Communication
Buchegger and Le Boudec (2005)	Reputation	Low	Low	Trust
Felegyhazi et al. (2006)	Utility	Low	Low	Receiver's payoff

Marbach and Qiu (2005) investigated a similar problem based on individual device pricing. However, the main differences are that each device is allowed to freely decide how much to charge for forwarding traffic (in previous researches, usually the unit price is the same for all device) and there is no budget constraint on all the devices.

Wang and Li (2005) proposed an auction-based scheme similar to the work by Gupta and Somani (2004). Specifically, each device in a wireless ad hoc network declares its cost for forwarding data when some other device wants to initiate a multihop transmission. After considering all possible paths that are able to reach the destination device, the least-cost path is chosen and the devices on the path are paid for their forwarding. Again using a Vickrey-Clarke-Groves (VCG) based analysis, it is shown that the dominant action for each device is to report its true cost of forwarding. Wang and Li also showed that no truthful mechanism can avoid collusion between two neighboring devices in the forwarding auction game.

Buchegger and Le Boudec (2005) observed that while economic incentives such as payment approaches can entice selfish users to help in routing and forwarding data, they may not be able to handle other types of misbehaviors, such as packet dropping, modification, fabrication, or timing problems. Thus, they proposed to use a reputation system in which every user provides "opinion" data to the network based on observing the behaviors of neighboring devices. After a user device has gathered such opinions (both from itself or from others, i.e., second-hand information), it can carry out a Bayesian estimation so as to classify the neighboring devices as malicious or normal. A neighboring device that is identified as a malicious user is then isolated from the network by rejecting its routing and forwarding requests.

Felegyhazi, Hubaux, and Buttyan (2006) reported an interesting game theoretic analysis of the forwarding problem in ad hoc networks. Instead of using a payment-based strategy, the model uses a purely utility concept in that a device's utility is equal to its payoff when it acts as a data source (i.e., the sender of a multihop traffic), minus the cost when it acts an intermediate device (i.e., a forwarder of other sender's traffic) in any time slot. Here both the payoff and the cost are defined in terms of data throughput. Thus, an important assumption in this model is that only the sender has a positive payoff, while all the intermediate devices enjoy no payoff but just incur forwarding costs. Specifically, the destination device (i.e., the receiver of the multihop traffic) also enjoys no payoff. This may not conform to a realistic situation. Simulations were done to estimate the probability that the conditions for a cooperative equilibrium hold in randomly generated network scenarios.

Table 3 gives a qualitative comparison of various data-forwarding approaches in wireless ad hoc networks. In general, some form of payment is required. However, as the devices in a wireless ad hoc networks are not under a centralized authority's control, it is very difficult to enforce a secure payment-clearance mechanism. Auction schemes are interesting but are also difficult to implement in practice because a highly trusted communication infrastructure is required for exchanging bidding information. Yet this is a paradoxical requirement, as the communication among wireless peers is itself the ultimate goal in data forwarding. Similarly, a reputation-based approach, while not difficult to implement in practice, could also lead to a paradoxical situation in the sense that the reputation values may not be trustworthy.

Wireless Information Sharing Systems

Wolfson, Xu, and Sistla (2004) investigated an interesting opportunistic wireless information exchange problem in which a moving vehicle transmits the information it has collected to encountered vehicles, thereby obtaining other information from those vehicles in exchange. The incentive mechanisms suggested are based on virtual currency. Specifically, each mobile user carries some virtual currency in the form of a protected counter. Two different mechanisms are considered: producer-paid and consumer-paid. The producer of information pays in the former, while the consumer pays in the latter. The price P of a piece of information item (e.g., availability information about a parking lot) is given by:

$$P = E - t - \frac{d}{v} \tag{12}$$

where E is the gross valuation of the information item, t is the time elapsed since the information item is created, d is the distance to travel before the user of the information can reach the relevant location (e.g., the parking space), and v is the speed of the user. Simulation results under a simple situation in which there are only one consumer

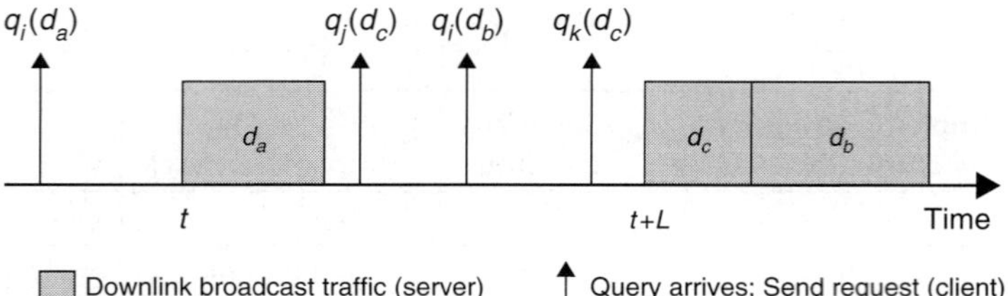

Figure 18: System model for wireless data access (based on Yeung and Kwok, *IEEE Transactions on Mobile Computing*, 2006)

and two parking spaces indicate that the proposed incentive mechanisms are effective.

Yeung and Kwok (*IEEE Transactions on Mobile Computing*, 2006) considered an interesting scenario in wireless data access: a number of mobile clients are interested in a set of data items kept at a common server. Each client independently sends a request to inform the server of its desired data items and the server replies in the broadcast channel. Yeung and Kwok investigated the energy consumption characteristics in such a scenario.

Figure 18 depicts the system model for wireless data access. It consists of a server and a set of clients, N. The clients are interested in a common set of data items, D, which are kept at the server. To request a specific data item, d_a, client i is required to inform the server by sending an uplink request, represented by $q_i(d_a)$. The server then replies with the content of the requested data item, d_a, in the common broadcast channel. This allows the data item to be shared among different clients. As illustrated in Figure 18, both clients j and k request the same data item, d_c, in the second interval. However, the server is required to broadcast the content of d_c only *once* in the next broadcast period, which reduces the bandwidth requirement.

To successfully complete a query, a client expends its energy in two different parts: (1) informing the server of the desired data item, E_{UL}; and (2) downloading the content of the data item from the common broadcast channel, E_{DL}. The energy cost of sending a request to the server is represented by E_s. If a client sends a request for each query, then E_{UL} would be the same as E_s. However, we show that clients need not send requests for each query even without caching. This implies that E_{UL} does not necessarily equal E_s. In general, the total energy required to complete a query E_Q, is given by:

$$E_Q = E_{UL} + E_{DL} \tag{13}$$

It is assumed that E_{DL} is the same for all clients, but its value depends on the size of a data item. In practice, E_s is a function of various quantities, including spatial separation, speed, instantaneous channel quality, bit-error rate requirement, etc. For simplicity, however, E_s is also assumed to be a fixed quantity.

Based on this model of wireless data access, a novel utility function for quantifying performance is defined as follows:

$$U_i - \frac{E_{total}}{E_Q^i} \tag{14}$$

where E_{total} is the total energy available. The objective is then to reduce the amount of energy consumed in the query process such that *every* client's utility (Equation 14) is increased.

Based on the utility function, Yeung and Kwok formulate wireless data access scheme as a noncooperative game—wireless data access (WDA) game. Game theoretic analysis shows that while the proposed scheme does not rely on client caching, clients do not always necessarily send requests to the server. Simulation results also suggest that the proposed scheme, compared with a simple always-request one, increases the utility and lifetime of every client while reducing the number of requests sent, at the cost of slightly larger average query delay. They also compared the performance of the proposed scheme with two popular schemes that use client caching. The simulation results show that caching only benefits clients with high query rates while resulting in both shorter lifetime and smaller utility in other clients.

Network Access Sharing

Efstathiou and Polyzos (2003) studied the problem of building a federation of wireless networks using a fully autonomous P2P approach. Specifically, in their system model, there are multiple wireless local area networks (WLANs), each of which is considered to be completely autonomous. When a user of one WLAN enters the domain of a different nearby WLAN, the latter would also admit the user based on reciprocity. To achieve this, each WLAN is equipped with a domain agent (DA), which is responsible for managing the roaming of foreign users. Each DA maintains a counter of tokens, which is increased when a foreign user is admitted to its WLAN and is decreased when a local user travels to a foreign WLAN. The DAs of different WLANs interact with each other in a pure P2P fashion. Thus, the advantage of this approach is that there is no need to set up prior pairwise administrative agreements among different WLANs.

Based on a prototype built using Cisco WLANs, it is found that the proposed P2P based roaming scheme is efficient.

Kang and Mutka (2005) considered an interesting problem in which peers share the access cost of wireless multimedia contents. Specifically, one peer in the network serves as a proxy, which pays a network server in order to download some multimedia contents in a wireless fashion. Other peers in the system then share the contents without incurring any cost. This is achieved by having the proxy broadcast the received multimedia data to the peers within its transmission range. For other distant

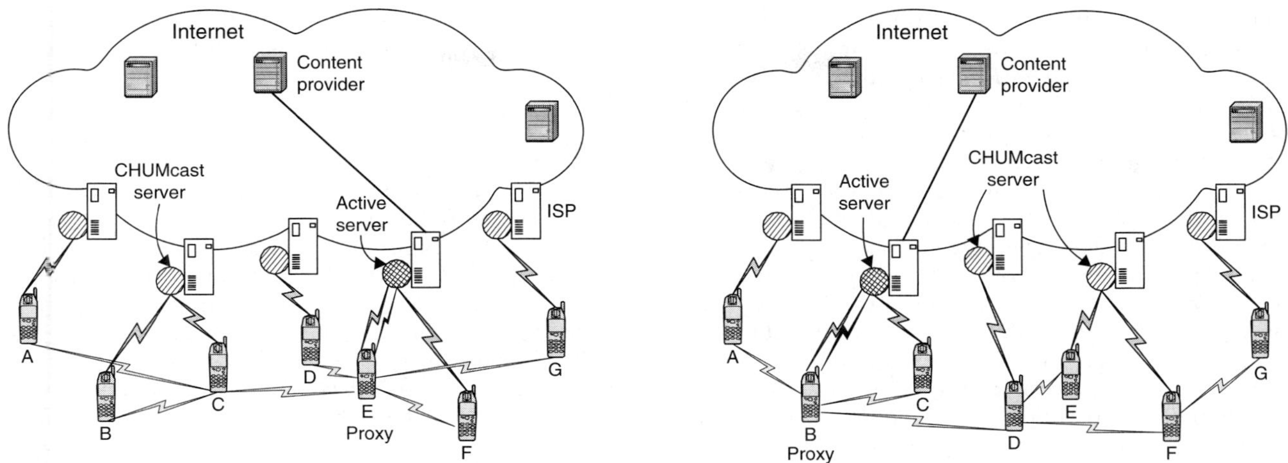

Figure 19: Illustration of network access cost sharing (left), and round-robin scheduling of proxy (right) (based on Kang and Mutka 2005)

peers, rebroadcasting by the edge peers is used to serve them. This is illustrated in Figure 19 (left side).

This idea of cost sharing in wireless data access is called CHUM (cooperating ad hoc networking to support messaging). A key component in such sharing is the cost sharing mechanism. In the CHUM system, the peers take turn, in a round-robin manner, to serve as the proxy. This is illustrated in Figure 19 (right side). It is assumed that the peers have the incentive to follow this round-robin rule based on the reciprocity concept. Simulation results indicate that 80% of network access cost is saved even with just six peers in the system.

DISCUSSION AND FUTURE WORK

We have seen that in both wired and wireless systems, the major techniques for providing incentives are payment (virtual or real), exchange (barter), reciprocity (pairwise), reputation (global), and game theoretic utility. Payment-based systems work by exploiting a user's incentive in increasing or even maximizing its "revenue." However, such an incentive may not be appropriate in some practical situations. For instance, a cellular phone user may not be interested in his or her income (from such sharing) but care more about the quality of service derived from the device. Exchange-based systems fit very well in file sharing applications because users have strong incentives for trading files of interest (e.g., music files). For other applications such as forwarding of data (e.g., in wireless ad hoc networks), it is debatable as to whether in practice a user would be interested in exchanging data-forwarding capabilities. Reciprocity (in a pairwise manner) is similar in spirit as an exchange-based mechanism. The major difference is that exchange is usually memoryless, in that every exchange transaction is treated as a rendezvous event, while general reciprocity is achieved when devices help each other at different times. Thus, such a difference leads to the requirement that users have to keep memory about the prior transactions so that users can "pay back" each other. Because of this history-based feature, reciprocity mechanisms suffer from one drawback—a user may be out of the system when he or she needs to pay back. Such a possible "future loss" may deter a user from genuinely contributing to the community for the fear of not getting deserved pay back. Reputation-based systems can be seen as a generalized form of reciprocity. Specifically, while reciprocity is about a particular user pair, a reputation value is a global assessment perceived by all users in the sense that the reputation value is computed by using observations made by many different users. By nature, similar to reciprocity mechanisms reputation systems require substantial memory, centralized or distributed, for recording the reputation values. Thus, it seems that such a system is more suitable for situations in which there is a persistent entity, which is logically external to the P2P system, for keeping track of the reputation values. For example, such an entity may be a centralized auctioneer in an electronic auction community, or the base station (access point) in a wireless network. Game theoretic incentive mechanisms are convincing in the sense that the utility function used can usually cover a multitude of important metrics. But the problem is that it is sometimes difficult to achieve an efficient distributed implementation of the resultant protocols.

Perhaps other than in an exchange-based system, which involves "stateless" interactions, all other incentive mechanisms could suffer from tampering or fabrication of the "incentive parameter" used: the money (virtual or real) in a payment-based system, the reciprocity metric, and the reputation value. Thus, additional mechanisms, usually based on cryptographic techniques, are needed to guard against such potential malicious attacks to the incentive mechanisms. In particular, whitewashing is widely considered to be a very low-cost technique for a selfish or malicious user to work around the incentive scheme.

Obviously, there is plenty of room for future research about incentive mechanisms in P2P sharing environments. Most notably, revenue maximizing (Yeung and Kwok, PIMRC 2006) in a hybrid P2P system (e.g., the so-called converged wireless architecture, in which an infrastructure-based cellular network is tightly coupled with P2P WLANs) is of a high practical interest because there are more and more cellular subscribers trying to share their resources without the intervention of the cellular service provider. In a data-sharing environment, server peer selection (Leung and Kwok, *Efficient and Practical Greedy Algorithm*, 2005) is another important direction because we believe that users care more about the quality of service achieved than about the revenue or cost they incur in participation. In economic terms, people, especially wired or wireless game players, are quite inelastic about the costs. Nevertheless, energy conservation (Leung and Kwok, *Energy Conservation*, 2005; *Community-based Asynchronous Wakeup Protocol*, 2005) is still of a prime concern in any wireless P2P sharing network because energy depletion cannot be compensated in any way by increased revenue generated in a payment-based sharing system. Thus, perhaps in a game theoretic setting, we should incorporate energy expenditure in the utility function. Finally, topology control (Leung and Kwok, *On Topology Control*, 2005) in a wired (overlay networks) or wireless (ad hoc networks) is also important in the sense that sharing is usually interest-based, meaning that users naturally form clusters with similar interests, and as such, related users would be more cooperative in following the incentive protocols. Consequently, building an interest-based sharing topology could be helpful in enhancing the effectiveness of sharing.

CONCLUSION

In this chapter, I have presented a detailed survey of incentive techniques for promoting sharing (discrete or continuous data) in a peer-to-peer system. I have considered well-known mechanisms that are proposed and have been deployed in the Internet environment. The techniques used can be classified into payment-based, exchange-based, reciprocity, reputation, and game theoretic. These techniques are also applicable in general to a wireless environment. However, a wireless P2P system, while still in its infancy, has a unique challenge—the connectivity among devices is by itself a crucial "sharing" problem (sharing of energy and bandwidth). Much more work needs to be done in related problems such as revenue maximizing (or pricing) in a hybrid wireless P2P system, intelligent peer selection in a data-sharing network, energy-aware incentive mechanisms, and interest-based topology control. Furthermore, in systems that require payments or some form of critical information items (e.g., reputation values), the security aspect needs to be properly addressed.

Finally, we can see that the amounts of work done in the areas of media streaming and wireless P2P systems are much smaller than that in the area of file sharing. This indicates that these two areas are wide open and are a fertile ground for further research.

ACKNOWLEDGMENT

This research was supported by the Hong Kong Research Grants Council (under project number HKU7157/04E). Thanks are due to Mr. Tyrone Kwok for his kind assistance in compiling the figures in this article. The author would also like to thank Professor Hossein Bidgoli for his professional advice in preparing this chapter. Finally the author would like to sincerely thank all the six anonymous reviewers for their insightful and constructive comments.

GLOSSARY

Altruism: A situation in which participants unselfishly contribute to the community.

Auction: A situation in which participants compete for ownership of an item by declaring a high price. The participant that gives the highest price wins the item.

Exchange: In the P2P computing context, the situation in which peers trade services in a rendezvous manner.

Free-Riding: Selfish participants in a community that only take advantage of others, without contributing.

Incentives: Valued entities that can motivate autonomous decision makers in a community to cooperate.

Nash Equilibrium: A situation in a strategy game in which no participant can benefit by unilaterally changing his or her decision.

P2P File Sharing: A peer-to-peer decentralized network of autonomous computers that share files among each other without intervention of any centralized authority.

P2P Media Streaming: A peer-to-peer decentralized network of autonomous computers that obtain media data from one or more peers in the network without intervention of any centralized authority.

Reciprocity: In the P2P computing context, the situation in which peer A "pays back" services to peer B who has previously contributed to peer A. That is, the return of a favor does not necessarily occur in a rendezvous manner.

CROSS REFERENCES

See Peer-to-Peer Network Applications; Peer-to-Peer Network Architecture.

REFERENCES

Anagnostakis, K. G., and M. B. Greenwald. 2004. "Exchange-based incentive mechanisms for peer-to-peer file sharing. *Proceedings of the 24th International Conference on Distributed Computing Systems*. Los Alamitos, CA: IEEE Computer Society.

Androutsellis-Theotokis, S., and D. Spinellis. 2004. A survey of peer-to-peer content distribution technologies, *ACM Computing Surveys* 36(4):335–71.

Becker, J. U., and M. Clement. 2004. The economic rationale of offering media files in peer-to-peer networks. *Proceeding of the 37th Hawaii International Conference on System Sciences*. Los Alamitos, CA: IEEE Computer Society.

Buchegger, S., and J. Y. Le Boudec. 2005. Self-policing mobile ad hoc networks by reputation systems. *IEEE Communications Magazine*, July: 101–7.

Castro, M., P. Druschel, A. Kermarrec, A. Nandi, A. Rowstron, and A. Singh. 2003. Splitstream: High-bandwidth multicast in cooperative environments. *Proceedings of the 19th ACM Symposium on Operating Systems Principles*. New York: ACM Press.

Chu, Y., and H. Zhang. 2004. Considering altruism in peer-to-peer Internet streaming broadcast. *Proceedings of NOSSDAV'04*, 10–5. New York: ACM Press.

Clarke, I., O. Sandberg, B. Wiley, and T. Hong. 2000. Freenet: A distributed anonymous information storage anonymity and retrieval system. *Proceedings of the Workshop on design issues in anonymous and unobservability*. Heidelberg, Germany: Springer Verlag.

Cohen, B. 2003. Incentives build robustness in BitTorrent. *Proceedings of the Workshop on Economics of Peer-to-Peer Systems*. New York: ACM Press.

Courcoubetis, C., and R. Weber. 2006. Incentives for large peer-to-peer systems. *IEEE Journal on Selected Areas in Communications* 24(5):1034–50.

Cui, Y., and K. Nahrstedt. 2003. Layered peer-to-peer streaming. *Proceedings of NOSSDAV'03*, 162–71. New York: ACM Press.

Efstathiou, E. C., and G. C. Polyzos. 2003. A peer-to-peer approach to wireless LAN roaming. *Proceedings of WMASH*, 10–8. New York: ACM Press.

Feldman, M., C. Papadimitriou, J. Chuang, and I. Stoica. 2004. Free-riding and whitewashing in peer-to-peer systems. *Proceedings of the 2004 SIGCOMM Workshop on Practice and Theory of Incentives in Networked Systems*, 228–235. New York: ACM Press.

Feldman, M., K. Lai, I. Stoica, and J. Chuang. 2004. Robust incentive techniques for peer-to-peer networks. *Proceedings of the 5th ACM conference on Electronic Commerce*, 102–11. New York: ACM Press.

Feldman, M., and J. Chuang. 2005. Overcoming free-riding behavior in peer-to-peer systems. *ACM SIGccom Exchanges* 5(4): 41–50.

Felegyhazi, M., J.-P. Hubaux, and L. Buttyan. 2006. Nash equilibria of packet forwarding strategies in wireless ad hoc networks. *IEEE Transactions on Mobile Computing*, 5(5):463–6.

Figueiredo, D., J. Shapiro, and D. Towsley. 2005. Incentives to promote availability in peer-to-peer anonymity systems. *Proceedings of the 13th IEEE International Conference on Network Protocols*. Los Alamitos, CA: IEEE Computer Society.

Gupta, R., and A. K. Somani. 2004. A pricing strategy for incentivizing selfish nodes to share resources in peer-to-peer (P2P) networks. *Proceedings of the IEEE International Conference on Networks*. IEEE Computer Society, Los Alamitos, CA, 624–629 vol.2.

Habib, A., and J. Chuang. 2006. Service differentiated peer selection: An incentive mechanism for peer-to-peer media streaming. *IEEE Transactions on Multimedia*, 8(3):601–21.

Hausheer, D., N. C. Liebau, A. Mauthe, R. Steinmetz, and B. Stiller. 2003. Token based accounting and distributed pricing to introduce market mechanisms in a peer-to-peer file sharing scenario. *Proceedings of the Third International Conference on Peer-to-Peer Computing* Los Alamitos, CA: IEEE Computer Society.

Hausheer, D., and B. Stiller. 2005. Decentralized auction-based pricing with PeerMart. *Proceedings of the 9th IFIP/IEEE International Symposium on Integrated Network Management*. Los Alamitos, CA: IEEE Computer Society.

Hefeeda, M., A. Habib, B. Botev, D. Xu, and B. Bhargava. 2003. PROMISE: peer-to-peer media streaming using CollectCast. *Proceedings of the ACM Multimedia*. New York: ACM Press.

Hsieh, H.-Y., and R. Sivakumar. 2004. On using peer-to-peer communication in cellular wireless data networks. *IEEE Transactions on Mobile Computing* 3(1):57–72.

Ileri, O., S.-C. Mau, and N. B. Mandayam. 2005. Pricing for enabling forwarding in self-configuring ad hoc networks. *IEEE Journal on Selected Areas in Communications*, 23(1):151–62.

Jia, Z., S. Tiange, H. Liansheng, and D. Yiqi. 2005. A new micropayment protocol based on P2P networks. *Proceedings of the 2005 IEEE International Conference on e-Business Engineering*. Los Alamitos, CA: IEEE Computer Society.

Jun, S., and M. Ahamad. 2005. Incentives in BitTorrent induce free riding. *Proceedings of the ACM SIGCOMM 2005 Workshop*. New York: ACM Press.

Jun, S., M. Ahamad, and J. Xu. 2005. Robust information dissemination in uncooperative environments. *Proceedings of the 25th IEEE International Conference on Distributed Computing Systems*. Los Alamitos, CA: IEEE Computer Society.

Kang, S. S., and M. W. Mutka. 2005. A mobile peer-to-peer approach for multimedia content sharing using 3G/WLAN dual mode channels. *Wireless Communications and Mobile Computing* 5:633.

Krishnana, R., M. D. Smith, and R. Telang. 2003. The economics of peer-to-peer networks. *Journal of Information Technology Theory and Application* 5(30):31–44.

Leung, A. K. H., and Y.-K. Kwok. 2005. An efficient and practical greedy algorithm for server-peer selection in wireless peer-to-peer file sharing networks. *Proceedings of the International Conference on Mobile Ad-hoc and Sensor Networks (MSN'2005)* 1016–25. New York: Springer Lecture Notes in Computer Science, 3794.

Leung, A. K. H., and Y.-K. Kwok. 2005. Energy conservation by peer-to-peer relaying in quasi-ad hoc networks. *Proceedings of IFIP International Conference on Network and Parallel Computing (NPC'2005)*, 451–60. Heidelberg, Germany: Springer Verlag Lecture Notes in Computer Science, 3779.

Leung, A. K. H., and Y.-K. Kwok. 2005. Community-based asynchronous wakeup protocol for wireless peer-to-peer file sharing networks. *Proceedings of the IEEE Second Annual International Conference on Mobile and Ubiquitous Systems: Networking and Services (MobiQuitous'2005)*, San Diego, California, 342–350. Los Alamitos, CA: IEEE Computer Society.

Leung, A. K. H., and Y.-K. Kwok. 2005. On topology control of wireless peer-to-peer file sharing networks: Energy efficiency, fairness and incentive. *Proceedings of the IEEE International Symposium on a World of Wireless, Mobile and Multimedia Networks (WoWMoM'2005). Taormina, Giardini Naxos, Italy*, 318–323. Los Alamitos, CA: IEEE Computer Society.

Ma, R. T. B., S. C. M. Lee, J. C. S. Lui, and D. K. Y. Ya. 2004. A game theoretic approach to provide incentive and service differentiation in P2P networks. *Proceedings of the SIGMETRICS*, 189–98. New York: ACM Press.

Ma, R. T. B., S. C. M. Lee, J. C. S. Lui, and D. K. Y. Ya. 2004. An incentive mechanism for P2P networks. *Proceedings of the 24th International Conference on Distributed Computing Systems*. IEEE Computer Society, Los Alamitos, CA, pp. 516–523.

Marbach, P., and Y. Qiu. 2005. Cooperation in wireless ad hoc networks: A market based approach. *IEEE/ACM Transactions on Networking* 13(6):1325–38.

Ngan, T. W. J., D. S. Wallach, and P. Druschel. 2004. Incentives-compatible peer-to-peer multicast. *Proceedings of the Workshop on Economics of Peer-to-Peer Systems*. New York ACM Press.

Osborne, M. J. 2004. *An introduction to game theory*. Oxford: Oxford University Press.

Qiu, D., and R. Srikant. 2004. Modeling and performance analysis of BitTorrent-like peer-to-peer networks. *Proceedings of the SIGCOMM*, 367–77. New York: ACM Press.

Ranganathan, K., M. Ripeanu, A. Sarin, and I. Foster. 2003. To share or not to share: An analysis of incentives to contribute in collaborative file-sharing environments. *Proceedings of the Workshop on Economics of Peer-to-Peer Systems*. New York: ACM Press.

Roussopoulos, M., M. Baker, D. Rosenthal, T. J. Giuli, P. Maniatis, and J. Mogul/2–4/2 P2P or not 2 P2P? *Proceedings of the Third International Workshop on Peer-to-Peer Systems (IPTPS '04)*, La Jolla, CA. Heidelberg, Germany: Springer Verlag.

Rowstron, A., and P. Druschel. 2001. Pastry: Scalable, distributed object address and routing for large-scale peer-to-peer systems. *Proceedings of the IFIP/ACM International Conference on Distributed Systems Platforms*. New York: ACM Press.

Saito, K., 2003. Peer-to-peer money: Free currency over the Internet. *Proceedings of the 2nd International Conference on Human.Society@Internet*. Heidelberg, Germany: Springer Verlag.

Saito, K., E. Morino, and J. Murai. 2005. Multiplication over time to facilitate peer-to-peer barter relationship. *Proceedings of the 16th International Workshop on Database and Expert Systems Applications*. Los Alamitos, CA: IEEE Computer Society.

Salem, N. B., L. Buttyan, J. P. Hubaux, and M. Jakobsson. 2006. Node cooperation in hybrid ad hoc networks. *IEEE Transactions on Mobile Computing* 5(4): 365–76.

Sanghavi, S., and B. Hajek. 2005. A new mechanism for the free-rider problem. *Proceedings of the SIGCOMM 2005 Workshop*. New York: ACM Press.

Schelling, T. C., 1978. *Micromotives and macrobehavior*. New York: Norton.

Shrivastava, V., and S. Banerjee. 2005. Natural selection in peer-to-peer streaming: From the cathedral to the bazaar. *Proceedings of the NOSSDAV'05*. New York: ACM Press.

Singh, S., S. Ramabhadran, F. Baboescu, and A. C. Snoeren. 2003. The case for service provider deployment of super-peers in peer-to-peer networks. *Proceedings of the Workshop on Economics of Peer-to-Peer Systems*. New York: ACM Press.

Stoica, I., R. Morris, D. Karger, M. F. Kaashoek, and H. Balakrishnan. 2001. Chord: A salable peer-to-peer lookup service for internet applications. *Proceedings of the ACM SIGCOMM 2001*, 149–60. New York: ACM Press.

Sun, Q., and H. Garcia-Molina. 2004. SLIC: A Selfish link-based incentive mechanism for unstructured peer-to-peer networks. *Proceedings of the 24th International Conference on Distributed Computing Systems*. Los Alamitos, CA: IEEE Computer Society.

Varian, H. R. 2003. The social cost of sharing. *Proceedings of the Workshop on Economics of Peer-to-Peer Systems*. New York: ACM Press.

Wang, W., and B. Li/2–5/Market-driven bandwidth allocation in selfish overlay networks. *Proceeding of the IEEE INFOCOM 2005*. Los Alamitos, CA: IEEE Computer Society.

Wolfson, O., B. Xu, and A. P. Sistla. 2004. An economic model for resource exchange in mobile peer to peer networks. *Proceedings of the 16th Int'l Conference on Scientific and Statistical Databased Management*. Heidelberg, Germany: Springer Verlag.

Wongrujira, K., and A. Seneviratne. 2005. Monetary incentive with reputation for virtual market-place based P2P. *Proceedings of the CoNEXT'05*. New York: ACM Press.

Xu, D., M. Hefeeda, S. Hambrusch, and B. Bhargava. 2002. On peer-to-peer media streaming. *Proceedings of the 22nd Int'l Conference on Distributed Computing Systems*. Los Alamitos, CA: IEEE Computer Society.

Xue, G.-T., M.-L. Li, Q.-N. Deng, and J.-Y. You. 2004. Stable group model in mobile peer-to-peer media streaming system. *Proceedings of the IEEE International Conference on Mobile Ad Hoc and Sensor Systems*, 334–39. Los Alamitos, CA: IEEE Computer Society.

Yang, B., and H. Garcia-Molina. 2003. PPay: Micropayments for peer-to-peer systems. *Proceedings of the 10th ACM Conference on Computer and Communication Security*, 300. New York: ACM Press.

Yang, M., Z. Zhang, X. Li, and Y. Dai. 2005. An empirical study of free-riding behavior in the Maze P2P file-sharing system. *Proceedings of IPTPS'05*. Heidelberg, Germany: Springer Verlag.

Ye, S., and F. Makedon. 2004. Collaboration-aware peer-to-peer media streaming. *Proceedings of MM'04*, 412–15. New York ACM: Press.

Yeung, M. K. H., and Y.-K. Kwok. 2006. On maximizing revenue for client-server based wireless data access in the presence of peer-to-peer sharing. *Proceedings of the 17th Annual IEEE International Symposium on Personal, Indoor, and Mobile Radio Communications (PIMRC'2006), Helsinki, Finland*. New York: IEEE Computer Society.

Yeung, M. K. H., and Y.-K. Kwok. 2006. A game theoretic approach to power aware wireless data access. *IEEE Transactions on Mobile Computing* 5(8).

Yu, B., and M. P. Singh. 2003. Incentive mechanisms for peer-to-peer systems. *Proceedings of the 2nd International Workshop on Agents and Peer-to-Peer Computing*. New York: ACM Press.

Storage Area Network Fundamentals

Vladimir V. Riabov, *Rivier College*

INTRODUCTION

The volume and value of enterprise data have been growing faster than the speed at which traditional backup utilities' effectiveness has been increasing. Enterprises have become more dependent on their online systems and cannot ensure the availability of these data by relying only on traditional, network-bottlenecked, server-attached storage systems. Solutions to this problem have been offered by storage area network (SAN) technology, which provides enterprises with serverless zero-time-windows backup. In this new backup approach, backed-up data are removed to a secondary remote storage device, and the enterprise server becomes off-loaded, permitting high-performance continuous access to both applications and data. The objective of a SAN is to allow multiple servers access to a pool of data storage in which any server can potentially access any storage unit. In this environment, management plays a large role in providing security guarantees (with authorization to access particular storage devices) and sequencing or serialization guarantees (with authorization to access a particular device at certain time-point) (Server Clusters 2003).

A SAN fabric is usually based on fibre-channel technology that allows up to 10-km long-distance connections. This feature has a significant advantage in a campus environment, where reliable backup resources can be shared among several divisions. For example, fibre-channel SANs for a health care enterprise allow 24/7 continuous operation, patient record backup, and medical image archiving (Farley 2001).

The SAN becomes a key element of the enterprise environment in which data availability, serviceability, and reliability are critical for a company's business. Many enterprise solutions (e.g., ATTO FibreBridge products, rack mount solutions, ATTO FibreCenter3400R/D, host bus adapters, the ATTO Diamond array, Compaq StorageWorks products, EMC Connectrix solutions, LSI Logic E4600 Storage System) are available today. They can be effectively used in multiple platform storage-infrastructure solutions for data-intensive applications such as e-commerce, online transaction processing, electronic vaulting, data warehousing, data mining, Internet/intranet browsing, multimedia audio/video editing, high-definition television (HDTV) streaming, and enterprise database management applications (Riabov 2004).

This chapter describes fundamentals of storage area networks (SANs), their architectural elements (interfaces, interconnects, and fabrics), technologies (fibre-channel-arbitrated loop transport protocol, Brocade's configurations, InfiniBand switched-fabric architecture, Crossroad systems with a storage router, virtual interface architecture, direct access file system, Internet protocol (IP) storage technologies, SANs over IP, fibre channel over IP, Internet fibre-channel protocol, Internet SCSI, storage over IP, fabric shortest path first protocol, storage resource management, and adaptive network storage archi-tecture), solutions, standards, associations, initiatives, forums, coalitions, vendors, and service providers.

SAN OVERVIEW

What Is a SAN?

A SAN (storage area network) is a networked high-speed infrastructure (subnetwork) that establishes direct access by servers to an interconnected group of heterogeneous data-storage devices such as optical disks, redundant arrays of inexpensive disks (RAIDs), and tape backups (or tape libraries). SANs are effective for storing large amounts of information and backing up data online in e-commerce, online transaction processing, electronic vaulting, data warehousing, data mining, multimedia Internet/intranet browsing, and enterprise-database-managing applications. SANs provide additional capabilities (fault tolerance, remote management, clustering, and topological flexibility) to mission-critical, data-intensive applications (Troppens, Erkens, and Müeller 2004). A SAN is typically a part of an enterprise network of computing resources (Sachdev and Arunkundram 2002). A simple model of the storage area network as a networked high-speed infrastructure is shown in Figure 1.

A SAN can be considered as an extended and shared storage bus within a data center, consisting of various storage devices and specific interfaces (e.g., fibre channel, enterprise system connection [ESCON], high-performance parallel interface [HIPPI], small computer system interface [SCSI], or serial storage architecture [SSA]) rather than Ethernet (Peterson 2006). In order to be connected to the enterprise network, the SAN uses technologies similar to those of local area networks (LANs) and wide area networks (WANs): switches, routers, gateways, and hubs (see Figure 1). WAN carrier technologies, such as asynchronous transfer mode (ATM) or synchronous optical networks (SONET), can be used for remote archival data storing and backup. As an important element of modern distributed networking architectures of storage-centric enterprise information processing, SAN technology represents a significant step toward a fully networked secure data storage infrastructure that is radically different from traditional server-attached storage (Clark 2003). In addition, SANs provide improved options for network storage, such as a creation of remote or local, dedicated or shared data storage networks with access capability faster than network attached storage (NAS) (Preston 2002).

A SAN can be divided into four separate segments (SAN School 2006): (1) all the hardware (e.g., switches, cables, disk arrays, tape libraries, etc.), (2) protocols (fibre-channel arbitrated loop [FC-AL] and fibre-channel switch fabric [FC-SW]) that are used for communicating between the hardware parts, (3) hardware and software vendors, and (4) various computer applications that benefit from using SAN. A SAN can be viewed as a composition of three layers (see Figure 1): (1) host layer that includes host bus adaptors (HBAs), drivers, host operating systems, and interface software, (2) fabric layer (hubs, switches, fabric operating systems, and cabling, and (3) storage layer (disks, tapes, and advanced storage software).

SANs are based on the storage-centric information-processing paradigm, which enables any-to-any connectivity of computers (servers) and storage devices over a high-speed enterprise network of interconnected fibre-channel switches that form the SAN fabric. The incidence of unconnected clusters of information is eliminated or significantly reduced by SANs. According to this concept, a SAN resides behind the server and provides any

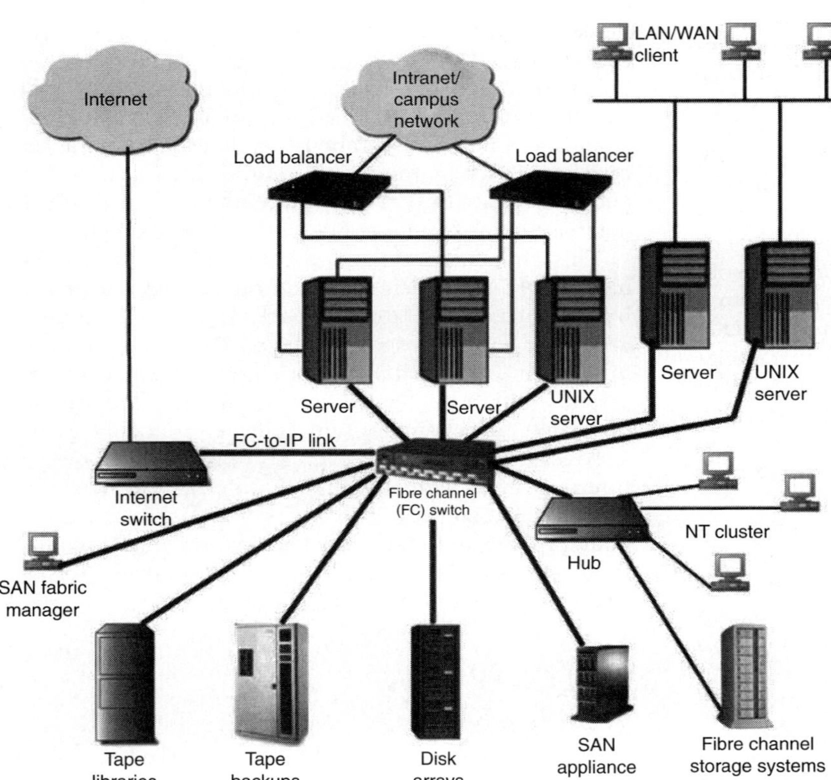

Figure 1: Storage area network as a networked high-speed enterprise infrastructure (NT = Windows NT)

users or devices on the enterprise network ("clients") with fast access to an array of data-storage devices. Multiple servers and workstations from various vendors, running different operating systems, can all be connected to a SAN by using fiber-optic cabling (either a single or dual connection) and a special fibre-channel card called a "host bus adaptor" (HBA) (Anderson 2006).

A SAN can be viewed as multihost connected-and-shared enterprise storage. Adding new storage devices and server elements resolves traditional network bottlenecks and small-scale problems of interfaces, such as SCSI and NAS, and can easily expand the scale of the SAN (Thornburgh and Schoenborn 2001). Another advantage of SAN technology is that backups can be made over the SAN fibre-channel subnet, and, in this case, backup traffic is totally removed from the enterprise network.

SANs can offer high availability of operations because of a fully redundant architecture supported by three building blocks: server clustering, multipathing, and storage replication (Anderson 2006). Server clustering, load balancing, and autorecovering after a primary server failure are the principal elements of high-availability computing with a SAN. Multi-pathing uses redundant components to guard against failure of any connection component (HBA, switch, cable, or array controller) by rerouting traffic from one component to the other. Small enterprises widely use storage replication between servers connected to a SAN over an IP network. This enables one-to-one, one-to-many, and many-to-many replication, and data are synchronized in incremental blocks to minimize network traffic.

The SAN represents a new segment of the information services industry called storage solution providers (SSP). However, isolated SANs cannot realize all SSP services, such as real-time data replication, storage hosting, and remote vaulting. A server cluster uses virtual servers to failover services from one server to another. A service runs on one server in the server cluster, and then if the server fails, another server loads the virtual server. The database must be located on shared storage that can be accessed by all servers in the server cluster.

Benefits of SANs

A SAN makes physical storage capacity a single, scalable resource and allows the flexible allocation of virtualized storage volumes (e.g., RAIDs, just a bunch of disks/drives [JBODs], and EMC, Sun, and Dell storage devices). Centralization of data storage into a single pool allows storage resources and server resources to grow independently, and allows storage to be dynamically assigned from the pool. The SAN can manage backup tasks that were a huge administrative and computer-resource burden under old storage architectures. Common infrastructure for attaching storage allows a single common management model for configuration and deployment (Server Clusters 2003). The storage management cost savings can be higher than 80%. A cost-effective, scalable SAN enhances overall system performance. It can integrate legacy SCSI devices, which allows increasing their systemwide effective usable capacity by up to 30% (InfraStor 2002).

SANs are an integral part of large financial services enterprises, Internet service providers (ISPs), government organization, research laboratories, electronic publishers, digital video production groups, TV-broadcasting stations moving to digital services, educational institutions, or any organization with increasing data storage needs.

There are several key reasons for implementing a SAN (InfraStor 2002). The first three concern business issues of return on the investment in data storage, as well as the protection of existing investments:

- SANs are cost-effective (reduced cost of storage management, including backup and recovery; increased user productivity; cost-effective implementations of high-availability disaster protection, using remote clusters and remote mirrored arrays).
- SANs reduce business risk (faster disaster recovery; reduced revenue loss from down-time; reduced lost-opportunity costs).
- Legacy investments are protected (SANs can be implemented without abandoning existing storage infrastructures such as devices using SCSI connections).

The next four reasons for using SANs address critical technical issues that face data-center managers at a time when the volume of data to be managed and made available in many organizations is increasing at an annual rate of 60% (InfraStor 2002):

- SANs provide scalability (add servers and storage independently).
- SANs allow flexibility (reconfigure storage and servers dynamically without interrupting their services; load sharing and redistribution); any additional tape or disk storage subsystems can be added to the SAN fabric dynamically.
- SANs enhance overall system performance (more effective use of existing server compute cycles; real-time backup without impacting LAN/WAN; multiple server-to-storage paths; networked storage arrays that can outperform bus-attached storage; compatibility with parallelized database applications).
- SANs are an integral part of any high-availability plan (facilitation of shared online spares and remote backup or mirroring; reduced down-time requirements; storage independent of the application and accessible through alternative data paths such as found in clustered systems).

With modern SAN architectures, enterprise data are available from 99.99% of the time to 99.999% of the time. This translates to down-time ranging from 53 minutes per year to 5 minutes per year. Also, the SAN implementation allows performing data replication to remote sites for significantly faster recovery in the event of a disaster. With SANs, data replication can be applied to storage at the controller, switch, or operating system level; this provides the capacity to create multiple copies of critical data and then move those copies to other parts of the SAN, or over a wide area network for remote protection (Storage Area Networks 2006).

The implementation of a SAN can realize significant overall cost savings in data-center operations and can increase user productivity. The opportunity to avoid escalating costs depends on decentralization of data and applications. A key element in the consolidation of data storage must include the implementation of a basic SAN infrastructure in order to provide the following (InfraStor 2002):

- Bandwidth to service clients;
- Maintenance of data availability without impacting LAN bandwidth;
- Scalability for long-term, rapid growth with protection of legacy investments
- Flexibility to provide optimal balance of server and storage capacity
- Manageability for ease of installation and maintainability
- Shared access to data resources for real-time backup and recovery
- Administrators can support over 40% more storage in a SAN environment than in direct-attached environments (Storage Area Networks 2006).

Distributed environments require high-cost maintenance in terms of staff resources. The consolidation of distributed NT-based storages to a virtualized SAN-based resource can save 80% or more of the costs of management (InfraStor 2002).

SAN Applications

SAN applications cover the following areas of data transfer (Peterson 2006): (1) externalization of data storage out of the server—SAN-attached storage (SAS) and NAS-with-SAN-interconnects network architectures; (2) clustering, a redundant process that provides failover, high availability, performance, and scalability through the use of multiple servers as a data pipe and allows data storage resources to be shared; (3) data protection solutions for backup, remote clustering, file mirroring, and replicating and journaling file systems by creating data storage redundancy on a dynamic basis; (4) data vaulting, which is the process of transferring archived data to less expensive media; (5) data interchange from one storage system to another or between different environments; and (6) disaster recovery, which is similar to data interchange, moving copies of data offsite, and is built on remote vaulting (backup) processes or on remote array mirroring or clustering.

Several new applications benefit from 2 Gb/s fibre-channel SANs (Hammond-Doel 2001): multimedia audio/video servers that provide the ability to stream higher-resolution files, medical imaging, prepress that speeds up design and file preparation, and video editing of uncompressed HDTV data.

The first effective application of SANs has been serverless backup, which provides enterprises with full-time information availability. All backup-related tasks have been relegated to the SAN. Large enterprises can store and manage huge amounts of information (several terabytes or more) in the SAN high-performance environment. Enterprise servers are connected to storage devices (e.g., RAIDs) via a high-speed interconnection, such as a fibre channel. The SAN any-to-any communication principle provides the ability to share storage resources and alternative paths from server to data storage device. A SAN is also able to share the resources among several consolidated servers (Riabov 2004).

A cluster of interconnected servers may be connected to common storage devices in the SAN environment and be accessible to all clients. Modern enterprises use this clustering technology to resolve several challenging application problems (Barker and Massiglia 2001, 244)—i.e., providing customers, partners, and employees with continuous application service, even if the enterprise systems fail, and supporting application performance growth as demand grows, without service disruption to customers. Clusters provide load balancing, high availability, and fault tolerance and support application scaling. In some implementations, the clustered servers can be managed from a single console. Clustering methods are effectively used in e-commerce, online-transaction processing, and other Web applications, which handle a high volume of requests.

SAN methods have their roots in two low-cost technologies: SCSI-based storage and the NAS-based concept. They both successfully implement storage-network links, but are limited to a low volume of data flows and rates. SCSI still remains the most popular "bus-attached" server-storage connection in SAS systems, especially at the stage of transition from SCSI bus devices to fibre-channel switches using the SCSI-fiber protocol converter in a new enterprise storage ("data center") environment. In a NAS system, storage elements (i.e., a disk array) are attached directly to any type of network via a LAN interface (e.g., Ethernet) and provide file access services to computer systems. If the NAS elements are connected to SANs, they can be considered as members of the SAS system. The stored data may be accessed by a host computer system using file access protocols such as network file system (NFS) or common Internet file system (CIFS).

SANs provide high-bandwidth block storage access over long distance via extended fibre-channel links. However, such links are generally restricted to connections between data centers. NAS access is less restricted by physical distance because communications are via TCP/IP (InfraStor 2001). NAS controls simple access to files via a standard TCP/IP link. A SAN provides storage access to client devices, but does not impose any inherent restrictions on the operating system or file system that may be used. For this reason, SANs are well suited to high-bandwidth storage access by transaction-processing and database-management system (DBMS) applications that manage storage access by themselves. NAS, which has the inherent ability to provide shared file-level access to multiple operating system (OS) environments, is well suited for requirements such as Web file services, computer-aided design (CAD) file access by combined WinNT/2000, UNIX, and LINUX devices, and wide-area streaming video distribution (InfraStor 2001). A balanced combination of these approaches will dominate in the future. See chapter on *Storage Area Networks: Architectures and Protocols*. Also see chapters on *Backup and Recovery System Requirements* and *Evaluating Storage Media Requirements*.

SAN Architecture and Infrastructure

SAN architectures have been changed evolutionarily, adapting to new application demands and expanding capacities. The original fibre-channel-based SANs were simple loop configurations based on the fibre-channel arbitrated loop (FC-AP) standard. Low-cost loops are easily expanded and combined with up to 126 hosts and devices, but they are difficult to deploy and have significant limitations on overall bandwidth. Requirements of scalability and new functionality had transformed SANs into fabric-based switching systems (fibre-channel switch fabric [FC-SW]) that could support up to 16 million hosts and devices. Numerous vendors offered different proprietary solutions of problems based on fabric switching. As a result, immature and competing standards created various interoperability problems. Homogeneous high-cost SANs were developed. Ottem (2001) refers to this phase as the "legacy proprietary fabric switch phase." The modern established architectural approach is associated with a standards-based "Open" 2-Gb fabric switch that provides all the benefits of fabric switching, but is based on new industry standards (FC-SW-2) and an interoperability architecture that runs at twice the speed of legacy fabric. The standards-based switches provide heterogeneous capability, fault isolation, and rerouting. The introduction of industry standards, as a substitute for proprietary standards, has reduced the price of SAN components and management costs of running a SAN.

The Open 2-Gb fibre channel allows doubled SAN speeds, enables greater flexibility in configuring SANs for a wide range of applications, and is especially useful for managing 1.5-Gb high-definition video data. In HDTV applications, a single fiber can carry a full high-definition video stream without having to cache, buffer, or compress the data. Other examples (Ottem 2001) include storage service providers that must deliver block data from and to users at the highest possible speeds and e-commerce companies that have to minimize transaction times. The 2-Gb fibre channel provides the high-speed backbone capability for fibre-channel networks, which can be used to interconnect two SAN switches. This configuration increases overall data throughput across the SAN even if servers and disk subsystems continue to operate via 1-Gb channels.

The fibre-channel (FC) data-storage industry has begun the transition to the 10-Gbps interface standard. The Technical Committee T11 of the International Committee for Information Technology Standards (INCITS) has developed the 10GFC project proposal (also known as FC-PI-2) that describes the fibre-channel physical layer for the transport of data at a rate of approximately 10 Gbps (Technical Committee T11 2006).

The new 4-Gbps technology for storage arrays has been announced (Lyon and Sturgeon 2006). It will significantly improve the sequential operations, such as database backups, long database loads, and streaming media. SAN implementations that make extensive use of interswitch links (ISLs) will also benefit from 4-Gbps technology (Business Brief 2006). It allows reducing the number of ISLs required and freeing up ports otherwise used for bandwidth aggregation.

Characteristics of four generations of SANs are summarized in Table 1.

A SAN system consists of software and hardware components that establish logical and physical paths between stored data and applications that request them (Sheldon 2001). The data transforms, which are located on the paths from storage device to application, are the four main abstract components (Barker and Massiglia 2001, 128): the disks (viewed through ESCON, FCP, HIPPI,

Table 1: Four Generations of SANs

	Fabric	Main Characteristics	Applications
First-Generation SANs	1-Gb loop	FC-AL protocol; 1-Gb speed; enabled first SANs	SCSI replacement
Second-Generation SANs	1-Gb proprietary; legacy fabric	FC-SW protocol; 1-Gb speed; proprietary switch-to-switch connections; expensive	LAN-free backup; high-availability clustering
Third-Generation SANs	2-Gb open fabric	Open FC-SW-2 protocol; 2-Gb speed; standards-based switch-to-switch connections; competition-driven price reductions	Serverless backup; heterogeneous storage consolidation; high-definition video data; virtualization
Fourth-Generation SANs	4–10-Gb fabric	10GFC-IP-2 protocol; 4–10-Gb speed	Medical imaging; streaming video; data mining; database backups; long database loads

SCSI, and SSA interfaces as abstract entities), volumes (logical/virtual disk-like storage entities that provide their clients with identified storage blocks of persistent/retrieved data), file systems, and application-independent database-management systems. In a system with a storage area network, five different combinations (Barker and Massiglia 2001) of these data transforms and corresponding transformation paths serve different applications and system architectures by various physical system elements. The disk abstraction is actually the physical disk drive. The abstract volume entity is realized as an external or embedded RAID controller, as an out-of-band or in-band SAN appliance, or as a volume manager serving a database or an application. Storage servers (such as NAS devices), database servers, and application servers may contain the abstract file systems. These devices and servers can be clustered to increase scaling and application availability. In that case, their volume file and management systems should be cluster-aware (Barker and Massiglia 2001).

Any SAN-based client–server system consists of three architectural components: interfaces, interconnects or network infrastructure components (switches, hubs, routers, bridges, gateways, multiplexers, extenders, and directors), and fabrics. The SAN interfaces are fibre channel, ESCON, HIPPI, SCSI, and SSA. The SAN interconnects link these storage interfaces together, making various network configurations.

The SAN infrastructure (fabric) includes the hardware, cabling, and software components that transmit data within the SAN. Fibre-channel switches and host bus adapters (HBAs) form the foundation, enabling servers and other storage devices to connect to one another (Anderson 2006). Since 1999, most HBAs support both FC-AL and FC-SW standards. However, HBA's configuration is not automatic in many cases, and it is important to verify from the switch side that the hosts are operating in the appropriate mode (Server Clusters 2003).

The fundamentally different fibre-channel topologies (point-to-point, FC-AL, and FC-SW) use different components to provide the infrastructure: (1) hubs, (2) switches, and (3) bridges and routers. Hubs are the simplest form of fibre-channel devices and are used to connect devices and hosts into arbitrated loop configurations. Hubs are typically half-duplex and have four, eight, twelve, or sixteen ports, allowing up to sixteen devices and hosts to be attached. However, the bandwidth on a hub is shared by all devices on the hub (Server Clusters 2003). Because of these performance constraints, hubs are used in small and/or low-bandwidth configurations.

Switches increase the overall SAN bandwidth by connecting system elements for data transmission and provide the advantages of the centralized storage repositories with shared applications and central management (IP Storage Area Networks 2006). A fabric switch provides the full fibre-channel bandwidth to each port independently. Typical switches allow ports to be configured in either an arbitrated-loop or a switched-mode fabric. In an arbitrated-loop configuration, the ports are typically full bandwidth and bidirectional, allowing devices and hosts to communicate at full fibre-channel speed in both directions simultaneously. Switches are the basic infrastructure used for large, point-to-point, switched fabrics. In this mode, a switch allows any device to communicate directly with any other device at full fibre-channel speed (1 Gbps or 2 Gbps) (Server Clusters 2003). Switches typically support 16, 32, 64, or even 128 ports. Switches can detect failed or congested connections and reroute data to the correct device. Linked (cascaded) switches increase the number of available SAN connections. This provides greater performance and resilience against individual connection failures (Anderson 2006).

Routers and bridges perform protocol transformations in SANs that allow different interconnect technologies to interoperate. The most common SAN fabrics are switched fibre channel, switched SCSI, and switched SSA, all of which physically link the interconnects and determine the SAN's performance and scalability (Simitci 2003). Some fabrics embed operating systems that provide for SAN security, monitoring, and management. Hosts are connected to the fibre-channel SAN through HBAs, which consist of hardware and interface drivers. Fibre-channel HBAs support negotiation with network-attached devices and switches and allow the host to minimize its CPU overhead.

SAN architectures are of two types: (1) "proprietary," those that are sourced from a single manufacturer who serves as the single point of contact for SAN hardware, software, and services, and (2) "open" architectures that consist of hardware and software from more than one manufacturer (Storage Area Networks 2003). Proprietary SAN architectures are usually limited in flexibility, because a hardware manufacturer could have limited experience in some specialized areas, such as tape library, software configuration, or storage management. Open-SAN architectures are more flexible. The issue of SAN integration with multivendor technologies is critical to ensure functionality, interoperability, and optimal performance. Ensuring data integrity guarantees and enforcing security policies for access rights to a particular storage device is a core part of the infrastructure (Server Clusters 2003). See chapter on *Storage Area Networks: Architectures and Protocols*.

SAN Design and Management Issues

The main benefit of SANs is that storage can be managed as a centralized pool of resources. The data storage infrastructure must be designed to provide highly available access so that the loss of one or more components in the storage fabric does not lead to servers being unable to access the application data. This principle is implemented in the following ways (Server Clusters 2003):

- There is no single point of failure of cables or components such as HBAs, switches, or storage controllers.
- Transparent and dynamic path detection and failover are implemented at the host. These features are supported by multipath drivers running on the host to present a single storage view to the application across multiple, independent HBAs.
- Almost all components (HBAs, switches, and controllers) have built-in hot-swap and hot-plug utilities for adopting interface cards, memory, CPUs, and disk drives.

Different SAN designs are based on the following topologies: (1) multiple independent fabrics, (2) federated fabrics, and (3) core backbone (Server Clusters 2003).

In the case of a multiple fabric configuration, each host or device is connected to multiple fabrics, but switches are not linked. In the event of the failure of one fabric, hosts and devices can communicate using the remaining fabric. In this configuration, each fabric should have the same zoning and security information to ensure a consistent view of the fabric regardless of the chosen communication port. Also, hosts and devices must have multiple adapters, which are treated as different storage buses. Additional multipathing software (e.g., EMC PowerPath™ or Compaq SecurePath™) is required to ensure that the host gets a single view of the devices across the two HBAs.

In the case of a federated fabric, individual hosts and devices are connected to at least two switches, which are linked together. This configuration has many management advantages (e.g., only one set of zoning information and one set of security information is managed; fabric itself can route around various link failures and switch failures, etc.). However, a disadvantage of this approach means that management errors can propagate to the entire fabric.

A core backbone configuration is frequently used (Server Clusters 2003). The core of the fabric is built using highly scalable, high-performance switches where the interswitch connections provide high-performance communication (e.g., 8 to 10 Gbps). Redundant edge switches can be cascaded from the core infrastructure to provide high numbers of ports for storage and hosts devices. As in the two previous configuration cases, additional multipathing software is required to ensure that the host gets a single view of the devices across the two HBAs. Also, management errors can propagate to the entire fabric.

SAN Operating System Software Components

The SAN software plays an important role in providing an environment for various business and management applications, called "system applications" (Barker and Massiglia 2001, 13). These include clustering, data replication, and data copying. The management applications (zoning, device discovery, allocation, RAID subsystems, and others) manage the complex environment of distributed systems. These applications can significantly reduce the cost and improve the quality of enterprise information services.

In particular, SAN management software provides the following services (Anderson 2006):

- Configuration and optimization of individual components of the best setup
- Monitoring of the entire network for performance bottlenecks and areas of potential failure
- Automation of time-consuming tasks such as data backup
- Management of all available storage system components as one virtual pool
- Statistics overview

Microsoft Corp. has launched the Simple SAN Program (Storage Management 2006) to ensure that customers deploying Windows Server 2003–based SANs have the appropriate tools for a simplified installation and management experience.

SAN Security Issues

The specific security issue of technology containment associated with a SAN also has to be addressed (Storage Area Networks 2003). For example, Windows NT servers would claim every available logical unit number (LUN) visible to them. Technology containment keeps servers from gaining unauthorized or accidental access to undesignated areas, such as data access and fabric management security, within the SAN.

The data access and security methodologies include: (1) fabric zoning, which provides a fabric port-and-host/storage-level point of logical partitioning and can help ensure that different OS types or applications are partitioned on the SAN (Server Clusters 2003); (2) LUN Masking, which is configured at the RAID storage subsystem level and helps ensure that only designated hosts assigned to that single storage port could access the specified RAID LUN; and (3) persistent binding, which forces a host to see a specific storage-subsystem port as a particular SCSI target and helps ensure that a specific storage-subsystem port on the SAN is always seen as the same SCSI target ID on the host, across the host and fabric, and throughout storage configuration changes. The advantages and disadvantages of these methods are described in Storage Area Network Security (2003).

The zoning security mechanism and access control are implemented at the switch level in the fabric. A port (either a host adapter or a storage controller port) can be configured as part of a zone. Only ports in a given zone can communicate with other ports in that zone. At the same time, the zoning mechanism also limits the traffic flow within a given SAN environment (Server Clusters 2003).

The fabric protection and management security technologies include: (1) fabric-to-fabric security technologies, which allow access control lists (ACLs) to permit or deny the addition of new switches to the fabric. The identity of the new switch may be validated by public key infrastructure (PKI) methods; (2) host-to-fabric security technologies, which apply ACLs at the port-level on the fabric, and permit or deny a particular host's FC HBA to attach to that port, and prevent an unauthorized intruder host from attaching to the fabric via any port; (3) management-to-fabric technologies, which use PKI and other encryption methods and ensure secure management in console-to-fabric communication; and (4) configuration integrity technologies, which ensure that propagated fabric configuration changes only come from one location at a time, and are correctly propagated to all switches on the SAN fabric with integrity. SAN security issues are discussed in Storage Area Network Security (2003) in detail.

SAN TECHNOLOGIES AND SOLUTIONS

The SAN infrastructures support multiple protocols, such as SCSI, simple network management protocol (SNMP), visual interface (VI), enterprise system connection/fiber connection (ESCON/FICON), TCP/IP, and session security authentication and initialization protocol (SSAIP), over a single physical connection. This unique capability provides the SAN system with the coupled functionality of an interface to storage devices and a server interconnect.

In the early 1990s, fibre channel was developed by the Fibre Channel Systems Initiative (FCSI) and adopted later by the American National Standards Institute (ANSI) X3T11 Committee as a high-speed interface for connecting storage devices to servers and other network configurations. These interconnect standards (FC-PH 2001) provide SANs with the vital properties of connectivity, bandwidth, interconnectivity, protocol efficiency, distance range, recoverability, failure tolerance, and cost options. The fibre-channel standards specify electrical and optical transmission media as well as conventions for signaling and transmission/functional protocols. Optical media (with SC, LC, and mechanical transfer registered jack [MT-RJ] connectors) support reliable signaling over long distances. Fibre channel provides data rates in the range from 133 Mbps to 4 Gbps over low-cost copper cabling (shielded twisted-pair wire or coaxial cable with serial communications d-shell connector, 9 pins [DB-9] and high-speed serial data connector [HSSDC]) or higher-cost multimode fiber-optic cable. Fibre-channel fabrics have transceivers, called "gigabit interface converters" (GBICs), which convert optical to electrical signals to cable connectors. Fibre-channel technology supports distances up to 10 km (see Table 2).

Optical and copper media are used in various SAN fibre-channel infrastructure applications (FCIA Roadmap 2006) including Inter Switch Links, SAN Edge Links, Back End Links, and Inter Device Links (see Table 3).

Fibre-channel Topologies

Fibre-channel methods have the means to implement three topologies: (1) point-to-point links, (2) shared bandwidth loop circuits known as fibre-channel arbitrated

Table 2: Maximum Distance for Fibre-channel Media Types

Data rate, MBps	12.5	25	50	100	200	400
Nominal signaling rate, Gbaut	0.133	0.266	0.531	1.063	2.126	4.252
T11 Specification completed, Year	1994	1994	1994	1996	2000	2003
Market availability, Year	1994	1994	1995	1997	2001	2005
9-μm single-mode fiber	–	–	–	10 km	10 km	10 km
50-μm multimode fiber	1.5 km	1.5 km	500 m	500 m	300 m	150 m
62.5-μm multimode fiber	1.5 km	1.5 km	350 m	300 m	150 m	70 m
Video coaxial cable	100 m	100 m	71 m	50 m	–	–
Miniature coaxial cable	42 m	28 m	19 m	14 m	–	–
Shielded twisted pair	80 m	57 m	46 m	28 m	–	–
Twinax	93 m	66 m	46 m	33 m	–	–

Sources: FC-PH (2001) and Stallings (2000).

Table 3: Fibre-channel Infrastructure Applications

Market	Length	Interswitch Link	SAN Edge Link	Back-End Link	Interdevice Link
Metropolitan Area Network [Fiber]	5 km and up	+			
Multi Building (campus) [Fiber]	300 m–5 km	+			
Single Building (Local) [Fiber]	30 m–5 km	+			
Datacenter or Rack [Fiber]	0 m–100 m	+	+	+	
Datacenter or Rack [Copper]	0 m–15 m	+	+	+	
Backplane [Copper]	0.6 m				+

Source: FCIA Roadmap (2006).

loops (FC-ALs), and (3) bandwidth-switched fibre-channel fabrics (FC-SW) that provide SANs with the ability to do bandwidth multiplexing by supporting simultaneous data transmission between various pairs of devices. Any storage device on the loop can be accessed through a fibre-channel switch (FC-SW) or hub. The fibre-channel switch can support entry-level (8 to 16 ports) to enterprise-level (64 to 128 ports) systems. Under ANSI X3T11 standards, up to 126 storage devices (nodes) can be linked in the fibre-channel arbitrated loop (FC-AL) configuration, with the storage interface bandwidth about 100 Mbps for transferring large files. More than seventy companies, including industry-leading vendors of disk arrays and computer and networking systems, support the FC-AL voluntary standards. FC-AL topology is used primarily to connect disk arrays and FC devices. Originally developed as the high-speed serial technology of choice for server-storage connectivity, the FC-AL method is extended to the FC-SL standard that supports isochronous and time-deterministic services, including methods of managing loop operational parameters and quality-of-service (QoS) definitions, as well as control. The FC-VI regulation establishes a fibre channel-virtual interface architecture (FC-VIA) mapping standard. See *Fibre Channel* for more information about various implementations of the technology in various network configurations, including SANs.

Because of the high cost of the FC interconnect components and separation of storage and servers at the wide area network scale (resulting in slow capabilities of WAN-SANs with fibre channel), alternatives to FC technologies have been developed. The ipStorage technology (Barker and Massiglia 2001, 187) uses TCP/IP as a storage interconnect. The Internet Engineering Task Force (IETF) has proposed the iSCSI (Internet SCSI) standards (Hufferd 2002) that address the issues of long distances (WAN-scale), reducing the interconnect cost, high security, and complex storage network topologies. The iSCSI is layered on top of the TCP/IP protocol hierarchy and can instantly access all modern transmission media and topologies. TCP/IP and related protocols have been implemented in the server-based systems that allow the most general storage networks to be constructed with the iSCSI method (iSCSI and IP-SAN Solutions 2006). The main challenge is a reduction of the iSCSI processor overhead of operating iSCSI packets below the fibre-channel overhead level. See more details in *Storage Area Networks: Architectures and Protocols*.

InfiniBand Solutions

InfiniBand is a new emerging interconnect technology, developed by the standards of the InfiniBand Trade Association (founded by Compaq, Dell, Hewlett-Packard, IBM, Intel, Microsoft, and Sun Microsystems) that offers the most general low-cost server system topologies (InfiniBand Trade Association 2006). It is expected that InfiniBand interfaces will be embedded into all Intel-based servers (Barker and Massiglia 2001, 188–92; Intel InfiniBand Architecture 2006) and will allow Windows and Linux servers to be available for resolving complex problems of data centers by adopting clusters and multiple-host enterprise RAID subsystems. InfiniBand technology implements a switched-fabric architecture with the packet-switching communication protocol (PSCP) that relates to the virtual interface (VI) architecture method. SANs, parallel processing systems, and systems area networks can effectively use InfiniBand as a high-performance/low-latency interconnect.

Crossroads Systems with a Storage Router

InfiniBand technology has been successfully implemented by Crossroads Systems, Inc., which promotes storage solutions based on protocol-independent connectivity at speeds of gigabit per second and unparalleled manageability for various storage devices. Crossroads' storage routers (e.g., Crossroads™ 10000) support peer operations between storage devices and multiprotocol servers on fibre-channel storage networks.

Brocade's Configurations

Brocade Communication Systems, Inc., has developed an intelligent fabric services architecture that creates a scalable and secure environment for enterprise mission-critical storage applications such as data backup and business continuity. The Brocade SANs (SilkWorm™ family of fabric switches and software) provide enterprises with any-server-to-any-storage-device connectivity and consolidate storage resources and servers, as well as sharing backup resources (Beauchamp, Judd, and Kuo 2002).

OTHER STORAGE NETWORKING TECHNOLOGIES

The following emerging technologies introduce new system architectural approaches in storage networking. SAN developers and users are trying to adapt them to a new enterprise environment that is characterized by host-level heterogeneous complexity, management flexibility, new TCP/IP network communication services, file-access-protocol developments, and the repartitioning of the functionality of file management systems.

VI (Virtual Interface) Architecture

The virtual interface (VI) architecture is a midlayer protocol specification that regulates virtual intercommunication between applications running on different remote servers (i.e., in a cluster). This method significantly reduces the latency and the volume of the system input/output (I/O) operations by using message and data buffer pools that are insensitive to the heterogeneous operating environment or other applications. The reduction of the I/O-related interrupts increases the CPUs' time for processing various other system tasks. Developers of the VIA technology (Compaq, Intel, Microsoft, etc.) use this architecture as an efficient way of message communication between the SAN nodes at the application level, creating only a small overhead of intercommunication between the remote applications. This method has been successfully implemented in database managers and NAS devices (Barker and Massiglia 2001, 189–90). Several efforts (i.e., the direct access file system and network file system initiatives) have been made to improve file system performance by using VIA-type advanced transport protocol features. The Emulex Corporation promotes the GN9000/VI™ 1 Gbps VI/IP PCI host bus adapter, which is based on the virtual interface (version 1.0) architecture, supports standard TCP/IP-reliable data delivery, IP routing, and the direct access file system standard, and speeds data access over standard Gigabit Ethernet networks.

Direct Access File System

The direct access file system (DAFS) is a new file access/transfer protocol that is based on CIFS/NFS characteristics and VIA-type transport protocol features. DAFS/VIA technology supports direct file transfer between the storage system and clients. In a SAN environment, data can be directly transferred among a number of servers.

IP Storage Technologies

Another *block-mode data* mechanism has been used by the IETF IP Storage Working Group in developing standards for a new IP-based transport-through-network technology that encapsulates fibre-channel and SCSI high-speed interfaces and provides direct access to data on disks, tapes, and optical storage devices. IP storage technology allows embedding low-cost SANs into IP-based enterprise infrastructures over existing Gigabit Ethernet networks. See chapter on *Ethernet LANs*.

SANs over IP

To avoid the distance limitation of the fibre-channel interconnects, enterprises build remote SANs that can be interconnected by means of the SAN-over-IP technology originally developed by the Computer Network Technology Corporation. The distant SANs appear as local storage entities. This technology improves enterprise management and data access, disaster recovery, business continuity, disk mirroring, electronic tape vaulting, and wide area clustering. The Storage Networking Industry Association (SNIA) offers three technologies for integrating fibre-channel SANs into the IP backbone. These methods include fibre channel over IP (FCIP), Internet fibre channel over IP (iFCP), and Internet SCSI (iSCSI). The FCIP, iFCP, and iSCSI transport protocol descriptions are presented in Clark (2002).

Fibre channel over IP (FCIP)

FCIP is the simplest point-to-point IP tunneling solution for intercommunicating remote SANs with fibre-channel fabrics. The FCIP gateways establish TCP/IP connections over a WAN path to transport the fibre-channel encapsulated frames. A typical discrepancy in data communication rates between an FCIP-attached WAN link and fibre-channel fabric generates various flow control issues that can be resolved by TCP sliding-window algorithms. Several FC-FCIP management issues cannot be properly determined for the FCIP pipes because the TCP/IP transport component ends at the external nodes of the fibre-channel network. These problems have been addressed and successfully resolved in the iFCP and iSCSI approaches.

Internet Fibre-channel Protocol (iFCP)

The gateway-to-gateway iFCP supports a means of integrating fibre-channel end devices into a single IP SAN. By using iFCP, the fibre-channel fabric services can be provided to the remote FC devices over a TCP/IP network. The iFCP IP storage switches can directly connect fibre-channel storage arrays, HBAs, hubs, switches, and routers. The iFCP is a protocol stack that can be implemented in an IP storage controller interface or integrated into Gigabit Ethernet IP storage network interface card (NIC) (known as ANSI X3T10 and X3T11 Standards) (Clark 2002, 126–39). It supports any-to-any IP routing of storage data. A mismatch in data communication rates between an iFCP-attached WAN link and fibre-channel fabric generates various flow-control issues that can be resolved by TCP sliding-window algorithms. The Internet protocol security (IPSec), public or private keys, and zoning methods can provide security across the Internet. One of the important applications of the iFCP technology is the support of multiple TCP/IP connections for concurrent storage transactions.

Internet SCSI (iSCSI)

In contrast to the FCIP concept, the iSCSI method, which follows the SCSI client/server model, is based on the implementation of a light-switch technology in IP storage networking (Clark 2002, 139–49) and excludes fibre-channel elements. The iSCSI servers (targets) are present in disk arrays and client nodes (initiators) that occupy host platforms. The iSCSI protocol over the TCP/IP layer is used for block data transport between these entities over the IP network. Data can be directly written into application memory through a steering and data synchronization layer located below the iSCSI sublayer. IPSec, Keyberos authentication, public key, and other methods can provide security across the Internet. SANs use the iSCSI adapters with TCP/IP offload engine (TOE) to minimize processing overhead and realize high-performance features of the iSCSI technology. The enterprise solutions with IP SANs can also support Gigabit and faster Ethernet on iSCSI-switch infrastructures (IP SAN Appliances 2006).

Storage over IP (SoIP)

Based on the SoIP remote storage technology, the Nishan Systems Corporation developed IP Storage switches of the IPS 4000 Series™ and a suite of storage management software that allows configuration and monitoring of large-scale storage networks.

Fabric Shortest Path First (FSPF)

FSPF is the open shortest path first (OSPF)-based standard routing protocol for fibre channel that determines the next shortest route for data traffic, updates the routing table, and detects the failed routes (Vacca 2002, 152). Optical, link, or switch failures can be effectively handled by FSPF with minimal impact on the interconnected devices in the FC/SAN environment.

Adaptive Network Storage Architecture (ANSA)

The Procom Technology Corporation has developed the ANSA approach, which delivers both block-level and file-level access to data. Procom's NetFORCE 3000™ Series provides filer functionality (together with advanced features of security, high stability, backup, and recovery) to enterprise storage that can result in high-performance information-management systems. The ANSA technology has been successfully applied to database management, data warehousing, e-mail delivering, and 24/7 rich-media applications.

Storage Resource Management (SRM)

The SRM technology provides applications for managing logical and physical storage-system resources (virtual devices, disk volumes, file resources, storage devices and elements, and appliances). SRM tools allow storage-system administrators to configure and monitor SANs and other storage resources. During the administrative monitoring, the transport or storage data remain unchanged. Vendors of the SRM tools, products, and services include SUN Microsystems (Sun StorEdge™), HighGround Systems, Inc. (Storage Resource Manager, Media Mirror), and Storage Computer Corp. (Storage Administrator) (Toigo 2001).

STANDARDS

American National Standards Institute (ANSI)

ANSI coordinates SAN voluntary standards (ANSI 2006). The ANSI X3T10 and X3T11 working committees are associated with storage networking issues, including SCSI I/O interface standards (X3T10) and fibre-channel interface standards (X3T11). The first set of fibre-channel standards (ANSI X.3230–1994) (Vacca 2002, 75–8) describes standards for a switch fabric (FC-SW2), the interconnect that supports high volumes of throughput and bandwidth for disk output and input, as well as a management information base (MIB) management standard that permits fibre-channel devices (switches) to be managed by any vendor's software, which includes an implementation of the simple network management protocol (SNMP). SAN users can find a brief description of other X3T11 fibre-channel standards in Barker and Massiglia (2001, 384–6).

Several FC SAN equipment vendors, including Brocade Communications Systems, have refined SAN standards in the areas of management, discovery, data transport, and WAN connectivity. This allows the fibre-channel SAN to become an integral part of the enterprise framework (Vacca 2002, 78–9).

Distributed Management Task Force (DMTF)

The DMTF has introduced management standards for computer systems and enterprise environment (DMTF 2006). The SAN-related management standards (Barker and Massiglia 2001, 386–7) cover a set of the Web-based enterprise management (WBEM) XML-based technologies. They support an object-oriented approach in developing a business's management environment, using the Common Information Model; architectures and frameworks for desktop, laptop, and server management (desktop management interface); standard data models for a network, its elements, policies, and rules (directory-enabled networks); and functional calls for transaction monitoring (known as the application response measurement [ARM] standard).

Storage Systems Standards Working Group (SSSWG)

As a division of the Institute of Electrical and Electronics Engineers (IEEE), the SSSWG develops models and architectures of storage systems, including SANs (SSSWG 2006). The SSSWG project authorization requests (Barker and Massiglia 2001, 387–8) include the "Guide to Storage System Design"; media management system (MMS) architecture; session security, authentication, initialization protocol (SSAIP) of the MMS; media management protocol (MMP) for both client and administrative applications; drive management protocol (DMP) of the MMS; library management protocol (LMP) of the MMS; the media manager interchange protocol (MMIP) for information exchange between autonomous media managers; the media manager control interface protocol (MMCIP); the C language procedural interface for implementation of the MMS's components; MMS User mount commands for establishing "command line interfaces" (CLI); MMS standard administrative and operational commands for administering and operating an MMS; and "MOVER" specifications of a storage system data mover architecture and its interfaces.

Internet Engineering Task Force (IETF)

The IETF defines a variety of the transmission control protocol/Internet protocol (TCP/IP) standards that are widely used in the enterprise environment with SANs (IETF 2006). The IETF standards related to storage networking (Barker and Massiglia 2001, 388) include the simple network management protocol (SNMP) for managing and monitoring devices and systems in a network; the Internet protocol over fibre channel (IPoFC); and a policy for quality of services (QoS).

STORAGE NETWORKING ASSOCIATIONS, INITIATIVES, FORUMS, AND COALITIONS

The organizations discussed below promote storage networking technologies and products, develop standards, undertake marketing activities in information technology industry, educate, train, and create the knowledge base for implementing SAN technology:

SNIA (Storage Networking Industry Association)

The SNIA, an international association of developers of storage and networking products, is focusing on the creation of a forum of IT companies, system integrators, and application vendors for delivering architectures, education, and services in storage networking, as well as defining the specifications and infrastructures, and proposing standards for storage networking systems, including SANs, SAN-attached storage (SAS), and network-attached storage (NAS) (SNIA 2006).

Fibre Channel Industry Association (FCIA)

The FCIA is an international organization of manufacturers, systems integrators, developers, systems vendors, industry professionals, and end users. In June 2002, this organization included more than 190 members and affiliates in the United States, Europe, and Japan. The FCIA is committed to delivering a broad base of fibre-channel infrastructure to support a wide array of industry applications within the mass storage and IT-based arenas. FCIA working groups focus on specific aspects of the technology that target markets, which include data storage networking and SAN management. The overview of fibre channel's SAN and networking applications and examples of fibre-channel solutions for high-performance networks of heterogeneous storage, server, and workstation resources can be found on the "technology" section of the FCIA Web site (FCIA 2006).

Fibre Alliance (FA)

The FA is the networking industry consortium originally founded by a group of storage networking companies, including EMC Corporation, to develop and implement standards for managing heterogeneous fibre-channel-based SANs. In collaboration with the IETF, this group develops the definition of simple network management protocol management information bases (SNMP MIB) for storage network and device management (Fibre Alliance 2006).

JIRO

Jiro is a Sun Microsystems technology that delivers intelligent management services for networked devices. Using the principles of Java and Jini platform-independent application development interfaces (Jini 2006), Jiro technology provides the architecture for connecting and managing complex distributed environments such as storage area networks. The Jiro technology brings higher levels of interoperability, adaptability, and manageability to enterprise networks with storage resources (Jiro 2002).

National Storage Industry Consortium (NSIC)

Since April 1991, the NSIC has consolidated the efforts of over fifty corporations, universities, and national labs in the field of digital information storage. The corporate members are major information storage manufacturers and companies from the storage industry infrastructure, including SANs. As a nonprofit organization, NSIC supports precompetitive joint research projects, involving collaboration among users and integrators of storage systems, storage system and device manufacturers, storage component and media manufacturers, suppliers, universities, and national laboratories (National Storage Industry Consortium 2006).

THE SAN MARKET, VENDORS, AND SERVICE PROVIDERS

Data storage management has become the primary issue for businesses in the past ten years. According to the International Data Corporation (IDC), the redundant array of independent disks (RAID) shipped in 2003 exceeded 250×10^{15} bytes (Storage Area Networks 2003). Data-rich businesses continue to seek effective data storage and management solutions to handle this data growth. SAN technologies allow existing enterprises to effectively manage more transactions, customers, suppliers, and services. Company operations are significantly improved by providing continuous high availability through uninterruptible access to data, increasing scalability through multiple-channel data transmission, and reducing the network and server's CPU overhead. Additional opportunities for the IT enterprises are also associated with the Internet, which allows them to increase the volume of data and rates of their transmission.

Evolution of the SAN Market

According to the Gartner's research study (Couture et al. 2006), the worldwide storage service market will grow from more than $23 billion in 2004 to more than $31 billion in 2009. The study conducted by the market research firm iSuppli Corporation (Gardner 2004) shows that the SAN enterprise market has been growing at an annual rate of 30% and promises to maintain that pace over the next five years. Among others, two growth factors will dominate: rapidly dropping prices on SAN solutions and better record-keeping practices mandated by federal legislation. By 2004, practically all large enterprises have installed SANs. Nowadays, SANs are being deployed by a growing number of midsized and smaller companies, including about 10% of enterprises with revenues of between $100 million and $300 million (Gardner 2004). Microsoft and other software providers have long viewed this market as a major growth opportunity, particularly for regulatory-compliant software packages that help protect confidentiality of patient records under the Health Insurance Portability and Accountability Act (HIPAA), which was introduced in April 2005 and requires the establishment of an IT infrastructure. Another factor of the future growing in the SAN installations is the Sarbanes-Oxley Act, which regulates how data are managed, archived, retrieved, and authenticated.

According to the Jupiter Media Metrix Corporation (Market Forecast Report 2002), the growth in Internet commerce is attributed to the increase in the U.S. online population by nearly 50%, from 141.5 million in 2001 to 210.8 million by 2006, as well as to the growth of U.S. online retail sales from $47.8 billion in 2002 to an estimated $130.3 billion in 2006. SANs have revolutionized the IT enterprise's infrastructure and improved its e-business applications, including e-commerce, e-mail, online transaction processing, data replication, and enterprise database management. Global continuous delivery of multimedia secured information has become the main service of modern e-business enterprises.

By adding networking and intelligence features to data storage, fibre-channel SAN switches enable the solution of several challenging e-business storage problems, such as linking high-performance workstation clusters, connecting high-performance tape storage on disk farms, giving server farms a high-speed data-transmission pipe, clustering disk farms, and linking Ethernet, fiber distributed data interface (FDDI), asynchronous transfer mode (ATM), and token ring LANs to the backbone. Intelligent SAN systems allow improving enterprise performance significantly, decreasing latency, supporting direct access to the storage shared by multiple servers, reducing network traffic on the front-end network, and removing storage management tasks from servers.

A new SAN market is open for small to medium businesses (SMBs) that need flexible and scalable storage systems to ensure critical data that can be accessed quickly, securely, and cost effectively (Storage Management 2006). According to New York–based market research firm Access Markets International (AMI) Partners Inc., SMBs in the United States spent $443 million on SANs in 2003, and this figure is expected to grow to $1.5 billion by 2008. Microsoft Corporation, together with business partners, has developed the Simple SAN Program that supports the iSCSI protocol, which allows SANs to be accessed over IP-based networks. New storage management capabilities have been built into Windows Server 2003 (Storage Management 2006).

SAN Vendors and Service Providers

Table 4 shows a list of SAN vendors, storage-networking service providers, and their products. The complete list of SAN deployment companies can be found in (Vacca 2002,

Table 4: SAN Vendors and Services

Company	Product Type	Source
ADVA Optical Storage Networking Technologies	Fiber Service Platform (FSP); DWDM system	(ADVA 2006)
ATTO Technology, Inc.	Fibre channel hub; Fibre channel, SCSI and IP storage solutions	(ATTO 2006)
Broadcom Corporation	SAN system core logic input/output chips	(Broadcom 2006)
Brocade Communication Systems, Inc.	Fabric switches; SAN solutions	(Brocade 2006)
Crossroads Systems, Inc.	Modular storage router	(Crossroads 2006)
Cutting Edge	Clustered failover; IP SAN solutions	(Cutting Edge 2006)
Dell Computer	Enterprise storage solutions; RAIDs	(Dell 2006)
EMC Corporation	Networked storage solutions	(EMC 2006)
Emulex Corporation	VI/IP PCI host bus adapters; SAN storage switchers	(Emulex 2006)
FalconStor Software, Inc.	Storage software; SAN infrastructure	(FalconStor 2006)
Fujitsu Ltd.	RAIDs	(Fujitsu 2006)
Hewlett-Packard	SAN management tools; storage systems	(Hewlett-Packard 2006)
Hitachi Data Systems/GST	SAN solutions	(Hitachi 2006)
IBM	Enterprise storage server; RAIDs; tape libraries; storage software	(IBM 2006)
Intel Corporation	iSCSI HBAs; GBICs; RAID controllers	(Intel Corporation 2006)
LSI Logic Storage Systems, Inc.	SAN solutions; RAID adapters	(LSI 2006)
McDATA	Enterprise FC management tools	(McDATA 2006)
Media Integration	Fibre channel SAN; iSCSI backup	(Media Integration 2006)
Microsoft Corporation	SAN management and backup software	(Microsoft 2006)
NEC Corporation	SAN support products	(NEC Corporation 2006)
Nishan Systems	IP storage switches	(Nishan Systems 2006)
QLogic Corp.	SAN management software; HBAs	(QLogic 2006)
SANRAD	iSCSI-SAN and IP-SAN solutions	(SANRAD 2006)
SUN Microsystems	Storage systems; RAIDs; disk backup	(Sun Microsystems 2006)
Unisys	SAN solutions	(Unisys 2006)
Xyratex	RAID systems	(Xyratex 2006)

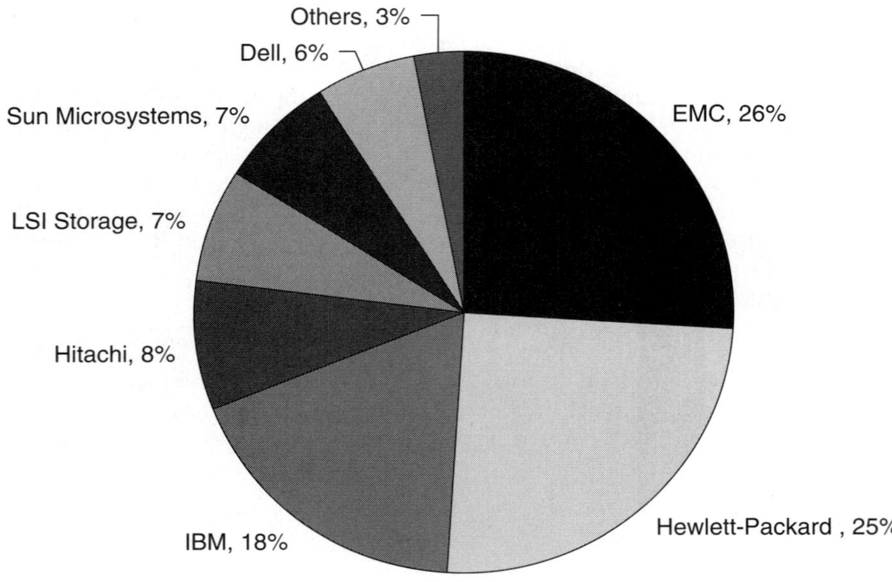

Figure 2: Shares of leading companies in the SAN market. (Data source: Gardner 2004)

495–7) and on the Network Buyers Guide Web site (Network Buyers Guide 2006).

The iSuppli survey (Gardner 2004) identifies seven leading providers of SAN solutions: EMC (26% of all shares), Hewlett-Packard (25%), IBM (18%), Hitachi (8%), LSI Storage (7%), Sun Microsystems (7%), and Dell (6%) (see Figure 2). The additional information (based on the revenue analyses) about the top 10 largest storage companies for the period from 1999 to 2005 can be found in (Kerekes 2005).

CONCLUSION

SANs, networked high-speed infrastructures, enable e-business enterprises to significantly improve their 24/7 continuous scalable services. They have become a critical part of the enterprise network infrastructure. The above-considered technologies and effective SAN solutions allow companies to shift their focus from numerous IT infrastructure problems to the successful performance of their businesses and services.

GLOSSARY

CIFS: Common Internet file system, also known as the Microsoft server message block protocol; a network file system access protocol that is primarily used by Windows clients to communicate file access requests to Windows servers.

CIM: Common information model; an object-oriented description of entities and relationships in the enterprise management environment.

DWDM: Dense wavelength division multiplexing; a method that allows more wavelengths to use the same fiber.

FC-AL: Fibre channel-arbitrated loop transport protocol.

FCSW: Fibre-channel switch.

FC-VIA: Fibre channel–virtual interface architecture.

FSPF: Fabric shortest path first; a routing protocol used by fibre-channel switches.

High-availability cluster: Also known as failover cluster, this computer cluster is implemented for the purpose of improving the availability of services that the cluster provides. The cluster includes a redundant computer that is used to provide services when system components fail.

IPoFC: Internet protocol over fibre channel.

iSCSI: Internet small computer systems interface.

JBOD: Just a bunch of disks; a term for a collection of disks configured as an arbitrated loop segment in a single chassis.

LC Connector: A small form-factor fiber-optic connector, which resembles a small SC connector. Lucent Technologies developed the LC connector for use in telecommunication environments. The LC connector has been standardized as FOCIS 10 (Fiber Optic Connector Intermateability Standards) in EIA/TIA-604-10.

NAS: Network-attached storage.

RAID: Redundant arrays of inexpensive disks; a technology for managing multiple disks.

SAN: Storage area network.

SAS: SAN-attached storage.

SC Connector: A fiber-optic connector with a push-pull latching mechanism that provides for quick insertion and removal while also ensuring a positive connection. The SC connector has been standardized as FOCIS 3 (Fiber Optic Connector Intermateability Standards) in EIA/TIA-604-03.

SoIP: Storage over IP; a storage technology developed by the Nishan Systems Corporation.

SSA: Serial storage architecture.

VI: Virtual interface architecture; a midlayer protocol specification.

CROSS REFERENCES

See *Fibre Channel; Storage Area Networks: Architectures and Protocols.*

REFERENCES

ADVA optical storage networking technologies. 2006. www.san.com (accessed April 4, 2006).

American National Standards Institute (ANSI). 2006. www.ansi.org (accessed April 4, 2006).

Anderson, N. 2006. Build your company's first SAN. White Paper. Hewlett-Packard, Inc. www.hp.com. (accessed April 4, 2006).

ATTO. 2006. *SAN solutions*. www.attotech.com/sans.html (accessed April 4, 2006).

Barker, R., and Massiglia, P. 2001. *Storage networking essentials: A complete guide to understanding and implementing SANs*. New York: Wiley.

Beauchamp, C., Judd J., and Kuo, B. 2002. *Building SANs with Brocade fibre channel fabric switches*. Rockland, MA: Syngress.

Broadcom Corporation. 2006. www.broadcom.com (accessed April 4, 2006).

Brocade Communication Systems, Inc. 2006. (see the SAN Info Center) www.brocade.com (accessed April 4, 2006).

Business Brief. 2006. SAN next generation—moving to 4 Gbps (2006). White paper. Hewlett-Packard, Inc. www.hp.com (accessed April 4, 2006).

Clark, T. 2003. *Designing storage area networks: A practical reference for implementing fibre channel and IP SANs*. Boston: Addison–Wesley.

Clark, T. 2002. *IP SANS: An introduction to iSCSI, iFCP, and FCIP protocols for storage area networks*. Boston: Addison–Wesley.

Couture, A., A. MacNeela, Y. Adachi, M, Caminos, and R. DeSouza. 2006 March 16. Forecast: IT Storage Services, Worldwide, 2003–2009. Stamford, CT: Gartner.

Crossroads Systems, Inc. 2006. www.crossroads.com/about (accessed April 4, 2006).

Cutting Edge, Inc. 2006. www.cuttedge.com (accessed April 4, 2006).

Dell, Inc. 2006. www.dell.com (accessed April 4, 2006).

Distributed Management Task Force (DMTF) 2006. www.dmtf.org (accessed April 4, 2006).

EMC Corporation. 2006. www.emc.com (accessed April 4, 2006).

Emulex Corporation. 2006. www.emulex.com (accessed April 4, 2006).

FalconStor Software, Inc. 2006. www.falconstor.com (accessed April 4, 2006).

Farley, M. 2001. *Building storage networks*, 2nd ed. New York: Osborne/McGraw–Hill.

FC-PH. 2001. Fibre channel physical interface, revision 13, December 9, 2001. www.t11.org/index.htm (accessed April 4, 2006).

FCIA (Fibre Channel Industry Association). 2006. www.fibrechannel.org (accessed April 4, 2006).

FCIA Roadmap. 2006. Fibre channel infrastructure application matrix, FCIA. www.fibrechannel.org/OVERVIEW/Roadmap.html (accessed April 4, 2006).

Fibre Alliance. 2006. www.fibrealliance.org (accessed April 4, 2006).

Fujitsu Ltd. 2006. *RAIDs*. www.fujitsu.com (accessed April 4, 2006).

Gardner, W. D. 2004 January 6. Falling prices, regulations drive SAN market. www.networkingpipeline.com (accessed April 4, 2006).

Hammond-Doel, T. 2001. *2 Gb/s fibre channel SANs*. Vixel Corporation. www.vixel.com/9000_docs/9000_wp.pdf (accessed March 24, 2003).

Hewlett-Packard, Inc. 2006. www.hp.com (accessed April 4, 2006).

Hitachi Data Systems. 2006. SAN Solutions. www.hds.com (accessed April 4, 2006).

Hufferd, J. L. 2002. iSCSI: *The universal storage connection*. Boston: Addison-Wesley.

IBM Enterprise SAN Solutions. 2006. www.storage.ibm.com/ibmsan (accessed April 4, 2006).

ILogic Corporation. 2006. www.ilogic.com (accessed April 4, 2006).

InfiniBand Trade Association. 2006. www.infinibandta.org/home (accessed April 4, 2006).

InfraStor Technology Corp. 2001. *SAN vs NAS*. www.infrastor.com/tech/sanvsnas.htm (accessed March 24, 2003).

InfraStor Technology Corp. 2002. *Introduction to SAN*. www.infrastor.com/tech/SANTechIntro.htm (accessed April 4, 2006).

Intel Corporation. 2006. *SAN systems*. www.intel.com (accessed April 4, 2006).

Intel InfiniBand Architecture. 2006. www.intel.com/technology/infiniband (accessed April 4, 2006).

Internet Engineering Task Force (IETF). 2006. www.ietf.org. (accessed April 4, 2006).

IP SAN Appliances. 2006. Celeros, Inc. www.celeros.com (accessed April 4, 2006).

IP Storage Area Networks. 2006. RADirect Inc. www.rad-direct.com/camp_ipsan_vswitch3000.html (accessed April 4, 2006).

iSCSI and IP-SAN Solutions. 2006. SANRAD Inc. www.sanrad.com (accessed April 4, 2006).

Jini 2006. www.jini.org (accessed April 4, 2006).

Jiro. 2002. www.sun.com/jiro (accessed September 12, 2002).

Kerekes, Z. 2005 May 26. *The top 10 biggest storage companies in 2008*. www.storagesearch.com/squeak-5.html (accessed April 4, 2006).

LSI Logic Storage Systems, Inc. 2006. www.lsilogicstorage.com (accessed April 4, 2006).

Lyon, C., and Sturgeon, S. 2006. FCIA showcases "fast and flexible" 4GFC products at SNW. www.fibrechannel.org/NEWS/fcia051018.html (accessed April 4, 2006).

Market Forecast Report. 2002. *E-commerce market size and trends*, 6. www.goecart.com/ecommerce_solutions_facts.asp (accessed April 23, 2006).

McDATA, Inc. 2006. www.mcdata.com (accessed April 4, 2006).

Media Integration, Inc. 2006. www.mediainc.com (accessed April 4, 2006).

Microsoft Corporation. 2006. www.microsoft.com/products (accessed April 4, 2006).

National Storage Industry Consortium. 2006. www.nsic.org (accessed April 4, 2006).

NEC Corporation. 2006. *SAN support products*. www.nec.com(accessed April 4, 2006).

Network Buyers Guide. 2006. http://networkbuyersguide.com (accessed April 4, 2006).

Nishan Systems. 2006. www.nishansystems.com (accessed April 4, 2006).

Ottem, E. 2001. *Third generation SANs: Open 2Gb fabric*. White Paper WP-2G0801. Gadzoox Networks, Inc. www.infrastor.com/downloads/2Gb_whitepaper.pdf (accessed April 4, 2006).

Peterson, M. 2006. *Embedded databases: Powering storage intelligence*. Santa Barbara, CA: Strategic articles.htm (accessed May 23, 2007)

Preston, W. C. 2002. Using SANs and NAS. Sebastopol, CA: O'Reilly.

QLogic Corporation. 2006. www.qlogic.com (accessed April 4, 2006).

Riabov, V. V. 2004. Storage area networks. In *The Internet encyclopedia*, Vol. 3, 329–39, edited by H. Bidgoli. New York: Wiley.

Sachdev, P., and Arunkundram, R. S. 2002. *Using storage area networks*. Special edition. Indianapolis: Que.

SANRAD. 2006. *iSCSI-SAN and IP-SAN solutions*. www.sanrad.com (accessed April 4, 2006).

SAN School. 2006. Search Storage Corp. www.searchstorage.com/SANSchool (accessed April 4, 2006).

Server Clusters: Storage Area Networks, Windows 2000 and Windows Server 2003. 2003. White paper. Microsoft Corporation. www.microsoft.com (accessed April 4, 2006)

Sheldon, T. 2001. *McGraw–Hill encyclopedia of networking and telecommunications*. New York: McGraw–Hill.

Simitci, H. 2003. *Storage network performance analysis*. New York: Wiley.

SNIA (Storage Networking Industry Association) 2006. www.snia.org (accessed April 4, 2006).

SSSWG (Storage Systems Standards Work Group) 2006. www.ssswg.org (accessed April 4, 2006).

Stallings, W. 2000. *Local and metropolitan area networks*. 6th ed. Upper Saddle River, NJ: Prentice Hall.

Storage Area Networks and Return on Investment. 2006. White paper. Datalink Corporation. www.datalink.com/whitepaper.cfm (accessed April 4, 2006).

Storage Area Network Security. 2003. Data access and fabric management. White paper. Datalink Corporation. www.datalink.com/whitepaper.cfm (accessed April 4, 2006).

Storage Management. 2006. Making SANs simple. In *Windows storage solutions*. SearchStorage www.SearchStorage.com/MicrosoftStorage (accessed April 4, 2006).

Sun Microsystems. 2006. *Data storage solutions*. www.sun.com/storage (accessed April 4, 2006).

Technical Committee T11. 2006. Fibre channel interfaces. www.t11.org/index.htm (accessed April 4, 2006).

Thornburgh, R. H., and Schoenborn, B. J. 2001. *Storage area networks: Designing and implementing a mass storage system*. Upper Saddle River, NJ: Prentice Hall.

Toigo, J. W. 2001. *The Holy Grail of data storage management*. Upper Saddle River, NJ: Prentice Hall.

Troppens, U., Erkens, R., and Müeller, W. 2004. *Storage networks explained: Basics and application of fibre channel SAN, NAS iSCSI and InfiniBand*. New York: Wiley.

Unisys. 2006. *SAN solutions*. www.unisys.com/index.htm (accessed April 4, 2006).

Vacca, J. 2002. *The essential guide to storage area networks*. Upper Saddle River, NJ: Prentice Hall.

Xyratex. 2006. *4Gb RAID systems*. www.xyratex.com (accessed April 4, 2006).

Fibre Channel

Jiying Zhao, *University of Ottawa, Canada*

INTRODUCTION TO FIBRE CHANNEL

The small computer system interface (SCSI) has been used widely so far for connecting different storage devices to high-end computer systems to provide high-speed parallel data transmission. The devices can be daisy-chained together with a terminator at both ends of the SCSI cable. However, the SCSI has the following limitations: (1) the maximum length of a SCSI bus is 25 m; (2) the maximum number of devices a SCSI bus can connect is 32; and (3) the maximum transmission bandwidth of a SCSI bus is 80 MBps. As a result of the development of computer and multimedia technologies, a greater speed of data transmission among more devices over longer distances has been increasingly required. As a solution, a storage area network (SAN) can be used to connect with high-speed computers and storage devices. Two primary protocols for building SAN are fibre channel and SCSI over TCP/IP (also known as iSCSI [Hufferd 2003]).

The iSCSI protocol enables a SAN solution whereby SCSI is transported over the top of TCP/IP. iSCSI uses TCP/IP to establish sessions between iSCSI initiator and iSCSI targets. An iSCSI session may consist of multiple TCP connections. However, any given SCSI exchange must be conducted on one TCP connection. Because of the ubiquity of IP networks, iSCSI can be used to transmit data over local area networks (LANs), wide area networks (WANs), or the Internet and can enable location-independent data storage and retrieval. However, in this chapter, we will only discuss fibre channel.

Fibre channel (FC), a highly reliable, one or more gigabit (10 Gb in the near future) serial interconnect technology, allows concurrent communications among workstations, mainframes, servers, data storage systems, and other peripherals using SCSI, Internet protocol (IP) and a wide range of other protocols to meet the needs of the data communication. Fibre channel was developed primarily to overcome the shortcomings of the current SCSI to provide higher speed and more scalable configuration. It turned out to be a technically attractive solution to the storage area network. Fibre channel can be used to implement SANs, to connect servers and high-performance workstations and mainframes, and to form the backbones between LANs. Currently, quite a number of manufactures provide various fibre-channel switches and end devices.

In order to help readers to understand fibre-channel technology, in the rest of the chapter, we will introduce fibre-channel protocol architecture, fibre-channel elements, fibre-channel transmission media and topologies, fibre-channel addressing, fibre-channel information transmission hierarchy, fibre-channel fabric routing, fibre-channel classes of service, fibre-channel flow control, mapping from other protocols to fibre channel, and fibre-channel distributed fabric services.

FIBRE-CHANNEL PROTOCOL ARCHITECTURE

Fibre channel is structured as a set of hierarchical functions. The American National Standards Institute (ANSI) FC-PI (fibre-channel physical interface) and ANSI FC-FS (fibre-channel framing and signaling) specifications define the fibre-channel layered-services model shown in Figure 1. As illustrated in Figure 1, the fibre-channel protocol consists of five layers: FC-0 (media and interface), FC-1 (transmission protocol), FC-2 (signaling protocol with link services), FC-3 (common services), and FC-4 (mapping from upper-layer protocols [ULPs] to fibre

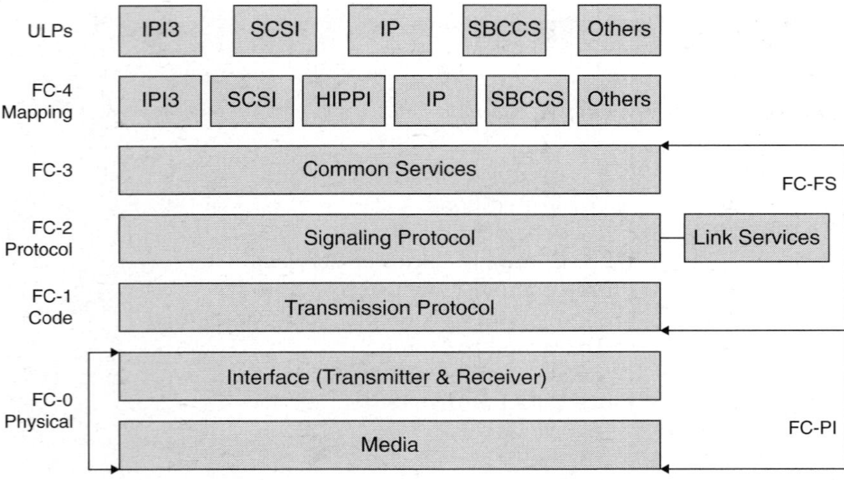

Figure 1: Fibre-channel structure (SBCCS = single-byte command code set)

channel). Each layer of this model provides services to the layer above and relies on the services provided by the layer below.

A fibre-channel node is functionally configured as illustrated in Figure 2: A node may support one or more N_Ports and one or more FC-4s. Each N_Port contains FC-0, FC-1, and FC-2 functions. FC-3 optionally provides the common services to multiple N_Ports and FC-4s. (Thornburgh 1999)

The following describes the layers in Figure 1 and Figure 2 (Ogletree 2003):

- FC-0: The FC-0 layer specifies the link between two ports. This consists of a pair of either optical fiber or electrical cables with transmitter and receiver circuitry, which work together to convert a stream of bits at one end of the link to a stream of bits at the other end. The FC-0 describes various kinds of media allowed, including single-mode and multi-mode optical fiber, as well as coaxial and twisted cables for shorter-distance links.
- FC-1: The FC-1 layer provides three primary functions: encoding and decoding data streams, managing ordered sets, and managing link-level protocols and states. The 8B/10B encoding scheme is used at FC-1 layer, which converts each 8-bit value into one of two possible 10-bit values. Each of the two 10-bit products of this conversion should have no more than six total 1's or 0's, about half will have an equal number of 1's and 0's. The 8B/10B encoding scheme can improve transmission characteristics on the link, and help receiver to recover clock, detect bit errors, and distinguish data bits from control bits. See the section below on 8B/10B Encoding.
- FC-2: The FC-2 layer is responsible for the functions associated with the establishment of communication between two ports. These functions include port login, the exchange, and associated frame sequences, flow control, and error control. The FC-2 layer also defined the fibre-channel frame format associated with all data and control frames. Link services defined in FC-2 are used to set up and manage links.
- FC-3: FC-3 (common services) provides a set of services that are common across multiple N_Ports and/or NL_Ports of a node. For example, services such as striping, hunt groups, and multicast are defined in FC-3. *Striping* is to multiply bandwidth using multiple N_ports in parallel to transmit a single information unit across multiple links. *Hunt groups* is the ability for more than one port to respond to the same alias address. This improves efficiency by decreasing the chance of reaching a busy N_Port. *Multicast* delivers a single transmission to multiple destination ports. This includes sending to all N_Ports on a fabric (broadcast) or to only a subset of the N_Ports on a fabric. FC-3 is under development.
- FC-4: The FC-4 layer defines how different higher-layer protocols are mapped to use fibre channel. The upper-layer protocols include intelligent peripheral interface (IPI), SCSI, high-performance parallel interface (HIPPI), IP, single-byte command code set (SBCCS) mapping, and others. Each of these protocols' commands, data,

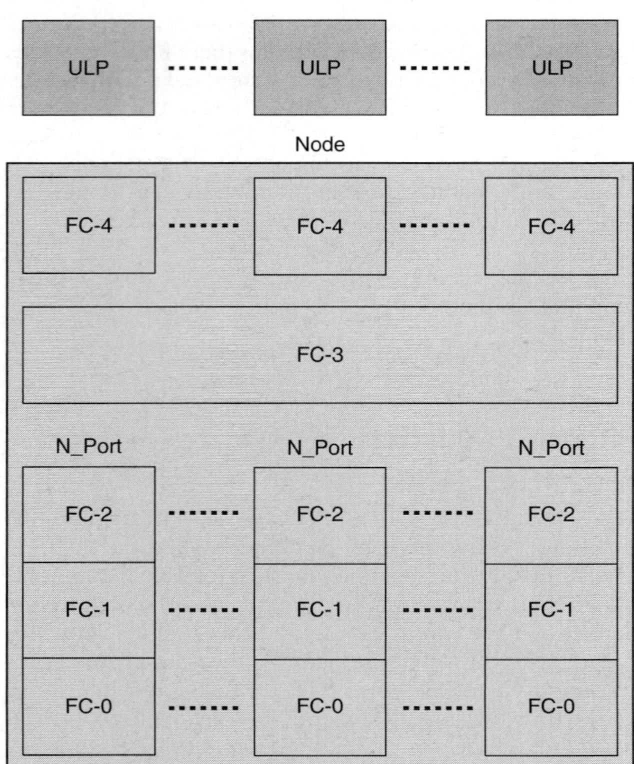

Figure 2: Node functional configuration

and status are mapped into information units that are then carried by fibre channel.

FIBRE-CHANNEL ELEMENTS

The key elements of a fibre-channel network are the end systems and the network itself. The end systems are called "nodes". A fibre-channel network consists of one or more switching elements. A switch is the smallest entity that may function as a switch-based fibre-channel fabric. A switch is composed of two or more switch ports; a switch construct, capable of either multiplexed frame switching or circuit switching, or both; an address manager; a path selector; a router; and a fabric controller. The collection of switching elements is called a "fabric." The following types of fibre-channel ports are defined in the Fibre channel standards:

- N_Port: An N_Port exists in an end device that is connected to an N_Port on another end device to form a point-to-point topology or an F_Port on a switch to form a switched-fabric topology. Multiple N_Ports can exist in a single physical device.
- NL_Port: An NL_Port exists in an end device attached to an NL_Port of another end device or a fibre-channel hub to form an arbitrated-loop topology. NL_Port can also connect to an FL_Port on a switch to form a public-loop topology.
- F_Port: An F_Port exists in a switch that directly connects to the N_Port of an end device.
- FL_Port: An FL_Port exists in a switched-fabric that directly connects to the NL_Port of an end device to form a public arbitrated-loop topology.
- E_Port: An E_Port, expansion port, exists in a switch that connects to an E_Port of another switch to form an interswitch link (ISL). In other words, switches are connected to form switched fabric through E_Ports.
- B_Port: A B_Port, bridge port, exists in a switched fabric that extends a fibre-channel ISL over a non–fibre-channel port.
- G_Port: A G_Port is a switch port that is capable of either operating as an E_Port or F_Port. A G_Port determines through port initialization whether it operates as an E_Port or as an F_Port.
- TL_Port: A TL_Port is a translative-loop port. It connects private loops to public loops or switches fabrics. A TL_Port acts as an address proxy for the private devices on the arbitrated loop.
- GL_Port: A GL_Port is a G_Port that is also capable of operating as an FL_Port.

Figure 3 illustrates how these types of ports can be used to connect switches and nodes to implement different possibilities (Cisco Systems 2004).

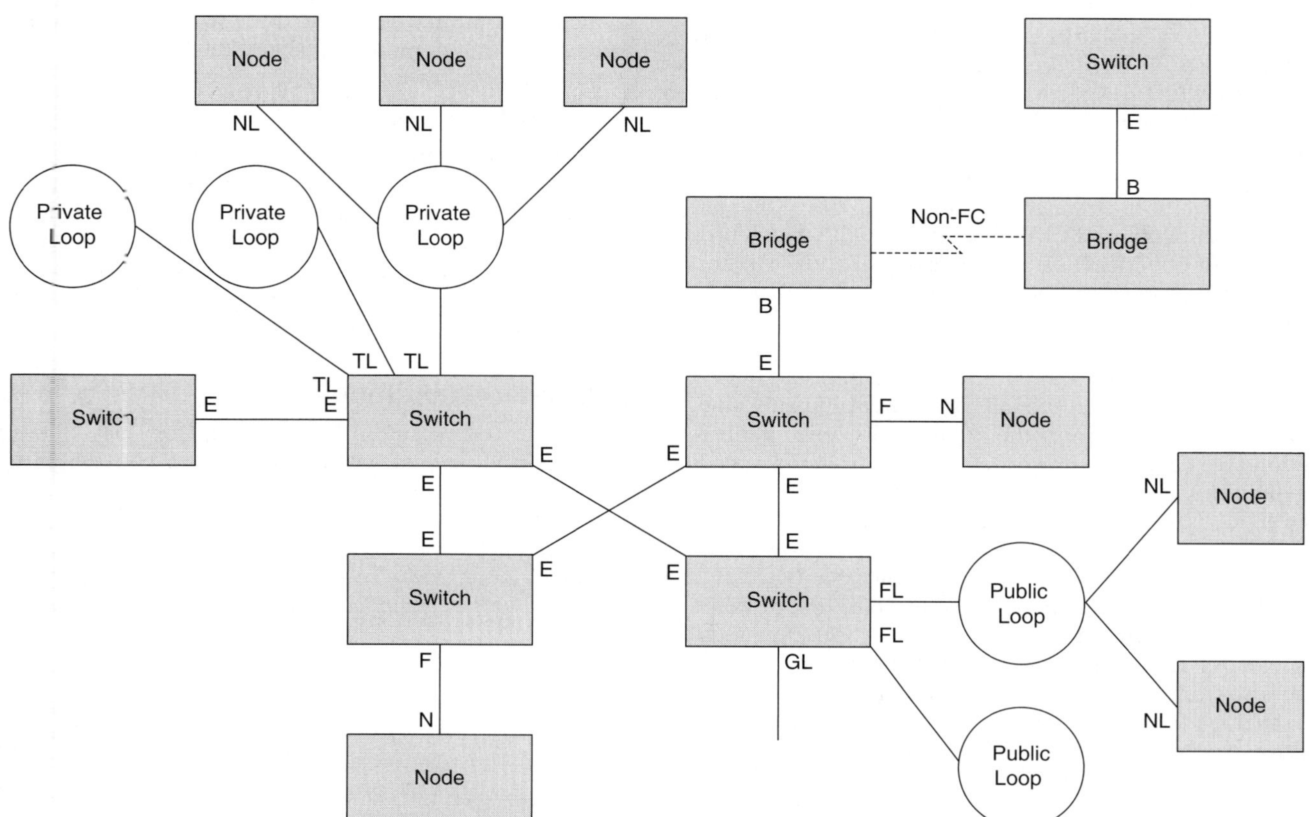

Figure 3: Fibre-channel connection modes

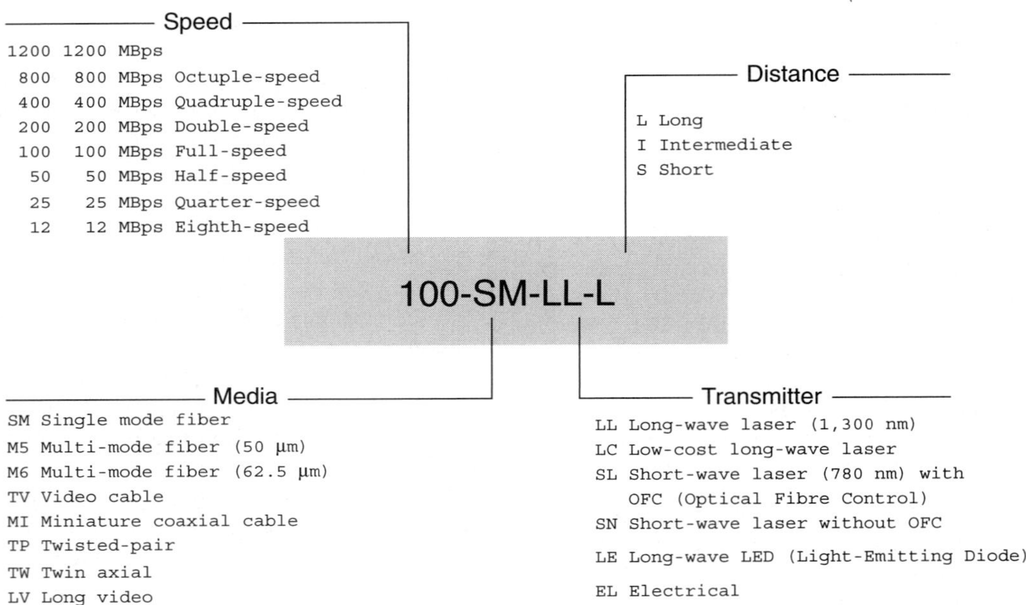

Figure 4: Fibre-channel variant nomenclature

FIBRE-CHANNEL TRANSMISSION MEDIA

The basic data rate over the fibre-channel link is just over 1 Gbps, with half-, quarter-, eighth-, double-, quadruple-speed and 10-Gbps links defined. The full-, double-, and quadruple-speed links are referred to as 1GFC, 2GFC, and 4GFC, which, respectively, provide a data-transmission bandwidth of about 100, 200, and 400 MBps. Using a different transmission code, the 10-Gbps link can provide about a 1200-MBps data-transmission bandwidth. To provide cost-effective fibre-channel migration, the Fibre Channel Industry Association (FCIA) introduced 8GFC, which provides about 800-MBps data-transmission bandwidth and full backward compatibility. Although the fibre-channel protocol is configured to match the transmission and technological characteristics of single- and multi-mode optical fibers, the physical medium used for transmission can also be copper twisted-pair, coaxial cable, or twin axial cable. For most of installations, the medium of choice is fiber-optic cable. Figure 4 illustrates the transmission speed, media, transmitter, and distance of fibre-channel technology (DeCusatis 2002). The fibre-channel standards define the maximum point-to-point transmission distance as 30 m for copper, and 10 km for optical fiber (www.t11.org). However, the maximum point-to-point link distance available in the market is reported to be 100 km (www.cisco.com). In the laboratory, the distance has reached 320 km while maintaining full throughput of the fibre channel at a 1-Gb line rate (www.cisco.com). Fibre-channel devices that support up to a 4-Gbps data rate are available in the market (www.cisco.com). Products with a bit rate of 8 or 10 Gbps are expected in the near future (www.fibrechannel.org).

FIBRE-CHANNEL TOPOLOGIES

Fibre channel is logically a bidirectional, point-to-point, serial data channel, structured for high-performance capability. A fibre-channel network may be implemented using any combination of the three topologies discussed below (Cisco Systems 2004) (Clark 2003).

Point-to-Point Topology

Point-to-point topology is used to directly connect two ports. As shown in Figure 5, the two fibre-channel-enabled devices, D1 and D2, are directly connected through two N_Ports without using any switch. The transmission between the two devices in the point-to-point topology is full-duplex, therefore point-to-point topology can be seen as a two-node loop topology.

Arbitrated-Loop Topology

Similar to token ring, arbitrated-loop topology is used to connected devices, each connected to two others by unidirectional transmission links to form a single closed path. As shown in Figure 6, the NL_Port of three end devices, D1, D2, and D3, are connected to form a unidirectional loop. Up to 127 nodes, including one possible hub port, can be supported in this topology. The loop is

Figure 5: Point-to-point topology

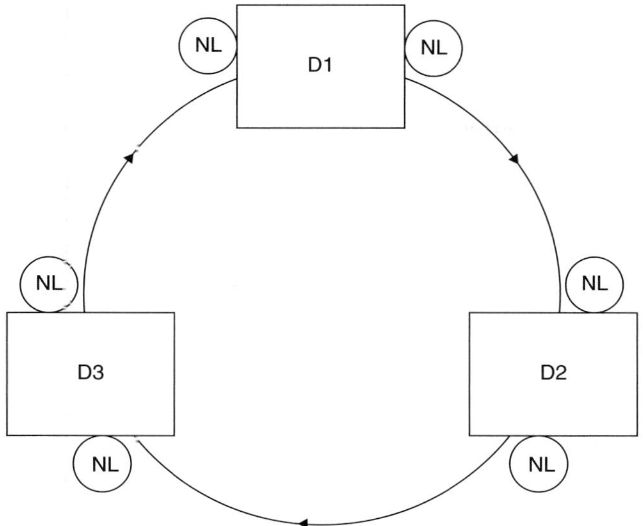

Figure 6: Arbitrated-loop topology

generally implemented using a fibre-channel hub for cable management.

Switched-Fabric Topology

Switched-fabric topology is the most general topology supported by fibre channel. At least one fibre-channel switch is needed in this topology, as shown in Figure 7. The "fabric" in Figure 7 can be one switch or multiple switches connected by interswitch links.

In applications, the three primary topologies (point-to-point, loop, and switched-fabric) can be connected to form a complex topology. For example, using a switch to connect multiple arbitrated loops allows one to bypass the 126-node limit that is inherent in using the single arbitrated-loop topology. Although each loop attached to a switch is still limited to 126 nodes, the switch makes a connection between these loops so that devices can communicate with each other, no matter which loop each device is connected to. One can also link multiple switches that have arbitrated loops attached. See Figure 3 for a more complex network topology that consists of point-to-point topology, arbitrated-loop topology, and switched-fabric topology.

FIBRE-CHANNEL ADDRESSING

Fibre channel has two types of addresses that are used to identify a device or switch port. The first is a globally unique assigned address called the worldwide name (WWN). The WWN is assigned by the manufacturer and is guaranteed to be globally unique.

The second type of address used in fibre channel is a dynamically assigned hierarchical address that lets frames be intelligently routed from one device to another. That is (called the "fibre-channel ID" [FC_ID]), the dynamic address contains information about where the device is connected to. In fibre-channel networks, the FC_ID is mapped to the WWN such that initiators can use the WWN to contact a device, and it will be translated to an FC_ID for communication.

The FC_ID addresses assigned to devices depend on the type of topology:

Point-to-Point: Point-to-point connections are actually implemented as a private loop with two devices. Because the devices are in a private loop, they use only an 8-bit arbitrated-loop physical address (AL_PA). The address is in the range of `0x000001h` to `0x0000EFh`.

Private Arbitrated Loop: Arbitrated loops can be implemented as private or public loops that determine the type of addresses assigned. In a private-loop topology, a standard AL_PA is assigned in a fashion similar to that of point-to-point topology. Each device on a private loop is assigned an address in the range of `0x000001h` to `0x0000EFh` (however only 126 devices may exist in a given arbitrated loop because of the 8B/10B encoding).

Public Arbitrated Loop: A public loop contains one or more FL_Ports that act as gateways to a switched fabric. As such, the addresses assigned to devices on a public loop contain a full 24-bit address. The first byte is the Domain_ID that is assigned to the switch. The second byte identifies the particular loop on the switch. The third byte is used for the AL_PA assigned to the devices on the loops. The FL_Port always has an AL_PA of `0x00h`. Therefore, the valid FC_ID address range for devices on a public arbitrated loop are `0xddllaa 0` (Cisco Systems 2004) where `dd` is the Domain_ID of the attached switch in the range of `0x01h` to `0xEFh` (1 to 239), `ll` is the loop identifier in the range of `0x00h` to `0xFFh`, and `aa` is the AL_PA in the

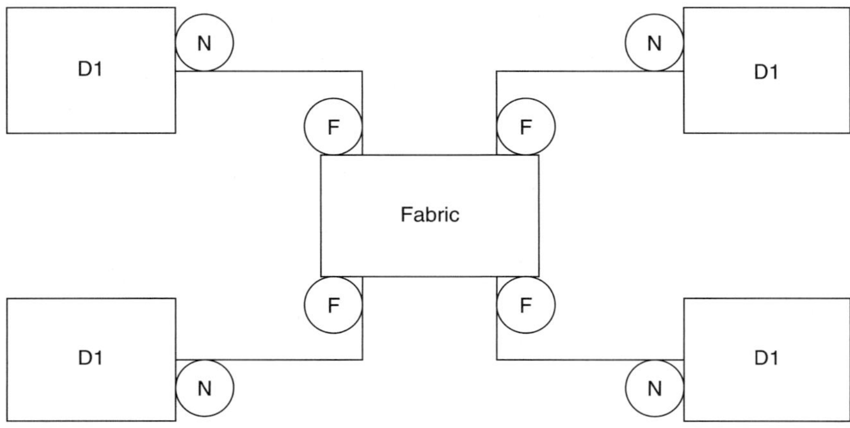

Figure 7: Switched-fabric topology

Table 1: Fibre channel Addressing

	8 bits	8 bits	8bits
Switch topology	Domain (01-EF)	Area (00-FF)	Device (00-FF)
Private loop topology	00	00	AL_PA (01-EF)
Public loop topology	Domain (01-EF)	Area (00-FF)	AL_PA (01-EF)

range of `0x01h` to `0xEFh`, where `0x00h` is reserved for the FL_Port. It is apparent that the format of the FC_ID, `0xddllaa`, can be used for facilitating routing in a way similar to netmask-based routing in IP.

Switched Fabric: A switched fabric address is based on FC_IDs that use the entire 24-bit address. Each switch within a switched fabric is assigned one or more Domain_IDs. This Domain_ID can be thought of as a routing prefix that the switch uses to route frames to devices connected to other switches. The first byte of a switched fabric FC_ID is the Domain_ID. It is in the range of `0x01h` to `0xEFh`. The second and third byte of a switched fabric FC_ID are called the Area_ID and Port_ID, respectively.

Table 1 gives the addressing ranges for the three different topologies.

FIBRE-CHANNEL INFORMATION TRANSMISSION HIERARCHY

The signaling-protocol (FC-2) level serves as the transport mechanism of fibre channel. To aid in the transport of data across the link, the following building blocks are defined by the FC-2 standard: ordered set, frame, sequence, and exchange. Figure 8 shows the relationship between frames, sequences, and exchanges. An exchange consists of one or more sequences, while a sequence in turn consists of one or more frames. A frame uses ordered sets to delimit its start and end. An ordered set consists of four 8B/10B encoded transmission characters. In the following, we will introduce the 8B/10B encoding, ordered set, frame, sequence, and exchange.

8B/10B Encoding

At FC-1 layer, information to be transmitted over a fibre channel is encoded 8 bits at a time into a 10-bit transmission character using the 8B/10B encoding scheme and then sent serially bit by bit across the link. Information received over the link is collected 10 bits at a time. The transmission characters that are used for data, called "data characters," are decoded into the correct 8-bit codes.

The 8B/10B encoding starts off with a process of assigning a letter to each bit in a single byte to be transmitted. As shown in Figure 9, letters H, G, F, E, D, C, B, and A are assigned to bits $b_7, b_6, b_5, b_4, b_3, b_2, b_1$, and b_0 of the byte to encode, respectively. Then `Zxx.y` notation is formed by calculating the decimal value `xx` using the lower 5 bits of the byte (letters EDCBA) and calculating decimal value `y` using the higher 3 bits of the byte (letters HGF). In other words:

$$\texttt{xx} = b_4 \times 2^4 + b_3 \times 2^3 + b_2 \times 2^2 + b_1 \times 2 + b_0$$

while

$$\texttt{y} = b_7 \times 2^2 + b_6 \times 2 + b_5$$

Let the letter `K` signify a special character and the letter `D` signify a data character. Then `Kxx.y` and `Dxx.y` represent a special character and a data character, respectively.

Refer to Figure 10, as an example, take `0xBCh` as the byte to encode: the corresponding `Zxx.y` notation is `Z28.5`, the data character is `D28.5`, and the special character is `K28.5`. Each transmission character (data or control) can have one of two possible binary values. By looking up the encoding table, `K28.5` has two possible 10-bit

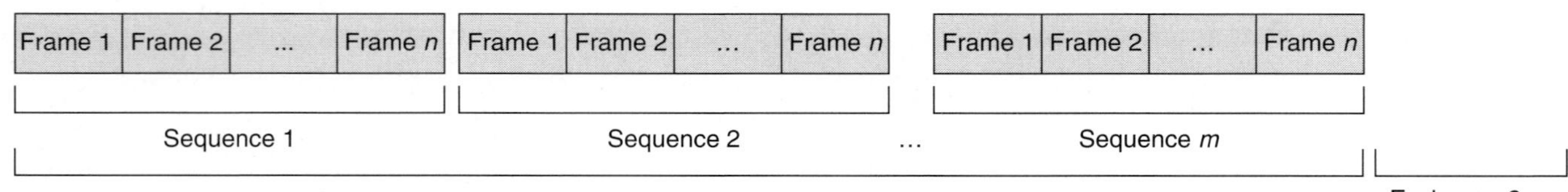

Figure 8: Relationship between frames, sequences, and exchanges

Order of bits to be encoded		b_7	b_6	b_5	b_4	b_3	b_2	b_1	b_0
8B/10B unencoded bit notation		H	G	F	E	D	C	B	A
`Zxx.y` notation	Z	E	D	C	B	A	H	G	F
		xx					*y*		

Figure 9: `Zxx.y` notation

Order of bits to be encoded		b_7	b_6	b_5	b_4	b_3	b_2	b_1	b_0
		1	0	1	1	1	1	0	0
8B/10B unencoded bit notation		H	G	F	E	D	C	B	A
		1	0	1	1	1	1	0	0
`Zxx.y` notation	Z	E	D	C	B	A	H	G	F
	K	1	1	1	0	0	1	0	1
		28					5		

Figure 10: Translation of `K.28.5`

values: `0011111010` (positive parity) and `1100000101` (negative parity). Which of the two possible binary values is transmitted depends on the disparity of the previously transmitted character. If a positive disparity character is transmitted, the next character issues should have negative parity. By monitoring the running disparity of the preceding event, the encoder can ensure that an overall balance of 1's and 0's is maintained in the serial stream.

The 10-bit transmission code supports all 256 eight-bit combinations. 12 of the remaining transmission characters, referred to as "special characters," are defined by the 8B/10B encoding scheme. However, only the `K.28.5` character is used in fibre channel, which is distinguishable from the contents of a frame and therefore can assist a receiver in achieving word alignment on the incoming bit stream.

The primary rationale for use of a transmission code is to improve the transmission characteristics of information to be transferred across a fibre channel. The encodings defined by the transmission code ensure that sufficient transitions are present in the serial bit stream to make clock recovery possible at the receiver. Such encoding also greatly increases the likelihood of detecting any single- or multiple-bit errors that may occur during transmission and reception of information.

Ordered Set

Ordered sets are a very important mechanism used in fibre-channel communications, and are used for many different purposes. An ordered set consists of four encoded bytes, which means 40 bits, because each byte is encoded into 10 bits by using 8B/10B encoding. Ordered sets can be classified into three basic categories:

- *Start of frame and end of frame delimiters:* Refer to Figure 11, one ordered set (SOF) is used to indicate the start of a frame, while another (EOF) is used to indicate the end of a frame. There are several different SOFs and EOFs defined in the fibre-channel standards. These SOF delimiters are also used to define the class of service to be used and whether the frame is the first in a series of frames. Like SOF, EOF can also be used to convey some other information about the frame.
- *Primitive signals:* The primitive signals are used for various purposes to initiate certain events on the transport medium. For example, when the medium is not being used, IDLEs signals are generated. Another type of primitive signal is the R_RDY (receive ready), which is used in buffer-to-buffer credit operations.
- *Primitive sequences:* The primitive sequences are used to control state changes on the fibre-channel link, such as initialization and recovery. An example of a primitive sequence is the set of LIP (loop initialization primitive) sequences used to initialize an arbitrated loop.

Frame

FC-2 framing protocol manages flow control so that data will be delivered with no collision or loss. This level defines the signaling protocol, including the frame and byte structure, which is the data-transport mechanism used by fibre channel. Frames transfer all information between nodes. The frames are normally constructed by the transmitting node's N_Port. A frame is the smallest unit of information transfer across a link. The format of a fibre-channel frame is shown in Figure 11.

It can be seen in Figure 11 that the size of a fibre-channel frame can be from 36 bytes to 2148 bytes, depending on the size of the data filed. IDLEs are used for synchronization and word alignment between transmitter and receiver. IDLEs indicate the readiness to transmit and are constantly transmitted when no other data are presented to send. An IDLE is actually a 4-byte ordered set. After the 4-byte SOF is the 24 byte frame header. The frame header includes fields such as the source FC_ID, destination FC_ID, and other necessary parameters. The data field consists of the actual upper-layer protocol data, which can range from 0 to 2112 bytes. Calculated using the frame header and the data field, the 4-byte cyclic redundancy check (CRC) code is used to check the correctness of the frame. The CRC used in fibre channel is a 32-bit polynomial:

$$x^{32} + x^{26} + x^{23} + x^{22} + x^{16} + x^{12} + x^{11} + x^{10} + x^{8} + x^{7} + x^{5} + x^{4} + x^{2} + x + 1$$

As shown in Figure 12, the 24-byte frame header is used to indicate the source and destination address of the

Figure 11: Fibre-channel frame format

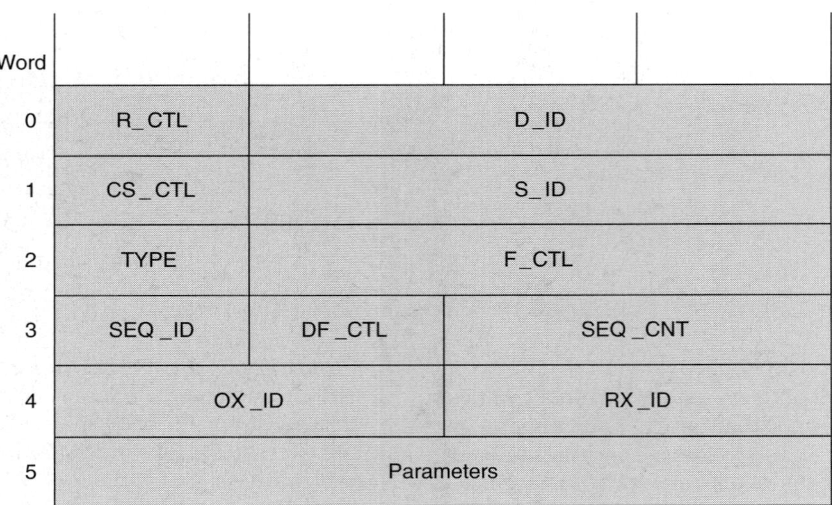

Figure 12: Fibre-channel frame header format

Table 2: Fields in Fibre channel Frame Header and Their Descriptions

Field	Length (bytes)	Description
R_CTL	1	Routing control contains routing bits and information bits to categorize the frame function. Routing bits differentiate frames based on function or service, such as data frames versus link control frames containing commands or status.
D_ID	3	Destination fibre-channel ID.
CS_CTL	1	Class-specific control contains management information for the class of service identified by the SOF. The meaning of the CS_CTL field is dependent on the class of service.
S_ID	3	Source fibre-channel ID.
Type	1	Type indicates the upper-level protocol carried in the frame payload, such as IP (TYPE is equal to `0x05h`) and SCSI (TYPE is equal to `0x0Ah`−`0x0Fh`).
F_CTL	3	Frame control contains a number of flags that control the flow of the sequence.
SEQ_ID	1	Sequence identifier uniquely identifies a given sequence within an exchange.
DF_CTL	1	Data field specifies the presence of optional headers at the beginning of the data field.
SEQ_CNT	2	Sequence count identifies the order of the transmission of frames within a sequence. It is used by a sequence recipient to account for all transmitted frames.
OX_ID	2	Originator exchange identifies an individual exchange. This identity is set by the originator of exchange.
RX_ID	2	Responder exchange identifies an individual exchange. This identity is set by the responder to exchange.
Parameters	4	The parameters field is dependent on the frame type, as identified in the R_CTL field.

frame, and also contains fields that are used to describe the content of frame. Table 2 describes briefly each field in the fibre-channel header.

Sequences and Exchanges

An exchange, unidirectional or bidirectional, is the fundamental mechanism for coordinating the interchange of information and data between two Nx_Ports. All data transmission is part of an exchange. An exchange is a set of one or more interrelated sequences, each of which flows unidirectionally between a pair of Nx_Ports. Within a single exchange, only one sequence will be active at any given time for a single initiating Nx_Port. A sequence is a data transmission that can contain one or more frames. The framing protocol is used to break sequences into individual frames for transmission, flow control, CRC generation, and various classes of service. As illustrated by Figure 8, by using the concept of an exchange, much of the overhead of setting up a connection—or terminating the connection—between two devices is made much simpler. To enable each of the communicating devices to distinguish between multiple sequences, a sequence ID is used. To keep track of exchange, an exchange ID is used.

Thus, for two devices communicating on a fibre-channel network, multiple transmissions of data (sequences) can be in process at the same time, contained within a single exchange.

Each frame is verified for validity during reception. The error recovery is done on the basis of sequence. Thus, if an error is detected with a sequence, then the entire sequence is retransmitted, without affecting other sequences in an exchange that are made up of multiple sequences. For classes of service that require an acknowledgment, the transmitter retransmits the sequence after a timer has expired, assuming that the sequence was not received intact.

FIBRE-CHANNEL FABRIC ROUTING

Routing is not needed for point-to-point topology and arbitrated-loop topology, since there exists only one possible route between any two devices.

In a switched-fabric topology, a dynamic routing protocol, called fabric shortest path first (FSPF), is used to route frames through the connected fabric. The FSPF is based on the widely used TCP/IP dynamic routing protocol open shortest path first (OSPF). The FSPF is a link-state protocol that requires all switches to exchange link-state information, including the operational state and routing metric for each direct ISL. The topology database is central to the operation of FSPF. It is a replicated database in which all switches in the fabric have the same exact copy of database at all times. Using this information stored in the local database, each switch performs the Dijkstra algorithm to compute the shortest path to every other Domain_ID, and then to build its own routing table. FSPF performs hop-by-hop routing, meaning that a switch only needs to know the next hop on the best path to the destination. A routing table entry minimally consists of a destination Domain_ID, and an E_Port to which frames are forwarded to the destination switch.

The FSPF has four major components:

1. A Hello protocol, used to establish connectivity with a neighbor switch, to establish the identity of the neighbor switch, and to exchange FSPF parameters and capabilities
2. A replicated topology database, with the protocols and mechanisms to keep the databases synchronized across the fabric
3. A path computation algorithm (with Dijkstra's algorithm being a possible candidate)
4. A routing table update (which is straightforward once the shortest path tree is generated)

The topology database synchronization in turn consists of two major components: an initial database synchronization and an update mechanism. The initial database synchronization is used when a switch is initialized, or when an ISL comes up. Reliable flooding is the mechanism by which topology changes are propagated throughout the fabric. Reliable flooding is used whenever any change of a switch link state occurs, but is not used for the initial database synchronization when an ISL between two switches initializes.

FIBRE-CHANNEL MEDIA ACCESS CONTROL

Fibre channel supports any combination of three primary topologies: point-to-point, arbitrated-loop, and switched fabric. Fibre channel uses a connection method that requires the setup of a channel between two devices before any data are exchanged. However, several steps must occur to establish a channel. After the channel has been established, communication between two end devices occurs according to a hierarchical model (see the section on Fibre-channel Information Transmission Hierarchy above). The following steps are required to establish communication between two devices using the different fibre-channel topologies discussed below.

Point-to-Point

Point-to-point topology is treated as an arbitrated-loop topology with two nodes in fibre channel. Devices connected point-to-point must first perform a loop initialization procedure (LIP) to determine that they are in a point-to-point configuration rather than an arbitrated-loop.

Arbitrated Loop

For arbitrated-loop topology, arbitration is used instead of a token that is used in Institute of Electrical and Electronics Engineers (IEEE) 802.5 protocol. Each device has a certain priority, based on its address. To gain access to the network, a device must "arbitrate" for it. If a loop is connected to a fabric switch port, then the FL_Port has the highest priority since it has the lowest AL_PA address (`0x00h`). Therefore, it can always win the arbitration and gain access to the loop when it needs to send frames.

Other devices must contend for loop access. They issue the arbitrate primitive, called `ARB(x)`, where `x` is the port address of the requestor on the network. IDLE primitive sequence circles the loop after the initialization process. When one or more nodes on the network send out an arbitration frame, a comparison is made by the nodes based on the priority of the `ARB(x)` frame received. If a node wanting to transmit data at the same time receives an `ARB(x)` frame that has lower priority than its own, then it simply discards that frame and does not retransmit it to the next node on the loop. Instead, the node sends out its own arbitration frame so that any other node issuing `ARB(x)` frames will know that it has won the arbitration process. Then the winner of the arbitration process receives the frame that it sent out, it knows it is the winner (because no other device wanting to transmit has a higher priority), and the node then transmits data frames on the loop.

When a member of the loop receives its own arbitration frame, it can then send an open frame onto the loop informing other nodes that it has arbitrated for access and wants to open a communication link with a specific target node.

The arbitration process allows for a fair access mechanism so that even devices with a low priority can eventually gain access to the loop. This is dependent on implementation. As far as the sender and receiver are concerned, they are now in a point-to-point connection, though the frames may be traveling through other nodes on the loop that are in the monitoring state, simply forwarding the frames. However, in most cases, the sender also monitors other frames traveling the loop and can tell if another node is trying to gain access to the loop. Although there is no specified number of frames the sender and the receiver can exchange, most devices try not to take a long time. Instead, most devices play in a fair manner and, after transmitting a number of frames, release their exclusive access to the loop to allow other members to make use of the shared media.

Switched Fabric

In switched-fabric topology, a dedicated connection between two connected ports is provided by switched fabric. Since bandwidth is not shared between ports, all ports can perform at full bidirectional speed for transmitting and receiving at all times.

FIBRE-CHANNEL CLASSES OF SERVICE

Fibre channel defines several classes of service. Each class of service is differentiated by its use of acknowledgment, flow control (refer to the section on Fibre-channel Flow Control below), and channel reservation:

- Class 1 is a connection-oriented service with confirmation of delivery or notification of nondelivery. A dedicated channel must be established from source to destination before the connection is granted. Once established, the two N_Ports can communicate using the full bandwidth of the connection, and no other traffic affects this communication. All the frames will follow the same connection. Because of this nature, frames are guaranteed to arrive in the order they were transmitted. Also, the media speeds must be the same for all links along the dedicated connection. There is no need for buffer-to-buffer flow control. Therefore, only end-to-end flow control is used in class 1 (see the section on Fibre-channel Flow Control below).
- Class 2 is a connectionless service between ports with confirmation of delivery or notification of nondelivery. A connectionless service does not need connection established. Instead, different frames may be sent through different paths depending on the present situation of the switched fabric. A port can transmit frames to and receive frames from more than one N_Port. As a result, the N_Ports share the bandwidth of the links with other network traffic. Multiplex may be involved in class 2 service. Frames are not guaranteed to arrive in the order they were transmitted, except for the point-to-point or loop topologies. In addition, the media speeds may vary for different links that make up the path. Both buffer-to-buffer and end-to-end flow control are used in class 2 (see the section on Fibre-channel Flow Control below).
- Class 3 is a connectionless service between ports with no confirmation of delivery or notification of nondelivery. Class 3 is very similar to class 2 except that it only uses buffer-to-buffer flow control (see the section on Fibre-channel Flow Control below). It is referred to as a datagram service.
- Class 4 provides fractional bandwidth allocation of resources of a path through a fabric that connects two N_Ports. This connection-oriented service provides a virtual circuit between N_Ports with confirmation of delivery or notification of nondelivery and guaranteed bandwidth. One N_Port will set up a virtual circuit by sending a request to the fabric indicating the remote N_Port as well as quality-of-service parameters. The resulting class 4 circuit will consist of two unidirectional virtual circuits between the two N_Ports. The virtual circuits need not have the same speed.
- Class 6 is a multicast variant of class 1 providing one-to-many service with confirmation of delivery or notification of nondelivery and guaranteed bandwidth. A device wanting to transmit frames to more than one N_Port at a time sets up a class 1 dedicated connection with the multicast server within the fabric at the well-known address of `0xFFFF5h`. The multicast server sets up individual dedicated connections between the original N_Port and the entire destination N_Ports. The multicast server is responsible for replicating and forwarding the frames to all other N_Ports in the multicast group. N_Ports become a member of a multicast group by registering with the alias server at the well-known address of `0xFFFF8h`.
- Intermix is an option of class 1 in which class 2 and class 3 frames may be transmitted at times when class 1 frames are not being transmitted.

FIBRE-CHANNEL FLOW CONTROL

Flow control is to ensure that the buffer of the recipient will not be overwhelmed by the initiator. Fibre-channel flow control is based on a permission system in which a device or port cannot transmit a frame unless it has a credit. Fibre channel as two flow control mechanisms—end-to-end and buffer-to-buffer.

End-to-end flow control is used to pace traffic between two end devices and can be used in class 1 and class 2 service. The end-to-end mechanism means that the intervening switches do not have to participate in the credit/acknowledgment scheme. Instead, when a connection is being set up between the initiator and the target device, the value used for the credit system is decided. This is usually based on the amount of buffer space that the recipient has installed on the adapter. When a frame is transmitted by an initiator, it subtracts one from the number of credits it has been granted. When an acknowledgment is received from the target device, the value of the credits is increased by one. This simple mechanism allows both ends of the connection to maintain a steady flow of data without overwhelming the recipient.

Buffer-to-buffer flow control takes place between every adjacent pair of ports along any given path in a fibre-channel network or between two devices on an arbitrated loop. Buffer credits relate to the number of input buffers that exist on the connected port. During a fabric log-in procedure, the number of buffer credits available to adjacent devices is exchanged. When an input buffer is emptied, a device generates a 4-byte R_RDY command and sends it to the neighboring feeder device, thereby incrementing the credit. The buffer-to-buffer flow control algorithm used in fibre channel is simpler than the sliding windows used in TCP/IP.

MAPPING OTHER PROTOCOLS TO FIBRE CHANNEL

Mapping is a set of rules that is defined to move information from ULP interfaces to the lower fibre-channel levels. The ULPs include IPI, SCSI, HIPPI, IP, SBCCS, and others. Each of these protocols' commands, data, and status are mapped into information units that are then carried by fibre channel. In the following, only IP over fibre channel and SCSI over fibre channel are introduced.

IP over Fibre channel

Establishing of IP communications with a remote node over fibre channel is accomplished by establishing an exchange. Each exchange established for IP is unidirectional. If two nodes wish to interchange IP datagrams, a separate exchange must be established for each direction. A set of IP datagrams to be transmitted is handled at the fibre channel as a sequence.

An address resolution protocol (ARP) server must be implemented to provide mapping between 4-byte IP addresses and 3-byte fibre-channel IDs. Generally, this ARP server will be implemented at the fabric level at the address of `0xFFFFFCh`.

SCSI over Fibre channel

The fibre channel acts as a data-transport mechanism for transmitting control blocks and data blocks in the SCSI format. A fibre-channel N_Port can operate as a SCSI source and target, generating or accepting and servicing SCSI commands received over the fibre-channel link. The fibre-channel fabric topology is more flexible than the SCSI bus topology, since multiple operations can occur simultaneously.

Each SCSI operation is mapped over the fibre channel as a bidirectional exchange. A SCSI operation requires several sequences. A read command, for example, requires: (1) a command from the source to the target, (2) possibly a message from the target to the source indicating that it is ready for the transfer, (3) a "data phase" set of data flowing from the target to the source, and (4) a status sequence, indicating the completion status of the command. Under fibre channel, each of these messages of the SCSI operation is a sequence of the bidirectional exchange.

FIBRE-CHANNEL DISTRIBUTED SERVICES

A distributed-services model in fibre channel is used to allow a switched fabric to provide consistent services to all attached N_Ports, to aid in the management, configuration, and security of a fibre-channel fabric. The following introduces fabric log-in, directory services, zone services, management services, and state change notification services.

Fabric Log-in

Fibre channel defines two types of log-in procedures: fabric and N_Port. With the exception of private NL_Ports, all other node ports must attempt to log in with the fabric. This is done after the link or the loop has been initialized, A fabric log-in starts by sending a fabric log-in (FLOGI) frame to the well-known fabric address of `0xFFFFFEh`. The following things can be accomplished through port log-in:

- It determines the presence or absence of a fabric.
- If a fabric is present, it provides a specific set of operating characteristics associated with the entire fabric, including which classes of service are supported.
- If a fabric is present, the N_Port that initiated the login can receive a fibre-channel address (FC_ID).
- If a fabric is present, it initializes the buffer-to-buffer credit.

Before an N_Port communicates with another N_Port, it must first log in to that N_Port. The port log-in (PLOGI) procedure can accomplish the following things:

- It provides a specific set of operating characteristics associated with the destination N_Port, including which classes of service are supported.
- It initializes the destination end-to-end credit.
- In a point-to-point topology, it initializes the buffer-to-buffer credit.

Both fabric log-in and N_Port log-in are intended to be long-lived. Once logged in, a device can stay logged in indefinitely, even if it has no further data to transmit at that time.

Directory Services

A fibre-channel switched fabric supports a distributed directory service called "name server." Since the FC_ID assigned in a fibre-channel fabric is dynamic, a service that can map a device's static WWN to its routable FC_ID is necessary. The name server is accessed by performing a port log-in (PLOGI) to a well-known address of `0xFFFFFCh`.

Zone Services

A fibre-channel fabric provides zone services to restrict communication between attached devices. A fibre-channel zone is a logical grouping of devices that are permitted to communicate. Because these devices may be attached to different switches, the zoning configuration is distributed between all switches in the fabric.

Management Services

The management service lets device attributes and configuration information be retrieved within the fabric.

This information may include attributes such as software versions, hardware versions, device capabilities, logical device names, and device-management IP addresses.

State-Change Notification Services

Because fabrics are a dynamic environment and may undergo topology changes when new devices are attached or previously active devices are taken off, it is useful if notification of changes can be provided to other participants. When events occur in the network, either accidentally or intentionally, registered state-change notifications (RSCNs) are generated to notify other devices of the event occurrence. Using the RSCN facility, devices can react much more quickly to failure events rather than waiting for timers to expire. RSCN is a voluntary function in that an N_Port or NL_Port must register its interest in being notified of network changes if another device alters state.

CONCLUSION

Fibre channel is backed by an industry group known as the Fibre Channel Association, and a variety of interface cards, storage devices, and switches for different applications are available. Being the major force for SANs, fibre channel has been most widely accepted as an improved peripheral device interconnection. It is a technically attractive solution to general high-speed LAN requirements but must compete with Gigabit Ethernet and asynchronous transfer mode (ATM) LAN. For implementing storage network, fibre channel will have to compete with iSCSI (internet SCSI) that uses TCP/IP to establish SCSI sessions across a long distance (Stallings 2004).

GLOSSARY

8B/10B Encoding: 8B/10B is a line code used in fibre channel, which maps 8-bit symbols to 10-bit symbols to achieve DC (direct current) balance and bounded disparity, and yet provide enough state changes to allow reasonable clock recovery.

Arbitrated Loop: A fibre-channel interconnection topology in which each port is connected to the next, forming a loop. At any instant, only one port in a fibre-channel arbitrated loop can transmit data. Before transmitting data, a port in an arbitrated loop must participate with all other ports in the loop in an arbitration to gain the right to transmit data.

Exchange: An exchange is a set of one or more nonconcurrent related sequences passing between a pair of fibre-channel ports. An exchange encapsulates a "conversation" such as SCSI task or an IP exchange. An exchange may be bidirectional.

Fibre Channel: Fibre channel is a gigabit enabling technology for SANs. An industry standard storage/networking interface, it connects host systems, storage devices, and others by means of a point-to-point bidirectional serial interface.

Frame: A frame, the basic unit of transmission on a network, is a collection of bits that contain both control information and data. A fibre-channel frame begins with a 4-bytes start of frame (SOF), ends with a 4-bytes end of frame (EOF), includes a 24-byte frame header and 4-byte Cyclic redundancy check (CRC), and can carry a variable data payload from 0 to 2112 bytes, the first 64 of which can be used for optional header.

iSCSI: iSCSI is Internet SCSI (also known as SCSI over TCP/IP), an Internet protocol (IP)–based storage networking standard for linking data storage facilities. By carrying SCSI commands over IP networks, iSCSI is used to facilitate data transfers over intranets and to manage storage over long distances.

Port: The hardware entity that connects a device to a fibre-channel topology. A device can contain one or more ports.

Private Loop: A fibre-channel arbitrated loop with no attachment to a switched fabric.

Public Loop: A fibre-channel arbitrated loop with an attachment to a switched fabric.

SCSI: Abbreviations for small computer system interface. It is a fast parallel bus structure for connecting a computer to peripheral devices such as disk drives, tape drives, CD-ROM drives, and printers.

Sequence: A sequence is a set of fibre-channel data frames with a common sequence ID, corresponding to one message element. Sequences are transmitted unidirectionally from initiator to recipient, with an acknowledgment transmitted from recipient to initiator.

Storage Area Network: A storage area network (SAN) is a high-speed dedicated network designed to connect computer storage devices to servers.

Switched Fabric: Switched fabric is a set of one or more fibre-channel switches interconnected by interswitch links (ISLs). Data can be transmitted physically between any two ports on any of the switches.

CROSS REFERENCES

See *Storage Area Network Fundamentals; Storage Area Networks: Architectures and Protocols.*

REFERENCES

Cisco Systems. 2004. *Internetworking technologies handbook*. 4th ed. Indianapolis: Cisco Press.

Clark, T. 2003. *Designing storage area networks*. 2nd ed. Upper Saddle River, NJ: Pearson Education.

DeCusatis, C. 2002. *Handbook of fiber optic data communication*. 2nd ed. New York: Academic Press.

Hufferd, J. H. 2003. *iSCSI: The universal storage connection*. Reading, MA: Addison-Wesley.

Ogletree, T. W. 2003. *Fundamentals of storage area networks*. Boston: Thomson Course Technology.

Stallings, W. 2004. *Data and computer communications*. 7th ed. Upper Saddle River, NJ: Prentice Hall.

Thornburgh, R. H. 1999. *Fibre channel for mass storage*. Upper Saddle River, NY: Prentice Hall.

Storage Area Networks: Architectures and Protocols

Nirwan Ansari and Si Yin, *New Jersey Institute of Technology*

INTRODUCTION

The rapid growth of data-intensive applications, such as multimedia, e-business, e-learning, and Internet protocol television (IPTV), is driving the demand for higher data-storage capacity. Companies and organizations want their data to be stored in such a way that the huge amount of data can be easily accessible and manageable. Furthermore, they also require the critical data to be securely transported, stored, and consolidated at high speeds (Ching 2000). Traditionally, on client/server systems, data are stored on devices either inside or directly attached to the server; this is thus known as direct attached storage (DAS). Next in the evolutionary scale comes network attached storage (NAS), which takes the storage devices away from the server and connects them directly to the network. Recently, storage area networks (SANs) push the network storage technology further by connecting storage devices into a separate network and allowing them to directly communicate with each other via a new protocol. SAN is emerging to become the choice of data-storage technology for its significant performance advantages, better scalability, and higher availability over the traditional SCSI buses, and DAS and NAS architecture (Phillips 1998; Farely 2001; Heath 2000; Clark 2003).

This section briefly reviews the early storage technologies, namely, DAS and NAS, and then provides an overview of fibre-channel (FC) SANs with regard to their concept, architecture, and characteristics.

Direct Attached Storage and Network Attached Storage

DAS is a traditional storage technology that uses a dedicated storage server that contains a file system to manage attached storage devices. It frees up the application server from storage management and allows users to share and back up important data. DAS does have drawbacks: first, it is likely to be a bottleneck if many servers and hosts access the same DAS simultaneously; second, data in a DAS system are accessed indirectly via the storage server; thus, DAS is not optimized for storage management. Figure 1 illustrates the architecture of DAS.

NAS, on the other hand, is a storage system directly connected to LAN and provides file-access services to the computer system. A NAS system usually includes a processor, one or more storage devices containing data, and an interface to LAN. NAS functions like a server that has its own network address. It processes file input/output (I/O) requests via file-access protocols such as the common Internet file system (CIFS) and network file system (NFS). NAS is normally used in enterprises where there is a need to manage a large amount of mission-critical data in a fast, efficient, and robust way. Figure 2 illustrates a typical architecture of NAS.

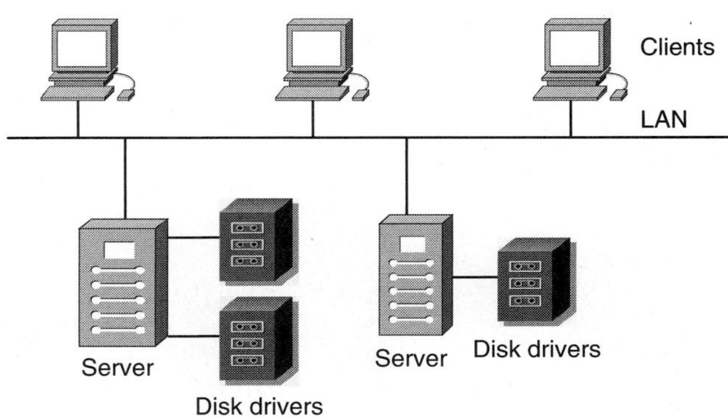

Figure 1: Illustration of direct attached storage

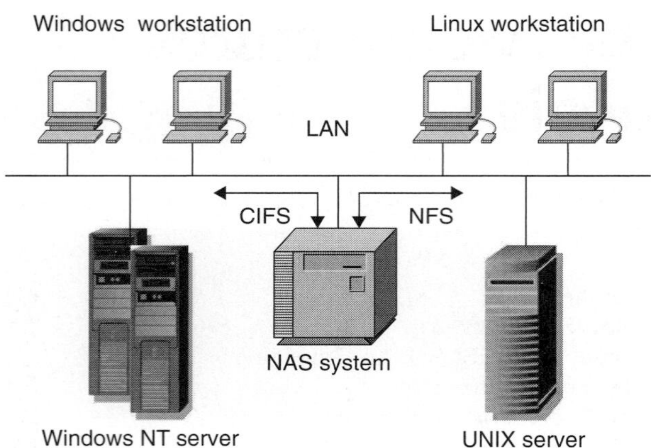

Figure 2: Illustration of network attached storage

Fibre-Channel Storage Area Network Overview

SAN, defined by the Storage Networking Industry Association (SNIA), is "a network whose primary purpose is the transfer of data between computer systems and storage elements and among storage elements" (Storage Networking Industry Association 2005). Unlike the traditional storage technologies, SAN takes the principle one step further by allowing storage devices to exist on their own separate network and communicate directly with each other at a very high speed. In SAN, clients in LAN access storage devices through servers, whereas servers interact with storage devices over SAN. Neither of these interactions is required to share the LAN's bandwidth, as was the case with earlier solutions such as DAS and NAS, thus greatly reducing the network traffic and congestion probability. SAN's highly flexible and scalable architecture simplifies the management of the ever-increasing storage capacity and reduces various information technology (IT) operating costs such as labor, maintenance, and expansion. Furthermore, the FC infrastructure, which forms the basis of SAN, guarantees faster data-transfer rates (up to 4 Gbps) than that of LAN. This is especially beneficial to e-commerce, for which fast data transactions are important to online companies that are aiming to attract online customers. Figure 3 shows a typical SAN environment.

Fibre channel is a generic name for the integrated set of standards developed by the American National Standard Institute (ANSI) (Technical Committee T11 2006). FC attempts to provide a means for the high-speed data transfer that supports several common transport protocols, including Internet protocol (IP), asynchronous transfer mode (ATM), and small computer system interface (SCSI).

FC first appeared in enterprise networking applications, including redundant array of independent disks (RAID) devices and mass storage subsystems. By the late 1990s, FC was quickly becoming the new connectivity standard for high-speed storage access and server clustering. FC specifications accommodate 133-Mbps, 266-Mbps, 532-Mbps, and 1 Gbps bandwidth (ANSI 2003). However, 4-Gbps FC products are currently available in the market, such as the 4-Gbps host bus adapters (HBAs) of LSI Logic Corporation. FC is unique in its support of multiple interoperable

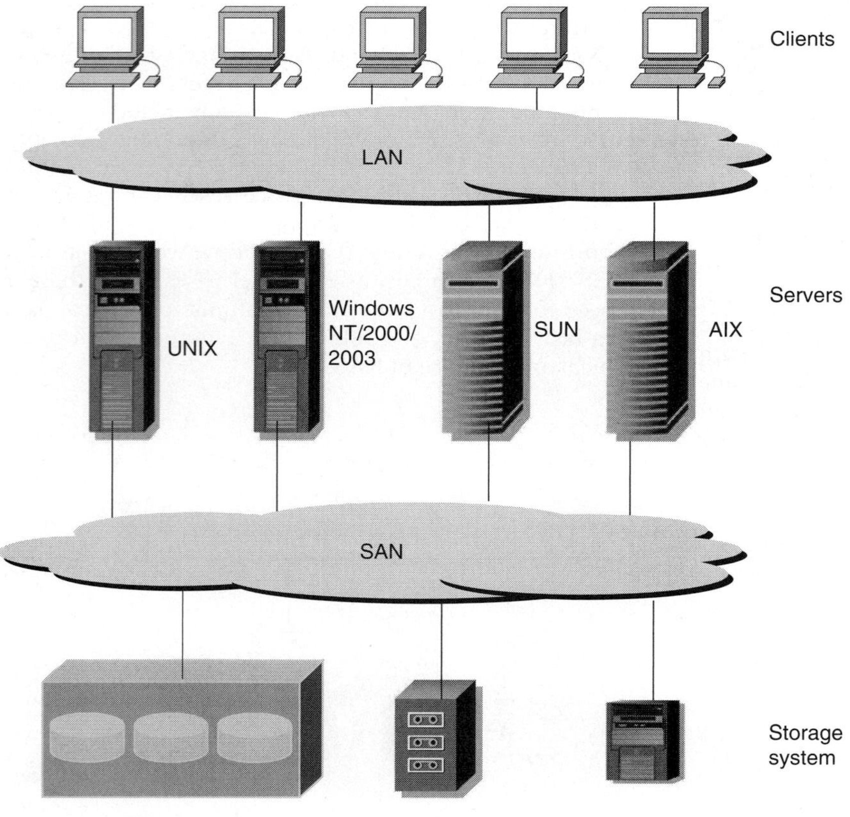

Figure 3: Illustration of storage area networks

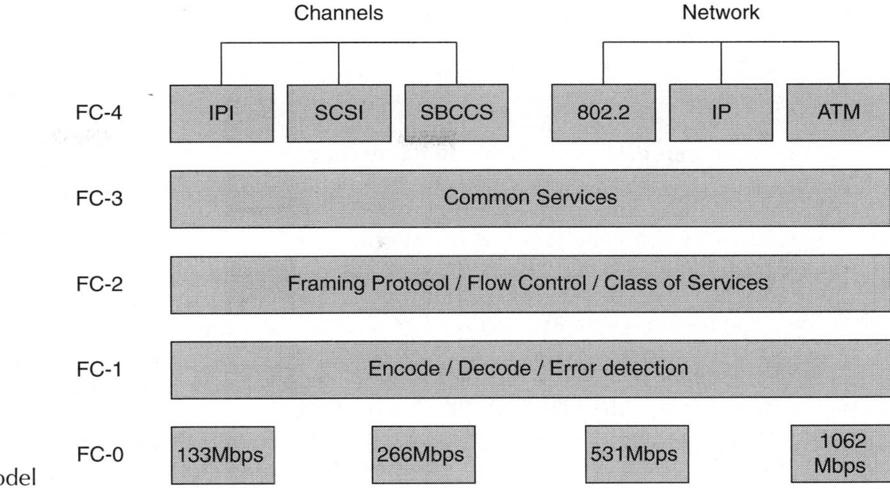

Figure 4: FC five-layer model

topologies, including point-to-point, arbitrated-loop, and switching, and it offers several classes of services (now six classes of services are defined in the new version of the FC standard) for network optimization. Furthermore, with its large frame sizes, FC is ideal for storage, video, graphics, and mass data-transfer applications (Benner 2001; Meggyesi 1994; Kembel 2000).

To clearly illustrate the functionalities of FC, the five-layer concept model is usually used to demonstrate the characteristics of FC, as shown in Figure 4.

This model is composed of five layers from FC-0 to FC-4, as detailed below:

FC-0—The lowest level, specifies the physical features of the media, including the cables, connectors, transmitter and receiver characteristics for a variety of data rates.

FC-1—Defines the transmission protocol, including the 8B/10B encoding/decoding rules used to integrate data with clock information required by serial transmission. In addition, error monitoring, link management, and low-level flow control are done at this layer.

FC-2—Defines the rules for data to be transferred between two ports, the format of FC frame, the mechanisms for controlling the various service classes, and the means of managing the sequence and exchange of a data transfer.

FC-3—Provides common services required for advanced features, such as the ability for more than one port to respond to the same alias address.

FC-4—Provides a set of interface standards to map existing protocols to FC layers.

So far, FC has become the dominant industry standard for SAN, commonly referred to as "fibre-channel SAN" by the SNIA (2005).

The rest of the chapter is organized as follows: in the section on Architectures and Protocols, we will discuss the FC protocol suite and its three typical topologies, in which detailed discussion regarding to characteristics and functionalities of FC layers will be presented. In the section on Applications, Challenges, and Solutions, we briefly introduce the applications of SAN and the challenges it faces. Subsequently, in the section on Internet SCSI (iSCSI), an emerging technology for SAN, iSCSI, is discussed in detail from its architecture to its security issues. Finally, we will draw conclusions and outline the future of SAN.

ARCHITECTURES AND PROTOCOLS

Fibre channel (FC) was developed as the first successful serial transport with gigabit-per-second rates to provide a practical, inexpensive, yet expandable way for quickly transferring data between workstations, mainframes, supercomputers, desktop computers, storage devices, displays, and other peripherals. Since the end of the past century, FC has been mainly adopted in block I/O applications, especially for SAN. "Fiber" in "fibre channel" refers to the FC's support for both fiber-optic and copper cabling. "Channel" refers to its role as a gigabit-per-second-rate, high-performance conduit to establish direct or switched point-to-point connection between the communicating devices.

On the other hand, fibre channel is also the generic name of an integrated set of standards developed by ANSI, that will be discussed in detail next.

FC Protocol Suite

The basic fibre-channel standard, fibre-channel physical and signaling interface (FC-PH) (ANSI 1994), defines a point-to-point device interconnection through a switched fabric (Sacks and Varma 1996; Heath 2000). The FC-PH standard also defines the physical layer, transmission, signaling, and framing protocols. The fibre-channel arbitrated loop (FC-AL) standard extends the FC-PH transmission and signaling functions to define a loop interconnection topology that does not require a fabric (ANSI, 1996, *Fibre channel arbitrated loop*).

In April 2003, ANSI approved fibre-channel framing and signaling (FC-FS) (ANSI 2003). Along with fibre-channel physical interface (FC-PI), the FC-FS standard combines FC-PH, its amendments 1 (ANSI 1996, *Fibre channel physical and signal interface*) and 2 (ANSI 1999), FC-PH-2 (ANSI 1996, *Fibre channel physical and signal protocol-2*), and FC-PH-3 (ANSI 1997) standards. The FC-FS standard deletes outdated functions and features from those standards and includes additional link services in support of new functions defined in the fibre-channel family of documents. FC-FS also includes new improvements and clarifications to the definitions of existing services, which are dictated by the experience of existing implementations. Above the FC-FS and FC-AL protocols layers are FC layer-4 standards, which consist of a set of protocols that map application protocols to the fibre-channel service. Among them, the most widely used application interface is SCSI, which is defined in the fibre-channel protocol for SCSI (FCP) (INCITS T10 2004). The FCP standard describes the protocol for transmitting SCSI commands, data, and status using FC-FS exchange and information units.

Currently, the fibre-channel community has circulated Request for Comment (RFC) documents regarding Internet fibre-channel protocol (Gibbons et al. 2006), fibre-channel management MIB (McCloghrie 2005), and securing block storage protocols over IP (Aboba et al. 2004). Interested readers may refer to the references for more details.

FC Topologies

There are three physical topologies available for FC SAN, namely, point to point, arbitrated loop, and switched fabric. Since the majority of FC SAN configurations in the current market are based on fabric switching, we will focus on the requirements and characteristics of switched fabric while briefly introducing point-to-point and arbitrated-loop topologies.

Point-to-Point Topology

Point-to-point topology is built on a dedicated, point-to-point connection between N_ports of two nodes (Figure 5). An FC port is the entity in the node or fabric of SAN that performs the data communication and transfer. It falls into several categories, including N_port, L_port, and F_port. N_port, known as "node port," is the node connection pertaining to hosts or storage devices in the point-to-point and fabric topology. L_port and F_port, on the other hand, are the entities that are used in the arbitrated loop and fabric loop, respectively.

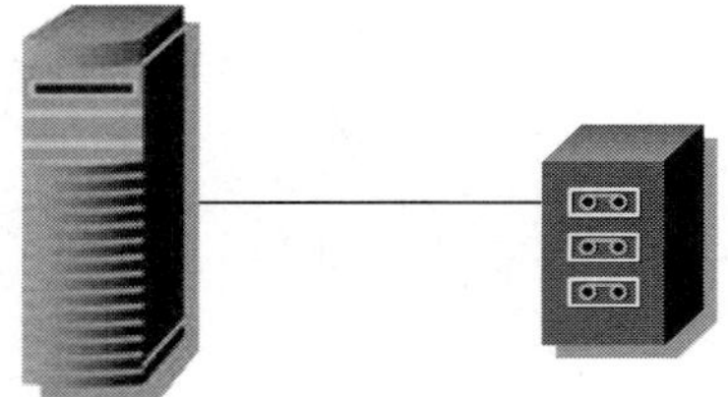

Figure 5: Point-to-point configuration

This topology creates dedicated bandwidth between the pair (normally, between a server and a storage device), with effective throughput of up to 1 Gbps in each direction (ANSI 2003). Before data transactions can be carried out, the two N_ports must perform an N_port log-in to assign N_port addresses or N_port IDs. Thereafter, a persistent connection is maintained, with utilization of the dedicated link determined by the application.

The scalability for the point-to-point topology is rather poor, and there is no resource sharing other than the two connected nodes. Currently, the point-to-point topology is adopted only for a very simple scenario.

Arbitrated Loop

Another way to connect FC nodes is by using an arbitrated loop (FC-AL) (ANSI 1996, *Fibre channel arbitrated loop*). Arbitrated loop allows more than two devices to communicate over a loop ring or hub, as shown in Figure 6.

In the daisy-chain type of an arbitrated loop ring, messages are transmitted from node to node until they reach the appropriate end user, and a fairness algorithm is implemented in FC-AL to ensure that no L_port is blocked from accessing the loop. In this way, a continuous data path exists through all the ports of each node, allowing any node to access any other node on the loop. However, should any link in the loop fail, communication between all L_ports is terminated. The daisy-chain type of FC-AL topology is illustrated in Figure 6a.

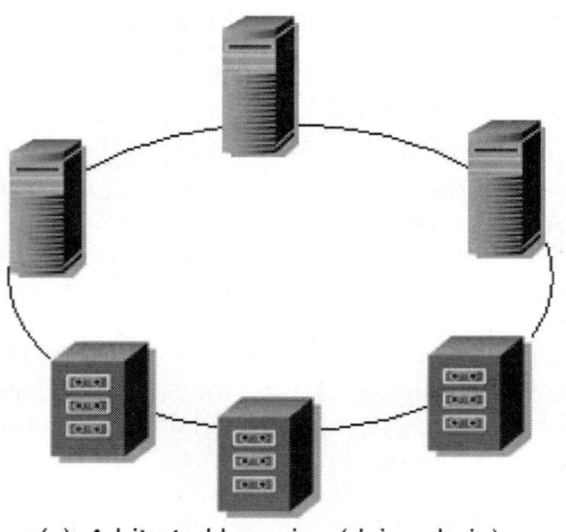

(a). Arbitrated loop ring (daisy chain)

(b). Arbitrated loop ring with central hub

Figure 6: Two primary FC-AL topologies

On the other hand, the arbitrated-loop hub helps continuous data communication even when one or more nodes fail. The mechanism lies in the internal architecture of a hub, which connects nodes on a port-by-port basis. The loop hub performs its functionality to sustain the persistent data communication by circumventing the disabled/disconnected node through its bypass circuitry at each port. However, the loop hub is not truly "plug-and-play." Any time a device is added or removed from the topology, the network must be reinitialized. Figure 6b illustrates the topology of an arbitrated-loop ring with loop hub.

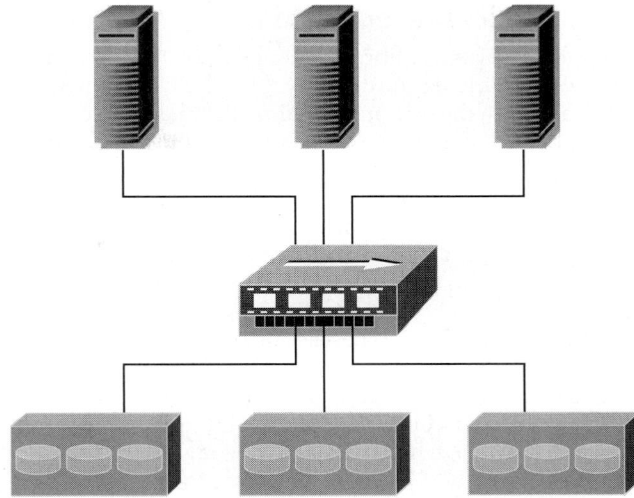

Figure 7: Switched-fabric topology

Switched Fabric

The switched-fabric configuration of FC is a routing architecture that delivers the FC frame to the intended receiver based on address information in the header of the FC frame. It provides multiple concurrent connections between any pair of devices using separate paths, thus efficiently reducing the congestion and enhancing the availability. Like a hub, an FC switch connects multiple servers to one FC port on the storage subsystem. With the FC switch, each server shares the bandwidth by rapidly switching from one connection to another, rather than by arbitrating for control of a shared loop. The congestion is hence reduced.

In the pure-loop topology, a host reset or device failure causes a loop initialization that resets all the other devices on the loop; this interrupts the loop's availability to other servers and storage devices. A switch can prevent this kind of error propagation and can also enable rapid isolation and repair of hardware device failures. Thus, the FC switch enhances availability. Figure 7 shows one possible switch configuration.

The switching mechanism typically used in fabrics is called "cut-through," which is used to speed packet routing by examining only the link-level destination ID of the FC frame. Based on the destination ID, a routing decision is made by its internal routing logic to switch the FC frame to the appropriate port. The destination ID resides in the first 4 bytes of the FC frame header, thus allowing cut-through to be accomplished quickly, without interpretation of anything other than the 4 bytes.

Another superior functionality for the FC switch is its capability to be cascaded to form a complex enterprise SAN, which supports a large number of system hosts and storage subsystems. When switches are connected, each switch's configuration information is to be copied into all other participating switches. Cascading provides switch topology scalable performance and increased redundancy. Figure 8 illustrates a typical scenario of cascaded FC switches.

All these superior characteristics popularize the switched fabric as the topology choice in the FC SAN industry.

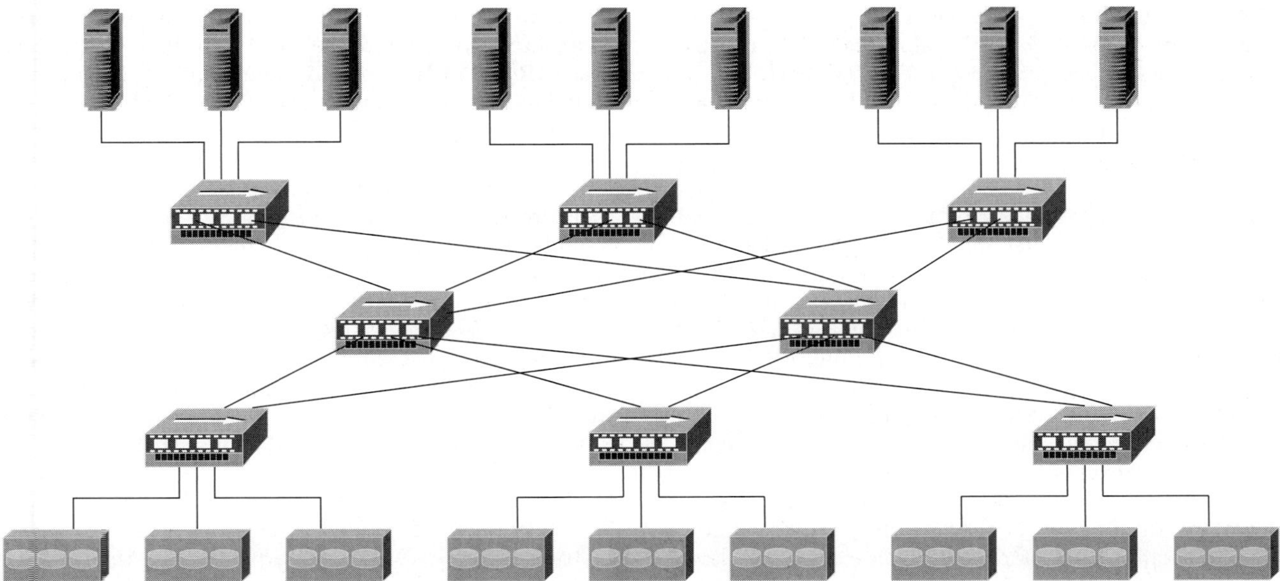

Figure 8: Cascaded FC switches

FC-0: Physical Layer Options

As mentioned above, fibre channel can be run over optical or copper media. At the lowest level, FC-0 defines the physical link in the system, including the fiber, connectors, and optical and electrical parameters for various data rates. At the physical layer, transceivers are devices that have combined transmitters and receivers for dealing with gigabit stream on the circuit boards of HBAs or controller cards. Different types of transceivers are available for both copper and optical media. For copper, transceivers simply perform the function of "electrical in, and electrical out," whereas for optical media, it performs the function that converts optical pulses into electrical signals, and vice versa. In today's market, the most widely used transceiver module is the gigabit interface converter (GBIC), which was developed by Compaq, Sun, Amp, and Vixel, and has become the de facto standard in the industry. GBICs are hot-swappable and can therefore be installed and removed while the card/shelf assembly is powered and running. There are two types of GBIC: optical and copper. Optical GBICs are classified into three categories: short-wave laser/multimode, with distance up to 500 m; long-wave laser/single mode, with distance up to 10 km; and extended long-wave laser, with distance up to 80 km. Copper GBICs, on the other hand, are available in two versions: passive (up to 13 m) and active (up to 30 m), and use DB-9 (serial communications D-shell connector, 9 pins) or HSSDC (high-speed serial direct connect) cable interfaces.

FC-1: Data Encoding

In FC, the encoding scheme is defined in the FC-1 layer, which prescribes the serial encoding and decoding rules, special characters, and error control. Owing to the gigabit and multigigabit speed of the FC, an efficient encoding scheme is especially important to achieve DC (direct current) balance and provide enough transitions for clock recovery. Currently, the IBM 8B/10B algorithm is the most widely used encoding scheme for FC. The basic idea of the 8B/10B encoding scheme is to convert every byte of data into one of two possible 10-bit values called "transmission characters." According to ANSI (1994), each byte of data is denoted in the form of `Dxx.y` where `D` indicates the byte being a data byte, `xx` is the decimal value ranging from 0 to 31, and `y` is the decimal value ranging from 0 to 7, before it is encoded. For example, `Hex xB7`, with the binary bit representation of `1011 0111`, is divided into the first 3 bits, `101` (decimal 5), followed by the byte's last 5 bits `10111` (decimal 23). Consequently, the 8B/10B notation refers to `xB7` as `D23.5`. This division illustrates the 8B/10B encoding scheme's internal operation. 8B/10B is realized by processing smaller 3B/4B and 5B/6B modules, followed by their combination to produce the 10-bit transmission character. ANSI (1994) also defines various command characters such as the `K28.5` command character, to be used exclusively for control purposes.

Since each of the 256 possible 8-bit words can be encoded in two different ways, the 8B/10B encoding scheme is able to achieve long-term DC balance in the datastream transmission. The 8B/10B encoding scheme also prescribes benefits of simplifying the design of receivers and transmitters, distinguishing control characters and ordinary data characters, helping clock synchronization, and improving error detection.

FC-2 Layer

The signaling protocol (FC-2) level serves as the transport mechanism for the fibre channel. The framing rules of the data to be transferred between ports, the different mechanisms for controlling the six service classes (see the section on Class of Service below), and the means of managing the sequence of a data transfer are defined by FC-2 (ANSI 2003; Clark 2003). In this section, we will mainly focus on the following five aspects of FC-2:

- Ordered sets
- Framing protocol
- Sequence and exchange
- Flow control
- Class of service

Ordered Sets

The ordered sets, with 40-bit-long command syntax, contain data and special characters that have a special meaning. Ordered sets are used to facilitate bit and word synchronization, as well as to establish word boundary alignment. The ordered sets fall into three general categories: frame delimiters, primitive signals, and primitive sequences.

The frame delimiters include start of frame (SOF) and end of frame (EOF) ordered sets. The SOF delimiter is used in a frame header to initiate a connectionless level of service. Following the SOF ordered set, up to 2112 bytes of data would compose the body of the frame. An EOF ordered set is used to indicate that the frame transmission is complete. Fibre channel defines eleven types of SOF ordered sets, and eight types of EOF ordered sets (ANSI 2003).

Primitive signals are ordered sets designated by the standard to indicate actions or events on the transport. there are two ordered sets: idle primitive and receiver ready (R_RDY) primitive. An idle primitive is a primitive signal used as a fill word between two data frames during the inactivity period. The R_RDY primitive, on the other hand, is used to indicate that the interface buffer is available for receiving further frames.

Primitive sequences are a group of ordered sets used to indicate or initiate state change on the port. Unlike primitive signals, primitive sequences require consecutive detection of three words before any action is taken. When a primitive sequence is received and recognized, a corresponding primitive sequence or idle needs to be transmitted in response. The primitive sequences supported by the FC standard are offline (OLS), not operational (NOS), link reset (LR), and link reset response (LRR).

Framing Protocol

The data must be framed as separated data packets to be transported in FC. The data packets are referred to as "FC frames." There are two types of frames in fibre channel: data frames and link-control frames. The two types

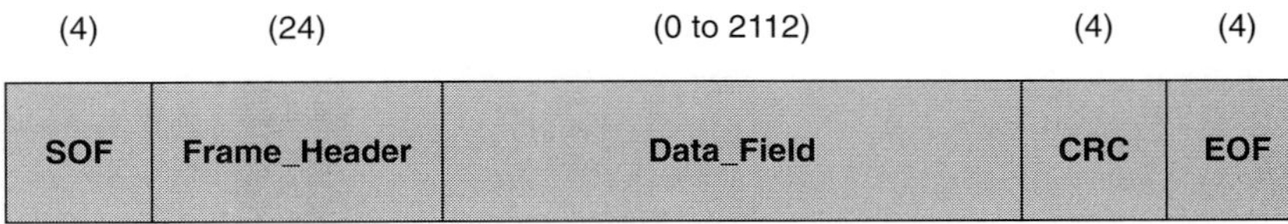

Figure 9: FC frame format

of frames have the same header format. The difference between the two frames is that link-control frames have no data payload, whereas the data frames can have as many as 2112 bytes of data after the header. Figure 9 illustrates the format of a FC frame.

As shown in Figure 9, frames are always started with an ordered set SOF. This is an encoded 4-byte word that defines the class of service and specifies whether or not the frame is the first in a series of related frames. Following the SOF, an encoded 24-byte frame header is used for link control and for detecting missing or out-of-order FC frames. Frame header contains eleven types of information, including destination identifier (D_ID), source identifier (S_ID), class specific control (CS_CTL), sequence identifier (SEQ_ID), and sequence count (SEQ_CNT) (ANSI 2003).

After the header, the data field varies from 0 to 2112 bytes. The variable length of the data fields facilitates FC's various applications to achieve an optimal trade-off between the frame overhead and the data payload. Following the data field, cyclic redundancy check (CRC) is used to check the data integrity within the frame. An EOF ordered set is finally appended to notify the recipients of the completion of the frame.

After the frame is assembled, the frames are delivered via a protocol hierarchy of the sequence and exchange, as discussed below.

Sequence and Exchange

A sequence is formed by a set of FC frames with a common sequence ID (SEQ_ID), corresponding to one message element, I/O block, or information unit. Sequences are transmitted from an initiator (usually an N_port) to a recipient, with an acknowledgment, if applicable. Error recovery is usually performed at the sequence level for efficiency. For example, if an FC frame fails the CRC check, it is more efficient to recover the entire sequence at gigabit speed than to embed the logic required to track and recover individual frames.

An exchange, on the other hand, is composed of one or more nonconcurrent sequences passing between two FC ports. An exchange usually corresponds to a single operation such as a SCSI task or an IP exchange and may be unidirectional or bidirectional. Sequences in an exchange have a common originator exchange identifier (OX_ID) and a responder exchange identifier (RX_ID), and only one sequence can be active at any one time. However, sequences of different exchanges may be concurrently active.

At the FC-2 layer, two nodes in the FC SAN system communicate with each other by establishing one or more exchanges simultaneously, with unique exchange IDs and sequence IDs registered in each FC frame. This nested structure maximizes the utilization of the link between two nodes, with minimal overhead for setting up and tearing down logical connections.

Flow Control

It takes finite time for a receiver to process incoming frames. If the second frame arrives while the receiver is still processing the first frame, it must be queued up in buffers. Since the amount of buffers is finite in each port of a receiver, the receiver must be able to regulate the rate at which frames are sent from the sender; otherwise, the port will be overwhelmed with frames. Thus, FC provides two flow-control mechanisms, buffer-to-buffer flow control and end-to-end flow control, based on a system of credits.

The concept of credits refers to the "permission" granted by a receiving port to a sending port to send a specified number of frames, and the number of frames that may be sent is referred to as the "available credit" of the receiving port. As long as a port has a nonzero available credit, it has permission to send a number of frames up to that of the available credit. When a frame is sent, the available credit is decremented by one. When a response is received, the available credit is incremented by one. If the available credit reaches zero, frame transmission is suspended until the available credit is refreshed to a nonzero value.

Just as there are two types of flow control, there are two types of credits: buffer-to-buffer (BB_Credit) and end-to-end credit (EE_Credit). Credit is granted during the log-in process and is based on the resources available in the receiving port.

Buffer-to-Buffer Flow Control. Buffer-to-buffer flow control, referred to as BB_Credit, is used by class 2 and class 3 services to ensure that the next node in the path has resources available to which it is attached. When one of the applicable frames is sent, the available BB_Credit is decremented by one, until the BB_Credit is exhausted to zero. The receiver will respond with the "receive ready" primitive R_RDY to the sender for every received FC frame. Accordingly, BB_Credit in the sender is incremented by one for each received R_RDY. However, the BB_Credit in no way guarantees that the final destination has the resources to process the frame; this task is fulfilled by end-to-end flow control. Figure 10 illustrates the scenario of buffer-to-buffer control for a pair of nearby nodes A and B with four available BB_credits.

End-to-End Flow Control. "End-to-end flow control" refers to the flow control between a source-node port and a destination-node port. Much like buffer-to-buffer flow

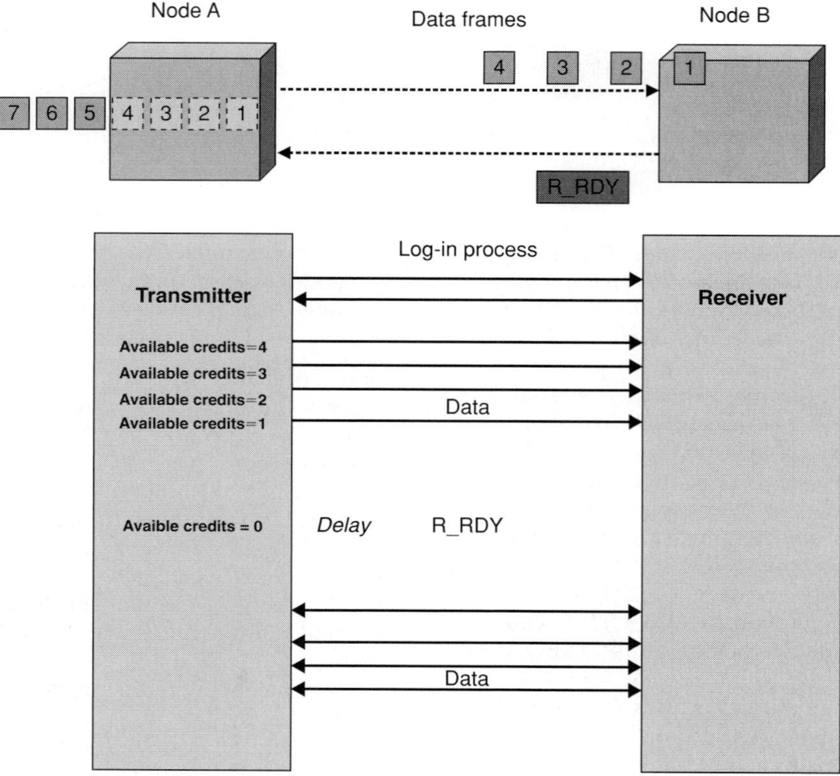

Figure 10: BB_Credit control with four available BB credits. Nodes A and B are a pair of nodes next to each other with buffer-to-buffer flow control. After the log-in process, four available BB credits are allocated to node A, which permits A to send up to four data frames (frames 1, 2, 3, and 4 in the figure). Node A decrements its BB_Credit by one for each frame sent, and is suspended for transmission after all four BB credits are exhausted (i.e., the available credit = 0). Thereafter, node A becomes idle until its BB_Credit is replenished by receiving R_RDY from node B.

control, during the log-in process, the destination node grants end-to-end credits (EE_Credit) to the source node. The EE_Credit is thereafter maintained by the source node for future communication. Unlike BB_Credit, the "Ready" signal in controlling EE_Credit is ACK, an FC frame with a full header and no data payload, rather than the R_RDY primitive. The source node decrements EE_Credit by one for each FC frame sent and increments EE_Credit by one for each ACK received. EE_Credit is used by class 1 and class 2 services. Figure 11 illustrates the EE_Credit control between a pair of source/destination nodes with four available credits.

Class of Service

A significant problem in designing a data communication system is to ensure proper data transmission that requires different levels of delivery guarantees, bandwidth, and connectivity between communicators. The concept of class of service is therefore proposed as an indication of what kind of service communicators request from the network. To address this issue, the FC protocol specifies six classes of service, namely, Class i, with $i = 1, 2, \ldots, 6$. Different classes of services determine different types of flow control and resource for regulating transmission:

Class 1 service—defines a dedicated connection between two devices with frame delivery acknowledgment. Because of the nature of the dedicated connection, there is no need for buffer-to-buffer flow control; the fabric does not need to buffer the frames as they are routed. Thus, only end-to-end flow control is used in class 1 and a heavy burden is placed on the FC switches. Furthermore, since class 1 is dedicated, established class 1 connections cannot be shared even when the connections are idle (i.e., no traffic). Thus, multiple connections of class 1 service would quickly consume the resource, and prevent the switch from serving other requests.

Class 2 service—is a connectionless class of service with confirmation of delivery, or notification of nondeliverability of frames, and no bandwidth is allocated or guaranteed. In the switched-fabric environment, it is the responsibility of the fabric to provide appropriate congestion control to prevent bandwidth hogging and starvation of ports. Class 2 is suitable for mission-critical applications that need verification via frame acknowledgments to guarantee data integrity.

Class 3 service—is a connectionless class of service providing a datagram-like delivery service with no confirmation of delivery and no notification when the frame is undeliverable. If a frame cannot be delivered or processed, it is discarded without notification. When such errors happen, class 3 relies on the upper level to recover the error. As compared with classes 1 and 2,

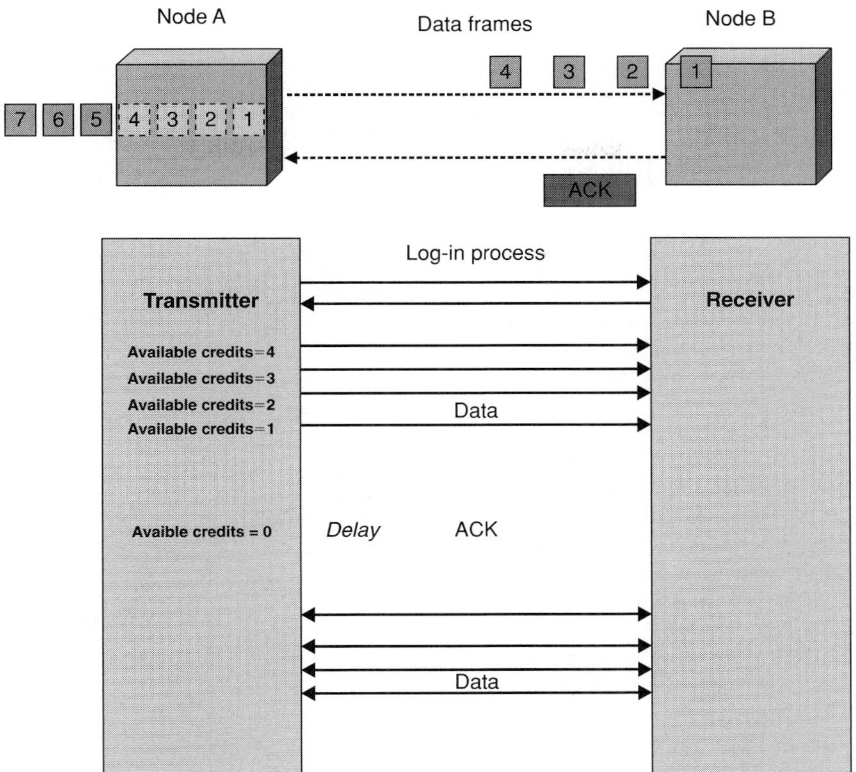

Figure 11: EE_Credit control with four available EE credits. Nodes A and B are a pair of source/destination nodes with end-to-end flow control. After the log-in process, four available EE credits are allocated to node A, which permits A to send up to four data frames (frames 1, 2, 3, and 4 in the figure). Node A decrements its EE_Credit by one for each frame sent, and is suspended for transmission after all four EE credits are exhausted (i.e., the available credit = 0). Thereafter, node A becomes idle until its EE_Credit is replenished by receiving ACK from node B.

class 3 provides the fastest transmission by sacrificing a certain degree of reliability. Class 3 service is best suited for time-critical applications such as real-time broadcasting.

Class 4 service—introduces the concept of virtual circuits for the FC architecture. Like class 1, class 4 service is connection-oriented. The difference is that, unlike class 1 service, which allocates the entire bandwidth to a communication pair, class 4 service provides fractional bandwidth as well as different quality of service (QoS) allocations. In addition, the multiple virtual circuits facilitate time-sensitive applications such as real-time videos. However, this functionality of class 4 service also poses challenges to the FC switch design, as the switch must maintain and monitor potentially hundreds of virtual circuits with variable QoS. The basic idea for Class 5 service is to provide isochronous, just-in-time service. However, it is still undefined, and possibly may be scrapped altogether. It is not mentioned in any of the FC-PH documents.

Class 6 service—provides support for multicast service with acknowledged delivery through a fabric. In the multicast scenario, if numerous target devices in the multicast group respond to the initiator with acknowledgments, thus flooding the initiator, the topology might be overwhelmed. Class 6 service alleviates this problem by placing a multicast server into the configuration. Class 6 service is also known as unidirectional dedicated connection service.

Although class 4 and class 6 services are described in detail in FC documents, they are actually not widely adopted in FC products. Class 2 and class 3 services, on the other hand, are the most widely used services because of their simplicity and efficiency. FC switches, for example, typically support only class 2 and class 3 services, an indication of the predominant market trend of the technology.

FC-3: Common Services

The FC-3 layer of the FC standard is still under deliberation and intended to provide the common services for advanced features, including striping, multicast data encryption, and data compression. For example, striping is used to increase the transmission rate of the data stream by transmitting data out of all N_ports simultaneously.

FC-4: Interface Layer

FC-4 establishes the interface between fibre-channel and upper-level applications, and specifies the mapping rules for upper-layer protocols to use the FC levels below. Fibre channel's FC-4 level has been documented in several standards describing how different upper-level protocols can make good use of the transport services provided by

FC-2, FC-1, and FC-0. These standards define the mapping of the following interface and protocols to FC:

- small computer system interface (SCSI)
- intelligent peripheral interface (IPI)
- high-performance parallel interface (HIPPI) framing protocol
- Internet protocol (IP)
- IEEE 802.2

Among these, the SCSI fibre-channel protocol (FCP) is most widely used (INCITS T10 2004; Wang et al. 2003). We will take SCSI FCP as an example to illustrate how the mapping scheme works.

The FCP initiator is responsible for mapping I/O traffic into FCP information units (IUs), and processes various IUs. The FCP-2 standard defines four FCP IUs: FCP_CMND, FCP_DATA, FCP_XFER_RDY, and FCP_RSP. All, except FCP_DATA, have well-defined packet formats.

When the SCSI request arrives at the FCP initiator, the FCP initiator fetches each coming request and encapsulates it into FCP_CMND. The FCP_CMND is then sent through the HBA and FC port. After having received FCP_CMND, the PCP target de-encapsulates PCP_CMND and processes the SCSI command.

In the case of the FCP read operation, the FCP target de-encapsulates the received FC frame into the SCSI request, and prepares for the requested data. When the data are ready, the FCP target will continuously transmit the requested data back to the FCP initiator until all the data are transferred. The FCP target will then immediately issue the completion message FCP_RSP to the initiator. With a FCP write operation, the FCP target will send out FCP_XFER_RDY to the FCP initiator after allocating sufficient space for coming data. When FCP initiator receives FCP_XFER_RDY, it will begin to transmit the write data until completion. Finally, when the target receives all the data successfully, it will send back FCP_RSP to the initiator indicating the completion of the FCP operation (Figure 12).

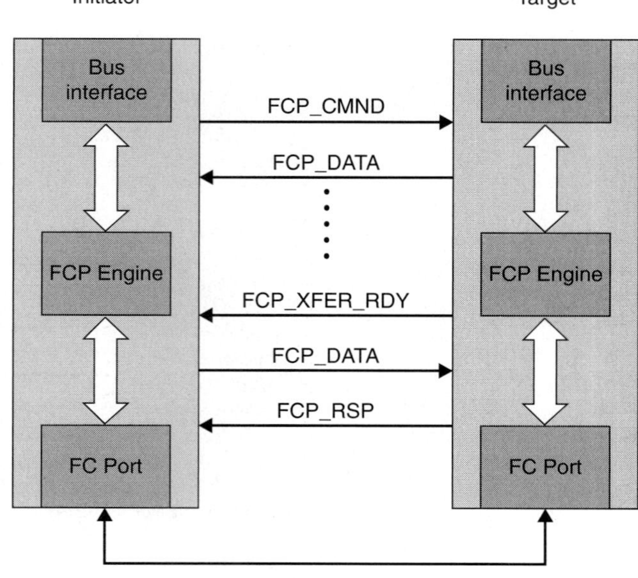

Figure 12: FCP operation

APPLICATIONS, CHALLENGES, AND SOLUTIONS

In this section, we will introduce some typical applications for FC SAN such as data consolidation and disaster recovery as well as challenges faced by FC SAN; some recently proposed solutions to meet the challenges are discussed in more detail.

Fibre-Channel Storage Area Network Applications

Although storage networks share common components in the form of servers, storage, and interconnection devices, the configuration of a SAN is determined by the upper-layer applications it supports. Currently, FC SAN is widely used in various applications such as storage consolidation, disaster recovery, server clustering, and remote data replication. In this section, we will take storage consolidation and disaster recovery as examples for illustration.

Storage Consolidation

Storage consolidation is performed by SAN to combine and consolidate the direct storage resources by each server, so that the maintenance cost is reduced and storage investment is more efficiently used. Traditionally, when an individual file or application server exhausts its storage resources, the IT administrator is forced to purchase a new storage device for more storage space. Over time, a data center is accumulated, with hundreds of servers, each with its own direct attached storage. This does not scale well, because a much larger IT staff is needed to maintain the servers for backups and updates. Moreover, since each server's utilization is not balanced, some may have a large percentage of free space while others may exceed their capacities; SANs offer a powerful solution for consolidating storage resources to improve the efficiency of the business environment, by breaking the direct connection between servers and storage, and combines both on a common network. SANs link multiple storage systems and servers over a high-speed network and allow the sharing of expensive tape devices and disk arrays. In this way, the storage devices can be constructed as separate, shared, and manageable resources (Figure 13).

Disaster recovery

Disaster recovery is the process of restoring operations of a business or organization in the event of a catastrophe. It is another important application of SAN. Traditionally, disaster recovery requires daily offsite backups. In a worst-case scenario, the offsite would be lagging by between 24 and 48 hours. In today's competitive economy, losing a day's worth of transactions may cause bankruptcy. The time between the last-stage backup and the point of failure is called the "recovery point." In contrast, recovery time includes the time elapsed from the time when the disaster occurs to the resumption of normal business

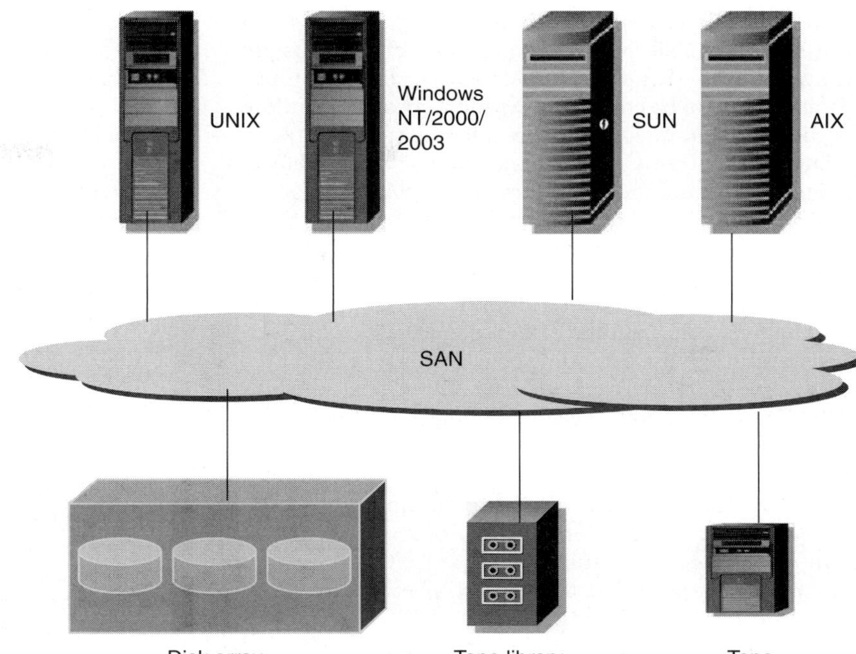

Figure 13: SAN solution for storage consolidation

activities. Currently, many organizations and companies have placed disaster recovery at a high priority, with IT administrators scrambling to implement disaster-recovery strategies within the confines of budget and personnel limitations.

Challenges

After 9/11, disaster recovery is becoming a critical part of IT spending for many companies. It was observed that even though a server machine may be very robust and highly fault-tolerant, it was still vulnerable to an unexpected catastrophe such as a natural disaster or a planned attack. All of the stored data and computing equipment could be wiped out instantly. Many companies have thus deployed FC SAN for data disaster recovery. Some of the applications currently supported by FC SAN, such as storage consolidation, data replication, backup, and recovery, have also been deployed.

FC SANs were, however, originally designed to operate within a limited distance such as a campus. This is not sufficient to safeguard corporate data. Owing to widespread power outages, caused by natural calamities such as earthquakes and by terrorist attacks, the distance expansion needed for robust disaster recovery planning has skyrocketed. The primary and secondary sites have to be physically separated by up to hundreds or thousands of miles, so that only one site will be affected in the event of a disaster.

The power-grid failure that occurred in Northeastern United States in August 2003 once again illustrates that a data disaster-recovery system within a small distance is not in keeping with business continuity. In this incident, the total business loss was estimated to be 2 billion dollars; the loss is in million dollars per hour during the 2 days' down time. From this incident, for more reliable data storage, companies need data recovery over long distances. Extending FC SAN over long distances (up to hundreds or thousands of miles) thus becomes the research focus of network storage.

The distance constraint of FC SAN is attributed to many factors, such as the flow-control protocol and application sensitivity to the round-trip time. New solutions are urgently sought to extend SAN islands into longer distances.

New Solutions

As mentioned in the previous section, an essential step in disaster recovery is to create a secondary site with the same capacity and performance as the primary site, and to make sure that primary and secondary SAN sites are geographically dispersed by long distances (up to hundreds or thousands of miles), so that only one site will be affected in the event of a disaster. SAN extension is hence becoming a significant technology for enterprise business continuity. An extended SAN increases the geographic distance allowed for SAN storage operation, in particular, for data replication and backup.

Consider further the requirements of FC SAN extension. For long-distance data replication and remote backup, there are a wide range of technologies involved, such as synchronous, asynchronous, and semisynchronous replication (Telikepalli et al. 2004). Of these technologies, synchronous data replication has a limitation on the distance between SAN islands because of its low tolerance to delays. Since synchronous replication implies real-time replication, the initiator must wait for an acknowledgment from the target in the remote site before the write operation is complete. This will cause longer round-trip times and slow down the available speed of writing data to the local devices. In asynchronous replication, the local write can be completed before receiving the acknowledgment from the remote site, thus making more efficient use of the available bandwidth. However, asynchronous replication also needs to be completed within a specified window, in order to avoid queuing that results in long data transfer latencies or frame loss. A huge amount of data has to be replicated within a few hours. Thus, SAN extensions must have adequate transfer capability to transport such an amount of data within the given time limit. Therefore, high throughput and low latency become the key requirements for the SAN extension solution.

Some new solutions have been proposed for FC SAN extension, such as extending FC SAN over IP-based technology, FC SAN over synchronous optical network (SONET), and FC SAN over wavelength-division multiplexing (WDM).

FC SAN Extension over IP-Based Technologies

IP-based extension solutions (Clark 2002) are emerging technologies that encapsulate SCSI and FC frames into standard IP frames to be transported over IP networks. Several protocols, including Internet SCSI (iSCSI), fibre channel over TCP/IP (FCIP), and Internet fibre-channel protocol (iFCP) have been introduced to transport the SCSI commands and responses, either by major vendors or the IP Storage Working Group of the Internet Engineering Task Force (IETF).

Internet SCSI (iSCSI). iSCSI is based on the SCSI protocol, which enables the host computer systems to perform data I/O operations with a variety of peripheral devices. iSCSI uses the TCP/IP suite for the transport of SCSI commands, and depends on a client/server architecture, with the clients being the SCSI initiators and the server being the SCSI target. The central mission of iSCSI is to encapsulate and reliably deliver data-block transactions between initiators and targets over TCP/IP networks.

iSCSI is currently being standardized by IETF (Bakke et al. 2005), in which iSCSI sessions, session management, and other aspects of iSCSI are being defined.

iSCSI is receiving more attention in recent years because it changes the price point of SAN so dramatically. It is hard to overstate how much different the world of SANs will become as iSCSI SANs become more popular. As such, in the next section, on Internet SCSI, we will have a more detailed discussion of iSCSI regarding its architecture, protocol-layer model, session management, and other relative issues.

Fibre Channel over TCP/IP. FCIP is a TCP/IP-based tunneling protocol for connecting geographically distributed FC SANs transparently to both FC and IP. FCIP gateways are located at the interface of the FC fabric and IP network, and are responsible for encapsulating and de-encapsulating FC frames. Essentially, the goal of FCIP is to interconnect geographically dispersed SANs through reliable high-speed links.

The first step of implementing FCIP is to encapsulate FC frames into IP packets and map FC fabric domains to IP addresses. Two sessions will be set up. One is an end-to-end session between FC devices that are based on the FC protocol. The other is the TCP/IP session between the gateways in the IP network. Unlike other IP-based technologies, which use native IP connections between individual storage devices, FCIP provides IP connections between FC SAN only at the FCIP tunneling devices at each end point of the IP network. The existence of the FCIP device and the IP network is transparent to the FC switches, whereas the FC connection buried in the IP datagram is transparent to the IP network. The FCIP protocol is compatible with ANSI FC standards and is being defined in an IETF draft (Natarajan and Rijhsinghani 2005). FCIP is illustrated in Figure 14.

Internet Fibre-Channel Protocol. iFCP is a gateway-to-gateway protocol to transport FC frames over TCP/IP switching and routing elements. According to the IETF draft (Gibbons et al. 2005), the protocol enables attachment of existing FC storage products to an IP network.

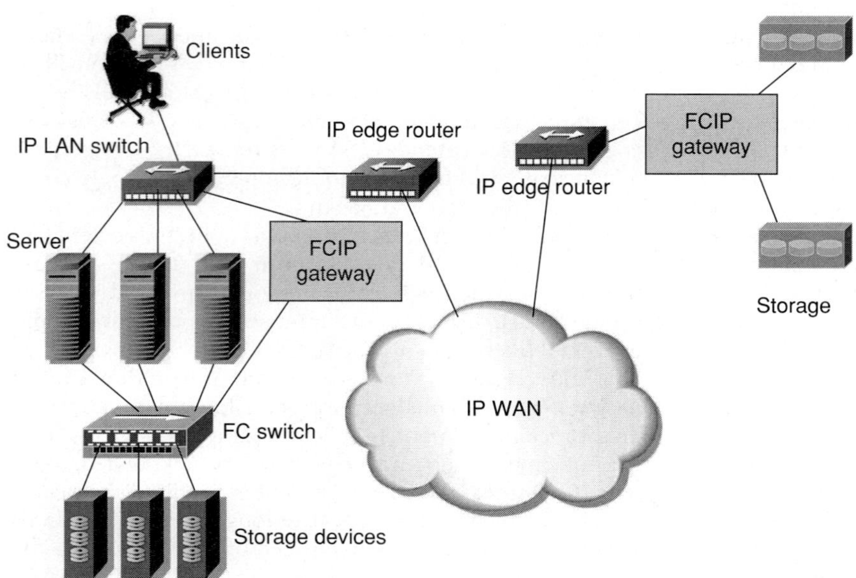

Figure 14: FCIP scenario

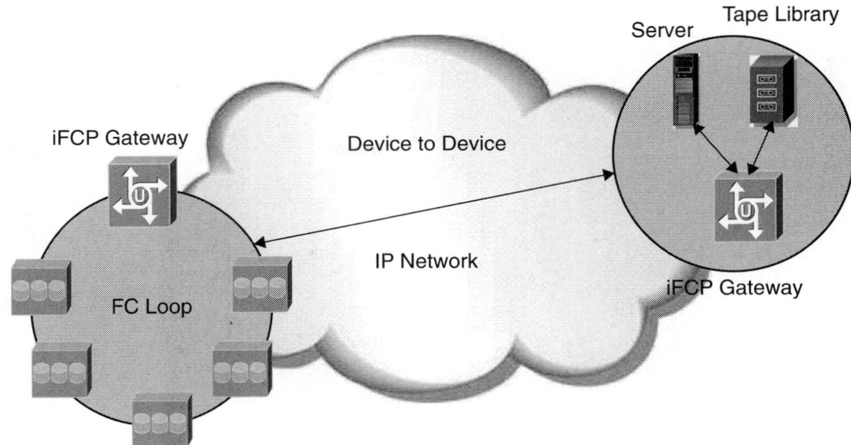

Figure 15: iFCP scenario

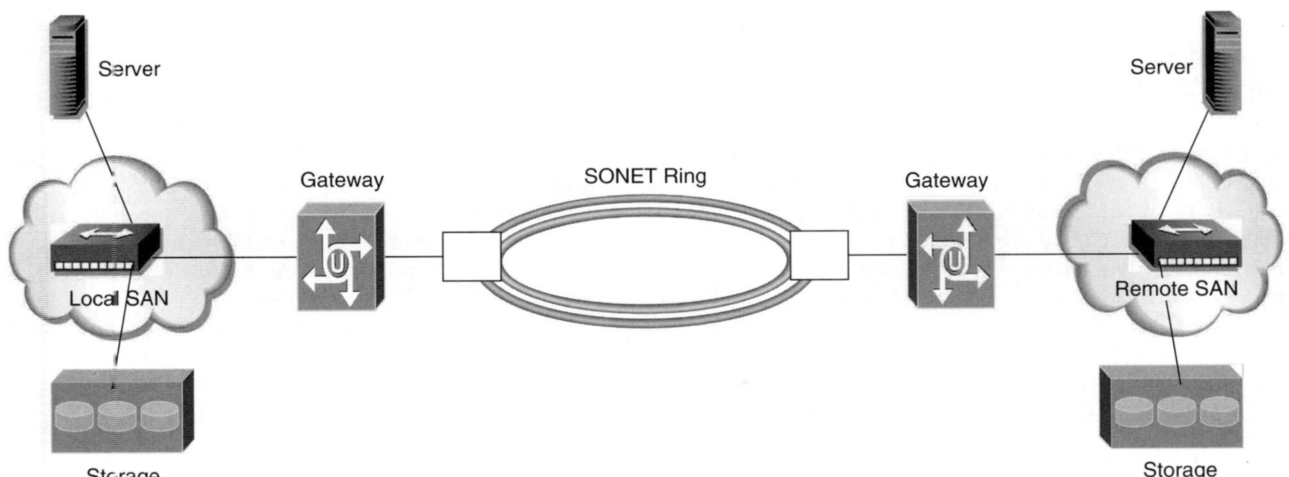

Figure 16: SAN extension over SONET

An iFCP fabric supports only classes 2 and 3 FC transport services.

iFCP assigns an IP address to each storage device in SAN. This allows communication between host and storage devices through standard IP switches and routers. In addition, iFCP provides flexible routing throughout the network, and servers from any locale can access storage resources on another. This facilitates remote mirroring and data-replication applications, as well as centralized backup and disaster recovery. The difference between FCIP and iFCP is that FC commands and data terminate in iFCP gateways, hence making the design of the iFCP gateway critical for achieving high application throughputs (Figure 15).

FC SAN Extension over Synchronous Optical Network

Synchronous optical network (SONET) is the transmission and multiplexing standard for high-speed traffic. SONET is mainly used in metro or backbone transport networks for transporting IP and ATM traffic.

The basic idea of extending FC SAN over SONET is to map FC frames onto SONET tributaries for transport across metro/regional add-drop (ring) and switching gateways. Other schemes have also added an intermediate ATM layer, so that FC frames will first be mapped into ATM cells before mapping onto SONET tributaries for transmission. In SONET, data are passed through dedicated channels at rates from 155 Mbps up to 4 Gbps. Data paths are not changed rapidly, as they are with routed IP networks. Instead, they are provisioned and remain rather static. Each dedicated channel is given a guaranteed fixed bandwidth for the data. SONET infrastructure is widely deployed, on top of which ATM and IP ride to provide voice and data transport, thus eliminating unnecessary overheads. Other advantages of the SONET-based extension solution include good availability and fast rebooting capability (Sorrento 2003; Helland 2002). Figure 16 illustrates the typical scenario of extending SAN over SONET.

FC SAN Extension over Wavelength-Division Multiplexing

Wavelength-division multiplexing (WDM) has emerged as a promising solution for the FC SAN extension. Compared with the existing technologies, extending FC SAN over WDM has the advantage of unsurpassed scalability, multiprotocol transparency, topological flexibility, and survivability (Murthy and Gurusamy 2001; Cisco Systems 2001; Telikepalli et al. 2004).

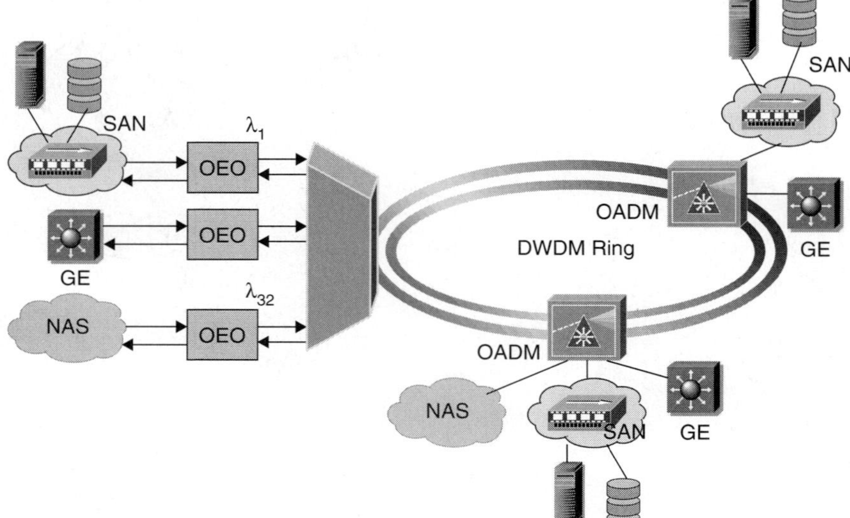

Figure 17: SAN extension over DWDM (GE = gigabit Ethernet; OEO = optical–electrical–optical; OADM = optical add/drop multiplexer)

WDM transmits multiple FC frame exchanges on a single fiber using different wavelengths. WDM is transparent because it will not change the original ways of transmission. Essentially, WDM provides virtual channels for FC transmission with path protection. WDM divides bandwidth on a fiber into several nonoverlapping channels (wavelengths) and realizes simultaneous message transmissions on different wavelengths on the same fiber. There are two types of WDM technologies: dense wavelength-division multiplexing (DWDM) and coarse wavelength-division multiplexing (CWDM).

FC extension over WDM can be used for either switch-to-switch or switch-to-node connectivity. As long as the link is stable, the connection presents no major difficulties. If the link fails, however, each node would undergo fabric reconfiguration, with all storage conversations suspended until each fabric is stabilized. Figure 17 illustrates FC SAN extension over a DWDM scenario.

INTERNET SCSI (ISCSI): AN EMERGING TECHNOLOGY FOR SAN

When we look at the various techniques for IP-based SANs, it is interesting to notice that FCIP is an extreme case of IP-based SANs, in the sense that it adopts many concepts of FC SAN and some from TCP/IP. In this sense, FCIP can be regarded as a simple extension of FC SAN, rather than a real migration from FC to IP-based storage. On the other hand, iSCSI protocol is another extreme case in the sense that it totally eliminates the FC concepts by replacing both FC fabrics and FC device interface with a native IP protocol. The development of iSCSI fulfills the market demand to leverage the available Ethernet and IP infrastructures, and has hence received much attention from all major storage and storage solutions providers (SNIA 2004; Zamer 2004; Clark 2003).

iSCSI Network Architecture

As illustrated by Figure 18, the goal of iSCSI is to establish SAN by using an initiator/target mechanism through IP networks. When an application or user issues a request for data, a file, or an application, the operating system generates the SCSI commands or data request. The command and request are then encapsulated, and a packet header is added. The packets are transmitted over an Ethernet connection. At the receiving end, the packet is disassembled, separating the SCSI commands and data. Finally, the SCSI commands and data are sent to the SCSI storage device.

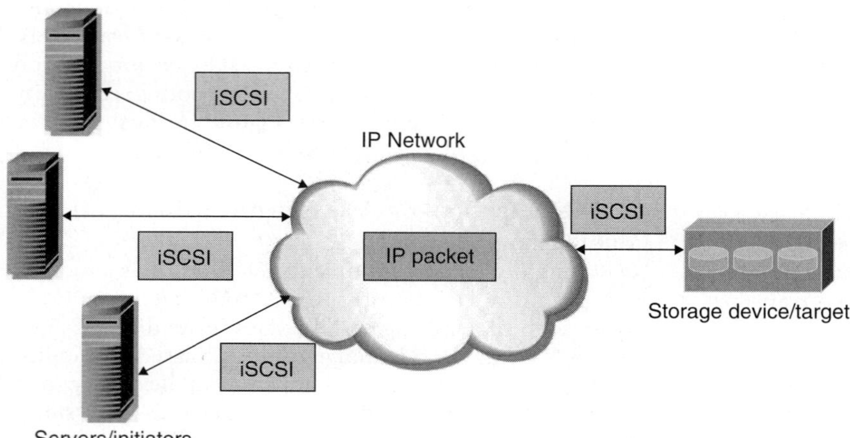

Figure 18: iSCSI scenario

One of the fundamental problems that iSCSI has to solve is the storage-relative network intelligence (Clark 2003). Unlike the FC SAN environment, in which FC devices provide network intelligence such as log in, device discovery, and state-change notification, iSCSI leverages on current Ethernet and IP infrastructures, which do not possess storage-specific intelligence. Therefore, an iSCSI device itself must install such intelligence to deal with all the storage relative requirements.

iSCSI Protocol-Layer Model

iSCSI uses TCP/IP for reliable data transmission over potentially unreliable networks. Figure 19 shows the iSCSI protocol-layer model, which provides an idea of an encapsulation order of SCSI commands for their delivery through a physical carrier. As illustrated by Figure 19, an initiator (server or workstation) initiates requests for data reading or writing from a target (a data-storage system). These requests are sent through a SCSI commands set, command descriptor block (CDB), in SCSI layer (INCITS 2004). The iSCSI layer then provides interfaces to the standard SCSI commands set and encapsulated CDB with data and status-reporting capacity. Encapsulation and reliable delivery of CDB transactions between initiators and targets through the TCP/IP network is the main function of the iSCSI, which is to be implemented in the potentially unreliable medium of IP networks.

The iSCSI protocol monitors the block data transfer and validates completion of the I/O operation. The data transfer is carried over one or more TCP connections between the initiator and target. Even though a single TCP connection is sufficient to establish communication between an initiator and a target, it is often advantageous to use multiple TCP connections (Meth and Satran 2003) for the following reasons:

- A single TCP connection is often not possible to achieve the maximum bandwidth of the underlying physical interconnect.
- A multiprocessor machine that allows separate threads running on the different processors may require simultaneous utilization of different TCP connections.
- When there are multiple target resources through different physical interconnects, their bandwidth can be aggregated by spreading multiple TCP connections over all the possible physical interconnects.

iSCSI Address and Naming Conventions

Because the iSCSI devices are participants in an IP network, they have individual network entities to identify their assigned network addresses. Each network entity can have one or several iSCSI nodes (Figure 20).

An iSCSI device is identified by a unique global iSCSI name. An iSCSI name is a 255-byte-long, human-readable identity for a storage device that is used to discover an I/O process and validate a device via the iSCSI log-in. An iSCSI name is usually composed of three parts: a type designator, a naming authority, and a unique identifier assigned by the naming authority. For example, "fqn.com.njit.storage.itdepartment.100" is a typical iSCSI name with "fqn" the designator, "(reversed) njit.com" the naming authority, and "storage.itdepartment.100" the unique identifier assigned by the naming authority. The iSCSI name is processed by the domain name system (DNS).

The iSCSI name, however, is not used for routing because its 255-byte length will greatly increase routers' burden. Instead, the iSCSI network portal is used to perform such a function. The iSCSI network portal is the combination of an iSCSI node's assigned IP address and TCP port number. Once the IP address and TCP port number are established for a specific iSCSI node, only the IP address/TCP port combination is required for handling data transfer.

The separation of the iSCSI name from the iSCSI network portal provides a correct identification of an iSCSI device irrespective of its physical location. Even if a storage device is moved and given a different IP address and

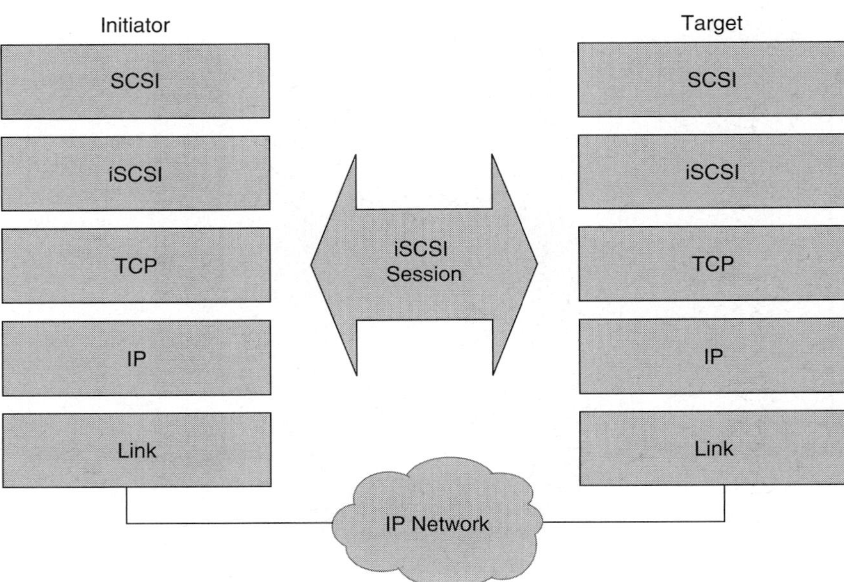

Figure 19: iSCSI protocol model

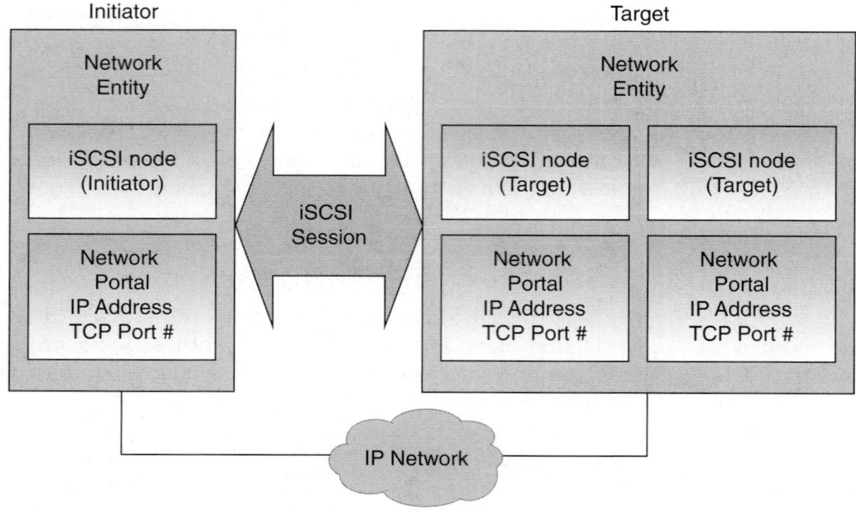

Figure 20: iSCSI name entities

TCP port number, its iSCSI name is always kept unaltered, thus allowing itself to be rediscovered. Moreover, the iSCSI network protocol together with iSCSI names provide a support for aliases that are reflected in the administration systems for better identification and management by system administrators.

Session Management

An iSCSI session is a collection of TCP connections between an iSCSI initiator and an iSCSI target used to pass SCSI commands and data. It consists of a log-in phase and a full-feature phase, which is completed with a special command.

In the log-in phase, the log-in negotiation is performed to exchange parameters and a corresponding range of values. After successful log-in (if not, the log-in is rejected and TCP connections are closed), the initiator will generate initiator session ID (ISID), which will be used together with its iSCSI name to uniquely identify this particular session. Likewise, the target will generate target session ID (TSID), together with its iSCSI name, to uniquely identify the session. Thereafter, one or multiple TCP connections will be set up for this ISID/TSID pair, which is illustrated in Figure 21.

Once the log-in phase is complete, the iSCSI session turns to the full-feature phase. If multiple TCP connections have been set up for that session, individual command/response pairs must flow over the same TCP connection, which is known as "connection allegiance." Connection allegiance policy is adopted to avoid extra overhead to monitor multiple TCP connections and to enhance the bandwidth utilization. An iSCSI read command, for example, is transmitted through a single TCP connection, until the completion of this transaction. Note that iSCSI connection allegiance is per command, not per task.

Error Handling

Unlike the SCSI protocol, which assumes an error-free environment because of its utilization of a dedicated parallel bus, the iSCSI protocol provides a great number

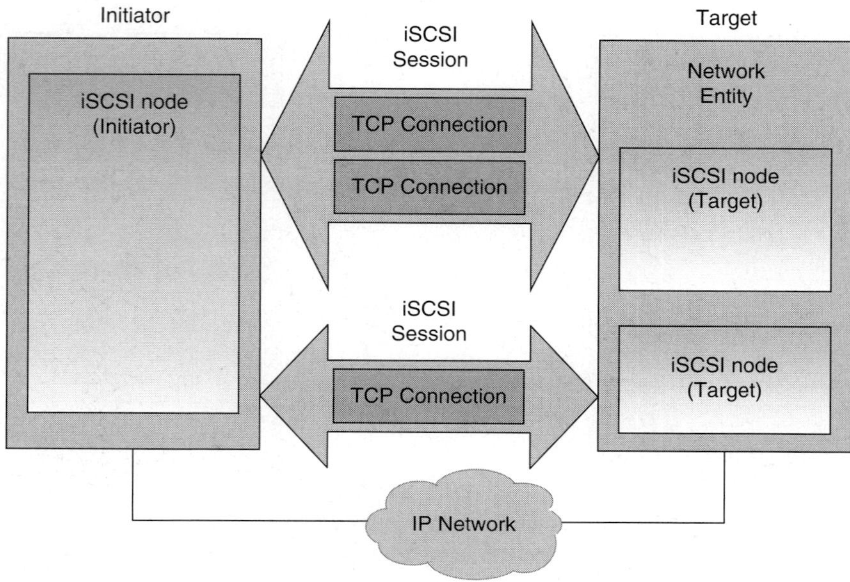

Figure 21: iSCSI session management

of measures for handling errors, owing to a high probability of errors in data delivery in some IP networks, especially WAN.

As such, iSCSI requires both the initiator and the target to have the ability to buffer commands and respond with acknowledgments. In case of protocol data units (PDUs) that are in error or are missing, the iSCSI end device must be able to retransmit the missing or corrupted PDUs.

iSCSI provisions a three-tier hierarchy of error handling and recovery. At the SCSI level, errors are recovered within a SCSI task, by repeating transfer of lost or damaged PDUs. Such errors occur infrequently because of the use of a parallel bus at the SCSI level. At the TCP level, a TCP connection may fail, in which case the TCP connection is recovered by a command restart. If multiple TCP connections are used for an iSCSI session, the reconstruction of each individual connection is required. Finally, the iSCSI session itself can be damaged. Termination and recovery of a session are usually not required unless both other levels fail to recover. Such a situation requires that all TCP connections be closed, all tasks terminated, and the session restarted via a repeated log-in.

Security

Because iSCSI data will go through WAN, the potentially insecure public IP network, data integrity and security become key issues. TCP itself can provide a basic level of end-to-end data integrity through the standard checksum. However, iSCSI will have to provide more data integrity and security options if stricter security requirements are needed.

IP security (IPSec) is transparent to higher levels, including iSCSI. Hence, iSCSI can leverage on IPSec to perform authentication between the initiator and target, authentication and data integrity, and finally, data encryption. Various solutions can be used for authentication, such as Kerberos or private keys exchange (Clark 2003).

CONCLUSION

In this chapter, we have provided an overview of the evolution from DAS and NAS to SAN. We have described the fundamentals of SAN—i.e., fibre channel protocol and its five-layer model. Moreover, we have presented the iSCSI protocol as the emerging technology for the next-generation SAN.

We first focused on the fibre channel by analyzing its protocol suite, topologies, and the five-layer model. We introduced the integrated set of FC standards defined by ANSI, and presented three types of FC topologies: point to point, arbitrated loop, and switched fabric. Thorough understanding of the five-layer model of the FC is essential for the study and design of SANs. We thus reviewed various aspects of the five-layer model, ranging from the physical-layer options of FC-0 to the mapping interface of FC-4.We then presented two typical applications of FC SAN, namely, data consolidation and disaster recovery, and introduced several proposed solutions for FC SAN extensions to mitigate the distance constraint.

As the newly emerging protocol for SAN, iSCSI has drawn much attention from all major storage vendors and storage solution providers. We thus provided a detailed discussion of various aspects of iSCSI, from the iSCSI network architecture to iSCSI security.

The future of SANs is being shaped by a spectrum of existing and emergent technologies, and the real-world applications they are designed to serve. We believe that two trends for SANs are emerging: first, the IP-based SAN technologies, especially iSCSI will play an increasingly important role in network storage; secondly, SAN will eventually be integrated with the mainstream core networking, as the core value of SANs is based on affordable and supportable by mainstream technologies.

GLOSSARY

ANSI: American National Standards Institute.

CIFS: Common Internet file system. CIFS is a network file system access protocol primarily used by Windows clients to communicate file access requests to Windows servers.

CRC: Cyclic redundancy check. CRC is used to check the correctness of transmitted data

DAS: Direct attached storage.

EOF: End of frame. EOF is used in the header of an FC frame to indicate the end of a FC frame.

Exchange: A set of non-concurrent sequences for a single I/O operation.

FC: Fibre Channel. FC is a collection of standards for high-speed data transmission. It supports point-to-point, arbitrated, and fabric topologies.

FCIP: Fibre channel over TCP/IP. FCIP is a TCP/IP-based tunneling protocol for connecting geographically distributed FC SANs transparently over IP.

F_port: The "fabric" port within an FC fabric switch.

GBIC: Gigabit interface converter. GBIC is the widely used transceiver to convert electrical signal in host bus adapters (HBAs) into optical or electrical signals for transmission.

iFCP: Internet fibre-channel protocol (iFCP). iFCP is a gateway-to-gateway protocol to transport FC frames over TCP/IP switching and routing elements.

iSCSI: Internet SCSI. iSCSI is based on the small computer systems interface (SCSI) protocol, which enables the host computer systems to perform data I/O operations with a variety of peripheral devices.

L_port: The "loop" port performing an arbitrated-loop function.

NAS: Network attached storage.

NFS: Network file system. NFS is a distributed file system originally developed by Sun Microsystems Computer Corporation.

N_port: Node connection associated with hosts or storage devices in the point-to-point and fabric topologies.

RAID: Redundant array of independent disks. RAID is a family of techniques for managing multiple disks to deliver desirable cost, data availability, and performance characteristics to host environments.

SAN: Storage area network.
Sequence: A set of related frames transmitted unidirectionally from one N_Port to another.
SNIA: Storage Networking Industry Association.
SOF: Start of frame. SOF is used in the header of a FC frame to indicate the start of a FC frame.
SONET: Synchronous optical network. SONET is a widely used transmission and multiplexing standard for high-speed traffic in North America.
WDM: Wavelength-division multiplexing.

CROSS REFERENCES

See *Fibre Channel*; *Storage Area Network Fundamentals*.

REFERENCES

Aboba, B., J. Tseng, J. Walker, V. Rangan, and F. Ftravostino. 2004. *RFC3723: Securing block storage protocols over IP*. www.ietf.org/rfc/rfc3723.txt (accessed June 8, 2006).

ANSI. 1994. *Fibre channel physical and signal interface (FC-PH)*. ANSI X3.230.

ANSI. 1996. *Fibre channel arbitrated loop (FC-AL)*. X3.272-1996.

ANSI. 1996. *Fibre channel physical and signal interface (FC-PH) Amendment 1*. 1.X3.230-1994/AM 1.

ANSI. 1996. *Fibre channel physical and signal protocol-2 (FC-PH-2)*. X3.297.

ANSI. 1997. *Fibre channel physical and signal protocol -3 (FC-PH-3)*. X3.303-1997.

ANSI. 1999. *Fibre channel physical and signal interface (FC-PH) Amendment 2*. X3.230-1994/AM 2.

ANSI. 2003. *Fibre channel framing and signaling interface (FC-FS)*. ANSI/INCITS 373.

Bakke, M., J. Muchow, M. Krueger, and T. McSweeney. 2005. *iSCSI, IETF*. draft-ietf-ips-iscsi-mib-11.txt. www.ietf.org/internet-drafts/draft-ietf-ips-iscsi-mib-11.txt (accessed January 20, 2006).

Benner, A. F. 2001. *Fibre channel for SANs*. New York: McGraw-Hill.

Ching, Y. Y. 2000. *Storage without boundaries-top predictions by industry gurus Gartner and IDC*. CNETAsia whitepaper. www.zdnetasia.com/itlibrary/whitepapers. (accessed January 22, 2006).

Cisco Systems. 2001. EMC and Cisco metro optical storage networking solutions. White paper. http://whitepapers.zdnet.co.uk/0,39025945,60031308p-39000566q,00.htm (accessed January 26, 2006).

Clark, T. 2002. *IP SANs: A guide to iSCSI, iFCP, and FCIP protocols for storage area networks*. Upper Saddle River, NJ: Pearson Education.

Clark, T. 2003. *Designing storage area networks*. 2nd ed. *A practical reference for implementing fibre channel and IP sans*. Reading, MA: Addison-Wesley.

Farely, M. 2001. *Building storage area networks*. 2nd ed. New York: McGraw-Hill.

Gibbons, K., C. Monia, J. Tseng, and F. Travostino. 2005. *iFCP—A protocol for Internet fibre channel storage networking*. IETF draft-ietf-ips-ifcp-mib-07.txt. www.ietf.org/internet-drafts/draft-ietf-ips-ifcp-mib-07.txt (accessed January 20, 2006).

Gibbons, et al. 2006. *RFC 4369: Definitions of Managed Objects for Internet Fibre Channel Protocol (iFCP)*. http://tools.ietf.org/html/4369 (accessed June 8, 2006).

Heath J. R. 2000. High-speed storage area networks using a fibre channel arbitrated loop interconnect. *IEEE Network* March:51–6.

Helland, A. 2002. The economics of large-scale data transfer: The benefits of fibre channel and SONET for high-performance, cost-effective data transport through WAN—storage networking. *Computer Technology Review* December.

INCITS Technical Committee of Accredited Standard Committee T10. 2004. *Fibre Channel Protocol for SCSI*. 3rd version (FCP-3).

Kembel, W. R. 2000. *Fibre channel: A comprehensive introduction*. Tucson, AZ: Northwest Learning Associates.

McCloghrie, K. 2005. *RFC 4044: Fibre Channel Management MIB*. http://tools.ietf.org/html/4044 (accessed June 8, 2006).

Meggyesi, Z. 1994, *Fibre channel overview*. http://hsi.web.cern.ch/HSI/fcs/spec/overview.htm (accessed December 15, 2005).

Meth, K. Z., and J. Satran. 2003. Features of the iSCSI protocol.x *IEEE Communication Magazine* August: 72–5.

Murthy, C. S. R., and M. Gurusamy. 2001. *WDM optical networks: Concepts, design, & algorithms*. Upper Saddle River, NJ: Prentice Hall.

Natarajan, R., and A. Rijhsinghani. 2005. *Fibre channel over TCP/IP (FCIP)*. IETF, draft-ietf-ips-fcip-mib-09.txt. www.ietf.org/internet-drafts/draft-ietf-ips-fcip-mib-09.txt (accessed January 2006).

Phillips, B. 1998. Have Storage area networks come of age? *IEEE Computer* 31(7):10–2.

Sacks, M., and A. Varma. 1996. Fibre channel and related standards. *IEEE Communication Magazine August*:40–50.

Sorrento Networks. 2003. *Storage networking extension in metro-regional domains*. Sorrento Networks Inc. white paper. www.sorrentonet.com (accessed September 21, 2003).

Storage Networking Industry Association. 2004. iSCSI technical review, white paper. www.snia.org/ipstorage/about/iscsi/iSCSI_Technical_whitepaper.PDF (accessed June 3, 2006).

Storage Networking Industry Association. 2005. www.snia.org. (accessed December 12, 2005).

Technical Committee T11. 2006. *FC project*. www.t11.org/index.html. (accessed December 1, 2006).

Telikepalli, R., T. Drwiega and J. Yan. 2004. Storage area network extension solutions and their performance assessment. *IEEE Communications Magazine* April:56–63.

Wang, C. Y., F. Zhou, Y.-L. Zhu, C. T. Chong, B. Hou, W.-Y. Xi. 2003. Simulation of fibre channel storage area network using SANSim. *Proceedings of the 11th IEEE International Conference on Networks (ICON2003), Sydney, Australia*: 349–354.Los Alamitos, CA: IEEE Press.

Zamer, A. 2004. *IPStorage tutorial*. Storage Networking Industry Association. www.snia.org/tech_activities/ip_storage/IPStorage_Tutorial_Primer_2.pdf (accessed June 5, 2006).

Distributed Intelligent Networks

G. N. Prezerakos, *Technological Education Institute of Piraeus, Greece*
I. S. Venieris, *National Technical University of Athens, Greece*

INTRODUCTION

The public switched telephone network (PSTN) was originally modeled along two major principles: (1) the offering of a single-service voice communication, between two parties, and (2) the fact that this service would be offered by means of a complex network equipped with rather simple terminal devices. This model worked well until the 1960s. when major network companies realized that advances in information technology (IT) could create additional revenue streams via the provision of services other than voice communication. Initially, the deployment of these extended services, such as call waiting, took place using stored program control (SPC) switching systems. SPC was a monolithic architecture that required programming of services in the switch.

In the mid 1970s, the common channel signaling network (CCSN)–more widely known as signaling system no. 7 (SS7)–was introduced. The CCSN architecture realized out-of-band signaling by providing separate network links for signaling and voice information. Also SS7 provided for a standardized switching protocol suite effectively liberating telecom operators from their dependence on specific switching equipment manufacturers. The IN concept was born out of SS7 in the early 1980s and became a very cost-effective solution for service provision in telephony because it allowed for extended services with minimum modifications in the network architecture.

From then on IN has successfully adapted to every major leap in either network or service provisioning technology. The following paragraphs detail the evolution from the original IN concept to the elaborate distributed intelligent broadband network (DIBN). Initially, the traditional IN model is presented in order to familiarize the reader with the relevant terminology as well as basic concepts. Consequently, the transition towards the intelligent broadband network (IBN) architecture is briefly presented, followed by an analysis of the incorporation of distributed processing and mobile code technologies, common object request broker architecture (CORBA) and mobile agents, to IBN resulting in the DIBN. Moreover, various approaches for open service provision via DIBN are analyzed, focusing on the adoption of the parlay APIs. As a final step, we discuss the gradual replacement of the IN concept in the context of the upcoming next generation networks (NGN).

INTELLIGENT NETWORK BASICS

The major innovation of IN was that it enabled operators to move the main bulk of service execution out of the switching elements and into a dedicated service-execution node. This way an operator could have a central point for managing and deploying services that was decoupled, to a certain extent, from the switching infrastructure.

Of course, for realizing the full potential of such a concept, certain international network standards had to be devised. An effort toward standardization was undertaken by the International Telecommunications Union (ITU) and the European Telecommunications Standards Institute (ETSI) and led to Intelligent Network Conceptual Model (INCM), which is described in the Q120x series of standards from the ITU. A similar effort was carried out in North America, resulting in the Advanced Intelligent Network (AIN) series of standards.

INCM prescribes four planes, which relate to IN implementations as shown in Figure 1. The INCM adopts a service-oriented approach; thus, the top plane is the service plane (ITU-T [Telecommunication Standardization Sector of the International Telecommunication Union] 1997 Q.1202). The service plane provides a view of the available IN services but with no implementation details.

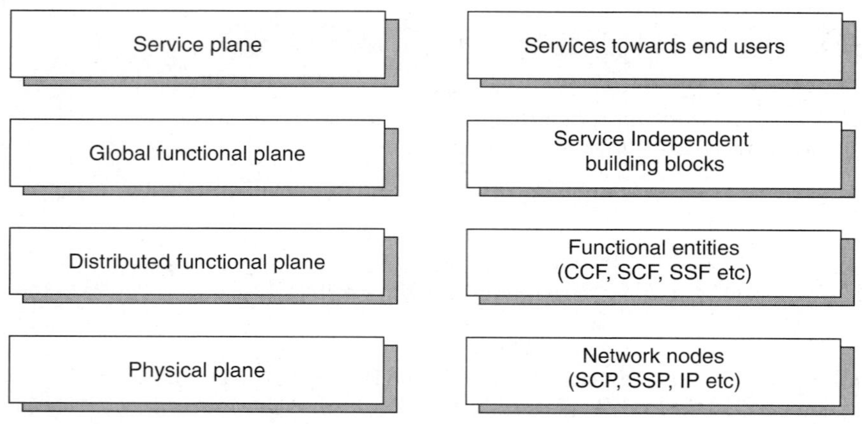

Figure 1: INCM and IN implementation (CCF = call control function; IP = Internet protocol; SCF = service control function; SCP = service control point; SSF = service switching function; SSP = service switching point)

Services are composed by service features (SFs), which are the smallest functions on this plane. The service plane is also concerned with the interaction between services as well as between service features as long as these interactions are implementation-independent. Avoiding undesired effects due to service and feature interaction is a major issue in telecommunications (Zave 1993).

SFs are mapped into Service independent Building blocks (SIBs), which are defined within the global functional plane (GFP) (ITU-T 1997, Q.1203). SIBs are the smallest building blocks in an IN, and are combined into concrete services or service logic programs (SLPs) by the global service logic (GSL).

The SIBs in the GFP are part of functional entities (FEs) that reside in the distributed functional plane (DFP) (ITU-T 1993, Q.1204). A SIB can be found in more than one FE, but it must be present in at least one. FEs provide the functional specifications that can be followed by specific IN implementations. Each FE may perform a variety of functional entity actions (FEAs), which, in turn, may be performed within different FEs. However, a given FEA may not be distributed across FEs. The communications between FEs takes place via information flows (IFs). Functional entities in the DFP include, among others, functions well known in modern telecommunication networks, such as the call control function (CCF), the service switching function (SSF), the service control function (SCF), the service data function (SDF) and the service resource function (SRF). The bottom plane of the INCM is the physical plane (ITU-T 1993, Q.1205) which models the physical aspects of an IN, including the detailed design of physical network elements, Physical entities (PEs), and communication protocols.

A short analysis of the CCF and SSF components is provided below, describing how IN functionality is implemented at the switching level. The basic call state model (BCSM) handles basic call state processing and provides a view of basic call states to the SSF. It includes points in call (PICs), which correspond to call states that might be of interest to an IN SLP, and detection points (DPs), which correspond to call states in which execution of a call can be transferred to an IN SLP. There is also a basic call unrelated state model (BCUSM), which models the call unrelated switching function (CUSF), and is concerned with the call unrelated interaction between the user and the service logic.

The SSF implements the switching state model (SSM), an object-oriented finite state machine that represents IN call control processing in terms of IN states. The SSM detects call-processing events that should be reported to active IN service logic instances or should trigger new ones. In addition, the SSM provides the SCF with a view of the SSF and CCF call-control activities.

The IN Protocol Stack

IN is implemented on top of the SS7 signaling network protocol stack. Figure 2 shows the relation between the open system interconnection (OSI) protocol layers and SS7.

The three levels of the message transfer part (MTP) provide for reliable transfer of messages between signaling nodes. The basic telephony functionality with respect to signaling (establishment, supervision, and termination of switched network connections) is provided by the integrated services digital network (ISDN) user part (ISUP). Therefore, ISUP controls the circuits used to carry either voice or data traffic.

IN related protocols sit on top of the MPT layer. The signaling connection control part (SCCP) enhances MTP level 3 with connection-oriented and connectionless network services as well as with address translation capabilities. Transaction capabilities application part (TCAP) makes use of SCCP functionality to support end-to-end transaction-based services between the various nodes in a network through a query/response interaction. In OSI terminology, TCAP is a remote operations service element (ROSE) protocol.

The IN application protocol (INAP) defines the IN application layer messages exchanges between the functional entities of an IN (SSF, SCF, and SRF). INAP defines an operation type in relation to each information flow exchanged between two communicating functional entities. The arguments of INAP operations are the information elements defined for the corresponding information flow.

Although IN can be implemented in a variety of architectures, the next section describes the most typical IN implementation that can be found in the majority of

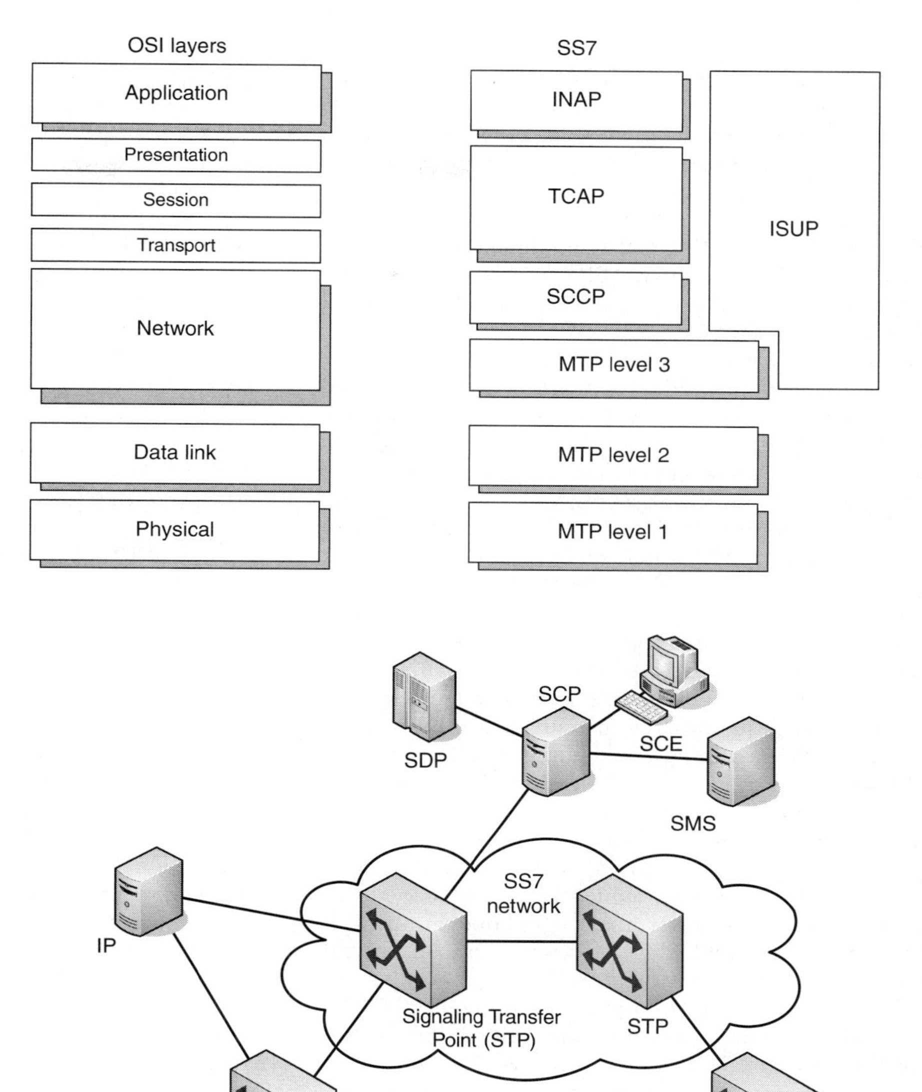

Figure 2: The IN protocol stack

Figure 3: Typical IN architecture (SMS = service management system)

modern networks. It involves a platform-based approach, in which the service control function (SCF) is implemented inside a dedicated network node known as service control point (SCP).

Figure 2 contains the network-to-network interface (NNI) signaling protocols. There is also the user-to-network interface (UNI) signaling functionality, which includes the Q.931 and Q.2931 protocols for ISDN and broadband integrated services digital network (B-ISDN), respectively. Intelligent networking in mobile networks implements the customized application for the mobile network enhanced logic (CAMEL) standard, which is also based on the INCM.

Physical Architecture

The IN architecture separates service logic from switching functionality; moreover, it realizes service provision by means of signaling only, before any end-to-end voice or data-related connections are established for a call.

A typical IN architecture is shown in Figure 3.

Within an SS7 network, several switches are upgraded to service switching points (SSPs). SSPs implement the service switching function (SSF) and the call control function (CCF). Therefore, SSPs perform basic call control and, in addition, can distinguish between simple voice and IN-related calls. Once an IN-related call is detected, the SSP informs a dedicated node called service control point (SCP). The SCP implements the service control function (SCF), which is responsible for service logic execution. The SCP contains service logic programs (SLPs) appropriately composed of groups of SIBs. The respective SLP is invoked and, according to the service logic structure, the SCP instructs the service switching points (SSPs) on how to process the call.

The IN architecture also includes the intelligent peripheral. This is a node that implements the specialized resource function. The intelligent peripheral is responsible for the communication between the users and the service. It can be used for digit collection, message playback, and voice recognition.

The data needed by the service logic are stored in the service data point (SDP) which implements the service data function. Although the SDP was specified as an independent node, many commercial implementations integrate it with the SCP.

A typical IN architecture also includes nodes dedicated to service management and to service creation. The service creation environment (SCE) is a platform that enables the graphical composition of IN services out of SIBs, which appear as visual components within the SCE. Several software engineering techniques can be applied for the design and verification of IN services, involving various methods of formal specification (Prezerakos, Anagnostakis, and Venieris 1999; Steffen and Margaria 1999). A detailed discussion on the origins and the evolution of the IN concept and standards can be found in Magedanz and Popescu-Zeletin (1996).

INs provide a vast variety of telephony services, such as free phone, localized weather forecast, televoting, routing by time/day/month, outgoing/incoming call restriction, do-not-disturb service, and many more. The free phone service constitutes a good example of the basic functionality behind an IN service. Free phone services involve the dialing of a nationwide number, usually starting with the digits 800, which is consequently translated by the respective IN service to an ordinary telephone number. Initially, a subscriber dials the free phone number. The call arrives at the SSP, which analyzes the called number and discovers that it starts with the digits 800, indicating that it is an IN call. Call execution is suspended and the SSP asks the SCP for instructions. The SCP analyzes the query and invokes the free phone SLP. The service logic translates the 800 number into the respective ordinary telephone number by querying a table in the SDP, which contains the associations between 800 and ordinary numbers. Finally the SCP instructs the SSP to setup a connection with that number, call processing is resumed, and the dialog between the two nodes ceases.

Benefits and Limitations of the Traditional Intelligent Network Architecture

The introduction of the intelligent network was regarded as a major step forward for telephony, since it provided network operators with several advantages, such as vendor independency, fast time to market, and easy service customization. But like every technological evolution, IN brought risks together with the advantages.

First, IN gives the SCP a leading role in service execution, effectively turning it into a single point of failure. If the SCP goes down, the services are unavailable to the entire network until the SCP is up again. Therefore, IN requires networks to provide for resilience mechanisms to the platform as well as to the network layer. Viewed from this angle, the IN concept is essentially non-distributed. Another IN shortcoming derived from its telephony heritage. IN was a concept well suited for networks providing voice and narrowband data transmission. During the beginning of the 1990s technologies such as asynchronous transfer mode (ATM) and fiber optics provided sufficient bandwidth for the transport of richer forms of information. Video and digital audio were paving the way for what is now known as broadband multimedia services. Although improved resilience was an issue that the technology available at that time could deal with, multimedia communication in broadband networks required an improved concept for service provisioning. An enhanced IN architecture was the evident candidate for such a purpose.

BEYOND TRADITIONAL INTELLIGENT NETWORKS

Intelligent Broadband Networks

The rise of multimedia services requiring multiparty and multi-point connections created the need for an architecture that would facilitate the provision of such services. The state of ITU standardization at the time could not cope with these requirements—e.g. the signaling capability set (SCS) 2.1 (under approval as late as 1997), supported only single connection, bidirectional point-to-point and unidirectional point-to-multipoint call/connections. Also, Internet-like architectures lacked the mechanisms for guaranteeing the quality of service (QoS) required by these services in contrast to other transport technologies available at the time, such as ATM. Evidently, the IN concept was perceived as an overlay architecture that would complement B-ISDN in multimedia service provision.

IN and B-ISDN integration was primarily investigated by the Advanced Communications Technologies and Services (ACTS) project INSIGNIA (IN and B-ISDN Signalling Integration on ATM Platforms). INSIGNIA (Prezerakos et al. 1998) was concerned with the definition and implementation of an intelligent broadband network (IBN) architecture by applying the IN concepts on top of the transport infrastructure provided by ATM technology using, where possible, standardized B-ISDN protocols. INSIGNIA replaced the functional entities in the distributed functional plane of the IN conceptual model, SSF, SCF, SRF, and SDF with broadband versions, creating the B-SSF, B-SCF, B-SRF, and B-SDF, respectively (Figure 4).

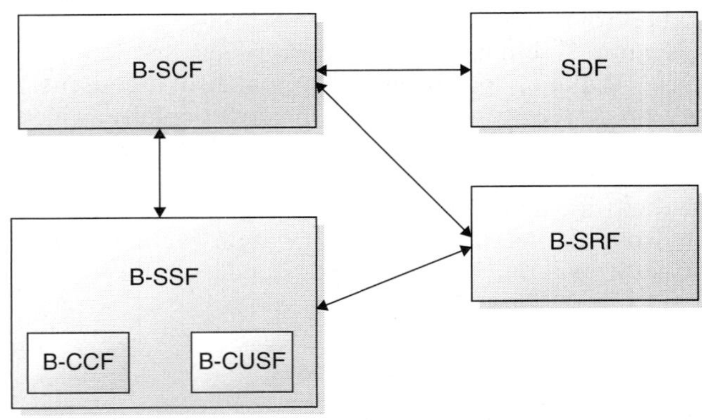

Figure 4: Functional entities of integrated IN/B-ISDN

The B-SSF also contains the broadband call control function (B-CCF) as well as the broadband call unrelated service function (B-CUSF).

Since IN services provided by this architecture were composed of multiple calls/connections and call unrelated associations (out-channel interaction between user terminal and service logic), a session management mechanism was imperative. To this end, INSIGNIA implemented an object-oriented session model for managing the complex topology of calls/connections and call unrelated associations. Session objects provided the B-SCF and B-SSF with a common view of each service instance. Moreover, the session model enabled the B-SCP to initiate call setups, a feature that was very useful for services such as multiparty broadband video-conferencing. It should be noted here that connection control in INSIGNIA involved the setup and termination of dynamic ATM connections. However, in the course of time, this has not been widely accepted, since ATM was ultimately perceived by the market mainly as a fast transport technology over permanent or semipermanent backbone network connections.

INSIGNIA also specified and implemented a broadband INAP (B-INAP) protocol for the communication between B-SSPs and B-SCPs and between B-SCPs and B-IPs. Broadband IN services were developed with the use of a commercial service creation environment enhanced with evolved versions of narrowband SIBs that were appropriately modified to support multimedia and multiparty requirements.

INSIGNIA made an important contribution to IN evolution because it proved that the IN concept could be enhanced in a cost-effective manner to support the demanding requirements posed by multimedia broadband services. It also introduced the term "intelligent broadband networks" (Venieris and Hussmann 1998), which gradually replaced plain IN within the research community. In terms of service distribution however, INSIGNIA retained the B-SCP as the central point of service logic execution. The rest of the article uses the IN term to refer also to intelligent broadband networks (IBNs).

Distributed Processing Technologies

At the beginning of the 1990s the widespread adoption of new software engineering technologies such as object orientation (OO) and component distribution started to affect the design and deployment of telecom services. These technologies provided for code reusability through software components that, although being distributed over heterogeneous platforms, could, at the same time, interact in a transparent manner. They also aimed at providing independence of application and service provision from specific hardware/software platforms. Two principal technologies in this area were the Common Object Request Broker Architecture (CORBA) (Object Management Group 2005) and the mobile agent technology (MAT). Eventually other similar technologies emerged such as the Distributed Component Object Model (DCOM) from Microsoft and the Java Remote Method Invocation (RMI) from Sun Microsystems. Both CORBA and MAT were immediately perceived as facilitators for the design and implementation of advanced services in fixed as well as wireless networks (Venieris, Zizza, and Magedanz 2000). Evidently, the question arose about whether the IN model could be adapted in order to take advantage of both CORBA and MAT. Dynamically deploying mobile code into a network using agents was a concept well beyond the state of the art; therefore, the introduction of CORBA was perceived as a more conventional way forward.

CORBA

The CORBA standard was developed under the auspices of the Object Management Group (OMG) as a response to the requirement for a distributed object framework. CORBA specifies the rules and the architecture by which a system or an application can be created out of software components (or objects) distributed in multiple platforms that interoperate in a fashion that is transparent to both developers and users.

Interoperability is ensured because CORBA objects are required to expose to client entities a standardized interface that is implementation-independent. Object interfaces are defined with the interface definition language (IDL), and they are consequently compiled into the stub (or skeleton) interfaces, which is the actual code that describes the objects methods. IDL can be mapped to a variety of programming languages, including C++, Java, C, Smalltalk, and others. Clients use this interface to request services from objects or, in other words, to make calls to methods publicly available via the objects. Client requests specify a reference to the object, the name of the requested operation, and the respective operation parameters.

CORBA provides for ways to discover objects at the network level, to standardize the format of object references, and to encode messages required for inter object communication. These features are the responsibility of the object request broker (ORB), which is a dedicated middleware present in every CORBA-compliant platform. ORBs work in conjunction with object adapters to deliver requests to objects and to activate objects. The process of object activation also makes use of the implementation repository, which provides information such as the object's location and operating environment.

Besides static invocation via IDL, CORBA also allows the dynamic (at run-time) invocation of objects without compile-time knowledge of the respective interfaces. This is accomplished via the dynamic invocation interface at the client side and the dynamic skeleton interface at the server side. In this case, the information required for forming as well as serving a request (such as reference to the object, the name of the requested operation and the respective operation parameters mentioned above) is retrieved from the interface repository.

An overview of the CORBA architecture is presented in Figure 5.

At the network level CORBA specifies the general inter-ORB protocol (GIOP) for transporting method invocations and replies through the network. In the same manner that IDL can be mapped to a variety of programming languages, GIOP can be mapped to a variety of network protocol suites. The proliferation of TCP/IP networks has made the respective GIOP mapping to IP, known as the

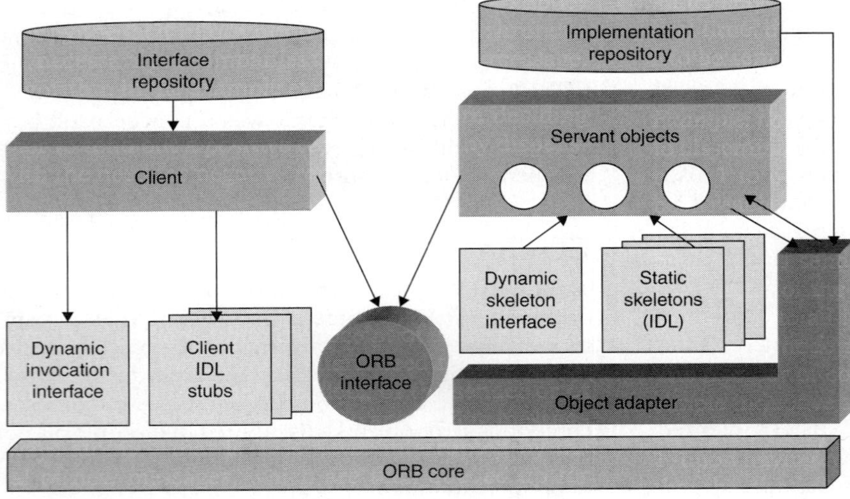

Figure 5: CORBA architecture

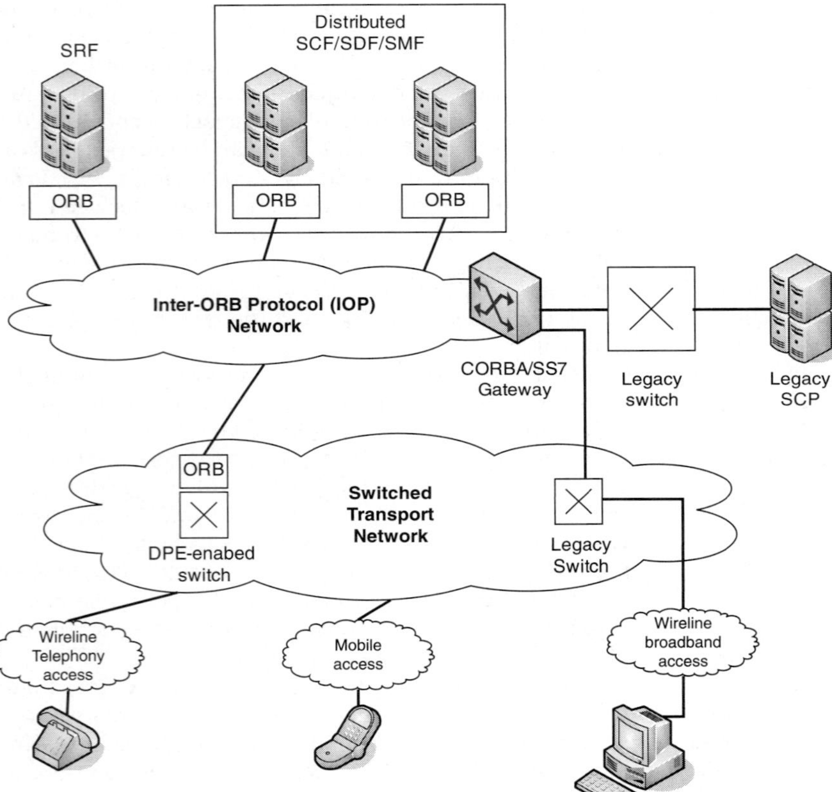

Figure 6: A CORBA-enabled IN architecture (DPE = distributed processing environment' SMF = service management framework)

Internet inter-ORB protocol (IIOP), the most popular inter-ORB protocol in the CORBA world.

Introducing Common Object Request Broker Architecture to Intelligent Network

The telecom industry saw in CORBA an interesting enabling technology for further IN enhancement. In particular, during 1996 and 1997, OMG issued a series of requests with respect to intelligent networking with CORBA (OMG 1996) as well as CORBA/IN interworking (OMG 1997). Blending the CORBA model into an IN architecture requires that the following three issues are challenged:

- Interoperability with existing IN systems based on SS7
- Mapping of the IN event/trigger model to a relevant computing paradigm based on CORBA
- High performance, reliability and real-time support

An ideal CORBA-compliant IN, depicted in Figure 6, was envisaged as based on a distributed middleware platform comprised of nodes (SSPs, SCPs, SRFs, etc.) built out of CORBA objects on top of respective ORBs.

The nodes would be connected via a resilient network similar to SS7 but based on some GIOP mapping. Service invocations would originate from terminals at the network edges (fixed and mobile phones, computing devices, etc.) using the typical user to UNI signaling protocols such Q.931 for N-ISDN or its broadband counterpart Q.2931 for B-ISDN.

CORBA-enabled SSPs translate these messages into object methods' invocations, which are consequently transferred to the CORBA-enabled IN nodes via IOP. The middleware architecture is complemented by several generic CORBA services, such as a naming service, and the generic CORBA event service as well as telecom-specific CORBA services such as a session-management service to handle the sessions established for the execution of different telecom services.

CORBA-enabled nodes would be able to use the IOP directly to communicate with one another. Non-CORBA-enabled nodes such as narrowband and broadband IN SSPs and SCPs would require a form of protocol conversion for communicating with the CORBA-enabled nodes. This functionality is provided by a dedicated network node, the CORBA/SS7 gateway. Such a gateway can be implemented with one of the three following options (Magedanz 1999):

1. INAP/CORBA gateway: In this case the gateway performs the conversion based on the mapping of INAP specifications into IDL-based interfaces. This mapping involves only IN services on top of TCAP; however, there are various INAP versions that deviate from the ITU-T standard. This is an interoperability problem that CORBA-based networks inherit from traditional IN.
2. TCAP/CORBA gateway: This is a more general solution for all TCAP/ROSE protocols (of which INAP is only one member along with e.g. MAP). The realization of a TCAP/CORBA gateway requires a conversion between resident operating system (ROS) constructs defined in abstract syntax notation One (ASN.1) and the corresponding CORBA structures expressed in IDL. This is a preferred solution, since it provides for CORBA interoperability with more application layer protocols than INAP.
3. Using SS7 as an IOP: This type of interworking, also called a "kernel transport network" (EURESCOM, 1997), allows distributed CORBA objects to communicate over the existing SS7 infrastructure by using SS7 as a transport mechanism. In AT&T, GMD FOKUS, IONA Technologies Plc, Nortel, Teltec DCU (2001) a GIOP mapping onto the signaling connection control part (SCCP) protocol of SS7 is defined for this purpose, which is called SCCP inter-ORB Protocol (SIOP).

The adoption of the distributed processing environment (DPE) principles in the telecoms world reached its peak with the consortium for a Telecommunications Information Networking Architecture (TINA). TINA (Barr, Boyd, and Inoue 1993) defined a framework for the development of service and network management applications in which service components are deployed on a distributed processing environment (DPE), which can be implemented on top of different network infrastructures. TINA services are provided by means of the interaction of computational objects (COs) that contain logic and data and offer specific operations. The communication between COs is supported by the DPE that allows the arbitrary distributions of COs. Migration from IN to TINA was expected to take place gradually by "TINA-rising" the IN elements by means of COs on top of a DPE (Herzog and Magedanz 1997). Initially, the TINA DPE was based on the International Standards Organization (ISO) open distributed processing (ODP) framework (ISO/IEC 1996) and was later migrated to CORBA.

Obviously the transition to TINA was expected to lead an intermediate state in which there would have been islands of TINA-rised networks in parallel to the traditional IN architecture. In the context of TINA/IN interworking, the IBIS project (Listanti and Salsano 1998) implemented a gateway based on principles as similar to those of the INAP/CORBA gateway. The proposed gateway was called adaptation unit (AU) and contained the interworking object (IwO). On the TINA side, the IwO interacted with the TINA user application (UAP) objects, while on the broadband IN side, the IwO interacted with a simplified B-SCF that handled the dialog with the B-SSFs, terminating the B-INAP protocol. For the services handled by the TINA service logic, the B-SCF could not make autonomous decisions, relaying all B-INAP messages to the IwO. Similar approaches involving TINA-endorsed AUs were discussed within OMG's TINA-IN-Workgroup created in April 1998.

Dynamic Code Deployment

The intelligent network control architecture (INCA) discussed in (Isaacs and Mortier 1999) moved one step further in terms of distributing processing. INCA exploited the features offered by the Tempest environment to provide IN services that could not have existed in either narrowband or broadband IN architectures.

The Tempest environment allows the partitioning of resources in the switching elements into one or more virtual networks managed by separate control architectures. INCA uses Tempest for realizing IN services that consist of dynamically loaded code in the form of service scripts. Service scripts are disseminated to the various parts of an active control architecture and cooperate for the provision of a certain IN service. INCA introduced features from the domain of active networking to the IN concept. However, this happens in an architecture that used proprietary network interfaces to a significant extent. Similar approaches to the same problem adopted a more coherent approach by adopting an active networking technology known as mobile agent technology (MAT).

INTELLIGENT BROADBAND NETWORKS AND MOBILE AGENTS

Mobile Agents

Although general consensus does not exist on a definition of the term "software agent" (Bradshaw 1997), one can say that an agent is an integrated software entity including code as well as data, with its own state, behavior, and with the ability to interact with other entities—including people, other agents, and legacy systems. Agents can be static, spending their entire life cycle within the same platform, or mobile, hence the term "mobile agent technology" (MAT). Services designed according to the MAT paradigm are composed of a set of mobile agents (MAs) that move from node to node inside a network. MAs can visit a node, execute several tasks, and then suspend execution and migrate to a new node, where their execution is resumed.

During service execution MAs can interact with other MAs in the same or a different node. MAT provides several benefits, such as autonomous task execution, reduction in network traffic due to local processing, automation of distributed processing, and increased resilience (Chess, Harrison, and Kershenbaum 1998). The most important aspect, though, with respect to service provision, especially for distributed IN, is the flexibility that MAs provide for on-demand service provisioning. Mobile agents can be used for the instant download of service segments to client and server nodes. Downloading and execution of MAs, however, requires a dedicated agent execution environment (AEE) or "agency" to be installed in the respective network nodes.

The obvious requirement for interoperability between agencies from different vendors as well as between agencies and several hardware/software combinations led to an international effort toward MAT standardization. This effort was undertaken by the Foundation for Intelligent Physical Agents (FIPA) as well as the OMG via a dedicated Agent Special Interest Group.

MAT became the core technology for service provision in wireline and wireless environments for numerous research projects (Raatikainen 1999). The following section discussed the results of the MARINE project, which combined MAT with CORBA to create a fully distributed intelligent broadband network (DIBN).

A Reference Architecture for Distributed Broadband Intelligent Network

MARINE (Faglia, Magedanz, and Papadakis 1999) expanded the broadband IN model in order to include the following innovations:

- Functional entities that controlled the exchange of service-related information (M-CUSF, SSF, SCF, and SRF) were developed using CORBA as a distributed processing environment (DPE).
- Several functionalities were consolidated in a single physical entity, thus creating a novel mapping of functional to physical entities.
- A computational model was defined that allowed CORBA objects to support IN services.
- Service logic programs (SLPs) at the SCP and at the intelligent peripheral level included service objects defined in the form of mobile agents.

In MARINE, switching and control functions are combined into SSCPs (service switching and control points), which correspond to an integrated SSP/SCP and SENs (service nodes), which correspond to an integrated SSP/SCP/IP. Therefore, MARINE abandons the concept of a centralized SCP and suggests the us of multiple small-scale SSCPs and/or SENs in parallel. MARINE connection control also relied, like INSIGNIA, on dynamic ATM connection handling.

Service logic programs (SLPs) can be hosted either at the SCCPs or at the SENs. This is partly due to the fact that the SSF, SCF, SRF, and M-CUSF are CORBA compliant; therefore, communication between those FEs takes place via the IIOP (Internet inter-RB protocol) providing location transparency. No modifications are required at the terminals, since the MARINE architecture communicates with terminals via standardized user-to-network signaling.

MARINE also defines objects belonging to the functional entities hosted on the DPE and specifies the information flows between them. This computational model allows an IDL (interface definition language) specification of single CORBA components, which are used to provide IN services. The model in question includes two broad categories of objects, service-specific objects (e.g., implementing specific service features in SLPs) and architecture-specific objects (e.g., the object that corresponds to the switching state model).

A percentage of these service-specific objects exist in MARINE in the form of mobile agents. The use of mobile agents enables these objects to roam between the service execution nodes (e.g., from a B-SCCP to a SEN and vice versa), realizing in essence a dynamic deployment of services. The deployment of services can also take place via the download of service agents from a service creation/management system to B-SCCPs and SENs. The use of mobile code in the form of agents requires the existence of an AEE (agent execution environment) into the respective nodes of MARINE. The selected MA platform for MARINE was Grasshopper (Bäumer and Magedanz 1999). All AEEs form collectively a DAE (distributed agent environment) in which the service agents may roam.

Service Execution

The MARINE B-SS&CP

The MARINE switching platform was an evolution of the INSIGNIA B-SSP, which has been enhanced to include a Java virtual machine, an agent execution platform and a DPE based on CORBA.

Physically, the B-SSCP comprises two systems: A server that is in charge of handling the IN signaling and a switching ATM matrix for handling switched voice and data connections. An Ethernet bus connects the two systems, allowing the server to request from the switch the establishment, modification, and release of switched connections according to the signaling information.

Figure 7 presents the B-SSCP architecture; it is obvious that the base signaling stack (UNI, NNI, B-INAP, CUSM) has remained the same. In general, the MARINE B-SS&CP could communicate with a B-INAP-based B-SCP, allowing it to work with broadband IN.

The DPE cooperates with the switching part of the B-SSCP via an appropriately modified switching state model (SSM). Moreover, a mobility basic call unrelated

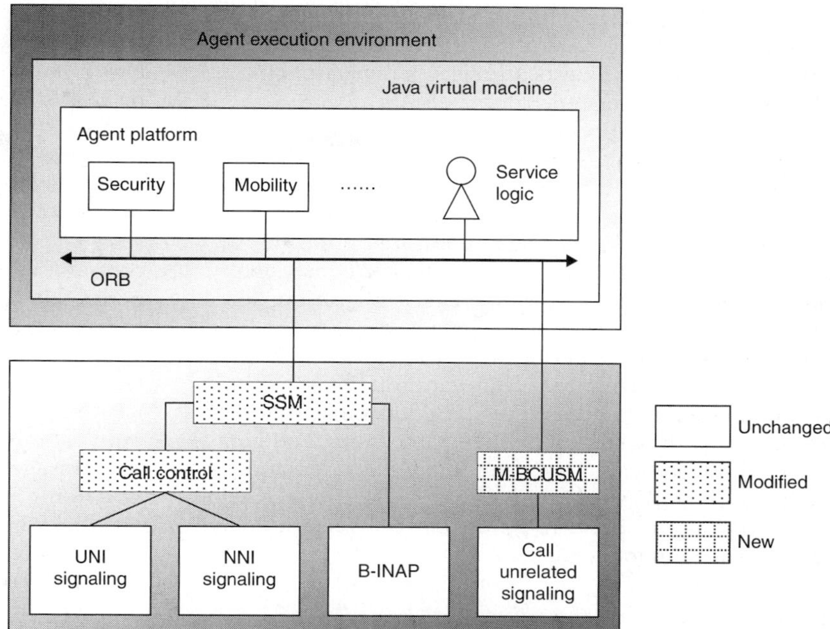

Figure 7: The MARINE B-SS&CP

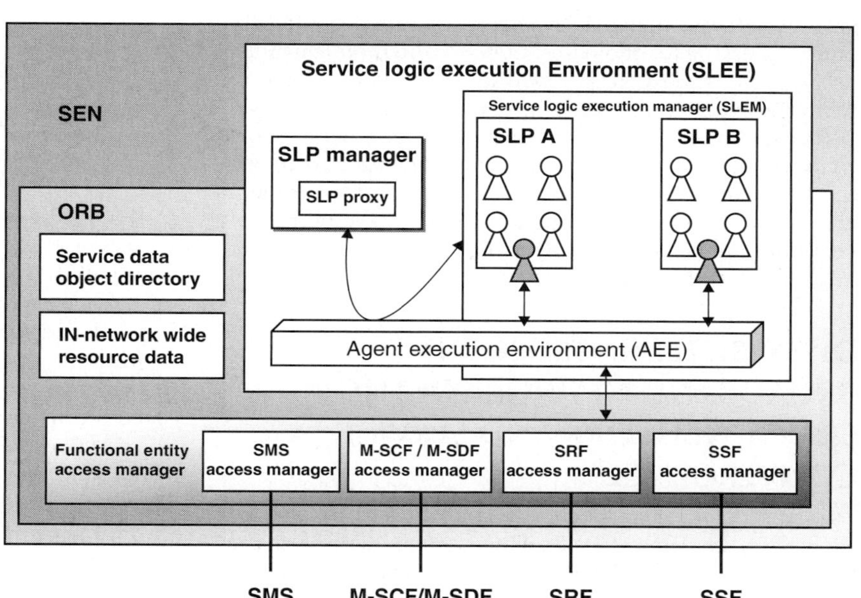

Figure 8: The MARINE service execution node

state machine (M-BCUSM) has been introduced that detects triggers and events related to mobility functions such as user registration.

The MARINE Service Execution Node

The service execution node (SEN) resulted from the integration of the B-SCP and the B-IP used in INSIGNIA and EXODUS projects–EXODUS (Francis et al. 1998) was a project focused on the transition from second-generation to third-generation mobile networks, and as such it performed research on the specification and implementation of IN functionalities that met third-generation requirements.

Like the B-SCCP, the MARINE SEN has been enhanced with both an AEE and a CORBA DPE. The SEN accommodates broadband IN functional entities (such as CCAF, B-SCF/SDF, B-SRF) as well as mobility-related functional entities (M-SCF/SDF). The SEN is shown in Figure 8, with the exception for the omission of the part that handles the communication with the subscriber's terminals.

The SEN establishes a switched connection with the terminal equipment (TE) in order to provide to the user the specialized resources required for the execution of a specific broadband service. The signaling communication between the SEN and the B-SS&CP is based on CORBA, specifically IIOP, or on the SS7 signaling stack for backward compatibility. In the latter case, a B-INAP-CORBA bridge is used. The MARINE SEN supports a B-INAP-based B-SSP, allowing the ability to work with broadband IN. Also the SEN communicates with the service management system (SMS) via IIOP in order to serve management requests and service deployment—i.e. the downloading of agents from the SMS.

The AEE in the SEN enables the local execution of the various mobile agents that are part of IN services. Depending on various criteria that can be satisfied during service execution, agents can migrate to B-SCCPs or to other SENs. These criteria are monitored either by the SMS or by the agents themselves, which consequently may decide to migrate. Usually, agent migration takes place because of perceived performance degradation. For example, an agent executing within a certain SEN may experience performance degradation when several B-SCCPs attempt to access the same service at the SEN concurrently, thus inducing a high processing and communication overhead. Migration to a less-loaded node is the recommended solution in this case. Agents can also migrate in case of connectivity loss or when user mobility has to be accommodated.

Beyond MAT

MARINE realized the concept of the distributed intelligent broadband network by means of two core distributed processing technologies, CORBA and mobile agents. As a result, almost every node in such an architecture (with the exception of terminals) was required to host an ORB as well as an agent execution environment. Especially the latter was something quite uncommon to telecom operators at that time. An answer to this problem was attempted by developing the service logic with conventional methods and using mobile agents only for the implementation of code mobility.

DISTRIBUTED INTELLIGENT BROADBAND NETWORK IN THE ERA OF NETWORK AND SERVICE CONVERGENCE

This approach taken by the IN concept and its various evolved forms (IBN, DIBN) seemed adequate up until the late 1990s, when the demand for a new service provisioning model re-emerged for the following reasons:

- Deregulation forced many operators to open up their networks to third-party service providers.
- The foreseen saturation of the voice communication market (especially in mobile telephony) reinstated value-added service provision as a necessity for sustained revenue growth.
- Technologies originating from the Internet became adopted by traditional networks and started to threaten long-established services (e.g., traditional voice calls) because of low cost and increased simplicity.

The most immediate threat to traditional telephony originated from the Voice over protocol (VoIP) technology. VoIP allows for the transport of packetized voice over the Internet's network layer. VoIP implements its own call state model in the equivalent of traditional switches, which are called "soft switches," since they are completely software-programmable. VoIP also incorporates signaling-like functionality by using dedicated application layer protocols. Recommendation H.323 (ITU-T 1998) and the session initiation protocol (SIP) (Schulzrinne and Rosenberg 2000) are two main frameworks regarding VoIP implementation and its interworking with PSTN. H.323 is a complex framework that specifies in detail a suite of protocols used for data, voice, audio, and video communication over IP. It also provides for specialized nodes, the gatekeepers, which map SS7 messages to the respective H.323 messages and vice versa. SIP, on the other hand, is an application-layer text-based protocol that is used only for session initiation, modification, and termination between two terminals. Again, when communication with the PSTN is required, a gateway is used for message translation. As of this writing, SIP seems to be gaining ground over H.323 because of SIP's increased simplicity in implementation.

This new reality called for a service provisioning framework that could satisfy the following requirements:

- Design and deployment of services that could be offered over multiple network technologies (fixed, mobile, wireless, etc.) with minimum modifications.
- Services should be offered either internally by the operator or externally by third-party providers without increased complexity in design and deployment.
- The time to market for these services should be minimized even further compared with IN.
- Services should be provided both via traditional networks as well as via the Internet with identical functionality.
- Services should be able to exploit both traditional networks as well as Internet resources during the same session.

Operators concluded that service provision would be simpler, cheaper, and faster if a high-level API could be offered to service providers that rendered the underlying network technologies transparent. Ideally, such an API would allow for one version of the service to be provided via any network or even across networks of different technologies. Such an API that stemmed from an international standardization effort is Parlay.

Introduction to Open Service Architecture/Parlay

The first activities regarding Parlay took place in 1998 by a group of companies including BT, Microsoft, Nortel, Siemens, and Ulticom, known as the Parlay Group. Their goal was to devise an API that would provide third parties with access to the network functions required for the creation and deployment of value-added services. Over the years, the Parlay Group has grown in popularity, and it currently has enlisted more than 10 full and more than 45 affiliate members.

Parlay (Parlay Group 2005) provides third parties with programming interfaces that are open, are language- and platform-independent, and include security provisions.

Thus, Parlay APIs can be supported on top of various middleware technologies, such as CORBA, DCOM, RMI, and simple object access protocol (SOAP). Parlay defines two roles in the process of service provision: the network operator and the application service provider (ASP). The network operator is typically perceived as deploying and operating the actual network infrastructure—e.g., switching and transmission equipment, access networks, etc. The ASP provides numerous networks with value-added services by gaining access to the network provider's resources via Parlay APIs. The services provided by the ASP are executed on respective application serers. The application servers become clients to one or more Parlay gateways, which reside at the network edge, offering service control functionality (SCF) to the client via the Parlay API. A high-level Parlay architecture is depicted in Figure 9.

In 2001, the Parlay standard was aligned with similar standards on OSA from the Third-Generation Partnership Project (3GPP) and became officially known as OSA/Parlay. The OSA/Parlay standard has currently reached version 5.0 and defines numerous APIs covering almost every aspect of mobile/fixed multimedia applications. The APIs that relate to call control and management, such as generic call control, multiparty call control, multimedia call control, and conference call control APIs are of particular importance for the provision of IN-like services.

The Role of Parlay in a Distributed Intelligent Network Architecture

Parlay in the context of the DIBN architecture was perceived as a solution for the provision of the so-called hybrid services—e.g., services originating from PSTN that require some sort of interaction with the Internet, or vice versa. A simple case of such a service is when a user would like to receive e-mails at his office about calls terminating at his home. This is not possible with any of the IN models presented so far; however, it can be achieved with Parlay. The following paragraphs describe this effort, which was undertaken in the context of the STARLITE research project.

The STARLITE Approach

The research effort undertaken within STARLITE (Chaniotakis et al. 2002) had the following goals:

- Retain the inherent flexibility of DIBN to move application code to various nodes in the network.
- Integrate the Parlay APIs with the DIBN concept.
- Exploit Parlay to realize service convergence between PSTN and the Internet by enabling the provision of "hybrid" services.

The STARLITE reference architecture is presented in Figure 10. It consists of the service creation environment (SCE), the service management system (SMS), the service switching and control points (SS&CP), and the Internet service node (ISN; not shown). The functionality of each entity is examined below.

Service Creation

Design, implementation, and testing of STARLITE service takes place via the SCE. Although the service provision models between PSTN and the Internet are significantly different, the SCE exploits the Parlay APIs in order to provide developers with a unified view of the network. The SCE consists of the SCE graphical user interface (SCE GUI) and the code generator.

The SCE GUI has been based on the rational rose (RR), which is a tool that allows the creation of system models that are based on the unified modeling language (UML). The RR's state diagram editor enables the initial description of services as finite state machines. The RR state diagram editor has been enhanced with several service independent building blocks (SIBs), which are represented within the GUI as shapes resembling specification and description language (SDL) constructs. The SIBs relate to the definition of methods that can be invoked from a service, to branching decisions as well as to the inclusion of Java code directly into an SLP. The SCE GUI produces a textual description of the service in XML, which is fed into the code generator.

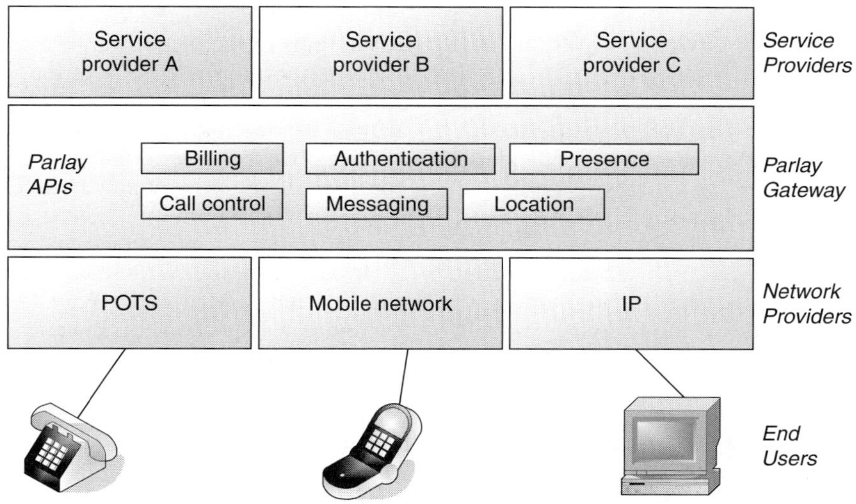

Figure 9: High-level PARLAY architecture (POTS = plain old telephone service)

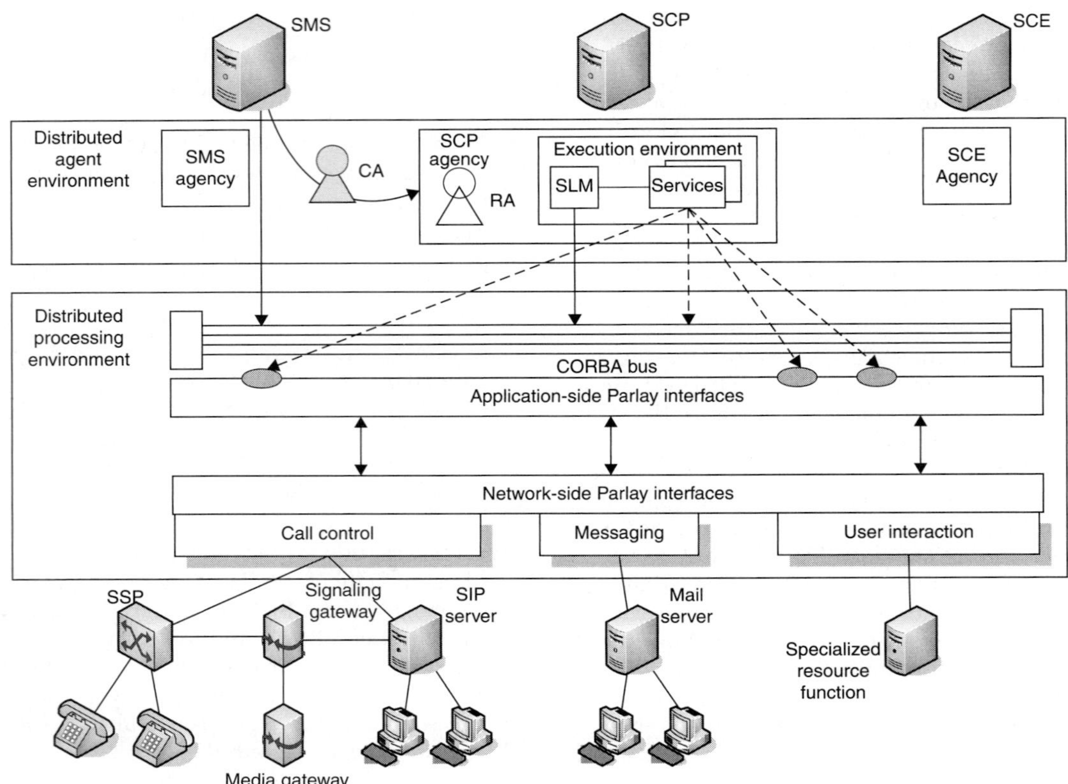

Figure 10: STARLITE reference architecture (CA = carrier agent; RA = receiver agent)

The code generator is a Java utility that makes use of the SLP's textual description to produce the final version of the service. The code generator provides its own GUI, which allows the developer to specify which service's textual description should be processed, as well as the triggering criteria for that service. These criteria are incorporated into the service code in the format of the appropriate Parlay data structure. Thus, the SCF components that are responsible for setting the triggers (detection points), can obtain this structure and arm the triggers via the invocation of the Parlay `enableCallNotification` method on the SSF. The output of the code generator is a Java application that can be compiled via a standard Java compiler.

Service Deployment

STARLITE inherits from DIBN the ability of an active service instance to migrate to the various network nodes. In contrast to MARINE, however, service logic is not implemented in the form of mobile agents, because this would have required mobile agents to implement Parlay interfaces. Instead, mobile agents are used for providing a carrier service for the uploading, transfer, and delivery of service instances to the various service control points.

Two types of agents are responsible for the implementation of code mobility, the carrier agents (CAs) and the receiver agents (RAs). The CA takes hold of a service instance via a common interface provided by the service base class. It is, however, totally unaware of the specific logic implemented by each service. Either the SCE or the SCP (in the case of migration) can trigger the SMS to deploy a CA instance. Upon triggering, the CA is informed about the address of the node hosting the SLP to be transported and the address of the node for which the SLP is destined.

Consequently, the CA transfers the SLP from the host to the destination node. Upon arrival at the destination node, the CA has no means of unloading the service, since it cannot obtain references to the local DPE components. Instead it communicates with the RA, which is a stationary agent, hosted in the destination node's local AEE, with references to the local DPE objects. Therefore, the RA obtains the service instance from the CA and passes it for execution to the node's components.

Consequently, the service binds to network resources via the service logic manager (SLM), which obtains the service's triggering criteria from the SLP and passes them to the network side managers in a structure compatible with Parlay specifications. This way, a service may receive events from the local SSP.

In addition, the STARLITE architecture incorporates the Internet service node (Papadakis et al. 2004) which serves as a front-end for Internet users wishing to use PSTN services and for phone users wishing to invoke Internet services.

One of the obvious advantages of using Parlay as an overlay to the DIBN architecture is the interoperability between Internet and PSTN-originating services. The same problem was tackled via SPIRITS, a similar approach that will be detailed in the following section.

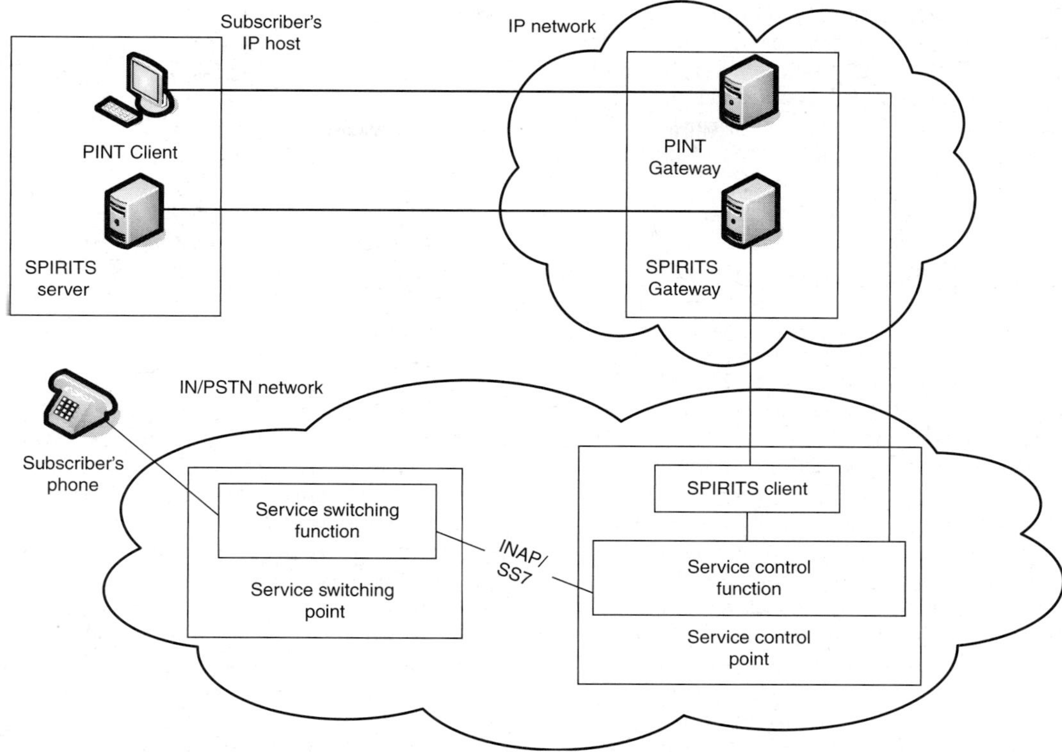

Figure 11: SPIRITS/PINT (PSTN and Internet networking) architecture

The Parlay/SPIRITS Approach

SPIRITS stands for "Service in the PSTN/IN Requesting Internet Service" (Faynberg et al. 2002). It supports services originating from the PSTN that require interactions between the PSTN and the Internet. In essence, SPIRITS allows SCPs to request the processing of IN services to be carried out on the IP network. The SCP is informed of the processing result and instructs the SSP accordingly on how to process the call.

The SPIRITS architecture consists of the SPIRITS client, the SPIRITS gateway, and the SPIRITS server. During an IN service invocation; the service request is transferred from the terminal to the SSF and from the SSF to the SCF. Consequently, the SCF forwards the request to the SPIRITS client, which in turn conveys the request to the gateway. The gateway converts the request to the SPIRIT protocol and forwards to the server, which performs the actual processing. The result is conveyed back to the SCF in the same fashion. Service invocations originating from the Internet are handled by the PINT framework (Petrack and Conroy 2000), which follows a philosophy similar to that of SPIRITS, including servers and gateways (Figure 11).

The Parlay/SPIRITS architecture proposed by Kozik, Unmehopa, and Vemuri (2003) replaces the SPIRITS server with a Parlay application server and turns the SPIRIT client into a Parlay-enabled node that can map INAP messages to Parlay-method invocations. Parlay parameters and methods are encoded in XML-based format and are transported as the payload of a SIP message from the SPIRITS client to the SPIRITS gateway. This way, developers can code SPIRITS applications using Parlay APIs, thus liberating themselves from the complexities of the underlying network. The SPIRITS/Parlay approach, although it lacks the advantages provided by the mobile code capabilities, is an alternative to STARLITE in terms of "hybrid" service provision.

Distributed Intelligent Network and Java

Parlay did not constitute the only effort toward the standardization of a high-level service-provision API. The wide adoption of Java as a programming language as well as an application development framework in conjunction with its developers' (Sun Microsystems) intention to promote it as a universal solution for both IT and Telecom gave birth to the Java API for integrated networks (JAIN).

JAIN (Tait, Keijzer, and Goedman 2000) defines a number of APIs for the provision of a wide range of value-added services over data, fixed, mobile, and wireless networks. As is the case with Parlay, JAIN promises service portability, network independency, open development, and telephony support. The JAIN service logic execution environment (JSLEE) constitutes the standard Java-based service platform. JSLEE exploits a set of JAIN APIs such as JSIP (Java SIP), JCC (Java call control), SAMS (server APIs for mobile systems), and mobile device management and monitoring (DM), creating a framework for service deployment over practically any network technology. These APIs are also known as resource adaptors 3 in JAIN terminology, since they interface the application logic with the underlying network resources.

JAIN can be viewed as a technology complimentary to OSA/Parlay. According to this perspective, the OSA/Parlay gateway is another JAIN resource adapter RA that interfaces the JSLEE with the IN architecture. There is also the contrary view0 that JAIN could possibly replace OSA/Parlay entirely as the framework of choice for open service provision.

Service Provision in Next-Generation Networks

In one of the first books on INAP-based Intelligent Networks, Jan Thörner (1994) included a section "The Term Intelligent Network will not be used beyond the 1990s." The reason given for this prediction was that by that time the IN concept would have become a commodity in commercial telecom networks. The author was correct in the sense that IN has indeed become a commodity, and therefore the term has ceased to become a buzzword when it comes to service provision. What could not have been predicted, however, was that widespread adoption of the Internet would initiate the process for the complete abolishment of IN as a service-provision architecture. Of course, IN represents a significant investment in networks today, and therefore it cannot be immediately replaced. But the time will come inevitably in the medium-term period.

The Internet architecture, in contrast to telephony, requires relatively simple routers and expects the intelligence required for service provision to be provided by hosts at the network edge. Developments in the past decade in all the layers of network technology (from physical up to the application) have initiated the gradual replacement of complex architectures in fixed and mobile networks by new-generation networking (NGN) architectures. There are several approaches to NGN by Open Mobile Alliance (OMA), 3GPP, W3C, the Parlay Group, and others. The common denominator in this transition is the existence of the Internet protocol (IP) as the prevalent protocol at the network layer for voice, data, and control information. Although few aspects of NGN have been currently standardized, future service-provision frameworks are expected to portray the following characteristics:

- Use of packet-based transfer mechanisms especially over IP
- Separated control functions for bearer resources, call/sessions, and services/applications
- Decoupling of service provisioning from specific network technologies via standardized APIs
- Decoupling of third-party service provision from specific operators via standardized APIs
- Service provision will be realized via distributed components
- Support for a wide range of services and information flows
- Support of user and terminal mobility
- Service-tailored QoS requirements
- Services will be context-aware and highly personalized
- New personalized services will be automatically composed out of existing services

Currently the Web services standard (W3C 2005) is gaining momentum as the enabling technology for distributed service provision in NGN. The Parlay Group has crafted a new set of specifications, termed Parlay-X, which realizes the Parlay functionality with the use of Web services. Moreover all major telecom equipment vendors have unveiled plans to work toward a new service layer architecture.

CONCLUSION

The IN concept has its own unique place in telecom history as the first attempt for a standardized service-provision framework in telephony. During the decades, it has successfully undergone several evolutionary cycles to comply with the requirements for broadband and distributed services. Distributed IN will continue to coexist with more modern service-provision frameworks until it will become obsolete as legacy architecture. In the meantime IN has managed to deliver the following very important lessons to the service engineering community:

- Control information, either as out-of-band signaling or in the form of a dedicated control protocol, can be exploited for service provision.
- Service provision should be cross-network, cross-platform, and dissociated from the underlying infrastructure.
- Service development is facilitated if service functionality can be grouped into high-level independent building blocks (SIBs) that can be distributed transparently across the network infrastructure.
- Code mobility can lead to increased performance and improve resource utilization in the network.

Unless a drastically different technology emerges, next-generation networks will surely be fully aligned with the above principles, which constitute the IN legacy to future service-provision frameworks.

GLOSSARY

Common Object Request Broker Architecture (CORBA): A standardized framework endorsed by the OMG (Object Management Group) that specifies the interaction between software objects in a distributed computing environment.

General Inter-Object Request Broker Protocol (GIOP): An abstract protocol for the communication of distributed objects in a CORBA architecture. GIOP can be mapped to various network layer protocols depending on the network technology used for connecting the distributed objects.

Intelligent Network (IN): An architecture, initially for the telephone network, in which the service logic for a call is located in a dedicated node outside the switch, allowing services to be added or modified independently of the switching equipment.

Intelligent Network Applications Part (INAP): The application layer protocol of the SS7 signaling stack. Used in the intelligent network architecture for the communication between service provisioning nodes.

Mobile Agent (MA): A piece of computer software that is able to move from host to host autonomously and continue its execution on the destination host.

Parlay: An open API for fixed and mobile voice and data networks.

Service Control Point (SCP): A resilient computer that enables operators to offer enhanced services by executing service logic programs that manipulate call connections and call-routing information. SCPs connect to signaling nodes called SSPs.

Service Switching Point (SSP): An enhanced switch that interoperates with SCPs for the provision of advanced services in an IN architecture.

Signaling System no. 7 (SS7): An international standardized suite of protocols that provide out-of-band signaling in the digital public switched network.

CROSS REFERENCES

See *Network Middleware*; *Web Services*; *Wireless Broadband Access*.

REFERENCES

AT&T, GMD FOKUS, IONA Technologies Plc, Nortel, Teltec DCU. 2001. *CORBA/TC interworking and SCCP inter-ORB protocol specification*. http://www.omg.org/docs/formal/01-01-01.pdf (accessed June 14, 2006).

Barr, W. J., T. Boyd and Y. Inoue. 1993. The TINA initiative. IEEE Communications Magazine. (3):70–631

Bäumer, C., and T. Magedanz. 1999. Grasshopper—A mobile agent platform for active telecommunication. *Proceedings of the Third International Workshop on Intelligent Agents for Telecommunication Applications*, 19-32. Heidelberg, Germany: Springer Verlag Lecture Notes in Computer Science, 1699.

Bradshaw, J. M. 1997. *Software agents*. Cambridge, MA: MIT Press.

Chaniotakis, E. S., A. E. Papadakis, N. D. Tselikas, G. A. Leoleis and I. S. Venieris, 2002. Parlay and mobile agents in a homogenized service provision architecture. *Proceedings of the European Conference on Universal Multiservice Networks (ECUMN02), Colmar, France, April 8-10, 2002*, 150-4. Los Alamitos, CA: IEEE.

Chess, D., C.G. Harrison, and A. Kershenbaum. 1998. *Mobile agents: Are they a good idea?* In *Mobile agents and security*, edited by G. Vigna, 25-47. Heidelberg, Germany: Springer Verlag Lecture Notes in Computer Science, 1419.

EURESCOM. 1997. *CORBA as an enabling factor for migration from IN to TINA: A EURESCOM-P508 perspective*. ftp://ftp.omg.org/pub/docs/telecom/97-01-01.pdf (accessed June 14, 2006).

Faglia, L., T. Magedanz, and A. Papadakis. 1999. Introduction of DOT/MAT into a broadband IN architecture for flexible service provision. *Proceedings of the 6th International Conference on Intelligence and Services in Networks*, 469-81. Heidelberg, Germany: Springer Verlag Lecture Notes in Computer Science, 1597.

Faynberg, I., J. Gato, H. Lu, and L. Slutsman. 2002. RFC 3298. Service in the public switched telephone network/intelligent network (PSTN/IN) requesting Internet service (SPIRITS) protocol requirements. www.rfc-archive.org/getrfc.php?rfc=3298 (accessed May 8, 2007).

Francis, J. C., D. V. Polymeros, G. L. Lyberopoulos, V. Vande Keere, A. Elberse, P. Rogl, and L. Vezzoli. 1998. Project EXODUS: Experimental mobile multimedia deployment in ATM networks. *Mobile Networks and Applications*, (1, Special Issue: Mobile Multimedia Communications):61-72.

Herzog, U., and T. Magedanz. 1997. From IN toward TINA–potential migration Steps. *Proceedings of the 4th International Conference on Intelligence in Services and Networks (IS&N), Como, Italy*, Heidelberg, Germany: Springer Verlag.

Isaacs, R., and R. Mortier. 1999. INCA: Support for IN using the Tempest. Globecom '99, 5-9 December 1999, Rio de Janeiro, Brazil, 812-6. Los Alamitos, CA: IEEE.

ISO/IEC 10746-2 1996. Open distributed processing—reference model: foundations.

ITU-T. 1993. Q.1204. Intelligent network distributed functional plane architecture.

ITU-T. 1993. Q.1205. Intelligent network physical plane architecture.

ITU-T. 1997. Q.1202. Intelligent network—Service plane architecture.

ITU-T. 1997. Q.1203. Intelligent network—Global functional plane architecture.

ITU-T. 1998. Recommendation H.323. Packet-Based Multimedia Communications Systems.

Kozik, J., M. R. Unmehopa, and K. V. Vemuri. 2003. A Parlay and SPIRITS-based architecture for service mediation. *Bell Labs Technical Journal* (4):105-22.

Listanti, M., and S. Salsano. 1998. IBIS: A testbed for the evolution of intelligent broadband networks toward TINA. *IEEE Communications Magazine* (3):78-86.

Magedanz, T. 1999. Tutorial: IN evolution—impact of Internet, CORBA, TINA, and mobile agent technologies. *Proceedings of the TINA '99 Conference, Hawaii*. http://www.tinac.com/conference/tina99/tutorial_p.pdf (accessed December 30, 2005).

Magedanz, T., and R. Popescu-Zeletin. 1996. *Intelligent networks—basic technology, standards and evolution*. London: International Thomson Computer Press.

Object Management Group. 2005. *CORBA basics*. http://www.omg.org/gettingstarted/corbafaq.htm (accessed June 14, 2006).

OMG 1996. *RFI on Issues for Intelligent Networking with CORBA*. Available at: ftp://ftp.omg.org/pub/docs/telecom/96-12-02.pdf (accessed June 14, 2006).

OMG 1997. *RFP on Interworking between CORBA and IN Systems*. Available at: ftp://ftp.omg.org/pub/docs/telecom/97-12-06.pdf (accessed June 14, 2006).

Papadakis, A. E., E .S. Chaniotakis, P. E. Giannakakis, N. D. Tselikas, and I. S. Venieris, 2004. Parlay-based service provision in circuit- and packet-switched telecommunications networks. *International Journal of Communication Systems* 17(1):63-83.

Parlay Group. 2005. Parlay Group home page. http://www.parlay.org (accessed June 14, 2006).

Petrack, S., and L. Conroy. 2000. RFC 2848. The PINT service protocol: Extensions to SIP and SDP for IP access to telephone call services. www.faqs.org/rfcs/rfc2848.html (accessed May 8, 2007).

Prezerakos, G. N., C. D. Anagnostakis, and I.S. Venieris. 1999. Stepwise creation of multimedia services for broadband intelligent networks. *Multimedia Tools and Applications* (3):251-75.

Prezerakos, G. N., S. Salsano, A.W. van der Vekens, and F. Zizza. 1998. INSIGNIA: A pan-European trial for the intelligent broadband network architecture. IEEE Communications Magazine (6):68-76.

Raatikainen, K. 1999. *Presentation: Agent technology in telecommunications*. http://www.cs.helsinki.fi/u/kraatika/Opetus/AT99S/99-10-04b.pdf (accessed June 14, 2006).

Schulzrinne, H. H., and J. Rosenberg. 2000. The SIP: Internet-centric signaling. *IEEE Communication Magazine* (10):134-41.

Steffen, B., and T. Margaria. 1999. *MetaFrame in practice: Design of intelligent network services. Correct system design, recent insight and advances,* 390-415. Springer Verlag Lecture Notes in Computer Science.

Tait, D., J.D. Keijzer, and R. Goedman. 2000. JAIN: A new approach to services in communication networks. *IEEE Communications Magazine* (1):94-9.

Thörner, J. 1994. *Intelligent Networks*. Boston: Artech House.

Venieris, I. S., and H. Hussmann, 1998. *Intelligent broadband networks*. New York: Wiley.

Venieris, I.S., F. Zizza, and T. Magedanz, 2000. Object oriented software technologies in telecommunications. New York: Wiley.

W3C. 2005. Web services activity. (accessed June 14, 2006).

Zave, P. 1993. Feature interactions and formal specifications in telecommunications. *IEEE Computer* (8):20-9.

Smart Cards: Communication Protocols and Applications

Michael Tunstall, *University College Cork, Ireland*
Konstantinos Markantonakis, *Royal Holloway, University of London, UK*
Damien Sauveron, *University of Limoges, France*
Keith Mayes, *Royal Holloway, University of London, UK*

INTRODUCTION

The sheer convenience of smart cards has contributed to their becoming more and more prevalent in a number of sectors today. We use them to withdraw money, to make telephone calls, to access buildings, to pay for goods, and to authenticate ourselves to a computer.

The Arrival of Smart Cards

Banking needs were the main driving force behind the introduction of the smart card's ancestor, the credit card (Rankl and Effing 2002). The main objective was to protect payment systems against fraud. The first credit cards were quite simple, and only included information such as the card's issuer and the cardholder's name, and the card number was printed or embossed on the card. These systems relied on a visual verification for security (security printing and signature field, for example), and as a consequence, the security of the system relied mainly on the traders that accepted the card. Because of the payment cards, increasing popularity, it became evident that this was not enough to prevent the system from being defrauded. The first improvement appeared with the addition of a magnetic stripe on the back of the card. This allowed data storage in a machine-readable form, making it easier to process transactions. The identification of a cardholder was achieved either via a signature or a PIN (personal identification number). Even though magnetic stripe cards are still commonly used worldwide, they suffer from a crucial weakness: data stored on them can be read, deleted, copied, and replaced easily with appropriate equipment. One solution would be to allow payment only when transactions can be validated online, but this is not always possible because of the high cost of the necessary infrastructure and the low speed of such transactions.

Patents were filed in several different countries at the end of the 1960 and the beginning of the 1970s on the idea of using plastic cards to carry microchips (Jürgen Dethloff and Helmut Grötrupp in Germany, and Roland Moreno in France). In 1974, the first prototype appeared, which functioned as a memory card. Two years later, the first microprocessor card based on a Motorola chip was developed. However, many new problems had to be solved before manufacturing in large quantities with acceptable quality and prices enabled the smart card to become a viable product.

The French telecommunications industry saw this new technology as an opportunity to reduce fraud and vandalism in coin-based phone booths. In 1980, the French General Direction of Telecommunication replaced all French phone booths with new ones equipped with a smart card reader. To make a telephone call a "telecarte" was required. It was initially credited with a fixed number of units that were reduced depending on the cost of each call made.

The telecarte's success convinced banking organizations that the smart card could be used in payment systems. In 1985, French banks agreed on a common payment system based on smart cards, resulting in the "Carte Bleu." The idea has since spread all around the world and was adopted by Europay, MasterCard, and Visa International in 1994.

Smart cards have also been used in health care, transport, pay TV, access control, electronic purse, and identity applications, and the number of different uses is always increasing.

More recent developments have introduced different types of embedded tokens that are based on the same technology as smart cards. Some examples of these are: RFID (ratio frequency identification) tags that are intended to act as a bar codes for commercial goods, and USB (universal serial bus) tokens (sometimes referred to as a "dongle") based on a secure microcontroller. The protocols will be discussed in terms of smart cards, as this is the predominant type of secure embedded token.

The Different Types of Smart Card

Since their first appearance smart cards have been compared with personal computers. In fact, the more complicated smart cards have a central processing unit (CPU), an operating system, and different types of memory, exactly like a computer. To satisfy the different requirements of the various applications, a number of different types of smart cards are in common use.

Memory-only cards: Memory cards consist of memory that can be written to once. These are mainly used to decrement units previously stored in memory—e.g. prepaid phone cards.

Memory cards with logic: Data stored in this type of card are protected with some hardwired logic. Such cards can be reloaded with updated values, since they include a high counting capacity, and are commonly used for public telephony. The logic present in the smart card can have an embedded cryptographic algorithm with a state machine to control it.

Microprocessor cards: In this case a microprocessor is embedded into the card to manage and compute data. Such cards contain a dedicated program, often referred to as an operating system (OS), in the read only memory (ROM), which manages other memory areas, such as the random access memory (RAM) and non-volatile memory, or the EEPROM (electrically erasable programmable read only memory), where personalization data is usually stored. The amount of ROM and EEPROM is very small and is usually expressed in kilobytes. The amount of memory available in smart cards is increasing all the time as advances in technology allow more transistors to be included in the same surface area. Some chip manufacturers also propose different types of memories, such as external RAM and Flash, granting extra data storage areas.

Contactless smart cards: Such cards can be either based on a microcontroller or a memory chip. Communication is performed via an antenna glued inside the card's plastic body, rather than directly via metal contacts. The different types of contactless smart card use various different radio frequencies and protocols, depending on the requirements of the application. For example, some frequencies require a card to be within 10 cm and others allow a card to be a few meters from a reader. Contactless cards are usually used in applications that require a high flow and low reader maintenance—e.g. transport or identification applications.

Dual interface cards: These cards are able to communicate both in contact and contactless modes. Two types of product are available:

1. Cards with two chips—one being a normal smart card chip and communicating via the normal contacts and the second a contactless chip with its own specific communication interface. These chips are independent and are used for different applications.
2. Cards with one chip that have both interfaces integrated on the silicon, although the interfaces may be separated logically within the chip.

Dual interface cards are generally designed to support more than one application—e.g. access-control cards with transport ticketing or e-purse.

Tamper Resistance

One of the most important features of a smart card is its tamper resistance. This means that the secrets stored within the smart card—e.g. cryptographic/authentication keys—are protected from unauthorized access. There are various attack methods that can be used on smart cards, and other embedded devices, to attempt to access secret information. Some of these methods are described below.

Hardware Attacks

The chip used in a smart card can be removed from its packaging to allow access to the surface of the chip using hot, fuming nitric acid to remove the resin around the chip to be able to directly access the chip. The information held on the chip can then potentially be accessed by directly reading the values held in the chips, memory. In practice, this is only ever possible on the ROM values, and current countermeasures (both the technology used and the scrambling of the data addresses) render this method of attack nearly impossible. Other possible methods of attack include disabling chip features, such as a random number generator, or attempting to reverse-engineer proprietary parts of a chip. Some examples of this type of attack are described in Anderson and Kuhn (1996).

Side Channel Analysis

As the protocols and cryptographic algorithms that are generally implemented in smart cards have been subjected to peer review and rigorous mathematical analysis, other methods have been sought to extract key information. The first example of this was the use of the time taken to execute certain public key algorithms (Kocher 1996).

This was followed by a method of deriving key information by performing a statistical analysis of the power consumption during the execution of an algorithm, called differential power analysis (DPA) (Kocher, Jaffe, and Jun 1999), by exploiting the small variations in power consumption (shown in Figure 1). The different levels of power consumption correspond to different values of the

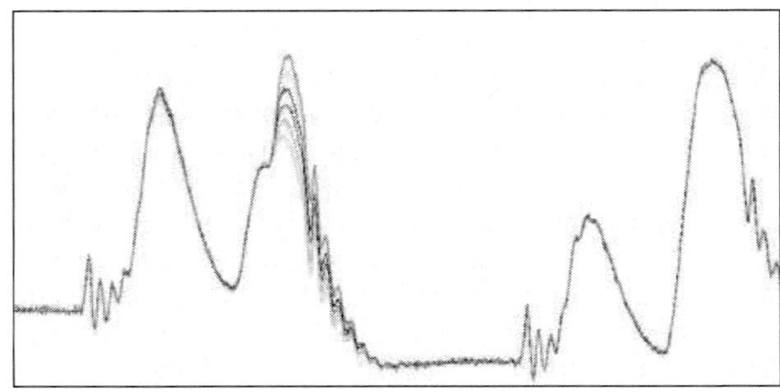

Figure 1: Overlaid acquisitions of the current consumption produced by the same instruction but with varying data

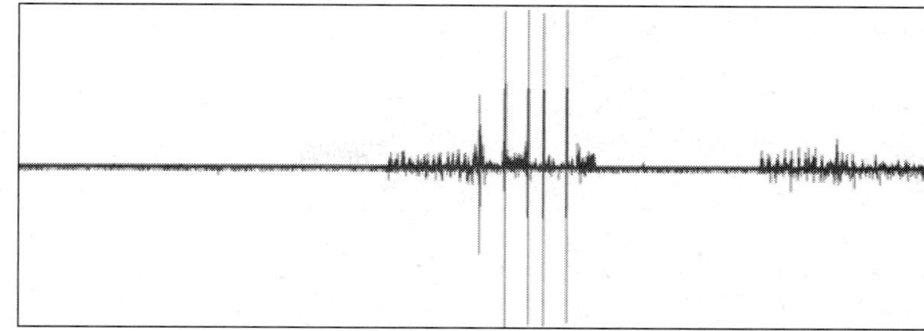

Figure 2: An example DPA trace showing the data dependence of the current consumption over time

Hamming weight of the data being manipulated by the chip under observation.

To attack a cryptographic algorithm, hypotheses can be made on portions of the secret key and the values of individual bits are predicted for a series of acquisitions. If a bit is correctly guessed for every acquisition, this can be made visible by using a statistical treatment on the acquisitions acquired. Figure 2 shows the DPA trace produced by correctly predicting the behavior of 1 bit of the output of the first S-box used in the DES algorithm (data encryption standard; Federal Information Processing Standards FIPS 46-3). The first peak corresponds to the output of the S-box; the four subsequent peaks correspond to the manipulation of the same bit during the P-permutation (a bitwise permutation used just after the S-boxes). An excellent tutorial on DPA can be found in Aigner and Oswald (2006).

Another example of a side channel attack is simple power analysis (SPA), which observes one trace or several to try to derive information by direct observation of the power consumption. The most well known example of this is against RSA (Rivest, Shamir, and Adleman 1978). If RSA is implemented using the square-and-multiply algorithm (Menezes, van Oorschot, and Vanstone, 1997) it may be possible to distinguish between the two functions that make up the algorithm, and therefore derive information on the key used. Examples of this are given in Joye and Olivier (2005).

Equivalent attacks can also be derived by observing the electromagnetic emanations generated by a chip while it is computing a cryptographic algorithm (Gandolfi, Mourtel, and Olivier 2001). Small probes can be used to acquire the electromagnetic emanations from a portion of a chip, allowing different results to be obtained.

Fault Attacks

Fault attacks are based on injecting a fault during the execution of a process in such a way that an attacker can derive information because of the effect of the fault. The first example of this type of attack was proposed against RSA when it is implemented using the Chinese remainder theorem (CRT) (DeMillo, Boneh, and Lipton 1997). The calculation of RSA using CRT involves calculating two modular exponentiations, and combining the results. This is a common optimization because it allows the calculation to take place about four times faster than directly calculating the modular exponentiation necessary for RSA. If a fault is injected in either of the exponentiations one of the primes used in RSA can be calculated by the computation of a GCD (greatest common denominator). A report of an implementation of this attack and some countermeasures are presented in Aumüller et al. (2002).

This was followed by fault attacks in secret key algorithms, where faults in DES can be treated in the same way that a differential cryptanalysis would be conducted (Biham and Shamir 1997). An implementation of this is discussed in Giraud and Thiebeauld (2004) and this principle has since been applied to other algorithms such as AES (Advanced Encryption Standard, FIPS 197), in which several different attacks have been proposed (Blömer and Seifert 2003; Giraud 2004).

Software Attacks

Initially, the embedded software on smart cards could not be modified (i.e., it did not allow code to be installed post-issuance). The potential for an attacker to mount a software attack was therefore limited. The attacks at the time were to try all the possible parameters for a service—i.e. to attempt all the possible valid application protocol data units (APDUs) for a given card. The aim was to try to find bugs, undocumented commands, or back doors that would allow an attack to be mounted. However, these kinds of attacks are quite inefficient because it is easy to remove the commands from an operating system (OS), and the number of possible commands is large. With modern smart cards it is possible to load software onto the smart card, in the form of applets, which has allowed for more aggressive software attacks. These are discussed in later sections of this chapter.

Countermeasures

There are numerous countermeasures that are used in embedded code to protect against the attacks outlined in this section. These vary from masking data to prevent the power consumption being visibly dependent with the values calculated (Chari et al. 1999), data randomization (Joye and Olivier 2005) to desynchronization techniques (Clavier, Coron, and Dabbous 2000). The design of new attacks and countermeasures for embedded devices is an area of vigorous research.

COMMUNICATION PROTOCOLS

There are various different communication protocols for the different types of smart card. This depends on the physical method used to communicate and the complexity of the device. All values given in this section are given in hexadecimal.

Smart Card Protocols

A smart card has five contacts that it uses to communicate with the outside world, defined in the ISO/IEC 7816-2 (International Organization for Standardization 1999). Two of these are taken by the power supply (usually 3 or 5 volts), referred to as Vcc, and the ground used to power the chip. Another contact is used to supply a clock, which is allowed to vary between 1 and 5 MHz but is usually set to 3.57 MHz. The remaining two contacts are used to communicate with the card. A sixth contact was originally used to provide a higher voltage to program the EEPROM (referred to as Vpp). This contact is no longer used, as this presented security problems if a smart card was unable change the values held in EEPROM (e.g., to decrement PIN counters). The layout of these contacts is shown in Figure 3.

One of the contacts used for communication is used to send commands to the chip in a smart card called the I/O. The protocols used to communicate with a smart cards are referred to as T = 0 and T = 1 and are defined in the ISO/IEC 7816-3 standard (International Organization for Standardization 1997). This section will describe both protocols, as they are nearly identical. The extra requirements of T = 1 are detailed where relevant.

The remaining contact is used to reset the smart card (there are two additional contacts defined in the ISO/IEC 7816-3 standard, but they are not currently used). This is a physical event (i.e., moving the voltage applied to this contact from 0 to 1) that will always provoke a response from the smart card and can occur at any time. The smart card will respond by sending an answer to reset (ATR) to the I/O contact, which is a string of bytes that defines the protocols the smart card can use, the speeds at which the smart card can communicate and the order in which bits are going to be sent during the session (i.e., most or least significant bit first). The smart card can also return up to fifteen historical bytes that have no impact on the protocol, but can be used to identify and distinguish one product from another. In the case of the T = 1 protocol, this is followed by a checksum on 1 byte that can be used to verify the integrity of the ATR. At this point the reader can change the protocol being used, within the bounds defined in the ATR, by sending a protocol type selection (PTS) to negotiate the parameters of the communication.

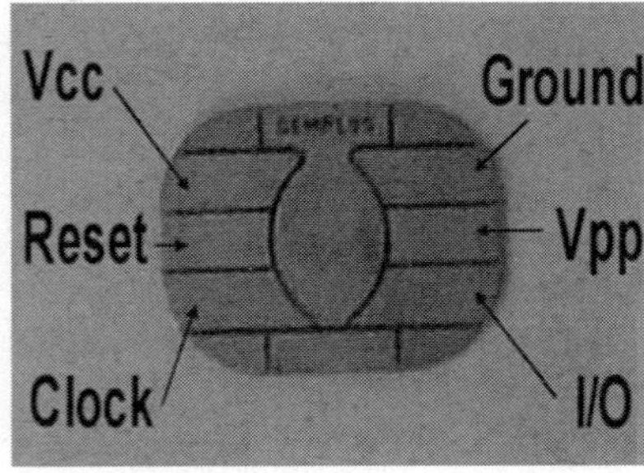

Figure 3: The six different smart card contacts, only five of which are currently used (I/O = input/output)

Each byte sent to or from the smart card is comprised of up to ten events on the I/O line—i.e. up to ten movements from 0 to 1 volts or vice versa, as shown in Figure 4. The voltage applied to the I/O line is set to 3 or 5 volts by the smart card reader before the reset is applied, so that either the card or the reader can pull this down to zero by connecting it to ground. The process starts by either the card or the reader pulling the line to zero for one elementary time unit (ETU—a length of time defined in the ATR that by default is 372 clock cycles). The byte is then sent over the I/O, where each bit is present for 1 ETU; whether the least or most significant bit is sent first is dictated by the ATR. This is followed by a parity bit that can be used to check the integrity of the byte sent. This is followed by at least 2 ETUs with no event on the I/O before the next byte can be sent. If the receiving party sends a signal of 1 or 2 ETUs on the line during the 2 end ETUs, this means that the byte was not correctly received. The misunderstood byte can then be resent.

The T = 0 and T = 1 protocols are half-duplex protocols, which means that data can flow in only one direction at a time. The reader initiates all the commands, and the smart card can only follow the instructions that it is sent. Each command consists of 5 bytes as shown in Table 1.

Each command sent by the reader will provoke a minimum of a 2-byte response from the smart card within a certain time, called the "status word". If the command has executed correctly, the status word will be 90 00, otherwise a value signifying an error is sent as defined in the ISO/IEC 7816-3 standard. If a smart card requires more time to process the command that it has been sent, it sends the value 60 on the I/O, known as a time request, that informs the reader that more time is required before the command can be terminated.

If data need to be sent to or from the smart card before the status word is sent, this is preceded by the procedure byte. This is a byte sent by the smart card to the reader that is equal to the INS byte of the command that signals to the reader that the smart card is ready to send

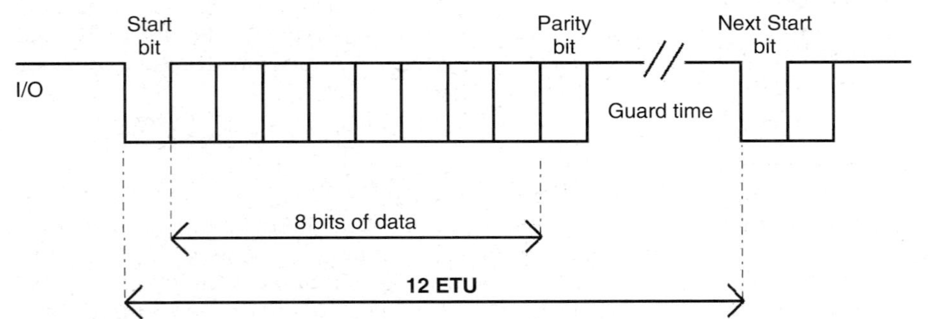

Figure 4: The signals needed to send a byte on the I/O, where the voltage can take the value applied to the Vcc or 0

Table 1: The Elements of an APDU Smart Card Command

Byte	Description
CLA	The first byte is the class of the command and defines the application. For example, the Global System for Mobile Communications (GSM) smart card application will always start with the CLA = A0.
INS	The second byte dictates the instruction being sent.
P1	A parameter byte that can be used to pass parameters for the command.
P2	A second byte that can be used to pass parameters.
P3	The last byte of the command is the number of bytes of data that will be sent or received by the smart card. The direction of the data is determined by the instruction that has been chosen. An alternative can be used in which 2 bytes are used for the length value to allow more data to be transferred.

or receive data. The data are then sent, and the card terminates the command with the status word. This is termed a transport protocol data unit (TPDU), and with the T = 1 protocol this process is followed by a checksum byte used for integrity purposes.

In general, a high-level approach is taken, and a user will use an APDU. This allows a user to assume that data can be sent and received from the smart card in one command. The bytes that can be sent to or from the smart card are summarized in Figure 5. The value for P3 is replaced with Lc (the number of inbound bytes) and Le (the number of outgoing bytes).

This means that it is possible for a user to request incoming and outgoing data in the same command. This

Reader command data:

CLA	INS	P1	P2	Lc	Inbound data	Le

Outgoing data sent by smart card:

Outgoing data	Status word

Figure 5: The structure of an APDU as defined in the ISO/IEC 7816-3 standard

is resolved at the TPDU level by breaking the APDU into two TPDUs. The first TPDU is a command that has data being sent from the reader to the smart card; the smart card then returns a status in which the first byte is equal to 65 (or 9F in the case of GSM cards) and the second byte is the amount of data waiting to be sent. This is followed by a get response (a specific TPDU in which the INS byte is set to C0) command that allows the data to be sent from the smart card to the reader.

Contactless Protocols

In a contactless device, a chip is embedded in a smart card or other device that contains an aerial that is used to communicate with a suitable reader. There is, therefore, only one path of communication between the chip and the outside world rather than one per contact. This aerial also needs to provide the clock and power supply to the embedded chip and enable the embedded chip to communicate with a suitable reader. A reader achieves this by emitting a varying electromagnetic field (a sine wave, referred to as a "carrier wave") that induces a current in the aerial of the smart card, which is used to power the chip and provide a clock. The communication relies on changing the modulation of the carrier wave used to power and clock the embedded chip. There are two types of contactless smart card, which are used for different purposes because of the different electrical properties of the cards. These are referred to as "proximity cards" and "vicinity cards".

Proximity Cards

The majority of contactless smart cards are proximity cards, which follow the ISO/IEC 14443 standard (International Organization for Standardization 2000). The signal used to communicate with the proximity card has a frequency of 13.56 MHz and a range of approximately 10 cm, and there can be numerous different smart cards within this range.

There are two types of card that can be used with this protocol, which are described as type A and type B. This determines the representation of data in the signal (i.e., the modulation) and the initialization method. The protocol for communicating with type A cards will be used as an example in this section. In contact protocols (see above) bits are sent across the I/O by changing the voltage from 0 to 1 or vice versa, but this is not possible with contactless cards. Instead the carrier wave emitted by the wave is modulated, as shown in Figure 6, although this does not represent a zero. Each bit is represented by the carrier wave being unmodulated and modulated for

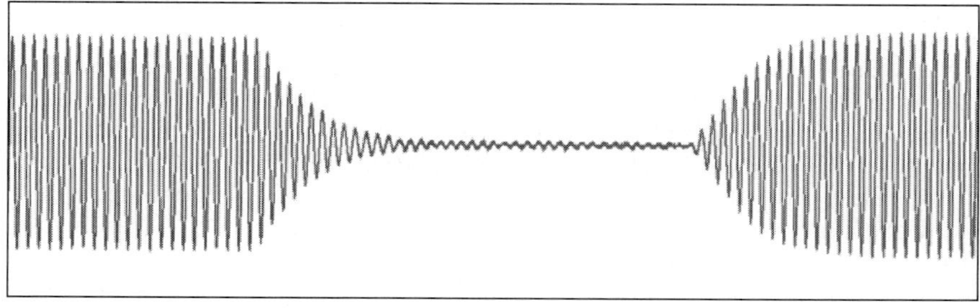

Figure 6: The change in the modulation of the carrier wave used to communicate with contactless smart cards

equal periods of time, where the order dictates whether a 0 or 1 is being sent. This is used to detect collisions when several cards are trying to communicate at the same time.

Because the reader does not know how many devices are present with the field, it needs to identify each device. This is achieved by emitting a request (REQA) that will be received by all devices in the reader's field. Each device will respond synchronously with an answer to request (ATQA) that will include 32 bits that uniquely identify each device. If two cards are trying to send different values, this can be detected, as, for a given bit, the modulation will last for the length of a whole bit rather than half a bit. The reader can deal with this by applying a mask to the number used to identify each smart card—e.g. it can ask that only cards whose most significant bit is equal to 1 to respond. This can be continued bit by bit to uniquely identify one of the smart cards present. The reader will then select this smart card (a SELECT command) and send a command to halt the smart card (a DESELECT command), which tells it to ignore all further REQA commands unless reselected or removed from the field and replaced. This process is then repeated for the remaining smart cards. Once all the smart cards have been identified one smart card can be selected for further communication.

This process of identifying all the cards present within a reader's field is universal for all cards of the correct type. After this, a smart card will either respond to a proprietary protocol or a protocol referred to as T = CL. Once a card has been selected, it is sent a request for answer to select (RATS) and responds with an answer to select (ATS). The ATS serves the same purpose as the ATR described in the previous section, and defines the parameters of the protocols that are supported by the device. This can be modified by a protocol and parameter selection (PPS) that is equivalent to the PTS used in T = 0 and T = 1. After this, the reader and the device can exchange information in a transparent manner with a small header and footer. After the reader and the device have finished exchanging information the session is ended with a DESELECT command.

There are three predominant types of proximity card, as described below:

Radio Frequency IDentification (RFID)—An RFID tag or transponder is an extremely small chip attached to an antenna. Unlike contactless smart cards the antenna is not set in a rigid plastic body, but is in a flexible sheet that can be stuck to any object. This tag responds to a contactless reader with an ID number than can be used to identify the object it is attached to. These data may also include other information, such as location information, product price, and date of purchase, etc.

Memory Cards—This is the most common type of contactless card, as most systems that use contactless cards do not require a large amount of processing power. One of the most common implementations of a proximity card is a MIFARE smart card (MIFARE 2006). These cards follow the anti-collision protocol defined above, but do not implement T = CL. The reader accesses areas of the chips, memory in either user or supervisor mode (with different rights to update or read different areas) using a proprietary protocol. All communication between the reader and the MIFARE card is enciphered using a proprietary algorithm owned by Philips. These cards are often used in transport systems because of the low cost per card; some examples include the Octopus card in Hong Kong (Octopus 2006) and the Oyster card in London (Oyster 2006).

Microcontroller Cards—If a microcontroller is present in the device, the T = CL is usually used as a wrapper to transport information. In the case of contactless smart card, the T = 0 or T = 1 protocol can be implemented within the payload of the T = CL protocol. In this case the ATS replaces the ATR required by the T = 0 and T = 1 protocols.

Vicinity Cards

Another type of contactless device is known as a vicinity card, and is defined in ISO/IEC 15693 (International Organization for Standardization 2000). The difference between these and proximity cards is that the reader has a range of 1 to 1.5 m. These use a protocol similar to that of proximity cards, with anticollision and transmission routines, based on modulating the fluctuating electromagnetic field. These are a common alternative for RFID tags, as they allow for lots of tags to be evaluated without having to move each tag. Another example of the use of vicinity cards is access control—e.g. SKIDATA (SKIDATA 2006).

INTERFACING WITH SMART CARD APPLICATIONS

A user does not have to implement the protocols described in the previous section. Platforms have been developed that help a user by acting as intermediaries between an application and a terminal. Two examples of interoperable smart card terminal specifications are the OpenCard Framework (OCF) (OpenCard Workgroup 2005) and the Personal Computer Smart Card (PC/SC) (PC/SC Workgroup 2005). These proposals have reached a relatively mature state, but the market has not yet converged on a single proposal. Moreover, a new standard enabling access to smart cards on embedded devices, called JSR177, has appeared. In the following sections, an overview of these standards will be presented.

Personal Computer Smart Card (PC/SC) Specification

The PC/SC working group (PC/SC Workgroup) was formed in 1996 by a number of smart card companies in order to enhance the adoption of smart card technology. The main aim of the PC/SC group was the long-term improvement of interoperability between smart cards and terminals, along with the smooth integration of terminals into PCs running the Windows operating system. The first documents became public in December 1996 and are formally known as "Interoperability Specifications for Integrated Circuit Cards (ICCs) and Personal Computers." As a group these documents are referred to as PC/SC and are decomposed into ten parts (see Figure 7).

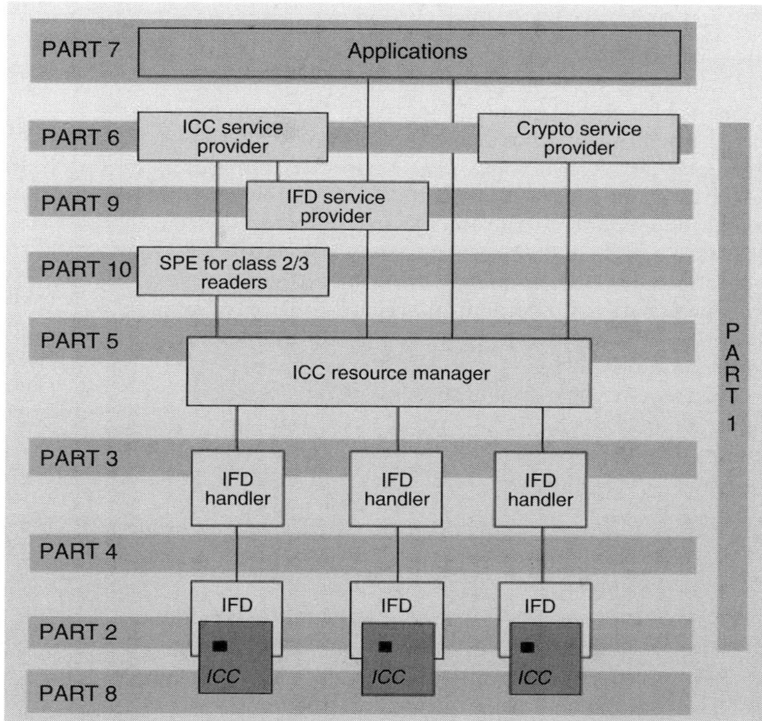

Figure 7: The PC/SC architecture Courtesy of PC/SC Workgroup, http://www.pcscworkgroup.com/specifications/overview.php)

Part 1 provides a general introduction and an overview of the overall PC/SC architecture. Part 2 provides characteristics and interoperability requirements for compatible smart cards (defined as integrated circuit cards [ICCs]) and smart card readers (defined as Interface Devices [IFDs]). For example, it describes the low-level characteristics of the smart card and reader in terms of the lower transport protocol and error-handling procedures. Part 3 describes the interface to, and required functionality for, compliant IFD devices. These components enable the higher layers (e.g., the Resource Manager) of PC/SC to communicate with smart card readers in a completely independent and transparent way. Part 4 provides other low-level design considerations—e.g. protocols for communicating with PS/2 keyboards with integrated smart card readers.

The main component of the PC/SC architecture is the Resource Manager (described in part 5). This is the most important component in the architecture and mediates access to the smart card and reader. In general, it is responsible for "ICC and IFD resources, controls shared access to these devices, and supports transaction management primitives."

Part 6 describes the service (e.g., ICC and Crypto) service provider models. The ICC service provider model offers all the necessary classes and context that will enable communication with a specific smart card. The optional Crypto service provider defines the necessary cryptographic functions that may be needed for accessing a smart card. Parts 7 and 8 contain advice on how to use the interface provided by the resource manager and how to handle information security operations (e.g., identification and secure storage) in a smart card solution. Parts 9 and 10 are considered recent additions to the overall PC/SC specification and contain information regarding the management of smart card readers with keypads that can be used for PIN entry and secure PIN entry, respectively.

Implementations

Microsoft was the first member of the workgroup to develop an implementation of the PC/SC specifications for its operating systems. Initially, this was an external program that fulfilled the role of resource manager, described above, and a high level library, called the "SCard Application Programming Interface" (API). Now the resource manager is an integral part of all Microsoft's operating systems (even Windows Mobile).

In the year 2000, David Corcoran and his colleagues initiated an open source project called "pcsc-lite" to provide better support for smart cards for the Unix-style operating system. The goal was to provide an implementation of PC/SC, and their efforts are gathered within MUSCLE (Movement for the Uses of Smart Card in A Linux Environment (MUSCLE)). In order to make transferring applications from Microsoft's operating systems as easy as possible, the interface used for the SCard API was adopted. Today, "pcsc-lite" functions on a great number of platforms: Linux, Solaris, Mac OS X, BSD, HP-UX, etc.

Wrappers

In order to enable the programming of applications communicating with the resource manager in languages other than C++, wrappers have been developed that allow PC/SC functions to be called from other programming languages. These wrappers use the FFI (Foreign Function Interfaces 2004) mechanisms of these various languages. These wrappers currently exist for Perl, Python, Prolog, Ruby, and Java. The wrapper for Java, referred to as JPC/SC, is thus a direct competitor of the OpenCard Framework, which is discussed below.

The OpenCard Framework (OCF)

The OpenCard consortium (OpenCard Workgroup) was founded in March 1997, predominantly by computer and smart card technology manufacturers. The main aim of the consortium, at an early stage, was to enable the use of smart card technology with networked computers. However, it was soon realized that the platform should not be dependent on the underlying operating system. OCF was therefore defined as an open standard that defines an architecture and a set of APIs that help application developers to implement smart card-based programs. OCF is written in Java to provide a platform-independent implementation.

The reference implementation of OCF, as presented in Figure 8, includes a set of Java classes, Java packages, and an API that contains all the necessary functionality. An application provider can take advantage of the interface offered by the API and develop the necessary services, which are then plugged into the framework. The core architecture of OCF is divided into the CardService and the CardTerminal layers.

The CardService layer makes it possible for OCF to incorporate a number of different smart card operating systems and the specific underlying technology they offer. "The core of the CardService component implements an API that maps smart card commands onto specific APDUs. A smart card's file system is standardized in Kaiserswerth (1998), an example of which is included in OCF called the FileSystemCardService. This implies that smart card vendors that support OCF are obliged to implement the FileSystemCardService class for each of their products." (Markantonakis 1999).

The CardTerminal layer contains all the classes that allow access to smart card readers. For example, using certain classes of this component, smart card insertion or removal can be tracked. Among the main advantages of OCF, apart from platform independence, is that it supports readers with multiple slots (a feature not available in PC/SC). The various classes within the CardTerminal are responsible for checking card presence or absence along with sending and receiving the commands in the form of APDUs.

Requirements for PC/SC and OCF

The goal of both PC/SC and OCF is to enhance the interoperability of smart cards, readers, and PC-based platforms and architectures. Most of the functionality is provided through the ICC service providers and CardService classes from within PC/SC and OCF, respectively. A relatively good overview of the similarities and differences of the aforementioned architectures is provided in Seliger (2000).

The main advantage of OCF is that it is completely independent of the underlying operating system and it can function on any system that supports Java. This makes OCF the preferred technology among the wide pool of Java programmers. On the other hand, PC/SC being integrated into Microsoft's operating system has aided its adoption. It is usually easy to find PC/SC drivers for a given smart card reader but this can be more difficult for OCF. However, the architecture of OCF can use PC/SC drivers to communicate where necessary, although it cannot take advantage of the service providers because of the architecture of the central resource manager.

JSR 177: The Security and Trust Services Application Programming Interface

The security and trust services specification, referred to as JSR 177 (JSR 177 Expert Group 2004) for the J2ME platforms (Java 2 Micro Edition) proposes a collection of APIs that provide security and trust services. This is achieved by integrating a component into a J2ME device called a security element (SE) that provides the following benefits:

- Secure storage of sensitive data—e.g. cryptographic keys, certificates, personal information, etc.

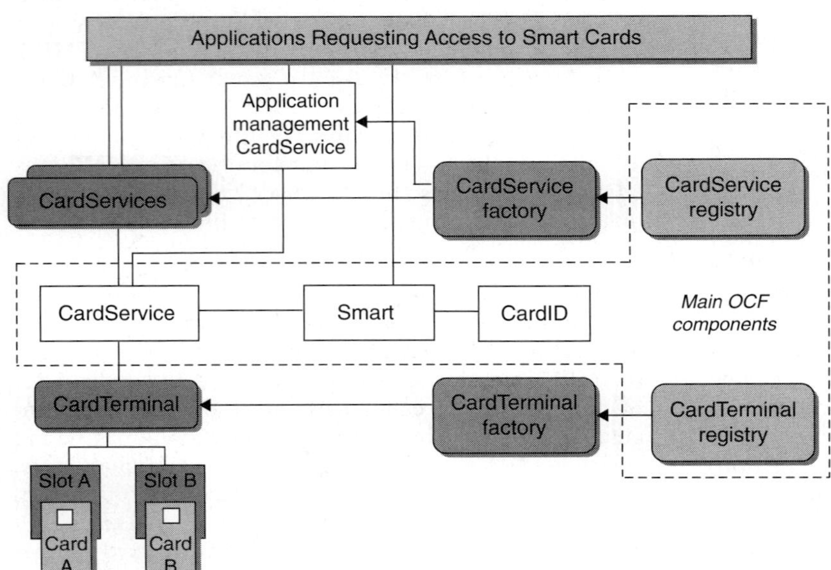

Figure 8: The OpenCard Framework Architecture (Markantonakis 1999)

- Support for cryptographic operations to enable payment protocols, data integrity, and data confidentiality
- A secure execution environment to deploy custom security features

An SE can be integrated into a variety of embedded devices. Smart cards provide a secure programmable environment and are the most widely deployed SE, and are used to deliver a broad range of security and trust services. These services can be continually upgraded with new and improved applications that can be installed on a smart card. They are widely deployed in mobile phones e.g. (SIM) cards in GSM phones. Alternatively, an SE may be entirely implemented in software on the J2ME device. The specification does not exclude any of the possible implementations of a SE, although some of the packages are optimized for implementation on a smart card.

The API in this specification is defined in four optional packages that can be implemented independently:

- *SATSA-APDU*—defines an API to support communication with smart card applications using APDUs.
- *SATSA-JCRMI*—defines a Java Card remote method invocation (RMI) client API that allows a J2ME application to invoke a method of a remote Java Card object.
- *SATSA-PKI*—defines an API to support application level digital signatures (but not verification) and basic user credential management.
- *SATSA-CRYPTO*—defines basic cryptographic operations to support hashing, signature verification, encryption, and decryption.

In short the JSR 177 provides two smart card access methods based on APDUs and a Java Card RMI protocol that allows a J2ME application to communicate with a smart card to leverage the security services deployed on it.

Comparison of the Architectures

The PC/SC architecture is the most deployed architecture across all the platforms. This is mainly because of the dominant position of Microsoft Windows, the open source implementation of PC/SC (pcsc-lite), and its adoption by Apple as reference implementation for their platforms. OCF is being used less and less, as the industrial consortium behind this standard no longer exists. However, JSR177 is a popular choice for embedded platforms, where the use of Java is well established. Table 2 gives a summary of the different architectures and the systems that support them.

Table 2: Architectures and the Systems That Support Them

	Windows		Network Computing		UNIX/Linux/BSD		Others	
	Classical	Embedded	Classical	Embedded	Classical	Embedded	Classical	Embedded
C++								
Java								
Other								

Key: PC/SC OCR JSR177

MANAGING MULTIPLE APPLICATIONS

Multi-application smart cards are a relatively new development, and have made it possible to implement several applications and to dynamically load new ones during a card's active life. These applications do not run simultaneously, because the smart card operating system has only a single thread, but new standards are beginning to propose multithreading.

Multi-Application Platforms

The two main standards for multi-application smart cards are Java Card (Chen 2000; Sun Microsystems 2006) and MULTOS (MAOSCO 2006). Two new technologies have joined them with the birth of Smartcard.NET (Hive Minded 2006; SmartCard Trends 2004) and of the Multi-Application BasicCard ZC6.5 (ZeitControl 2006). Windows for Smart Cards (Jurgensen and Guthery 2002) by Microsoft can also be cited, although it appears to no longer be supported by Microsoft.

The architecture of a smart card implementing these technologies consists of an embedded OS that supports the loading and the execution of different applications. The OS provides a run-time environment with a virtual machine (VM) that provides security features (e.g., a firewall between applications and inter application data-sharing mechanisms). The applications are interpreted by the VM, which enables applications to be independent of the underlying hardware and thus promotes interoperability. The following sections provide an overview of the types of multi-application smart card.

Java Card

Java Card enables applications (so-called applets) written in the Java Card language (a subset of the Java programming language) to run on smart cards. This technology is standardized by Sun Microsystems and the Java Card Forum, who produce the Java Card specifications.

Java Card is developed in the Java spirit of "write once, run anywhere." Java Card can support primitive data types such as `boolean`, `byte` and `short`, but not large data types such as `long`, `double` and `float`. Java Card supports one-dimensional arrays, packages, interfaces, and exceptions. Object-oriented programming paradigms are continued with support for inheritance, virtual methods, overloading, dynamic object creation, etc. However, not all the features are supported—e.g. strings, multi-dimensional arrays, dynamic class loading, security manager, and garbage collection. At the time of this writing, the currently available Java Cards comply with version 2.2.2. In future versions, starting with Java Card 3.0, other features will be supported, such as multithreading and a TCP/IP stack.

MULTOS

The MULTOS operating system is mostly confidential, as it was developed from the Mondex system for electronic purses and is controlled by the industrial MAOSCO Consortium. For application development, MULTOS proposes MEL (MULTOS Executable Language), which is an optimized language for smart cards based on Pascal, and runs on a virtual machine described with a well-defined and fixed API (Watt and Brown 2000). Applications are typically developed in another language (e.g., C or Java) and then translated into MEL.

Smartcard.NET

Smartcard.NET was developed to support the .NET framework on smart cards. In the spirit of the .NET philosophy, the intention is to give the developer the freedom to select the most appropriate language for development while allowing different language applications to interact via a common library. Thus, the .NET applications can be written in C#, VB.NET, J#, Jscript.NET, J#, etc. The virtual machine supports all the types except floating-point numbers, code checking, 64-bit integers and remoting (called "RPC" in .NET). The API includes all the types and all the methods required by the language to support .NET (including strings). It also manages the I/O, cryptography, synchronization between threads, etc.

Multi-Application BasicCard

BasicCard has existed since 1996, although it is only since April 2004 that ZeitControl proposed its first multi-application card: Multi-Application BasicCard ZC6.5. Applications for this smart card are written in ZeitControl BASIC, which contains the majority of commands present in the traditional BASIC language, such as strings and the functions to handle them, arrays, data structures defined by the user, etc. One of the differences with the other technologies is that BasicCard is the only one that has native support for floating-point numbers. It also proposes a file system similar to FAT and an API to manipulate the file structure.

Windows for Smart Cards

Windows for Smart Cards (WfSC) was proposed by Microsoft (Jurgensen and Guthery 2002) in 1998 and is no longer in use; it is included here for completeness. This operating system had a real FAT file system and rule-based access control list. The proposed API was a considerably reduced version of the Windows (Win32) API. These cards could be used in a file system mode, with access via the standard ISO/IEC 7816 protocol, or a multi-application mode where applications could be downloaded. Applications could be developed in Visual Basic or Visual C++ using Microsoft Visual Studio.

Multi-Application Platform Attacks

A common problem of all open multi-application smart cards is the potential to load a malicious application that would attack the security of the smart card. Such an application may attempt to:

- Identify available services on-card by collecting information and then trying to deduce the possible behavior of an official application (i.e., an application installed by some trustworthy organization, e.g. such as a banking application).
- Directly attack the VM and the firewall that is used to partition the resources between each applet.

The following sections describe how an attacker could attempt to attack a multi-application smart card.

Identification of Services and Collection of Information

The preliminary fundamental steps required to attack a card are the identification of the services that it offers and the collection of information regarding the OS and applications that have already been loaded. There are several ways that this can be achieved.

To identify the services offered by the card, any documentation is the first place to search for information. If this is not accessible, an attacker can try to load an application on the card to test every service defined in the specifications of the technologies supported by the card. For example, to identify the cryptographic services of a Java Card, an application can be loaded that uses `Cipher.getInstance` method (if the smart card supports the garbage-collection mechanism, this method can be called directly from anywhere in the code, otherwise the call should be inserted in the constructor). The application can be installed on the card and then be used to test whether the service is available with all the valid parameters, and then be removed to avoid any problem with an overflow in the heap due to multiple instances of the `Cipher` class.

If the smart card supports special mechanisms, similar to the GlobalPlatform management functions (e.g. the Get Status APDU command), the simplest way to collect information is to send the APDUs that reveal the required information. The attacker can also load an application on to a smart card to achieve this task. For example, to detect all the available applications on a Java Card and to determine whether they offer a service through the `Shareable` interface, all the possible parameters to the `JCSystem.getAppletShareableInterfaceObject` method can be exhausted. This particular method may return false negative results because of access control rules defined by the targeted application that determine whether services can be shared. If it is successful, and the attacker obtains `Shareable` interfaces, an attempt to apply illegal reference casting methods can be made (Montgomery and Krishna 1999).

Attacks against the VM and the Firewall

There exist many attacks directed against the VM and the firewall used in smart cards, but these are not covered here for brevity. Some attacks against the firewall mechanism, such as application identifier impersonation and illegal reference casting that provides access to all the interface methods of a class, are described in Montgomery and Krishna (1999) and are based on type confusion. Some examples of attacks on the VM are described in Witteman (2003), and some attacks that are derived from problems in the specifications are presented in Betarte et al. (2002).

Mixed Hardware and Software Attacks

To improve the efficiency of attacks on a smart card, it is possible to combine fault and software attacks. Using one of the fault-injection methods, it would be potentially possible to create faults in the software running on the smart card (e.g., to bypass verification, or bypass firewall checks). These modifications of the normal behavior could also be exploited by a loaded application to access unauthorized services or information.

One problem of this type of attack is the precision required to induce a usable faults—i.e. finding the precise point during a command at which a fault could have the desired effect. To help in determining where a fault should be injected, some physical characterization methods can be attempted, as described in Chaumette and Sauveron (2005).

An actual implementation of this type of attack is presented in Govindavajhala and Appel (2003), where an attack is conducted against the VM of a PC using a lamp to induce faults by raising the temperature of the RAM being used to execute the applet. This does not apply to smart cards, as this attack requires a strict control of the addressing of subfunctions in RAM that are then accessed when a fault is induced in a function call.

Multi-Application Security Mechanisms

A verifier is often not included because of the limited processing power and memory available in smart cards. Consequently, it is often not advisable to run uncertified applications that may be provided by someone who wishes to attack the assets of a platform or the applications being run on that platform.

Verifier and Firewall

Several examples of on-card verifiers have published (Cohen 1997; Rose and Rose 1998; Leroy 2001; Barthe et al. 2002; Casset, Burdy and Requet 2002; Deville and Grimaud 2002; Leroy 2002), and they are starting to be included in Java Cards. Three of the solutions that have been proposed (the defensive VM, the verifier based on code transformation, and the stand-alone verifier) allow an application to be loaded without requiring it to be signed by a third party without jeopardizing the card security. This can permit anyone to freely load their own applications—i.e. anyone can still load a rogue application but it will eventually be rejected by the verifier or blocked by the defensive VM. The verifier based on code transformations (Leroy 2001, 2002) requires an off-card program to normalize the application, whereas the other two (i.e., the defensive VM [Cohen 1997] and the stand-alone verifier [Deville and Grimaud 2002] is stand-alone. The two approaches are equivalent (Barthe et al. 2002), but the defensive VM dynamically checks each executed bytecode, whereas the stand-alone verifier statically checks the application once when the application is loaded, and it is associated with a VM that does not check the bytecode at execution time.

To enforce the security of multi-application smart cards, some other mechanisms have been added—e.g. the Java Card firewall. This firewall guarantees that each application loaded on to a Java Card is associated with a unique execution context, so that another application cannot access the objects created in this context. Exceptions can be created if explicitly stated in the application. This mechanism is orthogonal to the classical Java access rules.

Nevertheless, even though it is possible to have a real open multi-application smart card, issuers prefer to continue to support standards, such as GlobalPlatform (GlobalPlatform 2006), that enable applications to be securely managed on a smart card (as a set of cryptographic keys are required to authenticate a user before an application can be installed). This is likely to continue until the multi-application technologies are proven to be completely secure by formal methods. An example of this approach is the InspireD European project (InspireD 2006), which proposes modeling and verification tools that allow application developers to specify and to verify customizable security policies.

In the past, the FIPR (Foundation for Information Policy Research) thought that the multi-application cards were a bad idea, except in limited applications such as GSM SIM cards (Foundation for Information Policy Research 1999). Nevertheless, these cards are now a reality, even if they are currently available only as closed cards because of the constraints of GlobalPlatform. These open multi-application smart cards are not yet available on the market, but they are probably the future of smart cards because of the considerable amount of effort that is going into making them secure.

GlobalPlatform

International Visa initially developed the specifications of this standard within the Open Platform initiative, before being transferred to the GlobalPlatform consortium, where it is also supported by members of the banking and communications industries. The goal of the GlobalPlatform specifications is to bring a standard that, hitherto, was not present in the smart card arena: a specification to manage cards without any dependencies on hardware, manufacturers or applications. The actual GlobalPlatform specifications are related to the smart cards, the smart card terminals, and the global management of systems using smart cards. Only the on-card embedded GlobalPlatform architecture is presented in this chapter.

The GlobalPlatform card architecture is composed of a number of components that ensure hardware and vendor-neutral interfaces to applications and off-card management systems. GlobalPlatform does not mandate a specific run-time environment (RTE) technology and can be implemented on any multi-application technology. A user needs to conduct a mutual authentication with a smart card before applications can be loaded, so applications can be added only with the correct cryptographic keys for a given smart card.

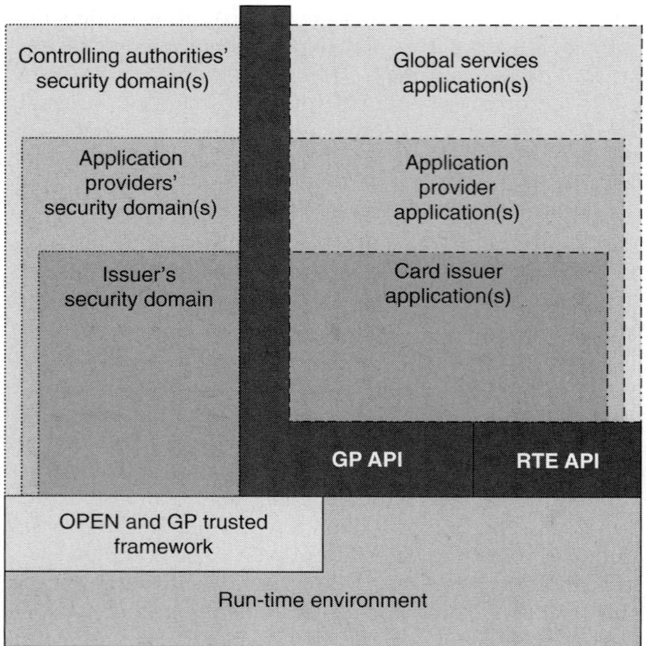

Figure 9: The GlobalPlatform (GP) card architecture

Figure 9 shows the components in an example card configuration, which includes one or more applications from the card issuer; one or more applications from one of the business partners of the card issuer (referred to as "application providers"), and one or more applications providing global services (e.g., cardholder verification method services) to other applications. The card manager (a generic term for the card management entities of a GlobalPlatform card) acts as the central administrator for a GlobalPlatform card.

Security domains are important to the security of GlobalPlatform, as security management applications are used that ensure complete separation of cryptographic keys between the card issuer and other security domains (generally owned by application providers). Security domains support security services such as key handling, encryption, decryption, digital-signature generation, and verification for their providers' (card issuer or application provider) applications. Each security domain is established on behalf of a card issuer or an application provider when these off-card entities require the use of keys that are completely isolated from each other. The applications interact with their related security domain via the GlobalPlatform API, which provides the aforementioned services (e.g., cardholder verification, personalization, or security services). GlobalPlatform cards may contain one or more trusted frameworks, which provide interapplication communication services between applications depending on the multi-application technology that the RTE implements (e.g., Sharing Interface Object of the Java Card technology).

APPLICATION SECURITY

The most common applications for smart cards are in the banking and telecommunications industries, where smart cards play an important role because of their security functionality, combined with tamper resistance. The following sections give details of Third Generation (3G) and EMV (Europay, Mastercard, Visa) standards for use in mobile networks and the role that is played by smart cards in these systems. In the case of 3G, a brief history of how the security of mobile telecommunications has evolved is also given.

Third-Generation Network Security

The requirement for an application security solution for 3G solutions suggests that the second- and first-generation solutions were not entirely satisfactory. This is not meant as a criticism of the legacy systems, as security solutions were implemented based on the needs and perceived threats at the time. If the old analog TACS (total access communication system) can be taken as an example of a first-generation system, then its goal was to ensure that only people with a valid account could make calls and when they did they would pay for them. The fact that TACS offered mobile communication was regarded as a wonder of radio engineering, and security was never the highest-priority topic. The outcome was that there was no encryption of call transmissions, and the caller's ID was simply their telephone number, which was also transmitted in clear. Confidentiality was therefore non-existent, and this led to some eavesdropping problems. However, there was at least an authentication method based on a serial number stored in the phone. An obvious problem was that the caller's ID was transmitted by phone and so could not be regarded as a secret. The only defense was that a mobile phone's serial number should only have been reprogrammed by authorized parties—but of course history has shown that this was not the case. The resulting escalation of phone cloning threatened to undermine mobile communication, and in a painful and practical way, taught the industry the importance of tamper-resistant security and confidentiality.

These lessons drove the European Technical Standards Institute (ETSI) to develop an enhanced solution for the new digital GSM system (referred to as second-generation [2G]), based on a tamper-resistant subscriber identity module (SIM) in the form of a smart card. The new protocols, underpinned by the SIM, supported confidentiality by using radio transmission encryption and temporary identities. Authentication was safeguarded by storing both a secret key (Ki) and an associated algorithm securely within a tamper-resistant SIM. The GSM solution has been very successful and has demonstrated the usefulness of tamper-resistant security modules; however, there are still some weaknesses. The priority with the 2G system was for users to reliably prove they had a valid account/SIM, so there was little consideration for the network to prove its authenticity to users. This led to the possibility of false-base-station or man-in-the-middle attacks that could also be used to turn off confidentiality measures. More widely known were attacks on the original authentication algorithm given as an example authentication algorithm called COMP128-1. It was a common misconception that COMP128-1 was "the" 2G authentication algorithm, as operators were free to develop and use their own designs. While the more technically competent operators took this precaution, others opted for the example algorithm suggested by the GSM Association—i.e. COMP128-1. The algorithm was vulnerable to attack, and too much reliance was placed on keeping it secret. The outcome was that the design was leaked, vulnerabilities were discovered, and it became possible to clone some cards. This was exacerbated by the gradual emergence of low-cost but sophisticated side-channel attacks. The main lessons learned from the 2G-application experience were that mutual authentication was needed, that algorithms should be robust even when exposed to public scrutiny, and that sophisticated attacks on tamper-resistant modules were practical and must be countered. A final but no less important lesson was that if there is a disaster scenario when things go badly wrong, it is very useful to have a back up authentication algorithm or mode plus the administrative means to select it.

At the end of 1998 several working groups were launched to specify the security of the 3G system. The aim was to provide a replacement for the 2G GSM network protocols. Most documents issued by these workgroups are available online at the 3GPP Web site (3GPP 2004) demonstrating a commitment to openness rather than reliance on secrecy of specifications.

In a 3G network, mutual authentication is performed (i.e., both user and network have to authenticate to each other). This is the most sensitive operation in a 3G network, as it identifies the client for billing purposes. To initiate an authentication handshake, a challenge is sent by the network (the operator) to the USIM (the smart card supporting the 3G standards, equivalent to the SIM used in GSM) via the phone, which is considered untrusted. The challenge consists of a random 128-bit random number (RAND) and an authentication token (AUTN). Figure 10 presents an overview of the handshake protocol. The USIM will take the values supplied by the network and calculate a response (RES) and some session keys for ciphering and integrity (CK and IK, respectively) that are passed back to the mobile equipment (ME) and the network. These values depend on a 128-bit key that is stored in the USIM and is known by the network. The response will also state whether the USIM was prepared to authenticate the network based on credentials supplied in the AUTN value, and assuming that this is the case, the network will then go on to check that the value for RES is the correct for the USIM in question.

The calculation of the RES value is done using an algorithm based on the AES (FIPS-197) called Milenage, although operators are free to replace this with a proprietary algorithm. The specification for this algorithm is also available on the 3GPP Web site, and the ETSI Security Algorithms Group of Experts (SAGE) group has made a "C" code version available. This represents a complete change in philosophy when compared to the 2G algorithms, which are still kept secret. The reason behind this is that the problems caused by COMP128-1 have left many network operators wary of trusting proprietary algorithms. However, each operator can customize Milenage (in a manner defined in the 3GPP technical report on the algorithm) so that a different version of the algorithm can be derived. This customization ultimately relies on global secrets, but only account-specific versions are stored within individual USIMs, and the operator can vary the customization across batches of cards.

Figure 11 shows the structure of the AUTN value sent by the network that contains the sequence number (SQN) (that may optionally be XOR (exclusive OR) -enciphered with the anonymity key [AK]), the 2-byte authentication

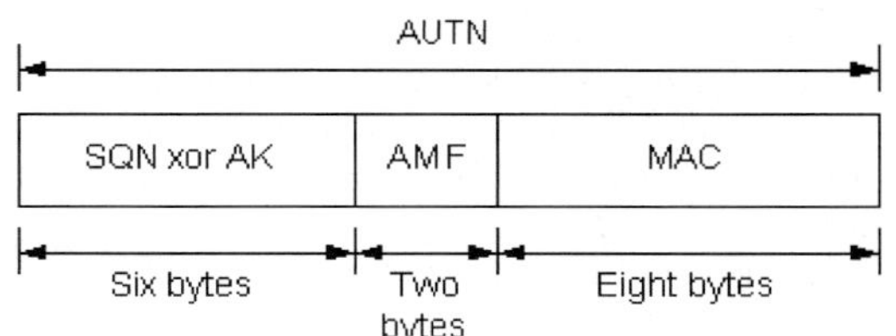

Figure 11: The authentication data sent to the USIM by the network

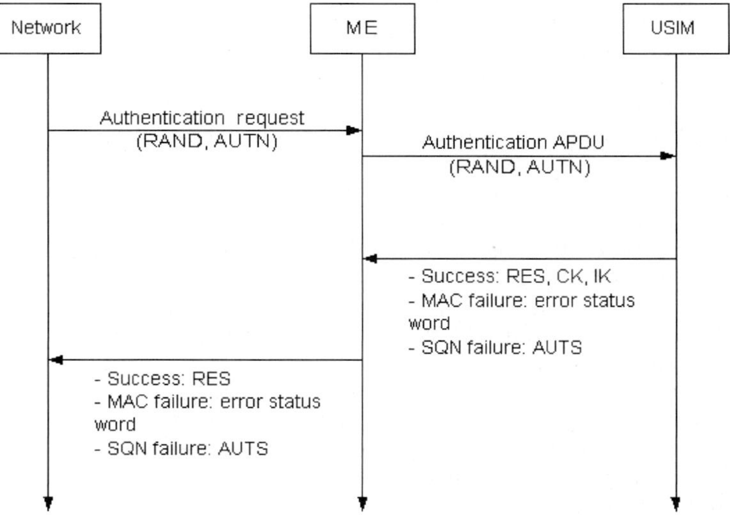

Figure 10: The 3G handshake protocol

management field (AMF), and the 8-byte message authentication code (MAC) field. These data are used by the USIM to authenticate the network as presented in Figure 11.

The AMF field is often overlooked, as it is not core to the description of the main 3G authentication process; however, it is important because it provides the means to control authentication. How it is used is not fully standardized, but a network operator could use it to select a backup algorithm or perhaps make changes to sequence-number generation. The MAC value is critical because it used by the USIM to verify the authenticity and the integrity of the network supplying the authentication challenge. The algorithm for generating this depends on the values of RAND, SQN, AMF, and the secret key held in both the USIM and the network authentication center. This makes it difficult to trick the card into thinking that it is communicating with a valid network, unless the secret key is known. The SQN value is a sequence number that prevents message sequences being replayed, as the card will return an error unless a new SQN value is presented, and that varies according to parameters determined by the network operator.

The SQN generator scheme is not fixed, and it is possible to have time-based and non–time-based methods, providing that both the network and USIM know which method is in use. The security benefit of using sequence numbers is well established; however, there are some management issues to deal with, particularly the case of lost synchronization between a network and a USIM. When challenged with an invalid SQN the USIM will respond with the AUTS field, which is basically the USIM suggested SQN plus a MAC to confirm the information is sourced by the USIM. When only one network entity is involved, a basic sequence number and resynchronization mechanism is quite adequate. However, 3G systems are a little more complex, the network may generate small batches of authentication challenges/vectors for distribution to regional subsystems. Within a region a USIM might simply check for an incrementing SQN, if there is a change of region, an older, yet valid, challenge may be presented and rejected because of the SQN. To overcome this, the 3G specifications define the use of an array of sequence number checkers that are indexed by the least significant bits (typically 5) of the SQN field.

After an authentication algorithm has taken place, session keys (CK and IK) are used to provide confidentiality and integrity using an algorithm based on Kasumi (available in the 3GPP specifications). This algorithm is implemented in the mobile device, primarily for performance reasons. Although the mobile device is not regarded as a trusted device, the exposed session keys only have short-term significance, as they are regularly refreshed by the network using the USIM-based tamper-resistant algorithms and secret keys.

Because of the critical importance of the long-term secret key held in the USIM, the 3G standards also specify that the smart card implementations of the Milenage algorithm must be resistant to side-channel analysis such as SPA or DPA. The underlying fear is that because side-channel attacks are low cost, they must not under any circumstances permit an attacker to clone client cards and then use or sell them.

The 3G security application is interesting because of its sophistication and also because just about every feature is justified by the lessons learned from previous generations. The USIM (smart card) is at the core because of its proven tamper-resistant storage and processing capabilities when compared with mobile devices. The resulting solution is a sophisticated example of a symmetric security application, with mutual authentication, confidentiality, and integrity protection. It combines the openness of good algorithm design with the customization and management functions needed by network operators.

The smart cards also provide a mechanism of personalizing mobile devices that is totally under the control of the network operator. This means that subscribers can be provided with mobile devices made in the same factory but that are made individual by smart cards owned and managed by the operator. USIM cards could in fact be used directly or as a model for nonmobile network applications, as they provide proven methods for mutual authentication, personalization, and the distribution of session keys.

Europay, Mastercard, Visa (EMV)

The requirement for additional security, in the banking card industry, was realized in the mid-1990s when the three major financial institutions (Europay, Mastercard and Visa—hence the choice of the abbreviation EMV) decided to work together to capitalize on the underlying tamper-resistance benefits of smart card technology. The requirement for credit cad fraud reduction was further enhanced in July 1996 with the release of a set of specifications, referred to as EMV 96 (EMV 1996). These standards cover a broad range of card characteristics (e.g., physical characteristics of the card, electrical signals to and from the card, etc.) along with the overall behavior of the credit and debit card resident applications. One of the goals of EMV was to further enhance the already existing credit/debit card architectures with the added functionality of additional on-card memory, processing power, and therefore, better risk management through online/offline authentication and authorization. In particular, the following processes are specified within the EMV standard:

- Offline PIN management
- Terminal/card risk management
- Online processing
- Card data authentication

Offline PIN management implies that, since the card offers tamper resistance, the PIN number can be verified by the underlying smart card microprocessor prior to a transaction being authorized. Terminal and card risk management processes ensure that both entities are provided with the necessary functionality that will enable it to decide when a transaction (e.g., high-value transactions or certain types of transactions) would go online for extra reassurance. For example, a card may decide to go online or even reject a transaction, always in line with the issuer's risk management policies. This will not only reduce communication costs for low value, and perhaps "less risky," transactions but at the same time offer the necessary reassurance.

Online processing is often described as the equivalent of the processing of magnetic stripe card transactions. The main difference is that the terminal can request from the smart card an application cryptogram (AC), which can be forwarded to the issuer in an authorization request message in order to further enhance the transaction authorization process.

With card data authentication the terminal verifies the authenticity of certain card resident data. The wo main processes described in the standard are tatic data authentication (SDA) and dynamic data authentication (DDA).

The main aim of SDA is for the card to prove to the terminal that certain card resident data, and therefore the actual card, has not been changed. The whole process is fundamentally based on the existence of a certification authority (often run by the actual financial scheme—e.g. Visa, Mastercard, etc.). This entity maintains a highly secure cryptographic facility that is responsible for signing, with the scheme's private key, the issuer's public key. The corresponding scheme's public key is placed in every card terminal conforming to the specifications. Subsequently, the issuer signs the aforementioned card resident data using the corresponding private key and places this signature in the card during personalization. Subsequently, the scheme's public key is used during verification to verify the issuer's public key and to verify the card resident data. If the process is completed with no problems, the terminal obtains the necessary reassurance that the card data are genuine and have not been modified during the card's lifetime. The actual process is described in Figure 12.

The DDA process is summarized in Figure 13. An EMV card capable of DDA also offers the aforementioned SDA process. The former is achieved using a unique private key that can be validated through a chain of certificates. More specifically, the terminal can receive a copy of the scheme's (i.e., fulfilled by the role of the certification authority) public key, which is used in verify the issuer public key (contained within the issuer public key certificate). During the next step the terminal verifies the card's public key by using the issuer public key (which is verified in the above step). The card's public key is used in order to subsequently verify a challenge. During this process the terminal can challenge the card with some data and request a signature as a response. By using the above process the terminal will be in a position to verify the actual signature through the verification of the aforementioned certificate chain.

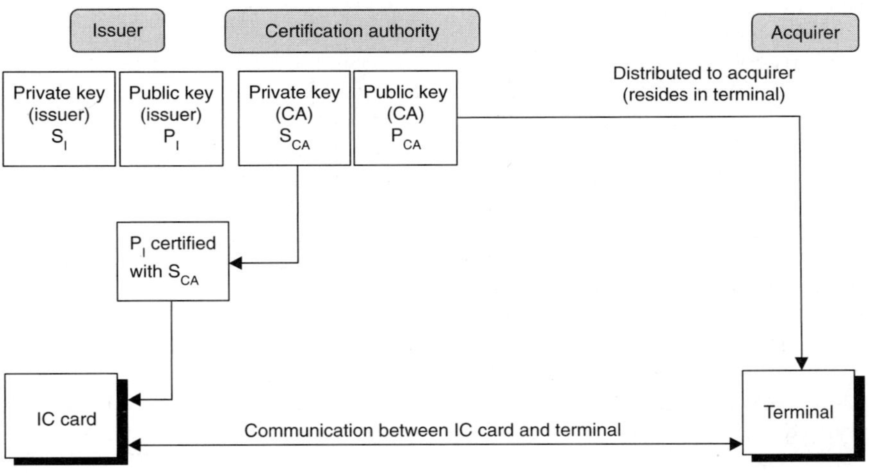

Figure 12: Diagram of static data authentication (Markantonakis and Rantos 1999)

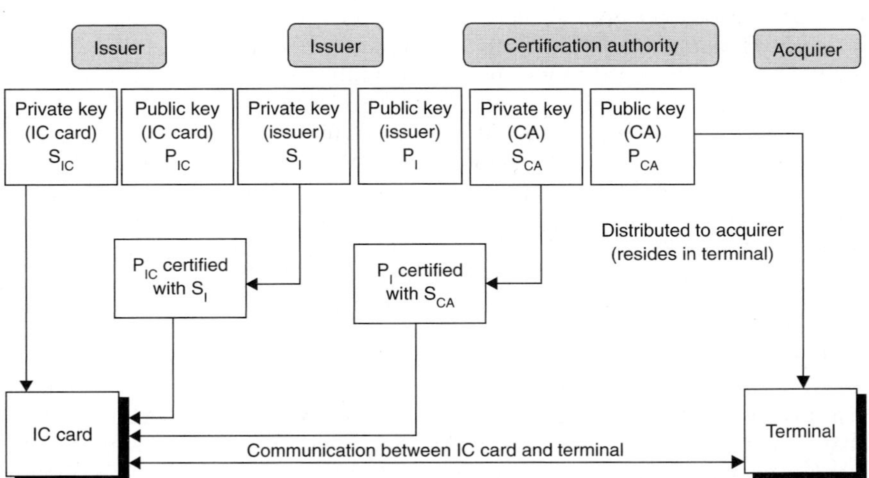

Figure 13: Diagram of dynamic data authentication (Markantonakis and Rantos 1999)

It appears that the major financial institutions are fully committed to the EMV standards, and they provide financial, operational, and planning assistance to their member banks in order to migrate from magnetic-stripe card technology into chip card technology. The EMV standards indicate examples of cryptographic algorithms, cryptographic key lengths, and crypto periods, but the details of the exact key-management processes are left entirely to the actual scheme operators. As a result, all major financial institutions provide their bank members with the necessary guidelines. However, the migration from a magnetic stripe card base to chip card technology is not a trivial step, and it requires thorough planning and implementation. It is often the case that member banks do not posses the right skills and expertise to successfully quantify the potential benefits from such a migration. However, the smart card industry is also offering assistance to banks seeking to migrate. As a result, a large number of banks have gradually changed their credit cards to chip card technology. It remains to be seen whether the fraud levels have dropped to a level that will justify the investment.

CONCLUSION

An overview of the different protocols that exist for smart cards has been presented. There are also devices that function as secure tokens that have a USB interface. These devices are often used to provide copy protection for software, whereby, the software will not run without the device being present. These devices have not been covered in detail, as the implementations are proprietary and the USB protocol is beyond the scope of this chapter.

Some chip manufacturers also propose smart cards with a USB interface that will allow for a larger bandwidth between a smart card and reader (STmicroelectronics 2002). These chips include a USB interface conforming to USB 1.1, which has taken the form of two extra contacts on the smart cards micromodule that handle the USB communication. The specification of an example smart card chip can be found at STmicroelectronics (2006) based on ST Microelectronic's ST19 chip family. This capability would allow smart cards to be more versatile because of the increased bandwidth offered by the USB protocol. However, industry has found these cards inadequate to increase the bandwidth between a smart card and reader because of the complexity of the host interface (Praca and Barral 2001), although advances in technology may have rendered this view invalid.

A more recent initiative is the Secure MultiMediaCards (Secure-MMC) (Giesecke and Devrient 2005) that aims to blend smart card technology with MultiMediaCards (MultiMediaCard Association 2006). These chips aim to provide secure storage in devices, such as mobile phones, principally for digital rights management. The MMC standard allows for a bandwidth of up to 416 Mbps, depending on the clock frequency and the size of the bus used. It is assumed that a Secure-MMC will be able to decipher several megabytes per second on-the-fly (Praca 2005). It will also be able to store large amounts of content in a secure manner and provide the same protection that is currently seen in smart cards. The Secure-MMC is a relatively new technology, so no specifications are currently available.

Two of the most common uses for smart cards using the standards banking and telecommunications have been described, where the smart card acts as a secure token. Another common use of smart card technology is in transport services (Oyster 2006; Octopus 2006), although the implementation on a smart card is simpler than the examples presented above.

GLOSSARY

APDU: Application protocol data unit. A command in the T=0 or T=1 protocol that con consist of 1 or 2 TPDUs.

API: Applications programming interface. A set of prewritten, and often standardized, functions that can be used by developers.

EEPROM: Electrically erasable and programmable memory, used in smart cards to store data special to a particular smart card. This process is referred to as "personalization."

ETU: Elementary time unit. The number of clock cycles required tosend 1 bit of information in the T=0 or T=1 protocol.

FAT: File allocation table. A commonly supported file system for computers developed by Microsoft for MS-DOS.

GSM: Global system for mobile communications. The most popular standard for mobile phones.

Hamming Weight: The number of bits set to 1 in a given bit string.

ICC: Integrated circuit card. A smart card.

IFD: Interface device. A smart card reader.

I/O: Input/output. Generally used to refer to the contact or pin used to pass information to or from a chip.

Micromodule: Term used to describe the chip used in a smart card when it has been attached to the metal plates that provide the contacts for communication and power supply.

PIN: Personal identification number. A four-digit number commonly used in smart cards to authenticate a user.

RAM: Random access memory. A fast access memory used in computers and smart cards alike to store variables and aid in calculation; it only holds its value while receiving power.

RFID: Radio frequency identification. A method of automatically identifying items by attaching a small tag or transponder that can communicate this identity using a contactless protocol.

RMI: Remote method invocation. A mechanism for invoking instance methods on objects located on remote virtual machines (i.e., a virtual machine other than that of the invoker).

RPC: Remote procedure call. Allows an application running on one platform to cause code to be executed on another platform.

RTE: Run-time environment. The implementation of a virtual machine that allows programs written for that virtual machine to run on a given platform.

S-Box: Used to refer to a substitution table in a cryptographic algorithm; these are a common feature of block ciphers.

TACS: Total access communication system. An early standard for mobile telecommunication.

TPDU: Transport protocol data unit. The basic command unit in the T = 0 or T = 1 protocol.

CROSS REFERENCES

See *Authentication; Code Division Multiple Access (CDMA); Fault Tolerant Systems; Firewalls.*

REFERENCES

3GPP Specifications 2004. www.3gpp.org/ftp/Specs/html-info/TSG-WG-S3.htm (accessed November 24, 2006).

Aigner, M. and E. Oswald. 2006. Power Analysis Tutorial. www.iaik.tugraz.at/aboutus/people/oswald/papers/dpa_tutorial.pdf (accessed November 24, 2006).

Anderson, R, and M. Kuhn. 1996. Tamper resistance—A cautionary note, In *the Second USENIX Workshop on Electronic Commerce Proceedings Oakland, CA,* 1–11. Berkeley, CA: Usenix.

Aumüller, C., P. Bier, P. Hofreiter, W. Fischer, and J.-P. Seifert. 2002. Fault attacks on RSA with CRT: Concrete results and practical countermeasures, In *Cryptographic hardware and embedded systems—CHES 2002,* edited by B. S. Kaliski, Ç. K. Koç, and C. Paar, 260–75. Heidelberg, Germany: Springer Verlag Lecture Notes in Computer Science, 2523.

Barthe G., G. Dufay, L. Jakubiec, and S. Melo de Sousa. 2002. A formal correspondence between offensive and defensive JavaCard virtual machines. In *Proceedings of the Verification, Model Chekcing, and Abstract Interpretation, Third VMCA/2002, Venice, Italy, January 21–22. 2002,* 32–45. Heidelberg, Germany: Notes in Computer Science, 2294.

Betarte G., E. Giménez, B. Chetali, and C. Loiseaux. 2002. FORMAVIE: Formal modelling and verification of Java Card 2.1.1 security architecture. In *Proceedings of the e-Smart 2002, Nice, France, September 19–20, 2002,* 215–29.

Biham, E. and A. Shamir. 1997. Differential fault analysis of secret key cryptosystems, In advances in Cryptology—CRYPTO '97, edited by B. S. Kaliski, 513–25. Heidelberg, Germany: Springer Verlag Lecture Notes in Computer Science, 1294.

Blömer, J. and J.-P. Seifert. 2003. Fault based cryptanalysis of the advanced encryption standard (AES), In Financial cryptography—FC 2003, edited by R. N. Wright, 162–81. Heidelberg, Germany: Springer Verlag Lecture Notes in Computer Science, 2742.

Casset L., L. Burdy, and A. Requet. 2002. Formal development of an embedded verifier for Java Card byte code. In *Proceedings of IEEE International Conference on Dependable Systems & Networks, June 2002, Washington, DC,* pp. 51–58, IEEE Press.

Chari, S., C. S. Jutla, J. R. Rao, and P. Rohatgi. 1999. Towards sound approaches to counteract power-analysis attacks. In *Advances in Cryptology—CRYPTO '99,* edited by M. Wiener, 398–412. Heidelberg, Germany: Springer Verlag Lecture Notes in Computer Science, 1666.

Chaumette S. and D. Sauveron. 2005. Some security problems raised by open multiapplication smart cards. In *Proceedings of the 10th Nordic Workshop on Secure IT-systems: NordSec, October 20–21. 2005, Tartu, Estonia.* Tartu University Press.

Chen Z. 2000. Java Card *technology for smart cards.* Reading, MA: Addison-Wesley.

Clavier, C, J.-S. Coron, and N. Dabbous, 2000. Differential power analysis in the presence of hardware countermeasures. In *Cryptographic Hardware and Embedded Systems—CHES 2000,* edited by Ç. K. Koç and C. Paar, 252–63. Heidelberg, Germany: Springer Verlag Lecture Notes in Computer Science, 1965.

Cohen R. M. 1997. Defensive Java virtual machine version 0.5 alpha. www.computationallogic.com/software/djvm (accessed November 24, 2006).

DeMillo, R. A., D. Boneh, and R. J. Lipton. 1997. On the importance of checking computations. In *Advances in Cryptology—EUROCRYPT '97* edited by W. Fumy, 37–55. Heidelberg, Germany: Springer Verlag Lecture Notes in Computer Science, 1233.

Deville, D., and G. Grimaud. 2002. Building an "impossible" verifier on a Java Card. In *Proceedings of 2nd USENIX Workshop on Industrial Experiences with Systems Software 2002, Boston.*

EMV 1996. EMV 3.1.1 specifications. www.emvco.com/specifications.asp?show=31 (accessed November 24, 2006).

Federal Information Processing Standards, Advanced Encryption Standard (AES), FIPS publication 197. http://csrc.nist.gov/publications/fips/fips197/fips-197.pdf (accessed November 24, 2006) 2004.

Federal Information Processing Standards, Data Encryption Standard (DES), FIPS publication 46–3. http://csrc.nist.gov/publications/fips/fips46-3/fips46-3.pdf (accessed November 24, 2006).

Foreign function interface. 2004. http://en.wikipedia.org/wiki/Foreign_function_interface (accessed May 1, 2007).

Foundation for Information Policy Research. 1999. Framework for smart card use in government—Consultation response. www.cl.cam.ac.uk/~rja14/Papers/smartcards-fipr.pdf (accessed August 24, 2006).

Gandolfi, K., C. Mourtel, and F. Olivier. 2001. Electromagnetic analysis: Concrete results. In *Cryptographic hardware and embedded systems—CHES 2001* edited by Ç. K. Koç, D. Naccache, and C. Paar, 251–61. Heidelberg, Germany: Springer Verlag Lecture Notes in Computer Science, 2162.

Giraud, C. and H. Thiebeauld. 2004. A survey on fault attacks. In *Smart card research and advanced applications VI—18th IFIPWorld Computer Congress,* edited by Y. Deswarte and A. A. El Kalam, 159–76. Boston: Kluwer.

Giraud, C. 2004. DFA on AES. In *4th International Conference Advanced Encryption Standard—AES 2004* , edited by H. Dobbertin, V. Rijmen, and A. Sowa, 27–41. Heidelberg, Germany: Springer Verlag Lecture Notes in Computer Science, 3373.

Giesecke and Devrient 2005. Secure and mobile storage media—the memory card with smart card technology. www.gi-de.com (accessed August 24, 2006).

GlobalPlatform. 2006. Global platform card specification. www.globalplatform.org/specificationview.asp?id=card (accessed November 24, 2006).

Govindavajhala S., and A. Appel 2003. Using memory errors to attack a virtual machine. In IEEE Symposium on Security and Privacy.

Hive Minded 2006. Smartcard.NET Technology Overview. www.hiveminded.com/docs/Smartcard. NET%201.0%20-%20A%20Technology%20Overview.pdf (accessed November 24, 2006).

International Organization for Standardization 1999. ISO/IEC 7816-2 Identification cards—Integrated circuit cards—part 2: Cards with contacts—dimensions and location of the contacts. Geneva, Switzerland: Author.

International Organization for Standardization 1997. ISO/IEC 7816-3 Identification cards—Integrated circuit(s) cards with contacts—part 3: Electronic signals and transmission protocols. Geneva, Switzerland: Author.

International Organization for Standardization 2000. ISO/IEC 14443 Identification cards—Contactless integrated circuit(s) cards—Proximity cards. Geneva, Switzerland: Author.

International Organization for Standardization 2000. ISO/IEC 15693 Identification cards—Contactless integrated circuit(s) cards—Vicinity cards. Geneva, Switzerland: Author.

Inspired 2006. Project overview. www.inspiredproject.com/index.php?rub=0&sub=4 (accessed November 24, 2006).

Joye, M. and F. Olivier. 2005. Side-channel attacks. In *Encyclopedia of cryptography and security*, 571—6. Boston: Kluwer.

JSR 177 Expert Group 2004. JSR 177: Security and trust services API for J2ME. http://jcp.org/en/jsr/detail?id=177 (accessed August 24, 2006).

Jurgensen T.M. and S.B. Guthery. 2002. Smart cards: The developer's toolkit. Upper Saddle River, NJ: Prentice Hall.

Kaiserswerth, M. 1998. The Open Card Framework and PC/SC, http://domino.watson.ibm.com/library/cyberdig.nsf/papers/2D63CAE9875AFB8A852565E9006BAB99/$File/RZ2999.pdf (accessed August 24, 2006).

Kocher, P. 1996. Timing attacks on implementations of Diffe-Hellman, RSA, DSS, and other systems. In *Advances in cryptology—CRYPTO '96*, edited by N. Koblitz, 104–13. Heidelberg, Germany: Springer Verlag Lecture Notes in Computer Science, 1109.

Kocher, P., J. Jaffe, and B. Jun. 1999. Differential power analysis. In *Advances in Cryptology—CRYPTO '99*, edited by M. Wiener, 388–97. Heidelberg, Germany: Springer Verlag Lecture Notes in Computer Science, 1666.

Leroy, X. 2001. On-card bytecode verification for Java Card. In *e-Smart 2001*, 150–164. Heidelberg, Germany: Springer-Verlag.

Leroy, X. 2002. Bytecode verification on Java smart cards. *Software-Practice & Experience 32* (pp. 319).

MAOSCO 2006. The MULTOS technology. www.multos.com/technology/ (accessed November 24, 2006).

Markantonakis, C. 1999. Interfacing with smart card applications (the PC/SC and OpenCard Framework). *Elsevier Information Security Technical Report* (2): 69–77.

Markantonakis, C., and K. Rantos. 1999. On the life cycle of the Certification authority key pairs in EMV '96. In *EUROMEDIA 99, April 25–28, 1999, Munich, Germany*, 125–30. Society for Computer Simulation Publication (SCS).

Menezes, A., P. van Oorschot, and S. Vanstone. 1997. Handbook of applied cryptography. Boca Raton, FL: CRC Press.

MIFARE. 2006. www.mifare.net/about/index.asp (accessed November 24, 2006).

Montgomery M., and K. Krishna. 1999. In *Proceedings of USENIX Workshop on Smartcard Technology (Smartcard '99), May 10–11, 1999, Chicago*.

MultiMediaCard Association. 2006. www.mmca.org/about/ (accessed November 24, 2006).

Octopus. 2006. www.hong-kong-travel.org/Octopus.asp (accessed November 24, 2006).

OpenCard Workgroup, OpenCard Framework, Retrieved November 24, 2006, from. 2005. www.opencard.org/overview.shtml

Oyster. 2006. www.tfl.gov.uk/tfl/fares-tickets/oyster/general.asp (accessed November 24, 2006).

PC/SC Workgroup. 2005. PC/SC Workgroup Specifications 2.01.3. www.pcscworkgroup.com/specifications/specdownload.php (accessed November 24, 2006).

Praca, D. 2005. *Next generation smart card: New features, new architecture and system integration. In 6th e-Smart Conference, Sophia Antipolis, France, September 2005*. www.gemplus.com/smart/rd/publications (accessed May 4, 2007).

Praca, D., and C. Barral. 2001. From smart cards to smart objects: The road to new smart card technologies. Computer Networks (4): 381–9.

Rankl, W., and W. Effing. 2002. Smart card handbook. 2nd ed. New York: Wiley.

Rivest, R.L., A. Shamir, and L. M. Adleman. 1978. Method for obtaining digital signatures and public-key cryptosystems, *Communications of the ACM 21* (2): 120–6.

Rose E. and K. Rose. 1998. Lightweight bytecode verification. In Workshop on Fundamental Underpinnings of Java, OOPSLA '98 edited by S. Eisenbach.

Seliger, F., 2000. OpenCard and PC/SC—Two new industry initiatives for smart cards, www.opencard.org/docs/ocfpcsc.pdf (accessed November 24, 2006).

SKIDATA. 2006. www.skidata.com/Solutions.2.0.html?&L=1 (accessed November 24, 2006).

SmartCard Trends. 2004. NET brings Web services to smart cards. *Smart Cards Trends* (April–May):. www.smartcardstrends.com/det_atc.php?idu=779 (accessed November 24, 2006).

STmicroelectronics 2002. *STmicroelectronics delivers world's first USB-certified smart card chips*. www.st.com (accessed August 24, 2006).

STmicroelectronics. 2006. *Smartcard solutions ST19 multi-application smartcard ICs*. www.st.com (accessed August 24, 2006).

Sun Microsystems. 2006. *Java Card 2.2.2 specifications*. java.sun.com/products/javacard/ (accessed November 24, 2006).

Watt D.A. and D.F. Brown. 2000. *Programming language processors in Java: compilers and interpreters*. Upper Saddle River, NJ: Prentice Hall.

Witteman M. 2003. Java card security. *Information Security Bulletin* 8:291

ZeitControl. 2006. BasicCard. www.basiccard.com/ (accessed November 24, 2006).

Fault-Tolerant Systems

Amiya Nayak, *University of Ottawa, Canada*

INTRODUCTION

The need for fault tolerance is becoming more evident as the complexity of digital systems continues to grow, with more and more transistors integrated on a single chip. With this development, the probability that some failure will occur is rising. It is hard to guarantee that the system is fault-free after production and testing, and that such faults will not occur later. Availability is also becoming progressively more important, as businesses continue to increase their reliance on information technology. Building fault-tolerant computer systems is now of paramount importance in many modern applications. In order for computers to reach a stage of acceptable dependability in the performance of modern applications, they must demonstrate the ability to produce correct results or actions in the presence of faults or other anomalous or unexpected conditions. Such fault-tolerant systems were first developed for robotics, process control, aerospace, and other mission-critical applications, for which the consequences of device failure could be catastrophic. Today, computers are playing a bigger role in everyday life and have left the clean environment of computer rooms for industrial and normal environments. They have to function normally even under many different environmental factors, such as temperature, humidity, electromagnetic interference, power supply, etc. Therefore, these systems have to be more robust and at the same time tolerate inadvertent user abuse. This coupled with the increasing complexity of modern computer-automated services demonstrates the need for ultra-reliable, highly available, fault-tolerant hardware and software. As hardware costs continue to decline and labor costs continue to escalate, the user cannot afford to have frequent service calls. To build fault-tolerant systems that can cope with the constant changes in environment and user requirements, it is essential to provide tools and techniques that enable developers to separate the concerns of fault-tolerant computing policies and mechanisms in applications.

FAULT-TOLERANCE TERMINOLOGIES

A computer system is generally constructed from a collection of software and hardware components, some of which may fail from time to time. A *fault* is simply any physical defect, imperfection, or flaw that occurs in hardware or software. The fault is a source that has the potential to generate errors. A fault may be dormant or active; a fault is active when it produces an error. An *error* is the manifestation of a fault within a program, a data structure, a component, or a system. The error is part of the system state that is liable to lead to a failure. A *failure* occurs when the delivered services deviates from the specification. Failures are caused by errors. These concepts are very well defined in Nelson (1990) and Rennels (1984). Faults, errors, and failures can be further classified as *permanent* (continuous, stable, or simply an irreversible physical change), *intermittent* (occasionally present because of unstable hardware or varying hardware or software state, such as a function of load or activity), and *transient* (resulting from temporary environmental conditions). A fault/error *latency* is the length of time between the occurrence of a fault/error and the appearance of an error/failure due to that fault/failure. Failures can be of different types: *crash failure* (in which the system simply halts, but was working correctly until that time), *omission failure* (in which the system fails to respond to a request), *timing failure* (in which the response lies outside an acceptable time interval), *response failure* (in which the response is simply incorrect), or *Byzantine failure* (in which arbitrary responses are produced at arbitrary times).

Fault tolerance is the attribute that enables a system to achieve fault-tolerant operation. It is the ability of a system to continue correct performance of its tasks and respond gracefully to an unexpected hardware or software failure. A *fault-tolerant system* is one that can continue to perform its specified tasks in the presence of hardware failures and software errors. The key to fault tolerance is redundancy. *Redundancy* is simply the addition of information, resources, or time beyond that needed for normal operation of the system. Many fault-tolerant computer systems mirror all operations; that is, every operation is performed on two or more duplicate systems, so if one fails the other can take over. *Fault-tolerant computing* describes the process of performing calculations, such as those performed by a computer, in a fault-tolerant manner.

Dependability of a system is defined as the quality of service provided by the system (Laprie 1985). This definition of dependability encompasses measures such as reliability and availability as distinct facets of a system specification. The *reliability* $R(t)$ of a component or a system is the probability that the component or the system will be operating correctly without failure in the interval from time 0 to t; that is, $R(t) = P(T > t)$, $t \geq 0$. The component or system unreliability $Q(t)$ is then $1 - R(t) = P(T \leq t)$. If the time to failure random variable T has the density function $f(t)$, we can then compute the reliability $R(t)$ from the failure density function $f(t)$ as follows:

$$R(t) = \int_t^{\infty} f(x)dx$$

The availability, $A(t)$, of a system is defined as the probability that the system is available at time t. Different from the reliability that focuses on a period when the system is free of failures, the availability is concerned with a point in time at which the system does not stay at the failed state. It can be viewed as the percentage of time the system is available to perform its expected task. A system can have low reliability but have high availability.

The failure rate function $z(t)$, or hazard function, specifies the rate of the system aging. The aging process of electronic components typically follows the so-called bathtub curve (burn-in phase, useful life, and burn-out phase) as shown in Figure 1. There is a period when the failure rate is approximately constant—what is considered to be the useful life of the component. Intuitively, the *failure rate is* the expected number of failures of a type of device or system per a given time period.

If $f(t)$ follows an exponential distribution with parameter λ, then the failure rate function is constant (i.e., $z(t) = \lambda$), which corresponds to the useful life of the component. Here, the parameter λ is considered to be the failure rate. The reliability in this case is known to be an exponential function of λ and is given by $R(t) = e^{-\lambda t}$. An important relationship relating $z(t)$, $f(t)$ and $R(t)$ is that $z(t) = f(t)/R(t)$.

Usually, we are interested in the expected time to next failure, termed "mean time to failure." The *mean time to failure* (*MTTF*) is defined as the expected value of the lifetime before a failure occurs. The *MTTF* can be computed from the reliability function as follows:

$$MTTF = \int_0^{\infty} R(t)dt$$

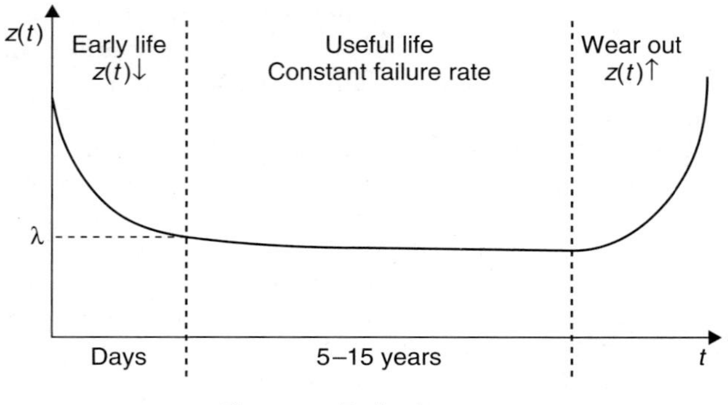

Figure 1: Bathtub curve

An important measure often used in maintenance studies is the mean time to repair (MTTR), or the mean downtime. MTTR is the expected value of the repair time, specified in terms of repair rate μ, which is the average number of repairs per unit time; that is, MTTR $= 1/\mu$. Another important measure in a repairable system is the mean time between failures (MTBF), which takes into account both MTTR and MTTF and can be computed as follows: MTBF = MTTR + MTTF. The maintainability $M(t)$ can be defined as the probability that the failed system can be restored to operation within time t. In terms of the repair rate, $M(t) = 1 - e^{-\mu t}$.

For a system with no possibility of repair, $A(t) = R(t)$. But, for a system with the possibility of repair:

$$A(t) = \frac{\mu}{\lambda + \mu} - \frac{\lambda}{\lambda + \mu} e^{-(\lambda+\mu)t}$$

In fact, we are mainly concerned with systems running for a long time. $A(t)$ has a simple steady-state or asymptotic expression. The steady-state or asymptotic availability A_{ss} is, therefore, given by

$$A_{ss} = \lim_{t \to \infty} A(t) = \frac{\mu}{\lambda + \mu} = \frac{MTTF}{MTTF + MTTR}$$

Coverage is defined as the ability of a system to perform fault detection, fault location, fault recovery, and fault containment. Coverage has two meanings: qualitative and quantitative. Quantitative coverage is concerned with how successful the recovery is from the specific type of failure, whereas qualitative coverage specifies the type of errors against which a particular scheme is meant.

Fault avoidance, fault masking, and fault tolerance are three main design philosophies to combat faults. *Fault avoidance* deals with ways to prevent, by construction, fault occurrence. It includes design reviews, component screening, testing, and quality-control methods.

Fault masking deals with ways to prevent faults from introducing errors. Triple modular redundancy (TMR) or majority voting and error correction in memory are some well-known fault masking techniques. *Fault tolerance* deals with ways to provide service complying with the specification in the presence of faults. It is achieved through redundancy in hardware, software, information, and/or computations. Fault detection, fault location, fault containment, fault recovery, and reconfiguration are typical methods. *Fault detection* is the process of recognizing that a fault has occurred. *Fault location* is the process of determining the location of the fault. *Fault containment* is the process of preventing the fault from propagating throughout the system. *Fault recovery* is the process of regaining operational status after the fault has occurred. *Reconfiguration* deals with eliminating a faulty unit from the system and restoring the system to some operational state.

MODELING FAULT-TOLERANT SYSTEMS

The modeling of fault-tolerant systems is primarily concerned with predicting system reliability and availability. A reliability model represents a clear picture of functional interdependencies, providing a means to trade off design alternatives and to identify areas for design improvement. System designers evaluate alternative architectures for their applications in terms of cost, performance, reliability, availability, or combinations of all of these. Reliability models can be used to help set and interpret system reliability requirements, predict the reliability of different system configurations, identify reliability bottlenecks (weak points) early in the product life cycle, and determine cost-effective sparing and maintenance strategies. Most reliability-modeling techniques are based on reliability block diagrams based on a combinatorial method, Markov chains, fault trees, etc. Detailed discussion on these models can be found in Shooman (2002) and Siewiorek and Swartz (1998). In this section, we will simply review the two most popular methods: combinatorial and the Markov approach.

Combinatorial Approach

Combinatorial models use probabilistic techniques to enumerate the different ways in which a system can remain operational. The reliability of a system is generally derived in terms of the reliability of the individual components of the system and the way the components are interconnected. Series and parallel systems are the two most commonly used models.

Series System

In a series system, each component of the system is required to operate correctly for the system to operate correctly. The reliability of the series system can be calculated as the probability that none of the components will fail. Another way to look at this is that the reliability of the series system is the probability that all of the elements are working properly. Consider the series system consisting of N components as shown in Figure 2.

Suppose that each component i satisfies the exponential failure law with failure rate λ_i, such that the reliability of each component is $R_i(t) = e^{-\lambda_i t}$. The reliability $R_S(t)$ of a series system is then

$$R_s(t) = R_1(t).R_2(t) \dots R_N(t) = \prod_{i=1}^{N} R_i(t) = e^{\sum_{i=1}^{N} \lambda_i t}$$

Note that the failure rate of a series system can be calculated by adding the failure rates of all the components that make up the series system.

Parallel System

In a parallel system, on the other hand, only one of several components must be operational for the system to be operational. Figure 3 shows the block diagram of a parallel system consisting of N components.

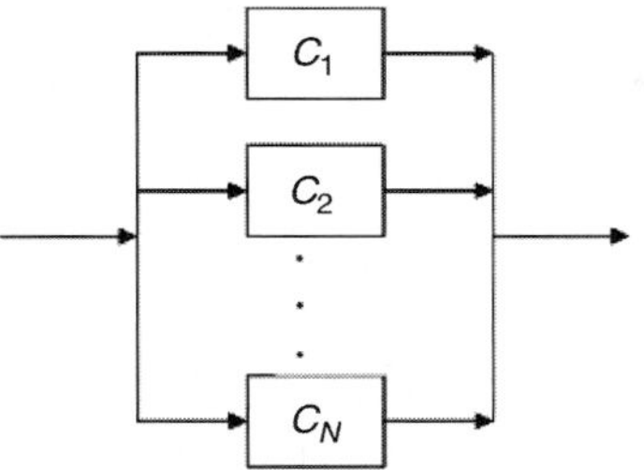

Figure 3: A parallel system

It is easier to compute the reliability of a parallel system by computing its unreliability first. The unreliability $Q_P(t)$ of a parallel system is the probability that all components will fail. In other words, $Q_P(t) = Q_1(t).\ Q_2(t) \dots Q_N(t)$. The unreliability $Q_i(t)$ of the component i is simply $1 - R_i(t)$. Thus, the reliability $R_P(t)$ of a parallel system can be shown to be

$$R_P(t) = 1 - Q_P(t) = 1 - \prod_{i=1}^{N} Q_i(t) = 1 - \prod_{i=1}^{N} (1 - R_i(t))$$

It should be noted that the equations for the parallel system assume that the failures of the individual elements that make up the parallel system are independent.

The generalization of a parallel system is the M-of-N system, in which there are N identical modules out of which M modules are required to work correctly for the system to be operational. The reliability of the M-of-N system is given by

$$R(t)_{MN} = \sum_{i=0}^{N-M} \binom{N}{i} R_m^{N-i}(t)\left(1 - R_m(t)\right)^i$$

A good example of the M-of-N system is the TMR system, which, in particular, is a 2-of-3 system with reliability $R_{TMR}(t) = 3R_m(t)^2 - 2R_m(t)^3$.

Combinatorial models are simple and can be used as long as the system block diagrams are in series or parallel form, for which we already have the reliability expression. Computer systems, in general, are very complex. We rarely come across systems whose components are either in series or in parallel; rather they come in a combination of both (series-parallel or non–series-parallel), in which case the system block diagram needs to be broken down into smaller series and/or parallel systems before combinatorial models can be applied. Combinatorial models are not suitable for modeling repair but it is possible to incorporate coverage. To see how coverage can be incorporated, consider a simple parallel system with two identical units U_1 and U_2 as shown in Figure 4. The secondary unit U_2 is switched on in the event of the failure of the primary U_1, if the system is able to detect the fault in U_1.

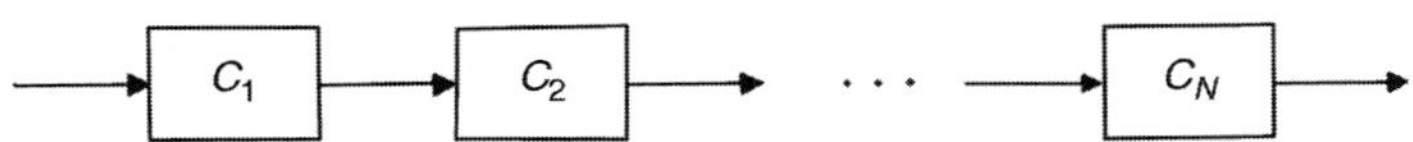

Figure 2: A series system

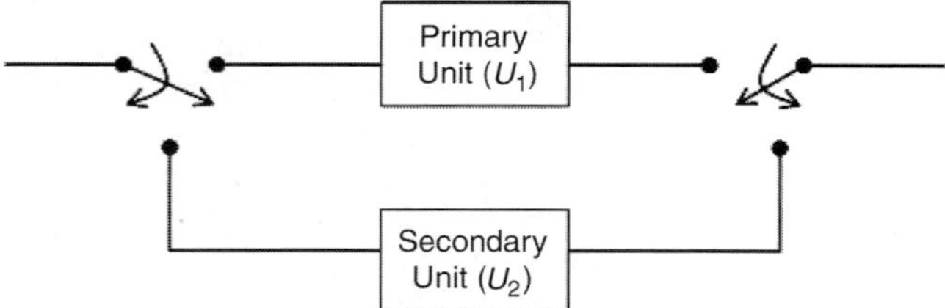

Figure 4: A simple parallel system (standby sparing)

Assuming that C_1 is the fault coverage of U_1, the reliability of this parallel system is given by $R_P(t) = R_1(t) + C_1(1 - R_1(t))R_2(t)$, where $R_i(t)$ is the reliability of unit U_i. Notice that in case of perfect coverage ($C_1 = 1$), we have $R_P(t) = R_1(t) + (1 - R_1(t))R_2(t) = 1 - (1 - R_1(t))(1 - R_2(t))$, which is the expression for a perfect parallel system. If $C_1 = 0$, $R_P(t)$ reduces to the reliability of a single unit (i.e., a simplex system).

Markov Approach

Markov modeling provides a systematic means of investigating system reliability for large and complex systems. One of the most significant advantages of the Markov models is that they allow us to model repair and coverage easily. Two main concepts of the Markov model are states and state transitions. The *state* describes the system at any given time with respect to component failures and the behavior of the system's redundancy-management strategy. Transitions govern the changes in state that occur in a system. Transitions from one state to another occur at given transition rates, which reflect component failure and repair rates. In this model, we calculate the probability of the system being in various states as a function of time. These state probabilities are then used to compute performance measures such as reliability and availability. For reliability modeling, we can use a first-order Markov model in which the present state depends only on the previous state and the state transition probability. Markov models can be of two types: discrete time and continuous time.

A set of differential equations define what is called a "continuous-time Markov model" (which is commonly used). This model can be solved to find the state probabilities. One of the most significant advantages of the Markov models is that they allow us to model repair and coverage easily. A major disadvantage is that the state space can grow exponentially with the number of components. We, therefore, need to find ways (such as grouping states, making assumptions, and/or simplifications) to render this problem tractable in many situations.

To illustrate the use of continuous-time Markov model, consider a simple redundant system with two identical components with failure rate λ and repair rate μ. The system is in operational state when both the components are operational, in half-operational state if one of the components has failed, and in failed state if both components have failed. Let P_O, P_H, and P_F denote the state probabilities; that is, the probability of the system is in operational state, half-operational state, and failed state, respectively. The state diagram for the Markov model is shown in Figure 5, assuming that we have perfect coverage and a single repair person.

The set of simultaneous differential equations (also called Chapman-Kolmogorov equations) that describe the system are given by

$$\dot{P}_O(t) = -2\lambda P_O(t) + \mu P_H(t),$$
$$\dot{P}_H(t) = 2\lambda P_O(t) - (\lambda + \mu)P_H(t) + \mu P_F(t),$$
$$\dot{P}_F(t) = \lambda P_H(t) - \mu P_F(t).$$

These equations can be solved using LaPlace transform with initial conditions $P_O(0) = 1$, $P_H(0) = 0$, and $P_H(0) = 0$ to obtain $P_O(t)$, $P_H(t)$, and $P_F(t)$. To get steady-state probability, we do not need to solve the differential equations. Instead, we solve the following equations to get P_O, P_H, and P_F:

$$\begin{aligned} 2\lambda P_O &= \mu P_H, \\ (\lambda + \mu) P_H &= 2\lambda P_O + \mu P_F, \\ \mu P_F &= \lambda P_H, \\ P_O + P_H + P_F &= 1. \end{aligned}$$

Thus, we have:

$$P_O = \frac{\lambda^2}{2\lambda^2 + 2\lambda\mu + \mu^2},$$
$$P_H = \frac{2\lambda\mu}{2\lambda^2 + 2\lambda\mu + \mu^2},$$
$$P_F = \frac{2\lambda^2}{2\lambda^2 + 2\lambda\mu + \mu^2}$$

The Markov technique can be used to model imperfect coverage. If we consider a coverage factor of C for the above example, the state diagram takes the form shown in Figure 6, where the arc from "Operational" to "Failed" represents a single component failure for which the fault-tolerance features cannot successfully reconfigure.

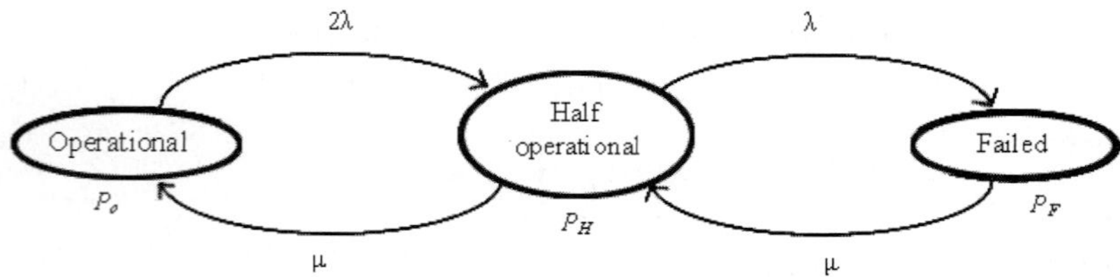

Figure 5: Markov model for a redundant system

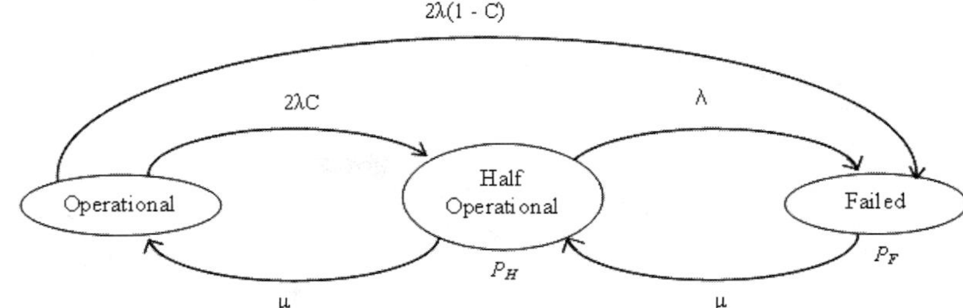

Figure 6: Markov model with coverage for a redundant system

FAULT-TOLERANCE TECHNIQUES

The key ingredient in all fault-tolerance techniques is redundancy. The redundancy may take several forms, including redundancies in information, hardware, software, and time. These techniques are summarized in this section. Detailed descriptions of various fault tolerance techniques can be found in Johnson (1989), Lyu (1995), Guerraoui and Schipper (1997), Pradhan (2003), Randell and Xu (1995), Hecht and Hecht (2003), Koo and Toueg (1987), Avizienis (1985), Torres-Pomales (2000), Nelson (1990), and Rennels (1984).

Hardware Redundancy

Hardware redundancy is the physical replication of hardware for the purpose of detecting and tolerating faults. This is perhaps the most common form of fault tolerance used in systems. A common form of this redundancy is the triple modular redundancy (TMR). In the TMR system three identical units perform identical functions, and a majority vote is performed by a voter on the output with the purpose of masking any single fault, as illustrated in Figure 7.

The general form of TMR is the *N*-modular redundancy (NMR). The voter in this scheme is, unfortunately, the single point of failure. In the case of NMR, *N* must be odd and such a system can tolerate $(N - 1)/2$ faults. The primary trade-off in NMR is the fault tolerance versus the hardware required. Power weight, cost, and size limitations very often determine the value of *N* in the NMR system. Other forms of hardware redundancy involve incorporating fault detection and fault recovery into the system at the expense of eliminating fault-masking capability. An example of this is the standby replacement. In this configuration, one unit is operational while one or more units are standbys. Various error-detection schemes are used to determine when the online unit has failed; if a failure is detected, the online unit is removed from operation and replaced with a standby. Hardware redundancy can be categorized in three schemes: *passive* (*static*), *active* (*dynamic*), and *hybrid*.

Passive (static) schemes use fault masking to hide the occurrence of faults and prevent the faults from resulting in errors. They rely on voting mechanism to mask the occurrence of faults. Passive redundancy schemes instantly correct errors and do not require higher system-level intervention to do so. The TMR and error-correcting codes are some examples of the static redundancy scheme.

Active (dynamic) schemes, on the other hand, achieve fault tolerance by detecting the existence of faults and performing some actions to remove the faulty hardware (using fault detection), fault location, and recovery. Active schemes require interruption of system availability while the fault is isolated. Once the fault is isolated, the redundant resource is switched on, and the system is recovered. For a real-time system, if the error occurs in the middle of an operation, some program rollback is necessary to discard the bad data and to recover as much good data as possible. The primary advantage of dynamic redundancy techniques is that they can be implemented with fewer resources. Examples of active redundancy are duplication with comparison, standby sparing, and watchdog timers. In duplication with comparison, if two processors disagree on the result found for the same job, obviously there is an error. The disadvantage of this technique is that if both results are incorrect, the error will go undetected. Another disadvantage is that the comparator may be faulty and signal an error when both results are correct.

In the standby sparing technique, one module is operational with one or more modules used as spares. When an error is detected in the operational module, it is removed from operation and is replaced by one of the spares. In hot standby sparing, spare modules operate in synchrony and are prepared to take over at any time. In cold standby sparing, spare modules are not powered until needed to replace the faulty module. An example of standby sparing is illustrated in Figure 4. Watchdog timers are one form of active redundancy used for detecting faults in a system. The idea of watchdog timers is that a lack of

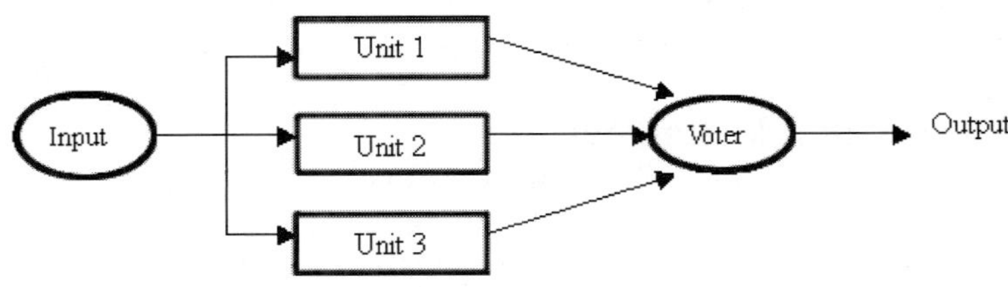

Figure 7: A TMR system

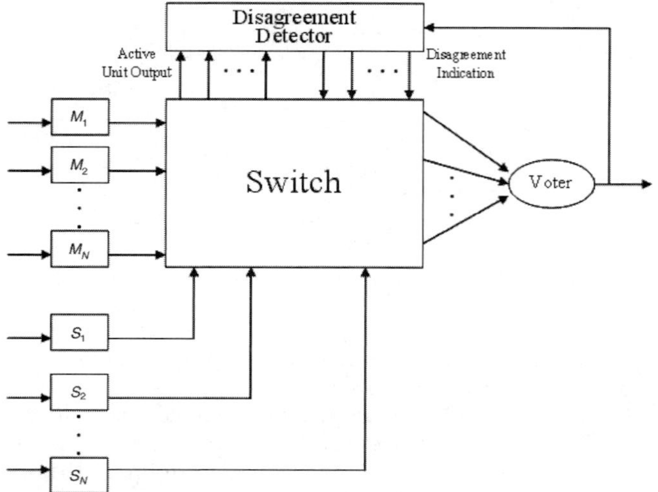

Figure 8: N-modular redundancy with spares

action indicates a fault. The timers may erroneously signal a fault if the module is slower than usual. The reason is that watchdog timers do not see any incoming results.

Hybrid schemes combine attractive features of both passive and active techniques. Static redundancy provides error masking and detecting capability. Dynamic redundancy provides a set of spares and a switching network for reconfiguration. Fault masking is used in hybrid systems to prevent erroneous results from being generated. Fault detection, location, and recovery are also used to improve fault tolerance by removing faulty hardware. This is a very expensive form of redundancy scheme to implement, and it is often used in critical applications, in which high reliability must be achieved. Examples of hybrid redundancy are *N*-modular redundancy with spares, self-purging redundancy, and triple-duplex architecture. The idea of *N*-modular redundancy with spares is to provide a core of *N* modules arranged in a voting configuration with additional spares to replace faulty units. A frequent configuration is three (redundant) modules with one or two spares. Figure 8 illustrates the operation of *N*-modular redundancy with spares. The self-purging redundancy approach is similar to the technique of *N*-modular redundancy with spares. The difference is that all units are active (no spares) at the same time. In this technique, each module can remove itself from the circuit if its output disagrees with the voted output of the system. This approach provides more fault tolerance but is more expensive as far as power consumption is concerned.

Triple-duplex architecture combines duplication with comparison and TMR. The use of TMR provides fault masking. The use of duplication with comparison allows for faults to be detected and then have faulty units removed from the system. In this configuration, each module of the TMR is duplicated (with a comparison scheme).

Information Redundancy

Information redundancy is concerned with the addition of redundant information to allow fault detection, fault masking, or possibly fault tolerance. Error-detecting and error-correcting codes (ECC Page 2002; Lin and Costello 1983) are good examples of information redundancy. Error-correcting codes enable data to be sent through a noisy communication channel without corruption. To accomplish this, the sender appends redundant information to the message, so that even if some of the original data are corrupted during transmission, the receiver can still recover the original message intact. Many computers now have error-correcting capabilities built into their random access memories; it is less expensive to compensate for errors through the use of error-correcting codes than to build highly reliable integrated circuits. Storage devices (compact disk, random access memory, dynamic random access memory), mobile communication (cellular telephones, wireless, microwave links), satellite communication, digital television, and high-speed modems (asymmetric digital subscriber line, x digital subscriber line) are other areas of computing in which error-correcting codes are used.

Instead of transmitting raw digital information, the data are encoded in the form of a "code word" with redundant information using a well-defined set of rules at the source. The code word is then transmitted, and the receiver can decode it to retrieve the desired information while being able to detect and possibly correct any error. A code word is said to be *valid* if it adheres to all of the rules that define the code; otherwise, the code word is said to be *invalid*. The *encoding* process determines the corresponding code word for a given data item, whereas the *decoding* process recovers the original data from the code word. If the code words are formed correctly, errors that are introduced during transmission can be detected during the decoding process at the destination because the code word would be transformed into an invalid code word. This is the basic concept of the *error-detecting codes*. The basic concept of the *error-correcting code* is that the code word is structured such that it is possible to determine the correct code word from the corrupted, or erroneous, code word. A fundamental concept in the characterization of codes is the *Hamming distance*, in which the distance between any two binary words is the number of bit positions in which the two words differ. The Hamming distance gives insight into the requirements of error-detecting codes and error-correcting codes. The *code distance* (C_d) is the minimum Hamming distance between any two valid code words. For a binary code (consisting of digits 0 and 1) to be able to detect up to d bit errors and to correct up to c bit errors, the code distance must be at least $d + 1$ and $2c + 1$, respectively. The same code can correct up to c bit errors and detect an additional d bit errors if and only if $C_d - 2c + d + 1$. For example, a code with a distance of 2 cannot provide any error correction but can detect single-bit errors. Similarly, a code with a distance of 3 can correct single-bit errors or detect a double-bit error. Separability is another fundamental concept in the characterization of codes. A code is *separable* if the code words are formed by appending the check bits to the original information bits. A code is *nonseparable* if the code words are not partitioned directly into information and check bits.

The simplest form of error-detection coding is the single-bit parity check. Single-bit parity codes require the addition of an extra bit to a binary word such that the resulting code word has either an even number of 1s (even parity) or an odd number of 1s (odd parity). The single-bit parity code (either odd or even) has a distance of 2; therefore, it allows any single-bit error to be detected but not corrected. Perhaps the most common extension of parity is the Hamming error-correcting code, which is designed to detect double errors and correct single errors. The Hamming code allows error correction because the minimum distance between any two *valid* code words is 3. Hamming codes are widely used most to protect memories. The reasons are that it is relatively inexpensive (10% to 40% of redundancy) and very efficient. The Hamming code is formed by partitioning information bits into parity groups. By overlapping the groups of bits, erroneous bits can be detected and corrected. Other forms of error detection coding are: *checksums* and *arithmetic codes* (Siewiorek and Swartz 1998).

Checksums are most applicable when blocks of data are to be transferred from one point to another. These are separable codes and perform error detection by appending extra information to the original data. They are often simple to implement but do not provide good error correction. The checksum is basically the sum of the original data and is appended to the original data. The checksum is then regenerated when the data are received at the destination. The original and the recomputed checksums are compared. An error is signaled if they differ.

Arithmetic codes are very useful when it is desired to check arithmetic operations such as addition, multiplication, and division. The data presented to the arithmetic operation are encoded before the operations are performed. After completing the arithmetic operations, the resulting code words are checked to make sure that they are valid. If the resulting code words are not valid, an error condition is signaled. The primary advantage of the arithmetic codes is that they allow hardware that performs arithmetic operations to be easily checked. The code must be invariant for a set of arithmetic operations. For instance, if an arithmetic code A is invariant for the multiplication, then $A(xy) = A(x).A(y)$, where x and y are operands, and $A(x)$ and $A(y)$ are the arithmetic code words for the operands x and y, respectively. The most common examples of arithmetic codes are the *AN* codes, residue codes, and the inverse residue codes. The *AN* code is formed by multiplying each data point, N, by a constant A. The *AN* codes are invariant to addition and subtractions but not multiplication and division. The correctness of an operation performed using an *AN* code can be checked by determining whether the result is evenly divisible by A; otherwise, it is signaled as an error. Selection of A is crucial to the effectiveness and efficiency of the resulting code. Moreover, the magnitude of A determines extra bits required to represent code words and the error-detection capability. For binary codes, A must not be a power of 2. The residue codes are separable arithmetic codes formed by appending the residue r (where r is the residue of N modulo m) of a number N for a given modulus m to that number. Encoding process determines the residue and appends the residue to the original data. Decoding process simply removes the residue. The inverse-residue codes are like residue codes, but rather than appending the residue, the inverse residue $m-r$ (where r is the residue of N modulo m) is calculated and appended.

Two other codes worth mentioning are *m-of-n codes* and *Berger codes*. The *m-of-n codes* are formed by creating code words of size n bits in which there are exactly m number of 1s. Any single-bit error forces the resulting erroneous word to have either $m+1$ or $m-1$ number of 1s. Not only can the error be detected, but also the direction of error (0 to 1 or 1 to 0) can be found. The *m-of-n codes* are conceptually simple, but the encoding, decoding, and detection processes are often difficult to perform. The *Berger codes* are separable codes formed by appending a special set of bits (check bits) to each word of information. The check bits are created based on the number of 0s in the original information. The code word is then formed by appending to the original information the binary representation of the number of 0s found. In general, if we have k information bits then we need $\lceil \log_2(k+1) \rceil$ check bits. The *Berger codes* use the fewest number of check bits of all separable codes.

Time Redundancy

Time redundancy uses additional time to provide fault detection and, sometimes, fault tolerance. It can be used to distinguish between permanent and transient failures. Time redundancy is extremely useful for detecting transient faults but not permanent faults. Simple retries allow for transient fault detection as well as their correction. This method attempts to reduce the amount of extra hardware at the expense of using additional time if that is readily available. The basic concept of time redundancy is to perform the same computation repeated times and compare the results to determine whether a discrepancy exists. If an error is detected, the computations can be performed again to see whether the disagreement remains or disappears. The processor performs the computations one or more times after detecting the first error; if the error condition clears, the processor can assume that the fault was transient. In another form of time redundancy, the same processor performs the same computations multiple times using different coding schemes in each case, with the assumption that the fault may manifest itself in different ways depending on the particular code being used. The main problem with many time-redundancy techniques is ensuring that the system has the same data to manipulate each time it redundantly performs a computation.

Software Redundancy

Unlike hardware, software is not subject to wear-out conditions that occur from aging, stress, or environmental factors. Thus, the only cause of software faults is improper specification or bad design and/or implementation of programs, which results in the inability of the software to meet its designed requirements or specifications under unforeseen circumstances or changes to the computing environment. Although, just like in fault-tolerant hardware, reliable software systems must be able to either eliminate or effectively tolerate and recover from faults. Because modern software systems are so complex, it is nearly impossible to eliminate all of the embedded faults;

therefore, development techniques that protect the entire system from incorrect operation should be used in cases in which program failure would have serious consequences. Like hardware, all software fault-tolerant techniques require redundancy to support the fault-tolerant features. Software redundancy is simply the addition of extra software to provide some fault-tolerance features. The type of redundancy may range from complete replication of software to the addition of small programs to perform validity checks, such as consistency and capability checks. A consistency check is based on prior knowledge of the computation results. If the result is not in a predefined range, then an error has occurred in the computation process. The capability-check technique verifies that a system possesses the capability expected. Apart from the validity checks, there are two important approaches to software fault tolerance: *recovery* and *redundancy*. The recovery is normally achieved through *recovery block* mechanisms, whereas design diversity such as the *N-version programming* is used to provide redundancy.

Error Recovery

Error recovery is a process that brings the system back to an error-free state. It is probably the most important phase of any fault-tolerance technique. There are two approaches to recovery: *backward recovery* and *forward recovery*.

Backward recovery restores the system to a previous safe state, which is referred to as a "recovery point." The act of establishing the recovery point is called "checkpointing," which is a process of checking and saving the current system state for recovery. The advantage of backward recovery is that the erroneous state is cleared, and no effort is needed to find the location and cause of the fault. Therefore, this approach is ideal for recovering from unanticipated faults, including design faults. Rollback is one of the backward-recovery mechanisms. Rollback is often used by database systems to return the system state from the unfinished transaction to the previous consistent state by undoing all the steps that have been done since the transaction started. To be able to recover, it is needed to store the system's state at the recovery point to a stable storage, such as a hard disk, so recovery needs space. Also, recovery takes time, and the whole process has to be prevented from proceeding by executing a recovery algorithm instead. In a real-time system, because of the tight time constraint to reach a certain state, recovery mechanisms might not be the possible solution to the detected errors.

Forward recovery attempts to continue from an erroneous state by making selective corrections to the system state. This includes making safe the controlled environment, which may be hazardous or damaged because of the failure. Upon the detection of a failure, the system discards the current erroneous state and determines the correct state without any loss of computation. It is system-specific and depends on accurate predictions of the location and cause of the errors (i.e., damage assessment). Exception handling is a forward-recovery mechanism, as there is no rollback to a previous state involved; instead, control is passed to the exception handler so that the recovery procedures can be initiated. There are two basic approaches to backward recovery: one that relies on hardware redundancy (both static and dynamic) and the other on software redundancy. Forward-recovery schemes based on static hardware redundancy mask the failures through redundancy and have very high hardware overhead, whereas forward recovery schemes that are based on dynamic redundancy and checkpointing have lower hardware overhead (Pradhan 2003). The software-redundancy-based approach for forward recovery requires a certain degree of software redundancy as well as hardware redundancy. Error detection is performed by acceptance tests, and the recovery is handled using the recovery block concept, described below.

Recovery Block

The recovery block (RB) mechanism (Randell and Xu 1995) combines the basics of the checkpoint and restart approach with multiple versions of a software component such that a different version is tried after an error is detected (see Figure 9). It detects errors through the

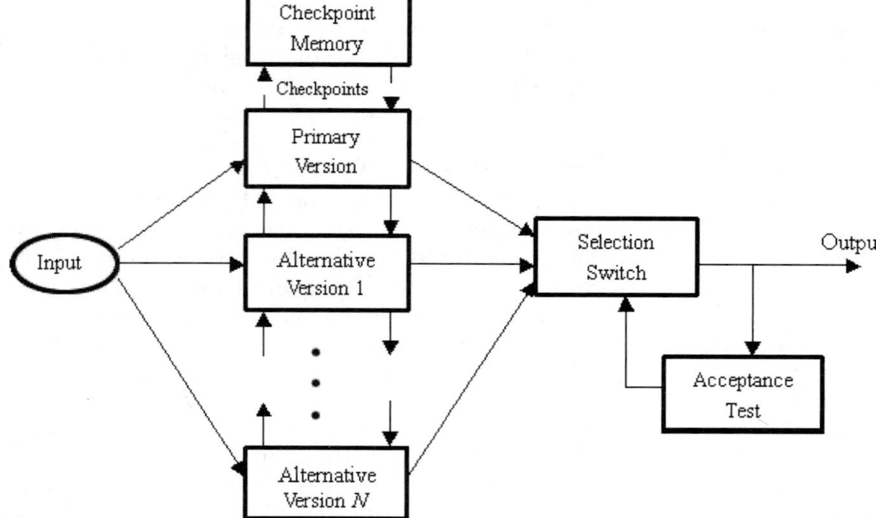

Figure 9: Recovery block

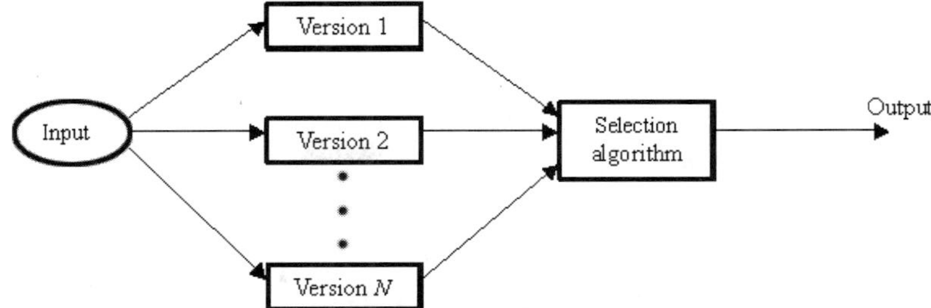

Figure 10: *N*-version programming

acceptance test after running each alternative. Checkpoints are created before a version executes and are needed to recover the state after a version fails. The recovery blocks use temporal redundancy (i.e., execution of a different version of software after an error has been detected) and software standby sparing. This provides protection against software-induced errors and hardware transient faults. Software is partitioned into several self-contained versions called "recovery blocks." Each recovery block is composed of a primary version, one or more alternative versions, and an acceptance test. The primary version contains the preferred algorithm for the task. The secondary versions act as standby spares that are designed and coded independently from the primary. The acceptance test is used to test whether the system is in an acceptable state after the first execution of the primary version. The failure of the acceptance test results in the program being restored to the recovery point and the second alternative version is executed. If the second version also fails the acceptance test, then the program is restored to the recovery point and yet another alternative version is executed. If all the alternatives are exhausted, the system fails.

Two issues must be considered when using the recovery-block mechanism (Torres-Pomales 2000):

- *Domino effect*: For two concurrent processes interacting with each other, one process rolling back to its recovery point might cause the other to roll back to its recovery point as well. This procedure could go on until the whole system returns to its original state. This phenomenon is called the "domino effect." The cause of this phenomenon is that each process is designed to have its own recovery point that does not consider others' recovery points. Carefully designing a consistent recovery point among all processes that are interacting with each other during execution could avoid this problem.
- *Logging*: Logging is the way used to keep track of modifications since last checkpointing, so the system will be able to roll back to the latest consistent state. Logs need to be saved in persistent storage to survive any crash.

N-Version Programming

The objective of *N*-version programming (NVP) is to provide fault tolerance through software design diversity. Design diversity assumes that multiple versions of software exist for a particular task and that each of these versions has been designed and coded by people working independently. The idea is that although each programmer is likely to make some error, all programmers will not make the same error. Hence, the results of running multiple versions of software can be voted upon in the same way that voting is conducted in hardware NMR. The rationale for the use of multiple versions is the expectation that components built differently should fail differently. The concept of NVP was developed by Algirdas Avizienis of UCLA (Avizienis 1985, 1995) to allow certain design flaws in software modules to be tolerated. In NVP, *N* versions of a software component are developed independently by different individuals/teams with different algorithms, techniques, programming languages, environments, and tools to ensure independent program versions. The *N*-version programs then run concurrently with the same inputs, and a driver process compares their results. The NVP concept is illustrated in Figure 10.

Another variation of multiversion programming is the *N*-self-checking programming (NSCP) (Lyu 1995), which is the use of multiple software versions combined with structural variations of RB and NVP. NSCP uses multiple versions of acceptance tests that are independently developed from common requirements. The use of separate acceptance tests for each version is the main difference between RB and NSCP. Like NSCP, other variations of RB also exist, the consensus recovery block (CRB) being one such variation. The CRB approach combines NVP and RB to improve reliability over any of these individual approaches. The CRB uses a decision algorithm similar to NVP as a first layer of decision. If the first layer declares a failure, a second layer using acceptance tests similar to those used in RB approach is used.

Algorithm-Based Fault Tolerance

Algorithm-based fault tolerance (ABFT) can be considered another form of software redundancy. It is based on the use of fault-detection and fault-tolerance techniques specific to an algorithm, which allows for errors in computations to be detected and corrected (Nair, Abraham, and Banerjee 1996). The ABFT techniques have been proposed for various signal-processing computations, such as matrix operations, fast Fourier transforms, factorization, etc. (Huang and Abraham 1984). For example, in a matrix operation, each matrix can be augmented with a row or column checksum. If the checksum is erroneous, the error will be detected, the location of the error can be identified, and the erroneous entry can be corrected. This can be illustrated with the following example.

Example: Suppose we want to multiply two 2 × 2 matrices A and B to get a 2 × 2 matrix C as given below:

$$A = \begin{pmatrix} 8 & 3 \\ 5 & 4 \end{pmatrix}, B = \begin{pmatrix} 2 & 4 \\ 6 & 7 \end{pmatrix}, C = AB = \begin{pmatrix} 34 & 53 \\ 34 & 48 \end{pmatrix}.$$

Instead of multiplying A and B to get C, we multiply A_{rcs} (the row checksum matrix of A) and B_{ccs} (the column checksum matrix of B) to get C_{cs} as shown below. C_{cs} happens to be the checksum matrix of C.

$$A_{rcs} \begin{pmatrix} 8 & 3 \\ 5 & 4 \\ 13 & 7 \end{pmatrix}, B_{ccs} = \begin{pmatrix} 2 & 4 & 6 \\ 6 & 7 & 13 \end{pmatrix}, C_{cs} = \begin{pmatrix} 34 & 53 & 87 \\ 34 & 48 & 82 \\ 68 & 101 & 169 \end{pmatrix}.$$

Now suppose that the (2,2) entry of C_{cs} is incorrect (say, 32 instead of 48). Not only can any single error be detected, the location of the error also be identified by taking the intersection of the row and column in which the checksums are erroneous. In our case, both row 2 checksum and column 2 checksum will signal an error, pointing to the error location (2,2), since $34 + 32 \neq 82$ and $53 + 32 \neq 101$. The erroneous entry can also be corrected with the value that will give the correct checksum in row 2 and column 2.

Self-Checking Design

As digital systems get more and more complex, it is becoming highly desirable to have systems that have self-checking capability. A circuit is called "self-checking" if it has the ability to automatically detect the existence of a fault without the need for externally applied test stimuli (Lala 1985). Self-checking design uses the error-detecting codes to encode the output. The basic idea behind this design is that during fault-free operation, the output of such a circuit is always a code word, and hence, an invalid code word at the output will signal the existence of a fault. Two concepts that define self-checking design need to be discussed. A circuit is said to be *fault-secure* for a given set of faults, if for any fault in the set, the circuit never produces an incorrect code word for any valid input code word. In other words, a circuit is fault-secure if the fault either has no effect on the output, or the output is affected such that it becomes an invalid code word. A circuit is said to be *self-testing*, if there exists at least one valid input code word that will produce an invalid output code word when a single fault is present. A circuit is *totally self-checking* if it is both fault-secure and self-testing. A totally self-checking circuit will always produce either the correct code word at the output or an invalid code word, and there will be at least one valid input code word that will produce an invalid output code word when any single fault is present. If the circuit is self-testing for a set N of normal inputs and a set F of faults, and is fault-secure for a subset of inputs and a subset of faults, then this circuit is called *partially self-checking*. A circuit is called *fail-safe* if the output is either correct or belongs to the set of safe outputs. The traffic light with a fail-safe output as flashing red on all sides is a good example of a fail-safe circuit. An application of the self-checking technique

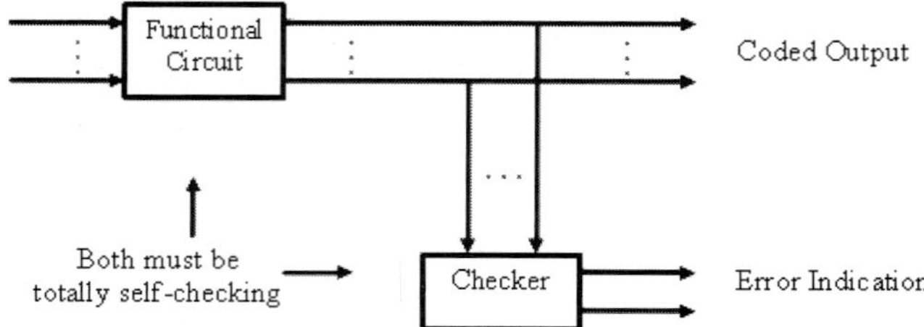

Figure 11: Basic structure of a totally self-checking circuit

is the programmable logic array, which is a common structure in very-large-scale integration (VLSI) designs. The basic structure of a totally self-checking circuit is shown in Figure 11.

In this figure, the function of a checker is to determine whether the output of the functional circuit is a valid code word. In addition, the checker must indicate if any fault has occurred in the checker itself. To accomplish both tasks, the output of the checker is encoded to produce an error signal. The checker has two bits of output. The outputs are complementary if the input to the checker is a valid code word and the checker is fault-free; otherwise, they are noncomplementary. The checker must possess *code disjoint* property, which means when the checker is fault-free, the valid code words on the checker's input lines must be mapped into valid error codes (the checker's outputs are complementary) on a checker's output lines. Likewise, invalid code words on a checker's input lines must be mapped into invalid error code words (the checker's outputs are noncomplementary) on the checker's output. There is no simple, systematic method to use in the design of totally self-checking checkers. The most common totally self-checking checker is the two-rail checker, as shown in Figure 12.

The two-rail checker is used to compare two words that should normally be complementary. It will produce complementary error signals e_1 and e_2 if the inputs are complementary; otherwise, the error signals will be non-complementary. The two-rail checker satisfies the fault-secure property for the following reason. Both e_1 and e_2 are generated by two physically separate circuits. Because the error signals are defined as complementary, any fault that affects one of the two signals will cause e_1 and e_2 to be noncomplementary. A fault either does not impact error signals or it forces error signals to no longer remain complementary. Faults on primary input to the checker simply appear to the checker as invalid code words and result in noncomplementary outputs. Similarly, it can be shown that the two-rail checker also satisfies the self-testing property, making it a totally self-checking checker. Totally

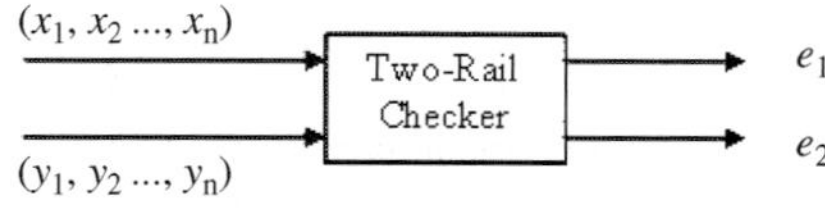

$e_1 = e_2'$ if and only if $x_i = y_i'$ for all i.

Figure 12: A two-rail checker

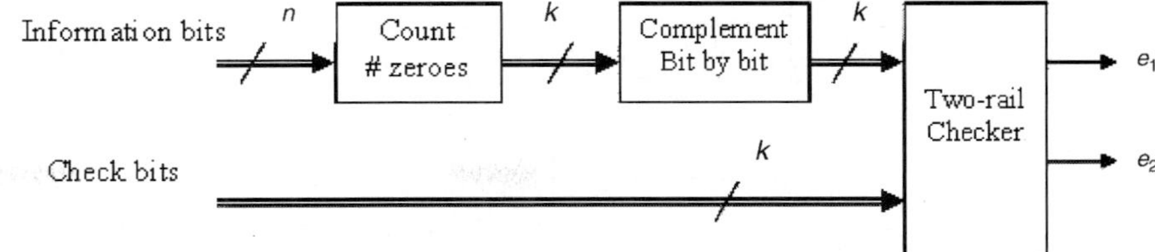

Figure 13: The general structure of a totally self-checking checker for the Berger code

self-checking checkers can be designed for any application. Figure 13 shows the general structure of a totally self-checking checker for the Berger code.

Survey of Fault-Tolerant Systems

Since the early 1950s, fault-tolerance techniques have been used to achieve highly reliable hardware operation. High reliability in computer design was first achieved through fault-avoidance techniques; these involved computer design that used high-quality, thoroughly tested components. Simple redundancy techniques were used to achieve limited fault tolerance. Examples of the first digital computers to use error-detection and fault-tolerance techniques to overcome the low reliability of their basic components are: the Bell Relay Computer (BRC), which had two CPUs; the IBM 650 and UNIVAC, which incorporated parity to check results of data transfer; and EDVAC, which was the first computer to have two arithmetic logic units (ALUs). With the advent of transistors, the emphasis of fault-tolerant computing decreased temporarily. It was not until computers began performing more critical tasks (for the U.S space program and in military applications) that fault tolerance again surfaced as a critical issue. Today, the increasing public dependence on automated services combined with the lower cost and increased performance of semiconductor technology has contributed to a renewed interest in fault-tolerant computing.

The major thrusts behind the development of fault-tolerant computing have been high reliability, high availability, reduced life-cycle cost, and long-life applications. Four major application areas of fault-tolerant systems are (ordered by increasingly stringent reliability requirements): general-purpose commercial applications, high-availability applications, long-life applications, and critical-computation applications. DEC VAX-11/780, IBM S/360-S/370-4300 family, Univac 1100/60 are some examples of general-purpose commercial applications. Banking and other time-shared systems are good examples of high-availability applications. Tandem (Dimmer 1985), Stratus (Webber and Beirne 1991), Pluribus (Katsuki et al. 1978), Electronic Switching System (ESS) (Toy 1978), and Intel 432 are some examples of high-availability applications. Users of these systems want to have a high probability of receiving service when it is requested. The Tandem NonStop transaction processing system is a good example of a system designed for high availability. The Intel 432 processor system is an example developed to support high availability in many general-purpose processing applications. The most common examples of long-life applications are unmanned space flight and satellites. The self-testing and repairing (STAR) computer (Avizienis et al. 1971), Pioneer, Voyager, Galileo, the fault-tolerant spaceborne computer (FTSC) (Burchby, Kern, and Sturm 1976), and the fault-tolerant building block computer (FTBBC) are some examples of long-life applications that have a system operating life over 5 years. These systems are highly redundant, with enough spares to survive the mission with required computational power. Typical long-life applications are to have 0.95 probability of being operational at the end of a 10-year period. Examples of critical-computation applications include aircraft flight-control systems, military systems, and certain types of industrial controllers. Examples of some critical-computation applications are the space shuttle computer (Sklaroff 1976), C.vmp (Siewiorek et al. 1978), the software-implemented fault-tolerance (SIFT) computer (Wensly et al. 1978), the fault-tolerant multiprocessor (FTMP) (Hopkins, Smith, and Lala 1978), aircraft-control systems, military systems, and industrial control systems. The design goal is the failure probability of less than 10^{-9} for a 10-hr mission. A typical requirement for a critical computation application is to have a reliability of 0.9999999 at the end of a 3-hr period. SIFT and FTMP are avionic computers designed to control dynamically unstable aircraft. In a critical computation application, computations must not only be correct, but recovery time from faults must be minimized. Specially designed hardware is implemented with concurrent error detection so that incorrect data never leave the faulty module.

In the remainder of this section, we will briefly review the main features of some of these fault-tolerant systems. Discussions on other fault-tolerant systems can be found in Pradhan (2003), Siewiorek and Swartz (1998), and Neil (2005). The features of a fault-tolerant storage device called the "redundant array of independent disks" (RAID), which uses multiple hard drives for sharing or replicating data among the drives to achieve fault tolerance, are also described as a related topic. In recent years, computer networks and the Internet have played an important role in modern society. Numerous network-based applications and services have made the availability and reliability of networks crucial. As a result, fault-tolerance ability is strongly needed by networks. This section will conclude with a discussion on fault tolerance in the context of networking and the Internet.

Tandem

Tandem computers (Dimmer 1985) were the early fault-tolerant computers built for high-availability applications to cope with the rising transaction-processing needs in banks, automatic teller machines (ATMs), stock exchanges, etc. The Tandem 16 NonStop System, built in 1976, supported up to sixteen processors in a multicomputer

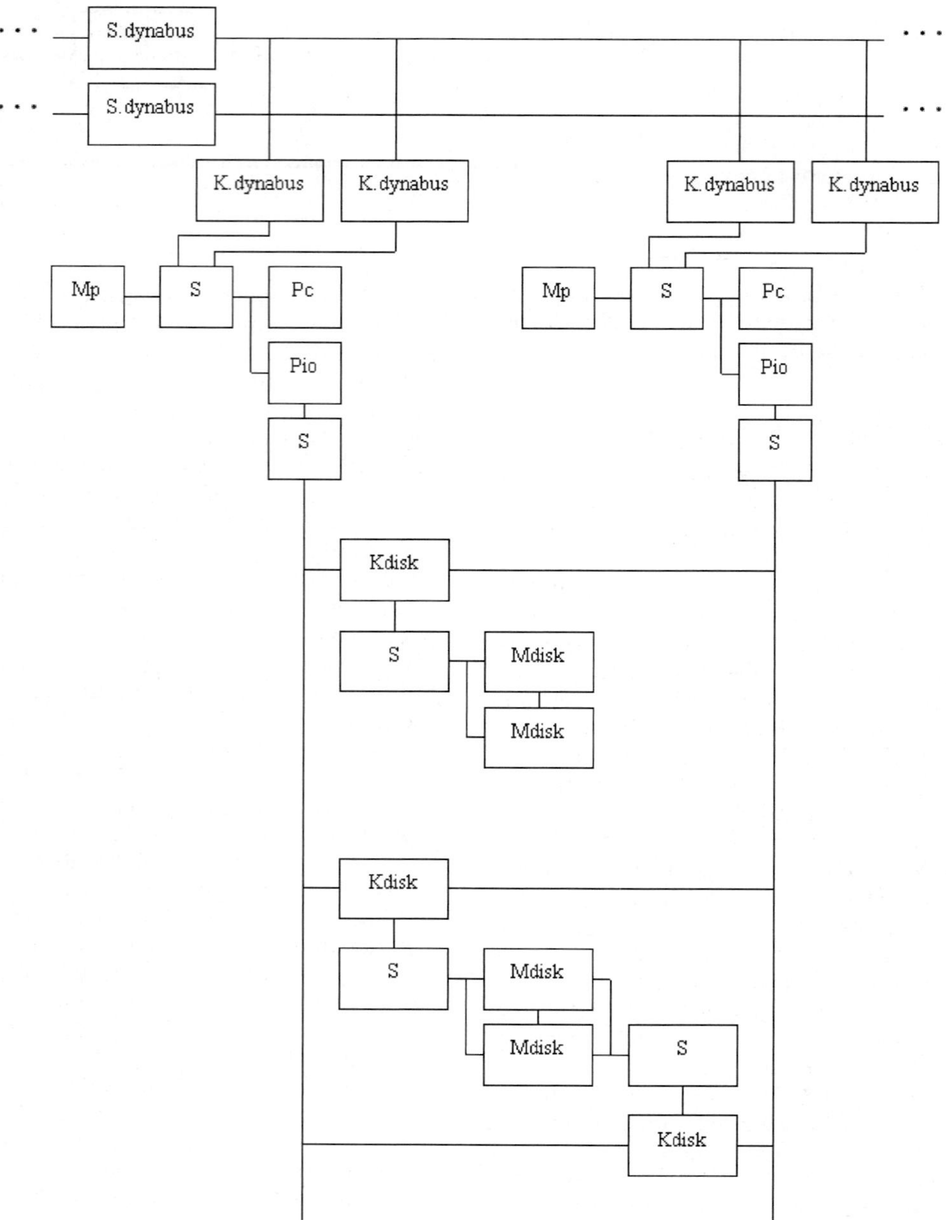

Figure 14: Tandem architecture

configuration. It was designed to provide autonomous fault detection, system reconfiguration, and system repair without interrupting the fault-free components within the system. The system contains a number of hardware-implemented fault-detection features, such as checksums on bus messages, parity error checking on data paths, error-correcting memories, and watchdog timers. The system eliminates single points of failure by means of dual paths to all system components, processor replication, redundant power supplies, and mirrored disks (see Figure 14). The Tandem system contains multiple CPUs, each with its own private memory and multiplexed input/output (I/O) channel. The processor modules communicate with one another over a pair of high-speed buses (called "Dynabus"). Peripheral-device controllers are connected to the I/O channel of two processor modules so that the device is accessible even if the CPU fails. Memories in Tandem systems use a modified Hamming code that allows for single-bit error correction and double-bit error detection. The NonStop hardware architecture and the Guardian 90 operating system architecture prevent a single hardware or software malfunction from disrupting system operations. In this parallel-processing architecture, the workload is divided among the processors, which perform multiple tasks simultaneously. This system architecture provides maximum throughput, since workloads are routed to the least congested processor. The key aspect of recovery in a Tandem system is checkpointing. Every process executing in the Tandem machine has an identical backup process (in standby mode) that resides in a different processor.

To guarantee that the backup process has the information to perform a required function, the primary process sends checkpoint messages to the backup process. The checkpoint messages specify the state of the primary process at certain critical points during the computation. If the primary process fails, the backup process is started using the most recent checkpoint information. Tandem systems use retry extensively to access I/O devices. For the past two decades Tandem systems have evolved considerably, and have been under the ownership of Compaq since 1997.

Space Shuttle Computer

In 1976, the space shuttle computer was probably the most difficult and complex machine ever built for critical-computation applications. The space shuttle computer system is responsible for providing flight-critical functions during the ascent, reentry, and descent of the spacecraft. The computer system consists of five identical IBM 32-bit general-purpose computers, each capable of performing critical and noncritical functions. In 1990, the original computers were replaced with IBM's upgraded model AP-101S, which has about 2.5 times the memory capacity (about 1 Mb) and three times the processor speed (about 1.2 million instructions per second). Each general-purpose computer consists of a CPU and an I/O processor. Four of these computers run a specialized software called the "primary avionics software set" (PASS) and are used as a redundant set during critical mission phases. The fifth computer, which acts as a backup to the primary system, runs a completely independent piece of software called the "backup flight software" (BFS) and performs noncritical tasks such as communications control and display processing. It sits in a "listen" mode, monitoring what is going on, unless it is commanded by the crew to take over. The four primary computers form an NMR arrangement, receive the same input, and perform the same computations. Each of these four computers listens to the output of the remaining three and compares those signals with its own. If one computer fails, the three functioning computers "vote" it out of the system. If a second of the three remaining computers fails, the system converts to a duplex system that can survive an additional computer failure by using comparison and self-tests to isolate the failure. The PASS was written by IBM, and the BFS was written by Rockwell International to minimize the probability of a common software error (Sklaroff 1976).

STAR

The self-testing and repairing (STAR) computer (Avizienis et al. 1971) was developed by the Jet Propulsion Laboratory (JPL), under the supervision of Algirdas Avizienis, for a 10-year mission to outer space. Although the design is over 30 years old, many of the techniques in this system are applicable today. The STAR computer was designed to handle guidance, control, and data acquisition on unmanned missions. It was desired to achieve a probability of 0.95 that the STAR computer would be completely operational at the end of 10 years. The designers of the STAR computer selected the dynamic redundancy method for achieving fault tolerance. The STAR computer uses cold standby sparing to achieve fault tolerance. Cold standby sparing incorporates active units with two spares. Error detection and reconfiguration are done by means of a special hardwired TMR test and repair processor (TARP) computer. The TARP computer uses triplication with voting and two spares to achieve fault masking and recovery. Each functional unit (control processor, logic processor, main arithmetic processor, and memory unit) performs its own fault detection. The TARP provides error checking on information transmitted over buses and reconfigures the system in the event of a unit failure. Error-detecting codes are used on all data and instruction words. The STAR system uses two primary types of error-detecting codes: the inverse residue code and the 2-of-4 code. However, the logic processor and the read/write memory use duplication and comparison for error detection. This scheme is defined as either shadow memory or mirrored memory. The TARP unit also operates as a watchdog timer. If a unit fails to send its periodic signal, the TARP computer considers the signal as a faulty unit and replaces it with a spare. The design of the STAR computer has been successful. It achieved a reliability of greater than 0.95 after 10 years of operation. A significant result of the STAR computer design was that it paved the way for future research in fault-tolerant computing. Many of the approaches tried and proven in the STAR design remain valid today.

Stratus

Founded in 1980, Stratus Computers competed mostly with Tandem Computers in transaction-processing applications. The Stratus systems are continuously checking between duplex components for detection of errors. The Stratus self-checking, duplicate-and-match architecture (see Figure 15) is composed of replicated power and backplane buses (StrataBus) into which a variety of boards are inserted. A Stratus computer system consists of up to thirty-two modules connected through a Stratus intermediate bus (StrataLink). Using StrataLink, the Stratus operating system provides a global system view of all devices in the system. The StrataLink consists of two independent coaxial links, each link running at 1.4 Mbps. The two processor boards (each containing a pair of multiprocessors) are self-checking modules used in a pair-and-spare configuration, each operating independently. Each half (A half or B half) of each board receives inputs from its own bus (bus A or bus B). The boards compare their two halves. Upon disagreement, a board signals malfunction and removes itself from service. The operating system executes diagnostics on the failed board to determine whether the error was due to a transient or a permanent fault. The Stratus hardware approach does not require online recovery from faults; the spare component continues processing until its faulty counterpart can be replaced. The fault-tolerant architecture isolates users from almost all hardware failures. System crashes are minimized with the use of software fault-recovery procedures.

RAID

RAID (redundant array of independent disks) is a family of techniques for managing multiple disks to provide desirable cost, data availability, and performance

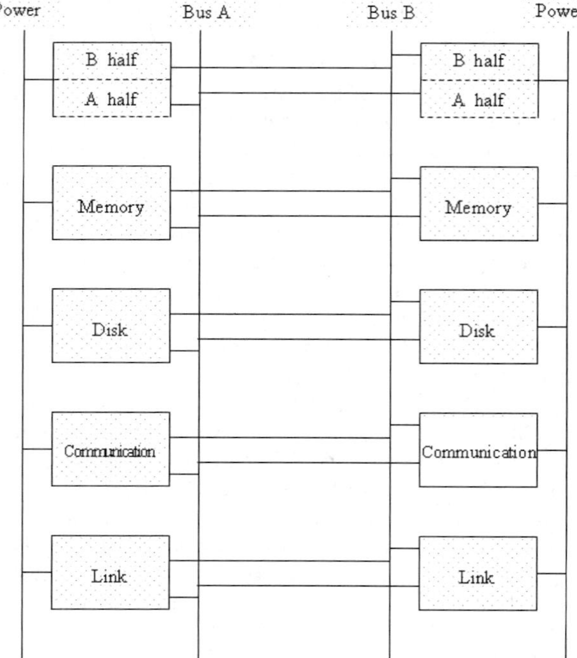

Figure 15: Stratus pair-and-spare architecture

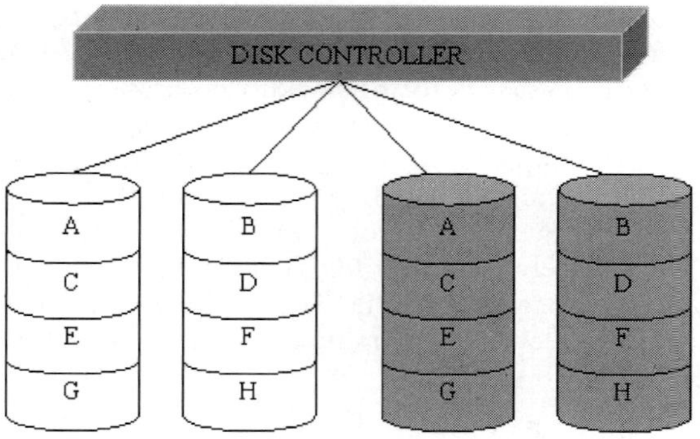

Figure 16: RAID-1 mirroring

characteristics to host environments. A RAID appears as a single drive. In principle, the same data are stored in many places on multiple disks to protect the data in the event of disk failure. RAID uses the technique of disk striping, which involves partitioning each drive's storage space into stripes that can be as small as one sector (a few bytes) or as large as several megabytes. The stripes of all the disks are interleaved in a round-robin fashion so that different stripes of the same file can reside in different physical drives. A disk controller in RAID manages the array of disk drives in such a way that data are protected. By mapping segments or by generating parity bits and storing them on the array, data can be regenerated if a disk drive fails. The manner in which data are placed onto the array provides for increased performance in different data structure environments.

There are many levels of RAID (AC&NC 2005; Chen et al. 1994), which are summarized below:

- *RAID*-0: This is the most basic level of RAID, which comes with striping but no redundancy. It is not a true fault-tolerant configuration, but it offers the best performance.
- *RAID*-1: This type is also known as *disk mirroring* and consists of at least two drives that duplicate the storage of data without any striping (see Figure 16). Read performance is improved, since either disk can be read at the same time. Write performance is the same as for single disk storage. RAID-1 provides the best performance and the best fault tolerance in a multi-user system, but it is most costly in terms of required disk overhead.
- *RAID*-2: This type uses striping across disks and handles the failed components with much less cost than mirroring by using error-correcting codes (ECC). This type uses striping across disks, with some disks storing ECC information. It uses the storage more efficiently than mirroring.
- *RAID*-3: This type introduces a more efficient way of storing data while still providing error correction. It uses striping, uses byte interleaved parity, stores parity information on a separate drive, and performs error checking. Data recovery is accomplished by calculating the exclusive OR (XOR) of the information recorded on the other drives. Since an I/O operation addresses all drives at the same time, RAID-3 cannot overlap I/O. For this reason, RAID-3 is best for single-user systems with long record applications.
- *RAID*-4: This type uses large stripes, which means one can read records from any single drive. This allows one to take advantage of overlapped I/O for read operations. Since all write operations have to update the parity drive, no I/O overlapping is possible.
- *RAID*-5: This type eliminates the parity disk bottleneck present in RAID-4 by distributing the parity uniformly over all the disks (rotating parity). Thus, all read and write operations can be overlapped. RAID-5 stores parity information but not redundant data (parity information is used to reconstruct data). RAID-5 requires at least three and usually five disks for the array. It is best for multi-user systems in which performance is not critical or which do few write operations.
- *RAID*-6: This type is similar to RAID-5 but includes a second parity scheme that is distributed across different drives, and thus offers extremely high fault- and drive-failure tolerance. The extra cost of additional space for parity drives has made RAID-6 rather unpopular.
- *RAID*-7: This type includes a real-time embedded operating system as a controller, caching via a high-speed bus, and other characteristics of a stand-alone computer.
- *RAID*-10 (*or RAID*-1+0): This hybrid configuration combines the best features of striping (RAID-0) and mirroring (RAID-1) to offer higher performance than RAID-1 but at much higher cost. This configuration comes in two forms: (1) RAID-0+1, in which data are organized as stripes across multiple disks, and then the striped disk sets are mirrored; and (2) RAID-1+0, in which the data are mirrored and the mirrors are striped.
- *RAID*-50 (*or RAID*-5+0): This type consists of a series of RAID-5 groups and striped in RAID-0 fashion to

improve RAID-5 performance without reducing data protection.
- *RAID*-53 (*or RAID*-5+3): This type uses striping (in RAID-0 style) for RAID-3's virtual disk blocks. This offers higher performance than RAID-3 but at much higher cost.

In summary, most RAID systems allow hot replacement of disks, which means that disks can be replaced while the system is running. When a disk is replaced, the parity information is used to rebuild the data on the disk. Rebuilding occurs while the operating system continues handling other operations, so there is some loss of performance during the rebuilding operation.

Fault-Tolerant Networking

The Internet has revolutionized the way people work and communicate. It is, therefore, important to ensure that the Internet continues to function reliably in the event of attacks and errors. In early packet switched network designs, the focus was on handling physical failures, such as link or node failure. More recently, the focus has shifted toward protecting routing protocols against more complex faults to ensure uninterrupted packet delivery. Many network vendors have already integrated fault-tolerance techniques into their systems or equipment.

A fundamental component of the Internet functionality is routing and therefore, it is critical to ensure its correctness and reliability. The abnormal routing behavior can happen because of compromised routers or by human error. Routing can be interrupted because of physical failures, operational faults, error in routing protocol design and/or implementation, compromised routers, and human error. Network resource exhaustion, which can be caused by software viruses, may also affect routing operation due to the in-line signaling nature of Internet routing protocols. Furthermore, malicious attacks can be directly aimed at routers, causing router overload and disrupting packet delivery. There are various defense schemes available against these attacks. Pei, Massey, and Zhang (2004) described a framework that divides defenses into different classes: cryptographic schemes, statistical anomaly detection, protocol syntax checking, and protocol semantic checking. Cryptographic mechanisms primarily aim at locking out external attackers. Anomaly detection, syntax, and semantics checking primarily provide essential detection mechanisms that notice when prevention has failed and also when unexpected faults occur. Secure neighbor-to-neighbor communication to prevent an outside entity from tampering with the messages exchanged between router, authentication to validate the identity of a legitimate router, and authorization to restrict the actions of a legitimate router are among the cryptographic protection schemes. These are all achieved through public-key cryptography. Statistical anomaly detection is based on statistical profiles to flag unexpected behavior. The abnormal routing behavior can happen because of compromised routers or by human error. Protocol syntax checking can be an effective means for detecting hardware faults and implementation error such as illegitimate message sequences. Protocol semantics checking can improve protocol behavior by monitoring the routing update messages among the routers.

The Internet was designed for fast packet delivery rather than reliability. The transmission in Internet is not fault-tolerant, but reliable delivery services are critical for certain applications, such as file transfer, database services, transaction processing, etc., which require every packet to be delivered. Though transport control protocol (TCP) provides reliable services, it depends on Internet protocol (IP) to deliver packets. IP sends and receives packets to and from IP addresses, but IP does not protect against data loss, data damage, packet out of order, or data duplication. IP is inherently unreliable, so TCP has to be responsible for verifying the correct delivery of data and requesting retransmissions. Several alternatives have been proposed for making TCP fault-tolerant, some of which are discussed below.

FT-TCP (fault-tolerant TCP) (Alvisi et al. 2001) allows the TCP connections to remain open until the faulty server recovers or is failed over to a backup, masking the failure from the client. To realize this, a wrapper software is used to surround the TCP layer and intercept all communication. Two wraps on both the IP and application sides communicate with a logger to record the state and cooperate to maintain or restore the TCP connection. FT-TCP does not need the modification of TCP protocol, nor does it affect the software running on a client, but the logger becomes a single point of failure. ST-TCP (server fault-tolerant TCP) (Marwah, Mishra, and Fetzer 2003) adopts the primary-backup approach, which uses an active backup server to tolerate TCP server failure by taking over the TCP connection. The backup server monitors the state of TCP connection between the client and the primary server and stores it as a replica of the primary application. No change or wrapper is required on the client machine, and the clients can connect to a ST-TCP server in the same way they connect to a standard TCP server. ST-TCP requires minor changes to the standard TCP server and can only tolerate single failure.

HARTs (high availability with redundant TCP stacks) (Shao et al. 2003) uses two or more servers as the primary servers to maintain redundant TCP connection stacks and to improve availability of TCP connections. Therefore, any failure in one of the server nodes does not interrupt the TCP connections. HARTs makes the redundant TCP connections as single networking, but multiple servers must be synchronized.

M-TCP (migratory TCP) (Sultan et al. 2002) also uses multiple servers. A client establishes a TCP connection with one of the servers, but the connection can migrate to another server depending on the migration policy used. The original server transfers the state of this connection to the new server, which starts a new TCP connection and restores the state, and then sends a message to the client to continue its operation. The migration is transparent to the client application. It may be triggered by conditions such as a server crash, network congestion, or degradation.

CONCLUSION

Fault-tolerant computing already has been playing a major role in communications, transportation, e-commerce, space, and many other areas that impact our lives. Computer architecture is changing because of development in the computer hardware and software design, which presents new challenges to the fault-tolerant industry. Many of its next advances are seen in new state-of-the-art systems such as massively parallel scalable computing, promising new unconventional architectures such as system-on-chip, processor-in-memory, or reconfigurable computing, mobile computing, and the other exciting new things that lie around the corner. Lately, there has been increasing focus on making applications fault-tolerant. Emerging multicast applications such as videoconferencing, distributed network games, telemedicine, distance learning, etc., need fault tolerance to ensure high levels of quality. Therefore, the interest in fault-tolerant systems, fault-tolerant computing, and fault-tolerant applications will keep increasing.

GLOSSARY

ABFT: Algorithm-based fault tolerance.

Availability, A(*t*): The probability that a system is operating correctly and is available to perform its functions at the instant of time *t*.

CRB: Consensus recovery block.

Dependability: The quality of service provided by a particular system.

Error: The occurrence of an incorrect value in some unit of information within a system.

Failure: A deviation in the expected performance of a system.

Fault: A physical defect, imperfection, or flaw that occurs in hardware or software.

Fault avoidance: A technique that attempts to prevent hardware failures and software errors from occurring in a system.

Fault Tolerance: The ability to continue the correct performance of functions in the presence of faults.

Fault-Tolerant Computing: The process of performing calculations, such as those performed by a computer, in a fault-tolerant manner.

Maintainability, M(*t*): The probability that the failed system can be restored to operation within time *t*.

MTBF: Mean time between failures.

MTTF: Mean time to failure.

MTTR: Mean time to repair.

NMR: N-modular redundancy.

NSCP: N-self-checking programming.

NVP: N-version programming.

RAID: Redundant array of independent disks.

RB: Recovery block.

Reliability, R(*t*): The conditional probability that a system has functioned correctly throughout an interval of time, [0,*t*], given that the system was performing correctly at time 0.

TMR: Triple modular redundancy.

CROSS REFERENCES

See *Computer Network Management; Network Reliability and Fault Tolerance; Network Traffic Management.*

REFERENCES

AC&NC—RAID.edu. 2005. RAID tutorial & benchmarking tools. www.raid.com/04_00.html (accessed December 10, 2005).

Alvisi, L., T. C. Bressoud, A. El-Khashab, K. Marzullo, and D. Zagorodnov. 2001. Wrapping server-side TCP to mask connection failures. *Proceedings of INFOCOM*, 329–37.

Avizienis, A. 1985. The N-version approach to fault-tolerant software. *IEEE Transactions on Software Engineering* SE-11:1491–501.

———. 1995. The methodology of N-version programming. In *Software fault tolerance*, edited by R. Lyu, 23–46. New York: Wiley.

Avizienis, A., G. C. Gilley, F. P. Mathur, D. A. Rennels, J. S. Rohr, and D. K. Rubin. 1971. The STAR (self-testing-and-repairing) computer: An investigation of the theory and practice of fault-tolerant computer design. *IEEE Transactions on Computers*, C-20:1312–21.

Burchby, D. D., L. W. Kern, and W. A. Sturm. 1976. Specification of the fault-tolerant spaceborne computer (FTSC). *Proceedings of the 6th International Symposium on Fault-Tolerant Computing* 129–33.

Chen, P. M., E. K. Lee, G. A. Gibson, R. H. Katz, and D. A. Patterson. 1994. RAID: High-performance, reliable secondary storage. *ACM Computing Surveys* 26:145–85.

Dimmer, C. I. 1985. The tandem non-stop system. In *Resilient computing systems*, edited by T. Anderson, 178–96. London: Wiley.

ECC (Error Correcting Codes) Page. www.eccpage.com (accessed February 1, 2002).

Guerraoui, R., and A. Schipper. 1997. Software-based replication for fault tolerance. *IEEE Computer* 30:68–74.

Hecht, H., and M. Hecht. 2003. Fault-tolerance in software. In *Fault-tolerant computer system design*, edited by D. K. Pradhan, 428–77. Upper Saddle River, NJ: Prentice Hall.

Hopkins, A. L., T. B. Smith, and J. H. Lala. 1978. FTMP—A highly reliable fault-tolerant multiprocessor for aircraft. *Proceedings of the IEEE* 66:1221–39.

Huang, K. H., and J. A. Abraham. 1984. Algorithm-based fault tolerance for matrix operations. *IEEE Transactions on Computer* C-33:518–28.

Johnson, B. W. 1989. *Design and analysis of fault-tolerant digital systems*. Reading, MA: Addison-Wesley.

Katsuki, D., E. S. Elsam, W. F. Mann, E. S. Roberts, J. C. Robinson, F. S. Skowronski, and E. W. Wolf 1978. Pluribus—An operational fault-tolerant multiprocessor. *Proceedings of the IEEE* 66:1146–59.

Koo, R., and S. Toueg, 1987. Checkpointing and rollback-recovery for distributed systems. *IEEE Transactions on Software Engineering*, SE-13:23–31.

Lala, P. K. 1985. *Fault tolerant and fault testable hardware design*. Englewood Cliffs, NJ: Prentice Hall.

Laprie, J. C. 1985. Dependable computing and fault tolerance: Concepts and terminology. *15th IEEE International Symposium on Fault-Tolerant Computing*, 2–11.

Lin, S., and D. J. Costello Jr. 1983. *Error control coding: Fundamentals and applications*. Englewood Cliffs, NJ: Prentice Hall.

Lyu, M. R. 1995. *Software fault tolerance*. New York: Wiley.

Marwah, M., S. Mishra, and C. Fetzer. 2003. TCP server fault tolerance using connection migration to a backup server. *Proceedings of the IEEE International Conference on Dependable Systems and Networks*, 373–82.

Nair, V. S. S., J. A. Abraham, and P. Banerjee. 1996. Efficient techniques for the analysis of algorithm-based fault tolerant (*ABFT*) schemes. *IEEE Transactions on Computers* C-45:499–502.

Neil's bibliography on Fault-tolerant systems. 2005. www.jjcc.com/Security/bib/fts.htm (accessed December 15, 2005).

Nelson, V. F. 1990. Fault-tolerant computing: Fundamental concepts. *IEEE Computer* 23:19–25.

Pei, D., D. Massey, and L. Zhang. 2004. A framework for resilient internet routing protocols. *IEEE Network* 18:5–12.

Pradhan, D. K. 2003. *Fault-tolerant computer system design*. Upper Saddle River, NJ: Prentice-Hall.

Randell, B., and J. Xu. 1995. The evolution of the recovery block concept. In *Software fault tolerance*, edited by M. R. Lyu, 1–21. New York: Wiley.

Rennels, D.A. 1984. Fault-tolerant computing—Concepts and examples. *IEEE Transactions on Computers* C-33:1116–29.

Shao, Z., H. Jin, B. Chen, J. Xu, and J. Yue. 2003. HARTS: High availability cluster architecture with redundant TCP stacks. *Proceedings of the International Performance Computing and Communication Conference*, 255–62.

Shooman, M. L. 2002. *Reliability of computer systems and networks: Fault tolerance, analysis and design*. New York: Wiley.

Siewiorek, D. P., V. Kini, H. Mashbum, S. McConnel, and M. Tsao. 1978. A case study of C.mmp, Cm*, and C.vmp: Part 1—Experiences with fault tolerance in multiprocessor systems. *Proceedings of the IEEE* 66:1178–99.

Siewiorek, D. P., Swartz, R. S. 1998. Reliable computer systems: Design and evaluation. Wellesley, MA: A K Peters.

Sklaroff, J. R. 1976. Redundancy management technique for space shuttle computers. *IBM Journal of Research and Development* 20:20–8.

Sultan, F., K. Srinivasan, D. Iyer, and L. Iftode. 2002. Migratory TCP: Connection migration for service continuity in the Internet. *Proceedings of the International Conference on Distributed Computing Systems*. 469–70.

Torres-Pomales, W. 2000. *Software fault tolerance: A tutorial*. NASA Technical Report, NASA/TM-2000-210616.

Toy, W. N. 1978. Fault-tolerant design of local ESS processors. *Proceedings of the IEEE* 66:1126–45.

Webber, S., and J. Beirne. 1991. The Stratus architecture. *Proceedings of the 1991 International Symposium on Fault-Tolerant Computing*, 79–87.

Wensly, J. H., L. Lamport, L. Goldberg, M. W. J. Green, K. N. Levitt, P. M. Melliar-Smith, R. E. Shostak, and C. B. Weinstock. 1978. SIFT: Design and analysis of a fault-tolerant computer for aircraft control. *Proceedings of the IEEE* 66:1240–55.

Distributed Algorithms

Valmir C. Barbosa, *Universidade Federal do Rio de Janeiro, Brazil*

> In mechanics we used only one clock. But this was not very convenient, because we had to take all measurements in the vicinity of this one clock. Looking at the clock from a distance, … we have always to remember that what we see now really happened earlier, just as we receive light from the sun eight minutes after it was emitted. We should have to make corrections, according to our distance from the clock, in all our time readings.
>
> —Einstein and Infeld (1938)

> Now what does that mean? If we look at the situation carefully we see that events that occur at two separated places at the same time, as seen by [an observer] in [a coordinate system], do *not* happen at the same time as viewed by [another observer] in [another coordinate system]. … This circumstance is called "failure of simultaneity at a distance,"…
>
> —Feynman, Leighton, and Sands (1963)

INTRODUCTION

Let G be a connected undirected graph with n nodes and m edges. Each node in G stands for a sequential processing element and each edge represents a bidirectional communication channel that allows for the point-to-point exchange of messages between its end nodes. G is then representative of a multitude of distributed-memory systems, such as computer networks and, more abstractly, systems of multiple agents that do not share memory. In this chapter, we understand a distributed algorithm to be any algorithm for execution by the nodes of G as concurrent sequential threads that communicate with one another by passing messages over the edges of G. We let nodes be numbered $1,\ldots,n$.

The field of distributed algorithms is an outgrowth of the research on concurrent programming that some decades ago was an essential part of the research on operating systems. The field evolved to encompass both the message-passing computations that are our subject matter in this chapter and computations on shared memory. Through the years, key representative problems have been identified, and a core collection of fundamental techniques has been put together for use in the design and analysis of the algorithms. In a space-constrained chapter such as this one, it is unavoidable that some topics be left out (such as the entire sub field of shared-memory computations) while others are only skimmed over (such as computations in the presence of faults, which we cover later only briefly). However, we are at present fortunate to have several texts on distributed algorithms available for in-depth study. Of these, we single out the books by Barbosa (1996), Lynch (1996), Peleg (2000), Tel (2000), and Attiya and Welch (2004). Each favors a different approach to the subject and has its particular choice of topics. Combined, they offer a comprehensive body of knowledge on the field.

Most of the research on distributed algorithms has had a strongly theoretical flavor and has striven for the rigorous establishment of correctness—and performance-related properties. As the reader will notice throughout the chapter, often the approach has been to concentrate efforts on a few paradigmatic problems whose definitions aim at capturing the practical issues pertaining to real-world problems. For readers of a handbook such as this, it is important to realize that this approach has been very successful and that many practical solutions exist that implement what has been discovered. Two important examples are the applications of leader-election algorithms, particularly within the asynchronous transfer mode (ATM) layers that lie at the Internet's backbone (Huang and McKinley 2000), and the use of algorithms to discover minimum-weight spanning trees on overlay networks for end-system multicast (Chu et al. 2002). Even conceptual problems whose treatment is fraught with difficulties, such as reaching agreement in faulty environments, have influenced real-world decisions: the four-way handshake that implements the closing of TCP connections (Kurose and Ross 2005), for example, is an attempt to handle the difficulties of such an agreement.

The two quotations that open this chapter are meant to stress what we deem to be the most fundamental issue underlying the study of distributed algorithms—that is, the issue of how to represent time, how to account for its passage, and how to refer to global entities without breaching any causality principles. We deal with this issue in the section on "Models of Computation," albeit still somewhat superficially, with the introduction of the so-called synchronous and asynchronous models of computation that we use throughout the chapter. The section also contains representative distributed algorithms for each model. The asynchronous algorithms, in particular, are expanded and generalized in the section on "The Quintessential Asynchronous Algorithm" to yield a template for any asynchronous algorithm. We then continue in the section on "An Asynchronous Building Block" with the introduction of an important building block to be used in the construction of asynchronous algorithms. This building block is intended for the asynchronous establishment on G of a rooted tree having certain desired properties.

In the section on "Events and Global States," we return to time-related modeling issues and expand on the asynchronous model by introducing details that eventually lead to the notion of a consistent global state of an asynchronous computation. This is followed by a section on "Other Asynchronous Building Blocks," in which two additional building blocks for the construction of asynchronous algorithms are discussed, namely the election of a leader and the distributed recording of a global state. Provisioned now with three important building blocks, we move in the next section to the description of an asynchronous algorithm that can be built out of some of them.

The issue of how to assess the computational complexity of a distributed algorithm is treated in the section on "Computational Complexity," in which we discuss both time- and communication-related measures. With these in hand, we are equipped not only to analyze the worst-case performance of the algorithms discussed up to that section, but mainly we can then return to the interplay between synchronism and asynchronism and describe how to safely translate a synchronous algorithm into an asynchronous one while being able to assess the unavoidable change in computational complexity. We do this in the next section, in which we discuss the so-called synchronizers.

The section titled "Additional Topics" is devoted to brief discussions of further topics of interest within the field both from a theoretical perspective (viz. lower bounds and impossibility results, computing on anonymous systems, topological awareness, self-stabilization, consensus problems, correctness proofs, and the emergence of an all-encompassing theory of distributed computing) and from an applications-related one (resource sharing and the design of asynchronous algorithms for wireless networks and for large unstructured networks of generally unknown topologies—the so-called complex networks). To finalize, we give conclusions and closing remarks.

MODELS OF COMPUTATION

We give each model of distributed computation by specifying how time elapses at each node of G, how the elapsing of time at one node relates to what happens at another node, and how the passing of messages relates to time. For most of the chapter we assume that nodes and edges never fail.

The Synchronous Model

The synchronous model of distributed computation is characterized by the existence of a single clock that makes all nodes work in lockstep at the occurrence of its pulses, numbered by the integer $s \geq 0$. The model also assumes that the local computation occurring at each node for each pulse takes no time, and also that messages sent between neighbors in G as part of the local computation for pulse s are delivered before the occurrence of pulse $s + 1$. The assumptions of the synchronous model are unrealistic, but allow for great simplifications in the design of distributed algorithms, as we exemplify next.

Example: breadth-first numbering This problem asks that each node i in G be labeled with the integer l_i such that the number of edges on the shortest path (i.e., the distance) from node i to node 1 is l_i. A synchronous algorithm to do this is initiated by node 1, which at pulse $s = 0$ lets $l_1 = 0$ and sends a message to all its neighbors. For $s > 0$, any node i receiving a message for the first time lets $l_i = s$ and also sends a message to all its neighbors. Clearly, the problem can be solved within diam(G) + 1 pulses, where diam(G) is the diameter (greatest distance between two nodes) of G. The number of messages used is $\sum_i d_i = 2m$, where d_i is the degree of node i.

Example: leader election in a complete graph When node i has an identification id_i that is distinct from all other nodes' and all identifications are totally ordered by $<$, this problem asks that all nodes in G determine the node k for which $id_k = \min_i id_i$. A nontrivial synchronous algorithm to do this on a complete graph is the following (Afek and Gafni 1991). Initially all nodes are candidates. At each even pulse, a node i that remains a candidate sends id_i to a new group of neighbors. At each odd pulse, every node compares all the identifications sent to it in the previous pulse to the least identification it has ever seen and, correspondingly, sends out at most one positive reply (to the owner of the new least identification, if any). A node remains a candidate if it receives positive replies to all identifications it sent out. If at pulse $s = 2z$, $z = 0,1,\ldots$, the group of neighbors to which a candidate's identification is sent has size 2^z, then clearly the number of pulses required to elect a leader is $O(\log n)$. As for the number of messages, notice that the number of candidates remaining at pulse $s = 2z$ for $z > 0$ is the number of nodes that were sent 2^{z-1} positive replies at pulse $s - 1$—that is, at most $n/2^{z-1}$. The overall number of messages includes the initial n identifications, the $(n/2^{z-1})2^z$ identifications sent for each $z > 0$, and finally the $O(n \log n)$ positive replies. These add up to $O(n \log n)$ messages.

Both examples take explicit advantage of the assumptions of the synchronous model. In the case of breadth-first numbering, this is revealed in the one-to-one correspondence between a node's distance to node 1 and the earliest pulse at which it can be reached by a message initially propagated by node 1. In the case of leader election when G is a complete graph, it is revealed in a subtler manner by the tacit information that, in the synchronous model, necessarily accompanies the absence of a message. The algorithm in the example exploits this by letting each node group all identifications sent to it before deciding whether to send out a positive reply, and also by dispensing with the need for negative replies.

The Asynchronous Model

In the asynchronous model, each node has its own local, independent clock, and computes, possibly sending out messages to its neighbors, upon the receipt of each message. Message delivery, even though guaranteed to occur, is in no way correlated to either the clock of the sender or of the receiver. The reactive response to an arriving message is always atomic—that is, it is never interrupted by the arrival of new messages, which are then queued up for future treatment. These assumptions, clearly, call for the existence of at least one initiator, that is, at least one node that performs some initial local computation, and sends out messages, without the need for an arriving message to respond to. We henceforth consider asynchronous algorithm nearly exclusively. They are in general more complex than synchronous algorithms; we start with very simple examples (Segall 1983).

Example: flooding Let I be a piece of information to be disseminated through the nodes of G from a single initiator, say node 1. In the absence of any further structure on G, one solution is to flood the graph: node 1 sends I to all its neighbors; all other nodes, upon receiving I for the first time, do the same. Clearly, this requires $2m$ copies of I to be sent out.

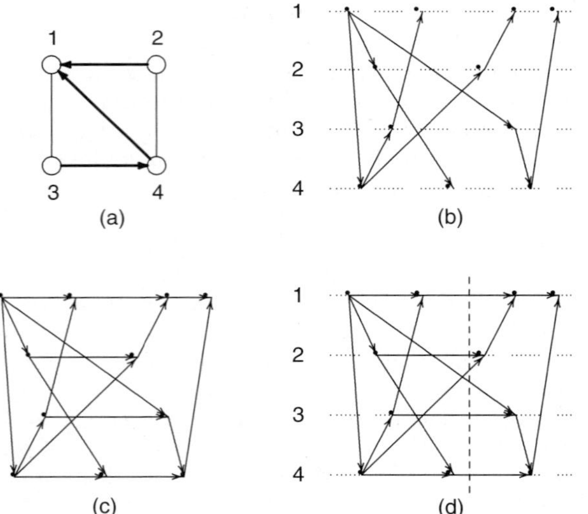

Figure 1 In the G of part a, directed edges are used to indicate a tree rooted at node 1 that may result from flooding the graph with feedback. The events of a possible execution leading to this tree are shown as filled circles in part b, where dotted lines indicate the nodes' local time axes (time progresses from left to right) and arrows depict messages. The B relation that corresponds to this execution is the edge set of the precedence graph of part c. One of the execution's global states is shown in part d, where the dashed line is used to indicate the corresponding partition of the event set. The only messages to be sent in the future of this global state are the copies of I that traverse tree edges root-ward to implement feedback.

Example: flooding with feedback Suppose that, in addition to disseminating I as in the previous example, we also want node 1 to be informed that all other nodes have already been reached by the dissemination when this happens. Let p_i be a variable local to node i. We use flooding with feedback: node 1 sends I to all its neighbors; node $i \neq 1$, upon receiving I for the first time, say from node j, lets $p_i = j$ and sends I on to all its neighbors but j; node j is sent I back only when node i has received I from all its neighbors. The number of copies of I required is still $2m$, but now a simple inductive argument on the spanning tree rooted at node 1 that the p_i variables establish on G shows that node 1, upon having received I from all its neighbors, is certain that the dissemination has finished (Figure 1(a)).

The first example is valid for any number of concurrent initiators. The second one, with its inherent ability to anchor the entire asynchronous computation, via the rooted tree, at the single initiator, gives rise to both a generic template for gracefully terminating asynchronous algorithms (cf. the section on "The Quintessential Asynchronous Algorithm") and also a fundamental building block for the development of asynchronous algorthms (cf. the section on "An Asynchronous Building Block").

THE QUINTESSENTIAL ASYNCHRONOUS ALGORITHM

Any asynchronous algorithm with one single initiator can be cast into the template we give in this section. In the case of algorithms that rely on the flexibility of multiple concurrent initiators, the same property continues to be ultimately valid in its essence, since conceptually we can always add a new node to G, connect this node to the desired initiators, and then let it be the sole initiator instead. Our template is based on the elegant method laid down by Dijkstra and Scholten (1980) for detecting the termination of asynchronous computations that have one single initiator.

We start with a generic template for an asynchronous computation with one single initiator that does not require the initiator to be informed of termination. Such a template requires that the initial action to be performed by the initiator be specified, and also that for all nodes (including the initiator) a specification be given as to how to respond to the reception of each possible message type during the computation. As a shorthand, we refer to such messages generically as *msg*, always bearing in mind that *msg* may stand for several different message types, each requiring a different treatment when received.

The generic template we seek in this section is an augmentation of the simple template we just outlined that aims at ensuring that the initiator be informed of termination when it occurs. It uses the same p_i variables of the flooding with feedback algorithm for basically the same purpose. In addition, it is based on the premise that every *msg* message is explicitly acknowledged—that is, for every *msg* that node i sends node j there has to correspond an acknowledgment message sent by node j to node i. We let such a message be generically denoted by *ack*. Deciding when to send each *ack* is the crux of the underlying method. For node i, a counter c_i, initially set to 0, is used to keep track of how many *ack* messages node i still expects to receive.

The following three actions specify the template asynchronous algorithm. As before, we let node 1 be the algorithm's sole initiator.

1. *Spontaneous initiation at node* 1—Perform some local computation, possibly sending out *msg* messages and incrementing c_1 by the number of messages sent.
2. *Upon the reception of msg from node j at node i*—Perform some local computation, possibly sending out *msg* messages and incrementing c_i by the number of messages sent. Then do one of the following:
   (a) If $c_i = 0$ held when *msg* was received and $c_i > 0$ holds now, then let $p_i = j$;
   (b) Otherwise, send *ack* to node j.
3. *Upon the reception of ack at node i*—Decrement c_i and check whether $c_i = 0$. In the affirmative case, conclude that termination has occurred if $i = 1$, or send *ack* to p_i if $i > 1$.

Any asynchronous computation conforming to this template spreads out from node 1 and, if termination ever occurs, eventually contracts back onto it. In the meantime, the computation remains anchored at node 1 through the tree rooted at node 1 that the variables p_i induce if $c_i > 0$. This tree grows with the incorporation of node $i > 1$ into it when in action 2(a) node i lets $p_i = j$; likewise, it contracts by shedding node $i > 1$ when in action 3 node i sends *ack* to p_i. As the computation progresses, such a node may enter and leave the tree several times, each time through a possibly different path from node 1 to it in G. For computations that do terminate, eventually the tree stops growing and then the same inductive argument used to demonstrate the correctness of flooding with feedback can be used.

AN ASYNCHRONOUS BUILDING BLOCK

This recurring idea that building trees on G asynchronously can be used to anchor asynchronous computations for proper termination signaling can be made more general and be applied to certain portions of the computation only. That is, it is possible to structure the tree-building procedure in such a way that it becomes a building block for the construction of more complex distributed algorithms. We specify such a building block now and use it to construct the algorithm in a later section as an example of its use.

Let N_i denote the set of neighbors of node i in G. Let N_i^- be a subset of N_i. Also, let S_i and T_i be Boolean conditions relative to node i, used respectively to indicate, when they become true, that node i is to be the sole initiator of the construction of a tree rooted at it, and that node i, not being the initiator, is to participate in such a construction as it is reached by its messages. The following three actions indicate how to grow and contract such a tree. We let node k be the assumed initiator of the algorithm and root of the tree. We use the same *msg* and *ack* messages as in the section on "The Quintessential Asynchronous Algorithm." Counter c_i is also used at each node i as in that section.

4. *Initiation at node k when S_k becomes true*—If $N_k^- \neq \emptyset$, then send *msg* to all nodes in N_k^- and increment c_k by $|N_k^-|$.
5. *Upon the reception of msg from node j at node i*—If $i \neq k$ and receiving *msg* has caused T_i to become true, and also $N_i^- \neq \emptyset$, then send *msg* to all nodes in N_i^-, increment c_i by $|N_i^-|$, and let $p_i = j$. Otherwise, send *ack* to node j.
6. *Upon the reception of ack at node i*—Decrement c_i and check whether $c_i = 0$. In the affirmative case, conclude that the tree has contracted back onto its root if $i = k$, or send *ack* to p_i if $i \neq k$.

Actions 4 to 6 promote the growth of a tree on G that is rooted at node k. Its creation starts when S_k becomes true and is joined by every node $i \neq k$ for which T_i becomes true as *msg* messages arrive and $N_i^- \neq \emptyset$. Its contraction is started concurrently at every node $i \neq k$ for which T_i never becomes true or $N_i^- = \emptyset$, and also as nodes receive copies of *msg* other than the first, and continues with the ensuing sending of the *ack* messages. Obviously, letting $N_i^- = N_i$ for all i and setting T_i to become true for all $i > 1$ as the first *msg* arrives yields the asynchronous algorithm for flooding with feedback. In this case, *msg* = *ack* = I and the flooding starts when S_1 becomes true.

EVENTS AND GLOBAL STATES

The design of an asynchronous algorithm must be resilient to any degree of the uncertainties that underlie the asynchronous model. Such uncertainties refer to the fact that local clocks are in no way correlated to one another, and also to the unpredictable delays that messages may undergo as they are transmitted on the edges of G. What this amounts to is that different executions of the same asynchronous algorithm may, from the local standpoint of a certain node, entail the reception of a different sequence of messages for each execution and therefore a different sequence of actions as well. Characterizing what is meant by an execution precisely is then crucial, as it affects directly the conception of certain asynchronous building blocks and also allows complexity measures to be defined correctly.

In what follows, and also in some of the forthcoming sections, we use a directed graph D in lieu of the undirected graph G we have been using. The nodes of D are the same as those of G, and its edges, by contrast, indicate the possibility of unidirectional communication between the nodes. We do this substitution for the sake of generality, since an undirected graph with the bidirectional-channel interpretation we have ascribed to the edges of G is equivalent to the particular case of D that has two directed edges between every two nodes that are neighbors in G, one in each direction. We let c denote the number of directed edges in D.

Our definition of an execution of an asynchronous algorithm is based on the seminal work of Lamport (1978). For an asynchronous algorithm A, we define an execution of A to be a set V_A of so-called events (Figure 1(b)). An event v is a sextuple containing the following elements:

node(v) is the node of D at which v happens;

time(v) is the time, as given by the local clock of *node*(v), right after the occurrence of v;

in_msg(v) is the message, if any, whose reception at *node*(v) triggers the occurrence of v;

Out_msgs(v) is the set of the messages, if any, that *node*(v) sends out as a consequence of the occurrence of v;

p_state(v) is the local state of *node*(v) that precedes the occurrence of v;

s_state(v) is the local state of *node*(v) that succeeds the occurrence of v, that is, at time *time*(v).

Clearly, this definition of an event captures the essential nature of an asynchronous algorithm, allowing for the first actions of initiators and for the subsequent processing by all nodes as they react to the reception of individual messages.

The events in V_A are obviously not independent of one another. In fact, the definition of the following binary relation, denoted by B, is quite natural. For v, $v' \in V_A$, we say that $(v, v') \in B$ if one of the two following possibilities holds: either $node(v) = node(v')$ and $time(v) < time(v')$ with no intervening events between them; or $node(v) \neq node(v')$ and $in\_msg(v') \in Out\_msgs(v)$. In other words, B characterizes the situations in which v is an immediate predecessor of v', either occurring in immediate succession at the same node, or occurring at different nodes, provided the message that triggers the occurrence of v' is sent as a consequence of the occurrence of v.

This relation B gives rise to two important entities. The first is an acyclic directed graph, called the precedence graph of execution V_A; its node set is V_A and its edge set is B (Figure 1(c)). The second important entity is the transitive closure B^+ of B, which is known as the happened-before relation; B^+ is a partial order on V_A and allows the precise definition of the past of an event v as $Past(v) = \{v' \in V_A \mid (v', v) \in B^+\}$ and of v's future as $Future(v) = \{v' \in V_A \mid (v, v') \in B^+\}$. It also allows concurrent events in V_A to be defined precisely: v, $v' \in V_A$ are concurrent if neither $(v, v') \in B^+$ nor $(v', v) \in B^+$.

The asynchronous model, by definition, precludes the precise treatment of global properties in time-related terms. This, of course, is because of the absence of a global clock, but the need remains for us to be able to refer to global properties. For example, the termination property that is detected as, in the algorithm of the section on "The Quintessential Asynchronous Algorithm," node 1 sets c_1 to 0 is a global property that makes sense even if we eliminate all *ack* messages from that algorithm: all this elimination achieves is that node 1 is no longer capable of detecting termination, but the notion of termination remains valid, and it is legitimate for us to want to refer to it globally. The way to achieve this is by defining precisely what a global state of the execution V_A is. We present this definition in two stages.

In the first stage, we first partition V_A into the sets $V_A(1),\ldots,V_A(n)$, where $V_A(i)$ is the set of events v for which $node(v) = i$. Then we further partition each $V_A(i)$ into $V_A^1(i)$ and $V_A^2(i)$ in such a way that $time(v) < time(v')$ for any $v \in V_A^1(i)$, $v' \in V_A^2(i)$. If we now regroup these sets into $V_A^1 = \cup_i V_A^1(i)$ and $V_A^2 = \cup_i V_A^2(i)$, then the new partition of V_A into V_A^1 and V_A^2 can be seen to define a global state of the system represented by the directed graph D. In this global state, the local state of node i is either its initial state (if $V_A^1(i) \neq \emptyset$) or *s_state*(v), where v is the event in $V_A^1(i)$ for which *time*(v) is greatest. The global state also includes messages in transit on the edges of D; these are the messages $in\_msg(v')$ such that $v' \in V_A^2$ and $in\_msg(v') \in Out\_msgs(v)$ for some $v \in V_A^1$.

Global states defined in this way can be easily seen to give rise to causal inconsistencies with respect to the partial order B^+. In the definition's second stage, we then complete it by requiring that $Past(v) \subseteq V_A^1$ for all $v \in V_A^1$ (an equivalent statement of this requirement is that $Future(v) \subseteq V_A^2$ for all $v \in V_A^2$). We sometimes refer to V_A^1 as the global state's past and to V_A^2 as its future. Global states are illustrated in Figure 1(d).

Vector Clocks and Beyond

This theory has been extended by the incorporation of several other time-related notions for asynchronous algorithms. These extensions can be found in the articles collected by Yang and Marsland (1994) and also elsewhere (e.g., Drummond and Barbosa 2003). One of the strongest motivations has been the design of algorithms for detecting various types of global predicates, such as the ones of Drummond and Barbosa (1996). We close this section by briefly discussing the notion of a vector clock. The vector clock of node i at time *time*(v), with v such that $node(v) = i$, is the size-n one-dimensional array K_i whose jth component is

$$K_i[j] = \begin{cases} time(v), & \text{if } j = i; \\ time(pred(v)), & \text{if } j \neq i, \end{cases}$$

where *pred*(v) is the latest predecessor of v at node j, that is, the event $v' \in V_A(j)$ such that $(v',v) \in B^+$ for which *time*(v') is greatest (if no such event exists, then we assume $time(pred(v)) = 0$). It is easy to see that there exists a global state of V_A of which K_i is the node-state part. Also, if every node attaches its current vector clock to all messages it sends, and furthermore updates its vector clock, whenever it receives a message, to the component-wise maximum of the vector clock that comes in the message and its own, then the result remains a valid vector clock. The extension of vector clocks to higher-dimensional matrix clocks follows similar principles and allows for consistent local representations of arbitrary-depth portions of an event's past in execution V_A.

OTHER ASYNCHRONOUS BUILDING BLOCKS

In addition to the tree-constructing asynchronous building block of the section on "An Asynchronous Building Block," two others are generally regarded as being just as fundamental. We discuss them next.

Leader Election

In the section on "Models of Computation," we introduced the leader-election problem as the problem of finding the node whose identification is the minimum. The problem is well posed, because we assumed that all nodes have distinct identifications totally ordered by $<$ and that all nodes are candidates initially. In this section we consider a more general definition of the problem: not only is G no longer assumed to be a complete graph, but also not all nodes are candidates initially. In addition, the problem does not ask for the candidate of least identification, but asks instead that all nodes agree on some candidate's identification.

When posed like this, the problem is very closely related to the problem of finding a minimum-weight spanning tree on G when edge weights are all distinct and totally ordered by $<$ (and hence G has a unique minimum-weight spanning tree). The reason that the two problems are so close to each other is that, in several solutions of the latter problem (Gallager, Humblet, and Spira 1983; Chin and Ting 1990), when the minimum-weight spanning tree is finally obtained, we automatically have a core edge whose end nodes, having distinct identifications, can decide between them which one becomes leader if at least one of them is a candidate. If neither is a candidate, then they can take upon themselves the task of deciding which of the candidates is to become leader. Obtaining their identifications and disseminating through all nodes the leader's identification is achieved rather simply by computing exclusively on the edges of the tree. The entire procedure, including finding the tree, can be designed so that the number of messages it requires is $O(m + n \log n)$.

It then remains for appropriate weights to be set for all edges of G. Any set of distinct weights ordered by $<$ will do, including the adoption of the ordered pair $(\min\{id_i, id_j\}, \max\{id_i, id_j\})$ as the weight of the edge between nodes i and j. In this case, weights are ordered lexicographically by $<$, and this is how comparisons are to be made as the minimum-weight spanning tree is built.

Global-State Recording

Consider an arbitrary execution V_A of an asynchronous algorithm A. Let X_A^1, X_A^2 and Y_A^1, Y_A^2 be distinct partitions of V_A that define global states as explained in the section on "Events and Global States." We say that the latter of these global states is in the future of the former one if $X_A^1 \subset Y_A^1$ (equivalently, if $Y_A^2 \subset X_A^2$). Now let P be a global predicate on execution V_A. We say that P is stable if P is true of all global states that are in the future of a global state of which P is true. One example of stable predicates is termination, which is true of a global state if and only if all nodes are idle and all edges are empty in that global state.

One possible approach to the detection of stable predicates is to repeatedly record global states of V_A until one is found of which the predicate is true. The ability to make such recordings is then crucial, and we now review an asynchronous algorithm to do it. As in the section on "Events and Global States," for the remainder of this section we revert to using the directed graph D in lieu of the undirected G.

The algorithm we give is the one of Chandy and Lamport (1985). Like all algorithms for recording global states, it is to be viewed as a separate computation that is superimposed on the computation whose execution is V_A (this execution is then referred to as a substrate). Even though A and the recording algorithm are separate entities, it is the interaction between them that allows for the recording of global states of V_A. So the two algorithms share the nodes of D (whose processing capabilities are split between the two as their actions are executed atomically) and also its edges.

Similarly to our earlier practice, we refer to each message of the substrate generically as *msg*. The recording algorithm uses *marker* messages exclusively, even though it also handles, without interpreting them, the *msg* messages. During recording, each node is responsible for recording its own local state and also the states, in the form of sequences of messages, of all edges that in D are directed toward it. We use $Msgs_i(j)$ to denote the sequence, initially empty, into which node i records messages it receives from j if (j, i) is a directed edge of D.

The recording admits any number of concurrent initiators. An initiator records its own local state and sends *marker* on all its outgoing edges. Any other node, upon receiving the first *marker*, does the same. From then on, node i (initiator or otherwise) monitors the *msg* messages it receives: if (j, i) is an edge of D, then every *msg* received from node j before a *marker* is received from that same node is appended to $Msgs_i(j)$.

This algorithm, evidently, is nothing but the obvious extension to directed graphs of the flooding algorithm of the section on "Models of Computation," naturally with the necessary provisions for node- and edge-state recording. If D is strongly connected, then assuredly all nodes participate in the recording and, overall, exactly c *marker*'s are sent. It is also possible to prove that, if in addition D's edges deliver messages in the first-in, first-out (FIFO) order, then all the information the algorithm records does indeed constitute a global state. In this global state, all (and only) messages recorded in $Msgs_i(j)$ have the following property: they were sent before node j's recording of its own local state and received after node i's. This property is the key to extending the algorithm to the case of non-FIFO message delivery.

AN EXAMPLE

We draw this section's example from the area of distributed computations for resource sharing. In this case, the nodes of G compete with one another for the use of shared resources, and we assume that the sharing policy they follow defines a dynamic subgraph of G that reflects, along the computation's global states, the wait of nodes for one another. Even though G is an undirected graph, this subgraph has directed edges: if the directed edge (i, j) is part of it in a certain global state, then in that global state node i is blocked and waiting for a signal from node j to help release it. We denote this subgraph of G by W. By the nature of W, its sinks (if any) are the only unblocked nodes, and the possibility of deadlocks is a reality.

A rich set of graph-theoretic concepts exists for the treatment of deadlocks in W (Barbosa 2002). In particular, since the existence of a deadlock in W is a stable property, recording a global state of the resource-sharing computation and checking the corresponding (static) W for the occurrence of some sufficient condition for deadlocks to occur is a common approach (we refer the reader to the example given by Misra and Chandy (1982), which is a clever, albeit concise, application of the template of the section on "The Quintessential Asynchronous Algorithm").

One example that illustrates the use of the tree-constructing building block of the section on "An Asynchronous Building Block" is the following (Bracha and Toueg 1987). Suppose that the resource-sharing computation is such that node i must receive at least x_i signals from its out-neighbors in W to be released. In order for node 1 to detect whether it is in deadlock according to a recorded W, it first builds a tree following actions 4 to 6 with: $k = 1$, S_1 becoming true when node 1 suspects it is in deadlock, T_i becoming true when node $i \neq k$ receives the first message, and finally $\overline{N_i}$ the set of out-neighbors of node i in W. This tree unfolds out from node 1 through the nodes' out-neighbors. If any sinks are reached, then each one builds another tree concurrently with the other sinks, before allowing the original tree to contract. Each sink-rooted tree follows actions 4 to 6 with: k the corresponding sink's number, S_k becoming true when node k is reached by the messages constructing the original tree, T_i becoming true when (nonsink) node $i \neq k$ has just received x_i of the messages used to expand the sink-rooted trees, and finally $\overline{N_i}$ the set of in-neighbors of node i in W. After the original tree contracts back on node 1, it decides for deadlock if and only if T_1 is false (note that T_1 is defined only for the sink-initiated tree constructions). This algorithm requires no more messages than twice the number of edges in W. An illustration is given in Figure 2.

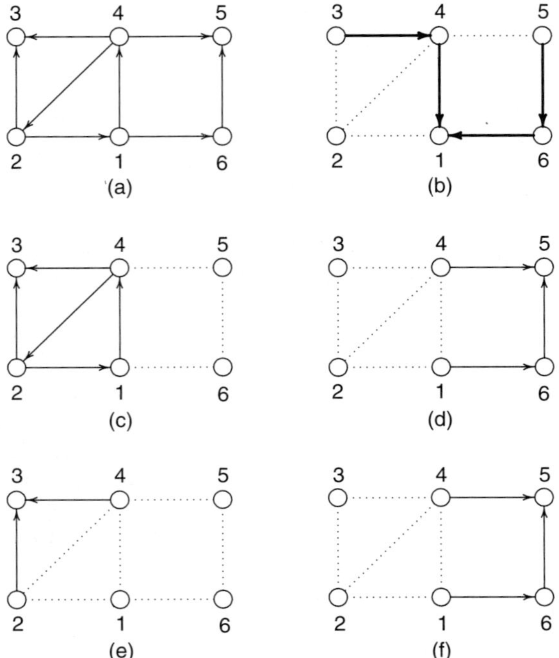

Figure 2 In the W of part a, x_i is equal to the number of out-neighbors of node i for $i \in \{1,2,3,5,6\}$. Part b shows one possibility for the tree rooted at node 1, at the stage in which its leaves are the sinks of W (nodes 3 and 5). For $x_4 = 2$, parts c and d show, respectively, the edges of W traversed by messages of the tree-building procedures started by nodes 3 and 5 (we assume that timing is such that node 4 is reached by a message from node 5 before being reached by one from node 3, and likewise node 1 from node 6 before node 4). Node 1 is reached once in each case (hence x_1 times overall) and concludes that it is not in deadlock in W. For $x_4 = 3$, on the other hand, the traversed edges are those shown in parts e and f, respectively for the tree-building procedures started by nodes 3 and 5 (timing conditions are in this case irrelevant). Node 1 is only reached once, and only by the edges that correspond to the latter procedure (hence less than x_1 times overall), so it concludes that it is in deadlock in W. For the sake of clarity, we omit from parts c and e any indication of the trees rooted at node 3, and similarly for parts d and f with respect to node 5.

COMPUTATIONAL COMPLEXITY

So far we have only superficially touched the issue of computational complexity. In the field of distributed computing, the complexity measures of interest are the time for completion of the algorithm and the overall number of messages used. In previous sections we have only given complete complexity figures for the two simple synchronous algorithms of the section on "Models of Computation"; for all asynchronous algorithms, we limited ourselves to discussing the number of messages used. We now give precise definitions in both cases; we concentrate on the case of worst-case figures, which is by far the most common, but it should become clear that extensions to average-case figures are straightforward. In what follows, we let $\mathbf{G}$ denote the class of all graphs for which a certain algorithm is designed (e.g., all connected graphs, all rings, etc.).

For an asynchronous algorithm A and a graph $G \in \mathbf{G}$, let $\mathbf{V}_A(G)$ be the set of all possible executions of A on G. In the section on "Events and Global States," we emphasized the possibility of multiple distinct executions of A as they stem from the inherent unpredictability of the asynchronous model, but clearly there can be variation due to differences in initial local conditions and also to probabilistic decisions. We denote the number of messages required for running A on G during execution V_A by $Messages(A,G,V_A)$. Clearly, assessing this number correctly is a matter of counting message exchanges during the execution. The worst-case message complexity of algorithm A, denoted by $MCompl(A)$, is defined as

$$MCompl(A) = \max_{G \in \mathbf{G}} \max_{V_A \in \mathbf{V}_A(G)} Messages(A,G,V_A).$$

That is, for fixed G we first find the number of messages exchanged during the execution of A on G that requires the most messages. Then we take the greatest of these numbers over $\mathbf{G}$. Naturally, the resulting figure depends on the parameters associated with at least one $G \in \mathbf{G}$, such as n, m, diam(G), or possibly others; here, and henceforth, we refrain from indicating this dependency explicitly for notational ease. All message complexities we have given heretofore in the chapter for asynchronous algorithms conform to this definition, as one may easily check.

A completely analogous definition can be given for the worst-case time complexity of A, which we denote by $TCompl(A)$:

$$TCompl(A) = \max_{G \in \mathbf{G}} \max_{V_A \in \mathbf{V}_A(G)} Time(A, G, V_A),$$

where $Time(A,G,V_A)$ is the time required for running A on G along execution V_A. The absence of a global clock in the asynchronous model requires that we approach the definition of this latter quantity with care. For cases in which the guarantee of a single initiator exists, a possibility one might think of would be to let this time be as given by the initiator's local clock. But this approach is avoided in general, because it makes the eventual time complexity depend on a specific clock and on the rate at which time progresses according to that clock.

A better approach is to recognize that the time expended by an asynchronous algorithm is determined primarily by the causal flow of messages on G during execution. For this reason, we assume local computation to take no time (just as in the synchronous model) and let $Time(A,G, V_A)$ be given by the length of the longest causal chain in V_A involving the reception of a message and the sending of another as a consequence. More precisely, we take the precedence graph of execution V_A and assign weights to each of its edges: either 1 (if it is a message-related edge) or 0. Then we let $Time(A,G,V_A)$ be the length of the longest weighted directed path on the precedence graph of V_A.

As we look back on the asynchronous algorithms seen previously in the chapter, we see that the flooding-based ones (both the two of the section on "Models of Computation" and the algorithm for global-state recording) all have an $O(n)$ worst-case time complexity. We also remark that it is possible to design an asynchronous algorithm for minimum-weight spanning trees that runs in $O(n \log^* n)$ time in the worst case ($\log^*$ denotes the number of successive applications of the log operator required to yield a number less than 1). As for the deadlock detection algorithm of the section above in which we give an example, it runs in $O(w)$ time in the worst case, where w is the number of nodes of W.

We finalize by pointing out that the case of synchronous algorithms is entirely analogous, provided we understand that the possibility of multiple executions has now nothing to do with the model of computation. Furthermore, the time required to run a synchronous algorithm S on G along a certain execution can be assessed by simply counting pulses. Henceforth, we let $MCompl(S)$ and $TCompl(S)$ denote, respectively, the worst-case message and time complexities of S.

SYNCHRONIZERS

As we remarked in the section on "Models of Computation," the synchronous model is unrealistic. The reason that it remains important despite this fact is that designing algorithms under its assumptions is often considerably simpler than designing for the asynchronous model. For example, the synchronous algorithm given in the previously mentioned section for numbering the nodes of G breadth-first is amazingly simple; an asynchronous algorithm, by comparison, would require considerable additional control and be significantly more complex.

But what really guarantees the place of the synchronous model in the study of distributed algorithms is the certainty that every synchronous algorithm can be correctly and automatically translated into an equivalent asynchronous one. This is achieved by transforming the operation of the synchronous algorithm at each pulse $s \geq 0$ into a fragment of an asynchronous algorithm. The desired asynchronous algorithm is obtained by piecing together these fragments for all values of s. Such fragments are known as synchronizers (Awerbuch 1985).

Let *Sync* be a synchronizer and suppose its worst-case message and time complexities (the latter in the asynchronous sense) per pulse are $M(Sync)$ and $T(Sync)$, respectively. Suppose also that initializing *Sync* requires $M_0(Sync)$ messages and $T_0(Sync)$ time at most. From the general description we have given so far of a synchronizer, it is clear that the asynchronous algorithm A resulting from transforming a synchronous algorithm S via synchronizer *Sync* has worst-case message and time complexities given, respectively, by

$$MCompl(A) = MCompl(S) + M_0(Sync) + TCompl(S)M(Sync)$$

and

$$TCompl(A) = T_0(Sync) + TCompl(S)T(Sync).$$

The essential property that needs to be guaranteed before a node executes its portion of the synchronous algorithm corresponding to pulse $s + 1$ for $s \geq 0$ is that all messages sent to it at pulse s have reached it. This can be taken for granted when the assumptions of the synchronous model are in effect, but lifting them requires special actions to ensure that the property continues to hold. Let us call a node safe with respect to pulse s when all messages it sends during that pulse have reached their destinations. Clearly, in order for a node to proceed to pulse $s + 1$ it suffices that all its neighbors be safe with respect to pulse s. The task of a synchronizer is to convey this safety information to all nodes for each pulse. We start by having all messages of S explicitly acknowledged by an *ack* message; clearly, this has no effect on $MCompl(S)$ or, provided no *ack* is ever withheld for later transmittal, on $TCompl(S)$.

Basic Synchronizers

The first basic synchronizer is called α and conveys the safety information directly between neighbors. When a node has received all *ack* messages corresponding to the messages it sent in pulse s it sends a *safe*(s) message to all its neighbors. Upon receiving a *safe*(s) message from all its neighbors, a node may proceed to pulse $s + 1$. We clearly have $M(\alpha) = O(m)$ and $T(\alpha) = O(1)$. Initializing synchronizer α requires that G be flooded with a signal for all nodes to start pulse 0, and so we have $M_0(\alpha) = O(m)$ and $T_0(\alpha) = O(n)$. Another basic synchronizer, called β, requires a rooted tree to have been built on G beforehand. The root floods the tree, with feedback, with successive signals for the nodes to execute the succession of pulses.

The feedback progresses past a node only when that node has received *ack* messages for all messages it sent during the current pulse. Clearly, $M(\beta) = T(\beta) = O(n)$. As for $M_0(\beta)$ and $T_0(\beta)$, they depend on the complexities of electing a leader (cf. the section on "Other Asynchronous Building Blocks").

A Parameterized Synchronizer

Synchronizers α and β may be combined in a parameterized way to yield another synchronizer. This combination requires the establishment on G of a rooted forest with a number k of trees and of preferential edges between neighboring trees. Synchronization takes place at two levels: inside each tree it works as synchronizer β; at a higher level, at which we consider a graph whose nodes are the trees' roots and whose edges join roots between which a simple path exists in G containing only tree edges and one preferential edge, it works as synchronizer α. If the largest tree has $O(f(G))$ edges, the number of preferential edges is $O(g(G))$, and moreover the greatest tree height is $O(h(G))$, then we have, letting γ denote this hybrid synchronizer, $M(\gamma) = O(kf(G) + g(G))$ and $T(\gamma) = O(h(G))$. The synchronizer γ of Awerbuch (1985) has $M(\gamma) = O(kn)$ and $T(\gamma) = O(\log n/\log k)$. It also has $M_0(\gamma) = O(kn^2)$ and $T_0(\gamma) = O(n \log n/\log k)$.

ADDITIONAL TOPICS

So far in this chapter we have aimed at characterizing what we judge to be the core aspects of the design and analysis of distributed algorithms. But progress has also been made along several other important avenues that are relevant from both a theoretical and an applications-related perspective. We devote this section to highlighting some of them.

Theoretical Aspects

Lower Bounds and Impossibility Results

An important issue that has persisted through the entire development of the field of distributed algorithms has been that of identifying what can and what cannot be computed distributedly, while asserting the minimum message and time complexities of the feasible computations whenever possible. Establishing such results depends on several factors, including the model of distributed computing that is assumed, the system's topology, the existence of distinct identifications for all nodes, and the possibility of failures. We refer the reader to the survey article by Fich and Ruppert (2003) for a comprehensive treatment.

Computing on Anonymous Systems

Anonymity means that the assumption of distinct node identifications does not hold. Although it may be argued that studying distributed computations on anonymous systems has in the past had little practical import, assuming anonymity is theoretically interesting because it highlights the influence of model- and topology-related characteristics on the possibilities of distributed computing. Electing a leader, for example, is naturally expected to be impossible under anonymity. What is curious, though, is that other problems that do not explicitly rely on node identifications also exist that cannot be solved distributedly if the system is anonymous. Several of the pertinent results refer to the consistent computation of functions from distributed inputs (Attiya, Snir, and Warmuth 1988; Attiya and Snir 1991; Yamashita and Kameda 1996), but there has also been recent interest in the impact of anonymity on other distributed tasks (e.g., routing in wireless sensor networks; cf. Dutra and Barbosa 2006).

Topological Awareness

Whenever a distributed algorithm is given for a graph G of unrestricted topology, the prevailing assumption in the field is that no node has built-in information on the structure of G. Such information can come only at the expense of messages and time, and this has to be weighed against any complexity-related advantage one may expect from knowing it locally. One interesting line of research has addressed the question of how to give nodes built-in information that, while still essentially local, has the potential of providing the desired topological awareness. Flocchini, Mans, and Santoro (2003) survey the successful approach known as sense of direction, which is based on labeling edges (locally at each node) in a globally consistent manner.

Self-Stabilization

Throughout the chapter we have concentrated solely on systems that do not fail. The study of failures, however, is an important part of the field of distributed algorithms. One aspect of it is the design and analysis of asynchronous algorithms that, regardless of how local variables are initialized, necessarily converge to some global state satisfying a preestablished property. These are then infinite computations that require no initialization and are resilient to local-state corruption to a certain degree. The characteristic of necessary convergence to a desired global state is called "self-stabilization." Its original introduction and also the first known examples are due to Dijkstra (1974); since then, the field has undergone considerable development (Dolev 2000).

Consensus Problems

These problems have a paradigmatic status in the study of failure-prone systems and ask that all nodes that do not fail reach some sort of agreement. In the asynchronous model, and considering node failures of the crash type only, the very influential study of Fischer, Lynch, and Paterson (1985) establishes the impossibility of agreement even if communication is fully reliable. In the synchronous model, by contrast, agreement can be reached even if we allow for the malicious (so-called Byzantine) failures in which nodes may fail by behaving unreliably instead of crashing (Pease, Shostak, and Lamport 1980; Lamport, Shostack, and Pease 1982), provided at least $2n/3 + 1$ of the n nodes do not fail. The reason for such a wide gap between what happens in the two models is that failure detection is trivial in the synchronous model but unattainable in the asynchronous model. However, in many real-world systems that do not adhere to the synchronous model, reaching agreement seems to be a definite possibility, as in fact demonstrated by the known solutions that adopt some sort of partially synchronous model or randomization (Gärtner 1999). The current framework within which these issues are studied was inaugurated by the work of Chandra and Toueg (1996) and its precursors by the same authors, and is centered on the notion of a failure detector: an imperfect distributed oracle that embodies the desired assumptions of partial synchronism. An introduction to the subject has been given by Raynal (2005).

Correctness Proofs

Similarly to what happens in all algorithm-oriented research areas, many researchers in the field of distributed algorithms have striven for the definition of frameworks that may ultimately lead to automatic correctness proofs. Input/output (I/O) automata and the various abstract structures through which they are combined are an example (Lynch et al. 1994). Another example is UNITY, originally introduced by Chandy and Misra (1988), comprising a programming notation and an associated logic. Ongoing progress on UNITY can be tracked through the PSP Group at UT Austin (2003), for example.

A Unifying Theory

As we generalize the synchronous and asynchronous models to encompass the possibility of failures and also communication by shared memory, the question of whether a unifying theory of computability and complexity for distributed computing can be constructed arises naturally. The surveys by Lamport and Lynch (1990) and Gafni (1999) offer two views of the issue separated by nearly a decade. A reasonable conclusion from the evolution of the field in the meantime between the two surveys seems to be that a theory has begun to emerge that focuses on the properties of complete problems—in a sense similar to that in which certain decision problems are NP-complete—using the tools of combinatorial topology (cf. Rajsbaum 2004 for the key references). Whether such a theory will be consolidated or remain a largely inchoate body of knowledge is yet to be seen.

Applications

Resource Sharing

Resource-sharing computations such as the one we used as an example above not only raise the safety-related issues (such as deadlock) of that example, but also are a source of important questions related to liveness issues and to the essential nature of synchronization procedures other than the synchronization for safety of the section on "Synchronizers" (Barbosa 2002). Answering these questions has led to the design of distributed schedulers targeted at deadlock- and lockout-free resource sharing. Such schedulers are rooted in the combinatorial properties that underlie all resource-sharing constraints, as can be seen, for example, in the seminal work of Chandy and Misra (1984) and in its further characterizations (Barbosa and Gafni 1989) and generalizations (Barbosa, Benevides, and França 2001).

Computing on Wireless Networks

The current ubiquity of wireless networks, including mobile ad hoc and sensor networks, has prompted researchers in the field to a whole new class of challenges. Depending on the nodes' degree of mobility in the network, even the seemingly simple task of determining their locations has required careful attention and resulted in the development of a special theory (Aspnes et al. 2006) to support the creation of location-independent algorithms, for example like the one for routing given by Fonseca et al. (2005). In a similar vein, for many of the envisaged applications of sensor networks it is expected that nodes will have to synchronize their local views of real time, and again special distributed algorithms, for which the works of Su and Akyildiz (2005) and Fan and Lynch (2006) provide the bases, will be needed. Of course, what prevents the direct use of the algorithms we have seen throughout the chapter is the dynamic character of G's topology. In such circumstances, even well-understood problems like determining a minimum-weight spanning tree distributedly may be impossible to solve exactly, which has motivated the first steps toward a theory of distributed approximability (Elkin 2004). Further applications-related considerations, like noisy environments and severe memory and processing limitations, also seem to be bringing the issues of anonymity and self-stabilization back to the fore (Angluin et al. 2005, Stably computable properties of network graphs; Angluin et al. 2005, Self-stabilizing population protocols).

Computing on Complex Networks

Networks like the Internet (and also several others; cf. Bornholdt and Schuster 2003 and Newman, Barabási, and Watts 2006) are examples of what we call a "complex network," that is, a large-scale, unstructured network of essentially unknown topology. Asynchronous algorithms designed to work on a generic graph G work also on such networks, but the networks' massive scale may lead to unacceptable complexity figures in the case of some algorithms. However, since the discovery that the Internet may be an instance of a random graph with known degree distribution (Faloutsos, Faloutsos, and Faloutsos 1999), the possibility has been opened up of designing asynchronous algorithms that take such a distribution into account and produce less costly approximations of the algorithms for generic G. Recent examples include probabilistic approximations of dissemination by flooding (Stauffer and Barbosa 2007), with applications (Stauffer and Barbosa 2006a), and also the probabilistic algorithm of Stauffer and Barbosa (2006b) to approximate the construction of a spanner (Kortsarz and Peleg 1998).

CONCLUSION

This chapter has concentrated on discussing the field of distributed algorithms from two main perspectives. The first perspective has been that of how to handle the notion of time under full asynchronism, and consequently how to approach the treatment of global properties. The second perspective has been that of designing asynchronous algorithms up from its constituent building blocks. Our treatment has included a discussion of some fundamental building blocks and also examples of their use.

It is important for the reader to bear in mind that the field is much broader than our limited selection of topics may have implied. The main role of the section on "Additional Topics" has been to single out and highlight some of the topics we have not treated in depth but are equally interesting and important.

ACKNOWLEDGMENT

The author acknowledges partial support from CNPq, CAPES, and a FAPERJ BBP grant.

GLOSSARY

Asynchronous Algorithm: A distributed algorithm for the asynchronous model.

Asynchronous Model: The model of distributed computing in which nodes are driven by independent, local clocks and messages suffer unpredictable, though finite, delays.

Atomic Action: The uninterrupted first action of an initiator, or the uninterrupted response to the arrival of a message, during a run of an asynchronous algorithm.

Event: A sextuple characterizing each atomic action of a run of an asynchronous algorithm.

Execution: A set of events characterizing a run of an asynchronous algorithm.

Global State: A two-set partition of an execution that is consistent with the happened-before relation.

Global-State Recording Algorithm: An asynchronous algorithm to record a global state.

Happened-Before Relation: A binary relation that gives the causal precedence among the events of an execution.

Initiator: A node that initiates a run of an asynchronous algorithm.

Leader-Election Algorithm: A distributed algorithm that identifies a unique node on whose identification all nodes agree.

Message Complexity: The worst-case number of messages required during a run of a distributed algorithm.

Synchronizer: An asynchronous-algorithm fragment for transforming a synchronous algorithm into an asynchronous one.

Synchronous Algorithm: A distributed algorithm for the synchronous model.

Synchronous Model: The model of distributed computing in which all nodes operate in lockstep with a global clock and messages suffer delays that are bounded by the duration between successive clock pulses.

Time Complexity: The worst-case time required for completion of a run of a distributed algorithm.

Tree-Constructing Algorithm: A distributed algorithm that constructs a tree rooted on its initiator.

CROSS REFERENCES

See *Fault Tolerant Systems; Principles and Applications of Ad Hoc and Sensor Networks*.

REFERENCES

Afek, Y., and E. Gafni. 1991. Time and message bounds for election in synchronous and asynchronous complete networks. *SIAM Journal on Computing* 20:376–94.

Angluin, D., J. Aspnes, M. Chan, M. J. Fischer, H. Jiang, and R. Peralta. 2005. Stably computable properties of network graphs. In *Distributed computing in sensor systems*, edited by V. K. Prasanna, S. Iyengar, P. Spirakis, and M. Welsh, 63–74. Berlin, Germany: Springer-Verlag Lecture Notes in Computer Science, 3560.

Angluin, D., J. Aspnes, M. J. Fischer, and H. Jiang. 2005. Self-stabilizing population protocols. In *Principles of distributed systems*, edited by J. H. Anderson, G. Prencipe, and R. Wattenhofer, 79–90. Berlin, Germany: Springer-Verlag Lecture Notes in Computer Science, 3974.

Aspnes, J., T. Eren, D. K. Goldenberg, A. S. Morse, W. Whiteley, Y. R. Yang, B. D. O. Anderson, and P. N. Belhumeur. 2006. A theory of network localization. *IEEE Transactions on Mobile Computing* 5:1663–78.

Attiya, H., and M. Snir. 1991. Better computing on the anonymous ring. *Journal of Algorithms* 12:204–38.

Attiya, H., M. Snir, and M. K. Warmuth. 1988. Computing on an anonymous ring. *Journal of the ACM* 35:845–75.

Attiya, H., and J. Welch. 2004. *Distributed computing: Fundamentals simulations and advanced topics*. 2nd ed. New York: Wiley.

Awerbuch, B. 1985. Complexity of network synchronization. *Journal of the ACM* 32:804–23.

Barbosa, V. C. 1996. *An introduction to distributed algorithms*. Cambridge, MA: MIT Press.

Barbosa, V. C. 2002. The combinatorics of resource sharing. In *Models for parallel and distributed computation: Theory, algorithmic techniques and applications*, edited by R. Corrêa. I. Dutra, M. Fiallos, and F. Gomes, 27–52. Dordrecht, The Netherlands: Kluwer.

Barbosa, V. C., M. R. F. Benevides, and F. M. G. França. 2001. Sharing resources at nonuniform access rates. *Theory of Computing Systems* 34:13–26.

Barbosa, V. C., and E. Gafni. 1989. Concurrency in heavily loaded neighborhood-constrained systems. *ACM Transactions on Programming Languages and Systems* 11:562–84.

Bornholdt, S., and H. G. Schuster. 2003. *Handbook of graphs and networks*. Weinheim, Germany: Wiley-VCH.

Bracha, G., and S. Toueg. 1987. Distributed deadlock detection. *Distributed Computing* 2:127–38.

Chandra, T. D., and S. Toueg. 1996. Unreliable failure detectors for reliable distributed systems. *Journal of the ACM* 43:225–67.

Chandy, K. M., and L. Lamport. 1985. Distributed snapshots: Determining global states of distributed systems. *ACM Transactions on Computer Systems* 3:63–75.

Chandy, K. M., and J. Misra. 1984. The drinking philosophers problem. *ACM Transactions on Programming Languages and Systems* 6:632–46.

Chandy, K. M., and J. Misra. 1988. *Parallel program design: A foundation*. Reading, MA: Addison-Wesley.

Chin, F., and H. F. Ting. 1990. Improving the time complexity of message-optimal distributed algorithms for minimum-weight spanning trees. *SIAM Journal on Computing* 19:612–26.

Chu, Y.-H., S. G. Rao, S. Seshan, and H. Zhang. 2002. A case for end system multicast. *IEEE Journal on Selected Areas in Communications* 20:1456–71.

Dijkstra, E. W. 1974. Self-stabilizing systems in spite of distributed control. *Communications of the ACM* 17:643–44.

Dijkstra, E. W., and C. S. Scholten. 1980. Termination detection for diffusing computations. *Information Processing Letters* 11:1–4.

Dolev, S. 2000. *Self-stabilization*. Cambridge, MA: MIT Press.

Drummond, L. M. A., and V. C. Barbosa. 1996. Distributed breakpoint detection in message-passing programs. *Journal of Parallel and Distributed Computing* 39:153–67.

Drummond, L. M. A., and V. C. Barbosa. 2003. On reducing the complexity of matrix clocks. *Parallel Computing* 29:895–905.

Dutra, R. C., and V. C. Barbosa. 2006. Finding routes in anonymous sensor networks. *Information Processing Letters* 98:139–44.

Einstein, A., and L. Infeld. 1938. *The evolution of physics*. New York: Simon & Schuster.

Elkin, M. 2004. Distributed approximation: A survey. *ACM SIGACT News* 35(4):40–57.

Faloutsos, M., P. Faloutsos, and C. Faloutsos. 1999. On power-law relationships of the Internet topology. In *Proceedings of the Conference on Applications, Technologies, Architectures, and Protocols for Computer Communication*, 251–62. New York: ACM Press.

Fan, R., and N. Lynch. 2006. Gradient clock synchronization. *Distributed Computing* 18:255–66.

Feynman, R. P., R. B. Leighton, and M. Sands. 1963. *The Feynman lectures on physics,* vol. I. Reading, MA: Addison-Wesley.

Fich, F., and E. Ruppert. 2003. Hundreds of impossibility results for distributed computing. *Distributed Computing* 16:121–63.

Fischer, M. J., N. A. Lynch, and M. S. Paterson. 1985. Impossibility of distributed consensus with one faulty process. *Journal of the ACM* 32:374–82.

Flocchini, P., B. Mans, and N. Santoro. 2003. Sense of direction in distributed computing. *Theoretical Computer Science* 291:29–53.

Fonseca, R., S. Ratnasamy, J. Zhao, C. T. Ee, D. Culler, S. Shenker, and I. Stoica. 2005. Beacon vector routing: Scalable point-to-point routing in wireless sensornets. In *Proceedings of the Second USENIX/ACM Symposium on Network Systems Design and Implementation*, 329–42. www.usenix.org/events/nsdi05/tech (accessed May 4, 2007).

Gafni, E. 1999. Distributed computing: A glimmer of a theory. In *Algorithms and theory of computation handbook*, edited by M. J. Atallah, chapter 48. Boca Raton, FL: CRC Press.

Gallager, R. G., P. A. Humblet, and P. M. Spira. 1983. A distributed algorithm for minimum weight spanning trees. *ACM Transactions on Programming Languages and Systems* 5:66–77.

Gärtner, F. C. 1999. Fundamentals of fault-tolerant distributed computing in asynchronous environments. *ACM Computing Surveys* 31:1–26.

Huang, Y., and P. K. McKinley. 2000. Group leader election under link-state routing. *Computer Communications* 23:653–66.

Kortsarz, G., and D. Peleg. 1998. Generating low-degree 2-spanners. *SIAM Journal on Computing* 30:1438–56.

Kurose, J. F., and K. W. Ross. 2005. *Computer networking*. 3rd ed. Boston: Addison-Wesley.

Lamport, L. 1978. Time, clocks, and the ordering of events in a distributed system. *Communications of the ACM* 21:558–65.

Lamport, L., and N. A. Lynch. 1990. Distributed computing: Models and methods. In *Handbook of theoretical computer science*, edited by J. van Leeuwen, vol. B, 1156–99. Cambridge, MA: MIT Press.

Lamport, L., S. Shostak, and M. Pease. 1982. The Byzantine generals problem. *ACM Transactions on Programming Languages and Systems* 4:382–401.

Lynch, N. A. 1996. *Distributed algorithms*. San Francisco: Morgan Kaufmann.

Lynch, N., M. Merritt, W. Weihl, and A. Fekete. 1994. *Atomic transactions.* San Mateo, CA: Morgan Kaufmann.

Misra, J., and K. M. Chandy. 1982. A distributed graph algorithm: Knot detection. *ACM Transactions on Programming Languages and Systems* 4:678–86.

Newman, M., A.-L. Barabási, and D. J. Watts. 2006. *The structure and dynamics of networks*. Princeton, NJ: Princeton University Press.

Pease, M., R. Shostak, and L. Lamport. 1980. Reaching agreement in the presence of faults. *Journal of the ACM* 27:228–34.

Peleg, D. 2000. *Distributed computing: A locality-sensitive approach*. Philadelphia: SIAM.

PSP Group at UT Austin. 2003. www.cs.utexas.edu/users/psp/ (accessed May 3, 2007).

Rajsbaum, S. 2004. ACM SIGACT News distributed computing column 15. *ACM SIGACT News* 35(3):46–57.

Raynal, M. 2005. A short introduction to failure detectors for asynchronous distributed systems. *ACM SIGACT News* 36(1):53–70.

Segall, A. 1983. Distributed network protocols. *IEEE Transactions on Information Theory* 29:23–35.

Stauffer, A. O., and V. C. Barbosa. 2006a. Dissemination strategy for immunizing scale-free networks. *Physical Review E* 74:056105.

———. 2006b. Local heuristics and the emergence of spanning subgraphs in complex networks. *Theoretical Computer Science* 355:80–95.

———. 2007. Probabilistic heuristics for disseminating information in networks. *IEEE/ACM Transactions on Networking* 15:425–35.

Su, W., and I. F. Akyildiz. 2005. Time-diffusion synchronization protocol for wireless sensor networks. *IEEE/ACM Transactions on Networking* 13:384–97.

Tel, G. 2000. *Introduction to distributed algorithms*. 2nd ed. Cambridge, UK: Cambridge University Press.

Yamashita, M., and T. Kameda. 1996. Computing functions on asynchronous anonymous networks. *Theory of Computing Systems* 29:331–56.

Yang, Z., and T. A. Marsland, eds. 1994. *Global states and time in distributed systems*. Los Alamitos, CA: IEEE Computer Society Press.

Distributed Databases

David Coquil and Harald Kosch, *University of Passau, Germany*

INTRODUCTION

A distributed database system (DDBS) considers interconnected sites, each containing a local database management system (DBMS), which interacts with the other sites through well-defined interfaces provided by the distributed database management system (DDBMS). It is widely recognized (Özsu and Valduriez 1999) that a key goal for DDBMSs is *transparency*: users must be able to interact with the system as if it were one single logical system.

Besides transparency, the expected benefits of DDBMSs compared to centralized DBMSs are the following:

- *Increased performance*: Data can be moved nearer to the points where they are mostly used and queries can be parallelized among several nodes.
- *Improved scalability*: When the amount of data increases, it can be easily further fragmented without having to change the rest of the system; moreover it is easier to integrate new databases.
- *Better reliability*: A fault in a node affects only that node, rather than the entire system.
- *Organizational structure is accurately reflected*: Data can be placed at the sites they relate to and be managed there, instead of being centrally managed.

However a DDBMS does not automatically grant these advantages; to benefit from them a number of issues must be addressed:

- *Architectural issues*: The component sites must be integrated into a single system. There are several options from which to choose in order to achieve this goal.
- *Distributed database design*: Additional issues are to be taken into account at the design stage with respect to central DBMSs. These include decisions about how relations should be partitioned (fragmentation) and where fragments should be stored (fragment allocation). Such decisions have a critical impact on query-execution times and thus dictate whether the DDBS actually improves performance.
- *Distributed query processing*: A DDBMS query processor must take into account the distribution of the data. This impacts the computation of query execution plans as well as query optimization, for which additional factors have to be considered (bandwidth, loads on the sites, etc.).
- *Reliability*: A DDBMS can improve reliability only if specific procedures have been designed for the cases in which one or more sites fail during the processing of a transaction.
- *Interoperability*: Such issues arise when the interconnected DBMSs are heterogeneous and/or have incompatible schemas.

The rest of this chapter is organized as follows. The next section describes the architectural alternatives for DDBMSs. Then we discuss the design issues specific to these systems. The following section outlines the topic of distributed query processing, and the next deals with the problem of reliability within DDBMSs, followed by a discussion of DDBMS interoperability. We then discuss Grid computing, more precisely Grid data management capabilities and the way they can be used to build and operate distributed databases. Finally, a summary of the subject is presented.

DISTRIBUTED DATABASE MANAGEMENT SYSTEMS ARCHITECTURES

Typology of Architectures

From an architectural point of view, DDBMSs can be characterized on the basis of three dimensions:

1. *Distribution* of data in the global system
2. *Autonomy* of the individual sites
3. *Heterogeneity* of the sites comprising the system

The resulting possibilities can be graphically displayed as a three-dimensional cube (see Figure 1). Each point corresponds to an architecture and represents its characteristics in the three dimensions. Let us first consider the alternatives for each dimension.

The possible options with respect to autonomy are:

1. *No autonomy*: The sites are tightly integrated and not capable of functioning independently.
2. *Partial autonomy*: The sites can function independently; however, the way they process queries is affected by cooperation. In this setting, the sites generally know about the existence of one another.
3. *Full autonomy*: The sites are fully independent, unaware of each other and unaffected by others.

The possible options with respect to distribution are:

- *No distribution*: All the data are located at a single site.
- *Partial distribution*: The data are distributed across some, but not all sites. A typical case is when participating machines are divided into servers, which hold data and process queries, and clients, which hold no data and access them only through queries to the servers.
- *Full distribution*: The data are spread across all sites. There is no distinction between the sites.

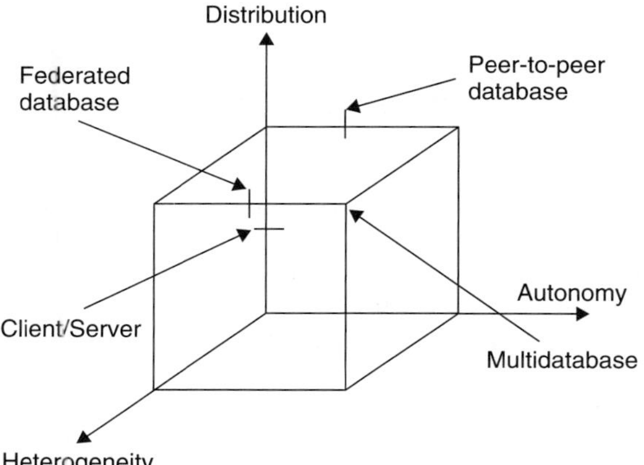

Figure 1: Dimensions of DDBMSs architectures; adopted and modified from Öszu and Valduriez (1999)

The possible cases in terms of heterogeneity are:

- *Homogeneity*: All machines and all sites are similar and connected through a homogeneous network. Minor differences in features that do not directly affect query processing are nevertheless possible.
- *Heterogeneity*: A system is considered heterogeneous when at least two sites differ in some characteristic that influences query processing. Heterogeneity factors include hardware architectures, operating systems, data managers, query languages and network access characteristics. Another heterogeneity factor is the existence of incompatible schemas in the component databases.

The main types of DDBS architectures with respect to these dimensions are:

- *Client/server*: No autonomy, partial distribution, homogeneity
- *Peer-to-peer*: Partial autonomy, full distribution, homogeneity
- *Multidatabases*: Full autonomy, full distribution, heterogeneity; *federated databases* are a semi-autonomous variant of multidatabases.

An important feature of DDBMSs architectures is the way they integrate separate databases so that they can be presented to users as a single database. One possibility is to create a global schema (the global conceptual schema, GCS) out of the local schemas. This issue is discussed in more detail in the section "Distributed Databases Interoperability."

Client/Server-Based Architectures

Client/server architectures for DDBSs come in two variants: multiple clients/single server, or multiple clients/multiple servers.

The single server architecture is similar to a centralized system. The only significant difference is that clients usually access the server through a wide-area network instead of a local network, which puts more emphasis on the need for clients to process a part of the queries locally.

The multiple servers/multiple clients architecture has two different configurations. In the first case, each client is tied to a "home server," to which it sends its queries. This server acts as a gateway to the other servers. The servers are therefore not fully autonomous as they need to cooperate when queries involve multiple servers. The clients are lightweight, because they can access their home server as in a single-server scenario. The communication between the servers is then of peer-to-peer nature, since each server can act both as a client (as a home server) and as a server (when processing queries from another server).

In the second case, each client directly contacts all servers involved in a query. In this case, the servers are fully autonomous, as they only receive queries. The clients are thick, because they need to have the capability to decompose queries into sub-queries (each sub-query being directed toward one server) and to reassemble the results.

Peer-to-Peer–Based Architectures

A peer-to-peer (P2P) system is an open-ended network of distributed computational peers, in which each peer can be both a client and a server—that is, it can provide *and* consume services or resources (see *Peer-to-Peer Network Architecture* and *Peer-to-Peer Network Applications* for more detail on P2P computing). There is no central authority in the network. Peers are autonomous, as they can freely decide the amount of data they make available, and enter and leave the system as they see fit (Schoder, Fischbach, and Schmitt 2005). P2P technology is mostly known for its use for distributed object sharing; however, it can also be used to serve as a foundation for the architecture of a DDBMS. As noted above, the system is autonomous per P2P definition (but only partially autonomous, as query processing requires cooperation between the peers), fully distributed, and homogeneous (in the sense that all peers communicate through identical P2P software, possibly hiding lower-level heterogeneity between them).

The mapping of P2P technology to DBMSs is not straightforward, as P2P systems lack a number of data management capabilities, such as managing complex data objects, content update, data semantics, and relationships between data (Roshelova 2004).

Especially, the existence of a global schema cannot be assumed because it would conflict with the autonomy of the peers. One solution to this problem is the mapping of local schemas on-the-fly during querying: query processing includes a schema-matching step in which schemas compatible with that of the query are looked for (Siong Ng, Ooi, and Zhou 2003). Alternatively, peers can coordinate themselves with their neighbors by mapping each others' schemas, new mappings being discovered via transitive relationships (Serafini et al. 2003).

Other problems related to peer-to-peer architectures include information redundancy, and the fact that the correctness and completeness of query results cannot be guaranteed (Ooi, Shu, and Tan 2003). At the time of the writing of this book, much of these remain open research issues, and productive peer-to-peer DBMSs are not available.

Multidatabases

Multidatabase systems correspond to the case in which a DDBMS is built on top of several existing DBMSs. In this case, heterogeneity is typically very high: operating systems, data formats, query languages and database manager software can all be different.

Given the nature of multidatabases, schema integration is a very important feature for allowing and optimizing query processing. This problem is described in more detail in the section on "Distributed Databases Interoperability".

Such systems can be further divided in two categories (Bright, Hurson, and Pakzadd 1992):

- *Global schema multidatabases*: A GCS is created and maintained by the distributed system; local DBMSs are unaware of the existence of each other, remaining completely autonomous. Queries are aimed at the GCS and translated into sub-queries, each of which concerning a single database.
- *Federated database systems*: In a federated system, each DBMS defines an export schema which represents the structure of the data it makes available to others. The queries are defined with respect to an import schema created by integrating several export schemas. These systems do not make use of a permanent GCS.

Comparison of the Architectures

Client/server-based systems are very widely used. They have several advantages:

- Users and database administrators are usually familiar with client/server technology.
- The technology is mature, and performance is known to be good.
- Many problems can be assimilated to similar ones of centralized DBMSs for which good solutions are known.

However:

- Client/server-based solutions cannot be applied in cases of heterogeneity: the participating databases must be fully compatible.
- A central point of administration is required.
- Adding and deleting nodes is a complex task.
- The participation to a client/server-based DDBMS has an influence on local query processing. The increased complexity might not be worth it for sites with mostly local queries.

Peer-to-peer–based systems have the following advantages:

- By design, there is no single point of failure.
- Administrative tasks are delegated to each node in the absence of central control. This can, however, turn into a problem in some cases, such as when updating the P2P software.
- Data are naturally replicated and cached locally, potentially improving performance.
- P2P systems scale well, as adding new nodes when needed is straightforward.

Their disadvantages are:

- The dynamic nature of the peers can be problematic, as it cannot be guaranteed that a node is available at a given moment.
- P2P systems are not adapted to all applications. For instance, when a node is not connected, its data are not available. This imposes limitations on the correctness and completeness of query results, which may be unacceptable for some applications.
- P2P databases are still a work in progress. Currently, there is no proof that a P2P DDBMS can deliver a performance similar to that of other architectures.

Multidatabase systems are difficult to compare with the other architectures because they provide solutions to cases in which other architectures cannot be used. These systems allow for the integration of very heterogeneous databases without the need for modifying them. The main problem of these systems is that of schema integration, which can be a very complex task.

DISTRIBUTED DATABASE MANAGEMENT SYSTEMS DESIGN

General Design Strategies

Distributed database design strategies generally fall into two major categories (Ceri, Pernici, and Wiederhold, 1987): top-down design and bottom-up design.

The choice of a design strategy is usually mandated by context: a top-down approach can only be applied when building a DDBMS from scratch, while a bottom-up approach is required when legacy systems are to be integrated.

The top-down design approach starts by identifying the system requirements (top-level goals). Two steps are then performed in parallel: view design, in which the required interfaces of the system are defined, and conceptual design, which identifies the basic elements of the schema. This results in a global conceptual schema. This global schema is then broken into a number of local conceptual schemas (distribution design), which in turn are mapped to physical storage (physical design).

A significant disadvantage of this approach is that it is suitable only for DDBSs designed from scratch. Although this is probably the ideal case for designing optimal DDBSs, it is not so common: in many cases, the idea of a DDBMS comes as an afterthought in order to integrate already existing systems. The top-down approach also makes it difficult to add new databases to the system.

The bottom-up approach is very common in the case of multidatabases, in which a distributed database is to be built out of legacy systems that are already in use. Such a design starts by examining existing resources, especially the schemas of the databases to be integrated, in order to create a global conceptual schema out of them. The main issue here is that of database interoperability, discussed in more detail in its own section below.

The bottom-up methods essentially build on the previous design of the existing databases that they are willing to integrate. As such, they do not involve design decisions that are specific to distributed environments. Contrary to the top-down approaches. In consequence, the remainder of this section describes issues and solutions in the context of a top-down design.

Fragmentation

Definition

Fragmentation is the process of dividing a relation into subrelations. The rationale for fragmentation is that applications generally deal with subsets of relations (views) rather than with entire relations. In the context of distributed database systems, these substes are therefore more convenient units of distribution than whole relations. More convenient units of distribution than whole relations (Özsu and Valduriez 1999). Cleverly defined fragments should also increase global performance, as they reduce the amount of irrelevant data to be dealt with and transferred between sites, and allow parallel processing (Lim and Ng 1996). On the other hand, bad fragmentation design can lead to degraded performance if typical transactions make use of many fragments that are distributed over many different sites.

There are three types of fragments:

- *Horizontal fragments* are subsets of the tuples of a relation.
- *Vertical fragments* are subsets of the attributes of a relation.
- *Mixed fragments* are fragments that are both horizontally and vertically fragmented.

All fragments are associated with a query that allows retrieval of their content when applied to the original relation.

Rules of Correctness

The fragmentation process should not change the semantic nature of the database. This can be ensured by checking that its result complies to a number of specific rules of correctness, which are defined below. All subsequent definitions assume that a relation R has been divided into a set of fragments $F=\{R1, R2, \ldots, R_n\}$. A data item is defined as a tuple for horizontal fragments and as a set of attributes for vertical fragments. The rules are the following:

- *Completeness*: For each data item d found in R, there should exist at least one R_i that contains d.
- *Reconstruction*: It must be possible to build a relational operator Δ such that

$$R=\Delta R_i, \forall R_i \in F$$

where Δ is the relational additive union operator for horizontal fragmentation, and the relational binary join operator for vertical fragmentation.

- *Disjointness*: A data item contained in a fragment must not appear in other fragments. There is an exception in the case of vertical fragmentation, for which the disjointness property applies only to non–primary key attributes. This is because a relation broken down vertically can only be rebuilt correctly from the fragments if they all include the primary key.

Horizontal Fragmentation Strategies

The horizontal fragmentation design choice can be divided into two categories:

- *Primary horizontal fragmentation*, in which tuples belong to fragments based on a predicate defined on the relation.
- *Derived horizontal fragmentation*, in which relations are partitioned with respect to the result of a predicate defined on another relation, e.g. the result of a join with another relation.

A horizontal fragmentation strategy must identify the "chunks" of the database that are accessed as units by applications; usually such chunks can be defined by a *minterm* predicate, which can be written as a conjunction of simple predicates of the form $p : A\Theta K$, where A is a single attribute, K a value comprised in the domain over which A is defined and Θ a comparison operator. Identifying such chunks and minterm predicates yields a list of candidates for horizontal fragmentation.

The "optimal" fragmentation plan should then be chosen from among these candidates. Important criteria for this choice are *completeness* and *minimality* (Ceri, Negri, and Pelagatti, 1982). A set of simple predicates is complete if and only if the probability of access by all applications is the same for each tuple belonging to any minterm fragment defined according to it. Minimality means that all fragments defined by the set of simple predicates are accessed differently If one of the simple predicates defines two fragments that are accessed exactly the same way by applications, then the fragmentation is not minimal, and this predicate should not be used as a basis for fragmentation.

Vertical Fragmentation Strategy

Vertical partitioning generally implies a very large number of alternatives, hence the use of heuristics rather than the search for optimal solutions. The main heuristics are variants of *splitting*, in which whole relations are considered one at a time in order to find a good fragmentation scheme with respect to previous access patterns (Navathe et al. 1984).

In order to choose a vertical fragmentation plan, the sets of attributes queried by each application and the frequency of occurence of the corresponding queries must be considered. This information can be summarized in an *attribute affinity matrix* which to each couple of attributes (A, B) associates a relative measurement of how often A and B are used in conjunction in queries. This matrix constitutes the input of an algorithm that produces a fragmentation plan clustering attributes of high affinity.

Fragment Allocation

Fragment allocation is the choice of placement of the fragments on each site of the distributed system. In order to compute a proper allocation plan, the following information must be known beforehand:

- Information about fragments: size and associated query
- Information about applications: which fragments each application may access and/or update, number of read/update to each fragment for each query
- Information about sites: temporary and secondary storage and processing capacities
- Information about the network: bandwidth, average latency, etc.

Note that fragment allocation alternatives depend on the degree of replication allowed. The DDBMS can *forbid replication*, in which case each fragment resides at only one site, implement *full replication*, in which each fragment exists at each site, or more commonly, allow *partial replication*, in which replication is neither forbidden nor compulsory.

The allocation process consists of defining binary values for x_{ij} variables, where $x_{ij} = 1$ if fragment F_i is stored at site S_j and 0 otherwise.

An allocation model can then be defined. Such a model is defined by its goals; for example in the model detailed in Özsu and Valduriez (1999), the main goal is to minimize processing and storage costs, with acceptable response time as a secondary objective. The goals are modeled as functions; in the example, a total cost function is defined, which outputs the sum of query processing and storage costs, themselves modeled as functions. Functions are further refined until functions depending on decisions of fragment allocation are identified.

Such a model allows a quantitative evaluation of an allocation scenario, but does not directly give an "optimal" solution, as the problem is NP-complete (Özsu and Valduriez 1999). Therefore heuristics methods based on plausible rules that produce nonoptimal but reasonably good results have to be used.

DISTRIBUTED QUERY PROCESSING

The query processing problem is more complicated in distributed environments than in centralized ones, as a larger number of factors can play a role. In particular, the relations of a DDBS are typically fragmented and distributed over distant sites, which may increase response times to queries involving several fragments; this also increases the number of possible execution strategies from which to choose.

Planning a processing strategy for a distributed query is comprised of three steps, which are detailed in the next sections:

1. Query decomposition: The high-level query submitted by the client is decomposed into a set of operations expressed in the relational algebra (the algebraic query).
2. Data localizatoin: The data that are accessed by the query is localized in the sites where they reside. The operations on global relations of the preceding step are transformed into operations on fragments.
3. Query optimization: This phase mainly amounts to choose the best execution plan with respect to predefined criterias.

Query Decomposition

Query decomposition is applied to global relations of the schema of a DDBS, and not to fragments. Its principles are, as such, identical for centralized and distributed databases (Kossmann 2000).

The process begins with the normalization of the high-level query. Usually, the submitted query is written in the structured query language (SQL); the main normalization operation is then the transformation of the WHERE clause. There are two types of normalized forms for such clauses, depending on whether precedence is awarded to the AND ($\wedge$) or to the OR ($\vee$) logical operator:

- The disjunctive normal form, where the clause is rewritten in the form:

$$(p_{1,1} \wedge p_{1,2} \wedge \ldots p_{1,n}) \vee \ldots \vee (p_{r,1} \wedge p_{r,2} \ldots \wedge p_{r,m})$$

the p_{ij}'s being simple predicates and r, n, m constants.

- The conjunctive normal form, represented as follows using the same conventions:

$$(p_{1,1} \vee p_{1,2} \vee \ldots p_{1,n}) \wedge \ldots \wedge (p_{r,1} \vee p_{r,2} \ldots \vee p_{r,m})$$

Rewriting a WHERE SQL clause in either form can be done easily using well-known transformation properties of the logical operators.

After the initial normalization, the query is analyzed, mainly to determine whether it is incorrect. Incorrect queries can either be type-incorrect or semantically incorrect. Type-incorrect queries use variables (attribute or relation names) not defined in the schema, or apply operators to attributes with which they are not compatible (e.g., a "greater than" operator applied to textual attributes). A query is semantically incorrect if some of its components do not contribute to the generation of the result. A typical example is that of a query on several relations in which no join clause has been specified.

The query is then parsed in order to eliminate redundancy. Simple predicates may need to be transformed using well-known idempotency properties in order to identify redundent statements.

The final step of the decomposition process consists of rewriting the query in the relational algebra—that is, in a form that uses only a set of operators (usually selection, projection, union, set difference anunion, set difference, and cartesian product) applied to relations. This query can be represented as an *operator tree*, with the relations involved in the query as leaves, and with internal nodes corresponding to the relational operators; these operators are connected to their operands by edges.

Data Localization

The goal of the data localization process is to transform an algebraic query on relations into an algebraic query on fragments (Ceri and Pelagatti 1982).

As discussed in the section on "Distributed Database Management Systems Design," fragments can be derived from the relations by applying fragmentation rules to them. Such rules can be written as relational queries. The reverse process is called a "localization program."

In this context, a simple method of data localization is to substitute each relation by its localization program in the input query. The result is called the "generic query." Although correct, the generic query is generally inefficient, and it is better to transform it using techniques specific to the type of fragmentation.

For horizontal fragments, the rules consist of identifying the parts of the generic query that produce empty relations. Typically, a selection or join operation applied to a fragment may contradict the fragmentation rule by which it is defined. Such operations can be written off the query. Similarly, in the case of vertical fragmentation, the query can be reduced by removing intermediary relations formed of projections with which the fragment has no common attribute.

Query Optimization

Though the previous steps have eliminated some obviously sub-optimal strategies, many query execution plans remain possible at this point. The goal of query optimization is to select one using a cost function as a choice criterion. Distributed query optimization in general is an NP-hard problem in the number of relations (Wang and Chen 1996), hence the motivation for using heuristics for selecting non-optimal but good plans.

At first a number of "good enough candidates" execution plans are generated. A large number of algorithms for this enumeration process have been proposed by the database community (Steinbrunn, Moerkotte, and Kemper 1997). Among them, the dynamic programming algorithm (Kossmann and Stocker 2000) is widely used, notably by popular commercial DBMSs. It consists in a dynamically pruning exhaustive search that constructs all alternative join trees by iterating on the number of relations joined so far. At each step, known rules are used in order to identify non-optimal trees and to prune them. The advantage of this algorithm is that it can guarantee to produce optimal or close-to-optimal plans with respect to the cost model that is used to assess the plans. Its problem is that it is of exponential computation time and space complexity, which makes it unsuitable for complex queries such as most of those submitted to a DDBMS. It can, however, be extended to use a simpler process for queries that are above a complexity threshold, producing "as good as possible plans" for complex queries with a reasonable computation time.

Choosing between the alternatives for the join trees in the query execution plan is a very important feature for a query optimizer. Indeed, the classical join operator being symmetrical, it is possible to permute the order of this join, and such permutations are known to have the most impact on the performance of the queries. In the case of DDBMSs, the normal way of processing a join between fragment A of site S_1 and fragment B of site S_2 is to transmit either A or B so that they are on the same site. Given the nature of distributed systems, the goal of join-ordering based optimization is to transmit the smallest operands of joins so as to minimize the network costs. This means that for complex queries with several joins, the size of the intermediate results involved in further joins in the query must be computed beforehand, which is generally a difficult and costly operation. Join operand ordering was the basis of the query optimizers of early experimental DDBMSs R and Distributed INGRES.

Semijoin programs were proposed as an alternative way of processing joins on fragments located on different sites (Bernstein et al. 1981). The semijoin of fragment A (of site 1) by fragment B (site 2) is defined as the subset of the tuples of A that participate in the join with B. The operator can be used to compute the join between A and B using the following sequences of operations:

1. The columns of A needed for the evaluation of the join predicate are sent from site 1 to site 2.
2. The set of tuples of B (noted B_j) that qualify the join is identified at site 2.
3. B_j is sent to site 1.
4. A is matched with B_j.

The argument for using semijoins in query execution plans is that they can reduce the amount of data that must be transmitted over the network. On the other hand, they increase the costs of processing, so they are traditionally considered useful when they induce communication costs savings that exceed the processing overhead that they create.

Candidate plans need to be evaluated using a cost model in order to determine the "best plan" with respect to predefined criteria. The main cost models for distributed queries are: the classic cost model and the response-time model.

The principle of the classic cost model is to estimate the resource consumption cost of every individual operation in the query and to add these costs up. The cost of an operation is composed of CPU, disk I/Os, and network consumption costs. The basic cost of a plan as evaluated by this model is thus its total resource consumption cost. The costs can be weighted according to the characteristics of the system (in order to take into account factors such as the average load on a site or the congestion on certain network links). Because it selects plans that use the least amount of resources, this model tends to increase the number of queries that can be performed simultaneously, maximizing site throughput.

The classic cost model does not favor intraquery parallelism; thus, it does not guarantee a minimal response time. Indeed, a plan with an optimal response time may be discarded if it consumes more resources. If response time is an important factor, it is advisable to use a different specific cost model (Ganguly, Hasan, and Krishnamurthy 1992). This model first computes the total resource consumption of each individual operation. Then, the total usage of every resource used by a group of operations that can be performed in parallel is calculated. The cost assigned to each group is defined as the maximum cost of all individual operations of the group. Intraquery parallelism is therefore taken into account, and the plan with the lowest expected time response should normally be selected. However, the model does not consider factors such as the load on each site, which may induce scheduling problems for heavily used sites and decrease the actual response time.

DISTRIBUTED DATABASE MANAGEMENT SYSTEMS RELIABILITY

As explained in the introduction, a potential benefit of a distributed DBMS is improved reliability: when a component of the system fails, some or all queries may still be processed, as opposed to a centralized DBMS, in which the failure of the central server leads to failure of the whole system. Of course, this benefit will be effective only if specific steps have been taken at the design level so that the system can take advantage of its inherent distribution in order to improve its reliability.

Typology of Failures in DDBMS

The failures that can occur in a DDBMS can be put into four categories (Özsu and Valduriez 1999):

- Transaction failures: abnormal termination of a transaction
- System failures: either hardware (disk, memory) or software (OS or database server) failures. This means that the parts of the database that might have been in main memory, called the "volatile database" (typically the results uncommitted operations) are lost, while the database stored on secondary storage (stable database) remains correct (thouh out of date).
- Media failures: a fault in secondary storage devices hosting a part of the database.
- Network failures: all problems related to the communication system. This type of failure is unique to DDBMSs with respect to centralized systems. Here we restrict ourselves to the network failures about which a DDBMS can take action as opposed to those that are the sole responsibility of the network. This means lost/undeliverable messages and line failures.

Local Reliability

One possibility to improve the reliability of a DDBMS is to use local a reliability manager (LRMs) on each DBMS comprising the system. The purpose of this component is to prevent the problems related to local system failures. As such, it is similar to its counterpart found in centralized DBMSs. This technique is based on the logging of all database operations, so that when a system failure occurs, previous operations can either be redone or undone, depending on the point of the transactions in which the failure occurred.

Media failures are another type of fatality that can be dealt with at the local level. Media failures are characterized by the fact that they cause data losses in the stable database and/or log. To counter this, the LRM can manage a backup of the database, and the log can be stored on a different secondary storage device. Many techniques have been developed for creating and maintaining such backups efficiently without affecting the performance of the stable database server (see Bhalla and Madnick 2004 for an overview).

Distributed-Reliability Protocols

The protocols relevant to reliability for DDBMSs are:

- *Commit*: the general commit procedure
- *Termination*: the action to be taken to terminate a transaction when one of the participating sites failed
- *Recovery*: how a site that failed in the middle of a distributed transaction can return to a stable state

Commit Protocols The two phase commit (2PC) (Lampson 1981) is meant to ensure the atomic commitment of distributed transactions—that is, the fact that a distributed transaction must either succeed or fail (in which case, all its proposed changes are discarded), in a context in which system failures may occur at sites.

2PC requires a central point of coordination (the coordinator) that can send sub transactions to each relevant site (the cohorts). Theoretically each site should answer to the coordinator that it will either commit or abort the transaction. Assuming that there is no site failure (that is, that the coordinator does receive answers from each cohort in the system), there are two possibilities:

- At least one site replied with an abort message: the distributed transaction must be aborted. The coordinator sends a global-abort (rollback) message to the cohorts, which abort their subtransactions accordingly.
- All sites replied with commit. The coordinator sends a global-commit message to the cohorts, which commit their corresponding subtransactions.

In both cases, the cohorts send an acknowledgment message to the coordinator after having complied with the final decision. The 2PC protocol can be divided into a voting phase, in which cohorts "vote" for acception or rejection of the transaction, and a completion phase, in which the transaction is actually executed or rejected hence, the "two-phase" name.

2PC has the drawback of inducing substantial cost overhead during normal transaction execution, because of its message complexity, as it requires a large number of messages between the coordinator and the cohorts, and because of the amount of log information that the coordinator and the cohorts must maintain during the transaction. Therefore, many proposals have been made in the literature to either optimize or replace 2PC. For example, recent years have seen a renewed interest in one-phase-commit (1PC) protocols (Abdallah, Guerraoui, and Pucheral 2002). These protocols manage to have only one phase by discarding the voting phase, overlapping it with the execution of operations in the cohorts.

While improving performance over 2PC, IPC protocols and other alternative distributed commit protocols usually make strong assumptions about how cohorts execute transactions and about the organization of the distributed system. This makes them impractical in several cases, which is probably the reason why 2PC remains the most widely used protocol despite its shortcomings: 2PC has been successfully used in large-scale distributed environments since the 1980s (Samaras et al. 1993) and is a universal feature of modern DBMSs (Greenwald, Stackowiak, and Stern 2004). Hence, we will assume 2PC to be the commit protocol for the remainder of this section. This is necessary because the termination and recovery protocols, which are described in the next paragraphs, are closely dependent on the commit protocol operated in the system.

Termination Protocol The 2PC protocol being synchronous, it mandates the use of time-outs so that failures can be identified and action subsequently taken. The termination protocols define what action to take in these cases. With 2PC there are two time-out cases to consider: time-outs at the coordinator and time-outs at a cohort.

For a coordinator, the time-out can either occur when waiting for votes, in which case it globally aborts the transaction, or when waiting for the acknowledgment of a global commit or global abort. In this case the only option is to repeatedly resend the message to the failed site, since the other cohorts have already processed the transaction.

For cohorts, the main problem is that of a time-out occurring while the site has already voted "commit" and is waiting for the decision of the coordinator. Because of the logic of 2PC, the site cannot decide to abort or commit the transaction on its own. If it can communicate only with the coordinator, it can only block indefinitely until the coordinator answers. As such it is desirable that cohorts have the possibility of communicating with one another. In this case, the site experiencing the time-out can query the other cohorts and take action depending on their responses.

Recovery Protocol The recovery protocol defines what a node of a distributed system must do when it has managed to restore itself to a stable state after experiencing a failure. For a coordinator, the main cases are the following:

- If it failed after sending an initial transaction message to the cohort, chances are it lost some answers and should therefore resend the message.
- If it failed after sending its commit or abort decision to the cohorts, it generally does not have anything to do.

For a cohort, the main cases are the following:

- If the failure occurred after the cohort received a transaction message from the coordinator but before it responded to it, it globally aborts the transaction. This is because of how coordinators handle time-outs in this case, as described in the preceding section.
- If the failure occurred after the cohort responded "abort," or after it received a global abort message, the site can resume normal operations, since it can assume that the transaction has been globally aborted.
- If the failure occurred after the cohort voted "commit," the cohort can treat it as a time-out and launch the termination protocol described in the previous section.

DISTRIBUTED DATABASES INTEROPERABILITY

Interoperability is a large problem, and a number of its aspects that are relevant to DDBMSs have solutions that are outside the scope of this chapter: standard network protocols allow heterogeneous operating systems to communicate, a standardized query language such as SQL allows distributed queries to be valid across different types of component databases, etc. In this section, we focus on the interoperability problems that is the most specific to DDBMSs, that of the resolution of heterogeneity at the schema level. This places us in the "multidatabases" case, as defined previously in the "architecture" section.

Schema Translation/Schema Integration

The problem of heterogeneity at the schema level can be addressed by a database integration process, the goal of which is to create a global schema of the distributed database. As previously explained, certain types of multidatabases do not necessarily need a global schema. Therefore, this process is relevant only to systems that do have one.

Database integration comprises two steps: schema translation, and schema integration.

Schema translation means transforming each component schema I to a common canonical representation.

This translation does not concern the semantics of the schemas, but the model in which they are expressed (such as relational, entity-relationship, object, ...).

Many techniques of schema translation from one specific data model to another have been developed. For a complete description of common cases of schema translation, see Silberschatz, Korth, and Sudarshan (2006). These techniques are widely used, though research on model-independent translation—that is, techniques that can be used for any translation regardless of the original and target model types—remains active (Atzeni, Cappellari, and Bernstein 2006).

Schema translation is followed by schema integration, which involves the following tasks:

1. Identifying the components of a database which are related to others.
2. Selecting an appropriate representation formalism for the global schema.
3. Actually integrating the initial schemas into a global conceptual schema.

Two types of approaches exist in terms of schema integration: the binary approach and the n-ary approaches (Batini, Lenzirini, and Navathe 1986).

In the binary approach, two different schemas are integrated into one at each step. This approach can either be balanced or stepwise. In balanced schema integration, schemas S_1 and S_2 are integrated into schema S_1', schemas S_3 and S_4 are integrated into schema S_2', and so on until all input schemas have been processed. The S_i's schemas are themselves pairwise integrated; the process is repeated until only one schema remains. A stepwise schema integration process starts by integrating two schemas. The resulting schema is then integrated with a third one, and so on until only one integrated schema remains.

With n-ary schema integration, more than two schemas are integrated at each step. The process can be either single-pass or iterative. A single-pass process integrates all schemas at once. In iterative n-ary schema integration, variable numbers of schemas are integrated at each step. There should be more than one step (otherwise the process falls into the single-pass case), and one of the steps should involve more than two schemas (otherwise it is equivalent to a binary schema integration).

Most available tools implement binary techniques, because they are easier to partly automate, while n-ary integration typically involves more complex cases. N-ary is advocated by researchers who argue that more information is available at each step, which can prevent poor intermediary decisions. To clarify matters, the next sections will assume a binary process applied to entity-relationship (ER) schemas.

Semantic Heterogeneity

A key issue in an integration process is that of the semantic heterogeneity. Although researchers do not agree on a precise definition of semantic heterogeneity, a generally accepted framework is the following: "variations in the manner in which data is specified and structured in different components" (Hammer & McLeod, 1993). Semantic heterogeneity is characterized by the existence of semantic conflicts between schemas. Transforming one or all schema(s) to resolve these conflicts is called homogenization. This process can be followed by integration, in which the homogenized schemas are combined.

Hammer and McLeod (1993) include a detailed taxonomy of semantic heterogeneity issues. The most prominent ones are naming conflicts, which can involve either homonyms or synonyms. Homonyms are database entities that have the same name but different meanings, while synonyms have different names but the same meaning.

Homonymy issues are usually easy to address: having different meanings, homonyms only have to be differentiated and not integrated. A common solution is to prefix the entities with their site and/or original relation names.

On the contrary, there exists no systematic way to resolve synonymy. In this context, ontologies have drawn much interest from the research community in the past few years (Wache et al. 2001), and have become the preferred way to deal with synonyms.

An ontology is basically a data model that represents a domain of knowledge. Ontologies are generally defined using four basic types:

- *Individuals*: objects (or instances)
- *Classes*: types of individuals. The notion is similar to that of object-oriented programming in particular inheritance is possible
- *Attributes*: features, properties, characteristics or parameters specific to an object
- *Relations*: characterization of relationships between objects

Ontologies provide a reference naming framework specific to a domain. In the context of semantic heterogeneity between schemas, if all schemas conform to the ontology related to their domain, their entities are named consistently, and synonymy issues can be avoided. As such, ontologies are the most useful when they are used at the design stage; however, they can also help resolve semantic heterogeneity between "ordinary" (non–ontology-based) schemas by providing a point of reference to which the entities of the schemas can be manually translated.

The problem of ontologies is that they are useful only if all experts of their domain agree on their content, a consensus that is generally hard to achieve. A typical example of this can be found in this very text: as noted above, experts do not agree on the exact definition of "semantic heterogeneity"!

Another source of semantic heterogeneity is the problem of structural conflicts between schemas. Four types of structural conflicts exist:

1. *Type conflicts*: for instance an attribute in one schema being modeled as an entity in another
2. *Dependency conflict*: identical relationships having different cardinalities
3. *Key conflicts*: identical relationships with different sets of candidate keys or primary keys
4. *Behavioral conflicts*: conflicts related to triggers, integrity constraints and other similar mechanisms

Methods of solving structural conflicts differ, depending on the data model in which the schemas are expressed (see, for example, Yang, Lee, and Ling 2003) for XML schemas). However, the idea is generally to transform entities, relationships, and attributes into one another. This generally requires human intervention to take the semantics of the schemas into account.

Homogenization of two schemas can be performed only once the relationships between them have been precisely determined. There are four possible types of relationships between schemas:

1. *Identity*: To each element of one schema corresponds one and only one element in the other schema.
2. *Inclusion*: One schema is a subset of the other.
3. *Overlapping*: Some elements of one schema are found in the other, but both have unique elements.
4. *Empty intersection*: The schemas are strictly disjoints.

As with many other parts of the homogenization process, identifying the relationship between two schemas requires human intervention, as the semantics of the schemas must be understood.

After homogenization, the actual integration into a single schema can be performed. This integration is fairly straightforward once all the issues described above have been resolved. Three dimensions have been identified in order to measure the quality of the outcome of an integration process (Batini et al. 1986):

1. *Completeness*: The whole semantics of the input schemas is retained in the global conceptual schema.
2. *Minimality*: The resulting schema should contain no redundant entity.
3. *Understandability*: The final schema should be easy to understand for a reasonably qualified observer. This should ideally be the main criterion of quality of a GCS; however, it is difficult to evaluate precisely because of its subjective nature.

DATAGRIDS

Datagrid Basics

Grid computing is an emerging computing model that was first formally introduced in 1998 by Foster and Kesselman (see *Grid Computing Fundamentals* and *Grid Computing Implementation* for more details on Grid computing). A Grid is a middleware system that takes advantage of the capabilities of a large number of heterogeneous interconnected computers in order to execute high performance computing applications. Typical Grid applications include scientific applications (high-energy physics, biology, meteorology, etc.) and business-oriented applications (complex financial modeling, highly distributed engineering projects, etc.).

The original "Grid book" (Foster and Kesselman 1998) defined a computational Grid as "a hardware and software infrastructure that provides dependable, consistent, pervasive, and inexpensive access to high-end computational capabilities." This definition insisted on the sharing of the computing power of a large number of internetworked devices. However, many computer scientists who followed up on the idea argued for a broader definition encompassing the sharing of resources in general, especially including storage resources and data. This prompted the development of Grid systems mainly concerned about data sharing as opposed to computing power sharing called datagrids (Rajasekar et al. 2003). By allowing the sharing of large data sets distributed across a large number of computer facilities and multiple administrative domains (called virtual organizations in Grid context), the Grid paradigm is a means through which the promises of DDBMSs as defined in the introduction of this chapter can be fulfilled (Stockinger 2001). Datagrids even go beyond these promises, since their "resource-sharing" philosophy allows the integration not only of structured data stored in DBMSs but also of unstructured data found in other data sources (file systems, directories, archives...).

Grid technology is a work in progress, with many practical issues still within the realm of research; however, commercial applications have started to appear. This trend is outlined by the fact that major DBMS vendors have introduced Grid facilities in the latest versions of their software.

Another important development in the Grid community is the introduction of Grid standards. With the large number of Grid projects springing up in the beginning of the 2000s, the need for Grid standards has quickly become obvious. This led to the foundation of the Global Grid Forum (GGF, www.gridforum.org), which issues standards for various aspects of Grid technology after extensive discussion in the community. Another major player in the Grid world is the Globus project (www.globus.org), which developed a toolkit that has become a de facto standard for Grid systems and applications development, implementing some of the GGF standards.

One very important trend in the latest Grid standards is their growing integration with Web services standards, in particular through the definition of the open Grid services architecture (OGSA, http://globus.org/ogsa). OGSA defines a service-oriented architecture through a set of core functionalities, including authentication, service discovery, service monitoring, etc. OGSA capabilities can be implemented as Web services with the Web Service Resource Framework (WSRF, www.globus.org/wsrf) specification.

General Grid Data Management Techniques

Datagrids need the following data management capabilities (Moore et al. 2004):

- Data-transfer mechanisms between nodes
- Replication mechanisms
- Metadata support
- Information repository abstraction for accessing multiple databases

Additional mechanisms are, of course, required for typical Grid system functioning (security, service-management capabilities, services related to distributed job execution, etc.)

but will not be detailed here, as they are not specific to data management.

Data Transfer

Grid data management requires efficient data-transfer services over wide area networks. A typical Grid transfer service is *GridFTP* from Globus, which defines a file transfer protocol (FTP)–like protocol with extensions taking advantage of the grid's characteristics: parallel transfers, partial transfers, reusable transfer channels. Globus also provides the reliable file transfer (RFT) service, a WSRF service that basically adds high fault tolerance to a GridFTP-like service.

Replica Management

Replication is a key technique for the design of efficient datagrids, as it can dramatically improve their performance: no matter how fast the network, strategically placed replica will always have a significant impact on query processing and retrieval times. Liberal replication also provides an additional level of fault tolerance: when a resource is unavailable, the data can still be accessed through its replicas.

Replication requires mechanisms for the definition of logical file names (LFNs), which are identifiers of a file replicated across the system. All replicas of a specific file share the same LFN. LFNs are opposed to physical file names (PFNs), which uniquely identify each file available in the Grid. A PFN is typically composed of the concatenation of the address of a storage resource with an LFN.

In this context, datagrids usually provide two replica management services: a replicator, which uses Grid data-transfer services to create copies of specified data at a specified location; and a replica location service (RLS), which can be queried to find the replicas of a given LFN. When creating replicas, the replicator registers them with the RLS. With current datagrids, replication is generally initiated by users; however, the transparency philosophy of the Grid should lead to the development of automatic replication by the middleware.

Metadata-Related Functions

Datagrids provide access to very large data sets. Many of these are described using metadata, implemented as a set of fields attached to data objects. Because the purpose of early datagrids was often to let members of a scientific community access large data resources relevant to their domain, the need for metadata integration arose quickly. This was usually performed with metadata catalogs. Grid metadata integration also first outlined the need for database integration into datagrids, as users needed to issue complex queries on metadata in order to discover interesting data.

Metadata can generally be divided into two categories: domain-related metadata (information relevant to only the members of a community), and domain-independent metadata (e.g. data size, owner, etc.). Ontologies are often used in order to define a naming space in which such information can be expressed consistently.

An example of a Grid metadata service is the Metadata Catalog Service (MCS) (Deelman et al. 2004), a Globus application built on top of OGSA-DAI (see below). Metadata related to files or collections of files are stored in a database. MCS provides a query interface to this database. For file-related metadata, the result of a query is a set of logical file names, which can be sent to the RLS to locate them. Metadata attributes can also be dynamically added by users.

Database Access

Early Grid applications were concerned mainly with the processing of scientific data, often stored as collections of files. As Grid application domains broadened over time, the need for the support of more structured data such as DBMSs repositories became quickly obvious.

This prompted much research in the field, mainly in two directions: providing a standard interface with which databases can be accessed through the Grid middleware, and defining an infrastructure using Grid resources in order to evaluate and execute distributed queries on grid-accessible DBMSs. This materialized with the *OGSA-DAI* (OGSA database access and integration [Antonioletti et al. 2005]) and *OGSA-DQP* (OGSA distributed guery processing [Alpdemir et al. 2003]) projects.

The main goal of OGSA-DAI is to provide a common interface to various types of data resources available on a datagrid. Its architecture comprises three types of services: Service Consumers, GDSF/GDS (Grid data service factories/Grid data services), DAISGR (DAI Service Group Registries). Service consumers are services trying to discover available data and to perform queries on them. A GDS service provides a data source abstraction, which allows access to data through consistent interfaces, regardless of their specific format. This is achieved thanks to plug-ins developped for each supported data-source type. There are plug-ins for all major DBMSs. A GDSF is responsible for creating a GDS when source appears and for publishing its availability to DAISGR services. The DAISGR services thus represent a directory of available data resources, which can be queried by service consumers.

OGSA-DQP is a framework for defining distributed query processors that can execute queries over data wrapped by OGSA-DAI. In accordance with the transparency philosophy of the Grid, the "orchestration" of the queries is left to the processor, which can have DQP services compile, optimize, and schedule queries. OGSA-DQP queries are written in object query language (OQL; Cattell et al. 2000). Client applications may use a translation service to translate queries into OQL. A query is separated into a number of partitions, each of which encapsulates the role of an individual service in the query evaluation and corresponds to a query execution plan. Queries are sent to a "query statement activity" service. This service parses queries, divides them into partitions, optimizes them, schedules them, and sends each partition to DQP evaluator services. These services can evaluate and execute a query plan provided as an input, and communicate with other evaluators for synchronization. These evaluators are included in "DQP resource," which encapsulate a distributed query management execution architecture: DQP evaluator, OGSA-DAI data services, etc. A DQP factor activity enables the creation and configuration of these resources so that a new infrastructure can easily be added.

SUMMARY

In this chapter, we have defined distributed database systems and presented the related issues with their usual state-of-the-art solutions: the choice of an architecture, the main options being client/server, peer-to-peer, and multidatabase; the design methods, especially in terms of fragmentation and fragment allocation; distributed query processing, dealing with how execution plans are computed and queries are optimized; DDBS reliability issues, especially how transactions can be committed in cases of site failures; and DDBS interoperability, notably the resolution of semantic heterogeneity issues when a global conceptual schema of the whole distributed database is wanted.

Distributed databases have been around for a long time. They represent a well-tested technology used daily by many large organizations. Despite this, research remains active in the field. One first type of research deals with specific issues of DDBMSs for which an optimal solution is not available (such as a number of NP-complete problems that were identified in this chapter). Perhaps most notably, the second type of research works results in introducing distributed databases in contexts in which they had not been used before:

- Peer-to-peer technologies allow a DDBMS to be built by aggregating to build the information carried by a very large number of lightweight clients.
- The Grid paradigm puts more power in the middleware, opening opportunities for an easier construction of DDBMSs, integrating various heterogeneous data sources.

Indeed, these new applications are characterized by the large number and heterogeneity of the data they integrate, as opposed to the handful of database servers comprising traditional distributed systems; hence the activity in the research related to semantic heterogeneity, upon which the success of this new breed of DDBMSs largely depends.

GLOSSARY

Component Database: Database participating in a distributed database system.

Datagrid: Middleware system taking advantage of a large number of interconnected computing resources with a focus on using them for data management purposes.

Fragmentation: Partitioning of a relation into subrelations to be distributed across the participating sites of a DDBMS. Horizontal fragmentation partitions relations into subsets of tuples, while vertical fragmentation divides them according to subsets of their attributes.

Global Conceptual Schema: Database schema encompassing a whole DDBMS even if it comprises component databases initially defined through their own independent schemas.

Localization: In the context of DDBMSs, localization is the process through which a distributed query expressed on global relations is translated to a query expressed on fragments.

Multidatabase: Distributed database management system built out of several existing databases.

Schema Integration: Process through which the schemas of several databases are combined into a single schema, that usually involves the resolution of semantic conflicts between the schemas to be combined.

Schema Translation: Process through which a database schema is transformed from a formalism of representation to another, with a view to a future integration with other schemas.

Semijoin: Relational operator that selects the tuples of a relation that participate in the natural join of this relation with another one. Semijoin operators are widely used by distributed query optimizers.

Transparency: Key feature of DDBMSs that allows users to interact with the system as if it were a single centralized DBMS, unaware of the geographical location and distribution of the data.

Two-Phase Commit Protocol: Distributed algorithm that ensures that all nodes of a DDBMS globally commit or globally abort a distributed transaction even in cases of failure of one or more participating node(s).

CROSS REFERENCES

See *Fault Tolerant Systems; Grid Computing Fundamentals; Groupware.*

REFERENCES

Abdallah, M., R. Guerraoui, and P. Pucheral. 2002. Dictatorial transaction processing: Atomic commitment without veto right. *Distributed and Parallel Databases* 11(3):239–68.

Alpdemir, M. N., A. Mukherjee, N. W. Paton, P. Watson, A. A. Fernandes, A. Gouranis, et al. 2003. Service-based distributed querying on the grid. In *First International Conference on Service Oriented Computing* 467–82. Heidelberg, Germany: Springer-Verlag Lecture Notes in Computer Science, 2910. www.cs.man.ac.uk/˜alvaro/publications/soc2003.pdf (accessed November 11, 2006).

Antonioletti, M., M. Atkinson, R. Baxter, A. Borley, N. Chue Hong, B. Coilins, et al. 2005. The design and implementation of grid database services in OGSA-DAI. *Concurrency and Computation: Practice and Experience* 17(2-4):357–76. www3.interscience.wiley.com/cgi-bin/abstract/109896161/ABSTRACT (accessed November 11, 2006).

Atzeni, P., P. Cappellari, and P. A. Bernstein. 2006. Model-independent schema and data translation. In *Proceedings of Advances in Database Technology—EDBT 2006, 10th International Conference on Extending Database Technology*, 368–385. Heidelberg, Germany: Springer-Verlag Lecture Notes in Computer Science, 3896.

Batini, C., M. Lenzirini, and S. B. Navathe. 1986. A comparative analysis of methodologies for database schema integration. *ACM Computer Surveys* 18(4):323–64.

Bernstein, P., N. Goodman, E. Wong, and J. Rothnie. 1981. Query processing in a system for distributed databases. *ACM Transactions on Database Systems* 6(4):602–25.

Bhalla, S., and S. E. Madnick. 2004. Asynchronous backup and initialization of a database server for replicated database systems. *The Journal of Super computing* 27(1):69–89.

Bright, M., A. Hurson, and S. Pakzadd. 1992. A taxonomy and current issues in multidatabase systems. *Computer* 25(3):50–60.

Cattell, R., D. Barry, M. Berler, J. Eastman, D. Jordan, C. Russell et al. 2000. Object query language. In *The object data standard: ODMG 3.0*, edited by R. Cattell and D. Barry. San Francisco: Morgan Kaufmann.

Ceri, S., M. Negri, and G. Pelagatti. 1982. Horizontal data partitioning in database design. In *ACM SIGMOD International Conference on Data Management* 128–36. New York: ACM Press.

Ceri, S., and G. Pelagatti. 1982. A solution method for the non-additive resource allocation problem in distributed system design. *Information Processing Letters*, 15(4):174–8.

Ceri, S., B. Pernici, and G. Wiederhold. 1987. Distributed database design methodologies. *Proceedings of the IEEE* 75(5):533–46 Deelman, E., G. Singh, M.P. Atkinson, A. Chervenak, N.P. Chue Hong, S. Patil.

Foster, I., and C. Kesselman. 1998. *The Grid: Blueprint for a new computing infrastructure*. San Francisco: Morgan Kaufmann.

Ganguly, W., S. Hasan, and R. Krishnamurthy. 1992. Query optimization for parallel execution. In *Proceedings of the ACM SIGMOD Conference on the Management of Data, San Diego, CA, USA*, edited by M. Stonebraker, 9–18. New York: ACM Press.

Greenwald, R., R. Stackowiak, and J. Stern. 2004. Distributed databases and distributed data. In *Oracle essentials*. 3rd ed., Chapter 12. Sebasopol, CA: O'Reilly.

Hammer, J., and D. McLeod. 1993. An approach to resolving semantic heterogeneity in a federation of autonomous, heterogeneous database systems. *Journal for Intelligent and Cooperative Information Systems* 2(1):51–83.

Kossmann, D. 2000. The state of the art in distributed query processing. *ACM Computer Surveys* 32(4):422–69. http://portal.acm.org/citation.cfm?doid=371578.371598 (accessed November 11, 2006).

Kossmann, D., and K. Stocker. 2000. Iterative dynamic programming: A new class of query optimization algorithms. *ACM Transactions on Database Systems* 25(1).

Lampson, B. W. 1981. Atomic transactions. *Distributed Systems: Architecture and Implementation-An Advanced Course* 105:246–65.

Lim, S. J., and Y.-K. Ng. 1996. A formal approach for horizontal fragmentation in distributed deductive database design. In *Database and Expert Systems Applications, 7th International Conference, DEXA '96*, 234. London: Springer-Verlag Lecture Notes in Computer Science, 1134.

Moore, R., A. S. Jagatheesan, A. Rajasekar, M. Wan, and W. Schroeder. 2004. Data grid management systems. In *21st IEEE/NASA Goddard Conference on Mass Storage Systems and Technologies, College Park, MD, USA*. http://romulus.gsfc.nasa.gov/msst/conf2004/Papers/MSST2004-01-Moore-a.pdf (accessed November 5, 2006).

Navathe, S., S. Ceri, G. Wiederhold, and J. Dou. 1984. Vertical partitioning algorithms for database design. *ACM Transactions on Database Systems* 9(4):680–710.

Ooi, B., Y. Shu, and K. Tan. 2003. Relational data sharing in peer-based data management systems. *ACM SIGMOD Record* 32(3):59–64.

Özsu, T., and P. Valduriez, 1999. *Distributed database systems*. 2nd ed. Englewood Cliffs, NJ: Prentice Hall.

Rajasekar, A., M. Wan, R. Moore, and T. Guptill. 2003. Data grids, collections and grid bricks. In *20th IEEE/NASA Goddard Conference on Mass Storage Systems & Technologies, San Diego, CA, USA*. http://storageconference.org/2003/papers/01-Rajasekar-Data.pdf (accessed July 27, 2006).

Roshelova, A. 2004. *A peer-to-peer database management system* (Technical Report no. DIT-04-057). Informatica e Telecomunicazioni, University of Trento, Italy. http://eprints.biblio.unitn.it/archive/00000585 (accessed November 18, 2006).

Samaras, G., K. Britton, A. Citron, and C. Mohan. 1993. Two-phase commit optimizations and tradeoffs in the commercial environment. In *Proceedings of the 9th IEEE International Conference on Data Engineering*. Washington, DC: IEEE Computer Society Press.

Schoder, D., K. Fischbach, and C. Schmitt. 2005. Core concepts in peer-to-peer technology. In *Peer to peer computing: The evolution of a disruptive technology*, edited by R. Subramanian and B. Goodman. Hershey, PA: Idea Group Inc. www.idea-group.com/books/additional.asp?id =4635&title=Book+ Excerpt&col=book_excerpt (accessed November 6, 2006).

Serafini, L., F. Giunchiglia, J. Mylopoulos, and P. Bernstein. 2003. Local relational model: A logical formalization of database coordination. In *Modeling and Using Context: 4th International and Interdisciplinary Conference CONTEXT 2003 Stanford, CA, USA*, 286–99. Heidelberg, Germany: Springer-Verlag Lecture Notes in Computer Science, 2680. http://sra.itc.it/people/serafini/distribution/lrm-context-03.pdf (accessed November 11, 2006).

Silberschatz, A., H. Korth, and S. Sudarshan. 2006. *Database system concepts*. 5th ed. New York: McGraw-Hill.

Siong Ng, W., B. Ooi, and A. Zhou. 2003. Peerdb: A P2P-based system for distributed data sharing. In *Proceedings of the Nineteenth International Conference on Data Engineering (ICDE'03), Bangalore, India*. Los Alamitos, CA, USA: IEEE Computer Society Press. http://xenal.ddns.comp.nus.edu.sg/p2p/peerdb.pdf (accessed November 10, 2006).

Steinbrunn, M., G. Moerkotte, and A. Kemper. 1997. Heuristic and randomized optimization for the join ordering problem. *The VLDB Journal* 6(3):191–208.

Stockinger, H. 2001. Distributed database management systems and the data grid. In *Proceedings of the Eighteenth IEEE Symposium on Mass Storage Systems and Technologies*. Washington, DC: IEEE Computer Society Press. http://storageconference.org/2001/2001CD/01stocki.pdf (accessed November 5, 2006).

Wache, H., T. Voegele, U. Visser, H. Stuckenschmidt, G. Schuster, H. Neumann, et al. 2001. Ontology-based integration of information—a survey of existing approaches. In *Proceedings of the Seventeenth International Joint Conference on Artificial Intelligence (IJCAI'01), Seattle, WA, USA*, 108–117. San Francisco: Morgan Kaufmann. www.informatik.uni-bremen.de/agki/www/buster/papers/SURVEY.pdf (accessed November 13, 2006).

Wang, C, and M.-S. Chen. 1996. On the complexity of distributed query optimization. *IEEE Transactions on Knowledge and Data Engineering*, 8(4).

Yang, X., M. L. Lee, and T. W. Ling. 2003. Resolving structural conflicts in the integration of XML schemas: A semantic approach. In *Conceptual Modeling—ER 2003*, 520–33. Heidelberg, Germany: Springer Verlag Lecture Notes in Computer Science, 2813.

FURTHER READING

The IEEE Computer Society offers in its distributed systems online Web site (http://dsonline.computer.org) a section specific to distributed databases, which is a good starting point for monitoring state-of-the-art research activity in the field. Particularly interesting are the pages on people working in the field, projects, and reference material. The other main online source of reference material on distributed databases is the DBLP computer science bibliography (www.informatik.uni-trier.de/~ley/db/), in particular with its "Database Systems" and "Distributed computing" entry points.

PART 2

Network Planning, Control, and Management

Network Capacity Planning

Priscilla Oppenheimer, *Southern Oregon University*

INTRODUCTION

Network capacity planning is the process of determining the resources that will be needed for a network to support the network traffic that is offered to it. Capacity planning is challenging because network capacity is affected by many factors, including the bandwidth of network links, the capabilities of network servers, and the performance of internetworking devices. Capacity planning is also difficult because it involves predicting the future. To accurately provision capacity, network engineers must try to learn what users are doing now, what they will be doing in the near future, and what they will be doing in a few years.

Despite the difficulties, capacity planning is one of the most important tasks an engineer will take on. Without enough capacity, a network experiences unwanted delay and errors, especially as load increases. Too much capacity wastes money and can result in problems in other parts of the network that cannot handle the extra traffic. The right amount of capacity, on the other hand, helps engineers meet current and future needs, achieve service-level objectives, minimize risks associated with unexpected traffic surges, and proactively identify bottlenecks. With a good plan, bottlenecks can be placed where they will cause the least disruption to the network, and internetworking devices can be configured to accurately prioritize traffic when there are bottlenecks.

This chapter presents capacity-planning terminology and principles, as well as recommendations for capacity planning processes. Capacity planning processes include gathering information about requirements, analyzing potential solutions, reviewing constraints and trade-offs, testing solutions, and gathering requirements information again. Capacity planning is not a linear step-by-step process. Rather, it is a creative, recursive process, in which multiple solutions are envisioned and evaluated. This chapter suggests possible ingredients for a good solution, but leaves it up to the reader to creatively select the right solutions based on actual requirements and constraints.

CAPACITY-PLANNING TERMINOLOGY

Planning is the act of designing a realization of a goal. Capacity planning involves designing the capacity that will be required of a network to meet the business and operational goals of the network users. Network capacity can be expressed in terms of network link bandwidth, network architecture and performance, server architecture and performance, router architecture and performance, application behavior, and so on. This section expands on these basic principles and defines capacity.

Definitions of Capacity

Capacity refers to the potential or suitability for holding, storing, or accommodating something. For example, the capacity of a bucket could be one gallon or the capacity of an auditorium could be 100 people. Networks hold (and convey) network traffic caused by network applications, such as Web browsing, file sharing, music downloading, video streaming, and searching for extraterrestrial intelligence (SETI). Network capacity is the potential for a network to accommodate the network traffic that is presented to it by network applications.

Sometimes the word *capacity* refers to the facility to produce something, such as the production capacity of a factory or the power-producing capacity of a generator. Networks do not really produce anything. Nonetheless, a network—and the networking devices that comprise it—does receive inputs and generate outputs (in the form of packets), and the rate at which it can do this has a major affect on network capacity.

Shannon's law, developed by Claude Shannon, a mathematician who helped build the foundations for modern computers, expresses capacity in terms of the maximum bits per second that a channel can carry in the presence of electrical noise. Shannon's law states that the highest obtainable error-free data rate, expressed in bits per second, is a function of the bandwidth (in Hertz) of the channel and the signal-to-noise ratio.

The broad concept to understand with Shannon's law is that raw frequency is not the only ingredient of capacity. Electrical noise affects capacity. To carry that concept a step further, it is also important to realize that capacity, as measured in raw bits per second, is not the only ingredient of network capacity. Network capacity is affected by network topologies, link characteristics, servers, routers, switches, firewalls, operating systems, and applications.

One final note with regard to definitions: Capacity should be distinguished from throughput. Throughput is a measure of how much actual traffic can be passed across a network path in a stated period of time (whereas capacity is the potential for a network to accommodate network traffic). *Throughput* usually refers to user data and is lower than capacity because it is affected by network congestion, server congestion, framing overhead, packet overhead, background traffic, and errors.

Network Capacity

In summary, the capacity of a network is provided by the following:

- The network topology
- The bandwidth (data rate in Mbps or Gbps) of local area network (LAN) links
- The bandwidth of wide area network (WAN) links
- The bandwidth of metropolitan area network (MAN) links
- The bandwidth, storage capacity, and disk access speed of storage area networks (SANs)
- The features of network servers, including CPU power, the amount of random access memory (RAM) and disk storage, RAM and storage access speed, bus speed, and operating system and application software behavior
- The features of internetworking devices (routers, bridges, switches, firewalls, wireless access points, concentrators, multiplexers, content switches, and load balancers), including CPU power, the amount of RAM and disk storage, RAM and storage access speed, bus speed, operating system and application software behavior, and packets-per-second (PPS) forwarding rate.

CAPACITY-PLANNING PROCESS

Capacity planning should be a structured, analytical process based on engineering design principles. Capacity planning requires gathering information about business and operational goals, applications, the current network's infrastructure and performance, and network traffic. After information is gathered, potential solutions should be developed and tested. Finally, a solution that is based on analysis and testing, and that is also flexible and modular so that changing needs can be met, should be selected and implemented. After the solution is implemented, it should be continually monitored to determine whether it is still working and meeting user needs. The job of a network engineer is never finished. Figure 1 illustrates the capacity-planning process discussed in this section.

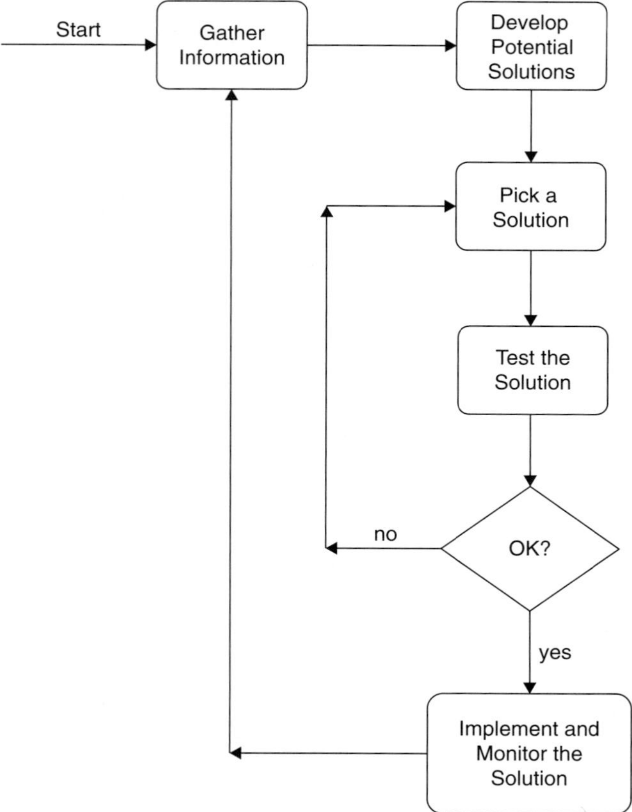

Figure 1: A capacity-planning process

Gathering Information

The first step for most planning projects is to gather information. Determining how much capacity a network will need requires gathering information about business drivers, applications, the current network, and traffic classes and patterns. These details are inputs to the capacity-planning process. A plan for a network with sufficient capacity is the output of the capacity-planning process. Figure 2 shows the inputs and outputs of a capacity-planning process.

Business Drivers

Computer networks exist because they solve a business or operational problem. Network upgrades are made not because some new technology sounds cool to the network engineers, but because they help an organization achieve its goals, whether the goals are to increase profits, gain market share, improve worker productivity, streamline processes, or something else unique to the organization. An important aspect of capacity planning is an analysis of the business or operational goals of the network. Likewise, an important aspect of a capacity-planning project is an analysis of the specific business or operational goals of the project. As part of this analysis, the engineer should gain an understanding of the scope of the capacity-planning project. Is the project related to a single network link, a set of LANs, a set of WANs or remote-access networks, or the entire internetwork?

Applications

Computer networks carry application data. While gathering information for a capacity plan, an engineer should identify user applications. Later, the engineer can characterize the applications' capacity requirements, as covered later in this chapter in the section on "Analyzing Network Traffic Patterns," but at this point, the engineer should

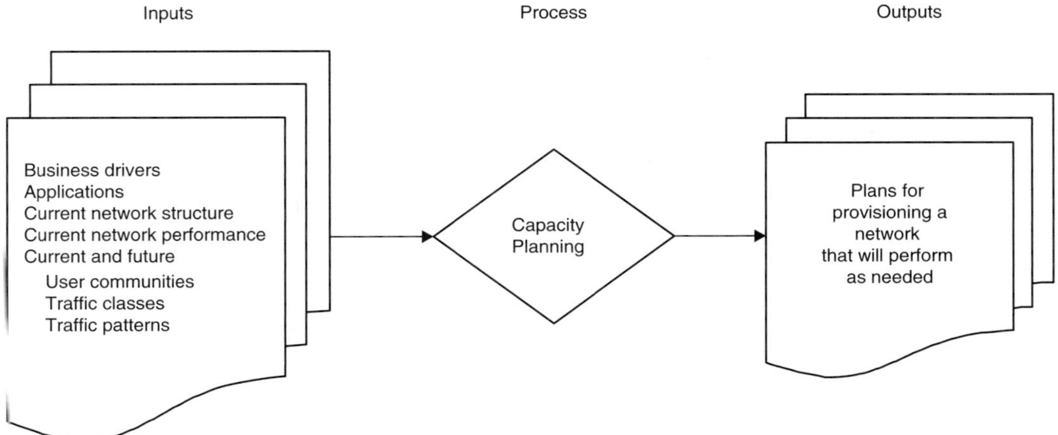

Figure 2: Inputs and outputs of a capacity-planning process

simply identify the major applications that offer traffic to the network, including e-mail, file-oriented applications, database access and updating, Web browsing, remote terminals, voice, video, network games, and so on. The above list is for user applications, but the capacity of the network must also support network services such as dynamic addressing, naming and name resolution, user authentication and authorization, remote booting, directory services, network backup, network management, software distribution, and so on.

Current Network Structure

An effective capacity-planning process starts with a characterization of the architecture of the current network. Engineers should learn the location of major network links, servers, server farms, and internetworking devices, and develop a set of detailed maps. If accurate maps already exist, they can be used, but often network documentation is out of date and should not be trusted without additional investigation.

While documenting the network structure, it is a good idea to take a step back from the detailed diagrams and try to characterize the logical topology of the network as well as its physical components. The logical topology depicts the overall design of a network; it can affect the upgrade of a network. For example, a flat topology, with no modularity or hierarchy, is hard to upgrade. A modular design, on the other hand, allows parts of a network to be upgraded without affecting the entire network.

Current Network Performance

Before engineers can decide how much additional capacity is needed for a network, they need to know how much it currently has, how much of that current amount is actually being used, and how well the network is performing with its current capacity. A baseline measure of the current performance of a network is an important input into the capacity-planning process. This measure should include information about bandwidth utilization, efficiency, availability, accuracy, response time and delay, and the status of major internetworking devices. (Oppenheimer 2004).

Bandwidth utilization is a measure of how much bandwidth is in use during a given time interval, usually specified as a percentage of the maximum theoretical bandwidth. For example, a measuring tool might specify that traffic is using 70 Mbps on a 100-Mbps Ethernet link—in other words, 70%. (Some tools might call this 35% of a full-duplex Ethernet link.)

Network monitoring tools use different time intervals for computing bandwidth utilization. Some tools let the user change the interval. Using a long interval (such as an hour or longer) can be useful for reducing the amount of data that the tool outputs, but granularity is sacrificed. Peaks in network traffic get averaged out. Using a time interval of a few minutes is a better plan, so that short-term peaks can be factored into the capacity-planning process. If practical, monitoring tools should run for at least a few days. If the project goals include improving performance during the busiest times, utilization should be measured during these times, not just on typical days. For example, an online store should measure utilization during the Christmas-shopping season.

Sometimes bandwidth is used inefficiently. One aspect of capacity planning is to determine whether there are any optimizations that can be done so that bandwidth is not wasted. Bandwidth utilization is optimized for efficiency when applications and protocols are configured to send large amounts of data per packet, thus minimizing the number of packets and round-trip delays required for a transaction. The number of packets needed for each transaction can also be minimized if the receiver is configured with a large receive window, allowing it to accept multiple packets before it must send an acknowledgment. The goal is to maximize the number of application-layer data bytes compared to the number of bytes in headers, acknowledgments, and other overhead information. (Note that an exception to this is networks with voice traffic and slow links. Voice uses small packets and works best when other applications also use small packets, so that the transmission time for outputting large packets does not cause extra delay for the voice applications. This is especially true for slow links.)

The availability of the network can be specified as a mean time between failures (MTBF) and a mean time to repair (MTTR). A baseline analysis of the current network should also include information about the accuracy of the network in terms of bit-error rates on WAN links, cyclic redundancy check (CRC) errors on LAN links, and dropped packets. If bandwidth is being wasted by retransmissions due to errors and dropped packets, these problems should be fixed, if possible, before more capacity is provided.

It is important to measure response time before and after a new capacity plan is implemented. Response time can be measured from a user's point of view by running representative applications on a user's workstation and measuring how long it takes to get a response. The time it takes to retrieve e-mail, send a file to a server, download a Web page, update a sales order, print a report, and so on, can be measured. In addition, the response time for network services should be measured. This includes measuring the time it takes to get an answer to a domain name system (DNS) query, a dynamic host configuration protocol (DHCP) request for an Internet protocol (IP) address, a user authentication request, and so on.

Another way to estimate response time and delay in a network is to send ping packets and measure the average round-trip time (RTT) to send a request and receive a response. Deviation from the average RTT can also be measured, which is important for applications that cannot tolerate jitter, such as voice and video. (*Jitter* in this context means a measure of the variability over time of the average delay across a network.)

The final step in analyzing the performance of the current network is to check the status of the servers and internetworking devices in the internetwork. It is not necessary to check every LAN switch, but the major switches, routers, firewalls, and servers should be checked. Checking the status includes determining how busy the device is (CPU utilization), how many packets it can process in a given time, how many packets it has dropped, and how efficiently it is using, creating, and deleting memory buffers. Checking utilization of storage and RAM is also important on some devices.

Analyzing Network Traffic Patterns

As mentioned above, network capacity can be defined as the potential for a network to accommodate the network traffic that is presented to it. To plan how much capacity is needed, the traffic must be understood. Both current and future traffic should be classified and studied so that capacity planning can be based on traffic behavior, flow, and load.

Network Traffic Classes

A broad categorization of network traffic is background versus transactional. Background traffic is a by-product of the protocols that are used on networks. For example, in a Windows environment, when a user maps a drive to a network share, the server message block (SMB) keepalive packets between the PC and server are background traffic. Transactional traffic is generated when a user performs a task. For example, when a bank teller enters a deposit for a customer, transactional traffic is generated (Baron 2005).

SMB is one of many protocols that send keepalives. Several voice-over-IP (VoIP) implementations send constant keepalives as a way of making sure that a session is available when it becomes necessary to ring the phone. Background traffic other than keepalives includes address resolution protocol (ARP) traffic, routing table updates, bridge protocol data units (BPDUs) sent by bridges and switches, and network management traffic. Network services background traffic associated with DNS, DHCP, user authentication, directory services, and so on must also be accommodated by a capacity plan.

Another categorization of network traffic is broadcast versus unicast. Broadcast traffic goes to all devices in the broadcast domain. It does not necessarily use more bandwidth than unicast traffic. (Broadcast packets are often smaller and less frequent than unicast packets.) However, broadcast traffic does disturb every station in the broadcast domain, which reduces the processing capacity that is available for other traffic, which is especially a problem for low-end devices. Broadcast domains should be limited in size, which can be accomplished with routers and virtual LANs (VLANs).

Network traffic can also be characterized with regard to the quality of service (QoS) that it requires. For example, the traffic might be especially sensitive to dropped packets, as in a bank transaction; or the traffic might be especially sensitive to delay, as in voice and video traffic; or the traffic might need high throughput, as in a file-upload application.

Some traffic requires a controlled-load service, as defined in RFC 2211 (Wroclawski 1997). With controlled-load service, the network provides a service that closely approximates the service that the traffic would receive on an unloaded network. The network is expected to apply admission control to ensure that the sensitive traffic receives the service it needs, even when the network is overloaded. An application that requests controlled-load service assumes that a very high percentage of transmitted packets are delivered and the transit delay by a very high percentage of traffic does not greatly exceed the minimum transit delay experienced by any successfully delivered packet. The controlled-load service is intended for applications that are highly sensitive to overload conditions. Important members of this class are "adaptive real-time applications" (Wroclawski 1997).

Some real-time applications are not adaptive and have stricter requirements with regard to delay and dropped packets than the controlled-load service can offer. The guaranteed service defined by RFC 2212 (Shenker, Partridge, and Guerin 1997) provides firm bounds on end-to-end packet-queuing delays. Guaranteed service is intended for applications that need a guarantee that a packet will arrive no later than a certain time after it was transmitted. With this service, the maximum queuing delay can be mathematically proven to be at a certain level. The guaranteed service does not attempt to minimize jitter. It is also not concerned with fixed delay, such as propagation delay across a network path, since there is not much it can do about the speed of light. Instead, guaranteed service guarantees that packets arrive within a guaranteed delivery time and that they are not discarded due to queue overflows.

According to RFC 2475 (Blake et al. 1998), IP packets can be marked with a differentiated services codepoint (DSCP) to influence queuing and packet-dropping decisions on an output interface of a router. The DSCP can have one of sixty-four possible values that specify how each router should handle the packet. Packets can be marked in such a way that a properly configured router implements controlled-load service, guaranteed services, and other QoS functionality. When conducting research for a capacity plan, if a network engineer discovers applications that are sensitive to delay and load, the plan must specify a need to deploy routers that support QoS features.

Network Traffic Behavior

Using a protocol analyzer and network modeling tools, an engineer can learn how network applications and protocols behave and use this information to plan capacity. How many and what types of packets do the applications and protocols send? How big are the packets? How quickly are the packets sent, and if not acknowledged, how quickly are they resent? Are the packets sent in bursts? Do the packets include lots of overhead?

As mentioned above, capacity planning should take into account network traffic that has not (or cannot be) optimized for packet-size efficiency. When network applications send small packets, a lot of capacity is consumed by packet headers. When possible, applications should be tuned to use large packets. Another contributor to capacity-usage inefficiency is applications that send numerous acknowledgments (acks), sometimes at multiple layers. For example, some implementations of Windows file sharing send acks at the SMB, NetBIOS, and transmission control protocol (TCP) layers. This may not be avoidable, but it is worth knowing about, as it affects capacity usage.

In some cases, capacity-usage inefficiencies can be avoided through the use of TCP extensions. For example, RFC 1323 (Jacobson, Braden, and Borman 1992) provides a method for scaling the TCP receive window beyond the maximum size that the 16-bit window size field in the TCP header nominally allows. As another example, RFC 2018 (Mathis et al. 1996) helps reduce capacity usage by optimizing error recovery and retransmission behavior.

Without RFC 2018, TCP acks are cumulative up to the point at which a problem occurs. If TCP segments are lost, the ACK number is one more than the number of the last byte that was received before the loss, even if more segments arrived after the loss. In other words, there is no way for a receiver to report a hole in the received data. This causes the sender to either wait a round-trip time to find out about each lost segment, or to unnecessarily retransmit segments that the recipient may have received correctly. With selective ACK, the TCP recipient fills in the selective ack option field in the TCP header to inform the sender of the noncontiguous blocks of data that have been received. The sender can then retransmit only the missing segments.

A protocol analyzer can help an engineer determine whether selective ACK is in use. A protocol analyzer can also be used to study other aspects of traffic behavior, including packet sizes, excessive overhead traffic, windowing and flow control, error-recovery mechanisms, broadcast rates, and so on. This information can be input into the capacity-planning process to ensure that solutions are selected that accommodate this traffic behavior (if the behavior cannot be changed to be more optimal.)

Network Traffic Flow

Accurately provisioning network capacity requires an analysis of traffic flow. An identification of the major sources and destinations of network traffic, and an analysis of the direction and volume of data traveling between them, helps the engineer comprehend traffic flow and correctly provision capacity.

To get a better understanding of traffic flow, network engineers should start with an analysis of the location and network-usage habits of user communities. A user community is a set of workers who use a particular application or set of applications. A user community could be a corporate department or a set of departments. However, in many organizations, application usage crosses departmental boundaries. It is generally more effective to characterize user communities by application and protocol usage, rather than by departmental boundary. User communities should be identified and located, and their applications should be analyzed for network traffic behavior and flow.

In addition to documenting user communities, characterizing traffic flow requires locating major data sources and sinks. A data source is a device, or group of devices, that mostly produces data. A data sink (sometimes called a "data store") is a device that mostly accepts data, acting as a data repository (McCabe 2003). Examples of data sources are devices that do a lot of computing, such as servers, mainframes, and computing clusters. Other examples, such as cameras, video-production equipment, and application servers, do not necessarily do a lot of computing, but can generate a lot of data. Data sinks include disks, tape backup units, SANs, and video-editing devices.

Analyzing traffic flow involves identifying and characterizing traffic flows between sources and sinks. In some cases, a traffic flow can be characterized as bidirectional and symmetric. Both ends of the flow send traffic at about the same rate. In other cases, a flow is bidirectional and asymmetric. Client stations send small queries and servers send large streams of data, for example. In a broadcast application, the flow is unidirectional and asymmetric. Figure 3 shows the differences between bidirectional, unidirectional, symmetric, and asymmetric traffic flows.

Network applications tend to fall into broad categories that can be characterized in terms of traffic flow. When conducting a capacity-planning project, a network engineer can categorize applications as being one of the following types: terminal/host, client/server, peer-to-peer, server/server, distributed computing, or broadcast. Once a high-level characterization is completed, a more detailed analysis of applications and their network traffic characteristics can be conducted using protocol analyzers and traffic modeling tools, but as a first step, Table 1 can be used to classify typical network application types.

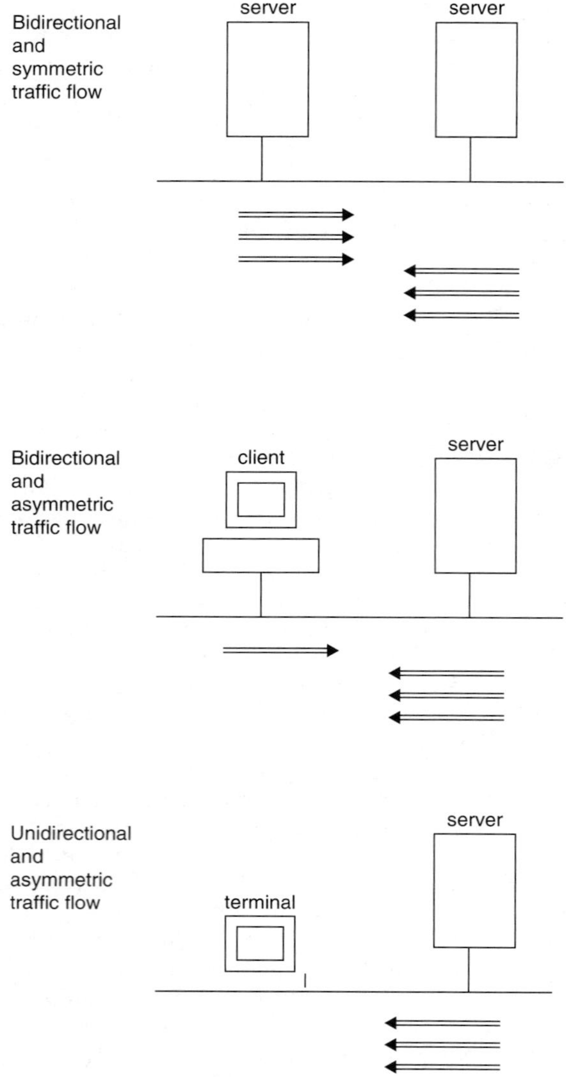

Figure 3. Traffic-flow examples

Network Traffic Load

After traffic flows between sources and destinations have been identified, their size needs to be measured or predicted, using protocol analyzers and traffic-modeling tools. In other words, the engineer has to analyze the volume of network traffic caused by traffic flows and how much of a load they will put on the network. Traffic load estimates are unlikely to be precise, but they can be reasonably accurate if they are based on an analysis of measured traffic and an extrapolation from the measurements for future requirements.

Protocol analyzers and modeling tools can be used to study the traffic load caused by a single user of an application. After the load caused by a single user is analyzed, the load can be scaled by the number of users of the application to get a better idea of capacity needs for the application. The analysis of the location and size of user communities, and the identification of data sources and sinks, can help make these calculations more accurate. Traffic-modeling tools can be used to automate the analyzing of traffic load.

Developing Potential Solutions

After engineers have analyzed business and operational goals, and gathered information about network traffic patterns (including traffic classes, behavior, flow, and load), they can start selecting capacity solutions. This section discusses options for network topology design, and LAN, WAN, MAN, and internetworking device capacity.

Network Topologies

Network topology is the arrangement of nodes and links in a network. A network's topology depicts the interconnectivity of major LAN and WAN segments, internetworking devices, servers, and user communities. Once the steps of analyzing traffic flow and load are completed, a network engineer can design a network topology that

Table 1: Types of Network Applications and Their Traffic Characteristics

Type	Flow	Symmetry	Comments	Examples
Terminal/host	Bidirectional	Asymmetric	Terminal sends just a few characters	Telnet, Secure Shell
Client/server	Bidirectional	Asymmetric	Clients send queries, servers send replies and bulk data	Web browsing, e-mail, SMB, network file system (NFS), file transfer protocol (FTP), voice call setup
Peer-to-peer	Bidirectional	Symmetric	Participants may put a large load on network	Small LANs in which every computer is a server, music and video sharing, real-time protocol for voice
Server/server	Bidirectional	Symmetric	Participants may put a large load on network	Network management, directory services, caching, backup
Distributed computing	Bidirectional	Asymmetric	Task manager tells computing nodes what to do	Graphics rendering, simulations, SETI@home
Broadcast	Unidirectional	Asymmetric	The flow of broadcasts can be contained through the use of routers and VLANs	Service announcement, service discovery, address resolution

connects the right devices and sites, and offers sufficient capacity, redundancy, and load balancing.

With complex networks, in which capacity planning is approached with some care, network engineers seek to design topologies that are modular so that parts of a network can be upgraded when needed without disrupting traffic flow on other parts of the network. Network solutions can be selected on a per-module basis, with obvious distinctions being made for different parts of the internetwork. These parts may include access networks in which users reside, server networks, e-commerce networks, network-management modules, campus backbones, remote-access networks, WANs, and so on. Modular network design helps minimize costs. A network engineer can purchase the appropriate internetworking devices for each module, thus avoiding spending money on unnecessary features. Modular design also makes testing easier, because there is clear and distinct functionality for each module.

One of the best modular architectures is one that is built in a hierarchical topology that caters to flexible communications and can be replaced in layers over time (Spohn 1997). Hierarchical networks evolved from early telephone networks that were once designed in a mesh, star, or multiple-star topology. Hierarchical networks brought order out of chaos and reduced the inputs and outputs on switches, permitting the handling of high traffic on certain routes where necessary, and allowing overflow and a means of recovery from problems (Freeman 1996).

With a hierarchical topology, instead of connecting numerous devices to each other in a mesh topology, or connecting all devices to a center device in a star topology, devices are connected in a layered tree structure. Devices and links closest to the root of the tree are provided with more capacity. Traffic between layers is forwarded toward the root, although optional routes are also possible for handling overflow and recovery from broken paths. Figure 4 shows the differences between a star, mesh, and hierarchical topology.

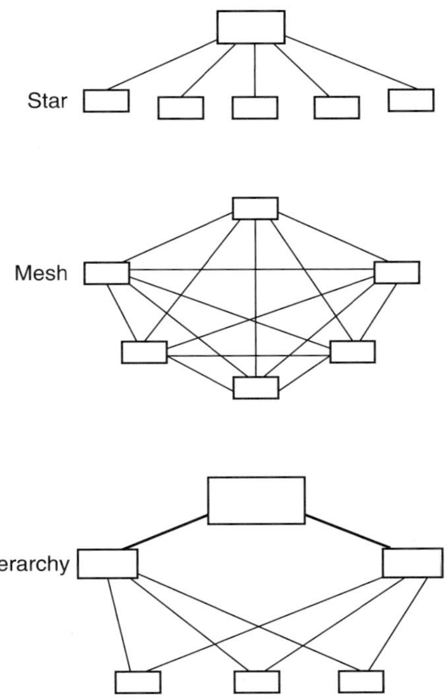

Figure 4. Network topologies

LAN Bandwidth

The amount of LAN bandwidth provided to clients and servers plays a major role in network capacity. This section mentions the typical options that are available for planning LAN capacity, starting with the least capable and moving to the most capable wired technologies, and then covering wireless options.

Half-duplex 10-Mbps Ethernet, using a hub or legacy bus topology, is obsolete and should not be recommended for a new network design, but it still exists in some networks and should be considered in an overall capacity plan if it will not get upgraded for monetary or other reasons. Full-duplex Ethernet uses a switch and allows the connected computer and the switch port to send at the same time. Full duplex is standard these days and should be recommended. Servers, especially, benefit from full duplex because they need the ability to send a response to a client while receiving another client request. 10-Mbps full-duplex Ethernet is possible but 100-Mbps full-duplex Ethernet is the better option.

Many computers are starting to support 1000-Mbps Ethernet (Gigabit Ethernet). Although most client computers do not need that much bandwidth yet, they will in the future, and many servers already do. 10-Gbps Ethernet is another option for servers, though it is rarely recommended for clients. As of this writing, 10-Gbps Ethernet uses only fiber-optic cabling, so it has not yet gained widespread popularity, though that will change.

Another option for servers (and the switch ports to which they attach) is Ethernet link aggregation. Link aggregation allows several Ethernet adapters to be aggregated to form a single Ethernet interface. A server that supports link aggregation considers the aggregated adapters to be one adapter and assigns one Internet protocol (IP) and one media access control (MAC) address to them, so they are treated by remote systems as one adapter. Link aggregation is standardized by the IEEE 802.3ad (IEEE P802.3ad Link Aggregation Task Force 2000) document and supported by many vendors, including Cisco Systems with its EtherChannel switch option.

The main benefit of link aggregation is that a server and switch can use the network bandwidth of all the connected adapters as one large pipe. So a single pipe could provide 800 Mbps, for example, if four full-duplex 100-Mbps adapters were linked. Another benefit of link aggregation is that capacity is still available when failures occur. If one adapter fails, network traffic is automatically sent to the next available adapter without disruption of user traffic. The capacity of the pipe is reduced but not eliminated.

The previous paragraphs discussed wired LAN technologies. Another option for users who need mobility is wireless connectivity. Wireless LANs (WLANs) do not offer as much bandwidth as wired LANs and should not be recommended unless the need for mobility outweighs the need for bandwidth. The amount of bandwidth available to a user depends on how many users are on the wireless network (it is a shared network), as well as how far away the user is from the wireless access point and antennas. Wireless bandwidth is reduced by environmental obstacles, such as steel girders, shelving units, and metal doors that cause signal reflection. The bandwidth is also reduced if the signal is absorbed by objects with high water content, including trees, wooden structures, and even people! Nonetheless, wireless options are appropriate for environments where users roam (conference rooms, cafeterias, lobbies) and where users deploy handheld units, such as on factory floors or in retail stores.

The IEEE 802.11 Working Group has standardized the following WLAN options:

- IEEE 802.11 supports 1 to 2 Mbps.
- IEEE 802.11a supports 54 Mbps.
- IEEE 802.11b supports 1, 2, 5.5, and 11 Mbps.
- IEEE 802.11g supports 54 Mbps and is backward-compatible with 802.11b.
- IEEE 802.11n (expected to be ratified in 2008) supports up to 540 Mbps, depending on the configuration.

Today, most WLANs use 802.11g but 802.11n is expected to catch on, as it will work across longer distances than the older standards and potentially support very high data throughput.

WAN Bandwidth

When connecting sites that are geographically dispersed, typical options include leased-line and frame relay circuits, using copper cabling, and leased-line, frame relay, and asynchronous transfer mode (ATM) circuits, using fiber-optic cabling. Wireless WAN solutions may also catch on, as service providers scramble to offer new options to cost-conscious users and users who cannot be reached by cables. Wireless WANs use satellite, cellular, microwave, or radio frequency (RF) technologies.

WAN bandwidth for copper cabling is specified in North America and other parts of the world using the North American Digital Hierarchy, which is shown in Table 2. A channel in the hierarchy is called a "digital stream" (DS). Digital streams are multiplexed together to form higher-speed WAN circuits. DS-1 and DS-3 are the most common capacities.

In Europe, the Committee of European Postal and Telephone (CEPT) standardizes the European Digital Hierarchy, which is shown in Table 3.

The synchronous digital hierarchy (SDH) is an international standard for transmission over fiber-optic cabling. SDH defines a standard transmission rate of 51.84 Mbps, which is also called synchronous transport signal level 1, or STS-1. Higher rates of transmission are a multiple of the STS-1 rate. The STS rates are the same as the SONET optical carrier (OC) levels, which are shown in Table 4.

MAN Bandwidth

It is becoming common for companies to connect their sites to each other and to the Internet using an Ethernet link, rather than the WAN technologies mentioned in the previous section. Both new providers and traditional providers, who once offered only classic WAN options such as dial-up, T1, and frame relay, now offer Ethernet connectivity, which is often called Metro Ethernet. Metro Ethernet blends the capabilities and behavior of WAN technologies with those of Ethernet.

A Metro Ethernet customer can use a standard 10/100-Mbps Ethernet interface, or a Gigabit or 10-Gbps interface, to access the provider's network. The customer can set up virtual circuits to reach other sites and to reach an Internet service provider (ISP). Metro Ethernet providers allow customers to add bandwidth as needed. Compared to adding WAN bandwidth, which can require months of negotiation with the provider, adding Metro Ethernet bandwidth often takes only a few minutes or hours. Metro Ethernet providers offer a wide range of bandwidth

Table 2: The North American Digital Hierarchy

Signal	Capacity	Number of DS-0s	Colloquial Name
DS-0	64 Kbps	1	Channel
DS-1	1.544 Mbps	24	T1
DS-1C	3.152 Mbps	48	T1C
DS-2	6.312 Mbps	96	T2
DS-3	44.736 Mbps	672	T3
DS-4	274.176 Mbps	4032	T4

Table 3: The European Digital Hierarchy

Signal	Capacity	Number of E1s
E0	64 Kbps	N/A
E1	2.048 Mbps	1
E2	8.448 Mbps	4
E3	34.368 Mbps	16
E4	139.264 Mbps	64

Table 4: The Synchronous Digital Hierarchy (SDH)

STS Rate	OC Level	Speed
STS-1	OC-1	51.84 Mbps
STS-3	OC-3	155.52 Mbps
STS-12	OC-12	622.08 Mbps
STS-48	OC-48	2.488 Gbps
STS-192	OC-192	9.953 Gbps
STS-768	OC-768	39.813 Gbps

options. In addition to the standard Ethernet data rates, many providers offer a 1-Mbps service and allow customers to add bandwidth in 1-Mbps increments.

Remote-Access Bandwidth

Remote offices (branch offices and telecommuters) may connect to an enterprise network using various remote-access technologies. The amount of bandwidth that these technologies offer depends on the provider and how much the user pays. It can also depend on physical constraints, such as how far the user is from the provider's central office and the condition of the wiring to the user's home. The bandwidth is generally sufficient for typical office applications, but may not be sufficient for bandwidth-intensive applications such as streaming video. Typical options include:

- A dial-up modem at 56 Kbps (a bad choice unless there is no other option)
- A cable modem at 256 Kbps upstream and 1 Mbps downstream
- Asymmetric digital subscriber link (ADSL) at 128 Kbps upstream and 256 Kbps downstream
- Symmetric DSL at 1.5 Mbps upstream and downstream
- Integrated services digital network basic rate interface (ISDN BRI) at 144-kbps upstream and downstream

Remote offices should connect to corporate headquarters via a virtual private network (VPN). At headquarters, a VPN concentrator must be carefully selected so that it has enough capacity to terminate VPN tunnels. As is the case with most internetworking devices, engineers should evaluate CPU speed and RAM-access speed. VPN concentrators can also benefit from specialized application specific integrated circuit (ASIC) hardware to speed up encryption and decryption of data sent across VPN tunnels.

Internetworking Device Capacity

The capacity of internetworking devices plays a major role in the overall capacity of a network. Internetworking devices include routers, bridges, switches, firewalls, wireless access points, concentrators, multiplexers, content switches, and load balancers. The capacity of an internetworking device is usually measured in packets-per-second (PPS) and means the number of packets in a second that the device can forward. The capacity of an internetworking device is affected by CPU power, the amount of RAM and disk storage, RAM and storage access speed, bus speed, and operating system and application software behavior. (Note that many internetworking devices do not have storage, so it may not be relevant.)

The software architecture of an internetworking device also affects its capacity. The speeds at which a device can handle buffering, queuing, dequeuing, matching addresses in tables such as routing tables, and applying differentiated services for high-priority traffic, all affect its capacity. The hardware architecture also affects capacity. For example, switches with a crossbar architecture are faster than older switches that used a shared bus.

Switches that avoid head-of-line blocking have higher capacity than those that do not. Head-of-line blocking is a problem of input-queued switches that occurs when a packet waiting for a busy output interface delays packets behind it in the input queue, even when those other packets are destined for an idle output interface. Head-of-line blocking is similar to a movie theatre complex that does not allow anyone into any theatre because the first person in line is waiting for a movie theatre that is not yet empty from the last showing. To avoid this problem, movie theatre complexes should let everyone in and shuffle the customers who cannot get into their movie yet to the candy and popcorn stands. Similarly, an internetworking device can have a buffer or a set of output queues in which it can place packets as they await the availability of their output interface. More advanced features for avoiding head-of-line blocking include parallel iterative matching (PIM), which schedules incoming packets using randomization, and iSLIP, which enhances PIM and avoids the need for generating numerous random numbers, which can be problematic at very high speeds (Varghese 2004).

The PPS capacity for an internetworking device is the maximum rate at which the device can forward packets without dropping any. Vendors of internetworking devices often publish PPS ratings for their products, based on their own testing and independent tests. To test an internetworking device, testers place the device between traffic generators and a traffic checker. The generators send Ethernet packets ranging in size from 64 to 1518 bytes. By running multiple generators, devices can be tested with multiple interfaces. In a typical testing scenario, the testers send bursts of traffic through the device at an initial rate that is half of what is theoretically possible. If all packets are received, the rate is increased. If all packets are not received, the rate is decreased. This process is repeated until the highest rate at which packets can be forwarded without loss is determined. PPS values for small packets are much higher than those for large packets (simply because more small packets fit in a period of time than large packets do), so, of course, vendors usually publish a PPS rating that is based on the smallest packet size.

High-end internetworking devices can often forward packets at the theoretical maximum rate for the types of links they connect. (This is called "wire-speed forwarding.") The theoretical maximum rate is calculated by dividing bandwidth by packet size. The packet size includes headers and any protocol-required preambles, start/end frame delimiters, inter-packet gaps, and so on. Table 5 shows the theoretical maximum PPS for 100-Mbps Ethernet, based on packet size.

Testing the Capacity Plan

Capacity solutions should be tested. Testing should measure functionality, response time, throughput, availability, errors, and dropped packets. Tests should be designed that will characterize network performance and behavior under normal loads and higher-than-normal loads. Testing can be accomplished with network modeling tools and by implementing a prototype or pilot project. A prototype can be implemented on a test network in a lab. A pilot project is usually implemented on a production network with real users—but not all users, in case there are problems.

Table 5: Theoretical Maximum Packets per Second (PPS) for 100-Mbps Ethernet

Packet Size (in bytes)	Maximum PPS
64	148,800
128	84,450
256	45,280
512	23,490
768	15,860
1,024	11,970
1,280	9,610
1,518	8,120

Engineers should develop test objectives, test methods and scripts, and acceptance criteria. The criteria for declaring that a test has been passed or failed should be clear and accepted by the testers and users of the network. There is nothing worse than running tests, agreeing on the results, but disagreeing on the interpretation of the results. The types of testing that should be conducted include application, throughput, availability, and regression testing.

Application testing measures performance from a user's point of view and verifies correct functionality and low response time as the user does typical tasks such as start an application, switch between screens, open and store files, search for data, and so on. The tester can watch actual users or simulate users with a modeling tool. The testing should start with a set number of users, then gradually increase the number of users to expose any problems related to high network or server load.

Throughput testing measures the bits- or bytes-per-second rate that applications can achieve with a new capacity plan. As in application testing, throughput testing should start with a set number of users and then gradually increase the number to analyze network and device behavior under load.

Availability testing makes sure the network does not fail (become unavailable) because of the changes related to the new capacity plan. It can also test for bit errors on WAN links, CRC errors on LAN links, and dropped packets. Finally, regression testing is also important, whereby the engineer tries to makes sure the new implementation will not break applications or devices that were known to work before the new plan was developed.

The results of testing the new capacity plan may call for some changes to the plan. If the plan was developed in a systematic way using the processes explained in this chapter, then it should not require major changes, but fine-tuning is often necessary. After the plan is implemented and users start maximizing their use of the network, then bigger changes may become necessary. Network capacity is like closet space—it is never enough.

Planning for the Future

After a capacity plan is implemented, it must be monitored. Network engineers need to be vigilant about measuring bandwidth utilization, throughput, availability, accuracy, delay and jitter, and response time. Engineers and their managers need to work with business and operational managers to learn about new applications and uses for the network that were not anticipated.

Parkinson's law applies to networks. Developed by C. Northcote Parkinson (1958), Parkinson's law states that "work expands so as to fill the time available for its completion." Parkinson based his law on his experiences in the British Civil Service, where he noted that the number of employees at the Colonial Office increased even though Britain's empire was no longer growing. In a more general sense, Parkinson's law means that the demand on a resource expands to match the supply of the resource. Parkinson's law is often used in the computer industry to call attention to the fact that the amount of data tends to grow to the point at which it fills the space available for storage; CPU power is consumed by new applications; and network traffic expands to fill the capacity available to it.

CONCLUSION

Capacity planning is the process of determining the resources that will be needed for a network to support the traffic that is offered to it. Resources include LAN and WAN bandwidth, server capacity, and internetworking device capacity. LAN and WAN bandwidth, as measured in bits-per-second rates, plays a major role in capacity planning, but it is not the only component of a good plan. Servers and internetworking devices also need sufficient CPU power, RAM and disk storage, and fast access to RAM and storage. They also need optimized architectures and the ability to process a high rate of packets per second. Capacity planning must take into account traffic behavior such as acknowledgments, broadcast packets, frame sizes, and windowing and flow-control mechanisms. Classifying network traffic as background versus transactional helps distinguish the types of traffic a network must carry. Classifying the service requirements of traffic helps determine the special processing that may be needed for some types of traffic.

Capacity planning is not an easy task. For one thing, it requires anticipating what users will do with the network in the future. In addition, network systems are complex, with many different components that can affect capacity. Nonetheless, by following a structured, systematic process that is based on gathering information about business drivers, applications, network architecture and performance, and the types of traffic and traffic patterns the network must support, effective capacity planning can be achieved. Capacity planning is also facilitated by a modular, hierarchical network topology in which future needs can be met by changing one layer of the architecture, rather than the entire structure.

Capacity planning does not stop with an implementation of the plan. Network usage tends to increase until the capacity of the network is reached. As it was said about the baseball diamond in the middle of Iowa in the movie *Field of Dreams,* "if you build it, they will come." Expect a well-functioning network to get used and overused to the point at which it needs more capacity. A network engineer's job is never done.

GLOSSARY

Bandwidth: The bits-per-second rate that a network can handle.

Capacity: The potential for a network to accommodate the network traffic that is offered to it.

Capacity Planning: The process of determining the resources that will be needed for a network to support the traffic that is offered to it.

Head-of-Line Blocking: A problem of input-queued switches that occurs when a packet waiting for a busy output delays packets behind it in the input queue, even when those other packets are destined for an idle output.

Jitter: A measure of the variability over time of the average delay across a network.

Packets per Second (PPS): The rate at which an internetworking device can forward packets.

Throughput: A measure of how much traffic can be passed across a network path in a stated period of time.

Wire-Speed Forwarding: Relaying packets at the theoretical maximum rate for the type of connected network.

CROSS REFERENCES

See *Computer Network Management*; *Network Reliability and Fault Tolerance*; *Network Security Risk Assessment and Management*; *Network Traffic Management*; *Network Traffic Modeling*.

REFERENCES

Baron, A. 2005. Strategies in network capacity planning and network optimization—AB Pound Co. www.microsoft.com/technet/archive/winntas/maintain/ntopt3.mspx (accessed December 13, 2005).

Blake, S., D. Black, M. Carlson, E. Davies, Z. Wang, and W. Weiss. 1998. *Request for comments 2475—An architecture for differentiated services*. www.ietf.org/rfc/rfc2475.txt (accessed May 5, 2007).

Freeman, R. L. 1996. *Telecommunication system engineering*. 3rd ed. New York: Wiley.

IEEE P802.3ad Link Aggregation Task Force. http://grouper.ieee.org/groups/802/3/ad/index.html (accessed May 5, 2007).

Jacobson, V., R. Braden, and D. Borman. 1992. Request for comments 1323—TCP extensions for high performance. www.ietf.org/rfc/rfc1323.txt (accessed May 5, 2007).

Mathis, M., J. Mahdavi, S. Floyd, and A. Romanow. 1996. *RFC 2018—TCP selective acknowledgment options*. http://www.faqs.org/rfcs/rfc2018.html (accessed May 5, 2007).

McCabe, J. D. 2003. *Network analysis, architecture and design*. 2nd ed. San Francisco: Morgan Kaufmann.

Oppenheimer, P. 2004. *Top-down network design*. 2nd ed. Indianapolis: Cisco Press.

Parkinson, C. N. 1958. *Parkinson's law: The pursuit of progress*. London: John Murray.

Shenker, S., C. Partridge, and R. Guerin. 1997. *Request for comments 2212—Specification of guaranteed quality of service*. www.faqs.org/rfcs/rfc2212.html (accessed May 5, 2007).

Spohn, D. L. 1997. *Data network design*. 2nd ed. New York: McGraw-Hill.

Varghese, G. 2004. *Network algorithmics: An interdisciplinary approach to designing fast networked devices*. San Francisco: Morgan Kaufmann.

Wroclawski, J. 1997. *Request for comments 2211—Specification of the controlled-load network element service*. www.faqs.org/rfcs/rfc2211.html (accessed May 5, 2007).

Network Traffic Modeling

Thomas M. Chen, *Southern Methodist University*

INTRODUCTION

Teletraffic theory is the application of mathematics to the measurement, modeling, and control of traffic in telecommunications networks (Willinger and Paxson 1998). The aim of traffic modeling is to find stochastic processes to represent the behavior of traffic. Working at the Copenhagen Telephone Company in the 1910s, A. K. Erlang famously characterized telephone traffic at the call level by certain probability distributions for arrivals of new calls and their holding times. Erlang applied the traffic models to estimate the telephone switch capacity needed to achieve a given call-blocking probability. The Erlang blocking formulas had tremendous practical interest for public carriers because telephone facilities (switching and transmission) involved considerable investments. Over several decades, Erlang's work stimulated the use of queuing theory, and applied probability in general, to engineer the public switched telephone network.

Packet-switched networks started to be deployed on a large scale in the 1970s. Like circuit-switched networks, packet networks are designed to handle a certain traffic capacity. Greater network capacity leads to better network performance and user satisfaction, but requires more investment by service providers. The network capacity is typically chosen to provide a target level of quality of service (QoS). QoS is the network performance seen by a packet flow, measured mainly in terms of end-to-end packet loss probability, maximum packet delay, and delay jitter or variation (Firoiu et al. 2002). The target QoS is derived from the requirements of applications. For example, a real-time application can tolerate end-to-end packet delays up to a maximum bound.

Unfortunately, teletraffic theory from traditional circuit-switched networks could not be applied directly to emerging packet-switched networks for a number of reasons. First, voice traffic is fairly consistent from call to call, and the aggregate behavior of telephone users does not vary much over time. However, packet networks carry more diverse data traffic, for example, e-mail, file transfers, remote log-in, and client/server transactions. Data applications are typically "bursty" (highly variable over time) and vary in behavior from one another. Also, the traffic diversity has increased with the growing number of multimedia applications. Second, traffic is controlled differently in circuit- and packet-switched networks. A circuit-switched telephone call proceeds at a constant bit rate after it is accepted by the network. It consumes a fixed amount of bandwidth at each telephone switch. In contrast, packet flows may be subjected to access control (rate enforcement at the network boundary); flow control (the destination slowing down the sender); congestion control (the network slowing down the sender); and contention within the network from other packet flows. Thus, packet traffic exhibits much more complex behavior than circuit-switched voice.

Teletraffic theory for packet networks has seen considerable progress in recent decades (Adas 1997; Frost and Melamed 1994; Michiel and Laevens 1997; Park and Willinger 2000). Significant advances have been made in long-range dependence, wavelet, and multifractal approaches. At the same time, traffic modeling continues to be challenged by evolving network technologies and new multimedia applications. For example, wireless technologies allow greater mobility of users. Mobility must be an additional consideration for modeling traffic in wireless networks (Thajchayapong and Peha 2006; Wu, Lin, and Lan 2002). Traffic modeling is clearly an ongoing process without a real end. Traffic models represent our best current understanding of traffic behavior, but our understanding will change and grow over time.

This chapter presents an overview of commonly used traffic models reflecting recent developments in the field. The first step in modeling is understanding the statistical characteristics of the traffic. The first section reviews common statistical measures such as burstiness, long-range dependence, and frequency analysis. Next, we examine common continuous-time and discrete-time source models. These models are sufficiently general to apply to any type of traffic, but application-specific models are tailored more closely to particular applications. We highlight studies of the major Internet applications: World Wide Web, peer-to-peer file sharing, and streaming video. In the last section, we examine two major ways that the network affects the source traffic. First, traffic sources can be "policed" at the network access. Second, the dynamics of TCP flows (the majority of Internet traffic) are affected by network congestion and active queue-management schemes at network nodes.

Packets, Flows, and Sessions

Some terminology should be introduced at this point because traffic can be viewed at different levels, as shown in Figure 1. When the need arises, a host will establish a session with another host. A session is associated with a human activity. For example, a client host will open a TCP connection to port 21 on a server to initiate a file transfer protocol (FTP) session. The TCP connection will be closed at the end of the FTP session. Or a session may be viewed as the time interval when a dial-up user is connected to an Internet service provider (ISP). For connection-oriented networks such as asynchronous transfer mode (ATM,) a session is a call established and terminated by signaling messages. Traffic modeling at the session (or call) level consists of characterizing the start times and duration of each session.

During a session, each host may transmit one or more packet flows to the other host (Roberts 2004). Although the term is used inconsistently in the literature, a *flow* is commonly considered to be a series of closely spaced packets in one direction between a specific pair of hosts. Packets in a flow usually have common packet header fields such as protocol ID and port numbers (in addition to source and destination addresses). For example, an FTP session involves two packet flows between a client and server: one flow is the control stream through TCP port 21, and the second flow is the data stream (through a negotiated TCP port). Traffic modeling at the flow level consists of characterizing the random start times and durations of each flow.

TCP flows have been called "elephants" or "mice," depending on their size. An elephant's duration is longer than the TCP slow start phase (the initial rate increase of a TCP connection until the first dropped packet). Because of their short duration, mice are subject to TCP's slow start but not to TCP's congestion-avoidance algorithm. Less-common terms are *dragonflies*, flows shorter than 2, and *tortoises*, flows longer than 15 minutes (Brownlee and Claffy 2002). Traffic measurements have suggested that 40 to 70% of Internet traffic consists of short flows, predominantly Web traffic. Long flows (mainly non-Web traffic) are a minority of the overall traffic, but have a significant effect because they can last hours to days.

Viewed in more detail, a flow may be made up of intermittent bursts, each burst consisting of consecutively transmitted packets. Bursts may arise in window-based protocols, in which a host is allowed to send a window of packets, then must wait to receive credit to send another window. Another example is an FTP session, in which a burst could result from each file transferred. If a file is large, it will be segmented into multiple packets. A third example is a talkspurt in packet voice. In normal conversations, a person alternates between speaking and listening. An interval of continuous talking is a talkspurt, which results in a burst of consecutive packets.

Finally, traffic can be viewed at the level of individual packets. This level is concerned only with the arrival process of packets and ignores any higher structure in the traffic (bursts, flows, sessions). The majority of research (and this chapter) address traffic models mainly at the packet level. Studies at the packet level are relatively straightforward because packets can be easily captured for minutes or hours.

Studies of traffic flows and sessions require collection and analysis of greater traffic volumes because flows and sessions change over minutes to hours, so hours or days of traffic need to be examined. For example, one analysis involved a few packet traces of several hours each (Barakat et al. 2003). Another study collected eight days of traffic (Brownlee and Claffy 2002).

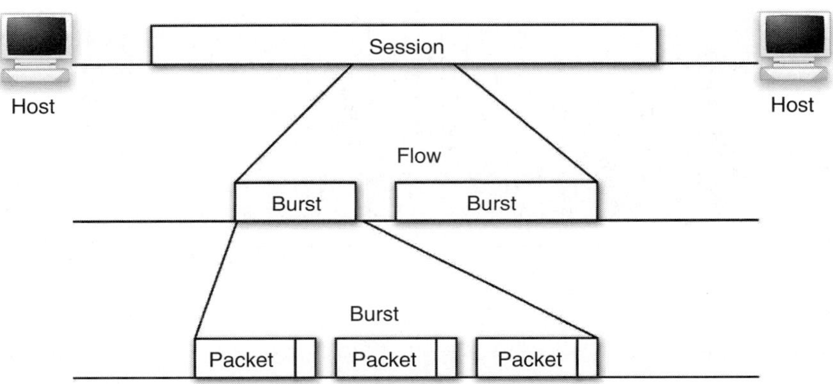

Figure 1: Levels of traffic

The Modeling Process

Traffic models reflect our best knowledge of traffic behavior. Traffic is easier to characterize at sources than within the network because flows of traffic mix together randomly within the network. When flows contend for limited bandwidth and buffer space, their interactions can be complex to model. The "shape" of a traffic flow can change unpredictably as the flow progresses along its route. On the other hand, source traffic depends only on the rate of data generated by a host independent of other sources.

Our knowledge is gained primarily from traces (measurements) of past traffic, consisting of packet arrival times, packet header fields, and packet sizes. A publicly available trace of Ethernet traffic recorded in 1989 is shown in Figure 2. A trace of *Star Wars IV* encoded by MPEG (Moving Picture Coding Experts Group) 4 at medium quality is shown in Figure 3 (data rate per frame). Traffic can be measured by packet sniffers or protocol analyzers, which are specialized pieces of hardware and software for recording packets at link rates (Thompson, Miller, and Wilder 1997). Common sniffers are tcpdump, Snort, and Ethereal. These can be easily connected to transmission links, local area networks, or mirrored ports on switches and routers. Also, traffic volume is routinely recorded by routers as part of the simple network management protocol (SNMP). In addition, some NetFlow-capable routers are able to record simple flow information (e.g., flow start/stop times, number of bytes, and number of packets).

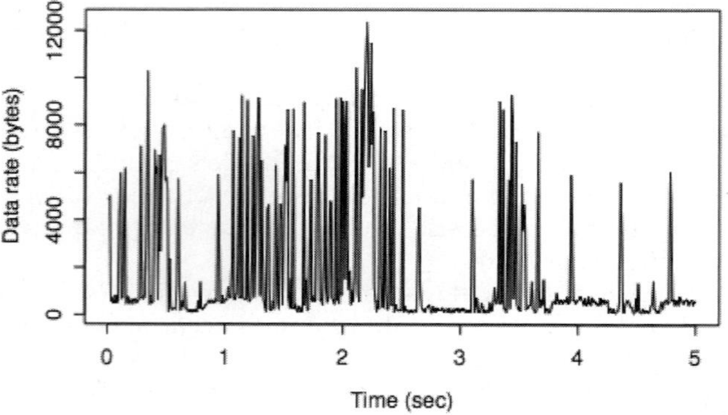

Figure 2: Ethernet traffic trace

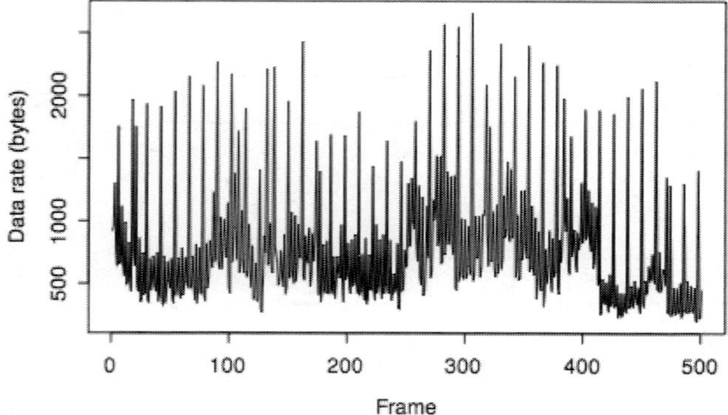

Figure 3: Trace of *Star Wars IV* encoded at medium quality MPEG-4

One of the practical difficulties in traffic modeling is collecting and analyzing large sets of traffic measurements. Traffic can be highly variable, even between two similar types of sources. For example, one video might have many scene changes, reflected by frequent spikes in the source rate, while another might have few scene changes, resulting in a smoother source rate. Therefore, it is good practice to collect measurements from many sources or over many time periods, and then look for common aspects in their behavior. In probabilistic terms, each traffic trace is a single realization or sample of the traffic behavior. A small sample set could give a misleading portrayal of the true traffic behavior.

A good choice for a stochastic model should exhibit accuracy and universality. *Accuracy* refers to a close fit between the model and actual traffic traces in statistical terms. Sometimes accuracy is judged by the usefulness of a model to predict future behavior of a traffic source. *Universality* refers to the suitability of a model for a wide range of sources. For example, an MPEG traffic model should be equally applicable to any particular video source, not just to *Star Wars* (although the parameter values of the model may need to change to fit different sources).

Our knowledge of traffic is augmented from analyses and simulations of protocols. For example, we know that TCP sources are limited by the TCP congestion-avoidance algorithm. The TCP congestion-avoidance algorithm has been analyzed extensively, and TCP sources have been simulated to investigate the interactions between multiple TCP flows to verify the stability and fairness of the algorithm.

Ultimately, a traffic model is a mathematical approximation for real traffic behavior. There is typically more than one possible model for the same traffic source, and the choice depends somewhat on subjective judgment. The choice often lies between simple, less accurate models and more complex, accurate models. An ideal traffic model would be both simple to use and accurate, but there is usually a trade-off between simplicity and accuracy. For example, a common time series model is the p-order autoregressive model (discussed later). As the order p increases, the autoregressive model can fit any data more accurately, but its complexity increases with the number of model parameters.

Uses of Traffic Models

Given the capability to capture traffic traces, a natural question is why traffic models are needed. Would not traffic measurements be sufficient to design, control, and manage networks? Indeed, measurements are useful and necessary for verifying the actual network performance. However, measurements do not have the level of abstraction that makes traffic models useful. Traffic models can be used for hypothetical problem solving, whereas traffic measurements only reflect current reality. In probabilistic terms, a traffic trace is a realization of a random process, whereas a traffic model is a random process. Thus, traffic models have universality. A traffic trace gives insight about a particular traffic source, but a traffic model gives insight about all traffic sources of that type.

Traffic models have many uses, but at least three major ones. One important use of traffic models is to allow proper dimensions for network resources for a target level of QoS. It was mentioned above that Erlang developed models of voice calls to estimate telephone switch capacity to achieve a target call-blocking probability. Similarly, models of packet traffic are needed to estimate the bandwidth and buffer resources to provide acceptable packet delays and packet-loss probability. Knowledge of the average traffic rate is not sufficient. It is known from queuing theory that queue lengths increase with the variability of traffic (Kleinrock 1976). Hence, an understanding of traffic burstiness or variability is needed to determine sufficient buffer sizes at nodes and link capacities (Barakat et al. 2003).

A second important use of traffic models is to verify network performance under specific traffic controls. For example, given a packet-scheduling algorithm, it would be possible to evaluate the network performance resulting from different traffic scenarios. For another example, a popular area of research is new improvements to the TCP congestion-avoidance algorithm. It is critical that any algorithm is stable and allows multiple hosts to share bandwidth fairly, while sustaining a high throughput. Effective evaluation of the stability, fairness, and throughput of new algorithms would not be possible without realistic source models.

A third important use of traffic models is admission control. In particular, connection-oriented networks such as ATM depend on admission control to block new connections to maintain QoS guarantees. A simple admission strategy could be based on the peak rate of a new connection; a new connection is admitted if the available bandwidth is greater than the peak rate. However, that strategy would be overly conservative because a variable bit-rate connection may need significantly less bandwidth than its peak rate. A more sophisticated admission strategy is based on effective bandwidths (Kelly 1996). The source traffic behavior is translated into an effective bandwidth between the peak rate and the average rate, which is the specific amount of bandwidth required to meet a given QoS constraint. The effective bandwidth depends on the variability of the source.

SOURCE TRAFFIC STATISTICS

This section gives an overview of general statistics to characterize source traffic. The traffic may be represented by its time-varying rate $X(t)$ in continuous time, or X_n in discrete time. In practice, we are often measuring the amount of data generated over short periodic intervals, and then the traffic rate is the discrete-time process X_n. A discrete-time process is also easier for computers to record and analyze (as a numerical vector) than a continuous-time process. On the other hand, it might be preferable to view the traffic rate as a continuous-time process $X(t)$ for analysis purposes, because the analysis in continuous time can be more elegant. For example, video source rates are usually characterized by the data per frame, so X_n would represent the amount of data generated for the nth frame. But X_n could be closely approximated by a suitable continuous-time process $X(t)$ for convenience, if analysis is easier in continuous time. Alternatively, traffic may be viewed as a point process defined by a set of packet arrival times $\{t_1, t_2,\ldots\}$ or equivalently a set of interarrival times $\tau_n = t_n - t_{n-1}$.

When a traffic trace is examined, one of the first analysis steps is calculation of various statistics. Statistics can suggest an appropriate traffic model. For example, an exponential autocorrelation function is suggestive of a first-order autoregressive process (discussed later).

Simple Statistics

The traffic rate is usually assumed to be a stationary or at least wide sense stationary (WSS) process for convenience, although stationarity of observed traffic is impossible to prove because it is a property over an infinite (and unobservable) time horizon. WSS means that the mean $E(X_t)$ is constant over all time t, and the autocovariance function:

$$R_X(t,s) = E[(X_t - E(X_t))(X_s - E(X_s))] \tag{1}$$

depends strictly on the lag $|t - s|$ and can be written as $R_X(t - s)$.

First-order statistics such as peak rate and mean rate are easy to measure. The marginal probability distribution function can be estimated by a histogram. Second-order statistics include the variance and autocorrelation function:

$$\rho_X(t - s) = R_X(t - s)/R_X(0). \tag{2}$$

An example of the autocorrelation function estimated for the Ethernet traffic from Figure 2 is shown in Figure 4 (lag is in units of 10 ms). The variance indicates the degree of variability in the source rate, while the autocorrelation function gives an indication of the persistence of bursts (long-range dependence is discussed below). The shape of the autocorrelation function is informative about the choice of a suitable time-series model (discussed below). Equivalently, the power spectral density function, which is the Fourier transform of the autocorrelation function, is just as informative.

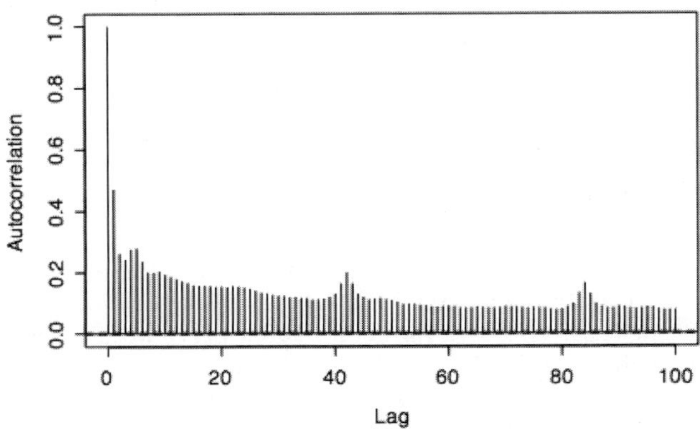

Figure 4: Autocorrelation function for Ethernet traffic

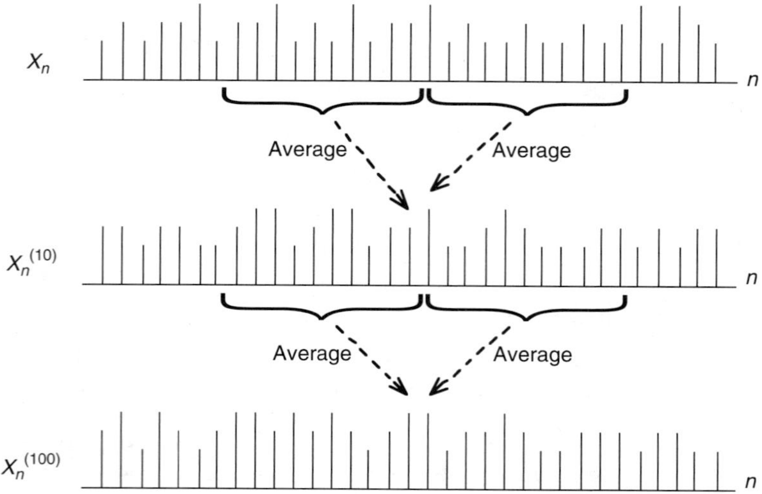

Figure 5: Construction of rescaled process by averaging over blocks

Burstiness Measures

For variable bit-rate sources, "burstiness" is a quantity reflecting the source's variability. While *burstiness* is easy to understand intuitively, there is unfortunately not a universally agreed-on definition. The simplest definition of *burstiness* is the ratio of peak rate to mean rate. This does not reveal much information about the source because it does not capture how long the peak rate can be sustained (which would have the greatest effect on queuing).

Another possibility is the squared coefficient of variation, treating the traffic rate as samples of a random variable X. The squared coefficient of variation $c^2(X) = \text{var}(X)/E^2(X)$ is a normalized version of the variance of X (normalized by dividing by the squared mean).

A related but more sophisticated measure is the index of dispersion of counts, or IDC, $I_c(t) = \text{var}(N(t))/E(N(t))$, the variance of the number of arrivals up to time t normalized by the mean number of arrivals (Gusella 1991). The number of arrivals up to time t, $N(t)$, is the number of interarrival times fitting in the interval $(0,t)$. Thus, the IDC captures similar but more time-scale–dependent information than the coefficient of variation $c^2(X)$.

Perhaps a more accurate measure is the index of dispersion of workload (IDW), $I_w(t) = \text{var}(Y(t))/E(Y(t))$, where $Y(t)$ is the total amount of data that has arrived up to time t. The workload takes into account the amount of data in packets, not only the number of packets (Fendick et al. 1991).

Long-Range Dependence and Self-Similarity

Measurements of Ethernet, MPEG video, and World Wide Web traffic have pointed out the importance of self-similarity in network traffic (Beran 1994; Crovella and Bestavros 1997; Erramilli et al. 2002; Leland et al. 1994; Paxson and Floyd 1995; Sahinoglu and Tekinay 1999). Suppose the traffic rate is a discrete-time WSS process X_n with mean $\bar{X}$ and autocorrelation function $\rho_X(k)$. For positive integer m, a new process $X_n^{(m)}$ is constructed as shown below by averaging the original process over nonoverlapping blocks of size m (Figure 5):

$$X_n^{(m)} = (X_{nm} + \cdots + X_{nm+m-1})/m. \tag{3}$$

The new process $X_n^{(m)}$ is WSS with mean $\bar{X}$ and autocorrelation function $\rho_X^{(m)}(k)$. The process X_n is asymptotically second-order self-similar if $\rho_X^{(m)}(k) = \rho_X(k)$ for large m and k. Essentially, self-similarity means that the rescaled process $a^{-H}X_{an}$ has the same statistical properties as the original process X_n over a wide range of scales $a > 0$ and some parameter $0 < H < 1$. This would not be true for a process such as the Poisson process, which tends to become smoother for large m. The Hurst parameter H is a measure of self-similarity.

Self-similarity is manifested by a slowly decaying autocorrelation function:

$$\rho_X(k) \sim ck^{2(H-1)} \tag{4}$$

for some $c > 0$ as $k \to \infty$. Self-similarity implies long-range dependence, which is a property of the asymptotic rate of decay of the autocorrelation function. A short-range dependent (SRD) process has an autocorrelation function that decays at least as fast as exponentially:

$$\rho_X(k) \sim \gamma^{-k} \tag{5}$$

for large k and some constant γ. Equivalently, the sum $\sum_k \rho_X(k)$ is finite. A long-range dependent (LRD) process has an autocorrelation function that decays slower than exponentially—for example,, hyperbolically $\rho_k(k) \to k^{2(H-1)}$ for $0.5 < H < 1$. In this case, the sum $\sum_k \rho_X(k)$ is infinite.

Self-similarity and long-range dependence are important statistical characteristics because they are believed to have a major effect on queuing performance (Erramilli et al. 2002). Essentially, bursts of LRD traffic tend to be more persistent, thereby causing longer queue lengths than estimated for traditional SRD traffic such as Poisson.

Multiresolution Time Scale

The establishment of long-range dependence in network traffic prompted interest in the analysis of self-similar processes using time-scale methods, particularly wavelets (Abry and Veitch 1998; Ma and Ji 2001). Wavelet transforms are a useful tool for examining processes with scaling behavior, referred to as multiresolution analysis. They are most easily approached and motivated from the familiar Fourier transform, which decomposes a process (or signal) into a weighted sum of sinusoids. That is, the Fourier transform gives information about the frequency components but not any time information (where the frequency components occur in time). This is well suited for stationary processes but not for nonstationary processes. In contrast, the wavelet transform gives both time and frequency information. The short-time Fourier transform can handle nonstationary processes by taking windows of the signal, but there is a trade-off between time and frequency resolution.

A continuous wavelet transform decomposes a process into a weighted sum of wavelet functions. The wavelet functions are derived from a "mother wavelet" $\psi(t)$—for example, the Haar wavelet, Morlet wavelet, Mexican Hat, or Daubechies family of wavelets. The set of wavelets is generated by dilating the mother wavelet

$$\psi_s(t) = \frac{1}{\sqrt{s}}\psi\left(\frac{t}{s}\right), \tag{6}$$

where s is the scale parameter. Larger scales correspond to dilated signals and give a global view of the process (low frequencies), while the opposite holds for smaller scales. The continuous wavelet transform of a process $X(t)$ is

$$CWT(b,s) = \frac{1}{\sqrt{|s|}}\int_{-\infty}^{\infty} X(t)\psi\left(\frac{t-b}{s}\right)dt, \tag{7}$$

where b is the translation parameter.

In order to facilitate computer processing, it is necessary to discretize the transform by sampling the time-frequency plane. The discrete wavelet transform (DWT) analyzes a process at dyadic scales using inner products at shifts equal to the length of the wavelet. It is computed by passing the process through a series or bank of filters. The first level consists of parallel low-pass and high-pass filters, followed by downsampling by two. The level 1 coefficients are output from the downsampled high-pass filter. The output of the low-pass filter goes again through another filter stage (with high- and low-pass filters, and downsampling) to increase the frequency resolution. The level 2 coefficients are output from the high-pass filter in the second stage, and additional stages of filters can be used in the same manner. The result is a set of coefficients that represent the process as a low-resolution approximation and additional approximations of increasing resolutions.

An early use of the DWT was estimation of the Hurst parameter (Abry and Veitch 1998; Roughan, Veitch, and Abry 2000). Wavelet transforms have been used to analyze video and Ethernet traffic for the purpose of accurately synthesizing traffic with both long- and short-range dependence (Ma and Ji 2001).

Scaling

Recent studies of network traffic have found complex scaling behavior at small time scales (Riedi et al. 1999; Gilbert, Willinger, and Feldmann 1999; Abry et al. 2002). Previous studies had focused on monofractal models, such as self-similar processes. These show invariance across a wide range of scales and can be characterized by a single scaling law, for example, the Hurst parameter H.

Multifractal models have been found to better explain scaling behavior at small time scales. Loosely speaking, multifractal models have local scaling properties dependent on a time-varying $h(t)$, the local Hölder exponent, instead of a constant Hurst parameter. Intervals during which $h(t) < 1$ show bursts, while intervals during which $h(t) > 1$ correspond to small fluctuations. In traffic measurements, the local scaling $h(t)$ appears to change randomly in time.

CONTINUOUS-TIME SOURCE MODELS

Traffic models can be continuous-time or discrete-time. In continuous time, we are interested in a stochastic process to represent the time-varying source rate $X(t)$ or the set of packet arrival times $\{t_1, t_2, \ldots\}$.

Traditional Poisson Process

In traditional queuing theory, the Poisson arrival process has been a favorite traffic model for data and voice. The traditional assumption of Poisson arrivals has often been justified by arguing that the aggregation of many independent and identically distributed renewal processes tends to a Poisson process when the number increases (Sriram and Whitt 1986). Poisson arrivals with mean rate λ are separated by interarrival times $\{\tau_1, \tau_2, \ldots\}$ that are i.i.d. (independent and identically distributed) according to an exponential probability distribution function $p(\tau) = \lambda e^{-\lambda\tau}$, $\tau \geq 0$. Equivalently, the number of arrivals up to time t is a Markov birth process with all birth rates of λ.

The Poisson arrival process has several properties that make it appealing for analysis.

- It is memoryless in the sense that, given that the previous arrival occurred T time ago, the time to the next arrival will be exponentially distributed with mean $1/\lambda$, regardless of T. In other words, the waiting time for the next arrival is independent of the time of the previous arrival. This memoryless property simplifies analysis because future arrivals do not need to take into account the history of the arrival process.
- The number of arrivals in any interval of length t will have a Poisson probability distribution with mean λt.
- The sum of two independent Poisson arrival processes with rates λ_1 and λ_2 is a Poisson process with rate $\lambda_1 + \lambda_2$. This is convenient for analysis because traffic flows are multiplexed in a network.
- Suppose a Poisson arrival process with rate λ is randomly split, meaning that each arrival is diverted to

a first process with probability p or a second process with probability $1 - p$. The first process is a Poisson arrival process with rate $p\lambda$ and the second process is another Poisson process with rate $(1 - p)\lambda$.

Despite the attractiveness of the Poisson model, its validity for real traffic has often been questioned. Barakat et al. (2003) offered evidence that flow arrivals on Internet backbone links are well matched by a Poisson process.

For large populations in which each user is independently contributing a small portion of the overall traffic, user sessions can be assumed to follow a Poisson arrival process (Roberts 2004). Based on traces of wide area TCP traffic, Poisson arrivals appear to be suitable for traffic at the session level when sessions are human-initiated—for example, interactive TELNET and FTP sessions (Paxson and Floyd 1995). However, the Poisson model does not hold for machine-initiated sessions or for any packet-level traffic.

Simple On/Off Model

The simple on/off model is motivated by sources that alternate between active and idle periods. An obvious example is speech, during which a person is either talking or listening. The time in the active state is exponentially distributed with mean $1/\alpha$, and the time in the idle state is exponentially distributed with mean $1/\beta$. The state of the source can be represented by the two-state continuous-time Markov chain shown in Figure 6.

In the active state, the source is generating packets at a constant rate $1/T$—that is, interarrival times between packets are a constant T. In the idle state, no packets are generated. This on/off model can be considered a simple example of a modulated process, which is a combination of two processes. The basic process is a steady stream of packets at a constant rate $1/T$. The basic process is multiplied by a modulating process, which is the Markov chain shown in Figure 6 (the active state is equivalent to 1, while the idle state is equivalent to 0). The modulation has the effect of canceling the packets during the idle state. The resulting on/off traffic is shown in Figure 7.

Suppose that packets are generated as a Poisson process with rate λ during active periods, instead of a constant rate process. This process is an interrupted Poisson process (IPP). The effect of the modulating process is to cancel or "interrupt" a normal Poisson process during idle states.

Markov Modulated Poisson Process

Although the Poisson process is attractive as a traffic model, it is obviously unrealistic in one aspect: the arrival rate λ is constant. If we consider the aggregate of multiple packet speech flows, the flow rate will not be constant because speech conversations are starting and terminating at random times. The flow rate will drop whenever a speech conversation stops and will increase whenever a new conversation begins.

Suppose N speech conversations are multiplexed, and each speech conversation is an IPP. The aggregate flow will be a Markov modulated Poisson process (MMPP) (Heffes and Lucantoni 1986). The basic process is a Poisson process with rate $\lambda(t)$. The rate is modulated as $\lambda(t) = n(t)\lambda$, where $n(t)$ is the number of speech conversations that are active at time t. In this case, $n(t)$ is the state of a continuous-time Markov chain (specifically, a birth-death process) shown in Figure 8. The MMPP preserves some of the memoryless property of the Poisson process and can be analyzed by Markov theory. However, the complexity of the analysis increases with N, so the value of N is usually small.

Stochastic Fluid Model

Fluid models depart from traditional point process models by ignoring the discrete nature of packets. Consider again the MMPP model. The traffic rate is $X(t) = n(t)\lambda$, where $n(t)$ is again the number of active sources at time t represented by the birth-death process in Figure 8. The packet process is a complicated point process if one attempts to characterize the packet arrival times $\{t_1, t_2, \ldots\}$ shown in Figure 9.

Instead, it is easier to simply use the process $X(t)$ as the traffic model for most purposes (Cassandras et al. 2002). According to the stochastic fluid model, an active source transmits data at a constant rate, λ like a fluid flow, instead of in discrete packets. The stochastic fluid model is the aggregation of N such fluid sources. The stochastic

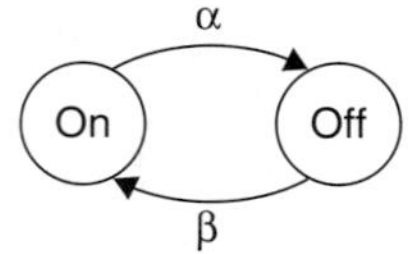

Figure 6: Two-state Markov chain

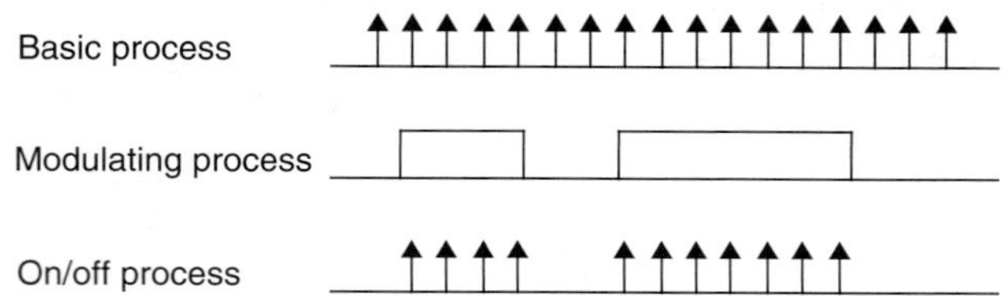

Figure 7: On/off traffic as example of a modulated process

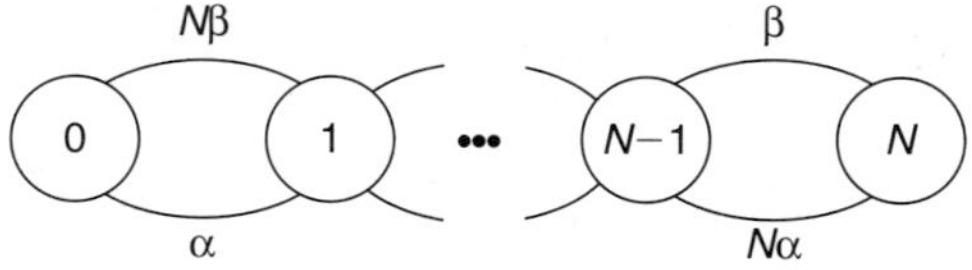

Figure 8: Birth-death process for number of active sources

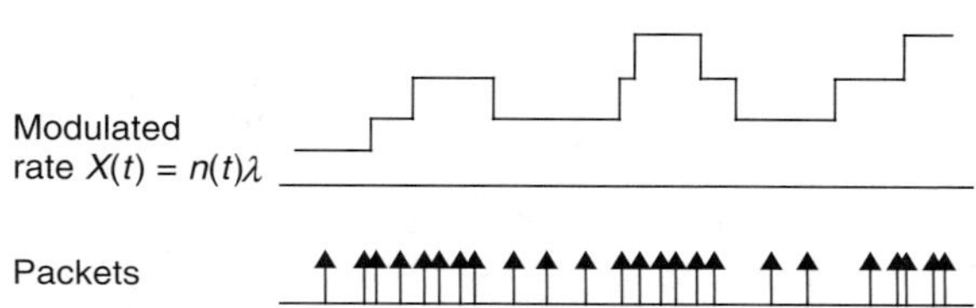

Figure 9: Packet arrivals in MMPP model

fluid buffer is attractive for its simplicity and tractability for fluid buffer flow analysis (Anick, Mitra, and Sondhi 1982).

Fractional Brownian Motion

The definition of fractional Brownian motion (FBM) is similar to the well-known Brownian motion except that it is generalized to depend on a Hurst parameter H. A fractional Brownian motion $X(t)$ is a Gaussian continuous process starting at $X(0) = 0$, with zero mean and variance $\text{var}(X(t)) = t^{2H}$, and has stationary increments that are normally distributed with zero mean and variance $\sigma^2 t^{2H}$. Its autocorrelation function is

$$R(s,t) = E(X(s)X(t)) = \tfrac{1}{2}(s^{2H} + t^{2H} - |s-t|^{2H}), \tag{8}$$

which shows that regular Brownian motion is a special case when $H = 0.5$. For $0.5 < H < 1$, the autocorrelation function exhibits long-range dependence with Hurst parameter H.

Fractional Brownian motion has been proposed as a model for "free traffic" (unconstrained by network resources) aggregated from many independent sources (Norros 1995). The model is attractive because it is fairly straightforward for analysis and characterization of long-range dependence. It is also tractable for queuing (fluid buffer) analysis, unlike most discrete-time models.

DISCRETE-TIME SOURCE MODELS

In discrete time, we are interested in a stochastic process X_n to represent the source rate sampled at discrete times $n = 1, 2, \ldots$. In a sense, there is little difference between continuous-time and discrete-time models because there are stochastic processes in continuous or discrete time that behave similarly to each other. Discrete-time processes can be closely approximated by continuous-time processes, and vice versa. Discrete-time models may be preferred when analysis is easier in discrete time, or when network simulations are carried out in discrete time (versus discrete-event simulations).

Time series are commonly assumed to be consecutive measurements of some random phenomenon taken at equally spaced time intervals. Classical time-series analysis using ARIMA (autoregressive integrated moving average) models largely follows the Box and Jenkins (1970) method.

Time Series

The simplest time-series model is perhaps the autoregressive (AR) process. A pth order autoregressive model, denoted AR(p), has the form:

$$X_n = (\alpha_1 X_{n-1} + \cdots + \alpha_p X_{n-p}) + e_n, \tag{9}$$

where $\{\alpha_1,\ldots,\alpha_p\}$ are coefficients and e_n is the residual process assumed to be i.i.d. zero-mean normal random variables. Each point in the process is a linear combination of previous points and a random noise. The coefficients are found by linear regression, or fitting the exponential autocorrelation function to the observed autocorrelation function.

AR models are particularly motivated by studies of packet video with low motion (e.g., videoconferencing), where X_n is the bit rate of the nth video frame (Maglaris et al. 1988). There is a strong correlation between the bit rates of successive frames because of the nature of low-motion video and interframe coding algorithms.

An autoregressive moving average (ARMA) model of order (p,q), denoted ARMA(p,q), has a more general form than the AR process:

$$X_n = (\alpha_1 X_{n-1} + \cdots + \alpha_p X_{n-p}) + (e_n + \beta_1 e_{n-1} + \cdots + \beta_q e_{n-q}), \tag{10}$$

where $\{\alpha_1,\ldots,\alpha_p, \beta_1,\ldots,\alpha_q$ are coefficients. The moving average terms constitute a linear combination of prior noise samples. The ARMA process has also been proposed for a video source model (Grunenfelder et al. 1991).

The autoregressive integrated moving average process, denoted ARIMA(p,d,q) with integer d, is a generalization of ARMA processes. Define B as the backward operator $BX_n = X_{n-1}$. A succinct representation of an ARMA process is

$$\phi(B)X_n = \theta(B)e_n, \tag{11}$$

where the polynomials are $\phi(B) = 1 - \alpha_1 B - \cdots - \alpha_p B^p$ and $\theta(B) = 1 + \beta_1 B + \cdots + \beta_q B^q$. In addition, define the difference operator $\nabla X_n = X_n - X_{n-1}$. An ARIMA($p,d,q$) process has the form:

$$\phi(B)\nabla^d X_n = \theta(B)e_n \tag{12}$$

The parameter d is the number of times that the time series is differenced (i.e., converting each ith element of the series into its difference from the (i–j)th element). The reason for differencing is usually to convert a nonstationary time series into a stationary series by removing seasonal dependencies. The parameters of the autoregressive and moving average components are computed for the series after the differencing is done.

A fractional ARIMA, denoted F-ARIMA(p,d,q), is a generalization of an ARIMA allowing noninteger values of d. With $0 < d < 0.5$, the F-ARIMA(p,d,q) is stationary with long-range dependence with Hurst parameter $H = d + 0.5$.

Box–Jenkins Method

The Box–Jenkins method proceeds in three stages: model identification, model estimation, and model validation. Model identification is perhaps the most challenging, and depends largely on the expert judgment of the analyst. The analyst needs to examine the stationarity of the time series, including seasonality (periodic components) and trends (nonperiodic linear or nonlinear components). Seasonality and trends are subtracted from the series in order to obtain a stationary process. Differencing is another technique to convert a nonstationary series into a stationary one. After stationarity is achieved, the analyst must decide on the order (p,q) of the ARMA model, largely based on examination of the autocorrelation function.

With the order of the ARMA process decided, the next step is estimation of the model parameters (coefficients). The most common methods are least squares regression or maximum likelihood estimation.

The last step examines the validity of the chosen ARMA model. If the model was fitted properly, the residuals should appear like white noise. That is, residuals should be stationary, mutually independent, and normally distributed.

APPLICATION-SPECIFIC MODELS

Network traffic is obviously driven by applications. The most common applications that come to mind might include Web, e-mail, peer-to-peer file sharing, and multimedia streaming. One traffic study of Internet backbone traffic showed that Web traffic is the single largest type of traffic, on the average more than 40% of total traffic (Fraleigh et al. 2003). However, on a minority of links, peer-to-peer traffic was the heaviest type of traffic, indicating a growing trend. Streaming traffic (e.g., video and audio) constitute a smaller but stable portion of the overall traffic. E-mail is an even smaller portion of the traffic.

It is possible to apply the general-purpose continuous-time and discrete-time traffic models from the previous section. However, it is logical that specialized traffic models may work better for particular applications. Therefore, traffic analysts have attempted to search for models tailored to the most common Internet applications (Web, peer-to-peer, and video).

Web Traffic

The World Wide Web is a familiar client/server application. Most studies have indicated that Web traffic is the single largest portion of overall Internet traffic, which is not surprising, considering that the Web browser has become the preferred user-friendly interface for e-mail, file transfers, remote data processing, commercial transactions, instant messages, multimedia streaming, and other applications.

An early study focused on the measurement of self-similarity in Web traffic (Crovella and Bestavros 1997). Self-similarity had already been found in Ethernet traffic. Based on days of traffic traces from hundreds of modified Mosaic Web browser clients, it was found that Web traffic exhibited self-similarity with the estimated Hurst parameter H in the range 0.7 to 0.8. More interestingly, it was theorized that Web clients could be characterized as on/off sources with heavy-tailed on periods. In previous studies, it had been demonstrated that self-similar traffic can arise from the aggregation of many on/off flows that have heavy-tailed on or off periods. A probability distribution is heavy-tailed if the asymptotic shape of the distribution is hyperbolic:

$$\Pr(X > x) \sim x^{-\gamma} \tag{13}$$

as $x \to \infty$, for $0 < \gamma < 2$. Heavy tails imply that very large values have non-negligible probability. For Web clients, on periods represent active transmissions of Web files, which were found to be heavy-tailed. The off periods were either "active off," when a user is inspecting the Web browser but not transmitting data, or "inactive off," when the user is not using the Web browser. Active off periods could be fit with a Weibull probability distribution, while inactive off periods could be fit by a Pareto probability distribution. The Pareto distribution is heavy-tailed. However, the self-similarity in Web traffic was attributed mainly to the heavy-tailed on periods (or essentially, the heavy-tailed distribution of Web files).

A study of 1900 Web-browser clients also characterized Web traffic with an on/off model (Choi and Limb 1999). Off periods include the user viewing the browser or doing something else. Off periods were fit with a Weibull probability distribution, consistent with earlier studies. The on period again represents a retrieved Web page, but the model was refined with a more detailed view of a Web page, as shown in Figure 10. A Web page consists of a main object, which is an HTML document, and multiple in-line objects that are linked to the main object. Both main object sizes and in-line object sizes were fit with (different) log-normal probability distributions. The number of in-line objects associated with the same main object was found to follow a gamma probability distribution. In the same Web page, the intervals between the start times of consecutive in-line objects was fit with a gamma probability distribution.

It has been argued that TCP flow models are more natural for Web traffic than are "page-based" models (Cao et al. 2004). Requests for TCP connections originate from a set of Web clients and go to one of multiple Web servers. A model parameter is the random time between new TCP connection requests. A TCP connection is held between a client and server for the duration of a random number of request/response transactions. Additional model parameters include sizes of request messages, server response delay, sizes of response messages, and delay until the next request message. Statistics for these model parameters were collected from days of traffic traces on two high-speed Internet access links.

Another study examined 24 hours of flow records from NetFlow-capable routers in the Abilene backbone network (Meiss, Menczer, and Vespignani 2005). Web traffic composed 4% (319 million flows) of the total observed traffic. The Web traffic flows were mapped to a graph of 18 million nodes (Web clients and servers) and 68 million links (flows between client/server pairs). The weight assigned to a link reflects the aggregate amount of data

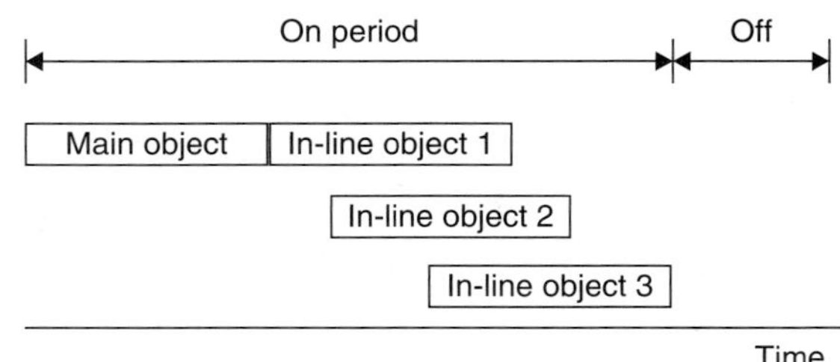

Figure 10: On/off model with Web page consisting of a main object linked to multiple in-line objects

between the nodes. The traffic study examined the probability distribution for number of servers contacted by a client, number of clients handled by a server, amount of data sent by a client, and amount of downloads handled by a server. One of the observations is that both client and server behaviors vary extremely widely, and therefore a "typical" client or server behavior is hard to characterize.

Peer-to-Peer Traffic

Peer-to-peer (P2P) traffic is often compared with Web traffic because P2P applications work in the opposite way from client/server applications, at least in theory. In actuality, P2P applications may use servers. P2P applications consist of a signaling scheme to query and search for file locations, and a data-transfer scheme to exchange data files. Whereas the data transfer is typically between peer and peer, sometimes the signaling is done in a client/server way (e.g., the original Napster kept a centralized index).

Since P2P applications have emerged in only the past few years, there are few traffic studies to date. Studies have understandably focused more on collecting statistics than on the harder problem of stochastic modeling. One study examined the statistics of traffic on a university campus network (Saroiu et al. 2002). The observed P2P applications were Kazaa and Gnutella. The bulk of P2P traffic was AVI (audio video interleaved) and MPEG video, and a small portion was MP3 audio. With this mix of traffic, the average P2P file was about 4 MB, three orders of magnitude larger than the average Web document. A significant portion of P2P was dominated by a few very large objects (around 700 MB) accessed ten to twenty times. In other words, a small number of P2P hosts are responsible for consuming a large portion of the total network bandwidth.

Another study collected P2P traffic traces from NetFlow-capable routers in an ISP backbone network (Sen and Wang 2004). The observed P2P applications were Gnutella, Kazaa, Grokster, Morpheus, and DirectConnect. Again, an extreme skew in the traffic was observed; a small number of P2P hosts (called "heavy hitters") accounted for much of the total traffic. The flow interarrival times, defined as the time between the host finishing one flow and then starting another flow, were found to be clustered at 1, 60, and 500 seconds. The very short (1 second) interarrival time could be the result of programmed sequential downloading of multiple files. The reason for the 60- and 500-second interarrival times was not clear.

Video

The literature on video-traffic modeling is vast because the problem is very challenging. The characteristics of compressed video can vary greatly depending on the type of video, which determines the amount of motion (from low-motion videoconferencing to high-motion broadcast video) and frequency of scene changes, and the specific intraframe and interframe video coding algorithms. Generally, interframe encoding takes the differences between consecutive frames, compensating for the estimated motion of objects in the scene. Hence, more motion means that the video traffic rate is more dynamic, and more frequent scene changes manifest as more "spikes" in the traffic rate.

Although many video coding algorithms exist, the greatest interest has been in the MPEG standards. Approved in 1992, MPEG-1 video coding was designed for reasonable-quality video at low bit rates. MPEG-2 video encoding at higher bit rates (such as DVDs) was approved in 1994. MPEG-4 approved in 1998 is highly efficient video coding for broadcast and interactive environments. In 2003, a more efficient coding method was approved jointly by the Telecommunication Standardization Sector of the International Telecommunication Union (ITU-T) as H.264 and MPEG as MPEG-4 Part 10 (also known as "advanced video coding").

Video source rates are typically measured frame by frame (which are usually 1/30 second apart). That is, X_n represents the bit rate of the nth video frame. Video source models address at least these statistical characteristics: the probability distribution for the amount of data per frame, the correlation structure between frames, times between scene changes, and the probability distribution for the length of video files.

Because of the wide range of video characteristics and available video coding techniques, it has seemed impossible to find a single universal video traffic model (Heyman and Lakshman 1996). The best model varies from video file to video file. A summary of research findings:

- The amount of data per frame have been fit to log normal, gamma, and Pareto probability distributions or combinations of them.
- The autocorrelation function for low-motion video is roughly exponential (Maglaris et al. 1988). The autocorrelation function for broadcast video is more complicated, exhibiting both short-range dependence at short lags and long-range dependence at much longer lags (Ma and Ji 2001). Time-series, Markov-modulated, and wavelet models are popular for capturing the autocorrelation structure (Dai and Loguinov 2005).
- The lengths of scenes usually follow Pareto, Weibull, or gamma probability distributions.
- The amounts of data in scene change frames are uncorrelated and follow Weibull, gamma, or unknown probability distributions.
- The lengths of streaming video found on the Web appear to have a long-tailed Pareto probability distribution (Li et al. 2005).

ACCESS-REGULATED SOURCES

Traffic sources cannot typically transmit data without any constraints. To be more realistic, traffic models must taking the limiting factors into account. For one thing, networks can regulate or "police" the rate of source traffic at the user-network interface in order to prevent congestion. Access policing is more common in networks in which connections are established by a signaling protocol. Signaling messages inform the network about traffic characteristics (e.g., peak rate, mean rate) and request a QoS. If a connection is accepted, the QoS is guaranteed as long as source traffic conforms to the given traffic parameters. A policer enforces conformance to given traffic parameters by limiting the source traffic as necessary.

Leaky-Bucket–Regulated Sources

The simplest policer enforces a peak rate defined by the shortest allowable interarrival time between two consecutive packets. If packets are arriving too closely in time, the second packet is nonconforming and therefore discarded. However, a policer with more tolerance for minor deviations from the peak rate is preferred.

The leaky-bucket algorithm is typically used for access policing because its enforcement is flexible, depending on the adjustment of two parameters: the bucket size B and a leak rate R. Packets are conforming and admitted into the network if they can increment the bucket contents by their payload size without overflowing. The contents of the bucket are emptied at the leak rate R. The leak rate R is the long-term average rate allowed. A larger bucket size allows greater variations from the rate R. A burst at a rate higher than R can still be conforming as long as the burst is not long enough to overflow the bucket. Hence, the maximum burst length b is directly related to the bucket size.

The maximum amount of traffic allowed by a leaky-bucket policer in an interval $(0,t)$ is represented by the deterministic (σ, ρ) calculus (Cruz 1991). The allowable traffic is deterministically bounded by

$$\int_0^t X(s)ds \leq \sigma + \rho t \tag{14}$$

where $\sigma > 0$, $\rho > 0$. From equation (14), it is clear that ρ is the long-term average rate, while σ is an allowable burst size.

Bounding-Interval-Length–Dependent Model

The deterministic bounding-interval-length–dependent (D-BIND) model characterizes traffic sources by multiple rate-interval pairs (R_k, I_k). R_k is the worst-case rate measured over every interval of length I_k. For practical applications, only a limited number of pairs would be used to characterize a source (Knightly and Zhang 1997).

S-BIND is a stochastic version in which a traffic source is similarly characterized by multiple pairs. In this case, R_k is a random variable that is stochastically larger than the rate over any interval of length I_k. Suppose r_k is the traffic rate in interval I_k, then $\Pr(R_k > x) \geq \Pr(r_k > x)$.

CONGESTION-DEPENDENT FLOWS

Traffic sources may be limited by access control or the level of network congestion. Some protocols limit the sending rates of hosts by means of sliding windows or closed-loop rate control. Clearly, traffic models must take such protocols into account in order to be realistic. Here we focus on TCP because TCP traffic constitutes the vast majority of Internet traffic. TCP uses a congestion-avoidance algorithm that infers the level of network congestion and adjusts the transmission rate of hosts accordingly. Even other protocols should be "TCP friendly," meaning that they interact fairly with TCP flows.

TCP Flows with Congestion Avoidance

TCP senders follow a self-limiting congestion-avoidance algorithm that adjusts the size of a congestion window according to the inferred level of congestion in the network. The congestion window is adjusted by so-called additive increase multiplicative decrease (AIMD). In the absence of congestion when packets are acknowledged before their retransmission time-out, the congestion window is allowed to expand linearly. If a retransmission timer expires, TCP assumes that the packet was lost and infers that the network is entering congestion. The congestion window is collapsed by a factor of a half. Thus, TCP flows generally have the classic "sawtooth" shape (Firoiu and Borden 2000; Paxson 1994).

Accurate models of TCP dynamics are important because of TCP's dominant effect on Internet performance and stability. Hence, many studies have attempted to model TCP dynamics (Mathis et al. 1997; Padhye et al. 2000; Barakat et al. 2003.) Simple equations for the average throughput exist, but the problem of characterizing the time-varying flow dynamics is generally difficult because of interdependence on many parameters, such as the TCP connection path length, round-trip time, probability of packet loss, link bandwidths, buffer sizes, packet sizes, and number of interacting TCP connections.

TCP Flows with Active Queue Management

The TCP congestion-avoidance algorithm has an unfortunate behavior whereby TCP flows tend to become synchronized. When a buffer overflows, it takes some time for TCP sources to detect a packet loss. In the meantime, the buffer continues to overflow, and packets will be discarded from multiple TCP flows. Thus, many TCP sources will detect packet loss and slow down at the same time. The synchronization phenomenon causes underutilization and large queues.

Active queue-management schemes, mainly random early detection (RED) and its many variants, eliminate the synchronization phenomenon and thereby try to achieve better utilization and shorter queue lengths (Floyd and Jacobson 1993; Firoiu and Borden 2000). Instead of waiting for the buffer to overflow, RED drops a packet randomly, with the goal of losing packets from multiple TCP flows at different times. Thus, TCP flows are unsynchronized, and their aggregate rate is smoother than before. From a queuing theory viewpoint, smooth traffic achieves the best utilization and shortest queue.

Active queue management has stimulated a number of control-theory approaches to understanding the stability, fairness issues, and flow dynamics (Tan et al. 2006; Srikant 2004).

CONCLUSION

Proper network design requires an understanding of the source traffic entering the network. Many continuous-time and discrete-time traffic models have been developed based on traffic-measurement data. The choice of traffic models involves at least two major considerations. The first is accuracy. Accurate traffic models should include not only source behavior but also possible policing or congestion avoidance. The second consideration is ease of queuing analysis. Traffic models are useful only if network performance can be evaluated. It is always possible to evaluate network performance via computer simulations, but analysis is preferred whenever analysis is tractable.

GLOSSARY

Access Policing: Regulation of ingress traffic at the user-network interface.

Active Queue Management (AQM): Intelligent buffer management strategies, mainly random early detection (RED) and its variants, enabling traffic sources to respond to congestion before buffers overflow.

Autoregressive Moving Average (ARMA): A general type of time-series model, including linear dependence on previous data samples and linear dependence on noise samples.

Burstiness: A measure of the variability of a traffic source rate.

Fluid Model: A view of data traffic ignoring the discrete nature of packets.

Fractional Brownian Motion (FBM): A long-range dependent Gaussian process with stationary increments including Brownian motion as a special case.

Leaky Bucket: A flexible algorithm for policing a specific traffic rate with an adjustable tolerance for deviation from that rate.

Long-Range Dependence (LRD): A property of stochastic processes with autocorrelation functions that decay more slowly than exponentially.

Markov Modulated Poisson Process (MMPP): A Poisson process in which the arrival rate varies according to a continuous-time Markov chain.

On/Off Model: A stochastic process with alternating active and idle states.

Poisson Process: A point process with interarrival times that are independent and identically distributed exponential random variables.

Quality of Service (QoS): The end-to-end network performance defined from the perspective of a specific user's connection.

Self-Similarity: A property of stochastic processes that preserve statistical characteristics over different time scales.

Time Series: A discrete-time stochastic process usually considered to represent measurements of a random phenomenon sampled at regularly spaced times.

Transmission Control Protocol (TCP): A transport layer protocol used over IP to ensure reliable data delivery between hosts.

CROSS REFERENCES

See *Computer Network Management*; *Network Capacity Planning*; *Network Reliability and Fault Tolerance*; *Network Security Risk Assessment and Management*; *Network Traffic Management*.

REFERENCES

Abry, P., R. Baraniuk, P. Flandrin, R. Riedi, and D. Veitch. 2002. Multiscale nature of network traffic. *IEEE Signal Processing Magazine* 19:28–46.

Abry, P., and D. Veitch. 1998. Wavelet analysis of long-range-dependent traffic. *IEEE Transactions on Information Theory* 44:2–15.

Adas, A. 1997. Traffic models in broadband networks. *IEEE Communications Magazine* 35:82–9.

Anick, D., D. Mitra, and M. Sondhi. 1982. Stochastic theory of a data-handling system with multiple sources. *Bell System Technical Journal* 61:1971–894.

Barakat, C., P. Thiran, G. Iannaccone, C. Diot, and P. Owezarski. 2003. Modeling Internet backbone traffic at the flow level. *IEEE Transactions on Signal Processing* 51:2111–24.

Beran, J. 1994. *Statistics for Long-Memory Processes*. London: Chapman and Hall.

Box, G., and G. Jenkins. 1970. *Time-series analysis, forecasting and control*. San Francisco: Holden-Day.

Brownlee, N., and K. Claffy. 2002. Understanding Internet traffic streams: dragonflies and tortoises. *IEEE Communications Magazine* 40:110–7.

Cao, J., W. Cleveland, Y. Gao, K. Jeffay, F. Smith, and M. Weigle. 2004. Stochastic models for generating synthetic HTTP source traffic. *In Proceedings of IEEE Infocom 2004*, 1546–57. Los Alamitos, CA: IEEE Press.

Cassandras, C., Y. Wardi, B. Melamed, G. Sun, and C. Panayiotou. 2002. Perturbation analysis for online control and optimization of stochastic fluid models. *IEEE Transactions on Automatic Control* 47:1234–48.

Choi, H. -K., and J. Limb. 1999. A behavioral model of Web traffic. In *Proceedings of the 7th International Conference on Network Protocols (ICNP'99)*, 327–34. Los Alamitos, CA: IEEE Press.

Crovella, M., and A. Bestavros. 1997. Self-similarity in World Wide Web traffic: evidence and possible causes. *IEEE/ACM Transactions on Networking* 5:835–46.

Cruz, R. 1991. A calculus for network delay, part I: Network elements in isolation. *IEEE Transactions on Information Theory* 37:114–31.

Dai, M., and D. Loguinov. 2005. Analysis and modeling of MPEG-4 and H.264 multi-layer video traffic. In *Proceedings of IEEE Infocom 2005*, 2257–67. Los Alamitos, CA: IEEE Press.

Erramilli, A., M. Roughan, D. Veitch, and W. Willinger. 2002. Self-similar traffic and network dynamics. *Proceedings of the IEEE* 90:800–19.

Fendick, K., V. Saksena, and W. Whitt. 1991. Investigating dependence in packet queues with the index of dispersion for work. *IEEE Transactions on Communications* 39:1231–44.

Firoiu, V., and M. Borden. 2000. A study of active queue management for congestion control. In *Proceedings of IEEE Infocom 2000*, 1435–44. Los Alamitos, CA: IEEE Press.

Firoiu, V., J.-Y. Le Boudec, D. Towsley, and Z.-L. Zhang. 2002. Theories and models for Internet quality of service. *Proceedings of the IEEE* 90:1565–91.

Floyd, S., and V. Jacobson. 1993. Random early detection gateways for congestion avoidance. *IEEE/ACM Transactions on Networking* 1:397–413.

Fraleigh, C., S. Moon, B. Lyles, C. Cotton, M. Khan, D. Moll, R. Rockell, T. Seely, and C. Diot. 2003. Packet-level traffic measurements from the Sprint IP backbone. *IEEE Network* 17:6–16.

Frost, V., and B. Melamed. 1994. Traffic modeling for telecommunications networks. *IEEE Communications Magazine* 32:70–81.

Gilbert, A., W. Willinger, and A. Feldman. 1999. Scaling analysis of conservative cascades, with applications to network traffic. *IEEE Transactions on Information Theory* 45:971–91.

Grunenfelder, R., J. Cosmas, S. Manthorpe, and A. Odinma-Okafor. 1991. Characterization of video codecs as autoregressive moving average processes and related queuing system performance. *IEEE Journal on Selected Areas in Communications* 9:284–93.

Gusella, R. 1991. Characterizing the variability of arrival processes with indexes of dispersion. *IEEE Journal on Selected Areas in Communications* 9:203–11.

Heffes, H., and D. Lucantoni. 1986. A Markov modulated characterization of packetized voice and data traffic and related statistical multiplexer performance. *IEEE Journal on Selected Areas in Communications* SAC-4:856–68.

Heyman, D., and T. Lakshman. 1996. Source models for VBR broadcast-video traffic. *IEEE/ACM Transactions on Networking* 4:40–8.

Kelly, F. 1996. Notes on effective bandwidths. In *Stochastic networks: Theory and applications*, 141–68. Oxford: Oxford University Press.

Kleinrock, L. 1976. *Queueing Systems Volume I*. New York: Wiley.

Knightly, E., and H. Zhang. 1997. D-BIND: An accurate traffic model for providing QoS guarantees to VBR traffic. *IEEE/ACM Transactions on Networking* 5:219–31.

Leland, W., M. Taqqu, W. Willinger, and D. Wilson. 1994. On the self-similar nature of Ethernet traffic (extended version). *IEEE/ACM Transactions on Networking* 2:1–15.

Li, M., M. Claypool, R. Kinicki, and J. Nichols. 2005. Characteristics of streaming media stored on the Web. *ACM Transactions on Internet Technology* 5:601–26.

Ma, S., and L. Ji. 2001. Modeling heterogeneous network traffic in wavelet domain. *IEEE/ACM Transactions on Networking* 9:634–49.

Maglaris, B., D. Anastassiou, P. Sen, G. Karlsson, and J. Robbins. 1988. Performance models of statistical multiplexing in packet video communications. *IEEE Transactions on Communications* 36:834–44.

Mathis, M., J. Semke, J. Mahdavi, and T. Ott. 1997. The macroscopic behavior of the TCP congestion avoidance algorithm. *Computer Communications Review* 27:67–82.

Meiss, M., F. Menczer, and A. Vespignani. 2005. On the lack of typical behavior in the global Web traffic network. In *Proceedings of the 14th International World Wide Web Conference*, 510–18. New York: ACM Press.

Michiel, H., and K. Laevens. 1997. Teletraffic engineering in a broadband era. Proceedings of the IEEE 85: 2007–33.

Norros, I. 1995. On the use of fractional Brownian motion in the theory of connectionless networks. *IEEE Journal on Selected Areas in Communications* 13:953–62.

Padhye, J., V. Firoiu, D. Towsley, and J. Kurose. 2000. Modeling TCP Reno performance: a simple model and its empirical validation. *IEEE/ACM Transactions on Networking* 8:133–45.

Park, K., and W. Willinger, eds. 2000. *Self-Similar Network Traffic and Performance Evaluation*. New York: Wiley.

Paxson, V. 1994. Empirically derived analytic models of wide-area TCP connections. *IEEE/ACM Transactions on Networking* 2:316–36.

Paxson, V., and S. Floyd. 1995. Wide area traffic: The failure of Poisson modeling. *IEEE/ACM Transactions on Networking* 3:226–44.

Riedi, R., M. Crouse, V. Ribeiro, and R. Baraniuk. 1999. A multifractal wavelet model with application to network traffic. *IEEE Transactions on Information Theory* 45:992–1018.

Roberts, J. 2004. Internet traffic, QoS, and pricing. *Proceedings of the IEEE* 92:1389–99.

Roughan, M., D. Veitch, and P. Abry. 2000. Real-time estimation of the parameters of long-range dependence. *IEEE/ACM Transactions on Networking* 8:467–78.

Sahinoglu, Z, and S. Tekinay. 1999. On multimedia networks: self-similar traffic and network performance. *IEEE Communications Magazine* 37:48–52.

Saroiu, S., K. Gummadi, R. Dunn, S. Gribble, and H. Levy. 2002. An analysis of Internet content delivery systems. *ACM SIGOPS Operating Systems Review* 36:315–27.

Sen, S., and J. Wang. 2004. Analyzing peer-to-peer traffic across large networks. *IEEE/ACM Transactions on Networking* 12:219–32.

Srikant, R. 2004. *The mathematics of Internet congestion control*. Boston: Birkhauser.

Sriram, K., and W. Whitt. 1986. Characterizing superposition arrival processes in packet multiplexers for voice and data. *IEEE Journal on Selected Areas in Communications* SAC-4:833–46.

Tan, L., W. Zhang, G. Peng, and G. Chen. 2006. Stability of TCP/RED systems in AQM routers. *IEEE Transactions on Automatic Control* 51:1393–8.

Thajchayapong, S., and J. Peha. 2006. Mobility patterns in microcellular wireless networks. *IEEE Transactions on Mobile Computing* 5:52–63.

Thompson, K., G. Miller, and R. Wilder. 1997. Wide-area Internet traffic patterns and characteristics. *IEEE Network* 11:10–23.

Willinger, W., and V. Paxson. 1998. Where mathematics meets the Internet. *Notices of the American Mathematical Society* 45:961–70.

Wu, C-H., H.-P. Lin, and L.-S. Lan. 2002. A new analytic framework for dynamic mobility management of PCS networks. *IEEE Transactions on Mobile Computing* 1:208–20.

FURTHER READING

The literature on traffic models is quite extensive, including references in which traffic models are discussed in combination with performance analysis. Examples of useful books covering both traffic modeling and performance analysis include:

Jain, R. 1991. *The art of computer systems performance analysis: Techniques for experimental design, measurement, simulation, and modeling*. New York: Wiley.

Krishna, M., V. Gadre, and U. Desai. 2003. *Multifractal based network traffic modeling*. Boston: Kluwer Academic.

Kumar, A., D. Manjunath, and J. Kuri. 2004. *Communication networking: An analytical approach*. San Francisco: Morgan Kaufmann.

A variety of traffic traces are publicly available on the Web. These can easily be found by searching. Popular collections include:

Internet Traffic Archive. http://ita.ee.lbl.gov/html/traces.html (accessed September 19, 2006).

NLANR network traffic packet header traces. http://pma.nlanr.net/Traces (accessed September 19, 2006).

MPEG-4 and H.263 video traces. http://www-tkn.ee.tu-berlin.de/research/trace/trace.html (accessed September 19, 2006).

Network Traffic Management

Thomas M. Chen, *Southern Methodist University*

INTRODUCTION

Although an analogy between computer networks and automobile highways is simplistic, the view of networks as a type of infrastructure points out the need for traffic control. Highways have a limited capacity, which can be exceeded when many people want to travel at the same time. Vehicles begin to slow down and back up in a congested area. The backup spreads if traffic approaches the congested area faster than traffic can leave it. Similarly, computer networks are designed to handle a certain amount of traffic with an acceptable level of network performance. Network performance will deteriorate if the offered traffic exceeds the given network capacity.

Packets will suffer long queuing delays at congested nodes and possibly packet loss if buffers overflow.

Traffic management refers to the set of traffic controls within the network that regulate traffic flows for the purpose of maintaining the usability of the network during conditions of congestion. Traffic management has multiple goals. First, it attempts to distinguish different types of traffic and handle each type in the appropriate way. For example, real-time traffic is forwarded with minimal delay, while best-effort traffic can afford to wait longer for any unused bandwidth. Second, traffic management responds to the onset of congestion. TCP is an example of a protocol that adapts the rate of TCP sources to avoid serious congestion. Third, traffic management seeks to maintain an acceptable level of network performance under heavy traffic conditions. The primary means of protection are admission control and access regulation (or policing), which limit the rate of traffic entering the network. By restricting the total amount of carried traffic, congestion will be avoided, and acceptable network performance will thus be sustained at the expense of blocking some amount of ingress traffic.

Quality of Service

Quality of service (QoS) is closely related to network performance, but QoS metrics are oriented toward a user's end-to-end experience (Gozdecki, Jajszczyk, and Stankiewicz 2003). Network performance is measured mainly from the network provider's viewpoint. Network performance metrics are defined to provide a meaningful portrait of network behavior to the network provider or network manager. Metrics can include end-to-end or hop-by-hop performance, and may be aggregated over the entire user population. Examples of network performance metrics may be average end-to-end packet delay or fraction of packets lost per hop observed over an interval of time. Although interesting to the network provider, these metrics do not mean that a particular user will see this network performance. Therefore, they are not that meaningful to users concerned with their application's requirements.

In contrast, QoS is the end-to-end network performance seen from the viewpoint of a user's particular connection. QoS parameters are defined to quantify the performance needed and experienced by a user's application. For example, a real-time application might require QoS guarantees such as an end-to-end packet delay of 10 msec and packet loss rate of 10^{-6}. The user would be assured that his or her application would see this level of performance. At the same time, a different user may require a different QoS from the same network. Ultimately, a certain amount of subjectivity is involved. A user will judge the QoS provided by the network according to how well his or her application seems to work.

QoS may not necessarily be quantified in specific terms. "Hard" QoS may refer to specific guarantees, whereas "soft" QoS involves specific parameters but no guarantees. An example of hard QoS is a guarantee that no more than 1% of packets will experience a delay of 100 msec. Hard QoS can be verifiable by measurements of the QoS parameters. Soft QoS may specify target QoS parameters but offers no guarantees that the QoS will be met; hence soft QoS is not verifiable by measurements. Soft QoS is often defined for one service relative to another service. An example is a high-priority service that is guaranteed to always have a shorter average packet delay than a low-priority service, but there are no absolute guarantees for either high- or low-priority service.

ATM has taken the approach of hard QoS guarantees. Table 1 lists the ATM definitions of QoS parameters (ATM Forum 1996). Although guarantees are offered on all QoS parameters, not all guarantees need to be specified explicitly. For example, it is assumed implicitly that the bit error rate in ATM (asynchronous transfer mode) networks will be very low, so the cell error ratio will be very low and therefore unnecessary to negotiate explicitly. Likewise, misinserted cells are considered to be very rare and negligible under normal operating conditions. The QoS parameters that are explicitly negotiated are mainly the cell loss ratio, cell transfer delay, and cell delay variation.

Similar QoS definitions have been standardized for IP (Internet protocol) networks (Seitz 2003). In the late 1990s, the IETF (Internet Engineering Task Force) IP Performance Metrics (IPPM) Working Group documented a set of QoS metrics for IP networks including one-way packet delay, round-trip packet delay, and one-way packet loss. More recently, the ITU-T (International Telecommunication Union, Telecommunication Standardization Sector) has standardized the set of IP performance metrics listed in Table 2 (ITU-T 1999).

Service-Level Agreements

Expectations for QoS may be specified in the form of a service-level agreement (SLA) between users and their network provider or between two network providers (Verma 2004). An SLA formally spells out expectations about the level of service in a way that allows monitoring and verification. SLAs often include terms for billing and financial compensation in case the received service level falls short of expectations. Hence, SLAs are legal contracts that must include clearly specified QoS metrics—typically availability, packet delay, jitter, packet loss, and throughput (Park, Baek, and Hong 2001). In common practice, SLAs are viewed more as insurance for unexpected lapses in network performance than as absolute guarantees, because of the practical difficulties of measuring and verifying QoS metrics.

Table 1: ATM Definitions of QoS Parameters

Aspect	Parameter	Definition
Accuracy	Cell error ratio	Fraction of cells delivered with bit errors
	Severely errored cell block ratio	Fraction of *N*-cell blocks delivered with *M* or more errored cells
	Cell misinsertion rate	Rate of appearance of misdirected cells from a different connection
Dependability	Cell loss ratio	Fraction of cells not delivered
Speed	Cell transfer delay	Maximum delay in delivering cells measured by *p*-percentile
	Cell delay variation (jitter)	Range between maximum and minimum cell delays, or deviation of cell delivery times from a reference pattern

Table 2: QoS Metrics for IP Networks

Aspect	Parameter	Definition
Accuracy	IP packet error ratio	Fraction of packets delivered with bit errors
	Spurious IP packet rate	Rate of appearance of misdirected packets at a network egress
Dependability	IP packet loss ratio	Fraction of packets not delivered
Speed	IP packet transfer delay	Mean or maximum delay in delivering packets
	IP packet delay variation (jitter)	Deviation in packet transfer delays from a reference packet transfer delay

SLAs typically share a few common elements: criteria to be used for measuring service levels; a method for reporting outages and service failures; timeframe for the network provider to respond to identified failures; a method for escalating network problems; and procedures for enforcement and compensation for failure to meet SLA goals.

SLAs are typically limited to a single provider network. However, routes through the Internet can cross multiple networks. SLAs can be negotiated between network providers, but the issue becomes how to guarantee the end-to-end QoS to users (Pongpaibool and Kim 2003).

General Principles

Traffic management is a difficult problem because it fundamentally involves a balance between conflicting objectives: statistical sharing versus isolation. At one extreme, statistical sharing of network resources without reservations is desirable to achieve a high efficiency. But since demand can exhaust resources, it is difficult (if not impossible) to guarantee QoS without reservations. At the other extreme, it is well known that QoS can be guaranteed by reserving resources for each traffic flow. Reservations isolate resources for each traffic flow so that flows do not have to compete for resources.

Another general principle is that traffic controls can be exercised simultaneously at various levels. At the node level, routers and switches are responsible for packet scheduling and selective packet discarding. Ingress nodes can perform access policing. Nodes may be capable of explicit congestion notification. At the network level, the network makes admission control decisions to accept or block new packet flows. At the higher level, transport or application layer protocols can be adaptive to the congestion level in the network.

Traffic control methods can be classified as preventive or reactive. Reactive methods are activated to ameliorate congestion after it is detected. For example, TCP reacts to congestion by reducing TCP source rates. A general principle is that prevention of congestion is preferred to reacting to congestion. If congestion occurs, packets will be lost, and it takes time to clear the queues in congested nodes. Preventive methods such as explicit congestion notification are preferred because congestion and packet loss may be avoided.

Overview of Methods

In practice, networks generally depend on a variety of traffic controls used at different points in the networks (El-Gendy, Bose, and Shin 2003). The main preventive traffic control is admission control. Admission control gives the network an opportunity to make a decision whether to accept or reject a new traffic flow before the flow begins. Admission control can be quite effective in protecting the network from congestion by blocking new traffic flows at the network ingress (Firoiu et al. 2002). Typically, admission control relies on a signaling protocol that allows applications to explicitly request a QoS or service class. Information about the new traffic flow (e.g., peak rate, average rate, burstiness) must be provided to the network at the same time so that sufficient resources can be allocated. A signaling protocol is not absolutely necessary if the required QoS can be inferred implicitly from knowledge about the traffic. For example, the telephone network uses admission control. Since every telephone call requires the same QoS, the required QoS does not have to be signaled explicitly.

Access or ingress policing is another preventive traffic control that typically accompanies admission control. Since admission control decisions are based on information about the accepted new traffic, it is important that source traffic conforms to the given parameters because excessive traffic could degrade network performance to the point of violating QoS guarantees. The most widely used algorithm for access policing is the leaky bucket. The leaky-bucket algorithm is simple to implement with counters, and allows adjustable tolerance for bursty traffic sources. For conforming traffic, the access policing should be invisible and make no difference. For excess traffic, three actions are possible: the excess traffic is admitted; it is admitted but marked with lower priority; or it is discarded immediately.

Packet scheduling is an essential traffic control because it recognizes that packets have different forwarding requirements. Packet scheduling should recognize different service priorities and give preferential treatment to packets with more stringent delay requirements.

Buffer management is a problem complementary to packet scheduling. Whereas packet scheduling deals with the order of packets to depart from a buffer, buffer management dictates how incoming packets should fill up limited buffer space. Buffer management should recognize different loss priorities and selectively discard packets of lower loss priority. In a way, loss priorities may be viewed as priorities related to space, while service priorities are related to time. In addition to simple loss priorities, packets may be discarded in coordination with higher-layer protocols. For example, random early detection (RED) is a random packet discarding strategy that takes advantage of the congestion-control algorithm in TCP to improve network throughput and stability (Floyd and Jacobson 1993).

Instead of simply discarding packets during congestion, it is better to avoid congestion entirely if possible. Congestion might be avoided by inferring the state of congestion in the network by watching for long packet delays and packet losses. This does not require the network to provide any congestion information. However, the most effective way to avoid congestion is explicit congestion notification by the network. Protocols such as ATM and frame relay allow switches to mark packets when congestion appears to be imminent. Traffic sources are given enough advance warning to slow down and prevent congestion. This so-called closed loop control works only for some adaptable applications that can adjust their transmission rate dynamically (in contrast, admission control is open loop control because sources are not controlled by feedback after they are accepted).

ADMISSION CONTROL

Admission control is one of the most effective means of congestion control. The objective is to prevent congestion by blocking new packet flows before the flow begins. If a new flow is accepted, the network is explicitly or implicitly agreeing to provide the required QoS for the duration of the flow. This agreement is explicit if the admission control is carried out with a signaling protocol.

Many approaches to admission control can be found in the literature (Firoiu et al. 2002). As shown in Figure 1, approaches can be classified according to where the acceptance decision is made: hop-by-hop, end-point or edge router, or centralized bandwidth broker (BB). Hop-by-hop admission control follows the traditional approach of telecommunications networks. A signaling message requesting resources attempts to find a path through the network. Each router or switch along the path has an opportunity to accept and forward the request or to reject and block the request. Although this is a natural approach, the complexity required for routers limits the scalability to large networks.

The second approach leaves the admission decision to the source end point (host) or an edge (ingress or egress) router (Elek, Karlsson, and Ronngre 2000). The decision can be based on data collected passively (without any extra effort) or actively by special probe packets. This approach simplifies the role of the core network, resulting in better scalability.

The third approach is also aimed at better scalability. Admission into each network domain is controlled by a centralized bandwidth broker (Zhang et al. 2000). The available resources of the domain are monitored by the BB, which makes all admission decisions and keeps track of accepted traffic flows. The BB concept has two potential advantages. It keeps the core network stateless for scalability. Also, it can make network-wide optimal resource allocation decisions.

In order to make an acceptance or rejection decision, the network must estimate the amount of bandwidth and buffer resources needed for a new traffic flow. The required resources are compared with the available resources. The network also estimates the hypothetical impact of the new traffic flow on the current network performance. There must be assurance that the new flow will not cause the QoS for current traffic flows to fall below acceptable levels.

Approaches for admission control can be alternatively classified by how the decision is made: deterministic, stochastic, or measurement-based (Perros and Elsayed 1996). Deterministic approaches use worst-case bounds. In contrast, stochastic approaches assume statistical characteristics of the traffic for more accurate estimation of required resources. However, the accuracy of stochastic approaches depends heavily on the choice of traffic models. Traffic modeling is a difficult problem because of the dynamic nature of network traffic. Measurement-based approaches attempt to avoid the modeling problem by using measurements of the actual traffic instead of assumed traffic models.

Hop-by-Hop Admission Control

As in traditional telecommunications networks, a signaling message is sent along a path to request resources. The signaling message carries information needed for routers and switches along the path to make decisions about whether sufficient resources are available. If a router or

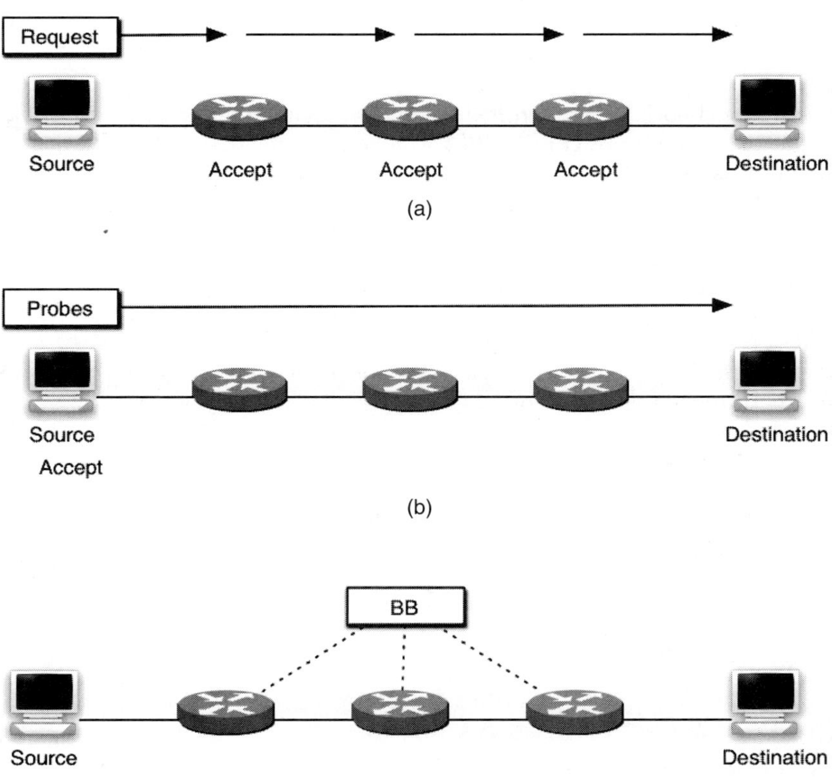

Figure 1: Hop-by-hop admission; (b) end-point admission; (c) centralized bandwidth broker

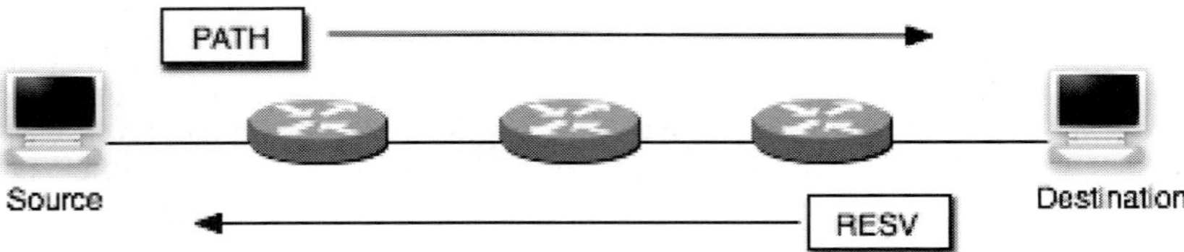

Figure 2: RSVP messages

switch has sufficient resources, it forwards the request to the next hop. If insufficient resources are available, it drops the request and notifies the source host by a "reject" signaling message.

RSVP (resource reservation protocol) is a well-known signaling protocol for IP networks capable of unicast or multicast reservations (Braden et al. 1997). In the basic reservation setup, a source sends an RSVP PATH message that is forwarded by each router, according to its routing table, until it reaches the destination, as shown in Figure 2. The most important element is a TSpec object that provides information about the source traffic characteristics. Traffic characteristics in the TSpec object are specified in token bucket parameters: token rate, token bucket size, peak rate, minimum policed unit, and maximum packet size.

The RSVP RESV message is returned from the destination to the source to request resources along the path traversed by the PATH message. In addition to a TSpec object, the RESV message can contain a controlled load or guaranteed load flow specification. Controlled load and guaranteed services are part of the IETF Integrated Services (IntServ) framework (Braden, Clark, and Shenker 1994). Controlled load service is intended for real-time applications that can tolerate a limited amount of packet loss and excessive packet delay. It can be viewed as "better than best-effort" and equivalent to QoS seen from an unloaded network. The controlled load flow specification in the RESV message consists of the token bucket parameters as in the TSpec object. Guaranteed service provides "hard" and measurable QoS guarantees in terms of throughput and maximum packet delay. The controlled load flow specification in the RESV message consists of token bucket parameters and an RSpec object, which includes a rate and a delay slack (delay variation) term.

RSVP suffers from two serious drawbacks: complexity and scalability (El-Gendy et al. 2003). Routers must be programmed to understand the signaling protocol and perform packet classification, packet scheduling, and admission control. The scalability problem is caused by the need for traditionally stateless routers to keep state information for each flow. RSVP uses soft state, meaning that reservation states are automatically deleted if not refreshed after some time. However, it is clear that the number of flows in the Internet will only be increasing over time, necessitating more state information to be maintained by RSVP-capable routers.

End-Point/Edge Admission Control

Hop-by-hop admission control suffers from two drawbacks: the need for a signaling protocol and the need for all routers or switches to keep track of flow reservations. An alternative idea is that the source host could probe the network to determine whether it can accommodate the new flow (Elek et al. 2000). For example, the source host (or ingress edge router) could inject a stream of probe packets at the same rate of the new flow and measure the packet delay and loss rate. This is a direct measurement of whether the new flow can be accommodated or not. The probe test may work better if routers along the path can mark the packets with congestion information (Gibbens and Key, 2001; Ganesh et al. 2006).

The probing method has been proposed for voice over IP (VoIP) calls (Mase 2004). It is claimed that the probing method over controls call admission, so the method is modified so that call requests failing the probe test can be accepted with some adjustable probability.

Egress admission control places the decision at the egress edge router (Cetinkaya, Kanodia, and Knightly 2001). The network is viewed as a black box, and the egress router just monitors data flows to infer the internal state of the network. The service capacity between ingress and egress end-points is estimated. If the new flow combined with the existing flows can be accommodated by the service capacity, the new flow is admitted. The advantage of the method is no need for probe packets.

Bandwidth Brokers

In differentiated services (Diffserv), the core routers are stateless for scalability, and complex traffic controls are pushed to the edge routers. Although ingress or egress routers could take responsibility for admission control, another idea is to centralize admission control in a BB entity (Nichols, Jacobson, and Zhang 1999). The BB keeps track of allocated and available resources in a Diffserv domain, makes all admission decisions, and configures the packet classifiers and traffic conditioners at the edges of the Diffserv domain to regulate incoming traffic.

The major advantage is scalability, because core routers are concerned only with packet forwarding. Another advantage is the network-wide view of the BB. This network-wide view should enable the BB to make optimal resource allocation decisions (e.g., balance traffic across the network). However, there may be a performance issue because the BB keeps all state information and makes all decisions. As a Diffserv domain grows larger, the BB could become a processing and communications bottleneck. It is also a single point of failure. To alleviate this problem, a hierarchy of BBs may be possible.

It is envisioned that bandwidth brokers in adjacent Diffserv domains could negotiate with each other to establish end-to-end services across multiple domains. However, an inter-BB protocol does not currently exist.

Deterministic Bounds

The deterministic approach to admission control assumes the worst-case traffic scenario, which is the peak rate for each traffic flow. A new flow is accepted if the sum of the peak rates for all flows is less than the physical capacity. It is obvious that traffic flows may be well below the peak rates in actuality, leading to considerable underutilization of capacity. However, this approach has appealing advantages. First, admission control is a simple decision. Second, the peak rate is always known, so the physical capacity will never be exceeded and QoS can be guaranteed.

Stochastic Bounds

For bursty traffic flows with random time-varying rates, it makes sense to allocate bandwidth less than the peak rates and assume that some capacity can be saved by statistical multiplexing (Firoiu et al. 2002). When a large number of flows are multiplexed, it is unlikely that all flows will be bursting at their peak rates simultaneously. Hence, an amount of bandwidth somewhat less than the sum of peak rates is needed.

The savings from statistical multiplexing is usually estimated from a finite-size queuing model. The queue represents the buffer in the switch or router making the admission control decision. The input to the queue is a stochastic process representing the random behavior of traffic sources. A number of traffic models have been proposed in the literature based on studies of historical traffic measurements (Michiel and Laevens 1997). Common traffic models include the Poisson process, interrupted Poisson process, simple on-off model, Markov modulated processes (such as the Markov modulated Poisson process), and ARMA (autoregressive moving averages) time series (Adas 1997). Due to the challenges of solving complex queueing systems, another popular model is the stochastic fluid buffer, where the input traffic is viewed as Markov modulated fluid flow instead of discrete packets. In any case, the delay through the queue and probability of buffer overflow are calculated for the hypothetical traffic. If the delay and buffer overflow probability meet the desired QoS, then the new traffic flow is accepted.

A popular alternative approach is to calculate the equivalent capacity for each traffic flow (Kelly 1996). The appeal of equivalent capacity is a simple admission control decision. The equivalent capacity for the total traffic is compared with the available physical capacity. The equivalent capacity for a source is derived by imagining the source as input into a finite queue. The equivalent capacity is the service rate resulting in the target buffer overflow probability. There are different expressions for equivalent capacity, depending on the source traffic characteristics. The equivalent capacity for multiple sources is derived similarly, whereby the aggregate traffic from the sources is the input into a finite queue. Generally, the equivalent capacity for multiple sources will be less than the sum of their individual equivalent capacities, due to the savings from statistical multiplexing.

Measurement-Based Admission Control

The accuracy of statistical admission control depends on correct assumptions for the source traffic models. Measurement-based admission control is motivated by the difficulty of choosing a traffic model for a new packet flow based on limited information. A traffic source may provide descriptive parameters but they may be inaccurate or uncertain. Measurement-based admission control avoids the need to assume a traffic model by characterizing sources by statistics measured from the actual traffic instead.

Several measurement-based methods have been proposed (Shiomoto, Yamanaka, and Takahashi 1999). The various methods all depend on measurements of the actual traffic made during a recent time window but differ in their usage of the measurements. For example, the measurements can be used to derive a marginal probability distribution for the source rates. The marginal probability distribution is then used to estimate the buffer overflow probability for a hypothetical finite queue. As a second example, the mean and variance of the source rates are measured. The effective capacity of the sources is derived from the mean and variance. As a third example, a frequency analysis of the source rates reveals the low-frequency and high-frequency components. Queuing is considered to accommodate high-frequency variations, and admission control is based on the low-frequency components.

ACCESS CONTROL

Access control, or *policing*, refers to regulation of ingress traffic at the user-network interface. There are reasons for regulating traffic at the network edge and not internally within the network. At the network boundary, excessive traffic can be blocked before consuming any network resources. Moreover, it is natural to verify conformance of the traffic as close to the source as possible before the traffic shape is affected by other packet flows. Finally, individual packet flows at the network edge are slower than multiplexed flows in the core network.

Traffic Contracts

When an admission control decision is made, that decision is based on traffic descriptors and QoS parameters provided by traffic sources. If the network admits a packet flow, it might be said that the user and network have agreed on a traffic contract. Unlike SLAs, traffic contracts are a misnomer because they are not legal agreements. A traffic contract is an implicit understanding between the network and sources that both sides are cooperating in admission control. Sources are obligated to conform to the traffic descriptors that they provided for the admission decision. Excessive traffic will consume more network resources and deteriorate the QoS seen by all users. In accepting a new flow, the network is obligated to provide and sustain the requested QoS.

Traffic Classification

Packets must be classified to determine their QoS requirements or which flow they belong to. In the Intserv framework, reservations are made for individual flows. Packets belonging to the same flow can be identified by these IP header fields: source IP address, destination IP address, source port number, destination port number, and protocol.

Packet classification is difficult for at least two reasons. First, routers must process terabytes of packets per second (Chao 2002). Thus, packet classification must be done very quickly and efficiently (Yu, Katz, and Lakshman 2005). Second, there may be an enormous number of flows going through a router. Classification of a packet to a particular flow essentially involves a table search, but the table could be enormous. Packet classification is an ongoing research problem that is central to router design (Van Lunteren and Engbersen 2003; Wang et al. 2004; Baboescu and Varghese 2005).

In the Diffserv framework, packets must be classified at the ingress to the Diffserv network such that an appropriate Diffserv codepoint (DSCP) can be assigned (Carpenter and Nichols 2002). The DSCP is encoded in the first six bits of the type of service (ToS) field in the IPv4 packet header. The DSCP identifies the per-hop behavior (PHB) to be applied to the packet.

Traffic Regulation

The rate of traffic entering the network can be regulated as a means of enforcing the traffic contract. Since admission control decisions are based on traffic parameters given for a packet flow, it is important that flows do not exceed their stated parameters because excessive traffic would deteriorate the network performance seen by all users.

The goal of traffic regulation is to differentiate between conforming and nonconforming packets (according to the traffic contract). Conforming packets should be allowed immediate entrance into the network as if the traffic policer was transparent. Nonconforming packets may be discarded immediately or allowed entrance with some kind of packet marking. The former is preferred if the network load is heavy, then it would be better to discard the nonconforming packets to avoid any wasted use of network resources. The idea behind packet marking is that the purpose of the network is to carry packets. If the network load is light, it does no harm to carry nonconforming traffic. If congestion is encountered anywhere, the marked packets can be discarded first.

In the Diffserv framework, packets may also be classified into flows that are subject to policing and marking according to a traffic conditioning agreement (TCA). The TCA includes traffic characteristics (such as token bucket parameters) and performance metrics (delay, throughput) as actions required for dropping out-of-profile packets (Longsong, Tianji, and Lo 2000). Out-of-profile packets are nonconforming packets, and they are either dropped or marked with a lower priority level.

Traffic Shaping

Traffic shaping can be done at the source prior to entrance into the network or within the network. Traffic shaping at the source is a means of self-regulation in order to ensure conformance to the traffic contract. Conformance is desirable, to minimize the amount of traffic discarded at the network ingress.

Traffic shaping within the network is not concerned with a traffic contract. The idea is that smooth traffic will cause smaller queues and hence incur shorter queuing delays and less delay jitter (Rexford et al. 1997). Since traffic shaping is done by buffering, some queuing delay is added by the traffic shaper, but then smooth traffic should flow more quickly along the rest of the path. Overall, network performance is improved by keeping traffic smooth (Elwalid and Mitra 1997).

Leaky-Bucket Algorithm

The leaky-bucket algorithm is widely used for access control. There are different versions. The basic version consists of a buffer (bucket) of size B and a leak rate R, as shown in Figure 3a. Packets are conforming if they can join the buffer without overflowing. The contents of the buffer are emptied at the leak rate R. A larger bucket size allows greater variations from the rate R. A burst at a higher rate can still be conforming as long as the burst is not long enough to overflow the bucket. Hence, the maximum burst length is directly related to the bucket size.

One variation is the token bucket. Tokens at some generation rate R can collect in a bucket size of B, as shown in Figure 3b. A packet is conforming if it can find and consume a token waiting in the bucket. Again, a larger bucket allows longer bursts to be conforming.

The leaky-bucket algorithm can be easily implemented by a counter. Another advantage is the simple use of dual leaky buckets in tandem to regulate both average rate and peak rate. For example, the first leaky bucket can regulate the peak rate, and the second leaky bucket can regulate the average rate.

PACKET SCHEDULING

Packet scheduling addresses the different needs of buffered packets contending for the same link bandwidth (El-Gendy et al. 2003). Packet scheduling should take into account the QoS requirements of each packet flow.

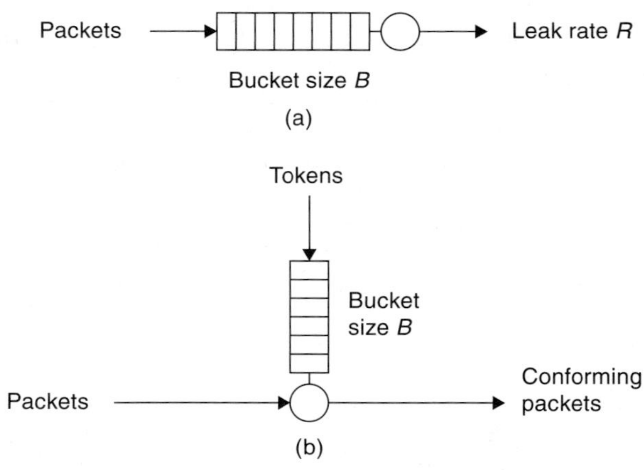

Figure 3: (a) Leaky-bucket policer; (b) token bucket

A packet flow may require a minimum throughput, maximum end-to-end delay, or maximum packet delay jitter.

A general principle of packet scheduling is that the average waiting time for all packets does not change under different schedules. In other words, giving higher priority to transmit one packet earlier comes at the expense of making other packets wait longer. Benefits to one packet's flow penalizes other packets. Hence, fairness is another issue when packet schedules are considered (Dua and Bambos 2005).

Priorities

A simple and intuitive packet schedule gives preferential treatment according to static priorities. Each packet belongs to one of priority levels 1 to N, where priority 1 is always transmitted first, priority 2 is transmitted when there are no priority 1 packets, and so on. The priority is static in the sense that a packet's priority never changes during its lifetime.

The advantage of static priorities is straightforward implementation. Different-priority packets may be queued in separate buffers, as shown in Figure 4. The priority buffers may be implemented as physically separate buffers or a single physical buffer separated into multiple virtual buffers.

A well-known disadvantage of static priorities is the possibility of starvation of low priorities. The high priority packets can consume all of the bandwidth and prevent low priority packets from receiving service. A possible solution to the starvation problem is dynamic priorities. For example, the priority of a packet can increase with its waiting time. As a packet is waiting, it will eventually receive service, ensuring some fairness. However, dynamic priorities are much more difficult to implement than simple priorities because the waiting times must be tracked for each packet.

Round Robin

Round robin is another simple and intuitive scheduling algorithm. Each packet flow is queued in a separate buffer, and the head of line 1 is transmitted, then the head of line 2, and so on, eventually back to line 1, as shown in Figure 5. Empty queues are skipped over immediately to avoid wasting bandwidth.

Round robin is intuitively fair because each packet flow takes equal turns during a round or cycle. However, it may not be entirely fair. First, packets may be unequal in size. If the packets of one flow are long, that flow will consume more bandwidth compared to flows with shorter packets.

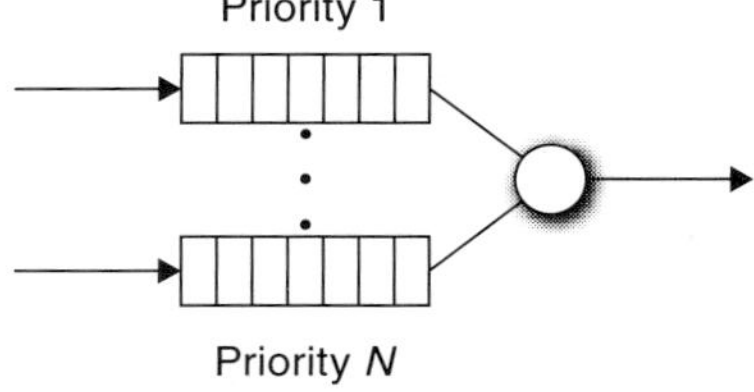

Figure 4: Priority buffers

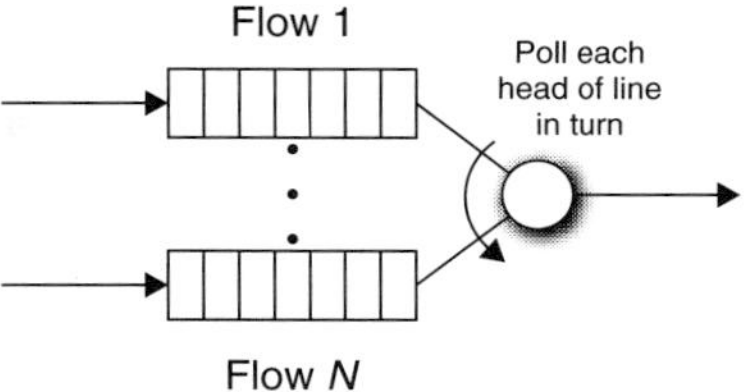

Figure 5: Round-robin scheduling

Second, certain flows may naturally require more bandwidth than other flows (e.g., video versus voice).

A simple modification is weighted round robin. The packet flows are assigned weights $w_1, w_2,.., w_N$. A higher weight means that more packets are transmitted from that buffer in each turn. For example, if $w_1 = 2w_2$, then twice as many packets are transmitted from queue 1 than from queue 2 in each turn. Sophisticated schemes can adapt the weights per flow based on the traffic behaviors (Wang, Shen, and Shin 2001).

Fair Queueing

Fair queueing is closely related to round robin. Recall that a potential cause of unfairness in round-robin scheduling is unequal packet sizes. A logical modification is round robin on the basis of bits instead of packets. Fair queuing might be considered as an approximation to bit-by-bit round robin. It is obvious that bit-by-bit fair queuing cannot be implemented in actuality because packets must be transmitted in their entirety, not piecemeal as separate bits.

In fair queuing, the hypothetical finishing time of each packet under bit-by-bit round robin is calculated and associated with that packet (Demers, Keshav, and Shenker 1989). The next packet chosen to transmit is always the packet waiting with the earliest hypothetical finishing time.

Along the same idea, weighted fair queuing (WFQ) is a packet-by-packet approximation to bit-by-bit weighted round robin. It is so-called fair in the sense that the ith packet flow is guaranteed a fraction of bandwidth equal to at least $w_i/(w_1 + \ldots + kw_N)$.

As a consequence of the guaranteed bandwidth, it may be expected that if a traffic source is rate-limited, then the delay through a queuing system with WFQ would be bounded (Parekh and Gallager 1993). Suppose each traffic flow is regulated by a token bucket with bucket size B_i and token rate R_i. Furthermore, assume that WFQ is used with relative weights $w_i = R_i$ for the flows. The maximum delay experienced by the ith flow through the node will be bounded by $D_i \leq B_i/R_i$. The bounded delay is an important advantage of WFQ because it means that admission control can guarantee a maximum end-to-end packet delay.

Deadline Scheduling

A widely studied class of scheduling algorithms is based on deadlines (Conway, Maxwell, and Miller 2003). When a packet arrives at the buffer, it is assigned a deadline

d, which is the time when it should be transmitted. For example, a real-time packet might have a deadline that is a short time after its arrival time a, whereas a non-real-time packet might have a deadline much farther in the future. The finishing time f of a packet is the sum $f = a + w + x$, where w is the waiting time before starting service, and x is its service time (i.e., transmission time). If a packet is transmitted by finishing time f, the packet's lateness is $l = f - d$. A packet with positive lateness has not met its deadline, whereas a packet with negative lateness is considered early. Typically, a penalty is associated with lateness but not with earliness.

A number of optimal schedules are known, depending on the criterion to optimize. The shortest processing time (SPT) discipline takes packets in order of increasing service time. That is, the next packet to transmit is always the packet waiting with the smallest service time. The SPT schedule is known to minimize the average waiting time and minimize the average lateness (averaged over all packets).

In certain cases, the most late packet is more important than the packet of average lateness. Another well-known optimal schedule is the earliest due date (EDD) or earliest deadline first (EDF) discipline. The next packet to transmit is always the packet waiting with the earliest deadline. The EDD schedule is known to minimize the maximum lateness. Suppose the packet that is most late under any schedule has lateness l_{max}. EDD is optimal in the sense that no other schedule will realize a smaller l_{max} than the EDD schedule.

BUFFER MANAGEMENT

Buffer management deals with how packets are given preferential access to limited buffer space. If packets are allowed into a full buffer, then packets already waiting in the buffer must be discarded to make space available. Hence, buffer management is also the problem of selective packet discarding (Labrador and Banerjee 1999).

Loss Priorities

In theory, packets may be marked with an explicit loss priority. ATM and frame relay are examples of protocols that include a bit in the packet header to indicate loss priority. The ATM cell header has a cell loss priority (CLP) bit, and cells with CLP = 1 are dropped first at congested switches. The frame relay header has a discard eligibility (DE) bit. Frames marked with DE = 1 are discarded before DE = 0 frames.

Although the ToS field in the IP packet header has a bit to maximize reliability (or presumably minimize the likelihood of dropping), the ToS field has ambiguous interpretations and has been preempted by the Diffserv codepoint. Thus, IP does not allow explicit loss priorities. However, strategies for discarding IP packets are an active area of research because packet loss affects TCP performance. These strategies are usually called "active queue management" (AQM) (Ryu, Rump, and Qiao 2003). The most important example, random early detection (RED), is discussed later in this chapter.

Push-Out Schemes

The simplest packet-discarding strategy is tail drop. When a buffer is full, arriving packets are dropped. This strategy has a potential "lock-out" problem, in which a subset of flows can monopolize the buffer space and prevent other flows from gaining access. In fact, higher-rate flows will gain more buffer space at the expense of lower-rate flows. Another drawback is that buffer congestion can continue for a long time when the traffic is TCP. TCP slows down when a dropped packet is detected by a retransmission time-out. A packet at the queue tail was transmitted later than a packet at the head of the queue. Therefore, a packet dropped from the tail will time-out at a later time than a packet dropped from the head. TCP sources will continue to transmit for a longer time before slowing down.

A third drawback is that simple tail drop does not recognize that packets have different loss priorities. If an arriving packet has high loss priority, it should be able to access the buffer space by discarding a packet of lower priority already in the buffer. The packet of lower priority is said to be pushed out (Roy and Panwar 2002). There are basically three push-out strategies: dropping low-priority packets near the head first, near the tail first, or randomly from anywhere in the buffer. For TCP traffic, dropping from the head of the queue works better (Lakshman, Neidhardt, and Ott 1996). In general though, optimal push-out schemes are not known (Sharma and Viniotis 1999).

Random Early Detection

The simple tail-drop strategy causes the undesirable phenomenon of global synchronization of TCP flows. TCP sources search for the proper sending rate by essentially increasing the rate until a dropped packet is detected by a retransmission time-out. The details of the TCP congestion-avoidance algorithm are described below. When a buffer overflows, it takes some time for TCP sources to detect a packet loss. In the meantime, the buffer continues to overflow, and packets will be discarded from multiple TCP flows. Thus, many TCP sources will detect packet loss and slow down at the same time. Even if the TCP sources were initially out of phase, they will become synchronized. The synchronization phenomenon causes underutilization and large queues. Underutilization occurs when all sources slow down (in "slow start"), then large queues are accumulated when all sources simultaneously increase their transmission rates.

RED eliminates the synchronization phenomenon and thereby achieves better utilization and smaller queues (Floyd and Jacobson 1993). A great advantage is that RED can be implemented as a buffer-management strategy with no change to the existing TCP protocol. Instead of waiting for the buffer to overflow, RED drops a packet randomly with the goal of losing packets from multiple TCP flows at different times. Therefore, the TCP flows slow down and ramp up at different times. Since they are unsynchronized, their aggregate rate is smoother than before. From a queue-theory viewpoint, smooth traffic achieves the best utilization and shortest queue.

RED keeps track of the average queue length, calculated as an exponentially weighted moving average of the

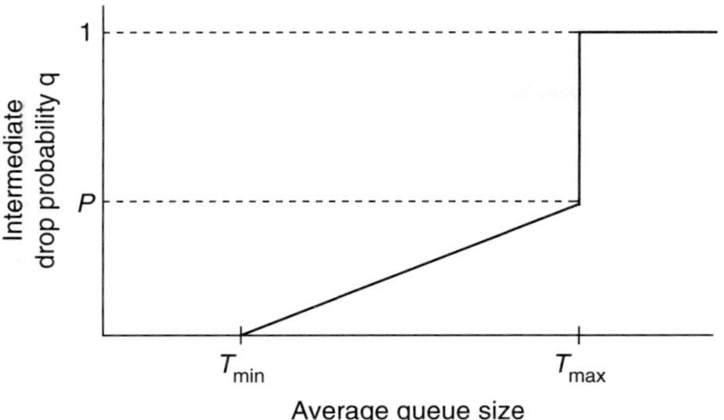

Figure 6: RED probabilities of discarding

instantaneous queue length. The average queue length is compared to a minimum threshold, T_{min}, and a maximum threshold, T_{max}. The packet-drop probability is calculated with the help of an intermediate drop probability q shown in Figure 6. Below T_{min}, no packets are dropped because the short queue means no congestion. Above T_{max}, all packets are discarded because the long queue is a sign of serious congestion. Between T_{min} and T_{max}, the intermediate drop probability q increases linearly to a maximum probability P. The actual drop probability p_{drop} is calculated as:

$$p_{drop} = \frac{q}{1 - q \cdot count}$$

where *count* is the number of undropped packets since the last dropped packet. In this way, RED attempts to drop packets in proportion to the rates of connections.

Since its introduction, RED has found wide commercial acceptance. Under certain traffic conditions, RED performs effectively if its parameters are properly tuned. However, it can be difficult to determine the proper parameters. Moreover, several problems can arise, depending on the traffic, such as unfairness, lowered throughput, and increased delay. Consequently, numerous variations have been proposed, including flow RED (FRED), weighted RED (WRED), stabilized RED (SRED) (Ott, Lakshman, and Wong 1999), BLUE (Feng et al. 2002), PURPLE (Pletka, Waldvogel, and Mannal 2003), adaptive virtual queue (AVQ) (Kunniyur and Srikant 2004), and predictive AQM (PAQM) (Gao, He, and Hou 2002), just to name a few. RED continues to be an active subject of research (Zhu et al. 2002; Bohacek et al. 2004).

CONGESTION CONTROL

Congestion control is a very broad term that is sometimes used interchangeably with *traffic control*. Here, *congestion control* refers to actions taken by hosts to prevent serious congestion. Congestion control can be classified as reactive or predictive (proactive). Reactive congestion control ameliorates congestion after it occurs. Generally, hosts observe the symptoms of congestion (packet loss and long packet delays) and then slow down. Predictive congestion control attempts to avoid congestion altogether by slowing down before the onset of congestion. Avoidance of congestion is obviously preferable, but predictive congestion control usually depends on explicit congestion information provided from the network.

Reactive Congestion Control

Reactive congestion control takes action when congestion is detected. A prime example of this approach is the congestion-avoidance algorithm in TCP. TCP takes responsibility for congestion control in the Internet because IP is too simple by design to handle congestion control. Strictly speaking, TCP does not actually avoid congestion. TCP pushes the network gently to the brink of congestion and then backs off. This is necessary because a TCP source does not know the appropriate transmission rate, and must search for it.

A TCP source limits itself by means of a congestion window. The congestion window is adjusted dynamically to the level of network congestion by an AIMD (additive increase, multiplicative decrease) algorithm (Jacobson 1988). The onset of congestion is detected by a retransmission time-out. As shown in Figure 7, a parameter *ssthresh* (slow start threshold) is set to half of the congestion window when congestion was encountered. The congestion window is closed to one TCP segment, and

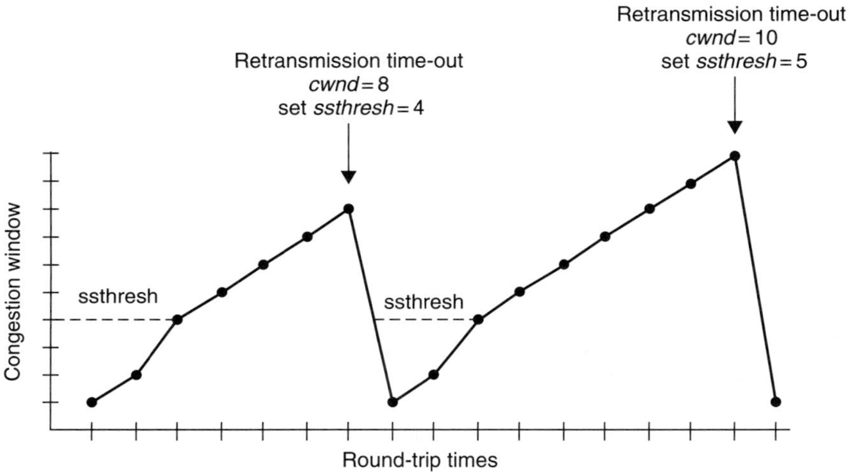

Figure 7: TCP congestion-control algorithm

the congestion control algorithm goes into slow-start. In the slow-start phase, the congestion window can increase at an exponential rate as long as acknowledgments for packets are returned promptly. When the congestion window size reaches *ssthresh*, the congestion-control algorithm enters the congestion-avoidance algorithm. In this phase, the congestion window (*cwnd*) increases by one segment for every round-trip time until congestion is encountered again. The idea is that linear increase during congestion avoidance is a cautious approach to the previous congestion point. When congestion is encountered, the *ssthresh* parameter is set to half of the congestion window, and the congestion-control algorithm repeats.

Predictive Congestion Avoidance

The congestion-avoidance algorithm in TCP is forced to probe for the appropriate transmission rate by pushing the network to the brink of congestion because the IP network is incapable of providing congestion information. A capability for explicit congestion notification is preferable as a method of "early warning." Protocols such as ATM and frame relay include explicit forward congestion indication (EFCI) and backward/forward explicit congestion notification (BECN/FECN), respectively.

Explicit congestion notification allows routers and switchers to give early warning to sources before congestion occurs. This advance warning can give sufficient time for traffic sources to reduce their rates in time to avoid congestion. This is a proactive approach to avoiding congestion instead of a reactive approach to ameliorate congestion. It has been shown that explicit congestion notification improves the performance of TCP with active queue management (Yan, Gao and Ozbay, 2005).

Explicit congestion notification in the forward direction refers to marking packets as they pass through a router or switch. Packets in the forward direction are delivered to the destination, and the destination must have a separate means of communicating congestion information to the source. The overall delay is one round-trip time. For efficiency, explicit congestion notification in the backward direction goes directly to the source. However, it is harder to implement because a router or switch must find and mark a packet going in the backward direction.

The current version of IP does not include a capability for explicit congestion notification but an IETF proposal calls for using the last two bits from the TOS field in the IP packet header (Ramakrishnan and Floyd 1999). One bit for explicit congestion notification (ECN) capable transport (ECT) would allow hosts to signal whether they are capable of making use of ECN. The second bit for congestion experienced (CE) would allow routers or switches to signal a state of congestion to hosts. An open research issue is how routers should choose packets to mark (Leung and Muppala 2001).

QOS MONITORING

Observability is a prerequisite for controllability. Measurements of QoS can verify the effectiveness of traffic management and provide evidence to validate SLAs. In addition, QoS monitoring can identify network performance problems and help to tune traffic controls (Jiang, Tham, and Ko 2000).

Network-Layer Performance Monitoring

Since the Internet has not historically supported QoS, there has not been a compelling need for sophisticated performance monitoring at the IP layer. By far, most methods and tools at the IP layer are based on *ping* (ICMP [Internet Control Message Protocol] echo and echo response messages) or *traceroute* (which exploits the time-to-live field in the IP packet header).

A few large-scale performance-monitoring projects use ping and traceroute to make regular measurements between multiple selected points in the Internet (Chen and Hu 2002). The basic idea is that performance measured on these selected routes will reflect the overall performance of the entire Internet if the monitoring points are numerous and geographically distributed. Repeated pings are an easy way to obtain a sample distribution function of round-trip time and an estimate of the packet-loss ratio (reflected by the fraction of unreturned pings). Although round-trip times measured by ping are important, especially for adaptive protocols such as TCP, ping is unable to measure one-way packet delays without additional means for clock synchronization among hosts such as a global positioning system (GPS). Another drawback to ping is the low priority or blocking given to pings by some networks, because pings are invasive and possibly involved in some types of security attacks.

Transport/Application-Layer Performance Monitoring

Another monitoring method is TCP bulk transfer between selected sites. One site acts as the source and another as the sink for TCP bulk transfer. The packets are recorded by *tcpdump* and analyzed for packet delay and loss.

Measurements at the transport layer are appealing because they are closer to the application's perspective. Moreover, they do not depend on ICMP or traceroute, which are not entirely reliable. At the transport layer, the idea is to run a program emulating a TCP session to send test traffic through the Internet. The performance of the TCP connection can be measured in terms of delay, loss, and throughput.

For example, *TReno* (traceroute Reno) is an emulation of TCP to measure throughput or bulk transfer capability. It combines traceroute and an idealized version of the flow-control algorithm in Reno TCP. Other examples are *ttcp* (throughput TCP) and *netperf*. Ttcp is a client/server benchmarking program to measure throughput and retransmissions. Netperf is a network performance benchmarking program for measuring bulk data transfer and request/response performance using TCP or UDP (user datagram protocol). One host runs netperf and another runs netserver. Tests can be a TCP stream performance test, UDP bulk transfer, or TCP request/response test.

Similarly, network performance can be measured at the application layer. For example, NetIQ's commercial Chariot or Qcheck software agents are installed and configured at hosts with scripts to emulate various applications and collect application-level performance (throughput, delay) measurements. Application-layer measurements have the advantage of measuring performance that is reflective of what applications are seeing. On the other hand, special software is needed at selected sites and it is an active monitoring method that adds traffic into the network.

CONCLUSION

As seen in this chapter, traffic management is a challenging problem covering an impressive breadth and depth. The breadth is due to various traffic controls that should work together. Moreover, many details are involved in engineering each control to work effectively.

Traffic management continues to be an active area of study, not because solutions are not possible but because many solutions are possible. The "optimal" solution continues to be elusive because many factors (fairness, effectiveness, efficiency, practicality) usually need to be considered, allowing for different opinions of optimality.

Even as next-generation networks provide more bandwidth, traffic management will still be an important problem. Next-generation networks will support a greater variety of applications. Different applications require different treatment by the network. The intelligence to recognize different traffic and their requirements implies the need for sophisticated traffic management.

GLOSSARY

Access Policing: Regulation of ingress traffic at the user-network interface.

Active Queue Management (AQM): Intelligent buffer management strategies enabling traffic sources to respond to congestion before buffers overflow.

Admission Control: An open loop control method to accept or block traffic flows before flows start.

Differentiated Services (Diffserv): An IETF framework supporting QoS classes by means of Diffserv code point marking, per-hop behaviors, and stateless core routers.

Explicit Congestion Notification: A proactive congestion-avoidance method involving routers or switches conveying congestion information to hosts.

Integrated Services (Intserv): An IETF framework supporting QoS based on RSVP reservations per flow.

Leaky Bucket: An algorithm for policing a specific traffic rate while allowing a limited variation around that rate.

Quality of Service (QoS): The end-to-end network performance defined from the perspective of a specific user's connection.

Random Early Detection (RED): An active queue management approach for preventing synchronization of TCP connections.

Resource Reservation Protocol (RSVP): An IETF standardized signaling protocol for IP networks.

Service-Level Agreement (SLA): A contract between users and a network provider or between two network providers specifying expectations about the level of service in a way that allows monitoring and verification.

Signaling Protocol: Rules for exchanging messages to request reservations of network resources.

Traffic Contract: An implicit agreement between users and the network to meet QoS requirements as long as ingress traffic conforms to specified traffic descriptors.

Traffic Shaping: Smoothing the traffic rate to improve network performance.

CROSS REFERENCES

See *Computer Network Management*; *Network Capacity Planning*; *Network Reliability and Fault Tolerance*; *Network Security Risk Assessment and Management*; *Network Traffic Modeling*.

REFERENCES

Adas, A. 1997. Traffic models in broadband networks. *IEEE Communications Magazine*, 35: 82–9.

ATM Forum Technical Committee 1996. *Traffic management specification version 4.1*. www.mfaforum.org/ftp/pub/approved-specs/af-tm-0056.000. pdf (accessed May 9, 2007).

Baboescu, F., and G. Varghese. 2005. Scalable packet classification. *IEEE/ACM Transactions on Networking* 13:2–14.

Bohacek, S., K. Shah, G. Arce, and M. Davis. 2004. Signal processing challenges in active queue management. *IEEE Signal Processing Magazine* 21:69–79.

Braden, R., D. Clark, and S. Shenker. 1994. Integrated services in the Internet architecture: an overview. IETF RFC 1633. www.apps.ietf.org/rfc/rfc1633.html (accessed May 9, 2007).

Braden, R., L. Zhang, S. Berson, S. Herzog, and S. Jamin. 1997. Resource reservation protocol (RSVP)–version 1, functional specification. *IETF RFC 2205*. www.apps.ietf.org/rfc/rfc2205.html (accessed May 9, 2007).

Carpenter, B., and K. Nichols. 2002. Differentiated services in the Internet. *Proceedings of the IEEE* 90:1479–94.

Cetinkaya, C., V. Kanodia, and E. Knightly. 2001. Scalable services via egress admission control. *IEEE Transactions on Multimedia* 3:69–81.

Chao, J. 2002. Next generation routers. *Proceedings of the IEEE* 90:1518–8.

Chen, T., and L. Hu. 2002. Internet performance monitoring. *Proceedings of the IEEE* 90:1592–603.

Conway, R., W. Maxwell, and L. Miller. 2003. *Theory of scheduling*. Mineola, NY: Dover Publications.

Demers, A., S. Keshav, and S. Shenker. 1989. Analysis and simulation of a fair queueing algorithm. In *Proceedings of ACM SIGCOMM 89*. New York: ACM Press.

Dua, A., and N. Bambos. 2005. On the fairness delay trade-off in wireless packet scheduling. In *proceedings of IEEE Globecom 2005*. Los Alamitos, CA: IEEE Press.

Elek, V., G. Karlsson, and R. Ronngre. 2000. Admission control based on end-to-end measurements. In *proceedings of IEEE INFOCOM'00*. Los Alamitos, CA: IEEE Press.

El-Gendy, A., A. Bose, and K. Shin. 2003. Evolution of the Internet QoS and support for soft real-time applications. *Proceedings of the IEEE* 91:1086–104.

Elwalid, A., and D. Mitra. 1997. Traffic shaping at a network node: theory, optimum design, admission control. In *proceedings of IEEE INFOCOM'97*, 444–54. Los Alamitos, CA: IEEE Press.

Feng, W.C., K. Shin, D. Kandlur, and D. Saha. 2002. The BLUE active queue management algorithms. *IEEE/ACM Transactions on Networking* 10: 513–28.

Firoiu, V., J. Y. Le Boudec, D. Towsley, and Z. L. Zhang. 2002. Theories and models for Internet quality of service. *Proceedings of the IEEE* 90:1565–91.

Floyd, S., and V. Jacobson. 1993. Random early detection gateways for congestion avoidance. *IEEE/ACM Transactions on Networking* 1:397–413.

Ganesh, A., P. Key, D. Polis, and R. Srikant. 2006. Congestion notification and probing mechanisms for endpoint admission control. *IEEE/ACM Transactions on Networking* 14:568–78.

Gao, Y., G. He, and J. Hou. 2002. On exploiting traffic predictability in active queue management. In *proceedings of IEEE INFOCOM'02*, 1415–24. Los Alamitos, CA: IEEE Press.

Gibbens, R., and P. Key. (2001). Distributed control and resource marking using best-effort routers. *IEEE Network* 15:54–9.

Gozdecki, J., A. Jajszczyk, and R. Stankiewicz. 2003. Quality of service terminology in IP networks. *IEEE Communications Magazine* 41:153–9.

ITU-T 1999. *Rec. I.380: Internet Protocol Data Communication Service—IP Packet Transfer and Availability Performance Parameters*.

Jacobson, V. 1988. Congestion avoidance and control. In *proceedings of ACM SIGCOMM'88*, 314–29. New York: ACM Press.

Jiang, Y., C. K. Tham, and C. C. Ko. 2000. Providing quality of service monitoring: challenges and approaches. In *proceedings of IEEE NOMS 2000*, 115–28. Los Alamitos, CA: IEEE Press.

Kelly, F. 1996. Notes on effective bandwidths. In *Stochastic networks: Theory and applications*, 141–68. Oxford: Oxford University Press.

Kunniyur, S., and R. Srikant. (2004). An adaptive virtual queue (AVQ) algorithm for active queue management. *IEEE/ACM Transactions on Networking* 12:286–99.

Labrador, M., and S. Banerjee. 1999. Packet dropping policies for ATM and IP networks. *IEEE Communications Surveys* 2: 2–14.

Lakshman, T., A. Neidhardt, and T. Ott. 1996. The drop from front strategy in TCP and in TCP over ATM. In *proceedings of IEEE INFOCOM'96*. Los Alamitos, CA: IEEE Press.

Leung, K., and J. Muppala. (2001). Effect of different marking strategies on explicit congestion notification (ECN) performance. In *proceedings of IEEE ICC 2001*, 1812–16. Los Alamitos, CA: IEEE Press.

Longsong, L., J. Tianji, and J. Lo. 2000. A generic traffic conditioning model for differentiated services. In *proceedings of ICC 2000*, 1305–09. Los Alamitos, CA: IEEE Press.

Mase, K. 2004. Toward scalable admission control for VoIP networks. *IEEE Communications Magazine* 42:42–7.

Michiel, H., and K. Laevens. 1997. Teletraffic engineering in a broadband era. *Proceedings of the IEEE* 85: 2007–33.

Nichols, K, V. Jacobson, and L. Zhang. 1999. A two-bit differentiated services architecture for the Internet. IETF RFC 2638. www.apps.ietf.org/rfc/rfc2638.html (accessed May 9, 2007).

Ott, T., T. Lakshman, and L. Wong. 1999. SRED: stabilized RED. In *proceedings of IEEE INFOCOM'99*, 1346–55. Los Alamitos, CA: IEEE Press.

Parekh, A., and R. Gallager. (1993). A generalized processor sharing approach to flow control in integrated services networks: the single node case. *IEEE/ACM Transactions on Networking* 1:344–57.

Park, L. T., J. W. Baek, and J. Hong. 2001. Management of service level agreements for multimedia Internet service using a utility model. *IEEE Communications Magazine* 39:100–6.

Perros, H., and K. Elsayed. (1996). Call admission control schemes: a review. *IEEE Communications Magazine* 34:82–91.

Pletka, R., M. Waldvogel, and S. Mannal. 2003. PURPLE: predictive active queue management utilizing congestion information. In *proceedings of IEEE LCN'03*, 21–30. Los Alamitos, CA: IEEE Press.

Pongpaibool, P., and H. Kim. 2003. Guaranteed service level agreements across multiple ISP networks. In *proceedings of the 4th International Workshop on Design of Reliable Communication Networks* (DRCN 2003), 325–32. Los Alamitos, CA: IEEE Press.

Ramakrishnan, K., and S. Floyd. 1999. A proposal to add explicit congestion notification (ECN) to IP. *IETF RFC 2481*. www.ietf.org/rfc/rfc2481.txt (accessed May 10, 2007).

Rexford, J., F. Bonomi, A. Greenberg, and A. Wong. 1997. Scalable architectures for integrated traffic shaping and link scheduling in high speed ATM switches. *IEEE Journal on Selected Areas in Communications* 15:938–50.

Roy, R., and S. Panwar. 2002. Efficient buffer sharing in shared memory ATM systems with space priority traffic. *IEEE Communications Letters* 6:162–4.

Ryu, S., C. Rump, and C. Qiao. 2003. Advances in Internet congestion control. *IEEE Communications and Surveys* 5:28–39.

Seitz, N. 2003. ITU-T QoS standards for IP-based networks. *IEEE Communications Magazine* 41:82–9.

Sharma, S., and Y. Viniotis. 1999. Optimal buffer management policies for shared-buffer ATM switches. *IEEE/ACM Transactions on Networking*, 7:575–87.

Shiomoto, K., N. Yamanaka, and T. Takahashi. 1999. Overview of measurement-based connection admission control schemes. *IEEE Communications Surveys* 2:2–13.

Van Lunteren, J., and T. Engbersen. (2003). Fast and scalable packet classification. *IEEE Journal on Selected Areas in Communication* 21:560–71.

Verma, D. 2004. Service level agreements on IP networks. *Proceedings of the IEEE* 92: 1382–8.

Wang, H., C. Shen, and K. Shin. (2001). Adaptive-weighted packet scheduling for premium service. In *proceedings of IEEE ICC 2001*, 1846–50. Los Alamitos, CA: IEEE Press.

Wang, P. C., C. T. Chan, S. C. Hu, C. L. Lee, and W. C. Tseng. 2004. High-speed packet classification for differentiated services in next-generation networks, *IEEE Transactions on Multimedia* 6:925–35.

Yan, P., Y. Gao, and H. Ozbay. 2005. A variable structure control approach to active queue management for TCP with ECN. *IEEE Transactions on Control Systems Technology* 13:203–15.

Yu, F., R. Katz, and T. Lakshman. 2005. Efficient multimatch packet classification and lookup with TCAM. *IEEE Micro* 25:50–9.

Zhang, Z. L., Z. Duan, L. Gao, and Y. Hou. 2000. Decoupling QoS control from core routers: A novel bandwidth broker architecture for scalable support of guaranteed services. In *proceedings of ACM SIGCOMM'00*. New York: ACM Press.

Zhu, C., O. Wang, J. Aweya, M. Ouellette, and D. Montuno. 2002. A comparison of active queue management algorithms using the OPNET modeler. *IEEE Communications Magazine* 40:158–67.

FURTHER READING

The literature on traffic management is quite extensive, due to its broad scope and allowance for different viewpoints. A number of useful books cover the topic of traffic management in depth, such as:

Chao, J., and X. Guo. (2002). *Quality of service control in high speed networks*. New York: Wiley.

Jha, S., and M. Hassan. 2002. *Engineering Internet QoS*, Norwood, MA: Artech House.

Wang, Z. 2001. *Internet QoS: Architectures and mechanisms for Quality of Service*. San Francisco: Morgan Kaufmann.

Network Security Risk Assessment and Management

Dan Port and Rick Kazman, *University of Hawaii, Manoa*
David Klappholz, *Stevens Institute of Technology*

INTRODUCTION

According to Williams, Pandelios, and Behrens (1999), "All projects have some level of risk associated with them." And as Carr et al. (1993) state, risks must be managed, and risk management must be part of any mature organization's overall management practices and management structure. They identify these primary activities for managing risk:

Identify: Risks must first be identified before they can be managed.

Analyze: Risks must be analyzed so that management can make prudent decisions about them.

Plan: For information about a risk to be turned into action, a detailed plan, outlining both present and potential future actions, must be created. These actions may mitigate the risk, avoid the risk, or even accept the risk.

Track: Risks, whether they have been acted on or not, must be tracked, so that management can continue to exercise diligence.

Control: Even if a risk has been identified and addressed, it must be continually controlled to monitor for any deviations.

The key activity tying all of these activities together is *assessment*. Assessment is considered central to the risk management process, underlying all of the other activities.

For the purposes of exposition, we follow Boehm's (1991) generic risk taxonomy, given in Figure 1. In this taxonomy, the activity of risk management has two major subactivities: risk assessment and risk control. Risk assessment is further divided into risk identification, risk analysis, and risk prioritization. Risk control is divided into risk-management planning, risk resolution, and risk monitoring. Although we broadly discuss several areas of risk management, our focus in this chapter is on risk assessment, as it applies to networking and, in particular, security issues in networking. Assessment is the starting point and forms the fundamental basis for all risk-management activities. Many risk-assessment methods and techniques have directly analogous application to risk control. In such cases we note this application without elaboration.

The terminology used in the field of risk management varies somewhat among the different business and engineering areas in which it is used; for example, see Boehm (1991), Carr (1993), and Hall (1998). It even varies among writers in the field of risk management. Although most people are unaware that they are doing it, we all engage in risk management on a daily basis. Consider, as an example, a decision, made on the way out the door, whether or not to stuff an umbrella into an uncomfortably heavy bag that will be taken on a 30-minute train ride, followed by a 10-minute walk[1] to the office. The decision is based on a quick, often almost unconscious assessment of the risks involved and how to control them.

On the one hand, there is the probability that the rain predicted by the TV forecaster will actually materialize, that it will be in progress during the drive to the train station and/or during the walk, and, if all goes as badly as it might, that it will cause damage, from the point of view

[1] This example, as well as a number of others in this section, is taken, albeit with considerably more detail, from National Institute of Standards and Technology (2002).

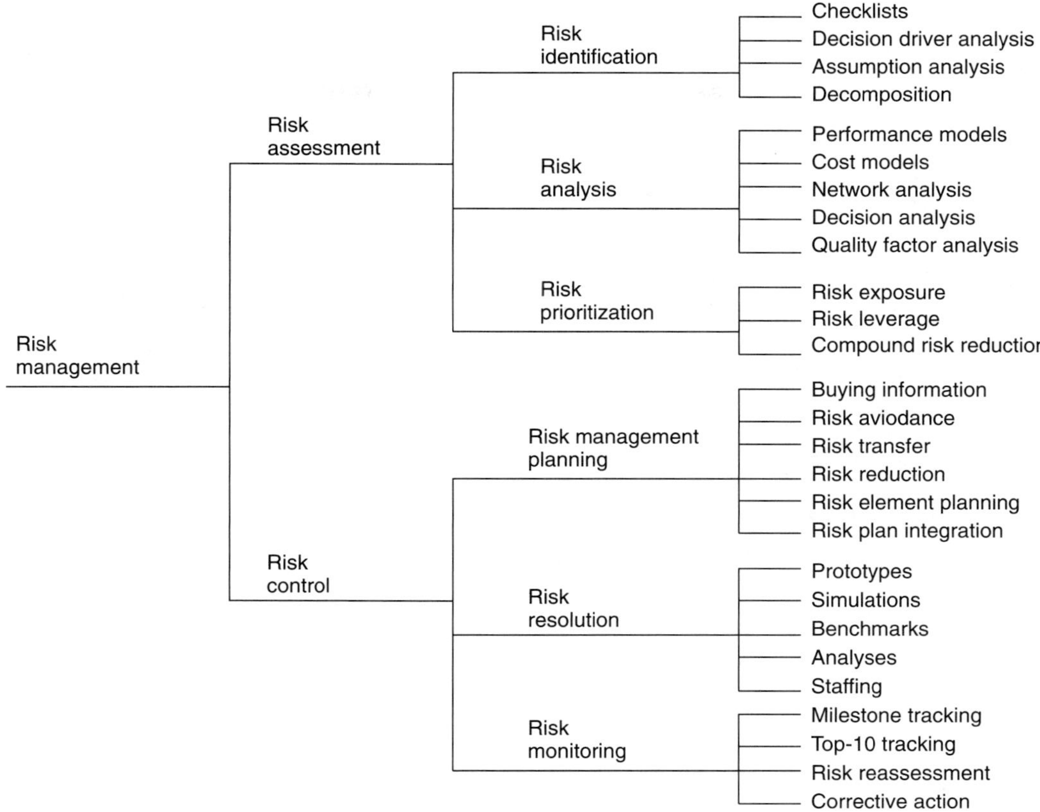

Figure 1: Boehm's risk-management taxonomy

of both walking in drenched clothing and possibly losing work time during the drying-out period. Balanced against all these risks, on the other hand, is the discomfort of carrying the extra weight, of the possibility of having the precariously situated umbrella drop out of the bag and, as it did last week, causing a spillage of hot coffee during the effort to pick it up. An additional consideration is the probability that carrying the umbrella will solve the problem, a consideration that depends on the expected strength of prevailing winds; if the wind proves to be too strong, the umbrella will provide no relief from the rain. An alternative possibility to consider, assuming it is an option, is to work at home all morning and to go to the office only after the rain or its unmaterialized threat has abated.

Network Security Risk Assessment

Networks run the modern business world. As such, networks must provide a high degree of security if those businesses are to survive and prosper. But networks are confronted with many security risks. The following are examples of the consequences that can result from the materialization of network security risks in the specific areas of confidentiality, integrity, and availability:

- Loss of confidentiality:
  - Personal embarrassment resulting from theft and publication of personal financial, health, or other data and possible prosecution and fines for individuals and the organization responsible for maintaining confidentiality
  - Corporate loss of earnings resulting from theft of prepatent technical data
  - Loss of life of a covert intelligence agent resulting from theft and revelation of name and address
- Loss of integrity:
  - Personal embarrassment and possibly fines and imprisonment resulting from insertion into a database of false financial data, implicating the subject in fraud or embezzlement
  - Loss of corporate auditors' ability to detect embezzlement and the attendant loss of funds, resulting from deliberate corruption of financial data by an embezzler
  - Loss of life resulting from changes to a database indicating that a subject is a covert agent when he or she is not
- Loss of availability:
  - Personal embarrassment caused by an inability to keep appointments resulting from temporary inability to use electronic calendar
  - Temporary inability of corporation to issue weekly paychecks to employees, with attendant anger and loss of productivity, resulting from temporary unavailability of hours-worked data

- Loss of initiative, armaments, and lives resulting from battlefield commander's inability to connect to field-support database

The terms *threat, threat source, vulnerability, impact*, and *risk exposure* are in common use in the field of information security assessment. Their application to the trip-to-work scenario is as follows:

- The *threat*, or *threat source*, is the onset of rain, at a sufficiently strong level, during an exposed part of the trip to work.
- The *vulnerability* is the fact that the person involved will get drenched if the threat materializes and the person has no form of shelter (e.g., an umbrella).
- The *impact* is the damage, measured in terms of discomfort and possibly of loss of productivity or even health, that will occur if the threat materializes.
- The *risk exposure* is an assessment, on either a numerical, perhaps monetary, scale or an ordinal scale (e.g., low, medium, or high), of the expected magnitude of the loss given the threat, the vulnerability to it, and its impact, should the threat materialize. In this example, the risk exposure might change if the person is wearing a water-resistant coat.

The first step in risk assessment is *risk identification*—the identification of potential threats, vulnerabilities to those threats, and impacts that would result should they materialize—all of which we presented for the scenario under discussion.

In the trip-to-work scenario, we are concerned with such intangibles as the threat of rain, the vulnerability to getting drenched, and the impact of discomfort, as well as with tangibles such as umbrellas. In the field of networking, we are concerned with systems that store, process, and transmit data/information. Information systems are sometimes localized and sometimes widely distributed; they involve computer hardware and software, as well as other physical and human assets. Tangibles include the various sorts of equipment and media and the sites in which they and staff are housed. Intangibles include notions such as organizational reputation, opportunity or loss of same, productivity or loss of same, etc.

Threat sources are of at least three varieties: natural, human, and environmental:

1. *Natural*: electrical storms, monsoons, hurricanes, tornadoes, floods, avalanches, volcanic eruptions
2. *Human*: incorrect data entry (unintentional), forgetting to lock door (unintentional), failure to unlock door to enable confederate to enter after hours (intentional), denial of service attack (intentional), creation and propagation of viruses (intentional)
3. *Environmental*: failure of roof or wall caused by the use of bad construction materials, seepage of toxic chemicals through ceiling, power outage

Vulnerabilities have various sources, including technical failings such as those reported in the public and professional presses on a daily basis.[2] Fred Cohen (Fred Cohen & Associates 2004) provides an excellent extensive taxonomy of threats and vulnerabilities in his Security Database. One unique aspect of this database is that threats (or causes) are cross-referenced against attack mechanisms to provide a linkage between the cause and the mechanisms used. The attack mechanisms are also cross-referenced against defense mechanisms to indicate which such mechanisms might be effective in some circumstances.

The second step in risk assessment is risk analysis, the estimation and calculation of the risk likelihoods (i.e., probabilities), magnitudes, impacts, and dependencies. This analysis is easy in the case of monetary impacts arising from threat-vulnerability pairs for which the probability of materializing can reasonably be computed, but is considerably harder in most other cases. Special care must be taken when assigning likelihoods, as the quality of the entire risk assessment is strongly dependent on the accuracy and realism of the assigned probabilities.

The final step in risk assessment is risk prioritization; that is, prioritizing all risks with respect to the organization's relative exposures to them. It is typically necessary to use techniques that enable risk comparison, such as calculating risk exposure in terms of potential loss. In the trip-to-work scenario, risks other than the ones discussed above might include the risk associated with not buckling the seat belt during the drive to the station, the risk of an accident during the drive, the risk of missing the train, etc. A meticulous person, one who always leaves the house earlier than necessary and who is very conscious of taking safety precautions, will likely rate these new risks as having far lower exposures than the rain risk: a less meticulous person might do otherwise. In a highly simplified version of a business situation, three threats might be volcanic eruption, late delivery of raw materials, and embezzlement. An organization located in Chicago would likely assign a lower priority to volcanic eruption than would one in southwestern Washington; an organization with suppliers that have never before been late would likely assign a lower priority to late delivery than would an organization using a supplier for the first time. Because there may be threats or vulnerabilities that you may not have included in your analysis, you should draw on the experiences of others to help build a library of threats and vulnerabilities.

Network Security Risk Control

During the risk control phase of the risk-management process, we are concerned with *safeguards*, also known as *controls*. Safeguards fit into at least three categories: technical, management, and operational:

1. *Technical*: authentication (prevention), authorization (prevention), access control (prevention), intrusion detection (detection), audit (detection), automatic backup (recovery), etc.

[2] A compilation of technical threats may be found at http://icat.nist.gov or www.cert.org.

2. *Management*: assign guards to critical venues (prevention) and institute user account initiation and termination procedures (prevention), need-to-know data access policy (prevention), periodic risk reassessment policy (prevention), and organizationwide security training (prevention and detection), etc.
3. *Operational*: secure network hardware from access to any but authorized network administrators and/or service personnel (prevention); bolt desktop PCs to desks (prevention); screen outsiders before permitting entry (prevention); set up and monitor motion alarms, sensors, and closed-circuit TV (detection of physical threat); set up and monitor smoke detectors, gas detectors, fire alarms (detection of environmental threats)

In the trip-to-work scenario, the safeguard that we have considered has a (fairly low-tech) technical component (i.e., the umbrella) and an operational component (i.e., carrying the umbrella). An alternative operational safeguard would be to work at home all morning, if that is an option, and to go to the office only after the rain or the threat of rain has abated.

During the risk-control phase of the risk-management process, we do the following:

- consider alternative individual safeguards and/or complexes of safeguards that might be used to eliminate/reduce/mitigate exposures to the various identified, analyzed, and prioritized threats (risk-management planning)
- perform the cost-benefit analysis required to decide which specific safeguards to use, and institute the relevant safeguards (risk resolution)
- institute a process for continuous monitoring of the network risk situation to detect and resolve problems as they arise and to decide, where and when necessary, to update or change the system of safeguards (risk monitoring)

In business and government organizations, there may be many possible alternative safeguards, including different vendors' hardware and/or software solutions to a particular threat or cluster of threats, alternative management or procedural safeguards, and alternative combinations of technical, management, and procedural safeguards. Complicating matters is the likelihood that different combinations of safeguards address different, overlapping clusters of threats.

Risk resolution begins with the cost-benefit analysis of the various possible safeguards and controls in lowering, to an acceptable level, the assessed risk exposures resulting from the various identified threats, vulnerabilities, and the attendant impacts. Just as we had to consider threats, vulnerabilities, and impacts during risk assessment, we must consider safeguards, their costs, and their efficacies during risk resolution. In the trip-to-work scenario, the marginal cost of the technical component of the umbrella-carrying safeguard is likely nil, as most people already own umbrellas; the operational cost is the discomfort of carrying a heavier bag. Even in this simple example, the safeguard's efficacy must be considered. For example, if the wind proves to be too strong, the umbrella will not reduce the exposure effectively.

Risk Management in Practice

The potential consequences of the materialization of a significant threat to a business or government organization and the obvious fact that risk management can greatly reduce those consequences make it eminently clear that organizations cannot afford *not* to engage in a serious risk-management effort. The smaller the organization and the simpler the threats, the less formal the organization's risk-management effort need be. For the small organization, such as a single retail store belonging to a family, very informal risk management may suffice. In many situations, legal statutes and acquisition policies give an organization no choice. The Hawthorne Principle states that productivity increases as a result of simply paying attention to workers' environments. It is likely, by analogy, that a simple concern with risk management produces significant, though certainly not optimal, results.

However, clearly risk management is rarely easy. In the case of the rare threat-vulnerability pair for which the probability can easily be assigned a numerical value, the impact can be assigned a precise monetary value, and there exists a safeguard with a cost and efficacy that can be pinned down numerically, there is no problem. In other cases, those in which one or more of the parameters can at best be placed on an ordinal scale, matters are more complicated, and approximate methods must be used. Consider, as examples the quantification of the impact of the following:

- personal embarrassment resulting from theft and publication of personal financial, health, or other data; insertion into database of false financial data implicating the subject in fraud or embezzlement; inability to keep appointments resulting from temporary inability to use electronic calendar
- corporate loss of earnings resulting from theft of prepatent technical data
- loss of corporate auditors' ability to detect embezzlement and attendant loss of funds, resulting from deliberate corruption of financial data by an embezzler
- temporary inability of a corporation to issue weekly paychecks to employees, with attendant anger and loss of productivity, resulting from temporary unavailability of hours-worked data
- loss of life of covert intelligence agent resulting from theft and revelation of name and address caused by changes to the database indicating that subject is a covert agent when he or she is not or by the battlefield commander's inability to connect to the field-support database

To aid in the identification and management of risks, a number of risk-management methods and risk taxonomies have been created. The Software Engineering Institute's (SEI) risk taxonomy, for example, divides risk into three classes: product engineering, development environment,

Table 1: Taxonomy of Software Development Risks (from Carr et al., 1993)

Product Engineering	Development Environment	Program Constraints
1. Requirements a. Stability b. Completeness c. Clarity d. Validity e. Feasibility f. Precedent g. Scale	1. Development process a. Formality b. Suitability c. Process control d. Familiarity e. Product Control	1. Resources a. Schedule b. Staff c. Budget d. Facilities
2. Design a. Functionality b. Difficulty c. Interfaces d. Performance e. Testability f. Hardware constraints g. Non-developmental software	2. Development system a. Capacity b. Suitability c. Usability d. Familiarity e. Reliability f. System support g. Deliverability	2. Contract a. Type of contract b. Restrictions c. Dependencies
3. Code and unit test a. Feasibility b. Testing c. Coding/implementation	3. Management process a. Planning b. Project organization c. Management experience d. Program interfaces	3. Program interfaces a. Customer b. Associate contractors c. Subcontractors d. Prime contractor e. Corporate management f. Vendors g. Politics
4. Integration and test a. Environment b. Product c. System	4. Management methods a. Monitoring b. Personnel management c. Quality assurance d. Configuration management	
5. Engineering Specialties a. Maintainability b. Reliability c. Safety d. Security e. Human Factors f. Specifications	5. Work environment a. Quality Attitude b. Cooperation c. Communication d. Morale	

and program constraints. The first level of decomposition of each of these classes is given in Table 1.

This taxonomy is used to "drive" a risk-assessment method. For each class (such as product engineering), and for each element within that class (such as design) and for each attribute of that element (such as performance), there are a set of questions that guide the risk analyst. Depending on the answers to these questions, the analyst might be guided to still further questions that probe the nature of the risk. For example, an analyst looking at performance risks would first ask whether a performance analysis has been done. If the answer is "yes," a follow-up question would ask about the level of confidence in this analysis. Note that security is just one attribute, located under the engineering specialties element. Clearly, to be able to manage security risks we need to delve more deeply into the elements and attributes that are particular to security. We give some examples of risk-management methods tailored for security in the next section.

NETWORK SECURITY RISK-ASSESSMENT METHODS

Risk management is the process of identifying, controlling, and minimizing or eliminating risks that may affect information systems, for an acceptable cost. This chapter has thus far addressed risk assessment. Now we turn to the broader topic of integrating risk assessment with risk management. The notion of risk management was briefly introduced in the previous section. In this section we examine and compare some of the most common and widely used assessment methods for network security risk management: the Operationally Critical Threat, Asset, and Vulnerability Evaluation (OCTAVE 2004) method, and the Survivable Network Analysis Method (Mead et al., 2000), both developed by the Computer Emergency Response Team (CERT) at Carnegie Mellon University (Alberts and Dorofee 2002); and the Facilitated Risk Assessment Process (FRAP), developed by Peltier and colleagues (2003).

There are other forms of risk assessment that may be applied to understanding risks in networks, such as fault tree analysis, probabilistic risk assessment, event trees, and so forth, but we will restrict our attention in this chapter to looking at network *security* risk, since that is the largest source of risk exposure for most organizations.

To facilitate comparison of these risk-assessment methods, we look at their steps and their organization, examining how they do the following:

- establish *context and goals* for the analysis
- *focus* the inquiry
- perform the *analysis*
- *close the loop*, tying analysis outcomes back to their original goals

By examining each of the analysis methods in terms of these categories, we can see where each method places its emphasis.

OCTAVE

The OCTAVE (2004) approach describes a family of security risk evaluation methods that, unlike many other security analysis methods, are aimed at finding *organizational* risk factors and strategic risk issues by examining an organization's security practices (Alberts and Dorofee 2002). Its focus is not on finding specific risks within specific systems, but rather to enable an organization to consider all dimensions of security risk so that it can determine strategic best practices. The OCTAVE approach thus needs to consider not only an organization's assets, threats, and vulnerabilities, as any security method would, but it also asks the stakeholders to explicitly consider and evaluate the organizational impact of security policies and practices. For this reason, an organization's evaluation team must be multidisciplinary, comprising both technical personnel and management.

The OCTAVE process is organized into three phases that are carried out in a series of workshops. In Phase 1—Build Asset-Based Threat Profiles—the team first determines the context and goals for the analysis by describing the information-related assets that it wants to protect. The team does this via a set of structured interviews with senior management, operational management, information technology (IT) staff, and general staff. The team then catalogs the current practices for protecting these assets. The OCTAVE approach then focuses the inquiry by selecting the most important of these assets as *critical assets*, which are the subject of the remainder of the analysis. The evaluation team identifies a set of threats for each critical asset.

In Phase 2—Identify Infrastructure Vulnerabilities—the analysis team performs the analysis by first identifying a set of components that are related to the critical assets and then determining the resistance (or vulnerability) of each component to being compromised. They do this analysis by running tools that probe the identified components for known vulnerabilities.

Finally, in Phase 3—Develop Security Strategy and Plans—the team closes the loop. It examines the impact of the threats associated with each of the critical assets based on the Phase 2 analysis, using a common evaluation basis (for example, a determination of high, medium, or low impact). Based on these evaluations the team determines a course of action for each: a risk-mitigation plan. Instead of merely determining a tactical response to these risks, the goal of the OCTAVE analysis is to determine an organizational "protection strategy" for the critical assets.

As an approach that is aimed at strategic organization-wide risk reduction, OCTAVE also includes activities to ensure that the organization monitors and improves its processes. These risk reduction activities revolve around planning in detail how to implement the protection strategy, implementing the plans, monitoring the plans as they are being implemented to ensure that they are on schedule and are effective, and finally correcting any problems encountered. Thus, the three phases of the OCTAVE approach can be seen as part of a larger picture, encompassing the activities shown in Figure 2.

The OCTAVE approach has been instantiated in two methods to date: OCTAVE and OCTAVE-S. OCTAVE is aimed at large organizations with large, complex information security requirements and infrastructures. OCTAVE-S, on the other hand, is aimed more at smaller

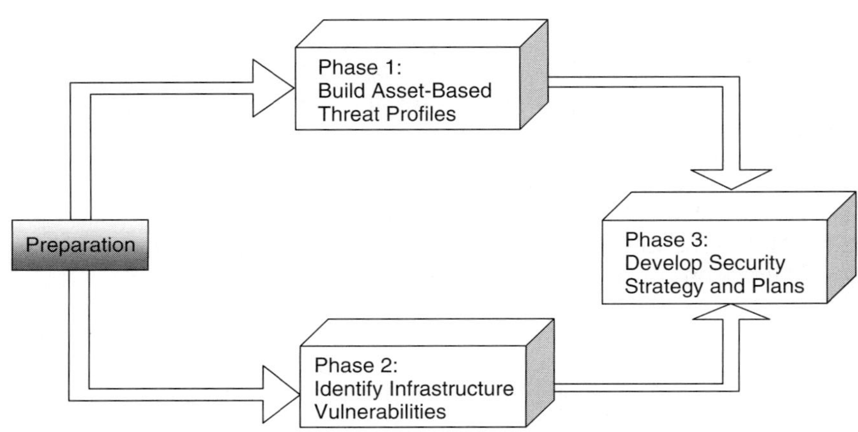

Figure 2: OCTAVE phases

organizations (or smaller subunits of large organizations) with simpler information security needs.

SNAM/SSAM

The SNAM (Survivable Network Analysis Method) (Mead et al. 2000), and its successor the SSAM (Survivable Systems Analysis Method) were created to systematically assess the survivability properties of complex systems. The method consists of a series of working sessions, in which analysts meet with system stakeholders, and results in a briefing on findings and recommendations.

The SNAM method is composed of four steps, as follows:

- Step 2, System Definition: To start, the business goals and mission objectives of the system, current set of requirements, details on the system architecture, and known risks from the operational environment are elicited from the system stakeholders. The capabilities and locations of system users, and the types and volumes of system transactions are recorded. Known system risks are reviewed.
- Step 2, Essential Capability Definition: Next, essential services and assets (assets whose integrity, confidentiality, availability, and other properties must be maintained during attack) are identified. These essential services and assets are characterized as *scenarios*. The scenarios are traced through the architecture to identify essential components whose survivability must be ensured.
- Step 3, Compromisable Capability Definition: A set of representative intrusion scenarios are selected based on assessment of the environment: both known risks and intruder capabilities. These scenarios are mapped onto the system architecture and their execution is traced through the system's representation as a means of identifying components that might be compromised (damaged by some intrusion).
- Step 4, Survivability Analysis: Finally, "soft spot" components of the architecture—components that are both essential and compromisable (based on the outputs of steps 2 and 3)—are now analyzed. These components are examined in terms of their "survivability" properties: resistance, recognition, and recovery. The analysis of these "three Rs" is summarized in a Survivability Map. The map enumerates, for every intrusion scenario and corresponding soft-spot effects, the current and recommended architecture strategies for resistance, recognition, and recovery. The Survivability Map provides feedback to the original architecture and system requirements, and gives management a roadmap for survivability evaluation and improvement.

The SNAM produces the following deliverable items for the system being analyzed:

- A list of system business and mission goals and key requirements
- An inventory of essential services and assets, and essential system architecture components
- A set of scenarios describing potential intrusions
- An identified set of compromisable system architecture components
- A list of architecture vulnerabilities and soft spots
- A determination of mitigation strategies for resistance, recognition, and recovery of each soft spot
- A system survivability map

These deliverables are provided in a final report and briefing, and provide a basis for risk analysis, cost-benefit trade-offs, and system improvement.

The Survivable Network Analysis method has helped organizations be proactive in defining, designing, and implementing system improvements to deal with inevitable intrusions and compromises. The SNAM process raises awareness of survivability exposures in systems; it helps avoid "unpleasant surprises" by providing a management roadmap for addressing exposures before the fact.

FRAP

The Facilitated Risk Assessment Program (FRAP) is a qualitative process developed by Thomas Peltier and colleagues (Peltier et al. 2003). In the FRAP, a system or a segment of a business process is examined by a team that includes both business/managerial and IT personnel. The FRAP guides them to brainstorm potential threats, vulnerabilities, and the potential damages to data integrity, confidentiality, and availability. Based on this brainstorming, the impacts to business operations are analyzed, and threats and risks are prioritized. The FRAP is purely qualitative, meaning that it makes no attempt to quantify risk probabilities and magnitudes. It has three phases, as discussed below.

Phase 1: The Pre-FRAP Meeting

In Phase 1, the initial team members are chosen, and the team determines the scope and mechanics of the review. This process establishes the context and goals of the inquiry. The outputs of Phase 1 are a scope statement, an identification of the team members (typically between 7 and 15 people), a visual model of the security process being reviewed, and a set of definitions. These definitions serve as an anchor to the rest of the process. The FRAP recommends that the team agrees on the following terms: *integrity, confidentiality, availability, risk, control, impact*, and *vulnerability*. Finally, the mechanics of the meeting need to be agreed on: location, schedule, materials, etc.

Phase 2: The FRAP Session

Phase 2 is divided into three parts. These three parts serve as the focusing activity, as well as the front end of the analysis activity. The first activity is to establish the logistics for the meeting: who will take what role (owner, team leader, scribe, facilitator, team member). Once this is done, the team reviews the outputs from Phase 1—the definitions, scope statement, and so forth—to ensure that all team members start from a common basis of understanding. The second activity is brainstorming, in which all of the team members contribute risks that are of concern to them. The third and final activity is prioritization.

Prioritization is ranked along two dimensions: vulnerability (low to high) and impact (low to high). When the risks are documented, the team also contributes suggested controls for at least the high-priority risks.

Phase 3: The Post-FRAP Meeting(s)

Phase 3 may be a single meeting or may be a series of meetings over many days. In this phase the bulk of the analysis work is done, as well as closing the loop. The outputs from the phase are a cross-reference sheet, an identification of existing controls, a set of recommendations on open risks and their identified controls, and a final report. Producing the cross-reference sheet is the most time-consuming activity. This sheet shows all the risks affected by each control, as well as any trade-offs between controls that have been identified. In addition to documenting everything that has been learned in the FRAP, the final report contains an action plan, describing the controls to implement.

Quantitative versus Qualitative Approaches

The security risk management methods described above differ in whether they attempt to quantify security risks or to assess and prioritize risks qualitatively. The OCTAVE process approaches the problem of identifying, analyzing, planning for, and managing security risks quantitatively (in the OCTAVE approach, quantitative analysis of risks is an optional element of phase 3). The FRAP, SNAM, and OCTAVE-S, on the other hand, are purely qualitative. What are the costs and benefits of each approach?

Neither approach is obviously superior to the other. Quantitative methods tend to be more expensive and time consuming to apply and require more front-end work, but they can produce more precise results. Such methods tend to be associated with higher-process mature organizations. Qualitative methods, on the other hand, are less time consuming (and therefore more agile to apply) and require less documentation. In addition, specific loss estimates are often not needed to make a determination to embark on a risk mitigation activity.

In the section on "Practical Strategic Risk Models," we will show how a quantitative security risk assessment practice can be implemented that is not unduly time or resource consuming.

RISK MODELS

At the start of this chapter the fundamental vocabulary and techniques of risk assessment and risk management were introduced. Now we discuss how risk assessment applies to risk management decision making. Our focus will be on "strategic" methods—methods that plan from the outset to achieve particular goals regardless of the circumstances rather than "tactical" methods, which attempt to make the best response in a given circumstance. To do this, we need to take some of the terms that we defined informally above and give them more precise definitions.

Definitions

A *risk*, from the network security perspective, is the potential of loss or damage from some threat that successfully exploits a vulnerability of the network. Risk generally has two dimensions—likelihood and size. The higher the likelihood that a threat will succeed, and the greater the size of the potential loss, the greater the risk to the network.

A *threat*, then, is a stimulus for a risk; it is *any* danger to the system; an undesirable event. A threat, however, might not be a person. The threat itself is not a risk, rather only the possible consequences of that threat incurs risk (i.e., empty threats have no risk). A "threat agent" is a person who initiates or instigates a threat. Typically a threat will take advantage of some network *vulnerability*—a condition in which the system is missing or improperly applying a safeguard or control. The vulnerability increases the likelihood of the threat or its impact, or possibly both. It is important to note that the "network" includes people, not just hardware and software.

The net effect of a vulnerability being exploited by a threat agent is to expose the organization's network-accessible assets to a potential loss. This loss might be in the form of a loss or disclosure of private information, a corruption of the organization's information (a loss of *integrity*), or a denial of services.

In the language of risk, we need to consider simultaneously the magnitude (size) and probability (likelihood) of a risk. A simple quantification of risk in terms of risk exposure (RE) (Boehm 1991) is:

$$RE = \text{probability(loss)} * \text{magnitude(loss)}$$

This is frequently written as $RE = P(L) * S(L)$. For example, if organization A calculates the probability of a key server being down for 2 hours as 10% due to denial of service attacks, and the resulting loss due to the down time to be $20,000, then the risk exposure facing A due to this loss is $2,000

Under general circumstances, we will see that the total potential loss due to a combination of risks is simply the sum of the individual RE. This leads to the *basic risk formula*, which frequently is presented as a summation of all sources of loss to which a network is exposed, therefore:

$$\text{Total RE} = \sum P(L_i) * S(L_i)$$

where L_i is the loss due to the ith risk. For example, if organization A has two other risks that they are facing, one with a probability of 50% and a loss of $1,000 and another with a probability of 0.1% and a loss of $1,000,000 then A's Total RE is:

$$\begin{aligned} &.1 * \$20{,}000 + .5 * \$1{,}000 + 0.001 * \$1{,}000{,}000 \\ &= \$2{,}000 + \$500 + \$1{,}000 \\ &= \$3{,}500 \end{aligned}$$

Related to the notion of RE is *risk reduction leverage* (RRL). RRL is a way of gauging the effectiveness or desirability of a risk reduction technique. The formula for RRL is:

$$RRL = (RE_{before} - RE_{after})/RRCost,$$

where RRCost stands for risk reduction cost. A similar formula can be used to compare the relative effectiveness of technique A with respect to B:

$$RRRL_{A,B} = (RE_B - RE_A)/(RRCost_A - RRCost_B),$$

where RE_A and RE_B are the risk exposures after using A and B, respectively (we assume that the RE before applying the techniques is the same for both techniques). We see that when $RRRL_{A,B} > 0$, technique A is more cost-effective than technique B.

Let us consider an example. Say an organization is considering ways of lowering its risk on a safety-critical network (such as an emergency communications network), and has identified a structured walkthrough or an IV&V (independent validation and verification) activity as two possible ways of finding vulnerabilities and hence reducing the risk. It may proceed as follows; first, it must establish a cost for each risk-reduction technique. Next, it must evaluate its current RE (which is its RE_{before}) and the RE that will result from the application of the technique (the RE_{after}). Let's assume that the organization is interested in the risk involved with the safety-critical network failing. Such a failure would result in a loss to the organization of $10,000,000, and currently the organization believes that there is a 5% likelihood of such an occurrence. Structured walkthroughs have, in the past, been shown to find 80% of the outstanding problems, reducing the probability of a loss to 1%. IV&V is even more effective at finding problems, and it is expected that this technique will reduce the probability of a loss to 0.01%. However, the structured walkthrough is relatively inexpensive, costing just $5,000 (the time of the employees involved). The IV&V, since it is independent, involves hiring a consultant, which will cost $100,000. The RRL for each technique can now be calculated as follows:

$$\begin{aligned} RRL_{inspection} &= (.05*10{,}000{,}000 - .01*10{,}000{,}000)/5{,}000 \\ &= (500{,}000 - 100{,}000)/5{,}000 \\ &= 80 \\ RRL_{IV\&V} &= (0.5*10{,}000{,}000 - .0001*10{,}000{,}000)/100{,}000 \\ &= (500{,}000 - 1{,}000)/100{,}000 \\ &= 4.99 \end{aligned}$$

Clearly, in this case the organization will want to choose to do the inspection first, as its RRL is far greater than the IV&V activity. However this could also be directly seen using:

$$\begin{aligned} RRRL_{inspection,IV\&V} &= (.0001*10{,}000{,}000 - .01*10{,}000{,}000)/(5{,}000 - 100{,}000) \\ &= (1{,}000 - 100{,}000)/(-95{,}000) \\ &= (-99{,}000)/(-95{,}000) = 1.042 > 0 \end{aligned}$$

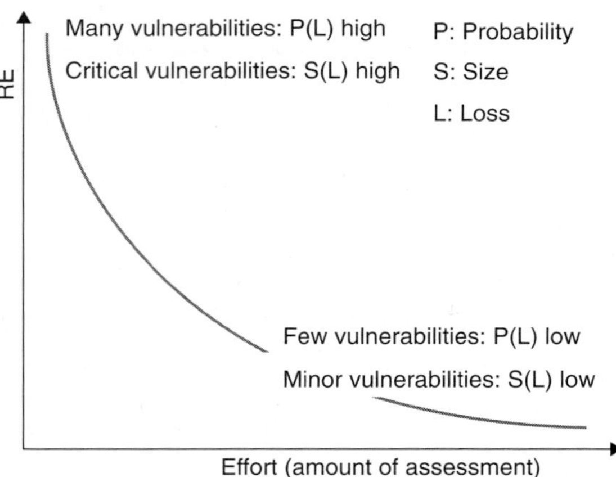

Figure 3: An idealized risk-reduction profile

It is often the case that a technique reduces only the likelihood of a risk and not its magnitude. In this case, the RRL reduces to the cost-benefit (CB):

$$CB = [P_{before}(L) - P_{after}(L)]*S(L)/RRCost = \Delta P(L)*S(L)/RRCost$$

Finally, another thing we can do with RE is to develop a *risk profile* (or *RE profile*) with respect to some measure of interest. For example, one can evaluate RE as a function of a monotonically increasing quantity such as elapsed time, cumulative effort, or cumulative cost. An illustrative risk profile is given in Figure 3.

Given this basis of understanding, we are now in a position to begin looking at specific techniques for strategic risk management.

Strategic Risk Models

Every network in operation will have some degree of security risk. Recall that security risks are possible situations or events that can cause a network harm and will incur some form of loss. Security risks range in impact from trivial to fatal and in likelihood from certain to improbable. Thus far we have only discussed risks that are either "identified," in that they arise from anticipated threats and known vulnerabilities; however, there are also *unidentified* risks, for which this is not the case. Similarly, the impact of an identified risk is either known, meaning the expected loss-potential has been assessed, or unknown, meaning the loss potential has not or cannot be assessed. Risks that are unidentified or have unknown impacts are sometimes loosely labeled as *risks due to uncertainty*. In the case of network security, risk considerations often must focus on uncertainty, since by design, identified known risks are either addressed or accepted as being within a "tolerable" level. Managing risks due to uncertainty is essentially the focus of sound *risk management*. Finally, note that a *risk model* describes risks and their impacts for a particular system.

We consider risk-profile models because risks are generally not static. Likelihoods and impacts change with a number of factors such as time, cost, network state, size, number of users, and so forth. As a consequence it is often desirable to consider risks with respect to a planned set of events such as assessment effort, network operation time, number of nodes, development investment, etc. Representations of risks that dynamically change over planned activities are called "strategic risk models." We would like to use these models to promote effective risk management.

As introduced above, we will use risk *profiling*. Recall that RE is computed as the product of the probability of loss and the size of that loss summed over all sources for a particular risk. Since security risk considerations greatly affect a network's operational value, it is important that these risks be investigated candidly and completely. Expressing network development and operation considerations in terms of risk profiles enables quantitative assessment of attributes that are typically specified only qualitatively. A useful property of RE is that if it is computed entirely within a particular system (i.e., no external loss sources), we may assume that all RE sources are *additive*. This will be true regardless of any complex dependencies and is analogous to mathematical expectation calculations within classic probability theory.

The additivity of RE can be exploited to analyze strategies for managing risk profiles for network security. Such analyses enable cost, schedule, and risk trade-off considerations that help identify effective risk-management strategies. In particular, this approach can help answer difficult questions such as: What particular methods should be used to assess these vulnerabilities? Which method should be used first? and How much is enough [risk assessment, risk mitigation, or risk control]? As in previous sections, our focus will be on risk assessment, noting that the methods presented often have analogous counterparts in risk control.

Strategic Risk Management Methods

The purpose of risk modeling is to aid in risk-management decision making. Management does not necessarily mean removing risk; this is not always possible or even practical. For any risk, there is usually only a limited degree to which that risk can be avoided, controlled, or mitigated (i.e., expected loss reduced). As indicated earlier, there are risks due to uncertainty that cannot be mitigated or even assessed. As such, risk management is the collection of activities used to address the identification, assessment, mitigation, avoidance, control, and continual reduction of risks within what is actually feasible under particular conditions and constraints. As such, the goal of risk management is one of "enlightened gambling," in which we seek an expected outcome that is positive (or as low-risk as practical), regardless of the circumstances. Assessment is the key starting point and, as stated earlier, the focus of this chapter. This includes gaining insight into the following:

- what the risks are and where there is risk due to uncertainty
- differentiating between development risks and operation risks
- avoidable versus unavoidable risks
- controllable versus uncontrollable risks
- cost and benefits of risk mitigation, avoidance, and control

Assessment enables a strategy to be chosen for the mitigation and control of risk. However, it is not obvious from the outset that any given assessment strategy will be effective (or even feasible). In fact, a poorly chosen strategy may actually *increase* overall risk. A strategic risk management method is one that produces a risk-management strategy that reduces overall risk with respect to a particular goal (e.g., most risk reduction at lowest cost). Having a particular goal here is firmly predicated on having acceptable, well-defined strategic risk models, as described above.

We will now describe models and methods for the strategic risk management of IT system security. Such models and methods will aid in making important "pre-crisis" risk-management decisions by determining how much effort (or time) should be invested assessing security risks with respect to project risk factors such as cost, schedule, launch (or operation) window, available skills and technology, uncontrollable external events, and so forth. In this way, we lay the foundation for a practical, economically feasible, empirically based approach for the strategic planning of risk-management efforts.

The Need for Strategic Risk Management Methods

To illustrate the need for strategic risk management we consider a general IT security risk assessment. The risk exposure corresponding to the cumulative potential loss from security violations in the operational network (e.g., intrusions) will be called $RE_{security}$. In the case of network security risk assessment, the more assessment that is done, the lower $RE_{security}$ is that results from unforeseen or uncontrolled vulnerabilities (i.e., uncertainty) such as those listed in Table 1. Assessed security attributes reduce both the size of loss due to "surprises" and the probability that surprises still remain. Prior to embarking on a security risk assessment, the network will likely contain many potential vulnerabilities, either known or from uncertainties. This results in an initially high (relative to the project) probability of loss—P(L)—value. In this, some may be critical, and so S(L), the size of the loss, will be high. Thus, without any assessment $RE_{security}$ initially will be high. When assessment has been used, the likelihood of unidentified vulnerabilities will be reduced. If assessment is done thoroughly (and identified vulnerabilities are addressed), most of the vulnerabilities remaining are likely to be minor, and $RE_{security}$ will be low.

It is generally not feasible to be totally exhaustive when performing a system assessment. As a result, the ideal assessment risk-reduction profile (as illustrated in Figure 3) is where $RE_{security}$ decreases as rapidly as possible at the beginning. This profile is ideal because it provides the maximum risk reduction for an arbitrary amount of security assessment effort. As stated previously, most strategies are nonideal, and the ideal profile must be expressly sought.

To give a concrete example of how a nonideal risk-reduction profile may occur, consider the data in Figure 4

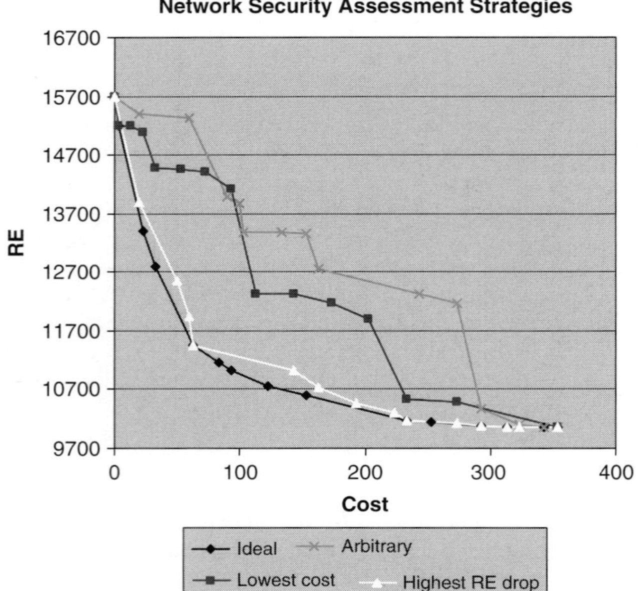

Figure 4: Example of $RE_{security}$ profiles

taken from a space systems ground-control network. The data were generated by assessing each relevant security attribute in Table 2 for S(L), in terms of percentage of the project value lost that would result from the exploitation of a vulnerability in this attribute; and ΔP(L) for the corresponding change in probability (as a percentage) of an exploitation occurring. These, in turn, are used to calculate the corresponding RE reductions if the attribute is fully assessed. The RE has been normalized to the fractional portion of the total known RE that can be reduced through assessment. The cost is effort in hours used to perform the assessment of the attribute. Each attribute was assessed using an extensive security review checklist for that attribute.

We see that some care must be taken in choosing the order (i.e., strategy) to perform the assessments to achieve the ideal risk reduction profile illustrated in Figure 3. Figure 4 compares the RE profiles of four strategies for performing the assessments. Each tick mark on the graph for each RE profile corresponds to the assessment of a particular attribute. Note that if the attributes are assessed in an arbitrarily order (i.e. the "arbitrary strategy"), the curve will typically look like the approximately linear curve indicated in the top of Figure 4 and clearly does not achieve the ideal of Figure 3. Another strategy is simply to do the least-cost assessments first. This generally results in the non-ideal $RE_{security}$ reduction profile indicated in the second to the top curve in Figure 4. A common recommended strategy is to prioritize the assessments from highest RE reductions first. Indeed, this will deliver a significant improvement over the other strategies discussed as indicated in the third to the top RE profile in Figure 4, however it is still not ideal. It is seen that performing the assessments in the order of highest cost-benefit (CB) will archive the desired $RE_{security}$ reduction profile. It can be shown that under fairly general circumstances, this will always be true.

We illustrated the strategic method with only risk assessment, but analogous methods exist for risk control. The important point here is that without a strategic approach, you are likely to end up with a less than ideal $RE_{security}$ reduction profile as indicated in Figure 4, resulting in inefficient use of your risk-management resources. This should not be taken lightly because frequently all assessment tasks are not, or cannot be, performed. Typically, assessment efforts are terminated when an arbitrarily defined budget is expended (rather than completed assessments), or when people "feel" as though enough risk has been reduced, or more commonly, when higher priority is given to tasks other than risk management. The outcome is a network with a high degree of risk due to uncertainty, resulting in the predictable consequences for "blind" risk taking (Basili and Boehm 2001; Tran and Liu 1997).

Table 2: Examples of Network Security Attributes

A1: Denial of service	A8: File deletions
A2: System crash	A9: Access to private data
A3: Message queue overflow	A10: Hardware Failure
	A11: Access to code
A4: System fault	A12: Resource utilization
A5: Misled operator	A13: Requirement consistency and completeness
A6: Unauthorized access	
A7: Unauthorized administrator	A14: Understandability

Practical Strategic Risk Models

In this section we look at how strategic methods may be applied in practice. This includes using strategic models to help make complex planning decisions such as "How much is enough risk assessment?" and extending the strategic method to account for multiple techniques.

Multitechnique Strategic Methods

To begin with, note that in our particular example the differences between risk-reduction strategies do not appear very pronounced. One reason for this is purely an artifact of the normalization of the RE scale. If *absolute* RE is used (that is, the actual risk is removed rather than the relative risk reduced), the difference will become more pronounced. There is a small concern that the absolute risk-reduction profile may not be consistent with the relative-risk reduction profile. However, under general circumstances it can be shown that an optimal relative risk-reduction implies an optimal absolute risk-reduction profile.

The application of a strategic method assumes that we are able to generate practical strategic risk models. From the above discussion it is clear that we always want to apply the most appropriate and effective risk-management approach for each risk. Allowing for multiple assessment techniques can greatly increase the risk-reduction cost-benefit ratio. How to do this in general is not entirely without complications. For example, in generating a multiple-attribute strategy we must account for the possibility that for some attributes, a particular assessment technique may not apply (e.g., model checking for unauthorized administrator) or may not be cost-effective (e.g., prototyping for misled operator). We now present an algorithm that generates a practical, cost-effective strategy for multiple attributes and respective assessment techniques. We assume that each attribute is to be assessed only once by exactly one technique (i.e., we do not allow partial assessment with one technique then further assessment with another). Our goal here is to first choose which technique is best to use for each particular attribute, then choose in which order to perform the techniques to achieve an ideal absolute risk reduction with respect to cost, as illustrated in Figure 3. The following algorithm will generate such a strategy:

Step 1: Identify the most significant system assessment attributes. Label them $A_1,\ldots, A_n$

Step 2: Identify the most significant assessment techniques (e.g., product testimonials, prototyping, etc.) applicable to the project and available resources (e.g., staff skills, tools). Label them $T_1,\ldots, T_n$

Step 3: Estimate the relative probabilities $P(A_i)$ and size $S(A_i)$ quantities for potential losses associated with attributes $i = 1, \ldots, n$ before any assessment. If desired $RE(A_i)$ can be estimated directly, perhaps from historical data.

Step 4: Estimate the cost $C(A_i,T_j)$, size $S(A_i,T_j)$, and probability $P(A_i,T_j)$ after assessment of A_i with T_j and the change in risk exposures $\Delta RE(A_i,T_j) = P(A_i) * S(A_i) - S(A_i,T_j) * P(A_i,T_j)$

Step 5: Calculate the benefit matrix $B(A_i,T_j) = \Delta RE(A_i,T_j) - C(A_i,T_j)$. For each A_i find the T_k where $B(A_i,T_k)$ is maximum. Set $c_i = k$.

Step 6: Calculate the RRL list, $RRL(A_i,Tc_i) = \Delta RE(A_i,Tc_i)/C(A_i,Tc_i)$ for $i = 1, \ldots, n$. Let $T(k) = (r_1,c_1)$ be the values for the corresponding attribute r_1, technique c_1 of the kth largest element in the RRL list. That is, $T(1)$ is the maximum $RRL(A_i,Tc_i)$ and $T(n)$ is the minimum.

Step 7: Graph the cumulative RE drop, $RE(n) = RE_{total} - \sum_{k=1}^{n} \Delta RE_{T(k)}$ versus cumulative effort $C(n) = \sum_{k=1}^{n} C_{T(k)}$.

The preceding process produces an ideal $RE_{security}$ risk-reduction strategy as presented, and it easily generalizes to risk-control management activities. The strategy dictates to perform $T(k)$ for $k = 1,2,3,\ldots$ until the cost outweighs the benefit (i.e. $RRL_{T(k)} < 1$) unless other risk reduction goals are desired (this will be discussed further in the next section). The algorithm assumes that the entire effort allocated for each $T(k)$ will be expended and then the attribute will not be assessed further. As a result, there may be more optimal strategies that allow for partial effort using multiple techniques per attribute. Multiple-attribute optimization techniques such as using simulated annealing could potentially be applied to find these but will not be discussed further here. Since the algorithm is somewhat involved, an example to illustrate it is presented in Tables 2a, 2b, 2c, 2d, and 2e, resulting in the $RE_{security}$ reduction strategy displayed in Figure 5. For a technique that is not applicable to a given attribute, an 'X' is placed in the relevant values and these are excluded from the calculations.

Although this appears to be somewhat complex at first, the algorithm is actually fairly straightforward to implement and use. For example, the all analysis for this example could be done completely within a spreadsheet.

Strategic Decision Making and Competing Risks

With strategic risk models, the strategic method can be used to provide practical answers to difficult questions such as "how much is enough?" risk assessment, mitigation, or control activities. This question is critically important because in practice it is not feasible to implement exhaustive risk reduction due to constraints on resources (e.g., budget, personnel, schedule, technology limitations). Even without such constraints, it is frequently impossible to reduce a risk to zero or even to determine all possible risks for any given system. The best we can strive for is to reduce risk as much as possible within the given resources and uncertainties.

Recall that as we saw in our example in Figure 4, in the single technique case ordering risk-reduction activity from highest to lowest RRL results in the "ideal" risk-reduction profile. It can be shown that, with respect to cost considerations, this is the optimal ordering for reducing risk when only a fraction of the risk-reduction activities will be performed. That is, if risk-reduction activity

Table 2a: Attribute Size and Probability of Loss (Steps 1, 2, and 3)

	misop	syscr	sysft	unacc	denos	RE_{total}
S(L)	500000	50000	20000	250000	90000	
P(L)	0.8	0.6	0.3	0.7	0.9	
RE	400000	30000	6000	175000	81000	692000

The following abbreviations are for all parts of Table 2: denos = denial of service; misop = misled operator; pdt = product testimonials; ppy = product prototyping; rvc = review checklist; syscr = system crash; sysft = system fault; unacc = unauthorized access.

Table 2b: (attribute *i*, technique *j*) Cost (step 4)

$C(A_i,T_j)$	pdt	rvc	ppy
misop	1000	3000	X
syscr	2000	10000	20000
sysft	X	6000	20000
unacc	2000	8000	X
denos	1000	4000	22000

Table 2c: (attribute *i*, technique *j*) RE Reduction (step 4)

$\Delta RE(A_i,T_j)$	pdt	rcv	ppy
misop	100000	150000	X
syscr	5000	10000	25000
sysft	X	2000	4000
unacc	25000	100000	X
denos	18000	9000	45000

Table 2d: (attribute *i*, technique *j*) Benefit (step 5)

$B(A_i,T_j)$	pdt	rcv	ppy
misop	99000	147000	X
syscr	3000	0	5000
sysft	X	−4000	−16000
unacc	23000	92000	X
denos	17000	5000	23000

Table 2e: (attribute *i*, technique *j*) Risk Reduction Leverage (step 6)

$RRL(A_i,T_j)$	pdt	rcv	ppy
misop	100	50	X
syscr	2.5	1	1.25
sysft	X	0.333	0.2
unacc	12.5	12.5	X
denos	18	2.25	2.045

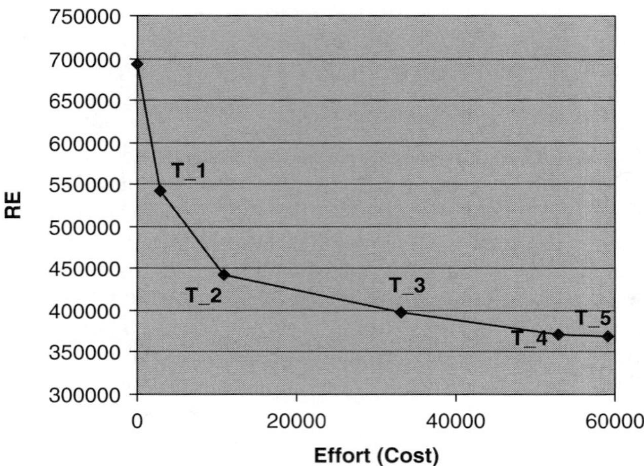

Figure 5: $RE_{security}$ reduction $T(k)$ (step 7)

is stopped at any point, there is no other ordering that reduces more risk and leaves less total risk when the remaining activities are not done. The algorithm described above extends this to the use of multiple techniques. In the strategic model if cost is the only consideration, then a natural answer to how much is enough is when the cost exceeds the risk reduction benefit. Since the ordering of RRL is decreasing, there will be no activity beyond this point that would decrease the risk more than the cost for any of the previous activities.

The difficulty with using this stopping point is that it only accounts for cost with respect to the investment in security risk reduction activity. Furthermore, it assumes that cost and risk are equally exchangeable. In practice, this is not typical, and moreover, management activities always imply direct or collateral risks. For example, a system patch may do a marvelous job plugging a critical network venerability for a type of operating system virus, but perhaps it also takes a long time to implement and disseminate, is difficult to install, and slows the system significantly or causes it to be unstable or keep important applications from running. The resulting loss in productivity to the installed base may prove significant. A more prudent action may be to quickly release a means of identifying and removing the particular virus threat at hand and perhaps delay the deployment of a

Table 2f: Strategic Order (attribute *i*, technique *j*) (step 6)

$T(k)$	Attribute	Technique	$\Delta RE_{T(k)}$	$Cost_{T(k)}$	$B_{T(k)}$	$CB_{T(k)}$	$RE_{total} - \sum \Delta RE_{T(k)}$	$\sum Cost_{T(k)}$
Start	None	None	None	None	None	None	692000	0
T_1	misop	rcv	150000	3000	147000	50	542000	3000
T_2	unacc	rcv	100000	8000	92000	12.5	442000	11000
T_3	syscr	pdt	45000	22000	23000	2.045	397000	33000
T_4	denos	ppy	25000	20000	5000	1.25	372000	53000
T_5	sysft	rcv	2000	6000	−4000	0.333	370000	59000

patch. In this example, the risk-reduction activity of developing and disseminating a patch may indirectly but consequently increase the overall system risk despite the worthy, cost-effective investment in its deployment. The challenge here is of *competing dependent risks*. That is, while one activity is reducing risk, there is another (event or activity) simultaneously increasing risk, and it is unclear which could be the cause of a loss. What is clear is that the benefits of risk reduction investments are negated when an increasing risk is greater than the decreasing risk, since in such cases the overall risk increases. When a competing dependent risk is simply proportional to the cost, it can be easily accounted for in $RE_{security}$ as an additional factor in its computation. This is typically an unrealistic assumption to make given that in general, increasing security decreases access in a disproportionate way. Such decreases in access, while often important from a security perspective, may also negatively impact the usability of a network, as will be elaborated next.

Usability Risk

Our system patch example is only one indication of competing dependent risks. There are a host of others that as a group impact the ability of users to make effective use of a network. For this exposition, we refer to such considerations collectively as *risk with respect to usability* or $RE_{usability}$ and these risks are of a fundamentally different nature than $RE_{security}$. Such risks can negatively impact or even paralyze a system to the point that the system will fail to meet its intended operational goals. $RE_{usability}$ may result in losses due to nonuse of the system when required or expected, from dissatisfied customers and users, or from productivity losses when system functions are inaccessible or unreliable. $RE_{usability}$ will monotonically increase since $RE_{usability}$ represents the cumulative potential losses resulting from the inability to make effective use of a network system. We assume that a system starts out with no risk of usability and that any network security risk management effort expended contributes to the overall increase in usability risk. Calculating $RE_{usability}$ can pose a considerable challenge, as usability concerns are often relative to the characteristics of the user (e.g., patience, attention to detail, urgency in job activities, etc.). Fortunately, for our needs a crude approximation of $RE_{usability}$ will be sufficient. To address this, we note that it has been empirically suggested that because of compounding of factors, $RE_{usability}$ increases supralinearly (Platt 1999). Owing to this, a reasonably good approximation of the $RE_{usability}$ risk profile can be generated through the identification of a few well-chosen successive data points. Here we consider the following three "critical points" to be relevant:

Point 1:—Usability problems identified (or identifiable). During the analysis and design of network security efforts, usability problems may be identified, but the full impact of these has not yet been assessed or experienced. This is early in the network security management effort (small cost investment) and increases overall usability risk moderately, as losses are not widely being realized.

Point 2:—Usability problems reported, After initial deployment of some network security measures, usability is notably impacted and losses are being realized.

Point 3:—System is effectively unusable. When overly aggressive network security measures are taken, the network may become unstable, effectively inaccessible, or too cumbersome to use (e.g., draconian access policies). The system no longer realizes its intended value by the users. When losses due to this are unrecoverable (e.g., corrupted data, shut-out users, missed business opportunities, etc.) then it is considered "effectively unusable."

The schedule for points 1, 2, 3 are necessarily sequential, and the amounts of time (in terms of effort or cost expended) to arrive at these points are cumulative; hence $RE_{usability}$ is successively nondecreasing at these points. Moreover, the change in $RE_{usability}$ between points 1 and 2 can never be less than that between the starting point and point 1; similarly for points 2 and 3. The critical points for our example project are contained in Table 3 and the resulting $RE_{usability}$ profile is illustrated in Figure 6.

As is evident in our example, creating appropriate risk models (e.g., $RE_{security}$, $RE_{usability}$) requires an organization to accumulate a fair amount of calibrated experience on the nature of the risks, their probabilities, and their magnitudes with respect to the risk-management effort (e.g., cost, duration). In general this can be challenging and costly; however, there are many practical approaches and software tools that address these topics specifically

Table 3: Example of $RE_{usability}$ Critical Points

Point	S(L)	P(L)	RE	Cost
Identified	138400	0.15	20760	8850
Exploited	311400	0.4	124560	29500
Total loss	622800	0.9	560520	64900

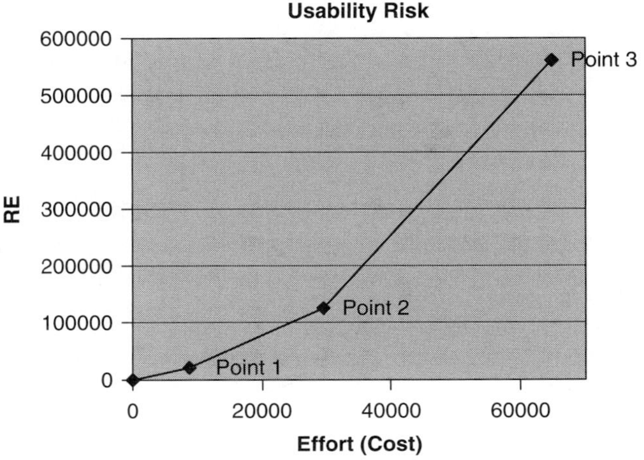

Figure 6: Example $RE_{usability}$ profile

(see, for example, Tran and Liu 1997; Ochs et al. 2001; Hall 1998; Boehm 1991).

Balancing Competing Risks for Strategic Network Security Planning

The general approach in answering a "how much is enough network security" question in the face of competing dependent risks is to optimize $RE_{security}$ with respect to $RE_{usability}$. Depending on the models used, this amounts to "balancing" the risk-reduction benefit of risk management and control activities with risk increases due to cost expenditures of dollars, effort, schedule, accessibility, and so forth.

Consider again our risk assessment example. We have noted previously that it is important to have an efficient strategy for reducing $RE_{security}$ and that such a strategy may be generated by assessing the attribute-technique pairs and applying the strategic method described in the section on "Multitechnique Strategic Methods." We have indicated that security measures reduce $RE_{security}$ by removing system vulnerabilities while simultaneously increasing $RE_{usability}$ due to their imposition on access. Too much security will put the system increasingly at risk, as it exceeds the $RE_{usability}$ critical points. However, too little security will leave the system with too much risk because of uncertainty within the vulnerabilities. The ideal security strategy decreases $RE_{security}$ but does not expend so much effort that this reduction is dominated by $RE_{usability}$. This is a formal response to the "how much is enough?" question. This derives directly from the general (yet often misunderstood) risk management principle:

> If it's risky to not secure, DO secure (e.g., uncertain, high loss potential, unprecedented);
>
> If it's risky to secure, DO NOT secure (e.g., well-established, well-known, highly tested, robust).
>
> (Boehm 1991)

The above principle provides a simple rationale for balancing $RE_{security}$ and $RE_{usability}$ and determining an effective amount of security *before* committing to a particular security strategy. Assuming we have generated a strategic $RE_{security}$ profile as described in the section on "Multitechnique Strategic Methods," then the optimal effort to expend will be where $RE_{security} + RE_{usability}$ is minimal. Although we know there are many dependencies among these risk factors, we are taking advantage of the remarkable previously mentioned fact that the REs are additive. As shown in Figure 7a, the decreasing $RE_{security}$ and increasing $RE_{usability}$ will have a minimum—the "sweet spot" at some intermediate point of effort. As a result of our risk-management principle, a strategic stopping point for the security effort is when this intermediate point has been reached. The sweet spot determination for the examples discussed in Figure 5 and Figure 6 is shown in Figure 7b. In this case, the purely cost-benefit analysis would recommend stopping security efforts at step T_4, however, accounting for $RE_{usability}$ indicates that T_3 is a more strategic stopping point.

The location of the sweet spot will vary by type of organization. For example, for the network in an internet service provider (ISP) in which $RE_{usability}$ increases rapidly because of high usability needs (e.g., market pressures and demanding customers with diverse needs), results in a sweet spot pushed to the left, indicating that less security effort should be expended. In contrast, a security-critical network, such as for a bank will have greater $RE_{security}$ because of larger potential losses. The sweet spot is pushed to the right, indicating that more security should be done. This is illustrated in Figure 7a.

Unsuitable Sweet Spots

There are situations in which the sweet spot is not an acceptable determination of how much assessment to perform. Acceptability is achieved only when (as indicated in Figure 7a) the RE at sweet spot is below a given risk tolerance and the effort at the sweet spot is less than the effort at critical point 3. Although, ideally, the assessment effort should be less than the effort at point 1, for most projects the additional risk incurred by passing this point is tolerable (Basili and Boehm 2001). In our example in Figure 7b we see the sweet spot is well past point 2. Because critical point 2 is where users have already begun reporting usability issues, depending on an organization's goals and policies, this may be unacceptable.

In Figure 7a there is an indication of an acceptable risk tolerance level, and the sweet spot lies below this level. What can be done if it lies above the acceptable risk tolerance level? There are two solutions: find another security approach (e.g., more cost-effective techniques) that can

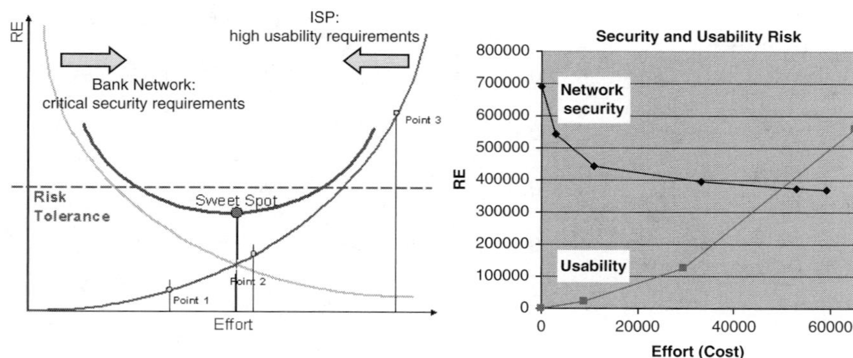

Figure 7: (a) Balancing $RE_{security}$ and $RE_{usability}$. (b) Sweet spot for example

lower $RE_{security}$, or mitigate potential losses due to usability (e.g., user training, faster hardware) in order to lower $RE_{usability}$. It is best if both approaches are applied simultaneously. If the sweet-spot effort exceeds the effort for point 2, the only reasonable approach is to find another security approach that can lower $RE_{security}$ more quickly or reconsider the organization's policies. Paradoxically, if $RE_{usability}$ were increased, say by imposing greater cost, schedule, or effort constraints, this too could potentially move the sweet-spot effort in front of point 2. However, the price to pay for this is a heavy increase in the overall risk, which likely will exceed the tolerable level.

PRACTICAL RISK EXPOSURE ESTIMATION

A risk-management program relies critically on the ability to estimate representative risk exposures. It is tempting to expend a large amount of effort to obtain precise results; however, this may prove untenable or impractical. Fortunately, for strategic method applications estimates do not have to be precise. In this section we will describe one practical approach to estimating risk exposures.

Qualitative Methods

Recall that calculating RE for a given risk involves estimating the probability of a potential loss P(L) and the size of that possible loss S(L). The challenge of estimating S(L) lies in quantifying intangibles such as "loss of reputation." There are numerous techniques that claim the ability to address this challenge; however, we have found that estimating highly subjective loss potentials is best accomplished by choosing a tangible "standard" within the particular context at hand and then establishing the remaining values relative to this standard. For example, an organization determined that because of lost sales they lost $1,000 for every minute their central sales system was down. If the sales system was down for more than 4 hours, their reputation as an "easy to buy from" company would be degraded and fewer customers would return. The minimum loss of 4*60*$1,000 = $240,000 was considered a "3" on a scale from 0 to 10 in terms of loss magnitude, and the loss of return customers was considered a 5 relative to this monetary loss. These size estimates can be used for RE calculations so long as all loss potentials are translated into loss magnitudes from 0 to 10 relative to the system down time.

In general it is difficult to calculate P(L) directly. This is primarily due to a lack of representative models that are able to generate an appropriate probability distribution. Even though there are many wonderful candidate parameter-based models, frequently there is not enough available data to calibrate and validate them.

One alternative to parametric models is to make use of a qualitative "betting analogy" as described in the following steps:

Step 1: For the risk under consideration, define a "satisfactory" level.

Step 2: Establish a personally meaningful amount of money, say, $100.

Step 3: Determine how much money you would be willing to risk in betting on a satisfactory level.

Step 4: Establish a proposition (e.g., Using a virus checker will avoid infection and loss of data).

Step 5: Establish betting odds (e.g., No loss of data: you win $100; infection and loss of data: you lose $500).

Step 6: Determine willingness to bet:

Willing: low probability

Unwilling: high probability

Not sure: there is risk due to uncertainty, so need to buy information

Express your willingness to bet with respect to the risk under consideration

e.g. We are likely to take this bet

For whatever qualifies your willingness-to-bet statement (in our example the qualification is "likely," use an adjective calibration chart such as the one illustrated in Figure 8 to get an estimate of the risk probability.

Empirical Approaches

Empirical methods rely on generating risk-exposure estimates based on observations, historical data, or experiments. One of the attractive properties of risk exposure is that it represents the expectation (or mean value) of the potential losses associated with a risk event. Under quite general conditions, this value can be approximated with the sample mean. Say you have losses $L_1, L_2, \ldots, L_n$ associated with a particular risk area, then

$$RE \approx \frac{1}{n}\sum_{i=1}^{n} L_i$$

Consult any college-level statistics book for further details on this. We can make use of this result in several ways, depending on whether or not historical risk loss data and risk event models are available. Historical risk loss data is the recorded losses realized from actual projects that were exposed to the risk (i.e., the risk actually occurred) under consideration. A risk-event model is a dynamic representation of all the possible losses and conditions under which those losses would occur.

Delphi Studies: No Historical Data, No Risk-Event Model

You may have noticed that the betting analogy relies on having a credible adjective-calibration table. These tables might have been based on surveying local experts. This technique can be used directly to estimate risk exposures. If a representative group of experts are available, a *Delphi study* (Helmer 1966) often provides workable risk-exposure estimates. Such a study would survey experts to estimate risk-exposure values and then calculate the sample mean as an estimate for the actual risk exposure. To avoid getting erroneous results, Delphi studies should not be undertaken haphazardly. There are a variety of well documented methods for conducting Delphi studies that should be followed to ensure valid results.

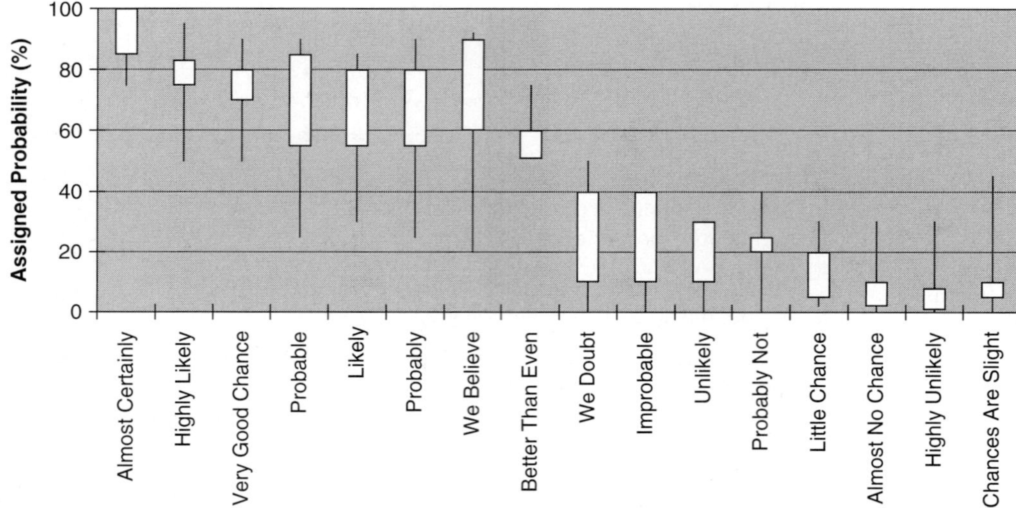

Figure 8: Probability adjective calibration table (what uncertainty statements mean to different readers)

Risk Sampling: Historical Data Available, No Risk-Event Model

If there is a reasonable amount of historical loss data available that is representative (unbiased) then risk sampling may be an effective means of estimating risk exposures. Calculate the estimated risk exposure by taking the sample mean of the historical data. However, it is likely that the data set will be small and the estimate may be poor. Under these conditions, bootstrapping and jackknifing methods (Effron and Gong 1983) may be used to improve estimates.

Risk-Event Simulation: No Historical Data Available, Risk-Event Model Available

When historical data are lacking (or nonexistent) and you are able to model the particular risk events under consideration, then risk-event simulation may provide a means of estimating risk exposures. Usually this amounts to creating a series of random events to run through the risk model and then calculate the sample mean to estimate the risk exposure. The idea here is to create a dynamic simulation of the risk events and run a series of experiments to get a representative collection of loss values. There are a host of powerful tools that can be of great use in creating and running these simulations. Two examples are the Simulink package for Matlab (www.mathworks.com) and also Modelica for Dymola (www.dynasim.com).

Pitfalls to Avoid

As indicated in the above discussions, there are many possible complications in estimating risk exposures, such as using insufficient or biased data. Of all the potential complications, perhaps the most common and troublesome is the problem of *compound risks*—a dependent combination of risks. Some examples are:

- Addressing more than one threat
- Managing threats with key staff shortages
- Vague vulnerability descriptions with ambitious security plans
- Untried operating system patches with ambitious release schedule

You must watch out for compound risks. The problem is that the dependencies complicate the probabilities in difficult-to-determine ways. When you identify a compound risk, it is best to reduce it to a noncompound risk, if possible. If the dependencies are too strong or complex, then this may not be possible. In this case you should plan to devote extra attention to containing such risks.

CONCLUSION

In this chapter, we have shown a number of network risk assessment and management techniques. This is a rich and growing field of inquiry, and it reaches deep into technical as well as organizational and managerial practices. The key insights that the reader should take away from this chapter are that: (1) network risk management is effective only to the degree that risk assessment is effective; and (2) it is not obvious how to go about applying individual security techniques (of which there are many) to ensure an optimal result at the level of the organization.

To address these issues we have described and demonstrated a strategic method for quantitatively assessing network risk that is probably optimal with respect to cost-benefit. This gives a manager a powerful tool for managing network risk.

GLOSSARY

FRAP: Facilitated Risk Assessment Program

OCTAVE: Operationally Critical Threat, Asset, and Vulnerability Evaluation

Risk: Possibility of loss or injury; a situation or event that can cause a project to fail to meet its goals

Risk Assessment: A set of activities aimed at quantifying the level of risk, consisting of risk identification, risk analysis, and risk prioritization.

Risk Control: A set of activities aimed at managing overall project risk, consisting of risk management planning, risk resolution, and risk monitoring

Risk Exposure: A quantification of the damage due to a risk, calculated as the product of the probability of a loss and the size of the loss, e.g., RE = Prob(loss) * Size(loss)

SNAM: Survivable Network Analysis Method

SSAM: Survivable Systems Analysis Method

CROSS REFERENCES

See *Computer Network Management*; *Network Capacity Planning*; *Network Reliability and Fault Tolerance*; *Network Traffic Management*; *Network Traffic Modeling*.

REFERENCES

Alberts, C., and A. Dorofee. 2002. *Managing information security risks*: The OCTAVE approach. Reading, MA: Addison-Wesley.

Basili, V., and B. Boehm. 2001. COTS-based systems top 10 list. *IEEE Computer* 34(5):91–5.

Boehm, B. 1991. Software risk management: Principles and practices. *IEEE Software* 8:32–41.

Carr, M. J., S. L. Konda, I. Monarch, F. C. Ulrich, and C. F. Walker. 1993. Taxonomy-based risk identification, Technical report CMU/SEI-93-TR-6. www.sei.cmu.edu/publications/documents/93.reports/93.tr.006.html (accessed May 7, 2007).

Fred Cohen & Associates. 2004. Security database. http://all.net (accessed May 7, 2007).

Effron, B., and G. Gong. 1983. A leisurely look at the bootstrap, the jackknife, and cross-validation. *The American Statistician* 37:36–48.

Hall, E. M. 1998. *Managing risk. Reading*, MA: Addison Wesley Longman.

Helmer, O. 1966. *Social technology*. New York: Basic Books.

Mead, N., R. Ellison, R. Linger, T. Longstaff, and J. McHugh. Survivable network analysis method. Technical report CMU/SEI-2000-TR-013. www.sei.cmu.edu/publications/documents/00.reports/00tr013.html (accessed May 7, 2007).

National Institute of Standards and Technology. 2002. Risk management guide for information technology systems. NIST Special Publication 800-30. http://csrc.nist.gov/publications/nistpubs/800-30/sp800-30.pdf (accessed May 7, 2007).

Ochs, M., D. Pfahl, G. Chrobok-Diening, and B. Nothelfer-Kolb. 2001. A method for efficient measurement-based COTS assessment and selection—Method description and evaluation results. http://csdl2.computer.org/persagen/DLAbsToc.jsp?resourcePath=/dl/proceedings/&toc=comp/proceedings/metrics/2001/1043/00/1043toc.xml&DOI=10.1109/METRIC.2001.915536 (accessed May 27, 2007).

Operationally Critical Threat, Asset, and Vulnerability Evaluation (OCTAVE). 2004. OCTAVE CERT Coordination Center, Software Engineering Institute at Carnegie Mellon University; www.cert.org/octave (accessed May 7, 2007).

Peltier, T., J. Peltier, and J. A. Blackley. 2003. *Managing a network vulnerability assessment*. Boca Raton, FL: Auerbach Publications.

Platt, A. 1999. The usability risk. In *Proceedings of the 18th IEEE Symposium on Reliable Distributed Systems*. Washington, DC: IEEE Computer Society.

Tran, V., and D.-B. Liu. 1997. A risk-mitigating model for the development of reliable and maintainable large-scale commercial-off-the-shelf integrated software systems. In *Proceedings of the 1997 Annual Reliability and Maintainability Symposium*, 361–7.

Williams, R. C., G. P. Pandelios, and S. G. Behrens. 1999. Software risk evaluation method description, version 2.0. Technical report CMU/SEI-99-TR-029. www.sei.cmu.edu/publications/documents/99.reports/99tr029/99tr029abstract.html (accessed May 7, 2007).

Network Reliability and Fault Tolerance

Matthew Liotine, *University of Illinois, Chicago*

INTRODUCTION

A computer network is deemed "reliable" when it has the ability to continue operations in spite of a disruption, regardless of the cause, while resources affected by the disruption are restored. Network reliability planning is the practice of prioritizing and assigning dollars to those portions of the network that are most mission-critical and whose interruption can directly affect service delivery. If not done properly or done indiscriminately, network upgrades intended to improve reliability can in fact be wasteful and could lead to ineffective solutions that produce a false sense of security. This is why an understanding of some basic reliability concepts is often the practitioner's best tool in planning and designing network upgrades to improve survivability and performance, without becoming overwhelmed by today's vast array of network technologies.

To this end, this chapter reviews some basic principles behind network reliability and fault tolerance. Although many of these concepts have been around for quite some time, in the past several years they have become more dominant in the planning and design of network infrastructure. Many of the concepts discussed here arose from developments in telecommunications, the space program, and the nuclear industry. They are applicable at almost any level of a network infrastructure—from component to network service, from software to hardware, from topology to operations. When used collectively and coupled with human judgment, these concepts can be an invaluable tool to characterize and understand network survivability and performance. More detailed discussions of many of these concepts can be found in Liotine (2003).

FUNDAMENTAL PRINCIPLES

Disruptions in a network operation occur mainly because of lack of preparation. Inadequacy in planning, infrastructure, enterprise-management tools, processes, systems, staff, and resources typically fuel disruption. Poor training or lack of expertise can lead to human error. Process errors result from poorly defined or documented procedures. System errors such as hardware faults, operating system hangs , and application failures are inevitable, as well as power outages or environmental disasters. Disruptions produce *down time* or *slow time*—periods of unproductive time resulting in undue cost. The conditions that lead to disruption can comprise one or many unplanned circumstances that could ultimately degrade a system to the point at which its performance is no longer acceptable. *Up time* is the opposite of down time; it is the time when an operation is fully productive. The meanings of up time, down time, and slow time are a function of the context of the service being provided. Many e-businesses view up time from the end user's perspective. Heavy-process businesses may view it in terms of production time, while financial firms view it in terms of transaction processing.

When a disruption occurs, several activities must take place (see Wrobel 1997):

- *Detection* is the process of discovering a fault, latent fault, or problem, after it happens or in advance. Quite often, a hidden problem can go undetected for a time, increasing the potential for damage. The longer it takes to discover a problem, the greater the possibility of extensive damage and increased recovery cost. Fault-detection mechanisms recognize certain behavioral patterns that forewarn that a fault has or is about to occur. Accurate fault detection involves reporting faults in a way that discriminates, classifies, and conveys priority. Valid faults should be distinguished from alerts stemming from nonfailing but affected devices. Although such accuracy may improve system reliability, it can also incur greater expense.
- *Containment* is the process that controls the effects of a disruption so that other systems are unaffected and end-user impact is minimized.
- *Failover* is the process of switching to a backup component, element, or operation while recovery from a

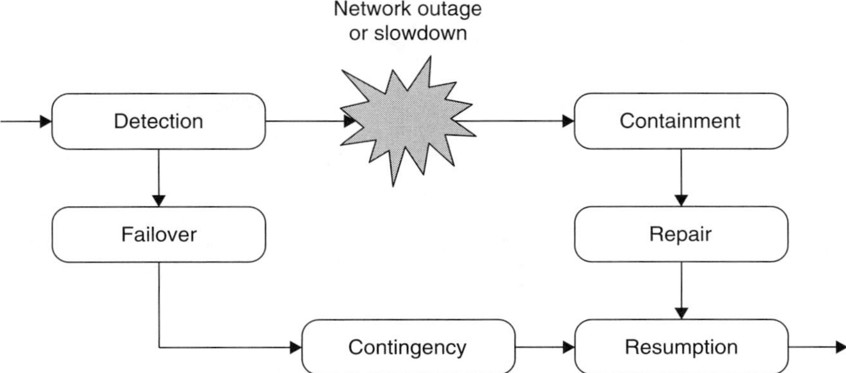

Figure 1: Network recovery processes

disruption is undertaken. *Hot* or *immediate failover* normally requires a running duplicate of a backup system to provide immediate recovery. *Cold failover*, on the other hand, uses a backup element with little or no information about the state of the primary system and must begin processing as if it were a new system upon failover. *Warm failover* uses a preinitialized backup that is not necessarily provided with all of primary system state information until a failover takes place.

- *Repair* is the activity of fixing a problematic component or system. Repair activity may not necessarily imply that the element has been returned to its operational state.
- *Contingency* is the activation of a backup element or process upon failover from the primary failed element. It can represent a backup component, system, network link or path, service provider, recovery data center or hot site.
- *Resumption* is the process of returning the repaired element back into operational service. It is the process of transferring operations over to the restored element, either gradually or instantaneously.

Figure 1 illustrates how these processes interact in relation to an adverse event. A detection process will identify that a network outage has occurred, or is about to occur. Once this happens, a failover process is invoked to activate and continue processing on a contingent network or system. While this is occurring, the process to contain and repair damaged systems is conducted. When this is completed, the resumption process gradually migrates the repaired components back into operation.

NETWORK TOLERANCE

Tolerance is the ability of an operation to withstand problems, whether at the component, system, application, network, or management level. Tolerance is often conveyed as *availability*, or the percentage of the time that a system or operation provides productive service. For example, a system with 99.9% (or three 9) availability will have about 8.8 hours of downtime per year. A system with 99.99% (or four 9) availability will have about 52 minutes of downtime per year. (Availability is discussed later in this chapter.) There are three general classes of tolerance often used to characterize computing and communication platforms, and are applicable to almost any level of network operation:

- *Fault tolerance* is a network's ability to automatically recover from problems. For this reason, it is usually associated with availability in the range of four to five 9s (or 99.99% to 99.999%). Such systems are designed with hot failover mechanisms, so that a single fault will not cause a system failure, thereby allowing applications to continue processing with virtually no transaction loss. It is typically achieved through component redundancy, continuous error checking, and automatic failover and recovery mechanisms.
- *Fault resilience* is used to characterize systems with availability of about four 9s (or 99.99%). A fault-resilient operation does not necessarily guarantee no transaction loss. It is usually achieved through warm failover mechanisms.
- *High availability* is typically associated with availability in the range of 99.5% to 99.9 %. Here, the expectation is that some transactional loss will occur during failover. Reliance on higher-level resources is typically expected to minimize disruptive impact.

As one might expect, fault-tolerant systems and operations are typically the most expensive to implement, and are usually found in mission-critical network applications, such as those involved with telecommunication and military operations. Critical factors in deciding the appropriate level of tolerance for an implementation are often cost and how problem correction and resolution are automated and allocated across network components.

NETWORK PROTECTION

Network protection is generally achieved by establishing redundancy through design and operation. Although multiple paths between critical network nodes could provide alternative routes for traffic to traverse if one path is congested or lost, the surviving path should have adequate capacity to handle the diverted traffic. Similarly, nodes or systems that are replicated for improved reliability but share common connectivity, infrastructure, or resources can be vulnerable to the same outage within those

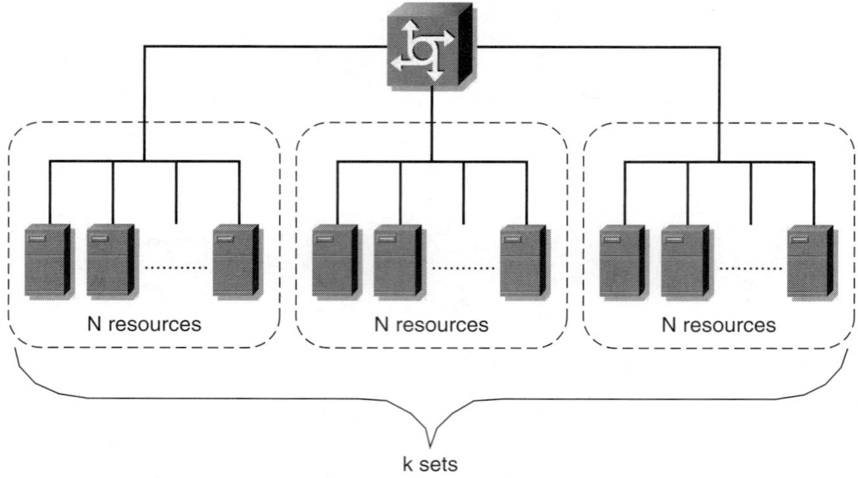

Figure 2: *kN* redundancy

elements. These scenarios typify false redundancies, which can artificially inflate network capital and operating costs while not providing additional levels of protection. In the end, protection must be applied appropriately and to those elements of the network infrastructure that are considered mission-critical. Concepts from graph theory such as two-terminal reliability, graph transformation, node-pair resilience and spanning trees have been used to intensively model communication networks, fault tolerance, and reliability (see Shooman 2002). Such concepts form the basis for much of the discussion that follows.

Redundancy

Redundancy is a network architectural feature in which multiple elements are used so that if one cannot provide service, the other will. Redundancy can be realized at many levels of a network in order to achieve service continuity. Network access, service distribution, alternative routing, system platforms, recovery data centers, and storage all can be instilled with some form of redundancy. It can also involve the use of redundant service providers, suppliers, staff, and even processes. Redundancy should be applied to critical resources required to run critical network operations. It should be introduced at multiple levels, including the network, device, system, and application levels.

Redundancy is best used to eliminate *single points of failure* (SPOFs). These can be any single isolated network element or resource that upon failure can disrupt a network's productive service. Fundamentally, redundancy involves using multiple elements to perform the same function as the SPOF. There are two fundamental types of redundancy that are often used, depending on the cost and level of need, where *N* is the number of resources needed to provide acceptable performance:

- *kN* redundancy, as illustrated in Figure 2, replicates *N* resources *k* times (i.e., *2N*, *3N*, *5N*, etc.). For example, if one ($N = 1$) network switch is sufficient to handle all network traffic, then *2N* redundant network switches allow one switch to continue switching traffic if the other fails or becomes isolated.

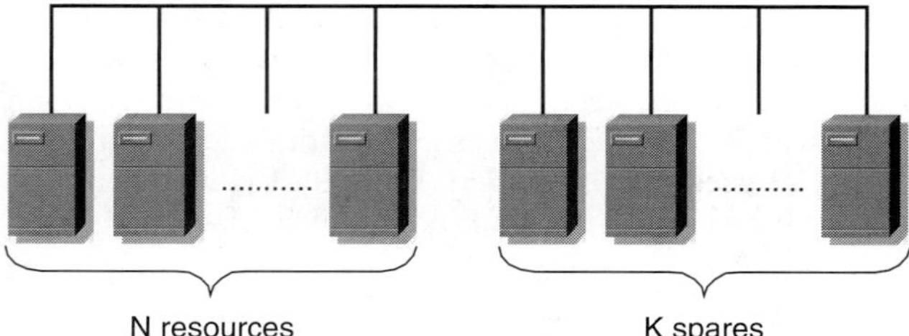

Figure 3: $N+K$ redundancy

- $N+K$ redundancy, as illustrated in Figure 3, involves having *K* spare resources for a set of *N* resources. If one of the *N* resources is removed, fails, or degrades, then one of the *K* spares takes over. For example, if a network requires 4 switches ($N = 4$) to process all traffic, then a network can be configured with 5 switches ($K = 1$) so that losing one switch does not affect service.

kN redundancy enables concurrent error detection and possible correction versus $N+K$ redundancy. $N+K$ arrangements can also be used in conjunction with *kN* arrangements, offering different granularities of protection. A *kN* arrangement can have *K* sets of resources, each having an $N+K$ arrangement to ensure a higher degree of reliability within a set.

NETWORK FAILURE

Networks are exposed to many types of threats. A threat can represent a broad range of adverse events that can produce damage, such as lost assets, productivity, or missed earnings or sales. Risk is the expected monetary loss or damage resulting from a particular threat. The greater the risk posed by a threat, the more important it becomes to mitigate that threat. A condition or event that could create much damage but has little chance of occurring can yet pose substantial risk if a network is not well protected against it. Threats can arise from all kinds of sources, typically human-made (e.g., mistakes, errors, design oversights, etc.), machine-made (e.g., breakdowns), and natural (e.g., weather, earthquakes, etc.). The nature of potential failures posing threats must be well understood in order to assess the reliability of a network.

Failures are adverse conditions that individually or collectively lead to delayed or immediate service disruption. *Self-healing failures* are those that are immediately correctable and may not require intervention to repair. Although they may have no observable impact on a system or operation, it is still important to log such instances, since they could conceal a more serious problem. *Intermittent failures* are chronic errors that often require some repair action. Persistent intermittent errors usually signal the need for some type of upgrade or repair.

Failures that occur in single isolated locations, components, connections, or some other piece of infrastructure are referred to as *simplex failures*. When not addressed, simplex failures can often create a chain reaction of additional failures, cascading into other network elements. These are referred to as *rolling failures* or *cascading failures*, often characterized by unsynchronized, out-of-sequence events that ultimately can be the most damaging.

Identifying a fault or problem in a network service often requires correlating information across different events or conditions at different network levels. Alarms or alerts might arise from individual or several devices or nodes, or perhaps no information is conveyed from a failing device. This latter case is sometimes referred to as a *fail-silent* fault model, in which a device will cease operating without communicating failure information to other devices. In emerging networks, transmissive fault models have become more prevalent. These involve dissemination of information among internal and external network devices. A *symmetric* fault is one that affects other devices in the same manner or conveys the same information to them. More common is the *asymmetric* fault, in which devices are not affected equally or are not given the same or correct information. Consequently, such faults are often more difficult to diagnose and require more information correlation. The following sections describe some fundamental parameters that are often used to characterize network failures.

Mean Time to Failure

Mean time to failure (MTTF) is the average time between placing a system or component in service until it fails. Ideally, to calculate MTTF accurately requires a system to be monitored for its expected useful lifetime, which can be quite long. Whether estimation of the MTTF involves monitoring a system for several years or a hundred years, accurate MTTF computation is often impractical to obtain. MTTF is viewed as an elapsed time. If a network element or system is not used all the time, but say at a periodic rate (every day only during business hours, for example), then the percent of time it is in operational use (or duty cycle) should be factored into the estimation.

Failure Rate

A *failure rate* is defined as the frequency of failure in terms of failures per unit time. System vendors might often state failure rates in terms of percent failures per 1000 hours, and will often use statistical sampling methods to estimate average failure rates over large populations of components. A failure rate can also be stated as 1/MTTF. In general, the failure rate conveys a system's propensity for failure over its operational lifetime. Many failure-estimation techniques assume an exponential distribution, in which the failure rate is constant with time.

Mean Time between Failures

The mean time between failures (MTBF) is a metric that conveys the mean or average life of a system, based on the frequency of system failures (see McCabe 1998). It is the average time between failures over the system's or network's operational life. It is somewhat different from MTTF, although the two are quite often used interchangeably. For example, if a system experiences 3 failures in 1000 hours of operational time, then the MTBF is approximately 333 hours. However, each failure may have occurred after 330 hours of operation, assuming a mean time to recovery (MTTR) of 3 hours. Figure 4 illustrates this relationship. MTTR is discussed further in this chapter.

The MTBF for a system or network can be estimated in various ways. If the MTBF is estimated as an arithmetic mean of observed MTBF values across numerous network nodes or systems, one could assume that MTBF represents the point in time at which approximately half of the systems have had a failure, assuming failure times are normally distributed (see Dooley 2002). Figure 5 illustrates the use of this assumption. For a network with a population of *N* nodes or systems, the MTBF would represent the median observed failure time. If the distribution of failure times is normal, this time would also convey the time corresponding to *N*/2 (or 50%) of the observed failure times. So, for example, in a large network with an estimated MTBF of 10 years, one would expect on average about half (or 50%) of the devices to have failed during that period, or 5% a year on average (50% ÷ 10 years).

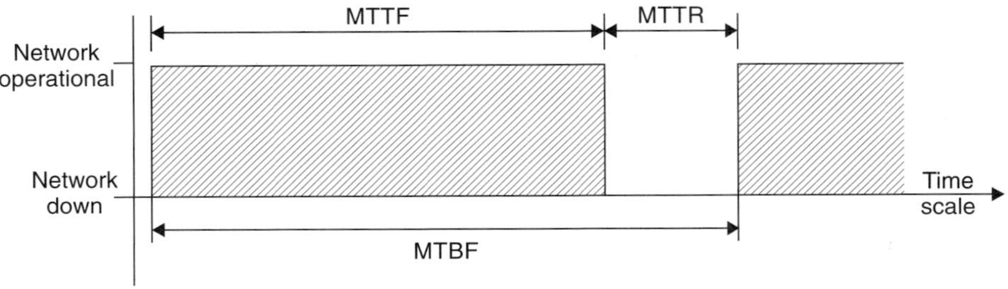

Figure 4: Relationship between mean time to failure (MTTF),mean time to recovery (MTTR), and mean time between failures (MTBF)

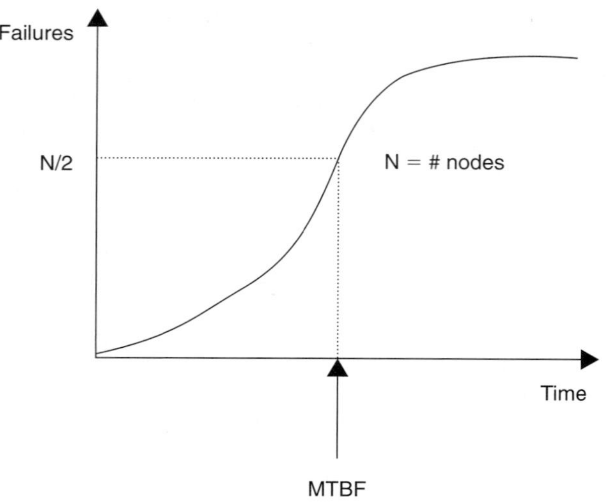

Figure 5: Failure approximation using MTBF

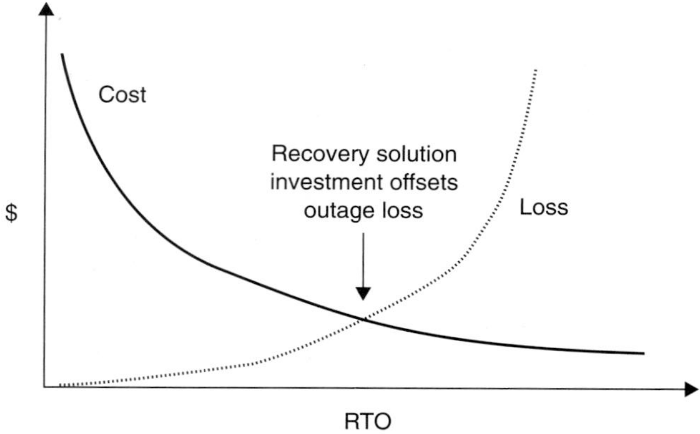

Figure 6: Relationships between RTO and cost

NETWORK RECOVERY

Recovery is comprised of all the activities that must occur from the time of an outage to the time service is restored. These will vary among organizations and depending on the context of use within a network environment. General recovery activities include declaration that an adverse event has occurred (or is about to occur), initialization of a failover process, repair activities, system restart, cutover, and resumption of service. It is important to distinguish between two types of recovery. *Service recovery* is the point at which a network continues to provide service, but not necessarily in the same way it did prior to an outage, yet in a manner that is satisfactory to end users. In this case, service is restored even if a problem has not been fixed. *Operational recovery* is the point at which a network delivers service in exactly the same fashion prior to the outage. The following sections describe some fundamental parameters that are often used to characterize network recovery operations.

Recovery Time Objective

The recovery time objective (RTO) is a target measure of the elapsed time interval between the point at which a disruption occurs and the point at which service is resumed. RTO is typically specified in units of time (hours, minutes, seconds, etc.) and represents an acceptable recovery time. The RTO can be applied to any network component—from an individual system even to an entire data center, depending on the case at hand. To define an RTO, one must determine how much service interruption can be tolerated. RTOs are usually in the range of 24 to 48 hours for large systems, but these numbers do not reflect any industry standard. Recovery cost is ultimately a deciding factor in determining an RTO objective. A high cost is required to achieve a low RTO for a particular process or operation. For example, to achieve an RTO close to zero would likely require expensive automated recovery and redundancy. As the RTO increases, the cost to achieve the RTO decreases. An RTO of long duration, while less expensive, invites greater transactional loss.

This relationship is illustrated in Figure 6. Here, the cost curve represents the cost of implementing a recovery solution versus the target RTO. Although the technology and operations costs to produce a corresponding solution decrease as the target RTO grows in size, outage losses will tend to accumulate. The point at which the two curves intersect represents that at which the investment in solution costs would be completely recaptured by way of recovered losses. Investments made prior to that point could be viewed as overspent relative to the small amount of recovered monetary loss, while those made beyond that point might be considered underspent, unless the monetary loss entailed is acceptable to an organization.

Specifying an RTO can be somewhat difficult, since a network recovery can involve many activities. An RTO specified for an entire network operation should account for all such activities. As an alternative, component activities can each be assigned their own RTO. Nevertheless, an RTO should include the time to detect and declare an adverse event, as the detection time interval can play a major role in the overall recovery effort.

It is important to distinguish between service and operational recovery to better characterize and analyze recovery viability. For this reason, recovery objectives should be specified at several levels. The recovery access objective (RAO), for example, is the tolerable time interval for failover to a redundant resource that provides the same application or service. It will typically be much lower than an RTO, sometimes on the order of seconds. This is in effect the tolerable disruption time from the end user's perspective, and characterizes service recovery. This distinction is important, since although failover mechanisms might enable reasonable continuation of service from the end user's perspective, full recovery is not achieved until a downed resource is restored to operation.

Recovery Point Objective

The recovery point objective (RPO) is used as a target metric for data recovery. It is the maximum tolerable elapsed time between the last safe data backup and the time of resumption. It is measured in terms of time, and refers to the maximum age of data required to restore operation following an adverse event. Data, in this context, might also include information regarding transactions not

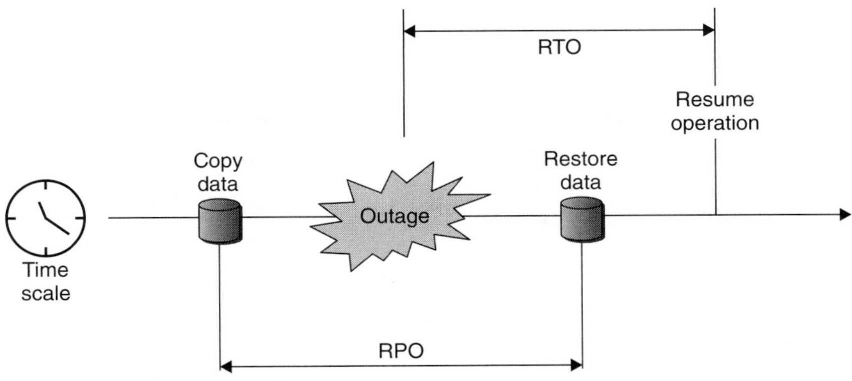

Figure 7: Relationship between RTO and RPO

recorded or captured during the outage. Like RTO, the smaller the RPO, the higher the expected data recovery cost. The RPO is the point in time to which the data must be recovered—sometimes referred to as the "freshness window." An organization that can tolerate no data loss (i.e., RPO = 0) requires their data to be restored instantaneously following an adverse event, implying the need for some type of continuous backup system.

RTO and RPO are loosely related to each other, as illustrated in Figure 7. Specifying an RTO that is short in duration does not necessarily imply a short RPO. For example, although a system can be restored with working data within an RTO of an hour following an adverse event, it could yet be acceptable for data to have an RPO of, say, four hours.

Mean Time to Recovery

Mean time to recovery (MTTR) is sometimes referred to as mean time to repair or restore. In either case, it conveys the average time required to restore operation in a network service or component that has stopped operating, or is not operating to satisfactory performance levels. It includes the total time it takes to restore the component to full operation. It could include things such as diagnosing a problem, repairing or replacing a faulty element, and system restart. MTTR is expressed in units of time. The time to diagnose can typically present the most uncertainty in estimating MTTR and can thus have a profound effect on MTTR, and ultimately, system availability. When inverted, 1/MTTR can be used to characterize a restoration or recoverability rate of a service or operation.

NETWORK RELIABILITY AND AVAILABILITY

Reliability is the probability of failure over time. In some applications, it is often characterized conversely as the likelihood that a system will continue to provide service without failure. *Reliability* is often used interchangeably with *availability*, but the two are quite different, as will be evident from the following discussion. *Availability* is concerned with the percent of time a network resource can provide operational service. So, for example, a network service that provides 99.99% availability may on the surface seem reliable. However, no implications can be made about the reliability of the service without considering the amount of failures experienced. In this case, while this availability level implies about 52 minutes of cumulative down time per year, there is no information regarding the number of failures that comprise this down time. Thus, this down time could have been the result of 3120 failures or service interruptions of one second each. In today's real-time-data–driven environment, interruptions of such short duration and volume could be quite destructive. End users typically require continuous access to uninterrupted network services. The following sections discuss these concepts in greater depth.

Reliability

Reliability is the probability that a system will work for some time period t without failure (see Blanchard 1981). The classic expression for reliability is given by:

$$R(t) = \exp(-t/MTBF) \quad (1)$$

where $R(t)$ is the reliability of a system at time t. This function assumes that the probability that a system will fail by a time t follows an exponential distribution. Although this assumption is commonly used in many system applications, there are a number of other well-known probability distributions that have been used to characterize system failures. Reliability at any point in time t is essentially the percent probability that a system with a particular MTBF will operate without a failure, or the percent of the systems that will still be operational at that point in time. Figure 8 illustrates the reliability function over time. The reliability, or probability that a system will not encounter a failure, decreases with time. As shown in Figure 8, this decrease is less pronounced for systems characterized by higher MTBFs.

Reliability block diagrams (RBDs) are a tool used for computing the reliability of a complex system or network of systems. Applying the laws of probability, a serial relationship between system reliabilities in a network of systems, or components within a system, implies that the system is operational only when all components are operating. Consequently, an upgrade that places an additional network component in series with others can actually reduce overall network reliability. When network components or platforms are connected in series, the overall system reliability could be reduced because it is the product of component system reliabilities (see Oggerino 2001).

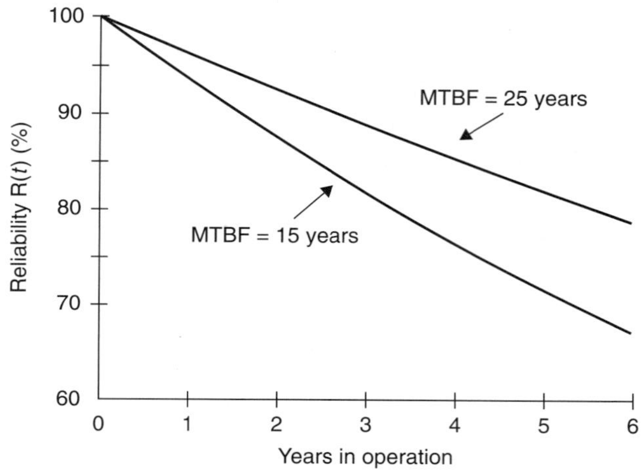

Figure 8: Reliability function over time

If the system or network is operational if either component is operating, then a parallel relationship is made. From the laws of probability, parallel reliability is obtained by subtracting from 1 the probability that all parallel components fail. Mathematically, this is done by multiplying the unreliability of each parallel component and then subtracting the result from 1 to obtain the reliability (see Hecht 2004). The following are the general formulas used to convey both the serial and parallel relationships for systems having *N* components:

Serial relationship (systems in series):

$$R(t) = \prod_{i=1}^{N} R_i(t) \tag{2}$$

Parallel relationship (systems in parallel):

$$R(t) = 1 - \prod_{i=1}^{N} [1 - R_i(t)] \tag{3}$$

Figures 9 and 10 illustrate example RBDs for these relationships. These relationships can also be used to assess the impact of *kN* and *N*+*K* arrangements as well. To calculate reliability for systems with components having a mix of parallel or series relationships, a recommended approach is to first calculate parallel reliability for the parallel components, and then combine these results in serial to compute the reliability of the serial components.

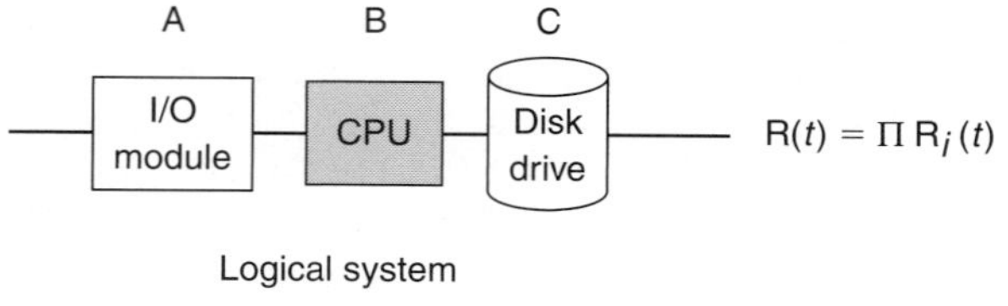

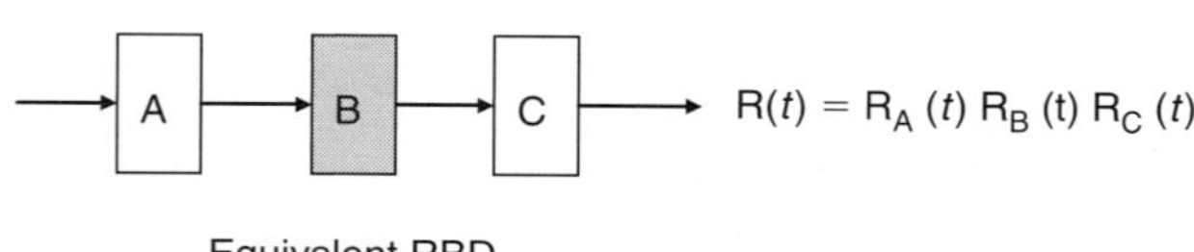

Figure 9: Serial relationship using reliability block diagrams

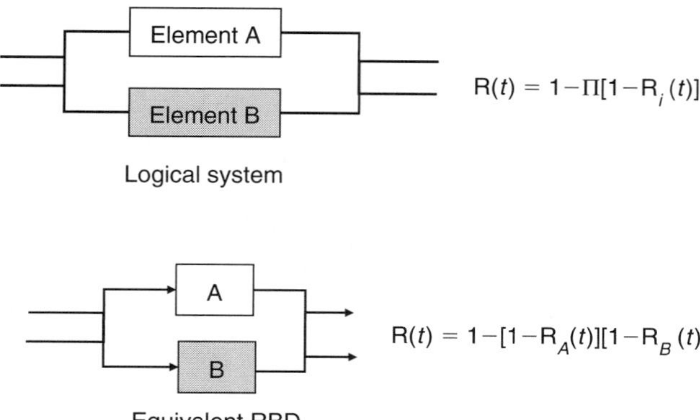

Figure 10: Parallel relationship using reliability block diagrams

Although this approach can work fairly well to evaluate RBDs for a system or network in which the component interactions are clear, it can become impractical when trying to model very large complex systems with many interactions. Alternative approaches can involve using statistical models, such as Markov chain models. These models, however, can be limited also by the numbers of components and operational or failure states of the network. A more popular approach is network simulation, which requires building a computerized model of a network, reflecting the network's topology and operations.

Availability

Availability is the probability or percent time that a system or network can provide service. The availability, *A*, of a system or component is calculated by the following:

$$A = \text{MTTF}/(\text{MTTF} + \text{MTTR}) \tag{4}$$

Consequently, the unavailability of a system or component is given by $1 - A$. As is often the case, obtaining the precise MTTF from system vendors for a particular network device can be difficult. In some cases, the MTBF can be more obtainable from either system vendors or field data. In such instances the MTBF can be used instead of the MTTF. Although this may not be totally accurate, in the end it makes little difference in the availability calculation (see Oggerino 2001). In this case, the expression to compute availability is:

$$A = \text{MTBF}/(\text{MTBF} + \text{MTTR}) \tag{5}$$

Figure 11 illustrates the effect of MTTR on availability. Availability is significantly affected by system or network recovery procedures. Since decreasing the MTTR can have a profound effect on improving availability, any improvement that can reduce the MTTR can in turn improve overall network availability. A high MTTR is usually indicative of the need for some kind of network redundancy or back up system.

Since the value *A* characterizes a probability, the serial and parallel relationship rules can be applied to multiple systems in the same fashion as calculating reliability. The relationship of availability among systems can be generalized in the same way as was the case for reliability.

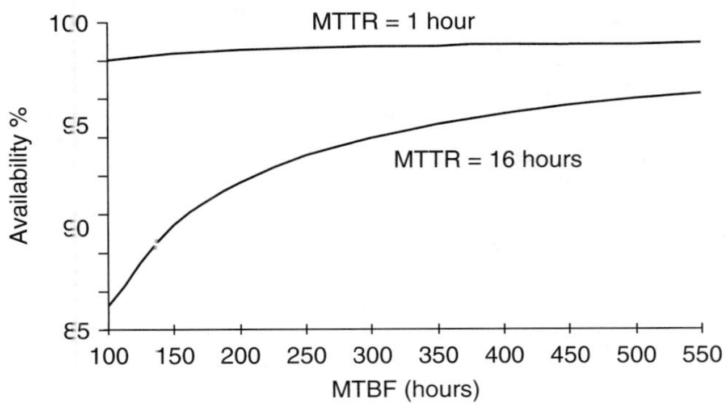

Figure 11: Effect of MTTR on availability

Thus, for a network or system having N components, the following formulas can be used:

Serial relationship (systems in series):

$$A = \prod_{i=1}^{N} A_i \tag{6}$$

Parallel relationship (systems in parallel):

$$A = 1 - \prod_{i=1}^{N} (1 - A_i) \tag{7}$$

Furthermore, for multiple systems or components, availability block diagrams (ABDs) can be constructed in the same manner as RBDs. Figures 12 and 13 illustrate example ABDs for these relationships. Although these resemble the RBDs that were discussed earlier, the RBDs were shown as time-dependent relationships.

Figure 14 shows a hypothetical example illustrating the effect of redundancy on availability. The example shows a Web site network configured with and without parallel server redundancy. By adding a second server in parallel to the first, as one might do in a cluster configuration, down time is significantly improved. It should be stressed that adding parallel redundancy to systems with low availability rates has greater impact than adding redundancy to systems that already have high availability. On the other hand, improving the availability of

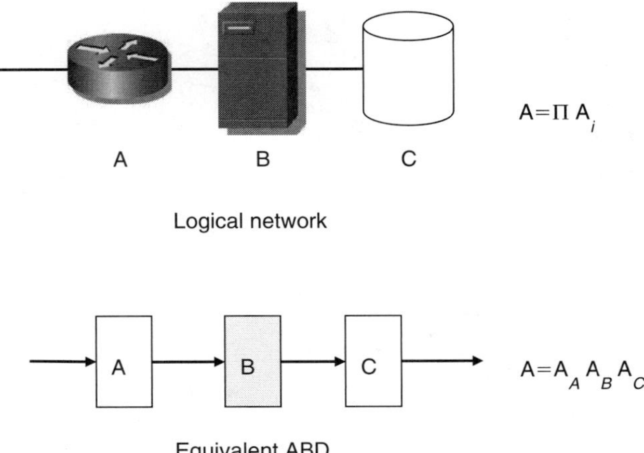

Figure 12: Serial relationship using availability block diagrams

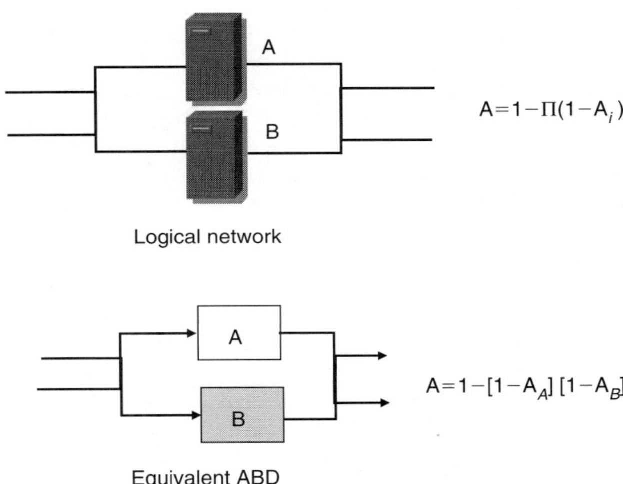

Figure 13: Parallel relationship using availability block diagrams

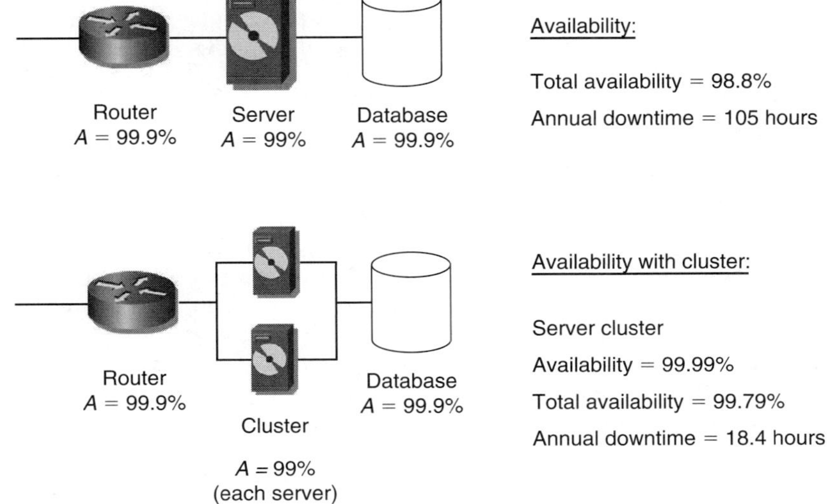

Figure 14: Example of availability

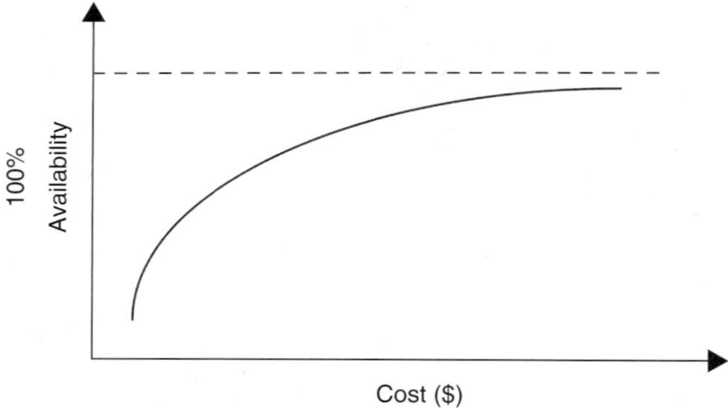

Figure 15: Cost versus availability

individual parallel systems can only marginally improve overall network availability.

Organizations will typically define their desired levels of availability according to the severity and impact on operations. The information technology industry has grown to recognize several known levels of availability. For example 99.999% availability is the typical standard for public switched telecommunication networks. This means, for example, that there could be one failure during a year that lasts just over five minutes, or there can be five failures that last one minute each; 99.5% is considered high availability, while 99.9% is often used for storage systems. Availability at 99.99% is considered fault resilient for reasons cited earlier.

Fundamental to achieving availability is the law of diminishing returns. The higher the level of availability, the greater is the cost of achieving a small improvement. A general rule of thumb is that the cost doubles to achieve each additional nine after the second nine in an availability value. Thus, for example, if the cost to achieve 99.9% availability was $250,000, then the cost to achieve 99.99% availability will likely be $500,000. As illustrated in Figure 15, improvements in availability diminish as one approaches 100%. Thus, achieving 100% availability is theoretically cost prohibitive—there is only so much availability that can be reasonably achieved.

Network Design Considerations for Reliability

Greater availability in a network can be achieved in several ways. First, improvement in recovery operations can help minimize down time, and consequently improve overall availability from the end user's perspective. Second, the availability of individual systems in a network can be improved through system upgrades, possibly bringing them to the level of fault-tolerant systems, as in the case of telecommunication networks. A third approach, which can be used in combination with the previous approaches, is to strategically place redundant systems or elements in parallel operation within the same network. By doing so, the percent of time the network is available is then equivalent to the percent of time either or both systems are operating. In each case, the effect is to keep the duration of outages as short as possible and reduce the overall MTTR, so that end users have uninterrupted access to service.

In the sections that follow, we will address some additional things that should be considered when planning availability improvements within a computing network. Specifically, we will discuss how network architectures and protocols can be leveraged to improve overall network survivability. A network architecture defines the ways in which nodes or elements of a network are interconnected. The links between nodes are governed by layered communication protocols. Inadequate network design and protocol recovery processes could further promote the potential for outages.

Network Architecture

Additional reliability can be manifested within a computing network through its architecture. The topology should be such that redundant paths or links lie between critical network nodes, at both the logical and physical layers. Even at this level of the network, the redundancy principles previously discussed can still apply. A redundant link design provides at least one alternative link between nodes so that information can be transported between them if a primary link fails. The protection can be achieved by duplicating the link over the same layer, creating a secondary link at a lower layer, or by creating completely different links using different physical or logical layers.

Protecting a path can be more complex than protecting a single link, since it implies more recovery intelligence in network elements. If a protection path is required, it is important to decide whether to define that path or route in real time (i.e., immediately after failure) or in advance. When paths are defined in real time, it implies that the network technology in use is focused primarily on maintaining connectivity in the event of a failure. An example of this is use of spanning tree protocols used in switches to compute multiple paths though a local area network (LAN), or open shortest path first (OSPF), used to compute multiple paths through a complex Internet protocol (IP) network. In such cases, it can take an inordinate amount of time to compute alternative paths in real time, depending on the protocol in use. Using preconfigured paths can better ensure performance levels, since these paths can be traffic-engineered beforehand. The multiprotocol label switching (MPLS) protocol, in fact, makes use of this capability (see Xiao et al. 1999).

The ability to define paths in a network, either statically or dynamically, is premised on whether the network topology can facilitate alternative path arrangements. Multiple paths are often appealing to further ensure reliability. However, such redundancy comes at a price, requiring design trade-offs between complete network connectivity and a hub-like structure. Quite often, greater network path redundancy will entail greater costs. For example, well-known topologies such as the *mesh* and *ring* each have survivability and protection characteristics. Mesh topologies are the most robust in eliminating SPOFs, since every node is connected to every other node to some degree, so that many alternative traffic routes can be defined. However, mesh networks are typically the most expensive to build. Ring topologies, on the other hand, are used as a less expensive option since they can

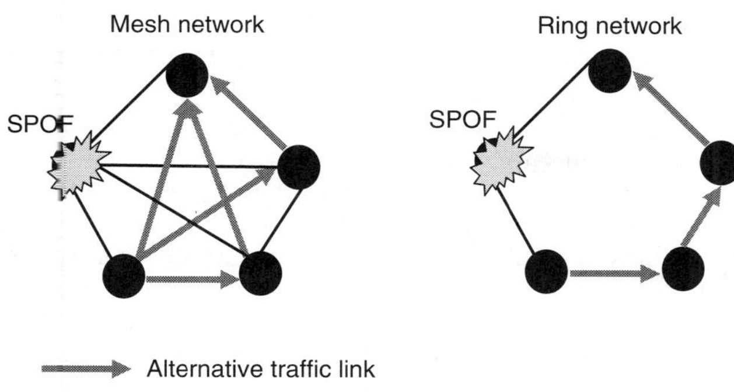

Figure 16: Examples of network SPOFs

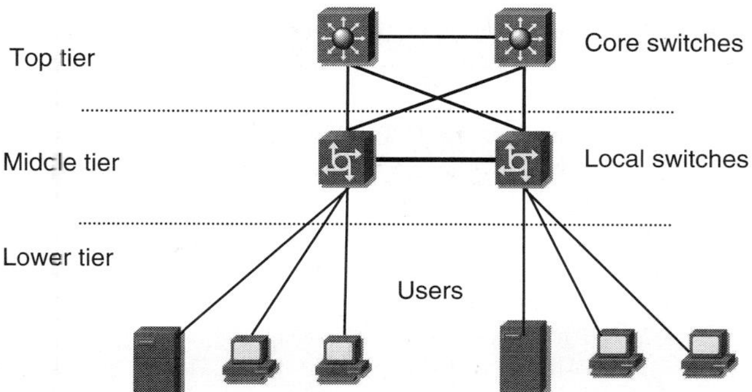

Figure 17: Example of a tiered network

protect against node and link failures as long as there is adequate link capacity to support redirected traffic. Figure 16 illustrates these points. Such is the case with synchronous optical network (SONET) and resilient packet ring (RPR) architectures.

Most computing networks are made up in a tiered fashion, with each tier using different types of topologies. Figure 17 illustrates a common tiered architecture that is often used in constructing a reliable network infrastructure. A sound approach to implementing network survivability is to optimize each tier for reliability as well as the connectivity between tiers. As traffic is aggregated going up the tiers, switches grow larger in capacity and require greater port utilization. Consequently, failures in either switches or links in the higher tiers can have more far-reaching effects. As a general rule, network links should be engineered to accommodate both their working traffic as well as additional traffic that is displaced should an outage occur.

The edge network is the access portion that connects remote end points, typically end users or other networks, to a main network. The edge network is usually the most vulnerable portion of a network. Efforts to improve the reliability of a network can be ineffective if the edge network is isolated in the event of a failure. Because edge nodes aggregate traffic onto a backbone network, they can be potential SPOFs if left unprotected. For example, if the edge network is home to a large number of LAN users who connect to a wide area network (WAN) or Internet through a switch or router, failure of that device or link can be catastrophic. Figure 18 illustrates this concept. A local network connecting to a WAN through one

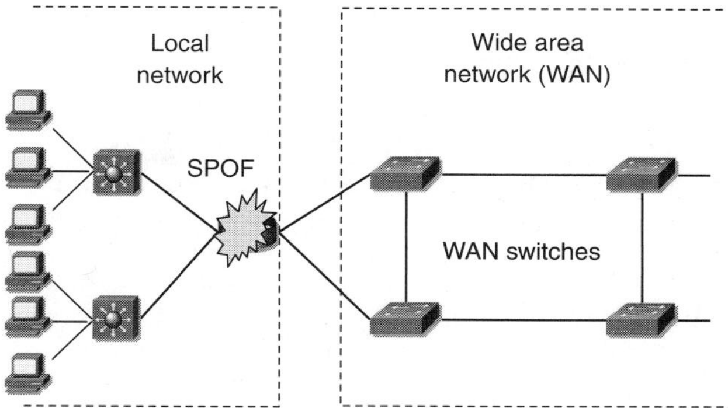

Figure 18: Example of an edge network

single device (a router) is immediately at risk, since that device is an SPOF. Failure of that device would prevent all local network user traffic from traversing the WAN.

Network Protocols

Computing networks rely on a multitude of protocols for their operation. There are numerous network protocols in use today, posing interoperability issues in using different systems and products. Extensive management coordination between the network protocol layers can introduce unwanted costs or resource consumption, as well as more network overhead. Network layer protocols usually have recovery features that come into play if a transmission link encounters high error rates or if a link or node fails. For example, reliability is important in each layer of open systems interconnection (OSI) and transmission control protocol/Internet protocol (TCP/IP) models. One will find many protocols in use across these layers and within these layers as well. Recovery requirements and inherent recovery mechanisms can vary widely across the many protocols and protocol layers depending on the type of network in which they are used. This phenomenon can often threaten interoperability and pose network vulnerability issues, raising the question as to how to provide proper protection at the right layers, yet avoid over protection or conflicting recovery mechanisms.

Use of a *parallel* strategy, which is quite common, simply allows every layer to apply its own protection or recovery mechanism. Although this can lead to overprotection, which can consume extra resources in other layers, it can also cause oscillations and unnecessarily throttle traffic. A general rule of thumb is to use a *sequential* strategy—that is, if a lower layer cannot provide needed protection, then apply protection at the next highest layer. Although this might seem like a sensible approach, survivability mechanisms between layers can yet create some undue problems. For example, if a physical link is cut between two switches, it is likely that layer 3 IP routing is unaffected, since recent strides in protocols, such as rapid spanning tree, can quickly reconstruct a spanning tree at layer 2. However, as IP switching times continue to decrease with improvements in technology, route oscillations could take place unless state information is exchanged between layers. This represents a *coordinated* strategy, a feature found in multilayer switching. Although this might seem like a sensible approach, it often can be difficult to achieve across different vendor products unless a single product line is used (see Breyer and Riley 1999).

SUMMARY AND CONCLUSION

Network recovery involves the specification of the RTO and RPO. The RTO is a target measure of the time interval between an outage and full restoration. The RPO, on the other hand, is used to specify the desired age of data required to restore operation following a service interruption. The MTTR is an observed average measure of the time required to restore operation. Network and system failures are conveyed using the frequency of failures and the MTTF. The MTBF measures the average life of a network component. Thus, a low MTBF could imply greater maintenance costs.

Network reliability conveys the ability to continue service even if a system or network resource becomes inoperable. It is best achieved using a mix of redundancy, reliable systems, and good network management. Although adding redundant systems in parallel can significantly improve network reliability, adding components in series could actually reduce it. Availability is the proportion of time service is provided. Availability as a measure can conceal outage frequency, so it should be interpreted carefully. Although *reliability* and *availability* are often used interchangeably, the two will differ slightly. *Reliability* is suggestive of failure frequency, whereas *availability* is indicative of service duration. The availability calculations presented can be used to estimate the contribution of each component or resource to the overall availability of a network. Although these estimates can never be precise, they can be used to evaluate the relative value of upgrade alternatives, and can help flag the areas of a network that require more attention.

Network reliability is typically improved by eliminating SPOFs through system upgrades, network redundancy, and improved recovery practices. At the system level, upgrades can be made to improve both the reliability and availability of the individual systems that comprise network nodes. At the network level, redundancy can be added by placing redundant systems in operation and/or establishing multiple paths between systems. This requires choosing appropriate network topologies and protocols to facilitate system failover and traffic redirection. Finally, recovery practices should involve detection, containment, failover, repair, contingency, and resumption procedures that can respond to adverse network or system events. In the end, achieving network reliability is often more art than science, involving trade-offs between cost, systems, topologies, and protocols.

GLOSSARY

Asymmetric Fault: A malfunction that impacts other devices differently or conveys different or incorrect information to them.

Availability: The probability or percent time that a system or network can provide service.

Containment: The process that controls the effects of a disruption so that other systems are unaffected and end-user impact is minimized.

Contingency: The activity of activating a backup element or process upon failover from a primary failed element.

Detection: The process of discovering a fault or problem after it happens or in advance.

Down Time: The period of time when a network service or element is unavailable.

Fail-Silent Fault: A failure whereby a network device will cease operating without communicating malfunction information to other devices.

Failover: The process of switching to a backup component, element, or operation while recovery from a disruption is undertaken.

Failure Rate: The frequency of failure in terms of failures per unit time.

Mean Time Between Failures (MTBF): The average time between failures over the system's or network's operational life.

Mean Time to Failure (MTTF): The average amount of time between placing a system or component in service until it fails.

Mean Time to Recovery (MTTR): The average time required to restore operation in a network component that has stopped operating, or that is not operating to a satisfactory performance level.

Recovery: All the activities that must occur from the time of an outage to the time service is restored.

Recovery Access Objective (RAO): The tolerable time interval for failover to a redundant resource that provides the same application or service.

Recovery Point Objective (RPO): A target metric referring to the age of data required to restore operation following an adverse event.

Recovery Time Objective (RTO): A target measure of the elapsed time interval between the point in time when a disruption occurs until service is resumed.

Reliability: The probability that a system will work for a designated time period without failure.

Repair: The activity of fixing a problematic component or system.

Resumption: The process of returning a repaired element to operational service and transferring operations over to that element, either gradually or instantaneously.

Self-Healing Failure: A failure that is immediately correctable and may not require intervention to repair.

Single Point of Failure (SPOF): Any single isolated network element, component, or connection that upon failure can disrupt a network's productive service.

Slow Time: The period of time when a network service or element's performance is such that productivity is reduced to unacceptable levels.

Symmetric Fault: A malfunction that impacts other devices in the same fashion, or conveys the same information to them.

CROSS REFERENCES

See *Computer Network Management*; *Fault Tolerant Systems*; *Network Capacity Planning*; *Network Security Risk Assessment and Management*; *Network Traffic Management*; *Network Traffic Modeling*.

REFERENCES

Blanchard, B. S. 1981. *Logistics engineering and management*. Englewood Cliffs, NJ: Prentice-Hall.

Breyer, R., and S. Riley. 1999. *Switched, fast, and gigabit Ethernet*. 3rd ed. New York: Macmillan Technical.

Dooley, K. 2002. *Designing large-scale LANs*. Sebastopol, CA: O'Reilly.

Liotine, M. 2003. *Mission-critical network planning*. Boston: Artech House.

Hecht, H. 2004. *Systems reliability and failure prevention*. Boston: Artech House.

McCabe, J. D. 1998. *Practical computer network analysis and design*. San Francisco: Morgan Kaufman.

Oggerino, C. 2001. *High availability network fundamentals*. Indianapolis: Cisco Press.

Shooman, M. L. 2002. *Reliability of computer systems and networks: Fault tolerance, analysis and design*. New York: Wiley.

Wrobel, L. A. 1997. *Business resumption planning*. Boston: Artech House.

Xiao, X., T. Irpan, R. Tsay, et al. 1999. Traffic engineering with MPLS. *America's Network* November 15:32–8.

Social Engineering

Benjamin Böck, Markus D. Klemen, and Edgar R. Weippl, *Secure Business Austria and Vienna University of Technology, Austria*

INTRODUCTION

Security is of prime importance for every business as security breaches can affect both a company's value and its reputation. The ever-rising need for business security leads to the development of new technological solutions on a regular basis. Companies often rely blindly on technology to eliminate as many risks as possible that occur in their work environment. Technology, however, leaves a gap; technical solutions are made by humans and administered by humans. The output of technical solutions is interpreted by humans. The entirety of these factors describes the biggest security issue: "the human factor" (Maris 2005).

Definition

Social engineering is a practice that may be used to exploit this "weakest link" in the security chain of an organization (Allen 2001). There are various definitions of social engineering contributed by different authors. Most of them agree that social engineering is an act of deceiving people into revealing private or otherwise confidential information or providing access to outsiders, sometimes called "hackers" or "crackers" (Allen subscribes to the common definition of "hackers" as interested people who don't intentionally inflict damage and "crackers" who set malicious actions). Social engineering can best be understood as "the art and science of getting people to comply to your wishes" (Harl 1997).

Following this argument, social engineering is not necessarily tied to technological aspects and settings; salespersons and confidence men may be dubbed "social engineers" as well.

Kevin Mitnick, a well-known hacker and cracker, provides a more detailed definition:

> Social Engineering uses influence and persuasion to deceive people by convincing them that the social engineer is someone she is not, or by manipulation. As a result, the social engineer is able to take advantage of people to obtain information with or without the use of technology. (Mitnick and Simon 2003)

For many, social engineering has an aura of mystery. Unlike technological tricks and tools, it is limited only by the hacker's imagination. The techniques take time to master and need a quick mind, practice, and intuition, especially when interacting directly with people. The efficiency of social engineering lies within people's perception that hackers master technology, not human behavior (Lafrance 2004).

Denning (2000) draws a line between technology and social engineering: "When they can't crack the technology, they use 'social engineering' to con employees into giving them access."

Motivation

What is the motivation behind social engineering? Once mastered, social engineering can be used to gain access on any system independent of the platform or the quality of hardware and software present. This also makes it the most difficult form of attack to defend against because hardware and software alone cannot stop it (Arthurs 2001).

The danger of social engineering lies in people's unawareness concerning the topic. Even though more people are aware of "crackers" in the technological field, only few anticipate them to target human behavior (Lafrance 2004).

PSYCHOLOGICAL BACKGROUND: WHY SOCIAL ENGINEERING WORKS

Social engineering exploits human vulnerabilities, such as ignorance or naiveté, and makes use of concepts such as authority, strong emotion, overloading, reciprocation, or deceptive relationships. Most attacks can be traced back to one of the six "weapons of influence" (reciprocity, commitment and consistency, social proof, linking, authority, and scarcity) that are used to motivate people (Cialdini 1993).

Positive values such as integrity and consistency or natural behavior such as curiosity and an individual's desire to be liked and helpful can be used against target persons to gain information (Arthurs 2001; Gragg 2003; Gulati 2003). It is a part of human nature that people usually trust easily and get satisfaction out of helping those in need (Dolan 2004).

Understanding the social and psychological background of social engineering is of utter importance to be able to develop a defense strategy. Because social engineering targets people rather than technology, technological countermeasures may be of only limited use, as outlined in a separate section below on "Password Problems," which may bring more problems than they can solve.

This section focuses on peculiarities of human behavior that can be exploited in order to gain information the target usually would not give away. These soft facts stand in contrast to technical knowledge that may be used for information gathering. The following subsections show some of the psychological concepts that make social engineering work.

Strong Emotion

Strong emotion is just a collective term for the reaction to a multitude of factors that may raise people to a heightened emotional state and thus make them more vulnerable to social-engineering attacks, as they will pay less attention to the "facts" or arguments presented. Strong emotion may be invoked by factors such as:

- *Anticipation*, such as the prospect of money or a substantial prize, makes people less suspicious. But it does not necessarily need a lot of cash. An example for a social-engineering attack abusing the trigger of anticipation is discussed in the section below on "Password Problems," where a survey is discussed that shows that people will reveal their passwords for a bar of chocolate or a cheap pen.

  Another example is "advanced fee fraud" mail scams. They involve requests for "up-front" money to secure your involvement in their transaction and promise great wealth in exchange. Nigeria gained notoriety in this area, the scheme is also known as "419," named after the relevant section of Nigerian penal code. The U.S. Secret Service even runs a Web site[1] targeting this special kind of fraud.
- *Stress*: Employees may be made to think that the decisions they have to make involve serious consequences. This leads to a high level of stress in the target that in turn, lowers the chance to notice false statements made by the attacker.
- *Other triggers, such as surprise, anger, fear, excitement, and panic*, that also lead to a heightened emotional state and thus make the target more vulnerable to a social-engineering attack.

The social engineer triggers strong emotion, which serves to interfere with the victim's ability to analyze and think closely, thereby aiding the attacker to persuade the victim and to reach the desired goal (Gragg 2003; Rusch 1999).

Overloading

Human beings can process only a limited amount of information at any given time. Even though the threshold may differ significantly among different persons it is only a matter of time and volume of data that has to be processed until an overload occurs.

The strategy of overloading works by simply providing more information to target persons than they can process in a timely manner. The rationale of this attack is that wrong statements are far less likely to be spotted when included with true ones. Another form of overloading can be stimulated through elements of surprise, such as bringing up arguments from an unexpected perspective. The target is not prepared for this new point of view and therefore needs time to think it through. Social engineers make sure this time is not available by continuing their strategy, thus reducing the target's ability to process or to analyze the received information. As a result, the target is more willing to accept opinions without questioning them (Gragg 2003).

Reciprocation

Reciprocation is most easily described as an automatic urge to respond to a gift or favor one receives. Individuals are far more likely to comply with a request if they have received something of value beforehand. This could be money (from a small present to full-blown bribery) or even immaterial presents such as information, advice, or assistance. Most notably, the sheer promise of a present can lead us to reciprocate (Gragg 2003).

Individuals may feel an urge to reciprocate if given or promised something. They may want to return the favor and often even want to "exceed" the original one. This also holds true for cases when the favor someone offers was not requested. Still, the person who is offered the favor may feel a strong obligation to comply with the favor the original person asks for in return. It is of capital importance to note that the returned favor may even be more costly than the original one (Rusch 1999). Moreover, this also holds true for intimate self-disclosure. If people first

[1] U.S. Secret Service, Web site about 419 "advance fee fraud": http://www.dced.state.ak.us/bsc/pub/publicawareness.pdf.

become recipients of such disclosures—whether true or not—they feel obligated to respond with a personal disclosure of equal intimacy (Nass and Moon 2000).

Reciprocation can also be used in another way. Behavioral experiments show that when two people disagree, if one will yield on some point, the other will feel compelled to yield as well, no matter how small the compromise is. This is what makes a compromise possible. A cracker can exploit this behavior by making additional requests and then by drawing them back. As a result, the target may feel pressure to accede to the original request (Gragg 2003).

An example for social engineering through reciprocation is given by Mitnick. He states that members of the Hare Krishna substantially increased the donations received by first giving people a book or flower as a gift without taking it back ("It is our gift to you") (Mitnick and Simon 2003).

The whole social system builds on the concept of giving and taking—and giving more the more one gets. That is what makes human beings so vulnerable to this kind of social-engineering attack. Thinking about the strange nature of reciprocation, "Do unto others as you would have others do unto you" is a saying, that inevitably crosses one's mind as well.

The concept of "tit-for-tat" is also an accepted (and often the best) strategy in games theory: some even call it "the only one Evolutionary Stable Strategy generated by cooperation within and between species."[2]

The best defense against the exploitation of the tendency of reciprocation is to be aware of reciprocation as a social engineering scheme. As Mitnick states:

> If a stranger does you a favor, then asks you for a favor, don't reciprocate without thinking carefully about what he's asking for. (Mitnick and Simon 2003)

Deceptive Relationships

The longer a relationship is established, the more trust the involved persons will express toward each other. If the goal seems worth it, social engineers may invest a lot of time and passion to reach it. Mitnick, for example, describes a "two-year hack" (Mitnick and Simon 2005). Thus, attackers may take the time to build and maintain a relationship with a target with the purpose of exploiting the other person.

Ways of building deceptive relationships may be information sharing or discussing a common enemy. Mitnick even describes a plot in which he makes friends via e-mail under a false name with an employee who has already become suspicious about him. Mitnick was sharing information and technology with the employee without asking for anything in return. One key element in bonding the relationship was talking negatively about "Kevin Mitnick" without the employee realizing that actually his pen pal was Mitnick himself. Mitnick was able to successfully exploit the established relationship by obtaining all kinds of information, essentially by simply badmouthing himself (Gragg 2003).

The concepts of liking and similarity can be abused to build deceptive relationships as well. It is a normal feature of human behavior to favor persons who have things in common with oneself. Examples are common places of birth, tastes in sports, music, art, and so on (Rusch 1999). Thus, one may trust that person even without legitimate motivation (Gragg 2003).

Authority

Another concept that can be exploited for social engineering purposes is authority. One's daily living and business in particular build on the notion of authority. People are far more likely to perform a certain action if the person asking them to do so is presumed to be in a position of authority (Gragg 2003; Rusch 1999).

The Milgram experiment is a famous study on the obedience to authority. It was conducted by Stanley Milgram, a psychologist at Yale University. The study was published in the *Journal of Abnormal and Social Psychology* in 1963. The setup was as follows: A participant was asked to take place in a learning experiment. Failure should be punished by applying electric shocks of increasing power. The victim was actually an accomplice of the experimenter and was not really exposed to electric shocks. The participant and the accomplice drew slips of paper from a hat to determine who would be the teacher and who would be the learner in the experiment. The drawing was manipulated so that the participant was always the teacher and the accomplice always the learner. During the experiment, the participant and the accomplice could not see each other as they were placed in different rooms. Whenever the accomplice gave a wrong answer to one of the questions the participant had read, the participant had to apply an electric shock on the victim. The voltage increased during the course of the experiment. There were thirty lever switches, labeled from 15 to 450 volts. They were also labeled in clear words in groups of four. After the group labeled "Danger: Severe Shock" the last two steps only carried a label of "XXX." When the voltage reached 300 volts, the accomplice would pound on the wall, which would be repeated at 315 volts. From this stage on, the learner would not react anymore at all. He would not answer the teacher's questions either. The experimenter would urge the participant to continue reading questions and applying shocks, though. He would, for example, assure the participant that the shocks would not cause "permanent tissue damage." The goal of the experiment was to find out how many of the participants would apply the highest amount of voltage to the learner, with the experimenter acting as source of authority. The outcome of the experiment was unsuspected: 65% (26 of 40) of experimental participants applied the final 450-volt shock, though many expressed being uncomfortable in doing so (Milgram 1963). The findings have been confirmed by other researchers around the world and are not tied to a specific time or location (Blass 1999). The fact that people respond so well to the concept of authority

[2] Tit-for-tat, the "Only Evolutionary Stable Strategy," which may be seen as a reason why social engineering through reciprocation is successful: www.abc.net.au/science/slab/tittat/story.htm.

that they even do things they have initially disapproved can be abused by a social engineer.

This also holds true for situations in which the person claiming to be in a position of authority is not physically present, as a study of three Midwestern hospitals shows (Rusch 1999). In the study, twenty-two nurses' stations were contacted by a researcher who identified himself untruthfully as a hospital physician. He asked the answering nurse to give a high dose of a prescription drug to a particular patient. The alarming result was that 95% of the nurses proceeded to carry out his instructions despite at least four factors should have kept them from doing so:

1. The order came from a doctor they had never met or even heard from.
2. It was communicated via telephone and not face-to-face, which is a clear violation of the hospital policy.
3. The drug concerned was not authorized for use on the wards.
4. The dosage indicated was much too high; almost double the usual daily dosage.

The fact that people react so well to the concept of authority—even when the person stating to be in a position of authority is not physically present—emphasizes the importance of policies and guidelines. The implementation of guidelines should go along with repetitive training of strict adherence, as discussed in a later section.

Integrity and Consistency

People have a tendency to believe others are articulating their true attitudes when they make a written statement unless there is strong evidence to the contrary. Furthermore, if the receiver of such a statement responds by writing a statement of one's own, it makes the writer believe in what one has written as well. This results in a feeling that both parties have expressed their true beliefs (Rusch 1999). Social-engineering attacks by means of written statements rely on this concept.

Another aspect of integrity and consistency is that people have an inclination to go through with commitments in the workplace even though they may have been wrong in the first place. People will even carry out commitments they believe were made by fellow employees (Gragg 2003).

This is the reason why automatic out-of-office e-mail replies may not a good idea; it also highlights why "innocuous information" such as vacation schedules can be abused as well and should thus be treated confidentially, too. By acquiring sensitive information like this, a social engineer knows which employees are currently away from work. In the next step, the attacker may impersonate the affected employees and ask their fellow employees to carry out commitments. They may comply because they assume the requests come from their original colleagues.

Social Proof

Instead of developing an opinion all by themselves,people usually rely to a certain degree on what other people are doing or saying. Even actions against one's self-interest may be taken if others do so as well without taking the time to properly think about them. Examples of this concept's power are cults from the Jonestown Temple to Heaven's Gate (Rusch 1999), though peer pressure might only be a component in these cases. The concept of social proof is also closely linked to the one of integrity and consistency mentioned above.

Mitnick instead uses the term *social validation*, which highlights one's acceptance of the action of others as validation that the behavior in question is the correct action (Mitnick and Simon 2003).

Lack of Reporting Due to Fear or Disinterest

Last but not least, one important, indirect cause of successful social engineering attacks is the lack of reporting of recognized or suspected attacks. An experiment among university students showed that they made little serious attempt to report incidents—some e-mails were even directed to the perpetrator himself (Greening 1996). These findings may stem from psychological concepts such as fear of punishment or exposure or plain disinterest.

TECHNIQUES

The following section provides an overview of some popular social engineering techniques. It is not an exhaustive enumeration of all existing methods; rather it is a selection of important ones.

Social-engineering techniques can be subdivided in several ways. An accepted approach of categorization is the subdivision into the two main categories of human-based attacks and computer-based attacks. This chapter does not follow this argument, as a successful attack often comprises multiple ingredients, some of them human-based and others with a technological background.

The following sections deal with some characteristic forms of social engineering.

Gathering Information with Google

An important step in the course of a social-engineering attack is gathering as much information as possible that can then be exploited in order to influence the target person or company. Gathering information is an area in which technical skills may come more into play than during the interaction with targets themselves. This section deals with Google[3] as an example of a search engine and the multitude of information it makes available to the experienced researcher.

The Internet

It is amazing how much information is available through open sources, most notably, the Internet. Just using one's favorite search engine, one can do a detailed survey on a target's interests, relations, habits, political orientation, and a lot of other potentially interesting facts—all this while conveniently sitting on one's sofa. Google, as the market leader, is the prime example and will therefore

[3] Google, world's most used Internet search engine: www.google.com.

be addressed specifically. It makes enormous amounts of private information about people available to everybody with an Internet connection with no questions asked. Thus, Google can be used as a mighty tool to pry into people's private lives, as more and more information becomes available online.

In 2005, Elinor Mills of CNET[4] (News.com[5]) showed exactly this when she researched and published personal information about Google CEO Eric Schmidt, including his salary, his hobby as an amateur pilot, his neighborhood, and his political donations (Mills 2005). Understandably, Google was not amused, and reacted with an interview ban on CNET reporters (as reported by CNET themselves), thereby essentially blackballing CNET (Westhoven 2005).

If used correctly, Google can be a powerful tool for gathering information relevant to social engineering. Sources to learn advanced search techniques are available for everybody—for example, the excellent *Google Hacks* (Calishain and Dornfest 2004). But Google can also be (ab)used as a tool for penetration testers (Long, Skoudis, and van Eijkelenborg 2004)—and thus as an attack tool for social engineers.

In the past few years, numerous news stories have been published about using Google to gain otherwise private information—for example, credit card data.[6] This could be accomplished through a simple trick, namely using a special operator Google provides for searching ranges of numbers. For example, "year numrange:1990–2000" will find instances of "year 1990" to "year 2000," a shortcut for the above shown numrange example is "year 1990..2000". Using the numrange operator, a multitude of valid credit card numbers was available online. This possibility may, of course, have existed before Google.

Another story in the popular press pointed out the danger of known URLs Web cams use by default.[7] Certain Web cam models use predefined URLs to make the images they record available online. If no precautions are taken and such a URL is accessible publicly from the Internet, Google's robot will assimilate the information when it scans the site. Thus, by searching for parts of the known default URL used by Web cams, publicly-accessible ones can easily be found. Who needs blast-proof walls, bullet-proof windows, and high-security authentication if everybody around the world can peek over your shoulder with the click of a button?

Newsgroups

The Usenet is an Internet-based bulletin board system that allows reading and posting of "news" in different "newsgroups." It is one of the largest and oldest cooperative networks, and it is still in heavy use today.

Google maintains archives of posts to newsgroups dating back to 1981. Knowing a target's e-mail address, the search engine can be used to gather information about a person's or company's interests. An example might be relations to other people, information about hobbies or even unlawful behavior, e.g. asking for a "crack" to an application in an adequate newsgroup.

But it does not stop there. Finding a Usenet post by a certain person via Google groups provides potential attackers with information about the IP address of the computer the post was issued from via the header field "NNTP-Posting-Host" and thereby:

- The target's Internet provider (type "nslookup IP" in a command shell).
- The geographical location the post originated from by tracing the route ("tracert" on Windows computers; may also be used as an alternative to "nslookup" on Windows 9x systems).
- The newsreader client the target is using can easily be found investigating the "X-Newsreader" header field of the post.
- Using the information about the newsreader, the operating system of a target can be guessed.

All of the above information may be fake, but most of the time, people either do not know or do not care about the risks arising from tracks they leave while surfing the Web or posting to newsgroups. In fact, a lot of people even consider it a good practice to use their real names in Usenet postings, which opens a point of attack for social engineers.

On the other hand, it is a justified argument that most of the Usenet information is very old in many cases. Considering the age of posts Google may return (back to 1981), it is likely that users may have changed addresses.

Phone Listings

The World Wide Web and Usenet are not the only sources of information Google provides. The "phonebook" operator searches both business and residential phone listings. Using the "rphonebook" and "bphonebook" operators, only residential and business, respectively. listings are searched. Phone listings other than those provided by Google may be used as well, of course.

If a social engineer knows the city a target lives in, phone listings provide a great opportunity to reveal not only the phone number but also, and more important, the target's address.

Google Maps

Using Google's free online map service Google Maps, a social engineer is able to map acquired address information to visual information about the target's surroundings. Given the target's home and working address, an attacker can even use the service to calculate a route between the two. Google Maps is able to show satellite data of a region that can be of great use for a social engineer who is not familiar with the place. The satellite pictures vary in age and detail but can be taken as a good first guess, though.

---

[4] CNET—Technology product reviews, price comparisons, tech video, and more: www.cnet.com.

[5] CNET News.com. News of change: www.news.com.

[6] CNET News.com. August 3, 2004. Google queries provide stolen credit cards: http://news.com.com/Google+queries+provide+stolen+credit+cards/ 2100-1029_3-5295661.html.

[7] The Register. January 8, 2005: Google exposes web surveillance cams: www.theregister.com/2005/01/08/web_surveillance_cams_open_to_all.

Social and Business Networking Sites

The growing popularity of MySpace.com[8] and other social networking sites is an acceptable gift to any potential attacker. MySpace.com hit the mark of 100 million accounts on August 9, 2006. On MySpace.com, users can create a profile for free in which they describe themselves. The data is searchable and can provide a wealth of information about a person or organization that can be abused by a social engineer. People reveal all sorts of personal information, such as age (sometimes birth dates), gender, location, marital status, education, sexual and political orientation, family/relatives, and preferences regarding books, music, movies, television, and so on. In addition, users can add other users to their "Friend Space," thus revealing interpersonal relationships. There is also the opportunity to add pictures and videos. With a bit of luck, a social engineer can extract valuable information about people and organizations that can be abused in ensuing attacks.

The fact that sites like MySpace "work" is confirmed by news stories that even police use the service successfully to solve criminal cases—for example, a triple homicide case[9] and the case of probation violation by a sexual offender.[10]

According to MySpace.com, the service is also used by businesspeople and coworkers interested in networking. Other providers, like openBC,[11] specialize in business networking. User profiles of business networking sites may provide information on current and previous companies, job title, language abilities, affiliated organizations, detail on education, earned degrees and certifications and, most important, contacts.

ZoomInfo[12] is another service that can provide valuable information about people and companies to an attacker. In contrast to the aforementioned solutions, ZoomInfo consists not only of a passive part ("BeFound"), where people can add their own profiles, but it actively searches and parses information from a wealth of sources, "such as Web sites, press releases, electronic news services and SEC filings." The service thus describes itself as "the premier summarization search engine" and promises comprehensive information on over 32 million business professionals and 2 million companies (September 2006). Information on people is often complete with portrait and details such as employment history, education, board membership and affiliations, and more. Information on companies contains key data such as address, telephone numbers, revenues, industry, and number of employees but also records on key people such CEOs, Chairpersons, and people with other important posts. ZoomInfo also provides links to Web references that usually contain more data. An upgrade from the free service to "BeFound Pro" enables even more sophisticated search opportunities—for example, all registered employees of a certain company can be listed, which may be a great source of information for an attacker who wants to conduct an impersonation attack. In a test conducted by us, ZoomInfo yielded information not only on U.S. but also (bigger) European and Asian companies.

In the past, an attacker may have had to steal an organizational chart to gain insight into a company's structure, However, nowadays a visit to Web sites such as openBC and ZoomInfo can suffice.

Social networking is a characteristic trait of humankind and has thus always been a "risk" when considered from a social engineering point of view. However, there are special risks attached to online social networks:

- Everyone can participate easily and within a short timeframe, no matter where one is located.
- Information on networks by different people may be combined. Information gathered through online social networks can be compared to the "traditional way" of stealing someone's address book—the combination of information from online networks of different people is equivalent to stealing the address books of all affected participants.
- Online social networks "are both vaster and have more weaker ties, on average, than offline social networks" (Gross, Acquisti, and Heinz 2005). People grant access to their online networks to rather unknown people.

On openBC, for example, there are users with several thousand confirmed direct (first-level) contacts. One may receive a "may i join?" message by such individuals minutes after registering and many users seem to comply, otherwise such "harvesters" would not have so many contacts. One should think twice before adding such users to one's "friends." Many online social networks allow for "privacy" settings according to different levels of information protection—for example, information may be:

- world-readable
- readable only by friends and oneself
- private: readable only by oneself.

Allowing foreign individuals access to the "inner circle" of friends is thus a potential security leak when the security level is set to level 2 (readable only by friends). Even worse, few users make use of limiting privacy preferences at all (Gross et al. 2005).

Weblogs, Blogs

Weblogs, which are usually called "blogs," are sites where individuals publish information such as news or comments on recent events. In the past few years there has been a steep rise in the use of blogs. Blogging can evidently lead to the same revelation of personal information as participating in online networking sites, with the exception that blogs usually are publicly accessible by design, providing not even the possibility of privacy preferences. Blogs and all their variations—like photoblogs and moblogs (blogs composed using mobile devices like

[8] MySpace.com, a social networking site: www.myspace.com.

[9] Thenewstribune.com, a news site. March 12, 2006. MySpace: Meet people, talk music, fight crime—Story about a triple homicide solved using MySpace: www.thenewstribune.com/news/story/5583466p-5021349c.html.

[10] MSNBC, news site. April 12, 2006. MySpace page puts teacher back in jail—Story about a sex offender arrested for probation violation caught using MySpace: www.msnbc.msn.com/id/12289591.

[11] openBC, a business networking site: www.openbc.com.

[12] ZoomInfo. People, companies, relationships—A business search engine addressing business professionals and companies: www.zoominfo.com.

PDAs)—may describe someone's life and social network (Nolan and Levesque 2005).

Internet Relay Chat and Instant Messaging

Other possible information sources are Internet relay chat (IRC) and instant messaging (IM) solutions. Both may disclose the IP of potential victims, for example. Tracking when a certain individual is "online" can be used to generate timetables of people's behavior. Information about when a certain employee is out of the office or at home may be used in impersonation attacks.

Companies' employees may gather in certain IRC channels, so that knowledge of one employee's nickname can lead to the discovery of other employees and their information. The channels an individual joins may indicate personal preferences. The private information and social network of a person may be uncovered.

Instant messaging solutions usually allow the creation of profiles, in which users can enter similar private information for those on online social networks, thus carrying the same risk.

But IRC and IM solutions can also be abused actively, as described in a CERT Incident Note; attackers may trick users into downloading and executing malicious software, for example (CERT 2002).

Spying and Eavesdropping

Spying and eavesdropping constitute an important source for social engineers in gathering information, either to find out what they are after directly or to gain more knowledge about a situation, environment, or victim in order to have a firmer basis for a pending attack.

The following discussion provides a brief overview of different technological and nontechnological approaches to spying and eavesdropping. Some of them are more obvious, some less:

"Shoulder surfing" denotes the easiest form of spying. It refers to using direct observation techniques in order to obtain the information sought. Therefore, it is particularly effective in crowded places, where it is easy to stay unnoticed when looking over someone's shoulder. A typical application for shoulder surfing attacks is when victims enter their pin code at an ATM and the attacker looks closely to remember the password. But it can also be done at a distance—using binoculars, for example—thus reducing the chance of getting caught or looking suspicious.

Shoulder surfing is an easy-to-conduct attack with a low risk attached to it. Countermeasures are as simple as they are effective: prying eyes are best fended off by simply shielding the confidential information from view—for example, by placing yourself between a camera and the information to protect or cupping your hand to hide your pin code while entering it using a keypad.

A study on shoulder surfing risks concerning graphical passwords (in this case, photos of faces have been used) shows differences in the vulnerability of the approach to shoulder surfing, compared to alphanumeric passwords. Graphical passwords that were entered via keyboard were significantly more difficult to spy on than those entered via mouse and both nondictionary and dictionary passwords (Tari, Ozok, and Holden 2006).

A more modern form of spying can be accomplished through technology such as miniature cameras, which can be hidden easily. Nowadays, tiny wireless spy cams are available online to everybody for as little as $50, complete with the option to record sound. Another kind of attack has already been mentioned, namely using an Internet search engine to find typical URLs of publicly available Web cams that have been placed by security-unaware people.

Using a "key logger," passwords can easily be spied on. They can be implemented as applications (software), which record the sequence of characters entered through the keyboard or as small devices (hardware), which are placed between the keyboard jack and the actual connector and store the keystrokes on internal memory.

Each of the approaches exhibits specific pros and cons. Software key loggers can be installed via malicious email attachments, for example, without the attacker needing to be physically present. Logs can be sent back via e-mail as well. On the other hand, they may easily be detected by security-aware users or antivirus scanners. Instead, hardware key loggers are absolutely invisible to software running on a computer and can therefore not be detected by antivirus scanners. But as they are hardware devices, they have to be planted in the first place and collected later for analysis, which makes access to the monitored system mandatory and thus poses a greater risk of discovery and punishment, if trespassing is involved.

A lot of different types of key-logging applications are available and they can be augmented with screen-capturing functions, instant messenger logging, etc. A famous representative is Spector[13], which has, for example, been mentioned in the news as a tool to catch cheating spouses.[14] The same holds true for hardware key loggers, which are available for different interfaces. KeyGhost[15] key-logger devices are available for PS2 and USB interfaces, for example.

Using a "sniffer" application, passwords and other confidential information can be extracted from the network environment. Access to the network is mandatory but can be gained through different measures—for example, by installing hidden software on a local PC or by hiding a "listening box" at the target site.

Ethereal[16] (and its successor, Wireshark[17]) is a free "protocol analyzer" that provides all the conveniences one can ask for of a good sniffer. It can capture data from many different interfaces, dissect more than 700 protocols, and read capture files by other popular sniffers. Filters can be set and output can be saved in different formats. Last but not least, it optionally makes available a nice graphical user interface (GUI).

---

[13] Spectorsoft Spector Pro Key Logger & Computer Spy Software: www.spector.com.

[14] A transcript of a CNN interview in which the software Spector is mentioned as a tool to catch cheating spouses: http://transcripts.cnn.com/TRANSCRIPTS/0505/07/cp.01.html.

[15] KeyGhost, key-logging hardware: www.keyghost.com.

[16] Ethereal, a free "protocol analyzer," the best-known free network sniffer: www.ethereal.com.

[17] Wireshark, successor to Ethereal, a free "protocol analyzer": www.wireshark.org.

Dsniff[18] takes the convenience one step further. It is a collection of tools for network auditing and penetration testing, which consists of several applications.

> dsniff, filesnarf, mailsnarf, msgsnarf, urlsnarf, and webspy passively monitor a network for interesting data (passwords, e-mail, files, etc.). arp-spoof, dnsspoof, and macof facilitate the interception of network traffic normally unavailable to an attacker (e.g., due to layer-2 switching). ssh-mitm and webmitm implement active monkey-in-the-middle attacks against redirected SSH and HTTPS sessions by exploiting weak bindings in ad-hoc PKI. (from the dsniff homepage)

Insufficiently secured wireless networks make sniffing even easier, as all an intruder needs is the right kind of equipment and to be within range of a wireless transmission. The signal can be picked up from outside the building, driving, or walking by. "Wardriving" and "warwalking," respectively, are coined from the term "wardialling" which refers to phoning lots of numbers in order to find out which ones did not answer with a dial but rather a data tone. If a target is not using wireless networking, an attacker can also gain access and plant a rogue wireless access point. Once installed, the intruder can attack safely from outside the building. The chance of discovery is low and even then, the wireless access point may be mistaken for a regular piece of hardware (Robinson 2002).

Telephone

Some kinds of social-engineering attacks are easier to pull off in person or via the telephone. The concept of overloading is much easier to apply and is far more likely to work when engaging someone in an oral debate than through an exchange of written e-mails, simply because the amount of information per time interval is higher in direct conversations. In addition, spoken words must be processed the instant they are received, whereas written messages can easily be skipped back on, in case something was not clearly understood. Even a live text chat does not provide the same level of interaction and information richness (and therefore, the potential of overloading) a personal conversation does.

One of hacker "Bernz's Social Engineering Tips" is:

> Try to be a woman: It's proven that women are more trusted over the phone. Use that to an advantage. Get a woman's help if needed. It's even better if you're actually a woman (a rarity in our biz). (Bernz 1995, Bernz's social engineering tips)

In another article, he even recommends voice changers in order to sound like a woman when on the phone. Because most people in the computer business are still men, posing as a woman can help a male social engineer reach his goal. "Sound helpless, they love it. (...) If you pretend to be a woman, they'll give you plenty of leeway" (Bernz 1995, The complete social engineering faq).

It is easy to pose as a woman in nonverbal conversation—for example via e-mail; however, it is difficult to make people believe you really are a woman, if you are not. Contrarily, it is easy to "prove" that you are a woman when on the phone (with the right voice) and harder to pose as one, if you are not.

Face-to-Face

A social engineer who is a master of the trade succeeds at face-to-face social engineering. It requires both nerves of steel and a quick mind in order to always have an answer ready, especially to unpleasant questions. Imagine lying to people's faces without showing the slightest hint of nervousness or scruples, against the background of the permanent danger of being caught, in person, on the spot. This may seem difficult to most people, but unfortunately there are many who are great at this.

Face-to-face social engineering usually goes along with impersonation. The attacker may pose as a fellow employee, a repairperson, a superior from a distant subsidiary, information technology (IT) support personnel, or another trusted third party, such as the vice president's secretary (Arthurs 2001).

A common technique is the forgery of badges. These are quickly printed, and with today's technology it is hard to tell the difference between an original and a fake if they are not secured in other ways (e.g., by incorporating a transponder chip).

Successful social engineers have a significant advantage; they usually have very attractive personalities. They are characteristically fast on their feet and quite eloquent (Mitnick and Simon 2003). Part of such charisma is inherent, part can be learned.

Dumpster Diving

"Dumpster diving" is a method used by intelligence agents and investigators all over the world. It is nothing more than the act of taking trash from dumpsters of an organization or individual in the hope of acquiring information. Dumpsters outside buildings are ideal targets, as they are usually far less secured than inside ones and no legal implications exist.

Depending on the amount, the trash is usually collected from the dumpster and taken off site for investigation. That way, the act of dumpster diving itself can be limited to screening the trash for promising findings, which makes the process far less time consuming. At a later stage, information may be recovered by applying thorough analysis.

Why would trash have value to anybody? It is amazing what one can learn about target persons/companies by sifting through their waste. People mindlessly throw away all kinds of materials, including but not limited to:

- bills
- financial statements
- credit card statements
- old checks

[18] Dsniff, a collection of tools for network auditing and testing: www.monkey.org/~dugsong/dsniff.

- medical prescription bottles
- work-related materials, such as memos, meeting agendas, and letters revealing names, telephone numbers, and other information (Lively 2003, Mitnick and Simon 2003)

Take a second and think about what social engineers might find in your trash even if they picked it up only for a short time. Many details, which may seem unimportant to insiders, can be valuable information to a social engineer. Organizational charts, for example, are a great source of information for a social-engineering attack as they reveal hierarchies of authority throughout the organization.

What is worse, and what makes dumpster diving an interesting form of acquiring knowledge about target persons or companies, is the low risk associated with it. It is not forbidden to search through someone else's trash, as long as one is not trespassing or violating the law in other ways. As the Defense Security Service's *Employee's Guide to Security Responsibilities* puts it, dumpster diving is perfectly legal in the United States:

> Stealing trash is not illegal. The Supreme Court ruled in 1988 that once an item is left for trash pickup, there is no expectation of privacy or continued ownership. (Defense Security Service 2002)

Local cities and counties may have specific laws that forbid dumpster diving, though. Circumventing a lock, trespassing, and leaving a mess are illegal.

A well-established countermeasure to dumpster diving is the practice of using shredders on classified documents before throwing them away. However, there are different ways shredders are built. Older and cheaper shredders cut documents only in one direction, resulting in spaghetti-like snippets. With enough time on hand (respectively, with the prospect of a positive cost-benefit equation) they can be reassembled quite easily. Crosscut shredders cut paper in two directions, vertically and horizontally. Still, this is no statement of quality on its own, as the residue may be of arbitrary size. This is why the *National Industrial Security Program Operating Manual* of the Department of Defense (DOD) demands a strict maximum size for the residue:

> Crosscut shredders shall be designed to produce residue particle size not exceeding 1/32 inch in width (with a 1/64 inch tolerance by 1/2 inch in length. (U.S. Department of Defense 1997, paragraph 5-705 "Methods of Destruction")

In the United States there are several federal regulations governing the proper disposal of personally identifiable information—for example, the Family Educational Rights and Privacy Act of 1974 (FERPA),[19] the Health Insurance Portability and Accountability Act of 1996 (HIPAA),[20] and the Gramm-Leach-Bliley Act of 1999 (GLBA).[21] FERPA covers the privacy of education and some medical records; HIPAA covers the privacy of personal health information; and GLBA covers the security of financial information.

Phishing

Phishing is most easily described as the practice of directing users to fraudulent Web sites. It is a problem despite all efforts to fight it as it is estimated that some phishing attacks have persuaded up to 5% of their audience to provide sensitive information to spoof Web sites (Dhamija, Tygar, and Hearst 2006).

Big names like AOL[22], eBay[23], PayPal[24] and a large number of financial institutions have been and still are targets for phishing attacks.

A social engineer phishing for passwords to bank accounts, for example, may imitate an e-mail by the victims' bank and ask them to log in as quickly as possible—for example, because of a fictitious "emergency." The e-mail mimics the looks of "real" e-mail by the financial institution—for example, by using the same colors and logos. The attacker provides a link to the "bank's Web site" inside the e-mail. However, the link only seems to point to the bank's Web site, while in truth it leads to a Web site controlled by the social engineer. As soon as the victims try to log on using their credentials, they actually send the confidential data to the attacker, who now has reached the goal of stealing the password. To perfect the masquerading process, the attacker may now output an error message "sorry, wrong password" and then redirect the victims to the real original Web site with which they believed they were interacting. This way, the victims are less likely to discover the scam and may think they just accidentally typed their password wrong the first time. As a result, they will not be alarmed and change their password, which gives the attacker more time to abuse the acquired information.

For example, phishing could be conducted by exploiting bugs or security holes in browsers and e-mail clients, most notably but not limited to Microsoft's Internet Explorer and Outlook and Outlook Express, as they are most commonly used today. Legitimate techniques such as JavaScript may be used in a malicious way. Because phishing relies on masquerading techniques, bugs that can be abused to cover the tracks of leading to Web site address other than the one of the real organization are popular among the phishing community. HTML e-mails (as opposed to plaintext e-mails) are a good example. If an e-mail is sent as HTML rather than plaintext, a link may show a different text than the address it is actually pointing to by using the "<A>" tag. This way, a link showing the text "www.myrealbank.com" may actually lead to the Web site "www.thefalsebank.com" when clicked on.

[19] Family Educational Rights and Privacy Act (FERPA): www.ed.gov/offices/OII/fpco/ferpa.

[20] Health Insurance Portability and Accountability Act of 1996 (HIPAA): www.hhs.gov/ocr/hipaa.

[21] Gramm-Leach-Bliley Act of 1999 (GLBA): www.ftc.gov/privacy/privacyinitiatives/glbact.html.

[22] America Online (AOL), a well-known Internet service provider (ISP): www.aol.com.

[23] Ebay, a big Internet auction platform: www.ebay.com.

[24] Paypal, a simple way of sending and receiving payments online: https://www.paypal.com.

Usually, hovering above the link will show the real destination in the status bar. A trick to spoof this occurrence as well may be of great use to attackers trying to deceive people. After clicking the link, a browser window may pop up and surf to the indicated address, thereby disclosing the false nature of the link. Again, a bug that allows hiding of the genuine events could be abused to cover the tracks of the attacker.

One early trick involved use of the "@" sign: a URL such as "www.thegoodurl.com@thebadurl.com" may trick people into believing they are visiting thegoodurl.com when actually everything before the "@" is just understood as a username by the Web server. If user "www.thegooodurl.com" does not exist, however, the page ("thebadurl.com") will load just as well. Fortunately, this potential security hole no longer works for most new browsers. The following list provides an overview of browser-specific behavior:

- The following browsers issue a security warning and asked the user if they should proceed:
  - Internet Explorer 6.x
  - Opera 8.x
  - Firefox 1.x
  - Netscape 8.x
- The following browser proceeds without asking:
  - Safari 2.0.3 on Apple

Currently, there are efforts to develop antiphishing techniques, in which one solution may be to detect phishing attacks by using fake responses that mimic real users (Chandrasekaran, Chinchani, and Upadhyaya 2006).

New or Creative Methods

Considering surprise and curiosity as two important concepts for successful social engineering attacks to rely on, the development of creative or new methods is a great opportunity for potential attackers. In June 2006, for example, a story on "Social Engineering, the USB Way" hit the news.[25] A security professional who had been hired for a security assessment described a new method to compromise companies' networks; it works by scattering specially prepared USB drives in the parking lot, smoking areas, and other areas frequented by employees. Nested between a set of assorted pictures, a Trojan was hidden on the drive. The idea was that curious employees who "found" the seeded devices would eventually plug them into their computers inside the company's network to watch the planted images, accidentally launching the Trojan that would phone home to the attacker. Fifteen of the twenty USB drives were found, and all of the found devices were plugged into employees' computers. Thus, the idea turned out to be a big success that also came along with other benefits for potential attackers: Apart from seeding the USB drives, which can be conducted in a rather unobtrusive way (e.g. at 6 A.M., as the author of the original article describes) social engineers do not even have to go near the company's building but can instead enjoy information sent out directly to their headquarters.

Another surprisingly easy way to conduct a social-engineering attack is to let go of most cover-up efforts and just ask users for their usernames and passwords, as described in the section on "Password Problems," below.

Reverse Social Engineering

Reverse social engineering (RSE) is an even more advanced form of social engineering. In contrast to traditional social engineering, in reverse social engineering, the cracker is thought to be on a higher level (e.g., a superior or administrator) than the legitimate user (Allen 2001). An example of RSE is when crackers cause a problem on the target's network or computer and then make themselves available to fix the problem. The trust they earn by helping the target can then be abused to obtain the information they are after (Gragg 2003). But the problem does not even have to be real; it may be sufficient to just make the victim think there is a problem (Mitnick and Simon 2003).

If the victim is the one acting and the actual attacker only *re*acts to a cry for help, the victim is a lot less likely to be suspicious. As Mitnick states:

> The attacker just sits and waits for the phone to ring, a tactic fondly known in the trade as reverse social engineering. An attacker who can make the target call him gains instant credibility: If I place a call to someone I think is on the help desk, I'm not going to start asking him to prove his identity. That's when the attacker has it made. (Mitnick and Simon 2003)

The victim asks the attacker for help, which the social engineer is able to provide easily, as the attacker has caused the incident. This leads the victim to trust the attacker, which is, in fact, nothing more than the acceptance of authority, which in this case (apparently) was confirmed by the demonstration of expertise.

PASSWORD PROBLEMS

A lot of social-engineering attacks try to steal passwords. This fact is rather unsurprising, as passwords are still the most commonly used authentication mechanism (Tari et al. 2006).

This section shows problems passwords entail and why they are partially inherent to the system.

The information presented stems from a survey[26] undertaken by the organizers of Infosecurity Europe[27] 2004 to find out more about the security consciousness of workers concerning company information stored on computers. The survey was conducted at Liverpool Street Station in London and consisted of a series of questions

[25] Darkreading, a security news site. June 7, 2006. "Social Engineering, the USB Way": http://www.darkreading.com/document.asp?doc_id=95556&WT.svl=column1_1—additional comment by the author at www.darkreading.com/boards/message.asp?msg_id=134658.

[26] Infosecurity Europe 2004 survey, results summarized in a mailing list thread: www.iwar.org.uk/pipermail/infocon/2004-April/001287.html.

[27] Homepage of Infosecurity Europe: www.infosec.co.uk.

that included the question "What is your password?" People were promised a chocolate bar for parting with their passwords (concept of anticipation). The results were quite alarming:

- A total of 37% of the 172 workers surveyed immediately gave their password when inquired about it. The number of people giving their password is alarming. It should be noted, though, that the sample size is small and it may thus be difficult to generalize the results.
- Another 34% initially refused but gave their password when being applied simple social engineering techniques on—"I bet it's to do with your pet or child's name."

This shows that social engineering can be easy at times; though some respondents may have cheated and it is hard to imagine that more than two thirds of people may give out their passwords so thoughtlessly, one can conclude that a considerable number of people do not require any social engineering at all. Just asking for their password—or promising them some chocolate might suffice.

The most common password categories were

- family names such as partners or children (15%)
- football teams (11%)
- and pets (8%)

In the 2003 survey, the most common password had been "password" (12%) and the most popular category their own name (16%) followed by their football team (11%) and date of birth (8%). Respondents had been promised a cheap pen in exchange for their passwords (Leyden 2003).

These might be worth a try for any social engineer struggling to find out the password of a given person. The results also show why people should be (made) aware about the risks of thoughtlessly giving out personal information. Even facts that seem unimportant can be of value to an attacker.

Only 53% of those surveyed said they would not give their password to someone calling from the IT department, as this could cause a security breach. This leaves more than half the workers vulnerable to one of the simplest (and thus most popular) social-engineering approach, the attacker pretending to be someone from the IT department and calling victims requesting their password in order to "solve a problem."

Four out of 10 colleagues knew their colleagues' passwords. This is an alarming finding as well, as many attacks originate from the inside of an organization. The *2005 CSI/FBI Computer Crime and Security Survey* states that incidents originating from outside and incidents originating from inside are roughly balanced, which is contrary to the popular belief that most attacks do originate from inside (Computer Security Institute 2006). However, the remaining share of about 50% of incidents originating from inside an organization should make people wary of telling their passwords to colleagues.

A total of 55% said they would give their password to their boss. The knowing reader immediately recognizes the concept of authority that was already mentioned in the section about the psychological background of social engineering. More than half the survey respondents would give their password to their boss—this underlines the danger posed by impersonating attackers.

Two thirds of workers use the same password they use for access to their company information for personal access for operations such as online banking and Web site access. This result clearly originates from the difficulties people have remembering passwords. This finding calls attention to the annoying fact that attackers might get even more than they asked for. With two thirds of people using the same password for multiple purposes, a password acquired for a computer account may also be the key to other "advantages" for the social engineer.

Respondents used an average of four passwords. This result shows that the problem of simple passwords is inherent to the system. The reason people choose simple passwords that present a security threat is because they have problems memorizing them.

The following facts were gathered concerning the duration of password use:

- A total of 51% of the passwords are changed monthly.
- A total of 3% of the passwords are changed weekly.
- A total of 2% of the workers change their passwords daily.
- A total of 10% change them each quarter.
- A total of 13% change them rarely.
- A total of 20% never change their passwords.

In addition, many workers who had to change their password on a regular basis wrote it down on a piece of paper or in a word-processing document in order not to forget it. Again, people's difficulties in remembering passwords make it simple for an attacker. With one fifth of them never changing their password, such targets represent easy victims.

The final finding to be mentioned here is the attitude toward passwords in general:

- A total of 80% of workers were fed up with using passwords.
- A total of 92% said they would prefer some sort of biometric technology to them, such as fingerprint and iris scanners, smartcards, or tokens. As pointed out later in this chapter, in Figure 3, in 2005 only 15% of the companies responding to a survey used biometrics. (Infosecurity Europe 2004)

A study conducted by researchers at Brigham Young University led to similar results—80% of the participants gave their username and 60% gave their password. An auditor gained physical access to the audited company and introduced himself as "performing a survey to assess the security of our network" (Orgill et al. 2004). One reason for the success of the mentioned audit may be the factor of surprise: The first three questions of the survey asked for name, username, and password of the participating employee. Who would suspect such a blatant approach to gain users' passwords, especially if the attacker is already inside the building and wearing a valid badge?

The difficulties in remembering multiple complicated passwords are usually described by basic human cognitive limitations from the psychology literature. A way to mitigate these problems may be the use of graphical passwords, which leads to an increase in memorability. Another surprising finding of the study is that dictionary passwords are less vulnerable to "shoulder surfing" (e.g., observation during password entry) than nondictionary passwords. This effect may be attributed to slower keyboard entry of nondictionary passwords (Tari et al. 2006).

In addition to people choosing weak passwords, there is always the risk of password-cracking tools, which can be used to find out passwords. Considering Microsoft Windows, for example, which is still by far the most used operating system for desktop computers, a multitude of tools is available. L0phtCrack[28] was the first well-known password cracker for Windows passwords and has since changed its image to an "award-winning password auditing and recovery application." It allows dictionary (using a set of words to try as a password) and brute-force attacks (trying all possible combinations of a set of given characters). Precomputed hash tables can be used as well. A Project called RainbowCrack[29] takes this last idea one step further. Precomputed hash tables for a wide range of characters are available online for free.

Considering the above-mentioned facts, it is no surprise even Bill Gates, founder of Microsoft, thinks the days of traditional passwords are numbered:

> There is no doubt that over time, people are going to rely less and less on passwords. People use the same password on different systems, they write them down and they just don't meet the challenge for anything you really want to secure. (Kotaida 2004)

The aforementioned facts show that the attempt to prevent social-engineering attacks by establishing technological countermeasures can lead to new, even more severe problems.

AN EXAMPLE: THE POSTMAN AS SENIOR PHYSICIAN

Well-trained social engineers have the potential to get almost everywhere they want. Some readers may not believe it. A trained postman posed as a doctor applying for a job in a psychiatric hospital. He got the job and worked as a senior physician for one and a half years. He prescribed drugs, held seminars in front of hundreds of "colleagues," invented new terminology, which was accepted without any doubt, and even appeared in court—not as a suspect but as an appraiser in more than twenty cases. He was awarded a professorship at a university, which he kindly turned down. This may sound impossible but it really happened.

Gert Postel's story sounds almost unbelievable—but it is true—a trained postman working as a senior physician in a Saxon psychiatric hospital for one and a half years. How did he manage to fool so many people, including doctors and politicians? The following section is based on an interview transcript provided on his homepage.[30]

Postel has a history of posing as a medical doctor, but this was his masterpiece, which ultimately got him four years in jail—but first things first.

The position had been advertised in medical newspapers. Postel applied normally and was picked out of thirty candidates. He had gathered a huge amount of knowledge on psychology by self-education and through two former girlfriends who had been studying medicine. This way, he managed to convince the board with a paper he had written, which was ironically discussing Thomas Mann's novel "Confessions of Felix Krull, Confidence Man," about a young man who recognizes that having a good appearance and a convincing attitude more than compensates for lack of experience or ability. With his appearance and (false) references he outwitted even experienced physicians.

Postel's acting was so convincing that he managed to keep up the masquerade for one and a half years—and he was discovered only because the parents of an assistant remembered his name from a prior coup. He remembers thinking, "Who actually is the fraud, me or them?"—for example, he introduced new terminology, terms that do not exist. In front of a hundred psychiatrists he talked about the "Bipolar Depression of the Third Degree"—a supposed psychiatric term that does not exist. No one asked a single question about it as Postel cleverly abused the concept of authority through knowledge: every one who had asked about the term would have implied their own incompetence. He used the same trick when during the job interview he was asked what his doctorate was in: he answered "Cognitive-Induced Distortions in the Stereotypical Formation of Judgment," which, he admits, "is nothing else than the stringing together of meaningless words."

Postel highlighted the importance of mastering the psychiatric jargon for making his way up to the top. By using the jargon, Postel applied three concepts of social engineering at the same time; he not only gained authority/credibility through (false) expertise but also lowered the chance of suspicion by invoking a feeling of "having something in common" and used the concept of overloading by exploiting the fact that human beings can process only a limited amount of information at any given time.

[28] L0phtCrack, an award-winning password auditing and recovery application for Microsoft Windows: www.atstake.com.

[29] RainbowCrack, a password cracker for Microsoft Windows (and other systems using vulnerable password hashes), which works by generating tables of precomputed passwords and then matching the encrypted passwords against these, which is much faster than trying to encrypt password guesses and then comparing them to the encrypted one: www.antsight.com/zsl/rainbowcrack.

[30] Homepage of Gert Postel, a trained postman successfully posing as a senior psychiatrist for one and a half years. English translation of a TV talk show: www.gert-postel.de/english.htm. Gert Postel's home page (German): www.gert-postel.de.

He also describes an exceptionally well conducted impersonating attack when remembering calling the senior consultant at the hospital as "Director of the University Clinic of Neurology in Muenster" and recommending "his assistant, Dr. Postel," for the position. Two hours later, the consultant was talking to "Dr. Postel" and referred to the earlier telephone conversation and how full of praise it had been, which Postel saucily dismissed as exaggeration.

Another anecdote concerns the police. When Postel had finally been unmasked and decided to flee from imminent arrest, the police managed to track down his exact location in a flat. But Postel had somehow smelled a rat and therefore pinned a note to the door: "Dear Simone, I'm with Steffi in Bremen. Will be back in a week. See you, yours..." With Postel looking through the spy hole and only ten centimeters between him and the police, they decided to leave again, as "he cannot be there if he is in Bremen." This can be seen as social engineering through surprise: the trick worked because the situation developed in such an unexpected way. No one believed a wanted criminal could act so impertinently.

But how did he manage to escape in the first place? Postel had built up a deceptive relationship with the senior consultant, who helped him to get away. Postel, looking back, says:

> the senior consultant told me that I was suspected of a serious offence. I was suspended until the next day. With incredible logic I concluded that finally the cat was out of the bag and that I should terminate my stay immediately. In fact, the senior consultant acted as accomplice (Gert Postel on his homepage).

The story even has a component of reverse social engineering in it: in the beginning, the hospital was searching for a senior physician. This can metaphorically be seen as a "cry for help," which Postel "answers" when he makes himself available after reading about the job advertisement in a medical newspaper. If you invite physicians you usually don't expect con men, that's another factor that made them so vulnerable to his attack.

As Mitnick states:

> Manipulative people usually have very attractive personalities. They are typically fast on their feet and quite articulate (Mitnick and Simon 2003).

This holds true for Postel, as a quote[31] in the German newspaper *Die Welt*[32] by his former boss shows: "The man immediately convinced me. His appearance, his references—I thought to myself, we cannot get a better physician."

Though Gert Postel's story is not specifically linked to computing, it illustrates a wealth of different social engineering attacks in just one real-world example.

DEFENDING AGAINST SOCIAL ENGINEERING

Because social engineering exploits the human factor as the weakest link in an organization's security chain, the most effective defenses rely on educating people. Nonetheless, technological approaches also have to be considered; phishing attacks, for example, might be a lot less successful if browsers and mail clients were designed in a more secure way.

A Multilayered Defensive Approach

In order to maximize abilities to prevent or detect social engineering attacks, a comprehensive approach is required. Requiring employees to sign a security policy on entry to the organization, for example, will not per se lead to an increase in security, because policies have to be reinforced and maintained. Thus, multiple layers of security should be introduced (Gragg 2003; Thornburgh 2004; Orgill et al. 2004). Gragg's concept, *A Multi-Level Defense against Social Engineering*, consists of the following levels of security:

- *Foundational Level*: Security policy addressing social engineering
- *Parameter Level*: Security-awareness training for all users
- *Fortress Level*: Resistance training for key personnel
- *Persistence Level*: Ongoing reminders
- *Gotcha Level*: Social engineering land mines (SELM)
- *Offensive Level*: Incident response (Gragg 2003)

The importance and roles of policies and security-awareness training will be highlighted in the following sections. Key personnel, such as helpdesk operators, who are likely to be targeted by social engineers should undergo resistance training in order to prepare for specific social engineering attacks. One of the essential features that should be instilled through resistance training is that employees must realize that they are personally vulnerable to such attacks. At the Persistence Level, personnel should regularly be reminded of the possibility of social engineering attacks. Social Engineering Land Mines (SELM) that are set at the Gotcha Level should assist in the defense against social engineering attempts. Examples for SELMs are callbacks by policy or bogus questions. Finally, there should be a well-defined process that employees can initiate as soon as they suspect something is wrong (Offensive Level). Incidents should be logged, the information may be used at the Persistence Level to remind employees of the possibility of attackers conducting social engineering attacks (Gragg 2003).

Policies

Security policies are the foundation of a successful defense strategy. In addition to a generic security policy, specific ones may be advisable, such as remote access. Employees are required to take note of the policies by acknowledging in written form, usually together with

[31] *Die Welt*, German newspaper. Article about the unbelievable story of Gert Postel, the trained postman posting as a senior psychiatrist: www.welt.de/data/1999/01/20/623409.html.

[32] *Die Welt*, German newspaper: www.welt.de.

signing their contract. Updates and enhancements have to be propagated in a correct manner so no one is missed.

In order to generate a sound security policy and before putting procedures into place, risk identification and assessment must take place, which consists roughly of the following steps[33]:

1. Identification of assets
2. Identification of risks/threats
3. Risk analysis—analysis of potential impact of the risks to the organization
4. Prioritization of risks
5. Planning and establishment of controls for risk mitigation
6. Monitoring

Policies have to target certain areas in order to provide a defense against social engineering—for example, they should address information-access controls, establishment and termination of accounts, management and approval of access rights, and password changes and complexity. However, physical security details such as locks, IDs, paper shredding (discussed in the section on "Dumpster Diving," above), and escorting of visitors need to be addressed. To decrease the chance of a dumpster-diving attack, for example, trash bins should be kept out of public access. People have to know how to respond to unusual requests. They should not be put in the situation of having to decide themselves whether information is allowed to be handed out (Gragg 2003).

Thus, a data-classification policy is of great importance as well. It helps to implement controls with respect to disclosing information (Mitnick and Simon 2003). Data not explicitly classified must retain a default state of confidential to minimize risk.

Security Awareness versus Technological Measures

Because social engineering targets the weakest link in the security chain of an organization—human beings—this is what countermeasures mainly have to focus on. People are simply unaware of the risks and dangers, which arise from security breaches like, for example, the leaking of classified or personal information. This is where the concept of *security awareness* emerges.

It is a widely accepted position that technological measures are of only very limited use against social engineering attacks. Even Gragg, in his *Multi-Level Defense against Social Engineering*, focuses only on policy and training issues (Gragg 2003).

> The truth is that there is no technology in the world that can prevent a social engineering attack (Mitnick and Simon 2003).

> In short: Do not rely only on security devices. To neutralize such hacker's techniques, one must use their own weapons against them: good old grey matter (Lafrance 2004).

Security awareness is the process of making people realize the importance of security and the consequences of security failure. Training on policies and procedures is important, but people will pay far more attention and will be far more likely to follow security policies if they know about the risks, which are targeted. Constant reminders and training make employees effective in identifying attacks and responding in an appropriate manner (Kratt 2005). That is why an ongoing awareness program is of great importance; some authorities recommend that 40% of a company's overall security budget be spent on security-awareness training (Mitnick and Simon 2003).

For example, it is a big problem that most people are not aware of the danger the exposure of personal information bears. "I've got nothing to hide" is a sentence one can hear quite often when asking people about freely available personal information about them. But each tiny bit of information can be abused for purposes of social engineering. A social engineer could call a target's neighbors to collect more information or even trick them to give away the key to the target's house they store for emergency cases. Names of family members and pets along with birth dates are often used as passwords, as surveys show (see section on "Password Problems," above). In addition, all of the above-mentioned information can be used to impersonate the target.

The Computer Security Institute (CSI)[34] conducts a yearly "Computer Crime and Security Survey" with the participation of the San Francisco Federal Bureau of Investigation's (FBI)[35] Computer Intrusion Squad. The following figures are based on data published in the 2006 survey and illustrate the significance of security awareness. Though the survey emphasizes computer security, and the term *social engineering* is used only with respect to information technology, the importance of security awareness holds true for other areas as well.

Because social engineering targets the human being as the weakest link in information society, security-awareness training is a key point in developing a proper defense against social engineering. The figures below emphasize the importance of the concept of security-awareness training. They give an overview of the components of and show the status quo of the investments in security-awareness training. Finally, commonly used security technologies are viewed from a social-engineering point of view.

Figure 1 shows the importance of security-awareness training that the 599 responding computer security practitioners in U.S. corporations, government agencies, financial institutions, and medical institutions attribute to various areas of security. For seven of the eight areas, training was seen as very important. The results indicate an overall substantial increase in the perception of

---

[33] Homepage of the Federal Financial Institutions Examination Council's (FFIEC). Information on Risk Identification and Assessment: www.ffiec.gov/ffiecinfobase/booklets/mang/07.html.

[34] Home page of the Computer Security Institute (CSI): www.gocsi.com.

[35] Home page of the Federal Bureau of Investigation (FBI): www.fbi.gov.

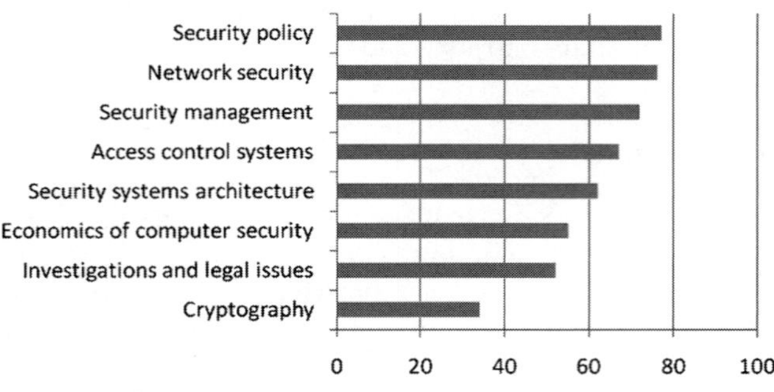

Figure 1: Importance of security-awareness training in specific areas (599 respondents) (Computer Security Institute 2006)

the importance of security-awareness training, compared to last year's result. Figure 1 shows the current figures (Computer Security Institute 2006).

Figure 2 gives a review of which organizations invest the most in security-awareness training. It is based on the replies of 483 respondents who were asked if their organization invested sufficiently in security-awareness training. The interesting result is that, "on average, respondents from 10 out of the 15 sectors do not believe that their organization invests enough in security awareness." The survey also presents numbers on the overall security operating expenditures and capital investment. In all but three sectors (federal government, utilities, and transportation), the perception that sufficient resources are being devoted to overall security and capital investment is much higher than security-awareness training. Thus, security-awareness training once more appears to be a prime area for additional funding (Computer Security Institute 2006).

The alarming fact is that most security practitioners know about the lack of investment in security-awareness training in their organizations and no substantial improvement has taken place over the past two years. This is an important finding to remember when discussing social engineering. Security awareness is the most important countermeasure to social engineering; security practitioners know that their organization is not investing enough on security awareness; still, there is no improvement, because decision makers obviously do not recognize the threat. As a conclusion, this means the door to social-engineering attacks remains wide open.

Figure 3 illustrates which security technologies are most commonly used. Compared to last year, the results shown in Figure 3 are approximately the same, apart from newly introduced categories. The use of biometrics increased from 15% to 20% compared to last year's results. Although the reported use of encryption for data in transit and reusable account/log-in passwords went down, the use of intrusion-prevention systems (IPSs) increased. The difference between IPSs and firewalls is the divergent approach: while firewalls use a so-called whitelist approach by blocking all traffic except the one they have a reason to pass, IPSs pass all traffic unless they have a reason to block it (Computer Security Institute 2006).

It is easy see that none of the top-listed technologies—neither firewalls nor antivirus software—are able to fend off a (nontechnical) social-engineering attack. This holds true for the other entries as well, since the "human factor" is neglected by purely technological measures. Security technology raises overall security, but neither cryptography nor passwords or biometrics can keep an employee from simply giving out proprietary information when deceived by a social engineer. Passwords as a

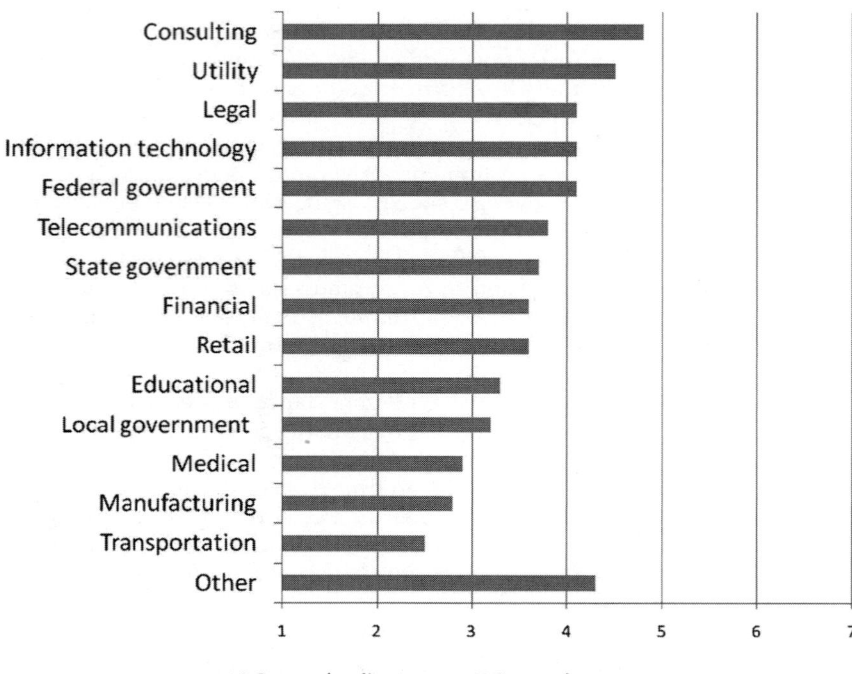

Figure 2: Responses of 483 security practitioners about whether their organization invests enough in security-awareness training (mean values reported on a seven-point scale) (Computer Security Institute 2006)

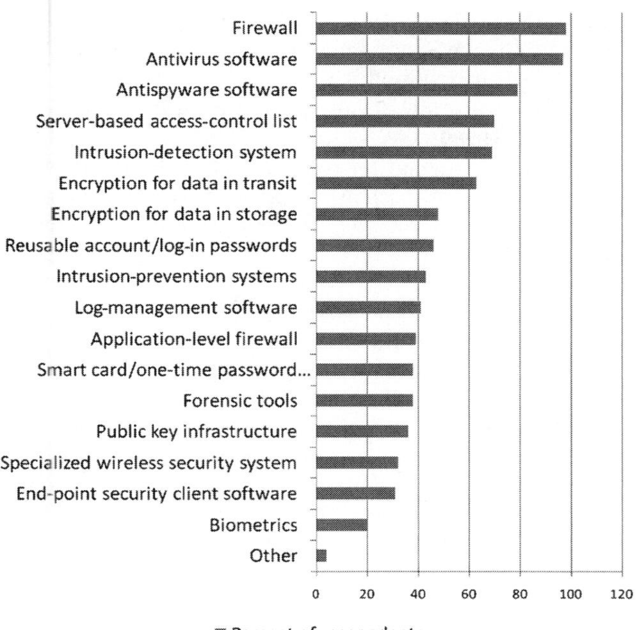

Figure 3: Security technologies used (616 respondents) (Computer Security Institute 2006)

special topic are discussed in the section on "Password Problems," above.

The newly introduced category of antispyware software ranks third, though. Certain technical approaches that may be used by an attacker to gain information (e.g., the use of key loggers to get users' passwords) may be tackled by technologies of this category, along with antivirus software, which is ranked second.

The following conclusion may be drawn from the above-mentioned information: Figure 3 points out that most respondents participating invest considerably in security technologies. Figure 1 illustrates that the perception of the importance of security-awareness training has increased in the past year, compared with last year's results, while Figure 2 shows that most security practitioners still sense a lack of investment in security-awareness training. As already stated, it is hardly possible to conquer social engineering using only technological measures. On the contrary, the findings show that organizations invest considerably in security technologies, while security practitioners sense a lack of security-awareness training, which most likely stems from decision makers' lack of perception of the importance of this training. Thus, as a conclusion, management should be more aware of the possibility and dangers of attacks like social engineering in order to grant adequate funds for security-awareness training.

Training

Policies are worth only the paper they are printed on if they are not enforced. The most important concept in dealing with human beings as the weakest link in an organization's security chain is education and training. An employee who is regularly required to attend security-awareness trainings is far less likely to fall for social-engineering attacks, and the mere signing of a security policy does not make the person more security-aware.

Incident Response

The issue of incident response is closely linked to the topic of continuous training. If an employee has uncovered a social-engineering attack, there must be a defined process for how to deal with the situation. Incidents have to be communicated through the entire organization in a timely manner so that the attacker does not have the chance of just looking for another victim who is less security-aware. Incidents should be tracked in a centralized way by a responsible person or department (Gragg 2003).

Termination Process

An organizational measure against social engineering is the establishment of a well-functioning termination process. The termination process ensures that employees have their user accounts and access rights removed in a timely manner once they leave the organization. This is of prime importance, as attacks may be conducted by disgruntled former workers. In addition to the danger of former employees still having access to sensitive information, a social engineer could deliberately try to guess the credentials of laid-off personnel.

While workers are on vacation their accounts could be locked instead of deleted in order to provide a higher level of security (Jones 2004). Locking instead of deletion makes sure there is no distraction from work once employees return, as the accounts can easily be unlocked again.

Technological Countermeasures

Although technological measures alone are not sufficient to provide a defense against social-engineering attacks, as discussed above, they can at least complicate an attack. The following list provides some examples; we will not discuss this topic in detail.

- *Network security*: The network should be protected against "sniffing" to prohibit easy spying on the data. Switches, for example, provide higher security than hubs by sending traffic only to the concerned computer ("unicast") rather than to all attached ones ("multicast"). However, this protection can be circumvented as well, for example with "arpspoof," which is part of the *dsniff*[18] package. A virtual private network (VPN) can add a layer of encryption in order to counter sniffing attacks. E-mails containing confidential information should be encrypted.
- *Virus scanners* provide a basic protection against malicious applications such as viruses, worms, and Trojan horses. They are available for different operating systems. There are also different types of virus scanners, which target servers, clients, and e-mail. Suspicious e-mail attachments can automatically be put in a vault and later released on request. Messages containing viruses can be deleted.

- *Intrusion-detection systems (IDS)* and *intrusion-prevention systems (IPS)*: Intrusion-detection systems detect unusual manipulations to systems by analyzing certain parameters like network traffic (network IDS) or logs and system calls (host-based IDS) for suspicious patterns. IDSs only issue warnings, whereas IPSs proactively respond to the assumed threat—for example by logging a user off (Rash et al. 2005). However, both systems must be finely adjusted in order to keep false positive results at a low level.
- *Media* containing confidential data must be handled suitably, which involves not only proper storage but also deletion processes. Data on magnetic storage media should be erased in a proper way, which includes wiping (overwriting data) or the use of degaussers.[36] Physical destruction like burning, grinding, or shredding should be considered for all media.

TESTING COUNTERMEASURES

Countermeasures and policies must be tested on an ongoing basis. They have to be maintained frequently; simulated attacks should be conducted regularly in order to find weak spots (Orgill et al. 2004, Allen 2001).

An interesting problem arises if employees are told that the level of security is satisfactory, as they may become complacent. Thus, both administration and employees will let their guard down. In fact, increased security measures even make psychological attacks easier because people think their data are safe (Dubin 2002). This always has to be kept in mind when testing countermeasures: negative findings may and will happen; however, they should not produce a bitter aftertaste. Instead, a communicated conclusion of "everything is great" may even lead to counterproductive results. Testing the compliance to the security policy and determining how vulnerable a company is to social engineering attacks is an important and complex topic. Hasle et al. (2005), for instance, propose a metric to measure the degree of vulnerability.

GUIDELINES

This section provides a brief set of guidelines (in random order) to identify and thus reduce the chance of a successful social-engineering attack.

- Follow the security policy; by doing so, no one will be able to accuse you of doing something wrong. Do not make exceptions.
- Know your fellow employees. By doing so, it is easy to spot suspicious unescorted visitors.
- Allow yourself to be mistrustful. Although being mistrustful complicates the process of making new friends, it may protect both you and them from damage and thus help in keeping old friends.
- Do not reciprocate mindlessly. If strangers do you a favor and then ask for a favor in return, think twice about what they are asking for.
- Ask unpleasant questions. Do not be rude to strangers or fellow employees you do not know and who are requesting information from you, but do ask them to identify themselves clearly. Bogus questions are a great opportunity to identify attackers in an early stage; an example is provided by Gragg:

> "Oh Mr. Smith, how is your daughter? Is she getting better from the accident?" If the caller says, "My daughter wasn't in an accident." or "I don't have a daughter," the caller has passed a single test. At this point the employee would apologize and explain that he or she must be mistaken. However, if the caller starts talking about the accident or lets the target talk about the accident, then the hacker has been hooked. (Gragg 2003)

- Take your time. Many social-engineering attacks work by applying some kind of pressure. Do not let an attacker fool you into revealing confidential information because of an "emergency case." There always has to be the time to thoroughly check whether a request is justified and the acting persons are authorized.
- Complying with authority is good; verification of authority is better. Though supervisors may react in an offended way when being asked for identification, it is even more important to do so. By strictly following the security policy even when "superiors" or their "secretaries" ask for information you demonstrate your correct understanding and awareness concerning security.
- Report recognized or suspected social-engineering attacks immediately.

CONCLUSION

Social engineering is a kind of attack, which cannot be remedied by technological measures, as it targets the weakest link in an organization's security chain, the human factor. You paradoxically fall for it because you believe in the good nature of human beings. It is a "soft" kind of attack and thus has to be countered by applying equivalent defense strategies. The most important step in doing so is to raise security awareness and keep it at a high level through continuous training, whereas purely technological countermeasures can be seen only as a supplement.

GLOSSARY

Dumpster Diving: The act of taking trash from dumpsters of an organization or individual in the hope of acquiring information.

Phishing: Most easily described as the practice of directing users to fraudulent Web sites.

Reciprocation: Most easily described as an automatic urge to respond to a gift or favor one receives.

Shoulder Surfing: Observation during password entry.

---

[36] Degaussers are able to completely erase all data from magnetic storage media, whereas overwriting does not erase all data. An example source for degaussers: www.veritysystems.com/degaussers/index.asp.

Social Proof: Instead of developing an opinion by themselves, people usually rely to a certain degree on what other people are doing or saying.

CROSS REFERENCES

See *Authentication*; *Computer Network Management*; *Network Attacks*.

REFERENCES

Allen, M. 2001. *The use of social engineering as a means of violating computer systems*. www.sans.org/reading_room/whitepapers/engineering/529.php (accessed May 12, 2007).

Arthurs, W. 2001. *A proactive defence to social engineering*. www.sans.org/reading_room/whitepapers/engineering/511.php (accessed May 12, 2007).

Bernz 1995. Bernz's social engineering tips. www.packetstormsecurity.org/docs/social-engineering/tips.html (accessed May 11, 2007).

Bernz 1995. The complete social engineering faq. http://morehouse.org/hin/blckcrwl/hack/soceng.txt (accessed May 11, 2007).

Blass, T. 1999. The Milgram paradigm after 35 years: Some things we now know about obedience to authority. *Journal of Applied Social Psychology* 25:955–78.

Calishain, T., and R. Dornfest, 2004. Google Hacks, 2nd ed. Sebastopol, CA: O'Reilly.

CERT. 2002, March 19. CERT® Incident Note IN-2002-03. Social engineering attacks via IRC and instant messaging. www.cert.org/incident_notes/IN-2002-03.html (accessed May 11, 2007).

Chandrasekaran, M., R. Chinchani, and Upadhyaya, S. 2006. PHONEY: Mimicking user response to detect phishing attacks. In *Proceedings of the 2006 International Symposium on the World of Wireless, Mobile and Multimedia Networks (June 26–29, 2006), International Workshop on Wireless Mobile Multimedia*. Washington, DC: IEEE Computer Society. DOI=http://dx.doi.org/10.1109/WOWMOM. 2006.87 (accessed May 11, 2007).

Cialdini, R. B. 1993. *Influence: The psychology of persuasion*. Revised ed. New York: Morrow.

Computer Security Institute (CSI) and FBI. 2006. CSI/FBI computer crime and security survey. www.gocsi.com (registration required)

Defense Security Service. 2002. *Employee's guide to security responsibilities*. www.dss.mil/training/csg/security/Home.htm (accessed May 11, 2007).

Denning, D. E. 2000, autumn. Cyberterrorism. In *Global Dialogue*. www.cs.georgetown.edu/~denning/infosec/cyberterror-GD.doc (accessed May 12, 2007).

Dhamija, R., J. D. Tygar, and M. Hearst. 2006. Why phishing works. In *Proceedings of the SIGCHI Conference on Human Factors in Computing Systems, Montréal, Québec, Canada, April 22–27, 2006. CHI '06*. New York: ACM Press. DOI=http://doi.acm.org/10.1145/1124772.1124861 (accessed May 11, 2007).

Dolan, A. 2004. Social engineering. www.sans.org/reading_room/whitepapers/engineering/1365.php (accessed May 12, 2007).

Dubin, L. 2002. *The enemy within: A system administrator's look at network security*. www.sans.org/rr/whitepapers/engineering/530.php (accessed May 11, 2007).

Gragg, D. 2003. *A multi-level defense against social engineering*. www.sans.org/reading_room/whitepapers/engineering/920.php (accessed May 12, 2007).

Greening, T. 1996. Ask and ye shall receive: A study in "social engineering." *ACM SIGSAC Review* 14(2):8–14. DOI=http://doi.acm.org/10.1145/228292.228295 (accessed May 11, 2007)..

Gross, R., A. Acquisti, and H. J. Heinz. III. 2005. Information revelation and privacy in online social networks. In *Proceedings of the 2005 ACM Workshop on Privacy in the Electronic Society, Alexandria, VA, USA*, 71–80. New York: ACM Press. DOI=http://doi.acm.org/10.1145/1102199.1102214 (accessed May 11, 2007).

Gulati, R. 2003. *The threat of social engineering and your defense against it*. www.sans.org/reading_room/whitepapers/engineering 1232.php (accessed May 12, 2007).

Harl, G. 1997. *People hacking: The psychology of social engineering*. Text of Harl's talk at *Access All Areas III, May 7, 1997*. http://library.cyber-punk.cc/files/se10.html (accessed May 12, 2007).

Hasle, H., Y. Kristiansen, K. Kintel, and E. Snekkenes. 2005. Measuring resistance to social engineering. In *Information security practice and experience* New York: Springer. www.springerlink.com/content/t0damd49w172l1wv (accessed May 11, 2007).

Infosecurity Europe. 2004. Office Workers Give Away Passwords for a chocolate bar. www.iwar.org.uk/pipermail/infocon/2004-April/001287.html (accessed May 11, 2007).

Jones, C. 2004. *Understanding and auditing*. www.sans.org/rr/whitepapers/engineering/1332.php (accessed May 11, 2007).

Kotaida, M. 2004, February 25. Gates predicts death of the password. ZDNet News, http://news.zdnet.co.uk/software/windows/0,39020396,39147336,00.htm (accessed May 11, 2007).

Kratt, H. 2005. The inside story: A disgruntled employee gets his revenge. www.sans.org/rr/whitepapers/engineering/1548.php (accessed May 11, 2007).

Lafrance, Y. 2004. *Psychology: A precious security tool*. www.sans.org/rr/whitepapers/engineering/1409.php (accessed May 11, 2007).

Leyden, J. 2003. Office workers give away passwords for a cheap pen. *The Register*. www.theregister.co.uk/2003/04/18/office_workers_give_away_passwords (accessed May 11, 2007).

Lively, C. E. Jr. 2003. Psychological based social engineering. www.giac.com/practical/GSEC/Charles_Lively_GSEC.pdf (accessed May 11, 2007).

Long, J., E. Skoudis, and A. van Eijkelenborg. 2004. Google hacking for penetration testers. Rockland, MA: Syngress Publishing.

Maris, K. 2005. *The human factor*. www.cccure.org/modules.php?name=Downloads&d_op=getit&lid=240 (accessed October 25, 2006).

Milgram, S. 1963. Behavioral study of obedience. Journal of Abnormal & Social Psychology 67:371–8.

Mills, E. 2005. Google balances privacy, reach. CNET News.com. http://news.com.com/Google+balances+privacy%2C+reach/2100-1032_3-5787483.html (accessed May 12, 2007).

Mitnick, K. D., and W. L. Simon. 2003. *The art of deception: Controlling the human element of security*. New York: Wiley.

Mitnick, K. D., and W. L. Simon. 2005. *The art of intrusion: The real stories behind the exploits of hackers, intruders & deceivers*. New York: Wiley.

Nass, C., and Y. Moon. 2000. Machines and mindlessness: Social responses to computers. *Journal of Social Issues* 56(1):81–103. www.blackwell-synergy.com/links/doi/10.1111/0022-4537.00153.

Nolan, J., and M. Levesque. 2005. Hacking human: data-archaeology and surveillance in social networks. *ACM SIGGROUP* Bulletin 25(2):33–7. DOI=http://doi.acm.org/10.1145/1067721.1067728.

Orgill, G. L., G. W. Romney, M. G. Bailey, and P. M. Orgill. 2004. The urgency for effective user privacy-education to counter social engineering attacks on secure computer systems. In *Proceedings of the 5th Conference on Information Technology Education, Salt Lake City, UT, USA, October 28–30, 2004. CITC5 '04*. New York: ACM Press. DOI=http://doi.acm.org/10.1145/1029533.1029577 (accessed May 11, 2007).

Rash, M., Angela D. Orebaugh, G. Clark, B. Pinkard, and J. Babbin. 2005. Intrusion prevention and active response: Deploying network and host IPS. Rockland, MA: Syngress Publishing.

Robinson, S. W. 2002. Corporate espionage 101. www.sans.org/rr/whitepapers/engineering/512.php (accessed May 11, 2007).

Rusch, J. J. 1999. *The "social engineering" of Internet fraud*. www.isoc.org/isoc/conferences/inet/99/proceedings/3g/3g_2.htm (accessed May 12, 2007).

Tari, F., A. A. Ozok, and S. H. Holden. 2006. A comparison of perceived and real shoulder-surfing risks between alphanumeric and graphical passwords. In *Proceedings of the Second Symposium on Usable Privacy and Security, Pittsburgh, Pennsylvania, July 12–14, 2006. SOUPS '06*, vol. 149. New York: ACM Press. DOI=http://doi.acm.org/10.1145/1143120.1143128 (accessed May 11, 2007).

Thornburgh, T. 2004. Social engineering: the "dark art." In *Proceedings of the 1st Annual Conference on information Security Curriculum Development, Kennesaw, Georgia. InfoSecCD '04*. New York: ACM Press DOI=http://doi.acm.org/10.1145/1059524.1059554

U.S. Department of Defense, Department of Energy, Nuclear Regulatory Commission, Central Intelligence Agency. 1997. DoD 5220.22-M National Industrial Security Program Operating Manual (NISPOM). January 1995. Includes change 1, July 31, 1997. www.usaid.gov/policy/ads/500/d522022m.pdf (accessed May 11, 2007).

Westhoven, J. 2005, August 5. CNN on CNET: We've been blackballed by Google—Tech news site says Google froze out its reporters for publishing Eric Schmidt's personal info. http://money.cnn.com/2005/08/05/technology/google_cnet (accessed May 11, 2007).

FURTHER READING

Denning, D. E. 1998. *Information warfare and security*. Reading, MA: Addison-Wesley Professional.

Mitnick, K. D. and W. L. Simon. 2003. *The art of deception: Controlling the human element of security*. New York: Wiley.

Mitnick, K. D. and W. L. Simon. 2005. *The art of intrusion: The real stories behind the exploits of hackers, intruders & deceivers*. New York: Wiley.

Intrusion-Detection Systems

Peng Ning, *North Carolina State University*
Sushil Jajodia, *George Mason Univesity*

INTRODUCTION

Intuitively, *intrusions* in an information system are the activities that violate the security policy of the system, and *intrusion detection* is the process used to identify intrusions. Intrusion detection has been studied for over 20 years, since Anderson's (1980) report. It is based on the beliefs that an intruder's behavior will be noticeably different from that of a legitimate user and that many unauthorized actions will be detectable.

Intrusion-detection systems (IDSs) are usually deployed along with other preventive security mechanisms, such as access control and authentication, as a second line of defense that protects information systems. There are several reasons that make intrusion detection a necessary part of the entire defense system. First, many traditional systems and applications were developed without security in mind. In other cases, systems and applications were developed to work in a different environment and may become vulnerable when deployed in the current environment. (For example, a system may be perfectly secure when it is isolated but become vulnerable when it is connected to the Internet.) Intrusion detection provides a way to identify and thus allow responses to attacks against these systems. Second, because of the limitations of information security and software engineering practice, computer systems and applications may have design flaws or bugs that could be used by an intruder to attack the systems or applications. As a result, certain preventive mechanisms (e.g., firewalls) may not be as effective as expected.

Intrusion detection complements these protective mechanisms to improve system security. Even if the preventive security mechanisms can protect information systems successfully, it is still desirable to know what intrusions have happened or are happening, so that we can understand the security threats and risks and thus be better prepared for future attacks. Ideally, intrusion detection can be used as the foundation for reactive measures. For example, when a denial of service (DoS) attack is detected, a firewall may be reconfigured to filter out the attack traffic. Moreover, intrusion detection can also be used to enforce accountability and compliance with security policy. This is particularly important to deal with threats from inside attackers, who are authorized to access the information system but may misuse their privileges to perform actions that violate the security policy.

In spite of their importance, IDSs are not replacements for preventive security mechanisms, such as access control and authentication. Indeed, IDSs themselves cannot provide sufficient protection for information systems. As an extreme example, if an attacker erases all the data in an information system, detecting the attacks cannot reduce the damage. Thus, IDSs should be deployed along with other preventive security mechanisms as a part of a comprehensive defense system.

Denning (1986) presented the first intrusion-detection model, which has six main components: subjects, objects, audit records, profiles, anomaly records, and activity rules. *Subjects* refer to the initiators of activity in an information system; they are usually normal users. *Objects* are the resources managed by the information system, such as files, commands, and devices. *Audit records* are those generated by the information system in response to actions performed or attempted by subjects on objects. Examples include user log-in, command execution, etc. *Profiles* are structures that characterize the behavior of subjects with respect to objectives in terms of statistical metrics and models of observed activity. *Anomaly records* are indications of abnormal behaviors when they are detected. Finally, *activity rules* specify actions to take when some conditions are satisfied, which update profiles, detect abnormal behaviors, relate anomalies to suspected intrusions, and produce reports.

Since Denning's (1986) model, intrusion-detection techniques have evolved into two classes: anomaly detection and misuse detection. *Anomaly detection* is based on the normal behavior of a subject (e.g., a user or a system); any action that significantly deviates from the normal behavior is considered intrusive. Denning's intrusion-detection model is an example of anomaly detection. *Misuse detection* catches intrusions in terms of the characteristics of known attacks or system vulnerabilities; any action that conforms to the pattern of a known attack or vulnerability is considered intrusive. The rationale of misuse detection is that with additional knowledge of known attacks or vulnerabilities, we can potentially detect these attacks more precisely and more quickly.

Alternatively, IDSs may be classified into host-based IDSs, distributed IDSs, and network-based IDSs according to the sources of the audit information used by each IDS. Host-based IDSs get audit data from host audit trails and usually aim at detecting attacks against a single host; distributed IDSs gather audit data from multiple hosts, and possibly the network that connects the hosts, aiming at detecting attacks involving multiple hosts. Network-based IDSs use network traffic as the audit data source, relieving the burden on the hosts that provide normal computing services.

This chapter starts with an overview of current intrusion-detection techniques. Next, it reviews the various types of anomaly-detection methods, such as statistical models and machine learning methods, followed by an overview of misuse-detection methods, including rule-based languages, the colored Petri-net-based method, and the abstraction-based method. The section following that describes techniques for automatically generating attack signatures, including a data-mining framework for learning attack signatures and recent advances in the automatic generation of worm signatures. This chapter continues to discuss host-based IDSs as well as additional techniques for intrusion detection in distributed systems, including distributed IDSs, network-based IDSs, and interoperation between (heterogeneous) IDSs. Finally, this chapter reviews intrusion-alert correlation techniques.

ANOMALY DETECTION

Statistical Models

Statistical modeling is among the earliest methods used for detecting intrusions in electronic information systems. It is assumed that an intruder's behavior is noticeably different from that of a normal user, and statistical models are used to aggregate the user's behavior and distinguish an attacker from a normal user. The techniques are applicable to other subjects, such as user groups and programs. In some cases, a simple threshold value is used to indicate the distinction (as with the common rule of raising an alarm if the password is mistyped three times); alternatively, more complex statistical models may be used. Here, we discuss two statistical models that have been proposed for anomaly detection: NIDES/STAT and Haystack.

NIDES/STAT

The Stanford Research Institute's next-generation real-time intrusion-detection expert system statistical component (NIDES/STAT) observes behaviors of subjects on a monitored computer system and adaptively learns what is normal for individual subjects, such as users and groups (Axelsson 1999). The observed behavior of a subject is flagged as a potential intrusion if it deviates significantly from the subject's expected behavior.

The expected behavior of a subject is stored in the subject's profile. Various measures are used to evaluate different aspects of a subject's behavior. When audit records are processed, the system periodically generates an overall statistic, T^2, that reflects the abnormality of the subject. This value is a function of the abnormality values of all the measures comprising the profile. Suppose that n measures $M_1, M_2, \ldots, M_n$ are used to model a subject's behavior. If $S_1, S_2, \ldots, S_n$ represent the abnormality values of M_1 through M_n, then the overall statistic T^2 is evaluated as follows, assuming that the n measures are independent of each other:

$$T^2 = S_1^2 + S_2^2 + \ldots + S_n^2.$$

The profile of a subject is updated to reflect the changes of the subject's behavior. To have the most recently observed behaviors influence the profile more strongly, NIDES/STAT multiplies the frequency table in each profile by an exponential decay factor before incorporating the new audit data. Thus, NIDES/STAT adaptively learns a subject's behavior patterns. This keeps human users from having to manually adjust the profiles; however, it also introduces the possibility of an attacker gradually "training" the profile to consider his/her intrusive activities as normal behavior.

Haystack

Haystack used a different statistical anomaly-detection algorithm, which was adopted as the core of the host monitor in the distributed intrusion-detection system (DIDS) (Axelsson 1999). This algorithm analyzes a user's activities according to a four-step process.

First, the algorithm generates a session vector to represent the activities of the user for a particular session. The session vector $\mathbf{X} = <x_1, x_2, \ldots, x_n>$ represents the counts for various attributes used to represent a user's activities for a single session. Examples of the attributes include session duration and number of files opened for reading.

Second, the algorithm generates a Bernoulli vector to represent the attributes that are out of range for a particular session. A threshold vector $\mathbf{T} = <t_1, t_2, \ldots, t_n>$, where t_i is a tuple of the form $<t_{i,min}, t_{i,max}>$, is used to assist this step. The threshold vector is stored in a user's profile. The Bernoulli vector $\mathbf{B} = <b_1, b_2, \ldots, b_n>$ is generated so that b_i is set to 1 if x_i falls outside the range t_i, and b_i is set to 0 otherwise.

Third, the algorithm generates a weighted intrusion score, for a particular intrusion type, from the Bernoulli vector and a weighted intrusion vector. Each group and intrusion type pair has a weighted intrusion vector $\mathbf{W} = <w_1, w_2, \ldots, w_n>$, in which each w_i relates the importance of the ith attribute in the Bernoulli vector to detecting the particular intrusion type. The weight intrusion score is simply the sum of all weights, w_i, where the ith attribute falls outside the range t_i. That is,

$$\text{the weighted intrusion score} = \sum_{i=1}^{n} b_i \cdot w_i \cdot$$

Finally, the algorithm generates a suspicion quotient to represent how suspicious this session is compared with all other sessions for a particular intrusion type. Specifically, the suspicion quotient is the probability that a random session's weighted intrusion score is less than or equal to the weighted intrusion score computed in the previous step.

Unlike NIDES/STAT, the Haystack algorithm has a step that determines resemblance to known attacks. The advantages are that more knowledge about the possible attacks can be derived from this step and better responses can follow the alarms. However, extra knowledge about possible intrusion types is required: We need to understand the impact of the intrusion types on the attributes of the session vectors and assign appropriate weights to these attributes to reflect the impact. In reality, the process of generating the weighted intrusion vectors is time consuming and error prone.

Machine-Learning and Data-Mining Techniques

A number of machine-learning and data-mining techniques have been investigated for the purpose of anomaly detection. The focus of these approaches is to "learn" the normal behaviors of the system automatically from the historic normal data. Such normal behaviors are represented in various forms and used as the basis for future anomaly detection. More of these approaches use "unsupervised" learning—that is, training anomaly detectors without requiring the training data be labeled. (By contrast, a supervised learning approach requires that each training data entry be labeled as normal or intrusive (or as a specific intrusion). In this section, we discuss several approaches in this category.

Time-Based Inductive Machine

Teng, Chen, and Lu (1990) proposed the use of a time-based inductive machine (TIM) to capture a user's behavior pattern. As a general-purpose tool, TIM discovers temporal sequential patterns in a sequence of events. The sequential patterns represent highly repetitive activities and are expected to provide predication. The temporal patterns, which are represented in the form of rules, are generated and modified from the input data using a logical inference called "inductive generalization." When applied to intrusion detection, the rules describe the behavior patterns of either a user or a group of users based on past audit history. Each rule describes a sequential event pattern that predicts the next event from a given sequence of events. An example of a simplified rule produced in TIM is

$$E1 - E2 - E3 \rightarrow (E4 = 95\%; E5 = 5\%),$$

where $E1$, $E2$, $E3$, $E4$, and $E5$ are security events.

This rule says that if $E1$ is followed by $E2$, and $E2$ is followed by $E3$, then there is a 95% chance (based on the previous observation) that $E4$ will follow, and a 5% chance that $E5$ will follow. TIM can produce more generalized rules than the above. For example, it may produce a rule in the form

$$E1 - * \rightarrow (E2 = 100\%),$$

where an asterisk matches any single event. Any number of asterisks is allowed in a rule.

The limitation of TIM is that it considers only the immediately following relationship between the observed events. That is, the rules represent only the event patterns in which events are adjacent to each other. However, a user may perform multiple tasks at the same time. For example, a user may check his/her e-mail during the editing of a document. The events involved in one application, which tend to have strong patterns embedded in the sequence of events, may be interleaved with events from other applications. As a result, it is very possible that the rules generated by TIM cannot precisely capture the user's behavior pattern. Nevertheless, TIM may be suitable for capturing the behavior patterns of entities such as programs that usually focus on single tasks.

Instance-Based Learning

Lane and Brodley (1998) applied instance-based learning (IBL) to learn entities' (e.g., users) normal behavior from temporal sequence data. IBL represents a concept of interest with a set of instances that exemplify the concept. The set of instances is called the "instance dictionary." A new instance is classified according to its relation to stored instances. IBL requires a notion of "distance" between the instances so that the similarity of different instances can be measured and used to classify the instances.

Lane and Brodley did several things to adapt IBL to anomaly detection. First, they transformed the observed sequential data into fixed-length vectors (called "feature vectors"). Specifically, they segmented a sequence of events (e.g., a sequence of user commands) into all possible overlapping sequences of length l, where l is an empirical parameter. (Thus, each event is considered the starting point of a feature vector, and each event is replicated l times.) Second, they defined a similarity measure between the feature vectors. For a length l, the similarity between feature vectors $\boldsymbol{X} = (x_0, x_1, \ldots, x_{l-1})$ and $\boldsymbol{Y} = (y_0, y_1, \ldots, y_{l-1})$ is defined by the functions

$$w(X,Y,i) = \begin{cases} 0 & \text{if } i < 0 \text{ or } x_i \neq y_i \\ 1 + w(X,Y,i-1), & \text{if } x_i = y_i \end{cases}$$

and

$$Sim(X,Y) = \sum_{i=0}^{l-1} w(X,Y,i).$$

The converse measure, distance, is defined as $\mathrm{Dist}(\boldsymbol{X},\boldsymbol{Y}) = Sim_{max} - Sim(\boldsymbol{X},\boldsymbol{Y})$, where $Sim_{max} = Sim(\boldsymbol{X},\boldsymbol{X})$. Intuitively, the function $w(\boldsymbol{X}, \boldsymbol{Y}, i)$ accumulates weights from the most recently consecutively matched subsequences between $\boldsymbol{X}$ and $\boldsymbol{Y}$ at position i, whereas $Sim(\boldsymbol{X},\boldsymbol{Y})$ is the integral of total weights.

A user profile is built to contain a collection of sequences, $\boldsymbol{D}$, selected from a user's observed actions (e.g., commands). The similarity between the profile and a newly observed sequence, $\boldsymbol{X}$, is defined as $Sim_D(\boldsymbol{X}) = \max_{Y \in D}\{Sim(\boldsymbol{Y}, \boldsymbol{X})\}$. That is, the similarity between $\boldsymbol{X}$ and $\boldsymbol{D}$ is defined as the similarity between $\boldsymbol{X}$ and a vector in $\boldsymbol{D}$ that is most similar to $\boldsymbol{X}$. Then a threshold r is chosen. If the similarity between an observed sequence $\boldsymbol{X}$ and the profile $\boldsymbol{D}$ is greater than r, $\boldsymbol{X}$ is considered normal; otherwise, $\boldsymbol{X}$ is abnormal.

To reduce the storage required by the profile, Lane and Brodley used the least-recently-used pruning strategy to keep the profile at a manageable size. As new instances are acquired and classification is performed, the profile instance selected as most similar is time stamped. Least-recently-used instances are removed when the profile is constrained to the desired size. In addition, they applied a clustering technique to group the instances in the profile, and they used a representative instance for each cluster.

This attempt shares a problem similar to that of TIM—that is, it tries to find patterns from sequences of consecutive events. As the authors have noted, a user may interrupt his/her normal work (e.g., programming) and do something different (e.g., answer an urgent e-mail) and thus yield a different sequence of actions from his/her profile. Lane and Brodley's (1998) solution is to use a time average of the similarity signals; however, such a solution may make real anomalies unnoticeable. In addition, the least-recently-used pruning strategy gives an attacker a chance to train the profile slowly, so that intrusive activities are considered normal ones.

Neural Network

Fox et al. (1990) were the first to attempt modeling system and user behaviors using neural networks. Their choice of neural network is Kohonen's (1982) self-organizing map (SOM), which is a type of unsupervised learning technique that can discover underlying structures of the data without prior examples of intrusive and nonintrusive activities.

They used SOM as a real-time background monitor that alerts a more complex expert system. In their prototype system, eleven system parameters accessible from the system's statistical performance data are identified as the input to the SOM model. These parameters include: (a) central processing unit (CPU) usage, (b) paging activity, (c) mailer activity, (d) disk accesses, (e) memory usage, (f) average session time, (g) number of users, (h) absentee jobs, (i) reads of "help" files, (j) failed log-ins, and (k) multiple log-ins. However, their study showed the results of only one simulated virus attack, which is not sufficient to draw serious conclusions.

In another attempt to apply neural network to anomaly detection, Ghosh, Wanken, and Charron (1998) proposed using a back-propagation network to monitor running programs. A back-propagation network is developed for supervised learning. That is, it needs examples of intrusive and nonintrusive activities (called "training data") to build the intrusion-detection model. Such a network consists of an input layer, at least one hidden layer (neurons that are not directly connected to the input or output nodes), and an output layer. Typically, there are no connections between neurons in the same layer or between those in one layer and those in a previous layer.

The training cycle of a back-propagation network works in two phases. In the first phase, the input is submitted to the network and propagated to the output through the network. In the second phase, the desired output is compared with the network's output. If the vectors do not agree, the network updates the weights starting at the output neurons. Then the changes in weights are calculated for the previous layer and cascade through the layers of neurons toward the input neurons.

Ghosh et al. proposed using program input and the program internal state as the input to the back-propagation network. One interesting result is that they improved the performance of detection by using randomly generated data as anomalous input. By considering randomly generated data as anomalous, the network gets more training data that is complementary to the actual training data.

Similarly to statistical anomaly detection models, deciding the input parameters for neural network anomaly detectors is a difficult problem. In addition, assigning the initial weights to the neural networks is also an unresolved question. The experiments by Ghosh et al. (1998) showed that different initial weights could lead to anomaly detectors with different performance. Nevertheless, research on applying neural networks to anomaly detection is still preliminary; more work is needed to explore the capability of neural networks.

Audit Data Analysis and Mining

Audit data analysis and mining (ADAM) proposes applying data-mining techniques to discover abnormal patterns in large amounts of audit data (e.g., network traffic collected by TCPdump, which is a program used to sniff and store packets transmitted in the network) (Barbara et al. 2001, 2002). (Lee and Stolfo [2000] use data-mining techniques for automatically generating misuse models; we will discuss it in the section on "Misuse Detection" later in this chapter.) In particular, the existing research focuses on the analysis of network audit data, such as the transmission control protocol (TCP) connections. Using data-mining techniques, ADAM has the potential to provide a flexible representation of the network traffic pattern, uncover some unknown patterns of attacks that cannot be detected by other techniques, and accommodate the large amount of network audit data that keeps growing in size.

ADAM uses several data-mining–related techniques to help detect abnormal network activities. The first technique ADAM uses is inspired by association rules. Given a set I of items, an association rule is a rule of the form $X \rightarrow Y$, where X and Y are subsets (called item sets) of I and $X \cap Y = \phi$. Association rules are usually discovered from a set T of transactions, where each transaction is a subset of I. The rule $X \rightarrow Y$ has a *support s* in the transaction set T if $s\%$ of the transactions in T contain $X \cup Y$, and it has a *confidence c* if $c\%$ of the transactions in T that contain X also contain Y.

However, ADAM does not use association rules directly; instead, it adopts the item sets that have large enough support (called "large item sets") to represent the pattern of network traffic. Specifically, it assumes that each network event (e.g., a TCP connection) is described by a set of attribute values and considers each event a transaction. The large item sets discovered from the network traffic then represent the frequent events in the network traffic. The power of such a mechanism lies in the flexible representation of events.

ADAM builds a profile of normal network activities in which the frequent events (represented by large item sets) are stored. During the detection time, it adopts a sliding-window method to incrementally examine the network events. Within each window, ADAM looks for the large item sets that do not appear in the profile and considers them suspicious.

The second technique ADAM uses is called "domain-level mining." Intuitively, it tries to generalize the event attribute values used to describe a network event. For example, an IP address that belongs to the subnet *ise.gmu.edu* can be generalized to *ise.gmu.edu*, *gmu.edu*. and *edu*. Then it discovers large item sets using the generalized attribute values. An advantage of this approach is that it provides a way to aggregate the events that have some commonality and may discover more attacks. However, the scheme used to generalize the attribute values is ad hoc; only generalization from IP addresses to subnets and from smaller subnets to larger subnets are studied.

The third technique ADAM uses is classification. ADAM is innovative in that classification is used to classify the output of the mining of large item sets. Four classification algorithms have been studied to date: C4.5 decision tree, naive Bayes, cascading classifier (which uses decision tree followed by naive Bayes and vice versa), and inductive rule learner. The results show that classification is quite effective in reducing false alarms.

Finally, ADAM uses the pseudo-Bayes estimator to accommodate unknown attacks. It is assumed that unknown attacks are those that have not been observed. The training data are represented as a set of vectors, each of which corresponds to an event and is labeled as normal or as a known class of attacks. An additional class is then considered to represent the unknown attacks. Because the unknown attacks have not been observed in the training data, the probability $P(x|\text{class} = \text{unknown})$, where x is a training vector, is zero. The pseudo-Bayes estimator is used to smooth all the conditional probabilities $P(x|\text{class})$ so that $P(x|\text{class} = \text{unknown})$ is assigned a (small) probability. These conditional probabilities are then used to build a naive Bayes classifier.

The limitation of ADAM is that it cannot detect stealthy attacks. In other words, it can detect an attack only when it involves a relatively large number of events during a short period of time. This limitation occurs because ADAM raises an alarm only when the support of an unexpected rule (i.e., association of event attributes) exceeds a threshold. Indeed, this limitation is not unique to ADAM; most of the anomaly-detection models and many of the misuse-detection models suffer from the same problem.

Computer Immunological Approach

The computer immunological approach is based on an analogy of the immune system's capability of distinguishing self from non-self (Hofmeyr, Forrest, and Somayaji 1998). This approach represents self as a collection of strings of length l, where l is a systemwide parameter. A string of length l is considered non-self if it does not match any string belonging to self. To generate detectors that can distinguish non-self from self, a naive approach is to randomly generate a string of length l and check whether it matches any self-string. If yes, the generated string is discarded; otherwise, it is used as a detector. However, the naive approach takes time exponential to the number of self-strings. To address this problem, Forrest et al. proposed an "r-contiguous-bits" matching rule to distinguish self from non-self: two l-bit strings match each other if they are identical in at least r contiguous positions. As a result, detectors can be generated more efficiently for this particular matching rule.

Hofmeyr et al. proposed using short sequences of system calls to distinguish self from non-self for anomaly detection. Given a program in a particular installation, the immunological approach collects a database of all unique system call sequences of a certain length made by the program over a period of normal operation. During the detection time, it monitors the system call sequences and compares them with the sequences in the aforementioned database. For an observed sequence of system calls, this approach extracts all sub-sequences of length l and computes the distance $d_{\min}(i)$ between each sub-sequence i and the normal database as $d_{\min}(i) = \min\{d(i,j)$ for all sequences j in the normal database$\}$, where $d(i,j)$ is the Hamming distance between sequences i and j (i.e., the number of different bits in sequences i and j). The anomaly score of the observed sequence of system calls is then the maximum $d_{\min}(i)$ normalized by dividing the length of the sequence. This approach raises an alarm if the anomaly score is above a certain threshold.

The advantage of this approach is that it has a high probability of detecting anomalies using a small set of self-strings based on short sequences of system calls. In addition, it does not require any prior knowledge about attacks. The disadvantage is that it requires self to be well understood. That is, it requires a complete set of self-strings in order not to mistake self for non-self. This requirement may be trivial for applications such as virus detection, but it is very difficult for intrusion detection, for which some normal behaviors cannot be foreseen when the detectors are being generated.

Sekar et al. 2001 further improve the computer immunological method by using an automaton to represent a program's normal behavior. The program counter is used as the state of the automaton, and the system calls made by the program are used as the events that cause the state transitions. As a result, the automaton representation can accommodate more information about the programs' normal behavior and, thus, reduce the false-alert rate and improve the detection rate. In addition, the automaton representation is more compact than the previous alternative. Consequently, such automata are easier to build and more efficient to use for intrusion detection.

The research on the computer immunological method has led to the development of an anomaly-detection system called STIDE (sequence time-delay embedding). People have independently and consistently found that a sequence length of six makes STIDE capable of detecting anomalies. Tan and Maxion (2002) investigated this problem by establishing a framework of three sequence types: rare, common, and foreign. A rare (or common) sequence is one that occurs infrequently (or frequently) in the training data that defines the normal behavior. A foreign sequence is one that never occurs in the training data. A minimal foreign sequence is a foreign sequence having the property that all of its proper subsequences already exist in the training data. Tan and Maxion discovered that STIDE requires a sequence length of at least six because in all the data traces used for evaluating STIDE the length of the smallest minimal foreign sequence is six.

Specification-Based Methods

Ko, Ruschitzka, and Levitt (1997) proposed a specification-based approach for intrusion detection. The idea is to use *traces*, ordered sequences of execution events, to specify the intended behaviors of concurrent programs in distributed system. A specification describes valid operation sequences of the execution of one or more programs, collectively called a "(monitored) subject." A sequence of operations performed by the subject that does not conform to the specification is considered a security violation. Each specification is called a "trace policy." A grammar called "parallel environment grammars" (PE-grammars) was developed for specifying trace policies.

The advantage of this approach is that in theory, it should be able to detect some types of attacks that intruders will invent in the future. In particular, if a new attack causes a program to behave in a way outside the specification, then it will be flagged as a potential attack. The drawback of this approach is that substantial work is required to specify accurately the behavior of the many privileged system programs, and these specifications will be operating-system–specific. To address this issue, Ko (2000) proposed the use of *inductive logic programming* to synthesize specifications from valid traces. The automatically generated specifications may be combined with manual rules to reduce the work involved in specification of valid program behaviors.

Wagner and Dean (2001) further advanced the specification-based approach. The basic idea is to automatically generate the specification of a program by deriving an abstract model of the programs from the source or binary code. Wagner and Dean studied several alternative models, including the call-graph model and the abstract-stack model. Central to these models is the control flow graph of a program; these models adopt different ways to represent the possible system call traces according to the control flow graph. Attractive features of this approach are that it has the potential to detect unknown patterns of attacks and that it has no false alerts, although it may miss some attacks. Moreover, the specification-based methods also offer an opportunity to stop ongoing attacks. For example, it is possible to automatically embed code (e.g., embedded sensors by Zamboni [2001]) into an existing program, which forces the program to quit when certain specifications are violated.

Information-Theoretic Measures

Lee and Xiang (2001) proposed the use of information-theoretic measures to help understand the characteristics of audit data and build anomaly-detection models. The well-known concept of *entropy* is the first information-theoretic measure. Given a set of classes C_X and a data set X, where each data item belongs to a class x C_X, the entropy of X relative to C_X is defined as

$$H(X) = \sum_{x \in C_X} P(x) \log \frac{1}{P(x)},$$

where $P(x)$ is the probability of x in X. For anomaly detection, entropy reveals the regularity of audit data with respect to some given classes.

The second information-theoretic measure is *conditional entropy*. The conditional entropy of X given Y is the entropy of the probability distribution $P(x|y)$; that is,

$$H(X / Y) = \sum_{x,y \in C_X, C_Y} P(x) \log \frac{1}{P(x \mid y)},$$

where $P(x,y)$ is the joint probability of x and y and $P(x|y)$ is the conditional probability of x given y. The conditional entropy is proposed to measure the temporal or sequential characteristics of audit data. Let X be a collection of sequences in which each is a sequence of n audit events and Y is the collection of prefixes of the sequences in X that are of length k. Then $H(X|Y)$ indicates the uncertainty that remains for the rest of the audit events in a sequence x after we have seen the first k events of x. For anomaly detection, conditional entropy can be used as a measure of regularity of sequential dependencies.

The limitation of conditional entropy is that it measures only the sequential regularity of contiguous events. For example, a program may generate highly regular sequences of events; however, if these events are interleaved with other sequences of events, the conditional entropy will be very high, failing to reflect the regularity embedded in the interleaved sequences.

The third information-theoretic measure, *relative entropy*, measures the distance of the regularities between two data sets. The relative entropy between two probability distributions $p(x)$ and $q(x)$ that are defined over the same $x \in C_X$ is

$$\text{relEntropy}(p \mid q) = \sum_{x \in C_X} p(x) \log \frac{p(x)}{q(x)}.$$

The fourth information-theoretic measure, *relative conditional entropy*, measures the distance of the regularities with respect to the sequential dependency between two data sets. The relative entropy between two probability distributions $p(x|y)$ and $q(x|y)$ that are defined over the same $x \in C_X$ and $y \in C_Y$ is

$$\text{relCondEntropy}(p \mid q) = \sum_{x,y \in C_X C_Y} p(x) \log \frac{p(x \mid y)}{q(x \mid y)}.$$

Viewing intrusion detection as a classification problem, Lee and Xiang proposed the fifth information-theoretic measure, *information gain*, to measure the performance of using some features for classification. The information gain of attribute (i.e., feature) A on data set X is

$$\text{Gain}(X, A) = H(X) - \sum_{v \in \text{Values}(A)} \frac{|X_v|}{|X|} H(X_v),$$

where Values(A) is the set of values of A and X_v is the subset of X where A has value v. This measure can help choose the right features (i.e., the features that have high information gain) to build intrusion-detection models. The limitation of information gain is that it requires a relatively complete data set to help choose the right features for the classification model. Nevertheless, an intrusion-detection model cannot be better than the data set from which it is built.

Limitation of Anomaly Detection

Although anomaly detection can accommodate unknown patterns of attacks, it also suffers from several limitations. A common problem of all anomaly-detection approaches, with the exception of the specification-based approach, is that the subject's normal behavior is modeled on the basis of the (audit) data collected over a period of normal operation. If undiscovered intrusive activities occur during this period, they will be considered normal activities. A relevant issue is the progression of anomaly-detection models. Because a subject's normal behavior may change over time (for example, a user's behavior may change when he moves from one project to another), the IDSs that use some of the above approaches may allow the subject's profile to change gradually. This may give an intruder the chance to gradually train the IDS and trick it into accepting intrusive activities as normal. Thus, any profile change in an anomaly-detection system must be carefully performed to avoid such problems. Also, because these approaches are all based on summarized information, they are insensitive to stealthy attacks. The specification-based approaches do not suffer from the problems in training datasets. However, they may also have problems due to mistakes in (manual) specifications, and in some cases, it is difficult to develop specifications that precisely characterize the normal behaviors. Finally, because of some technical reasons, most of the current anomaly-detection approaches suffer from a high false-alarm rate.

Another difficult problem in building anomaly-detection models is how to decide the features to be used as the input of the models (e.g., the statistical models). In the existing models, the input parameters are usually decided by domain experts (e.g., network security experts) in ad hoc ways. It is not guaranteed that all and only the features related to intrusion detection will be selected as input parameters. Although missing important intrusion-related features makes it difficult to distinguish attacks from normal activities, having non-intrusion-related features could introduce "noise" into the models and thus affect the detection performance.

MISUSE DETECTION

Misuse detection is considered complementary to anomaly detection. The rationale is that known attack patterns can be detected more effectively and efficiently by using explicit knowledge of them. Thus, misuse-detection systems look for well-defined patterns of known attacks or vulnerabilities; they can catch an intrusive activity even if it is so negligible that the anomaly-detection approaches tend to ignore it. Commercial systems often combine both misuse- and anomaly-detection approaches.

The major problems in misuse detection are the representation of known attack patterns and the difficulty of detecting new attacks. Another problem is an inherent limitation of misuse detection: While misuse-detection algorithms may sometimes detect variations of known attacks, they cannot identify truly new attacks since no pattern may be provided for them. Existing work on misuse detection is mostly aimed at the first problem, the representation of known attacks. The detection algorithms usually follow directly from the representation mechanisms. In this section, we discuss the typical ways to represent attacks.

Rule-Based Languages

The rule-based expert system is the most widely used approach for misuse detection. The patterns of known attacks are specified as rule sets, and a forward-chaining expert system is usually used to look for signs of intrusions. Here we discuss two rule-based languages, rule-based sequence evaluation language (RUSSEL) (Mounji et al. 1995) and production-based expert system tool set (P-BEST) (Lindqvist and Porras 1999). Other rule-based languages exist, but they are all similar in the sense that they all specify known attack patterns as event patterns.

RUSSEL

RUSSEL is the language used in the advanced security audit trail analysis on UNIX (ASAX) project (Mounji et al. 1995). It is a language specifically tailored to the problem of searching arbitrary patterns of records in sequential files. The language provides common control structures, such as conditional, repetitive, and compound actions. Primitive actions include assignment, external routine call, and rule triggering. A RUSSEL program simply consists of a set of rule declarations that are made of a rule name, a list of formal parameters and local variables, and an action part. RUSSEL also supports modules sharing global variables and exported rule declarations.

When intrusion detection is being enforced, the system analyzes the audit records one by one. For each audit record, the system executes all the active rules. The execution of an active rule may trigger (activate) new rules, raise alarms, write report messages, or alter global variables, for example. A rule can be triggered to be active for the current or the next record. In general, a rule is active for the current record because a prefix of a particular sequence of audit records has been detected. When all the rules active for the current record have been executed, the next record is read and the rules triggered for it in the previous step are executed in turn. User-defined and built-in C-routines can be called from a rule body.

RUSSEL is quite flexible in describing sequential event patterns and corresponding actions. The ability to work with user-defined C-routines gives the users the power to describe almost anything that can be specified in a programming language. The disadvantage is that it is a low-level language. Specifying an attack pattern is similar to writing a program, although it provides a general condition-trigger framework and is declarative in nature. The feature that rules can share global variables introduces the possibility of bugs along with the convenience of sharing information among different rules.

P-Best

P-BEST was developed for the multiplexed information and computing service (Multics) intrusion-detection and alerting system (MIDAS) and later used by the intrusion-detection expert system (IDES), NIDES, and the event monitoring enabling responses to anomalous live disturbances (EMERALD) (Lindqvist and Porras 1999). The P-BEST toolset consists of a rule translator, a library of run-time routines, and a set of garbage-collection routines. Rules and facts in P-BEST are written in production-rule specification language. The rule translator is then used to translate the specification into an expert system program in C language, which can then be compiled into either a stand-alone, self-contained executable program or a set of library routines that can be linked to a larger software framework.

The P-BEST language is quite small and intuitive. In P-BEST, the user specifies the structure of a fact (e.g., an audit record) through a template definition referred to as a *pattern type*. For example, an event consisting of four fields—*event_type* (an integer), *return_code* (an integer), *username* (a string), and *hostname* (a string)—can be defined as ptype[event *event_type*: int, *return_code*: int, *username*: string, *hostname*: string].

Thus, P-BEST does not depend on the structure of the input data. One important advantage of P-BEST is that it is a language preprocessor (i.e., it generates a precompiled expert system) and can extend its ability by invoking external C functions. However, it shares a similar problem with RUSSEL: It is a low-level language. Specification of attack patterns in P-BEST is time consuming. When many related rules are included in a system, correctness of the rules is difficult to check due to the interaction of these rules.

State-Transition Analysis Toolkit

Though rule-based languages are flexible and expressive in describing attack patterns for misuse detection, in practice, they are usually difficult to use. As observed in Ilgun, Kemmerer, and Porras (1995), "in general, expert rule-bases tend to be non-intuitive, requiring the skills of experienced rule-base programmers to update them." STAT was developed to address this problem.

In STAT, state-transition analysis technique was adopted to facilitate the specification of the patterns of known attacks (Ilgun et al. 1995). It is based on the assumption that all penetrations share two common features. First, penetrations require the attacker to possess some minimum prerequisite access to the target system. Second, all penetrations lead to the acquisition of some ability that the attacker does not have prior to the attacks. Thus, STAT views an attack as a sequence of actions performed by an attacker that leads from some initial state on a system to a target-compromised state, where a *state* is a snapshot of the system representing the values of all memory locations on the system. Accordingly, STAT models attack as a series of state changes that lead from an initial secure state to a target-compromised state.

To represent attacks, STAT requires some critical actions to be identified. These *signature actions* refer to the actions that, if omitted from the execution of an attack scenario, would prevent the attack from successful completion. With the series of state changes and the signature actions that cause the state changes, an attack scenario is then represented as a state-transition diagram, where the states in the diagram are specified by assertions of certain conditions and the signature actions are events observable from, for example, audit data.

STAT has been applied for misuse detection in UNIX systems, distributed systems, and networks. USTAT is the first prototype of STAT, which is aimed at misuse detection in UNIX systems (Ilgun et al. 1995). It relies on Sun Microsystems' C2- Basic Security Module (BSM) to collect audit records. In addition to detecting attacks, USTAT is designed to be a real-time system that can preempt an attack before any damage can be done. USTAT was later extended to process audit data collected on multiple UNIX hosts. The resulting system is NSTAT, which runs multiple daemon programs on the hosts being protected to read and forward audit data to a centralized server, which performs STAT analysis on all data.

A later application of STAT to network-based misuse detection resulted in another system, named *NetSTAT* (Vigna and Kemmerer 1999). In this work, the network topology is further modeled as a hypergraph. Network interfaces, hosts, and links are considered the constituent elements of hypergraphs, with interfaces as the nodes, and hosts and links as hyperedges. Using the network-topology model and the state-transition description of network-based attacks, NetSTAT can map intrusion scenarios to specific network configurations and generate and distribute the activities to be monitored at certain places in a network.

STAT was intended to be a high-level tool to help specify attack patterns. Using STAT, the task of describing an attack scenario is expected to be easier than using rule-based languages, although the analysis required to understand the nature of attacks remains the same. In the implementations of STAT techniques (i.e., USTAT, NSTAT, and NetSTAT), the attack scenarios are transformed into rule bases, which are enforced by a forward-chaining inference engine.

Colored Petri Automata

Kumar and Spafford (1994) and Kumar (1995) viewed misuse detection as a pattern-matching process. They proposed an abstract hierarchy for classifying intrusion signatures (i.e., attack patterns) based on the structural interrelationships among the events that compose the signature. Events in such a hierarchy are high-level events that can be defined in terms of low-level audit trail events and used to instantiate the abstract hierarchy into a concrete one. A benefit of this classification scheme is that it clarifies the complexity of detecting the signatures in each level of the hierarchy. In addition, it also identifies the requirements that patterns in all categories of the classification must meet to represent the full range of commonly occurring intrusions (i.e., the specification of context, actions, and invariants in intrusion patterns).

Kumar and Spafford adopted colored Petri nets to represent attack signatures, with guards to represent signature contexts and vertices to represent system states. User-specified actions (e.g., assignments to variables) may be associated with such patterns and then executed when patterns are matched. The adapted colored Petri nets are called "colored Petri automata" (CPA). A CPA represents the transition of system states along paths that lead to intruded states. A CPA is also associated with pre- and postconditions that must be satisfied before and after the match, as well as invariants (i.e., conditions) that must be satisfied while the pattern is being matched. CPA has been implemented in a prototype misuse-detection system called intrusion detection in our time (IDIOT).

CPA is quite expressive; it provides the ability to specify partial orders, which in turn subsume sequences and regular expressions. However, if improperly used, the expressiveness may lead to potential problems: If the intrusions are described in every detail, the attacker may be able to change his/her attacking strategy and bypass the IDSs. Nevertheless, CPA is not the root of the problem.

Abstraction-Based Intrusion Detection

Many misuse-detection approaches share a common problem in their implementation: Each system is written for a single environment and has proved difficult to use in other environments that may have similar policies and concerns. The primary goal of abstraction-based intrusion detection is to address this problem.

The initial attempt of the abstraction-based approach is a misuse-detection system named the adaptable real-time misuse-detection system (ARMD) (Lin, Wang, and Jajodia 1998). ARMD provides a high-level language for abstract misuse signatures, called MuSigs, and a mechanism to translate MuSigs into a monitoring program. With the notion of abstract events, the high-level language specifies a MuSig as a pattern over a sequence of abstract events, which is described as conditions that the abstract event attributes must satisfy. The gap between abstract events and audit records is bridged by an audit subsystem, which transforms the actual audit records into abstract events. In addition, on the basis of MuSigs, the available audit trail, and the strategy costs, ARMD uses a strategy generator to automatically generate monitoring strategies to govern the misuse-detection process.

ARMD is a host-based misuse-detection system. In addition to the features mentioned above, it also uses database query-optimization techniques to speed up the processing of audit events. The experiences with ARMD show that knowing the characteristics of the audit trail helps estimate the cost of performing misuse detection and gives the security officers the opportunity to tune the misuse-detection system.

A limitation of ARMD is that it requires users to have a precise understanding of the attacks and to make careful plans for the abstraction of events. This planning is not an easy job, especially when a user does not know how his/her MuSigs may be used. In particular, unforeseen attacks may invalidate previously defined abstract events and MuSigs, thus forcing the redevelopment of some or all of the MuSigs.

The work by Ning, Jajodia, and Wang (2001) further extends the result in ARMD to address the aforementioned limitation. It provides a framework for distributed attack specification and event abstraction. In this framework, abstraction is considered an ongoing process. The structures of abstract events are represented as system views, and attack signatures are represented as generic patterns on the basis of system views. This new approach allows the semantics of a system view to be modified by defining new signatures and view definitions without changing the specifications of the views or the signatures specified on the basis of the system views. As a result, signatures in this model can potentially accommodate unknown variants of known attack patterns. Although the specification of attack signatures and the choice of right abstraction still partially depend on the users' skill, this framework provides guidance and alleviates the burden of writing and maintaining signatures.

Automatic Generation of Attack Signatures

Most commercial IDSs are misuse-detection systems that rely on attack signatures to identify attacks. The ability of an IDS to detect attacks is highly affected by the quality of the attack signatures used for detection. Most signatures used in existing IDSs were manually crafted by human users after they understood the nature of the attacks. However, it has been commonly agreed that manually generating attacks signatures is time-consuming and error-prone. In particular, there is no hope of manually generating attack signatures for fast-spreading attacks such as worms to effectively detect and stop such attacks. In this section, we discuss several attempts to generate attack signatures automatically, starting with the influential work by Lee and Stolfo.

Data Mining Framework for Building Attack Models

Lee and Stolfo (2000) looked at intrusion detection as a data-analysis process and applied several data-mining techniques to build misuse-detection models. The research efforts were conducted under a project entitled JAM, the Java Agent for Meta-learning (meta-learning is a general strategy that provides the means of learning how to combine and integrate a number of separately learned classifiers or models). In particular, association rules and frequent episodes are used to automatically discover features that should be used to model a subject's behavior, and the meta classification is used to combine the results of different classifiers to get better classification results. This framework uses a "supervised" learning approach to build attack models. In other words, it requires that records of the training datasets used for building attack modes be labeled as either normal or intrusive.

Lee and Stolfo extended the original association rules to take into account the "order of importance" relations among the system features (the notion of an association rule was discussed above regarding ADAM). *Axis* refers to the features that are important to intrusion detection; only the association rules involving axis features are considered. For example, in the shell command records, the command is likely to reflect the intrusive activities and thus be identified as an axis feature. In some sense, axis features incorporate expert knowledge into the system and thus improve the effectiveness of association rules.

To represent frequent sequential patterns of network events, Lee and Stolfo (2000) extended frequent episodes, which was originally proposed by Mannila, Toivonen, and Verkamo (1995), to represent the sequential interaudit record patterns. Their algorithm finds frequent sequential patterns in two phases. First, it finds the frequent associations among event attributes using the axis attributes, and then it generates the frequent sequential patterns from these associations. The algorithm also takes advantage of the "reference" relations among the system features. That is, when forming an episode, the event records covered by the constituent item sets of the episode share the same value for a given feature attribute. The mined frequent episodes are used to construct temporal statistical features, which are used to build classification models. Thus, new features can be derived from the training data set and then used for generating better intrusion-detection models.

Another innovation of the JAM project is meta classification, which combines the output of several base classifiers and generates the best results out of them. Specifically, from the predictions of base classifiers and the correct classes, a meta classifier learns which base classifier can make the best prediction for each type of input. It then chooses the prediction of the best base classifier for different inputs and combines the powers of the base classifiers.

Lee and Stolfo (2000) advanced state-of-the-art knowledge of intrusion detection by introducing the MADAMID (mining audit data for automated models for intrusion detection) framework that helps generate intrusion-detection models automatically. The limitation is that the framework depends on the volume of the evidences. That is, intrusive activities must generate a relatively noticeable set of events so the association of event attributes or frequent episodes can reflect them. Thus, the generated models must work with some other complementary systems, such as STAT.

Automatic Signature Generation and Intrusion Prevention

Fast-spreading worms (e.g., Code Red, SQL Slammer, Blaster) motivated the investigation of more efficient and effective defense mechanisms that can stop such attacks. Initial attempts include Autograph (Kim and Karp 2004), EarlyBird (Singh et al. 2004), and Polygraph (Newsome, Karp, and Song 2005). One common goal of these approaches is to automatically and quickly generate attack signatures from worm attack traffic, so that these attack signatures can be deployed at content-based firewalls elsewhere to stop the spread of (previously unknown) worm attacks. Despite the difference in technical details, these approaches share some common features. Given a set of worm traffic, all these approaches identify the byte sequences that are common to this type of traffic, and use such byte sequences as signatures for the worms. A limitation of these approaches is that they all extract signatures in a syntactic manner, while ignoring the semantics of the attacks. This limitation makes these approaches vulnerable to polymorphic and metamorphic worms. Polymorphic worms change their binary representations while they spread through semantic manipulation of their code representation. Similarly, metamorphic worms evade detection via encryption (with different keys) while they spread. As a result, the worm traffic may not have common substrings that are good enough to distinguish them from normal traffic, thus making these syntactic approaches not as effective as expected.

Several recent approaches attempt to generate attack signatures by exploiting the semantics of victim programs and attacks to address the aforementioned problem. A notable approach is TaintCheck (Newsome, Karp, and Song 2005), which performs dynamic taint analysis (via binary program emulation) to track the propagation of network input data, and raise alerts (and at the same time stop the attacks) when such data are directly or indirectly used illegitimately (e.g., a network input is used as the target of a jump instruction). TaintCheck generates semantic-based attack signatures from the network input data that eventually leads to an alert. Because TaintCheck has access to the history of the program execution, it has the information to pinpoint the invariable content (e.g., vulnerable memory address to be exploited) in attack packets, and thus can potentially generate attack signatures more precisely than the aforementioned syntactic approaches. Another example is the automatic diagnosis and response mechanism studied by Xu et al. 2005. This method is aimed at automatically identifying (unknown) memory corruption vulnerabilities, which are the dominant target of worm attacks. Based on the observation that a randomized program usually has an extremely high probability of crashing upon such attacks, this method uses a crash of a randomized program as a trigger to start the automatic diagnosis of memory corruption vulnerabilities, and traces back to the vulnerable instructions that corrupts memory data upon a memory corruption attack. The output of the diagnostic process includes the instruction exploited by the attacker to corrupt critical program data, the stack trace at the time of the memory corruption, the history that the corrupted data is propagated after the initial data corruption, and a signature of the attack exploiting the vulnerabilities. Such a signature consists of the program state at the time of attack and the memory address values used in the attack, allowing efficient and effective protection of the vulnerable program by filtering out future attacks. Wang, Cretu, and Stolfo (2005) took a different approach to automatically generating attack signatures by correlating (and identifying the longest common subsequence of) ingress and egress malicious payloads. Though most of these approaches are still works in progress, they certainly have demonstrated the potential of semantic-based signatures. We expect to see substantial advances in this direction in the next few years.

A closely related issue is evaluation of attack signatures. That is, how well can an attack signature detect attacks (including their variations)? Vigna et al. (2004) developed an approach to evaluating attack signatures by generating variations of known attacks (called "mutant attacks") through manipulating attack packets. Rubin, Jha, and Miller (2004) developed an approach to inferring all variations of an attack using language-based techniques. We refer readers to these papers.

Limitation of Misuse Detection

Current misuse-detection systems usually work better than anomaly-detection systems for known attacks. That is, misuse-detection systems detect patterns of known attacks more accurately and generate much fewer false alarms. This better performance occurs because misuse-detection systems take advantage of explicit knowledge of the attacks.

The limitation of misuse detection is that it cannot detect novel or unknown attacks. As a result, the computer systems protected solely by misuse-detection systems face the risk of being compromised without detecting the attacks. In addition, because of the requirement of explicit representation of attacks, misuse detection requires the nature of the attacks to be well understood. This implies that human experts must work on the analysis and representation of attacks, which is usually time consuming and error prone. Several ongoing works (e.g., Lee and Stolfo 2000; Newsome, Karp, and Song 2005; Xu et al. 2005) are targeting this problem by automatically generating attack signatures and preventing attacks in-progress.

INTRUSION-DETECTION SYSTEMS

Host-Based Intrusion-Detection Systems

As discussed earlier in the chapter, host-based IDSs get security audit data from individual hosts, and usually are aimed at detecting attacks against a single host. Several techniques we have discussed in earlier sections can be used for host-based IDSs—for example, the statistical models, the specification-based method, and the computer immunological approach. There are both advantages and disadvantages of using host-based IDSs. On the positive side, host-based IDSs can access more information on the host, and thus can usually make more accurate decisions about attacks. On the negative side, running a host-based IDS on an operational machine that runs critical services will add performance overheads to the host, thus degrading the performance.

There have been a lot of debates about whether host-based IDSs should be adopted or entirely discarded. Advances in attacks and detection techniques seem to indicate that host-based IDSs are necessary parts of a comprehensive defense system. There are two reasons. First, as discussed earlier, worms have adopted polymorphic and metamorphic techniques to evade detection. In both cases, it is difficult to identify patterns of worm attack traffic that do not match normal network traffic. Second, protocols with encryption (such as secure socket shell [SSH] and secure sockets layer [SSL]) are more and more widely adopted by Internet users. It is impossible to detect attacks carried in encrypted payloads through network-based IDSs. In contrast, it is convenient for host-based IDSs to get precise information about attacks, including the semantics of the programs that are potentially attacked.

Intrusion Detection in Distributed Systems

The rapid growth of the Internet not only provides the means for resource and information sharing, but it also brings new challenges to the intrusion-detection community. Because of the complexity and the amount of audit data generated by large-scale systems, host-based IDSs, though helpful for protecting large-scale systems through protection of individual hosts, are not sufficient by themselves. It is highly desirable to have complementary techniques that can detect and respond to attacks against large-scale systems.

Research on intrusion detection in distributed systems has been focused on two essential issues: *scalability* and *heterogeneity*. The IDSs in large distributed systems need to be scalable to accommodate the large amount of audit data in such systems. In addition, such IDSs must be able to deal with heterogeneous information from component systems of different types and that constitute large distributed systems and can cooperate with other types of IDSs.

Research on distributed intrusion detection is being conducted in three main areas. First, people are building scalable, distributed IDSs or are extending existing IDSs to make them capable of being scaled up for large systems. Second, network-based IDSs are being developed to take advantage of the standard network protocols to avoid heterogeneous audit data from different platforms. Third, standards and techniques are being developed to facilitate information sharing among different, possibly heterogeneous IDSs.

Distributed Intrusion Detection Systems

Early distributed IDSs collect audit data in a distributed manner but analyze the data in a centralized place—for example DIDS (Snapp et al. 1991) and ASAX (Mounji et al. 1995). Although audit data are usually reduced before being sent to the central analysis unit, the scalability of such systems is still limited. When the size of the distributed system grows large, not only might audit data have to travel long distances before arriving at the central place, but the central analysis component of the IDS may be overwhelmed by large amounts of audit data being generated.

Systems such as EMERALD (Lindqvist and Porras 1999), GrIDS (graph-based intrusion detection systems; Axelsson 1999), and AAFID (the autonomous agents for intrusion detection system; Spafford and Zamboni 2000), pay more attention to the scalability issue. To scale up to large distributed systems, these systems place IDS components in various places in a distributed system. Each of these components receives audit data or alerts from a limited number of sources (e.g., hosts or other IDS components), so the system is not overwhelmed by large amounts of audit data. Different components are often organized hierarchically in a tree structure; lower-level IDS components disseminate their detection results to higher-level components, so the intrusion-related information from different locations can be correlated together.

Although most of the recent distributed IDSs are designed to be scalable, they provide only a partial solution to the scalability problem. The IDS components are either coordinated in an ad hoc way or are organized hierarchically. Although coordinating the IDS components in an ad hoc way is certainly not a general solution, organizing the components hierarchically does not always provide an efficient solution, especially when the suspicious activities are spread in different, unpredictable locations in a large system. In a hierarchical system, when the activities involved in a distributed attack fall beyond the scope of one IDS component, the audit data possibly related to the attack will have to be forwarded to a higher-level IDS component to be correlated with data from other places. In a worst-case scenario, the audit data may have to be forwarded several times before arriving at a place where the data can finally be correlated with the related information. This process not only wastes the network's bandwidth, it also limits the scalability of the detection of distributed attacks.

Abstraction-based intrusion detection (Ning, Jajodia, and Wang 2001) addresses this problem by generating a hierarchy of IDS components dynamically rather than statically. Intuitively, this method defines attack signatures as generic patterns (called "generic signatures") of abstract events that may be observed in different places in a distributed system. When a particular type of attack is to be detected in a distributed system, the corresponding generic signature is mapped to the specific systems. The resulting signature is called a "specific signature." This method then decomposes the specific signature into components called "detection tasks," each of which corresponds to the intrusion-detection activities required to process a type of event involved in the attack. A coordination mechanism is developed to arrange the messages passing between the detection tasks, so the distributed detection of attacks is equivalent to having all events processed in a central place. The abstraction-based method is more flexible and more efficient than the previous methods; however, it is limited in that it is applicable only to misuse detection.

Network-Based Intrusion-Detection Systems

Network-based IDSs collect audit data from the network traffic, in contrast to host-based IDSs, which usually collect audit data from host audit trails. Examples of network-based IDSs include NSM (Network Security Monitor; Axelsson 1999), NetSTAT (Vigna and Kemmerer 1999), and Bro (Axelsson 1999).

One challenge that network-based intrusion detection is facing is the speed of high-performance networks, which makes it very difficult to capture the network traffic, let alone perform intrusion detection in real time. Several efforts have addressed enabling intrusion detection in high-speed networks. Snort, an open source IDS that specializes in network intrusion detection (Snort 2002), was developed by Roesch (1999). It uses a fast pattern-matching algorithm to detect network misuse. However, early versions of Snort detected attacks individually, and its performance degrades when the number of attack signatures (rules) increases. Since version 1.9, Snort has incorporated new pattern-matching algorithms to address this problem.

Sekar et al. (1999) developed a high-performance network-IDS-based on an efficient pattern-matching algorithm. A distinguishing feature is that the performance of the system is independent of the number of misuse rules (signatures).

Kruegel et al. (2002) proposed a partition approach to intrusion detection that supports misuse detection on high-speed network links. This approach is based on a slicing mechanism that divides the overall network traffic into subsets of manageable size. Thus, each subset can be processed by one or several misuse-detection systems. The traffic partitioning is done such that each subset of the network traffic contains all the evidence necessary to detect a specific attack.

Network-based IDSs offer several advantages. First, network-based IDSs can take advantage of the standard structure of network protocols, such as TCP/IP. This is a good way to avoid the confusion resulting from heterogeneity in a distributed system. Second, network-based IDSs usually run on a separate (dedicated) computer; thus, they do not consume the resources of the computers that are being protected.

Conversely, network-based IDS are not silver bullets. First, because these IDSs do not use host-based information, they may miss the opportunity to detect some attacks. For example, network-based IDSs cannot detect an attack launched from a console. Second, the standard network protocols do not solve the entire problem related to the heterogeneity of distributed systems because of the variety of application protocols and systems that use these protocols. For example, network-based IDSs must understand the UNIX shell commands if their goal is to monitor intrusive remote log-ins. As another example, network-based IDSs usually describe the suspicious network activities using the structure of the packet that standard network protocols such as TCP/IP support, which makes the specification of the suspicious activities to be detected very difficult.

Network-based IDSs have the same scalability problem as do general distributed IDSs. For example, existing network-based IDSs analyze network traffic data in a centralized place, as was done by the early distributed IDSs, although they may collect data from various places in the network. This structure limits the scale of the distributed systems that such IDSs can protect.

Sharing Information among Intrusion-Detection Systems

With the deployment of so many commercial IDSs, these IDSs must be able to share information so that they can interact and thus achieve better performance than if they were operating in isolation. Research and development activities are currently under way to enable different, possibly heterogeneous, IDSs to share information.

The common intrusion-detection framework (CIDF) was developed to enable different intrusion detection and response (IDR) components to interoperate and share information and resources (Porras et al. 1999). It began as a part of the Defense Advanced Research Project Agency (DARPA) Information Survivability program, with a focus on allowing DARPA projects to work together. CIDF considers IDR systems as composed of four types of components that communicate via message passing: event generators (E-boxes), event analyzers (A-boxes), event databases (D-boxes), and response units (R-boxes). A communication framework and a common intrusion-specification language are provided to assist the interoperation among CIDF components.

Researchers involved in CIDF started an Intrusion Detection Working Group (IDWG) in the Internet Engineering Task Force (IETF), trying to bring the impact of CIDF to a broader community. The IDWG has been working to develop data formats and exchange procedures for sharing information among IDSs, response systems, and management systems. The extensible markup language (XML) has been chosen to provide the common format, and an intrusion-detection message exchange format (IDMEF) has been defined in an Internet draft. The IDWG uses the blocks extensible exchange protocol (BEEP) as the application protocol framework for exchanging intrusion-detection messages between different systems; an intrusion-detection exchange protocol (IDXP) is specified as a BEEP profile, and a tunnel profile is provided to enable different systems to exchange messages through firewalls.

Another effort in sharing information among different IDSs is the Hummer project (Fringke et al. 1998). In particular, the relationships among different IDSs (e.g., peer, friend, manager/subordinate) and policy issues (e.g., access-control policy, cooperation policy) were studied, and a prototype system, HummingBird, was developed to address these issues. A limitation of the Hummer project is that it addresses only the general data-sharing issue; what information needs to be shared and how the information would be used are out of its scope. Thus, it should be used along with mechanisms such as IDIAN (Feiertag et al. 2000) and the decentralized coordination mechanism in the abstraction-based approach (Ning, Jajodia, and Wang 2001).

There are several ongoing efforts to facilitate the sharing of intrusion related data. Examples include DShield (http://www.dshield.org) and the PREDICT project (http://www.predict.org). A common goal of these projects is to collect data about intrusions from different regions and different organizations to facilitate intrusion analysis. However, these activities also raised legal and privacy concerns of the organizations that provide such data. Several research groups have investigated techniques that can allow access to the valuable information and at the same time can protect the privacy of the data providers (Lincoln et al. 2004; Xu and Ning 2005)

INTRUSION-ALERT CORRELATION

Traditional IDSs focus on low-level attacks or anomalies, and raise alerts independently, though there may be logical connections between them. In situations in which there are intensive attacks, not only will actual alerts be mixed with false alerts, but the number of alerts will also become unmanageable. As a result, it is difficult for human users or intrusion-response systems to understand the alerts and take appropriate actions. Therefore, it is necessary to develop techniques to correlate IDS alerts and construct attack scenarios (i.e., steps that attackers use in their attacks) to facilitate intrusion analysis.

In this section, we first give a brief overview of the techniques for intrusion-alert correlation, and then present in more detail one approach that correlates intrusion alerts based on prerequisites and consequences of known attacks.

Techniques for intrusion-alert correlation can be divided into several classes. The first class of approaches (e.g., Spice [Staniford, Hoagland, and McAlerney 2002] and probabilistic alert correlation [Valdes and Skinner 2001]) correlates IDS alerts based on the similarities between alert attributes. They usually require a distance function to measure the similarity between two IDS alerts based on the alert attribute values, and correlate two alerts together if the distance between them is less than a certain threshold. Though they are effective for clustering similar alerts (e.g., alerts with the same source and destination IP addresses), they cannot fully discover the causal relationships between related alerts.

The second class of methods (e.g., correlation based on STATL [Eckmann, Vigna, and Kemmerer, 2002]) performs alert correlation based on attack scenarios specified by human users, or learned from training data sets. Such methods are essentially extensions to misuse detection. Similar to misuse detection, intrusion-alert correlation based on known scenarios are effective in recognizing known attack scenarios, but are also restricted to known attack scenarios, or those that can be generalized from known scenarios. A variation in this class uses a consequence mechanism to specify what types of attacks may follow a given attack, partially addressing this problem (Debar and Wespi, 2001).

The third class of methods (e.g., JIGSAW [Templeton and Levitt 2000], the MIRADOR correlation method [Cuppens and Miege 2002], and the correlation method based on prerequisites and consequences of attacks [Ning, Cui, and Reeves, 2002]) targets recognition of multistage attacks; it correlates alerts if the prerequisites of some later alerts are satisfied by the consequences of some earlier alerts. Such methods can potentially uncover the causal relationship between alerts, and are not restricted to known attack scenarios. We will discuss one such method in detail later in this chapter.

The fourth class of methods attempts to correlate alerts (including IDS alerts) from multiple sources, using potentially complementary information to improve the understanding of possible intrusions. A formal model named M2D2 was proposed in Morin et al. (2002) to correlate alerts by using multiple information sources, including the characteristics of the monitored systems, the vulnerability information, the information about the monitoring tools, and information of the observed events. Because of the multiple information sources used in alert correlation, this method can potentially lead to better results than those simply looking at intrusion alerts. A mission-impact-based approach was proposed by Porras, Fong, and Valdes (2002) to correlate alerts raised by information security devices such as IDSs and firewalls. A distinguishing feature of this approach is that it correlates the alerts with the importance of system assets so that attention can be focused on critical resources. Though methods in this class are still in their preliminary stage, we believe techniques in this class will eventually provide the most support for intrusion-alert analysis.

Intrusion-Alert Correlation Based on Prerequisites and Consequences of Attacks

To further illustrate intrusion-alert correlation techniques, we give additional details about the alert correlation method based on prerequisites and consequences of attacks (Ning, Cui, & Reeves 2002), which one of us was involved in developing.

The alert-correlation model is based on the observation that in series of attacks, the component attacks are usually not isolated, but related as different stages of the attacks, with the early ones preparing for the later ones. For example, an attacker has to install distributed denial of service (DDoS) daemon programs before he can launch a DDoS attack. To take advantage of this observation, it correlates alerts using prerequisites and consequences of the corresponding attacks. Intuitively, the *prerequisite* of an attack is the necessary condition for the attack to be successful. For example, the existence of a vulnerable service is the prerequisite of a remote buffer overflow attack against the service. Moreover, an attacker may make progress (e.g., install a Trojan horse program) as a result of an attack. Informally, the possible outcome of an attack is called the *consequence* of the attack. In a series of attacks in which earlier ones are launched to prepare for later ones, there are usually connections between the consequences of the earlier attacks and the prerequisites of the later ones. Accordingly, this method identifies the prerequisites (e.g., existence of vulnerable services) and the consequences (e.g., discovery of vulnerable services) of attacks, and correlates detected attacks (i.e., alerts) by matching the consequences of previous alerts and the prerequisites of later ones.

Predicates are used as basic constructs to represent prerequisites and consequences of attacks. For example, a scanning attack may discover UDP (user datagram protocol) services vulnerable to certain buffer overflow attacks. We can use the predicate *UDPVulnerableToBOF* (*VictimIP*, *VictimPort*) to represent this discovery. In general, a logical formula (i.e., a logical combination of predicates) is used to represent the prerequisite of an attack. Thus, we may have a prerequisite of the form *UDPVulnerableToBOF* (*VictimIP*, *VictimPort*) ^ *UDPAccessibleViaFirewall* (*VictimIP*, *VictimPort*). Similarly, a set of logical formulas is used to represent the consequence of an attack.

With predicates as basic constructs, a *hyper-alert type* is used to encode our knowledge about each type of attack. A *hyper-alert type T* is a triple (*fact, prerequisite, consequence*) in which: (1) *fact* is a set of attribute names, each with an associated domain of values, (2) *prerequisite* is a logical formula whose free variables are all in *fact*, and (3) *consequence* is a set of logical formulas such that all the free variables in *consequence* are in *fact*. Intuitively, the *fact* component of a hyper-alert type gives the information associated with the alert, *prerequisite* specifies what must be true for the attack to be successful, and *consequence* describes what could be true if the attack indeed happens. For brevity, we omit the domains associated with attribute names when they are clear from context.

Given a hyper-alert type T = (*fact*, *prerequisite*, *consequence*), a *hyper-alert* (*instance*) *h of type T* is a finite set of tuples on *fact*, where each tuple is associated with an interval-based timestamp [begin_time, end_time]. The hyper-alert h implies that *prerequisite* must evaluate to True and all the logical formulas in *consequence* might evaluate to True for each of the tuples. The *fact* component of a hyper-alert type is essentially a relation schema (as in relational databases), and a hyper-alert is a relation instance of this schema. A hyper-alert *instantiates* its *prerequisite* and *consequence* by replacing the free variables in *prerequisite* and *consequence* with its specific values. Note that *prerequisite* and *consequence* can be instantiated multiple times if *fact* consists of multiple tuples. For example, if an IPSweep attack involves several IP addresses, the *prerequisite* and *consequence* of the corresponding hyper-alert type will be instantiated for each of these addresses.

To correlate hyper-alerts, this method checks whether an earlier hyper-alert contributes to the prerequisite of a later one. Specifically, it decomposes the prerequisite of a hyper-alert into parts of predicates and tests whether the consequence of an earlier hyper-alert makes some parts of the prerequisite True (i.e., makes the prerequisite easier to satisfy). If the result is positive, then the hyper-alerts are correlated together. In the formal model, given an instance h of the hyper-alert type T = (*fact, prerequisite, consequence*), the *prerequisite set* (*or consequence set*) of h, denoted $P(h)$ (or $C(h)$), is the set of all such predicates that appear in *prerequisite* (or *consequence*) whose arguments are replaced with the corresponding attribute values of each tuple in h. Each element in $P(h)$ (or $C(h)$) is associated with the timestamp of the corresponding tuple in h. A hyper-alert h_1 *prepares for* hyper-alert h_2 if there exist $p \in P(h_2)$ and $C \subseteq C(h_1)$ such that for all $c \in C$, c.end_time $< p$.begin_time and the conjunction of all the logical formulas in C implies p.

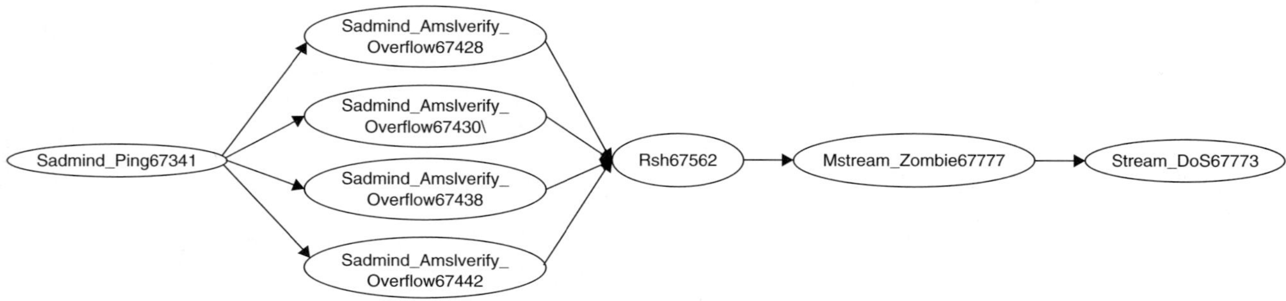

Figure 1: A hyper-alert correlation graph

Given a sequence S of hyper-alerts, a hyper-alert h in S is a *correlated hyper-alert* if there exists another hyper-alert h' such that either h prepares for h' or h' prepares for h. A *hyper-alert correlation graph* is used to represent a set of correlated hyper-alerts. Specifically, a *hyper-alert correlation graph* $CG = (N, E)$ is a connected graph, where N is a set of hyper-alerts and for each pair $n_1, n_2 \in N$, there is a directed edge from n_1 to n_2 in E if and only if n_1 prepares for n_2.

Figure 1 shows one of the hyper-alert correlation graphs discovered in an experiment with the 2000 DARPA intrusion-detection evaluation data sets. Each node in Figure 1 represents a hyper-alert, where the label inside the node is the hyper-alert type followed by the hyper-alert ID. This hyper-alert correlation graph shows an attack scenario in which the attacker probes for vulnerable *Sadmind* service, compromises the vulnerable service using a buffer overflow attack, copies some file with *Rsh*, starts a DDoS daemon program named *mstream*, and finally launch a DDOS attack.

CONCLUSION

Intrusion detection continues to be an active research field, and it is undergoing a fast transition. Even after over 20 years of research, the intrusion-detection community still faces several difficult problems. How to detect unknown patterns of attacks without generating too many false alerts remains an unresolved problem, although several results have shown there is a potential resolution to this problem. The evaluation and benchmarking of IDSs is also an important problem, which, once solved, may provide useful guidance for organizational decision makers and end users. (Some results on evaluating IDSs can be found in McHugh [2000].) Reconstructing attack scenarios from intrusion alerts and integration of IDSs will improve both the usability and the performance of IDSs. How to prevent attacks while detecting these attacks (i.e., intrusion prevention) is also a critical issue affecting the deployment of IDSs. Many researchers and practitioners are actively addressing these problems. We expect intrusion detection to become a practical and effective solution for protecting information systems.

This chapter is by no means a complete reference for intrusion-detection systems; many important issues have not been included because of space constraints. Further readings are suggested at the end of this chapter.

GLOSSARY

Anomaly Detection: One of the two methods of intrusion detection. Anomaly detection is based on the normal behavior of a subject (e.g., a user or a system); any action that significantly deviates from the normal behavior is considered intrusive. More generally, anomaly detection refers to identification of potential system security policy violations based on observation that some action or other characteristics deviate from normal. The underlying philosophy is that "normal" or acceptable behaviors and other features can be described, and deviations from them recognized. The other method is misuse detection.

Audit Trail: Records a chronology of system-resource usage. This includes user log-in, file access, other various activities, and whether any actual or attempted security violations occurred.

False Negative: An actual misuse action that the system allows to pass as non-misuse behavior.

False Positive: Classification of an action as anomalous (a possible instance of misuse) when it is legitimate.

IDS: Intrusion detection system.

Intrusion: Any activity that violates the security policy of an information system, normally ascribed to a system outsider who "enters" the system to perform this behavior, but sometimes used more generally to cover any violation of policy. Also referred to as "misuse."

Intrusion Detection: The process of identifying intrusions or other misuses by observing security logs, audit data, or other information available in computer systems and/or networks.

Intrusion-Alert Correlation: The process to identify related intrusion alerts and the relationship between them. The goal is often to reconstruct the attack scenarios (i.e., steps of attacks) from the intrusion alerts reported by the IDS; alternatively, it may be used to recognize broad-based attacks even without regard to specific steps.

Misuse Detection: One of the two methods of intrusion detection, often but not necessarily used to scrutinize representations of behavior. Catches intrusions in terms of the characteristics of known patterns of attacks or system vulnerabilities; any action that conforms to the pattern of a known attack or vulnerability is considered intrusive. More generally, misuse detection refers to identification of violations of system-security policy based on recognizing actions or other characteristics known to be associated with such violations. The philosophy behind misuse detection is that inappropriate activities or behaviors can be characterized, and used to detect policy violations. The other method is anomaly detection.

Misuse Signature: A known pattern or attack or vulnerability, usually specified in a certain attack-specification language.

Profile: A set of parameters used to represent the pattern of a subject's (e.g., a user or a program) normal behavior. It is normally used to conduct anomaly detection.

Security Policy: A set of rules and procedures regulating the use of information, including its processing, storage, distribution, and presentation.

CROSS REFERENCES

See *Authentication;Denial of Service Attacks;Virtual Private Networks*.

REFERENCES

Anderson, J. P. 1980. *Computer security threat monitoring and surveillance*. Technical report. Fort Washington, PA: James P. Anderson.

Axelsson, S. 1999. *Research in intrusion-detection systems: A survey*. Technical report TR 98-17. Göteborg, Sweden: Department of Computer Engineering, Chalmers University of Technology.

Bace, B. 1999. *Intrusion detection*. New York: Macmillan Technical Publications.

Barbara, D., J. Couto, S, Jajodia, and N. Wu. 2001. ADAM: A testbed for exploring the use of data mining in intrusion detection. *ACM SIGMOD Record* 30(4):15–24.

———. 2002. An architecture for anomaly detection. In *Applications of data mining in computer security*, edited by D. Barbara and S. Jajodia, 63–76. Boston: Kluwer Academic.

Cuppens, F., and A. Miege. 2002. Alert correlation in a cooperative intrusion detection framework. In *Proceedings of the 2002 IEEE Symposium on Security and Privacy*, 202–15. Los Alamitos, CA: IEEE Computer Society.

Debar, H., and A. Wespi. 2001. Aggregation and correlation of intrusion-detection alerts. *Proceedings of Recent Advances in Intrusion Detection*, 85–103. New York: Springer-Verlag Lecture Notes in Computer Science, 2212.

Denning, D. 1986. An intrusion-detection model. In *Proceedings of 1986 IEEE Symposium on Security and Privacy*, 118–31. Los Alamitos, CA: IEEE Computer Society.

Eckmann, S., G. Vigna, and R. Kemmerer. 2002. STATL: An attack language for state-based intrusion detection. *Journal of Computer Security* 10:71–104.

Feiertag, R., S. Rho, L. Benzinger, S. Wu, T. Redmond, C. Zhang, K. Levitt, D. Peticolas, M. Heckman, S. Staniford, and J. McAlerney. 2000. Intrusion detection inter-component adaptive negotiation. *Computer Networks* 34(4):605–21.

Fox, K. L., R. R. Henning, J. H. Reed, and R. P. Simonian. 1990. A neural network approach towards intrusion detection. In *Proceedings of 13th National Computer Security Conference*, 125–34. Baltimore: National Institute of Standards and Technology (NIST).

Frincke, D., D. Tobin, J. McConnell, J. Marconi, and D. Polla. 1998. A framework for cooperative intrusion detection. In *Proceedings of the 21st National Information Systems Security Conference*, 361–73. Baltimore: National Institute of Standards and Technology (NIST).

Ghosh, A. K., J. Wanken, and F. Charron. 1998. Detecting anomalous and unknown intrusions against programs. In *Proceedings of the 14th Annual Computer Security Applications Conference*, edited by K. Keus, 259–67. Los Alamitos, CA: IEEE Computer Society.

Hofmeyr, S., S. Forrest, and A. Somayaji. 1998. Intrusion detection using sequences of system calls. *Journal of Computer Security* 6:151–80.

Ilgun, K., R. A. Kemmerer, and P. A. Porras. 1995. State transition analysis: A rule-based intrusion detection approach. *IEEE Transactions on Software Engineering* 21(3):181–99.

Kim, H., and B. Karp. 2004. Autograph: toward automated, distributed worm signature detection. *Proceedings of 2004 USENIX Security Symposium*, 271–86. Berkeley, CA: USENIX.

Ko, C. 2000. Logic induction of valid behavior specifications for intrusion detection. In *Proceedings of 2000 IEEE symposium of security and privacy*, edited by M. Reiter and R. Needham, 142–53. Los Alamitos, CA: IEEE Computer Society.

Ko, C., M. Ruschitzka, and K. Levitt. 1997. Execution monitoring of security-critical programs in distributed systems: a specification-based approach. In *Proceedings of 1997 IEEE Symposium on Security and Privacy*, edited by G. Dinolt and P. Karger, 175–87. Los Alamitos, CA: IEEE Computer Society.

Kohonen, T. 1982. Self-organizing formation of topologically correct feature maps. *Biological Cybernetics* 43(1):59–69.

Kruegel, C., F. Valeur, G. Vigna, and R. Kemmerer. 2002. Stateful intrusion detection for high-speed networks. In *Proceedings of 2002 IEEE Symposium on Security and Privacy*. edited by M. Abadi and S. Bellovin, 285–93. Los Alamitos, CA: IEEE Computer Society.

Kumar, S. 1995. *Classification and detection of computer intrusions*. Unpublished doctoral dissertation. West Lafayette, IN: Purdue University.

Kumar, S., and E. H. Spafford. 1994. A pattern-matching model for misuse intrusion detection. In *Proceedings of the 17th National Computer Security Conference*, 11–21. Baltimore: National Institute of Standards and Technology (NIST).

Lane, T., and C. E. Brodley. 1998. Temporal sequence learning and data reduction for anomaly detection. In *Proceedings of 5th Conference on Computer and Communications Security*, edited by L. Gong and M. Reiter, 150–8. New York: ACM Press.

Lee, W., and S. J. Stolfo. 2000. A framework for constructing features and models for intrusion detection systems. *ACM Transactions on Information and System Security* 3(4):227–61.

Lee, W., and D. Xiang. 2001. Information-theoretic measures for anomaly detection. In *Proceedings of 2001 IEEE Symposium on Security and Privacy*, edited by R. Needham and M. Abadi, 130–43. Los Alamitos, CA: IEEE Computer Society.

Lin, J., X. S. Wang, and S. Jajodia. 1998. Abstraction-based misuse detection: High-level specifications and adaptable strategies. In *Proceedings of the 11th Computer Security Foundations Workshop*, edited by S. Foley, 190–201. Los Alamitos, CA: IEEE Computer Society.

Lincoln, P. P. Porras, and V. Shmatikov. 2004. Privacy-preserving sharing and correlation of security alerts. In *Proceedings of 13th USENIX Security Symposium*, 239–54. Berkeley, CA: USENIX.

Lindqvist, U., and P. A. Porras. 1999. Detecting computer and network misuse through the production-based expert system toolset (P-BEST). In *Proceedings of the 1999 IEEE Symposium on Security and Privacy*, edited by L. Gong and M. Reiter, 146–61. Los Alamitos, CA IEEE Computer Society.

Mannila, H., H. Toivonen, and A. I. Verkamo. 1995. Discovering frequent episodes in sequences. In *Proceedings of the 1st Conference on Knowledge Discovery and Data Mining*, edited by U. Fayyad and R. Uthurusamy, 210–5. Menlo Park, CA: AAAI Press.

McHugh, J. 2000. Testing intrusion detection systems: a critique of the 1998 and 1999 DARPA intrusion detection system evaluations as performed by Lincoln laboratory. *ACM Transactions on Information and System Security* 3(4):262–94.

Morin, B., L. Mé, H. Debar, and M. Ducassé. 2002. M2D2: A formal data model for IDS alert correlation. In *Proceedings of the 5th International Symposium on Recent Advances in Intrusion Detection*, 115–37. New York: Springer-Verlag.

Mounji, A., B. L. Charlier, D. Zampuniéris, and N. Habra. 1995. Distributed audit trail analysis. In *Proceedings of the ISOC'95 Symposium on Network and Distributed System Security*. edited by D. Balenson and R. Shirey, 102–12. Los Alamitos, CA: IEEE Computer Society.

Newsome, J., B. Karp, and D. Song. 2005. Polygraph: automatically generating signatures for polymorphic worms. In *Proceedings of 2005 IEEE Symposium on Security and Privacy*, 226–41. Los Alamitos, CA: IEEE Computer Society.

Ning, P., Y. Cui, and D. S. Reeves. 2002. Constructing attack scenarios through correlation of intrusion alerts. In *Proceedings of the 9th ACM Conference on Computer and Communications Security*, 245–54. Washington, DC: ACM Press, Washington, D.C.

Ning, P., S. Jajodia, and X. S. Wang. 2001. Abstraction-based intrusion detection in distributed environments. *ACM Transactions on Information and System Security* 4(4):407–52.

Northcutt, S. and J. Novak. 2002. *Network intrusion detection*. New York: Sams.

Porras, P., M. Fong, and A. Valdes. 2002. A mission-impact-based approach to INFOSEC alarm correlation, In *Proceedings of the 5th International Symposium on Recent Advances in Intrusion Detection*, 95–114. New York: Springer-Verlag.

Porras, P., D. Schnackenberg, S. Staniford-Chen, M. Stillman, and F. Wu. 1999. *Common Intrusion Detection Framework Architecture*. http://www.isi.edu/gost/cidf (accessed February 13, 2003).

Roesch, M. 1999. Snort—Lightweight intrusion detection for networks. In *Proceedings of the 13th Systems Administration Conference*, edited by D. Parter. www.usenix.org/publications/library/proceedings/lisa99/technical.html (accessed February 13, 2003).

Rubin, S., S. Jha, and B. P. Miller. 2004. Automatic generation and analysis of NIDS attacks. In *Proceedings of 20th Annual Computer Security Applications Conference*, 28–48. Los Alamitos, CA: IEEE Computer Society.

Sekar, R., M. Bendre, D. Dhurjati, and P. Bollineni, P. 2001. A fast automaton-based method for detecting anomalous program behaviors. In *Proceedings of 2001 IEEE Symposium on Security and Privacy*, edited by R. Needham & M. Abadi, 144–55. Los Alamitos, CA: IEEE Computer Society.

Sekar, R., Y. Guang, S. Verma, and T. Shanbhag. 1999. A high-performance network intrusion detection system. In *Proceedings of the 6th ACM Conference on Computer and Communications Security*, edited by J. Motiwalla and G. Tsudik, 8–17. New York: ACM Press.

Singh, S., C. Estan, G. Varghese, and S. Savage. 2004. Automated worm fingerprinting. *Proceedings of 2004 ACM/USENIX Symposium on Operating Systems Design and Implementation*, 45–60. Berkeley, CA: USENIX.

Snapp, S. R., J. Brentano, G. V. Dias, et al. 1991. DIDS (distributed intrusion detection system)—Motivation, architecture, and an early prototype. In *Proceedings of 14th national computer security conference*, 167–76. New York: ACM Press.

Snort—The open source intrusion detection system. 2002. http://www.snort.org (accessed February 13, 2003).

Spafford, E. H., and D. Zamboni. 2000. Intrusion detection using autonomous agents. *Computer Networks* 34:547–70.

Staniford, S., J. Hoagland, and J. McAlerney. 2002. Practical automated detection of stealthy portscans. *Journal of Computer Security* 10(1–2):105–36.

Tan, L., and R. Maxion. 2002 "Why 6?" Defining the operational limits of STIDE, an anomaly-based intrusion detector. In *Proceedings of IEEE Symposium on Security and Privacy*, 188–201. Los Alamitos, CA: IEEE Computer Society.

Templeton, S., and K. Levitt. 2000. A requires/provides model for computer attacks. In *Proceedings of New Security Paradigms Workshop*, 31–8. New York: ACM Press.

Teng, H. S., K. Chen, and S. C. Lu. 1990. Adaptive real-time anomaly detection using inductively generated sequential patterns. In *Proceedings of 1990 IEEE Symposium on Security and Privacy*, 278–84). Los Alamitos, CA: IEEE Computer Society.

Vigna, G., and R. A. Kemmerer. 1999. NetSTAT: A network-based intrusion detection system. *Journal of Computer Security* 7(1):37–71.

Vigna, G., W. Robertson, and D. Balzarotti. 2004. Testing network-based intrusion detection signatures using mutant exploits. In *Proceedings of 2004 ACM Conference on Computer and Communications Security*, 21–30 Washington, DC: ACM Press.

Valdes, A. and K. Skinner. 2001. Probabilistic alert correlation, *Proceedings of the 4th International Symposium on Recent Advances in Intrusion Detection*, 54–68. New York: Springer-Verlag.

Wagner, D., and D. Dean. 2001. Intrusion detection via static analysis. In *Proceedings of 2001 IEEE Symposium on Security and Privacy*, edited by R. Needham and M. Abadi, 156–68. Los Alamitos, CA: IEEE Computer Society.

Wang, K., G. Cretu, and S. Stolfo. 2005. Anomalous payload-based worm detection and signature generation. In *Proceedings of the Eighth International Symposium on Recent Advances in Intrusion Detection*. New York: Springer.

Xu, D., and P. Ning. 2005. Privacy-preserving alert correlation: A concept hierarchy based approach. In *Proceedings of the 21st Annual Computer Security Applications Conference*, Los Alamitos, CA: IEEE Computer Society.

Xu, J., P. Ning, C. Kil, Y. Zhai, and C. Bookholt. 2005. Automatic diagnosis and response to memory corruption vulnerabilities. In *Proceedings of 2005 ACM Conference on Computer and Communications Security*, 223–4. Washington, DC: ACM Press.

Zamboni, D. 2001. *Using internal sensors for computer intrusion detection*. Unpublished doctoral dissertation, West Lafayette, IN: Purdue University.

FURTHER READING

This chapter serves as an introduction to intrusion detection. The reader may want to read more on this subject to gain a full picture of the state of the art of intrusion detection. A book titled *Intrusion Detection* (Bace 1999) gives a nice overview of intrusion-detection techniques and systems prior to the late 1990s. Another book, titled *Network Intrusion Detection* (Northcutt and Novak 2002) provides a wonderful guideline for practical network intrusion detection. DARPA (Defense Advanced Research Projects Agency) provided substantial support for intrusion-detection research in the late 1990s and early 2000s, including the 1998 and 1999 DARPA Intrusion Detection Evaluation program led by researchers at the MIT Lincoln Laboratory. DARPA-supported researchers made substantial progresses in intrusion detection, which were mostly reported in the Proceedings of DARPA Information Survivability Conference and Exposition (DISCEX) (http://csdl2.computer.org/persagen/DLPublication.jsp?pubtype=p&acronym=DISCEX). Another good source for the recent advances in intrusion-detection research is the Proceedings of the International Symposia on Recent Advances in Intrusion Detection (RAID) (http://www.raid-symposium.org/).

Network Attacks

Mohamed Hamdi and Noureddine Boudriga, *University of 7th of November, Carthage, Tunisia*

INTRODUCTION

The last decades of the twentieth century were characterized by the rise of new technologies that support most of the strategic and critical activities. Energy, manufacturing, water resources, geology, and press are just few applications that are evolving by leaps and bounds on the impulse of the computer and communication locomotive. Having followed the mechanical and industrial revolutions, these developments have been so important that their traces are ever-present. The widespread use of advanced computer and network technologies has allowed the automation of certain key processes and the fast transmission of important data. Obviously, this has resulted in a noteworthy gain, especially in terms of time and effort, which magnifies productivity. Nevertheless, advances in these areas have also been linked to huge losses because of the improper use of the network computing infrastructure. The functionalities provided by the modern networked information systems have been exploited by attackers and victims alike. Even though the existing protection infrastructures are being continuously improved, they are overawed by the power of the attackers' capabilities.

The purpose of this chapter is to convey to the reader the problems of defining and modeling network attacks, the pervasiveness and impact of these attacks, and how one can develop a cost-effective security platform when encountering such security incidents.

The remainder of this chapter is structured as follows. The section on security incidents introduces the basic terminology that is used throughout the chapter and points out the main features of network attacks. The next section reviews the importance of the attack outcome analysis. It also identifies several new attack trends. We next focus on various attack techniques and discusses some useful attack taxonomies. The next section explains the need for building attack models to achieve different objectives (e.g., detection, prevention, reaction). And the subsequent section analyzes the features of two types of models: the preventive models and reactive models. Next, three major aspects of network attack response are covered: building the security policy, monitoring the network state, and handling security incidents. A set of general guidelines to choose the more suitable security solutions is given in the section titled "Countermeasure-Selection Guidelines." The final section examines the most relevant challenges faced by the security community.

DESCRIPTION OF SECURITY INCIDENTS

Intrusions, threats, and alerts are three concepts that are similar in the sense that they represent attacks; but they are also different because they actually refer to different aspects of the attack process. In this section, a set of definitions that highlight the slight differences between attacks, intrusions, threats, and alerts are proposed. In addition, the characteristics of the information conveyed by each of these terms are investigated.

Threats, Alerts, and Intrusions

A *threat* is any event that can result in a loss for the target system. It can be malevolent, accidental, or even due to a natural disaster. Threat modeling is an important practice that provides the capability to secure a network environment. It is critical to be aware of the types of threats and how to reduce or mitigate the risk both in systems and applications on network devices. In fact, reaching an accurate description of a specific threat clearly allows identifying the best techniques that protect the system against it. Modeling a threat mainly includes identifying the vulnerabilities to which it relates, and structuring incidents in a way that facilitates the communication of threat information throughout the network computing environment. This turns out to be a difficult process because the security analyst should look for the events that might occur and anticipate how the malicious user could harm the protected system. Typically, the information that should be associated with a specific threat breaks into three components: probability, outcome, and exploited vulnerability.

An *alert* can be loosely defined as a description of an attack that is achieved by monitoring several system parameters. Alert generation is an event triggered by the occurrence of a network attack. The main role of alert generation is that it allows the security analyst to identify the attacks that are carried out against the system to proceed to the appropriate reaction. However, the alert-attack association is never certain, and a single alert can be related to more than one attack. Hence, mechanisms to determine the *most probable* attack linked to a specific alert should be available. Generally, the decision errors that confuse the alert-based incident response break into two categories: (1) false positives (i.e., an alert is generated in the absence of a network attack), and (2) false negatives (i.e., no alert is generated when an attack did occur). Obviously, both of these errors result in a loss, and their probability should be therefore minimized to enhance the efficiency of the intrusion-detection process. *Probability* defines the amount of uncertainty related to the attack event, and *impact* provides an idea about the severity of a specific threat. It is often assessed on the basis of the nature of the victim network asset. Generally, threats that are characterized by important probability and impact values are prioritized. The exploited vulnerability should be included in the threat information to facilitate the countermeasure-selection process.

To explain what an intrusion is, some fundamentals about security policy should be given. In its broadest definition, a *security policy* consists of a set of rules that define how critical assets should be secured. Based on this definition, an intrusion in an information system can be thought of as an activity that does not respect the system's security policy. In other terms, an action that violates one or more security property (i.e., confidentiality, integrity, availability) of the protected system is considered as an intrusion. As an extension to this reasoning, an attack against a communication network is not perceived as an intrusion if it does not violate the security rules of the target system. In this case, the attack is not detected at the time and the only information available for the response team is the intrusion outcome; consequently, novel rules should be appended to the security policy to prevent future occurrences of the experienced attack. Typically, when a system experiences an attack that has not been noticed by the detection infrastructure, a forensic activity should be conducted in order to reconstitute the instruction scheme and decide the novel rules to append.

Basic Attack Features

It comes from the previous subsection that a network attack is rather an abstract concept, which is represented by some pieces of information that may vary according to the situation. For instance, in the context of threat analysis, the information one is seeking is the knowledge of whether a security breach has been experienced, and, if the answer is yes, what are the probability and the impact. Conversely, when studying an alert, the main concern is to identify the malicious action that is being carried out in order to react at the convenient moment and in a cost-effective manner. Despite the pervasiveness of network attacks, several fundamental characteristics should be taken into consideration independently from the way the attack is viewed. Analyzing those common features is helpful in the sense that it conveys a better understanding of both the attacker behavior and the defense capabilities. The most prominent attack characteristics can be summarized in the following points:

Coordination

To achieve a major objective, the attacker often combines multiple elementary attacks or uses several external resources. This is because organized attacks aiming at disrupting critical infrastructure are beyond the capabilities of a single attacker. Therefore, multiple attackers can cooperate by resource sharing, task allocation, and time synchronization. Obviously, such attacks are more difficult to detect and to counter. The most important problems associated with these attacks are given in the following:

Coordinated attacks are difficult to detect: Many intrusion-detection systems (IDSs) can be defeated by coordinated attacks capable of breaking the attack scheme into many apparently inoffensive actions. For instance, if we consider a large set of users, hosts, processes, and threads with few attackers hiding a coordinated attack plan, it is practically impossible to discern individual attackers because of the huge amount of data that would be analyzed. In addition, many of those attackers would appear to perform innocuous actions.

Differentiating between decoy and actual attacks is difficult: Often, numerous attacks are conducted against a system in a nearly simultaneous manner. In order to mislead the IDS, all but a small number of these attacks are designed to be decoys, meaning that they are carried out for the sole purpose of distracting the intrusion-response system and consuming its resources. Decoy attacks may have different goals. They could: create simultaneous alerts in order to alter the efficiency of the intrusion response system; waste system response resources on decoy goals; or perform a denial-of-service attack on the IDS.

There is a large variety of coordinated attacks: Intruders may attack single or multiple victims. Some attacks could be automatically replicated in order to accumulate more power. Other attacks may be carried out in parallel from multiple attackers (or network nodes that are under the control of the attacker) targeting a single victim.

Incomplete Knowledge

Threats and alerts, which are often used to select the optimal set of countermeasures for a specific attack scenario, are characterized by an amount of uncertainty. This uncertainty should be taken into consideration when making decisions based on threat or alert representation of network attacks. Practically, threats and alerts are used to select the best set of countermeasures according to a cost-benefit balance. On the one hand, modeling a threat allows thwarting the attack before its occurrence by adding rules to the security policy. On the other hand, alerts provide a strong means for reacting against intrusions. Models used to represent threats and alerts should therefore integrate uncertainty-handling mechanisms (e.g., probabilistic, fuzzy logic–based) to measure the lack of information about the original attack. Most of the algorithms proposed in the literature to deal with this aspect rely on uncertain decision making by associating a probability of occurrence to a specific threat and a measure of efficiency to the intrusion-detection tool (Lee et al. 2002; Wei et al. 2001).

Handling the Attack Information

At this level, the reader may be wondering about the practical use of the aforementioned attack-related concepts. Actually, threats and alerts are two key components of the risk-management framework, which consists of integrating security in the business process of the enterprise. Both threats and alerts are helpful for conducting an efficient and cost-effective decision-making process. In the following, we underline the importance of threat and alert analysis in the risk-management process.

Generally, risk analysis breaks into three elementary activities (Hamdi and Boudriga 2005, Computer and network security risk management): (1) threat analysis, which consists of estimating the probability, outcome, and exploited vulnerability associated with a threat, (2) business impact analysis (BIA), which consists of evaluating the effect of the occurrence an attack against a given asset, and (3) cost-benefit analysis (CBA), which consists of comparing the cost and the benefit of the available countermeasures to select the most convenient ones. The two last aspects are beyond the scope of this chapter, and will not be detailed.

Peltier (2001) affirmed that threat analysis should involve the examination of three basic elements: (1) the agent, which is the entity that carries out the attack, (2) the motive, which is the reason that causes the agent to act, and (3) the results, which are the outcomes of the occurrence of the attack. Another element that can be added to the aforementioned ones is the attack mechanism. This key factor can serve to differentiate between threats that share the same agent, motive, and results by highlighting the weakness that would be exploited by the attacker. In addition, analyzing the steps to carry out a harmful action is helpful for automating several tasks, such as the selection of appropriate solutions. Threat modeling has often been linked to the vulnerability-analysis process, which consists of identifying the security breaches in a specific system. This encompasses a security assessment that takes into account operating systems (OSs), applications, protocols, and network topologies. Consequently, a huge amount of data must be accurately collected and scanned. Unfortunately, most of the existing risk-management (RM) methods reduce vulnerability analysis to vulnerability identification and thus subordinate many key issues. For example, OCTAVE (Alberts and Dorofee 2002) defines this activity as "running vulnerability evaluation tools on selected infrastructure components." A similar definition has been given by Ozier (1999): "*This task includes the qualitative identification of vulnerabilities that could increase the frequency or impact of threat event(s) affecting the target environment*." It appears from these definitions that the goal of vulnerability analysis has been commonly viewed as ascertaining the existence of a set of vulnerabilities in several components of a given system. In other terms, the risk analyst has to map some elements of the vulnerability library to each asset of the studied system. Nevertheless, this task can be more skillfully applied by considering the following concepts:

Vulnerability-Detection Strategies

Security specialists should be aware of the various testing methods that can be applied to detect vulnerabilities. The choice of a testing strategy depends on the nature of the weakness and the characteristics of the target system. Automated vulnerability testing strategies break into two categories: black-box testing and white-box testing. The former consists of evaluating the behavior of the system without having a precise idea about its constituency, while the latter presupposes that the source code of the tested entity (e.g., piece of software, OS, and communication protocol) is available. Most of the existing vulnerability-detection methods belong to the black-box class (e.g., rule-based testing, penetration-based testing, and inference-based testing).

Vulnerability-Identification Techniques

Many vulnerability-detection mechanisms are available. Thus, the most convenient ones should be selected according to the need of the risk analyst. Many static white-box testing techniques have been evolved and discussed. The more basic one is related to the use of the **gets()** function within C programs. This function normally captures strings from the standard input, but it has been demonstrated to be vulnerable to buffer-overflow errors because it does not test the size of this input (Krsul, Spafford, and Tripunitara 1998). Likewise, Bishop and Dilger (1996) focused on a specific type of software errors called "time-of-check-to-time-of-use" (TOCTTOU). These race-condition errors occur when a function or a piece of program is executed without checking to see whether it yields a secure state. A known example resides in set user ID (SUID)-root programs in UNIX-based environments that check the access permissions to a file and modify it directly without checking to see whether this security property still holds after the modification. Viega et al. (2000) give 12 rules that prevent several errors in Java code. Ghosh et al. (1996) proposed a white-box dynamic security-testing technique that relies on two main principles: random input generation and fault injection. Input generation gives the risk analyst the ability to generate a set of test values that will be submitted to the analyzed program as inputs in order to study its behavior. Fault injection is the process of perturbing the execution of a program by introducing several insecure states.

Vulnerability-Library Structure

The vulnerability library can contain thousands of security weaknesses. Therefore, it must be structured in a manner to support various types of queries. Vulnerability information is customary structured in various manners, including traditional (i.e., relational) databases, mailing lists, and newsletters. The most important vulnerability databases (VDBs) are the following:

The Computer Emergency Response Team (CERT) Advisories: CERTs publish warnings related to the most important, and most recent, vulnerabilities. They collect information about different types of security incidents. After analyzing these events, a report including the possible exploits and the related countermeasures is established.

The MITRE Common Vulnerability and Exposures (CVE) list: CVE is defined as a "standardized list of names for vulnerabilities and other information security exposures." Substantially, CVE is not a database; nevertheless, it is very helpful when the risk analyst uses data from different VDBs. Practically, within the risk-management framework, multiple vulnerability scanners are used for a more complete list of detected weaknesses. In this case, CVE can serve to fuse the data emanating from those tools into a unified list.

The Bugtraq mailing list: This archive basically consists of a mailing list that allows security specialists to exchange information and to share their knowledge. Its main limitation is that the focused vulnerabilities and exploits concern only Windows-based operating systems.

The NIST meta-base: The National Vulnerability Database is a CVE-based VDB that offers interesting search possibilities. It may link the user to other vulnerability databases where more detailed information can be found, or it can even redirect the user toward Web resources where accurate defense solutions can be found. ICAT is probably the most complete VDB, as it "indexes the information available in CERT advisories, ISS X-Force, Security Focus, NTBugtraq, Bugtraq, and a variety of vendor security and patch bulletins." Hence, it would be considered as a meta-base that can be use as a search engine rather than a VDB itself.

ANALYZING THE ATTACKER'S OBJECTIVES

The number of services that are (partially or completely) provided via modern communication infrastructures and information systems is growing explosively. Unfortunately, as these systems get more sophisticated, so do the attacks carried out against them. Effectively, it appears that every attack is linked to one or more specific services. This section addresses the relationship between the attacker's goals and the characteristics of the target service. More precisely, several factors, such as the proportionality of the complexity of the attack process to the budget spent to conduct it will be investigated. Finally, novel attack trends will be explored based on intruder activity during recent years.

The Attack/Service Relationship

Several services offered by networked infrastructures are more vulnerable than others. This subsection provides a detailed discussion of the characteristics that might increase the attractiveness of a service to the attacker.

First, the weakness of a service is linked to its scalability. In fact, if a service is intended for a large number of users, the authentication and access-control mechanisms that are used to protect are rarely strict. This is mainly for three reasons:

1. When the number of users is important, the client community becomes heterogeneous and the enterprise that manages the service should deal with a mixing of specialists and nonexperts And nonspecialists often feel reluctant to adhere to strong security policies, especially when they there are additional costs involved as compared with the intrinsic cost of the service. The enterprise then chooses simple authentication schemes, which are not necessarily in conformance with its security objectives. In addition, a wider and heterogeneous client community is more likely to include malicious users.
2. The cost of handling the authentication credentials and the access-control system increases with respect to the size of the client population. In other words, the scalability of the security infrastructure itself should be considered. Hence, enterprises tend to avoid complex security mechanisms that become hard to administer for a large network.
3. If the service is distributed among multiple countries, the legal aspects should be discussed, and this sometimes weakens the security level of the policy rules. For instance, consider the case in which a virtual private network (VPN) is used to interconnect internationally distributed subsidiary companies, and suppose that the VPN nodes are authenticated on the basis of digital certificates. The problem that may arise in such situations is that a cross-certification agreement must exist between the certification authorities that generate the different certificates. Such agreement is not usually easy to achieve because of the divergence of local certification laws, architectures, and policies.

Furthermore, it appears that distributed services are more vulnerable to network attacks. This is due to the lack of security at the distributed-component level. Enterprises seldom dedicate additional security equipment or skilled staff to these components, which become key elements to launch various types of attacks.

In the Arbor Worldwide ISP [Internet service provider] Security Survey (Arbor Networks 2005), the majority of respondents indicated that gambling and adult content Web sites are the most frequent targets of denial of service attacks. Internet relay chat (IRC) infrastructures are also often attacked. This means that the nature of the population that connects to a specific Web site can also be an indicator of the threat likelihood.

Correlating Attack Complexity and Attack Severity

The Arbor Worldwide ISP Security Survey cited two major threats facing network operators:

***Distributed Denial of Service* (DDoS)**—The survey states that "Despite concern in the press and research communities about the evolving complexity of backbone attacks, most providers reported that the majority of DDoS attacks exhibited relatively simple brute-force attack vectors." Effectively, more than 90 percent of the respondents reported that transmission control protocol (TCP) synchronization (SYN) and user datagram protocol (UDP) flooding attacks, which are among the simplest DoS techniques, are the primary source of threats against their infrastructures;

Worms—Worms rank second in the list of the most reported attacks (Arbor Networks 2005). According to ISPs, the actual loss related to worms does not reside in their payload but rather in the network congestions they cause. It has been noticed that the flow corresponding to a single attack may range from 500 Mbps to 8 Gbps.

Simple attacks continue to constitute the greatest source of damage, despite the appearance of sophisticated protection tools. This idea is reinforced by the analysis of the dollar amount losses by type of attack reported in the 2005 CSI/FBI threat report (Gordon et al. 2005). The results, which are summarized in Figure 1 show that viruses generated the most important losses during 2005. It should be also pointed out that "Unauthorized access" and "Proprietary information theft" have been the source of significant damages.

Available protection strategies have not been very successful in limiting the impact of the attacks. One of the key factors is that multiple security mechanisms are needed to ensure an acceptable security level. These mechanisms should be distributed on all the network components. In fact, several attacks, such as worms, must be stopped at the client level (by installing patches and antivirus programs) but also at the ISP level to avoid congestion. Security solutions should also be associated with strategies and guidelines that are necessary to promote the awareness of the enterprises' personnel. This view regarding security problems encompasses a division of the global networked infrastructure into domains that should be secured using different techniques. For instance, each enterprise would be responsible for the security of its domain, consisting of the assets belonging to its private network.

Noteworthy Shifts in Network Attack Techniques

In addition to the aforementioned surveys, other studies and surveys (Australian High Tech Crime Centre 2005; Department of Trade and Industry (UK) 2004) have shown that new trends are emerging with the appearance of novel attack categories and the decay of other categories. In the following, six trends that have shaped the attackers' behavior are discussed.

Trend 1: Virus-Based Attacks Are Deceasing

Figure 2 shows that the number of virus-based attacks has decreased considerably in the United States. This is confirmed by other surveys carried out in other countries (e.g., the United Kingdom and Australia). However, malicious codes, and worms in particular, have sustained the outcome of most of the remaining threats, especially from a network perspective. This means that antivirus programs are no longer sufficient to counter this type of

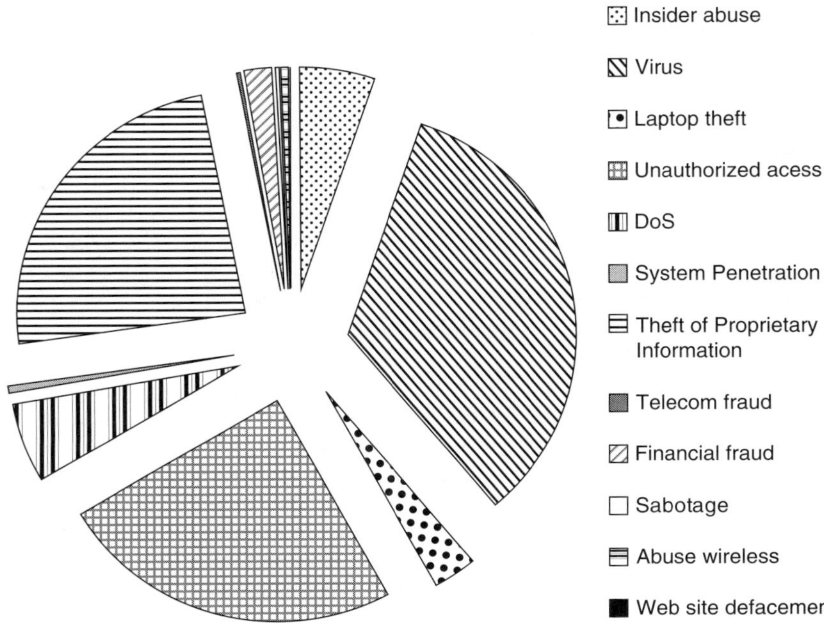

Figure 1: Dollar amount losses by threat type in the United States. Source: 2005 CSI/FBI threat annual report

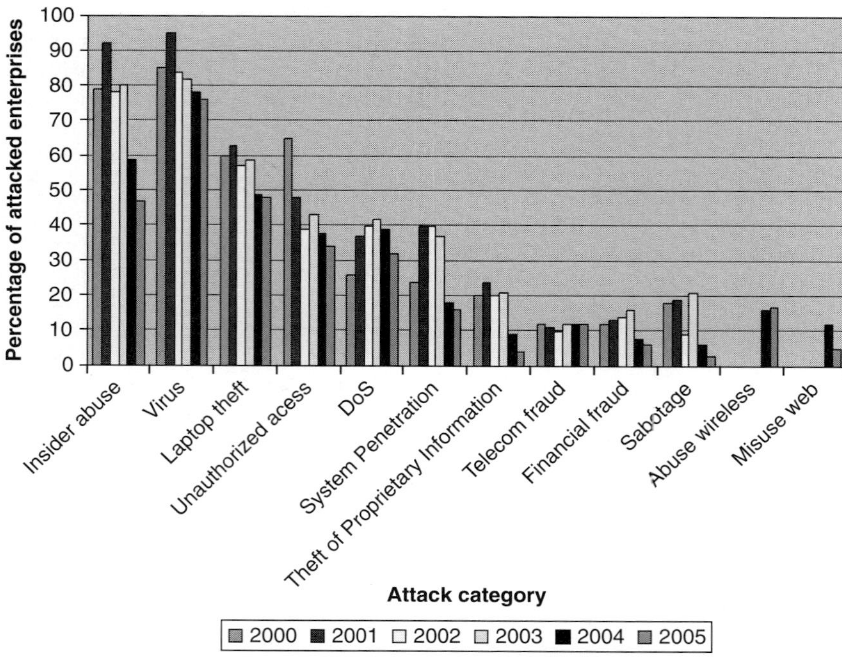

Figure 2: Types of attacks experienced by U.S. enterprises. *Source:* CSI/FBI Annual Report, 2000–2005

digital attack. Network-anomaly-based monitoring tools should be used to enhance defense capabilities.

Trend 2: Attack Tools Are Increasingly Sophisticated

The level of automation in attack tools continues to increase. Automated attacks commonly involve four phases, each of which is changing.

1. Scanning for potential weaknesses. Widespread scanning has been common since 1997. Today, scanning tools are using more advanced scanning patterns to maximize impact and speed.
2. Compromising vulnerable systems. Previously, the scanning activity was limited to vulnerability identification. To perform effective intrusions, attackers had to look for separate autonomous programs and scripts. Now, attack tools exploit vulnerabilities as a part of the scanning activity, which increases the speed of propagation.
3. Propagating the outcome. Before 2000, attack tools required a person to initiate additional attack cycles. Today, attack tools can self-initiate new attack cycles. Tools like Code Red and Nimda, for example, self-propagate to a point of global saturation in less than 18 hours.
4. Using composite attacks. Since 1999, with the advent of distributed attack tools, attackers have been able to manage and coordinate large numbers of deployed attack tools distributed across many Internet systems. Today, distributed attack tools are capable of launching denial of service attacks more efficiently, scanning for potential victims and compromising vulnerable systems. Coordination functions now take advantage of readily available, public communications protocols such as Internet relay chat (IRC) and instant messaging (IM).

Trend 3: Attacks Are Becoming More Robust against Detection Mechanisms

Attack-tool developers are using more advanced techniques than previously. Attack-tool signatures are more difficult to discover through analysis and more difficult to detect through signature-based systems such as antivirus software and intrusion-detection systems. Three important characteristics are the antiforensic nature, dynamic behavior, and modularity of the tools.

1. Antiforensics. Attackers use techniques that obfuscate the nature of attack tools. This makes it more difficult and time consuming for security experts to analyze new attack tools and to understand new and rapidly developing threats. Analysis often includes laboratory testing and reverse engineering.
2. Dynamic behavior. Early attack tools performed attack steps in single defined sequences. Today's automated attack tools can vary their patterns and behaviors based on random selection, predefined decision paths, or through direct intruder management.
3. Modularity of attack tools. Unlike early attack tools that implemented one type of attack, tools now can be changed quickly by upgrading or replacing portions of the tool. This causes rapidly evolving attacks and, at the extreme, polymorphic tools that self-evolve to be different in each instance.

In addition, attack tools are more commonly being developed to execute on multiple operating system platforms. As an example of the difficulties posed by sophisticated attack tools, many common tools use protocols like IRC or HTTP (hypertext transfer protocol) to send data or commands from the intruder to compromised hosts. As a result, it has become increasingly difficult to distinguish attack signatures from normal, legitimate network traffic.

Security of a networked system is, by nature, highly dependent on the security of the elementary components. Each Internet system's exposure to attack depends on the state of security of the rest of the systems attached to the global Internet. Because of the advances in attack technology, a single attacker can relatively easily use a large number of distributed systems to launch devastating attacks against a single victim. As the automation of deployment and the sophistication of attack-tool management both increase, the asymmetric nature of the emerging threats will continue to grow. There are three basic types of asymmetric attacks:

- consumption of computational resources, such as bandwidth, disk space, or CPU time
- disruption of configuration information, such as routing information
- disruption of physical network components

Trend 4: Firewalls and IDSs Are Increasingly Permeable

Firewalls are often relied on to provide primary protection from intruders. However, technologies are being designed to bypass typical firewall configurations; for example, IPP (the Internet printing protocol) and WebDAV (Web-based distributed authoring and versioning). In addition, some protocols marketed as being "firewall-friendly" are, in reality, designed to bypass typical firewall configurations.

Certain aspects of "mobile-code" (ActiveX controls, Java, and JavaScript) make it difficult for vulnerable systems to be protected and malicious software to be discovered. Furthermore, IDSs are being continuously targeted by several evasive attacks. Evasion is not only the process of totally concealing an attack but it can also be a technique to make an attack appear less threatening than it really is. Attacks based on basic string matching weaknesses are among the easiest to implement and understand. Signature-based IDS devices rely almost entirely on string matching, and breaking the string match of a poorly written signature is trivial. Polymorphic shell code is a more dangerous, recently developed evasion tactic that IDS devices cannot so easily defend against. This technique is limited to buffer overflows, and is much more effective against signature-based systems than against anomaly-based or protocol analysis–based systems.

Trend 5: Decreasing Threat from Internal Attacks

Figure 3 shows that the number of attacks from outside the victim enterprises decreased in the United States during 2005. The Australian 2005 threat report corroborates this result, as the sources of 81 percent of attacks against Australian enterprises were external versus internal (37 percent). Nonetheless, fewer respondents experienced external incidents as compared with 2004 and 2003 (88 percent and 90 percent, respectively).

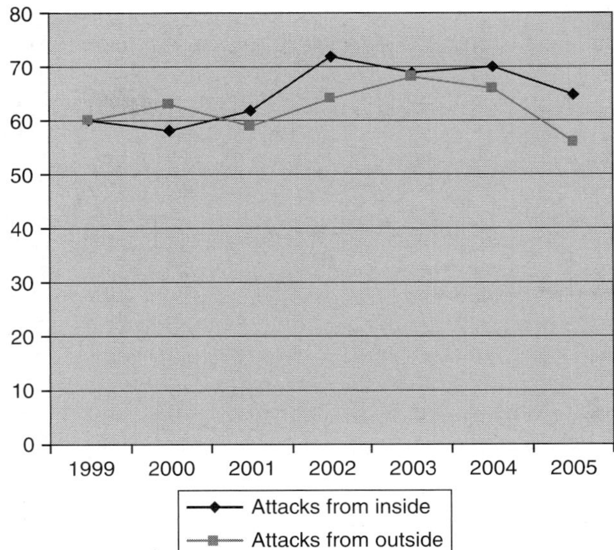

Figure 3: Number of attacks from inside and outside sources

Trend 6: Increasing Threat from Infrastructure Attacks

Infrastructure attacks broadly affect key components of the Internet. They are of increasing concern because of the number of organizations and users on the Internet and their increasing dependency on the Internet to carry out day-to-day business. Four types of infrastructure attacks are described briefly below.

Attack 1: Distributed denial of service. Denial-of-service attacks use multiple systems to attack one or more victim systems with the intent of denying service to legitimate users of those systems. The degree of automation in attack tools enables a single attacker to install their tools and control tens of thousands of compromised systems for use in attacks.

Intruders often search address blocks known to contain high concentrations of vulnerable systems with high-speed connections. Cable modem, digital subscriber line (DSL), and university address blocks are increasingly targeted by intruders planning to install their attack tools. Denial-of-service attacks are effective because the Internet is composed of limited and consumable resources, and Internet security is highly interdependent.

Attack 2: Worms. A worm is self-propagating malicious code. Unlike a virus, which requires a user to do something to continue the propagation, a worm can propagate by itself. The highly automated nature of the worms coupled with the relatively widespread nature of the vulnerabilities they exploit allows a large number of systems to be compromised within a matter of hours (for example, Code Red infected more than 250,000 systems in just 9 hours on July 19, 2001). Some worms include built-in denial-of-service attack payloads (e.g., Code Red) or Website defacement payloads (sadmind/IIS, Code Red); and others have dynamic configuration capabilities (W32/Leaves). But the biggest impact of these worms is that their propagation effectively creates a denial of service in many parts of the Internet because of the huge amounts of scan traffic generated, and they cause much collateral damage (examples include DSL routers that crash; cable modem ISPs whose networks are completely overloaded, not by the scanning itself but by the burst of underlying network-management traffic that the scanning triggers; and printers that crash or print reams of junk output).

Attack 3: Attacks on the Internet Domain Name System (DNS). DNS is the distributed, hierarchical global directory that translates names (www.example.com) to numeric IP addresses (192.168.13.2). The top two layers of the hierarchy are critical to the operation of the Internet. In the top layer are thirteen root-name servers. Next are the top-level domain (TLD) servers, which are authoritative for .com, .net, etc., as well as the country code TLDs (ccTLDs—.us, .uk, .tn, etc). Threats to DNS include the following:

Cache poisoning: If DNS is made to cache bogus information, the attacker can redirect traffic intended for a legitimate site to a site under the attacker's control. A survey by the CERT/Coordination Center shows that over 80 percent of the TLDs are running on servers that are potentially vulnerable to this form of attack.

Compromised data: Attackers compromise vulnerable DNS servers, giving the attackers the ability to modify the data served to users. Many of the TLD servers run a software program called Berkeley Internet Name Domain, in which vulnerabilities are discovered regularly. A CERT/Coordination Center survey indicates that at least 20 percent of TLDs are running on vulnerable servers; another 70 percent are "status unknown."

Denial of service: A large denial-of-service attack on some of the name servers for a TLD (for example, .com) could cause widespread Internet slowdowns or effective outages.

Domain hijacking: By leveraging insecure mechanisms used by customers to update their domain registration information, attackers can co-opt the domain registration processes to take control of legitimate domains.

Attack 4: Attacks Against or Using Routers. Routers are specialized computers that direct traffic on the Internet (similar to mail-routing facilities in the postal service). Threats fall into the following categories:

Routers as attack platforms: Intruders use poorly secured routers as platforms for generating attack traffic at other sites, or for scanning or reconnaissance.

Denial of service: Although routers are designed to pass large amounts of traffic through them, they often are not capable of handling the same amount of traffic directed at them. (Think of it as the difference between sorting mail and reading it.) Intruders take advantage of this characteristic by attacking the routers that lead into a network rather than attacking the systems on the network directly.

Exploitation of trust relationship between routers: For routers to do their job, they have to know where to send the traffic they receive. They do this by sharing routing information between them, which requires the routers to trust the information they receive from their peers. As a result, it would be relatively easy for an attacker to modify, delete, or inject routes into the global Internet routing tables to redirect traffic destined for one network to another, effectively causing a denial of service to both (one because no traffic is being routed to it, and the other because it is getting more traffic than it should). Although the technology has been widely available for some time, many networks (ISPs and large corporations) do not protect themselves with the strong encryption and authentication features available on the routers.

ATTACK TECHNIQUES

This section discusses some of the most known attack schemes and shows, through concrete examples, how these attacks can be combined. For a more extensive idea about these attacks, the reader should refer to Anderson (2001) and Huang and Lee (2004).

Most-Cited Attacks

The most-cited attacks can be classified into six categories based on the technique they use.

Flooding Attacks

These attacks use the nature of a communication protocol and flood a target with a specific packet. Three flooding attacks can be considered:

- *SYN flood*: The SYN flood attack consists simply of sending a large number of SYN packets and never acknowledging any of the replies (i.e., SYN-ACK). This violation of the TCP handshake leads the recipient to accumulate more records of SYN packets than the software (implementing the TCP/IP stack) can handle. The most popular version of the attack does not reveal the actual IP address of the hacker. In fact, the return address associated with the initial SYN packets is in this case not valid; therefore, the victim would return the SYN-ACK packet to an address that does not respond or even does not exist.

  A technical fix, called SYNcookie, has been found and incorporated in the Linux OS in 1996 (since, it has been extended to some other OSs). Rather than keeping a copy of the incoming SYN packet, the victim simply uses a sequence number that is derived from the sequence number of the attacker (i.e., the host that initiates the connection).
- *Smurf attack*: This attack exploits the Internet control message protocol (ICMP), which enables users to send an echo packet to a remote host to check whether it is alive. The problem arises with broadcast addresses that correspond to more than one host. Some implementations of the Internet protocols respond to pings to both the broadcast address and their local address (the idea was to test a local area network [LAN] to gather the hosts that are alive). The attack is to construct a packet with the source address forged to be that of the victim, and send it to a number of Smurf amplifiers that will each respond (if alive) by sending a packet to the target; this can swamp the target with more packets than it can cope with.

- *Tribe Flood Network* (TFN): TFN is made up of client and daemon programs, which implement a distributed network denial of service tool capable of waging ICMP flood, SYN flood, UDP flood, and Smurf style attacks. The attacker(s) control one or more clients, each of which can control many daemons. The daemons are all instructed to coordinate a packet-based attack against one or more victim systems by the client. This reduces the chances of the victim to "survive" the flooding attack because it would face hundreds (even thousands) of machines instead of a single attacker. This type of attack also hides the identity of the attack source.

Buffer-Overflow Attacks

The attacks exploit the procedure call flow to execute nonauthorized commands. From one point of view, a procedure call alters the flow of control just as a jump does, but unlike a jump, when finished performing its task, a function returns control to the statement or instruction following the call. Basically, a buffer overflow is the result of stuffing more data into a buffer than it can handle. It allows the attacker to change the return address of a function so that the attacker can change the flow of execution of the program. Typically, the return pointer of a given function is replaced by the address of the nonauthorized process (or command) that the attacker wants to execute.

Spoofing Attacks

In a spoofing attack, a user appears to be someone else—that is, the attacker fakes his identity to be that of a legitimate user. Because of spoofing, that attacker is able to manipulate packets so that they appear to come from another system or network. Thus, spoofing could include spoofing an internal network IP address or return e-mail address. This attack technique is customarily used to prepare for perpetrating flooding or other denial-of-service attacks. Spoofing covers a large category of computer attacks. It basically stands for identity falsification or masquerading. This attack class includes IP address spoofing, session highjacking, DNS spoofing, sequence-number spoofing, and replay attacks.

For example, in the case of sequence-number spoofing, the attacker must monitor the packets sent from A to B and then guess the sequence number of the packets. Then the attacker knocks out A with spoofed packets, claiming to have the address of A. A's firewall can defend against spoof attacks when it has been configured with knowledge of all the IP addresses connected to each of its interfaces. It can then detect a spoofed packet if it arrives from an interface that is not known to be connected to that interface. Many carelessly designed protocols are subject to spoof attacks, including many of those used on the Internet.

Another kind of spoofing is "Web page spoofing," also known as *phishing*. In this attack, a Web page is made to look like a legitimate server, but is owned and operated by someone else. This attack is intended to make victims think that they are connected to a trusted site. Typically, a payment system's log-in page might be spoofed, allowing the attacker to harvest user names and passwords. This is often performed with the aid of DNS cache poisoning in order to direct the user away from the legitimate site and to the false one. Once the user puts in her password, the attack-code reports a password error, and then redirects the user back to the legitimate site.

Sniffing Attacks

Sniffing attacks use protocol analyzers to capture network traffic for passwords and other confidential data. In many network setups, it is possible for any machine on a given network to hear the traffic for every machine on that network. This is true for most Ethernet-based networks, and Ethernet is by far the most common LAN technology in use today. This characteristic of Ethernet is especially dangerous, because most of the protocols in use today are unencrypted. As a result, the data sent and received are there for anybody to snoop on. These data include files accessed via network file systems, passwords sent to remote systems during Telnet, file transfer protocol (FTP), and rlogin sessions; e-mail sent and received; and so on. A password sniffer is a program that takes advantage of this characteristic to monitor all of the IP traffic on its part of the network. By capturing the first 128 bytes of every FTP or Telnet session, for example, password sniffers can easily pick up your username and password as you type them. Password sniffers may use programs provided for network debugging as building blocks, or may be written to use the services directly. Special-purpose password sniffing toolkits are widely available to attackers.

The danger of password sniffing attacks is in their rapid spread. Favorite targets for sniffers are network providers and public access systems, in which the volume of Telnet and FTP connections is huge. One sniffer on large public access systems can collect thousands of sniffed account names and passwords, and then compromise every system accessed. Even if your systems are as secure as possible and your user passwords are not guessable, you can be infected by a packet sniffer running at any site that your users can log in from, or at any site their packets will cross to get to you.

Sniffing attacks are among the most difficult to handle because the use of sniffing software can seldom be prohibited. Sniffers have many legitimate uses that system administrators should be aware of. They can be used to find what computers on the network are causing problems, such as using too much bandwidth, having the wrong network settings, or running malware.

Scanning Attacks

A port scan is one of the most popular reconnaissance techniques attackers use to discover services they can break into. All machines connected to a LAN or Internet run many services that listen at well-known and not-so-well-known ports. A port scan helps the attacker find which ports are available (i.e., what service might be listing to a port). Essentially, a port scan consists of sending a message to each port, one at a time. The kind of response received indicates whether the port is used and can therefore be probed further for weakness.

Routing Attacks in Mobile Ad Hoc Networks

In an ad hoc network, a malicious node intentionally drops control packets, misroutes data, or disseminates incorrect information about its neighbors and/or its prediscovered routing capabilities to particular destinations. An attacker might try to:

- forge messages by spoofing originator or destination addresses
- signal false route errors or modify route error messages
- alter or replace originator, destination or sender addresses in routed messages

The attacker might also try to consume network resources by:

- initiating large numbers of route requests to bogus destinations in order to exhaust the resources of the network
- playing the "gray hole attack" or "selective dropping" of packets, resulting in increased numbers of route requests from neighbor nodes that have limited routing capabilities, exhausting neighbors' resources

Network Attack Taxonomies

In the early security approaches, security incidents were broken into categories of disclosure of confidential information (loss of confidentiality), loss of integrity, and denial-of-service (DoS [loss of availability]) attacks (Amoroso 1994). However, with the spread of sophisticated attack techniques, one could assert that some other form of taxonomies needed to be developed. This section will review the most important taxonomies in the literature describing types of computer misuse and the perpetrators who perform that misuse. The taxonomies of Anderson (1980) and Neumann and Parker (1989) are covered; as well as the extension of Neumann and Parker made by Lindqvist and Jonsson (1998) and the network security taxonomy of Jayaram and Morse (1997).

Anderson's Penetration Matrix

This taxonomy develops a four-cell matrix that covers the types of penetrators, based on whether they are authorized to use the computer and the data/program source. Relying on this idea, three major attack classes have been considered:

Class A: External Penetration, referring to attacks that are sourced from the protected system itself

Class B: Internal Penetration, referring to attacks that are sourced from outside the protected system:

a. The masquerader (defeats procedural controls)
b. The legitimate user
c. The clandestine user (defeats logical controls)

Class C: Misfeasance (authorized action in an improper way)

Neumann and Parker's Method

In 1989, Neumann and Parker published, "A Summary of Computer Misuse Techniques," in which they outlined a series of classes of computer misuse from their data of about 3000 cases over nearly twenty years. Nine categories of computer misuse, referred to as NP1 to NP9 have been considered. They mainly address the source or technique used to achieve a misuse:

NP1: external
NP2: hardware misuse
NP3: masquerading
NP4: pest programs
NP5: bypasses
NP6: active misuse
NP7: passive misuse
NP8: inactive misuse
NP9: indirect misuse

Lindqvist's Extension

Lindqvist and Jonsson (1998) extended Neumann and Parker's method by expanding categories NP5 (bypassing intended controls), NP6 (active misuse of resources), and NP7 (passive misuse of resources). They introduced the concept of dimension: attacks have certain intrusion techniques and certain intrusion results. Their extensions of Neumann and Parker's categories NP5 to NP7, along with their intrusion techniques is given in Lindqvist and Johnsson (1997).

Jayaram and Morse's Network Security Taxonomy

Jayaram and Morse (1997) developed a taxonomy of security threats to networks including five classes:

Physical: Security breach arising from the theft of components and systems, often perpetrated through impersonation.

System Weak Spots: Weak spots in operating systems or other system software that a perpetrator exploits for unauthorized access to the systems.

Malign Programs: A perpetrator embeds malevolent programs (viruses, for example) in a system with the intention of causing destruction to the information carried by the system.

Access Rights: Legitimate user's identity usurped by "acquiring" user's access rights through password traps, password cracking, etc. to gain illegitimate access to system resources.

Communication-based Network connectivity opens up opportunities for illegal information access through such means as eavesdropping, spoofing, etc.

NEED FOR ATTACK MODELS

Attack models are mainly needed to prevent the occurrence of threats, to react against network intrusions, or to perform a digital investigation after an intrusion has occurred. These models should particularly allow:

- Representing complex attacks by combining elementary attacks and addressing the dependencies that may be noticed between the actions engaged by a complex attack.
- Selecting the appropriate security decisions that prevent threats from occurring based on a decision-making process using various criteria.

- Identifying the reactions that make the system recover to its initial state after a security incident has occurred.
- Detecting the occurrence of harmful events by allowing the management of metrics monitoring system activity and reasoning about sensor performances.
- Proving evidence of harmful intrusions by tracing activities, marking activities, inspecting logs, storing appropriate events, and considering relations with legal issues.

Representing attacks against computer networks is among the most challenging tasks of the risk analyst. The representation should cope with the nature of the link between the actions composing an attack, the number of actions, and the size of the target systems. This stems from the intrinsic complexity of these attacks, which can be reduced to the following points:

1. A corresponding predictive model would be hard to evolve because network attacks are conducted by humans. Unlike most of the natural behaviors, human thoughts cannot be easily translated into a formal representation. Most of the existing methods assume the existence of an attack database without addressing this issue.
2. Attacks are seldom performed in a single step. Attackers often follow a structured method to achieve malicious acts. Hence, the risk analyst should establish various kinds of links between elementary threats (e.g., causality, time precedence). The major shortcoming of the traditional approaches is that they do not integrate security countermeasures and enterprise resources as a part of the expert knowledge related to attack scenarios.
3. Attacks belonging to the same scenario could be spatially and temporally distributed. Some attacks that constitute part of a scenario will not be represented in the alert stream. This could be due to missing sensor coverage or because the attack—albeit part of an attack scenario—is indistinguishable from normal benign activity.

Digital investigation is another challenging task that a security manager needs to face, since this manager's objectives are to gather evidence and analyze it to apprehend attackers. To build a strong link between the evidence and the attacker, the representation model should integrate enough knowledge of the applicable legal framework and the security policy enforced in the system to protect (Hamdi and Boudriga 2005, Security policy guidelines). Identification, for example, is a complex task to manage because of the huge volume of data that may need to be analyzed (Reith, Carr, and Gunch 2002).

Correlation handling is a third primary concern that network attack modeling should address. To be able to secure assets, effective detection is needed. Most existing models on intrusion detection focus on activities generated by a single source, which has resulted in many false positives and undetected attacks. Overcoming this requires correlating activities from all involved components and analyzing logs together. This is because an intrusion typically leaves multiple signs of presence that are correlated somehow.

STRUCTURAL MODELS

A set of techniques modeling the structure of network attacks is presented in this section. The richness of each of these techniques is evaluated and some implementation issues are also investigated. Two major attack model categories—preventive models and reactive models—will be considered to address risk management, protection mechanisms, and effective response to intrusions.

Preventive Models

Modeling attacks before their occurrence is a crucial task because a priori information about an adversary's behavior is hard to obtain and because attacks are gaining in complexity and evolving tremendously. Particularly, the probability and the impact, which are among the most important attack attributes, cannot be precisely determined.

One of the most important issues is to model the gradual evolution of the attacker's plan to reach the main objective. It has been remarked that attackers often proceed through multiple steps in order to fulfill their malicious intentions. Tree structures have therefore been introduced to capture those steps. Indeed, fault trees, which have been used for a long time to analyze the failure conditions of complex systems, have been adapted to the computer network security context. Several risk-management approaches, such as CORAS (Stolen et al. 2003) rely on fault-tree analysis (FTA) to evaluate and prioritize risks. Two concepts have been especially focused: minimal cut sets and top event frequencies. The former identifies attack scenarios (or composite attacks) while the latter allows the computation of the frequency of the main attack with respect to the frequencies of the elementary threats. Helmer et al. (2006) also proposed using FTA to model attacks within the frame of an intrusion-detection approach.

Attack trees, which were first introduced by Schneier (2001) and extended by Tidwell et al. (2001), can be seen as a transposition of FTA into the computer security field. Their purpose is to determine and assess the possible sequences of events that would lead to the occurrence of a main attack. The root of a tree represents the main objective of an attacker while the subordinate nodes represent the elementary attacks necessary to perform in order to achieve the global goal. Writing a global threat as the conjunction of multiple threat scenarios offers a useful tool to the risk analyst, who can henceforth describe the various manners for achieving the main attack.

A substantial attack library has been proposed by Moore et al. (2001). This approach relies on attack patterns, which are essentially used to build generic representations of attack scenarios. The constituents of an attack pattern are mainly: (1) the goal of the attack, (2) a list of preconditions (i.e., hypotheses that should be verified by the system so that the attack succeeds), (3) the attack mechanism (i.e., the steps followed by the attacker to reach the objective), and (4) a list of postconditions (changes to the system state resulting from the occurrence of the attack). Attack patterns are in turn organized into attack profiles that introduce variants (i.e., abstract parameters that can be instantiated with concrete values). Moreover, the approach develops the concept of attack tree refinement to enrich the library of a particular organization. Generic attack profiles are used to this purpose. If the analyzed system presents a set of values that match with several variants parameters, then the attack profile is said to be consistent with the system architecture. Then, the instantiation principle is applied to determine which attack pattern has the same goal as the identified attack. Based on this reasoning, three enriching mechanisms have been defined: (1) leaf-node application, (2) non-leaf-node application to OR-decomposition, and (3) non-leaf-node application to AND-decomposition.

McDermott (2000) has presented *Attack Net*, an attack modeling approach relying on Petri nets. A Petri net is customarily composed of places, transitions, arcs, and tokens. Places are the equivalent of graph nodes while a transition is a token move between two places. According to this analogy, attack steps are represented by places that are similar to nodes in attack trees. Basically, an attack net consists of a set of places and a set of transitions representing, respectively, the various states of the target system and the events that may trigger state changes. Moreover, tokens are used to evaluate the progression of a given attack through the study of a set of moves within the attack net. Attack nets combine the advantages of hypothetical flaws and attack trees. The main difference with these concepts is that attack events (i.e., transitions) are described separately from the system states (i.e., places). On the opposite side, attack trees merge the preconditions, the postconditions, and the running steps of a given attack into a single node. McDermott asserts that "Attack nets are better than attack trees for top-down testing of poorly documented operational systems.". Furthermore, transitions can catch a vast variety of relationships between system states. As a passing remark, transitions turn out to be more efficient than AND/OR operators to build attack libraries. In fact, these traditional logical operators exhibit some important limits, especially when enriching an existing state. For instance, adding an AND branch to a set of alternatives (OR node) cannot be achieved without restructuring the child nodes.

Recently, more sophisticated models have been developed. In Steffan and Schumacher (2002), attack nets have been combined with the WikiWeb system to enable knowledge sharing. Moreover, Wiki pages can contain customized descriptions of the formal objects (i.e., places, transitions, tokens). This gives more flexibility with respect to the rigorous attack nets. Particularly, this allows building attack libraries through a collaborative process that involves many security experts. Of course, this means that managing attack libraries using this framework (called *AtiKi*) makes them richer.

Reactive Models

When reacting to a security incident, the attack damages may inadvertently increase. Stopping a machine or counterattacking the attack source may worsen the system state. Hence, reactions should be selected according to a sound method. The most prominent criteria to model attacks in this context are given in the following:

Detection cost: Prior to the generation of a security alert by an analyzer, the corresponding sensor should have captured the required parameters appropriately (e.g., metric value, packet header fields). Then, the analyzer inspects these data to decide whether an intrusion occurred. Both of these operations have a cost that must be taken into account when computing the total cost of the incident. That cost is often supposed to be intrinsic to the elementary IDS components (consisting of an analyzer and a sensor); therefore, it does not depend on the nature of the generated alert.

Cost of reaction: Each of the potential reactions has a cost that depends heavily on the reaction itself. This cost can be expressed in terms of different attributes such as monetary units, processing resources, or time to repair.

Attack impact: Carrying out a malicious act on an information system causes various kinds of undesirable effects. To this purpose, the impact representing these effects should be represented by multiple attributes. Furthermore, a novel concept, called "progression factor," has been introduced in (Fessi et al. 2007) to have a more suitable representation of the benefit of a given reaction. In fact, the system can react before or after the attack occurs. Each of these reactions has a different benefit. The former aims at stopping the complete execution of the attack after receiving signals that reveal it, while the objective of the latter is to make the system recover at the right time.

IDS efficiency: Efficiency represents a fundamental topic in reactive attack modeling. It should detect a substantial percentage of intrusion into the supervised system while still keeping the false alarm rate at an acceptable level. In our case, it relies on two factors: the alert and the related attack.

TOWARD AN ATTACK-RESPONSE STRATEGY

The available security surveys show that a wide proportion of the enterprises that have been subjected to security incidents did possess, at the moment they were attacked, some security components. Hence, firewalls, intrusion-detection systems (IDSs), and antivirus programs, to name just a few, are not sufficient to attain an acceptable security level. Consistent strategies should be built for this purpose. In particular, we will point out three components that are often missed by security officers.

Security Policy

The need of an enterprise for a security policy (SP) can be driven by various reasons, which depend essentially on the organization's nature, the organization's business, and the context in which it operates. They can be divided into two major categories: business-oriented objectives and regulatory objectives (Hamdi and Boudriga 2005, Forensic computing).

Business-Oriented Objectives

The reasons beyond developing and implementing SPs should align with the basic organizational objectives. The benefits from having a SP can be either direct or indirect. Some can be easily assessed in monetary terms (e.g., preventing critical assets from being attacked) while the others are rather nonconcrete (e.g., preserving the reputation of the enterprise). The most important among the business-oriented objectives are:

- The measures of the SP should maintain the security of critical components at an acceptable level. In other terms, the SP helps enterprises in reducing the amount of risk related to harmful adverse events, and augment employee awareness.
- The SP must include some response schemes that make the system recover if an incident occurs (e.g., security attack, natural disaster). It also must develop appropriate procedures in conformance with the enforced law and the risks related to the organization's activity. Individual responsibilities and consequences must be defined in a SP.
- The SP must, whenever an incident occurs, ensure the continuity of the critical processes conducted by an enterprise. It should contain recovery plans and be accompanied by a set security guidelines to ensure efficient continuity and recovery.

Regulatory Objectives

The security measures of the SP are often developed as a regulatory obligation. Organizations that operate in sensitive sectors are particularly concerned with this issue. In the following, we will illustrate our reasoning by using two significant examples: banks and CAs (certification authorities). The former are accountable for the operations they carry out while the latter handle various types of critical information (e.g., key pairs, private user information). Among others, the following principles have to be respected:

- *Duty of loyalty*: When carrying her charges, an employee must place the employer's interest above her own. The relationship between the enterprise and the employee should be based on honesty and faith.
- *Conflict of interest*: A conflict of interest occurs in a situation in which the impact of a given action is positive for a category of employees and negative for others. The SP should guarantee that the security rules do not include such discriminatory clauses.
- *Duty of care*: The employees should proceed with caution when performing critical tasks. For example, the internal security auditing team should adequately protect the resources to which it has access (e.g., log files, personal information) to avoid divulging confidential information.
- *Accountability*: In order to be accounted for, employees should be uniquely identified and authenticated. When the responsibility of an employee has a legal aspect, which is often the case, the identification and authentication have to be compliant with the regulation. More precisely, credentials used for authentication purposes must conform to legislation. For instance, when asymmetric cryptographic keys are of use in this context, SP developers should verify that protocols (e.g., generation protocols, encryption protocols), format, and key lengths do not conflict with the regulatory framework.

Monitoring

This monitoring task is often reduced to a continuous control of the system state and the collection of simple events that the system triggers when specific things occur. However, it seems inadvisable to confine monitoring to its pure security facets. It should provide for an efficient analysis of collected events, rapid generation of alerts, enhanced capability of learning, and incidence response. Incident response, for instance, should be enriched by a set of models allowing the accurate measurement of an incident's impact, and the selection of the appropriate reactions. At least three reasons confirm this idea:

- New vulnerabilities, exploits, and attack mechanisms can be discovered,
- Violations can be detected at the right time,
- Effective countermeasures can be reviewed to see whether they are as sufficient as they were thought to be at the design stage.

Security monitoring is customarily performed through the use of IDSs using two detection techniques: pattern-based monitoring and behavior-based monitoring. Pattern-based monitoring, also referred to as "misuse detection," attempts to characterize known patterns of security violations. This basically requires a sensor network, a signature database, and an analyzer. Sensors are deployed at the strategic segments of the monitored network to collect the needed data. Obviously, an engineering activity should be conducted before setting those sensors to ensure that the target information can be gathered without introducing a considerable overhead at the communication flow level (i.e., without affecting the quality of service). Signatures consist of descriptions of the known intrusions. An appropriate language is always needed for this representation. Finally, the analyzer matches the collected data with the existing signatures to decide whether an attack did occur. In addition to the description language, another important aspect that greatly affects the efficiency of pattern-based monitoring consists of identifying the parameters that should be controlled by the sensors. Because it is not possible to specify the behavior of the system with full confidence, the security analyst should define exactly what should be monitored. Among the most relevant issues that should be taken into account when defining attack signatures are the following:

Access to the information system objects: The access policy to the system assets (e.g., files, hosts) should be first expressed in a machine language. Then, the access events to critical resources should be logged and checked. For instance, in UNIX-based operating systems, the execution of the system command *ls* from a user account into /root/ directory should be detected. Moreover, the access policy corresponding to a malicious action can be specified.

A relevant example is to associate the existence of a Trojan horse to an open port.

Operations sequencing: The order in which some operations are executed is sometimes a good indicator of the legitimacy of an access. For example, the execution of some critical commands after being logged in as a normal user is prohibited. This shows how a signature can be based on a sequence of two, or more, events.

Protocol violation: Many signatures rely on detecting a communication flow that does not conform to the rules of a given protocol. For example, looking for IP packets in which the source and the destination addresses are the same permits the detection of a Land attack (which consists of sending a packet in which the source and destination IP addresses are identical). Likewise, checking the conformance of the fragmentation fields with the corresponding requests for comments (RFCs) allows thwarting fragmentation attacks such as Teardrop (which consists of sending two or more interleaving fragmented IP packets).

A behavior-based IDS, also referred to as an anomaly-based IDS, looks at actions, attempting to identify attacks by monitoring system or network activity and flagging any activity that does not seem to fit in. Anomaly detectors identify abnormal or unusual behavior (anomalies) on a host or network. They function on the assumption that attacks are different from "normal" (or legitimate) activity and can therefore be detected by systems that identify these differences. Anomaly detectors construct profiles representing normal behavior of users, hosts, or network connections. These profiles are constructed from historical data collected over a period of normal operation. The detectors then collect event data and use a variety of measures to determine when monitored activity deviates from the norm. The most used techniques in anomaly detection include:

Threshold detection, in which certain attributes of user and system behavior are expressed in terms of counts, with some level established as permissible. Such behavior attributes can include the number of files accessed by a user in a given period of time, the number of failed attempts to log in to the system, the amount of CPU space used by a process, etc. This level can be static or adaptive (i.e., designed to change with actual values observed over time).

Statistical measures—both parametric, in which the distribution of the profiled attributes is assumed to fit a particular pattern, and nonparametric, in which the distribution of the profiled attributes is "learned" from a set of historical values, observed over time.

Rule-based measures, which are similar to nonparametric statistical measures in that observed data define acceptable usage patterns, but differ in that those patterns are specified as rules, not numeric quantities.

Techniques belonging to the first class are categorized by two major shortcuts. First, they are not able to detect previously unknown attacks because it is often impossible to map them to any existing signature. Second, as different manners can exist to carry out a specific attack, it might be difficult to build signatures that cover all the variants of such intrusions.

Anomaly detectors often produce a large number of false alarms, as normal patterns of user and system behavior can vary wildly. Despite this shortcoming, researchers assert that anomaly-based IDSs are able to detect new attack forms, unlike signature-based IDSs, which rely on matching patterns of past attacks. Furthermore, some forms of anomaly detection produce output that can in turn be used as information sources for misuse detectors. For example, a threshold-based anomaly detector can generate a figure representing the "normal" number of files accessed by a particular user; the misuse detector can use this figure as part of a detection signature that says "if the number of files accessed by this user exceeds this "normal" figure by ten percent, trigger an alarm."

A significant problem with security-incident detection and response systems is the high number of false alarms. Various techniques are therefore developed to assist the security manager in understanding security faults and attacks. Visualization is perhaps the most renowned monitoring-assistance approach. It can be defined as a translation of the abstract data generated by the IDS to a visual interactive data set. Generally, the visualization process consists of three steps:

1. Data transformation: Consists of mapping raw data generated by the detection system to structured data, called "data tables." This can range from relational description techniques to metadata extraction,
2. Visual mapping: Extracts visual structures of the data tables based on spatial substrates, marks, and graphical properties,
3. Visual transformation: Allows building views by fixing graphical parameters (e.g., position, scaling, clipping).

The reader can find more information about these tasks in Axelsson (2004).

Another important aspect of security state monitoring is the use of honeypots, which are traps set to detect and trace attack-related activities. Honeypots also provide a useful tool to build accurate statistics about specific threats. Traditionally, they consist of isolated subnetworks that are seemingly important and sensitive. Therefore, they constitute good targets for malicious users. However, they are appropriately protected so that the attack damage is confined to the isolated perimeter. Honeypots have also been used to benchmark several detection mechanisms as in the DARPA-MIT Lincoln IDS evaluation project (www.ll.mit.edu/IST/ideval/index.html).

Incident Response

Accurate and fast response to attacks should be implemented. This process is hard to put in place because it is a hybrid, in the sense that it involves both human and automated reasoning. It is worth mentioning that the response strategy should be built based on the attacks that threaten the target system.

When an incident has been detected and analyzed, it is important to contain it before the spread of the incident overwhelms resources or the damage increases. Most incidents require containment, so it is important to consider it early in the course of handling each incident. An essential part of containment is decision making (e.g., shut down a system, disconnect it from a wired or wireless network, disconnect its modem cable, disable certain functions). Such decisions are much easier to make if strategies and procedures for containing the incident have been predetermined.

Another key task related to the incident-response process is evidence gathering and source tracing. Although the primary reason for gathering evidence during an incident is to resolve the incident, it may also be needed for legal proceedings. In such cases, it is important to clearly document how all evidence, including compromised systems, has been preserved. Evidence should be collected according to procedures that meet all applicable laws and regulations, developed from previous discussions with legal staff and appropriate law-enforcement agencies, so that it would be admissible in court. In addition, evidence should be accounted for at all times; whenever evidence is transferred from person to person, chain of custody forms should detail the transfer and include each party's signature. A detailed log should be kept for all evidence, including the following:

Identifying information (e.g., the location, serial number, model number, hostname, media access control (MAC) address, IP address of a computer)

Name, title and phone number of each individual who collected or handled the evidence during the investigation

Time and date (including time zone) of each occurrence of evidence handling

Locations where the evidence was stored

Multiple techniques have been proposed by Casey (2001) to identify an attacker. Identifying the attacker can be a time-consuming and futile process that can prevent a team from achieving its primary goal—minimizing the business impact. The following items describe the most commonly performed activities for attacker identification:

Validating the Attacker's IP Address

New incident handlers often focus on the attacker's IP address. The handler may attempt to validate that the address was not spoofed by using pings, traceroutes, or other methods of verifying connectivity. However, this is not helpful because at best it indicates that a host at that address responds to the requests. A failure to respond does not mean the address is not real—for example, a host may be configured to ignore pings and traceroutes. The attacker may have received a dynamic address (e.g., from a dial-up modem pool) that has already been reassigned to someone else. More importantly, if the IP address is real and the team pings it, the attacker may be tipped off that the organization has detected the activity. If this occurs before the incident has been fully contained, the attacker could cause additional damage, such as wiping out hard drives that contain evidence of the attack. The team should consider acquiring and using IP addresses from another organization (e.g., an ISP) when performing actions such as address validation so that the true origin of the activity is concealed from the attacker.

Scanning the Attacker's System

Some incident handlers do more than perform pings and traceroutes to check an attacking IP address. They may run port scanners, vulnerability scanners, and other tools to attempt to gather more information on the attacker. For example, the scans may indicate that Trojan horses are listening on the system, implying that the attacking host itself has been compromised. Incident handlers should discuss this issue with legal representatives before performing such scans because the scans may violate organization policies or even break the law.

Researching the Attacker through Search Engines

In most attacks, incident handlers may have at least a few pieces of data regarding the possible identity of the attacker, such as a source IP address, an e-mail address, or an IRC nickname. Performing an Internet search using these data may lead to more information on the attacker—for example, a mailing list message regarding a similar attack, or even the attacker's Web site. Research such as this generally does not need to be performed before the incident has been fully contained.

Using Incident Databases

Several groups collect and consolidate intrusion detection and firewall log data from various organizations into incident databases. Some of these databases allow people to search for records corresponding to a particular IP address. Incident handlers could use the databases to see if other organizations are reporting suspicious activity from the same source. The organization can also check its own incident-tracking system or database for related activity.

Monitoring Possible Attacker Communication Channels

Another method that some incident handlers use to identify an attacker is to monitor communication channels that may be used by an attacker. For example, the attacker may congregate on certain IRC channels to brag about Web sites that they have defaced. However, incident handlers should treat any such information that they acquire only as a potential lead to be further investigated and verified, not as fact.

COUNTERMEASURE-SELECTION GUIDELINES

Practical measures (security solutions) are given in this section to maintain the protected system at an acceptable security level. These solutions will be either preventive or reactive. They can be implemented at the different vulnerable points of the system. Mainly, the security of the assets listed below will be addressed:

Desktop workstations

Public and private servers

Storage and archival servers

Wireless LANs

Among others, the countermeasures presented in these guidelines will allow:

The secure configuration of the crucial assets
The accurate and fast detection of harmful events
The efficient response to the detected incidents
The precise identification of attack sources

Most of the proposed guidelines have appeared in the CERT security guidelines series.

Desktop Workstation Security

Security of a desktop workstation is mainly the responsibility of users. Their daily work usually requires that protected information resources be accessed, manipulated, modified, and transmitted across networks. However, it also requires considerable planning activity at the management level. The following points (Allen 2001) highlight the most important actions that should be implemented to secure workstations:

- Develop a computer deployment plan that includes security issues.
- Keep operating systems and applications software up to date.
- Configure computers for user authentication.
- Configure computer operating systems with appropriate object, device, and file access controls.
- Identify data that characterize systems and aid in detecting signs of suspicious behavior.
- Manage logging and other data-collection mechanisms.
- Configure computers for file backups.
- Protect computers from viruses and similar programmed threats.
- Configure computers for secure remote administration.
- Configure computers to provide only selected network services.
- Configure network service clients to enhance security.
- Configure multiple computers using a tested model configuration and a secure replication procedure.
- Allow only appropriate physical access to computers.

Public and Private Server Security

Public servers require special attention when being protected because their security needs differ from normal network nodes. The following actions (Allen 2001) represent the core of a set of recommended practices allowing securing public servers:

- Isolate the server from public networks and your organizations internal networks.
- Configure the server with appropriate object, device, and file-access controls.
- Identify and enable server-specific logging mechanisms.
- Consider security implications before selecting programs, scripts, and plug-ins for the public server.
- Configure the server to minimize the functionality of programs, scripts, and plug-ins.
- Configure the server to use authentication and encryption technologies, where required.
- Maintain the authoritative copy of your site content on a secure host.
- Protect the public server against common attacks.

Storage and Archival Server Security

Because of their focal role, it is common for servers to store many of an organization's most valuable and confidential information resources. They also are often deployed to provide a centralized capability for an entire organization, such as communication (e-mail) or user authentication. Security breaches on a network server can result in the disclosure of critical information or the loss of a capability that can affect the entire organization (Rekhis, Boudriga, and Obaidat 2005). Therefore, securing network servers should be a significant part of the organization's network and information security strategy. Several important guidelines for storage and archival servers are given below (Allen 2001):

- Develop a computer deployment plan that includes security issues.
- Include explicit security requirements when selecting servers.
- Keep operating systems and applications software up to date.
- Offer only essential network services and operating system services on the server host machine.
- Configure computers for user authentication.
- Configure computer operating systems with appropriate object, device, and file access controls.
- Identify data that characterize systems and aid in detecting signs of suspicious behavior.
- Manage logging and other data-collection mechanisms.
- Configure computers for file backups.
- Protect computers from viruses and similar programmed threats.
- Configure computers for secure remote administration.
- Allow only appropriate physical access to computers.

Wireless LAN Security

Wireless LANs (WLANs) are inherently less secure than wired networks because:

The signal is broadcast, the network is shared, and any network device can listen to network traffic for any other network device in range, making privacy and authentication difficult

The signal spreads outside buildings, so physical security is ineffective and it could be very difficult to locate a rogue device

Mistakes were made in designing wireless network standards so that the built in WEP (wired equivalent privacy) is effectively useless—it gives no assurance of privacy;

Efficient operation of wireless networks depends on a planned approach to the allocation of the limited spectrum available in the 2.4-Ghz band and rogue wireless equipment may interfere with and degrade the performance of authorized services.

There are different alternatives for securing a connection: end-to-end security at the application level, end-to-end security at the transport layer and link security at the link layer. Several useful protection techniques for wireless networks are listed in the following:

Authentication: An authentication method for wireless networks has to be mutual, self-protecting, and immune to dictionary attacks. This means that it must: (1) provide mutual authentication—that is, the authenticator must authenticate the user, but the user must be able to authenticate the authenticator as well; (2) protect itself from eavesdropping since the physical medium is not secure; and (3) be robust against online or offline dictionary attacks. An online attack is one in which the imposter must make repeated tries against the authenticator "online." These can be thwarted by limiting the number of failed authentication attempts a user can have. An offline attack is one in which attackers can make repeated tries on their own computers, very rapidly, and without the knowledge of the authenticator. Simple challenge/response methods are susceptible to offline attacks because if attackers capture a single challenge/response pair, they can try all the passwords in the dictionary to see if one produces the desired response.

Encryption: Encryption software can be used to protect the confidentiality of sensitive information stored on handheld devices and mirrored on the desktop PC. The information on add-on backup storage modules should also be encrypted and the modules securely stored when not in use. This additional level of security can be added to provide an extra layer of defense to further protect sensitive information stored on handheld devices. Many software programs are freely available to help users encrypt these types of files for an added layer of security.

Antivirus software: Malicious codes are often used to compromise handled devices. Antivirus software should therefore be used to scan the content of the mobile devices and to remove harmful components.

Public Key Infrastructures: Using certified asymmetric keys to protect networks is among the most secure techniques. A certification authority is needed to achieve this task. A regulatory framework should also be available to set the dues of the different parties participating in the wireless electronic transactions. Wireless public key infrastructure (PKI) should take into account the mobility of the handled devices.

VPNs: A VPN creates a virtual private network between the handheld device and the organization's network by sharing the public network infrastructure. VPN technology offers the security of a private network through access control and encryption, while taking advantage of the economies of scale and built-in management facilities of large public networks. This technique is widely used in wired networks and is being extended to wireless networks. A VPN can be used to authenticate access points at the network and link layers, and to encrypt the packets exchanged between handled devices.

MAJOR CHALLENGES

This section covers the most important challenges that are currently faced by the security community. Three main aspects are underlined:

Need for new response methods: Decision making to thwart security attacks is guided by many requirements (e.g., cost-effectiveness, real-time). Therefore, new security structures and processes are needed. Structured libraries seem to be an accurate choice to address this need. They allow to: (1) share the knowledge of security experts, (2) reuse security countermeasures that were implemented in the past, when similar security challenges are faced, and (3) make useful security-related information available for different user categories.

Secure protocol design: Most of the attacks discussed in the section on "Analyzing the Attacker's Objectives" are due to several weaknesses characterizing most of the network protocols. This emphasizes the need for integrating security at the earliest phases of protocol design. To this end, risk-analysis step, allowing the selection of the most efficient security solutions, should be conducted.

Quality of Service (QoS) versus security: Setting the QoS requirements for an application involving computing and communication infrastructures may turn out to conflict with the security objectives. Effectively, the application of strong security policies often induces delays and overhead. This renders QoS requirements hard to satisfy.

Attacks against new-generation networks: Mobility, which is among the most important characteristics of the new-generation networks, has introduced some novel topologies, in which some critical (from security point of view) tasks can be delegated by operators to normal users. This introduces some important security concerns that should be considered.

GLOSSARY

Alert: An alert is an attack description that is achieved by monitoring several system parameters. It provides the capability to detect and identify the potential intrusions that are carried out on the victim assets.

Attack: An attack is an action conducted in order to harm a networked system. Attackers' objectives vary from disrupting a vital service to accessing private information.

Firewall: Network firewalls are devices or systems that control the flow of network traffic between networks using differing security postures. In most modern applications, firewalls and firewall environments are discussed in the context of Internet connectivity and the TCP/IP suite. Firewalls are typically categorized into a few types: packet filters, stateful inspection firewalls, and application proxies.

Incident Response: A process involving the actions that should be executed to limit the impact of an attack that has occurred. Time and cost-benefit are the most important parameters involved in this process.

Intrusion: Any activity that violates the security policy can be qualified as an intrusion. Hence, an attack does not necessarily correspond to an intrusion. In fact, because of some lacks at the security policy level, several attacks cannot be mapped to intrusion schemes.

Intrusion-Detection System (IDS): Software or hardware systems that automate the process of monitoring the events occurring in a computer system or network, analyzing them for signs of security problems.

Security Policy: A set of rules that define how critical assets should be secured within a networked system.

System Monitoring: Monitoring consists of performing a continuous control of the system's security state. It allows detecting new vulnerabilities, detecting security policy violations, and reacting in a convenient manner.

Threat: Any event that can result in a loss for a sensitive system. It can be malevolent, accidental, or even due to natural disaster. A threat is generally characterized by a probability of occurrence and an outcome.

Virus: A program or piece of code that is introduced into a computer and runs against the security policy. Viruses have the ability to replicate themselves, they are therefore dangerous because they can use all available disk and memory resources, bringing the system to a halt.

Worm: A program or algorithm that replicates itself over a computer network and usually performs malicious actions. A worm is generally characterized by a payload defining the malicious action(s) that it can perform.

CROSS REFERENCES

See *Computer Network Management*; *Denial of Service Attacks*; *E-Mail Threats and Vulnerabilities*; *Intrusion Detection Systems*; *Social Engineering*; *Worms and Viruses*.

REFERENCES

Alberts, J., and J. Dorofee. 2002. *Managing information security risks*. Reading, MA: Addison Wesley Professional.

Allen, J. 2001. *CERT® guide to system and network security practices*. Reading, MA: Addison Wesley Professional.

Amoroso, E. 1994. *Fundamentals of computer security technology*. Upper Saddle River, NJ: Prentice-Hall.

Anderson, J. 1980. *Computer security threat monitoring and surveillance*. Technical Report Contract 79F296400. Fort Washington, PA: James Anderson.

Anderson, J. 2001. *Security engineering—A guide to building dependable distributed systems*. New York: Wiley.

Arbor Networks. 2005. Worldwide ISP Security Report. www.arbornetworks.com (accessed May 15, 2007).

Australian High Tech Crime Centre. 2005. *Computer crime and security survey*. www.auscert.org.au/images/ACCSS2005.pdf (accessed May 15, 2007).

Axelsson, S. 2004. Visualizing intrusions: Watching the WebServer. In *Proceedings of the 19th IFIP International Information Security Conference (SEC 2004), Toulouse, France*. Dordrecht, The Netherlands: Kluwer Academic.

Bishop, M., and M. Dilger. 1996. *Checking for race conditions in file accesses*, 131–52. Berkeley, CA: Usenix.

Casey, E. 2001. Handbook of computer crime investigation: Forensic tools and technology. New York: Academic Press.

Department of Trade and Industry (UK). 2004. *Information security breaches survey*. www.dti.gov.uk/files/file9990.pdf (accessed May 15, 2007.)

Fessi, B. A., M. Hamdi, S. Benabdallah, and N. Boudriga. 2007. A decisional framework system for computer network intrusion detection. *European Journal of Operational Research* 177(3):1824–38.

Ghosh, A. K., G. E. McGraw, F. H. Charron, and M. E. Shatz. 1996. Towards analyzing security critical software during development. Technical report RSTR-96-023-01. Charlotte, NC: RST Corporation.

Gordon, L., M. Loeb, W. Lucyshyn, and R. Richardson. 2005. *Computer crime and security survey*. Computer Security Institute. www.gocsi.com (accessed May 15, 2007).

Hamdi, M., and N. Boudriga. 2005. Computer and network security risk management: theory, challenges, and countermeasures. *International Journal of Communication Systems* 18(8):763–93.

Hamdi, M., and N. Boudriga. 2005. Forensic computing. In *Handbook of information security.* Volume 2: *Information warfare, social, legal, and international issues and security foundations*. Edited by H. Bidgoli. New York: Wiley.

Hamdi, M., and N. Boudriga. 2005. Security policy guidelines. In *Handbook of information security*. Volume 3: *Threats, vulnerabilities, prevention, detection, and management*. Edited by H. Bidgoli. New York: Wiley..

Helmer, G., J. Wong, M. Slagell, V. Honavar, L. Miller, and R. Lutz. 2006. Software fault tree and colored Petri net based specification, design, and implementation of agent-based intrusion detection systems. *International Journal of Information and Computer Security* 1(1):109–42.

Huang, Y., and W. Lee. 2004. Attack analysis and detection for ad hoc routing protocols. In *Recent Advances in Intrusion Detection Symposium*, 125–45., Berlin: Springer Verlag.

Jayaram, N., and P. Morse. 1997. Network security—A taxonomic view. In *Proceedings of the IEEE European Conference on Security and Detection*, 124–7. London: IEEE Publishing.

Krsul, I., E. Spafford, and M. Tripunitara. 1998. *Computer vulnerability analysis*. West Lafayette, IN: Purdue University.

Lee, W., M. Miller, S. Stolfo, K. Jallad, C. Park, and C. Zadok. 2002. Toward Cost-sensitive modeling for intrusion detection. *Journal of Computer Security* 10(1):5–22.

Lindqvist, U., and E. Jonsson. 1998. A map of security risks associated with using cots. *Computer* 31(6):60–6.

McDermott, J. 2000 Attack net penetration testing. In *Proceedings of the 2000 New Security Paradigms*

Workshop. Ballycotton, Country Cork, Ireland. New York: ACM Press.

Moore, A. P., R. J. Ellison, and R. C. Linger. 2001 *Attack modeling for information security and survivability*. CMU/SEI Technical Report, CMU/SEI-2001-TN-01 www.sei.cmu.edu/about/website/indexes/siteIndex/siteIndexTR.html (accessed May 16, 2007).

Neumann, P., and D. Parker. 1989. A summary of computer misuse techniques. In *Proceedings of the 12th National Computer Security Conference*, 396–407. Gaithersburg, MD: National Institute of Standards and Technology

Peltier, T. R. 2001. *Information security risk analysis*. Boca Raton, FL: Auerbach.

Ozier, W. 1999. *Risk analysis and assessment: The handbook of information security*. Volume 3, Chapter 15, Boca Raton, FL: Auerbach.

Reith, M., M. Carr, and G. Gunch. 2002. An examination of digital forensic models. *International Journal of Digital Evidence* 2(3). www.utica.edu/academic/institutes/ecii/publications/articles/A04A40DC-A6F6-F2C1-98F94F16AF57232D.pdf (accessed May 28, 2007).

Rekhis, S., N. Boudriga, and M. S. Obaidat. 2005. Server-side security. *Handbook of information security*. Volume 3, Chapter 159. New York: Wiley.

Schneier, B. 2001. *Secrets and lies: Digital security in a networked world*. New York: Wiley.

Steffan, J., and M. Schumacher. 2002. Collaborative attack modeling. In *Proceedings of the 2002 ACM Symposium on Applied Computing, Madrid, Spain*, 253–9. www.ito.tu-darmstadt.de/publs/pdf/sac2002.pdf (accessed May 28, 2007).

Stolen, K., K. den Braber, T. Dimitrakos, R. Fredriksen, B. Gran, S.-H. Houmb, Y. C. Stamatiou, and J. O. Aagedal. 2003. Model-based risk assessment in a component-based software engineering process: The CORAS approach to identify security risks. In *Business component-based software engineering*, edited by F. Barbier, 189–207. Boston: Kluwer.

Tidwell, T., R. Larson, K. Fitch, and J. Hale. 2001. Modeling Internet attacks. In *Proceedings of the 2001 IEEE Workshop on Information Assurance and Security, West Point, NY*. www.itoc.usma.edu/Workshop/2001/Authors/Submitted_Abstracts/paperT1C1(50).pdf (accessed May 28, 2007).

Viega, J., T. Mutdosh, and G. McGraw. 2000. Statically scanning JAVA code: Finding security vulnerabilities. *IEEE Software* 17(5): 68–74.

Wei, H., D. Frinke, O. Carter, and C. Ritter. 2001. Cost-benefit analysis for network intrusion detection systems. In CSI 28th *Annual Computer Security Conference*, Washington D.C, http://www.csds.uidaho.edu/deb/costbenefit.pdf (accessed May 28, 2007).

Computer Viruses and Worms

Robert Slade, *Independent Consultant, Canada*

INTRODUCTION

Computer viruses are unique among the many security problems because the fact that someone else is infected increases the risk to you. However, viruses also seem to be surrounded by myths and misunderstandings. In this chapter we will help to set the record straight.

History of Computer Viruses and Worms

Many claims have been made for the existence of viruses prior to the 1980s, but so far these claims have not been accompanied by proof. The Core Wars programming contests, frequently cited as early examples of virus-like computer programs, did involve self-replicating code, but usually within a structured and artificial environment. Primarily on the basis of a "copyright" date of 1986 included in the code of the Brain virus, 2006 has been hailed as the 20th anniversary of computer viruses.

The general perception of computer viruses, even among security professionals, has concentrated on their existence in personal computers, and particularly "Wintel"- type systems. This is despite the fact that Fred Cohen's (1984) seminal academic work took place on mainframe and minicomputers in the mid-1980s. The first e-mail virus was spread in 1987. The first virus hoax message (then termed a "metavirus") was proposed in 1988. Even so, virus and malware research has been neglected, possibly because malware does not fit easily into the traditional access-control security models.

At least two Apple II viruses are known to have been created in the early 1980s. However, it was not until the end of the decade (and 1987 in particular) that knowledge of real viruses became widespread, even among security experts. For many years boot-sector infectors and file infectors were the only types of common viruses. These programs spread relatively slowly, primarily distributed on floppy disks, and were thus slow to disseminate geographically. However, these viruses tended to be very long lived.

During the early 1990s virus writers started experimenting with various functions intended to defeat detection. (Some forms had seen limited trials earlier.) Among these were polymorphism (to change form in order to defeat scanners) and stealth (to attempt to confound any type of detection). None of these virus technologies had a significant impact. Most viruses using these "advanced" technologies were easier to detect because of a necessary increase in program size. (Although various detection-avoidance technologies may make detection of viruses difficult, and possibly computationally expensive, it is impossible to make a virus that cannot be detected by some means. At the same time, Fred Cohen's work, noted later in this article, has proven that a "perfect" antivirus, which can detect all possible viruses without ever making an error, is not going to happen. Therefore, we are faced with a situation in which we cannot know, with complete assurance, that all viruses have been found, but we likewise know that no virus can reliably evade detection.)

Although demonstration programs had been created earlier, the mid-1990s saw the introduction of macro and script viruses in the wild. These were initially confined to word-processing files, particularly files associated with the Microsoft Office Suite. However, the inclusion of programming capabilities in office productivity applications eventually led to macro and script viruses in many objects that would normally be considered to contain data only, such as Excel spreadsheets, PowerPoint presentation files, and e-mail messages. This fact led to greatly increased demands for computer resources among antiviral systems, since many more objects had to be tested, and Windows OLE (object linking and embedding) format data files presented substantial complexity to scanners. Macro viruses also increase new variant forms very quickly, since the virus carries its own source code, and anyone who obtains a copy can generally modify it and create a new member of the virus family.

E-mail viruses became the major new form in the late 1990s and early 2000s. These viruses may use macro capabilities, scripting, or executable attachments to create e-mail messages or attachments send out to e-mail addresses harvested from the infected machine. E-mail viruses spread extremely rapidly, distributing themselves worldwide in a matter of hours. Some versions create so many copies of themselves that corporate and even service provider mail servers become flooded and cease to function. E-mail viruses are very visible, and so tend to be identified within a short time, but many are macros or scripts, and so generate many variants.

With the strong integration of the Microsoft Windows operating system with its Internet Explorer browser, Outlook mailer, Office suite, and system scripting, recent viruses have started to blur the normal distinctions. A document sent as an e-mail file attachment can make a call to a Web site that starts active content that installs a remote-access tool acting as a portal for the client portion of a distributed denial-of-service network. Indeed, not only are viruses starting to show characteristics that are similar to each other, but functions from completely different types of malware are beginning to be found together in the same programs, leading to a type of malware convergence.

Many security specialists have stated that the virus threat is decreasing, since, despite the total number of virus infections being seen, the prevalent viruses are now almost universally e-mail viruses, and therefore constitute a single threat with a single fix. This ignores the fact that, although almost all major viruses now use e-mail as a distribution and reproduction mechanism, there are a great many variations in the way e-mail is used. For example, many viruses use Microsoft Outlook mailer to spread, and reproduction can be prevented simply by removing Outlook from the system. However, other viruses may make direct calls to the mail application programming interface (MAPI), which is used by a number of mail-user programs, while others carry the code for mail server functions within their own body. A number of e-mail viruses distribute themselves to e-mail addresses found in the Microsoft Outlook address book files, while others may harvest addresses from anywhere on the computer hard drive, or may actually take control of the Internet network connection and collect contact data from any source viewed online.

Because virus research has had to deal with detailed analysis of low-level code, it has led to significant advances in the field of forensic programming. However, to date computer forensic work has concentrated on file recovery and decryption, so the contributions in this area likely still lie in the future.

With regard to current threat levels, a 2005 FBI computer crime survey (authored by Special Agent Bruce Verduyn and publicly posted on the Web, but no longer available on the Web at the time of writing) noted that not only were malware attacks the largest single class of computer crimes, but they were responsible for fully one-third of the financial damage resulting from all computer crime. According to the figures collected in the report, in 2004/2005, malware attacks resulted in an estimated loss of six million dollars per hour in the United States alone. According to many other reports and studies, the threat continues to grow.

Many computer pundits, as well as some security experts, have proposed that computer viruses are a result of the fact that currently popular desktop operating systems have only nominal security provisions. They further suggest that viruses will disappear as security functions are added to operating systems. This thesis ignores the fact, well established by Cohen's research and subsequently confirmed, that viruses use the most basic of computer functions, and that a perfect defense against viruses is impossible. This is not to say that an increase in security measures by operating-system vendors could not reduce the risk of viruses: the current danger could be drastically reduced with relatively minor modifications to system functions.

It is going too far to say (as some have) that the very existence of virus programs, and the fact that both viral strains and the numbers of individual infections are growing, means that computers are finished. At the present time, the general public is not well informed about the virus threat, and so more copies of virus programs are being produced than are being destroyed.

Indeed, no less an authority than Fred Cohen has championed the idea that virus programs can be used to great effect. An application using a viral form can improve performance in the same way that computer hardware benefits from parallel processors. It is, however, unlikely that virus programs can operate effectively and usefully in the current computer environment without substantial protective measures being built into them. A number of virus and worm programs have been written with the obvious intent of proving that viruses could carry a useful payload, and some have even had a payload that could be said to enhance security. Unfortunately, all such viruses have created serious problems themselves.

Virus Definition

A computer virus is a program written with functions and intent to copy and disperse itself without the knowledge and cooperation of the owner or user of the computer. A final definition has not yet been agreed on by all researchers. A common definition is, "a program that modifies other programs to contain a possibly altered version of itself." This definition is generally attributed to Fred Cohen from his seminal research in the mid-1980s, although Dr. Cohen's actual definition is in mathematical form. Another possible definition is "an entity that uses the resources of the host (system or computer) to reproduce itself and spread, without informed operator action."

Cohen is generally held to have defined the term *computer virus* in his thesis (published in 1984). (The suggestion for the use of the term virus is credited to Len Adleman, his seminar advisor.) However, his original definition covers only those sections of code that, when active, attach themselves to other programs. This, however, neglects many of the programs that have been most successful "in the wild".

Many researchers still insist on Cohen's definition and use other terms such as "worm" and "bacterium" for virus programs that do not attack other programs. Currently, viruses are generally held to attach themselves to some object, although the object may be a program, disk, document, e-mail message, computer system, or other information entity.

Computer virus programs are not a "natural" occurrence. Viruses are programs written by programmers. They do not just appear through some kind of electronic evolution—they are written, deliberately, by people. However, the definition of "program" may include many items not normally thought of in terms of programming, such as disk boot sectors, and Microsoft Office documents or data files that also contain macro programming.

Many people have the impression that anything that goes wrong with a computer is caused by a virus. From hardware failures to errors in use, everything is blamed on a virus. A virus is not just any damaging condition. Similarly, it is now popularly believed that any program that may do damage to your data or your access to computing resources is a virus. Virus programs are not simply programs that do damage. Indeed, virus programs are not always damaging, at least not in the sense of being deliberately designed to erase data or disrupt operations. Most virus programs seem to have been designed to be a kind of electronic graffiti: intended to make the writer's mark in the world, if not with his or her name. In some cases a name is displayed, on occasion an address, phone number, company name, or political party.

Is My Computer Infected? What Should I Do?

In many books and articles you will find lists of symptoms to watch for in order to determine whether your computer is infected. These signs include things like running out of memory space, running out of disk space, the computer operating more slowly than normal, files changing size, and so forth. In fact, many factors will create these same effects, and current viruses seldom do. The best way to determine whether your computer has been infected by a virus is to get and use an antivirus scanner. In fact, get more than one. With the rapid generation of new viruses these days, it is quite possible for a maker of antivirus software to make mistakes in updating signatures. Therefore, having a second check on a suspected virus is always a good idea.

One scanner for the Wintel platform is F-PROT. It is available in a DOS version, free of charge from www.f-secure.com. (Look under "Downloads" and "Tools.") Although a DOS scanner has some limitations in a Windows environment (particularly with an NTFS [new technology file system] in Windows XP), it will still be able to identify infected files, and is quite good at picking out virus infections within e-mail system files (the files of messages held on your computer).

Another scanner available free is AVG (antivirus Grisoft), from www.grisoft.com.. This one also does a good job of scanning, and will even update itself automatically (although that feature is problematic on some machines).

The various commercial antivirus program producers generally release trial versions of their software, usually limited in some way. Sophos and Avast have been very good in this regard.

Considering the suggestion to use more than one scanner, it should be noted that a number of successful software publishers have included functions that conflict with software from other vendors. These products should be avoided, because of the previously noted possibility of failure in a single protection program. The use of "free" software, and purchase of software from companies that provide such free versions, is recommended, since the existence of these free scanners, and their use by other people, actually reduces your risk, since there will be fewer instances of viruses reproducing and trying to spread. (In this situation I am speaking of software for which no fee is charged, rather than specifically open source "free" software.)

Readers may be surprised at the recommendation to use software that is free of charge: there is a general assumption that commercial software must be superior to that provided free. It should be noted that I am a specialist in the evaluation of security and, particularly, antivirus software, and I have published more reviews of antivirus software than any other individual. The reader can be assured that it can be proven that, in the case of antivirus software, free software is as effective, and in some cases superior to, many very expensive products.

TROJAN HORSES, VIRUSES, WORMS, RATs, AND OTHER BEASTS

Malware is a relatively new term in the security field. It was created to address the need to discuss software or programs that are intentionally designed to include functions for penetrating a system, breaking security policies, or carrying malicious or damaging payloads. Since this type of software has started to develop a bewildering variety of forms—such as backdoors, data diddlers, DDoS (distributed denial of service), hoax warnings, logic bombs, pranks, RATs (remote-access Trojans), Trojans, viruses, worms, zombies, etc.—the term has come to be used for the collective class of *mal*icious soft*ware*. The term is, however, often used very loosely simply as a synonym for virus, in the same way that virus is often used simply as a description of any type of computer problem. I will attempt to define the virus and worm problem more accurately, and to do this I need to describe the various other types of malware.

Viruses are the largest class of malware, both in terms of numbers of known entities, and in impact in the current computing environment. Viruses, therefore, tend to be synonymous, in the public mind, with all forms of malware. Programming bugs or errors are generally not included in the definition of malware, although it is sometimes difficult to make a hard and fast distinction between malware and bugs. For example, if a programmer left a buffer overflow in a system and it creates a loophole that can be used as a backdoor or a maintenance hook, did he do it deliberately? This question cannot be answered technically, although we might be able to guess at it, given the relative ease of use of a given vulnerability.

In addition, it should be noted that malware is not just a collection of utilities for the attacker. Once launched, malware can continue an attack without reference to the author or user, and in some cases will expand the attack to other systems. There is a qualitative difference between malware and the attack tools, kits, or scripts, that have to operate under an attacker's control, and which are not considered to fall within the definition of malware. There are gray areas in this aspect as well, since RATs and DDoS zombies provide unattended access to systems, but need to be commanded in order to deliver a payload.

Trojans

Trojans, or Trojan horse programs, are the largest class of malware in terms of numbers of different entities produced. However, the term is subject to much confusion, particularly in relation to computer viruses.

A Trojan is a program that pretends to do one thing while performing another, unwanted action. The extent of the "pretense" may vary greatly. Many of the early PC Trojans relied merely on the filename and a description on a bulletin board. Log-in Trojans, popular among university student mainframe users, mimicked the screen display and the prompts of the normal log-in program and could, in fact, pass the username and password along to the valid log-in program at the same time as they stole the user data. Some Trojans may contain actual code that does what it is supposed to be doing while performing additional nasty acts that it does not tell you about.

Another confusion with viruses involves Trojan horse programs that may be spread by e-mail. In years past, a Trojan program had to be posted on an electronic bulletin board system or a file archive site. Because of the static posting, a malicious program would soon be identified and eliminated. More recently, Trojan programs have been distributed by mass e-mail campaigns, by posting on Usenet newsgroup discussion groups, or through automated distribution agents (bots) on Internet relay chat (IRC) channels. Since source identification in these communications channels can be easily hidden, Trojan programs can be redistributed in a number of disguises, and specific identification of a malicious program has become much more difficult.

Some data security writers consider that a virus is simply a specific example of the class of Trojan horse programs. There is some validity to this classification, since a virus is an unknown quantity that is hidden and transmitted along with a legitimate disk or program, and any program can be turned into a Trojan by infecting it with a virus. However, the term *virus* more properly refers to the added, infectious code rather than the virus/target combination. Therefore, the term *Trojan* refers to a deliberately misleading or modified program that does not reproduce itself.

A major aspect of Trojan design is the social engineering (fraudulent or deceptive) component. Trojan programs are advertised (in some sense) as having a positive component. The term *positive* can be disputed, since a great many Trojans promise pornography or access to pornography, and this still seems to be depressingly effective.

However, other promises can be made as well. A recent e-mail virus, in generating its messages, carried a list of a huge variety of subject lines, promising pornography, humor, virus information, an antivirus program, and information about abuse of the recipient's email account.

Sometimes the message is simply vague, and relies on curiosity. Social engineering really is nothing more than a fancy name for the type of fraud and confidence games that have existed since snakes started selling apples. Security types tend to prefer a more academic-sounding definition, such as the use of nontechnical means to circumvent security policies and procedures. Social engineering can range from simple lying (such as a false description of the function of a file), to bullying and intimidation (in order to pressure a low-level employee into disclosing information), to association with a trusted source (such as the username from an infected machine).

Worms

A worm reproduces and spreads, like a virus, and unlike other forms of malware. Worms are distinct from viruses, though they may have similar results. Most simply, a worm may be thought of as a virus with the capacity to propagate independently of user action. In other words, they do not rely on (usually) human-initiated transfer of data between systems for propagation, but instead spread across networks of their own accord, primarily by exploiting known vulnerabilities (such as buffer overflows) in common software.

Originally, the distinction was made that worms used networks and communications links to spread, and that a worm, unlike a virus, did not directly attach to an executable file. In early research into computer viruses, the terms *worm* and *virus* tended to be used synonymously, it being felt that the technical distinction was unimportant to most users. The technical origin of the term *worm program* matched that of modern distributed processing experiments: a program with "segments" working on different computers, all communicating over a network (Shoch and Hupp 1982).

The first worm to garner significant attention was the Internet Worm of 1988, discussed in detail in the section on "Worms (First and Third Generation)." Recently, many of the most prolific virus infections have not been strictly viruses, but have used a combination of viral and worm techniques to spread more rapidly and effectively. LoveLetter was an example of this convergence of reproductive technologies. Although infected e-mail attachments were perhaps the most widely publicized vector of infection, LoveLetter also spread by actively scanning attached network drives, infecting a variety of common file types. This convergence of technologies will be an increasing problem in the future. Code Red and a number of Linux programs (such as Lion) are modern examples of worms. (Nimda is an example of a worm, but it also spreads in a number of other ways, so it could be considered to be an e-mail virus and multipartite as well.)

Viruses

A virus is defined by its ability to reproduce and spread. A virus is not just anything that goes wrong with a computer, and *virus* is not simply another name for *malware*. Trojan horse programs and logic bombs do not reproduce themselves.

A worm, which is sometimes seen as a specialized type of virus, is currently distinguished from a virus since a virus generally requires an action on the part of the user to trigger or aid reproduction and spread. The action on the part of the user is generally a common function, and the user usually does not realize the danger of the action, or the fact that he or she is assisting the virus.

The only requirement that defines a program as a virus is that it reproduces. It is not necessary that the virus carry a payload, although a number of viruses do. In many cases (in most cases of "successful" viruses), the payload is limited to some kind of message. A deliberately damaging payload, such as erasure of the disk, or system files, usually restricts the ability of the virus to spread, since the virus uses the resources of the host system. In some cases, a virus may carry a logic bomb or time bomb that triggers a damaging payload on a certain date or under a specific, often delayed, condition.

Because a virus spreads and uses the resources of the host, it affords a kind of power to software that parallel processors provide to hardware. Therefore, some have theorized that viral programs could be used for beneficial purposes, similar to the experiments in distributed processing that are testing the limits of cryptographic strength. (Various types of network-management functions, and updating of system software, are seen as candidates.) However, the fact that viruses change systems and applications is seen as problematic in its own right. Many viruses that carry no overtly damaging payload still create problems with systems. A number of virus and worm programs have been written with the obvious intent of proving that viruses could carry a useful payload, and some have even had a payload that could be said to enhance security. Unfortunately, all such viruses have created serious problems themselves. The difficulties of controlling virus programs have been addressed in theory, but the solutions are also known to have faults and loopholes.

Logic Bombs

Logic bombs are software modules set up to run in a quiescent state, but to monitor for a specific condition, or set of conditions, and to activate their payload under those conditions. A logic bomb is generally implanted in or coded as part of an application under development or maintenance. Unlike a RAT or Trojan it is difficult to implant a logic bomb after the fact. There are numerous examples of this type of activity, usually based on actions taken by a programmer to deprive a company of needed resources if the programmer's employment is terminated.

A Trojan or a virus may contain a logic bomb as part of the payload. A logic bomb involves no reproduction, no social engineering. A persistent legend with regard to logic bombs involves what is known as the salami scam. According to the story, this involves the siphoning off of small amounts on money (in some versions, fractions of a cent) credited to the account of the programmer, over a very large number of transactions. Despite the fact that these stories appear in a number of computer security texts, the author has a standing challenge to anyone to come up with a documented case of such a scam. Over a period of eight years, the closest anyone has come is a story about a fast-food clerk who diddled the display on a drive through window, and collected an extra dime or quarter from most customers.

Other Related Terms

Hoax virus warnings or alerts have an odd double relation to viruses. First, hoaxes are usually warnings about "new" viruses: new viruses that do not, of course, exist. Second, hoaxes generally carry a directive to the user to forward the warning to all addresses available to them. Thus, these descendants of chain letters form a kind of self-perpetuating spam.

Hoaxes use an odd kind of social engineering, relying on people's naturally gregarious nature and desire to communicate, and on a sense of urgency and importance, using the ambition that people have to be the first to provide important new information. Hoaxes do, however, have common characteristics that can be used to determine whether their warnings may or may not be valid:

- Hoaxes generally ask the reader to forward the message.
- Hoaxes make reference to false authorities such as Microsoft, AOL, IBM, and the FCC (none of which issue virus alerts) or to completely false entities.
- Hoaxes do not give specific information about the individual or office responsible for analyzing the virus or issuing the alert.
- Hoaxes generally state that the new virus is unknown to authorities or researchers.
- Hoaxes often state that there is no means of detecting or removing the virus; many of the original hoax warnings stated only that you should not open a message with a certain phrase in the subject line. (The warning, of course, usually contained that phrase in the subject line. Subject-line filtering is known to be a very poor method of detecting malware.)
- Hoaxes often state that the virus does tremendous damage, and is incredibly virulent.
- Hoax warnings very often contain A LOT OF CAPITAL LETTER SHOUTING AND EXCLAMATION MARKS!!!!!!!!!!
- Hoaxes often contain technical sounding nonsense (technobabble), such as references to nonexistent technologies like "*n*th complexity binary loops."

It is wise, in the current environment, to doubt all virus warnings, unless they come from a known and historically accurate source, such as a vendor with a proven record of providing reliable and accurate virus alert information, or preferably an independent researcher or group. It is best to check any warnings received against known virus encyclopedia sites. It is best to check more than one such site: in the initial phases of a "fast burner" attack some sites may not have had time to analyze samples to their own satisfaction, and the better sites will not post information they are not sure about.

Remote-access Trojans (RATs) are programs designed to be installed, usually remotely, after systems are installed and working (and not in development, as is the case with logic bombs and backdoors). Their authors would generally like to have the programs referred to as remote administration tools, in order to convey a sense of legitimacy.

When a RAT program has been run on a computer, it will install itself in such a way as to be active every time the computer is started subsequent to the installation. Information is sent back to the controlling computer (sometimes via an anonymous channel such as IRC) noting that the system is active. The user of the command computer is now able to explore the target, escalate access to other resources, and install other software, such as DDoS zombies, if so desired.

DDoS (distributed denial of service) is a modified denial of service (DoS) attack. DoS attacks do not attempt to destroy or corrupt data, but attempt to use up a computing resource to the point at which normal work cannot proceed. The structure of a DDoS attack requires a master computer to control the attack, a target of the attack, and a number of computers in the middle that the master computer uses to generate the attack. These computers between the master and the target are variously called "agents" or "clients," but are usually referred to as running "zombie" programs. The existence of a large number of agent computers in a DDoS attack acts to multiply the effect of the attack, and also helps to hide the identity of the originator of the attack.

Closely related to RATs and DDoS zombie clients are bot clients. Originally, bots were automated tools, frequently used on chat circuits for automatic administrative functions. However, various functions have been coded into pieces of malware for distribution to a large number of computers. One of the largest classes of bots are spambots, used to subvert a number of normal user computers into a spambotnet. As the name implies, these machines are used to generate and distribute spam. However, since the spambotnet is composed of a large number of disparate computers, it is much harder to isolate or shut down than a normal mail relay server. Many of these spambotnets are used to distribute advance-fee fraud messages, identity-theft solicitations (usually known as phishing), and new versions of malware and viruses.

There is a lot of controversy over a number of technologies generally described as adware or spyware. Most people would agree that the marketing functions are not specifically malicious, but what one person sees as "aggressive selling" another will see as an intrusion or invasion of privacy.

Shareware or freeware programs may have advertising for a commercial version or a related product, and users may be asked to provide some personal information for registration or to download the product. For example, an unregistered copy of the WinZip archiving program typically asks the user to register when the program is started, and the free version of the QuickTime video player asks the user to buy the commercial version every time the software is invoked. Adware, however, is generally a separate program installed at the same time as a given utility or package, and continues to advertise products even when the desired program is not running. Spyware is, again, a system distinct from the software the user installed, and passes more information than simply a username and address back to the vendor: often these packages will report on Web sites visited or other software installed on the computer, and possibly compile detailed inventories of the interests and activities of a user.

The discussion of spyware often makes reference to cookies or Web bugs. Cookies are small pieces of information in regard to persistent transactions between the user and a Web site, but the information can be greater than the user realizes—for example, in the case of a company that provides content, such as banner ads, to a large number of sites. Cookies, limited to text data, are not malware, and can have no executable malicious content. Web bugs are links on Web pages or embedded in e-mail messages that contain links to different Web sites. A Web bug, therefore, passes a call, and information, unknown to the user, to a remote site. Most commonly a Web bug is either invisible or unnoticeable (typically it is one pixel in size) in order not to alert the user to its presence.

There is a persistent chain letter hoax that tells people to forward the message because it is part of a test of an e-mail tracking system. Although to date all such chain letter reports are false, such a system has been implemented and does use Web bug technology. The system is not reliable: Web bugs in e-mail rely on an e-mail system calling a Web browser function, and, while this typically happens automatically with systems like Microsoft Outlook and Internet Explorer, a mailer like Pegasus requires the function call to be established by the user, and warns the user when it is being invoked.

On susceptible systems, however, a good deal of information can be obtained: the mail system noted can frequently obtain the IP address of the user, the type and version of browser being used, the operating system of the computer, and the time the message was read.

Pranks are very much a part of the computer culture. So much so that you can now buy commercially produced joke packages that allow you to perform "Stupid Mac (or PC, or Windows) Tricks." There are countless pranks available as shareware. Some make the computer appear to insult the user; some use sound effects or voices; some use special visual effects. A fairly common thread running through most pranks is that the computer is, in some way, nonfunctional. Many pretend to have detected some kind of fault in the computer (and some pretend to rectify such faults, of course making things worse). One entry in the virus field is PARASCAN, the paranoid scanner. It pretends to find large numbers of infected files, although it does not actually check for any infections.

Generally speaking, pranks that create some kind of announcement are not malware: viruses that generate a screen or audio display are actually quite rare. The distinction between jokes and Trojans is harder to make, but pranks are intended for amusement. Joke programs may, of course, result in a denial of service if people find the prank message frightening.

One specific type of joke is the "easter egg," a function hidden in a program, and generally accessible only by some arcane sequence of commands. These may be seen as harmless, but note that they do consume resources, even if only disk space, and also make the task of ensuring program integrity very much more difficult.

FIRST-GENERATION VIRUSES

Many of the books and articles that are currently available to explain viruses were written based on the research that was done on the first generation of viruses. While these programs are still of interest to those who study the internal structures of operating systems, they operated much differently from the current crop of malicious software. First-generation viruses tended to spread very slowly, but to hang around in the environment for a long time. Later viruses tended to spread very rapidly, but also to die out relatively quickly.

Boot-Sector Viruses

Viruses are generally partly classified by the objects to which they attach. Worms may be seen as a type of virus that attaches to nothing. Most desktop computer operating systems have some form of boot sector, a specific location on the hard disk that contains programming to bootstrap the startup of a computer. Boot-sector infectors (BSIs) replace or redirect this programming in order to have the virus invoked, usually as the first programming running on the computer. Because the minimal built-in programming of the computer simply starts to read and execute material from a specific location on the disk, any code that occupies this location is run. BSIs copy themselves onto this location whenever they encounter any new disk.

BSIs would not appear to fit the definition of a virus infecting another program, since BSIs can be spread by disks that do not contain any program files. However, the boot sector of a normal MS-DOS disk, whether or not it is a "system" or bootable disk, always contains a program (even if it only states that the disk is not bootable), and so it can be said that a BSI is a "true" virus.

The terminology of BSIs comes from MS-DOS systems, and this leads to some additional confusion. The physical "first sector" on a hard drive is not the operating-system boot sector. On a hard drive the boot sector is the first "logical" sector. The number one position on a hard drive is the master boot record (MBR). Some viral programs, such as the Stoned virus, always attack the physical first sector: the boot sector on floppy disks and the master boot record on hard disks.

Thus, viral programs that always attack the boot sector might be termed "pure" BSIs, whereas programs like Stoned might be referred to as an "MBR type" of BSI. The term *boot-sector infector* is used for all of them, though, since all of them infect the boot sector on floppy disks.

File-Infecting Viruses

A file infector infects program (object) files. System infectors that infect operating system program files (such as COMMAND.COM in DOS) are also file infectors. File infectors can attach to the front of the object file (prependers), attach to the back of the file and create a jump at the front of the file to the virus code (appenders), or overwrite the file or portions of it (overwriters). A classic is Jerusalem. A bug in early versions caused it to add itself over and over again to files, making the increase in file length detectable. (This has given rise to the persistent myth that it is a characteristic of a virus that it will fill up all disk space eventually; however, by far, the majority of file infectors add only minimally to file lengths.)

Polymorphic Viruses

Polymorphism (literally "many forms") refers to a number of techniques that attempt to change the code string on each generation of a virus. These vary from using modules that can be rearranged to encrypting the virus code itself, leaving only a stub of code that can decrypt the body of the virus program when invoked. Polymorphism is sometimes also known as "self-encryption" or "self-garbling," but these terms are imprecise and not recommended. Examples of viruses using polymorphism are Whale and Tremor. Many polymorphic viruses use standard "mutation engines" such as MtE. These pieces of code actually aid detection because they have a known signature.

Some authors have demonstrated that, in theory, polymorphic viruses cannot be perfectly detected. However, it is also theoretically true that no virus can be perfectly detected. In practical terms, polymorphic viruses present no particular problem, aside from the additional processing burden that algorithmic signature detection places on the scan.

A number of viruses also demonstrate some form of active detection avoidance, which may range from disabling of on-access scanners in memory to deletion of antivirus and other security software (Zonealarm is a favorite target) from the disk.

Virus-Creation Kits

The term *kit* usually refers to a program used to produce a virus from a menu or a list of characteristics. Use of a virus kit involves no skill on the part of the user. Fortunately, most virus kits produce easily identifiable code. Packages of antiviral utilities are sometimes referred to as tool kits, occasionally leading to confusion of the terms.

MACRO VIRUSES

A macro virus uses macro programming of an application such as a word processor. (Most known macro viruses use Visual BASIC for Applications [VBA] in Microsoft Word: some are able to cross between applications and function in, for example, a PowerPoint presentation and a Word document, but this ability is rare.) Macro viruses infect data files, and tend to remain resident in the application itself by infecting a configuration template such as MS Word's NORMAL.DOT.

Although macro viruses infect data files, they are not generally considered to be file infectors: a distinction is generally made between program and data files. Macro viruses can operate across hardware or operating system platforms as long as the required application platform is present. (For example, many MS Word macro viruses can operate on both the Windows and Macintosh versions of MS Word.) Examples are Concept and CAP. Melissa is also a macro virus, in addition to being an e-mail virus: it mailed itself around as an infected document.

Viruses contained in test or data files had been both theorized and tested prior to the macro viruses that used VBA. DOS batch files had been created that would copy themselves onto other batch files, and self-reproducing code had been created with the macro capabilities of the Lotus 1-2-3 spreadsheet program, but these were primarily academic exercises.

Macro viruses are not currently a major class of malware, and are certainly nothing in comparison to e-mail viruses and network worms. However, increasing numbers of applications have macro programming capabilities, and it is possible that macro viruses may become a problem again as the computing environment changes.

What Is a Macro?

As noted above, a macro is a small piece of programming contained in a larger data file. This differentiates it from a script virus that is usually a stand-alone file that can be executed by an interpreter, such as Microsoft Windows Script Host (.vbs files). A script virus file can be seen as a data file in that it is generally a simple text file, but it usually does not contain other data, and generally has some indicator (such as the .vbs extension) that it is executable. LoveLetter is a script virus.

Free Technology to Avoid Macro Viruses

A recommended defense is MacroList, written by A. Padgett Peterson. This is a macro itself, available for both Wintel and Macintosh machines. It will list all the macros in a document. Since most documents should not contain macros, any document that does should either have a really good reason for it, or be looked at with suspicion.

E-MAIL VIRUSES (THIRD GENERATION)

With the addition of programmable functions to a standard e-mail user agent (usually Microsoft Outlook), it became possible for viruses to spread worldwide in mere hours, as opposed to months.

The "Start" of E-Mail Viruses: Melissa

Melissa was far from the first e-mail virus. The first e-mail virus to successfully spread in the wild was CHRISTMA exec, in the fall of 1987. However, Melissa was certainly the first of the "fast burner" e-mail viruses, and the first to come to wide public attention.

The virus, generally referred to as W97M.Melissa is a Microsoft Word macro virus. The name *Melissa* comes from the class module that contains the virus. The name is also used in the registry flag set by the virus. The virus is spread, of course, by infected Word documents. What has made it the "bug du jour" is that it spreads itself via e-mail.

Melissa was originally posted to the alt.sex newsgroup. At that time it was LIST.DOC, and purported to be a list of passwords for sex sites. If you get a message with a Melissa infected document, and do whatever you need to do to "invoke" the attachment, and have Word on your system as the default program for .doc files, Word starts up, reads in the document, and the macro is ready to start. Assuming that the macro starts executing, several things happen. The virus first checks to see if Word 97 (Word 8) or Word 2000 (Word 9) is running. If so, it reduces the level of the security warnings on Word so that you will receive no future warnings. In Word97, the virus disables the Tools/Macro menu commands, the Confirm Conversions option, the MS Word macro virus protection, and the Save Normal Template prompt. It "upconverts" to Word 2000 quite nicely, and there disables the Tools/Macro/Security menu.

Specifically, under Word 97 it blocks access to the Tools/Macro menu item, meaning you cannot check any macros. It also turns off the warnings for conversion, macro detection, and to save modifications to the NORMAL.DOT file. Under Word 2000 it blocks access to the menu item that allows you to raise your security level, and sets your macro virus detection to the lowest level—that is, none. Since the access to the macro security menu item is blocked, you must delete the infected NORMAL.DOT file in order to regain control of your security settings. Note that this will also lose all of your global templates and macros. Word users who make extensive use of macros are advised to keep a separate backup copy of a clean NORMAL.DOT in some safe location to avoid problems with macro virus infections.

After this, the virus checks for the HKEY_CURRENT_USER\Software\Microsoft\Office\Melissa?\ registry key with a value of "... by Kwyjibo". (The "kwyjibo" entry seems to be a reference to the "Bart the Genius" episode of the "Simpsons" television program where this word was used to win a Scrabble match.) If this is the first time you have been infected, then the macro starts up Outlook 98 or higher, in the background, and sends itself as an attachment to the "top" fifty names in each of your address lists. (Melissa will not use Outlook Express. Also, Outlook 97 will not work.) Most people have only one (the default is "Contacts"), but if you have more than one, then Out-look will send more than fifty copies of the message. Outlook also sorts address lists such that mailing lists are at the top of the list, so this can get a much wider dispersal than just fifty copies of the message/virus.

Once the messages have been sent, the virus sets the Melissa flag in the registry, and looks for it to check whether to send itself out on subsequent infections. If the flag does not persist, then there will be subsequent mass mailings. Because the key is set in HKEY_CURRENT_USER, system administrators may have set permissions such that changes made are not saved, and thus the key will not persist. In addition, multiple users on the same machine will likely each trigger a separate mailout, and the probability of cross infection on a common machine is very high.

Since it is a macro virus, Melissa will infect your NORMAL.DOT, and will infect all documents thereafter. The macro within NORMAL.DOT is "Document_Close()" so that any document that is worked on (or created) will be infected when it is closed. When a document is infected the macro inserted is "Document_Open()" so that the macro runs when the document is opened.

Note that not using Outlook does not protect you from the virus, it only means that the fifty copies will not be automatically sent out. If you use Word but not Outlook, you will still be infected, and may still send out infected documents on your own. Originally the virus would not invoke the mailout on Macintosh systems. However, infected documents would be stored, and, recently, when Outlook became available for Macs, there was a second wave of Melissa mailings.

The message appears to come from the person just infected, of course, since it really is sent from that machine. This means that when you get an "infected" message it will probably appear to come from someone you know and deal with. The subject line is "Important Message From: [name of sender]" with the name taken from the registration settings in Word. The text of the body states "Here is that document you asked for ... don't show anyone else ;-)". Thus, the message is easily identifiable: that subject line, the very brief message, and an attached Word document (file with a .doc extension to the filename).

However, note that, as with any Microsoft Word macro virus, the source code travels with the infection, and it was very easy for people to create variations of Melissa. Within days of Melissa there was a similar Excel macro virus, called "Papa."

One rather important point: the document passed is the active document, not necessarily the original posted on alt.sex. So, for example, if I am infected, and prepare some confidential information for you in Word, and send you an attachment with the Word document, containing sensitive information that neither you nor I want made public and you read it in Word, and you have Outlook on your machine, then that document will be mailed out to the top fifty people in your address book, and so forth.

How to Avoid E-Mail Viruses

It really is very simple to avoid e-mail viruses: don't double click on any attachments that come with your e-mail. We used to say not to run any programs that came from someone you do not know, but many e-mail viruses spread using the identity of the owner of the infected computer, so that is no longer any protection. Do not run anything you receive, unless you know, from some separate verification, that this person intended to send you something, and that it is something you need, and that the person sending it is capable of protecting themselves from infection.

It is also somewhat safer to use a mail program other than Outlook, since some versions of Outlook allowed attachments to run even before the user reads the message to which they are attached.

Worms (First and Third Generation)

In autumn 1988, the Internet/UNIX/Morris Worm did not actually bring the Internet in general and email in particular to the proverbial grinding halt. It was able to run and propagate only on machines running specific versions of the UNIX operating system on specific hardware platforms. However, given that the machines that are connected to the Internet also comprise the transport mechanism for the Internet, a "minority group" of server-class machines, thus affected, degraded the performance of the Net as a whole. Indeed, it can be argued that despite the greater volumes of mail generated by Melissa and LoveLetter and the tendency of some types of mail servers to achieve meltdown when faced with the consequent traffic, the Internet as a whole has proved to be somewhat more resilient in recent years.

During the 1988 mailstorm, a sufficient number of machines had been affected to impair e-mail and distribution-list mailings. Some mail was lost, either by mailers that could not handle the large volumes that "backed up," or by mail queues being dumped in an effort to disinfect systems. Most mail was substantially delayed. In some cases, mail would have been rerouted via a possibly less efficient path after a certain time. In other cases, backbone machines, affected by the problem, were simply much slower at processing mail. In still others, mail-routing software would crash or be taken out of service, with a consequent delay in mail delivery. Ironically, electronic mail was the primary means that the various parties attempting to deal with the trouble were trying to use to contact each other.

In many ways, the Internet Worm is the story of data security in miniature. The Worm used "trusted" links, password cracking, security "holes" in standard programs, standard and default operations, and, of course, the power of virus replication.

"Big Iron" mainframes and other multi-user server systems are generally designed to run constantly, and execute various types of programs and procedures in the absence of operator intervention. Many hundreds of functions and processes may be running all the time, expressly designed neither to require nor to report to an operator. Some such processes cooperate with each other; others run independently.

In the UNIX world, such small utility programs are referred to as "daemons," after the supposedly subordinate entities that take over mundane tasks and extend the power of the "wizard," or skilled operator. Many of these utility programs deal with the communications between systems. "Mail," in the network sense, covers much more than the delivery of text messages between users. Network mail between systems may deal with file transfers, the routing of information for reaching remote systems, or even upgrades and patches to system software.

When the Internet Worm was well established on a machine, it would try to infect another. On many systems, this attempt was all too easy, since computers on the Internet are meant to generate activity on each other, and some had no protection in terms of the type of access and activity allowed.

The finger program is one that allows a user to obtain information about another user. The server program, fingerd, is the daemon that listens for calls from the finger client. The version of fingerd common at the time of the Internet Worm had a minor problem: it did not check how much information it was given. It would take as much as it could hold and leave the rest to overflow. "The rest," unfortunately, could be used to start a process on the computer, and this process was used as part of the attack. This kind of buffer overflow attack continues to be very common, taking advantage of similar weaknesses in a wide range of applications and utilities.

The sendmail program is the engine of most mail-oriented processes on UNIX systems connected to the Internet. In principle, it should only allow data received from another system to be passed to a user address. However, there is a debug mode, which allows commands to be passed to the system. Some versions of UNIX were shipped with the debug mode enabled by default. Even worse, the debug mode was often enabled during installation of sendmail for testing and then never turned off.

When the Worm accessed a system, it was fed with the main program from the previously infected site. Two programs were used, one for each infected platform. If neither program could work, the Worm would erase itself. If the new host was suitable, the Worm looked for further hosts and connections. The program also tried to break into user accounts on the infected machine. It used standard password-cracking techniques such as simple variations on the name of the account and the user. It carried a dictionary of words likely to be used as passwords, and would also look for a dictionary on the new machine and attempt to use that as well. If an account was "cracked," the Worm would look for accounts that this user had on other computers, using standard UNIX tools.

Following the Internet Worm, and a few similar examples in late 1988 and early 1989, worm examples were very infrequent during the 1990s. By spring 2001, a number of examples of Linux malware had been seen. Interestingly, while the Windows viruses generally followed the CHRISTMA exec style of having users run the scripts and programs, the new Linux worms were similar to the Internet/Morris/UNIX worm in that they rely primarily on bugs in automatic networking software.

The Ramen worm makes use of security vulnerabilities in default installations of Red Hat Linux 6.2 and 7.0 using specific versions of the wu-ftp, rpc.statd, and LPRng programs. The worm defaces Web servers by replacing index.html, and scans for other vulnerable systems. It does this initially by opening an ftp connection and checking the remote system's ftp banner message. If the system is vulnerable, the worm uses one of the exploitable services to create a working directory, and then downloads a copy of itself from the local (attacking) system.

Lion uses a buffer overflow vulnerability in the bind program to spread. When it infects, Lion sends a copy of output from the ifconfig command, /etc/passwd, and /etc/shadow to an e-mail address in the china.com domain. Next the worm adds an entry to etc/inetd.conf and restarts inetd. This entry would allow Lion to download components from a (now closed) Web server located in China. Subsequently, Lion scans random class B subnets in much the same way as Ramen, looking for vulnerable hosts. The worm may install a rootkit onto infected systems. This backdoor disables the syslogd daemon and adds a trojanized ssh (secure shell) daemon.

Code Red uses a known vulnerability to target Microsoft IIS (Internet information server) Web servers. Despite the fact that a patch for the loophole had been available for five months prior to the release of Code Red, the worm managed to infect 350,000 servers within nine to thirteen hours. When a host is infected it starts to scan for other hosts to infect. It probes random IP addresses but the code is flawed by always using the same seed for the random number generator. Therefore, each infected server starts probing the same addresses that have been done before. (It was this bug that allowed the establishment of such a precise count for the number of infections.) During a certain period of time the worm only spreads, but then it initiates a DoS attack against www1.whitehouse.gov. However, since this particular machine name was only an overflow server, it was taken offline prior to the attack and no disruptions resulted. The worm changed the front page of an infected server to display certain text and a background color of red, hence the name of the worm.

Code Red definitely became a media virus. Although it infected at least 350,000 machines within hours, it had probably almost exhausted its target population by that time. In spite of this, the FBI held a press conference to warn of the worm. Code Red seems to have spawned quite a family, each variant improving slightly on the random probing mechanism. In fact, there is considerable evidence that Nimda is a descendent of Code Red.

Nimda variants all use a number of means to spread. Like Code Red, Nimda searches random IP addresses for unpatched Microsoft IIS machines. Nimda will also alter Web pages in order to download and install itself on computers browsing an infected Web site using a known exploit in Microsoft Internet Explorer's handling of Java. Nimda will also mail itself as a file attachment and will install itself on any computer on which the file attachment is executed. Nimda is normally e-mailed in HTML format, and may install automatically when viewed using a known exploit in Microsoft Internet Explorer. Nimda will also create e-mail and news files on network shares and will install itself if these files are opened.

Although Nimda would attack both servers and desktop machines, it did so through the use of a variety of vectors, and is known as a multipartite virus. The most successful "pure" worm was probably Blaster. It made a direct connection to any machine on the Internet, including desktops, since it used a vulnerability in Microsoft's DCOM function, which was enabled by default on all versions of Windows. At the height of the Blaster attacks, an unprotected machine exposed to the Internet would be infected within two minutes.

DETECTION TECHNIQUES

All antiviral technologies are based on the three classes outlined by Fred Cohen in his early research. The first type performs an ongoing assessment of the functions taking place in the computer, looking for operations known to be dangerous. The second checks regularly for changes in the computer system, where changes should occur only infrequently. The third examines files for known code found in previous viruses.

Within these three basic types of antivirus software, implementation details vary greatly. Some systems are meant only for use on stand-alone systems, while others provide support for centralized operation on a network. With Internet connections being so important now, many packages can be run in conjunction with content scanning gateways or firewalls.

String Search (Signature-Based)

Scanners examine files, boot sectors and/or memory for evidence of viral infection. They generally look for viral signatures, sections of program code that are known to be in specific virus programs but not in most other programs. Because of this, scanning software will generally detect only known viruses and must be updated regularly. Some scanning software has resident versions that check each file as it is run.

In years past, search strings were generally found during a general analysis of the code of the virus. Currently, most antivirus companies have automated systems that run suspected programs on "goat" machines, in order to assess changes made. Goat machines are sometimes created by running virtual machines inside other platforms, such as running an emulator of a Microsoft Windows computer on a Linux computer platform. In this case, even if a Windows-based virus escapes from the controls in the virtual machine, it will find itself in an unfamiliar platform, and is therefore unable to proceed further.

Scanners have generally been the most popular form of antiviral software, probably because they make a specific identification. In fact, scanners offer somewhat weak protection, since they require regular updating. Scanner identification of a virus may not always be dependable: a number of scanner products have been known to identify viruses based on common families rather than definitive signatures.

Change Detection (Integrity Checking)

Change detection software examines system and/or program files and configuration, stores the information, and compares it against the actual configuration at a later time. Most of these programs perform a checksum or cyclic redundancy check (CRC) that will detect changes to a file even if the length is unchanged. Some programs will even use sophisticated encryption techniques to generate a signature that is, if not absolutely immune to malicious attack, prohibitively expensive, in processing terms, from the point of view of a piece of malware.

Change-detection software should also note the addition of completely new entities to a system. It has been noted that some programs have not done this, and allowed the addition of virus infections or malware. Change-detection software is also often referred to as integrity-checking software, but this term may be somewhat misleading. The integrity of a system may have been compromised before the establishment of the initial baseline of comparison.

A sufficiently advanced change-detection system, which takes all factors including system areas of the disk and the computer memory into account, has the best chance of detecting all current and future viral strains. However, change detection also has the highest probability of false alarms, since it will not know whether a change is viral or valid. The addition of intelligent analysis of the changes detected may assist with this failing.

Most antivirus companies and vendors now use change-detection systems for automated assessment of viruses. The virus is allowed to run in a restricted environment such as a virtual machine, and modifications to the system are noted. Generally this information is used to create signatures for scanning programs.

Real-Time Scanning

Real-time, or on-access, scanning is not really a separate type of antivirus technology. It uses standard signature scanning, but attempts to deal with each file or object as it is accessed, or comes into the machine. Because on-access scanning can affect the performance of the machine, vendors generally try to take shortcuts in order to reduce the delay when a file is read. Therefore, real-time scanning is significantly less effective at identifying virus infections than a normal signature scan of all files.

Real-time scanning is one way to protect against viruses on an ongoing basis, but it should be backed up with regular full scans.

Heuristic Scanning

A recent addition to scanners is intelligent analysis of unknown code, currently referred to as "heuristic scanning." It should be noted that heuristic scanning does not represent a new type of antivirus software. More closely akin to activity monitoring functions than traditional signature scanning, this looks for "suspicious" sections of code that are generally found in virus programs. Although it is possible for normal programs to want to "go resident," look for other program files, or even modify their own code, such activities are telltale signs that can help an informed user come to some decision about the advisability of running or installing a given new and unknown program. Heuristics, however, may generate a lot of false alarms, and may either scare novice users, or give them a false sense of security after "wolf" has been cried too often.

Permanent Protection

The ultimate object, for computer users, is to find some kind of antiviral system that you can set and forget: that will take care of the problem without further work or attention on your part. Unfortunately, as previously noted, it has been proved that such protection is impossible. On a more practical level, every new advance in computer technology brings more opportunity for viruses and malicious software. As it has been said in political and social terms, so too the price of safe computing is constant vigilance.

Vaccination

In the early days of antiviral technologies, some programs attempted to add change detection to every program on the disk. Unfortunately, these packages, frequently called "vaccines," sometimes ran afoul of different functions within normal program which were designed to detect accidental corruption on a disk. No program has been found that can fully protect a computer system in more recent operating environments.

Some vendors have experimented with an "autoimmune" system, whereby an unknown program can be sent for assessment, and, if found to be malicious, a new set of signatures created and distributed automatically. This type of activity does show promise, but there are significant problems to be overcome.

Activity Monitoring (Behavior-Based)

An activity monitor performs a task very similar to an automated form of traditional auditing: it watches for suspicious activity. It may, for example, check for any calls to format a disk or attempts to alter or delete a program file while a program other than the operating system is in control. It may be more sophisticated, and check for any program that performs "direct" activities with hardware, without using the standard system calls.

Activity monitors represent some of the oldest examples of antivirus software, and are usually effective against more than just viruses. Generally speaking, such programs followed in the footsteps of the earlier anti-Trojan software, such as BOMBSQAD and WORMCHEK in the MS-DOS arena, which used the same "check what the program tries to do" approach. This tactic can be startlingly effective, particularly given the fact that so much malware is slavishly derivative and tends to use the same functions over and over again.

It is, however, very hard to tell the difference between a word processor updating a file and a virus infecting a file. Activity-monitoring programs may be more trouble than they are worth because they can continually ask for confirmation of valid activities. The annals of computer virus research are littered with suggestions for virusproof computers and systems that basically all boil down to the same thing: if the operations that a computer can perform are restricted, virus programs can be eliminated. Unfortunately, so is most of the usefulness of the computer.

PREVENTION AND PROTECTION TECHNIQUES

In regard to protection against viruses, it is germane to mention the legal situation with regard to viruses. Note that a virus may be created in one place and still spread worldwide, so issues of legal jurisdiction may be confused. In addition, specific activity may have a bearing: in the United States it may be legal to write a virus, but illegal to release it. However, in the first sixteen years of the existence of viruses as a serious occurrence in the computing environment, only five people have been convicted of writing computer viruses, and in all five cases the defendants entered guilty pleas. Therefore, it is as well not to rely on criminal prosecutions as a defense against viruses.

The converse, however, is not true. If you are infected with a virus, and it can be demonstrated that your system subsequently sent a message that infected someone else, you may be legally liable. Thus, it is important to protect yourself from infection, even if the infection will not inconvenience you or cause loss to your business.

Training and some basic policies can greatly reduce the danger of infection. A few guidelines that can really help in the current environment are:

- Don't double-click on attachments.
- When sending attachments, be really specific when describing them.
- Do not blindly use Microsoft products as a company standard.
- Disable Windows Script Host.
- Disable ActiveX.
- Disable VBScript.
- Disable JavaScript.
- Don't send HTML-formatted e-mail.
- Use more than one scanner, and scan everything.

There are now companies that will provide insurance against virus attacks. This insurance is generally an extensive of "business loss of use" insurance, and potential buyers would do well to examine the policies very closely to see the requirements for making a claim against it, and also conditions that may invalidate payment.

Unfortunately, the price of safe computing is constant vigilance. Until 1995 it was thought that data files could not be used to transport a virus. Until 1998 it was thought that e-mail could not be used to automatically infect a machine. Advances in technology are providing new viruses with new means of reproduction and spread. Two online virus encyclopedias (F-Secure/Data Fellows Virus Encyclopedia; Sophos Virus Encyclopedia) are in the reference list, and information about new viruses can be reliably determined at these sites.

NON-PC-PLATFORM VIRUSES

As noted, many see viruses only in terms of DOS or Windows-based programs on the Intel platform. Although there are many more PC viruses than on other platforms (primarily because there are more PCs in use than other computers), other platforms have many examples of viruses. Indeed, I pointed out earlier that the first successful viruses were probably created on the Apple II computer.

CHRISTMA exec, the Christmas Tree Virus/Worm, sometimes referred to as the "BITNET chain letter," was probably the first major malware attack across networks. It was launched on December 9, 1987 and spread widely on BITNET, EARN, and IBM's internal network (VNet). It has a number of claims to a small place in history. It was written, unusually, in REXX, a scripting system used to aid with automating of simple user processes. It was mainframe-hosted (on VM/CMS systems) rather than microcomputer-hosted, quaint though that distinction sounds nowadays when the humblest PC can run UNIX.

CHRISTMA presented itself as a chain letter inviting the recipient to execute its code. This involvement of the user leads to the definition of the first e-mail virus, rather than a worm. When it was executed, the program drew a Christmas tree and mailed a copy of itself to everyone in the account holder's equivalent to an address book, the user files NAMES and NETLOG. Conceptually, there is a direct line of succession from this worm to the social engineering worm/Trojan hybrids of today.

In the beginning of the existence of computer viruses actually proliferating in the wild, the Macintosh computer seemed to have as many interesting viruses as those in the DOS world. The Brandau, or "Peace" virus, became the first to infect commercially distributed software, while the nVIR virus sometimes infected as many as 30 percent of the computers in a given area. However, over time it has become evident that any computer can be made to spread a virus, and the fact that certain systems have more than others seems to be simply a factor of the number of computers, of a given type, in use.

CONCLUSION

Malware is a problem that is not going away. Unless systems are designed with security as an explicit business requirement, which current businesses are not supporting through their purchasing decisions, malware will be an increasingly significant problem for networked systems.

It is the nature of networks that what is a problem for a neighboring machine may well become a problem for local systems. In order to prevent this, it is critical that the information security professional help business leaders recognize the risks incurred by their decisions, and help to mitigate those risks as effectively and economically as possible. With computer viruses and similar phenomena, each system that is inadequately protected increases the risk to all systems to which it is connected. Each system that is compromised can become a system that infects others. If you are not part of the solution, in the world of malware, you are most definitely part of the problem.

GLOSSARY

Terms derived from the "Glossary of Communications, Computer, Data, and Information Security Terms," posted online at http://victoria.tc.ca/techrev/secgloss.htm.

Activity Monitor A type of antiviral software that checks for signs of suspicious activity, such as attempts to rewrite program files, format disks, and so forth. Some versions of activity monitors will generate an alert for such operations, while others will block the behavior.

Change Detection Antiviral software that looks for changes in the computer system. A virus must change something, and it is assumed that program files, disk system areas and certain areas of memory should not change. This software is very often referred to as "integrity-checking" software, but it does not necessarily protect the integrity of data, nor does it always assess the reasons for a possibly valid change. Change detection using strong encryption is sometimes also known as "authentication software."

False Negative There are two types of "false" reports from antiviral software. A false negative report is when an antivirus program reports no viral activity or presence when a virus is present. References to false negatives are usually made only in technical reports. Most people simply refer to an antivirus program "missing" a virus. In general security terms, a false negative is called a "false acceptance," or "Type II error."

False Positive The second kind of false report that an antiviral can make is to report the activity or presence of a virus when there is, in fact, no virus. False positive has come to be very widely used among those who know about virus and antivirus programs. Very few use the analogous term, "false alarm." In general security terms, a false positive is known as a "false rejection," or a "Type I error."

Heuristic In general, *heuristic* refer to trial-and-error or seat-of-the-pants thinking rather than formal rules. In antivirus jargon, however, the term has developed a specific meaning regarding the examination of program code for functions or opcode strings known to be associated with viral activity. In most cases this is similar to activity monitoring but without actually executing the program; in other cases, code is run under some type of emulation. In recent years, the meaning has expanded to include generic signature scanning meant to catch a group of viruses without making definite identifications.

Macro Virus A macro is a small piece of programming in a simple language, used to perform a simple, repetitive function. Microsoft's Word Basic and Visual BASIC for Applications (VBA) macro languages can include macros in data files, and have sufficient functionality to write complete viruses.

Malware A general term used to refer to all forms of malicious or damaging software, including virus programs, Trojans, logic bombs and the like.

Multipartite Formerly, a virus program that would infect both boot sectors and files; now refers to a virus that will infect multiple types of objects or that reproduces in multiple ways.

Payload Used to describe the code in a viral program that is not concerned with reproduction or detection avoidance. The payload is often a message but is sometimes coded to corrupt or erase data.

Polymorphism Techniques that use some system of changing the "form" of the virus on each infection to try to avoid detection by signature-scanning software. Less sophisticated systems are referred to as "self-encrypting."

Rootkit A script, set of scripts, or package of modified system programs used for gaining unauthorized root privileges (or equivalent supervisory powers) on a compromised system. Recently, media usage has expanded this definition to include any software that can hide software or processes on a system, but this usage is vague and should be avoided.

Scanner A program that reads the contents of a file looking for code known to exist in specific virus programs. Also known as a "signature scanner."

Stealth Various technologies used by virus programs to avoid detection on disk. The term properly refers to the technology, and not a particular virus.

Trojan Horse A program that either pretends to have or is described as having a (beneficial) set of features but that either instead of or in addition to that contains a damaging payload. Most frequently the usage is shortened to Trojan.

Virus A final definition has not yet been agreed on by all researchers. A common definition is, "a program that modifies other programs to contain a possibly altered version of itself." This definition is generally attributed to Fred Cohen, although Dr. Cohen's actual definition is in mathematical form. Another possible definition is, "an entity that uses the resources of the host (system or computer) to reproduce itself and spread, without informed operator action."

Wild, in the A jargon reference to virus programs that have been released into, and successfully spread in, the normal computer user community and environment. It is used to distinguish viral programs that are written and tested in a controlled research environment, without escaping, from those that are uncontrolled "in the wild."

Worm A self-reproducing program that is distinguished from a virus by copying itself without being attached to a program file, or that spreads over computer networks, particularly via e-mail. A recent refinement is the definition of a worm as spreading without user action, for example by taking advantage of loopholes and trapdoors in software.

CROSS REFERENCES

See *Authentication*; *Computer Network Management*; *E-Mail Threats and Vulnerabilities*; *Firewalls*; *Network Attacks*.

REFERENCES

F-Secure/Data Fellows Virus Encyclopedia. www.f-secure.com/v-descs (accessed May 19, 2007).

Shoch, J. F., and J. A. Hupp. 1982. The "worm" programs—Early experience with a distributed computation *Communications of the ACM*. 25(3):172–80.

Sophos Virus Encyclopedia. www.sophos.com/virusinfo/analyses (accessed May 19, 2007).

FURTHER READING

Bidgoli, H. (ed.), 2002, *Encyclopedia of information systems*. New York: Academic Press

Cohen, F. 1994. *A short course on computer viruses*, 2nd ed. New York: Wiley.

Ferbrache, D. 1992. *A pathology of computer viruses*. London: Springer-Verlag.

Harley, D., R. Slade, and U. Gattiker. 2001. *Viruses revealed*. New York: McGraw-Hill.

Highland, H. J. 1990. *Computer virus handbook*. New York: Elsevier Advanced Technology.

Hruska, J. 1992. *Computer viruses and anti-virus warfare*. 2nd ed. London: Ellis Horwood.

IBM Research Papers www.research.ibm.com/antivirus (accessed May 19, 2007)

Kane, P., 1994. *PC security and virus protection handbook*. New York: M&T Books.

Lammer, V. 1993. *Survivor's guide to computer viruses*. Abingdon, UK: Virus Bulletin.

Slade, R. M. 1996. *Robert Slade's Guide to Computer Viruses*, 2nd ed., New York: Springer-Verlag.

Slade, R. M. 2004. *Software forensics*. New York: McGraw-Hill.

Solomon, A. 1991. *PC viruses: Detection, analysis and cure*. London: Springer-Verlag.

Solomon, A. 1995. *Dr. Solomon's virus encyclopedia*. Aylesbury, UK: S&S International.

Szor, P. 2005. *The art of computer virus research and defense*. Boston: Addison-Wesley.

Tipton, H., and M. Krause (eds.). 2003. *Information security management handbook*. 4thd ed. Vol. 4, Boca Raton, FL: Auerbach.

Vibert, R. S. 2000. *The enterprise anti-virus book*. Braeside, Ontario, Canada: Segura Solutions.

Denial of Service Attacks

Qijun Gu, *Texas State University*
Peng Liu, *Pennsylvania State University*

INTRODUCTION

Denial of service (DoS) attacks have become a major threat to current computer networks. Early DoS attacks were technical games played among underground attackers. For example, an attacker might want to get control of an Internet relay chat (IRC) channel by performing DoS attacks against the channel owner. Attackers could get recognition in the underground community via taking down popular Web sites. Because easy-to-use DoS tools, such as Trinoo (Dittrich 1999), can be easily downloaded from the Internet, normal computer users can become DoS attackers as well. They sometime coordinately expressed their views by launching DoS attacks against organizations whose policies they disagreed with. DoS attacks also appeared in illegal actions. Companies might use DoS attacks to knock off their competitors in the market. Extortion via DoS attacks were on rise in the past years (Pappalardo and Messmer 2005). Attackers threatened online businesses with DoS attacks and requested payments for protection.

Known DoS attacks in the Internet generally conquer the target by exhausting its resources, which can be anything related to network computing and service performance, such as link bandwidth, TCP connection buffers, application/service buffer, CPU cycles, etc. Individual attackers can also exploit vulnerability, break into target servers, and then bring down services. Because it is difficult for attackers to overload the target's resource from a single computer, many recent DoS attacks have been launched via a large number of distributed attacking hosts in the Internet. These attacks are called "distributed denial of service" (DDoS) attacks. In a DDoS attack, because the aggregation of the attacking traffic can be tremendous compared with the victim's resources, the attack can force the victim to significantly downgrade its service performance or even stop delivering any service. Compared with conventional DoS attacks that could be addressed by securing service systems better prohibiting unauthorized remote or local access, DDoS attacks are more complex and harder to prevent. Since many unwitting hosts are involved in DDoS attacks, it is challenging to distinguish the attacking hosts and react against them. In recent years, DDoS attacks have increased in frequency, sophistication, and severity because computer vulnerabilities are increasing quickly (CERT 2006; Houle and Weaver 2001), which enable attackers to break into and install various attacking tools in many computers.

Wireless networks also suffer from DoS attacks because mobile nodes (such as laptops, cell phones, etc.) share the same physical media for transmitting and receiving signals; and mobile computing resources (such as bandwidth, CPU, and power) are usually more constrained than those available to wired nodes. In a wireless network, a single attacker can easily forge, modify, or inject packets to disrupt connections between legitimate mobile nodes and cause DoS effects.

In this chapter, we will provide an overview on existing DoS attacks and major defense technologies. The chapter is organized as follows. In the next section we present an overview of major DoS attack techniques on the Internet. We also discuss the reasons why a DoS attack can succeed and why defense is difficult. In the subsequent section, a taxonomy of DDoS attacks is discussed according to several major attack characteristics. Then we present an overview of recent DDoS defense technologies according to their deployment locations. Then we discuss DoS attacks and defenses in wireless networks according to different network layers. Finally, we present our conclusions.

OVERVIEW OF DOS ATTACKS ON THE INTERNET

In this section, we overview the common DDoS attack techniques and discuss why attacks succeed fundamentally.

Attack Techniques

Many attack techniques can be used for DoS purposes as long as they can disable service or downgrade service performance by exhausting resources for providing services. Although it is impossible to enumerate all existing attack techniques, we describe several representative network-based and host-based attacks in this section to illustrate attack principles. Readers can also find complementary information on DoS attacks in Handley and Rescorla (2006) and Mirkovic et al. (2005).

Network-Based Attacks

TCP SYN Flooding. DoS attacks often exploit stateful network protocols (Jian 2000; Shannon, Moore, and Claffy 2002), because these protocols consume resources to maintain states. TCP SYN flooding is one such attack and has had a wide impact on many systems. When a client attempts to establish a TCP connection to a server, the client first sends a SYN (synchronize) message to the server. The server then acknowledges by sending a SYN-ACK (synchronize-acknowledgment) message to the client. The client completes the establishment by responding with an ACK message. The connection between the client and the server is then opened, and the service-specific data can be exchanged. The abuse arises at the half-open state, when the server is waiting for the client's ACK message after sending the SYN-ACK message to the client (CERT 1996). The server needs to allocate memory for storing the information of the half-open connection. The memory will not be released until either the server receives the final ACK message or the half-open connection expires. Attacking hosts can easily create half-open connections via spoofing source IPs in SYN messages or ignoring SYN-ACKs. The consequence is that the final ACK message will never be sent to the victim. Because the victim normally allocates only a limited space in its process table, too many half-open connections will soon fill the space. Even though the half-open connections will eventually expire because of the time-out, zombies can aggressively send spoofed TCP SYN packets requesting connections at a much higher rate than the expiration rate. Finally, the victim will be unable to accept any new incoming connection and thus cannot provide services.

ICMP Smurf Flooding. ICMP (Internet control message protocol) is often used to determine whether a computer on the Internet is responding. To achieve this task, an ICMP echo request packet is sent to a computer. If the computer receives the request packet, it will return an ICMP echo reply packet. In a smurf attack, attacking hosts forge ICMP echo requests having the victim's address as the source address and the broadcast address of these remote networks as the destination address (CERT 1998). As depicted in Figure 1, if the firewall or router of the remote network does not filter the special crafted packets, they will be delivered (broadcast) to all computers on that network. These computers will then send ICMP echo reply packets back to the source (i.e., the victim) carried in the request packets. The victim's network is thus congested.

User Datagram (UDP) Flooding. By patching or redesigning the implementation of TCP and ICMP protocols, current networks and systems have incorporated new security features to prevent TCP and ICMP attacks. Nevertheless, attackers may simply send a large number of UDP packets toward a victim. Since an intermediate network can deliver higher traffic volume than the victim's network can handle, the flooding traffic can exhaust the victim's connection resources. Pure flooding can be done with any type of packets. Attackers can also choose to flood service requests so that the victim cannot handle all requests with its constrained resources (i.e., service memory or CPU cycles). Note that UDP flooding is similar to flash crowds that occur when a large number of users try to access the same server simultaneously. However, the intent and the triggering mechanisms for DDoS attacks and flash crowds are different.

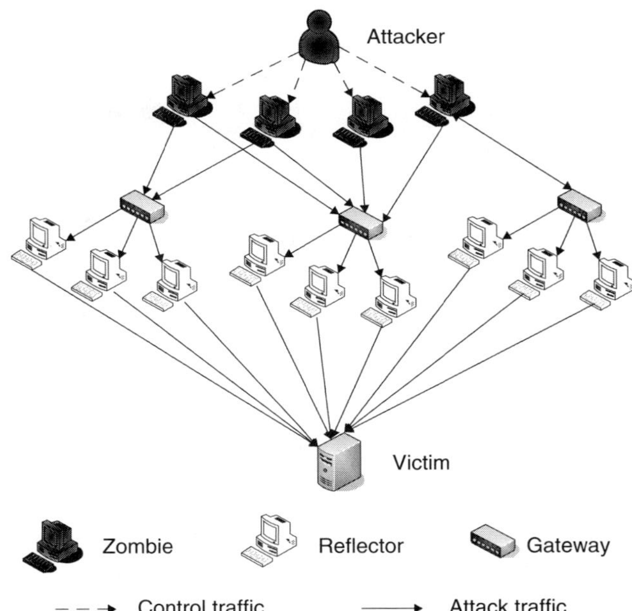

Figure 1: ICMP smurf attack

Intermittent Flooding. Attackers can further tune their flooding actions to reduce the average flooding rate to a very low level while achieving equivalent attack impacts on legitimate TCP connections. In shrew attacks (Kuzmanovic and Knightly 2003), attacking hosts can flood packets in a burst to congest and disrupt existing TCP connections. Since all disrupted TCP connections will wait a specific period (called "retransmission time out" [RTO]) to retransmit lost packets, attacking hosts can flood packets at the next RTO to disrupt retransmission. Thereby, attacking hosts can synchronize their flooding at the following RTOs and disable legitimate TCP connections, as depicted in Figure 2. Such collaboration among attacking hosts not only reduces overall flooding traffic, but also helps avoid detection. Similar attack techniques targeting services with congestion control mechanisms for quality of service (QoS) have been discovered by Guirguis et al. (2005). When a QoS-enabled server receives a burst of service requests, it will temporarily throttle incoming requests for a period until previous requests have been processed. Thus, attackers can flood requests at a

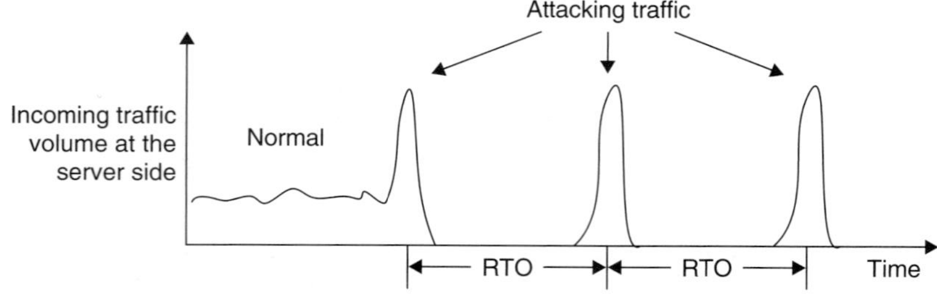

Figure 2: Low-rate intermittent flooding

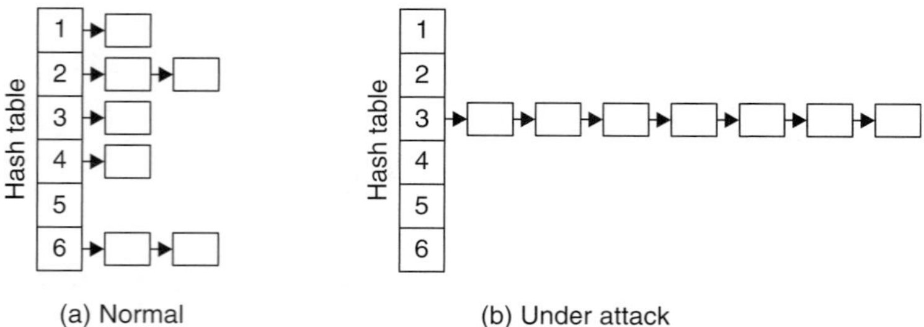

Figure 3: An example of attack against application deficiency

pace to keep the server throttling the incoming requests and achieve the DoS effect. Guirguis's study showed that a burst of 800 requests can bring down a Web server for 200 seconds, and thereby the average flooding rate could be as low as four requests per second.

Host-Based Attacks

In addition to misusing network protocols, attackers can also launch DoS attacks via exploiting vulnerabilities in target's applications and systems. Different from network-based attacks, this type of attack is application-specific—that is, it exploits particular algorithms (Crosby and Wallach 2003), memory structure (Cowan et al. 2003), authentication protocols (Dean and Stubblefield 2001, Zhang and Chen 2005), implementation (CERT 1997), etc. Attacks can be launched either from a single host as a conventional intrusion or from a number of hosts as a network based-DDoS attack. The traffic of host-based attacks may not be as high as that of network-based attacks, because application flaws and deficiencies can easily crash applications or consume a tremendous amount of computer resources. Several example attacks are described as follows.

Dean and Stubblefield (2001) identified that attackers could easily arrange an attack such that e-commerce Web sites remain available, but clients are unable to complete any purchase. Such an attack is based on going after the secure server that processes credit card payments. In such e-commerce applications, the secure sockets layer/transport layer security (SSL/TLS) protocol is used to make secure connections between clients and servers. The protocol allows a client to request the server to perform an RSA decryption. RSA decryption is an expensive operation. For instance, a large secure Web site can process a few thousand RSA decryptions per second. If a secure sockets layer (SSL) handshake request takes 200 bytes and a server can process 5000 decryptions per second, 1 MBps of requests is sufficient to paralyze an e-commerce site, which is a hard-to-notice small amount of traffic. Attackers can also send large modulo values via client certificates to increase the RSA computation per authentication. Consequently, mutual authentication cannot be done quickly and service performance is downgraded.

Researchers also found that attackers could exploit algorithmic deficiencies in many applications' data structures to launch low-bandwidth DoS attacks (Crosby and Wallach 2003). Because many frequently used data structures have an "average-case" expected running time that is far more efficient than the worst case, attackers can carefully choose inputs to produce the worst scenario in data structures. Crosby and Wallach demonstrated this kind of DoS attack against the hash-table implementations. Normally, inserting n inputs into a hash table requires $O(n)$ computation on average (Figure 3a). However, inputs could collide if they have the same hash value. Then, some applications use open addressing to solve the collision following a deterministic strategy to probe for empty hash-table entries. In the worst case, in which all n inputs collide, $O(n^2)$ computation will be required (Figure 3b). Crosby and Wallach found that attackers can easily figure out such collision inputs in some hash algorithms, and demonstrated that attackers could bring down two versions of Perl, the Squid Web proxy, and the Bro intrusion-detection system via inputting strings that collide to crash the critical hash tables in these applications.

Attack Network

Many recent DoS attacks (also called "DDoS attacks") were launched from distributed attacking hosts. A DDoS attack is launched in two phases. First, an attacker builds an attack network that is distributed and consists of thousands of compromised computers (called zombies, bots, or attacking hosts). Then, the attacking hosts flood a tremendous volume of traffic towards victims either under the command of the attacker or automatically.

To build an attack network, the attacker looks for computers that are poorly secured, such as those not having

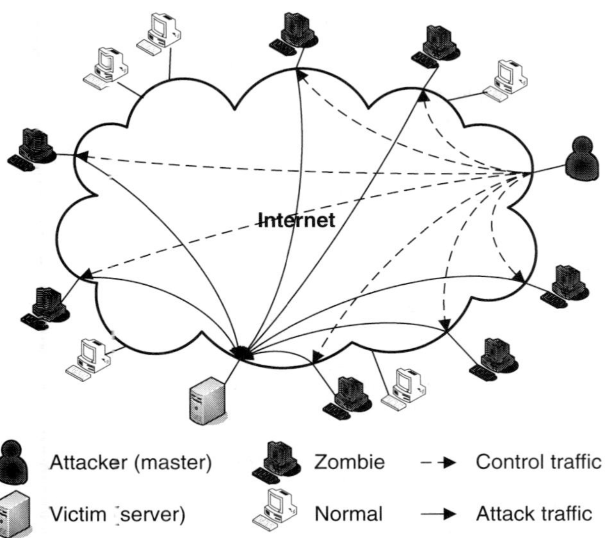

Figure 4: Attack network (botnet)

been properly patched. In general, a vulnerable host can be compromised via two types of approaches. One is to entice users to run malicious programs, such as a virus, a spyware, or a Trojan horse carried in malicious e-mails, files, or Web pages. The other approach is via automated malicious programs, such as worms that can automatically scan vulnerable remote computers. The vulnerability in these computers is then exploited to allow the attacker to break into and install DoS attacking programs that further scan other hosts, install backdoors, and flood packets. The attacker is thus called the master of these compromised computers (zombies). Some DoS programs have the ability to register the compromised computer as a member in the attack network controlled by the attacker. In addition, the newly compromised computers will automatically repeat the scanning and exploiting process to look for other vulnerable computers. Because of the self-propagation, a large attack network can quickly be built to include hundreds or thousands of computers.

A botnet (Honeynet 2005) is an example of attack networks (depicted in Figure 4) in which an attacker controls a large number of zombies. In the attack network, zombies are called "bots." They can be used to scan and subvert other vulnerable computers to new bots. They can communicate with the attacker and synchronize their actions via covert channels. For instance, Internet relay chat (IRC) is a legitimate communication service, and the attacker sends commands via an IRC channel to control the zombies. Nevertheless, the attacker usually disguises his control packets as legitimate chat traffic. The discovery of a zombie may not reveal the identification of other zombies or the attacker. To further avoid discovery, the attacker can frequently switch IRC channels. In addition, because IRC service is maintained in a distributed manner, an IRC server can host a particular IRC channel anywhere in the world. Investigation in the IRC channel thus faces many practical issues.

MyDoom virus provides another example of building such a DoS attack network (CERT 2004). Different from botnets, the attack network was not solely built through technological vulnerabilities. One variant of MyDoom could coax computer users into executing a malicious program that was sent either as an e-mail attachment or as a file downloaded from a peer-to-peer (P2P) network. The attacking program in compromised computers was designed to automatically and simultaneously flood toward www.sco.com on February 1, 2004, and www.microsoft.com on February 3, 2004.

Why a DoS/DDoS Attack May Succeed

The design of the Internet is one of the fundamental reasons for successful DoS attacks. The Internet is designed to run end-to-end applications. Routers are expected to provide the best-effort packet forwarding, while the sender and the receiver are responsible for achieving desired service guarantees such as quality of service and security. Accordingly, different amounts of resources are allocated to different roles. Routers are designed to handle large throughput that leads to the design of high-bandwidth pathways in the intermediate network. On the contrary, end hosts may be assigned only as much bandwidth as they need for their own applications. Consequently, each end host has less bandwidth than do routers. Attackers can misuse the abundant resources in routers for delivery of numerous packets to a target.

The control and management of the Internet is distributed. Each component network is run according to local policies designed by its owners. No deployment of security mechanisms or security policy can be globally enforced. Because DoS attacks are commonly launched from systems that are subverted through security-related compromises, the susceptibility of the victim to DoS attacks depends on the state of security on the rest of the global Internet, regardless of how well the victim may be secured. Furthermore, it is often impossible to investigate cross-network traffic behaviors in such a distributed management. If one party in a two-way communication (sender or receiver) misbehaves, it can cause arbitrary damage to its peer. No third party will step in to stop it.

The design of the Internet also hinders the advancement of DDoS defenses. Many solutions have been proposed to require routers and source networks, together with victims, to participate in constructing a distributed and coordinated defense system. However, the Internet is administered in a distributed manner. Besides the difference of individual security policies, many entities (source networks and routers) in the Internet may not directly suffer from DDoS attacks. Hence, they may not have enough incentive to provide their own resources in the cooperative defense system.

Finally, the scale of the Internet requires more effort to get a defense system benchmark and test bed to evaluate and compare proposed defense technologies. Defense systems should be evaluated with large-scale experiments, data should be collected from extensive simulations, and cooperation is indispensable among different platforms and networks. Researchers, industries, and the U.S. government are trying to develop a large-scale cyber security test bed (DETER 2005) and design benchmarking suites and measurement methods (EMIST 2005) for security systems evaluation.

TAXONOMY OF DOS/DDOS ATTACKS ON THE INTERNET

In this section, DoS attacks are classified based on the material presented by Mirkovic and Reiher (2004). Interested readers can obtain further information on DDoS attacks from Mirkovic et al.'s (2005) book. The classification is according to the major characteristics of DDoS attacks: (1) how attackers (or zombies) scan vulnerable computers, (2) how attack packets are spoofed, (3) what attack targets are, and (4) what attack impacts are.

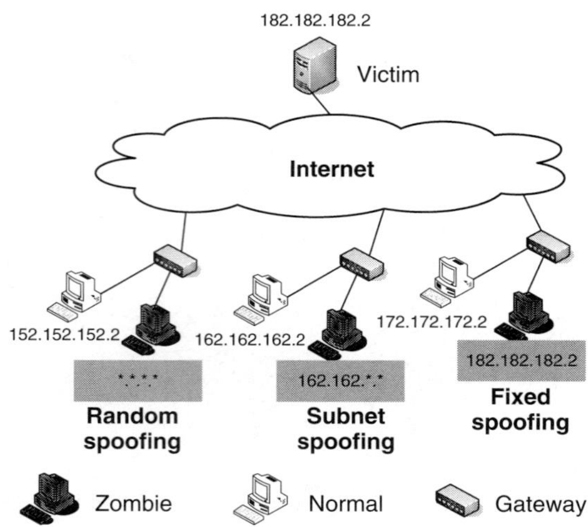

Figure 5: Source-address spoofing

Scanning

In the past, an attacker manually scanned remote computers for vulnerability and installed attack programs. Now, the scanning has been automated by worms (Staniford, Paxson, and Weaver 2002) to help attackers quickly probe potentially vulnerable computers. Attackers can also control the scanning behavior to find vulnerable computers in a slow and stealthy manner. Worm scanning may have secondary impacts on address resolution protocol (ARP) (CISCO 2001) and multicast (Hamadeh et al. 2005) because of high router CPU utilization and memory demand.

Random Scanning

In random scanning, each compromised computer probes random addresses in either global or local IP address space. Because scanning attempts are not synchronized among attacking hosts, there are often duplicate probes to the same addresses. Thereby, a high volume of scanning traffic may be present, especially when most of the vulnerable computers on the Internet are infected.

Hitlist Scanning

A compromised computer performs hitlist scanning according to an externally supplied list. When it detects a vulnerable computer, it sends a portion of the hitlist to the recipient. A complete hitlist allows an attacker to infect the entire susceptible population within 30 seconds (Staniford et al. 2002). Nevertheless, the hitlist needs to be assembled in advance via other reconnaissance and scanning approaches. In addition, the list might be long. Thus, the transmission of the hitlist between two hosts might create a high volume of traffic.

Signpost Scanning

Signpost scanning takes advantage of habitual communication patterns of the compromised host to select new targets. E-mail worms use the information from the address books of compromised machines for their propagation. A Web-based worm could be propagated by infecting every vulnerable client that clicks on the server's Web page. Signpost scanning does not generate a high traffic load. The drawback is that the propagation speed depends on user behavior and is not controllable by the attacker.

Permutation Scanning

This type of scanning requires all compromised computers to share a common pseudo-random permutation of the IP address space, and each IP address is mapped to an index in this permutation. Permutation scanning is preceded by a small-hitlist scanning. A computer infected in the hitlist then scans through the permutation, starting with its IP address. A computer compromised by permutation scanning starts from a random point in the permutation. Whenever a scanning host sees an already-infected machine, it chooses a new random starting point. The scanning host will become dormant to avoid collision after encountering some threshold number of infected hosts. The analysis (Staniford et al. 2002) shows that the propagation speed could be on the order of 15 minutes if a 10,000-entry hitlist is used and a worm generates 100 scans per second. As infection progresses, a large percentage of infected machines become dormant, which hinders detection because of the low duplicate scans.

Spoofing

Spoofing techniques define how the attacker chooses the spoofed source address in its attack packets. Spoofing attackers can choose one of three approaches, as depicted in Figure 5.

Random Spoofing

Attackers can spoof random source addresses in attack packets, since this can simply be achieved by generating random 32-bit numbers and stamping packets with them. Attackers may also choose more sophisticated spoofing techniques, such as subnet spoofing, to defeat some anti-spoofing firewalls and routers using ingress filtering (Ferguson and Senie 1998) and route-based filtering (Li et al. 2002).

Subnet Spoofing

In subnet spoofing, the attacker spoofs a random address within the address space of the sub-network. For example, a computer in a C-class network could spoof any address with the same prefix. It is impossible to detect this type of spoofing anywhere on the Internet. Subnet spoofing is useful for the attackers that compromise machines on networks running ingress filtering. A possible defense against this type of spoofing is to bind the IP address, the media access control (MAC) address, and the network port of each computer in the subnetwork.

Fixed Spoofing

Different from the other two spoofing techniques, the spoofed address is the address of the target. For example, an attacker performing a smurf attack spoofs the victim's address so that ICMP ECHO packets will be reflected to the victim.

Target

Although most DoS attacks work via exhausting resources, the actual target for which to deny services varies. The target could be the server application, the network access, or the network infrastructure.

Server Application

An application attack targets a given application on the victim (normally a server), thus disabling legitimate clients to use the service and possibly tying up resources of the host machine. Nevertheless, if the victim can well separate the resources for different applications, other applications and services in the victim should still be accessible to users. For example, a signature attack on an authentication server can send a large volume of authentication requests to exhaust the victim's resources of the signature verification and thus bring down the service. Nevertheless, if the victim can separate resources for applications, the victim can still have resources for other applications that do not require authenticated access. Consequently, the victim may need to enforce defense in each application, instead of only in its network access or its operating system.

Network Access

This type of attack disables access to the victim's computer or network by crashing it or overloading its communication mechanism. An example of this type of attack is the UDP flooding attack. All attack packets carry the destination address of the target host without concerning the content of the target service. The high packet volume consumes network resources of the victim. At the same time, the attack traffic in fact facilitates detection, but the host cannot defend against these attacks alone. It must request help from some upstream routers and firewalls.

Infrastructure

Infrastructure attacks target some critical services that are crucial for global Internet operation. Examples include the attacks on domain name servers, core routers, certificate servers, etc. The key feature of these attacks is not the attack mechanism, but the attack target and the attack impact.

Impact

Depending on the impact of a DDoS attack on the victim, the attacks are classified as disruptive and degrading.

Disruptive

The objective of disruptive attacks is to completely stall or crash the victim's service. For instance, the victim network is completely congested under attack, or the victim server crashes or halts under attack. Consequently, clients cannot access the service.

Degrading

The objective of degrading attacks is to consume some portion of a victim's resources to seriously downgrade the service performance. For example, an attack sends a high volume of authentication requests that can significantly consume computing resources in the target server. This attack can slow down the service response to legitimate customers. If customers are dissatisfied with the service quality, they may change their service provider.

DDOS DEFENSES ON THE INTERNET

In this section, we provide an overview of products that have been deployed with an emphasis on their functionalities and principles. Then, we will focus our discussion on recent defense technologies proposed by researchers, and categorize them according to where they could be deployed.

Defense Technologies in Deployment

In response to DDoS attacks, a variety of commercial products have been developed and deployed by networking and security manufacturers, mainly including intrusion-detection systems (IDSs), firewalls, and security-enhanced routers. These devices are normally deployed between the Internet and servers so that they can monitor incoming and outgoing traffic and take appropriate actions to protect servers. Fundamental technologies inside these devices include traffic analysis, access control, packet filtering, address blocking, redundancy, etc.

IDSs typically log incoming traffic and make statistics from traffic traces. For example, CISCO IOS NetFlow (2006) can account for network traffic and usage and provide valuable information about network users and applications, peak usage times, and traffic routing. Traffic traces and statistics can be compared to baseline traffic profiles to identify potential DoS attacks. In the past, most DDoS attacks caught attention because of abnormal conditions of the victim network, such as high traffic volume targeting at a certain port, slowing down of target servers, or high dropping rates of service requests. In addition, well-known DoS attack signatures (e.g., TCP SYN flooding) can also be captured to raise alerts.

Firewalls are widely deployed in the defense against DoS attacks. With correct configurations, firewalls are used to inspect ingress and egress packets and filter unwanted packets. Firewalls allow or deny certain packets according to protocols, ports, IP addresses, payloads, connection states, etc. The information is usually defined in access-control lists and filtering rules in firewalls. Some firewalls and IDSs (CISCO PIX 500 Series Security Appliances 2006; Bro 2006) can conduct stateful inspection so that only legitimate packets for ongoing connections can be passed into networks, and only legitimate TCP connections can be established and maintained. Firewalls can also create profiles (idle duration, data rate, etc.) for connections and conduct real-time analysis to detect and forbid malicious attempts (Thomas et al. 2003). Several products (MAZU 2006, CISCO Guard DDoS Mitigation Appliances 2006) integrate intrusion detection and firewall functions, and give more DDoS-specific visibility of the network for administration. Security measures in routers can push the defense frontline further away from the target, so that internal networks will not be directly impacted by DDoS flooding traffic. Similar to firewalls, many routers have access-control lists, and can filter or rate-limit traffic. Routers can quickly filter packets having bogus and unwanted IP addresses, while firewalls can more closely examine packet payloads.

Service providers can also increase redundancy of network and service infrastructure (Handley and Rescorla 2006). Service content can be backed up in redundant servers. When a server fails, redundant servers can take it over. Failure due to DoS attacks, in this case, is the same as a regular failure. Service access points can be distributed across network as well. Since DoS attacks may target only a single network link, redundant network accesses can alternatively provide services. Nevertheless, redundancy solutions may not be as effective as expected against DoS attacks. First, redundancy asks for additional computing resources to handle incoming traffic. It could be costly for service providers to maintain enough computing resources. Second, attackers can easily find a large number of attacking agents in the Internet (refer to the section on "Attack Techniques," above) to overwhelm the capability of redundant equipments.

Although a few practical solutions and products have been deployed, many problems still exist. First, it is hard to distinguish flash crowds from flooding traffic. For example, firewalls may not prevent attacks against port 80 (Web service) of servers, because many packets are just surfing traffic to the Web sites hosted by the target servers. Second, when flooding traffic is mitigated through filtering and rate-limiting mechanisms, some portion of the legitimate traffic may also be discarded. Access-control lists may be set up on wrong information as well, because flooding packets may spoof addresses. Third, firewalls and routers can be easily overwhelmed under DDoS attack. They may be slowed down or congested. If they cannot forward incoming packets to servers, attackers also achieve DoS effects. Fourth, existing products act on their own without any control over other routers. Even if a border router or firewall has identified the upstream routers from which flooding packets are coming, it is not easy to ask the owners of upstream routers (e.g., telecom companies or Internet service providers) to throttle some specific traffic flows. Observing these problems, researchers have proposed quite a few DDoS defense technologies. In the following, we present them according to the location where they could be deployed.

Attacker-Side Defenses

Since source address spoofing plays an important role in DDoS attacks, restricting the source address of the traffic to known prefixes is a straightforward idea. Ingress filtering is a representative technique (Ferguson and Senie 1998) based on this idea. As depicted in Figure 5, an attacker resides within a C-class network 152.152.152.0/24. The gateway of the network, which provides connectivity to the attacker's network, allows only traffic originating from source addresses with the 152.152.152.0/24 prefix, while prohibiting an attacker from using "invalid" source addresses that reside outside this prefix range (e.g., 192.100.201.20). This technique can well prevent random address spoofing and fixed address spoofing. The idea of filtering packets according to their source addresses is also applicable in Internet routers (Li et al. 2002; Park and Lee 2001). SAVE (Li et al. 2002) enforces routers to build and maintain an incoming table for verifying whether each packet arrives at the expected interface. Obviously, ingress filtering does not preclude an attacker using a forged source address of another host within the permitted prefix filter range (i.e., subnet address spoofing). Nevertheless, when an attack of subnet address spoofing occurs, a network administrator can be sure that the attack is actually originating from within the known prefixes that are being advertised.

D-WARD (Mirkovic, Prier, and Reiher 2002) is another technique on the attacker side that prevents the machines from participating in DDoS attacks. D-WARD monitors two-way traffic between the internal addresses and the rest of the Internet. Statistics of active traffic are kept in a connection hash table and compared to predefined models of normal traffic, and noncomplying flows are rate-limited. The imposed rate limit is dynamically adjusted as flow behavior changes, in order to facilitate fast recovery of misclassified legitimate flows and severely limit ill-behaved aggressive flows that are likely to be a part of an attack. Because of the limited size of the hash table, D-WARD can possibly discard packets of legitimate traffic during a DDoS attack in which many malicious flows are present. D-WARD also needs to be able to monitor traffic in both incoming and outgoing directions, which may be not realistic when a network has several border routers. D-WARD, similar to other attacker-side defense systems, can limit attack traffic only from the networks from which it is deployed. Attackers can still perform successful DDoS attacks from networks that are not equipped with the D-WARD system. Because attacking sources are randomly distributed, it is thus necessary to deploy attack-side defense systems in as many networks as possible so that DDoS attacks can be fully controlled at the source.

Victim-Side Defenses

Many defense systems are proposed at the victim side (Gil and Poletter 2001, Wang, Zhang, and Shin 2002) since victims suffer the greatest impact of DoS attacks and are therefore most motivated to enforce defenses. Jin, Wang, and Shin (2003) proposed hop-count filtering based on the observation that most randomly spoofed packets do not carry hop-count values that are consistent with the spoofed addresses. Thereby, time-to-live (TTL) value in packets can be used to decide if a packet is spoofed. A router decreases the TTL value of an in-transit IP packet by one before forwarding it to the next-hop. The final TTL value when a packet reaches its destination is the initial TTL subtracted by the number of intermediate hops (i.e., hop-count). However, the final TTL value that the destination can see does not directly reveal the hop-count. Fortunately, most modern OSs use only a few selected initial TTL values—30, 32, 60, 64, 128, and 255. This set of initial TTL values covers most of the popular OSs, such as Microsoft Windows, Linux, BSD, and many commercial Unix systems. In addition, few Internet hosts are apart by more than 30 hops (Cheswick, Burch, and Branigan 2000). Hence, one can determine the initial TTL value of a packet by selecting the smallest initial value in the set that is larger than its final TTL. For example, if the final TTL value is 112, the initial TTL value is 128 (i.e., the smaller one of the two possible initial values, 128 and 255). A hop-count filtering system first builds an IP-to-hop-count mapping table, and clusters address prefixes based on hop-count. With the table, the system works in two running states: alert and action. Under normal condition, the system stays in alert state, watching for abnormal TTL behaviors without discarding any packet. Even if a legitimate packet is incorrectly identified as a spoofed one, it will not be dropped. Therefore, there is no collateral damage in the alert state. Upon detection of an attack, the system switches to action state, in which the system discards IP packets with mismatching hop-counts. The inspection algorithm extracts the source IP address and the final TTL value from each IP packet. The algorithm infers the initial TTL value and subtracts the final TTL value to obtain the hop-count. The source IP address serves as the index into the table to retrieve the correct hop-count for this IP address. If the computed hop-count does not match the stored hop-count, the packet is classified as spoofed.

Hop-count filtering cannot recognize forged packets whose source IP addresses have the same hop-count value as that of a zombie, a diverse hop-count distribution is critical to effective filtering. Jin et al. (2003) found that the Gaussian distribution is a good first-order approximation. The largest percentage of IP addresses that have a common hop-count value is 10 perent. The analysis using network measurement data shows that hop-count-filtering can recognize nearly 90 percent of spoofed IP packets. The stability in hop-counts between a server and its clients is also crucial for hop-count filtering to work correctly and effectively. Frequent changes in the hop-count between the server and each of its clients can lead to excessive mapping updates. Paxson (1997) found that the Internet paths are dominated by a few prevalent routes, and about two thirds of them have routes persisting for either days or weeks. Jin et al. (2003) also made measurements and found that 95 percent of paths had fewer than five observable daily changes. Hence, the hop-count filtering approach needs to update the IP-to-hop-count mapping table daily. Hop-count filtering is designed to filter spoofed packets. It does not prevent an attacker from flooding packets with true sources and correct TTL values. Hence, it cannot protect victims from recent DDoS attacks using bots that do not necessarily spoof source addresses.

Defenses in Transit Networks

DDoS defense mechanisms deployed at the intermediate network provide infrastructural defense to a large number of Internet hosts. They usually ask routers to collaboratively monitor and exchange certain information to defend against DDoS attacks. Distributed congestion puzzle (Wang and Reiter 2004), pushback (Mahajan et al. 2002, Ioannidis and Bellovin 2002) and traceback (Yaar, Perrig, and Song 2005; Savage et al. 2000; Snoeren et al. 2001), and capability filtering (Anderson et al. 2003, Yaar, Perrig, and Song 2004; Yang, Wetherall, and Anderson 2005) techniques are representative intermediate network mechanisms.

Defenses Using Puzzles

Client puzzles have been proposed to defend against DoS attacks in TCP (Juels and Brainard 1999), SYN cookie (Bernstein 1996), authentication protocols (Aura, Nikander, and Leiwo 2000), TLS (Dean and Stubblefield 2001), graphic Turing test (Kandula et al. 2005), application traffic control (Walfish et al.2006), etc. In brief, when a client requests a service, the server first asks the client to solve a problem before accepting the service request. Then, the client needs to send an answer back to the server. Usually, solving the problem takes a certain amount of computing resources, while resource demand for verifying an answer is negligible. The server will discard service requests if either the client does not reply or the answer is incorrect. Most of these protocols involve only clients and servers in the puzzle-solving mechanisms. In contrast, Wang and Reiter (2004) proposed a distributed puzzle mechanism (DPM) to defend against bandwidth-exhaustion DDoS attacks in which routers take the main role in solving puzzles and verifying puzzle solutions. In DPM, a typical puzzle is composed of a moderately hard function (such as hash function MD5); solving the puzzle requires a brute-force search in the solution space. The hash takes three parameters: a server nonce Ns created by the congested router, a client nonce Nc created by the client, and a solution X computed by the client. The solution of the puzzle satisfies that the first d bits of h(Ns,Nc,X) are zeros. d is called the puzzle difficulty. DPM requests routers on the puzzle distribution paths to generate their own path nonces and attach them to the congestion notification during the puzzle distribution phase. By using path nonces, DPM gives different responders different puzzles (nonce sequences), thus preventing the adversary from replaying the solutions via different paths. For example, in Figure 6, R2 and R3 treat NsN1 as the server nonce and append their own nonces to the nonce sequence; R1 treats N2Na and N3Nb as the client nonces from R2 and R3. Once a link adjacent to a router is congested, the router requires the clients to solve the puzzle and thereby imposes a computational burden on clients who transmit via this router. The computation demand is tied to the bandwidth consumed by a puzzle-based rate-limiter implemented in the router.

DPM requires a participating router to keep puzzles for a period to verify solutions and prevent reusing puzzles. Hence, it might be demanding for a high-throughput router to be equipped with a large memory for keeping nonces and a fast CPU for verifying solutions. Probabilistic verification is applied to reduce the computational load of verification. Based on the arriving packet rate, a DPM router dynamically adjusts the sampling rate to selectively verify solution packets and prevents the router's CPU from being overloaded. In addition, a DPM router uses bloom filters to reduce the memory demand from 80 MB to 1 MB. Although DPM distributes computation

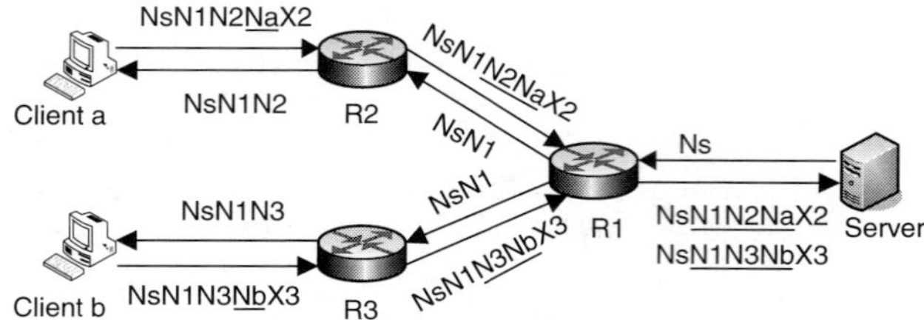

Figure 6: Distributed congestion puzzle

loads to the clients via intermediate routers, it still causes unfairness among traffic because powerful clients need less time to solve a puzzle and make a DPM router pass more traffic. DPM routers may themselves suffer from DoS attacks, because they need to maintain puzzles and status of connections. Attackers can deplete the routers' resources via flooding bogus puzzles. DPM, similar to other puzzle-solving defense approaches, is not effective in defending against connectionless flooding that does not need interaction between clients and servers.

Pushback

Mahajan et al. (2002) proposed an aggregate-based congestion-control (ACC) method that manages packet flows at a finer granularity. An aggregate is defined as a collection of packets that share some properties. ACC provides a mechanism for detecting and controlling aggregates at a router using attack signatures and a pushback mechanism to propagate aggregate control requests (and attack signatures) to upstream routers. ACC mechanisms are triggered when a router experiences sustained congestion. The router first attempts to identify the aggregates responsible for the congestion. Then, the router asks its adjacent upstream routers to rate-limit the aggregates. Since the neighbors sending more traffic within the aggregate are more likely to be carrying attack traffic, this request is sent only to the neighbors that send a significant fraction of the aggregate traffic. The receiving routers can recursively propagate pushback further upstream. As illustrated in Figure 7, assuming L0 is highly congested because of a high-bandwidth aggregate, and R0 identifies the responsible aggregate L2 and L3, R0 can then pushback to R2 and

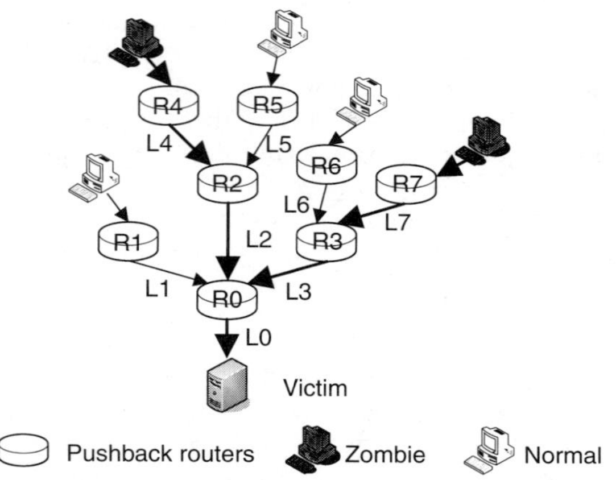

Figure 7: Aggregate-based congestion control

R3 and subsequently to R4 and R7. Therefore, traffic from L1, L5, and L6 are protected.

In pushback, the ACC mechanism divides the rate limit among the contributing neighbors. In general, the contributing neighbors do not contribute the same amount. It is challenging to determine which contributing neighbor should be rate-limited and by how much. The heuristic of ACC is that the link that carries more traffic in the aggregate is more likely to be sending attack traffic. Hence, more traffic should be dropped from it. After computing the limit for each contributing neighbor, a pushback request message is sent to them. The recipients begin rate-limiting the aggregate with the specified limit. Therefore, pushback not only saves upstream bandwidth through early dropping of packets that would be dropped downstream at the congested router, but also helps to focus rate-limiting on the attack traffic within the aggregate. Note that the enforcement of pushback will change the traffic distribution in upstream routers. Thereby, a dynamic adjustment of rate-limiting should be integrated into ACC. However, pushback routers need to be continuously deployed in the Internet. Rate-limit requests cannot be pushed back to legacy routers that do not understand the pushback approach. Pushback cannot protect legitimate traffic sharing the same path of attacking traffic either, because ACC does not distinguish traffic in the same path.

IP Traceback

Packets forwarded by routers can carry information to help victims reconstruct the attack path. Routers can add extra information as a header or an extra payload to packets so that the border router of the victim can identify the routes close to the attacking sources and ask these routers to filter flooding packets (Argyraki and Cheriton 2005). Routers can also embed information into IP headers (Dean, Franklin, and Stubblefield 2002, Savage et al. 2000, Snoeren et al. 2001, Song and Perrig 2001, Yaar, Perrig, and Song 2003, 2005; Aljifri, Smets, and Pons 2003) to help victims trace back the true attacking sources. Fast Internet traceback (FIT) (Yaar et al. 2005) has been proposed as one of the probabilistic packet-marking traceback schemes and consists of two major parts: a packet-marking scheme to be deployed at routers, and path reconstruction algorithms used by end hosts receiving packet markings. As other probabilistic marking schemes, FIT requires routers to mark the 16-bit IP Identification (IP ID) field of the IPv4 header of a small percentage of the packets that they forward. An FIT router marks a forwarded packet with a certain probability, q (0.04 for the best marking over 20 hops), which is a global constant among all FIT enabled routers. As depicted in Figure 8, FIT packet markings contain three elements: a fragment of the hash of the marking router's IP address (hash_frag), the number of the hash fragment marked in the packet (frag#), and a distance field (b). Each FIT router precalculates a hash of its IP address and splits the hash into n fragment (e.g., $n = 4$ in Figure 8). When marking a packet, a router randomly selects a fragment of its IP address hash to mark into the hash_frag field, and its corresponding fragment number into the frag# field. Then, the router also sets the five least significant bits of the packet's TTL to a global constant c, and stores the sixth bit of the

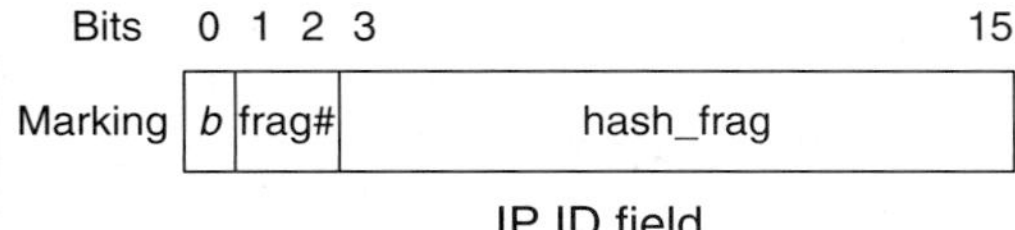

Figure 8: FIT packet marking

TTL in the distance field b. Yaar et al. (2005) shows that $c = 22$ is the best parameter for traceback. This last step allows the next FIT-enabled router, or the packet receiver, to determine the distance from the router's mark.

In FIT, an end host first computes hashes of all IP addresses, which can be done in hours. Then, the end host obtains distances and IP hashes of upstream routers from marked packets. Therefore, the end host can set up a table (map) of IP, hash, and distance of upstream routers. The map is normally constructed prior to the attack and updated according to normal incoming traffic. When an attack occurs, the end host obtains the hash segment and the distance from a marked packet to determine from which router the packet comes. FIT uses node marking instead of the commonly used edge marking (Dean et al. 2002; Savage et al. 2000; Snoeren et al. 2001). Hence, FIT avoids incrementally reconstructing the attack paths. Node marking also enables the end host to reconstruct the attack paths from much fewer packets (hundreds in contrast to thousands in edge marking). Furthermore, an FIT router does not require the next router to be an FIT router. Therefore, FIT is an incrementally deployable scheme. However, FIT does not stop an ongoing attack. When true attacking sources are identified, attacking traffic should be filtered. At the victim side, it is impossible to filter attacking packets, because they may not carry true sources. Hence, victims will need to ask routers closing to the true attacking sources to filter the attacking traffic or stop attacking hosts. Unfortunately, such a counterattack would need a complex and coordinated defense system deployed throughout the Internet.

Capability Filtering

The design principles of the Internet overlooked the receivers' capability. In many cases, routers are designed to forward packets from senders, regardless of whether or not the packets are desired by receivers. Although several aforementioned approaches (Mahajan et al. 2002; Argyraki and Cheriton 2005; Li et al. 2002) have been proposed to filter unwanted packets at upstream routers before they can consume the resources of destinations, these approaches act without knowing the allowance of destinations. As a consequence, these approaches may block legitimate traffic, because routers cannot discriminate attacking traffic from other traffic, especially when attackers can compose packets with contents of their choosing. To solve this problem, researchers proposed the approach of putting a token of capability into each data packet to prove that packets were requested by receivers (Anderson et al. 2003; Yaar et al. 2004; Yang et al. 2005). This category of filtering approaches takes two steps. First, a sender requests permission to send; after verifying the sender is valid, the receiver provides a token of capability. Then, routers along the path from the sender to the receiver can verify packets carrying the token and forward the packets with valid tokens.

In the first step (capability handshake), capabilities are obtained using request packets that do not have capabilities. A request is sent as a part of the TCP SYN packet. If the request is authorized, a token of capability is piggybacked in the TCP SYN/ACK packet. Thereby, routers are also notified of the capability. Once the sender receives the capability, the communication is bootstrapped. To identify paths, each router at the ingress of a trust boundary tags requests with a unique value (flow nonce) derived from its incoming interface. Routers not at trust boundaries do not tag requests, but fair-queue requests using their tags as unique path identities. Thereby, an attacker that composes arbitrary requests can, at most, cause contention in one queue that is corresponding to the edge router of the attacker. At the same time, request packets compromise only a small fraction of traffic. Hence, it is difficult for attackers to manipulate the capability handshake step.

Capability is bound to a specific network path, including source and destination addresses, in a specific duration. Each router that forwards a request packet generates its own precapability and attaches it to the packet. The precapability consists of a time stamp and a cryptographic hash of the time stamp, the source and destination IP addresses, and a secret known only to the router. Each router can verify for itself that a purported precapability attached to a packet is valid by recomputing the hash. The precapability is hard to forge without knowing the router secret. The destination receives an ordered list of precapabilities that corresponds to a specific network path with fixed source and destination IP end points. The destination adopts fine-grained capabilities that grant the right to send up to N bytes along a path within the next T seconds. The destination converts the precapabilities it receives from routers to full capabilities by hashing them with N and T. If the destination wishes to authorize the request, it returns the ordered list of full capability, together with N and T, to the sender. Routers along the path verify their portion of the capabilities by recomputing the hashes and the validity of time. Routers cache their capabilities and the flow nonce for verification later. For longer flows, senders should renew these capabilities before they reach their limits. Finally, all packets carry a capability header that is implemented as a shim layer above IP so that there are no separate capability packets. Regular packets have two formats: packets that carry both a flow nonce and a list of valid capabilities and packets that carry only a flow nonce. A regular packet with a list of capabilities may be used to request a new set of capabilities. A few problems might exist because of the dynamic nature of the Internet. First, routes could change. Packets in this case are handled by demoting them to low priority as legacy traffic. These packets are likely to reach the destination only when there is little congestion. Second, routes could be asymmetric, and thus capability handshake cannot be achieved and communication cannot be established. Third, the approach is not applicable when partially deployed on the Internet, because a router without implementing capability filtering still forwards as many packets as possible.

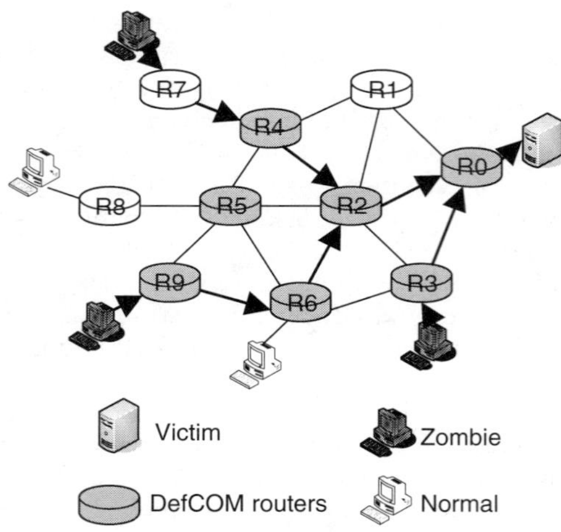

Figure 9: Architecture of DefCOM

Defenses Using Overlay Networks

Aforementioned defense technologies require homogeneous system design. However, no single defense mechanism can guarantee wide deployment, as deployment depends on market conditions and social aspects. Therefore, Mirkovic et al. (2003) proposed defensive cooperative overlay mesh (DefCOM) as a new deployment paradigm, which uses a peer-to-peer network to integrate heterogeneous systems. Nodes in DefCOM are classified as three types: alert-generator nodes that detect attacks and deliver attack signatures to the rest of the peer network; core nodes that rate-limit high-volume transit traffic-matching signatures; and classifiers that perform selective rate-limiting, differentiate between legitimate flows and attack flows, and cooperate with other defense nodes to ensure preferential service for legitimate traffic. As demonstrated in Figure 9, alert-generator node R0 detects a DDoS attack on the victim, and informs all other defense nodes through the DefCOM network. The notified nodes then identify the upstream-downstream relationship between peers and cooperate to trace out the topology of the victim-rooted traffic tree. Knowing the tree, the classifiers can differentiate legitimate traffic from attack streams and devise the appropriate rate limits to restrain the attack traffic. DefCOM allows heterogeneous systems to cooperate to achieve a better overall defense, instead of every defense system operating in isolation. Each system would autonomously perform the defense functions that it is best at and compensate for its weaker traits through cooperation with other systems. Division of work would enable nodes to become more specialized, leading to better overall performance. The wide deployment necessary to handle diffuse attacks would be achieved by incorporating existing defense nodes in the framework. As the attacks evolve, new systems could join and either replace or enhance the functionality of the old ones. Nevertheless, the design of interface in the overlay network for different defense systems to cooperate is still open.

Overlay network also provides an infrastructure to deploy distributed DDoS defense system. Secure overlay services (SOS); (Keromytis, Misra, and Rubenstein 2004) prevents DoS attacks on critical servers via an overlay network. In general, a defense system, such as a firewall, should be able to filter malicious traffic. To avoid the effects of a DoS attack against the firewall connectivity, expensive processing tasks of a firewall, such as access control and cryptographic protocol handling, are distributed to a large number of nodes in an overlay network. Thus, SOS becomes a large distributed firewall that distinguishes "good" (authorized) traffic from "bad" (unauthorized) traffic. Service requests from authenticated clients are routed to the protected servers via the overlay network, while nonauthenticated requests are filtered. Mayday (Andersen 2003) generalizes the idea of SOS and uses a distributed set of overlay nodes that are trusted (or semi-trusted) to distinguish legitimate traffic from attack traffic. To protect a server from DDoS traffic, Mayday prevents general Internet hosts from communicating directly with the server by imposing a router-based, network-layer filter ring around the server. Clients communicate with overlay nodes that verify whether a client is permitted to use the service. These overlay nodes then use an easily implemented lightweight authenticator to get through the filter ring. Within this framework, SOS represents a particular choice of authenticator and overlay routing, using distributed hash table lookups for routing among overlay nodes and using the source address of the overlay node as the authenticator. Since these overlay-based defense techniques work at the application layer, their deployment requires client systems to modify the access model of applications so that client systems are aware of the overlay and use it to access the target.

DOS ATTACKS AND DEFENSES IN WIRELESS NETWORKS

Wireless networks are taking a more important role today. As these networks gain popularity, providing security and trustworthiness will become an issue of critical importance. In this section, we discuss DoS attacks and defense in wireless networks according to the three lower network layers. Attacks at and above the transport layer in wireless network are similar to attacks on the Internet. Note that our focus is on IEEE 802.11-based wireless networks, which is a family of physical and MAC protocols used in many hotspot, ad hoc, and sensor networks.

Physical-Layer Attacks and Defenses

The shared nature of the wireless medium allows attackers to easily observe communications between wireless devices and launch simple DoS attacks against wireless networks by jamming or interfering with communication. Such attacks in the physical layer cannot be addressed through conventional security mechanisms. An attacker can simply disregard the medium access protocol and continually transmit in a wireless channel. By doing so, the attacker either prevents users from being able to commit legitimate MAC operations or introduces packet collisions that force repeated backoffs. Xu et al. (2005) studied four jamming attack models that can be used by an adversary to disable the operation of a wireless network and observed that signal strength and carrier sensing time are unable to conclusively detect the presence of a jammer. It is also found that the packet-delivery ratio may help differentiate between congestion and jamming scenarios but cannot help defenders to conclude whether poor link utility is due to jamming or to the mobility of nodes. To address the jamming attacks, Xu et al. (2005) proposed two enhanced detection protocols. One scheme uses signal strength measurements as a reactive consistency check for poor packet-delivery ratios, and the other uses location information to serve as the consistency check.

MAC-Layer Attacks and Defenses

In the MAC layer, the defects of MAC protocol messages and procedures of a MAC protocol can be exploited by attackers. Bellardo and Savage (2003) discussed the vulnerabilities of authentication and carrier sense and showed that attackers can provide bogus information or misuse the carrier sense mechanism to deceive normal nodes. For example, attackers can forge deauthentication or disassociation packets to break the connections between nodes and access points or send ready-to send (RTS) and clear-to-send packets with a forged duration to suppress the transmission of nearby nodes. Attackers can disobey the backoff procedure so that they always get the first chance to send RTS right after the end of last transmission. Gu, Liu, and Chu (2004) analyzed how the attackers can exhaust bandwidth by using large junk packets without breaking the MAC protocol. The attackers can use certain packet generation and transmission behavior to obtain more bandwidth than other normal nodes. Wullems et al. (2004) identified that attackers can exploit the Clear Channel Assessment function of the 802.11 protocol to suppress other nodes with the illusion of a busy channel. Bellardo and Savage (2003) suggested that extending explicit authentication to 802.11 control packets would be a solution to prevent attackers from easily forging the protocol control packets.

Networking-Layer Attacks and Defenses

DoS attacks in the network layer focus mainly on exploiting routing and forwarding protocols in wireless networks. In particular, ad hoc and sensor networks are susceptible to these attacks. It is also noticed that network-layer DoS attacks on wireless networks are very different from the attacks in the Internet. Because routers in wireless networks are computers that could be compromised as end hosts, network-layer DoS attacks in wireless networks can be launched by any computer in the network. In addition, DoS defense techniques on the Internet that demand the cooperation of routers are no longer valid.

Routing Attacks and Defenses

Researchers have shown that attackers can manipulate ad hoc network routing protocols (such as DSR [Johnson, Maltz, and Hu 2002] and AODV [Perkins, Belding-Royer, and Das 2002]) to break valid routes and connections (Hu, Perrig, and Johnson 2002, 2003). For example, if attackers change the destination IP address in the route request message, the victim cannot establish a route to its destination and thus cannot access services. Hence, the security of routing protocols is the solution for defending routing-based DoS attacks. In order to prevent attackers from exploiting the security flaws in routing protocols, several secure routing protocols have been proposed to protect the routing messages and thus prevent DoS attacks. For example, Hu et al. (2002) proposed to use TESLA (Perrig et al. 2002), which is a symmetric broadcast-authentication protocol, in routing discovery to secure routing protocols. When a source sends a route request, it authenticates the request with its own TESLA to prevent attackers from forging or modifying the request.

Forwarding Attacks and Defenses

Similar to routing attacks, attackers can also exploit forwarding behavior. Typical attacking approaches include injecting junk packets, dropping packets, and disorder packets in legitimate packets. Attackers can use spoofed packets to disguise their attacking behavior, or find partners to deceive defenders. The objective is to exhaust bandwidth (Gu et al. 2005) or disrupt connection (Aad, Hubaux, and Knightly 2004) so that service cannot be delivered.

To prevent attackers from spoofing and flooding packets in wireless networks, hop-by-hop source authentication is needed so that every node participates in the protection of the network. Ye et al. (2004) proposed a statistic filtering scheme that allows en route nodes to filter out false data packets with some probability. This approach will not filter packets that do not carry keys that the en-route nodes have, but will discard them at the destination. Zhu et al. (2004) proposed an interleaved hop-by-hop authentication scheme that guarantees that false data packets will be detected and dropped within a certain number of hops, although the scheme does not tolerate the change of routers. Gu et al. (2005) proposed another hop-by-hop source authentication approach with a higher overhead to ensure that a packet can be verified when a route is changed because of unreliability in wireless networks. In this approach, the routing node at which a new route diverges from the old route takes the responsibility of authenticating the packets. The routing nodes in the new route can then verify the packets based on the new authentication information.

CONCLUSION

In this chapter we presented an overview of existing DoS attacks and defense technologies on the Internet and on wireless networks. DoS attackers exploit flaws in protocols and systems to deny access of target services. Attackers also control a large number of compromised hosts to launch DDoS attacks. Simply securing servers is no longer enough to make service available under attack, since DoS attack techniques are more complicated and many unwitting hosts are involved in DoS attacks. By reviewing several existing DoS attack techniques and classifying them, this chapter highlighted challenges of DoS defense from characteristics of DoS attacks. For defenders, it is difficult to decide whether a packet is spoofed, to prevent a host from being compromised and controlled, to ask upstream routers to filter unwanted traffic, and to keep defenders themselves from DoS attacks.

This chapter reviewed current DoS defense solutions in deployment and in research. These solutions are trying to address one or several problems in DoS defense, for instance, how to distinguish legitimate traffic from flooding traffic, how to identify or trace true attacking hosts, how to filter or control flooding traffic as close as possible to attacking sources, and how to allow routers to collaborate in defense. These solutions can handle some but not all DoS attacks because of their design principles, deployment issues, etc. New DoS attack techniques may also invalidate these solutions. This chapter acknowledged these innovative ideas and provided a fundamental understanding for developing new solutions.

Different from the Internet, wireless networks have their own unique DoS attacks because wireless is an open communication approach and mobile devices can function as routers in wireless networks. DoS attacks in wireless networks extend to a scope not viable on the Internet. The existing defense approaches illustrate that security countermeasures should be studied and incorporated into wireless protocols at lower layers, and mobile hosts should actively and collaboratively participate in protecting their wireless networks.

ACKNOWLEDGMENT

Peng Liu was supported in part by NSF and DHS through NRT-0335241.

GLOSSARY

Access control: A range of security methods to permit or deny the use of an object by a subject. An object refers to a resource in a system. A subject refers to an entity that performs actions. Access control methods decide whether a subject can access an object based on the subject's identity and a predefined access control matrix.

Ad hoc network: A type of network that does not have an infrastructure. Normally, a host in the network should forward packets as a router even though the packets are neither originated nor destined to the host. The host can also ask other hosts to forward its packet via routing protocols.

Bot: A type of malicious program that functions as a backdoor in the host and accepts commands from its master. It is more organized than other malicious programs in that many bots often form a network via certain communication mechanisms. Such a network is called BotNet.

CTS: In an 802.11 network, a receiving computer sends a clear-to-send (CTS) packet to a sending computer to indicate the shared wireless channel is cleared for transmission and inform all other computers in the receiver's transmission range to suspend transmission to avoid collision.

DoS: A type of attack that targets disabling service, denying service access, or downgrading service performance. DoS attack techniques vary as long as the attack objective can be achieved. Many recent DoS attacks try to exhaust resources for providing services.

MD5: A cryptographic hash function designed by Ronald Rivest in 1991. The algorithm processes a variable-length message and generates a fixed-length hash output of 128 bits.

Overlay Network: A network that runs above the network layer and consists of end hosts forwarding packets as routers. The underlying communication between end hosts is unicast, even when an end host communicates with several other end hosts. The network is normally application-oriented.

RSA: A public key encryption/decryption algorithm invented by Ron Rivest, Adi Shamir and Leonard Adleman in 1977. RSA are the initials of their last names.

RTS: In an 802.11 network, a sending computer sends a ready-to-send (RTS) packet to inform a receiving computer that a data packet is ready for transmission. The RTS packet is used for competing the wireless transmission channel that is shared with other computers.

Scan: In a network, scanning refers to a technique in which a computer sends a number of packets with various destination addresses and then gathers information of computers at the destination addresses according to received response packets.

Spoof: A technique to replace the originator's identity with another identity. Normally, in a network attack, an attacker puts another (any) address as the source address field in the IP header of an attack packet.

TTL: Time-To-Live field in the IP header of a packet. It is decremented by a router when the packet goes through it. It is used to prevent the packet from staying forever in the Internet because the packet will be discarded when its TTL is reduced to 0.

Worm: A type of malicious program that can be propagated by itself from one infected host to another vulnerable host. When a host is infected by a worm, the worm starts to scan other vulnerable hosts. Once a vulnerable host is found, it compromises the host by exploiting the vulnerability, and copies its code to the host. Then, the worm in the new infected host starts its own propagation.

CROSS REFERENCES

See *Authentication*; *Computer Network Management*; *Firewalls*; *Intrusion Detection Systems*; *Network Attacks*.

REFERENCES

Aad, I., J. P. Hubaux, and E. Knightly. 2004. Denial of service resilience in ad hoc networks. In *Proceedings of ACM Mobicom*. New York: ACM Press.

Aljifri, H., M. Smets, and A. Pons. 2003. IP traceback using header compression. *Computers & Security*, 22(2):136–51.

Andersen, D. G. 2003. Mayday: Distributed filtering for Internet services. In *Proceedings of the 4th USENIX Symposium on Internet Technologies and Systems*. Berkeley, CA: USENIX Press.

Anderson, T., T. Roscoe, and D. Wetherall. 2003. Preventing Internet denial of service with capabilities. In *Proceedings of HotNets-II*. New York: ACM Press.

Argyraki, K., and D. R. Cheriton. 2005. Active Internet traffic filtering: Real-time response to denial-of-service attacks. In *Proceedings of the USENIX Annual Technical Conference*. Berkeley, CA: USENIX Press.

Aura, T., P. Nikander, and J. Leiwo. 2000. DoS-resistant authentication with client puzzles. *Proceedings of Security Protocols Workshop, Lecture Notes in Computer Science*, 213(33):170–81.

Bellardo, J., and S. Savage. 2003. 802.11 denial-of-service attacks: real vulnerabilities and practical solutions. In *Proceedings of USENIX Security Symposium*, 15–28. Berkeley, CA: USENIX Press.

Bernstein, D. J. 1996. SYN cookies. http://cr.yp.to/syncookies.html (accessed October 31, 2006).

Bro. 2006. Bro Intrusion Detection System. http://bro-ids.org/ (accessed October 31, 2006).

CERT. 1996. CERT Advisory CA-1996-21 TCP SYN flooding and IP spoofing attacks. www.cert.org/advisories/CA-1996-21.html (accessed January 2, 2006).

CERT. 1997. CERT Advisory CA-1997-28 IP Denial-of-Service Attacks. www.cert.org/advisories/CA-1997-28.html (accessed August 20, 2006).

CERT. 1998. CERT Advisory CA-1998-01 Smurf IP denial-of-service attacks. www.cert.org/advisories/CA-1998-01.html (accessed January 2, 2006).

CERT. 2004. Technical Cyber Security Alert TA04-028A, W32/MyDoom.B virus. www.us-cert.gov/cas/techalerts/TA04-028A.html (accessed January 2, 2006).

CERT. 2006. CERT/CC Statistics 1988–2005. www.cert.org/stats/#incidents (accessed January 2, 2006).

Cheswick, B., H. Burch, and S. Branigan. 2000. Mapping and visualizing the internet. In *Proceedings of USENIX Annual Technical Conference*. Berkeley, CA: USENIX Press.

CISCO. 2001. Dealing with malloc fail and high CPU utilization resulting from the code red worm. www.cisco.com/warp/public/63/ts_codred_worm.shtml (accessed April 15, 2006).

CISCO. (2006). CISCO IOS NetFlow. www.cisco.com/en/US/products/ps6601/products_ios_protocol_group_home.html (accessed August 20, 2006).

CISCO. (2006). CISCO PIX 500 Series Security Appliances. www.cisco.com/en/US/products/hw/vpndevc/ps2030/index.html (accessed August 20, 2006)

CISCO. (2006). Cisco Guard DDoS Mitigation Appliances. www.cisco.com/en/US/products/ps5888/index.html (accessed August 20, 2006).

Cowan, C., S. Beattie, J. Johansen, and P. Wagle. 2003. PointGuard: Protecting pointers from buffer overflow vulnerabilities. In *Proceedings of the 12th USENIX Security Symposium*. Berkeley, CA: USENIX Press

Crosby, S. A., and D. S. Wallach. 2003. Denial of service via algorithmic complexity attacks. In *Proceedings of the 12th USENIX Security Symposium*, 29–44. Berkeley, CA: USENIX Press.

Dean, D., and A. Stubblefield. 2001. Using client puzzles to protect TLS. In *Proceedings of the 10th Annual USENIX Security Symposium*. Berkeley, CA: USENIX Press.

Dean, D., M. Franklin, and A. Stubblefield. 2002. An algebraic approach to IP traceback. *ACM Transactions on Information and System Security*, 5(2):119–37.

DETER 2005. Cyber Defense Technology Experimental Research. www.isi.edu/deter (accessed January 2, 2006).

Dittrich, D. 1999. The DoS Project's "trinoo" distributed denial of service attack tool. http://staff.washington.edu/dittrich/misc/trinoo.analysis (accessed January 2, 2006).

EMIST. 2005. Evaluation methods for Internet security technology. www.isi.edu/deter/emist.temp.html (accessed January 2, 2006).

Ferguson, P., and D. Senie. 1998. RFC 2267—Network ingress filtering: Defeating denial of service attacks which employ IP source address spoofing. www.faqs.org/rfcs/rfc2267.html (accessed January 2, 2006)

Gil, T. M., and M. Poletter. 2001. Multops: A data-structure for bandwidth attack detection. In *Proceedings of USENIX Security Symposium*. Berkeley, CA: USENIX Press.

Gu, Q., P. Liu, and C. Chu. 2004. Tactical bandwidth exhaustion in ad hoc networks. In *Proceedings of the 5th Annual IEEE Information Assurance Workshop*, 257–64. New York: IEEE Press.

Gu, Q., P. Liu, S. Zhu, and C. H. Chu. 2005. Defending against packet injection attacks in unreliable ad hoc networks. *Proceedings of IEEE Globecom*. New York: IEEE Press.

Guirguis, M., A. Bestavros I. Matta and Y. Zhang. 2005. Reduction of quality (RoQ) attacks on Internet end systems. *Proceedings of INFOCOM*. New York: IEEE Press.

Hamadeh, I., J. Hart, G. Kesidis, and V. Pothamsetty. 2005. A preliminary simulation of the effect of scanning worm activity on multicast. In *Proceedings of the 19th Workshop on Principles of Advanced and Distributed Simulation*. Washington, DC: IEEE Computer Society.

Handley, M. and E. Rescorla. 2006. Internet denial of service considerations. http://tools.ietf.org/html/draft-iab-dos-05 (accessed October 31, 2006).

Honeynet 2005. Know your enemy: Tracking botnets. www.honeynet.org/papers/bots/ (accessed January 2, 2006).

Houle, K. J., and G. M. Weaver. 2001. Trends in denial of service attack technology. www.cert.org/archive/pdf/DoS_trends.pdf (accessed January 2, 2006).

Hu, Y. C., A Perrig, and D. B. Johnson. 2002. Ariadne: a secure on-demand routing protocol for ad hoc networks. In *Proceedings of ACM Mobicom*, 12–23. New York: ACM Press.

Hu, Y. C., A Perrig, and D. B. Johnson. 2003. SEAD: Secure efficient distance vector routing for mobile wireless ad hoc networks. *Ad Hoc Networks* 1(1):175–92.

Ioannidis, J., S. M. Bellovin. 2002. Implementing pushback: Router-based defense against DDoS attacks. In *Proceedings of NDSS*. Reston, VA: The Internet Society.

Jian, W. 2000. A possible LAST_ACK DoS attack and fix. www.ussg.iu.edu/hypermail/linux/kernel/0004.1/0105.html (accessed October 31, 2006).

Jin, C., H. Wang, and K. G. Shin. (2003). Hop-count filtering: an effective defense against spoofed DDoS traffic. In *Proceedings of ACM CCS*, 30–41. New York: ACM Press.

Johnson, D. B., D. A. Maltz, and Y-C. Hu. 2002. The dynamic source routing protocol for mobile ad hoc networks (DSR). www3.ietf.org/proceedings/04mar/I-D/draft-ietf-manet-dsr-09.txt (accessed May 23, 2007).

Juels, A., and J. Brainard. 1999. Client puzzle: A cryptographic defense against connection depletion attacks. In *Proceedings of NDSS*, 151–65. Reston, VA: The Internet Society.

Kandula S., D. Katabi, M. Jacob, and A. Berger. 2005. Botz-4-Sale: Surviving organized DDoS attacks that mimic flash crowds. In *Proceedings of the 2nd Symposium on Networked Systems Design and Implementation*. Berkeley, CA: USENIX Press.

Keromytis, A. D., V. Misra, and D. Rubenstein. 2004. SOS: An architecture for mitigating DDoS attacks. *IEEE Journal on Selected Areas of Communications*, 33(3):413–26.

Kuzmanovic, A., and E. W. Knightly. 2003. Low-rate TCP-targeted denial of service attacks. *Proceedings of ACM SIGCOMM*, 75–86. New York: ACM Press.

Li, J., J. Mirkovic, M. Wang, P. Reiher, and L. Zhang. 2002. Save: Source address validity enforcement protocol. *Proceedings of IEEE Infocom* 3: 1557–66.

Mahajan, R., S. M. Bellovin, S. Floyd, J. Ioannidis, V. Paxson, and S. Shenker. 2002. Controlling high bandwidth aggregates in the network. *ACM SIGCOMM Computer Communications Review* 32(3):62–73.

MAZU. 2006. MAZU Enforcer. www.mazunetworks.com/products/mazu-enforcer.php. (accessed January 2, 2006).

Mirkovic, J., G. Prier, and P. Reiher. 2002. Attacking DDoS at the source. *Proceedings of IEEE ICNP*, 312–21. New York: IEEE Press.

Mirkovic, J., M. Robinson, P. Reiher, and G. Kuenning. 2003. Alliance formation for DDoS defense. In *Proceedings of the New Security Paradigms Workshop in ACM SIGSAC*. New York: ACM Press.

Mirkovic, J., and P. Reiher, 2004. A taxonomy of DDoS attack and DDoS defense mechanisms. *ACM SIGCOMM Computer Communication Review* 34(2):39–53.

Mirkovic, J., S. Dietrich, D. Dittrich, and P. Reiher. 2005. *Internet denial of service: Attack and defense mechanisms*. Upper Saddle River, NJ: Prentice Hall.

Pappalardo, D., and E. Messmer. 2005. Extortion via DDoS on the rise. www.techworld.com/security/features/index.cfm?featureid=1452 (accessed October 31, 2006).

Park, K., and H. Lee. 2001. On the effectiveness of route-based packet filtering for distributed DoS attack prevention in power-law Internets. In *Proceedings of ACM SI*. New York: ACM Press.

Paxson, V. 1997. End-to-end routing behavior on the Internet. *IEEE/ACM Transactions on Networking*, 5(5).

Perkins, C.E., E.M. Belding-Royer, and S. R. Das. 2002. Ad hoc on-demand distance vector (AODV) routing. http://tools.ietf.org/html/draft-ietf-manet-aodv-11 (accessed May 23, 2007).

Perrig, A., R. Canetti, D. Tygar, and D. Song. 2002. The TESLA broadcast authentication protocol. *Cryptobytes*, 5(2):2–13.

Savage, S., D. Wetherall, A. Karlin, and T. Anderson. 2000. Practical network support for IP traceback. In *Proceedings of ACM SIGCOMM*, 295–306. New York: ACM Press.

Shannon, C., D. Moore, and K.C. Claffy, 2002. Beyond folklore: Observations on fragmented traffic. *IEEE/ACM Transactions on Networking*, 10(6):709–20.

Snoeren, A. C., C. Partridge, L. A. Sanchez, C. E. Jones, F. Tchakountio, S. T. Kent, and W. T. Strayer. 2001. Hash-based IP traceback. In *Proceedings of ACM SIGCOMM*. New York: ACM Press.

Song, D., and A. Perrig. 2001. Advanced and authenticated marking schemes for IP traceback. In *Proceedings of IEEE INFOCOM*. New York: IEEE Press.

Staniford, S., V. Paxson, and N. Weaver. 2002. How to own the internet in your spare time. In *Proceedings of the 11th USENIX Security Symposium*, 207–13. Berkeley, CA: USENIX Press.

Thomas, R., B. Mark, T. Johnson, and J. Croall. 2003. NetBouncer: Client-legitimacy-based high-performance DDoS filtering. In *Proceedings of DARPA Information Survivability Conference and Exposition*, 1:14.

Walfish M., M. Vutukuru, H. Balakrishnan, D. Karger, and S. Shenker. 2006. DoS defense by offense. In *Proceedings of ACM SIGCOMM*. New York: ACM Press.

Wang, H., D. Zhang, and K. G. Shin. 2002. Detecting SYN flooding attacks. In *Proceedings of IEEE Infocom*. New York: IEEE Press.

Wang, X., and M. K. Reiter. 2004. Mitigating bandwidth-exhaustion attacks using congestion puzzles. In *Proceedings of ACM CCS*, 257–67. New York: ACM Press.

Wullems, C., K. Tham, J. Smith, and M. Looi. 2004. Technical summary of denial of service attack against IEEE 802.11 DSSS based wireless LANs. www.isi.qut.edu.au/research/publications/technical/wlan.php (accessed January 2, 2006).

Xu, W., W. Trappe, Y. Zhang, and T. Wood. 2005. The feasibility of launching and detecting jamming attacks in wireless networks. In *Proceeding of ACM Mobihoc*, 46–57. New York: ACM Press.

Yaar, A., A. Perrig, and D. Song. 2003. Pi: A path identification mechanism to defend against DoS attacks. In *Proceedings of IEEE Symposium on Security and Privacy*. New York IEEE Press.

Yaar, A., A. Perrig, and D. Song. 2004. SIFF: A stateless internet flow filter to mitigate DDoS flooding attacks. In *Proceedings of IEEE Symposium on Security and Privacy*. New York: IEEE Press.

Yaar, A., Perrig, A., and Song, D. 2005. FIT: Fast internet traceback. In *Proceedings of IEEE Infocom*. New York: IEEE Press.

Yang, X., D. Wetherall, and T. Anderson. 2005. A DoS-limiting network architecture. In *Proceedings of ACM SIGCOMM*. New York: ACM Press.

Ye, F., H. Luo, S. Lu, and L. Zhang. 2004. Statistical en-route detection and filtering of injected false data in sensor networks. In *Proceedings of IEEE INFOCOM*. New York: IEEE Press.

Zhang, R., and K. Chen. 2005. Improvements on the WTLS protocol to avoid denial of service attacks. *Computers & Security*, 24(1):76–82.

Zhu, S., S. Setia, S. Jajodia, and P. Ning. 2004. An interleaved hop-by-hop authentication scheme for filtering false data in sensor networks. In *Proceedings of IEEE Symposium on Security and Privacy*. New York: IEEE Press.

E-Mail Threats and Vulnerabilities

David Harley, *Small Blue-Green World, UK*

INTRODUCTION

The classic IT (Information Technology) security tripod model (integrity, confidentiality, and availability) applies as much to e-mail as it does to other areas of information management, and the medium is subject to a range of security problems. Johnson (2000) categorizes these as follows:

- Eavesdropping (susceptibility to network sniffing and other breaches of confidentiality)
- Impersonation/Identity Theft. Even though well-managed organizations use authentication to regulate access to services, many e-mail-related Internet services such as Simple Mail Transfer Protocol (SMTP) are highly vulnerable to abuses such as impersonation by forging e-mail headers. Although identity theft is an ongoing and increasing problem, the rather less glamorous problems of impersonation by spam, fraudulent e-mail such as phishing, and malware remain a constant drain on resources and patience.
- Denial of service (DoS), either by deliberate action such as e-mail traffic volume attacks (mail bombing and subscription bombing, for example) or as an accidental result of inappropriate action by legitimate software or authorized users (mail loops, poorly configured filters, inappropriate mass mailing), or incidental action such as direct harvesting attacks (DHA) by spamming software. In the latter case, the intention is not normally to bring down systems deliberately, but the sheer volume of traffic may result in unavailability of services. At times, of course, there might be an intention to mount a secondary DoS attack from compromised systems, such as distributed denial of service (DDoS) attacks, often on sites with high profiles and low popularity: the W32/MyDoom@mm (Novarg) virus, for instance, attempted to launch attacks from infected machines on a number of vendor sites, including Microsoft and SCO (F-Secure 2004), and attacks on anti-spam sites are commonplace (Hypponen 2003).
- Overzealous Domain Name System (DNS) blacklists (or blocklists or poor practice in the use of such blacklists by end-sites) constitute a significant problem, amounting to a denial of e-mail service on some sites. Blacklists are a primitive form of reputation service (Harley 2006). IP addresses or ranges appear in such lists on a range of criteria: for instance, known open relays, known open proxies, sites deemed not to be compliant with RFCs (Requests For Comment), and so forth. Many sites block mail from any IP address found on blacklists to which they subscribe. However, while some blacklists are professionally conceived and administered, others are run by amateurs and vigilantes who have no particular incentive to take into account high volumes of false positives. One blacklist, for instance, has included all German addresses with a .de suffix for over a year, and has refused to address the problem. Use of professional and well-conceived blacklist and reputation services reduces the problem, but some sites continue to prefer a free service, even one with a high volume of false positives.
- System integrity may be impaired in a number of ways by e-mail attacks, notably by the transmission of and subsequent or consequent infection by malicious software.

Johnson (2000) describes a number of technologies, such as encryption, authentication, anonymity protocols, and technologies that are considered elsewhere in this book. In this overview chapter, however, we deal primarily with technologies that address direct e-mail abuse such as malicious software and spam.

SOCIAL AND ANTISOCIAL E-MAIL ISSUES

As Michel Kabay (1996) points out, there are also a number of social issues associated with e-mail use and management:

- "Flaming" (intemperate language in the heat of the moment), inappropriately targeted humor or vulgarity, gossip and other indiscretions can result in bad feeling, communications breakdowns, and even implication of the employer in libel action.

- Careless targeting of e-mail responses can result in inappropriate leakage of confidential and/or sensitive information inside and beyond the organization's perimeter.
- Relations between the employer and the employed can be damaged by unclear policies and perceived rights to individual privacy.
- End users can send unconsidered mail that puts them in breach of copyright, data protection, and other legislation that restricts how data can be used and re-used.

Many of these problems are best dealt with on a policy level, and we include a consideration of e-mail-related policy management at the end of the chapter.

Malware

A full taxonomy of malware (*Mal*icious soft*ware*) types is beyond the scope of this chapter, which considers them only in the context of e-mail transmission. Fuller taxonomical issues are addressed by Harley, Slade, and Gattiker (2001), while Thompson (2002) and Szor (2005) address specific virus taxonomies. Other chapters in this book also deal at length with other malware issues.

E-Mail and Early Viruses

Although e-mail as a virus vector is most popularly associated with recent mass mailer epidemics, viruses have actually been associated with e-mail almost since the first replicative malware.

Boot Sector Infectors (BSIs)

Most of the effective early viruses were boot sector infectors and master boot record (MBR) infectors. Some of these are still occasionally reported; however, they do not normally spread via e-mail, but when a system is booted with an infected diskette. However, it is possible to transport such viruses in dropper form or as a disk image. These methods are normally associated with intentional transfer by mutual consent, but it is not impossible or unknown for malware to use them as a direct propagation channel.

File Viruses (Parasitic Viruses)

File viruses infect files by attaching themselves to them in some way, so that when the file is run, the virus code is also run. They are far less common than in the early days, but are still found in the wild, and can be spread by e-mail. An interesting phenomenon sometimes reported is the infection of a modern mass mailer virus/worm by an older parasitic virus such as W95/CIH, perhaps better known but misleadingly renamed as Chernobyl (Symantec 2004). (There is no evidence that the date of activation of some variants is intended to coincide with the anniversary of the Chernobyl disaster.) Some types of virus such as companion viruses and cluster viruses use somewhat different infection mechanisms, but the precise mechanics need not concern us here.

File and Boot (Multipartite) Viruses

File and boot viruses, since they use both methods of infection, in many cases can, in principle, be spread by e-mail. These are often referred to as multipartite viruses, though strictly speaking this term refers to a virus that uses more than one infection method, and is not restricted to viruses that infect program files and boot sectors only (Harley et al. 2001).

Macro Viruses

Macro viruses normally infect documents: technically, they might be regarded as a special case of file virus. Most macro viruses infect Microsoft Word or Excel documents, but there are other vulnerable applications, not all of which are Microsoft Office applications. They can be multiplatform—most of the very few viruses to cause problems on Macintoshes in recent years have been macro viruses rather than Macintosh-specific malware (Harley 1997)—and some can affect more than one application. Macro viruses are particularly likely to be a problem in relation to applications that, like most Microsoft Office applications, store macros in data files rather than in separate macro files. Macro viruses are still commonly found transmitted by e-mail, but are much less prevalent than they were in the mid-to-late 1990s. However, it has been reported that targeted Trojan attacks of the kind reported in several CERT/CC advisories (CPNI 2005) frequently use attached Word documents containing malicious embedded executables.

Script Viruses

Script viruses are self-contained mini-programs in VBscript, Javascript, and so on, and are often found as embedded scripts in some form of HTML (HyperText Markup Language) file (as well as in some types of formatted e-mail). They may also be transmitted as e-mail attachments.

Mass Mailers

Mass mailers are a class of malware designed explicitly to spread via e-mail that maximize their own spread by seeking new target addresses from a victim's address book, files on an infected system, and other sources such as Web pages; these are considered at length below. They generally rely on social engineering (a term applied to a variety of attacks exploiting human weakness and gullibility rather than technological loopholes) to persuade the recipient to execute the malicious program. Recent examples of social engineering in mass mailer dissemination are included in the next section, and involve a form of impersonation on the part of the virus (the real sender of the e-mail) to dupe the recipient into thinking the attachment is safe to open, or at least interesting enough to be worth the risk.

Nearly all recent mass mailers are spoofing viruses: that is, they forge e-mail headers.

Spoofing Viruses

The term *spoofing* was formerly applied to viruses that exploit a characteristic of an antivirus program so as to hide their presence from that program. The term is now more often applied to e-mail viruses/worms that forge message headers (especially the "From:" and "Reply-to:" fields to obscure the real source of the viral e-mail, or to dupe the recipient into running the viral attachment. The term is often abbreviated to spoofer, and the antonym is non-spoofer or non-spoofing virus. Spoofing viruses often insert addresses they find in the Windows address book or elsewhere on the infected hard disk, or an address from a list carried in the body of the virus, or an address simply made up. Thus, the message arrives looking as if it were sent by person A, when it really comes from person B. This not only causes mischief by blaming the wrong person for having an infected PC, it also makes it harder to trace the owner of the system that is *really* infected. Sometimes, though, a different form of spoofing is used. A popular alternative form is for the message to masquerade as a message from a vendor (especially Microsoft!) or a system administrator, passing off the attachment as a systems or application patch, or as an important message. Yet another alternative is to disguise the message as being from someone the recipient does not know and being intended for a completely different recipient, but suggesting that the content of the attachment is something particularly interesting or desirable. Popular forms of this particular trick include suggesting that the attachment consists of erotic photographs. It may also be suggested that the attachment is a returned message from the targeted recipient to the apparent, or that it contains information pertaining to their being investigated by a law enforcement agency, or a photograph of themselves, or password information, or a mail message to them received in error by the apparent sender. Although antivirus vendor sites such as www.f-secure.com/v-descs/ (F-Secure), http://vil.nai.com/vil/ (McAfee/AVERT), and http://securityresponse.symantec.com/ (Symantec) include information about specific forms of message used by individual mass mailers such as Sobig, MyDoom, Bagle, and Netsky in order to trick the recipient into opening the attachment, it is not feasible to address all the possible social engineering tricks available to an imaginative writer of viruses and other malware.

"Traditional" mass mailers have declined in numbers in recent years. Indeed, replicative malware in general has declined in volume and impact since the beginning of the twenty-first century (Mashevsky 2005). In part, this is a consequence of the general professionalization of virus writing. Malicious software in general has become less the province of the "hobbyist" coder. Instead, it has become a major addition to the arsenal of the professional cybercriminal. However, this class of malefactor is less likely to make use of the "pure" mass mailer, intended merely to self-propagate. Instead, mass mailers are used as a means of disseminating other malware, for example by installing other malicious programs on a compromised system, or by opening a channel between the compromised system and a system hosting such programs. Such a system might be a malicious Web site or another compromised system, for instance one of the bot-infested machines on a botnet. Although botnets are not wholly or even primarily an e-mail security issue, they certainly affect messaging across several dimensions, and are discussed later in this chapter.

Network Worms

Network worms are usually distinguished from e-mail viruses, as well as from conventional viruses, by the fact that they do not attach themselves to a legitimate program, though they do replicate across networks. However, this distinction is somewhat contentious. Network worms are usually self-launching—they do not require direct user action in order to execute—and do not spread by e-mail, or not only by e-mail. (Network worms that also spread by e-mail would be better described as hybrid.) Examples include the Code Red family, Slammer, Blaster, and Welchia/Nachi. Mass mailers are also frequently referred to as worms, but are not usually self-launching, though some e-mail viruses do exploit misconfigured or unpatched mail software to execute without direct human intervention. They are, however, usually nonparasitic—that is, they do not attach to other programs, in the sense that file viruses do.

Hybrid and Multipolar Malware

Although Nimda is sometimes taken to be part of the Code Red family, it is actually a hybrid virus, a network worm that can also be spread by e-mail. Malware like this, combining multiple attack vectors, is sometimes referred to as convergent, blended, or multipolar (Harley 2002, The future of malicious code). Blended threats are a major factor in the current spread and impact of bots and botnets.

E-Mail Viruses and Worms

Most mass mailers—the type of virus most commonly encountered currently in the context of e-mail—occupy somewhat fuzzy middle ground between conventional viruses (because they replicate), worms (because they do not attach themselves to a legitimate program), and Trojans (because they trick the recipient into running malicious programs, thinking they do something desirable). In fact, there can be considerable overlap between these types. (Trojans are considered in more detail below.) Melissa, for example, was a macro virus but also one of the first effective e-mail worm/mass mailers (though claims that it was *the* first are untenable). It tricked the recipient into opening a document that then ran code, much as the CHRISTMA EXEC worm had in 1987 (Slade 1996). It infected other documents (and so can be described as a true virus), but also made use of e-mail to trick the recipient into furthering its spread. More recent mass mailers tend to rely on persuading the victim to run stand-alone code, but some also use software vulnerabilities as an additional entry point, and some mass mailers are also viruses, or drop viruses or other malware—especially Trojans such as keyloggers and backdoors—as part of the replicative mechanism.

The mass mailer problem has been seriously compounded by the poor option sets or local configuration of some filtering and antivirus products and services, especially gateway products. There are many circumstances under which generation of multiple alerts or any alert at all is incorrect behavior, most notably when the message that accompanies a mass mailer is known to forge message headers. An infected message should be returned to the sender only if it can be ascertained with reasonable certainty that the address in the From: and Reply-To: fields is not forged. Even then, it should not be returned with the uncleaned attachment, as often happens with filters that do not recognize specific viruses (either generic filters or mail transfer agents (MTAs) bouncing an undeliverable message). However, it is not possible for automated software to ascertain the real sender with this degree of confidence in the case of most modern spoofing viruses. Indeed, even inspection by eye often fails to do this reliably. As a result, poorly configured antivirus services may inform the wrong person that their system is infected, and similarly mislead the intended recipient, leading to panic on the part of the wrongly blamed system's owner, to ill-feeling between the apparent sender and intended recipient, and maybe even to legal action (Harley 2003, Fact, fiction and managed anti-malware services).

Fortunately, antivirus companies have become much more aware of these problems, and are less likely to configure such behavior as a default. However, they are often reluctant to remove these configuration options altogether, so customers who do not understand the problem sometimes introduce inappropriate reconfigurations. Third-party managed e-mail antivirus providers may also reconfigure inappropriately, and may not have hooks to all the functionality of the core antivirus product.

A very high proportion of current infected e-mail traffic carries spoofing malware, so while it is responsible behavior to advise someone with an infected system of the fact when there is no doubt about the correct identification of the infected system, it is appropriate to do so only when the detected malware is known not to spoof headers. Many products and services cannot discriminate between viruses in this sense, even though they can identify the actual name of the virus correctly. The recipient should receive a message only if the removal of the viral code leaves a disinfected and useful object to be forwarded (as is the case with macro viruses), or if the forwarded message is a legitimate and intended communication from the sender. Most e-mail-borne viruses are not "infective" in the sense of attaching to a legitimate object. The message is initiated and controlled by the virus (or, more correctly, by the virus author who coded the message-generation mechanism), not the owner of the infected system, who is usually unaware of the presence and transmission of the malware. The "infected" file contains no legitimate code, so disinfection is effectively the same as deletion. There is, therefore, no reason to forward the message and no point (except advertising the product) in advising the intended recipient of the interception, certainly if the originating e-mail account cannot be accurately ascertained.

Unfortunately, many scanning services cannot distinguish cases in which it is not appropriate to send an alert or forward a message, or in which the malware is known to forge headers, and are not therefore able to modify their own behavior accordingly. In fact, some services cannot even be configured to stop alerts or forwarding at all. As a result, it can happen at times that the impact of secondary traffic from filtering and antivirus services vastly exceeds that of "real" mass-mailers and spam. (Harley 2004)

The Malware Author's Dilemma

The malware writer has a significant barrier to overcome if his program is to spread beyond his own development environment. Malicious programs are harmless unless they are executed. How does he get his code to run on someone else's system? All malware exploits one or more vulnerabilities. These may consist of programming bugs and errors and other software vulnerabilities in a victim system, or of a lack of caution and skepticism in human victims, allowing them to be tricked into running unsafe programs, or in some cases, of a combination of the two.

"Self-launching" code exploits bugs such as buffer overflows, which can allow code to be run where it should not be. No action from the victim is necessary (Harley et al. 2001). The "Internet Worm" or "Morris Worm" of 1988 is as good an example as the far more recent MSBlaster or Code Red worms: possibly better, in that one of the vulnerabilities it exploited was in sendmail (Hruska 1992), whereas recent network worms have tended to exploit vulnerabilities in nonmail applications, such as IIS or SQL-Server. Mass mailers, however, have in some cases exploited vulnerabilities in mail applications, notably Outlook and Outlook Express (Microsoft 1999). There is a minor distinction to be drawn here between instances in which malware exploits miscoding and instances in which malware exploits (not necessarily intentionally) incautiously configured systems (as when office applications are set to allow macros to auto-execute, or mail clients are set to run attachments automatically).

"User-launched" code relies on persuading the victim to execute a malicious program, using social engineering in the general sense of psychological manipulation (Harley et al. 2001). Most e-mail-borne malware is user-launched or hybrid. Hybrid malware combines both the self-launching and user-launched approaches, thus maximizing the potential for spread. E-mail-borne malware is sometimes hybrid: it uses a bug such as those in some versions of Outlook that allow code to be run just by previewing a message, or the facility for auto-executing macros in Word or Excel, and thus requiring no intervention from the victim, but also hedges its bets by using what is often called social engineering to persuade victims to conspire in their own downfall by running an attachment. Such manipulation might persuade an unwary or unsophisticated computer user to open an executable file under the impression that it is a game or screensaver or even a data file. Most data files cannot carry executable code but Microsoft Office documents can, in the form of macros, and a Postscript file contains both programming instructions and data. This issue has long been recognized in antivirus circles, but has recently been revisited in more general security circles, notably on some specialist mailing lists. Not everyone realizes (for instance) that a screensaver (.SCR) is an executable program with the same format as an .EXE file, not a simple graphics file, and there are a multitude of well-documented ways in which an executable file might be "disguised" as a data file. For example, by using the "double filename extension" technique (examplefile.doc.scr) to hide the real file-type, or by presenting it as a self-extracting or self-decrypting archive file.

Trojan Horses

A Trojan horse (or simply a Trojan) tricks the victim into running its code by masquerading as something else (a desirable program). Most e-mail worms also do this, so they meet the definition of a Trojan, but they also replicate, so they belong in the virus family. (In fact, there is an argument for claiming that viruses belong to the Trojan family, though to do so is not particularly helpful in practical terms, since it tends to increase confusion among nonexperts.)

Classic Trojans tend either to be destructive to data or to cause leakage of information (or both). They may include among other payloads:

- Damage to or loss of files and file systems
- Allowing access to the network via network shares
- Opening ports to allow traffic through the Internet gateway
- Sending passwords or data back to an unauthorized person
- Altering the configuration of a victim system
- Causing advertisements to pop up
- "Recruiting" compromised systems for use in botnets
- Track which Web sites victims visit, and which passwords they use.

Trojans' main weakness as an e-mail-borne threat is that they are usually reliant on the quality of the social engineering in the accompanying message to gain a foothold into the system, and they cannot self-replicate even when they do gain a foothold (Harley 2002, Trojans). They include a wide variety of subclasses according to functionality, including among others:

- Destructive (Trojans that trash or overwrite files or file systems, most commonly)
- Backdoors (Trojans that attempt to open a connection to the victim computer from a remote system, for whatever purpose)
- Password stealers and keyloggers
- Porndialers and other dialers (programs that use the modem on the infected machine to dial pornographic or other services, usually using premium rates and long-distance call charges).
- Distributed denial of service (DDoS) agents
- Rootkits (Trojanized versions of system files and other tools for concealing the presence of an intruder on a compromised system)
- Bots (in the sense of backdoor Trojans linked in a "botnet" that communicate and are controlled through Internet Relay Chat [IRC]).

Grimes (2001) also considers a class of program he calls parasites. Although these include such privacy-invasive nuisances as programs that "call home" and pass marketer-friendly data (often installed as part of a more-or-less legitimate and authorized program installation), there is also an argument for including objects with similar potential functionality such as adware, single-pixel GIFs, malicious cookies, and web bugs that can be accessed via e-mail incorporating active-content (PC Mag, 2006).

Bots and Botnets

The term *bot* is an abbreviated version of "robot." In the context of software, it usually refers to some kind of agent for remote control or information gathering (Overton 2005). In terms of e-mail threats, the term may be used to refer to "crawlers" that are used to seek out e-mail addresses (James 2005). However, bots (usually in the form of scripts) have long been used to automate processes on IRC (Canavan 2005). Such agents have long been used for legitimate and for malicious purposes. However, since 1999, when the PrettyPark worm used IRC as a channel for remote control and communication, and 2002, when SDbot and Agobot, among others, pioneered the emergence of binaries incorporating an IRC client (Harley and Bradley 2007), the impact of IRC bots on computing in general and messaging (and other security threats) in particular has grown alarmingly (Schiller & Binkley 2007). So-called zombie systems (PCs compromised by bot infestation), especially when combined into "botnets" under the control of a Bot Master (also known as a Zombie Master, Bot Herder, or Botmeister, among other terms), can be used for any number of malicious activities, from DDoS (distributed denial of service) attacks to spam, phish, and malware dissemination, updating of malware, hosting of blind drop servers (for the collection and storing of phishing data), and so on. Similarly, bots can have a wide range of capabilities—vulnerability scanning; channel, UDP (User Datagram Protocol) and ping flooding; rootkit functionality, and password sniffing, for instance. Bots may be disseminated as e-mail (as attachments or as malicious hyperlinks), but are often distributed by other means. Nevertheless, they have a considerable secondary effect on messaging security.

Anti-Malware Solutions

The most effective answer to viruses is, of course, antivirus software, deployed not only at the desktop, but also on Web servers, file servers, and, most relevantly to this chapter, at the e-mail gateway. Unfortunately, this rather glib statement does not take into account all the realities of twenty-first century malware management. Old-fashioned viruses have declined significantly in volume and impact, while Trojans and blended threats constitute an increasing proportion of current malware problems (Braverman 2006). Although virus detection using both proactive and reactive techniques has attained an impressive technical level, there are limitations on the detection of nonviral threats that affect all antivirus products that extend their service to cover other forms of malware (nearly all of them, nowadays). These issues are considered further below. However, the virus threat has also changed, in that virus writers have moved away from hitting as many machines as possible and as quickly as possible with a single variant, to stealthier models of distribution (short spamming/seeding runs, frequent releases of repacked subvariants).

There are two main approaches to e-mail gateway-hosted virus management: generic and virus-specific. Generic virus management consists largely of discarding or quarantining objects that are capable of carrying or consisting entirely of a predetermined range of malicious code. In e-mail terms, this range usually consists of file attachments of file types often used by the writers of mass mailer viruses, including .PIF, .SCR, .VBS, .EXE, .BAT, .COM and so on, though exactly which file types are blocked will depend partly on local usage. For instance, most sites do not block Microsoft Office documents, even though they are commonly associated with the passing of macro viruses, since legitimate business processes would suffer seriously from the blocking of legitimate documents. Table 1 classifies common attachment types by risk level (Harley 2004). Issues regarding the relative risks of common file types are also examined in considerably more detail in a Technical Note published by the UK's Centre for Protection of National Infrastructure (CPNI 2004).

Virus-specific software detects (obviously) known, specific viruses. A consideration of the precise mechanisms for such detection is beyond the scope of this chapter, but is based on a process of comparing code-bearing objects to a database of definitions, so that (in principle) a new definition (or search string) is required for each new virus or variant. In practice, the use of augmented detection by heuristic analysis and of generic drivers that are capable of catching some currently unknown variations and variants, sometimes lessens the impact of brand-new malware. However, the need still exists for updating antivirus software with the latest definitions (sometimes not altogether correctly referred to as signatures) as soon as they become available. Gateway systems and services should also be implemented with due regard to the need for configurability and appropriate alerting and forwarding mechanisms arising from the increase in header-spoofing mass mailers and allied problems, as described above and (at far greater length) by Harley (2003, Fact, fiction and managed anti-malware services). Modern antivirus programs often use advanced heuristic technology capable of detecting a very high percentage of new, unknown viruses and worms. However, it can be much harder to detect related forms of malware (especially nonreplicative malware) heuristically. Unfortunately, although the major vendors do exchange samples in order to maximize detection of known malware, changes in malware dissemination patterns mean that it is possible for some variants to remain undetected for a considerable length of time, sometimes months (James 2005).

The range and speed of spread of malicious code (e-mail-borne or not) also necessitates good systems and software patching practice at the server, desktop, and application levels and supplementary measures such as the blocking of vulnerable ports and services whenever possible and applicable; and it is no longer possible to consider virus management in complete isolation from other security technologies such as perimeter and desktop firewalls, intrusion-detection systems, and intrusion-prevention software. Policy and education remain a sometimes neglected but nonetheless essential component of a holistic security posture.

Although encryption is an essential adjunct to confidentiality in e-mail, it may also form part of the problem as regards the transfer of malicious code, and virus writers have made frequent use of the popular confusion between "encrypted" and "safe." The fact that a message or attachment is encrypted tells us nothing about whether it is infected. In most environments, encryption can be a barrier to effective gateway scanning, forcing the enterprise to rely on desktop scanning as a last-ditch defense, notwithstanding the difficulties of maintaining desktop security products in large or fragmented corporate environments. Viruses such as Netsky and Bagle that present as encrypted .ZIP files indicate that even a comparatively trivial form of encryption can present challenges to conventional antivirus that have not yet been completely addressed. Indeed, generic filters that regulate the introduction of executable attachments can often be circumvented simply by zipping the viral program.

Public key infrastructure (PKI) can, if rigorously applied, have benefits in terms of control of mass mailers and some forms of spam, by making it harder for a message using deception and forgery as a means of delivery to survive an authentication mechanism. Applied purely as a means of managing e-mail abuse, however, it constitutes a somewhat expensive form of whitelisting (i.e., allowing only mail from approved addresses to reach the protected mailbox).

Anti-Trojan Software

Most antivirus software detects a reasonable proportion of all Trojans, joke programs, and similar nuisances, but antivirus vendors are not usually brave enough to claim that they can detect all known Trojans. There are a number of reasons for this, including:

- Difficulties in formal definition—the definition of a Trojan relies, in part, on the perception of the victim, a factor often not susceptible to automated code or text analysis.
- The fact that it is immeasurably easier to write trivial nonreplicative malware and introduce minor variants.
- The lack of a more-or-less universal Trojan-specific mechanism for sharing samples with trusted vendors and researchers comparable to those that exist for virus sample sharing.

Unfortunately, the same caveats tend to apply to the producers of Trojan-specific scanners, and rivalry between some Trojan specialists and the antivirus industry further complicates the issue. Similar problems are encountered in the detection of specific forms of Trojan such as bots, spyware, and adware.

SPAM AND RELATED E-MAIL ABUSE

The name *spam* is applied to a number of abuses involving the indiscriminate use of e-mail or newsgroup postings, though the use of the term as applied to newsgroup abuse is largely overlooked nowadays except by Usenet junkies.

E-mail spam includes the following:

- UCE—unsolicited commercial e-mail (junk mail): this term is applied to any unsolicited advertising. Most spam is disseminated with the intention of advertising a product or service, but other motivations may apply. Although the term can be and is applied to all unsolicited advertising, it is useful to discriminate between "honest" advertising (from more-or-less legitimate and

Table 1: Categorization of Attachment Types by Risk Level

Risk Level	Attachment Type
Very high risk	File types almost never exchanged legitimately by e-mail but are executable file types used by mail-borne malware: e.g. .PIF, .LNK, .BAT, .COM, .CMD, .SHS. These file types should, therefore, be blocked in all but the most exceptional circumstances. The .EXE file type is also heavily used by mass mailers and other malware, and is very frequently blocked by generic filters for this reason (and with good reason). However, it is included in the high-risk category rather than very-high-risk because it is possible and may be convenient for legitimate .EXE files to be exchanged, so blocking must remain a local decision. Filenames with double extensions, especially when one type is a nonexecutable and the last one(the one that matters) is executable: for instance. myfile.txt.pif. File types that do not match the filename extension, when the file type is more dangerous than the filename extension suggests Filenames with double or multiple extensions for which an attempt has been made to mask the presence of the real file type, for example by inserting several spaces between the penultimate extension and the real, final extension Files with a deceptive icon suggesting a nonexecutable file type Filenames that include the characters {}, suggesting an attempt to disguise an executable file type by using its CLSID (class ID extension)
Medium high risk	This category includes file types that are heavily used by mass mailers, but may also be exchanged legitimately (e.g., .EXE, .SCR, .VBS). It may be decided locally not to block these types for the following reasons: .EXE attachments may denote data rather than a "real" executable, but in the form of a program file—for example, self-decompressing archive files and self-decrypting files are often convenient because they do not oblige the recipient to own the archiving or encryption utility that generated them. It is hard to imagine that any organization still considers the attractions of exchanging fluffy screensavers to be worth the risk of allowing .SCR files, but again, the final decision must be local. Earlier mass mailers were very often VBScript files, and new .VBS mass mailers (and more current malware types) are still seen from time to time, but it can also happen that such scripts are used to install system patches, for example. Nonetheless, it is strongly recommended that if any of these file types must be allowed and exchanged by e-mail, that stringent precautions be taken to ensure that only trusted and trustworthy code is allowed through. Compressed archive files, especially the .ZIP file type characteristic of PKZip and WinZip, pose a significant risk, convenient as they are. Indeed, in the early years of the present decade, the use of encrypted .ZIPs and .RARs to transport mass mailers posed a major problem for mail administrators, though the problem has diminished as the mass mailer problem has diminished. Some generic filters are unable to check inside a compressed file for the presence of archived executables, though virus-specific software is almost always capable of scanning the contents of a .ZIP file (and a variety of other archive formats). However, virus-specific scanners are not able to scan the contents of encrypted archives in real time and have been forced to apply less satisfactory search criteria as more viruses have exploited this loophole. Also, multiply nested archives containing unusually large compressed files may constitute an effective denial of service attack on antivirus scanners and e-mail servers.
Medium risk	This class includes file types not frequently used by mass mailers, but capable of carrying executable/malicious code. Most file infectors, Trojans, etc. would be caught by the previous categories, but documents that can contain macros (especially Office documents) fall here. Note that exchange of some documents will often be seen as impacting too heavily on normal business practices to override the moderate increase in security (.DOC, .XLS), but others may be borderline high risk, such as those file types associated with Microsoft Access. People do not exchange full databases as often as they do more concise forms of data. Note, also, that the incidence of macro viruses has subsided. This trend may well be influenced by the fact that Microsoft applications no longer enable execution of unsigned macros by default.
Medium-low risk	This category includes executable files of types not currently associated with virus action, or only with extinct viruses, or zoo viruses (especially proof-of-concept viruses that exist only "to show it's possible")

(continued)

Table 1: *(continued)*

Risk Level	Attachment Type
Low risk	Nonexecutables. Technically, this should be "no risk." However, it is impractical to prove automatically that a file contains no executable code.
Uncategorized	Files whose executability or infective status is presently unknown, or cannot be determined or assumed Files of unknown file type (or no explicit file type: Macintosh users are frequently penalized by generic checkers for the fact that Mac data files are often not given a filename extension) Encrypted files Archives that cannot be unpacked (fully or at all) for scanning Note that the last two categories can be said to include some file types in preceding categories: however, no presumptions are made in this case about filename extensions.

reputable organizations using more-or-less legitimate direct-marketing techniques) and advertising that includes a degree of deception not only in the content, but in the delivery mechanism. Reputable organizations generally conform to regulatory legislation. As well as being reasonably restrained in their claims regarding the products they are advertising, they obey (increasingly restrictive) laws.

- UBE—unsolicited bulk e-mail—is sent in bulk to many addresses. It may be and often is commercial, so is essentially a superset of UCE.
- NCE (nonresponsive commercial e-mail) is a term sometimes applied to spam sent by a company that fails to honor a user's request to unsubscribe (James 2005).

The term is applied by many people to many divergent forms of unsolicited bulk e-mail. Most sources (especially antispam vendors!) suggest that well over 50 percent of all e-mail is now junk mail (some estimates suggest a much higher proportion, and almost all sources indicate continuing growth).

The term is still applied to bulk postings to Internet newsgroups (Usenet), but is now most commonly applied to unsolicited commercial and other bulk e-mail. It often involves advertising products or services, but may also be applied to many other types of unsolicited mail, including the following (some of these categories often overlap with other categories of e-mail abuse considered below, and may not always be considered "real" spam):

- Financial marketing messages that may or may not be genuine
- Product-oriented messages (general goods or services ranging from antivirus products to fake diplomas and qualifications to septic tanks and timeshare apartments)
- Illegal products or services (illicit drugs, pirated software etc.)
- Pornographic spam:
  - Hardcore
  - Softcore
  - Deviant
  - Legal/illegal. The implications of legality may be far-reaching: for instance, processing of pedophilic content can, if not conducted in accordance with law enforcement guidelines, expose the recipient of such material to legal action.
- Offers of spamming software and services
- Health (diet-related, "improvement" of physical assets, medical supplies)
- "Spiritualist"/organized religion
- Other "soapboxing" from individuals with bees in their bonnets, religious, moral or otherwise.
- Fraud:
  - Pyramid and MLM (multilevel marketing) schemes
  - 419s (see below)
  - Credit card scams and other phishing attacks
- Leisure messages (prizes, online games, electronic greetings cards using wormlike replicative techniques to spread)
- Surveys
- Begging letters

Some find it useful to distinguish between "amateur" spam or unsolicited junk mail (commercial or otherwise) and "professional" or "hardcore" spam, which is not only unsolicited but includes a degree of deception, not only in its content, but as regards its origin.

I have proposed the following definition of "professional" spam elsewhere (Harley 2007) and will use it here, in the absence of a universally accepted standard: "Unsolicited and usually unwanted mail, often for advertising purposes, sometimes fraudulent, and generally including some degree of deception as to the source and purpose of the mail, such as forged From: fields, misleading Subject: fields, fake 'opt-out' mechanisms that don't work or are used only to validate the address as a potential spam target, misleading pseudo-legal statements, and obfuscation of the originator of the spam mail." Other commentators have made similar implicit assumptions about the nature of spam (Schwartz and Garfinkel 1998). Paul Vixie makes an excellent point—actually, several.

(see http://tqmcube.com/contrib.php). His definition has three dimensions to it:

1. The recipient's individual identity is irrelevant (the message is not personalized or significantly targeted).
2. The message is completely unsolicited.
3. From the recipient's point of view, the message gives a "disproportionate benefit to the sender."

Vixie's definition requires all three dimensions to be present.

Revenge spamming is a term sometimes applied to the implication of a disliked person (especially an antispammer) in spamming activities by using their site as a relay, fraudulently inserting their details into the mail headers, using their details in the body of the message, and so on. The victim of this sort of revenge spam subsequently becomes the victim of various sanctions applied by groups and individuals who are violently opposed to spamming. This form of abuse is closely allied to other forms of impersonation in which offensive or inappropriate mail is manipulated to make it look as if it came from someone else.

Some junk mail is clearly not expected to achieve anything other than to annoy or in some way distress the recipient, though in some instances it may be sent as a "probe" to test spamming software or to validate an address.

Malware writers also make use of spamming techniques to inject viruses, worms, and Trojan horses into the wild. Not only do they use deceptive headers and content to trick the recipient into opening the mail and running the malicious program attached, but they use spammer-like forgery of mail headers to disguise the true whereabouts and ownership of the infected system. They also use built-in SMTP servers to cover their tracks and maximize spread, in a manner highly reminiscent of some spamming tools, as well as using botnets.

Spam and Malware

A correlation has been noted between virus writing and spamming. (Hypponen 2003) Some mass mailers, bots, and other Trojans install software on infected systems that allow them to be used as open relays or open proxies by spammers, so that infected machines can be used to relay spam, increasing the potential spam-processing rate and the difficulty of tracing the real source of a spammed message. Since most corporate organizations nowadays maintain reasonable antivirus precautions—at least on the e-mail gateway, and hopefully on the desktop too—home computer systems are far more vulnerable to being exploited in this way. As long as most home computer users fail to install, configure, or maintain antivirus software correctly, it is probable that spammers will continue to make use of this approach. In fact, although home users do seem to be more aware of the risks and to be making attempts to protect their systems properly, it is increasingly difficult for antivirus companies to maintain the near-100 percent protection, not only from viruses and worms but from all other forms of malware, that antivirus users often expect.

Some malware is also known to install Web server processes on infected home (and other vulnerable) machines for the distribution and advertising of products and services that in themselves are often illegal. There have also been reports of infected systems being used to mount DoS attacks against antispam sites. Some malware forwards e-mail addresses and other information that may be used subsequently for spamming purposes.

However, mass-mailing malware also uses techniques analogous to those used by spambots to harvest target e-mail addresses not only from the victim's Windows address book, but often from other files and system areas such as Word documents, HTML files, web caches and so on. Mass mailers often use header forgery to spoof addresses and disguise the source of the infected mail and avoid early detection by gateway filters by using varying ("polymorphic") subject lines, message content, and made-up source addresses. The use by mass-mailer viruses of their own internal SMTP engines or known relays to self-disseminate also makes it harder to trace the source of infective mail or the footprint of the virus in the infected mail system. These spam-like techniques are symptomatic of increasing cross-pollination not only between virus/malware technology and spamming technology, but between malware authors, spammer communities, and phishing gangs (EEMA 2003; F-Secure 2005).

Chain Letters, Chain E-Mails, and Hoaxes

A chain letter is, in its broadest sense, any message that includes a request for the recipient to forward it. Terrestrial chain letters usually ask the recipient to forward a set number of copies, but chain e-mail usually asks the recipient to forward to "everyone they know" or "everyone in their address book" or "everyone who might use the Internet." The common denominator is that circulation increases in a geometric progression.

Chain letters are not necessarily hoaxes, but frequently contain some deceptive content, either through a deliberate attempt to mislead or because of a misunderstanding of the issue in question. Very frequently, fact is mixed in with fiction to add circumstantial credibility. It is possible for purely factual material to be forwarded in this way, of course, but in general, responsible (or for-fee!) distributors of quality information tend to use less intrusive forms of dissemination. The forwarding of messages by victims of pyramid scams is addressed in the later section on e-mail fraud, rather than as a form of chain letter, though there are certainly similarities between these two nuisances.

On their Hoaxbusters Web site, CIAC (2004) describe the chain letter as having a tripartite structure: hook, threat, and request. Although it is not always straightforward to separate these elements, they do seem to be common to most chain letters, electronic or otherwise.

The *hook* is there, like a riff in a popular song, to catch the recipient's interest, and consists of an eye-catching tag like "Free trainers!" or "Virus alert," and perhaps some expansion of the theme. It exploits some basic psychological issue like greed and self-interest, fear of technology and its consequences, or sympathy with the unfortunate (Harley 2000).

The *threat* pressures the recipient into passing on the message. Sometimes, the threat is simply that if the mark doesn't forward the mail, they will miss out on some personal advantage: for instance offers of free cell phones, sports gear, and so forth in return for meeting or exceeding a required number of forwardings. Less blatantly, a chain mail may exploit the desire to please or to earn brownie points or competitive advantage while doing something responsible and helpful, or the fear of being thought mean or uncharitable or unsympathetic (Harley and Gattiker 2002).

Direct threats may be used, somewhat in the fashion of older terrestrial chain mail that describe how recipients who did not forward met with misfortune or even death. More modern, less superstitious variations include threats to deluge the target's mailbox with spam or viruses.

It is more common for chain e-mail to use indirect threats that are not necessarily explicitly stated. For instance, behind virus hoaxes, there is the implicit threat of widespread damage and inconvenience personally and to all Internet users.

Some chain mail makes an overt emotional appeal such as that made by political petitions (such as those concerning the treatment of Afghan women under the Taliban, or opposing war with Iraq) or solicitations to forward e-mail to attract funding for cancer research. The threat is that if the mail is not forwarded, political injustice, cancer, or the suffering of an individual will continue unchecked, or a little boy's dying wish will not be granted, or child victims of a natural disaster like the 2004 tsunami will remain isolated from their parents or other family members. The common denominator is that all representatives of this class of nuisance ask the recipient to keep the chain going by forwarding e-mail, so that some undesirable outcome will be avoided.

The *request* expresses the "core function" of the chain letter: that is, to replicate by forwarding. The use of the term *replicate* is not accidental: chain letters, especially virus hoaxes, are sometimes considered to be "memetic viruses" (Gordon, Ford, and Wells 1997), or "viruses of the mind" (these commonly-used expressions and concepts largely originate in the writings and theories of biologist Richard Dawkins). Instead of the code used by computer viruses, which replicate by infection, chain letters rely on persuading the recipient to pass the message on to others. They often have a "payload" that results in the useless consumption of bandwidth through the replication of hoax e-mail, personal fear caused by scare stories with no basis in fact, and in some instances the erasure of legitimate software incorrectly identified as "viruses." However, they masquerade as an appeal to "help" others by disseminating "information," whereas cancer victim hoaxes ask you to generate money for medical research by forwarding identical messages, and others appeal to self-interest by offering money or free goods or services (clothes, cell phones, holidays, and so on).

Chain letters can be said to fall into three main classes:

- Pure fiction, intended to trick the victim into forwarding a chain letter and bolster the self-image of the originator by "proving" the stupidity of others. This class includes many virus hoaxes and other hoaxes related to security—sometimes to other aspects of information security, but often to personal security such as vulnerability to robbery or personal attack. This latter class of hoax includes elements of the urban legend, especially those urban legends that have a gory or otherwise horrific element.
- Some hoaxes might be better described as semi-hoaxes, as they may be based on misunderstanding a real issue. Some virus hoaxes may fall into this class, but so do other hoaxes, such as widespread stories about highway speed cameras, telephone scams, and tsunami victims. However, a hoax with no basis in fact may nevertheless acquire a patina of circumstantial support as it passes from person to person. Such messages often originate from or are perpetuated by (for example) consultants, journalists, and others who are perceived, often inaccurately, as speaking authoritatively or from a position of exceptional knowledge. Rosenberger and others sometimes describe this as False Authority Syndrome, though this term is usually used in the context of virus hoaxes (Harley et al. 2001).
- More rarely, a security alert or other form of chain letter may be reasonably accurate in its content, but the form of transmission is inappropriate. Hoaxes and chain letters are not easy to manage using automatic software, though some sites do attempt to manage it using keyword filtering and Bayesian and other analytical techniques. However, these can lead to an unacceptably high false positive rate. In general, this is an area in which good policy and education works best, with good information resources as backup.

E-Mail Fraud

The following subclassifications are by no means all-inclusive, but do include some major current abuses.

Password Stealing

Attempts to gain password information, either by social engineering, the enclosure of some form of Trojan horse, or a combination of both, have long been associated with e-mail (Gordon and Chess 1998) and the use of particular ISPs—AOL users have been particularly victimized. However, this class of abuse is by no means ISP-specific, and can involve attempts to gain other types of information.

Phishing

This form of fraud, though it may be regarded in some instances as a special case of the preceding category, is also associated with malware distribution, and has become increasingly prevalent in recent years. In its most usual current form, it masquerades as a communication from a banking or other financial establishment (eBay and PayPal are very popular targets, but less obvious targets such as the IRS are increasingly exploited) asking the recipient to re-enter their banking details or other sensitive information into a form that appears to be generated at a legitimate Web site, or attaching (or persuading the recipient to download and run) malicious software such as keyloggers and bots. The scammer's intentions may include directly plundering the victim's bank or credit card account, but may also be developed into more advanced forms of identity theft, such as taking out loans and mortgages in the victim's name.

Refinements of phishing technique include the exploitation of cross-site scripting vulnerabilities and setting up spoof Web sites. Spoofed Web sites and forms are often referenced by misleading and camouflaged Web links. Approaches involving the redirection of browser requests from legitimate to phish sites using DNS cache poisoning, corruption of the local "hosts" file, and so on, is sometimes referred to as "pharming."

Although some definitions emphasize the element of Web-site spoofing, there is a certain amount of crossover here between several types of e-mail abuse. At the moment, the efficacy of such frauds is often diluted by ineffective targeting, but it would be naïve to assume that fraudsters will not find ways of improving their credibility. Some reports (James 2005) suggest a much lower current response rate (between 0.01 percent and 0.1 percent), compared to that seen during the first half of the decade, but the return on investment (ROI) still provides massive incentive to phishing gangs to continue their activities. This type of identity fraud is extending into other business areas, and targets other types of data. Research by the Anti-Phishing Working Group (APWG 2006) and others (James 2005) suggests that the volume of dissemination of phishing scams has risen very quickly indeed, and that targeting and presentation of phishing mails have improved dramatically. The transmission of highly targeted phishing mails is sometimes termed "spear phishing."

Anti-phishing countermeasures include advanced content filtering, two- and three-factor mutual authentication between the end user and legitimate Web sites, and improving the quality of legitimate communications from phished organizations, to make them less easy to spoof. Some links to organizations working on improving consumer education and incident response are included in the "Further Reading" section at the end of this chapter.

Money Laundering and Mule Recruitment

Phishing is often associated with money-laundering activities (Rivner 2006), and e-mails intended to offer "jobs" described as "financial management" or "financial operations" usually turn out to be attempts to recruit "money mules" to sanitize funds stolen from phished accounts. Mules are needed to receive and forward money or goods acquired fraudulently from banks or credit card accounts. Like phishing mails, mule recruitment mails are often backed up by carefully constructed but fraudulent Web sites, and some mules do not realize that they are involved in money laundering until law enforcement agencies catch up with them. Unfortunately, this type of mail often manages to evade spam filters that are fairly effective at blocking phish mails, and this problem remains somewhat underreported and underestimated.

Pump and Dump Fraud

Pump and Dump (Penny Stocks, Pennystox, Hype and Dump) spam, though it relates to a very American form of trading in shares worth up to $5 apiece, has been widely reported in the United Kingdom and elsewhere since about 2004. An increasing proportion of this spam has proved to be intended to perpetuate stock fraud, to the benefit of organized crime (Wallener 2006; Harley and Lee 2007). These mails tend to use classic-spam-filter evasion techniques, such as image spam, with notable success. The basic spam is based on artificially inflating the price of low-priced stock the scammer holds by predicting a massive upward movement. As the victims rush to buy in, the stock value does indeed climb. When the scammer sells, however, and stops hyping the stock, the price plummets.

Pyramid Schemes and Multilevel Marketing

Pyramid schemes are based on the principle that the recipient of the e-mail sends money to a number of people, who send money to more people, who send money to more people ad infinitum. The idea is that eventually the recipient's name will rise to the top so that they too will receive money. They are generally associated with the selling of some token product or service. However, they make a profit only for the originator of the scam. Such scams often claim to be more-or-less legitimate multilevel marketing (MLM) operations. Ponzi schemes are another type of fake "investment" widely advertised by e-mail. Note that scam e-mails of this sort are often widely spammed, though they will usually need to point to a temporary but legitimate mailbox somewhere to which the money is directed. The mathematical model of some pyramid schemes resembles the model for the distribution of chain letters, especially those that specify the number of addresses to which you should forward them. This class of abuse is considered at some length by Barrett (1996).

Advance-Fee Fraud (419s)

Advance-fee frauds, better known as 419s or Nigerian scams (the name 419 derives from the section of the Nigerian Criminal Code dealing with fraud) are a long-standing type of scam that can be disseminated by fax, letter, etc. but is nowadays most often seen as e-mail. They constitute the largest proportion of current e-mail fraud, and work, broadly, as follows. The target receives an unsolicited communication containing a business proposal that often involves some form of money laundering or similar illegal operation, though if the proposal is obviously illegal, it often includes an attempt at moral justification and a comical plea to the recipient to act with honesty and integrity. Variations are endless, but may include:

- A request for help from a political refugee to get their family and their money out of a war-torn (usually African) country
- A request for help with the distribution of money for charitable purposes
- A request for assistance from a bank or other official with transferring money obtained more or less illicitly from the government
- A request to stand as "next of kin" for the purposes of claiming the estate of a dead foreigner who has died intestate
- Notification of a lottery win
- Phish-influenced offers of "jobs" that are likely to be linked to money laundering.

At some point, the victim is asked to pay advance fees of some sort (for example, for taxes, legal fees, or bribes or as evidence of good faith) or to give sensitive information about their own financial accounts. Some individuals have lost very large sums of money in this way.

These communications often but by no means always derive from Nigeria or another African state, but may originate or appear to originate from any part of the world. They often offer a URL pointing to a convincing but not necessarily relevant or genuine news item or other Web site, as circumstantial evidence.

These 419s are often regarded as indistinguishable from spam, and there are indeed many points of similarity. Like spammers, 419 perpetrators use target addresses harvested directly or indirectly from Web sites, newsgroups, mailing lists, and so on. However, they tend not to manipulate message headers so heavily, possibly because they need to maintain some sort of contact with the victim, though the contact point may be buried in the body of the message rather than the header, which may contain a forged address. They also make heavy use of "disposable" free e-mail accounts from Web mail providers: these are easily blocked when complaints are received, but are also quite difficult to trace, and less susceptible to automatic detection by filters that rely on header anomalies. They are, however, fairly susceptible to detection by filtering on keywords and phrases. Address information, text, and scam ideas are heavily recycled and exchanged, and some kinds of stereotyped "business English," names and event information are frequently re-encountered by the dedicated 419-trapper.

Like spammers, 419 fraudsters generally use a scattergun approach. The messages are mailed to anyone whose address is harvested, irrespective of their likely interest, on the assumption that one or two potential victims will bite and make it worth the minimal initial investment required from the perpetrator.

However, there seem to be many "gangs," individuals and countries operating this form of organized crime. It is strongly recommended that individuals, and the organizations they belong to, should *not* respond directly to such communications unless asked to by law-enforcement agencies.

There are a number of possibilities for dealing directly with 419s received. Individuals may be encouraged simply to delete them, of course, or report them to their local IT helpdesk or security administrator, who may be authorized to take immediate action to block, send alerts, and advise law enforcement, as well as finding it useful to monitor incoming fraudulent mail in order to keep records and to track trends in 419 technology and psychology. If a reporting mechanism exists, it is useful to include the whole message and full headers, but the From:, To:, and Subject: fields are the minimum likely to be needed for reactive blocking by domain or sender.

Possible direct action includes the following:

- Forward the e-mail to the abuse@[domain] account for the domains mentioned in the e-mail headers and in the message body, including full message headers.
- Forward to an appropriate law-enforcement agency: any local agency will give advice on how best to do this, but some national resources are included in the Further Reading section at the end of this chapter. The 419 Coalition (2004) Web site includes contact addresses for several countries.
- In the event of a 419 with a likely Nigerian connection, file a complaint with the Nigerian Embassy or High Commission and with the Central Bank of Nigeria (info@cenbank.org).
- Where loss has occurred, a complaint can be filed with the Nigerian Economic and Financial Crimes Commission (EFCC) (info@efccnigeria.org). In many countries, it is also possible to report cases of contact and actual loss to national law-enforcement agencies, as well as to the local police. However, the sheer scale of this problem means that none of these parties will necessarily take action in every case, and if there has been no return communication with the fraudster, it's unlikely that there will be any direct response.

Threats and Extortion

There are as many possibilities for persuading or bullying an e-mail recipient into inappropriate and self-destructive behavior as human ingenuity and gullibility can accommodate. A common attack on individuals (especially those within corporate environments) is to send mail claiming to be able to take over their system and threatening to delete files or to unleash viruses or pornographic e-mail onto the individual's machine unless they pay a (sometimes comparatively small) sum (CNN 2003).

This form of attack is difficult to address by technical means, and is better addressed by corporate policy and education. It is noteworthy that the efficacy of this particular attack relies implicitly on organizational security being draconian and blame-oriented. Security is often improved by encouraging the end user to report incidents and breaches without fear of unjust retribution (Harley 1998).

Mail Bombing

This term is applied when an individual (or sometimes a site) is bombarded with e-mail messages, constituting a form of denial of service attack and invasion of privacy.

Subscription Bombing

This term is applied when rather than directly bombarding a target individual or site with e-mail, as in mail bombing, the target is subscribed to numerous mailing lists, especially high-volume lists. List-processing software nowadays includes a verification/confirmation mechanism by which an applicant subscriber is required to confirm their wish to subscribe. However, commercial mailing lists are not always so scrupulous.

E-Mail Abuse and Policy-Based Solutions

The following suggested policy outlines will not work for everyone in all respects, but highlight and to some extent address most of the core issues (Harley et al. 2001).

Acceptable Use of Facilities and Resources

Policies addressing the use and abuse of company resources may cover the use of e-mail, instant messaging, and access to the World Wide Web and other resources owned by the employer, specifying that they are intended for work purposes only, or for non-work purposes in moderation, according to local practice. Access should not be permitted to resources that customarily carry pornographic material, pirated software, and other illegitimate information and resources, such as malicious software (binaries or source code), including viruses, Trojan horses, backdoor/remote access tools, password-cracking tools, and hacking tools. Special considerations may apply as regards the use of Web-hosted mail services (and related or somewhat similar services such as Usenet, IRC, etc.)

All use of company facilities should be required to be in accordance with:

- All binding laws, including but not restricted to:
  - Data-protection legislation
  - Copyright legislation
  - Legislation concerned with unauthorized access or modification to systems or data
  - Trade-secrets legislation
  - Antidiscrimination legislation
  - Obscenity/pornography legislation, especially legislation relating to child pornography and pedophilia. Reporting and processing of problems relating to pedophilia is likely to require careful and unambiguous guidance, in order to conform with what is often complex and contradictory legislation.
- All internal policies
- Other policies and agreements by which the company is bound.

It might be considered appropriate here to proscribe the use of company resources for administration of private business ventures.

Acceptable Use of E-Mail

Staff using a company e-mail account, or other messaging facility, need to be aware that what they write will often be seen to represent the views and policies of the company. They should therefore be required to conform to appropriate standards of accuracy, courtesy, decency, and ethical behavior and to refrain from the dissemination of inappropriate mail content. Sending of bulk e-mail within the company or beyond should be consistent with internal policy, ethical practice, and legal and mandatory requirements.

Inappropriate behavior exposes the employee and the company to accusations of libel/defamation, harassment/discrimination, copyright infringement, invasion of privacy and so on. Employees are therefore required to act in accordance with the company's published policies as well as all applicable legislation and other binding agreements.

The company is probably not able or obliged to maintain constant surveillance of employees' use of its facilities, especially where use is not specifically authorized or is misused, but employees should not assume an automatic right to privacy. Mail may be monitored or checked from time to time for reasons of maintaining network support, security, or other reasons, as well as for ensuring that it meets prescribed standards of conduct.

E-mail should not be used as if it were a secure communications channel for the transmission of sensitive information or messages. Use of encryption, however, should be in accordance with the company's policy and practice.

There should be no sharing of games, joke programs, screensavers etc. Any attachment is potentially hostile, irrespective of what it is claimed to be or the perceived trustworthiness of the source.

On no account should an end user be allowed to disable or reduce the functionality of security software without authorization.

End users should be expected to use the corporate standard antivirus package. Systems running unsupported security packages and other applications should be regarded as unprotected: this may have general support implications, as well as the obvious security implications.

Anti-Hoax and Chain Mail Policy

Chain e-mail is a drain on network resources, system resources, and support staff. Any mail that includes a request to forward widely and inappropriately should be regarded with suspicion and promptly reported, especially if it states or implies any sort of threat. Originating or forwarding mail that carries some sort of threat against recipients who do not forward it in turn should be regarded as a disciplinable offense. On no account should mail that warns of viruses, Trojan horses, and other security threats be forwarded without checking and authorization from the local IT unit, however apparently trustworthy or senior the source, unless they are specifically qualified and authorized to do so. Consider mandating the digital signing of such warnings or authorization, given how easy it is to forge headers. A number of recent spear phishes are manipulated so that they appear to be sent internally.

Some virus hoaxes may have been intended to discourage the forwarding of previously existing chain letters. This is *not* an acceptable reason for passing on a hoax or chain letter, and it may be worth addressing the issue specifically.

Passing on warnings about hoax warnings can be a difficult area. Some individuals and groups have recommended passing on information about hoaxes and chain letters back to other recipients of a hoax or chain letter, and in some extreme instances, to everyone in the recipient's address book.

- Passing on an anti-hoax message with instructions to the recipient to forward indiscriminately (or to a fixed number of people) is simply a chain letter, and should not be regarded as acceptable.
- Passing back an anti-hoax message to other hoax recipients may be justifiable if there are only a few of them

and if it is reasonable to assume that they will receive more benefit than annoyance from the information. Even then, the information should be accurate and subject to the approval of the appropriate manager.

- Not all hoaxes are security-related. Appeals to forward mail to raise money for a worthy cause (for example), even if not actually a hoax, may not be an appropriate use of company resources. End users should be educated to be skeptical, rather than believing that everything heard from Web sites, colleagues, newsgroups, or the media is true, or completely true.

Anti-Spam Policies

Employees should be strictly forbidden to use company resources for the dissemination of inappropriate mass e-mail for private or work-related purposes. Mailing lists specifically set up for dissemination of particular types of work-related information are an exception, if the type of information broadcast is appropriate to the list. However, spamming a mailing list should never be considered appropriate. Employees should be expected to react appropriately to spam and related nuisances. Advice should be available on when it is appropriate simply to trash messages and when it is required to report and (where appropriate) forwarding them to the appropriate quarter and following their advice on what further action to take, if any. Direct response to spam (including angry replies or following instructions to unsubscribe) can cause more damage than ignoring or simply deleting offending messages, and should be discouraged or controlled, subject to local policy. Spam that may have pedophilic content, for instance, may be subject to special handling considerations, depending on local legal frameworks.

"Spoofing," "munging," or forging mail headers in the headers of e-mail or news postings should be forbidden, whether as a means of disguising the source of mass e-mail (there is no legitimate business reason for doing this) or as a means of making it more difficult for spammers to harvest an address. Exceptions may be made for manipulating the address as in the interpolation of spaces or the substitution of AT and DOT for @ or the period character to make it harder for automatic harvesting software to recognize a valid address. (However, the effectiveness of such trivial manipulations against modern harvesting tools is likely to be disappointing.) Spoofing likely to ease the spoofer's burden of junk mail at the expense of other legitimate users should be seriously discouraged. The use of anonymous e-mail should be considered specifically and according to local practice.

Advice should be available to end users on minimizing exposure to junk mail. Some research (Centre for Democracy and Technology 2003) suggests that the most common means for address harvesting is from the Web, so measures that might be explored include:

- Not publishing e-mail addresses unnecessarily on the Web, and obfuscating addresses where they *do* need to be published on Web sites. (This is a measure to avoid the automated harvesting of e-mail addresses by spammers, and should not be confused with the forging of e-mail headers, which is generally deprecated.)
- Restrictions on membership of and specific posts to newsgroups, Web forums and mailing-lists from work addresses except as required for work purposes.

It also makes sense at an administrative and technical level to consider mitigating the impact of direct harvesting attacks by mandating account names that may be less susceptible to automated guessing (dictionary) attacks than obvious formats like [firstname][surname-initial]@ or [firstname-initial][surname]@, and by specifying appropriate Mail Transfer Agent (MTA) configurations to counteract brute-force guessing attacks (e.g., by flagging traffic patterns that suggest such an attack preparatory to blocking the domain).

Codes of Conduct

All staff should be required to meet prescribed ethical standards, but particular attention should be paid to staff with special skill sets and corresponding privileges (technical management, MIS [Management Information Systems] personnel). It might be specified that all staff are expected to conform with the following strictures, which are staples of many codes of conduct used by IT professional peer organizations:

- Promote public health and safety
- Respect the legitimate rights of others—property rights, copyrights, intellectual property, and so on
- Comply with and maintain knowledge of standards, policies, and legislation
- Exert due care and diligence
- Refuse inducements
- Avoid disclosing confidential information
- Avoid conflicts of interest
- Conform to and maintain relevant professional standards in e-mail
- Advance public/customer knowledge
- Support fellow professionals
- Do not exceed their own expertise or authority
- Upgrade skills when opportunities exist
- Accept professional responsibility. Follow through and do not offload inappropriately or evade responsibility by blaming others.
- Access systems, data, resources only when authorized and when appropriate.

CONCLUSION

Even as the rest of us have taken to the Internet in general and e-mail in particular, the bad guys have quickly spotted the potential for exploitation, to the point at which legitimate traffic is increasingly swamped by e-mail abuse. These problems are accentuated by the essential insecurity of core messaging protocols, though the impact of these vulnerabilities can be mitigated by the application of encryption and authentication protocols such as TLS (Transport Layer Security), further supported by abuse-specific technologies such as antivirus (in its many forms) and anti-spam technologies such as those described in this article. However, it can be assumed that spammers, virus writers, scammers, and other undesirables will continue to waste their energy and creativity on new ways to evade these technologies, at least as long as home users fail to protect themselves and businesses fail to supplement technical measures with education and policy.

GLOSSARY

419 (Nigerian Scam, Advance-Fee Fraud): A fraudulent communication, nowadays mostly e-mail, that attempts to persuade the target to take part in a (sometimes frankly illegal) scheme to transfer large sums of money to an account in the target's country, in return for a percentage of those funds. However, the victim is persuaded to part with sensitive financial information or sizable funds up front for taxes, bribes etc. and never sees any return. A common variation is to persuade the victim that they have won a lottery, but are required to pay local taxes before they receive their "winnings."

AUP (Acceptable Use Policy): Guidelines for users on what constitutes acceptable usage of a system, network services, etc.

Blacklisting: In spam management, the blocking or other special treatment of messages with particular attributes (e.g. originating from a known spam-friendly e-mail address or domain). A DNS blacklist (DNSBL) is a list of mail sources (usually IP addresses) associated with spam, and (ideally) continuously maintained by the addition and removal of addresses as appropriate, as a commercial or voluntary service. However, badly conceived and/or implemented blacklists can generate considerable false positive problems. (See also RBL).

Chain Letter: Originally a letter promising good luck if you pass it on to others or misfortune if you do not, thus breaking the chain. Hoax virus alerts are a special case of electronic chain mail: the recipient is urged to pass on the warning to everyone he or she knows.

Denial of Service (DoS) Attack: An attack that compromises the availability of system services and therefore data. DoS attacks in the e-mail context often consist of attempts to overwhelm a mail server or an individual's ability to handle mail by sheer volume of traffic, or to exceed an individual's quota of incoming e-mail (e.g. by mail-bombing or subscription bombing). When an attack is amplified by the use of many machines (as when linked in a botnet), the attack is referred to as a "distributed denial of service" (DDoS) attack.

Direct Harvest Attack (DHA): An attempt to harvest target e-mail addresses for spam or virus dissemination purposes, often by brute-force guessing of account names.

Ethics: Moral philosophy, dealing with human conduct and character. In the context of practical computer ethics, we are mostly concerned with "normative ethics," the establishment of a code of values based on accepted social norms, but applied specifically to the use of computers.

False Positive: Term used when software incorrectly diagnoses the presence of malicious software. In anti-spam terms, it is usually applied to a message incorrectly identified as spam—such messages are sometimes referred to as "ham."

File Type: In the virus context, especially with reference to mass mailers, the important characteristic of a file type is whether it is executable—that is, whether it contains executable code, and that is the use of the term here. The file type may be indicated by the filename extension, and much generic filtering is based on checking that attribute, but a virus writer can change the extension to mislead the target. Some filters check file headers, which is generally more accurate but requires considerably more work and maintenance.

Hybrid Malware: Malware that can gain a foothold and execute on a target system both by exploiting a vulnerability in software and by using social engineering to track the system user, thus combining both the self-launching and user-launched approaches.

Malware: Malicious code (*mal*icious soft*ware*) such as viruses and Trojan horses.

Mass Mailer: A malicious program whose main or only infection mechanism is to mail itself out to e-mail addresses found on an infected system in the hope of persuading the recipient by social engineering into executing an attached copy of the mass mailer. (Some mass mailers may also use software vulnerabilities to force execution of embedded code without the intervention of the recipient.)

Message Headers: The part of an e-mail message that contains information about the identities of the sender and the intended recipient, where replies should be sent, and information about the route the message has taken to get from one party to the other. However, a very high proportion of e-mail abuse is enabled by the ease with which headers can be forged (either manually or automatically).

Ponzi Schemes: A fraudulent scheme by which the victim is persuaded to "invest" money. As the number of participants increases, the fraudster uses money sent by later investors to pay off early investors and build up numbers and confidence in the scheme, until he chooses to disappear with the money. The Internet offers virtually cost-less administration of such schemes.

POP: Post office protocol: allows a client machine to transfer e-mail from a server. Mail received via this protocol evades central anti-malware measures if applied only to an SMTP service, and unless the client machine has an up-to-date desktop antivirus program, it becomes vulnerable to mass mailers and other incoming e-mail abuse. Some organizations address this potential weakness by blocking port 110, thus disabling the service.

Pyramid Schemes: An allegedly profitable scheme by which one person sends money to a number of people who send money to a number of people ad infinitum. A common variation is to disguise this (generally illegal) scheme as a "legitimate" scheme to buy and sell mailing lists, software, t-shirts and so on.

Realtime Blackhole List (RBL): RBL is actually a service mark of MAPS LLC, but the term is often applied incorrectly to other DNS blacklists (DNSBLs).

Scam: An attempt to con money or services or information out of the victim. Scams always involve an element of deception, and may be distributed as a chain letter, among other means (including spam); 419s and phishing scams are particularly common at time of writing.

Self-Launching Malware: Malware, especially a worm, that exploits a vulnerability in software or operating systems rather than social engineering to gain a foothold and execute on a target system.

Signature: See "Virus Definition"

SMTP: Simple Mail Transfer Protocol. A core e-mail standard that is not, in itself, significantly secured against header forgery or breaches of confidentiality, and therefore open to a variety of forms of e-mail abuse.

Social Engineering: A term applied to a variety of attacks that rely on exploiting human weakness rather than technological loopholes. Often specifically applied to: (1) password stealing, and (2) manipulation of an e-mail recipient into running an attached malicious program, but has many other applications.

Spam: Unsolicited e-mail, especially commercial/junk e-mail. Also applied to the practice of posting large numbers of identical messages to multiple newsgroups. "Hardcore" or "professional" spam are terms sometimes applied to junk mail including a measure of deception (forged headers, misleading or even fraudulent content) and incorporates techniques intended to evade gateway filters and other anti-spam measures. The term derives, probably via a Monty Python sketch, from the canned meat marketed by Hormel who are understandably sensitive about the use of the name in the context of e-mail abuse.

UBE: Unsolicited bulk e-mail. The term is sometimes used synonymously with "spam."

UCE: Unsolicited commercial e-mail. Large subset of UBE with an overt commercial agenda. This term is also sometimes used synonymously with "spam."

User-Launched Malware: Malware that relies on social engineering to persuade a human victim to execute it.

Virus Definition: A scan string or algorithm used by a virus-specific scanner to recognize a known virus. Sometimes (but not altogether correctly) referred to as a signature, which in antivirus is usually taken to refer to matching a static string, a technique that has not been much used in that context for many years.

Virus-Specific Scanner: An antivirus scanner that checks an infectable object for indications that it is infected by a known virus, rather than for generic indications of possible infection. Essentially, it looks for matches to a virus definitions database. Sometimes referred to as a known virus scanner, or, less correctly, as a signature scanner.

Vulnerability: Condition of an asset in which a risk-reducing safeguard has not been applied, or is not fully effective in reducing risk. Sometimes used less formally to refer simply to a flaw, especially a programming error, which may require application of a patch.

Web Mail: A generic term applied to e-mail that, irrespective of the underlying mail transfer protocol, is accessed via a Web interface. Some mail services are accessible only by this means (Hotmail, Bigfoot etc.), but many ISPs include an additional Web interface facility as a courtesy to allow their customers to access their mail on systems other than their own PCs. From a security standpoint, a major corporate problem with Web mail stems from the fact that it is less susceptible to central filtering for viruses and other forms of abuse. However, many of the bigger providers apply their own antivirus and/or anti-spam measures.

Worm: A replicative, malicious program. The term is particularly applied to malware that spreads across networks and does not infect another program parasitically (as opposed to "true" viruses). The term is also often applied to mass mailers.

CROSS REFERENCES

See *Authentication*; *Computer Network Management*; *Firewalls*; *Intrusion Detection Systems*; *Worms and Viruses*.

REFERENCES

419 Coalition. 2004. http://home.rica.net/alphae/419coal (accessed June 8, 2007).

APWG. 2006. www.antiphishing.org (accessed June 7, 2007).

Barrett, D. J. 1996. *Bandits on the information superhighway*. Sebastopol, CA: O'Reilly.

Braverman M. 2006. The Windows malicious software removal tool: Progress made, trends observed. http://go.microsoft.com/fwlink/?linkid=67998 (accessed June 8, 2007).

Canavan J. 2005. The evolution of malicious IRC bots. In *Proceedings of the 15th Virus Bulletin International Conference*. Abingdon, UK: Sophos.

Centre for Democracy and Technology. 2003. www.cdt.org/speech/spam/030319spamreport.shtml (accessed June 17, 2007).

CIAC. 2004. http://hoaxbusters.ciac.org/HBHoaxInfo.html#what (accessed June 8, 2007).

CNN. 2003. www.cnn.com/2003/TECH/internet/12/29/cyber.blackmail.reut (accessed June 8, 2007).

CPNI. 2004. *Guidance on handling files with possible malicious content*. Technical Note 03/04 Issued 19 March 2004. www.cpni.gov.uk/Products/technicalnotes/default.aspx?id=tn-20040319-00147.xml (accessed June 7, 2007).

CPNI. 2005. *Targeted Trojan e-mail attacks*. NISCC Briefing 455/2005 Issued 16 June 2005. www.cpni.gov.uk/docs/ttea.pdf (accessed June 7, 2007).

EEMA. 2003. Spam and e-mail abuse management. Available to members at: http://www.eema.org/ (accessed June 16, 2006).

F-Secure. 2005. www.f-secure.com/2005/2 (accessed June 8, 2007).

F-Secure. 2004. www.f-secure.com/v-descs/novarg.shtml (accessed May 19, 2007).

www.f-secure.com/v-descs/mydoom_b.shtml (accessed June 8, 2007).

Gordon S., and D. Chess. 1998. Where there's smoke, there's mirrors: The truth about Trojan horses on the Internet. www.research.ibm.com/antivirus/SciPapers/Smoke/smoke.html (accessed June 8, 2007).

Gordon S., R. Ford, and J. Wells. 1997. Hoaxes and hypes. In *Proceedings of the Seventh Virus Bulletin International Conference*, 49–66. Abingdon, UK: Virus Bulletin.

Grimes R. A. 2001. *Malicious mobile code—virus protection for Windows*. Sebastopol, CA: O'Reilly.

Harley, D. A. 1997. Macs and macros: the state of the Macintosh nation. In *Proceedings of the Seventh International Virus Bulletin Conference*, 67–98. Abingdon: UK: Virus Bulletin.

———. 1998. Refloating the Titanic—Dealing with social engineering attacks. In *EICAR 98 Conference Proceedings (CD)*. Munich, Germany: EICAR.

———. 2000. The e-mail of the species—Worms, chain-letters, spam and other abuses. Reserve paper for 2000 Virus Bulletin International Conference. Available at: mailto:dharley@smallblue-greenworld.co.uk.

———. 2002. The future of malicious code: predictions on blended threats, e-mail exploits, social engineering and more. *Information Security* 5(5):36–8.

———. 2002. Trojans. In *Maximum security*, 351–77. Indianapolis: SAMS.

———. 2003. Fact, fiction and managed anti-malware services—Vendors, resellers, and customers divided by a common language. In *Proceedings of the 13th Virus Bulletin International Conference*. Abingdon, UK: Virus Bulletin.

———. 2004. Fighting the epidemic. *SC Magazine* January:28–9.

——— 2006. *Reputation services and spam control report*. http://ferris.com/view_content.php?o=Spam+Control&id=1591 (accessed July 27, 2006).

Harley D. A., and U. Gattiker. 2002. Man, myth, memetics and malware. In *Proceedings of the 2002 EICAR conference*. Munich, Germany: EICAR.

Harley, D. A., R. M. Slade, and U. Gattiker. 2001. *Viruses revealed*. Berkeley, CA: Osborne.

Harley D.A. 2007. Stalkers on your Desktop. In *The AVIEN Guide to Managing Malware in the Enterprise*, Rockland MA. Syngress (In press.)

Harley D.A., and T. Bradley. 2007. Big Bad Botnets. In *The AVIEN Guide to Managing Malware in the Enterprise*, edited by D. Harley, Rockland MA. Syngress (In press.)

Harley D.A. and A. Lee. 2007. A Pretty Kettle of Phish. (In press. Will be available at www.eset.com/download/whitepapers.php.)

Hruska, J. 1992. *Computer viruses and anti-virus warfare*. Chichester, UK: Ellis Horwood.

Hypponen, M. 2003. F-Secure Corporation's Data Security Summary for 2003: The Year of the worm. www.f-secure.com/2003/ (accessed June 8, 2007).

James L. 2005. *Phishing exposed*. Rockland, MA: Syngress.

Johnson, K. 2000. *Internet e-mail protocols—A developer's guide*. Reading, MA: Addison-Wesley.

Kabay, M. E. 1996. *The NCSA guide to enterprise security*. New York: McGraw-Hill.

Mashevsky, Y. 2005. Watershed in malicious code evolution. www.viruslist.com/en/analysis?pubid=167798878 (accessed June 8, 2007).

Microsoft. 1999 *Windows security update, 7th December 1999*. www.microsoft.com/windows98/downloads/contents/wucritical/scriptlet/default.asp (accessed June 16, 2006).

Overton, M. 2005. *Bots and botnets: Risks, issues and prevention*. Abingdon, UK: Virus Bulletin. http://arachnid.homeip.net/papers/VB2005-Bots_and_Botnets-1.0.2.pdf (accessed June 8, 2007).

PC Mag. 2006. Definition of Web bug. www.pcmag.com/encyclopedia_term/0,2542,t=Web+bug&i=54280,00.asp (accessed June 8, 2007).

Rivner, U. 2006. Phishing supply chain parts 1 & 2. www.rsasecurity.com/blog/entry.asp?id=1088; www.rsasecurity.com/blog/entry.asp?id=1090 (accessed June 8, 2007).

Schiller, C., J. Binkley, D. Harley, G. Evron, T. Bradley, C. Willems, and M. Cross. 2007. *Botnets: the Killer Web App*. Rockland MA: Syngress

Schwartz, A., and S. Garfinkel, S. 1998. *Stopping Spam*. Sebastopol, CA: O'Reilly.

Slade, R. 1996. *Robert Slade's guide to computer viruses*. New York: Springer.

Symantec. 2004. http://securityresponse.symantec.com/avcenter/venc/data/cih.html (accessed June 8, 2007).

Szor, P. 2005. *The art of computer virus research and defense*. Upper Saddle River, NJ: Symantec/Addison-Wesley.

Thompson, R. 2002. Virus varieties. In *Computer security handbook*, 4th ed. Edited by S. Bosworth and M. E. Kabay, 9.4–9.8. New York: Wiley.

Wallener, D. 2006. What is penny stock fraud? www.wisegeek.com/what-is-penny-stock-fraud.htm (accessed June 8, 2007).

FURTHER READING

Hughes, L. 1998. *Internet e-mail: Protocols, standards, and implementation*. Norwood, MA Artech.

Loshin, P, and P. Hoffman. 2000. *Essential e-mail standards: RFCs and protocols made practical*. New York: Wiley.

Rhoton, J. 2000. *Programmer's guide to internet mail*. Woburn, MA: Digital Press.

419 Information

419 samples and lottery winner variants: www.data-wales.co.uk/nigerian.htm (accessed June 8, 2007).

The 419 Coalition Web site: http://home.rica.net/alphae/419coal (accessed June 8, 2007).

UK Metropolitan Police general fraud information: www.met.police.uk/fraudalert; their 419 information page is at www.met.police.uk/fraudalert/419.htm (accessed June 8, 2007).

www.superhighway.is/iis/index.asp (accessed June 8, 2007).

E-Mail Cryptography/Confidentiality Resources

Blum, R. 2002. *Open source e-mail security*. Indianapolis: SAMS.

Schneier, B. 1995. *E-mail security*. New York: Wiley.

Hoaxes, Urban Legends, and Memetic Malware (Web Pages)

http://hoaxbusters.ciac.org/ (accessed June 8, 2007).

http://urbanlegends.about.com (accessed June 8, 2007).

www.f-secure.com/hoaxes/ (accessed June 8, 2007).

www.korova.com/virus/hoax.htm (accessed June 8, 2007).

www.mcafee.com (accessed June 8, 2007).

www.securitycritics.org (accessed June 8, 2007).

www.snopes.com (accessed June 8, 2007).

www.sophos.com (accessed June 8, 2007).

www.symantec.com/ (accessed June 8, 2007).

Memetics

Blackmore, S. 1999. *The meme machine*. Oxford: Oxford University Press.

Brodie, R. 1996. *Virus of the mind: The new science of the meme*. Seattle, WA: Integral Press.

Dawkins, R. Oxford University Press, Oxford, 1976. *The selfish gene: River out of Eden* (Phoenix, London, 1995), and *Unweaving the rainbow.* 1998, Penguin, Harmondsworth UK (Social biology, memetics, and specific material on chain letters. Also: *Viruses of the mind*. http://cscs.umich.edu/~crshalizi/Dawkins/viruses-of-the-mind.html. (accessed June 8, 2007).

Harley, D. 1997. *Dealing with Internet hoaxes/alerts*. http://cluestick.me.uk/hoax/harley_hoaxes.txt (accessed June 8, 2007).

http://arachnid.homeip.net/papers/VB2001_Electronic_Ephemera-1.01.pdf (accessed June 8, 2007).

http://arachnid.homeip.net/papers/VB2005-Bots_and_Botnets-1.0.2.pdf (accessed June 8, 2007).

http://cluestick.me.uk/hoax/index.htm#papers (accessed June 8, 2007).

Kaminski, J. 1997. Multiplatform Attack—In the land of hoaxes. In *Proceedings of the 1997 Virus Bulletin International Conference*. Abingdon UK: Virus Bulletin.

Overton, M. 2000. Safe hex in the 21st century—Part 1. *Virus Bulletin* June:16–7.

Overton, M. (2000). Safe hex in the 21st century—Part 2. *Virus Bulletin* July:14–5.

Multilevel Marketing

www.mlmwatch.org/

www.mlmsurvivor.com/ (accessed June 8, 2007)

www.quackwatch.org/01QuackeryRelatedTopics/mlm.html (accessed June 8, 2007)

Newsgroups

All other spam issues: news.admin.net-abuse.misc

Discussion of how to combat Spam: news.admin.net-abuse.policy

Discussion of usenet spam: news.admin.net-abuse.usenet

Discussion of e-mail spams: news.admin.net-abuse.e-mail

Phishing

Anti-Phishing Best Practices for ISPs and Mailbox Providers: www.antiphishing.org/reports/bestpracticesforisps.pdf (accessed June 8, 2007)

Anti-Phishing Working Group: www.antiphishing.org/apwg.htm (accessed June 8, 2007).

Dedicated anti-phishing service: www.millersmiles.co.uk/ (accessed June 8, 2007).

Harley D.A., A. Lee. Phish Phodder: is User Education Helping or Hindering? In *Proceedings of the 17th Virus Bulletin International Conference*. Abingdon, UK: Virus Bulletin.

Phishing Incident Reporting and Termination (PIRT) Squad: www.castlecops.com/pirt (accessed June 8, 2007).

Quizzes and tips on phish recognition: www.sonicwall.com/phishing/quiztest.html (accessed June 8, 2007).

Policy Resources

Flynn, N. 2001. The ePolicy handbook. New York: Amacom.

Flynn, N., and R. Kahn. 2003. *E-mail rules: A business guide to managing policies, security, and legal issues for e-mail and digital communications*. New York: Amacom.

Overley, M. R. 1999. *E-policy: How to develop computer, e-mail and Internet guidelines to protect your company and its assets*. New York: Amacom.

Wood, C. C. 2006. *Information security policies made easy* www.informationshield.com (accessed May 19, 2007).

Spam

Mailscanner (free, highly configurable antispam product from University of Southampton, includes capacity to plug in antivirus scanning and works with SpamAssassin): www.sng.ecs.soton.ac.uk/mailscanner (accessed June 8, 2007).

MessageLabs (Anti-Virus and Anti-spam managed services): www.messagelabs.com. (accessed June 8, 2007).

Reading e-mail headers: www.spamcop.net/fom-serve/cache/19.html (accessed June 10, 2007) and www.haltabuse.org/help/headers/ (accessed June 8, 2007).

SpamAssassin open source filtering product: http://eu.spamassassin.org/index.html (accessed June 10, 2007).

Spamcop (Spam reporting, spam blocking service) FAQ: www.spamcop.net/fom-serve/cache/1.html (accessed June 8, 2007).

Spam management information, discussion and resources: www.cauce.org (accessed June 8, 2007), www.euro.cauce.org (accessed June 8, 2007), www.claws-and-paws.

com/spam-l (accessed June 8, 2007), www.spamhaus.org (accessed June 8, 2007), www.elsop.com/wrc/complain.htm (accessed June 8, 2007), and www.junkbusters.com. (accessed June 8, 2007).

Spoofing Mass Mailers

Burrell, R. 2004. *The plague of viruses that send e-mail with forged "from:" fields*. www.itd.umich.edu/virusbusters/forged_from.html (accessed May 19, 2007).

Information on E-mail Spoofing: www.cert.org/tech_tips/e-mail_spoofing.html (accessed June 8, 2007). www.itd.umich.edu/virusbusters/forged_spam.html (accessed June 8, 2007).

Trojan Information Resources

This site was comprehensive but no longer seems to be updated: www.simovits.com/trojans/trojans.html (accessed June 8, 2007). Other sites specializing in Trojans and related issues include: www.moosoft.com/products/cleaner/search (accessed June 8, 2007) and www.chebucto.ns.ca/~rakerman/trojan-port-table.html (accessed June 8, 2007).

Virus Information Resources

Microsoft's Antivirus Defense-in-Depth Guide is available at www.microsoft.com/technet/security/guidance/avdind_0.mspx (accessed June 8, 2007).

Virus Bulletin is a specialist monthly publication that runs a major yearly virus and spam-related conference. The following page from their Web site links to a wide range of resources, including antivirus vendors, virus information databases, and so on: www.virusbtn.com/resources/links/index.xml (accessed June 8, 2007).

WildList International tracks viruses in the wild: www.wildlist.org (accessed June 8, 2007). The following antivirus vendor sites include virus information databases. Since specific page URLs tend to change over time, only top-level site URLs are given: www.sophos.com (accessed June 8, 2007) www.eset.com (accessed June 8, 2007).

www.f-secure.com (accessed June 8, 2007), http://viruslist.com (accessed June 8, 2007), www.symantec.com (accessed June 8, 2007), www.mcafee.com (accessed June 8, 2007), and www.complex.is (accessed June 8, 2007).

Virtual Private Networks

G. I. Papadimitriou, *Aristotle University, Thessaloniki, Greece,* M. S. Obaidat, *Monmouth University,*
C. Papazoglou, A. S. Pomportsis, *Aristotle University, Thessaloniki, Greece*

INTRODUCTION

The best way to come up with a definition of the term *virtual private network* (VPN) is to analyze each word separately. Having done that, Ferguson and Huston (1998) came up with the following definition:

> A VPN is a communications environment in which access is controlled to permit peer connections only within a defined community of interest, and is constructed through some form of partitioning of a common underlying communications medium, where this underlying communications medium provides services to the network on a non-exclusive basis.

Ferguson and Huston also provided a simpler and less formal description of a VPN as a private network constructed within a public network infrastructure, such as the global Internet. Others define a VPN as a network that allows two or more private networks to be connected over a publicly accessed network. It is similar to wide area networks (WANs) or a securely encrypted tunnel. The chief feature of VPNs is that they use public networks like the Internet rather than using expensive, private leased lines while having similar security and encryption features as a private network (Obaidat and Boudriga 2007).

VPNs have evolved as a compromise for enterprises desiring the convenience and cost-effectiveness offered by shared networks, but requiring the strong security offered by private networks. Whereas closed WANs use isolation to ensure that data are secure, VPNs use a combination of encryption, authentication, access management and tunneling to provide access only to authorized parties and to protect data while in transit (Hunt and Rodgers 2003). To emulate a point-to-point link, data are encapsulated, or wrapped, with a header that provides routing information allowing it to traverse the shared or public internetworks to reach its end point. To emulate a private link, the data being sent are encrypted for confidentiality. Packets that are intercepted on the shared or public network are indecipherable without the encryption keys (Arora, Vemuganti, and Allani 2001).

In order to enable the use of VPN functions, special software can be added on top of a general computing platform, such as a UNIX or Windows operating system. Alternatively, special hardware augmented with software can be used to provide VPN functions. Sometimes, VPN functions are added to a hardware-based network device such as a router or a firewall. In other cases, VPN functions are built from the ground up and routing and firewall capabilities are added. A corporation can either create and manage the VPN itself or purchase VPN services from a service provider (Strayer and Yuan 2001).

VPNs first appeared in 1984, when the service was offered to U.S. users by Sprint, with MCI and AT&T producing competing products soon after. In their initial form, VPNs were offered as a flexible, cost-effective approach to the problem of connecting large, dispersed groups of users. Private networks were the main alternative, and although equivalent functionality could be achieved via the public switched telephone network (PSTN), this was a limited solution because of the length of full national telephone numbers and the lack of in-dialing capabilities from the PSTN. Such a VPN acted as a PSTN emulation of a dedicated private network, using the resources of the PSTN in a time-sharing arrangement with other traffic (Hunt and Rodgers 2003).

Many forms of VPNs have existed in the technology's relatively short lifetime. The level of variety has resulted from the distinct domains of expertise of the companies developing and marketing VPN solutions. For example, hardware manufacturers may offer customer premise equipment-based solutions (i.e. devices installed at the company's headquarters and subdivisions), whereas an Internet service provider (ISP) would be more likely to offer a network-based solution (Hunt and Rodgers 2003).

The level of confusion and lack of interoperability between competing products led to the submission of a VPN framework to the Internet Engineering Task Force (IETF) in 1999, which defined VPNs as "the emulation of a private WAN facility using IP facilities." A number of VPN implementations have been proposed to operate over a variety of underlying infrastructures and protocols, including asynchronous transfer mode (ATM), multiprotocol label switching (MPLS), Ethernet, IP, and heterogeneous backbones (Hunt and Rodgers 2003).

Traditional private networks facilitate connectivity among various network entities through a set of links comprised of dedicated circuits. These may be leased from public telecommunication carriers or may be privately installed wiring. The capacity of these links is available at all times, albeit fixed and inflexible. The traffic on these private networks belongs only to the enterprise or company deploying the network. Therefore, there is an assured level of performance associated with the network. Such assurances come with a price.

The drawbacks of this approach are:

> Traditional private networks are not cheap to plan and deploy. The costs associated with dedicated links are especially high when they involve international locations [and security concerns are exacerbated due to the international transport of information]. The planning phase of such networks involves detailed estimates of the applications, their traffic patterns and their growth rates. Also, the planning periods are long because of the work involved in calculating these estimates. (Arora et al. 2001)

Further, dedicated links take time to install. It is not unusual that telecommunication carriers take sixty to ninety days to install and activate a dedicated link. Such a long waiting period adversely affects the company's ability to react to the quick changes in these areas (Arora et al. 2001).

Another trend is the mobility of today's workforce. Portable computing facilities such as laptops and palm-based devices have made it easy for people to work without being physically present in their offices. This also makes less investment into real estate (Arora et al. 2001).

To support the increase in home offices, companies need to provide a reliable information technology (IT) infrastructure so that employees can access a company's information from remote locations. This has resulted in large modem pools for employees to dial in. The cost keeps increasing because of the complexity of managing and maintaining the large modem pools. An additional cost with the mobile users is the long-distance calls or toll-free numbers paid for by the company. The costs are much higher if we consider international calling. For companies with a large mobile workforce, these expenses add up to significant numbers (Arora et al. 2001).

In addition, in the case of the private network, the company has to manage the network and all its associated elements, invest capital in network switching infrastructure, hire trained staff, and assume complete responsibility for the provisioning and ongoing maintenance of the network service. Such a dedicated use of transport services, equipment, and staff is often difficult to justify for many small-to-medium-sized organizations, and while the functionality of a private network system is required, the expressed desire is to reduce the cost of the service through the use of shared transport services, equipment, and management (Ferguson and Huston 1998).

In this direction, VPNs promise to help organizations support sales over the Internet more economically, tying business partners and suppliers together, linking branch offices, and supporting telecommuter access to corporate network resources. A VPN can reduce costs by replacing multiple communication links and legacy equipment with a single connection and one piece of equipment for each location (Younglove 2000). In order to extend the reach of a company's intranet(s), a VPN over the Internet promises two benefits: cost efficiency and global reachability. However there are three major concerns about VPN technology: security, manageability, and performance (Günter 2001).

Security

In order for Virtual Private Networks to be private the transmitted data must be encrypted before entering the Internet, since the Internet is considered an untrusted network. Everybody can connect to the Internet and there is no guaranty that participants stick to any policy or rule. However, protecting the traveling data will not protect the information inside the Intranet from unauthorized access (Obaidat and Boudriga 2007; Günter 2001).

Manageability of VPNs

A company's telecommunication requirements and equipment evolve at a high speed. The VPN management must be able to cope with these changes while avoiding high expenses. VPNs are connected to many different entities that even by themselves are hard to manage and that constantly evolve. Such entities include the company's physical network (eventually featuring unregistered IP addresses), the company's security policy, the company's electronic services, and the company's ISPs (Günter 2001).

Performance of VPNs

Since ISPs deliver IP packets still on a "best effort" basis, the transport performance of a VPN over the Internet cannot be predicted, it is variable. Furthermore, security measures (encryption and authentication) can decrease transport performance significantly. This also points out two management problems: The clients must be enabled to (a) measure the performance, and (b) customize the VPN (e.g., the security options) in order to optimize it (Günter 2001).

A VPN solution consists of multiple, appropriately configured VPN devices that are placed in the appropriate locations within the network. As with any network, after all the VPN devices are installed and configured, the network should be continually monitored and managed (Strayer and Yuan 2001).

The most common VPN device is the VPN gateway, which acts as the gatekeeper for network traffic to and from protected resources. Tunnels are established from the VPN gateway to other appropriate VPN devices serving as tunnel end points. A VPN gateway is usually located at the corporate network perimeter, and it acts on behalf of the protected network resources within the corporate intranet to negotiate and render security services. The gateway assembles the tunneling, authentication, access control, and data security functions into a single device. The details of how these functions are integrated within a VPN gateway are specific to a vendor's implementation. Sometimes these functions can be integrated into existing router or firewall products. Sometimes a VPN gateway can be a stand-alone device that performs pure VPN functions, without firewall or dynamic routing exchange capabilities (Strayer and Yuan 2001).

The data traffic coming from the public interfaces (inbound traffic) is thoroughly examined by the gateway according to the security policies. Usually, only the traffic from the established secure tunnels should be processed by the VPN gateway. If no secure tunnel is found, the traffic should be dropped immediately, unless its purpose is to negotiate and establish a secure tunnel. Depending on the implementation, an alert or alarm can be generated to notify the network management station (Strayer and Yuan 2001).

The data traffic coming from the private interfaces and exiting to the public interface (outbound traffic) is deemed secure a priori, even though many network attacks are generated within a corporate network. The outbound traffic is examined according to a set of policies on the gateway. If secure tunneling is required for the traffic, the VPN gateway first determines whether such a tunnel is already in place. If it is not, the gateway attempts to establish a new tunnel with the intended device—either another VPN gateway or simply some other device with secure tunneling capabilities. After the tunnel is established, the traffic is processed according to the tunnel rules and is sent into the tunnel. The traffic from the private interface can also be dropped if a policy cannot be found. Depending on how quickly a secure tunnel can be established, the VPN gateway may buffer the outbound packet before the secure tunnel is in place (Strayer and Yuan 2001).

The VPN client is software used for remote VPN access for a single computer or user. Unlike the VPN gateway, which is a specialized device and can protect multiple network resources at the same time, the VPN client software is usually installed on an individual computer and serves that computer only. Generally, VPN client software creates a secure path from the client computer to a designated VPN gateway. The secure tunnel enables the client computer to obtain IP connectivity to access the network resources protected by that particular VPN gateway.

VPN client software also must implement the same functions as VPN gateways—tunneling, authentication, access control, and data security—although these implementations may be simpler or have fewer options. For example, the VPN software usually implements only one of the tunneling protocols. Because the remote computer does not act on behalf of any other users or resources, the access control can also be less complex.

Unlike the VPN gateway, in which all of the gateway's hardware and software is geared toward the VPN functionality, VPN client software is usually just an application running on a general-purpose operating system on the remote computer. Consequently, the client software should carefully consider its interactions with the operating system.

One of the important concerns regarding VPN client software is the simplicity of installation and operation. Because client software is expected to be deployed widely on end users' machines, it must be easily installed and easily operated by regular computer users who may not know much about the operating system, software compatibility, remote access, or VPNs. A VPN gateway, on the other hand, is usually deployed on the company's corporate network site and is managed by IT professionals.

VPN client software must work within the constraints of host computers' operating systems, whether the software is deeply integrated with the operating system or runs as an application. Because networking is a major function of today's computers, almost all modern operating systems have built-in networking functionality. However, few have strong support for VPN capabilities integrated into the operating system. As a result, separate VPN client software must be written for those operating systems that lack the VPN functionality. Furthermore, the same VPN client software may need to be ported to different operating systems, even for different release versions of the same operating system (Yuan 2002).

There are two fundamental architectures for implementing network-based VPNs: virtual routers (VRs) and piggybacking. The main difference between the two architectures resides in the model used to achieve VPN reachability and membership functions. In the VR model, each VR in the VPN domain is running an instance of routing protocol responsible for disseminating VPN reachability information between VRs. Therefore, VPN membership and VPN reachability are treated as separate functions, and separate mechanisms are used to implement these functions. VPN reachability is carried out by a per-VPN instance of routing, and a range of mechanisms is possible for determining membership. In the piggyback model the VPN network layer is terminated at the edge of the backbone, and a backbone routing protocol (i.e., extended border gateway protocol-4, BGP-4) is responsible for disseminating the VPN membership and reachability information between provider edge (PE) routers for all the VPNs configured on the PE (Ould-Brahim et al. 2003).

TYPES OF VPN SERVICES

A variety of VPN implementations and configurations exists to cater to a variety of needs (Metz 2003). Organizations may require their VPN to offer dial-up access or to allow third parties such as customers or suppliers to access specific components of their VPN (Hunt and Rodgers 2003). VPNs can be classified into three broad categories: intranet, extranet, and remote-access VPNs. VPNs can be classified into three broad categories, which are illustrated in Figure 1: intranet, extranet and remote-access VPNs.

Intranet VPNs

An intranet VPN connects a number of local area networks (intranets) located in multiple geographic areas over the shared network infrastructure (Venkateswaran

2001). Typically, this service is used to connect multiple geographic locations of a single company (Arora et al. 2001). An intranet VPN enables the sharing of information and resources among dispersed employees. For example, branch offices can access the network at the head office, typically including key resources such as product or customer databases. Intranet access is strictly limited to these networks, and connections are authenticated. Differing levels of access may be allocated to different sites on the intranet, depending on their purpose (Hunt and Rodgers 2003). Since an Intranet VPN is formed by connecting two or more trusted sites (corporate LANs), which will certainly be protected by firewalls, most security concerns are alleviated.

Extranet VPNs

An extranet VPN extends limited access to corporate computing resources to business partners, such as customers or suppliers, enabling access to shared information (Wright 2000). Such users are restricted to specific areas of the intranet, usually denoted as the demilitarized zone (DMZ). It is the responsibility of the firewall and authentication and access-management facilities to distinguish between company employees and other users, and differentiate their access privileges accordingly; employee connections should be directed to the company intranet, whereas recognized third-party connections should be directed to the DMZ (Hunt and Rodgers 2003). An extranet VPN helps provide connectivity to new external suppliers and customers within a short time. In addition, an extranet VPN supports a number of important e-commerce initiatives, providing opportunities for significant cost savings and efficiency gains.

A number of possible extranet configurations exist, which vary in their level of security and access. The most common examples, in order from most to least secure, are listed below (Hunt and Rodgers 2003).

1. *Private extranet*. Access to a private Extranet is strictly for members only, with no use made of shared networks. Such a configuration cannot be considered a VPN, as it is physically private.
2. *Hybrid extranet*. A hybrid extranet is equivalent in operation to a private extranet, except that it uses one or more shared network to provide connectivity. Membership is restricted, and access to private resources is limited to relevant resources only.
3. *Extranet service provider*. This configuration is offered by an ISP, which builds extranet services based on its backbone network. This is a type of provider-provisioned VPN.
4. *Public extranet*. A public extranet provides data that are globally accessible. An example is a company that provides a public Web site and possibly a public FTP (file transfer protocol) site that Web users are free to access. Such facilities are normally distinct and separate from private file servers, so that public servers cannot be used as staging points for compromising the private component of the extranet.

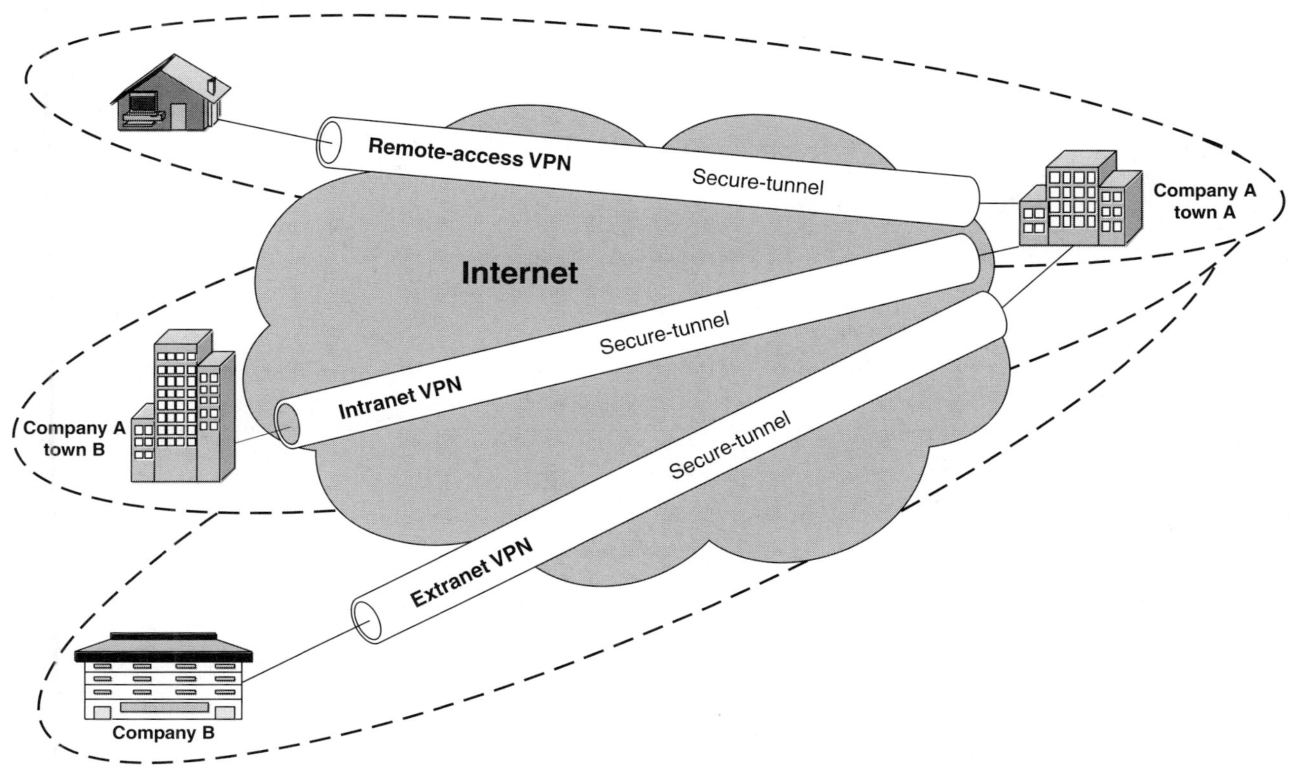

Figure 1: Types of VPN services

Remote-Access VPNs

A remote-access VPN connects telecommuters and mobile users to corporate networks. An ideal VPN enables the remote user to work as if he or she were at a workstation in the office. Deployment of a remote-access VPN can result in considerable cost savings, eliminating the need for the company to manage large modem pools, and replacing the need for toll calls to these modems with calls to local ISP accounts. By taking advantage of a high-speed access infrastructure such as DSL (digital subscriber line), cable modem, or ISDN (integrated services digital network), some of the performance limitations typically associated with remote access can be diminished (Hunt and Rodgers 2003). In addition, wireless networks enable computers to achieve network connectivity with a reasonable amount of bandwidth without a physical connection (Ribeiro, Silva, and Zuquete 2004).

The deployment of remote-access VPNs also gives rise to several security concerns. Precautions must be taken to ensure that the corporate network is not compromised by an insecure remote user. The enforcement of company security policies on remote users is a necessary step in this direction, especially regarding virus protection. It must be noted that the increased flexibility of wireless networks raises additional security issues. On one hand, given the ubiquitous nature of the communication channel, clients of the infrastructure must be authenticated, in order to avoid unauthorized users gaining access to network resources. On the other hand, since any wireless device may listen on the communication channel, data encryption must be enforced if some level of data protection and confidentiality is desired. The security concerns relating to VPNs are discussed in more detail in the following sections.

Table 1 summarizes the characteristics of the types of VPNs that were discussed above.

TUNNELING

Tunneling is defined as the encapsulation of a certain data packet (the original or inner packet) into another data packet (the encapsulating, or outer packet) so that the inner packet is opaque to the network over which the outer packet is routed (Strayer and Yuan 2001).

The need for tunneling arises when it is not appropriate for the inner packet to travel directly across the network for various reasons. For example, tunneling can be used to transport multiple protocols over a network based on some other protocol, or it can be used to hide source and destination addresses of the original packet. When tunneling is used for security services, an unsecured packet is put into a secure, usually encrypted, packet (Strayer and Yuan 2001).

Tunneling allows network traffic from many sources to travel via separate channels across the same infrastructure, and it enables network protocols to traverse incompatible infrastructures. Tunneling also allows traffic from many sources to be differentiated, so that it can be directed to specific destinations and receive specific levels of service (Wright 2000). Two components can uniquely determine a network tunnel: the end points of the tunnel and the encapsulation protocol used to transport the original data packet within the tunnel (Strayer and Yuan 2001).

Tunneling is the most important mechanism used by VPNs. The idea behind this concept is that a part of the route between the originator and the target of the packet is determined independently of the destination IP address. The importance of tunneling in the context of access VPNs in broadband access networks is twofold (Cohen 2003). First, the destination address field of a packet sent in an access VPN may indicate a non-globally-unique IP address of a corporate internal server. Such an address must not be exposed to the Internet routers because these routers do not know how to route such packets. Second, very often a packet sent by a user of an access VPN should be forwarded first to the ISP of this user, and only then from the ISP toward the corporate network. In such a case, the first leg of the routing between the host and the ISP cannot be performed based on the destination IP address of the packet, even if this address is globally unique (Cohen 2003).

The devices at one or both ends of a tunnel could be network address translation (NAT) devices. NAT is another important mechanism used by VPNs. The need for IP address translation arises when a network's internal IP addresses cannot be used outside the network either because they are invalid for use outside or because the internal addressing must be kept private from the external network. Address translation allows hosts in a private

Table 1: Types of VPN Services

	Intranet VPN	Extranet VPN	Remote-Access VPN
Typical scenario	Multiple geograhical locations of a single company	Two or more companies have networked access to a limited amount of each other's corporate data	Mobile users connecting to corporate networks
Typical Users	Employees working in branch offices	Customers, suppliers	Employees working at home or on the road
Security Concerns	Minor	Medium	Major
Implementation	Two or more connected LANs	A company LAN connected to another company's DMZ	Remote users dial up to the corporate network

network to transparently communicate with destinations on an external network and vice versa. NAT is a method by which IP addresses are mapped from one address realm (i.e., network domain) to another, providing transparent routing to end hosts (Srisuresh and Holdrege 1999).

Two main types of tunneling techniques are used by VPNs (Hunt and Rodgers 2003):

- *End-to-end tunneling (also known as "transport model" tunneling)*. The VPN devices at each end of the connection are responsible for tunnel creation and encryption of the data transferred between the two sites, so the tunnel may extend through edge devices such as firewalls to the computers sending and receiving the traffic. Secure sockets layer/transaction layer security (SSL/TLS) is an example of a protocol that uses end-to-end tunneling. This solution is extremely secure, because the data never appear on the network in clear-text form. However, performing encryption at the end hosts increases the complexity of the process of enforcing security policies. The network gateways, which would normally be responsible for enforcing security policy, are used only for forwarding the packets to their destination in this scenario, and as such, they possess no knowledge of the content or purpose of the traffic. This is particularly problematic for filtering programs installed at the gateway.
- *Node-to-node tunneling*. Node-to-node tunnel creation and termination occurs at the gateway devices comprising the edge of the networks, which are typically firewalls. In this model, transport within the LANs remains unchanged, as it is assumed that internal traffic is inaccessible from outside the LAN. Once traffic reaches the gateway, it is encrypted and sent via a dynamically established tunnel to the equivalent device on the receiving LAN, where the data are decrypted to recover their original format, and transmitted over the LAN to the intended recipient. This has an additional security advantage, in that an attacker operating a network analyzer at some point on the network between the two tunnel servers would see IP packets with the source and destination addresses corresponding to those two servers—the true source and destinations are hidden in the encrypted payload of these packets. Since this information is hidden, the would-be attacker does not gain any indication as to which traffic is heading to or from a particular machine, and so will not know which traffic is worth attempting to decrypt. This also eliminates the need for NAT to convert between public and private address spaces, and moves the responsibility for performing encryption to a central server, so intensive encryption work does not need to be performed by workstations. This is especially important when using costly encryption algorithms such as 3-DES (triple data encryption standard), which requires hardware encryption support in order to operate without limiting the effective bandwidth.

There are two main drawbacks associated with node-to-node tunneling (Hunt and Rodgers 2003):

1. *Poor scalability*. The number of tunnels required for a VPN increases geometrically as the number of VPN nodes increases, and that has serious performance ramifications for large VPNs.
2. *Suboptimal routing*. Since tunnels represent only the end points and not the path taken to reach the other end of the tunnel, the paths taken across the shared network may not be optimal, which may cause performance problems.

One can also distinguish two different tunneling modes—that is, "voluntary" and "compulsory" tunneling. *Voluntary tunneling* is a method in which the tunnel is created at the request of the user for a specific purpose, while *compulsory tunneling* is when the tunnel is created without any action from the user, and without allowing the user any choice in the matter (Ferguson and Huston 1998). The concepts of compulsory and voluntary tunneling are illustrated in Figures 2 and 3, respectively. In both figures, a host is attempting to connect to a corporate network using a dial-up connection to a network access server.

There are a number of desirable characteristics for a VPN tunneling mechanism. These include (Gleeson et al. 2000; Rosenbaum, Lau, and Jha 2003):

- *Multiplexing*. There are cases in which multiple VPN tunnels may be needed between the same two IP end points. This may be needed, for instance, in cases in which the VPNs are network-based, and each end point supports multiple customers. Traffic for different customers travels over separate tunnels between the same two physical devices. A multiplexing field is needed to distinguish which packets belong to which tunnel. Sharing a tunnel in this manner may also reduce the latency and processing burden of tunnel setup.
- *Signaling protocol*. There is some configuration information that must be known by an end point in advance of the tunnel establishment, such as the IP address of

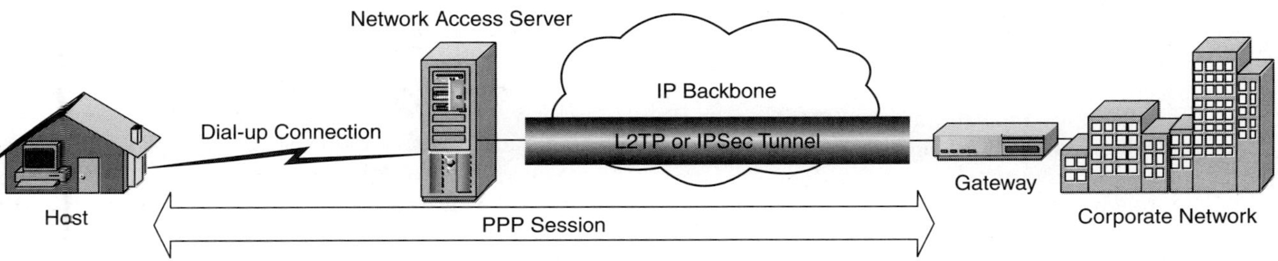

Figure 2: Compulsory tunneling scenario

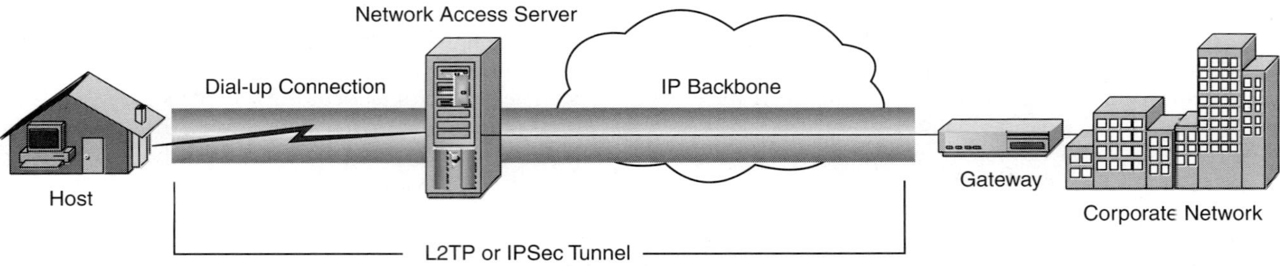

Figure 3: Voluntary tunneling scenario

the remote end point, and any relevant tunnel attributes required, such as the level of security needed. Once this information is available, the actual tunnel establishment can be completed in one of two ways—via a management operation or via a signaling protocol that allows tunnels to be established dynamically. Using a signaling protocol can significantly reduce the management burden, however, and as such, is essential in many deployment scenarios. It reduces the number of configurations needed, and also reduces the management coordination needed if a VPN spans multiple administrative domains.

- *Data security*. A VPN tunneling protocol must support mechanisms to allow for whatever level of security may be desired by customers, including authentication and/or encryption of various strengths. If some form of signaling mechanism is used by one VPN end point to dynamically establish a tunnel with another end point, then there is a requirement to be able to authenticate the party attempting the tunnel establishment.
- *Multiprotocol transport*. In many applications of VPNs, the VPN may carry opaque, multiprotocol traffic. As such, the tunneling protocol used must also support multiprotocol transport.
- *Frame sequencing*. Sequencing may be required for the efficient operation of particular end-to-end protocols or applications. In order to implement frame sequencing, the tunneling mechanism must support a sequencing field.
- *Tunnel maintenance*. The VPN end points must monitor the operation of the VPN tunnels to ensure that connectivity has not been lost, and to take appropriate action, such as route recalculation, if there has been a failure.
- *Support for large maximum transmission units (MTUs)*. If the tunnel's MTU is larger than the MTU of one or more individual hops along the path between tunnel end points, some form of frame fragmentation will be required within the tunnel. If the frame to be transferred is mapped into one IP datagram, normal IP fragmentation will occur when the IP datagram reaches a hop with an MTU smaller than the IP tunnel's MTU. This can have undesirable performance implications at the router performing such midtunnel fragmentation. An alternative approach is for the tunneling protocol itself to incorporate a segmentation and reassembly capability that operates at the tunnel level. This avoids IP level fragmentation within the tunnel itself.
- *Minimization of tunnel overhead*. Minimizing the overhead of the tunneling mechanism is beneficial, particularly for the transport of jitter and latency sensitive traffic such as packetized voice and video. On the other hand, the security mechanisms that are applied impose their own overhead; hence, the objective should be to minimize overhead over and above that needed for security, and to not burden those tunnels in which security is not mandatory with unnecessary overhead.
- *Quality of service (QoS)/traffic management*. Customers are expected to require that VPNs yield similar behavior to physical leased lines or dedicated connections with respect to QoS parameters such as loss rates, jitter, latency, and bandwidth guarantees. How such guarantees could be delivered will, in general, be a function of the traffic management characteristics of the VPN nodes themselves, and the access and backbone networks across which they are connected.

Three major tunneling protocol suites have been developed for building VPNs: point-to-point tunneling protocol (PPTP), layer two tunneling protocol (L2TP), and Internet protocol security (IPSec). These protocols are discussed later in this chapter.

SECURITY CONCERNS

Security concerns that arise when transmitting data over shared networks can be divided into the following categories (Hunt and Rodgers 2003):

1. *Privacy*. Can unauthorized parties gain access to private VPN traffic? Privacy can be achieved through the use of encryption.
2. *Integrity*. Can VPN traffic be altered without detection? Integrity is generally achieved through the use of checksums.
3. *Authentication*. Can I be certain that the sender or recipient is really who they claim to be? Authentication is usually performed by confirming that the other party has knowledge of or is in possession of some shared secret or unique key.
4. *Nonrepudiation*. Can the sender or receiver later deny their involvement in a transaction? Nonrepudiation, also known as data origin verification, is often achieved through the use of digital signatures. When nonrepudiation measures are in place, the recipient cannot deny

having received the transaction, nor can the sender deny having sent it (Hunt and Rodgers 2003).

There are two main trust models applicable to the use of a shared backbone network (Hunt and Rodgers 2003):

1. *Untrusted service provider*. In this scenario, the customer does not trust their service provider to provide security for VPN traffic, preferring instead to use devices that implement firewall functionality, passing data between these devices using secure tunnels. The role of the service provider in this scenario is solely that of a connectivity provider.
2. *Trusted service provider*. In this scenario, the customer trusts the service provider to provide a secure, managed VPN service. Specifically, the customer trusts that VPN packets will not be misdirected, that their contents will not be inspected or modified while in transit, and that they will not be subjected to traffic analysis by unauthorized parties.

Cryptography

Cryptographic algorithms are essential for achieving secure communications over shared networks, as a would-be attacker may obtain and store all the packets of a data stream belonging to a specific communication as it traverses the shared network. There are a number of encryption algorithms available, many of which support varying levels of security. The algorithms most commonly applied to VPNs are the data encryption standard (DES) and triple DES (3-DES). DES has been the de facto standard in data communications for a number of years, but the ever-increasing processing capacity of computers has reached the point at which only the larger key lengths supported by DES should be considered secure (Hunt and Rodgers 2003).

Increased security generally comes at the cost of reduced performance, so a balance between efficiency and security must be achieved when applying encryption; the expected time for an attacker to complete a brute-force cipher attack should exceed the length of time for which the data remain valuable. If this requirement cannot be met effectively, alternative options such as dynamic key renegotiation within a given data stream may improve security without necessarily having a significant impact on performance. Such a process forces an attacker to decrypt small blocks of data at a time, dramatically increasing the difficulty of retrieving the clear-text for the entire message (Hunt and Rodgers 2003).

Integrity Checksums

A checksum is a series of bits of fixed length, whose value is derived from a given block of data. Checksums are often appended to a block of data prior to transmission, so that the receiver can verify that the data were received in the exact condition in which they were sent (Hunt and Rodgers 2003). Simple checksums are merely a count of the number of bits in a transmission unit, which is insufficient for security purposes, as it provides no means of verifying the integrity of the received data, only that it is of the correct size. Hash functions introduce a greater computational overhead than a simple tally, but allow verification that the transmission was received successfully, free from transmission errors or deliberate tampering en route. The hash value, also known as a message digest, concisely represents the longer message or document from which it was derived. A message digest acts as a form of "digital fingerprint" of the original document, and can be made public without revealing the contents of the corresponding document (Hunt and Rodgers 2003).

Authentication

Authentication of VPN users is generally performed by confirming the knowledge of some shared secret. Passwords are the most user-friendly option, although the process may incorporate tokens or smart cards if enhanced security is required. Digital certificates are a reliable way of providing strong authentication for large groups of users (Hunt and Rodgers 2003). Because passwords can be cracked or sniffed, authentication methods that use static password authentication should be considered insecure, particularly if the authentication session is not encrypted (Hunt and Rodgers 2003).

There are three distinct factors for authentication (Hunt and Rodgers 2003):

1. *What do you know?* This fact should be known only by the user and the verifier, and should be infeasible to guess or derive. A common application of this factor in VPNs is an alphanumeric password, which is verified by an authentication server using an authentication protocol.
2. *What do you have?* In VPNs, this factor will typically be some form of identification card, smart card, or token. Such items should be unique and difficult to forge.
3. *What you are*. This refers to some unique attribute of the user, such as a fingerprint or voiceprint, that is impractical to forge or imitate. Such authentication methods are rarely used in VPNs at this time.

Access Management

It is not always sufficient merely to authenticate a user; too often it is assumed that once a user has been granted access, he or she should have widespread access to almost all resources on the VPN (Hunt and Rodgers 2003). This is a potentially dangerous assumption, since insiders can pose as great a threat to the security of an organization as outsiders; they may have various advantages beyond privileges and access rights, such as a superior knowledge of system vulnerabilities and the whereabouts of sensitive information. Despite the risks involved, the problem of protecting a VPN and its resources from insiders is often assigned a relatively low priority, if it is not ignored altogether (Hunt and Rodgers 2003).

This is where access management techniques can be a valuable tool. Using access management tools, such as Kerberos (a hardware and/or software implementation), an enterprise can ensure that insiders are granted access only to resources for which they have been explicitly assigned access rights. Usually, the process of managing and

Table 2: VPN Security Concerns

Security Concern	Privacy	Integrity	Authentication	Nonrepudiation
Relevant Question	Can unauthorized parties gain access to private VPN traffic?	Can VPN tranffic be altered without detection?	Can I be certain that the sender or recipient is really who they claim to be?	Can the sender or receiver later deny their involvement in a transaction?
Solution	Encryption	Checksums	Possession of secret key	Digital signatures

restricting access to VPN resources involves maintaining an access control list (ACL) for each of the resources for which use is restricted to specific users or groups of users. When a user attempts to access a given resource, the access management tool consults the ACL for that resource, and will subsequently grant access only if that user is represented in the list (Hunt and Rodgers 2003).

Security concerns relating to VPNs are summarized in Table 2.

VPN IMPLEMENTATIONS

One can distinguish between two fundamental VPN models, namely the peer and the overlay model. In the peer model, the network-layer forwarding path computation is implemented on a hop-by-hop basis, in which each node in the intermediate data transit path is a peer with a next-hop node. In contrast, in the overlay model, the network-layer forwarding path computation is not implemented on a hop-by-hop basis, but rather, the intermediate-link-layer network is used as a "cut-through" to another edge node on the other side of a large cloud (Ferguson and Huston 1998). The overlay model introduces some serious scaling concerns in cases in which large numbers of egress peers are required. This is because the number of adjacencies increases in direct relationship with the number of peers; thus, the amount of computational and performance overhead required to maintain routing state, adjacency information, and other detailed packet forwarding and routing information for each peer becomes a liability in very large networks. If all egress nodes in a cut-through network become peers, in an effort to make all egress nodes one "layer 3" hop away from one another, this limits the scalability of the VPN overlay model quite remarkably (Ferguson and Huston 1998).

A number of approaches may be taken to the problem of providing VPN links and services. In particular, a VPN may be implemented and secured at a number of layers of the TCP/IP protocol stack (Knight and Lewis, 2004). The most significant of the currently available approaches are described below.

Network-layer VPNs (Hunt and Rodgers 2003): Network layer VPNs, based primarily on IP, are implemented using network-layer encryption, and possibly tunneling. Packets entering the shared network are appended with an additional IP header containing a destination address, which corresponds to the other end of the tunnel. When this node receives the packet, the header is removed and the original packet, which is addressed to some location within the given network, is recovered. Because of this encapsulation, the original packets could be based on any network-layer protocol without affecting their transport across the shared network.

Data-link-layer VPNs (Hunt and Rodgers 2003): Data-link-layer VPNs use a shared backbone network based on a switched-link-layer technology such as frame relay (FR) or ATM. Links between VPN nodes are implemented as virtual circuits, which are inexpensive, flexible, and can offer some level of ensured performance. Link-layer VPNs are most appropriate for providing intranet services; dial-up access is not well supported, as most ISPs provide connectivity using IP. Most of the cost savings associated with VPNs are the result of the use of ISPs. Therefore, IP-based network-layer VPNs are more attractive than link-layer VPNs if dial-up access is required. Virtual-circuit based VPNs face scalability issues similar to those of node-to-node tunneled VPNs, so a full-mesh architecture may not be possible. Alternatives such as partial meshes or hub-and-spoke configurations address this limitation to some extent, but these solutions may produce suboptimal behavior, especially for routing, introducing performance concerns.

Application-layer VPNs (Hunt and Rodgers 2003): Application-layer VPNs are implemented in software, whereby workstations and servers are required to perform tasks such as encryption, rather than assigning these tasks to specialized hardware. As a result, software VPNs are inexpensive to implement but can have a significant impact on performance, limiting network throughput and producing high CPU usage, particularly over high-bandwidth connections.

Non-IP VPNs (Ferguson and Huston 1998): It is widely recognized that multiprotocol networks may also have requirements for VPNs. The most pervasive method of constructing VPNs in multiprotocol networks is to rely on application-layer encryption, and as such, are generally vendor proprietary, although some would contend that one of the most pervasive examples of this approach was the mainstay of the emergent Internet in the 1970s and 1980s—that of the UUCP (UNIX-to-UNIX copy protocol) network, which was (and remains) an open technology.

Hardware Components

A number of hardware devices are required to implement the various types of VPNs discussed above. Many of these devices are common to standard networks, but some have additional burdens and responsibilities placed on them when applied to VPNs and their specific requirements. The main hardware devices used by VPNs, and the implications of any additional processing that they must perform are discussed below (Hunt and Rodgers 2003).

Firewalls: VPNs must be protected from other users of the backbone network. This is typically achieved using a firewall, which provides critical services such as tunneling, cryptography, and route and content filtering (Hunt and Rodgers 2003).

Routers: Adding VPN functionality to existing routers can have an unacceptable performance impact, particularly at network stress points. Specifically, multiprotocol label switching (MPLS) VPNs address this problem by making only the perimeter (PE) routers VPN-aware, so the core routers need not maintain the multiple routing tables that introduce so much overhead on PE routers (Hunt and Rodgers 2003).

Switches: Some switches offer facilities for increased separation of traffic by allowing a physical network to be partitioned into a number of virtual LANs (V-LANs). On a normal switch, all ports are part of the same network, whereas a V-LAN switch can treat different ports as parts of different networks if desired (Hunt and Rodgers 2003).

Tunnel servers: This service may be provided by a VPN router or a firewall. Assigning an existing network component this additional responsibility may have a serious impact on performance (Hunt and Rodgers 2003).

Cryptocards: Encryption algorithms that provide strong encryption, such as 3-DES, are computationally expensive and can limit effective bandwidth to around 100 Mbps unless specialized cryptographic hardware is used. On a workstation, this specialized hardware is provided in the form of an expansion card, which may be separate or integrated with the network interface card. Some firewalls also offer hardware support for various encryption algorithms (Hunt and Rodgers 2003).

PROTOCOLS USED BY VPNs

Point-to-Point Tunneling Protocol

The point-to-point tunneling protocol (PPTP) (Pall et al. 1999) allows the point-to-point protocol (PPP) (Network Working Group 1994), to be tunneled through an IP network. PPTP does not specify any changes to the PPP protocol, but rather describes a new vehicle for carrying PPP. The PPTP network server (PNS) is meant to run on a general-purpose operating system while the client, referred to as a PPTP access concentrator (PAC), operates on a dial access platform. PPTP specifies a call control and management protocol that allows the server to control access for dial-in circuit switched calls originating from a PSTN or ISDN or to initiate outbound circuit-switched connections. A network access server (NAS) provides temporary, on-demand network access to users. This access is point-to-point using PSTN or ISDN lines.

PPTP uses an extended version of the generic routing encapsulation mechanism (Hanks et al. 1994) to carry user PPP packets. These enhancements allow for low-level congestion and flow control to be provided on the tunnels used to carry user data between PAC and PNS. This mechanism allows for efficient use of the bandwidth available for the tunnels and avoids unnecessary retransmissions and buffer overruns. PPTP does not dictate the particular algorithms to be used for this low-level control, but it does define the parameters that must be communicated in order to allow such algorithms to work (Pall et al. 1999). PPTP allows existing NAS functions to be separated using a client/server architecture. Traditionally, the following functions are implemented by an NAS (Pall et al. 1999):

1. Physical native interfacing to PSTN or ISDN and control of external modems or terminal adapters
2. Logical termination of a PPP link control protocol (LCP) session
3. Participation in PPP authentication protocols
4. Channel aggregation and bundle management for PPP multilink protocol
5. Logical termination of various PPP network control protocols (NCPs)
6. Multiprotocol routing and bridging between NAS interfaces

PPTP divides these functions between the PPTP access concentrator (PAC) and the PNS. The PAC is responsible for functions 1, 2, and possibly 3. The PNS may be responsible for function 3 and is responsible for functions 4, 5, and 6. The decoupling of NAS functions offers the following benefits (Pall et al. 1999):

- *Flexible IP address management*. Dial-in users may maintain a single IP address as they dial into different PACs as long as they are served from a common PNS.
- *Support of non-IP protocols for dial networks behind IP networks*.
- *A solution to the "multilink hunt-group splitting" problem*. Multilink PPP, typically used to aggregate ISDN B channels, requires that all the channels composing a multi-link bundle be grouped at a single NAS. Since a multilink PPP bundle can be handled by a single PNS, the channels comprising the bundle may be spread across multiple PACs.

The PPTP protocol is implemented only by the PAC and PNS. No other systems need to be aware of PPTP. Dial-up networks may be connected to a PAC without being aware of PPTP. Standard PPP client software should continue to operate on tunneled PPP links. PPTP can also be used to tunnel a PPP session over an IP network. In this configuration the PPTP tunnel and the PPP session run between the same two machines with the caller acting as a PNS (Pall et al. 1999).

A tunnel is defined by a PNS-PAC pair. The tunnel protocol is defined by a modified version of GRE. The tunnel carries PPP datagrams between the PAC and the PNS. Many sessions are multiplexed on a single tunnel. A control connection operating over TCP controls the establishment, release, and maintenance of sessions and of the tunnel itself (Pall et al. 1999).

The security of user data passed over the tunneled PPP connection is addressed by PPP, as is authentication of the PPP peers. Because the PPTP control channel messages are neither authenticated nor integrity-protected, it might be possible for an attacker to hijack the underlying TCP connection. It is also possible to manufacture false control channel messages and alter genuine messages in transit without detection. The GRE packets forming the tunnel itself are not cryptographically protected. Because the PPP negotiations are carried out over the tunnel, it may be possible for an attacker to eavesdrop on and modify those negotiations. Unless the PPP payload data are cryptographically protected, it can be captured and read or modified (Pall et al. 1999).

PPTP is limited in usage. It offers remote connections to a single point. It does not support multiple connections, nor does it easily support network-to-network connections. PPTP's security is also limited. It does not offer protection from substitution or playback attacks, nor does it provide perfect forward secrecy. PPTP has no clear mechanism for renegotiation if connectivity to the server is lost (Günter 2001).

Layer Two Tunneling Protocol

Layer two tunneling protocol L2TP (Townsley et al. 1999) facilitates the tunneling of PPP packets across an intervening network in a way that is as transparent as possible to both end users and applications. PPP defines an encapsulation mechanism for transporting multiprotocol packets across layer two (L2) point-to-point links. Typically, a user obtains an L2 connection to an NAS using one of a number of techniques (e.g., dial-up through the telephone system, ISDN, asymmetric digital subscriber line [ADSL], etc.) and then runs PPP over that connection. In such a configuration, the L2 termination point and PPP session end point reside on the same physical device (i.e., the NAS) (Townsley et al. 1999).

L2TP extends the PPP model by allowing the L2 and PPP endpoints to reside on different devices interconnected by a packet-switched network. With L2TP, a user has an L2 connection to an access concentrator (e.g., modem bank, ADSL access multiplexer, etc.), and the concentrator then tunnels individual PPP frames to the NAS. This allows the actual processing of PPP packets to be divorced from the termination of the L2 circuit. One obvious benefit of such a separation is that instead of requiring the L2 connection terminate at the NAS (which may require a long-distance toll charge), the connection may terminate at a (local) circuit concentrator, which then extends the logical PPP session over a shared infrastructure such as frame relay circuit or the Internet. From the user's perspective, there is no functional difference between having the L2 circuit terminate in an NAS directly or using L2TP (Townsley et al. 1999).

L2TP has inherent support for the multiplexing of multiple calls from different users over a single link. Between the same two IP end points, there can be multiple L2TP tunnels, as identified by a tunnel-id, and multiple sessions within a tunnel, as identified by a session-id. Signaling is supported via the built-in control connection protocol, allowing both tunnels and sessions to be established dynamically (Rosenbaum et al. 2003).

L2TP transports PPP packets (and only PPP packets) and thus can be used to carry multiprotocol traffic, since PPP itself is multiprotocol. L2TP also supports sequenced delivery of packets. This is a capability that can be negotiated at session establishment, and that can be turned on and off during a session. Concerning tunnel maintenance, L2TP uses a keepalive protocol in order to distinguish between a tunnel outage and prolonged periods of tunnel inactivity (Rosenbaum et al. 2003).

L2TP as used over IP networks runs over UDP (user datagram protocol) and must be used to carry PPP traffic. This results in a significant amount of overhead both in the data plane, with UDP, L2TP and PPP headers, and in the control plane, with the L2TP and PPP control protocols (Rosenbaum et al. 2003). An L2TP header contains a 1-bit priority field, which can be set for packets that may need preferential treatment during local queuing and transmission. Also by transparently extending PPP, L2TP has inherent support for PPP mechanisms such as multilink PPP and its associated control protocols, which allow for bandwidth on demand to meet user requirements (Rosenbaum et al. 2003).

Security Considerations

The L2TP tunnel end points may optionally perform an authentication procedure of one another during tunnel establishment. This authentication provides reasonable protection against replay and snooping during the tunnel-establishment process. This mechanism is not designed to provide any authentication beyond tunnel establishment; it is fairly simple for a malicious user to inject packets once an authenticated tunnel has been established successfully (Obaidat and Boudriga 2007; Townsley et al. 1999).

Securing L2TP (Patel et al. 2001) requires that the underlying transport make available encryption, integrity, and authentication services for all L2TP traffic. This secure transport operates on the entire L2TP packet and is functionally independent of PPP and the protocol being carried by PPP. As such, L2TP is concerned only with confidentiality, authenticity, and integrity of the L2TP packets between its tunnel end points. L2TP is similar to PPTP, and they both target the remote access scenario. L2TP delegates security features toward IP Security (IPsec), which is presented later in this chapter. Also, it suffers from the same drawbacks as PPTP (Günter 2001).

The choice between PPTP and L2TP for deployment in a VPN depends on whether the control needs to lie with the service provider or with the subscriber (Ferguson and Huston 1998). Indeed, the difference can be characterized as to the client of the VPN, in which the L2TP model is one of a "wholesale" access provider who has a number of configured client service providers who appear as VPNs on the common dial-up access system, while the PPTP model is one of distributed private access, in which the client is an individual end user and the VPN structure is that of end-to-end tunnels. One might also suggest that the difference is also a matter of economics, since the L2TP model allows the service provider to actually provide a value-added service, beyond basic IP-level connectivity, and charge their subscribers accordingly for the privilege of using it, thus creating new revenue streams.

On the other hand, the PPTP model enables distributed reach of the VPN at a much more atomic level, enabling corporate VPNs to extend access capabilities without the need for explicit service contracts with a multitude of network access providers (Ferguson and Huston 1998).

IP Security

IP security (IPSec) is an open architecture for IP-packet encryption and authentication, thus it is located in the network layer (Man 2003). IPSec adds further headers/trailers to an IP packet and can encapsulate (tunnel) IP packets in new ones (Cohen 2003). A number of security services are provided by IPSec, including access control, connectionless integrity, nonrepudiation, protection against replay attacks, confidentiality, and limited traffic flow confidentiality. These services are provided at the transport layer, offering protection for IP and upper-layer protocols (Hunt and Rodgers 2003). There are three main functionalities of IPSec, separated into three protocols—authentication through an authentication header (AH), encryption through an encapsulating security payload (ESP), and automated key management through the Internet key exchange (IKE) protocol. IPSec provides an architecture for key management, encryption, authentication, and tunneling (Cohen 2003). IPSec was designed to be algorithm-independent. It supports several encryption and authentication algorithms, which allow the companies using VPN to select the desired security level for each VPN (Obaidat and Boudriga 2007; Younglove 2000).

IPSec is an optimal solution for trusted LAN-to-LAN VPNs (Günter 2001). IPsec can ensure authentication, privacy, and data integrity. It is open to a wide variety of encryption mechanisms. It is application-transparent and a natural IP extension, thus ensuring interoperability among VPNs over the Internet. Router vendors and VPN hardware vendors support IPsec. Nevertheless, there are disadvantages of IPsec. It is bound to the TCP/IP stack. IP addressing is part of IPsec's authentication algorithm. This is less secure than higher-layer approaches, and it is a problem in dynamic address environments, which are common to ISPs. Moreover, it requires a public key infrastructure, which is still subject to current research, and it does not specify a method for access control beyond simple packet filtering (Günter 2001).

The Encapsulating Security Payload

The encapsulating security payload (ESP) protocol is responsible for packet encryption. An ESP header is inserted into the packet between the IP header and the packet contents. The header contains a security parameter index (SPI), which specifies to the receiver the appropriate security association (SA) for processing the packet. Also included in the ESP header is a sequence number that is a counter that increases each time a packet is sent to the same address using the same SPI and that indicates the number of packets that have been sent with the same group of parameters. The sequence number provides protection against replay attacks, in which an attacker copies a packet and sends it out of sequence to confuse communicating nodes. Packet data are encrypted prior to transmission. ESP allows multiple methods of encryption, with DES as its default. ESP also can be used for data authentication. Included in the ESP header is an optional authentication field, which contains a cryptographic checksum that is computed over the ESP packet when encryption is complete. The ESP's authentication services do not protect the IP header that precedes the ESP packet.

ESP can be used in two different modes. In transport mode, the packet's data, but not the IP header, are encrypted and, optionally, authenticated. Although transport-mode ESP is sufficient for protecting the contents of a packet against eavesdropping, it leaves the source and destination IP addresses open to modification if the packet is intercepted. In tunnel mode, the packet's contents and the IP header are encrypted and, optionally, authenticated. Then, a new IP header is generated for routing the secured packets from sender to receiver. Although tunnel-mode ESP provides more security than transport-mode ESP, some types of traffic analysis are still possible. For example, the IP addresses of the sending and receiving gateways could still be determined by examining the packet headers (Obaidat and Boudriga 2007).

Key Management

There are two ways to handle key management within IPSec's architecture: manual keying and Internet key exchange. Manual keying involves face-to-face key exchanges (e.g. trading keys on paper or magnetic disk) or sending keys via a bonded courier or e-mail. Although manual keying is suitable for a small number of sites, automated key management is required to accommodate on-demand creation of keys for SAs. IPSec's default automated key management protocol is Internet key exchange (IKE), which was formed by combining the Internet security association key management protocol (ISAKMP), which defines procedures and packet formats to establish, negotiate, modify, and delete SAs, with the Oakley key determination protocol, which is a key exchange protocol based on the Diffie-Hellman algorithm (Diffie and Hellman 1976).

Because key exchange is closely related to the management of SAs, part of the key-management procedure is handled by SAs, and the SPI values that refer to the SAs, in each IPSec packet. Whenever an SA is created, keys must be exchanged. IKE's structure combines these functions by requiring the initiating node to specify:

- an encryption algorithm to protect data
- a hash algorithm to reduce data for signing
- an authentication method for signing the data
- information about the material needed to generate the keys, over which a Diffie-Hellman exchange is performed

A pseudo-random function used to hash certain values during the key exchange for verification purposes may also be specified.

Packet Authentication

In IPSec's architecture, the AH provides data integrity and authentication services for IP packets. The data integrity feature prevents the undetected modification of a packet's contents while the packet is in transit, and the authentication feature prevents address spoofing and replay attacks, and enables the receiver to authenticate the application and filter traffic accordingly (Wright 2000). Like the ESP header, the AH is inserted into the packet between the IP header and the packet contents. The AH also contains an SPI, which specifies to the receiver the security protocols the sender is using for communications. The authentication provided by the AH differs from that provided by the ESP. AH services protect the external IP header that precedes the ESP header, along with the entire contents of the ESP packet. The AH contains authentication data, obtained by applying the hash algorithm defined by the SPI to the packet's contents. Two algorithms are supported: hash-based message authentication code with message digest version 5 (HMAC-MD5) and secure hash algorithm version 1 (SHA-1) (Wright 2000).

The AH can be used in the same two modes as ESP. In transport mode, the packet's data and the original IP header are authenticated. In tunnel mode, the entire IP packet—data, original IP header, and outer IP header—are authenticated. In addition to applying either AH or ESP to an IP packet in transport or tunnel modes, IPSec supports combinations of these modes. Several combinations are possible, among them (Wright 2000):

- ESP could be used in transport mode without the authentication option (to encrypt the packet's data), then AH could be applied in transport mode (to authenticate the ESP header, the packet's data, and the original IP header).
- AH could be used in transport mode to authenticate the packet's data and the original IP header, then ESP could be applied in tunnel mode to encrypt the entire, authenticated inner packet and to add a new IP header for routing the packet from sender to receiver.
- ESP could be used in tunnel mode to encrypt and, optionally, authenticate a packet and its original header, then AH could be applied in transport mode to authenticate the packet's data, original IP header, and outer IP header.

User Authentication

A VPN must be able to reliably authenticate users in order to control access to enterprise resources and keep unauthorized users out of corporate networks (Wright 2000). Three protocols are described here: PAP, CHAP, and RADIUS.

Password Authentication Protocol. The password authentication protocol (PAP) was originally designed as a simple way for one computer to authenticate itself to another computer when PPP is used as the communication's protocol. PAP is a two-way handshaking protocol. When the PPP link is established, the client system sends the plaintext user ID and password pair to the destination system (the authenticator). The authenticator either accepts the pair or terminates the connection. PAP is not a secure means of user authentication. The authentication information is transmitted in the clear, and there is nothing to protect against playback attacks or excessive attempts by attackers to guess valid user ID/password pairs (Wright 2000).

Challenge Handshake Authentication Protocol. The challenge handshake authentication protocol (CHAP) is a more secure method for authenticating users. CHAP is a three-way handshaking protocol. Instead of the simple, two-step user ID/password approval process used by PAP, CHAP uses a three-step process to produce a verified PPP link (Wright 2000):

- The authenticator sends a challenge message to the client system.
- The client system calculates a value using a one-way hash function and sends the value back to the authenticator.
- The authenticator acknowledges authentication if the response matches the expected value.

CHAP removes the possibility that an attacker can try repeatedly to log in over the same connection (a weakness inherent in PAP). However, PAP and CHAP share some disadvantages. Both protocols rely on a secret password that must be stored on the remote user's computer and the local computer. If either computer comes under the control of a network attacker, the password will be compromised. Also, both PAP and CHAP allow only one set of privileges to be assigned to a specific computer. This prevents different network access privileges from being assigned to different remote users who use the same remote host (Wright 2000).

Remote Authentication Dial-In User Service. The remote authentication dial-in user service (RADIUS) protocol provides greater flexibility for administering remote network connection users and sessions. RADIUS uses a client/server model to authenticate users, determine access levels, and maintain all necessary auditing and accounting data. The RADIUS protocol uses an NAS to accept user connection requests, to obtain user ID and password information, and to pass the encrypted information securely to the RADIUS server. The RADIUS server returns the authentication status (approved or denied), along with any configuration data required for the NAS to provide services to the user. User authentication and access to services are managed by the RADIUS server, enabling a remote user to gain access to the same services from any communications server that can communicate with the RADIUS server (Obaidat and Boudriga 2007; Wright 2000).

The services and protocols of IPSec are summarized in Figure 4.

SOCKS v5 and Secure Sockets Layer

SOCKS v5 was originally approved by the IETF as a standard protocol for authenticated firewall traversal (Günter 2001). When combined with the secure sockets layer (SSL) it provides the foundation for building highly secure VPNs that are compatible with any firewall. SOCKS v5's strength is access control; it controls the flow of data at the session layer (open system interconnection [OSI] layer 5). It establishes a circuit

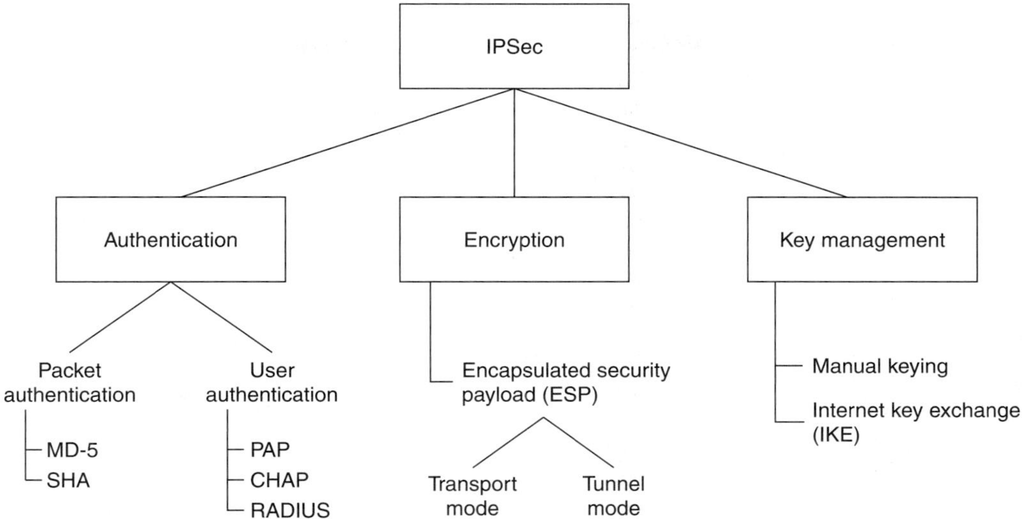

Figure 4: Summary of IPSec (MD-5 = message-digest algorithm 5; PAP = password authentication protocol; SHA = secure hash algorithm)

between a client and a host on a session-by-session basis. Thus, it can provide more detailed access control than protocols in the lower layers without the need to reconfigure each application. SOCKS v5 and SSL can interoperate on top of IPv4, IPsec, PPTP, L2TP, or any other lower-level VPN protocol. A session-layer solution does not have to interfere with the networking transport components; thus, the clients are nonintrusive. SOCKS v5 provides plug-and-play capabilities, including access control, protocol filtering, content filtering, traffic monitoring, reporting, and administration applications. On the minus side, SOCKS v5 decreases performance. Also, client software is required to build a connection through the firewall to transmit all TCP/IP data through the proxy server (Günter 2001).

Multiprotocol Label Switching

Multiprotocol label switching (MPLS) is deployed in an ISP's IP backbone network that uses IP routers at the edges of the network and ATM switches controlled by an MPLS component in the inside (Günter 2001). The basic idea is to do (intelligent) layer three routing at the edges of the backbone network and to do fast layer two forwarding inside the backbone network. Incoming IP packets get an attached MPLS header, they are labeled according to IP header information (mainly the target address, but also type of service and other fields). A label switched path is set up for each route or path through the network. Once this is done, all subsequent nodes may simply forward the packet along the label-switched path identified by the label at the front of the packet. Negotiations of labels between nodes are done by the label distribution protocol of MPLS. An ATM connection is set up for each label-switched path. Thus, MPLS can support quality of service. MPLS makes the underlying backbone infrastructure invisible to the layer three mechanisms. This lightweight tunneling provides an extendable foundation that provides VPN and other service capabilities. Furthermore, the MPLS architecture enables network operators to define explicit routes (Günter 2001). MPLS technologies are useful for ISPs that want to offer their customers a wide band of IP services. The ISPs add value to their service, for example, by offering the complete management of the customers' VPN. Obviously, the more the customers outsource their VPN management, the more crucial network management becomes to the ISP (Günter 2001).

MPLS VPNs provide a highly scalable technology for ISPs that want to offer layer three VPN services to their customers (Chou 2004). BGP-4 (Rekhter, Watson and Li 1995) is a scalable protocol and is widely accepted in the industry. Furthermore, it is also very well-suited to carrying additional information in its routing updates, which is required in the MPLS VPN architecture (Obaidat and Boudriga 2007; Tomsu and Wieser 2002).

QUALITY-OF-SERVICE SUPPORT

Apart from creating a segregated address environmentto allow private communications, there is also the expectation that the VPN environment will be in a position to support a set of service levels (Zeng and Ansari 2003; Braun et al. 1999). Such per-VPN service levels may be specified either in terms of a defined service level on which the VPN can rely at all times, or in terms of a level of differentiation that ensures that the VPN can draw on the common platform resource with some level of priority of resource allocation (Ferguson and Huston 1998). Efforts within the Integrated Services Working Group of the IETF have resulted in a set of specifications for the support of guaranteed and controlled load end-to-end traffic profiles using a mechanism that loads per-flow state into the switching elements of the network. There are a number of caveats regarding the use of these mechanisms, in particular relating to the ability to support the number of flows that will be encountered on the public Internet. Such caveats tend to suggest that these mechanisms will not be the ones ultimately adopted to support service levels for VPNs in very large networking environments (Ferguson and Huston 1998).

The differentiated services (DiffServ) approach tries to provide a solution for quality of service (QoS) support with better scalability than integrated services (IntServ). Differentiated services can provide two or more QoS levels without maintaining per-flow state at every router. The idea of the DiffServ approach is to use the DiffServ field in the IP header to designate the appropriate DiffServ level that the packet should receive. DiffServ can provide scalability by aggregating the flows into a small number of DiffServ classes and by implementing traffic conditioning at the boundary routers of a network or an administrative domain (Cohen 2003).

It must be noted that QoS and VPN techniques introduce new challenges. They need extensive configurations in the routers. The local configurations have to be consistent across the network. Many companies may not have the knowledge and resources to deploy and manage enhanced Internet services by themselves. Rather, they will outsource the service management to their ISP (Braun, Günter, and Khalil, 2001).

The traditional model for specifying QoS arrangements involves drawing a set of network service requirements between ordered pair of customer sites. The ordered pair defines a direction of data flow, and the whole set is termed the "traffic matrices." The traffic matrices model gives the customer fine granularity of control over the traffic flows between customer sites, and the network provider can offer stringent service guarantee for each data flow. However, maintaining the traffic matrices can become complicated as the VPN grows in size (Harding 2003).

Recent developments in VPN technologies have introduced a new QoS specification model, called the "hose model," that may be desirable to the VPN customers (Kumar et al. 2002). In this model, two hoses are given to the customer with one hose used for sending traffic out of the network and the other used for receiving traffic from the network. This means that the network provider offers aggregate traffic service in which all traffic going toward the customer site must fit within the receiving hose capacity and all the traffic going out of the customer site must be within the sending hose capacity (Harding 2003). The hose specification contains the egress bandwidth (outbound traffic) and the ingress bandwidth (inbound traffic) pair for every customer site that takes part in the VPN. The major advantages of this model from the customer's perspective are that specification is made simple and there is a high potential for multiplexing gain for using aggregate requirements rather than traffic matrices. The simple specification allows changes to be made easily, including changes in the VPN membership. However, the customer in this model loses control of the data flow between sites, and the service guarantee is on an aggregate basis, resulting in a coarser service guarantee level (Harding 2003). From a network provider's perspective, the traffic matrices model specifies heavy constraints, which restrict the network optimization that can be achieved. The hose model specifies aggregate requirements that are lighter in constraints, thus giving the network provider more flexibility to perform network optimization. Network optimization involves mechanisms to improve bandwidth efficiency, load balancing, and traffic multiplexing (Harding 2003).

CONCLUSION

People increasingly depend on remote access to do their jobs, and demand is growing for access to large volumes of corporate information. Moreover, the upsurge of e-commerce means that companies are implementing business applications that share information among sites, extending the reach of their business to partners, contractors, and supply chain. In all these areas, VPNs promise to reduce recurring telecommunications charges, minimize the amount of access equipment required, and give managers better control over their networks (Younglove 2000). Organizations are struggling to meet the escalating demand for remote connectivity, and they are having difficulty dealing with the resulting increase in network complexity and end-user support costs. VPNs offer a more affordable, scalable way to meet the demands of a growing community of remote users and to manage branch office connectivity. They can help to accommodate the pace and unpredictability of business by linking customers and business partners into extranets on an ad hoc basis. VPNs can provide access to networked resources without compromising security. Virtual private networking offers the capability of enhanced and secure corporate communications, with the promise of future cost savings (Wright 2000).

The pertinent conclusion here is that while a VPN can take many forms, there are some basic common problems that a VPN is built to solve. These are virtualization of services and segregation of communications to a closed community of interest, while simultaneously exploiting the financial opportunity of economies of scale of the underlying common host communications system. Each solution has a number of strengths and also a number of weaknesses and vulnerabilities. There is no single mechanism for VPNs that will supplant all others in the months and years to come, but instead we will continue to see a diversity of technology choices in this area of VPN support (Ferguson and Huston 1998).

GLOSSARY

Border Gateway Protocol (BGP): A routing protocol that facilitates the exchange of network reachability information between systems.

Challenge Handshake Authentication Protocol (CHAP): A three-way handshaking authentication protocol that can be applied to produce a verified PPP link. CHAP is a more secure authentication protocol than PAP.

Extranet VPN: A VPN that extends limited access to corporate computing resources to business partners, such as customers or suppliers.

Generic Routing Encapsulation (GRE): A simple, general purpose encapsulation mechanism.

Internet Key Exchange (IKE): The default automated key management protocol of IPSec.

Intranet VPN: A VPN that connects a number of local area networks located in multiple geographic areas over a shared network infrastructure.

IP Security (IPSec): An open architecture for IP-packet encryption and authentication, and key management.

IPSec adds additional headers/trailers to an IP packet and can encapsulate (tunnel) IP packets in new ones.

Layer Two Tunneling Protocol (L2TP): A tunneling protocol that facilitates the tunneling of PPP packets across an intervening network in a way that is as transparent as possible to both end users and applications.

Network Address Translation (NAT): A method by which IP addresses are mapped from one address realm (i.e., network domain) to another, providing transparent routing to end hosts.

Password Authentication Protocol (PAP): A simple two-way handshaking authentication protocol that allows one computer to authenticate itself to another computer when the point-to-point protocol is used as the communication's protocol.

Point-to-Point Protocol (PPP): A protocol that defines an encapsulation mechanism for transporting multiprotocol packets across layer two point-to-point links.

Point-to-Point Tunneling Protocol (PPTP): A tunneling protocol used by VPNs that allows the point-to-point protocol to be tunneled through an IP network.

Remote-Access VPN: A VPN that connects telecommuters and mobile users to corporate networks.

Remote Authentication Dial-In User Service (RADIUS): A user authentication protocol that uses a client/server model to authenticate users, determine access levels, and maintain all necessary audit and accounting data.

Virtual Private Network (VPN): A private network constructed within a public network infrastructure, such as the global Internet.

CROSS REFERENCES

See *Access Control*; *Authentication*; *Cryptography*; *Network QoS*.

REFERENCES

Arora, P., P. R. Vemuganti, and P. Allani, P. 2001. Comparison of VPN protocols—IPSec, PPTP, and L2TP. Project Report ECE 646, Fall 2001. http://ece.gmu.edu/courses/ECE543/project/reports_2001/arveal.pdf (accessed June 4, 2007).

Braun, T., M. Günter, and I. Khalil. 2001. Management of quality of service enabled VPNs. *IEEE Communications Magazine* 39(5):90–8.

Braun, T., M. Günter, M. Kasumi, and I. Khalil. 1999. Virtual private network architecture. CATI Project Deliverable, January 1999, available at http://www.tik.ee.ethz.ch/~cati/deliverables.html (accessed May 25, 2007).

Chou, C. T. 2004. Traffic engineering for MPLS-based virtual private networks. *Elsevier Computer Networks* 44(3):319–33.

Cohen, R. 2003. On the establishment of an access VPN in broadband access networks. *IEEE Communications Magazine* 41(2):156–63.

Diffie, W., and M. Hellman. 1976. New directions in cryptography. *IEEE Transactions on Information Theory* 22(6):644–54.

Ferguson, P., and G. Huston. 1998. What is a VPN? White paper. http://www.potaroo.net/papers/1998-3-vpn/vpn.pdf (accessed June 4, 2007).

Gleeson, B., A. Lin, J. Heinanen, G. Armitage, and A. Malis. 2000. A framework for IP based virtual private networks. 2764, February 2000. http://tools.ietf.org/html/rfc2764 (accessed June 4, 2007).

Günter, M. 2001. Virtual private networks over the Internet. http://citeseer.ist.psu.edu/480338.html (accessed June 4, 2007).

Hanks, S., T. Li, D. Farinacci, and P. Traina. 1994. Generic routing encapsulation (GRE). 1701, October1994. www.faqs.org/rfcs/rfc1701.html (accessed May 25, 2007).

Harding, A. 2003. SSL virtual private networks. *Computers & Security* 22(5):416–20.

Hunt, R., and C. Rodgers. 2003. Virtual private networks: Strong security at what cost? http://citeseer.ist.psu.edu/555428.html (accessed June 4, 2007).

Knight, P., and C. Lewis. 2004. Layer 2 and 3 virtual private networks: Taxonomy, technology, and standardization efforts. *IEEE Communications Magazine* 42(6):124–31.

Kumar, A., R. Rastogi, A. Silberschatz, and B. Yener. 2002. Algorithms for provisioning virtual private networks in the hose model. *IEEE/ACM Transactions on Networking*.10(4):565–78.

Man, L. 2003. Policy-based IPsec management. *IEEE Network* 17(6):36–43.

Metz, C. 2003. The latest in virtual private networks: Part I. *IEEE Internet Computing* 7(1):87–91.

Network Working Group. 1994. The point-to-point protocol (PPP). Edited by W. Simpson. 1661, July 1994. www.faqs.org/rfcs/rfc1661.html (accessed May 25, 2007).

Obaidat, M. S., and N. Boudriga. 2007. Security of e-Systems and computer networks. Cambridge: Cambridge University Press.

Ould-Brahim, H., G. Wright, B. Gleeson, R. Bach, T. Sloane, A. Young, R. Bubenik, L. Fang, C. Sargor, C. Weber, I. Negusse, and J. J. Yu. 2003. Network based IP VPN architecture using virtual routers. http://tools.ietf.org/id/draft-ietf-ppvpn-vpn-vr-04.txt (accessed May 25, 2007).

Pall, G., W. Verthein, J. Taarud, W. Little, and G. Zorn. 1999. Point-to-point tunneling protocol (PPTP). 2637, July 1999. www.faqs.org/rfcs/rfc2637.html (accessed May 25, 2007).

Patel, B., A. Aboba W. Dixon G. Zorn, and S. Booth. 2001. Securing L2TP using IPsec. 3193, November 2001. www.ietf.org/rfc/rfc3193.txt (accessed May 25, 2007).

Rekhter, Y., T. J. Watson, and T. Li 1995. A border gateway protocol 4 (BGP-4). 1771, March 1995. www.ietf.org/rfc/rfc1771.txt (accessed May 25, 2007).

Ribeiro, S., F. Silva, and A. Zuquete. 2004. A roaming authentication solution for Wifi using IPSec VPNs with client certificates. In *TERENA Networking Conference*, June 2004. www.terena.org/publications/tnc2004-proceedings/papers/ribiero.pdf (accessed May 25, 2007).

Rosenbaum, G., W. Lau, and S. Jha. 2003. Recent directions in virtual private network solutions. In *IEEE*

International Conference on Networks (ICON 2003), September 2003. http://ieeexplore.ieee.org/Xplore/login.jsp?url=/iel5/8945/28322/01266193.pdf (accessed May 25, 2007).

Srisuresh, P., and M. Holdrege. 1999. IP network address translator (NAT) terminology and considerations. 2663, August 1999. www.faqs.org/rfcs/rfc2663.html (accessed May 25, 2007).

Strayer, W. T., and R. Yuan. 2001. Introduction to virtual private networks. http://www.awprofessional.com/articles/article.asp?p=167809&rl=1 (accessed June 4, 2007).

Tomsu, P., and G. Wieser. 2002. MPLS-based VPNs—Designing advanced virtual networks. Upper Saddle River, NJ: Prentice-Hall.

Townsley, W., A. Valencia, A. Rubens, G. Pall, G. Zorn, and B, Palter. 1999. Layer two tunneling protocol. 2661, August 1999. www.faqs.org/rfcs/rfc2661.html (accessed May 25, 2007).

Venkateswaran, R. 2001. Virtual private networks. *IEEE Potentials* 20(1):11–5.

Wright, M. A. 2000. Virtual private network security. *Network-Security* July:11–4.

Younglove, R. 2000. Virtual private networks: Secure access for e-business. *IEEE Internet Computing* 4(4):96.

Yuan, R. 2002. The VPN client and the Windows operating system www.awprofessional.com/articles/article.asp?p=25042&rl=1 (accessed June 4, 2007).

Zeng J., and N. Ansari. 2003. Toward IP virtual private network quality of service: A service provider perspective. *IEEE Communications Magazine* 41(4):113–9.

Cryptography

Ari Juels, *RSA Laboratories*

INTRODUCTION

For most people, the word *cryptography* evokes one of two images. There is the classical, somewhat outdated idea of crabbed documents, full of symbols, tucked into books or carried by spies on microfiche. Then there is the updated notion of computers performing arcane calculations that protect everything from secrets of state to credit-card numbers. Both ideas have an element of truth. Indeed, the word *cryptography* derives from the Greek for "secret writing." Today, however, the science of cryptography has overflowed its etymological confines, and means much more than the mere transmission of secret messages and concealment of data. Cryptography, in its fullest contemporary sense, is the science of communicating in the presence of adversaries. To put it another way, cryptography is about enforcing fair play in information exchange in potentially hostile environments.

A couple of examples help illustrate the broad scope of the field. Consider two people, Alice and Bob. (Alice and Bob are the stock characters of storytelling among cryptographers—i.e., scientists who study cryptography.) Alice and Bob each have a list of favorite movies, denoted A and B, respectively. Together they would like to determine which favorite movies they have in common—that is, the intersection $A \cap B$. They do not want to reveal their full lists to one another, however, as they consider these lists to be highly personal. Alice and Bob's goal here is indeed to keep information hidden, as in the classical view of cryptography; however, they also want to reveal information to one another on a selective basis. If you take a moment to reflect on how Alice and Bob can together learn $A \cap B$ without revealing any other data to one another, you may well find it far from obvious. It may even seem impossible without outside help. Contemporary cryptographic techniques, however, make such tasks possible. In fact, tasks like privacy-preserving partial matching of lists are useful in a variety of fields. Health care is one example; a group of hospitals may wish to know the names of any patients making multiple (fraudulent) insurance claims, but are not at liberty to disclose their patient lists to one another.

Here is another example. Alice is sending e-mail to Bob regarding a large financial transaction. She is concerned that her e-mail could be altered in transit or by unscrupulous people in Bob's office. (Even the change of a single digit, e.g., a change from $100,000 to $1,000,000 could, of course, have very serious implications.) Alice would like to ensure that her message is secure against tampering. A cryptographic tool called a "digital signature"—supported, in fact, in many e-mail clients—can achieve exactly this goal, and ensure the integrity of Alice's message to Bob.

At a broader level, the design of electronic voting systems—polling-site machines and apparatus for central tabulation—poses an instructive collection of surprisingly formidable cryptographic challenges. The underlying goal is easy to state. A voting system should permit every registered voter to cast a single, private vote, and should yield a certifiably correct tally. Mechanical systems to accomplish this goal have existed since the classical period of Greek history. In an electronic environment, however, many complications arise. For example, many polling sites today use computers that allow voters to input their choices on touch screens and output a local tally at the end of the voting period. But how can voters be assured that these machines operate correctly? It is easily conceivable that in a race between candidate A and candidate B that an electronic voting machine could be programmed (either accidentally or with malicious intent) to discard half of the votes cast for candidate A. Indeed, experts have noted grave concerns about existing voting systems, and have proposed a range of cryptographic solutions. Here again, cryptography can achieve an almost paradoxical proposition. It permits the creation of a system in which voters' choices remain anonymized, but the system yields a publicly verifiable, mathematical proof of correctness of a centralized tally.

These examples illustrate the very broad purview of cryptography and its relevance not merely in military and diplomatic circles, but to everyday users of computing systems. As I explain, strong cryptographic algorithms are present in the basic software of nearly every computer sold today, and play a large, if often hidden role, in e-commerce and basic computer security. Often without knowing it, active users of the Internet use encryption to conceal data on a regular basis. When accepting credit-card information or processing other financial transactions, most Web servers initiate encryption sessions with clients. The form of encryption used to support sessions of this kind on the Web is very strong—so strong that it is generally believed to be effectively unbreakable by even the most powerful computers. In most browsers, the appearance of an icon representing a closed padlock on the bottom of the screen indicates the use of encryption in a protocol known as SSL (secure sockets layer). By clicking on this padlock, a user can learn detailed information about the encryption session, much of which is explained in further depth in this chapter.

Although the science of constructing systems to protect data is called "cryptography," the science of analyzing and attempting to find weaknesses in cryptographic systems is called "cryptanalysis." Together, the two complementary sciences are known as cryptology. In this chapter, I focus mainly on encryption, one of the most widespread applications of cryptography, and in many respects the most accessible. (I draw heavily on my chapter, entitled "Encryption," published in the *Handbook of Information Security* [Juels 2006]). I also briefly discuss digital signatures and data integrity. For readers interested in more advanced applications of cryptography, I suggest the further readings at the end of this chapter.

A Brief Historical Note

An exciting subject of study in its own right, the history of cryptography—and cryptology—is also intimately associated with the birth of the digital computer. During WWII, the efforts of British signals intelligence to break the German Enigma cipher led to the development of mechanical devices known as "bombes," so called because of the ticking sounds they made in testing possible cipher keys. The bombes and the later generation of Colossus machines arising from these efforts were important precursors of the modern computer. Moreover, the man overseeing the immensely successful Enigma break was Alan Turing, a progenitor of the field of computer science.

SYMMETRIC-KEY CRYPTOGRAPHY

Encryption is the most basic and historically important operation in the field of cryptography. It is the procedure of rendering a message into a concealed form so that it is decipherable exclusively by a particular recipient or recipients. The message in its original state is known as a *plaintext* (or *cleartext*); in its encrypted form, it is known as a *ciphertext*. Historically, the aim of encryption has been to enable two parties to exchange messages confidentially, even in the presence of an eavesdropper capable of intercepting most or all of their communications. The use of encryption has been confined chiefly to diplomatic and military circles in the past, but its scope in everyday life has broadened enormously in recent years. Thanks to the rise of the Internet, it is estimated that over half a billion personal computers are equipped today with strong encryption capabilities in their Web-browsing software. This includes nearly every new computer sold today.

An encryption algorithm is considered to be secure when an adversary—traditionally referred to in cryptographic circles as Eve—cannot feasibly distinguish between the encryptions of two different plaintexts. This should hold even in cases in which Eve has the ability to manipulate the messages transmitted between Alice and Bob in various ways. For example, suppose that Eve can cause Alice to generate and reveal ciphertexts A and B computed on messages X and Y in a random order. Eve should nonetheless be unable to tell whether A is an encryption of X or of Y.

The operational basis of an encryption algorithm, or cipher, is a piece of information known as a key. A key serves as input to the encryption process that Alice and Bob have agreed to use. The encryption process consists of a series of instructions on how Alice, for instance, should convert a plaintext into a ciphertext. The key serves as a parameter guiding the instructions. The reverse process, whereby Bob converts a ciphertext back into a plaintext, is also guided by a key, one that may or may not be the same as Alice's. The security of traditional ciphers—that is, the privacy of the messages they encrypt—depends on a shared key that is kept secret. For example, in one form of folklore encryption, Alice and Bob each have copies of the same edition of a particular novel. They share the identity of this novel as a secret between them. Alice encrypts a plaintext by finding a random example of each letter of her message in the novel. She writes down the page, line, and ordinal position of each of these letters in turn. The result of this process constitutes the ciphertext. Bob, of course, can reverse the process and obtain the original plaintext by referring to his copy of the shared novel. In this case, the novel itself serves as a key—one that is quite long, of course, running potentially to hundreds of pages. In the forms of cryptography used on computers today, the key is much shorter, typically equivalent in length to several words or sentences.

Symmetric-Key Encryption

When Alice and Bob make use of the same key for encryption and decryption, as in our example above, this is referred to as symmetric encryption, or symmetric-key encryption. Figure 1 gives a basic operational schematic of symmetric-key encryption.

Let us consider another folklore cipher, in which each letter of a message is replaced with another letter according to a fixed set of random, predetermined assignments. For example, the message, "MEET ME UNDER THE BRIDGE" might be encrypted as: ZKKO ZK BWIKQ OPK UQMIFK.

This form of encryption is known as a substitution cipher. It is, in fact, quite easy for a skilled cryptanalyst—or even just a good puzzle solver—to break. Edgar Allen Poe, for instance, challenged readers of a newspaper in 1839 to submit English-language ciphertexts produced by letter substitution. He published the plaintexts of many such challenge ciphertexts in subsequent issues of the newspaper. Knowing, for example, that *e* is the most common letter in the English language, one would be tempted—quite

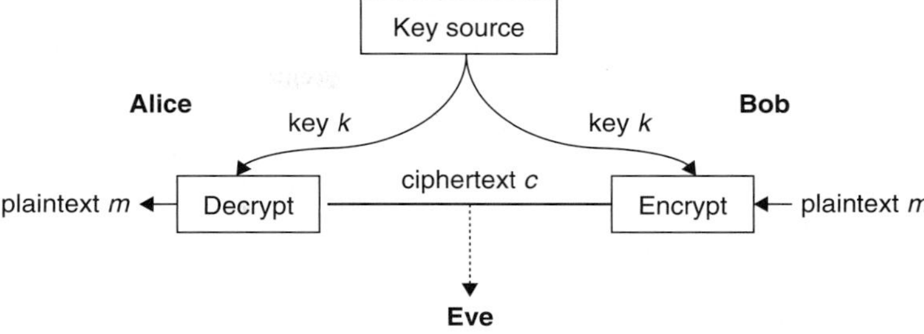

Figure 1: Symmetric-key encryption. Bob wishes to transmit plaintext message m securely to Alice over a channel subject to eavesdropping. He encrypts it under shared symmetric key k to obtain ciphertex c, and transmits c. Eavesdropper Eve learns the ciphertext c, but should not learn m if the cipher is constructed and used properly

correctly—to identify the letter *K*, which appears most frequently in the above ciphertext, with the letter *e* in the plaintext. More sophisticated cryptanalytic techniques for attacking substitution ciphers focus on the frequency statistics not just for single letters, but also for letter pairs and triples.

Knowing that their cipher is subject to cryptanalytic attacks of this kind, Alice and Bob might be tempted to use a different, perhaps more complex cipher, and to hide from Eve not just their key, but also the workings of the cipher. This is equivalent in effect to making the choice of the cipher a part of the key itself. An important principle enunciated by the nineteenth-century cryptologist Auguste Kerckhoffs (1883) discourages this approach. Adhered to by contemporary cryptologists, this principle may be stated as follows: The security of a cipher should reside in the key alone, not in the secrecy of the process of encryption. The motivations behind Kerckhoffs's principle are several. First of all, widespread use of a good cipher requires that its workings be divulged in some form. Even if a cipher is disseminated only through software, for example, the underlying instructions can be reverse-engineered. Thus, it is fair to assume that an attacker can learn the mechanics of the cipher. Moreover, despite the oft-demonstrated inventiveness of the cryptographic community, there is time enough to devise and refine only a limited number of basic techniques for strong new ciphers. A poorly designed cipher, even when its workings are hidden from view, is vulnerable to attack by means of an arsenal of analytic techniques refined by the cryptanalytic community over many years. These techniques are roughly analogous in spirit to the idea that leads to the discovery of the letter *e* in the example ciphertext above, but rely on more sophisticated forms of statistical analysis.

The basic unit of information in the computer and the fundamental unit for the encoding of digital messages is not the letter, but the bit. For this reason, contemporary symmetric-key ciphers operate through the manipulation of bits, rather than lexicographic units. One of the earliest ciphers designed from this perspective is known as the one-time pad. Invented during World War I, the one-time pad is also of interest as the only cipher whose security is provable in the strictest mathematical sense. Formal understanding of its properties emerged in 1948–1949, with the publication of seminal work by Claude Shannon (1948). (The security analysis of other ciphers, as I shall explain, has a strong, but less complete or rigorous mathematical basis).

A one-time pad is a key shared by Alice and Bob consisting of a perfectly random string of bits as long as the message that Alice wishes to transmit to Bob. To encrypt her message, Alice aligns the pad with the message so that there is a one-to-one correspondence between the bits in both. Where the pad contains a 1, Alice flips the corresponding bit in her plaintext. She leaves the other bits of the plaintext unchanged. This simple process yields the ciphertext. As may be proven mathematically—and perhaps grasped intuitively—this ciphertext is indistinguishable to Eve from a completely random string. Indeed, from her perspective, it is a completely random string. This is to say that Eve can learn no information at all from the ciphertext, no matter how powerful her cryptanalytic capabilities. Apart from its requirement of perfect randomness, though, the one-time pad carries another strong caveat. The term *one-time* refers to the fact that if Alice uses the same key to encrypt more than one message, she loses the security properties of the cipher. This makes the one-time pad impractical for most purposes, as it requires that Alice and Bob generate, exchange, and store many random bits in advance of their communications. Nonetheless, the one-time pad has seen practical use. For example, the "hot-line" established between the United States and the Soviet Union in the wake of the Cuban missile crisis used a one-time pad system to ensure confidentiality, with tapes containing random keying material exchanged via the embassies of the two countries.

Symmetric-Key Encryption in Practice

The symmetric-key ciphers in common use today are designed to use relatively short keys, typically 128 to 256 bits in length. Moreover, these ciphers retain their security properties even when individual keys are used to encrypt many messages over long periods. Indeed, a well-designed symmetric-key cipher should permit only one effective avenue of attack, described by cryptographers as "exhaustive search" or "brute force." By this, it is meant that an attacker familiar with the cipher makes random guesses at the key until successful. If Eve wishes to mount a brute-force attack against a ciphertext sent by Alice to Bob, she will repeatedly guess their shared key and try to decrypt the message, until she obtains the correct plaintext.

Given use of a 128-bit-long key, Eve will on average have to make well more than a trillion trillion trillion guesses before she is successful! This is more, for example, than the total number of atoms composing all of the human beings in the world. The most powerful computers available today could not be expected to mount a successful brute-force attack against a well-designed cipher using a key of this length, even over the course of many years. It should be observed that the difficulty of breaking a key doubles for every additional bit in length. Thus, for instance, a 128-bit key is not twice as hard to break as a 64-bit key, but over a million trillion times harder.

The first widely embraced cipher using the strong design principles in use today was the data encryption standard, or DES (pronounced "dehz"). Developed at IBM, the DES cipher was published as a federal standard in 1976 by what is now the National Institute of Standards (NIST) of the U.S. government. DES and security-enhanced variants are still widely deployed, particularly in the banking industry. DES uses a 56-bit key, operating on a basic unit of encryption consisting of a 64-bit block. This is to say that in order to encrypt a long message using DES, Alice first subdivides the message into 64-bit (i.e., 8-byte) blocks, each of which she enciphers individually. Ciphers that operate in this fashion are referred to as block ciphers.

Brute-force attack on a 56-bit key requires substantial computational effort, very likely beyond the reach of most organizations at the time of invention of DES. Today, however, such capability is attainable with networks of ordinary workstations. This was first demonstrated in 1997, when a successful attack was mounted against a DES-encrypted ciphertext by a network of thousands of computers over the course of 39 days, and subsequently duplicated by a single, special-purpose computer in less than a day. (It should be noted that even today, DES is still not easy to break without considerable resources.) Earlier concerns about the strength of DES had already prompted many organizations to use a strengthened version involving application of DES operations not once, but three times to each input block, and typically using two distinct DES keys. Known as triple-DES (3-DES), this enhanced version offers considerably stronger security than DES, with what may be viewed as an effective key strength of up to 112 bits.

With DES in its basic form approaching the end of its serviceable lifetime, the cryptographic community began in 1999 to lend its efforts to the development of a new standard cipher to serve as a successor. The advanced encryption standard, or AES (pronounced letter by letter), emerged as the result of an open competition conducted by NIST. After a period of rigorous scrutiny by the research community and government agencies, a cipher known as Rijndael (of which one recognized pronunciation is "Rhine dahl") was selected as the AES. Designed by two Belgian researchers, Joan Daemen and Vincent Rijmen, the AES is seeing internationally widespread deployment. Rijndael is a block cipher designed to accommodate key lengths of 128, 196, or 256 bits and operate on data blocks of 128, 196, or 256 bits in any of the nine possible combinations. In its standardization as the AES, however, only a 128-bit data block size is accommodated. Rijndael, like many contemporary symmetric-key ciphers, is capable of very fast encryption—easily supporting broadband connection speeds on typical PCs. The code sizes for AES implementations can be less than 1 kb. The size of a basic ciphertext yielded by AES, as with any block cipher, is roughly the size of the plaintext. A little extra space—less than the block size—may also be needed to accommodate added randomness and the fact the plaintext generally cannot be divided into data blocks of exactly the right size.

Another symmetric-key cipher deserving discussion is RC4. RC4 was designed by Ronald L. Rivest, one of the co-inventors of the RSA cryptosystem, which I discuss later in this chapter. The letters *RC* stand for "Ron's code," and the number 4 denotes Rivest's fourth cipher design. In contrast to the block ciphers described above, RC4 is known as a stream cipher. It does not operate by encrypting individual blocks of data. Rather, the only fixed-length input to RC4 is a key, typically 128 bits in length. The output of the cipher is a string of random-looking bits that serves to encrypt messages. This string may be made as long as desired by the user. In order to encrypt a message for Bob, Alice inputs a shared key to RC4 and generates a string as long as the message. Although not a one-time pad, this string is used by Alice to encrypt the message in exactly the same manner as a one-time pad—that is, using the same system of bit alignment and flipping. In addition, the output string of RC4 for a particular key has the "one-time" restriction, which is to say that the string can be safely used for encryption only once. The fact that RC4 can generate a string of arbitrary length, however, means that different portions of the string can be used for different messages. Also, encipherment under RC4 is naturally capable of yielding a ciphertext identical in length to the plaintext.

This said, the output string of RC4 on a given key is not in fact a one-time pad, because it is not fully random. This may be seen in the fact that Alice and Bob know the process that generated the string, because they know their shared input key to RC4. In particular, they can write a short set of instructions describing to someone else how to generate exactly the same output string from RC4. If k denotes their shared key, these instructions would simply say, "Give the key k as input to RC4." They could not do this in the case of a truly random string. Suppose, for instance, that Alice and Bob generated a shared random string—that is, a one-time pad—by flipping a coin many times. If they gave the instructions "Flip a coin" to Carol, it is almost certain that Carol, in following the same instructions, would generate a very different-looking string. Obviously, though, RC4 is much more convenient for Alice and Bob to use than a one-time pad, because it requires of them only that they share a key of, say, 128 bits in length. For all intents and purposes, this is true no matter how long the messages they wish to encrypt.

The security of the RC4 cipher comes from the fact that from the perspective of Eve, who does not know the key, the output of RC4 is indistinguishable from a one-time pad. That is, if Alice were to give an RC4 output string to Eve (rather than using it for encipherment), and were also to give Eve a truly random string of the same length, Eve would not be able to tell the difference. Thus, as far as Eve is concerned, when Alice and Bob encrypt their messages using RC4, they might as well be using a one-time pad. This, at any rate, is a rough expression of the conclusion that cryptanalysts have arrived at after many years of statistical study of the RC4 cipher. They express this belief by describing the output of RC4 as being pseudo-random. Strong block ciphers like AES are also believed to possess this property of pseudo-randomness, but in a different form.

RC4 is of particular interest because it is one of the most commonly used ciphers in the world and included in the software of nearly every new PC sold today. It is generally a component of the SSL encryption system used for secure credit-card transactions on the Internet. In other words, the closed padlock on a browser screen mentioned earlier in this chapter indicates that the RC4 cipher is being used.

The design principal for RC4, like that of most symmetric ciphers, is a delicate sequencing of a few very basic mathematical instructions. In RC4, the operations are the swapping of integer elements in a small array representing a permutation and addition of small integers (in fact, modular addition, an operation explained later in this chapter). Others of Rivest's suite of cipher designs are also in common use, namely RC2, which forms the basis of many e-mail encryption programs, and also RC5. Apart from DES, 3-DES, AES, and the RC series, there are a number of other popular ciphers used in various systems today. These include IDEA, CAST-128, and Blowfish, to name just a few.

Encryption and Passwords

Symmetric-key ciphers are used not only to protect communications, but also commonly to protect files against unauthorized access. Many users rely on encryption software to protect files on their hard drives against exposure to hackers or to protect sensitive data in case of laptop theft. For these purposes, it is common for the user to use a password. The encryption software converts this password into a key for use with a standard symmetric-key cipher such as AES. Because users typically use passwords consisting of or closely related to words in their native languages, there is generally less randomness in the key generated by a password than in a randomly generated symmetric key. One well-known means for a hacker to attack password-encrypted files in a particular encryption system, therefore, is to compile a large lexicon of common passwords. The hacker converts each entry in the lexicon into a symmetric key in the same manner as the encryption system and then uses each such key in a brute-force attack against individual users using that system. This is known as a dictionary attack. One way to reduce vulnerability to dictionary attacks is to use salt. This is a random string of bits generated for each password individually and combined with the password in the generation of a symmetric key. The use of salt renders dictionary attacks more difficult, as it effectively forces an attacker to recompile the base lexicon for each target password. It should be understood nevertheless that salt is a limited countermeasure, and does not compensate for poor selection of passwords.

Passwords are, of course, also the most common way for users to authenticate when logging into accounts over the Internet. In this context, however, the password is typically not used as an encryption key. Instead, the server to which the user is attempting to connect checks processed password information against a database entry for the requested account.

Message Integrity: Hash Functions and Message Authentication Codes

A critical problem that encryption alone does not solve is that of message integrity. When Bob sends a message to Alice encrypted using, for example, RC4, he may be reasonably well assured of the privacy of his communication if he uses the cipher correctly. When Alice receives his message, however, how does she know that Eve has not tampered with the message en route, by changing a few bits or words? Indeed, how does she even know that Bob is the one who sent the message? For this type of assurance, some additional cryptographic apparatus is required.

One of the workhorses of the cryptographic world is an algorithm known as a hash function, which is a form of cryptographic compression algorithm. It takes as input a message m of arbitrary length and produces a message digest of fixed length—typically on the order of a few hundred bits. This message digest is essentially a kind of fingerprint or checksum for the message m. Modifying even a single bit of m renders the checksum invalid. Thus, a message digest can detect message transmission errors. As a cryptographic primitive, however, a hash function offers much stronger properties than the mere error detection afforded by a simple checksum. A well-designed hash function yields message digests that resist message modifications by sophisticated and powerful adversaries.

A good hash function has the property of collision resistance, which means that it is infeasible—even using massive computing power—to find two messages, m_1 and m_2 that have an identical message digest. (Since a hash function takes inputs of arbitrary length, but has a fixed-length output, a simple counting argument shows that message collisions do exist. They are just hard to find.) The property of collision resistance implies another, subtly different property called "preimage resistance." Given a particular message m_1, it is hard to find a second message m_2 with an identical message digest.

Message digests can serve effectively as uniquely identifying, compact digital tags for messages or documents. One application, for example, is integrity assurance for software. Suppose that Alice's company wants to ensure that every new computer sent to an employee is configured in exactly the right way and contains no unauthorized programs, Trojans, or viruses. The IT (information technology) department might apply a hash function f to the hard-drive contents of an exemplar machine, obtaining a 256-bit message digest, which they publish on the company intranet. To inspect a new machine and ensure that it is configured identically with the exemplar, a company employee can download its hard-drive contents onto a trusted computer, apply the hash function f, and check that the resulting message digest is the same as that published by the IT department.

The most common hash functions in use today are MD5 (message digest 5), developed by Rivest, and SHA-1 (secure hash algorithm), developed by NIST. Recently uncovered, serious weaknesses in these two hash functions, however, are prompting industry migration to such hash functions as SHA-256 (so called because its digest length is 256 bits), a successor to SHA-1.

Hash functions are unusual cryptographic algorithms in that they have no secret keys associated with them. Alice might think of appending a message digest z to her e-mail message m to Bob as a way of ensuring that Eve does not tamper with it. Eve, however, can simply swap in a new message m' of her choice, compute and append a new message digest z', deceiving Bob into thinking that the message originates with Alice.

It is possible, however, to combine a hash function with a secret key in precisely this setting so as to prevent message tampering. In particular, a tool known as a message authentication code (MAC) provides message integrity in symmetric-key settings. A MAC is essentially a hash function applied to a message *with* a secret key; viewed another way, it is like a cryptographically keyed checksum. Making use of a shared secret key, Alice can append a MAC to her messages to Bob so as to enable Bob to be sure that Eve has not tampered with them. MACs can be combined with encryption to achieve message confidentiality and integrity simultaneously.

In practice, naïve ways of combining hash functions with secret keys to build MACs do not achieve the rigorous technical assurances desired for well-designed cryptographic systems. Instead, well-designed industry applications today generally use HMAC, an algorithm developed by Bellare, Canetti, and Krawczyk (1996), whose security is based on strong theoretical underpinnings.

More on the Security of Symmetric-Key Cryptography

As already explained, in the area of encryption, cryptologists know of a truly complete mathematical proof of security only for the one-time pad. For DES, 3-DES, AES, RC4, and kindred ciphers, cryptographers have no such security proofs. Strong proof for these ciphers is not possible at present; belief in their security, however, rests on fairly well-explored (if heuristic) mathematical foundations. The same lack of fundamental proof applies to other cryptographic algorithms, such as hash functions. In fact, as mentioned above, the most common hash functions in use today have been recently shown to contain design weaknesses.

Shortly after the publication of DES, two cryptologists—Eli Biham and Adi Shamir (1991)—developed a technique called "differential cryptanalysis." Roughly speaking, differential cryptanalysis involves statistical analysis of a cipher based on the way particular bits change (or do not change) in output ciphertexts when bits in certain positions are flipped in input plaintexts. The technique of differential cryptanalysis helped to confirm the strength of DES and to inform the design of later ciphers. (Some time after the academic development of differential cryptanalysis, it was publicly revealed that the technique had already been familiar to the government intelligence community, and had indeed helped guide the design of DES.)

Subsequently developed cryptanalytic techniques have further enhanced the collection of tools available to the cryptanalyst, influencing new designs for cryptographic algorithms in the process.

In analyzing the security of a cipher or MAC, one might consider Eve as an inert eavesdropper, attempting to decipher or modify the messages sent between Alice to Bob by harvesting and analyzing the ciphertexts they exchange. In fact, cryptologists also consider a range of ways in which Eve might try to tamper with or otherwise influence what messages Alice and Bob exchange in the hope of learning additional information. For example, if Alice encrypts all of her e-mail, then Eve might send a note containing a petition to Alice, and ask Alice to forward it to her friends. If Alice sends the petition to Bob while Eve is eavesdropping, then Eve learns a ciphertext for which she herself has selected the corresponding plaintext. In other words, Eve is able to perform active experimentation on the cipher. If Alice and Bob use a cipher that is poorly designed, then Eve may be able to gain information about their key in this way, or about messages they have exchanged with one another. This type of attack is known as a chosen-plaintext attack. It is an example of one of the types of attack against which cryptographers must ensure that their cipher designs are resistant. Analogous attacks against MACs are possible.

Even if a cryptographic primitive like a cipher is well designed, it must still be used with great care. Consider another example. Suppose that Alice and Bob always use a strong block cipher such as AES with a random 128-bit key to encrypt their communications. They perform encryption simply by dividing their messages into blocks and encrypting each block individually under their key. But suppose further that Eve knows that Alice and Bob exchange stock tips, and that these regularly take the form of simple buy and sell orders. Eve might then pass some stock tips to Alice, such as "Buy ABC, Inc." and "Sell DEF Corp.," and suggest that these be forwarded to Bob. If Eve eavesdrops while these stock tips are forwarded, then she learns what the corresponding ciphertexts look like. Thus, if Alice later sends the message "Buy ABC, Inc." to Bob, Eve will be able to recognize the ciphertext and identify the corresponding buy or sell order. In other words, even though Alice and Bob are using a very strong cipher, Eve will be able to identify (and effectively, to decrypt) any of a small set of target messages!

The way that Alice and Bob use a block cipher is known as a mode of operation. The naïve example I just described is known as electronic code book (ECB) mode, a form whose use is avoided today in part because of the problem I have just described. To prevent Eve from learning what particular ciphertexts look like, Alice may adopt a mode of operation that involves the introduction of random bits into the message. One popular mode of operation today is known as cipher block chaining (CBC) mode. In this system, Alice divides her plaintext into blocks and inserts some freshly generated random bits at the beginning to serve as the first block. Alice then uses a principle of "chaining," in which the encryption of one block is affected by the encryption of the previous one, thereby causing the randomness in the first block to propagate through the ciphertext. Although the architectural motivations behind this mode are somewhat complex, its basic impact on message privacy is easy to understand. The fact that Alice introduces randomness into her ciphertexts means that the same plaintext is not encrypted twice the same way, and thus that Eve cannot trick Alice so as to recognize the stock tips or other plaintexts that Alice encrypts. Other modes of encryption aim at formally achieving additional security aims like message authentication. In particular, they enable Alice and Bob to ensure that the origin of messages is legitimate, and that the messages do not include spurious insertions or modifications made by Eve.

PUBLIC-KEY CRYPTOGRAPHY

Many years of research have led to the widespread deployment of strong symmetric-key ciphers and MACs capable of supporting high communication speeds. One might be tempted to believe that the basic problem of private communications has been solved and that the science of cryptology has run its course. Even if a symmetric-key cipher, hash function, or MAC is unbreakable, however, there remains a fundamental problem. I have assumed in this discussion that Alice and Bob share knowledge of a secret key. The question is: How do they obtain this key to begin with?

If Alice and Bob can meet face to face, in the absence of the eavesdropper Eve, then they may generate their shared key by repeatedly flipping a coin, or Alice may simply hand Bob a key written on a piece of paper or stored on a floppy disk. What if Alice and Bob wish to communicate privately over the Internet, however, without ever meeting? Alternatively, what if a commercial site on the Web wishes to enable any customer, new or old, to submit an order and credit-card number securely from anywhere in the world? The administrator of the Web site cannot possibly hope to communicate keys in private to all customers before they log in. To simplify the formidable difficulties that secure key distribution can pose, cryptographers have devised a form of mathematical magic known as public-key encryption or cryptography (also known as asymmetric-key cryptography, in contrast to symmetric-key cryptography). Using public-key cryptography, Alice and Bob can send each other encrypted messages securely, even if they have never met, and even if Eve has eavesdropped on all of their communications!

In a public-key cryptosystem, Alice possesses not one, but two keys. The first is known as her public key. Alice makes this key known to everyone; she may publish it on her Web page, in Internet directories, or in any other public place. Her second, mathematically related key is known as a private key. Alice keeps this key secret. She does not divulge it to anyone else, even people with whom she wishes to communicate privately. Together, the public key and private key are referred to as a key pair. Bob sends a private message to Alice by performing a computation using her public key, and perhaps a private key of his own as well.

Public-key cryptography is a powerful tool—indeed, one whose feasibility may at first seem counterintuitive. Even if Eve knows Alice and Bob's public keys, it is possible for Alice and Bob to communicate privately using public-key cryptography. Moreover, with public-key cryptography, not only Bob, but Carol or any other party can achieve private communication with Alice over a public communication medium like the Internet.

Public-key cryptography can serve, moreover, not simply for encryption, but also for data integrity. Alice can use her private key not only to decrypt messages that people send her, but also to create digital signatures on messages—encrypted or unencrypted—that she sends others. Using Alice's public key, anyone can check the correctness of a message to which she has applied a digital signature. As I explain below, when a message bears a correct digital signature from Alice, it carries a very high assurance that not a single bit was modified by any other party subsequent to Alice's creation of the message.

Diffie-Hellman Key Exchange

Public-key encryption was the brainchild of Ralph Merkle, who in 1974 conceived a plausible, but somewhat impractical initial scheme. The idea saw its first practical form in 1976 in a seminal paper by Whitfield Diffie and Martin Hellman entitled "New Directions in Cryptography." Diffie and Hellman proposed a system in which Alice can combine her private key with the public key of Bob, and vice versa, such that each of them obtains the same secret key. Eve cannot figure out this secret key, even with knowledge of the public keys of both Alice and Bob. This system has come to be known as Diffie-Hellman key exchange, abbreviated D-H.

D-H exploits a form of mathematics known as modular arithmetic. Modular arithmetic is a way of restricting the outcome of basic mathematical operations to a set of integers with an upper bound. It is familiar to many schoolchildren as "clock arithmetic." Consider a clock on military time, by which hours are measured only in the range from zero to twenty-three, with zero corresponding to midnight and twenty-three to 11 o'clock at night. In this system, an advance of 25 hours on 3 o'clock brings us not to 28 o'clock, for example, but full circle to 4 o'clock (because $25 + 3 = 28$ and $28 - 24 = 4$). Similarly, an advance of 55 hours on 1 o'clock brings us to 8 o'clock (because $55 + 1 = 56$ and $56 - (2 \times 24) = 8$). In this case, the number 24, an upper bound on operations involving the measurement of hours, is referred to as a modulus. When a calculation involving hours on a clock yields a large number, we subtract the number 24 until we obtain an integer between 0 and 23, a process known as modular reduction. This idea can be extended to moduli of different sizes. For example, in the modulus 10, the sum of 5 and 7 would not be 12, which is larger than 10, but 2, because modular reduction yields $12 - 10 = 2$. We say that an arithmetic operation is modular when modular reduction is applied to its result. For example, modular multiplication is simply ordinary multiplication followed by modular reduction. We write mod p to denote reduction under modulus p. Thus, for example, it is easily seen that $3 \times 4 \bmod 10 = 2$.

Diffie and Hellman proposed a public-key cryptosystem based on modular multiplication, or more precisely, on modular exponentiation—that is, the repeated application of modular multiplication. Their scheme depends for its security on the use of a modulus that is a very large number. In the systems used today, the modulus is typically an integer that is 1024 bits in length—that is, a little more than 300 decimal digits. It is also generally prime, which is to say that apart from the number 1, it is not divisible by any smaller integers. There are some additional, technical restrictions on the form of the modulus that I shall not explore here.

The security of D-H is based on the following idea. Suppose that p is a large modulus and g is an integer less than p (again, with some additional technical restrictions). Suppose that Alice selects a random integer a, also less than p. She then computes the integer $y = g^a \bmod p$ and gives the integers p, g, and y to Eve. It is believed by cryptologists that with this information alone, it is infeasible for Eve to figure out the value a. The task of figuring out a is known as the discrete logarithm problem, one that has been the subject of many years of study by mathematicians and cryptographers. Although the security of D-H is not directly based on the discrete logarithm problem, it is very closely related.

In D-H, the values p and g are standard, public values. They may be conveyed in some widely distributed piece of software, such as a browser. Alice selects a random integer a less than p as her private key and computes $y_{Alice} = g^a \bmod p$ as her public key—that is, the key that she publishes. Bob similarly selects a random integer b, also less than p, as his own private key, and computes $y_{Bob} = g^b \bmod p$ as his public key. Using her private key a, Alice can take the public key y_{Bob} and compute a value $k = (y_{Bob})^a \bmod p$. Bob, similarly, can compute exactly the same value k using y_{Alice} in combination with his own private key b. In particular, it is also the case that $k = (y_{Alice})^b \bmod p$ (thanks to the commutative properties of modular exponentiation). Eve, however, cannot figure out the secret k. This, at least, is the belief of cryptologists, based on the idea that Eve knows neither of the private keys a and b and on the difficulty of the discrete logarithm problem. Thus, if Alice and Bob use the secret k as the basis for private communication using a symmetric-key cipher like AES, Eve will be unable to eavesdrop successfully on their communications. This is a capsule summary of the idea behind the Diffie-Hellman cryptosystem. There are other details involved in making D-H a secure, workable system, which I gloss over in this description. I also note in passing that an attractive feature of D-H is the fact that variants may be implemented over algebraic structures known as elliptic curves. This results in more compact key lengths and faster running times.

D-H is used, among other places, in some versions of PGP (pretty good privacy), a popular piece of encryption software used to secure Internet communications such as e-mail, and available as freeware in some versions.

The RSA Cryptosystem

A year after the publication of Diffie and Hellman's key exchange system, three faculty members at MIT proposed a new public-key cryptosystem. This cryptosystem is called RSA after its three inventors, Ronald Rivest, Adi Shamir, and Leonard Adleman. RSA is now the most widely deployed cryptosystem in the world (RSA Laboratories 2007).

Use of the RSA cryptosystem for encryption is very similar to the use of D-H. One superficial difference is that in the RSA cryptosystem, Bob can send an encrypted message to Alice without having a public key of his own. In particular, Bob can encrypt a message directly under Alice's public key in such a way that Alice can decrypt the ciphertext using her private key. Figure 2 diagrams this operation of RSA and similar public-key encryption schemes. (Much the same functionality can be achieved with D-H by having Bob generate a temporary key pair on the fly and using this as the basis for encryption of a message for Alice.)

There are two rather more important differences between the two cryptosystems. The first lies in the speed of their respective operations. In RSA, encryption is a very fast operation; it generally requires less computational effort than a D-H key exchange. Decryption, however, is several times slower for RSA than for key exchange in D-H. Another important difference between the two is a feature present in RSA. RSA can also be used to perform digital signing, an operation not covered in this chapter, but of central importance in cryptography. Digital signing achieves the goal of authenticating messages—that is, proving their origin, rather than concealing their contents.

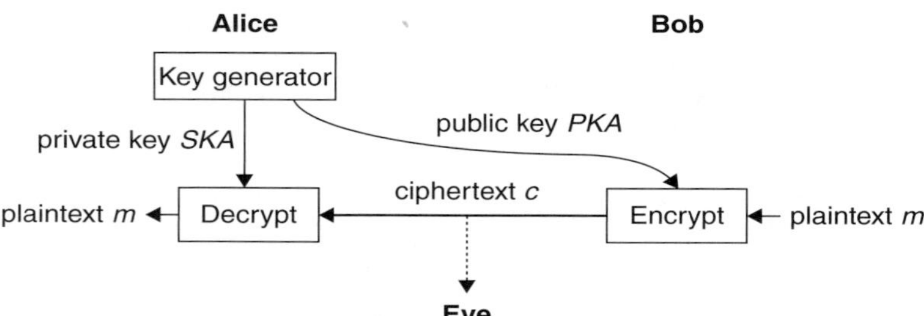

Figure 2: Public-key encryption (e.g., RSA). Alice generates for herself a private key SK_A and corresponding public key PK_A. Suppose then that Bob wishes to transmit plaintext message m securely to Alice over a channel subject to eavesdropping. Bob encrypts m under public key PK_A to obtain ciphertext *c*, which the transmits to Alice. Eavesdropper Eve learns the ciphertext *c* and may also learn PK_A, as it is a public value. If the public-key encryption algorithm is well constructed and properly used, however, Eve should be unable to learn *m*

The RSA system uses modular arithmetic, the same type of mathematical basis as for Diffie-Hellman key exchange. In D-H, the modulus is a published value that may be used by any party to construct his or her key pair. In RSA, however, every party uses a different modulus, published as part of his or her public key. Thus, if Bob wishes to encrypt a message for Alice, he uses a modulus N_{Alice} unique to the public key of Alice; if he wants to encrypt a message for Carol, he uses a different modulus, N_{Carol}. The reason for the use of different moduli is the fact that the value of the modulus in the RSA cryptosystem relates directly to that of the private key.

A modulus N in the RSA cryptosystem has a special form. It is the product of two large prime integers, generally denoted by p and q. In other words, $N = p \times q$. The pair of primes p and q are treated as private values in the RSA cryptosystem; they are used to compute the private key for the modulus N. Thus, the security of RSA is related very closely to the difficulty of determining the secret primes p and q given knowledge of the modulus N. This is known as the problem of factoring and is believed to be extremely difficult when p and q are large. In typical systems today, p and q are chosen to be primes of about 512 bits in length, so that N is an integer of about 1024 bits, the same length as generally selected for a Diffie-Hellman modulus. Factoring is the only effective method known for attacking RSA when the cryptosystem is used properly.

Among its many other uses, the RSA cryptosystem (along with RC4) is used as the basis for SSL, the encryption system in most Web browsers today, and also in some versions of PGP software.

More Technical Detail on RSA

I now describe in more mathematical detail how the RSA cryptosystem works. Unable as we are to delve further into the underlying mathematics, I provide only prescriptive formulae, without explaining the rationale behind them. For further information, the reader is directed to a good textbook (e.g., Menezes, van Oorschot, and Vanstone 2001).

To compute her public key, Alice selects two random primes p_{Alice} and q_{Alice}, both of roughly equal length in bits (e.g., 512 bits long). The product

$$N_{\text{Alice}} = p_{\text{Alice}} \times q_{\text{Alice}}$$

is the modulus used by Alice in her public key. She also selects a small odd integer e_{Alice}; generally, this value is more or less standardized in a given system, the integer 65535 being a common choice. An additional restriction on e_{Alice} is that it must not have a factor in common with $p_{\text{Alice}} - 1$ or $q_{\text{Alice}} - 1$, a criterion considered in the selection of primes. Together, the pair of values $(e_{\text{Alice}}, N_{\text{Alice}})$ constitutes Alice's public key. Her private key is computed as follows. Let $\Phi(N_{\text{Alice}}) = (p_{\text{Alice}} - 1) \times (q_{\text{Alice}} - 1)$. Alice computes her private key, generally denoted by d_{Alice}, in such a way that $e_{\text{Alice}}\, d_{\text{Alice}} = 1 \bmod \Phi(N_{\text{Alice}})$. The bit-length of the private key d_{Alice} here is typically quite close to that of N_{Alice}.

A message in the RSA cryptosystem consists of a positive integer m less than N_{Alice}. To encrypt m, Bob computes the ciphertext

$$c = m^{e_{Alice}} \bmod N_{Alice}.$$

As a technical restriction required to achieve good security, the plaintext m is formatted so as to be about equal in length to the modulus, resulting in a ciphertext that is similarly so. To decrypt the ciphertext, Alice applies her private key and computes

$$m = c^{d_{Alice}} \bmod N^{Alice}.$$

An Example

Let us consider a small example to provide some flavor of how the RSA cryptosystem works. For illustrative purposes, we consider integers much smaller than those needed for true, secure use of RSA. Suppose that p_{Alice} and q_{Alice} are 5 and 11, respectively. Then $N_{Alice} = 5 \times 11 = 55$. Observe that $e_{\text{Alice}} = 3$ does not divide $p_{\text{Alice}} - 1$ or $q_{\text{Alice}} - 1$. Thus, Alice can use $(e_{\text{Alice}}, N_{\text{Alice}}) = (3,55)$ as her public key. A valid private key for Alice is $d_{\text{Alice}} = 27$, because $\Phi(\text{N}_{\text{Alice}}) = (p_{Alice} - 1) \times (q_{Alice} - 1) = (5 - 1) \times (10 - 1) = 40$, and $e_{Alice} \times 27 = 81 = 1 \bmod 40$.

To encrypt the message $m = 7$, Bob computes the ciphertext $c = 7^3 \bmod 55 = 343 \bmod 55 = 13$. Alice decrypts the ciphertext $c = 13$ by computing $13^{27} \bmod 55$. Using a pocket calculator, the reader can easily verify that the result of this decryption operation is indeed the original plaintext $m = 7$.

The security of RSA requires some special, technical restrictions on the value of m. In fact, as the RSA cryptosystem is generally used, the message m is itself the key for a symmetric-key cryptosystem such as AES, and is specially formatted prior to encryption. Public-key cryptosystems are generally used in conjunction with symmetric-key cryptosystems, as discussed below.

With a 1024-bit RSA modulus, a Pentium Celeron processor running at about 2 GHz can perform roughly 150 RSA decryption operations per second, and about 2250 encryption operations per second under the public exponent $e = 65535$. (These speeds, of course, can vary enormously depending on the particular software implementation and system configuration.)

As explained above, the security of the RSA cryptosystem is closely related to the difficulty of factoring the product of two large primes. Security guidelines for RSA thus depend on advances in the factoring problem made by researchers, as well as the cost and availability of computing power to a potential attacker. According to guidelines issued in April 2005 by NIST, 1024-bit RSA moduli may be used for most data-security applications through 2009. For more sensitive data, or for security needs beyond that date, a 2048-bit RSA modulus is recommended instead. Although there is substantial debate and uncertainty among cryptographers as to the exact ongoing security level afforded by RSA, there is general agreement as to the rough accuracy of these predictive guidelines. To avoid a common misconception, it should be emphasized that the mathematical basis for the RSA cryptosystem means that the recommended modulus lengths, and thus the public and private keys, are substantially longer than the 128- to 256-bit key lengths prescribed for symmetric-key ciphers.

How Public-Key Encryption Is Used

Encryption of a large quantity of data is generally much slower using a public-key cryptosystem than using a symmetric-key cipher. On the other hand, public-key encryption offers an elegant approach to the problem of distributing keys that is unavailable in symmetric-key ciphers. It is common in practice, therefore, to combine the two types of encryption systems in order to obtain the best properties of both. This is achieved by use of a simple principle known as enveloping. Enveloping involves use of a public-key cryptosystem such as RSA as a vehicle for transporting a secret key, which is itself then used for encryption with a symmetric-key cipher. To send a megabyte-long file to Alice, for example, Bob might select a random 128-bit RC4 key k and encrypt the file under k. He would then send this ciphertext of the file to Alice, along with an RSA encryption of k under Alice's public key. In effect, enveloping is a way of making a public-key cryptosystem faster. Enveloping yields much the same data flows as in Figure 2. The only difference is that a symmetric key k is encrypted rather than an ordinary plaintext m; in addition to the public-key ciphertext c, Bob also transmits a symmetric-key ciphertext c', namely the message m encrypted under k using a symmetric-key cipher.

As with symmetric-key ciphers, cryptologists aim to design public-key cryptosystems to withstand a wide range of possible attacks, involving some very strong ones in which, for example, Eve can persuade Alice to decrypt a range of ciphertexts that Eve herself selects. Like symmetric-key block ciphers, when used in a naïve manner, RSA has a limitation in that encryption of the same plaintext always yields the same ciphertext; it also has the additional weakness of leaking some bits of a plaintext. Prior to encryption under RSA, therefore, it is common practice to subject a message to a special type of formatting that involves the addition of random bits. Loosely speaking, this incorporation of randomness serves much the same purpose as in the case of cipher-block chaining for symmetric-key block ciphers, as described above. Other aspects of the formatting process permit the RSA cryptosystem to withstand other forms of attack, and to do so with guarantees that are subject to rigorous mathematical justification.

Most public-key encryption systems have an additional advantage over symmetric-key systems, in that they permit a flexible approach to distributed storage of the private key, known as secret sharing. This is a way of mathematically splitting a private key into a number of elements known as shares. To achieve a decryption operation, each of these shares may be applied individually to a ciphertext, without the need to assemble the shares themselves in a single place. Thus, a cryptosystem can be set up so that compromise of any one share does not expose the full decryption key itself. For example, Alice can divide her private key into, say, three shares, keeping one for herself and giving one each to her friends Bob and Carol. To decrypt a ciphertext, Alice can ask Bob and Carol to apply their shares and to send her the result. Alice can then complete the decryption with her own share, without Bob or Carol seeing the resulting plaintext. If an attacker breaks into Alice's computer and obtains her share, the attacker will still be unable to decrypt ciphertexts directed to Alice (without also obtaining the assistance of Bob and Carol). The system can even be set up so that decryption is possible given particular sets of shares. Thus, for example, Alice might be able to achieve decryption of her ciphertexts even if Bob or Carol is on vacation.

Despite its great flexibility, public-key cryptography does not directly address all the challenges of key distribution. For example, we have said that Alice can safely disseminate her public key as widely as she likes, publishing it in Internet directories and so forth. But when Bob obtains a copy of Alice's public key, how does he really know it belongs to Alice, and is not, for example, a spurious key published by Eve to entrap him? To solve problems of this kind, we appeal to a public-key infrastructure (PKI), as explained in detail in, for example, Perlman (2006) Another issue worth mentioning—and a pitfall for many system designers—is the problem of finding an appropriate source of randomness for generating keys. Good generation of random bits is the cornerstone of cryptographic security and requires careful attention.

DIGITAL SIGNATURES

Public-key cryptography can be used not only for encryption, but also for message integrity. A digital signature is the public-key analog of a message authentication code. In fact, the RSA cryptosystem itself can be used to perform message signing, and is the most commonly used algorithm for that purpose. To apply a digital signature to a message m, Alice executes an RSA operation using her private key SK_A. That is to say that (setting aside low-level differences) Alice performs a decryption operation on m—i.e., exponentiation by d_{Alice}—to produce a digital signature Σ_m. Anyone with access to Alice's public key PK_A can verify the signature Σ_m on m. The verification procedure is essentially like that of encryption—that is, it involves exponentiation by e_{Alice}.

Of course, the need to apply digital signatures to long messages is as common as that of encrypting long messages. Digital signing, therefore, requires a procedure analogous to enveloping so that a single application of the RSA algorithm suffices to sign a long message. In the case of digital signatures, messages are compressed prior to signing by means of a hash function. This is to say that in generating Σ_m, Alice does not apply the RSA algorithm directly to m, but instead to a specially processed message digest m.

A message digest is in fact padded prior to signing. *Padding* is a randomized transform that meets the bit-length requirements of the RSA algorithm and also provides important security assurances. The optimal asymmetric encryption padding (OAEP) of Bellare and Rogaway (1994) is the most common form of padding in use with RSA today.

Certificates

As explained above, public-key encryption addresses the problem of key management—that is, the distribution of secret keys between communicating parties. Simply by exchanging their respective public keys, PK_A and PK_B, Alice and Bob can communicate privately without ever meeting in secret. But even public-key cryptography leaves an unresolved problem. When Bob receives a public key from Alice—via e-mail, for instance—how does he know that it is authentic? How does he know, for example, that Eve has not impersonated Alice and sent him her own public key PK_E, so that she can decrypt messages that Bob sends to Alice?

Digital signatures support a tool for secure distribution of public keys. Suppose that Alice and Bob both possess the public key PK_T of a mutually trusted third party, Trent. Trent can help Alice and Bob exchange public keys by certifying their correctness. Suppose that Trent creates a digital signature $\Sigma_{T,A}$, on a message that includes Alice's key PK_A as well as her name, "Alice." If Bob receives PK_A along with Trent's signature $\Sigma_{T,A}$, then by verifying the correctness of $\Sigma_{T,A}$, he can leverage his trust in Trent to assure himself that he has indeed received a correct key for Alice. The digital signature $\Sigma_{T,A}$, which binds Alice's key to her name, is known as a *certificate*.

Certificates are very flexible. They can support diverse sets of trust relationships. To assure Bob that PK_T itself is valid, for example, Trent might obtain a certificate binding PK_T to the name "Trent" from a trusted organization—for example, a town government. To provide further assurance, the town government might have its own certificate digitally signed by a state government, and so forth. A sequence of certificates of this kind is called a "certificate chain." Bob's trust in the certificate at the bottom of chain—Alice's, in this example—relies on Bob's trust of the public key (or certificate) at the top of the chain. Bob's trust in the chain, therefore, depends on his preexisting trust in the certificate at the top of the chain. Thus, a network of certificates and public keys relies on a small set of universally trusted public keys against which certificate chains may be anchored. These public keys are called "root keys." A system of public-key cryptography with supporting certificates is called a "public-key infrastructure" (PKI).

Certificates play an important role in Web browser security. Web sites that implement SSL present their public keys to the browsers of visiting users in the form of certificates. (By clicking on the lock appearing in the browser during an SSL session, you can obtain information about the certificate, including the name of the entity that owns it, and various cryptographic characteristics, like the associated RSA-key length.) Browser certificates bind public keys to the identities (domain names) of the sites that possess them. To permit the verification of SSL certificates, browsers come with preinstalled set of root keys.

CONCLUSION

Encryption algorithms, hash functions, message authentication codes, and digital signatures, as described above, are the most commonly deployed cryptographic primitives, but are just the tip of the iceberg. Just a few other notable cryptographic tools are:

Challenge-response authentication—A MAC or digital signature can serve not just to authenticate a message, but also to authenticate a device. For example, many automobile ignition keys today contain tiny wireless devices that perform a digital authentication protocol with a reader inside the vehicle. (This procedure serves as a countermeasure to hot-wiring and to undesirable copying of keys.) The reader shares a secret key k with the ignition key. When the ignition key is placed in the key slot by the steering column, the reader transmits a random value c—referred to as a challenge—to the ignition key. The ignition key computes a MAC z on the challenge c, and returns z to the reader. Only if the MAC is correct does the automobile start. Many other wireless devices, like payment tokens, use similar protocols, and some devices use public-key variants involving digital signatures.

Identity-based encryption (IBE)—IBE is a form of encryption developed by Boneh and Franklin in 2001 (Boneh and Franklin 2003). It permits the transmission of encrypted messages without the need for a sender to look up the public key or associated certificate of a receiver. In this system, the name of the receiver, or associated information like her e-mail address, *is* in fact her public key. (The system does require distribution of a master key, however.) The mathematics underlying IBE is quite elegant and useful for minimizing communication in other cryptographic applications.

Digital rights management (DRM)—Designers of systems to restrict unauthorized dissemination of media have pressed a range of cryptographic tools into service. One example is broadcast encryption, a set of techniques that permits content to be encrypted for a dynamically changing set of entities. For example, cable television providers wish to encrypt their broadcasts so as to prevent pirating of their content. They would like valid set-top boxes to be able to decrypt content, but would also like to be able to render content inaccessible to consumers whose subscriptions have lapsed or to pirated set-top boxes. Sophisticated schemes for distributing cryptographic keys can support the dynamic access privileges required in such an environment. In addition, some broadcast encryption schemes support a complementary process of traitor tracing, namely the ability on examining a set-top box to determine which keys it contains and thereby implicate the sets of valid set-top boxes involved in the creation of pirate boxes.

At the frontiers of cryptology are ideas beyond the traditional conceptual and physical boundaries of computing systems. In some cases, for instance, a clever attacker can extract a secret key from a device by observing side information, like computing time and power consumption. The field of side-channel analysis involves the development of countermeasures to these devious attacks. Some researchers are casting much farther afield, and considering technologies that may play a role in cryptology in decades to come, such as computers and networks that operate on quantum-mechanical principles.

GLOSSARY

AES: The advanced encryption standard, a symmetric-key cipher known as Rijndael, serving as a successor to DES.

Asymmetric: In the context of encryption, a type of cryptographic system in which a participant publishes an encryption key and keeps private a separate decryption key. These keys are respectively referred to as public and private. RSA and D-H are examples of asymmetric systems. *Asymmetric* is synonymous with *public-key*.

Certificate: A digitally signed public key and associated information; a certificate generally creates an authenticated binding of a key to an owner.

Ciphertext: The data conveying an encrypted message.

Cryptanalysis: The science of analyzing weaknesses in cryptographic systems.

Cryptography: The science of constructing mathematical systems for securing data.

Cryptology: The combination of the complementary sciences of cryptography and cryptanalysis.

Cryptosystem: A complete system of encryption and decryption, typically used to describe a public-key cryptographic system.

Decryption: The process of obtaining a readable message (a *plaintext*) from an encrypted transformation of the message (a *ciphertext*).

DES: The data encryption standard, an existing form of symmetric cipher in wide use today, often in a strengthened variant known as triple DES.

Diffie-Hellman (D-H): A public-key cryptosystem used to exchange a secret (symmetric) key.

Digital Signature: Information appended to a message that ensures its integrity and authenticity; generally used to describe information derived from a public-key cryptosystem.

Encryption: The process of rendering a message (a *plaintext*) into a data string (a *ciphertext*) with the aim of transmitting it privately in a potentially hostile environment.

Enveloping: A method for using a symmetric-key cipher in combination with a public-key cryptosystem to exploit simultaneously the advantages of the two respective systems.

Hash Function: A cryptographic algorithm that compresses a message of arbitrary length into a fixed-length *message digest*.

HMAC: A commonly used MAC scheme.

Key: A short data string parameterizing the operations within a cipher or cryptosystem, and whose distribution determines relationships of privacy and integrity among communicating parties.

Key Pair: The combination of a public and private key.

Message Authentication Code (MAC): Information appended to a message that ensures its integrity and authenticity; generally used to describe information derived from a symmetric-key cryptographic algorithm.

Message Digest: The output yielded by a hash function; a message digest serves as a cryptographic checksum or fingerprint on a digital message.

Plaintext: A message in readable form, prior to encryption or subsequent to successful decryption.

Private Key: In an asymmetric or public-key cryptosystem, the key that a communicating party holds privately and uses for decryption or completion of a key exchange.

Public Key: In an asymmetric or public-key cryptosystem, the key that a communicating party disseminates publicly.

Public Key: In the context of encryption, a type of cryptographic system in which a participant publishes an encryption key and keeps private a separate decryption key. These keys are respectively referred to as public and private. RSA and D-H are examples of public-key systems. *Public key* is synonymous with *asymmetric*.

RC4: A symmetric-key cipher of the type known as a stream cipher. Used widely in the SSL (secure sockets layer) protocol.

RSA: A public-key cryptosystem in very wide use today, as in the SSL (secure sockets layer) protocol. RSA can also be used to create and verify digital signatures.

Symmetric: A type of cryptographic system in which communicating parties use shared secret keys. The term is also used to refer to the keys used in such a system.

CROSS REFERENCES

See *Access Control*; *Authentication*; *Biometrics*.

REFERENCES

Anderson, R. J. 2001. *Security engineering: A guide to building dependable distributed security systems*. New York: Wiley.

Bellare, M., and P. Rogaway. 1994. Optimal asymmetric encryption—How to encrypt with RSA. In *Advances in Cryptology—Eurocrypt '94*, 92–111. New York: Springer Verlag.

Bellare, M., R. Canetti, and H. Krawczyk. 1996. Keying hash functions for message authentication. *Advances in Cryptology—CRYPTO '96*. New York: Springer-Verlag Lecture Notes in Computer Science, 1109:1–15.

Biham, E., and A. Shamir. 1991. Differential cryptanalysis of DES-like cryptosystems. *Journal of Cryptology* 4(1).

Boneh, D., and M. Franklin. 2003. Identity based encryption from the Weil pairing. *SIAM Journal of Computing* 32(3):586–615.

Daeman, J., and V. Rijmen. 2002. *The design of Rijndael*. New York: Springer-Verlag.

Electronic Privacy Information Center. 2006. Web page on Cryptography Policy. www.epic.org/crypto (accessed May 27, 2007).

Goldreich, O. 2000. *Foundations of Cryptography: Basic tools*. Cambridge, UK: Cambridge University Press.

Goldreich, O. 2004. *Foundations of cryptography: Basic applications*. Cambridge, UK: Cambridge University Press.

Juels, A. 2006. Encryption. In *Handbook of Information Security*, edited by H. Bidgoli. New York: Wiley.

Kahn, D. 1996. *The codebreakers: The story of secret writing*. New York: Simon & Schuster.

Kaufman, C., R. Perlman, and M. Speciner. 2002. *Network security: Private communication in a public world*. 2nd ed. Englewood Cliffs, NJ: Prentice–Hall.

Kerckhoffs, A. 1883. La cryptographie militaire. *Journal des Sciences Militaires* 9:5–83, 161–91.

International Association for Cryptologic Research (IACR). 2006. www.iacr.org (accessed May 27, 2007).

Menezes, A. J., P. C. van Oorschot, and S. A. Vanstone. 2001. *Handbook of applied cryptography*. Boca Raton, FL: CRC Press.

Perlman, R. 2006. PKI (public key infrastructure). In *Handbook of Information Security*, edited by H Bidgoli. New York: Wiley.

RSA Laboratories. 2007. *Frequently asked questions about today's cryptography*, version 4.1. http://www.rsa.com/rsalabs/node.asp?id=2152 (accessed June 26, 2007).

Schneier, B. 2002. *Applied cryptography: Protocols, algorithms, and source code in C*. 2nd ed. New York: Wiley.

Schneier, B. 2004. *Secrets and lies: Digital security in a networked world*. New York: Wiley.

Shannon, C. E. 1948. A mathematical theory of communication. *Bell System Technical Journal* 27:379–423, 623–56.

Singh, S. 2000. *The science of secrecy from ancient Egypt to quantum cryptography*. New York: Knopf.

Stallings, W. 2002. *Cryptography and network security: Principles and practice*. 3rd ed. Englewood Cliffs, NJ: Prentice Hall.

Stinson, D. 2005. *Cryptography: Theory and practice*. 3rd ed. Boca Raton, FL: CRC/C&H.

FURTHER READING

Two broad and accessible introductory books on the field of cryptology are *Applied Cryptography*, by Bruce Schneier (2002), and the online compendium *Frequently Asked Questions about Today's Cryptography* (RSA Laboratories 2006). A more detailed technical treatment of cryptographic techniques and concepts, along with an extensive bibliography, may be found in the excellent *Handbook of Applied Cryptography*, by Alfred J. Menezes, Paul C. van Oorschot, and Scott A. Vanstone (2001). Detailed information on the AES algorithm (Rijndael) is available in *The Design of Rijndael*, by Joan Daeman and Vincent Rijmen (2002).

Readers interested in the practical application of cryptography in real-world systems may wish to consult *Network Security: Private Communication in a Public World*, by Charlie Kaufman, Radia Perlman, and Mike Speciner (2002) and *Cryptography and Network Security: Principles and Practice*, by William Stallings (2002). For a more comprehensive view of security engineering, an excellent work is Ross Anderson's *Security Engineering: A Guide to Building Dependable Distributed Systems* (2001). Of similar interest is Bruce Schneier's *Secrets and Lies* (2004), which offers some caveats regarding the limitations of cryptography and other security tools.

A good introductory textbook of a more academic flavor is *Cryptography: Theory and Practice*, by Douglas Stinson (2005). For information on the foundational mathematics and theory of cryptology, an important work is *Foundations of Cryptography* by Oded Goldreich; this evolving series now includes two volumes: *Foundations of Cryptography: Basic Tools* (2000) and *Foundations of Cryptography: Basic Applications* (2004). For a historical overview of cryptology, the classic text is *The Codebreakers*, by David Kahn (1996). More up-to-date, although less exhaustive, is *The Science of Secrecy from Ancient Egypt to Quantum Cryptography*, by Simon Singh (2000).

The use and export of products containing strong cryptographic algorithms were at one time strongly restricted by regulations of the U.S. government and other nations. The U.S. government dramatically relaxed its restrictions in 2000, however, as did many other nations at around the same time. Some countries, such as China, still retain strong regulations around both domestic use and import and export of cryptographically enabled products. While regulations treating the use of cryptography are in frequent flux, readers may refer to Electronic Privacy Information Center (2006) for historical and current information on this topic.

Many cryptologists are members of the International Association for Cryptologic Research (IACR), whose home page (IACR 2006) lists publications and conferences devoted to advanced research in cryptography and cryptanalysis.

Access Control

Sabrina De Capitani di Vimercati, Sara Foresti, *University of Milan, Italy,*
Stefano Paraboschi, *University of Bergamo, Italy,* Pierangela Samarati, *University of Milan, Italy*

INTRODUCTION

An important requirement of any system is to protect its data and resources against unauthorized disclosure (secrecy or confidentiality) and unauthorized or improper modifications (integrity), while at the same time ensuring their availability to legitimate users (no denial-of-service or availability) (Samarati and De Capitani di Vimercati 2001). The problem of ensuring protection has existed since information has been managed. However, as technology advances and information management systems become more and more powerful, the problem of enforcing information security also becomes more critical. The development of information technology in the past few years has led to the widespread use of computer systems to store and manipulate information and has greatly increased the availability, the processing power, and the storage power of information systems. However, it has also posed new serious security threats and has increased the potential damage that violations may cause. More than ever today, organizations depend on the information they manage. A violation to the security of the information may jeopardize the whole system and cause serious damages. Hospitals, banks, public administrations, private organizations—all of them depend on the accuracy, availability, and confidentiality of the information they manage. Just imagine what could happen, for example, if an organization's data were improperly modified, were not available to the legitimate users because of a violation blocking access to the resources, or were disclosed to the public. For instance, imagine the damage that could be caused by the improper modification of a prescription for a medication.

A fundamental component in enforcing protection is represented by the access control service whose task is to control every access to a system and its resources and ensure that all and only authorized accesses can take place. Access control usually requires authentication (i.e., the process of certifying the identity of one party to another) as a prerequisite. In general, when considering an access control system, it is necessary to make a distinction among access control policies, access control models, and access control mechanisms. A policy defines the (high-level) rules, expressed using an adequate language, according to which access control must be regulated. A model provides a formal representation of the access control security policy and its working. The formalization allows the proof of properties of the security provided by the access control system being designed. A mechanism defines the low-level (software and hardware) functions that implement the controls imposed by the policy and formally stated in the model. Access control policies may be grouped into three main classes: discretionary, mandatory, and role-based (described in the section on "Access Control Policies").

In the remainder of this chapter, we start with a brief overview of the basic approaches to access control policies, and continue with a discussion of the main desiderata for an access control system. We then survey the access control services provided by some of the most popular operating systems, database management systems, and network solutions. Although clearly their characteristics will vary from one class to the other as their focus is different (e.g., database management systems focus on the data and rely on the operating systems for low-level support), we will comment on how they accommodate (or do not accommodate) the features introduced in the section on desiderata. Also, while covering a feature in some way, some systems take unclear solutions that may have side effects in terms of security or applicability, aspects that should be taken into account when using the systems. We therefore present an overview of different access control solutions, outlining their strengths and limitations. This can serve as an interesting reference for readers involved in access control development and access control specifications. It is, however, important to highlight that no solution is more secure in absolute terms; each solution has to be evaluated depending on the specific context and protection requirements that need to be enforced.

ACCESS CONTROL POLICIES

Access control policies can be grouped into three main classes: discretionary, mandatory, and role-based (Castano et al. 1995). We now briefly describe the main characteristics of these policies.

	Invoice	Order	Program
Ann	Own, Read, Write	Read	Read, Execute
Bob	Read, Write		Execute
Carol		Own, Read, Write	

Figure 1: Example of an access matrix

The discretionary access control (DAC) policies control access based on users' identities and on a set of rules, called "authorizations," explicitly stating which subjects can execute which actions on which resources. Early approaches to authorization specifications use authorization triples (s, o, a) stating that user s can execute action a on object o. One of the first models that provided a framework for describing DAC policies is the access matrix model (Lampson 1974). In this model, the state of the system is represented through a triple (S, O, A), where S is the set of subjects, O is the set of objects, and A is a matrix with a row for each subject $s \in$ S and a column for each object $o \in$ O. Each entry A[s,o] contains the set of actions that subject s is allowed to perform over object o. Figure 1 illustrates an example of access matrix. The access control matrix is usually not very suitable for direct implementation because it is likely to be sparse. For this reason, the access matrix is typically implemented according to the following three mechanisms.

- *Authorization table.* Nonempty entries in A are stored in a table with three columns: user, action, and object.
- *Capabilities.* Capabilities correspond to rows of the access matrix. Each subject is associated with a list of objects, together with the set of actions she can perform on each of them.
- *Access control lists (ACLs).* ACLs correspond to columns of the access matrix. Each object is associated with a list of subjects, together with the set of actions they can perform on the object.

Figure 2 shows the authorization table, capabilities, and access control lists, respectively, corresponding to the access matrix in Figure 1. Note, however, that recent access control approaches support authorizations more complex than the simple authorization triple (s, o, a). These approaches allow conditions to be associated with authorizations to restrict their validity, and support the concept of user groups, which greatly simplifies management of authorizations, since a single authorization granted to a group can be enjoyed by all its members. Also, since there will be many cases in which exceptions (i.e., authorizations applicable to all members of a group but few) will need to be supported, modern access control solutions support both positive and negative authorizations (Samarati and De Capitani di Vimercati 2001).

The main problem of DAC policies is that they ignore the distinction between a user (a human entity interacting with the system) and a subject (a process generated by a user). This implies that all requests submitted by a process running on behalf of some user are evaluated against the authorizations of the user. This aspect makes discretionary policies vulnerable to Trojan horses. A Trojan horse is a computer program with an apparently useful function, which contains a piece of malicious code. This piece of code is hidden to the user and exploits the authorizations of the invoking user to make actions it would not be allowed to. As an example, consider two users, namely Alice and Bob, and suppose that Alice is the owner of a file, namely file A, that contains highly sensitive data and such that no users other than Alice are authorized to access the file. Bob wants to read the content of such a file and implements a useful utility program. In this utility program, Bob embeds a hidden function that reads file A and copies the contents into a file, namely file B. File B has an ACL associated with it that allows processes executing on Alice's behalf to write to it, while allowing Bob's processes to read it. When Alice executes the utility program, it assumes her identity and thus her access rights to file A. The utility program then copies the contents of file A to file B. This copying takes place within the constraints of the DAC policy, and Alice is unaware of what is happening.

The problem of Trojan horses is solved by mandatory access control (MAC) policies. In general, these policies control access based on mandated regulations determined by a central authority. The most common form of MAC policies is the multilevel security policy, based on classifications associated with subjects and objects. An access class is usually composed of two elements: a security level and a set of categories. Security levels are an ordered set of elements, while categories are an unordered set of elements that define the area of competence of users and data. Consequently, access classes form a partially ordered set, in which the dominance relationship, which defines the partial order among access classes, is defined as follows: class c_1 dominates class c_2 if the security level of c_1 is greater than or equal to the security level of c_2 and the set of categories in c_2 is a subset of or is equal to the set of categories in c_1. The set of access classes together with the dominance relationship form a lattice.

For instance, consider a system with two security levels, Top Secret (TS) and Secret (S), where TS>S, and two categories, Economic and Financial. The corresponding lattice has eight access classes, as illustrated in Figure 3. The top element of the lattice is `<TS,{Economic, Financial}>`, while the bottom element is `<S,{}>`. Access requests are granted or denied on the basis of the relationship between the classes of the requesting subjects and of the requested objects. In particular, there are two kinds of multilevel mandatory security policy: secrecy-based (Bell and LaPadula 1973) and integrity-based (Biba 1977).

User	Action	Object
Ann	Own	Invoice
Ann	Read	Invoice
Ann	Write	Invoice
Ann	Read	Order
Ann	Read	Program
Ann	Execute	Program
Bob	Read	Invoice
Bob	Write	Invoice
Bob	Execute	Program
Carol	Own	Order
Carol	Read	Order
Carol	Write	Order

(a)

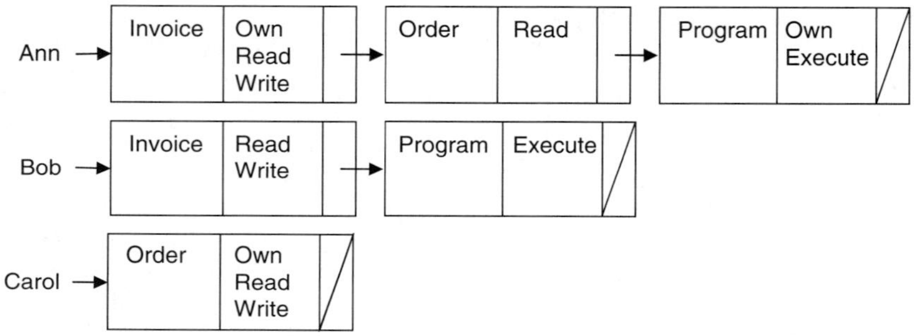

Ann →	Invoice	Own Read Write	→ Order	Read	→ Program	Own Execute
Bob →	Invoice	Read Write	→ Program	Execute		
Carol →	Order	Own Read Write				

(b)

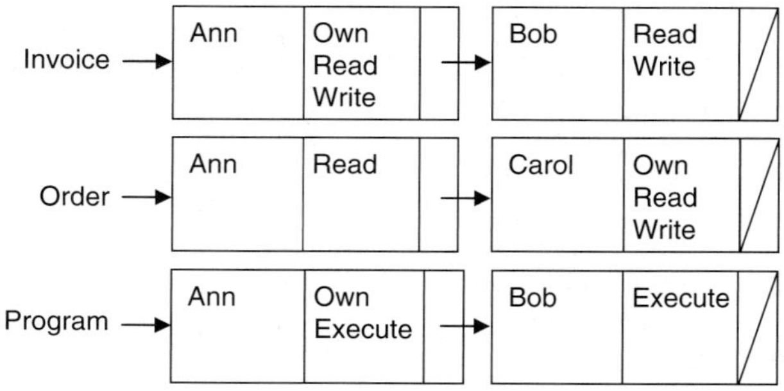

Invoice →	Ann	Own Read Write	→ Bob	Read Write
Order →	Ann	Read	→ Carol	Own Read Write
Program →	Ann	Own Execute	→ Bob	Execute

(c)

Figure 2: Authorization table (a), capabilities (b), and access control lists (c) corresponding to the access matrix in Figure 1

The goal of a secrecy mandatory policy is to protect data confidentiality. The security level of the access class associated with an object reflects the sensitivity of the information it contains. The security level of the access class associated with a subject, called "clearance," reflects the degree of trust placed in the subject not to disclose sensitive information to users not cleared to see it. This policy prevents flows of information from high- to low-level access classes by applying the no-read-up and no-write-down principles, first formulated by Bell and La Padula (1973). According to these two principles, a subject can read objects with access classes dominated by her

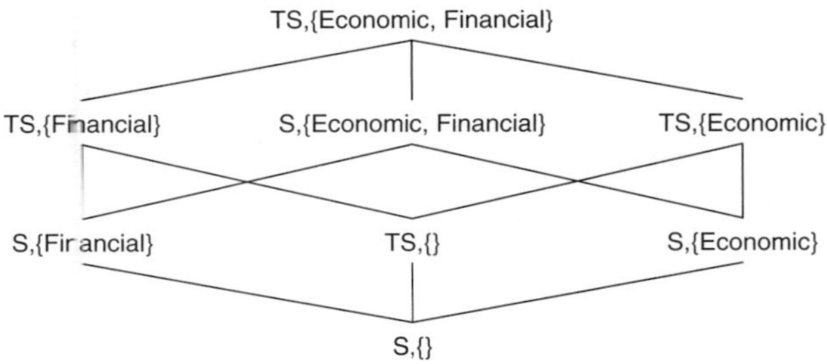

Figure 3: Example of a security lattice

classification and can write objects with access classes that dominate her classification. It is easy to see that the secrecy mandatory policy is robust against Trojan horse attacks. Consider the scenario previously described, and suppose that the system now implements a secrecy mandatory policy with two security levels, namely TS and S, with TS>S. For the sake of simplicity, we ignore the set of categories. Alice operates at level TS, and the security level associated with file A is TS. Bob operates at level S because he is not allowed to access sensitive data, and the security level associated with file B is S. As before, Bob's Trojan horse program is executed by Alice. Within the constraints of the mandatory policy, the utility program reads file A. However, when the Trojan horse tries to write the sensitive data into file B, this operation is not allowed because it violates the no-write-down principle.

The goal of an integrity mandatory policy is to protect data integrity. As for secrecy, each subject and object is associated with an integrity class. The integrity classes and the dominance relationship are defined as before. In this case, the integrity level of the integrity class associated with an object reflects the degree of trust placed on the information stored in the object and the potential damage that could derive from unauthorized modifications. The integrity level of the integrity class associated with a subject reflects instead the degree of trust placed in the subject to manipulate sensitive objects. This policy prevents flows of information from low- to high-level access classes by applying the no-read-down and no-write-up principles. According to these two principles, a subject can read objects with access classes that dominate her classification and can write objects with access classes dominated by her classification.

Role-based access control (RBAC) policies (Sandhu et al. 1996) are based on the observation that access privileges are usually assigned to users not on the basis of their identity, but depending on the organizational activities and responsibility that the users have in the considered organization. The central notion of RBAC is therefore that authorizations are associated with roles and users are assigned to appropriate roles. Roles are created for the various activities in the organization and users are assigned to roles according to their responsibilities (see Figure 4). This greatly simplifies the management of authorizations because the authorization specification task is partitioned into two subtasks: (1) assignment of roles to users, and (2) assignment of authorizations to roles.

In general, a user can play different roles on different occasions, and a role can be played by different users, possibly simultaneously. Sophisticated approaches for RBAC support the definition of relations between roles as well as between authorizations and roles and between users and roles. For instance, two roles can be defined as mutually exclusive; thus, the same user is not allowed to play both roles (separation of duties principle). RBAC also has other advantages. It can easily support the concept of least privilege, which requires the identification of the user's job functions, the definition of the minimum set of privileges required to perform those functions, and the restriction for the user to play only the role with which those privileges are associated, and nothing more. In real applications, users who can play different roles may need to perform common operations. For instance, some general operations can be executed by all employees. In this situation, it would be inefficient to specify these general operations for each role. A role hierarchy can be then exploited for authorization implication. Figure 5 illustrates an example of a role hierarchy, where each role is represented as a node and there is an arc between a specialized role and its generalization. Authorizations granted to roles can be propagated to their specializations (e.g., the secretary role can be allowed all authorizations granted to admin_staff). Authorization implication can also be enforced on role assignments, by allowing users to activate all generalizations of the roles assigned to them.

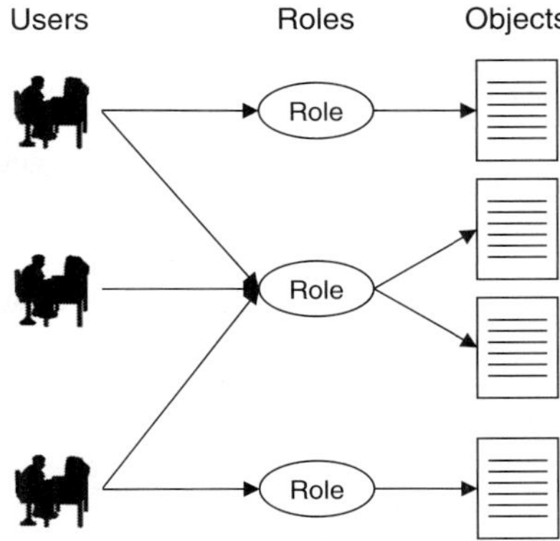

Figure 4: Role-based access control

RBAC represents therefore a useful paradigm for many commercial and governmental organizations. The strong interest in RBAC is also visible in the standard arena. For instance, roles are part of the SQL:2003 standard for database management systems (see section on "Access Control in Database Management Systems").

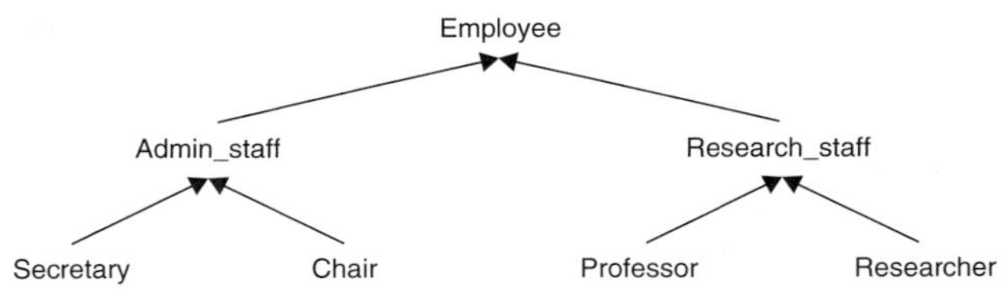

Figure 5: Example of role hierarchy

DESIDERATA FOR AN ACCESS CONTROL SYSTEM

The definition of access control policies to be fed into the access control system is far from being a trivial process. One of the major difficulties lies in the interpretation of often complex and sometimes ambiguous, real-world security policies and in their translation in well-defined unambiguous rules enforceable by the computer system. Many real-world situations have complex policies, in which access decisions depend on the application of different rules coming, for example, from law practices, and organizational regulations. A security policy must capture all the different regulations to be enforced and, in addition, must consider all possible additional threats due to the use of computer systems. Given the complexity of the scenario, it is therefore important that the access control service provided by the computer system is expressive and flexible enough to accommodate all the different requirements that may need to be expressed, while at the same time it should be simple both in terms of use (so that specifications can be kept under control) and implementation (so to allow for its verification).

An access control system should include support for the following concepts/features.

- *Accountability and reliable input*. Access control must rely on a proper input. This simple principle is not always obeyed by systems, allowing access control rules to be evaluated on the basis of possibly unreliable information. This is, for example, the case of location-based access control restrictions, in which the access decision may depend on the IP from which a request originates, information that can be easily faked in a local network, thus fooling access control (allowing nonlegitimate users to acquire access despite the proper rule enforcement). This observation has been traditionally at the basis of requiring proper user authentication as a prerequisite for access control enforcement (Sandhu and Samarati 1997). Although more recent approaches may remove the assumption that every user is authenticated (e.g., credential-based access control), the assumption that the information on which access decision is taken must be correct continues to hold.
- *Support for fine- and coarse-specifications*. The access control system should allow rules to be referred to specific accesses, providing fine-grained reference to the subjects and objects in the system. However, fine-grained specifications should be supported, but not forced. In fact, requiring the specification of access rules with reference to every single user and object in the system would make the administrative task a heavy burden. Besides, groups of users and collections of objects often share the same access control requirements. The access control system should then provide support for authorizations specified for groups of users, groups of objects, and possibly even groups of actions (Jajodia et al. 2001). Also, in many organizational scenarios, access needs may be naturally associated with organizational activities; the access control system should then support authorizations reflecting organizational roles (Sandhu et al. 1996).
- *Conditional authorizations*. Protection requirements may need to depend on the evaluation of some conditions (Samarati and De Capitani di Vimercati 2001). Conditions can be in the simple form of system's predicates, such as the date or the location of an access (e.g., "Employee can access the system from 9 A.M. to 5 P.M."). Conditions can also make access dependent on the information being accessed (e.g., "Managers can read payroll data of the employees they manage.").
- *Least privilege*. The least privilege principle mandates that every subject (active entity operating in the system) should always operate with the least possible set of privileges needed to perform its task. Obedience of the least privilege principle requires both static (policy specification) and dynamic (policy enforcement) support from the access control system. At a static level, least privilege requires support of fine-grained authorizations, granting to each specific subject only those specific accesses it needs. At a dynamic level, least privilege requires restricting processes to operate within a confined set of privileges. Least privilege is partially supported within the context of RBAC (see above). Authorizations granted to a role apply only when the role is active for a user (i.e., when needed to perform the tasks associated with the role) (Gong 1999). Hence, users authorized for powerful roles do not need to exercise them until those privileges are actually required. This minimizes the danger of damages due to inadvertent errors or to intruders masquerading as legitimate users. Least privilege also requires the access control system to discriminate between different processes, even if executed by the same user—for example, by supporting authorizations referred to programs or applicable only within the execution of specific programs. A robust implementation of the least privilege principle is needed in order to avoid the threat coming from privilege escalation, in which a user starts from a limited authorized access and obtains greater privileges, typically exploiting a vulnerability unavailable to outside users.
- *Separation of duty*. Separation of duty refers to the principle that no user should be given enough privilege to misuse the system on her own (Sandhu 1990). While separation of duty is better classified as a policy specification constraint (i.e., a guideline to be followed by those in charge of specifying access control rules), support of separation of duty requires the security system to be expressive and flexible enough to enforce the constraints. At a minimum, fine-grained specifications and least privilege should be supported; history-based authorizations, making one's ability to access a system dependent on previously executed accesses, are also a convenient means to support separation of duty.
- *Multiple policies and exceptions*. Traditionally, discretionary policies have been seen as distinguished into two classes: closed and open (Samarati and De Capitani di Vimercati 2001). In the most popular closed policy, only accesses to be authorized are specified; each request is controlled against the authorizations and allowed only if an authorization exists for it. By contrast, in the open policy, (negative) authorizations specify the accesses that should not be allowed. By default, all access requests

for which no negative authorization is specified are allowed.

- *Policy combination and conflict-resolution*. If multiple modules (e.g., for different authorities or different domains) exist for the specification of access control rules, the access control system should provide a means for users to specify how the different modules should interact—for example, if their union (maximum privilege) or their intersection (minimum privilege) should be considered. Also, when both permissions and denials can be specified, the problem naturally arises of how to deal with incompleteness (existence of accesses for which no rule is specified) and inconsistency (existence of accesses for which both a denial and a permission are specified). Dealing with incompleteness—requiring the authorizations to be complete would be very impractical—requires support of a default policy either imposed by the system or specified by the users. Dealing with inconsistencies requires support of conflict-resolution policies. Different conflict-resolution approaches can be taken, such as the simple denials take precedence (in the case of doubt, access is denied) or most specific criteria that make the authorization referred to the more specific element (e.g., a user is more specific than a group, and a file is more specific than a directory) takes precedence. Although among the different conflict-resolution policies that can be thought of (see Samarati and De Capitani di Vimercati 2001 for a deeper treatment), some solutions may appear more natural than others, none of them represents "the perfect solution." Whichever approach we take, we will always find one situation for which the approach does not fit. On the one side, support of negative authorizations does not come free; there is a price to pay in terms of authorization management and less clarity of the specifications. On the other side, the complications brought by negative authorizations are not due to negative authorizations themselves, but to the different semantics that the presence of permissions and denials can have—that is, to the complexity of the different real-world scenarios and requirements that may need to be captured. There is, therefore, a trade-off between expressiveness and simplicity. Consequently, current systems try to keep it simple by adopting negative authorizations for exception support, imposing specific conflict-resolution policies, or supporting a limited form of conflict resolution.
- *Administrative policies*. Because access control systems are based on access rules defining which accesses are (or are not) to be allowed, an administrative policy is needed to regulate the specification of such rules—that is, define who can add, delete, or modify them. Administrative policies are one of the most important, though less understood, aspects in access control. Indeed, they have usually received little consideration, and, while it is true that a simple administrative policy would suffice for many applications, it is also true that new applications (and organizational environments) would benefit from the enrichment of administrative policies. In theory, discretionary systems can support different kinds of administrative policies: centralized, in which a privileged user or group of users is reserved the privilege of granting and revoking authorizations; hierarchical/cooperative, in which a set of authorized users is reserved the privilege of granting and revoking authorizations; ownership, in which each object is associated with an owner (generally the object's creator), who can grant to and revoke from others the authorizations on its objects; and decentralized, in which, extending the previous approaches, the owner of an object (or its administrators) can delegate to other users the privilege of specifying authorizations, possibly with the ability of further delegating it. For its simplicity and large applicability the ownership policy is the most popular choice in today's systems (see section on desiderata, above). Decentralized administration approaches can be instead found in the database management system contexts (see section on "Access Control in Database Management Systems"). Decentralized administration is convenient since it allows users to delegate administrative privileges to others. Delegation, however, complicates the authorization management. In particular, it becomes more difficult for users to keep track of who can access their objects. Furthermore, revocation of authorizations becomes more complex.

ACCESS CONTROL IN OPERATING SYSTEMS

We describe access control services in two of the most popular operating systems: Linux (e.g., www.redhat.com, www.suse.com) and Microsoft Windows 2000/XP (www.microsoft.com).

Access Control in Linux

We use Linux as a modern representative of the large family of operating systems deriving from UNIX. We signal the features of Linux that are absent in other operating systems of the same family.

Apart from specific privileges such as access to protected TCP ports, the most significant access control services in Linux are the ones offered by the file system. The file system has a central role in all the operating systems of the UNIX family, as files are used as an abstraction for most of the system resources.

User Identifiers and Group Identifiers

Access control is based on a user identifier (UID) and group identifier (GID) associated with each process. A UID is an integer value unique for each username (log-in name), the associations between usernames and UIDs is described in file /etc/passwd. A user connecting to a Linux system is typically authenticated by the log-in process, invoked by the program managing the communication line used to connect to the system (getty for serial lines, telnetd for remote telnet sessions). The log-in process asks the user for a username and a password and checks the password with its hash stored in read-protected file /etc/shadow; a less secure and older alternative stores hashed password in the readable-by-all file /etc/passwd. When authentication is successful, the login process sets the UID to that of the authenticated user, before starting an instance of the program listed in /etc/passwd and associated with the specific user entry (typically the program is a shell, such as /bin/bash). Users in Linux are members of groups. Every time a user connects to the system, together with the UID, a primary GID is set. The value of the primary GID to use at log in is defined in file /etc/passwd. Group names and additional memberships in groups are instead defined in file /etc/group. Command newgrp allows users to switch to a new primary GID. If the user is listed in /etc/group as belonging to the group she chooses as the new primary GID, the request is immediately executed; otherwise, for groups having a hashed password stored in /etc/group, the primary GID can be changed after the password has been correctly returned. However, group passwords are deprecated, as they easily lead to lapses in password management.

Processes are usually assigned the UIDs and GIDs of their parent processes, which implies that each process acquires the UID and GID associated with the log-in name with which the session was started. The process UID is the central piece of information for the evaluation of the permitted actions. There are many operations in the system that are allowed only to the root user, whose value of UID is equal to zero. The *root* user represents the owner of the system who supervises all the activities. For instance, the TCP implementation allows user *root* only to open ports below 1024.

Files and Privileges

In the Linux file system, each file is associated with a UID and a GID, which typically represent the UID and the primary GID of the process that created the file. UID and GID associated with a file can be changed by commands *chown* and *chgrp*. The privileges associated with each file are nine: three groups of three privileges each, that is *read*, *write*, and *execute* privileges are defined at level of *user*, *group*, and *other*. The privileges defined at the level of *user* are the actions that will be permitted to processes having the same UID as the file; the privileges defined at the level of *group* are granted to processes having the same GID as the file; the privileges at the level of *other* are for processes that share neither the UID nor the GID with the file. The privileges are commonly represented, in the result of *ls -l* command, as a string of nine characters (preceded by a character representing the file type). The string presents first the three *user* privileges, then *group*, and finally *other*, in the order: *read*, *write*, and *execute*. Each privilege is represented by a single letter: *r* for *read;* *w* for *write;* and *x* for *execute;* the absence of the privilege is represented by character -. For instance, rwxr-xr-- means that a process having as UID the same UID as the file has all the three privileges, a process with the same GID can read and execute (but not write) the file, and remaining processes can only read the file. When a user belongs to many groups, all the corresponding GIDs are stored in a list in the process descriptor of her processes beside the primary GID. When the policy needs to be evaluated, all the groups in the list are considered: if the GID of the file is the primary GID, or appears anywhere in the list, group access privileges apply. It is important to note that some operating systems of the UNIX family store only the primary GID within the process descriptor.

The semantics of privileges may be different depending on the type of the file on which they are specified. In particular, for directories, the *execute* privilege represents the privilege to access the directory; *read* and *write* privileges permit, respectively, to read the directory content and to modify it (adding, removing, and renaming files). Privileges associated with a file can be updated via the *chmod* command, which is usable by the file owner and by user *root*.

Additional Security Specifications

The file system offers three other privileges on files: *save text image (sticky bit)*, *set user ID (setuid)*, and *set group ID (setgid)*. The *sticky bit* privilege is useful only for directories, and it allows only the owner of the file, the owner of the directory, and the root to remove or rename the files contained in the directory, even if the directory is writable by all. The *setuid* and *setgid* privileges are particularly useful for executable files, in which they permit setting the UID and the GID, respectively, of the process that executes the file to that of the file itself. These privileges are often used for applications that require a higher level of privileges to accomplish their task (e.g., users change their passwords with the *passwd* program, which needs read and write access on file /etc/shadow). Without the use of these bits, enabling a process started by a normal user to change the user's password would require explicitly granting the user the write privilege on the file /etc/shadow. Such a privilege could, however, be misused by users who could access the file through different programs and tamper with it. The *setuid* and *setgid* bits, by allowing the *passwd* program to run with root privilege, avoid such a security exposure. It is worth noticing that, while providing a necessary security feature, the *setuid* and *setgid* solutions are themselves vulnerable, as the specified programs run with root privileges—in contrast to the least privilege principle, they are not confined to the accesses needed to execute their task—and it is therefore important that these programs are *trusted* (Samarati and De Capitani di Vimercati 2001).

The *ext2* and *ext3* file systems, the most common ones in Linux implementations, offer additional Boolean attributes on files. Among them, there are attributes focused on low-level optimizations (e.g., a bit requiring a compressed representation of the file on the disk) and two privileges that extend access control services: *immutable* and *append-only*. The *immutable* bit specifies that no change is allowed on the file; only the user *root* can set or clear this attribute. The *append-only* bit specifies that the file can be extended only by additions at the end; this attribute can also be set only by *root*. Attributes are listed by command *lsattr* and can be modified by command *chattr*.

IP-Based Security

Linux offers several utilities exploiting IP addresses for authentication purposes. All of these solutions should be used with care, as IP addresses can be easily spoofed in a local network (Fielding et al. 1999) and therefore fool the access control system. For this reason, they are not enabled by default. Among these utilities, *rsh* executes remote shells on behalf of users; *rcp* executes copies involving the file systems of machines in a network; and *nfs* permits sharing of portions of the file system on the network. For these applications, access control typically is based on a few relatively simple text files, which describe the computers that can use the service and the scope of the service; patterns can be used to identify ranges of names or addresses, and groups may be defined, but overall the access control features are basic. Secure solutions of the above applications (like the *ssh* application and the *scp* program offered within the same package) offer a greater degree of security, at the expense of computational resources, configuration effort, and in general less availability.

Security-Enhanced Linux

An important initiative in the context of access control for Linux is the Security-Enhanced Linux (SELinux) kernel module (Loscocco and Smalley 2001). This component, originally developed within a project sponsored by the National Security Agency, aims at introducing the services of mandatory access control (MAC) within the Linux environment. Access control in SELinux is realized extending the services of the traditional (DAC) Linux model, which uses the pair `<UID,GID>` of the process to evaluate the ACL of the requested resource; in SELinux, each access request, coming by a process characterized by its "process label" and operating on a resource characterized by its "resource label," is allowed if it also satisfies the centralized mandatory policy (see the section on "Access Control Policies" for a brief overview on mandatory access control policies).

The policy is composed of a set of rules, following a relatively rich syntax. Rules specify the set of labels and the initial assignment of labels to resources and processes; rules also specify how labels can be changed and which are the constraints that every operation has to satisfy. Using the rule syntax, SELinux permits the specification of a fine-grained access control policy; in this way, Linux can adequately support the principle of "least privilege," giving each process access only to the set of resources that the process needs to execute its function. The policy usually classifies applications into many distinct domains, each characterized by a label, providing to each application access only to the resources that are needed to fulfill its task. This is particularly important for the configuration of processes realizing network services, which are exposed to the input of external users and have often been used to gain access to a system, exploiting errors in the input processing functions. When a process managing a server is constrained to access only the resources that are needed to realize the service, the risk deriving from an error in the code is considerably reduced, and its exploitation by a malicious user is considerably more difficult.

A few obstacles have slowed the adoption of SELinux. The most important current issue is the complexity of the policy-definition phase. Moreover, users are often surprised by the denial of requests that are legitimate in the DAC model, but that now violate MAC policy rules. In some cases the policy was too strict; in others, the user behavior did not take into account the features of the novel access control model. Fortunately, Linux distributions are providing continuously improved policies, which come preconfigured with the system in order to protect traditional services, and users are acquiring familiarity with the system. In addition, SELinux is going to be enriched by tools that will allow relatively easy access and manipulation of policies, in order to facilitate the adaptation of a predefined policy to the specific needs of a given environment.

In conclusion, SELinux is an interesting solution, which promises to have a significant impact on the security of the Linux operating system, as is testified by its growing presence; several important Linux distributions already provide this kernel module, activated by default. Also, the SELinux model is flexible enough to permit the realization of sophisticated MAC solutions, such as multilevel security, which can be of interest in several environments, such as databases (Jajodia and Sandhu 1991).

Access Control in Windows

We now describe the characteristics of the access control model of the Microsoft Windows 2000/XP operating system (msdn.microsoft.com). Most of the features we present were already part of the design of Microsoft Windows NT; we will clarify the features that were not present in Windows NT and that were introduced in Windows 2000. We use the term *Windows* to refer to this family of operating systems. We do not consider the family of Windows 95/98/ME operating systems.

Security Descriptor

One of the most important characteristics of the Windows operating system is its object-oriented design. Every component of the system is represented as an object, with attributes and methods. Any subject that can operate on an object (user, group, log-on session, and so on) is represented in Windows by a security identifier (SID), with a rich structure that manages the variety of active entities. In this scheme, it is natural to base access control on the notion that objects can be securable—that is, they can be characterized by a security descriptor that specifies the security requirements for the object (this corresponds to implementing access control with an access control list approach [Samarati and De Capitani di Vimercati 2001]). The main components of the security descriptor are the SIDs of the owner and of the primary group of the object, a discretionary access control list (DACL), and a system access control list (SACL). Almost all of the system objects are securable: files, processes, threads, named pipes, shared memory areas, registry entries, and so on. The same access control mechanism applies to all of them.

Access Control Entry

Each access control list consists of a sequence of access control entries (ACEs). An ACE is an elementary authorization on the object, with which it is associated by way of the ACL; the ACE describes the subject, the action, the type (allow, deny, or audit), and several flags (to specify the propagation and other ACE properties). The subject, called "trustee" in Windows, is represented by a SID. The action is specified by an access mask, a 32-bit vector (only part of the bits are currently used; many bits are left unspecified for future extensions). Half of the bits are associated with access rights that are the same for every object type; these access rights can be divided into three families:

- *generic*: *read*, *write*, *execute*, and the union of all of them;
- *standard*: *delete*, *read_control* (to read the security descriptor), *synchronize* (to wait on the object until a signal is generated on it), *write_dac* (to change the DACL), and *write_owner* (to change the object's owner);
- *SACL*: *access_system_security* (a single access right to modify the SACL; the right is not sufficient, as the subject must also have the SE_SECURITY_NAME privilege). It cannot appear in a DACL.

The remaining 16 bits are used to represent access rights specific for the object type (directory, file, process, thread, and so on). For instance, for directories, access rights *open*, *create_child*, *delete_child*, *list*, *read_prop*, and *write_prop* apply.

Access Token

Each process or thread executed in the system is associated with an access token—that is, an object describing the security context. An access token describing the user is created after the user has been authenticated and it is then associated with every process executed on behalf of the user. The access token contains: the SID of the user's account; SIDs of the groups that have the user as a member; a log-on SID identifying the current logon session; a list of the privileges held by the user or by the groups; an owner SID; the SID of the primary group; and the default DACL, used when a process creates a new object without specifying a security descriptor. In addition, there are other components that are used for changing the identifiers associated with a process (called "impersonation" in Windows), and to apply restrictions.

Evaluation of ACLs

When a thread makes a request to access an object, its access token is compared with the DACL in the security descriptor of the resource. If the DACL is not present in the security descriptor, the system assumes that the object is accessible without restrictions. Otherwise, the ACEs in the DACL are considered one after the other, and for each one the user and group SIDs in the access token are compared with the one in the ACE. If there is a match, the ACE is applied. The order of ACEs in the DACL is extremely important, in fact the first ACE that matches will allow or deny the access rights in it. The following matching ACEs will only be able to allow or deny the remaining access rights. If the analysis of the DACL terminates and no allow/deny result has been obtained for a given access right, the system assumes that the right is denied (closed policy). As an example, with reference to Figure 6, for user Bob the second ACE will apply (as it matches the group Nurse in the thread's access token) denying Bob the execute and write accesses on object 1. The approach of applying the first ACE encountered corresponds to the use of a "position-based" criterion for resolving possible conflicts

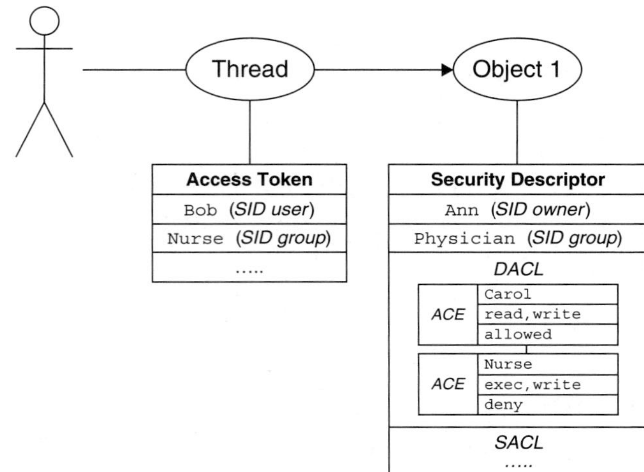

Figure 6: Access control in Windows

(Samarati and De Capitani di Vimercati 2001). Although simple, this solution is quite limiting. First, it gives the users specifying the policy the complete burden of solving each specific conflict that may arise (not allowing them to specify generic high-level rules for conflicts). Second, it is not suitable if a decentralized administration (where several users can specify authorizations) has to be accommodated. Also, users should have explicit direct write privilege on the DACL to properly order the ACEs. However, doing so it would be possible for them to abuse the privilege and set the ACL in an uncontrolled way.

It is worth noting that an empty DACL (which returns no permissions) will deny all users the access to the object, whereas a null DACL (which returns no restrictions) would grant them all. Therefore, attention must be paid to the difference between the two.

The DACL is set by the object creator. When no DACL is specified, the default DACL in the access token is used by the system. The SACL is a sequence of ACEs like the DACL, but it can be modified only by a user who has the administrative privilege SE_SECURITY_NAME, and describes the actions that have to be logged by the system (i.e., if the ACE for a given right and SID is positive, the action must be logged; if it is negative, no trace will be kept); the access control system records access requests that have been successful, rejected, or both, depending on the value of the flags in the ACE elements in the SACL. Each monitored access request produces a new entry in the security event log.

System Privileges

A system privilege in Windows is the right to execute privileged operations, such as making a backup, debugging a process, increasing the priority of a process, increasing the storage quota, and creating accounts. All these operations are not directly associated with a specific system object, and they cannot conveniently be represented by ACEs in an object security descriptor. System privileges can be considered as authorizations without an explicit object. System privileges can be associated with user and group accounts. When a user is authenticated by the system, the access token is created; the access token contains the system privileges of the user and of the groups in which the user is a member. Every time a user tries to execute a system's privileged operation, the system checks whether the access token contains the adequate system privilege. System privileges are evaluated locally: a user can have different system privileges on different nodes of the network.

Impersonation and Restricted Tokens

Impersonation is a mechanism that permits threads to acquire the access rights of a different user. This feature is similar to the *setuid* and *setgid* services of Linux, in which the change in user and group identifiers permits programs invoked by a user to access protected resources. In Windows, impersonation is also an important tool for client/server architectures. The server uses impersonation to acquire the security context of the client when a request arrives. The advantage is that, in a network environment, a user will be able to consistently access the resources for which the user is authorized, and the system will be better protected from errors in the protocol used for service invocation or in the server application.

Each process has an access token (created at log on) built from the profile of the authenticated user. An impersonating thread has two access tokens, the primary access token that describes the access token of the parent process, and the impersonation access token that represents the security context of a different user. Impersonation requires an adequate system privilege and it can be a very useful tool; Windows Server 2003 has introduced the possibility for applications to set restrictions on delegation, to minimize the risk that a server receiving the impersonation access token accidentally forwards it to another untrusted party, giving access to resources that would otherwise be protected.

Windows 2000 introduced primitives for the creation of restricted tokens. A restricted token is an access token for which some privileges have been removed, or restricting SIDs have been added. A restricting SID is used to limit the capabilities of an access token. When an access request is made and the access token is compared with the ACEs in the ACL, each time there is a match between the restricting SID in the token and the SID in an ACE, the ACE is considered only if it denies access rights on the object.

Inheritance

Some important securable objects contain other securable objects. As an example, folders in the New Technology File System (NTFS) file system contain files and other folders; registry keys contain subkeys. This containment hierarchy puts in the same container objects that are often characterized by the same security requirements. The hierarchy results are then extremely convenient because they permit an automatic propagation of security descriptions from an object to all the objects contained within it (see the section on desiderata). This feature is realized in Windows by access control inheritance.

A difference exists between Windows NT and Windows 2000 (and later) with respect to inheritance. In Windows NT there is no distinction between direct and inherited ACEs: inherited ACEs are directly copied into the object's ACL when the object is created or when a new ACL is applied to an object. The result is that a change in an object's ACL is not propagated down the hierarchy to the objects that inherit it. In Windows 2000 (and later), ACL inheritance is managed "by reference," obtaining an automatic propagation of ACL updates to the inheriting objects (as users would probably expect). Also, Windows 2000 gives higher priority to ACEs directly defined on specific objects, by putting the inherited ACEs at the end of the DACL.

In Windows 2000 (and later), every ACE is characterized by three flags. The first flag is active if the ACE has to be propagated to descendant objects. The second and third flags are active only if the first flag is active. The second flag is active when the ACE is propagated to children objects without activating the first flag, thus blocking propagation to the first level. The third flag is active when the ACE is not applied to the object itself. In addition, in the security descriptor of a securable object there is a flag that permits the disabling of the application of inherited ACEs to the object.

ACCESS CONTROL IN DATABASE MANAGEMENT SYSTEMS

DataBase Management Systems (DBMSs) usually provide access control services in addition to those provided by the underlying operating systems (Bellovin 1989). DBMS access control allows references to the data model concepts and the consequent specification of authorizations dependent on the data and on the applications. Most of the existing DBMSs (e.g., Oracle Server, IBM DB2, Microsoft SQL Server, and PostgreSQL) are based on the relational data model and on the use of SQL (Structured Query Language) as the data definition and manipulation language (Bellovin 1989). The SQL standard provides commands for the specification of access restrictions on the objects managed by the DBMS. Here we illustrate the main SQL facilities with reference to the current version of the language, namely SQL:2003 (Database Language SQL 2003).

Security Features of SQL

SQL access control is based on user and role identifiers (Atzeni et al. 1999). User identifiers correspond to log-in names with which users open the DBMS sessions. DBMS users are defined by the DMBS in an implementation-dependent way and are usually independent from the usernames managed by the operating system; SQL does not define how OS users are mapped to SQL users. Roles, introduced in the SQL standard with SQL:1999, are "named collections of privileges" (Sandhu, Ferraiolo, and Kuhn 2000)—that is, named virtual entities to which privileges are assigned. By activating a role, users are enabled to execute the privileges associated with the role.

Users and roles can be granted authorizations on any object managed by the DBMS, namely: tables, views, columns of tables and views, domains, assertions, and user-defined constructs such as user-defined types, triggers, and SQL-invoked routines. Authorizations can also be granted to the public, meaning that they apply to all the user and role identifiers in the SQL environment. Apart from the drop and alter statements—which permit deletion and modification of the schema of an object and whose execution is reserved for the object's owner—authorizations can be specified for any of the commands supported by SQL, namely: *select, insert, update*, and *delete* for tables and views (where the first three can refer to specific columns), and *execute* for SQL-invoked routines. In addition, other actions allow controlling references to resources; they are: *reference, usage, under*, and *trigger*. The *reference* privilege, associated with tables or attributes within, allows referring to tables/attributes in an integrity constraint: a constraint cannot be checked unless the owner of the schema in which the constraint appears has the *reference* privilege for all the objects involved in the constraint. This is because constraints may affect the availability of the objects on which they are defined, and therefore their specification should be reserved for those explicitly authorized. The *usage* privilege, which can be applied to domains, user-defined types, character sets, collations, and translations, allows the use of the object in one's own declarations. The *under* privilege can be applied to a user-defined type and allows subjects to define a subtype of the specified type. The *trigger* privilege, referring to a table, allows the definition of a trigger on the table.

In addition to authorizations to execute privileges on the different objects of the database management system, SQL also supports authorizations for roles. In particular, roles can be granted to other users and roles. Granting a role to a user means allowing the user to activate the role. Granting a role r' to another role r means permitting r to enjoy the privileges granted to r'. Intuitively, authorizations on roles granted to roles introduce chains of roles through which privileges can flow. For instance, consider the case in Figure 7, in which the rightmost three nodes are users, the remaining three nodes are roles, and an arc corresponds to an authorization of the incident node on the role source of the arc (e.g., Ann has an authorization for the Admin_Supervisor role). Although each of the users will be allowed to activate the role for which Ann has the authorization (directly connected in our illustration) she will enjoy the principles of all the roles reachable through a chain. For instance, when activating role Admin_Supervisor, Ann will enjoy, in addition to the privileges granted to this role, also the privileges granted to roles Secretary and Accountant.

Access Control Enforcement

The subject making a request is always identified by a pair <*uid, rid*>, where *uid* is the SQL-session user identifier (which can never be null) and *rid* is a role name, whose value is initially null. Both the user identifier and the role identifier can be changed via the commands *set session authorization* and *set role*, respectively, whose successful execution depends on the specified authorizations. In particular, enabling a role requires the current user to have the authorization for the role. The current pair <*uid, rid*> can also change on execution of a SQL-invoked routine, where it is set to the owner of the routine (see the section on "Views and Invoked Routines"). An *authorization stack* (maintained using a "last-in, first-out" strategy) keeps track of the sequence of pairs <*uid, rid*> for a session. Every request is controlled against the authorizations of the top element of the stack. Although the subject is a pair, like for authorizations and ownership, access control always refers to either a user or a role identifier in mutual exclusion: it is performed against the authorizations for *uid* if the *rid* is null; it is performed against the authorizations for *rid*, otherwise. In other words, by activating a role a user can enjoy the privileges of the role while disabling her own. Moreover, at most one role at a time can be active: the setting to a new role rewrites the *rid* element to be the new role specified.

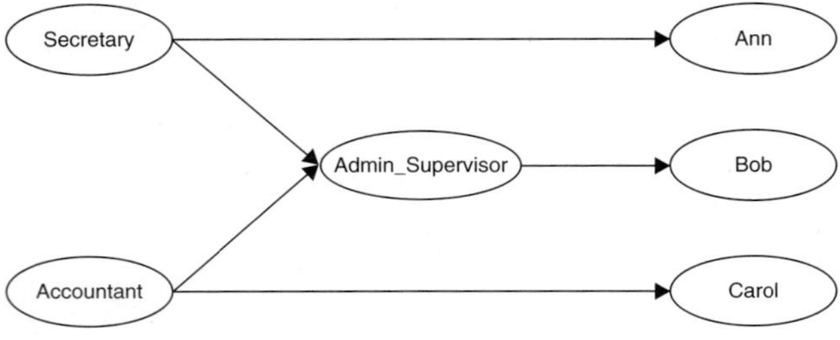

Figure 7: An example of role chains in SQL

Administration

Every object in SQL has an owner, typically its creator (which can be set to either the current_user or current_role). The owner of an object can execute all privileges on it, or a subset of them in case of views and SQL-invoked routines (see the section on "Views and Invoked Routines"). The owner is also reserved the privilege to drop the object and to alter (i.e., modify) it. Apart from the drop and alter privileges, the execution of which is reserved for the object's owner, the owner can grant authorizations for any privilege on its objects, together with the ability to pass such authorizations to others (grant option).

A *grant* command, whose syntax is illustrated in Figure 8, allows the granting of new authorizations for roles (enabling their activation) or for privileges on objects. Successful execution of the command requires the grantor to be the owner of the object on which the privilege is granted, or to hold the grant option for it. The specification of all privileges, instead of an explicit privilege list, is equivalent to the specification of all the privileges, on the object, for which the grantor has the grant option. The with hierarchy option (possible only for the *select* privilege on tables) automatically implies granting the grantee the *select* privilege on all the (either existing or future) subtables of the table on which the privilege is granted. The *with grant option* clause (called *with admin option* for roles) allows the grantee to grant others the received authorization (as well as the grant option on it). No cycles of role grants are allowed.

The *revoke* statement allows revocation of (administrative or access) privileges previously granted by the revoker (which can be set to the current_user or current_role). Because of the use of the grant option, and the existence of derived objects (see the section on "Views and Invoked Routines"), revocation of a privilege can possibly have side effects, since there may be other authorizations that depend on the one being revoked. The options *cascade* and *restrict* dictate how the revocation procedure should behave in such a case: *cascade* recursively revokes all the authorizations that should not exist anymore if the requested

```
grant all privileges | <action>
on [ table ] | domain | collation | character set | translation | type <object name>
to <grantee> [{<comma> <grantee>}...]
[ with hierarchy option ]
[ with grant option ]
[ granted by <grantor> ]
```

```
grant <role granted> [{<comma><role granted>}...]
to <grantee> [{<comma><grantee>}...]
[ with admin option ]
[ granted by <grantor>]
```

```
revoke [ grant option for | hierarchy option for ] <action>
on [ table ] | domain | collation | character set | translation | type <object name>
from <grantee> [{<comma><grantee>}...]
[ granted by <grantor> ]
cascade | restrict
```

```
revoke [ admin option for ]
<role revoked> [{<comma><role revoked> }... ]
from <grantee> [{<comma><grantee> }... ]
[ granted by <grantor> ]
cascade | restrict
```

Figure 8: Syntax of the grant and revoke SQL statements

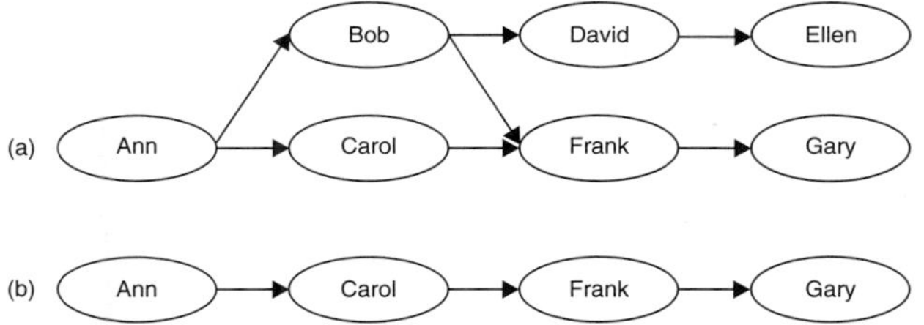

Figure 9: Authorizations before (a) and after (b) the cascade revocation of Bob's privilege

privilege is revoked; *restrict* rejects the execution of the revoke operation if other authorizations depend on it. To illustrate, consider the case in which user Ann creates a table and grants the select privilege, and the grant option on it, to Bob and Carol. Bob grants it to David, who grants it to Ellen, who grants it to Gary. Carol also grants the authorization to Frank. Assume for simplicity that all these grant statements include the grant option. Figure 9a illustrates the resulting authorizations and their dependencies, with a node for every user and an arc from the grantor to the grantee for every authorization. Consider now a request by Ann to revoke the privilege from Bob. If the revoke is requested with the option *cascade*, also the authorizations granted by Bob (who would no longer hold the grant option for the privilege) will be revoked, causing the revocation of David's authorization, which will recursively cause the revocation of the authorization David granted to Ellen. The resulting authorizations (and their dependencies) are illustrated in Figure 9b. Note that no recursive revocation is activated for Frank, because even if the authorization he received from Bob is deleted, Frank still holds the privilege with the grant option (received from Carol). By contrast, if Ann were to request the revoke operation with the restrict option, the operation would be refused because of the authorizations dependent on it (those which would be revoked with the cascade option).

Views and Invoked Routines

Special consideration must be taken for authorizations for derived objects (views) and SQL-invoked routines, for which the owner creating them does not own the underlying objects used in their definition.

A view is a *virtual* table derived from base tables and/or other views. A view definition is an SQL statement whose result defines the content of the view. The view is virtual since its content is not explicitly stored, but it is derived, at the time the view is accessed, by executing the corresponding SQL statement on the underlying tables. A user/role can create a view only if it has the necessary privilege on all the views, or base tables, directly referenced by the view. The creator receives on the view the privileges that it holds on all the tables directly referenced by the view. Also, it receives the grant option for a privilege only if it has the grant option for the privilege on all the tables directly referenced by the view. If it holds a privilege on the view with the grant option, the creator can grant the privilege (and the grant option) to others. The grantees of such privileges need not hold the privileges on the underlying tables to access the view; access to the view requires only the existence of privileges on the view. Intuitively, the execution of the query computing the view is controlled against the authorizations of the view's owner (similarly to what the *suid* bit does in UNIX). Also, views provide a way to enforce finer-grained access (on specific tuples). For instance, a user can define a view EU_Employees on table Employees containing only those rows for which the value of attribute nationality is equal to EU. She can then grant other users the *select* privilege on the view, thus allowing (and restricting) them access to information on employees within the European Union. Views are the only means to bypass an *all tuples* or *no tuple* access on tables. Although convenient, views are simply a trick for enforcing content-dependent fine-grained access control (which is not the main reason why they were developed), and as such limit results for this purpose: a different view should be defined for any possible content-dependent access restriction that should be enforced.

An SQL-invoked routine is an SQL-invoked procedure, or an SQL-invoked function, characterized by a header and a body. The header consists of a name and a, possibly empty, list of parameters. The body may be specified in SQL or, in the case of external routines, written in a host programming language. At object creation time, a user is designated as the *owner* of the routine. Analogously to what is required for views, to create an SQL-invoked routine, the owner needs to have the necessary privileges for the successful execution of the routine. The routine is dropped if at any time the owner loses any of the privileges necessary to execute the body of the routine. When a routine is created, the creator receives the *execute* privilege on it, with the grant option if it has the grant option for all the privileges necessary for the routine to run. If the creator of a routine has the *execute* privilege with the grant option, she can grant such a privilege, and the grant option on it, to other users/roles. The *execute* privilege on an SQL routine is sufficient for the users/roles gaining the privilege to run the routine (they need not have the privileges necessary for the routine to run; only the creator does). Intuitively, SQL routines provide a service similar to the *setuid/setgid* privileges in Linux and impersonation in Windows (controlling privileges with respect to the owner instead of the caller of a procedure).

ACCESS CONTROL FOR INTERNET-BASED SOLUTIONS

We here survey the most common security features for Internet-based solutions. Again, we illustrate the most popular representative of the different families. We will therefore look at the XACML access control language for regulating information and e-service accesses; Apache for Web-based solutions; and the Java 2 security model.

XML-Based Access Control Languages

An essential requirement of new Internet-wide security standards is that they should be able to apply to content created using also eXtensible Markup Language (XML) (Bradley 2002). XML has been adopted widely for a great variety of applications and types of content. Examples of XML-based markup languages are Security Assertion Markup Language (SAML) used to exchange security credentials among different parties, Geography Markup Language (GML), Wireless Markup Language (WML), Physical Markup Language (PML), and Mathematical Markup Language (MathML), just to name a few. XML is also at the basis of interoperability protocols used to integrate applications across the Internet, such as Web Services protocols (e.g., SOAP [Simple Object Access Protocol], WSDL [Web Services Description Language], and UDDI [Universal Description, Discovery, and Integration] [Newcomer 2002]). It is therefore of paramount importance to provide integrity, confidentiality and other security benefits to entire XML documents or portions of these documents in a way that does not prevent further processing by standard XML tools.

Traditionally, XML security has developed along two distinct though related lines of research, corresponding to two facets of the XML security notion. The first facet defines XML security as a set of security techniques (access control [Samarati and De Capitani di Vimercati 2001], differential encryption [XML Encryption Syntax and Processing, W3C Recommendation 2002], digital signature [XML-Signature Syntax and Processing, W3C Recommendation 2002]) tightly coupled with XML to maintain the main features of the XML semistructured data model while adding to it all the necessary security capabilities. A second important facet of XML security deals with models and languages specifying and exchanging access control policies to generic resources, which may or may not comply with the XML data model. Initially, XML-based access control languages were introduced only for the protection of resources that were themselves XML files (Damiani et al. 2002; Gabillon 2004). Some proposals instead use XML to define languages for expressing protection requirements on any kind of data/resources (Ardagna et al. 2004; Godik and Moses 2004). One of the most relevant XML-based access control languages is the eXtensible Access Control Markup Language (XACML) (Godik and Moses 2004; Moses 2005). XACML is the result of an OASIS standardization effort proposing an XML-based language to express and interchange access control policies. XACML is designed to express authorization policies in XML against objects that can themselves be identified in XML.

XACML

The main concepts of interest in the XACML policy language are: policy, policy set, and rule.

Policy Syntax and Semantics. An XACML policy has, as the root element, either Policy or PolicySet. A PolicySet is a collection of Policy or PolicySet. An XACML policy consists of a target, a set of rules, a rule combining algorithm, and an optional set of obligations. A target consists of a simplified set of conditions for the subject, resource, and action that must be satisfied for a policy to be applicable to a given request. If a policy applies to all entities of a given type, that is, all subjects, actions, or resources, an empty element, named AnySubject, AnyAction, or AnyResource, respectively, is used. The components of a rule are target, effect, and condition. The optional target element defines the set of resources, subjects, and actions to which the rule is intended to apply. The effect of the rule can be permit or deny. The condition represents a Boolean expression that may further refine the applicability of the rule. A rule-combining algorithm is used for reconciling the decisions each rule makes. The final decision value, called "authorization decision," is the value of the policy as defined by the rule-combining algorithm. XACML defines the following different combining algorithms.

- *Deny overrides*. It states that if there exists a rule that evaluates to deny or if all rules evaluate to not applicable, the result is deny. If all rules evaluate to permit, the result is permit. If some rules evaluate to permit and some evaluate to not applicable, the result is permit.
- *Permit overrides*. It states that if there exists a rule that evaluates to permit, the result is permit. If all rules evaluate to not applicable, the result is deny. If some rules evaluate to deny and some evaluate to not applicable, the result is deny.
- *First applicable*. It states that each rule has to be evaluated in the order in which it appears in the policy. For each rule, if the target matches and the conditions evaluate to true, the result is the effect (permit or deny) of such a rule.
- *Only-one-applicable*. It states that if more than one rule applies, the result is indeterminate. If no rule applies, the result is not applicable. If only one policy applies, the result coincides with the result of evaluating that rule.

According to the selected combining algorithm, the authorization decision can be permit, deny, not applicable (when no applicable policies or rules could be found), or indeterminate (when some errors occurred during the access control process). An obligation is an action that has to be performed in conjunction with the enforcement of an authorization decision. For instance, an obligation can state that all accesses on medical data have to be logged. Note that only policies that are evaluated and have returned a response of permit or deny can return obligations. In other words, obligations associated with a policy that evaluates indeterminate or not applicable are ignored.

An important feature of XACML is that a rule is based on the definition of attributes corresponding to specific characteristics of a subject, resource, action, or environment. Attributes are identified by the Subject Attribute Designator, ResourceAttributeDesignator, Action Attribute Designator, and EnvironmentAttributeDesignator elements. These elements use the AttributeValue element to define the requested value of a particular attribute. Alternatively, the AttributeSelector element can be used to specify where to retrieve a particular attribute. Note that both the attribute designator and AttributeSelector elements can return multiple values. For this reason, XACML provides an attribute type, called "bag," corresponding to an unordered collection of values that can contain duplicated values for a particular attribute. In addition, XACML defines other standard value types such as string, Boolean, integer, time, and so on. Together with these attribute types, XACML also defines operations to be performed on the different types such as equality operation, comparison operation, string manipulation, and so on.

Policy example. As an example of an XACML policy, suppose that an e-commerce site defines a high-level policy stating that "any user playing the role Subscribers can read the discount_products if the Acme fidelity card is attached to the request." Figure 10 illustrates the XACML policy corresponding to this high-level policy. The policy applies to requests on the www.example.com/products/discount.html resource. The policy has one rule with a target that requires a read action, a subject with role Subscribers, and a condition that applies only if the subject has the Acme fidelity card.

Apache Access Control

The Apache HTTP server (www.apache.org) allows the specification of access control rules via a per-directory configuration file usually called .htaccess (Apache HTTP server version 1.3). The .htaccess file is a text file including access control rules (called "directives" in Apache) that affect the directory in which the .htaccess file is placed and, recursively, directories below it (see the section on "Evaluation of .htaccess Files" for more details). Figure 11 illustrates a simple example of an .htaccess file.

Access control directives, whose specification is enabled via module mod_access, can be either host-based (they can refer to the client's host name and IP address, or other characteristics of the request) or user-based (they can refer to usernames and groups thereof). We start by describing such directives and then we illustrate how the .htaccess files including them are evaluated.

Host-Based Access Control

Both permissions and denials can be specified, by using the Allow (for permissions) and Deny (for denials) directives, which can refer to location properties or environment variables of the request. *Location-based* specifications have the form:

Allow from *host-or-network*/all
Deny from *host-or-network*/all

where *host-or-network* can be: a domain name (e.g., acme.com); an IP address or IP pattern (e.g., 155.50.); a network/netmask pair (e.g., 10.0.0.0/255.0.0.0); or a network/n CIDR mask size, where *n* is a number between 1 and 32 specifying the number of high-order 1 bits in the netmask. For instance, 10.0.0.0/8 is the same as 10.0.0.0/255.0.0.0. Alternatively, value all denotes all hosts on the network.

Variable-based specifications have the form:

Allow from env = *env-variable*
Deny from env =*env-variable*

where *env-variable* denotes an environment variable. The semantics is that the directive (allow or deny) applies if *env-variable* exists. Apache permits the setting of environment variables based on different attributes of the HTTP client request using the directives provided by module

```
<Policy PolicyId="Pol1"RuleCombiningAlgId="urn:oasis:names:tc:xacml:1.0:rule-combining-algorithm:permit-overrides">
<Target>
 <Subjects> <AnySubject/> </Subjects>
 <Resources>
  <Resource>
   <ResourceMatch MatchId="urn:oasis:names:tc:xacml:1.0:function:stringmatch">
    <AttributeValue DataType="http://www.w3.org/2001/XMLSchema#string">
   http://www.example.com/products/discount.html
    </AttributeValue>
    <ResourceAttributeDesignator
   DataType="http://www.w3.org/2001/XMLSchema#string"
   AttributeId="urn:oasis:names:tc:xacml:1.0:resource:target-namespace"/>
    </ResourceMatch>
  </Resource>
 </Resources>
 <Actions> <AnyAction/> </Actions>
</Target>
<Rule RuleId="ReadRule" Effect="Permit">
 <Target>
  <Subjects>
   <Subject>
    <SubjectMatch MatchId="urn:oasis:names:tc:xacml:1.0:function:string-equal">
     <AttributeValue DataType="http://www.w3.org/2001/XMLSchema#string">
     Subscribers
     </AttributeValue>
     <SubjectAttributeDesignator AttributeId=
    "urn:oasis:names:tc:xacml:2.0:example:attribute:role"
    DataType="http://www.w3.org/2001/XMLSchema#string"/>
    </SubjectMatch>
   </Subject>
  </Subjects>
  <Resources> <AnyResource/> </Resources>
  <Actions>
   <Action>
    <ActionMatch MatchId="urn:oasis:names:tc:xacml:1.0:function:string-equal">
     <AttributeValue DataType="http://www.w3.org/2001/XMLSchema#string">
     read
     </AttributeValue>
     <ActionAttributeDesignator
     DataType="http://www.w3.org/2001/XMLSchema#string"
     AttributeId="urn:oasis:names:tc:xacml:1.0:action:action-id"/>
    </ActionMatch>
   </Action>
  </Actions>
 </Target>
 <Condition FunctionId="urn:oasis:names:tc:xacml:1.0:function:string-equal">
  <SubjectAttributeDesignator
  DataType="http://www.w3.org/2001/XMLSchema#string"
  AttributeId="urn:oasis:names:tc:xacml:1.0:subject:fidelitycardID"/>
  <AttributeValue DataType="http://www.w3.org/2001/XMLSchema#string">
  ACME
  </AttributeValue>
 </Condition>
</Rule>
</Policy>
```

Figure 10: A simple example of an XACML policy

mod_setenvif. The attributes may correspond to various HTTP request header fields (see RFC 2616 [Fielding et al. 1999]) or to other aspects of the request. The most commonly used request header field names include: User-Agent (the user agent originating the request) and Referer (the Uniform Resource Identifier [URI] of the document from which the URI in the request was obtained). For instance, in Figure 11, directive SetEnvIf sets "internal_site" if the

```
SetEnvIf Referer www.mydomain.org internal_site
AuthName "user-based restriction"
AuthType Basic
AuthUserFile /home/mylogin/.htpasswd
AuthGroupFile /home/mylogin/.htgroup
Order Deny,Allow
Deny from all
Allow from acme.com
Allow from env= internal_site
Require valid-user
Satisfy any
<FilesMatch public_access.html>
Allow from all
</FilesMatch>
```

Figure 11: A simple example of an .htaccess file

referring page was in the www.mydomain.org Web site. The "Allow from env = internal_site" directive, then, permits access if the referring page matches the given URI.

Access control evaluates the content of file .htaccess to determine whether a request should be granted or denied. The Order directive controls the order in which the Deny and Allow directives must be evaluated (thus allowing users to dictate the conflict resolution policy to be applied) and defines the default access state. There are three possible orderings:

- Deny,Allow. The deny directives are evaluated first, and access is allowed by default (open policy). Any client that does not match a deny directive *or* matches an allow directive is granted access.
- Allow,Deny. The allow directives are evaluated first and access is denied by default (closed policy). Any client that does not match an allow directive *or* matches a deny directive is denied access.
- Mutual-failure. Only clients that do not match any Deny directive *and* match an Allow directive are allowed access.

For instance, the .htaccess file in Figure 11 states that all hosts in the acme.com domain and requests with a referring page in the www.mydomain.org Web site are allowed access; all other hosts are denied access.

User-Based Access Control

Besides host-based access control rules, Apache includes a module, called mod_auth, that enables user authentication (based on usernames and passwords) and enforcement of user-based access control rules. Usernames and associated passwords are stored in a text *user file*, reporting pairs of the form "*username:MD5-encrypted password*." Command htpasswd is used to modify the file (i.e., add new users or change passwords) as well as to create/rewrite it (a -c flag rewrites the file as new). The command has the form:

htpasswd [-c] *filename username*

where *filename* is the full path name of the user file and *username* is the name of the user we are creating. Upon entering the command, the system will ask to specify the password (as usual asking its input twice to avoid insertion errors). An alternative to the text user file provided by module mod_auth, is given by modules mod_auth_db and mod_auth_dbm. With these modules, the usernames and passwords are stored in Berkeley DB files and DBM type database files, respectively.

To define user-based restrictions, a name can be given to the portion of the file system access that requires authentication. This portion, called "realm," corresponds to the subtree rooted at the directory containing the .htaccess file.

The main directives to create realms are:

- AuthName, to give a name to the realm. The realm name will be communicated to users when prompted for the log-in dialog.
- AuthType, to specify the type of authentication to be used. The most common method, implemented by mod_auth is Basic, which sends the password from the client to the server unencrypted (with a base64-encoding). A more secure, but less common alternative is the Digest authentication method, implemented by module mod_auth_digest, which sends the server a one-way hash (MD5 digest) of the username:password pair, combined with a nonce provided by the server. This Digest authentication method is supported by all recent versions of common browsers (e.g., MS Internet Explorer, Mozilla Firefox, and Opera).
- AuthUserFile, to specify the absolute path of the file that contains usernames and passwords. Note that the user file containing names and passwords does not need to be in the same directory as the .htaccess file.
- AuthGroupFile, to specify the location of a *group file*, and therefore provide support for access rules specified for groups. The group file is a list of entries of the form

group-name: username1 username2 username3......

where *group-name* is the name associated with the group to which the specified usernames are declared to belong, and each of the usernames appearing in the list must be in the user file (i.e., be an existing username).

The four directives above allow the server to know where to find the usernames and passwords and which authentication protocol has to be used. User-based access rules are specified with a directive "require" that can take three forms:

- require user *username1 username2 ...usernameN*—only usernames "*username1 username2...usernameN*" are allowed access;
- require group *group1 group2...groupM*—only usernames in groups "*group1 group2...groupM*" are allowed access;
- require valid-user—any username in the user file is allowed access.

Host-Based and User-Based Interactions and Finer-Grained Specifications

Host- and user-based access directives are not mutually exclusive, and they can both be used to control access to the same resource. The directive *satisfy* allows the specification of how the two sets of directives should interact. Satisfy takes one argument whose value can be either all or any. Value *all* requires both user-based and host-based directives to be satisfied for access to be granted, whereas for value *any*, it is sufficient that either one is satisfied for access to be granted.

As already stated, all the directives specified in .htaccess apply to the file system subtree rooted at the directory that contains the specific .htaccess file unless overridden. In other words, an .htaccess file in a directory applies to all the files directly contained in the directory and recursively propagates to all its subdirectories unless an .htaccess has been specified for them (most specific takes precedence). Apache 1.2 (and later) supports finer-grained rules allowing the specification of access directives on a per-file basis by including FilesMatch section of the form "`<FilesMatch` *`reg-exp`*`>`*directives*`</FilesMatch>`," with the semantics that the directives included in the FilesMatch section apply only to the files with a name matching the regular expression specified. Also, directives can be specified on a per-method basis, by using a Limit section of the form "`<Limit` *`list of access methods`*`>`*directives* `</Limit>`," with the semantics that the directives included in the Limit section apply only to the accesses listed (again overriding the directives specified in the .htaccess file). As an example, directive

```
<Limit get post put>
        require valid-user
</Limit>
```

would allow any authenticated user to execute methods get, post, and put. The directive does not apply to other operations.

Evaluation of .htaccess Files

As mentioned previously, the file .htaccess is used to control accesses to the files in a directory. Therefore, whenever an access request to a file is submitted, the Apache HTTP server starts checking in the top directory for an .htaccess file, and then checks each subdirectory until it reaches the directory that contains the requested file appears (Coar 2001). All .htaccess files found during this process (called "directory walk") are processed and merged, thus resulting in a set of directives that apply to the requested file. More precisely, the directives specified in the .htaccess files have to be processed if they belong to the categories (AuthConfig, FileInfo, Indexes, Limit, and Options) listed in the AllowOverride list specified in a server configuration file. These directives are then merged according to the most specific principle—that is, directives within .htaccess files in subdirectories may change or nullify the effects of the directives within .htaccess files of parent directories. As an example, suppose that the access request for http://acme.com/Department1/welcome.html resolves to the file /home/myaccount/www/Department1/welcome and that statement AllowOverride All has been specified. In this case, the Apache HTTP server merges *all* directives included in the .htaccess files of directories: /; /home; /home/myaccount; /home/myaccount/www; and /home/myaccount/www/Department1.

Java 2 Security Model

Java is both a modern object-oriented programming language and a complex software architecture. Java has been developed by Sun Microsystems and is currently one of the most important solutions for the construction of applications in a network environment. Java offers sophisticated solutions for the design of distributed and mobile applications, in which the software can be partitioned on distinct nodes and downloaded from one node to be executed on another.

Since its introduction, Java designers have carefully considered the security implications of an architecture for which executable code could be downloaded from the network, possibly from untrusted hosts. The first security model of Java, the one associated with Java Development Kit version 1.0 (JDK 1.0), was based on the construction of a *sandbox*, a restricted environment for the execution of downloaded code, with rigid restrictions on the set of local resources that could be used (e.g., with no access to the file system and with limits on network access).

The main problem of the JDK 1.0 security model was the limited granularity and the availability of a single policy for all downloaded code. JDK 1.0 would let programmers revise the access control services and implement their own version; but the implementation of access control services is complex, expensive, and delicate, making it unfeasible for most applications.

The evolution of Java to version 2 gave the opportunity to revise the security model and significantly improve it. We describe the Java 2 Security Architecture. A full and authoritative description of the architecture appears in (Gong 1999).

We observe that the security services of Java are not related to the access control system of the host operating system. This design choice derives from the requirement to make Java a fully portable execution environment, which does not depend on the services of the underlying system. The Java environment will have to be properly protected on the host system, as write access to the implementation of the Java Virtual Machine, or to its configuration, would permit the bypassing of any security mechanism within the Java environment.

We focus our presentation on the security model that associates permissions with pieces of Java code. This code-centric model adequately supports the security of mobile code. We do not describe the Java Authentication and Authorization Service (JAAS, since Java 2 v. 1.4 integrated with the JDK), a set of Java packages that offer services for user authentication and management of access control rights. JAAS extends the native Java 2 security model, using all the mechanisms presented here.

It is important to observe that the Microsoft .NET architecture presents many features that are similar to those offered by Java, with a standard virtual machine environment (the common language runtime, CLR) responsible for the execution of portable code in a network-centered environment. In terms of security, the design of the .NET architecture has taken advantage of the experience in the design of Java and offers a security model that presents most of the functions appearing in the Java 2 model; a distinctive feature is the strong integration of the .NET security services with all the features of the Windows access control model. We refer the reader to the description available on the Microsoft Web site; the understanding of the services of the Java 2 model should greatly facilitate the comprehension of the design of the .NET security model.

Security Policy

The security policy describes the behavior that a Java program should exhibit. Each security policy is composed of a list of entries (an access control list) that defines the permissions associated with Java classes and applications. There is a standard security policy defined for the whole Java installation, and each user can personalize it extending the ACL in several ways—for example, writing a specific file in the personal home directory. The security policy is represented by a Policy object.

Each entry in the security policy describes a piece of Java code and the permissions that are granted to it. Each piece of Java code is described by a URL and a list of signatures (represented in Java by a CodeSource object). The URL can be used to identify both local and remote code; with a single URL it is also possible to characterize single classes or complete collections (packages, Java Archive [JAR] files, directory trees). The signatures may be applied on the complete URL or on a single class within a collection. Because URLs may identify collections, it is important to support implication among CodeSource objects (e.g., www.xmlsec.org/classes/ implies www.xmlsec.org/classes/xml.jar).

Permissions

Permissions describe the access rights that are granted to pieces of Java code. Each permission is represented by an instance of the abstract class Permission. Permissions are typically represented by a target and an action (e.g., file target /tmp/javaAppl/buffer and action write). There are permissions that are characterized only by the target, with no action (e.g., target exitVM for the execution of System.exit). The Permission class is specialized by many concrete classes, which define a hierarchy. Direct descendants of Permission are FilePermission (used to represent access rights on files), SocketPermission (used to control access to network ports), AllPermission (used to represent with a single permission the collection of all permissions), and BasicPermission (typically used as the base class for permissions with no action).

The current security model considers only positive authorizations. The rationale is that the evaluation is more efficient and the model is clearer for the programmer. However, no fundamental restriction has been introduced, and the model could evolve to support negative authorizations (in a future version of Java, or in an ad hoc security mechanism built for a specific application).

It is also interesting to note that permissions refer to classes and not to instance objects. A model granting permissions to objects would have offered finer granularity, but it would have also been more difficult to manage. Specifically, objects exist only at run-time, whereas the security policy is static, and it is not convenient to specify in it permissions at the level of objects.

To manage sets of permission, the Java model offers class PermissionCollection, which groups permissions of the same category (e.g., file permissions). Class Permissions represents collections of PermissionCollection objects, that is, collections of Permission objects.

Access Control

In the Java 2 architecture, permissions, which are represented by various Permission objects, are not directly associated with classes. Class ProtectionDomain realizes the link between classes and permissions. A protection domain contains classes and objects that inherit the permissions granted to the domain itself. For instance, a protection domain can be defined as follows:

```
ProtectionDomain domain =
        new ProtectionDomain(codesource,permissions);
```

This piece of code creates a new ProtectionDomain with the given codesource and permissions.

The security policy specifies permissions for a URL that may correspond to many classes; all the classes refer to the same protection domain. There is a predefined *system* domain that associates permission AllPermissions to all the classes in the core of the Java architecture.

In Java 2, access control is realized at two levels: SecurityManager and AccessController. At the higher level, class SecurityManager is responsible for evaluating access restrictions and is invoked whenever permissions have to be verified. In JDK 1.0 the class was abstract, forcing each Java implementation to provide its own realization. In Java 2 the class is concrete, and a standard implementation is part of the run-time environment. The main method of class SecurityManager is checkPermission. In JDK 1.0 the check on permissions was realized by ad hoc methods (e.g., to check for read permission on a file, method checkRead was used). Java 2 maintains all the previous methods for backward compatibility, but it uses a single method, checkPermission, for every permission type. This increases the flexibility of the security model, as the introduction of novel permissions can be managed with relative ease, without the need to modify the implementation of the SecurityManager.

The method checkPermission determines whether the permission that appears as the first parameter of the method is granted. If the check is successful, the method returns the control to the caller, otherwise it generates a security exception.

The method checkPermission in the standard SecurityManager immediately calls the method checkPermission of the class AccessController. The class AccessController is a final (i.e., unmodifiable) class that represents the security policy that Java 2 supports by default. This distinction into two levels is motivated by two conflicting requirements, each managed at a separate level. On the one hand, there is the need for flexibility, for applications that may need a different security policy; for these applications it would be possible to realize a specialized implementation of the Security Manager class, which would then be automatically invoked for security checks by Java classes, that call the services of the SecurityManager. On the other hand, applications may prefer to have a guarantee that the security model used is the default one for Java 2; in this case, applications may opt to refer directly to the services of the AccessController class.

Access control is evaluated in the execution environment, which is characterized by an array of ProtectionDomain objects. There may be more than one ProtectionDomain object, as Java classes may invoke the services of classes that belong to different domains. The problem is then to decide how to consider the permissions of different domains in the execution environment. The solution used in Java 2 is to consider as applicable permissions only those that belong to the intersection of all the domains. Consequently, when checkPermission runs, it considers all the ProtectionDomain objects, and if there is at least one domain that has not been granted the permission being checked, a security exception is generated. The rationale for this policy is that this is the safest approach, realizing the minimum privilege principle.

There is an exception to the above behavior, which requires the use of the method doPrivileged of the class AccessController. The method doPrivileged creates a separate execution environment, which considers only the permissions of the ProtectionDomain associated with the code itself. The goal of this method is analogous to that of the *setuid* mechanism in Linux, in which the privileges of the owner of the code are granted to the user executing it. For instance, a changePassword method that requires write permission on a password file can be realized within a doPrivileged method. The advantage of this mechanism with respect to the *setuid* mechanism is that in Java it is possible to restrict with a very fine granularity the Java statements that have to be executed in a privileged mode, whereas in Linux the privileges of the owner are available to the executor for the complete run of the program (in contrast to the least privilege). Finally, we consider how the security model integrates with the inheritance mechanism that characterized the Java object model. Two classes, one of which is a specialization of the other may belong to distinct domains. When a method of a subclass is invoked, the effective ProtectionDomain is the one for which the method is implemented; if the method is simply inherited from the superclass, with no redefinition, the domain of the superclass is considered; if the method is redefined in the subclass, the domain of the subclass is instead used by the checkPermission method.

DISCUSSION AND CONCLUSION

In this chapter, we discussed the basic concepts of access control and illustrated the main features of the access control services provided by some of the most popular operating systems, database management systems, and network-based solutions. Recent proposals addressing access control in open and dynamic environments take into consideration the fact that a server may receive requests not just from the local community of users, but also from remote, previously unknown users. The traditional separation between authentication and access control cannot be therefore applied in this context, and alternative access control solutions should be devised.

To this purpose, trust management has received considerable attention in the research community. In this case, access control is no longer based on users' identities, but on their attributes/properties (Bonatti and Samarati 2002). These properties are typically represented through digital certificates (credentials). A digital certificate is basically a statement certified by a given entity that can be used to establish properties of the certificate holder. Trust between two interacting parties is then established on the basis of parties' properties, which are proven through the disclosure of digital certificates.

To adopt digital certificates for access control, it is necessary to develop authorization languages and systems, for which parties must be able to state and enforce access rules based on credentials and communicate these rules to their counterpart to correctly establish a negotiation. The negotiation consists of a series of requests for credentials and counter-requests on the basis of the parties' policies. Different trust negotiation strategies have been proposed in the past few years, which try to balance two different needs (Seamons, Winslett, and Yu 2001). On the one hand, the user is willing not to release credentials to the remote and unknown server if it is not necessary for accessing the requested resource, as credentials may contain sensitive information. On the other hand, the server does not want to communicate to the unknown user the policies it is enforcing for granting access to the resources. It is therefore necessary to introduce the definition of policies, both client and server side, to control the release of credentials, and to establish a negotiation process between the parties to gain an agreement.

Although current solutions supporting credential-based policies are technically mature enough to be used in practical scenarios, there are still issues that need to be investigated to enable more complex applications such as (De Capitani di Vimercati and Samarati 2005): the definition of common languages, dictionaries, and ontologies to provide parties with a means to understand each other with respect to the properties they enjoy (or request the counterpart to enjoy); the development of a mechanism that explains why access requests are eventually denied, or—better—how to obtain the desired permissions; and the development of a mechanism that returns the information about which conditions need to be satisfied for the access to be granted, without disclosing "too much" of the underlying security policy, which might also be regarded as sensitive information.

GLOSSARY

Authentication: Means of establishing the validity of a claimed identity.

Authorization: The right granted to a user to exercise an action (e.g., read, write, create, delete, and execute) on certain objects.

Availability: A requirement intended to guarantee that information and system resources are accessible to authorized users when needed.

Confidentiality: The assurance that private or confidential information not be disclosed to unauthorized users.

Credential: Certified property of the holder, issued by an authorized party.

DAC: Discretionary Access Control.

Data Integrity: A requirement that information is not modified improperly.

Group: A set of users.

Integrity: Information has integrity when it is accurate, complete, and consistent. (See *Data Integrity* and *System Integrity*).

MAC: Mandatory Access Control.

RBAC: Role-Based Access Control.

Role: A job function within an organization that describes the authority and responsibility related to the execution of an activity.

Secrecy: A requirement that released information be protected from improper or unauthorized release.

Security: The combination of integrity, availability, and secrecy.

Security Mechanism: Low-level software and/or hardware functions that implement security policies.

Security Policy: High-level guidelines establishing rules that regulate access to resources.

SELinux: Security-Enhanced Linux.

Subject: An active entity that can exercise access to the resources of the system.

User: A person who interacts directly with a system.

XACML: eXtensible Access Control Markup Language.

XML: eXtensible Markup Language.

CROSS REFERENCES

See *Authentication*; *Cryptography*; *Password Authentication*.

REFERENCES

Apache HTTP server version 1.3. http://httpd.apache.org/docs (accessed May 27, 2007).

Ardagna, C. A., E. Damiani, S. De Capitani di Vimercati, and P. Samarati. 2004. XML-based access control languages. http://seclab.dti.unimi.it/Papers/RI-3.pdf (accessed May 27, 2007).

Atzeni, P., S. Ceri, S. Paraboschi, and R. Torlone. 1999. *Database systems—Concepts, languages and architectures*. New York: McGraw-Hill.

Bell, D. and L. LaPadula. 1973. Secure computer systems: Mathematical foundations. Technical Report MTR-2547, vol. 1, Bedford, MA: MITRE.

Bellovin, S. M. 1989 Security problems in the TCP/IP protocol suite. *Computer Communication Review* 19(2):32–48.

Biba, K. J. 1977. Integrity considerations for secure computer systems. Technical Report MTR-3153, rev., Bedford, MA: MITRE.

Bonatti, P., and P. Samarati. 2002. A unified framework for regulating access and information release on the Web. *Journal of Computer Security* 10(3):241–72.

Bradley, N. 2002. *The XML companion*. 3rd ed. Reading, MA: Addison Wesley.

Castano, S., M. G. Fugini, G. Martella, and P. Samarati. 1995. *Database security*. Reading, MA: Addison-Wesley.

Coar, K. 2001. Using .htaccess files with Apache. http://apache-server.com/tutorials/ATusing-htaccess.html (accessed May 27, 2007).

Damiani, E., S. De Capitani di Vimercati, S. Paraboschi, and P. Samarati. 2002. A fine-grained access control system for XML documents. *ACM Transactions on Information and System Security* (TISSEC) 5(2): 169–202.

Database Language SQL—Parts 1–5. 2003. ISO International Standard, ISO/IEC 9075:2003. www-compsci.swan.ac.uk/~csroger/StandardSQL.doc (accessed May 27, 2007).

De Capitani di Vimercati, S., and P. Samarati. 2005 New directions in access control. In *Cyberspace security and defense: Research issues*. Boston: Kluwer Academic.

Fielding, R., J. Gettys, J. Mogul, H. Frystyk, L. Masinter, P. Leach, and T. Berners-Lee. 1999. *Hypertext transfer protocol -HTTP/1.1*. www.rfc-editor.org/rfc/rfc2616.txt (accessed May 27, 2007).

Gabillon, A. 2004. An authorization model for XML databases. In *Proceedings of the ACM Workshop Secure Web Services, George Mason University, Fairfax, VA*, October 2004. New York: ACM Press.

Godik, S., and T. Moses. 2004. eXtensible access control markup language (XACML) www.oasis-open.org/committees/xacml/repository/cs-xacml-specification-1.1.pdf (accessed May 27, 2007).

Gong, L. 1999. *Inside Java 2 platform security*. Reading, MA: Addison-Wesley.

Jajodia, S., P. Samarati, M. L. Sapino, and V. S. Subrahmanian. 2001. Flexible support for multiple access control policies. *ACM Transactions on Database Systems* 26(2):18–28.

Jajodia, S., and R. S. Sandhu. 1991. Toward a multilevel secure relational data model. In *Proceedings of the ACM SIGMOD International Conference on Management of Data, Denver, CO*, 50–9. New York: ACM Press.

Lampson, B. W. 1974. Protection. *ACM Operating Systems Review* 8(1):18–24.

Loscocco, P., and S. Smalley. 2001. Integrating flexible support for security policies into the Linux operating system. www.nsa.gov/seLinux/papers/freenix01.pdf (accessed May 27, 2007).

Moses T. 2005 eXtensible Access Control Markup Language (XACML) Version 2.0 http:// docs.oasis-open.org/xacml/2.0/XACML-2.0-OS-NORMATIVE.zip (accessed June 1, 2007).

Newcomer, E. 2002. *Understanding Web services : XML, WSDL, SOAP, and UDDI*. Reading, MA: Addison Wesley.

Samarati, P., and S. De Capitani di Vimercati. 2001. Access control: Policies, models, and mechanisms. In *Foundations of Security Analysis and Design*, edited by R. Focardi and R. Gorrieri. New York: Springer-Verlag Lecture Notes in Computer Science, 2171.

Sandhu, R. 1990. Separation of duties in computerized information systems. http://www.list.gmu.edu/confrnc/ifip/i90sep.pdf (accessed May 27, 2007).

Sandhu, R., D. Ferraiolo, and R. Kuhn. 2000. The NIST model for role-based access control: Towards a unified standard. In *Proceedings of the Fifth ACM Workshop on Role-Based Access Control, Berlin Germany, July 2000*, 47–63, New York: ACM Press.

Sandhu, R., and P. Samarati. 1997. Authentication, access control and intrusion detection. In *CRC Handbook of Computer Science and Engineering*, 1929–48. Boca Raton, FL: CRC Press.

Sandhu, R., E. J. Coyne, H. L. Feinstein, and C. E. Youman. 1996. Role-based access control models. *IEEE Computer* 29(2):38–47.

Seamons, K., M. Winslett, and T. Yu. 2001. Limiting the disclosure of access control policies during automated trust negotiation. In *Proceedings of the Network and Distributed System Security Symposium (NDSS 2001), San Diego, CA, USA, 2001*. New York: ACM Press.

XML Encryption Syntax and Processing, W3C Recommendation. 2002. www.w3.org/TR/xmlenc-core (accessed May 27, 2007).

XML-Signature Syntax and Processing, W3C Recommendation. 2002. www.w3.org/TR/xmldsig-core (accessed May 27, 2007).

Biometrics

James L. Wayman, *San Jose State University*

INTRODUCTION

The importance of data security in networked computer environments has been emphasized since the beginning of such networks (IBM 1970; National Bureau of Standards 1977; Wasserman 1969). One long-recognized key to maintaining data security is the "consistent verification of both the identification and authorization of the individual subject and terminal, depending upon the degree of security required, *each time* an attempt is made to access restricted data" (IBM 1970). IBM listed "three basic ways to identify a terminal subject: 1) By something he knows or memorizes, ... 2) By something he carries, ... 3) By a personal physical characteristic." The process of recognizing subjects by personal physical characteristics is now referred to as "biometric authentication," or more simply "biometrics." These technologies have become far more available and practical since first being introduced in the 1960s and are now important alternatives to "something he knows or memorizes" (personal identification numbers [PINs] and passwords) or "something he carries" (fob, key, or badge) for recognizing individual network subjects and connecting them with their authorizations. In this chapter, we will look at these technologies in general, and give case studies of some specific applications of biometrics to computer network security.

FUNDAMENTAL CONCEPTS

"Biometric authentication" can be defined as the automated recognition of individual persons based on distinguishing biological (usually anatomical) and behavioral traits. The field is a subset of the broader field of human identification science. At the current level of technology, DNA analysis is a laboratory technique not fully automated and requiring human processing, so it is not considered "biometric authentication" under this definition. Examples of technologies currently in use to control access to computer networks or physical spaces containing computer network hardware include: fingerprint, speaker, face, hand geometry, hand vein, and iris recognition. Some techniques (such as iris recognition) are more biologically based, some (such as speaker recognition) are more behaviorally based, but all techniques are influenced by both behavioral and biological elements.

"Biometric authentication" is frequently referred to simply as "biometrics," although this word has historically been associated with the statistical analysis of general biological data. *Biometrics,* like *genetics,* is usually treated as singular. It first appeared in the vocabulary of physical and information security around 1980 (Pollack 1981) as a substitute for the earlier descriptor, "automatic personal identification," in use in the 1970s. Biometric systems recognize "individual persons" by recognizing "bodies." The distinction between person and body is subtle (Baker 2000; Martin and Barresi 2003), but it is of key importance in understanding the inherent capabilities and limitations of these technologies. In this chapter, we will adopt the conventional terms *individual, person,* and *subject,* although we really mean "body." In our context, biometrics deals with computer recognition of signal patterns created by body behaviors and biological structures and is usually associated more with the field of computer engineering and statistical pattern analysis than with the behavioral or biological sciences.

The perfect biometric measure for all applications would possess the following five properties:

Distinctive: Different from individual to individual
Repeatable: Similar across time for each individual
Accessible: Easily displayed to a sensor
Acceptable: Not objectionable to persons
Universal: Possessed by and observable on all people

Unfortunately, no biometric measure has all of the above properties: there are great similarities among the sensor patterns generated by different individuals; measures associated with each individual change over time; some physical limitations prevent display; "acceptability" is in the mind of the subject; not all people have all characteristics. Practical biometric technologies must compromise on every point. Consequently, the challenge of biometric deployments is to develop robust systems to deal with the vagaries and variations of discernible characteristics of human beings.

All biometric systems verify claims (test hypotheses) regarding the source of a biometric pattern in the database. In application to computer network access control, the claim is a positive one, as in "I am the source of a biometric data record in the database," and will be accompanied by the submission of a "live" sample of the biometric pattern to be compared to the stored biometric record. This stored record is called the "biometric reference." Claims can be made specific, such as "I am the source of the biometric reference for subject A in the database," or can remain unspecified, requiring the computer to search the database for a matching reference. Claims need not involve a person's "real" name, so biometrics can be used anonymously. Implicit in the application of biometric recognition to computer network security is that the biometric data will be linked to a subject record, containing the network authorizations established at the time the biometric reference was created. Recognizing the person establishes a link to the authorizations and perhaps other data, such as a legal name, network usage records, and the like. In this chapter, we will call the subject data associated with an enrollment record an "identity" and will use the terms identity and *enrollment record* interchangeably. There is no need, however, for this identity to correspond to any identity for the same person in any other system. Biometrics is agnostic as to whom a person "really is" and cannot resolve the philosophical and moral issues of who a person "should be".

This approach to person recognition can be contrasted with the use of "something he knows" or "something he carries" in that biometrics links recognition to the person's body, not to knowledge or possessions, which are easily transferred (intentionally or unintentionally) to nonauthorized persons. Consequently, biometrics can be considered more secure than other forms of person recognition. But, in contrast to knowledge or possessions, biometric patterns cannot be replaced if compromised and are subject, like other forms of person recognition, to forgery and replay attacks (Geller et al. 1999; van der Putte and Keuning 2000; Lewis and Statham 2004; Matsumoto et al. 2002). Like "something he carries" biometrics will generally require specialized collection hardware at each point of service (keystroke and speaker recognition being possible exceptions). This is in contrast to "something he knows," which can be communicated to the network via an existing keyboard or numeric pad.

More general applications of biometrics also include verification of negative claims, such as "I am not the source of any biometric reference in the database," Social service and driver licensing systems make use of negative-claim biometric components to prevent multiple enrollments of a single individual. Whereas positive-claim systems can restrict each network identity to a single human subject, negative-claim systems can restrict each human subject to a single identity within the network, if that function is required.

Systems requiring a positive subject claim to a specific identity treat the biometric reference as an attribute of the enrollment record. These systems "verify" that the biometric reference in the claimed enrollment record matches the sample submitted by the subject and are called "verification" systems. Some systems, such as those for social service and driver licensing, verify a negative claim by a subject of having no identity record already in the database by treating the biometric pattern as a record identifier or pointer. These systems search the database of biometric pointers to find one matching the submitted sample and are called "identification" systems. However, the act of finding an identifier (or pointer) in a list of identifiers also verifies an unspecific claim of enrollment in the database, and not finding a pointer verifies a negative claim of no enrollment. Consequently, the differentiation between "identification" and "verification" systems is not always clear, and these terms are not mutually exclusive.

In the simplest systems, "verification" of a positive claim to a specific identity in the network might require the comparison of submitted samples to only the biometric references in the single claimed identity record. For example, a person might claim to be a specific, authorized network user. To prove this, she would type in an identity record identifier (perhaps a name or ID number), then place her finger on a glass platen of an electronic imaging device. The system would compare the sample fingerprint against the fingerprint reference in the claimed identity record. If the two were reasonably close, the system would conclude that the subject is indeed connected to the identity record and therefore should be afforded the rights and privileges associated with that identity.

Simple identification, done without a specific claim by the subject to an enrolled identity record, might require the comparison of the submitted biometric samples to all of the biometric references stored in the database. A personal computer log-on, for instance, can be implemented simply by the placement of the finger onto a scanner embedded in the keyboard. If the fingerprint matches any of those enrolled in the log-on database, that identity record is opened and its authorizations are granted.

Other "identification" applications, however, are much more complex. The State of California requires applicants for social service benefits to verify the negative claim of no previous enrollment in the system by submitting fingerprints from both index fingers to the Statewide Finger Imaging System. Depending on the specific automated search strategy, these fingerprints might be searched against the entire database of enrolled benefit recipients to verify that there are no matching fingerprints already in the system. If matching fingerprints are found, the enrollment record associated with those fingerprints is returned to the system administrator to confirm the rejection of the applicant's claim of no previous enrollment.

These are examples of the simplest systems. More advanced systems might use comparisons with multiple enrolled references for verification of linkage to a single, claimed identity or only a very limited number of comparisons when there is no claim to a specific enrolled reference. There is no dependable relationship between "verification" or "identification" and the number of comparisons that the system is required to make.

Network security systems generally use biometrics to verify positive subject claims to a specific or nonspecific identity in the database. These systems are commonly called "verification" systems regardless of the search strategy or architecture used. If a claim to an enrolled identity is verified, authorizations contained in the verified or identified enrollment record can then be applied with confidence to the requested activities, such as a computer log-on. Although hybrid systems are also possible, such as those that verify the negative claim that a subject does not already have an identity in the database at the time of enrollment and then verify in later encounters positive claims to an existing identity in the database, they are not currently widespread.

Biometric technologies are playing a growing role in computer network security today to connect persons to system authorizations through verification of claims of enrolled identity. The argument can be made that biometric measures more closely link the authentication process to the human network user than "what you have" or "what you know." Biometric measures are not as easy to transfer, forget, or steal as PINs, passwords, and tokens, so they may increase the security level of systems using them. Biometrics can be combined with PINs and tokens into multifactor systems for added security should the PINs or tokens be stolen or compromised.

A SHORT HISTORY

The science of recognizing people based on physical measurements was invented by the French police clerk, Alphonse Bertillon, who began his work in the late 1870s (Beavan 2001; Cole 2001). The Bertillon system involved multiple measurements, including height, weight, the length and width of the head, width of the cheeks, and the lengths of the trunk, feet, ears, forearms, and middle and little fingers. Categorization of iris color and pattern was also included in the system. By the 1880s, the Bertillon system was in use in France to identify repeat criminal offenders. Use of the system in the United States for the identification of prisoners began shortly thereafter and continued into the 1920s.

Although research on fingerprinting by a British colonial magistrate in India, William Herschel, began in the late 1850s, knowledge of the technique did not become known in the Western world until the 1880s (Faulds 1880; Herschel, 1880) when it was popularized scientifically by Sir Francis Galton (1888) and in literature by Mark Twain (1893). Galton's work also included the identification of persons from profile facial measurements.

By the mid-1920s, fingerprinting had completely replaced the Bertillon system within the U.S. Bureau of Investigation (later to become the Federal Bureau of Investigation). Research on new methods of human identification continued, however, in the scientific world. Handwriting analysis was recognized by 1929 (Osborn, 1929) and retinal identification was suggested in 1935 (Simon and Goldstein 1935).

These techniques were not automatic, however, so none of them meets the definition of "biometric authentication" being used in this chapter. Automatic techniques require automatic computation. Work in automatic speaker recognition can be traced directly to experiments with analog filters conducted in the 1940s (Potter, Kopp, and Green 1947) and early 1950s (Chang, Pihl, and Essignmann 1951). With the increasing availability of industrial and government computers in the 1960s, speech (Pruzansky 1963) and fingerprint (Trauring 1963, On the automatic comparison) pattern recognition were among the very first applications in automatic signal processing. By 1963, a "wide, diverse market" for automatic fingerprint recognition was identified, with potential applications in "credit systems" and "industrial and military security systems" and for "personal locks" (Trauring 1963, Automatic comparison). Computerized facial recognition research followed (Bledsoe 1966; Goldstein, Harmon, and Lesk 1971). In the 1970s, the first operational fingerprint and hand geometry systems were fielded, results from formal biometric system tests were reported (Wegstein 1970), measures from multiple biometric devices were being combined (Messner et al. 1974; Fejfar 1978) and government testing guidelines were published (National Bureau of Standards 1977). In the 1980s, fingerprint scanners and speaker recognition systems were being connected to personal computers to control access to stored information. Based on a concept patented in the 1980s (Flom and Safir 1987), iris recognition systems became available in the mid-1990s (Daugman 1993; Siedlarz et al. 1995). Today there are over a dozen approaches used in commercially available systems, using hand and finger geometry, iris and fingerprint patterns, face images, voice and signature dynamics, computer keystroke, and hand vein patterns.

SYSTEM DESCRIPTION

Overview

Given the variety of applications and technologies, it might seem difficult to draw any generalizations about biometric systems. However, all such systems have many elements in common. Biometric samples are acquired from a person (the "subject") by a sensor. During enrollment, these samples can be stored directly as the references for that subject. More commonly, the sensor output is sent to a processor, which extracts the distinctive but repeatable measures of the signal (the "features"), discarding all other components. If the subject is claiming no previous enrollment, the features can be compared to references from all enrolled subjects to verify this claim before a new identity record is created and the features are accepted as the reference "template" for the new record. Features might be processed further to produce a more complex statistical "model" to be stored as the subject reference instead of a template. An enrolled subject seeking access to a network will generally submit biometric samples to be compared to an enrolled reference in a claimed identity record linking the subject to network authorizations. The subject may identify the claimed identity record by entering a PIN, or through a token of some type, containing a pointer to the centrally stored, claimed record and its biometric reference. Alternatively, the claimed identity and its biometric reference might be stored on a token in the subject's possession so that the subject supplies both

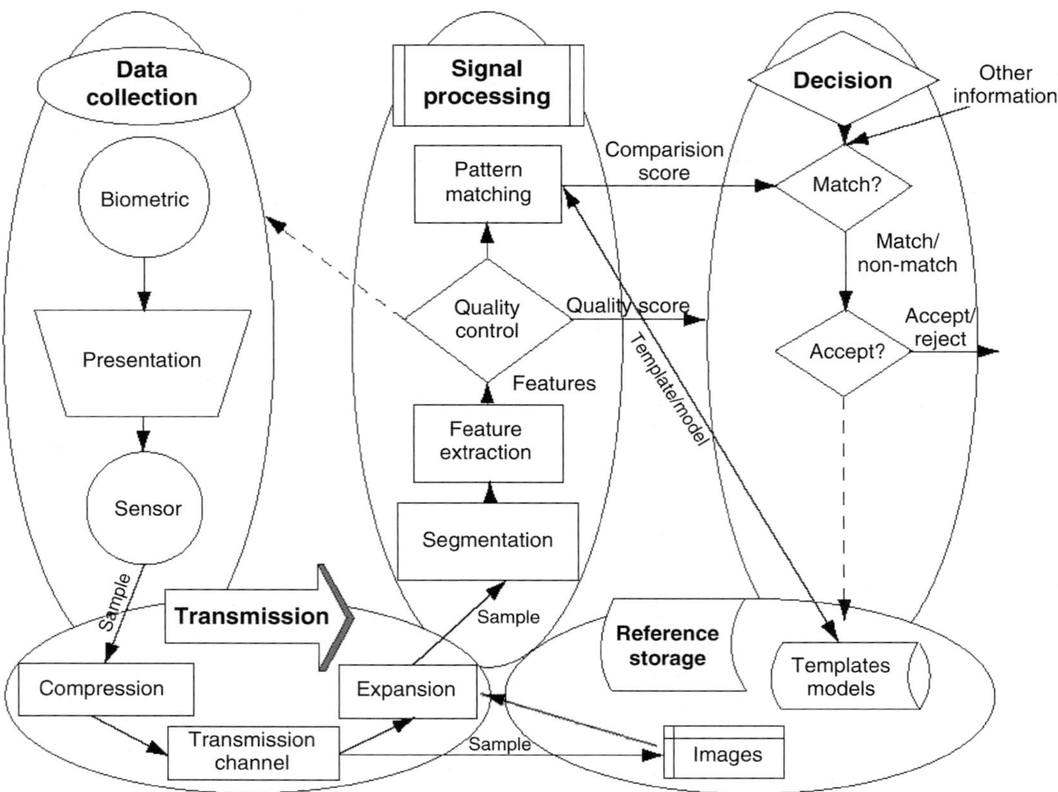

Figure 1: Example of a biometric system

a biometric sample to a sensor and a token from which the stored reference is read. Some highly distinctive biometric patterns, such as those of fingerprints or irises, may be submitted without the claim to a specific enrollment reference, thus necessitating a search of all references in a centralized database to find a "match" and thereby link to the appropriate subject authorizations.

Figure 1 illustrates this information flow, showing a general biometric system consisting of data collection, transmission, signal processing, reference storage, and decision subsystems. This diagram illustrates both enrollment and operation of systems designed for verifying specific or unspecific, positive or negative claims of enrollment. In the following sections, we will go through each of these subsystems in detail.

Data Collection

Biometric systems begin with the collection of a signal from a behavioral/biological characteristic. As data from a biometric sensor can be one-dimensional (speech), two-dimensional (fingerprint), or multidimensional (handwriting dynamics), we are not generally dealing with "images." To simplify our vocabulary, we refer to the sensor output simply as "samples."

Key to all systems is the underlying assumption that the signal from the biometric characteristic being observed is both distinctive between individuals and repeatable over time for the same individual. Therefore, it is desirable that there be as much variation between individuals, and as little variation between multiple samples from the same individual, as possible. The challenges of controlling these sample variations begin in the data-collection subsystem.

The subject's biometric characteristic must be observed by a sensor, such as a microphone, CCD (charge-coupled device)-based fingerprint scanning chip, or digital camera. In systems in which a subject seeks verification of a positive claim to an enrolled identity, the subject can cooperatively present the characteristic to the sensor. The act of presenting a biometric characteristic to a sensor introduces a behavioral component to every biometric method, as the subject must interact with the sensor in the collection environment. The output of the sensor is the combination of: (1) the biometric characteristic; (2) the way the characteristic is presented; and (3) the technical properties of the sensor. All measurements and decisions made by the system will be based on this sensor output. Both the repeatability and the distinctiveness of the measurement are negatively impacted by changes in any of these three factors. We must emphasize the importance of good ergonomic design on item 2, allowing users of the system to easily and quickly present biometric characteristics. If a system is to exchange data with other systems, the presentation constraints and sensor properties must be standardized (International Standards Organization 2005, Parts 2, 4, 5, and 6) to ensure that biometric characteristics collected with one system will match those collected on the same individual by another system.

Transmission

Some biometric systems collect samples at one location but process them at another. If a great amount of data is involved, data compression may be required to conserve transmission bandwidth. Systems storing unprocessed biometric samples as the references do so in a compressed format. Figure 1 shows compression and transmission occurring before signal processing or sample storage. The transmitted or stored compressed data must be expanded before further use. The process of compression and expansion generally causes quality loss in the restored sample, with loss increasing with higher compression ratios. An interesting area of research is in finding, for a given biometric technique, compression methods with minimum negative impact on the subsequent signal-processing activities. Interestingly, limited compression has been observed, in many cases, to improve the performance of the pattern-recognition software (Watson and Wilson 2005), as information loss in the original signal is generally in the less repeatable high-frequency components.

Signal Processing

The biometrics signal-processing subsystem is composed of four modules: segmentation, feature extraction, quality control, and pattern matching. The segmentation module must determine whether any biometric signals exist in the received data stream (signal detection) and, if so, extract the signal from the surrounding noise. If the segmentation module fails to properly detect or extract a biometric signal, we say that a "failure-to-acquire" has occurred.

The feature-extraction module must process the signal in some way to preserve or enhance the between-individual variation (distinctiveness) while minimizing the within-individual variation (nonrepeatability). The output of this module is numbers that, although called biometric "features," may not have direct biological or behavioral interpretation. For example, the numerical values developed by a facial recognition system do not indicate the width of the lips, length of the nose, or the distance between the eyes and the mouth, but rather represent the face in a more abstract, mathematically based way, such as by "decomposing" the face into "basis" faces. In this process, a preset collection (perhaps 128) of generic "basis" faces can be combined with determined intensities to approximate the face being decomposed. The values of these intensities are the numbers by which the face will be recognized.

The quality-control module must do a statistical "sanity check" on the extracted features to make sure they are not outside population statistical norms. If the sanity check is not successfully passed, the system may be able to alert the subject to resubmit the biometric pattern. If the biometric system is ultimately unable to produce an acceptable feature set from a subject, a "failure-to-enroll" or a "failure-to-acquire" will have occurred. Failure-to-enroll/acquire may be due to failure of the segmentation algorithm, in which case no feature set will be produced. The quality-control module might even impact the decision process, directing the decision subsystem to adopt higher requirements for matching a poor-quality input sample, for instance.

The pattern-matching module compares sample feature data with previously enrolled feature data ("templates") or feature data models (such as neural network or Gaussian mixture models) from the database and produces a numerical "comparison score." When both the reference and features are vectors, the comparison score may be as simple as a Euclidean distance. In more complex systems, statistical measures, such as likelihood ratios, might be used instead. Some pattern-matching modules may even direct the adaptive recomputation of features from the input data to see whether better matches might be made through small adjustments to the input data. Regardless of what pattern-matching technique is used, references and features from samples will never exactly match because of the repeatability issues already discussed. Consequently, the comparison scores determined by the pattern-matching module will have to be interpreted by the decision subsystem.

Decision

The decision subsystem is considered separately from the pattern-matching module. The decision subsystem might make a simple "match" or "no match" determination by comparing the output score from the pattern-matching module against a predetermined threshold value. A subject claim of an identity within a system will be accepted if a match is determined. A subject claim of no identity within a system will be rejected if a match is determined. Consequently, relating "match" and "no match" decisions to claim "acceptance" or "rejection" will depend on the claim being made. System policy may require that the ultimate "acceptance" or "rejection" of a subject's claim be based on multiple "match/no match" decisions from multiple measures or from some dynamically determined, subject-dependent or measure-dependent decision criterion. For instance, common decision policies will accept a subject claim to an identity record if a match occurs in any of three attempts or against any one of several stored references.

The decision module might also direct operations to the stored database, storing features as reference templates during enrollment, updating references in the database after a successful transaction, calling up additional references for comparison in the pattern-matching module, or directing a database search.

Because input samples and stored references will never exactly match, the decision modules will make mistakes—wrongly rejecting a correctly claimed identity of an enrolled subject or wrongly accepting the identity claim of an impostor. Thus, there are two types of errors: false rejection and false acceptance. In systems verifying positive subject claims to identity, these errors can be traded off against one another to a limited extent: decreasing false rejections at the cost of increased false acceptances and vice versa. In practice, however, inherent within-individual variation (nonrepeatability) limits the extent to which false rejections can be reduced, short of accepting all comparisons. The decision policies regarding match/no match and the accept/reject criteria are specific to the operational and security requirements of the system and reflect the ultimate cost and likelihood of errors of both types. These errors can be reduced if the sample size is increased—that is, a number of repeated data inputs are taken from the subject.

Because of the inevitability of false rejections, all biometric systems must have exception-handling mechanisms in place. If exception-handling mechanisms are not as strong as the basic biometric security system, vulnerability will result. High numbers of falsely rejected transactions may overload even strong exception-handling mechanisms and lower the responsiveness of system management to potential attacks on the system. Consequently, a high false rejection rate can lead not only to subject inconvenience and operational delays, but to a compromise in system security as well.

In a system assessing a positive claim, the false acceptance rate measures the percentage of "zero effort" impostor transactions that result in access to the system. The false acceptance rate should never be confused with the probability that a successful transaction is actually fraudulent. This latter probability depends on both the false acceptance rate and the percentage of all transaction attempts that are actually by impostors. Depending on the application and how alarms are handled, even a 20 percent false acceptance rate (which indicates an 80 percent probability of intercepting an impostor) may be low enough to decrease the frequency of attacks on the biometric system to the point at which there are no successful impostor transactions. Truly determined fraudulent persons might find other entry points, including the exception-handling mechanism, more appealing than the biometric portal.

Consequently, the security level provided by a biometric system might be as sensitive to the false rejection rate as it is to the false acceptance rate. Sound practice would indicate that we do not rely only on a single biometric safeguard to catch every impostor, do not place extreme emphasis on attaining near-zero false acceptance rates, and continue to couple biometrics with other methods, such as PINs and passwords.

Reference Storage

The remaining subsystem to be considered is that of reference storage. Submitted samples, extracted features, or the feature-generated model of each enrolled subject is stored in an identity record in the database for future comparison by the pattern matcher to incoming samples. Systems for verifying negative claims of identity require a centralized database (or the equivalent—linked decentralized databases) of all enrolled references to verify a claim that a person does not have an identity in the system. Such systems generally return the records of any enrollments found, and so are called "identification" systems, as previously discussed. Large-scale identification systems generally partition the database using factors such as gender or age so that not all centrally stored references need be examined to establish that a person is not in the database. Such systems are sometimes loosely called "one-to-N" or "one-to-many" to indicate that a submitted sample must be compared to multiple identity records.

For systems only verifying positive claims to a specific identity, the database of references may be distributed on magnetic stripe, optically read, or smart cards carried by each enrolled subject; no centralized database need exist. Such positive verification systems are sometimes loosely called "one-to-one," to indicate that biometric samples might be compared to the references of only the single claimed identity. However, verification systems based on likelihood-estimation techniques compare samples not only to the claimed references, but also to the references of other subjects or to "background models," and therefore might not be strictly "one-to-one" with regard to the total number of comparisons required.

Although distributed storage is possible, positive claim verification systems might use a centralized, encrypted database to prevent creation of counterfeit cards or to reissue lost cards without re-collecting the biometric data.

The original biometric measurement, such as a fingerprint pattern, is generally not reconstructable from its stored reference, unless that reference is in the form of a compressed sample. However, if access can be had to unencrypted references of any type, it is quite possible for a knowledgeable hacker in possession of an identical system to construct an artifact capable of matching the compromised reference. Unlike PINs and passwords, however, biometric data cannot be changed at the request of the subject. For this reason, biometric references must always be protected as sensitive data and will generally require encryption, even when stored on user-controlled cards. Several forms of encryption specific to biometric data have been proposed in the literature (Kumar, Khosla, and Savvides 2004; Ratha, Connell, and Bolle 2001; Hao, Anderson, and Daugman 2005). The decision to maintain a centralized reference database for verification applications should be done with an assessment of the privacy and security risks should the database be compromised.

Table 1 shows some examples of unencrypted template sizes for various biometric devices.

PERFORMANCE TESTING

Biometric devices and systems might be tested in many different ways. Types of testing include:

Technical performance
Reliability, availability, and maintainability (RAM)
Vulnerability
Security
User acceptance
Human factors
Cost/benefit
Privacy regulation compliance

Table 1: Biometric Template Sizes

Device	Size in Bytes
Fingerprint	200–1000
Speaker	100–6000
Finger geometry	14–48
Hand geometry	9–72
Face	100–3500
Iris	512

Technical performance has been the most common form of testing in the past four decades. Technical tests are generally conducted with the goal of predicting system performance with a target population in a target environment, but historically, extrapolation of results from a test environment to the "real world" has been difficult. This may be largely due to the variability of human performance between the lab and the field. Ultimately "technical performance" is a measure of how well people perform when interacting with these technologies.

Technical tests can be either "closed-set" or "open-set". A "closed-set" test assumes that all subjects are enrolled in the system and does not acknowledge the existence of impostors. A closed-set test returns the rank of the true comparison when an input sample is compared to all of the enrolled patterns. Closed-set tests measure the probability that the true pattern was found at rank k or better in the search against the database of size N. In any test, the rank k probability is dependent on the database size, decreasing as the database size (i.e., number of references) increases.

An "open-set" test does not require that all input samples be represented by a reference in the enrolled database and measures all comparison scores against a score threshold. An open-set test returns, as a function of the threshold, the probability of either missing a true comparison (the false nonmatch rate) or matching on a wrong comparison (the false match rate). Open-set measures are independent of the size of the database searched, converging to the correct estimator as the test size increases. Examples of both open-set and closed-set tests are found in the literature, but since most applications must acknowledge the potential for impostors, open-set results are of greater practical value to the system designer or analyst.

To make test results more predictive of real-world performance, testing "best practices" (Mansfield and Wayman 2002) and standards (International Standards Organization 2006) have been developed. Metrics generally collected in open-set technical tests are: failure-to-enroll, failure-to-acquire, false nonmatch, false match, false acceptance, false rejection, and throughput rates. Failure-to-enroll rate is determined as the percentage of all persons presenting themselves to the system in "good faith" for enrollment who are unable to do so because of system or human failure. Failure-to-acquire rate is determined as the percentage of "good faith" presentations by all enrolled persons who are not acknowledged by the system. The false nonmatch rate is the probability that a single sample from a randomly chosen, "good faith" subject will not match his own reference. The false match rate is the probability that a single biometric sample from a randomly chosen subject (acting in "good faith" to match her own reference) will be wrongly matched to a single reference of a different, randomly chosen subject.

In biometric systems in which subjects make a positive claim to linkage with an identity, such as access control to computer networks, the false rejection rate is the percentage of all subjects whose claim to identity is not accepted by the system after some number of attempts. This will include failed enrollments and failed acquisitions, as well as false nonmatches against the subject's stored reference. The false acceptance rate for positive claim systems is the rate at which "zero-effort" impostors making no attempt at impersonation are incorrectly matched, after some number of attempts, to a single, randomly chosen false identity. Because false acceptance/rejection (as well as false match/nonmatch rates) are competing measures, they can be displayed together on a "decision error tradeoff" (DET) curve.

The throughput rate is the number of persons processed by the system per minute, and includes both the human-machine interaction time and the computational processing time of the system. Ultimately, the throughput and error rates will be dependent on the interaction of the humans with the technology. This implies that not only will good ergonomic design be of great importance, but so will subject attitudes and perceptions.

Types of Technical Tests

Three types of technical tests have been described: technology, scenario, and operational (Phillips et al. 2000; International Standards Organization 2006; Wayman et al. 2005).

Technology Test

The goal of a technology test is to compare competing algorithms from a single technology, such as fingerprinting, against a standardized database collected with a "universal" sensor. There are competitive, government-sponsored technology tests in speaker verification (Martin, Przybocki, and Campbell 2005; NIST 2006), facial recognition (Phillips et al. 2005), and fingerprinting (Maio et al. 2002; Wilson et al. 2004; Watson et al. 2005; Capelli et al. 2006).

Scenario Test

Whereas the goal of technology testing is to assess the algorithm, the goal of scenario testing is to assess the performance of the subjects as they interact with the complete system in an environment that models a "real-world" application. Each system tested will have its own acquisition sensor and so will receive slightly different data. Scenario testing has been performed by a number of groups, but few results have been published openly (Fejfar and Myers 1977; Rodriguez, Bouchier, and Ruehie 1993; Bouchier, Ahrens, and Wells 1996; Mansfield et al. 2001). Scenarios may differ with regard to variables such as the level of subject habituation, cooperation and supervision, the physical environment of enrollment and collection (i.e., indoor/outdoor), whether subjects are from the general or more restricted populations, and whether references are collected on the same system or collected elsewhere and imported.

Operational Test

The goal of operational testing is to determine the performance of a target population in a specific application environment with a complete biometric system. In general, operational test results will not be repeatable because of unknown and undocumented differences between operational environments. Further, "ground truth" (i.e., who was actually presenting a "good faith" biometric measure) will be difficult to ascertain. Because of the sensitivity of information regarding error rates of operational systems, few results have been reported in the open literature (Wayman 2000).

Regardless of the type of test, all biometric authentication techniques require human interaction with a data-collection device, either standing alone (as in technology testing) or as part of an automatic system (as in scenario and operational testing). Consequently, humans are a key component in all system assessments. Error, failure-to-enroll/acquire, and throughput rates are determined by the human interaction, which in turn depends on the specifics of the collection environment. Therefore, little can be said beyond the context of the test about the performance of biometric systems, or more accurately, about the performance of the humans as they interact with biometrics systems.

The National Physical Lab Tests

A study by the U.K. National Physical Laboratory (Mansfield et al. 2001) looked at eight commercially available biometric products in a scenario test designed to emulate access control to computer networks or physical spaces by scientific professionals in a quiet office environment. A more detailed description of the products, test environment and volunteer population is available in the original report.

The false accept/false reject DET under a "three-tries" decision policy for this test is shown in Figure 2. The false rejection rate includes failure-to-enroll/acquire rates in its calculation.

Figure 2 allows estimation of the false rejection rate for each of the tested products for any required false acceptance rate, but only for this test environment and this set of test subjects. The figure does not show the decision thresholds required to attain those false acceptance rates. The tested products may not be representative of the technology in general and it is not possible to extrapolate these results to any other application environment or set of test subjects. For example, the figure shows that it is possible for National Physical Laboratory subjects using hand geometry to attain a 1 percent false rejection rate at a 0.1 percent false acceptance rate in this environment. A failure-to-enroll was considered as a "false rejection" in the computation of this figure. These results relate to the average error rates over all subjects. Individuals may have error rates considerably above or below the averages.

It is also important to note that the National Physical Laboratory results do not tell us about the subject error rates with technologies such as PINs and tokens, generally thought to be competitors of biometrics. Determining the strength of biometrics relative to the other mechanisms for personal identification is an unresolved research issue.

The National Physical Laboratory study also established the access control transaction times for the above subjects with the various biometric devices in this office environment as shown in Table 2.

In Table 2, the term "PIN?" indicates whether the transaction time included the manual entry of a four-digit identification number by the subject. These times referred only to the use of the biometric device and did not include actually accessing a restricted area.

BIOMETRICS AND COMPUTER NETWORK SECURITY

Biometrics can have an important role in computer network security, being much more closely linked to an individual and more difficult to forget, give away, or lose than a token, a PIN, or a password. Use of biometrics can provide additional evidence that an authorization credential is being presented by the person to whom it was issued. However, biometric technologies do not represent a silver bullet, eliminating PINs, passwords, and tokens while resolving all security issues.

In devising a system architecture for verifying a positive claim to identity, we must decide whether each biometric reference will be carried by the persons themselves on a token, or whether all references will be stored centrally in a database linked to the point of service by a communications system. The former approach has positive implications for privacy (Kent and Millett 2003), but will require some form of key, such as a PIN or a password, to unlock the biometric measure that will be encrypted on the token. Consequently, all the general issues regarding data security on tokens still exist.

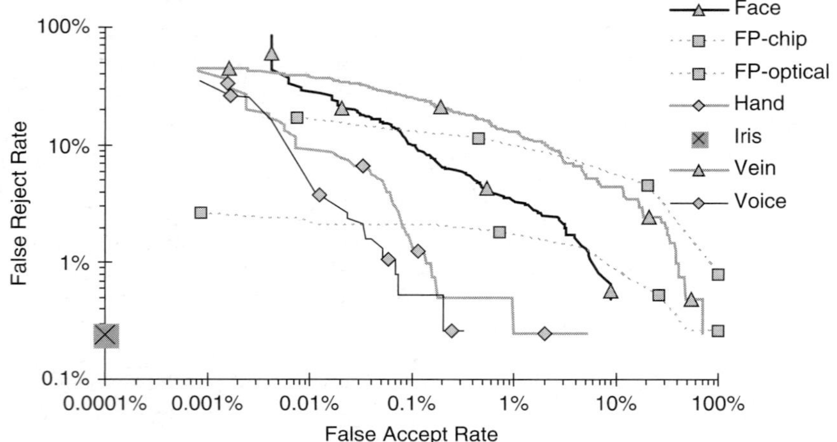

Figure 2: Detection error trade-off curve: best of three attempts

Table 2: Transaction Times in Office Environment

Device	Transaction Time (seconds)			PIN?
	Mean	Median	Minimum	
Face	15	14	10	No
Fingerprint— optical	9	8	2	No
Fingerprint—chip	19	15	9	No
Hand	10	8	4	Yes
Iris	12	10	4	Yes
Vein	18	16	11	Yes
Speaker	12	11	10	No

If biometric references are stored centrally, several questions arise:

1. Will the biometric sample be sent to the central system, or will the central system pass the reference to the point of service for processing? In either case, some strong form of encryption will be required to protect the data during transmission.
2. if the input data is sent from the point of service to the central site, will it be in raw form or processed into features? If processed into features prior to transmission, computational power and knowledge of the feature extraction algorithm will be required at each point of service but transmission bandwidth will be reduced.
3. How will the encrypted data be unencrypted when necessary for comparison?
4. How will the subject judge the point of service to be legitimate and not to be storing the biometric data after transmission?

Although these problems are not insurmountable, they demonstrate that use of biometrics does not eliminate the usual security issues.

It has been well known since the 1970s that biometric devices can be fooled by forgeries (Lummis and Rosenberg, 1972; Raphael and Young 1974; National Bureau of Standards 1977). In a system for verifying positive claims of identity, "spoofing" is the use of a forgery of another person's biometric measures. In a system for verifying a negative claim, spoofing is an attempt to disguise one's own biometric measure. Forging biometric measures of another person is more difficult than disguising one's own measures, but is quite possible nonetheless. Several studies (Blackburn et al. 2000; van der Putte and Keuning 2000; Matsumoto et al. 2002; Thalheim, Krissler, and Ziegler 2002) discuss ways by which facial, fingerprint, and iris biometrics can be forged. Speaker recognition systems can make forgery difficult by requesting the subject to say numbers randomly chosen by computer. However, the current state of technology does not provide reliable "liveness testing" to ensure that the biometric measure is both from a living person *and* not a forgery.

The use of biometrics does not reduce the need to fully scrutinize all applicants for authorizations. A biometric system can neither verify the external truth of the enrolled identity itself nor establish the link automatically to an identity record with complete certainty. Determining an individual's "true" identity, if required, is done at the time of enrollment through trusted external documentation, such as a birth certificate or driver's license. The biometric measures link the individual to an enrolled identity and associated authorizations that are only as valid as the original determination process.

Not all systems, however, have a requirement to know an individual's "true" name or identity. Biometric measures can be used as anonymous and pseudo-anonymous identifiers, and consequently, have intriguing potential for privacy enhancement of authorization systems.

All biometric measures may change over time, because of aging, injury, or disease. Therefore, reenrollment may be required. If "true" identity or continuity of identity is required by the system, reenrollment must necessitate presentation of trusted external documentation. Both enrollment and reenrollment also require the physical presence of the enrolling person before the enrolling authority. Otherwise, there is no way to determine that the enrolled biometric measure came from the body of the person presenting it.

EXAMPLE APPLICATIONS

San Jose State University

San Jose State University has been using hand geometry readers for around-the-clock controlled, secure access to the Computer and Telecommunications Center since 1993. About 125 employees are enrolled in the system and log a combined 500 entrance events each day at the three entrances. The system records all events on a central PC, allowing management to audit after-hours access to the Center.

Employees enter a four-digit PIN into the system and place their right hand down on a reflective platen. Infrared light reflects vertically off the platen, but not the skin, allowing a "shadow" of the hand without the skin texture information to be imaged. In addition, a mirror reflects light horizontally across the top of the hand, supplying a second two-dimensional shadow of the side of the hand. Both of these two-dimensional images are reduced using image-processing techniques to a 9-byte feature vector, the values of which cannot be directly related to finger lengths, widths, or other anatomical measures. If the sample is "close enough" in Euclidean distance to the 9-byte template stored at enrollment, the door strike opens and access is permitted. Upon successful use, the system automatically updates the stored template by averaging in the newly acquired sample. The threshold used to determine "close enough" can be set individually, if necessary, to accommodate anyone having unusual difficulty using the system. The entire access process takes just a few seconds and the false rejection of daily, habituated system users is exceedingly rare.

Impostors would need both a valid PIN and the correct hand shape to gain access to the system. PIN guessing can be prevented by locking the system or sounding an alarm after some number of consecutive access failures.

The hand readers at each door cost about $1,500 in 2006. Some additional items, such as electrically activated door strikes, cabling, and "request to exit" switches were purchased and installed, as well. The door strikes are controlled and powered directly from the hand reader unit. Although the units can stand alone, a central PC is used for event logging and for networking multiple units into a single reference database. University management has been quite pleased with the cost, efficiency, and security of the system.

We can classify this as an application to verify a positive claim of identity, with trained, habituated subjects in an unsupervised office environment. The system is used only by employees of the Computer and Telecommunications Center, so is not a public application. It serves as a good cost, performance, and procedure model only for proposed applications with these same characteristics.

Purdue Employees Federal Credit Union

Since 1997, Purdue Employees Federal Credit Union (PEFCU) in West Lafayette, Indiana, has been using fingerprint verification to replace PINs at five automatic teller machine (ATM) kiosks. About 11,500 customers (20 percent of the PEFCU membership) are enrolled in the system, generating about 28,000 biometrically enabled transactions per month. Customers electing to use fingerprinting can enroll in the system at the central office by presenting any two fingers to an optical scanner. Customers with poor fingerprints due to age or occupation, and customers not wishing to participate, can continue to use traditional PINs at all PEFCU ATMs.

The scanner takes a digital image of the fingerprint, which is converted into "minutiae features," a numerical structure based on the patterns in the fingerprint ridges. These features, but not the original fingerprint image, are stored in a central database. After enrollment, customers can withdraw or deposit cash or apply for loans presenting their ATM card with either enrolled fingerprint to the kiosk scanner. No PIN entry is required. To guide customers in the proper placement of the finger, a display screen on the kiosk shows the customer the image of the presented fingerprint and an image of an ideally placed finger. The features extracted from the presented fingerprint are compared to those in the reference stored in the central database under the entered customer name. Close similarity between the stored and presented features verifies that the customer is the source of the claimed enrollment record and is, therefore, the authorized ATM card holder.

The fingerprinting technology is estimated to represent only a small fraction of the total $70,000 cost of the ATM kiosk. No case of fraud owing to misuse of the fingerprinting system has ever been reported. Incidence of fraud originating from fingerprint-equipped ATMs is currently less than 5 percent of the fraud rate on other ATMs operated by PEFCU. The credit union is currently expanding the fingerprint system to traditional teller lines to eliminate the need for enrolled customers to present photo identification when making cash withdrawals.

We can classify this use by PEFCU as an application to verify a positive claim of identity, with habituated and nonhabituated customers in an unsupervised indoor or outdoor environment. The system is used by a wide cross section of credit union customers, so can be called a public application. Consequently, we would expect the PEFCU application to be more challenging than the San Jose State University Computer Center application, with its more controlled population and environment.

BIOMETRICS AND PRIVACY

The concept of "privacy" is highly culturally dependent. Legal definitions vary from country to country and, in the United States, even from state to state (Alderman and Kennedy 1995). A classic definition is the intrinsic "right to be let alone" (Warren and Brandeis 1890), but more modern definitions include informational privacy: the right of individuals "to determine for themselves when, how and to what extent information about them is communicated to others" (Westin 1967). Both types of privacy can be impacted positively or negatively by biometric technology.

Intrinsic (or Physical) Privacy

Some people see the use of biometric devices as an intrusion on intrinsic privacy. Touching a publicly used biometric device, such as a fingerprint or hand geometry reader, may seem physically intrusive, even though there is no evidence that disease can spread any more easily by these devices than by door handles. People may also object to being asked to look into cameras or to stand still while giving an iris or facial image.

Not all biometric methods require physical contact. A biometric application that replaced the use of a keypad with the imaging of an iris, for instance, might be seen as an enhancement of physical privacy.

If biometrics is used to limit access to private spaces, then biometrics can be more enhancing to intrinsic privacy than other forms of access control, such as keys, which are not as closely linked to the holder.

There are people who object to the use of biometrics on religious grounds: Some Muslim women object to displaying their face to a camera and some Christians object to hand biometrics as the Biblical "the sign of the beast." In response, it has been noted (Siedlarz 1998) that a theistic interpretation would more properly consider biometric patterns to be marks given by God.

It can be argued (Locke 1690; Baker 2000) that a physical body is not identical to the person that inhabits it. Whereas PINs and passwords identify persons, biometrics identifies the body. Some people are uncomfortable with biometrics because of this connection to the physical manifestation of human identity, the possibility of nonconsensual collection, and the impossibility of changing biometric measures if stolen. Biometric measures could allow linking of the various "persons" or psychological identities that each of us choose to manifest in our separate dealings within our social structures. Biometrics, if universally collected without adequate controls, could aid in linking employment records to health history and church membership, for example. This leads us to the concept of "informational privacy."

Informational Privacy

With notably minor qualifications, biometric features contain no personal information whatsoever about the subject. This includes no information about health status, age, nationality, ethnicity, or gender. Consequently, this also limits the power of biometrics to prevent underage access to pornography on the Internet or to detect voting registration by noncitizens.

No single biometric measure has been demonstrated to be distinctive or repeatable enough to allow the selection of a single person out of a very large database. However, when aggregated with other data, such as name, telephone area code, or other even weakly identifying attributes, biometric measures can lead to *unique* identification within a large population. For this reason, databases of biometric information must be treated as personally identifiable information and protected accordingly.

Biometrics can be directly used to enhance informational privacy. Use to control access to and promote accountability with databases containing personal and personally identifiable data can enhance informational privacy. The use of biometric measures, in place of name or social security number, to make personal data anonymous, enhances privacy.

SUGGESTED RULES FOR SECURE USE OF BIOMETRICS

From what has been discussed thus far, we can develop some reasonable rules for the use of biometrics for logical and physical access control, and similar applications.

1. Never participate in a biometric system that allows either remote enrollment or reenrollment. Such systems have no way of connecting a subject with the enrolled biometric data, so the purpose of using biometrics to connect the subject more closely to the authentication mechanism is lost.
2. Biometric measures can reveal your "real" identity only if they are linked at enrollment to your name, social security number, or other closely identifying information. Without that linkage, your biometric measures are anonymous.
3. Remember that biometric measures cannot be reissued if stolen or sold. Do not enroll in a biometric system unless you have complete trust in the system administration.
4. All biometric access control systems must have exception-handling mechanisms for those that either cannot enroll or cannot reliably use the system. If you are uncomfortable with enrolling in a biometric system for verifying positive claims of identity, insist on routinely using the exception-handling mechanism instead.
5. The most privacy-enhancing biometric systems are those in which each subject controls his/her own reference.
6. Because biometric measures are not perfectly repeatable, are not completely distinctive, and require specialized data collection hardware, biometric systems are not useful for tracking people within large populations. Anyone who really wants to physically track the movements of a person in a large population will use credit card or phone records or cell phone emanations instead. But over a small population, biometric measures are distinctive and repeatable enough to provide accountability for activities such as accessing stored information. Consequently, the technology itself should not be feared. In the proper applications, biometrics can be used as a strongly privacy-enhancing technology.

CONCLUSION

Automated methods for human identification have a history predating the digital computer age. For decades, mass adoption of biometric technologies has appeared to be just a few years away (Raphael and Young 1974), yet even today, difficulties remain in establishing a strong business case, in motivating consumer demand, and in creating a single system usable by all sizes and shapes of persons. Nonetheless, the biometric industry has grown at a steady pace as consumers, industry, and government have found appropriate applications for these technologies, particularly in the area of computer security. Although the privacy implications continue to be debated, biometrics can be used in privacy-enhancing applications. At the current level of development, biometric technologies seem to be a reasonable alternative to PINs and passwords in some applications associated with computer network security.

GLOSSARY

Biometric Reference: Stored biometric data used as a pointer to, or an attribute of, an enrollment record for an individual. Data can be in the form of a raw sample, a template consisting of mathematical features extracted from a sample(s), or as a model based on extracted features.

Biometrics: The automatic recognition of individuals based on distinguishing biological and behavioral traits.

Comparison Score: A measure of similarity or dissimilarity between a presented sample and a stored biometric reference.

Decision: A determination of probable validity of an individual's claim to an identity or no identity in the system.

Enrollment: The presentation of an individual to an biometric system for the first time, creating an identity record within the system, and collecting biometric samples for the creation of a biometric reference to that identity.

Failure-to-Acquire Rate: The percentage of transactions for which the system cannot obtain a usable biometric sample.

Failure-to-Enroll Rate: The percentage of a potential system's users for which the system cannot create a usable biometric reference.

False Acceptance rate (FAR): The expected proportion of transactions with wrongful claims of identity (in a positive ID system) or nonidentity (in a negative ID system) that are incorrectly confirmed. In applications to verify positive claims, the FAR will depend on the false match rate and the system policy specifying how many attempts will be allowed to prove the claimed identity. In negative identification systems, the FAR may include the failure-to-acquire rate and the false nonmatch rate.

False Match Rate (FMR): The false match rate is the expected probability that a sample acquired from a individual will be falsely declared to match to a single reference from a different, randomly selected individual.

False Nonmatch Rate (FNMR): The false nonmatch rate is the expected probability that an acquired sample will be falsely declared not to match a reference from the same individual.

False Rejection Rate (FRR): The expected proportion of transactions with truthful claims of identity (in a positive ID system) or nonidentity (in a negative ID system) that are incorrectly denied. In positive identification systems, the FRR will include the failure-to-enroll and the failure-to-acquire rates, as well as the false nonmatch rate.

Features: A mathematical representation of the information extracted from the presented sample by the signal processing subsystem that will be used to construct or compare against biometric references. Biometric features generally have no direct anatomical meaning.

Identifier: An identity pointer, such as a biometric reference, a PIN (personal identification number) or a name.

Identity: An information record about a person, perhaps including attributes or authorizations, or other pointers, such as names or identifying numbers.

Models: Biometric references derived through further mathematical processing of biometric features, perhaps indicative of the feature-generating process.

Negative Claim of Identity: The claim that an individual is neither known to nor enrolled in the system. As an example, social service systems open only to those not already enrolled require all applicants to make negative claims to any existing identity in the system.

Positive Claim of Identity: The claim that an individual is enrolled in or known to the system. A specific positive claim of identity will be accompanied by an identifier in the form of a name, PIN, or identification number. Common access control systems are an example. A nonspecific positive claim of identity will not require any identifier be given other than the biometric sample. "PIN-less" verification systems are an example.

Sample: A biometric signal derived from an individual and captured by the data collection subsystem. (Voice signals, fingerprints, and face images are samples)

Template: A stored reference consisting of features extracted from biometric samples.

Transaction: An attempt by an individual to prove a claim of identity or nonidentity by consecutively submitting one or more samples, as allowed by the system policy.

Verification: Proving as truthful an individual's claim to an identity in the system.

Zero-Effort Impostor: A fraudulent or opportunistic an individual who submits their own biometric measure without alteration in an attempt to make a positive claim to another, randomly chosen identity.

CROSS REFERENCES

See *Authentication; Cryptography; Password Authentication; Smart Cards: Communication Protocols and Applications.*

REFERENCES

Alderman, E., and C. Kennedy. 1995. *The right to privacy*. New York: Vintage.

Baker, L. R. 2000. Persons and bodies: A constitution view. Cambridge, UK: Cambridge University Press.

Beavan, C. 2001. *Fingerprints.* New York: Hyperion.

Blackburn, D. M., J. M. Bone, and P. J. Philips. 2001. Facial vendor recognition test 2000. DoD Counterdrug Technology Development Program Office. http://face.nist.gov/frvt/frvt2000/FRVT_2000.pdf (accessed July 26, 2007).

Bledsoe, W. W. 1966. *Man-machine facial recognition: Report on a large-scale experiment*. Palo Alto, CA: Panoramic Research.

Bouchier, F., J. Ahrens, and G. Wells. 1996. Laboratory evaluation of the IriScan Prototype Biometric Identifier.http://infoserve.library.sandia.gov/sand_doc/1996/961033.pdf (accessed April 21, 2006).

Capelli, R., D. Maio, D. Maltoni, J. Wayman, and A. Jain. 2006. Performance evaluation of state-of-the-art fingerprint verification systems., *Transactions on Pattern Analysis and Machine Intelligence* 28(1):3–18.

Chang, S. H., G. E. Pihl, and M. W. Essignmann. 1951. Representations of speech sounds and some of their statistical properties. *Proceedings of the Institute of Radio Engineers* 39(2):147–53.

Cole, S. 2001. *Suspect identities.* Cambridge, MA: Harvard University Press

Daugman, J. 1993. High confidence visual recognition of persons by a test of statistical independence.

Transactions on Pattern Analysis and Machine Intelligence 15:1148–61 www.cl.cam.ac.uk/users/jgd1000/PAMI93.pdf (accessed April 21, 2006).

Faulds, H. 1880. On the skin furrows of the hand. *Nature* 22:605. www.scafo.org/library/100101.html (accessed April 21, 2006).

Fejfar, A., and J. W. Myers. 1977. The testing of three automatic identity verification techniques. In *Proceedings of the International Conference On Crime Countermeasures,Oxford., July. 25–29, 1977*. Oxford, UK: Oxford University Press.

Fejfar, A. 1978. Combining techniques to improve security in automated entry control. In *Carnahan Conference on Crime Countermeasures*. New York: IEEE Press.

Flom, L. and A. Safir, A. 1987. Iris recognition system. U.S. Patent 4,641,349.

Galton, F. 1888. On personal identification and description. *Nature* 21/28:201–2. www.scafo.org/library/100801.html (accessed May 30, 2006).

Geller, B., J. Almog, P. Margot, and E. Springer. 1999. A chronological review of fingerprint forgery. *Journal of Forensic Sciences* 44(5):963–8.

Goldstein, A. J., L. D. Harmon, and A. B. Lesk. 1971. Identification of human faces. *Proceedings of the Institute of Electrical and Electronic Engineers* 59:748–60.

Hao, F., R. Anderson, and J. Daugman. 2005. *Combining cryptography with biometrics effectively*. Cambridge Computer Laboratory Technical report UCAM-CL-TR-640. www.cl.cam.ac.uk/TechReports/UCAM-CL-TR-640.html (accessed June 10, 2006).

Herschel, W. J. 1880. Skin furrows of the hand. *Nature* 23:76.

IBM. 1970. The considerations of data security in a computer environment. Report G520-2169, White Plains, NY: IBM.

International Standards Organization. 2005. Information technology. Biometric data interchange formats—Part 2: Finger image data. ISO/IEC 19794-2:2005.

International Standards Organization. 2005. Information technology Biometric data interchange formats—Part 4: Finger image data. ISO/IEC 19794-4:2005.

International Standards Organization. 2005. Information technology. Biometric data interchange formats—Part 5: Finger image data. ISO/IEC 19794-5:2005.

International Standards Organization. 2005. Information technology. Biometric data interchange formats—Part 6: Finger image data. ISO/IEC 19794-6:2005.

International Standards Organization. 2006. Information technology. Biometric system testing and reporting—Part 1: Principles and framework, ISO/IEC 19795-1:2006.

Kent, S. T. and L. I. Millett. 2003. *Who goes there? Authentication through the lens of privacy*. Washington, DC: National Academies Press. http://books.nap.edu/html/whogoes/ (accessed April 21, 2006).

Kumar, B. V. K., P. K. Khosla, and M. Savvides. 2004. Cancelable biometric filters for face recognition. In *International Conference of Pattern Recognition, ICPR 2004*. August, 3: 922–925.

Lewis, M., and P. Statham. 2004, CESG Biometric Security Capabilities Programme: Method, results and research challenges. *Biometric Consortium Conference, Arlington, VA*. www.biometrics.org/bc2004/Presentations/Conference/2%20Tuesday%20September%2021/Tue_Ballroom%20A/6%20Special%20Topics/1%20Lewis_presentation.pdf (accessed May 30, 2006).

Locke, J. 1690. *An Essay Concerning Human Understanding*, Book 2, Chapter 27. http://www.ilt.columbia.edu/publications/locke_understanding.html (accessed May 30, 2006).

Lummis, R. C., and A. Rosenberg. 1972. Test of an ASV method with intensively trained professional mimics, *Journal of the Acoustical Society of America* 51:131.

Maio, D., D. Maltoni, J. Wayman, and A. Jain. 2002. FVC2000: Fingerprint verification competition Transactions on Pattern Analysis and Machine Intelligence 24:402–11.

Mansfield, A. J., G. Kelly, D. Chandler, and J. Kane. 2001. *Biometric product testing final report*. www.cesg.gov.uk/site/ast/biometrics/media/BiometricTestReportpt1.pdf (accessed May 30, 2006).

Mansfield, A. J,. and J. L. Wayman. 2002. Best practices for testing and reporting biometric device performance, Issue 2.0, U.K. Biometrics Working Group. www.cesg.gov.uk/site/ast/biometrics/media/BestPractice.pdf (accessed May 30, 2006).

Martin, R., and J. Barresi. 2003. *Personal identity*. Malden, MA: Blackwell.

Martin, A., M. Przybocki, and J. P. Campbell. 2005. The NIST speaker recognition evaluation program. In *Biometric systems: Technology, design and performance evaluation*, edited by Wayman, J. L, et al. London: Springer-Verlag.

Matsumoto, T., H. Matsumoto, Y. Yamada, and S. Hoshino. 2002. Impact of artificial "gummy" fingers on fingerprint systems Washington. *Proceedings SPIE* 4677:275–89.

Messner, W. K., C. A. Cleciwa, G. O. T. H. Kibbler, and W. L. Parlee. 1974. Research and development of personal identify verification systems. In *Proceedings of the 1974 Carnahan and International Crime Countermeasures Conference, University of Kentucky*. Lexington, KY, April 16–19, 1974.

National Bureau of Standards. 1977. Guidelines for evaluation of techniques for automated personal identification, Federal Information Processing Standard Publication; 48. Springfield, VA: National Technical Information Service.

National Institute of Standards and Technology. 2006. Speaker recognition evaluation. www.nist.gov/speech/tests/spk/2006/index.htm (accessed May 30, 2006).

Osborn, S. 1929. *Questioned documents*. Chicago: Nelson-Hall.

Phillips, J. P., D. Blackburn, P. Grother, P. Newton, and J. M. Bone. 2005. Methods for assessing progress in face recognition. In *Biometric systems: Technology, design and performance evaluation*, edited by J. L. Wayman, et al. London: Springer-Verlag.

Phillips, P. J., A. Martin, C. L. Wilson, and M. Przybocki. 2000. An introduction to evaluating biometric systems. *Computer* 33:56–63. www.frvt.org/DLs/FERET7.pdf (accessed May 30, 2006).

Pollack, A. 1981, September 24. Recognizing the real you. *New York Times* D1:2.

Potter, R. K., G. A. Kopp, and H. C. Green. 1947. *Visible speech*. New York: van Nostrand.

Pruzansky, S. 1963. Pattern-matching procedure for automatic talker recognition. *Journal of the Acoustical Society of America* 26:403–6.

Raphael, D. E., and J. R. Young. 1974. *Automated personal identification*. Palo Alto: SRI International.

Ratha, N., J. Connell, and R. Bolle. 2001. Enhancing security and privacy in biometrics-based authentication systems. *IBM Systems Journal* 40(3):614–34.

Rodriguez, J. R., F. Bouchier, and M. Ruehie. 1993. Performance evaluation of biometric identification devices. *Sandia National Laboratory Report SAND93-1930*,Albuquerque: Sandia National Laboratory.

Siedlarz, J. E., C. B. Kuhla, G. O. Williams, J. H. Lee, J. T. McHugh, and D. R. Richards. 1995. Biometric verification/identification brassboard proof-of-concept system: Phase II. *Defense Nuclear Agency*, DNA-TR-95-18.Alexandria, VA: Defense Nuclear Agency.

Siedlarz, J. 1998, April 6. Letter to the Editor. *Philadelphia Inquirer*.

Simon, C., and I. Goldstein. 1935. A new scientific method of identification. *New York State Journal of Medicine* 35:901–6.

Thalheim, L., J. Krissler, and P. Ziegler. 2002. Biometric access protection devices and their programs put to the test. *C'T Magazine* 11. www.heise.de/ct/english/02/11/114 (accessed May 30, 2006).

Trauring, M. 1963. On the automatic comparison of finger ridge patterns. *Nature* 197:938–40.

Trauring, M. 1963. Automatic comparison of finger ridge patterns. Hughes Research Laboratory Report 190. Malibu, CA. Hughes Research Laboratory.

Twain, M. 1893. Pudd'nhead Wilson. *The Century*, serialized 47(2)–48(2). New York: The Century Company.

van der Putte, T. and J. Keuning. 2000. Biometrical fingerprint recognition: Don't get your fingers burned, *IFIP TC8/WG.8., Fourth Working Group Conference on Smart Card Research and Advanced Applications*, 289–303. www.keuning.com/biometry/Biometrical_Fingerprint_Recognition.pdf (accessed May 30, 2006).

Warren, S., and L. Brandeis. 1890. The right of privacy. *Harvard Law Review* 4. www.louisville.edu/library/law/brandeis/privacy.html (accessed May 30, 2006).

Wasserman, J. J. 1969. Plugging the leaks in computer security. *Harvard Business Review* 47:119–29.

Watson, C., C. Wilson, K. Marshall, M. Indovina, and R. Snelick. 2005. Studies of one-to-one fingerprint matching with vendor SDK matchers. National Institute of Standards and Technology, NISTIR 7221. http://fingerprint.nist.gov/SDK/ir_7221.pdf (accessed June 10, 2006).

Watson, C. I., and C. L. Wilson. 2005. Effect of image size and compression on one-to-one fingerprint matching. National Institutes of Standards and Technology, NISTIR7201. ftp://sequoyah.nist.gov/pub/nist_internal_reports/ ir_7201.pdf (accessed April 21, 2006).

Wayman, J. L 2000. Evaluation of the INSPASS Hand Geometry Data. In *U.S.National Biometric Test Center Collected Works: 1997-2000*, edited by J. L. Wayman. San Jose: San Jose State University. www.engr.sjsu.edu/biometrics/nbtccw.pdf (accessed May 30, 2006).

Wayman, J. L., A. K. Jain, D. Maltoni, and D. Maio. 2005. *Biometric systems: Technology, design and performance evaluation*. London: Springer-Verlag.

Wegstein, J. 1970. Automated fingerprint identification. National Bureau of Standards Technical Note 538. Washington, DC: Government Printing Office.

Westin, A. 1967. *Privacy and freedom*. Boston: Atheneum.

Wilson, C. L., et al. 2004 Fingerprint Vendor Technology Evaluation 2003: Summary of results and analysis report. National Institute of Standards and Technology, NISTIR 7123. fpvte.nist.gov (accessed June 10, 2006).

Firewalls

James E. Goldman, *Purdue University*

INTRODUCTION

When an organization or individual links to the Internet, a two-way access point out of and in to their information systems is created. To prevent unauthorized activities between the Internet and the private network, a specialized hardware, software, or software-hardware combination known as a firewall is often deployed.

Overall Firewall Functionality

Firewall software often runs on a dedicated server between the Internet and the protected network. Firmware-based firewalls and single-purpose dedicated firewall appliances are situated in a similar location on a network and provide similar functionality to the software-based firewall. All network traffic entering the firewall is examined, and possibly filtered, to ensure that only authorized activities take place. This process may be limited to verifying authorized access to requested files or services, or it may delve more deeply into content, location, time, date, day of week, participants, or other criteria of interest. Firewalls usually provide a layer of isolation between the inside, sometimes referred to as the "clean" network, and the outside or "dirty" network. They are also used, although less frequently, to separate multiple subnetworks so as to control interactions between them. Figure 1 illustrates a typical installation of a firewall in a perimeter security configuration.

A common underlying assumption in such a design scenario is that all of the threats come from outside the network or from the Internet, but many modern firewalls provide protection against insiders acting inappropriately and against accidental harm that could result from internal configuration errors, viruses, or experimental implementations. Research consistently indicates that 70 to 80 percent of malicious activity originates from insiders who would normally have access to systems both inside and outside the firewall. In addition, outside threats may be able to circumvent the firewall entirely if dial-up modem access remains uncontrolled or unmonitored, if wireless LANs (local area networks) or similar wireless technology is used, or if other methods can be used to

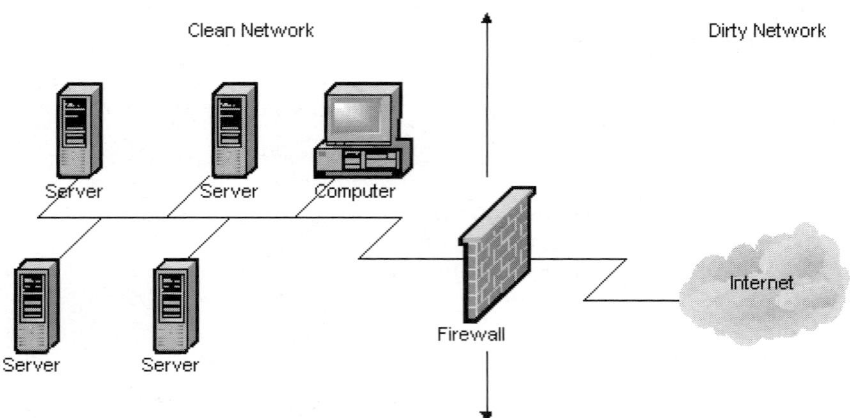

Figure 1: Typical installation of a firewall in a perimeter security configuration

co-opt an insider, to subvert the integrity of systems within the firewall, or to otherwise bypass the firewall as a route for communications. Incorrectly implemented firewalls can exacerbate this situation by creating new, and sometimes undetected, security holes or by creating such an impediment to legitimate uses that insiders subvert its mechanisms intentionally. It is often said that an incorrectly configured and maintained firewall is worse than no firewall at all because it gives a false sense of security.

Advantages

- When properly configured and monitored, firewalls can be an effective way to protect network and information resources.
- Firewalls are often used to reduce the costs associated with protecting larger numbers of computers that are located inside it.
- Firewalls provide a control point that can be used for other protective purposes.

Disadvantages

- Firewalls can be complex devices with complicated rule sets.
- Firewalls must be configured, managed, and monitored by properly trained personnel.
- A misconfigured firewall gives the illusion of security.
- Even a properly configured firewall is not sufficient or complete as a perimeter security solution. A total security solution typically also includes intrusion-detection/prevention systems, vulnerability assessment technology, and antivirus technology. Eighty percent of successful network attacks either penetrate or avoid firewall security.
- The processing of packets by a firewall inevitably introduces latency that, in some cases, can be significant.
- Firewalls often interfere with network applications that may expect direct connections to end user workstations such as voice over Internet protocol (VoIP) phones and VPNs (virtual private networks) as well as some collaborative tools such as instant messenger and video and audio conferencing software.
- The level to which firewalls inspect the data contained with packets varies widely. While some firewalls filter packets based only on source and destination addresses, other firewalls perform much more comprehensive packet inspection on the contents of those packets.
- Firewalls cannot prevent vulnerabilities introduced directly at client computers, such as malicious code, e-mail attacks, and Web-based Trojans. Trojan programs can then launch attacks within the internal network, undetected by the perimeter-based firewall.

FIREWALL FUNCTIONALITY

Background

Network communication between computers, whether or not that communication is through a firewall, is most often organized into layers according to the OSI (open systems interconnect) model. Figure 2 illustrates basic firewall functionality and technology categories in terms of the OSI model.

Firewalls were initially introduced as application-level programs running over standard operating systems. As a result, these firewall programs were easily bypassed by directly attacking the vulnerabilities of the underlying TCP/IP (or network protocol) stack and native operating system over which these firewall applications were executing. Such operating systems were often default installations and were sometimes referred to as nonhardened operating systems. Firewall application software conforming to this type of configuration is sometimes referred to as first-generation firewalls.

Today, most firewalls use hardened operating systems and are run as single programs on a dedicated computing device or hardware firewall appliance. As a result, it is more difficult to attack firewalls through the underlying vulnerabilities of operating systems and network protocols. Firewalls conforming to this architecture are sometimes referred to as second-generation firewalls.

Firewalls basically act as filters. They either allow or disallow a given packet based on rules contained in a filter table. At the highest level, filtering is either positive or negative. Positive filters allow traffic to pass through the firewall if those packets meet the criteria listed in the filter table and block all traffic that does not. Negative filters prevent any traffic that meets criteria on filter tables from passing through the firewall and allows all traffic to pass that does not. Firewall rules are processed in a serial

OSI Model Layer	Firewall Functionality	Firewall Technology	
7—Application	Application-level proxies, forward and reverse proxies	Proxy servers	Switched firewalls
6—Presentation		Firewall	Air gap technology
5—Session	Stateful firewall	Appliances	
4—Transport: TCP/UDP	Port filtering, circuit-level proxy		
3—Network—IP	Packet filtering, address filtering, packet filtering firewall	Router or layer three firewall	
2—Data link		Bridging or transparent firewalls	
1—Physical			

Figure 2: Basic firewall functionality and technology versus the OSI model

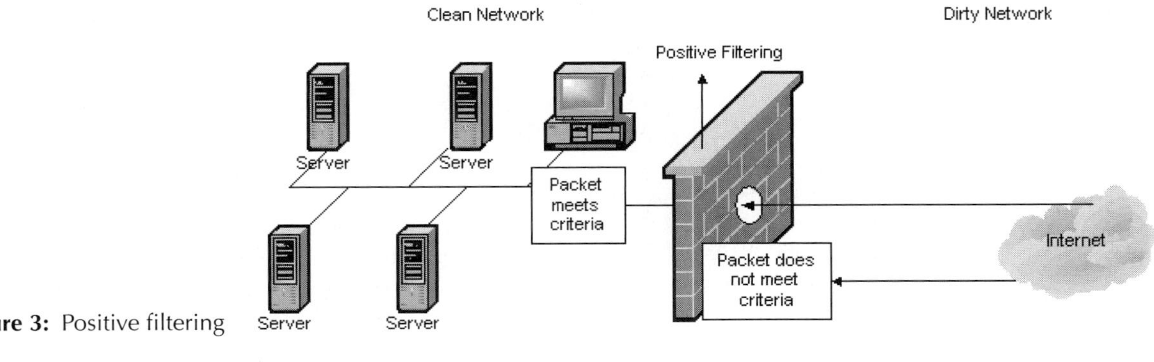

Figure 3: Positive filtering

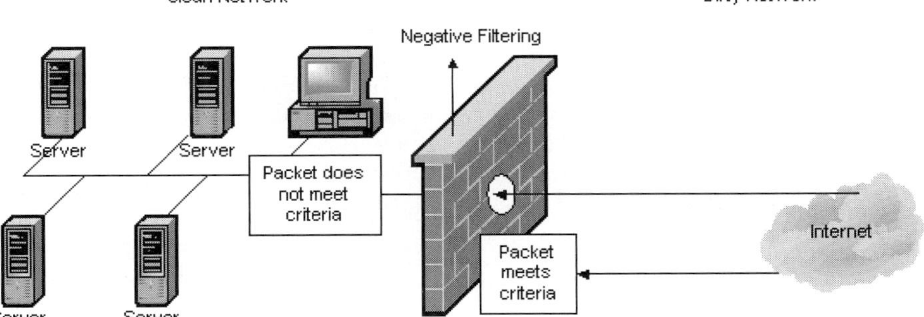

Figure 4: Negative filtering

fashion. Initially, the first rule in a firewall is generally to block all traffic, followed by exception rules allowing through the packets specified in the filter table (positive filtering). Conversely, the first rule could be to allow all traffic to pass through the firewall, followed by exception rules in a filter table specifying which traffic must be blocked (negative filtering). Filters can be applied as easily to traffic going from internal (secure) networks to the Internet (nonsecure) as they can be from the Internet into the secure internal networks. Which packets are allowed and disallowed in either direction can vary based on the order in which the firewall rules are processed. As a result, firewall rule logic can be extremely complicated and must be tested carefully.

Figure 3 illustrates positive filtering, in which only packets meeting the criteria of the firewall's filter tables are allowed through the firewall. Figure 4 illustrates negative filtering, whereby any packet meeting the criteria of the firewall's filter table is blocked and prevented from passing through the firewall.

A given firewall may, but does not necessarily, offer any or all of the functions discussed below.

Bad-Packet Filtering

The first type of filtering normally done is to remove bad packets, sometimes also referred to as misshapen packets. Such abnormal packets are often used to look for vulnerabilities or to launch attacks such as denial-of-service attacks or distributed-denial-of-service attacks. Bad packet filtering can be, and often is, implemented in an edge router, sometimes referred to as a filtering router, that faces the dirty network. However, it is highlighted here as an initial firewall function to ensure that it is not overlooked. More specific examples of bad packets are packet fragments, packets with abnormally set flags, time to live

(TTL) fields, abnormal packet length, or Internet control message protocol (ICMP) packets. The overall purpose in removing such "trash" initially is that the processing-intensive firewall can spend its time looking only at legitimate (although not necessarily authorized) packets. In this manner, bad packets are removed by the edge routers before reaching the firewall, thereby freeing the firewall from ever having to deal with these bad packets.

Address Filtering

This function can, and perhaps should, be performed by a device other than the firewall, such as a border router. Based on address filter tables containing allowed or disallowed individual or groups (subnets) or addresses, address filtering blocks all traffic that contains either disallowed source or destination addresses. Address filtering by itself may not provide adequate protection because it has too large a granularity for some protective requirements, but it does provide a first line of defense against attack techniques such as address spoofing.

Port Filtering

Port filtering goes beyond address filtering, examining to which function or program a given packet applies. For example, file transfer protocol (FTP) typically uses ports 20 and 21, inbound electronic mail (simple mail transfer protocol, or SMTP) typically uses port 25, and inbound nonencrypted Web traffic (hypertext transfer protocol, or HTTP) typically uses port 80. Attacks are often targeted and designed for specific ports. Port filtering can be used to ensure that all ports are disabled except those that must remain open and active to support programs and protocols required by the owners of the inside network. Static port filtering leaves authorized ports open to all traffic all the time, whereas dynamic port filtering opens and closes portions of protocols associated with authorized ports over time as required for the specifics of the protocols.

Domain Filtering

Domain filtering applies to outbound traffic headed through the firewall to the Internet. It can block traffic with domains that are not authorized for communications or can be designed to permit exchanges only with authorized "outside" domains.

Network Address Translation

When organizations connect to the Internet, the addresses they send out must be globally unique. In most cases, an organization's Internet service provider specifies these globally unique addresses. Most organizations have relatively few globally unique public addresses compared with the actual number of network nodes on their entire network.

The Internet Assigned Numbers Authority has set aside the following private address ranges for use by private networks:

10.0.0.0 to 10.255.255.255
172.16.0.0 to 172. 31.255.255
192.168.0.0 to 192.168.255.255

Traffic using any of these "private" addresses must remain on the organization's private network to interoperate properly with the rest of the Internet. Because anyone is welcome to use these address ranges, they are not globally unique and therefore cannot be used reliably over the Internet. Computers on a network using the private IP address space can still send and receive traffic to and from the Internet by using network address translation (NAT). An added benefit of NAT is that the organization's private network is not as readily visible from the Internet.

All of the workstations on a private network can share a single or small number of globally unique assigned public IP address(es) because the NAT mechanism maintains a table that provides for translation between internal addresses and ports and external addresses and ports. The combination of the shared public IP address and a port number that is translated into internal address and port numbers via the translation table allows computers on the private network to communicate with the Internet through the firewall. NAT can also run on routers, dedicated servers, or other similar devices, and "gateway" computers often provide a similar function.

Dynamic NAT entries are created automatically in the NAT table as the firewall or router receives packets that require NAT translation. Dynamic NAT entries are purged after a preset period. For mapping addresses on a more permanent basis through the firewall, static NAT entries can be manually entered into the NAT table and must be manually removed as well. Most firewalls provide some type of NAT functionality as illustrated in Figure 5.

Data Inspection

The primary role of many firewalls is to inspect the data passing through it using a set of rules that define what is and is not allowed through the firewall and then to act appropriately on packets that meet required criteria. The various types of firewalls, described in the next section, differ primarily in what portions of the overall data packet are inspected, the types of inspections that can be done, and what sorts of actions are taken with respect to that data. Among the data elements that are commonly inspected are the following:

- IP address
- TCP port number
- User datagram protocol port number
- Data field contents

Contents of specific protocol payloads, such as HTTP, can be inspected in order to subsequently filter out certain classes of traffic (e.g., streaming video, voice, music, etc.). Other data-field content that can be checked for and filtered includes access requests to restricted Web sites, information with specific markings (e.g., proprietary information), or content with certain words or page names.

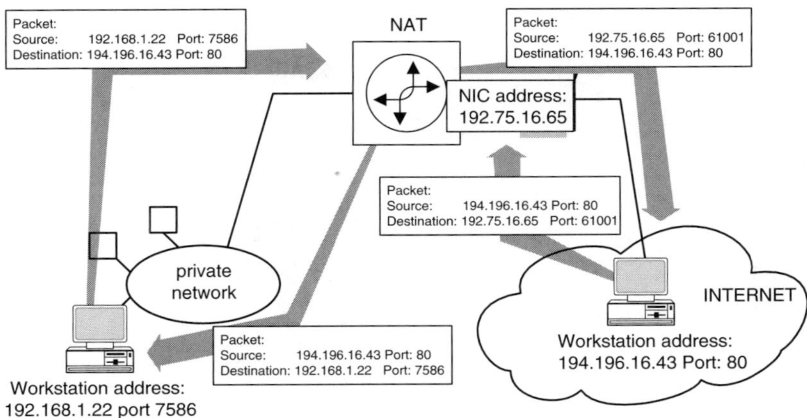

NAT Source/Destination Table

Private Source IP Addres	Private Source Assigned Port ID
192.168.1.22	61001
192.168.1.23	61002
192.168.1.24	61003
192.168.1.25	61004
and so on...	and so on...

GOLDMAN & RAWLES: ADC3e
FIG. 09-13

Figure 5: NAT functionality

Virus Scanning and Intrusion Detection

Some firewalls also offer functionality such as virus scanning and intrusion detection. Advantages of such firewalls include the following:

- "One-stop shopping" for a wide range of requirements
- Reduced overhead from centralization of services
- Reduced training and maintenance

Disadvantages include the following:

- Increased processing load requirements
- Single point of failure for security devices
- Increased device complexity
- Potential for reduced performance over customized subsolutions

Other Functions

Some firewalls also offer functions such as the following:

- VPN (virtual private networks): VPN functionality, allowing secure communication over the Internet, was typically provided by separate, dedicated devices. VPN traffic would have to be decrypted from the VPN tunnel and then passed through a separate firewall for filtering. By combining the VPN functionality with the firewall functionality on a single box, the process is somewhat simplified.
- Usage monitoring, traffic monitoring, and traffic logging: These functions provide usage statistics that can be valuable for capacity planning and also provide information to troubleshoot problems or spot potential abuse.
- Protection against some forms of IP address spoofing
- Protection against denial-of-service attacks
- Quality of service (QoS): QoS management provides differentiated levels of service (bandwidth, delay, routes) for different types of network traffic

FIREWALL TYPES

Another difficulty with firewalls is that there are no standards for firewall types, configuration, or interoperability. As a result, users must often be aware of how firewalls work to use them, and owners must be aware of these issues to evaluate potential firewall technology purchases. Many different devices can all be called firewalls, but that does not imply that these devices provide identical or even similar functionality. Firewall types and configuration are explained in the next few sections.

Bastion Host

Many firewalls, whether software- or hardware-based, include a bastion host—a specially hardened server or a trusted system designed so that the functionality of the device cannot be compromised by attacking vulnerabilities in the underlying operating system software over which its firewall application software runs. Specifically, the bastion host uses a secure version of the operating system with the most recent patches, security updates, and minimum number of applications to avoid known and unknown vulnerabilities. A bastion host is nothing more than the platform on which the firewall software is installed,

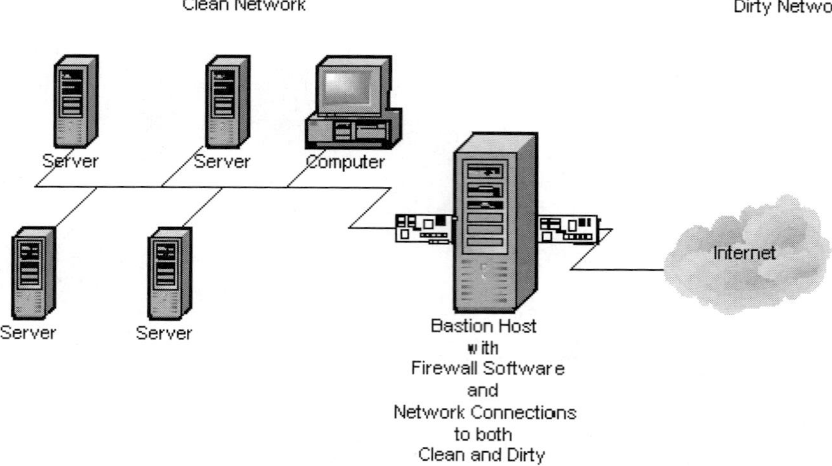

Figure 6: Bastion host

configured, and executed. Once configured with firewall software, the bastion host sits between clean and dirty networks providing a perimeter defense, as illustrated in Figure 6.

Bridging or Transparent Firewalls

Typical firewalls are installed between two or more subnetworks in order to filter traffic between those networks. Multiple network interface cards reside in the firewall and have IP addresses that belong to the respective subnetworks connected to the firewall via a given network interface card. These typical, or layer three, firewalls always must have network interface cards that are assigned IP addresses from surrounding networks. This presents a problem when a layer three firewall needs to be added to an existing network. Addressing schemes and routing tables must be adjusted in such a case. This can be a very time consuming and complex task.

Fortunately, there is a simpler way to add a firewall to an existing network. A layer two or transparent or bridging firewall works at layer two of the OSI model. The network interface cards in a transparent firewall do not require IP addresses. As a result, the network interface cards in these firewalls cannot be accessed directly from the outside, hence the term *"transparent" firewall*. Transparent or bridging firewalls can be created in at least two ways. Operating systems such as Linux and OpenBSD provide support for configuring a bridging firewall. Router-based or layer three firewalls also often can support transparent bridging firewalls in addition to layer three functionality. The key benefits of a bridging or transparent firewall are ease of installation and configuration, and the added security offered by the transparency of such devices.

Packet-Filtering Firewalls or Layer Three Firewalls

Every packet of data on the Internet can be identified by a source address (IP address) normally associated with the computer that issued the message and the destination address (IP address) normally associated with the computer to which the message is bound. These addresses are included in a portion of the packet called the header.

A packet filter can be used to examine the source and destination address of every packet. Network access devices known as routers are among the commonly used devices capable of filtering data packets. Filter tables are lists of addresses with data packets and embedded messages that are either allowed or prohibited from proceeding through the firewall. Filter tables may also limit the access of certain IP addresses to certain services and subservices. This is how anonymous FTP users are restricted to only certain information resources. It takes time for a firewall server to examine the addresses of each packet and compare those addresses to filter table entries. This filtering time introduces latency to the overall transmission time and may create a bottleneck to high volumes of traffic. Hardware implementations of such filters are often used to provide low latency and high throughput.

A filtering program that only examines source and destination addresses and determines access based on the entries in a filter table is known as a network-level filter or packet filter. The term *network level* or *network layer* in this case refers to the network layer or layer three of the OSI Model (see Figure 2), where IP addresses reside in the TCP/IP protocol stack.

Packet-filter gateways can be implemented on routers. This means that an existing piece of technology can be used for dual purposes. Maintaining filter tables and access rules on multiple routers is not a simple task, and packet filtering of this sort is limited in what it can accomplish because it examines only certain areas of each packet. Dedicated packet-filtering firewalls are usually easier to configure and require less in-depth knowledge of protocols to be filtered or examined. One easy way that many packet filters can be defeated by attackers is a technique known as IP spoofing. Because these simple packet filters make all filtering decisions based on IP source and destination addresses, an attacker can often create a packet designed to appear to come from an authorized or trusted IP address, which will then pass through such a firewall unimpeded.

Circuit-Level Gateways and Proxies

Circuit-level proxies, or circuit-level gateways, provide proxy services for transport layer (layer four) protocols such as TCP. Socks, an example of such a proxy server, creates proxy data channels to application servers on behalf of the application client. Socks uniquely identifies and keeps track of individual connections between the client and server ends of an application communication over a network. Like other proxy servers, both a client and a server portion of the Socks proxy are required to create the Socks tunnel. Some Web browsers have the client portion of Socks included, whereas the server portion can be added as a further application to a server functioning as a proxy server. The Socks server would be located inside an organization's firewall and can block or allow connection requests, based on the requested Internet destination, TCP port ID, or user identification. Once Socks approves and establishes the connection through the proxy server, it does not care which protocols flow through the established connection. This is in contrast to other more protocol-specific proxies such as Web proxy, which allows only HTTP to be transported, or WinSock Proxy, which allows only Windows application protocols to be transported.

Because all data go through Socks, it can audit, screen, and filter all traffic in between the application client and server. Socks can control traffic by disabling or enabling communication according to TCP port numbers. Socks4 allowed outgoing firewall applications, whereas Socks5 supports both incoming and outgoing firewall applications, as well as authentication.

The key negative characteristic of Socks is that applications must be "socksified" to communicate with the Socks protocol and server. In the case of Socks4, this meant that local applications had to be recompiled using a Socks library that replaced its normal library functions. However, with Socks5, a launcher is used that avoids "socksification" and recompilation of client programs that in most cases do not natively support Socks. Socks5 also uses a private routing table and hides internal network addresses from outside networks.

Application Gateways

Application gateways are concerned with what services or applications a message is requesting in addition to who is making that request. Connections between requesting clients and service providing servers are created only after the application gateway is satisfied as to the legitimacy of the request. Even once the legitimacy of the request has been established, only proxy clients and servers actually communicate with each other. A gateway firewall does not allow actual internal IP addresses or names to be transported to the external nonsecure network, except as this information is contained within content that the proxy does not control. To the external network, the proxy application on the firewall appears to be the actual source or destination, as may be the case.

Application-level filters, sometimes called "assured pipelines," "application gateways," or "proxy servers," go beyond port-level filters in their attempts to control packet flows. Whereas port-level filters determine the legitimacy of the IP addresses and ports within packets, application-level filters are intended to provide increased assurance of the validity of packet content in context. Application-level filters typically examine the entire request for data rather than just the source and destination addresses. This ability to examine the entire contents of a data packet in the context of its intended application is sometimes referred to as deep packet inspection. Controlled files can be marked as such, and application-level filters can be designed to prevent those files from being transferred, even within packets authorized by port-level filters. Of course, this increased level of scrutiny comes at the cost of a slower or more expensive firewall.

Proxies are also capable of approving or denying connections based on directionality. Users may be allowed to upload but not download files. Some application-level gateways have the ability to encrypt communications over these established connections. The level of difficulty associated with configuring application-level gateways versus router-based packet filters is debatable. Router-based gateways tend to require a more intimate knowledge of protocol behavior, whereas application-level gateways deal predominantly at the application layer of the protocol stack. Proxies tend to introduce increased latency compared with port-level filtering. The key weaknesses of an application-level gateway is their inability to detect embedded malicious code such as Trojan horse programs or macro viruses and the requirement of more complex and resource-intensive operation than lower-level filters.

Certain application-level protocol commands that are typically used for probing or attacking systems can be identified, trapped, and removed. For example, SMTP is an e-mail interoperability protocol that is a member of the TCP/IP family and used widely over the Internet. It is often used to mask attacks or intrusions. Multipurpose Internet mail extension (MIME) is another method that is often used to hide or encapsulate malicious code such as Java applets or ActiveX components. Other application protocols that may require monitoring include but are not limited to World Wide Web protocols such as HTTP, telnet, FTP, gopher, and Real Audio. Each of these application protocols may require its own proxy, and each application-specific proxy must be designed to be intimately familiar with the commands within each application that will need to be trapped and examined. For example an SMTP proxy should be able to filter SMTP packets according to e-mail content, message length, and type of attachments. A given application gateway may not include proxies for all potential application-layer protocols.

Trusted Gateway

A trusted gateway or trusted application gateway seeks to relieve all the reliance on the application gateway for all communication, both inbound and outbound. In a trusted gateway, certain applications are identified as trusted and are able to bypass the application gateway entirely and are able to establish connections directly rather than be executed by proxy. In this way, outside users can access information servers and Web servers without tying up the proxy applications on the application gateway. These servers are typically placed in a demilitarized zone (DMZ)

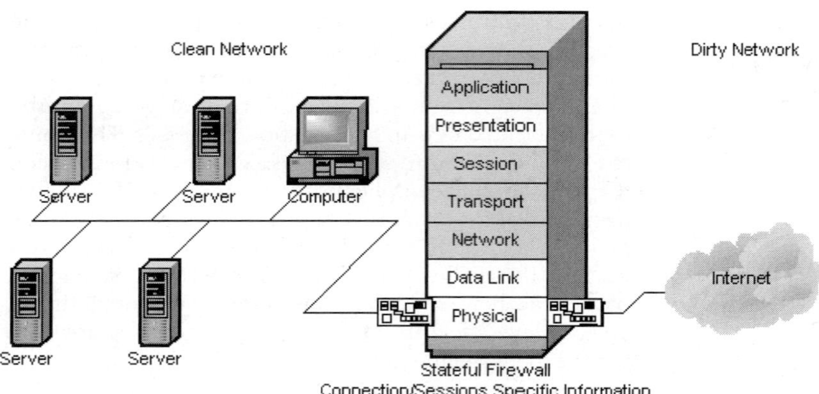

Figure 7: Stateful firewall

so that any failures in the application servers will grant only limited additional access to other systems.

Stateful Firewalls

Rather than simply examining packets individually without the context of previously transmitted packets from the same source, stateful firewalls, sometimes referred to as stateful multi-layer inspection firewalls, store information about past activities and use this information to test future packets attempting to pass through. Stateful firewalls typically review the same packet information as normal simple packet filtering firewalls such as source address, destination address, protocol, port, and flags; however, they also record this information in a connection state table, also referred to as a dynamic state table, before sending the packet on. This table will have an entry for each valid connection established over a particular reference frame. The multi-layer aspect of their functionality refers to the fact that they filter packets at the network, transport, session (connection), and application layers. Although stateful firewalls filter applications and evaluate application packet contents, they do not provide application-specific proxies. They combine the functionality of network packet filters, circuit-level gateways, and application-level gateways while adding the connection-oriented stateful inspection.

Some stateful firewalls keep sequence number information to validate packets even further, so as to protect against some session-hijacking attacks. As each packet arrives to a stateful firewall, it is checked against the connection table to determine whether it is part of an existing connection. The source address, destination address, source port, and destination port of the new packet must match the table entry. If the communication has already been authorized, there is no need to authorize it again and the packet is passed. If a packet can be confirmed to belong to an established connection, it is much less costly to send it on its way based on the connection table rather than to reexamine the entire firewall rule set. This makes a stateful firewall faster than a simple packet-filtering firewall for certain types of traffic patterns, since the packet-filtering firewall treats each connection as a new connection. In addition, because there is a "history" in the state tables, flags can be analyzed to ensure the proper sequence as in the TCP connection handshake, and the stateful firewall can drop or return packets that are clearly not a genuine response to a request.

As a result, stateful firewalls are better able to prevent some sorts of session hijacking and man-in-the-middle attacks. Session hijacking is very similar to IP spoofing, described earlier, except that it hijacks the session by sending forged acknowledgment (ack) packets so that the victimized computer still thinks it is talking to the legitimate intended recipient of the session. A man-in-the-middle attack could be seen as two simultaneous session hijackings. In this scenario, the hacker hijacks both sides of the session and keeps both sides active and appearing to talk directly to each other when, in fact, the man-in-the middle is examining and potentially modifying any packet that flows in either direction of the session. Figure 7 illustrates the basic functionality of a stateful firewall.

Internal Firewalls

Not all threats to a network are perpetrated from the Internet by anonymous attackers, and firewalls are not a stand-alone, technology-based quick fix for network security. In response to the reality that most losses due to computer crime involve someone with inside access, internal firewalls have been applied with increasing frequency. Internal firewalls include filters that work on the data-link, network, and application layers to examine communications that occur only within internal networks. Internal firewalls also act as access control mechanisms, denying access to applications for which a user does not have specific access approval. To ensure the confidentiality and integrity of private information, encryption and authentication may also be supported by firewalls, even during internal communications.

Virtual Firewalls and Network Based Firewall Services

Virtual firewalls, also known as virtual firewall systems, provide a single, centralized point of control over multiple distributed firewalls. As enterprise networks have grown in both scale and complexity, it has become more difficult to manage increasing numbers of firewalls on an individual basis. As a result, centralized firewall-management systems have been developed. Each individual firewall is able to be configured uniquely with its own policies and rule sets. The area of protection provided by each firewall is referred to as its security domain or risk domain. All of the configuration for the distributed firewalls can be done from a single, centralized location. A third-party service provider, such as an Internet VPN provider, may provide virtual firewall services, otherwise known as network-based firewall services.

SWITCHED FIREWALLS—AIR GAP TECHNOLOGY

Some vendors try to assert the strength of their protection by using widely known terms such as *switched firewalls* and *air gap* to characterize their protective mechanisms. One example of such a technology provides the same separation of the clean and dirty networks as firewalls. A hardware-based network switch is at the heart of this technology. The premise of creating a physical disconnection between the clean or secure network (intranet) and the nonsecure or dirty network (Internet) is accomplished by connecting a server on the Internet connection that will receive all incoming requests. This server will connect to an electronic switch that strips the TCP headers and stores the packet in a memory bank, and then the switch disconnects from the external server and connects with the internal server. Once the connection is made, the internal server recreates the TCP header and transmits the packet to the intended server. Responses are made in the reverse order. The physical separation of the networks and the stripping of the TCP headers remove many of the vulnerabilities in the TCP connection-oriented protocol. Of course this provides little additional protection over other firewalls at the content level because content-level attacks are passed through the so-called air gap and responses are returned.

By using high-speed switches for rule checking and packet forwarding, switched firewalls, also known as switch-accelerated firewalls are able to filter and forward packets at multigigabit speeds. In some switched firewall architectures, separate dedicated devices, sometimes referred to as switched firewall directors perform firewall control functions such as policy and session management, connection-table management, and packet-handling rules specification, thus freeing the dedicated separate switched firewall to perform only rule checking and packet forwarding. In some cases, application-specific filtering is provided on the air gap technology. Such devices may be referred to as application firewall appliances or air gap application firewalls. Figure 8 illustrates air gap functionality.

A protective device that is highly effective at limiting information flow to one direction—so-called digital diode technology—is applied in situations in which the sole requirement is that no information be permitted to leak from one area to the other while information is permitted to flow in the other direction. An example would be the requirement for weather information to be available to military planning computers without the military plans being leaked to the weather stations. This sort of protection typically uses a physical technology such as a fiber-optic device with only a transmitter on one end and a receiver on the other end to provide high assurance of traffic directionality.

SMALL OFFICE, HOME OFFICE FIREWALLS

As telecommuting has boomed and independent consultants have set up shop in home offices, the need for firewalls for the small office, home office (SOHO) market has grown as well. These devices are often integrated with integrated services digital network–based multiprotocol routers that supply bandwidth on demand capabilities for Internet access. Some of these SOHO firewalls offer sophisticated features such as support for VPNs at a reasonable price. The most expensive of these costs less than $3,000 and some simpler filtering firewalls cost as little as $100. Some of these devices combine additional functionality such as NAT, built in hub and switch ports, and load balancing in a combined hardware-software device known as a security appliance. Often DSLs (digital subscriber lines) or cable modems include firewall functionality because of their “always on” connection status.

Software-only solutions are also available. These products are installed on every computer and provide firewall-like functionality to each workstation, thereby effectively eliminating client-side vulnerabilities that may bypass server-based or perimeter firewalls. Additional benefits are that each workstation has an extremely inexpensive solution and that protection can be customized at the system level. A potential problem is that some software-only solutions require all users to be firewall administrators for their computers, losing the economy of scale that was one of the original benefits associated with firewalls, while in other cases, distributed desktop firewall configuration is handled from a centralized control point.

FIREWALL FUNCTIONALITY AND TECHNOLOGY ANALYSIS

Commercially available firewalls usually use either packet filtering or proxies as firewall architecture and add an easy-to-use graphical user interface (GUI) to ease the configuration and implementation tasks. Some firewalls even use industry standard Web browsers as their GUIs. Several certifying bodies and internationally accepted criteria are available to certify various aspects of firewall technology. Common Criteria Evaluation Assurance Level (EAL) 4 has been certified on some firewalls. These evaluation criteria are officially known as “Common Criteria for Information Technology Security Evaluation” ISO/IEC 15408 (National Security Agency and National Institute of Standards and Technology 2006). In addition, ICSA (International Computer Security Association) Labs, a division of TruSecure Corporation offers certification of a variety of security technology including firewalls.

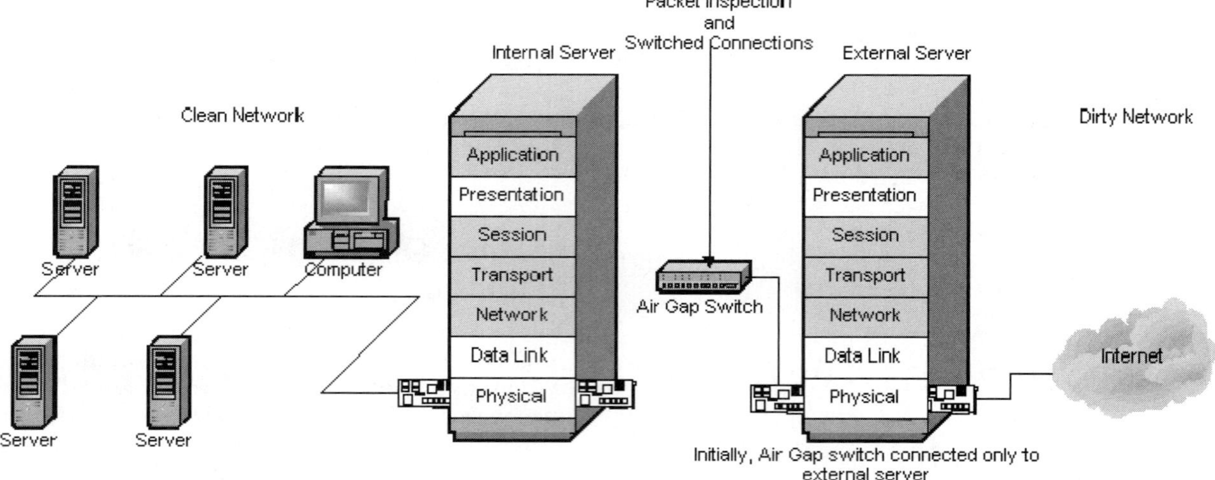

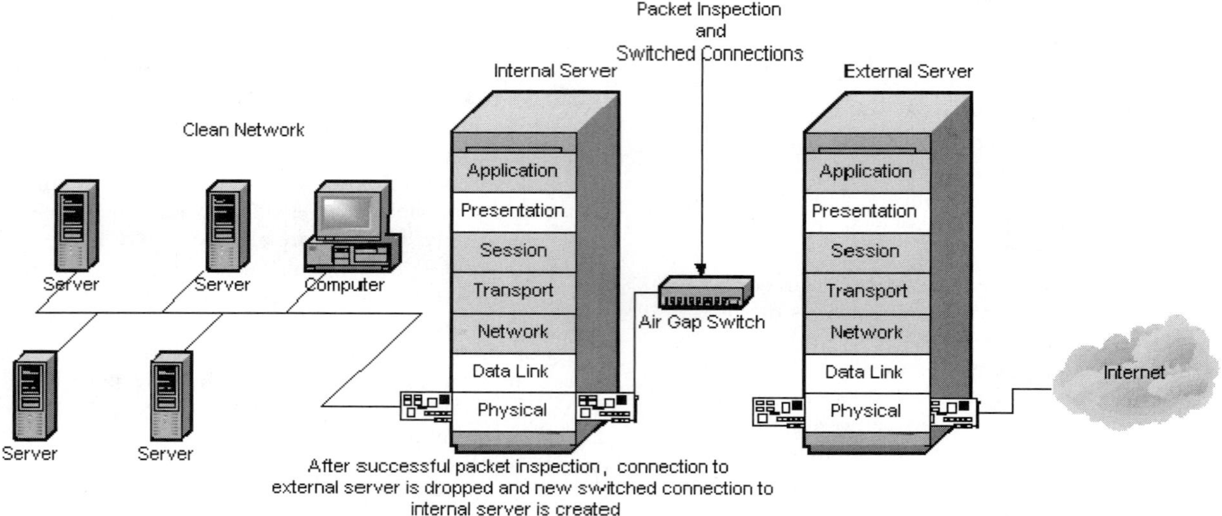

Figure 8: Air gap functionality

In general, certification seeks to ensure the following:

- That firewalls meet the minimum requirements for reliable protection
- That firewalls perform as advertised
- That Internet applications perform as expected through the firewall

Table 1 summarizes some of the key functional characteristics of firewall technology.

ENTERPRISE FIREWALL ARCHITECTURES

Conceptual Design Options of Firewall Architectures

Firewalls, or any security technologies for that matter, are virtually useless without associated security policies and the requisite education and communication that are associated with those policies. Before considering alternative enterprise firewall architectures, the information security analyst must be sure that the policies to be implemented on that enterprise firewall architecture are clearly understood and rigorously enforced.

Before the correct physical firewall architecture for a given situation can be determined, alternative conceptual design options for firewall architectures must be analyzed. At a high level, there are really two alternative conceptual philosophies to firewall architecture design: (1) defense in depth security, and (2) perimeter security.

Defense in Depth

A defense in depth design philosophy proposes multiple levels of security devices such as firewalls and intrusion-detection devices. The greater the value of the information assets within a given risk domain, the greater the number of layers of security technology must be penetrated in order to reach those information assets. Such a philosophy would seem to assume that intrusion or attack is as likely to come from someone inside a corporate network as from outside that network. Defense in depth at

Table 1: Sample Functional Characteristics of Firewall Technology

FIREWALL FUNCTIONAL CHARACTERISTIC	EXPLANATION/IMPORTANCE
Encryption	Allows secure communication through firewall Encryption schemes supported: DES, 3-DES, AES Encryption key length supported: 40, 56, 128, 168, and 256 bits.
Virtual private network (VPN) support	Allows secure communication over the Internet in a VPN topology VPN security protocols supported: IPSEC, SSL
Application proxies supported	How many application proxies are supported? Internet application protocols (HTTP, SMTP, FTP, telnet, NNTP, WAIS, SNMP, rlogin, ping traceroute)? Real Audio? How many controls or commands are supported for each application?
Proxy isolation	In some cases, proxies are executed in their own protected domains to prevent penetration of other proxies or the firewall operating system should a given proxy be breached.
Operating systems supported	UNIX and varieties; Windows NT, 2000, XP,
Virus scanning included	Because many viruses enter through Internet connections, the firewall is a logical place to scan for viruses.
Web tracking	To ensure compliance with corporate policy regarding use of the World Wide Web, some firewalls provide Web-tracking software. The placement of the software in the firewall makes sense because all Web access must pass through the firewall. Access to certain uniform resource locators (URLs) can be filtered.
Violation notification	How does the firewall react when access violations are detected? Options include SNMP traps, e-mail, pop-up windows, pagers, reports.
Authentication supported	As a major network access point, the firewall must support popular authentication protocols and technology.
Network interfaces supported	Which network interfaces and associated data-link-layer protocols are supported?
System monitoring	Are graphical systems monitoring utilities available to display statistics such as disk usage or network activity by interface?
Auditing and logging	Is auditing and logging supporting? How many types of events can be logged? Are user-defined events supported? Can logged events be sent to SNMP managers?
Attack protection	Following is a sample of the types of attacks that a firewall should be able to guard against: TCP denial-of-service attack, TCP sequence number prediction, source routing and RIP attacks, EGP infiltration and ICMP attacks, authentication server attacks, finger access, PCMAIL access, DNS access, FTP authentication attacks, anonymous FTP access, SNMP access, remote access, remote booting from outside networks; IP, MAC and ARP spoofing and broadcast storms; trivial FTP and filter to and from the firewall, reserved port attacks, TCP wrappers, gopher spoofing, and MIME spoofing.
Attack retaliation/counterattack	Some firewalls can launch specific counterattacks or investigative actions if the firewall detects specific types of intrusions.
Administration interface	Is the administration interface graphical in nature? Is it forms based?

ARP = address resolution protocol; DNS = domain name server; EGP = exterior gateway protocol; DES = data encryption standard; FTP = file transfer protocol; HTTP = hypertext transfer protocol; ICMP = Internet control message protocol; IP = Internet protocol; MAC = media access control; MIME = multipurpose internet mail extension; NNTP = network news transfer protocol; RIP = routing information protocol; SMTP = simple mail transfer protocol; SNMP = simple network management protocol; TCP = transmission control protocol. WAIS = wide area information services.

its extreme would propose server-specific firewalls protecting individual servers. In a physical or building security metaphor, defense in depth would propose biometric locks on every door throughout a building, not just on the outside doors.

Perimeter Security

A perimeter security design philosophy draws an imaginary line, or moat, around the perimeter of the risk domain it is seeking to protect. An underlying design assumption in perimeter security is that threats to the information assets within the protected risk domain are likely to come only from outside that risk domain. Individual servers within a risk domain are typically not specifically or individually protected. All of the emphasis is on building impenetrable perimeter security architecture. In a physical or building security metaphor, perimeter security would have biometric access to the outside doors or armed guards protecting the entrance to the building, but no further security within the building.

Firewall Architecture Design Elements

Once an overall security or firewall philosophy has been determined, key decisions remain to be made regarding the number and location of these firewalls in relation to the Internet and a corporation's public and private information resources. Each of the alternative enterprise firewall architectures explored in this section attempt to segregate three distinct networks or risk domains:

1. The Internet or other "dirty" networks: contain legitimate customers and business partners as well as hackers
2. The DMZ(s), otherwise known as the screened subnet, neutral zone, or external private network: contains Web servers and mail servers among other information assets
3. The internal private network, otherwise known as the secure network or intranet: contains most valuable corporate information

The firewall architectures described in the following sections represent generalized designs or approaches to firewall architecture design. They are not necessarily mutually exclusive. Elements of various firewall architectures described below may be combined in order to properly meet the security requirements of a particular risk domain. For example, packet-filtering routers could easily, and correctly, be added to any of the other firewall architectures described. Likewise, server- or host-specific firewalls could easily be added to other firewall architectures as well.

PACKET-FILTERING ROUTERS

Functionality

Packets-filtering routers or border routers are often the first devices that face the Internet or dirty network from an organization network perspective. These packet-filtering routers first remove all types of traffic that should not even be passed to the firewalls. This process is typically fast and inexpensive because it involves only simple processes that are implemented in relatively low-cost hardware. Examples of removed packets include packet fragments, packets with abnormally set flags, TTL, abnormal packet length, or ICMP packets, all of which could potentially be used for attacks or to exploit known vulnerabilities and packets from or to unauthorized addresses and ports. Figure 9 illustrates a packet-filtering router architecture.

Advantages

- Perimeter routers can easily perform this task.
- Fast processing
- No additional expense or specialized equipment
- Filter tables listing bad packets to remove is relatively static; not a lot of maintenance involved.

Disadvantages

- Should not be mistaken as a replacement for a firewall
- Processor speed and memory on the router must be properly sized to handle required throughput.
- Filter tables must be manually maintained.

PERIMETER FIREWALL ARCHITECTURE

Functionality

The perimeter firewall architecture represents the physical implementation of the perimeter security conceptual design described previously. It was, and in some cases still is, the most commonly implemented firewall architecture. All rules processing and packet filtering is performed on the perimeter firewall. It is very important that firewall rules are carefully configured and tested, since there is no additional security provided once past the perimeter firewall. A perimeter firewall architecture implies that all information assets within a risk domain protected in this manner are of equal value and face equal risk. Figure 10 illustrates a perimeter firewall architecture.

Advantages

- Relatively simple to configure and manage

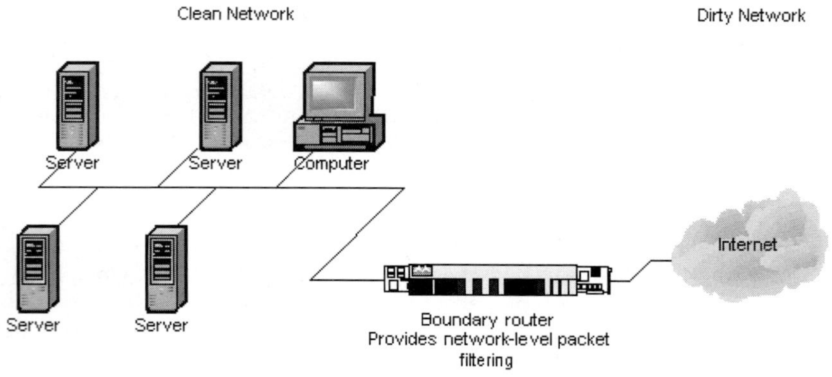

Figure 9: Packet-filtering router architecture

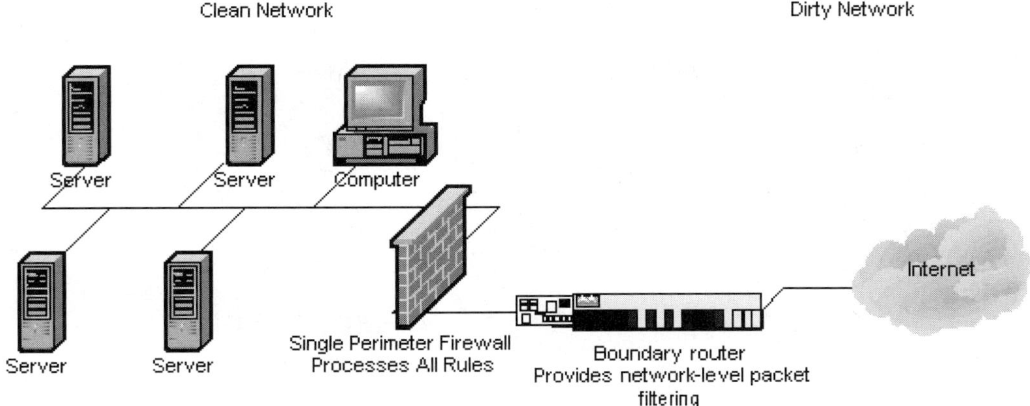

Figure 10: Perimeter firewall architecture

Disadvantages

- Single point of security implies a single point of failure.
- All information assets within risk domain are at risk if perimeter security is breached.

SERVER/HOST FIREWALL ARCHITECTURE

Functionality

The server/host firewall architecture is also known as a screened host architecture. This architecture can be used in combination with other architectures such as the perimeter, DMZ, and multitiered DMZ. A server/host firewall is often software-based and resides/executes on the application server that it is protecting. It is sort of a personal bodyguard for the application server within an otherwise secure environment.

TCPWrapper is just one example of a UNIX-based program that could be considered a limited-function server/host firewall software program. It is a utility that can intercept and log any requests for TCP services. It could be considered a "shim" program, much like a proxy server that sits between the computer connection requesting the service and the actual service itself on the server computer. Server/host firewall software programs such as TCPWrapper may provide some or all of the following functionality:

- Attempts to detect IP address spoofing by performing what is known as a double-reverse lookup of the IP address to ensure that the IP address and hostname match the domain name service (DNS) entry. DNS is a service that translates between commonly remembered names such as www.wiley.com and an IP address such as 128.210.114.39.
- Performs address and service filtering to be sure that the requested connection is allowed or authorized
- Logs the connection
- Completes the connection to the requested service

Server/host firewalls such as TCPWrapper often run directly on application servers. Microsoft's ISA (Internet Security & Acceleration) server, formerly known as Microsoft Proxy Server, is another example of a software-based firewall package that can run on an application server. This makes them distinct from other software-based firewalls that require a dedicated server. Figure 11 illustrates a server/host firewall architecture.

Advantages

- Relatively easy to install and configure
- Adds server-specific incremental protection to other firewall architectures

Disadvantages

- Ongoing maintenance/management can become difficult as the numbers of individual server/host firewalls are installed unless some type of centralized firewall management system is used.

SCREENED SUBNET (DMZ) FIREWALL ARCHITECTURE

Functionality

Rather than using only the packet-filtering router as the front door to the DMZ, a second firewall is added behind the packet-filtering router to further inspect all traffic bound to or from the DMZ. The initial application gateway or firewall still protects the perimeter between the DMZ and the intranet or secure internal network.

A DMZ is considered a neutral or safe zone. Outbound communications from the clean network to the Internet can go through proxy servers in the DMZ. The general public accessing this network from the Internet would be able to access only servers located in the DMZ. The DMZ contains mail, Web, and often e-commerce servers. Servers located behind the DMZ firewall on the clean network behind the DMZ would not be accessible by the general public from the Internet. Figure 12 illustrates a screened subnet (DMZ) firewall architecture. Although this logical diagram would suggest that multiple distinct firewalls are required to establish a DMZ, this is actually not the case. Numerous vendors sell "multilegged" (multiple interface)

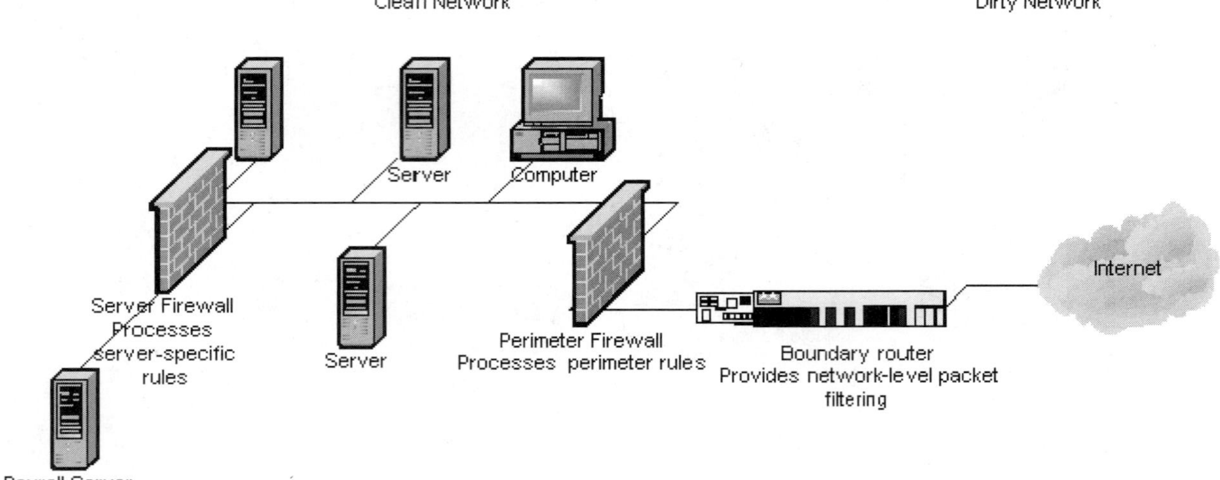

Figure 11: Server/host firewall architecture

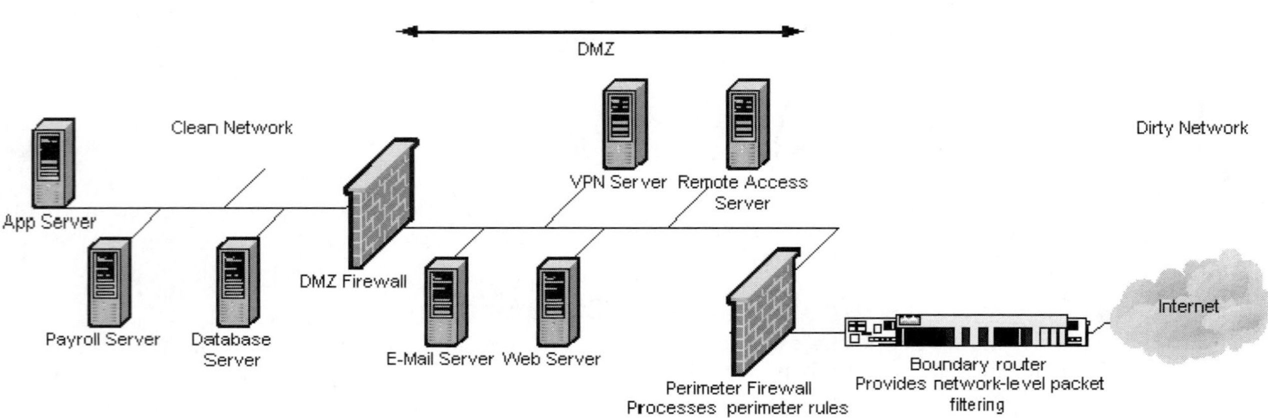

Figure 12: Screened subnet (DMZ) firewall architecture

firewalls that allow both DMZ or Internet-accessible networks as well as clean or protected networks to be physically attached to a single firewall device.

Advantages

- Provides flexibility especially for Internet-based applications such as e-mail, Web services, and e-commerce
- Allows servers that must be accessible to the Internet while still protecting back-office services on the secure internal network or Intranet

Disadvantages

- More complicated rule configuration means more likelihood of errors.
- Applications running in DMZ may still need access to servers/resources in the secure internal network.
- Once through the server between the DMZ and the Internal network, there is no further protection or differentiated levels of security.

MULTITIERED/DISTRIBUTED DMZ ARCHITECTURE

Functionality

As e-commerce and e-business have proliferated, the need for e-commerce servers to access more and more secure information from database and transaction servers within the secure intranet has increased proportionately. As a result, the number of connections allowed through firewalls into the most secure areas of corporate networks has increased dramatically. In response to this phenomenon, the model of a multitiered DMZ has developed. Such a scenario really builds on the screened subnet firewall (DMZ) architecture by adding additional tiers to the DMZ, each protected from other tiers by additional firewalls. Typically, the first tier of the DMZ closest to the Internet would contain only the presentation or Web portion of the e-commerce application running on Web servers.

A firewall would separate that first tier of the DMZ from the second tier that would house the business logic and application portions of the e-commerce application

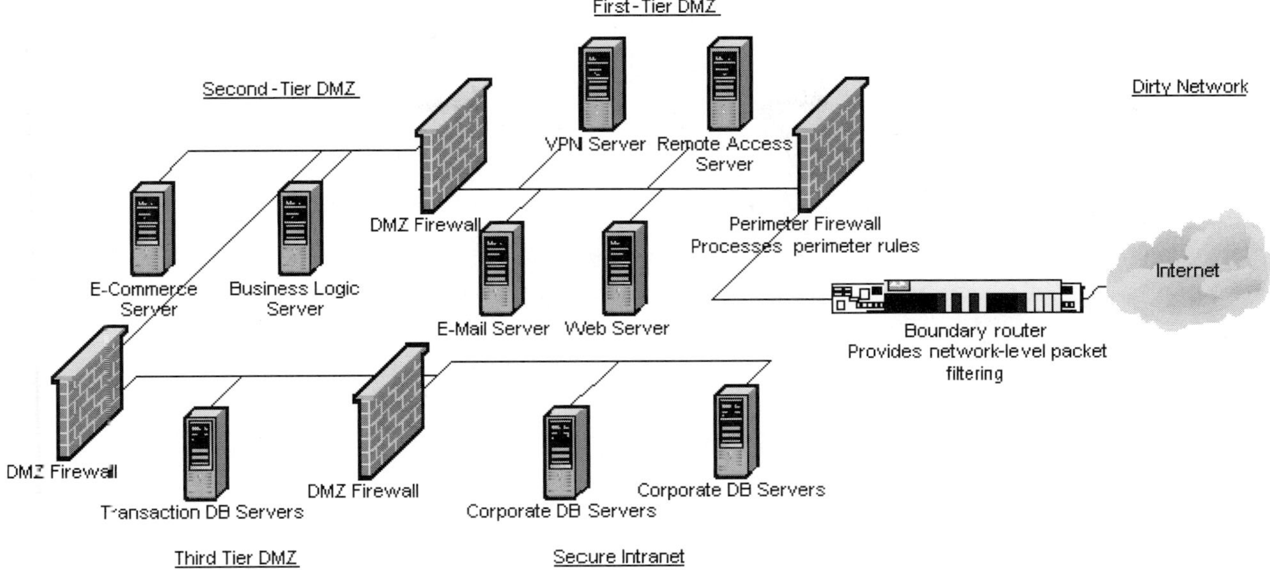

Figure 13: Multitiered/distributed DMZ architecture (DB 5 database)

typically running on transaction servers. This firewall would have rules defined to allow only packets from certain applications on certain servers with certain types of requests through from the first-tier DMZ to the second-tier DMZ. The third (most secure) tier of the DMZ is similarly protected from the second tier by a separate firewall. The servers in the third-tier DMZ would be database servers and should contain only the data necessary to complete requested e-commerce transactions. Finally, as in the screened subnet firewall architecture, a firewall would separate the third-tier DMZ from the intranet, or most secure corporate network. Figure 13 illustrates the multitiered/distributed firewall architecture.

Advantages

- When combined with screened host/server specific firewalls, a multitiered DMZ firewall architecture provides good protection for back-office systems such as payroll and inventory servers.
- A multitiered DMZ system provides the greatest level of flexibility and highest number of risk domains, thus providing the ability for optimal placement of information resources

Disadvantages

- Each additional level of firewalls adds a level of complexity in terms of rule configuration and opportunity for configuration errors that can lead to security breaches.
- There is obviously a proportional increase in expense for each level of security/DMZ added.

AIR GAP ARCHITECTURE

Functionality

A hardware-based network switch is at the heart of the air gap architecture. The premise of creating a physical disconnection between the clean or secure network (intranet) and the nonsecure or dirty network (Internet) is accomplished by placing a server on the Internet connection that will receive all incoming requests. This server will connect to an electronic switch that strips the TCP headers and stores the packet in a memory bank, and then the switch disconnects from the external server and connects with the internal server. Once the connection is made, the internal server recreates the TCP header and transmits the packet to the intended server. Responses are made in the reverse order. The physical separation of the networks and the stripping of the TCP headers remove many of the vulnerabilities in the TCP connection-oriented protocol. Of course this provides little additional protection over other firewalls at the content level because content-level attacks are passed through the so-called air gap and responses are returned.

By using high-speed switches for the rule checking and packet forwarding, switched firewalls, also known as switch-accelerated firewalls are able to filter and forward packets at multigigabit speeds. In some switched firewall architectures, separate dedicated devices, sometimes referred to as switched firewall directors, perform firewall control functions such as policy and session management, connection-table management, and packet-handling rules specification, thus freeing the dedicated separate switched firewall to perform only rule checking and packet forwarding. In some cases, application-specific filtering is provided on the air gap technology. Such devices may be referred to as application firewall appliances or air gap application firewalls. Figure 14 illustrates an air gap architecture.

Advantages

- Provides switched connections between clean and dirty network thereby creating a physical gap or moat between the two.

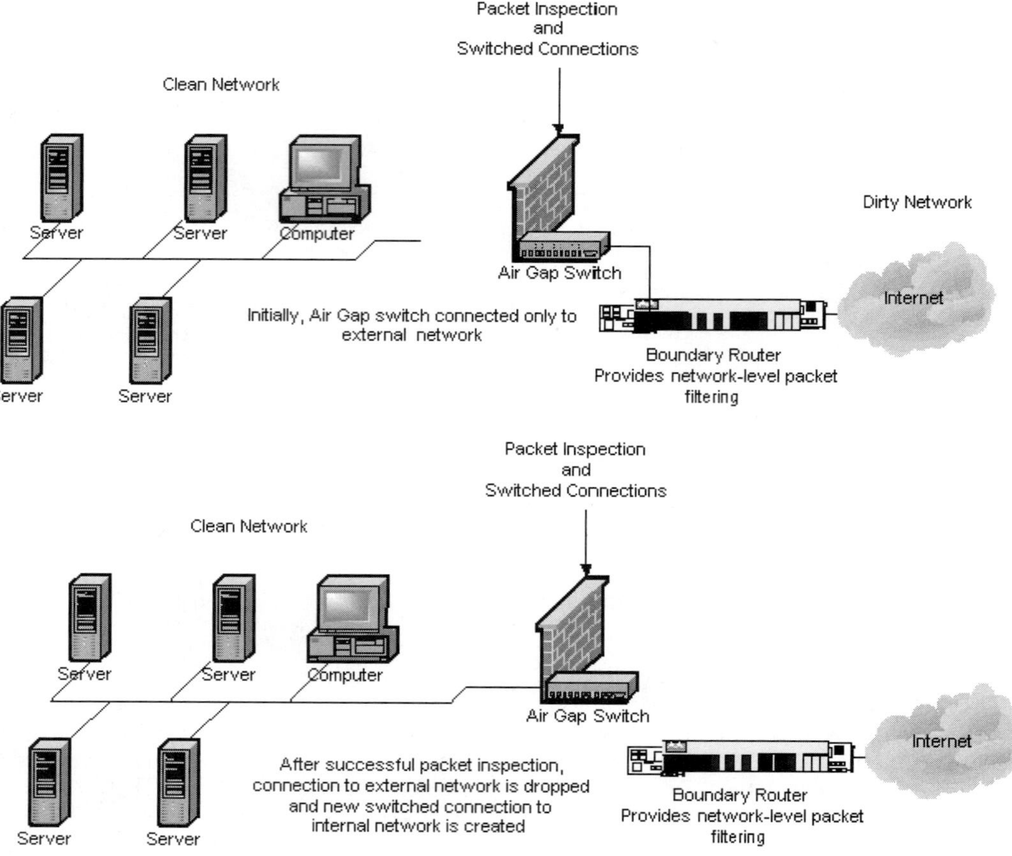

Figure 14: Air gap architecture

- High-speed network switches at the heart of the air gap architecture provide high throughput.

Disadvantages

- Effectiveness of the architecture is still dependent on the effectiveness of the packet filtering rules within the air gap device.
- Deep packet inspection or content/application-specific inspection cannot be assumed.
- Vendors loosely interpret the term *air gap technology*. Specific functionality of any given device should not be assumed.

CONCLUSION

Firewalls are an essential and basic element of many organizations' security architecture. Nonetheless, technology must be chosen carefully to ensure that it offers the required functionality, and firewalls must be arranged into properly designed enterprise firewall architectures and properly configured, maintained, and monitored. Even in the best circumstances, firewalls should be seen as a relatively small solution within the overall information-protection challenge and should not be considered sufficient on their own.

There is no single firewall architecture that is the correct choice for all security scenarios. Firewall architectures vary primarily in the number of firewalls used and the placement of those firewalls relative to each other, the information resources they are trying to protect, and the dirty networks or threats they are trying to protect the information resources from. A thorough security-requirements analysis is prerequisite to firewall architecture choice. Such an analysis must start with a detailed understanding of the applications that must be secured. Firewalls, and their arrangement in a particular architecture, are just one piece of the overall security framework puzzle.

GLOSSARY

Address Filtering: A firewall's ability to block or allow packets based on Internet protocol addresses.

Air Gap Technology: Switched connections established to connect external and internal networks that are not otherwise physically connected.

Application-Level Gateway: Application-level filters examine the entire request for data rather than only the source and destination addresses.

Bastion Host: Hardened server with trusted operating system that serves as the basis of the firewall.

Circuit-Level Proxies: Proxy servers that work at the circuit level by proxying protocols such as file transfer protocol.

Demilitarized Zone (DMZ): A neutral zone between firewalls or between a packet filtering router and a firewall in which mail and Web servers are often located.

Domain Filtering: A firewall's ability to block outbound access to restricted sites.

Dual-Homed Host: A host firewall with two or more network interface cards with direct access to two or more networks.

Ephemeral Ports: Port numbers that are temporarily assigned to client-side connections from a predetermined range of available port numbers.

Firewall: A network device capable of filtering unwanted traffic from a connection between networks.

Internal Firewalls: Firewalls that include filters that work on the data-link, network, and application layers to examine communications that occur only on an organization's internal network, inside the reach of traditional firewalls.

Multitiered DMZ: A DMZ that segments access areas with multiple layers of firewalls.

Network Address Translation: A firewall's ability to translate between private and public globally unique Internet protocol addresses.

Packet-Filtering Gateway: A firewall that allows or blocks packet transmission based on source and destination Internet protocol addresses.

Port Filtering: A firewall's ability to block or allow packets based on transmission control protocol port number.

Proxy Server: Servers that break direct connections between clients and servers and offer application- and circuit-layer-specific proxy services to inspect and control such communications.

Screened Subnet: Enterprise firewall architecture that creates a DMZ.

Stateful Firewall: A firewall that monitors connections and records packet information in state tables to make forwarding decisions in the context of previous transmitted packets over a given connection.

Trusted Gateway: In a trusted gateway, certain applications are identified as trusted, are able to bypass the application gateway entirely, and are able to establish connections directly rather than by proxy.

CROSS REFERENCES

See *Authentication; Cryptography; Intrusion Detection Systems; Password Authentication; Smart Cards: Communication Protocols and Applications.*

REFERENCES

National Security Agency and National Institute of Standards and Technology. 2006, September. *Common methodology for information technology security evaluation*, version 3.1. Rockville, MD: National Security Agency and National Institute of Standards and Technology.

FURTHER READING

Cheswick, W. R., S. Bellovin, and A. Rubin.2003. *Firewalls & internet security: Repelling the wily hacker*. 2nd ed. Boston: Addison-Wesley.

Dubrawsky, I. 2003, July. *Firewall evolution—deep packet inspection*. www.securityfocus.com/infocus/1716 (accessed June 1, 2007).

e-Gap application firewall appliance: A technical overview. 2003, January. www.whalecommunications.com (accessed June 1, 2007).

Garfinkel, S., and G. Spafford. 2003. *Practical Unix and Internet Security*. 3rd ed. Sebastopol CA: O'Reilly

Goldman, J. E., and P. T. Rawles. 2004. *Applied data communications: A business oriented approach*. 4th ed.. New York: Wiley.

Hucaby, D. 2005. *Cisco ASA and PIX firewall handbook*. San Jose, CA: Cisco Press.

Mercadet, R. *From DMZ to DdMZ*. 2003, February. www.evidian.com (accessed June 1, 2007).

PIX 500 Series Firewalls. Cisco Systems. 2003. www.cisco.com.

Poynter, I., and B. Doctor. 2003, January. *Beyond the firewall: The next level of network security*. www.stillsecure.com (accessed June 1, 2007).

Ramsey, J. 2003, July. *Client-side vulnerabilities: meet your network's weakest link*. www.secureworks.com (accessed June 1, 2007).

Strassberg, K., G. Rollie, and R. Gondek.2002. *Firewalls: The complete reference*. New York: McGraw-Hill.

Suehring, S., and R. Ziegler. 2005. *Linux firewalls*. 3rd ed. Indianapolis: New Riders

Tanase, M. Transparent, bridging firewall devices. 2006, June. www.securityfocus.com (accessed June 1, 2007).

Transparent Cisco IOS Firewall. 2006, June. www.cisco.com.

Wireless Firewall Gateway White Paper. 2003, September. http://www.nas.nasa.gov/Research/Tasks/Networks/Wireless/whitepaper.html (accessed June 1, 2007).

Authentication

Patrick McDaniel, *Pennsylvania State University*

INTRODUCTION

An authentication process establishes the identity of some entity under scrutiny. For example, a traveler authenticates herself to a border guard by presenting a passport. Possession of the passport and resemblance to the attached photograph are deemed sufficient proof that the traveler is the identified person. The act of validating the passport (by checking a database of known passport serial numbers) and assessing the resemblance of the traveler to the photograph is a form of authentication.

On the Internet, authentication is somewhat more complex; network entities do not typically have physical access to the parties they are authenticating. Malicious users or programs may attempt to obtain sensitive information, disrupt service, or forge data by impersonating valid entities. Distinguishing these malicious parties from valid entities is the role of authentication, and is essential to security.

Successful authentication does not imply that the authenticated entity is given access. An authorization process uses authentication, possibly with other information, to make decisions about whom to give access. For example, not all authenticated travelers will be permitted to enter the country. Other factors, such as the existence of visas, past criminal record, and political climate will determine which travelers are allowed to enter the country.

Although the proceeding has focused on entity authentication, it is important to note that other forms of authentication exist. In particular, message authentication is the process by which a particular message is associated with some sending entity. Message authentication is a continuous process, in which the sender of each new message must be constantly evaluated. Such evaluation is typically performed with respect to some identity previously authenticated—that is, through entity authentication. This chapter restricts itself to entity authentication, deferring discussion of forms to other entries in this book.

Introducing Alice and Bob

Authentication is often illustrated through the introduction of two protagonists, Alice and Bob. In these descriptions, Alice attempts to authenticate herself to Bob. Note that in practice, Alice and Bob may not be users, but computers. For example, a computer must authenticate itself to a file server prior to being given access to its contents. Independent of whether Alice is a computer or person, she must present evidence of her identity. Bob evaluates this evidence, commonly referred to as a credential. Alice is deemed authentic (is authenticated) by Bob if the evidence is consistent with information associated with her claimed identity. The form of Alice's credential determines the strength and semantics of authentication.

The most widely used authentication credential is a password. To illustrate, UNIX passwords configured by system administrators reside in the /etc/passwd file. During the log-in process, Alice (a UNIX user) types her password into the host console. Bob (the authenticating UNIX operating system) compares the input to the known password. Bob assumes that Alice is the only entity in possession of the password. Hence, Bob deems Alice authentic because she is the only one who could present the password credential.

Note that Bob's assertion that Alice is the only entity who could have supplied the password is not strictly accurate. Passwords are subject to *guessing* attacks. Such an attack continually retries different passwords until the authentication is successful. Many systems combat this problem by disabling authentication of that identity after a threshold of failed authentication attempts. The more serious *dictionary* attack makes use of the UNIX password file itself. Passwords are not stored in their original form. The password and a random salt value are cryptographically hashed when the result is stored. Because the hash function is guaranteed to be noninvertible, someone who gains access to the password file cannot trivially recover the passwords. However, a malicious party who obtains the password file can mount a dictionary attack by comparing hashed, salted password guesses against the password file's contents. Such an attack debilitates the authentication service, and hence is difficult to combat. Recent systems have sought to mitigate attacks on the password file by placing the password hash values in a highly restricted *shadow password* file.

Passwords are subject to more fundamental attacks. In one such attack, the adversary simply obtains the password from Alice directly. This can occur where Alice "shares" her password with others, or when she records it in some obvious place (e.g., on her PDA). Such attacks illustrate an axiom of security: a system is only as secure as the protection afforded to its secrets. In the case of authentication, failure to adequately protect credentials from misuse can result in compromise of the system.

Particularly in cases in which the substance of the interaction has monetary value, it is important for Alice and Bob to perform *mutual authentication:* not only must Alice prove her identity to Bob, but Bob must also prove his identity to Alice. If this bidirectional authentication is not performed, any adversary can exploit Alice by pretending to be Bob. In fact, attacks on the lack of effective mutual authentication lie at the heart of one of the most dangerous and costly attacks on the Internet today, phishing. In a phishing attack, the adversary uses some medium, such as e-mail, to pose as some important entity, and then uses fake Web sites and other means to coerce the victim into exposing authenticating information such as passwords. Attacks in which the adversary interposes himself between the victim and the real authority fall into the class of *man-in-the-middle* attacks.

The definition of *identity* has historically been controversial. This is largely because authentication does not truly identify physical entities, but associates some secret or (presumably) unforgeable information with a virtual identity. Hence, for the purposes of authentication, any entity in possession of Alice's password is Alice. The strength of authentication is determined by the difficulty with which a malicious party can circumvent the authentication process and incorrectly assume an identity. In our above example, the strength of the authentication process is largely determined by the difficulty of guessing Alice's password. Note that other factors, such as whether Alice chooses a poor password or writes it on the front of the monitor, will determine the effectiveness of authentication. The lesson here is that authentication is as strong as the weakest link; failure to protect the password by either Alice or the host limits the effectiveness of the solution.

Authentication on the Internet is often more complex than suggested by the previous example. Often, Alice and Bob are not physically colocated. Hence, both parties will wish to authenticate each other. In our above example, Alice will wish to ensure that she is communicating with Bob. However, no formal process is needed; because Alice is sitting at the terminal, she assumes that Bob (the host) is authentic.

On the Internet, it is not always reasonable to assume that Alice and Bob have established (or can establish) some relationship prior to communication. For example, consider the case in which Alice is purchasing goods on the Internet. Alice goes to Bob's Web server, identifies the goods she wishes to purchase, provides her credit card information, and submits the transaction. Alice, being a cautious customer, wants to ensure that this information is being given only to Bob's Web server (i.e., she wants to authenticate the Web server). In general, however, requiring Alice to establish a direct relationship with each vendor from whom she may purchase goods is not feasible (e.g., it is not feasible to establish passwords for each Web site out of band).

Enter Trent, the trusted third party. Logically, Alice appeals to Trent for authentication information relating to Bob. Trent is trusted by Alice to assert Bob's authenticity. Therefore, Bob need only establish a relationship with Trent to begin communicating with Alice—that is, Trent vouches for the identity of Bob. Because the number of widely used trusted third parties is small (on the order of tens), and every Web site establishes a relationship with at least one of them, Alice can authenticate virtually every vendor on the Internet.

CREDENTIALS

Authentication is performed by the evaluation of credentials supplied by the user (i.e., Alice). Such credentials can take the form of something you know (e.g., password), something you have (e.g., smart card), or something you are (e.g., fingerprint). The credential type is specific to the authentication service, and reflects some direct or indirect relationship between the user and the authentication service.

Credentials often take the form of shared secret knowledge. Users authenticate themselves by proving knowledge of the secret. In the UNIX example above, knowledge of the password is deemed sufficient evidence to prove user identity. In general, such secrets need not be statically defined passwords. For example, users in one-time password authentication systems do not present knowledge of secret text, but identify a numeric value valid only for a single authentication. Users need not present the secret directly, but demonstrate knowledge of it (e.g., by presenting evidence that could only be derived from it).

Secrets are often long random numbers, and thus cannot be easily remembered by users. For example, a typical RSA private key is a 1024-digit binary number. Requiring a user to remember this number is, at the very least, unreasonable. Such information is frequently stored in a file on a user's host computer, a PDA, or other nonvolatile storage. The private key is used during authentication by accessing the appropriate file. However, private keys can be considered "secret knowledge" because the user presents evidence external to the authentication system (e.g., from the file system).

Credentials may also be physical objects. For example, a smart card may be required to gain access to a host. Authenticity in these systems is inferred from possession, rather than from knowledge. Note that there is often a subtle difference between the knowledge- and possession-based credentials. For example, it is often the case that a user-specific private key is stored on an authenticating smart card. In this case, however, the user has no ability to view or modify the private key. The user can be authenticated only via the smart card issued to the user. Hence, for the purposes of authentication, the smart card is identity; no amount of effort can modify the identity encoded in the smart card.[1]

Biometric devices measure physical characteristics of the human body. An individual is deemed authentic if the measured aspect matches previously recorded data. The accuracy of matching determines the quality of authentication. Contemporary biometric devices include fingerprint, retina, or iris scanners, and face-recognition software. However, biometric devices are primarily useful only when the scanning device is trusted—that is, under control of the authentication service. Although biometric authentication has seen limited use in the Internet, it is increasingly used to support authentication associated with physical security (i.e., governing clean-room access).

Credential use is subject to eavesdropping and replay. For example, any adversary can watch a user type a password from across the room. The adversary later uses the password to gain access to the system. This problem only gets worse in networks: anyone who can get access to the messages used to authenticate users could potentially reuse the data to masquerade as a legitimate user. Such attacks are mitigated in authentication systems by requiring *freshness*. Freshness guarantees that the use of a credential is bounded in time, and hence could not possibly be replayed. The following sections demonstrate several methods for achieving freshness.

Multifactor authentication systems use more than one system to authenticate the user. For example, some systems require both a password and a token to prove identity. These systems can significantly increase the difficulty of attacks on the authentication. It is much harder to both eavesdrop a password and steal a token than it is to do only one or the other. Multifactor systems have been seen as a valuable way to increase security while maintaining the simplicity and ease of use of traditional authentication mechanisms, and have been widely adopted in corporate environments. However, these mechanisms are only as strong as the underlying systems—that is, if the underlying mechanisms are vulnerable, so is the multifactor system.

Credentials need not identify a particular entity, but can be used to prove some characteristic of a community. For example, a concert ticket serves as a credential that the owner has paid or received permission to attend the show. *Reverse turning tests* use tasks that cannot easily be performed by a computer, such as extracting text from complex images. The correct answer shows that a human was involved. Such tests are useful in preventing online "scripted" attacks.

Authentication Services

A number of general-purpose services have been developed to support authentication, credential maintenance, access control, and accounting. For example, RADIUS, DIAMETER, and LDAP-based authentication services have been widely deployed on the Internet. Networks subscribing to these services defer all authentication-related activities to these centralized services. Each such system can support a range of authentication services and protocols appropriate for the served environment.

In addition to authentication, these services typically implement access control, which regulates access to valued infrastructure or data, for the controlled environment. For example, all users are authenticated when entering most networks. However, this (typically) does not give total access to the entire network. An access control service determines, based on the identity established via authentication, which services that entity user has a right to access (e.g., file servers, printers, etc.). How access control is performed and results presented to the network is beyond the scope of this chapter.

Authentication services exist to simplify network management. Because of the way technology has evolved, the diverse services comprising a network often require different methods of authentication. Supporting the many authentication methods required by an environment (or many instantiations of a single authentication service) can be enormously costly. Administrators can vastly simplify the administrative process by managing a single database of identities in the authentication services. The services can use whatever credentials are deemed necessary, so long as they are supported by the authentication service. Similarly, new applications can be developed and easily integrated with the existing authentication service through well-defined interfaces. Existing authentication services (nearly) universally support the authentication services defined in this chapter.

Biometrics

Biometrics are a class of authentication systems that exploit the unique physical or behavioral characteristics of users. These services measure characteristics such as fingerprints, hand measurements, face recognition, irises, (walking) gait, or others to determine their identity. The measurements are compared for similarity to previously recorded samples using apparatus specialized for the particular biometric system—for example, fingerprint scanners and video cameras. People whose characteristics are "close enough" to the previously recorded measurement are deemed authentic and associated with the appropriate user identity.

Biometrics are often referred to as "something you are" credentials. That is, the credential is an artifact of your person or behavior. This has the advantage that the user does not need to possess or remember the credential, nor can it be lost. Biometrics are limited in the same way: once the characteristic is lost, it cannot be revoked. For example, unlike other credentials such as public keys, a user whose signature is forged cannot change it later. Hence, in practice it is essential to protect the measurements and apparatus from exposure to adversaries.

In practice, the quality of the apparatus used to measure biometric features varies widely. Hence, error is introduced into the process of measurement. For example, mood, lack of sleep, or aging can significantly affect the quality of measurement in a face-recognition system. The similarity of the measurements to the original is

[1]In practice, contemporary smart cards can be modified or probed. However, because such manipulation often takes considerable effort and sophistication (e.g., use of an electron microscope), such attacks are beyond the abilities of the vast majority of attackers.

used, rather than an exact match. Biometrics systems compare the measured distance or existence of features between the previously recorded and measured samples. The measured sample is authentic if the distance is small enough or the number of features is large enough based on a system-specific threshold.

The quality of a biometric system is measured in the rate of false positives and false negatives. A false positive occurs when an inauthentic sample is deemed authentic, and a false negative occurs when a authentic sample is deemed inauthentic. These features are in direct proportion to each other and a direct reflection of the threshold value. A high threshold will prevent false positives but incur more false negatives. Conversely, a low threshold will prevent false negatives but incur more false positives. How one selects a threshold (and more broadly a type of biometric system) is dependent on the needs of the environment, the frequency of authentication, and the value of the protected system.

WEB AUTHENTICATION

One of the most prevalent uses of the Internet is Web browsing. Users access the Web via specialized protocols that communicate HTML and XML requests and content. The requesting user's Web browser renders received content. However, it is often necessary to restrict access to Web content. Moreover, the interactions between the user and a Web server are often required to be private. One aspect of securing content is the use of authentication to establish the true or virtual identity of clients and Web servers.

Password-Based Web Access

Web servers initially adopted well-known technologies for user authentication. Foremost among these was the use of passwords. To illustrate the use of passwords on the Web, the following describes the configuration and use of basic authentication in the Apache Web server (Apache 2002). Note that the use of basic authentication in other Web servers is largely similar.

Access to content protected by basic authentication in the Apache Web server is indirectly governed by the password file. Web site administrators create the password file (whose location is defined by the Web site administrator) by entering user and password information using the htpasswd utility. It is assumed that the passwords are given to the users using an out-of-band channel (e.g., via e-mail, phone).

In addition to specifying passwords, the Web server must identify the subset of Web content to be password-protected (e.g., set of protected URLs). This is commonly performed by creating an .htaccess file in the directory to be protected. The .htaccess file defines the authentication type and specifies the location of the relevant password file. For example, located in the content root directory, the following .htaccess file restricts access to users who are authenticated via password.

```
AuthName "Restricted Area"
AuthType Basic
AuthUserFile /var/www/webaccess
require valid-user
```

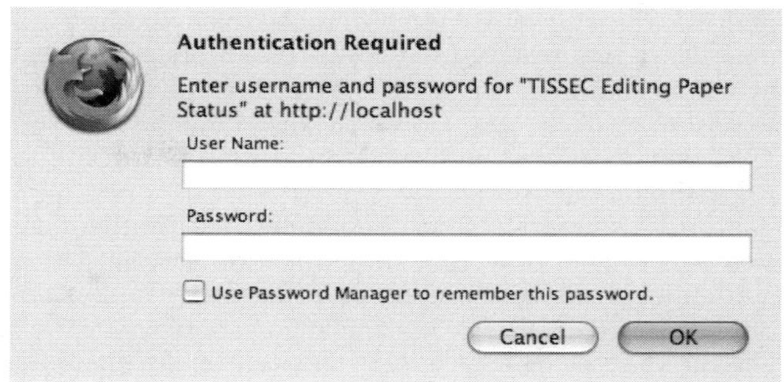

Figure 1: Password authentication on the Web

Users accessing protected content (via a browser) are presented with a password dialog (e.g., similar to the dialog depicted in Figure 1). The user enters the appropriate username and password, and if correct, is given access to the Web content.

Because basic authentication sends passwords over the Internet in cleartext, it is relatively simple to recover them by eavesdropping on the HTTP communication. Hence, basic authentication is sufficient to protect content from casual misuse, but should not be used to protect valuable or sensitive data. However, as is commonly found on commercial Web sites, performing basic authentication over more secure protocols (e.g., secure sockets layer [SSL], see below) can mitigate or eliminate many of the negative properties of basic authentication.

Many password-protected Web sites store user passwords (in encrypted form) in cookies the first time a user is authenticated. In these cases, the browser automatically submits the cookie to the Web site with each request. This approach eliminates the need for the user to be authenticated every time she visits the Web site. However, this convenience has a price. In most single-user operating systems, any entity using the same host will be logged in as the user. Moreover, the cookies can be easily captured and replayed back to the Web site (Fu et al. 2001).

Digest authentication uses challenges to mitigate the limitations of password-based authentication (Franks et al. 1999). Challenges allow authenticating parties to prove knowledge of secrets without exposing (transmitting) them. In digest authentication, Bob sends a random number (nonce) to Alice. Alice responds with a hash of the random number and her password. Bob uses Alice's password (which only he and Alice know) to compute the correct response, and compares it to the one received from Alice. Alice is deemed authentic if the computed and received responses match (because only Alice could have enerated the response). Because the hash, rather than the secret, is sent, no adversary can obtain Alice's password from the response.

Single Sign-on

Password authentication is the predominant authentication method on the Web. Users register a username and password with each retailer or service provider with which they do business. Hence, users are often faced with the difficult and error-prone task of maintaining a long list of usernames and passwords. In practice, users avoid this maintenance headache by using the same passwords on all Web sites. However, this allows adversaries who gain access to the user information on one site to impersonate the user on many others.

A single sign-on (SSO) system defers user authentication to a single, universal authentication service. Users authenticate themselves to the SSO once per session. Subsequently, each service requiring user authentication is redirected to an SSO server that vouches for the user. Hence, the user is required to maintain only a single authentication credential (e.g., SSO password). Note that the services themselves do not possess user credentials (e.g., passwords), but simply trust the SSO to state which users are authentic.

Although SSO services have been used for many years (e.g., see the section on "Kerberos" below), the lack of universal adoption and cost of integration has made their use in Web applications highly undesirable. These difficulties have led to the creation of SSO services targeted specifically to authentication on the Web. One of the most popular of these systems is the Microsoft Passport service (Microsoft 2002). Passport provides a single authentication service and repository of user information. Web sites and users initially negotiate secrets during the Passport registration process (i.e., user passwords and Web site secret keys). In all cases, these secrets are known only to the Passport servers and the registering entity.

Passport authentication proceeds as follows. Users requesting a protected Web page (i.e., page that requires authentication) are redirected to a Passport server. The user is authenticated via a Passport-supplied log-in screen. If successful, the user is redirected back to the original Web site with an authentication cookie specific to that site. The cookie contains user information and site-specific information encrypted with a secret key known only to the site and the Passport server. The Web site decrypts and validates the received cookie contents. If successful, the user is deemed authentic and the session proceeds. Subsequent user authentication (with other sites) proceeds similarly, except that the log-in step is avoided. Successful completion of the initial log-in is noted in a session cookie stored at the user browser and presented to the Passport server with later authentication requests.

Although SSO systems solve many of the problems of authentication on the Web, they are not a panacea. By definition, SSO systems introduce a single point of trust for all users in the system. Hence, ensuring that the SSO is not poorly implemented, poorly administered, or malicious is essential to its safe use. For example, Passport has been shown to have several crucial flaws (Kormann and Rubin 2000). Note that although existing Web-oriented SSO systems may be extended to support mutual authentication, the vast majority have yet to do so.

Certificates

Although passwords are appropriate for restricting access to Web content, they are not appropriate for more general Internet authentication needs. Consider the Web site for an online bookstore examplebooks.com. Users wishing to purchase books from this site must be able to determine that the Web site is authentic. If not authenticated, a malicious party may impersonate examplebooks.com and fool the user into exposing his credit card information.

Note that most Web-enabled commercial transactions do not authenticate the user directly. The use of credit card information is deemed sufficient evidence of the user's identity. However, such evidence is typically evaluated through the credit card issuer service (e.g., checking that the credit card is valid and has not exceeded its spending limit) before the purchased goods are provided to the buyer.

The dominant technology used for Internet Web site authentication is public key certificates. Certificates provide a convenient and scalable mechanism for authentication in large distributed environments (such as the Internet). Note that certificates are used to enable authentication of a vast array of other non-Web services. For example, certificates are often used to authenticate electronic mail messages (see the section on "Pretty Good Privacy," below).

Certificates are used to document an association between an identity and a cryptographic key. Keys in public key cryptography are generated in pairs; a public key and a private key (Diffie and Hellman 1976). As the name would suggest, the public key is distributed freely, and the private key is kept secret. To simplify, any data signed (using a digital signature algorithm) by the private key can be validated using the public key. A valid digital signature can be mapped to exactly one private key. Therefore, any valid signature can be generated only by some entity in possession of the private key. Conversely, keys in secret cryptography use a single shared secret key. Although it is often more efficient than public key algorithms, secret key cryptography requires the communicating parties to negotiate a secret before communicating.

Certificates are issued by certification authorities (CAs). The CA issues a certificate by signing an identity (e.g., domain name of the Web site), validity dates, and a Web site's public key. The certificate is then freely distributed. A user validates a received certificate by checking the CA's digital signature. Note that most browsers are installed with a collection of CA certificates that are invariantly trusted (i.e., do not need to be validated). For example, many Web sites publish certificates issued by the VeriSign CA (VeriSign 2002), whose certificate is installed with most browsers. In its most general form, a system used to distribute and validate certificates is called a "public key infrastructure" (PKI).

Certificate technologies such as those supported by pretty good privacy (PGP) are the basis of secure multipurpose Internet mail extension S/MIME standards (Dusse et al. 1998). S/MIME defines protocols, data structures, and certificate management infrastructures for authentication and confidentiality of MIME data. These standards are being widely adopted as a means to secure personal and enterprise e-mail.

Secure Sockets Layer

Introduced by Netscape in 1994, the secure sockets layer (SSL) protocol uses certificates to authenticate Web content. In addition to authenticating users and Web sites,

Figure 2: The SSL protocol: Alice (the client) and Bob (the server) exchange an initial handshake identifying the kind of authentication and configuration of the subsequent session security. As dictated by the authentication requirements identified in the handshake, Alice and Bob may exchange and authenticate certificates. The protocol completes by establishing a session-specific key used to secure (e.g., encrypt) later communication

the SSL protocol negotiates an ephemeral secret key. This key is subsequently used to protect the integrity and confidentiality of all messages (e.g., by encrypting the messages sent between the Web server and the client). SSL continues to evolve. For example, the standardized and widely deployed TLS (transport-layer security) protocol is directly derived from SSL version 3.0.

The use of SSL is signaled to the browser and Web site through the https URL protocol identifier. For example, Alice enters the following URL to access a Web site of interest:

https://www.example.com

In response to this request, Alice's browser will initiate an SSL handshake protocol. If the Web site is correctly authenticated via SSL, the browser will retrieve and render Web site content in a manner similar to HTTP. Authentication is achieved in SSL by validating statements signed by private keys associated with the authenticated party's public key certificate.

Figure 2 depicts the operation of the SSL authentication and key agreement process. The SSL handshake protocol authenticates one or both parties, negotiates the cipher-suite policy for subsequent communication (e.g., selecting cryptographic algorithms and parameters), and establishes a master secret. All messages occurring after the initial handshake are protected using cryptographic keys derived from the master secret.

The handshake protocol begins with both Alice (the end-user browser) and Bob (the Web server) identifying a cipher suite policy and session identifying information. In the second phase, Alice and Bob exchange certificates. Note that policy will determine which entities require authentication: as dictated by policy, Alice and/or Bob will request an authenticating certificate. The certificate is validated on reception (e.g., issuance signature checked against CAs whose certificate is installed with the browser). Note that in almost all cases, Bob will be authenticated, but Alice will not. In these cases, Bob typically authenticates Alice using some external means (only when it becomes necessary). For example, online shopping Web sites will not authenticate Alice until she expresses a desire to purchase goods, and her credit card number is used to validate her identity at the point of purchase.

Interleaved with the certificate requests and responses is the server and client key exchange. This process authenticates each side by signing information used to negotiate a session key. The signature is generated using the private key associated with the certificate of the party to be authenticated. A valid signature is deemed sufficient evidence because only an entity in possession of the private key could have generated it. Hence, signed data can be accepted as proof of authenticity. The session key is derived from the signed data, and the protocol completes with Alice and Bob sending *finished* messages.

HOST AUTHENTICATION

Most computers on the Internet provide some form of remote access, which access allows users or programs to access resources on a given computer from anywhere on the Internet. This access enables a promise of the Internet: independence from physical location. However, remote access has often been the source of many security vulnerabilities. Hence, protecting these computers from unauthorized use is essential. The means by which host authentication is performed in large part determines the degree to which an enterprise or user is protected from malicious parties lurking in the dark corners of the Internet. This section reviews the design and use of the predominant methods providing host authentication.

Remote Log-in

Embodying the small, isolated UNIX networks of old, remote log-in utilities allow administrators to identify the set of hosts and users that are deemed "trusted." Trusted hosts are authenticated by source IP address, hostname, and/or username only. Hence, trusted users and hosts need not provide a username or password.

The rlogin and rsh programs are used to access hosts. Configured by local administrators, the /etc/hosts.equiv file enumerates hosts/users that are trusted. Similarly, the .rhosts file contained in each user's home directory identifies the set of hosts trusted by an individual user. When a user connects to a remote host with a remote log-in utility, the remote log-in server (running on the accessed host) scans the hosts.equiv configuration file for the address and username of the connecting host. If found, the user is deemed authentic and allowed access. If not, the .rhosts file of the accessing user (identified in the connection request) is scanned, and access is granted where the source address and username are matched.

The remote access utilities do not provide strong authentication. Malicious parties may trivially forge IP addresses, domain name service (DNS) records, and usernames (called "spoofing"). Although attempts have been made to address the security limitations of the IP protocol stack (e.g., IPsec, DNSsec), this information is widely accepted as untrustworthy. Remote access tools trade off security for ease of access. In practice, these tools often weaken the security of network environments by providing a vulnerable authentication mechanism. Hence, the use of such tools in any environment connected to the Internet is considered extremely dangerous.

Secure Shell

The early standards for remote access—telnet and ftp—authenticated users by UNIX password. Although the means of authentication were similar to terminal log-in, their use on an open network introduces new vulnerabilities. Primarily, these utilities are vulnerable to password sniffing. Such attacks passively listen on the network for communication between the host and the remote user.[2] Because passwords are sent in the clear (unencrypted), user-specific authentication information could be recovered. For this reason, the use of these utilities as a primary means of user access has largely been abandoned.[3]

The secure shell (SSH) (Ylonen 1996) combats the limitations of standard tools by performing cryptographically supported host and/or user authentication. Similar to SSL, a by-product of the authentication is a cryptographic key used to obscure and protect communication between the user and remote host. SSH is not vulnerable to sniffing attacks, and has been widely adopted as a replacement for the standard remote access tools.

SSH uses public key cryptography for authentication. Upon installation, each server host (host allowing remote access via SSH) generates a public key pair. The public key is manually stored at each initiating host (host from which a user will remotely connect). Note that unlike SSL, SSH uses public keys directly, rather than issued certificates. Hence, SSH authentication relies on the due diligence of host administrators to maintain the correct set of host keys.

SSH initiates a session in two phases. In the first phase, the server host is authenticated. The initiating host creates the SSH session by requesting remote access. To simplify, the requesting host generates a random session key, encrypts it with the received host public key of the server, and forwards it back to the server.[4] The server recovers the session key using its host private key. Subsequent communication between the hosts is protected using the session key. Because only someone in possession of the host private key could have recovered the session key, the server is deemed authentic.

The second phase of the SSH session initialization authenticates the user. Dictated by the configured policy, the server will use one of the following methods to authenticate the user:

- *.rhosts file*: As described for the remote access utilities above, simply tests whether the accessing user identifier is present in the .rhosts file located in the home directory of the user.
- *.rhosts with RSA*: Similar to above, but requires that the accessing host is authenticated via a known and trusted RSA public key.
- *password authentication*: Prompts the user for a local system password. The strength of this approach is determined by the extent to which the user keeps the password private.
- *RSA user authentication*: Authenticates via a user-specific RSA public key. Of course, this requires that the server be configured with the public key generated for each user.

Note that it is not always feasible to obtain the public key of each host that a user will access. Host keys may change frequently (as based on an administrative policy), be compromised, or be accidentally deleted. Hence, when the remote host key is not known (and the configured policy allows it), SSH will simply transmit it during session initialization. The user is asked if the received key should be accepted. If accepted, the key is stored in the local environment and is subsequently used to authenticate the host.

Although the automated key distribution mode does provide additional protection over conventional remote access utilities (e.g., eavesdropping prevention), the authentication mechanism provides few guarantees. A user accepting the public key knows little about its origin (e.g., it may be subject to forgery, man-in-the-middle attacks, etc.). Hence, this mode may be undesirable for some environments.

One-Time Passwords

In a very different approach to combating password sniffing, the S/Key system (Haller 1994) limits the usefulness of recovered passwords. Passwords in the S/Key system are valid only for a single authentication. Hence, a malicious party gains nothing by recovering a previous password (e.g., via eavesdropping of a telnet log-in). Although on the surface the one-time password approach may seem to require that the password be changed following each log-in, the way in which passwords are generated alleviates the need for repeated coordination between the user and remote host.

The S/Key system establishes an ordered list of passwords. Each password is used in order and only once, then discarded. Although the maintenance of the password list may seem like an unreasonable burden to place on a user, the way in which the passwords are generated makes it conceptually simple. Essentially, passwords are

[2]The physical media over which many local network communication occurs is Ethernet. Because Ethernet is a broadcast technology, all hosts on the local network (subnet) receive every bit of transmitted data. Obviously, this approach simplifies communication eavesdropping. Although eavesdropping may be more difficult over nonbroadcast media (e.g., switched networks), it is by no means impossible.

[3]ftp is frequently used on the Web to transfer files. When used in this context, ftp generally operates in *anonymous* mode. ftp performs no authentication in this mode, and the users are often restricted to file retrieval only.

[4]In reality, the server initially transmits a short-term public key in addition to the host key. The requesting host encrypts the random value response with both keys. The use of the short-term keys prevents adversaries from recovering the content of past sessions should the host key become compromised.

created such that the knowledge of a past password provides no information on future passwords. However, if one knows a secret value (called a "seed value"), then all passwords are easily computable. Hence, whereas an authentic user can supply passwords as they are needed, a malicious adversary can supply only passwords that have been previously used (and are no longer valid).

In essence, the S/Key system allows the user to prove knowledge of the password without explicitly stating it. Over time, this relatively simple approach has been found to be extremely powerful, and is used as the basis of many authentication services. For example, RSA's widely used SecurID combines a physical token with one-time password protocols to authenticate users (RSA 2002).

Kerberos

The Kerberos system (Neuman and Ts'o 1994) performs trusted third-party authentication. In Kerberos, users, host, and services defer authentication to a mutually trusted key distribution center (KDC). All users implicitly trust the KDC to act in their best interest. Hence, this approach is appropriate for localized environments (e.g., campus, enterprise), but does not scale well to large, loosely coupled communities. Note that this is not just an artifact of the Kerberos system, but is true of any trusted third-party approach; loosely coupled communities are unlikely to universally trust any single authority.

Depicted in Figure 3, the Kerberos system performs mediated authentication between Alice and Bob through a two-phase exchange with the KDC. When logging onto the system, Alice enters her username and password.

Alice's host sends the KDC her identity. In response, the KDC sends Alice information that can be understood only by someone in possession of the password—that is, it is encrypted with a key derived from the password. Included in this information is a TGT used later by Alice to initiate a session with Bob. Alice is deemed authentic because she is able to recover the TGT.

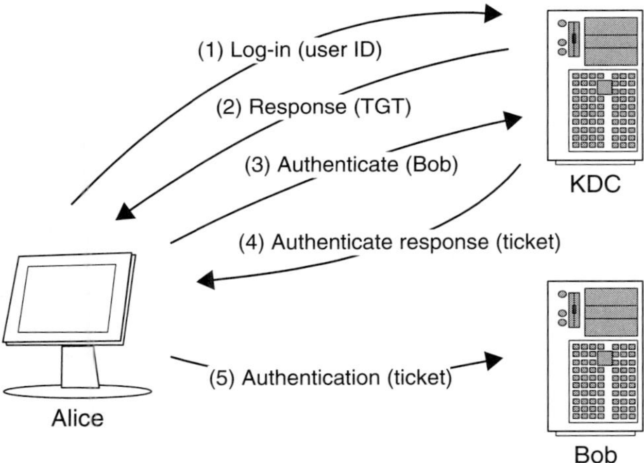

Figure 3: Kerberos authentication: Alice receives a ticket-granting ticket (TGT) after successfully logging into the Kerberos KDC. Alice performs mutual authentication with Bob by presenting a ticket obtained from the KDC to Bob. Note that Bob need not communicate with the KDC directly; the contents of the ticket serve as proof of Alice's identity

At some later point, Alice wishes to perform mutual authentication with another entity, Bob. Alice informs the KDC of this desire by identifying Bob and presenting the previously obtained TGT. Alice receives a message from the KDC containing the session key and a ticket for Bob. Encrypting the message with a key known only to Alice ensures that its contents remain confidential.

Alice then presents the ticket included in the message to Bob. Note that the ticket returned to Alice is opaque; its contents are encrypted using a key derived from Bob's password. Therefore, Bob is the only entity that can retrieve the contents of the ticket. Because later communication between Alice and Bob uses the session key (given to Alice and contained in the ticket presented to Bob), Alice is assured that Bob is authentic. Bob is assured that Alice is authentic because Bob's ticket explicitly contains Alice's identity.

One might ask why Kerberos uses a two-phase process. Over the course of a session, Alice may frequently need to authenticate a number of entities. In Kerberos, because Alice obtains a TGT at log-in, later authentication can be performed automatically. Thus, the repeated authentication of users and services occurring over time does not require human intervention; Alice types in her password only once.

Note that a KDC authenticates users only within its realm. Users and services in different realms would seem not to be able to authenticate each other. However, protocol extensions allow interrealm authentication by cross registering KDCs. A user contacts its local KDC, which acts as an introducer to the foreign KDC, which in turn enables authentication of the entities as above.

Because of its elegant design and technical maturity, the Kerberos system has been widely accepted in local environments. Historically common in UNIX environments, it has recently been introduced into other operating systems—for example, Windows 2000 and XP.

Pretty Good Privacy

As indicated by the previous discussion of trusted third parties, it is often true that two parties on the Internet will not have a direct means of performing authentication. For example, a programmer in Great Britain may not have any formal relationship with a student in California. Hence, no trusted third party exists to which both can defer authentication. A number of attempts have been made to address this problem by establishing a single public key infrastructure spanning the Internet. However, these structures require users to directly or indirectly trust CAs whose operation they know nothing about. Such assumptions are inherently dangerous, and have been largely rejected by user communities.

The pretty good privacy system (PGP; Zimmermann 1994) takes advantage of social and organizational relationships between users on the Internet. In PGP, each user creates a self-signed PGP certificate identifying a public key and identity information (e.g., e-mail address, phone number, name). Users use the key to sign the keys of users whom they trust. In addition, they obtain signatures from users who trust them. The PGP signing process is not defined by PGP. Users commonly will exchange signatures with friends and colleagues.

The keys and signatures defined for a set of users defines a web of trust. Upon reception of a key from a previously unknown source, an entity will make a judgment of whether to accept the certificate based on the presence of signatures by known entities. A certificate will likely be accepted if a signature generated by a trusted party (with known and acceptable signing practices) is present. Such assessment can span multiple certificates, in which signatures create trusted linkage between acceptable certificates. However, because trust is not frequently transitive, less trust is associated with long chains. PGP certificates are primarily used for e-mail and software distribution validation, but have been extended to support a wide range of data-exchange systems (e.g., Internet newsgroups).

Internet Protocol Security

Internet protocol security (IPsec; Kent and Atkinson 1998) is emerging as an important service for providing security on the Internet. IPsec is not just an authentication service, but provides a complete set of protocols and tools for securing IP-based communication. The IPsec suite of protocols provides host-to-host security within the operating system implementation of the IP protocol stack. This has the advantage of being transparent to applications running on the hosts. A disadvantage of IPsec is that it does not differentiate between users on the host. Hence, while communication passing between the hosts is secure (as determined by policy), little can be ascertained as to the true identity of users on those hosts.

The central goal of IPsec was the construction of a general-purpose security infrastructure supporting many network environments. Hence, IPsec supports the use of an array of authentication mechanisms. IPsec authentication can be performed manually or automatically. Manually authenticated hosts share secrets distributed via administrators (i.e., configured manually at each host). Identity is inferred from knowledge of the secret. Session keys are directly or indirectly derived from the configured secret.

The Internet security association key management protocol (ISAKMP) defines an architecture for automatic authentication and key management used to support the IPsec suite of protocols. Built on ISAKMP, the Internet key exchange (IKE) protocol implements several protocols for authentication and session key negotiation. In these protocols, IKE negotiates a shared secret and policy between authenticated end points of an IPsec connection. The resulting IPsec security association (SA) records the result of IKE negotiation, and is used to drive later communication between the end points.

The specifics of how authentication information is conveyed to a host are a matter of policy and implementation. However, in all implementations, each host must identify the keys or certificates to be used by IKE authentication. For example, Windows XP provides dialogs used to enter preshared keys. These keys are stored in the Windows registry, and are later used by IKE for authentication and session key negotiation. Note that how the host stores secrets is of paramount importance. As with any security solution, users should carefully read all documentation and related security bulletins when using such interfaces.

Wireless Networks

Wireless networks are quickly becoming ubiquitous. The ability to get access to the Internet anywhere and at any time is permitting new applications and easing our online and physical lives. However, wireless networks introduce enormous security risks. The omnipresence of wireless permits anyone within range some level of access to sensitive assets. In short, the security perimeter upon which much of traditional network security is based has completely disappeared. This has caused security personnel, developers, and researchers to reevaluate the methods and policies used to govern the digital domain. This is particularly true of authentication.

Wireless networks are defined by the mode in which they operate. There are two predominant modes in use today: ad hoc and infrastructure. In an ad hoc mode, the hosts in the wireless network form a peer-to-peer physical routing infrastructure. That is, each host acts as a router for the other hosts in the network by passing packets between themselves and local access points (devices that route packets between wireless and physical networks). In infrastructure mode, every host must communicate directly with an access point. Because it introduces fewer security and performance concerns and is generally simpler to administer, infrastructure mode is more popular. Independent of the mode, either the access points or peer hosts authenticate new hosts before they are allowed entry into a secure wireless network.

The simplest form of wireless authentication is MAC (media access control) authentication. Each physical network device (e.g., network card) is programmed with a unique MAC address. Because this is guaranteed to be unique, it can be used to identify the devices that should be allowed on the network (e.g., employee laptops). The authenticating device simply looks at the MAC address included in each packet. If it is on the list of approved devices, the packet is allowed. Note that this is not very secure, but it does prevent hosts from inadvertently gaining access to the network. MAC addresses can be trivially spoofed, and moderately sophisticated users easily bypass such authentication measures.

The wired equivalent privacy (WEP) protocol was introduced to solve some of the security issues associated with wireless networks. The WEP protocol aims only to prevent unauthorized parties from gaining access to the network or manipulating packets on the network. WEP assumes that all authorized entities have access to a cryptographic key shared by all authorized parties. In practice, this key is typically generated from a password or pass-phrase entered into some host configuration dialog. WEP specifies how the key is used to encrypt and provide integrity checks for the packet payload. Hence, the WEP key (or password) is used as a credential—access to the password is deemed sufficient proof of identity as an authorized user.

WEP suffers from two central limitations. First, the protocol has a critical design flaw that leaves the WEP key vulnerable to exposure. This exploit is available in several widely available hacker tools, and has led to the decline of the protocol's use. A second limitation is that the protocol does not identify a particular user or host. Hence, it is difficult to perform accounting and user logging in environments that use WEP as the sole authentication mechanism.

The 802.11i (also known as WPA) standards are designed to address the security limitations of WEP. In addition to addressing transport security (e.g., encryption key management), these standards define a framework for wireless authentication. The authentication framework standard, called 801.1x, provides an architecture in which centralized services authenticate hosts through access points Existing authentication services can be used for authenticating the hosts (e.g., Kerberos, certificates, etc.), and the standard defines how these methods will be performed in the wireless network.

The centerpiece of the 802.1x standard is the EAP (Extensible Authentication Protocol). EAP is a challenge-response protocol run over secured transport service such as TLS/SSL Once the secure transport protocol is established, other authentication services such as Kerberos or RADIUS are used to complete authentication. Developed by the CISCO Corporation, LEAP is an instance of the EAP protocol. Wireless clients (e.g., laptops, PC, handhelds) use the LEAP protocol to communicate with RADIUS-enabled gateway devices. Typically, the gateway devices are wireless base stations that connect the wireless network to local wired networks.

Interactive Media

The growth of the Internet has spawned many new ways of communicating. Internet messaging, voice over IP, digital conferencing, collaborative tools, and other media have hastened changes in the way we interact with people all over the globe. However, with these new media comes the need for authentication: we must ensure that we are exposing our data and ourselves only to authenticated users and services.

The H.323 protocol is the dominant tool for interactive media on the Internet. H.323 is a suite of media protocols that control the signaling and data transmission in media calls. The session initialization protocol (SIP) is an evolving framework for IP-based media signaling, and is seen as a replacement for much of H.323. Both H.323 and SIP allow the gatekeeper servers to integrate external authentication services such as RADIUS (remote authentication dial-in user service). Hence, as is the trend on general computing systems, the media applications most frequently defer authentication to specialized services.

CONCLUSION

The preceding sections described but a small fraction of the vast array of available authentication services. Given the huge number of alternatives, one might ask, "which one of these systems is right for my environment?" The following presents several guidelines for the integration of an authentication service with applications and environments.

- *Don't try to build a custom authentication service*. Designing and coding an authentication service is inherently difficult. This fact has been repeatedly demonstrated on the Internet; bugs and design flaws are occasionally found in widely deployed systems, and several custom authentication services have been broken in a matter of hours. It is highly likely that there exists an authentication service that is appropriate for a given environment. For all these reasons, one should use services that have been time-tested.
- *Understand who is trusted by whom*. Any authentication system should accurately reflect the trust held by all parties. For example, a system that authenticates students in a campus environment may take advantage of local authorities. In practice, such authorities are unlikely to be trusted by arbitrary end points in the Internet. Failure to match the trust existing in the physical world has ultimately led to the failure of many services.
- *Evaluate the value of the resources being protected and the strength of the surrounding security infrastructure*. Authentication is useful only when used to protect access to a resource of some value. Hence, the authentication service should accurately reflect the value of the resources being protected. Moreover, the strength of the surrounding security infrastructure should be matched by the authentication service. One wants to avoid "putting a steel door in a straw house." Conversely, a weak or flawed authentication service can be used to circumvent the protection afforded by the surrounding security infrastructure.
- *Understand who or what is being identified*. Identity can mean many things to many people. Any authentication service should model identity as is appropriate for the target domain. For many applications, it is often not necessary to map a user to a physical person or computer, but may treat them as distinct, largely anonymous entities. Such approaches are likely to simplify authentication, and provide opportunities for privacy protection.
- *Establish credentials securely*. Credential establishment is often the weakest point of a security infrastructure. For example, many Web registration services establish passwords through unprotected forms (i.e., via HTTP). Malicious parties can trivially sniff such passwords and impersonate valid users. Hence, these sites are vulnerable even if every other aspect of security is correctly designed and implemented. Moreover, the limitations of many credential establishment mechanisms are often subtle. One should be careful to understand the strengths, weaknesses, and applicability of any solution to the target environment.
- *Authenticate all hosts in wireless environments*. Wireless networks vastly complicate network security. The loss of the traditional security perimeter caused by ubiquitous access mandates that strong protections be put in place to prevent authorized entities from gaining access. Authentication is a necessary component of such protections.

In the end analysis, an authentication service is one aspect of a larger framework for network security. Hence, it is necessary to consider the many factors that contribute to the design of the security infrastructure. It is only from this larger view that the requirements, models, and design of an authentication system emerge.

GLOSSARY

Authentication: The process of establishing the identity of an online entity.

Authorization: The process of establishing the set of rights associated with an entity.

Certificate: A digitally signed statement associating a set of attributes with a public key. Most frequently used to associate a public key with a virtual or real identity (i.e., identity certificate).

Credential: Evidence used to prove identity or access rights.

Malicious Party: Entity on the Internet attempting to gain unauthorized access, disrupt service, or eavesdrop on sensitive communication (synonyms: adversary, hacker).

Secret: Information known only to and accessible by a specified (and presumably small) set of entities (e.g., passwords, cryptographic keys).

Trusted Third Party: An entity mutually trusted (typically by two end points) to assert authenticity or authorization, or perform conflict resolution. Trusted third parties are also often used to aid in secret negotiation (e.g., cryptographic keys).

Web of Trust: Self-regulated certification system constructed through the creation of ad hoc relationships between members of a user community. Webs are typically defined through the exchange of user certificates and signatures within the pretty good privacy (PGP) system.

CROSS REFERENCES

See *Cryptography*; *Password Authentication*; *Smart Cards: Communication Protocols and Applications*.

REFERENCES

Apache 2002. http://httpd.apache.org (accessed August 1, 2007).

Diffie, W., and M. E. Hellman. 1976. New directions in cryptography. *IEEE Transactions on Information Theory* 6:644–54.

Dusse, S., P. Hoffman, B. Ramsdell, L. Lundblade, and L. Repka. 1998, March. S/MIME version 2, Message specification. Internet Engineering Task Force, RFC 2311. www.faqs.org/rfcs/rfc2311.html (accessed June 2, 2007).

Franks, J., P. Hallam-Baker, J. Hostetler, S. Lawrence, P. Leach, A. Luotonen, and L. Stewart. 1999. HTTP authentication: Basic and digest access authentication. Internet Engineering Task Force, RFC 2617. www.faqs.org/rfcs/rfc2617.html (accessed June 2, 2007).

Fu, K., E. Sit, K. Smith, and N. Feamster. 2001. Dos and don'ts of client authentication on the Web. 10th USENIX Security Symposium, 2001. http://pdos.csail.mit.edu/papers/webauth:sec10.pdf (accessed June 2, 2007).

Haller, N. M. 1994. The S/Key one-time password system. In *Proceedings of the 1994 Internet Society Symposium on Network and Distributed System Security*, 151–7. www.cs.utk.edu/~dunigan/cns04/skey.pdf (accessed June 2, 2007).

Kent, S., and R. Atkinson. 1998. Security architecture for the Internet protocol. Internet Engineering Task Force, RFC 2401. http://www.faqs.org/rfcs/rfc2401.html (accessed June 2, 2007).

Kormann, D. P., and A. D. Rubin. *Risks of the Passport single signon protocol* www.avirubin.com/passport.html (accessed June 2, 2007).

Neuman, B. C., and T. Ts'o. 1994. Kerberos: An authentication service for computer networks. *IEEE Communications* 32(9):33–8.

RSA. 2002. www.rsasecurity.com/products/securid (accessed August 1, 2007).

VeriSign. 2002. http://www.verisign.com (accessed August 1, 2007).

Ylonen, T. 1996. SSH—Secure login connections over the Internet. In *Proceedings of 6th USENIX Security Symposium*, 37–42. San Francisco: USENIX Association.

Zimmermann, P. 1994. *PGP user's guide.* Cambridge, MA: MIT Press.

Password Authentication

Jeremy L. Rasmussen, *Sypris Electronics*

INTRODUCTION

The ancient folk tale of Ali Baba and the Forty Thieves mentions the use of a password. In this story, Ali Baba finds that the phrase "Open Sesame" magically opens the entrance to a cave where the thieves have hidden their treasure. Similarly, modern computer systems use passwords to authenticate users and allow them entrance to system resources and data shares on an automated basis. The use of passwords in computer systems can be traced to the earliest multi-user time-sharing and dial-up networks. There is no evidence that passwords were used before this in purely batch-job systems.

The security provided by a password system depends on the passwords being kept secret at all times. Thus, a password is vulnerable to compromise whenever it is used, stored, or even known. In a password-based authentication mechanism implemented on a computer system, passwords are vulnerable to compromise because of the following exposure areas (Brotman 1985):

1. Passwords are initially assigned to users when they are enrolled on the system. The threat here is that a default password can be guessed and used by an attacker before it is changed by the authorized user. In addition, an attacker could trick a system administrator or user to reset an account password to a default state, allowing an avenue for compromise.
2. Passwords are stored in a "password database" by the system. If an attacker could access the database, he could compromise the security of the passwords stored in it.
3. Users must remember their passwords. Because of the limitations of human memory, users are prone to choose weak or easily guessed passwords, or else they write down their passwords. Either can lead to compromise by attackers.
4. Users must enter passwords into the system to authenticate. Whenever passwords are entered, an attacker could use a keystroke logger, sniffer, or other device to capture the password and perhaps replay it later.

Because of these factors, a number of protection schemes have been developed for maintaining password security. These include implementing policies and mechanisms to ensure "strong" passwords, encrypting the password database, and simplifying the sign-on and password synchronization processes. Without a "defense-in-depth" approach to securing passwords—that is, implementing all of these methods to provide several layers of security—security administrators will be leaving their systems at risk.

TYPES OF IDENTIFICATION/AUTHENTICATION

There are three basic ways to verify the identity of users on a system: (1) what they have (e.g., smartcard or hardware token), (2) what they are (e.g., biometric fingerprint [see Figure 1] or iris pattern), and (3) what they know (e.g., personal identification number [PIN] or password).

Of all identity verification methods, passwords are probably weakest because of the exposure factors enumerated above; yet they are still the most widely used method in systems today because password-verification schemes are easily programmed and maintained in automated systems. In order to guarantee strong authentication, a system ought to combine two or more of the verification factors. For example, in order to access an ATM, someone must have a bank card and know her PIN.

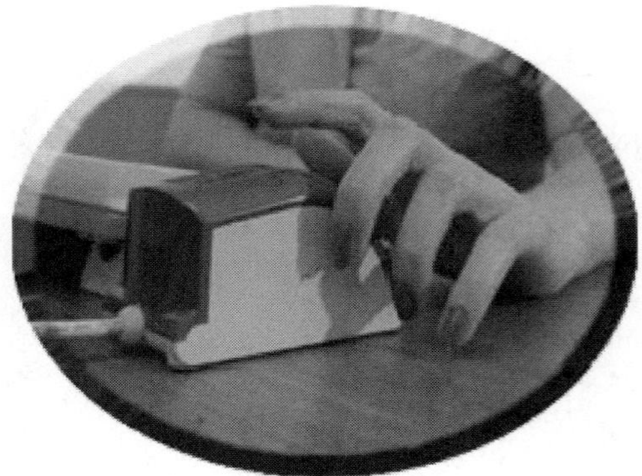

Figure 1: A biometric fingerprint reader (photo courtesy of Biometric Access Company)

The manner in which these verification methods are implemented in a system include hardware or software features, operating procedures, management procedures, or a combination of these.

HISTORY OF PASSWORDS IN MODERN COMPUTING

Conjecture as to which system was the first to incorporate passwords was discussed by several computing pioneers on the Cyberspace History List-Server (CYHIST), the archives of which are now maintained by West Virginia University (www.clc.wvu.edu). However, no one ever provided any concrete evidence to support one system or another as being the progenitor. The consensus opinion favors the Compatible Time-Sharing System (CTSS) developed at the Massachusetts Institute of Technology (MIT) Computation Center beginning in 1961. As part of Project MAC (multiple access computer) under the direction of Professor Fernando J. ("Corby") Corbató, the system was implemented on an IBM 7094 and reportedly began using passwords by 1963.

According to researcher Norman Hardy, who worked on the project, the security of passwords immediately became an issue as well: "I can vouch for some version of CTSS having passwords. It was in the second edition of the CTSS manual, I think, that illustrated the login command. It had Corby's user name and password. It worked—and he changed it the same day" (personal e-mail communication to the author of this chapter).

Passwords were widely in use by the early 1970s as the "hacker" culture began to develop, possibly in tacit opposition to the ARPANET (the precursor to the Internet). By the 1980s, there were published accounts of how passwords had been used to access systems either by guessing or using system default passwords. In the 1990s, sophisticated password-cracking tools began to appear. Incidentally, the technical knowledge required to use such tools did not increase. On the contrary, these tools are simple to use and widely available for free on the Internet (see Figure 2). Now, with the explosion of the World Wide Web, the use of passwords and the quantity of confidential data that those passwords protect have grown exponentially.

However, just as the forty thieves' password protection system was breached (the cave could not differentiate between Ali Baba's voice and those of the thieves), computer password systems have also been plagued by a number of vulnerabilities. The history of password authentication is replete with examples of weak, easily compromised systems. In general, "weak" authentication systems are characterized by protocols that either leak the password directly over the network or leak sufficient information while performing authentication to allow intruders to deduce or guess at the password.

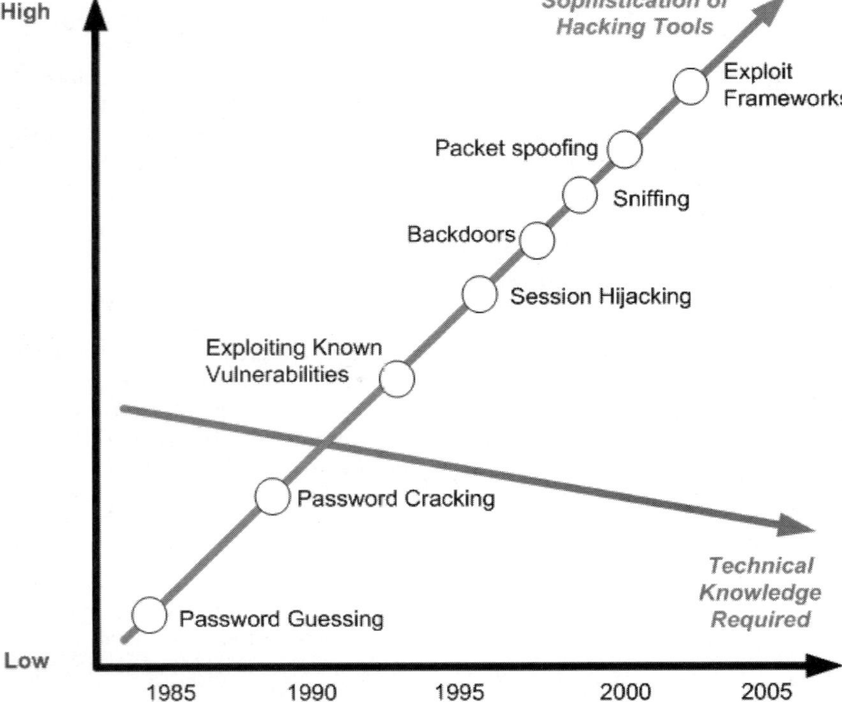

Figure 2: Proliferation of hacking tools

The U.S. Department of Defense Computer Security Center (CSC) recognized this problem and published the *Password Management Guideline* (also known as the "Green Book") in 1985 "to assist in providing that much needed credibility of user identity by presenting a set of good practices related to the design, implementation and use of password-based user authentication mechanisms." The Green Book outlined a number of steps that system security administrators should take to ensure password security and suggests that, whenever possible, they be automated. These include the following "Ten Commandments" of passwords:

1. System security administrators should change the passwords for all standard user IDs before allowing the general user population to access the system.
2. A new user should always appear to the system as having an "expired password," which will require the user to change the password by the usual procedure before receiving authorization to access the system.
3. Each user ID should be assigned to only one person. No two people should ever have the same user ID at the same time, or even at different times. It should be considered a security violation when two or more people know the password for a user ID.
4. Users need to be aware of their responsibility to keep passwords private and to report changes in their user status or suspected security violations. Users should also be required to sign a statement to acknowledge understanding of these responsibilities.
5. Passwords should be changed on a periodic basis to counter the possibility of undetected password compromise.
6. Users should memorize their passwords and not write them on any medium. If passwords must be written, they should be protected in a manner that is consistent with the damage that could be caused by their compromise.
7. Stored passwords should be protected by access controls provided by the system, by password encryption, or by both.
8. Passwords should be encrypted immediately after entry, and the memory containing the plaintext password should be erased immediately after encryption.
9. Only the encrypted password should be used in comparisons. There is no need to be able to decrypt passwords. Comparisons can be made by encrypting the password entered at log-in and comparing the encrypted form with the encrypted password stored in the password database.
10. The system should not echo passwords that users type in, or at least it should mask the entered password (e.g., with asterisks).

PASSWORD SECURITY—BACKGROUND

Information Theory

According to fundamental work in information theory performed by Claude Shannon (1948), we find that a password is only as good as its entropy, or apparent "randomness." According to Shannon's theorems, the quality of a password (i.e., that which keeps an attacker from guessing it) is not necessarily a function of the length of a password or the number of symbols used in it. Rather, it is determined by how many different possible passwords there are and how frequently each is used. The following illustrates this.

Say a user is filling out a form on a Web page (see Figure 3). The form has a space for "Sex," and leaves six characters for entering either "female" or "male" before

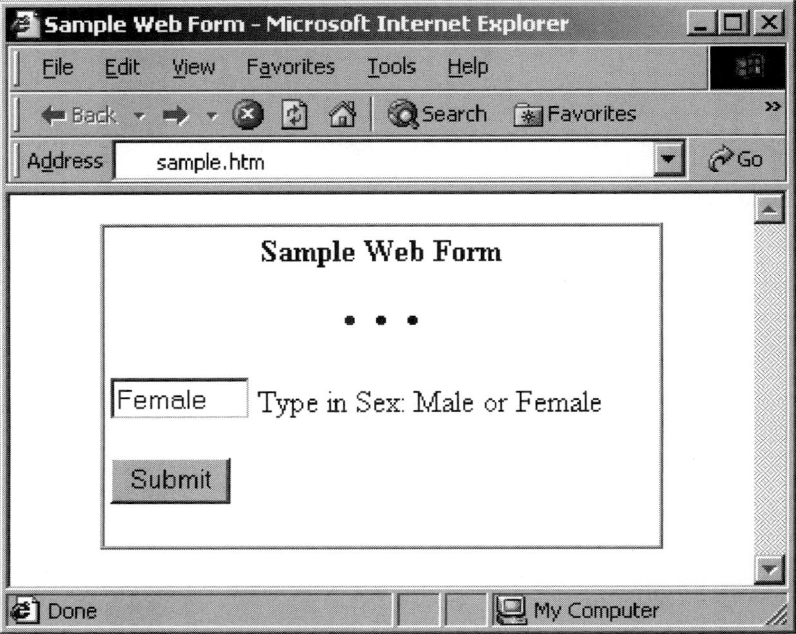

Figure 3: Sample Web page entry form

the entry is encrypted and sent to the server. If we consider each character is a byte (8 bits), then $6 \times 8 = 48$ bits will be sent for this response. Is this how much information is actually contained in the field, though? Clearly, there is only 1 *bit* of data represented by the entry—a binary value—either male or female. That means there is only 1 bit of entropy (or uncertainty), and there are 47 bits of redundancy in the field. This redundancy could be used by a cryptanalyst (someone who analyzes crypto-systems) to find regularities between the unencrypted and encrypted text, perhaps allowing him to crack the key and reveal the entire entry.

The same concept applies to password security. A longer password is not necessarily a better password. Rather, a password that is difficult to guess (i.e., one that has high entropy or appears random) is best. This usually comes from a combination of factors (see "Guidelines for Selecting a Strong Password," below). The probability that any single attempt at guessing a password will be successful is one of the most critical factors in a password system. This probability depends on the size of the password space and the statistical distribution within that space of passwords that are actually used.

However, over the past several decades, Moore's law (see Glossary) has made it possible to use brute-force methods (i.e., trying all combinations a keyboard can provide) to crack password spaces of larger and larger entropy. This, combined with the fact that there is a limit to the entropy that the average user can remember, means that nowadays passwords are more at risk than ever. A user cannot typically remember a completely random-looking 32-character password—but that is what is required to have the equivalent strength of a 128-bit (i.e., strong) encryption key. Password-cracking tools have advanced to the point of being able to crack nearly anything a system could reasonably expect a user to memorize (see "Password Length and Human Memory," below).

Cryptographic Protection of Passwords

In early password systems, the most basic and least secure method of authentication was to store passwords in plaintext in a database on a server. During authentication, the client would send his or her password to the server, and the server would compare this against the stored value. Obviously, however, if the password file were accessible to unauthorized users, the security of the system could easily be compromised.

In later systems, developers discovered that a server did not need to store a user's password in plaintext form in order to perform password authentication. Instead, the password could be transformed through a one-way function, such as a hash function, into a random-looking sequence of bytes. Such a function would be difficult to invert. In other words, given a password, it would be easy to compute its hash, but given a hash, it would be computationally infeasible to derive the password from it (see "Hashing," below). Authentication would consist merely of performing the hash function over the client's password and comparing it to the stored value. The password database itself could be made accessible to all users without fear of an intruder being able to steal passwords from it.

According to Cambridge University professor of computing Roger Needham, the Cambridge Multiple Access System (CMAS), which was an integrated online-offline terminal or regular input-driven system, may have been among the earliest to implement such one-way functions. It first went online in 1967, and incorporated password protection. According to Needham: "In 1966, we conceived the use of one-way functions to protect the password file, and this was an implemented feature from day one" (personal e-mail communication to the author of this article).

Hashing

A hash function is an algorithm that takes a variable-length string as input and produces a fixed-length value (the hash) as output. The challenge for a hashing algorithm is to make this process irreversible; that is, finding a string that produces a given hash value should be very difficult. It should also be difficult to find two arbitrary strings that produce the same hash value. This is called a "collision."

Also called "message digests" or "fingerprints," several one-way hash functions are in common use today. Among these are Message Digest Algorithm 5 (MD5) and Secure Hash Algorithm 1 (SHA-1). The former was developed by Ron Rivest for RSA Security, Inc., and produces 128-bit hash values. See Table 1 for an example of output generated by MD5. SHA-1 was developed by the U.S. National Institute of Standards and Technology (NIST) and the National Security Agency (NSA), and produces 160-bit hash values. SHA-1 is generally considered more secure than MD5 because of its longer hash value. The longer the output, the harder it is to find a collision.

Microsoft Windows XP uses one-way hash functions to store password information in the security account manager (SAM). There are no Windows32 applications programming interface (API) function calls to retrieve user passwords because the system does not store them. It stores only hash values. However, even a hash-encrypted password in a database is not entirely secure. A cracking tool can compile a list of, say, the one million most commonly used passwords and compute hash functions from all of them. Then the tool can obtain the system account database and compare the hashed passwords in the database with its own list to see what matches. This is called a "dictionary attack" (see "Password-Cracking Tools," below).

To make dictionary attacks more difficult, some systems use what is called a "salt." A salt is a random string that is concatenated with a password before it is operated on by the hashing function. The salt value is then stored in the user database, together with the result of the hash function. Using a salt makes dictionary attacks more difficult, as a cracker would have to compute the hashes for all possible salt values.

A simple example of a salt would be to add the time of day; for example, if a user logs in at noon using the password "pass," the string that would be encrypted might be "1p2a0s0s." By adding this randomness to the password, the hash will actually be different every time the user logs in (unless he logs in at noon every day). Whether a salt is used and what the salt is depends on the operating system and the encryption algorithm being used. In the FreeBSD

Table 1: Output from the MD5 Test Suite

For the input string	The output message digest is
""(no password)	d41d8cd98f00b204e9800998ecf8427e
"a"	0cc175b9c0f1b6a831c399e269772661
"abc"	900150983cd24fb0d6963f7d28e17f72
"message digest"	f96b697d7cb7938d525a2f31aaf161d0
"abcdefghijklmnopqrstuvwxyz"	c3fcd3d76192e4007dfb496cca67e13b
"ABCDEFGHIJKLMNOPQRSTUVWXYZab cdefghijklmnipqrstuvwxyz0123456789"	d174ab98d277d9f5a5611c2c9f419d9f
"12345678901234567890123456789012345678901234567890123456789012345678901234567890"	57edf4a22be3c955ac49da2e2107b67a

operating system, for example, there is a function called "crypt" that uses the DES (data encryption standard), MD5, or Blowfish algorithms to hash passwords and can also use three forms of salts.

Hashing addresses the secure storage issue, but it does not address another weakness in a networked environment—it is difficult to transmit the password securely to the server for verification without it being captured and reused, perhaps in a replay attack. To avoid revealing passwords directly over an untrusted network, computer scientists have developed "challenge and response" systems. At their simplest, the server sends the user some sort of challenge, which would typically be a random string of characters called a "nonce" (contraction of "number used once") that changes with time. The user then computes a response, usually some function based on both the challenge and the password. This way, even if the intruder captured a valid challenge/response pair, it would not help her gain access to the system, because future challenges would be different and require different responses.

These challenge/response systems are sometimes referred to as one-time password (OTP) systems. Bellcore's S/KEY is one such system in which a one-time password is calculated by combining a seed with a secret password known only to the user and then applying a secure hashing algorithm a number of times equal to the sequence number. Each time the user is authenticated, the sequence number expected by the system is decremented, thus eliminating the possibility of an attacker trying a replay attack using the same password again.

PASSWORD-CRACKING TOOLS

Password-Cracking Approaches

As mentioned above, passwords are typically stored as values hashed with one-way functions. In other words, this entire book could be hashed and represented as 8 bytes of gibberish. There would be no way to use these 8 bytes of data to obtain the original text. However, password crackers know that people do not use whole books as their passwords. The majority of passwords are four to twelve characters in length. Passwords are also, in general, not just random strings of symbols. Because users need to remember them, passwords are usually words or phrases of significance to the user. This is an opportunity for the attacker to reduce the search space.

An attacker might steal a password file, or sniff the network segment and capture the user ID/password hash pairs during log-on, and then run a password-cracking tool on them. Because it is impossible to decrypt a hash back to a password, these programs will try a dictionary attack approach first. The program guesses a password; for instance, the word "Dilbert." The program then hashes "Dilbert" and compares the hash to one of the hashed entries in the password file. If it matches, then that password hash represents the password "Dilbert." If the hash does not match, the program takes another guess. Depending on the tool, a password cracker will try all the words in a dictionary, all the names in a phone book, and so on. Again, the attacker does not need to know the original password, just a password that hashes to the same value.

This is analogous to the "birthday paradox," which is an old parlor trick that says, "If you get 25 people together in a room, the odds are better than 50/50 that two of them will have the same birthday." How does this work? Imagine a person meeting another on the street and asking him his birthday. The chances of the two having the same birthday are only 1/365 (0.27 percent). Even if one person asks 25 people, the probability is still low. But with 25 people in a room together, each of the 25 is asking the other 24 about their birthdays. Each person only has a small (less than 5 percent) chance of success, but trying it 25 times increases the probability significantly.

In a room with 25 people, there are 300 possible pairs (25*24/2). Each pair has a probability of success of 1/365 = 0.27 percent, and a probability of failure of 1 − 0.27 percent = 99.726 percent. Calculating the probability of failure: 99.726 percent^{300} = 44 percent. The probability of success is then 100 percent − 44 percent = 56 percent. So a birthday match will actually be found five out of nine times. In a room with 42 people, the odds of finding a birthday match rise to 9 out of 10. Thus, the birthday paradox is that it is much easier to find two arbitrary values that match than it is to find a match to some particular value.

If the first wave of dictionary guesses fails to produce any passwords for the attacker, the cracking program will try a hybrid approach of different combinations, such as forward and backward spellings of dictionary words, additional numbers and special characters, or sequences of characters. The goal here again is to reduce the cracker's search space by trying "likely" combinations of known words. Note that cracking programs are very clever about guessing hacker jargon; so, do not assume that "h@ck0rz" would be a sufficiently obscure form of "hackers," if that were your password.

After exhausting both of these avenues, the cracking program would start in on an exhaustive or "brute-force" attack on the entire password space. The program also remembers the passwords it has already tried and will not need to recheck these during the search.

Rainbow Tables

An alternative to cracking passwords is simply to know all of them ahead of time. Modern techniques make use of prodigiously large tables that list all possible password hash values and allow quick lookup and retrieval. These are known as rainbow tables. The idea here is that you are trading space for time. You could implement a hash-and-check operation with a very small amount of memory; however, you are at the mercy of your processing speed. Conversely, with enough storage space, you could access a table of every possible hash value for passwords of a given length and on a particular system (for example, all of the older LanMan-type Windows passwords), and then processing speed would be inconsequential. There are techniques for looking up things very quickly in large tables. Computer scientist Philippe Oechslin (2003) demonstrated this at the Crypto 2003 Conference. Using 1.4 GB of data (two CD-ROMs), he showed that he could crack 99.9 percent of all alphanumerical Windows password hashes in 13.6 seconds. Subsequently, Zhu Shuanglei published code and a tool called RainbowCrack that allows anyone to generate his or her own rainbow tables for all sorts of hashing algorithms. There are Web sites where you can download the rainbow tables people have generated using RainbowCrack, and there are various forums where people trade rainbow tables they have custom-generated.

Password-Retrieving Approaches

Before password-cracking can commence, an attacker must first retrieve the password hashes for his program to decipher. Several programs, such as L0phtcrack,[1] have built-in mechanisms to do this. A sophisticated attacker will not try to guess passwords by entering them through the standard user interface, because the time to do so is prohibitive, and most systems can be configured to lock out a user after too many wrong guesses.

On Microsoft Windows systems, obtaining the password hashes requires the "Administrator" privilege to read them from the database in which they are stored. This is usually somewhere in the system registry. In order to access them, a cracking tool will attempt to dump the password hashes from the Windows registry on the local machine or over the network if the remote machine allows network registry access. The latter requires a target Windows machine name or IP address.

Another method is to access the password hashes directly from the file system. On Microsoft Windows systems, this is the SAM. Because Windows locks the SAM file where the password hashes are stored in the file system with an encryption mechanism known as SYSKEY, it is impossible to read them from this file while the system is running. However, sometimes there is a backup of this file on tape, on an emergency repair disk (ERD), or in the repair directory of the system's hard drive. Alternatively, a user may boot from a floppy disk running another operating system such as Linux and be able to read password hashes directly from the file system. This is why security administrators should never neglect the physical security of systems. If an attacker can physically access a machine, he or she can bypass the built-in file system security mechanisms (see "Bypassing Password Security").

Todd Sabin released a free utility called PWDUMP2 that can dump the password hashes on a local machine if the SAM has been encrypted with the SYSKEY utility that was introduced in Windows NT Service Pack 3 and is also used in Windows 2000 and XP. Once a user downloads the utility, he or she can follow the instructions on the Web page to retrieve the password hashes, load the hashes into a tool such as L0phtcrack, and begin cracking them.

Password Sniffing

Instead of capturing the system user file (SAM on Windows or /etc/passwd or /etc/shadow on UNIX/Linux), another way of collecting user IDs and passwords is through sniffing network traffic. Sniffing uses some sort of software or hardware wiretap device to eavesdrop on network com- munications, usually by capturing and deciphering communications packets. According to Peiter "Mudge" Zatko (1999), who authored L0phtcrack: "Sniffing is slang for placing a network card into promiscuous mode so that it actually looks at all of the traffic coming along the line and not just the packets that are addressed to it. By doing this one can catch passwords, login names, confidential information, etc."

L0phtcrack offers an "SMB Packet Capture" function to capture encrypted hashes transmitted over a Windows network segment. On a switched network, a cracker will be able to sniff only sessions originating from the local machine or connecting to that machine. As server message block (SMB) session authentication messages are captured by the tool, they are displayed in the SMB Packet Capture window. The display shows the source and destination IP addresses, the username, the SMB challenge, the encrypted LAN manager hash, and the encrypted NT LAN manager hash, if any. To crack these hashes, the tool saves the session and then works on the captured file.

Note that the L0phtcrack application was acquired by Symantec Corporation in 2004. Symantec has since stopped selling this tool to new customers, citing

[1]Note that Symantec stopped shipping its L0phtcrack product in March 2006, and stopped supporting it as of December 16, 2006. www.eweek.com/article2/0,1895,1935696,00.asp.

U.S. government export regulations, and announced that they have discontinued support as of the end of 2006 (Narain 2006).

Bypassing Password Security

Limiting physical access to computer systems is still an important way to protect password-enabled systems. Norwegian software developer Petter Nordahl-Hagen developed a tool called "The Offline NT Password Editor" for recovering Windows passwords on workstations. His approach bypasses the NTFS (new technology file system) file permissions of Windows NT, 2000, and XP by using a Linux boot disk that allows one to reset the Administrator password on a system by replacing the hash stored in the SAM with a user-selected hash. His program has even been shown to work on Windows XP systems with SYSKEY enabled. An MS-DOS version also exists, as do versions that boot either from a CD-ROM or USB thumb drive. Thus, physical access to the workstation can mean instant compromise, unless perhaps the system BIOS settings are also password-protected and do not allow a user to boot from floppy or CD-ROM. However, several attacks against BIOS settings have also been published. These include the following (LabMice.net 2003):

- Using a manufacturer's backdoor password to access the BIOS
- Using password-cracking software
- Resetting the CMOS (complementary metal oxide semiconductor) using the jumpers or solder beads
- Removing the CMOS battery for at least 10 minutes
- Overloading the keyboard buffer
- Using a professional service

Types of Password-Cracking Tools

Password-cracking tools can be divided into two categories—those that attempt to retrieve system-level log-in passwords and those that attack the password-protection mechanisms of specific applications. The first type includes programs such as L0phtcrack, Cain & Abel, and John the Ripper. Some sites for obtaining password-cracking tools for various platforms, operating systems, and applications are included in the "Software Tool References" section at the end of this chapter.

The Russian company ElcomSoft has developed a range of programs that can crack application passwords for Microsoft Office encrypted files, WinZip or PKZip archived files, or Adobe Acrobat (PDF) files. The U.S. government charged ElcomSoft with violating the Digital Millennium Copyright Act of 1998 for selling a program that allowed people to disable encryption software from Adobe Systems that is used to protect electronic books. The case drew attention after ElcomSoft programmer Dmitry Sklyarov was arrested at the DefCon 2001 convention in July 2001. A jury later acquitted Sklyarov and ElcomSoft. Although the jury agreed that ElcomSoft's product was illegal, they decided to acquit because they believed the company did not mean to violate U.S. law.

PASSWORD SECURITY ISSUES AND EFFECTIVE MANAGEMENT

Enforcing Password Guidelines

The FBI and the Systems Administration and Networking Security (SANS) Institute (2006) maintain a Web page summarizing the "Twenty Most Critical Internet Security Vulnerabilities." The majority of successful attacks on computer systems via the Internet can be traced to exploitation of security flaws on this list. One of the items on this list is "accounts with no passwords or weak passwords." In general, these accounts should be removed or assigned stronger passwords.

In addition, accounts with built-in or default passwords that have never been reconfigured create vulnerabilities because they usually have the same password across installations of the software. Attackers will look for these accounts, having found the commonly known passwords published on hacking Web sites or some other public forum. Therefore, any default or built-in accounts also need to be identified and removed from the system or reconfigured with stronger passwords.

With the proliferation of wireless systems, the default configuration vulnerability has become an even bigger issue. For instance, a user who installs a new wireless router at her home and keeps the out-of-the-box settings is susceptible to being compromised. The device will likely have a default service set identifier (SSID), which would attract would-be snoopers because it shows the system has not been customized. Next, after gaining access to the unsuspecting user's network, the interloper could point his browser to the default network address for configuring the router and use the default UserID/Password that is published on the vendor's Web site. Within moments, the attacker could have changed the router settings, created a denial of service, or performed other malicious acts because the user never changed her default settings.

The list of common vulnerabilities and exposures (CVEs) maintained by the MITRE Corporation (www.cve.mitre.org) provides a taxonomy for more than 3000 well-known attacker exploits (and some 14,000 others that are currently under consideration). Among these, more than 1100 have to do with password insecurities. The following provides a few examples across many platforms:

- CVE-1999–0366: "In some cases, Service Pack 4 for Windows NT 4.0 can allow access to network shares using a blank password, through a problem with a null NT hash value."
- CVE-1999–1104: "Windows 95 uses weak encryption for the password list (.pwl) file used when password caching is enabled, which allows local users to gain privileges by decrypting the passwords."
- CVE-1999–1298: "Sysinstall in FreeBSD 2.2.1 and earlier, when configuring anonymous FTP, creates the ftp user without a password and with/bin/date as the shell, which could allow attackers to gain access to certain system resources."
- CVE-2000–0267: "Cisco Catalyst 5.4.x allows a user to gain access to the 'enable' mode without a password."

- CVE-2000–0981: "MySQL Database Engine uses a weak authentication method which leaks information that could be used by a remote attacker to recover the password."
- CVE-2001–0465: "TurboTax saves passwords in a temporary file when a user imports investment tax information from a financial institution, which could allow local users to obtain sensitive information."
- CVE-2002-0911: "Caldera Volution Manager 1.1 stores the Directory Administrator password in cleartext in the slapd.conf file, which could allow local users to gain privileges."
- CVE-2003-0601: "Workgroup Manager in Apple Mac OS X Server 10.2 through 10.2.6 does not disable a password for a new account before it is saved for the first time, which allows remote attackers to gain unauthorized access via the new account before it is saved."
- CVE-2003-0745: "SNMPc 6.0.8 and earlier performs authentication to the server on the client side, which allows remote attackers to gain privileges by decrypting the password that is returned by the server."
- CVE-2004-0031: "PHPGEDVIEW 2.61 allows remote attackers to reinstall the software and change the administrator password via a direct HTTP request to edit-config.php."
- CVE-2005-3595: "By default Microsoft Windows XP Home Edition installs with a blank password for the Administrator account, which allows remote attackers to gain control of the computer."
- CVE-2006-2229: "OpenVPN 2.0.7 and earlier, when configured to use the management option with an IP that is not 127.0.0.1, uses a cleartext password for TCP sessions to the management interface, which might allow remote attackers to view sensitive information or cause a denial of service."

SANS suggests that to determine whether your system is vulnerable to such attacks, you need to be cognizant of all the user accounts on the system. First, the system security administrator must inventory the accounts on the system and create a master list. This list should include even intermediate systems, such as routers and gateways, as well as any Internet-connected printers and print controllers. Second, the administrator should develop procedures for adding authorized accounts to the list and for removing accounts when they are no longer in use. The master list should be validated on a regular basis. In addition, the administrator should run some password-strength-checking tool against the accounts to look for weak or nonexistent passwords. A sample of these tools is noted in the "Software Tool References" section at the end of this chapter.

Many organizations supplement password-control programs with procedural or administrative controls that ensure that passwords are changed regularly and that old passwords are not reused. If password aging is used, the system should give users a warning and the opportunity to change their passwords before they expire. In addition, administrators should set account lockout policies that lock out a user after a number of unsuccessful log-in attempts, and cause him have his password reset.

Microsoft Windows XP, Server 2003, and Vista include built-in password constraint options in the "Group Policy" settings. An administrator can configure the network so that user passwords must have a minimum length, complexity, minimum and maximum age, and other constraints. It is important to require a minimum age of a password.

Guidelines for Selecting a Strong Password

The following outlines the minimal criteria for selecting "strong" passwords:

- The goal is to select something easily remembered but not easily guessed.
- Length:
  - Windows systems: seven characters or longer
  - UNIX, Linux systems: eight characters or longer
- Composition:
  - Mixture of alphabetic, numeric, and special characters (e.g., #, @, or !)
  - Mixture of upper- and lower-case characters
  - No words found in a dictionary
  - No personal information about the user (e.g., any part of the user's name, a family member's name, or the user's date of birth, Social Security number, phone number, license plate number, etc.)
  - No information that is easily obtained about the user, especially any part of the user ID
  - No commonly used proper names such as local sports teams or celebrities
  - No easily recognized keyboard patterns such as 12345, sssss, or qwerty
  - Try misspelling or abbreviating a word that has some meaning to the user (e.g., "How to select a good password?" becomes "H2sagP?")

Password Aging and Reuse

Users should be required to change their passwords regularly to limit the usefulness of compromised passwords. Many systems force users to change their passwords when they log in for the first time, and again if they have not changed their passwords for an extended period (say, 90 days). In addition, users should not reuse previous passwords. Some systems support this by recording the old passwords, ensuring that users cannot change their passwords back to previously used values, and ensuring that the users' new passwords are significantly different from their previous passwords. Unfortunately, such systems usually have a finite memory (say, the past 10 passwords), and users can circumvent the filtering controls by changing their password 10 times in a row until it is the same as the previously used password.

At a predetermined time prior to their password expiration, users should be notified by the system that they will need to change their password. A user who logs in with an ID having an expired password should be required to change the password before further access to the system is permitted. If a password is not changed before the end of its maximum lifetime, the user ID should be locked by the system, and no log-in should be permitted until a system administrator unlocks it. After a password has been changed, the lifetime period for the password should be reset to the maximum value established by the system.

Social Engineering

Despite advances in technology, the oldest way to attack a password-based security system is still the easiest: coercion, bribery, or trickery against the users of the system. Social engineering is an attack against people, rather than machines. It is an outsider's use of psychological tricks on legitimate users of a computer system, usually to gain the information (e.g., user IDs and passwords) needed to access a system. The notorious "hacker" Kevin Mitnick, who was convicted on charges of computer and wire fraud and spent 59 months in federal prison, told a congressional panel that he rarely used technology to gain information; he used social engineering techniques almost exclusively.

According to a study by British psychologists (Brown 2002), people often base their passwords on something obvious and easily guessed by a social engineer. About 50 percent of computer users base them on the name of a family member, a partner, or a pet. Another 30 percent use a pop idol or sporting hero. Another 10 percent of users pick passwords that reflect some kind of fantasy, often containing some sexual reference. The study showed that only 10 percent use cryptic combinations that follow all the rules of "tough" passwords.

The best countermeasures to social engineering attacks are education and awareness. Users should be instructed never to tell anyone their passwords; doing so destroys accountability. A system administrator should never need to know it either. In addition, users should never write down their passwords. A clever social engineer will find it if it is "hidden" under a mouse pad or inside a desk drawer.

Some Examples of Social Engineering Attacks

"Appeal to Authority" Attack. This is impersonating an authority figure or else identifying a key individual as a supposed acquaintance in order to demand information. For example: A secretary receives a phone call from someone claiming to be the "IT Manager." He requests her user ID and password, or gives her a value to reset her password immediately because "there has been a server crash in the computer center and we need to reset everyone's account." Once she has complied, he now has a valid user ID and password to access the system.

"Fake Web Site" Attack. The same password should not be used for multiple applications. Once a frequently used password is compromised, all of the user's accounts could be compromised. A good social engineering attack might be to put up an attractive Web site with titillating content, requiring users to register a username and password in order to access the "free" information. The attacker would record all passwords (even incorrect ones, which a user might have mistakenly entered thinking of another account), and then use those to attack the other systems frequented by the user. The Web site could even solicit information from the users about their accounts—for example, what online brokerage, banking, and e-mail accounts they use. Web-site operators can always keep a log of IP addresses used to access the site and could go back to attack the originating system directly.

"Phishing" Attack. Similar to the fake Web site, phishing schemes typically send an official-looking e-mail to the victim informing him about a security problem with his bank or e-mail account, and asking him to reconfirm his personal data via a secure link. The URL appears as if it takes him to the correct Web site, but it actually redirects him to the ISP of the attacker, where the attacker collects his user id, password, and sometimes other private data such as credit card or Social Security numbers.

In 2006, Bank of America implemented a user validation system called SiteKey which was intended to protect people from phishing sites. SiteKey has users enroll by answering a series of challenge/response questions and selecting an image from a gallery. If the user logs on to a Web site purporting to be Bank of America, but he does not recognize his previously chosen picture, he should not proceed. It is likely a rogue site masquerading as the bank www.bankofamerica.com/privacy/sitekey).

"Dumpster Diving" Attack. Many serious compromises are still caused by contractors and third parties throwing away draft instruction manuals or development notes with user IDs and passwords in them. Social engineers may use "dumpster diving"—digging through paper printouts in the trash looking for such significant information—to gain system access.

Single Sign-on and Password Synchronization

One issue that has irritated users in large secure environments is the increasing number of passwords they have to remember to access various applications. A user might need one password to log in to her workstation, another to access the network, and yet another for a particular server. Ideally, a user should be able to sign on once, with a single password, and be able to access all the other systems on which he or she has authorization.

Some have called this notion of single sign-on the "Holy Grail" of computer security. The goal is admirable—to create a common enterprise security infrastructure to replace a heterogeneous one. It is currently being attempted by several vendors through technologies such as the Open Group's Distributed Computing Environment (DCE), MIT's Kerberos, Microsoft's Active Directory, and public key infrastructure (PKI)–based systems. However, few, if any, enterprises have actually achieved their goal. Unfortunately, the task of changing all existing applications to use a common security infrastructure is very difficult, and this has further been hampered by a lack of consensus on a common security infrastructure. As a result, the disparate proprietary and standards-based solutions cannot be applied to every system. In addition, there is a risk of a single point of failure. Should one user's password be compromised, it is not just his local system that can be breached but the entire enterprise.

Password synchronization is another means of trying to help users maintain the passwords that they use to log on to disparate systems. In this scheme, when users periodically change their passwords, the new password is applied to every account the user has, rather than just one. The main objective of password synchronization is to help users remember a single, strong password. Password synchronization purports to improve security because synchronized passwords are subjected to a strong password policy, and users who remember their passwords are less likely to write them down.

The following guidelines should be used to mitigate the risk of a single system compromise being leveraged by an intruder into a network-wide attack:

- Very insecure systems should not participate in a password-synchronization system.
- Synchronized passwords should be changed regularly.
- Users should be required to select strong (hard to guess) passwords when synchronization is introduced.

UNIX/Linux-Specific Password Issues

Traditionally, on UNIX and Linux platforms, user information (including passwords) was kept in a system file called /etc/passwd. The password for each user is stored as a hash value. Despite the password being encoded with a one-way hash function and a salt as described earlier, a password cracker could still compromise system security if he or she obtained access to the /etc/passwd file and used a successful dictionary attack. This vulnerability has been mitigated simply by moving the passwords in the /etc/passwd file to another file, usually named /etc/shadow, and making this file readable only by those who have administrator (also called "root") access to the system.

In addition, UNIX or Linux administrators should examine their password file (as well as the shadow password file when applicable) on a regular basis for potential account-level security problems. In particular, it should be examined for:

- Accounts without passwords
- User IDs of 0 for accounts other than root (which are also superuser accounts)
- Group IDs of 0 for accounts other than root (Generally, users do not have group 0 as their primary group.)
- Other types of invalid or improperly formatted entries

Note: Usernames and group names in UNIX and Linux are mapped into numeric forms (UIDs and GIDs, respectively). All file ownership and processes use these numerical names for access control and identity determination throughout the operating system kernel and drivers.

Under many UNIX and Linux implementations (via a shadow package), the command pwck will perform some simple syntax checking on the password file and can identify some security problems with it. pwck will report invalid usernames, UIDs and GIDs, null or nonexistent home directories, invalid shells, and entries with the wrong number of fields (often indicating extra or missing colons and other typos).

Since 2003, Linux has implemented a security service called "pluggable authentication module" (pam), which governs enforcement of password complexity, including length, and minimum number of upper and lower case letters, digits, and special characters. Whenever a password for a given user ID is set or changed, it is checked versus the configuration settings in pam_cracklib to ensure it has the appropriate complexity and does not contain a dictionary word.

Windows-Specific Password Issues

Windows uses two password functions; a stronger one designed for Windows NT and later systems, and a weaker one, the LAN Manager hash, designed for backward compatibility with older Windows 9X networking log-in protocols. The latter is case-insensitive and does not allow passwords to be much stronger than seven characters, even though they may be much longer. These passwords are extremely vulnerable to cracking. There is an article on how to prevent Windows from storing a LAN manager hash of your password in Active Directory and local SAM databases (http://support.microsoft.com/?id=299656).

On a standard desktop PC, for example, L0phtcrack can try every short alphanumeric password in a few minutes and every possible keyboard password (except for special ALT-characters) within a few days. Some security administrators have dealt with this problem by requiring stronger and stronger passwords; however, this comes at a cost (see "An Argument for Simplified Passwords." below).

In addition to implementing policies that require users to choose strong passwords, the Computer Emergency Response Team (CERT) Coordination Center provides guidelines for securing passwords on Windows systems (CERT Coordination Center 2003):

- Using SYSKEY enables the private password data stored in the registry to be encrypted using a 128-bit cryptographic key. This is a unique key for each system. However, as mentioned in "Bypassing Password Security" above, physical access to the computer and an alternate boot disk can bypass this protection.
- By default, the administrator account is never locked out; so it is generally a target for brute-force log-on attempts of intruders. It is recommended to rename the account in User Manager. It may also be desirable to lock out the administrator account after a set number of failed attempts over the network. The NT Resource Kit provides an application called "passprop.exe" that enables Administrator account lockout except for interactive log-ons on a domain controller.
- Another alternative that avoids all accounts belonging to the Administrator group being locked over the network is to create a local account that belongs to the Administrator group, but is not allowed to log on over the network. This account may then be used at the console to unlock the other accounts.
- The Guest account should be disabled. If this account is enabled, anonymous connections can be made to Windows computers.
- The emergency repair disk should be secured, as it contains a copy of the entire SAM database. If a malicious user has access to the disk, he or she may be able to launch a crack attack against it.

How Long Should Your Password Be?

Say you use a typical password of six characters. When you enter this into your computer's authentication mechanism, it is hashed and stored in a database. Because an attacker cannot try to guess passwords at a high rate through the standard user interface (the time to enter them is prohibitive, and most systems can be configured to lock the user out after a consecutive number of incorrect attempts), one may assume that the attacker will get them either by capturing the system password file or by sniffing the network to capture log-in packets.

There are, of course, many other factors to be considered here. What operating system is it? What algorithm is being used for the hash? Is there a salt? What characters will be used for inputting the password? None of these, however, will greatly affect the time needed for brute forcing all possible combinations of passwords. All an attacker really needs is one password to gain entry to a system. If there are 1000 users on the system, he needs only to capture 0.1 percent of the passwords to gain entry.

Nevertheless, let us make an assumption about which characters will be used as input for a password. Each character in a password is a byte. The keyboard has 95 possible choices for each of the six password characters; this makes the password space $95^6 = 735{,}091{,}890{,}625$ combinations.

According to the Web site www.top500.org, several supercomputer clusters in the world can perform in excess of teraflops; that is, a million million floating point operations per second. That is only the publicized machines. It has been conjectured that agencies such as the National Security Agency (NSA) have code-breaking machines that could hash and check passwords at a rate in excess of 1 billion per second, assuming there are 1000 floating point operations required to perform a hash-and-check operation. The actual number, given an elegant implementation, could be somewhat lower than this. Note, as discussed in the "Rainbow Tables" section above, if it is possible to generate a rainbow table for the hashes used in the system, the time to "crack" passwords will be an order of magnitude faster—perhaps only a few seconds. However, many systems, such as Linux, use a salt to randomize the stored password hash. The time-memory trade-off technique used in generating rainbow tables is not practical when this type of hash is used.

How fast could a high-powered attacker check every possible combination of six-character passwords? 735,091,-890,625/1,000,000,000 = about 12 min (see Table 2).

Keep in mind that this is the time needed to use brute force for every possible combination of passwords. As we said earlier, password crackers will first use dictionary and hybrid attacks before resorting to brute force. Thus, if your password is weak (that is, easily guessed and not sufficiently random), the time to crack it could be much shorter.

What if the system forces users to have a seven-character password? Then it would take the attacker 19 hours to use brute force for every possible password. Many Windows networks fall under this category because of backward-compatibility issues. Passwords on these systems cannot be much stronger than seven characters. Thus, it can be assumed that every password sent on a Windows system using the old LAN Manager hashes could be cracked within a day.

Table 2: Password Cracking Times of a Mythical Teraflop Supercomputer*

Chars	Combinations	Time to crack (hrs)
0	1	0.0
1	95	0.0
2	9025	0.0
3	857375	0.0
4	81450625	0.0
5	7737809375	0.0
6	735091890625	0.2
7	69833729609375	19.4
8	6634204312890620	1842.8
9	6.E+17	2.E+05
10	6.E+19	2.E+07
11	6.E+21	2.E+09
12	5.E+23	2.E+11
13	5.E+25	1.E+13
14	5.E+27	1.E+15
15	5.E+29	1.E+17
16	4.E+31	1.E+19

*Printable ASCII characters are in codes 32 through 126. ASCII codes 0–31 and 127 are unprintable characters, and 128–255 are special ALT characters that are not generally used for passwords. This leaves 95 printable ASCII characters that are usually used for password generation.

What if the system enforces eight-character passwords? Then it would take the attacker 77 days to use brute-force to obtain them all. If a system's standard policy is to require users to change passwords every 90 days, this would not be sufficient. So, it appears a nine-character password should be sufficient, for today. Fortunately, this is still within the constraints of human memory.

PASSWORD LENGTH AND HUMAN MEMORY

Choosing a longer password does not help much on systems with limitations such as the LAN Manager hash issue. It also does not help if a password is susceptible to a dictionary or hybrid attack. It only works if the password appears to be a random string of symbols, but this type of password can be difficult to remember. A classic study by psychologist George Miller (1956) showed that humans work best with the magic number 7 (plus or minus 2). So it stands to reason that once a password exceeds nine characters, the user is going to have a hard time remembering it.

Here is one idea for remembering a longer password. Security professionals generally advise people never to write down their passwords. But the user could write down half of it—the part that looks like random letters and numbers—and keep it in a wallet or desk drawer.

The other part could be memorized—perhaps it could be a misspelled dictionary word or the initials for an acquaintance, or something similarly memorable. When concatenated together, the resulting password could be much longer than nine characters, and therefore presumably stronger.

Some research has shown that the brain remembers images more easily than letters or numbers. Thus, a number of new schemes use sequences of graphical symbols for passwords. For example, a system called PassFaces replaces the letters and numbers in passwords with sequences or groups of human faces. It is one of several applications that rely on graphical images for the purpose of authentication. Another company, Passlogix, has a system in which users can mix drinks in a virtual saloon or concoct chemical compounds using an onscreen periodic table of elements as a way to log on to computer networks.

AN ARGUMENT FOR SIMPLIFIED PASSWORDS

Using all of the guidelines for a strong password (length, mix of upper and lower case, numbers, punctuation, no dictionary words, no personal information, etc.) as outlined in this chapter may not be necessary after all.

According to security expert and TruSecure Chief Technology Officer Peter Tippett (2001), statistics show that strong password policies only work for smaller organizations. Suppose a 1000-user organization has implemented such a strong-password policy. On average, only half of the users will actually use passwords that satisfy the policy. Perhaps if the organization frequently reminds its users of the policy, and implements special software that will not allow users to have "weak" passwords, this figure can be increased to 90 percent. It is rare that such software can be deployed on all devices that use passwords for authentication; thus, there are always loopholes. Even with 90 percent compliance, this still leaves 100 easily guessed user/ID password pairs. Is 100 better than 500? No, because either way, an attacker can gain access. When it comes to strong passwords, anything less than 100 percent compliance allows an attacker entry to the system.

Second, with modern processing power, even strong passwords are no match for current password crackers. The combination of 2.5-gHz clock speed desktop computers and constantly improving hash dictionaries and algorithms means that, even if 100 percent of the 1000 users had passwords that met the policy, a password cracker might still be able to defeat them. Although some user ID/password pairs may take days or weeks to crack, approximately 150 of the 1000, or 15 percent, can usually be "brute-forced" in a few hours.

In addition, strong passwords are expensive to maintain. Organizations spend a great deal of money supporting strong passwords. One of the highest costs of maintaining IT help desks is related to resetting forgotten user passwords. Typically, the stronger the password (i.e., the more random), the harder it is to remember. The harder it is to remember, the more help desk calls result. Help desk calls require staffing, and staffing costs money. According to estimates from technology analysts such as the Gartner Group and MetaGroup, the cost to businesses for resetting passwords is between $50 and $300 per computer user each year.

So, for most organizations, the following might be a better idea than implementing a strong password policy: Simply recognize that 95 percent of users could use simple (but not basic) passwords—that is, good enough to keep a casual attacker (not a sophisticated password cracker) from guessing them within five attempts while sitting at a keyboard. These could be four or five characters (no names or initials) and changed perhaps once a year. In practical terms, this type of password is equivalent to the current "strong" passwords. The benefit is that it is much easier and cheaper to maintain.

Under this scenario, a system could still reserve stronger passwords for the 5 percent of system administrators who wield extensive control over many accounts or devices. In addition, a system should make the password file very difficult to steal. Security administrators should also introduce measures to mitigate sniffing, such as network segmentation and desktop automated inventory for sniffers and other tools. Finally, for the strongest security, a system could encrypt all network traffic with IPSec on every desktop and server.

Dr. Tippett states: "If the Promised Land is robust authentication, you can't get there with passwords alone, no matter how 'strong' they are. If you want to cut costs and solve problems, think clearly about the vulnerability, threat and cost of each risk, as well as the costs of the purported mitigation. Then find a way to make mitigation cheaper with more of a security impact."

CONCLUSION

Passwords have been widely used in computing systems since the 1960s, and password security issues have followed closely behind. Now, the increased and very real threat of cyber crime necessitates higher security for many networks that previously seemed safe. Guaranteeing accountability on networks—that is, uniquely identifying and authenticating users' identities—is a fundamental need for modern e-commerce. Strengthening password security should be a major goal in an organization's overall security framework. Basic precautions (policies, procedures, filtering mechanisms, encryption) can help reduce risks from password weaknesses. However, lack of user buy-in and the rapid growth of sophisticated cracking tools may make any measure taken short-lived. Additional measures, such as biometrics, certificates, tokens, smart cards, and other means can be very effective for strengthening authentication, but the tradeoff is additional financial burden and overhead. It is not always an easy task to convince management of inherent return on these technologies, relative to other system priorities. In these instances, organizations must secure their passwords accordingly and do the best they can with available resources.

GLOSSARY

Access Control: The process of limiting access to system information or resources to authorized users.

Accountability: The property of systems security that enables activities on a system to be traced to individuals who can then be held responsible for their actions.

ARPANET: The network first constructed by the Advanced Research Projects Agency of the U.S. Department of Defense (ARPA), which eventually developed into the Internet.

Biometrics: Technologies for measuring and analyzing living human characteristics, such as fingerprints, especially for authentication purposes. Biometrics is seen as a replacement for or augmentation of password security.

Birthday Paradox: The concept that it is easier to find two unspecified values that match than it is to find a match to some particular value. For example, in a room of 25 people, if 1 person tried to find another person with the same birthday, there would be little chance of a match. However, there is a very good chance that some pair of people in the room will have the same birthday.

Brute Force: A method of breaking decryption by trying every possible key. The feasibility of a brute-force attack depends on the key length of the cipher and on the amount of computational power available to the attacker. In password cracking, tools typically use brute force to crack password hashes after attempting dictionary and hybrid attacks to try every remaining possible combination of characters.

Cipher: A cryptographic algorithm that encodes units of plaintext into encrypted text (or *ciphertext*) through various methods of diffusion and substitution.

Ciphertext: An encrypted file or message. After plaintext has undergone encryption to disguise its contents, it becomes ciphertext.

Compatible Time-Sharing System: An IBM 7094 time-sharing operating system created at MIT Project MAC and first demonstrated in 1961. May have been the first system to use passwords.

Computer Emergency Response Team: An organization that provides Internet security expertise to the public. CERT is located at the Software Engineering Institute, a federally funded research and development center operated by Carnegie Mellon University. Its work includes handling computer security incidents and vulnerabilities and publishing security alerts.

Crack, Cracking: Traditionally, using illicit (unauthorized) actions to break into a computer system for malicious purposes. More recently, either the art or science of trying to guess passwords or copying commercial software illegally by breaking its copy protection.

Dictionary Attack: A password-cracking technique in which the cracker creates or obtains a list of words, names, and so on, derives hashes from the words in the list, and compares the hashes with those captured from a system user database or by sniffing.

Entropy: In information theory, a measure of uncertainty or randomness. The work of Claude Shannon defines it in bits per symbol.

Green Book: The 1985 U.S. Department of Defense CSC-STD-002-85 publication *Password Management Guideline,* which defines good practices for safe handling of passwords in a computer system.

Hybrid Attack: A password-cracking technique that usually takes place after a dictionary attack. In this attack, a tool will typically iterate through its word list again, adding certain combinations of a few characters to the beginning and end of each word prior to hashing. This attempt gleans any passwords that a user has created by simply appending random characters to a common word.

Kerberos: A network authentication protocol developed at MIT to provide strong authentication for client/server applications using secret key cryptography. It keeps passwords from being sent in the clear during network communications and requires users to obtain "tickets" to use network services.

Message Authentication Code: A small block of data derived by using a cryptographic algorithm and a secret key that provide a cryptographic checksum for the input data. MACs based on cryptographic hash functions are known as HMACs.

Moore's Law: An observation named for Intel cofounder Gordon Moore that the number of transistors per square inch of an integrated circuit has doubled every year since integrated circuits were invented. This "law" has also variously been applied to processor speed, memory size, and so on.

Nonce: A random number that is used once in a challenge/response handshake and then discarded. The one-time use ensures that an attacker cannot inject messages from a previous exchange and appear to be a legitimate user (see *Replay Attack*).

One-Way Hash: A fixed-sized string derived from some arbitrarily long string of text, generated by a formula in such a way that it is extremely unlikely that other texts will produce the same hash value.

One-Time Password: Also called OTP. A system that requires authentication that is secure against passive attacks based on replaying captured reusable passwords. In the modern sense, OTP evolved from Bellcore's S/KEY and is described in RFC 1938.

Orange Book: 1983 U.S. Department of Defense 5200.28-STD publication, *Trusted Computer System Evaluation Criteria,* which defined the assurance requirements for security protection of computer systems processing classified or other sensitive information. Superseded by the Common Criteria.

Password Synchronization: A scheme to ensure that a known password is propagated to other target applications. If a user's password changes for one application, it also changes for the other applications that the user is allowed to log on to.

Phishing: A play on "fishing"; the idea that bait is thrown out in the hope that some victim will be tempted into biting. In a phishing scheme, an attacker sends an e-mail falsely claiming to be an established legitimate enterprise in an attempt to entice the user into providing private information that will be used for identity theft.

Plaintext: A message or file to be encrypted. After it is encrypted, it becomes *ciphertext*.

Promiscuous Mode: A manner of running a network device (especially a monitoring device or sniffer) in such a way that it is able to intercept and read every network packet, regardless of its destination address. Contrast with nonpromiscuous mode, in which a device accepts and reads only packets that are addressed to it.

Rainbow Table: Based on the work of Philippe Oechslin and Zhu Shuanglei, a lookup table that takes advantage of the time-memory trade-off to break passwords. In other words, by listing every possible hash value and providing a quick means for lookup/retrieval, it can break any possible password for a particular system and algorithm.

Replay Attack: An attack in which a valid data transmission is captured and retransmitted in an attempt to circumvent an authentication protocol.

Salt: A random string that is concatenated with a password before it is operated on by a one-way hashing function. It can prevent collisions by uniquely identifying a user's password, even if another user has the same password. It also makes hash-matching attack strategies more difficult because it prevents an attacker from testing known dictionary words across an entire system.

Secure Shell: An application that allows users to log in to another computer over a network and execute remote commands (as in rlogin and rsh) and move files (as in FTP). It provides strong authentication and secure communications over unsecured channels.

Secure Sockets Layer (SSL): A network-session-layer protocol developed by Netscape Communications Corp. to provide security and privacy over the Internet. It supports server and client authentication, primarily for HTTP communications. SSL is able to negotiate encryption keys as well as to authenticate the server to the client before data are exchanged.

Security Account Manager (SAM): On Windows systems, the secure portion of the system registry that stores user account information, including a hash of the user account password. The SAM is restricted via access control measures to administrators only and may be further protected using SYSKEY.

Shadow Password File: In UNIX or Linux, a system file in which encrypted user passwords are stored so they are inaccessible to unauthorized users.

Single Sign-on: A mechanism whereby a single action of user authentication and authorization can permit a user to access all computers and systems on which that user has access permission, without the need to enter multiple passwords.

Sniffing: The process of monitoring communications on a network segment via a wire-tap device (either software or hardware). Typically, a sniffer also has some sort of "protocol analyzer" that allows it to decode the computer traffic on which it is eavesdropping and make sense of it.

Social Engineering: An outside hacker's use of psychological tricks on legitimate users of a computer system to obtain the information (e.g., user IDs and passwords) needed to gain access to a system.

SYSKEY: On Windows systems, a tool that provides encryption of account password hash information to prevent administrators from intentionally or unintentionally accessing these hashes using system registry programming interfaces.

CROSS REFERENCES

See *Access Control*; *Authentication*; *Biometrics*.

REFERENCES

Brotman, R. L. 1985. *Password management guideline (Green Book)*. Baltimore: Department of Defense Computer Security Center.

Brown, A. 2002. *U.K. study: Passwords often easy to crack*. www.cnn.com/2002/TECH/ptech/03/13/dangerous.passwords/index.html (accessed May 19, 2006).

CERT Coordination Center. 2003. *Windows NT configuration guidelines*. www.cert.org/tech_tips/win_configuration_guidelines.html (accessed May 19, 2006).

LabMice.net. 2003. *How to bypass BIOS passwords*. http://labmice.techtarget.com/articles/BIOS_hack.htm (accessed May 19, 2006).

Miller, G. A. 1956. The magical number seven, plus or minus two: Some limits on our capacity for processing information. *Psychological Review* 63:81–97

Narain, R. 2006. *Symantec pulls plug on L0phtcrack*. www.eweek.com/article2/0,1895,1935696,00.asp (accessed January 30, 2007).

SANS Institute. 2006. *The twenty most critical Internet security vulnerabilities*. www.sans.org/top20.htm (accessed May 19, 2006).

Tippett, P. 2001. *Stronger passwords aren't. Information Security*. www.infosecuritymag.com/articles/june01/columns_executive_view.shtml (accessed May 19, 2006).

Zatko, P. "Mudge." 1999. *L0phtCrack 2.5 Readme.doc*. Boston: L0pht Heavy Industries, Inc. [now Symantec Corp.].

SOFTWARE TOOL REFERENCES

Cain & Abel (computer software). www.oxid.it (accessed 2006).

Cracklib and associated PAM modules (user manual). www.kernel.org/pub/linux/libs/pam/Linux-PAM-html/pam.html (accessed 2006).

ElcomSoft (computer software). www.elcomsoft.com/prs.html (accessed 2006).

Intertek (computer software). www.intertek.org.uk/downloads (accessed 2006).

John the Ripper (computer software). www.openwall.com/john (accessed 2006).

Microsoft Baseline Security Analyzer 2.0 (computer software). www.microsoft.com/technet/security/tools/mbsahome.mspx (accessed 2006).

Npasswd (Computer software for SunOS 4/5, Digital UNIX, HP/UX, and AIX). www.utexas.edu/cc/unix/software/npasswd (accessed 2006).

Offline NT Password & Registry Editor (computer software). http://home.eunet.no/~pnordahl/ntpasswd (accessed 2006).

Pandora (computer software). www.nmrc.org/project/pandora/index.html (accessed 2006).

PassFaces (computer software). www.passfaces.com/products/passfaces.htm (accessed 2006).

Passfilt (computer software). http://support.microsoft.com/kb/q161990 (accessed 2006).

Passlogix (computer software). www.passlogix.com (accessed 2006).

Project RainbowCrack (computer software). www.antsight.com/zsl/rainbowcrack (accessed 2006).

PWDUMP2 (computer software). www.bindview.com/Support/RAZOR/Utilities/Windows/pwdump2_readme.cfm (accessed 2006).

FURTHER READING

Barbalace, R. J. 1999. *How to choose a good password (and why you should).* www.mit.edu/afs/sipb/project/doc/passwords/passwords.html (accessed May 19, 2006).

Bobby, P. 2000. *Password cracking using focused dictionaries.* www.totse.com/en/hack/hack_attack/162116.html (accessed May 19, 2006).

Botzum, K. 2001. *Single sign on—A contrarian view.* http://www7b.software.ibm.com/wsdd/library/techarticles/0108_botzum/botzum.html (accessed May 19, 2006).

Curry, D. A. 1990. *Improving the security of your UNIX system.* www.alw.nih.gov/Security/Docs/unix-security.html (accessed May 19, 2006).

CYHIST. 2006. *Cyberspace history list-server.* www.clc.wvu.edu (accessed May 19, 2006).

Donovan, C. 2000. *Strong passwords.* www.giac.org/pratical/GSEC/Craig_Donovan_GSEC.pdf (accessed May 19, 2006).

Frisch, A. 2002. *Essential system administration.* 3rd ed. Sebastopol, CA: O'Reilly.

Jablon, D. P. 1997. Extended password key exchange protocols immune to dictionary attack. In *Proceedings of the 6th Workshop on Enabling Technologies Infrastructure for Collaborative Enterprises*, Institute of Electrical and Electronics Engineers. http://csdl2.computer.org/persagen/DLAbsToc.jsp?resourcePath=/dl/proceedings/&toc=comp/proceedings/wetice/1997/7967/00/7967toc.xml&DOI=10.1109/ENABL.1997.630822 (accessed May 19, 2006).

Litchfield, D. 2002. *Hackproofing Oracle application server (a guide to securing Oracle 9).* www.cgisecurity.com/lib/hpoas.pdf (accessed May 19, 2006).

Luby, M., and C. Rackoff. 1989. A study of password security. *Journal of Cryptology* 1(3):151–8.

McGraw, G., and J. Viega. 2000. *Protecting passwords: Part 1.* http://www-106.ibm.com/developerworks/library/s-pass1 (accessed May 19, 2006).

Morris, R. T., and K. Thompson. 1979. Password security: A case history. *Communications of the ACM* 22(11). http://portal.acm.org/citation.cfm?id=359168.359172 (accessed May 19, 2006).

Narain, R. 2006, March 8. Symantec pulls plug on L0phtCrack. *eWeek*, http://www.eweek.com/article2/0,1759,1935616,00. asp.

Netscape. 2005. *Choosing a good password.* http://browser.netscape.com/ns8/help/privacy_help.jsp#good_password (accessed May 19, 2006).

Nomad, S. 1997. *The unofficial NT hack FAQ.* www.secinf.net/windows_security/The_Unofficial_NT_Hack_FAQ (accessed May 19, 2006).

Oechslin, P. 2003. *Making a faster cryptanalytic time-memory trade-off.* http://lasecwww.epfl.ch/pub/lasec/doc/Oech03.pdf (accessed August 1, 2005).

Raymond, E. S. 1998. A brief history of hackerdom. In DiBona, C, S. Ockma, and M. Stone, eds. *Voices from the open source revolution.* Sebastopol, CA: O'Reilly.

Russell, R. (ed.). 2002. *Hack proofing your network.* Rockland, MA: Syngress.

Sanjour, J., A. Arensburger, and A. Brink. 2000. *Choosing a good password.* www.cs.umd.edu/faq/Passwords.shtml (accessed May 19, 2006).

Schneier, B. 2000. *Secrets & lies: Digital security in a networked world.* New York: Wiley.

Shannon, C. 1948. A mathematical theory of communication. *Bell System Technical Journal* 27:379–423, 623–56.

Smith, R. E. 2001. *Authentication: From passwords to public keys.* Boston: Addison Wesley Longman.

Zatko, P. "Mudge." 1999. *Vulnerabilities in the S/KEY one time password system.* www.UNIX.geek.org.uk/~arny/junk/skeyflaws.html (accessed May 19, 2006).

Physical Security Threats and Measures

Mark Michael, *Research in Motion Limited, Canada*

INTRODUCTION

The first concern of classical physical security was to preclude unauthorized access to fixed assets; it did so by enclosing the assets in layers: put the jewels in a safe, in a locked room, in a castle with guards outside, surrounded by a wall and then a moat. A second concern was to maintain the assets in their desired state, protected from fire, flood, wind, mildew, and the like. As time went on, assets became more mobile, and the list of threats grew and became more diverse, including some, such as biological and radiological hazards, that are injurious primarily to people—the most valuable asset to be protected. When the asset is information, there is the further threat that the information may be appropriated and endlessly duplicated even while it remains in place.

The physical assets associated with supporting network operations—storage media, information-processing equipment, facilities, personnel, and transmission media—are not as easy to corral as jewels. Figure 1 illustrates in a "geographic Venn diagram" how these various assets may, in sixteen different combinations, be co-located. Facilities, once the universe of classical physical security concerns, no longer contain all the other assets, viz., the storage media, equipment, and personnel. For example, a company employee may carry beyond company premises storage media within a mobile computing device, as well as crucial personal knowledge capable of supporting or damaging network operations. The transmission media crucial to network operations may reach even where people cannot go, with wireless transmissions reaching virtually everywhere.

Not only has the perimeter to be guarded become more complex and indeterminate, the boundary between physical security and cybersecurity is becoming increasingly blurred. Cybersecurity protects information assets in the form of ones and zeroes against threats that come in the form of other ones and zeroes designed to cause un-authorized changes in or to make unauthorized use of an information asset. A virus is an example of a cyberthreat, and virus-protection software is a corresponding cyberdefense. At some point, physical security ends and cyberdefenses such as encryption must take over. But the classic view (see, for example, Microsoft 2006) that physical security (itself multilayered) forms the "lowest" layer of defense in depth is now a bit simplistic. There are many points at which physical security and cybersecurity work together or converge. A password that should serve as a cyberdefense may be compromised if it is written down. Physical access can be controlled by biometrics and smartcards. Tracking software can help recover a stolen laptop.

As with cybersecurity, being "equipped" for physical security is not enough—faithful adherence to proper practices is also required. Good behavior cannot replace expensive security equipment, but bad behavior can render that equipment useless. Conduct conducive to physical security begins with the establishment of policies, followed by appropriate education, enforcement, and communication of management's commitment to the importance of the policies.

Unlike cybersecurity, physical security faces threats to which there are no adequate countermeasures. For instance, although one absolute defense against unauthorized

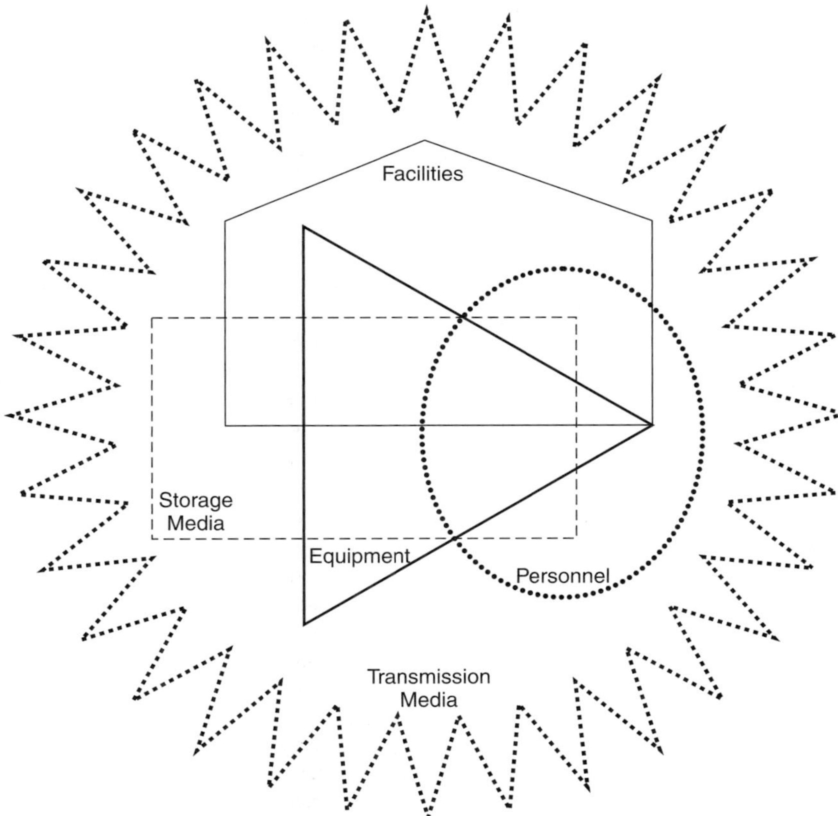

Figure 1: Co-location of resources

modification of a file by a cyberattack is to store the file on a CD-ROM, we cannot stop a rocket-propelled grenade from destroying the disk; we could preemptively save a backup copy at a distant location, but if an employee is forced at gunpoint to turn it over, any confidential information on it will be irreversibly compromised. This illustrates that, while physical security may be better understood than cybersecurity, maintaining physical security is, in a way, an intractable problem.

That being said, the prevention and mitigation of breaches of physical security are, nevertheless, deserving of investments of money and effort commensurate with the considerable potential benefits. Compromises of confidential customer information (that have come to light) have received much attention, and their financial impact has been analyzed; see, for example, Ponemon Institute (2006) for one study of the cost of data breaches. Given that a single patent-infringement judgment or settlement can run into hundreds of millions of dollars, the theft of trade secrets may easily erase a competitive advantage of comparable magnitude, though such crimes are less likely to receive the attention that accompanies a breach of customer privacy. Even the premature release of information about or the public display of an invention intended to be patented can make it unpatentable in most jurisdictions, regardless of who is responsible for the revelation.

PHYSICAL SECURITY FOR STORAGE MEDIA

Networks exist to provide information and services across a distance. Those information and services depend on data and computer code, not all of which can reside in active computer memory at all times. Much of it must be saved to nonvolatile storage media at some point.

Magnetic Storage Media

For magnetic storage media such as tapes and disks, the most obvious threat is to the orientation of the ferromagnetic particles within the media. Although physical shocks can partially rearrange particles, a far more common cause for magnetic realignment is, of course, magnetic fields. The Earth's magnetic field, averaging about 0.5 Gauss at the surface, is too weak to cause short-term or even long-term damage to magnetic media. Certain electrical devices pose hazards to magnetic media; among these are electromagnets, motors, transformers, magnetic imaging devices, metal detectors, and devices for activating or deactivating inventory surveillance tags. (X-ray scanners and inventory surveillance antennae do not pose a threat.) Degaussers (bulk erasers) can produce fields in excess of 4000 Gauss, strong enough to affect nearby media not intended for erasure. Although the intensity of most magnetic fields decreases rapidly with distance, to shield against them requires a container made of a metal that is highly permeable (in the sense of being susceptible to magnetization). The container will attract lines of magnetic force, thereby protecting the magnetic media within the container from an external magnetic field. Steel, cobalt, and certain alloys are such metals.

Electrical currents and electrostatic discharge are a related threat to magnetic media. As a precaution against lightning, magnetic media (and sensitive equipment) should be kept away from metal objects, especially structural

Table 1: Temperature Thresholds for Damage to Computing Resources

Component or Medium	Sustained Ambient Temperature at Which Damage may Begin
Flexible disks, magnetic tapes, etc.	38°C (100°F)
Optical media	49°C (120°F)
Hard-disk media	66°C (150°F)
Computer equipment	79°C (175°F)
Thermoplastic insulation on wires carrying hazardous voltage	125°C (257°F)
Paper products	177°C (350°F)

Source: Data taken from National Fire Protection Association (2003, *Standard for the protection of electronic computer/data processing equipment*).

steel and the components of a lightning-arresting system. On the other hand, items within a metal container are protected by the skin effect, so called because the current passes only through the outer skin of the metal.

High temperatures can affect magnetism, but damage to magnetic media occurs at much lower temperatures in the carrier and binding materials. See Table 1.

Arguably the most prevalent threat to removable magnetic media is humidity. Again, the carrier and binding materials are most at risk. Magnetic media deteriorate by hydrolysis, in which polymers "consume" water; the binder ceases to bind magnetic particles to the carrier and sheds a sticky material (which is particularly bad for tapes). Obviously, the rate of decay increases with humidity (and, as for any chemical process, temperature). If condensation forms, the damage is even worse.

The reading of magnetic media can be adversely affected by dirt on the media, but read-write heads for magnetic media typically need to be cleaned far more often than the media that moves by them. However, dirty magnetic tape can actually stick and break. Magnetic tapes that are subjected to repeated reuse (say, for backing up data) should be periodically removed from service to be tested on a tape certifier, which writes sample data to the tape and reads it back to detect any errors; some models incorporate selective cleaning as an option.

For long-term storage of data (e.g., vital statistics and legal records), the guidelines for acceptable humidity, temperature, and temperature changes are far stricter than for ordinary usage. Magnetic media, both tapes and disks, should be stored upright (i.e., with their axes of rotation horizontal) in containers that will not chemically interact with the media. Projected life spans (before any bit reversals) for properly archived magnetic media are considered to be 5 to 10 years for floppy diskettes and 10 to 30 years for magnetic tapes. See International Advisory Committee for the UNESCO Memory of the World Programme (2000) for detailed preservation guidelines.

Optical Storage Media

The first concern with optical media is that they be readable. Any scratches, cracks, dust, or dirt on the bottom side of a disk (the side facing the laser) will interfere with reading data. CDs are actually more easily damaged by scratching on the seemingly "safe" top side (where a label or marking might appear), since there is very little protecting the data layer from that side. Claims have been made that DVDs' more robust error-correction schemes (with increased proportion of nondata bits) should, in theory, more than compensate for the increased data density (i.e., increased number of bits effected by a given scratch), making them more forgiving of a scratch than would be a CD. In practice, anecdotal experience of lending libraries seems to indicate that DVDs are more problematic with regard to scratching.

There are commercial products and services for repairing scratched disks by polishing the bottom side. Likewise, there are products for cleaning optical media. Compressed air should not be used to remove dirt, as the resulting drop in temperature produces a thermal shock (rapid temperature change) for the disk.

Although some chemicals can be safely used to clean disks, others can have a detrimental effect on plastics. DVDs seem to be more sensitive to chemicals in the form of markers and label adhesives. If markers are used on the top side, they should be ones designed specifically for chemical compatibility with optical media.

Attached labels are best avoided. A minute off-centering of an attached label may cause instability and, therefore, a greater likelihood of data error. This is more likely with a DVD than with a CD because of the former's higher rotational speed. The alternative is to use specialized equipment to print labels directly on DVDs.

Optical media can be damaged by bending, even if they appear to return to their original shape, because of microscopic cracking or delamination (separation of layers). Cracks or delamination may also allow the incursion of air and the subsequent deterioration of the reflective layer. In this regard, DVDs are more susceptible to flexing than are CDs; this is because DVDs have protective layers on both sides of the data layer whereas a CD has a single, sturdier protective layer (but little protection on the other side). Hence, DVDs should never be stored in CD cases, as they do not provide adequate support. Furthermore, care should be taken to fully depress the button of the hub lock before attempting to remove a DVD from its case and to avoid any flexing of the disk.

Both DVDs and CDs should be stored vertically and should not be stored in envelopes (especially ones with plastic windows). See Svensson (2004).

High humidity can result in corrosion of the metallic reflective layer of optical media, especially if there has been any cracking or delamination. High humidity can also promote the growth of mold and mildew, which can obstruct reading from optical media. In tropical regions, there are even documented cases of fungi burrowing into CDs and corrupting data.

Projected life spans for properly archived optical media are considered to be 20 to 30 years. However, since optical media are relatively new, this expectation is extrapolated from accelerated aging tests based on assumptions and end-of-life criteria that may be invalid. Numerous factors other than temperature and humidity influence longevity. Optical media incorporating dyes are also subject to degradation from exposure to light, even at safe temperatures. Write-once formats have greater life expectancies than rewriteable formats. It is known that the bit-encoding dye phthalocyanine (appearing gold or yellowish green) is less susceptible than cyanine (green or blue-green) to damage from light after data have been written.

What appears to be a major determiner of longevity is the original quality of the stored data. This in turn depends on the quality of the blank disk (which can vary greatly), the quality of the machine writing the data, and the speed at which data was written. For example, recording data at a slower speed does not necessarily imply that a better job will be done; lasers calibrated for high-speed recording will "overburn" at a very low recording speed. Actual testing is necessary to ensure that the machine and batch of media being used is producing a good representation of the data. Hartke (1998, 2001) gives an enlightening look at the complexities of this and related issues.

Solid-State Storage Media

Small solid-state forms of removable storage such as USB flash memory are becoming increasing popular. Although not a major locus of primary or backup storage of information needed for access by a network, removable solid-state storage media may one day take over some of the roles currently played by magnetic and optical media because of the apparently unlimited longevity of information stored in solid-state media.

As the data density of removable storage media increases, so does the volume of information that can be stored on one item and, therefore, the ease with which a vast amount of information can be stolen or misplaced. Small, unattached items are the easiest to lose, either through theft or accident. In the information-processing domain, removable storage media fit this description. Particularly at risk to accidental loss are the tiny solid-state forms of removable storage, such as USB flash memory.

Solid-state memory devices typically have cases that can easily admit water and other foreign substances. Some models of USB flash memory designed for resistance to crushing are now being produced.

Nondigital Storage Media

The loss of more old-fashioned forms of media can still affect operations. For instance, a map of an intranet's topology may be easier to scan visually from a giant printout than from an electronic version. In some facilities, plastic photographic media such as microfiche still serve a purpose. In some cases, crucial information may have been written down and never stored online. Perhaps more importantly, for any information that *is* stored in "soft copy" (digitally), there may be a corresponding "hard copy" that could be subject to unauthorized access. This in turn could lead to theft or duplication of the information. In the case of a password written down, a larger breach of network security could result from someone seeing the password, memorizing it, and using it to obtain access to some resource.

As with other media, nondigital storage media may be adversely affected by temperature and humidity. Formation of mold and mildew can damage paper-based records and plastics. Water in particular is a threat to paper documents, the most vulnerable being documents printed with water-soluble inks (the type more commonly used in ink-jet printers). Plastics may further be damaged by heat or light. Paper products actually are more resistant to heat than other forms of storage media (see Table 1).

Physical Access Control for Storage Media

Like most tangible assets, storage media can be stolen. Unlike most assets, information is also subject to theft by copying—the original copy remains, another copy is expropriated—making it a special security challenge. In particular, a person who gains access to storage media of an organization may either copy information from the organization's media onto his/her own media on site or may temporarily borrow the organization's media to make a copy elsewhere, retuning it later; in either case, there is likely no intrinsic evidence that the theft by copying took place.

In a later section on "Physical Access Control for Equipment," a number of strategies are enumerated, some of which could also apply to precluding unauthorized contact with storage media. For now, the discussion will be limited to controlling the physical movement of storage media.

It is self-evident that the extreme physical portability of storage media, especially since the rise of solid-state storage media, works to the disadvantage of those protecting the physical security of those media. Controlling the movement of media owned by an organization can be tracked within a contiguous area physically controlled, for example, by the organization by the use of a radio-frequency identification (RFID) tag. A more "invasive" procedure—such as the use of an x-ray machine, a metal detector, or a manual search—would be needed to prevent the use of untagged media, camera phones, and the like from being brought in by an outsider or an insider to take away a copy of information. The motive of an insider may be benign (perhaps copying information for convenience, not subterfuge), but the result may still pose a potential hazard.

The extreme portability of data may be turned to an advantage, in the case of mobile devices, such as laptop computers. If the loss of information within a computer is more devastating than the loss of the computer itself, one approach to safeguarding information is to "sacrifice" hardware but preserve the confidentiality of information by storing data only on removable storage media so that theft of the machine from a vehicle or room will not compromise the data. There are several problems with this. First, it may be difficult to ensure that no remnant of the data is stored with or within the device, as operating systems may create "echoes" of files. If there really is no copy of a file on a machine, then the machine is removed as a locus of backup data.

The smallness that makes portable media so convenient to carry also makes them easy to lose. To counter this, some versions have been worn as a necklace or incorporated in larger items such as pens, watches, and Swiss Army knives, which makes them a little harder to misplace.

Storage Media Disposal and Reuse

At some time, every piece of storage media of every type will cease to play its current role. It may be reused to store new information, it may be recycled into a new object, or it may be "destroyed" in some sense (probably not as thoroughly as by incineration). If it is to be used by another individual not authorized to access the old information stored within it, the user of that information may very well think to purge the information. If it is to be "recycled" or "destroyed," its original user may assume that no attempt to access the old information will be made after it leaves his or her possession. This is a foolhardy assumption.

The term *dumpster diving* usually refers to an outsider pillaging items that have been "thrown out" and are no longer in a secure area, although perhaps still on an organization's property. (The legal remedies with respect to dumpster diving will depend on local laws, legal precedents, and especially the circumstances under which an item was discarded and recovered.) However, a similar threat to data confidentiality can come from an insider scrounging within a trash receptacle within a building for discarded documents, media, and equipment to recover information. At the other extreme, recovery could, in theory, take place thousands of miles from the point at which an object was initially discarded. A large fraction of the purportedly "recycled" components from industrialized countries actually end up in trash heaps in Third World countries. Thus, media must be carefully sanitized regardless of whether it is to be reused or discarded. The only difference is that care must be taken not to damage the media in the former case.

For magnetic media, it is fairly well known that "deleting" a file really only changes a pointer to the file; the ones and zeroes of the file remain unchanged. There are commercial, shareware, and freeware tools for overwriting files so that all the bits are replaced with, for example, all ones, then all zeroes, than random bits. Echoes of the original information may remain in other system files, however. Another potential problem is that sectors that have been flagged as bad might not be susceptible to overwriting. Special, drive-specific software should be used to overwrite hard drives because each has its own way of using hidden and reserved sectors.

Even after all sensitive bytes have been overwritten by software, there may still be recoverable data, termed "magnetic remanence." One reason is that write heads shift position over time so that where new bytes are written does not perfectly match where the old bytes were written. Hence the use of a degausser is generally recommended. Some models can accommodate a wide range of magnetic media, including hard drives, reel or cartridge tape, and boxed diskettes. Degaussers are rated in Gauss (measuring the strength of the field they emit), in Oersteds (measuring the strength of the field within the media they can erase), or in dB (measuring on a logarithmic scale the ratio of the remaining signal to the original signal on the media). A degausser generates heat rapidly and cannot be operated continuously for long periods; it should be equipped with an automatic shutoff feature to prevent overheating. Even degaussing may leave information retrievable by an adversary with special equipment. If a hard drive is not to be reused, then grinding off the surface is an option. For more information on magnetic remanence, see National Computer Security Center (1991).

Guidelines for sanitizing write-once or rewritable optical media are not as clear. In theory, even write-once disks can be overwritten. But from what has been said about magnetic media, it is inadvisable for any optical media to be erased for reuse. Two "folk remedies," breaking the disk or placing it in a microwave oven for two seconds, should not be used. Another suggestion, scratching, may be ineffective because there are commercial products and services for repairing scratched disks by polishing. Therefore, if complete destruction of the disk is not possible, it should be ground to the point of obliterating the layer on which the data are actually stored.

For printed media holding sensitive information, reuse is not an option. Some shredders are worthless, slicing pages into parallel strips, which can be visually "reassembled." At the other extreme is government equipment that liquefies documents to the point at which they cannot be recycled (because the paper fibers are destroyed). In between are crosscut shredders that produce tiny pieces of documents, a reasonable approach.

An increasingly common practice is for an organization to outsource their shredding to a company specializing in document disposal. It goes without saying that the organization is now dependent on the honesty and competence of the document disposal company. Moreover, documents destined to be picked up by the document disposal company are often deposited by organization personnel in centrally located boxes. The security of such a box, particularly if documents remain there overnight (as is often the case), may be questionable. The construction may involve flimsy materials and locks, and the slot for allowing the insertion of documents may also allow retrieval of them if they stack up high enough within the boxes.

Regardless of whether shredding is handled internally or outsourced, some personnel choose to accumulate sensitive documents in containers or in piles on desks with signage indicating "To be shredded." This is an example of counterproductive security signage; to an attacker, the translation is: "This is the good stuff!"

For maximum security in reusing or disposing of media, learn to think forensically. If a government agency could recover information from your media, so could a sufficiently sophisticated adversary.

Redundancy of Storage Media

Redundancy is the safety net for ensuring integrity and availability of resources. Confidentiality, on the other hand, cannot be "backed up"; some damage, such as the revelation of personal information, can never be repaired. Redundancy can be viewed as a preventive measure in that it prevents a permanent or extended loss of information and/or services. In fact, redundancy only pays dividends when other defenses have failed to prevent some calamity. In that sense, exploiting redundancy is a reactive measure. Redundancy cannot succeed without a combination of foresight and discipline. An organization must envision the potential need for redundancy and must consistently adhere to proper practices.

Perhaps the first type of redundancy that springs to mind is to back up data. If only a single copy of information exists, it may be difficult, if not impossible, to reconstruct it with complete confidence in its validity. Not to be overlooked are system software and configurations and any documents needed to restore systems expeditiously.

There are a wide variety of schemes for creating backups. Many are based on some type of high-density tape. Capacities for some are measured in terabytes. The backup procedure can be either manual or automated. However, the former approach is subject to human error or simple neglect. The latter approach is safer, but should issue a notification if it encounters problems while performing its duties. Backups can be made, managed, and used remotely. Some systems allow access to other cartridges while one cartridge is receiving data. Reliability and scalability are important features to consider when choosing a system. As mentioned earlier, tapes that are subjected to repeated reuse should periodically be tested and, if necessary, cleaned by a tape certifier.

Ideally, backups should be kept far enough away from the site of origin that a single storm, forest fire, earthquake, or dirty bomb could not damage both locations. At a bare minimum, backups should be kept in a safe that is fireproof, explosion-resistant, and insulated so that heat is not conducted to its contents. Backups that are going off-site (perhaps via the Internet) should be encrypted. In all cases, access to backups should be restricted to authorized personnel.

Point-in-time recovery requires not only periodic backups but also continual logging of changes to the data since the last complete backup so that files can be reconstructed to match their most recent version. Although the need to back up digital information is well recognized, essential printed documents are sometimes overlooked. These can be converted to a more compact medium (e.g., microfiche).

See also "Backup and Recovery System Requirements" for more details.

Time

Time is the enemy of all things made by humans, and stored information is no exception. Time is the ally of all threats that have hidden, cumulative effects, especially inappropriate temperature and humidity. As has already been discussed, even atmospheric conditions that would be acceptable for day-to-day storage and usage of media in the short run will degrade media of all types in the long run. All archived data of critical importance should be sampled periodically and backed up well before the rate of correctable errors indicates that data might be unrecoverable at the next sampling.

Although the physical degradation of information has been around since the days of cave art, a new threat has emerged now that the Information Age is decades old: technological obsolescence. Even physically perfect data has been effectively lost because it outlived the software or hardware needed to read it. Successive generations of information storage technology have resulted in data lost because no one thought to convert the data to a new format when the hardware, supporting software, or human expertise associated with the old storage format faded into oblivion. Therefore, before its storage format becomes obsolete, the data must be converted to an actively supported format.

Official records of births, deaths, marriages, legal proceedings, and transfers of property ownership, all of which should obviously be kept in perpetuity, are easy to keep in mind when a new storage format comes along; although the costs of converting to the new format may be high, there are always benefits in terms of storage space, access time, and possibly searching capabilities. Data gathered for other reasons, perhaps as part of a scientific or socioeconomic study, are very susceptible to eventual loss because of (temporary) disinterest. Human knowledge often follows a waterfall model, dropping from current/interesting to outdated/uninteresting to archaic/irretrievable. In many cases, the old information then becomes of interest again, precisely because it *is* old. Unfortunately, it is not always possible to anticipate which information will someday be useful, perhaps after being ignored for several techno-generations.

PHYSICAL SECURITY FOR INFORMATION-PROCESSING EQUIPMENT

Equipment for processing information has certain physical requirements for its continued (unimpaired) functioning. These include an appropriate supply of basic utilities (electrical power, telecommunications services, and water) and an environment free of inappropriate temperature, humidity, substances, and forces.

Physical security must not only ensure the availability of the equipment for legitimate use, but must also control physical access to the equipment to guard against damage, theft, and unauthorized usage of it.

Utilities

Sustaining information requires electrical power, telecommunication services, and water. In most cases, an organization is at the mercy of one or more external agencies for these utilities. Each agency may be a cooperative venture, may be directly controlled by a government, may be a corporate monopoly operating with government oversight, or may be one among many competing companies. The dependability of these agencies and the likelihood of interruptions due to forces of nature vary widely from region to region, even from neighborhood to neighborhood. Some elements of the world's infrastructure—roads, bridges, railroads, and buildings—age in ways obvious to the casual observer. Others, such as water, sewer, telecommunications, and electrical networks, age more invisibly and often receive less attention as a result. In the United States, deregulation of and competition among electric companies has fostered the unwillingness of companies to upgrade transmission capacity that can be used by its competitors.

Municipal

Obviously, a complete loss of municipal power (discussed earlier) precludes the operation of electrical devices and causes the loss of any information stored in volatile memory. Although a few electrical utilities are "islands," most are tied into a massive grid. The conundrum is this: The large, interconnected networks fashioned to allow power demands to be met by sharing power resources are precisely the same thing that allows one mountain climber to bring down all the other climbers roped together. The year 2003 brought reminders of this when a massive power outage in North America affecting 50 million people was followed soon afterward by blackouts in the United Kingdom and Italy. Many had thought power disruptions on this scale were no longer a threat. In fact, the strain placed on the world's aging electrical systems seems only to worsen.

In the case of the North American blackout, human errors have been well documented as a contributing factor. (See U.S.-Canada Power System Outage Task Force 2004.) Obviously, human error will never be eliminated; utilities can only strive to prevent, catch, or compensate for such errors. Perhaps the most important lesson to be learned is that there will always be some new combination of circumstances that may fall outside the range of what the best system can handle. Deliberate sabotage, either by physical or computer attack, has long been feared as a possibility. Certainly, there are many natural events that can cause power failures on a variety of scales regardless of the system, including the following:

- ice storms and snow storms
- wind storms (including tornadoes and hurricanes)
- earthquakes
- fires
- solar flares (see the section on "Electromagnetic Interference," below)

A generalization that can be made is that large-scale outages tend to take longer to fix and, therefore, produce even more bad consequences. One is that battery-based backup power supplies (discussed below in the section on "Uninterruptible Power Supply") are more likely to fail before power is restored. If the outage lasts days, even backup generators may run out of fuel if it must be pumped from holding tanks to delivery trucks; generators fueled by piped-in natural gas are less susceptible to such a problem.

There is, of course, no guarantee that a continuous supply of backup power will be enough to weather a widespread blackout. Just getting to work may be a challenge for employees who normally depend on electric trains or traffic signals. Therefore, it may be necessary to house critical employees on-site. Even if one company has done its part to stay operational, its continued functioning may be impossible or moot if another company has not had the same foresight.

Telecommunications Service

By definition, telecommunications service of some sort is an essential part of any computer network. Loss of telecommunications capabilities effectively nullifies any facility whose sole purpose is to provide information and service to the outside world. Although maintaining connectivity to perform that role is the highest priority, maintenance of communications for voice and for external notification of alarm conditions is still necessary to support that role.

A telecommunication difficulty may originate internally or externally. In the latter case, an organization must depend on the problem-solving efficiency of another company. In situations in which voice and data are carried by two separate systems, each is a possible point of failure.

Despite the interconnected nature of telecommunication systems, problems typically do not cascade the way electrical problems do. Hence, they rarely strike an entire system. The exceptions (e.g., the loss of all toll-free service by one phone company) have tended to be the result of a software problem. On certain holidays (for example Mother's Day in the United States), a spike in the number of calls taxes transmission capacity.

Regional disruptions in telecommunications service can result from weather, at the surface or in space. It is not uncommon for large areas to experience lines downed by wind or ice storms. Satellite dishes may be damaged by wind or rendered temporarily inoperable by a thick blanket of snow or ice. Solar flares (discussed below) can affect satellite and radio communications, especially at high latitudes. A widespread disruption of Internet service in 2001 resulted from such a train derailment and ensuing fire in a tunnel in Baltimore.

On a local scale, service disruptions are frequently due to underground lines being accidentally dug up by construction workers. In local emergencies, phone lines typically become clogged, and this can have a ripple effect as calls are rerouted. This applies even to cellular communications. Or cellular services could be shut down, as occurred on September 11, 2001, for fear they might be used to trigger bombs (a technique used 2½ years later in Madrid).

Whereas the robustness of an intranet is often under an organization's own control, communication beyond a single campus typically depends on an Internet service provider (ISP). Politically, operationally, and economically, it may make sense to have a single ISP. From the standpoint of robustness, however, it is better to have at least two service providers and to have their respective cables exit the organization's physical perimeter by different routes (so that any careless excavation cannot damage both lines). Internally, the organization must be able to switch critical services promptly from one provider to the other.

Less glamorous but also essential is basic voice communication. Even if network communication is entirely internal to an organization and not dependent on an external provider of telecommunication services, the physical security of that internal network does not stop at the door. Events outside—riots, dust storms, rolling brownouts—can disturb operations inside. Physical security policies must provide for timely, two-way flow of information (e.g., monitoring of weather forecasts and prompt reporting of internal incidents to relevant authorities). Increasingly, voice communication may be handled by VoIP (voice over Internet protocol). Thus, a lack of Internet service automatically implies a lack of voice communication, a fact to be taken into consideration when weighing the benefits of VoIP.

Phone service is a resource that may be misappropriated on a large scale (as opposed to the occasional personal phone call). Although less common now, some types of PBX (private branch exchange) can be "hacked," allowing an attacker to obtain free long-distance service or to mount modem-based attacks from a "spoofed" phone number.

As already mentioned, cellular communications may also fail in an emergency. Another alternative emergency communication system would be a battery-powered, two-way radio that broadcasts on a frequency monitored by emergency agencies; this may require a governmental license. In any case, RF-emitting devices must not be active near equipment that could suffer from the emissions. Chapter 12 of Garcia (2001) discusses the use of radios as a standard tool of security guards and suggests a minimum of four to six channels as a defense against jamming.

Water

Although water is often looked on as a threat to computer network equipment, the lack of water can also be a threat. As was the case with storage media, information-processing equipment will suffer from excessively high temperatures. In some facilities, heating, ventilation, and air conditioning (HVAC) equipment is an essential support component for information-processing equipment. After the attack on the Pentagon, the maintenance of computer operations hinged on stopping the hemorrhage of chilled water used for climate control.

Water is also required for human sanitation needs and for many fire-suppression systems, even in areas with sensitive equipment (as will be detailed later).

Electrical Anomalies

As discussed earlier, electrical equipment cannot function without power, but the quantity and quality of electricity supplied to equipment are important, too. The term *power conditioning* refers to smoothing out the irregularities of the power supply. Although maintaining power is clearly the highest priority, we introduce power conditioning first, as power maintenance devices can also condition power.

Electrical anomalies that affect equipment need not arrive via the power supply. Others result from the buildup and discharge of static electricity. Still others arise when one electrical device broadcasts "information" in conflict with the digital information being processed by another device.

Power Conditioning

Low-voltage equipment such as telephones, modems, and networks are susceptible to small changes in voltage. Integrated circuits operate on very low currents (measured in milliamps); they can be damaged by minute changes in current. Power fluctuations can have a cumulative effect on circuitry over time, termed "electronic rust." Of the data losses due to power fluctuations, about three-fourths of culpable events are drops in power.

Even under normal conditions, the power grid will deliver transients created as part of the continual balancing act performed in distributing power. Abnormalities in the power supply are also caused by loose connections, wind, tree limbs, and errant drivers. Another source of surges is lightning; even cloud-to-cloud bolts can induce voltage on power lines.

Both the power grid and communications can be affected by so-called space weather. The Earth's magnetic field captures high-energy particles from the solar wind, shielding most of the planet while focusing it near the magnetic poles. Communications satellites passing between oppositely charged "sheets" of particles (seen as the Aurorae Borealis and Australis) may suffer induced currents, even arcing; one was permanently disabled in 1997. A surge (sudden increase in current) due to a 1989 geomagnetic storm blew a transformer, which in turn brought down the entire HydroQuébec electric grid in 90 seconds. The periods of most intense solar activity generally coincide with Solar Max, when the cycle of sunspot activity peaks every 10.8 years (on the average). The most recent peak was in July 2000. That said, some of the largest flares ever recorded occurred in October 2003 (and did adversely affect air-traffic control at high latitudes). It should be noted that the span of recorded history of solar weather disrupting human activity is very short; a solar anomaly of unprecedented scale could blow out transformers at all latitudes.

Although external sources are the obvious culprits, the reality is that most power fluctuations originate within a facility. A common circumstance is when a device that draws a large inductive load is turned off or on; thermostatically controlled devices, such as fans and compressors for cooling equipment, may turn off and on frequently.

Surge protection ideally has three layers: lightning arresters, circuit breakers, and surge protectors and/or line filters. Uninterruptible power supplies can also provide surge protection.

Lightning Precautions. The most devastating form of power surge is from a direct or nearby lightning strike. In addition, the heat from lightning can ignite a fire or can physically destroy by explosive expansion. But few businesses would be willing to disconnect from the municipal power supply whenever the potential for lightning exists. Nor would that prevent all problems. Lightning can be surprisingly invasive, penetrating where rain and wind do not. In addition to direct hits on power lines or a building, near misses can travel through the ground and enter a building via pipes, telecommunication lines, or nails in walls. Moreover, lightning does not always hit the most "logical" target, and it can arrive unexpectedly.

Consequently, the first line of defense for a large building should be a lightning protection system. Although properly a defense applied at the level of facilities, it is discussed here because of its relation to surge protection. See National Fire Protection Association (2000, *Standard for installation of lightning protection systems*) and International Electrotechnical Commission (1993) for different viewpoints on lightning protection systems.

For homes, there are surge protectors for power, telephone, and cable TV lines; however, during an electrical storm, there is no substitute for disconnecting computers from both the electric grid and communication lines.

Surge Protectors and Line Filters. A surge protector is designed to protect against sudden increases in current. Ideally, it forms a third line of defense, the circuit breaker being the second, and a lightning protection system the first.

Surge protectors are currently based on four technologies, described in Table 2.

Metal oxide varistor (MOV), gas tube, and silicon avalanche diode (SAD) surge protectors short-out the surge and isolate it from the protected equipment. The reactive-circuit type uses a large inductance to spread a surge out over time. All should have lights to indicate whether they are in functioning order. MOVs and SADs are the types preferred for computing environments because of their reaction times. All surge protectors require a properly grounded electrical system in order to do their job.

Line filters clean power at a finer level, removing electrical noise entering through the line power. Their concern is not extreme peaks and valleys in the alternating current (AC) sine wave, but modulation of that wave. Their goal is to restore the optimal sine shape. Power purity can also be fostered by adding circuits rather than filters. The most important precaution is to keep large machinery off any circuit powering computing equipment. If possible, it is preferable to have each computer on a separate circuit.

Uninterruptible Power Supply (UPS)

An uninterruptible power supply counteracts a loss of power for equipment whose continued functioning is crucial. Often forgotten is that power supply is also crucial for support equipment, such as HVAC and some types of monitoring devices. For some equipment, power may need to be maintained only long enough for a graceful shutdown without loss of data.

An uninterruptible power supply typically provides surge protection as well as power continuity. This is accomplished by means of separate input and output circuits, the input circuit inducing current in the output circuit. A UPS may also incorporate noise filtering. UPS systems fall into three categories.

An online system separates the input and output with a buffer, a battery that is constantly in use and (almost) constantly being charged. This is analogous to a water tank providing consistent water pressure, regardless of whether water is being added to it. This is the original and most reliable design for a UPS. In the strictest sense, this is the only truly uninterruptible power supply; its transfer time (defined below) is 0 msec.

An offline system sends the primary current straight through in normal circumstances, but transfers to backup power if its detection circuit recognizes a problem with the primary power. The problem might be a complete drop in primary power, but it might also be a spike, a surge, a sag (drop in voltage), or electrical noise.

A line interactive system is similar to an offline system, but its output waveform will be a sine wave (as is the input waveform) rather than a square or step wave.

Aside from its basic type, the most important characteristics of a UPS are its

- capacity—how much of a load it can support (measured in volt-amps or watts)
- voltage—the electromotive force with which the current is flowing (measured in volts)
- efficiency—the ratio of output current to input current (expressed as a percentage)
- backup time—the duration during which it can provide peak current (a few minutes to several hours)
- transfer time—the time from the drop in primary power until the battery takes over (measured in milliseconds)

Table 2: Comparison of Types of Surge Protectors

Surge Protector Type	Characteristics
MOV (metal oxide varistor)	Inexpensive, easy to use, but progressively degrades from even minor surges (possibly leading to a fiery demise)
Gas tube	Reacts quickly, can handle big surges, but may not deactivate until an alternating circuit polarity flip (which may mean the computer shuts down in the meantime)
SAD (silicon avalanche diode)	Faster than an MOV (1 nsec vs. 5 nsec), but has a limited power capacity
Reactive circuit	Also smoothes out noise but can only handle normal-mode surges (between hot and neutral lines) and may actually cause a common-mode surge (between neutral and ground lines), which is thought to be the more dangerous type of surge for desktop computers

- battery life span—how long it is rated to perform as advertised;
- battery type—a small Ni-MH (nickel metal hydride) battery may support an individual machine, whereas lead-acid batteries for an entire facility may require a room of their own
- output waveform—sine, square, or step (also known as a modified sine) wave

Another consideration is the intended load: resistive (as a lamp), capacitive (as a computer), or inductive (as a motor). Because of the high starting current of an inductive load, the components of an offline UPS (with its square or step wave output) would be severely damaged. Actually, an inductive load will have a similar but less severe effect on other types of UPS systems (with sine-wave output).

Some UPS systems have features such as scalability, redundant batteries, or redundant circuitry. Especially important is interface software, which can do any or all of the following:

- indicate the present condition of the battery and the main power source
- alert users when backup power is in operation, so that they can shut down normally
- actually initiate a controlled shutdown of equipment prior to exhaustion of backup power

This last feature is critical on those occasions (e.g., fires and floods) when power must suddenly be cut; this includes disconnecting a UPS from its load. (Emergency lighting and fire detection and suppression systems must, of course, have self-contained power sources and remain on.). Any intentional disruption of power should be coordinated with computers via software to allow them to power down gracefully.

The existence of any UPS becomes moot whenever someone accidentally flips the wrong switch. The low-cost, low-tech deterrent is switch covers, available in stock and custom sizes.

Large battery systems may generate hydrogen gas, pose a fire hazard, or leak acid. Even a sealed, maintenance-free battery must be used correctly. It should never be fully discharged, it should always be recharged immediately after use, and it should be tested periodically.

Many UPS systems have backup times designed only to allow controlled shutdown of the system so that no data are lost and no equipment is damaged. For continued operation during extended blackouts, a backup generator system will also be necessary. It is tempting to place large UPS systems and generators in a basement, but that can backfire if the power outage is concurrent with water entering the building. It is important to anticipate plausible combinations of calamities.

A UPS should come with a warranty for equipment connected to it. However, the value of any lost data is typically not covered.

When limited resources do not allow for all equipment to be on a UPS, the process of deciding which equipment is most critical and therefore most deserving of guaranteed power continuity should consider two questions. First, if power is lost, will appropriate personnel still receive automated notification of this event? Second, is the continued functioning of one piece of equipment moot if another component loses power?

See Kozierok (2004) for a sequence of Web pages introducing the various aspects of the subject.

Electrostatic Discharge

A type of electrical anomaly worthy of special note can be created on a very local scale. Triboelectricity (static electricity) results from the same segregation of positive and negative charges that spawns lightning. It typically is generated by friction. Among factors contributing to a static-prone environment are low relative humidity (possibly a consequence of heating) and synthetic fibers in floor coverings, upholstery, and clothing. Even when not discharged, static electricity poses a risk because it can attract contaminants.

An electrostatic discharge (ESD) of static electricity, though highly localized, is nevertheless a potentially serious form of excess power. It can produce electromagnetic interference (see the next section) or a spike (momentary increase in voltage) of surprisingly high voltage. Especially at risk is integrated circuitry that has been removed from its antistatic packaging just before installation. In actuality, just opening the cover of a computer increases the vulnerability of the components inside. Estimates on the voltage threshold at which damage to electronic circuitry can occur vary by an order of magnitude—not surprising given the variety of circuits in use. Intel (2003) says, "Many of the more sophisticated electronic components can be damaged by charges as low as 10 volts." Next-generation technology in development will be even more sensitive to discharges. At a few thousand volts, monitors, disk drives, and printers can malfunction and a computer system may shut down.

There is more agreement on voltage thresholds that relate to human perception. The minimum voltages at which a discharge can be felt and heard are in the ranges of 1500 to 3000 and 3000 to 5000 volts, respectively. Humans can generate over 10,000 volts, enough to produce a visible blue spark. The point is this: The most likely delivery system for a discharge is a human, and a human may deliver a charge that is both damaging and imperceptible. See Electrostatic Discharge Association (2001) for a thorough introduction to ESD.

The dangers of static electricity can be reduced by inhibiting its buildup, providing ways for it to dissipate gradually (rather than discharge suddenly), or insulating vulnerable items. General techniques for discouraging the buildup of static electricity include the following:

- Properly bond components and ground equipment.
- Keep the relative humidity from dropping too low (i.e., below 40 percent).
- Avoid the use of carpets and upholstery with synthetic fibers, or spray them with antistatic sprays.
- Use antistatic tiles or carpets on floors.
- Do not wear synthetic clothing and shoes with soles prone to generating charges.

- Use an ionizer, which sends both positive and negative ions into the air as a neutralizing influence.

It is also advisable to keep computers away from metal surfaces or to cover metal surfaces with dissipative mats or coverings.

Electronic circuitry becomes exposed to a possible ESD from a human as soon as the case of a computer is open. It is most at risk when it is encased in neither a computer nor its antistatic shipping container. The following precautions should be taken when installing integrated circuits and cards:

- Work on an antistatic mat.
- Use an antistatic "garment" such as a bracelet or strap for wrists and ankles, glove, finger cot, or smock.
- Attach the computer, antistatic mat, and antistatic garment to a common, reliable ground.
- Avoid touching any conducting surface of a card or chip.
- Do not set a component on a synthetic or other static-prone surface.

See Electrostatic Discharge Association (2001) for a sequence of Web pages introducing ESD and its control.

Electromagnetic Interference

Digital and analog information is transmitted over conductive media by modulating an electrical current or is broadcast by modulating an electromagnetic wave. Even information intended to remain within one device, however, may become electromagnetic interference (EMI) for another device. Any energized wire emits electromagnetic radiation, and any wire (energized or not) can act as an antenna. Thus, electrical devices have an inherent potential to interfere with one another by broadcasting and receiving conflicting "information." The "messages" may have no more meaning than the "snow" on a television screen. Even with millions of wireless communications devices on the loose, much of the "electromagnetic smog" is incidental, produced by devices not designed to broadcast information.

The terms EMI and RFI (radio-frequency interference) are used somewhat interchangeably. The term electrical noise usually indicates interference introduced via the power input, though radiated energy may have been among the original sources of the noise; this term is also used with regard to small spikes. EMC (electromagnetic compatibility) is a measure of a component's ability neither to radiate electromagnetic energy nor to be adversely affected by electromagnetic energy originating externally. Good EMC makes for good neighbors. The simplest example of incompatibility is cross talk, when information from one cable is picked up by another cable. By its nature, a digital signal is more likely to be received noise-free than an analog signal.

EMI from natural sources is typically insignificant (background radiation) or sporadic (like the pop of distant lightning heard on an amplitude-modulated radio). Occasionally, solar flares can muddle or even jam radio communications on a planetary scale, especially at Solar Max. Fortunately, a 12-hour window for such a disruption can be predicted days in advance. It is now possible to receive automated alerts regarding impending adverse space weather—that is, electromagnetic anomalies originating with solar flares and potentially disruptive of communications and power networks (especially at high latitudes). The service can be tailored with regard to the means of notification (e-mail, fax, or pager), the type of event expected (radio burst, geomagnetic impulse, and so forth), and the threshold at which a warning should be reported. See Space Environment Center (2002).

Most EMI results from electrical devices or the wires between them. Modulating power supply lines to synchronize wall clocks within a facility can have the side effect of interfering with the proper functioning of computer systems. For radiated interference, mobile phones and other devices designed to transmit signals are a major hazard; according to Garfinkel (2002), they have triggered explosive charges in fire-extinguisher systems. Major high-voltage power lines generate fields so powerful that their potential impact on human health has been called into question. Motors are infamous sources of conducted noise, although they can radiate interference as well.

Government regulations limit how much RF (radio-frequency) radiation computers and other electronic devices may emit and where they may be used. To achieve EMC in components, there are specially designed, conductive enclosures, gaskets, meshes, pipes, tapes, and sprays. The simplest measure for achieving EMC is to use shielded cables and to keep them separated to prevent cross talk. Devices designed to be RF emitters, such as mobile phones, should be kept away from computers with sensitive data.

For an annotated bibliography of EMC publications, see Gerke (2003). An especially important reference regarding grounding and EMC is Institute of Electrical and Electronic Engineers (1999).

On a related note, some equipment can also be damaged by strong magnetic fields.

Environmental Conditions

As with storage media, the physical security of network equipment includes maintaining an environment free of inappropriate temperature, humidity, substances, and forces.

Temperature and Humidity

Most individual pieces of electrical equipment have no control over humidity and possess merely a fan for temperature control. Thus, in many facilities, dedicated HVAC (heating, ventilation, and air-conditioning) equipment is an essential support component for maintaining the security of information. As mentioned earlier, after the attack on the Pentagon, continued computer operations hinged on stopping the hemorrhage of chilled water for climate control. Because HVAC systems generally serve rooms and buildings rather than individual pieces of equipment, discussion of HVAC will be deferred until the major section on facilities. For now, the focus is primarily on the threats to equipment.

Most electrical equipment is designed for use at low to moderate humidity. High humidity has a long-term corrosive effect. On the other hand, very low humidity may change the shape of some materials, thereby affecting performance. A more serious concern, noted earlier, is that static electricity is more likely to build up in a dry atmosphere. If not actively controlled, humidity tends to drop when air is heated.

The internal temperature of equipment can be significantly higher than that of the room air. Although increasing densities have brought decreasing currents at the integrated-circuit level, dissipation of heat is still a major concern. If a cooling system fails, a vent is blocked, or moving parts create abnormal friction, temperature levels can rise rapidly.

Well below the point at which permanent damage begins (see Table 1), high temperatures can decrease computer performance, sometimes in ways that are not immediately evident; the resources might continue to operate, but with unreliable results. The severity of permanent damage increases with temperature and exposure time. Silicon—the foundation of current integrated circuitry—will lose its semiconductor properties at significantly lower temperatures than what it takes to melt the solder that connects a chip to the rest of the computer.

For perspective, some heat-activated fire-suppression systems are triggered by ambient temperatures (at the sensor) as high as 71°C (160°F). Even in temperate climates, the passenger compartment of a sealed automobile baking in sunlight can reach temperatures in excess of 60°C (140°F). If a mobile computer is directly in sunlight and absorbing radiant energy, the heating is more rapid and pronounced, especially if the encasing material is a dark color, which, in the shade, would help radiate heat.

Although excessive heat is the more common culprit, computing equipment also has a minimum temperature for operation. Frigid temperatures can permanently damage mobile components (e.g., the rechargeable battery of a laptop computer), even (in fact, *especially*) when they are not in use. Plastics can also become more brittle and subject to cracking with little or no impact.

Foreign Substances

Foreign substances—those that do not belong in the information-processing environment—range from insects down to molecules. They can damage equipment and storage media in subtle, perhaps unseen, ways. Often damage results from the combination of a normal motion (e.g., rotation of a disk) and an inappropriate substance.

The most prevalent threat is dust. Even fibers from fabric and paper are abrasive and slightly conductive. Worse are finer, granular dirt particles. Manufacturing byproducts, especially metal particles with jagged shapes, are worse yet. Magnetic and optical storage media become a moving part when used in equipment. It is the combination of motion with foreign particles that is particularly damaging. Rotating media can be ground repeatedly by a single particle; a hard-drive head crash is one possible outcome.

A massive influx of foreign particles can overwhelm the air-filtering capability of HVAC systems, which can in turn result in adverse temperature and/or humidity. The potential causes include the following:

- Controlled implosion of a nearby building
- Catastrophic collapse (such as occurred near the World Trade Center)
- Volcanic eruption
- Dust storm
- Massive wildfire
- Wind storm carrying debris left over from a massive wildfire (as happened weeks after the major fires in California in 2003)

Dust surges that originate within a facility because of construction or maintenance work are not only more likely than nearby catastrophes, they can also be more difficult to deal with because there may be no air filter between the source and the endangered equipment. A common problem occurs when the panels of a suspended ceiling are lifted and particles rain down.

Keyboards are convenient input devices—for dust and worse. The temptation to eat or drink while typing only grows as people increasingly multitask. Food crumbs are stickier and more difficult to remove than ordinary dust. Carbonated drinks are not only sticky, but also far more corrosive than water. In industrial contexts, other handborne substances may also enter.

Smoke consists of gases, particulates, and possibly aerosols resulting from combustion (rapid oxidation, usually accompanied by glow or flame) or pyrolysis (heat-induced physicochemical transformation of material, often prior to combustion). The components of smoke, including that from tobacco products, pose all the hazards of dust and may be corrosive as well.

Some airborne particles are liquid droplets, or aerosols. Those produced by industrial processes may be highly corrosive. A more common and particularly pernicious aerosol is grease particles from cooking, perhaps in an employee lunchroom; the resulting residue may be less obvious than dust and may cling more tenaciously.

Water—whether it flows in (from below or above), wafts in (as an aerosol), or condenses (because of high humidity)—is a critical problem in energized electrical equipment. Water's conductive nature (assuming, as is likely, that it is not distilled water) can cause a short circuit (a current that flows outside the intended path). When the improper route cannot handle the current, the result is heat, which will be intense if there is arcing (a luminous discharge from an electric current bridging a gap between objects). This may melt or damage items and may even spawn an electrical fire.

Inappropriate Forces

Although computers and their components have improved considerably in shock resistance, there are still many points of potential failure due to shock. Hard drives and laptop LCD (liquid crystal display) screens remain particularly susceptible.

More insidious are protracted, chronic vibrations. These can occur if fixed equipment must be located near machinery, such as HVAC equipment or a printer.

If sensitive equipment cannot be located away from these sources of vibration, vibration-absorbing mats can be placed under the sensitive equipment or under the offending device. Mobile equipment that is frequently in transit is also at higher risk. Persistent vibrations can loosen things, notably screws, that would not be dislodged by a sharp blow. Even low-grade vibrations will eventually misalign read-write heads.

With the upsurge in mobile computing has come an increased incidence of damage from shock, vibration, dust, water, and extremes of temperature and humidity. One survey found that 18 percent of corporate laptops in "*non*rugged" applications had suffered substantial damage (averaging about half the purchase price). Several precautions that should be taken with a laptop are:

- transporting it only in a case designed for that purpose
- making sure it is off (not just in standby mode) when it is stored in its case (to avoid overheating)
- avoiding leaving it where it is subjected to temperature extremes (such as an unoccupied car)
- not subjecting it to moisture, dust, food, or drink
- being careful not drop, bang, or jostle it

Ruggedization of Equipment

An alternative to pampering a device is to make it more resistant to hazards. Laptops and other mobile devices can be "ruggedized" by adding characteristics such as the following:

- having an extra-sturdy metal chassis, possibly encased in rubber
- being shock- and vibration-resistant (with a floating LCD panel or gel-mounted hard drive)
- being rainproof, resistant to high humidity, and tolerant of salt fog
- being dustproof (with an overlay panel for the LCD screen)
- being able to withstand temperature extremes and thermal shock
- being able to operate at high altitude

Touch screens, port replicators, glare-resistant coatings for the LCD screen, and modular components are available on some models. Some portable ruggedized units resemble a suitcase more than a modern laptop.

Ruggedization techniques can also be used for any computer that must remain in areas where explosions or other harsh conditions may be encountered. Accessories available are ruggedized disk drives, mouse covers, transparent keyboard covers, and sealed keyboards (some of which can be rolled up). Some biometric devices can be used in demanding environments.

The term *industrial Ethernet* refers to the use of Ethernet to connect factory floor operations with front-office data systems. Ruggedization aspects associated with this include hardened cable systems, sealed RJ 45 connectors, and M12-4 "D" connectors for tight spaces. Some equipment is designed to operate continuously at 5 to 40°C (41 to 104°F) and 5 to 85 percent humidity and, for periods up to 72 hours, at even wider temperature and humidity ranges. Seismic racks are specially designed with internal bracing and/or shock absorption to hold servers as well as keyboards and monitors. A commonly applied standard for ruggedization is Bellcore GR-63-CORE.

Physical Access Control for Equipment

It is self-evident that access to equipment must be limited to authorized personnel to prevent vandalism, theft, and inappropriate use.

By comparison with stealing storage media, stealing hardware usually involves removing bigger, more obvious objects, such as computers and peripherals, with the outcome being more apparent to the victim. Garfinkel (2002), however, reports thefts of random access memory (RAM). If not all the RAM is removed from a machine, the loss in performance might not be noticed immediately.

At some facilities, only entrance to areas and/or contact with resources—equipment and storage media—is controlled. When removal of resources (or copies thereof) by persons authorized to have contact with them is a concern, control of egress should be equally important. (See also the comments on the need for and challenges of allowing emergency egress in the later section on "Fire Preparedness.") There are several philosophical approaches to controlling physical contact with and movement of resources. These methods can be used in combination with one another.

- Physical contact with a resource is restricted by putting it in a locked cabinet, safe, or room; this would deter even vandalism.
- A machine may be accessed, but it is secured (perhaps permanently bolted) to an object difficult to move; this would deter theft. In a variation of this, movement of an object is allowed, but a motion-sensored alarm sounds.
- Contact with a machine is allowed, but a security device controls the power switch.
- A machine can be turned on, but logging on requires a user identification process, possibly involving a password or a biometric device. Related to this is the idea of having the computer "locked" by software (perhaps a password-protected screensaver) while the user is away from the machine.
- A resource is equipped with a tracking device, such as an RFID tag, so that a sensing portal can alert security personnel or trigger an automated barrier to prevent the object from being moved out of its proper security area.
- An object, either a resource or a person, is equipped with a tracking device so that his, her, or its current position can be monitored continually.
- Resources are merely checked in and out by employees, for example by scanning barcodes on items and ID cards, so that administrators know at all times who has what, but not necessarily where they have it.

Specific hardware for controlling physical access is discussed in the major section on facilities because most devices protect spaces rather than individual pieces of equipment.

Worthy of note here, however, are laptop computers. Because it is often beyond an organization's ability to control access to the space it is in, a laptop provides increased opportunity for theft. According to Gordon et al. (2006) the third costliest category of computer crime for businesses is theft of laptop computers. Rittinghouse and Hancock (2003) suggest that employees sign an acknowledgment of additional precautions to be taken with off-site use of mobile devices. When a laptop must be left unattended, it should be kept it in a locked cabinet or car trunk or, at the very least, hidden from the view of passersby. The suggestion to "disguise" a laptop by *not* carrying it in a case designed for it runs contrary to proper practice for protecting the machine from accidental blows, etc. Some hardware devices specific to deterring laptop theft are security cables (for locking the laptop to a less movable object) and alarms.

The prudent assumption is that a laptop will eventually be accessed by an unauthorized person. In addition to hardware and/or software controls for logging in, portable machines should have all stored sensitive data encrypted. There are also software products for helping recover or control stolen laptops. One application has the laptop periodically report its serial number to a central monitoring center. If necessary, the laptop can be traced to its current location. The software is supposed to remain hidden and resident, even if a drive is formatted or the operating system is reinstalled. (See Absolute Software, 2003.)

It is sometimes appropriate for an organization to allow public physical access to some of its computers. In such case, certain cyberprecautions should be taken. Such computers should be on a separate LAN, isolated from sensitive resources. Furthermore, to avoid any liability issues, the public should not be afforded unrestricted access to the Internet.

PHYSICAL SECURITY FOR FACILITIES

Much of the control of physical security for the network resources already discussed—storage media and information-processing equipment—actually takes place at the level of facilities. In particular, control of physical access to spaces, most environmental controls, and most preparations for fire, flood, and damaging forces are done at this level. Each control put in place typically protects multiple pieces of equipment and storage media.

Physical Access Control for Spaces

Controlling physical access to buildings and rooms can be crudely broken down into three aspects: first, barriers and openings; second, lighting and surveillance; and third, detectors and alarms.

Barriers and Openings

The most fundamental protection against intruders is to put obstacles in their way. In doing so, we must not unreasonably impede authorized access or emergency egress. In theory, barriers are preventive measures. In reality, they are merely deterrents. To paraphrase General George C. Patton, any security device designed by humans can be defeated by humans. Each has its own weaknesses to attacks by stealth or force. The context will determine which type of attack is more likely. Stealthy attacks usually require more expertise and time. Forceful attacks are simpler, but typically are noisier and require larger tools. POA Publishing LLC (2003) has numerous comparisons (some the result of research at Sandia Laboratories) of the time required for and the noise produced by various types of attacks on different kinds of walls, doors, windows, and locks.

The openings required for the passage of people, air, and utilities are the most obvious potential weak points where penetration by people, foreign particles, and fire is easier. In some cases, however, walls have turned out to be easier to breach than locked doors. Doors tend to get the most attention when it comes to protection, but windows, even if sealed shut, are relatively "open" compared to the more impermeable surrounding walls. Some of the unseen openings are easy to overlook, especially below raised floors (common in computing centers) and above suspended ceilings (common in many rooms). These include passages for power and communication lines, water and sewer lines, and ventilation.

The barriers to intrusion form layers, from the campus boundary to buildings to rooms to safes. Using each layer effectively to protect the information-processing environment provides defense in depth.

The outermost barrier can be established at the property line. The sensitivity of a facility may require a wall or fencing. If vehicles must be permitted on the property, the potential for car or truck bombs may require strict control of which vehicles can drive or park where; permanent barriers, pop-up barriers, swing-down arms, "wrong-way" tire-puncturing spikes, and guard houses are possible traffic controls.

The second barrier is buildings. Exterior architecture and landscaping should avoid providing easy access to windows and roofs or obscuring public view of entrances. Regional and seasonal considerations should influence grounds maintenance. In colder climes, security-aware architecture may be nullified if snow is allowed to drift up toward windows or near entrances. In all climates, external construction materials should inhibit ignition by external fires. In dry regions, special care should be taken to keep away from buildings any vegetation with the potential to fuel wildfires. Roofs often have service hatches—for example, to afford servicing of external components of an air-conditioning system. Any roof or windows that might reasonably be accessed via a portable ladder should be protected accordingly.

The third barrier is the surfaces of individual rooms. Floors and ceilings are often forgotten. In the case of a dropped ceiling or a raised floor, the hidden space should not extend above or below multiple rooms if the intention is that access to each room be controlled separately. It is at the level of rooms or groups of rooms that fire divisions (discussed later) are created.

The fourth barrier, within rooms, is vaults, safes, or locked cabinets for storing specific resources. Such containers may serve double duty, providing not only safety from unauthorized access, but also from certain environmental threats (fire, moisture, electrical fields, magnetic fields, etc.). A safe typically has a combination lock, which may be either mechanical or electrical. The locking mechanism may be a time-delay lock (which cannot be opened until a fixed duration of time after the correct combination has been dialed or pressed) or a time lock (which cannot be opened except during certain predetermined periods). Although these theft-deterrent features are most common when protecting money, they may have wider application as well. Safes are rated by certification agencies (such as Underwriters Laboratories) based on the time it would take for a skilled and suitably equipped safe-cracker to compromise it; the safe, if not monitored remotely, should be visited by a guard patrol at intervals less than the rated time of the safe.

These layers need not restrict access the same way. In some settings, stringent controls at the outermost layer may obviate the need to "recheck" people once they are inside. A more orthodox scheme is to tighten security closer to sensitive resources.

There are a multitude of devices for keeping people out of areas or containers, ranging from padlocks to enclosures with two doors. Fundamental to most systems are the following:

- an immovable barrier (e.g., a wall) with an opening
- a door or comparable part that can be moved to block or to expose the opening
- a way of securing the "door" to the barrier, typically with a bolt or latch

The bolt used to secure a door is usually either a latchbolt or a deadbolt. The former provides greater convenience as it is spring-loaded and beveled, so it slides into the strike when the door is pulled closed. The latter provides greater security, as it requires an additional separate action after the door is closed to move the bolt into the strike. Bolts controlled electrically may be either fail-safe (opening if power fails) or fail-secure (remaining closed if power fails).

Traditional mechanical locks using metal keys are still common and may be adequate in certain situations. They certainly are better than nothing (as is often the case with wiring cabinets). As with encryption, security is no better than key management. Policy guidelines in this connection include the following:

- special security for the key cabinet
- logs of who has which key(s)
- periodic inventories of keys, duplicates, and blanks
- stampings of "Do not duplicate" on keys
- the absence of room or name identification on keys

Comparable precautions must be taken with combinations, personal identification numbers, badges, and cards of various types.

Electronic access control (EAC) systems typically involve a central point of control and monitoring. EAC systems may provide the security practitioner the following capabilities:

- being able to lock and unlock doors remotely
- being able to log who has entered
- being able to preclude access by specific persons (perhaps everyone)
- knowing when a room is legitimately occupied so intrusion-detection devices can be deactivated (preferably automatically)
- knowing in times of emergency where people still remain

The actual identification mechanism may be the use of some kind of card and/or PIN (personal identification number). The most promising new technology appears to be biometric devices. A major advantage of these is that they depend on a physiological or behavioral characteristic, which cannot be forgotten or lost and which is difficult to forge. There are a wide range of available technologies, which are the subject of the chapter "Biometrics;" consequently, we do not detail the many types of biometric devices in Table 3.

Table 3 lists a selection of the more common components of physical access control systems. Some, such as door closers, must be used in combination with other things.

It is not practical here to enumerate the various techniques for defeating each of the various access control devices listed in Table 3. POA Publishing LLC (2003, 60) lists the average time it takes to surreptitiously neutralize several different kinds of standard locks via different techniques. Whereas most of us probably think of picking a lock or shimming a latchbolt (stereotypically, with a credit card) as the usual attacks on locks, most people do not have the right skills and/or tools for a stealthy attack. Consequently, most attacks are by force. The most vulnerable type of lock is the kind that incorporates the key mechanism in the door knob, common in residential use, as it can easily succumb to an attack by force.

All parts of an opening and its closure are fair game for attacks. Exposed hinges are easy to remove. A strike that is weak or weakly attached will give way under the force of a quickly moving shoulder. The bolt can be exposed by prying a flimsy door jam or "peeling" poorly constructed doors or walls. The locking mechanism itself can succumb to particular types of drilling, punching, hammering, and wrenching.

In assessing a candidate architecture with respect to barriers and openings, the time, resources, and sophistication of a likely hypothetical attacker must be correlated with both the assets it protects (the bigger the prize, the greater the enticement to attack) and the overall security scheme. Of particular note with regard to that overall security scheme is how the choice of openings and barriers should be made in concert with the choice of lighting and surveillance, discussed in the following section. A well-lit, well-observed point of potential attack may not need to be as resistant to the type of attack requiring privacy for an extended time.

Table 3: Physical Access Control Components

Access Control Type	Characteristics
Badge, visitor's pass	Worn by authorized persons, checked by security guards (and perhaps other employees). For employees, should feature a photograph. Features to prevent forgery should be incorporated.
Mechanical key lock	Requires inserting and turning a metal key with a specific configuration. Among various subtypes, pin-tumbler offers better protection than warded, wafer, or lever locks.
Combination lock	Mechanical version involves turning a dial to certain positions. Electronic version requires typing a specific sequence on a keypad.
Card reader	Activated upon insertion of a smartcard or swiping of a card with a magnetic strip or bar code. May also incorporate a keypad for entering a personal identification number. Alternatively, may sense a proximity card without contact.
Hollerith card	Holes in card are read by passage of light or contact brushes. Now used only for hotel security.
Swipe card	Slid through a reader. Can use a magnetic strip or a bar code. Can be used in conjunction with a personal identification number. Magnetic watermarked subtype has magnetic strip embedded, not added on to outside. Infrared shadow subtype is transparent to infrared light, has embedded bar code.
Proximity card	Embedded circuitry emits frequencies that can be detected by a reader when the card is near. Reader can be hidden in a wall. Card can remain inside clothing. Suffers less wear than a swipe card. Same principle can be applied to automobile access.
Memory card	Contains memory circuitry to carry a user's identification information. Intelligent (or protected or segmented) subtype has logic to control memory access.
Smartcard	Contains both memory for a user's identification information and processing power to run related security protocols.
Biometric device	Many subtypes, exploiting physiological and/or behavioral characteristics of the user. (See "Biometrics".)
Stairtower lock	Frame-mounted hybrid electric device. Allows door handle to operate if power fails. Designed for emergency egress.
Magnetic lock	Electromagnet installed on door frame plus strike plate on door. Always a fail-safe device. Direct-hold subtype is surface-mounted on the secure side of door and door frame. Shear (or concealed) subtype in embedded within door and door frame.
Electric strike lock	Solenoid moves a strike from door frame into door. No wiring in door required. Can be fail-safe or fail-secure, use a latch bolt or deadbolt.
Electric lockset	Similar to a mechanical lockset, but with solenoid action in place of key action. Can be fail-safe or fail-secure.
Door closer	Automatically pulls a door shut after it has been opened.
Turnstiles, revolving doors	Used as a choke point (possible with a programmed time delay and sensors in walls) to prevent entry by two people at once ("piggybacking" or "tailgating").
Mantrap (or double-vestibule portal)	Glass enclosure with two doors that cannot be opened simultaneously. Prevents "piggybacking."
Dispensable barriers	Foam, fog, or entangling devices deployed when intrusion is detected. (A "reactive-preventive" measure.)

With regard to the interplay between barriers and surveillance, it is appropriate to single out for comment one particular, common workplace design: a large room with numerous cubicles. The relatively open architecture of cubicles discourages certain types of behavior. On the other hand, the "space" of each cubicle is not lockable as a room is. Removable materials are thus more likely to be left unattended and insecure during the work day. Even at the end of each day, it is more inconvenient (and perhaps impractical) for a cubicle occupant to secure all sensitive materials. Even if materials are secured, they may be in a type of cabinet offering little resistance to an attack. However, a locked door may give an office occupant a false sense of security; cleaning staff will likely have access to individual offices. Therefore, at least outside normal working hours, security within an office should be treated as if it were in a cubicle.

Lighting and Surveillance

Whereas barriers can be an obstacle to intrusion, they can also be an aid to it. If, for example, an entrance is sheltered, an intruder has a better chance of picking a lock unobserved. Consequently, one of the principles of crime prevention through environmental design (CPTED) is to increase the perception of natural surveillance—that is, a clear line of sight between the honest and the dishonest. There are several applications of this principle. Outside, fences, doors, and windows should not be obscured by hedges. The architectural design should also present an unobstructed view of doors and windows. Within the workplace, an open design can discourage certain kinds of activities. See Crowe (2004) for a broader discussion of CPTED.

Organized surveillance can be done in person (by stationed or roving guards) or remotely (by camera). In any case, if potential perpetrators are aware of the surveillance, then it can serve as a deterrent, not just as a reactive measure.

Closed-circuit television (CCTV) or digital cameras may or may not be monitored by humans in real time, but some form of recording should be done in any case (to preserve evidence, perhaps for legal proceedings). Recording can be done on analog tape or digitally on hard drives. Real-time monitoring in some form is necessary to interrupt malfeasance before it is completed. For digital cameras, the tedious task of monitoring cameras—perhaps many in number—can be aided by integrating the camera system with motion-detection software or even intelligent software that can recognize suspicious activity or "hot" license plates (of cars known to be stolen or associated with criminals). See [U.K.] Department of Trade and Industry (2005). To the extent possible, care should be taken to install cameras in a way that makes it difficult to disable them or their communication link with a monitor or recorder.

Lighting and surveillance go hand in hand. Whether achieved remotely by cameras or in person, surveillance is aided by lighting. Therefore, good lighting is a deterrent to crime. Although continual illumination is generally preferred, motion-triggered lighting may have more of a deterrent effect in situations in which its activation would be noticed by others more readily than would be the actions of an intruder; an example would be where there are rows of shelving or equipment racks blocking natural surveillance. The most effective type of lighting to support color CCTV cameras is metal halide lamps because they imitate daylight well; however, they are the most expensive type to install and maintain. See Chapter 5 of Cumming (1992) for a comprehensive introduction to CCTV and types of lighting.

Even if surveillance is not a concern, to help prevent accidents, some lighting should remain on outside business hours; it should remain on even if the municipal power supply fails and should not be controllable by any publicly accessible switches. Moreover, additional lighting triggered by a fire or other emergency should aid escape despite the presence of smoke.

Detectors and Alarms

When prevention and deterrence fail, the next line of defense is to discover, report, and react to fire or unauthorized access. Whether for intrusion or fire, all alarms systems should adhere to the following principles:

- The functioning of detectors and alarms should not depend on the municipal power supply, which can be disrupted; the control unit should indicate the status of both municipal and backup power.
- The remote reporting by detectors should not depend on exposed communication lines that can be cut; alternatives available include radio, microwave, cellular, and satellite communication links.
- Sensing and reporting should be zoned, meaning that responders know an event's location within a facility; ideally, the monitor panel should provide specific information, such as whether a door is still ajar.

A wide variety of devices are available for detecting unwanted intrusions in the form of unauthorized entry or activity. Table 4 outlines the basic characteristics of the main types. Devices should be chosen based on their reliability, features, and cost and on the kind of threat anticipated. The primary consideration, however, is the intended protection pattern. Some devices are strictly for monitoring outdoor areas, perimeters, indoor areas, or items, whereas other types can be used in multiple applications.

Not indicated in Table 4 is the full litany of strengths and weaknesses of the various types of sensors—that is, what causes them to issue false alarms or to ignore suspect events. A very thorough reference for explicit characteristics of sensors is Cumming (1992). Table 11-1 in Fennelly (2004) shows recommendations based on an extensive list of factors affecting sensor usage.

Many sensors have added or optional features (not listed here) that improve their sophistication. It should be noted that the integration—not simply the usage—of two or more technologies can dramatically improve reliability—that is, the likelihood of detecting all and only unwanted intrusions.

Security guards are not listed in Table 3 as an access control device (though they are often used to check badges) or in Table 4 as a detection device (though they often search articles brought in or out). They can be used in both capacities and can also be used to respond to unauthorized entry or behavior. In the present era of hypersensitivity to potential terrorism, behavior is now beginning to be monitored by specially trained security guards for possible indicators of hostile intent. This approach is new and still fraught with false positives (and ensuing indignant reactions by those erroneously suspected), especially in situations (such as in the travel industry) where people may already be under stress.

Guard service is frequently outsourced, a practice that requires depending on the competence and trustworthiness of another organization. Choosing good security guards directly may be a riskier proposition, as determining the reputation of an established security firm is easier

Table 4: Comparison of Types of Intrusion-Detection Sensors

Sensor Type	Characteristics
PIR (passive infrared)	"Sees" change in heat characteristic of human movement. Limited range.
Glass break	"Hears" 3- to 5-kHz sound frequencies and "feels" 200-Hz seismic shock frequencies characteristic of glass breaking; has replaced foil strips previously common on windows.
Acoustic	Microprocessor analyzes shapes of sound frequency to discriminate between breaking glass and other sounds. Best when placed opposite the window to be protected.
Audio	Reacts to and perhaps records the audible range (20–20,000 Hz). Can be attached to a fence to "hear" the sound of it being cut.
Shock	Attached directly to pane of glass. Subtype generating piezoelectric current can protect only one pane. Subtype in which a circuit is "shaken" open can protect nearby panes as well.
Vibration	Reacts to vibrations from forced entry (other than glass breaking).
Electromechanical	Motion breaks or completes an electrical circuit. Largely obsolete. Many subtypes, including pressure mats, metallic foil on windows, door or window switches, and window screens, wooden lattices, or door paneling incorporating fine, easily broken wires.
Ultrasonic	Uses the Doppler effect to detect motion by noting changes in reflections of 19.2-kHz sounds. Limited range. (Can be adjusted to detect air convection from fire, but may be triggered by ventilation system.) Not fooled by movement outside protected room.
Microwave	Similar in principle to an ultrasonic sensor, but using higher-frequency waves, which will penetrate nonmetallic construction. Can be used outside without being inhibited by weather. Can protect perimeters (narrow beam) or areas (wide beam).
Capacitance	Detects changes in capacitive coupling between a ground and an energy-radiating antenna. Very limited range, obsolete except for protecting an individual object.
Photoelectric	Reacts to interference with a beam of light, preferably infrared. Outdoors, weather can interfere with its proper operation.
Chemical	Detects human effluvia. Vapor trace analyzer subtype can test for explosives, inflammables, and drugs.
Balanced pressure	Notes changes in differential pressure in liquid-filled tubes buried under soil. Hard (e.g., frozen) soil may prevent triggering. Nearby traffic may cause false alarms.
Leaky coax	Detects changes in standing pattern of electronic signal emitted by a buried coaxial cable with (partially) stripped shielding. More reliable than balanced pressure sensor.
Fiber-optic cable vibration	Cable can be attached to fences, walls, rooftops, ducts, or pipes or can be buried in ground. Software monitoring changes in signal transmitted through the cable can be "tuned" to ignore certain types of vibrations. Protection extends the entire length of the cable.

than checking the background of each applicant for a security position. Moreover, agencies specializing in physical security provide extensive experience and specialized knowledge, not just expediency. Rittinghouse and Hancock (2003) report that it is "extremely rare" that an outsourcing security company is the problem when there is an internal or external breach of security.

The principle of natural surveillance effectively makes every employee (or, for that matter, helpful nonemployee) a quasi-guard. Those whose primary job function is not security can use a duress alarm to send a signal to a security specialist or law enforcement agency to indicate that help is needed. This can be of a fixed nature, such as a hidden button a bank teller might use, or can be on a wearable, wireless device. All employees need to know how intruders might enter, how to recognize intruders, and how to react—whom to call and what to do until help arrives. Dealing with intruders is a lengthy subject in itself. A comprehensive list of appropriate actions is given in Chapter 143 of Tyska and Fennelly (2000).

Custodial personnel may need additional training and oversight. They often work at night, a time favored by certain types of intruders. Cleaning crews also are prone to breach security protocols to streamline their work, for example, by leaving offices open and unattended for periods of time. For this reason, education should be reinforced by spot checks to see what is actually going on.

Environmental Control

As mentioned before, maintaining environmental control may be as critical as maintaining power or telecommunication service. As such, if network equipment is to be kept running despite a loss of municipal power the continuity of HVAC systems' own utilities—power and, if required, water—must be maintained.

HVAC systems should have independently controlled temperature and relative humidity settings. Each variable should be monitored by a system that can issue alerts when problems arise. Ideally, HVAC units should be installed in pairs, with each unit being able to carry the load of the other should it malfunction.

For large, critical facilities, HVAC should be protected from sabotage or "misappropriation" for nefarious ends. In particular, air intakes should be viewed as potential entry points for dangerous airborne substances.

Keeping a computing area free of foreign particles actually requires multiple defenses. Air filters should remove fine dust particles because outdoor dust is brought in on clothes and shoes. Filters must be cleaned or replaced on a regular schedule. Periodically, air-heating equipment should be turned on briefly even when not needed. This is to incrementally burn off dust that would otherwise accumulate and be converted to an appreciable amount of smoke when the equipment is activated for the first time after a long period of disuse. Vacuuming of rooms and equipment should also involve filters. Food, drink, and tobacco products should be banned from the computing area. Maintenance and construction workers (whether they are employees or not) must be made of aware of the dangers posed by dust, even from something as simple as accessing the space above a suspended ceiling. When dust-producing activities are anticipated, other employees should know to take precautions, such as installing dust covers on equipment.

Fire Preparedness

Throughout history, fire has been one of the most important threats to human life, property, and activity when measured in terms of frequency, potential magnitude, and rapidity of spread. Fire presents a bundle of the previously mentioned environmental threats. By definition, combustion involves chemical and physical changes in matter, in other words, destruction of what was. Even away from the site of actual combustion, heat can do damage, as detailed earlier. If water is the suppressing agent, it can wreak havoc on adjacent rooms or lower floors that suffered no fire damage. Smoke can damage objects far from the site of combustion, even, in the case of wildfires, after traveling great distances. More critical are smoke's irritant, toxic, asphyxial, and carcinogenic effects on humans; smoke, not heat, is most often the killer in a fire. With the advent of modern synthetic materials, fires can now produce deadlier toxins. Hydrogen cyanide, for instance, is approximately twenty-five times more toxic than carbon monoxide. Some modern fire suppressants themselves decompose into dangerous substances, as is discussed in the section on "Halon," below. Even the smoke from a single fire has been responsible for chronic illness and cancer in firefighters.

It follows that one of the oldest roles of physical security has been to deal with the threat of fire. There are several sides to this issue: emergency egress, prevention, mitigation, detection, and suppression. Some aspects of fire control pertain specifically to the facilities housing information-processing equipment. Measures that might be adequate in a general setting would be inappropriate for the protection of delicate equipment and media.

A comprehensive tome on fire is Cote (2003).

Emergency Egress

Preservation of human life is the highest priority in fire preparedness. Knowing how to escape from a fire is of the utmost importance because human life has greater value than any information assets. Fire evacuation maps and procedures should be posted and evacuation should be practiced. When the general power supply is cut, signs pointing toward exits must stay illuminated, and some of the lighting along escape routes should also stay on. Ideally, lighting should also come on when a fire has been detected to help evacuees see through smoke.

Fire doors must be latched in fail-safe mode, require only a single action to use, and must incorporate door closers. In particular, emergency exits cannot consist of a sequence of two doors (as in a mantrap, for instance).

Despite good design, instances continue to occur in which well-marked emergency exits have been found to be blocked or locked when the need for them arises. One reason for nullifying a door's panic hardware is that the doors were being used for other reasons, perhaps being propped open, thereby creating the threat of unauthorized entry. If emergency doors are alarmed, misuse of the doors should be rare. If misuse of the doors cannot be prevented by connecting them to alarms, then personnel must be educated as to the threats from misuse. In any case, all employees must know where the emergency exits are, and maintenance personnel must understand the importance of keeping those exits functional.

Governmental regulations may mandate accommodations for persons who have problems with mobility. In the United States, the Americans with Disabilities Act requires that sight-impaired people be able to understand what to do upon touching door hardware, that exit signage meet certain visibility criteria, that exits be usable by weak and wheelchair-bound persons, and that doorways provide at least 32 inches of clearance.

It is possible to install a delayed-egress device on a fire door. The delay can be as long as 15 seconds. A CCTV and remote control of the exit by a guard can be implemented. In such case, the CCTV signal should not be delayed by transmission over low-bandwidth voice communication lines. See Konicek and Little (1997) and National Fire Protection Association (2003, *Life safety code*).

To this point, we have dodged a ticklish issue: The same principles of controlling entrance to areas can be applied to controlling egress—except in times of fire or other emergency. Allowing quick escape is inherently at odds with checking to see who and what is leaving a building. With an EAC, a person would not be required to use a swipe card to exit; therefore, there would be no record of precisely who exited.

Fire Prevention

In attempting to prevent an accidental fire from ever getting started, the two things best to avoid are high temperatures and low ignition points. It is usually possible to exclude highly flammable materials from the computing environment. Overheating, on the other hand, is a possibility in almost any electrical device and many mechanical devices. In some cases a cooling system has failed or has been handicapped. In other cases, a defective component generates abnormal friction. The biggest threat comes from short circuits; the resulting resistance may create a small electric heater or incite arcing.

Some factors that may lead to a fire, such as short circuits within a machine or a wall, are beyond our control. Yet many precautions can be taken to lessen the chances of a fire. Vents should be kept unobstructed and air filters clean. Power circuits should not be asked to carry loads in excess of their rated capacity. Whenever possible, wires should run below a raised floor rather than on top of it. If wires must lie on a floor where they could be stepped on, a sturdy protective cover must be installed. In any case, wires should be protected from fatiguing or fraying. See National Fire Protection Association (2003, *Standard for the protection of electronic computer/data processing equipment*) for fire prevention guidelines for the computing environment. As of this writing, the newest electrical code pertaining specifically to computing equipment is from the International Electrotechnical Commission (2001).

Many fires are actually the culmination of a protracted process. In some cases, a material smolders for hours before the first flame appears. Therefore, another preventive measure is for employees to use their eyes, ears, noses, and brains. Damage to a power cord can be observed if potential trouble spots are checked. Uncharacteristic noises from a component may be symptomatic of a malfunction. The odor of baking thermoplastic insulation is a sign that things are heating up.

A common, sudden cause of fire is lightning. See the section on "Lightning Precautions," above, for references on lightning-protection systems.

Fire Detection

Automatic fire detectors should be placed on the ceilings of rooms as well as in hidden spaces (e.g., below raised floors and above suspended ceilings). The number and positioning of detectors should take into account the location of critical items, the location of potential ignition sources, and the type of detector. Fire detectors are based on several technologies, outlined in Table 5.

Of the technologies listed, the continuous air-sampling smoke detector is particularly appropriate for computing facilities, as it can detect very low smoke concentrations and report different alarm levels.

For high-hazard areas, there are also automatic devices for detecting the presence of combustible vapors or abnormal operating conditions likely to produce fire. Said another way, they sound an alarm *before* a fire starts.

Some fire detectors, especially the fusible type, are integrated into an automatic fire-suppression system. This means that the first alarm could be the actual release of an extinguishing agent (hence the water-flow detector).

Table 5: Comparison of Types of Fire-Detection Technology

Detector Type	Characteristics
Fixed-temperature	Triggered at a specific temperature. Fusible subtype has metal with a low melting temperature. Quartzoid bulb subtype completes an electrical circuit when a liquid-filled bulb breaks. Line subtype completes an electrical circuit when insulation melts. Bimetallic subtype completes a circuit by bending of bonded metals that expand differently.
Rate-compensation	Triggers at a lower temperature if the temperature rise is faster and at a higher temperature if the temperature rise is slower.
Rate-of-rise	Reacts to a rapid temperature rise, typically 7–8°C (12–15°F) per minute.
Electronic spot type thermal	Uses electronic circuitry to respond to a temperature rise.
Flame	"Sees" radiant energy. Good in high-hazard areas. Infrared subtype may be fooled by sunlight. Ultraviolet subtype may be affected by smoke.
Smoke	Usually detect fires more rapidly than heat detectors. Ionizing subtype uses a small radioactive source (common in residences). Photoelectric subtype detects obscuring or scattering of a light beam. Cloud chamber subtype detects formation of droplets around particles in high-humidity. Continuous air-sampling subtype can detect very low smoke concentrations.
Water flow	Reacts to the activation (or malfunction) of a sprinkler system.

Because an event triggering a fire may also disrupt the electrical supply, fire detectors must be able to function during a power outage. Many fire detectors are powered by small batteries, which should be replaced on a regular schedule. Some components of detectors, such as the radioisotope in an ionizing smoke detector, have a finite life span; the viability of such a detector cannot be determined by pushing the "test" button, which merely verifies the health of the battery. Such detectors must be replaced according to the manufacturer's schedule.

Fire Mitigation

While fire prevention typically receives more attention in the media, fire mitigation is arguably more important. This is because, despite the best precautions to prevent the accidental ignition of a fire within a facility, a fire may have an external or deliberate origin. Mitigation requires greater planning and expense. The key ideas are to erect fire-resistant barriers and to limit fuel for the fire between the barriers.

For computing environments, the choice of construction materials, design, and techniques for mitigating the spread of fire should exceed the minimum standards dictated by local building codes. Because fires can spread through unseen open spaces, including ventilation systems, a computing area is defined to be all spaces served by the same HVAC (heating, ventilation, and air-conditioning) system as a computing room. Air ducts within that system should have smoke dampers. The computing area must be isolated in a separate fire division. This means the walls must extend from the structural floor to the structural ceiling of the computer area and have a 1-hour rating (resistance to an external fire for 1 hour). Care should be taken to ensure that openings where pipe and cables pass through the fire-resistant boundaries of the separate fire division are sealed with material that is equally fire-resistant.

Many fires affecting a computer area do not actually originate in that area. Even if a fire does not technically spread into a computing area, its products—heat, smoke, and soot (carbon deposits)—may. Consequently, the level of fire protection beyond the computing area is still of critical concern. Fully sprinklered buildings (protected by sprinkler systems throughout) are recommended. Concern should extend beyond the building if it is located in an area with high hazards, such as chemical storage or periodically dry vegetation. In the latter case, an important barrier to fire is a firebreak around the building created by removal of any vegetation likely to fuel a fire.

The standards prescribed by the National Fire Protection Association (2003, *Standard for the protection of electronic computer/data processing equipment*) for fire protection of computing equipment put forth specifications for wall coverings, carpet, and furnishings (which are relaxed in fully sprinklered buildings). Additional prescribed limitations on what other materials can be present in a computer area do not take into account that even high-hazard areas have computers present. In interpreting those standards, one should determine which dangerous materials are absolutely essential for operations, and work to minimize any unnecessary hazards. Because of their potential contribution to fire (as well as being a more likely starting point for a fire), materials that could contribute to a Class B fire (including solvents, paints, etc.) should not be stored in a computing area except in a fireproof enclosure. Materials that could contribute to a Class A fire (including paper) should be kept to the minimum necessary.

Raised floors are standard features of many computer facilities, allowing for cables to connect equipment without the need to cover cables to prevent fraying and electrical shorting. The use of junction boxes below the floor should be minimized, however. The needed equipment for lifting the heavy removable panels to gain access to the space between the raised floor and the structural floor must be easy to locate, even in the event of a fire.

Fire Suppression

The delicate nature of information resources presents special challenges for firefighting. It is preferable to extinguish a fire with specialized, on-site equipment rather than high-volume fire hoses. Local fire departments should always be informed of any special fire hazards they might encounter on a call. Likewise, they should be made aware of sensitive equipment and media, as well as the fire controls in place. (Newman 2003). Depending on how many operations are automatic, certain employees (enough so that an adequate number are always on duty) must be trained to perform extra duties, including:

- calling emergency officials
- shutting off electricity and natural gas
- altering the air flow (if HVAC is powered from outside the immediate area) so that either smoke is exhausted or it is prevented from spreading inside
- operating special fire systems (hoses, wheeled portable units, manually controlled sprinklers, etc.)

Fire-suppression systems generally release water, dry chemical, or gaseous agents. The release can be from portable devices, from a centralized distribution system of pipes (perhaps with hoses that will be manually directed), or from modular devices in fixed locations. Fire can be extinguished by displacing oxygen, by breaking the chemical reaction, by cooling the fire's fuel below its point of ignition, or by a combination of these.

Any fire in a computing environment should be considered a Class C fire because of the presence of electricity. Electrical power should be cut as soon as possible, regardless of whether a conductive fire-suppression agent is used, because any electrical shorting will work against the suppressant. Obviously, automatic fire-suppression systems must be able to function independently of the facility's main power supply.

When possible, it is preferable to extinguish a fire immediately with portable extinguishers aimed at the base of the fire before it can grow. Each device should have one or more letters on the label, indicating the class(es) of fires on which it can be used. For most computing facilities, a dry chemical extinguisher rated A-B-C will cover all situations. The dry chemical will leave a residue, but if the fire can be caught early, this is a small price to pay. All personnel should be acquainted with the location and proper use of portable fire-suppression devices. If more than one type is available, they must know which type is suitable for which kinds of fires.

Countermeasures must match the potential conflagration, both in quantity and quality. The presence of flammable materials requires greater suppression capacity. In addition, special tools and techniques are needed for special fires. A Class D fire, involving combustible metals such as magnesium, requires the application of a metal-specific dry powder, so named to distinguish its purpose from that of ordinary dry chemical with B-C or A-B-C ratings. (Rechargeable batteries in laptops do not contain enough lithium to require special treatment in case of a fire.) Recently certified, specialized (wet chemical) extinguishing equipment should be installed if there is the potential of a Class K fire, involving cooking equipment using oils and fats at high temperature.

Total Flooding with Gaseous Agents

Total flooding seeks to release enough of a gaseous agent to alter the entire atmosphere of a sealed area (with openings totaling no more than 1 percent of the total surface area of the enclosure). The term *clean agent* is often used to indicate that the gas itself leaves no residue (although its decomposition by-products will). Ordinarily, the air-agent mixture alone would be safe for humans, but fires always produce toxic smoke.

Consequently, the best protocol is to have an alarm continuously announce the impending release of a flooding agent, allow a reasonable time period for personnel to evacuate and seal the area, and sound a second alarm to announce the actual release. Occupants of those areas must understand the different alarms, must know how to proceed when the first alarm sounds, and must appreciate the seriousness of that environment. (A short science lesson might help.) Doors must be self-closing and have "panic hardware" for easy exit. Warning signs must proclaim the special nature of the area. Self-contained breathing equipment must be available for rescuing people.

The sudden release of a highly pressurized gaseous agent has several side effects. The gas undergoes a dramatic decrease in its temperature. Reportedly, skin in direct contact with a release could suffer frostbite. Equipment could suffer as well. The force of the exhaust is considerable and should be taken into account when placing the vents. The noise of a release is loud, but does not impair hearing.

Gaseous fire-suppression systems can be either centralized or decentralized. Centralized systems are generally custom-fitted for a particular installation. A network of pipes delivers the suppressant from a single tank to multiple nozzles operating simultaneously. This is the more traditional and common approach.

Decentralized systems are modular, so there is greater flexibility in placing the individual units or repositioning them (guided by expert advice) if the layout of a facility changes. Independent units each have a tank, triggering device, and nozzle; they can be equipped for remote triggering or monitoring. On the negative side, the individual units, being self-contained, are heavier and bulkier than the outlets and pipes of a centralized system. Therefore, they must be supported from a structural ceiling rather than a suspended ceiling. Moreover, each cylinder must be anchored very securely to prevent the force of release from turning the cylinder into a projectile subsequent to the release of gas.

Gaseous agents that have been used in total flooding fire-suppression systems in computing facilities include carbon dioxide, argon, nitrogen, halogenated agents (halons), newer replacements for halons, and mixtures of these. (Pure CO_2 at the concentration needed for total flooding is hazardous to humans.)

Halon. For decades, the fire-suppression technique of choice in computing facilities was total flooding with Halon 1301—also known as bromotrifluoromethane or $CBrF_3$. (Halon 1211, a liquid streaming agent, was also used in portable extinguishers.) Because of their ozone-depleting nature, proportionally worse than chlorofluorocarbons (CFCs), halons were banned by the Montréal Protocol of 1987. Disposal and recycling of Halon 1301 must be performed by experts, because it is contained under high pressure. Consult Halon Recycling Corporation (HRC 2002) for advice and contacts. Although no new halons are being produced, existing systems may remain in place, and the use of recycled Halon 1301 in new systems is still allowed by the protocol (on a case-by-case basis) for "essential" use (not synonymous with "critical" as used by the HRC). Because the world's supply has been decreasing since 1994, a concern when relying on Halon 1301 is its future availability.

Halon 1301's effectiveness is legendary. One factor is its high thermal capacity (ability to absorb heat). More important, it also appears to break the chemical chain reaction of combustion. Although the mechanism by which it does this is not perfectly understood (nor, for that matter, is the chemistry of combustion), the dominant theory proposes that the toxins into which it decomposes at about 482°C (900°F) are essential for chemical inhibition. The chemistry and other aspects of halons are discussed in the chapter on Halogenated Agents and Systems in Cote (2003).

In low-hazard environments, a concentration of approximately 5 percent Halon 1301 by volume suffices. Short-term exposure at this level is considered safe but not recommended for humans; dizziness and tingling may result. An even lower concentration is adequate when the Halon 1301 is delivered with a dry chemical that inhibits reignition. Regardless of the concentration applied, immediately after exposure to Halon 1301 (perhaps from an accidental discharge), a victim should not be given adrenaline-like drugs because of possibly increased cardiosensitivity. The real risk comes when fire decomposes Halon 1301 into deadly hydrogen fluoride, hydrogen chloride, and free bromine. Fortunately, these gases, being extremely acrid, are easy to smell at concentrations of just a few parts per million.

Gaseous Alternatives to Halon. In addition to the natural inert gases, there are numerous gaseous replacements for Halon 1301 in the general category of halocarbon agents. Subcategories include: hydrofluorocarbons (HFCs), hydrochlorofluorocarbons (HCFCs), perfluorocarbons (PFCs and FCs), and fluoroiocarbons (FICs). None of these or blends of them seem to be as effective as halons—that is, more of the substance is needed to achieve the same end. The search for better clean agents continues. See National Fire Protection Association (2000, *Standard for clean agent fire extinguishing systems*) for guidelines regarding clean agents and [U.S.] Environmental Protection Agency (2003) for a listing of alternatives.

Water-Based Suppression. Despite its reputation for doing as much damage as fire, water is coming back in favor—more so in Europe than in North America—even for areas with computer equipment. (For areas without such equipment, water is still the preferred, cost-effective response.) Because water's corrosive action (in the absence of other compounds) is slow, computer equipment that has been sprinkled is not necessarily damaged beyond repair. In fact, cleanup from water can be much simpler and more successful than from other agents. Water also has an outstanding thermal capacity.

Misting with water is now used as an alternative to Halon 1301. The decreased droplet size in mists (compared to ordinary sprays) makes them more effective in extracting heat. The explosive expansion of the steam contributes to displacing oxygen at the place where the water is being converted to steam, namely, the fire. (Steam itself has been used as a suppressant.) See, for example, Fleming (1999).

There has also been research with chemically enhanced water mists, but this is not yet in common use.

To reduce the risk of accidental leakage, recommendations have traditionally specified dry pipe systems, in which pipes for hose, sprinkler, or mist systems remain dry until needed. In fact, leakage from wet pipe systems is very rare; damage from washroom incidents is far more likely. See, for instance, Mangan (2002).

Fire Recovery

Even when a fire has been put out, new problems arise—and can intensify as time passes. By-products of the fire, perhaps because of the type of suppressant used, may be toxic to humans or corrosive to equipment. As soon as practical after a fire has been extinguished, thorough ventilation should take place. Only appropriately trained and equipped experts should enter to begin this dangerous procedure. Aside from the initial health hazard, improper procedures may worsen the situation. For example, active HVAC equipment and elevators might spread contamination to additional areas.

Once air quality has returned to a safe level, resources should be rehabilitated. In some cases, equipment will never again be suitable for regular use; however, it may be brought to a condition from which any unique data can be backed up. The same is true of removable storage media. Paper documents can be restored provided they have not become brittle.

The combustion by-products most devastating to electronic equipment are corrosive chloride and sulfur compounds. These reside in particulate residue, regardless of whether dry chemical (which itself leaves a film) or a clean agent (a somewhat misleading term) was applied. In either case, time is of the essence in preventing the progression of damage. Some types of spray solvents may be used for preliminary cleanup. In the case of fire suppression by water, the procedures outlined below should be followed.

Flood Preparedness

As many have learned too late, much flood damage occurs in areas not considered flood-prone. Flooding, in the broad sense used here, is simply invasive water, whether rising from below, falling from above, or striking laterally. It need not originate in a body of water, and it may be the result of nature or human action. Breaks in water mains can occur at any time, but especially during excavation or winter freeze-thaw cycles. Fire hydrants can be damaged by vehicles. Pipes can leak or commodes overflow. Roofs can be damaged by wind, fallen trees, or snow overburden. Therefore, all facilities should take precautions against flooding from both rising and falling water.

The force of moving water and debris can do structural damage directly or indirectly, by eroding foundations. In some cases, natural gas lines are broken, thus feeding electrical fires started by short-circuiting.

Most flood damage, however, comes from the water's suspended load of particles. Whereas falling water, say from a water sprinkler or a leaking roof, is fairly pure and relatively easy to clean up, floodwater is almost always muddy. Fine particles (clays) cling tenaciously, making cleanup a nightmare. A dangerous biological component may be present if sewage removal or treatment systems back up or overflow or if initially safe water is not drained promptly. Another hazard is chemicals that may have escaped containment far upstream.

When flooding or subsequent fire has disabled HVAC systems in the winter, ice formation has sometimes added further complications. Freezing water wedges items apart. Obviously, recovery is delayed further by the need to first thaw the ice.

Flood Anticipation

Assessing flood risk is no mean task. Government maps depicting flood potential are not necessarily useful in assessing risk because they can quickly become outdated. One reason is construction in areas with no recorded flood history. Another is that urbanization itself changes drainage patterns and reduces natural absorption of water.

Small streams react first and most rapidly to rainfall or snowmelt. Even a very localized rain event can have a profound effect on an unnoticed creek. Perhaps the most dangerous situation is in arid regions, where an intermittent stream may be dry or nearly dry on the surface for much of the year. A year's worth of rain may arrive in an hour. Because such flash floods may come decades apart, the threat may be unrecognized or cost-prohibitive to address.

Usually, advance warning of floods along large rivers is better than for the small rivers that feed them. Because they have a larger watershed, large rivers react more slowly to excessive rain or rapidly melting snow. Formation of ice jams, breaking of ice jams, structural failure of dams, and landslides or avalanches into lakes, however, can cause a sudden, unexpected rise in the level of a sizable river. People far inland have also been caught by surprise when the less-windy but still-moisture-laden remnant of a hurricane suddenly stalls and quickly inundates a region unaccustomed to or equipped to handle a tropical downpour.

Coastal areas are occasionally subjected to two other types of flooding. The storm surge associated with a hurricane-like storm (in any season) can produce profound and widespread damage, but advance warning is usually good enough to allow for appropriate preparations. Moving at 725 km (450 miles) per hour on the open ocean, tsunamis (seismic sea waves) caused by undersea earthquakes or landslides can be higher than storm surges. Monitors at sea together with computer modeling have aided in posting or canceling some tsunami warnings. However, near-shore events allow little time for warnings. Tsunamis most often strike coastlines on the Pacific Rim since the "Ring of Fire" is responsible for much of the Earth's strongest seismic activity. However, the largest recorded tsunami occurred in the Indian Ocean on December 26, 2004. An even larger (and rarer) mega-tsunami would affect much of the Atlantic if a particular volcano in the Canary Islands collapses all at once. As the world learned in the 2004 disaster, tsunami warning systems based on ocean buoys are not in place worldwide, and seismic monitoring stations are poorly equipped to alert authorities in all areas in imminent peril. Moreover, some submarine fault lines are so close to land that inhabitants would be inundated within 15 minutes of a quake.

Any urban area is served by an artificial drainage system, the maintenance of which is often at the mercy of a municipality. A violent storm can itself create enough debris to greatly diminish the system's drainage capacity.

Flood Detection and Mitigation

Water detectors should be placed above and below a raised floor to monitor the rise of water. A sensor that is lower than the lowest energized wire should trigger an automatic power shutdown.

All facilities—but especially those in flood-prone areas—should keep critical resources out of the lowest level or any level below ground level or any known prior flood level. Although safest from rising water, the top floor is the first affected if the roof leaks, collapses, or is blown away. Likewise, the area near a window will be most affected by rain if the window is damaged during a storm.

To mitigate damage from falling water, fitted covers for equipment can, if readily available, be quickly deployed in anticipation of or in immediate response to a damaged roof, overhead pipe leaks, or sprinkler systems. They can also be used as dust covers when equipment is moved or stored, during construction work, or when the panels of a suspended ceiling need to be lifted.

Flood Recovery

The first rule of rehabilitating electrical equipment exposed to water is to disconnect it from its power source. Energizing equipment before it is thoroughly dried may cause shorting, damage, and fire. The second rule is to expedite the drying process to prevent the onset of corrosion. Low ambient humidity speeds drying, whereas high humidity (and, even more so, dampness) speeds the corrosive action of any contaminants. If the HVAC system cannot (or should not) be used to achieve a relative humidity of 40 to 50 percent, then wet items should be moved to a location where this can be done. Actively applying heat significantly above room temperature must be done with caution. (See the Table 1 for temperatures at which damage can occur to media and equipment.) Handheld dryers can be used on low settings. An alternative is aerosol sprays that have a drying effect. Even room-temperature air moved by fans or compressed air at no more than 3.4 bar (50 psi) can be helpful. In any case, equipment should be opened up as much as possible for the greatest effect. Conversely, equipment should not be sealed, because this may cause condensation to develop inside. Low-lint cotton-tipped swabs may be used to dab water from hard-to-reach areas.

Preparedness for Wind, Seismic, and Explosive Forces

Both wind forces and seismic forces can damage facilities and what lies within them either directly or indirectly—that is, by impelling or toppling a "projectile." Explosive forces can create both wind forces and seismic forces. Facilities located in regions prone to damaging winds or earthquakes, those that house or are near potentially explosive materials, and those that might invite deliberate acts of sabotage should be "hardened" against such threats. This can be done in a structural sense (preferably at the time of construction) and/or by internal design. In times of impending disaster, additional protective measures can be taken. To the extent practical, all facilities should take similar measures. This is because earthquake-like force and destructive weather can occur anywhere. For example, buildings have collapsed for a wide variety of reasons, ranging from snow accumulation above to water main breaks below; a nearby collapse has a seismic impact on the immediate vicinity. (Even the initial crashes into the World Trade Center registered on seismographs.)

Many regions of the world are subject to seasons when monsoons, hurricanes (typhoons), tornadoes, damaging hail, ice storms, or blizzards are more likely to occur. But global climate change has already resulted in more frequent extreme weather events and more of them occurring outside their customary seasons and regions.

Even if a weather event arrives in its proper season, that arrival may be unexpected. In general, the larger the scale of the weather event, the farther in advance it can be anticipated. Despite dramatic advances in the accuracy and detail of regional forecasting, the granularity of current weather models does not allow precise forecasting of highly localized phenomena beyond saying, "Small bad things may happen within this larger area." As the probability of any specific point in that area being hit with severe weather is small, such generalized warnings often go unheeded. Even if a warning is noted, there may not be time to "board up the windows."

Consequently, some standing precautions should be taken regardless of the severe-weather history of a locale. These precautions can serve in case of other disasters as well. As stated before, fitted covers for equipment can be quickly deployed to protect against falling water from a damaged roof, overhead pipe leaks, or sprinkler systems. They can also be used as dust covers when equipment is moved or stored, during construction work, or when the panels of a suspended ceiling need to be lifted. Keeping critical resources away from windows and off top floors is a good precaution in any location, but particularly in areas where fierce winds could breach the windows, walls, or roofs.

Hurricane-prone jurisdictions are increasingly requiring ever sturdier construction; design consideration should also be given to efficiently protecting windows in advance of an approaching storm. Advanced warning of hurricanes is now adequate to evacuate personnel, crucial media, and perhaps small equipment. In fact, one suite of hurricane-related commercial products can predict peak winds, wind direction, and the arrival time of damaging winds at specific locations.

Facilities in tornado-prone regions should provide for emergency shelter. This involves two things. The first is to construct or at least identify a safe place within the facility, preferably within each building, so people are not required to walk far, especially outside. The other requisite is universal knowledge of where to go. Since tornadoes still, on occasion, arrive with little or no warning, everyone must be ready to move on a moment's notice.

The actual formation of small, intense weather events can be detected by modern radar, and warnings of potential and imminent danger can be obtained through a variety of means. There are radio receivers that respond specifically to warnings transmitted by meteorological agencies or civil authorities. The Internet itself can be the messenger. One mode of notification is e-mail. Other services run in the background on a client machine, checking with a specific site for the latest information. Some of these services are free (though accompanied by advertising banners).

Earthquakes can have widespread effects on infrastructure. The damage to an individual structure may depend more on *where* it was built than on *how*. Buildings on fill dirt are at greater risk because of potential liquefaction, in which the ground behaves like a liquid. Earthquake predictions are currently vague as to time and location.

In regions of the world having a well-known history of frequent earthquakes, planning for the inevitable is second nature. Complacency prevails where damaging earthquakes strike decades or centuries apart; earthquake survivability features may not be required by building codes or may not be calculated to be cost-effective. Fortunately, some cities in seismically dormant areas are waking up to the importance of earthquake precautions.

Regardless of construction techniques, how the occupants furnish buildings is largely their own responsibility. Some precautions can be taken with relatively little expense or intrusion to normal operations. Following are three suggestions from Garfinkel (2002) based on the simple principle that objects will move and perhaps fall from high places to lower places:

- Place computers under sturdy tables, not on high surfaces or near windows.
- Do not place heavy objects so that they could fall onto computers.
- Restrain the possible movement of computers with bolts and other equipment.

The first two recommendations also help in case damaging wind or the force of an external explosion blows out a window or damages a roof. The last could also serve as a theft deterrent, depending on the type of restraint used. There are also relatively easy ways to secure things other than computers. For example, bookcases can be bolted to walls so they cannot topple, and books can be restrained by removable bars or straps. In the newly opened Computer History Museum in Mountain View, CA (10 miles from the infamous San Andreas Fault), some fragile items are bolted down and others are prevented from shaking off shelves by fittings on the front of the shelves (Ward 2004).

Currently, the forecasting of earthquakes is not well focused in space or time. The only certainty is that major shocks are always followed by aftershocks. Therefore, a partially damaged building should not be entered without professional advice on how it is likely to react to an aftershock that could be nearly as strong as the original quake.

Preparedness for Other Disasters

There are a multitude of assorted disasters other than those detailed already. Without attempting to be exhaustive, these include volcanic eruptions, landslides and mudslides, and releases and spills of dangerous substances.

Volcanic ash is one of the most abrasive substances in nature. It can occasionally be carried great distances and in great quantities. If it does not thoroughly clog up HVAC air filters between outside and inside air domains, it may still be tracked in by people. Most volcanic eruptions can now be anticipated with some accuracy, and advanced warning of eruptions has saved lives. Precautions to protect against an influx of ash may be required hundreds of kilometers downwind of an explosive eruption. The Japanese have had some success with constructing structures to divert lava flows, but this is a massive undertaking beyond the means of most organizations. In most areas that might be engulfed by lava, evacuation is the only defense.

Landslides and mudslides may not have the heat (and eventual permanence) of lava, but they can move more rapidly, arrive with less warning, and occur in many more locations than lava. Landslides and mudslides are more common after earthquakes and rainstorms, but they can occur with no obvious triggering event. Often, there is evidence of slow, subtle movement before a collapse. Monitoring of weather, soil conditions, and any changes in potentially threatening slopes may give enough warning to evacuate. Anticipating where slides could occur in the future may require professional geological consultation. As an illustration, a cliff with layers of clay dipping toward the face of the cliff is an accident waiting to happen.

Facilities housing hazardous materials are required to take extra precautions, not the least of which is training personnel in handling the materials and dealing with mishaps. Every organization should endeavor to determine what hazardous materials are located in nearby enterprises so precautions can be taken as well. Unfortunately, any nearby major transportation route will likely carry a wider array of substances with toxic, corrosive, or explosive potential, and it is impossible to know in advance what might leak or ignite in case of an accident.

Because of the tremendous variety of characteristics of modern contaminants, a facility contaminated by chemical, biological, or radiological agents should not be reentered until local authorities and appropriately trained professionals give clearance. Some contaminants, such as sarin gas, dissipate on their own. Some, such as anthrax spores, require weeks of specialized decontamination. Others, such as radiation, effectively close down an area indefinitely. One helpful action that can be taken during egress or remotely as soon as possible is to shut down air-circulation equipment, as it will tend to distribute airborne particles or molecules.

PHYSICAL SECURITY FOR PERSONNEL

Much of what was said with respect to physical access control for storage media, for information-processing equipment, and for facilities relates to keeping people—insiders and outsiders—from obtaining unauthorized access to information and services. Now we turn to the physical security issues related to personnel (in the broad sense—employees, contractors, and others with "insider" privileges) who have been granted access to information and services to achieve the goals of the organization. As such, they are often referred to as "the weak link." This usually laments the fact that humans are "human"—that is, fallible. But they can also be a deliberate adversary, potentially the most dangerous of all.

Personnel as Resources

Human beings are the ultimate reason we build networks, and certain humans are employed for the express purpose of keeping those networks running; they are every bit as essential a resource as electrical power and telecommunications service. The protection of humans is mandated by laws, regulations, insurance companies, and basic economics. Even the temporary absence or decreased productivity of individuals soon adds up to a major business expense. For these reasons, employers are increasingly paying attention to environmental hazards and ergonomics in the workplace.

Personnel Availability

The value of human beings was once again evidenced by the fact that response to the New Orleans flood was more influenced by the actions of humans than by planning and equipment. See, for example, Denning (2006) with respect to human behavior in crises.

Although personnel have always been recognized as an essential resource, before the attacks on New York and Washington, the sudden, permanent disappearance of personnel in large numbers was not generally anticipated. Now, business-continuity planners and disaster-recovery planners, whether focused on preservation of processes or assets, realize that such an occurrence is possible.

Aside from mass slaughter, there are other circumstances in which the availability of human resources may be lacking. Severe weather may preclude employees from getting to work. Labor disputes may result in strikes. These may be beyond the direct control of an organization if the problems are with a vendor from whom equipment has been bought or leased or with a contractor to whom services have been outsourced. A different kind of discontinuity in human expertise can come with a change of vendors or contractors or with the replacement of a large group of workers in one country with workers in another country.

Environmental Hazards

As with storage media and information-processing equipment, humans need reasonable environmental conditions, but humans have their own set of susceptibilities. Employers may be held responsible for a wide range of occupational health and safety issues. Some concerns are common to any indoor workplace. Sick building syndrome may be manifested by a variety of symptoms, including nausea, headaches, dizziness, fatigue, and irritations of the eyes, nose, and throat. The most common cause is poor ventilation combined with indoor air pollution from office supplies and equipment as well as furnishings and construction materials, notably insulation. Minimizing the sources of such pollution may not be as practical as improving ventilation and air filtration, either by means of the HVAC system or stand-alone devices. Another threat is the growth of bacteria or toxic mold from excessive humidity, possibly localized to areas such as washrooms. Eradication of toxic mold can be an expensive, disruptive process. On the other hand, maintaining the proper humidity and ventilation can result in Legionnaire's disease, a form of pneumonia transmitted via mist and sometimes associated with large air conditioning systems; contaminated water in these systems is the suspected source of the *Legionella pneumophila* bacteria.

There is currently no consensus on the long-term effects of extremely low-frequency (ELF) emissions (below 300 Hz)—magnetic fields emitted by a variety of devices, including high-tension lines and cathode ray tube monitors (but not LCD displays). Laboratory tests with animals have found that prolonged exposure to ELF fields may cause cancer or reproductive problems. Studies of pregnant CRT users have produced conflicting data. Pending conclusive evidence, some recommend keeping 60 cm (2 ft) away from such monitors, which may not be practical.

Health worries with regard to cellular phones had mostly been dispelled. But a report of the [U.K.] Health Protection Agency (2005) calls for caution and continued research. Specific concerns are: third-generation (3G) phones, which emit higher levels of radiation; greater sensitivity of children and other groups to radio waves; longer lifetime exposures for those who begin using cellular phones in childhood; and a lack of very long-term data because of the newness of the technology. It has been suggested that children limit use of the devices for voice communication and rely primarily on text-messaging.

Although the World Health Organization acknowledges the need for continued research in certain areas, its latest position is that there is no evidence of health risks associated with exposures to electromagnetic fields below the levels set forth by the International Commission on Non-Ionizing Radiation Protection (1998).

It is known that people with pacemakers should avoid devices creating strong magnetic fields, such as degaussers.

The heat produced by a laptop computer is sufficient that warnings have been issued against using one on bare skin and against falling asleep while having one in a lap. One study done at the State University of New York in Stony Brook indicated that the heat could affect male fertility. (Human Reproduction 2004.)

There is an ever-growing list of potential chemical, biological, and radiological contaminants—each posing its own set of dangers to humans. Most are eventually involved in storage or transportation mishaps. More and more are intentionally used in a destructive fashion. Even if humans are the only component of the computing environment that is threatened, normal operations at a facility must cease until any life- or health-threatening contamination is removed.

Ergonomics

It has been long recognized that the repetitive motions and static positions of workers in many occupations pose health risks. Ergonomically related hazards specific to the computing environment include:

- carpal tunnel syndrome (from repetitive actions, notably typing)
- back and neck pain (from extended use of improper seating)
- eye strain and headaches (from staring at a computer screen for long periods)
- pooling of blood in the legs and increased intraspinal pressure (from sitting for extended periods)

The defense against these is to combine proper equipment, proper relative positioning of equipment and body parts, and proper use of body parts.

Human-friendly appointments pertinent to an information-processing facility include the following:

- a negative-tilt platform for the keyboard and/or mouse
- a specially shaped keyboard or mouse (preferably large and not curved)
- a comfortable, adjustable chair with lumbar support
- appropriately aimed or diffused lighting, a matted working surface, a monitor hood, and/or a screen covering that reduce glare (and, therefore, eyestrain)
- a working surface that can be moved (possibly by means of a motor) to various levels, even to allow use at a standing position
- a movable support to position the monitor
- a document holder, positioned in line with the monitor

Among behavior patterns beneficial to healthy computer usage are:

- sitting at arms' length from the monitor with feet flat on the floor and thighs parallel to the ground
- dynamic sitting—that is, not staying in a fixed position for a long time
- keeping shoulders, arms, hands, and fingers relaxed
- using arm motion (from the elbow) rather than wrist motion to move a mouse
- taking frequent microbreaks, resting on palm supports
- proper relative positioning of chair, monitor, and input devices
- perhaps most importantly, being continually aware of one's own body

Two extensive sources of information on computer workstation ergonomics can be found at the [U.S] Centers for Disease Control and Prevention (2000) and Cornell Human Factors and Ergonomics Research Group (2004).

Personnel as Threats

Obviously, many of the security threats discussed up until now can be mounted by human beings, and for most of those threats, personnel (employees, contractors, and others with "insider" access) are in a better position to mount the threats (intentionally or accidentally) than are outsiders. The focus now is on two additional areas in which personnel can threaten information and services as outsiders cannot. The first area deals with knowledge that personnel possess as a legitimate part of their job function. The second deals with services to which personnel have access as a legitimate part of their job function.

In numerous surveys, statistics on what percentages of information security incidents and monetary losses are due to insiders and to outsiders vary according to the country, the size, and the performance level (whether "best in class" or not) of the organizations surveyed—not to mention the way in which questions were asked in the various surveys. Moreover, not all studies on information security explicitly distinguish among purely physical attacks, cyberattacks based on physical access, and remote cyberattacks. For a "mid-Atlantic" perspective, compare the surveys by the [U.S.] Computer Security Institute/Federal Bureau of Investigation (Gordon et al. 2006) and the [U.K.] Department of Trade and Industry (PricewaterhouseCoopers 2006), newer editions of which will exist subsequent to this writing. It is generally recognized that insiders are a major (and, by some accounts, the predominant) source of breaches of physical security. While human error is often cited as the leading insider threat, misuse of confidential information and Internet access rank high. Clearly, authorized access to information resources not only increases the opportunity for attacks, but also allows for attacks requiring less sophistication, equipment, and daring.

Mention was made earlier of attempts to gauge malicious intent by observing behavior at checkpoints. Even observing the overall behavior of an insider may be an exercise in futility. Crume (2000) relates how the characteristics of a model employee may as easily be the characteristics of a corporate spy.

For the threats arising from human failings, the articulation, implementation, and enforcement of a security policy and a thorough security awareness training program are essential. Smaller institutions in which everyone knows everyone else are especially likely to have coworkers who are overly trusting of one another. The corporate culture should foster "collegial paranoia" without breeding mistrust among coworkers. Physical security is just another problem that needs to be attacked with teamwork—a highly valued corporate virtue. That means that everyone should expect cooperation from everyone else in adhering to physical security protocols. For instance, anyone asking to "borrow" someone else's account should expect to be turned down. Policies must be communicated and justified. Policies that are considered to be frivolous or unnecessarily restrictive tend to be ignored or circumvented. For instance, doors will be propped open when convenience is considered more important than security.

Human-borne Information

Human knowledge is an asset less tangible than data on a disk, but potentially of great value to someone planning to mount a physical attack or a cyberattack. Human-borne information transcends space and time in the sense that personnel can carry potentially compromising knowledge within them to places where there are no corporate laptops or disks, and they may maintain that knowledge beyond their employment at (or even the existence of) an organization.

Human-borne information can be roughly lumped into two categories. Primary information is the lifeblood of the organization, the information that is the main security objective. Secondary information is that which relates to securing the primary information.

Primary information may include customer information, confidentiality of which may be mandated by government legislation and regulation, such as, in the United States, for example, the Sarbanes-Oxley (SOX) Act, the Gramm-Leach-Bliley Act, the Health Insurance Portability and Accountability Act (HIPAA), and California Senate Bill 1386 (which governs persons or businesses that conduct business in California). Primary information may include product development and marketing plans, revelation of which might forfeit a competitive advantage. It may also include trade secrets.

Secondary information may include passwords, but also information about how an internal network is configured, whether there are hidden cameras, when security guards make rounds, etc. Although not the focus of the security effort, a compromise of the secondary information could clearly lead to a compromise of the primary information.

The threat of human-borne information's falling into the wrong hands can come in several forms. An employee may directly leak information by their willful or inadvertent action or inaction. Or he or she may be duped or coerced by someone (not necessarily an outsider) into yielding information or access to services. In still other cases, it may be possible to glean from public sources information that may aid an attack.

Passwords

Some of the best-known breaches of security involve network-access passwords. A password written down on paper invites a crime of opportunity to anyone who finds the paper. The same effect can be achieved by "shoulder surfing" even if the password is not written down. Employee voice mail, even personal voice mail at home, has been compromised for the purpose of obtaining sensitive information such as reset passwords. A password that is predictable based on the life of the associated employee (birth date, spouse's name, etc.) does not require physical access to a piece of paper, but rather personal acquaintance with the employee. Of course, if a computer has been left unattended while logged on, or if one employee willingly "shares" an account with someone else, no password is needed for an attacker to establish a foothold.

The defense is the establishment and enforcement of policies mandating strong passwords, banning the writing down of passwords, requiring "locking" a computer (by reverting to the password-protected log-in screen) when unattended, and prohibiting the sharing of an individual account or the assigning of a common account name and password to a group of people (because this complicates tracing malfeasance to a single person). This highlights the challenges of what is often called personnel security. Automatic, iron-clad cyberenforcement of policies dictating the length, composition, or life span of passwords is trivial. On the other hand, enforcing a policy such as, "Eat it if you write it down," is essentially impossible to enforce. At the same time, stringent password policies commonly result in passwords that are hard to remember and short-lived, thereby provoking users to write them down.

Social Engineering. A deliberate way of gaining unauthorized access to resources is social engineering, the art of conning others into acting on one's behalf to achieve one's own, illegitimate end. The victim usually realizes the information is privileged, but the perpetrator—who may or may not be an outsider—successfully impersonates an insider having some privileges ("I forgot my password ..."). The request may be for privileged information ("Please remind me of my password...") or for an action requiring greater privileges ("Please reset my password..."). Of course, the information or action sought need not involve passwords.

Larger organizations are more easily victimized by social engineering because no one knows everyone in the firm. Social engineering can be done in person, over the phone, or via the Internet.

The defense is to institute social engineering awareness training that provides sample scenarios. Some interesting examples of engineering attacks both by phone and by e-mail can be found in the penetration testing checklist of Orrey and Lawson (2006).

See also "Social Engineering" for a thorough treatment of this area.

Information Mining. Less famous than social engineering are methods of mining public information posted by personnel, either in an official or an unofficial capacity. Some information must necessarily remain public, some should not be revealed, and some should be obfuscated.

Domain name service information related to an organization—domain names, IP (Internet protocol) addresses, and contact information for key information technology (IT) personnel—must be stored in an online "whois" database. If the name of a server is imprudently chosen, it may reveal the machine's maker, software, or role. Such information makes the IP addresses more useful for cyberattacks. Knowing the key IT personnel may make it easier to pose as an insider for social engineering purposes.

Currently, the most obvious place to look for public information is an organization's own Web site. Unless access is controlled so that only specific users can view specific pages, anyone might learn about corporate hardware, software, vendors, and clients. The organizational chart and other, subtler clues about corporate culture may also aid a social engineering attack. Of course, this information and more may be available in print.

Another dimension of the Internet in which one can snoop is newsgroup bulletin boards. By passively searching these public discussions ("lurking"), an attacker might infer which company is running which software on which hardware. He or she may instead fish actively for information. An even more active approach is to provide disinformation, leading someone to incorrectly configure a system.

All employees who know anything that might be useful to a potential attacker should be given awareness training with regard to indiscreet usage of newsgroup bulletin boards, etc. As with social engineering, sample scenarios should be described.

Appropriate Use. An increasingly nagging and complex issue is the personal use of network resources by those who are authorized to use the resources as an essential part of their work-related duties. It is typically done without malice or any thought that it has any significant adverse impact on the organization. Current attitudes toward intellectual property rights are a major societal problem. A pilferer of "excess" computing power may view his or her actions as a "victimless crime."

Before the digital age, infractions would have been on the level of personal phone calls and photocopying. Now there are far more ways to misappropriate resources, and inappropriate use of network resources has far more legal and ethical implications than older forms of misbehavior. Acts of misappropriation by personnel may compromise confidentiality, authentication, and authorization and may even have impact on availability and integrity.

Currently, one of the most pressing problems is how employees abuse Internet access in the workplace. Volonino and Robinson (2004) cite two studies that quantify the magnitude of the problem. One, by IDC Research, estimates that 30 to 40 percent of workplace Internet usage in 2003 was not work-related. In another, Websence claims that cyberslacking costs U.S. businesses $85 billion per year in lost productivity. It should come as no surprise, then, that surveys of U.S. companies indicate the proportion monitoring employees' Internet activities is about 63 percent, 80 percent for larger companies.

Forms of inappropriate use of network resources include:

- accessing confidential data for personal reasons
- downloading pirated music or software
- launching cyberattacks or enabling resources to become launching points for attacks by others
- downloading child pornography
- creating a hostile work environment because of downloaded materials
- exchanging information in connection with criminal activities—for example, fraud or money-laundering

The consequences of these inappropriate uses include:

- lost productivit.y due to time misspent
- expended bandwidth and, therefore, reduced speed for appropriate, work-related actiivities
- legal action based on employee claims of a hostile work environment
- legal action based on violation of intellectual property rights
- legal action based on the use of resources (even if by outsiders) in illegal activities
- damage to an organization's reputation

Beyond the obvious waste of time for which employees are being compensated, there may also be a significant impact on an organization's available bandwidth. In academic institutions with lax controls over student usage, the (often illegal) downloading of entertainment media has, in some cases, exceeded the volume of all other Internet traffic. From a practical standpoint, inbound or outbound Internet traffic can be selectively blocked, filtered, or shaped; the last is the least intrusive because it limits the portion of bandwidth that can be consumed by certain services while not prohibiting them entirely.

The direct impact on the bottom line is not the only consequence of improper use. Legal precedent has established that a company that does not actively prevent inappropriate behavior by its employees within the job's time-space domain is seen as promoting that misconduct and may be held liable for it; this is the principle of respondeat superior. Violation of intellectual property rights is one concern. When the Internet activity of some employees offends other employees, a company is likely to incur legal action for neglecting its duty of care obligations to employees by allowing the creation of a hostile work environment.

PHYSICAL SECURITY FOR TRANSMISSION MEDIA

Of the various resources critical to network communication, the resource most far-flung and arguably hardest to secure is transmission media. It is often largely beyond the control of an individual organization.

The availability of telecommunication service was dealt with earlier. The remaining issue is controlling physical access to transmission media at and between standard access points. Unguided transmission media such as microwave (whether terrestrial or satellite), radio (the easiest to intercept), and infrared (the hardest to intercept) should be considered fair game for outsiders to intercept at the air interface. Because of their inherent vulnerability to eavesdropping, wireless digital transmissions should be encrypted (a cyberdefense) and analog voice communication should be scrambled if confidentiality, integrity, or authentication is desired. Therefore, interception between standard access points will be considered only for guided transmission media.

Standard Access Points

Connecting to a network, whether copper-based or fiber optic, is easiest at (unguarded) standard points of access. Examples are: a live, unused local area network (LAN) wall jack; a live, unused hub port; and a LAN-connected computer that no longer has a regular user. For the perpetrator, these approaches involve varying degrees of difficulty and risk. The second approach may be particularly easy, safe, and reliable if the hub is in an unsecured closet, the connection is used for sniffing only, and no one has the patience to check the haystack for one interloping needle. Defenses are to secure wiring cabinets and to establish and enforce policies that remove or nullify access points as soon as they are not needed; computers that are no longer needed on the LAN should be locked away and have their hard drives sanitized.

A slightly different issue is employees' installing unauthorized modems, sometimes to facilitate work-related activities either at home or, in some cases, at the office (Skoudis 2000). These can provide entrée to an outsider who would otherwise be stopped by a corporate firewall. Even IT administrators, who should know better, leave "back-door" modems in place, sometimes with trivial or no password protection. Checking for rogue modems can be done either by visually inspecting every computer or by "war-dialing" all possible company extensions.

A related issue is the risk posed by broadband access by home users; depending on how the laptop's access to the Internet and access to corporate information are controlled, a compromising of a laptop while used at home by an employee may lead to the compromising of corporate information.

Although more related to cybersecurity, it is worth noting in passing that a computer user may transform the nature of a standard access point by installing software (e.g., Skype) that uses a "rogue" VoIP protocol, which establishes a direct connection with other computers. Reconnex (2006) discusses the dangers of and solutions to this type of access.

As mentioned above, a particularly easy attack is to use a computer to which an authorized user has already logged on or to which one has been able to learn the password. One way to learn a password or any other information typed on keyboard is with a keyboard monitor, a small device interposed between a computer and its keyboard that records all keystrokes. The attacker (or suspicious employer) must physically install the item and access it to retrieve stored data. (Hence, keyboard logging is more often accomplished by software.)

Wiretapping Guided Transmission Media

Aside from outright damage to guided transmission media, typically via a construction misadventure, the primary security concern associated with guided transmission media is wiretapping. The term originally referred to making a surreptitious (perhaps legal) connection with telephone lines, often with a transmitting device. See the chapter "Voice Communication Systems." We simply point out that more sophisticated equipment (e.g., a nonlinear junction detector or a telephone analyzer) is generally expensive. See Purpura (2002). In the more general sense intended here, *wiretapping* refers to making physical contact with transmission media at points other than standard access points for the purposes of intercepting information.

Copper-wired media are relatively easy to tap. Visual inspection of all exposed wires may be difficult. A more practical reactive measure is to detect a tap using time-domain reflectometry (sending a pulse down the wire and analyzing the signal that bounces back) together with a baseline reading of cable in an "inviolate" state. A preventive measure is to enclose in pipes all cables that are not in secured spaces; the pipes should themselves be protected against tampering.

According to Oyster Optics (2003), "Although it was initially thought that these optical fibre systems would be inherently secure, it has been discovered that the extraction of information from optical fibers is relatively simple and is aided by the increasing sophistication and availability of standard test and maintenance equipment," This can be accomplished by bleeding off less than 1 percent of the light, an amount less than normal operational variations. There are two ways to do this. Macro-bending involves flexing the cable in the way a road would curve, then suitably aligning an optical detector. Micro-bending consists of creating ripples in the surface of an otherwise straight (and perhaps fully coated) cable by clamping onto it a device with ridges; the optical detector is incorporated into the clamp.

One defense against this is to use optical time-domain reflectometry, which is analogous to the electronic version mentioned above. However, this may not be able to detect the small loss of light required to obtain meaningful information from a line. An alternative is a relatively new technique to detect physical disturbances in the cable that do not even involve a loss of light. (The same principle can be used to protect a variety of items, even very large ones, by attaching a nondata fiber-optic cable; see the last line in Table 4.) This form of defense is described by Future Fibre Technologies™ (2005).

Incidental Compromising Emissions

As mentioned with respect to EMI, all electrical devices and wires emit electromagnetic radiation. Even electronic equipment *not* designed to broadcast information may produce unintended emanations containing recoverable information. Unshielded twisted-pair cabling emits most readily. Fiber-optic cable stands alone for its inability to radiate or induce any signal detectable without contact. Mobile detectors have been used to locate radios and televisions (where licensing is required) or to determine the stations to which they are tuned. Video displays (including those of laptops) are notorious emitters; inexpensive equipment can easily capture scan lines, even from the video cable to an inactive screen.

Electronic emissions are considered "compromising" if they contain sensitive recoverable information. The term *tempest* originated as the codename for a U.S. government program to prevent compromising emissions. (Governments are highly secretive in this area; contractors need security clearance to learn the specifications for equipment to be tempest-certified.) Related compromising phenomena are as follows:

- hijack—signals conducted through wires (and perhaps the ground, as was noted during World War I)
- teapot—emissions intentionally caused by an adversary (possibly by implanted software)
- nonstop—emissions accidentally induced by nearby radio-frequency (RF) sources

One attack is to irradiate a target to provoke resonant emissions—in other words, intentional nonstop. (This is analogous to how an infrared beam can expropriate acoustic information.) Interestingly, equipment certified against passive tempest eavesdropping is not necessarily immune to this more active attack, Although these emissions were formerly the concern only of governments, increasingly less expensive and more sophisticated equipment is making corporate espionage a growing temptation and concern. An excellent introduction to this area is Chapter 15 of Anderson (2001). A well-known portal for tempest information is McNamara (2002).

PHYSICAL SECURITY PLANNING

Physical security planning involves gathering information about the assets to be protected and potential threats to them, determining and implementing appropriate preventive practices, and planning for recovery if a disaster nevertheless occurs.

Physical Asset Identification

The first and most obvious question to pose during security planning is: What are the assets to be guarded? Physical security seeks to protect the five major networking components featured in Figure 1: storage media, information-processing equipment, facilities, personnel, and transmission media. It will be appreciated that an attack on any of these that results in a breach of the confidentiality, integrity, availability, or usage authorization of information or services associated with an organization may also be an attack on other, less tangible assets, such as an organization's reputation, which in turn may ultimately be an attack on the organization's bottom line and survival. Thus, a starting point may be to think backward, from the mission of the organization to the role networking resources play in achieving that mission.

Formerly, to answer the question of what assets needed to be guarded, one relied entirely on a manual inventory. Now there are asset management tools that can track the location and migration of hardware and software. These can manage software licenses and monitor security policy violations, such as unauthorized software or outdated virus definitions. See, for example, Absolute Software (2003).

The natural follow-up or concurrent question is: Where are the assets located? Clearly, the location of any asset influences which defenses can be put in place. For example, the options for guarding a laptop are different than for guarding a server. More important is how the location of an asset influences the risks associated with it and therefore the defenses that should be used.

Physical Threat Assessment

Having determined what is to be protected, the logical question to answer is: What is likely to go wrong in the future? Unfortunately, it is human nature to dwell on answering a simpler question: What has gone wrong in the past? Since looking back in time is infinitely easier than looking forward, the temptation is to "fight the last war," a trap that has snared many a general; a reminder is the sequence of low-tech forms of attack mounted by Iraqis seeking to expel high-tech invaders. An understanding of past glitches and disasters is essential, but not sufficient. Not all that *will* happen (in your neighborhood or in the world) *has* happened. Many events are common enough that we can reasonably trust probability tables constructed for them. Others calamities have yet to be invented. To expand George Santayana's famous quote, those who are ignorant of history are doomed to repeat it, but those who live in the past are also doomed.

The apocalypse in New Orleans is a reminder of another saying: "None are so blind as those who will not see." Despite decades of dire predictions and days of forewarning, officials at all levels stared at an oncoming Category 5 Hurricane Katrina (which was only at Category 3 strength when its weaker side hit New Orleans) and refused to see that *everyone*, even those without cars, needed to be evacuated *before* the storm arrived.

Similarly, there are large institutions that, despite abundant experience with blizzards, blackouts, and other calamities of regional scale, blindly insist on having their backup facilities in the same metropolitan area as their primary facilities.

The key to preventing physical breaches of confidentiality, integrity, and availability of network resources is to anticipate as many bad scenarios as possible. A common flaw is to overlook plausible combinations of concurrent problems, such as the incursion of water at the same time backup power is needed. Another error is to become frozen in time, forgetting that, to cite another cliché, nothing is constant except change. Periodically, the threat space (and, therefore, the assets) must be reassessed.

Physical Security Practice

Having determined the physical assets to be protected and the threats to those assets, physical security can be put into practice by identifying appropriate countermeasures and then establishing and implementing a preventive physical security policy for personnel. Periodically, the effectiveness of the countermeasures chosen and the actual implementation of the established policies by personnel must be tested. Terms such as *computer security audit* and *penetration testing* have come to be applied more to cybersecurity than to physical security, but the same general principles apply to each. *Auditing* is a more general term that can include interviews of personnel, analysis of systems, review of logged incidents, and testing. Black box, white box, and various levels of gray box testing are performed with no, complete, and partial information, respectively, of the security system in place. Audits and testing can be performed by regulatory agencies, specialized security companies, or internal staff.

Physical Security Measure Identification

Determining the appropriate physical security precautions to take begins with the information obtained in the physical security audit, knowledge of the defensive countermeasures presented above and in other chapters, and a large dose of pragmatism. The past has taught us that preventing *all* bad events is impossible, regardless of the time, effort, and money invested in preventive measures. There *will* be failures. For integrity and availability of resources, redundancy can be used as a remedy when the worst-case scenario becomes reality, allowing one to "go back in time" to some extent. Unfortunately, there is no comparable way to undo a breach of confidentiality.

The inherent intractability of physical security requires one to approach it in a pragmatic and fiscally responsible way. This cannot be done without answering another question: What are the guarded assets worth? It may be natural to ask this question when the assets are identified, but it is mentioned here because the answer may depend on the particular threat to an asset. It is simplistic to say that the cost of protecting an asset should not exceed the value of the asset. It is more precise to say that the cost of protecting an asset against a particular type of attack should not exceed the liability if the attack succeeds. That liability may be many orders of magnitude greater than the cost of the asset. The marginal cost of creating a customer's bank account may be relatively small. The impact could be huge if an unauthorized person were to drain the account or if sensitive financial information were revealed to the public. An organization failing to exercise due diligence may be subject to lawsuits, fines, and/or other legal sanctions. Even the financial losses directly related to a failure to maintain physical security may be small compared to the later consequences of a widespread loss of clients' confidence in an organization. Admittedly, an estimation of an asset's value may be fairly unreliable, especially for a less tangible asset. But measuring a potential loss in monetary terms helps justify an investment in security measures.

As a practical matter, the probability of each type of potential breach of physical security must also be factored in when comparing the potential liability incurred by the breach and the expense of preventing that particular event. This allows one to compute the (probabilistically) expected benefit of adopting a security measure. As mentioned above, the probabilities of some events will be more difficult to estimate than others. According to Gordon (2006), most organizations use either return on investment (ROI), internal rate of return (IRR), or net present value (NPV) to evaluate the cost-effectiveness of security expenditures.

Physical Security Policy for Personnel

Physical security measures comprise two disparate components—suitable objects (perhaps incorporating software) and suitable practices by personnel. Action items in a physical security plan may be discrete events that support physical security measures, such as the installation of a lock on a door or the instatement of a policy that the door should be locked. On the other hand, there is the continual vigilance needed to consistently abide by the policy and use the lock. A classical view is that corporate respect for the importance of security must start at the top of the organization and be communicated downward through the chain of command.

At its inception, a physical security policy is established and articulated through employee education. Thereafter, it must be implemented and enforced. Periodically, the policy must be reviewed and revised, with concomitant reeducation.

A particularly tricky issue is establishment of an acceptable-use policy that strikes the right balance. Some employers prohibit even personal e-mail to an employee's spouse saying, "I have to work late"—a practice this spouse has found to be both ironic and very inconvenient. Others seem not to care about misuse of resources until glaring abuses arise. Neither policy extreme is optimal; research has shown that productivity is actually best when employees are allowed modest time for personal e-mail and Internet access. To install a favorite snapshot on an employee's computer desktop screen is considered a de facto right as much as to place a family photo on his/her desk. A thorough introduction to the subject is contained in Chapter 6 (Acceptable-Use Policies) of Volonino and Robinson (2004).

Depending on the jurisdiction and circumstances, companies may be required to announce monitoring of employees' usage of their resources. For example, under the U.K. Data Protection Act of 1998, covert monitoring is allowed only if there are clear grounds for suspecting criminal activity. If activity monitoring is used, the notification of employees (whether legally required or not) may create some animosity, but much less so than when it is eventually discovered that secret monitoring has been in effect. It is best to spell out both what an employer expects in the way of behavior and what employees might expect with regard to what they may see as their "privacy." In practice, monitoring should be used to control problems before they get out of hand, not to ambush employees.

Corporations have taken a number of approaches to enhance security awareness, including the following:

- publishing policies in handbooks, memos, etc.
- requiring courses (perhaps self-study) before activating user accounts
- periodically testing employees for knowledge of policies

For physical security, implementation and enforcement of a policy is far more difficult than establishing the policy and training personnel.

Checking on employees' computer usage is easy. Best practices on choosing passwords can be rigidly enforced. Storage areas on workstations and on servers can be checked to see that all stored content is work-related. In addition to monitoring e-mail passing through their hardware, companies use activity monitors, software to record keystrokes, to capture screen displays, or log time spent on Internet chatting, game playing, etc. Some activity monitors can be set up to alert administrators to inappropriate behavior or to block use of certain applications or Web sites. Some products claim they cannot be detected, located, deactivated, or removed, even by experienced users. Other products exist to detect or even block any key-logging software.

The problem is that computer usage monitoring as described actually covers a small fraction of the spectrum of security-related behavior. So much of physical security is *not* about keystrokes and mouse clicks. It is about not writing down passwords, not talking to strangers, not propping doors open, etc.

Chapter 8 of Wylder (2004) discusses the various past approaches to enforcement and the problems each has encountered. He advocates and details a bottom-up approach that emphasizes personal accountability; in a nutshell, a personal security plan is created and incorporated into employee performance assessments. This approach makes security more analogous to occupational health and safety, for which employers and employees share responsibility for maintaining an appropriate work environment.

Ultimately, the employees' competence and trustworthiness are invaluable defenses. The former is much easier to ensure than the latter. Managers at all levels must appreciate the potential for attacks from within, understand the various motivations for such attacks, and guard against provoking negative attitudes toward the organization either by how they treat subordinates or by how they themselves behave in the workplace.

It goes without saying that once his or her employment with an organization has ceased, an ex-employee is not under the same type of control by his or her former employer. But while admonitions and disciplinary actions (even the threat of a pink slip) might no longer be available to the ex-employer as options for applying security-compliance leverage, the organization may still have legal recourse (and, therefore, a measure of leverage)—provided restrictive covenants were included in the employment contract. See, for example, Ogilvy Renault (2006) for general guidelines for increasing the likelihood that a restrictive covenant will be legally enforceable.

Along the same lines, "insiders" who are not employees—contractors, vendors, clients, corporate partners, and the like—are inherently more detached from an organization's control than is a full-fledged employee. Again, the organization must proactively use legal means to protect any of its intellectual property that must be revealed to said insiders. A nondisclosure agreement (NDA) between the organization on the one hand and the insider and/or the insider's employer on the other hand must be signed before the transfer to the insider of any confidential materials or information to be covered by the NDA. NDAs should be drawn up by legal counsel cognizant of what intellectual property should be covered, who must sign, and what legal remedy may apply if the terms of the agreement are broken. Even when an NDA is in place, confidential information should be shared only on a need-to-know basis (a basic security principle that should apply even within an organization).

Disaster Recovery Planning

Disaster is in the eye of the beholder. If it is *your* hard drive that crashes while holding unique data, it is a disaster. Other events, such as the destruction of an entire building, may be far more disastrous in one sense; yet, with the proper planning, an organization might continue to function with no loss of data or services.

Disaster recovery can take as many forms as the disasters themselves. A single event may be handled in different ways or may require a combination of remedies. Data and services replicated elsewhere may be called into service. Media and equipment may be rehabilitated on- or off-site. Simultaneously, operations may be (partially) restored on-site or transferred off-site. In most disaster recovery planning, the first priority is maintaining operations or restoring them as soon as possible. There are a variety of services that can be contracted to resume operations or to rehabilitate damaged media, equipment, and buildings. Some are mobile facilities. See the chapter "Business Continuity Planning."

We concentrate here on the physical aspects of rehabilitating buildings, equipment, and media. Professional disaster-recovery services should always be used for this purpose. Because such specialized companies are not based in every city, however, their response time does not match that of emergency personnel. Yet for many physical disasters, the first 24 hours are the most important in limiting progressive damage, for example, from water and smoke. Consequently, knowledge of what to do during that crucial time is essential. Good references in this regard are McDaniel (2001) and the three separate links on "What to do in the first 24 hours!" (for electronics; for magnetic, optical, information media; and for documents and vital records) at the press releases Website of BMS Catastrophe (2002).

CONCLUSION

The scope of physical security is wider than is immediately evident. It concerns an organization's resources, wherever they go. An asset often forgotten is employees' knowledge. Equally important are their intentions. Thus, any employee has the potential to pose or mitigate a physical threat.

In the realm of security for computer networks, physical security tends to receive less attention than cybersecurity. Yet the two sides of security must work together to defeat malicious insiders and outsiders. Ultimately, physical security is the greater challenge, because nature can be the biggest foe, and insiders with authorized access are the most prevalent threat.

Physical security has grown from its simple, ancient roots into a modern, highly complex field involving a broad range of topics outside the normal sphere of IT expertise. Consequently, to obtain the best protection, professionals in other fields should be consulted with regard to HVAC, fire detection and suppression, power maintenance and conditioning, physical access control, forensic science, managerial science, and disaster recovery. A basic understanding of how these areas relate to physical security facilitates communication with consultants. Combining knowledge with the imagination to expect the unexpected leads to better physical security planning and practice.

GLOSSARY

Bolt: A bar that slides into a *strike* to attach a movable object (e.g., a door) to an immovable object (e.g., a door frame).

Class A Fire: Fire involving ordinary *combustibles* (e.g., wood, paper, and some plastics).

Class B Fire: Fire involving *flammable* or *combustible* liquid or gas (e.g., most solvents).

Class C Fire: *Class A* or *Class B* fire amid energized electrical wiring or equipment, which precludes the use of extinguishing agents of a conductive nature (e.g., water or foam).

Clean Agent: Gaseous fire suppressant that technically leaves no residue; residues will result when the agent breaks down under the heat of combustion.

Combustible: Capable of burning at normal ambient temperature (perhaps without a flame).

Degausser or Bulk Eraser: Alternating current–powered device for removing magnetism. (*Degausser* is often applied specifically to wands that rid cathode-ray-tube monitors of problems displaying colors. The term *bulk eraser* indicates that data are wiped en masse rather than sequentially.)

Electrical Noise: Electromagnetic interference, especially interference conducted through the power input, or minor *spikes*.

Electromagnetic Interference (EMI): Undesired electrical anomalies (imperfections in the desired waveform) due to externally originating electromagnetic energy, either conducted or radiated.

Flammable: Capable of burning with a flame; for liquids, having a flash point below 38°C (100°F).

Halon or Halogenated Agent: *Clean agent* formed when one or more atoms of the halogen series (including bromine and fluorine) replace hydrogen atoms in a hydrocarbon (e.g., methane).

Heating Ventilation Air Conditioning (HVAC): Equipment for maintaining environmental air characteristics suitable for humans and equipment.

Line Filter: Device for "conditioning" a primary power source (i.e., removing *electrical noise*).

Nondisclosure Agreement (NDA): Legal contract governing the use and disclosure of one party's confidential information by another party.

Radio-Frequency Interference (RFI): Sometimes used as a synonym for *EMI*, but technically the subset of EMI due to energy in the "radio" range (which includes frequencies also classified as microwave energy).

Sag or Brownout: Drop in voltage.

Smoke: Gaseous, particulate, and aerosol by-products of (imperfect) combustion.

Spike or Transient or Transient Voltage Surge (TVS): Momentary (less than one cycle) increase in voltage.

Strike: The socket into which a *bolt* slides when locking a door, etc.

Surge: Sudden increase in electrical current; also used for *spike*, because the two often arrive together.

Tempest or Compromising Emissions: Electromagnetic emanations from electrical equipment that carry recoverable information, popularly referred to by the code word for a US government program to combat the problem.

Uninterruptible Power Supply (UPS): Device to provide battery power as a backup in case the primary source of power fails.

CROSS REFERENCES

See *Access Control*; *Authentication*; *Password Authentication*.

REFERENCES

Absolute Software. 2003. *AbsoluteTrack: Secure computer asset tracking solution*. http://www.absolute.com/PDF/AbsoluteTrack_WP.pdf (accessed November 11, 2006).

Anderson, R. 2001. Security engineering: *A guide to building dependable distributed systems*. New York: Wiley.

BMS Catastrophe. 2002. *BMS CAT response: What to do in the first 24 hours*. http://www.bmscat.com/were/press.shtml (accessed November 11, 2006).

Centers for Disease Control and Prevention. 2000. *Computer workstation ergonomics*. http://www.cdc.gov/od/ohs/Ergonomics/compergo.htm (accessed November 11, 2006).

Cornell Human Factors and Ergonomics Research Group. 2004. *Cornell University ergonomics Web site*. http://ergo.human.cornell.edu (accessed November 11, 2006).

Cote, A. E. (Ed.). 2003. *Fire Protection Handbook (2003 ed.)*. Quincy, MA: National Fire Protection Association.

Crowe, T. 2004. Crime prevention through environmental design strategies and applications. In Fennelly, L. J. (Ed.). *Effective physical security*, 3rd ed., 49–99. Burlington, MA: Elsevier Butterworth-Heinemann.

Crume, J. 2000. *Inside Internet security: What hackers don't want you to know*. Toronto: Pearson Education.

Cumming, N. 1992. *Security: A guide to security system design and equipment selection and installation*. Stoneham, MA: Butterworth-Heinemann.

Denning, P. 2006. Hastily formed networks. *Communications of the ACM* 49(4):15–20.

Department of Trade and Industry. 2005. *Security equipment in the UK: A guide to UK capability, 2005/6 edition*. http://www.dti.gov.uk/files/file11403.pdf (accessed November 29, 2006).

Electrostatic Discharge Association. 2001. *Fundamentals of ESD*. http://www.esda.org/basics/part1.cfm (accessed November 11, 2006).

Environmental Protection Agency. 2003. *Halon substitutes under SNAP as of August 21, 2003*. http://www.

epa.gov/ozone/snap/fire/halo.pdf (accessed November 11, 2006).

Fennelly, L. J. 2004. *Effective physical security*. 3rd ed. Burlington, MA: Elsevier Butterworth-Heinemann.

Fleming, J. W. 1999. Chemical fire suppressants: How can we replace halon? *Proceedings of the Fall Technical Meeting of the Eastern States Section of the Combustion Institute, Raleigh, NC*, 16–23.

Future Fibre Technologies™ Pty Ltd. 2005. *FFT Secure Link™*. http://www.fft.com.au/pages/product_link.htm (accessed November 11, 2006).

Garcia, M. L. 2001. *The effective evaluation of physical protection systems*. Woburn, MA: Butterworth-Heinemann.

Garfinkel, S. with G. Spafford. 2002. *Web security, privacy, and commerce*. Sebastopol, CA: O'Reilly.

Gerke, K. 2003. *Bibliography of EMC publications*. http://emiguru.com/bibliog.htm (accessed November 11, 2006).

Gordon, L, et al. 2006. *2006 CSI/FBI computer crime and security survey*. http://www.gosci.com/forms/fbi/csi_fbi_survey.jhtml (accessed November 29, 2006).

Halon Recycling Corporation. 2002. *Halon Recycling Corporation homepage*. http://www.halon.org (accessed November 11, 2006).

Hartke, J. 1998. *Duplication quality tips*. 2nd ed. Marlborough, MA: Media Sciences.

Hartke, J. 2001. *Measures of CD-R longevity*. http://www.mscience.com/longev.html (accessed October 23, 2004).

Health Protection Agency. 2005. *Mobile phones and health*. http://www.hpa.org.uk/hpa/news/nrpb_archive/press_releases/2005/press_release_02_05.htm (accessed November 11, 2006).

Human Reproduction. 2004. *Increase in scrotal temperature in laptop computer users*. http://humrep.oxfordjournals.org/cgi/content/abstract/deh616v1 (accessed June 18, 2007).

Institute of Electrical and Electronic Engineers. 1999. *Recommended practice for powering and grounding electronic equipment, IEEE Standard 1100-1999*. Piscataway, NJ: IEEE Standards Department.

Intel. (2003) *Electrostatic discharge(ESD) safety guidelines*. http://resource.intel.com/telecom/support/install/config/esd/esd.pdf (accessed November 11, 2006).

International Advisory Committee for the UNESCO Memory of the World Programme staff, 2000. *Safeguarding the documentary heritage*. http://webworld.unesco.org/safeguarding/en (accessed November 11, 2006).

International Commission on Non-Ionizing Radiation Protection. 1998. Guidelines for limiting exposure to time-varying electric, magnetic, and electromagnetic fields (up to 300 GHz). *Health Physics* 75(4):494–522. http://www.icnirp.de/documents/emfgdl.pdf (accessed November 11, 2006).

International Electrotechnical Commission. 1993. *Information technology equipment-safety—Part 1: General principles, section 1: Guide A: Selection and protection levels for lightning protection systems [IEC 61024–1–1 – Ed. 1.0]*. Geneva: International Electrotechnical Commission.

International Electrotechnical Commission. 2001. *Information technology equipment-safety—Part 1: General requirements [IEC 60950–1—Ed. 1]*. Geneva: International Electrotechnical Commission.

Konicek, J., and K. Little. 1997. *Security, ID systems and locks: the book on electronic access control*. Woburn, MA: Butterworth-Heinemann.

Kozierok, C. M. 2004. *Uninterruptible power supplies*. http://www.pcguide.com/ref/power/ext/ups/index-c.html. (accessed November 11, 2006).

Mangan, J. F. 2002. Cutting edge protection for information technology hardware is old hat. *Insurance Advocate*, 111(43):12.

McDaniel, L. D. D. (Ed.). 2001. *Disaster Restoration guide for disaster recovery planners (revision no. 10)*. Fort Worth: Blackman-Mooring Steamatic Catastrophe.

McNamara, J. 2002. *The unofficial tempest information Page*. http://www.eskimo.com/~joelm/tempest.html (accessed December 6, 2003).

Microsoft. 2006. *Server and domain isolation using IPsec and group policy, Appendix D: IT threat categories*. http://www.microsoft.com/technet/security/topics/architectureanddesign/ipsec/ipsecapd.mspx (accessed October 10, 2006).

National Computer Security Center. 1991. *A guide to understanding data remanence in automated information systems, version 2 [NCSC-TG-025]*. http://www.fas.org/irp/nsa/rainbow/tg025-2.htm (accessed November 11, 2006).

National Fire Protection Association. 2000. *Standard for installation of lightning protection systems (NFPA 780; 2000 ed.)*. Quincy, MA: National Fire Protection Association.

National Fire Protection Association. 2000. *Standard for clean agent fire extinguishing systems (NFPA 2001; 2000 ed.)*. Quincy, MA: National Fire Protection Association.

National Fire Protection Association. 2003. *Standard for the protection of electronic computer/data processing equipment (NFPA 75; 2003 ed.)*. Quincy, MA: National Fire Protection Association.

National Fire Protection Association. 2003. *Life safety code (NFPA 101; 2003 ed.)*. Quincy, MA: National Fire Protection Association.

Newman, R. C. 2003. *Enterprise security*. Upper Saddle River, NJ: Prentice Hall.

Ogilvy Renault LLP. 2006. *In Canada—Don't be vulnerable to a departing employee*. http://www.ogilvyrenault.com/WebControls/GetResource.aspx?id=4726 (accessed November 23, 2006).

Orrey, K., and L. J. Lawson. 2006. *Penetration testing framework 0.23*. http://www.vulnerabilityassessment.co.uk/Penetration%20Test.html (accessed November 30, 2006).

Oyster Optics Inc. 2003. *Securing fiber optic communications against optical tapping methods*. http://www.rootsecure.net/content/downloads/pdf/fiber_optic_taps.pdf (accessed November 11, 2006).

POA Publishing LLC. 2003. *Asset protection and security management handbook*. Boca Raton, FL: Auerbach.

Ponemon Institute, LLC. 2006. *2006 annual study: Cost of a data breach*. http://www.vontu.com/uploadedFiles/

global/2006_Cost_of_Data_Breach_Report.pdf. (accessed November 28, 2006).

PricewaterhouseCoopers LLP. 2006. *DTI information security breaches survey 2006*. http://www.dti.gov.uk/files/file28343.pdf (accessed November 29, 2006).

Purpura, P. 2002. *Security and loss prevention*. 4th ed. Woburn, MA: Butterworth-Heinemann.

Reconnex Corp. 2006. *Reconnex insider threat index Q1 06*. http://www.reconnex.net/Threat/pdf/InsiderThreatQ106v2.pdf (accessed November 11, 2006).

Rittinghouse, J. W., and W. M. Hancock. 2003. *Cybersecurity operations handbook*. Burlington, MA: Elsevier Digital Press.

Skoudis, E. 2002. *Counter hack: A step-by-step guide to computer attacks and effective defenses*. Upper Saddle River, NJ: Prentice Hall PTR.

Space Environment Center. 2002. *Space Environment Center space weather alerts*. http://www.sec.noaa.gov/alerts (accessed November 11, 2006).

Svensson, P. 2004. *CDs and DVDs not so immortal after all*. http://www.usatoday.com/tech/news/2004-05-05-disc-rot_x.htm. (accessed November 11, 2006).

Tyska, L. A., and L. J. Fennelly. 2000. *Physical Security: 150 things you should know*. Woburn, MA: Butterworth-Heinemann.

U.S.-Canada Power System Outage Task Force. 2004. *Final report on the August 14, 2003 blackout in the United States and Canada: Causes and recommendations*. https://reports.energy.gov/BlackoutFinal-Web.pdf (accessed November 11, 2006).

Volonino, L. and S. R. Robinson. 2004. *Principles and practices of information security*. Upper Saddle River, NJ: Pearson Prentice Hall.

Ward, B. (Ed.). 2004. Silicon Valley museum celebrates history of computing. *Computer*, 37(10):15–9.

Wylder, J. 2004. *Strategic information security*. Boca Raton, FL: Auerbach.

FURTHER READING

International Standards Organization. (2000). Information Technology—*Code of Practice for Information Management [ISO/IEC 17799:2000]*. Geneva, Switzerland: ISO.

Computer Security Incident Response Teams (CSIRTs)

Raymond R. Panko, *University of Hawaii, Manoa*

INTRODUCTION

Almost all corporations today protect themselves with layered defenses consisting of firewalls, antivirus systems, hardened hosts, and other protections. Even so, security incidents (also called security breaches) sometimes occur.

The firm's on-duty staff may be tasked to handle minor incidents because they can respond immediately and generally effectively. For major incidents, however, such as a major virus attack, a major denial-of-service attack, or the hacking (takeover) of important servers, the firm needs a team approach to stop the breach and get the firm back to normal. To handle major incidents, many firms create computer security incident response teams (CSIRTs), also known as computer emergency response teams (CERTs) and computer incident response teams (CIRTs). The term *computer emergency response team* (CERT) is a registered trademark of the CERT/Coordination Center at Carnegie-Mellon University (www.cert.org) and may be used only with permission.

A critical success factor for any CSIRT is speed of response. During a major security breach, a corporation's operations are likely to be disrupted. This can result in the loss of immediate revenues and the imposition of penalties by business partners and regulators and by a loss in customer or investor confidence.

During emergencies, human beings often are not at their best cognitively. Instead of ensuring that they understand the situation well, they often fixate on a single possible solution that eventually turns out to be fatally flawed. They also tend to make mistakes and work slowly when they are handling complex and difficult tasks for the first time. In addition, teams with members who are unfamiliar with the way their coworkers operate often have communication breakdowns.

Consequently, it is extremely important for CSIRTs to be organized before an incident and to conduct live rehearsals regularly. Although first attempts may not be satisfactory, live rehearsals will identify problems that can be corrected so that performance is good during real incidents.

Once a real security breach occurs, the CSIRT's work must proceed through a series of well-considered steps (Panko 2004). These are the discovery of an incident and its escalation to the status of major incident, the analysis of the incident to understand it, the containment of the attack to stop the spread of damage, repair to get damaged systems cleaned up and operational, possible punishment of the attacker, hardening of damaged systems against new attacks, and postmortem analysis.

BEFORE THE INCIDENT

Justifying the CSIRT

CSIRTs are expensive. It is important to be able to justify the cost of having one to senior management. It is also important to be able to justify requiring participation from a number of departments, including during live rehearsals, which are very time-consuming.

The normal way to justify a CSIRT is to collect data on the frequency of attacks and the damage caused by attacks. One excellent general source is the Computer Emergency Response Team/Coordination Center (www.cert.org). Other good general sources are SecurityFocus (www.securityfocus.com) and the SANS Institute (www.sans.org). The Federal Bureau of Investigation (FBI) and the Computer Security Institute conduct an annual survey of corporations to assess the frequencies of various kinds of attacks (www.gocsi.com). A good source of data on viruses and spam is MessageLabs (www.messagelabs.com). In presenting summary information to top management, it is good to have data on both general trends and some examples of serious problems caused by incidents in specific corporations.

This information should be combined with estimates of how much major attacks of various types would cost the firm and, if possible, how having rapid detection and containment through the use of a CSIRT could reduce these costs.

Organizing the CSIRT

The first step is to create the CSIRT. Information technology (IT) security incidents can affect several functional groups in a firm. It usually also takes the staff from several functional areas to handle major IT security incidents. Consequently, the CSIRT must draw on several functional areas for its membership (Panko 2004): the IT security staff, the IT staff, functional line managers, public relations, the legal department, and external organizations, such as outsourcers and law enforcement agencies.

The IT Security Staff

Obviously, the IT security staff needs to be involved and may lead the CSIRT. Most firms have very small IT security staffs, and for these firms, it is normal for the entire IT security staff to be on the CSIRT.

The IT Staff

Sometimes, the IT security staff is under the information technology director. This arrangement is not ideal because a large fraction of all IT security breaches are committed by the IT staff. It is better for accountability if IT security is a parallel operation. Another reason for keeping the IT security staff separate is that the IT staff sometimes focuses primarily on technology, whereas the IT security staff must focus more broadly on organizational issues. On the negative side, separating IT security from IT can result in friction between the two groups in terms of the ownership of server logs and other important matters. In addition, a separated IT security staff cannot "order" the IT staff to take action, and separation frees the IT department from accountability for security.

In CSIRTs, it is important to have members of the IT staff be involved, however IT security and IT relate organizationally. It is also important to have operational levels of IT represented as well as IT management because operational employees often have a better picture of what is happening at a detailed level, whereas IT managers have the broader perspective needed to understand what is happening across systems and needed to understand the corporate implications of IT security breaches and alternative remedies.

Functional Line Managers

Fixing an IT security breach is not simply a technical matter. For example, the simplest and most effective way to contain a hacking intrusion is to terminate a victim computer's network or Internet connection. The business implications of "pulling the plug" can be horrendous, however. Functional line managers in critical areas must be involved in and must approve the CSIRT's actions.

Public Relations

One non-IT group that needs to be strongly involved in an adverse incident is the company's public relations department. If there is a serious problem, the company will want to manage communication with the outside world to cause as little damage as possible to public relations. Under no circumstances should an IT or IT security employee talk to the media directly. Many firms also work with external public relations companies, and there are even public relations companies that specialize in incident handling.

Legal Department

It is critical to have members of the legal department on the CSIRT. Lawyers have the specialized knowledge needed for prosecution and to defend the company against liability. (If an attacker compromises a corporate computer and uses it to attack another corporation, the company whose computer was compromised and used may be liable.)

IT Outsourcers

Most companies outsource at least some of their IT activities, and many companies outsource most of their IT. In such cases, the IT outsourcing vendor will have to work closely with the CSIRT. Beyond that, the IT outsourcer must have good internal incident response capabilities, and expertise in incident handling may be a factor in selecting an outsourcer.

Some firms turn to IT security outsourcers to detect problems in internal systems and to provide expertise and actual work in the case of security incidents. One advantage of using IT security outsourcers is that they have constant experience with handling attacks, whereas internal CSIRTs may handle only a handful of attacks each year.

In any IT outsourcing, it is important to have outsourcers intimately connected to the CSIRT, including participating in rehearsals for security incidents.

Software Contractors

Many information systems today are developed by contractors. In some cases, systems are custom-built. In other cases, they are commercial off-the-shelf (COTS) products. In many cases, they are COTS products customized to a corporation's needs. During an incident, the CSIRT may need help from software developers. The CSIRT should have contact information for the contractors of all major systems, and in the case of pervasive organization-wide tools, such as enterprise resource planning (ERP) systems, a contractor employee may rehearse with the CSIRT during major planning exercises.

Law Enforcement Agencies

Although law enforcement agencies will not actually be part of the CSIRT, their expertise is invaluable if action is to be taken against the attacker. It is important for the CSIRT to understand how to interact with law enforcement agencies and to know what services law enforcement agencies can provide, such as the copying and protection of evidence. Law enforcement officers may even participate in CSIRT rehearsals.

Live Rehearsals

Once the CSIRT is formed, it must engage in rehearsals that take it through realistic emergencies. As noted earlier, during crises, people are not at their best cognitively. Rehearsals bring the practice needed for correct actions to become habitual so that they will be effective even during the stresses of crises. In addition, you would not expect a football team to execute plays without repetitive practice. In fact, the first time that teams try to execute a play in practice, it is usually painful to watch.

The simplest way to rehearse is to conduct a desktop exercise. In this type of exercise, the CSIRT members sit around a table and are given a series of crisis situations to consider. They then describe each step they would take during each crisis. Desktop exercises are useful during the early stages of a CSIRT's life. During these desk exercises, the CSIRT's members may discover that they are missing representation from an important functional area, that their approaches to recovery are not viable, that they have misunderstandings about authority and terminology, and so forth.

To really develop their skills, however, CSIRTs need to move to live rehearsals, in which they actually conduct the steps needed to address various types of incidents. Live rehearsals identify many problems that the best desktop exercises cannot address. In addition, live rehearsals bring the practice needed for habituated responses and build confidence and speed. The military maintains the importance of "training the way you fight." The same is true for CSIRTs.

Technology Base

The CSIRT will need some technology to do its job. Some of it the firm already has; some must be purchased separately.

Protection Technology

By definition, incidents occur when protection technology (firewalls, antivirus, server hardening, etc.) breaks down. Good protection technology may, however, be able to reduce the severity of an attack. Protections are discussed extensively in other chapters in this book.

Intrusion-Detection Systems (IDSs)

Technologies can also help in the response phase of incidents. Most obviously, intrusion detection systems can alert firms to attacks. In addition, IDS log files can help the firm analyze what has happened during an attack. This chapter does not look at IDSs because they are covered in detail elsewhere in this book.

File-Integrity Checkers

To respond to an incident involving a server compromise, it is important to be able to know what changes the attacker has made. File-integrity checkers periodically create message digests of important system programs. Tripwire is a popular file-integrity checker. After an attack, message digests are again computed and compared with message digests before the attack to see which programs have been changed. Unfortunately, few firms use file-integrity checkers because they are difficult to use successfully. A serious problem with these tools is that many critical system files change during normal operation. Consequently, it takes a great deal of knowledge to select the specific system files to which file-integrity checkers should be applied.

Evidence-Collection Technology

Evidence-collection technology allows a firm to capture evidence during an attack. If evidence is not collected rapidly and carefully, it will become almost impossible to prosecute attackers or even to understand the attack well. One action is to back up the hard drive on the compromised computer. In addition, transient information stored in RAM (random access memory) during an attack may be crucial to understanding the attack and prosecuting attackers. Special-purpose software can handle backups and capture this transient information in ways that will preserve evidence for presentation in court if necessary. Again, this chapter does not discuss evidence-collection technology because this topic is covered in several chapters dealing with forensics in this book.

The Problem of Communication

One inevitable problem in CSIRTs is communication. During an attack, e-mail may be compromised, and even if it is not, it is likely to be too slow for important functions. The CSIRT organizer must maintain up-to-date lists of office telephone numbers, home telephone numbers, pager numbers, short message service cellular telephone numbers, e-mail addresses, and other contact information for each member of the CSIRT. This contact information changes so rapidly that it must be updated frequently and aggressively.

In the same vein, each CSIRT member must designate an alternate team member if he or she is unavailable. The CSIRT leader needs to maintain up-to-date contact information for these alternates as well. Ideally, alternates should participate in tests.

The Decision to Prosecute

One issue should be considered carefully before any incident occurs: whether to attempt to punish the attacker. For internal employees, this usually is a fairly straightforward decision because termination and lesser punishments are easy and usually legally safe to administer.

For external hackers, however, prosecution is difficult, especially if the attacker is a minor. Furthermore, pursuing prosecution may open up the firm to negative publicity and consequent losses in customer and investor confidence. Before attacks occur, the company should develop a policy regarding external (and internal) prosecution with the aid of the corporate legal department and senior managers.

One consideration in developing prosecution policies is that successful prosecution will require the CSIRT to take certain actions discussed later in this chapter. Evidence must be carefully protected and preserved. In addition, during the attack, it may be necessary to allow the attack to continue long enough to gather sufficient evidence for conviction instead of cutting off the attacker as soon as possible.

DURING THE ATTACK

Although preparation before a security incident is important, how well the CSIRT responds to actual security incidents is the litmus test for success.

Discovery and Escalation

First the attack must be discovered. Often, the employee who discovers the attack is a low-level IT employee or an employee in a functional area such as marketing. A key question to ask any firm to assess its state of security is, "Do your employees know the telephone number for reporting security concerns?" A sticker with this number should be on every telephone in the organization. Often, this is the telephone number of the firm's general security office. Delays in reporting suspected security breaches often result in severe damage before the CSIRT can even start its work.

In other cases, someone on the IT security or general IT staff detects the incident. Often, the firm's intrusion-detection system sets off an alarm when there is suspicious activity in the system.

In addition, the IDS maintains log files of events relevant to security. During the later analysis phase, analyzing these log files is crucial in understanding the nature of the incident.

The on-duty IT and IT security staff members typically handle small incidents. However, the on-duty staff manager must have clear guidelines for when to escalate an incident—that is, when to declare the situation sufficiently dangerous or damaging to convene the CSIRT. In particular, the firm must have good guidelines for classifying attacks as minor or major.

Initial Analysis (Triage)

The first action of the CSIRT must be to analyze the situation. There is a tendency to act precipitously even when little information is available. A short initial period of incident analysis is critical for later success. This is similar to the medical concept of triage (the initial analysis of a patient's condition) and is, in fact, often called triage.

The first step is to classify the security incident. Typically, there are three types of security incidents—widespread virus or worm outbreaks, denial-of-service attacks, and hacking attacks. Hacking is the access of a protected resource without authorization or in excess of authorization. Hacking, in other words, is breaking into a client, server, switch, router, or other computer.

The second step is to understand the attack. What vulnerability allowed the hacker to break into the computer? What has he or she already done? How sophisticated does the attack appear to be? In the case of virus or worm outbreaks, how is the virus or worm propagating, and how rapidly is it propagating?

Although analysis typically focuses on internal data in computer and intrusion-detection system log files, the CSIRT may also contact other organizations, including the Computer Emergency Response Team/Coordination Center (www.cert.org), which maintains information about common hacking breaches and virus attacks. There is a good chance that the current attack uses a method that has been common in recent attacks, that the method is well understood, and that there are good defenses and recovery techniques already known.

Containment

The next step is containment, which means stopping the attack. As noted earlier, the simplest approach to containment is to unplug affected computers. Although this is effective and may even prove to be necessary, it is a drastic step that can have important implications for the firm as a whole if an affected server is vital to the firm's operations. Effectively, unplugging a computer is a self-administered denial-of-service attack.

In addition, it may be desirable to allow the attacker to continue working so that the attack can be better understood. Containing attackers too soon may simply keep them out for a few minutes, after which they may be able to get back in using the same method they used to gain entry in the first place. In a virus or worm attack, containment before understanding may result in immediate reinfection through the same vulnerability.

If legal prosecution is a goal, furthermore, it may be important to continue gathering evidence. On the negative side, if hackers are given sufficient time, they can scatter backdoor attack programs throughout a server's directories, read sensitive information, and take steps to make themselves difficult to detect. Consequently, containment should be initiated as soon as possible.

Recovery

Recovery, also called repair, means getting the computer system back to the state it was in before the attack. This means removing programs the attacker placed on the computer and cleaning up any altered data files.

Recovery usually focuses on program files, because hackers and virus and worms often litter the computer with attack programs that must be rooted out. Attackers also Trojanize legitimate system programs by replacing them with an attack program but keeping the name the same. To recover the system of program files on the computer, there are three main options: repair during continued operation, restoration from backup tapes, and reinstallation from original installation media.

Repair during Continued Operation

If a company has a good way to recognize attack programs, it may be able to make program file repairs while the computer is still operational. However, this presumes that the firm has done such things as keep message digests for all program files so that changes can be detected. This seldom is done.

Recovery from Backup Tapes

It is more common to reinstall all system and other program files from the last clean backup tape. This can be effective, but it is important to know when the attack began, because the backup files may themselves be suspect. In addition, the restoration of program files from backup tapes often requires the system to be taken offline at least temporarily.

Reinstallation from Original Installation Media

In the worst case, the computer's software will have to be reinstalled using original software installation media. It is important to have these media readily available for such eventualities. It is also important to document all configuration changes made during and since the last installation. For instance, patches frequently need to be applied to remove known vulnerabilities, and there usually are many company-specific and computer-specific configuration changes made for other reasons. Reinstallation from original media typically takes the computer down for several hours.

Data Files

The CSIRT will face special problems if the attack damaged data files. Although restoration from the last clean backup tape will work for older files, all data entered since the last backup will be lost unless a real-time journal of changes has been maintained (which is rare). Laboriously, online files can be compared with backup files to identify safe files and files that must be looked at carefully.

Protection against Subsequent Attacks

The last action of any CSIRT during an attack is to protect the firm against subsequent attacks. Obviously, the specific vulnerability that allowed the attack to succeed must be fixed. In addition, firewalls should be tuned to stop such attacks if possible, and intrusion-detection systems must get filters to warn of subsequent attacks that are conducted in the way the current breach was created.

Second, and more subtly, the server that was attacked must be especially hardened against reattacks. Hardening involves the application of all patches to the system and the general configuring of the system for maximum security.

Internet hackers, to demonstrate their successes, often invite other hackers to get into your system. For some period of time after an attack, your "famous" server will continue to be attacked by hackers. If you repair the specific exploit used in the first place, hackers will attempt to find other vulnerabilities to prove that they could break into the server in ways that the original hacker could not.

AFTER THE ATTACK

Sanctions

Sanctions are punishments that a firm directs at attackers. Although anger usually makes a firm eager to sanction attackers, it is not always practical to do so.

Punishing Employees

If the attacker is a current employee, the firm must weigh the benefits of prosecution against the simple expedient of firing the employee. (For minor incidents, milder sanctions may be appropriate.) Firing an employee typically can be done with no publicity, especially if the employee agrees to either keep quiet or face legal prosecution. In addition, although prosecution is difficult, employment usually can be terminated fairly easily for attacking IT resources, and it usually is legally safe to terminate employment (however, state laws differ in the United States, international laws vary greatly, and union agreements may make sanctions difficult to apply in some firms).

Prosecuting Attackers

Prosecuting employees, ex-employees, or other, outside, attackers in courts of law requires a firm to prove that a particular person committed the attack. This can be difficult, especially if the attacker is using a spoofed IP address or attacked indirectly from a computer previously compromised instead of from his or her own computer.

In addition, as noted earlier, the attacker must be traced doing a series of actions (individual actions may not convince a jury), and this may require allowing the attack to continue longer than it would if prosecution were not a goal.

Successful prosecution will depend heavily on the quality of evidence collected. As soon as possible, crucial information on the attacked computer must be documented or backed up. Otherwise, the defense will argue that the evidence is tainted and that many things could have caused later changes.

In addition, the CSIRT needs to document carefully how and by whom evidence was collected. The firm also must maintain a clear chain-of-evidence documenting who had the evidence at all times and how it was collected and protected after collection. Any breakdown in documentation can ruin a case. Judges often will not even allow a jury to see evidence that does not meet strict legal evidence requirements.

For prosecution, it is critical to train the CSIRT beforehand in evidence collection and preservation. In fact, it is highly desirable to call in local authorities or the FBI. They can make backups of your hard drives and collect other information in a way likely to get a conviction. Other chapters in this book contain detailed discussions of forensic data collection.

Lawsuits

For attacks that produce only modest amounts of damage, the authorities often are reluctant to prosecute. A firm may still be able to act through the legal system by suing the attacker for actual damages and perhaps for punitive damages as well. These damages and the attacker's cost of legal defense may be a satisfactory way to exact some measure of revenge. However, lawsuits are expensive and reveal the attack to the public. In addition, if the hacker community views the lawsuit as "lame," the firm may become a popular target of revenge attacks by other hackers.

Reprisal Attacks

One option is to attack the attacker in return—essentially, hacking the attacker's computer. This may seem attractive, but it is almost always a very bad idea. First, attackers often use intermediate victim computers to launch attacks. Reprisal attacks are likely to hurt an innocent victim. (If a firm feels that companies that allow their computers to be hacked are not innocent, it should keep in mind that it has just been hacked itself.)

Of course, more fundamentally, reprisal attacks are almost always illegal. The jailing of members of the CSIRT is not a goal of incident response. Also, a CSIRT is an official organization within the firm; liability for a reprisal attack is likely to extend to senior officers and even the board of directors.

Postmortem Analysis

After things have stabilized, it is important to conduct a postmortem analysis to review what happened during the incident. The goal is to improve future responses to incidents. Things that worked well should be noted, but problems also should be highlighted and fixes created for the future. After the exhaustion of an incident and the need to catch up on work postponed during the incident, it is difficult to motivate the CSIRT team members to undertake a postmortem analysis. However, given the valuable information gained during the actual incident, as opposed to simple live rehearsals, the information gathered in the postmortem analysis can produce strong benefits.

There should also be a follow-up analysis 1 to 6 months later to determine which recommendations made during a postmortem analysis have been implemented and which have not.

CONCLUSION

When major IT security incidents happen, companies cannot sit back and wonder what they should do. Before the attack, companies need to organize and train cross-disciplinary computer security incident response teams—also called computer emergency response teams. Training using realistic rehearsals is important for ensuring adequate and rapid CSIRT responses during an emergency.

During an attack, once an incident is discovered and escalated by the on-duty staff to a major incident, the CSIRT is activated. The CSIRT analyzes the attack so that appropriate responses can be made, contains the attack to prevent further damage, recovers program files and perhaps data files, gathers information needed for internal punishment or legal prosecution, hardens the system to prevent reattacks, and conducts a postmortem analysis to refine its incident response abilities.

GLOSSARY

Analysis: Incident response phase just after discovery phase. The CSIRT determines how the attack was made and what was done to affected systems.

Breach: Another name for a *Security Incident*.

Computer Emergency Response Team (CERT): Another name for *Computer Security Incident Response Team*.

Computer Incident Response Team (CIRT): Another name for *Computer Security Incident Response Team*.

Computer Security Incident Response Team (CSIRT): Cross-disciplinary team created to respond to major security incidents.

Containment: The phase in incident response in which the damage to systems is stopped.

Desktop Exercise: A process in which the CSIRT members sit around a table and discuss in detail the steps each member would take during a response.

Discovery: The phase in incident response in which a security incident is first discovered and reported.

Escalation: The act of determining that a particular security incident is a major breach and that the CSIRT must be activated.

Forensics: The application of science to criminal investigations.

Hacking: Taking over a computer; intentionally using a computer without authorization or in excess of authorization.

Hardening: Removing vulnerabilities from a host computer and configuring the computer for high security.

Incident: Another name for a *Security Incident*.

Incident Response: The multiphase process of responding to a security incident.

Information Technology (IT): Computer hardware, computer software, networking, and data.

Intrusion-Detection System: Tool that signals that an attack appears to be underway and that collects data in log files for analysis during and after an incident.

IT Security: Security of the IT function, as opposed to physical and building security.

IT Security Staff: The IT staff given responsibility for IT security, as opposed to physical and building security.

Live Rehearsal: An exercise in which the CSIRT team members go through a sample incident, implementing each step along the way.

Outsourcer: External company that provides IT services to a firm.

Postmortem Analysis: Assessment conducted after a security incident to determine how to respond better in the future.

Prosecution: The attempt to convict an attacker in a court of law.

Public Relations: Department in a firm charged with communicating with the public and the media on behalf of the firm.

Punishment: Taking action against an attacker; both sanctioning employee attackers and prosecuting and suing external attackers.

Repair: Phase in incident response in which the damaged system is brought back to correct operation.

Reprisal Attack: Attacking the attacker (usually illegal).

Security Breach: Another name for a *Security Incident*.

Security Incident: A virus attack, denial-of-service attack, or hack (computer break-in).

Trojanize: To replace a legitimate file by an attacker's file, giving the attacker's file the same name as the legitimate file.

CROSS REFERENCES

See *Business Continuity Planning*; *Cryptography*; *Denial of Service Attacks*; *Intrusion Detection Systems*; *Network Attacks*.

REFERENCES

Panko, R. R. 2004. *Corporate computer and network security*. Upper Saddle River, NJ: Prentice Hall.

FURTHER READING

CERT (Computer Emergency Response Team), Carnegie Mellon University. www.cert.org (accessed April 2005). Provides a broad range of information services for CSIRTs, including detailed reports on specific aspects of CSIRT management and operation.

Kruse, W. G., II, and J. G. Heiser. 2002. *Computer forensics: Incident response essentials*. Boston: Addison-Wesley.

Lucas, J., and B. Moeller. 2004. *The effective incident response team*. Boston: Addison-Wesley.

Mandia, K., and C. Prosise. 2001. *Incident response*. New York: Osborne/McGraw-Hill.

Northcutt, S., and J. Novak. 2001. *Network intrusion detection: An analyst's handbook*. Indianapolis: New Riders.

Prosise, C., and K. Mandia. 2001. *Incident response: Investigating computer crime*. Emeryville, CA: McGraw-Hill Osborne Media.

Schultz, E. E., and R. Shumway. 2002. *Incident response*. Indianapolis: New Riders.

Schweitzer, D. 2003. *Incident response: computer forensics toolkit*. Upper Saddle River, NJ: Prentice Hall.

West-Brown, M. J., D. Stikvort, K. P. Kossakowski, G. Killcrece, R. Ruefle, and M. Kajicek. 2003. *Handbook for computer security incident response teams*. 2nd ed. Pittsburgh: Carnegie Mellon Software Engineering Institute. www.cert.org/archive/pdf/csirt-handbook.pdf (accessed April 2005).

Whitman, M. E., and H. J. Mattord. 2006. *Principles of incident response and disaster recovery*. Boston: Thompson Course Technologies.

Backup and Recovery System Requirements

David R. Reavis, *Texas A&M University, Texarkana*

INTRODUCTION

As organizations work to determine how to protect their data, they face the challenge of quantifying the value of their data, then determining the most effective way to back up their data so that it can be restored in an acceptable time frame if a disaster occurs. This chapter addresses issues important to identifying backup and recovery requirements.

GENERAL BACKUP AND RECOVERY REQUIREMENTS

Requirements Planning Team

Planning for backup and recovery activities is often done in the context of a disaster-recovery planning project. The requirements for backup and recovery systems have technical, logistical, business, and operational components. Because the potential impact of any data loss is so broad, the planning for backup and recovery requirements should involve a cross-functional team. Candidates for the planning team include computer operators, application developers, key customer representatives, physical security personnel, database administrators, and stakeholders in the organization. As with any successful IT project, the support of an executive sponsor will greatly increase the likelihood of developing a robust backup and recovery system (Schiesser 2002, 300–4).

Operating Systems

One factor that influences every aspect of the backup and recovery process is the operating system. Operating systems dictate the terminology, thought processes, and operating procedures used in any IT environment. The operating system is the foundation on which backup and recovery system requirements are built.

There are a few areas in which the backup and recovery system requirements will be similar regardless of the operating system in use. These areas include job scheduling, scripting, and native backup utilities. Regardless of the operating system, most backup systems require a job scheduler to automate the backup process. This ensures that backups are done at the proper time and with the proper frequency. Job schedulers provide similar features across platforms and allow administrators to verify that backups are running on schedule. Every operating environment provides a means for creating scripts or sequencing commands as part of a backup procedure. The terminology for this process may be a script, a job control language program, or a batch program, but in many operating environments, the script is used to start the backups. Another similarity among operating systems is that each provides the administrator with utilities or commands that are specific to the operating system, and may be used for creating backups. These operating-system-specific utilities are sometimes used by third-party vendors as the basis for creating backups. An example of this is AMANDA, the Advanced Maryland Automated Network Disk Archiver, a public domain utility developed at the University of Maryland. AMANDA uses the UNIX tar utility to facilitate partial backups on systems running UNIX (Preston 1999).

Data Types

Different types of data hold different levels of value for the organization. Mission-critical data should be backed up frequently, and other data vary in value from important to unnecessary and may require a lower backup frequency (McDowell 2001). To develop backup and recovery system requirements, it is essential to understand the value of different data types. Assessing the current storage requirements will help to determine backup needs, appropriate methods, and the most effective strategies for backup and recovery procedures. As various data types are evaluated, the amount of each type of data on the system, along with the volatility of the data type should be documented. Volatility refers to the frequency with which data change or

Table 1: Data Type Assessment

Data Type	Size in Megabytes	Volatility	Value to Organization
Operating system		Low	High
Database		Medium to high	High
Applications		Low	High
E-mail		High	Medium to high
User files		Medium to high	Low-medium to high
Log files		High	Medium
Other			

are added to or deleted from the database. Data that do not change frequently, such as archived files, could be described as having low volatility, while files that are updated hourly would be considered to have high volatility. Table 1 is representative of the types of data that could be considered in a storage requirements assessment.

Another benefit of the storage requirements assessment is that obsolete data may be identified in any of the data types. Cleaning up obsolete data before determining backup requirements will provide a better picture of overall backup needs (Barth 2004). Archiving data implies that data have been moved from dynamic production databases to a static system. The static system will require different backup and recovery strategies because it changes less frequently (Mensching and Corbitt 2004).

One way to estimate the value of data is to determine how much effort would be required to re-create the data if they were lost. A similar approach is to estimate how much time and effort has been spent to create the data that are stored on a given system. Either of these approaches can provide insight into the true value of a data set to the organization (Wells 2003, 538). In addition to determining the value of data, one should also consider how critical certain systems are to ongoing operations. Data that may be easily created may appear to have a lower value, but if the data are critical to operations, the value increases (D'Amico 2004).

Databases

Most organizations consider the information stored in their databases to be among their most valuable assets. In some organizations, the database information is a key component of daily operations. Organizations such as financial institutions rely on their databases to provide critical information for almost every transaction. The critical nature of this information store requires careful planning to mitigate the risk of loss of the data. The simplest way to backup databases is to copy the entire database to backup media; however, this method can be time-consuming and expensive for large databases. More frequently, databases are backed up using a full backup followed by incremental backups or differential backups during a given period (Qian, Nakamura, and Nakagawa 2002).

Security Data

Different operating systems provide various capabilities for backing up sensitive information such as user IDs, passwords, permissions, and group memberships. Backing up these data is vital to the system backup, and sometimes overlooked. A complete backup plan should include provisions for backing up security data, along with guidelines about how the media should be handled, and how the restoration will be executed. Many organizations back up the security data in tandem with the operating system backup.

E-Mail

E-mail is an area in which backups are sometimes confused with archives. Archiving e-mail is the process of moving e-mail messages from the e-mail system to a record-retention system designed to archive electronic documents and messages. This is in contrast to backups, which are created to mitigate the risk of the loss of the data in the event of a disaster. Some experts recommend that e-mail be kept in the e-mail system for a minimal amount of time, then moved to a permanent archival system (Stephens and Wallace 2000). One of the legal concerns of backing up e-mail is the potential for electronic discovery. Electronic discovery is a request from a court of law to produce electronic documents for participants in a lawsuit. If an electronic discovery request is made, the company must make all e-mail messages available for inspection. The e-mail messages that exist on backup media are also subject to an electronic discovery request (Lange 2002).

User Files

User files may be overlooked or ignored in the backup plan of a data center because they exist on computer hard drives in each user's machine. One approach to backing up user files is to make users responsible for their own backups. User files saved to a file server are more likely to be backed up on a regular basis because they are readily accessible via the network. The analysis of user files should include a review of the file types and age of the files. Most users do not delete files unless they are prompted to do so because of disk quotas or other policy requirements. Asking users to remove documents they do not need can streamline the backup process. User files should also be analyzed to determine whether their existence on the network complies with company policy. If company policy prohibits storage of music files such as MP3 files, then these files will only impede the backup and recovery process without adding value to the data backup and restore process (Barth 2004).

Log Files

When assessing data types in an information system, it may be difficult to assess the value of certain data types. Log files are a typical example. Log files that were produced during a software installation process that occurred in the distant past may need to be purged from the system, while other log files should be treated with care and an eye toward preservation. In some cases, organizations may be required to analyze and retain log file data to comply with regulatory compliance rules such as the Sarbanes-Oxley Act (Zhen 2005). Log files are also variable in volatility. They may contain information about a single event, such as a software configuration change, or information that is updated by the system on a regular basis. Evaluating the backup requirements for log files is likely to require input from technically adept staff members. Finding the balance between backing up all log files and backing up only the most critical log files is a challenge that should be addressed in the context of a limited backup window and the need to meet the business and regulatory requirements of the environment.

Configuration Data

Many of the files on any computer specify how the computer functions. These files are normally backed up along with the operating system files or the security data. It is important to note that configuration files may also reside on network devices. Each piece of network hardware—such as switches, routers, and hubs—contain tables, configuration information, and security information that are critical to network operations. This configuration information is normally not highly volatile and may only be changed when new equipment is added or existing network configurations are updated. A system to back up these data should be considered as part of the overall disaster recovery plan, and the requirements for backup and recovery of network components are different from the requirements for other types of data. If an organization has previously ignored the backup and recovery issues for network devices, then the steps below may be used to develop an initial starting point for protecting this critical data.

1. Inventory network equipment: In many organizations an inventory of network components has already been done. Usually the purpose for such an inventory is to track the value of each component as a financial asset, or to monitor network performance to aid in troubleshooting network problems. Using either of these types of inventories is an excellent starting place.
2. Determine backup needs: The most important aspect of the inventory for backup and recovery requirements planning is to determine whether there are configuration data that need to be backed up on each device. The next most important piece of information is the actual function of the device. An Ethernet hub may not contain any special configuration data, but its existence should be documented so that in the event it is destroyed, the physical network configuration can be recreated. A network switch is more likely to have specific information about network segments, Internet protocol (IP) addresses, and traffic routing that should be saved in the event that the switch is destroyed.
3. Create initial backups: For devices that have custom configuration information, create initial backups. Many devices provide the ability to copy configuration information to a personal computer, where the configuration file can be modified, copied to external media, or printed.
4. Specify backup format: One of the risks associated with network equipment is that a replacement unit may not use the exact same configuration format that the original unit used. In fact it is very likely that any replacement for network equipment will be significantly different from an original unit. Network technology advances at high speed, and the improvements are incorporated into new products frequently. Because of this risk, it is prudent to consider creating backup documentation for certain network equipment other than simply backing up the configuration files. The meaning of the configuration parameters for a complicated switch should be committed to a designated format so that in the event the equipment is destroyed, and the replacement is significantly different, the new equipment can be configured to operate effectively in its new environment.
5. Handle with care: Keeping a duplicate copy of the configuration files and associated documentation on a personal computer is a good first step. Backing up these configuration files and storing them in a secondary location can further reduce the risk of loss.

The requirements for continued backup and recovery of network devices should be determined based on the volatility of the configuration files. Two approaches to backing up this type of data are the periodic approach and the change trigger approach. In the periodic approach, backups are created based on set time periods. Weekly or monthly backups are created; documentation is updated, backed up, and stored in an alternate location. In the change trigger approach, any time a network device configuration is changed, or new equipment is installed, the backup process is triggered.

It is difficult to plan all aspects of restoring data to network components. The major reason for the difficulty is that network components are frequently replaced by more advanced components with added features and different capabilities. The part of the plan that can be successfully created is the retrieval of all configuration information from the backup documentation. If the configuration files can be used by the new equipment, then the recovery will be faster, but if the replacement equipment requires information in a different format, or new specifications, then the alternate documentation must be used to initiate the new device. The Network Reliability and Interoperability Council (NRIC), an organization comprised of telecommunications industry representatives, has developed over 750 best practices that deal with backup and recovery of telecommunications equipment. These procedures address a variety of issues in network reliability and promote automated backup procedures for telecommunications equipment (Lennert et al. 2004).

Recovery Requirements

Because backups usually occur frequently and recovery occurs much less frequently, many organizations put more effort into the backup process than into the planning of the recovery process. Both are important. A poorly planned recovery process can make a great backup plan look terrible, because the backup is only half of the overall process. To determine the requirements for the recovery system, some critical measures must be analyzed.

The first is the recovery time objective (RTO). RTO is a measure of how long the organization can effectively function without the system. If the system is a convenience system that is only used for occasional reference, then the organization may be able to function for days or weeks without access. The RTO for such a system might be expressed in days. If the system is a mission-critical, real-time, transaction-oriented system that the organization relies on to do business 24 hours a day, then the RTO might be expressed in seconds. Determining the RTO for each system is important, because these numbers will ultimately contribute to the recovery requirements for the organization.

Another measure that should be determined for each system is the recovery-point objective (RPO). RPO is expressed in terms of how much data the organization can afford to lose if the system fails. Less volatile systems generally have a higher RPO than more volatile systems. Mission-critical, online systems usually have an RPO that approaches zero (Preston 2005). Recovery issues need to be addressed in planning the backup strategy. RTO and RPO measures will influence the way backups are scheduled and executed.

A COMPARISON OF BACKUP METHODS

Hot versus Cold

The hot or cold approach to backups is directly related to the system availability requirement in the organization. Hot backups are those that take place while the system is operating; cold backups take place while the system has been made inaccessible to users. If an organization cannot tolerate any down time, then a hot backup scheme is usually implemented. In a hot backup scenario, data may be copied to a fast tape drive or secondary disk while data files are actually in use. This may require data to be buffered and databases to take advantage of journaling, and it may slow down the overall performance of the system during the backup process. In a cold backup scenario, the backup window is normally defined as a time when minimal usage is likely such as in the early hours of the morning—for example, 2:00 A.M. Shortly before the scheduled backup time a notice may be sent to any users logged on the system informing them that the system will be going down for scheduled backups. At the appointed time, interactive users are logged out of the system and batch programs are ended or suspended. When all interactive processes are stopped, the system is identified as a "quiet" system and can be backed up. The backup is then executed and verified before allowing users to log in to the system. This sequence is important because if one of the tapes cannot be verified, the backup set may be corrupt. The following checklist shows the correct sequence of events in a cold backup scenario:

1. Notify any users on the system that the system will be unavailable beginning in a set amount of time (usually 10 to 15 minutes).
2. At the scheduled time, disable the ability for users to log into the system interactively.
3. At the scheduled time, remove any users from the system who have not logged out.
4. Start the backup job at the designated time and monitor the job for successful completion.
5. Verify the readability of the tapes or other backup media.
6. If the backup media prove to be readable, then allow users to log in. If the backup media fails, take action to redo the backup or log that the backup media failed. (McDowell 2001).

Online versus Offline

During recent years, changes in telecommunications technology have allowed some new backup methods to thrive. Improvements in the quality of service, bandwidth, and cost of telecommunications have made it possible to backup computer systems over telecommunications links. This is referred to as an online backup. Online backups are becoming more cost-effective when compared to the traditional method, in which all of the costs of the traditional method are considered. Traditional backup costs include tape drives, media, personnel, off-site courier expenses, and physical storage space. Expenses for online backups include the telecommunication link and associated hardware, along with a service provider's software and service fees. In many cases an existing telecommunication link is used, provided there is enough available bandwidth. One concern that should be addressed is the security of sensitive data traveling over telecommunication lines. If data are encrypted before being sent, the security issue is handled, but encryption requires CPU cycles and will consume system resources on the system being backed up (Stoddard 2004).

Backup Types

There are several types of backups that can be performed with any data type. Three commonly used backup techniques are the full backup, the incremental backup, and the differential backup. The full backup captures all of the files specified in the system or subsystem. These files are stored on a single media set, and this type of backup provides the fastest and cleanest restore scenario. The negative aspects of the full backup are that it takes more time to perform than other types of backups and in some cases files are backed up that rarely or never change, resulting in unnecessary media storage requirements.

An incremental backup establishes a repetitive cycle that begins with a full backup, then on subsequent periods (usually days) backs up only the data that have changed since the last backup, including previous incremental backups.

The backups made after the full backup normally require fewer media, less time, and less computer resources than the full backup. The negative aspects of this strategy are that the restoration process may require multiple media sets, and the time to restore data will be longer than the full-backup method. For example, suppose a full backup is run on Monday, followed by incremental backups on Tuesday and Wednesday. On Thursday morning the server crashes, requiring a new disk to be installed. To restore the system the full backup set would have to be restored, then the media set created on Tuesday would have to be restored, followed by the Wednesday media set restoration. Therefore the time required for restoring the data increases as the time since the last full backup increases.

A differential backup also begins with a full backup, then in subsequent periods, backups are run to back up any files that have been created or modified since the last full backup. This method may require fewer media sets to restore data because all changes since the last full backup are saved in each subsequent backup. In the scenario mentioned above, the Monday backup set would have to be restored, and then the most recent differential backup would have to be restored. This would result in a more streamlined restore process than used in the incremental strategy (Swanson et al. 2002).

Generational backups refer to a system of media rotation in which three media sets (usually tapes) are used for backups. Typically the first set (set A) is referred to as the grandfather, the second set (set B) is referred to as the father, and the third set (set C) is referred to as the son. Set A normally consists of a full backup tape(s) and all incremental or differential tapes used until the next full backup is scheduled. When the time to create the next full backup occurs, set A is set aside and set B is used for the next rotation. In the third cycle set C is used for the full and subsequent incremental or differential backups. In some cases, set A is then reused for the next cycle, and in some cases the grandfather (set A) is permanently retired and archived in an off-site location. One benefit of this practice is that if one media set is corrupted or damaged, then the previous media set still exists and can be used to recover the data, although it may not be as up to date as the most current media set (Marakas 2006, 303).

SOLUTION OPTIONS

Since the majority of computer systems are a mixture of heterogeneous systems, the requirements for any single organization are likely to be a mixture of methods and techniques that support the individual organization. In this section several issues are discussed that highlight concerns in diverse environment.

Third-Party Backup and Recovery Product Requirements

There are many backup and recovery tools on the market. Several of these tools provide the user with options that are beyond the capabilities of their operating systems and offer excellent value by improving the backup and recovery process. A complete evaluation of third-party backup software is beyond the scope of this chapter; however, a discussion of some of the important features that are available is in order to provide some insight into how to evaluate various backup and recovery packages. The following checklist can be used to evaluate potential backup and recovery software. Requirements for specific organizations may be more or less rigorous than those listed, but this checklist should provide a good starting point for any product evaluation.

1. Easy installation and configuration: The product should be easy to install and configure. If the configuration is overly complex, the risk of improper configuration rises and along with it, the risk of getting an incomplete backup rises proportionally. This issue increases in importance when an entire system is lost and the backup software must be reinstalled to do a complete restore. If the installation process is complicated and lengthy, the recovery time will be extended.
2. User interface: The user interface for a backup and recovery tool should be easy enough for a user with limited training to use. Some of the tools available allow the user to select wizards to streamline various processes, and others require a step-by-step sequence of menu options. Remember that the recovery may be performed by someone other than the most highly trained operations staff, and in some cases under difficult circumstances. A simple user interface can make the restore process easier and increase the likelihood of success for a backup and disaster recovery team member.
3. Support: Support for backup and recovery software may be available via online documentation, a built-in help facility, printed manuals, or via e-mail or telephone. One way to test the response of a vendor is to call the help line prior to buying the software and evaluate the response prior to purchasing the product. If you have to navigate complicated electronic response screening software before speaking to a live support person, you should know that before the purchase. Evaluating the overall help features of a product is important in determining whether the product is well supported.
4. Multiple device support: Many backup and restore products support specific drive types and not others. Another related issue is that you may be backing up on tape today and DVDs tomorrow. The best products support many backup devices and have the ability to span across multiple media to create a media set.
5. Validation: Most backup products provide validation for the external media. An important consideration regarding validation is the time required for the validation process. Some organizations opt not to validate the backup media because of the time it takes. This risky behavior reduces the chances of a complete and accurate backup. The time required is a function of the speed of the backup device, but the software can function efficiently or poorly in validating the integrity of the media.
6. Compression: Backup and restore software usually provides the ability to compress data before storing it on the backup media. This reduces the number of tapes required, but may extend the time required for the backup and slow down the system during the

backup process. This feature may be important depending on the backup method chosen and the speed of the processor.

7. Encryption: The ability to encrypt data provides an additional layer of security for the organization's data. Some organizations protect their computers effectively with authentication, physical security, and other safeguards, but do not consider security as important for their backup media. This mistake can be avoided by encrypting backup data.
8. Reporting: Backup and restore software should provide reporting for problems that occur during the backup or recovery process, successful operations, and configuration information. The reporting information should be easy to understand and as jargon-free as possible. A lack of robust reporting features is a good reason to avoid certain third-party backup products.
9. Flexibility: Backup and restore software should allow files to be backed up from selected locations, volumes, and in groups defined by the administrator. It should support full backups, incremental backups, differential backups, and on-demand or ad-hoc backups. The software should also support restoring single files from a backup media set, and restoring files to any location.

Third-party backup and restore software vendors offer numerous products that will effectively manage the backup and restore process. It is important to evaluate an organization's specific needs to determine which product most closely meets those needs. In addition to evaluating product literature, the organization should evaluate independent product reviews that are frequently available in trade publications or magazines (Vella 2005).

Media

Regardless of the platform, operating system, or data type, when backups are performed on any removable media (such as magnetic tape or CDs) the procedures for handling the media should be documented. Removable media may be kept on-site or off-site. If the media are stored off-site, the storage facility needs to be physically secure, environmentally controlled, and accessible during potential recovery windows. Contact information for the off-site storage facility should be available to IT staff who may require the media to restore files during and after normal business hours. The off-site storage facility should be far enough away from the data center that potential weather or other disasters would not affect both locations and therefore reduce the potential for recovery. Table 2 is a planning checklist for media requirements. The checklist is designed to help determine how much media is required for individual backup situations. The checklist assumes a full backup weekly, followed by incremental backups on a daily basis. The table should be modified to reflect specific backup strategies.

Tape versus Disk

Magnetic tape is still one of the most popular media for backing up information systems. It is relatively inexpensive, based on proven, stable technology and supported by numerous hardware and software vendors as a viable backup technology. Magnetic tape also has some drawbacks. One of the primary drawbacks of using tape is that data recorded to tape is recorded and retrieved sequentially. This can extend the time required to find and retrieve single files on a tape or tape set. Another drawback is that tapes tend to wear out with use, and a worn tape can be unreliable. Various vendors provide software to verify the contents of a tape after it is written, and this improves reliability, but errors may still occur. Even when a tape has been recorded and verified, a break in the tape can render the tape or the tape set useless. These are some of the disadvantages or risks of using tape, but with these risks noted, using tape is still a widely accepted method for backups.

Another option for saving important data is to copy the data to disk-based storage on another system or subsystem. This may be accomplished using a variety of techniques such as network-attached storage (NAS) or storage area networks (SANs). These technologies are discussed later, but in contrast to using tape as a storage medium, their common advantages will be noted here. The most important advantage of storing the data to disk instead of tape is a faster rate of transfer. Transfer rates for disk-to-disk copies are significantly faster than for disk-to-tape. This can

Table 2: Media Requirements Planning Checklist

A	Total amount of data to be backed-up (full backup)	115 Gb
B	Capacity of individual media (assume tape)	40 Gb
C	Tapes required for full backup	3
D	Tapes required for incremental backup (estimated average per day * 4 days)	(1 * 4) = 4
E	Number of generations of tapes	3
F	Total number of active tapes (C + D) * E	(3 + 4) * 3 = 21
G	Tapes in reserve (in case of tape failure)	4
H	Tapes required for monthly archive	2
I	Total number of tapes for backup system (F + G + H)	(21 + 4 + 2) = 27

reduce the amount of time required for both backup and recovery processes. Transfer rates are also impacted by the speed of communications between the source of the data and the target storage device. Most experts recommend that a dedicated network be used to transfer backup data between servers and backup devices. This allows maximum throughput and reduces the potential for slowdowns on networks that are used in normal work environments. Disk access is not limited to sequential access methods. Any file can be restored without having to read through other files in the backup set. This is significantly better than searching a ten-tape set for a file that may be located on the eighth tape in the set (Qu et al. 2004). A disadvantage of storing backup data on disk is that it is not usually practical to store the disk off-site. If the target storage disk is in the same physical data center, then some significant risks are still unaddressed. These risks include fire, tornado, flood, and other natural phenomena that can impact the data center. To address these risks, some organizations take advantage of both disk-to-disk backups and tape backups. This can be done by backing up the system using disk-to-disk technology and taking advantage of the shorter backup window, faster transfer rates, and more convenient restore methods, then backing up the target system to tape. The tapes can be made without interrupting online availability of the production system because they are backing up the backup system. The tapes can be moved off-site to mitigate the risk of natural disaster in the data center.

Other Media

Media other than disks and tapes are used in some backup scenarios. These include CD drives and flash drives. Organizations must evaluate the cost and capacity of each of these media to determine whether they are viable options for backup media.

CD-ROM media is a type of CD that may be used as a backup media. ROM is an acronym for read-only memory. If CD-ROMs are used to backup data, then the media may be used only once. The CD-ROMs must then be stored and kept until it is determined that the data are no longer viable as a backup. A similar alternative is CD-RW (read/write) technology, in which the CD may be used multiple times. Since the media can be used multiple times, the cost of this medium is much less than CD-ROM technology. Another alternative to CD technology is DVD, which is also available with read-only or read and write capabilities. DVD drives provide larger capacity than CD drives. DVD media may hold up to 50 Gb of data, whereas CD drives commonly hold 850 Mb of data. Flash drives (also called thumb drives or USB drives) may be used in certain cases for backups. These devices typically plug into an open USB port and appear to the system as a disk drive. The capacity for these devices is constantly increasing, and their potential for use in backup scenarios increases as the capacity increases. One advantage of a flash drive is that it has a small physical size and is therefore easily transported. Another advantage is that no special software is required to install the drive on a different machine in the event of the loss of a computer. These advantages also become disadvantages when considered in light of data security. The small size would potentially allow the data to be more easily stolen, and the ease of getting the data off of the flash drive by simply plugging it into another computer exposes the organization to increased risk of loss. These risks can be mitigated by using encryption, which is discussed in more detail later in this chapter.

Desktop Computers

There are some specific steps that can be taken to clarify the backup and recovery requirements for desktop systems. The first step is to encourage individual users to participate in a standardized scheme of file storage on their desktop computers. As an example, Microsoft has created standard folders for each user such as My Documents and My Pictures. If every user stores their documents under this (or another standard) scheme, then the backup process can be simplified. Desktop computers may be backed up via network connections, or by using removable media on each computer. Network backups are more consistent because they are usually administered by IT operations. If individuals are responsible for backing up their own desktop computer, they should be trained in the process and understand how to back up their files, along with being told why it is important to do so. Another practice that streamlines the backup and recovery process is to standardize hardware and software for the organization's desktops. Most organizations attempt to standardize as much as possible, but inconsistencies in desktop computer models and brands contribute to complexity in developing an effective backup and recovery system (Swanson et al. 2002). The goals of an effective user training program should include providing the user with an understanding of the organization's approved backup and recovery methods and tools, an introduction to the media supported by the organization's policies and procedures, and access to a list of parties to be notified in various cases of data loss.

File and Application Servers

Some of the same considerations for the desktop environment apply to file and application servers. Standardization for hardware, software, and peripherals can reduce the time needed to recover from equipment failure. One of the key differences between the server and the desktop computer is that many servers are equipped with redundant components such as power supplies, disk arrays, and tape drives. Servers may also be configured with an uninterruptible power supply (UPS) to allow the system to operate during a power outage.

A common redundant component is RAID technology. Using a redundant array of inexpensive disks (RAID) is a way to create real-time backups. Although a full discussion of various RAID levels is beyond the scope of this chapter, a brief description of RAID will help in understanding how RAID may fulfill some of the organizations backup and recovery requirements.

Mirroring

Mirroring occurs when a system is equipped with two different disk drives or disk arrays. When data are written to one disk, they are automatically and immediately written to the other disk. This creates two copies of all data. If one disk fails, the other disk can provide access to the data. In many cases, mirrored drives are hot-swappable, meaning they can be removed and replaced without interrupting system activity. Once the new drive is installed, the two drives are automatically synchronized and no other intervention is needed. The danger of this type of technology is that it gives some IT managers a false sense of security. Since events may occur that can render the server inoperable, a backup on removable media will further reduce the risk of losing the data. Mirroring is also referred to as RAID Level 1.

Parity

Parity is a technique that is used to determine whether data have been lost. Parity is created by summing the number of bits in a given data stream then adding a parity bit of 1 or 0 to make the sum odd or even. A system may use even parity or odd parity. In even parity the bits are summed then, if the number is odd, 1 is added to the sum to create even parity. The RAID system can determine whether there is damage to the file if the parity is supposed to be even, but during recalculation, determines that the parity is odd. In a RAID configuration, several types of parity schemes are possible. Parity requires multiple drives and does not store a complete second copy of the data as mirroring does (Dean 2006). This popular technique is a safeguard against losing a single disk drive on the server.

Striping

Striping improves performance by distributing data across multiple drives. RAID techniques use a variety of striping and parity techniques to achieve different levels of speed and redundancy (Swanson et al. 2002). Striping data across multiple drives is used in RAID Level 3 (see Figure 1). RAID Level 3 uses a disk controller to write data for a given file across multiple drives and then writes the parity information on a separate drive. The advantage of this technique is that it provides a high transfer rate and can automatically detect and correct errors related to data storage.

RAID Level 5 is similar to RAID Level 3, but instead of storing the parity information on a separate drive, the parity information is stored on multiple disks in the disk array (see Figure 2). This technique provides a higher level of fault tolerance and is a popular technique for data protection.

Outsourcing Backup and Recovery Functions

Many organizations are looking for ways to streamline technical processes while continuing to meet their organizational objectives. An option that is popular for some organizations is to outsource certain IT functions to a third party. This is frequently done for Web-site hosting because of the intense requirements of the Web hosting environment. Many of the requirements for backup and recovery functions can also be met with outsourcing. Foskett and Tobin (2005) describe three basic mechanisms for outsourcing backups as insourcing, online backup, and hosted backup services.

Insourcing refers to inviting a qualified vendor to manage the backup process using the resources of the organization. The benefits of this approach include maintaining physical control of the data and media and taking advantage of expertise in backup and recovery management without the overhead of having full-time operational employees. This service is available with various amounts of actual on-site support and may include some remote monitoring of the backup process.

Online backups are usually an effective choice for smaller organizations. In this scenario, the data are transferred (in an encrypted format) via telecommunications

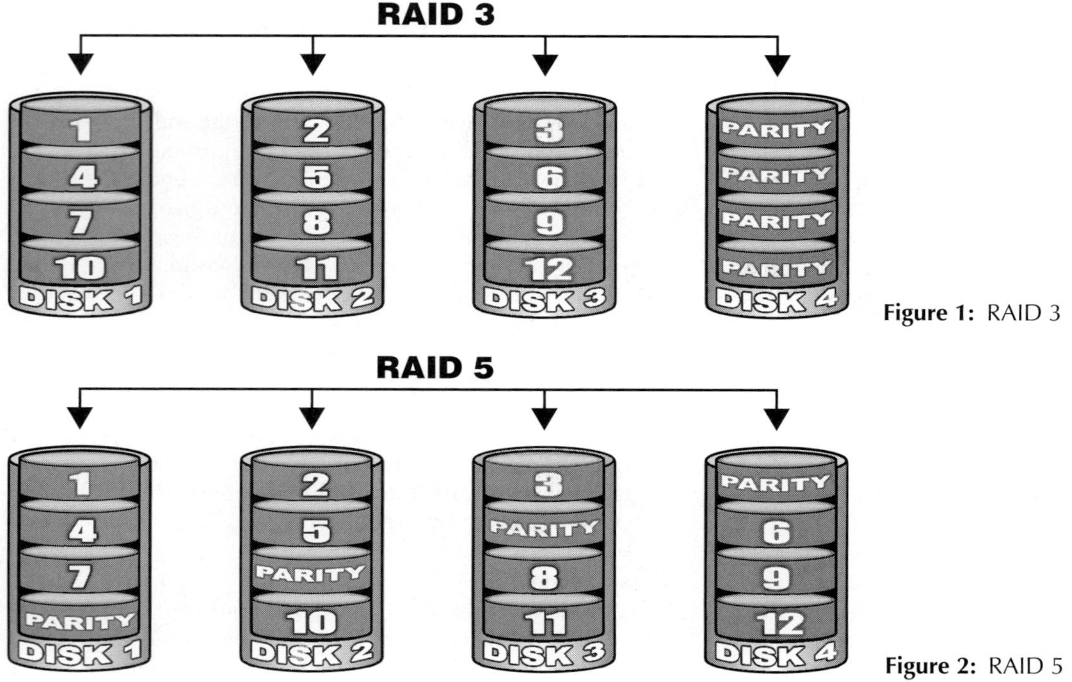

Figure 1: RAID 3

Figure 2: RAID 5

systems (usually the Internet) and stored in a remote location. This option is attractive for smaller organizations because they can take advantage of professionally managed backup services without the investment in infrastructure that might otherwise be required. The disadvantage of this option is that when the time comes to restore the data, connectivity and coordination with the service provider must be fully in place.

Hosted backup services are described as backup services for organizations in which most or all of the IT functions are already hosted by a third party. This option is easily selected when the majority of IT operations are hosted off-site because retaining this complex function in-house when the data are elsewhere is difficult to justify (Foskett and Tobin 2005).

There are variations on each of these three themes, and when an organization is considering their options, each of these should be considered. Telecommunications technology advances continue to create new options for moving data from point A to point B, and improvements in outsourcing options are likely to make these and other techniques more attractive as technology improves.

In the broader context of disaster recovery, whether an organization uses in-house employees or contracted third-party vendors for backup and recovery services, there are some services that will usually be performed by an outside company. These services include electrical contractors, water-removal specialists, tree-removal services, and data-recovery services. In documenting the backup and recovery requirements, a list of service providers and their contact information is an important part of the disaster-recovery plan (Erbschloe 2003, 169).

Snapshots

When traditional methods of backup are no longer sufficient, there are some newer technologies that may provide the necessary speed to restore large volumes of data without the expense of long backup windows. One such technology is the snapshot. A snapshot is a virtual copy of a file system that includes all the data in the given file system. The virtual copy of the file system must be backed up to recover from physical failures, but creating a snapshot of a file system will allow for a very short recovery window in many types of failures. The network data management protocol (NDMP) and Microsoft Corp.'s Volume Shadow Copy Service (VSS) are examples of products that support snapshot capabilities (Preston 2005).

NAS and SANs

During the early 1990s, organizations began adopting the client/server model of computing, in which desktop PCs were connected to file servers. This configuration allowed users to store important files on the server so that backups could be centralized and managed. The next step in storage innovation was the movement of storage devices onto specialized appliances directly attached to file servers. This network-attached storage (NAS) took advantage of the widespread availability of various protocols such as Novell's Network File System (NFS). NAS systems are normally deployed using tools and utilities supplied by the vendor (Morris and Truskowski 2003). NAS may also provide a centralized storage location from which backups can be completed.

Advancements in storage technology have resulted in a system of hardware and software components that interconnect file servers and storage systems (Zheng, Wang, and Zhang 2003). This technology is referred to as a storage area network (SAN). The interconnection may be over an existing data network or via a separate physical network, but is usually high-speed and frequently based on fiber-optic connections. SANs take advantage of multiple storage subsystems by pooling the storage area and allowing multiple file servers to use the free space available on the SAN (Sarkar et al. 2003). Although SANs are sometimes touted as sophisticated storage solutions, the sophistication may also mean complexity. Radding (2005) cites issues such as interoperability problems, latency, and a lack of robust design tools on the market as reasons for SAN adoption roadblocks. Both NAS and SAN technology are attractive for purposes of identifying backup system requirements. The fewer physical data storage devices that contain data to be backed up, the easier it is to plan for how, when, and why the data will be backed up.

Encryption

Many organizations maintain information in their computer systems that represent large investments of time, money, and effort. In addition to the value of the information, some data may be sensitive in terms of Human Resources, or competitive strategies. Most organizations protect their information systems by granting access permission to those members who need access to perform their duties and denying access to everyone else. This approach works well when the data are locked up in a secure data center with limited physical access. The authentication process can break down when the organization's valuable data are stored on removable media such as tape. The size of a tape cartridge makes it easy to carry off-site, thus protecting the organization from the risk of loss due to fire, flood, or other natural disasters. This same feature also provides an easy target for removing critical data from the organization for someone with sinister motives. In some cases, it is much easier to remove a backup tape from the company than to break into the computer system.

One of the ways that some organizations have addressed this risk is by encryption. If the data on a backup tape are encrypted, then in the event it is lost or stolen, the data will still be secure. The majority of organizations do not encrypt their backups, but a trend toward targeting backup tapes for theft is causing concern among those who are required by government regulators to protect their data (Lock 2005). Two of the methods used for encryption are encryption on the data as it resides on the system and encryption done at the time the backup is created through software or hardware. When data are encrypted on the system through database encryption or through an operating system utility, then the data will be encrypted on the tape, meeting the objective of a secure tape. This approach provides an additional layer of security during operation. A drawback of this approach is that ongoing encryption of a database or data files can be expensive in terms of CPU cycles. Some organizations do not want to encrypt their data on the system, but want to encrypt their backup tapes to reduce the risk of losing their data because of theft (Haber 2005). Encrypting the data on the tapes can be accomplished using software utilities, or hardware appliances. Many software utilities provide encryption capabilities. Third-party backup software may allow the administrator to select the type of encryption and key length among the options for encryption. This type of encryption may require significant computing resources, and it can potentially lengthen the backup and recovery time requirement. Another option is to include an encryption appliance in the system. The encryption appliance sits between the computer system and the tape drive, and encrypts (or decrypts) the data as they are passed from one device to the other. Since the data are encrypted by the appliance, fewer CPU cycles are required of the host system, speeding up the backup process.

One reason that this approach is not widely used is that administrators are concerned about the possibility of not being able to restore the encrypted data. In the event that fire destroys the data center, careful planning must be in place to make sure that encryption keys are available to restore data from backup tapes. If an external appliance is used, then provision for replacing the device and its hardware key are important to recovery. These issues add complexity to the disaster-recovery requirements and must be weighed against the risk of losing the information on backup tapes.

CONCLUSION

Many organizations rely on their data to effectively run daily operations. Because the value of data in most organizations is so high, safeguarding the information is vital to the organization's existence. One important aspect of making sure information is available to users is the backup and recovery systems that ensure data availability, even when computers or network hardware components fail. The requirements for an operational backup and recovery system are built on the foundation of a data and systems assessment. A data assessment identifies and documents various data types, the systems using the data, and other critical system elements such as the operating system and security data. Once the data that need to be protected are identified, the method for backup and recovery can be selected from numerous technologies and procedures. Choices for backup and recovery techniques include third-party solutions or internal solutions, media determination, and frequency determination. Some areas that may be overlooked include backing up network hardware configuration and data residing on desktops throughout the organization. Determining the requirements for backup and recovery systems will help mitigate the potential loss of data for many organizations relying on information to run operations.

GLOSSARY

Data Compression: Storing data in a format that takes less space than it would take under normal storage conditions.

Differential Backup: A backup procedure that copies files that have changed since the last full backup.

Encryption: The process of encoding or obscuring information so only a person (or computer) with the key can decrypt the information.

Full Backup: A backup procedure that copies every file on the system to another media or disk regardless of whether the files have changed since the previous backup.

Incremental Backup: A backup procedure that copies files that have changed since the last backup (of any kind) to another media or disk.

Job Scheduling: The IT function concerned with ensuring the efficient queuing and processing of data at a predetermined time.

Media: Data storage technologies used to store backed-up data. Media may include floppy disks, magnetic tape, Compact disk (CD), or digital versatile disk (DVD).

Parity: The characteristic of a number in which the sum of the digits is either odd or even. This characteristic is used in error checking in RAID drive configurations.

RAID: An acronym for redundant array of inexpensive (or independent) disks. These disk drives are configured to use two or more drives in combination to improve fault tolerance and performance.

Recovery-Point Objective (RPO): RPO is expressed in terms of how much data the organization can afford to lose if the system fails. For example, if backups were run each night, the recovery point objective would be the end of the previous day's activity. In this case, any data that were entered or processed between the point of failure and the most recent backup would be lost.

Recovery Time Objective (RTO): A measure of how long the organization can effectively function without the computer system.

Striping: A technique for writing data onto multiple disk drives for improved fault tolerance and performance.

Volatility: The rate of change of the values of data in a database or file.

CROSS REFERENCES

See *Business Continuity Planning*; *Business Requirements of Backup Systems*; *Evaluating Storage Media Requirements*.

REFERENCES

Barth, K. 2004, March. Better backup and recovery: Know your data and your storage. *Computer Technology Review*. www.findarticles.com/p/articles/mi_m0BRZ/is_3_24/ai_n6017379 (accessed November 15, 2005).

D'Amico, V. 2004. Ten steps for surviving a disaster! *Handbook of Business Strategy* 5(1):173–8.

Dean, T. 2006. *Network+ Guide to Networks*. 4th ed. Boston: Thompson, Course Technology.

Erbschloe, M. 2003. *Guide to disaster recovery*. Boston: Thompson, Course Technology.

Foskett S., and M. Tobin. 2005. Three ways to outsource backups. *Storage Magazine*. http://storagemagazine.techtarget.com/magItem/1,291266,sid35_gci1096485,00.html (accessed October 27, 2005).

Haber, L. 2005, September 15. Financial firm finds safety in encryption. *Internetnews.com*. www.internetnews.com/storage/article.php/3549026 (accessed October 26, 2005).

Lange, M. 2002. Document retention policies can help pare legal bills. *Financial Executive* 18(9):3–45.

Lennert, J., W. Retzner, M. Rodgers, B. Ruel, S. Sundararajan, and P. Wolfson. 2004. The automated backup solution—Safeguarding the communications network infrastructure. *Bell Labs Technical Journal* 9(2):59–84.

Lock, T. 2005, July 21. Why are you not encrypting your backup tapes? *IT-Director.com*. www.it-director.com/article.php?articleid=12816 (accessed October 25, 2005).

Marakas, G. 2006. *Systems analysis and design*. 2nd ed. Boston: McGraw-Hill Irwin.

McDowell, R. D. 2001. Computer (in)security -2: Computer system backup and recovery. *Quality Assurance Journal* 5:149–55.

Mensching, J., and G. Corbitt. 2004. ERP data archiving—critical analysis. *Journal of Enterprise Information Management* 17(2):131–41.

Morris, R. J., and B. J. Truskowski. 2003. The evolution of storage systems. *IBM Systems Journal* 42(2):205–17.

Preston, W. C. 1999. Unix Backup and Recovery. Sebastopol, CA: O'Reilly.

Preston, W. C. 2005, June. New backup strategies. *Storage Magazine*. http://storagemagazine.techtarget.com/magItem/1,291266,sid35_gci1096485,00.html (accessed October 22, 2005).

Qian, C., S. Nakamura, and T. Nakagawa. 2002. Optimal backup policies for a database system with incremental backup. *Electronics and Communications in Japan* 84(4):1–9.

Qu, Z., Y. Chen, Z. Zhang, and Y. Boon-Lock. 2004, June. Efficient data restoration for a disk-based network backup system. *Proceedings of the IEEE International Conference on Mechatronics*, 452–8. Istanbul, Turkey: IEEE Xplore.

Radding, A. 2005, February. No-sweat SAN design. *Storage Magazine*. http://storagemagazine.techtarget.com/magItem/1,291266,sid35_gci1052906,00.html (accessed October 25, 2005).

Sarkar, P., K. Voruganti, K. Meth, O. Biran, and J. Satran. 2003. Internet protocol storage area networks. *IBM Systems Journal* 42(2):218–31.

Schiesser, R. 2002. *IT systems management*. Upper Saddle River, NJ: Prentice Hall.

Stephens, D. O., and R. C. Wallace. 2000. Electronic records retention: Fourteen basic principles. *Information Management Journal* 34(4):38–47.

Stoddard, B. 2004, March. Online data backup and recovery takes hold: Outsourcing better addresses data protection. *Computer Technology Review*. www.findarticles.com/p/articles/mi_m0BRZ/is_3_24/ai_n6017377 (accessed October 30, 2005).

Swanson, M., A. Wohl, L. Pope, T. Grance, J. Hash, and R. Thomas. 2002. Contingency planning guide for information technology systems: recommendations of the National Institute of Standards and Technology. NIST Special Publication 800-34. Technology Administration, U.S. Department of Commerce. http://csrc.nist.gov/publications/nistpubs/800-34/sp800-34.pdf (accessed November 12, 2005).

Vella, K. 2005. How to go about the backup software purchase decision? Liutilities.com. www.liutilities.com/news/articles/article32 (accessed November 30, 2005).

Wells, N. 2003. Guide to Linux installation and administration. Boston: Thompson, Course Technology.

Zhen, J. 2005, June 22. 10 essentials of MSP log management. *Computer World*. www.computerworld.com/securitytopics/security/story/0,,102657,00.html (accessed November 15, 2005).

Zheng, W., F. Wang, and Y. Zhang. 2003. A new backup model based on SAN system. *The 8th International Conference on Computer Supported Cooperative Work in Design Proceedings*, 702–7. Xiamen, China: IEEE Xplore.

Business Requirements of Backup Systems

Markus Klemen, Thomas Neubauer and Edgar R. Weippl, *Vienna University of Technology, Vienna, Austria*

INTRODUCTION

As businesses across all industries grow more dependent on information technology (IT) infrastructure, high availability and backup of IT systems becomes an increasingly strategic business concern. Having the right information at the right time can be the edge to make the difference between profits and losses. But, as the complexity of the IT infrastructure grows, so do the risks. Failures can incur high costs and damage a company's reputation. Especially during unpredictable disruptions or disasters, critical system must be available to prevent the loss of competitive advantages. Therefore, high availability and backup aim at mitigating these risks to ensure continuous availability of critical systems. The mitigation of risks comprises the definition of a business continuity strategy or what traditionally has been referred to as disaster recovery. The business continuity strategy should be aligned with the corporate strategy to allow the optimal consideration of the business requirements. Business requirements generally influence the backup strategy by defining how often specific data must be backed up, how many copies of the data must be retained, or how long different types of data must be stored. The main aim of business continuity is to minimize interruptions of the business processes due to technical difficulties. For achieving these goals, comprehensive planning and commitment of resources are necessary. Typical risks of insufficient business continuity procedures and neglecting the appropriate definition of business requirements include:

- Interruption of critical business processes: Business processes allow the operationalization of the business strategy. Thus, the frictionless execution of business processes is the precondition for generating business value and competitive advantages.
- Loss of corporate data: Often as a result of insufficient security measures or poor IT—or backup—systems the loss of data may result in severe financial or reputational losses and thus in customer dissatisfaction.
- Failure to meet regulatory or legal requirements: Recent corporate financial and reporting scandals (Enron, WorldCom, ImClone) resulted in new regulations, such as SOX (Sarbanes-Oxley Act, July 30, 2002), HIPAA (Health Insurance Portability and Accountability Act of 1996, Public Law 104-19), or Basel II will require organizations to align their infrastructure with the ability of fulfilling these regulations.
- Failure to meet service-level agreement and recovery time objectives as well as recovery point objectives: This aspect includes backup and recovery guarantees and the definition of times for recovery.

As the saying "all business is local" has been made obsolete by the ongoing revolution in IT, the new challenge facing IT managers is to interconnect previously local networks into one global one. Businesses operating on a global scale no longer have off-hours at night for performing maintenance operations or for restoring backups unnoticed. Online businesses run around-the-clock. Taking all these aspects into account, what are the main concerns for IT managers when dealing with backup systems? Aside from the obvious technical aspects, the focus must be on business requirements such as legal, organizational, enterprise risk management, and security aspects, because these have a strong influence on the definition of backup and restore strategies and the way that storage resources are structured and managed.

OVERVIEW

In this section, we clarify the meaning of certain terms that are related to backups. Figure 1 is a visual overview of all these terms. This initial, simplified overview is meant to foster understanding of the subsequent definitions and explanations. Some of the terms will be covered only in this section. They are mentioned to provide a semantic context for the actual key terms and, consequently, to define the topic of this article. Moreover, the descriptions serve as a starting point for exploring the terms in more detail.

Business Continuity Management

According to the Business Continuity Institute (www.thebci.org), business continuity management (BCM)

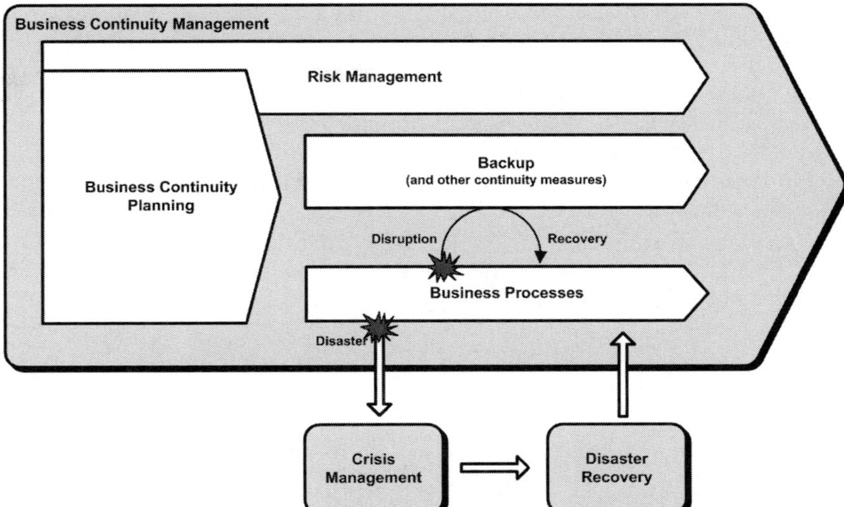

Figure 1: Overview of terms

"is a holistic management process that identifies potential impacts that threaten an organization and provides a framework for building resilience and the capability for an effective response that safeguards the interests of its key stakeholders, reputation, brand, and value creating activities. BCM must be owned and fully integrated into the organization as an embedded management process." In other words, the purpose of BCM is to guarantee that an organization can keep its business going at all times, even in cases of serious disruptions, which means that BCM is about the continuity of business processes. The most important element of BCM is business continuity planning, which is covered briefly in the following section. Management, however, certainly involves more than just planning; the plan must also be executed and involves organizing, leading, coordinating, and controlling.

Risk management is the most important management aspect of BCM. This process begins in the planning phase as risk analysis, and it accompanies every business process through to completion. A short explanation of risk management can be found in the corresponding section below; the interdependence of risk analysis and backups will be covered in more detail in conjunction with the business continuity planning process. One of BCM's major elements with regard to information systems is the backup process. Later in this chapter we will present a fairly detailed discussion of the backup function from a management point of view. Chapter 175 in this book provides a technical perspective on backups.

A very important distinction must be made between the terms *BCM, crisis management,* and *disaster recovery.* The difference lies in the gravity of a given problem. If a business process is affected by a disturbance that was detected in advance and thus earmarked as a potential threat during the risk analysis process of the planning phase, it is regarded as a mere disruption and can be treated and neutralized within the boundaries of the BCM process, since appropriate countermeasures would have been developed and prepared; thus, recovery is relatively easy to achieve. This holds true even in cases in which the disturbance would usually be considered a disaster by common standards.

In contrast, if a business process is affected by a disturbance that was not detected in the course of the risk analysis or, although aware of the threat, no precautions were taken for some reason (e.g., costs), the incident has to be regarded as a disaster for the organization, even if it would not be considered a disaster by common standards. In this case, the required reaction is no longer a matter concerning BCM. Instead, the BCM sphere is exited, and the first step is to conduct crisis management in order to survive the disaster or mitigate its effects. As soon as the situation is stabilized, the disaster recovery procedure is initiated for the purpose of returning to business as usual and moving back into the BCM sphere. These two topics, crisis management and disaster recovery, will be covered briefly at the end of this overview section.

Business Continuity Planning

Business continuity planning (BCP) is a process that intends to set the stage for a reduction of a company's business risks resulting from disruptions of major IT system functions or operations. As already stated, it is the main element of the BCM process. The BCP process usually consists of the following planning steps, which will be covered in more detail later in this chapter:

1. Initiation
2. Business impact analysis
3. Development of a business continuity plan
4. Training and awareness program
5. Implementing and testing the plan
6. Monitoring and improving procedures

Risk Management

Risk management (RM) is a generic concept that can be applied in quite different contexts, such as, enterprise RM or project RM (see Peltier [2001] for a more detailed description). The basic idea of RM is to deal with the given risks in a planned and controlled manner. Therefore, a systematic approach should be pursued, which commonly includes the following steps:

1. Establishing the context: This step defines the scope and the focus of RM. These goals should reflect the business requirements for the continuity and information security of the main business functions relevant for information security.
2. Risk identification: This is the process of identifying risks regarding the most critical business processes. Typical reasons for failure include sabotage, terrorism, fire, accidents, IT failure, and power loss.
3. Risk analysis (RA): This is the process determining how often the identified risks occur and estimating the magnitude of their likely consequences.
4. Risk evaluation: This is the process of determining priorities by comparing the identified level of risk against target risk levels or predetermined standards.
5. Risk treatment: According to Peltier (2001) risk can be treated in the following four ways: (a) Risk can be transferred to another party, typically by contracting insurance. (b) Risk can be avoided, which means that the probability that an unwanted incident occurs is systematically reduced. (c) The negative effect of an unwanted incident can be mitigated in advance. (d) The risk can be accepted without special precautions.

Risk analysis will be discussed in more detail in this chapter, as part of the "Business Impact Analysis" phase in the section on "Business Continuity Planning."

Backup

In the context of computer engineering, the term *backup* usually refers to data backup, which means copying data in order to have an additional instance of the original source. Backups are typically stored at a physical distance from operational data to protect them against events that destroy operational data. If the backup is done properly, loss of or damage to the original data can be neutralized or at least mitigated by copying back the data from the backup medium. The latter process is known as data recovery, or data restoring. The data in question can either be data as such (text, image, or audio files, etc.) or stored program code. In both cases, the backup and recovery processes work the same way. The difference between a backup and an archive is that archiving data usually does not involve duplication, whereas backup does.

Of course, the general term *backup* can have a much broader meaning than described above. In all kinds of organizations, it is possible (and reasonable) to back up not only data but also other resources. For example, it is quite common to have backup hardware for critical parts of the system. Likewise, there can be backup provisions for especially important infrastructure elements, such as extra data transmission lines, power supply from an alternate substation, or emergency power supply. Apart from physical backups, it is also wise to define backups of organizational elements. Replacement policies within the staff are fairly common, for instance. Job rotation and mandatory vacation policies not only help to detect fraud but also enable employees to replace each other. It is also conceivable to set up alternative processes for certain essential business functions in order to compensate for a temporary failure of the primary processes caused by extraordinary external influences. In the case of a rather unstable procurement situation, the availability of proper backup providers for important externally purchased services must be granted.

However, in most cases *backup* refers to data backup, whereas its wider meaning is covered by the expressions "business continuity management" and "business continuity planning." Because *backup* refers to data backup in this chapter, the rest of this section will give an overview of the characteristics of data backup (for further reading see Bishop [2002]).

Guidelines for Backup

A thoroughly established backup strategy is more than just arbitrarily copying data from time to time. It takes careful planning and adherence to certain guidelines focusing on the following aspects:

- The responsibility to perform backups must be clearly assigned by defining an organizational role.
- Backups must be carried out on a regular basis. To fulfill this requirement, backups should be automated (e.g., within a networked storage infrastructure) in order to require only minimal human intervention. Storage area networks (SANs) are replacing direct attached storage (DAS) because they allow the centralization of the storage systems and provide a higher security level. Furthermore, the regular verification of the backups must be ensured.
- The backup medium should be kept at a different location from the original data. This secondary location should be as safe and as secure as the primary location. If removable media are used for backups, the availability of the corresponding drives has to be guaranteed. Therefore, data backup may demand hardware backup as well.
- Backup media have to be tested at regular intervals to ensure that they are still readable. When the life cycle of the technology used is about to reach its end, the data should be transferred to a different medium. Further note that backups should use well-established standard formats.
- The users of the system should be made aware of all relevant parameters of the backup process. In particular, they should know how to request the recovery of lost data.

Apart from these minimum requirements, there are also other guidelines that should be followed to further improve the quality of the backup function. These measures might cause higher initial costs, but most could save a lot of time and money in the case of a more serious disruption:

- The procedure of performing a backup should be defined as simply as possible.

- Carrying out a backup run should be possible without interrupting normal day-to-day business.
- For each piece of data, at least two copies should be made. These copies should be stored on different media and kept at different locations. An effective backup rotation scheme should be applied, which means keeping backup images of several points in time of the recent past and gradually fewer of the older states.
- The backup should have a certain degree of deliberate redundancy, such as checksums or hashes, in order to facilitate the validation of the copy's integrity without needing the original data.
- Different kinds of data usually have different update frequencies and should consequently have different backup frequencies as well. If a backup is distributed over multiple volumes, recovery should not need all volumes to be readable or present.

Data Recovery

The term *data recovery* refers to the process of restoring data from a backup medium in case the original source of data has been damaged or destroyed. Data recovery is not the same as data salvaging. The latter refers to the process of rescuing data directly from a damaged or destroyed storage medium. Every backup without an appropriate recovery strategy is practically useless. For example, if the software that is needed to read and restore the backup data is destroyed along with the original data, the copy is rendered worthless.

In principle, there are two scenarios in which data recovery might be necessary. First, in the more grave one, a complete data carrier, or a considerable part of it, is damaged or destroyed. Here, the backup usually has to be restored in order to bring the system back to an operational state. Examples would be the loss of a hard disk or the file system getting corrupted so badly it can no longer be read. The second scenario, which is sometimes overlooked, although it is more common, is the need to recover a single file, directory or data set, lost by accidental deletion or corrupted by a program.

Scope for Decisions

In contrast to the guidelines above, which we suggest applying in all cases, there are some important decisions about backup for which no general recommendations can be made. They simply depend on the situation and various environmental parameters. Two of the most relevant aspects involving more than cost alone will be presented in this section. The first is which type of media to use as backup data carrier. The possibilities are subject to change over time. In the late 1980s and the 1990s, floppy disks and magnetic tape were common. Nowadays, hard disks and optical disks serve as backup media. In areas (e.g. the health sector, digital libraries) for which terabytes and even petabytes must be saved, newer generations of tapes (such as digital linear tape [DLT] and linear tape-open [LTO]) are still one of the most reliable solutions. With widespread broadband network access, a new trend emerges: remote backup, also referred to as online backup or Internet-based backup. In this case, the customer of the backup service does not know the actual type of storage media used.

The most appropriate medium depends on certain criteria. First of all, the price per gigabyte is a crucial aspect. Second, the specific technical properties of the medium, such as speed, reliability, and ease of use must be considered. In the past a considerable disadvantage of magnetic tape was that it could be read only sequentially. Nowadays magnetic tape provides structures that allow fast recovery of single files. Also of particular relevance is whether a medium can be written on only once or many times. The advantage of a rewritable data carrier is that it can be reused, which saves costs and facilitates the implementation of a proper rotation scheme. On the other hand, a write-once medium is better from a security perspective or when revision-proof archiving is needed, as the data cannot be manipulated later. Third, durability is an important issue, because with new storage technologies one has to be aware that the life expectancy of the medium can only be estimated and is far from certain. Conventional magneto-optical WORM (write-once, read-many) disks guarantee readability for up to 40 years, but they are slow compared with magnetic tapes and several times more expensive. As previously stated, backups must be recopied to new types of storage media to avoid obsolete technology.

Another important decision concerns whether or not to compress backup data. From the technical point of view it would be better not to compress the data, as uncompressed data can be recovered more easily in case of damage or corruption of the backup media. Considering the cost aspect and the increasing data volume, on the other hand, compression makes sense. Still, this decision is not just a matter of cost. It should be considered in connection with the possible encryption of the backup data for security reasons, as this would also be some kind of manipulation to the data. So, if the data need to be encrypted, it can also be compressed since today's block ciphers usually operate in cipher block chaining (CBC) mode. The encryption of sensitive data should be an integral part of the security strategy, because the backup tape is a mirror of the server's contents. The chronological order of encrypting and compressing is important, as compression algorithms are not working effectively on encrypted data. In addition, key management should match the corporate business processes—for example, to grant that the keys expire when data expire. However, the total cost of encryption must be compared to potential risks and the likelihood of a security breach to determine the cost-benefit ratio of encrypting backups. In addition, decision makers have to consider that it can take longer to complete an encrypted backup than a comparable nonencrypted backup. The time needed for encryption depends on the type of data, the encryption algorithms, and the type of encryption software or hardware as well as the underlying infrastructure such as disks, tapes, or processors. Today, many vendors of tape backups provide built-in encryption capabilities in their products. This solution has additional overhead, and key management is very basic. The latest storage encryption methods use hardware-accelerated appliances that are located in the SAN. They offer very good performance but have higher costs than other solutions.

The secret keys of the appliances can be stored on a set of smartcards that can be distributed to selected people. Encrypted data can be deleted by destroying selected encryption keys.

Best Practices for High Availability

Along with the gradually expanding availability requirements of today's businesses, making backups is increasingly tricky. It is obvious that any kind of maintenance work, including backup, can be performed more easily if the corresponding business process is regularly halted for a certain amount of time, such as over the weekend. With the need for 24/7 availability, this so-called batch or backup window is no longer available. However, there are some techniques that help in carrying out backups even within a very small or (for the system as a whole) practically nonexistent time frame:

- *Partitioning* the source data, for example a large database, makes it possible to back up only a small part, an individual partition, of the source data at a time, thus providing increased operational flexibility.
- *Incremental backup* is a technique in which only changes of the data via a certain base copy, the so-called deltas, are stored. Consequently, the elapsed time to complete a backup or recovery operation can be reduced in comparison to full backup.
- *Parallel processing* is a divide-and-conquer approach, in which backup is performed for multiple partitions of the source data at the same time. Naturally, for this technique, multiple data carriers need to be available in parallel, which usually means multiple drives of some kind. The advantage of parallel processing is an increased bandwidth of the backup (and restore) activity.
- *Concurrent backup* is a technology offered by most database vendors that allows backup even of data structures that are still online and in use. Consequently, no business process has to be interrupted, which leads to extended availability.

BUSINESS CONTINUITY PLANNING

This section describes the steps of the BCP process in detail (see Figure 2) and focuses on the business impact analysis as the most important element of the BCP process. Although the last three steps of the process are to be executed after the plan has been developed, their realization still needs to be planned beforehand, which is why they are covered as part of the planning process. Analyzing business processes and the impact of nonavailable data is of paramount importance to implement a backup scheme that efficiently supports business objectives.

Initiation

First, the BCP project has to be initiated. Although it might appear somewhat trivial at first, this phase is very important. The following points must be considered when launching the project:

- Support and involvement of the organization's senior management and board have to be obtained and confirmed.
- Senior staff support, especially from key business and technical stakeholders, has to be obtained and confirmed.
- The BCP project team has to be formed. There should be representatives from all critical business functions, such as human resources, accounting, IT, etc.
- Objectives and constraints of the project need to be defined and transformed into a roadmap with strategic milestones.
- A draft version of the overall business continuity policy has to be defined and communicated to the project staff.

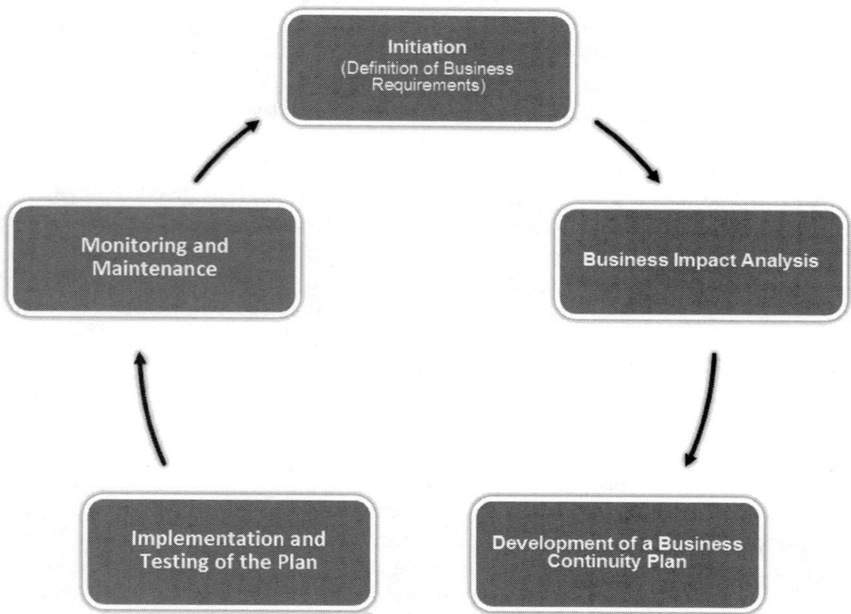

Figure 2: Business continuity planning life cycle

Business Impact Analysis

Business impact analysis (BIA) comprises the assessment of each of the business requirements and their ranking according to their importance to the company. A typical business impact analysis will consist of the steps defined in the following sections. The BIA measures the severity of the impact on the company according to multiple objectives such as operating costs, regulatory fines, and financial losses or loss of reputation if certain business functions become unavailable.

Prior to implementing any backup solution, to ensure continuity a business case study must be made. Since simply backing up data cannot guarantee recovery of critical data, many additional measures have to be considered, such as testing of backups, establishing alternative processing sites, and security policies for offsite storage of backups. Moreover, one has to make sure that only truly necessary data are backed up. Storing and recovering unnecessary data adds additional costs and time for recovery.

Business Process Analysis

In this step, all business processes must be identified and then ranked according to how critical they are. Knowing how crucial processes are is important for determining the most appropriate backup scenario. For accurately categorizing the business processes the following questions should be considered:

- Are the processes main contributors to revenue?
- What is the relationship between length of interruption of processes and consequences (loss of customers, loss of revenue, loss of reputation)?
- Do the processes deal with sensitive data?
- Are the processes related to safety or health of people (nuclear power plant maintenance, traffic control systems)?
- Which legal requirements (SAS 70 [Statement on Auditing Standards No. 70: Service Organizations], SOX) must be considered?

IT Infrastructure Mapping

In the penultimate step, the relationship between business processes and IT infrastructure must be established. Therefore the following question must be considered:

- Which systems are necessary to execute certain core processes?
- Which systems can go offline without interrupting normal business process operations?

This is the most important and most underappreciated step. In many cases, system functions that are not deemed critical may still have a negative influence on critical systems in cases of system interruption. The most appropriate safeguard to alleviate this is an identical test system, which can be used to simulate various failures. Still, most test systems—especially in smaller companies—are not completely identical, because of cost restrictions. Therefore, the analysis of system interdependencies is crucial to ensure that business continuity scenarios are consistent with reality. The identified systems may be classified using the following framework shown in Table 1.

Risk Analysis

In companies that depend heavily on IT systems, attaining security attributes (confidentiality, integrity, and availability) is a major goal of management. For example,

Table 1: Analysis of System Interdependencies

Classification	Description
Nonsensitive	Even when interrupted for a prolonged time span or when done manually, the business impact is minimal. Resuming requires little or no catching up.
	Examples: very small companies, typical office application that can easily be relocated to other workstations
Sensitive	These functions can be done manually and for an extended period, though at considerably higher costs than normal operations. Additional staff may be required.
	Examples: mass mailings, computer-supported accounting for smaller companies
Vital	For a brief period, these services can be done manually. Usually, if operations are restored within a timeframe of up to 7 days, the costs are still within reasonable limits and much lower than for critical systems.
	Examples: access to central file servers, e-mail, or other resources
Critical	These services cannot be done manually and require virtually identical infrastructure capabilities. Tolerance to interruptions is low, cost of interruption is high.
	Examples: accounting systems of financial institutions, databases or Web servers of large Web stores

a hacker who attacks and crashes a server reduces the availability of this server. If there is no appropriate recovery procedure, the server crash will have a major impact on the department's or even the entire company's efficiency. The loss caused by the resulting failure of a business process that requires the crashed server will affect the decision whether to buy a backup system or to implement mirror processing at a remote site. However, if the server is used for noncritical tasks and the business process can also be performed manually at a tolerable cost, expensive recovery mechanisms make little sense. In this case, the cost of implementing a backup system may exceed the potential benefits resulting from minimizing loss.

Therefore, the process of risk analysis must focus on identifying risks that negatively affect the execution of critical and strategic business processes. A company must develop a clear understanding of potential threats causing business process interruptions and their ramifications. Risks need to be sorted by impact and likelihood, and must also be categorized (see Neubauer, Stummer, and Weippl [2006] for a description of workshop-based risk analysis). The following risk categories must be considered in the process of risk analysis (Peltier 2001):

- External factors: The interactions with clients, business partners, and environment are referred to as external factors. This also includes criminal activities—for example, by hackers—as well as services and deliveries provided by external partners.
- People: The entire staff—from top management to the operational level—that are needed for the execution of the corporate business processes.
- Systems: This area comprises the entire technical infrastructure—with a special focus on IT and telecommunications—needed for the optimal execution of the critical business processes.

There are various approaches for efficiently performing a risk analysis. Basically, all of these approaches can be divided into qualitative and quantitative approaches.

Qualitative Risk Analysis

Qualitative risk analysis uses relative values for evaluating potential threats. Methods such as questionnaires, checklists, and workshops with experts from different departments of the organization are commonly used. Therefore, this method strongly relies on people's experience, opinions, and intuitions. The advantage of qualitative risk analysis is that it is easier to reach consensus as compared with quantitative methods. Thus, results are available sooner and at lower cost. The drawback of qualitative methods is that the relative values are not applicable for (for example) conducting an accurate cost-benefit analysis. Commonly used techniques are the following:

The Delphi technique—The Delphi technique (Gupta and Clarke 1996) is used for eliciting information and judgments from a small group of participants and achieving consensus among these experts. This method is often used when there are insufficient or unreliable data. The objective of this method is to isolate the inputs of each expert to prevent the influence of rank or of strong personalities. Therefore, there is no direct communication between the team members, and the participants do not sit together in a meeting. Instead, information is exchanged via mail, fax, or e-mail. The facilitator coordinates the whole process and provides support to the team members. The facilitator defines the issue and prepares and sends the first questionnaire to the participants. Each participant returns his or her ideas and thoughts to the facilitator, who compiles the ideas and sends a second questionnaire. The process continues until no new ideas emerge and all strengths, weaknesses, and opinions have been identified and discussed.

Risk (rating) matrix—The risk matrix is a table that shows the relationship between likelihood, impact, and level of risk. As stated before, the level of risk comprises the combination of the impact and the likelihood of the threat occurring. The matrix contains a description of the risk, a unique ID for each risk, a likelihood of occurrence, an impact, and the risk that is the product of likelihood and impact. Therefore, levels of risk can be determined by using a risk matrix. To categorize likelihood, impact, and levels of risk, the National Institute of Standards and Technology (NIST) uses three terms (low, medium, and high). NZ(AS/NZS 4360, 1999, 2004) uses five levels of categorizing likelihood (almost certain, likely, possible, unlikely, and rare/almost never), five levels of impact (catastrophic, major, severe, moderate, and minor), and four levels of risk (low, medium, high, and critical). The risk levels are prioritized in order of magnitude from low to high.

Threat Trees

Threat (or attack) trees (see Figure 3) provide a formal, methodical way of describing the security of systems, based on different attacks (Schneier 2000); the potential threats to a system are described in a tree structure. The root node of the tree shows the goal of the attack, whereas leaves describe different ways of achieving the goal. These nodes can be defined as OR nodes for describing alternatives or AND nodes for representing a state in which it is necessary to fulfill more than one subgoal in order to achieve the goal. An attack path is a route from a leaf to the root, taking AND nodes (and their subtrees) into account (Swiderski and Snyder 2004).

Quantitative Risk Analysis. The goal of quantitative approaches is to calculate numeric values for all assets and potential threats. Therefore, two fundamental key figures are used: First, the *probability* of the occurrence of an event and, second, the *impact* of its occurrence.

For all identified threats, corporate decision makers have to assign reasonable values to both categories. Moreover, they have to valuate the assets at risk. There are many ways to estimate the value of an asset, such as profit loss due to lost productivity or reputation, or cost to recover. The drawbacks of this approach are, on the one hand, that the so-called accuracy of the calculation hides the fact that the numbers are based solely on imprecise estimates.

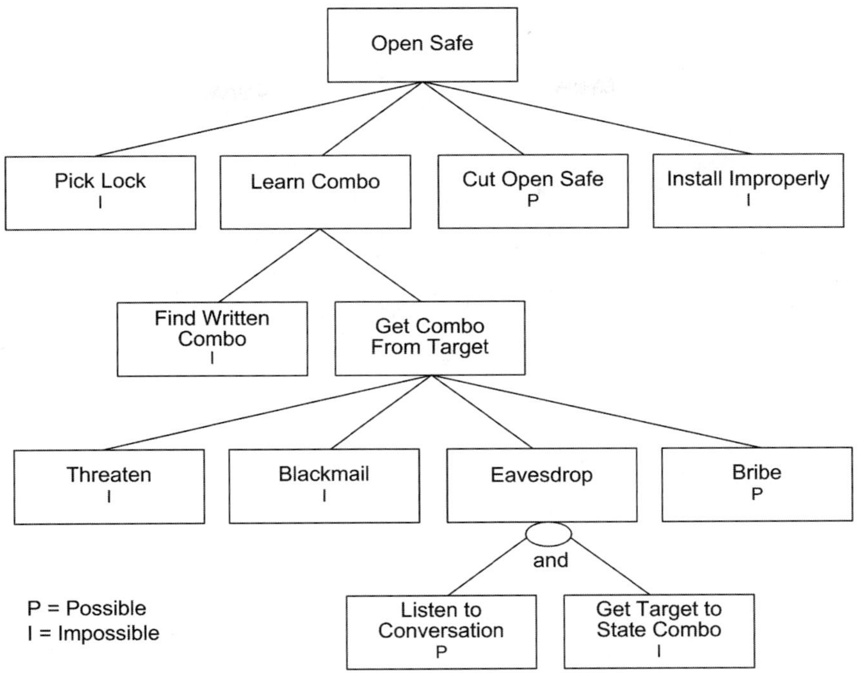

Figure 3: Example of an attack tree (Schneier 2000)

To partly overcome this weakness, historical data can be used, if available. On the other hand, the use of quantitative approaches can be very costly, involve many stakeholders, and take a long time. Nevertheless, the use of concrete numbers allows the objective comparison of results, and thus serves as a basis for a cost-benefit analysis. Quantitative risk analysis is essential for decision making and must be based on financial figures. Examples for methods of quantitative risk analysis are the following:

Annual loss expectancy—Annual loss expectancy (ALE) (Federal Information Processing Standard 1979) is a method for calculating a company's potential losses caused by security breaches. Loss values are compared to the investments needed for their mitigation. ALE is calculated by multiplying the expected loss of an event with its rate of occurrence. The single loss expectancy (SLE) is the monetary value that is lost if the risk occurs once. This value includes the costs for fixing or replacing the asset, and, in addition, the wages for the person fixing the problem and for the employees who are unable to work during this time. Beside the impact of a security breach, the likelihood of a risk occurring within a year—the annualized rate of occurrence (ARO)—must be determined.

For example, a Web server hosting an e-commerce site that generates revenue of $ 20,000/hour is down for 3 hours because of an attack by a hacker. (We assume that buyers do not return for the intended purchase if the site is not available, and that their choice of where to shop the next time is not influenced.) We assume that the rate of such an event is 0.5 (i.e., once in 2 years) and the costs for replacing the server are $5,000. So, the SLE of the risk is $65,000. ALE is calculated using this formula: ALE = SLE ARO. Thus, the ALE for the example with the Web server would be $32,500. Based on this value, decision makers can determine whether it is beneficial in terms of monetary value to purchase (for example) a firewall for protecting the Web server.

Extended ALE approaches—In addition to the typical problems of quantitative approaches, a major drawback of ALE is its combination of impact and rate of occurrence into a single number. That makes it impossible to distinguish between events with high frequency and low impact and events with low frequency and high impact. Hoo (2000) uses an approach based on ALE to calculate the benefits of additional investments in security safeguards.

Multiobjective portfolio selection—Traditionally, security safeguards are evaluated through a single (aggregated) criterion, such as return on investment. These approaches may no longer be sufficient as economic and legal requirements force top management to consider security issues in a more differentiated way. Most real-life issues have multiple risks and uncertainties; multiple objectives need to be achieved, although they are often mutually exclusive, such as minimizing costs while enhancing protection. In addition, different and changing preferences of several stakeholders must be taken into account. Existing approaches stem from Guan et al. (2003), who apply methods from multicriteria decision support to risk management. Gupta and Clarke (1996) propose a decision-support approach based on a genetic algorithm for security portfolio selection; Strauss and Stummer (2002) introduce a

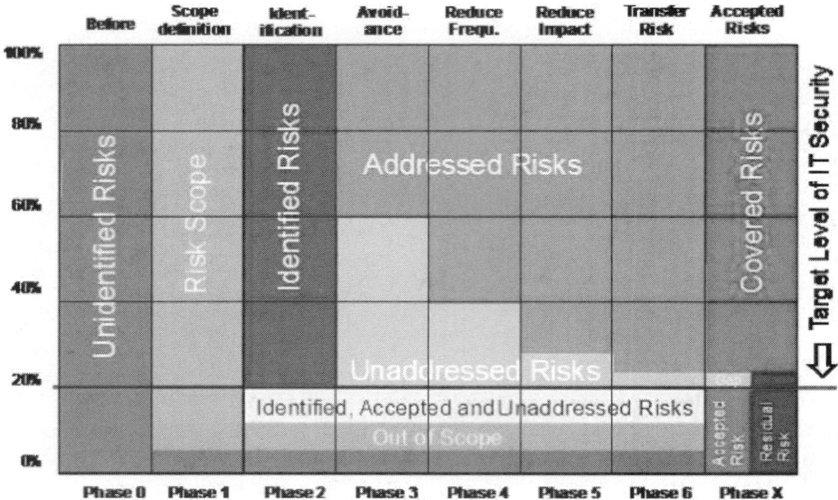

Figure 4: Multistep approach to addressing risks

two-step interactive multiobjective decision support approach for selecting portfolios of measures in IT risk management. Their approach interactively assists IT managers in reducing a given risk by evaluating and selecting pareto-optimal (an allocation in which there is no feasible reallocation that would be strictly preferred by all agents [http://en.wikipedia.org/wiki/Pareto_efficiency]) portfolios of security measures. This approach is extended in Neubauer et al. (2006) by defining a workshop environment for the multiobjective selection of security safeguards.

Risk Evaluation

Once all risks have been identified, they need to be addressed in a step-by-step process. Figure 4 shows an iterative approach for addressing risks that comprise the following steps:

1. **Scope definition:** First, the scope of the risk analysis must be established. Some major catastrophic events, such as nuclear fallout or a hit from a meteor, might be considered out of scope and therefore discarded.
2. **Identification:** In the next step, a list of potential risks is created. Popular methods are questionnaires, interviews, and workshops.
3. **Avoidance:** Some risks might simply be avoided. This might reduce or limit business to a certain degree, but usually does not generate any additional costs.
4. **Reducing frequency:** In IT, reducing the frequency of major risks usually implies improving the hardware equipment by investing in redundancy or high-availability (HA) systems.
5. **Reducing impact:** In the case of business continuity planning, backup procedures are the most common way to reduce the impact of all kinds of risks resulting in data loss.
6. **Transferring risks:** Typically, risks that cannot be avoided or reduced are mitigated by contracting the appropriate insurance.
7. **Accepting risks:** In some cases, all available options to avoid, reduce, or mitigate a risk might be unacceptably expensive. In these cases, the risks are accepted, though not covered.

Development of a Business Continuity Plan

By correlating the business requirements with the current IT infrastructure and combining it with the results of the risk analysis, a first outline of the business continuity plan becomes apparent. The plan has to be elaborated in more detail by developing policies and procedures for each of the critical business functions. In the first step, the preferred business continuity service levels must be defined for every important business process. This measure includes establishing profiles for continuity and recovery. The recovery objectives must be quantified in terms of recovery time objectives (RTOs) and recovery point objectives (RPOs). RTOs define the time it takes to restore the business function to an operational level. RPOs define the specific point in time to which the data need to be restored in order to effect a successful recovery. A more detailed discussion of recovery objectives can be found below.

The second step includes the development of possible continuity approaches for each threat, according to the continuity service levels set before. The threats are those that have been identified in the course of the business impact analysis. Now, the available approaches must be evaluated in terms of time, cost, and benefits. After the best approach for each threat has been determined, corresponding continuity procedures can be worked out in detail. In principle, the plan comprises the entire collection of policies and procedures.

Recovery Objectives

A major step when designing and implementing backup systems is the identification of various recovery strategies and available alternatives for recovering from an interruption. The selection of the appropriate strategy is based on the business impact analysis and criticality analysis. There are two metrics that help identify and determine the recovery strategies; the recovery point objective (RPO) and the recovery time objective (RTO). The RPO is determined based on the acceptable data loss in case of disruption of operations. It indicates the earliest point in time at which it is acceptable to recover the data. For example, if losing the data up to 12 hours prior to the disruption can be afforded, then a backup no older than 12 hours must be available. The transactions between the RPO and the interruption need to be entered manually after recovery or may be omitted entirely. Moreover, the RPO clearly quantifies the amount of accepted data loss in case of interruption.

Unlike RPO, the RTO is based on the acceptable down time in case of a disruption of operations. This value indicates the latest point in time at which the business operations must be resumed after an interruption. However, both metrics are based on time parameters. The lower the time requirements, the higher the cost of recovery strategies,; for example, if the RPO is a matter of minutes, then data mirroring or duplexing should be implemented as the recovery strategy. If the RTO is less, then an alternative site might be preferred over a hot site[1] contract. The lower the RTO, the lower the interruption tolerance. Interruption tolerance is the time gap within which the business can accept nonavailability of IT facilities.

In order to ensure an effective recovery, a recovery strategy should be established by the organization. A recovery strategy combines preventive, detective, and corrective measures. The main actions are as follows:

- Remove all possible threats
- Minimize the likelihood of occurrence
- Minimize the effect of occurrence

Removing threats and minimizing the risk of occurrence can be addressed through implementing physical and environmental security measures. Minimizing the effect can be achieved by implementing built-in resilience through alternative routing and redundancy. In the first step of creating a recovery strategy, prospective resilience mechanisms should be evaluated by taking built-in solutions into account. The future disruption recovery procedure will address the restoration of affected facilities that are obviously not covered by resilience concepts but are identified as significant for business functionality by senior management.

The recovery strategy identifies and describes the best ways to recover a system in case of interruption or failure. It can be seen as a guidance document that includes detailed recovery procedures that can be used in different strategies, including alternatives. The alternatives should be documented and presented to senior management. Finally, it is a management responsibility to identify the most appropriate strategy from the alternatives provided. The selected strategy should be used to further develop the detailed business continuity plan. When senior management decides which alternative to identify, the selection of the strategy depends on the following four criteria:

- Criticality of the business process and the corresponding application
- Cost of the recovery solution
- Time required to recover the service
- Security considerations when compromising the established security architecture by implementing new systems

Of course, there will be various strategies for recovering critical information resources. However, the appropriate strategy is the one with a reasonable cost for an acceptable recovery time as compared with the impact and the likelihood of occurrence as determined in the business impact analysis. The cost factors also have an impact on senior management's decision. The cost of recovery is the cost of preparing for possible disruptions (e.g., purchasing, maintaining, and testing all duplicate and redundant facilities and systems), as well as the cost of putting these into use in the event of a disruption. The latter costs can often be insured against, but the former generally cannot. The premiums for disaster insurance will usually be lower for an organization with an appropriate plan.

Every platform that runs and supports a business-critical application (i.e., one that is required for a critical business process or function) will need a documented and approved recovery strategy. Strategies would need to be developed for facilities such as the following:

- Hot site
- Warm site
- Cold site
- Duplicate site
- Mobile site

Training and Awareness Program

In order for a business continuity plan (BC plan) to work effectively in an organization, staff must receive the appropriate instructions. Consequently, thoroughly planning and realizing a training and awareness program for business continuity is an imperative step in the process. However, the inspiration of a continuity culture within the organization is not without obstacles, as organizational priorities of day-to-day business usually appear more important to the employees. It is therefore fairly difficult to maintain a high level of awareness if no major business disruptions occur. Therefore, BCP exercises need to be conducted on a regular basis in order to establish this issue as a high organizational priority. Another means to

[1] "A hot site is a commercial disaster recovery service that allows a business to continue computer and network operations in the event of a computer or equipment disaster. For example, if an enterprise's data processing center becomes inoperable, that enterprise can move all data processing operations to a hot site. A hot site has all the equipment needed for the enterprise to continue operation, including office space and furniture, telephone jacks, and computer equipment." Verbatim quote from http://searchcio.techtarget.com/sDefinition/0,290660,sid19_gci557324,00.html.

raise awareness is the frequent involvement of employees in periodic review and evaluation of the policies and procedures of the BC plan. One might even try to inspire people to transfer the basic ideas of BCP to their personal lives, thus stimulating intrinsic interest in the subject.

Implementing and Testing the Plan

Unlike newly developed software, in the case of BCP, it is not feasible to set up a complete test environment, as this would mean duplicating the entire organization. Therefore, before testing, the plan needs to be implemented, at least in some small sector of the organization. The easiest way to implement the plan, from the point of view of the BCP responsible, is to distribute the BC plan to all department managers and then hold them responsible for its realization in their particular areas of competence. Of course, proper support must be provided along with this measure.

After implementation, the plan must be tested. Since acceptance criteria are basically defined by the required service levels of the BC plan, formulation of a matching test schedule with major testing milestones is all that is necessary. Basically, testing the BC plan involves simulating possible disruptions and documenting the results of the corresponding continuity measures. Finally, the test run has to be evaluated; this is the next step in the process.

Monitoring and Improving the Procedures

Every plan should be reviewed from time to time. Naturally, the same is true for a BC plan. The first occasion for reviewing the BC plan is the initial test run. Depending on the acquired results, necessary improvements to the plan should be carried out and communicated to the employees. After this first review, an iterative monitoring-and-improving cycle must be set up as a permanent facility. This way, changes in the contexts or properties of the critical business processes, which can very well be anticipated in today's dynamic world, can be detected in due time, making it possible to formulate appropriate changes to the BC plan before a disruption. In addition, there are certain occasions when special reviews of the plan are highly recommended: following a BCP exercise by the regular staff training program and, even more, after a real disruption or disaster.

CONCLUSION

The general public may see backup of data as the solution to availability requirements. There is, however, no business requirement for backups—it is the successful recovery of business-relevant data after disruptions that should interest management. Preparing for complex recovery procedures adds considerable costs to the operation of the IT infrastructure. It is therefore essential to apply due diligence in the planning process in order to identify critical data and critical systems, as well as to estimate acceptable RPOs and RTOs. The planning has to start with the business strategy that serves as the basis for defining the business requirements of the backup strategy. For defining business requirements decision makers have to focus on business processes, regulatory and legal requirements, or service-level agreements. This chapter defines the major parts of business continuity management and describes the process of business continuity planning as an integral part of business continuity management in detail.

GLOSSARY

Business Continuity Management (BCM): The purpose of BCM is to guarantee that an organization can keep its business going even in cases of serious disruptions.

Business Continuity Planning (BCP): BCP is a process that intends to set the stage for lowering a company's business risks resulting from disruptions of major IT system functions or operations. It is the main element of the BCM process.

Risk Management (RM): The most important management aspect of BCM is risk management. The basic idea of RM is to deal with the given risks in a planned and controlled manner.

Recovery Point Objective (RPO): The earliest point in time at which it is acceptable to recover the data.

Recovery Time Objective (RTO): This value indicates the latest point in time at which the business operations must be resumed after an interruption.

CROSS REFERENCES

See *Backup and Recovery System Requirements*; *Business Continuity Planning*; *Evaluating Storage Media Requirements*.

REFERENCES

AS/NZS 4360. 1999. AS/NZS 4360:1999: Risk management. April 1999.

AS/NZS 4360. 2004. Risk management, OB-007. August 2004, 3rd ed.

Federal Information Processing Standard (FIPS). 1979. *Guideline for automatic data processing risk analysis* (withdrawn in 1995). Gaithersburg, MD: National Institute of Standards and Technology.

Guan, B.-C., C.-C. Lo, W. Ping, J.-S. Hwang. 2003. Evaluation of information security related risk of an organization: The application of the MCDM method. *Proceedings IEEE 37th Annual 2003 International Carnahan Conference,* pp. 168–175.

Gupta, U. G., and R. E. Clarke. 1996. Theory and applications of the Delphi technique: A bibliography (1975–1994). *Technological Forecasting and Social Change* 53(2):185–211.

Hoo, K. J. S. 2000. How much is enough? A risk-management approach to computer security. Working Paper. Stanford, CA: Consortium for Research on Information Security and Policy (CRISP). http://iis-db.stanford.edu/pubs/11900/soohoo.pdf

Neubauer, T., C. Stummer, and E. Weippl. 2006. Workshop-based multiobjective security safeguard selection. In *Proceedings of the First International Conference on Availability, Reliability and Security ARES 2006*. IEEE CS.

Peltier, T. R. 2001. *Information security risk analysis*. Boca Raton, FL: Auerbach.

Schneier, B. 2000. *Secrets and lies: Digital security in a networked world*. New York: Wiley.

Strauss, C., and C. Stummer. 2002. Multiobjective decision support in it-risk management. *International Journal of Information Technology & Decision Making* 1(2):251–68.

Swiderski, F., and W. Snyder. 2004. *Threat modeling*. Redmond, WA: Microsoft Press.

FURTHER READING

Bishop, M. 2002. *Computer security: Art and science*. Reading, MA: Addison-Wesley-Longman.

Evaluating Storage Media Requirements

David R. Reavis, *Texas A&M University, Texarkana*

INTRODUCTION

As technology advances, some improvements provide a greater positive impact than do others. The improvements in electronic storage media, such as magnetic tape, hard disks, and flash drives are allowing organizations to be more flexible in choosing the media for various applications such as daily backups, disaster recovery, and long-term data archiving. This chapter discusses the issues that are important to consider when evaluating media options for electronic data storage. While capacity (the amount of data that a particular medium will hold) is usually the first consideration, other factors—such as longevity, reusability, and cost—should also be determined before making a choice. Evaluating each of the characteristics discussed in this chapter with organizational goals in mind will help in selecting the optimal medium for any application.

SELECTION ISSUES

Longevity

When selecting media for storing electronic data, one of the important considerations is determining how long the media will be viable. Certain storage media, such as magnetic tape, are frequently warranted for 10 years or longer, but usage factors—including frequency of use, storage conditions, and condition of the drive in which the tape is used—can dramatically alter the usable life of individual tapes. The same caution is true for other media. In most cases, the longevity of the medium is related to the conditions in which it is used and stored.

Longevity should be viewed in the long term for archival purposes, and in the short term for backup purposes. If the purpose of storing data is to maintain a long-term archive so that the data may be (accessed years after it was initially created, then the user should consider the likelihood that the technology used to read and write the media will be available years in the future. In long-term data archives, the drives used to record data may become obsolete before the physical deterioration of the storage media (Brown 2003).

If the purpose of storing data is to mitigate the risk of data loss due to system failure, as in the case of periodic backups, more consideration should be given to usage issues such as whether the medium is reusable or prone to physical damage or failure as a result of environmental conditions. Media life may be extended by adopting techniques that prescribe frequent media rotation. For example, rotating through a set of five daily backup tapes (one for each business day) would extend the usable life of each tape over rotating through three backup tapes. During a normal month, a single tape would be used four times as part of a five-tape set versus seven times as part of a three-tape set.

When comparing longevity among various technologies, it is important to note the rate of improvement for every aspect of technology. As with all the characteristics described in this chapter, comparisons among different options should be viewed as relative to one another and not absolute. Kryder's law states that hard disk drives are improving in the density of information at an exponential rate (Walter 2005). Although this phenomenon is not consistent among all types of storage, it demonstrates the rapid pace of change in storage technology. Comparisons of various storage characteristics in this chapter represent the relative capabilities of different media options, and will likely change as technology improves. The comparisons are presented (in as up-to-date terms as possible) so that the user can identify key benchmarks for various media choices.

Capacity

The amount of data that can be stored on a particular device such as a disk or tape defines its capacity. When choosing the media for backups or archives, fewer media

Table 1: Removable Media Capacity

Media	Estimated Capacity
Floppy disk	1.44 Mb
Removable disk	100 Mb to 35 Gb
Compact disk (CD)	184 to 870 Mb
Digital video disk (DVD)	1.46 to 4.7 Gb (per side)
Magnetic tape	20 to 800+ Gb
USB flash drive	128 Mb to 64 Gb

per session is more efficient. Table 1 shows some relative capacities for removable media that could potentially be used for backups.

The capacity of a removable medium is more important when a backup of large amounts of data is necessary. If the amount of data being backed up exceeds the capacity of a single medium, then multiple media sets (i.e., two or more tapes) must be used. This requires human intervention to remove one medium and insert subsequent media, or the use of an automated loader. Automatic tape loaders are readily available and widely used for managing large backup jobs. A drawback to using an automated loader is that the device adds a level of complexity to the process and provides another risk of failure to the backup and recovery system.

Data Growth

A careful assessment of capacity needs should include an analysis of the growth rate for data created by the organization. Some obvious areas in which the amount of data increases consistently may include transactional databases or operational data. Growth in other areas, such as e-mail and e-commerce data, may outpace these traditional data sources. Growth in the context of media capacity may be defined as the increase in capacity required to store electronic data. As more data are entered, generated, or acquired by the system, more storage capacity is required. The storage requirements for e-mail and e-commerce applications generally increase at a faster pace than that of some other applications (Lee 2002). When determining the most effective medium for archiving data, growth is an important consideration. Ignoring the increase in data over time could lead to excessive wear on removable media, added complexity in managing and storing media, and loss of efficiency in backup operations.

Data Transfer Rate

The transfer rate refers to the amount of data that can be transferred from one location (usually the primary medium, such as a hard drive) to another location (usually a secondary medium such as tape) in a given period of time. Some estimates for data transfer rates for tape drives range from below 10 Gb/hour up to over 300 Gb/hour. The transfer rate of the device used for backups and archiving is important, because with a fast transfer rate, the backup can be completed in less time, and the system will return to full operation sooner. For example, if the size of the data set to be backed up is 100 Gb and the tape drive is able to transfer the data at 300 gigabits per hour (Gbph), then the backup can be completed in 20 minutes. If the tape drive is slower, and can transfer data at only 10 Gbph the same data set would require 10 hours to back up. Another issue that should be considered is how fast the data can be supplied to the backup device. If the data are being backed up via a 10BaseT Ethernet network, then the maximum throughput could not exceed 10 megabits per second (Mbps). In this application, using a tape drive that is capable of a 30-Mbps transfer rate would not be supplied with data at a rate fast enough to run continuously. The drive may start the tape, empty its buffer (to the tape), then stop the tape while waiting for more data from the Ethernet network. This start-stop-start action would significantly reduce the life span and reliability of the tapes (Yamagaki, Tode, and Murakami 2005). Transfer rates that could "starve" the device are not generally a problem for nontape media. Optical media such as CDs or DVDs can buffer the data, and not experience significant problems when transfer capacity exceeds the system's ability to supply data.

Integrity

Data integrity implies that the data stored on a particular medium is correct. When data are corrupted during transfer from one storage medium to another, an integrity violation occurs. Integrity violations can occur because of hardware malfunction, software errors, or physical media problems. Methods used to reduce the risk of integrity violations include checksumming, cyclical redundancy checks, and error correction code (Sivathanu, Wright, and Zadok 2005). Most backup and archival software provides features to test media immediately after a backup using one or more of these techniques. If an error is detected, then the data is rewritten and tested again, or a message is generated to inform the user of the error. Testing the medium after a backup process is sometimes optional, and adds additional time to the overall backup process, but skipping the verification step adds to the potential risk of having an unusable backup medium.

Reliability

This chapter is concerned primarily with media, but most media are closely tied to the drive from which the media are read and written. Tape and disk drives vary in their ability to operate effectively over time. To quantify this ability, manufacturers have developed two measures of product reliability. The first is mean-time-between-failures (MTBF). This is a number, frequently expressed in hours, that indicates the average time that a drive will operate without failing. The second measure, the annualized failure rate (AFR) is a measure of the probable percentage of failures per year when compared to the total number of installed drives of the same type and same manufacturer.

It is important to identify the duty cycle for any reliability measure. The *duty cycle* generally describes how much of the time a drive operates during a given period.

If a tape drive were used only for backups, which take 2 hours per day, then the duty cycle would be about 8 percent. When describing various drives, manufacturer's claims of reliability should be examined to determine the duty cycle of the product. Manufacturers' MTBF claims can range from a 10 percent to a 100 percent duty cycle.

Other factors that may affect reliability include operating conditions such as temperature and humidity, frequency of cleaning the drive (in the case of tape drives), and the quality of the medium used in the drive (De Graaf 2001).

Obsolescence

Media used for data storage and its supporting hardware should be based on mature technology. Mature technology is more likely to be supported by open standards, multiple vendors, and a sustainable marketplace for support and supplies (Brown 2003). As changes in technology occur, some methods and products will experience brief success then vanish from the market. It is important to attempt to quantify the lifespan of the media and drive technology under consideration before adopting any specific solution. In many cases the drive technology will become obsolete before the media itself becomes unusable. In his article titled "The Digital Dark Age," John Huxley (2005) describes a scenario in which 50 years in the future, two children discover a CD-ROM along with a letter explaining the data it contains. The children have never seen a CD-ROM and have no way of retrieving the data. Although a 50-year window may be a long time for backups or most archival purposes, the scenario may prompt one to consider what the realistic operational life span may be for the technology used to preserve company data. Another way to gain perspective on the potential problem of obsolescence is to try to find a computer that will allow you to retrieve data from a 5.25-inch floppy disk or listen to your favorite 8-track audio tape.

Cost

The total cost of ownership (TCO) for various media must be calculated for several potential areas. The first is the medium itself. Media costs include media that will be used in a rotational scheme, such as daily backups, and media that will be used for archival purposes, such as monthly, quarterly, or annual backups. Purchasing media in bulk quantities may provide some cost savings. The potential for damaged media (i.e., broken tapes or scratched CDs) should be considered, so that enough media are on hand to perform the required tasks.

Another cost associated with media is the hardware or device used to access it. Hardware costs for various drives should include the cost of the device and the cost of maintenance for the device. Maintenance should take into account supplies such as cleaning kits or cartridges and contracts for repair. Any special software used in backups and archiving should be evaluated, along with software maintenance fees.

Media must be stored in a climatically controlled environment to continue to be viable over time. Climatically controlled floor space costs should be determined and the amount of space required should be part of the cost of choosing a given medium. Options such as robotic tape-manipulation devices, which maintain large tape libraries with near-online access require much more floor space than optical disk technologies. These costs may be significant or insignificant based on the cost of the building, rent, or other floor space costs.

Finally, the cost of using one medium over another is influenced by operational costs. Operational costs may include the time required to load and unload media, time to configure and administer the software operations, and time required to restore backups or retrieve information from archives. Additional time may be required to label media and format media for use. Table 2 provides a simple worksheet that demonstrates a cost comparison between 4-mm tape cartridges and CD-ROM disks, for an example. The costs given in the table are for demonstration only.

Table 2: Media Cost Comparison

Cost Factor	4 mm Tape Cartridge	CD-ROM
Media cost/year	$289.00	$236.00
Hardware	800.00	300.00
Hardware maintenance	180.00	65.00
Software	625.00	425.00
Software maintenance	50.00	30.00
Floor space cost/year	680.00	600.00
Operational costs/year	800.00	1030.00
Total	$3424.00	$2686.00

Access Methods

Tape drives access data sequentially. This means that data are written to the tape and read from the tape as the tape passes the read/write heads on the device. To retrieve data from the tape, the drive must read the tape sequentially to find specific records for retrieval. This means that if a certain file or record is stored near the end of the tape, the access time will be longer than that for a file or record stored near the beginning of the tape.

Other storage media, such as disk drives, flash drives, and Zip drives store files in a way that allows random access. This means that a catalog is kept on the disk and the operating system can access the catalog to determine the exact location of the file so that retrieval time is minimized.

Summary

Some criteria for selecting storage media are more important than others. As an example, many organizations tend to focus on cost issues, but in some organizations, better operational reliability may be a more important factor than cost. Each of the criteria listed above should be considered with the perspective of the organization and its goals, to determine the weight of each factor on the ultimate decision.

MEDIA OPTIONS

Magnetic Tape

Technology breakthroughs in storage density and improvements in capacity occur frequently. Magnetic tape has been a reliable alternative for backups for many years, and despite improvement in other storage alternatives, tape continues to provide high-capacity, cost-effective, secure, easily portable data storage that meets the requirements for backup storage media in many organizations (Hein 2005).

Tape has the benefit of being a mature technology. As such, it is defined by industry standards such as the International Organization for Standardization (ISO) 1001:1986, which specifies volume and file structures, basic characteristics of blocks with records forming a file, recorded labels for files, and conditions for processes within information systems using recorded magnetic tapes. Tape is also available in a variety of formats, which are supported by multiple vendors, in several capacity and price ranges. Table 3 lists some of the tape formats available. The list is not exhaustive, but it shows some of the variety of options available.

Magnetic tape drives must be cleaned regularly. Each manufacturer provides guidelines for cleaning their drives. Normally the cleaning requires a special tape-cleaning cartridge and may require cleaning fluids as well. Tape cartridges are also susceptible to data loss if they are exposed to a magnetic field. Magnetic fields are generated by a variety of appliances, computer monitors, clocks, and desk lamps. It is important to store tapes in an environment away from magnetic fields, in a temperature- and humidity-controlled storage area (IBM 2003).

Optical Disks

Optical disks are manufactured in a variety of formats. Initially, optical disks allowed only one write operation, with the media being read as many times as necessary. This is referred to as write-once-read-many, or WORM, technology. Further developments in optical drives and media have produced optical devices that can be used multiple times.

Two popular formats for optical drives are compact disk (CD) and digital versatile disk (DVD). Both of these optical disk types are available in write-once and rewritable media.

The technology used in writing data to an optical disk incorporates some reflective media upon which a laser acts to change the reflectivity of the media. The reflective component of a CD-R disk is usually a silver, gold, or platinum alloy. The reflective element is coated with a dye, which changes the amount of light reflected by the laser, thus representing digital data. Dyes currently in use include cyanine, phthalocyanine, metalized azo, and hybrid dyes made from these three basic types. Each of these dyes has a different color characteristic when "burned" by the recording laser light and are patented by various companies that produce the media (McFadden 2006).

Media used in optical disk burners are different from media used in software or movie distribution. Media used to distribute software are created by mechanically pressing an image onto the media. This process is much more precise and accurate than the laser burning method used in current systems.

Optical media products vary in quality and reliability. One of the major differences in determining the quality of

Table 3: Magnetic Tape Format Options

Format	Brief Description
9-Track open reel tape	Virtually obsolete ½-inch tape
½-Inch data cartridge	Includes IBM 3480, Imation 9940, and other products
DLT (digital linear tape) cartridge	DLT tape is advertised to safely archive data for up to 30 years. DLT data cartridges hold up to 160 GB of data
SDLT (super digital linear tape)	SDLT storage media is ideally suited for data center and departmental backups for which capacity, performance and cost are critical. SDLT technology offers up to 300 GB of native storage capacity
LTO (linear tape-open) cartridge, −1, −2, and −3	LTO cartridges use linear multichannel, bidirectional formats with data compression, track layout and error correction code to optimize capacity, speed, and reliability. Storage capacity is generally rated up to 800 GB
DAT (digital audio tape)	Available from 12 GB up to 36 GB native capacity.Ideally suited for backup operations in small and medium-sized systems. DAT is a popular 4-mm helical scan medium for network and other backups. The DAT format supports random data reads and writes
Travan	Travan uses linear recording technology. Data tracks are recorded longitudinally in the direction of tape movement; this is the same technology as used by DLT tape drives. Only one motor is required to drive the tape, and the head moves only to change tracks at the beginning and end of the multiple recording passes. Capacity is rated up to 40 GB

the media is the quality of the dye used in the manufacturing process. Better dyes tend to be more stable over time, and provide a longer life for the media. Less expensive dyes result in a shorter life span and produce a larger percentage of rejected or unusable media (Laskey 2004). In addition to the initial quality of the dye, imperfections in the way the dye was applied to the medium during manufacturing can cause quality issues. If the dye was not spread uniformly over the medium, a condition known as dye thinning may occur. When the dye is not applied all the way to the edge of the medium (short spreading) the outer edges of the medium do not work properly. These dye-related problems usually cause the medium to be rejected during the recording or verifying stage, but may be realized only upon attempting to read the data later. Another problem with some poor-quality media is that some dyes cannot handle high-speed burns, and immediately deteriorate. Many of these problems can be avoided by using high-quality, branded optical disks for data storage (DigitalFAQ 2005). Fake, generic, and low-quality optical media are available from numerous sources, but the increased risk of losing data or monitoring every recording session for bad media frequently justifies the cost of first-class media.

Optical media should be stored in a temperature-controlled environment to prevent the deterioration of the dyes used in the media. Most manufacturers recommend temperatures between 20°C (68°F) and 4°C (39°F). Recordable optical media should be labeled using a non-solvent-based permanent marker, since adding paper labels to a medium can affect the balance of the medium and cause vibration and potential read errors when the medium is read. Bending or flexing optical disks can form stress patterns in the polycarbonate and may deform the reflective or recording layer of the disk, so care should be taken when removing the disk from a protective sleeve or jewel case (McFadden 2006).

Optical technology, like magnetic tape, is a relatively mature technology. It is also an evolving technology with advances in capacity, speed, and life span occurring regularly. When selecting any optical technology, it is important to consider how long the media will be stored. For example, daily backups are viable for only a short time, while archived information may need to be accessible for several years. As with any storage technology, as improvements are made, current practices should be evaluated in light of the availability of support for existing products. When newer products become more widely used, a migration strategy to the newer technology should be developed and implemented.

Hard Disks

Hard disk technology was originally developed in the 1950s. Since that time, the capacity and performance of hard disks has improved dramatically, and although the technology is mature, improvements are still occurring. Data are stored on a hard disk by dividing the disk into sections, then magnetically charging tiny segments of the disk surface. The magnetic charges represent digital data. There are some specific terms used to describe how a disk is divided. A hard disk contains multiple *platters*. Each platter is a thin, circular surface that is logically divided into concentric circles, or *sectors*. Each sector is divided into smaller units called *tracks*. Each track is formatted to hold a specific number of bytes of data. Figure 1 illustrates the sector and track concept.

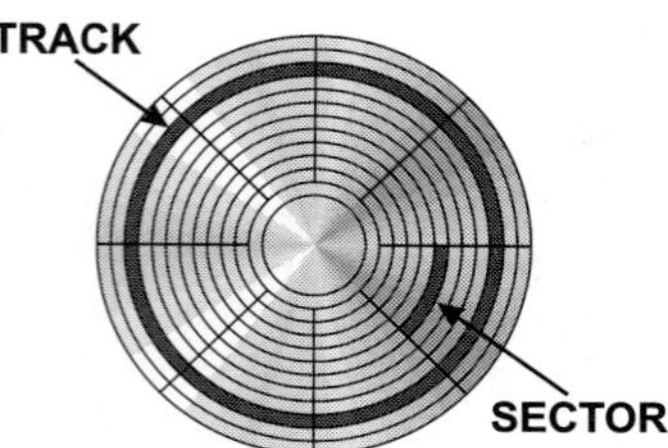

Figure 1: Hard-disk platter

Two of the important characteristics of hard disks are capacity and performance. Capacity is currently measured in gigabytes. Desktop computers are commonly available with hard disks ranging from 80 to 500 Gb per drive. Servers and large multi-user systems may have access to hard-disk capacity up to several terabytes of data. Hard-disk performance is based on the ability of the drive to transfer data to and from the disk to the computer. High-performance drives can transfer data at speeds of 80 Mbps and faster using data caches and wide data channels. The major limiting factor in data transfer speed is the rotational speed of the disk platter. The data can only be read from or written to the disk as the platter spins. Drive rotational speed is measured in revolutions per minute (RPM), and disks are currently available with speeds between 7200 and 15,000 rpm. Hard disks can be arranged in various configurations that provide fault tolerance, high capacity, and high performance. Some of the techniques for these arrangements are discussed in "Storage Area Networks Fundamentals" and "Storage Area Networks: Architectures and Protocols." A discussion of fault-tolerant technology for disk drives is in "Backup and Recovery System Requirements."

Hard disks are very reliable. A common measure of reliability for hard disks is mean (average) time between failures (MTBF). MTBF is calculated using one of two widely accepted standards. Most government programs use the MIL-HDBK (Military Handbook for Reliability Prediction of Electronic Equipment)-217 standard, developed by the military, and the Bellcore standard, which is based on the MIL-HDBK-217 standard, is used for other drive reliability predictions. MTBF calculations are based on predictions of failures of the components of a hard disk, not on actual failures (Case 2000).

Another aspect of hard-disk technology is that the disk must be formatted for use in a way that is compatible with the operating system. Part of the formatting process is determining which file system will be used by the disk. Some of the choices are listed in Table 4, with a brief description of each.

File systems provide several functions that make hard disks usable. One of the functions of a file system is user access. The file system works with the operating system to allow or deny access to files on the disk. Different operating system/file system combinations provide different levels of security, but the file system is an integral part of data security. Another function of the file system is that the file system determines the logical characteristics of

Table 4: File Systems for Hard Disks

File System	Brief Description
FAT32	File allocation table 32. Older file system for Microsoft Windows
NTFS	New Technology File System for Windows. Supports more security features, disk quotas, and larger volumes than FAT32
Ext2	Second Extended File System. Used in Linux systems
Ext3	Third Extended File System. Used in Linux systems. Provides support for journaling
GPFS	General Parallel File System. Proprietary to IBM. Scalable high-performance parallel file system for AIX 5L and Linux clusters

the disk. These logical characteristics include the maximum volume size, partition size, and number of levels of hierarchical structure that are supported by the disk. The file system may also handle read/write errors on the disk, and manage user quotas with information provided by the operating system (Shah 2001, 195).

Hard disks are used to store data from a variety of applications. In the desktop environment, personal computer applications and files are stored on the personal computer hard disk along with the operating system and utility programs. Organizations frequently use hard disks on a file server to store enterprise data such as databases and mission-critical application data (i.e., spreadsheets and policy documents). Larger computer systems store data on hard disks, including all of the previously listed files, and often use large disks for archival purposes.

Hard disks may also be used as a target medium for backing up large data sets. The advantage of using hard disks for backups is that transferring data between two hard drives is fast. The high throughput available by copying data from one hard disk to another hard disk tends to minimize the amount of time needed to complete the backup. Hard disks are also very reliable, and the risk of losing data because of media failure is minute. A disadvantage of using a hard disk for backups is that hard disks are less portable than other media. Disks with the fastest transfer rates and largest capacity are usually mounted in a computer or special appliance that is not easily transported offsite. This disadvantage may be overcome by transferring the data over a network to a remote site.

One of the choices available for remote storage, in a data storage or backup scenario is subscribing to data storage services from a storage service provider (SSP). An SSP provides remote disk space to an organization for a fee. SSPs offer security through encryption, guaranteed up-time, recovery services in case of disaster at the client site and archiving services. Other advantages include not having to incur the overhead associated with having the actual disk drives on site, such as power consumption, hardware maintenance, space considerations, and human resource costs (Cummings 2006).

Removable Disks

This discussion of removable disks will be broken into three categories. The first category is the Zip disk. Introduced by Iomega in 1994, the Zip disk works like a floppy disk, but has a much larger capacity. Zip disks are available in 100-, 250-, and 750-Mb capacities. The disk requires a Zip drive, which can be permanently installed in the computer or can be attached via a universal serial bus (USB) port (Delaney 2002). Iomega currently markets REV drives with removable disks rated at 35 Gb. These disks are frequently used for backups. The benefit of this technology is that the disks have a large capacity (up to 90 Gb when compression is used) and are easily transportable.

Another category of removable disk is a configuration in which a bay to receive the disk drive is installed into a computer or peripheral device, and the drive can be removed from the bay and reinserted without shutting down the computer (Miles 2003). This is also referred to as a hot-swappable drive configuration. This type of removable drive is frequently used in a RAID configuration. (RAID is discussed in more detail in Chapter 175, "Backup and Recovery System Requirements.") This category of removable drive is not usually used for backup and recovery purposes. The benefit of the device is that when a single drive fails, it can be replaced with a similar drive without interrupting system functions.

The third category of removable drives is the external disk drive. This drive is attached to the computer via a USB port or FireWire connection. Capacities for these external drives are comparable to those of internal drives. Although this type of drive could be used for disaster recovery, backups, and archives, many manufacturers market this category of drives as a medium for storing music, photos, computer games, and videos (Shaw 2006).

Static Memory

One of the most recent developments in data storage is the flash drive. This device is also known as a memory stick, USB drive, JumpDrive, Pocket drive, Pen drive, and Thumb drive. Flash drives are currently available in capacities up to 2 Gb. An advantage of a flash drive is that it can be used on any computer that is equipped with a USB port. Most computers sold today are manufactured with several USB ports. This means that the flash drive can be used on most computers, without the need for a drive such as a floppy disk drive or a removable hard disk drive. The device is about the same size as a car key and some users carry their flash drive on their key ring.

Some of the features provided in flash drives include a strap for carrying the device, a write protect switch (similar to the write protect switch on a floppy disk), and support to make the device bootable. Some flash drives also include encryption software. Most manufacturers do not specify an MTBF for their products, but offer warranties ranging from 1 year to a lifetime (Woodward 2005).

Some of the common uses for flash drives are storing data that need to be accessed from multiple computers, backing up small amounts of data, and storing data that may not be allowed (because of policy or space restrictions) on a user's desktop computer. Users frequently use a flash drive for storing files that they need to access from multiple computers. If someone needs to take a spreadsheet home from work, a flash drive is a convenient way to transport the file home, and then bring the updated file back to work the next day. Flash drives are an effective backup device for small backup jobs. They are relatively inexpensive, fast, and easily transportable. In some organizations, certain files, such as music files are not allowed on employees' computers. In some cases, the organization may allow music files to be accessed from flash drives because this does not use up the hard disk storage space on the employee's personal computer.

Two of the security issues for flash drives are that the small size provides an easy method for stealing data, and the data on the drive itself may be accessed by anyone in possession of the drive. The first issue must be addressed by safeguards in the organization similar to safeguards used to protect data against theft from a floppy disk. These safeguards include hiring reliable employees, protecting access to data by requiring passwords, and encrypting data when necessary. It is also possible to reduce the risk of data loss by "locking down" USB ports on personal computers through operating-system-based security tools (Mellor 2005). Some manufacturers have addressed the second issue by password-protecting access to the data on the flash drive. In some flash drives, there is an area for storage on the drive that cannot be accessed without a password. Data may also be encrypted when stored on a flash drive for additional protection. Flash drives may also be a source of computer virus infection. One method that has been successful is to put a virus on a flash drive, then leave the drive in an area where it can be easily found. The natural response is for someone to plug the drive into their computer to see if they can identify the owner of the device. Opening a document on the device can spread a virus and the computer user could then spread the virus throughout the organization (Mullins 2005).

Summary

Each of the media options discussed above is suitable for different applications. Large data sets can be backed up using hard disks, or tape, and smaller data sets could use other options such as a flash drive or removable disk. When determining the best alternative, each of the selection issues discussed in the first section of this chapter should be considered.

HANDLING REMOVABLE MEDIA

The physical environment where media, particularly removable media such as tape and floppy disks are stored, can affect the viability of the media and the length of time the media can reliably store data.

Recommendations

The following guidelines may be helpful in getting the maximum life and reliability from removable media. Each media type has specific requirements, and the packaging should be consulted for recommended storage temperatures and operating conditions, but the following general guidelines apply to most removable media:

1. Store the media in a controlled environment. The ideal area is temperature- and humidity-controlled according to the specifications from the media manufacturer. For optical media, avoid sunlight and ultraviolet light, and store the disks in a dark area.
2. Return the medium to its storage case or container immediately after use. This helps keep the surface clean and free of dust and other matter that could damage the recording surface or drive.
3. Leave new media in the original packaging until it is needed. This protects the media from contamination from foreign objects or materials.
4. Avoid storing media near devices that might emit a magnetic field.
5. Before using a tape or disk, inspect it to make sure that there is no dust or dirt on the recording surface. If contamination is found, clean it according to the manufacturer's instructions before use.
6. Label the medium so that it can be easily found if needed. Special care must be taken with optical media (Byers 2003).

Media Rotation

Media used for backup or archival purposes should be evaluated periodically so that it is not kept in service past its ability to provide reliable data retention. In the case of a backup medium, it is common to reuse it several times, overwriting the existing data each time. This practice saves time and money, but if the medium is used repeatedly, it will eventually wear out or become unstable. Some backup software provides error logging, which can be useful in evaluating media. One option to consider is a planned number of passes or uses for a given medium. As an example, suppose the backup system for an organization uses tape cartridges. The manager, after consulting the manufacturer's specifications, might decide to designate five tapes for daily backups, one for each day of the work week. In order to provide an extra level of reliability, the manager may designate that the five-tape set will be totally replaced two times each year and the old tapes will be removed from service. This practice increases the probability that the tapes in service are viable. Other media rotation planning options should be considered based on the media used.

Security

One of the major advantages of removable media is that it can be easily transported. This advantage also increases the risk that valuable data might be compromised. Since it is very difficult to ensure that valuable data are not transported away from authorized areas, many security specialists recommend that data be encrypted when stored on removable media. Of course, the encryption is useless if the perpetrator is able to obtain the encryption key, but this added level of security will protect against the loss of data from many potential threats. For a complete discussion of physical security, see "Physical Security Threats and Measures."

GLOSSARY

Checksumming: A mechanism that computes a value for a message packet, based on the data it contains, and passes it along with the data to authenticate that the data have not been tampered with. The recipient of the data recomputes the cryptographic checksum and compares it with the cryptographic checksum passed with the data; if they match, it is "probabilistic" proof the data were not tampered with during transmission. The important property of a cryptographic checksum is that, without knowing the secret key, a malicious interceptor has only an infinitesimally small chance of being able to construct an altered message with a valid corresponding checksum (Smith 1999, 270).

Cyclical Redundancy Check (CRC): A method of detecting errors in the transmission of data between two devices. A value is calculated for each block of data before it is sent and then the value is sent along with the data. A new value is calculated on the receiving device for the data. If the new value does not match the one that has been sent with the data, then a CRC error is reported.

Data Transfer Rate: The speed at which a device can write digital data to another storage device. The data transfer rates represent the highest maintainable speed at which the storage device can move data to the target media.

Disk Volume: A logical division of a physical disk. Usually a partition contains one volume. See *Partition*.

Duty Cycle: The proportion of time during which a device or system is used. The duty cycle may be expressed as a ratio (i.e., 2 hr/24 hr) or as a percentage (i.e., 20%).

FireWire: FireWire is Apple Computer's version of the IEEE 1394 standard for a high-performance serial bus, used in connecting devices to a computer. FireWire provides a single plug-and-socket connection on which up to sixty-three devices can be attached with data transfer speeds up to 800 Mbps (megabits per second). The standard describes a serial bus or pathway between one or more peripheral devices and your computer's microprocessor. Many peripheral devices now come equipped to meet IEEE 1394 (Sabetti 2003).

Partition: A logical division of a physical disk. In cases in which the user needs to organize his data into separate spaces, a hard disk can be set up to contain multiple partitions. In many cases, a hard disk is set up with a single partition.

CROSS REFERENCES

See *Backup and Recovery System Requirements; Business Continuity Planning; Business Requirements of Backup Systems*.

REFERENCES

Brown, A. 2003. Selecting storage media for long-term preservation. www.nationalarchives.gov.uk/documents/selecting_storage_media.pdf (accessed June 15, 2007).

Byers, F. 2003. *Care and handling of CDs and DVDs, a guide for librarians and archivists*. NIST special publication 500-252. Washington, DC: National Institute of Standards and Technology.

Case, D. 2000. *MTBF revisited, a tutorial*. www.evaluationengineering.com/archive/articles/0500analyz.htm (accessed June 17, 2006).

Cummings, J. 2006. Managed storage comes of age. *Networkworld* 23:60–4.

DeGraaf, C. 2001. *Tape drive technology comparison*. www.spectralogic.com/index.cfm?fuseaction=home.displayFile&DocID=161 (accessed April 26, 2006).

Delaney, J. 2002. Zip triples capacity, doubles speed. *PC Magazine*. www.findarticles.com/p/articles/mi_zdpcm/is_200208/ai_ziff30329 (accessed June 17, 2006).

DigitalFAQ. 2005. *DVD media guides*. www.digitalfaq.com/media/dvdmedia.pdf (accessed May 6, 2006).

Hein, B. 2005. Disk + tape = smarter libraries. Computerworld.www.snwonline.com/behind/disk_plus_tape_06-06-05.asp?article_id=562 (accessed April 14, 2006).

Huxley, J. 2005, September 23. The digital dark age. *The Sydney Morning Herald*. www.smh.com.au/news/technology/the-digital-dark-age/2005/09/22/1126982184206.html (accessed April 26, 2006).

IBM. 2003. Tape backup—Media operation and care considerations. *International Business Machines*. http://www-307.ibm.com/pc/support/site.wss/document.do?lndocid=VLAR-42XRPP (accessed May 5, 2006).

Laskey, I. 2004. CD-R media lifespan. *PC Computing*. www.practicalpc.co.uk/computing/storage/cdrlifespan.htm (accessed May 9, 2006).

Lee, J. 2002. Active archiving minimizes data growth. *ComputerWorld*. www.snwonline.com/tech_edge/active_archiving_09-23-02.asp?article_id=161 (accessed April 25, 2006).

McFadden, A. 2006. What kinds of media are there? CD-recordable FAQ—Section 7. www.cdrfaq.org/faq07.html#S7-1 (accessed May 3, 2006).

Mellor, C. 2005. *USB flash drive security risk removed*. www.techworld.com/storage/features/index.cfm?featureid=2051 (accessed June 8, 2006).

Miles, J. 2003. Hard drives hit the road. *Government Computer News*. www.gcn.com/print/22_18/22678-1.html (accessed June 8, 2006).

Mullins, M. 2005. Shore up USB flash drive security. http://techrepublic.com.com/5100-1009_11-5695113.html (accessed June 8, 2006).

Sabetti, E. 2003. FireWire. Whatis.com. http://searchnetworking.techtarget.com/sDefinition/0,,sid7_gci212126,00.html (accessed June 18, 2006).

Shah, S. 2001. *Linux administration, a beginner's guide*. New York: Osborne/McGraw-Hill.

Shaw, K. 2006. *Seagate launches 750Gb external drive*. www.networkworld.com/community/?q=node/5614 (accessed June 17, 2006).

Sivathanu, G. , C. Wright, and E. Zadok. 2005. Ensuring data integrity in storage: Techniques and applications.

Proceedings of the 2005 ACM workshop on storage security and survivability, Fairfax, VA, USA. 26-26. Fairfax, VA: Association for Computing Machinery.

Smith, R. 1999. *Oracle advanced security administrator's guide*. Redwood City, CA: Oracle Corporation.

Walter, C. 2005, July 25. Kryder's law: The doubling of processor speed every 18 months is a snail's pace compared with rising hard-disk capacity, and Mark Kryder plans to squeeze in even more bits. www.scientificamerican.com/article.cfm?chanID=sa001&articleID=000B0C22-0805-12D8-BDFD83414B7F0000&pageNumber=2&catID=2 (accessed April 12, 2006).

Woodward, M. 2005. *Son of the USB 2.0 hi-speed flash drive roundup*. http://arstechnica.com/reviews/hardware/flash2005.ars/1 (accessed June 17, 2006).

Yamagaki, N. , H.Tode, and K. Murakami. 2005. Dual metrics fair queuing: Improving fairness and file transfer time. In *2005 Symposium on Applications and the Internet, (SAINT'05)*. 150–6. Trento, Italy: IEEE Computer Society.

Business Continuity Planning

Marco Cremonini and Pierangela Samarati, *University of Milan, Italy*

INTRODUCTION

The concept of business continuity planning (BCP) identifies a set of technical, administrative, and management activities aimed at planning the steps to recover and restore critical business assets after an unforeseen event has impaired corporate functions. The BCP field has its roots in the 1970s, when mainframes and centralized data centers were designed so that the environment, access, and security could be controlled. Another advantage of this centralized approach provided a central environment that could be managed in such a way as to mitigate the consequences of external catastrophes (e.g., floods, fires, or earthquakes). For a couple of decades, such procedures and techniques took the name of disaster recovery (DR), emphasizing the fact that recovery and restoration activities were mostly focused on information technology (IT) physical facilities and assets that could have been damaged.

In the past decade, however, the way in which companies are organized and managed has changed dramatically, and DR requirements have changed accordingly to meet the new business requirements. In particular, the very nature of business assets has changed, first with the advent of personal computers and distributed systems, then with the expansion of Internet-based service-oriented companies, shifting from the provision of physical tangible goods alone to providing functions and services that could be operated in a wide range of different ways. Consequently, the former field of DR has grown in complexity to handle both old and new requirements and to comply with newer business models. For these reasons, since the focus has shifted from techniques solely to secure IT physical assets to procedures and management strategies for ensuring the continuation of the business in its entirety, BCP has replaced DR as the discipline that describes how to face those unforeseen events that may impair the functions of modern networked organizations.

The goal today is the continuous availability of the business and its processes in its entirety—with the technology infrastructure taking a critical but no longer exclusive role—which gives an enormous importance to the time factor. That is, if down-time periods must be the shortest possible, then recovery and restoration must be as quick as possible.

This chapter is organized as follows. First, we discuss how the growing dependence of business-critical activities on the IT infrastructure affects BCP. The causes of down time are then explored, and in particular, we point out that modern organizations continue to be concerned with so-called small disasters (e.g., system failures, power outages, telecommunication interruption, and so on) and their management, which has modified the BCP focus in most cases. We then present the main characteristics of BCP and introduce the importance of a business impact analysis (BIA) as a fundamental activity for understanding the business needs of an organization and thus providing sound technical measures for recovering from disasters. In the context of BCP, we introduce the notion of risk management, which includes the need for analyzing and mitigating risks. We then present backups and alternate sites as the traditional techniques for data recovery and business continuity after the advent of failures. Emerging technologies like disk-to-disk backups and iSCSI (Internet SCSI [small computer system interface]) are also discussed. Important laws and regulations in the field of BCP are introduced. Finally, we discuss how BCP is evolving toward the more comprehensive notion of business resilience.

FROM DISASTER RECOVERY TO BUSINESS CONTINUITY PLANNING

For many years, corporations have placed most of their critical information assets into automated systems, and more recently, they have adopted business models largely based on the Internet. Although they provide more efficiency, cost reduction, and competitive advantage, these developments have also increased corporations' dependence on the IT infrastructure and therefore increased the potential economic losses caused by its failure. More than ever, a loss of access to the IT infrastructure will prove to be, in many cases, fatal for the business of affected companies. It is therefore crucial for companies to consider precise plans for counteracting possible events that may cause such interruptions. Examples of companies that failed to recover their businesses after a prolonged interruption of IT functions, caused by floods or fires, for example, are well known and documented (Hiles 2002; Kaye 2001; Noakes-Fry and Diamond 2001; Toigo 1999, 2001, *Fighting fires on the Web*).

E-business and Internet connections are shortening recovery time objectives (RTOs) and changing the way we think about DR planning; full 24/7 operations and zero down time are now commonly seen as business necessities. Although traditional countermeasures to natural disasters should still be provided (e.g., keeping backup data in locations out of the area possibly affected by natural disasters), a wide spectrum of other risks (e.g., cyberattacks) have to be considered. In addition, critical business processes must be analyzed and recovered much faster than in the past: down times of days (the usual time window for natural disasters) are definitely no longer sustainable for any company in general, and Internet-based businesses in particular.

Nevertheless, many enterprises still have minimal contingency plans in place to ensure business continuity for their business requirements. Managers fail to plan for DR in the new project development life cycle, which results in more risks and exposures than in the past. From a technological standpoint, some managers and planners still do not understand the intrinsic fragility of the new architectures for the e-commerce business to which they are migrating. Consequently, they do not understand fully the increased requirements for business continuity, do not plan for the inevitable failures, do not mitigate the risks, and are not prepared to sustain the consequences.

Downtimes in Business Services

Down times in business services might be caused by several things: equipment failure (e.g., disk crashes); disruption of power supply or telecommunications (e.g., blackouts, brownouts, or digging in areas where telecommunications/electrical lines are located); application failures or database corruption (e.g., inaccurate configurations or improper maintenance); human error (e.g., improper technical actions); insufficient technical staff (e.g., strikes or coincident emergencies); malicious software (e.g., viruses or worms); hacking and Internet intrusions (e.g., random targets or specifically selected targets); fire; natural disasters (e.g., floods, earthquakes, or hurricanes).

Clearly, down times might be the effect of or worsened by a combination of causes. For instance, an emergency that could have been managed well without losses for the company may become catastrophic if it happens when key technical personnel are unavailable or are already busy solving another failure and recovery plans are nonexistent. Problems may even arise as a side effect of events that do not affect a company directly. For instance, if a nearby company has an emergency, this event may impair the proper functioning or physical access to all locations in a certain area (e.g., incidents in chemical plants); this is called a "regional disaster."

Causes of failure can be characterized further based on two aspects: (1) the likelihood of occurrence and (2) the potential damage that they can provoke. These two properties reflect, respectively, a probabilistic and a quantitative description. For instance, events such as sabotage, floods, or fire, which are usually considered in traditional DR plans, are rare, but when they happen, they are often catastrophic. On the other hand, events such as equipment failures or software errors are less catastrophic in nature, but occur more frequently and represent almost day-to-day problems for system administrators.

Usually, these failures are not devastating for a company, and in the past (in the pre-Internet age), they were not included in DR planning. However, with today's companies relying more and more on networked systems, complex distributed multicomponent architectures, and the Internet as a primary business enabler, short but frequent down-time periods can become a major problem in terms of competition, reputation, and revenue losses (Bounds 2003; Toigo 2001, Storage disaster).

How to strike a balance in investing decisions between prevention measures focused on rare but catastrophic events and those focused on frequent but less severe failures is one of the most difficult challenges faced by modern BCP. In the old days, DR was focused only on the former; modern information security and system/network administration techniques are focused only on the latter. BCP should encompass both, thereby planning for all risks that may affect a company.

According to a study by the Gartner Group (Scott and Natis 2000), only 20 percent of down time is caused by technology failures including hardware (servers and network devices), environmental factors (e.g., cooling and power outages), and natural disasters. By contrast, 40 percent of down time is caused by application failures, which include software bugs, operating system crashes, performance slowdowns, incorrect updates, and changes to software. The remaining 40 percent of failures are due to human errors. In other words, according to these results, failures are mainly due to people and process issues, including software, whereas infrastructural components are more robust and reliable (Kaye 2001; Noakes-Fry and Diamond 2001, 2002).

These results should come as no surprise, actually. Applications frequently fail because of all sorts of problems, including code bugs, bad design, weak requirement analysis, inconsistent tests, misconfigurations, erroneous installation or deployment, incompatibility with the run-time environment, and conflicts with other applications. Connectivity instead fails because of misconfiguration of devices such as routers, switches, or domain name systems (DNSs), sometimes caused by the company's staff and other times by Internet service providers (ISPs) and application service providers (ASPs).

Based on these figures, many experienced business continuity planners suggest that organizations select products and vendors with a good reputation of robustness and be skeptical about the latest products, because these products often provide exciting new features but at the price of less reliability and are less able to be recovered if a disruption occurs. Adopting a prudent approach is important for software products because they have been one of the principal causes of small disasters, but is of particular significance for infrastructural hardware components whose robustness and reliability impact on the whole organization.

BUSINESS CONTINUITY MANAGEMENT

Business continuity management (BCM) consists of a set of activities aimed at identifying the impact of potential losses, defining and realizing viable recovery strategies, and developing recovery plans for ensuring the continuity of business services. Disaster recovery planning is one of the components of a BCM plan and encompasses a set of activities aimed at reducing the likelihood and the impact of disaster events on critical business assets (NIST 2002; Toigo 1999; Wold 2002, Disaster recovery planning process—Parts I, II, and III). BCM planning is as complicated as any major system development project, with many stages of analysis and an overall activity set encompassing all critical assets, business functions, and technological solutions.

Convincing corporate management to invest in BCM planning is often a challenge greater than dealing with the technical problems of backing up critical systems, minimizing down time, and maintaining network connectivity. To complicate matters, investing in BCM capabilities is not a one-time event, but must be sustained over time, because every BCM plan needs to be tested, reviewed, and updated regularly to be effective. In addition, BCM planning needs to be managed, improved, and updated in synch with modifications to the company, its business environment, its IT infrastructure and critical assets, government and industry requirements, as well as personnel changes. For these reasons, management consensus is vital for every BCM plan that, in the best of circumstances, will enable failure avoidance, detecting and reacting to potential problems before they become disasters.

BCM plans should be documented adequately with an in-depth analysis of the risks addressed in the plan, the benefits for the corporation, the possible impact on revenues of an insufficient BCM plan, the estimates of the cost of down time, and the possible savings on insurance costs (Kaye 2001; Toigo 1999).

The process of managing business continuity, in a classification scheme inspired by the *Business Continuity Management—Good Practice Guidelines* (BCI 2005) of the Business Continuity Institute, has these five phases:

1. understanding the company's business
2. recognizing the risks to business activities
3. developing recovery strategies, such as backup, alternate site, or replication
4. exercising, rehearsing, and periodically reviewing the DR-BC plan
5. creating a BCM plan

Understanding the Company's Business

Understanding a company's business requires an analysis of the operational aspects of the company. This analysis should determine what are the key business objectives and the products or services of the business objectives, when the business objectives should be achieved, who is involved in the achievement of business objectives, and how the business objectives are achieved. This analysis should result in the clear identification of mission-critical activities. Elements of mission-critical activities are human resources, stakeholders, suppliers, customers, facilities, functions, processes, materials, technology, telecommunications, and data. In addition, for each mission-critical activity, it is necessary to identify single points of failure—elements or components for which no alternatives exist.

The business impact analysis (BIA) and the risk assessment and analysis (RA) jointly address all these issues.

Business Impact Analysis

The BIA encompasses activities aimed at identifying, quantifying, and qualifying the business impact and other effects of a mission-critical activity failure on a company. The fundamental outcome of the BIA is the identification of the minimum level of resources needed to accomplish the company's business objectives in terms of an acceptable recovery time—recovery time objectives (RTO)—and an acceptable recovery status of assets: recovery point objectives (RPO). The outcomes of the BIA can then be summarized as follows:

- Identification of mission-critical activities, along with their dependencies and single points of failure
- Financial and nonfinancial impacts of a disruption, failure, or loss of one or more mission-critical activities for a given time frame
- Recovery priorities for each mission-critical activity based on the criticality of resources and on the associated sustainable time window and cost considerations (Prioritizing recovery strategies can optimize allocations and expenditures for the recovery process.)
- Recovery objectives in terms of RTOs, RPOs, and the minimum level of acceptable business continuity to sustain the company's operations
- Work area recovery, the minimum level of resources necessary to achieve the recovery objectives according to the resource recovery objectives of each mission-critical activity

The BIA should involve staff members from most, if not all, areas of the company. For instance, business managers are better able to analyze business impacts, either financial or nonfinancial, and should provide initial input as to the recovery priorities required by their business areas. Senior management should be involved in making the final determination of the recovery priorities among mission-critical activities.

Evaluation of Losses: Tangible and Intangible Costs

To evaluate how much down-time periods may cost, companies must consider all the components that comprise their business and how each may be affected by system failures, including not only lost current revenues but also the loss of any future or potential revenues. Because many companies today have structured their organization across interdependent business units and have extended their supply chains, the impact of down time may spread through many interconnections, and hence grow rapidly. No longer restricted to a core business, businesses may experience the effects of down time on related businesses, partners, and customers all along the value chain.

Moreover, companies' increasing reliance on a few business-critical technologies is another aspect that increases the severity of the impact of down time. Internet-based companies, which require connectivity and availability of their Web sites 24 hours a day, 7 days a week, 365 days a year, are in such a situation—they are completely based on Internet connectivity for their business, which has made them the victim of unforeseen problems. In the past few years they have suffered all sorts of system and/or network outages and have been threatened by distributed denial-of-service attacks. A classification of costs should divide them into tangible and intangible costs (Merchantz 2002), which we discuss next.

Tangible Costs

Tangible costs are easily identified and are often (though not always) easily measured, and may include the following:

- *Lost revenue*: This is the most obvious cost, as the company cannot conduct business, and balance sheets state that unmistakably. Just looking at normal hourly sales and then multiplying that figure by the number of hours of down time provides a good estimate of lost revenues. However, this must be regarded as only one component of the total cost of down time and, taken singularly, normally underestimates the true loss greatly. E-commerce companies amplify the problem because a company normally has no alternative way of conducting business and depends entirely on system availability.
- *Lost productivity*: During down time, production is blocked, and productivity lowers to zero. The same applies even when production is not blocked completely, but is just impaired, because employee productivity is still affected. Evaluating lost productivity is difficult because production normally does not stop completely and employees might then engage in different duties. One way to obtain an estimate is to compute the cost of salaries and wages for the time frame of the down-time. Productivity value is normally higher than labor costs; hence, this figure represents a conservative evaluation of what a company has lost during down time. In addition to pure labor costs during down-time hours, one should consider that, after the recovery effort is completed, employees will not simply go back to their normal duties, but some will probably be in charge of other recovery actions (e.g., data reentry). This represents either additional costs (e.g., if done on an overtime basis) or less productivity (e.g., if done by taking time away from usual work).
- *Late fees and penalties*: Some companies work under contracts, normally called "service-level agreements," that include penalties for late deliveries. If system down time causes these companies to miss their contracted delivery dates or users cannot access data made available by an Internet-based company, the penalties incurred are another cost of down time.
- *Legal costs*: Depending on the nature of the affected systems, there could be legal costs associated with down time. For example, a drop in the share price may induce shareholders to initiate a class-action suit if they believe that management was negligent in protecting vital assets. Other examples of legal costs are cases of business partnerships in which the failure of one company affects the business of the others or of defective products delivered as a consequence of a system failure. In addition, some public utility companies could be considered legally responsible for the suspension of a public service because of a lack of sufficient precautions and failure prevention. Evaluating possible legal costs is extremely difficult because legal aspects are complex and are strictly related to the specificities of any single case. Experiences or historical data from companies in the same business sector could give a broad estimate. For a more specific evaluation, a legal consultant should analyze in detail the risks the company may face.
- *Other costs*: Many other costs could arise, which are often specific to the particular industrial sector. For example, a fresh food producer could be forced to discard perishable goods, a manufacturer may incur costs when restarting automatic machines, a construction company may have leased machines for which the leasing period must be prolonged, and so forth.

Intangible Costs

Intangible costs, by nature, are neither easy to identify nor easy to measure, but they affect the business just like tangible ones and have been the most critical cost factor in recent years in the BCM field. Think, for instance, about the impact of a system failure on the company's brand and reputation. The brand value does not appear in any balance sheet, but it is often one of a business's most valuable assets. There are statistics and analyses (Hiles 2002) that correlate how the devaluation of a reputation of a company suffering a disaster affects the share price. According to these studies, the share price of a corporation suffering a disaster falls by about 5 to 8 percent within the first few days after a disaster. This decline is reasonable, because stakeholders may consider their investments to be in danger.

What is interesting is how recovery of the share price depends on the efficiency in recovering critical business functions. Past cases have shown that efficient recovery has enabled companies to regain the confidence of financial analysts quickly, and their share values have climbed back to the prices preceding the disaster, even increasing by 10 to 15 percent in the following 100 days. Companies that recovered with many difficulties, instead, were penalized with declining share values, about 15 percent on average (Hiles 2002). These facts demonstrate how a company's reputation affects tangible items such as the share price, not only permitting a company to rapidly regain share prices held before a disaster but even improving on those quotes. An inefficient recovery, in contrast, harms the company's reputation, which may have a perverse effect on share prices.

Another intangible cost is lost opportunities. During a down-time period, potential customers who would have been conducting business with the company suffering the failure may choose a competitor. This lost opportunity not only causes an immediate loss but also may have persistent negative effects because those customers could be lost forever. Calculating such loss of future revenue is very difficult. Historical data showing the rate of new customers in a given period could provide a broad estimate.

After recovery, the company's management might be forced to initiate an expensive corporate image and marketing campaign and a promotional campaign with significant price discounts to regain the confidence of customers and rebuild its reputation. The cost of such promotional and marketing campaigns can be evaluated precisely and must be taken into account as possible additional costs of down time.

RISK MANAGEMENT

Risk is defined as the possibility of suffering harm or loss, and *risk management* is the process of planning for such eventuality (Wold and Shriver 2002). The goal of risk management is not to eliminate all risks (which would be impossible in practice), but rather to find an acceptable balance between reducing risk and preparing the organization for losses. The risk management process has three steps:

1. *Risk analysis*: Identify the types of losses that may occur, determine the causes and the likelihood that a loss will occur, and estimate the resulting cost for the organization.
2. *Risk mitigation*: Identify actions to reduce or eliminate the likelihood of occurrence of each risk, determine the cost of those actions, and produce a cost-benefit analysis of the actions for each risk and loss.
3. *Risk transfer*: Address the losses that may occur despite preventive actions and consider transferring those losses to insurers or third parties, such as service providers, vendors, or outsourcers in general.

Risk Analysis

A risk analysis includes these activities:

- Identify existing risks to mission-critical activities resulting from the BIA. For each mission-critical activity, threats and their possible sources should be identified.
- Establish the likelihood and impact of each possible threat. This analysis is needed for defining priorities and planning for preventive measures and recovery actions. The clear identification of the relationship between the likelihood and the impact of each risk is a key component.

Define BCM strategies for each failure cause, which means that the BCM planner must define approaches to manage the risk and estimate the trade-off between sustaining the possible losses and implementing a preventive strategy.

Risk Mitigation

Risk mitigation is a process aimed at limiting the likelihood of risks and the potential losses those risks can cause (Kaye 2001). The process of mitigating risks can be summarized as follows:

- *Avoid the causes*. Make conservative and prudent technology choices for critical assets: avoid technology risks by developing services in a robust manner and with the support of reliable platforms instead of adopting the latest technology without testing it for reliability (which is usually riskier), unless it has been proven to give a sensible competitive advantage.
- *Reduce the frequency*. All IT infrastructure components should be chosen based on their ability to ensure a low rate of failure. Operating systems and software/hardware platforms of different vendors (or different versions produced by the same vendor) often have different failure frequencies. To enforce the risk-management strategy, reliability, and not just performance and features, should be evaluated carefully when purchasing technology.
- *Minimize the impact*. Because the frequency of failures and outages can never be reduced to zero, a risk-mitigation strategy should analyze all the possible single points of failure, the failure of which may cause major losses in terms of down time and extent of service interruption. Redundancy is the typical strategy that can be applied to servers, network devices, and internal components.
- *Reduce the duration*. Minimizing the duration of down time is the ultimate goal of every DR plan—the longer the down time, the greater the loss of revenue. Many strategies can be adopted to speed up the recovery of data and functions. These may involve onsite hardware spares, onsite staff, efficient backup solutions, and alternative operating locations.

Risk Transfer

Risks that cannot be sustained by a company can be transferred to a third party that then assumes the risks in exchange for a service fee (Kaye 2001). Hiles (2002) estimated that, on average, up to 40 percent of actual losses could be transferred, but no more than that. Risk transfer can assume two forms: insurance or outsourcing.

Insurance is the traditional way of transferring risks that cannot be mitigated with in-house solutions or transferred by purchasing the service outside. Most insurers offer coverage even for risks related to Internet-based threats, such as intrusions or denial-of-service attacks.

With outsourcing, a third party provides a specific service in place of an in-house solution. This third party can then assume the risk of losses that the company may incur, either by refunding the fee paid by the company (as in the case of Web-hosting services) or reimbursing the losses (as in the case of vendors). Risk transfer is established via a contract that usually includes a service-level agreement (SLA) that should guarantee a minimum level of service to the company that purchases the service.

Risk transfer is a suitable solution in many situations, but the trade-off between the cost of possible down time, if the service is realized in-house, and the cost of the purchased service with a certain quality level should be evaluated carefully. A careful evaluation of the return on the outsourcing investment should therefore be completed to determine whether the strategy is convenient (down-time costs versus service fees). Consider, for example, networked services, Web hosting, and mainframe hosting, for which outsourcing is the common choice today.

When purchasing a critical service from a vendor instead of managing it in-house, the company signs an agreement concerning the level of service guaranteed. The parties agree on a certain up-time guarantee, expressed as a percentage of time of availability (usually a value between 99 and 100 percent) of the purchased service. Clearly, the higher the up-time guarantee, the more costly the service, and after a certain percentage of up-time guarantee, the cost that a company would pay for a given service level is not worth the benefit gained. Penalty clauses are normally defined in the SLA, which charges the ISP with monetary fines if it is unable to comply with the up-time guarantee. However, because there are loopholes in SLAs that can be exploited for the benefit of the service provider, legal clauses defined in the SLA should be reviewed carefully. Many ISPs promise an up time of 99.99 percent, but do not actually comply with their claim because of a host of limitations related to infrastructure, government policies, inefficient resources, etc.

BACKUP, RECOVERY STRATEGIES, AND CONTINUOUS DATA PROTECTION

Traditionally, backup has been seen as a batch process, running during night hours, which stores on tapes all relevant information produced during that workday. Although this process is still used and is necessary for the majority of organizations, in many other cases it is now outdated. With the increase in Web-based services and service-oriented architectures (SOAs), applications and business processes tend to be active on a 24/7 basis. Therefore, there is no longer the notion of "night hours," which was meant to be that window of inactivity of business transactions perfectly suited to take a snapshot of data. In many real-world scenarios, transactions are always running, and information is always accessed and possibly updated. In addition, the amount of data to be managed is growing every year at a terrific rate. Many commentators refer to the ever-growing amount of data that need to be managed, backed up, and restored as "the explosion of data," to emphasize both its impressive growth and chaotic nature (Campbell 2000; Kaye 2001; Nicolett and Berg, 1999; Toigo 2001, *Fighting fires on the Web*).

Recovery strategies are one of the most dynamic areas of BCP. Beyond traditional backup and recovery solutions, more sophisticated data storage and network recovery technologies are emerging, pushed by recovery speed and data availability requirements that are becoming increasingly severe. Continuous data protection (CDP) is the newest concept and most ambitious goal of BCP for what concerns data availability and recovery strategies. Despite the lack of a rigorous definition of CDP and formal standards—the Storage Networking Industry Association's (SNIA) Data Management Forum (DMF) is still working on such a definition—vendors are stressing CDP as an essential BCP practice for modern enterprises. For example, CDP has been described as "fine-grain, point-in-time views of data and applications for the purposes of data recovery," or as a function that lets "data [be] protected as close to instantaneously as [possible] after creation, and should the primary copy become unavailable, the system needs to automatically and transparently fetch one or more copies of that data" (Kerner 2005). The purpose of CDP is evident from these two statements: the highest granularity, both in time and in content, in the selection of data to be recovered; and the immediate availability of data when needed, achieved with the highest degree of automation and transparency. In more detail, what makes CDP different from previous recovery strategies is that CDP should provide continuous recovery points, so that it should be possible to roll back from *any* point in time, instead of from a *single* point in time as for traditional recovery technologies. Considering technologies, CDP is not seen as a revolutionary idea that would bring solution alternatives to the current ones. Instead, it is perceived as the concept that could drive the development of the next generation of recovery technologies, incrementally enhancing current solutions, like data snapshots and virtual tapes, and integrating them in coherent CDP-oriented data-protection frameworks. By means of such frameworks, the traditional batch-mode way of dealing with data recovery should be abandoned in favor of more proactive systems able to meet those data availability requirements needed by modern business models. The CDP's goal is ambitious, indeed, and although it is still not clear how achievable it will be, for which contexts it will be well suited (business categories, enterprise types, etc.), and to what extent it will be worth it (in particular, analyses investigating the economic and financial basis of such recovery solutions are yet to come), most of the advances in storage technologies are based on CDP premises.

Fundamentals of Backup and Recovery

Key to an effective recovery of business functions is the availability of all the company's data, as well as the reconfiguration of all critical components of the IT infrastructure (e.g., backup of servers and network devices configuration, patches, passwords, routing tables, and firewall rules).

Backup and recovery of data should achieve two fundamental goals:

- Backup should be completed with a minimal impact on the production environment and, ideally, should be performed without blocking transaction execution.
- Recovery should be efficient, so as to minimize the time necessary to restore the data and bring the system back to its operational state. The efficiency of the recovery process is a key factor for the effective restoration of the company's business functions, as a delay in recovery could cause a severe loss of market share.

Although the need to maintain backup copies of data is well recognized, many companies overlook the need to make a copy of system configurations. This requirement is overlooked so frequently because of its intrinsic organizational nature: system management and day-to-day administration of the IT infrastructure, such as a change in routing tables or firewall rules, installation of patches, or the like, must always be documented fully to be backed up. In addition, procedures should be put in place to make sure that every modification to system components—the ones needed by mission-critical activities, at least—is reported in backup copies.

Some consideration should be devoted to the particular backup requirements of desktop computers and portable systems, which have some peculiarities with respect to servers. Often the data backup process for these systems is not automated (e.g., saving data on backed-up file servers), so it is a duty of users to manually save critical data on backed-up servers. This good practice should be governed by an appropriate usage policy (i.e., a documentation possibly subscribed to by each user stating, among other things, that each user should take care of saving his or her critical data on a backed-up server and not locally). Intermediate managers should enforce this policy, devoting particular attention to having training sessions during which users should be instructed about the importance of this recovery requirement. Providing an automatic backup and restoration process for personal computers requires interoperability and platform standardization. Usually recommended are homogeneous platform operating systems, configurations, and applications among the organization's personal computers and portable devices (NIST 2002).

Alternate Sites Strategy

In addition to the safe storage of data backups, it is necessary to provide an organization with a plan for the continuation of its business functions if its primary site suffers severe damage. A DR plan should then include a strategy to recover and perform system operations at an alternate facility. Generally, three types of alternate site strategies are possible (NIST 2002):

- dedicated site owned or operated by the organization
- reciprocal agreement with an external entity (e.g., a business partner)
- commercial leased facility

As prospective alternate sites are evaluated, the DR planner should ensure that the system's security, management, operational, and technical controls are compatible with the prospective site. Controls may include measures for network security, such as firewalls and intrusion-detection systems, and physical access controls. If the service is purchased from a vendor, an SLA must be negotiated carefully. It must clearly state all conditions, such as testing time; workspace; security, hardware, and telecommunication requirements; locations of facilities; support services; declaration procedures; and recovery time frame.

The DR planners should be aware that a commercial facility usually hosts many customers, which may all be affected by the same natural disaster simultaneously. Hence, the commercial facility could be asked to recover several customers simultaneously, but might not have enough resources to do so properly. In that case, the commercial facility would tend to set priorities among its customers and not treat all of them at the same level of service. Unfortunately, this scenario is realistic, and for this reason it is extremely important to negotiate a clear and extremely detailed SLA with the commercial vendor, with defined legal and penalty clauses that address how possible disasters will be handled and how priority status is determined.

Regardless of the type of alternate site strategy used, commercial facilities provide different services and have different levels of readiness with respect to the goal of immediate resumption of all business functions. The following classification of facilities also reflects the different commercial services offered on the market (NIST 2002; Nicolett and Berg 1999; Toigo 1999):

- A cold site typically consists of a facility with adequate space and infrastructure (electric power, telecommunication connections, and environmental control) to support the IT infrastructure. However, the cold site contains neither IT equipment nor office automation equipment, such as telephones, fax machines, or copiers. The organization leasing a cold site needs to provide all the necessary equipment.
- A warm site is a partially equipped office space containing some hardware, software, telecommunication connections, and power sources. The warm site is kept in an operational state so it can be promptly made fully operative in the event of a disaster at the company's main site.
- A hot site is a fully functional and immediately ready facility equipped with all the needed hardware, software, telecommunication connections and equipment, and power sources. Hot sites are usually staffed 24 hours a day, 7 days a week. Recovery of business functions is guaranteed to be extremely fast.
- A mobile site is a self-contained, transportable shell equipped to restore immediately the subset of the most critical business functions, including telecommunication facilities. Major commercial vendors lease these mobile sites and keep them located in strategic places to enable them to reach most of the industrial plants in a relatively short time. However, to guarantee an on-time recovery, a company should sign agreements with vendors to have the mobile site ready in a time frame compatible with its business requirements.

- A mirrored site maintains an almost exact replica of the IT infrastructure of the company's main site and is always ready to recover all the business functions. Recovery is almost immediate through a mirrored site. It is usually owned and operated by the company, given the high degree of customization and specificity required.

The above solutions differ in terms of their cost and timeliness. Cold sites are less expensive to maintain, but require that the business expend considerable time to acquire and install the necessary equipment. Going down the list, we find solutions that are more expensive, but provide greater availability.

Trade-offs in the Offsite Location Choice

Backups should be kept in a safe place, where they cannot be affected by the consequences of a disaster; doing so enables their recovery in the event of a disaster that compromises or makes their original data unavailable. This has been for decades DR's golden rule, especially for mainframe-centric IT infrastructures. Effective recovery requires that in addition to data, even media for custom and purchased software together with their license information be kept offsite. Last, but not least, all documentation related to the BCM and DR plan should be backed up. It may seem obvious that BCM documentation and plans need to be available when an emergency calls for its activation, but this might not be the case if they are not kept in a safe and reachable place (e.g., offline at an alternate site).

However, although the necessity of maintaining backed up assets in a safe place is unanimously recognized, how to evaluate the safety of the offsite location, and in particular how to balance the trade-off between safety of the alternate location and physical availability of recovery data, accessibility of the secondary site, and costs of the offsite setup has proved to be not that clear. Anecdotal experience shows that it is easy to find apparently illogical situations like, for example, secondary sites two blocks away from the primary site—and likely to be affected by the same consequences in case of disasters—or offsite locations hundreds of miles far from the main one or in locations difficult to reach and poor of IT infrastructures, so that while safety is achieved in case of a disaster, the same cannot be said about the ability to effectively restore business operations at the secondary location.

There is not an unanimously recognized standard; however, as a rule of thumb, a distance of about 35 miles between the primary and the secondary sites—which is almost the size of an MAN (metropolitan area network)—is a reference value accepted by many (Robb 2005). That reference value should, of course, be considered as a gross estimation of the needed distance, which could vary considerably according to the risks that are taken into account. For instance, if risks are those derived by small disasters, that distance could be greatly reduced because it is extremely unlikely that the same small disaster is able to hit both sites at the same time. More in general, and considering especially those risks typical of disaster recovery situations, there could be cases in which a distance of about 35 miles is not sufficient. Devastation provoked by Hurricane Katrina is only the latest example of a disaster that hit an area much larger than 35 miles. Another documented case was when after the events of September 11, 2001, several U.S. agencies suggested a 200-mile plus separation between the primary and secondary facilities.

Despite these counterexamples, the point that must be stressed once again is that safety is not the only requirement. Availability, costs, and technological limitations must be taken into account. For instance, about the 200-mile plus recommendation, there was an inescapable problem in complying with it because of the fact that there were no technological solutions able to support such a distance—or if a few could be close by, they came at enormous costs—providing not simply backup copies' safety but also backup efficiency, recovery availability, and synchronous updates of large-scale transactional databases and other applications without a large performance hit. Only very recently have advances in IP SAN (Internet protocol storage area network), which we will discuss in the following, have been able to reach distances of several hundred miles, providing, at the same time, good efficiency. Costs for such solutions are, however, still very high. This simple case witnesses one of the biggest difficulties of modern BCP: solutions are no longer specific for a single requirement (e.g., data safety) as they were, sometimes, for DR in the past. On the contrary, BCP must strike a balance between many different and often contradictory requirements, maximum safety and easy accessibility, immediate availability and affordable costs, and best efficiency and high level of integration, to name just the main ones. BCP solutions inevitably have to accommodate all these needs, and from here it is easy to see why in the BCP field, more and more people stress the fact that there are no "one-size-fits-all" solutions (solutions not tailored to the needs of the specific context in which they will be applied). This way, all the trade-offs between different requirements are resolved without taking into account the peculiarities of the business, of the organization, of the market, and of the environment, leading to a BCP solution that inevitably does not fit with the context to which it will be applied.

STORAGE TECHNOLOGIES FOR DATA BACKUP AND RECOVERY

Well-Established Technologies

Some of the conventional, well-established, and experimental technologies for backing up data are summarized by Toigo (1999) as follows:

- *Server image backup*: Image backup creates a physical image of an entire disk. It operates at the physical disk level by transferring sectors of physical data storage blocks from hard disk to tape. It has fast transfer rates and provides complete server backup by transferring the entire contents of the hard disk as a single unit. This technology requires the system to be inactive during the backup.
- *Snapshot or versioning backup*: This technique is fast because, after an initial complete image backup,

it proceeds incrementally by backing up the modifications only. It works with block-level copies on a partition basis. It is widely used in traditional tape-based backup systems.

- *Full volume backup on a file-by-file basis*: Complete data sets are copied over the production network to backup devices. A process controlled by the server initiates the transfer to backup devices.
- *Incremental or differential file backup*: Files are compared with their version in the preceding backup, and only the changed files are backed up again. Differential backup keeps separate versions of the same backed-up files, whereas incremental backup keeps just the newer version.
- *Backup using object replication*: Software defines logical objects, including disk partition tables, boot volume, security information, system volume, and user data volumes. Logical objects are regarded as a single logical unit, and all data can be copied at once.
- *Electronic tape vaulting*: This process replaces the manual procedures for handling tapes stored in off-site storage facilities and for moving tapes between locations. To provide for immediate access to data stored on tapes, it exploits a wide area network (WAN) connection between the company facility and the offsite facility where the tapes are stored. Technologies such as shadowing and multiplexing controllers allow the simultaneous duplication of backup data streams in two or more tape devices. This way a company could make both a local backup (for complete recovery in the event of a disaster) and an electronic vaulting on a remote storage facility (to preserve data from a disaster, such as a flood or fire that affects the company site).
- *Remote disk mirroring*: This is another alternative to handling tapes physically. The content of disks is duplicated in near real time to a remote disk volume. The same concept is applied to redundant array of inexpensive disks (RAID) technology as a means of fault tolerance, rather than disaster recovery.

Making use of an offsite storage facility is the safest choice for preserving backups. The remote storage facility should be in a location that is unlikely to be affected by the same disasters that might affect the main company site. It could be a branch of the company or a commercial system recovery facility offering this service. Although companies with decentralized sites could choose to keep backups in their different sites, commercial storage facilities offer backup storage as a service, including media transportation, safe storage, and recovery (Nicolett and Berg 1999; NIST 2002; Toigo 1999).

Remote Mirroring

Remote mirroring techniques form the basis of many commercial systems aiming at safeguarding corporate data and providing fast recovery. However, sometimes the expectations that planners place on remote mirroring solutions are not realistic. In addition, solutions based on remote mirroring tend to be complex, both architecturally and in data management, so that they can satisfy the high requirements from companies. This complexity may lead to a lack of robustness of the recovery system, incorrect configuration, and improper array maintenance. The consequence could be the loss of synchrony between arrays or the storage of corrupted data. If this happens, a recovery could result in a multiplication of the disaster because it runs the risk of recovering corrupted or incoherent data (Kaye 2001; Toigo 2001, *Fighting fires on the Web*, 2001, Storage disaster). In addition, remote mirroring does not allow zero down time, which is considered a requirement by some senior managers. Remote mirroring, if configured properly and implemented with high-level technology, can be much faster than many other recovery alternatives, but it cannot reduce the down time to zero. Hence, remote mirroring is not the panacea that makes the nightmare of down time disappear: risk management and DR planning are still mandatory. Moreover, remote mirroring is subject to data gaps, because some sort of asynchrony is usually implemented (e.g., the mirroring between the secondary and the tertiary arrays of Figure 1). Possible consequences of incoherent recovered data should be analyzed carefully in the planning stage. Such data may provoke the loss of commercial orders, payments, or shipments, if data gaps are not identified and handled properly. Solutions designed to be completely synchronous do exist, but come at high prices in terms of performances and system latency. In fact, the problem in remote mirroring has traditionally been the latency caused by the distance, possibly many hundreds of miles, between the sites, in particular when the mirroring is synchronous (i.e., writes to production disks wait for the mirrored writes to be completed and acknowledged).

Starting from the mid-1990s, the cost of high-speed bandwidth WAN decreased and vendors realized architectures that made remote mirroring one of the best solutions at an affordable cost for many companies. The typical improvement provided for three arrays, adding an intermediate site between the company and the final remote storage facility (Toigo 1999). Figure 1 shows the traditional and the enhanced schema for remote mirroring. The benefit of the enhanced schema is twofold. First, the link between the company site and the secondary array could be a high-speed serial one, thus reducing the latency in synchronous mirroring. Second, the mirroring between

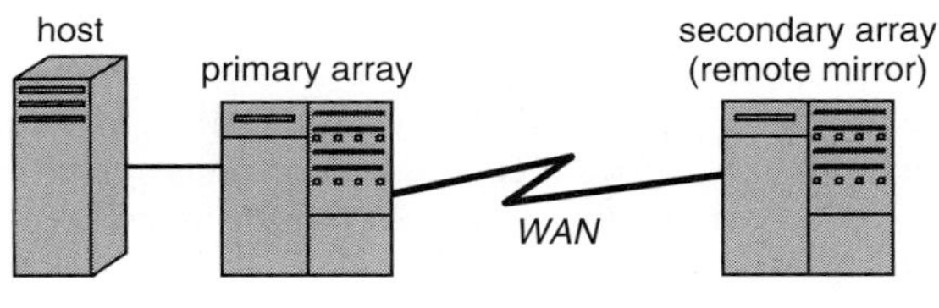

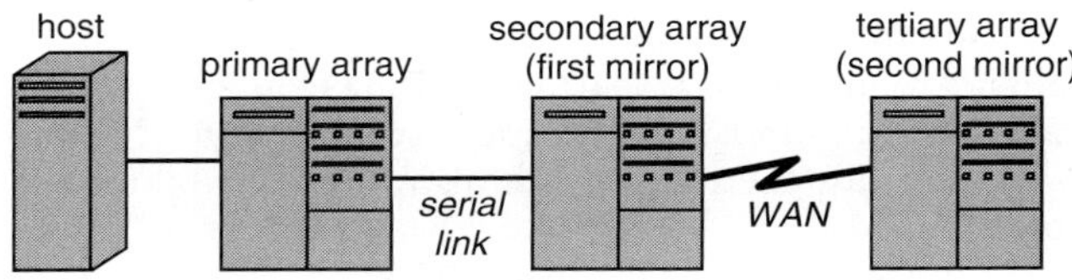

Figure 1: Remote mirroring configurations

the secondary and the final arrays, connected with a WAN, could be realized asynchronously, hence optimizing the mirror operation while not affecting the robustness of the DR solution.

Disk-to-Disk Backup

Disk-to-disk (D2D) backup technology is fast, efficient, and automatic and is able to respond to most of the current need for speed in terms of business continuance. D2D is the practice of protecting data using hard disk as a primary backup medium rather than tape technology. This contrasts with traditional approaches to backup that consist of a backup application, a backup server, tape libraries, tape drives, and media. D2D backup solutions, instead, integrate hard-disk technology and systems into the backup function to serve as the primary target of the backup application, complementing tape drives and libraries that focus on the archive function. The performance advantage is evident in terms of speed of backup and speed of restoration of backed-up data. It should be noted, however, that D2D technologies are not really new, because hard disks, the serial advanced technology attachment (ATA), and tape emulation have been IT tools at least since 1992, with products designed for block-level mirroring for quick restore and incremental backup. What makes today's D2D solutions attractive is the new emphasis on BCP and the ever-growing call for more speed and cost containment. D2D integrates tape-based backup architectures by inserting a new level of backup that fosters speed in storage and recovery. Then, on the backup disk, data can be filtered and managed so that only selected information, for instance, is then subsequently moved to tapes.

Cost of D2D solutions is the other motivating factor. In fact, the major complaint about D2D—its expense—has no more reason to hold with the advent of increasingly resilient and decreasingly expensive ATA and serial ATA arrays. Decreasing costs combined with innovative features of D2D technologies benefit from new algorithms that factor out replicated data on multiple primary disk platforms, copying only one occurrence of the data and thereby reducing the size of the data set that needs protection. A metadata repository of the data that is mirrored is normally maintained so that it becomes possible to roll back to any point in time and to return data to a usable form.

In a sense, the D2D approach, especially when combined with technology to replicate data in caching appliances at multiple locations within the enterprise network, represents the new generation of remote mirroring solutions, in which the very concept of mirroring is surpassed in favor of a vision of systems as synchronized caches that afford fault tolerance to the entire enterprise environment.

However, D2D solutions have not yet come into the mainstream, and the many promised benefits still have to be demonstrated. In particular, D2D technology must be tested in complex and critical scenarios in order to prove not just their speed but also their reliability and robustness.

To this end, what happened in 2002 is not encouraging. Vendors concerned with the many configurations of D2D founded the EBSI (Enhanced Backup Solutions Initiative). EBSI gained wide consensus among consumers, but was first blocked, then absorbed, by SNIA. Little has been done since to evaluate and compare data-protection solutions appearing in the market.

Storage Area Networking

Let us introduce some basic definitions of the key network-based storage technologies (Steinberg 2002, Kaye 2001):

- *Direct Attached Storage (DAS)*: DAS requires that all storage access methods involve a central processing unit (CPU)/server, with requests sent over an input/output (I/O) bus such as SCSI or integrated device electronics (IDE). As a result, DAS storage devices are tightly coupled with the host computer's operating system, and distance limitations come into play. DAS devices can be physically inside a server or external to it.
- *Network Attached Storage (NAS)*: NAS describes a specialized file server and storage device connected to a local area network (LAN) hub or switch. Client machines mount volumes (i.e., disks of the server) to transfer data files to local machines.
- *Storage Area Network (SAN)*: A SAN is a dedicated, high-performance network infrastructure optimized to move large amounts of data for applications that require optimal performance, redundancy, and availability. SANs provides scalability, accessibility, manageability, and fine-grained data selection. Most of all, SANs greatly extend the distance of a peripheral channel with respect to NASs that are bounded to LANs.

Among storage technologies, the SANs in particular have gained wide acceptance—SANs amount to almost 50 percent of the current storage solutions on the market. A SAN is a specialized, high-speed network attaching servers and storage devices using network devices, such as routers, gateways, hubs, and switches. Its main benefit is that it eliminates dedicated connections between servers and storage devices. The most common SAN technology is fibre-channel networking with the SCSI command set. A typical fibre-channel SAN is made up of a number of fibre-channel switches that are connected together to form a fabric or network. Moreover, a SAN also eliminates all restrictions on the amount of data that a server can access. A server is enabled to share a common storage environment, which may comprise many storage devices, including disk, tape, and optical storage. SAN solutions often use a dedicated network behind the servers, based primarily on fiber-channel architecture. Fiber channel provides a highly scalable bandwidth over long distances with the ability to offer full redundancy, high availability, and high performance. A SAN normally supports direct high-speed transfers between servers and storage devices in the following ways:

- *Server to storage*: This is the common method of interaction with storage devices. The SAN advantage is that the same storage device may be accessed serially or concurrently by multiple servers.

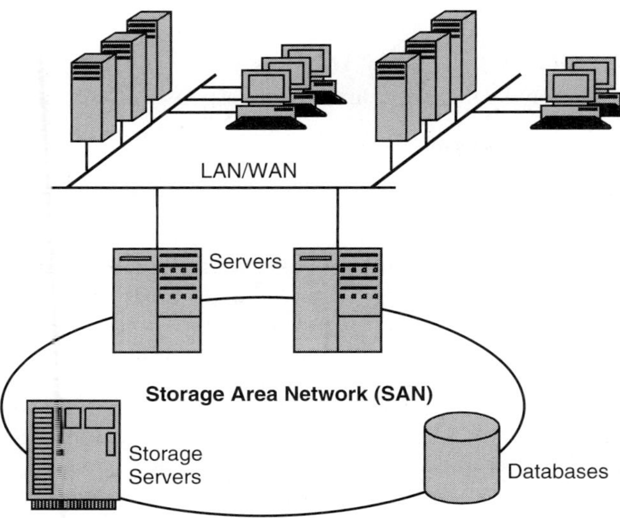

Figure 2: Storage area network (SAN) reference architecture

- *Server to server*: In this case, a SAN is used to enable high-speed and high-volume communications between servers.
- *Storage to storage*: With this configuration, a disk array could back up its data directly to tape across the SAN without processor intervention. Alternatively, a device could be mirrored remotely across the SAN.

Figure 2 shows the typical SAN architecture.

However, even SANs do not come without problems and limitations. For instance, network managers are often concerned with interoperability because vendors have designed proprietary products to maintain a competitive advantage. Despite the promise of interoperability, there are no standards for a heterogeneous storage environment, and this on the one side introduces restrictions in the technology choice, while on the other it often leads to less-than-optimal solutions, either for functionalities or for costs. Other factors that affect interoperability of SANs are related to the difficulty in making use of efficient management software and diagnostic tools. Some of the main vendors, like IBM and HP, are offering complete SAN frameworks, in which the storage technology is integrated with management and diagnostic tools provided by the vendor. However, these solutions often look like the one-size-fits-all solutions that we previously mentioned, most of the time tailored for large network infrastructures, difficult if not impossible to integrate with existing technologies, limited to a single family line of products and one single vendor, and usually extremely expensive.

SAN Security Issues

Another issue that is often disregarded when SANs are deployed is security (Rhodes 2005). As Haron (2002) points out, since SAN is usually used in highly critical systems that require high availability, confidentiality, and integrity, organizations must be aware of all potential points at which a security breach might occur and include these considerations when designing SAN security solutions. In other terms, this observation means that all the usual security problems, risks, threats, and countermeasures apply to SANs too, despite the fact that the adoption of consolidated security solutions is still not so common in the BCP field.

In addition to security considerations based on the networked nature of SANs and the value of information usually transmitted on SAN infrastructures, laws such as the Sarbanes-Oxley Act of 2002 and the Health Insurance Portability and Accountability Act of 1996 (HIPAA)—to name the main U.S. related laws; similar laws have been promulgated in the European Union and in other countries—make an organization accountable for how information is processed and stored.

Threats to SANs can be summarized in three basic categories:

- *Unintentional and due to accidents or mistakes*: These are what we have called small disasters, which can happen often, may have limited consequences when considered singularly, but may become one of the most serious causes of down time because of their frequency. Precautions must be taken as for all critical network components. For instance, SAN switches have ports that can be restricted to management purposes only. Next, the physical access to the SAN can be restricted by configuring dedicated management networks—a common design choice in modern network layouts. Access to the management network can be controlled by means of corporate firewalls and virtual private networks. Finally, access control lists at the application level should be used to authenticate and authorize users accessing the SAN configuration. In short, all common solutions for the correct management of a critical IT asset, as a SAN is, should be put in place. Finally, encryption for both data in transit and data kept in storage must be used.
- *Simple malicious attack that uses existing equipment and possibly some easily obtained information*: These attacks usually come from internal sources, such as disgruntled employees looking to destroy information or someone looking to gain profit or an advantage from the information obtained. Security measures applied to address the previous point are effective here too, but often are not sufficient. There are numerous ways an internal source can obtain sensitive information under false pretenses—the main one is posing as an authorized user or device—and could result in gaining access to the SAN. To counter these risks, authentication requirements should apply to users, to the devices, and to applications. However, although authentication is the main mechanism for preventing the impersonation of other identities, it has limitations, mostly related to the quality of the implementation and the strength of credentials. If the credentials are weak, or if authentication data are exposed because of faulty implementation, the mechanism itself can and will be defeated. For these reasons, architectural countermeasures are normally adopted. These rely on the fact that the networked architecture must be designed to minimize the possibility of spreading an intrusion into the network. The basic means to achieve this goal is zoning, which is a method of arranging SAN devices into logical groups over the physical configuration

of the fabric. Zoning adds another level of security to a SAN because it controls access to a SAN from a host device. Only devices that are authorized to access a particular storage resource are allowed to do so.

- *Large-scale attack on SAN infrastructures*: Although attacks of this type have been extremely rare in SANs today, with the increasingly diffusion of SANs and the augmented value of information traversing and stored on SANs, it is likely that even SANs will become targets of external attacks, as many of the network components of an IT infrastructure currently are. Solutions to be applied are the ones studied and adopted to protect large and complex IT networks. SANs must be considered as other critical assets, just as corporate databases or application servers. This is a strong reason for a better and enlarged convergence between BCP and security planning.

Internet SCSI

An alternative, and more recent (Satran et al. 2004), SAN protocol is iSCSI, which uses the same SCSI command set over TCP/IP (and, typically, Ethernet). In this case, the switches are Ethernet switches and the network is not referred to as a fabric. The iSCSI protocol uses TCP/IP for its data transfer. Unlike other network storage protocols, such as fibre channel (which is the foundation of most SANs), it requires only the simple and ubiquitous Ethernet interface (or any other TCP/IP-capable network) to operate. This enables low-cost centralization of storage without all of the expense and incompatibility normally associated with fibre-channel storage area networks. The other benefit that iSCSI promises to bring is a lower implementation and management complexity with respect to fiber-channel SANs.

However, again, as already seen for other emergent technologies, the early hype faded and problems emerged to slow down the adoption. Critics noted that one misguided expectation about iSCSI was that it could be the SAN protocol that would quickly replace fiber channel. This did not happen, and vendors, such as IBM, that initially targeted the same market segment of fiber-channel SAN, have modified their offering of iSCSI solutions from big high-end premium products to entry-level storage devices for mid-sized businesses. According to these indications, iSCSI seems to find its place as a solution aimed at those companies that could not afford the enormous costs of high-end fiber-channel SANs. There are actually signs that the shift of iSCSI from a competitor of fiber-channel SAN to a complementary solution able to lower the entry barrier has been the right move. IDC, a leading provider of global IT research and advice, has forecast that by 2009, over 30 percent of all SAN disk storage systems revenue and almost 50 percent of SAN revenue in price bands 1 to 4 (systems with average selling price of $1 to $49,900) will be generated from storage systems based on iSCSI technology. From 2004 to 2009, the iSCSI SAN market will grow at a compound annual growth rate of 107 percent. If this trend is confirmed, it can be welcomed as an efficient, sophisticated, and reasonably priced SAN solution for mid-sized enterprises that have so far been excluded from adopting SAN technology.

TRAINING AND TESTING

Business Continuity Training

Operational continuity, emergency response, and security plans should be exercised twice a year. For example, many companies, such as Texas Instruments and Hewlett Packard, operate out of their backup data centers periodically, so that security experts are prepared for any disasters that may hamper normal business operations. Updated plans alone are not enough to ensure continuity if recovery team members do not exercise them and therefore do not know exactly what they are supposed to do. Team members should receive training in recovery concepts in general and their team's functions in particular. This way, needed improvements in strategies and plans are discovered, and team members may acquire valuable experience in dealing with their duties in the event of a recovery scenario.

An organization should review the following plan elements during the exercise:

- *Recovery team alert list*: Commonly known as a "calling tree," this is contact information for all personnel assigned to the team. Because this list can change frequently, team leaders should update it regularly and communicate changes to each team member.
- *Critical functions list*: This is a list of critical functions that each team must accomplish in a recovery scenario.
- *Team recovery steps*: Strategies for recovery of critical functions must be reviewed to ensure that they meet the objectives stated in the BIA.
- *Functional recovery steps:* Procedures to complete all operational recoveries must be reviewed and validated to determine effectiveness and efficiency.
- *Vendor and customer list*: This contact information for critical vendors and customers must be reviewed to determine its accuracy and completeness.
- *Offsite storage list*: Critical facilities or resources stored offsite must be reviewed to determine their operational status and completeness.

Testing Processes and Procedures

To determine which business processes to test and in which order, the BIA analysis should be at hand, because it is the BIA that states mission-critical activities and defines recovery requirements, such as the RTO and RPO. The most challenging aspect of exercising and testing a BCM plan is devising a testing method and implementation schedule such that the following occur:

- The BCM and DR plans are tested to the fullest extent possible, according to the BIA.
- The costs are sustainable and well documented.
- Interruptions of normal business operations are minimal or nonexistent.
- The tests provide a high degree of assurance in recovery capability.
- Evaluation of test results provide quality feedback for maintaining BCM and DR plans.

One of the most common methods for testing BCM and DR plans involves using checklists, performing simulations, tabletop exercises, checking the procedures in parallel between the main and an alternate site, and fully testing the DR plan by interrupting operations.

Checklist Testing

Checklists are the primary tools for testing a plan, because they are inexpensive to implement and maintain. A checklist should be subdivided into groups of checklists dedicated to the different business units or organization areas involved in the DR plan. They should be specific and appropriate for each business unit and for the phases of mission-critical activities in which they are involved. In addition, the experience of each business unit should be used in preparing and updating checklists. A checklist test can be used to validate multiple components of the DR plan; for example, key procedures validation, hardware and software configuration, documentation completeness and update status, availability of process-specific resources, and data backup correctness and reliability.

Simulation Testing

The purpose of simulating a failure is to evaluate the effectiveness of the BCM plan without interfering with normal business operations. Hardware, software, personnel, communications, procedures, documentation, transportation, utilities, and alternate site processing should be included in a simulation test. Factors such as traveling, moving equipment, or coordinating activities with external agencies may not be feasible during a simulated test. However, checklists can provide a reasonable level of assurance for many of these scenarios.

Tabletop Exercise

According to the Disaster Recovery Institute International (DRII), a tabletop exercise is "one method of exercising teams in which participants review and discuss the actions they would take per their plans, but do not perform any of these actions. The exercise can be conducted with a single team, or multiple teams, typically under the guidance of exercise facilitators." A tabletop exercise is a convenient way of testing a BCM plan; however, to be effective, it requires careful planning. First, the BCP or BCP sections that are to be tested must be identified. Then, members of the recovery team, those responsible for business processes whose BCP will be exercised and observers (e.g., senior managers, auditors, etc.) are called to participate. The tabletop exercise must then be focused on one or two disruption scenarios, such as failures to support services, to the IT infrastructure, or to key software applications (Hayes 2000).

Parallel Testing

In parallel tests, historical transactions, such as the prior business day's transactions, are processed against the preceding day's backup files at the replicated or hot site. All reports produced at the alternate site should agree with those produced at the main site.

Full-Interruption Testing

A full-interruption test activates the DR plan in its entirety. It is clearly the most meaningful test and also the most expensive and intrusive. It could disrupt normal operations and result in losses to the company.

BUSINESS CONTINUITY LAWS AND REGULATIONS

The matter of BCM has been the subject of several laws and regulations in the past decade. Such laws and regulations are often specific to an industry sector, and specify requirements for business continuity and disaster recovery planning. Requirements vary among industry sectors, although they all seem to be inspired by general best practices and guidelines—similar to the ones described in this chapter—developed over the past decade. The bottom line for all these laws and regulations is to force organizations to exercise due care to ensure that necessary data are available. Noakes-Fry, Baum, and Runyon (2005) presented a comprehensive list of BCM/DR related laws and regulation for the four key industry sectors: health care, government, finance, and utilities. Table 1 lists the main U.S. laws and regulations.

BUSINESS CONTINUITY AND INVESTMENT DECISIONS

BCM and DR solutions are usually expensive. For comprehensive solutions, costs were high in the old days of data centers and continue to be high today in the world of networked resources, replicated servers, and mirrored sites. A review by Toigo (2004) in *Network Computing* presented solutions from some vendors that address the needs of a reference fictional retailer taken as the test case. Costs for those solutions began at approximately $300,000, rose to $700,000, surpassed $1 million, and reached $6 million for the most expensive. Indeed, business continuity is not compatible with low budgets, especially because by its nature business continuity is organization-wide and not modular.

Widup (2003) raises an interesting question in her SANS Institute GSEC Practical: because economic difficulties have severely affected the development of BCM plans, why is BCM still proposed as an organization-wide plan instead of developing less monolithic and more modular approaches and less comprehensive and more affordable projects to comply with reduced investments? This is more a business than a technical trade-off that is rarely addressed in the BCM literature and online publications. Often statistics are presented about the percentage of companies that do not have any kind of BCM plan in place, do not perform any kind of testing and maintenance of plans, or do not invest in BCM planning. This is evidence that the perceived importance of BCM has diminished rather than increased. For instance, Widup (2003) discussed the results of a poll conducted by *InformationWeek* (D'Antoni 2003), that of the 300 business technology executives interviewed about their 2003 budget plans and IT strategies, 65 percent said that BCM planning and improved disaster preparedness are priorities. This is a decrease from 77 percent the previous year. Moreover, some 61 percent of executives at small companies reported a continued commitment to

Table 1: BCM/DR-Related Laws and Regulations

Industry Sector	Laws and Regulations	Requirements for BCM
Health care	Health Insurance Portability and Accountability Act (HIPAA) of 1996	Requires data backup plan, DR plan, and emergency-mode operation plan, as well as appropriate measures relative to the size, complexity, and resources of the organization.
	Food and Drug Administration (FDA) Code of Federal Regulations (CFR), Title XXI, 1999	Requires electronic records and electronic signatures.
Government	Federal Information Security Act (FISMA) of 2002, Title III of the E-Government Act of 2002 (PL 107-347, December 2002)	Mostly focused on data security rather than BCM/DR.
	Continuity of Operations (COOP) and Continuity of Government (COG). Federal Preparedness Circular 69, July 26, 1999	Requires planning considerations for federal government operations. BCP must be implemented even without warning and operational no more than 12 hours after activation, and sustainable for up to 30 days.
	National Institute of Standards and Technology (NIST) Special Publication (SP) 800-34, *Contingency Planning Guide for Information Technology Systems,* 2002	Specifies detailed recommendations from NIST, requiring contingency, DR, and COOP plans.
	NIST 800-53, Recommended Security Controls for Federal Information Systems, February 2005	Provides guidelines and requirements for BC planning policy and procedures, plan, training, plan testing, and updating.
Finance	Federal Financial Institutions Examination Council (FFIEC) Handbook, 2003–2004 (Chapter 10)	Requires managers to be accountable for organization-wide contingency planning and for timely resumption of operations in the event of a disaster.
	Basel II, Basel Committee on Banking Supervision, *Sound Practices for Management and Supervision, 2003*	Requires banks to put in place BC and DR plans to ensure continuous operation and to limit losses.
	Interagency Paper on Sound Practices to Strengthen the Resilience of the U.S. Financial System, 2003	Focused on systemic risk as a result of the World Trade Center disaster. Requires BCPs to be upgraded and tested to incorporate new risk categories. Authorizes actions against banks that fail to comply with specified requirements.
Utilities	Governmental Accounting Standards Board (GASB) Statement No. 34, June 1999	Requires a BCP to ensure that an agency's mission continues in a time of crisis. Applies to all government entities that operate utilities.
	North American Electric Reliability Council (NERC) Cyber Security Standards, 2006	Formerly NERC 1300, replaces NERC 1200. Defines mandatory obligations for recovery plans.
	Federal Energy Regulatory Commission (FERC) RM01-12-00 (Appendix G), 2003	Mandates recovery plans. Does not apply to Rural Utilities Service (RUS) borrowers and limited distribution cooperatives.
	RUS 7 CFR Part 1730, 2005	Emergency restoration plan required as condition of continued borrowing. Applies to all rural *utility* borrowers.
	Telecommunications Act of 1996, Section 256, Coordination for Interconnectivity	Requires the Federal Communications Commission (FCC) to establish procedures to oversee coordinated network planning by carriers and other providers.

BCM planning, a drop of 14 percent compared with the year before. Responses among managers at mid-sized companies showed a similar decline, and larger sites were down 7 percent from the previous year.

Given the costs presented in Toigo (2004) and the current economic difficulties, it is no surprise that small and mid-sized companies have severely cut spending on BCM plans. Nevertheless, the BCM field seems to have no adequate proposal to face this situation. This demonstrates a weakness of BCM planning, which has made it very difficult to formulate proposals well suited for small and mid-sized companies, which often simply rely on basic tape-based backups and other low-cost precautions.

One way to make BCM solutions more attractive to small and mid-sized companies is to make them more modular; for example, there should be different modules for different business functions, instead of imposing an organization-wide approach. Modular solutions are easier to integrate with existing infrastructures and technology. Most of the expense of BCM solutions comes from the purchase of dedicated equipment, substitution of existing technology/components, and the impossibility of preserving previous IT investments that often cannot be integrated or reused with BCM solutions. Moreover, initial expenditures are not the only barrier to adopting BCM solutions. If those solutions are not made less expensive to maintain and update, the natural consequence of each period of economic difficulty will be the reduction of investments in BCM and in the maintenance and development of existing plans. Floods, fire, and power outages become secondary thoughts, and BCM budgets get smaller. We should admit openly that from a risk-management perspective it does make sense.

However, it is clear that modularizing a BCM plan and supporting only some functions instead of *all* mission-critical functions means having plans that are generally inadequate to sustain business continuity in the event of severe disasters. The coherence of an enterprise-wide plan, based on enterprise-wide analyses, developments, and tests, would be lost, as well as the performance and effectiveness of the more sophisticated technology in place today that is able to satisfy continuous-availability requirements. Nevertheless, BCM analysts should consider that in most cases, cutting expenditures on BCM is not merely done because of the shortsightedness of a company's management; instead it may be the result of a realistic calculation in situations in which financial shortages are the primary reason why a company goes out of business.

In these situations, BCM analysts and vendors should make efforts to demonstrate the cost-effectiveness of solutions, to consider the trade-off between BCM investments and other technologies from the perspective of corporate management, and to be able to scale down solutions when circumstances need it.

Finally, to foster the adoption of complex BCM solutions, some BCM literature, especially online literature and marketing communications, seems sometimes to stress excessively the potential consequences of catastrophic and tragic events on business. Unfortunately, these consequences are sometimes presented without a corresponding realistic analysis of the likelihood of occurrence of those events, which actually is extremely low for the great majority of organizations. This literature has much in common with many marketing campaigns about cyberattacks in the information security area: both tend to focus on short-term emotional reactions instead of demonstrating cost-effectiveness and the technical soundness of solutions. Information to enable a correct cost-benefit analysis is not provided to the customers, which turns out to be a shortsighted strategy in the mid- to long-term period when economic considerations become paramount for investment decisions.

BEYOND BUSINESS CONTINUITY: BUSINESS RESILIENCE

The world of business continuity is a lively world, indeed. We have just moved from disaster recovery to business continuity management, considerably enlarging the scope of the discipline, and many are already calling for a new step ahead (critics would say that yet another buzzword is taking the scene). Business resilience (BR) is the new goal. Before introducing a definition, we cannot avoid observing that literally, *resilience* means "an ability to recover from or adjust easily to misfortune or change" (from the *Merriam-Webster Dictionary*), which looks exactly like what we have discussed in BCM. Apparently, critics are not without their arguments. However, the notion of BR is the topic of many new publications in the BCM field (Cocchiara 2005; Owens 2004; Ross 2004) and has been emphasized in the last BCM (Business Continuity Management) World 2005 Conference, whose Web page (www.bcmworld.net/conference.htm) states: "Business resilience [can be defined] as the ability of an organization's business operations to rapidly adapt and respond to internal and external dynamic changes and continue operations with limited impact to business." It is hard to distinguish BR from BC reading this definition, but luckily the same Web page specifies that "Business Continuity has evolved over the years, taking shape under the influence of many parts including IT disaster recovery (DR), contingency planning, crisis and emergency management to name a few. Today, the scope of business and continuity management has broadened in discipline to encompass 'Business Resilience.' Business resilience moves us forward along the continuum of business continuity planning from the sense of reacting to recover from an event to becoming immune to the event." Thus, BR is about assuming an aggressive, offensive posture toward events that may impair business operations, in contrast to the defensive approach assumed so far.

Although the definition still seems a little too vague to be operational, some consequences can be derived. An "offensive posture" translates into more planning, more organization, and more readiness. If an organization wants to become immune to events that may provoke failures, then mitigation and recovery strategies are no longer the focus of the process because the goal shifts from deploying the fastest and most effective recovery strategies to organizing the whole business and infrastructure to not require any recovery at all. The change in the perspective could be enormous, as well as the efforts and investments required to achieve it. That is probably even the best argument for critics: whether achieving a real business resilience will require such an amount of work, time, and money, it is likely that very few will be able to do that, while for the great majority, business resilience will simply turn into the new buzzword used in revamping old solutions.

Principles of Business Resilience

A better definition of BR's goal can be found in Owens (2004). Key to BR seems to be that it is not just about surviving a disaster or recovery from a failure. The perspective is larger than that because at the core, BR is about the ability to deal with sudden change. It is impossible to account for and prepare for every possible eventuality, of course; it is nevertheless possible to design for resilience and to train for dealing with disruption. Thus, BR is about dealing with sudden change, which may or may not be negative or destructive change. They could be positive changes, as well, such as technological improvements, reorganizations, and so forth. This represents the enlarged perspective and the most challenging goal, because ultimately BR represents a shift from the traditional field of disaster recovery and business continuity, which are about system failures and business losses, to change management, agile organizations, and preparedness in a dynamic context.

Ingredients proposed for an effective BR stem from efficient communication and collaboration among people, strict dependency from the "weakest link" (i.e., the weakest component in the organization is likely to provoke the failure), profound knowledge and in-depth analysis of the context in which a business is operated (this because failures most of the time do not happen randomly), actual measures of key factors (characteristics such as the availability of a critical system must be measured with precise metrics, not by means of gross, subjective estimates), and interchangeability of infrastructural components. Finally, BR must be an approach, so training is of fundamental importance.

A Business Resilience Framework

IBM, for example, has proposed a framework for BR that includes five major attribute classes associated with improved business resilience:

- *Control and comply*: the attributes necessary to anticipate, evaluate, and control risks associated with complying with industry and government regulations, as well as those risks associated with environmental, social, technical, and economic factors
- *Predict and detect*: the attributes necessary to predict, detect, estimate, measure, and report events to ensure security, privacy, and protection of critical data, enabling the business to respond to any threats that may jeopardize business operations
- *Deflect and solidify*: the attributes necessary to create a solid physical and logical topology to deflect problems and ensure continuity of operations through reliability, redundancy, and failover
- *Adapt and optimize*: the attributes necessary to ensure adaptable, efficient, and flexible integrated risk-mitigation strategies, technologies, and processes
- *Protect and preserve*: the attributes necessary to ensure that the business is preserved and protected against accidental and intentional damage, alteration, or misuse.

Together with the five attribute classes, the IBM framework identifies six object layers related to the business resilience. Those layers model the corresponding layers of most business organizations. They are:

- *Strategy*: objects related to the strategies used by the business to complete day-to-day activities while ensuring continuous operations, such as financial, manufacturing, and disaster recovery strategies
- *Organization*: objects related to the structure, skills, communications, and responsibilities of your employees (Examples include human resources, training, and internal and external communications.)
- *Applications and data*: objects related to the software necessary to enable business operations, as well as the method used to develop that software (Examples include customer relationship management (CRM) applications, enterprise resource planning (ERP) applications, databases, and transaction processors.)
- *Processes*: objects related to the critical business processes necessary to run the business, as well as the IT processes used to ensure smooth operations (Examples include accounts receivable, accounts payable, change management, and problem management.)
- *Technology*: objects related to the systems, network, and industry-specific technology necessary to enable your applications and data (Examples include host systems, workstations, and IP networks.)
- *Facilities*: objects related to the buildings, factories, and offices necessary to house your organization and your production or service technologies (Examples include data centers, office buildings, and physical security operations.)

IBM uses its business resilience framework as a logical representation that provides an examination of a business that is both comprehensive and modular. The six object layers expand into more than 140 objects examined by means of the five attribute classes for a complete analysis of resilience capabilities.

It must be noted, however, that the framework for BR has many similarities with traditional risk management and BC/DR plans. For instance, considering the attribute classes, "Control and comply" are issues that a risk analysis takes into account, as well as "Predict and detect," which is partially covered by a BIA, too. Next, "Deflect and solidify" looks like a different way to name recovery solutions. Considering the six object layers, instead, it is evident that they identify subjects that have always been considered in BCM.

In this regard, it seems that criticisms concerning the difficulty of clearly identifying the innovative nature of BR are confirmed.

CONCLUSION

Internet connections have driven the development of new business models that have enlarged and modified the scope of DR since the days of mainframe-based data centers. This amplified discipline has taken the name of *business continuity management*, of which DR is today one aspect of a greater process aimed at ensuring the continuity of mission-critical business activities. A requirement that follows this evolution in business models is the need for immediate recovery and continuous operations with zero down time as their ultimate goal. Although the zero-down-time goal is still extremely difficult to achieve, and this should be stated clearly in each BCM project, the BCM field has developed new planning methods and techniques to match these requirements. As a consequence, the process of putting in place an effective BCM plan uses sophisticated technologies, but the many interconnections with both the IT infrastructure and the business functions of a company make it more complex. Companies could suffer severe losses if they experience one of the many risks, not just traditional disasters, but even so-called small disasters, which include failures of the IT infrastructure, telecommunications, power outages, and human errors. E-commerce business models can no longer sustain those frequent downtimes or network outages as in the past, when companies accepted RTOs of some days in the event of an IT failure and RPOs that restored resources to the previous status.

Processes that enable a more efficient recovery phase in the event of a disaster, such as the business impact analysis, the work area recovery, risk analysis, and the innovative backup and recovery techniques, therefore assume great importance.

GLOSSARY

Activation: The implementation of business continuity procedures, activities, and plans in response to an emergency, disaster, or incident.

Alternate Site: A location, other than the normal facility, used to process data and conduct critical business functions in the event of a disaster.

Backup: The process of copying data (paper-based or electronic) so as to make the data available for use if the original data are lost, destroyed, or corrupted.

Business Continuity Management (BCM): A management process that identifies potential impacts that threaten an organization and provides a framework for ensuring the continuity of business operations in the event of a disaster, failure, or unplanned incident.

Business Continuity Plan: A clearly and formally defined plan to use in the event of an emergency, incident, or failure. Typically, it includes the description of all key personnel, resources, services, and actions required to manage a BCM process.

Business Continuity Planning: The process of planning for the identification of potential losses, prevention measures, viable recovery strategies, and training/testing/maintenance activities provided by the BCM process.

Business Impact Analysis (BIA): The management analysis that addresses financial and nonfinancial effects that might result in the event of a disaster or failure. The BIA represents the basis for every BCM strategy and solution.

Data Mirroring: A process that permits the copying of data instantaneously to another location.

Disaster: Any event that can cause an organization to be unable to provide critical business functions for a certain period of time. Also commonly known as a *Disruption*.

Disaster Recovery: An integral part of the BCM plan aimed at recovering and restoring an organization's capabilities (e.g., IT and telecommunications) after a disaster.

Electronic Vaulting: Transfer of data to an off-site storage facility via a communication link or a different portable medium.

Facility: Location containing equipment and infrastructure to perform normal business functions.

Loss: The financial or nonfinancial consequence resulting from a disaster/failure.

Mission-Critical Activities: The critical operational or business activities necessary to the organization's ability to achieve its business objectives.

Network Outage: The interruption of system availability as a result of a communication failure affecting a network.

Offsite Storage Facility: A secure and remote location where backups of hardware, software, data files, documents, or equipment are stored.

Risk Assessment: The overall process of risk identification, analysis, and evaluation.

Risk Management: The processes and structures put in place to effectively manage negative events to minimize adverse effects and reduce damages or losses to an acceptable level.

Service-Level Agreement (SLA): A formal agreement between a service provider and the client that specifies all conditions of service provision.

System Outage: An unplanned interruption in system availability resulting from operational problems or hardware/software failures.

Work Area Recovery: The identification of the minimum level of resources (e.g., personnel, hardware, software, data, or telecommunications) required after a failure that permits an organization to conduct its mission-critical activities at a minimum level of service.

CROSS REFERENCES

See *Backup and Recovery System Requirements*; *Business Requirements of Backup Systems*; *Computer Security Incident Response Teams (CSIRTs)*; *Evaluating Storage Media Requirements*.

REFERENCES

BCI. 2005. Business continuity management—Good practice guidelines. *The Business Continuity Institute*. www.thebci.org/goodpracticeguidetoBCM.pdf (accessed February 1, 2005).

Bounds, G. 2003. Preparing for the worst: A best practices guide to disaster recovery planning. *Contingency Planning Magazine*. www.contingencyplanning.com/archives/2003/apr/index.aspx (accessed July 1, 2005).

Campbell, R. 2000. *Continuity planning in the new millenium—The convergence of disciplines*. www.disaster-resource.com/cgi-bin/article_search.cgi?id='16' (accessed February 1, 2006).

Cocchiara, R. 2005. *Beyond disaster recovery: Becoming a resilient business*. IBM Global Service. Somers, NY. http://www-1.ibm.com/services/us/bcrs/pdf/wp_becoming-a-resilient-business.pdf (accessed February 1, 2006).

D'Antoni, H. 2003. Business continuity slides down the priority scale. *InformationWeek*. www.informationweek.com/story/IWK20030109S0002 (accessed February 1, 2006).

Haron, M. 2002. *Is your storage area network secure? An overview of storage area network from security perspective*. www.sans.org/rr/whitepapers/storage/516.php (accessed February 1, 2006).

Hayes, J. M. 2000. Business continuity planning tabletop exercise white paper. *Disaster Recovery Journal*. www.drj.com/new2dr/toolchest/tabletop.pdf (accessed June 30, 2006).

Hiles, A. 2002. *Business impact analysis: What's your downside?* www.rothstein.com/articles/busimpact.html (accessed February 1, 2006).

Kaye, D. 2001. *Strategies for Web hosting and managed services*. New York: Wiley.

Kerner, S. M. 2005. *A new beginning for backup*. www.enterprisestorageforum.com/continuity/features/article.php/3546911 (accessed February 1, 2006).

Merchantz, B. 2002. The true cost of downtime. *Contingency Planning & Management*. www.contingencyplanning.com/archives/2002/mayjun/index.aspx (accessed July 1, 2006).

Nicolett, M., and T. Berg. 1999. *Storage backup and recovery for distributed systems* (Strategic Analyses Report R-09-3148). Stamford, CT: Gartner Group.

NIST. 2002. *Contingency planning guide for information technology systems*. NIST Special Publication 800-34. csrc.nist.gov/publications/nistpubs/800-34/sp800-34.pdf (accessed May 25, 2007).

Noakes-Fry, K., and T. Diamond. 2001. *Business continuity recovery planning and management: Perspective* (Technology Overview DPRO-100862). Stamford, CT: Gartner Group.

Noakes-Fry, K., and T. Diamond. 2002. *Business continuity planning software: Perspective* (Technology Overview DPRO-100469). Stamford, CT: Gartner Group.

Noakes-Fry, K., C. H. Baum, and B. Runyon. 2005. *Laws influence business continuity and disaster recovery planning among industries*. Stamford, CT: Gartner Group.

Owens, C. 2004 *Fostering business resilience*. Boston: Interisle Consulting Group.

Rhodes, C. 2005 *Security considerations for storage area networks*. www.infosecwriters.com/text_resources/pdf/SAN_CRhodes.pdf (accessed February 1, 2006).

Robb, D. 2005. *Disaster recovery sites: How far away is far enough?* www.enterprisestorageforum.com/continuity/features/article.php/3552971 (accessed February 1, 2006).

Ross, S. J. 2004. *Modeling resiliency*. www.isaca.org/Template.cfm?Section=Home&Template=/ContentManagement/ContentDisplay.cfm&ContentID=19737 (accessed February 1, 2006).

Satran, J., K. Meth, C. Sapuntzakis, M. Chadalapaka, and E. Zeidner. 2004. *Internet small computer systems interface (iSCSI), RfC 3720*. www.ietf.org/rfc/rfc3720.txt (accessed June 15, 2007).

Scott, D., and Y. Natis. 2000. *Building continuous availability into e-applications* (Research Note COM-12-1325). Stamford, CT: Gartner Group.

Steinberg, M. 2002. *Storage area networking: An essential guide to SANs as a component of business continuation*. www.hill.com/archive/pub/papers/2002/09 (accessed February 1, 2006).

Toigo, J. W. 1999. *Disaster recovery planning: Strategies for protecting critical information assets*. 2nd ed. Englewood Cliffs, NJ: Prentice Hall PTR.

Toigo, J. W. 2001. *Fighting fires on the Web*. www.esj.com/Features/article.aspx?EditorialsID=60 (accessed February 1, 2006).

Toigo, J. W. 2001. Storage disaster: Will you recover? *Network Computing*. www.networkcomputing.com/1205/1205f1.html (accessed February 1, 2006).

Toigo, J. W. 2004. Natural selection. *Network Computing*. www.nwc.com/showitem.jhtml?articleID=17301530&pgno=6 (accessed February 1, 2006).

Widup, S. 2003. *Business continuity planning in difficult economic times* (GSEC Practical, Security Reading Room, SANS Institute). http://www.sans.org/rr/whitepapers/recovery/1114.php> (accessed February 1, 2006).

Wold, G. H. 2002. Disaster recovery planning process—Part I. *Disaster Recovery Journal*. www.drj.com/new2dr/w2_002.htm (accessed February 1, 2006).

Wold, G. H. 2002. Disaster recovery planning process—Part II. *Disaster Recovery Journal*. www.drj.com/new2dr/w2_003.htm (accessed July 15, 2004).

Wold, G. H. 2002. Disaster recovery planning process—Part III. *Disaster Recovery Journal*. rom www.drj.com/new2dr/w2_004.htm (accessed February 1, 2006).

Wold, G. H., and R. F. Shriver. 2002. Risk analysis techniques. *Disaster Recovery Journal*. www.drj.com/new2dr/w3_030.htm (accessed February 1, 2006).

FURTHER READING

Takemura, R., and R. M. Taylor. 1996. *The increasing need for client/server contingency planning*. www.disaster-resource.com/cgi-bin/article_search.cgi?id='36' (accessed July 15, 2004).

E-Mail and Internet Use Policies

Nancy J. King, *Oregon State University*

INTRODUCTION

Surveys highlight for employers the importance of having a well-drafted e-mail and Internet use policy. These surveys show that the majority of employers adopt e-mail and Internet use policies for important business reasons that range from addressing employee productivity to preventing hostile work environments. For example, the American Management Association's *Electronic Monitoring & Surveillance Survey* (2005) (hereafter referred to as the 2005 AMA Survey) reported that 84 percent of the organizations in their survey had written policies concerning personal e-mail use and 81 percent had written policies concerning personal Internet use. Although less common, organizations also reported they had written policies covering personal instant messenger (IM) use (42 percent), operation of personal Web sites on company time (34 percent), personal postings on corporate blogs (23 percent), operation of personal blogs on company time (20 percent), and use of cell phones in the office (27 percent). In its 2003 *E-Mail Rules, Policies and Practices Survey* (hereafter referred to as the 2003 AMA Survey), the American Management Association reported that more than one third of respondents had experienced problems related to their e-mail systems, including having their computer systems disabled for a time, having their businesses interrupted for a time, and having computer viruses enter their systems through e-mail. Other surveys have demonstrated that employees' misuse of Internet access may also be a serious business concern for employers. It has been reported that many employees use the Internet at work for nonbusiness reasons such as viewing pornography, analyzing their investment portfolios, making personal travel arrangements, locating friends, following sports teams, and shopping for merchandise (Burgunder 2004). Clearly the use of e-mail and Internet access by employees in the workplace calls for well-designed e-mail and Internet policies to prevent abuse of work time and to minimize other business and legal risks.

Although there are valid business reasons for employers to carefully craft e-mail and Internet use policies to avert abuses by some employees, it is likely that the vast majority of employees do not engage in misconduct or abuse the privilege of using the employers' communications equipment. Furthermore, employers benefit from employees' enhanced productivity made possible by e-mail and Internet access in the workplace. In addition, employees have legal rights related to the workplace that need to be considered when employers draft e-mail and Internet use policies. This chapter endeavors to help employers draft and enforce e-mail and Internet use policies that achieve an appropriate balance between preventing abuses and protecting employees' rights in the workplace.

PURPOSE AND FUNCTION OF E-MAIL AND INTERNET USE POLICIES

An employer's policy covering e-mail and Internet use is a key workplace management tool. When the policy is properly drafted, effectively communicated to employees, and consistently enforced, it enables the employer to establish guidelines for acceptable and unacceptable workplace behavior involving the use of e-mail and Internet access (Page 2002). An employer's e-mail and Internet access policy should notify employees of acceptable and unacceptable workplace behavior (Page 2002). Another advantage of an effective policy is that it may prevent losses to the employer that may result from employees deliberately or carelessly misusing e-mail and Internet access. These losses may include misappropriations of intellectual property and employer liability for civil damages or criminal sanctions. An effective e-mail and Internet use policy helps an employer achieve legal compliance with myriad workplace laws that protect employees' rights and restrict the employer's and employees' actions related to e-mail and Internet systems, provided the employer follows the policy, applies it fairly, and trains its managers on implementation of the policy (Harmon 1982, 23). Finally, an effective e-mail and Internet use policy reserves the employer's property and management rights, including the right to monitor the employer's equipment and systems for a variety of business reasons and the right to discipline or terminate employees for violating the policy (Harper Business 1990, 340–2). See Table 1 for a description of important policy issues and drafting suggestions.

Table 1: Drafting E-Mail and Internet Use Policies

Important Policy Issues	Drafting Suggestions
Establishing the purpose of providing employee use of company-provided e-mail and Internet access	Company-provided e-mail and Internet access and related systems and equipment are provided to employees for the purpose of conducting company business.
Defining the scope of the e-mail and Internet use policy broadly	This policy covers e-mail access and the contents of e-mail messages, Internet or intranet communications, records of Internet or intranet access, and other electronic communications, files, and data of any kind stored or transmitted by or on company-owned or leased systems or equipment. The policy covers wireless access to the company's equipment and systems. It also covers remote access to company systems and equipment.
Establishing company ownership of electronic communications, files, and data	Electronic communications, files, and data covered by this policy remain company property even when transferred to equipment that is not owned by the company.
Clarifying that employees have no expectation of privacy in their use of company-provided e-mail or Internet access and that all information communicated on the company's systems is company property	Employees should *not* consider any communications made using company-provided e-mail or Internet access to be private, even if those communications are personal in nature. Except as provided by law, all information communicated on any of the company's systems or equipment, including e-mail or use of Internet access, is company property.
Establishing a standard for employees' use of company-provided e-mail and Internet access	Employees are authorized to use e-mail and Internet access for company work-related purposes and consistent with company policies and procedures. Employees are expected to use good judgment and act courteously and professionally when using company-provided e-mail and Internet access.
Permitting employees to make reasonable personal use of company-provided e-mail and Internet access while protecting company business interests	Employees may make reasonable personal use of company-provided e-mail and Internet access so long as the use does not interfere with the work duties of any employee, violate company policy, or unduly burden the company's equipment or systems, and does not undermine the company's business interests.

(*continued*)

Table 1: *(Continued)*

Important Policy Issues	**Drafting Suggestions**
	The permission to make reasonable personal use of company-provided e-mail and Internet systems may be revoked or revised at any time.
Prohibiting employees from using company-provided e-mail and Internet access for unlawful reasons	Employees may not use company-provided e-mail and Internet access for any illegal purpose. Uses that are illegal include violating copyright or trade secret laws; spam laws; child pornography laws; antitrust laws; laws restricting exports of information or other products for national security reasons; laws prohibiting online gambling, etc. Unauthorized installation of adware or spyware on another's computer, unauthorized access of another's computer, and improper acquisition, use, or disclosure of personally identifying information related to customers, employees, or other persons may also be unlawful and/or in violation of company policy. Be aware of special restrictions on access, use, or disclosure of personally identifying information related to children, especially those under 13 years of age.
Requiring employees to follow security procedures regarding use of e-mail and Internet access	Employees must follow security procedures established by the company related to the use of company-provided information systems and equipment including e-mail and Internet access. No person shall use any other user's identification or password or attempt to bypass security features to access information that the person is not authorized to access.
Prohibiting employees from using company-provided e-mail and Internet access for reasons that violate company policy	Employees may not use company-provided e-mail and Internet access for any reason that violates company policy. Company policy prohibits viewing, storing, or distributing pornography, sexually offensive materials, or other materials inappropriate for the workplace. It is also a violation of company policy to make or distribute harassing or discriminatory communications related to sex, gender, race, religion, national origin, age, or disability. In all communications, including e-mail and Internet chat, employees must follow company policies regarding improper disclosures of trade secrets and confidential or proprietary information.
Requiring employees who make electronic communications about the company or work-related matters in blogs, Internet chat rooms, instant messages, or by e-mail, etc. to clarify the personal nature of their comments and not to disclose confidential company information	Employees must exercise caution and protect company interests in all communications they make with persons outside the company that are made outside their job responsibilities (personal communications). For example, employees who participate in instant messaging, e-mails, Internet chats, and blog postings, etc. must state that any opinions expressed in such communications about work-related matters are the employees' own and have not been reviewed or approved by the company. In such communications, employees are prohibited from disclosing company trade secrets and confidential or proprietary information of the company. Employees may not disclose insider information that may violate securities laws and regulations. Employees may not post copyrighted material in such communications without authorization of the copyright holder, and should be aware that doing so may lead to civil and criminal penalties. Company logos and trademarks may not be reproduced within employees' personal communications as described above. In addition, employees should be respectful in their communications with persons outside the company and must consider the impact of their statements on others including the company, its products, company managers and supervisors, the employees' coworkers, and the company's competitors. Employees' communications are subject to these rules even if the employee uses no company-provided equipment and is not communicating on company time.

(continued)

Table 1: *(Continued)*

Important Policy Issues	Drafting Suggestions
Prohibiting employees from sending mass e-mail for personal reasons that may burden the company's information technology systems	Employees may not send spam or other mass e-mails for personal reasons that are not related to their work. A mass e-mail is a message sent simultaneously to more than ______ recipients (enter employer's threshold, e.g., 50).
Reserving the company's right to access or to retrieve communications, files, and other electronic data, use of computer forensics, or use of blocking software	The company may access, monitor, intercept, block access, inspect, copy, disclose, use, destroy, delete, recover using computer forensics or other techniques, and/or retain any communications, files, or other data covered by this policy, except as required by law. Such company actions may occur at any time and with no advance notice. Employees are required to provide passwords requested by the company to enable access to company property.
Anticipating the company's obligations to respond to government requests for electronic communications and other documents	The company may access, monitor, intercept, and/or disclose communications, files, or other data covered by this policy in relation to government investigations for national security or law enforcement purposes, without further notice.
Reserving the company's right to discipline or terminate employees for violations of the e-mail and Internet use policy.	Violations of this policy may result in immediate termination of employment or other discipline that the company determines is appropriate under the circumstances.
Reserving the right to take action against company contractors whose employees violate this policy	This policy applies to the employees of contractors who are authorized by the company to use company-provided e-mail and Internet access. Contractors are responsible for ensuring compliance with this policy by their employees. The company reserves the right to exclude contractor's employees who violate this policy from further dealings with the company.

Note: This table has been prepared from the perspective of a private-sector, nonunion employer in the United States that employs at-will employees, referred to here as "the company." The information in the table does not provide legal advice for policy drafters. All workplace policies should be reviewed by the organization's legal counsel.

BALANCING BUSINESSES' NEEDS AND EMPLOYEES' PRIVACY RIGHTS

A well-drafted policy serves as a legal compliance mechanism for management, such that following the policy will avoid violating laws that protect employee rights. A well-drafted policy will be enforceable legally because it will at least provide the minimum protection for an employee that is required by a multitude of laws regulating the employment relationship. Today, one of the greatest challenges for employers is to draft an e-mail and Internet use policy that balances the business's needs with employees' privacy rights consistent with applicable privacy and data protection laws. Given the different regulatory approaches for workplace privacy and data protection, this is not an easy task.

The Global Perspective

When drafting e-mail and Internet use policies, employers with employees outside the United States need to be aware of privacy and data protection laws in other countries that may be far more protective of employees' rights than U.S. laws. For example, in the twenty-seven member countries of the European Union, privacy and data protection are considered to be fundamental rights of individuals (Lasprogata, King, and Pillay 2004). These countries have laws that afford individuals residing in these countries significantly heightened privacy and data protection rights. In addition, even if a company has only U.S. employees, multinational companies need to be aware that the same privacy and data protection laws may apply to customer communications and restrict the company's ability to collect, use, or disclose personally identifying information about their international customers.

Europe has a long history of treating personal privacy as a fundamental right. As Article 8 of the European Convention for the Protection of Human Rights and Fundamental Freedoms (1950) (ECHR) provides: "Everyone has the right to respect for his private and family life, his home and his correspondence." The Treaty of the European Union recognizes the ECHR and requires members of the European Union to respect the fundamental rights guaranteed by the Convention (Treaty Establishing the European Community 1992). Electronic communications are a form of personal correspondence. For example, people in Europe have fundamental rights to privacy in their e-mail communications, even when the communications are made using the employer's e-mail system (*Halford v. United Kingdom* 1997).

More recently, personal data protection has also been recognized as separate but related fundamental right in the European Union. The Charter of Fundamental Rights of the European Union (2000) (EU Charter 2000) provides: "Everyone has the right to the protection of personal data concerning him or her." Further, the European Union's

Data Protection Directive (Directive 95/46/EC 1995) requires EU member states to adopt data protection legislation regulating the processing of personal data and the free movement of such data (Directive 95/46/EC 1995). The Data Protection Directive expressly refers to the fundamental rights of privacy that are contained in the abovementioned conventions and treaties and states the intention to regulate the processing of personal data consistent with these fundamental rights (Directive 95/46/EC 1995, preamble, p. 10). The Data Protection Directive defines *personal data* as information relating to an identified or identifiable natural person (Directive 95/46/EC 1995, article 2a). Examples of personal data related to e-mail and Internet communications include the sender's and receiver's names, as well as their e-mail or Internet addresses, postal addresses, phone numbers, etc. Although privacy as a fundamental right is also recognized in international law, there is no specific recognition in international law of data protection as a fundamental right similar to that found in the European Union (International Covenant on Civil and Political Rights 1966, article 17).

There is no universally recognized standard for protecting personal data as a fundamental human right. However, the EU approach provides a system that comprehensively regulates the processing of personal data consistent with fair information practices (EU Charter 2000, article 8(2)). Fair information practices include: (1) defining the obligations of those using personal data and limiting the use of personal data; (2) mandating transparent data-processing systems; (3) providing at least minimum procedural and substantive rights for data subjects; and (4) providing external oversight of data-processing activities by a governmental or other independent body (Schwartz 1999).

The EU Model of Workplace Privacy Rights

In the European Union, employees have privacy and data protection rights according to the national laws of the country in which they live, including workplace-specific laws and personal data protection legislation implementing the EU's Data Protection Directive (Delbar, Mormont, and Schots 2003; Lasprogata, King, and Pillay 2004). Workplace-specific laws in EU member countries that protect the privacy of employees' e-mail and Internet communications are found in:

- labor statutes
- labor agreements (which may be national in scope)
- criminal statutes that protect the secrecy of private e-mail messages (as opposed to business enterprise–related messages) and may require consent for monitoring
- civil statutes that apply when an employer has permitted private e-mail and Internet use by employees
- court decisions (including those requiring employers to have issued clear policies or instructions on e-mail and Internet use before disciplining employees for misuse)

In some countries, works councils and other employee representatives may have legal rights to agree to or to be informed and consulted about workplace privacy policies and procedures, including the right to be consulted before new technology such as e-mail or Internet monitoring equipment is introduced in a workplace.

Each country in the European Union is also required to adopt legislation to implement the EU Data Protection Directive. This Directive protects the privacy of individuals (referred to as "data subjects") when their personal data are processed. The EU Data Protection Directive regulates the quality of personal data, requiring that it be processed fairly and lawfully, be collected for legitimate purposes, be relevant, be accurate, and be kept in a form that permits identification of data subjects for no longer than is necessary for the purposes of the collection (George, Lynch, and Marsnik 2001). The EU Data Protection Directive also sets criteria for legitimate processing of personal data. To process personal data of employees or customers, in some cases employers are required to obtain consent from the data subject. In other cases, consent is not required, but the employer may process personal data only when it is necessary for performance of a contract with the data subject, necessary for the controller of the personal data to meet its legal obligations, or allowed for other specified reasons. There are special rules that severely limit the processing of special categories of personal data that would reveal race, ethnic origin, political opinions, religious or philosophical beliefs, trade union membership, health, or sex life. The EU Data Protection Directive requires collectors of personal data to inform the data subject about the processing of data and to give the person access to data about themselves. The party responsible for processing personal data must make sure the processing is confidential and secure and notify a designated government monitoring authority prior to processing.

In the EU there are restrictions on the transfer of personal data outside the EU that impact e-mail and Internet use policies. For example, General Motors Company ("GMC") found that its plan to update its electronic company phone book to include office phone numbers for employees around the world was covered by the EU Data Protection Directive because it involved sending the employees' office phone numbers outside the EU (Scheer 2003). To comply with the EU Data Protection Directive, GMC was required to get the approval of the government privacy agency in the European countries where its employees worked and to satisfy rigorous personal data transfer rules before issuing the global phone book. Among other obligations under the EU Data Protection Directive, GMC was required to make disclosures to employees whose personal data would be included in the phone book and to consult with employees' labor representatives where appropriate. There is no reason to believe that employees' e-mail addresses would be treated differently than their office phone numbers, so the EU Directive would apply to global e-mail directories as well.

Since the EU has determined that the laws of the United States do not provide an adequate level of privacy protection consistent with the Data Protection Directive, transfer of personal data about customers or employees from the European Union to the United States is severely restricted. Generally, to make such a transfer, the recipient in the United States must make a commitment to follow the Safe

Harbor Agreement of the U.S. Department of Commerce (U.S. Department of Commerce 2000). Alternatively, the transfer of data from the European Union must be subject to a contract that includes EU-approved model contractual clauses designed to provide an adequate level of privacy protection for the personal data of EU residents.

Despite the existence of comprehensive privacy and data protection rules in the European Union, there is little employment-specific legislation related to policies and practices covering workplace privacy and e-mail or Internet use. For more specific guidance, employers drafting workplace e-mail or Internet use policies may also consult guidance and opinions issued by government bodies in the European Union on privacy in the workplace and employees' e-mail and Internet use (Lasprogata, King, and Pillay 2004). For example, the Information Commissioner in the United Kingdom published *The Employment Practices Data Protection Code* to provide guidance to employers on the process of complying with the United Kingdom's personal data protection act and offers good practice recommendations for employers (United Kingdom Information Commissioner 2006).

The U.S. Perspective on Workplace Privacy

Unlike the European approach, the U.S. has no comprehensive privacy or data protection regulation that applies to workplace privacy. When drafting an e-mail or Internet use policy for employees in the United States, employers need to be aware of myriad laws, including common law privacy tort law, laws related to employment relationships, and federal and state privacy legislation. However, taking all these laws into account, U.S. employees have significantly fewer workplace privacy and data protection rights than their European counterparts.

U.S. tort law gives employees working in the private sector only limited privacy rights. The privacy tort that is most frequently applied to workplace privacy issues is the tort of intrusion into seclusion, which covers employers' intrusions into employees' private affairs (Rothstein 2000). If an employer intentionally intrudes, physically or otherwise, upon the solitude or seclusion of the employee in her private affairs or concerns, and a reasonable person would find the intrusion highly offensive, the employee may be able to recover damages for invasion of privacy under tort law (Rothstein 2000). However, courts have generally found that private-sector employees in the United States have no reasonable expectation of privacy that prevents their employers from engaging in intrusive behavior in the workplace, such as monitoring and other surveillance. The rationale of courts is that employees give up workplace privacy rights by agreeing to work for their employers. Also, sound business reasons often are found to justify actions by employers that are viewed by employees as invasions of privacy, such as the need to investigate complaints that employees have used employers' e-mail systems to harass other employees. When an employer has a company policy that prohibits misuse of its e-mail or Internet system, the policy may serve to reduce expectations of privacy by employees in their use of e-mail or Internet systems, thus helping the employer defend privacy tort cases. For example, in *Garrity v. John Hancock Mutual Life Insurance Company* (2002) the court dismissed employees' claims of invasion of privacy based on their employer's reading of their e-mail on the employer's computer system. The court held that the employer's policy prohibited employees from using the employer's e-mail system to send or receive sexually explicit material and the employees had violated the employer's policy by sending and receiving sexually explicit e-mail messages; thus the employees had no reasonable expectation of privacy in their office e-mail.

The laws governing employment relationships also provide U.S. employees with few workplace privacy rights related to e-mail and Internet use policies. The basic rule is that unless private-sector employees have statutory or contractual rights to privacy, they have no privacy rights that limit their employer's ability to impose e-mail or Internet use policies or to engage in electronic monitoring of e-mail and Internet use in the workplace (Cottone 2002). In contrast, employees covered by collective bargaining agreements may have contractual rights to privacy that arise from those agreements. Collective-bargaining agreements may also restrict employers' rights to terminate employees without just cause, notice, and procedural process (Cottone 2002; National Labor Relations Act of 1935). Also in contrast to private-sector employees, public employees may have rights to privacy and protections from arbitrary termination that are based on civil service legislation and state or federal constitutions (Cottone 2002; *U.S. v. Simmons* 2000).

Unlike employees in most other countries, employees in the United States are often employed "at will." Under employment at will, employers may discipline or discharge an employee for almost any reason or for no reason, as long as the discharge is not contrary to law (including law established by statutes, court decision, and/or contracts) (Cottone 2002). Many exceptions to at-will employment have been developed in statutes or by the courts, and these exceptions limit an employer's prerogatives to discipline employees and terminate their employment. For example, it is unlawful under federal discrimination statutes for an employer to treat employees differently with respect to terms and conditions of employment based on their sex, race, color, national origin, religion, age, or disability (Title VII of the Civil Rights Act of 1964; Age Discrimination in Employment Act of 1967; Americans with Disabilities Act of 1990). At-will employees are also protected from wrongful discharge for reasons that violate public policy, such as exercising a legal right to file a workers' compensation claim, to serve jury duty, or to come to the aid of a person known to be in serious danger (*Frampton v. Central Indiana Gas Co*. 1973; *Garner v. Loomis Armored, Inc*. 1996). Another exception to at-will employment protects employees covered by individual employment contracts that provide contractual rights greater than at-will employment, such as a right to be discharged only for just cause (Cottone 2002; Leonard 1988).

Typically, at-will employees have no privacy or other employment rights that limit their employers' ability to impose and enforce e-mail or Internet use policies or engage in electronic monitoring of the workplace (Cottone 2002).

In contrast, in unionized workplaces in the United States, where employers generally have an obligation to bargain over terms and conditions of employment, employers may not be able to unilaterally impose e-mail or Internet use policies, at least if unionized employees may be disciplined for violations of the policy. In addition, once collective bargaining agreements are in place, unionized employees may have contractual rights to privacy that arise from the collective bargaining agreements, and their collective bargaining agreements may also restrict employers' rights to terminate employees without just cause, notice, and procedural process, including arbitration to resolve any disputes (Cottone 2002; National Labor Relations Act of 1935). Also, in contrast to at-will employees, public employees (those working for government employers) may have rights to privacy and protections from arbitrary termination that are based on civil service legislation and state or federal constitutions (Cottone 2002; *U.S. v. Simmons* 2000).

When drafting e-mail and Internet use policies, at-will employers often document the at-will employment relationships they have with employees in policy language and will include disclaimers designed to limit the likelihood that courts will interpret the policies to create contractual obligations other than at-will employment. Sometimes, at-will language and disclaimers will be included in the body of e-mail and Internet use policies. In other cases, when employers' e-mail and Internet use policies are included in employee handbooks containing other policies, at-will language and disclaimers will often be found in the introductory sections of the handbooks to avoid repetition in individual policies. At-will language typically states that employment at a company is at will and clarifies that either employers or employees may terminate the employment relationship at any time, without advance notice, and for any reason except one prohibited by law. Disclaimer statements for at-will employees generally state that policies and/or handbooks are only a guideline for employees and supervisors and do not create contractual relationships that differ from at-will employment.

Whether employees in the United States are at will, covered by a collective-bargaining agreement or other employment contract, or working for public employers, federal and state privacy statutes may impose privacy requirements on employers that are related to drafting e-mail and Internet use policies. However, federal statutes designed to protect the privacy of electronic communications provide only limited privacy protection for employees in the context of e-mail and Internet communications in the workplace (Lasprogata, King, and Pillay 2004). The Electronic Communications Privacy Act of 1986 (ECPA) is the primary federal law that protects the privacy of electronic communications, including the contents of e-mail and Internet chat. The ECPA prohibits wiretapping and unauthorized access to communications in electronic storage (*Konop v. Hawaiian Airlines* 2002). Under these federal privacy statutes, it is unlawful for anyone, including an employer, to intentionally "intercept" the content of a wire, oral, or electronic communication (Title I violations) (ECPA 1986). It is also a federal crime for anyone to "access" a facility providing electronic communication service without "authorization" and thereby obtain access to a wire or electronic communication while it is in electronic storage (Title II violations) (ECPA 1986).

Unless the interception or unauthorized access of a wire, oral, or electronic communication is covered by one of several statutory exemptions or authorized or required by law or a government order, violation of these statutes is a federal crime. Fortunately for employers, there are many exceptions to the ECPA that permit employers to adopt e-mail and Internet use policies and reserve the right to monitor the use of their equipment and systems. For example, Title I contains exceptions for "business use in the ordinary course of business," "providers of communication systems," and "consent" (Kesan 2002; Sidbury 2001). Title II contains exceptions for "providers of communications" and "authorization by users of communications systems" (Kesan 2002; Sidbury 2001). Employers who want to reserve the right to monitor their employees' use of e-mail and Internet access systems need to consider the ECPA and its exemptions when drafting their policies.

Although the ECPA restricts access only to the contents of electronic communications, the distinction between the contents of an e-mail and other information related to the e-mail communication may not be obvious. The ECPA does not restrict the employer's access to information about e-mail or Internet communications that is analogous to the addressing information on the outside of a letter sent through the U.S. mail. But is the subject line of an e-mail content or addressing information? A Federal Circuit Court of Appeals recently held that interception of Internet search queries was covered by the ECPA (*In re Pharmatrak, Inc. Privacy Litigation* 2002). For example, an Internet search query containing the key word "breast cancer" may reveal a lot about the subject of an employee's Internet search, particularly if it is captured along with personally identifying information about the sender of the query, like the sender's name. Fortunately for Pharmatrak, the case was remanded to the district court to determine whether Pharmatrak intended to intercept the contents of electronic communications, a necessary element of an ECPA violation. The court found there was no evidence that Pharmatrak intentionally intercepted the electronic communications, and dismissed the case. Based on the *In re Pharmatrak, Inc. Privacy Litigation*, employers would be wise to view personal information contained in Internet queries as contents of employees' communications, rather than mere addressing information that would not be covered by the ECPA.

In addition, employers who adopt e-mail and Internet use policies and communicate those policies to employees may qualify for the ECPA's exemptions covering interception or access to electronic communications with employees' consent. Additional tips for compliance with the ECPA exemptions are found later in this chapter in the section on "Reserving the Employer's Right to Conduct Electronic Monitoring." Finally, the exemption for interceptions of electronic communications in the ordinary course of business also permits some employer monitoring of e-mail and Internet access. However, in the context of telephone communications, courts have held that this exemption does not permit the employer to listen to personal conversations, and the employer must stop listening when a communication is found to be personal

(*Fischer v. Mt. Olive Lutheran Church* 2002). In *Fischer*, the court held that once the employer became aware that an employee, a youth counselor, was having a sexually explicit conversation with another adult and not a minor, the employer should have known the employee's conversation was not job-related. At that point, listening in on the employee's conversation was no longer covered by the ECPA's exemption for interceptions in the ordinary course of business and was therefore a violation of the ECPA.

The ECPA sets a minimum privacy protection for electronic communications, including those of employees. However, state wire-tapping statutes may be more protective of electronic communications privacy rights (United States Government Accounting Office 2002) and should also be reviewed when drafting a policy. For example, Florida's Security of Communications Act is stricter than the ECPA and prohibits intercepting or disclosing the contents of any electronic communication without obtaining the consent of both the sender and the recipient. The Florida statute covers interceptions and disclosures of workplace communications even when the employer provides the e-mail system (Florida Statute 2005 §934.01 *et seq*.; Safon 2000). In addition, some states have statutes that specifically restrict the employer's ability to monitor e-mail without employee consent (Burgunder 2004; Safon 2000). These workplace-specific laws are discussed next.

In addition to state tort laws related to privacy and state wiretapping statutes similar to the ECPA, some states have specific statutes that affect employment policies such as e-mail and Internet policies. For example, Connecticut has a statute that prohibits employers from electronically monitoring employees' e-mail without giving employees prior written notice, except in certain circumstances. One of the exceptions allows employers to electronically monitor employees' e-mail when there are reasonable grounds to believe an employee has violated the law or engaged in conduct that creates a hostile work environment (Connecticut General Statutes 2005). Other states have statutes that prohibit monitoring e-mail without employee consent (Burgunder 2004; Safon 2000, 101, 102). Finally, some states have statutes that prohibit employers from using employees' lawful, off-duty conduct as a reason for termination (see, e.g., Cardi 2004). It is not a far stretch to imagine a court interpreting state laws that protect employees' lawful, off-duty conduct from invalidating discipline or discharge of employees for violating an employer's e-mail and Internet use policy when that policy seeks to regulate the employees' off-duty use of e-mail and Internet access. Under these statutes, employees discharged for off-duty conduct that violates employers' e-mail and Internet use policies may have a remedy for wrongful termination.

Designing Global Policies for Multinational Employers

Multinational employers face special challenges when designing e-mail and Internet use policies. Outside the United States, employment at will is less likely to be a legally recognized employment relationship—even if employment at will is lawful, employees often have heightened privacy and data protection rights under national laws and regional agreements. One of the challenges for private businesses that are multinational employers is designing e-mail and Internet use policies that are consistent with employees' privacy and data protection rights in countries other than the United States. The European Union is recognized as the leader in providing the greatest level of privacy and data protection for employees in the workplace (George, Lynch, and Marsnik 2001). Because the European Union has the most rigorous privacy and personal data protection laws, multinational employers may choose to comply with EU rules when drafting e-mail and Internet use policies in order to have uniform global policies. For an example of a global privacy policy adopted by a multinational company with operations in the EU, see Hewlett-Packard's global master privacy policy (Hewlett-Packard 2006) (this global privacy policy is not specific to the context of e-mail and Internet use). Because of the increasingly global nature of business today, employers in the United States may eventually be subject to regulations that require providing privacy and personal data protections for workplace communications consistent with the principles found in EU law. In addition, adopting a global e-mail and Internet use policy consistent with EU privacy protections may make sense for many multinational companies because other countries are adopting privacy laws consistent with those of the European Union, including Canada, Australia, New Zealand, South America, and parts of Asia (Scheer 2003).

SCOPE OF E-MAIL AND INTERNET USE POLICIES

An important strategic decision that an employer must make when drafting an e-mail and Internet use policy is the scope of the policy. An initial scope issue is the breadth of technologies to cover, including wireless access, cell phones, instant messaging, blogs and other communications avenues, and tools currently available or under development (2005 AMA Survey). The scope of the policy will also be expanded or limited by the employer's decisions regarding whether to permit personal use of its e-mail and Internet systems, whether to limit application of the policy to employer-provided equipment and systems, and whether to cover off-premises use of its e-mail and Internet systems.

Evolving Forms of Electronic Communications

An employer's policy should be drafted to cover the multitude of communications devices and technologies that can be used by employees to send and receive e-mail and access the Internet (Honda and Martin 2002). Currently, this means the employer's policy should cover the use of cell phones and personal digital assistants (PDAs) supported by wireless technology and the use of instant messaging capability (2005 AMA Survey). To avoid having its policy become technologically outdated, the employer's policy should be worded to encompass new technologies as they become available even if wireless or other e-mail and Internet access capabilities are not currently provided by the employer for its employees' use. This is because wireless technology permits employees to access e-mail and the Internet from the workplace with or without using the employer's e-mail or Internet access equipment or systems. For example, employees with a personal cell phone or personal PDA with Internet capability can send or receive e-mail or access the Internet to chat and send text or instant messages while in the workplace and without using the employer's systems or equipment (Honda and Martin 2002). Employees may have their own communications equipment in the workplace, enabling them to download pornography or copyrighted music in the workplace or to send messages containing the employer's trade secrets from within the workplace to an outsider.

Cell phone use in the United States is ubiquitous and is growing globally. One survey showed that 59 percent of people in the United States use cell phones, more at work than at any other location (Smith 2005). In Europe, where the device is more likely to be called a mobile phone, the rate of cell phone use is even higher. Approximately 88 percent of Europeans use mobile phones (European Mobile Statistics 2004). The use of cell phones on the job for work or personal reasons can be expected to grow.

Although it is estimated that less than one in five U.S. employees use instant messaging, internationally the practice may be more widespread. For example, it is estimated that about 65 percent of employees in the United Kingdom use instant messaging (that may be communicated with or without using wireless devices). Potential uses of instant messaging with workplace ramifications include "flirting with colleagues, scheming against the boss and gossiping about coworkers," or even sending "sensitive information about major corporate projects" to competitors (Reuters 2003). Many employees who use instant messaging wrongly assume that instant messages cannot be monitored by the boss (Reuters 2003). Also troubling for employers is the risk that employees will use instant messaging in unprofessional or even discriminatory ways, such as logging on as "cutelilpixiechick" or sending sexual jokes through instant messaging (McClure 2003, 31). Thus, the use of wireless technology and/or instant messaging should be covered by an employer's e-mail and Internet use policy and raises valid productivity and legal risk considerations for employers.

At a minimum, the employer's e-mail and Internet use policy should cover the use of wireless technology by employees while they are at work, whether the wireless technology is provided by the employer or the employee. In the policy, the employer should also address scope issues in the context of wireless devices, including whether to:permit reasonable personal e-mail and Internet access on the job using wireless devices; apply the policy to e-mail and Internet access using wireless devices if employees are not on the employer's premises; or cover wireless access that also involves use of the employer's systems and equipment. In the policy, the employer also should anticipate that new ways of communicating electronically will be used by employees, such as text messaging, instant messaging capability, or Voice over the Internet Protocol (VoIP). See the next section for a discussion of some important legal constraints on imposing a policy with a broad scope.

Business Use versus Personal Use

An important question for employers to answer is whether to limit employees' use of the employer's e-mail and Internet systems to "business use only," thus excluding any personal use of these systems provided by the employer. Generally, employees have no legal "right" to use the employer's e-mail and Internet systems for personal reasons, so an employer may lawfully adopt a business-use-only policy (King 2003, Labor law for managers). However, in view of the fact that many people work long hours, some advocates for privacy in the workplace argue that it has become accepted that there will be a certain amount of personal business that will be done during business hours, including personal e-mail communications (Sidbury 2001). Realistically, some employees will use e-mail and Internet communications for some personal use regardless of the prohibitions found in any employment policy (Anandarajan and Simmers 2004).

An advantage of permitting some personal use is that employees may be better able to balance work and family conflicts by having access to e-mail and Internet systems for some personal uses, such as family emergencies, monitoring the after-school activities of children, checking in with a spouse, and so forth. Personal use of e-mail and Internet access for these types of reasons may be less disruptive in the workplace than employees' use of telephones and/or cell phones, because the communications are generally "silent" and less likely to disrupt the work of other employees. Furthermore, allowing reasonable personal use of e-mail and Internet access may result in less loss of work time by reducing absenteeism at little or no additional cost to the employer. Allowing reasonable personal use of the employer's e-mail and Internet access may generate positive employee morale and may also encourage employees to keep abreast of technological developments. Current research supports the conclusion that there are some positive beneficial side effects of permitting employees to surf the Web at work (Anandarajan and Simmers 2003).

On the other hand, limiting e-mail and Internet access to business-use-only policies may discourage employees' abuse of work time for personal reasons, reduce the need for management to supervise employees' use of e-mail and the Internet to prevent excessive personal use, and limit the likelihood that employees opening personal e-mail on their employer's systems will infect the employer's system with computer viruses.

Blurring of Workplace Boundaries: Virtual Workplaces

One of the advantages of e-mail and Internet technology is that it permits work to be done by employees from just about anywhere. For employees who conduct business using the Internet and Web sites or using a cell phone or other mobile wireless technology, the workplace is primarily a virtual workplace as opposed to a physical one. The blurring of workplace boundaries and emergence of virtual workplaces challenge policy drafters to clearly define the scope of policies. A question for policy drafters to consider is whether there are special concerns when an employee works in a virtual workplace. For example, do virtual workers have stronger arguments in favor of reasonable personal use of employer-provided Internet access or e-mail via cell phones because the virtual workplace is their primary workplace? Of course, employees may carry personal cell phones or PDAs to use for personal communications, so perhaps business-use-only policies related to employer-provided equipment will be justified even in virtual workplace scenarios because such policies do not foreclose use of personal communications devices. Even when employers adopt business-use-only policies, the use of personal cell phones by employees in the workplace and the impact on work time and productivity are issues to be addressed in the employers' policies.

Even for employees in traditional workplaces, communications technology has blurred workplace boundaries. Should the employer's e-mail and Internet use policy also cover e-mail and Internet access by employees on their home computer systems and conducted on their own time? If on the employees' own time, and from their homes, employees use their laptops and their own Internet service providers (ISPs) to send e-mail messages to their coworkers' personal e-mail accounts, should the employers' policy apply? If one assumes that the employees' e-mail messages may expose the employers' trade secrets in an insecure environment, it seems clear that employers have valid business interests in applying their policies. What if employees use their own laptops and ISPs to chat online and in so doing make derogatory statements about their bosses that members of the public may access, potentially harming the employers' reputations with their customers? In both of these situations, the employees are not using the employers' systems or equipment or making the communication on work time, but the online conversations arguably relate to their workplaces and involve legitimate employers' interests. From a management perspective, considering the potential harm to the employers' businesses, these types of communications probably should be covered by the employers' policies. However, caution should be exercised when drafting policies that regulate employees' use of e-mail or the Internet outside the workplace. In Europe and other countries that protect individual privacy as a fundamental human right, employers who regulate employees' personal communications will be viewed as interfering with individual rights, such as the individual right everyone has "to respect for his private and family life, his home and his correspondence" (ECHR, Article 8, 1950; (ICCPR, Article 17, 1966). In 2007, the European Court of Human Rights ruled that a public-sector employee was entitled to damages and court costs from her employer, the U.K. government, for monitoring that violated Article 8 of the Convention on Human Rights. In that case, a college monitored the employee's personal Internet usage and telephone calls without informing her in advance that her communications might be monitored (*Copland v. United Kingdom* 2007; Espiner 2007).

Non-union, private-sector employees in the United States do not generally have legally recognized fundamental rights of privacy in their personal communications. However, in some states, private-sector employees have constitutional free speech rights or rights to engage in lawful off-duty conduct that protect them from intrusive private-sector employers (Safon 2000). In addition, public-sector employees have free speech rights with respect to their governmental employment under the U.S. Constitution (*O'Connor v. Ortega* 1987).

Many e-mail and Internet use issues also involve employees using their own computer systems and ISPs to access the employer's computer systems. This was the case in *Smyth v. Pillsbury Co*. (1996), in which an employee sent an e-mail from his home to another employee by accessing the company's e-mail system. In his e-mail message, the employee made derogatory references about another manager that included a threat to "kill the backstabbing bastard" and compared an upcoming holiday party to a "Jim Jones Kool-Aid Affair." The employer obtained copies of the employee's e-mail and, not surprisingly, terminated his employment for inappropriate use of the company's e-mail system. The court in *Smyth v Pillsbury* held that the employee lost any reasonable expectation of privacy by sending his e-mail over the employer's e-mail system, and denied the employee's claim that his discharge was in violation of public policy.

Outside the United States, the outcome of a similar case would not be so predictable if brought by employees who have legally recognized personal privacy rights even when they use their employer's e-mail systems for personal communications. For example, in *Halford v. United Kingdom* (1997), the European Court of Human Rights (ECHR) rejected an employer's argument that the employee had no reasonable expectation of privacy when she made personal telephone calls from business premises using a company phone. The court held that the employee's calls were covered by notions of "private life" and "correspondence" that are fundamental individual privacy rights in Europe, particularly since the employee had no warning that her calls could be intercepted.

In *Smyth v. Pillsbury*, both employer- and employee-provided equipment and systems were being used and the communication was both personal and work-related. Such situations involving blurred workplace boundaries are likely to be increasingly frequent as e-mail and Internet access become increasingly pervasive in our society. To help prevent misuse of e-mail and Internet systems that may harm employers' legitimate business interests, employers' policies may, and probably should, cover any use of employer-provided computer equipment, e-mail, or Internet access, even if employee-provided equipment and/or systems are also used, and even if the communications are "personal." The employer's interest in including these types of communications within its e-mail and Internet use policy is stronger if the employer has provided at least some of the e-mail and Internet equipment or systems. In addition, contemporary workplace violence and harassment concerns merit a broadly worded policy. However, drafting a policy to address improper use of e-mail and the Internet is difficult. Drafters need to consider how to define misconduct under the policy, the consequences for policy violations, and whether the policy will enable an employer to engage in electronic monitoring to investigate noncompliance. As this chapter explores, employers' prerogatives to set workplace rules for e-mail and Internet use and to investigate and discipline employees for improper use often depends on the laws of the countries where employees work. Employers will have relatively more latitude to do these things in the United States and in other countries where employees do not have extensive privacy and other legal rights in the workplace. On the other hand, employers will have less latitude in drafting workplace e-mail and Internet use policies in Europe and other countries where employees have extensive privacy and other legal protections related to their e-mail and Internet communications.

Employee Blogging

One of the most recent challenges to managing a workforce is employee "blogging" (Gutman 2003). "A blog, short for web log, is a journal or diary posted on the Internet" (Cobey and Gordon 2005). It is estimated that 10 million Americans maintain their own blog, which can serve many purposes, such as political commentary, recruitment, venting, or commenting on a person's work life and coworkers (Cobey and Gordon 2005). Although some employers have discouraged blogging by their employees, others have embraced blogging as a means of promoting employee creativity and constructive dialog about the workplace (Cobey and Gordon 2005). Blogging by an employee may create broad employment liability concerns for employers, including employer liability for employees' blogging that is criminal, defamatory, or violates copyright laws (Gutman 2003, 150). Employees' blogging may disclose confidential business information or undermine a company's public image (Cobey and Gordon 2005). Some employers have been fired because they have posted harmful content on their blogs, including a flight attendant who described herself as "Queen of the Sky" and posted pictures of herself in her uniform showing more skin than usual, and a U.S. Senate staff member whose blog contained thinly disguised descriptions of the sexual escapades of her coworkers (Cobey and Gordon 2005). To prevent employees from blogging in ways that harm company interests and create company liability, employers should address these concerns in their Internet use policies. Employers should also prohibit blogging that would violate the law. For example, employees' disclosure of confidential information about the company on a blog could cause a drop in a publicly traded company's stock price, potentially violating U.S. securities laws.

Recent litigation by Apple Computer illustrates the risk that employees may use blogs to improperly disclose companies' trade secrets. Apple subpoenaed records related to a lawsuit claiming unknown persons (DOEs) had violated Apple Computer's trade secrets by communicating the trade secrets to online publishers who then published the trade secrets (*Apple Computer v. DOE 1-25* 2005). Apple Computer's subpoena sought evidence that could reveal the identities of the people who supplied the company's trade secrets to the online publishers. The trade secrets included details of a new product to be produced by Apple that had not yet been publicly announced. The trial court considered a motion by the online publishers to dismiss the subpoena. Although the trial court initially ruled in favor of Apple, ordering the enforcement of the subpoena, the California Court of Appeal reversed, ordering the trial court to grant a protective order to prevent Apple from issuing subpoenas to identify the sources of stories (*O'Grady v. Superior Court (Apple Computer, Inc., Real Party in Interest)* 2006; Hiltzik 2005). The appellate decision is consistent with protecting the free speech rights of the online publishers not to reveal news sources (Hiltzik 2005), but impacts the ability of companies to discover the identities of employees and former employees who anonymously post online messages that disclose confidential company information in violation of company policies.

The determination of whether the scope of the employer's policy should include e-mail and Internet access involving employee-provided equipment, communications made outside the employee's work time, and personal as opposed to work-related communications involves weighing management as well as legal concerns. For more discussion of U.S. legal constraints on the scope of e-mail and Internet use policies, see "Additional Tips on Complying with U.S. Employment Laws in Table 1."

COORDINATING E-MAIL AND INTERNET USE POLICIES WITH OTHER POLICIES

E-mail and Internet use policies typically involve issues that are related to other business practices and policies. The most obvious connection is between e-mail and Internet use policies and the company's privacy practices and policies. Because of the number of privacy issues related to e-mail and Internet use policies, a company should consider drafting a company privacy policy that covers employee privacy. With a general privacy policy in place, a company may refer to it in its e-mail and Internet use policy.

Another area of coordination between company practices and policies involves the retention of stored e-mail and Internet access records and a company's document-retention policies. There are obvious risks related to retaining e-mail and Internet use records indefinitely, including the risk that the company will be required to sort and produce e-mail and Internet use records in litigation that may be filed in the future against the company. On the other hand, the company needs to be able to retain and produce e-mail and Internet use records related to discovery requests in pending or threatened litigation. For these reasons, a company's e-mail and Internet use policy should be consistent with its document-retention policies for electronic documents and records.

A company's e-mail and Internet use policy also involves issues of confidentiality of employees' records, including policies for granting access to e-mail communications and Internet access information. Employees are often concerned about the privacy of their e-mail communications and favor limiting their employer's access to records about their e-mail and Internet use. The employer often favors broad employer access to employees' electronic communications and records of Internet access for valid business reasons. Valid business reasons to reserve employer access to employees' electronic communications and Internet access records include investigating complaints of misconduct, responding to discovery requests related to litigation, and monitoring misuse of e-mail and Internet systems. If the company has a separate policy regarding confidentiality of employee records, it should be consistent with the company's e-mail and Internet use policy.

A serious concern of businesses today is violence in the workplace and national security threats. Many companies have separate policies prohibiting violence in the workplace and requiring employees to report threats of violence in the workplace and other threats. It is important to consider that threats of violence may be communicated by e-mail or Internet chat, and the employer and/or law enforcement may need access to e-mail and Internet systems to respond to threats of violence. On a broader scale, national security threats may also involve the use of e-mail and Internet systems. Coordination of e-mail and Internet use policies with workplace violence policies and national security interests is crucial to enable appropriate responses to threats of violence and other security issues.

COMMUNICATING E-MAIL AND INTERNET USE POLICIES TO EMPLOYEES

A critical component of being able to enforce an e-mail and Internet use policy is communicating the policy to employees and others covered by the policy, such as independent contractors. There are various ways to communicate an e-mail and Internet use policy to the people who will be covered by the policy. A traditional way to communicate a workplace policy is to distribute a paper copy of the policy and to require written acknowledgment from the user that he or she has read and understands the policy. The user's acknowledgment generally becomes part of company records. Some employers electronically distribute their e-mail and Internet use policy to users of their e-mail and Internet use systems on a regular basis. To proceed and use the e-mail or Internet system, users of the system may periodically be required to scroll through the policy and to "click" on a statement indicating that the user has read and understands the employer's e-mail and Internet use policy. Electronic records of the user's acknowledgment of receipt of the policy may then be kept.

Another method of communicating an employer's e-mail and Internet use policy is to provide training for users of the system. The training may be part of new employee orientation. Training may also be provided for existing employees and other systems users on a periodic basis. The possibility of providing online training about using the employer's e-mail and Internet systems should also be considered. Certainly managers and supervisors responsible for implementing the e-mail and Internet use policy should receive training on administering the policy. A key component of training for managers and supervisors is to communicate the employer's philosophy about respecting employees' privacy consistent with protection of the employer's legitimate interests.

A critical issue regarding communication of the employer's e-mail and Internet use policy is to make sure it is communicated to all covered users of the employer's systems, including the employees of independent contractors that use the company's e-mail and Internet systems. Compliance with the employer's e-mail and Internet use policy should be referenced in any written agreements with independent contractors, staffing services, or other users of the employer's systems.

ENFORCING THE POLICY

A key point related to designing and implementing effective e-mail and Internet use policies is that even the best-designed policy will fail if it is not enforced consistently and fairly. A policy that is not followed consistently by the employer may lead to discrimination complaints when an attempt is made to enforce the policy. Such discrimination complaints may protest inconsistent enforcement of a policy against members of any legally protected class, including classes of persons based on race, sex, national origin, disability, or age. In addition, even in nonunion workplaces, employees may file unfair labor practices complaints when an employer enforces an e-mail or Internet use policy in a way that discriminates against employees who are engaging in collective action related to their terms and conditions of employment. For example, selective discipline of an e-mail "griper" who sends an e-mail to coworkers complaining about the employer's new vacation policy may turn into an unfair labor practice complaint. If the employer's e-mail and Internet use policy prohibits all nonbusiness use of its e-mail and Internet systems, this type of e-mail message would violate the policy. However, if the employer disciplines the "griper" for sending personal e-mails but has not disciplined other employees for making personal use of its systems, it has inconsistently enforced the policy. In these types of situations, a court or administrative agency may reverse the discipline and order damages, effectively preventing the employer from enforcing its policy. See the discussion of discrimination and harassment concerns and federal labor law issues found in the section on "Additional Tips on Complying with U.S. Employment Laws."

PROTECTING THE EMPLOYER'S TRADE SECRETS AND OTHER PROPRIETARY INFORMATION

An e-mail and Internet use policy is an important tool to protect a company's trade secrets, such as marketing strategies, customer lists, price lists, expansion plans, and other company documents containing confidential and proprietary information that a company would like to keep secret from its competitors. When a company's trade secrets have been made publicly available, the information may lose its protection under trade secret law because it is no longer secret. This is because an essential component of the law's protection for a company's proprietary information is that the information is in fact not public knowledge. The employer's e-mail and Internet use policy should also prohibit employees from pirating trade secrets from former employers or competitors, thus exposing the current employer to litigation for trade secret infringement lawsuits under state trade secret laws. Trade secret theft is also a federal crime under the Economic Espionage Act of 1996, which provides for fines up to 5 million dollars against corporations as well as imprisonment and hefty fines for individuals.

Agreements Covering Employees

An e-mail and Internet use policy is often supplemented by other preventive steps that may reduce the risk of loss of the company's trade secrets and the risk of liability for infringing on the trade secrets of other companies. For example, an employer may develop written noncompetition and/or nondisclosure (confidentiality) agreements for employees to sign (Garrison and Stevens 2003). An employer may also require job applicants or new employees to sign statements that they are not bound by noncompetition or confidentiality agreements related to former employers and to agree that they will not use information that belongs to others, including information protected by trade secret laws. In the United States, because employees owe fiduciary duties of loyalty to their employers under state agency laws even when they have not signed a formal written agreement, a written agreement may not be required for employers to address breaches of confidentiality by employees. A contemporary issue involves the inevitable disclosure doctrine, which provides a remedy for employers similar to an unwritten noncompetition agreement in circumstances in which employees leaving the workplace to work for a new employer cannot avoid sharing or relying on trade secrets from their former employer (Frauenheim 2005). In states that accept the inevitable disclosure doctrine, employers can sue former employees using this doctrine even if they have signed only a nondisclosure agreement or if they have not signed any agreement (Frauenheim 2005).

Agreements Covering Nonemployees

Employers using the services of independent contractors or their employees should also consider requiring noncompetition agreements or nondisclosure agreements to protect company trade secrets. When nonemployees are given access to company e-mail or Internet access, the employer has valid concerns that can be protected by requiring nonemployees to sign these types of agreements. If the employer's e-mail and Internet use policy covers nonemployees, the employer should make sure to clarify that requiring nonemployees to comply with the policy does not create any employment rights or change the nonemployees' status as independent contractors.

Noncompetition agreements and nondisclosure agreements also have an important role to play in protecting the privacy and personal data stored in the employers' databases. For a discussion of the legal risks and obligations to protect the privacy and personal data of customers, employees and others, see the sections on "Protecting the Employer's Computer Networks" and "Protecting the Personal Data of Third Parties."

PROTECTING THE EMPLOYER'S COMPUTER NETWORKS

E-mail and Internet use policies have an important role to play in protecting the employer's computer networks from threats such as spam, spyware, and unauthorized access by outsiders. Employees' use of e-mail and Internet access may expose the employer's computer networks to these threats. Thus, the employer's policy is a tool to educate employees about the threats and what they can do to help prevent damage to the employer's computer networks.

SPAM

Spam, unsolicited e-mail communications, is analogous to junk mail sent through regular mail. Spam may be sent for commercial purposes, including advertising goods and services, or to solicit donations for nonprofit organizations or political campaigns. Because spam is often sent through mass e-mailings to a large number of recipients, it may overburden companies' e-mail systems. Spam e-mail may also be used to deliver fraudulent solicitations. A "phishing" e-mail is an example of fraudulent spam (Stewart 2004). The "phisher" sends an e-mail to someone pretending to be a legitimate business with an existing relationship with the recipient but seeking to obtain personal information from that recipient that can be used for unlawful purposes such as identity theft or to gain a password that enables unauthorized access to a computer network or data, such as an online bank account.

Spam is more highly regulated in the United States than regular junk mail. Under federal law, Controlling the Assault of Non-Solicited Pornography and Marketing Act of 2003 (CAN-SPAM), deceptive forms of commercial spam are prohibited. For example, it is unlawful to send commercial e-mail ads that disguise the identity of the sender by using a false or misleading e-mail header. CAN-SPAM applies only to commercial spam and does not cover the sending of spam for nonprofit or political purposes. The general rule under CAN-SPAM is that nondeceptive commercial e-mail solicitations may lawfully be sent to recipients without their advance consent as long as the recipients are given the option to "opt-out" of receiving future e-mail solicitations from the sender and have not already made an "opt-out" request. Any spam that includes sexually oriented material must be labeled "SEXUALLY EXPLICIT" in the subject line. There are numerous other technical and disclosure requirements under CAN-SPAM with which companies engaged in advertising by e-mail must comply. CAN-SPAM regulates the sending of commercial solicitations even if sent to only one recipient (i.e., it need not be a bulk or mass e-mail to be covered by CAN-SPAM), so employees engaged in e-mail advertising for a company need to be well aware of the CAN-SPAM Act and its prohibitions. Both civil and criminal penalties are provided under CAN-SPAM (Fingerman 2004). CAN-SPAM supersedes inconsistent state spam laws, but it allows state spam laws to continue to apply to the extent that they provide additional remedies for false and deceptive spam. Other state laws, such as state tort laws, continue to apply after CAN-SPAM and may provide additional remedies for spam victims.

Spyware

Spyware is any software that is placed on a user's computer without his or her knowledge that takes control of the user's computer and/or Internet connections (Report to U.S. Congress 2005). For example, spyware may collect information about a computer user's activities and transmit it to another person. Some spyware is related to advertising and direct marketing and enables advertisers to measure effective placement of ads on others' Web sites or cause pop-up ads to appear (in this context spyware is called "adware," and is arguably legitimate, at least when the computer user is informed in advance that adware is being installed on their computer). But spyware may be used for more malicious purposes, such as capturing the key strokes of the user (key logging), thus enabling surreptitious collection of passwords and other personal information that may be used for identity theft or other crimes (Report to U.S. Congress 2005). A computer user acquires spyware in various ways, including downloading free or purchased software programs from the Internet or from a disk. Free screen-saving programs and free games have been used to deliver spyware to unknowing computer users. There are commercially available anti-spyware programs that detect and remove spyware.

Several bills have been proposed in Congress to regulate spyware (Report to U.S. Congress 2005). As of this writing, no federal law specifically regulating spyware has been passed; however, some existing laws can be used to fight deceptive uses of spyware and provide remedies for its victims. Both federal and state laws prohibit false or misleading advertising and deceptive business practices. These laws have been used as a basis for lawsuits against those who install spyware on users' computers without adequate notice and consent. For example, the New York Attorney General filed a lawsuit against a company that created and used spyware programs under New York's general business law. Like most states, New York law prohibits companies from creating false advertising and engaging in deceptive business practices (Hines 2005). The lawsuit claims the defendant in the case installed advertising software on home computers without informing the user that it was doing so. The software involved in the case redirected Web addresses, added toolbars, and delivered pop-up ads (Hines 2005).

Unauthorized Access to Computer Networks

Employees using Internet access on the job to access computerized information need to be aware of criminal laws that prohibit unauthorized access to computers or computer networks. The leading federal law on this issue in the United States is the Computer Fraud and Abuse Act of 1984 (Computer Fraud and Abuse Act). State laws also address unauthorized access to computer behavior, commonly referred to as computer hacking and cracking. Under the Computer Fraud and Abuse Act, it is a crime to access a computer without authority and to take data that is restricted or protected. Unauthorized access includes circumventing password or other access restrictions. The law protects financial and credit records, medical records, legal files, and other confidential information in government or private computers.

Policy Implications

As discussed above, spam, spyware, and computer hacking raise data security, online privacy, and network and computer performance issues that should be considered in drafting an e-mail and Internet use policy. The policy should prohibit company employees from engaging in these types of unlawful behavior and make it clear that unlawful behavior can never be justified as a competitive business practice.

PROTECTING THE PERSONAL DATA OF THIRD PARTIES

This section explores data security and online privacy issues as they relate to protecting the personal data of third parties, such as customers. The same legal protections apply to employees' personal data.

Protecting Customers' Personal Data

The personal data of customers includes information that can be used to individually identify them, such as their names, mailing addresses, e-mail addresses, phone numbers, credit card numbers, and details of their online purchases. Multinational companies that conduct global business (including online business) and/or have employees working outside the United States need to be aware of privacy and data protection laws in other countries. These laws may be far more protective of customers' privacy than U.S. laws. Even if a company has only U.S. employees, multinational companies need to be aware that the same privacy and data protection laws may restrict their ability to collect, use, or disclose personally identifying information (PII) about their customers or other persons who reside outside the United States. See the privacy and data protection discussion in the section on "The Global Perspective." The EU Data Protection Directive and member states' privacy laws mandate a high level of privacy and data protection for the PII of customers as well as employees.

Unlike the laws in many other countries, including the European Union, there is no generally applicable data protection law in the United States that protects the privacy of customers' personal data. However, there are U.S. laws that regulate the privacy of certain kinds of personal data, and these laws may require businesses to protect customers' personal data. Even when no specific statute requires a company to protect customers' personal information, tort or contract law may provide protection and remedies to U.S. customers for privacy and data protection breaches.

Special Issues Related to Collecting Children's Personal Data

The Children's Online Privacy Protection Act of 1998 (COPPA) regulates the online collection of personal data about children. Operators of commercial Web sites or online services that are directed at children under the age of 13 and operators of other Web sites or online services who have actual knowledge that they collect personal information from children online must comply with COPPA. COPPA requires the operators of these types of Web sites or online services to obtain verifiable parental consent before collecting, using, or disclosing personal information from children under age 13. If an employer's business involves operating a Web site or online service that could or does collect personal data from children, its e-mail and Internet use policy should address compliance with COPPA.

Regulation of Commercial Solicitations, Including Spamming

Employers and employees need to be aware of the laws regulating spam because even one advertising e-mail sent to one customer on behalf of a company may violate U.S. spam laws. In this way, CAN-SPAM differs from foreign spam laws because U.S. law is not limited to bulk or mass unsolicited e-mail (Fingerman 2004). Generally, CAN-SPAM permits businesses to send at least one unsolicited commercial e-mail to someone without his or her advance consent as long as it is truthful and nondeceptive and the recipient has the right to opt out of receiving future solicitations. There is no general exception to CAN-SPAM that allows a business to send commercial e-mail to lists of existing customers without complying with the form requirements in CAN-SPAM, and the business must honor requests by recipients to opt out of receiving further e-mail from the sender. Further, to send a spam message to a cell phone or other wireless device, the sender needs the recipient's consent in advance of sending even one commercial solicitation message.

CAN-SPAM primarily covers false and deceptive commercial e-mail. It prohibits using false or misleading e-mail headers, thus requiring spammers to identify themselves. It also prohibits the sender from misleading the recipient about the contents of the message and requires the sender to use the label "SEXUALLY EXPLICIT" if such material is included in the message. Further, CAN-SPAM requires the sender to include meaningful opt-out mechanisms in e-mail messages, including a physical postal address of the sender, so that recipients can opt out of receiving future e-mails from the sender. The sender must honor opt-out requests within 10 days of receipt. The requirement to honor opt-out requests gives the recipient the right to control whether his or her personal data may be used by the sender for commercial solicitations.

There are both civil and criminal remedies for violation of CAN-SPAM. For example, statutory damages of $250 per violation up to $2 million are available for spamming (Fingerman 2004). Further, CAN-SPAM imposes vicarious liability on parties for spam sent by other people, so a business that is promoted in an illegal e-mail by another entity may be liable for violations of CAN-SPAM. Thus, a business must exercise care in selecting advertising services to avoid liability for advertisers' violations of CAN-SPAM on behalf of the business.

PREVENTING EMPLOYEES FROM ENGAGING IN CRIMINAL ACTIVITY

A company's e-mail and Internet policy should also prohibit use of company systems and property for criminal activity including violation of criminal laws. Criminal acts involving spamming, spyware, and unauthorized access to protected computers have already been discussed in previous sections of this chapter and should be covered in the policy. There are many other criminal laws that apply to employees' use of e-mail or Internet access. For example, criminal laws prohibit acquiring or distributing child pornography and make downloading copyrighted material (without permission of the copyright holders and in excess of "fair use" exceptions) a criminal act.

Workplace Access of Pornography

One survey revealed that nearly half of human resource professionals reported that they have discovered pornography on company computers used by employees (Bachman 2003). Although employees' access of pornography involving adults is generally not a crime, these activities pose serious risk for employers because they may create a hostile work environment, may lead to embarrassing public relations problems, and may constitute a waste of work time when employees view pornography on the job. However, when employees view or distribute pornography involving children using company e-mail and Internet access, they violate criminal laws. A Boeing worker was recently arrested on suspicion of violating laws related to child pornography (Biggs 2003). The Boeing worker was arrested by police after Boeing's security staff told police they suspected the employee had been viewing child pornography via the Internet while at work. Acquiring or distributing child pornography violates state and federal laws that prohibit the exploitation of children. For example, a federal criminal statute prohibits the sexual exploitation of children, including receiving, distributing, or reproducing child pornography (Sexual Exploitation of Children 2005).

Downloading Copyrighted Material Without Permission

With the advent of MP3 technology that enables easy downloading of music, video, and other electronic files, there is an increase in the ability of employees to engage in copyright-infringing activities using the employer's computer systems and Internet access. Infringement can result in civil suits for damages against employers that may be found vicariously liable for copyright infringement by employees. Copyright violations may also lead to criminal penalties under federal copyright laws. The No Electronic Theft Act of 1997 expanded the criminal remedies for copyright violations to include circumstances in which copyright infringements are not motivated by financial gain, as long as the unlawful copies made have a total retail value of more than $1000 in any 180-day period. Today, even employees who are ignorant of the copyright laws can be criminally responsible for making unauthorized copies of music, videos, or other copyrighted works in the workplace. Likewise, employees who manage to circumvent copyright protection systems that are designed to control access to copyrighted work may violate the Digital Millennium Copyright Act of 1998. Thus, an employer's e-mail and Internet use policy should prohibit "hacking" into copyright protected materials as well as copying or distributing (e.g., forwarding e-mail containing copyright-protect material) without authorization. An effective policy alone may not be enough to deter copyright infringement by employees. Another survey revealed that employees are still swapping music and other files on peer-to-peer applications at work, despite threats of lawsuits for copyright infringement by the music industry (Reuters 2004). Careful hiring, proper training of employees and supervisors, and monitoring to detect violations are also steps employers should take to prevent copyright violations.

RESERVING THE EMPLOYER'S RIGHT TO CONDUCT ELECTRONIC MONITORING

Electronic monitoring allows an employer to observe what employees do on the job and to review employee communications, including e-mail and Internet activity, and enables employers to capture and review communications that employees consider private. Electronic monitoring also includes the use of computer forensics, a relatively new science and an important advancement in the broader field of electronic monitoring and computer evidence. There are many good business justifications for employers to electronically monitor employees in the workplace. Key reasons for monitoring are to assess worker productivity, to protect company assets from misappropriation, and to ensure compliance with workplace policies. The importance of electronic monitoring to enforcement of the employer's e-mail and Internet use policy is the focus of this section.

The term *electronic monitoring* is used here to encompass three different concepts. First, it includes employer use of electronic devices to review and measure the work performance of employees. For example, an employer may use a computer to retrieve and review an employee's e-mail messages sent to and received from customers to evaluate the employee's performance as a customer service representative. Second, it includes electronic surveillance in the form of an employer's use of electronic devices to observe the actions of employees while employees are not directly engaged in the performance of work duties, or for a purpose other than to measure their work performance. For example, an employer may electronically review an employee's e-mail messages as part of an investigation of a sexual harassment complaint. Third, it includes employer use of computer forensics, the electronic recovery and reconstruction of electronic data after deletion, concealment, or attempted destruction of the data (New Technologies 2006). For example, an employer may use specialized computer forensics software to retrieve or recover e-mail messages stored on the employer's computer hard drive that relate to an investigation of alleged theft of its trade secrets by an employee. Recovery may be possible even if the employee has deleted the messages or reformatted the hard drive.

In countries such as the United States, where electronic workplace monitoring is generally lawful, an e-mail and Internet use policy should reserve the right of the employer to conduct electronic monitoring for the following business reasons:

1. to investigate employee or former employee misconduct
2. to investigate complaints by employees or former employees
3. to respond to litigation discovery requests and requests by government administrative agencies for information and documents

The policy should also reserve the right of the employer to use a broad range of electronic monitoring techniques and technology, including the following:

1. to conduct historical and real-time monitoring
2. to use computer forensics techniques
3. to monitor off-site communications related to the employer's business

By reserving the full panoply of employer rights to conduct electronic monitoring, the employer makes it clear that employees should not have expectations of privacy related to workplace use of e-mail and Internet access. This is a critical component of preventing and defending invasion of privacy claims by employees and others who may be covered by the policy, including former employees and independent contractors.

RESPONDING TO GOVERNMENT REQUESTS FOR ELECTRONIC INFORMATION

Government requests for electronic information may come in a variety of forms. For example, government administrative agencies may request or subpoena information, including electronic documents and other information, in relation to discrimination, workplace safety, environmental, and other complaints. The information requested may include digital documents and electronic communications such as e-mail and Internet chat.

In recent years, because of national security concerns, an important concern for employers is the possibility of being required to respond to government requests for information about their employees or customers that relates to criminal and foreign intelligence investigations. Electronic monitoring of computer systems, including workplace e-mail and Internet access, can be used to discover electronic evidence related to terrorism, computer hacking, and other crimes (King 2003, Electronic monitoring). However, there are important privacy issues for employees that relate to employer monitoring for national security concerns (King 2003, Electronic monitoring). In October 2001, the Uniting and Strengthening America by Providing Appropriate Tools Required to Intercept and Obstruct Terrorism Act (USA PATRIOT Act 2001) amended provisions of the ECPA that prohibit interception of oral, wire, and electronic communications and restrict access to stored wire and electronic communications. As a result of the USA PATRIOT Act's amendments to these federal laws, employers may likely be asked, and in some cases compelled, to provide private information about employees and former employees to law enforcement and other government agencies (King 2003, Electronic monitoring). The employers' expanded legal obligations include the possibility of employers receiving government requests to produce information about a former or current employee in conjunction with a criminal investigation or government intelligence surveillance of potential terrorism activities. Government orders and requests can take various forms, including search warrants, court wiretap orders, pen-register and trap and trace orders, and subpoenas. The expanded employer legal obligations under the USA PATRIOT Act are essentially obligations to engage in electronic monitoring and/or to produce electronic communications, raising workplace privacy concerns. In some cases, the government order to conduct electronic monitoring of an employer's electronic communications system requires the employer to keep its participation secret even from the employee who is being monitored (King 2003, Electronic monitoring).

For the above-listed reasons, an employer's e-mail and Internet policy should anticipate that the employer may be required to monitor its system and to secretly produce electronic communications and documents to the government under government order. Accordingly, an employer should not promise that it will notify employees if their e-mail or Internet access is disclosed to the government—current federal law may make it unlawful to keep this promise.

RESERVING THE EMPLOYER'S RIGHT TO DISCIPLINE EMPLOYEES FOR MISUSE

An important component of an e-mail and Internet use policy is to reserve the employer's right to discipline employees for violation of the policy. The policy should provide employees with a warning that violations of the policy may lead to discipline up to and including termination from employment, thus serving to notify employees of the consequences of violating the policy. Certainly some misconduct or criminal activity engaged in by employees in violation of the employer's e-mail and Internet use policy may lead to immediate discharge. For example, an employee found to have distributed child pornography using the employer's computer system may face criminal prosecution as well as discipline for violating the employer's policy. Such a policy violation may clearly merit discharge from employment. However, other violations of the employer's policy may appear less serious and merit discipline short of discharge but that is designed to punish the offender and to set an example for other employees that may deter similar policy violations. For example, an employee found to have engaged in excessive personal, but lawful, use of the employer's e-mail or Internet access may be warned, placed on probation, or otherwise disciplined for the policy infraction, but would rarely be discharged for a first offense. A well-drafted e-mail and Internet use policy will reserve the right of the employer to discipline employees appropriately under the circumstances.

In countries where employees have fundamental rights of privacy even in private-sector workplaces, discipline of employees who violate their employers' e-mail and Internet use policies may be restricted to protect employees' privacy rights. For example, in *Onuf v. Nikon* (2001), the French Supreme Court considered the discharge of an employee for alleged improper use of work time. Evidence of the employee's misconduct included e-mail messages he had sent at work and marked "personal." The French court held the employer was not permitted to read the employee's personal e-mail and that "doing so is a violation of the fundamental right of secrecy in one's private correspondence even when that correspondence is conducted via an employer's e-mail system and in violation of company policy" (Finken 2000, 313 [quoting the French court]).

ADDITIONAL TIPS ON COMPLYING WITH U.S. EMPLOYMENT LAWS

In addition to the key legal concerns discussed earlier in this chapter, including employees' privacy, there are many other legal issues that relate to drafting and enforcing e-mail and Internet use policies. This section addresses some of the other legal concerns related to drafting and enforcing e-mail and Internet use policies for employees in the United States. Similar legal concerns may apply to drafting policies covering non-U.S. employees, and should be explored with local legal counsel.

Discrimination and Harassment Concerns

An important component of an e-mail and Internet use policy is to prohibit unlawful discrimination and harassment. The risk that employees will harass or make discriminatory statements using e-mail or in an Internet chat room is significant, and has been the focus of several lawsuits against employers. In *Blakey v. Cont'l Airlines, Inc.* (2000), an airline captain complained of sexual harassment and a hostile work environment after coworkers placed derogatory messages referring to her gender on an electronic bulletin board that the employer provided for its employees' use. The fact that the electronic bulletin board was operated by CompuServe, a third-party provider, was not a good defense for the employer—an appellate court ordered the trial court to consider whether the electronic bulletin board was so closely related to the workplace that it should be regarded as part of the workplace.

An employer's policy may also be a proactive tool to avoid liability for harassment and discrimination if it prohibits harassment or discrimination on the part of coworkers and the employer takes prompt remedial action to remedy any harassment once a complaint is made. For example, in *Schwenn v. Anheuser-Busch, Inc.* (1998), an employee lost a sexual harassment suit based on receipt of sexually harassing e-mail from coworkers on her office computer. Shortly after she complained, Anheuser-Busch investigated the complaint and took corrective action—it held two employee meetings to tell employees that its company sexual harassment policy prohibited harassment via e-mail and advised employees it would monitor e-mail messages and would discipline or discharge employees who violated the policies. In another case, an employee lost a lawsuit claiming that the employer negligently allowed employees to use the company e-mail system to send racially harassing e-mail (*Daniels v. Worldcom Corp.* 1998). The employer in *Daniels* was found not to have been negligent because, upon learning of misuse of its e-mail system, it organized employee meetings to discuss proper use of the e-mail system and disciplined the employees who had improperly used it.

All forms of unlawful discrimination and harassment prohibited by state and federal laws applicable to the employer should be prohibited in the employer's e-mail and Internet use policy. Actually, unlawful harassment is a form of unlawful discrimination. For example, unwanted derogatory comments about a person's gender or pregnancy, sexual jokes, and comments of a sexual nature are forms of sex discrimination that are prohibited by law when they generate a hostile work environment. Federal law prohibits discrimination and harassment in the workplace on the basis of gender or sex, race or color, national origin, religion, age, and disability (Title VII of the Civil Rights Act of 1964; the Age Discrimination in Employment Act of 1967; the Americans with Disabilities Act of 1990). An employer may also be required to prohibit other forms of discrimination and harassment, such as sexual orientation discrimination or harassment, because they are prohibited by state law (e.g., *Tanner v. OHSU* 1998), or because the employer has adopted a voluntary policy to prohibit such forms of harassment.

Disability and Medical Confidentiality Concerns

The primary source of federal law that requires employers to protect the confidentiality of medical information related to employees is the Americans with Disabilities Act of 1990 (ADA). The ADA applies to all employment practices and policies of employers with more than fifteen employees, including workplace e-mail and Internet use policies. The ADA's medical confidentiality rules protect all applicants and employees of a covered employer, even if the individual does not have a disability as defined by the ADA. It is likely, however, that the employer's liability under the ADA is limited by the employee's need to show he or she has an actual disability, a record of a disability, or has been regarded as having a disability by the employer in order to recover damages (*Sutton v. United Airlines, Inc.* 1999). The ADA requires employers to keep disability-related information confidential. In essence, the ADA prohibits companies from disclosing information about applicants' and employees' medical conditions, physical or mental impairments, and medical treatments to anyone inside or outside the company, except when permitted for specified purposes set out in the ADA (United States Equal Employment Opportunity Commission 2000).

The ADA also limits the inquiries that an employer may lawfully make about an applicant's or an employee's medical condition or disability. For example, prior to making a conditional offer of employment, an employer is prohibited from asking job applicants any questions that would reveal a physical or mental disability. In the pre-employment stage, after making a conditional offer of employment, the employer is free to delve into an applicant's medical history and medical condition, although the employer may only use such information for job-related reasons. After employment begins, an employer is prohibited from asking employees any questions about their medical conditions or disabilities unless the questions are job-related and necessary. Details of an employee's medical treatment or condition are rarely job-related or necessary, and the ADA generally prohibits employers from prying into the employee's medical condition to the extent the employer is seeking disability-related information. This rule generally limits the employer from seeking employee medical information beyond assessing the employee's ability to perform job functions, need for accommodation, or need for time away from work. Family and medical leave laws also restrict the amount of information that an employer may request from the employee or the employee's doctor to substantiate an employee's leave request and require employers to keep an employee's medical reasons for taking family and medical leave confidential (see, e.g., Federal Family and Medical Leave Act of 1993).

An employer's e-mail and Internet use policy should prohibit uses of the employer's systems that would violate disability discrimination laws. In the policy or training related to the policy, employers should train supervisors on appropriate use of e-mail in light of the ADA and family and medical leave laws. Such training should include instruction not to use e-mail to ask applicants or employees for "disability-related" information prohibited by the ADA or for medical information that would violate family and medical leave laws. Employers also need to be cognizant that the digital form of electronic communications creates significant additional litigation risk for employers. For example, e-mail records of improper disability-related inquiries may exist in the employer's computer systems and files for lengthy periods. These electronic records may also be recoverable using computer forensics techniques. Electronic records may provide damaging evidence of ADA violations in disability discrimination or family and medical leave claims and lawsuits.

Another concern is whether e-mail or Internet communications from applicants or employees contain confidential medical information. The ADA or family and medical leave laws require employers to keep this type of information in separate confidential files and not to disclose it except as authorized by law. There is the potential for the employer to violate medical confidentiality laws whenever employees communicate with their supervisors about their medical conditions. For example, a supervisor may send an e-mail to ask the employee for information that the employer is not entitled to request, such as details about an employee's medical diagnosis or prognosis that are unnecessary to determine whether the employee is currently able to do his or her job or to process a request for a family or medical leave. Or an employee may voluntarily provide confidential medical information to a supervisor by e-mail, but the supervisor may unlawfully forward the e-mail message containing confidential medical information to coworkers or clients who are not entitled to have access to the information. The employer should also be concerned with the security of electronically stored e-mail and Internet communications, particularly the need to protect confidential medical information from snooping coworkers or hackers.

Health care providers, including self-insured employers who provide medical insurance directly for their employees, should also be aware of the medical confidentiality rules of the Health Insurance Portability and Accountability Act of 1996 (HIPAA). Administrative rules interpreting HIPAA require privacy for customers of health care providers including employees covered by self-insured plans

(HIPAA Privacy Regulations 2005). The HIPAA Privacy Regulations apply when a health care provider transmits health care information electronically. Under these regulations, the data subject is required to give permission for use or disclosure of health care data unless a statutory exclusion applies (Manny 2003).

Federal Labor Law Protections

Most employees working for private businesses have some protections under Section 7 of the federal National Labor Relations Act of 1935 (Section 7 and NLRA), even if they are not represented by a union (King 2003, Labor law for managers). For example, if nonunion or union-represented employees in private-sector workplaces communicate with each other about their workplaces, including discussions about wages or other terms and conditions of employment, Section 7 of the NLRA may protect their communications from employer interference as "protected concerted activity" (King 2003, Labor law for managers). If an employer's e-mail and Internet use policy is broadly worded to prohibit employees from engaging in Section 7 activities, it will violate the NLRA. A policy that violates Section 7 of the NLRA is not enforceable and gives employees the right to file unfair labor practices charges against the employer with the National Labor Relations Board (NLRB). Employees are entitled to seek remedies such as back pay and reinstatement if they are disciplined or discharged under policies that violate the NLRA. Employment policies such as confidentiality policies and wage-secrecy policies also are unenforceable under Section 7 if they are too broadly worded. For example, workplace policies that prohibit nonsupervisory employees from talking with each other about their wages generally violate Section 7. Therefore, e-mail or Internet use policies that include overly broad confidentiality or wage-secrecy provisions may violate Section 7.

An issue that is hotly debated is whether an employer's e-mail and Internet use policy may prohibit all nonbusiness use of the employer's systems, even use by employees to communicate about matters that would be protected by Section 7 of the NLRA. Current federal labor law seems to support the view that the employer may prohibit employees from engaging in *all* personal use of its e-mail or Internet access. In other words, an employer may have a business-use-only e-mail and Internet access policy, providing it enforces the policy in a nondiscriminatory way and prohibits all personal use, not just use for union-related matters or Section 7 protected matters (King 2003, Labor law for managers). However, if the employer's e-mail and Internet use policy permits some personal use of the employer's systems by employees, it must also permit employees to use the employer's systems and equipment to discuss matters that fall under the umbrella of "protected concerted activity." Protected concerted activity includes discussion between employees of union matters, wages, or other matters of mutual concern to employees.

Employers may have valid business reasons to limit personal e-mail or Internet use by employees, even when the employer's policy permits reasonable personal use. For example, if the employer can show that certain types of personal e-mail or Internet use by employees unduly burden its systems, the employer may restrict the personal use for valid business reasons. Mass e-mails sent by employees that overburden an employer's computer systems and personal e-mails that expose the employer's systems to computer viruses are valid business reasons for an employer to limit employees' personal use of a company's systems. Also, even if an employer permits employees to make reasonable personal use of its e-mail and Internet systems, it need not permit employees to use work time for this purpose. The employer has a legitimate right to prevent loss of work time by employees sending and receiving e-mails for personal reasons (King 2003, Labor law for managers).

For a discussion of bargaining and enforcing a policy covering union employees, see the section on "Special Issues Related to Union-Represented Employees," found later in this chapter.

Respecting Constitutional Rights

Generally, employers in the private sector may adopt e-mail and Internet policies without worrying about federal or state constitutional restrictions because private-sector employment practices are not covered by the U.S. Constitution or by most state constitutions (Burgunder 2004). A few states have constitutions that protect the privacy of employees in private-sector workplaces (Safon 2000). California is one of these states (California Constitution 2005). For issues of constitutional law that relate to drafting policies for government employees, see the discussion of this topic in the section on "Special Issues Related to Government Employees," found later in this chapter.

Respecting Employment Contracts

Although at-will employment is common in private-sector employment in the United States, it is not the only type of employment relationship that is possible. Union-represented and government employees typically are not at-will employees, but rather have greater contractual rights related to their employment (see the next section). But even employees in private-sector workplaces may be covered by employment contracts that give them contractual rights that are greater than at-will employment, such as a right to be discharged only for just cause (Cottone 2002; Leonard 1988). Such employees have express or implied contractual rights that are found in their individual employment contracts, including implied contractual rights that arise from employer policies, whether written or not. Whether employees have express or implied employment rights greater than those of an at-will employee depends on whether a court, interpreting the employment contract, finds the employer's promises, which may be in the form of a policy, are enforceable and confer greater rights than at-will employment. For example, promises made in workplace policies established by employers may be enforced as "implied contracts" by the courts (*Toussaint v. Blue Cross & Blue Shield of Michigan* 1980; *Berube v. Fashion Centre Ltd*. 1989). In *Toussaint* and *Berube*, written disciplinary policies promising not to discharge the employees except for cause gave employees rights to sue their employers for breach of contract when their employment was terminated. Employers who make oral or written promises to employees of privacy and data protection related to e-mail and Internet use can expect to have those promises enforced. Discipline of employees or termination of their employment for reasons that violate implied contracts may be a breach of those contracts and a violation of the legal rights of employees, and gives employees the right to recover damages or perhaps seek reinstatement. Exercising caution as a policy drafter or in other communications with employees is essential to avoid making unintended but binding contractual promises to employees.

Often the critical policy-drafting issue for employers is to avoid inadvertently creating implied legal rights that employees would not otherwise have under existing laws. To illustrate, if an employer's e-mail and Internet use policy promises employees that their personal communications will not be read by the employer, the policy may create a contractual promise of personal privacy in the workplace—a privacy right that at-will employees in U.S. workforces do not otherwise have (King, 2003, Electronic monitoring). If the employer then violates its own policy by reading the personal e-mail of employees and terminates employees for the contents of the e-mail, the employees may be able to successfully argue in court that their termination is a breach of an implied employment contract.

Although implied contracts have been enforced in employment situations, employees have not prevailed on this claim in any reported case that relates to e-mail and Internet access. One court even disregarded an oral promise of privacy made by an employer, finding the promise created no privacy rights or, even if it did, the employer acted reasonably in the circumstances. In this case, the employer suspended the employee for investigation of misconduct. The employer then successfully bypassed a password set by the employee that protected his personal files stored on the employer's computers, read the files, discovered evidence of misconduct, and then terminated his employment for misconduct (*McLaren v. Microsoft Corporation*, 1999). Employees have, however, prevailed in similar cases involving implied contracts based on other types of workplace policies. For example, in *Woolley v. Hoffmann-La Roche, Inc.* (1985), express and implied promises in the defendant's employment manual created an employment contract under which an employee could not be fired at will, but rather only for cause, and then only after the procedures outlined in the manual were followed. For this reason, employers should be careful not to make promises in e-mail and Internet use policies that they are not prepared to keep. It is also a good idea to add a disclaimer in a policy, or in a handbook containing policies, to make it clear that the employer's policy does not create express or implied contractual rights for employees (*Federal Express Corp. v. Dutschmann* 1993). In *Federal Express* the court held that an employee handbook expressly stating that employment at the company was at will and disclaiming any other contractual employment rights was binding and precluded recovery of damages for breach of contract by an employee.

Special Issues Related to Union-Represented Employees

In workplaces where employees are represented by a labor union, the employer generally must bargain with the employees' union representative before introducing a new or a substantially revised policy regarding employees' use of informational technologies when employees may be disciplined under the policy (*King Soopers, Inc.* 2003). This is because imposition of a new or substantially revised workplace policy that establishes a basis for employee discipline is a mandatory subject of bargaining under the National Labor Relations Act. Although there is little definitive guidance on the topic, imposition of a new e-mail or Internet policy covering union employees must be bargained if employees may be disciplined for failing to follow the policy (Lieber 1998). A requirement to bargain with the union does not require the employer and union to agree on the terms of the policy. However, the employer is required to bargain in good faith about the effects of imposing the policy until a bargaining impasse is reached—only then may the employer unilaterally impose its proposed workplace policy. An employer may also have an obligation to bargain with the union over imposition of electronic monitoring or other surveillance practices or policies that are designed to detect violations of the e-mail and Internet policy. For example, an employer was required to bargain with union representatives over the imposition of new package-inspection practices designed to prevent employee theft (*Edgar P. Benjamin Healthcare Center* 1996). So, by analogy, an employer may be required to bargain about electronic monitoring practices designed to prevent employee abuse of its computer systems and violations of its e-mail and Internet use policy.

If an employer implements a workplace policy without bargaining with the union or obtaining the union's waiver of its right to bargain, either the union or employees may file an unfair labor practice charge with the NLRB. Also, even if the policy is lawfully implemented, when disputes about e-mail and Internet use or employer monitoring arise, employers may have obligations under collective bargaining agreements to arbitrate these disputes. Such disputes may include disputes about employee discipline for violating the e-mail and Internet use policy or disputes about whether the employer's electronic monitoring violates the collective-bargaining agreement.

Special Issues Related to Government Employees

Government employees may have constitutional rights to privacy under federal or state laws that employees in the private sector generally do not have, including a Fourth Amendment right to be free from unreasonable searches and seizures by their government employer (*O'Connor v. Ortega* 1987). However, even when a constitutional right to privacy claim may be made, employers have generally prevailed on invasion of privacy claims. In *Kelleher v. City of Reading* (2002), a city employee lost a claim for invasion of privacy against the city for allegedly publicizing her e-mail and other purportedly private information relating to her suspension by the city. And in *U.S. v. Simmons*

(2000), the federal government used electronic monitoring to examine the records of Web sites visited by a federal employee and then examined files saved on his computer. The court recognized that public-sector employees may have constitutional or statutory privacy rights in e-mail communications in some circumstances. However, the court said this employee did not have an objectively reasonable expectation of privacy in electronic communications made in the workplace in light of the employer's monitoring policy. The employer's policy specified the types of data that would be monitored, including e-mail, Internet, and electronic file transfers, and specified the ways in which the data would be retrieved, including audit and inspection. However, even if public employees' e-mail messages are public records that a public employer may monitor, courts have issued injunctions to prevent public disclosure of the contents of personal e-mail as personal information (*Tiberino v. Spokane County* 2000). Although most constitutional invasion of privacy claims relate to public employees, states such as California have also extended state constitutional rights to privacy to private-sector employees (Safon 2000; California Constitution 2005).

A number of important issues have been discussed in this chapter that relate to drafting an effective e-mail and Internet use policy. A summary of some of these issues is provided in Table 1. Table 1 also includes drafting suggestions for policies covering at-will employees working in private sector nonunion workplaces in the United States.

CONCLUSION

The reassuring news for employers about drafting e-mail and Internet use policies is that well-drafted policies educate employees about the proper ways to use e-mail and the Internet, help protect employers' property and trade secrets, and help prevent expensive lawsuits related to misuse of the employers' systems. One of the challenges for employers is to comply with the multitude of laws that protect employee rights in this situation. It is true that private-sector employers in the United States have the most latitude to draft policies that do not expand employee privacy and other legal rights, yet reserve employer rights to monitor and enforce their policies. Multinational companies with employees and customers in the European Union and other countries that have adopted privacy laws similar to those of the European Union face the greatest challenges as they seek to comply with laws protecting the privacy of personal information and electronic communications, while preserving employer rights to monitor their systems and enforce their policies.

A key challenge for policy drafters is to keep abreast of the developments in laws that protect employee rights in the workplace and regulate improper uses of e-mail and Internet access by company employees. Because business is increasingly global, drafting a company policy for e-mail and Internet use that is consistent with the laws in the countries where the company operates is a key challenge for multinational companies. Countries other than those in the European Union are following the lead of the European Union in establishing workplace privacy and data protection rights for employees related to e-mail and Internet communications. In addition, employees commonly use the personal data of others, including customers and employees, in the process of using e-mail and Internet access on the job. In many countries, including the United States and EU member countries, the use of customers' personal data in conjunction with the use of e-mail and Internet access is increasingly regulated. So, employees' using their employers' e-mail and Internet access to do their jobs may run afoul of civil and criminal laws such as those addressing spam or communications with children.

A well-drafted e-mail and Internet use policy also needs to be effectively communicated to users who will be required to follow the policy. However, having a policy is no substitute for good management practices and consistent enforcement of the policy. Finally, all e-mail and Internet use policies should be reviewed by the company's legal counsel. Although this chapter provides much insight into the legal issues of which policy drafters and enforcers should be aware, it does not provide specific legal advice for any company related to its e-mail and Internet use policy and is not a substitute for consulting legal counsel.

GLOSSARY

At-Will Employment: The traditional view of the employment relationship in the United States, in which either the employee or the employer may terminate the employment at any time, without advance notice, and for any lawful reason. There are many exceptions to at-will employment that have been created in contracts, statutes, constitutions, or in some cases by courts. The major exceptions include prohibitions on the termination of an at-will employee for reasons that violate public policy (prohibiting termination for serving on jury duty, filing workers' compensation claims, etc.); for reasons that violate discrimination statutes (prohibiting race, color, sex, religion, national origin, age, disability, pregnancy, harassment, and other forms of unlawful discrimination); for engaging in protected concerted activity under federal or state labor laws; for reporting unsafe working conditions; and for reporting criminal or other wrongful activity in the workplace (whistle-blowing). Employees in the private sector are presumed to be at will in the United States unless they are covered by an employment contract that promises employees greater protection from discipline or termination, such as a promise to be terminated only for "just cause." Union-represented employees covered by collective bargaining agreements generally have a right to be disciplined or terminated only for just cause, and thus are not at-will employees.

Computer Forensics: The electronic recovery and reconstruction of electronic data after deletion, concealment, or attempted destruction of the data, generally from the hard drive of a computer.

Contract: An agreement between two or more parties creating obligations that a court will enforce. The agreement may be oral or written and may also be implied from the parties' conduct rather than their words. For example, an implied employment contract may be based on an employment handbook or employment policy that has been communicated to employees.

Copyright: A property right of an author of an original work that has been fixed in a tangible medium, including literary, musical, artistic, photographic, or film works. The holder of a copyright has the exclusive right to reproduce, distribute, perform, and display the work.

Disabled Person: A person is protected by federal disability laws if that person has a physical or mental impairment that substantially limits one or more major life activities, has a record of a substantially limiting physical or mental impairment, or is perceived by others as having such impairment. Under federal disability laws, all applicants and employees are entitled to medical confidentiality from their employers even if they are not disabled.

Disclaimer: A statement repudiating or renouncing the legal rights of another. For example, an employer may include a disclaimer in an employment policy or handbook to disavow the creation of any contractual rights on the part of employees and to attempt to retain an at-will employment relationship.

Electronic Workplace Monitoring: Use of electronic devices and/or computer software to measure or observe the work performance of employees, to conduct electronic surveillance of the workplace, including observation of the actions and communications of others, and the use of computer forensics to recover or reconstruct evidence of the actions or communications of employees and others related to the workplace.

European Data Protection Directive: Requires member states of the European Union to enact national laws consistent with the European Data Protection Directive (Directive 95/46/EC of the European Parliament and of the Council of 24 October 1995) to protect the privacy of personal data when it is processed by another person or company, including an employer. Requires that processing of personal data be fair and lawful and that data be collected for legitimate purposes, be relevant, be accurate, and be kept in a form that permits identification of data subjects for no longer than is necessary for the purposes of the collection of the data. Provides that data subjects are entitled to access data about themselves and have rights to correct data about themselves. Applies to both consumer and workplace data protection issues. Restricts transfer of personal data about European residents to countries outside the European Union that have privacy laws that fail to provide an adequate level of data protection.

Fair Use: An exception under the U.S. Copyright Act that allows one who does not own a copyright to make limited "fair use" of the copyrighted work for purposes such as criticism, comment, news reporting, teaching, scholarship, or research without being liable for copyright infringement. Fair use is primarily an affirmative defense to a claim of copyright infringement. Qualification for the affirmative defense is determined by courts on a case-by-case basis and depends on: (1) the purpose and character of the use, including whether the use is of a commercial nature or for nonprofit, educational purposes; (2) the nature of the copyrighted work; (3) the amount and substantiality of the portion of the copyrighted work that is used in relation to the whole of the copyrighted work; and (4) the effect of the use on the potential market for or the value of the copyrighted work.

Family and Medical Leave: A form of protected leave from employment that is protected by federal and some state laws. The leave is available for an employee's serious health condition, for the birth or adoption of a child, and for the serious health condition of a family member, defined as a parent, spouse, or child. A person is not required to be disabled within the meaning of federal or state law to qualify for family and medical leave. Persons on family and medical leave are entitled to medical confidentiality from their employers.

Hostile Work Environment: A form of harassment prohibited by U.S. federal and state discrimination laws. A hostile work environment is unlawful when it is based on an employee's sex (or gender), race, color, national origin, religion, age, or disability (prohibited classifications). Although federal laws do not protect employees from sexual orientation or marital discrimination, state and local laws may prohibit harassment and discrimination for these reasons. Words or conduct of coworkers, supervisors, managers, or third parties that occurs in or is associated with the workplace are unlawful discrimination when the words or conduct are based on one or more of the prohibited classifications, are unwelcome, and are sufficiently serious or pervasive.

Noncompetition Agreements: An agreement between an employer and an employee or an independent contractor that restricts the ability of the employee or independent contractor from working for a competitor and/or competing directly through his own business with his employer. Such agreements are generally disfavored under the law because they restrict competition. However, depending on state law, noncompetition agreements may be enforceable if reasonable. Factors considered by courts in determining reasonableness include the scope of the noncompetition activity covered by the agreement, the term of the agreement, and the size of the geographic area in which noncompetition is restricted.

Nondisclosure Agreements: An agreement between an employer and an employee or an independent contractor that restricts the ability of the employee or independent contractor to disclose confidential or proprietary information of the employer. Such agreements are likely to be enforceable under state law and are consistent with the fiduciary duty that an agent owes a principal to be loyal to the principal in carrying out his responsibilities. This duty may extend beyond termination of the employment and/or the agency relationship.

Tort: The breach of a legal duty established by law that causes injury or damage to another. This is a civil wrong that does not arise from a contract. One who violates a civil duty and injures another may be required to pay damages to the person injured. Examples of torts include defamation, assault, battery, wrongful interference by a third party with a contractual relationship, and invasion of privacy.

Trade Secret: A formula, process, device, or other business information that is kept confidential to maintain a competitive advantage.

CROSS REFERENCES

See *Computer Network Management*; *E-mail and Instant Messaging*; *Network Attacks*; *The Internet Fundamentals*.

REFERENCES

Age Discrimination in Employment Act of 1967. 1967. 29 U S.C.S. §§621 et seq.

American Management Association. 2005. *2005 Electronic monitoring & surveillance survey (2005)*. www.amanet.org (accessed December 28, 2005).

American Management Association. 2003. *2003 E-mail rules, policies and practices survey*. www.amanet.org (accessed March 15, 2004).

Americans with Disabilities Act of 1990. 2005. 12 U.S.C.S. §§12101 et seq.

Anandarajan, M., and C. A. Simmers. 2004. *Personal web usage in the workplace: A guide to effective human resources management*. Hershey, PA: Information Science.

Apple Computer, Inc. v. DOE 1-25 2005. 2005 WL 578641, 74. U.S.P.Q.2d 1191 (unpublished opinion).

Bachman, J. 2003, October 23. Survey: Porn found often on work computers. *SiliconValley.com*. www.siliconvalley.com (accessed March 15, 2004).

Berube v. Fashion Centre Ltd. 1989. 771 P.2d 1033, Utah.

Biggs, P. 2003, September 23. Mesa man accused of molestation via web cam. *The Arizona Republic*, B5.

Blakey v. Cont'l Airlines, Inc. 2000. 751 A.2d 538, New Jersey.

Burgunder, L. 2004. *Legal aspects of managing technology*. 3rd ed., 616, 619. Mason, OH: Thomson Corporation/West Legal Studies in Business.

California Constitution. 2005. Article 1, Section 1.

Cardi, M., Employer control of employee's off-duty conduct. 2004. West's Colorado Practice Series, Methods of Practice, §19.21. 4th ed.

Charter of Fundamental Rights of the European Union, Article 8, December 7, 2000, O.J. (C 364/1) 1 2000 (EU Charter).

Children's Online Privacy Protection Act of 1998 (COPPA). 15 U.S.C. Sections 6501 et seq.

Cobey, C. E., and P. L. Gordon. 2005, June. *Dooces wild: How employers can survive the new technological poker game of employee blogging*. LawMemo.com (accessed August 8, 2005).

Computer Fraud and Abuse Act of 1984 (Computer Fraud and Abuse Act), as amended by the National Infrastructure Protection Act of 1996. 18 U.S.C. Section 1030.

Connecticut General Statutes. 2005. §§31–48d.

Controlling the Assault of Non-Solicited Pornography and Marketing Act of 2003 (CAN-SPAM). 2003. Public Law No. 108-187.

Copland v United Kingdom, European Court of Human Rights. 2007, April 3. www.echr.coe.int/echr. (accessed June 22, 2007).

Cottone, E. R. 2002. Employee protection from unjust discharge: A proposal for judicial reversal of the terminable-at-will doctrine. *Santa Clara Law Review* 42:1259.

Daniels v. Worldcom Corp. 1998. No. CIV.A.3:97-CV-0721-P, 1998 WL 91261 at *4, Northern District of Texas.

Delbar, C., M. Mormont, and M. Schots. 2003. *New technology and respect for privacy at the workplace* (EU Study). Institut des Sciences du Travail, European Industrial Relations Observatory Online. www.eiro.eurofound.eu.int/2003/07/study/TN0307101S.html (accessed January 14, 2006).

Digital Millennium Copyright Act of 1998. 2005. Pub. L., 17 U.S.C.S. § 1201.

Directive 95/46/EC of the European Parliament and of the Council of 24 October 1995 on the protection of individuals with regard to the processing of personal data and on the free movement of such data. 1995. Council Directive 95/46, Arts. 22–23, O.J. (L281) 31 (Data Protection Directive).

Economic Espionage Act of 1996. 2005. 18 U.S.C.S. § 1831 et seq.

Edgar P. Benjamin Healthcare Center 1996. Case 1-CA-32505, 322 N.L.R.B. No. 128.

Electronic Communications Privacy Act of 1986 ECPA. 2005. Pub. L. No. 99-508, 100 Stat. 1848 (1986). Title I of the ECPA amended the Wiretap Act of 1968 and is codified at 18 U.S.C.S. §§2510 et seq. 2005; Title II of the ECPA created the Stored Communications Act and is codified at 18 U.S.C.S. §§2701–2711.

Espiner, T. 2007, April 11. Email monitoring may contravene European laws. http://news.zdnet.co.uk/itmanagement/0,1000000308,39286674,00.htm (accessed June 22, 2007).

European Convention for the Protection of Human Rights and Fundamental Freedoms. 1950. Art. 8, para. 1, 213 U.N.T.S. 221 (ECHR).

European Mobile Statistics August 2004. http://cellular.co.za/stats/stats-europe.htm (accessed May 27, 2006).

Federal Express Corp. v. Dutschmann. 1993. 846 S.W. 2d 282, Texas.

Federal Family and Medical Leave Act of 1993. 2005. 29 U.S.C.S. §2601 et seq.

Finken, M. 2000. Privacy and employment law. *Comparative Labor Law and Policy Journal* 21:813, 814.

Fingerman, D. 2004. Spam canned throughout the land? Summary of CAN-SPAM Act with commentary. *Journal of Internet Law* 7(8):1.

Fischer v. Mt. Olive Lutheran Church. 2002. 207 F. Supp. 2d 914, 922, 928, W. D. Wisconsin.

Florida Statute. 2005. §934.01 et seq.

Frampton v. Central Indiana Gas Co. 1973. 260 Ind. 249, 297 N. E. 2d 425.

Frauenheim, E. 2005. Legal argument could hamper high-tech job-changers. CNETNews.com (accessed August 30, 2005).

Garner v. Loomis Armored, Inc. 1996. 913 P.2d 377, 1996 Wash. LEXIS 109.

Garrison, M. J., and C. D. Stevens. 2003. Sign this agreement not to compete or you're fired! Noncompete agreements and the public policy exception to employment at will. *Employee Responsibilities and Rights Journal* 15(3):105.

Garrity v. John Hancock Mutual Life Insurance Company 2002. 2002 WL 974676 at *1, D. Massachusetts.

George, B. C., P. Lynch, and S. F. Marsnik. 2001. U.S. multinational employers: Navigating through the "safe harbor" principles to comply with the EU Data Privacy Directive. *American Business Law Journal* 38:735.

Gutman, P. S. 2003. Say what?: Blogging and employment law in conflict. *Columbia Journal of Law and the Arts* 27:145.

Halford v. United Kingdom 1997. 24 Eur. Ct. H.R. 523.

Harmon, R. E. 1982. *Improving administrative manuals*. New York: American Management Association.

Harper Business. 1990. *The company policy manual: A complete guide to legal and effective company policies*. New York: HarperCollins.

Health Insurance Portability and Accountability Act of 1996. 2005. Public Law 104-191, codified at 42 U.S.C.S. §201 et seq.

Hewlett-Packard. 2006. Global master privacy policy. www.hp.com/hpinfo/globalcitizenship/privacy/masterpolicy.html (accessed January 14, 2006).

Hiltzik, M. 2005, April 27. Apple lawsuit takes a bite out of First Amendment. *The Houston Chronicle* B11.

Hines, M. 2005, April 28. Intermix hit with spyware suit. From CNET News.com, http://news.com.com/2102-7348_3-5688609.html?tag=st.util.print (accessed June 28, 2005).

HIPAA Privacy Regulations. 2005. *Privacy of individually identifiable health information*. 45 C.F.R. §164.101 et seq.

Honda, G. and K. Martin. 2002. *The essential guide to Internet business technology*, 36, 37. Upper Saddle River, NJ: Prentice Hall.

International Covenant on Civil and Political Rights. 1966. GA Res. 220, U.N. GAOR, 21st Sess., Supp. No. 16, UN Doc A/6316, 993 U.N.T.S. 171, and its Optional Protocol, GA Res. 2200, U.N. GAOR, 21st Sess., Supp. No. 16, UN Doc. A/6316 (ICCPR).

In re Pharmatrak, Inc. Privacy Litigation. 2002. 220 F.Supp.2d 4, D. Massachusetts.; reversed by 329 F.3d 9 (1st. Cir. 2003); on remand, 292 F.Supp.2d 263 (D. Massachusetts 2003) (dismissing the case on summary judgment).

Kelleher v. City of Reading. 2002. 2002 WL 1067422, E. D. Pennsylvania.

Kesan, J. P. 2002. Cyber-working or cyber-shirking: A first principles examination of electronic privacy in the workplace. *Florida Law Review* 54:296.

King, N. J. 2003. Electronic monitoring to promote national security impacts workplace privacy. *Employee Responsibilities and Rights Journal* 15(3):127.

King, N. J. 2003. Labor law for managers of non-union employees in traditional and cyber workplaces. *American Business Law Journal* 40(4):827.

King Soopers, Inc. 2003. 27-CA-16965, 340 N.L.R.B. No. 75.

Konop v. Hawaiian Airlines. 2002. 302 F.3d 868, 870, 9th Cir.

Lasprogata, G., N. J. King, and S. Pillay. 2004. Regulation of electronic employee monitoring: Identifying fundamental principles of employee privacy through a comparative study of data privacy legislation in the European Union, United States and Canada. *Stanford Technology Law Review* 4, ¶ 24 et seq.

Leonard, A. S. 1988. A new common law of employment termination. *North Carolina Law Review* 66:631.

Lieber, E. 1998. Picketing the information superhighway: Must employers bargain with a union over their e-mail policy? *1998 Annual Survey of American Law* 517.

Manny, C. 2003. Privacy protection for health information transferred between the European Union and the U.S.: A comparison of legal frameworks. *Business Law Review* 36:107.

McClure, J. 2003, November 17. U R hereby fired! *Newsweek*, 31.

McLaren v. Microsoft Corporation. 1999. 1999 WL 339015, Texas App. (unpublished opinion).

National Labor Relations Act of 1935. 2005. 29 U.S.C.S. §§151–169.

New Technologies. 2006. Computer forensics defined. www.forensics-intl.com/def4.html (accessed January 14, 2006).

No Electronic Theft Act of 1997. 2005. PL 105-147 (HR 2265), codified at 17 U.S.C.S. § 506.

O'Connor v. Ortega. 1987. 480 U.S. 709.

O'Grady v. Superior Court (Apple Computer, Inc., Real Party in Interest), 44 Cal. Rptr.3d 72 (2006).

Onuf v. Nikon, Arret No. 4164 (Fr. Oct. 2, 2001).

Page, S. B. 2002. *Establishing a system of policies and procedures*, pp. 2–9. Westerfield, OH: Process Improvement Publishing.

Report to U.S. Congress. 2005, May 18. Spyware: background and policy issues for Congress. www.opencrs.com (accessed January 14, 2006).

Reuters. 2003, September 15. Survey: Forget work, IM is for scheming, flirting, gossip. Yahoo! News.

Reuters. 2004, March 4. Employees still swapping files at work. *Reuters.com*. www.reuters.com.

Rothstein, L. E. 2000. Privacy or dignity: Electronic monitoring in the workplace. *New York Law Journal of International and Comparative Law* 19:379.

Safon, D. M. 2000. *Workplace privacy, real answers and practical solutions*, pp. 101–3, 105–12. Tampa, FL: Thompson.

Scheer, D. 2003, October 10. Europe's new high-tech role: Playing privacy cop to world, U.S. firms run afoul of EU laws on sharing and collection of data. *The Wall Street Journal*, section A, page 1, column 5.

Schwartz, P. M. 1999. Privacy and democracy in cyberspace. *Vanderbilt Law Review* 52:1609–14.

Schwenn v. Anheuser-Busch, Inc. 1998. No. CIVA95CV716, 1998 WL 166845 at *1, N. D. New York.

Sexual Exploitation of Children. 2005. 18 U.S.C.S. §2251 et seq.

Sidbury, B. F. 2001. You've got mail … and your boss knows it: Rethinking the scope of the employer e-mail monitoring exceptions to the Electronic Communications Privacy Act. *U.C.L.A. Journal of Law and Technology* 5.

Smith, E. D. 2005, September 26. Media madness: study reveals America's media usage. *The Indianapolis Star* (Indiana).

Smyth v. Pillsbury Co. 1996. 914 F. Supp. 97, E.D. Pennsylvania.

Stewart, C. 2004. *How to avoid getting hooked by pfishing*. http://ezinearticles.com/?How-To-Avoid-Getting-Hooked-By-Pfishing&id=5933 (accessed December 30, 2005).

Sutton v. United Airlines, Inc. 1999. 527 U.S. 471, 482–83, U S. Supreme Court.

Tanner v. OHSU. 1998. 971 P.2d 435, 437, Oregon App.

Tiberino v. Spokane County. 2000. 13 P.3d 1104, Washington Ct. App.

Title VII of the Civil Rights Act of 1964, as amended. 2005. 42 U.S.C.S. §2000d.

Toussaint v. Blue Cross & Blue Shield of Michigan. 1980. 292 N.W.2d 880, Michigan.

Treaty Establishing the European Community. 1992, February 7. O.J. (C224).

United Kingdom Information Commissioner. 2006.. *Codes of practice* (employment parts I–IV). www.informationcommissioner.gov.uk/eventual.aspx?id=437 (accessed January 14, 2006).

United States Equal Employment Opportunity Commission. 2000, July 27. *EEOC enforcement guidance: Disability-related inquiries and medical examinations of employees under the Americans with Disabilities Act, number 915.002*. http://eeoc.gov (accessed January 14, 2006).

United States Government Accounting Office. 2002. Employee privacy, computer-use monitoring practices and policies of selected companies (Report to the Ranking Minority Member, Subcommittee on 21st Century Competitiveness, Committee on Education and the Workforce, House of Representatives). www.gao.gov/new.items/d02717.pdf (accessed January 14, 2006).

Uniting and Strengthening America by Providing Appropriate Tools Required to Intercept and Obstruct Terrorism Act of 2001 (USA PATRIOT Act). 2001, October 26. Pub. L. No. 107-56, 115 Stat. 272.

U.S. Department of Commerce, Safe Harbor Documents. 2000. www.export.gov/safeharbor/SafeHarborDocuments.htm (accessed May 13, 2006).

U.S. v. Simmons. 2000. 206 F.3d 392, 4th Cir.

Woolley v. Hoffmann-La Roche, Inc. 1985. 491 A.2d 1257, New Jersey; modified, 499 A.2d 515, New Jersey.

Computer Network Management

Jian Ren, *Michigan State University*

INTRODUCTION

Network management, in general, is a service that uses a variety of protocols, tools, applications, and devices to assist human network managers in monitoring and controlling the proper network resources, both hardware and software, to address service needs and the network objectives. This includes performing functions such as initial network planning, frequency allocation, predetermined traffic routing to support load balancing, cryptographic key distribution authorization, configuration management, fault management, security management, performance management, bandwidth management, and accounting management.

When transmission control protocol/Internet protocol (TCP/IP) was developed, little thought was given to network management. Prior to the 1980s, the practice of network management was largely proprietary because of the high cost of development. The rapid movement in the 1980s toward larger and more complex networks caused a significant diffusion of network management technologies. The starting point in providing specific network management tools was in November 1987, when simple gateway monitoring protocol (SGMP) was issued. In early 1988, the Internet Architecture Board (IAB) approved a simple network management protocol (SNMP) as a short-term solution for network management. Standards like SNMP and common management information protocol (CMIP) paved the way for standardized network management and the development of innovative network management tools and applications.

However, these protocols were not designed for wireless networks. The wireless-specific mobility management, including handoff management and location management, were not addressed in these protocols.

Network management system (NMS) refers to a collection of applications that enable network components to be monitored and controlled. In general, network management systems have the basic architecture shown in Figure 1. The architecture consists of two key elements: a managing device, called a "management station," or a "manager," and the managed devices, called "management agents," or simply "agents." A management station serves as the interface between the human network manager and the network management system. It is also the platform for management applications to perform management functions through interactions with the management agents. The management agent responds to the requests from the management station and also provides the management station with unsolicited information.

Given the diversity of managed elements, such as routers, bridges, switches, hubs, and so on, and the wide variety of operating systems and programming interfaces, a management protocol is critical for the management station to communicate with the management agents effectively. SNMP and CMIP are two well-known network management protocols. A network management system is generally described using the open system interconnection (OSI) network management model. As an OSI network management protocol, CMIP was proposed as a replacement for the simple but less sophisticated SNMP; however, it has not been widely adopted. For this reason, we will focus in this chapter on SNMP.

OSI Network Management Model

The OSI network management comprises four major models:

- The **organization model** defines the manager, agent, and managed object. It describes the components of a network management system, the components' functions, and its infrastructure.

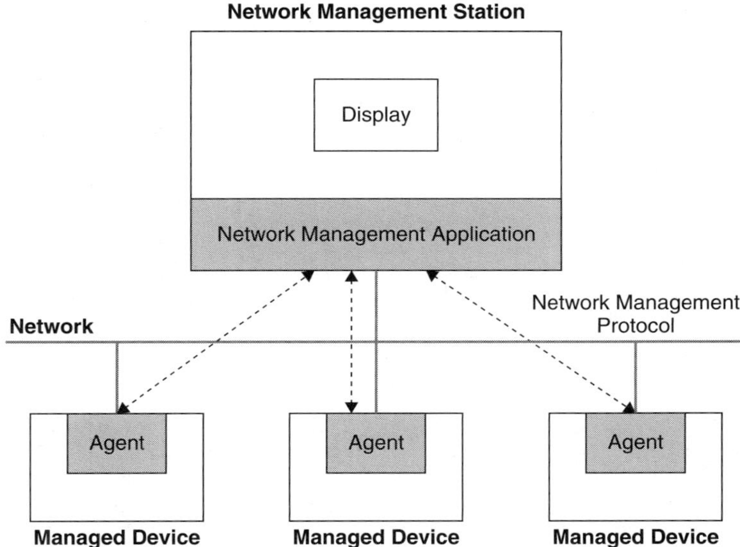

Figure 1: Typical network management architecture (Cisco Systems 2002)

- The **information model** is concerned with the information structure and storage. It specifies the information base used to describe the managed objects and their relationships. The structure of management information (SMI) defines the syntax and semantics of management information stored in the management information base (MIB). The MIB is used by both the agent process and the manager process for management information exchange and storage.
- The **communication model** deals with the way information is exchanged between the agent and the manager and between the managers. There are three key elements in the communication model: the transport protocol, the application protocol, and the actual message to be communicated.
- The **functional model** comprises five functional areas of network management, which are discussed in more detail in the next section.

Network Management Layers

Two protocol architectures have served as the bases for the development of interoperable communications standards: the International Organization for Standardization (ISO) OSI reference model and the TCP/IP reference model, which are compared in Figure 2 (Tanenbaum 2003). The OSI reference model was developed based on the premise that different layers of the protocol provide different services and functions. It provides a conceptual framework for communications among different network elements. The OSI model has seven layers. Network communication occurs at different layers, from the application layer to the physical layer; however, each layer can communicate only with its adjacent layers. The primary functions and services of the OSI layers are described in Table 1.

The OSI and TCP/IP reference models have much in common. Both are based on the concept of a stack of independent protocols. Also, the functionality of the corresponding layers is roughly similar.

However, differences do exist between the two reference models. The concepts that are central to the OSI model include service, interface, and protocol. The OSI reference model makes the distinction among these three concepts explicit. The TCP/IP model, however, does not clearly distinguish among these three concepts. As a consequence, the protocols in the OSI model are better hidden than in the TCP/IP model and can be replaced relatively easily as the technology changes. The OSI model was devised before the corresponding protocols were invented;

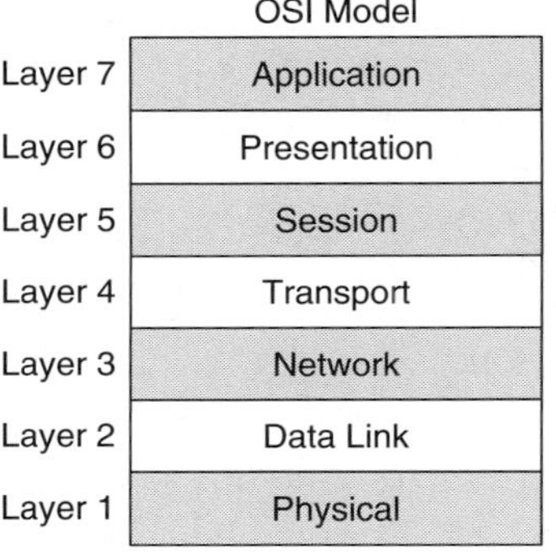

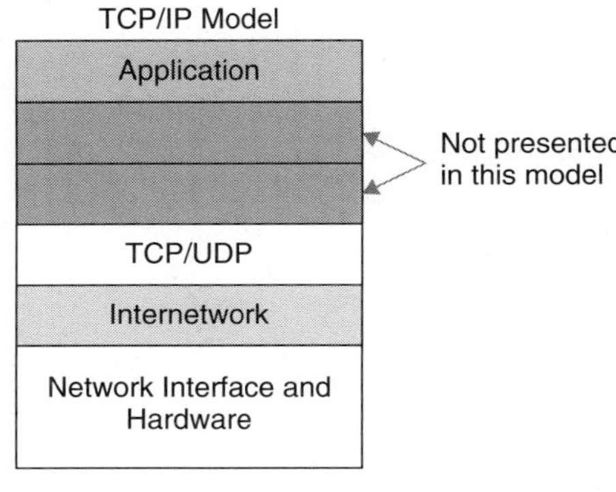

Figure 2: The OSI and TCP/IP reference models

Table 1: OSI layers and functions

Layer	Functions
Application	• Provides the user application process with access to OSI facilities
Presentation	• Responsible for data representation, data compression, and data encryption and decryption • Ensures communication between systems with different data representations • Allows the application layer to access the session layer services
Session	• Allows users on different machines to establish sessions between them • Establishes and maintains connections between processes, and data-transfer services
Transport	• Provides reliable, transparent data transfer between end systems, or hosts • Provides end-to-end error recovery and flow control • Multiplexes and de-multiplexes messages from applications
Network	• Establishes, maintains, and terminates connections between end systems • Builds end-to-end route through the network
Data Link	• Composed of two sublayers: logical link control (LLC) and media access control (MAC) • Provides a well-defined service interface to the network layer • Deals with transmission errors • Regulates data flow
Physical	• Handles the interface to the communication medium • Deals with various medium characteristics

therefore, it is not biased toward one particular set of protocols, which makes it quite general. With TCP/IP, the reverse is true: the protocols came first, and the model was really just a description of the existing protocols. Consequently, this model does not fit any other protocol stacks (Tanenbaum 2003).

The rest of the chapter is organized as follows. In the next section, ISO network management functions are briefly described. Network management protocols are discussed in the subsequent section. This is followed by a section on network management tools and then by a section on policy-based network management, followed by our conclusions.

ISO NETWORK MANAGEMENT FUNCTIONS

To ensure rapid and consistent progress on network management functions, including operations, administration, and maintenance (OAM), ISO has grouped the management functions into five areas: (1) configuration management, (2) fault management, (3) security management, (4) accounting management, and (5) performance management. The ISO classification has gained broad acceptance for both standardized and proprietary network management systems. A description of each management function is provided in the following subsections.

Configuration Management

Configuration management is concerned with initializing a network, provisioning the network resources and services, and monitoring and controlling the network. More specifically, the responsibilities of configuration management include setting, maintaining, adding to, and updating the relationship among components and the status of the components during network operation.

Configuration management consists of both device configuration and network configuration. Device configuration can be performed either locally or remotely. Automated network configuration, such as dynamic host configuration protocol (DHCP) and domain name services (DNS), plays a key role in network management.

Fault Management

Fault management involves detection, isolation, and correction of abnormal operations that may cause the failure of the OSI network. The major goal of fault management is to ensure that the network is always available and that when a fault occurs, it can be fixed as rapidly as possible.

Faults should be distinct from errors. An error is generally a single event, whereas a fault is an abnormal condition that requires management attention to fix. For example, the physical communication line cut is a fault, while a single-bit error on a communication line is an error.

Security Management

Security management protects the networks and systems from unauthorized access and security attacks. The mechanisms for security management include authentication, encryption, and authorization. Security management is also concerned with generation, distribution, and storage of encryption keys as well as other security-related information. Security management may include security systems such as firewalls and intrusion-detection systems that provide real-time event monitoring and event logging.

Accounting Management

Accounting management enables the charge for the use of managed objects to be measured and the cost for such use to be determined. The measure may include the resources consumed, the facilities used to collect accounting data and set billing parameters for the services used by customers, the maintenance of the databases used for billing purposes, and the preparation of resource usage and billing reports.

Performance Management

Performance management is concerned with evaluating and reporting the behavior and the effectiveness of the managed network objects. A network monitoring system can measure and display the status of the network, such as gathering the statistical information on traffic volume, network availability, response times, and throughput.

NETWORK MANAGEMENT PROTOCOLS

In this section, different versions of SNMP and RMON will be introduced. SNMP is the most widely used data network management protocol. Most of the network components used in enterprise network systems have built-in network agents that can respond to an SNMP network management system. This enables the new components to be monitored automatically. Remote network monitoring is, on the other hand, the most important addition to the basic set of SNMP standards. It defines a remote network monitoring MIB that supplements MIB-II and provides the network manager with vital information about the internetwork.

SNMP

The objective of network management is to build a single protocol that manages both OSI and TCP/IP networks. Based on this goal, SNMP, or SNMPv1 (Case et al. 1990; McCloghrie and Rose 1991; Rose and McCloghrie 1990), was first recommended as an interim set of specifications for use as the basis of common network management throughout the system, whereas the ISO CMIP over TCP/IP (CMOT) was recommended as the long-term solution (Cerf 1988, 1989).

SNMP consists of three specifications: the SMI, which describes how managed objects contained in the MIB are defined; the MIB, which describes the managed objects contained in the MIB; and the SNMP itself, which defines the protocol used to manage these objects.

SNMP Architecture

The model of network management that is used for TCP/IP network management includes the following key elements:

- **Management station**: hosts the network management applications.
- **Management agent**: provides information contained in the MIB to management applications and accepts control information from the management station.
- **Management information base**: defines the information that can be collected and controlled by the management application.
- **Network management protocol**: defines the protocol used to link the management station and the management agents.

The architecture of SNMP, shown in Figure 3, demonstrates the key elements of a network management

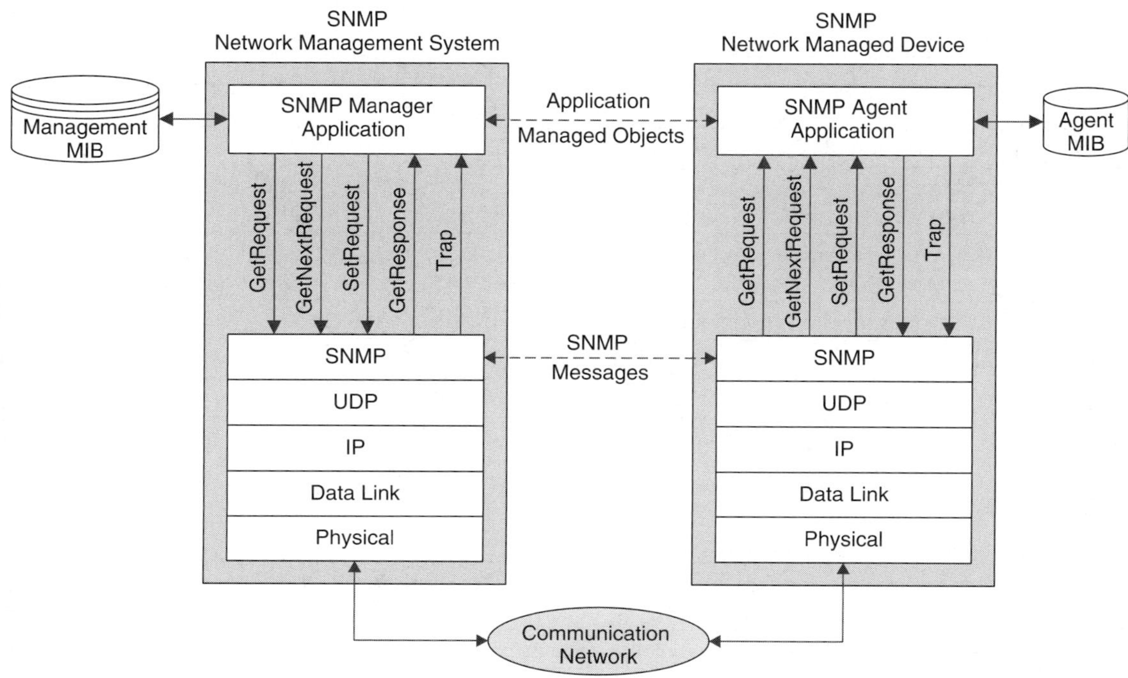

Figure 3: SNMP network management architecture

(a) SNMP message

PDU Type	RequestID	ErrorStatus	ErrorIndex	VariableBindings				
				Name 1	Value 1	...	Name N	Value N

(b) `Get/Set` Type of PDUs

PDU Type	Enterprise	Agent-Address	Generic-Trap	Specific-Trap	Timestamp	VariableBindings				
						Name 1	Value 1	...	Name N	Value N

(c) `Trap` PDUs

Figure 4: SNMP message formats

environment. SNMP is designed to be a simple message-based application-layer protocol. The manager process achieves network management using SNMP, which is implemented over the user datagram protocol (UDP) (Postel 1980; Bidgoli 2006). An SNMP agent must also implement SNMP and UDP protocols. Because UDP is a connectionless protocol, SNMP is itself a connectionless protocol. No outgoing connections are maintained between a management station and its agents. This design minimizes the complexity of the management agents.

Figure 3 also shows that SNMP supports five types of protocol data units (PDUs). The manager can issue three types of PDUs on behalf of a management application: `GetRequest`, `GetNextRequest`, and `SetRequest`. The first two are variations of the `get` function. All three messages are acknowledged by the agent in the form of a `GetResponse` message, which is passed up to the management application. Another message that the agent generates is `trap`– an unsolicited message that is generated when an event that affects the normal operations of the MIB and the underlying managed resources occurs.

SNMP Protocol Specifications

The SNMP message package communicated between a management station and an agent consists of a version identifier indicating the version of the SNMP protocol, an SNMP community name to be used for this message package, and an SNMP PDU. The message structure is shown in Figure 4, and each field is explained in Table 2.

Structure of Management Information

Figure 3 shows the information exchange between a single manager and agent pair. In a real network environment, there are multiple managers and many agents. The foundation of a network management system is a management information base (MIB) containing a set of network objects

Table 2: SNMP Message Fields

Field	Functions
Version	SNMP version (RFC 1157 is version 1)
Community Name	A pairing of an SNMP agent with some arbitrary set of SNMP application entities (Community Name serves as the password to authenticate the SNMP message)
PDU Type	The PDU type for the five messages is application data type, which is defined in RFC 1157 as `GetRequest (0), GetNextRequest (1), SetRequest (2), GetResponse (3), trap (4)`
`RequestID`	Used to distinguish among outstanding requests by the unique ID
`ErrorStatus`	A non-zero `ErrorStatus` is used to indicate that an exception occurred while processing a request
`ErrorIndex`	Used to provide additional information on the error status
`Variable-Bindings`	A list of variable names and corresponding values
`Enterprise`	Type of object generating trap
`AgentAddress`	Address of object generating trap
`GenericTrap`	Generic trap type; values are `coldStart (0), warmStart (1), linkDown (2), linkUp (3), authenticationFailure (4), egpNeighborLoss (5), enterpriseSpecific (6)`
`SpecificTrap`	Specific trap code not covered by the `enterpriseSpecific` type
`Timestamp`	Time elapsed since last reinitialization

to be managed. Each managed resource is represented as an object. The MIB is in fact a database structure of such objects in the form of a tree (Stallings 1998). Each system in a network environment maintains an MIB that keeps the status of the resources to be managed at that system. The information can be used by the network management entity for resource monitoring and controlling. SMI defines the syntax and semantics used to describe the SNMP management information (McCloghrie 1999).

MIB Structure

For simplicity and extensibility, SMI avoids complex data types. Each type of object in an MIB has a name, syntax, and an encoding scheme. An object is uniquely identified by an `OBJECT IDENTIFIER`. The identifier is also used to identify the structure of object types. The term `OBJECT DESCRIPTOR` may also be used to refer to the object type (McCloghrie and Rose 1991). The syntax of an object type is defined using Abstract Syntax Notation One (ASN.1) (International Organization for Standardization 1987). Basic encoding rules (BER) have been adopted as the encoding scheme for data type transfer between network entities.

The set of defined objects has a tree structure. Beginning with the root of the object identifier tree, each object identifier component value identifies an arc in the tree. The root has three nodes: `itu (0), iso (1), and joint-iso-itu (2)`. Some of the nodes in the SMI object tree, starting from the root, are shown in Figure 5. The identifier is constructed by the set of numbers, separated by a dot, that defines the path to the object from the root. Thus, the `internet` node, for example, has its `OBJECT IDENTIFIER` value of `1.3.6.1`. It can also be defined as follows:

```
internet OBJECT IDENTIFIER ::={ iso (1) org (3) dod (6) 1 }.
```

Any object in the `internet` node will start with the prefix `1.3.6.1` or simply `internet`.

SMI defines four nodes under `internet: directory, mgmt, experimental`, and `private`. The `mgmt` subtree contains the definitions of MIBs that have been approved by the IAB. Two versions of the MIB with the same object identifier have been developed, `mib-1` and its extension `mib-2`. Additional objects can be defined in one of the following three mechanisms (Case et al. 1990; Stallings 1998):

1. The `mib-2` subtree can be expanded or replaced by a completely new revision.
2. An experimental MIB can be constructed for a particular application. Such objects may subsequently be moved to the `mgmt` subtree.
3. Private extensions can be added to the `Private` subtree.

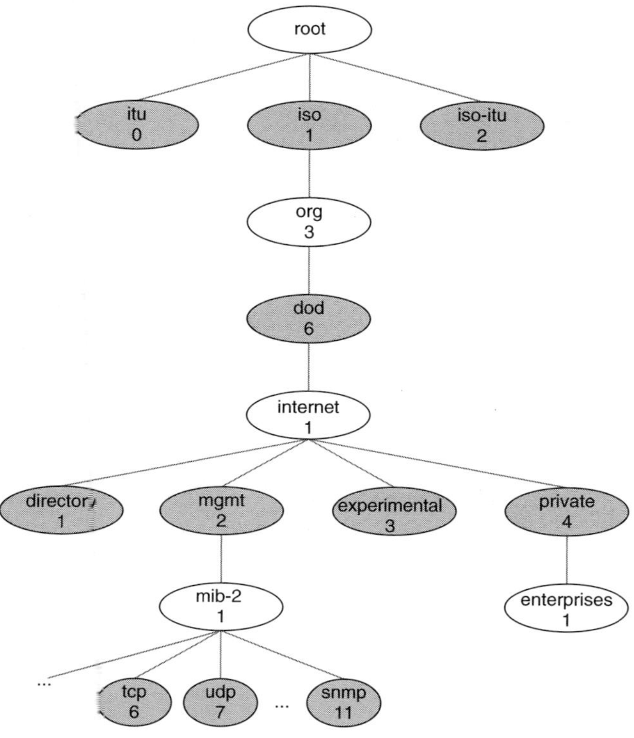

Figure 5: Management Information Tree

Object Syntax. The syntax of an object type defines the abstract data structure corresponding to that object type. ASN.1 is used to define each individual object and the entire MIB structure. The definition of an object in SNMP contains the data type, its allowable forms and value ranges, and its relationship with other objects within the MIB.

Encoding. Objects in the MIB are encoded using the BER associated with ASN.1. Although it is not the most compact or efficient form of encoding, BER is a widely used, standardized encoding scheme. BER specifies a method for encoding values of each ASN.1 type as a string of octets for transmitting to another system.

Management Information Base

Two versions of MIBs have been defined: MIB-I and MIB-II. MIB-II is a superset of MIB-I, with some additional objects and groups. MIB-II contains only essential elements; none of the objects is optional. The objects are arranged into groups as shown in Table 3.

Security Weaknesses

The only security feature that SNMP offers is through the Community Name contained in the SNMP message as shown in Figure 4. Community Name serves as the password to authenticate the SNMP message. Without encryption, this feature essentially offers no security at all, since the Community Name can be readily eavesdropped as it passes from the managed systems to the management system. Furthermore, SNMP cannot authenticate the source of a management message. Therefore, it is possible for unauthorized users to exercise SNMP network management functions and to eavesdrop on management information as it passes from the managed systems to the management system. Because of these deficiencies, many SNMP implementations have chosen not to implement the `Set` command. This reduces their utility to that of a network monitor, and no network control applications can be supported.

Table 3: Objects Contained in MIB-II

Groups	Description
system	Contains system description and administrative information.
interfaces	Contains information about each of the interfaces from the system to a subnet.
at	Contains address translation table for Internet-to-subnet address mapping. This group is deprecated in MIB-II and is included solely for compatibility with MIB-I nodes.
ip	Contains information relevant to the implementation and operation of IP at a node.
icmp	Contains information relevant to the implementation and operation of ICMP at a node.
tcp	Contains information relevant to the implementation and operation of TCP at a node.
udp	Contains information relevant to the implementation and operation of UDP at a node.
egp	Contains information relevant to the implementation and operation of EGP at a node.
transmission	Contains information about the transmission schemes and access protocols at each system interface.
snmp	Contains information relevant to the implementation and operation of SNMP on this system.

SNMPv2

SNMP was originally developed as an interim management protocol, while CMIP over TCP/IP (CMOT), which essentially enables the OSI system management protocols to operate on top of the TCP protocol, was developed as the ultimate network management protocol. However, the latter goal never came about in reality. At the same time, SNMP has been incorporated widely, and enhancement is expected. SNMPv2 was developed when it was obvious that the OSI network management standards were not going to be widely adopted in the foreseeable future.

Major Changes in SNMPv2

The SNMPv2 system architecture is essentially the same as that of SNMP. The key enhancement in SNMPv2 can be summarized as follows:

- **Bulk data transfer capability**: The most noticeable change in SNMPv2 is the inclusion of two new PDUs. The first PDU is the `GetBulkRequest` PDU, which enables the manager to retrieve large blocks of data efficiently, and therefore speeds up the `GetNextRequest` process.
- **Manager-to-manager capability**: The second PDU is the `InformRequest` PDU, which enables one manager to send trap type of information to another, and thus makes network management systems interoperable.
- **Structure of management information**: The SMI defined in SNMP has been consolidated and rewritten.

SNMPv2 Protocol Specifications

To improve the efficiency and performance of message exchange between systems, the PDU data structure in SNMPv2 has been standardized to a common format for all messages, given in Figure 6. In the `GetBulkRequest` PDU, the `NonRepeaters` field indicates the number of non-repetitive field values requested and the `MaxRepetitions` field designates the maximum number of table rows requested.

SNMPv2 Structure of Management Information

The SMI for SNMPv2 is based on the SMI for SNMP. It is nearly a proper superset of the SNMP SMI. The SNMPv2 SMI is divided into three parts: module definitions, object definitions, and notification definitions.

Module definitions are used to describe information modules. An ASN.1 macro, `MODULE-IDENTITY`, is used to concisely convey the semantics of an information module. Object definitions are used to describe managed objects. `Object-Type` is used to concisely convey both syntax and semantics of a managed object. Notification definitions are used to describe unsolicited transmissions of management information. Notification in SNMPv2 is

PDU Type	RequestID	ErrorStatus	ErrorIndex	VariableBindings				
				Name 1	Value 1	...	Name N	Value N

(a) All but Bulk Type of PDUs

PDU Type	RequestID	NonRepeaters	MaxRepetitions	VariableBindings				
				Name 1	Value 1	...	Name N	Value N

(b) `GetBulkRequest` PDU

Figure 6: SNMP entity

equivalent to trap in SNMP SMI. NOTIFICATION-TYPE conveys both syntax and semantics.

SNMPv2 Management Information Base

The SNMPv2 MIB defines objects that describe the behavior of an SNMPv2 entity. It consists of three groups:

- **System group**: An expansion of the original MIB-II system group. It includes a collection of objects that allow an SNMPv2 entity to act in an agent role to describe its dynamic configurable object resources.
- **SNMP group**: A refinement to the original MIB-II snmp group. It consists of objects that provide the basic instrumentation of the protocol activity.
- **MIB objects group**: A collection of objects that deal with SNMPv2Trap PDUs and that allow several cooperating SNMPv2 entities, each acting in a manager role, to coordinate their use of the SNMPv2 set operations.

Security Weaknesses

Similar to SNMP, SNMPv2 fails in providing any security services. The security of SNMPv2 remains the same as the SNMP. Therefore, it is still vulnerable to security attacks such as masquerade, information modification, and information disclosure.

SNMPv3

The security deficiency in SNMP and SNMPv2 significantly limits their utility. To remedy this problem, SNMPv3 was developed (Blumenthal and Wijnen 2002; Case et al. 2002; Harrington, Presuhn, and Wijnen 2002; Levi, Meyere, and Stewart 2002; Wijnen, Presuhn, and McCloghrie 2002). The SNMPv3 configuration can be set remotely with secure communication links. SNMPv3 also provides a framework for all three versions of SNMP and future development in SNMP with minimum impact on existing operations.

SNMPv3 Architecture

An SNMP management network consists of a distributed, interacting collection of SNMP entities. Each entity consists of a collection of modules that interact with each other to provide services. The architecture of an entity is defined as the elements of that entity and the names associated with them. There are three kinds of naming: naming of entities, naming of identities, and naming of management information.

SNMP Entities

The elements of the architecture associated with an SNMP entity, shown in Figure 7, consist of an SNMP engine, named snmpEngineID, and a set of applications that use the services provided by the SNMP engine. A brief description of each of the modules is given below.

- **Dispatcher**: Allows for concurrent support of multiple versions of SNMP messages in the SNMP engine. It performs three sets of functions. First, it sends and receives SNMP messages from the network. Second, it determines the version of the message and interacts with the corresponding message-processing model. Third, it provides an abstract interface to SNMP applications to deliver an incoming PDU to the local application, and to send a PDU from the local application to a remote entity.
- **Message-processing subsystem**: Responsible for preparing messages for sending, and extracting data from received messages.
- **Security subsystem**: Provides security services such as authentication and privacy of messages. It potentially contains multiple security models.
- **Access control subsystem**: Provides authorization services by means of one or more access control models.

SNMP Names. The names associated with the identities include principal, securityName, and a model-dependent security ID. A principal indicates to "whom" services are provided. A principal can be either a person or an application. A securityName is a human-readable string that represents a principal. A model-dependent security ID is the model-specific representation of a securityName within a particular security model.

A management entity can be responsible for more than one managed object. Each object is called a "context"

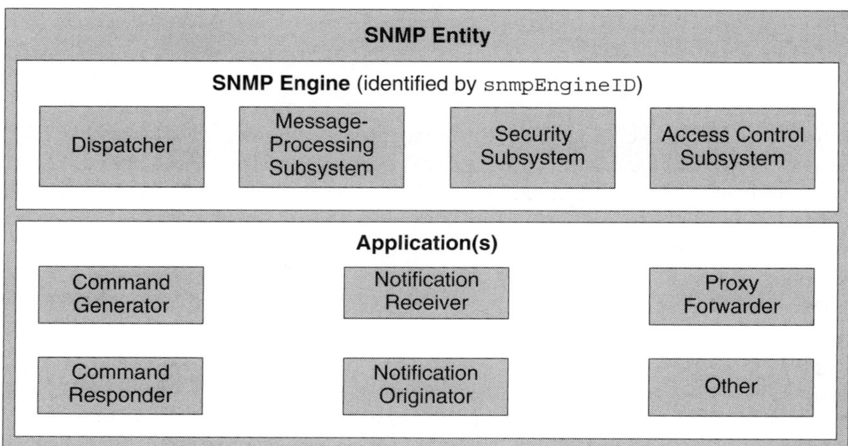

Figure 7: SNMPv2 PDU formats

Table 4: List of Primitives

Component	Primitive	Service Provided
Dispatcher	sendPdu	Sends an SNMP request or notification to another SNMP entity
	processPdu	Passes an incoming SNMP PDU to an application
	returnResponsePdu	Returns an SNMP response PDU to the PDU dispatcher
	processResponsePdu	Passes an incoming SNMP response PDU to an application
	registerContextEngineID	Registers responsibility for a specific contextEngineID, for specific pduTypes
	unregisterContext-EngineID	Unregisters responsibility for a specific contextEngineID, for specific pduTypes
Message Process Subsystem	prepareOutgoingMessage	Prepares an outgoing SNMP request or notification message
	prepareResponseMessage	Prepares an outgoing SNMP response message
	prepareDataElements	Prepares the abstract data elements from an incoming SNMP message
Access Control Subsystem	isAccessAllowed	Checks whether access is allowed
Security Subsystem	generateRequestMsg	Generates a request or notification message
	processIncomingMsg	Processes an incoming message
	generateResponseMsg	Generates a response message
User-Based Security Model	authenticateOutgoingMsg	Authenticates an outgoing message
	authenticateIncomingMsg	Authenticates an incoming message
	encryptData	Encrypts data
	decryptData	Decrypts data

and has a contextEngineID and a contextName. A scopePDU is a block of data containing a contextEngineID, a contextName, and a PDU.

Abstract Service Interfaces. Abstract service interfaces describe the conceptual interfaces between the various subsystems within an SNMP entity and are defined by a set of primitives and the abstract data elements. A primitive specifies the function to be performed and the parameters to be used to pass data and control information. Table 4 lists the primitives that have been defined for the various subsystems.

SNMPv3 Applications

SNMPv3 formally defines five types of applications. These applications make use of the services provided by the SNMP engine. SNMPv3 defines the procedures followed by each type of application when generating PDUs for transmission or processing incoming PDUs. The procedures are defined in terms of interaction with the dispatcher by means of the dispatcher primitives.

Command Generator. The command generator application makes use of the sendPdu and processResponsePdu dispatcher primitive to generate GetRequest, GetNext-Request, GetBulk, and SetRequest messages. It also processes the response to the command sent. The sendPdu provides the dispatcher with information about the intended destination, security parameters, and the actual PDU to be sent. The dispatcher then invokes the message-processing model, which in turn invokes the security model, to prepare the message. The dispatcher delivers each incoming response PDU to the correct command generator application, using the processResponsePdu primitive.

Command Responder. A command responder application makes use of four dispatcher primitives (registerContextEngineID, unregisterContextEngineID, processPdu, and returnResponsePdu) and one access control subsystem primitive (isAccessAllowed) to receive and process SNMP Get and Set requests. It also sends response messages. The dispatcher delivers each incoming request PDU to the correct command responder application, using the processPDU primitive. The command generator uses returnResponsePdu to deliver the message back to the dispatcher.

Notification Originators. A notification-originator application follows the same general procedures used for a command-generator application to generate either a trap or an Inform. If an Inform PDU is to be sent, both the sendPDU and processResponse primitives are used. If a trap PDU is to be sent, only the sendPDU primitive is used.

Notification Receiver. A notification receiver application follows a subset of the general procedures as for a command responder application to receive SNMP notification messages. Both types of PDUs are received by means of a `processPdu` primitive. For an `Inform PDU`, a `returnResponsePdu` primitive is used to respond.

Proxy Forwarder. A proxy-forwarder application makes use of dispatcher primitives to forward SNMP messages. The proxy-forwarder application handles four types of messages: messages containing PDU types generated by a command-generator application, messages containing PDU types generated by a command-responder application, messages containing PDU types generated by a notification-originator application, and messages containing a `report` indicator.

SNMPv3 Management Information Base

Three separate MIB modules have been defined by Levi et al. (2002) to support SNMPv3 applications: the management target MIB, the notification MIB, and the proxy MIB.

The `SNMP-TARGET-MIB` module contains objects for defining management targets. It consists of two tables. The first table, the `snmpTargetAddrTable`, contains information about transport domains and addresses. The second table, the `snmpTargetParamsTable`, contains information about SNMP version and security information to be used when sending messages to particular transport domains and addresses.

The `SNMP-NOTIFICATION-MIB` module contains objects for remote configuration of the parameters used by an SNMP entity for the generation of notifications. It consists of three tables. The first table, the `snmpNotifyTable`, selects one or more entries in `snmpTargetAddrTable` to be used for the generation of notifications. The second table, the `snmpNotifyFilterProfileTable`, sparsely augments the `snmpTargetParamsTable` so as to associate a set of filters with a particular management target. The third table, the `snmpNotifyFilterTable`, defines filters used to limit the number of notifications generated for a particular management target.

The `SNMP-PROXY-MIB` contains objects for the remote configuration of the parameters used by an SNMP entity for proxy-forwarding operations. It contains a single table, `snmpProxyTable`, which is used to define the translations between management targets for forwarding messages.

SNMPv3 Message Format

Each SNMPv3 message includes four data groups: `msgVersion`, `msgGlobaData`, `msgSecurityParameters`, and `msgPDU`, as shown in Figure 8.

The `msgVersion` field is set to `snmpv3 (3)` and identifies the message as an SNMP version 3 Message. The `msgGlobaGata` field contains the header information. The `msgSecurityParameters` field is used exclusively by the security model. The contents and format of the data are defined by the security model. The `msgData` is the scoped PDU field containing information to identify an administratively unique context and a PDU.

Security Enhancement

One of the main objectives in developing SNMPv3 is the addition of security services for network management. SNMPv3 is intended to address four types of security threats: modification of information, masquerade, disclosure, and message-stream modification. The first two are identified as principal threats, while the last two are identified as secondary threats. A user-based security model (USM) is proposed in SNMPv3. This model reflects the traditional concept of a user identified by a `userName` (Blumenthal and Wijnen 2002).

User-Based Security Model (USM)

The USM encompasses three different security modules: the authentication module, the timeliness module, and the privacy module.

In order to protect against message replay, delay, and redirection, when two management entities communicate, one of the SNMP engines is designated to be the authoritative SNMP engine. Particularly, when an SNMP message contains a payload that expects a response, then the receiver of such messages is authoritative. When an SNMP message contains a payload that does not expect a response, then the sender of such a message is authoritative.

The message process model invokes the USM in the security subsystem. Based on the security level set in the message, the USM in turn invokes the authentication modules, privacy modules, and timeliness module. The USM allows for different protocols to be used instead of, or concurrent with, the protocols described by Blumenthal

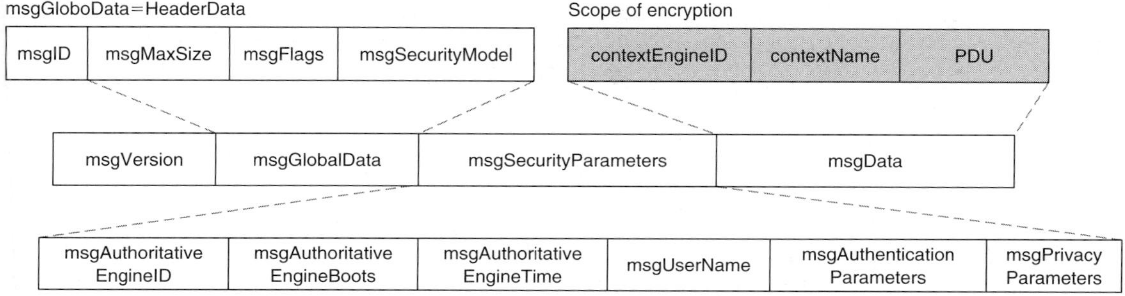

Figure 8: SNMPv3 message format

and Wijnen (2002) and Wijnen, Presuhn, and McCloghrie (2002).

Authentication. USM uses one of two alternative authentication protocols to achieve data integrity and data origin authentication: HMAC-MD5-96 and HMAC-SHA-96. HMAC uses a secure hash function and a secret key to produce a message authentication code (Stallings 1998; Krawczyk, Bellare, and Canetti 1997). In this case, the secret key is the localized user's private authentication key `authKey`. The value of `authKey` is not accessible via SNMP. For HMAC-MD5-96, MD5 is used as the underlying hash function. The `authKey` is 16 octets in length. The algorithm produces a 128-bit output, which is truncated to 12 octets (96 bits). For HMAC-SHA-96, the underlying hash function is SHA-1. The `authKey` is 20 octets in length. The algorithm produces a 20-octet output, which is again truncated to 12 octets.

Encryption. USM uses a cipher block chaining data encryption standard (CBC-DES) symmetric encryption protocol to protect against disclosure of the message payload (Stallings 1998; Krawczyk et al. 1997). A 16-octet `privKey` is provided as the input to the encryption protocol. The first 8 octets (64 bits) of this `privKey` are used as a DES key. Since DES uses only 56 bits, the least significant bit in each octet is disregarded. For CBC mode, a 64-bit initialization vector (IV) is required. The last 8 octets of the `privKey` contain a value that is used to generate this IV.

In order to ensure that the IVs for two different packets encrypted by the same key are not identical, an 8-octet string called "salt" is XOR-ed with the pre-IV to obtain the IV.

View-Based Access Control Model (VACM). The access control subsystem of an SNMP engine has the responsibility for checking whether a specific type of access (read, write, notify) to a particular object (instance) is allowed.
Access control occurs in an SNMP entity when processing SNMP retrieval or modification request messages from an SNMP entity and when an SNMP notification message is generated.

The VACM defines a set of services that an application can use for checking access rights. It is the responsibility of the application to make the proper service calls for access checking.

Remote Network Monitoring (RMON)

Remote network monitoring devices, often called "monitors" or "probes," are instruments that exist for the purpose of managing a network. The RMON can produce summary information of the managed objects, including error statistics, performance statistics, and traffic statistics. Based on the statistics information, the status of the managed objects can be observed and analyzed.

RMON1 Groups

The RMON1 specification is primarily a definition of an MIB, defined by Waldbusser (1993, 2000). RMON1 delivers management information in nine groups of monitoring elements; each provides specific sets of data to meet common network-monitoring requirements. Some RMON1 groups require the support of other RMON1 groups to function properly. Table 5 summarizes the nine monitoring groups specified in Waldbusser (1997).

RMON2

RMON2 as defined by Waldbusser (1997) enables network statistics and analysis to be provided from the network layer up to the application layer. The most visible and most beneficial capability in RMON2 is monitoring

Table 5: RMON1 MIBs

RMON Group	Functions
Statistics	Contains statistics measured by the probe for each monitored interface on this device.
History	Records periodic statistical samples from a network and stores them for later retrieval.
Alarm	Takes statistical samples periodically from variables in the probe and compares them with previously configured thresholds. If the monitored variable crosses a threshold, an event is generated.
Host	Contains statistics associated with each host discovered on the network.
HostTopN	Prepares statistics about the top *N* hosts on a subnetwork based on the available parameters.
Matrix	Stores statistics for conversations between sets of two addresses. As the device detects a new conversation, it creates a new entry in its table.
Filters	Enables packets to be matched by a filter equation. These matched packets form a data stream that may be captured or may generate events.
Packet capture	Enables packets to be captured after they flow through a channel.
Events	Controls the generation and notification of events from a device.
Token ring extensions	Contains four groups to define some additional monitoring functions specified for token ring. They are the ring station group, the ring station order group, the ring station configuration group, and the source routing statistics group.

Table 6: RMON2 MIBs

RMON2 MIB Group	Functions
Protocol directory	Presents an inventory of protocol types capable of monitoring.
Protocol distribution	Collects the relative amounts of octets and packets.
Address mapping	Provides address translation between MAC addresses and network addresses on the interface.
Network-layer host	Provides network host traffic statistics.
Network-layer matrix	Provides traffic analysis between each pair of network hosts.
Application-layer host	Reports on protocol usage at the network layer or higher.
Application-layer matrix	Provides protocol traffic analysis between pairs of network hosts.
User history collection	Provides user-specified history collection on alarm and configuration history.
Probe configuration	Controls the configuration of probe parameters.
RMON conformance	Describes the conformance requirements to RMON2 MIB.

above the MAC layer, which supports protocol distribution and provides a view of the whole network rather than a single local area network (LAN) segment. RMON2 also enables host traffic for particular applications to be recorded. The managed objects in RMON2 are arranged into groups, as shown in Table 6.

Mobility Management in Wireless Networks

The major feature of wireless communication is that it supports user mobility. Handoff management and location management are two key components in mobility management of wireless networks (Mark and Zhuang 2003).

Handoff Management. Wireless networks have the flexibility to support user roaming. To facilitate user roaming, there must be an effective and efficient handoff mechanism so that the mobile's connection can be transferred from one access point to another access point with continued service.

An effective handoff scheme should have the following features: (1) fast and lossless, (2) minimal number of control signals, (3) scalable with network size, and (4) capable of recovering from link failures.

Location Management. For identification purposes, each wireless subscriber must register with its home network. The subscriber's identity is a permanent address that resides in the database of a location register, called the subscriber's home location register (HLR). When the subscriber moves away from his/her home network, the new address the mobile enters is a visitor network. It must update its registration with the home location register through its visitor location register (VLR) in order to facilitate message delivery to the mobile in its new location. The procedure of maintaining an association between the mobile and its HLR when it is away from its home network is referred to as location management.

Location management is achieved mainly through location update and paging. The location update procedure allows the system to keep location knowledge in order to find the user for incoming calls. The paging process achieved by the system consists of sending paging messages in all cells in which the mobile terminal could be located.

NETWORK MANAGEMENT TOOLS AND SYSTEMS

The tremendous growth in scale and diversity of computer networks has made network management a complex and challenging task for network administrators. To manage computer networks tangibly and efficiently, specific management tools and systems must be used to seamlessly monitor the network activities and to preemptively determine and control the network behaviors.

The catalog of network management tools and systems is extensive, and it is far beyond the scope of this chapter. Network management tools are usually based on particular network management protocols. Most tools use open protocols; however, some network management tools are based on vendor-specific proprietary protocols. The network management capabilities provided with the tools are usually based on the functionality supported by the network management protocols.

In this section, we will briefly describe network management tools in several categories, including network monitors, network scanners, and packet filters, along with two network management systems.

Network Monitors

One of the fundamental responsibilities of a network administrator is network monitoring. Network monitors are responsible for collecting and analyzing network traffic. A good system should be able to generate log files and performance charts that detail the system capabilities and responses. With these data, the network configuration can be optimized and better prepared for faults. Some network monitors are designed with SNMP management capability to offer full view of the fundamental network issues. Based on the observation of network monitors, network configuration can be optimized, and the administrators can be better prepared for faults. To minimize the network down time, effective network monitoring will alert the presence of a network anomaly immediately.

Numerous network monitoring tools are available today. Based on the functionalities, network monitoring tools may be further divided into the following categories:

- **Network and system monitoring** can enhance commercial network and system performance. Representative examples of network and system monitoring include ActiveXperts Network Monitor (www.activexperts.com/activmonitor), AdventNet OpManager (http://manageengine.adventnet.com/products/opmanager), GFI Network Server Monitor (www.gfi.com/nsm), and ipMonitor (www.ipmonitor.com/default.aspx).
- **Network traffic monitoring** can monitor traffic flows through and between critical network devices as well as collect utilization statistics. Examples of network traffic monitoring tools include Colasoft EtherLook (www.etherlook.com) and TracePlus Ethernet (www.sstinc.com/ethernet.html).
- **Protocol analyzing and packet capturing** provide packet capture, network sniffers, performance monitors and so on. Distinct Network Monitor (www.distinct.com), WildPackets' Etherpeek (www.wildpackets.com/products/etherpeek/overview), and Network Probe (www.objectplanet.com/probe) are some examples in this category.
- **Security monitoring** provides security monitoring of workstations and servers. Activeworx Security Center (www.activeworx.com/products/asc/index.html) and NetOp Desktop Firewall (www.netop.com/netop-14.htm) are two examples in this category.

Network Scanners

Network security vulnerabilities are being detected on a daily basis. A network scanner is one of the key elements of network security. It checks network system, operating system, and applications running on the network to identify vulnerabilities and possible security flaws that could expose the network to security compromise. To protect online assets and eliminate the risk to the business, some network scanners can also automate vulnerability assessment. Some representative network security scanners include Internet Scanner, Nessus Network Vulnerability Scanner, SAINT Vulnerability Scanner, Retina Network Security Scanner, NetIQ Vulnerability Manager, and GFI LANguard Network Security Scanner.

Packet Filters

Packet filters control access of data packets to a network by scanning the contents of the packet headers. A packet filter determines whether a packet should be allowed to go through a given point based on certain access control policies.

Packet filtering is most commonly used as the first line of defense against attacks from machines outside the network. It has become a common and inexpensive mechanism for security protection. However, packet filtering does not guarantee the security of the network and internal data.

Dynamic packet filtering, also referred to as stateful inspection, is a firewall architecture that works at the network layer. Stateful inspection tracks each connection traversing all interfaces of the firewall and makes sure they are valid. A stateful firewall may examine the contents of the packet up through the application layer in order to get more information about the packet other than its source and destination. A stateful inspection firewall also monitors the state of the connection and compiles the information in a state table. As a result, filtering decisions are based not only on administrator-defined rules but also on context that has been established by prior packets passed through the firewall.

Simple packet filters are implemented in most routers and operating systems. Some well-known packet filters include netfilter (Linux) (www.netfilter.org), PF (OpenBSD) (www.openbsd.org/faq/pf), ipfilter (Unix) (http://coombs.anu.edu.au/~avalon), and SmartSniff (Windows) (www.nirsoft.net/utils/smsniff.html).

Network Management Systems

A network management system (NMS) is an automated system tool that helps networking personnel perform their functions efficiently. Many network management systems are available today. In this section, three network management systems will be briefly introduced.

- **HP OpenView** (http://h20229.www2.hp.com) is HP's network management platform. It is most commonly described as a suite of software applications that allow large-scale system and network management of an organization's IT assets. It includes hundreds of optional modules from HP as well as thousands of third parties that connect within the well-defined framework and communicate with one another.
- **Network Node Manager (NNM)** is the network system built on the HP OpenView platform. The HP OpenView platform provides the common management services that are accessed through standard application programming interfaces (APIs). NNM is also used in its own right to manage networks, possibly in conjunction with other products, such as Cisco CiscoWorks.
- **IBM Tivoli** (http://222-306.ibm.com/software/tivoli) is a systems management platform from IBM. It is a CORBA-based architecture that allows the platform to manage large numbers of remote locations or devices. Tivoli includes a huge list of software tools in providing management functions. These tools can be largely divided into four major categories, including business service management, security management, storage management, and system management.

POLICY-BASED NETWORK MANAGEMENT–SOLUTIONS FOR THE NEXT GENERATION

Policy-based network management (PBNM) (Strassner 2004) is a way to manage the configuration and behavior

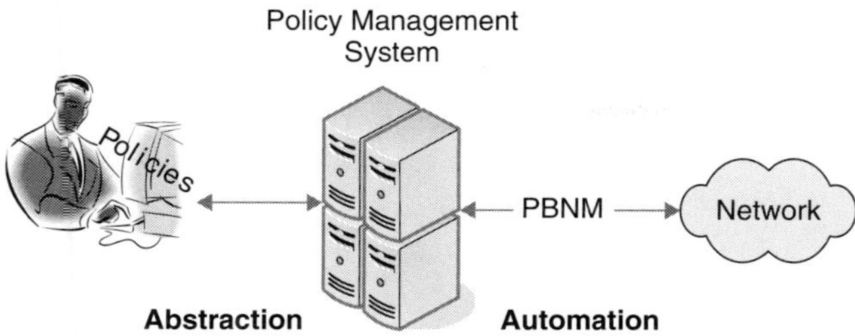

Figure 9: The basic model of policy-based management

of one or more entities based on business needs and policies. PBNM systems enable business rules and procedures to be translated into policies that configure and control the network and its services. PBNM can also be defined as a condition-action response mechanism. The general form is:

```
ON <event>
IF <conditions>
THEN <actions>
```

PBNM enables an automatic response to conditions in the network according to predefined policies. By automating the network management, the entire network can be managed as an entity itself. The essence of PBNM is portrayed in Figure 9.

Policy-based network management (PBNM) will redefine the way networks are being managed. Policy management is necessary to administer network QoS (quality of service), security, and resources throughout the enterprise.

What Is a Policy?

Policy is typically defined as a set of operating rules that manage and control access to network resources. It allows a network to be managed through a descriptive language. Policy can be represented at different levels, ranging from business goals to device-specific configuration parameters.

Policy management is the use of operating rules to accomplish decisions. It forms a bridge between the service-level agreement (SLA) and the network entities. Business goals and policies can be defined as a separate business management layer on top of the service management layer that provides services such as QoS, as shown in Figure 10 (Erfani et al. 1999).

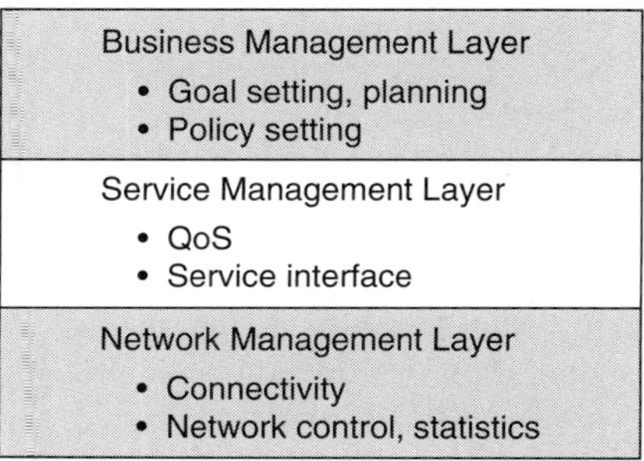

Figure 10: Network management—layered view

With the growth in scale and complexity of computer networks, QoS and security are becoming very challenging management issues. PBNM is emerging as a promising solution in simplifying the management of QoS and security.

Benefits of PBNM

The appealing part of PBNM is that through abstractions, the network management QoS and security mechanisms can be simplified so that the majority of network management tasks are simple in nature. PBNM also enables system behavior to be changed without modifying the implementation. More specifically, the benefit of PBNM can be summarized as follows (Strassner 2004; Hewlett-Packard 1999):

- **Optimizes network resource intelligently**: The automation of management tasks intelligently optimizes both the use of network infrastructure and the network policies. PBNM reduces the need for adding bandwidth to congested links.
- **Simplifies network and service management**: PBNM users are no longer required to be specialists in order to perform network management functions. Another aspect is that changes in business policies do not necessarily require any low-layer development, which makes management updating painless.
- **Manages complex traffic and services intelligently**: PBNM can manage applications with competing demand for shared resources using the predicated traffic information. Unauthorized and unwanted applications can be controlled or eliminated, while mission-critical applications can be assigned with special priority.
- **Performs time-critical functions efficiently**: PBNM can simplify and better implement the time-critical functions, such as changing device configurations within a specific time window and performing scheduled provisioning functions.
- **Provides better security**: PBNM can help categorize traffic into expected and unexpected types and assign rules to deal with each type. PBNM can also be used to determine whether a particular user can access a resource or not.

Architecture of a PBNM System

The general architecture for a policy-management system is shown in Figure 11. This architecture contains four major components (Hewlett-Packard 1999; Westerinen et al. 2001):

- **Policy Management Console**: The user interface to construct policies, deploy policies, and monitor the status of policy-managed environment.
- **Policy Repository**: A database that stores the policy rules, their conditions and actions, and related policy data. It can also be defined as a model abstraction representing an administratively defined, logical container for reusable policy elements.

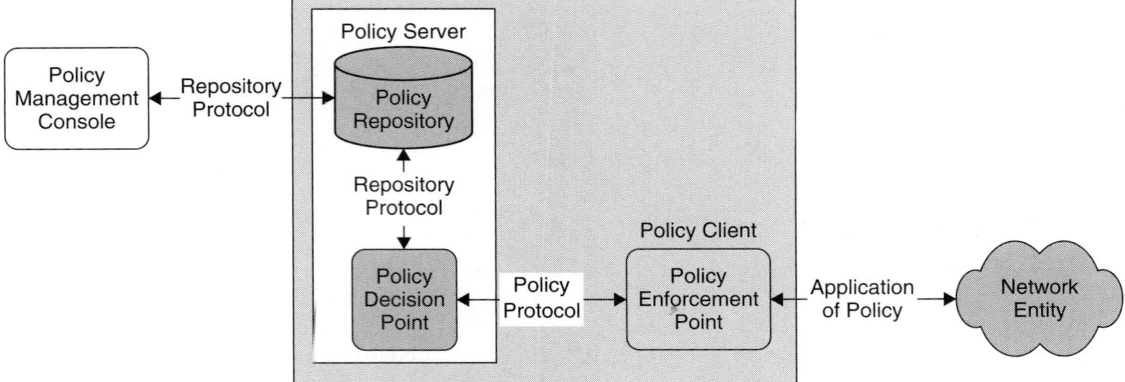

Figure 11: A logic architecture for PBNM

- **Policy Decision Point (PDP)**: A logical process that makes decisions based on the policy rules and the conditions under which the policy rules are applied.
- **Policy Enforcement Point (PEP)**: A logical entity that executes policy decisions and/or makes a configuration change.
- **Policy Communication Protocols**: Needed for data exchange between entities in the policy management system. The common object policy service protocol (COPS) is often mentioned to support the communication between the PDP and the PEP.

CONCLUSION

In this chapter, after a brief introduction of the network management system, the evolution of the two most widely used network management standards, SNMP and RMON, is reviewed along with the rapid development in computer and communication networks. Network management tools and systems, which have become an indispensable element in network management, are then briefly introduced. As a promising solution for the next generation of network management, the architecture of PBNM is also discussed. The popularity of SNMP and RMON is due largely to their simplicity in architecture and implementation; however, the simplicity comes with limitations as well. The versatile expertise required for the administrators and the reality that even a slight change in business policy may require complex development at lower layers, prevent these standards from further development. To overcome these disadvantages, PBNM is proposed to ensure efficient network management and smooth network services upgrade. Although PBNM is not yet fully mature, its promising features make it very appealing and convincing for a rosy future.

GLOSSARY

Account Management: One of the five OSI systems management functional areas. Consists of facilities that enable cost allocation based on the use of network resources.

Common Management Information Protocol (CMIP): An object-oriented OSI standard management protocol.

Configuration Management: One of the five OSI systems management functional areas. Consists of facilities that set and change the configuration of networks and network components.

Fault Management: One of the five OSI systems management functional areas. Consists of facilities that detect, isolate, and correct the abnormal operation of the OSI environment.

HMAC Protocols: Message authentication protocols used for the authentication scheme in security management. It is based on hashing algorithms to derive the message access code (MAC). Two common algorithms used in SNMP security management are HMAC-MD5-96 and HMAC-SHA-96.

Managed Object: A network device that can be managed remotely by a network management system.

Management Information Base (MIB): An abstract definition of the management information available through a management interface in a system.

Network Management System (NMS): The platform that houses the network manager module. It monitors and controls the network components from a centralized operation.

Network Monitoring: Network monitoring describes the use of a system that constantly monitors a computer network for slow or failing systems and that notifies the network administrator of outages via e-mail, pager, or other alarms.

Network Scanner: Network scanner describes the systems used to check the network system, the operating system, and applications running on the network to identify vulnerabilities and possible security flaws that could expose the network to security compromise.

Packet Filter: A packet filter determines whether a packet is allowed to go through a given point based on certain access control policies.

Performance Management: One of the five OSI systems management functional areas. Consists of facilities that evaluate the behavior of managed objects and the performance of network activities.

Policy-Based Network Management (PBNM): Manages the configuration and behavior of networks based on business needs and policies.

Remote Network Monitoring (RMON): Remotely monitoring the network with a probe.

Security Management: One of the five OSI systems management functional areas. Consists of facilities that provide security services essential to operate OSI network management correctly and to protect managed objects.

Simple Network Management Protocol (SNMP): An application layer protocol that facilitates the exchange of management information between network devices.

Structure of Management Information (SMI): Defines managed objects and their characteristics, as well as the relationship between the objects.

Trap: An alarm or an event generated by a management agent and sent in an unsolicited manner to a network management system.

User-Based Access Control Model (UACM): The access control scheme defined in SNMPv3. It is more secure and flexible than the simple access policy defined in SNMP.

CROSS REFERENCES

See *Backup and Recovery System Requirements*; *Business Continuity Planning*; *E-Mail and Internet Use Policies*; *Network Attacks*.

REFERENCES

Bidgoli, H., editor. 2006. *The handbook of computer networks*, Volume 2, "TCP/IP suite." Hoboken, NJ: John Wiley & Sons, Inc.

Blumenthal, U., and B. Wijnen. 2002, December. RFC3414: User-based Security Model (USM) for Version 3 of the simple network management protocol (SNMPv3). www.rfc-editor.org/rfc/rfc3414.txt (accessed June 19, 2007).

Case, J., D. Harrington, R. Presuhn, and B. Wijnen. 2002, December. RFC3412: Message processing and dispatching for the simple network management protocol (SNMP). www.rfc-editor.org/rfc/rfc3412.txt (accessed June 19, 2007).

Case, J., M. Fedor, M. Schoffstall, and J. Davin. 1990, May. RFC1157: A simple network management protocol (SNMP). www.rfc-editor.org/rfc/rfc1157.txt (accessed June 19, 2007).

Cerf., V. 1988. RFC1052: IAB Recommendations for the development of Internet network management standards. http://www.rfc-editor.org/rfc/rfc1052.txt (accessed June 19, 2007).

Cerf., V. 1989. RFC1109: Report of the Second Ad Hoc Network Management Review Group. www.rfc-editor.org/rfc/rfc1109.txt (accessed June 19, 2007).

Cisco Systems. 2002, February. Network management basics. www.cisco.com/univercd/cc/td/doc/cisintwk/ito_doc/nmbasics.htm (accessed June 19, 2007).

Erfani, S., V. B. Lawrence, M. Malek, and B. Sugla. 1999. Network management: Emerging trends and challenges. *Bell Labs Technical Journal*, October–December.

Harrington, R. Presuhn, and B. Wijnen. 2002, December. RFC3411: An architecture for describing simple network management protocol (SNMP) management frameworks. www.rfc-editor.org/rfc/rfc3411.txt (accessed June 19, 2007).

Hewlett-Packard. 1999, September 24. A primer on policy-based network management. www.openview.hp.com/Uploads/primer_on_policy-based_network_mgmt.pdf (accessed June 22, 2007).

International Organization for Standardization. 1987, December. Specification of Abstract Syntax Notation One (ASN.1). International Standard 8824.

Krawczyk, H., M. Bellare, and R. Canetti. 1997, February. RFC2104: HMAC: Keyed-hashing for message authentication. www.rfc-editor.org/rfc/rfc2104.txt (accessed June 22, 2007).

Levi, D., P. Meyer, and B. Stewart. 2002, December. RFC3413: Simple network management protocol (SNMP) applications. www.rfc-editor.org/rfc/rfc3413.txt (accessed June 22, 2007).

Mark, J. W., and W. Zhuang. 2003. *Wireless communications and networking*. Upper Saddle River, NJ: Prentice Hall/Pearson Education.

McCloghrie and M. Rose. 1991, March. RFC1213: Management information base for network management of TCP/IP-based internets: MIB-II. http://www.rfc-editor.org/rfc/rfc1213.txt (accessed June 19, 2007).

McCloghrie, K., D. Perkins, and J. Schoenwaelder. 1999. Structure of management information version 2 (SMIv2). www.rfc-editor.org/rfc/rfc2819.txt (accessed June 19, 2007).

Postel, J. 1980. RFC768: User datagram protocol. www.rfc-editor.org/rfc/rfc768.txt (accessed June 19, 2007).

Rose, M., and K. McCloghrie. 1990. RFC1155: Structure and identification of management information for TCP/IP-based internets. http://www.rfc-editor.org/rfc/rfc1155.txt (accessed June 19, 2007).

Stallings, W. 1998. *SNMP, SNMPv2, SNMPv3 and RMON 1 and 2*. 3rd ed. Reading, MA: Addison Wesley.

Strassner, J. C. 2004. *Policy based network management—Solutions for the next generation*. Boston: Morgan Kaufmann.

Subramanian, M. 2000. *Network management—Principles and practice*. Reading, MA: Addison Wesley.

Tanenbaum, A. S. 2003. *Computer networks*. 4th ed. Upper Saddle River, NJ: Prentice Hall.

Wijnen, B., R. Presuhn, and K. McCloghrie. 2002, December. RFC3415: View-based access control model (VACM) for the simple network management protocol (SNMP). www.rfc-editor.org/rfc/rfc3415.txt (accessed June 22, 2007).

Waldbusser, S. 2000, May. RFC2819: Remote network monitoring management information base. www.rfc-editor.org/rfc/rfc2819.txt (accessed June 22, 2007).

Waldbusser, S. 1993, September. RFC1513: Token ring extensions to the remote network monitoring MIB. www.rfc-editor.org/rfc/rfc1513.txt (accessed June 22, 2007).

Waldbusser, S. 1997, January. RFC2021: Remote network monitoring management information base version 2 using SMIv2. www.rfc-editor.org/rfc/rfc2021.txt (accessed June 22, 2007).

Westerinen, A., J. Schnizlein, J. Strassner, M. Scherling, B. Quinn, S. Herzog, A. Huynh, M. Carlson, J. Perry, and S. Waldbusser. 2001, November. RFC3198: Terminology for policy-based management. www.rfc-editor.org/rfc/rfc3198.txt (accessed June 22, 2007).

ACRONYMS

ASN.1 Abstract Syntax Notation One
BER basic encoding rules
CBC cipher block chaining
CMIP common management information protocol
CMOT CMIP over TCP/IP
COPS common object policy service protocol
DES data encryption standard
DHCP dynamic host configuration protocol
DNS domain name services
EGP external gateway protocol
HMAC hashed message authentication code
IAB Internet Architecture Board
IP Internet protocol
ISO International Organization for Standardization
IV initialization vector
MD message digest
MAC media access control
MTU maximum transmission unit
MIB management information base
NMS network management system
OSI open systems interconnection
PBNM policy-based network management
PDP policy decision point
PDU protocol data unit
PEP policy enforcement point
QoS quality of service
RFC Request for Comments
RMON remote network monitoring
SGMP simple gateway monitoring protocol
SHA secure hash algorithm
SLA service level agreement
SMI structure of management information
SNMP simple network management protocol
TCP transmission control protocol
UDP user datagram protocol

Part 3

Computer Network Popular Applications and Future Directions

E-Mail and Instant Messaging

Bhagyavati, *DeSales University*

INTRODUCTION

E-mail and IM systems are the two main categories of software described in this chapter, and emphasis is placed on security issues and solutions. After a brief introduction to electronic mail and instant messaging, a more detailed look at each system is presented. In today's world of increasing cybercrime, security in e-mail and IM environments is an important concern. Security issues and possible solutions are examined in depth for both e-mail and IM. Following this discussion, e-mail and IM usage policies are suggested. The conclusion is followed by a glossary of key terms and a list of references.

ELECTRONIC MAIL

Electronic mail is ubiquitous in communication today. Before the usefulness of e-mail was perceived, the Internet was widely used initially for military and academic purposes. The growth in popularity of the Internet was due, in part, to e-mail. Compared to other modes of communication, such as postal mail, e-mail is cheaper, faster, and more convenient. The ability to forward communications to many people and to address more than one recipient, as well as the asynchronous nature of the communication, makes e-mail popular. The advent of mailing lists and address books added convenience and ease of use, leading to an upsurge in the use of e-mail.

Definition of E-Mail

Per the popular usage of the term, e-mail can be defined as mail sent via electronic means. According to Lombardi (2003), e-mail messages use standard conventions for addressing and delivering content across the public Internet. An e-mail has two mandatory parts: a header and a message. Other components, including attachments, are optional. In the beginning of e-mail history, all e-mails were in text format. As e-mail systems evolved, formatting styles other than plain text began to be used. The e-mail header contains information on where the e-mail originated, the route it has traveled, and to whom it is addressed. Although most e-mail users may dismiss the header as irrelevant to their communication, technical staff need to know the source, destination, and route of the e-mail in case of problems.

Brief History of E-Mail

Ray Tomlinson adapted an existing internal e-mail program to the ARPAnet file transfer technology and sent the first e-mail message from one computer to another in 1971 (Griffiths 2002). After the first message, "Testing 1-2-3," was successfully sent and received by two different computers, Tomlinson sent a message to all ARPAnet users and gave them instructions for sending and receiving electronic mail. The convention username@hostname, which is the basis for e-mail today, dates from this time.

Initially, e-mail was cumbersome and not user-friendly. However, most of the modern e-mail features were implemented within a year of the first e-mail transmission (Griffiths 2002). The ability to delete, forward, and save messages, together with a standard protocol to transfer messages between programs, was established by 1972. Thus, e-mail evolved along with the network now known as the Internet. In 1977, a standard specification of e-mail was published in a document called RFC 733, which was revised in 1982 to describe domain name syntax explicitly for the first time (Crocker 2003).

Eric Allman developed the sendmail program in the 1980s, which was derived from e-mail relaying on the UNIX operating system at the University of California at Berkeley. In 1988, Vinton Cerf sent the first commercial e-mail by connecting MCI Mail to the NSFnet (National Science Foundation network). This event marked a milestone in the history of e-mail because it paved the way for the network service providers America Online and Delphi to connect their proprietary e-mail systems to the Internet. The exponential growth in e-mail use can be traced to this moment when the benefits of e-mail were globally recognized.

Advantages and Features of E-Mail

Some people consider one of the advantages of e-mail to be its informal style of communication. Although people expect typed letters to be formal and perfect, no such expectations exist for e-mail. E-mail became more popular because of its relatively low cost, high reliability, and almost instantaneous delivery as compared with regular mail (Living Internet 2003). E-mail provides a high level of informality, a sense of community and sharing, wide tolerance of spelling and typographical errors, and brevity of expression. It has been theorized that the style of e-mail communication was a factor in its early and continued success. Also, unlike the telephone, e-mail does not demand an immediate response (Griffiths 2002).

Scientists and researchers working in the ARPAnet (precursor to the Internet) community started to recognize the immense promise of e-mail to change the way people communicate in all sectors of society, including the academic, business, and cultural sectors (Myer and Dodds 1976). Productivity gains were realized by businesses through the use of e-mail. Today, e-mail has become indispensable in academic, governmental, and business organizations around the world because of ease of use, convenience, low cost, asynchronous nature, range of features, and communication efficiency.

Current E-mail Systems

An e-mail system has three components: the transport agent and the delivery agent on the server, and the user agent or client (Preetham 2002). Popular graphical-user-interface (GUI)-based e-mail clients such as Eudora, Google mail, Mozilla Thunderbird, Microsoft's Outlook and Outlook Express, and Pegasus incorporate features such as e-mail forwarding, read receipts, e-mail filtering, and spam blocking. Web-based clients such as Hotmail and Yahoo are also popularly used. While Web-based clients do not require software downloads onto people's personal computers, non-Web-based GUI e-mail clients such as Eudora require downloads.

Besides the GUI-based e-mail clients mentioned previously, popular text-based e-mail clients include elm and pine. An e-mail client can use either the post office protocol (POP) or the Internet mail access protocol (IMAP). POP copies e-mails from the server to the computer on which the client resides, whereas IMAP works by copying e-mail headers to the client computer—actual e-mail messages are not copied unless selected (Nevis 2004).

On Outlook for Microsoft Exchange server, messaging application programming interface (MAPI) can be used for retrieving e-mail. For sending e-mail, simple mail transfer protocol (SMTP) is the de facto standard for transmission, whereas multipurpose Internet mail extensions (MIME) is another popular protocol available for e-mail clients (Wikipedia 2006). For server software, Exchange and sendmail protocols are popularly used. On Linux, qmail is a widely used protocol on the e-mail server. Howstuffworks.com has simple diagrams that provide a clearer understanding of the e-mail transfer process and SMTP protocol.

MIME is a protocol that provides the ability to transmit nontext data such as graphics and audio through e-mail. Text-based encoding is used so that the nontext data can be transported through text-based e-mail gateways. The specifications for the MIME protocol are documented in RFC 1521 and RFC 1522; these documents also specify the standard representation for "complex" message bodies (ELook.org 2006). A complex message body is the body of an e-mail message that does not follow a human-readable ASCII format of default e-mail messages. Digitally signed e-mail messages and file attachments sent with textual e-mail are some examples of complex message bodies.

E-mail addresses can be grouped together into mailing lists. A manager program automates the tedious maintenance of the list by adding, modifying, and deleting users and their e-mail addresses. Most corporations use standard naming procedures to make e-mail administration and management easier (Tittel 2002). Popular e-mail server software can be categorized into proprietary intranet solutions such as Microsoft's Exchange program and the Internet-based sendmail program. Web-based e-mail software abounds, and providers make these clients available to users for free. For instance, Yahoo! and Hotmail provide free e-mail quotas of 250 MB to each user. Google mail (Gmail) provides more than 2 GB to each user.

Disadvantages and Vulnerabilities of E-mail

Although more detail can be found in "E-Mail Threats and Vulnerabilities," this chapter provides a high-level perspective on e-mail vulnerabilities and disadvantages. The very advantages of e-mail can be construed as disadvantages under certain circumstances. The asynchronous nature of e-mail results in disadvantages such as the lack of face-to-face presence that is vital to effective communication. Terse messages can mislead the recipient, especially if previous threads to an e-mail conversation are not attached. E-mail is hampered by the lack of visual cues that are sometimes necessary to understand what the sender really means (Counseling 2003). Some people find it ineffective to communicate solely via e-mail because its asynchronous nature means there is an absence of immediate, real-time responses.

Today's e-mail systems are more vulnerable to attacks than earlier ones because of the many additions made to the basic model. Advanced formatting such as hypertext markup language (HTML) and the sending of attachments via e-mail contribute to the propagation of viruses and spam. It is also easy to impersonate others via e-mail. Recipients may be led to believe that the e-mail is from someone they know, but the sender's name and e-mail address could have been impersonated by a crook.

Standard procedures and default configurations are vulnerabilities in e-mail systems. For example, standard naming procedures that ease e-mail management are predictable and thus exploited by hackers. Malicious users hide their identities by using anonymous addresses of publicly available Web-based e-mail providers such as GMail, Yahoo!, and Hotmail (Kruse and Heiser 2002). Source addresses can be spoofed. Even if the sender's Internet protocol (IP) address is logged, it may not be of much use because the hacker may be using a computer in a public place such as a library or an airport.

Other threats to e-mail include interception and modification of messages and distortion of message headers and content to hide the source and route of traversal (Pfleeger 1997). Sophisticated protection systems exist today to resolve these threats. E-mail filters work in conjunction with firewalls and intrusion-protection systems to create layers of blocking measures for potential malicious software. Sender identity and e-mail privacy are resolved by security measures such as public/private key encryption and digital signatures. "Cryptography," has detailed information about encryption.

Spam, or unsolicited e-mail (often undesirable), is an ever-growing problem and has surpassed legitimate e-mail in volume. Because spam constitutes over 60 percent of all email in 2006 as of the date of this writing (Barracuda Networks 2006), spam filtering for e-mail is a must, especially in the enterprise, if employee productivity and network bandwidth are to be protected against the adverse effects of spam. Commercial implementations of spam filters include SpamAssasin, Spamihilator, SpamBouncer, SPAMfighter, Spam Bully, and Barracuda Spam Firewall. Spam filters use many techniques for preventing false positives, that is, legitimate e-mails flagged as spam. Bayesian learning techniques, bouncing spam back to the sender, Turing test filters, IP address black listing, and e-mail stamps have been used successfully against spam.

The Bayesian spam filter has an initial time period to "learn" user preferences about spam e-mails and legitimate e-mails (Graham 2002). Spam filters also exist that can send a fake bounce message to the spammer after simulating an e-mail delivery failure. The Turing test filter requests a human response for a potential spam e-mail before placing it in the inbox (Knight 2003). With e-mail stamps, a charge can be imposed before allowing the spam messages to go through to the sender. Other spam blocking techniques are surveyed in a Barracuda Networks white paper (Barracuda Networks 2006).

Malicious people such as virus writers usually exploit the features of e-mails to spread their destructive payload. An e-mail virus usually spreads from computer to computer by automatically mailing itself to all the e-mail addresses in the victim's address book. The Melissa virus of 1999 spread through Microsoft Word documents attached via e-mails (Brain 2004). Social engineering attacks are also common via e-mail. The "I Love You" virus that spread in 2000 was an example.

The virus writers exploited the trust that prompted readers to open the e-mail message because the subject line contained the phrase "I Love You." Thus, e-mail readers inadvertently spread the malicious virus. Until this virus was released, most e-mail was trusted, especially ones that came from a trusted source such as a coworker or spouse (Miller 2000). Some people also thought that it may have been a joke because e-mail was popularly used for distributing jokes. The Love bug virus, as it came to be known, caused damage that was expensive to repair, both in terms of money and lost time/productivity and in terms of eroding trust in e-mailed messages.

Another example is the recent spate of "phishing" attacks that exploit e-mail's ubiquity in order to harvest confidential data of unsuspecting users who click on an apparently genuine URL in an e-mail purportedly from a legitimate authority (FTC 2003). Phishing and pharming attacks are on the rise today, and continue to be one of the areas of concern in e-mail security.

A key concern is the confidentiality of e-mail communication. Because an e-mail can pass through many servers from source to destination, it can be stored and/or retrieved at any point along its route. Network administrators and high-level managers have the right to read all e-mail passing through their networks. Employees may not be aware that e-mail communication is neither private nor confidential. Law enforcement officials can confiscate e-mail on servers and backups for investigative purposes. Later in this chapter, e-mail use policies are described that elaborate on the procedures necessary to alert employees about e-mail communication.

Safeguards for E-mail: Filters and Usage Policies

Several vulnerabilities posed by e-mail communication make the presence of monitoring systems inevitable today, especially in large corporate environments. The process of monitoring e-mail and taking certain actions based on predefined criteria is referred to as e-mail filtering. E-mail that is monitored can be incoming or outgoing; messages need to match predefined criteria, which can be changed at any time. E-mail filters can help sort, forward, and delete incoming and outgoing e-mail. On an organization-wide level, e-mail filters might be installed:

- to disinfect viruses from attachments
- to block unsolicited e-mail (spam)
- to block confidential information from going outside the company,
- to block incoming and outgoing offensive content
- to prevent unauthorized usage of corporate e-mail systems (Bhagyavati and Yang 2004).

E-mail filtering software is currently available from Lyris, ePrism, MailMate, SurfControl, and SpamAssasin. Although e-mail filters are necessary to monitor spam and offensive e-mail, their implementation can have unintended consequences, such as blocking legitimate e-mail or blacklisting naïve users accused of sending unsolicited e-mail. Cross-compatibility issues among e-mail filters and antivirus software may cause unintentional propagation of viruses.

Monitoring and matching measures add extra time to the delivery of e-mail. These security measures also inhibit the free flow of communication that is vital for research and creativity in organizations. The unintended effect of these filters could cause a shift away from e-mail by annoyed employees.

Because e-mail is frequently used to communicate with colleagues, peers, and superiors, a lack of usage guidelines can lead to confusion over appropriate content and message form. Lack of an e-mail use policy can have serious consequences in cases of inappropriate communication. If corporations do not have policies on e-mail use, employees can misuse corporate-owned e-mail systems without fear of consequences. In creating a written e-mail policy, all "do's and don'ts" need to be included.

Employees must also be trained to understand fully why policies are important. Implementation of the rules can be monitored by management tools (EmailReplies.com 2001). Professionalism, efficiency, and liability protection are the primary reasons for an organization to implement etiquette rules and train its employees on them. Sending e-mails in uppercase letters, attaching unnecessary files, making grammatical and spelling errors, and requesting read receipts frequently are all etiquette policy violations.

Consequences for policy violations vary widely by state and by the type of organization. For example, the consequences for violations in a not-for-profit organization run by volunteers may be different from the consequences faced by employees in traditional businesses. Also, the penalties may range from reprimand to termination, depending on the severity of the offense, the scope and definition of the policy, and the enforcement mandated within the company. Sample policy guidelines are as follows (SANS 2006):

1. Office e-mail may not be used for commercial purposes or for personal gain. Distribution of spam or flame e-mails is not tolerated from office computers.
2. Confidential and sensitive information should not be sent via e-mail, unless it is encrypted. Because e-mail communication is free and open, anyone can obtain such sensitive information. Encryption makes the message impossible to read if the deciphering key is not available.
3. E-mail communications on office systems will be monitored for appropriateness of use.
4. Due diligence needs to be practiced while communicating via e-mail; although an e-mail has been deleted by the recipient, it can be retrieved and used against the sender or the workplace.
5. Inappropriate and offensive material, which is not suitable for distribution otherwise, should not be transmitted through e-mail. For example, off-color remarks, racist comments, pornographic material, and other unsuitable material should not be sent through office e-mail.
6. E-mail communication needs to be concise and work-related. Incidental personal use is permitted only if it does not interfere with office operations.
7. E-mail recipients should be limited only to those with a need to know the contents of the communication. Forwarding and copying to everyone in the workplace should be avoided.
8. If copyrighted information or trademarks are sent via e-mail, the recipient must have a need to know the information and should be able to securely receive the e-mail.
9. Use of office e-mail implies that the sender acts as an agent on behalf of the employer. Appropriateness of tone, style, content, and form of e-mail will ensure that high standards of work and professionalism are maintained.

INSTANT MESSAGING

Instant messaging systems extended the chat service available on time-shared computers to the Internet. IM client programs on users' computers connect to specialized servers that monitor all IM users and maintain buddy lists for each user. America Online (AOL) popularized the IM service with its AIM (AOL Instant Messenger), which is freely available for download from its Web site. IM can be thought of as an online, real-time version of e-mail (Day, Rosenberg, and Sugano 2000). In today's fast-paced corporate environment, employees do not wish to wait for recipients to check e-mails and then respond; instead, real-time and interactive responses are expected. The use of instant messaging grew exponentially in the late 1990s (Ralston, Reilly, and Hemmendinger 2003).

Definition of IM

Instant messaging is a type of real-time communication via the Internet that enables a user to create a private chat room with another user (Webopedia 2006). Whereas e-mail can be compared to postal mail, IM can be compared to a telephone conversation. However, a telephone conversation is voice-based, whereas an IM conversation is largely text-based. The IM system allows a user to create and maintain a buddy list of other users; the system alerts the user when any of the buddies is online. The user is then free to initiate an IM session with the buddy. For IM to work, both users must download and install an IM client, and both users must be logged on to the Internet at the same time.

Brief History of IM

Internet relay chat (IRC) was a messaging program invented in 1988 that was IM-like in its functionality. More about IRC can be found in "Internet Relay Chat (IRC)." In November 1996, four Israeli programmers introduced ICQ ("I seek you"), which was a free instant-messaging utility that anyone could use by downloading a client capable of real-time communication (Tyson 2004). Because of the sense of community it created, online services were popular even before the growth in popularity of the Internet.

America Online, long considered the pioneer of the online community, had provided chat rooms for its users before it introduced AIM, its version of IM services. Although AIM uses proprietary protocols to enable users to IM each other, non-AOL users can talk to AOL users; this explains the dominance of AIM in the IM marketplace. The development of standards and protocol specifications by the Internet Engineering Task Force popularized the use of IM and pushed the technology to the mainstream (Day, Rosenberg, and Sugano 2000).

The future of instant messaging appears promising because of heightened interest among the business and common user community. The fact that 85 percent of all businesses today acknowledge the use of IM within their organizations is testimony to the growing popularity of instant messaging solutions. Since IM software is going to be downloaded and used by employees, companies want to control the deployment process and manage security as well.

Advantages and Features of IM

IM appears attractive to people on projects that require more real-time interaction than e-mail can provide. Employees on team projects need not check their e-mails frequently; instant messaging provides interactive and real-time contact among them (Deutschle 2003). Synergies of work and a boost in productivity are usually reported when an organization deploys IM. Communicating in real-time streamlines interactions and saves time and money. In addition, free IM client software implies reduced licensing and contractual fees for communication. Employee frustration can also be minimized because IM facilitates immediate access to colleagues.

Long-distance telephone bills can be reduced by using IM. Spam can be reduced because the sender and recipient communicate in real time. IM provides an opportunity for employees to hold conferences and chats (IM-Age 2006). It also speeds up internal and external communications and provides network-independent access to communication. However, several corporations are hesitant to deploy IM because of inadequate security. Corporate policy sometimes may not deter employees from using public-domain IM clients without IT approval. This activity may result in inadvertent disclosure of confidential corporate information.

Current IM Systems

Although AIM and ICQ are the leaders in the IM race, other popular IM systems include Microsoft's MSN Messenger, the open-source multiprotocol GAIM, Google Talk, and Yahoo! Messenger (YM). Utilities such as Odigo and Omni allow the user to combine multiple IM services in one application (Tyson 2004). MSN Messenger and YM allow users to talk via IM just like via the telephone, provided both parties have the necessary equipment, such as microphone and speakers, to access the voice feature.

Today's IM programs also incorporate file-sharing and file-transfer capabilities. Mobile devices such as handhelds, tablet personal computers (PCs), and Internet-enabled cellular telephones are capable of communicating via instant messaging systems. There are two main categories of second-generation secure IM products: (a) IM clients with security features built in and (b) IM management software that can monitor any of the products currently popular among users. Zone Labs' product "Integrity IM Security," FaceTime Communications' "IMAuditor," and IM-Age's "Policy Manager" management solution belong to the latter category.

These products do more than secure IM; they handle policy management and provide centralized security (Zone Labs 2006; FaceTime Communications, 2006; IM-Age 2006). For example, Zone Labs' IM Policy Manager authenticates internal IM users, blocks file transfers, and monitors employee communications. Niksun's "NetDetector" can detect anomalies, reconstruct IM sessions, and archive IM for long-term storage (Niksun 2002). Microsoft Communicator is another IM system that allows corporate entities to secure their IM environments. It also allows IM communication with other popular IM systems. The Internet has diagrammatic representations of instant messaging concepts—the diagram that appears on Learnthenet.com is one such example.

Disadvantages and Vulnerabilities of IM

Basic IM is not a secure way to communicate. The content of instant messages and information about user (network) connections are maintained on servers controlled by the IM provider. Although most of the large IM providers offer encryption, user logs have been captured by malicious hackers in the past (Deutschle 2003). The perception among employers is that IM is uncontrollable; therefore, the whole network becomes compromised. Buffer overflow vulnerabilities in IM clients can lead to attacks that result in denial of service and/or execution of arbitrary code. Open ports can be found by hackers via file transfer on IM. Malware can be spread using file sharing and transfer.

Proprietary client software, word limits on messages and sessions, potential for employee misuse, and security concerns have managed to restrain the popularity of IM in the business environment. Because IM does not leave an audit trail, the corporation cannot monitor the conversation. Proprietary consumer products such as MSN Messenger and ICQ are unsuited for enterprises because they allow unencrypted data and bypass the virus protection at the corporate network's gateway servers. The file-transfer capability of IM is especially insecure in this regard. Service providers such as AOL and Sprint have developed separate enterprise versions of their proprietary IM solutions that address corporate security concerns.

Safeguards for IM, and Usage Policies

Buffer overflow vulnerabilities found in popular instant messaging applications such as Yahoo! Messenger and AIM serve as a reminder that hackers can take control over other machines for coordinated attacks at a later time (Weber 2004). Because consumer-level IM programs do not use encryption, these programs cannot be used in corporate environments without modification. IM also allows hackers to become aware of user presence—that is, whether the user is online or offline. Social engineering, which can lead to identity theft, is also common because of poor authentication practices. Security concerns are, therefore, paramount in presence-aware IM environments.

According to security experts, insecure IM is the new target for hackers who seek to steal sensitive corporate information. Firewalls and intrusion-detection systems are not useful unless they are integrated with IM-security software (Gaudin 2002). Employees sending noncorporate information on IM can waste network bandwidth. IM can also cause easy distraction and loss in productivity. Offensive jokes propagated through IM can led to harassment suits. Because of legal and ethical ramifications of IM use, an enterprise needs to structure IM use policies and train employees before deploying the IM solution. Sample policies include the following:

1. Confidential and sensitive information should not be sent via IM unless it is encrypted. Because IM communication is insecure, anyone can obtain such sensitive information.
2. IM communications on office systems will be monitored for appropriateness of use.
3. Inappropriate and offensive material, which is not suitable for distribution otherwise, should not be transmitted through IM. For example, off-color remarks, racist comments, pornographic material, and other unsuitable material should not be sent through office IM.
4. IM communication needs to be concise and work-related. Incidental personal use is permitted only if it does not interfere with office operations.
5. Use of office IM implies that the sender acts as an agent on behalf of the employer. Appropriateness of tone, style, content, and form of IM will ensure that high standards of work and professionalism are maintained.

SECURITY IN E-MAIL AND IM ENVIRONMENTS

Security is a significant area of concern in an e-mail environment because e-mail is the most crucial form of communication medium available on the Internet (Preetham 2002). To ensure the integrity of e-mail communication, various measures have been implemented. Not caring about e-mail security could result in the sender's identity being compromised, the recipient's identity being compromised, or leakage of sensitive information. If the transfer agent and client of an e-mail system can be secured on the network, the service provider can secure the delivery agent. Encryption software can ensure security on the communication channel. Security measures can also guard against address spoofing and anonymous e-mail.

Features of secure environments include confidentiality of message content, authentication of sender and recipient, and assurance of message integrity (Kurose and Ross 2003). Public key cryptography (more detail in "Cryptography"), symmetric key cryptography, digital signatures, message digests, message integrity checks, trusted key distribution, and certificate validating authority are essential to secure all e-mail communication within the environment. Because IM clients are used on mobile handheld devices such as PDAs and cellular telephones in addition to desktop and laptop computers, the security risks are higher because of the inherent vulnerabilities of wireless transmission. The lack of secure environments exacts a productivity and monetary toll.

E-Mail Security: Issues and Practices

User awareness and training are probably the most important tools to secure e-mail. Deleting unsolicited messages, not opening suspicious attachments, encrypting sensitive information sent via e-mail, and using spam filters are effective practices for ensuring the security of e-mail communications (Weber 2004). Corporate policies will not amount to much if users are not trained on implementing the policies and made aware of the consequences of violations. Security-savvy users can thwart social engineering attacks that try to obtain log-in and password information from them.

Other security measures to follow in an e-mail environment include using proxy servers to forward e-mail to the clients and using an updated antivirus program to check all incoming and outgoing e-mail. Modern antivirus programs are capable of heuristic analysis of viruses by safely monitoring their behavior under controlled conditions (Sandhu 2002). Installation of antivirus software must be augmented by prompt updating of virus definitions and patterns; otherwise, the antivirus software will not be effective against newly generated viruses and other malware, such as Trojan horses and worms, which may infect application software.

IM Security: Issues and Practices

Patch management and avoidance of spying software are the first steps in securing IM systems. Antivirus software and intrusion-detection and intrusion-protection programs will limit the security vulnerabilities of IM systems. However, corporate entities can ensure IM security by not allowing their employees to use public-domain IM systems such as AIM and YM. Proprietary solutions combined with end-to-end security provide a better defense than freeware.

Solutions from FaceTime Communications, IMlogic, Akonix Systems, and MessageLabs provide software and hardware to manage IM systems in enterprises (Hoover 2006). These providers claim that viruses sent through IM will be detected, unintentional transmission of sensitive information will be controlled, and the IM security solution will be integrated with preexisting antispam, content scanning, and encryption programs (FaceTime Communications 2006). For example, if unauthorized IM or P2P (peer-to-peer) connections are detected, they are blocked and logged.

Realizing that the corporate environment was not ready to accept insecure IM systems, service providers such as AOL and Sprint developed enterprise versions of their IM clients, specifically tightening or adding security features. AOL's Enterprise AIM service allows system administrators to manage IM use from behind the corporate firewall (Deutschle 2003). Although the security features come at a steeper price than the virtually free consumer versions, companies are expected to invest in IM's long-term advantages. Other security-hardened IM products include IBM's Lotus Sametime and Bantu's Presence Platform. An encrypted version of Sametime is used by the U.S. military and some academic institutions.

Security providers such as Zone Labs have developed management platforms for securing IM in the enterprise and ensuring privacy for IM communications (Zone Labs 2006). This program is independent of the IM client and can execute equally well on AIM, MSN Messenger, and YM. According to Zone Labs, this product is compatible with its firewall product, so both can be integrated to form an end-to-end solution. Featuring IM encryption, spam blocking, password protection, and security logging, this product is geared toward the security-conscious corporate marketplace. Other vendors such as IM-Age and Niksun have also developed secure IM products or IM management software.

CONCLUSION

E-mail has become one of the primary means of communication for people today (Tyson 2004). E-mail clients that allow users to send, receive, and manage their messages evolved from different formats and storage systems. E-mail clients differ in how they track e-mail and where they store archived data (Nelson et al. 2004). Hence, no single security solution can be provided for their varying vulnerabilities and differing reactions to threats.

Because of its ubiquitous nature, several viruses now use e-mail as a distribution and reproduction mechanism because of its potential for rapid, worldwide spread. Security concerns must be weighed critically before sending confidential data through the system. Behavior-based monitoring of virus activity, integrity checks, detection of changes in content and sources and destinations of e-mail, signature-based searches, and heuristic, real-time scanning can mitigate security risks (Slade 2004).

The Gartner Group, in October 2001, opined that IM, like e-mail, could cause a company to operate as a real-time enterprise if it is properly managed and integrated into the underlying infrastructure. Today, IM is being used by 85 percent of all businesses (Hoover 2006). Although IM is perceived to be ephemeral, every message can be stored by the service provider or the organization. These archives can be monitored and even used in evidence. Hence, it is prudent to exercise care in sending e-mail and IM messages.

GLOSSARY

Antivirus Software: Software programs that detect and eliminate viruses, worms, Trojan horses, and other malware.

Authentication: The process of ensuring that the individual is who she says she is.

Confidentiality: The act of keeping sensitive information secretive.

Demilitarized Zone (DMZ): A computer or a subnetwork that is installed between a trusted internal network and an untrusted external network.

Digital Certificate: An attachment to an e-mail used for security purposes such as verifying the sender's identity to the receiver.

E-Mail: An asynchronous communication tool analogous to postal mail; it is used to transmit messages via the Internet.

Encryption: The process of translating data into a secret code; it is the most effective way to achieve data confidentiality.

Filter: Software or hardware that monitors and blocks incoming and outgoing e-mail traffic.

Firewall: Hardware and/or software designed to prevent unauthorized access to or from a private network.

Instant Messaging: An interactive, synchronous tool for engaging in real-time communication via the Internet.

Intrusion-Detection System: A system that inspects all inbound and outbound network activity to identify suspicious patterns that may indicate an attack.

Malware and Spyware: Malicious software designed to damage a system. Spyware is software that gathers user information through the Internet connection without his or her knowledge, usually for advertising purposes.

Message Integrity: This refers to the validity of e-mail transmissions.

Nonrepudiation: When the recipient of a communication has the ability to ensure that the sender is unable to deny the sending of the message or the authenticity of its signature on the communication.

Patch Management: Process of updating and managing patches and temporary fixes on a frequent and regular basis so as to remain current on the latest updates of the software.

Proxy Server: A server that sits between a client application and another server; it intercepts all requests to the actual server. Proxy servers improve efficiency and filter harmful traffic.

Spam: Electronic junk mail or unsolicited, targeted advertisement via e-mail.

Use Policies: Policies regarding employee use of organization-owned computers for e-mail and IM.

Virtual Private Networks: A private network developed by using public wires to connect nodes. A virtual private network uses encryption and other security mechanisms, thus ensuring that corporate data are safe traveling on the public Internet.

Viruses, Worms, and Trojan Horses: Malicious software that infect a host computer, then replicate and spread to other computers via the network to cause more damage.

Vulnerabilities and Threat Assessment: A process of proactively identifying vulnerabilities (weaknesses) in computers of a network to determine if and where a system can be exploited and/or threatened (attacked).

CROSS REFERENCES

See *Computer Network Management*; *E-mail and Internet Use Policies*.

REFERENCES

Barracuda Networks. 2006. *An overview of spam blocking techniques*. www.barracudanetworks.com/ns/downloads/barracuda_spam_blocking_techniques.pdf (accessed September 5, 2006).

Bhagyavati, R., N., and M. Yang. January 5, 2004. *Email filters can adversely affect free and open flow of communication*. Paper presented at the Winter International Symposium on Information and Communication Technologies, WISICT 2004, Cancun, Mexico.

Brain, M. 2004. *How computer viruses work*. http://computer.howstuffworks.com/virus.htm/printable (accessed September 5, 2006).

Crocker, D. 2003 *Email history: Living Internet*. http://livinginternet.com/e/ei.htm (accessed September 5, 2006).

Counseling. 2003 *Disadvantages of counselling by email.* http://counsellingresource.com/counselling-service/online-disadvantages.html (accessed September 5, 2006).

Day, M., J. Rosenberg, and H. Sugano. 2000, February. *A model for presence and instant messaging* (RFC 2778). Internet Engineering Task Force. www.ietf.org/rfc/rfc2778.txt?number=2778 (accessed September 5, 2006).

Deutschle, S. 2003, August 8. *Security issues keep instant messaging out of workplace*. In Depth: Tech & Telecom. www.bizjournals.com/columbus/stories/2003/08/11/focus3.html (accessed September 5, 2006).

ELook.org. 2006. *MIME Protocol Overview*. www.emailreplies.com (accessed September 5, 2006).

EmailReplies.com. 2001. *Email etiquette*. www.emailreplies.com (accessed September 5, 2006).

FaceTime Communications 2006. *Instant messaging security*. www.facetime.com/Solutions/security.aspx (accessed September 5, 2006).

FTC. 2003, July. *FTC consumer alert: How not to get hooked by a "phishing" scam*. www.ftc.gov/bcp/conline/pubs/alerts/phishingalrt.htm (accessed September 5, 2006).

Gaudin, S. 2002, September 6. *IM security risks spark workplace monitoring debate*. http://itmanagement.earthweb.com/secu/article.php/1458241 (accessed September 5, 2006).

Graham, P. 2002, August. *A plan for spam*. www.paulgraham.com/spam.html (accessed September 5, 2006).

Griffiths, R. T. 2002, October 11. *Chapter three: History of electronic mail*. www.let.leidenuniv.nl/history/ivh/chap3.htm (accessed September 5, 2006).

Hoover, N. 2006, January 9. Your IM buddy, or a hacker? It's getting harder to tell. *Information Week*, p. 30. www.informationweek.com/story/showArticle.jhtml?articleID=175802139 (accessed September 5, 2006).

IM-Age. 2006. *IM-Policy Manager v4.0*. www.im-age.com/_product/policy.html (accessed September 5, 2006).

Knight, W. 2003, January 3. *Turing tests filter spam email*. www.newscientist.com/news/news.jsp?id=ns99993227 (accessed September 5, 2006).

Kruse, W. G., II, and J. G. Heiser. 2002. Computer forensics: Incident response essentials. New York: Addison-Wesley.

Kurose, J. F., & Ross, K. W. 2003. Computer networking: A top-down approach featuring the Internet. Boston: Pearson Education.

Living Internet. 2003. *Electronic mail (Email)*. http://livinginternet.com/ttoc_e.htm (accessed September 5, 2006).

Lombardi, J. V. 2003. *Managing universities: The Internet and glossary*. http://courses.umass.edu/lombardi/edu03/gloss.html#Email (accessed September 5, 2006).

Miller, T. 2000, June 19. *Social Engineering*. SecurityFocus.com. www.securityfocus.com/infocus/1229 (accessed September 5, 2006).

Myer, T. H., and D. W. Dodds, D. W. 1976. *Notes on the development of message technology*. Paper presented at the Berkeley Workshop on Distributed Data Management and Computer Networks (LBL-5315). Berkeley, CA: Lawrence Berkeley Laboratories,

Nelson, B., A. Phillips, F. Enfinger, and C. Steuat. 2004. *Guide to computer forensics and investigations*. Hoboken, NJ: Course Technology, Thomson Learning.

Nevis. 2004. *Nevis POP versus IMAP guide*. www.nevis.columbia.edu/mail/pop-vs-imap.html (accessed September 5, 2006).

Niksun. 2002. *Is Instant messaging a threat to your network?*. (White paper). www.niksun.com/Instant_Messaging.htm (accessed September 5, 2006).

Pfleeger, C. P. 1997. *Security in computing*. Upper Saddle River, NJ: Prentice Hall PTR.

Preetham, V. V. 2002. *Internet security and firewalls*. Cincinnati: Premier Press.

Ralston, A., E. D. Reilly, and D. Hemmendinger. 2003. *Encyclopedia of computer science*. 4th ed., 1284. New York: Wiley.

Sandhu, R. J. 2002. *Disaster recovery planning*. Cincinnati: Premier Press.

SANS. 2006. *Email use policy*. SANS Institute. www.sans.org/resources/policies/Email_Policy.pdf (accessed September 5, 2006).

Slade, R. 2004. *Software forensics: Collecting evidence from the scene of a digital crime*. Columbus, OH: McGraw-Hill.

Tittel, E. 2002. *Schaum's outlines: Computer networking*. Columbus, OH: McGraw-Hill.

Tyson, J. 2004. *How instant messaging works*. http://computer.howstuffworks.com/instant-messaging.htm (accessed September 5, 2006).

Weber, M. J. 2004. *Invasion of privacy: Big brother and the company hackers*. Cincinnati: Premier Press,.

Webopedia. 2006. *What is instant messaging*? www.webopedia.com/TERM/I/instant_messaging.html (accessed September 5, 2006).

Wikipedia. 2006. *The free encyclopedia*. http://en.wikipedia.org/wiki/Instant_messaging (accessed September 5, 2006).

Zone Labs. 2006. *Integrity IM security: Comprehensive IM protection*. www.checkpoint.com/products/integrity_im/index.html (accessed September 5, 2006).

FURTHER READING

Babu, M. 2000. *Instant messaging: The future of communication?* www.expressitpeople.com/20021007/abroad1.shtml (accessed September 5, 2006).

Burkhardt, J., H. Henn, S. Hepper, K. Rintdorff, and T. Schack, T. 2002. *Pervasive computing: Technology and architecture of mobile Internet applications*. Boston: Pearson Education.

Goldsborough, R. 2004, August 1. *Instant messaging: Managing the risks and rewards*. www.infotoday.com/linkup/lud080104-goldsborough.shtml (accessed September 5, 2006).

Hardy, I. R. 1996. *The evolution of ARPANET email*. www.ifla.org/documents/internet/hari1.txt (accessed September 5, 2006).

Holden, G. 2003. *Guide to network defense and countermeasures*. Hoboken, NJ: Course Technology, Thomson Learning.

IEEE Computer: News Briefs 2006, February. New worm chats up its victims. *IEEE Computer Magazine*

February:22. www.computer.org/portal/cms_docs_computer/computer/homepage/0206/r2021.pdf (accessed September 5, 2006).

Learn the Net. 2006, January 6. *Conferencing: Instant messaging*. www.learnthenet.com/english/html/32im.htm (accessed September 5, 2006).

Licklider, J. C. R., and A. Vezza. 1978, November. Applications of information networks. *Proceedings of the IEEE* 66(11):1330–46.

Russell, D., and G. T. Gangemi Sr. 1991. *Computer security basics*. Sebastopol, CA: O'Reilly.

Sullivan, B. 2003, August 6. *Has the spam dam really burst?* MSNBC News: Spam Wars—How Unwanted E-mail is Burying the Internet. http://msnbc.msn.com/id/3078649 (accessed September 5, 2006).

Application Service Providers (ASPs)

Bandula Jayatilaka, *Binghamton University, SUNY*

INTRODUCTION

Application service providers (ASPs) have become acceptable external sources of software services for many organizations. In the basic ASP model, a vendor hosts an application required by a client and delivers the application services over a network. In one variation of the basic ASP model, application services are not customized. In another variation of this model, as in managed service provisioning (MSP), more customized services are provided. In fact, a variant of the ASP model in which software services were obtained from a vendor was in existence during the early days of computing, and this was called time-sharing (Braunstein 1999). However, with advances in networking and data communications technologies, ASP has become more widely used as a viable alternative to in-house IT departments and other forms of outsourcing (Dibbern et al. 2004) for obtaining IT applications (Currie 2004). According to a recent Gartner research study "almost one third of US companies currently use application service providers and another 22 percent plan to do so in the next two years" (Betts 2005). This trend in the use of ASPs follows a previous period of decline from 2001 to 2004 that occurred with the bursting of the "dot com bubble."

Traditionally, a company purchasing application software from a vendor installed the software in the company's own systems, either on a network or in a single system, and maintained the software and user data. This traditional approach can become too costly for some companies, or a company may not possess enough technical skills and suitable technologies to implement and manage the purchased software. In such cases, companies may instead decide to contract with an ASP. In contrast to the traditional approach, a company seeking services from an ASP will obtain the services of the application from the vendor's servers, which hosts the applications. In this ASP arrangement, the customer company pays the vendor a periodic fee for the use of the software. Such an arrangement can benefit companies when they do not want to spend money to purchase software outright or to set up the infrastructure for hosting the software. Although cost is a main advantage for a company seeking ASP services, risks such as data security and lack of control over the application still exist when using an ASP. The objective of this chapter is to discuss the ASP model, the types and characteristics of ASP arrangements, and the benefits and risks of ASPs.

In general, many digital or electronic business services offered by vendors are described using terms ending with "SP." In their attempts to use a generic term, some people have coined the term 'xSP' to refer to the different service providers (Means 2004; Dickerson 2002). Because of the wide spectrum of services falling under this category of xSPs, it is necessary to define the scope of the topic of this chapter. Obtaining IT services related to networking from external sources can be referred to as "netsourcing" (Kern, Lacity, and Willcocks 2002, Netsourcing). The netsourcing spectrum includes application service providers (ASPs), business service providers (BSPs), commerce service providers (CSPs), ExSourcers, full-service providers (FSPs), managed service providers (MSPs), and storage service providers (SSPs). Although some explanations in this chapter are applicable to more than one type of service providers, our intent here is to cover only the ASP area.

Network configurations and capabilities are critical for the successful use of any ASP, and specific network configuration requirements and capacities will vary, depending on the client's demands. The network-configuration-related technical capabilities are only one type of factor essential for success. A client's demand for ASP depends on many nontechnical determinants. The nontechnical determinants for using an ASP in an organization can be classified as economic, strategic, and knowledge-related. Before explaining the organizational criteria for choosing an ASP and the associated applications, we need to discuss the ASP model, the network hardware and software making the ASPs possible, and ASP configurations. Finally, the feasibility assessment criteria for choosing an ASP are also discussed.

ASP BUSINESS MODELS

This section examines the important factors in ASP business models—technical infrastructure, vendor-customer relationship management, support staff, and contract. As mentioned in the introduction, current studies indicate increased use of ASPs in the future (Betts 2005). The expected increase in demand is due to the potential benefits of the ASP model. The ASP sourcing option is capable of delivering best-of-breed business applications in a scalable and flexible manner. Typically, an organization can obtain these services in exchange for a periodic fee (e.g., either a monthly or an annual fee) based on the number of transactions generated and/or the number of users at a customer's site. In addition, some vendors provide free online application services such as Yahoo's calendar, e-mail, and file-management applications in My Yahoo.

The types of ASPs have grown since the early days, when vendors primarily rented software to their clients (Tebboune 2003). One of the early definitions of *application service provider* was "a form of selective sourcing where a third-party organization rents generally available packaged software and related services" (Bennett and Timbrell 2000). Today, the application services have evolved to encompass different types of services. ASPs are no longer limited solely to renting software packages. The vendors can host and manage applications developed by customers, or the vendors can be other software developers who provide their services to customers.

Many popular software products of independent software vendors (ISVs) can be rented from the ASPs. Rented software products range from organizationwide enterprise resource planning (ERP) applications such as packages from JD Edwards, Oracle, Peoplesoft, and SAP to individual-level applications such as personal productivity software from Google, Microsoft, and Netscape. At a functional level, ASPs provide e-commerce and e-business software for specific business functions such as supplier relationship management (from CommerceOne), customer relationship management, and sales force automation (from salesforce.com and SSA Global). Because of the availability of many different ASP options, taxonomies of ASPs can help clarify the world of ASPs. Before examining the taxonomies of ASPs, an examination of generic models will be helpful in understanding the specific available service options. Several elements are common to all of the different ASP arrangements. The fundamental elements are the clients or customers who need application software services and the service providers or vendors who possess the resources to provide these services.

Vendor-Client Relationship

Some of the essential elements of an ASP arrangement are: (1) delivery of the services, (2) integration of the ASP service with the rest of the client organization as needed, and (3) management and operations necessary for providing/obtaining services and enabling the services appropriately. Delivery of the services requires infrastructure providing connectivity between the clients and the vendor. Integration with the rest of the organizational activities requires software compatibility, suitable technical infrastructure, as well as business processes that can be integrated with ASP services. Delivery, integration, management and operations, and enablement require technology and human resources.

The ownership of resources is an important aspect of the vendor-client relationship that must be examined when obtaining software services from vendors. Typically, the software package and the data reside at the vendor location, and the client personnel access the software from their own location. This spatial separation of vendor and client necessitates some infrastructure to be at the vendor and some infrastructure to be at the client. Based on these infrastructure requirements, most of the resources in these ASP arrangements are owned by the service providers. The vendor must have: (1) the software package, (2) infrastructure to host and deliver the services to the client location, (3) the resources for storage and management of the data related to the application, and (4) the resources necessary to manage the application and networks. At the client end, the ownership will often be limited to the workstations and client network connectivity.

The essential components of an ASP arrangement are depicted in Figure 1. The model shows the relationships between the ASP and the clients in terms of the nontechnical factors. In the figure, a vendor supports many clients through a network. The network connecting the vendor and clients can be the Internet or a proprietary wide area network (WAN); therefore, the network is shown as a cloud shape in Figure 1. The network configurations will be discussed more specifically in the next section. At the vendor site, software, hardware, and networking capabilities enable providing the services to the clients. In addition, adequate managerial and technical support must be available at the vendor site. Clients need connectivity within their organization to distribute the application services as necessary and workstations to interface with the vendor systems. Moreover, proper vendor relationship management efforts at the client side can ensure success of the sourcing arrangement. Finally, both client and vendor behavior occur within the terms, conditions, and service levels stipulated in the contracts defining the ASP services to be delivered. Contract and service levels are discussed later in this section, and the contract is only one means to ensure receiving an efficient and effective service from the vendor.

Hosting applications and providing services to customers must be done efficiently and effectively. Typically, this means that the services should be available on demand. The application runs on the vendor server, and it is possible that the server performance is poor. Because of the server's poor performance, the application may not respond when a user needs to use it. For example, a user at the client end may want to make a customer service decision that requires information generated by the vendor application. If the application does not respond on time the user will not be able to make a timely decision. Such slow response may cause customer dissatisfaction. In addition to the server, other components such as communication media, switches, and protocols can also impact performance and availability. Because of the service-on-demand objectives and the likelihood of experiencing unacceptable performance, mechanisms to ensure quality of service (QoS) meeting the demands on time must be implemented. Providing quality and service levels requires enabling managerial processes and structures.

Managerial processes and structures for management of the applications and the networks are critical mechanisms for the success of ASPs. One managerial activity essential for the success of an ASP is proper IT operations management. The management must ensure that

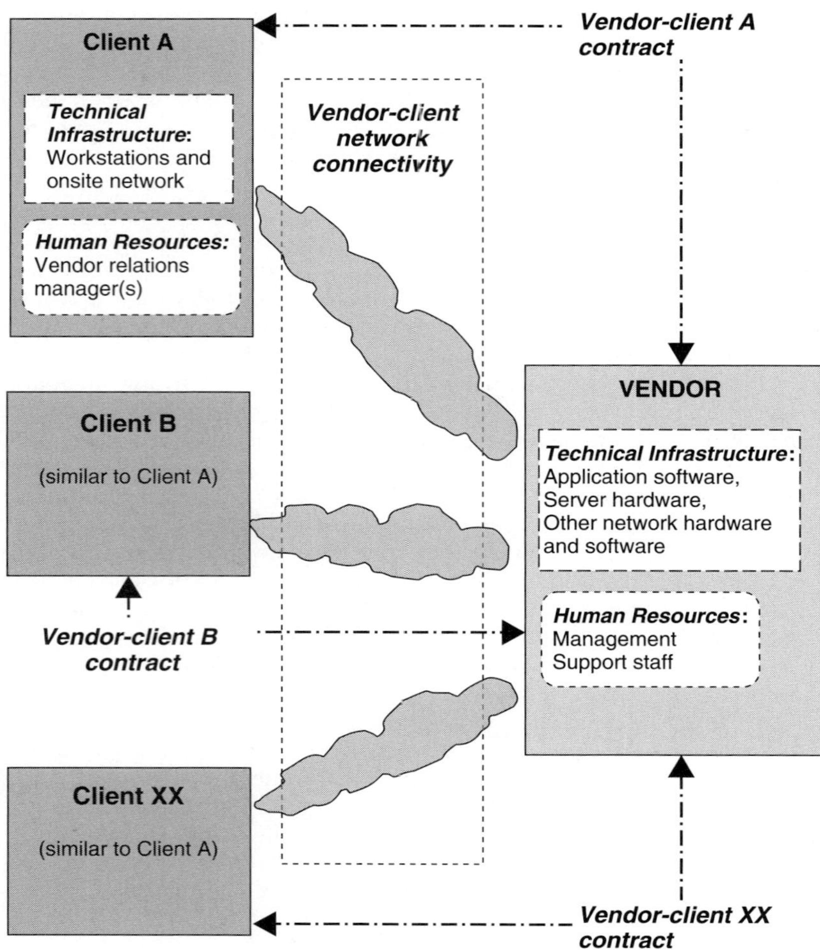

Figure 1: One-to-many ASP model

applications are running on the server when needed, the data residing at the ASP are backed up and kept securely, the servers are running uninterrupted without glitches, recovery from failures is done appropriately, and the networks are performing efficiently. It is the responsibility of the vendor to put these managerial structures in place, including adequate support staff to ensure that the services are delivered at the anticipated levels. Therefore, the ASP support staff must reside mostly at the vendor site rather than at the customer site. On the client side, a client needs a management structure in place to manage its relationship with the vendor. The complexity of this structure may depend on the extent of services obtained from external vendors. As an example, if it is a single vendor and a single application, the existing internal IT managers at the client may be able to effectively oversee the relationship with the vendor. On the other hand, if a company obtains many services from several different ASPs, it may be more effective to set up a formal management structure dedicated to managing all the relationships with the ASPs.

The vendor provides services to the clients within a contractual framework, incorporating the essential aspects of service provisioning, terms, and conditions in the contract. The contract should be specific and adequately detailed to provide the framework for providing the services at the acceptable levels and to establish an appropriate fee structure (Oakes 2005; Weblaw 2003). Obviously, the contract must stipulate the basics, such as fees to be paid by the client, the extent of service to be provided by the service provider, and the acceptable levels of service. The extent of service refers to the number of users given access to the application and the number of workstations that will have connectivity to the application's server. Service levels must specify the performance levels such as the availability of the application, down time, and acceptable time for fixing a problem so that the application will be up and running before the acceptable time elapses.

A service-level agreement (SLA) provides a framework for the delivery of services and for the measurement of service quality. More specifically, an SLA specifies services to be delivered, service availability, performance measures, arrangement for managing problems and performance, and the costs, as well as the penalties if the vendor does not meet stipulated service levels. The penalties may not be directly stated but often will be in the form of reduced payment for partial fulfillment of services. Oakes (2005) suggests that at least the following items must be addressed by an SLA.

- Customer and vendor responsibilities
- Problem definition, prioritization, and problem tracking

- Roles and responsibilities of each entity, such as network management and client network personnel
- Detailed information regarding help-desk services
- Problem escalation procedures—that is, procedures describing how and when problem solving moves to the next level and what the next level is if a problem is not solved by the first level of technicians or personnel
- Performance monitoring and reporting
- Quality-of-service guarantee
- Dispute-resolution procedures
- Security issues—such as data security and network security
- Termination of service provisions

In addition to these stipulations, other clauses must be included in an ASP contract to mitigate the risks. Details of the risks are discussed later in this chapter. For example, the contract should include clauses indicating the actions that must be taken if the vendor or the client needs to withdraw from the contract prematurely. Another important contractual specification relates to penalties if the service levels or the contractual terms are not met by either party (i.e., vendor or customer). As an illustration, consider a vendor who made the application available only 80 percent of the time and the client company has agreed to 95 percent as an acceptable availability. The contract should stipulate the amount of penalty for the reduction of availability by 15 percent experienced by the client.

In general, based on the number of vendors and clients in an ASP vendor-client relationship, there are four possible ASP arrangements: many-to-one, many-to-many, one-to-many, and one-to-one. Although many different vendors in a consortium can provide services to one client or an alliance of clients (forming many-to-one and many-to-many relationships), one-to-one and one-to-many occur more commonly. This section describes the latter two. Often, a single vendor serves many client companies with the same application. This scenario establishes one-to-many client-vendor relationships. The one-to-many relationship when providing the software implies that there will be no or minimal customization of the software.

Taxonomies of ASPs

Figure 1 demonstrates the basic one-to-many ASP model. In reality, this model is too simplistic to characterize the many complexities in the ASP industry. One way to understand the complexities in ASP business models is to classify all the different ASP arrangements that occur in practice (Currie, Desai, and Khan 2004; Kern, Lacity, and Willcocks 2002, Application service provision). According to a taxonomy based on the type of services provided (Currie et al. 2004), four types of ASPs are identifiable: (1) enterprise, (2) vertical, (3) horizontal, and (4) pure-play. In addition to these four types of ASPs providing their services directly to the clients, there are many ASP enablers who provide hardware, telecommunications, or Internet connectivity.

Enterprise ASPs provide enterprise-wide applications software, which usually can be used in different divisions or groups in an organization. An example of applications offered by an enterprise ASP is enterprise resource planning (ERP) software (such as Peoplesoft, JD Edwards), which integrates manufacturing, accounting, and other functional areas. The enterprise ASPs do not restrict their solutions to the Internet only and thus could be offered over other WANs as well. Pure-play ASPs, on the other hand, offer Web-enabled applications only (e.g., salesforce.com offering sales force management and customer relationship management [CRM] software only over the Internet).

A vertical ASP offers services to a specific industrial sector. Two examples of vertical ASPs are: Trizetto (an ASP offering services to the health sector) and Constructware (an ASP offering application services to the construction industry). Other business sectors in which vertical ASPs offer services are engineering, hospitality management, insurance, finance, legal, transportation, retail, and wholesale (ASP directory 2000; Tebboune 2003). Another way to look at the different service providers is to examine the entities required for obtaining application services such as software, network infrastructure, and management (Ekanayake, Currie, and Seltsikas 2003). In contrast to the vertical ASPs that specialize in a specific sector, horizontal ASPs can cater to different industries using a specific application. For example, salesforce.com is a horizontal ASP offering sales force application software services across different vertical markets. From the vendor side, there are disadvantages and advantages to the different types of ASPs because of the limitation in their markets and the ability to specialize. A vertical ASP has a market limited to their specialization, but on the other hand, they will have better expertise in a given industry. A vendor providing services to the construction industry has a client base limited to construction companies, but the vendor will have the expertise to provide the necessary services to the construction industry.

Different players are necessary to implement ASPs successfully, and it is possible to classify these vendors taxonomically. According to this taxonomy, there are: ASP resellers, ASP developers, ASP aggregators, hosting services, and managed service providers (Currie et al. 2004). ASP resellers offer software from other developers for rent over networks. Applications for ERP and CRM are typical packages offered by ASP resellers. Some ASPs have developed their own software and deliver them over the networks. For example, Employease (Employease 2006) rents their human resource information/management software over the Internet. ASP aggregators integrate and market packages developed by ASP developers and ISVs. For example, Jamcracker (Jamcracker 2006) offers solutions for service management, user management, and access management solutions to service providers. A hosting service hosts a client's application. A hosting service is responsible for providing the server to host the application.

In a one-to-many ASP business model customers are offered software that is not customized—all the customers use the same software. However, businesses often have their own idiosyncratic needs that must be met. In such cases, ASP vendors have to customize the applications according to the customers' requirements. Such customization makes the one-to-many ASP model inapplicable. Instead, with customization we can see a model that can be called a one-to-one model, although it may not be a strictly one-to-one model in which each customer is served with a specific application (or an application with specific features). Figure 2 shows the modified ASP model to represent the one-to-one vendor-client relationship. Figure 2 is somewhat similar to Figure 1. The main difference is that the vendor now provides customized versions of applications X and Y to the clients. A variant of an ASP model is emerging, called "managed service providers" (MSPs), and according to this model the vendor provides more-customized services (Collett 2005). In addition to the application services, MSP provides other services such as network management. For this reason, MSP is not explicitly addressed in this chapter.

Note that taxonomies are based on certain criteria used for classifications, and those discussed above are not the only possible classifications. For example, according to Webopedia (Webopedia 2006), ASPnews.com classifies ASPs as: enterprise ASPs, local/regional ASPs, specialist ASPs, vertical ASPs, and volume business ASPs.

NETWORK COMPONENTS AND ASP CONFIGURATIONS

Successful ASPs depend on cost-effective communications and reliable services. We now examine the network components of such a communications system. Before discussing the network requirements of an ASP, let us look at a typical scenario of an ASP user. The ASP user signs on to a workstation or to a local computer that is connected to a network. Once the local computer is running, the user selects the remote application program to run or signs on to the service provider before selecting the remote program. Typically, the actual location of the application is transparent to the user. The server at the vendor end runs the application and sends responses to the user's requests back to the user interface at the local computer. The user at the local computer uses her keyboard and mouse to interact with the program. Depending on the type of application, the user may save data on the local computer or at the vendor's site. Applications that work with large volumes

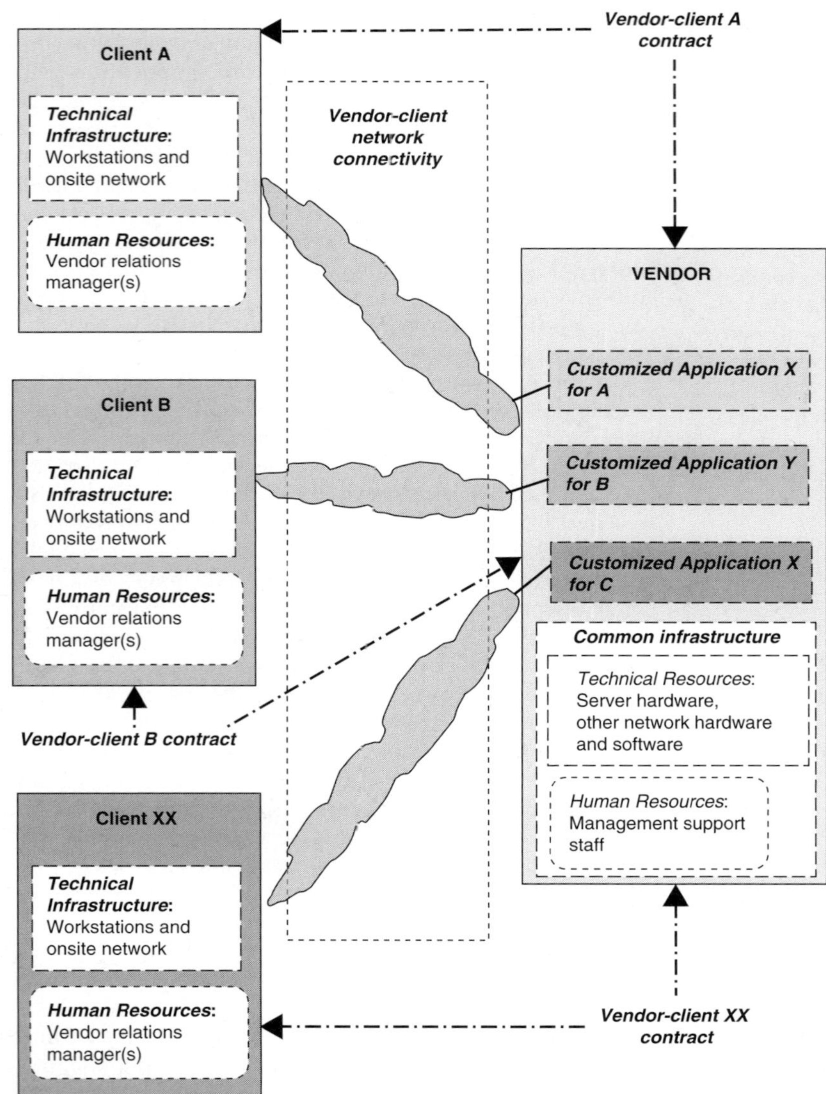

Figure 2: One-to-one ASP model with customized applications

of data are often stored at the vendor's site. However, this arrangement depends on the user needs and the resources of the user. In both cases, some data will be stored at the vendor location.

An ASP configuration implementing the described scenario is a typical client-server configuration, in which certain hardware and software needs to be at both the vendor and customer sites. The customer uses an interface, which can be either a common Internet browser or an application-specific interface depending on the software. At the customer site, the client systems run their own operating systems on suitable hardware. The operating system can be A/UX, Linux, Mac OS X, or Microsoft Windows (XP, 2000, etc.) or other Unix versions that run on a compatible platform (i.e., Apple Macintosh or PC). Similarly, the customer's hardware platform can be any type, conditional on compatibility between the operating system and the hardware. The users' client systems at the customer end must be compatible with the ASP's systems so they can be connected to the vendor's server through a communications network. Often, the customer systems are on a local area network (LAN). Some companies may also have a wide area network (WAN) that connects their systems and networks. Figure 3 shows the client systems at the customer end with a user's hardware platform connected to a customer's network infrastructure, in which the network infrastructure can be a LAN or a WAN. Figure 3 is given here to complete the description; more on LANs and WANs can be found in separate chapters in this handbook. The components at the client site are shown as a stack, in which client workstation hardware and software are connected to the network infrastructure. At the client site, a user interface to the application appears and the operating system, which ultimately runs on the hardware platform, supports the interface.

The vendor's application runs on a server providing accessibility, efficiency, and security. Although the server's operating system need not be the same type as that of the users, the vendor's server must be running an operating system capable of providing reliable, efficient, effective, secure, and on-demand access to the application. As mentioned earlier, the server needs to run an application that properly enables access from many different types of systems at the workstations or client systems that the users are using. Such accessibility from different client

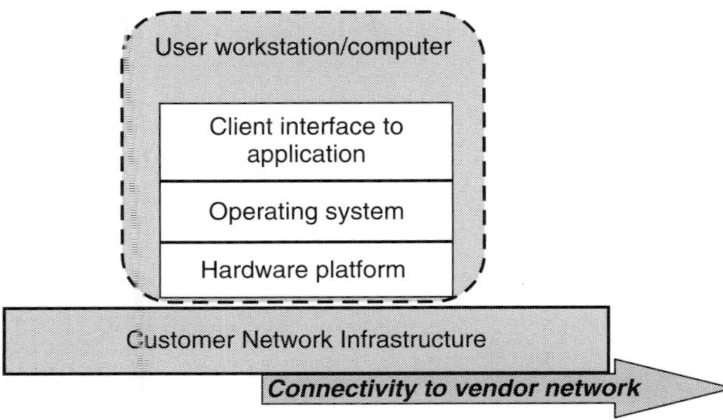

Figure 3: Customer/user end—client

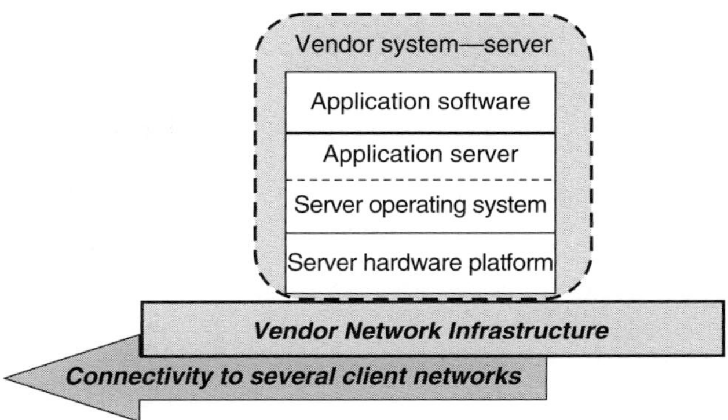

Figure 4: Vendor end—server

systems requires proper application server software. A comparison of application server software is available at TheServerSide.com (Serverside 2006), and some vendors have their own solutions for application servicing (Citrix 2006). The application server software runs on the server operating system (Fitzgerald and Dennis 2005; PC World 2006) and the server-hosting hardware platform runs the operating system. The server operating system provides a platform for applications to run on, and the operating system must possess the features to enable access requests coming from many different types of clients. Definitely, the server operating system must possess multi-user capabilities as well as features providing security and stability. The server hardware platform is connected to the local network infrastructure at the vendor, which in turn must be linked to a network connecting to the customer's networks. The vendors' system can be represented as a stack, shown in Figure 4. Similar to Figure 3, Figure 4 is given here to complete the description. The essential feature of the system in the application server is the facility for serving remote users in different system environments. The server must meet the essential performance levels in terms of response time, throughput, availability, reliability, and in some cases, the ability to handle time-dependent/critical user interactions. Moreover, the server system must provide facilities for user management, including keeping user accounts and data and security management.

As mentioned earlier, for customers to use the applications at the vendor site, connectivity must exist between the vendor and customer networks. The necessary connectivity can be achieved through the Internet. Theoretically, any WAN that provides communications facilities between the customers and vendors can be used, as shown in Figure 5. Secure communications between the customers and vendors are necessary.

In these situations, the vendor and the customer can connect through secure networks such as virtual private networks (VPNs). In using a VPN, the Internet can provide the underlying physical communications capabilities while the VPN offers the secure connectivity required. The Internet often provides a more cost-effective way to connect vendor and customer networks. Figure 6 shows the connection between several customers and a vendor network through the Internet and through a VPN. In Figure 6, Customer X is using a more secure VPN to

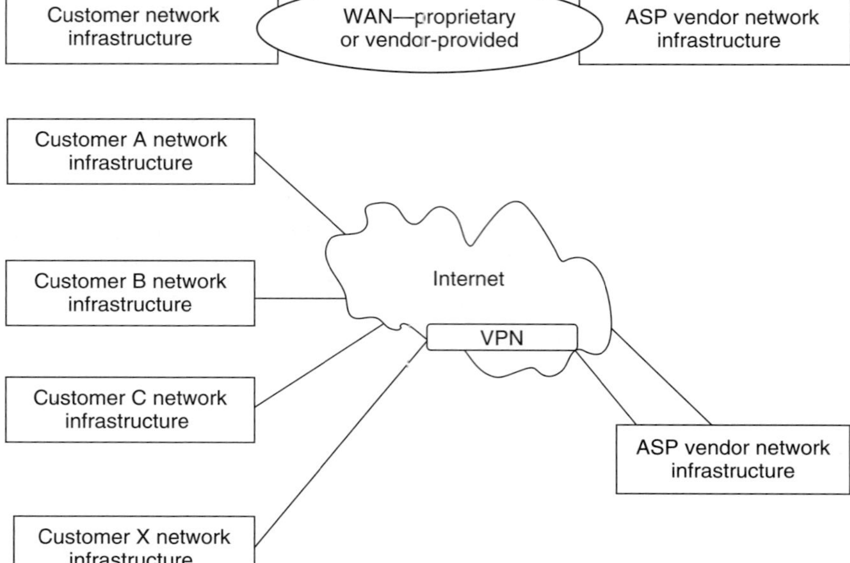

Figure 5: Vendor-customers networking through WAN

Figure 6: Vendor-customers networking

connect to the ASP while the other customers communicate through the Internet.

The Internet, instead of another type of proprietary or customized WAN, offers both advantages and disadvantages. The Internet offers an inexpensive method of communications between the vendor and clients, but the communications are more vulnerable to external threats. Moreover, both the vendor and the client have to depend on other organizations for availability of the network (e.g., sometimes the Internet may go down and an Internet service provider (ISP) may be slow to respond). Another problem with the current Internet is the unpredictable performance. At times, because of heavy use and the type of data being transferred, the user might experience slow response time while using an application via the Internet. In such situations, time-critical applications might not perform as desired. Performance degradation caused by the Internet may be beyond the control of the ASP.

A proprietary or customized WAN is more costly, and is maintained by either the vendor or the client. With direct involvement of the vendor, the client, or both in maintaining the WAN, both parties will have more control over the network, allowing for more secure networks versus using the Internet. By considering these benefits and problems of the network configurations, one can evaluate whether to use a specific delivery network. The other organizational and business issues that need to be considered prior to making ASP decisions will be discussed later. The following section describes the ASP configuration in general and associates it with the different types of vendors, for each type of activity.

ASP MODEL ELEMENTS AND RELATED VENDORS

ASPs are not always vendors just offering their applications to customers over networks. As described in the previous section, the ASPs can serve as many different types of ASPs in the vendor market. We now examine the overall ASP infrastructure in terms of its components and relate the components to the different vendors in the market. The following infrastructure elements are necessary for ASPs: (1) technology for development, deployment, and management; (2) software; (3) delivery infrastructure for data needs; (4) business activities for establishing and managing ASP customer relationships; (5) communications networks; and (6) end users.

The hardware and software necessary for application development and deployment are technologies necessary for ASPs. These technologies can come from other software and technology companies that act in partnership with the ASP. Application software meeting business needs, such as ERP, can come either from ISVs or from ASPs. The delivery infrastructure must ensure the bandwidth capabilities both at the user and the vendor ends. In addition, the delivery infrastructure must ensure the data security and data center services such as proper backup and restoration.

Sometimes the ASPs are not capable of providing these services by themselves. In such cases, the ASPs may have to work with other software infrastructure partners who provide data center services or provide the necessary bandwidth. For example, initial customer-vendor relationships are established through marketing and sales. Once the initial contacts are established, there are other activities that must be performed. After the vendor and the customer enter into an agreement through the contract there will be a necessity for after-sales services such as customization, billing, and maintenance. ASP aggregators often offer these after-sales services to other ASPs. The ASP network infrastructure can be provided by ISPs or other third-party network service providers in the case of WAN architectures other than the Internet. Along with the networking elements, it often will be necessary to have services for managing the networks to ensure optimal performance to meet an application's run-time needs and user needs.

Kern, Willcocks, and Lacity (2002, Netsourcing) present these elements in a similar manner by focusing on the service provided by networking alone. They use the term *netsourcing*, which they broadly define as provisioning of IT infrastructure services over networks, to refer to this service; it includes ASPs (Kern et al. 2002). Their definition of the netsourcing stack consists of the elements or components in an ASP. The components are: (1) network connectivity services, (2) network services—monitoring and management, (3) hosting infrastructure services, (4) application operating infrastructure services—middleware for remotely accessing applications, (5) standard application access services, (6) customized application access and support services, and (7) business process delivery services.

DETERMINANTS OF CUSTOMER ASP CHOICE

In the early days of ASP, the ASP market did not grow as anticipated. Not all companies considered ASPs to be an appropriate means for obtaining application software services. In particular, large companies often did not use ASP services. Thus, many of the ASP vendors targeted small and medium-sized enterprises (SMEs). Researchers have shown the suitability of ASPs for SMEs (Currie and Seltsikas 2001). SMEs may not have enough resources to set up their own applications, delivery infrastructures, and data centers. For SMEs, renting applications from service providers can be less costly than setting up their own facilities. Suitability of ASPs for SMEs does not imply that large companies will not benefit from ASPs. Large companies also may find applications and requirements that ASPs can fulfill because of the variety of ASPs on the market. For example, a large company may not find that an ASP reseller meets the company's needs because of its large user base. Yet it may find an ASP that can provide application services required by a specific group or an organizational unit within the company. Table 1 shows a set of potential determinants for using an ASP's services.

Often, companies compare the costs of developing and deploying application software internally to the costs of renting the application from an ASP reseller or a developer. Nevertheless, factors other than costs must be considered when determining the use of ASPs (Jayatilaka, Schwarz, and Hirschheim 2003). The factors acting as determinants for using ASPs are cost advantages, availability of external resources, lack of internal resources, strategic reasons, and business knowledge associated with the application.

Implementation of application software is a task that can be costly and complex. According to the traditional systems development method, a software or systems life cycle consists of the following stages: preliminary investigation (including feasibility analysis), requirements analysis, design, development, testing, and maintenance. Prior to developing software, systems developers go through requirements gathering, analysis, and design stages regardless of the approach they use for development of the software. Once these activities are performed, actual software development (writing the code and testing) may require technical and human resources as well as financial resources, which are needed for acquiring and using other resources. After development, the software has to

Table 1: Possible Determinants of an ASP Choice

Determinant Category	Associated Determinants
Cost	Applications development
	Capital costs for infrastructures—servers, data centers
	Management costs—server management, data-center management, and some of the communications network management
	Maintenance costs—server maintenance, data-center maintenance, and some communication network maintenance
	Operations costs—data-center operations
	Support staff—application maintenance and help desk
Internal resources	Lacks personnel for development and supporting applications
	Lacks hardware, software, and networking resources
	Inability to keep up with the rapid changes in technologies
External resources	Needed applications, technologies, and vendor for obtaining application services available in market
	Rapid changes in technologies
Strategy/competition	Need for timely entry into a market/product/service
	Gain efficiency over competitors

be deployed and made available to the users in the operations and production stage. Once the application is in production, it needs to be properly managed for optimal effectiveness and efficiency. Making the application accessible over a company's network will require a network infrastructure, which includes communications software and hardware, server hardware and software, personnel for installation of the application, and operation and management of the network. If a company performs all these activities internally when implementing the systems, the company also has to manage the development and deployment process.

Essentially, a company has to incur technical, personnel, operational, and managerial costs for development and deployment by an internal IT department (often referred to as in-house development and deployment). However, if a company rents the application from an ASP, the company will not need to spend capital on development, deployment, management, and maintenance of the application. Providing help to the users is another essential task when an application is implemented within a company. In addition to the application costs, costs due to the server, data, and networks must be taken into consideration. Those costs are: (1) server management and maintenance, (2) data center management and maintenance, (3) data center operations, and (4) communications infrastructure management and maintenance. The applications must run on servers accessible to the users in a client company. Data generated through the use of the application must be properly maintained and managed. Proper management and maintenance requires making regular backups and allowing proper access to data. In addition, the servers and the networks delivering the application to the users must be managed and maintained.

Even if a company decides to use an ASP, the company still has to spend money for doing a preliminary investigation, gathering requirements, and analyzing and determining the specifications. The specifications of the needed systems may be found only during the design of business solutions. Once these initial activities are completed, the company will be able to find a suitable application package in the market and find an ASP that offers those application services. If the overall costs of in-house development and deployment of the application is higher than renting it from an ASP, a company may consider renting from the ASP. Although the cost is a primary determinant for many companies to choose an ASP vendor, it is advisable for them to consider other factors as well.

From a resource viewpoint, application development, deployment, and management consume scarce resources. Two essential types of such resources are technical and human. Even with the necessary financial resources, a company may not have the necessary technical resources or may not want to allocate existing resources to implement an application. As a possible scenario, consider a company that does not have a server capable of supporting an application with a large user base. If the installation and management of a new server requires more technical and personnel resources, the lack of resources presents a resource gap, and the company may have to seek the resources from an ASP vendor.

Vendors with the capabilities must exist in the market for a company to obtain application services. As discussed earlier, the services may need to come from more than just one vendor who can provide all the necessary infrastructure and services. The application may have to be obtained from one vendor (i.e., an ASP developer or reseller), while the hosting services and data center services may have to be obtained from another or the same vendor. Meanwhile, networking services such as the infrastructure and management services may have to be obtained from yet another vendor. Alternatively, it might be possible to obtain all the services from a single ASP. Whichever arrangement of sources is sought, the necessary capabilities must be available in the market. Then the costs of obtaining these available capabilities from the market must be evaluated. On the other hand, a company may already have some in-house capabilities and skills and thus be able to deliver the same application. In this case, it will be necessary to evaluate and compare the costs of using the internal resources versus the costs of using an ASP vendor. In some cases, a resource gap may exist, and a company may try to acquire the resource to implement the application. The estimated in-house costs will have to include acquisition of the needed resources as well.

Data communications and other information technologies are changing at a rapid pace because of innovations. With the rapid pace of change in the technologies, decision makers may perceive a rapidly diminishing effectiveness in their in-house software applications. They may find it necessary to upgrade the technologies frequently. In contrast, if a company obtains the services from an ASP, the burden of upgrading the technologies as the innovations occur shifts to the vendor. The vendor will be in a better position to perform the necessary upgrades to their applications and the associated technologies because they are directly related to their core competency. Therefore, if a company wants to mitigate the risks of technological obsolescence or diminishing effectiveness due to rapid changes in technologies, the company may seek the services of an ASP.

Cost and unavailability of resources are not the only drivers for using an ASP. A company may have a need for an application implemented by its competitors as well. When a short time for implementing the application is a critical factor, a company may find it quicker to obtain the services of an ASP. An ASP may be able to offer the application more quickly to better support the company's strategy. Sometimes a company may have an application that performs efficiently with a quick response time. For example, in order to support a large sales force in the field competitively, it may be necessary to have an application that provides quick responses to sales personnel's requests. An in-house IT department may not be able to provide the high performance needed, whereas an ASP may be able to provide the application services at the performance level required. Therefore, in this case the ASP will be able to support the competitive advantage through its sales-force support application. Of course, when considering the strategic importance of an application, an ASP may not always provide a strategic advantage. Although a vendor offers a strategically important application, renting an application from an ASP may involve risks also. The next section examines this risk from ASPs.

RISKS IN ASPs

Several risks are associated with the use of ASPs. However, knowing the potential risks can help both vendors and customers to mitigate those risks. Sometimes the risks may be considered as disadvantages at an aggregated level (NTAP 2006), but the risks can arise for several reasons. Because of the different types of risks, the risk factors must be considered individually, and proper analysis of these risks is necessary (Kern et al. 2002, Application service provision). There are organizational risks and technical risks. In some situations, these two types of risks may need a comprehensive approach. Although some risks are primarily technical in nature, some need proper organizational as well as technical solutions. Table 2 shows the risks associated with ASPs and their two primary categories—technical and organizational. This categorization attempts to make it easy to identify the risks.

Security of data, or the lack of security, is one of the major risks of ASPs. In the ASP model, customers' data are stored at the vendor's data center. The vendor is responsible for management of the data, and the vendor has more control over the data. The customer risks loss of confidential company information or specific business processes of the company. In some cases, the data resulting from the use of an application may divulge information about the business processes of the customer company. Therefore, the security of the data is a critical issue that must be taken into consideration. Data security has to be ensured at two stages of the application-use process: (1) when data are transmitted over the networks, and (2) when the data are archived or stored at the data centers. If customer data are strategically critical and security is essential, security must be guaranteed all the time. During the initial customer vendor negotiations, it is necessary to discuss how the data will be secured by the vendor and what guarantees the vendor can provide about the security of the data. Some of the specific important aspects of security are: (1) access privileges, (2) access controls, (3) data transmission security, (4) disaster management, (5) intrusion detection and reporting, and (6) communication of data security status to customers.

One critical technical risk is the poor performance of the application itself. The performance of an application depends on the network performance as well as the software performance. Network performance is often defined in terms of measures such as response time, availability, reliability, and throughput. From the customer view, users must be able to get fast responses and the applications must be available when they are needed. ASPs must be able to provide information on their performance related to specific applications. Such prior knowledge about the ASP's performance will help clients mitigate future risks due to poor performance. One method to mitigate the risk due to poor performance is to implement proper

Table 2: Risks Associated with ASPs

Category	Risk	Mitigation
Technical	Data security • Lack of secure transmission channels • Lack of security at data center and data resources not properly secured	Proper analysis of vendor and network service provider capabilities and technologies Ensuring the following are clearly specified, understood and agreed to by vendors and customers: • access privileges • access controls • data transmission security • disaster management • intrusion detection and reporting • communication of data security status to customers
	Performance—inadequate or not meeting expectations	Proper analysis of vendor and network service provider capabilities and technologies
	Failure of systems	Determining the tolerable failures Ensuring that proper procedures for recovery are in place
Organizational	Data security—possibility of application data divulging strategically important information to competitors through the vendor	Inclusion of necessary conditions, procedures, and policies in the contract
	Vendor going out of business	Evaluating tenure and past performance of the vendor before selecting
	Vendor not performing as expected	Contract stipulations and monitoring
	Vendor subcontracting	Include in the vendor negotiations
	Customers' unrealistic expectations	Educate customers about capabilities, problems, and risks
	Customer immaturity/lack of knowledge	Same as above

monitoring and management of the networks and servers so that optimal performance can be obtained (Fitzgerald and Dennis 2005; Goldman and Rawles 2004).

Failures of network and server are technical in nature; however, they are risks that are similar to the other issues to be foreseen and prevented. Organizational mechanisms must be put in place to mitigate the risks due to failure. Any system, server, or network is subject to failing or crash. However, it is necessary to take appropriate steps to recover from failure and minimize the damage or problems due to failures. To avoid failures of servers, fault-tolerant systems and duplicate systems can be used. Similarly, the networks can have duplicate resources to handle a failure. Yet having redundant resources can be too costly sometimes; fail-proof services may not always be required. In such cases, it will be necessary to bring up the applications properly after a failure and restore the data so minimal disruptions occur in the business processes.

Other major risks are due to organizational and managerial issues (Kern et al. 2002, Application service provision). ASPs may oversell their capabilities, knowingly or unknowingly. This risk can be mitigated by properly analyzing the ASP proposals and capabilities prior to signing the agreements. As we saw earlier, the breadth of players in the ASP arena may result in the possibility of the primary provider subcontracting some tasks of an ASP arrangement to other vendors. Subcontracting can give rise to problems (Kern et al. 2002, Application service provision). Therefore, the customer company should make sure to identify the subcontracts within an ASP and to evaluate their performance and records prior to deciding on a specific ASP. Just as in any other product, a risk exists because of the possibility of a vendor going out of business. Sometimes, because of turbulent times, this failure may not be predictable. Nevertheless, it is better to be aware that such a likelihood exists. Customers should gather information on the tenure of the vendor and their past performance. Such information on the vendor may provide some indications of the likelihood of failure. From the customer side, the risks can occur because of a customer's unrealistic expectations, getting into incomplete contracts, and lack of experience of the customer (Kern et al. 2002, Application service provision).

FEASIBILITY ASSESSMENT OF ASP—MAKING A BUSINESS CASE

Every company should perform a complete feasibility analysis before deciding on an ASP. The feasibility analysis must include economic feasibility, technical feasibility, operational feasibility, and legal feasibility. Other feasibilities may be considered, depending on the business/organizational or market conditions. In some cases, it may be necessary to consider political feasibility in certain countries or in certain organizations before using an ASP. The technical components, risks, and the business model discussed earlier in this chapter must be considered when examining the technical feasibility. Basically, a company needs to evaluate whether the technologies necessary for the application and delivery of services as required are available within the organization or if they should be outsourced. Operational feasibility involves determining whether it is possible to use the ASP services within the company's operational context. This section examines factors necessary for evaluating economic feasibility and other nonfinancial factors that impact technical, operational, and other feasibilities.

Economic feasibility is the examination of the cost-effectiveness of the ASP. As discussed earlier, the costs of using an internal IT department and the ASP must be evaluated and compared. These cost factors will be incurred in internal sourcing and usually this can be called the total cost of ownership (TCO) of an application. Cost comparisons for internal sourcing of applications and using external ASP services are shown in Table 3, which shows costs as static factors; however, it is also necessary to consider the expected period of the use of the ASP application. For example, the cumulative cost of renting ASP software for the expected period of use must be calculated.

The other factors are not directly related to the costs and may not be financially quantifiable. Organizational level factors that need to be considered are as follows:

- Specificity of the application (Does the ASP offer customization?)
- Ability of the ASP to serve the user base in the company
- Need for control of the application
- Strategic importance of the application

Table 3: Costs to Be Included in an Economic Feasibility Study

Cost of Internal Sourcing	Costs of Using an ASP Vendor
• Analysis costs • Total cost of ownership: – Application development or purchasing cost – Server costs: initial purchasing, management and/or maintenance – Network costs – Application maintenance costs – Data center costs	• Analysis costs • Rent and other fees • External network use costs—delivery infrastructure (Internet or other WAN) • Early termination fees & costs to be incurred due to risks (not always) • Vendor relationship management costs

- Time criticality of the application services
- Need for integration with the rest of the organization
- Need for focusing on strategic or core activities rather than implementing the application in-house.
- Handling of failures and recovery policies

At the individual user level, the following factors need to be considered:

- User interfaces—commonly used Internet browsers or application specific interfaces
- User training (Does the ASP provide training?)
- User support—availability of help-desk facilities
- Customer service in general

In addition to the above, a business or organization may have questions that are specific to that organization's context. The topic of feasibility analysis of ASPs is extensive, spanning the feasibility of IT in general. As such, this section is limited to pointing out the important factors.

CONCLUSION

Obtaining an ASP's services shows marked differences from traditional outsourcing because of its dependence on computer networks, although both types of sourcing use external vendors to obtain IT services. ASP is limited to application-software services only, whereas traditional outsourcing covers the whole range of IT activities. Because of the cost benefits provided by ASP arrangements and the capabilities of vendors, many companies will seek ASPs to obtain application services. Because of the ability of an ASP to serve many customers, an ASP will have the advantage of the economy of scale and will be able to provide solutions to customers at an acceptable cost (i.e., at a cost lower than if the customer were to develop and host its own application). Also, a vendor may have the technical expertise to implement and manage network applications. In particular, the development and broad availability of networking technologies are making ASP arrangements more attractive than ever before. Today's networks carry more bandwidth, provide better security, and will continue to improve in the future.

Researchers have been examining the ASP phenomenon, but it is not as extensively researched as traditional outsourcing (Dibbern et al. 2004). ASP can be treated as an evolutionary step in the traditional outsourcing (Currie and Selstikas 2001; Tebboune 2003). This chapter presented the basics of application service providers. When deciding whether to use an ASP, it is necessary to consider the factors applicable to the specific business/organizational context and to evaluate the available vendor services properly (Currie et al. 2004; Jayatilaka et al. 2003). For clients to see the fit between business needs and benefits of an ASP, the client's evaluation of their needs is inadequate. The vendor must give appropriate value propositions to the clients (Currie 2004; Currie et al. 2004). The vendors will be able to provide clients with appropriate value propositions if they understand the clients' needs properly. Therefore, the vendors' perceptions of the clients are critical.

GLOSSARY

Application: A computer program used by an organization to perform tasks to achieve a given objective.

ASP (Application Service Provider): A vendor providing application services to customers for a fee.

ASP (Application Service Provisioning): Act of providing application services for a fee.

Enterprise ASP: An independent software vendor who deploys their own application to deliver the application services directly to the customers.

Feasibility Assessment (ASP Feasibility): Determining whether the use of an ASP can be done with the available technologies and whether vendors are available with the necessary capabilities. Different feasibility categories include economic feasibility, legal feasibility, operational feasibility, political feasibility, schedule feasibility, and technical feasibility.

Horizontal ASP: A vendor who provides an application service that cuts across industries but is specific to a given application—e.g., e-mail.

Netsourcing: Obtaining IT services over computer networks.

MSP (Managed Service Providers): A vendor who provides a variety of managed services, sometimes including application services. These types of vendors also provide other services such as network management services.

Pure-Play ASP: A vendor who takes on the responsibility for all of the requirements for delivering the application services.

Vertical ASP: A vendor who provides all of the applications required by a specific industry.

VPN (Virtual Private Network): A secure network established over a public network such as the Internet or over a more open wide area network. This network is called "virtual" because only a secure channel is provided over an existing physical network, while no separate physical network exists for the private network.

WAN (Wide Area Networks): A network that spans more than a single building or work area.

xSP: An abbreviation referring to service provisioning in general.

CROSS REFERENCES

See *Network Security Risk Assessment and Management*; *Web Hosting*; *Web Services*.

REFERENCES

ASP Directory. 2000. Directory of vertical market applications. www.asp-directory.com/directory/vertical_market/index4.shtml (accessed January 5, 2006).

Bennett, C., and G. Timbrell. 2000. Application service providers: Will they succeed? *Information Systems Frontiers* 2:195–211.

Betts, M. 2005. Application service providers are back for a second act. *Computerworld* 39:61.

Braunstein, A. 1999. The state of ASPs. www.cio.com/analyst/122799_rfgonline_content.html (accessed January 5, 2006).

Citrix. 2006. www.citrix.com/lang/English/home.asp (accessed January 5, 2006).

Collett, S. 2005. The making of an MSP. *Computerworld* 39:64.

Currie, W. 2004. Value creation from application service provider e-business model: The experience of four firms. *Journal of Enterprise Information Management* 17:117–30.

Currie, W., B. Desai, and N. Khan. 2004. Customer evaluation of application service provisioning in five vertical sectors. *Information and Organization* 19:39–58.

Currie, W., and P. Seltsikas. 2001. Exploring the supply-side of IT outsourcing: Evaluating the emerging role of application service providers. *European Journal of Information Systems* 10:123–34.

Dibbern, J., T. Goles, R. Hirschheim, and B. Jayatilaka. 2004. Information systems outsourcing: A survey and analysis of literature. *DATABASE for Advancement of Information System*, 35:6–99.

Dickerson, C. 2002. xSP expectations. *InfoWorld* 24:46.

Ekanayake, Y., W. Currie, and P. Seltsikas. 2003. Evaluating applicant service providers. *Benchmarking* 10(4):343–54.

Employease. 2006. www.employease.com (accessed January 5, 2006).

Fitzgerald, J., and A. Dennis. 2005. *Business data communications and networking*. New York: Wiley.

Goldman, J. E., and P. T. Rawles. 2004. *Applied data communications: A business-oriented approach*. New York: Wiley.

Jamcracker. 2006, www.jamcracker.com/productoverview.htm (accessed January 5, 2006).

Jayatilaka, B., B. Schwarz, and R. Hirschheim. 2003. Determinants of ASP choice: An integrated perspective. *European Journal of Information Systems* 12(3):210–24.

Kern, T., M. Lacity, and L. Willcocks. 2002. Application service provision: Risk assessment and mitigation. *MIS Quarterly Executive* 1:113–26.

———. 2002. *Netsourcing: Renting business applications and services over a network*. Upper Saddle River, NJ: Financial Times Prentice Hall.

Means, P. 2004. How xSPs can use data backup to develop a new profit center. *Computer Technology Review* 24:46.

NTAP. 2006. *Online training module*. http://lstech.org/ntap/trainings/modules/CMS202/index_html?start:int=26 (accessed January 5, 2006).

Oakes, R. 2005. Key to successful IT outsourcing. *LIMRA's Market Facts Quarterly* 24:82–3.

PC World. 2006. www.pcworld.idg.com.au/index.php/id;1327251104 (accessed January 5, 2006).

Salesforce. 2006. www.salesforce.com (accessed January 5, 2006) _

Serverside. 2006. www.theserverside.com/reviews/matrix.tss (accessed January 5, 2006).

Tebboune, D. E. S. 2003. Application service provision: origins and development. *Business Process Management Journal* 9(6):722–34.

Weblaw. 2003. Application service provider (ASP) contract. www.weblaw.co.uk/aspheads.php. (accessed January 5, 2006).

Webopedia. 2006. www.webopedia.com/TERM/A/Application_Service_Provider.html (accessed January 5, 2006)

Videoconferencing

Ketan Mayer-Patel, *University of North Carolina, Chapel Hill*

INTRODUCTION

Videoconferencing has been widely hailed both for its incredible potential to change the way we work and interact as well as for its arguably ongoing failure to actually live up to that potential (Egido 1988). The myriad potential uses of videoconferencing that have been touted over the years include:

- *Interpersonal communication:* This use of videoconferencing extends the traditional telephone model with video.
- *Business meetings:* By connecting multiple individuals or small groups located in different offices, videoconferencing can potentially provide greater flexibility to employees in terms of where they conduct business as well as potentially reduce costs to employers by eliminating the need for relatively expensive and slow business travel.
- *Distance learning:* Videoconferencing could allow educators to meet interactively with remotely located students either individually or as a group. Descriptions of videoconferencing in a distance learning setting often include the integrated use of other collaboration tools such as online whiteboards and shared document editing.
- *Telemedicine:* By allowing doctors to consult interactively with other doctors and patients, videoconferencing could potentially improve access to health care for rural areas where access to expert care is otherwise limited and cumbersome.

Although videoconferencing is used more widely than ever and that use is growing, there is still a gap between its real and potential impact. The exact reasons for the failure of videoconferencing to become the next "killer app" are difficult to distill, and there is little to no consensus among developers or potential users as to what obstacles remain. It may be a matter of usability and thus point toward issues of user interface and session management. Alternatively, it may be a larger-scale social issue of how people interact with visual images, in which case the future of videoconferencing may lie in improving the sense of presence created by videoconferencing technologies. Videoconferencing may fall into a natural dead spot between the need to communicate quickly, satisfied by e-mail and telephony, and the need to communicate more deeply and spontaneously over longer timescales, satisfied by actually traveling in order to be physically co-located. Or it may simply be a matter of time before we find that videoconferencing does live up to all our expectations. Whatever the reason, videoconferencing remains an important application area both for its current growing impact and its future unrealized potential.

What makes videoconferencing a particularly interesting technical case study is that almost all of the difficult technical issues have largely been solved. Although early videoconferencing systems suffered from a lack of processing power at the client end and limited end-to-end bandwidth, advances in processor speeds and the wide-scale deployment of broadband networks have obviated many of these resource limitations. A notable exception is the failure of Internet protocol (IP)–based multicast that would have greatly enhanced the development of many videoconferencing systems.

A simple definition of videoconferencing is that it is an application that allows two or more remotely located participants (or groups of participants) to communicate in real time using video and audio. It is important to draw a distinction between video conferencing and video streaming and voice over IP (VoIP) telephony. Clearly, elements of both of these other application domains exist within the domain of videoconferencing. The difference between conferencing and streaming revolve mostly around the latency requirements of conferencing. Although streaming applications can often afford a startup delay of several seconds in order to provide spacious buffers for smooth and synchronized video delivery, the same is not true in a conferencing application. Another important difference is that each participant both produces and consumes a number of media streams.

The main difference with IP telephony is the addition of a video stream that generally dwarfs the associated audio stream in computational complexity and bandwidth requirements. Both application domains require session control and setup protocols. In fact, there is little in these session-control protocols that is video-specific, and our treatment here will omit discussion of session control altogether to avoid duplication with other chapters that deal with VoIP as an application. Both the H.323 standard published by the International Telecommunication Union (ITU) and the SIP standard published by the Internet Engineering Task Force (IETF) are widely used for both VoIP and videoconferencing (ITU 2006; Rosenberg 2002).

In this chapter, we examine a number of aspects of videoconferencing. Although usability and interface issues may be the key for harnessing the untapped potential of videoconferencing as an application, our goal here is to concentrate on the technical aspects of the application. Thus, we focus our attention on its technical challenges and the current state-of-the-art solutions for IP-based videoconferencing. We begin with a brief history of various notable videoconferencing systems that have been developed over the years. We then discuss the various human factors involved and the requirements these factors place on videoconferencing systems in general (especially with regard to end-to-end latency limits). A taxonomy of different videoconferencing architectures is presented to provide an overview of the design space and to provide context for many of the technical challenges. Following this, we include sections that focus on the networking and video-encoding aspects of videoconferencing. A brief section describing various audio standards follows. Finally, the chapter concludes with a discussion of the future of videoconferencing and current research efforts in tele-immersion. Throughout this chapter, the focus of our attention is on IP-based videoconferencing via the Internet.

HISTORY

Early videoconferencing systems dating back to the late 1960s and early 1970s were largely developed as extensions of the telephone. AT&T and Ericsson both demonstrated video phone products in the late 1960s and early 1970s. Neither was able to attract much commercial success. Large companies began to develop in-house analog videoconferencing capabilities between dedicated meeting rooms as way of facilitating remote collaboration in the 1970s. Notable efforts include those of Nippon Telegraph and Telephone and IBM. These were closed systems that were engineered and developed for specific sites and were not developed as commercial products.

The first reasonably successful commercial product was the PictureTel system introduced in the early 1980s. This system included dedicated hardware operating over leased lines and at $80,000 was remarkably expensive (although much cheaper than any other solution at the time). As PictureTel continued to develop and improve its product, costs were lowered and quality improved. By 1991, a PictureTel system could be purchased for approximately $20,000 with $30/hour line charges. PictureTel systems were marketed to businesses and were typically installed in meeting rooms as a way of connecting groups of people.

With the development and deployment of the Internet, videoconferencing for individuals using digital packet video and audio on a PC became a reality. The CU-SeeMe system developed at Cornell University in 1992, however, was the first system to really tap into the potential of videoconferencing on the Internet (Dorcey 1995). Although the video quality provided by CU-SeeMe was very limited (initially 160×120 4-bit grayscale), the system benefited tremendously by the fact that the program was free. This allowed ordinary users, developers, and enthusiasts to experiment with videoconferencing. CU-SeeMe was developed first for the Macintosh, and a Windows version followed within a few years.

At around the same time, development of IP-multicast and the initial deployment of multicast via the MBone led to the development of a number of UNIX-based videoconferencing systems. These systems were largely experimental research systems and included NetVideo or *nv* from Xerox PARC (Fredricks 1992), the INRIA Videoconferencing System, also known as *ivs* (Turletti 1994), and LBL's suite of videoconferencing tools *vic*, *vat*, and *wb* (McCanne and Jacobson 1995), which, respectively, provided videoconferencing, audio conferencing, and shared whiteboard functionality. All of these systems are notable for their pioneering use of the real-time protocol (RTP) and the real-time control protocol (RTCP) developed within the Audio/Video Transport working group of the IETF.

In conjunction with the development and use of these research systems, standards were developed to address various facets of videoconferencing. These included various standards for video codecs such as H.261, H.263, and more recently H.264; audio codecs such as G.711, G.722, and G.728; and session control such as H.323 and SIP. The standards process is particularly important for videoconferencing as an application domain in order to promote interoperability among different systems.

Low-cost standards-based commercial desktop videoconferencing emerged in the early 1990s with Intel's ProShare system and Microsoft's NetMeeting. Since then, the number of IP-based desktop videoconferencing solutions has exploded, and any number of commercial, freeware, shareware, and open source solutions are available (Woolley 2006). NetMeeting is now bundled with Microsoft's WindowsXP operating system. Similarly, Apple bundles a version of their videoconferencing system, iChat, with the OS X operating system. The availability of feature-rich, standards-based videoconferencing as part and parcel of the standard software delivered with the operating system is further evidence of the maturation of videoconferencing as an application. Recently, Skype has received a great deal of attention as a peer-to-peer VoIP and video conferencing solution (Krim 2005). The main technical innovation of Skype is its very robust and turnkey handling of network address translation (NAT) devices.

HUMAN FACTORS

The effectiveness of videoconferencing is determined by the user's perceived quality of the experience. This in turn is directly related to a number of different human factors governing the utility of both the video and audio channels and the overall usability of the system. In this section, we highlight several of these factors, including communication latency and jitter, audio quality, video quality, intermedia issues, and usability.

Latency

Latency is generally considered the number one factor in determining the perceived quality of a videoconference. It has been shown that the effects of latency on interactive communication is noticeable as latency exceeds 100 msec, is significantly disruptive as latency approaches 250 msec, and is crippling as latency exceeds 500 msec (Krauss and Bricker 1967). Thus, latency control is a key issue for videoconferencing systems. Another factor affecting the perceived quality of video is media jitter. In general, smooth delivery of video frames at an even slower rate is perceived as being of higher quality than delivery of video frames at an uneven higher frame rate (Calyam et al. 2004).

Quality Metrics

Although the audio stream portion of a videoconference consumes significantly less bandwidth than the video portion, paradoxically, it is generally much more important to the overall quality of the video conference and can be much more sensitive to dynamic network conditions. From a human factors point of view, however, the quality requirements imposed on the audio stream are quite modest, as the audio content for a video conference is most often human speech. Thus, basic telephonic audio transmission rates and fidelity suffice to support most communication needs.

The relationship between video quality and the overall quality of experience provided by videoconferencing is much more difficult to determine. This is because assessing the impact of video quality is greatly affected by the metrics used to measure the quality of the conference itself. If the metric used is too simplistic (e.g., were participants able to effectively communicate some specific piece of information), the value of the video channel as a whole may be negligible or the effect of video quality may be immaterial. In other words, even though the metric is well defined and easy to quantify, the metric may be measuring a quality that is not greatly influenced by the visual information provided by the video channel. If, instead, one focuses on the value of nonverbal communication such as the ability to express understanding (e.g., nodding or shaking one's head), interest level (e.g., smiling, attentiveness), or gestures, the quality of the video channel becomes much more important (Isaacs and Tang 1994). Often, this nonverbal communication is described as the "sense of presence." One can qualitatively judge the sense of presence created by a videoconference relative to the experience of actually being physically co-located, but quantifying this sense of presence and deriving a relationship of it to analytical measures of video quality (e.g., peak signal-to-noise ratio or frame rate) remains very difficult.

Audio versus Video

As a rule of thumb, audio is more important to the basic communication needs of videoconferencing participants than is video. A videoconference in which the video channel ceases to function essentially (and automatically) becomes the same as a telephone call. A conference in which the audio channel ceases to function, on the other hand, becomes almost meaningless. Another intermedia issue is that of synchronization. Whereas synchronized delivery of video and audio certainly benefits the perceived quality of both channels, doing so may be to the detriment of end-to-end latency.

Usability

The usability of a videoconferencing system in large part reflects the culture of the organization and whether the conference is being used to support informal, interpersonal communication or more formal, intergroup communication. Videoconferencing as an informal, interpersonal communication channel requires an organizational culture that provides the necessary equipment and resources to enough people such that a critical mass is achieved and people can expect to communicate via conferencing (Fish et al. 1992). Usability and effectiveness in such a setting can then be measured by examining the circumstances in which participants choose conferencing instead of other communication methods such as e-mail and/or the telephone. Conferencing for intergroup communication is often realized by constructing specific meeting rooms in which conference facilities have been installed. Usability in these settings is dominated by ease of setup, configuration, and control.

CONFERENCING ARCHITECTURES

The architecture of most IP-based videoconferencing systems is primarily organized in one of two ways. The first is a centralized architecture in which all media data are sent from all conference participants to a single location and then rebroadcast to participants. The second is a decentralized architecture in which participants distribute their video and audio streams directly to each other. This section describes each of these architectures in greater detail, noting their relative strengths and weaknesses. A noteworthy special case is a videoconference that involves only two participants. In this case the participants directly exchange media streams. Although this situation can be clearly classified as an instance of a decentralized architecture, it can almost as easily be considered an instance of a centralized architecture in which one of the participants is deemed a "master" to the other. The difference in this case is purely one of semantics.

Centralized

A centralized conferencing architecture relies on the existence of a single rendezvous point to serve as the destination

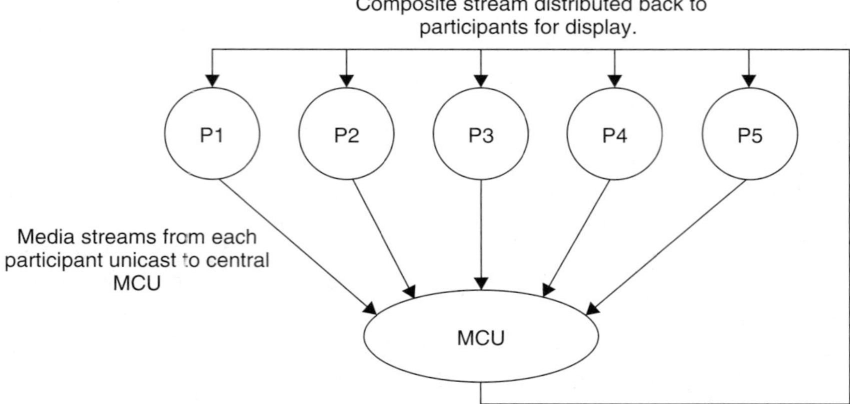

Figure 1: Logical relationships between participants and an MCU in a centralized conferencing architecture

for all of the media streams produced by all participants and is the source of media streams received by participants for display to the user. Such an architecture is illustrated in Figure 1. A common name for this centralized service is a multipoint control unit (MCU). Although it is conceivable that the MCU may in fact be co-located with one of the participants, in general the advantages of a MCU-based architecture are more easily realized if this service exists within the networking infrastructure on a well-provisioned host or as a special-purpose device dedicated to the task. The MCU is responsible for synchronizing the media streams from each participant and redistributing one or more media streams to the participants for presentation.

There are a number of advantages to a MCU-based architecture. First, the MCU can synchronize and mix together all of the audio streams into a single, coherent audio stream. This ensures that all participants hear each other in the same way. This is particularly important if the audio levels of different participants vary, since the MCU can then normalize the different streams by applying a participant-specific gain function. Second, if conference participants are able to reasonably receive only a limited number of video streams because of bandwidth considerations, the MCU can effectively negotiate competing interests and ensure that each participant is watching the same stream in order to realize a measure of floor control. Third, if the conference participants have heterogeneous capabilities, the MCU can tailor the streams distributed to participants in order to match client capabilities. Fourth, the MCU provides a convenient billing model for third-party conference services that may require differential pricing based on the number of participants and/or duration of the conference. Finally, the MCU provides a convenient framework within which to implement security and authentication measures if the media streams require encryption.

Decentralized

A decentralized conferencing architecture relies on the participants themselves to distribute the media streams directly to each other as peers, and in fact videoconferencing is an early example of a peer-to-peer application, even predating wide use of that term. Such an architecture is illustrated in Figure 2. A decentralized architecture is best suited for participants that are reasonably homogenous in client capabilities and network connectivity. As will be discussed in more detail later, the availability of multicast can greatly facilitate the effectiveness of a decentralized approach. One advantage of a decentralized approach by definition is that it does not rely on the deployment and availability of an MCU infrastructure. A second advantage of a decentralized approach is the ability to optimize each media stream for the dynamic network conditions that may exist between participants on a pairwise basis. This may be especially important if one of the participants is located relatively far away (e.g., on the other side of a long-latency satellite link) from the other participants. A third advantage is that the decentralized approach provides more flexibility to individual users in determining exactly which media streams to receive and display and to whom their own media streams are distributed.

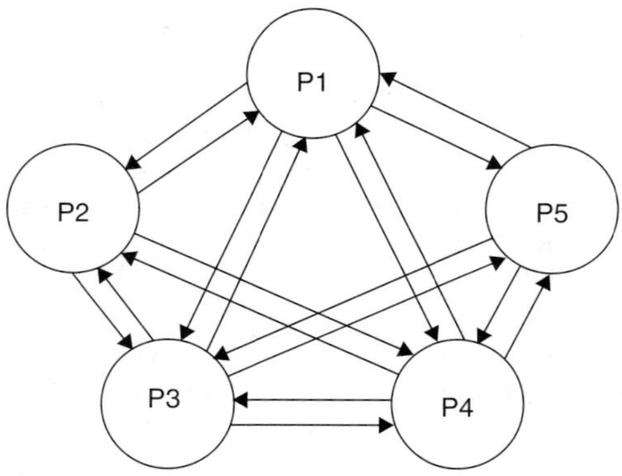

Figure 2: Logical relationships among participants in a decentralized architecture

NETWORKING ISSUES

This section reviews a number of networking protocols, mechanisms, and techniques that are important to videoconferencing systems. Because other chapters in this volume deal with many of these same topics in greater depth, the treatment here concentrates on how these concepts specifically relate to videoconferencing as an application. General descriptions of protocols that are covered elsewhere in this volume will be kept brief and informal in order to provide only the context necessary.

Multicast

Multicast is a natural fit for multiparty videoconferencing and can greatly improve a system's ability to scale to accommodate more participants. As originally envisioned, IP multicast establishes per group state in the routing infrastructure in order to discover and maintain a source-specific distribution tree spanning the participants of a multicast (Deering 1988). A class D IP address is used to address the multicast group. A host controls membership in an IP multicast group with `join` and `leave` messages that update the distribution tree accordingly. Packets addressed to the group traverse the distribution tree with routers replicating the packet as necessary at branch points.

The service model associated with IP multicast is strictly best effort, with no guarantee of delivery. Without application-level feedback, IP multicast does not provide the sender with any information about whether a packet was delivered to all, none, or some subset of the participants. Neither does IP multicast maintain any sort of group membership list. In fact, any number of hosts can act as sources of packets for an IP multicast group, and a source is not required to join the IP multicast as a participant.

Although powerful, IP multicast has proven difficult to deploy. In part, this has been due to a number of technical challenges inherent in multicast routing and tree maintenance. To address some of these challenges, later developments of IP multicast introduced the idea of single-source multicast (Holbrook and Cheriton 1999). In single-source IP multicast, the root of the distribution tree is placed at a single host that is the only source of packets allowed for that particular multicast group. Single-source IP multicast greatly simplifies routing and tree maintenance, does not require periodic flooding of multicast packets as occurred in the original IP multicast service, and allows group size and membership to be more strictly monitored and controlled. Furthermore, single-source IP multicast provides a scalable way to solicit feedback from participants about dynamic network characteristics such as latency, loss, and jitter.

In a centralized videoconferencing architecture, unicast transmission can be used to send media streams from each participant to the MCU. The MCU, in turn, can send a composite result back to the participants via multicast. This is a particularly good fit for single-source IP multicast, since the MCU is the only component of such an architecture that requires the ability to send IP multicast packets. Furthermore, the MCU can leverage the feedback facilities of single-source IP multicast to monitor performance in order to group participants by the quality of service experienced. This allows the MCU to tailor the encoding and transmission of the media streams (e.g., lowering video quality or frame rate for bandwidth-constrained hosts) to best fit the encountered conditions.

In a decentralized architecture, a multicast group can be associated with a particular media type (i.e., one group for all video information from all participants and one group for all of the audio), a particular participant (i.e., each participant creates one multicast group for distributing its video and its audio), or both. The capabilities of the multicast service available will obviously constrain the design choice. For example, if single-source IP multicast is being used, then grouping media by type is not an option. Although soliciting feedback from participants and dynamically grouping participants by loss and latency characteristics is possible in a decentralized system, the complexity of doing so is greatly increased by the fact that every participant is also a source of multicast packets.

Sadly, IP multicast, either in its originally envisioned form or single source, is likely never to be widely deployed on the Internet at large. The barrier to deployment has little to do with the technical challenges faced but instead seems to revolve around economic issues that result in very little incentive for Internet service providers (ISPs) to deploy multicast. Despite this, multicast is still a viable option for intranets within an organization that enjoys full control over its administrative domain. For organizations with a number of different locations, the combination of virtual private networks (VPNs) and locally administered IP multicast can be used to support videoconferencing within the organization. Another option is to rely on the services of a content distribution network (CDN). A CDN is an overlay network established by third-party organizations that is distributed across many different ISPs with nodes strategically located at various peering points (Verma 2002). Multicast can then be implemented as a service within a CDN.

Furthermore, in the past several years a number of application-level multicast technologies have been developed. Application-level multicast (ALM) does not rely on router support for maintaining the distribution tree and replicating packets. Instead, the participants themselves are organized into a distribution tree and packets are unicast in a peer-to-peer fashion (Banerjee, Bhattacharjee, and Kommareddy 2002; Chu et al. 2001; Zhang and Hu 2003; Kostić et al. 2003; Ratnasamy et al. 2001). ALM schemes are often evaluated in terms of stress and stretch (Chu, Rao, and Zhang 2000). Stress is defined as the number of copies of a particular packet that must traverse an underlying physical link given the ALM distribution tree that is created. *Stretch* measures the ratio between the costs (generally in terms of latency or hop count) of the path from source to a participant in the ALM scheme compared to the direct unicast path between those hosts.

Several issues must be addressed if an ALM scheme is to be used for videoconferencing. Because videoconferencing is very sensitive to latency, managing stretch will be a prime concern. Since the number and location of participants in a video conference is usually reasonably stable, much of the complexity of ALM protocols for dealing with participants joining and leaving, also known as *churn*, may be avoided by precomputing an optimal distribution tree of the known participants and tailoring with as much knowledge about client capabilities and available bandwidth as possible. Since each peer will now be responsible for replicating packets for one or more children in the distribution tree, limiting the number of such media streams that need to be distributed will probably be necessary. This implies that floor control should be done in a centralized manner to select the media streams to be distributed to all participants.

Jitter Control

Jitter can be defined as the variance of the interarrival separation of a stream of packets. In other words, jitter is a measure of the latency variance experienced by packets transmitted through the Internet. The primary cause of jitter is the dynamic growing and shrinking of queues encountered in routers along the forwarding path. Thus, while a stream of packets originally transmitted at an even rate can be expected to arrive at that same average rate over some sufficiently long time scale, at shorter time scales, the packet arrival rate will fluctuate.

A subtle, but important, distinction needs to be made between packet jitter and media jitter. For media data types in which the natural application data unit is quite small relative to packet size, many samples of the media are generally packed into a single packet. For example, the natural data unit for audio data is a single audio sample. In the case of a monaural representation, this may be as small as 1 byte. In this case, packet-level jitter manifests itself as jitter between frames of audio data, where each frame is a collection of audio samples. For media data types in which the natural application data unit is larger relative to packet size, a media data unit is necessarily fragmented into two or more packets. For example, video frames, even when compressed, often do not fit into a single packet. Typically the packets that comprise a single video frame are sent with little to no separation followed by a delay between the last packet of one video frame and the first packet of the next. In this case, packet-level jitter does not directly translate into frame-level jitter. A videoconferencing system is ultimately most concerned with media jitter. To the degree that media jitter is a function of and reflects packet jitter, we can discuss the issue relative to packet jitter without belaboring the point.

Controlling jitter is important because users are sensitive to the smoothness of media playback. To control jitter, videoconferencing systems use a jitter buffer, which essentially delays playback of a media data unit in order to ensure that the next media unit arrives by the time it needs to be played. This additional delay is often referred to as the playout delay.

Synchronized clocks are not necessary to measure jitter and determine playout delay. Instead, a method based on modeling the difference between two unsynchronized clocks can be used. In this method, each media unit is timestamped by the sending host with the system time of its transmission. Upon the arrival of the first media unit, the receiving host calculates the clock offset as the difference between its system time and the time stamp carried by the media unit itself. This initial calculation of offset is shown in Equation 1.

$$offset = t_{current} - t_{media} \quad (1)$$

Using this offset value, the playout time in terms of the local system clock for this media unit and all subsequent media units is calculated using Equation 2.

$$playout = speed * t_{media} + offset \quad (2)$$

In this formula, the speed term represents the playback rate relative to the natural media rate. Values larger than one correspond to playing faster (i.e., fast forward) while values smaller than one correspond to playing slower (i.e., slow motion). For videoconferencing applications, this term is nearly always set to the value one. The value of offset models the end-to-end display latency. In our formulation above, this is initially determined by the first media unit, which, according to the formula in Equation 2, would be displayed immediately.

The key issue for this method is appropriately setting and adaptively changing the value of offset to accommodate dynamic network conditions. Naylor and Kleinrock (1982) first articulated the spectrum of choices for jitter buffers as lying between two policies that they call the "I-policy" and the "E-policy." The I-policy attempts to permanently set offset to a reasonably representative value and discards all media units that do not arrive by the calculated display times. At the other end of the spectrum, the E-policy resets the value of offset to accommodate the largest observed offset, ensuring that no subsequent media units that experience smaller delays will ever miss the calculated display time. Between the two extremes is any number of adaptive solutions.

Since offset models both the large-time-scale average network delay that the system must accommodate as well as an allowance for any small time-scale jitter, setting it based solely on the first media unit is insufficient, as the delay experienced by the first media unit may or may not be a representative value. Typically, offset is recalculated periodically as an exponential weighted moving average (EWMA) of the observed clock differences. Although this helps to smooth out the estimate for offset, the choice of gain coefficients of the EWMA filter still represents a design choice between an estimator that is very stable, but not particularly agile, and an estimator that is very agile, but not as stable (Kim and Noble 2001). Another technique is to recalculate the value of offset implicitly by monitoring the queue length of media units waiting to be displayed (Stone and Jeffay 1994). In other words, if the current value of offset results in a persistent queue of media units that arrive before the appropriate display time, offset is recalculated to effectively reduce the queue length.

Media elasticity is another issue that must be considered when designing an adaptive jitter buffer algorithm. *Elasticity* refers to the quality degradation associated with a media data type due to lost or discarded media units and/or presentation of those data units at a rate other than the natural media data rate. For example, video is a highly elastic data type, since the marginal effect on perceived quality of a missing frame is low. Furthermore, video can be displayed either at a faster or a slower rate than its natural frame rate without greatly affecting quality. This sort of time dilation and compression is almost imperceptible if it is within 10 percent of the natural frame rate. Audio, on the other hand, is not particularly elastic. Missing audio samples cause highly perceptible pops and other annoying artifacts, and it is much more difficult to play audio frames at any rate other than its natural rate without either causing gaps between audio frames sent to the audio device, perceptibly changing the pitch of the audio, and/or causing audio samples to be destructively played on top of each other.

The elasticity characteristics of the media type determine to what extent jitter buffer adjustments can be made and when. Jitter buffer adjustments for video can be done at almost any granularity and at almost any time because they can be implemented by taking advantage of the elastic nature of video as a media type. The same cannot be said of audio. Instead, a common technique for videoconferencing in which the audio is almost always human conversation is to take advantage of talkspurts. A talkspurt is a sequence of audio frames that represent continuous talking by one of the participants. Generally, talkspurts are separated by some amount of silence created by the natural back and forth between participants in the conversation and/or thinking times and breathing pauses between statements. These silence periods can be lengthened and/or shortened without any effect on the perceived quality of the audio stream, and thus represent the best opportunity to make adaptive changes to playout delay (Moon, Kurose, and Towsley 1998).

Transport Protocols

The development of early videoconferencing systems such as the vic/vat suite was done in conjunction with efforts by the IETF Audio/Visual Transport Working Group to develop suitable transport-level protocols for such systems. The results were definitions for the real-time protocol (RTP) and its companion real-time control protocol (RTCP) (Schulzrinne et al. 1996). Although intended to be used together and to support multicast, multiparty applications, either protocol can be effectively used separately and in unicast environments as well. Both of these protocols continue to be used in media streaming applications of all sorts, including videoconferencing. Because these protocols are described in greater detail elsewhere in this book, we only briefly review their main design features here in the context of videoconferencing.

The design of RTP and RTCP is firmly grounded in the principle of application layer framing (Clark and Tennenhouse 1990). This design principle stresses the concept that the application is in the best position to understand how the underlying constraints of the protocol stack (e.g., minimum/maximum packet size, etc.) and network dynamics (e.g., loss, delay, etc.) affect the overall quality of experience within the application. Toward this end, hidden costs and constraints should be exposed to the application, which can in turn adapt how it represents and frames data to achieve application-level goals. By applying this principle to the design of RTP and RTCP, its creators have purposefully underspecified many key elements of the protocol. Thus, the protocol specifications are incomplete and must be augmented with additional specifications to fill out the exact semantics of various header fields and the format and layout of data packets for a particular data type within the context of a particular application.

RTP provides a very thin header to support a number of basic media unit framing and transport tasks. The header includes the following fields:

- *Sequence number:* This 16-bit field is expected to monotonically increase, and numbers each packet in sequence in order to support loss detection.
- *Payload type:* This media-type-specific field identifies the data type encapsulated by the packet. The exact semantics of the time stamp field (described below) and the format and layout of data in the payload of this packet are determined by the value of this field.
- *Time stamp:* This field provides timing information for the media data unit represented by this packet. The granularity of the time stamp and its exact semantics is type-specific. For example, for audio data types, this time stamp essentially identifies the sample number of the first audio sample contained in the packet. For video data types, however, the time stamp represents the acquisition time of the video frame and is sampled from a 90-kHz clock.
- *Marker bit:* The semantics of this 1-bit field is also media-type-specific. For audio data types, the recommended use of the marker bit is to indicate talkspurt boundaries. For video data types, the recommended use of the marker bit is to indicate the last of a sequence of packets that all contribute to the same media data unit.
- *Synchronization source identifier (SSRC):* This 32-bit field is used to globally identify the participant associated with this media stream. By using the same SSRC for all RTP streams associated with this participant, the application can associate related streams, such as which video stream belongs to which audio stream.

RTCP is used to provide feedback on the quality of a received media stream and to distribute timing information that can be used to synchronize media streams from different participants and make jitter buffer adjustments. RTCP also supports distributing identifying information associated with a SSRC such as a human-readable canonical name, e-mail address, geographic location, etc. Finally, RTCP can be extended in application-specific ways to provide other types of control information such as floor control, capability negotiation, and other session-control mechanisms. The RTCP specification provides recommendations and algorithms for determining the frequency of RTCP report packets by monitoring the rate of received RTCP packets from other participants. This decentralized approach was motivated by the characteristics of the IP multicast service model, in which the exact number of participants in a multicast group may not be exactly known.

VIDEO REPRESENTATIONS

To some degree, the choice of video compression algorithm to be used within a videoconferencing system is somewhat arbitrary. While keeping bandwidth requirements as small as possible motivates compression, any number of video representations will do. At the same time, however, the computational costs and compression benefits of various compression techniques make some video representations better for videoconferencing than others. In this section, we first describe several general video compression techniques and discuss their suitability for video conferencing applications. Then we quickly review a number of specific video compression standards that were either specifically designed for videoconferencing or have been found to be useful for videoconferencing.

General Video Compression Techniques

At the heart of almost every video compression algorithm is some sort of transform-based encoding that converts the spatial-domain representation of a block of pixels into an equivalent frequency-domain representation of those pixels. The most widely used transform is the discrete cosine transform (DCT). The primary benefits of using a frequency transform is to concentrate the energy of the pixel information into a small number of coefficients. A second benefit is that different coefficients that correspond to different frequency bands can be quantized separately in order to selectively preserve more information in coefficients representing lower frequencies and possibly eliminate coefficients that represent higher frequencies. Although doing so necessitates a loss of information, the human visual system is less sensitive to the loss of high-frequency information. The DCT is particularly useful, since very efficient implementations of the 8×8 2D DCT have been developed.

Motion compensation is another key technique used by most video compression algorithms. Motion compensation exploits the temporal coherence between video frames. Block-based motion compensation tiles the pixel data into non-overlapping blocks of the same size and searches for a motion vector that selects a region of pixels within some reference frame to use a predictive basis for the pixels to be encoded. The residual error values are calculated as the difference between the target pixel values to be encoded and the reference region selected. The motion vector and an encoding of the residual values are then sent instead of the original pixel values.

Although motion compensation is effective, it creates an encoding dependency between a frame and the reference frame(s) from which the predictive pixel values are selected. This becomes problematic if a frame that serves as a reference frame is lost or contains errors due to packet loss. The use of motion compensation will propagate this error to future frames or even prevent future frames from being decoded at all. In some video compression algorithms, most notably the various MPEG standards, frames are classified by their use of motion compensation. I-frames use no motion compensation at all, and thus in the event of a catastrophic loss of packets, decoding can always be resumed at the next I-frame. P-frames use the previous I- or P-frame as a reference frame. A sequence of P-frames forms a dependency chain, which, if broken or damaged, will propagate errors until an I-frame is encountered. B-frames can use both the previous I- or P-frame as well as the next I- or P-frame as possible reference frames. Since B-frames are not used as a reference frame by any other frame, errors are not propagated. Because B-frames may depend on future frames, however, the encoding and decoding order of the frames is not the same as the display order of the frames. For videoconferencing application in which end-to-end latency is key, B-frames are almost never used because they require additional coding latency in order to encode the future reference frame first. Instead, a sequence of P-frames between periodic I-frames in order to provide error control is most common. Figure 3 illustrates these concepts.

Furthermore, the search for the best motion vector can be very expensive if a large window of motion is considered. Again, this is problematic for a videoconferencing application, in which latency must be kept to a minimum. Fortunately, the video characteristics within a conferencing application lend itself to a number of heuristics. Since the camera rarely moves in a videoconferencing application, global motion due to camera movement is generally absent. Usually pixels are either part of the background or part of a coherent foreground (i.e., the face and body of the participant). Finally, participant motion is generally smooth and reasonably small, so the search for a good motion vector can be abbreviated to a smaller window.

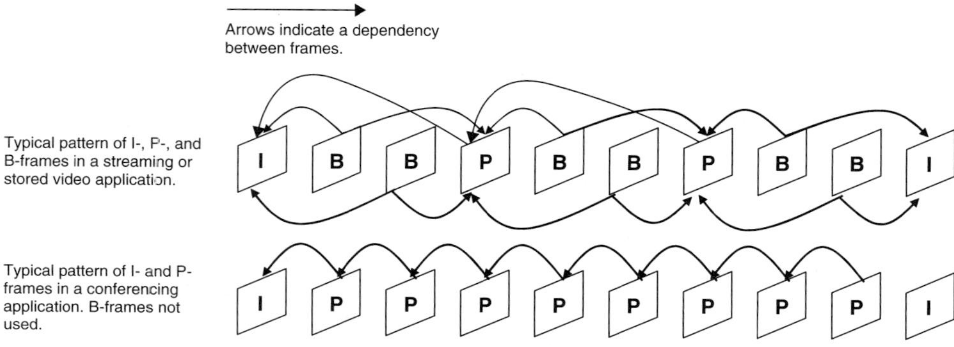

Figure 3: I-, P-, and B-frame relationships

Video Compression Standards

One of the earliest video compression standards specifically designed to support videoconferencing applications was the ITU standard H.261, also sometimes referred to as p*64 kbs (ITU 1993). First published in 1990, this standard contains support for two different frame sizes: CIF (352 pixels wide by 288 pixels high) and QCIF (176 pixels wide by 144 pixels high). Pixel data are organized into three planes, with one luminance plane and two subsampled chrominance planes. The standard uses DCT-based transform encoding and forward-only motion compensation. This standard was designed to support videoconferencing over integrated services digital network (ISDN) lines. A variant of H.261, called "intra-H.261," was developed as part of the early vic/vat suite. In this variant, the use of motion compensation is reduced strictly to either reusing the same block of pixels from the prior frame (i.e., a zero motion vector) or replacing the block entirely with a transform-encoded block of pixels (i.e., not using motion compensation at all).

Experience from the development and use of H.261 led to the evolutionary development of H.263 in 1995 (ITU 2005, H.263). The main improvements included a much wider set of supported frame sizes, the use of arithmetic coding as a final entropy encoding step, wider options on motion vector search, and half-pixel resolution for its motion compensation algorithm. Further improvements were published in 1997 as a series of annexes to the original H.263 algorithm resulting in what is known as H.263v2 or H.263+. The most significant of these was the ability to signal which of several previously transmitted frames was to be used as a reference frame. This scheme, known as NEWPRED, allowed the encoder to use only frames that were known via feedback from the receiver to be properly received as reference frames for future frames. While some temporal coherence is forfeited, the scheme prevents errors in reference streams from being propagated to future frames, thus supporting very long sequences of P-frames.

The most recent video compression standard to emerge for video conferencing is H.264 (ITU 2005, H.264). This standard was developed jointly by the ITU and the MPEG consortium and is also published under the name MPEG-4/Part 10. The standard is also known as the advanced video coding (AVC) standard. This standard was published in 2003 and is the culmination of years of experience and research from both the prior H.26x standards as well as the MPEG-1 and MPEG-2 standards. It has been shown to be capable of providing excellent video quality at a very wide range of bit rates. As a result, many industry experts believe that H.264 will quickly become the industry standard for most video applications including streaming and conferencing. The standard is incredibly feature-rich, and different feature sets are specified in a profile and level system in order to allow different levels of interoperability and to trim the feature set to only those appropriate for a particular application domain. For videoconferencing, the baseline profile (BP) is most appropriate. This profile includes support for forward (but not backward) motion compensation, multiple reference frames, a deblocking filter, context-based arithmetic coding, and redundant slices, which is a form of forward error correction.

AUDIO REPRESENTATIONS

The data rates associated with audio streams are generally much smaller than the associated video data rates. Similarly, audio encoding is computationally less complex than video compression. This section briefly describes several different audio standards defined by the ITU that have been used in various videoconferencing systems over the years. Since the techniques of representing and transmitting audio in a videoconferencing system are almost identical to those used in VoIP applications, our treatment here is very brief.

G.711

The G.711 standard is an 8-bit-per-sample pulse code modulation (PCM) scheme that uses a simple type of compression called "companding," which provides approximately the same quality as an uncompressed signal using 12 or 16 bits per sample. This standard was originally published in 1972 for use in telephony (ITU 1988, G7.11). The basic idea behind companding is to use a logarithmic scale instead of a linear scale to provide greater resolution for sample values with relatively small amplitudes compared to sample values with relatively large amplitudes. Two main algorithms are defined in the standard, and these variants are commonly called mu-law and A-law. Both variants work in approximately the same way, but the coefficients and constants used by A-law have been specifically selected in order to be numerically easier to manipulate with a computer using binary arithmetic.

G.722

The G.722 standard uses an adaptive differential pulse code modulation (ADPCM) scheme in which the difference between successive samples is encoded instead of the sample values themselves (ITU 1988, G.722). The scheme is adaptive in that the granularity with which these differences are represented is changed depending on the relative size of recent differences. The target bit rate of G.722 is 32 to 64 kbps. Variants of G.722 intended to support even lower bitrates include G.722.1 and G.722.2. All of these variants sample data at 16 kHz, which is about twice that of the standard telephone rate.

G.728

The G.728 standard is a speech-specific codec that uses low delay code excited linear prediction, or LD-CELP (ITU 1992). This method is an example of a vocoder, which attempts to model speech as an underlying fundamental frequency and as set of filter coefficients that modify it. The main feature of the G.728 standard is that it incurs a very small encoding delay and operates at 16 kbps.

THE FUTURE OF VIDEOCONFERENCING

Gaze Awareness

The most recent advances in videoconferencing have been in the direction of increasing the sense of presence experienced by the participants. One way to do so is to provide participants with gaze awareness and eye contact. A common shortcoming of many videoconferencing systems is that because participants are looking at the screen in order to see the other participants and not looking directly at the camera, each participant appears to be looking away at something off to the side or in the distance. Since this occurs for all participants, no one appears to be looking at each other, even though they are clearly talking directly with each other. In multi-party systems, this effect can be particularly noticeable, since gaze awareness (i.e., whom each participant is looking at) is the basis for how people naturally negotiate floor control in a group conversation. One way to incorporate gaze awareness and eye contact into a videoconferencing system is to warp the video image to make it appear as if participants are looking directly at each other (Wa et al. 2003; Gemmell and Zhu 2002; Grayson and Monk 2003). This may require calculating (or at least approximating) the geometric relationship between the camera, the screen, and the participant. Another way to achieve this effect in a meeting room setting is to use pinhole cameras set into a projection screen. In this case, the effect of eye contact is achieved directly.

Another approach to increasing the sense of presence in a multi-party conference is to create a virtual meeting room by combining the video streams of many participants together as if each participant was in the same room. Such a system presents each with a rendering of the virtual space from an appropriate viewpoint. The experimental Coliseum system developed by Hewlett-Packard is an excellent example of this kind of system (Baker et al. 2005). Coliseum used several cameras to capture each participant from several different angles simultaneously. Using these video streams, the system was able to do background separation and calculate a visual hull as a rough approximation of each participant's head and shoulders. This rough geometric information was used to warp the foreground image into a virtual meeting space and render views of this virtual meeting space for each participant.

Tele-Immersion

Whereas Coliseum takes a 2.5-dimensional approach to providing a sense of presence, other research efforts are investigating true 3-dimensional approaches. These systems are often referred to as tele-immersion systems (Kauff and Schreer 2002; Gross et al. 2003; Sadagic et al. 2001). A tele-immersion systems captures the imagery of a relatively small (i.e., room-sized) environment from a number of different cameras placed at different viewpoints. These systems may then extract per-pixel information from the video streams using algorithms developed for computer vision. Alternatively, the video streams may be used to form an approximation of the plenoptic function. The plenoptic function models all of the light rays passing through a volume. Several representations of the plenoptic function have been developed, including light fields (Levoy and Hanrahan 1996), layered depth images (Shade et al. 1998), and concentric mosaics (Shum and He 1999). These systems may also make use of polygonal geometric models derived either from the imagery itself or provided a priori for known structures within the room (e.g., walls, furniture, etc.). At the remote site, all of this information is then recombined into a three-dimensional rendering of the environment. This may be accomplished with head-mounted stereo displays, autostereoscopic displays, stereo project displays, or display caves.

The computational demands and bandwidth requirements of tele-immersion systems are obviously much greater than traditional, single-camera videoconferencing. Although one can easily realize a simple videoconferencing application with commodity off-the-shelf components, a tele-immersion system once again requires complex experimental software, hardware, and networking components. It may be reasonable to ask whether the failure of videoconferencing to live up to its potential foretells a similar fate for tele-immersion. In fact, it is the relative failure of videoconferencing as an application that motivates much of the work in tele-immersion. The argument put forth by many tele-immersion researchers is that videoconferencing does not provide a sufficient marginal advantage over simple audio conferencing to warrant its use. If the sense of presence achieved by a tele-immersion system was compelling to the point of people truly feeling that they were within a shared space, the marginal utility of using such a system would increase. Furthermore, tele-immersion systems would then find use in situations that demand such a compelling sense of presence such as battleground operations or surgical procedures.

GLOSSARY

Application-Level Framing (ALF): A design principle that argues that hidden costs and limitations of the network should be exposed to the application in order to best adjust the packetization and framing of application data units.

Application-Level Multicast (ALM): An implementation of multicast that does not rely on in-network support for packet replication and forwarding but organizes the participants of the multicast group themselves into a peer-to-peer distribution tree.

Arithmetic Coding: A form of lossless entropy encoding that produces near-optimal compression given a specific model of symbol frequencies.

B-Frame: A video frame that uses motion compensation using reference frames from either the near past and/or the near future but does not serve as a reference frame itself.

Churn: A term used to characterize the dynamics of multicast or peer-to-peer group membership.

Content Distribution Network (CDN): An overlay network embedded within the Internet using provisioned resources carefully located at strategic peering points.

Discrete Cosine Transform (DCT): A transform coding technique that represents a one- or two-dimensional field of pixel values in the frequency domain using cosine functions that form an orthonormal basis.

Elasticity: The degree to which a media type can be displayed at rates that deviate from the original sampling rate with little observable decrease in quality.

Entropy Coding: A data-compression technique in which variable-length codes are assigned to input symbols in order to take advantage of an uneven distribution of symbol frequencies.

E-Policy: One end of the spectrum of jitter buffer policies in which the playout delay is adjusted to accommodate the largest observed delay.

Exponential Weighted Moving Average (EWMA): A technique for estimating a long-term average from spot sample values of a noisy signal in which the contribution of a spot value decays over time.

Floor Control: A mechanism for determining which participant in a conference is the primary speaker at any given time.

Forward Error Correction: A technique for proactively sending redundant representations of previously transmitted information in order to guard against possible packet loss.

Gaze Awareness: The ability (either simulated or real) for a conferencing participant to establish eye contact with another participant.

I-Frame: A video frame that is encoded without use of motion compensation such that it can be decoded correctly whether or not previous frames have been received or contain errors.

IP Multicast: An in-network forwarding service that allows a packet to be sent to a group of receivers by replicating the packet at routers in order to traverse a distribution tree.

I-Policy: One end of the spectrum of jitter buffer policies in which the jitter buffer is never adjusted after a playout delay has been established, despite future variations in delay.

Jitter: The variance of transmission latency experienced in a packet network.

Jitter Buffer: A receiver-side mechanism for ameliorating the effects of jitter.

Motion Compensation: A video-compression technique that uses past (or possibly future) frames to predict the value of blocks of pixels by discovering global or local motion within the scene and transmitting only the residual difference.

Multipoint Control Unit (MCU): A component of a centralized conferencing architecture that is responsible for receiving the media streams of each participant and transmitting a composite stream back to each participant for display.

P-Frame: A video frame that uses forward-only motion compensation from a past reference frame and may serve as a reference frame for other frames.

Peer-to-Peer (P2P): A decentralized application architecture in which peers participate with equivalent or similar capacity and communicate directly with each other.

Playout Delay: The end-to-end delay target used to schedule the display of a media unit.

Plenoptic Function: A function that models all light passing through a volume in space.

Real-Time Control Protocol (RTCP): The IETF-developed control and feedback protocol designed to be used in conjunction with RTP in conferencing and streaming systems.

Real-Time Protocol (RTP): An IETF-developed transport protocol based on the principles of application-level framing used in videoconferencing and streaming systems.

Single-Source Multicast: An alternative to IP multicast that limits each multicast group to have exactly one prespecified source of packets.

Stress: A metric used to evaluate how often a duplicate packet traverses any given link using an application-level multicast scheme.

Stretch: A metric used to evaluate the latency penalty of the path from source to receiver in an application-level multicast scheme as compared to the shortest unicast path available.

Talkspurt: A period of audio samples that correspond to continuous speech separated from the next and previous talkspurts by silence associated with natural breath pauses and/or changes in who is speaking.

Tele-Immersion: An advanced form of videoconferencing in which three-dimensional information and multiple camera angles are used to provide a heightened sense of presence.

Vocoder: An audio-compression technique designed for human speech that analyzes an input signal in order to derive coefficients and parameters for a corresponding synthesis process.

CROSS REFERENCES

See *Computer Conferencing and Distance Learning*; *IP Multicast*; *Video Compression*.

REFERENCES

Baker, H. H., N. Bhatti, D. Tanguay, I. Sobel, D. Gelb, M. E. Goss, W. B. Culbertson, and T. Malzbender. 2005. Understanding performance in coliseum, an immersive videoconferencing system. *ACM Transactions Multimedia Computing and Communication Applications* 1(2):190–210.

Banerjee, S., B. Bhattacharjee, and C. Kommareddy. 2002. Scalable application layer multicast. In *Proceedings of the 2002 Conference on Applications, Technologies, Architectures, and Protocols for Computer Communications, Pittsburgh, Pennsylvania, USA, August 19–23, 2002*, 205–17. New York: ACM Press.

Calyam, P., M. Sridharan, W. Mandrawa, and P. Schopis. 2004. Performance measurement and analysis of H.323 traffic. In *Proceedings of the 5th International Workshop on Passive and Active Network Measurement* (Antibes Juan-les-Pins, France, April 19–20, 2004). New York: Springer Lecture Notes in Computer Science 3015.

Chu, Y., S. G. Rao, and H. Zhang. 2000. A case for end system multicast (keynote address). In *Proceedings of the 2000 ACM SIGMETRICS International Conference on Measurement and Modeling of Computer Systems.*

Santa Clara, California, United States, June 18–21, 2000, 1–12. New York: ACM Press.

Chu, Y., S. Rao, Seshan, S. and H. Zhang. 2001. Enabling conferencing applications on the internet using an overlay multicast architecture. In *Proceedings of the 2001 Conference on Applications, Technologies, Architectures, and Protocols For Computer Communications, San Diego, California, United States,* 55–67. New York: ACM Press.

Clark, D. D., and D. L. Tennenhouse. 1990. Architectural considerations for a new generation of protocols. In *Proceedings of the ACM Symposium on Communications Architectures & Protocols. Philadelphia, Pennsylvania, United States, September 26–28, 1990*, 200–8. New York: ACM Press.

Deering, S. E. 1988. Multicast routing in internetworks and extended LANs. In *Symposium Proceedings on Communications Architectures and Protocols, Stanford, California, United States, August 16–18, 1988*, edited by V. Cerf, 55–64. New York: ACM Press.

Dorcey, T. 1995. The CU-SeeMe desktop videoconferencing software. *ConneXions* 9(3):42–5.

Egido, C. 1988. Video conferencing as a technology to support group work: a review of its failures. In *Proceedings of the 1988 ACM Conference on Computer-Supported Cooperative Work, Portland, Oregon, United States, September 26–28, 1988,* 13–24. New York: ACM Press.

Fish, R. S., R. E. Kraut, R. W. Root, and R. E. Rice. 1992. Evaluating video as a technology for informal communication. In *Proceedings of the SIGCHI Conference on Human Factors in Computing Systems, Monterey, California, United States, May 3–7, 1992*, edited by P. Bauersfeld, J. Bennett, and G. Lynch, 37–48. New York: ACM Press.

Fredricks, R. 1992. *nv: Network Video Tool*. Page from the manual distributed with Unix.

Gemmell, J., and D. Zhu. 2002. Implementing gaze-corrected videoconferencing. In *Proceedings of the IASTED International Conference on Communications Internet and Information Technology*, 382–7. Anaheim, CA: ACTA Press.

Grayson, D. M., and A. F. Monk. 2003. Are you looking at me? Eye contact and desktop video conferencing. *ACM Transactions in Computer-Human Interaction* 10(3):221–43.

Gross, M., S. Würmlin, M. Naef, E. Lamboray, C. Spagno, A. Kunz, E. Koller-Meier, T. Svoboda, L. Van Gool, S. Lang, K. Strehlke, A. V. Moere, and O. Staadt. 2003. Blue-c: A spatially immersive display and 3D video portal for telepresence. *ACM Transactions on Graphics* 22(3):819–27.

Holbrook, H. W., and D. R. Cheriton. 1999. IP multicast channels: EXPRESS support for large-scale single-source applications. In *Proceedings of the Conference on Applications, Technologies, Architectures, and Protocols for Computer Communication, Cambridge, Massachusetts, United States, August 30–September 3, 1999*, 65–78. New York: ACM Press.

Isaacs, E., and J. C. Tang. 1994. What video can and cannot do for collaboration. *Journal of Multimedia Systems*, vol. 2, 63–73. New York: Springer-Verlag.

ITU. 1988. *G.711: Pulse code modulation (PCM) of voice frequencies*. www.itu.int/rec/T-REC-G.711 (accessed June 23, 2007).

ITU. 1988. *G.722: 7 kHz audio-coding within 64 kbits/s*. www.itu.int/rec/T-REC-G.722 (accessed June 23, 2007).

ITU. 1992. *G.728: Coding of speech at 16 kbit/s using low-delay code excited linear prediction* www.itu.int/rec/T-REC-G.728 (accessed June 23, 2007).

ITU. 1993. *H.261: Video codec for audiovisual services at* $p \times 64$ *kbit/s*. www.itu.int/rec/T-REC-H.261 (accessed June 23, 2007).

ITU. 2005. *H.263: Video coding for low bit rate communication*. www.itu.int/rec/T-REC-H.263 (accessed June 23, 2007).

ITU. 2005. *H.264: Advanced video coding for generic audiovisual services*. www.itu.int/rec/T-REC-H.264 (accessed June 23, 2007).

ITU. 2006. *H.323v6: Packet-based multimedia communications systems*. www.itu.int/rec/T-REC-H.323 (accessed June 23, 2007).

Kauff, P., and O. Schreer. 2002. An immersive 3D videoconferencing system using shared virtual team user environments. In *Proceedings of the 4th International Conference on Collaborative Virtual Environments, Bonn, Germany, September 30–October 02, 2002*, 105–12. New York: ACM Press.

Kim, M., and B. Noble. 2001. Mobile network estimation. In *Proceedings of the 7th Annual International Conference on Mobile Computing and Networking, Rome, Italy*, 298–309. New York: ACM Press.

Kostić, D., A. Rodriguez, J. Albrecht, and A. Vahdat. 2003. Bullet: High bandwidth data dissemination using an overlay mesh. In *Proceedings of the Nineteenth ACM Symposium on Operating Systems Principles, Bolton Landing, NY, USA, October 19–22, 2003)*, 282–97. New York: ACM Press.

Krauss, R. M., and P. D. Bricker. 1967. Effects of transmission delay and access delay on the efficiency of verbal communication. *Journal of the Acoustical Society of America* 41:286–92.

Krim, J. 2005, September 13. EBay to acquire internet phone leader. *The Washington Post*, D01.

Levoy, M., and P. Hanrahan. 1996. Light field rendering. In *Proceedings of the 23rd Annual Conference on Computer Graphics and Interactive Techniques*, 31–42. New York: ACM Press.

McCanne, S., and V. Jacobson. 1995. vic: A flexible framework for packet video. In *Proceedings of the Third ACM International Conference on Multimedia, San Francisco, California, United States, November 5–9, 1995*, 511–22. New York: ACM Press.

Moon, S. B., J. Kurose, and D. Towsley. 1998. Packet audio playout delay adjustment: performance bounds and algorithms. *Multimedia Systems* 6(1):17–28.

Naylor, W. E., and L. Kleinrock. 1982. Stream traffic communication in packet-switched networks: Destination buffering considerations. *IEEE Transactions on Communications* 30(12):2527–34.

Ratnasamy, S., M. Handley, R. Karp, and S. Shanker. 2001. Application-level multicast using content-addressable networks. In *Proceedings of the 3rd International Workshop on Networked Group Communication*. Berlin, Germany: Springer-Verlag.

Rosenberg, J., H. Schulzerinne, G. Camarillo, A. Johnston, J. Pertson, R. Sparks, M. Handley, and E. Schooler. 2002. *SIP: Session Initiation Protocol*, Internet Engineering Task Force RFC 3261. www.ietf.org/rfc/rfc3261.txt (accessed June 23, 2007).

Sadagic, A., H. Towles, J. Lanier, H. Fuchs, A. Van Dam, K. Daniilidis, J. Mulligan, L. Holden, and B. Zeleznik. 2001. National tele-immersion initiative: Towards compelling tele-immersive collaborative environments. Presentation given at Medicine Meets Virtual Reality 2001 Conference.

Schulzrinne, H., S. Casner, R. Frederick, and V. Jacobson, 1996. *RTP:A transport protocol for real-time applications*. Internet Engineering Task Force RFC 1889.

Shade, J., S. Gortler, L. He, and R. Szeliski. 1998. Layered depth images. In *Proceedings of the 25th Annual Conference on Computer Graphics and Interactive Techniques*, 231–42. New York: ACM Press.

Shum, H., and L. He. 1999. Rendering with concentric mosaics. In *Proceedings of the 26th Annual Conference on Computer Graphics and Interactive Techniques*, 299–306. New York: ACM Press/Addison-Wesley.

Stone, D., and K. Jeffay. 1994. Queue monitoring: A delay jitter management policy. In *Proceedings of the 4th International Workshop on Network and Operating System Support for Digital Audio and Video (NOSSDAV)*, edited by D. Shepherd et al., 149–216. New York: Springer Lecture Notes in Computer Science, 846.

Turletti, T. 1994. The INRIA videoconferencing system (IVS). *ConneXions* 8(10):20–4.

Verma, D. 2002. *Content distribution networks: An engineering approach*. New York: Wiley.

Wa, J., R. Renaud, A. Vincent, et al. 2003. Stereoscopic video telephony: naturalness and sense of presence. *Proceedings of the SPIE—The International Society for Optical Engineering* 5243(1):19–29.

Woolley, D. R. 2006. *Video conferencing and conference calling: An independent guide to video conferencing and phone conferencing products and services*. www.thinkofit.com/webconf/video.htm (accessed June 23, 2007).

Zhang, R., and Y. C. Hu. 2003. Borg: A hybrid protocol for scalable application-level multicast in peer-to-peer networks. In *Proceedings of the 13th International Workshop on Network and Operating Systems Support for Digital Audio and Video, Monterey, CA, USA, June 1–3, 2003*, 172–9. New York: ACM Press.

Computer Conferencing: Protocols and Applications

William R. Gillis and Colleen Taugher, *WSU Center to Bridge the Digital Divide*

INTRODUCTION

The history of communications is filled with examples of a nearly insatiable demand for connectedness. As dispersed work has become more common practice among business and public institutions, so too has the need for computer-facilitated solutions that enable efficient work collaboration among those separated by distance or responsibilities within business enterprise functions.

Computer conferencing systems are an evolving family of information communication technologies supported through a variety of protocols, which can be selected depending on the communication functions desired by those involved in the conferencing application (Table 1). For example, network voice protocols (NVPs) can enable computer conferencing functions as simple as a telephone conference that is scheduled and monitored by a computer. When conferencing communication requires rapid online text interchange, Internet relay chat (H.323 IRC) can provide the needed functionality. A growing number of computer conferencing applications are optimized with voice over Internet protocols (VoIPs) combined with an interactive Web site where multiple users manipulate documents through a common database, share screens and talk with the group, instant message, or a combination of these. Real-time transport protocols (RTPs) enable opportunities for more complex communications by adding multimedia communication connecting supporting digital interaction among multiple users. Increasingly, computer conference participants are beginning to add Web cams into the mix, effectively blurring the lines between a computer conference

Table 1: Computer Conferencing Protocols

Protocol	Description
VoIP (voice over Internet protocol)	VoIP routes voice conversations over the Internet over an IP-based network using a packet switched network rather than telephone lines.
H.323, IRC (Internet relay chat [IRC])	IRC is a plaintext, open protocol used for instant communication over the Internet. Users initiate the protocol by connecting a client to an IRC server.
RTP (real-time transport protocol)	RTP is a standardized packet format for delivering audio and video data over the Internet using a dynamic port range.
SIP (session initiation protocol)	SIP is a protocol designed for initiating, modifying, and ending user sessions using interactive media such as online games, video, voice, instant messaging, and virtual reality.
NVP (network voice protocol)	NVP is an early protocol for transporting voice communications over the Internet via packets. It can be viewed as a precursor to VoIP.

and a videoconference. These are just several examples of common protocols that facilitate today's computer conferencing applications.

Although evolving protocols enable increasingly rich interactions, the more basic computer conferencing technologies have been available for many years. Both real-time and asynchronous text communication, in fact, have been around since the very earliest days of the Web and continue to play a role in computer conferencing today. First-generation online technologies such as e-mail, listservs, and bulletin boards were a valuable step forward for collaborative computing; however, the functionality of these early technologies lacked the complexity needed for many distributed team collaboration applications. For example, e-mail is optimized for one-on-one communication and listservs and bulletin boards lack the dynamic and targeted communication functions often desired for teamwork.

NetMeeting was the first true Web conferencing application that allowed screen sharing, file sharing, and real-time communication and a much richer experience than a simple text discussion. NetMeeting was introduced by Microsoft in the mid-1990s as a free download that relied on peer-to-peer communication to function. Since then, many vendors—such as IBM, Cisco, WebX, GoToMeeting, and Genesys—have entered the market.

New generations of computer conferencing tools are designed to meet the need of enhanced integrated communication that provides a rich collaborative work environment for participants working from multiple locations and with potentially very different communication needs and abilities. Evolving open standards based on Internet protocols such as session initiation protocol (SIP) are rapidly enabling more complex and rich integrated computer conferencing flexibility than early generations of software. Today's Web conferencing tools typically include things such as text conferencing and videoconferencing capabilities, shared calendars, discussion forums, document sharing, instant messaging, and whiteboard features, either offered individually or in combination. They allow for both real-time and asynchronous communication.

Under optimal circumstances, computer conferencing and Web collaboration tools are both easy to use and rich enough in functionality to support more complex integrated voice, video, and data communication interactions. Unfortunately, the reality is that there is generally a trade-off between ease of use and the degree of communication functionality that can be supported by computer conferencing software. Conferencing software that can support complex integrated communication functions often can be difficult to use, and especially complicated to maintain and integrate, with users operating from multiple platforms and with diverse experience. It is not probable that online collaboration can ever fully replace face-to-face communication. Nevertheless, the future is a promising one, in which computer conferencing software continues to make inroads into supporting complex business and social communication needs.

This chapter explores the origins of computer conferencing, its value in application, as well as emerging protocols important to the future of conferencing and collaboration in the digital world.

THE PARADIGM SHIFT TO COLLABORATIVE COMPUTING

Computer conferencing and Web collaboration are a mainstay of human interaction within today's workplace ; however, they are relatively recent within the history of computation. Indeed, computing began as a solitary task. From the inception in 1940s until the late 1960s, the fledgling computational machines filled entire rooms and were accessible by only one user and one program at a time. Tracing the history of collaborative computing, Laiserin (2000) notes it was not until the introduction of AT&T Bell Lab's UNIX platform in 1969 that a paradigm shift emerged with an engineering transformation to support the sharing of simple files for real-time collaboration among multiple users. David Wooley (1994) identifies the origins of computer conferencing to have occurred as early as 1973 with the creation of PLATO, which was among the early systems to pioneer online forums and message boards, e-mail, chat rooms, instant messaging, remote screen sharing, and multiplayer games, leading to the emergence of what was perhaps the world's first online community.

In the 1960s and 1970s, most computing was accomplished with large mainframe computers shared by multiple users. However, the mainframe computing environment at that time was still relatively inaccessible and available to only an elite few in universities and large research organizations. Consequently, although collaborative computing was technically enabled in the early 1970s, the number of people with equipment and knowledge to engage in such collaboration was relatively small.

DEC delivered its first production version of the PDP-1 microcomputer early in 1961. In his detailed history of personal computing technology, Alan (2001) observes that the term *personal computer* was coined to make a distinction from the shared mainframe devices to recognize a computer made for use by one individual. Although the personal computer (PC) began to gather greater commercial significance and became more affordable to ordinary people later in the 1970s, the technology was not an immediate catalyst for collaborative computing. Rather, PCs were used as smaller personal versions of the early mainframe devices, with single users accessing stored files from their personal digital storage space at a given time. In the 1980s, the practice of computing as an independent solitary task was eventually overtaken by a growing value being found in the early UNIX-based Internet, which was transformed to be accessible to PC users. However, it was not until the following decade and the acceptance of Tim Berners-Lee's World Wide Web as the system of standards that would enable computer owners throughout the world to share and exchange information in a common format that the paradigm of collaborative computing began to truly accelerate (Berners-Lee and Fischetti 2000).

EMERGENCE OF VALUE: A NEW GENERATION OF INTERACTIVE DIGITAL NETWORKS

Ultimately, the value of computer conferencing hinges critically on the availability of a robust and cost-effective digital communications network over which conferencing applications can be conducted. George Gilder (1993) coined the phrase *Metcalf's law*, recognizing the groundbreaking work of Robert Metcalf in creating a formula to predict the value of communication network technologies. Specifically, the value of a network equals the square of the number of users, while the value of an individual is proportional only to the number of users.

Prior to 1990, the value of computer conferencing was limited in part because an accessible interconnected network did not exist. With the Internet and eventually the World Wide Web well established to support the interconnectivity needs of the growing number of businesses, public institutions, and households owning PCs, the necessary foundation for the takeoff of computer conferencing and associated Web collaboration tools was in place by the early 1990s. Businesses, public institutions, and to a lesser extent, ordinary households became aware of the power and value of being able to communicate and share data with others around the world using connections through the Internet.

Along with the recognition of value came new consumer demands for both software and hardware to improve the versatility, functionality, accessibility, and affordability of computer conferencing and collaboration. Not only was there a growing demand for digital tools, enabling the productive sharing of data, voice conversations, and video images, but also there was a growing demand for real-time access to desired digital information 24 hours a day, 7 days a week using multiple information communication devices from a variety of locations.

With expanded recognition of the potential value of modern computation as an "always-on" information communication network, computer equipment and software engineers moved into high gear in the 1990s. Initially, new products and services catered to the business customer who wanted to communicate, real-time and anytime, with customers and business partners around the globe using a full suite of integrated digital data conferencing, voice conferencing, and videoconferencing capabilities. The rapidly growing suite of digital computer conferencing tools, designed first for global business purposes, very quickly evolved to meet the needs of small businesses, schools, health care organizations, and individuals.

As advances and affordability of microchip technologies continued, various innovative computer conferencing technologies quickly came to market, including videoconferencing shared digital workspaces for project collaboration, instant text messaging, asynchronous text conferencing, enterprise information portals, real-time digital whiteboards, shared data storage applications, and others. This, along with a variety of Web-application service providers that were available to help business and individual customers use and cost-effectively integrate and apply the growing suite of computer conferencing tools, provided customized solutions to individual challenges.

Further catalyzing the demand for computer conferencing products and services was the concurrent expansion of mobile computing and communication technologies, beginning with mobile phones and morphing quickly into new personal digital devices with the computing power of desktop PCs only a few years earlier. Historical telecommunications data published by CellularOnline (2006) indicate that in 1992, there were only about 200,000 handheld mobile phone units in use worldwide. By 2004, there were well over 1.5 billion handheld mobile phones in use throughout the world. In addition to these handheld devices, ownership and use of powerful laptop computers has skyrocketed over the past decade, further enabling computer conferencing and digital work collaboration to be possible almost anyplace an Internet connection is feasible.

Another critical technological enabler catalyzing the value of computer conferencing is the wider availability of high-speed Internet connection points. Broadband wireless technologies continue to proliferate both within and outside of the United States, making 24/7 high-speed Internet connections for computer conferencing available not only at the usual place of work, but also in airports, hotels, coffeehouses, and other locations where computer users may gather.

A final and important network enabler of computer conferencing is the growing universal availability of free or low-cost voice over Internet protocol (VoIP). VoIP can be expected to have a transformative impact on computer conferencing capability by providing a critical link of fully compatible video, data, and voice connections to be cost-effectively integrated over a single Internet communications backbone.

TECHNOLOGY EVOLUTION

Although Web-based communication tools have been with us for a number of years, there has been a recent shift in their design that changes the way people can work together over the Internet. Table 2 illustrates the transformation from first-generation Web tools to new tools that allow a different attitude about collaborative work. In each instance, there is a change from a hierarchical management system controlled by a select group of people to fully collaborative and personalized creative work spaces.

Online tools have evolved over the past several years to improve the perceived value of computer conferencing for collaborating colleagues. Taxonomies and BitTorrent, for example, allow participants working from diverse contexts, to more easily customize conferencing applications to their unique scenarios. Wikis and blogging enable content development from multiple participants without hierarchical filters to more closely match the way work is actually accomplished in many organizational settings. Web services enable more effective collaboration among participants working from different organizations or remotely in different time zones to effectively participate in conferencing. These are just several of the positive recent trends improving the relevance and the likely acceptance of computer conferencing within the business setting.

THE TRANSFORMATION OF WORKPLACE

Computer conferencing has significantly changed the business paradigm and the way work is accomplished in much of the industrialized world. Francis Cairncross

Table 2: Evolution of Collaborative Online Tools

First-Generation Closed Systems for Managing Internet-Based Tools	Second-Generation Open Systems for Facilitating Internet-Based Work
Directories: Content organized by database developer trying to second guess keywords that users will need.	**Taxonomies**: Users post their own content to the database and write keywords themselves.
Akamai: Content caching for large files such as applications or videos that are downloaded via http.	**BitTorrent**: Content caching and file sharing via a peer-to-peer swarm that can handle much larger files than Akamai can.
Top-down content management: Content is given to a select individual (or small group) who then edits, organizes, and publishes approved content.	**Content management through wikis**: All participants organize and publish directly to the Web site.
Screen scraping: Content-capturing technique involving crawling and capturing data not intended for sharing beyond its original publication.	**Web services**: A more sophisticated content-capturing technique that supports a decentralized machine-to-machine interaction over a network.
Single-source publishing: A Web site published by an individual at a single URL.	**Mash-ups**: Content as well as layout are gathered from multiple Web sites and reassembled into something new.
Personal Web sites: Single-source publishing that can be viewed through a Web browser. The site designer controls how viewers see the information.	**Blogs**: Allow interactivity through comments. Allow users to customize their experience through sorting, filtering, saving individual posts, and managing posts through RSS readers.
Streaming Web seminars: Individuals follow along as they listen to others speak.	**Collaborative online tools**: Individuals can interact with the speaker, comment, share files, and talk with other participants.

(1995) writing for *The Economist,* characterized the social and economic impact of the new generation of digital networks combined with emerging computer conferencing applications with the coining of the phrase "The Death of Distance." In today's accessible and affordable digital collaboration, geographic proximity to customers, suppliers, markets, and business partners is much less critical than in the days prior to accessible and affordable computer conferencing.

Nicholas Economides (2004) has traced the evolution of the pricing structure of digital information and communication channels. Prior to the development and rapid adoption of the World Wide Web, the cost of communicating internationally or between cities increased with distance. However, with a growing array of competitive communication options, including VoIP, both voice and data communication costs very little extra today to communicate over long distances than over short ones. Consequently, the historical advantage of being located close to customers, suppliers, or even a specific workforce is much less relevant today than was the case prior to broad availability and acceptance of computer conferencing.

Concurrent with the advances in favorable economics for dispersed work has been a steady shift of workforce functions away from manual occupations to occupations that focus on the creation and processing of knowledge. Using federal census data from 1950 to 2000, Wolff (2005) found that the proportion of the U.S. workforce engaged primarily in "information work" increased from 37 percent of the work force in 1950 to 59 percent in 2000.

Sophisticated computer conferencing tools translate into new opportunities for business and professional people all over the world. Because many tasks can now be accomplished over the Internet, businesses can hire workers anywhere there is adequate communications connectivity. The result is savings on wages and real estate costs as well as opportunities to recruit the best talent any place in the world without need for relocation. If a company's best talent is no longer concentrated in a single city or even a single building, disruption in services due to natural disasters is no longer an issue. Employees distributed geographically can carry on with business as usual despite any disruptive event in a particular geographic location.

Because many computer conferencing systems allow a great deal of collaboration and real-time interaction, companies can enjoy savings by eliminating the need to squander time and money on endless travel for meetings. Talented peers can work together across thousands of miles and many time zones. In some instances, workers across the world can collaborate in a way that keeps project development moving around the clock.

THE NEXT FRONTIER: PEOPLE

The dot-com financial boom of the 1990s—driven in part by the perceived productivity gains that could be obtained through computer conferencing and collaboration—took a tumble in the early years of the new millennium. A number of factors contributed to the bursting of the dot-com bubble, one of which was that technological advances proceeded at a pace ahead of people's ability to effectively manage and use the emerging information and communication technologies.

In an analysis of collaborative computing practices within 41 large businesses, Brynjolfsson (2005) documents that many corporate executives were forced to come to terms with the reality that technology investments of the 1990s were not producing the expected productivity gains. Innovation in the application of information technology to business processes proved insufficient to realize the full potential for productivity gain. The perceived value of computer conferencing equipment and services enabled by a new generation of digital networks deflated as meaningful business evaluations were brought to the boardroom. The lesson to be learned is that companies and public institutions must make complementary organizational investments in addition to IT investments to fully take advantage of the power of computer conferencing.

As a result of these lessons learned, today multidisciplinary teams are more likely to join with engineers in the design of future generations of computer conferencing and online collaboration tools. For example, leading companies within the software and microprocessor industry have hired and expanded teams of ethnographers to join with product development teams. "Social computing" is recognized for its important commercial value within corporate research divisions as well as in major research universities. Consequently, a comprehensive survey of the current state of computer conferencing protocols and applications would be incomplete without careful consideration of the emerging challenges of understanding how people desire to relate to and use their technology, and how business processes must be reshaped to fully take advantage of productivity gains that can be achieved through computer conferencing.

WORKPLACE IMPLEMENTATION CHALLENGES

As the reliance on information and communications technology for workplace interactions has expanded, so too have the challenges of meeting the needs of people who are required to use those technologies. Galinsky et. al. (2004) document in a study by the Families and Work Institute that 56 percent of North American workers say they typically have to work on too many tasks simultaneously or are interrupted in the work day so many times that they find it difficult to get work done. An in-depth study of 24 information workers by Gonzalez and Harris (2005) reached similar conclusions, with 57 percent reporting frequent work interruptions largely attributed to managing multiple simultaneous task using technological work systems.

In many workplaces, the aggregate number of electronic communications—e-mails, instant messages, calendaring requests, and so forth are rising at a rapid pace. Farhoomand and Drury (2002) found that the two most common sources of information overload were an excessive volume of information (reported by 79 percent of respondents) and difficulty or impossibility of managing it (reported by 62 percent of respondents). A Microsoft white paper (2005) says that information workers spend up to 30 percent of their working day just looking for data they need. When the volume and pace of information becomes so great that it exceeds the ability of people to process and use that information, digital collaboration can undermine rather than enhance worker productivity.

Whatever their skill level, many people develop their own methods for dealing with the expanding volumes of online workplace communication. Some of those methods may be the digital equivalent of duct tape and bailing wire. But however ineffective, they are also familiar, and getting busy people to change habits and learn new skills can be a daunting task. For example, Bellotti et al. (2005) provide detailed surveys documenting task overload and loss of productivity that occurs for knowledge workers as a result of overreliance on e-mail to accomplish collaborative communication, especially as the range of people and topics of communication expand. The implication for employers seeking productivity and efficiency gains from computer conferencing is that no matter how user-friendly or comprehensive the solutions offered by software vendors, organizational systems that create a workplace environment in which people are likely to accept and use those solutions must be in place first.

Computer conferencing tools are designed to enable collaboration among coworkers. But as organizational leadership analysts Thompson and Good (2005) observe, within many organizations, a culture of collaboration is dangerously lacking, and many workers are challenged with digital collaboration scenarios that are largely new and unfamiliar. Today it is uncommon for workers to know, share common space with, and work the same hours or even for the same organization as all the people with whom they collaborate. This, of course, is the precise scenario in which computer conferencing tools can potentially add the greatest benefit. But in the end, it is the motivation, skills, and comfort level of people using those tools that makes collaboration in a modern heterogeneous, dispersed, asynchronous work environment possible.

The motivation, skills, and comfort levels in using the tools of digital collaboration are in no small measure linked to the organization's management culture. A study by MIT's Center for eBusiness concluded that organizational culture was a defining factor among corporations most successful in achieving desired productivity gains from investments in collaborative computational technologies (Brynjolfsson 2005). Notable computer conferencing tools are most applicable to organizations that instill and practice core values that include open communication, decentralized decision authority, and teamwork. The technology tools themselves cannot produce the intended benefits of collaboration. However, well-designed computer conferencing tools can enable organizations to be successful when those organizations have made a commitment to practices that empower dispersed decision-making authority and human organizational processes consistent with effective virtual team collaboration.

Organizations seeking to reinvent themselves with a commitment to open information sharing and dispersed decision making are often quickly faced with the need to deal with additional challenges of information overload. If not addressed, this becomes a new fatal flaw beyond that which can be addressed through technology design alone. In his cross-industry research on collaborative computing use, Brynjolfsson (2005) found that the most successful organizations deal with these competing goals through support, training, and merit reward systems that help workers make good choices both with respect to specific technology tools to use in specific situations and rules of engagement for the efficient sharing of information among collaborative teams. He notes Cisco as an example of a company that has been successful by instituting a comprehensive workforce development process that uses merit rewards to encourage virtual team collaboration and intranet "dashboards" that help employees access the information most relevant to their jobs.

Nardi (1996) provides a comprehensive analysis of ethnological and anthropological research to demonstrate the inseparable connection between the human context of communication needs and successful application of computer and Web tools in the workplace. For information professionals responsible for the design and ultimate adoption of computer conferencing and work collaboration systems, the implications are clear. A holistic systems approach that empowers the organization with a culture of collaboration, technology support and training appropriate for busy people, and a refocusing of management skills to meet needs of dispersed teams are all required to achieve the hoped-for productivity gains promised by computer conferencing.

CONFERENCING TECHNOLOGY SYSTEMS DESIGN WITH PEOPLE IN MIND

Genevieve Bell, an anthropologist, was charged by Intel to travel throughout Asia and observe how people from different cultures choose to use computers and computer devices. Oanh Ha (2004) notes some of Bell's surprising observations, including Muslims using global positioning system technology to find Mecca at prayer time, elderly Indian grannies using text messaging to keep in contact with relatives around the world, and cell phones being blessed at temples because they are such an integral part of people's lives and identities.

Bell is one of a growing number of anthropologists trained in ethnographic methods hired today by both hardware and software design companies. This is because it is widely recognized that information technology managers within organizations, as well as those who design the digital tools, need to begin with an understanding of how people desire to use those technologies. Within the domain of computer conferencing, this basic principle is of even greater importance because the systems must be designed to accommodate collaborating participants, often with very diverse levels of technology skills, experience, motivation, time demands, and cultural perspectives.

Collaboration tools that are not broadly accessible and able to be used by all members of the group for which collaboration is desired will ultimately be counterproductive. In practice, the concept of accessibility is complex, with multiple facets, but they can be grouped into two broad categories of consideration: (1) participants must have the ability to access and the ability to use required computer conferencing software and (2) participants must have the motivation, skills, and knowledge required to use the available conferencing and collaboration tools.

These two broad sets of issues are important considerations for both those who create computer conferencing software and those responsible for the design of systems to optimize the use of available computer conferencing tools within organizations. Because of the diversity of needs, skills, and experience of potential computer conferencing participants, system designs must be able to flexibly accommodate diverse circumstances without adding unnecessary complexity. Examples of critical design considerations include:

- Degree of interoperability across multiple platforms
- Potential restrictions of lower communication bandwidth
- Data and information security
- Ability to easily integrate into group work habits
- Simplicity of use and training requirements
- Universal design accommodating persons with disabilities

The workplace communication tools required by today's information workers must continue to evolve to meet new needs and provide new capabilities. For example, information workers today are much more likely to be required to collaborate with colleagues from other organizations and with a broader set of business enterprises within their own organizations. With continued economic globalization, computer conferencing increasingly must accommodate persons collaborating from multiple time zones and differing standards of underlying telecommunications. Business analyst I.M. Weinstein (2005) observes that broadening collaboration is a trend among information workers to rely on multiple communication devices operable from multiple locations. Today's workers are often highly mobile, using a combination of office desktop computers, notebook computers, handheld devices, and desktop computers from remote locations in accomplishing their work.

Consequently, designers of computer conferencing solutions are faced with the challenge of creating solutions that work across multiple platforms and with equipment supported by highly variable underlying communication capabilities. As a result, there is a much higher premium on computer conferencing capabilities that are interoperable across multiple platforms without unacceptable loss of key functionality when the underlying digital communication bandwidth is limited.

Yamauchi and his colleagues (2000) document a growing trend toward open source computer conferencing solutions as a potential avenue for organizations to address the pressing need for greater interoperability allowing work teams to customize work collaboration tools to meet needs and provide cost-effective access to those tools to participants from multiple organizations. However, open source solutions may also come with the additional challenge of requiring members of the work team to have code-writing expertise to customize software tools with adequate functionality to meet specific workforce needs.

Although the expense of proprietary computer conferencing solutions is a potential barrier to access, they often come with more user-friendly interfaces and customer support, making initial implementation easier. Whether proprietary or not, the challenge of enabling organizations to flexibly meet the diverse conferencing scenarios typical of today's information work are best met through open XML standards and available development tools that empower users to build and extend applications as needed.

As computer conferencing software developers continue to expand options for open information sharing across platforms, new potential security and privacy threats arise. Information technology (IT) managers who address these threats with stronger corporate firewall protections requiring manual registration and authorization of all participating users may unintentionally erect new barriers to collaboration as employees are unwilling to take the additional time and effort needed to include colleagues from outside the organization, even when policies allow for such inclusion and opportunities invite the collaboration.

The trend toward software developers relying on open XML standards offers opportunities not otherwise possible for corporate IT managers to customize applications to improve security, reliability, and manageability in a manner most consistent with the working style and needs of the organization's information workers. Potential solutions are also found in a new generation of Web services, which make it possible for organizations to share information with partners by creating a common understanding of how data are structured, shared, and secured.

A repeated theme emphasized throughout this chapter is that the success of computer conferencing in addressing desired work collaboration goals hinges critically on technology solutions that are appropriate for the way members of an organization desire to work and that minimize the challenge of participants in using the conferencing software. For a solution to be successful, software designers must provide users with access to basic features such as Web conferencing, shared calendars, discussions, shared workspaces, document sharing, instant messaging, and whiteboards in a format that minimizes training requirements.

Drawing on the ethnological and anthropological research described earlier, it is critical that designers integrate knowledge about the real-world work practices and behaviors of knowledge workers into their design efforts. The most powerful computer conferencing solutions are not necessarily the best solutions. Design solutions that use Web interfaces with a look and functionality familiar to most users of the conferencing software add value by enhancing the probability of widespread use.

The accessibility of computer conferencing software is also enhanced with designs that recognize the need to include populations with disabilities. In the United States, 18.1 percent of people are impacted by a disability compromising their vision, hearing, mobility, or learning. (Steinmetz 2002). This number is projected to rise significantly as the global population ages and the current growth in the incidence of diabetes continues to take its toll. Employment is the most significant challenge facing persons with disabilities.

Stodden and Dowrick (1999) found less than 30 percent of working-age adults with disabilities have even part-time employment. The Internet supported with computer conferencing tools has the potential to serve as an equalizer, creating opportunities to tap talent, ideas, and contributions from those with disabilities that make it difficult to leave home. Many persons with disabilities, who would not be able to participate fully in a face-to-face meeting because of physical limitations or because of simple prejudice, can fully participate in interactive Web-based events using adaptive technologies. In addition to benefiting from the previously hidden talent of this growing segment of our population, and providing employment opportunities, there is the added opportunity to change attitudes about disabilities among the rest of the population.

None of this is possible, however, unless developers create products that meet basic accessibility standards. With appropriate up-front consideration and planning, it is entirely feasible to accommodate the communication needs of populations with disabilities. Such modifications in design can also result in many secondary benefits for the enabled population as well. This is a basic principle of the universal design concept; it applies broadly to products and environments made usable by anyone regardless of disability. For example, curb cuts that were built to accommodate wheelchairs are much appreciated by parents pushing strollers and people on bicycles. The same is true for Web applications. A site that is fully accessible to a text reader also downloads easily to handheld devices. Images with alternative text tags are welcome to users with slow connections or those who prefer to disable images in their browsers. Accessibility principles applied on the Web make Internet tools more flexible, easily personalized, and usable for everyone.

CONCLUSION AND THE DIRECTION FORWARD

Wellman (2001) notes that computer networks are inherently social networks, linking people, organizations, and knowledge. The value of IT systems must be considered in the context of the lives of people who use those systems.

The ability to personalize our online work experience, collaborate, and co-create with colleagues anywhere in the world continues to improve with each revision of new computer conferencing tools. These tools continue to transform into operational frameworks that are more intuitive, flexible, and inclusive. However, technological innovation as well as organizational systems innovations must continue to evolve before the envisioned benefits for business productivity gains and effective collaborative work can be fully realized.

Research conducted by Benford and his colleagues (2001) documents that most people who collaborate online today do so with a customized collection of tools they assemble to meet their specific needs. Although collaborative computing technology can enable productive and meaningful interactions, ultimately it is human beings who make meaning and connections from the information that is shared. Contemporary Internet tools are limited because they are designed to parse content as raw material for humans to sort out.

Today, computer software programs can organize headings and links, they can sort information according to keywords, and they can provide text boxes for people to communicate in. However, they cannot prioritize or connect the meaning or semantics of any shared information. It is up to people to make meaning that leads to decisions. Henderson (2005) found that knowledge workers working on the same job and with the same software systems typically have significant variance in their selected hierarchical file structure for storing digital documents. Such variances in the way people choose to organize their personal digital documents can be a substantial barrier to effective work collaboration. The most dramatic future advances in computer conferencing will most likely be in the domain of managing information among workgroups.

The originator of the World Wide Web, Tim Berners-Lee (2001) envisions the emerging Semantic Web as a transformative technology in which information is given well-defined meaning, better enabling computers and people to work in cooperation. To envision the transformative potential of the Semantic Web for productive collaboration, imagine a company that needs to find a php programmer to develop a Web site. Using a variety of online databases available today, it is feasible to quickly develop a list of names and resumes of potential candidates. But the online process ends at this point and a new round of communication through e-mail or telephone must be initiated after reviewing the candidate pool.

With the addition of a Semantic Web agent, the online search process would not end with the passive process of identifying a pool of trustworthy programmer candidates matching the desired skill base. The online process would be enabled to continue beyond the first step of identifying possible employee candidates. For example, the Web-enabled decision process could continue by making an appointment for the assigned company representative to have a VoIP meeting at a time that fits into both persons' calendars. In many cases, the manager conducting the search may desire to consult and obtain views of other colleagues before initiating contact with potential programmers with the desired skill set. The Semantic Web agents of colleagues within the organization would be linked to contribute their perspectives and possibly to volunteer them to participate in the interview meeting as well.

This is just one example of the potential of the Semantic Web to enhance computer conferencing as a tool for meaningful work collaboration. Human interaction is, of course, still required. However, the information will be stored, tagged, and parsed in a way that is easy for machines to communicate with one another and for semantic software agents to discern meaning for the individual requesting the information to adjust and improve the quality of the information based on the human user's interaction with it. Microsoft founder Bill Gates (2005) envisions a near-term business environment in which software will play an important role in replacing the complexity of the workplace with contextual information needed for decisions involving joint interaction among people from multiple organizations working from many different locations.

This vision for the future of computer conferencing is much more than an improved and more powerful tool for the sharing of data and information. It is a vision in which computer conferencing will provide colleagues in the workplace with the ability to make real-time decisions with comprehensive knowledge of how their work connects with others within the same organization and others with connected work outside the organization. The ultimate benefit of computer conferencing will hinge on success in creating flexible, intelligent software systems that reflect the way colleagues in the workplace desire to interact for decision making rather than requiring people to change the way they must interact to meet the requirements of the conferencing software.

GLOSSARY

Asynchronous Communication: Any method of communication that does not demand real-time responses from participants. Individuals contribute to a dialog at any time and place that is personally convenient. Examples include message boards, e-mail, listservs, and Web-based threaded discussions.

Information Communication Technology (ICT): Any technology that enables the sharing of data, text, images, or voice communication. Computers and cellular telephones both fall within this category.

Open Standards: Nonproprietary and publicly available, allowing anyone with the expertise to implement them. They are designed using an open and collaborative method by teams of experts. Applying open standards ensures compatibility with various hardware, software, and vendors that design with open standards.

Persons with Disabilities: The definition of a disability varies depending on the source. A broad definition includes any physical or mental impairment that significantly interferes with ordinary day-to-day activities such as blindness, a missing limb, or a learning disability. A social definition of *disability* refers to barriers in society in relation to a person's impairment—the idea being that the limits of an impairment are socially imposed.

Semantic Web: A World Wide Web Consortium–sponsored project that seeks to develop intelligent systems for machine-to-machine communication that will self-adapt and refine its processes based on user behavior.

Social Computing: The software that supports the growing trend in ICT for social interaction, collaboration, and communication.

Web Application: A software application tool that is accessible over the Internet through a browser instead of through one's local hard drive.

Whiteboard: Whiteboard software replicates whiteboard writing surfaces commonly used in schools and offices. Electronic whiteboards allow users to draw pictures and write freehand messages that can easily be erased and modified. They are a common feature in collaborative virtual meeting software and instant messaging.

XML: The extensible markup language (XML) is a standard developed by the World Wide Web Consortium (W3C) designed for cross-platform machine-to-machine communication and capable of describing many kinds of data.

CROSS REFERENCES

See *Computer Conferencing and Distance Learning*; *Telecommuting and Telework*; *Video Conferencing*.

REFERENCES

Alan, R. A. 2001. *A history of the personal computer: The people and the technology*. London, ON: Alan Publishing.

Bellotti, V., et al. 2005. Quality versus quantity: E-mail centric task management and its relation with overload. *Human Computer Interaction* 20(1/2):89–138.

Benford, X. X., et al. 2001. Collaborative virtual environments. *Communications of the ACM* 44:79–85.

Berners-Lee, T. 2001. The Semantic Web. *Scientific American .Com* www.scientificamerican.com/article.cfm?articleID=00048144-10D2-1C70-84A9809EC588EF21&catID=2 (accessed June 15, 2006).

Berners-Lee, T., and M. Fischetti. 2000. *Weaving the Web: The original design and ultimate destiny of the World Wide Web*. New York: HarperCollins.

Brynjolfsson, E. 2005. VII pillars of productivity. *Optimize* 22:26–31.

Cairncross, F. 1995. The death of distance: A survey of telecommunications. *The Economist* 336:27–8.

CellularOnline. 2006. Latest global, hand set, base station and cellular statistics. www.cellular.co.za (accessed June 23, 2007).

Economides, N. 2004. Telecommunications regulation: An introduction. NET Institute Working Paper No. 04–20. http://ssrn.com/abstract=465020 (accessed June 23, 2007).

Farhoomand, A. F., and D. H. Drury. 2002. Managerial information overload. *Communications of ACM* 45:127–31.

Galinsky, E., et al. 2004. Overwork in America: When the way of work becomes too much. Work Life Research Report of the Families and Work Institute. http://familiesandwork.org/summary/overwork2005.pdf (accessed June 23, 2007).

Gates, B. 2005. *The new world of work*, speech at Microsoft CEO Summit. www.finfacts.com/irelandbusinessnews/publish/printer_10001879.shtml (accessed June 23, 2007).

Gilder, G. 1993. *Metcalf's law and legacy*. www.seas.upenn.edu/~gaj1/metgg.html (accessed June 23, 2007).

Gonzalez, M. G., and V. M. Harris. 2005. No task left behind? Examining the nature of fragmented work. In *Proceedings of CHI 2005 Conference, Portland, OR*, 321–30. CHI 2005 Technology, Safety, Community: Conference on Human Factors in Computing Systems.

Henderson, S. 2005. Genre, task, topic and time: Facets of personal document management. In *Proceedings of CHINZ 2005 Conference, Auckland, NZ*, 75–82. ACM SIGCHI New Zealand Chapter's International Conference on Computer-Human Interaction.

Laiserin, J. 2000. On-line collaboration: The pre-history of internet collaboration. *Cadence Channel* 15:59–61.

Microsoft. 2005. *Digital workstyle: The new world of work. A Microsoft White Paper.* www.microsoft.no/div/files/office/New%20World%20of%20Work%20Whitepaper%20Local.pdf (accessed June 23, 2007).

Nardi, B. A., editor. 1996. *Context and consciousness: Activity and theory in human interaction*. Cambridge MA: MIT Press.

Oanh Ha, K. 2004, August 9. Anthropologists dig into business. *The Mercury News*.

Stodden, R. A., and P. W. Dowrick. 1999. Postsecondary education and employment of adults with disabilities. *American Rehabilitation* 25:19–20.

Steinmetz, E. Current population reports: Americans with disabilities: 2002, issued May 2006. www.census.gov/prod/2006pubs/p70–107.pdf (accessed June 23, 2007).

Thompson, K., and R. Good. 2005. *The bioteaming manifesto: A new paradigm for virtual business networked teams.* http://changethis.com/19.BioteamingManifesto (accessed June 23, 2007).

Weinstein, I. M. 2005. *The arrival of the virtual office*. Duxbury, MA: Wainhouse Research.

Wellman, B. 2001. Computer networks as social networks. *Science* 293:2031–4.

Wolff, E. N. 2005. The growth of information workers in the U.S. economy. *Communications of the ACM* 48:37–42.

Wooley, D. 1994. *PLATO: The emergence of on-line community.* http://thinkofit.com/plato/dwplato.htm (accessed June 23, 2007).

Yamauchi, Y., et al. 2000. Collaboration with lean media: How open-source software succeeds. In *ACM 2000 Conference on Computer Supported Cooperative Work*, 2–6, 329–38. Philadelphia: ACM Press.

Telecommuting and Telework

Michael Workman, *Florida Institute of Technology*

TELECOMMUTING AND TELEWORK

As a result of the World Wide Web phenomenon a wellspring of new terminology has made its way into the common vernacular such as *blog* and *mudding*, and many of us have participated online in discussion boards or chat rooms used by *virtual communities*. At one time or another, most of us have been online gathering information or transacting business. Contemporary society is being shaped around the emerging technologically mediated ways of interacting, and there are a growing number of online transactions in which telecommunications are substituted for in-person acquisition or performance of services. Examples include online or distance education, online shopping, online banking, telemedicine, telejustice, teletaxes, televoting, and virtual entertainment (Bureau of Transportation Statistics 1992). And events, such as 9/11, and disasters such as the Northridge earthquake in California, have caused some to wonder if telework might serve as a potential mitigation or disaster recovery option. It is only natural then to expect that new forms of telework would emerge. It is important, however, to distinguish various forms of online transactions (or what might be called "telebusiness" or "e-business") from telework because telework carries with it a variety of unique characteristics beyond transacting online.

The term *telework* is typically applied to an arrangement in which someone works from a remote location away from a traditional office building or on the go in a mobile environment (Hertel, Konradt, and Orlikowski 2004). It began as telecommuting, where someone would work from home on a part-time basis (Nilles et al. 1976). Today, with transnational organizations proliferating along with globalization we are seeing the emergence of new forms of telework, such as virtual teaming, particularly among organizations involved in knowledge work (ITAA 2003). These forms of virtual work enable corporations to transcend geographies and time zones and get closer to customers, suppliers, and trading partners, and more effectively respond to turbulent business environments through their "instantaneity"—anytime, anywhere work (Baruch and Nicholson 1997). In this chapter we examine some of the forms of virtual work, their relative advantages and disadvantages, and some of the managerial and employee issues and questions that must be addressed. We also look at some of the social, legal, and technological implications and various roles technologies are playing in the emergence of virtual work.

Forms of Virtual Work

In his book *The Third Wave*, Alvin Toffler (1980) wrote about a growing phenomenon in which people would work from home in what he called "electronic cottages." The practice of working from home was not a new concept in the 1980s, but it had not yet been widely recognized as a formal working arrangement. The term *telecommuting* was coined (Nilles et al. 1976) and has since become a lexicon in modern society to describe a variety of work settings that involve people who work from their homes on an occasional basis. By the late 1980s in offices around corporate America it was not uncommon to hear someone comment that he or she would telecommute on a given day.

Since that time, more specialized strains of telecommuting have evolved and have acquired their own monikers to denote a specific form of telecommuting. The term *telework*, for example, has traditionally indicated a formal telecommuting arrangement in which someone works full-time in a location outside a corporate center, which may include home, remote, or satellite office, or even "on the go" (Fritz, Higa, and Narasimhan 1995), although some research (Orlikowski and Barley 2001) has shown that the boundaries between working at home and working at the office have become blurred. The term *virtual* is often used to define the forms of distributed work that use information and communications technologies, or ICT, predominantly for communication and coordination (Lipnack and Stamps 1997) (Figure 1).

Because of its flexibility, virtual work is implemented in a variety of ways. The notion of "hotelling" grew out of a concept in which teleworking sales personnel, consultants, or repair technicians would share cubicles or offices with other teleworkers who may work in the office only

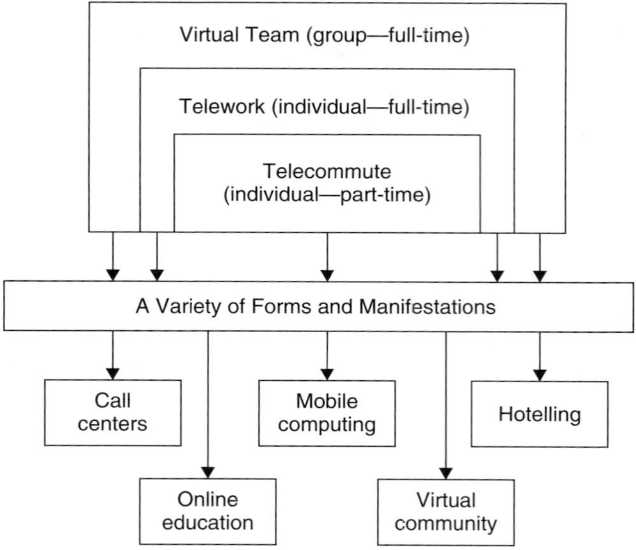

Figure 1: Virtuality and manifestations

a few hours a week. At Bank of America, for example, mobile loan processors travel to applicants' residences or places of business armed with laptop computers and document scanners to initiate loan applications. After a day's work, they return to the office to upload the applications data to the central loan office computer for further processing (Frigault 2000). In other arrangements, virtual workers have no permanent work location at all. At Kablelink, computer repair technicians work entirely from their trucks or vans equipped with GPS and are dispatched by operators who work full-time from their homes. The corporate office consists only of a receptionist, some computers, and a bank of telecommunications equipment used for handling and dispatching calls through the company's networks and mobile communications technology.

Many teleworkers work in "virtual teams," in which members are geographically and temporally dispersed. France Telecom's Orange division is a transnational organization serving in over 220 countries and territories and covering more than 140 nationalities speaking 70 languages. Orange employs a staff of over 4300 people who work in virtual teams on information technology solutions around the world. Because of its global reach and the dynamic nature of its business and geographically dispersed client base, Orange uses virtual teams for projects ranging from a few months to over a year that require specific expertise in a particular geography (Hyde 2004).

When Delta Airlines appoints Orange to install a network application at the airport in Auckland, New Zealand, a virtual team consisting of network engineers, security specialists, system architects and designers, network administrators, software designers and developers, business analysts, database analysts, hardware specialists, and a virtual team manager from various parts of the world, including France, Italy, India, Australia, the United States and the United Kingdom will collaborate from their respective parts of the world on the project using a variety of technologies ranging from e-mail to video teleconferencing. The virtual team will use a software application known as a "change control system" to track and coordinate the changes each member of the virtual team makes to the system under development, along with technologies used in managing software and network revisions, called a "source control system." These technologies enable the various virtual team members to coordinate the technical aspects of their work, such as who is working on which task at a given time.

In "virtual communities" geographically dispersed people, or people who are homebound, who have shared interests and common goals participate with each other using the Internet (Wellman 1997). Unlike virtual teams, virtual communities are not a formal organizational structure but are instead informally initiated organically by community members, such as in open source software projects (Moon and Sproull 2002) or scientific collaborations (Finholt 2002). People may belong to many virtual communities, and their memberships may change regularly. Virtual communities emerge "when enough people carry on public discussions long enough, with sufficient human feeling, to form webs of personal relationships in cyberspace" (Rheingold 1994, 5).

The Rise of Telework and Telework on the Rise

From its inception, telecommuting offered many benefits to employees, business, and society at large. Employees generally experienced less interruption in their tasks and concentration, they spent less time commuting, and found a better balance between work and family life (Hill et al. 1998). Coupled with rising facilities costs and fueled by tax incentives resulting from legislation such as the Federal Clean Air Act of 1990 and the Intermodal Surface Transportation Efficiency Act of 1991, business executives saw virtual work as a means for gaining efficiencies, and the flexible work environment enabled companies to get closer to their customers, yielding a strategic advantage (Katz 1997; Lococo and Yen 1998). Many companies reported productivity increases by as much as 34 percent and increases in revenues by as much as 19 percent (Katz 1997; Turban, McLean, and Wetherbe 1996). Yet it was not until the mid-1990s, when technologies and remote working processes had matured sufficiently to effectively support virtual work, that they evolved into more formal arrangements and flourished (Chakravarthy 1997).

Now, with more than 10 million in the United States alone, estimates are that over 34 million people throughout the world are full-time teleworkers, a phenomenon that is experiencing an annual growth rate of between 5 and 10 percent (Bureau of Transportation Statistics 1992; Gartner Group 2000) with the vast majority of teleworkers working in virtual teams (Earley and Mosakowski 2000; Miller 1999; Wallace 1998). Virtual teams are becoming so pervasive that they are being called a "workplace revolution" (Daniels, Lamond, and Standen 2001) and are now commonplace in the United States, United Kingdom, and Western Europe (Hertel et al. 2004; O'Hara-Devereau and Johansen 1994), and they are emerging in India and Asia and many other parts of the world (Gartner Group 2000; Gibson, Zellmer-Bruhn, and Schwab 2003). Indeed, the traditional exclusively proximal team is becoming increasingly rare in organizations, and most professional teams now consist of mixtures or degrees of virtual work (Bell and Kozlowski 2002; Martins, Gilson, and Maynard 2004).

Although the developments of telework and virtual teams have been impressive, they have not been without problems. Implementation rates have fallen short of many projections (Ruppel and Howard 1998), and between 25 and 50 percent have failed to live up to either employee or employer expectations (Fusaro 1997; Jarvenpaa and Leidner 1999; Wallace 1998). In some cases, employees who had been successful in a traditional proximally located team were unable to cope in a telework or virtual team environment, and employers reverted from using virtual work back to a traditional office setting (Workman, Kahnweiler, and Bommer 2003).

Although there are many reasons to expect businesses to escalate the implementation of telework and virtual teams, problems are expected to persist when there is a mismatch between employee and environment fit, or the proper steps are not taken to adequately support the virtual work or worker (Kozma 1991; Wieland 1999). As Toffler (1980, 215) warned, "One should not underestimate the difficulties entailed in transferring work from its locations in factory and office to its location in the home. Problems of motivation and management, of corporate and social reorganization will make the shift both prolonged and, perhaps, painful. [And] not all communication can be handled vicariously." To capitalize on the benefits and mitigate the pitfalls of virtual work, we must draw on explanatory theory to help us better understand both their strengths and their weaknesses.

THEORETICAL FOUNDATIONS AND THE NATURE OF TELEWORK

In most cases, people do not work entirely alone. Even those who are self-employed communicate with customers, vendors, or other trading partners. It is just as likely that people in organizations work in groups or teams. The membership in these teams may be stable or transient, and the durations of their assignments may be temporary or permanent (Mohammed, Mathieu, and Bartlett 2002). As people work together, the extent to which they are interdependent on one another is a product of the complexity of the tasks they perform accompanied by the degrees or intensity of the communications shared (Griffin, Patterson, and West 2001; Mohammed et al. 2002). Different levels of task complexity may require certain forms of team structures such as pooled, sequential, or reciprocal (Bell and Kozlowski 2002), which in turn rely on certain kinds of collaborative relationships to succeed (Shaw and Barrett-Power 1998).

However, it is becoming commonly recognized that the nature of telework differs from the traditional office environment, where workers are proximally located, and therefore differing team characteristics may be needed to support collaboration. One of the contributing factors comes from the technology media used to support collaboration that may span geographies, cultures, time, and time zones (Malhotra, Majchrzak, and Carman 2001; Townsend, DeMarie, and Hendrickson 1996). Hence, it is often distance that necessitates the use of technology media for collaboration, and not necessarily social or convenience preferences. The resulting constraints on the collaboration may not always be a matter of choice. Therefore, it is important to understand how these collaborative conditions affect perceptions and performance in virtual work.

When people collaborate, information is conveyed through various channels linguistically with the words we say, paralinguistically through intonations and verbal patterns in speech, and nonlinguistically with eye gaze, posture, gestures, and signs such as blushing. For instance, a shift in eye gaze may signal turn taking or it may mean disinterest in the conversation. Having more information by way of the various channels helps us to fully grasp the meaning. Together, these channels create a shared communicative context (Fussell and Benimoff 1995), and drawing from this context our collaboration evolves from communicating information and ideas into negotiating the meanings and ultimately into a consolidation of shared understanding (Jehng 1997).

In a seminal study of computer-mediated collaboration, Murninghan (1981) identified a number of outcomes in proximal interaction versus communication over a technology medium. Specifically, as proximal contact decreased and technological intermediation increased, the number and quality of ideas increased. However, the number of conflicts also increased along with increased task (versus relationship) focus of the collaborators, while social pressures and group cohesion decreased. Carrying over into virtual work, three theories help to explain these phenomena and define the nature of telework. These are discussed below.

Theory Foundations

The ICT used in virtual work broadly include those such as e-mail, instant messaging, video teleconferencing, digital libraries, and databases, along with a host of applications for planning, managing, and executing work. One of the key aspects of contemporary ICT is the addition of interactivity in data processing and communications functions. The ICT mechanisms differ, however, in their capacities to transfer information. Information richness theory (Daft and Lengel 1986) explains how technology media affects collaborative exchanges in virtual work. Some forms of media are inherently richer than others owing to their capabilities to convey information. As an example, the telephone is capable of transmitting only about 37 percent of the sound frequency that the human voice can emit (Carr and Snyder 1997); thus, it can be difficult in some telephone conversations to detect subtle emotive nuances such as the difference between excitement and agitation, or boredom and relaxation, particularly without a visual component (Raghuram 1996).

An ICT such as video teleconferencing is considered a rich medium according to information richness theory, because it conveys many channels of information and more closely resembles face-to-face interaction than a leaner technology medium. By contrast, lean media such as e-mail have few channels through which information is passed (Daft and Lengel 1986). Media used in collaboration therefore places various constraints, and to varying degrees, on the communicative context shared by collaborators. However, it is important to note that people, depending on their personal and social characteristics, differentially perceive this truncation of communicative context. For example, Carlson and Zmud (1999) expanded on the media richness concept by suggesting that one's experience with the technology and with those with whom one communicates means that more expressive messages can be transmitted over lean media, enhancing the perceptions of richness (Ngwenyama and Lee 1997). The communicative constraints in a virtual environment can elevate the level of ambiguity in the mental concepts people form during collaboration while other aspects attenuate social forces (Workman 2005). As an illustration, in telephone conversations more cognitive effort is spent making inferences about information that otherwise comes from visual cues and paralinguistic voice channels truncated in the telephone transmissions, which can raise the levels of ambiguity about both tasks and interpersonal relationships as we try to figure out "where the other person is coming from."

The impact of ICT on cognition and social activity is partly explainable by social influence theory (Deutch and Gerard 1955), which postulates two forms of social influences: normative influences that are used to levy or gain approval or avoid rejection such as with peer pressure, and informational influence that stems from efforts to acquire accurate perceptions such as when seeking expert advice. The power of social influence increases as the intensity of the interaction with one another increases (Shaw and Barrett-Power 1998; Suzuki 1997; Workman 2001), and this governs communication and cooperative behavior (Hertel et al. 2004; Kraut et al. 1998).

As people cooperatively interact, they undergo a variety of social influences that shape perceptions as well as performance (Shaw and Barrett-Power 1998; Smith 2005). Social influences determine how shared meaning is co-created and structured using the participants' social systems as they collaborate (Suzuki 1997). As the intensity of interaction increases, people tend to become increasingly cohesive and their ideas become increasingly congruent (Jehng 1997).

Where social influence theory explains the collaborative behavior within groups, social forces also help to govern collaborative behavior across both formal and informal groups. Social identity theory (Tajfel and Turner 1986) explains how in-group/out-group boundaries are defined (Chen, Brockner, and Katz 1998; Heald et al. 1998) and is concerned with three components: categorization, identification, and comparison (Tajfel and Turner 1986). Social identity theory thus determines the "thickness" of group boundaries that divide an in-group from out-groups, and this helps to determine how cooperative people are in their behavior. As group members are socialized into a group, they undergo deindividuation, resulting in a loss of individual identity concomitant with acquisition of a group identity (Zajonc 1969). As such, social identity defines the ways in which and the extent to which people collaborate and cooperate with those outside the group.

As a consequence, the degree to which people cooperate and comply with the demands of a group depends on the weighting they place between personal and social knowledge acquired from the group's socialization processes (Gass and Seiter 1999; Zajonc 1969). When technology media intervenes, it reduces the channels of information to varying degrees that enable group identity to form and the extent to which social influences affect one's perceptions and behavior.

A side effect of the information channels constraint with ICT is that it sometimes conspires to depersonalize the social environment, which can lead to objectification (Moscovici 1984), and objectification amplifies comparative dissimilarity in which people categorize others who they perceive to be unlike themselves in abstract terms or stereotypes (Tajfel and Turner 1986). As such, low social identity and low social influence result in more conflicts within the group, whereas high social influence and identity result in more conflicts with out-groups (Heald et al. 1998; Shaw and Barrett-Power 1998). Combined, these factors help to define the nature of virtual work.

The Nature of Virtual Work

As suggested by the theory, research (Martins et al. 2004) has shown that the nature of virtual work is more solitary than traditional office-based work due in part to the fact that there are reduced formal and informal interactions in virtual work than would normally take place in an office setting (Ellison 1999), and that the interactions that do take place are somewhat different from those in a typical office setting because of the constraints placed on how people communicate and coordinate their work (Jehng 1997; Raghuram 1996). Although people react differently to this environment, some virtual workers have reported that this solitary environment sometimes creates in them a feeling of remote isolation (Konradt and Schmook 1999; Turban et al. 1996), and there are tendencies for people to objectify virtual others, sometimes causing unusual hostility and alienation (Hertel et al. 2004; Wellman et al. 1996), while others are quick to trust and form rapid ties in a virtual setting (Jarvenpaa and Leidner 1999).

In addition to having the potential to increase solitude, virtual work is also less externally structured. Since virtual work is typically done remotely and communication is constrained to varying degrees by the richness or leanness of ICT, there are fewer opportunities for virtual workers to share or model coworkers' approaches to tasks. This necessitates individual approaches to doing things (Hill et al. 1998; Jehng 1997; Wieland 1999). As Baruch and Nicholson (1997, 23) found, "Some people may feel anxious and ill-at-ease without the reassurance of feedback from locally present management. Individuals with high needs for certainty may feel disoriented when confronted with the high discretionary environment of homeworking."

In addition to the more solitary and unstructured nature of virtual work there are also increased levels of ambiguity in terms of tasks and interpersonal relationships (Workman 2005; Workman et al. 2003). As people collaborate on problems, they use the information they gather to help formulate mental concepts and understanding to guide their choices and decisions. The varying amounts of information constriction from ICT have some universal effects in raising cognitive ambiguity (Kraut et al. 1998; Montgomery 1999) but there are also differences in how people react individually to these effects (Lim and Benbasat 2000; Montgomery 1999). It is interesting to note that while sometimes ICT-mediated interaction may lead to objectification and greater levels of conflict than in a proximal setting, at other times people may form unqualified and unbridled intimacy with virtual others (Workman 2007).

HOW DOES TELE- WORK?

Since there are so many different ways virtual work can be conceptualized and implemented, for the purpose of simplification let us define "virtualization" as the degree of technological intermediation versus proximal interaction. Technological intermediation subsumes interdependence and communications intensity regardless of whether one is self-employed, working only with a superior or subordinate, or working in a group or team; or whether the reasons for virtual work are geographical, organizational, or for convenience. Working from this definition we can imagine a variety of implications for the individual, organization, and society from the personal and social effects from increasing virtualization as identified by Murninghan (1981) (Figure 2).

When virtualization increases, some people tend to perceive higher degrees of flexibility and control over their time, along with greater empowerment and increased responsibilities, although there may be increases in misunderstandings and greater role ambiguity and goal conflict (Hertel, Geister, and Konradt 2005). Organizationally, there may be greater efficiencies, lower overhead costs, and better responsiveness to customers or pressing needs. However, there may be greater complications in overseeing and managing the dispersed community of resources

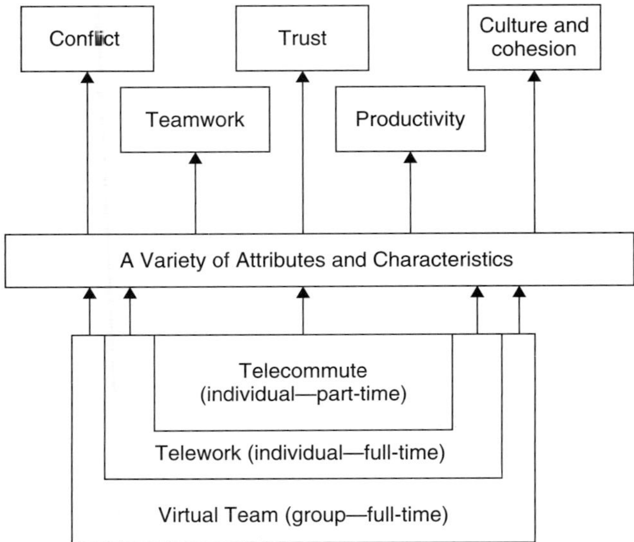

Figure 2: Attributes and characteristics

in terms of people, information, and equipment (Lipnack and Stamps 1997). On a societal scale, virtual work may serve to better integrate disadvantaged persons or those with family care commitments into the workforce, and it may reduce environmental impacts from commuting traffic, gasoline consumption, and air pollution. On the other hand, it may also serve to further divide those who have from those who do not have the educational or other resources to work independently from home or on the go (the so-called digital divide). It may also place in greater jeopardy the security of information or other vital societal resources (Davis and Botkin 1995).

Managerial Oversight

To help maintain the balance among the multiple competing forces and address the complications with virtualization, managerial oversight is crucial. Traditional proximally located work and virtual work share many characteristics. Workers must communicate, plan, and allocate subtasks; sequence, schedule, and coordinate the work; problem-solve; derive products or solutions; and monitor performance (Bell and Kozlowski 2002), and their effectiveness is frequently based on productivity, efficiency, and adaptability (Chakravarthy 1997). Still, because of the nature of virtual work, there are some unique managerial considerations regarding individuals and teams as virtualization increases (Bailey and Kurland 2002). A useful managerial framework is called the GRIP model, representing goals, relationships, information, and processes (Hofstede 1998; O'Hara-Devereau and Johansen 1994) (Table 1).

Process-oriented teams are mechanistic in nature (Burns and Stalker 1961) and are concerned with the means by which goals are pursued. Their focus is on process improvement, and they tend to have many elaborate written processes and procedures stipulating how work is to be carried out. They work to standardize, eliminate variance, and reduce ambiguity (Hofstede 1998). On the other hand, results-oriented teams are concerned with the end products or services, and are organic in nature (Burns and Stalker 1961). Their focuses are on action and end goals, and their work is such that ends may justify the means (Daft 1998; Hofstede 1998).

Studies of proximal work (Daft 1998; Wageman 1995) have suggested that results-oriented teams may be more suitable than process-oriented ones because they enable tasks to be adjusted and redefined according to situational variables. However, this assumption relies heavily on the ability to make quick and effective decisions about courses of action (Daft and Lengel 1986). As indicated earlier concerning the nature of virtual work, virtual teams have less externally supplied structure than do proximal teams because of physical distance and time lags in communications, as well as constrictions of media richness by various technology bandwidths that facilitate remote communication (Workman et al. 2003). Also in virtual teams, both formal and informal interactions are reduced, which may elevate the ambiguity of some tasks and may increase indecision about courses of action (Jehng 1997; Wieland 1999).

To help compensate for this heightened ambiguity, people often turn to formal structures such as rules and

Table 1: GRIP Characteristics

Dimension		Attributes	Outcomes
Goals and processes			
	Process-oriented	Many written procedures	Highly structured, means-oriented
	Results-oriented	Few written procedures	Low structure, ends-oriented
Managerial/company relationships			
	Tight control	Centralized decision making	Strict hierarchies, formal
	Loose control	Decentralized decision making	Autonomy, informal
Employee relationships			
	Employee-centered	Collectivistic	Negotiation and consensus, feedback from others
	Job-centered	Individualistic	Independence, feedback from nonsocial sources, e.g., documentation
Information flows			
	Open teams	Thin, permeable team boundaries	Highly interdependent, much intra-team information flows
	Closed teams	Thick, impermeable team boundaries	Low interdependence, little intra-team information flows

procedures. However, when rules and procedures are lacking in an organization, people tend to use the organizational hierarchy as the primary method for managing group goals, and disputes are settled by referring problems to a common superior (Daft 1998; Griffin et al. 2001). In the absence of these supports, people find their own way through the system to figure out what to do. Because the interaction among virtual team workers and management is constrained by the nature of virtual work, increasing the specificity of the goals, processes, rules, and regulations augments the structure within the virtual team (Griffith, Sawyer, and Neale 2003; Montoya-Weiss, Massey, and Song 2001). Stated simply, the increased ambiguity and solitary nature of virtual work elevates the need for increasing process and procedural specificity. Unlike proximal teams, in which members often freely interact to derive team norms and behaviors and their contemporaneous nature better facilitates agility, effective virtual team performance requires specification "not only of individual team member roles but also the interrelationships between the roles of team members" (Bell and Kozlowski 2002, 41).

In a similar fashion, tighter control is also important in virtual teams. Tightly controlled teams have strict management hierarchies, and decision making tends to be centralized, whereas loosely controlled groups are more autonomous. Decision-making authority tends to be decentralized when loosely controlled and the decisions tend to be emergent and adaptive (Hofstede 1998; Moses and Stahelski 1999; Murninghan 1981). As autonomy increases, ambiguity increases concomitantly in a setting mediated by technology (Jehng 1997; Lim and Benbasat 2000), and this can have a negative impact on virtual team performance (Conner 2003; Montoya-Weiss et al. 2001).

Because virtual teamwork is less structured than proximal teamwork, and there are greater degrees of uncertainty, virtual team leaders must provide additional clarity and direction than might be necessary in a proximal setting (Workman 2005). The tighter control enables virtual team leaders to clarify contextual factors critical to performance management, including the ability to address work processes conducted by virtual team members with disparate worldviews (O'Hara-Devereau and Johansen 1994). According to Bell and Kozlowski (2002, 27), virtual team leaders must "closely monitor any changes in the environmental conditions. Because virtual team members are distributed, they are less aware of the broader situation and the dynamics of the overall team environment. So, as external conditions change such as in the case of modified task specifications or a new deadline or changes in the team's goals, managers need to facilitate adaptive and appropriate changes within their team."

When it comes to working relationships, employee-centered teams operate on the principle of consensus and are collectivistic in nature. They derive feedback from teammates and work together on problem solving, and in employee-centered teams, work sequencing tends to be negotiated (Hofstede 1998). On the other hand, job-centered teams sequence work according to management directives or by means of expert power (Eby and Dobbins 1997). They are individualistic in nature, operate on the principles of efficiency, cost, and time (Hofstede 1998), and derive feedback from nonsocial sources such as a computer or documentation while people work by themselves on problems and tasks (Workman 2001).

These types of relationship interdependencies flow over into the information intensity of the team. Research (see, e.g., Griffith et al. 2003) shows that to compensate for informational gaps created by technology mediation, distance, and time lags, more attempts are made at peer-group referencing in a virtual setting "as compared with individuals working within proximity of similar comparison others; [and] individuals within a virtual context will engage in more attempts at selecting referents outside of the organization" (Conner 2003, 141) to assess the distribution of workload, task progress, and fairness in relation to distributive justice (Conner 2003; Lipnack and Stamps 1997). This increases the need for horizontal and spatial linkages, which are dependent on how open a team is to cooperating and sharing information.

In a closed team there are thick boundaries between in-group and out-groups. They are highly compartmentalized, with few linkages, which constrain interdependence (Suzuki 1997). The thick boundaries between a closed team and other organizational units regulate the information flows, reducing information intensity horizontally and spatially. An open team is transcendent, has many information-intensive linkages among groups, and facilitates interdependence. Boundaries between the in-group and its out-groups are thin and permeable, intensifying the exchange of information horizontally and spatially (Hertel et al. 2004; Hofstede 1998; Mohammed et al. 2002).

Since virtual teams must rapidly assemble and import eclectic information to accomplish their tasks across functional, divisional, geographical, and time spans (Griffith et al. 2003; O'Hara-Devereau and Johansen 1994), and since virtual team assembly occurs with the involvement of many departments, such as human resources and line managers (Hyde 2004), open teams with permeable boundaries best facilitate information flows to support the dynamic nature of virtual work (Bell and Kozlowski 2002; Cole, Schaninger, and Harris 2002).

Employee Development

As discussed previously, research (Ellingson and Wiethoff 2002; Jarvenpaa and Leidner 1999; Maruping and Agarwal 2004) on the nature of virtual work and the person-environment fit suggest supplementing the virtual environment by providing additional structure and specificity to that typically found in a proximal work setting. Beyond these environmental factors, employee development is an important consideration both in terms of preparing people for virtual work as well as during virtual work (Hertel et al. 2005). Preparatory development may involve the knowledge, skills, and abilities that are specifically related to the virtual work environment, while ongoing development may include supplementing occupational knowledge and skills ordinarily acquired from observational modeling and other proximal learning.

In addition to the competencies needed for work in general, virtual workers may also benefit from the development of "telecooperation" skills (Duarte and Snyder 2001; Ellingson and Wiethoff 2002; Jarvenpaa and Leidner 1999; Lipnack and Stamps 1997) acquired through self-management training and by providing substitutes for leadership along with acculturating mutual trust. Self-management is comprised of independence, persistence, and creativity (Staples, Hulland, and Higgins 1999). An independent worker is self-motivated and is able to plan and organize activities with little external support. Persistent workers have high endurance toward goal achievement and continue working after interruptions (Hertel et al. 2005). Creativity involves the ability to work with novelty and derive unconventional solutions to unconventional problems (Jehng 1997; Kozma 1991; Wieland 1999), which is an important coping mechanism, given that the nature of virtual work makes observational modeling difficult and produces a highly novel working environment (Workman et al. 2003).

With increasing virtuality, mutual trust is reduced (Maruping and Agarwal 2004); therefore, building trust is especially important to the potential success of virtual teams. Trust-building techniques include face-to-face kick-off workshops (Duarte and Snyder 2001), sponsoring and facilitating informal communications (Saphiere 1996), and clarifying rules, roles, and structure to reduce potential conflicts (Duarte and Snyder 2001; Hertel et al. 2005). These techniques generally require a significant amount of time, so their effectiveness is improved when team members have predispositions for trust that aid the development of a positive team climate (Hertel et al. 2005).

Regulatory Compliance, Laws, and Corporate Policy

Accompanying oversight and employee development are specifications of regulatory compliance and policy. There are many regulations and laws that govern various aspects of home offices and home-based worksites. Some of these address criminal activity, some civil, and others sociopolitical elements of the law. International work laws vary widely, and in the United States they are changing rapidly. Managers should investigate the laws and regulations for their locale and jurisdiction. Some public policies and regulations that affect telework in the United States are specified by the federal Department of Labor. This body oversees regulatory agencies such as OSHA, Bureau of Labor Statistics, and Worker's Compensation. Although there are other agencies (mainly at the state level), the federal Department of Labor has the primary responsibility for public regulation of telework at large. State agencies (the state departments of labor, for example) should also be consulted about specifics for a given state. There are some legal considerations, such as privacy and ownership rights, to consider as well. In addition, there may be policies that affect telework in a specific industry defined by the Environmental Protection Agency, the Department of Energy, the National Telecommunications and Information Administration, and the Bureau of Transportation.

For the purposes of this chapter, the following brief discussion will be confined to some key regulatory and legal issues regarding electronic transmission of information, official records, video teleconferencing, and surveillance. As with many of these issues, a concern for a traditional office environment is a concern as well for virtual work; however, in terms of information ownership and chain of custody, information that might not normally pass over a public wire may be more subject to this mode of transmission in virtual work.

It is important to note that international work laws and regulations vary widely, and in the United States, the laws that affect virtual work are changing rapidly. In the United States, the federal Department of Labor specifies many of the public policies and regulations that affect virtual work. State agencies such as state departments of labor may also define virtual work regulations, and there are regulations that affect virtual work in a specific industry such as the Health Insurance Portability and Accountability Act (HIPAA). Local zoning laws may also apply.

Most messaging systems use store-and-forward, and the World Wide Web caches files on intermediate servers. These media create multiple intended and unintended recipients of information copies, which create several potential problems for virtual work. The precise effects and importance of these problems depend largely on the kinds of virtual work done, the industry, and the kinds of information being used. For instance, there will be a greater impact if virtual workers are operating with sensitive or official information such as government, financial, or health care records than if they are simply reporting their time over the Internet.

Because electronic information products are intangible (Borrull and Oppenheim 2004), there is no good way to determine whether they have been altered unless digital signatures are used. Sensitive information may "fall into the wrong hands." In the case of store-and-forward messaging, the legal recourse and process of adjudication is complicated, and in some cases unclear, especially if an infringement occurs across international boundaries. For instance, unless information is protected with encryption, it has not been legally determined what limitations and liabilities are applicable to redistribution of information by intermediaries on the Internet (Bureau of Transportation Statistics 1992; Akdeniz, Walker, and Wall 2000). As suggested, the best safeguards against most of these problems are to use digital signatures and cryptography, although this is not always possible. For certain kinds of documents the techniques used in digital rights management such as watermarking and recording document usage may be beneficial.

Another issue for virtual work involves official "records" and e-mail. In most traditional office settings the messaging infrastructure is under the control of the company, but in a virtual work setting the control often falls under Internet service providers. For example, the National Archives and Records Administration (NARA) has created regulations under the Federal Records Act (FRA) to prevent shredding or deleting certain kinds of e-mail. These regulations may have implications not only for e-mail considered federal records but also for a range of message types in the wake of the Microsoft antitrust litigation and the Sarbanes-Oxley Act (Borrull and Oppenheim 2004).

Some of the regulations address retention requirements, but several problems have not yet been resolved and include the fact that to comply, e-mail has to be modified to distinguish whether or not a document is a matter of federal record. Also, it has not been legally decided where responsibilities lie with regard to maintaining detailed audit trails of messages that traverse systems in the Internet. In addition, organizations that fall under the FRA regulation must specify locations of all documents. This is a problem for distributed databases, home or remote locations, intermediaries, if data is mirrored, if documents have multiple parts or attachments, or if they are WAV, GIF, or JPEG files (Matteson and Feldstein 2005).

In terms of videoconferencing and surveillance, one of the central issues concerns the right to privacy versus the right to know. Laws have tended to support the rights of corporations to inspect and monitor work and workers, which arises from needs related to business emergencies and the corporation's rights over its assets and to protect its interests (Borrull and Oppenheim 2004). Employees may use e-mail or the Web inappropriately for purposes such as disseminating harmful information, infringing on copyrighted or patented materials, harassment, corporate espionage or insider trading, or acquiring child pornography. In these instances, the courts have leaned on the principle of discovery to allow inspection, granting any party or potential party to a suit, including those outside the company, access to certain information, such as e-mail and backups of databases, even to reconstruction of deleted files. The idea has now evolved to the use of video for surveillance (Bureau of Transportation Statistics 1992).

The Electronic Communications Privacy Act defines an "electronic communication" as any transfer of signs, signals, writing, images, sounds, data, or intelligence of any nature transmitted in whole or in part by a wire, radio, electromagnetic, photoelectronic, or photooptical system that affects interstate or foreign commerce, but it does not include the radio portion of a cordless telephone communication that is transmitted between the cordless telephone handset and base unit, wireless networks, any wire or oral or video communication, any communication made through a tone-only paging device, or any communication from a tracking device (Losey 1998). The original intent was to protect people from the interception of communications not otherwise subject to interception. However, the U.S. Patriot Act (HR 3162) has vastly expanded the powers of government and enforcement agencies to conduct surveillance and communications interception pertaining to criminal activity (Borrull and Oppenheim 2004).

Beyond the criminal concerns about virtual workers' activities, in some cases employers have chosen to use video teleconferencing to monitor worker productivity. Although surveillance in home offices carries special right-to-privacy considerations (Theuman 2005), from a virtual work standpoint, the use of video teleconferencing to monitor work activity may be supported by an analogy to the "plain view" doctrine, which allows the rights of a company to monitor employees in plain sight as long as the company takes overt action to notify its employees (Borrull and Oppenheim 2004).

The extent of an employee's expectation of privacy often turns on the nature of an intended intrusion. With the exception of personal containers, there is little reasonable expectation of privacy that attends to the work area. That is, a worker may have reasonable expectation of privacy in personal possessions such as a handbag in the office, but the law holds that employers possess a legitimate interest in the efficient operation of the workplace and one aspect of this interest is that supervisors may monitor at will that which is in plain view within an open work area (Braithwaite and Drahos 2000). This position is strengthened if an employer acts overtly in notifying its workforce in advance that video cameras would be installed and used for that purpose. Consequently, it might be legally possible to use video teleconferencing for monitoring work activity in the home as long as certain safeguards are observed (Akdeniz et al. 2000).

Security

In many if not most cases, virtual workers are provided with company-owned computer equipment and software and have in their possession documents and data and other information that may be proprietary or confidential. In addition to the obvious and well-publicized damages that can occur from security breaches, one of the key issues concerns downstream liability, in which companies may be held liable for surreptitious actions that are taken using their equipment, even if those actions are not known to the company or are unauthorized by them. This liability may well extend to virtual work settings unless there is a due diligence effort to preclude it from happening (Borrull and Oppenheim 2004). As a result, there are important considerations for virtual work that include how to control access to networked resources both resident on virtual workers' machines and the ones they may access at corporate locations. Basic security technologies such as firewalls, cryptography and authentication software, and virus and spyware scanners are important in the defense arsenal. Yet, although many security controls exist to help maintain information security, people frequently do not use these technologies to secure their systems even when they know how to use them and that they are readily and often freely available (Hochhauser 2004; Ives, Walsh, and Schneider 2004).

When people lack the skills necessary to use security technology and indicate that they would be willing to pay a fee to have their information protected by a third party, in practice they often do not avail themselves of the opportunity (Acquisti and Grossklags 2003). Thus, there exists a classic "knowing-doing" gap relative to information security, which is exacerbated in a virtual work setting.

Research (Woon, Tan, and Low 2005) has shown that people implement security measures with greater consistency when the security threat is perceived as more severe than when a threat is seen as innocuous, especially when a severe threat is also perceived as imminent. Other important factors in whether virtual workers implement security measures include whether they feel that their security actions will help prevent a security incident (Pahnila, Siponen and Mahmood 2007).

One of the greatest security threats comes from covert actions taken inside a company by its own employees (Blackwell 1998; Bresz 2004). Employees have the greatest access to sensitive information, and company insiders may also have extra motivation and opportunity for committing crimes using private business information.

Thus, managers of virtual teams must first increase employee awareness of security threats (Calluzzo and Cante 2004), provide training on security technology, processes, and procedures (Straub and Nance 1990), inculcate ethics and spell out clearly the consequences for misbehavior (Harrington 1996; Hsu and Kuo 2003; Kurland 1995), and develop clear and comprehensive security policies that govern the behaviors of individuals within organizations as well as the technological defenses (Schlarman 2002).

The SANS Security Policy Project (SANS 2005) provides common security practices, and beyond the technological components, its recommendations include ethics and information security awareness as well as enforcement and punishment that attend to contravention from insiders. In any case, security policies need to address both behavioral and technological components of information security for virtual workers (Stanton et al. 2005).

Employee Agreements and Ways of Working

As ad hoc formation of norms might be constrained by the nature of the virtual environment, formalizing rules and behaviors will increase structure, leading to better performance (Daniels et al. 2001; Griffin et al. 2001; Montoya-Weiss et al. 2001). A way to accomplish this is to use employee agreements (Frigault 2000) and to develop policies and procedures that define ways of working (Hyde 2004). The contributions derive from formalizing preparations, establishing virtual project launch activities, developing guidelines for performance management, and laying out plans for team behaviors and development (Hertel et al. 2005). Other essential ingredients in successful virtual working are the identification of dependencies; ensuring that priorities in the project are well understood; making sure that financial, budgetary, and purchasing processes are identified; gaining a clear understanding of time and expense reporting; assessing risks; and determining the training, rollout, and support plans (Hyde 2004).

Thus, the best way to address the potential legal and other problems besides increasing process and political structure, training, and using security technology is to establish guidelines and have clear written policies and procedures that cover both employer and employee responsibilities (Frigault 2000; Hyde 2004). Corporate policies may include virtual worker responsibilities and assumed liabilities related to conducting work on behalf of the company from home, on the road, or in a remote facility including customer locations. These policies often delineate insurance coverage and liability, for example, that specify who is responsible for loss or damage to data or equipment used at home and who should be responsible for injury to third parties on virtual workers' premises. The use of personal versus corporate equipment, ownership of intellectual property, and information security are also generally addressed. It is common to designate aspects of the home office environment in a virtual work policy, and if policies include home inspections it is important to include how and when virtual workers are notified about inspections. Guidelines that govern landlord/tenant relationships in each state might prove to be useful, although inspections may increase employer liability if the company "certifies" a home office safe and a virtual worker is subsequently injured (Akdeniz et al. 2000).

In addition to covering the legal aspects of virtual work, many companies establish policies and procedures that define how employees are selected for or assigned to virtual work, how they are evaluated, how work is allocated and coordinated among virtual collaborators, and how time and production are managed and monitored (Baruch and Nicholson 1997). In virtual projects, kickoff meetings are seen as crucial for educating virtual workers about policies, setting clear expectations, clarifying roles, and laying the groundwork for how the virtual project will be conducted (Lipnack and Stamps 1997). It is important to note that there are many instances in which good policies and procedures were "on the books" but were either improperly implemented or were not enforced. Unless established policies and procedures are enforceable and enforced, they are a detriment. Companies need to enforce the policies to protect business interests and themselves. If a company does not properly implement and enforce its policies, it opens itself up to claims of discrimination. Simply having a policy on the books is not an absolute defense.

IMPLICATIONS AND DIRECTIONS—CONCLUDING THOUGHTS

As technologies continue to mature, virtual work continues to develop into increasingly sophisticated forms. The maturation and richness of the technology is giving rise to the term *telepresence* to describe simulated environmental realism. By simulating a familiar environment and context, virtual workers become more comfortable with the computer-mediated form of work. The shared context also improves the consolidation of shared understanding (Jehng 1997) to better facilitate collaboration in virtual work. An example of telepresence is *KMi Stadium*, a suite of software applications used at the Open University's Knowledge Media Institute in the United Kingdom to model live events that give remote participants on the Internet a feeling of "being there." Auditory cues such as clapping, laughing, shouting, and whispering are embedded in the video stream to simulate the presence of a live crowd (Scott 2002).

By combining digital technologies, telecommunications and computer companies are creating new low-cost interactive multimedia products and services that provide voice telephony through cable networks, analog and premium TV broadcast, pay-per-view, and video-on-demand entertainment with teleshopping and telebanking businesses, which create new industries and business opportunities. These business models are incipient prototypes for virtual work. For example, when enLeague patented its new technology, company managers, programmers, systems architects, and patent attorneys across the United States used videoconferencing and streaming video to map out the schematics together; and for planning the Windward live-and-work community in Alpharetta, Georgia, cartographers, planners, and building contractors were better able to visualize landscapes and simulate noise levels using telepresence.

The delivery of broadband networking to the home and remote office has cheaply and reliably enabled commercial-grade communications from the home or remote work center, and multimode technologies that make use of these high-bandwidth communications allow virtual workers to choose the medium that best fits their tasks and preferences. An example of this type of multimode flexibility involves the different uses of video teleconferencing in which people who prefer the full richness of the medium may have their conversational partners use the entire range of the visual, voice, and textual capabilities. For those who prefer leaner media, the shutter of the camera may be closed, leaving the voice and textual components, or the microphone may be turned off, and only the "whiteboard" capability of the medium used (Webster 1998).

Video teleconferencing technology is becoming widely available for the home user and ranges from sophisticated, multi-user technologies such as VSGI to inexpensive simple, single-user systems such as Intel's PC camera. In addition, rather than using traditional telephone service, virtual workers are frequently using the Internet for voice over IP, or VoIP, with applications such as Skype and Vonage, and new VoIP technologies are emerging to carry increasing amounts of data along with policy-based routing protocols to better support the nature of voice and video transmission.

There are interesting trends in wireless technologies also. Blackberry and Palm represent forms of powerful wireless personal mobile computing systems (PCS), and many of these devices come equipped to operate with products such as TeamCenter and Symantec's pcANYWHERE and pcTELECOMMUTE to support Web-based project management for overseeing access, tasks, projects, and teams. When the Best Buy company contracts technicians from InitiaTEK to install a new line of point-of-sale computers throughout its store chain, technicians log into a secure portal on the InitiaTEK Web site and use their Dell Axim PCS enter the project status, where it can be tracked over the World Wide Web by managers at both companies.

Applications in cellular phones currently support e-mail, Internet access, facsimile, and other basic services, and palmtop computers and IP phones are becoming powerful enough that they will soon be able to take the place of laptops for many applications. As third-generation or "3G" cellular phones and WiMAX take hold, there will be support for broadband services for mobile phones to enable fast Web access, streaming music, on-demand video programming, and videoconferencing.

The increasing sophistication of technology and the need for faster, better, cheaper business operations are co-evolving. The demand for richer and more flexible technology is enabling virtual work, which is creating a greater demand for richer and more flexible technology. This co-evolutionary drive toward more robust technology and more responsive business models is redefining what we have come to think of as "work." Fuzzier dimensions are supplanting the traditional boundaries that have defined the workplace, the designation of work times, and the fixed roles in normative occupational relations. Along with this new agility come risks that include a reduction in the ability to manage one's time, difficulties in supervising the health and safety of remote and mobile workers, constant intrusions from the myriad new communications media, and alienation from vital social and instructional ties at work. The success of virtual work in the future might quite literally hang in the balance.

GLOSSARY

3G: A third-generation mobile telephone technology associated with the ability to transfer both voice data (a telephone call) and nonvoice data such as downloading information, exchanging e-mail, and instant messaging.

802.1(X): An IEEE standard that defines port-based, network access control to provide authenticated network access for Ethernet networks.

Blog: Web log in which virtual community members post comments about a given topic.

Chat: A program that enables dynamic (instantaneous) conversations using text messaging.

Information and Communications Technologies (ICT): Includes e-mail, instant messaging, video teleconferencing, digital libraries, and databases.

MUD (and MUDding): MUD stands for multiple user dimension, multiple user dungeon, or multiple user dialogue. It is a computer program in which users log in to and explore a textual theme, story, pretense, or game using a computerized persona called an "avatar."

Skype: A proprietary peer-to-peer protocol used for VoIP communications.

Spyware: A broad category of malicious software intended to intercept or take partial control of a computer's operation without the user's informed consent.

Text Messaging: A two-way conversation using textual forms of communications over a telecommunications medium.

Virus: A self-replicating program (in the classification of malicious software, or malware) that spreads by inserting copies of itself into other executable code or documents; typically used for causing damage to computer files.

VoIP: Voice over Internet protocol (also called IP telephony, Internet telephony, and digital phone) is the routing of voice conversations over the Internet or any other IP-based network. Voice data flow over a general-purpose packet-switched network instead of traditional dedicated, circuit-switched voice transmission lines.

Vonage: A commercial voice over IP (VoIP) network that provides telephone service via a broadband connection.

WiMAX: Acronym for worldwide interoperability for microwave access, a certification mark for products that pass conformity and interoperability tests for the IEEE 802.16 standards.

CROSS REFERENCES

See *Computer Conferencing and Distance Learning*; *Computer Conferencing: Protocols and Applications*; *Video Conferencing*.

REFERENCES

Acquisti, A., and J. Grossklags. 2003. *Losses, gains, and hyperbolic discounting: An experimental approach to information security attitudes and behavior*. Berkeley, CA: 2nd Annual Workshop on Economics and Information Security.

Akdeniz, Y., C. Walker, and D. Wall. 2000. *The Internet, law, and society*. Harlow, UK: Pearson.

Bailey, D. E., and N. B. Kurland. 2002. A review of telework research: Findings, new directions, and lessons for the study of modern work. *Journal of Organizational Behavior* 23:383–400.

Baruch, Y., and N. Nicholson. 1997. Home, sweet work: Requirements for effective home working. *Journal of General Management* 23:15–31.

Bell, B. S., and S. W. Kozlowski. 2002. A typology of virtual teams: Implications for effective leadership. *Group and Organization Management* 27:14–49.

Blackwell, E. 1998. Building a solid foundation for Intranet security. *Information Systems Management* 5:26–33.

Borrull, A. L., and C. Oppenheim. 2004. Legal aspects of the Web. In *Annual Review of Information Science and Technology, 38*, edited by B. Cronin, 483–548. Medford, NJ: Information Today.

Braithwaite, J., and P. Drahos. 2000. *Global business regulation*. Cambridge, UK: Cambridge University Press.

Bresz, F. P. 2004. People—Often the weakest link in security, but one of the best places to start. *Journal of Health Care Compliance,* July–August:57–60.

Bureau of Transportation Statistics. 1992. *Transportation implications of telecommuting*. Washington, DC: National Transportation Association. http://ntl.bts.gov/DOCS/telecommute.html (accessed June 23, 2007).

Burns, T., and G. M. Stalker. 1961. *The management of innovation*. London: Tavistock.

Calluzzo, V. J., and C. J. Cante. 2004. Ethics in information technology and software use. *Journal of Business Ethics* 52:301–12.

Carlson, J., and R. Zmud. 1999. Channel expansion theory and the experiential nature of media richness perceptions. *Academy of Management Journal* 42:153–70.

Carr, H. H., and C. A. Snyder. 1997. *The management of telecommunications*, Boston: Irwin.

Chakravarthy B. 1997. A new strategy framework for coping with turbulence. *Sloan Management Review* Winter: 69–82.

Chen, Y., J. Brokner, and J. Katz. 1998. Toward an explanation of cultural differences in in-group favoritism: The role of individual versus collective primacy. *Journal of Personality and Social Psychology* 75:1490–502.

Civin, M. A. 1999. On the vicissitudes of cyberspace as potential space. *Journal of Human Relations* 52:485–506.

Cole, M. S., W. S. Schaninger, and S. G. Harris. 2002. The workplace social exchange network: A multilevel, conceptual examination. *Group and Organization Management* 27:142–67.

Conner, D. S. 2003. Social comparison in virtual work environments: An examination of contemporary referent selection. *Journal of Occupational and Organizational Psychology* 76:133–47.

Daft, R. L. 1998. *Essentials of organization theory and design*. Cincinnati: South-Western College.

Daft, R. L., and R. H. Lengel. 1986. Organizational information requirements. Media richness and structural design. *Management Science* 32:554–70.

Daniels, K., D. Lamond, and P. Standen. 2001. Teleworking: Frameworks for organizational research. *Journal of Management Studies* 38:1158–85.

Davis, S., and J. Botkin. 1995. *The monster under the bed*. New York: Touchstone.

Deutch, M., and H. B. Gerard. 1955. A study of normative and informational social influence upon judgment. *Journal of Abnormal and Social Psychology* 51:629–36.

Duarte, D. L., and N. T. Snyder. 2001. *Mastering virtual teams*. San Francisco: Jossey-Bass.

Earley, P. C., and E. Mosakowski 2000. Creating hybrid team cultures: An empirical test of transnational team functioning. *Academy of Management Journal* 43:26–49.

Eby, L. T., and G. H. Dobbins. 1997. Collectivistic orientation in teams: An individual and group-level analysis. *Journal of Organizational Behavior* 18:275–95.

Ellingson, J. E., and C. Wiethoff. 2002. From traditional to virtual: Staffing the organization of the future today. In *Human resource management in virtual organizations*, edited by R. L. Henemann and D. B. Greenberger, 141–77. Greenwich, CT: Information Age Publishing.

Ellison, N. B. 1999. Social impacts—New perspectives on telework. *Social Science Computer Review* 17:338–56.

Finholt, T. A. 2002. Collaboratories. *Annual Review of Information Science and Technology* 36:73–107.

Frigault, L. 2000. *A manager's guide to virtual teaming*. Charlotte, NC: A Bank of America White Paper.

Fritz, M. B. W., K. Higa, and S. Narasimhan. 1995. Toward a telework taxonomy and test for suitability: A synthesis of the literature. *Group Decision and Negotiation* 4:311–34.

Fusaro, B. 1997. How do we set up a telecommuting program that really works? *PC World* 15:238–47.

Fussell, S. R., and I. Benimoff. 1995. Social and cognitive processes in interpersonal communication: Implications for advanced telecommunications technologies. *Human Factors* 37:228–50.

Gartner Group. 2000. Telecommuting trends. *The Gartner Report*. www.businesswire.com (accessed June 24, 2007).

Gass, R. H., and J. S. Seiter. 1999. *Persuasion, social influence, and compliance gaining*. Needham Heights, MA: Allyn and Bacon.

Gibson, C. B., M. E. Zellmer-Bruhn, and D. P. Schwab. 2003. Team effectiveness in multinational organizations: Evaluation across contexts. *Group and Organization Management* 28:444–74.

Griffin, M. A., M. G. Patterson, and M. A. West. 2001. Job satisfaction and teamwork: The role of supervisor support. *Journal of Organizational Behavior* 22:537–50.

Griffith, T. L., J. E. Sawyer, and M. A. Neale. 2003. Virtualness and knowledge in teams: Managing the love triangle of organizations, individuals, and information technology. *MIS Quarterly* 27:265–87.

Harrington, S. J. 1996. The effect of codes of ethics and personal denial of responsibility on computer abuse judgments and intentions. *MIS Quarterly* 20:257–78.

Heald, M. R., N. S. Contractor, L. M. Koehly, and S. Wasserman. 1998. Formal and emergent predictors of coworkers' perceptual congruence on an organization's social structure. *Human Communication Research* 24:536–63.

Hertel, G., S. Geister, and U. Konradt. 2005. Managing virtual teams: A review of current empirical research. *Human Resource Management Review* 15:69–95.

Hertel, G., U. Konradt, and B. Orlikowski. 2004. Managing distance by interdependence: Goal setting, task interdependence, and team-based rewards in virtual teams. *European Journal of Work and Organizational Psychology* 13:1–28.

Hill, E. J., B. C. Miller, S. P. Weiner, and J. Colihan. 1998. Influences of the virtual office on aspects of work and work/life balance. *Personnel Psychology* 51:667–83.

Hochhauser, M. 2004. Smart executives, dumb decisions. *Journal of Risk Management* 51:64–73.

Hofstede, G. 1998. Identifying organizational subcultures: An empirical approach. *Journal of Management Studies* 35:1–12.

Hsu, M.-H., and F.-Y. Kuo. 2003. An investigation of volitional control in information ethics. *Behavior and Information Technology* 22:53–62.

Hyde, L. 2004. *Virtual team handbook: A way of working*. Paris: A France Telecom Technical White Paper.

ITAA. 2003. *2003 workforce survey*. Arlington, VA: ITAA. www.itaa.org/workforce/studies/03execsumm.pdf (accessed June 24, 2007).

Ives, B., K. R. Walsh, and H. Schneider. 2004. The domino effect of password reuse. *Communications of the ACM* 47:75–8.

Jarvenpaa, S. L., and D. E. Leidner. 1999. Communication and trust in global virtual teams. *Organization Science* 10:791–815.

Jehng, J. J. 1997. The psycho-social processes and cognitive effects of peer-based collaborative interactions with computers. *Journal of Educational Computing Research* 17:19–46.

Katz, J. E. 1997. Social and organizational consequences of wireless communication: A selective analysis of residential and business sectors in the United States. *Telematics and Informatics* 14:233–56.

Konradt, U., and R. Schmook. 1999. Telework: Stress and strain in a longitudinal study. *Zeitschrift für Arbeits- und Organisationspsychologie* 43:142–50.

Kozma, R. B. 1991. Learning with media. *Review of Educational Research* 61:179–211.

Kraut, R. E., R. E. Rice, C. Cool, and R. S. Fish. 1998. Varieties of social influence: The role of utility and norms in the success of a new communication medium. *Organization Science* 9:437–53.

Kurland, N. B. 1995. Ethical intentions and the theories of reasoned action and planned behavior. *Journal of Applied Social Psychology* 25:297–313.

Lim, K. H., and I. Benbasat. 2000. The effect of multimedia on perceived equivocality and perceived usefulness of information systems. *MIS Quarterly* 24:449–71.

Lipnack, J., and J. Stamps. 1997. *Virtual teams: Reaching across space, time, and organizations with technology*. New York: Wiley.

Lococo, A., and D. C. Yen. 1998. Groupware: Computer supported collaboration. *Telematics & Informatics* 15:85–101.

Losey, R. C. 1998. The electronic communications privacy act: United States Code. Orlando, FL: The Information Law Web at http://floridalawfirm.com/privacy.html (accessed June 24, 2007).

Malhotra, A., A. Majchrzak, and R. Carman. 2001. Radical innovation without collocation: A case study at Boeing-Rocketdyne. *MIS Quarterly* 25:46–63.

Martins, L. L., L. L. Gilson, and M. T. Maynard. 2004. Virtual teams: What do we know and where do we go from here? *Journal of Management* 30:805–35.

Maruping, L. M., and R. Agarwal. 2004. Managing team interpersonal processes through technology: A task-technology fit perspective. *Journal of Applied Psychology* 89:975–90.

Matteson, L., and X. X. Feldstein. 2005. A synopsis of the Federal Records Act with implications for electronic document transmission. *Journal of Law and Social Issues* 34:122–49.

Miller, T. E. 1999. Research backgrounder: Telecommuting boosted in 1998 by internet & economy. *Cyber Dialogue*. www.cyberdialogue.com (accessed June 24, 2007).

Mohammed, S., J. E. Mathieu, and A. L. Bartlett. 2002. Technical-administrative task performance, leadership task performance, and contextual performance: Considering the influence of team- and task-related composition variables. *Journal of Organizational Behavior* 23:795–814.

Montgomery, D. A. 1999. Human sensitivity to variability information in detection decisions. *Human Factors* 41:90–105.

Montoya-Weiss, M. M., A. P. Massey, and M. Song. 2001. Getting IT together: Temporal coordination and conflict management in global virtual teams. *Academy of Management Journal* 44:1251–62.

Moon, J. Y., and L. Sproull. 2002. Essence of distributed work: The case of the Linux kernel. In *Distributed work*, edited by P. Hinds and S. Kiesler, 381–404). Cambridge, MA: MIT Press.

Moscovici, S. 1984. The phenomenon of social representations. In *Social representations*, edited by R. M. Farr and S. Moscovici. Cambridge, England: Cambridge University Press.

Moses, T. P., and A. J. Stahelski. 1999. A productivity evaluation of teamwork at an aluminum manufacturing plant. *Group and Organization Management* 24:391–412.

Murninghan, J. K. 1981. Group decision-making: What strategies should you use? *Management Review* February:51–71

Ngwenyama, O. K., and A. S. Lee. 1997. Communication richness in electronic mail: Critical social theory and the contextuality of meaning. *MIS Quarterly* June:145–66.

Nilles, J. M., F. R. Carlson, Jr., P. Gray, and G. J. Hanneman. 1976. *The telecommunications-transportation tradeoff: Options for tomorrow*. New York: Wiley.

O'Hara-Devereaux, M., and R. Johansen. 1994. *Globalwork: Bridging distance, culture & time*. San Francisco: Jossey-Bass.

Orlikowski, W. J., and S. R. Barley. 2001. Technology and institutions: What can research on information technology and research on organizations learn from each other? *MIS Quarterly,* 25, 145–165.

Pahnila, S., M., Siponen, and A. Mahmood. 2007. Employees' behavior towards IS security policy compliance. In *Proceedings from the 40th Hawaii International Conference on System Sciences, HICSS'07*, 1–10.

Raghuram, S. 1996. Knowledge creation in the telework context. *International Journal of Technology Management* 11:859–70.

Rheingold, H. 1994. *The virtual community: Finding connection in a computerized world*. London: Minerva.

Ruppel, C. P., and G. S. Howard. 1998. The effect of environmental factors on the adoption and diffusion of telework. *Journal of End User Computing* 10:33–43.

SANS. 2005. *The SANS security policy project*. Bethesda, MD: SANS Institute.

Saphiere, D. M. H. 1996. Productive behaviors of global business teams. *International Journal of Intercultural Relations* 20:227–59.

Schlarman, S. 2002. The case for a security information system. *Information Systems Security* 11:44–50.

Scott, P. J. 2002. *An Internet stadium*. Milton Keynes, UK: The Knowledge Media Institute, The Open University. http://cnm.open.ac.uk/projects/stadium/papers.htm (accessed June 24, 2007).

Shaw, J. B., and E. Barrett-Power. 1998. The effects of diversity on small work group processes and performance. *Human Relations* 51:1307–35.

Smith, M. K. 2005. *Bruce W. Tuckman—Forming, storming, norming and performing in groups*, The Encyclopedia of Informal Education. New York: Porter-Jones.

Stanton, J. M., K. R. Stam, P. Mastrangelo, and J. Jolton. 2005. Analysis of end user security behaviors. *Journal of Computers & Security* 24:124–33.

Staples, D. S., J. S. Hulland, and C. A. Higgins. 1999. A self-efficacy theory explanation for the management of remote workers in virtual organizations. *Organization Science* 10:758–76.

Straub, D. W., and W. D. Nance. 1990. Discovering and disciplining computer abuse in organizations: A field study. *MIS Quarterly* 14:45–60.

Suzuki, S. 1997. Cultural transmission in international organizations. Impact on interpersonal communication patterns in intergroup contexts. *Human Communication Research* 24:147–80.

Tajfel, H., and J. C. Turner. 1986. The social identity theory of inter-group behavior. In *Psychology of intergroup relations*, edited by S. Worchel and L. W. Austin. Chicago: Nelson-Hall.

Theuman, J. E. 2005. Constitutionality of secret video surveillance. *American Law Review* 91:585–648.

Toffler, A. 1980. *The third wave*. New York: Morrow.

Townsend, A., S. M. DeMarie, and A. R. Hendrickson. 1996. Are you ready for virtual teams? *HR Magazine* 41:22–45.

Turban, E., E. McLean, and J. Wetherbe. 1996. *Information technology for management: Improving quality and productivity*. New York: Wiley.

Wageman, R. 1995. Interdependence and group effectiveness. *Administrative Science Quarterly* 40:145–80.

Wallace, C. 1998. Gartner group forecast: By 2000, only half of all first-time remote-access pilot programs will succeed. *Business Wire* April:1–2. www.businesswire.com (accessed June 24, 2007).

Webster, J. 1998. Desktop videoteleconferencing: Experiences of complete users, wary users, and non-users. *MIS Quarterly* September:257–86.

Wellman, B. 1997. An electronic group is virtually a social network. In *Culture of the Internet*, edited by S. Kiesler, 179–208. Mahwah, NJ: Erlbaum.

Wellman, B., J. Salaff, D. Dimitrova, L. Garton. M. Gulia, and C. Haythornthwaite. 1996. Computer networks as social networks: Collaborative work, telework, and virtual community. *Annual Review of Sociology* 22: 213–38.

Wieland, R. 1999. Mental workload in VDU-assisted office work: Consequences for the design of telework. *Zeitschrift für Arbeits- und Organisationaspsychologie* 43:153–8.

Woon, I. M. Y., G. W. Tan, and R. T. Low. 2005. A protection motivation theory approach to home wireless security, *Proceedings of the Twenty-Sixth International Conference on Information systems, Las Vegas*: 367–380.

Workman, M. 2001. Collectivism, individualism, and cohesion in a team-based occupation, *Journal of Vocational Behavior* 58:82–97.

Workman, M. 2005. Virtual team culture and the amplification of team boundary permeability on performance, *Human Resource Development Quarterly* 16:435–58.

Workman, M. 2007. Virtual team performance and the proximal-virtual team continuum. *Journal of American Society for Information Science and Technology* 58:729–44.

Workman, M., W. Kahnweiler, and W. Bommer. 2003. The effects of cognitive style and media on commitment to telework and virtual teams. *Journal of Vocational Behavior* 63:199–19.

Zajonc, R. B. 1968, Attitudinal effects of mere exposure. *Journal of Personality and Social Psychology*, 9:Monograph supplement 2, part 2.

Online Banking

Ronnie J. Phillips, *Colorado State University*

INTRODUCTION: WHAT IS ONLINE BANKING?

Online banking is the use of the Internet to obtain financial services. Its origins can be found in the early 1980s, when many larger financial institutions began to provide access to some banking services through the telephone. With the spread of the personal computer in the 1980s and the emergence of the World Wide Web, online banking became a reality. At first, banks distributed proprietary software that had to be installed on the customer's computer. However, the proprietary approach is problematic: software had to be written for different operating systems such as Microsoft, Apple, and Linux, and the bank had to address all the issues of difficulty and compatibility that arose for their customers.

Online banking changed significantly in the mid-1990s, when Wells Fargo allowed its customers to access some banking services through the Internet, and Security First Network Bank became the first Internet-only financial institution. As the security and simplicity of use of Web browsers improved, virtually all institutions offering online banking migrated to a system that requires a customer only to have a secure Web browser, regardless of the underlying operating system. Since the Web browser is the primary way by which most individuals interact on the Internet, the adoption of this technology for online banking has served to increase the number of individuals willing to engage in online banking.

Banks serve a useful function in offering payment services to facilitate the exchange of goods and services between two parties. An important component of online banking is the provision of payment services. Banks are involved in the entire supply chain of payment services, from providing payment instruments to clearing and settlement. Indeed, because of legal restrictions in most countries, only chartered and regulated banks can be involved in the final clearing of payments through the Central Bank. However, banks face competition from nonbanks in other elements of the payment supply chain. In particular, nonbanks have been prominent in facilitating Internet payments. A significant example is PayPal, which designed a front end for payment services on the Internet and tied it to flexible back-end processing, which can clear a payment using credit cards, the automated clearinghouse, or other alternatives. The success of PayPal and other nonbank payments providers on the Internet suggests that there are characteristics of Internet retailing that opened up opportunities for providing online payments that banks have yet to exploit (Paunov and Vickery 2004).

The economic analysis of payment systems differs from that of most goods and services because payment systems are two-sided platforms. As Evans and Schmalensee (2005, 78) note, such "businesses are intermediaries that add value if and only if they can appropriately coordinate the demands of two distinct groups of customers." The implication is that consumers and merchants will use banks for payments only if they are willing to pay some or all of the costs of the transaction. The market price for the payments transaction service is also contingent on the acceptability of this form of payment to the other party (Baxter 1983, 543–4).

In Baxter's analysis, there are four parties to the transaction: a purchaser (P), a merchant (M), the purchaser's bank (P bank), and the merchant's bank (M bank). M and P have a demand for transactional services, and M bank and P bank supply those services. Though it may appear that transactional services are private goods, the aggregate demand for them cannot be found by horizontally summing the individual consumer demands. Though P's marginal valuation of the additional unit of transactional services may differ from M's, the valuations cannot be independent of each other. This is because for every purchaser, there must be a payee. Hence, the marginal valuation of a transaction service by one party is contingent on the acceptability of this form of payment to the other party (Baxter 1983, 543–4). The key point for such markets is that there is a price level that induces the transaction to occur, but also a price structure—the ratio of the price paid by the two parties. Competition for provision of Internet payment services is, in part, a search for a price ratio that determines how the cost of payment services is split between merchants and consumers. Nonbank providers of Internet payment services may be successful because, compared to banks, they have found a better solution to this pricing problem (Federal Reserve Bank of Kansas City 2005).

By definition, online banking would not exist without the Internet. The simplest form of online banking merely provides account information; for example, electronic delivery of statements or transfers between accounts within one institution. Table 1 contains a list of the features of bank Web sites. The transactional features are used by bank customers to replace in-person transactions at a brick-and-mortar bank site. Bill-pay services are very

Table 1: Generic List of Web-Site Features

Informational	General bank information and history Financial education information Employment information Interest rate quotes Financial calculators Current bank and local news
Administrative	Account information access Applications for services—opening accounts Personal finance software applications
Transactional	Account transfer capabilities Bill-pay services Corporate services Online insurance services Online brokerage services Online trust services
Portal	Links to financial information Links to community information Links to local business Links to nonlocal businesses (and/or advertisers)
Others	Wireless capabilities Search function

Source: Southard and Siau (2004).

popular with customers. Customers may pay a variety of bills from utility companies, credit card companies, and most other companies that accept electronic payments. Customers may also make direct payments from their accounts. Electronic bill presentment and payment (EBPP) is a form of bill payment by which bills are presented to a customer online, via either e-mail or a notice in an e-banking account. After presentment, the customer may pay the bill online when convenient. The payment is electronically deducted from the customer's account. Most bank customers can now use the automated clearinghouse (ACH) through the online banking services provided by their financial institution. The advent of electronic check conversion has also eliminated the need to physically transfer pieces of paper. ACH was created in the early 1970s to help reduce the volume of paper checks. In 1974, the regional ACH associations formed the National Automated Clearing House Association (NACHA) to facilitate the nationwide clearing of ACH payments. The system originally relied on magnetic tapes and diskettes to exchange ACH files, which required the physical transport of tapes among the ACH participants. The ACH system can process large volumes of individual payments electronically, and it has become the largest payment system in the country. The Federal Reserve processes approximately 75 percent of all the items handled by ACHs in the United States. There is only one private ACH operator in the United States (www.theclearinghouse.org/home.php). Though developed for recurring credit payments, such as a home mortgage payment, developments in technology have increased the frequency of its use and reduced the number of transactions that go through ACH. In 1994, the Federal Reserve mandated that all ACH payments would have to be done electronically. This requires that all financial institutions dealing with the Federal Reserve directly must have an electronic link to a mainframe computer or personal computer to participate in the ACH.

Informational features replace the need for the banks to provide paper copies to the customer available at the brick-and-mortar bank site (though banks may do both). The administrative features include access to account information and any software that may be needed to conduct financial services. Finally, the Web site can be a portal to provide links to other Web sites and information (Sullivan 2001).

A special category of Internet-only banks also exists (DeYoung 2001, The Financial Performance, 2001, Learning-by-Doing). Unlike traditional banks with a physical brick-and-mortar location, these banks have no physical offices where customers can engage in traditional banking services. One example of an Internet-only bank currently operating is the First Internet Bank of Indiana (www.firstib.com). Though the bank claims a cost advantage because "we don't have a costly branch network to support," lower costs do not necessarily mean higher profits. Internet-only banks likely represent a niche market whose customers would be only the most sophisticated and computer-savvy users who also were not bothered by being unable to visit a physical location (Evans 2004). Though there would be some cost savings from not having physical offices, it is not clear that the Internet-only strategy would be as profitable when compared with an institution that could offer both traditional and online banking (DeYoung 2001, The Financial Performance). As DeYoung observes, the introduction of online banking has parallels to the introduction of automated teller machines (ATMs), which provided a convenient way to engage in traditional banking transactions. Perhaps the most important feature of traditional banking that is missing with online banking is that a customer cannot get cash online. An important point that DeYoung makes is that Internet-only banks have a harder time obtaining higher-yield assets such as loans. The lack of a branch network for online banks therefore hurts relationship lending.

Cash had long been an important component of the payment services provided by banks. Indeed, for the average person in the nineteenth and early twentieth centuries, traditional banking meant using banknotes as a means of payment; personal loans from banks were rare. Today, traditional banking means the use of a checking or NOW account (demand deposit) or savings account (time deposit). Individuals also expect a role for the government (state or federal) in ensuring the safety and soundness of banks.

Online banking uses new technology in the delivery of banking services, but it does not entail a basic change in the nature of those services. This is because much of banking is information-related and can therefore be delivered electronically (Nickerson and Sullivan 2003). Referring to Table 1, it is apparent that so far banks have not tried to do something different; customers have no new service to them that is not provided by a traditional bank. Banks have had to provide technical support to consumers and have had to be prepared to make corrections when customer errors occur. The best banks adapt quickly to these new services. Banks also help with the accounting and monitoring of accounts through making the customer's bank information available for download into software such as Quicken or Money. This service enables the customer to monitor and track transactions, and also helps in the preparation of income taxes. The development and widespread use of software such as Quicken and Money has meant that banks often provide the ability to download account information into a format that can readily be imported into the customer's financial planning software (Furst and Nolle 2004).

Online banking is only part of the electronic revolution in banking. Examples of electronic banking include direct deposit of pay directly into a bank account, ATM cards, debit cards, and preauthorized debits, which allow customers to have regular, recurring bills paid automatically (Anguelov, Hilgert, and Hogarth 2004). There are also products that are not connected to a bank account, such as stored-value cards and smart cards; these have a preloaded value that need not be deducted directly from a bank account. Though these are important parts of the change in the payments system, the focus of this chapter will be those activities specifically connected to a bank account through the use of the Internet.

WHO USES ONLINE BANKING?

The diffusion of new technologies in society is an important topic (Bradley and Stewart 2003). There are both supply and demand considerations that affect the rate at which a new technology is adopted in society (Dinlersoz and Hernandez-Murillo 2005). In the case of banking, as more individuals and firms adopt the technology, there is a greater incentive for others to adopt it as well.

An important impact of online banking has been on the costs of doing banking for the banks and their customers (both individuals and businesses) (Bauer and Hein 2005). Online banking has reduced many of the costs of providing payments and lending services (trips to the bank), but it may have raised other costs such as account monitoring by individuals (Kim, Widdows, and Yilmazer 2005). The most immediate way that online banking differs from traditional banking is that transactions occur without the need to interact face to face with a bank employee. For banks, this typically means fewer interactions with bank tellers or loan officers. The use of tellers to conduct business is costly, as banks have known for some time. One estimate is that branch banking costs \$1.07 per transaction, telephone transactions 55 cents each, ATMs 27 cents, and online banking about 1 cent per transaction (DeYoung 2001, The Internet's Place). These estimates give an idea of the magnitude of the potential cost savings for banks with greater use of online banking.

One reason banks are considered "special" is the customer relationship that is fostered through the use of the teller and personal loan officers. On the one hand, the adoption of online banking is an effort by banks to reduce their costs, but on the other hand, it may put in jeopardy that special customer relationship. Thus, benefits for the bank on the cost side may also impact the revenue side if customers no longer perceive banks as "special" providers of payments and lending services. Online banking creates new pieces to the customer relationship. When a customer gets accustomed to using a bank's online system, much of the customer's routine payment information may get entered into a bank's online system. It becomes easier to switch into other products the bank offers, and the bank's Web site provides it with new, low-cost opportunities to supply information to customers about banking products they might want. These features of online banking could make a relationship more important and would add a whole new set of complications that a customer would have to go to the trouble of changing if he or she moved to another bank.

Banks will offer online banking if they believe it will ultimately improve their profits. Given competition, they may be forced to adopt the technology though it may not be profitable in the short-run. Lang, Nolle, and Furst (2002) found that though the more profitable banks were the ones more likely to adopt Internet banking after Quarter 2 1998, they were less likely to be the first institutions to adopt Internet banking. They also found that among banks with assets over \$100 million, institutions with transactional Internet banking were generally more profitable and tended to rely less heavily on traditional banking activities. Further, for banks with less than \$100 million in assets, there was no statistical difference in profitability among mature Internet and non-Internet banks. One important finding for online banking was that the startup Internet banks were significantly less profitable than startup non-Internet banks (Lang, Nolle, and Furst 2002).

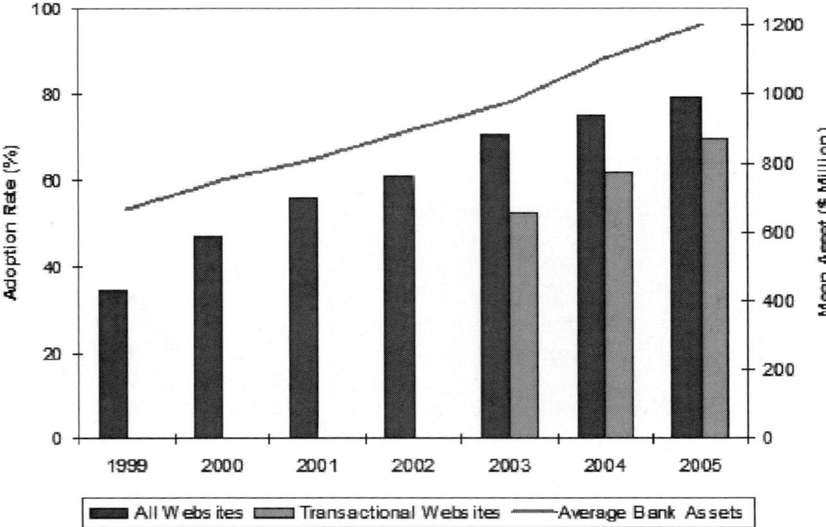

Figure 1: The Diffusion of Internet Banking 1999–2005 (Sullivan and Wang 2005)

Figure 1 plots the diffusion trends of Internet banking. It shows that 35 percent of depository institutions reported a Web site address in 1999, rising to 79 percent in 2005. Moreover, 53 percent of depository institutions reported Web sites with transaction capabilities in 2003, rising to 70 percent in 2005. Though data on transactional Web sites are not available for the whole sample of commercial banks before 2003, an independent survey conducted by the Office of the Comptroller of the Currency (OCC) shows that 6 percent of national banks adopted transactional Web sites in 1998, and the proportion rose to 37 percent in 2000 (Sullivan and Wang 2005; Chang 2005).

An interesting comparison for the diffusion of online banking is to consider the number of years it took for various types of technology to reach 30 percent penetration of the U.S. market. For the telephone, it was 38 years, television 17 years, personal computers 13 years, and the Internet 7 years. Sullivan (2004), in a survey of Tenth Federal Reserve District banks, found that fewer than 3 percent of the banks had transactional Web sites in 1999, but by 2004, nearly 46 percent had such sites that allowed customers to access and execute transactions on their accounts. Though banks have offered transactional services, estimates for the entire United States show that households using online payments grew from 2.6 percent in 1998 to 25 percent in 2003 (Sullivan 2004).

Individuals respond to relative prices, but they also have preferences that are determined by habits and other factors that influence their decisions on whether to adopt new technologies (Anguelov et al. 2004). Today, about 40 million U.S. households actively use online banking accounts (Wang 2006). Those who were already computer- and Internet-savvy were quick to adopt online banking. These are individuals with some sophistication in computer usage, who trust the security of online transactions, and who can conduct business without necessarily needing to visit brick-and-mortar banking offices. The distribution of this group varies with education, income, and other factors, including access to a personal computer (Sarel and Marmorstein 2004).

The demographic characteristics of those who were early users of computer banking can be seen in Table 2. The category of computer banking users is somewhat broader than online banking users, since the former could include those who may be using modem access to dial directly into the financial institution's computer and using proprietary software to access those financial services. However, the demographic characteristics of computer versus online banking users would likely be very similar.

In general, users of computer banking had higher incomes, were younger, and were more educated than nonusers. In addition, more users were white, married, held a job, and owned their own home. As costs fall and computers are more widely available, a greater portion of the population is able to use computer banking. The differences between users and nonusers provide some guidance on where banks should focus for new customers and also as a guide for public policy to increase access to financial services for a wider range of constituents.

There is also some evidence that rather than online banking being a substitute for traditional ways of delivering banking services, it is in fact a complement (DeYoung 2001, The Internet's Place). Though there has been a decline in check usage as the use of online banking has grown, banks have also increased the number of offices. In addition to the now-familiar ATMs, banks have also used automated banking machines (ABMs), which combine ATM and online services through the use of "kiosks" (DeYoung 2001, The Internet's Place).

WHAT ARE THE RISK AND SECURITY ISSUES IN ONLINE BANKING?

Today, most online bank users are able to access their bank accounts through the use of a Web browser such as Internet Explorer, Mozilla, Firefox, Safari, and others. As Sullivan (2004) notes, there are changes in both the technical and procedural ways in which online banks do business that expose them to operational risks. By providing access over the Internet, there is the risk that information

Table 2: Demographic Characteristics of Users and Nonusers of Computers Banking

	1995		2001	
	Users	Nonusers	Users	Nonusers
Household median income (2001 dollars)	53,168	38,950	71,953	38,032
Household financial assets, median (2001 dollars)	35,714	18,504	81,350	21,500
Age of head of household, median (years)	40	46	42	49
Education of head of household, median (years)	15	13	16	12
Race/ethnicity of head of household, distribution (percent)				
White	81	83	87	78
Black	15	9	7	13
Hispanic	3	5	2	7
Other	2	4	5	2
Marital status of head of household, distribution (percent)				
Married	65	61	74	60
Single female	20	26	13	27
Single male	15	13	14	13
Employment status of head of household, distribution (percent)				
Working	89	69	89	70
Retired	7	20	7	22
Unemployed, looking for job	1	3	2	2
Unemployed, not looking for job	2	8	2	6
Homeownership status, distribution (percent)				
Own home	71	71	77	71
Do not own home	29	29	23	29

Source: Anguelov et al. (2004).

may be acquired by an unauthorized person. The online user must be authenticated by the security system. Banks must work to ensure that they allow only authorized access to the system and can protect against account fraud and identity theft.

There is concern that customers could give out their account information inadvertently. Through various means, customers may be persuaded to provide account and password information or be directed to fake Internet sites. *Phishing* is a scam that involves the obtaining and using of an individual's personal or financial information, usually through an e-mail sent from what appears to be a financial institution, government agency, or other entity that requests personal information. The e-mail often contains a link that directs the recipient to a phony Web site. Once the individual goes to this Web site, personal information such as Social Security number, account numbers, passwords, and so on, may be requested. If the consumer provides this information, it can be used fraudulently to access consumer accounts or assume the person's identity.

Pharming refers to the redirection to an illegitimate Web site through technical means that may redirect a consumer when trying to access his or her bank's Web site (FDIC [Federal Deposit Insurance Corporation] 2005). Pharming can occur through static domain name "spooking." An example of spooking is when a pharmer may direct a user to anybnk.com instead of anybank.com, the site the consumer intended to access. Also, malicious software in the form of viruses or "Trojans" can intercept a user's request to visit a particular site and redirect the user to a site that the pharmer has set up. A hacker may also steal or hijack a company's legitimate Web site, allowing the hacker to redirect all legitimate Internet traffic to the fraudulent site. This is referred to as "domain hijacking," and can be done by slamming (submitting a domain transfer request from one registrar to another) or through the failure of a legitimate company to maintain the lease on the Web site. The most dangerous form of pharming is when the domain name server (DNS) translates the phrase entered into the Web browser into an Internet protocol address (IPA) and the user's connection is routed to a site other than that requested. This DNS poisoning can occur as a result of misconfiguration, network vulnerabilities, or malicious software (referred to as malware) installed on the server. For the entire Internet, there are thirteen root DNS servers that are closely protected and controlled. If a hacker were to penetrate one or more of these root servers, the Internet could be severely compromised (FDIC 2005). Banks and their customers can take steps to prevent such phishing and pharming attacks. These include digital certificates used by legitimate Web sites to differentiate themselves from illegitimate sites. Financial institutions need to be vigilant in renewing their domain names and must investigate the possibility of registering similar names to avoid unauthorized domain slamming and investigate any anomalies about their Web site to ensure that DNS poisoning attacks are addressed promptly. Consumer education is also essential to maintaining a safe system (FDIC 2005).

One example of large-scale Internet fraud is what happened to the Swedish bank Nordea. It lost up to $1.1 million in what security company McAfee is describing as the "biggest ever" online bank heist. The attack was a tailor-made Trojan sent in the name of the bank that encouraged clients to download a "spam-fighting" application. Users who downloaded the attached file, called raking.zip or raking.exe, were infected by the Trojan. Once installed, the program recorded keystrokes, and users were redirected to a false home page, where they entered important log-in information, including log-in numbers; then an error message appeared saying that the site was experiencing technical problems. The data were then harvested by the criminals, who used it at the real Nordea Web site to remove money from customer accounts. Bank spokespersons reported that the problem was not a lack of security at the Nordea site, but rather customers opening the Trojan virus and not having updated antivirus software installed on their computers. The bank refunded losses to its customers (Espiner 2007).

Once financial institutions have taken all precautions to maintain the integrity of their DNS, then the most important security measures concern log-ins to the site by their customers. This is done through various methods of authenticating the user. This process must be secure. Transport layer security (TLS) is a cryptographic protocol that provides secure communications on the Internet for financial transactions and other data transfers. It replaces an earlier protocol, secure socket layers (SSL). The TLS protocol allows client/server applications to communicate to prevent eavesdropping, tampering, and message forgery. 3-D Secure™ is an XML-based protocol to allow authentication of cardholders of credit-card companies in electronic payment transactions. The protocol ties the financial authorization process with an online authentication. In order for a member bank to use the service, it must operate a compliant software that supports the latest protocol specifications.

The authentication factor is typically something that customers provide as a means of identification. These factors are either something a person knows (such as a personal identification number, or PIN), something a person has (such as a physical device that has to be attached to the computer—e.g., a USB token device), or something a person is (such as a fingerprint, voice pattern, or pattern of veins in the user's eye). The latter type of identification is referred to as "biometrics" (FFIEC [Federal Financial Institutions Examination Council] 2005).

The authentication methods vary from a simple one-factor method requiring a password, to double-factor methods requiring a password and additional information input or a physical device or card. To meet the standards set by the bank regulatory agencies, banks have increasingly moved to multifactor authentication. On the initial log-in page, the customer may be asked to input a log-in name and also a series of numbers that appear at random below the log-in name. After clicking to go to the next page of the log-on process, the customer is presented with a customer preselected image and a place to input the account password. Such log-in procedures increase the level of security, but also require more time and effort from the customer. Missouri-based Midwest Independent Bank's system presents customers with nine faces in a tic-tac-toe-like grid and requires them to identify the right one and click on it. All of the bank's customers are required to choose a stranger's face and remember that face. Another large institution, Wachovia Bank, requires customers to enter separate access codes in addition to log-in names and passwords. SunTrust Banks Inc.'s new security will be written into software used behind the scenes that most customers will not notice (Matthews 2007). Because individuals do not always have all of their financial assets in a single firm; they may be faced with a bewildering collection of log-in names, passwords, images, and other such log-in authentication factors. The banks must find a balance between enhanced security, which their customers and the regulatory agencies both require, while maintaining the high level of convenience and ease afforded by online banking.

Of course, the security of a particular method depends on the integrity of its implementation. In addition to using passwords and PINs, other types of information-based authentication include online questions or queries that require a specific answer. These security methods can be enhanced if there is also the requirement that they be periodically changed. This may be an unwanted inconvenience for the customer, but Web browsers can retain passwords and information can be stored on the personal computer or elsewhere for quick reference, though this may raise concerns about security on the individual's computer.

The use of physical devices such as a USB token that plugs directly into a computer's USB port does not require any special hardware on the user's computer. Such a device provides additional security, especially if used in combination with something that a person knows, such as a password. Again, as the level of security increases, it may require greater responsibility from the individual not to lose such a device or token. The USB tokens are one-piece, injection-molded devices that can store digital certificates that can be used in a public key infrastructure (PKI) environment (FFIEC 2005). To date, a small number of large banks are using this technology.

Two other physical devices that can be used are smart cards and password-generating tokens. Though not currently in widespread use, they represent alternative technologies. Smart cards can be inserted into a compatible reader that is attached to a customer's computer. Such cards are hard to duplicate, are tamper-resistant, and are easily portable. A password-generating token ensures that the same one-time password (OTP) is not used consecutively. The OTP is displayed on a small screen on the token after the customer enters a user name and password. Authentication requires that the regular password and the new OTP match those on the authentication server. Because of the element of randomness, such devices increase the difficulty for a cyber thief attempting to break into a system (FFIEC 2005).

One of the most recent methods for authentication, biometric technology, is based on identifying physiological characteristic such as fingerprints, iris configuration, or facial structure. At present, these technologies are being tested by a few institutions involving very large financial transactions (hundreds of millions of dollars). The process of introducing people into a biometrics-based system is referred to as "enrollment." During enrollment, a sample of data is taken from one or more physiological or physical characteristics and the samples are converted into a mathematical model or template. Once the information is stored in a database, a software application can be used to perform the analysis. The customer then interacts through a live scan that is compared with the registered template stored in the system. Provided there is a match, the person is authenticated. In addition to the identifiers already mentioned, other possibilities are voice recognition, keystroke recognition, handwriting recognition, and finger and hand geometry (FFIEC 2005).

Two biometric techniques available are fingerprint and face scans. Fingerprints have long been used, prior to the computer age, and fingerprint biometrics is generally considered easier to install and use than iris scanning. The FFIEC recommends fingerprint technology for large-dollar transaction accounts. Face recognition, a newer technology, focuses on specific features of the face and makes a two-dimensional map of the face. Obtaining good scans requires proper lighting and placement of the video device for collecting the image. Several cameras may collect image data, and tests for authenticity can also be included to eliminate the chance that the person is using a photograph of an authorized person.

Though the above methods require an increasing level of sophistication on both the hardware and software sides, lower-level technologies are also available. These include the use of scratch cards as a low-tech version of the OTP tokens. Another method is to use the telephone or fax or regular mail to confirm a transaction. The customer's response to this confirmation request may require an additional password or other identifying information. Another low-cost way to verify a customer is to know the identity of the person at a specific IPA. There may, however, be problems with verifying IPAs, because they may be changed frequently or they could be fake. There are software fixes for such problems, but again there are problems associated with using proprietary software written for a particular platform. Geo-location software inspects and analyzes the small bits of time required for Internet communications to move through a network. Distances can be calculated and compared with those known for the user, and if they seem unreasonable, the user will not be authenticated. One other level of authentication is that banks could provide authentication to their customers before sending sensitive information. This would help deal with the problems encountered when customers are directed (through e-mails or otherwise) to false Web sites that look like the actual sites but are intended only to collect the user's information (FFIEC 2005).

One other method that banks can use is to have the customer verify information that the bank has on record or can obtain from a third party. In making online loans, banks will want to ensure that they have the right person, so they can match up credit information or geographical location with information from a third party such as a credit rating agency. Banks can also verify that address, area code, and ZIP code information are consistent. Banks can also use information regarding known fraudulent behavior to screen customers (FFIEC 2005).

As a result of the guidance issued by the FFIEC, many U.S. financial institutions redid their authentication protocol in 2006. Banks are supposed to tailor authentication efforts to risks of transactions (FFIEC 2005). It appears that the method of choice that financial institutions have adopted is a challenge-and-response system. Customers are first asked to provide answers to a random set of questions, which are stored on the financial institution's computer system. If the financial institution's Internet banking system detects a security risk, it can challenge the user and ask for the answers to one of these questions. One security risk, for example, is when a funds transfer is requested. Also, computer profiling has become common; the Internet banking system can detect characteristics of the user's computer. An Internet banking session is considered lower risk if it is initiated from a computer with a profile with which the system is familiar. If it is initiated from an unfamiliar computer, it would trigger the challenge-and-response mechanism.

Though customers access their accounts via the Web, the actual software used by banks is dominated by only a handful of vendors. Sullivan (2004) reports that in the Tenth Federal Reserve District (Kansas City headquarters), the top software vendor accounted for 20 percent of the online banking software used by banks in the district. Hence, if the software used by a large number of firms were compromised, the impact could be dramatic, and could intensify any fraudulent transactions problems. Because of the potential for large losses, there is a strong incentive for both the software vendors and the banks to be vigilant in security measures.

The Regulation of Financial Institutions

Though banks have a self-interest motive to protect their customers, there are also government regulations and laws with which banks must comply. Most recently there are the various regulations of the Gramm-Leach Bliley Act, the USA Patriot Act (section 326), and the Sarbanes-Oxley Act. These laws require that banks and savings associations safeguard the information of all persons who obtain financial services through a federally insured institution. Similar legislation covers credit unions and many other types of financial institutions as well (Mann 2006; Sullivan 2006).

The bank regulatory agencies have been aggressive in promoting online banking security. The Federal Financial Institutions Examination Council (www.ffiec.gov) provides a centralized source of information on the safety and security directives and information from the federal regulatory agencies such as the OCC, the FDIC, and the Federal Reserve. These responsibilities come from the basic mandate for bank regulatory agencies to maintain the safety and soundness of the financial system (Spong 2000). The government agencies are either part of the Central Bank or the Treasury Department (or Ministry of Finance). In the United States, the Federal Reserve System both provides liquidity to financial institutions in times of localized or systemic crisis and regulates and supervises financial institutions. The FDIC is the agency responsible for resolving any solvency questions and oversees the bank insurance fund, while the OCC charters and regulates national banks. One important reason government began to regulate banking was to protect the depositor against losses incurred by the bank in the event of a liquidity or solvency crisis. The creation of the FDIC in 1933 was a direct result of the problems of bank runs and bank failures (Rogers 2005).

Bank runs occur when depositors withdraw their money from their accounts. In the United States, regular accounts are insured up to $100,000. Economists make a distinction between "lobby run" and "clearinghouse" run. Lobby runs, initiated by small depositors, are no longer important because of deposit insurance. Clearinghouse runs (which apparently occurred when Continental Illinois failed in the 1980s) are still important, because large depositors are uninsured. With the advent of the Internet, clearinghouse runs could occur more quickly as large depositors execute withdrawals through their online connections.

The widespread use of online banking, with its implied increased monitoring by bank customers, could help reduce the need for monitoring by bank regulatory authorities. Such a development would reduce the regulatory burden on banks and help promote a safe banking system. Though online banking could reduce monitoring costs, Berentsen (1996) believes that today banks are more vulnerable to bank runs because news and rumors spread quickly over public computer networks. The problem is one of contagion; one bank may have problems, and the public may assume that this means other banks also have problems. When information is accurate, the potential for a bank run is a disciplining factor on banks, but if the information is incorrect, it may have a strong negative impact on the stability of the banking system.

CONCLUSION: WHAT IS THE FUTURE OF ONLINE BANKING?

Over the past decade and a half, legislation and technological advances have resulted in fewer numbers of bank charters. The demise of geographical restrictions on bank offices and branches due to legislation passed in 1994 has meant a consolidation of the banking industry into a smaller numbers of firms. At the same time, economic growth has increased the demand for financial services. Though online banking will likely continue to grow for the foreseeable future, this does not mean that traditional banking will disappear anytime soon. Evidence of this is that over the past decade, as the Internet and online banking have expanded, so has the growth in the number of bank branches. As previously noted, this indicates that online banking is a complement to the more traditional methods of delivering financial services.

The use of the Internet for payments may call into question the special role of banks. Banks have traditionally been at the front end of payments (interacting with the consumer), which has been aided by their monopoly access to the payments system. But now many nonbanks, such as PayPal, are taking the front-end role. They provide payment initiation and banks are relegated to the (less visible) back-end processing of payments. Nonbanks, in fact, are important sources of payment innovation. But this may also mean that the bank monopoly on access to payments is less important in terms of customer relationships. There is a concern, however, that nonbank access to payments could bring new risks to payments. Restricting access to banks has arguably kept payments relatively safe because risk control is easier with a closed, homogeneous system. Allowing nonbank access to the payments system may be desirable public policy but it would need to be done carefully (Quinn and Roberds 2003).

The challenges facing online banking for banks, customers, and government regulators are different but intertwined. Though there appear to be great cost savings from the point of view of banks when it comes to using online services, from the point of view of someone who wishes to make a payment transaction, the use of cash is most often the quickest and lowest-cost. The reason for this is that cash is readily available, it is convenient to carry, and most daily transactions are in small amounts. One factor important in the spread of online banking is to find a means of payment that will induce payers to use an electronic means of payment instead of cash (McGrath 2005). At present cash remains a useful means of payment for many transactions—and not all of those are necessarily illegal. If it becomes possible to transfer value from a checking account to a cash card, then this could change the future evolution of the payments system dramatically.

GLOSSARY

ACH: The Automated Clearing House, which processes payments electronically, was designed to reduce the use of paper checks for routine payments.

Authentication: The process of verifying the identity of a person or entity using online banking services.

Computer Banking: Banking services that consumers can access, by using an Internet connection to a bank's computer center, in order to perform banking tasks, receive and pay bills, and so forth.

Direct Deposit: A form of payment by which an organization (such as an employer or a government agency) pays funds (such as pay or benefits) via an electronic transfer. The funds are transferred directly into a consumer's bank account.

Direct Payment (also Electronic Bill Payment): A form of payment that allows a consumer to pay bills through electronic fund transfers. Funds are electronically transferred from the consumer's account to the creditor's account. A direct payment differs from a preauthorized debit in that the consumer must initiate each direct payment transaction.

Electronic Check Conversion: The process by which information from a check (routing number, account number, and amount of the transaction) is converted into an electronic format in order to make a one-time electronic fund transfer from an account.

Multifactor Authentication: A method to combat bank fraud that requires something the user possesses (i.e., the card) combined with something the user knows (i.e., PIN) before access to financial account information is allowed.

Smart Card: A type of stored-value card in which one or more chips or microprocessors are embedded, making the card capable of storing data, performing calculations, or performing special-purpose processing (to validate personal identification numbers, authorize purchases, verify account balances, and store personal records).

Stored-Value Card: A card on which monetary value is stored, through either prepayment by a consumer or deposit by an employer or other entity. For a single-purpose stored-value card, the card issuer and acceptor are generally the same entity, and the funds on the card represent prepayment for specific goods and services (for example, a phone card). A limited-purpose card is generally restricted to well-identified points of sale within a given location (e.g., vending machines at a university).

CROSS REFERENCES

See *Authentication*; *Social Engineering*; *The Internet Fundamentals*.

REFERENCES

Anguelov, C. E., M. A. Hilgert, and J. M. Hogarth. 2004. US consumers and electronic banking, 1995–2003. *Federal Reserve Bulletin* 90:1–18.

Bauer, K., and Hein, S. E. 2005. The effect of heterogeneous risk on the early adoption of Internet banking technologies. http://ssrn.com/abstract=772185 (accessed June 24, 2007).

Baxter, W. F. 1983. Bank interchange of transactional paper: Legal and economic perspectives. *Journal of Law and Economics* 26(3):541–88.

Berentsen, A. 1998. Supervision and regulation of network banks. www.firstmonday.org/issues/issue2_8/berentsen (accessed July 20, 2006).

Bradley, L., and K. Stewart. 2003. The diffusion of online banking. *Journal of Marketing Management* 19:1087–109.

Chang, Y. T. 2005. Dynamics of Internet banking adoption. http://ssrn.com/abstract=911602 (accessed June 25, 2007).

DeYoung, R. 2001. The financial performance of pure play Internet banks. *Federal Reserve Bank of Chicago. Economic Perspectives* 25(1):60–78.

DeYoung, R. 2001. Learning-by-doing, scale efficiencies, and financial performance at Internet-only banks. *Federal Reserve Bank of Chicago Working Papers Series*. WP-01-06.

DeYoung, R. 2001, March. The Internet's place in the banking industry. *Federal Reserve Bank of Chicago. Chicago Fed Letter*.

DeYoung, R. 2006. The performance of Internet-based business models: Evidence from the banking industry. http://ssrn.com/abstract=376821 (accessed June 25, 2007).

Dinlersoz, E. M., and R. Hernandez-Murillo. 2005. The diffusion of electronic business in the United States. *Federal Reserve Bank of St. Louis. Review* 87(1):11–34.

Espiner, T. 2007, January 19. Swedish bank hit by "biggest ever" online heist. *New York Times*.

Evans, D. S., and R, Schmalensee. 2005. The economics of interchange fees and their regulation: An overview. In *Interchange fees*. Federal Reserve Bank of Kansas City.

Evans, G. L. 2004. Old-fashioned banking in a high-tech medium: Internet-only banks. *Federal Reserve Bank of Chicago Proceedings* 83–9.

FDIC. 2005. Pharming: Guidance on how financial institutions can protect against pharming attacks. Financial Institute Letter July 18. FIL-64-2005. www.fdic.gov/news/news/financial/2005/fil6405.pdf (accessed June 25, 2007).

Federal Reserve Bank of Kansas City. 2005. *Interchange Fees in Credit and Debit Card Industries*. Kansas City, MO: Author.

FFIEC [Federal Financial Institutions Examination Council]. 2005. Authentication in an Internet banking environment. www.ffiec.gov/ffiecinfobase/resources/info_sec/2006/fdi-fil-103-2005.pdf (accessed January 20, 2007).

Furst, K., and D. E. Nolle. (2004). Technological innovation in retail payments: Key developments and implications for banks. *Journal of Financial Transformation* 12:93–101.

Hernandez-Murillo, R., and D. Roisman. 2004, October. Point and click, or mortar and brick? A look at Internet banking in the Eighth District. *Federal Reserve Bank of St. Louis. The Regional Economist*. St. Louis.

Kim, B.-M., R. Widdows, and T. Yilmazer. 2005. The determinants of consumers' adoption of Internet banking. *Federal Reserve Bank of Boston. Conference Series Proceedings*.

Lang, W., D. E. Nolle, and K. Furst. 2002. Internet banking. *Journal of Financial Services Research* 22(1&2).

Mann, R. J. 2006. Regulating Internet payment intermediaries. U of Texas Law, Public Law Research Paper No. 54; and U of Texas Law, Law and Econ Research Paper No. 007 http://ssrn.com/abstract=446420 (accessed June 25, 2007).

Matthews, R. G. 2007, January 2,. How safe is your online bank? *Wall Street Journal*, D2.

McGrath, J. C. 2005. *Will online bill payment spell the demise of paper checks?* Federal Reserve Bank of

Philadelphia. Payment Cards Center Discussion Paper. 05-08.

Nickerson, D. B., and R. Sullivan. 2003, November. *Financial innovation, strategic real options and endogenous competition: Theory and an application to Internet banking*. Federal Reserve Bank of Kansas City. Payments System Research Working Paper. PSR WP 03-01.

Paunov, C., and G. Vickery. 2004. Online payments systems for e-commerce. *Journal of Financial Transformation* 12:49–54.

Quinn, S. F., and W. Roberds. 2003. Are on-line currencies virtual banknotes? *Federal Reserve Bank of Atlanta. Economic Review* 2:1–15.

Rogers, J. S. 2005. *The new old law of electronic money.* Boston College Law School Research Paper No. 62. http://ssrn.com/abstract=680803 (accessed June 25, 2007).

Sarel, D., and H. Marmorstein. 2004. Marketing online banking to the indifferent consumer: A longitudinal analysis of banks' actions. *Journal of Financial Services Marketing* 8:231–43.

Southard, P. B., and K. Siau. 2004. A survey of online e-banking retail initiatives. *Communications of the ACM* 47:99–102.

Spong, K. 2000. *Banking regulation*. Kansas City, MO: Federal Reserve Bank of Kansas City.

Steeves, B. 2006. Wave good-bye to swiping. *Federal Reserve Bank of Kansas City Ten* Spring:6–9.

Sullivan, R. J. 2001. Performance and operation of commercial bank Websites. *Federal Reserve Bank of Kansas City. Financial Industry Perspective* December:23–33.

Sullivan, R. J. 2004, August. Payment services and the evolution of Internet banking. *Federal Reserve Bank of Kansas City. Payments System Research Briefing*.

Sullivan, R. J. 2006. The supervisory framework surrounding nonbank participation in the US retail payments system: An overview. *Federal Reserve Bank of Kansas City. Payments System Research Working Paper*. PSR WP 04-03.

Sullivan, R. J., and Z. Wang. 2005. Internet banking: An exploration in technology diffusion and impact. *Federal Reserve Bank of Kansas City. Payments System Research Working Paper*. PSR WP 05-05.

Wang, Z. 2006. Online banking comes of age. *Federal Reserve Bank of Kansas City Ten* Winter:22–3.

Digital Libraries

Cavan McCarthy, *Louisiana State University*

INTRODUCTION

Defining Digital Libraries

Digital libraries take advantage of the networking facilities of the Internet to offer quality content from authoritative sources, such as libraries and universities; they can be characterized as the "high end" of the Internet: that sector of the Internet that maintains a tradition of shared resources and easy access.

A major textbook for the field offers the following definition of a digital library:

> First, the digital library must have content. It can either be new material prepared digitally or old material converted to digital form. It can be bought, donated, or converted locally from previously purchased items. Content then needs to be stored and retrieved. Information is widely found in the form of text stored as characters, and images stored as scans. These images are frequently scans of printed pages, as well as illustrations or photographs. More recently, audio, video, and interactive material is accumulating rapidly in digital form, both newly generated and converted from older material. Once stored, the content must be made accessible. Retrieval systems are needed to let users find things; this is relatively straightforward for text and still a subject of research for pictures, sounds, and video. Content must then be delivered to the user; a digital library must contain interface software that lets people see and hear its contents. A digital library must also have a "preservation department" of sorts; there must be some process to ensure that what is available today will still be available tomorrow. (Lesk 2005, 2)

A digital library must contain and manage content; a system that simply points to outside information resources cannot be considered a true digital library. The literature uses three parallel terms: *digital, electronic,* and *virtual libraries;* these terms are normally used interchangeably (Saffady 1995). In current usage, *digital library* is preferred in North America whereas Europeans tend to use *electronic library;* the blanket term, *digital collections,* is little used. Definitions of digital libraries have been intensively discussed, notably in a survey by Schwartz (2000), in which she discovered sixty-four formal and informal definitions of *digital library*, and in a chapter by Borgman (2000, 40–4), which examined various approaches to the terminology. An entire chapter of Chowdhury and Chowdhury's (2003) textbook *Introduction to Digital Libraries* was dedicated to definitions and characteristics of the field.

Institutional and Informational Resources in the Digital Library Field

The Digital Library Federation, based in Washington D.C., is a consortium of thirty-nine major libraries, plus related institutions (www.diglib.org). It maintains a Digital Collections Registry at http://dlf.grainger.uiuc.edu/DLFCollectionsRegistry/browse. This offers simple or advanced searching of the descriptions of more than 750 digital libraries.

Resource pages for the digital library field are maintained by Ben Gross at the University of Illinois (http://bengross.com/dl), Candy Schwartz at Simmons (http://web.simmons.edu/~schwartz/dl.html), and at the University of California at Berkeley's SunSITE (http://sunsite.berkeley.edu). Major textbooks for the field have been authored by Lesk (2005), Chowdhury and Chowdhury (2003), and Arms (2000). A book by Tedd and Large (2005) discusses digital libraries in a global environment. Overviews of the field have been produced by Fox and Urs (2002) and McCarthy (2004). Chowdhury and Chowdhury (2000) compared the information-retrieval features of twenty important digital libraries. Greenstein and Thorin

(2002) prepared a biography of the digital library, based on six case studies.

Special government grants are a major source of financing in the digital library field. The National Science Foundation's Digital Libraries Initiative was of great importance to digital library development in the United States. Projects financed in Phase 1, 1994–1998, can be seen at www.dli2.nsf.gov/dlione; they were discussed by Fox (1999). Phase 2 projects are available at www.dli2.nsf.gov; they were summarized by Lesk (1999). One of the most important sources at the moment for the financing of digitization projects in the United States is the Institute of Museum and Library Services (IMLS; www.imls.gov). For examples of projects that have received IMLS support, go to www.imls.gov/search.asp and search for grants in areas such as "Preservation or digitization."

The Inventory of Canadian Digital Initiatives lists and describes Canadian information resources created for the Web (www.collectionscanada.ca/initiatives/index-e.html). The EnrichUK program (www.enrichuk.net), supported by British lottery funds, provides free access to 150 sites displaying the country's cultural, artistic and community resources. For a description, see Nicholson and MacGregor (2003). McCarthy and Cunha (2003) discuss digital library development in Brazil.

Digital library research was first reviewed by Chowdhury and Chowdhury (1999). This was updated by the chapter on "Digital Library Research" in Chowdhury and Chowdhury's *Introduction to Digital Libraries* (2003, 35–66). It is natural that the digital library area is well served by e-journals. In the United States, the major e-journal is *D-Lib Magazine* (www.dlib.org; Figure 1).

Other journals are *Ariadne* (www.ariadne.ac.uk), from Britain, and the *Journal of Digital Information* (JoDI; http://journals.tdl.org/jodi), from Texas. The major U.S. conference for this area is the Joint Conference on Digital Libraries (JCDL; www.jcdl.org); it is sponsored by Association for Computing Machinery (ACM) and the Institute of Electrical and Electronics Engineers (IEEE). European professionals participate in the European Conference on Research and Advanced Technology for Digital Libraries (ECDL), while Asian professionals go to the International Conference on Asian Digital Libraries (ICADL).

Digital libraries already demonstrate remarkable diversity, despite their short history. The next section presents an abbreviated overview of categories of digital libraries; for more detailed discussions, see my article in *The Internet Encyclopedia* (McCarthy 2004), or "A World Tour of Digital Libraries," in Lesk's *Understanding Digital Libraries* (2005, 321–60).

CATEGORIES OF DIGITAL LIBRARIES

Image-Oriented Digital Libraries

An important proportion of digital library materials consists of photographs and still images. These are relatively easy to digitize; they may avoid some of the copyright problems related to printed texts and can easily become the basis of attractive Internet presentations. For a major example see the 160,000 black-and-white Farm Security Administration photographs at the Library of Congress, which offer a picture of American rural life during the Depression (http://memory.loc.gov/ammem/fsowhome.html; Figure 2); keyword, subject, creator, and geographic indexes are available.

Another major collection is at the Bancroft Library, the University of California, Berkeley, which makes available the 37,000 image California Heritage Collection (http://sunsite.berkeley.edu/CalHeritage). Smaller collections have been digitized in numerous cities and states worldwide; historical photographs support local

D-Lib® Magazine

Search

Go

About D-Lib Magazine
Current Issue
Table of Contents
Featured Collection
In Brief
Clips & Pointers
Indexes
Back Issues
Author Index
Title Index
Subscriptions
Search Guidelines
Mirror Sites
Author Guidelines
Contact D-Lib
•••
DOI
10.1045/dlib.magazine

ISSN
1082-9873
•••
RSS D-Lib via RSS

In the Current Issue
Full-length Features

November 2005
Vol. 11 No. 11
Table of Contents
•••
EDITORIAL
Designing for Success
by Bonita Wilson, *CNRI*
•••
LETTERS
To the Editor
•••
OPINION
Public Domain Art in an Age of Easier Mechanical Reproducibility
by Kenneth Hamma, *J. Paul Getty Trust*
doi:10.1045/november2005-hamma
•••
COMMENTARY
What is a Digital Library Anymore, Anyway? Beyond Search and Access in the NSDL
by Carl Lagoze, Dean B. Krafft, and Sandy Payette, Cornell University, and Susan Jesuroga, UCAR-NSDL
doi:10.1045/november2005-lagoze

Also This Month
Digital Collections
FEATURED COLLECTION
Historic Pittsburgh Image Collections
Historic Pittsburgh features books, real estate maps, census records and images, that explores the history of Pittsburgh and the surrounding Western Pennsylvania area.
[Charles "Teenie" Harris Collection. Carnegie Museum of Art, Pittsburgh; Gift of the Estate of Charles "Teenie" Harris. Used with permission.]
Digital Library Community Activities
In Brief
Short items of current awareness.
In the News
Recent press releases and announcements.
Clips & Pointers
Documents, deadlines, calls for participation.
Archives
Back Issues and Indexes

Figure 1: An issue of DLib Magazine, a leading electronic journal for the digital library field

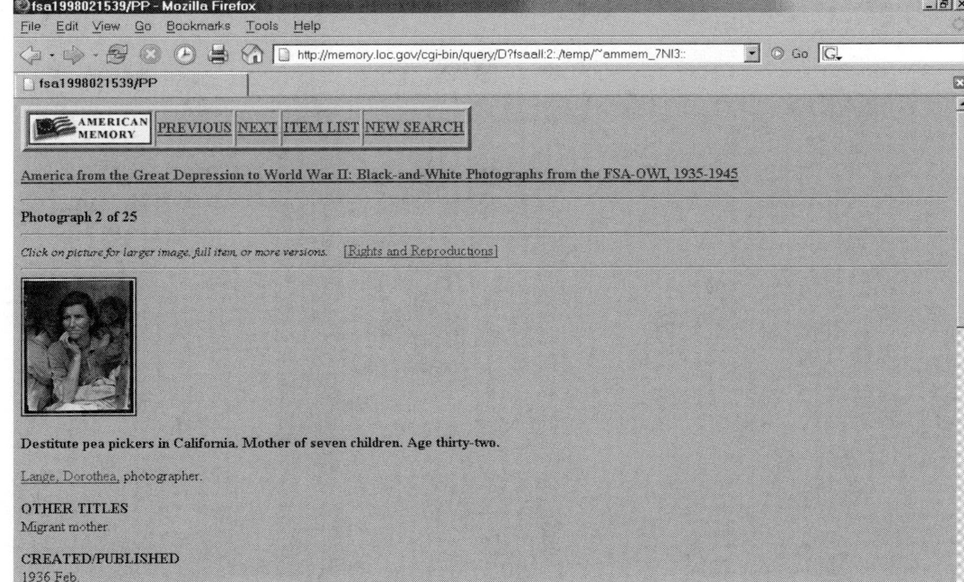

Figure 2: Photograph from the Farm Security Administration collection at the Library of Congress. Taken by Dorothea Lang, this photograph is usually referred to as the "Migrant Mother"

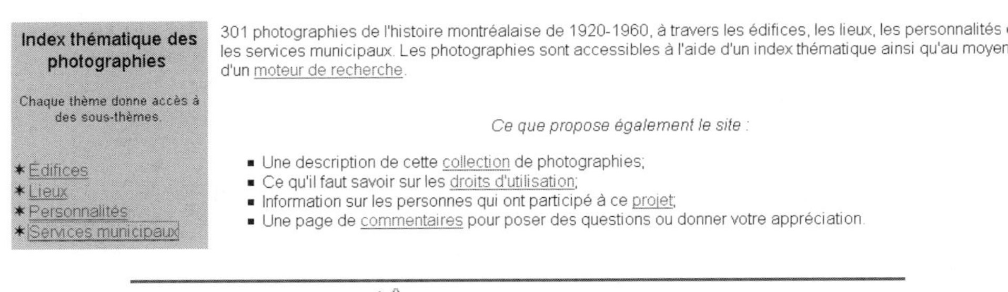

Figure 3: Historical photographs from Montréal city archives

community feelings. For a typical example, see the photographs from the Montréal city archives in *Montréal: Municipalité-Métropole 1920–1960* (http://epe.lac-bac.gc.ca/100/205/301/ic/cdc/mtl/default.htm; Figure 3).

Other types of images can also be made available in digital library collections. Visually stunning Spanish Civil War posters have been digitized at the University of California at San Diego (http://orpheus.ucsd.edu/speccoll/visfront; Figure 4).

Book-Oriented Digital Libraries

Project Gutenberg, often considered the first significant digital library, has always concentrated on simple presentations of books (www.gutenberg.net). It was founded in 1971 at the University of Illinois, and originally offered FTP downloads of "plain vanilla" ASCII texts, readable on almost any platform. Many of Project Gutenberg's 20,000 free texts are now available in HTML; input is processed by volunteers. The University of Michigan is responsible for several significant book-oriented projects, notably *Making of America* (http://quod.lib.umich.edu/m/moagrp/; Figure 5). This contains approximately 10,000 books and 50,000 journal articles on nineteenth-century American social history from the Antebellum period through Reconstruction. Sophisticated software offers a choice of image, text, and PDF files, in normal, large, and small size.

Figure 4: Spanish Civil War poster, digitized at the University of California, San Diego

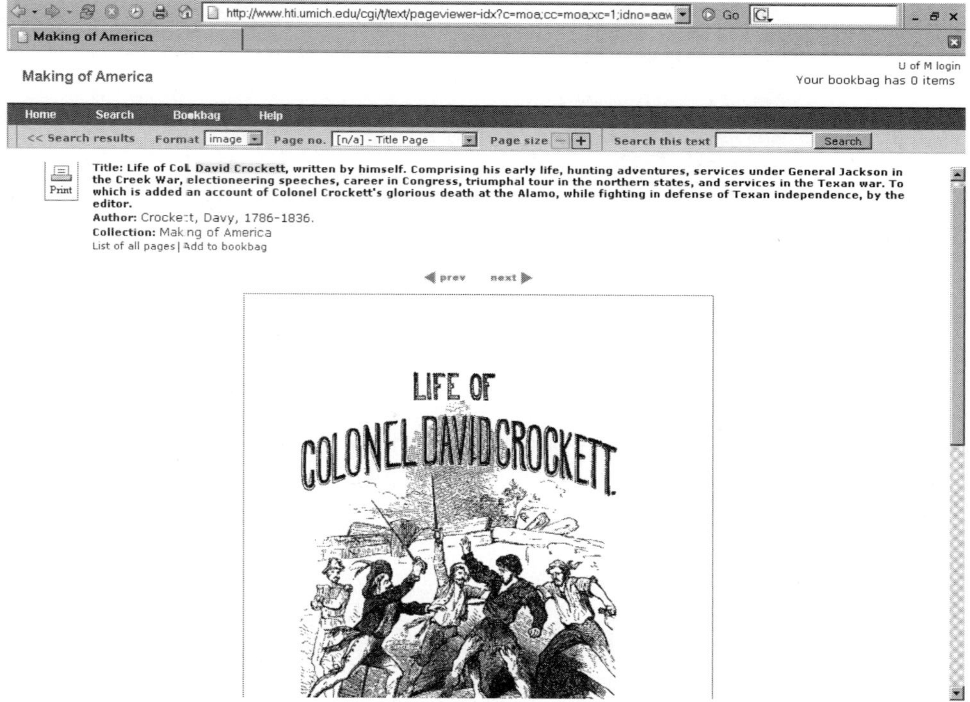

Figure 5: Screen from the Making of America Collection, the University of Michigan. Note bibliographic data, "Format" settings (image, text, PDF), "page size" buttons and controls to move from page to page

The University of Virginia Electronic Text Center (http://etext.lib.virginia.edu), founded in 1992, offers major resources in the humanities, including 10,000 publicly available online texts, and over 160,000 images. This attracts more than a million visitors each month; the Etext Center is also a valuable source of information on digitization procedures. It is important to note that digital libraries today exclude most modern commercially published books and the majority of copyright-protected items. These are exactly the texts that would be in high demand. The Digital Book Index (www.digitalbookindex.com) claims to list more than 130,000 English-language book texts, of which more than 90,000 are said to be free, but many texts are available in multiple versions. The Online Books Page (http://digital.library.upenn.edu/books), a wide-ranging catalog of online books, covers more than 25,000 titles.

Many early book-oriented digital libraries were established by universities and libraries for cultural motives. Commercially oriented digital libraries soon began to appear. One of the most successful in the North American market is NetLibrary, which has always concentrated on selling through libraries; it now offers more than 100,000 titles (www.netlibrary.com; Figure 6). It is so library-oriented that it permits access to only a limited number of copies of a book at any one time. This might appear unusual, because the Internet permits simultaneous access to an unlimited number of digital copies, but this limitation encourages publishers to join the scheme. The software does not permit rapid printing of multiple pages. NetLibrary is a subsidiary of OCLC (Online Computer Library Center; www.oclc.org), a cooperative system that supplies cataloging data and related digital services to more than 57,000 libraries in 112 countries and territories around the world.

Questia (www.questia.com) digitized core collections in the social sciences and humanities, and now offers over 67,000 books and 1.5 million articles through a sophisticated software interface. Questia is based in Houston, and sells subscriptions to the general public. Paid access services in the area of computing are dominated by the Association for Computing Machinery (ACM) Digital Library (http://portal.acm.org/portal.cfm). The ACM has been extremely successful in leveraging its informational resources to an audience with a high level of computer literacy. Another source for texts in the same area is Safari Tech Books Online (http://safari.oreilly.com), which offers digital versions of texts on computer science and programming from O'Reilly and other companies.

The systems cited above use Internet browsers as a distribution system, but some important commercial alternatives deserve mention. In the year 2000, half a million people downloaded Stephen King's e-book, *Riding the Bullet;* this can be considered the beginning of the commercially produced e-book. Numerous formats are offered, including Adobe Acrobat PDF (portable document format), Microsoft's downloadable e-book software, MS Reader, and the Palm and Mobipocket formats for mobile devices and PDAs. A major company in the field is Rosetta Books (www.rosettabooks.com; Figure 7), which offers e-books in all four formats. This publisher won a legal victory in 2001 when Random House objected to them distributing electronic versions of texts by William Styron, Kurt Vonnegut, and others. The judge considered that e-books constitute a separate medium from the original printed products, because they offer additional electronic advantages, such as full-text searching and hyperlinking (Stein 2001). Contracts in which authors had assigned rights to publish "books" would, therefore, not automatically cover the electronic texts.

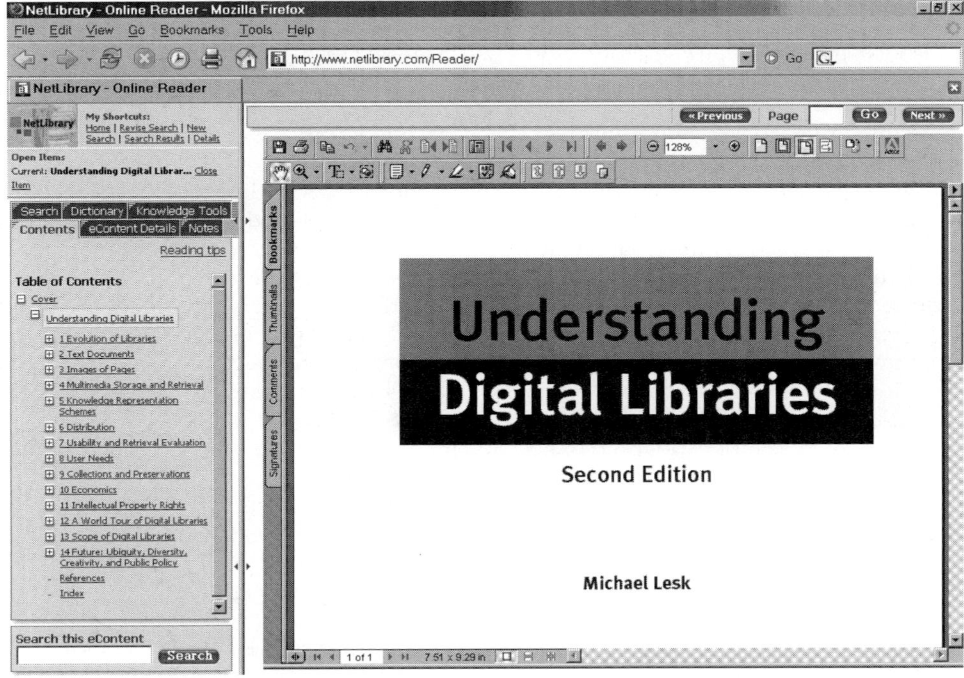

Figure 6: A sample screen from NetLibrary

Figure 7: Opening screen of Rosetta Books, a major e-book publisher

According to its banner, eReader.com is the world's largest e-bookstore (www.ereader.com); it sells more than 17,000 texts. Manybooks (www.manybooks.net) offers over 17,000 public domain e-books, for free reading on Palm, PocketPC, or other devices. An academic initiative, the University of Virginia Electronic Text Center, makes available more than 2000 downloadable books for MS Reader or Palm Pilots (http://etext.lib.virginia.edu/ebooks/ebooklist.html). The variety of formats has been a significant factor in deterring readers from purchasing texts (Crawford 2000). Also, consumers have been most unwilling to invest in specially designed e-book readers. The major bookseller, Barnes & Noble.com (www.barnesandnoble.com), announced the closure of its e-bookstore in 2003 (Albanese 2003). Publishers stated that the decision would not affect their e-book programs, which are still showing steady growth. Amazon (www.amazon.com/) maintains its e-books division, where it now offers *Amazon Shorts*, brief texts available for only 49 cents (www.amazon.com/shorts). Readers have to install a special plug-in to use ebrary (www.ebrary.com/), which offers 120,000 e-books and other titles. Major publishers, such as McGraw-Hill and Random House, finance ebrary, which, like NetLibrary, emphasizes sales to libraries. But it also offers ebrary Discover, which permits individual credit card holders to open an account and read 20,000 books free, paying only to print or copy text (http://shop.ebrary.com/). In Amherst, Massachusetts, the National Yiddish Book Center (www.yiddishbookcenter.org/) maintains the Steven Spielberg Digital Yiddish Library, with 14,000 texts. Digital versions are not available, but paper copies are produced on demand. As a result of the Book Center's efforts, Yiddish went from the threat of extinction, to being the language that has the highest proportion of its literature immediately available.

There has been major growth in digital library systems offered by search engines or major e-commerce sites. Consumers in traditional bookstores have always had the right to flip through a few pages of the text. Amazon.com (www.amazon.com) began to permit this in a digital archive, initially of 120,000 books (Wolf 2003). Users can search the entire text, but printing is impossible and only a few pages can be viewed at any one time. The system is available only to persons whose credit cards are registered with Amazon.com; these restrictions make it acceptable to publishers. Google (www.google.com) has also been responsible for a variety of interrelated activities in the book digitization area. These were originally referred to as Google Print, but the general title Google Book Search was adopted in November 2005 (http://googleblog.blogspot.com/2005/11/judging-book-search-by-its-cover.html). This offers three levels of presentation of text: snippet view, which displays a few sentences and information about the book; sample pages view, displaying a few pages; and finally, full book view (http://print.google.com/googlebooks/about.html). The texts come from two sources: the first is a well-established partner program, in which publishers authorize Google to display sample pages from their books; this offers publishers useful publicity, on terms that they control, and has generally been successful. The second source of texts is the library project, under which Google intends to scan millions of books; this was announced late in 2004 and initiated in five major libraries (Carlson and Young 2004). Despite the boldness of the vision, which can be seen as a major step toward reaching the goal of "universal access to human knowledge" (President's Information Technology Advisory Council 2001), the initiative was soon questioned (Quint 2004). Over the next few months positive aspects of the initiative were overshadowed by concerns of publishers over the legality of Google's plan to scan copyrighted texts and present snippets to the public (Young 2005). Google claims that this is covered by the "fair use" provisions of U.S. copyright law, and is no different from indexing; publishers view it as an infringement, and it seems probable that the question will ultimately be decided by the courts. Despite the controversy, numerous libraries have adhered to Google's program (http://books.google.com/googlebooks/partners.html); DeBonis (2007) cites a Japanese library as the twenty-sixth to join.

Meanwhile, the publicity given to Google's plans attracted the attention of other major players in the highly competitive search-engine world. Late in 2005 the Open Content Alliance brought together Yahoo!, Microsoft, the

Internet Archive, Hewlett-Packard, Adobe, and major universities (Quint 2005). They plan major book digitization at the Open Library project (www.openlibrary.org); Microsoft Network (MSN), for instance, has pledged $5 million to digitize approximately 150,000 books. Copyrighted texts will be included only with the agreement of the publisher; it will be possible to order hard copies through a Print-on-Demand service. Also late in 2005, a World Digital Library was announced by the Library of Congress; this would make available online rare and unique cultural materials held in U.S. and Western repositories, together with those of other great cultures beyond Europe, such as Asia, the Islamic world, and Africa (Library of Congress 2005). The first private-sector partner in this undertaking was Google.

Electronic Journals (E-Journals)

Digital penetration in the area of e-journals has been intense, and can often be both controversial and commercially driven. Three main areas of activity can be distinguished: commercial, semicommercial, and free e-journals.

During the second half of the twentieth century, the production of scientific and technical journals came to be dominated by a small number of commercially oriented companies. These became known for constantly increasing prices, but libraries maintained their subscriptions because researchers and professors considered the journals essential for their research. At the end of the past century, e-journals began to appear, but they offered libraries little relief. Major journal publishers began to offer both electronic and paper versions of their titles, but subscribers often found little advantage in subscribing to only the electronic editions. Titles are bundled, publishers discourage cancellation of individual titles, and libraries are forced to take titles of little interest to them while the prices of the bundles increase steadily. Discussions of these problems (Knight 2003; Carnevale 2003) frequently mentioned journals published by Elsevier (www.elsevier.com). The Association of Research Libraries has mounted the "Create Change" campaign, in favor of the digital sharing of research results (www.arl.org/create/index.html). Elsevier electronic journals are available through Science Direct (www.sciencedirect.com), which offers controlled access to more than 2000 titles and 8 million articles. Elsevier is part of Reed Elsevier, a major Anglo-Dutch conglomerate (www.reed-elsevier.com). An important U.S. source for e-journal subscriptions is Ebsco, established decades ago to fulfill library journal subscriptions. It now permits libraries to access more than 12,000 e-journals and more than 6 million articles (http://ejournals.ebsco.com/ejournals/ejsbro.pdf).

Librarians and researchers see semicommercial approaches as the solution. The Public Library of Science (PLoS) is a nonprofit organization of scientists and physicians that treats the costs of publication as the final step of the research funding process (www.publiclibraryofscience.org). Its first title was *PLoS Biology*, launched in 2003; it is also responsible for *PLoS Medicine* and a series of other titles. All of its publications are subject to an open access license. Similar principles have been adopted by SPARC, the Scholarly Publishing and Academic Resources Coalition (www.arl.org/sparc/index.html), a collaborative system for academic e-journal production supported by the Association of Research Libraries. A Brazilian initiative, SciELO, Scientific Electronic Library Online, offers access to medical and scientific periodicals from Brazil, Chile, Spain, and other countries (www.scielo.org; Figure 8). It is based at the Regional Medical Library (BIREME) in São Paulo; more than 270 journals are available.

Figure 8: Opening screen of SciELO, Scientific Electronic Library Online, São Paulo, Brazil

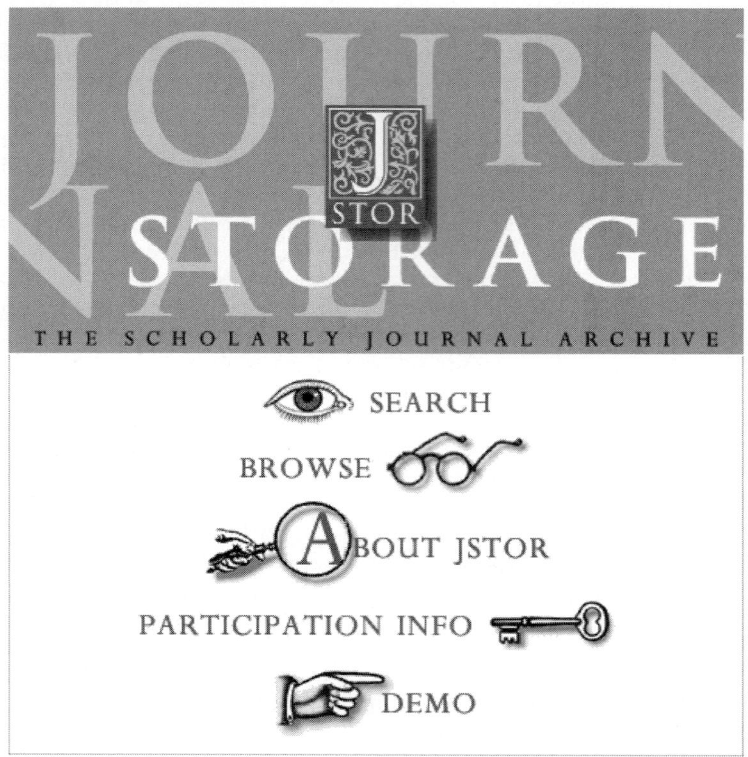

Figure 9: Opening screen of JSTOR, the Scholarly Journal Archive, from the University of Michigan

Two major university initiatives offer members of participating academic institutions reasonably priced access to journals. More than 300 titles from sixty scholarly publishers are available from Project Muse, of Johns Hopkins University Press (http://muse.jhu.edu). Over 700 titles are available from JSTOR, the scholarly journal archive, organized by the University of Michigan (www.jstor.org; Figure 9).

There has also been a rapid expansion of free e-journals. The Internet Public Library (www.ipl.org/div/serials) describes numerous titles, arranged in carefully constructed subject categories. The World Wide Web Virtual Library offers an additional list of e-journals (www.e-journals.org). Preprint archive systems are also relevant in this context; arXiv (http://arxiv.org) permits rapid access to preprints in physics, science, and mathematics.

Digital Newspaper Collections

Nearly 70 million indexed newspaper pages are available online from NewspaperArchive for a monthly subscription (www.newspaperarchive.com). This Cedar Rapids company claims to add 2.5 million pages each month. Olive ActivePaper Archive software offers dynamic newspaper viewing capability (www.olivesoftware.com). This permits its users to click on any article, photograph, or advertisement, which is then enlarged and presented in a separate window. For an example, see The Missouri Historical Newspapers Collection (http://newspapers.umsystem.edu/archive/Skins/Missouri/navigator.asp). Newspaper clippings are relatively easy to handle, and several collections are now available. For an indexed collection of clippings from newspapers published in the Pacific Northwest, see http://content.wsulibs.wsu.edu/pncc/pncc.htm. A collection of more than 144,000 Canadian newspaper articles, covering the Second World War, has been digitized and indexed at www.warmuseum.ca/cwm/newspapers/index.html.

Electronic Theses and Dissertations

The Networked Digital Library of Theses and Dissertations (NDLTD; www.ndltd.org) is the central organization for this field. For a practical example, see Virginia Tech, which offers nearly 10,000 digital theses (http://scholar.lib.vt.edu/theses). Experience suggests that digital availability stimulates use and promotes the author's reputation. West Virginia University reports more than 4 million hits on its digital theses (www.wvu.edu/~thesis/etd-faq.html); one notable thesis has already been downloaded more than 15,000 times. UMI Dissertation Publishing, of Ann Arbor, archives over 2 million doctoral dissertations and master's theses, and sells copies on demand. UMI, part of ProQuest, now accepts electronic submission of theses (http://wwwlib.umi.com/dissertations/about_etds).

Manuscripts and Ephemera

In a digital environment, there is no longer a clear line between libraries and archives. Papers of major personages in American history are available digitally from the Library of Congress. The papers of George Washington total 65,000 items (http://memory.loc.gov/ammem/gwhtml/gwhome.html); those of Abraham Lincoln total 20,000 (http://memory.loc.gov/ammem/alhtml/malhome.html). In 2003, 10,000 documents of Wilbur and Orville Wright were added to commemorate the centennial of their first flight (http://memory.loc.gov/ammem/wrighthtml/wrighthome.html). The Internet is an appropriate medium for the transmission of ephemeral materials; therefore it is not surprising to find digital libraries that preserve and disseminate ephemera. One of Britain's oldest libraries, the Bodleian Library of Oxford University, offers a well-organized Broadside Ballads collection (www.bodley.ox.ac.uk/ballads), which contains more than 30,000 items. Three thousand items of Historic American Sheet Music, including numerous items related to the Civil War from the collections of Duke University, can be found at http://memory.loc.gov/ammem/award97/ncdhtml/hasmhome.html.

Multimedia, Audio, and Video Digital Libraries

Digital libraries use computers for their interface, and therefore can present a variety of materials, such as books, photographs, film, and audio, with equal facility. The American Memory project of the Library of Congress (http://memory.loc.gov; Figure 10) is a major multimedia collection and one of the world's most important digital libraries. It now includes more than 9 million items organized into more than 100 thematic collections; digital materials include rare books, manuscripts, photographs, maps, sound recordings, and moving pictures.

Another important multimedia collection is ibiblio (http://ibiblio.org/index.html), whose objective is to make information freely available for the public domain. It offers software, music, literature, art, history, science, politics, and cultural documentation and is supported by the Center for the Public Domain and the University of North Carolina at Chapel Hill. Apart from written texts, it also includes music and poetry archives, sports statistics, large text database projects, and software archives.

Fascinating materials from the dawn of the cinema can be found among the Early Motion Pictures of the American Memory collection (http://memory.loc.gov/ammem/vshtml/vsfilm.html). The Prelinger Archives of Ephemeral Films, nearly 2000 short films, illustrating aspects of American life in the twentieth century, is available from the Internet Archive (www.archive.org/details/prelinger). History and Politics Out Loud is a major site dedicated to audio files (www.hpol.org), with speeches of Roosevelt, Churchill, and many others. The Open Video Project, from the School of Library and Information Science, University of North Carolina at Chapel Hill, offers more nearly 4000 video segments, retrievable by keyword or category (www.open-video.org).

CONSTRUCTING DIGITAL LIBRARIES

Digital libraries are complex structures that need to be carefully planned and designed. Their construction requires attention to a series of related considerations from the technical, legal, intellectual, and even aesthetic area.

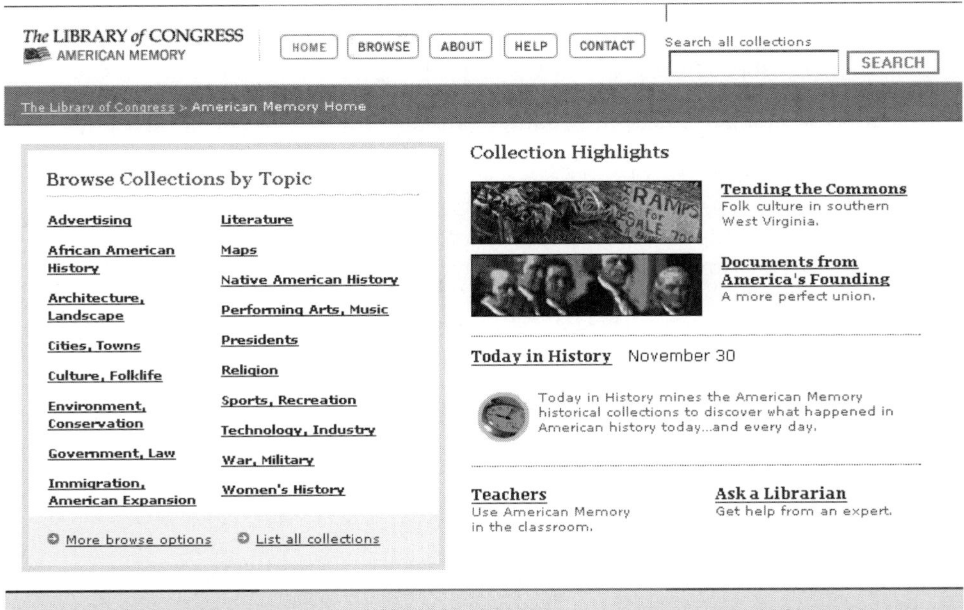

Figure 10: Opening screen, American Memory, Library of Congress (http://memory.loc.gov/ammem)

Copyright and Digital Libraries

Copyright law was originally formulated to control the dissemination of printed materials. It adapts poorly to digital environments and creates a major constraint for digital library activities. Lesk's *Understanding Digital Libraries* includes an entire chapter on "Intellectual Property Rights (2005, 293–319). The U.S. Constitution grants copyright for "limited times," but copyright terms have been constantly extended, in recent years largely to protect the interest of film studios. The Sonny Bono Copyright Term Extension Act, 1998, fixed copyright in the United States at the life of the author plus 70 years. Pre-1978 works in copyright are protected for 95 years from the date copyright was first secured. Most materials published in 1923 or after are protected by copyright. For details, see the Public Domain and Copyright page of Project Gutenberg (http://promo.net/pg/vol/pd.html) or When Works Pass into the Public Domain (www.unc.edu/~unclng/public-d.htm). Copyright protects everything fixed in tangible form: books, journals, newspapers, photographs, films, ephemera, and computer files, whether or not anybody is interested in protecting rights to these materials. About 10,000 books were published in the United States in 1930; today fewer than 200 are available from publishers (*Brief* 2002). The other 9800 could include texts that could usefully be digitized and disseminated, but the texts continue under copyright until 2019. They cannot be digitized, because copyright holders might appear. Contracts for most books published in the United States in the twentieth century stated that rights would return to the authors a few years after the book goes out of print (Lynch 2001). Should the authors die, their rights pass to their descendents, creating a huge category of "orphan books," for which no rights-holder can be traced. The situation is even more complex for photographs, sheet music, and ephemera. Eric Eldred, who founded the Eldritch Press (www.ibiblio.org/eldritch) to freely disseminate public domain texts, mounted a challenge to the copyright term extension laws, but lost in the Supreme Court. CNN reported: "Decision seen as victory for movie, recording industry" (Mears 2003). The problems refuse to go away, however, and in 2005, the U.S. Copyright Office undertook a full inquiry into the status of orphan works (www.copyright.gov/orphan/index.html). But the results offered little concrete in support of digital libraries. The Chronicle of Higher Education headline read: "Copyright Office Sides with Publishers in Proposal for Handling 'Orphan' Works"; the Copyright Office's recommendations were described as "unlikely to please archivists or scholars" (Foster 2006). Meanwhile, the Copyright Board of Canada has been operating a licensing system for orphan works since 1990 (www.cb-cda.gc.ca/unlocatable/index-e.html): fewer than 200 licenses have been requested, and most were granted.

In practice, it is much simpler for digital libraries to limit themselves to pre-1923 materials, to avoid having to identify rights-holders. Even when rights-holders can be traced, the digital library would have to negotiate for rights, a lengthy, expensive, and often fruitless process. Covey (2005) discusses acquiring copyright permission to digitize and provide open access to books. A possible solution would be to operate within the "fair use" provisions of U.S. copyright law. These provisions might be invoked when a nonprofit library or archive makes materials available for research and private study. The legal situation is complex, and the institution should emphasize that it does not condone further distribution, such as commercial use or print publication. Relevant disclaimers can be seen on many digital library sites. See, for example, the Library of Congress (www.loc.gov/homepage/legal.html) or Duke University's Rare Book, Manuscript, and Special Collections Library (http://scriptorium.lib.duke.edu/copyright.html).

Contracts between freelance authors and newspapers or magazines did not, until recently, mention the right to disseminate their work via databases. This market was nonexistent in the pre-electronic age. The Supreme Court in 2001 handed down the *Tasini* decision (*New York Times* 2001), which recognized that these authors had rights in this area. Dissemination via a database, in which materials could be consulted individually, was considered separate from print or microfilm publication. As a result, the *New York Times* was said to have removed 115,000 articles by 27,000 writers from its database (Stern 2001). Since the mid-1990s, newspaper and journal publishers retain digital rights over freelance articles.

When copyrighted materials have been posted to the Internet, there must be a mechanism to remove them, either against a formal demand made under the Digital Millennium Copyright Act or an informal request. "Take down" or "cease and desist" orders are rarely invoked against digital libraries, which offer mainly cultural and historical materials. Authors are, in effect, asking to be removed from the historical record. Search engines are more likely to receive "cease and desist" orders; see the Chilling Effects Clearinghouse (www.chillingeffects.org) for sample demands.

A possible solution for digital libraries is to work with copyright-free materials. Southern Methodist University mounted a digital library of government publications from World War II (http://worldwar2.smu.edu); this is legal because there is no copyright on U.S. government publications. The National Library of Medicine maintains PubMed, disseminating over 17 million items of medical literature (www.ncbi.nlm.nih.gov/entrez/query.fcgi). There are no copyright restrictions here, because the system delivers abstracts, rather than full text.

Interesting new possibilities are presented by open licensing systems, such as Creative Commons (http://creativecommons.org); works subject to this license can be made freely available, but attribution can be required, commercial use can be prohibited, and the original creator can insist that derivative works must also be publicly available. The license relieves authors of liability or implication of warranties and is in many ways similar to open-source licensing in the software area. In November 2005, Google Advanced Search began to permit users to limit their searches to items that could be freely used or shared.

Selection of Materials for Digital Libraries

For an overview of the problems of selecting research materials for digitization, see Hazen, Horrell, and

Merrill-Oldham (1998). Their first criterion is, unsurprisingly, copyright. Next, they recommend carefully analyzing the intellectual content of the resources, and estimating current and potential use. This permits the definition of the nature and format of the digital product. Metadata must be created and delivered alongside the digital images, while archival copies must be carefully preserved. It is also important to examine the relationship to other digitization projects; finally, costs and benefits need to be carefully weighed. Projects that score well on these considerations should receive priority. Chowdhury and Chowdhury dedicate a chapter of their *Introduction to Digital Libraries* to "Collection Management" (2003, 89–102).

Digitization of Materials for Digital Libraries

The classic method of offering access to individual visual resources, such as photographs, posters, or drawings, is by a series of three images. A high-quality archive image is produced on a scanner; this is then used to create an access or working image for use by the general public. The third image is a small thumbnail, used for quick reference (Boss 2001; Lee 2001). These terms are described in more detail below.

Archive Image

This is a high-quality image that was scanned directly from the original; it is normal to use an uncompressed TIFF (tagged image file format) for this purpose. This system preserves high-quality images; a resolution of 600 dpi (dots per inch) is commonly adopted. The archive image has significant value, because scanning is an expensive procedure, which may subject the originals to damage; it will therefore be carefully preserved. All digitization procedures must produce archive images, but these are often not available to the end user. TIFF files occupy significant space on servers and can be slow to download. An additional consideration is that some digital libraries will wish to profit from selling their own prints of quality images. For a discussion of the technical standards adopted in the digital imaging of photographic collections, see Frey (1997).

Access Image or Working Image

This must be adequate for a consultation by serious users. It is normal to use a high-quality JPG (Joint Photographic Experts Group) image, which is generated from the archival TIFF. JPG files offer quality spatial and color reproduction, and a high compression ratio; they are in wide use on the Internet. A digital library may, for instance, generate JPG images at a resolution of 300 dpi and a size of 640 × 480 pixels.

Thumbnail Image

This gives the user a quick preliminary overview of the access image. Thumbnails are typically produced as a medium- or low-quality JPG, about one-tenth of the size of the access image, at a resolution of 72 dpi. Alternatively, thumbnails can be generated using GIF (graphic interchange format) files.

Practitioners in this area offer detailed advice; see *Digital Projects Guidelines* from Arizona State Library, Archives and Public Records (http://www.lib.az.us/digitalProjectsGuidelines.pdf), or the *Western States Digital Imaging Best Practices* from the Colorado Digitization Program (www.cdpheritage.org/digital/scanning/documents/WSDIBP_v1.pdf); both of these include useful summary tables. See also Washington State Library's *Digital Best Practices* (http://digitalwa.statelib.wa.gov/newsite/best.htm), *Moving Theory into Practice: Digital Imaging Tutorial* from Cornell University Library (www.library.cornell.edu/preservation/tutorial/index.html), and *Benchmark for the Faithful Reproduction of Monographs and Serials* from the Digital Library Federation (www.diglib.org/standards/bmarkfin.htm). The *Image Quality Calculator* from the Digital Services Development Unit of the University of Illinois at Urbana-Champaign permits calculation of file sizes and recommended resolutions for a wide range of materials (http://images.library.uiuc.edu/projects/calculator). For a comparative discussion of file types for images, audio, video, etc., see the *University of Virginia Community Digitization Guidelines*, from the University of Virginia Library (www.lib.virginia.edu/digital/reports/uva_digitization_guidelines.pdf).

Further standardization and development can be expected in this field; notably, there is increasing interest in a major upgrade of the original JPG format, known as JPEG 2000 (www.jpeg.org/jpeg2000/index.html). JPEG 2000 images offer high quality and excellent compression; they are gaining acceptance for video reproduction and could possibly displace TIFFs for the archiving of still images. They use various file extensions—for example, .jp2, .jpx, .jpc. Sending the first part of a JPEG 2000 file can result in a version similar to the original .jpg; continuing to transmit the file results in the fidelity improving until the original image is restored. For a comprehensive account, see Acharya and Tsai (2005). OCLC has made available an extension to CONTENTdm digital library software, facilitating the viewing of JPEG 2000 images (www.oclc.org/news/announcements/announcement139.htm).

Low-value books may be disbound and the pages stack-fed through a scanner. But this process may take longer than anticipated, because of the dust generated by the paper, and will almost certainly render the original unusable. Rare materials, older books, and fragile items cannot be disbound and will demand gentle handling. The newest development is automated digitization machines, which carefully turn pages of books and even of newspaper volumes. 4DigitalBooks (www.4digitalbooks.com; Figures 11 and 12) offers equipment approximately the size of a sports utility vehicle that can now process up to 1800 pages an hour. This Swiss-designed robot is considered cost-effective for projects that involve more than 5.5 million pages (Markoff 2003).

For a smaller automated digitizer, based on a system developed by Xerox, see Kirtas Technologies (www.kirtas-tech.com; Figure 13). An animated graphic of their page-turning system can be seen on their home page. They claim that their page-turning process is more gentle than the human hand and can process 1200 pages per hour. Kirtas equipment is also being used in the Open Content Alliance digitization initiative (Quint 2005).

When digital libraries offer textual content, they need to convert page images to text that can be indexed

Figure 11: Automated digitizer, developed by 4DigitalBooks; illustration from www.4digitalbooks.com/photogallery/photo0001.jpg

Figure 12: Close-up of the automated digitizer, from 4DigitalBooks; illustration from www.4digitalbooks.com/photogallery/152_5300_b.jpg

and manipulated. Some early systems, such as Project Gutenberg, began by offering plain ASCII text files, which were keyboarded by hand. It is now normal to present HTML text that has been generated by OCR (optical character recognition) software. Relevant OCR products include OmniPage Pro from Nuance (www.nuance.com), formerly ScanSoft, or the Russian ABBYY (www.abbyy.com). Even the best scanning software can sometimes confuse certain terms; for example, modern/modem or clean/dean. Digital libraries face special difficulties. They strive to offer accurate conversion, but they handle large numbers of old and specialized books, which include antique fonts, unusual spellings, rare terms, and soiled pages. For a general discussion

Figure 13: Automated digitizer, developed by Kirtas Technologies; illustration from www.kirtas-tech.com/APT_1200/productphotos.asp

of these problems, see the text-scanning helpsheet from the University of Virginia (http://etext.lib.virginia.edu/services/helpsheets/scan/scantext.html). Text destined for digital libraries must be carefully proofread, but this requires qualified and dedicated personnel. Project Gutenberg has developed a system whereby new text is proofread page by page, by teams of volunteers (www.pgdp.net/c/default.php).

In order to guarantee textual integrity to the user, it is common for digital libraries to offer two versions of a text: page image and HTML. The image can be a medium-quality JPG; this is often adequate for plain text, without illustrations. An alternative is to offer the text in portable document format (PDF). This generally gives satisfactory results, and the images accurately represent the original. It is possible to include security measures—for example, to inhibit printing—and most Internet users are familiar with the free Adobe Reader. An archival version of PDF, known as PDF/A, is being developed by the International Standards Organization (www.digitalpreservation.gov/formats/fdd/fdd000125.shtml). Both text and page-image formats are available in digital libraries such as the University of Michigan's *Making of America* (http://quod.lib.umich.edu/m/moagrp). Here, users have a choice of image, text, or .pdf files, which can be presented in normal, large, or small size. The *Digital Quaker Collection* (http://esr.earlham.edu/dqc) offers full text and page images of more than 500 seventeenth- and eighteenth-century Quaker texts.

Software for Digital Libraries

Standard HTML can be used to hand code small-scale digital collections. Major systems can use commercial enterprise-level software, such as Oracle, used for the New York Public Library Digital Gallery (http://digitalgallery.nypl.org/nypldigital/dgabout.cfm). But it is now common to adopt software specifically designed for digital libraries for digital library development. Principal options, in alphabetical order, are:

CONTENTdm: Digital Collection Management Software is rapidly gaining ground as a high-performance storage and retrieval system for multimedia cultural collections (http://www.oclc.org/contentdm). Originally developed at the University of Washington, CONTENTdm was acquired in 2006 by OCLC, the major supplier of cataloging data to libraries (www.oclc.org). Numerous cultural collections have already adopted CONTENTdm (http://contentdm.com/customers/index.html); typical users include the Louisiana Digital Library (http://louisdl.louislibraries.org) and the American Indians of the Pacific Northwest Collection at the University of Washington Libraries (http://content.lib.washington.edu/aipnw/index.html).

DigiTool: This is an enterprise solution for the management of digital assets in libraries and academic environments, enabling institutions to create, manage, preserve, and share locally administered digital collections, such as institutional repositories, collections of educational materials, and special collections (www.exlibrisgroup.com/digitool.htm). It is used by the Digital Library Center at the Florida State University Libraries (http://digitool3.lib.fsu.edu). DigiTool is part the Ex Libris library automation software suite, internationally known for its multilingual and multiscript capacity (www.exlibrisgroup.com).

DLXS: This was developed by the University of Michigan Digital Library eXtension Service; its strength is in the indexing and presentation of multi-page documents (www.dlxs.org). It was used for the approximately 10,000 books and 50,000 journal articles of the University of Michigan's *Making of America* collection, mentioned above (http://quod.lib.umich.edu/m/moagrp). An additional 3000 books are available in the *Wright American Fiction Collection, 1851–1875* (www.letrs.indiana.edu/web/w/wright2).

DSpace: This captures, stores, indexes, distributes, and preserves digital research materials for academic institutions (http://dspace.org). A joint project of MIT Libraries and Hewlett-Packard, the original DSpace can be searched at https://dspace.mit.edu/index.jsp; PDF is used for full-text documents. DSpace is an open-source software that can be downloaded from http://sourceforge.net/projects/dspace (Atwood 2002).

eXist: This is an open-source XML database system from Germany (http://exist.sourceforge.net or http://exist-db.org). It was used for a major database of historical documents, *The Proceedings of the Old Bailey, 1674 to 1834* (www.oldbaileyonline.org). These describe more than 100,000 criminal trials held at London's central criminal court; it is probably the largest collection of historical texts relating to the lives of ordinary people.

Greenstone Digital Library: This software is an open-source system for building and distributing digital library collections (www.greenstone.org). It automatically generates organized digital collections and gives them a standard interface; full text indexes and lists of titles are created automatically (Witten and Bainbridge 2002). It is capable of handling large document collections, in various formats, and functions at server or desktop level. It will even export to CD-ROMs and can handle a variety of languages and scripts, including Arabic and Chinese. It was developed in New Zealand at the University of Waikato, and was used for the *New Zealand Digital Library* (www.nzdl.org; Figure 14), which offers significant United Nations and humanitarian collections. Greenstone is distributed under the GNU Public License, and can be downloaded freely from www.greenstone.org/cgi-bin/library?a=p&p=download.

Hyperion Digital Media Archive: This offers full-text indexing, storing, and accessing of nonbook materials in digital form (www.sirsi.com/Sirsiproducts/hyperion.html). It is a product of SirsiDynix, an Alabama conglomerate, a

Figure 14: Opening screen of the New Zealand Digital Library, created using Greenstone open-source software

major supplier of automated systems to libraries. For an example, see the Hekman Digital Archive at Calvin College in Grand Rapids, Michigan (www.calvin.edu/library/researchhelp/hda).

Insight: This is an image management and delivery software from Luna Imaging, produced in collaboration with the J. Paul Getty Trust, California, and Eastman Kodak (www.luna-imaging.com). It is noted for the high quality of its images and its powerful zoom capacity; it is generally used for photographs, maps, and art objects. For sample collections, see www.luna-imaging.com/community/collectionsharing.html. One collection, the *David Rumsey Historical Map Collection* (www.davidrumsey.com), won a Webby Award in 2002; it features nearly 16,000 maps.

Olive ActivePaper: This archive software creates fully searchable collections of historical newspapers, which can be scanned from the original or from microfilm. Readers can click on any item in the newspaper, such as an article or advertisement; this is enlarged in a separate window. For an example, see the *Pennsylvania Civil War Newspapers* at Penn State University (http://digitalnewspapers.libraries.psu.edu/Archive/Skins/civilwar/welcome.asp). Olive Software is widely used by newspapers, magazines, and libraries (www.olivesoftware.com).

Open-source software is frequently used for server-site software, especially in academic environments. It has, therefore, found applications in the digital library area. For a discussion of open-source software for the management of digital content, see Zhang and Gourley (2003). SQL (structured query language) is the best-known database language; in digital library applications, it is normally used via open-source serverside software, such as PostgreSQL or MySQL. Combinations of MySQL with PHP have also been found to be valuable. PHP (www.php.net) can be described as a serverside Web-scripting language that can easily interface with MySQL via a predefined function set. Another alternative is Macromedia's ColdFusion (http://www.adobe.com/products/coldfusion). The *Digital Library Toolkit* (Noerr 2003) offers a general review of software for the area. For a discussion of digital workflow management, with a diagram, see Choudhury and colleagues (2000). People working on projects that involve querying traditional library catalogs will wish to adopt software compliant with the Z39.50 standard, which permits Boolean searching and truncation. A resource center for this standard is maintained by the Library of Congress (www.loc.gov/z3950/agency).

Metadata and Digital Libraries

The value of digital objects is significantly increased by the addition of metadata, or subject terms and descriptive elements characterizing the digital object. Figure 15, from the *LOUISiana Digital Library* (http://louisdl.louislibraries.org) demonstrates the value of metadata.

The metadata elements locate the photograph geographically, define its subject, identify the photographer, and give additional information. What might have been simply an attractive photograph becomes a resource that researchers can identify and retrieve. Note that metadata is hyperlinked; users who wish to examine other illustrations of wrought iron can jump directly to them.

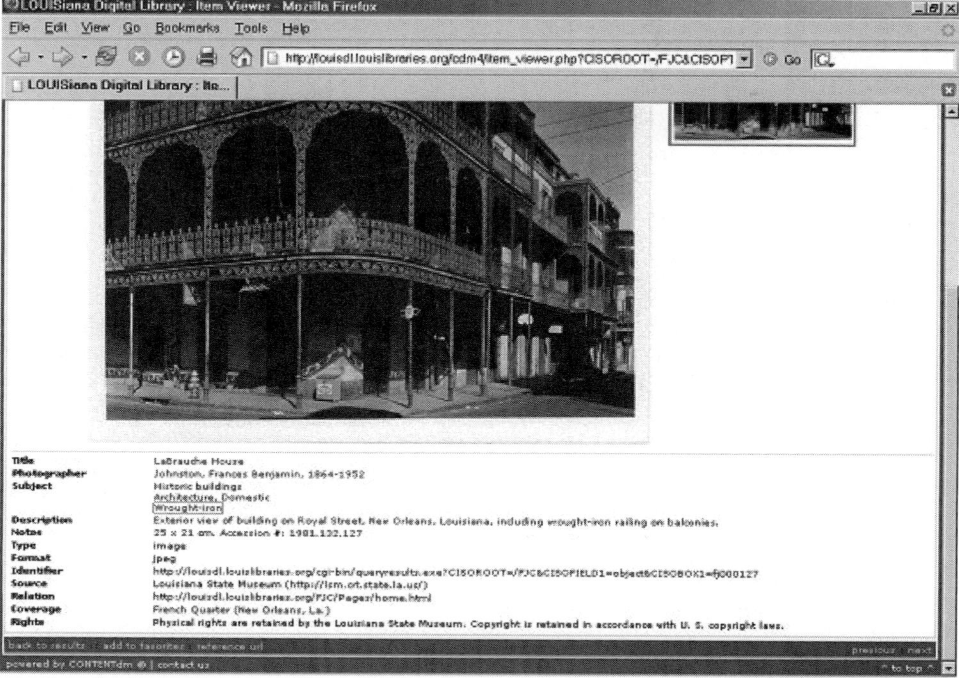

Figure 15: Photograph of a building in the French Quarter of New Orleans, digitized by the LOUISiana Digital Library, with metadata

It is possible to distinguish various types of metadata:

Descriptive Metadata: Author, title, abstract, subject headings, and so forth; the data used to index, discover, and identify digital resources.

Structural Metadata: Structural metadata include the structural divisions of a resource (i.e., the chapters of a book) or sub-object relationships (such as the individual diary entries in a diary).This is used to record information on the internal organization of the digital resource; it permits navigation within the resource, and display of specific digital objects.

Administrative Metadata: Management information for the digital object, such as the information needed to access and display the resource; this might include technical information, such as the hardware and software used in producing the image, the resolution at which the image was scanned, compression information, pixel dimensions, and so forth (Dublin Core 2005, 6). Technical metadata must be recorded accurately and consistently to ensure that the image files remain usable well into the future; standards are currently being developed (www.niso.org/committees/committee_au.html). Digital rights management information, such as contact information and rules for appropriate use of the data, is another important element of administrative metadata. Correct legal language must be employed to specify digital rights.

Metadata can be:

- embedded within the resource to which it relates; for example, as HTML metatags
- stored in a data management database separate from, but linked to the resource
- included in a resource discovery service, such as a library catalogue, with a link to the resource (National Library of Australia 2002).

Vellucci (1998) prepared an in-depth discussion of metadata for the *Annual Review of Information Science and Technology*. Traditional archive or library systems can include entire collections of photographs, listed on a single catalog or container record. Digital presentation, however, will require the application of detailed metadata. The Dublin Core is the best-known metadata system; it was specifically developed for digital environments at a 1995 meeting in Dublin, Ohio. The Dublin Core metadata element set (http://dublincore.org/documents/dces) specifies metadata elements such as title, creator, subject, date, and format; it also includes digital rights management information. Dublin Core metadata best practices have been published by the Collaborative Digitization Program (Dublin Core 2005). Metadata are applied by professionals known as metadata analysts, who normally work with a list of acceptable terms. Established sources include *The Art and Architecture Thesaurus Online* from the Getty Museum (www.getty.edu/research/conducting_research/vocabularies/aat) and the *Thesaurus for Graphic Materials*, from the Library of Congress Prints and Photographs Division (www.loc.gov/rr/print/tgm1). The *Library of Congress Subject Headings* are firmly established in traditional libraries and have been widely used in digital environments, such as the *American Memory* collections. Metadata analysts must avoid inconsistent vocabulary and take care with locally created terms, so as to maximize retrieval. Metadata creation adds significantly to both the value and the cost of systems; good metadata may be responsible for half or more of project costs. Metadata can facilitate retrieval of resources by major search engines, permitting the contents of digital libraries to be easily accessed by a wide audience, instead of becoming lost in the "deep Web" or "invisible Web."

The Open Archives Initiative (OAI; www.openarchives.org) makes metadata widely available in digital environments. This is based on harvester/server architecture: participating data repositories make metadata available in standardized format; information systems harvest the metadata automatically and use it to power subject gateways. For an outline of the origins and development of the OAI, see Digital Library Federation (2001) or Lagoze and Van de Sompel (2001). OAI harvesting from the *NASA Technical Reports Server* (http://ntrs.nasa.gov) is described by Nelson and colleagues (2003). An important initiative is OAIster, from the University of Michigan, which is a sophisticated search interface to a variety of freely available, academically oriented digital resources (http://oaister.umdl.umich.edu/o/oaister). OAIster indexes more than 12 million items from more than 850 institutions. A registry of OAI providers is available from the Grainger Engineering Library, University of Illinois at Urbana-Champaign (http://gita.grainger.uiuc.edu/registry/searchform.asp). Kepler (http://kepler.cs.odu.edu) permits research teams or individual researchers to easily self-archive their own publications within an OAI-compliant digital library framework.

Indexing and Retrieval in Digital Libraries

Digital library users normally have a choice between browse and search access. Browse access, or directory-based access, offers a menu of choices, such as alphabetically organized lists of titles or authors, or lists categorized by subject, location, etc. Broad subjects can be subdivided by using nesting menus. This is simple to organize, even by manual procedures, and is typically offered by digital libraries from the opening page. Search access is via a search box, which permits the user to query an index generated by specialized software. Search boxes are prominent features of digital libraries, and can be quite sophisticated. For an example of a retrieval system with multiple boxes, see Gallica, the digital library of the National Library of France (http://gallica.bnf.fr; Figure 16). In this case, browsing by alphabetical subject terms is also available from the search page.

Word-by-word text indexing is one of the most valuable features of digital libraries. Specialized software includes the XPAT search engine, part of the University of Michigan Digital Library eXtension Service (DLXS) system (www.dlxs.org). For a working example, on a large file, see the Legacy National Tobacco Documents Library (LNTDL); this collection of more than 7 million documents, relating to the manufacture and marketing of cigarettes, was

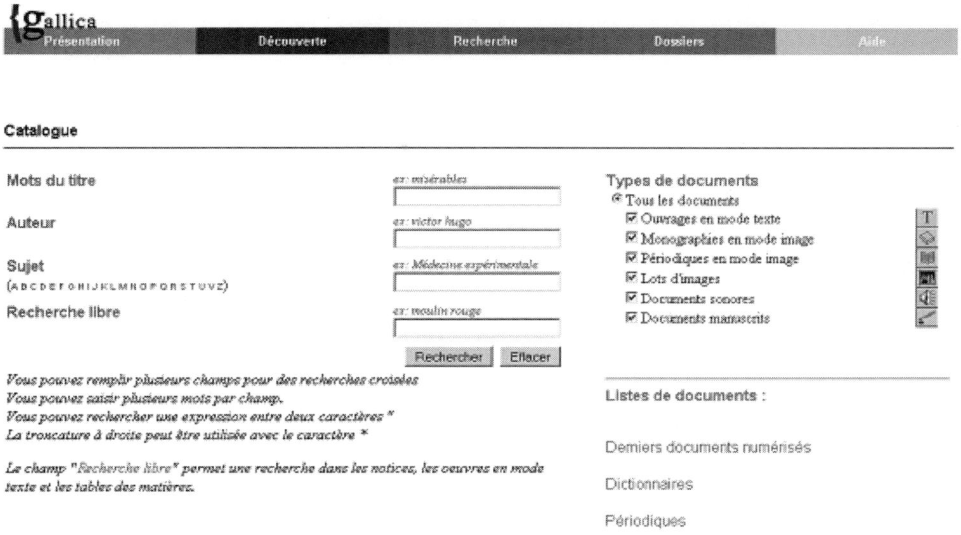

Figure 16: Search boxes on Gallica, digital library of the National Library of France

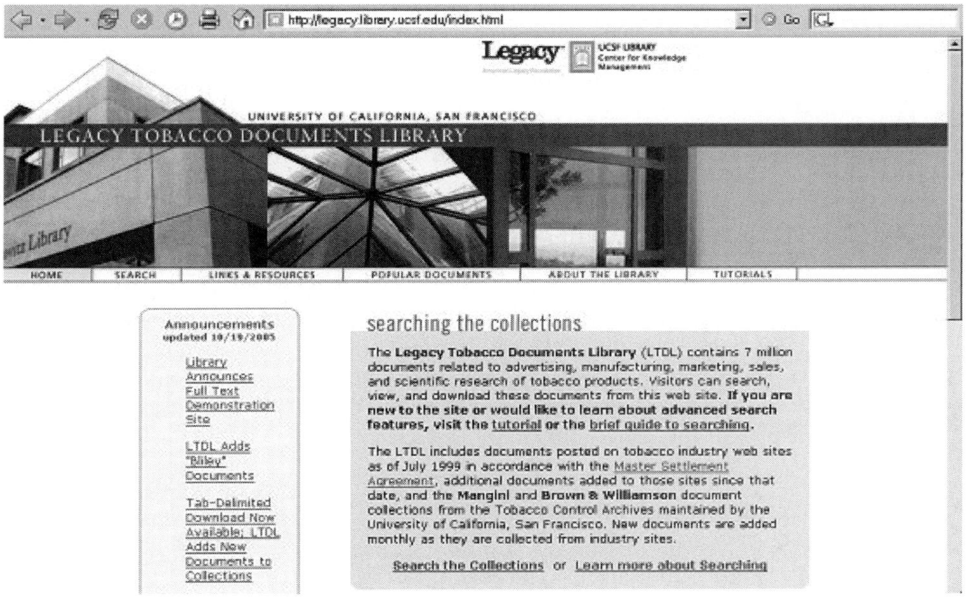

Figure 17: Opening screen of the Legacy Tobacco Documents Library, from the University of California, San Francisco

obtained through legal discovery in relation to a lawsuit (http://legacy.library.ucsf.edu; Figure 17).

Simple Web Indexing System for Humans—Enhanced (SWISH-E; http://swish-e.org) is an open-source software that enables full-text indexing. It can be seen in use at many locations, including the Berkeley Digital Library SunSITE (http://sunsite.berkeley.edu/cgi-bin/search.pl), and the Apache Web server site (http://search.apache.org). An additional option is WebGlimpse (http://webglimpse.net), originally developed at the University of Arizona. A free version is available for educational or U.S. government users; it can be seen in the index to the papers of President George Bush, Senior (http://bushlibrary.tamu.edu/research/paper.html; test with "saddam"). Fluid Dynamics Software (www.xav.com/scripts/search) is widely used; for example, see the Encyclopedia Titanica (www.encyclopedia-titanica.org/index.php), a fascinating collection of documents relating to the sinking of the Titanic. Indexing software from Master.com (www.master.com/texis/master/app/home.html) offers advanced Boolean search (AND, OR, NOT) capability; for a relevant example, see the Chicago Women's Liberation Union (http://cwluherstory.master.com/texis/master/search/?q=CWLU&s=SS&cmd=Options). MG is a freely available, open-source full-text retrieval system developed by the team responsible for the Greenstone library software (Witten, Moffat, and Bell 1999). It makes efficient use of disk resources by storing the index, and the text that is indexed, in compressed form (www.nzdl.org/html/mg.html). The Apache Lucene open-source Java text search engine (http://lucene.apache.org/java/docs/index.html) is used to power the DSpace digital

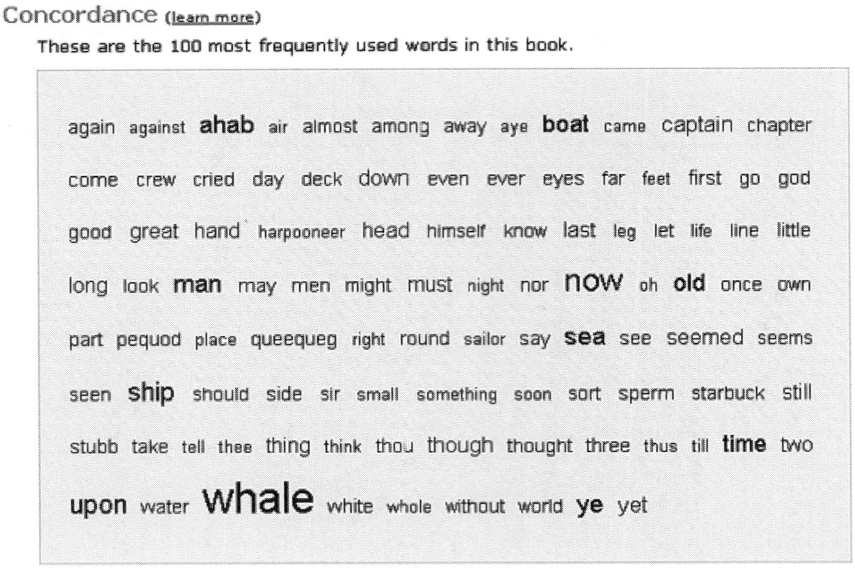

Concordance (learn more)

These are the 100 most frequently used words in this book.

again against ahab air almost among away aye boat came captain chapter come crew cried day deck down even ever eyes far feet first go god good great hand harpooneer head himself know last leg let life line little long look man may men might must night nor now oh old once own part pequod place queequeg right round sailor say sea see seemed seems seen ship should side sir small something soon sort sperm starbuck still stubb take tell thee thing think thou though thought three thus till time two upon water whale white whole without world ye yet

Figure 18: Concordance of the 100 most frequently used words in *Moby Dick,* generated by Amazon.com

repository system (www.dspace.crg/technology/system-docs/functional.html).

Amazon.com (www.amazon.com) has recently been experimenting with the in-depth indexing of the books they have digitized. They automatically generate "statistically improbable phrases" or SIPs, the most distinctive phrases in the book; SIPs for Herman Melvilles's *Moby Dick* include "pagan harpooners" and "ivory leg." The "Capitalized Phrases" or CAPs, are people, places, events, or important topics frequently mentioned in the text; examples from Moby Dick include "Captain Peleg" and "Cape Horn." They also generate concordances of the 100 most frequently used words in a book; Figure 18 shows an Amazon.com display of the concordance for *Moby Dick.*

Networking and Digital Libraries

Networking is a common feature in digital libraries, Borbinha and Delgado (1996) discuss the concept in general and point out the potential of the networked digital library to not only function as an information repository, but to become an active partner of the researcher, stimulating, supporting, and registering the process of the creation of knowledge. Fox and Marchionini (1998) expand the concept to a world-wide level, where barriers to interoperability and multilingual processing are being gradually overcome. The result will be the creation of a digital library system that can contribute significantly to global understanding and cooperation. A distributed digital library model, in which materials on separate machines are connected via a network, is frequently adopted (Adams, Jansen, and Howard 1998).

Networking of this type is a common feature in digital libraries, although it is often done in a manner not immediately perceptible by users. Probably the best-known examples of networked digital library collections are those produced for the American Memory as a collaborative effort between the Library of Congress and major libraries, historical societies, and similar institutions. This program lasted from 1996 to 1999, and was known as the Library of Congress/Ameritech National Digital Library Competition (http://memory.loc.gov/ammem/award/online.html). For a typical example, see "The Chinese in California, 1850–1925" (http://memory.loc.gov/ammem/award99/cubhtml; Figure 19).

The initial page (Figure 19) clearly acknowledges that the "materials in this online compilation are drawn from collections at The Bancroft Library, University of California, Berkeley, The Ethnic Studies Library, University of California, Berkeley, and the California Historical Society, San Francisco." The file is on a server at http://memory.loc.gov.

Figure 20 shows a thumbnail image and metadata from that collection; this is still on the Library of Congress server. The working or access image (Figure 21), however, is held on a server at the University of California, Berkeley. The system is fully networked, but functions so smoothly that few users will notice the change of server.

Networking features are very obvious to the users of PictureAustralia, maintained by the National Library of Australia (www.pictureaustralia.org/index.html). The initial page (Figure 22) is very clear: "Search for people, places, and events in the collections of libraries, museums, galleries, archives, universities, and other cultural agencies, in Australia and abroad - all at the same time. View the originals on the member agency web sites and order quality prints." The initial page welcomes new participants, and includes a link for those who would like to make their picture collections available through PictureAustralia. (It is also interesting to note the disclaimer typical of Australian image collections: "Indigenous Australians are advised that PictureAustralia may include images or names of people now deceased.").

Search results come from a wide range of libraries. Figure 23 shows hits from the State Library of Victoria, the State Library of Queensland, the State Library of

Figure 19: Opening screen of the Chinese in California collection, from the Library of Congress

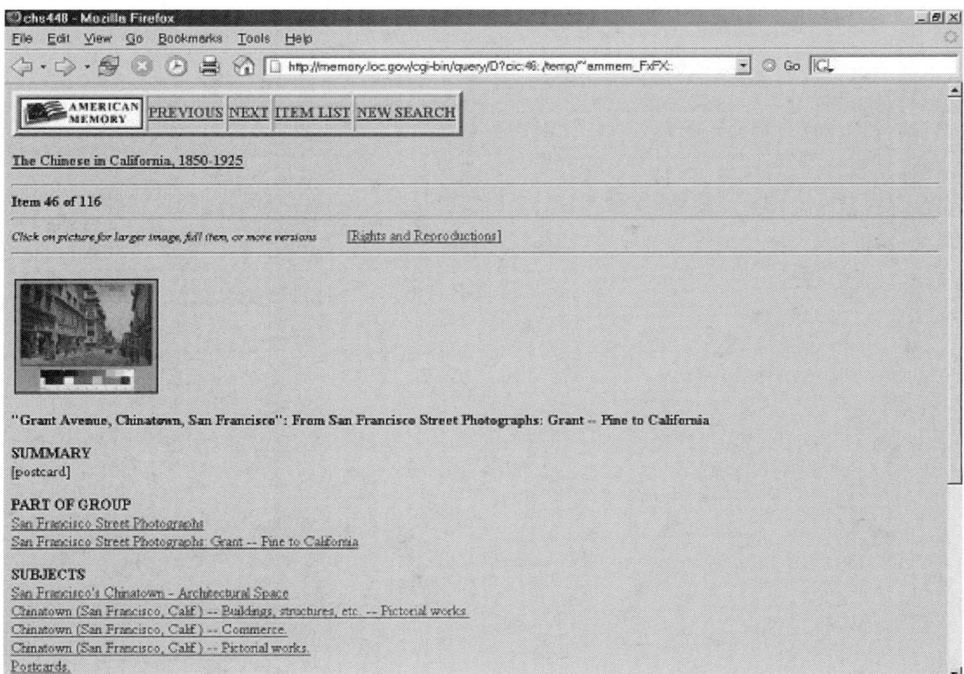

Figure 20: Thumbnail and metadata for an image in the Chinese in California collection, from the Library of Congress

New South Wales, Logan City Council Libraries, and the Australian Heritage Photo Library.

It is possible to see metadata of specific items by following the link to "More information" (Figure 24).

A link from the "More information" page takes the user to the original image; in this example, it is held on the server of the State Library of Queensland (Figure 25).

Witten, McNab, Jones, and colleagues (1999) discuss the sophisticated distributed digital library system set up for the New Zealand Digital Library (www.nzdl.org). This covers twenty collections that use different indexing and browsing structures, can be accessed by computers in different locations, can accept queries in various languages, and contain text, images, and audio.

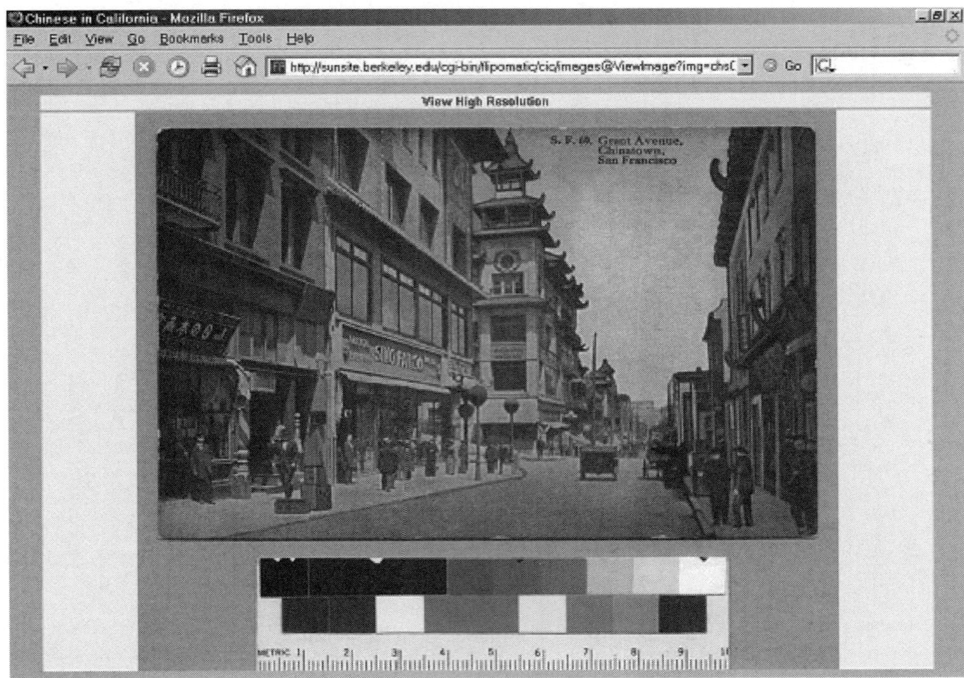

Figure 21: Working or access image from the Chinese in California collection. This image is held on the server of the University of California, Berkeley.

Figure 22: Initial page of PictureAustralia, from the National Library of Australia

The use of mirror sites constitutes a common alternative form of networking to digital libraries; they reduce load on the central server, and the existence of multiple sites offers increased data security. Project Gutenberg (www.gutenberg.org/wiki/Main_Page) is widely mirrored and offers a page of instructions on how to set up a mirror site (www.gutenberg.org/wiki/Gutenberg:Mirroring_How-To). A static IP address and a T1 network connection are minimum requirements; Project Gutenberg occupies 150 GB, a total of 100,000 files in twenty-three formats. Mirrors are expected to update files nightly; forty sites currently mirror Project Gutenberg (www.gutenberg.org/MIRRORS.ALL). The New Zealand Digital Library (www.nzdl.org) is mirrored by the Southern Alberta Digital Library Centre, at the University of Lethbridge (www.sadl.uleth.ca/gsdl/cgi-bin/library). Attempts to link from North America to www.nzdl.org are automatically redirected to www.sadl.uleth.ca. The Perseus Digital Library of classical literature (www.perseus.tufts.edu) is based at Tufts University, Somerville, Massachusetts, but is mirrored in Chicago and Berlin. WiderNet (www.widernet.org), based at the University of Iowa, offers a creative solution for

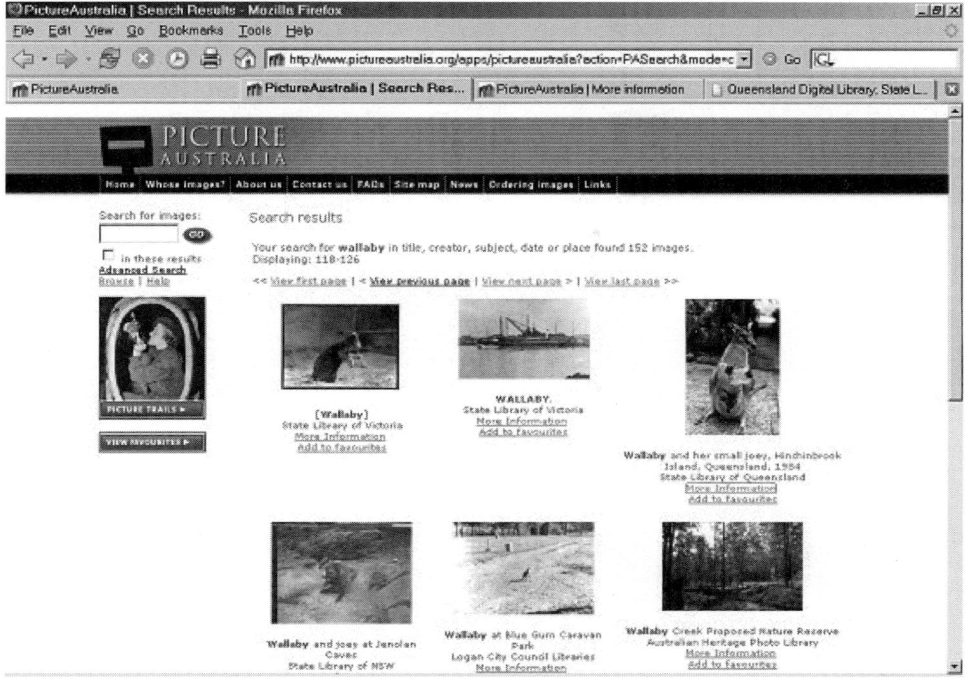

Figure 23: Search results from PictureAustralia, from the National Library of Australia

Figure 24: Thumbnail image and metadata from PictureAustralia, from the National Library of Australia

locations in Africa and elsewhere that suffer chronic connectivity problems. This is the eGranary Digital Library Appliance, a server preloaded with over 5 million relevant documents, which can be slotted into any local area network (www.widernet.org/digitalLibrary/index.htm). This can be searched like the Internet and offers Lucene indexing; there is also 20 GB for local documentation, which is indexed alongside the preloaded documents.

MAINTAINING DIGITAL LIBRARIES

Security and Digital Libraries

Digital libraries offer a valuable contribution to document security because they generate and disseminate multiple copies; experience has shown that documents available in numerous copies are more likely to survive.

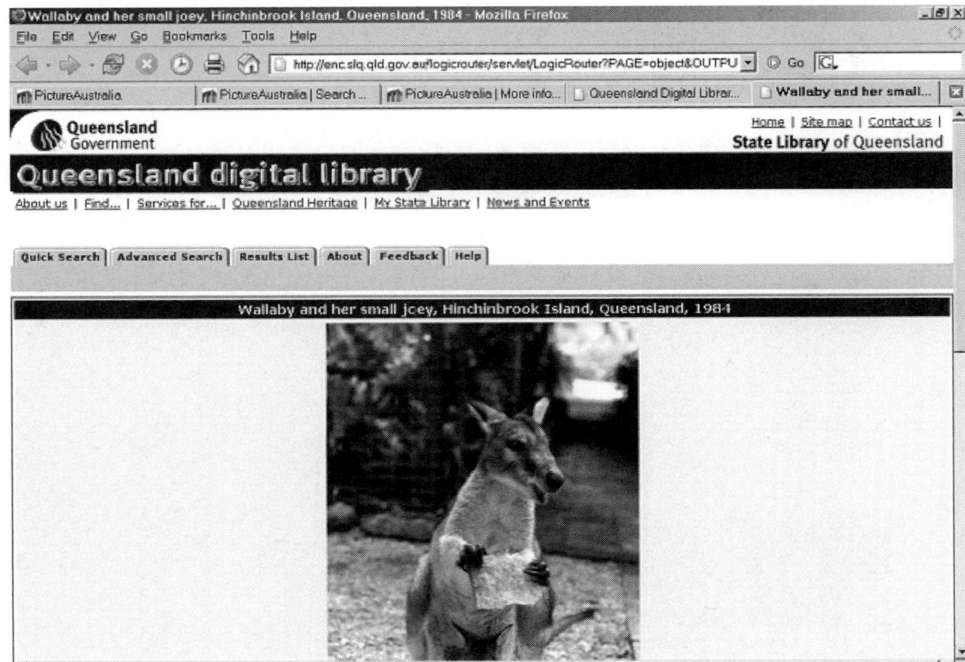

Figure 25: Full-size image, held on the server of the State Library of Queensland

Security problems during digitization are similar to those that occur during microfilming. Special care must be taken with old, fragile documents. It is normal to digitize valuable materials on site to avoid the risks of transportation. All items must be carefully counted and numbered before they are processed. Some projects have outsourced digitization to countries such as the Philippines or India, but this is possible only for materials that can be replaced.

Lesk's *Understanding Digital Libraries* devotes part of a chapter to security (Lesk 2005, 174–80); he discusses basic security, sensible administration, and the use of firewalls and passwords. Even digital libraries that make their materials publicly available will need to take precautions against hackers, crackers, or persons who attempt to download major proportions of their content. The materials within digital libraries constitute the best of an institution's resources. Older materials may be in the public domain and could possibly be redistributed. If users can steal an image, the institution may possibly lose publication fees.

Access-management policies must be established to determine who can access information, and under what terms and conditions. Access management is required because of copyright, trade secrets, obscenity, privacy, or donor restrictions. Commercial environments or secure government systems also require appropriate access formalities. It is common to restrict digital library materials to users of specific institutions; this is frequently achieved by Internet Protocol (IP) identification, which limits access to specific computers. An additional possibility is the use of passwords. Arms devotes a chapter of his textbook, *Digital Libraries,* to access management and security (Arms 2000, 123–42). Access management begins when users identify themselves; specific procedures then validate the users, verifying their true identities. Digital resources also have to be authenticated, while specific categories of materials may require special restrictions.

So far, only one significant example of violation of an institutional digital library has come to light. 50,000 articles were illegally downloaded from *JSTOR* (www.jstor.org), the University of Michigan's scholarly journal archive, by an intruder who used a false IP address (Olsen 2003). *JSTOR* posted a strong statement concerning unauthorized access (www.jstor.org/about/unauthorized.html). It is also testing new open-source software, Shibboleth, which guarantees the security of online services and restricts access to digital content (http://shibboleth.internet2.edu). Shibboleth is being developed by Internet2 researchers with National Science Foundation support, and is being evaluated or adopted by numerous institutions. Systems such as Blackboard, Ebsco, Elsevier, OCLC, and Thomson Gale are now Shibboleth-enabled (https://wiki.internet2.edu/confluence/display/seas/Home).

Watermarks are used as a security measure for paper currency, and can also be incorporated in digital objects, in which a subsidiary visible image can be inserted in a protected image. Visible watermarks are in common use to mark sample images in catalogs of commercial photograph collections; see the *New York Times* (www.nytstore.com/ProdCode.aspx?prodcode=791; Figure 26) or Corbis (http://pro.corbis.com).

Herzberg (1998) discusses charging for content by digital libraries, analyzing a variety of different charging mechanisms, both existing and proposed. Credit-card payments are not appropriate for very small purchases, and advertising revenues are limited in the digital library area. It is also possible to sell subscriptions, but in practice few users are willing to subscribe, and fees have to be shared with middlemen. Considerable interest has been

Figure 26: This image of a facsimile Audubon print, offered for sale by the *New York Times,* has been protected by a clearly visible watermark. The print shows an American White Pelican

shown in micropayments, whose value is too small to justify the use of a credit card (e.g., less than one dollar). In theory, they are an attractive option, but their widespread use depends on mechanisms that can rapidly transfer small amounts of money at a low cost.

The other side of digital library security is the privacy of users. Sturges and colleagues (2003) point out that with digital technology, libraries can archive detailed information on users; this is normally considered confidential, but could be relevant for security, law enforcement, or commercial organizations. Saeednia (2000) examined problems of privacy and authentication in digital libraries, and proposed practical solutions, such as a key exchange protocol and an identification scheme, based on computing discrete logarithms and factoring large integers.

Preservation and Digital Libraries

Despite the fact that their major objective is to increase access, digital libraries also perform important preservation functions; for instance, they reduce the need to handle original resources. There are two related considerations: preservation of the original materials and preservation of the digital surrogates.

It is normal to retain the originals of photographs and broadsides, even after digitization. It can be more difficult to preserve books, which may be printed on brittle paper and will possibly have been disbound to facilitate processing. Microfilm is sometimes seen as the solution for long-term preservation, but libraries have been roundly criticized for not preserving the originals of microfilmed newspapers (Baker 2001). Libraries will feel an obligation to preserve originals after digitization, especially when they are the last copies. Some difficult decisions will have to be made. Should the project include minor restoration, such as mending tears? Digital library projects rarely cover costs of restoration. Should images be processed to restore their original color? Normally, digitizers will aim to faithfully reproduce the object as it is now.

Protection of digital resources is equally essential in digital library management. Even when the public has access only to working JPG images, the system must guarantee the long-term storage of the high-quality archival images. Libraries traditionally think in terms of centuries, while computer software is frequently replaced, often by incompatible systems. This poses a risk to all types of digital information. File formats and versions constantly change, while hardware and software become obsolete; important data therefore becomes unusable. This process can affect even simple data formats and even high-quality information resources, such as databases and e-journals, can be jeopardized. When the problem is finally detected, it may be too late (Ray et al. 2002).

Arms devotes a chapter of his *Digital Libraries* to repositories and archives (Arms 2000, 245–62), in which he suggests criteria for the evaluation of repositories and the storage of metadata. He discusses digital archeology, which can be defined as recovering data from superseded systems, and views digital archival operations in terms of refreshing and migrating data. Arms distinguishes carefully between:

Migration: The "preservation of digital content, where the underlying information is retained but older formats and internal structures are replaced by newer," and

Emulation: "[T]he replication of a computing system to process programs and data from an early system that is no longer available" (Arms 2000, 276–9).

The *Introduction to Digital Libraries* by Chowdhury and Chowdhury also includes a chapter on digital library archiving and preservation (2003, 214–26). Problems and strategies for digital preservation are outlined and principal projects in the area are discussed. For a general overview of preservation problems, see the discussion by Smith (2004), published by the Council on Library and Information Resources (CLIR). The fundamental questions of stewardship, such as which resources are to be collected and preserved, by whom, for how long, and for whom, have undergone a major change. We now face key questions such as, Is it possible or desirable to select or preserve the rapidly growing Web? Can institutions collaborate in collection development, the creation of metadata, or preservation activities? Can institutions, such as libraries, preserve digital information that is owned by commercial companies and licensed to the library? Who will be responsible for paying for the preservation of digital resources?

Gould and Ebdon (1999) surveyed the digitization and preservation policies of major libraries and archives worldwide. Of those that digitized materials, 64 percent had a preservation policy for digitized documents. The majority, 83 percent, allowed access to the original document after digitization, while 67 percent of the institutions surveyed stored their originals in special conditions. Just over half of the respondents had established a policy for migrating data to recent platforms; when migration was undertaken, all data were migrated. Data migration was never contracted out; it was always an internal activity. The survey was conducted for the International Federation of Library Associations (IFLA) and the United Nations Educational, Scientific and Cultural Organization (UNESCO).

The Digital Library SunSITE at Berkeley suggested four levels of collecting, each of which implied a different commitment to preservation:

Archived: The material is hosted here, and the library intends to keep the intellectual content of the material available on a permanent basis.

Served: The material resides here, but the library has not (yet) made the level of commitment to keeping it available that it has for "archived" materials.

Mirrored: A copy of material residing elsewhere is hosted here, and the library makes no commitment to archiving. Also, an institution other than the library has primary responsibility for the content and its maintenance.

Linked: The material is hosted elsewhere and the library points to it at that location. Therefore, the library has no control over the information (http://sunsite.berkeley.edu/Admin/collection.html).

Material in any category except for the first, "Archived," may be reallocated from one level to another to meet changing information needs, access to or responsiveness of remote servers, local demands, and so forth. Material designated as "Archived" cannot be downgraded. The Digital Library SunSITE at Berkeley also offers additional preservation resources at http://sunsite.berkeley.edu/Preservation.

Disaster protection in digital libraries is discussed by Tennant (2001). RAID (redundant array of inexpensive [or independent] disks) technology is commonly used. RAID level one involves mirroring data or making one complete copy; level five distributes data between several physical disks. Necessary infrastructure includes uninterruptible power supplies and fire and alarm systems. He also recommends backing up data to a distant location.

The National Digital Information Infrastructure and Preservation Program (NDIIPP), led by the Library of Congress, is actively developing an infrastructure for collecting and preserving digital resources (www.digitalpreservation.gov). It is working with a variety of partners to collect and preserve specific types of digital content that will be used for generations to come. The National Library of Australia offers much valuable documentation on digital preservation at PADI: Preserving Access to Digital Information (www.nla.gov.au/padi). This covers strategies and standards, and links to a variety of relevant information sources. In the United States, the Online Computer Library Center (OCLC) maintains a digital archive that enables members to store digital assets, either item by item or as collections (www.oclc.org/digitalarchive/default.htm).

The Internet Archive and the Wayback Machine (www.archive.org; Figure 27) offer access to a wide variety of resources, and also permit surfing through Web pages from several years ago. Because they have an important role in the preservation of the Internet, it is relevant to discuss their archiving procedures. They operate on PCs with clusters of IDE (integrated device electronics) hard drives. For storage they use DLT (digital linear tape) and hard drives in various formats (www.archive.org/about/about.php). DLT is rated to last 30 years; for additional security, industry practice is to migrate data every decade. The Internet Archive, however, plans more frequent migrations. It also collects software and emulators that will assist future researchers and historians in analyzing the development of the Internet.

At a library level, copies of electronic journals can be automatically archived by LOCKSS, or Lots of Copies Keep Stuff Safe, from Stanford University (http://lockss.stanford.edu/index.html). This open-source system regularly polls the Web journals subscribed to by the library; new material is preserved in a local cache.

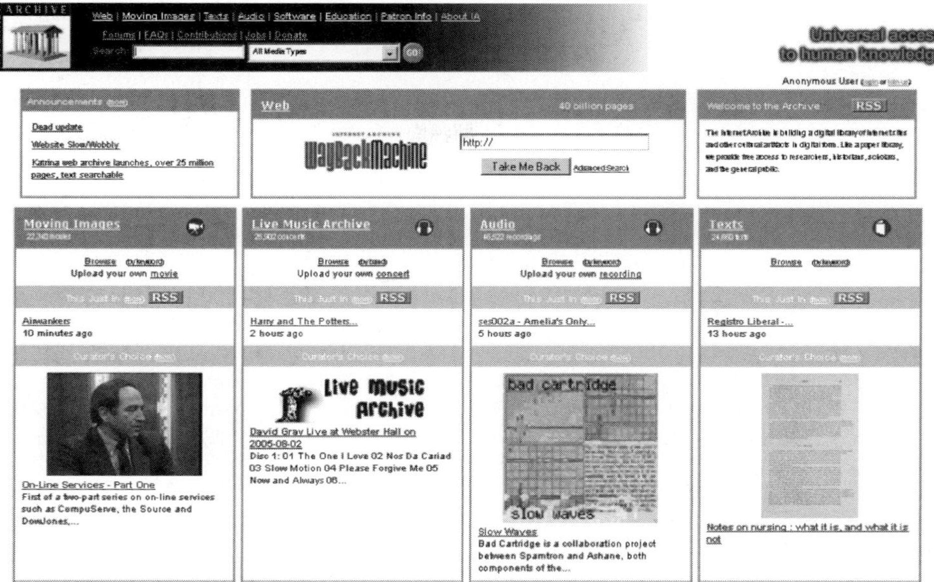

Figure 27: The Internet Archive and the Wayback Machine

It is possible to find resources that represent the same document at different sites. Digital library professionals must therefore concern themselves with the authenticity of their digital resources. For a discussion of this problem, see Bearman and Trant (1998). As part of this process, it is essential to be able to analyze the methods used to digitize the original, and to be able to determine the integrity of a specific digital copy.

The archival TIFF files that digital libraries produce directly from original resources must be carefully preserved; at the moment they are frequently archived on sets of CD-Rs. A relatively small digital library can easily be responsible for more than a thousand CD-Rs. For a comprehensive guide to the handling of CDs and DVDs by librarians and archivists, see Byers (2003), which covers the types of media used, and their manufacture, care, and operation, with special attention to their longevity and conditions of storage. Digital libraries typically use "write-once" CD-Rs to record digital data; these should survive for at least a century if correctly stored. CD-Rs and DVD-Rs incorporate silver, silver alloy, or gold reflective layers; gold lasts longer, but is also more expensive (Byers 2003, 10). The problems are much more serious with mass-produced audio CDs, which use aluminum reflective layers; these may last for only twenty years, even when carefully looked after. The problem recently came to the attention of a wide public when an enthusiast noted that 15 to 20 percent of his audio CDs would not play because of "CD rot" (Baig 2004). The Library of Congress's Preservation Research and Testing Division is actively engaged in this area (Library of Congress 2003). Even when preservation is guaranteed, a digital library will often possess thousands of CD-Rs; numbering and file naming rules will have to be drawn up, so that specific images can be easily retrieved.

The basis of book preservation has always been the legal deposit of copies at national libraries; this concept is gradually being applied to digital resources. UNESCO issued an important *Draft Charter on the Preservation of the Digital Heritage* (UNESCO 2003). Member nations need to create appropriate legal and institutional machinery to secure and preserve their digital heritage. Key elements of national preservation policy are legal or voluntary deposit in libraries, archives, and similar repositories. Adequate access to digital heritage materials that have been legally deposited should be ensured. Appropriate legal and technical structures must be established to guarantee authenticity and prevent manipulation of digital resources. The British Library has begun a project that may eventually lead to the archiving of all U.K. Web sites (Marson 2004). The U.K. Web Archiving Consortium, led by the British Library, and including the National Archives and the Scottish and Welsh national libraries, has processed more than a thousand British Web sites for preservation (http://info.webarchive.org.uk/index.html). The British Library does not censor the materials; ultimately, it aims to archive all British Web sites. The software used for the archiving system was developed by PANDORA (Preserving and Accessing Networked Documentary Resources of Australia), established by the National Library of Australia in 1996 (http://pandora.nla.gov.au/index.html). PANDORA now covers nearly 15,000 Web sites. Because of the lack of legal deposit provisions covering online publications in Australia, PANDORA seeks permission from publishers before including materials in the Archive (http://pandora.nla.gov.au/legaldeposit.html). In a wider initiative, the National Library of Australia contracted the Internet Archive to harvest the entire Australian Web domain for six weeks during June and July 2005; 185 million unique documents were archived from more than 800,000 hosts. Because Australia lacks legal deposit provisions for online materials, it is still uncertain what access can be provided to this collection (http://pandora.nla.gov.au/panfaqs.html). It is interesting to compare digital and audio materials in this context: the United States introduced legal deposit for sound recordings only in the

1970s; as a result, many early recordings are not in the Library of Congress (Lesk 2005, 240).

Continuity of Digital Libraries

The existence of "dead links" is a common problem on the Internet, of special concern to digital libraries that link to outside materials. Links need to be checked frequently, and dead links have to be updated or removed. A possible solution is offered by persistent identifiers, PURLs or persistent URLs (http://purl.oclc.org). To a user, a PURL looks and works just like a URL, but it does not point to an Internet page, but to an intermediate service. This PURL resolution service switches the client seamlessly to the current URL. The most widely established identification system for individual digital library items is the digital object identifier (DOI; www.doi.org/index.html). A DOI persistently identifies a content-bearing entity in a digital environment, permitting localization, links between users and content suppliers, and management of intellectual property rights. The DOI will remain the same even if the object's network location changes. The standard DOI format is "DOI:Prefix/Suffix"; for example: "DOI:10.1045/june2003-paskin," where the prefix, "DOI:10.1045" indicates a DOI issued by *D-Lib Magazine.* That journal is responsible for the suffix, which identifies a June 2003 article by Norman Paskin, the director of the International DOI Foundation (Paskin 2003). A search engine, such as Google, can use the DOI to retrieve the paper. CrossRef, the official DOI registration agency for scholarly and professional publications (www.crossref.org), has registered over 20 million DOIs (CrossRef 2006). The OpenURL standard uses Web-transportable packages of metadata to switch users to relevant versions of digital materials (www.niso.org/committees/committee_ax.html); for instance, a user who retrieves an article citation can obtain immediate access to the "most appropriate" copy of that object via a linking service (www.exlibrisgroup.com/sfx_openurl.htm).

Digital libraries have a short history and are frequently established by solid institutions, such as universities. Most of the systems implanted are apparently still functioning. Notess (2005) lists more than twenty dead search engines, but there is no list of dead digital libraries. The few closures that have come to public attention all seem related to changes in government policies. PubScience (formerly at http://pubsci.osti.gov) enabled researchers to examine more than a thousand peer-reviewed journals free of charge through a single interface. It was part of the U.S. Department of Energy's Office of Scientific and Technical Information, but was closed because it duplicated commercial services (Foster 2002). Government policies also had a major impact on the ERIC database (www.eric.ed.gov). This collection of 1.2 million documents and journal articles on educational topics has established itself as a primary source since its foundation in 1966. In 2003–2004, it was heavily modified; the previous model, based on decentralized clearinghouses, was abandoned in favor of a centralized system (Viadero 2004). A chain of pioneering virtual hospitals was managed from the University of Iowa for many years (www.vh.org or www.vh.org/pediatric/index.html); content was either contributed by faculty of the University of Iowa or taken from U.S. government or other noncopyrighted sources. The system was supported by U.S. Navy funding for the parallel Virtual Naval Hospital, but this funding was withdrawn at the beginning of 2006 (www.vnh.org). The virtual hospitals continue to exist, but only in highly truncated form.

Sustainability is frequently discussed in the digital library field, where it covers a variety of topics, from the technical problems of digital preservation, to the social impact of long-term accessibility of resources (McArthur 2003). The Framework of Guidance for Building Good Digital Collections, developed by the National Information Standards Organization (NISO) states as the third principle of successful collection building that "A collection should be sustainable over time. In particular, digital collections built with special internal or external funding should have a plan for their continued usability beyond the funded period" (www.niso.org/framework/Framework2.html). Funding proposals submitted to the Institute for Museum and Library Services (IMLS) typically include sustainability; for an example, see *Connecticut History Online* (http://www.cthistoryonline.org/cdm-cho/cho/project/IMLSproposal.htm#sustainability).

CONCLUSION—THE FUTURE OF DIGITAL LIBRARIES

The future of digital libraries seems assured. They offer a series of advantages in relation to traditional libraries: it is not necessary to travel to a library to access information; two or more people can access the same item simultaneously; they are available beyond the often restricted opening hours of traditional libraries; digital texts can easily be copied, updated, corrected, and even manipulated when copyright permits; they can also be indexed word-for-word; older, rarer materials can be made available, and repeatedly examined, without risk to the originals; and links to related materials can easily be established (McCarthy 2004). Traditional libraries cannot easily compete on any of these features.

Like any new technology, digital libraries do have constraints and limitations. A seminal paper by Lynch (2001) drew attention to the potentially significant social cost of digital technologies, which permit increased levels of monitoring and control. The use of digital books can be regulated in a manner that would be totally impossible with traditional books. At the same time, unless publishers are able to establish levels of control that they consider appropriate, they will not permit in-print texts to move to digital form. Migration of this nature has been notably slow up until now. An increase has been noted in e-book sales (Becker 2004), but the process continues to be slow because of the traditional and decentralized nature of the publishing business. While publishers hesitate, they risk being sidelined by new entrants to the digital arena. Over the past year or so, major digitally based initiatives such as Google, Yahoo!, and MSN have begun to pay significant attention to book digitization. Early activities have been hindered by a lack of standardization and clear business models, but players of this importance can be expected to invest significantly in the solution to these problems. It is probable, therefore, that large-scale book digitization activities will have a major impact in the near future.

The relationship between traditional and digital libraries will also become more clearly defined in the future. How far will digital libraries be linked with or integrated into library cataloging systems? It is necessary to remember that libraries face several digital challenges at the same time: digital libraries, online article databases, federated searching, link resolvers, and other systems; it is uncertain exactly how digital libraries will work within a larger library automation structure.

Even more exciting developments can be expected from the impact on digital libraries of the latest trends in Internet technology. The small orange buttons that denote RSS (really simple syndication) feeds are now common on dynamic Web sites and are beginning to turn up in digital libraries such as ibiblio (www.ibiblio.org/rss/ibiblio.rss), the Internet Archive (www.archive.org/services/collection-rss.php), and Project Gutenberg (www.gutenberg.org/feeds/today.rss). PubMed (www.ncbi.nlm.nih.gov/entrez/query.fcgi?DB=pubmed) now permits users to create personalized RSS feeds for medical literature (www.nlm.nih.gov/pubs/techbull/mj05/mj05_rss.html). Personalization is also occurring in other digital library applications. The British Library's Online Gallery permits sending e-cards with illustrations from the library's collections (www.bl.uk/ecards/index.html). The ingenious system offers 30,000 images from Britain's Science Museum and other museums (www.ingenious.org.uk); free registration permits users to save images, send e-cards, and create Web galleries. The updated version of the ERIC Educational Resources Information Center (www.eric.ed.gov) permits users, after free registration, to save searches and search results, and to submit documents for possible inclusion in the database. I have already noted the collaboration between the National Library of Australia's image-sharing system, PictureAustralia (www.pictureaustralia.org), and the Flickr photo-sharing system (www.flickr.com), which is part of Yahoo! Flickr permits users to load their own materials, leave comments about the photographs of others, and report abuse of the system. O'Reilly (2005) discusses the concept of Web 2.0 systems such as Flickr, which are based on sharing, tagging, reputation, and trust. Of interest to the digital library field are sites like YouTube (www.youtube.com), a video-sharing system, or Digg (www.digg.com), for distribution of technical news; both of these permit participants to vote dynamically for or to promote specific items. Another technology central to Web 2.0 is peer-to-peer distribution, which has had a major impact on popular systems, and has been adopted as the basis for the European Commission's BRICKS: Building Resources for Integrated Cultural Knowledge Services project (www.brickscommunity.org). Web 2.0 services may well have a significant future impact on digital libraries.

At the moment, readers view e-text on devices they already have: desktop PCs, laptops, or personal digital assistants (PDAs). The desktop area has been fairly stable recently, but there have been many major changes in the area of small electronic devices. Cell phones are daily becoming more powerful, and the iPod was transformed from a novelty into an everyday object in a couple of years. The author expects that the convergence between a cut-down laptop and an improved iPod will shortly produce a universal digital tool that will also serve as a widely acceptable platform for text. Kurzweil's seminal book, *The Age of Spiritual Machines,* forecast that printed books and paper documents would become rare by the year 2019, and that all multimedia and documents would be fully digitized by 2029 (Kurzweil 1999). The role of libraries will, no doubt, be to continue to guarantee access to quality and older materials. Institutions such as libraries and archives have contributed much in the past decade toward the digitization of cultural materials. This is an important step toward achieving a major medium-term objective of humanity, the digitization of the cultural heritage of civilization.

GLOSSARY

American Memory: The Historical Collections of the National Digital Library, maintained by the Library of Congress (http://memory.loc.gov); one of the world's largest digital libraries, with more than 100 collections, a total of 9 million digital items, including photographs, manuscripts, rare books, maps, sound recordings, and moving pictures.

Digital Library: "A managed collection of information, with associated services, where the information is stored in digital formats . . . organized on computers and available over a network, with procedures to select the materials in the collections, to organize it, to make it available to users, and to archive it" (Arms 2000, 2).

Digital Preservation: Process of guaranteeing the long-term preservation of digital objects, by storage of files in secure repositories, migration to other platforms, and other means.

Digital Rights Management: Procedures that ensure that holders of digital rights are clearly identified and receive the stipulated payment for their materials; they may also impose additional restrictions on use of digital objects—for example, inhibiting printing or prohibiting further distribution.

Digitization: Process of converting analog documents (such as paper, photographs, film, maps) to digital form.

Electronic Journals (E-Journals): Journals, such as scientific and professional journals, available in digital form.

Electronic Theses and Dissertations (ETDs): Theses and dissertations available in digital form.

Indexing: The process of systematically generating pointers or keys to the content of texts, permitting readers to go directly to locations that contain specific words or deal with specific topics.

Metadata: Data about data. Keys, guides, or indications of the content of a document or data set and stipulations of appropriate use.

Migration: Transfer of digital data from one format or platform to another; normally, digital data are migrated from an older format or platform to a newer format or platform, to guarantee preservation.

Multimedia Digital Library: Digital library that delivers content in a variety of formats: text, photographic images, audio, short films, and so forth.

Project Gutenberg: One of the longest-running digital libraries (http://www.gutenberg.org/wiki/Main_Page), founded in 1971. It has always concentrated on simple, copyright-free texts that can be read on almost any computing platform. Now offers more than 20,000 texts and is supported by a network of mirror sites.

Sustainability: The capacity of a digital system to continue operating for the foreseeable future. Sustainability depends on factors such as organizational or governmental commitment, a secure financial model, adequate protection from external attack, use of appropriate formats and platforms, and collections that are of lasting interest or are capable of being updated.

CROSS REFERENCES

See *Online News*; *The Internet Fundamentals*.

REFERENCES

Acharya, T., and P. S. Tsai. 2005. *JPEG2000 standard for image compression: Concepts, algorithms and VLSI architectures.* Hoboken, NJ: Wiley.

Adams, W. J., B. J. Jansen, and R. Howard. 1998. Distributed digital library architecture: the key to success for distance learning. In *Proceedings of the 1998 8th International Workshop on Research Issues Data Engineering (RIDE), Orlando, FL., Feb. 23–24 1998.* Los Alamitos, CA: IEEE.

Albanese, A. 2003, September 22. Barnes & Noble drops ebooks citing sales, unwieldy devices. *Library Hotline: The Weekly Newsletter from Library Journal and School Library Journal* 32(38):1.

Arms, W. Y. 2000. *Digital libraries*. (Digital libraries and electronic publishing). Cambridge, MA: MIT Press.

Atwood, S. 2002. MIT's superarchive: A digital repository will revolutionize the way research is shared and preserved. *Technology Review* 104(12). www.technologyreview.com/articles/02/12/atwood1202.asp (accessed July 15, 2007).

Baig, E. C. 2004, July 7. Life has gotten even shorter in digital age. *USA Today.* www.usatoday.com/tech/news/2004–07–26-longevity_x.htm?POE=click-refer (accessed July 15, 2007).

Baker, N. 2001. *Double fold: Libraries and the assault on paper.* New York: Random House.

Bearman, D., and J. Trant. 1998. Authenticity of digital resources: Towards a statement of requirements in the research process. *D-Lib Magazine* 4(6). www.dlib.org/dlib/june98/06bearman.html (accessed July 15, 2007).

Becker, D. 2004, August 27. Have e-books turned a page? *CNET News.com*. http://news.zdnet.com/2100–3513_22–5326015.html?tag=zdfd.newsfeed (accessed July 15, 2007).

Borbinha, J. L. B., and J. C. M. Delgado. 1996. Networked digital libraries. *Microcomputers for Information Management* 13(3–4):195–215.

Borgman, C. L. 2000. *From Gutenberg to the global information infrastructure: Access to information in the networked world.* (Digital libraries and electronic publishing). Cambridge, MA: MIT Press.

Boss, R. W. 2001. Imaging for libraries and information centers. *Library Technology Reports* 37(1):1–59.

Brief of amici curiae: The Internet archive: Filed on behalf of petitioners. 2002. http://cyber.law.harvard.edu/openlaw/eldredvashcroft/cert/archive-amicus.html (accessed July 15, 2007).

Byers, F. R. 2003. *Care and handling of CDs and DVDs: A guide for librarians and archivists.* Washington, DC: Council on Library and Information Resources (CLIR). www.clir.org/pubs/abstract/pub121abst.html (accessed July 15, 2007).

Carlson, S., and J. R. Young. 2004, December 14. Google will digitize and search millions of books from 5 leading research libraries. *The Chronicle of Higher Education.* http://chronicle.com/free/2004/12/2004121401n.htm (accessed July 15, 2007).

Carnevale, D. 2003, December 19. Libraries with tight budgets renew complaints about Elsevier's online pricing. *The Chronicle of Higher Education* 50(17):A33.

Choudhury, G. S., et al. 2000. Digital workflow management: The Lester S. Levy Digitized Collection of Sheet Music. *First Monday* 5(6). www.firstmonday.org/issues/issue5_6/choudhury/index.html (accessed July 15, 2007).

Chowdhury, G. G., and S. Chowdhury. 1999. Digital library research: Major issues and trends. *Journal of Documentation* 55(4):409–48.

Chowdhury, G. G., and S. Chowdhury. 2000. An overview of the information retrieval features of twenty digital libraries. *Program* 34(4):341–73.

Chowdhury, G. G., and S. Chowdhury. 2003. *Introduction to digital libraries*. London: Facet.

Covey, D. T. 2005. *Acquiring copyright permission to digitize and provide open access to books.* Washington, DC: Digital Library Federation and Council on Library and Information Resources. http://purl.oclc.org/dlf/trollcovey0509 (accessed July 15, 2007).

Crawford, W. 2000. Nine models, one name: Untangling the e-book muddle. *American Libraries* 31(8):56–9.

CrossRef surpasses 20 million DOI mark: press release. 2006. Lynnfield, MA: CrossRef. www.crossref.org/01company/pr/press042606.htm (accessed July 15, 2007).

DeBonis, L. 2007. Keio University joins Google's Library Project. *Inside Google Book Search.* http://booksearch.blogspot.com/2007/07/keio-university-joins-googles-library.html (accessed July 15, 2007).

Digital Library Federation. 2001. *A new approach to finding research materials on the web*. www.diglib.org/architectures/vision.htm (accessed July 15, 2007).

Dublin Core metadata best practices version 2.1. 2005. Denver: University of Denver; Collaborative Digitization Program. www.cdpheritage.org/cdp/documents/CDPDCMBP.pdf (accessed July 15, 2007).

Foster, A. L. 2002, September 6. Energy Department seeks to close Web site that searches scientific journals. *The Chronicle of Higher Education* 49(2):A46.

Foster, A. L. 2006, February 17. Copyright office sides with publishers in proposal for handling "orphan" works. *The Chronicle of Higher Education* 52(24):A39.

Fox, E., 1999. Digital Libraries Initiative (DLI) projects 1994–1999. *Bulletin of the American Society for Information Science* 26(1):7–11. www.asis.org/Bulletin/Oct-99/fox.html (accessed July 15, 2007).

Fox, E. and G. Marchionini. 1998. Toward a worldwide digital library. *Communications of the ACM* 41(4): 28–32.

Fox, E., and S. Urs. 2002. Digital libraries. *Annual Review of Information Science and Technology* 36:503–89.

Frey, F. 1997. Digital imaging for photographic collections: Foundations for technical standards. *RLG DigiNews* 1(3). www.rlg.org/preserv/diginews/diginews3.html#com (accessed July 15, 2007).

Gould, S., and R. Ebdon. 1999. *IFLA/UNESCO survey on digitisation and preservation.* (International preservation issues; 2). Wetherby, West Yorkshire, UK: IFLA Offices for UAP and International Lending. www.unesco.org/webworld/mdm/survey_index_en.html (accessed July 15, 2007).

Greenstein, D., and S. E. Thorin. 2002. *The digital library: A biography.* Washington, DC: Digital Library Federation, Council on Library and Information Resources. www.clir.org/pubs/reports/pub109/pub109.pdf (accessed July 15, 2007).

Hazen, D., J. Horrell, and J. Merrill-Oldham. 1998. *Selecting research collections for digitization.* Washington, DC: Council on Library and Information Resources. www.clir.org/pubs/reports/hazen/pub74.html (accessed July 15, 2007).

Herzberg, A. 1998. Safeguarding digital library contents: Charging for online content. *D-Lib Magazine* 5(1). www.dlib.org/dlib/january98/ibm/01herzberg.html (accessed July 15, 2007).

Knight, J. 2003. Cornell axes Elsevier journals as prices rise. *Nature* 426(6964):217.

Kurzweil, R. 1999. *The age of spiritual machines: When computers exceed human intelligence.* New York: Penguin.

Lagoze, C., and H. Van de Sompel. 2001. The Open Archives Initiative: Building a low-barrier interoperability framework. In *Proceedings of the First ACM/IEEE-CS Joint Conference on Digital Libraries (JCDL 2001); Roanoke, VA., June 24–28, 2001,* 54–62). New York: Association for Computing Machinery (ACM).

Lee, S. D. 2001. *Digital imaging: A practical handbook.* New York: Neal-Schuman.

Lesk, M. 1999. Perspectives on DLI-2—Growing the field. *D-Lib Magazine* 5(7–8). www.dlib.org/dlib/july99/07lesk.html (accessed July 15, 2007).

———. 2005. *Understanding digital libraries.* 2nd ed. (The Morgan Kaufmann series in multimedia information and systems). San Francisco: Morgan Kaufmann.

Library of Congress. Preservation Research & Testing Division. 2003. *Compact disc preservation.* www.loc.gov/preserv/rt/#cd (accessed July 15, 2007).

Library of Congress. 2005, November 22. *Library of Congress launches effort to create World Digital Library: Google is first private-sector partner with funding of $3 million.* Washington, DC: Author. www.loc.gov/today/pr/2005/05–250.html (accessed July 15, 2007).

Lynch, C. 2001. The battle to define the future of the book in the digital world. *First Monday* 6(6). www.firstmonday.org/issues/issue6_6/lynch/index.html (accessed July 15, 2007).

Markoff, J. 2003, May 12. The Evelyn Wood of digitized book scanners. *New York Times on the Web.* www.nytimes.com/2003/05/12/technology/12TURN.html (accessed July 15, 2007).

Marson, I. 2004, June 24. British Library plans to archive whole UK web. *ZDNet UK.* http://news.zdnet.co.uk/internet/0,39020369,39158517,00.htm (accessed July 15, 2007).

McArthur, D. J., S. Giersch, and H. Burrows. 2003. Sustainability issues and activities for the NSDL. In *Proceedings of the Third ACM/IEEE-CS Joint Conference on Digital Libraries (JCDL 2003); Houston, TX., May 27–31, 2003,* 395. New York: Association for Computing Machinery (ACM).

McCarthy, C. 2004. Digital libraries. In *The Internet encyclopedia,* Vol. 1. Edited H. Bidgoli, 505–25. Hoboken, NJ: Wiley.

McCarthy, C., and M. B. Cunha. 2003. Digital library development in Brazil. *OCLC Systems and Services Journal* 19(3):114–9.

Mears, W. 2003, January 15. Supreme Court upholds copyright extensions: Decision seen as victory for movie, recording industry. *CNN.com.* www.cnn.com/2003/LAW/01/15/scotus.copyrights/index.html (accessed July 15, 2007).

National Library of Australia. 2002. *Safeguarding Australia's Web resources: Guidelines for creators and publishers.* www.nla.gov.au/guidelines/webresources.html (accessed July 15, 2007).

Nelson, M. L., J. Rocker, and T. L. Harrison. 2003. OAI and NASA's scientific and technical information. *Library Hi Tech* 21(2):140–50. http://techreports.larc.nasa.gov/ltrs/PDF/2003/jp/NASA-2003-lht-mln.pdf (accessed July 15, 2007).

New York Times Co. Inc., et al. v. Tasini et al. 2001, June 25. *Certiorari to the United States Court of Appeals for the Second Circuit.* http://straylight.law.cornell.edu/supct/html/00–201.ZS.html (accessed July 15, 2007).

Nicholson, D., and G. MacGregor. 2003. Distributed digital libraries; "NOF-Digi": Putting UK culture online. *OCLC Systems and Services* 19(3):96–9.

Noerr, P. 2003. *The digital library toolkit.* 3rd ed. www.sun.com/products-n-solutions/edu/whitepapers/pdf/digital_library_toolkit.pdf (accessed July 15, 2007).

Notess, G. 2005. *Search engine showdown reviews.* http://searchengineshowdown.com/reviews (accessed July 15, 2007).

Olsen, F. 2003, March 21. Seeking additional security after a big theft, JSTOR tests Internet2's Shibboleth. *The Chronicle of Higher Education* 49(30):A35.

O'Reilly, T. 2005. *What is Web 2.0? Design patterns and business models for the next generation of software.* O'Reilly Network. www.oreillynet.com/lpt/a/6228 (accessed July 15, 2007).

Paskin, N. 2003. DOI: A 2003 progress report. *D-Lib Magazine* 9(6). www.dlib.org/dlib/june03/paskin/06paskin.html (accessed July 15, 2007).

President's Information Technology Advisory Council. Panel on Digital Libraries. 2001. *Digital libraries:*

Universal access to human knowledge: Report to the President. Washington, DC: Author.

Quint, B. 2004, December 27. Google's Library Project: Questions, questions, questions. *Information Today.* www.infotoday.com/newsbreaks/nb041227–2.shtml (accessed July 15, 2007).

Quint, B. 2005, October 31. Open Content Alliance expands rapidly; Reveals operational details. *Information Today*. www.infotoday.com/newsbreaks/nb051031–1.shtml (accessed July 15, 2007).

Ray, J., et al. 2002. Panel on digital preservation. In *Proceedings of the Second ACM/IEEE-CS Joint Conference on Digital Libraries (JCDL 2002); Portland, OR, July 14–18, 2002*, 365–7. New York: Association for Computing Machinery (ACM).

Saeednia, S. 2000. How to maintain both privacy and authentication in digital libraries. *International Journal on Digital Libraries* 2:251–8.

Saffady, W. 1995. Digital library concepts and technologies for the management of library collections: An analysis of methods and costs. *Library Technology Reports* 31:221–380.

Schwartz, C. S. 2000. Digital libraries: An overview. *Journal of Academic Librarianship* 26(6):385–93.

Smith, A. 2004. *Access in the future tense*. Washington, DC: Council on Library and Information Resources (CLIR). www.clir.org/pubs/abstract/pub126abst.html (accessed July 15, 2007).

Stein, S. H. (U.S. District Judge) 2001. *Random House, Inc. v. Rosetta Books LLC; F. Supp. 2nd, 2001 U.S. Dist. Lexis 9456* (S.D.N.Y. 2001). www.law.cornell.edu/copyright/cases/ebooks.htm (accessed July 15, 2007).

Stern, C. 2001, June 26. Freelancers win fight over reuse of works; Justices say databases require permission. *Washington Post* E1.

Sturges, P., et al. 2003. User privacy in the digital library environment: An investigation of policies and preparedness. *Library Management*, 24(1–2):44–50.

Tedd, L. A., and J. A. Large. 2005 *Digital libraries: Principles and practice in a global environment*. Munich, Germany: K.G. Saur.

Tennant, R. 2001. Coping with disasters. *Library Journal* 126(19):26.

UNESCO. 2003. *Draft charter on the preservation of the digital heritage* (Document 32 C/28). http://unesdoc.unesco.org/images/0013/001311/131178e.pdf (accessed July 15, 2007).

Vellucci, S. L. 1998. Metadata. *Annual Review of Information Science and Technology* 33:187–222.

Viadero, D. 2004, September 15. ERIC Education Library's new look debuts online. *Education Week* 24(3):29.

Witten, I. H., and D. Bainbridge. 2002. *How to build a digital library.* San Francisco: Morgan Kaufmann.

Witten, I. H., R. J. McNab, S. Jones, M. Apperley, D. Bainbridge, and S. J. Cunningham. 1999. Managing complexity in a distributed digital library. *Computer* 32(2):74–9.

Witten, I. H., A. Moffat, and T. Bell. 1999. *Managing gigabytes: Compressing and indexing documents and images.* 2nd ed. San Francisco: Morgan Kaufmann.

Wolf, G. 2003. The great library of Amazonia. *Wired* 11(12). http://www.wired.com/techbiz/media/news/2003/10/60948 (accessed July 15, 2007).

Young, J. R. 2005, June 21. Publishers' group asks Google to stop scanning copyrighted works for 6 months. *The Chronicle of Higher Education.* http://chronicle.com/free/2005/06/2005062101t.htm (accessed July 15, 2007).

Zhang, A., and D. Gourley. 2003. A digital collections management system based on open source software. In *Proceedings of the Third ACM/IEEE-CS Joint Conference on Digital Libraries (JCDL 2003); Houston, TX, May 27–31, 2003*.381). New York: Association for Computing Machinery (ACM).

Computer Conferencing and Distance Learning

Liam Rourke, *Nanyang Technological University, Singapore*
Heather Kanuka, *Athabasca University, Canada*

INTRODUCTION

To a large extent, distance learning derives its ability to exist as a recognized form of educational delivery from the technologies it uses. When print packages and postal services were the predominant technologies, distance learning was often referred to as "correspondence study," in which teaching and learning consisted of tutors and students exchanging instructional packages and completed assignments through the mail. With the current set of sophisticated information and communication technologies (ICT), distance learning is increasingly referred to as "e-learning." Teaching and learning activities regularly include lectures, whole-group discussions, small-group collaborative activities, mentoring relationships between students and their advisors, and informal chats among students and instructors. In the inaugural issue of the *Journal of Distance Education*, several authors identified computer conferencing as the harbinger of these profound changes.

Since text-based, asynchronous, computer conferencing was introduced to distance learning settings in the mid-1980s, many innovations have surpassed its sophistication (e.g., blogs, wiki, podcasts, Web-based audio conferencing and videoconferencing); still, computer conferencing retains a central position in distance education, while newer innovations continue to remain marginalized. Students, instructors, administrators, and learning theorists each find in it unique advantages; however, it is its ability to provide communication that removes access barriers (e.g., temporal, geographical, situational) in a manner that is generally considered cost-effective for students, instructors, and institutions—as well as being transparent and ubiquitous.

In addition to being cost-effective (unlike older models of audio conferencing and videoconferencing) and easy to use (unlike many newer innovations), computer conferencing provides mediated interaction (unlike paper-based correspondence). It is this last element (mediated communication) that is central to providing an effective learning environment and the focus of our discussion. In particular, computer conferencing enables students to interact with each other and their instructor, but it does not force them to be at a particular place at a particular time; it allows instructors to incorporate discussion in their courses, but in a way that allows participants to deliberate over others' opinions, reflect on their own, and articulate cogent responses. It supports many-to-many communication, but it is inexpensive and simple for people to master.

In this chapter, we discuss the presence of computer conferencing and its ability to provide mediated interaction in distance learning. Our practice and our research are situated in higher education settings, and our discussion will reflect this perspective. We begin with definitions of our key terms and then move to a historical approach to understanding computer conferencing's position in distance learning. This approach provides a rich context for discussions of the learning theories, instructional activities, and proposed outcomes that are associated with computer conferencing in distance learning. We also provide substantial attention to empirical studies that have investigated each of these topics. A historical approach, we feel, provides some unique insights into an area that has been the subject of excellent reviews, including definitive reviews by Romiszowski and Mason (2004, 1996).

DEFINITIONS

Computer Conferencing

For the participants in distance learning, *computer conferencing* is a sort of robust e-mail that facilitates textual, asynchronous, group communication. By *textual*, we mean that message production is limited to the characters on a computer keyboard, and by *asynchronous* we mean that the communication is somewhat liberated from the temporal and orchestral constraints of face-to-face communication. It is one tool among a set that tutors, course designers, and students encounter in their learning management systems (e.g., Blackboard, Moodle, WebCT). In taxonomies of educational technologies, it is grouped in the category of computer-mediated communication systems, along with synchronous chat systems, listservs, bulletin board systems, e-mail, desktop videoconferencing, and voice over Internet protocol systems (VoIP). Those who have studied and worked in the field of distance learning for years regard it as one of three forms of conferencing that also include audio conferencing and videoconferencing. Others position it as the fulcrum on which distance learning rises from its second generation to its third—from learners as consumers of packaged media (e.g., print, audio tapes, and videotapes) to learners as participants in interactive media (Nipper 1989). These are some of the meanings of computer conferencing in the context of distance learning.

Distance Learning

Distance learning too has an assortment of meanings, but each overlaps to some extent with Keegan's (1990) definition of *distance education*. Seeking to delimit the field, Keegan compiled the following parameters that set distance education off from on-campus education and further distinguished it from what many saw as related activities such as continuing education or informal learning:

> Distance education is a form of education characterized by a) the quasi-permanent separation of teacher and learner throughout the length of the learning process, b) the influence of an educational organization, c) the use of technical media, d) the provision of two way communication, and e) the quasi-permanent absence of the learning group throughout the length of the learning process. (Keegan 1990, 44)

As is predictable in a field involving ICT, this definition was being undermined before it made it to print—largely by computer conferencing. Soon, all that remained of Keegan's essences were items b and c (i.e., the influence of an educational organization and the use of technical media).

Even the term *education* was proving to be a moving target. Simultaneous with the growing presence of ICT in the field, a pedagogical movement was afoot that regarded the term *education* with disapproval. Bringing together themes from progressive education, humanistic psychology, andragogy, and cognitive and social constructivism, many argued that the very term *education* linguistically positioned instructors and content at the center of education, a position that rightly should be occupied by students and learning. Distance educators responded to this discourse, and *distance education* became, for many, *distance learning*.

After losing three of Keegan's five essences, and then the term *education*, the concept *distance* became a focus of dispute. Moore (1972) deconstructed the term *distance*, questioning whether geographic separation had any influence on learning, and whether the real distance—the psychological, social, and cognitive separation between students and instructors—was any less salient in, for instance, the large lecture halls of conventional universities.

After much reflection and dialogue, the contours of the field, which we refer to as *distance learning* in the rest of this chapter, are probably less certain than they were before Keegan attempted to consolidate the field, which coincided with the introduction of the disruptive technology, computer conferencing.

HISTORY OF MEDIATED INTERACTION IN DISTANCE EDUCATION

To appreciate the role of mediated interaction via computer conferencing in distance learning, it is helpful to know something about the history of this union. In this section, we examine the ways in which this technology has been construed in the distance learning literature. We provide brief sketches of the views of Holmberg (1983), Moore (1991, 1983, 1972), Garrison, Anderson, and Archer (2001, 2000), Laurillard (2002), Evans and Nation (1989), Gunawardena, Lowe, and Anderson (1997), and Murphy (2004, 2003). Although there are others who have made important contributions to computer conferencing, these theorists have made the most significant contributions within the field of distance learning. From their writings, we abstract the learning activities and educational outcomes they associate with mediated interaction, and the larger theoretical frameworks they draw on to work out a role for computer conferencing in distance learning.

Holmberg and the Guided Didactic Conversation

One of the first to conceive of a role for interaction in distance learning was Holmberg (1983). He began writing in what is now referred to as the first generation of distance education (Nipper 1989), the era of correspondence study. Apropos of this system, Holmberg understood learning as "primarily an individual activity" (p. 116). Despite this understanding and the rudimentary communication technologies available to distance learning at the time (e.g., print packages, telephones, and postal services), he was already considering a role for interaction among students and members of the supporting educational institution.

Holmberg (1983) identified two forms of interaction that would be helpful to students studying at a distance. The first he characterized as *real*, in which conversational partners included students and members of the supporting institution. This type of conversation was realized when students submitted assignments and received feedback from their tutor. Because it was one of the few avenues of interaction available to distance learners, Holmberg urged that student assessment should be more like a conversation than an examination, and students' submissions, therefore, should be treated as a springboard for prescriptive feedback, not simply grading.

Holmberg (1983) characterized the second form of interaction as *simulated*, in which the conversational partners were the students' existing knowledge, the new course content, and the voice of the tutor that was becoming increasingly internalized. To facilitate this type of interaction, Holmberg suggested that course material be composed in an accessible, exoteric tone rather than the esoteric tone typical of scholarly texts.

He envisioned three outcomes arising from, in his terms, "guided didactic conversations." The first was improved retention of information (he wrote specifically of recall and recognition). A second, higher-level outcome would be the students' ability to weigh new information, to consider it, and to think critically about it. A third outcome also central in Holmberg's theory were the feelings of study pleasure and motivation that would arise as students developed personal relationships with members of the supporting institution.

The theoretical links between these educational outcomes and the literal and figurative forms of interaction can be found in the cognitive, humanistic, and sociocultural psychology movements that were influencing education at the time. Cognitive psychologists, building on the work of Piaget (1977), were arguing for the importance of interaction among peers and adults in generating the perturbation necessary for intellectual development (Perret-Clairmont, Perret, and Bell 1989). Sociocultural psychologists were advancing notions of *thinking* as an internalized conversation with the generalized other (Vygotsky 1984), and humanistic psychologists were stressing the importance of a warm, receptive, supportive environment for learning (Rogers and Freiberg 1993).

In 1983, Holmberg reviewed a set of studies that tested several conjectures emanating from his theory. His summary of the results was pessimistic, "The investigations," he concluded, "cannot be said to have given any conclusive evidence in favor of my hypotheses" (p. 34). Garrison (2000) has offered a similar evaluation of Holmberg's theory, in which he suggests that the results are an inherent aspect of correspondence study and its associated media and communicative processes:

> The question arises as to whether an inert learning package, regardless of how well it is written, is a sufficient substitute for real sustained communication with the teacher as both content and learning expert. The role of the teacher was largely simulated by way of written instructions and commentary. In sum, the organizational assumptions and principles of the industrial model and the dependence upon written communication seriously constrain and limit the role of conversation and the full emergence of a transactional perspective. (Garrison 2000, 29)

In Garrison's larger discussion, and in several other analyses, the assessment that emerges of Holmberg's ideas is that they were sound, but unable to be realized because of the constraints of the technology and the modes of distance learning. The communicative learning activities, the educational outcomes, and the role of mediated interaction that he envisioned were prescient. Each continues to be represented prominently, in modern forms, in current research on computer conferencing. Several researchers continue to demonstrate that: (a) for many students, peer communication makes distance learning more enjoyable; (b) the interaction among students, instructors, and peers can foster critical, reflective thinking; and (c) acculturation to a discipline can be enhanced by interaction in computer conferencing.

Moore and Dialogue

Moore (1991, 1983, 1973) was influenced by the North American andragogical movement in adult education (e.g., Knowles 1990). Premised on a few of the central tenets of andragogy, such as the assumptions that adults are autonomous and self-directed learners, Moore developed a model of interaction in distance settings. Whereas Holmberg's model arose in the context of correspondence study, Moore's, with its central positioning of two-way communication technologies, was reflective of a second- or third-generation model (Nipper 1989). An additional distinction between Moore's and Holmberg's models is that the latter was constrained by convention and by technology to figurative uses of the term *conversation*, whereas Moore began formulating a literal conceptualization of the role of dialogue in distance education.

To Holmberg's (1983) two forms of interaction (learner-to-content and learner-to-tutor), Moore (1983) added a third—learner-to-learner. Unfortunately, Moore is vague about the specific types of interaction that count as *dialogue* between learners. In 1991, Moore offered the following explanation in a review of his model:

> *Dialogue* describes the interaction between the teacher and learner when one gives instruction and the other responds. The extent and nature of this dialogue is determined by the educational philosophy of the individual or group responsible for the design of the course, by the personalities of teacher and learner, by the subject matter of the course, and by environmental factors. (p. 3)

Subsequent studies of his model have been equally equivocal. Chen and Willits (1999) studied Moore's three forms of interaction without providing an operational definition of dialogue, and Haughey and Fenwick (1996) studied the construct *participation*, which colloquially seems to signify something different than dialogue. Saba and Schearer's (1994) substantive study of Moore's theory included the following definition of *dialogue*: "the extent to which, in any educational program, learner and educator are able to respond to each other" (p. 42).

More recently, research by Kanuka, Collett, and Caswell (2002) sought to gain a greater understanding of the topics of feedback, emotional distance, and structure using the two dimensions within the theory of transactional distance (structure and dialogue, and autonomy). *Dialogue* was defined as the interaction between the instructor and learners with computer conferencing as the communication medium. The results of this study revealed that most instructors and students continue to experience a tension between structure, dialogue, and autonomy. However, how these issues should be addressed depends on the characteristics of the learners. Their findings showed that if learners are autonomous, they will tolerate emotional distance and be less dependent on feedback, and a high level of transactional distance is fine; if learners are not autonomous, a low level of transactional distance is most appropriate. Thus, using this rationale, the results of this study indicate that there is a need for instructors to assess learner autonomy. In keeping with Moore's theory, if the learners are not autonomous, then instructors will need to address the issues of feedback, emotional distance, and structure.

These findings support Moore's (1983) theory that dialogue, when defined as interaction with computer conferencing between the instructor and students, could close the *transactional distance*, which he defined as the subjective feeling students have of the social, psychological, and cognitive separation from their teacher and the subject matter. Moore's goal was to deconstruct unfavorable comparisons between distance education and face-to-face education. In a phenomenological vein (though he does not use this term), Moore argued that a student's experience of distance was more important than an objective assessment of geographic separation.

Andragogy, a perspective of adult learning first articulated by Knowles (1990), plays an important role in Moore's thinking. Synthesizing motifs from humanistic psychology with the unique situation of mature students, Knowles formulated a perspective on how best to assist adults in their efforts toward continuing education. Moore saw a fortuitous relationship between Knowles' notion of learner-centeredness and distance education. Unlike immature learners, adults can independently assess gaps in their current knowledge, identify resources that will fill these gaps, motivate themselves to progress through difficult material, and evaluate their progress toward a learning goal. This construction of autonomous, independent students looking to formal education as a resource for their self-directed efforts was congenial to the form of education offered at a distance.

Moore's theory has been subjected to two systematic empirical tests. Using the path analysis technique, Saba and Shearer (1994) found that dialogue was inversely related to transactional distance. Chen and Willits (1998) studied a course delivered via interactive television and found that in-class discussion contributed to student achievement. The relationship, however, is complex. Some students report that student-to-student interactions are not critical to their success and are the least important form of interaction (Kelsey and D'souza 2005). The instructor that Kelsey and D'souza interviewed mused: "To be honest, my feeling was that distance students really didn't want contact and were not interested in communicating" (p. 36). Gorsky, Caspi, and Tuvi-Arad (2004) studied the role of learner-to-learner and learner-to-instructor dialogue in distance education using naturalistic methods. When an online forum was available but not required, they found that students contacted one another only when they experienced conceptual difficulties. They concluded, "Theories like Moore's often assign to interpersonal dialogue an importance that may not be realized in practice" (p. 17).

Garrison and the Community of Inquiry

Garrison (1997) moved the discourse begun by Holmberg (1983) and Moore (1983) squarely into the third generation of distance education, the era in which information and communication technologies (ICT) became commonplace. He was one of the first to begin writing specifically about computer conferencing and its role in distance education. Like Moore, his focus was on adult learners. But more like Holmberg, he was skeptical about the level of independence and self-directedness that one should expect of students. Garrison adopted Moore's concern with several configurations of learner, content, and instructor interaction.

It was with authors such as Garrison, Anderson, and Archer (2001, 2000) that constructs such as Holmberg's *conversation* or Moore's *dialogue* began to take on a specific definition in terms of its observable, constituent, conversational actions. Garrison et al. proposed a four-phase process for online discussion and identified conversational actions characteristic of each phase. The phases and processes include:

Triggering Event: Presenting background information that culminates in a question

Exploration: Presenting opinions, sharing anecdotes, contradicting previous ideas

Integration: Building on others' ideas, articulating evidentiary hypotheses

Resolution: Applying knowledge, testing and defending solutions

Garrison et al. caution that this is an idealized sequence, and that actual discussions are less formalized.

Critical thinking and higher-order learning have preoccupied Garrison's writing throughout his career, and it is these outcomes that he associates with computer conferencing's role in distance learning. He and his colleagues define critical thinking as "the acquisition of deep and meaningful understanding as well as content-specific critical inquiry abilities, skills, and dispositions" (Garrison et al. 2000, 4). The way to achieve these goals with computer conferencing they wrote is through *critical discourse*:

> For a computer conference to serve as an educational environment, it must be more than undirected, unreflective, random exchanges and dumps of opinion. Higher-order learning requires systematic and sustained critical discourse where dissonance and problems are resolved through exploration, integration, and testing. (p. 21)

Garrison has identified critical thinking as the hallmark of higher education, and he sees critical discourse in computer conferencing as a way to enact this in distance-learning settings.

Resonating in Garrison et al.'s (2001, 2000) model is the sociocognitive account of learning that originated with Piaget (1977) and was developed further by European researchers including Perret-Clairmont et al. (1989). Essentially, Garrison et al. envisioned student's unreflective assumptions and inchoate ideas becoming clear, precise, and defensible through antagonistic interaction with other students and their instructor in computer conferences. This is an important departure from Holmberg (1983) and Moore (1983, 1972), who envisioned mediated conversations or dialogues leading to increased study pleasure, motivation, engagement, and thereby achievement.

Like Holmberg's (1983) and Moore's (1983) models, Garrison et al.'s (2001, 2000) model has generated much interest, and is currently used extensively as a theoretical framework for research in the field of distance learning. However, there are few empirical tests of its central claims. Garrison has participated in three studies, and there have been others that explore the relationships he envisioned (Garrison and Cleveland-Innes 2005; Garrison, Cleveland-Innes, and Fung 2004; Garrison et al. 2001; Kanuka, Rourke, and Laflamme 2006; Vaughan and Garrison 2005). Consistent in these studies is the following problem: researchers are unable to assess the relationship between critical discourse and critical thinking because of the virtual absence of critical discourse. Garrison et al.'s (2001) own findings are representative. Summarizing their analysis of a graduate level computer conference, they report:

> The highest frequency (42%) of contributions to the conference was categorized as *exploration*, the brainstorming phase where people share information. The frequency of the contributions fell-off rapidly at the next stage, *integration* (13%). This issue is worthy of special consideration. There was a virtual absence of responses (4%) associated with the highest phase of critical discourse, *resolution*. (p. 6)

Observers of interaction as it takes shape in computer conferencing rarely report significant instances of critical discourse, dissenting opinion, challenges to others, or expressions of difference. This makes it difficult to assess the relationship between the types of discursive activity promoted by Garrison et al. (2000) and their hypothesized outcomes.

Laurillard and the Conversational Framework

Laurillard (2002) is another writer who proposes a role for mediated discussion, supported by computer conferencing, in distance learning. Like Holmberg (1983), her use of the term *conversation* is both literal and figurative. In its literal sense, *conversation* connotes the verbal interaction that students have with each other and with their tutors. In its figurative sense, *conversation* connotes a type of educational cybernetics.

The relevant notion of cybernetics is that existing actions are perfected based on the continuous assessment of their current state versus a goal state. Pask (1976) saw in this process an analogue to the coaching that takes place between an adult and a child. Building on these ideas, Pask devised a *conversational theory* of education, which, though complex and dotted with neologisms, can be conveyed as follows. First, a subject-matter expert devises a detailed conceptual map of a topic. Next, he or she (or it—computer-assisted instruction is quite suitable in this function) presents this representation to students. Students then acquire this representation and demonstrate the accuracy of their acquisition through assessment.

With minor variations, this is the model that Laurillard (2002) uses to understand the role of computer conferencing in higher education. Her general model positions the tutor and the student in an adaptive relationship. Tutors and students exchange their understandings of course topics, and during these exchanges, tutors tailor their authoritative, expert presentations to the students' existing constructions. The students modify their constructions so that they become successively more accurate representations of the tutors' (Allan 2004; Hannon 2002; Laurillard 2002). There are also opportunities for self-assessment as students articulate and argue their interpretations with their peers. These are presented as secondary in importance however, with Laurillard worrying about students "floundering in mutually progressive ignorance" (1993, 172).

Unfortunately, Laurillard (2002) has not conducted empirical studies of computer conferencing. Her empirical work focuses mainly on videodisk technology, with the bulk of her writing being of a reflective sort. Allan (2004), however, has also argued that adaptive feedback from a perceptive tutor will always be more effective than the best artificial-intelligence tutors: "No simulation or technology is able to give truly intrinsic or fully customized feedback," she declares. "Online tests, self-assessment questions, and other artificial sources of formative feedback cannot provide the degree of depth or insight required for customized learning assistance in the ways a human tutor can" (p. 11). Rowntree (1997) adds, "Personal feedback is the key to quality in education and training. It is what enables us all to learn from our experience. A response from another human being that challenges or confirms our understanding, helps us overcome errors, and encourages us toward new insights" (p. 58). Hannon's (2002) research suggests that feedback is also related to student satisfaction: "Students want (and expect) quick and detailed responses to their questions and concerns, as well as timely, qualitative feedback on their work" she concluded:

> Students in distance learning courses apparently expect active interaction with their teachers. Students who felt that these expectations were met tended to be positive about the course, and about distance learning in general. These expectations can be time consuming for professors and teaching assistants to meet, but there are possible compromises that will satisfy both teachers and students, such as posting ideal responses to exam questions and using a course listserv to answer common questions. Student and faculty evaluations of more recent versions of the online courses reveal that these measures have improved satisfaction with distance learning for both parties. (Hannon 2002, 42)

Although the specifics of Laurillard's model have not been investigated empirically, there is support for the principles on which it is based, and it has been highly influential within the field of distance learning literature and research.

Gunawardena, Lowe, and Anderson and Meaning Making

Gunawardena worked through several of the models we have described in order to understand the role of computer conferencing in the distance learning courses she taught. From her practical perspective, she encountered difficulties with each of the models: Either they presented ambiguous conceptualizations of interaction that were difficult to implement as an instructor, or they were rooted in teacher-centered, instructivist perspectives of education (Gunawardena, Carabajal, and Lowe 2000). To address these limitations Gunawardena et al. (1997) developed their own model. Like Garrison et al.'s (2000) and Laurillard's (2002) models, it arose at a time when conferencing was widespread, and it found an audience for whom the distinction between distance learning and on-campus education was beginning to blur.

Gunawardena et al. (1997) believed that computer conferencing should be used to engage students in five types of conversational activities. The activities occur in a developmental sequence and move students through a five phase process of knowledge co-construction:

- Sharing and comparing information
- Discovering and exploring dissonance
- Negotiating meaning
- Testing new knowledge
- Establishing a consensus and applying knowledge

Unlike the models described previously, the space between these conversational actions and the purported learning outcomes does not present a large and inferential gap. Through conversation with their peers and the instructor, students will build networks for subsequent collaboration, enhance the information provided in course materials with additional information and alternative interpretations, and make the topics personally meaningful.

This model reflects a social constructivist understanding of learning and instruction. Koschmann and colleagues (1996) describe the role of computer conferencing in the social constructivist models:

> It is in the process of articulating, reflecting and negotiating that we engage in a meaning making or knowledge construction process. This process can become even more powerful when communication among peers is done in written form, because writing, done without the immediate feedback of another person as in oral communication, requires a fuller elaboration in order to successfully convey meaning. (p. 83)

With its foundation in social constructivism, Gunawardena et al.'s model of computer conferencing is notably different from the previous models. Gunawardena et al.'s (1997) model, like the others we have reviewed, has received little empirical substantiation. When studies are conducted, a familiar problem reappears: conference participants rarely engage in anything beyond the lowest levels of interaction (i.e., sharing-and-comparing information). The elements of discussion that are essential to meaning making and knowledge construction—elements such as exploring dissonance and negotiating meaning with peers and the instructor—are absent. Gunawardena et al. (2001) summarize the results of several applications of the model:

> As the model has been applied to a succession of conferences, it has brought to light indications that many, probably most, conferences do not proceed beyond the lowest phases of knowledge co-construction. Participants share and compare their experiences and viewpoints on course topics but when they find areas of disagreement, instead of negotiating meaning as the social constructivist theory would suggest, they appear to agree to disagree. (p. 8)

One of the studies that Gunawardena et al. are referring to may have been Kanuka and Anderson's (1997), in which the authors report:

> Evidence from surveys, telephone interviews, and transcript analysis indicates that most of the interaction is of a sharing and comparing nature. Dissonance and inconsistency are not actively explored, there is little testing of evidence against experience or the literature, and rarely do participants state the relevance or application of new knowledge that might have been created. (p. 45)

In a similar study of computer conferencing in an undergraduate setting, Thomas (2002) reports:

> The quality of interaction was insufficient to promote the levels of interpersonal communication necessary for a truly conversational mode of learning. While there was evidence of some interaction with students building upon or presenting arguments against other students' contributions, there was no real co-operative development of ideas between groups of students. (p. 359)

De Laat (2001) found similar results in her content analysis of an online discussion. Using Gunawardena et al.'s (1997) interaction analysis scheme, she found many initiations to which there were no replies. Gunawardena et al. (2001) observed that dissonance and the testing and modification of proposed co-constructions were almost absent in the conferences that she studied. Further substantiation of these results are provided by Davis and Rouzie (2002), Pena-Shaff and Nicholls (2004), and Yakimovicz and Murphy (1995), among others.

Murphy and Solving Problems in Collaborative Environments (SPICE)

Murphy (2000) developed a model of computer conferencing that, like that of Gunawardena et al. (1997), presents an alternative to the teacher-centered, instructivist perspective of teaching and learning in distance settings. Murphy stipulates a specific learning activity for which conferencing should be used. As we have in previous sections, we will describe that activity, the types of outcomes with which it is associated, Murphy's account of the relationship between the activities and outcomes, and the empirical evidence that she and her colleagues have brought to bear on the model.

Murphy (2000) regards computer conferencing as a medium that allows students studying at a distance to engage in purposive, collaborative activities, namely, problem solving. She envisions group problem solving as occurring in a developmental sequence that begins with superficial interaction and culminates in the production of a shared artifact. Murphy has identified six stages in this sequence and a corollary set of conversational actions for each stage (Murphy 2004, 2000). They are:

Social presence: Sharing personal information, complimenting others, expressing appreciation

Articulating individual perspectives: Stating personal opinions, summarizing/reporting on content

Accommodating others' perspectives: Challenging others' statements

Co-constructing meaning: Seeking clarification/elaboration, responding to questions

Building shared goals and purposes: Proposing a shared goal, working toward a shared goal

Producing shared artifacts: Producing a document or other artifact collaboratively

Murphy sees the strength of computer conferencing as a forum in which students can debate, wrestle, and argue with each other over individual interpretations. However, she is aware of the virtual absence of these processes in most instances of conferencing. That is why she introduces collaborative problem solving as an essential activity for computer conferencing. Where others assumed that any type of interaction in an asynchronous, textual environment would automatically be valuable, Murphy argues that small group, collaborative problem-solving activities compel students to contend with each other's opinions and interpretations.

A strength of Murphy's model is the sustained program of empirical study that informs her conceptual framework and her claims about computer conferencing. In a series of projects, she has examined the validity of her conceptualization of the problem-formation/problem-resolution process, the validity of the instrument used to assess students' engagement in the six-stage process, and the students' experience of the learning activity (Murphy 2004, 2003, 2000). The results of the empirical investigations support the findings of Garrison et al. (2001), Gunawardena et al. (1997), Kanuka and Anderson (1997), and others who have looked for the social construction of knowledge in computer conferencing. Murphy (2004) summarizes these results:

> Students engage primarily in processes related to *social presence* and *articulating individual perspectives* and do not reach a stage of sharing goals and producing shared artefacts. Few messages show evidence of collaborative processes such as *accommodating others' perspectives*, *reflecting others' perspectives*, or *co-constructing shared perspectives and meanings*. Still fewer messages show any attempt to *build shared goals and purposes*, and no messages show evidence of *producing shared artifacts.* (pp. 427–8)

Empirical observations of computer conferencing in distance learning consistently find a predominance of monologues, relational communication, or superficial interaction and a meager amount of collaboration and knowledge co-construction. Murphy hypothesized that a learning activity that compels students to interact in meaningful ways—collaborative problem solving—would change this; however, she has found little evidence to support this hypothesis so far.

In 1992, Mason called on distance educators to develop a conceptual and empirical rationale to guide the use of computer conferencing in distance learning, and since that time there has been a proliferation of models. The models we have reviewed represent important developments in the conceptualization of the role of computer conferencing in distance learning. Our review has certainly not been exhaustive. We have excluded some notable efforts that have been reviewed extensively in the literature and whose principles have been incorporated into the models we did review.

DISCUSSION

Many models for the role of computer conferencing in distance learning have been developed. Table 1 provides an overview of the most noteworthy models described in this chapter. Upon examination of the types of learning activities and educational outcomes prescribed in these models, we can see that they can be grouped into two broad categories: (1) Dialectical models, in which computer conferencing is regarded as a forum in which students engage in critical discourse and thereby critical thinking, and (2) dialogical models in which students engage in collaborative meaning making and thereby social knowledge construction. Unfortunately, both models are more successful at prescribing what teachers and students should or might do than they are at describing what they actually do. Neither set of models receives consistent support in systematic observations of students and instructors.

Of collaborative meaning making, Pena-Shaff and Nicholls (2004) provide the following evaluation:

> Conversations online are more like people standing up and taking the floor one by one and speaking as long as they want. Whoever speaks next may talk about anything. It is like conversing in soliloquies or, in centuries past, through letters carried by horse and driver to distant colonies. Others have little influence on one's thoughts at the time of writing. (p. 257)

Table 1: Noteworthy Contributions to Models of Computer Conferencing in Distance Education

Theorist	Theory	Brief Description
B. Holmberg	Guided didactic conversation	One of the first to theorize a role for interaction of distance education Proposed two forms of interaction: *Real* conversations (learner to tutor) *Simulated* conversation (learner to content)
M. G. Moore	Theory of interaction	Proposed that three forms of interaction should be present in distance education for effective learning: Learner-learner Learner-content Learner-tutor/teacher
D. R. Garrison T. Anderson W. Archer	Community of inquiry	Some of the first theorists to specifically write about the use of computer conferencing in distance education Proposed a four-phase process of critical discourse in computer conferencing as necessary to enact critical thinking skills. The phases are as follows: *Triggering Event:* presenting background information that culminates in a question *Exploration:* Presenting opinions, sharing anecdotes, contradicting previous ideas *Integration:* Building on others' ideas, articulating evidentiary hypotheses *Resolution:* Applying knowledge, testing and defending solutions.
D. Laurillard	Conversational framework	Developed a model for effective computer conferencing as being: *Discursive:* There needs to be some dialogue between the learner and instructor about why the topic is important *Adaptive:* The instructor must be prepared to shift the focus to reflect how the learners are doing *Interactive:* Learners must engage in the topic at a practical level and receive feedback on their actions *Reflective:* Learners must connect the feedback they received from their actions back to the topic and articulate it back to the instructor in an essay or project of some kind exhibiting their new understanding
C. Gunawardena C. Lowe T. Anderson	Model for meaning making	One of the first models proposed in distance education using computer conferencing based on social constructivism. This model proposed five phases of knowledge co-construction: Sharing and comparing information Discovering and exploring dissonance Negotiating meaning Testing new knowledge Establishing a consensus and applying knowledge
E. Murphy	Solving problems in collaborative environments (SPICE)	Identified six stages of group problem solving that occur in sequence, and a corollary set of conversational actions for each stage: *Social presence:* sharing personal information, complimenting others, expressing appreciation *Articulating individual perspectives:* stating personal opinions, summarizing/reporting on content *Accommodating others' perspectives:* challenging others' statements *Co-constructing meaning:* seeking clarification/elaboration, responding to questions *Building shared goals and purposes:* proposing a shared goal, working toward a shared goal *Producing shared artifacts:* producing a document or other artifact collaboratively

Of critical discourse, Marttunen (1998) provides this assessment:

> Results reveal that the majority of students' messages are non-interactive in nature. In particular, real interaction, including responses to responses, is very rare. In addition, interaction between students turns out to be mainly non-argumentative in nature: only a small percentage of students' references to each others' texts express opinions opposed to those of fellow students, and only a smaller fraction indicate grounded disagreement. The results suggest that the pedagogical aim of our studies, to engage students in argumentative interaction, is not realized very well. (p. 397)

Fortunately, solutions are arising among the dozens of researchers who have recorded similar observations. The first of three that we will discuss is discussion facilitation.

The role of a facilitator in an online discussion is perhaps the most written about topic in this domain. Dozens of authors have studied and written about the roles and responsibilities of a successful facilitator (Berge 2002; Garrison et al. 2000; Heimstra 1994; Paulson 1995; Salmon 2000; Shea, Swann, and Pickett 2005). Consistently, a positive correlation is identified between the quality of facilitation, student satisfaction, and student perceptions of learning. These findings and the reflective suggestions of dozens of distance educators suggest strongly that skilled and energetic moderators play an important role in facilitating critical discourse and collaborative meaning making.

For various reasons (some more defensible than others), the role is not always taken up successfully. This gives rise to an alternative means of addressing the essential roles and responsibilities. Sophisticated conferencing systems, referred to as computer support for collaborative learning (CSCL) systems, provide technological proxies for responsible facilitation. Duffy, Dueber, and Hawley (1998) developed a conferencing system that compels students to participate in a circumscribed manner. In place of the generic options for posting a message offered by most conferencing systems (e.g., post, reply), their system offers options such as rebut, add evidence, and challenge assumption. Jonassen and Kwon (2001) have studied the use of a similar system. The system, which they refer to as a "computer-supported collaborative argumentation system" (CSCA), is designed to scaffold argumentation among students. It offers the following conversational ontology: hypothesis, data, and principles, along with for and against. When using this system, Jonassen and Kwon found that students were able to construct coherent arguments more often than students using a conventional conferencing system. They analyzed students' interactions using Toulmin's (1958) familiar system of informal argumentation and found significantly more evidence of claims, grounds, and rebuttals among the CSCA group. Knowledge Forum™ is probably the most widely known effort to guide student interaction into a particular conversational genre. Scardemalia and Bereiter's (1994) CSCA delimits student interaction to patterns that are characteristic in scientific research communities, including: my theory, I need to understand, new information, this theory cannot explain, a better theory, and putting our knowledge together. Dozens of studies demonstrate the efficacy of this product in the K–12 settings for which it was designed (e.g., Scardemalia and Bereiter 1994), and similar work has begun in postsecondary settings (van Aalst and Chan 2002).

Discussion facilitation, through either skilled and energetic instructors or technological proxies, is one means of addressing the lack of critical discourse or collaborative meaning making in computer conferencing. The final suggestion we explore is implementation of appropriate learning activities.

Looking closely at the types of learning activities that underlie reports of computer conferencing, Rourke and Conrad (2004) found two common designs. In the most prevalent, students engage in week-long, whole-group, open-ended forums. Consistently, this design is associated with low levels of participation and interaction and few instances of critical discourse or collaborative meaning making. In the second design, a whole class is divided into small groups of students who engage in purposive collaboration (e.g., case-based learning, problem-based learning). This design is associated consistently with high levels of participation, participation that is predominantly interactive, and many instances of knowledge co-construction. Villalba and Romiszkowski (2000), Kanuka (2005), and Kanuka, Rourke, and Laflamme (2006) report similar findings. Villalba and Romiszkowski, for example, performed a comparative analysis of online courses and found that few emphasize collaborative, small-group learning. Most offered a relatively unstructured online group discussion. Assessing these courses, the authors conclude:

> There is little if any research indicating that such environments are conducive to in-depth reflective discussions of the type required to develop critical and creative thinking skills. And there are some studies that suggest they are singularly ineffective in this respect. (p. 405)

Pena-Shaff and Nicholls' (2004) research sheds light on why small-group purposive collaboration can be more valuable than open-ended, whole-group forums:

> In the open forums, if one student disagreed with another, she/he could simply ignore the comment. The small group activity, however, required the students to reach some degree of consensus about their project. If they disagreed with someone, or felt someone else's argument was not well developed, it was more important for them to challenge or contradict them to ensure the presentation would be coherent. (p. 64)

Together, the results of Kanuka, 2005; Kanuka, Rourke, and Laflamme (2006), Pena-Shaff (2000), Rourke and Conrad (2004), and Villalba and Romiszowski (2000) remind distance educators of a conclusion that is well established throughout the literature: Instructional methods have a greater effect on teaching and learning than instructional media (Clark 1994). Hopefully, our review has reminded readers that computer conferencing, in and of itself, is not a pedagogy. Our developmental review indicates that it has taken over twenty years for teachers, students, and researchers to fashion a role for computer conferencing in distance learning.

CONCLUSION

Computer conferencing was invented in the early 1970s (Hiltz and Turoff 1993) and made its way into distance learning in the mid-1980s (Harasim 1990). The union represented the intersection of two growing movements that we remain in the midst of: (1) the maturation of networked computing as a stable and diffuse technology, and (2) a growing recognition of the importance of interaction for learning. The asynchronous mode of communication presented by computer conferencing provides distance learners with a means of interaction while preserving the "anywhere anytime" quality that draws many students to this type of formal education. Since its introduction thirty years ago, there have been many advances in computer networks, communication software, and learning theories; yet computer conferencing continues to expand its role in many levels and types of education.

Therefore, it is important for us to conclude by revisiting some of the problems that persist across the models we reviewed and to see how they are being addressed. The problem, generally, is the students' reluctance to use this technology to engage in either critical discourse or collaborative meaning making—two sets of conversational activities that provide the rationale for including computer conferencing in a course. Documented solutions to this general problem, which we sketch below, include: (1) skilled and energetic facilitation of online discussions, (2) sophisticated conferencing systems that assume some of the roles and responsibilities of successful facilitators, and (3) learning activities that encourage critical discourse and collaborative meaning making.

We conclude that the prescribed processes and outcomes—that is, critical discourse and collaborative meaning making, are unlikely to materialize in the absence of (1) skilled and energetic facilitation, (2) sophisticated conferencing systems that assume some of the responsibilities of successful facilitators, or (3) learning activities that encourage productive and meaningful communication.

GLOSSARY

Andragogy: With the rise of social phenomena such as lifelong learning, educational theorists began to make categorical distinctions between teaching and learning with children, referred to as *pedagogy*, and teaching and learning among adults, referred to in some quarters as *andragogy*.

Asynchronous Communication, Textual: In the context of educational computer conferencing, *textual* refers to message production that is limited to the characters on a computer keyboard; *asynchronous* refers to communication is somewhat liberated from the temporal and orchestral constraints of face-to-face communication.

Computer-Assisted Instruction: For many, the adoption of computer conferencing signaled a shift in the way computers were used in distance learning. In contrast to this communicative function, they had previously been used in a limited way to present structured, preprogrammed learning materials. This was referred to as *computer-assisted instruction*, and is easily distinguishable from *computer-mediated communication*.

Correspondence Education: Sometimes referred to as *first-generation distance education*, correspondence education involved courses of study in which students and teachers communicated by mail.

Critical Discourse: A particular pattern of interaction in computer conferencing that advocates associate with favorable learning outcomes. In Wegerif's description, it involves interaction in which partners engage critically but constructively with each other's ideas. Relevant information is offered for joint consideration. Proposals may be challenged and counterchallenged, but if so. reasons are given and alternatives are offered. Agreement is sought on a basis for joint progress. Knowledge is made publicly accountable and reasoning is visible in the talk.

Distance Learning: In Keegan's definitive conceptualization, distance learning is a form of education characterized by: (a) the quasi-permanent separation of teacher and learner throughout the length of the learning process, (b) the influence of an educational organization, (c) the use of technical media, (d) the provision of two-way communication, and (e) the quasi-permanent absence of the learning group throughout the length of the learning process.

Technological Characteristics Perspective: A variant of technological determinism specific to the study of communication technologies. Stated briefly, attributes of media exercise a predictable causal influence on users' actions. One of the central projects of this perspective was to rationally and efficiently match the properties of a medium to the characteristics of a communication task.

Technological Determinism: The notion that user behavior is determined by particular features of a technology, which in turn is regarded as an autonomous agent outside the influence of human beings.

Tutors: Content specialists (but not necessarily at the level of subject-matter experts in the course design team) who provide instructional guidance to students during a distance education course. Tutors typically provide feedback to students on their assignments, but are not involved in the course design.

CROSS REFERENCES

See *Computer Conferencing: Protocols and Applications; E-mail and Instant Messaging; Telecommuting and Telework; Video Conferencing; Web-Based Training.*

REFERENCES

Allan, M. 2004. A peek into the life of online learning discussion forums: Implications for web based higher education. *International Review of Research in Open and Distance Learning* 5(2). www.irrodl.org/content/v5.2/allan.html (accessed March 2, 2005).

Berge, Z. 2002. Active, interactive, and reflective eLearning. *Quarterly Review of Distance Education* 3(2):181–90.

Chen, Y., and F. Willits. 1999. Dimensions of educational transactions in a videoconferencing learning environment. *The American Journal of Distance Education* 13(1):45–59.

Clark, R. E. 1994. Media will never influence learning. *Educational Technology Research and Development* 42(2):21–9.

Davis, M., and A. Rouzie. 2002. Cooperation vs. deliberation: Computer mediated conferencing and the problem of argument in international distance education. *International Review of Research in Open and Distance Learning* 3(1). www.irrodl.org/content/v3.1/davis.html. (accessed December 23, 2005).

De Laat, M. 2001. *Network and content analysis in an online community discourse. CSCL-ware in practice*. New York: Kluwer.

Duffy, T., B. Duber, and C. Hawley. 1998. Critical thinking in a distributed environment: A pedagogical base for the design of conferencing systems. In *Electronic collaborators: Learner centered technologies for literacy, apprenticeship, and discourse* Edited by C. Bonk, 51–78. Mahwah, NJ: Lawrence Erlbaum.

Evans, T., and D. Nation. 1989. *Critical reflections on distance education*. London: Farmer Press.

Garrison, D. R. 1997. Self-directed learning: Toward a comprehensive model. *Adult Education Quarterly* 48(1):18–32.

Garrison, D. R. 2000. Theoretical challenges for distance education in the 21st century: A shift from structural to transactional issues. *International Review of Research in Open and Distant Learning* 1(1). www.irrodl.org/content/v1.1/randy.html (accessed February 21, 2006).

Garrison, D. R., T. Anderson, and W. Archer. 2000. Critical thinking in a community of inquiry. *Educational Media International* 1(1):1–24.

———. 2001. Critical thinking, cognitive presence, and computer conferencing in distance education. *American Journal of Distance Education* 15(1):7–23.

Garrison, D. R., and M. Cleveland-Innes. 2005, May. *Going beyond online discussion*. Paper presented at the annual conference of the Canadian Association of Distance Education. Vancouver Canada.

Garrison, D. R., M. Cleveland-Innes, and T. Fung. 2004. Student role adjustment in online communities of inquiry: Model and instrument validation. *Journal of Asynchronous Learning Networks* 8(2):61–74.

Gorsky, P., A. Caspi, and I. Tuvi-Arad. 2004. Use of instructional dialogue by university students in a distance education chemistry course. *Journal of Distance Education* 19(1):1–19. http://cade.athabascau.ca/vol19.1/GORSKY_et_al_article.pdf (accessed February 21, 2006).

Gunawardena, C. N., K. Carabajal, and C. Lowe. 2000, April. *Critical analysis of models and methods used to evaluate online learning networks*. Paper presented at the annual conference of the American Educational Research Association, Seattle, USA.

Gunawardena, C. N., C. Lowe, and T. Anderson. 1997. Interaction analysis of a global on-line debate and the development of a constructivist interaction analysis model for computer conferencing. *Journal of Educational Computing Research* 17(4):395–429.

Hannon, P. 2002. Gagne and Laurillard's models of instruction applied to distance education: A theoretically driven evaluation of an online curriculum in public health. *International Review of Research in Open and Distance Learning* 3(2). www.irrodl.org/content/v3.2/hannon.html (accessed December 30, 2005).

Harasim, L. 1990. *Online education: Perspectives*. London: Praeger.

Haughey, M., and T. Fenwick. 1996. Issues in forming school district consortia to provide distance education: lessons from Alberta. *Journal of Distance Education* http://cade.athabascau.ca/vol11.1/haugheyfenwick.html (accessed February 21, 2006).

Heimstra, R. 1994. Computerized distance education: The role for facilitators. *Journal of Adult Education* 22(2):11–23.

Hiltz, R., and M. Turoff. 1993. *The network nation: Human communication via computer*. Cambridge, MA: MIT Press.

Holmberg, B. 1983. Guided didactic conversation in distance education. In *Distance education: International perspectives,* edited by D. Sewart, D. Keegan, and B. Holmberg, 114–22. New York: St. Martin's Press.

Jonassen, D., and H. Kwon. 2001. Communication patterns in computer-mediated vs. face-to-face group problem solving. *Educational Technology: Research and Development* 49(10):35–52.

Kanuka, H. 2005. An exploration into facilitating higher levels of learning in a text-based Internet learning environment using diverse instructional strategies. *Journal of Computer Mediated Communication* 10(3). http://jcmc.indiana.edu/vol10/issue3/kanuka.html (accessed July 22, 2007).

Kanuka, H., and T. Anderson. 1997. On-line forums: New platforms for professional development and group collaboration. *Journal of Computer Mediated Communication* 3(3). www.ascusc.org/jcmc/vol3/issue3/anderson.html (accessed December 30, 2005).

Kanuka, H., D. Collett, and C. Caswell. 2002. University instructor perceptions of the use of asynchronous text-based discussion in distance courses. *The American Journal of Distance Education* 16(3):151–67.

Kanuka, H., L. Rourke, and E. Laflamme. 2006, in press. The influence of instructional methods on the quality of online discussion. *British Journal of Educational Technology*.

Keegan, D. 1990. *The foundations of distance education*. 2nd ed. London: Routledge.

Kelsey, K., and A. D'souza. 2005. Student motivation for learning at a distance: Does interaction matter? www.westga.edu/~distance/ojdla/summer72/kelsey72.html (accessed December 30, 2005).

Knowles, M. 1990. *Fostering critical reflection in adulthood: A guide to transformative and emancipatory learning*. London: Jossey Bass.

Koschmann, T., A. C. Kelson, P. J. Feltovich, and H. S. Barrows. 1996. Computer-supported problem-based learning: A principled approach to the use of computers in collaborative learning. In *CSCL: Theory &*

practice in an emerging paradigm, edited by T. Koschmann, 83–124 Mahwah, NJ: Lawrence Erlbaum.

Laurillard, D. 1993. *Rethinking university teaching: A framework for the effective use of educational technology*. London: Routledge.

Laurillard, D. 2002. *Rethinking university teaching: A conversational framework for the effective use of learning technologies*. London: Farmer Press.

Marttunen, M. 1998. Electronic mail as a forum for argumentative interaction in higher education studies. *Journal of Educational Computing Research* 18(4):387–405.

Mason, R. 1992. The textuality of computer networking. In *Computer conferencing: The last word,* edited by R. Mason. Victoria, BC: Beach Holme.

Moore, M. 1972. Towards a theory of independent learning and teaching. *Journal of Higher Education* 44(9):661–79.

Moore, M. 1983. On a theory of independent study. In *Distance education: International perspectives,* edited by D. Sewart, D. Keegan, B. Holmberg, 68–94. London: Croom Helm.

Moore, M. 1991. Distance education theory. *American Journal of Distance Education* 5(3). www.ajde.com/Contents/vol5_3.htm#editorial. (accessed February 21, 2006).

Murphy, E. 2000. SPICE: Solving problems in collaborative environments: Unpublished Web-based learning module. Memorial University of Newfoundland, St. John's, Canada.

Murphy, E. 2003. Moving from theory to practice in the design of web-based learning from the perspective of constructivism. *Journal of Interactive Online Learning* 1(4). www.ncolr.org/jiol/archives/2003/spring/4/MS02028.pdf (accessed December 30, 2005).

Murphy, E. 2004. Recognizing and promoting collaboration in an online asynchronous discussion. *British Journal of Educational Technology* 35(4):421–31.

Nipper, S. 1989. Third generation distance learning and computer conferencing. In *Mindweave: Communication, computers and distance education,* edited by R. Mason and A. Kaye, 53–73. Oxford: Pergamon.

Pask, G. 1976. Conversational techniques in the study and practice of education. *British Journal of Educational Psychology* 46(1):12–25.

Paulson, M. 1995. Moderating educational computer conferences. In *Computer mediated communication and the online classroom in distance education,* Z. Berge and M. Collins. Cresskill, NJ: Hampton Press.

Pena-Shaff, J., and C. Nicholls. 2004. Analyzing student interactions and meaning construction in computer bulletin board (BBS) discussions. *Computers and Education* 42:243–65.

Perret-Clairmont, A., J. Perret, and N. Bell. 1989. The social construction of meaning and cognitive activity of elementary school children. In *Perspectives on socially-shared cognition,* edited by L. Resnick, J. Levine, S. Teasley, 41–62. Washington, DC: American Psychological Association.

Piaget, J.1977. *The development of thought: Equilibration of cognitive structures*. New York: Viking.

Rogers, C., and H. J. Freiberg. 1993. *Freedom to learn*. 3rd ed. New York: Merrill.

Romiszowski, A., and R. Mason. 1996. Computer mediated communication. In *Handbook of research on educational communications and technology: A project of the association for educational communications and technology,* edited by D. Jonassen, 438–53. New York: MacMillan.

Romiszowski, A., and R. Mason. 2004. Computer mediated communication. In *Handbook of research on educational communications and technology: A project of the association for educational communications and technology.* 2nd ed., edited by D. Jonassen, 397–432. Mahwah, NJ: Lawrence Erlbaum.

Rourke, L., and D. Conrad 2004, May. Constructing computer conferencing in distance education journals. Paper presented at the annual conference of the Canadian Association of Distance Education, Toronto, Canada.

Rowntree, D. 1997. *Making materials-based learning work*. London: Kogan Page.

Saba, F., and R. Shearer. 1994. Verifying key theoretical concepts in a dynamic model of distance education. *American Journal of Distance Education* 8(1):36–56.

Salmon, G. 2000. *E-moderating: The key to teaching and learning online*. London: Kogan Page.

Scardemalia, M., and C. Bereiter. 1994. Computer support for knowledge-building communities. *The Journal of the Learning Sciences* 3(3):256–83.

Shea, P., K. Swan, and A. Pickett. 2005. Teaching presence and establishment of community in online learning environments. www.sloanconsortium.org/summerworkshop2004/papers.htm (accessed December 30, 2005).

Thomas, M. 2002. Learning within incoherent structures: The space of online discussion forums. *Journal of Computer Assisted Learning* 18:351–66.

Toulmin, S. E. 1958. *The uses of argument*. Cambridge, UK: Cambridge University Press.

Van Aalst, J., and C. Chan. 2002. Beyond "sitting next to each other": A design experiment on knowledge building in teacher education. In *Proceedings of the first European conference on computer-supported collaborative learning, Maastricht, March 22-24, 2001*, edited by P. Dillenbourg, A. Eurelings, and K. Hakkarainen, 20–28. Maastricht, the Netherlands: The University of Maastricht.

Vaughan, N., and D. R. Garrison. 2005. Creating cognitive presence in a blended faculty development community. *Internet and Higher Education* 8(1):1–12.

Villalba, C., and A. Romiszowski. 2000. Structural communication and Web based instruction. In *Proceedings of EdMedia 2000,* edited by J. Bourdeau & R. Heller, 1111–6. Montreal, Canada: Association for the Advancement of Computing in Education.

Vygotsky, L. 1984. *Thought and language*. Cambridge, MA: MIT Press.

Yakimovicz, A.D., and K. L. Murphy. 1995. Constructivism and collaboration on the Internet: Case study of a graduate class experience. *Computers in Education* 24(3):203–9.

Electronic Commerce

Charles Steinfield, *Michigan State University*

INTRODUCTION

The term *electronic commerce* came into widespread usage after the first graphical Web browser—Mosaic—was developed in 1993 and freely distributed around the world. Drawn by the ease of use of the browser, millions of home consumers, businesses, and educators connected to the Internet, creating the conditions for Internet-based commerce. Indeed, Nielsen/Netratings estimates that there are nearly half a billion people worldwide who have access to the Internet from home as of December 2006 (this number rises if we also include those who access the Internet from work or other public settings; see www.nielsen-netratings.com for the latest monthly estimates). Businesses, often backed by venture capital from investors enamored with the new opportunities created by Internet-based business, flocked to the Internet, attracted by the ease of setting up electronic storefronts and the potential access to a global market of Internet subscribers. For example, Laudon and Traver (2003) estimate that more $120 billion was invested in 12,450 Internet start-up companies between 1998 and 2000, a period of significant growth in e-commerce. Impressively, despite the highly publicized dot-com failures in 2000 and 2001, Internet sales of goods and services to consumers (i.e., business-to-consumer, or B2C, e-commerce) have grown steadily, exceeding $88 billion in 2005 and expected to easily surpass $100 billion in 2006 in the United States (U.S. Department of Commerce 2007). Growth in other parts of the world, and especially Europe, is equally impressive. Forrester (www.forrester.com) estimates that 2006 online sales in Europe exceeded €100 billion with a growth rate that is even higher than that in the United States. Even more dramatic has been the extent to which businesses have adopted e-commerce to support exchanges with other firms, such as suppliers and business customers, referred to as business-to-business (B2B) trade. The U. S. Department of Commerce (2006) has reported that e-commerce shipments accounted for over 21 percent of the total value of manufacturing shipments, or $843 billion in 2003, while nearly 17 percent, or $730 billion, of all merchant wholesaler sales were accomplished via e-commerce in the United States in 2003. In Europe, across twenty industry sectors, 48 percent of firms report placing orders for supplies online (e-Business Watch 2006).

Chapter Overview and Themes

This chapter examines the ongoing development of e-commerce and its influences on the way that companies work with their suppliers and market their products to customers. The next section begins with a look at the historical development of e-commerce, which suggests that it emerged as a powerful force only once a truly open and standard data network—the Internet—was coupled with easy-to-use software—the graphical Web browser. The section on e-commerce development continues by noting that despite the dot-com bust in 2000 and 2001, e-commerce usage has increased steadily, and affects a growing proportion of economic activity in the industrialized world. The next section explores aspects of the basic technological infrastructure that supports e-commerce, focusing on the increasing emphasis on the role of standards, especially for B2B transactions, evolving methods in the ongoing battle against security threats, the explosion in both broadband and wireless access, and the rapid emergence of a range of new approaches to e-commerce models and designs, often termed Web 2.0. Then we explore e-commerce from a business opportunity perspective, noting that thousands of Internet-based companies have flocked to capitalize on this new platform, equipped with innovative, albeit at times not all that effective, business models. Then we take a closer look at approaches to online retailing, focusing on the increasingly clever marketing strategies used by e-commerce companies. The next section provides a brief look at B2B e-commerce, exploring the role of this evolving exchange medium in the supply chain. We go on to examine one area in particular in which e-commerce has had an enormous impact—the content industries—in which new models for the sale of online content have challenged traditional print, music, and video publishing. Next is a brief review of research on a number of anticipated impacts of e-commerce, highlighting the need to critically assess the early hype about the effect of e-commerce on market structures, prices of goods and services, and problems of trust in the relationships between an online business and its stakeholders. The chapter concludes by summarizing key themes and issues for further research.

DEFINITION, HISTORY, AND CURRENT STATUS

What Is E-Commerce?

Today the term *electronic commerce* (or *e-commerce*) most commonly refers to the process of buying and selling goods—both information and tangible products—and services over the Internet. Earlier definitions (e.g., Clarke 1999) emphasized the "conduct of commerce in goods and services using telecommunications-based tools." More recent definitions (e.g., Laudon and Traver 2003, 10) emphasize the "use of the Internet and the Web to transact business" in what they call "digitally enabled commercial transactions," in which there is some "exchange of value across organizational or individual boundaries in return for products and services." Narrower definitions require that complete transactions, including ordering and payment, occur entirely via the Internet, while broader definitions include information exchange in support of transactions, even if the actual payment occurs outside the Internet (often called "offline" payment). Intermediate approaches, such as the one used by the U.S. Department of Commerce, require that an order occur online, although payment may still be made offline.

The term *e-business* is also used frequently, which refers more broadly to the conduct of business over computer networks. E-business includes activities that are not purely commercial transactions, such as when two firms use the Internet to collaborate on product development or research, or a firm provides customer service online. Some (e.g., Laudon and Traver 2003) consider e-business to include only internal applications of a firm's computer network, and not transactions that span to other firms. Here we will consider *e-business* to be a broader term, referring to a range of intraorganizational and interorganizational interactions over computer networks, including but not limited to e-commerce. *E-commerce*, then, refers to the process of buying and selling goods and services over a computer network.

In most e-commerce research and discussion, business-to-consumer (B2C) transactions are considered as a distinct topic from business-to-business (B2B) exchange. There are good reasons for this, as B2C exchanges are often ephemeral retail transactions that are typically smaller in value, and involve customers with whom there is little to no long-term relationship. B2B exchanges are typically larger in value, are structured by contracts, and are often shaped by existing relations between buyer and seller. Although some B2B exchanges resemble retail trade, on the whole, it makes good sense to study the kinds of buyer-supplier and buyer-distributor electronic exchanges through a different lens than one would study online shopping by consumers.

History of E-Commerce

Long before the World Wide Web, electronic networks were used to support transactions between businesses and their various external constituents (e.g. suppliers or customers). In the 1970s, forward-thinking manufacturers and wholesalers deployed proprietary data networks and simple terminal-based remote ordering systems to the premises of business customers. The value of computer networks to link business buyers and sellers was soon well established, and efforts to create standard electronic documents to support trade were occurring across many industries. These latter standards were collectively called EDI (electronic document interchange). In some industries, such as automobile manufacturing and chemical production, EDI transactions proliferated because large dominant manufacturers mandated their use. However, because EDI standards were complex and costly to implement, especially for small businesses, the extent of its diffusion was limited (Markus et al. 2006).

There were precursors to consumer-based e-commerce as well. The Home Shopping Network on cable television and the many 1980s-era electronic information services collectively known as videotex in Europe and the United States resembled Web-based electronic retailing. The most successful of these systems in Europe was the French system popularly known as Minitel, named after the small terminal that initially was freely distributed to telephone subscribers. Beginning in 1983, French telephone subscribers could use their Minitels to look up a wealth of information, engage in home banking, and order a wide range of goods and services, such as tickets, groceries, and other consumer products. Like the Internet, these services were offered over a public network to which anyone could connect, used a single standard, and relied extensively on graphical content. Unlike the Internet, a clear payment model was implemented, with France Telecom (at the time, the public administration responsible for the provision of all telecommunications networks and services in France) providing a "billing and collection" service for all companies that wished to sell via the Minitel. Consumers received the bill for their Minitel use on their regular phone bill, and France Telecom in turn paid the various service providers (Steinfield, Kraut, and Plummer 1995).

In contrast, American electronic information services of the 1980s were still based on closed, rather than open systems, using what has been called a "walled garden" approach. That is, services like CompuServe and America Online (which are now merged) used their own proprietary networks, and their content and services were available only to their subscribers. It was not until commercial traffic was permitted on the Internet that consumer-oriented e-commerce as we know it today was born.

The early years of e-commerce had all the characteristics of a gold rush, as companies flocked to the Web to set up their electronic storefronts. Lured by the rapid growth of first movers like Amazon.com, more than $125 billion in investment capital was poured into Internet initial public offerings (IPOs) between 1996 and 2000 (Laudon and Traver 2003). The birth of a new digital economy was proclaimed, characterized by seemingly unending growth in productivity rooted in the supposedly frictionless commerce afforded by the Internet. The new Web-based businesses theoretically offered benefits such as access to a larger potential market, lower inventory and building costs, more flexibility in sourcing inputs, improved transaction automation and data mining capabilities, an ability to bypass intermediaries that added costs but little value, lower costs for adjusting prices (known as a menu costs), enabling more rapid response to market changes, increased ease of bundling complementary products, 24/7 access, and no limitation on depth of information provided to potential customers (Steinfield, Mahler, and Bauer 1999). With all these advantages, and the reduced search costs faced by consumers, prices were expected to be lower, and Internet firms would prosper.

Despite the rosy projections for e-commerce, in late 2000 and early 2001 many of the dot-com companies began to fail. Few ever made any profits, as their business approach revolved around scaling up to increase market share (Hawkins 2004). This approach was based on the belief that Internet businesses would enjoy positive network externalities—implying that the more people who used a site, the more value it would have for each user. The dot-coms that could rapidly attract the largest number of users would thus have an insurmountable competitive edge. In search of the required scale, Internet firms kept prices too low and quickly burned through the cash raised from venture capitalists. At the same time, the U.S. economy began to slip into a recession, and venture capitalists began to lose faith in the viability of start-ups that failed to return any profits. Stock prices, which were far too high by normal investment standards, dropped precipitously, and the venture capital community lost interest in dot-com businesses. By the end of 2001, the dot-com era was over, and by one estimate only about 10 percent of the dot-coms created since 1995 still survived (Laudon and Traver 2003).

B2B-oriented dot-coms experienced much the same fate. Large numbers of B2B electronic marketplaces were created to help match buyers and sellers in many industries, and by early 2000, more than 750 B2B e-markets were operating worldwide (U.S. Department of Commerce 2000). Yet most of the new dot-coms in this arena failed as well.

Current Status

Despite the problems of the dot-coms, statistics on e-commerce use do show steady gains, particularly as traditional companies have moved to enhance their offerings with Internet-based sales channels. According to U.S. Census figures, even as the dot-coms were failing and the economy went through a recession, retail e-commerce sales in the United States grew at a brisk pace (see Figure 1). Annual U.S. retail e-commerce sales have more than tripled between 2000, the first full year that the government tracked this statistic, and 2005, rising from approximately $27.8 billion to more than $88 billion (U.S. Department of Commerce 2007), and today is estimated to account for approximately 3 percent of all retail sales. In the all important fourth quarter, during which holiday shopping occurs, online sales exceeded $27 billion in 2005, more than five times the total in the fourth quarter of 1999. Even more telling is the fact that online sales growth is far higher than the rate of growth in traditional retail formats, averaging more than 28 percent for the same quarter across years compared to just 4.6 percent for total retail sales. These census figures are a low estimate, since they do not include sales from online travel, financial brokers, and online ticket sales.

U.S. B2B online trade dwarfs B2C e-commerce, accounting for over 94 percent of all e-commerce activity, according to Commerce Department statistics. It has also grown more rapidly than offline trade. Manufacturing

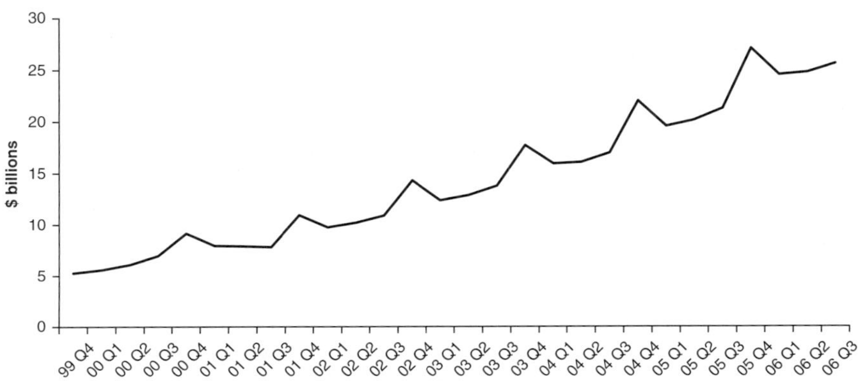

Figure 1: Quarterly U.S. Retail E-commerce Sales, Fourth Quarter 1999 to Third Quarter 2006 (*Source:* U.S. Department of Commerce 2007)

online sales, for example, grew at a greater than 12 percent rate from 2002 to 2003, while offline sales grew only 1.5 percent (U.S. Department of Commerce 2006).

Global Trends

The United States was an early adopter of Internet-based commerce, but now this commerce is growing rapidly in other parts of the world. As noted earlier, Forrester estimates that European retail e-commerce to total more than €100 billion for 2006. The OECD (2006, Measuring the information economy) provides estimates illustrating how e-commerce use varies considerably across countries (Figure 2). Outside the United States, e-commerce use in 2005 was heaviest in Northern Europe, Canada, the advanced Asian economies, and Australia and New Zealand. Southern and Eastern European countries, less developed regions of Asia, Central and South American countries, and African countries have lagged beyond, largely because of the lack of the requisite infrastructure to support e-commerce. Analyses of global e-commerce trends point to differences in policies toward the Internet and broadband deployment; cultural differences in terms of shopping preferences, use of credit cards, and perceptions of privacy; and other geographical and economic factors to explain these differences (Kraemer, Dedrick, and Melville, 2006).

Increasingly, e-commerce is being seen as a crucial benchmark for determining the strength of national economies. Since 2001, for example, the World Economic Forum has published an annual Global Information Technology Report in order to track the progress that countries have made in using ICT to enhance productivity in business. The 2005–2006 report includes a "networked readiness index" to compare the world's economies on how well they incorporate use of the Internet and other ICT by businesses, governments, and individual consumers. Their most recent report reveals the startling progress in some of the formerly least developed countries with regard to online commerce, especially India, while noting that the most competitive countries remain the traditionally strong Internet using nations such as the United States, Singapore, and the Nordic countries in Europe (Dutta, Lopez-Claros, and Mia 2006). The OECD devotes an entire chapter in the 2006 Information Technology Outlook to the dramatic growth of the Internet and e-commerce in China, although most of the growth is in the eastern coastal cities (OECD 2006, *Information Technology Outlook 2006*). In Europe, policy makers have established the e-Business Watch, an annual assessment of the evergrowing penetration of ICT-enabled business within the European context. Their detailed annual surveys reveal the spread of e-commerce for both B2C and B2B trade in twenty industries (e-Business Watch 2006). Nearly half (48 percent) of all firms order supplies online, and 25 percent now accept orders from customers online. Since larger firms are more likely to use e-commerce, these numbers increase to 57 percent and 35 percent when evaluated by percent of employees rather than percent of firms. Clearly, e-commerce is a global phenomenon, but requires strong national policies favoring the deployment of the underlying telecommunications infrastructure, a financial infrastructure, and a cultural environment that is compatible.

THE CHANGING NATURE OF E-COMMERCE INFRASTRUCTURE, TECHNOLOGY, AND TECHNIQUE

The infrastructure to support e-commerce is constantly evolving, and includes the underlying wired and wireless networks that carry traffic as well as the devices that connect to these networks; the protocols, software, and scripting languages that define how information is carried and how e-commerce applications are built,

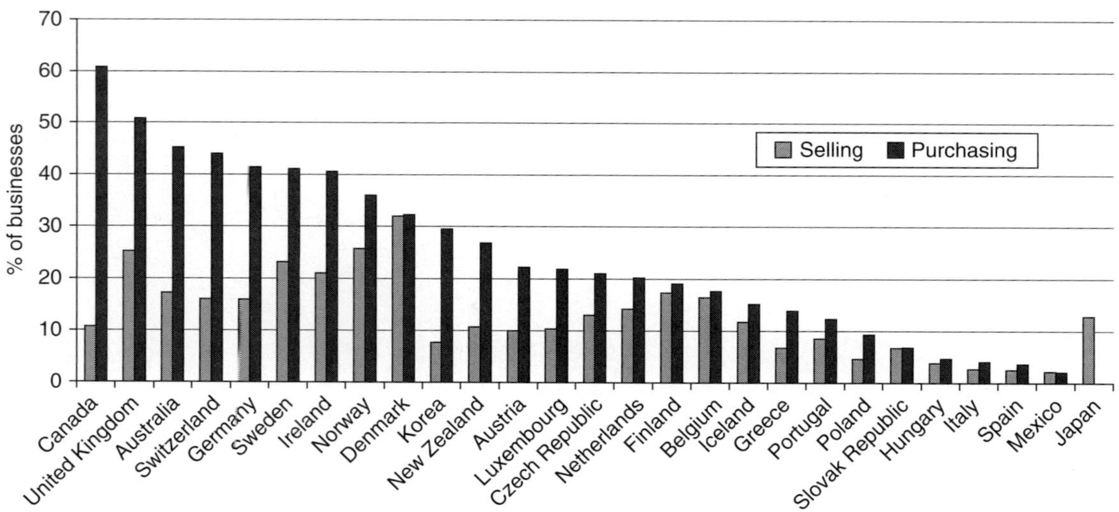

Figure 2: Percent of business with more than 10 persons using the Internet for selling and purchasing in selected countries in 2005 (No data were available for Internet business purchasing in Japan; data for New Zealand are from 2001, from Switzerland 2002, from Iceland and Mexico 2003, and from Australia 2004–2005.) (*Source:* OECD 2006, Measuring the information economy)

including a focus on standards to enable interoperability across e-commerce applications built by individual firms; technical approaches to providing a secure and private environment within which transactions can be made; and changing business and interface logics enabled by these technical developments. A brief introduction to some of the evolving topics in this area follows.

Broadband Wired and Wireless Networks and E-Commerce

The technologies that support e-commerce are constantly evolving, creating new capabilities and opportunities. Although space does not permit a review of all of the many technological developments that are shaping the future of e-commerce, the continued development of both wired and wireless access networks has strong implications because of their effect on improving customer experiences and spreading access to mobile customers.

The Internet-using population across the world is continuing to transition from slower dial-up lines to broadband access using DSL (digital subscriber line) and cable modem technology providing at least 256 kbps (OECD 2006, Telecommunications and Internet policy). Across the 30 OECD countries, the number of broadband subscribers went from 13.6 per 100 inhabitants in December 2005 to 15.5 in June of 2006, with some countries, like Denmark and the Netherlands, having a broadband subscriber population of nearly 30 of every 100 people (see Figure 3). Since households typically have more than one person, the actual proportion of the population with direct broadband access is quite high.

In the United States, broadband penetration is high, with more than two-thirds of active Internet users subscribing, according to statistics released by Nielsen/Netratings through February 2006.

In addition to wireline access, there has been tremendous innovation in the area of wireless network infrastructure, improving the bandwidth of connections as well as capabilities of handheld and portable devices. Next-generation cellular networks (often termed 3G, or third generation) have been deployed across the world, and broadband connections are increasingly available. Moreover, wireless local area networks (LANs) based on the Wireless Fidelity (Wi-Fi) (i.e., IEEE 802.11) family of standards are widely deployed with a range of subscription and ad hoc access from many public venues. Cellular and Wi-Fi wireless infrastructures are complemented by newer WiMax (IEEE 802.16) standards that provide broadband access over wider areas where the economics make sense (e.g., rural areas not currently served by 3G cellular, DSL, or cable broadband networks). Mobile handset manufacturers are increasingly building handsets with enhanced data capabilities, including some mobiles that switch between cellular and Wi-Fi, as well as other wireless standards for nearer-field connections such as Bluetooth. As next-generation cellular infrastructures speed up access times, people will no longer be tied to a desktop computer in order to surf the Internet and shop online. They are free to engage in e-commerce anytime and anyplace.

How will e-commerce be impacted by these new mobile capabilities? Surprisingly, even before Web-enabled phones have achieved widespread adoption, early forms of mobile commerce have occurred with simple text messaging (e.g., via short message service, or SMS). Cell phone users simply made purchase requests or responded to advertisements by sending SMS messages to special numbers. Today, broadband wireless is mainly impacting the sale of content, through the downloading of ringtones, music, video, and information. New approaches that better integrate other forms of

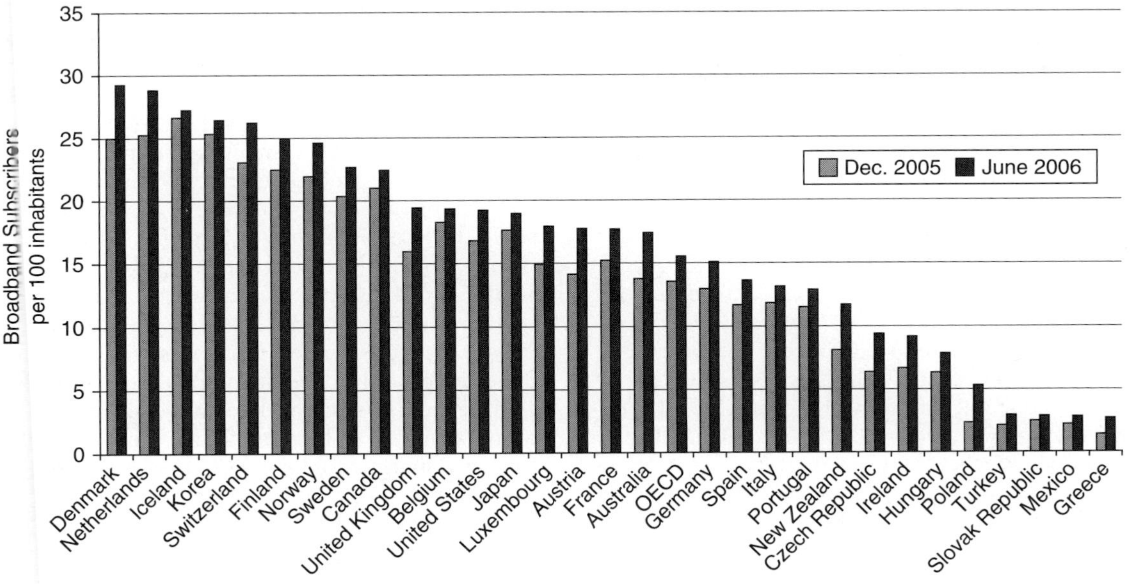

Figure 3: Broadband Subscribers in OECD Countries per 100 Inhabitants: December 2005 and June 2006 (*Source:* OECD 2006, Telecommunications and Internet policy)

e-commerce with mobile devices are appearing, for example, in areas such as mobile payment and location-based services. Indeed, many mobile e-commerce (or m-commerce) services will be based on the particular location of shoppers, allowing someone in a car, for example, to find the nearest vendor of a particular product (Steinfield 2004). In the United States, the Federal Communications Commission (FCC) has mandated that all cellular operators be capable of determining the location of cell phone users in order to support emergency 911 services. However, numerous e-commerce uses of location data, and a wide range of services, beginning first with navigation support, are now, or will soon be available. Users may use their mobile device to search for available vendors in an area, receive directions from their current location to a vendor, make payments at the point of sale, and receive advertisements based on their interests when they near particular locations. Location-based services thus blend e-commerce and physical commerce in new ways, blurring the traditional online/offline distinctions of the past.

The integration of wireless devices into e-commerce is extending beyond mobile phones, leading to innovative applications for tracking inventory and product usage. Radio-frequency identification (RFID) tags, for example, can enhance supply-chain performance, and are being adopted by some of the world's largest retailers, albeit with some concerns about market power and intrusiveness (McGinty 2004). Tags may be embedded in products, so that information can be transmitted from a customer to a reader in many different locations. An RFID tag on prescription drugs in an Internet-enabled cabinet might trigger an automatic reorder from a pharmacy after a specific date has passed, for example.

The Internet and E-Commerce Standards

E-commerce use exploded in 1994, built on an open, standard computer network—the Internet. The mandated use of the TCP/IP standard ensured data connectivity while markup standards such as hypertext markup language (HTML) ensured some degree of consistency in the presentation of information. Continuing development of markup languages, and in particular, languages that deal with semantic issues in addition to presentation, has altered the e-commerce landscape. Extensible markup language (XML) has had a significant impact on e-commerce, especially between businesses, helping to move it from a basic presentation focus to a transactional focus. Like HTML, XML relies on tags to mark up text files. However, the emphasis is not on tags that define how information is to be formatted and presented, but on tags to describe data (see Dorfman [2004], for a detailed description of how XML works). Moreover, users can define their own tags (hence, the notion of "extensible") based on the data they are providing. XML makes databases portable over the Internet, and has been the basis for a growing family of transaction standards. As more firms use XML-based standards, particularly for B2B transactions, a new opportunity has arisen to develop industry-wide data standards. Essentially, XML has become an enabler for EDI over the Internet. Markus and colleagues (2006), have documented the growth of vertical industry standards using XML, illustrating the many challenges that industries face in agreeing on such factors as data definitions, transaction formats, and the like.

Building on XML, another e-commerce infrastructure development to highlight here is the growth in Web services. Web services are self-contained, modular e-commerce applications built on standardized protocols, made available over the Internet to e-commerce users and vendors through standardized XML messaging (Ritsko and Davis 2002). For example, a shopping cart function is a common Web service that a merchant may use to support its e-commerce site, rather than writing its own cart software. In order to enable Web services, standards for making XML-based requests (simple object access protocol [SOAP]), describing the services that are available (Web services description language [WSDL]), and publishing service descriptions in online directories in a manner that permits requesters to search for needed services (universal description, discovery, and integration [UDDI]) are required (Gottshalk et al. 2002). Some of the most famous Web vendors now enable business partners to link to their service via a Web services architecture (e.g., see Amazon.com's Web services offerings at www.amazon.com). As the notion of Web services continues to expand, so too do efforts by major software vendors to provide development platforms to speed up service deployment. Microsoft's .NET platform and Sun's J2EE are the two most well known today (Sahai, Graupner, and Kim 2004).

Encryption Methods in E-Commerce

Another fundamental part of the e-commerce infrastructure is the set of technologies aimed at ensuring the security of online transactions. Lack of trust in an online store, fear of financial loss through theft of a credit card or other banking information, and other concerns over the privacy of information transmitted to and stored by an online store are just some of the concerns faced by consumers in e-commerce transactions. In the earliest years of e-commerce, fears that credit-card information would be intercepted while in transit over the Internet prompted most online stores to implement secure servers relying on secure sockets layer (SSL) transmission. However, e-commerce security involves much more than secure transmissions. Among the many requirements are needs to authenticate both consumers and online stores, preserve the confidentiality of information related to online transactions, and ensure the integrity of transaction-related information. Public and symmetric key encryption systems are two fundamental techniques for accomplishing these needs, which then must be incorporated into a broader public key infrastructure (Juels 2004). In a symmetric key system, the same code is used to encrypt a message (i.e., the credit-card number or the order for a product) as to decrypt it. Hence, the sender and receiver must both possess the secret key needed to decode the encrypted text (also called ciphertext, as opposed to a plaintext message). The main problem with symmetric key approaches is that it is difficult to distribute the secret key safely. In public key encryption systems, a pair of codes is needed to encrypt a plaintext message into ciphertext and then decrypt it to plaintext again. A person or a store is assigned both a public key that is published and available to anyone (often called a "certificate"), and the matching private key that only its holder possesses. In this way, public key encryption systems are able to accomplish the needs for authentication and confidentiality noted above, without suffering from the problem of how to send secret keys over the insecure Internet. To ensure confidentiality, buyers use an online store's public key to encrypt the message. Then, only the store would possess the matching private key, ensuring that only it would be able to decrypt the order. Buyers using their private key authenticate themselves, since only their public key decrypts the order. In practice, public key encryption is processing-intensive, and is therefore impractical for large transmissions. The solution is to use a combination of systems, with symmetric keys used for much of the encryption, but public keys used to encrypt the symmetric keys for transmission.

Public Key Infrastructure

To enable fuller use of public key encryption systems in practice requires a trusted system to assign the keys in the first place, and make sure that only the rightful owners obtain them. In addition, keys may need to be revoked in the event they are abused or appropriated by the wrong entities. Such a trusted party is often called a "certificate authority," and the system to accomplish this is called a "public key infrastructure" (PKI) (Housley and Polk 2001).

Encryption technology is evolving to help establish a more secure line of communication between online vendors and their buyers. However, some of the most-well-known breaches of security have occurred outside the buyer-seller transaction link. In particular, one critical issue is the need to secure buyer information, such as a credit-card number, once the vendor receives it. Servers storing thousands of credit-card numbers are more desirable targets for hackers than an individual transaction. In fact, one of the most widely publicized e-commerce security breaches to date occurred when a hacker compromised CD Universe's database, reportedly stealing 350,000 credit-card numbers (Wolverton 2000). The hacker attempted to extort $100,000 from CD Universe, and when that failed, posted thousands of stolen card numbers on a public Web site. This illustrates that e-commerce security encompasses more than secure transactions, and must include a broad range of security practices that protect customers' information even after purchases take place.

Changing Interface and Business Logics: Web 2.0

Web 2.0 is a broad collection of ideas, techniques, and applications with a label derived from an influential conference about the emergence of the Web as a platform for businesses and services (O'Reilly 2005). Among the themes, some of which have already been mentioned in this chapter are:

- Richer, more interactive interfaces on the Web. For example, site developers have increased their use of programming strategies like Asynchronous Javascript and XML (AJAX) that allows animation and new content to appear without the tedious process of a new page load. The Gap, for example, recently re-engineered their entire e-commerce site (www.gap.com) to take advantage of this technique, allowing customers to view product details without ever leaving the product category page.
- Leveraging the long tail. *Long tail* refers to the traditional "power law" distribution that has been used to describe the popularity or frequency of occurrence of things like Web-site page views (Adamic and Huberman 2001). A small number of pages are viewed by a large number of Internet users, for example, while a very large number of pages are viewed by a very small number of people. For merchants, this can mean that a small number of products will be popular with large numbers of shoppers, while many products are desired by only a few people. In a traditional store, inventory costs militate against holding these less-popular products, but on the Internet, they can be offered without holding them in inventory. Industry observers now argue that e-commerce will reshape business inventory practices, as merchants benefit from the increased sales by offering more than the blockbuster hits, and aggregating across the many items in the long tail (Anderson 2006).
- Capitalizing on user co-production and harnessing collective intelligence. Users can increase the value of an e-commerce business by contributing their own content such as product usage know-how that enhances any business's offerings. E-commerce businesses are increasingly adding community tools to their sites for this purpose.
- Using interfaces that enable syndication and "mash-ups." Syndication tools like RSS (meaning either "rich site summary" or "really simple syndication") enable sites to keep users up to date without requiring them to check in regularly. Mash-ups allow a site to create new services by combining its content (e.g., maps) with another site's content (e.g. houses for sale that can then be located on a map, such as HousingMaps.com that represents a mash-up between Craigslist and Google Maps). Tagging of content such as photos and videos allows it to be searched and more easily incorporated into other sites (e.g., users' photos from a photo-sharing site like Flickr might be brought into a news site to enhance coverage).

E-COMMERCE BUSINESS MODELS

Many innovative methods of doing business were created in the early years of e-commerce, which collectively came to be called "Internet business models." Exactly what constituted a business model was the subject of much debate, as was the issue of which models were successful. Rappa (2004), for example, defines a business model as the "method of doing business by which a company can sustain itself—that is, generate revenue. The business model spells out how a company makes money by specifying where it is positioned in the value chain." Timmers (1998) considers a business model to include three basic components: (1) the architecture for the product, services, and information flows, (2) the potential benefits for the various business actors, and (3) the sources of revenues. Weill and Vitale (2001) characterize models as the roles and relationships among a firm's major stakeholders that result in flows of products, information, and money, leading to benefits for the participants. Other scholars offer what might be called an *ingredients* perspective on Internet business models, suggesting that they each contain many facets, such as: a value proposition, sources of revenue, a market opportunity, a competitive landscape, a competitive advantage, a strategy for promotion in the market, an organizational development plan, and a management team (Afuah and Tucci 2001; Laudon and Traver 2003).

Along with the numerous definitions of business models can be found many taxonomies of models that are commonly seen on the Internet. Three well-known taxonomies are summarized in Table 1. Although direct comparisons of models are difficult, given the varying perspectives the authors have used in forming categories (Wang and Chan 2003), these models do illustrate the range of approaches stimulated by e-commerce capabilities, ranging from simple translations of offline retail practices to complex match-making services in brokerage configurations to emerging community-based models supported by users and/or advertising.

Table 1: Taxonomies of Internet Business Models

Author(s)	Internet Business Models	Comments
Timmers (1998)	E-Shop E-Auction E-Mall Third-Party Marketplace E-Procurement Virtual Communities Value-Chain Integrators Collaboration Platforms Value-Chain Service Provider Information Brokerage Trust Services	In this early typology, Timmers organized observed models along two dimensions: (1) the degree of innovation (i.e., difference from traditional business models), and (2) the degree of functional integration. E-shops are simple translations from offline models, with low innovation and low integration of functions. Third-party marketplaces provide a number of functions for both buyers and sellers, and are seen as relatively more innovative.
Rappa (2004)	Brokerage Advertising Infomediaries Merchant Manufacturer Affiliate Community Subscription Utility	These models are largely organized by the primary source of revenue. For example, brokerage models such as eBay rely on fees or commissions. Infomediaries give discounted or free goods or services, while they collect consumer information and sell to marketers. Affiliates derive revenue by referring customers to other e-commerce firms, who then provide a sales commission. Utility models refer to firms that charge customers on a metered, or pay-per-use basis. In some cases, the models refer to a primary way in which value for customers is created—e.g. community models rely on users with common interests to provide content, so that they can charge for advertising. Also, within each model, Rappa defines many subtypes, such as the click and mortar vs. virtual merchant business models in the merchant category.
Laudon and Traver 2003	B2C Portal E-Tailer Content Provider Transaction Broker Market Creator Service Provider Community Provider B2B E-Distributor E-Procurement Exchange Industry Consortia Private Industrial Networks	These authors divide models by their consumer vs. business focus. Within model types they describe the value proposition, as well as the many subtypes. For example, portals offer an integrated package of content and services, and can be horizontal (targeting all users) or vertical (focused on a specific subject matter or market segment). Moreover, they illustrate that many Internet business models combine a number of sources of revenue, including advertising, subscription fees, transaction fees, margins on sales, and affiliate fees. In the B2B arena, they further illustrate the importance of private networks and industry consortia—models that suggest that existing business relationships are essential, even for Internet-based transactions.

After the dot-com crash, attempts to list the many observed Internet business models gave way to analyses focusing on what was wrong with the models. For example, early in the e-commerce boom years, many felt that revenue from advertising would sustain e-commerce. This made some sense for content firms, such as online newspapers, magazines, radio stations, and other media-oriented companies that were accustomed to reliance on sponsors to bring down the costs for their viewers, listeners, and readers. However, one failed Internet business model, pursued somewhat by Buy.com, involved the use of advertising revenue to subsidize product sales, so that consumers could buy products at heavily discounted prices. Another problematic business model in the B2C arena involved manufacturers of products selling directly to end consumers and bypassing wholesale and traditional retail channels. Levis, for example, attempted to sell its blue jeans directly to online shoppers. Existing retailers, however, threatened retaliation. Given the relatively small percentage of sales generated by the Internet, Levis soon gave up on the direct-sale model and now uses its Web site mainly to promote sales of Levis at traditional retail outlets or to sell online through its retailers' Web sites.

Hawkins (2004) criticizes the notion that the Internet required altogether new business models, arguing instead that it simply enabled some firms to apply models that heretofore had not been used by them in their particular market, but that had been common in markets for other types of goods and services. Moreover, he argued that a model does not convey competitive advantage in and of itself, but only if there were reasons to expect that a firm could prevent others from easily imitating it.

Critics of the early business model literature also point out that the dominant focus on revenue streams can encourage firms to ignore other benefits that e-commerce offers, such as cost reductions, improved customer relations, or enhanced performance of traditional channels (Steinfield, Bouwman, and Adelaar 2002). For example, a virtual merchant may be able to offer goods at lower prices because of its lower inventory holding costs and lower selling costs. On the other hand, a click-and-brick firm may use its Web site to help generate more traffic in its physical stores by offering coupons or searches of in-store inventory (Steinfield 2005).

Despite the critiques, it is clear that the development of online commerce has enabled the application of many innovative strategies. One way to view the dot-com crash was simply as an inevitable shakeout that always follows the rapid entry of firms into a new area of business. In this perspective, the models that survived represent the winning approaches, promising significant opportunity for the firms that have successfully adopted them.

ONLINE RETAIL MARKETING STRATEGIES

E-commerce gives merchants many opportunities to enhance the way products are marketed to customers, stemming from the information capture and manipulation capabilities of computer-mediated commerce, as well as the networking and community-enabling affordances of the online world. These affordances make it possible to personalize and customize interactions with consumers in much more sophisticated ways than heretofore possible, at least by larger retailers. They provide better tools to match products and product features with consumer preferences, and enable joint efforts among vendors of complementary products to meet demand. Through creative application of data on past purchases, buyer loyalty and incentive programs can increase switching costs and lock-in. Moreover, by connecting with customers in new ways, through multiple channels including customer to customer interactions, e-commerce can capitalize on multichannel and viral marketing opportunities and give buyers access to a wealth of untapped knowledge.

Personalization, Customization, and Recommendation Systems

By supplying information about preferences, as well as information from purchase histories to online vendors, either directly through interaction with the Web site, or indirectly through marketing intermediaries, it is possible to tailor offerings more directly to individual buyers. Dynamically constructed pages can reflect customer information and preference in what some call a one-to-one marketing relationship. In addition to personalizing the interaction to enhance the relationship with customers, the two-way interaction supported by the Web, coupled with back-end intelligence about what features and accessories go with selected products, provides the potential for product customization. Many e-commerce vendors offer customers a "build-to-order" option that allows some degree of customization of the products to suit buyer tastes. This is common for computer vendors, but other types of e-commerce companies have also used e-commerce to offer this value-added service to customers. Lands' End, for example, offers hem-to-order pants. Even Levis, in their initial foray into e-commerce, attempted a "made-to-measure" blue jean product.

Collective intelligence mined from data on the population of customers further adds to online merchants' abilities to meet customer needs through sophisticated recommendation systems (Schafer, Konstan, and Riedl 2001). Recommendations can range from using simple automated rules to suggest related products that can complement a product in a customer's order—often termed "cross-selling"—to more complex mining techniques that integrate customer purchase histories, the profiles and purchases of other customers, and association rules. This latter technique, often termed "collaborative filtering," can lead to ever more accurate recommendations as the population of buyers grows larger. Amazon was one of the first to implement such a service with their now famous recommendation services for related books. Such systems can also enhance up-selling practices, where more expensive alternatives are suggested.

Incentive and Loyalty Programs

In an effort to inspire greater customer loyalty, many e-commerce sites followed the lead of airlines and offered various types of incentive marketing programs. Frequent shoppers can accumulate points on many sites that entitle them to discounts and other benefits. Because all transactions are automated and it is so easy to collect information via the Web, these types of programs became much more accessible to all online merchants. As with airline frequent flyer programs, these techniques create switching costs, since customers who do not return know they will lose accumulated benefits.

Direct E-Mail, Viral, and Multichannel Marketing

The Internet affords merchants new channels with which they can interact and sell to consumers, even beyond their own Web sites. For example, e-mail, the most popular application of the Internet, has been a valuable e-commerce marketing tool. Companies obtain e-mail addresses of visitors and customers, and regularly send targeted letters with new product information, announcements of sales, and other promotional content. Although diminished in usefulness today because of the overwhelming presence of spam, customers may still opt-in to receive information on product updates via e-mail.

Perhaps more important than direct e-mail from merchant to consumer is the interaction between customers that can be facilitated in the online context. Increasingly, companies rely on customers to help spread the word about their products and services. Such a strategy is known as viral marketing, because the marketing material is carried by customers and spread throughout a target population. Often, dissemination is accomplished by giving users access to free services or games, which require the participation of others. Paypal, for example, lets its customer send payments to others for free. Recipients must open an account with Paypal in order to transfer the funds into their regular bank account. This strategy has helped grow the number of Paypal account holders, which in turn entices more merchants to accept Paypal payments. Merchants, however, do pay a fee to receive funds.

Such customer-to-customer interactions may also occur in new social network communities, perhaps with some sponsoring activity by vendors. Online social network services like MySpace and Facebook enable users to construct rich profiles and then to make explicit connections (friends) with other site users. These so-called articulated friendship networks (Donath and Boyd 2004) are visible, so one user can see his or her friends' friends. This can help foster new connections and help users judge someone they do not yet know based on the implicit warranting done by mutual acquaintances. E-commerce companies have discovered that such online social networks can be valuable marketing tools, for purposes such as viral marketing campaigns, obtaining product feedback from user discussions through sponsored groups, or simply mining profile data to better target product advertising.

Channels to reach potential buyers can extend to other online business, in what have been called "affiliate relationships," as well as into the offline world. In the former situation, vendors use the wider Web community to help sell products. This involves more than simple reciprocal linking, and can include payments to Web affiliates that refer a customer who purchases a product. Amazon was a pioneer in this area as well, allowing virtually anyone with a Web site to become an Amazon affiliate. For example, an author might provide a link from his or her personal Web site to the book's purchase page on Amazon. The link is coded to identify the referrer, who then earns a slight commission on any purchase originating from the referring site. Multichannel e-commerce extending to the offline world has expanded considerably in the past decade. In most cases, these retailers have both a physical store and a virtual one, and seek to meet diverse customer needs with this combined offering. For example, a multichannel—or click-and-brick—retailer can provide detailed product information online, immediate pick-up in a store, and extensive support after the purchase online. Catalogue companies can refer to their Web site in every printed catalogue mailed to customers. In this way, they can gain the benefit of a regular reminder to look at their merchandise, with the cost savings that accrue when customers fill out online forms instead of calling a call center. Such examples highlight how click-and-brick firms and catalogue companies capitalize on the synergies that arise from the integration of traditional and online channels (Steinfield et al. 2002; Steinfield 2006). Such synergies may not come without problems, as channel conflicts may surface, in the form of undue competition across channels, cannibalization of sales, and lack of seamless interoperability that frustrates customers.

BUSINESS-TO-BUSINESS E-COMMERCE

Although business-to-consumer (B2C) e-commerce captures much of the headlines, business-to-business e-commerce volume is vastly larger—representing 94 percent of all U.S. online transactions in 2003, as noted earlier.

B2B e-commerce typically is divided into two main categories based on characteristics of the infrastructure and interfirm relationships of the participants: private industrial networks and Internet-based marketplaces (Laudon and Traver 2003). Private industrial networks are typically organized over proprietary network arrangements and involve existing trading partners in established trading relationships. Internet-based marketplaces rely on public network arrangements and hence can be open to new participants.

B2B Internet marketplaces have further been classified according to two important dimensions of business purchasing: how businesses buy and what businesses buy (Kaplan and Sawhney 2000). The "how" dimension distinguishes between spot purchasing to fill an immediate need, and systematic purchasing for planned, long-term needs. The former is often done using ephemeral, market-based transactions, without long-term contracts. The latter is often done after significant negotiation, and is often used for purchasing in large volumes from trusted trading partners. The "what" dimension normally distinguishes between vertical (also called "direct" or "manufacturing") inputs that relate to the core products of a firm and horizontal (often called "indirect" or "MRO" [for maintenance, repair, and operating]) inputs, such as office supplies, that are acquired by all firms.

Laudon and Traver (2003) distinguish the following four types of Internet-based B2B marketplaces.

- E-distributors (support spot purchasing for horizontal inputs), such as Grainger.com or Staples.com, offer electronic catalogues representing thousands of suppliers. Laudon and Traver (2003) call them the Amazon.com for industry since they operate much like retailers. The main benefit for buyers is simply the reduced search cost, although additional services such as credit and account management are offered to help further reduce transaction costs.
- E-procurement services such as Ariba.com also offer MRO supplies, but focus on systematic purchasing rather than spot purchasing. Such B2B intermediaries offer a range of procurement services, including the licensing of procurement software that supports a range of value-added services. They do not own the supplies, but offer the catalogues of thousands of suppliers from whom they also obtain fees and commissions. They theoretically bring value by aggregating both buyers and sellers, decreasing search costs for both parties, and therefore are subject to significant positive network externalities (the more buyers they attract, the more suppliers will join, and vice versa).
- Exchanges, such as E-steel.com, are intermediaries that focus on bringing together buyers and sellers within a particular industry, and concentrate on the spot purchasing of manufacturing inputs. They charge commissions, but offer a range of purchasing services to buyers and sellers, supporting price negotiations, auctions, and other forms of bidding in addition to normal fixed-price selling. Buyers benefit from greater choice and lower prices, while sellers gain access to large numbers of buyers. Often these vertical markets are used to unload surplus materials (for example, via auction). They are also subject to network externalities.
- Industry consortia are best represented by Covisint, the electronic procurement system developed by the leading automobile manufacturers. These exchanges are typically jointly owned by large buying firms seeking to rely on electronic networks to support long-term relationships with their suppliers. Entrance is by invitation only, and the buying clout of the founders influences suppliers to make the investments needed to participate.

In general, Laudon and Traver (2003) note that private industrial networks remain far more commonplace than Internet-based B2B markets. This is perhaps due to the need to make investments in the hardware, software, and business process re-engineering necessary to accomplish B2B transactions electronically. Companies need to be sure there is a payoff for these investments, and hence engage in them to serve established trading partners (Kraut et al. 1999). Moreover, as e-commerce becomes a more important part of the supply chain, greater amounts of strategic information (e.g., provision of forthcoming product designs to help suppliers prepare for new orders and better integrate their components), then concerns over the protection of information, lead firms to restrict electronic transactions to trusted trading partners.

ONLINE CONTENT DISTRIBUTION

The content industries have been dramatically affected by e-commerce. Because content today is created, stored, and increasingly distributed digitally, it is ideally suited for e-commerce. Content is a classic example of an information good, with its unique economic characteristics (Shapiro and Varian 1999). It is nonrivaled in that consumption by one user does not necessarily prevent consumption by another. Content producers traditionally face high first-copy costs for quality content, but near-zero marginal costs of digital reproduction and dissemination. These characteristics can encourage illegal copying and piracy, which can ultimately result in lower incentives to produce good content. New strategies are required, therefore, of content producers, since the Internet could easily render older business models obsolete (Evans and Wurster 2000). Online content business models are appearing, including on-demand (e.g., iTunes), subscription (e.g., Rhapsody), advertiser-supported (e.g., New York Times Electronic Edition), and various combination models (e.g., free or advertiser-supported basic content with premium paid content). The content industries face many challenges related to e-commerce. First, because of the legacy expectation that content on the Internet should be free, many content providers, especially in the online news arena, have felt compelled to find ways to provide online content without subscription or per-use charges. In the case of newspapers and magazines, this means that companies face the risk that online versions will cannibalize sales of offline subscriptions. The empirical evidence is mixed on this topic. Simon (2005) found that magazine subscriptions decline by 3 percent following the introduction of a Web site, while Kaiser and Kongsted (2005) found a complementary effect, with offline circulation increasing following the establishment of a companion Web site.

Content producers and distributors also face severe challenges from piracy, especially in the context of peer-to-peer file-sharing services (Premkumar 2003). Premkumar noted in 2003 that more than half of all U.S. teenagers had downloaded free music over the Internet. Today, the availability of legitimate Internet-based on-demand and subscription-based services offering music, TV shows, and movies, coupled with aggressive prosecution of copyright violations has alleviated the damage to some extent. Digital rights management (DRM) software is used to limit consumers' abilities to upload online-purchased digital music to free filesharing sites. Yet it also limits consumers' abilities to use their purchased content on multiple devices, creating some backlash against the DRM schemes in use.

Another new development facing content producers seeking to make gains from e-commerce is the rise in user-generated content. Some news-related weblogs (blogs) and video weblogs (vlogs) have become quite established, attracting many readers and viewers (Rainie 2005). User-generated video is also increasing in popularity, with a number of sites appearing that aggregate online user-generated video into new Internet "channels," such as YouTube (www.youtube.com), iFilm (www.ifilm.com), and Democracy (www.getdemocracy.com). These sites compete for viewers' attention, potentially taking revenue from traditional content producers and distributors.

However, established TV and movie producers are increasing their use of the Internet and finding ways to generate new revenues. They are placing trailers on free sites to help promote their content, and rather than make the same mistake as the music industry did, are beginning to embrace the Internet for legitimate purchases. For-pay downloads of video content are provided through online stores such as iTunes, or movie distribution sites such as CinemaNow. Revenue models are evolving beyond one-time purchase and ongoing subscription to also include time-limited rentals using DRM software. Content distribution is also extending to mobile devices as well, using services such as Verizon's VCast and other mobile content platforms. Sites that host user-generated content are also being viewed as sources of new talent by traditional content providers. Some merchants have even experimented with user-generated ads for their products, not only showing them online, but through mainstream media as well. These new strategies highlight the increasing convergence between old and new media.

ECONOMIC IMPACTS OF E-COMMERCE

Research on e-commerce has identified a wide range of economic impacts that stem from the new business models, costs of accessing customers and markets, supply-chain integration, and marketing and pricing strategies. One recurring theme found in the literature on e-commerce is the potential that it offers for a dramatic reconfiguration of the value chain in industry after industry. Reduced costs for accessing consumers can encourage producers to bypass middlemen, resulting in disintermediation. Online retailers may bypass traditional wholesalers and distributors and work directly with manufacturers. A second recurring theme is the effect of e-commerce on information asymmetries that formerly characterized many markets. Both of these themes are played out in the effect of e-commerce on market structures and prices, on relations between buyers and sellers, on pricing strategies, and on online merchants' abilities to establish trust. A brief overview of e-commerce research on these topics is provided below.

Effects on Markets and Prices

E-commerce research has long focused on the ways it may influence markets, such as encouraging the bypass, or disintermediation, of traditional middlemen, and altering buyer-seller relations, and creating downward pressure on prices in general. One of the key mechanisms behind these hypothesized impacts is the effect of e-commerce on the costs of doing business. E-commerce helps companies reduce costs and enable the entry into new markets by reducing what economists call transaction costs (Williamson 1975, 1985). Every commercial exchange, including those between consumers and businesses, and business-to-business exchanges, is a transaction that can be broken into a number of discernible stages, each with its own set of costs to the participants. At the simplest level, we can consider any purchase to require an information or prepurchase phase, a purchase phase, and an after-sales, or postpurchase phase. During the information phase, for example, buyers face search costs, while sellers have costs to supply purchase information to buyers. During the purchase phase, other costs are associated with negotiation, monitoring contracts, and actual financial settlement. Postpurchase costs include repairs, returns, and other types of customer services. When transaction costs get too high, markets become inefficient, and prices can be higher than they should be. For example, imagine a small town with one seller of some product. Without the Internet, customers in this town face high search costs (e.g., driving to another city to look in stores there) with uncertain payoff. So they pay the higher prices charged by the local monopoly provider. With the Internet, customers' search costs for finding lower-priced suppliers are dramatically reduced, forcing the local monopoly seller to lower its prices. Because of this effect, many economists believe that the Internet will help reduce prices across all industries (Bakos 1997). Indeed, it became popular to talk about the "death of distance" as a barrier to commerce due to the reduced transaction costs afforded by e-commerce.

One oft-mentioned market structure impact of the reductions in transactions costs offered by e-commerce is its potential to enable producers of goods and services to bypass intermediary firms like wholesalers and retailers and sell directly to end customers (Benjamin and Wigand 1995). Many producers were swayed by this logic, and began to sell products directly from their Web sites. For some companies, such as Dell Computer and Cisco, the direct-sale business model made a great deal of sense, and the Internet provided a cost-effective way to manage it. Most of their customers were businesses already connected to the Internet, and accustomed to doing business in this way. For others, especially those selling to consumers, this approach made less sense. Sarkar, Butler, and Steinfield (1995) showed early on that, in fact, the Internet provided as much or more opportunity for new forms of intermediation, and also helped to strengthen the role of existing intermediary firms. Indeed, some of the most famous Internet companies, such as Amazon and eBay, are examples of the new types of intermediation made possible by e-commerce. Sarkar and colleagues argued that intermediaries' transaction costs have also been reduced, and the gains they get from e-commerce may negate any advantages producers might gain. They also note that intermediaries provide many functions to both buyers and sellers, such as needs assessment and evaluation, market information, and risk reduction, which are critical for many purchases. Many subsequent analyses demonstrated the fallacy of the disintermediation hypothesis (e.g., Schmitz 2000). Marketing theorists caution that while any particular intermediary might be eliminated, their functions cannot be, suggesting that a role remains for intermediaries even in the age of e-commerce (Stern, El-Ansary, and Coughlan 1996).

Buyer-Seller Relations

Another market effect of e-commerce related to transaction costs in general, and search costs in particular, is the potential for companies to find new trading partners rather than remain locked in to existing relationships. If transaction costs can be reduced, then market mechanisms may be used where they were not feasible beforehand, based on an early theoretical argument proposed by Malone, Yates, and Benjamin (1987). For example, suppose a company needed a very specific type of input, available from only one particular supplier in its area. In the past, this company was at a disadvantage. Because of information asymmetries (the supplier knew what it cost to make the goods, but the buying company did not), and lack of alternative providers, the supplier could charge higher prices. However, the reduced search costs and greater information available on the Internet reduce these asymmetries, and increase choice. Hence, firms can avoid being locked into long-term relationships, and use more spot-market buying behavior to source the inputs they need. The theoretical prediction was that such uses of e-commerce would give rise to large electronic marketplaces in which businesses could buy inputs based purely on the best available offers.

Although e-commerce did result in the formation of large B2B electronic marketplaces that offered both manufacturing (vertical) inputs and commodities (horizontal) supplies, the above prediction has not been entirely supported. First, most of the third-party developed B2B markets have failed (Laudon and Traver 2003). Substantial empirical evidence suggests that firms are more likely to use e-commerce to increase the efficiency of transactions with trusted suppliers than to enable spot transactions with new suppliers (Steinfield, Kraut, and Plummer 1995). Hence, they were less likely to allow new third-party firms to position themselves as profit-making intermediaries in these well-established relationships. Instead, the bulk of B2B e-commerce occurs over private industrial networks typically organized by larger buyers or sellers. Often a large company will function as the leader in a value network that encompasses firms up and down the value chain. These value networks compete with other value networks, as an extension of simple firm-to-firm competition. The B2B e-commerce links permit more than just simple buy and sell transactions—they enable collaborative e-commerce among networks of firms, allowing activities such as co-design of components, joint marketing efforts, and the like.

Pricing

As noted above, because of the reduction in transaction costs, and access to information about prices of alternative vendors, a primary effect of e-commerce was supposed to be lower and more homogenous prices relative to traditional channels. Up to now, the evidence for lower prices is rather mixed, especially when the added costs for shipping are taken into account. Moreover, price dispersion remains high, contrary to the expectations of economists (Smith, Bailey, and Brynjolfsson 2000). It appears that because it is so easy to change prices (referred to as menu costs), Internet companies make more changes in smaller increments in order to respond to the market.

Another reason there is variability in prices is that e-commerce makes it easier to engage in price discrimination, whereby vendors sell the same product to different customers at different prices. The goal, of course, is to learn what each customer is willing to pay, and then charge him or her that price. One way that this can happen is through auction pricing, which allows customers to submit their willingness to pay in the form of bids. Another popular price-discrimination approach is to charge different prices for different versions of the same product or service (e.g., a student version of software vs. a professional version) (Shapiro and Varian 1999). Sometimes e-commerce companies have tried to estimate willingness to pay based on some aspect of online behavior. Amazon, for example, once angered its customers when it was revealed that the online vendor had attempted to charge higher prices to returning customers, based on the assumption that these loyal customers would be less likely to switch to other online sellers. They soon stopped this practice. Another method of price discrimination is to make assumptions about willingness to pay based on the referring site. Thus, if a shopper arrives at an online retail site by way of a comparison shopping agent or a discount shopping site, he or she may be presented with a lower price than a shopper who had clicked on an ad in an upscale investment journal.

In summary, much of the market impact literature related to e-commerce overlooks many important influences on the price of any product, including the fact that online products differ in many ways from their counterparts in a store. Online products are not immediately available, cannot be touched, smelled, or otherwise physically examined, and perceived risks—for example, ease of returns—may be higher. It further ignores the importance of established relations between buyers and sellers, as well as the use of e-commerce in ways that lock in trading partners rather than reducing so-called market frictions that make it easier to switch vendors. For example, companies that gather information from customers, and then use this to help offer highly personalized services, or that provide incentives to keep customers returning to their Web site, create what has been called "sticky" e-commerce (Shapiro and Varian 1999). In this way, e-commerce raises customers' switching costs (the costs to move to a different supplier of a good or service), raising a new barrier that can help prevent other firms from successfully attacking a particular market. Network externalities, which create positive feedback loops so that the larger the service, the more attractive it is, also work to make it difficult for new firms to attack established players. For example, eBay is so attractive because its large user base increases the likelihood that people can always find the specific product they are seeking. This in turn draws more sellers, which attracts more buyers, and so on. Smaller systems have trouble competing with this dynamic. Such differentiation effects demonstrate that e-commerce does not make exchanges frictionless, and this result would not, in any case, be in the interest of merchants.

Alternative perspectives point out other reasons why new entrants may find it difficult to dislodge incumbents in any industry. Afuah and Tucci (2001) point out that incumbent firms normally possess crucial resources that new entrants may not have. These are often called "complementary assets," and include factors such as established relationships with suppliers, experience, access to retailers, powerful information systems, and strong distribution networks. Indeed, the rise of click-and-brick e-commerce show forcefully how incumbent retailers can better capitalize on e-commerce than the new dot-coms that do not possess the required complementary assets.

Trust, Security, and Privacy

How to establish trust in online commerce is one of the most heavily researched e-commerce areas, becoming an issue when thousands of new and unfamiliar dot-com companies flooded the Internet (Grabner-Kräuter and Kaluscha 2003; Koufaris and Hampton-Sosa 2004; Tan and Thoen 2002). Consumers are reluctant to shop at unfamiliar online stores for fear that their orders may not be fulfilled or that they may not be able to return defective merchandise. The same problem prevents businesses from buying from unfamiliar suppliers, who have not proved that they are both trustworthy and competent to handle the business. Much of the research has attempted to identify factors that influence the formation of trust, such as Web-site quality, presence of Web assurance seals (verification from trusted third parties—firms like VeriSign or Trust-E that vouch for the legitimacy of an online vendor), use of secure servers for transactions, and specification of privacy policies (Kim et al. 2004). To some extent, the growing familiarity of e-commerce brands, and movement of established firms into e-commerce has helped. However, consumers have new concerns about how e-commerce companies will use the information they collect. This is a privacy issue on its face, but also reflects a lack of trust that online vendors will behave responsibly.

A related issue is the fear that many online users have over the security of online transactions. Theft of credit-card numbers and personal information are chief concerns, and statistics on online fraud supplied by the Federal Trade Commission (2004) suggest that trust and security remain a significant problem. Clearly, the continued use of strong encryption measures, such as those outlined above in the section on "Encryption Methods in E-Commerce," will help bridge the trust gap. Secure transactions are not enough; they must be accompanied by sound information security practices in all aspects of a firm's infrastructure. The cases of hackers breaking into corporate networks and stealing entire databases of credit-card numbers stored on servers reminds us of the importance of an overall information security policy (Laudon and Traver 2003). Other measures for establishing trust, however, are also needed for consumer-to-consumer markets like eBay, as noted above. Reputation and feedback systems, as well as escrow systems, are some of the measures used to generate trust among strangers in such auction markets (Resnick et al. 2000).

Finally, for many purchases, e-commerce may not be the best approach, given consumers' needs, desires, or home situations (Steinfield et al. 1999). For example, when someone needs a product immediately, they are much more likely to pick it up at a local store than wait one or more days for delivery. Click-and-brick firms such as Best Buy recognize this need, and now offer in-store inventory search and pick-up options for online shoppers. Other consumers see shopping as a social and entertainment activity, and a visit to the mall with friends is hardly replaceable by e-commerce. Finally, some services simply require too much of consumers to be viable. For example, in order to buy groceries including perishable items online, someone needs to be home at the time of delivery. This scheduling may be difficult, and to get around it, some companies attempted to use refrigerators in garages to which deliverymen had access. Yet this also requires consumers to open up their private space to strangers, and the costs of installing appliances at customer premises proved to be impractical. Moreover, not everyone had a garage, which limits the market. These are just a sampling of shopping situations in which e-commerce might not be the best option.

CONCLUSION

This chapter has provided a broad overview of e-commerce and showed how the creation of a ubiquitous, easy-to-use, and open data network helped e-commerce emerge as a powerful force from the many precursor systems and technologies. As evolving technologies such as broadband access via wired and wireless networks, new markup standards, encryption systems, and new interfaces, extend the reach of e-commerce, its influence on the structure of commerce throughout the world grows stronger. E-commerce is continuing to spread throughout the economies of the world, with the pace determined by national policy contexts, infrastructure availability, and cultural factors.

The dot-com bust may have caused some to be pessimistic, but it can also be viewed as a normal evolutionary process at the start of any new industry. Poor business models have failed, but viable ones have survived and are now prospering. Moreover, the entry of established companies into e-commerce is lending more legitimacy to the sector, and is helping to overcome trust problems, as is the increasing use of powerful public key encryption systems to protect transaction data. These firms also have the resources and alternative sources of income to enable their e-commerce channels to develop appropriately, without reckless moves aimed at capturing market share at the expense of profits.

Online commerce fundamentally changes businesses practices in many industries, enabling customization where it was not possible before, creating long-tail markets for goods and services that could not previously be offered in a profitable way, and opening up markets to new competitors coming from different locations and industries. Value chains are experiencing reconfiguration, as the costs of reaching suppliers and customers are reduced and information asymmetries lessened. Efficiencies in the supply chain encourage globalization, and lower prices for consumers.

As e-commerce becomes even more pervasive, new research issues continue to surface. The extension of data capture through mobile devices, for example, requires much new work on how to provide services without intrusions into personal privacy. The increasing sophistication of pricing strategies requires greater understanding of their effects on both sellers and buyers. The growth of multichannel retailing requires more understanding of how to manage channel conflicts and identify synergy opportunities. New interface techniques are being deployed without adequate understanding of their effects on users. The implications of new online practices such as mash-ups, user-generated content, and social networking services for e-commerce are not fully understood. Clearly, there is a rich future for research in the broad new field of e-commerce.

GLOSSARY

B2B Electronic Hub: Electronic marketplaces in which business buyers can acquire goods from suppliers. Vertical hubs focus on the provision of manufacturing inputs bringing together firms operating at various stages inside a particular industry value chain. Horizontal hubs focus across industries, bringing buyers and sellers of a wide range of maintenance, repair, and operation goods (MRO) to the market.

Collaborative E-Commerce: A form of B2B e-commerce among cooperating networks of firms that involves more than just purchases, but also such activities as the co-design of components and joint marketing efforts.

Complementary Assets: Resources possessed by a firm that enable it to take better advantage of innovations such as e-commerce. These resources include established relationships, product know-how, existing business processes and systems, and distribution systems.

Disintermediation: An effect of e-commerce whereby producing firms bypass traditional intermediaries in order to sell directly to end consumers. Hence, intermediaries such as wholesalers or retailers (see below) find their position in the market, and thus their very survival, threatened.

Dot-Com: A name given to Internet companies because their network name ended in ".com."

EDI: Electronic document interchange, a standard for transmitting business documents over computer networks.

Intermediary: An entity that facilitates trade between buyers and sellers in markets. Wholesalers and retailers are considered to be intermediaries that help manufacturers sell their products to end consumers. Real estate agents are intermediaries who bring together home buyers and sellers.

Internet Business Model: A generic term referring to a variety of specific methods of doing business and generating revenue on the Internet.

Network Externalities: A term describing the changes in benefit that an agent receives from a good or service due to changes in the number of other people using that good or service. The word *externality* implies that these benefits are not "internalized" by the seller (i.e., captured in the price). They may be negative (e.g., congestion effects) or positive (e.g., more potential contacts). Often the term *network effect* is used to refer to the increasing benefits to customers associated with a larger user base in an online business.

Price Discrimination: A pricing strategy whereby vendors sell the same product to different customers at different prices in an attempt to maximize overall revenue by matching prices to customers' willingness to pay.

Public Key Encryption: An asymmetric method of encryption that requires two separate keys: one public and one private. Data encrypted with a public key can be decrypted only by the corresponding private key, and vice versa. Asymmetric systems are in contrast to symmetric, or private, key systems, which use the same key at both ends to decrypt transmissions. Public key systems solve the problem of sending keys over an insecure network, and they are often used in concert with symmetric systems—encrypting the symmetric key prior to sending to the other party.

Switching Costs: In e-commerce, such costs are the additional costs a user (or buyer) faces when changing to a different supplier of a good or service, caused by such factors as learning costs, loss of accumulated benefits, contract requirements, and so forth.

Transaction Cost: Costs incurred by buyers and sellers as they complete a commercial exchange, including search and information-gathering costs, monitoring and settlement costs, and after-sales and service costs.

CROSS REFERENCES

See *Electronic Data Interchange (EDI); Electronic Payment Systems; Mobile Commerce; The Internet Fundamentals*.

REFERENCES

Adamic, L., and B.Huberman. 2001. The Web's hidden order. *Communications of the ACM* 44(9):55–60.

Afuah, A., and C. Tucci (2001). *Internet business models and strategies: Text and cases*. New York, NY: McGraw-Hill Irwin.

Anderson, C. 2006. *The long tail: Why the future of business is selling less of more*. New York: Hyperion.

Benjamin, R., and R. Wigand. 1995. Electronic markets and virtual value chains on the information highway. *Sloan Management Review* 36(2):62–72.

Bakos, J. Y. 1997. Reducing buyer search costs: Implications for electronic marketplaces. *Management Science* 43(12):1676–92.

Clarke, R. 1999. Electronic commerce definitions. www.anu.edu.au/people/Roger.Clarke/EC/ECDefns.html#EC (accessed October 6, 2004).

Donath, J., and D. Boyd. 2004. Public displays of connection. *BT Technology Journal* 22(4):71.

Dorfman, R. 2004. Extensible markup language (XML). In *The Internet encyclopedia*, Vol. 1, no. 7, edited by H. Bidgoli, 32–754. New York: Wiley.

Dutta, S., A. Lopez-Claros, and I. Mia (eds.) 2006. *The global information technology report 2005–2006*. 5th ed. *Levering ICT for development*. London: Palgrave Macmillan.

e-Business Watch. 2006. The European e-business report, 2006/2007 edition, Brussels: European Commission, www.ebusiness-watch.org/resources/documents/EBR06.pdf (accessed February 1, 2007).

Evans, P., and T. Wurster. 2000. *Blow to bits: How the new economics of information transforms strategy*. Boston: Harvard Business School Press.

Federal Trade Commission. 2004. National and state trends in fraud and identity theft: January–December 2003. www.consumer.gov/idtheft/stats.html (accessed October 6, 2004).

Gottshalk, K., S. Graham, H. Kreger, and J. Snell. 2002. Introduction to Web services architecture. *IBM Systems Journal* 41(2):170–7. www.research.ibm.com/journal/sj41–2.html (accessed October 6, 2004).

Grabner-Kräuter, S., and E. Kaluscha. 2003. Empirical research in on-line trust: A review and critical assessment. *International Journal of Human-Computer Studies* 58(6):783–812.

Hawkins, R. 2004. Looking beyond the dot-com bubble: Exploring the form and function of business models in the electronic marketplace. In *E-life after the dot-com bust*, edited by B. Priessl, H. Bouwman, and C. Steinfield, 65–81. Heidelberg: Physica-Verlag.

Housley, R., and J. Polk. 2001. *Planning for PKI: Best practices for deploying a public key infrastructure*. New York: Wiley.

Juels, A. 2004. Encryption. In *The Internet encyclopedia*, Vol. 1, edited by H. Bidgoli, 686–94. New York: Wiley.

Kaiser, U., and H. Kongsted. 2005. Do magazines' "companion websites" cannibalize the demand for the print version? Center for Applied Microeconomics Working Paper, University of Copenhagen. www.econ.ku.dk/CAM/Files/workingpapers/2005/2005–07.pdf (accessed July 6, 2006).

Kaplan, S. N., and M. Sawhney 2000. E-hubs: The new B2B marketplaces. *Harvard Business Review* 78:97–103.

Kim, D. J., N. Sivasailam, and H. R. Rao. 2004. Information assurance in B2C Websites for information goods/services. *Electronic Markets* 14(4):344–59.

Koufaris, M., and W. Hampton-Sosa. 2004. The development of initial trust in an online company by new customers. *Information and Management* 41(3):377–97.

Kraemer, K., J. Dedrick, and N. Melville. 2006. Globalization and national diversity: e-commerce diffusion and impacts across nations. In *Global e-commerce: Impacts of national environment and policy*, edited by K. Kraemer, J, Dedrick, N. Melville, and K. Zhu, 13–61. Cambridge, UK: Cambridge University Press.

Kraut, R., C. Steinfield, A. Chan, B. Butler, and A. Hoag. 1999. Coordination and virtualization: The role of electronic networks and personal relationships. *Organization Science* 10(6):722–40.

Laudon, K., and C. Traver. 2003. *E-commerce: Business, technology, society*. 2nd ed. Boston: Addison-Wesley.

Malone, T., J. Yates, and R. Benjamin. 1987. Electronic markets and electronic hierarchies: Effects of information technology on market structure and corporate strategies. *Communications of the ACM* 30(6):484–97.

Markus, M. L., C. Steinfield, R. Wigand, and G. Minton. 2006, August. Industry-wide information systems standardization: The case of the U.S. residential mortgage industry. *MIS Quarterly* 30 (Special Issue on Standard Making):439–65.

McGinty, M. 2004. RFID: Is this game of tag fair play? *Communications of the ACM* 47(1):15–8.

OECD. 2006. Measuring the information economy: OECD Key ICT Indicators. www.oecd.org/sti/ICTindicators (accessed February 1, 2007).

OECD. 2006. *OECD Information Technology Outlook 2006*. Paris: Organization for Economic Cooperation and Development.

OECD. 2006. Telecommunications and Internet policy: OECD broadband statistics to June 2006. www.oecd.org/sti/ict/broadband (accessed February 1, 2007).

O'Reilly, T. 2005. What is Web 2.0? Design patterns and business models for the next generation of software. www.oreillynet.com/pub/a/oreilly/tim/news/2005/09/30/what-is-web-20.html (accessed July 6, 2006).

Premkumar, G. P. 2003. Alternative distribution strategies for digital music. *Communications of the ACM* 46(9):89–95.

Rainie, L. 2005. The state of blogging. Pew Internet and American Life Project. www.pewinternet.org/pdfs/PIP_blogging_data.pdf (accessed July 6, 2006).

Rappa, M. 2004. Business models on the Web. North Carolina State University Web page. http://digitalenterprise.org/models/models.html (accessed October 6, 2004).

Resnick, P., K. Kuwabara, R. Zeckhauser, and E. Friedman. 2000. Reputation systems. *Communications of the ACM* 43(12):45–8.

Ritsko, J., and A. Davis. 2002. Preface to special issue on new developments in Web services and e-commerce. *IBM Systems Journal* 41(2):168–9. www.research.ibm.com/journal/sj41–2.html (accessed October 6, 2004).

Sahai, A., S. Graupner, and W. Kim. 2004. Web services. In *The Internet encyclopedia*, Vol. 3, edited by H. Bidgoli, 754–66. New York: Wiley.

Sarkar, M., B. Butler, and C. Steinfield. 1995. Intermediaries and cybermediaries: A continuing role for mediating players in the electronic marketplace. *Journal of Computer Mediated Communication* 1(3). www.ascusc.org/jcmc/vol1/issue3/vol1no3.html (accessed October 6, 2002).

Schafer, J., J. Konstan, and J. Riedl. 2001. Electronic commerce recommender applications. *Journal of Data Mining and Knowledge Discovery* 5(1–2):115–52.

Schmitz, S. 2000. The effects of electronic commerce on the structure of intermediation. *Journal of Computer Mediated Communication* 5(3). www.ascusc.org/jcmc/vol5/issue3/ (accessed October 6, 2002).

Shapiro, M., and H. Varian. 1999. *Information rules: A strategic guide to the network economy*. Boston: Harvard Business School Press.

Simon, D. H. 2005, April 1. The effect of a magazine's digital content on its print circulation: Cannibalization or complementarity? http://ssrn.com/abstract=689522 (accessed July 6, 2006).

Smith, M., J. Bailey, and E. Brynjolfsson. 2000. Understanding digital markets: Review and assessment. In *Understanding the digital economy*, edited by E. Brynjolfsson and B. Kahin, 99–136. Cambridge, MA: MIT Press.

Steinfield, C. 2004. The development of location based services in mobile commerce. In *E-life after the dot-com bust*, edited by B. Priessl, H. Bouwman, and C. Steinfield, 177–97. Heidelberg: Physica-Verlag.

Steinfield, C. 2005. Click and brick electronic commerce. In *The handbook of information security*, *Volume* 1. edited by H. Bidgoli, 242–53. New York: Wiley.

Steinfield, C., H. Bouwman, and T. Adelaar. 2002. The dynamics of click-and-mortar e-commerce: Opportunities and management strategies. *International Journal of Electronic Commerce* 6(5):93–119.

Steinfield, C., R. Kraut, and A. Plummer. 1995. The effect of networks on buyer-seller relations. *Journal of Computer Mediated Communication* 1(3). www.ascusc.org/jcmc/vol1/issue3/vol1no3.html (accessed October 6, 2002).

Steinfield, C., A. Mahler, and J. Bauer. 1999. Electronic commerce and the local merchant: Opportunities for synergy between physical and Web presence. *Electronic Markets* 9(1):51–7.

Stern, L. W., A. I. El-Ansary, and A. T. Coughlan. 1996. *Marketing channels*. Upper Saddle River, N.J.: Prentice Hall-International.

Tan, Y., and W. Thoen. 2002. Formal aspects of a generic model of trust for electronic commerce. *Decision Support Systems* 33(3):233–46.

Timmers, P. 1998. Business models for electronic markets. *Electronic Markets* 8(2):3–8. www.electronicmarkets.org/modules/pub/view.php/electronicmarkets-183 (accessed November 1, 2002).

U.S. Department of Commerce. 2000. *Digital economy 2000*. https://www.esa.doc.gov/Reports/DIGITAL.pdf (accessed July 6, 2006).

U.S. Department of Commerce. 2006. 2004 e-commerce multi-sector report. *U.S. Census Bureau E-Stats*. www.census.gov/eos/www/papers/2004/2004reportfinal.pdf (accessed July 6, 2006).

U.S. Department of Commerce. 2007. Quarterly retail e-commerce sales: 3rd Quarter 2006. *U.S. Census Bureau News*. www.census.gov/mrts/www/data/html/06Q3.html (accessed February 1, 2007).

Wang, C. P., and K. C. Chan. 2003. Analyzing the taxonomy of Internet business models using graphs. *First Monday* 8(6). www.firstmonday.dk/issues/issue8_6/wang (accessed July 6, 2006).

Weill, P., and M. Vitale. 2001. *Place to space: Migrating to e-business models*. Boston: Harvard Business School Press.

Williamson, O. 1975. *Markets and hierarchies: Analysis and antitrust implications*. New York: Free Press.

———. 1985. *The economic institutions of capitalism*. New York: Free Press.

Wolverton, T. 2000, January 10. FBI probes extortion case at CD store. *CNET News.com*. http://news.com.com/2100–1017–235418.html (accessed March 1, 2004).

Electronic Data Interchange (EDI)

Matthew K. McGowan, *Bradley University*

INTRODUCTION

Electronic data interchange (EDI) is the exchange of business transactions from computer to computer using standardized formats. EDI usually involves an electronic link from one organization to another, but it can also be used for transactions from one division of an organization to another division of the same organization. EDI is classified as a type of interorganizational information system (IOIS). There are more than 100,000 companies in the United States (Cooke 2002; Witte, Grunhagen, and Clarke 2003) and more than 200,000 worldwide (Angeles et al. 2001) using EDI. The U.S. Census Bureau reported that for the year 2000, manufacturers were the largest business users of electronic commerce, conducting 18.4 percent of their orders as electronic transactions.

EDI is a form of business-to-business (B2B) electronic commerce, and is considered one of the earliest forms of e-commerce. B2B is the largest portion of electronic commerce. Some studies have reported that EDI accounts for over 80 percent of B2B electronic commerce (Down 2002; Laudon and Laudon 2006).

EDI processing involves the translation of transactions into standard EDI formats. These formatted transactions are sent electronically to a trading partner, and the trading partner translates the transactions from the standard format into the format required for processing by its systems. EDI started in the early 1970s, when the transportation industry created the Transportation Data Coordinating Committee to develop standards for forty-five common types of transactions (Hsieh and Lin 2004). The earliest forms of EDI used private networks to link with trading partners, in some cases going through value-added network (VAN) service providers. The availability of the Internet has motivated organizations to move much of their EDI traffic to the Internet to reduce communication costs. It is estimated that Internet EDI transactions are increasing at an annual rate of about 50 percent (Zuckerman 2004).

EDI is an enabling technology: it enables businesses to send and receive business transactions electronically. EDI not only results in greater accuracy and faster processing of transactions, but it can also permit the full business-to-business integration of information systems. Researchers have observed that the use of EDI has revolutionized the ways in which organizations conduct business in recent years (Arunachalam 2004; Lee, Lee, and Kang 2005). EDI is moving beyond dyadic (between two trading partners) implementations and toward networked configurations (Arunachalam 2004; Christiaanse 2005) that enable even greater levels of benefits.

BUSINESS APPLICATIONS OF EDI

The business applications of EDI have increased as EDI has grown and evolved. Like other applications of computer technology, EDI started out as an efficiency improvement. The number of types of transactions defined by EDI standards has increased since its introduction. Its role in business has similarly expanded. This section explains how the motivation for businesses to use EDI has changed since the inception of EDI, and identifies the ways in which EDI can support various business strategies.

Motivation for Using EDI

EDI began at a time when computing technology was mainframe-based and proprietary; few common communication protocols existed among vendors, and data representation also varied by vendor (Hsieh and Lin 2004). Companies did recognize the limitations of paper-based transaction systems (Down 2002): it is labor-intensive and inefficient; it does not permit easy tracking; it requires long lead times for processing; there are many opportunities for errors; it may require data entry multiple times for the same data; and it does not provide visibility into the process. EDI evolved as a way to overcome these problems. The first industries to develop EDI solutions were those with high volumes of transactions: transportation, automotive, grocery, and retail (Hsieh and Lin 2004; Witte et al. 2003).

The early EDI adopters identified standards for common types of transactions such as shipping notices, orders, and other transactions to support trade, and invoices, payments, and other financial transactions. Many of the reasons for initially adopting EDI were to improve efficiency. Some small and medium-size businesses have adopted EDI as a requirement for doing business with a larger trading partner (Hart and Saunders 1998; Iacovou, Benbasat, and Dexter 1995). Today, EDI is frequently used to support business strategies such as just-in-time (JIT) inventory management and continuous replenishment process (CRP), and is important in supply chain management (SCM). The motivation for using EDI now extends to integrating business processes and optimizing business operations (Arunachalam 2004; Down 2002).

Business Strategies Supported through EDI

EDI can be applied to many functional areas, from logistics to management (Hsieh and Lin 2004). Banerjee and Kumar (2002) identify the following business objectives that can be supported through the use of electronic business data interchange: reduced raw material inventory, reduced finished goods inventory, reduced cost of quality, reduced shipping costs, improved cash flow, increased sales opportunities, reduced data entry and paper costs, improved customer service, and faster response to changing product demand. Companies frequently initiate EDI to support JIT inventory management systems (Hsieh and Lin 2004), which can lead to reduced inventories.

Campbell used EDI to support a CRP strategy with the grocery retail chains that it supplies (Lee, Clark, and Tam 1999). Although Campbell had previously used EDI with the retail chains, the chains managed their own inventories. Under the new system, Campbell managed the inventories, a major change for the business. The arrangement led to improved inventory turns and reduced stockouts for the retail chains, and improved sales for Campbell.

Smaller companies may be coerced into using EDI in order to satisfy the demands of a larger company that they supply. For these companies, using EDI may be a necessity to ensure survival. Companies should plan their EDI implementations with trading partners in order to avoid alienating them (Iacovou et al. 1995). Research has found that the level of trust in trading partner relations is positively correlated with successful EDI implementation (Ruppel, Underwood-Queen, and Harrington 2003). Hart and Saunders (1998) found that companies that used cooperative strategies and built trust in trading relationships experienced a greater volume and variety of EDI transactions than companies that used coercion. Companies may need to provide technical assistance to trading partners to help them implement EDI (Iacovou et al. 1995; McGowan and Madey 1998).

The use of the Internet for EDI has led to new opportunities for EDI applications. Traditionally, EDI has been used primarily to support dyadic trading relationships, ones in which a company buys a product from one of a handful of suppliers (Choudhury 1997). EDI can now be used to support highly coordinated trading communities (Arunachalam 2004; Christiaanse 2005; Down 2002; Elgarah et al. 2005) instead of being limited to dyadic trading relationships. The chemical industry is using EDI to support marketplaces and hubs within the industry, enabling companies to connect upstream supply channel functions with channel functions both inside and outside organizational boundaries (Christiaanse 2005). The potential benefits of using EDI are explained in the following section.

ADVANTAGES AND POTENTIAL LIMITATIONS OF USING EDI

There are many benefits that companies have attributed to the use of EDI. However, because some of those benefits are not realized unless a company uses EDI for a high number of transactions, there are some companies whose benefits are limited or go unrealized.

Benefits of Using EDI

Companies have received numerous benefits from the use of EDI. The benefits of EDI include: reduced data entry and paper costs, more timely information, improved information integrity, ability to handle a greater business volume, reduced logistics costs, improved information consistency and integrity, better business communications, improved business processes, and improved security (Banerjee and Kumar 2002; Copeland and Hwang 1997; Hsieh and Lin 2004; Mount 2003; Raghunathan and Yeh 2001; Witte et al. 2003).

Properly implemented, an EDI transaction is entered once by one trading partner and electronically transmitted to the corresponding trading partner. Because the information comes in a standard electronic form, there is no need to re-key the information into the receiving system. EDI often results in more frequent communications with trading partner, which allows faster response to quality problems (Banerjee and Kumar 2002). The electronic transmission is more timely than mail, phone, or fax communications, which EDI replaced. RJR Nabisco reports that its cost to process a purchase order via EDI is only $1, compared with $70 for a paper-based purchase order (Witte et al. 2003).

Early EDI systems were targeted toward achieving improved efficiencies through automation of existing processes (Down 2002). The benefits of such systems included reduced transaction costs and improved timeliness of information. Many new implementations of EDI are focused on improving business processes and business operations (Down 2002). Capturing data in electronic form permits businesses to distribute that information to multiple systems for other purposes (Witte et al. 2003).

EDI implementation is a multifaceted concept; one can look at the breadth (number of trading partners using EDI with the organization), diversity (number of different types of EDI transactions supported), and depth (extent to which EDI is integrated with other systems) in measuring EDI implementation (Massetti and Zmud 1996). Some companies have managed to extend integration beyond their boundaries to obtain benefits from EDI. Organizations in some industries have been able to realize network effects by using EDI to more tightly integrate operations across firms, thus extending efficiencies to all participants (Christiaanse 2005).

Potential Problems and Limitations of EDI

EDI has several potential drawbacks: high implementation costs, high operational costs, and the need to keep up with standards or maintain multiple standards (Witte et al. 2003). EDI implementation requires effective controls to prevent intentional or unintentional errors in the system (Lee et al. 2005). Smaller companies may perceive a lack of control in whether or how their trading partners use EDI (Riggins and Mukhopadhyay 1994). New versions of the EDI standards are released every few years, and not all trading partners may upgrade at the same time (Down 2002; Witte et al. 2003). This can lead to difficulties in keeping EDI running smoothly, and adds troubleshooting costs to the costs of using EDI.

The cost of implementing and operating EDI systems can be high (Mount 2003; Witte et al. 2003). Mount estimates that the cost to purchase and install EDI software could cost a midsized company \$120,000, and that operation costs, including communications costs for transactions, could reach \$400,000 for a midsized company. For companies performing high volumes of transactions, the benefits may far exceed the costs, but they may not for small companies (Down 2002; Lee et al. 2005; Mount 2003). The costs of implementing EDI will vary with the type of technology used (Banerjee and Kumar 2002).

EDI has both administrative and technical components. Organizations that possess greater levels of technical knowledge have been able to achieve greater levels of EDI implementation than organizations with lower levels of technical knowledge (McGowan and Madey 1998). EDI users may fail to realize the benefits of EDI if they do not adequately integrate EDI systems with other systems (Copeland and Hwang 1997). This level of integration may require a company to use business process reengineering to modify the business operations involved with EDI (Lee et al. 1999).

HOW THE EDI PROCESS WORKS

Overview

Recall that EDI is the computer-to-computer exchange of business transactions in standardized formats. The EDI process for a customer sending a purchase order to one of its suppliers is illustrated in Figure 1. Assuming that the customer has already entered the purchase orders into the purchasing system, the first step in the process is for a program to extract and format the purchase order information from the purchasing system. The extracted information is then translated into an EDI-standard format, often done by commercial EDI software. Next, the purchase order information, now in the standard format, is packaged for transmission, also frequently done by commercial software. The packaged purchase orders are then transmitted electronically to the supplier. Various communications alternatives are discussed later in this section. The supplier receives the packaged purchase order documents and uses its EDI document management system to parse the packaged documents into their component documents before running them through the translation software. The resulting translated documents are then formatted to match the supplier's order system and loaded into the order system. The entire process is automated and electronic, so there is no need for human intervention.

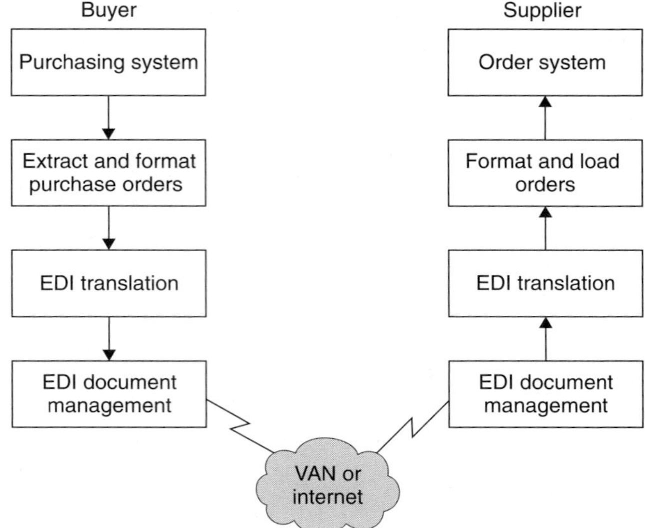

Figure 1: Steps in the EDI process

It is possible to outsource various steps in the EDI process. For example, some customers use a network service provider to perform the translation and EDI document management. Other companies may choose a less sophisticated approach to EDI. Commercial software is available that would allow a customer to enter the purchase order information; the software would translate the information into the EDI standard format and package it for delivery. Similarly, there is commercial software to receive EDI information, parse it into documents, and print the documents. Companies that use this technique often do not receive the full benefits of EDI.

The major EDI standards are discussed later in this chapter. There are two common communications network alternative for EDI: traditional EDI and Internet-based EDI. These two approaches are discussed in the remainder of this section.

Traditional EDI Communications

The earliest EDI communications configurations used proprietary protocols, which meant that EDI could take place only between trading partners with compatible systems (Witte et al. 2003). Some larger companies established their own systems for processing whereby their trading partners would connect directly to the host company to transmit and receive EDI transactions over dial-up or leased lines. The larger company acted as a hub, and its trading partners would link to it, much as spokes connect to a hub on a wheel (Arunachalam 2004). This arrangement created a problem for trading partners who might need special equipment to communicate using multiple independent spokes to connect to multiple hubs. This led to the development of value-added network (VAN) service providers.

One of the primary services offered by VANs is to serve as an exchange for EDI transactions among various trading partners. The VAN offers electronic mailboxes and distribution services to its customers. A trading partner can send its EDI transactions to the VAN over a communications link. The VAN will store the EDI transactions in the electronic mailbox of trading partners who subscribe to the same service, or forward the transactions to the service provider used by the trading partner. In addition to the electronic mailbox, VAN services can include translation services, connectivity, security, and an audit trail (Copeland and Hwang 1997). The mailbox feature means that a trading partner does not need to have a spoke to each of its trading partners, it needs only one spoke to its VAN service provider. The VAN can also provide immediate notification to companies or forward documents to companies to ensure that event-driven processes run smoothly (Copeland and Hwang 1997).

Traditional EDI has used leased lines or dial-up for trading partners to connect to their VAN service providers. This mechanism replaced the early proprietary systems, in which a large company would maintain its own mailbox system. The growth of the Internet as a ubiquitous, low-cost communications network has led to the development of Internet-based EDI alternatives.

Internet-Based EDI Communications

Multiple technical EDI implementation alternatives are possible through the Internet. There is not a single approach to Internet-based EDI that has become a standard. Some companies have tried to bypass expensive VAN providers by using the Internet to connect directly with trading partners. Since the Internet uses a common protocol, this approach does not carry the burden of supporting multiple proprietary communications configurations that created expense under the original proprietary approaches to EDI. Some companies still value the services provided by VANs, and have migrated their communications with their VAN over to the Internet.

Companies are using various approaches to conduct EDI over the Internet. One approach is to use EDI formats and then transmit them using protocols such as file transfer protocol (FTP) (dmx.com 2002) or electronic mail (Chan 2002). Another approach is having trading partners enter transactions directly into forms (Mount 2003), a technique that is sometimes labeled WebEDI or electronic forms interchange (EFI). Companies also use extensible markup language (XML) (Mount 2003; Zuckerman 2004) for exchanging business documents. The Internet is becoming the transmission medium of choice for EDI (Zuckerman 2004).

One issue common to all Internet alternatives is that of security. The Internet is a public network. Many companies are using encryption services such as secure hypertext transfer protocol (https) or virtual private networks (VPNs) to limit exposure. Security considerations are discussed further in a later section of this chapter.

Chan (2002) describes a technique for using electronic mail multipurpose Internet mail extension (MIME) protocol and traditional EDI standards to exchange business transactions. This approach involves an additional step at both the sending and receiving ends: the formatted EDI documents need to be converted to MIME at the sending side and back at the receiving end.

Global Exchange Services, a VAN service provider, offers software that allows companies to create forms online for its trading partners to enter information; the form is then converted to EDI format and sent to the company for processing (Mount 2003). Such arrangements can reduce the amount of technical expertise required of trading partners while still providing the benefits of EDI to the company hosting the Web site.

XML has become increasingly popular for exchanging documents over the Internet (Mount 2003). XML is a language that is used to define documents containing data. It separates the structure of the data from the content and display of the data, so it offers significant advantages compared to HTML. XML allows the definition of various document types, and then those document definitions can be used to transmit data over the Internet. XML document definitions could be established containing elements similar to EDI documents.

Similarly to EDI messages, XML/EDI messages could be sent via email, FTP, or other Internet communications protocol (Hsieh and Lin 2004). However, XML is slower than traditional EDI (Witte et al. 2003). Since XML messages are as much as nineteen times larger than traditional EDI messages, the difference is especially noticeable in larger transactions (Witte et al. 2003). Since XML can be read by Web browsers, it is expected that many small and medium-sized enterprises (SMEs) will use Web-based forms to read and create XML/EDI documents (Witte et al. 2003) Another problem of using XML is that most implementations do not use traditional EDI formats (Mount 2003; Zuckerman 2004). Some companies have mandated that their suppliers continue supporting traditional EDI formats (Zuckerman 2004).

EDI STANDARDS

Since EDI involves the electronic exchange of transactions in standard formats, it is necessary to develop standard formats for EDI to take place. Early EDI systems use proprietary standards. Proprietary standards created problems for companies that had to support multiple standards of different trading partners (Chan 2002). In the early 1970s, the transportation industry formed the Transportation Data Coordinating Committee (TDCC) to develop common standards for the industry (Hsieh and Lin 2004). The American National Standards Institute formed the Accredited Standards Committee X12 in

1979, and that group adopted the TDCC standards as the basis for national standards, now referred to as the X12 standards (Hsieh and Lin 2004). The X12 standards are widely used throughout the United States.

The X12 Standard

The X12 standard defines over 100 different types of transactions. The standard specifies the data content, structure, sequencing, and syntax for business transactions. Each type of business document is considered a transaction set. The X12 standard includes specifications for business documents such as invoice, payment order, request for quotation, response to request for quotation, and many more. The organization responsible for managing EDI standards in the United States is the Data Interchange Standards Association (DISA) (www.disa.org). In addition to updating the X12 standards, the organization is also involved with the development of international standards.

The X12 standard specifies data segments, groups of related data elements, for each transaction set. A data segment for a shipping notice could include the data elements related to the shipping address, and another for the billing address. The X12 standard also specifies a data dictionary for each transaction set that defines the exact content of the data elements.

The X12 standard also specifies transmission control standards for the electronic envelope used to interchange data. It is possible to include several types of transaction groups destined for the same recipient in a single interchange envelope. An example of the X12 interchange structure is shown in Figure 2. In this example, a single interchange envelope contains two purchase orders and one invoice grouped together for transmission to the same destination (customer). The interchange envelope is like a courier envelope that is sent from a source to a destination location; it includes address and tracking information. The envelope contains two groups of transactions: the first group contains two purchase orders, and the second group contains one invoice. Groups of the same type of transaction are bounded by headers and trailers. Similarly, each transaction is delineated by a header and trailer. Only one functional group header is needed for the purchase orders, but each purchase order has its own transaction set header and transaction set trailer to separate the documents. The invoice group has its own group header and footer, and the invoice transaction has a transaction header and trailer to mark its boundaries.

UN/EDIFACT Standards

In 1986, the United Nations created a group to develop international standards for EDI, the United Nations Electronic Data Interchange for Administration, Commerce, and Transport (UN/EDIFACT) (Hsieh and Lin 2004). The UN/EDIFACT standard combined the X12 standard from the United States with the Trade Data Interchange (TDI) standard developed in the United Kingdom (Chan 2002), and includes components similar to the X12 standard. Some users claim that one standard has technical advantages over the other. In practice, many U.S. companies still rely on the X12 standard. However, UN/EDIFACT is in widespread use, and companies that want to compete internationally may need to support it (Witte et al. 2003). UN/EDIFACT is widely used in finance and banking, in transport and logistic chains, and in fast-moving consumer goods, and is recommended by the World Customs Organization for customs documents. There are many companies that support both standards.

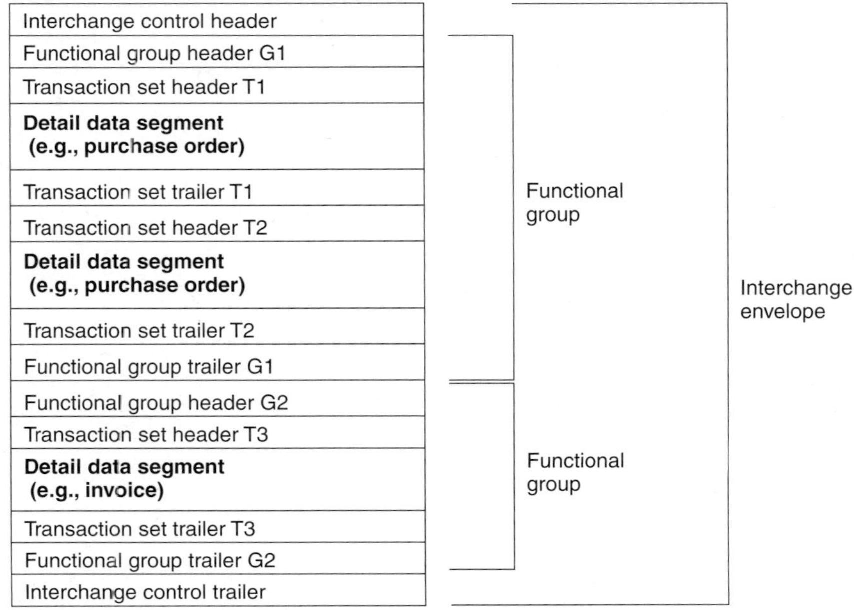

Figure 2: X12 EDI interchange structure

Other Standards

The growth of Internet-based EDI has seen the call for new EDI standards. One of the impediments to using XML for EDI has been the lack of standards, or, more accurately, the proliferation of standards (Zuckerman 2004). Although some companies are using traditional EDI standards and simply using the Internet as the communications network, others want to design standards that might be better suited to the Internet.

Today there are efforts to develop extensions to XML that will provide standard mechanisms for XML/EDI. DISA is working to develop extensions, based on the X12 standard, to support XML/EDI. Another standard being developed for EDI is electronic business XML (ebXML) The development of ebXML is being led by the United Nations Centre for Trade Facilitation and Electronic Business (UN/CEFACT) and the United Nations Economic Commission for Europe (UNECE), in coordination with the Organization for the Advancement of Structured Information Standards (OASIS) (Butterly and Misovicova 2006). The ebXML standard may replace UN/EDIFACT in the long term, especially for SME trading partners (Hsieh and Lin 2004). It is already widely used in Europe and Asia, and the U.S. Department of Defense and automobile industry are adopting it (Babcock 2004). One goal of the developers is to develop an electronic exchange standard that would be affordable by both large and small companies, including companies that cannot afford EDI's complexity and expense (Babcock 2004). If this goal can be achieved, it would mean that e-business could be done throughout the world by large and small businesses alike.

Industry Conventions

Although EDI standards specify common formats for transactions, many industries have adopted conventions for how they will implement those standard formats. In some cases an industry may use an older version of the standard to ensure that companies use common conventions (Hsieh and Lin 2004). The automotive, airline, and chemical industries have each developed a set of conventions to specify how EDI standards should be implemented in their respective industries. Having a common understanding of how to implement EDI can make EDI implementation faster and less costly.

EDI IMPLEMENTATION AND BEST PRACTICES

This section provides guidelines for the successful implementation of EDI. Before proceeding with EDI implementation, a company must examine its EDI strategy. More accurately, the company must look at how its information systems (IS) strategy will support its business strategy, and how EDI can play a part. For example, a logistics transport company that has a business strategy to reduce delivery times might implement EDI for customs forms to help support that strategy.

When companies consider using EDI, they should first evaluate the underlying business processes in order to be able to obtain EDI's full benefits (Down 2002). Business process reengineering may be required. As mentioned earlier, entire industries are changing processes to improve business performance.

Successful implementation relies on the development of strong relationships with trustworthy trading partners. Developing trust with trading partners is important to successful EDI implementation (Ruppel et al. 2003). Traditionally, EDI has taken place between companies that are already trading partners before engaging in EDI between themselves. Companies need to assess the preparedness of trading partners to use EDI. Trading partners in the SME category may need technical, administrative, or financial assistance. Doing business electronically may impose new concerns, and a part of many EDI solutions is a trading partner agreement (TPA) (Down 2002).

Using EDI in certain industries may dictate particular standards and influence the choice of hardware and software. A company that deals with many SMEs may choose to use Web-based forms to reduce the technical complexity for its trading partners.

Companies need to pay careful attention to implementation in order to obtain the full range of benefits possible through EDI (Angeles et al. 2001). Technical details of implementation are important because they affect costs, benefits, and security issues (Banerjee and Kumar 2002). Technical issues of implementation include selecting the EDI technologies, developing the infrastructure to support EDI, and interfacing EDI tools with existing systems.

Companies also need to identify and assess potential security risks. Certain types of data may be more inviting targets, or may result in more severe consequences if compromised. Some trading partners may not have adequate security measures in place. Technical or administrative assistance may be necessary with some trading partners. Companies should promote the benefits of EDI both internally and with trading partners.

Proper administrative and technical security controls need to be included in EDI implementation. User training is often required to prevent accidental errors. System controls should be evaluated and tested prior to implementation and reviewed after implementation.

EDI SECURITY

Since EDI involves both technical and administrative components, EDI security must involve both technical and administrative controls. Research has found that adequate security is one of the factors that contributes to successful EDI implementation by U.S. firms for both domestic and international EDI (Angeles et al. 2001). The discussion in this section provides an overview of the steps necessary to secure EDI applications. For a more comprehensive understanding of EDI and its underlying technologies, the reader should refer to *The Handbook of Information Security* (Bidgoli 2006), which includes a chapter on EDI security and chapters on many of the technologies used to implement EDI.

EDI Threats

The primary threats to EDI systems are: (1) interception (unauthorized access to data), (2) interruption (prevention of transaction completion), (3) modification (intentional or unintentional loss or destruction of data), and (4) fabrication (fraudulent transactions). EDI data can be intercepted at any point in the EDI process. The greatest interception threats occur when data are in transit, particularly if the Internet is used as the communications network. Data interception can also take place while data reside on a computer accessible to the Internet during the EDI process. The EDI process is also susceptible to interception. Since the EDI process involves multiple software packages and multiple hardware platforms, any one of these components could be attacked or fail.

Modification of EDI data can be intentional or unintentional. Unintentional modifications could include incorrect information coming from the originating system or incorrect extraction and formatting of the data, or errors in transmission. The most likely threats of intentional modification are from people who work with the systems from which the data originate or ultimately reside. Fraudulent transactions are a great threat to EDI systems (Smith 2005). The threat comes from a lack of proper administrative controls and system controls in systems that originate EDI data. The following section suggests some ways to deal with these threats.

EDI Security Mechanisms

There are five general types of security mechanisms for reducing the security risks for EDI systems: access control; authentication (originator and receiver); nonrepudiation (originator and receiver); data integrity (content and sequence); and auditable history/paper trail. The EDI security mechanisms are summarized in Table 1.

The issue of who is able to obtain and view the transaction and under what circumstances is the central focus of access control. Access controls must be in place for: (1) transaction origination, (2) the duration of the transaction transmission, and (3) transaction receipt. Transaction origination and receipt should be restricted to authorized users or applications. Organizations frequently use controls requiring user identification and a password to gain access to such systems. Encryption is one technique for securing data in transit.

Authentication concerns the verification that a transaction is genuine and authorized. Techniques used for authentication include digital signatures or digital certificates. The use of user IDs and passwords may also be part of authorization. Using acknowledgments of transactions can also help with authentication. Nonrepudiation (of transaction origination) provides the recipient of the message with proof that a message has been sent, and the proof should withstand any attempt by the originator to deny sending the message (Humphreys 1995). Similarly, there is a need for authentication on the receiver side of the exchange so that the receiver cannot deny that it received the transaction. Trading partners can use acknowledgments (and save these) as proof of transactions.

Data integrity means the content and sequence of the message is valid, accurate, and complete. Transmission errors are possible with EDI transactions. It is also possible that someone could tamper with EDI transactions. The EDI transaction process needs to ensure data integrity. The document-handling software that receives EDI messages with traditional EDI can check that the message is a valid EDI message. The translation software can also perform some checking. Some EDI systems are set up to use hash totals that are calculated by the originator and then recalculated and checked by the receiver (Sterling Commerce 2003; Waksmunski 1996).

The last security mechanism that can be used is to ensure there is an auditable history maintained so that one can verify the entire transaction process. This may be necessary for accounting purposes. Since EDI involves electronic exchanges, it offers little in the way of a paper trail.

Table 1: Mechanisms EDI Security

Mechanism	Description
Access control	Limit who is able to obtain and view the transaction and under what circumstances.
Authentication	Verify that the transaction is genuine and authorized by the trading partner.
Nonrepudiation	Validate through undeniable proof that the partner participated in the transaction.
Data integrity	Ensure the content and sequence of the transaction is valid, accurate, and complete.
Auditable history	Maintain a complete record of the transaction process.

EDI APPLICATIONS

EDI applications have been in use for more than 30 years. During that time, new standards have emerged and new technologies have been used to implement EDI. The two applications described in this section portray the evolution of EDI applications and illustrate the latest direction in EDI applications.

EDI at Sega

The description of EDI applications at Sega is summarized from a description provided by Cohen (2005). Sega is a maker of gaming software that runs on other manufacturers' game consoles; it first implemented an EDI system in 1994. Sega found that its original system had become obsolete and could not keep up with the 7000 orders per month that came from customers that included Target, Wal-Mart, Toys R Us, and Circuit City. Sega's old system used a slow, 9600-baud modem that could take nearly 2 hours to send order information to Sega's warehouses. Several years before Sega converted its EDI system, it invested in an 18-month project to upgrade to a new version of its EDI system. In 2004, before the conversion of the EDI system, information had to be batch loaded into Sega's enterprise resource planning (ERP) system.

The business need that drove Sega to convert its system was Wal-Mart's requirement that it support AS2 (applicability statement 2), an Internet-based EDI standard that uses MIME and HTTP for real-time process-to-process EDI (Down 2002). Sega evaluated various vendors' alternatives and ultimately selected one because it had existing adapters and reusable templates that would reduce the time needed to customize the application. The system was also designed to work tightly with its ERP system, had a graphical user interface, and could break a purchase order from a single retailer into multiple separate orders for different locations.

With the help of its EDI solution vendor, Sega was able to do its initial implementation of the new system in 3 months, including customizing document templates for eight types of documents, and meet the EDI formats required by twenty-five trading partners. By the end of 9 months, Sega had phased in all of its other trading partners. Compared to its pervious EDI system, Sega has saved money on transaction costs by eliminating its VAN, improved the processing time for EDI transactions, and achieved tighter integration in its business processes. The new system also had a shorter training time for educating its EDI specialists.

EDI in the Chemical Industry

The description of EDI applications in the chemical industry is summarized from a description provided by Vinas (2005). This example also provides some historical perspective on the development of EDI. Researchers have suggested that this is the direction for future growth of EDI (Arunachalam 2004; Christiaanse 2005).

The chemical industry was one of the first to adopt EDI due, in part, to pressure from the auto industry. The Chemical Industry Data Exchange (CIDX) was formed in 1985 to develop standards for the exchange of data within the industry. Since that time, the group has developed its fourth version of its standards, Chem eStandards, for electronic commerce among chemical companies.

The chemical industry moved to EDI in order to lower costs; many chemicals are commodities and have low margins. The chemical industry is characterized by many chemical companies trading with other chemical companies, a characteristic that made adoption and implementation of EDI less costly and more beneficial. Most chemical sales take place via EDI today, but much of that is Internet-based EDI.

The chemical industry is now moving to Elemica, an exchange formed in the early 2000s, that uses the Chem eStandards. Elemica is a vertical industry hub for the chemical industry (Christiaanse 2005). The collaborative effort has resulted in further efficiencies in industry trading (Christiaanse 2005), and is characteristic of the new EDI configurations. Elemica accounts for about 10 percent of sales within the chemical industry. The industry is considering shifting to XML, but many companies are reluctant to give up their investments in EDI.

CONCLUSION

Electronic data interchange has been in use for over 30 years. Early applications of EDI used proprietary protocols and focused on efficiency improvements. Since that time, national and international standards for EDI have evolved, and new communications technologies are available for implementing EDI network applications. Much EDI activity has moved to the Internet, and Internet-based EDI is the fastest-growing type of EDI. The development of EDI standards and conventions for Internet-based EDI will increase the rate of EDI applications, though EDI already accounts for over 80 percent of B2B e-commerce.

Although EDI offers benefits of efficiency to large users of EDI, smaller companies are also able to benefit from EDI. Companies are using EDI to support a variety of business strategies, including JIT inventory management, SCM, and CRP. Since EDI involves both technical and administrative aspects, companies need to pay attention to technical details of implementation as well as to administrative arrangements. Administrative issues include trading partner agreements, developing trust in trading partner relationships, and reengineering business processes. Ensuring the security of EDI network applications requires both technical and administrative controls.

Traditional users of EDI, such as Sega, are upgrading their infrastructures to obtain greater benefits from EDI, often reducing the costs of EDI at the same time. The chemical industry is at the forefront of EDI. Network applications of EDI in the chemical industry are expanding beyond dyadic relationships to include marketplace hubs that will provide even higher levels of benefits to participating companies.

GLOSSARY

DISA (Data Interchange Standards Association): The organization responsible for the development of EDI standards in the United States.

ebXML (Electronic Business XML): An extension to XML designed to accommodate electronic business.

EDI Electronic data interchange, the computer-to-computer exchange of business transactions in standardized formats.

Internet-Based EDI: The use of the Internet as the communications mechanism for electronic data interchange.

IOIS (Interorganizational Information Systems): Automated information systems that involve information sharing between two organizations.

UN/EDIFACT: A set of standard formats for EDI transactions developed by a committee from the United Nations (UN).

VAN (value-added network): A company that provides a network and various other services for EDI.

CROSS REFERENCES

See *Electronic Payment Systems; Terrestrial Wide Area Networks; The Internet Fundamentals*.

REFERENCES

Angeles, R., C. L. Corritore, S. C. Basu, and R. Nath. 2001. Success factors for domestic and international electronic data interchange (EDI) implementation for US firms. *International Journal of Information Management* 21:329–47.

Arunachalam, V. 2004. Electronic data interchange: An evaluation of alternative organizational forms. *Accounting, Organizations and Society* 29(3)4:227–41.

Babcock, C. 2004, March 1. What's behind electronic business XML. *Information Week*. www.informationweek.com/story/showArticle.jhtml?articleID=18201094 (accessed June 2, 2004).

Banerjee, S., and R. L. Kumar. 2002 Managing electronic interchange of business documents. *Communications of the ACM* 45(7):96–102.

Bidgoli, H., ed. 2006 *Handbook of information security*. Hoboken, NJ: Wiley.

Butterly, T., and M. Misovicova. 2006. List of UNECE UN/CEFACT Recommendations on Trade Facilitation. www.UNECU.org/cefact/recommentations/rec_summary.pdf (accessed July 3, 2006).

Chan, S. C. 2002. Introduction to electronic data interchange (EDI). home.hkstar.com/~alanchan/papers/edi (accessed May 15, 2002).

Choudhury, V. 1997. Strategic choices in the development of interorganizational information systems. *Information Systems Research* 8(1):1–24.

Christiaanse, E. 2005 Performance benefits through integration hubs. *Communications of the ACM* 48(4):95–100.

Cohen, R. C. 2005 EDI platform upgrade keeps Sega at top of game. *Frontline Solutions* June:37–8.

Cooke, J. A. 2002 Is XML the next big thing? (Maybe not for a while). *Logistics Management & Distribution Report* 41(5):53, 55–6.

Copeland, K. W., and C. J. Hwang. 1997. Electronic data interchange: Concepts and effects. In *INET 97 Proceedings*. www.isoc.org/inet97/proceedings/c5/c5_1.htm (accessed May 22, 2002).

dmx.com. 2002. The basics of electronic commerce and electronic data interchange. www.dmx.com/edibasic.html. (accessed May 17, 2002).

Down, A. 2002. Integrating EDI systems across and beyond your enterprise. IBM White Papers. www-3.ibm.com/software/integration/wdi/library/whitepapers/edi_v1c.pdf. (accessed January 6, 2005).

Elgarah, W., N. Falaleeva, C. S. Saunders, V. Ilie, J. T. Shim, and J. F. Courtney. 2005. Data exchange in interorganizational relationships: Review through multiple conceptual lenses. *The Data Base for Advances in Information Systems* 36(1):8–29.

Hart, P. J., and C. S. Saunders. 1998. Emerging electronic partnerships: Antecedents and dimensions of EDI use from the supplier's perspective. *Journal of Management Information Systems* 14(4):87–111.

Hsieh, C., and B. Lin. 2004. Impact of standardization on EDI in B2B development. *Industrial Management & Data Systems* 104(1/2):68–77.

Humphreys, T. 1995. Electronic data interchange (EDI) messaging security. In *Information security: An integrated collection of essays*, edited by M. D. Abrams, S. Jajodia, and H. J. Podell, 423–38. Los Alamitos, CA: IEEE Computer Society Press. www.acsac.org/secshelf/book001/18.pdf (accessed July 9, 2007).

Iacovou, C. L., I. Benbasat, and A. S. Dexter. 1995. Electronic data interchange and small organizations: Adoption and impact of technology. *MIS Quarterly* 19(4):465–85.

Laudon, K. C., and J. P. Laudon. 2006. *Management information systems: Managing the digital firm*. 9th ed. Upper Saddle River, NJ: Pearson Education.

Lee, H. G., T. Clark, and K. Y. Tam. 1999. Research report: Can EDI benefit adopters? *Information Systems Research* 10(2):186–95.

Lee, S., K. Lee, and I. W. Kang. 2005. Efficiency analysis of controls in EDI applications. *Information & Management* 45(3):425–39.

Massetti, B., and R. W. Zmud. 1996. Measuring the extent of EDI usage in complex organizations: Strategies and illustrative examples. *MIS Quarterly* 17(1):63–84.

McGowan, M. K., and G. R. Madey. 1998. The influence of organization structure and organizational learning factors on the extent of EDI implementation in U.S. firms. *Information Resources Management Journal* 11(3):17–27.

Mount, I. 2003, August 1. Why EDI won't die. *Business 2.0*. http://money.cnn.com/magazines/business2/business2_archive/2003/08/01/346303/index.htm (accessed January 6, 2005).

Raghunathan, S., and A. B. Yeh. 2001. Beyond EDI: Impact of continuous replenishment program (CRP) between a manufacturer and its retailers. *Information Systems Research* 12(4):406–19.

Riggins, R. J., and T. Mukhopadhyay. 1994. Interdependent benefits from interorganizational systems: Opportunities for business partner reengineering. *Journal of Management Information Systems* 11(2):37–57.

Ruppel, C., L. Underwood-Queen, and S. Harrington. 2003. The roles of trust, security, and type of e-commerce involvement. *e-Service Journal* 2(2):25–45.

Smith, A. D. 2005. Accountability in EDI systems to prevent employee fraud. *Information Systems Journal* Spring:30–8.

Sterling Commerce. 2003. E-business data exchange: Surviving the security audit, www.sterlingcommerce.com/apps/WhitePapers/DownloadPaper.asp?ID=6 (accessed September 9, 2003).

Vinas, T. 2005. E-commerce early bird. *Industry Week* 254(4):60–1.

Waksmunski, D. 1996. Electronic data interchange security and information assurance. In *A View to the Future: 1996*, www.gitec.org/pubs/view96 (accessed May 17, 2002).

Witte, C. L., M. Grunhagen, and R. L. Clarke. 2003. The integration of EDI and the Internet. *Information Systems Management* 20(4):58–65.

Zuckerman, A. 2004. EDI messages still keep info flowing along the global supply chain. *World Trade* 17(10):60–4.

Electronic Payment Systems

Indrajit Ray, *Colorado State University*

INTRODUCTION

Throughout the ages, from ancient times to the present, money has played a very important role in the ordinary business of the life of different people. Money can be best defined as "anything that is widely used for making payment and accounting for debts and credits"(Davies 2002). All sorts of things have been used as money at different times in the history of mankind, including amber, beads, cowries, drums, eggs, feathers, gongs, hoes, ivory, jade, kettles, leather, mats, nails, oxen, pigs, quartz, rice, salt, thimbles, umiacs, vodka, wampum, yarns, and zappozats (decorated axes) (Davies 2002). In recent times, we are witnessing the emergence of a more intangible form of money—namely, electronic money. In fact, although much of the money used by individuals in their day-to-day transactions is still in the form of notes and coins, its quantity is minuscule compared to the intangible electronic money that exists only as records in the books of financial institutions. With the progression of technology we can envision a society, in the not-too-distant future, in which physical money in the form of notes and coins will become as obsolete as amber and beads and cowry shells.

In this chapter, we look at electronic payment systems. These systems enable the payment for goods and services over a computer network using some form of electronic money. We begin by identifying the requirements for such systems. We observe that the major technical challenge for developing such a system is ensuring its security. We discuss the different types of electronic payment schemes that are available, identifying, in the process, any special security or network requirement for each. However, we do not cover the different technologies that are used to provide these services. These are covered elsewhere in this book. Interested readers are directed to Volume II, Parts 2 (The Internet, Global Networks, and VoIP) and 3 (Cellular and Wireless Networks), and Volume III, Part 2 (Network Planning, Control, and Management). We discuss some of the more important commercial/research products available today. Finally, we conclude by providing pointers to some of the resources that are available today to learn more about electronic payment systems.

REQUIREMENTS FOR ELECTRONIC PAYMENT SYSTEMS

Electronic payment systems have more or less the same set of requirements as traditional paper-based systems. The difference is that owing to the unique nature of electronic payment transactions, these requirements impose different types of challenges on the payment system design and the infrastructure support. Security is of paramount importance in electronic payment systems, more so probably than in traditional paper-based system. The reasons for this are numerous. First, a major portion of these transactions is carried out over networks, which are rather easy to eavesdrop on even with limited resources. Thus, confidential financial information may no longer remain confidential if adequate protection mechanisms are not implemented. Second, since the transacting parties can remain faceless, it is quite easy to forge identities of end users and systems in the Internet. Anybody can masquerade as somebody else and continue on a transaction with impunity. Gathering evidence of a crime is, thus, more difficult in such an environment. Third, electronic payments are often carried out over inherently unreliable communication media. This implies that messages that are exchanged for execution of the transaction can be corrupted or altered during transit, resulting in unforeseen results. Last, but not least, electronic payment transactions can span both geographical and judicial boundaries. While this is also possible for traditional payment transactions, the implications for electronic payments are different. It is more difficult to identify a felon in an electronic payment crime and bring her or him to justice.

We begin by summarizing the requirements for electronic payment systems. These challenges can be categorized as network bandwidth requirements (including availability requirements) and security requirements. We observe that while bandwidth and availability requirements are important issues for electronic payment systems, security requirements by far pose the biggest challenge to the widespread deployment of electronic payment systems. In later sections, as we discuss different types of payment systems, we identify specific challenges for each.

Network Requirements

To increase productivity and competitiveness, financial institutions are increasingly relying on computer networks to connect offices, partners, suppliers, and most importantly, customers. As the volume of financial transaction increases, the payment infrastructure must scale up with it appropriately. Servers must be powerful enough to support the rapidly expanding customer base. Communication channels with higher bandwidths need to be established to support the high volume of traffic. To support the real-time requirements of most financial transactions, networks supporting high transmission speeds are also needed. In addition, any disruption of telecommunications services critically affects financial-services processes. Without telecommunications capabilities being always available most financial services companies will be able to provide nothing better than the barest minimum of services. Thus, network resiliency is an important consideration for the financial sector.

Network availability can be compromised because of failures in the network as well as malicious attacks. The first step toward achieving resiliency is to have redundancy in the network. Redundancy ensures that a single point of failure does not disrupt services. Redundancy is achieved by having multiple routes for network traffic from the source to the destination, multiple telecommunications circuits, and/or alternative communications technologies. Although redundancy ensures a significant degree of fault tolerance, by itself it cannot ensure availability in the face of deliberate attacks. To protect against attacks, diversity needs to be incorporated into the network infrastructure. Proper diversity management can ensure that redundant assets do not share common vulnerabilities, thus protecting a network from intentional attacks. Diversity in the network can be achieved through a number of means—(a) obtaining network services from a number of different providers, (b) including alternative communication means (e.g., wired, microwave, radio wave, or satellite), and (c) providing physically and logically separate routes for a transmission. However, even with these measures, failures can still occur. Thus, the network should be able to recover from these failures in a proper manner. This ensures that the affected financial service is restored after a transient failure. Response time is the most important parameter for recovery procedures. A number of measures can help with the recovery process, including proper network management control and using synchronous optical network technology (see the chapter "SONET/SDH Networks").

Security Requirements

Need to Ensure Integrity for Payer, Payee, and Payment System

The first major rules of thumb in designing any payment systems is to ensure that (1) nothing happens without authorization, and (2) nothing happens without generating sufficient pieces of evidence. Moreover, technical and legal procedures for dispute handling should be made part of the system.

Ensuring proper authorization by itself is not a very big challenge. All that is needed is a provision for signatures, maybe notarized, at the right place for the authorization to be recorded. (The reader is referred to the chapter "Cryptography" for discussion on techniques for obtaining digital signatures.) This needs to be accompanied by proper identification of the signatory and correct association of the signature to the signatory. (Techniques for authentication and authorization are discussed in more detail in the chapters "Access Control" and "Biometrics".) However, in the context of electronic payment systems, authentication and authorization is more easily said than done. To begin with, although a digital counterpart of traditional signatures has been available for some time, some with even stronger non-forgeability properties than traditional signatures, the technology and infrastructure for these are not yet widely available. Many communities have yet to establish laws that recognize the validity of such digital signatures.[1] Compounding the problem is the technical difficulty associated with identifying and authenticating the signatory. Users of computer systems remain faceless throughout a transaction. Thus, although it is easy to authenticate the process that is used in the transaction, it is extremely difficult to associate the process with a real-life entity. This implies that it is quite easy for the digital signatory of a document to refute a signature later.

Generating sufficient pieces of evidence for electronic payments is also considerably difficult. This requires a proper audit trail of a transaction to be maintained during the entire transaction life cycle and until such time as it is no longer needed. In addition, we must ensure that such audit trails are not tampered with after generation. This is quite difficult to ensure, especially if we impose the requirement that such audit trails and other associated information may often need to be transmitted over open, unreliable networks. With currently available technology, it is not possible to completely prevent tampering with audit trails. We must accept that there will be times when such tampering occurs. Obviously, this creates a number of technical challenges when disputes need to be handled based on audit-trail data. Thus, in the event of audit-trail tampering, we should be able to detect and prove the tampering. Further, we should have proper contingency plans for such an eventuality. Although the technology to perform these individually has been available for many years, an integrated mechanism that incorporates the

[1]Currently, there are only handful of countries that recognize digital signatures as legal. The Digital Signature Law Survey at http://dsls.law.uvt.nl provides comprehensive information about countries that have enacted statutes concerning digital signatures or are in the process of doing so.

individual technologies into a cohesive framework that is also supported by proper legal and procedural methodologies is still not widely available.

Privacy for Payer and Payee

The requirement for ensuring payer and payee privacy arises in much the same way in electronic payment systems as in traditional payment systems. Users of the electronic payment system need the assurance that their financial information remains confidential throughout the transaction—that only such information as the user deems necessary to reveal is actually revealed. Further, the user needs the assurance that the recipient does not use the piece of confidential information that is revealed in an improper manner. Each of these requirements is extremely difficult to ensure in the electronic world.

To begin with, many electronic payment transactions are carried over open networks such as the Internet. Such networks are susceptible to eavesdropping. Thus, if appropriate precautions are not adopted, any financial information that is transmitted is available to whoever is eavesdropping. The solution to this problem is to encrypt the information in an appropriate manner before transmission. Many people believe that proper encryption is the panacea for all confidentiality problems. This, however, is not really the case. To begin with, we need to remember that a brute-force approach can always, in principle, break the strongest of currently available encryption technology. This is assuming that there is no hidden trapdoor in the encryption algorithm that makes the technique vulnerable. We can take some solace from the fact that such a brute-force approach is beyond the technical and physical capabilities of even the most powerful. However, we should realize that it is extremely difficult to prove formally that an encryption algorithm is strong. In fact, there is no theory that guarantees the strength of any conventional cryptographic systems. Traditionally, encryption systems have been considered strong when they have been used and tested for a reasonably long time without anybody knowing how to break them efficiently, in a practical and practicable manner. Such testing can prove the weakness of a particular scheme for a given level of effort; this cannot prove that there is no simpler approach to breaking the scheme. In addition, encryption technology is sometimes implemented incorrectly, just as buggy software. Thus, there can be loopholes in the software that performs the encryption operation that can be exploited to breach confidentiality. Ensuring that encryption software is foolproof is not an easy task.

Assuming that we can protect confidential information from prying eyes while in transit, we note that it is extremely difficult to ensure that the recipient treats confidential information in a confidential manner. For example, many of us use credit cards for purchasing services. The merchant stores such credit-card numbers electronically in its computer system. However, there is no guarantee that the merchant's computer systems are adequately protected. Although this is also the case for traditional financial transactions, we at least know to whom we are revealing confidential information. In the electronic world, the end parties are faceless. We may easily be led to believe that we are revealing information to trusted parties when we are not. In addition, we do not know whether the recipient handles the information in an appropriate manner.

A related problem is how to ensure the anonymity of the user of the electronic payment system. A user may want that not only that his or her financial information remain confidential but also that he or she remain anonymous in the transaction. If a user is using traditional cash in a transaction, the user remains anonymous. It is not possible to link a transaction that has been paid for by traditional cash to a particular customer. It is also not possible to derive any personal information about the customer from this transaction. In the electronic world, this is more difficult to achieve. Part of the reason is that every message that is used in the transaction can be traced to a source address. Complex cryptographic protocols are needed to achieve such anonymity or unlinkability. At the same time allowing anonymity creates additional problems, namely in the way of ensuring authenticity, proper authorization, and fair exchange.

Fair Exchange

In the classical business environment, a transaction essentially involves fulfillment of some obligation by two parties; a contract describes the penalties if either party fails to meet its obligation. Since each transacting party has an identifiable place of doing business, if any party behaves unfairly, that party can be physically approached and held accountable for its unfair behavior. In the electronic world, on the other hand, a party does not always have a physically identifiable place for doing business. After behaving unfairly in the electronic transaction, a party can simply vanish without a trace. In such cases, it may be next to impossible to enforce the penalties of the contract, leading to losses for the other party. For example, a customer buys a product from a merchant. The customer pays for the product in some electronic manner. However, once the merchant receives the payment the merchant never delivers the product. This causes financial loss for the customer. Thus, any electronic payment scheme must ensure that at the end of the protocol execution, either each transacting party receives the other's product or neither does. This is often referred to as the problem of fair exchange, and it is quite difficult to achieve, particularly if this needs to be accompanied by anonymity for the payer or the payee.

In summary, it is fair to say that though electronic payment systems make it easier to perform commercial transactions over the Internet, there are a number of challenges remaining to make the scheme successful. In the following section, we discuss some of the types of electronic payment systems available today. We also discuss some of the challenges unique to each scheme.

TYPES OF ELECTRONIC PAYMENT SYSTEMS

Electronic payment systems broadly use one of three forms of electronic money: (1) token money, (2) notational money, and (3) hybrid money.

Token money is similar to real cash. It is used in token-based or cash-like system. Transactions are performed with token money that has a certain value and must be brought to a central authority before consumers are able to make any transaction. These systems do not support the notion of debt. Electronic cash and electronic purse are the two major types of token money systems.

Notational money is used in credit/debit systems. The system consists of having an account and a central authority keeping a record of the amount in that account. Consumers exchange documents that are equivalent to value transfers. These exchanges consist of debiting the consumer's account and crediting the merchant's account. Systems using notational money can support the concept of fiscal debt. Electronic payment orders over the Internet and credit-card billing over the Internet are the two most well known systems that use notational money.

Hybrid money combines the features of both token money and notational money. Automated clearinghouses and electronic checks form the major system using hybrid money. In the following, we discuss each of these systems in more details.

Electronic Bill Presentment and Payment Systems

These systems allow companies to bill customers for their services and in turn receive payments from them electronically over the Internet. There are two types of presentment models:

1. Direct model—A company (that is, a seller of a service) delivers the bill to customers (buyers of services) via either the company's own site (seller-direct model) or the customer's site (buyer-direct model).
2. Consolidator model—Bills from multiple issuers are delivered to a single site to be presented later in aggregate to the consumer for payment. A consolidator acts as an intermediary, collecting or aggregating invoices from multiple sellers for multiple consumers. Consolidators are generally third parties who may additionally provide a variety of financial services such as escrow, insurance, credit ratings, etc.

The following steps are involved in a system based on the direct model.

1. Enrollment—For the seller-direct model, the consumer enrolls in the company's bill-processing system using a standard Web interface. For the buyer-direct model, the seller enrolls in the customer's Web site that has been set up for this purpose. The site at which bill information is exchanged is henceforth called the bill processor.
2. Presentment—This occurs in the following steps:
   a. The seller generates and/or transfers the invoice information to the bill processor.
   b. The consumer is informed that a bill is ready.
   c. The consumer accesses the bill-processing site to review and analyze the invoice information.
3. Dispute handling—The consumer may dispute a bill. To do this, the consumer contacts the seller for review of the bill.
4. Payment—This occurs in the following steps:
   a. The consumer authorizes either full or partial payment for the bill.
   b. If it is the seller-direct model, then the seller's financial institution processes the payment transaction; otherwise, the buyer's financial institution processes the transaction.
   c. The appropriate financial institution confirms payment execution—credit to account for seller-direct model and debit from account for buyer-direct model.
   d. The respective financial institution reports payment return or rejection information.

The consolidator model is very similar to the direct models. The differences are as follows:

1. Enrollment—Both the seller and the buyer have to register at the consolidator's bill-processing system.
2. Presentment and dispute handling are done using the consolidator as the intermediary.
3. Payment—The following steps are performed:
   a. The consolidator initiates the payment and reports the activity to the buyer and the seller.
   b. The payment transaction is processed by either the buyer's or the seller's financial institution. Sometimes, the consolidator assumes the role of a financial institution.
   c. The financial institutions confirm execution of the payment.
   d. Payment return or rejection information may be reported to both buyer and seller by their respective financial institutions.

Electronic bill or invoice presentment and payment systems are gaining considerable popularity among both buyers and sellers. The major reason is that these are much faster and more efficient than traditional systems. The advantage of the consolidator model over the direct model is that in this model both the seller and the buyer reduce the number of bill-processing sites with which each has to interact. The disadvantage is that each may have to pay a fee to the consolidator to avail of its services.

Credit-Card-Based Systems

Credit cards are by far the most popular form of online payments for consumers. Credit cards are widely accepted by merchants around the world. They offer a number of benefits for both the consumer and the merchant. A consumer is protected by a grace period during which he or she can dispute a credit-card purchase. A merchant has a high degree of confidence that a credit card can be safely accepted from an unknown and not trusted purchaser. Using a credit card to pay for online purchases is just as easy as using it for a conventional purchase from a store. Merchants who already accept credit cards in an offline store can accept them immediately for online payment because they already have a merchant credit-card account. Online purchases require an extra degree of security. This is because a credit-card holder is not present and cannot be identified as easily as he or she can be when standing at the cash register. Online credit-card services must somehow authenticate the purchaser as well as protect sensitive information as it is transmitted on the Internet.

A credit card, such as that offered by Visa or MasterCard, has a preset spending limit based on the user's credit limit; the credit limit is determined by the customer's credit history, income level, and total wealth. The limit ranges from a few hundred to several thousand dollars. The user uses these cards to purchase goods and services or obtain cash from participating financial institutions. The user is required to pay his or her debt during the payment period. He or she can pay off the entire credit balance or pay a minimum amount each billing period. Thus, the credit provided by a credit card is a revolving credit. Credit-card issuers, however, charge interest on any unpaid balance.

A purchase card, on the other hand, is a special-purpose credit card that provides a nonrevolving credit line to the bearer. Purchase cards are issued by employers to employees for the sole purpose of facilitating payment for purchases made by the employee on behalf of the employer.

A charge card, such as one from American Express, is similar to a credit card except that it does not carry a preset spending limit, and the entire amount charged to the card is due at the end of the billing period. Charge cards do not involve lines of credit and do not accumulate interest charges. The distinction between credit cards and charge cards is unimportant in the discussion of processing credit and charge cards for electronic payment; the collective term *credit card* is used here to refer to both types.

Payment using credit cards generally involves one or more financial institutions for the processing of payment information. For some credit-card systems, banks and other financial institutions serve as a broker between card users and the merchants accepting the cards. These types of arrangements are called closed-loop systems because no other institution (local bank, national bank, or other clearinghouse) is involved in the transaction. American Express and Discover are examples of closed-loop systems because there is exactly one franchise for each of those systems. Open-loop systems can involve three or more parties. Besides the customer's and the merchant's banks, a third party, called an "acquiring bank," is involved. The acquiring bank passes authorization requests from the merchant's bank to the customer's bank to obtain authorization for the credit purchase from the customer's bank. A response is sent back to the acquiring bank and on to the merchant. Similarly, the acquiring bank is responsible for contacting the merchant's bank and the many customers' banks to process sales drafts. The merchant's bank usually plays the role of the acquiring bank. Systems using Visa or MasterCard are the most visible examples of open-loop systems because many banks issue both cards. Unlike American Express or Discover, neither Visa nor MasterCard issues cards directly to consumers. Member banks are responsible for handling all the details of establishing customer credit limits. For this discussion, we will assume that there are four players involved in a payment-card transaction: the customer who uses a credit card, the merchant that accepts a credit card toward a payment, the acquiring bank, and the issuing bank.

The following steps are involved in credit-card processing:

1. The customer provides the credit-card information to the merchant using a secure online communication channel. The communication channel needs to be previously established between the customer, and the merchant and needs to provide security services such as authentication, confidentiality, and integrity.
2. The merchant processes credit-card payments using software provided by the acquiring bank. The software enables the merchant to submit the credit-card information electronically to the acquiring bank. Usually the merchant submits this information via a dedicated communication channel.
3. The acquiring bank sends a request to the issuing bank authorizing payment for the particular charge incurred by the customer. This request is typically sent over a protected financial services network.
4. The issuing bank either approves or declines the charge. If the charge is approved, the issuing bank puts a hold on the customer's account for the funds needed to satisfy the current charge and forwards an approval code to the issuing bank. If it is declined the issuing bank is notified.
5. The issuing bank sends the transaction (either the approval code or the decline information) back to the merchant.
6. The merchant completes the payment transaction.

Credit cards have several features that make them an attractive and popular choice to both consumers and merchants in online and offline transactions. For merchants, credit cards provide fraud protection. When a merchant accepts credit cards for online payment, he or she can authenticate and authorize purchases using a credit-card-processing network. For consumers, credit cards are advantageous because various consumer credit protection acts limit the cardholder's liability to small amounts if a card is used fraudulently.

The biggest advantage of using credit cards is their worldwide acceptance. A user can pay for goods with credit cards anywhere in the world, and the currency conversion, if needed, is handled by the card issuer. For online transactions, credit cards are particularly advantageous. When a consumer reaches the electronic checkout, he or she enters the credit-card number and his or her shipping and billing information in the appropriate fields to complete the transaction. The consumer does not need any special hardware or software to complete the transaction.

Credit cards have very few disadvantages, but they do have one when compared with cash. Credit-card service companies charge merchants per-transaction fees and monthly processing fees. For example, MasterCard charges $0.29 plus 2 percent of the transaction value for each transaction. This is in addition to any fee that the acquiring bank may charge the merchant. Thus, credit-card transactions are quite expensive. However, online (and offline) merchants view them as a cost of doing business. Any merchant that does not accept credit cards for purchases is probably losing a significant number of sales because of it. In addition, credit cards typically provide a built-in safety net for merchants, as they have a higher degree of assurance that they will be paid through companies that issue credit cards. This makes credit cards generally lucrative to merchants for online payments. The consumer often does not pay any direct fees for using credit cards (there may be some fees, for example, when a credit card is used in a transaction in a foreign country requiring currency conversion), but the prices of goods and services are slightly higher than they would be in an environment altogether free of credit cards. A second disadvantage over cash is that obtaining a credit card is not trivial. The onus is on the consumer to demonstrate creditworthiness in order to get a credit card; thus, many may not qualify for credit cards, while anyone can get and use cash.

Debit-Card-Based Systems

Debit cards are another form of electronic payment system that falls somewhere between credit cards and personal checks. Though they look very much like credit cards, they operate differently. Unlike credit cards, which make funds available through a financial institution, debit cards are a way to pay now and to subtract money automatically from the cardholder's bank account. There are two types of debit cards—PIN-based or online debit cards, and signature-based or offline debit cards. They differ in the ways debit payments are processed.

PIN-based debit transactions are fast, convenient, and secure. It calls for customers to endorse payments by submitting a personal identification number (PIN) at the point of sale. The transaction is authorized in real time. Funds in the customer's account are set aside immediately to pay for the transaction. The money is transferred into the merchant's account in 2 to 3 business days. Merchants pay a nominal transaction fee, much lower than a typical credit-card transaction. The fact that customers authorize charges with PINs that are known only to them virtually eliminates the risk to merchants of charge backs. However, this type of debit transaction is currently available only in the physical world. This is because customers need access to a physical, discrete PIN-entry device (the PIN pad) that has to be integrated with the payment system. A number of financial institutions are introducing technologies that attempt to mimic the functionality of PIN pads. However, widely accepted operating standards have yet to be established.

Signature-based debit cards do not involve PINs. These are typically offered by credit-card companies, and may be used everywhere that credit cards are accepted. Merchants complete the debit sale in much the same way as credit sales. The transaction is processed through a credit-card-processing network for authorization. The customer signs the sales draft that authorizes the merchants to charge the customers' accounts. Transactions normally settle in 2 to 3 business days. Because these transactions are processed through the same networks as credit cards, they often incur the same transaction fees for the merchant.

Electronic Funds Transfer

The discussion of electronic payment systems would be incomplete without discussing electronic funds transfer (EFT) systems. An EFT transaction provides for electronic payment and collection. It is transfer of funds initiated through an electronic terminal, electronic mail, telephone, computer, or magnetic tape. It is comprised of the generation and delivery of instructions that directs a financial institution to either credit or debit a consumer's asset account. The term *EFT* itself does not refer to a specific product. Rather, it is a descriptor that defines payment vehicles that use electronic networks to conduct a transaction. Historically, the core of consumer EFT networks has been the automated teller machine and associated access cards. Currently, an EFT transaction involves payment processing through one or more of the electronic payment systems discussed earlier. The following are the most common EFT systems.

1. *Automated Teller Machines, or 24-Hour Tellers.* These electronic terminals let a customer perform banking at almost any time. Services offered through these computer systems, though limited, are quite comprehensive. Customers can withdraw cash, make deposits, query account balances, or transfer funds between accounts at the same bank. The customer initiates the transaction by inserting an ATM card and entering a PIN. The ATM card is encoded with the customer's account information on a magnetic strip. This information is transmitted to the bank's central computer by modem over either a dedicated telephone line or a normal dial-up telephone line. The information is protected via encryption during transmission. After proper authentication, the bank's central computer allows the ATM to complete the transaction. Banks have formed global networks so that a customer of one bank can use an ATM of another. Often ATM networks are also connected to credit-card and debit-card-processing networks. In these cases, the ATM machine allows a customer to use a credit or debit card; however, the customer is limited to withdrawing cash. Such transactions are processed as typical credit-card or debit-card transactions.
2. *Direct Deposit.* This lets the customer authorize specific deposits such as paychecks, stock dividends, and pensions to the customer's bank account either on a regular basis or on an ad hoc basis. It also allows the customer to preauthorize direct withdrawals so that recurring bills such as insurance premiums, mortgages, and utility bills are paid automatically. By completing

a standard enrollment form, a customer authorizes a company or organization to make a credit payment to or a debit payment from one or more of his or her accounts. The actual transaction is then processed over the automated clearinghouse (ACH) system as an ACH transaction.

3. *Pay-by-Phone Systems.* These systems let a customer call his or her financial institution with instructions to pay certain bills or to transfer funds between accounts. The customer must have a previous agreement with the bank for such transactions. Usually these transactions are limited to within the customer's own bank—that is, the customer cannot use a pay-by-phone system to transfer money between accounts at different banks. For services such as bill-pay, the bank uses a system such as ACH to complete the transaction. To use pay-by-phone, the customer dials a special phone number on a touch-tone phone to access the central computer of the bank. After proper authentication of the customer, usually through a PIN, the computer allows the customer to proceed with the rest of the transaction. Pay-by-phone systems typically offer a limited number of services. Moreover, these systems are not very secure. This is because of the inherent vulnerability of the public telephone network. The popularity of these systems is gradually waning and being replaced by personal computer banking.
4. *Personal Computer Banking.* This allows the customer to handle many banking transactions over the Internet via a remote computer. The system works very much like the pay-by-phone system. The customer uses a computer to connect to the central computer of his or her bank. After proper authentication, the customer is allowed to view account balances, request transfers between accounts, and pay bills electronically. Bill payment is processed offline as ACH transactions. The ability to use strong cryptographic techniques makes these systems more secure than pay-by-phone systems.
5. *E-Mail-Based Person-to-Person Payment.* This allows the customer to send a one-time payment instruction to a financial institution using e-mail. The financial institution authenticates the payment instruction by presenting some kind of a challenge to the payer. Once the challenge has been responded to in an appropriate manner, the financial institution credits the payee's account with the appropriate amount.
6. *Electronic Check Conversion.* This system converts a paper check into an electronic payment at the point of sale or elsewhere, such as when a company receives the customer's check in the mail. Electronic check conversion links two existing technologies—a magnetic ink character recognition (MICR) scanner and the ACH network. The paper check is processed through a MICR scanner to capture the check number, the number that identifies the customer's bank, and the customer's account number. The information is used to make a one-time electronic payment from the customer's account. The check itself is not the method of payment. This means that the cancelled check is not returned to the customer with his or her account statement.

Electronic Cash

Electronic cash (or e-cash) (Weber 1998) is a method of payment in which a unique number or identifier is associated with a given amount of money at a financial institution. It is often suggested as an alternative method to credit cards for purchases made over the Internet. Some definitions of electronic cash are much broader, describing it as any form of "prepaid, stored value that can be used for electronic purchases" (van Slyke and Belanger 2002). However, these systems are better categorized as electronic purse systems. The use of electronic cash requires the customer to open an account in a bank and then deposit money to this account. The bank provides the customer with a unique digital coin (essentially a unique identifier) that is used for all electronic payments.

Any electronic cash system needs to possess five characteristics if it is to be usable and universally accepted. First, it must be ensured that the electronic cash is spendable only once; that is, double spending should be prevented at all costs. This is needed to ensure that both parties involved in the transaction knows that the e-cash currency being received is not counterfeit or being used in two different transactions. Second, the e-cash system has to be independent of any particular proprietary storage or transmission mechanism. Third, electronic cash must be portable; it should be able to pass transparently across international borders and be automatically convertible to the recipient country's currency in all forms of peer-to-peer transactions. Fourth, electronic cash must be divisible. Divisibility determines the size of payment units. Both the number of different electronic cash units and their values can be defined independently of real currency. The denominations are up to the definers and are not limited to the typical breakdowns of a traditional cash system. Finally, e-cash systems should be anonymous, very much like their paper-world counterpart. The consumer (and sometimes the seller) should be able to use e-cash without revealing her or his identity. However, as explained later, ensuring the last property also makes the prevention of double spending rather difficult.

Double spending is extremely difficult to detect and/or prevent with truly anonymous electronic cash. Anonymous electronic cash is electronic cash that, like bills and coins, cannot be traced back to the person who spent it. To ensure anonymity or unlinkability of the customer, the payment protocol cannot associate any form of customer's identification mark with the cash system—much in the same way as in traditional cash systems. This implies that the bit string that represents electronic cash is not traceable to the customer who spends it. Since it is rather trivial to make multiple copies of the bit string representing cash, anybody can make counterfeit electronic cash, without fear of being caught and prosecuted. One way to be able to trace electronic cash (to prevent money laundering) is to attach a serial number to each electronic cash transaction. That way, cash can be positively associated with a particular consumer. This does not, however, solve the double spending problem completely. While a single issuing bank can detect whether two deposits of the same electronic cash are about to occur, it is impossible to ascertain who is at fault—the consumer or the merchant. If the duplicate electronic coins are presented to two different banks, the problem is exacerbated. Further, it is not easy to develop an electronic cash system in which the cash can be traced back to its origin. Complex cryptographic algorithms are needed to create tamperproof electronic cash that can also be traced back. Electronic cash containing serial numbers also raises a number of privacy issues, because merchants could use the serial number to track spending habits of consumers. The whole purpose of electronic cash systems—namely the ability of a customer to remain anonymous—is lost. It is important that a procedure is available both to protect the anonymity of electronic cash users and to provide built-in safeguards to prevent double spending.

One advantage of electronic cash is that like real cash it tends to be less costly to both merchants and consumers. This can make micropayments (where the value of the payment is comparable to or even less than the cost of the transaction) using electronic cash feasible. Micropayment fundamentally creates a new billing model, under which the individual items purchased can be billed separately and individually. With micropayment methods, consumers can download a song or a chapter of a book and be billed as little as 50 cents or a dollar, with that small amount being charged to their Internet service provider (ISP) or phone bill. Security issues with micropayments are primarily centered on the premise that a small charge would not require extensive use of encryption technology or other means of fraud prevention. The widespread use of micropayments is a potential breeding ground for fraud that today is not apparent. The lack of an authoritative infrastructure standard, coupled with strong network externalities, has limited micropayments from becoming a dominant means of value transfer.

Micropayment

Micropayment is a new model of electronic payment for goods or services in situations in which the cost to transact the payment by conventional means, such as credit cards or electronic checks, far exceeds the value of the actual payment. To make payments in a cost-effective manner, micropayment systems gather a large number of small payments intended for a specific merchant and batch process them for financial institutions as one single transaction. Micropayment systems are designed to support large numbers of small payments with the help of an intermediary broker. The broker acts on behalf of the merchant (maybe several merchants) to collect payment. Micropayment protocols can afford to have lesser security features for individual payments. This is because the amount of money lost on a single payment is considered within the range of tolerable risks.

Electronic Purse or Stored-Value Card

An electronic purse, as defined by the United Kingdom Banking Code, is "any card or function of a card which contains real value in the form of electronic money which someone has paid for in advance, and which can be reloaded with further funds and which can be used for a range of purposes." These are essentially prepaid stored-value cards. As with electronic cash systems, the consumer needs to deposit real money with the issuer of the purse. The amount of money deposited is then encoded into the card. As purchases are made using the electronic purse, the value in the card is reduced and the amount is credited to the merchant's account. The development of electronic purses has been driven almost wholly by commercial and technological organizations rather than by demand from consumers. The organizations operating electronic purse systems gain from the use of the money stored on the cards. For banks, there are advantages in reducing the handling of cash and checks, which have to be transported securely and are labor-intensive to handle. For the retailer, the advantages are the reduction in handling of currency and checks. This includes reducing the delay in money being credited to the retailer's bank account. Another advantage is reducing the risk of theft.

A stored-value card can be as elaborate as a smart card or as simple as a plastic card with a magnetic strip. One of the most common stored-value cards is a prepaid phone, copy, subway, or bus card. These cards can be recharged with more value by inserting them into special machines, inserting currency into the machine, and withdrawing the card. Another example is the retail store "gift card." These cards can be purchased at retailers for a fixed denomination. Most of the time, they cannot be recharged. Unlike smart cards, magnetic strip cards are passive. That is, they cannot send information such as a customer's digital certificate, nor can they receive and automatically increment or decrement the value of cash stored on the card. Smart cards evolved from magnetic strip cards. Instead of encoding and storing data using a magnetic strip, a computer microchip is embedded on the card itself, containing information about the owner, such as financial facts, private encryption keys, account information, credit card numbers, and so on. Like magnetic-strip cards, smart cards can be used online and offline. Smart cards are better suited for Internet payment transactions because they have more processing capability than the magnetic stripe cards.

Electronic purses have gradually become one of the most widely used electronic payment systems for consumers. The advantages include ease of use, ability to pay the exact amount without searching for change, no authorization requirement, and the possibility of depositing additional value as and when required. However, a major disadvantage from the consumer's point of view is that the purse is as good as real money. If it is lost or stolen, the consumer loses. To protect against such losses, smart-card technology is now being more widely used that allows units of credit to be reloaded. Another disadvantage, especially with retail store gift cards, is that they often come with expiration dates. If the card is not used within this period, the money is lost to the consumer. This provides a significant benefit to the issuer, however. A final shortcoming is that seldom is the card completely spent in one transaction. If the card is not rechargeable and the balance left in the card is not sufficient for another transaction, then the balance is, more or less, money lost to the consumer.

Electronic Wallets

Today's online shoppers have begun to tire of repeatedly entering details about shipping and payment information each time they make an online purchase. Research has shown that filling out forms rank high on online customers' lists of grievances about online shopping. Electronic wallet technology is intended to solve this problem. At the same time, an electronic wallet provides a secure storage place for credit-card data and electronic cash. In short, an electronic wallet (or e-wallet), serves a function similar to a physical wallet; it holds credit cards, electronic cash, owner identification, and owner contact information and provides that information at an electronic commerce site's checkout counter. Occasionally, an e-wallet may contain an address book. Some wallets also hold an encrypted digital certificate, which securely identifies the wallet's owner. E-wallets make shopping more efficient. An e-wallet simplifies the online checkout process. A simple click inserts the e-wallet information into the payment forms on the merchant's site. E-wallets can also provide many additional services. They can keep track of the owner's purchases by saving receipts. An enhanced digital wallet can even suggest where a consumer may find the best price on an item that he or she purchases on a regular basis.

E-wallets are of two types based on where they are stored. A client-side e-wallet stores a consumer's information on the consumer's own computer. This shifts the responsibility for ensuring the e-wallet's security to the end user. This can be regarded as both an advantage as well as a disadvantage. It is an advantage because the user has more control in keeping the e-wallet secure; it is a disadvantage because users may not always take appropriate measures. Many of early e-wallets were client-side wallets and required lengthy downloads, which was one of their chief disadvantages. Another disadvantage of client-side e-wallets is that they are not portable. They are not available when the owner is making a purchase at a location other than the computer on which the wallet resides. A server-side electronic wallet alleviates this problem; it stores a customer's information on a remote server belonging to a particular merchant or belonging to the wallet's publisher. The main weakness of server-side e-wallet is that a server-side security breach could reveal personal information for thousands of users. Server-side e-wallet systems typically use strong security measures that minimize or eliminate the possibility of unauthorized disclosure.

For a wallet to be useful at many online sites, it should be able to populate the data fields in any merchant's form at any site that the customer visits. This accessibility means that the e-wallet manufacturer and merchants from many sites must coordinate their efforts so that a wallet can recognize what consumer information goes into each of a given merchant's forms.

Electronic Checks

Electronic checks are a comparatively new and still emerging technology that combines high security, speed, convenience, and processing efficiencies for online transactions. They are based on the premise that electronic documents can be substituted for paper and public-key-cryptography-based digital signatures can replace handwritten signatures. Thus, the attraction is that electronic checks can replace paper checks without the need to create a new payment instrument, together with the implied legal, regulatory, and commercial practice changes. The technology promises several advantages. It leverages the time-tested paper-based check payment system and uses the same legal and business protocols. It works like a paper check but in a pure electronic form, with all the associated efficiency. It can be used by all bank customers who have check-signing privileges. Last but not least, it includes enhanced security features that allow automatic verification of content and validity, thereby helping to reduce check fraud.

Electronic checks work the same way as a traditional paper check does (see Figure 1.). The steps involved in electronic check processing can be summarized as follows:

1. The payer retrieves an "electronic check" from an "electronic checkbook" and electronically fills in the check just as he or she would fill in a paper check.

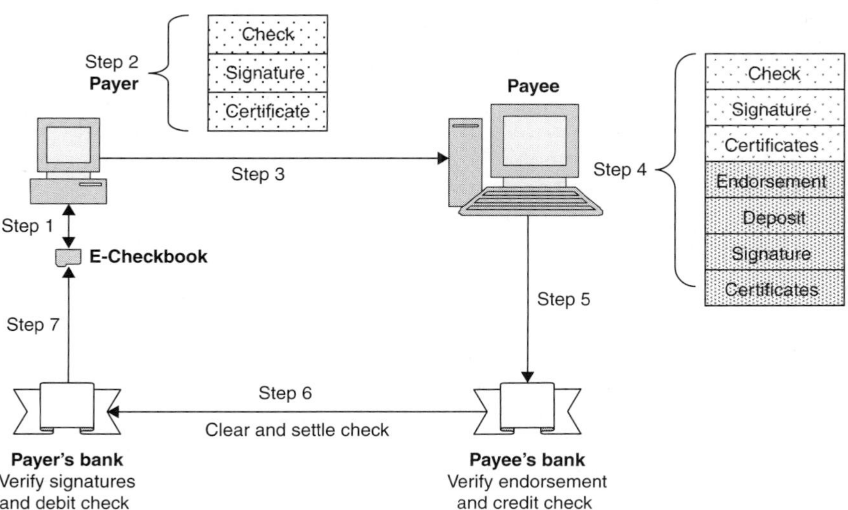

Figure 1: Steps involved in payment using electronic checks

2. The payer digitally signs the check and includes any necessary certificates with the check.
3. The payer then gives the electronic check to the payee using one of several secure electronic means (e.g., through secure e-mail or over secure Web connections).
4. The payee endorses the electronic check by putting its digital signature on the check.
5. The payee then electronically deposits the endorsed check in the payee's bank and receives credit.
6. The payee's bank submits (also electronically) the electronic check to the paying bank for clearing.
7. The paying bank validates the electronic check and then charges the payer's account for the check.

Mobile Payment System

With the rapid growth of wireless technologies (see Volume II, Part 3—Cellular and Wireless Networks) the financial industry is increasingly aiming toward providing mobile financial services to the end user. The vision is that the mobile communications channels will be used in financial transactions not only to complement communications over wired channels but also to usher in newer services that only mobility can enable. For example, stock alerts can be sent to wireless personal digital assistants (PDAs) so that the active trader can conduct transactions while on the move, independent of space and time constraints. Or, for example, the user can use a cellular phone for buying snacks from a vending machine. The rationale for such a vision is that mobile devices like cellular phones, wireless-enabled PDAs, and so on will increasingly become the platform of choice for users for managing their finances (e.g., accessing their bank accounts or investing in the stock market), making purchases in local environments (e.g., within a store) and remote environments (e.g., over the Internet), and securing authenticated access to various services.

Mobility can be accorded to electronic payment systems in one of three ways: (1) using wireless communication technology as a substitute for standard wired communication channels, and (2) using the new paradigm of contact-less payment. The first method is used mostly for traditional financial transactions like purchasing over the Internet. Broadband wireless access (see the chapter "Wireless Broadband Access") is typically used to support wireless access to data networks when this method is used from mobile laptops. When network access is desired using slower carrier-based mobile communication technology like global system for mobile (GSM) or code division multiple access (CDMA) communications as in PDAs or cellular phones, a still evolving standard called WAP (wireless application protocol—see the chapter "Wireless Application Protocol (WAP)") is used to support these applications. There are no major changes to the underlying payment protocols, and hence this method will not be discussed further in this section. The second method, on the other hand, is a relatively newer model of noncash electronic payment that has been enabled by emerging technologies such as Bluetooth (see the chapter "Bluetooth Technology") and wireless infrared communication (see the chapter "Indoor Wireless Infrared Communications"). The major characteristic of these technologies is the relative short communication range offered (typically in the range of a few centimeters for radio-frequency devices to tens of meters for Bluetooth-enabled devices). Thus, the second method finds widest adoption at retail point-of-sale terminals. Sometimes this method of payment is complemented by carrier-based mobile technologies such as CDMA and GSM.

Contact-less payment is based on establishing a wireless communication between a user's payment device that stores one of the forms of electronic money discussed earlier and a point-of-sale payment terminal or infrastructure device. The technology can be broadly classified into five major categories depending on the wireless communication method used—radio waves or infrared light. These are:

1. ISO 14443 proximity card standard–based methods
2. ISO 15693 vicinity card standard–based protocols
3. Proprietary radio-frequency technology–based protocols
4. Bluetooth-based systems
5. Payment systems by cellular service providers
6. Infrared communication based protocols

The first three use radio waves at different frequency levels for communication. The fourth and fifth technologies use microwaves, and the last uses line-of-sight infrared beams for communication.

ISO 14443–Based Proximity Devices

The ISO 14443 specifications provide the standard for contact-less smart cards that usually use the standard credit-card form defined by ISO 7810 ID-1. However, other forms are also used, such as watches and mobile phones. These devices use either low-frequency radio waves in the 125-KHz band (rare) or high-frequency radio waves in the 13.56-MHz band (most common) with a transmission speed in the range of 106 to 424 Kbps. The fast transmission speed allows the devices to be present in the proximity for a very short while for the transaction to be completed. The operational range of these devices is on the order of tens of centimeters. This means that the customer's payment device has to be in close proximity to the point-of-sale payment terminal. Thus, the customer cannot repudiate an intention to pay at a later time. In addition, although radio-wave communication is a broadcast technology in the sense that anyone with a suitable receiver can eavesdrop on the communication, the close proximity of the two devices helps limit unintended communication significantly. Broadcasting brings with it one more challenge—that of collisions. If more than one such device is placed within the communication field at the same time, there may be collisions among the packets transmitted between the different devices. ISO 14443 specifies how such collisions are handled.

Typically, these proximity devices are used as stored-value cards. They are widely used in automatic fare collection for mass-transit systems and offline purchases in vending machines. In recent years, smart cards have been provided with built-in microprocessors. These smart cards provide strong cryptographic protection of the communication channels and thus enable all the functionalities of contact smart cards. A number of credit-card providers, including Visa and MasterCard, are offering such ISO 14443–based smart cards that are also equipped with conventional magnetic stripes. These cards allow all the features of the conventional credit and debit cards from these groups in a contact-less manner.

ISO 15693–Based Vicinity Devices

The ISO 15693 specifications provide the standard for contact-less "vicinity cards." These devices come in various forms , such as key fobs, car tags, and plastic cards. Typically, these operate in the 13.56-MHz high-frequency range, like the ISO 14443 devices. However, they have a much slower transmission rate—typically around 20 Kbps. Thus, the devices need to be in the vicinity of the communicating device for a longer period for the transaction to be completed. The operation range of these devices is between 1 and 1.5 m. Although this can be a benefit for a number of applications, like parking and vending, it also brings in added security risks. Unlike ISO 14443 devices, ISO 15693 devices do not convey any payment intention on the part of the user. Thus, a user can repudiate a payment with the claim that a malicious attacker with a similar device had been in the vicinity and falsely made the charge. The possibility of eavesdropping increases for these devices, as does the possibility of unintended communications. This requires additional security measures to be incorporated within the devices. These devices broadcast the transmission like ISO 14443 devices. The ISO 15693 specifications address the problem of collisions during communication.

Vicinity devices find major application as electronic debit cards in closed systems like toll collection, gas pumps, and vending machines.

Proprietary Radio-Frequency Technology Systems

There have been attempts to develop proprietary contact-less payment devices for use in various closed systems. These use radio waves at different frequency bands: 100–300 KHz, 13.56 MHz, and 900–928 MHz. The operating ranges of these devices vary significantly. For example, the devices in the 13.56-MHz frequency range operate as proximity devices, while those operating in the ultra-high-frequency range (900+ MHz) provide an operating range of several meters. All the problems of the ISO 14443– and ISO 15693–compatible devices are also observed among these devices, and similar solutions have been proposed. Because of a lack of standardization, these devices have yet to find widespread usage.

Bluetooth-Based Systems

Bluetooth is a wireless technology that can be used to interconnect devices such as PDAs, laptops, digital cameras, mobile phones, etc. using a secure globally unlicensed short-range radio frequency. Bluetooth-enabled devices come in various power ranges (from 1 to 100 mW) that provide them with operating ranges of up to 100 m. There have been some attempts to develop payment applications based on Bluetooth. However, two major technical challenges impede the wide adoption of this technology for payment. First, Bluetooth does not provide a wide enough operating range to be used as an alternative to cellular services. They are primarily intended to facilitate IEEE 802.15–based personal area networks. This signifies that they can be used only for vicinity payment systems. In this context also, Bluetooth suffers because it does not offer any point-to-point localization, which is the second technical challenge.

Payment System by Mobile Carriers

The rapid growth of high-speed data networks, like 2.5 and 3G, has opened up the possibility of carrier-based mobile devices being used for electronic payment. A number of mobile service providers have teamed up with the financial services industry to form the Mobile Payment Forum (www.mobilepaymentforum.org), which is "dedicated to realizing the full potential of mobile commerce." Various technologies have been proposed, including using short/medium message service (SMS/MMS) messages for payment authorization and integrating mobile phones with ISO 14443/ISO 15693/proprietary radio-frequency devices. There is a continuing active interest in this area. However, as of today no significant system exists that provides contact-less payment using a carrier-based system. Lack of interoperability and the high total cost of ownership are often cited as the primary reasons why these systems have not become popular.

Infrared Communications–Based Protocols

The Infrared channel is one of the oldest wireless communication technologies. It provides a line-of-sight communication protocol—that is, the two communicating devices need to have an unobstructed view of each other in order to communicate. Infrared devices can theoretically communicate over several meters; however, an operational range of 20 to 30 cm is more practical and consumes very little power. Thus, infrared-enabled devices such as PDAs and mobile phones offer opportunities to be used as electronic "vicinity" payment devices. A number of projects have looked into maintaining mobile wallets in these devices. Customers can beam payment information from these wallets to point-of-sales terminals at physical retailers. A major advantage of infrared wireless communication is that the line-of-sight property provides some degree of protection from eavesdropping, although application-level security in terms of encryption and authentication must still be provided for protecting the payment information from other types of attacks. Lack of interoperability standards among various infrared-enabled devices is the major hurdle in the wide adoption of this technology.

REPRESENTATIVE TECHNOLOGIES

Electronic Bill Presentment and Payment Systems

CheckFree

CheckFree (www.checkfree.com) is the largest online bill processor. It provides online-payment-processing services to both large corporations and individual Internet users. CheckFree Corporation provides a wide range of electronic commerce solutions, including online share portfolio management in conjunction with the PAWWS system (www.pawws.com) and general online bill payment systems. CheckFree provides the infrastructure and software to permit users to pay all their bills with online electronic checks. It offers an electronic check payment service as a replacement for traditional paper checks. This payment system results in a service similar to money orders. Their software is compatible with the wallet software from Cybercash. For bill processing, the customer receives a bill from a service provider and sends the payment information to CheckFree. The customer creates an account with CheckFree that is linked by direct debit to the customer's bank account. CheckFree pays the bill on the customer's behalf in the form of electronic checks. If required, CheckFree can also pay the bill in the form of a traditional paper check.

Electronic Wallet Systems

Many electronic wallet systems are commercially available for pocket, palm-sized, handheld, and desktop PCs. The current technology trend is to produce electronic wallets in the smart card. In the electronic payment system developed in the CAFE (Conditional Access For Europe) project, the electronic wallet can be either in the form of a small portable computer with an internal power source or in the form of a smart card. Electronic money can be loaded into the wallets online and used for payments at point-of-sale (POS) terminals. Examples of e-wallet applications include Microsoft's Passport (Microsoft Corporation 2004) (the system is used mainly as a form of single-sign-on framework rather than as an electronic payment system), Ilium Software's eWallet (Ilium Software 2004), VeriFone's Vwallet (www.verifone.com—now integrated into its Integrated Payment Solutions payment software), and Qwallet.com's Q*Wallet (Qwallet.com 2004). Numerous banks and companies have now developed their own e-wallets, such as AT&T's e-wallet or MasterCard's e-wallet.

Credit-Card-Based Systems

Secure Electronic Transaction (SET) Protocol

Secure electronic transaction, or SET, is a secure protocol jointly developed in 1996 by MasterCard and Visa with the backing of Microsoft, Netscape, IBM, GTE, SAIC, and other companies, to facilitate credit-card transactions over the Internet (Schneider 2006). SET specifications were published in 1997 as an open standard, which allows all companies developing related applications to use this protocol and make their products work together successfully.

The objective of SET is to provide security for credit-card payments as they traverse the Internet from the customer to the merchant sites and on to the processing banks. SET has been developed to secure the entire credit-card-payment process, including verifying that the consumer is indeed the owner of the credit card. While Visa and MasterCard have publicly stated that the goal of proposing the SET protocol is to establish a single method for consumers and merchants to conduct payment-card transactions on the Internet, acceptance of the standard has been slow. SET Co. is the consortium that manages and promotes the SET standard. The SET protocol assumes an already established public key infrastructure. The SET specification uses public key cryptography and digital certificates for validating all participants in the transaction. In contrast to the secure sockets layer (SSL) protocol, which provides only confidentiality and integrity of credit-card information while in transit, the SET protocol provides confidentiality of information, payment data integrity, user and merchant authentication, consumer nonrepudiation, and payment clearinghouses (certificates).

The major components of SET are as follows:

1. The issuer (or customer's bank) is a financial institution that issues bankcards (credit cards or debit cards).
2. The customer (or cardholder) is an authorized user of the bank card, who is registered with SET. The customer participates in the SET transaction by using an electronic wallet. SET calls this the "cardholder wallet." This is where the customer/consumer's credit-card information is stored in an encrypted manner. The wallet software is able to communicate and interoperate with other SET components.
3. The merchant is the seller of goods and services. The merchant uses the merchant server software to automatically process credit-card authorizations and payments.
4. The payment gateway processes merchant authorization requests and payment messages, including payment instructions from cardholders. It is operated by either an acquirer or some other party that supports acquirers (for example, the merchant's bank). It interfaces with financial networks to support the capture of SET transactions.
5. One or more certification authorities issue and verify digital certificates related to public keys of customers, merchants, and/or the acquirers or their gateways. The SET public key infrastructure proposes a top-down hierarchy of certification authorities comprising the following types:

    - *Root certification authority:* All certification paths start with this authority's public key. It is operated by an organization that the entire industry agrees to trust. The initial root-key is built in to the SET software with a provision for replacing it in the future. It issues certificates to brand certification authorities.
    - *Brand certification authority:* These authorities are operated by different credit-card brand owners like Visa and MasterCard. Each brand has considerable autonomy as to how it manages the certificate subtree rooted at it.

- *Geopolitical certification authority:* This is an optional level of certification authority. It allows a brand to distribute responsibility for managing lower-level certificates across different geographic or political regions. This is to account for variations in how financial systems operate in different regions.
- *Cardholder certification authority:* These authorities generate and distribute cardholder certificates to cardholders. Depending on brand rules, the certification authority maybe operated by an issuer or another party.
- *Merchant certification authority:* These authorities issue certificates to merchants based on approval by an acquirer.

The SET infrastructure is deliberately planned not to interoperate with any payment infrastructure other than the bank-card system. Although this may be considered a restriction of SET, it ensures that the operating organizations are not subjected to any unknown risks. The main steps of SET are described in the Figure 2. The sequence can be summarized as follows:

1. *Customer and merchant registration:* In this step (messages labeled 0 in Figure 2), the customer and the merchant acquire relevant certificates from the corresponding authorities that will allow them to participate in the transaction. This needs to be done once before any SET transaction and needs to be reexecuted if the certificates expire or are revoked.
2. *Browse and negotiate purchase:* This step (message 1) proceeds separately from the main protocol; it allows the customer to select the product and negotiate on a price. SET is not involved in this phase.
3. *Purchase request:* Once the customer has completed the product selection process, it invokes the cardholder wallet software on its machine. This is where the main SET protocol starts (message 2). The cardholder wallet initiates a SET session with the merchant server; it sends its certificate to the merchant and requests a copy of the merchant's certificate and the payment gateway's certificate. On receipt of these, the cardholder wallet creates payment information (PI) and order information (OI). The PI includes the cardholder's credit-card account information and public key certificate, among others. The OI includes necessary information about the order. Two digests are computed, one each for PI and OI. They are concatenated and signed by the customer's private key. The PI is encrypted with payment gateway's public key. Next, the OI and encrypted PI are together encrypted with the merchant's public key. Finally, the entire message is signed and sent to the merchant server. The merchant server verifies the cardholder's certificate. It verifies the signature on the PI and OI. If it agrees to the OI, it forwards the encrypted PI to the payment gateway (PG) for authorization (message 3). While waiting for authorization, the merchant prepares an order confirmation (OC), signs it with its private key, and sends it encrypted with the customer's public key.
4. *Payment authorization:* To request payment authorization, the merchant sends the encrypted PI (received in step 3) signed with its private key (message 3) to the payment gateway. The payment gateway verifies the merchant's signature on the message, decrypts the PI with its private key, and retrieves the customer's certificate. It then verifies the relevant signature, and performs an authorization at the issuer (message 4).

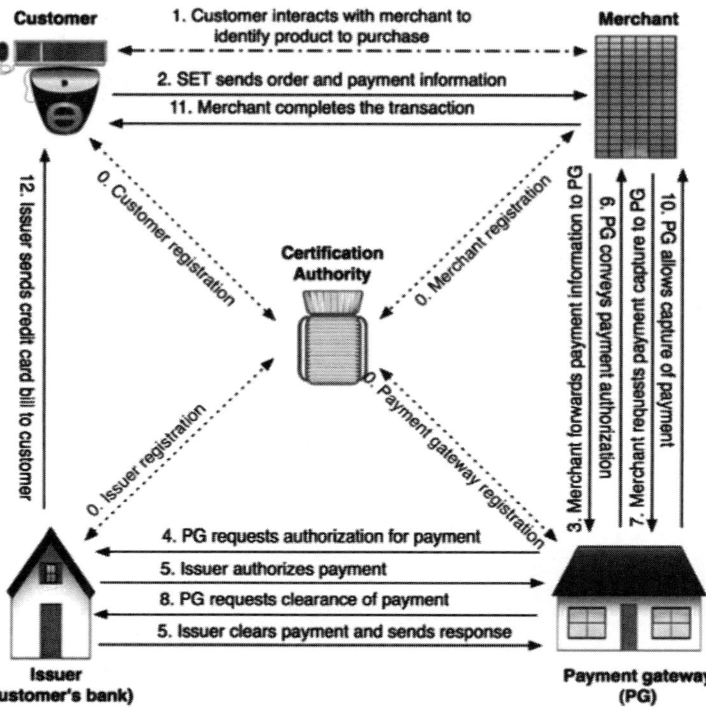

Figure 2 : Steps involved in a SET transaction

When the issuer authorizes payment (message 5), the payment gateway generates an authorization response (AR) and a capture token (CT). Both are signed by the payment gateway's private key and sent to merchant encrypted with the latter's public key. The merchant, on receipt, stores the payment authorization response and capture token for later use.

5. *Payment capture:* The merchant prepares a payment capture request with the transaction identifier from the original OI and the CT obtained earlier. It signs the capture request (CR) and sends it encrypted with the PG's public key (message 7). The payment gateway verifies the CR message and sends a clearing request (CLR) message to the issuer (message 8). When the issuer clears the payment (message 9), the payment gateway generates a CR and sends it encrypted with the merchant's public key. The merchant stores the CR and completes the transaction with customer.

A major advantage of using SET for electronic credit card payment over using the SSL protocol to do the same is that SET does not allow the merchant to view the customer's credit-card information. This provides an additional degree of protection to credit-card information. This is unlike SSL, in which the merchant has the complete credit-card information. In addition, SET prevents the payment gateway and/or the issuer bank from being able to view the terms of the transaction established between the merchant and the customer. This way the privacy of the customer is also enhanced. However, SET has received a lukewarm reception in the United States and, so far, has not attracted a large number of merchants and consumers, though it seems to be the "best" protocol for securing payment over the otherwise unsecured Internet. The major SET activities are in Asian and European nations. Part of the problem with the acceptance of SET is that apparently, it is not as easy to implement or as inexpensive as most banks and merchants had expected. The typical reaction of many banks to SET is that it is clumsy—not tried and tested. The future might prove brighter for SET, though. After a few years of testing and trials, SET's supporters believe it is ready for widespread deployment.

Electronic Funds Transfer Systems

Automated Clearinghouse

The automated clearinghouse (ACH) system was developed in the United States in the 1970s by the banking industry in an effort to allow automatic funds transfer by replacing the paper check. The ACH system supports both debit and credit transactions. ACH payments include direct deposit of payroll and social security and other government benefits tax refunds; direct payment of consumer bills such as mortgages, loans, utility bills, and insurance premiums; business-to-business payments; E-checks; and e-commerce payments.

The ACH system is a batch processing store-and-forward system. Transactions received by the financial institution during the day are stored and processed later in batch mode. ACH transactions are accumulated and sorted by destination for transmission. Typically, five participants are involved in an ACH transaction (see Figure 3). (1) The originating company or individual (Originator) initiates a fund transfer from its account. (2) The Originating Depository Financial Institution (ODFI) receives a payment instruction from an originator and forwards it to the ACH Operator. (3) The Receiving Depository Financial Institution (RDFI) receives ACH entries from the ACH operator and posts the entries to the accounts of receivers. (4) The receiving company, employee, or customer (Receiver) authorizes an originator to initiate an ACH entry to the receiver's account with the RDFI. (5) The ACH Operator is the central clearing facility to or from which participating depository financial institutions transmit or receive ACH entries.

PayPal

PayPal (eBay Inc. 2002) operates very differently from ACH. It originally began as a payment system for person-to-person (P2P) payments via e-mail. Of late, it has become a very popular method for consumers to pay for online purchases. Owned by eBay Inc. and touted as the world's first e-mail payment service, PayPal.com is a free service that earns a profit on the float, which is money that is deposited in PayPal accounts. PayPal is very popular with eBay auction customers—it is currently the

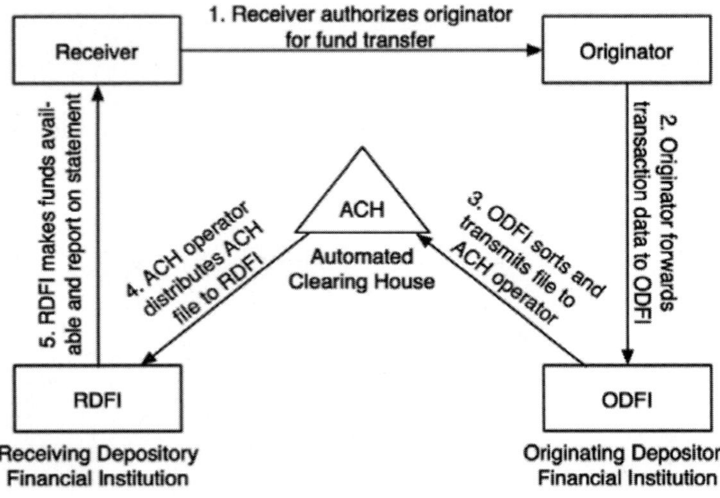

Figure 3: Steps involved in an ACH transaction (Courtesy of NACHA—The Electronic Payments Association [www.nacha.org/what_is_ach.htm])

number one electronic cash system used by eBay. PayPal eliminates the need to pay for online purchases by writing and mailing checks or using credit cards. PayPal allows consumers to send money instantly and securely to anyone with an e-mail address, including an online merchant. PayPal is a convenient way for auction bidders to pay for their purchases, and sellers like it because it eliminates the risks of accepting other types of online payments. PayPal transactions clear instantly so that the sender's account is reduced and the receiver's account is credited when the transaction occurs. Anyone with a PayPal account—online merchants and eBay auction participants alike—can withdraw cash from their PayPal accounts at any time.

To use PayPal, merchants and consumers first must register for a PayPal account. There is no minimum amount that a PayPal account must contain. Customers add money to their PayPal accounts by sending a check or using a credit card. Once members' payments are approved and deposited into their PayPal accounts, they can use their PayPal money to pay for purchases. Merchants must have PayPal accounts to accept PayPal payments, but consumer-to-consumer markets such as eBay are more flexible. Using PayPal to pay for auction purchases is very popular. A consumer can use PayPal to pay a seller for purchases even if the seller does not have a PayPal account. When one uses PayPal to pay for purchases from a seller or merchant who does not have a PayPal account, the PayPal service sends the seller or merchant an e-mail message indicating that a payment is waiting at the PayPal Web site. To collect PayPal cash, the seller or merchant who received the e-mail message must register and provide PayPal with payment instructions.

ELECTRONIC CASH SYSTEMS

CAFE

The European Union project CAFE (Conditional Access For Europe) (European Community's ESPRIT Program 1995) is an offline direct cash–like scheme that guarantees customer anonymity. The CAFE project ended in mid-1997, but has been continued in the follow-up project, OPERA. The partners in OPERA—that is, banks that support CAFE—are continuing the trial of and improving the CAFE system. About thirteen partners from several European countries were involved in the project, DigiCash[2] and Siemens among them. The system is designed for use in shops rather than over the Internet. In a way, it is the offline, portable versions of the DigiCash ECash system. It is based on the system proposed by Brand's cash. The protocol is disclosed for public review. An important feature of CAFE is the multiparty security. No mutual trust between parties of conflicting interest is assumed.

CAFE is an open secure system. It supports multiple issuers of electronic value and multiple currencies, including currency exchange during a payment. It provides the customer with a history log of their payments. The system uses public key signature and encryption and allows for offline purchase transactions. The basic purchase transaction mode is anonymous and untraceable for the customer and performed offline; there is no need to connect to a third party online. Withdrawals and deposits are identified, traceable, and online. If payments exceeding a certain level must be confirmed, then some online interaction becomes necessary.

CAFE provides recovery of lost, stolen, and damaged cards. Although prepaid, it is loss-tolerant and allows customers to recover their money if they lose their cards, because an encrypted version of all tokens issued to the customer is held in a safe place. The customer must surrender his or her anonymity and untraceability, then the issued token backup can be decrypted and matched against the redeemed token database. To provide some loss tolerance for stolen cards, the customer must authenticate himself or herself via a pass phrase (PIN) prior to a purchase.

The device receives coins by withdrawing them from the issuer account via an ATM using the blind signature method known from ECash. CAFE is prepaid, and the tokens on the device do not exist as currency anywhere else. When the customer spends money, the device transmits one or more tokens to the merchant and marks on the device them as spent. Transmissions are performed contact-less via infrared channels. The merchant then owns the value of those tokens, which need to be deposited with an acquirer and accepted by the issuer for that value to be realized for the merchant. Thus, the primary flow of value in CAFE is that of withdraw, pay, and deposit—that is, the payment model is the typical direct cash–like approach.

The basic hardware device is a pocket calculator–like electronic wallet, to be used for customer payments, to access information services, and for identification. It aims to be nonproprietary. The electronic wallets and smart cards—that is, the hardware—should become standardized and be available in shops just like other electronic consumer goods. The wallet contains a so-called guardian, a smart card with a dedicated cryptographic processor. The wallet protects the interests of the customer, the guardian protects the interests of the money issuer, and both are holding part of each token withdrawn. No transactions are possible without the cooperation of the guardian; the guardian maintains a record of all the tokens spent to avoid double spending. The guardian chip authorizes each payment by signing it. CAFE tokens do not remain in circulation like real cash tokens do. Re-spendability is broken explicitly—the wallet signs to whom it pays a token, so only that payee can deposit the token.

As a fallback, when the guardian is compromised CAFE uses so-called offline digital coins that provide a once-concealed, twice-revealed feature. The money is encrypted, and the identity of the customer signed by that customer is encoded into the token number. This is done in a way that the identity of the customer can be recovered only if the customer double spends. This feature works as follows: When the customer uses a token in payment, it is challenged by the merchant to reveal a

[2]DigiCash is the company that pioneered electronic cash systems. It was founded by David Chaum, who is widely credited with being the first to propose an anonymous electronic cash system. Interested readers are directed to articles by Chaum (1982) and Chaum, Fiat, and Naor (1988).

certain part of the encoded customer identity. One part on its own does not reveal anything useful. If, however, the customer tries to re-spend the same token, another part of the customer identity is revealed to the merchant; now, with a high probability, the identity of the customer can be traced. In order to do this, the issuer must hold a database of all reimbursed tokens that it already needs for the fault-tolerance feature.

As a fixed-denomination token system that distinguishes between customers and merchants, CAFE needs to address the problem of making change. It allows the construction of coins that can be split into smaller coins if need be and of coins that—being more expensive than their denomination—may be spent more than once. These measurements reduce the unlinkability of the payments but not their integrity. For repeated very small payments to the same merchant, so-called phone ticks, CAFE provides a special way of surrendering a token in installments.

In CAFE, transactions appear atomic to the user but not to the merchant. The tokens a merchant accepts in payment must be deposited with an acquirer and accepted by the issuer before their monetary value can be realized by the merchant. The value leaves the customer, but does not immediately arrive at the merchant.

Micropayment Systems

MilliCent

MilliCent (Manasse 1997) is the most widely known micropayment scheme. MilliCent is a proprietary voucher-based digital micro commerce system from the erstwhile Digital Equipment Corporation (acquired by Compaq and now part of HP Invent). It aims at the micropayment segment of electronic commerce and supports transactions with values of fractions of a cent. MilliCent considers that coins are treated differently than paper money, in the same manner that small-denomination notes are treated differently than high-denomination notes. Because MilliCent represents very small coins, it uses lightweight security measures. A public trial of the MilliCent system involving toy money started in December 1997.

The system uses merchant-specific vouchers, the so-called scrip, which is a form of token that is valid only with a particular merchant for a limited period. Brokers act as intermediaries between merchants and customers. The fact that any type of scrip is valid only at a particular merchant means that the merchant does not need to connect to a central issuer to validate the token. This reduces network traffic and the validation cost. To avoid customers having to maintain separate accounts with the individual merchants for mostly short-term relationships, brokers act as intermediaries. The long-term relationships are between brokers and customers, and brokers and merchants. Consumers register with one broker and buy broker scrips in bulk—generic scrip. Brokers receive payment from consumers in a variety of ways, but the most common way the consumers pay is with a credit card. When a consumer locates a product on a merchant's Web site that he or she would like to purchase, the consumer converts the broker scrip into vendor-specific scrip. Vendor-specific scrip is scrip that a particular merchant will accept. The consumer's new scrip is stored in an electronic wallet on the consumer's computer. Paying for an item involves simply transferring a merchant's scrip, which is in a consumer's wallet, to the merchant in exchange for a purchased item. Merchants can then send a broker their own scrip and obtain a check. The basic sequence of interactions is as follows:

1. The customer obtains a quantity of broker scrip at the outset.
2. The customer requests some specific vendor scrip, which they will pay for later with the broker scrip.
3. The broker obtains the required vendor scrip from the vendor.
4. The broker sells the vendor scrip to the customer.
5. The customer buys the service with the vendor scrip.
6. The vendor gives change in vendor scrip.

Steps 1 to 4 are not required for every transaction; the customer can buy sufficient scrip from the broker for a period. Likewise, the broker can store enough vendor scrip to serve many customer requests or it can have a license from the vendor to create that vendor scrip directly. Although at first glance a lot of message passing seems to be required, there is no bottleneck like one single currency issuer to be contacted during each transaction, especially once steps 1 to 4 are completed. Experiments at Digital indicate that MilliCent is efficient enough for transactions as low as one-tenth of a cent. A broker is required in the protocol for two reasons. First, the system of very small payments works because transactions can be aggregated so they are significant. That is, when a consumer buys a few dollars worth of scrip, there is little profit in the deal. However, when several consumers purchase scrip, the aggregate amount—even discounted so that the broker can make money—does make economic sense. The second reason for a broker is that it makes the entire system easier to use. A consumer has to deal with only one broker to satisfy his or her scrip needs for many merchants. The broker buys the scrip in bulk and does all the hard work of organizing the retail selling to customers.

A significant feature of the MilliCent protocol is the trade-offs attempted at different points in the design. For example, MilliCent offers three protocol versions—"private and secure," "secure without encryption," and "scrip in the clear." The least secure is "scrip in the clear." Here, the scrip is transferred between customer and vendor without any encryption or protection; thus, the protocol is the most efficient and cheapest to implement. However, this allows any observer to change the scrip or replay it and spend it itself. Thus, the customer can potentially suffer a financial loss. Although amounts stolen this way will be quite small, it can be rather annoying to the customer to find their small change to be invalid. The next level of security is provided by "secure without encryption." Here, personal information about the customer that is carried by a field in the scrip is available to the player involved in the scrip system; however, the scrip itself is protected from replays that allow an observer to spend the scrip itself. The most secure is the "private and secure" version of the protocol.

However, it too uses lightweight encryption technology, which is probably not too difficult to break. The philosophy is that the cost of breaking the protocol should be greater than the value of the scrip itself. Scrips can be minted at very low value. Thus, loss of scrip due to confidentiality or integrity breaches does not cause significant financial loss to the end user.

Stored-Value Card Systems

MONDEX

The most well known example of an electronic purse or stored-value card system is the MONDEX smart card—a service of MasterCard International (2004). It was introduced in the early 1990s; it is the largest pilot program of an electronic purse product to date. The MONDEX smart card contains a microcomputer chip. The card can accept electronic cash directly from a user's bank account. Cardholders can spend their electronic cash with any merchant who has a MONDEX card reader. Two cardholders can even transfer cash between their cards over a telephone line. A single card works in both the online world of the Internet and the offline world of ordinary merchant stores while simultaneously being impervious to the theft threats of credit cards. Another advantage of MONDEX is that the cardholder always has the correct change for vending machines of various types. MONDEX electronic cash supports micropayments as small as 3 cents. MONDEX has lower per-transaction costs than credit or debit cards, since value transfers take place locally, just as for cash. Thus, it is a good choice for minipayments and micropayments. Finally, MONDEX has the ability to provide user anonymity. This is because, just like cash systems, MONDEX does not maintain any audit record. MONDEX has some disadvantages, too. The card carries real cash in electronic form, and the risk of theft of the card may deter users from loading it with a significant amount of money. Moreover, MONDEX cannot compare with credit cards in the area of deferred payment. One can defer paying his or her charge or credit card bill for almost a month without incurring any interest. MONDEX cards dispense their cash immediately. Last but not least, a MONDEX card requires special equipment; merchants who accept it must have a specific card reader at their checkout counter. A MONDEX card must also be in physical contact with a special card reading and writing device during a merchant or recharge transaction. Internet users can transfer cash over the Internet using MONDEX, but they must attach a MONDEX reader with their PC in order to use the card. These requirements have proven to be barriers to the widespread use and success of MONDEX.

A MONDEX transaction consists of several steps. These steps ensure that the transferred cash reaches the correct destination in a safe and secure manner. Following are the steps to transfer electronic cash from the buyer to the seller.

1. The card user inserts the MONDEX card into a reader. The merchant and the card user are both validated to ensure that both the user and the merchant are still authorized to make transactions.
2. The merchant's terminal requests payment while simultaneously transmitting the merchant's digital signature.
3. The customer's card checks the merchant's digital signature. If the signature is valid, then the transaction amount is deducted from the cardholder's card.
4. The merchant's terminal checks the customer's just-sent customer digital signature for authenticity. If the cardholder's signature is validated, the merchant's terminal acknowledges the cardholder's signature by again sending back to the cardholder's card the merchant's signature.
5. Once the electronic cash is deducted form the cardholder's card, the same amount is credited to the merchant's electronic cash account. Serializing the debit and credit events before completing a transaction eliminates the creation or loss of cash if the system malfunctions in the middle of the process.

Currently, only a few cities in the United States accept MONDEX. Worldwide, MONDEX is available in several countries on the North and South American continents, Europe, Africa, the Middle East, Asia, Australia, and New Zealand. As a whole, stored-value cards are not yet very popular in the United States, where people still prefer credit cards rather than smart cards.

Electronic Check Systems

ECheck

The most well known among the electronic check systems is eCheck (Financial Services Technology Consortium 2002). It combines "the security, speed and processing efficiencies of all-electronic transactions with the familiar and well-developed legal infrastructures and business processes associated with paper checks" (www.echeck.org). An eCheck is the electronic version of a standard paper check. It contains the same information as paper checks contain. It is based on the financial services markup language (FSML). It provides strong authentication, strong encryption, and duplicate detection features. It can be used with existing checking accounts, has unlimited but controlled information-carrying capability, and has some enhanced capabilities, such as effective dating, that are not provided in traditional checks. In addition, eCheck is often considered more secure than traditional paper checks. In eCheck, each electronic checkbook is assigned a unique eCheck account number that only the bank can map into the actual underlying account number. This account number is part of the distinguished name in the bank-issued account certificate, so it cannot be modified but is easily verified by anyone who receives an eCheck. Thus, compromise of an eCheck does not lead to possible compromise of the underlying account. Revoking an eCheck account number has no impact on the underlying account.

ECheck is the first and only electronic payment mechanism chosen by the U.S. Treasury to make high-value payments over the Internet. It is currently under enhancement in Singapore and is being considered for many online systems.

Mobile Payment Systems

FeliCa Card

The FeliCa card is a contact-less smart card developed by SONY Corporation to be used as an electronic purse. It operates in the 13.56-MHz frequency range and has an operation range of a few centimeters. It uses the ISO 7810 form for credit cards. The FeliCa card was first used in the Hong Kong Octopus card system for public transportation. Later it was used in many other systems, including EZ-link in Singapore, most mass-transit system in Japan, and the New Delhi Metro in India. Mobile FeliCa is a modification of FeliCa for use in mobile phones. Mobile FeliCa–equipped mobile phones can potentially be used as prepaid electronic cash, tickets, membership cards for clubs, and credit and debit cards. Pilot projects are currently under way in Japan. However, the proprietary technology is hindering widespread adoption.

ExxonMobil Speedpass

ExxonMobil was one of the first to introduce a contact-less electronic payment system to help consumers make retail purchase. Called Speedpass, it uses a proprietary radio-frequency communication technology and is a proximity card. A customer opens a Speedpass account that is linked to the customer's credit or check card. The radio-frequency payment device comes as a key fob, a watch. or a transponder affixed to the customer's vehicle's rear window. The payment terminal is integrated into the gas pump. At the beginning of a transaction, the payment terminal authenticates the Speedpass device and authorizes a charge. The charge gets reflected directly into the user's credit/check card account. Although initially intended for purchases made at a pump, Speedpass is increasingly being accepted at convenience stores for retail purchase.

CONCLUSION AND FURTHER READING

In this chapter, we presented an overview of electronic payment systems. One of our objectives was to identify the technical challenges, mostly security-related, that hinder the widespread deployment of such systems. We also surveyed some of the more well known instances of electronic payment systems. Our survey is by no means complete. Many new systems are proposed on a regular basis. The majority of them do not survive market forces. Those that do frequently are acquired by the bigger players, and their initial business focus gets lost.

A good source of information for electronic payment systems is Dr. Phillip M. Hallam-Baker's Web page on *Electronic Payment Schemes* (Hallam-Baker 2004) on the W3 Consortium. This page categorizes electronic payment schemes along two dimensions—the level of abstraction for the payment scheme (namely, *policy,* the semantics of the payment scheme; *data flow,* the requirements for storage of data and communication between parties; and *mechanism,* the security methods used), and the payment model for the protocol (namely, cash, check, or card). The Web page contains a comprehensive list of Internet payment schemes and protocols. The author makes an earnest effort to keep the list as up-to-date as possible; however, this may not always be possible. The CAFE project of the European Community's ESPRIT program (1995) and the SEMPER project of the European Commission's ACTS Program (2000) are two important European projects that provide valuable information on electronic payment systems. The list maintained by the SIRENE (2004) group is also a valuable resource for electronic payment systems. Leo Van Hove's (2004) database on E-purse provides a collection of links and references on electronic purses (and related issues). The E-money mini FAQ page (Miller 2004) written by Jim Miller and maintained by Roy Davies, provides answers to some frequently asked questions about electronic money and digital cash. Roy Davies also maintains a comprehensive information resource for electronic money and digital cash (Davies 2004). The Financial Services Technology Consortium (FSTC) has several projects (both past and present) aimed at developing technologies that facilitate electronic payment systems. Information about these projects can be found from the FSTC Projects Web page at www.fstc.org/projects. For a comprehensive (although somewhat dated) overview of contact-less payment systems, readers are directed to the Smart Card Alliance (www.smartcardalliance.org) report PT-03002, dated March 2003, "Contactless Payment and the Retail Point of Sale: Applications, Technologies and Transaction Models." Finally, some useful reference books for electronic commerce and electronic payment systems, are the books by Bidgoli (2002), Schneider (2006), Turban et al. (2005), and van Slyke and Belanger (2002).

GLOSSARY

Acquirer: The entity or entities that hold(s) deposit accounts for card acceptors (merchants) and to which the card acceptor transmits the data relating to the transaction; the acquirer is responsible for the collection of transaction information and settlement with acceptors.

Audit Trail: A sequential record of events that have occurred in a system.

Automated Clearinghouse: An electronic rendezvous for financial institutions where payment orders are exchanged among the financial institutions primarily via magnetic media or communications network. Commonly known as ACH.

Automated Teller Machine: An electromechanical device that permits authorized users to use machine-readable plastic cards to withdraw cash from their accounts at a particular financial institution and/or access other services, such as account balance enquiries, transfer funds between accounts, or deposit money into accounts.

Batch Processing: The transmission or processing of a group of payment orders as a set at discrete intervals of time.

Card: A general term used to describe several types of payment systems, including ATM card or cash card, check guarantee card, chip card (or smart card), credit card, charge card, debit card, delayed debit card, prepaid card, retailer card, and stored-value card.

Cash Card: Card for use only in ATMs or cash dispensers.

Certificate: A document (physical or electronic) that evidences the undertakings of an issuer.
Charge Card: Card issued by nonbanks indicating that the holder has been granted a line of credit. It enables the holder to make purchases but does not offer extended credit, the full amount of the debt incurred having to be settled at the end of a specified period. Typically issued by the travel and entertainment industry to their customers.
Check: A written order from one party (the drawer) to another (the drawee, normally a bank) requiring the drawee to pay a specified sum on demand to the drawer or a third party of the drawer's choosing. Checks may be used for settling debts and withdrawing money from banks.
Check Card: A card issued as part of a check guarantee system.
Check Guarantee System: A system to guarantee checks, typically up to a specified amount by the issuer of the guarantee card.
Chip Card: See *Smart Card.*
Clearing/Clearance: The process of transmitting, reconciling, and, in some cases, confirming payment orders or security transfer instructions prior to settlement.
Credit Card: A card indicating that the holder has been granted a line of credit. It enables the holder to make purchases and/or withdraw cash up to a prearranged ceiling; the credit granted can be settled in full by the end of a specified period or can be settled in part, with the balance taken as extended credit.
Credit-Card Company: A company that owns the trademark of a particular credit card, and may also provide a number of marketing, processing, or other services to its members using the card services.
Debit Card: A card that enables the holder to have his/her purchases directly charged to funds available in his/her account at a deposit-taking financial institution.
Delayed Debit Card: A card issued by banks indicating that the holder may charge his/her account up to an authorized limit. It enables the holder to make purchases but does not offer extended credit; the full amount of the debt incurred needs to be settled at the end of the specified period.
Electronic Fund Transfer System: A formal arrangement based on private contract or statute law with multiple membership, common rules, and standardized arrangements, for the electronic transmission and settlement of monetary obligations.
Electronic Payment System: An electronic system consisting of a set of instruments, banking procedures, and typically interbank fund transfer systems that ensure the circulation of money.
Electronic Purse: A reloadable multipurpose prepaid card that may be used for small retail or other payments instead of coins.
Electronic Wallet: A computer device used in some electronic payment systems to store information that is needed to undertake a financial transaction.
Magnetic Ink Character Recognition: A technique using machine-readable characters imprinted on a document using an ink with magnetic properties by which information on the document is interpreted by machines for electronic processing. Also known as MICR.
Micropayment: A method of payment for very small sums of money where the cost of making the payment using traditional means—like check, credit or debit cards, etc.—far exceeds the value conveyed in the payment. Typically, the amount transacted is on the order of several cents to at most a few dollars (<10) only.
Payment: The process of the payer's transfer of a monetary claim on a party acceptable to the payee.
PIN: A numeric code that a cardholder may need to quote for verification of identity. It is often seen as the equivalent of a signature.
Prepaid Card: A card on which value is stored and for which the holder has paid the issuer in advance. Also known as stored-value card.
Provider: The operator who establishes the hardware and software conditions for the conduct of transactions with electronic money without necessarily being the issuer of the electronic money units.
Scrip: A form of micropayment token (voucher) that is valid only with a particular merchant for a limited period.
Settlement: The act of discharging obligations with respect to fund transfers between two or more parties.
Smart Card: A card with a built-in microprocessor and memory that is capable of performing calculations and storing information.
SSL: Secure sockets layer. A cryptographic protocol used for exchanging information between a client and a server over the Internet in a secure and authenticated manner.

CROSS REFERENCES

See *Electronic Commerce*; *Electronic Data Interchange (EDI)*; *Mobile Commerce*; *The Internet Fundamentals*.

REFERENCES

Bidgoli, H. 2002. *Electronic commerce: Principles and practice*. New York: Academic Press.
Chaum, D. 1982. Blind signatures for untraceable payments. *Advances in Cryptology, Proceedings of Crypto '82*. New York: Plenum.
Chaum, D., A. Fiat, and M. Naor. 1988. Untraceable electronic cash. *Advances in Cryptology, Proceedings of Crypto '88*. New York: Springer-Verlag.
Davies, G. 2002. *A history of money from ancient times to the present day*. 3rd ed. Cardiff: University of Wales Press.
Davies, R. 2004. *Electronic money, or e-money, and digital cash*. www.ex.ac.uk/~RDavies/arian/emoney.html (accessed July 5, 2007).
EBay Inc. 2002. *PayPal*. www.paypal.com/cgi-bin/webscr?cmd=p/gen/about-outside (accessed July 5, 2007).
European Commission's ACTS Program. 2000. *SEMPER—Secure Electronic Marketplace for Europe*. www.semper.org/index.html (accessed July 5, 2007).

European Community's ESPRIT Program. 1995. CAFE—Conditional Access For Europe. www.semper.org/sirene/projects/cafe/index.html (accessed July 5, 2007).

Financial Services Technology Consortium 2002. *eCheck*. www.echeck.org (accessed July 5, 2007).

Hallam-Baker, P. M. 2004. *Electronic payment schemes*. http://www.w3.org/ECommerce/roadmap.html (accessed July 5, 2007).

Ilium Software. 2004. *eWallet*. www.iliumsoft.com/ew/ewallet.htm (accessed July 4, 2007).

Manasse, M. 1997 *Millicent*. http://research.compaq.com/SRC/articles/199705/Millicent.html (accessed October 4, 2005).

MasterCard International. 2004. *Mondex electronic cash*. www.mondexusa.com (accessed July 5, 2007).

Microsoft Corporation. 2004. *Microsoft .NET Passport*. www.passport.net/Consumer/default.asp?lc=1033 (accessed July 4, 2007).

Miller, J. 2004. *E-money Mini FAQ (release 2.0)*. www.ex.ac.uk/~RDavies/arian/emoneyfaq.html (accessed August 16, 2007).

Qwallet.com. 2004. *Q*Wallet Home*. http://qwallet.com/index.shtml (accessed July 4, 2007).

Schneider, G. P. 2006. *Electronic commerce*. 7th ed. Boston: Thomson Course Technology.

SIRENE. 2004. *Electronic commerce, payment systems, and security*. www.semper.org/sirene/pointers_complete.html (accessed July 5, 2007).

Turban, E., D. King, J. K. Lee, J. Lee, and D. Viehland. 2005. *Electronic commerce: A managerial perspective 2006*. Upper Saddle River, NJ: Prentice Hall.

Van Hove, L. 2004. Leo Van Hove's DB on E-purse http://epso.intrasoft.lu/inventory/indexvanhove.cfm (accessed August 16, 2007).

van Slyke, C., and F. Belanger. 2002. *E-business technologies: Supporting the net-enhanced organization*. New York: Wiley.

Weber, R. 1998. *Chablis—Market analysis of digital payment systems*. Report No. TUM-I9819. Munich, Germany: Technische Universität München.

Internet Relay Chat (IRC)

James M. Hudson, *PayPal, an eBay, Inc. company*
Paul L. Witt, *Texas Christian University*

A SOCIAL HISTORY OF INTERNET RELAY CHAT

From the earliest days of Internet-based communication, Unix systems have included a variant of the *talk* program. This program simply divides two users' computer terminals in half. Each user types in one half of the screen, and the other user immediately sees these keystrokes. Over time, the talk program evolved into *ytalk,* which allowed more than two users to communicate at one time. In 1988, Jarkko Oikarinen (n.d.) built on this idea to create Internet relay chat (IRC). Although Oikarinen points out that earlier chat programs existed, this is largely recognized as the beginning of Internet chat. Chat has evolved in a number of ways since the creation of IRC (e.g., Churchill et al. 2000; Farnham et al. 2000; Erickson et al. 2002; Smith, Cadiz, and Burkhalter 2002), the fundamental features have not changed.

In text-based chat programs like IRC, a number of users can connect into the same virtual space and communicate with one another in near real time using text. Unlike *talk* and *ytalk*, IRC sends completed messages over the network, rather than individual keystrokes. In other words, most chat programs allow interlocutors to compose comments in private, which are not revealed to others until the user presses the *Enter* key. As we will describe in more detail later, this design feature has significant implications for the psychology of interaction in IRC. In the conversation window, new comments are typically placed on the bottom of the screen when they arrive, causing older messages to scroll off of the top of the screen.

Created in 1988, IRC's popularity grew enormously during the early 1990s. IRC gained notoriety as a strategic global communication system in 1991, when real-time messages were received from IRC users inside Kuwait during the Iraqi occupation. In 1993, IRC enabled computer users in Moscow to communicate with outsiders during the uprising against President Yeltsin. Following the terrorist attacks in New York and Washington in September 2001, IRC networks became extremely active, initially to support communication with survivors and rescue workers, and later to allow users from around the globe to vent their feelings, rally support for victims, and engage in political and ideological debate. When other communication systems failed or became congested during these international crises, computer users with access to the Internet used IRC for up-to-the-minute interaction with external parties. In recent years, however, easy-to-use Web-based chat systems and instant messaging have largely contributed to a significant decline in IRC's popularity. Unfortunately, because of the distributed nature of IRC networks, few concrete statistics exist about its popularity and use.

TECHNICAL DETAILS

Servers, Networks, and Channels

IRC is built on a fairly standard client/server framework. The IRC server is the central point of communication through which all messages pass en route to individual client computers. In the simplest IRC network structure, each user's computer runs a client program to connect to a common server. The server runs an application called an IRC daemon (IRCD), which allows connections from individual users and relays messages from one client to another by passing them through the server. Some IRC chat systems consist of a simple network in which a single server manages connections and communications among all its clients. However, most IRC servers are connected to other IRC servers, thus opening the IRC system to potential communication among all users with connections to all the servers on the network.

The details of the communication protocol were originally laid out in RFC 1459 in 1993. Seven years later, this protocol was updated to RFC 2810, RFC 2811, RFC 2812, and RFC 2813, reflecting the growing use of file sharing and other enhancements. Although IRC technically refers to any system built using this communication protocol, most people use the term to refer to a handful of large networks of servers, such as EFnet or IRCnet. Originally, there was only one IRC network, consisting of a few servers, but as IRC grew in popularity and complexity, it splintered into multiple networks. Today there are hundreds of IRC networks that are constantly evolving through expansion and redefinition. They range in size from very small, family-oriented chat networks, to such

Table 1: Some of the Largest IRC Networks

	Number of Servers	Help Site and Server List
Efnet	40	www.efnet.org
IRCnet	>120	www.ircnet.com
DALnet	30	www.dal.net
Undernet	40	www.undernet.org
GalaxyNet	30	www.galaxynet.org
WebNet	15	www.webchat.org
NewNet	15	www.newnet.net
ChatNet	15	www.chatnet.com

global networks as EFnet or the expansive IRCnet, which links well over 100 servers and supports thousands of chat groups, or *channels* (see Table 1).

To engage in IRC, users select an IRC network and connect to one of the available servers, using a nickname (e.g., *SuperTig*) rather than their real name. Unlike many modern communication systems, however, users do not have to register their nickname. Instead, they can choose any nickname they want as long as no one else on the network is already using that nickname. Until 1994, there was a system called NickServ, however, that allowed users to register nicknames, but it worked a little differently than might be expected. If a nickname was registered, any user could still log onto an IRC network with that nickname. If the registered owner of that nickname happened to log onto that same network, however, he or she could reclaim this nickname and force the other user to change his or her nickname to something else. There is no evidence that NickServ will resume.

Upon logging onto an IRC network, users typically receive the MOTD (message of the day) containing some basic information from the server's database about the channel's current activity (topic, nicknames of current users, etc.). Using the */list* command, users can consult a list of public chat rooms, known as channels, currently available on that server, which can they can join using the command */join #channelname*. The channels listed as *#channelname* are global and can be accessed through any server on the network; channels listed as *&channelname* are available through that server alone. Some channels are designated "secret" and are not open to others. Channels exist only when they are used. In other words, users can create new channels simply by attempting to join one that does not exist. Similarly, channels disappear when the last user leaves. Having joined a channel, the new user is then ready to communicate with others by sending a message that will appear more or less synchronously on the screens of all channel participants (see Figure 1). The command */leave* or */part* will terminate the connection to the channel, and the command */quit* will terminate the connection to the network.

In reality, connecting to an IRC server is not always simple, especially for newcomers. Connection may be prevented if the user enters an incorrect server name, chooses an unacceptable nickname, or has been *K-lined* (specifically banned from the server for some reason). Users who connect to the Internet through large, popular ISPs (Internet service providers) may find some channels closed to them, based on the stereotype that

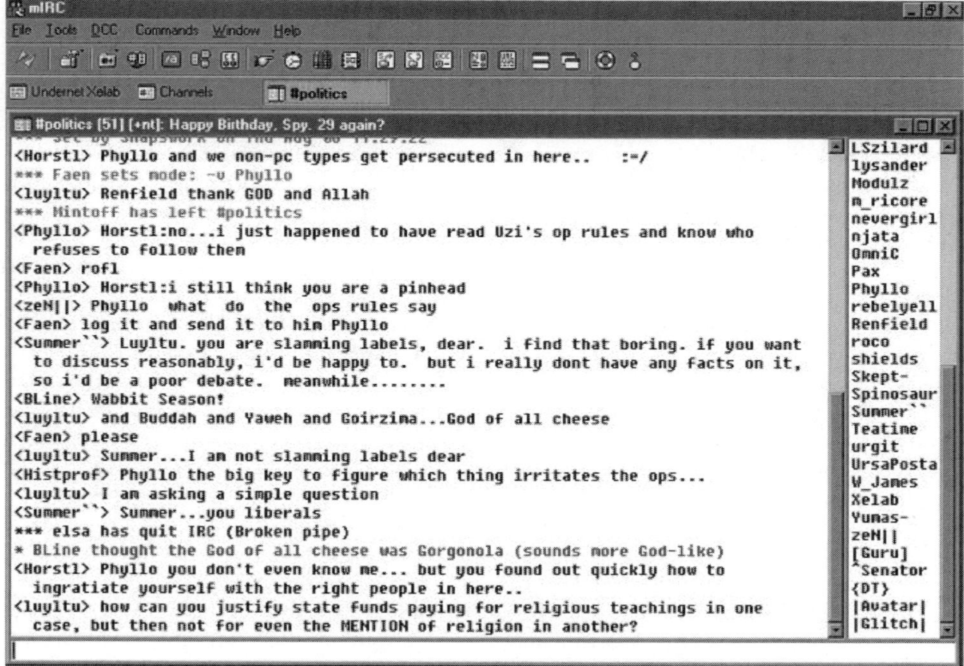

Figure 1: Screenshot of online interaction using mIRC

such subscribers are probably newbies and therefore unwelcome on certain channels.

IRC networks are not immune to problems of congestion or breakdown. As with all other packet-switching Internet communication systems, users sometimes experience delays in the transmission of electronic messages. This delay (known to IRC users as "lag") is irritating to all Internet users, but it is especially problematic in synchronous communication systems characterized by real-time interaction. A 10-second lag can dramatically change the timing and effectiveness of some types of online interaction, as threads of conversation become entangled and users appear to be "talking over" one another. The jumble of multiple conversations is a common characteristic of interaction on public IRC channels (Herring 1999, Interactional coherence in CMC), and lag serves to exacerbate the problem. Increased lag may be caused by heavy traffic on the Internet or IRC network, a malfunctioning server, flooding, or a denial of service attack (see below). Lag is sometimes related to a netsplit, which occurs when one or more IRC servers lose their connection to the network. Netsplits fracture the network and effectively create separate network fragments that may or may not continue to operate separately. Netsplits often result in a buildup of packets queued for delivery to servers that are no longer available. After a netsplit, servers sometimes reconnect to the network and are able to update the server with activity that occurred during the netsplit. Sometimes a netsplit results when an IRC operator revises the network's connection to other servers in order to achieve a more efficient or more desirable network configuration.

Although IRC communication was intended to flow through servers, a new form of communication, known as direct client connection (DCC), emerged in the late 1990s. Two clients who are connected to the same IRC network can initiate a direct connection between each other. IP (Internet protocol) addresses are typically used to establish the DCC connection, and messages or shared files pass directly from one client to the other without being relayed by the IRC server. Many of the more experienced users prefer to use DCC for their one-on-one interactions and file transfers, because DCC frequently results in faster message exchange, a higher degree of privacy, and avoidance of network problems such as lags and netsplits.

IRC Client Software

In order to engage in online communication using IRC, users need access to the Internet through an ISP or direct network connection. They must also install a communications software program called an IRC client. The client software serves as the interface between the individual computer (the client) and the IRC server (serving the needs of multiple clients). The IRC client processes the commands that are typed or clicked by the user and then uses network protocols, such as TCP/IP (transfer control protocol/Internet protocol) to transmit them to the server.

IRC supports communication across different operating platforms, enabling the flow of messages between PC and Macintosh computers, as well as UNIX-based computing systems. IRC clients for these and other operating systems are readily available, and free downloads or demonstration copies can be found on most of the major FTP (file transfer protocol) sites on the Internet. Some IRC clients are available as shareware, meaning that after a free trial period, if users wish to continue using it, they are asked to purchase the software or pay a modest registration fee. Generally, the cost of IRC client software is quite reasonable.

Text-Based IRC Clients

Early IRC users were almost exclusively UNIX-based, and the majority of today's IRC servers are UNIX servers. Individual computer users who use a terminal-emulation program to establish a dial-in connection to an organization for Internet access effectively turn their computer into a terminal making use of a shell account on the UNIX system. The most common IRC client for UNIX and related systems (such as shell accounts and Linux) is IRCII. This full-featured, text-based client was the first widely used IRC client and still serves as a reference standard for essential commands and functions. More advanced users sometimes use IRCII's scripting language to create scripts that streamline complex processes, generate customized output, or perform certain functions automatically when prescribed conditions occur.

Graphical Interface IRC Clients

The majority of online communicators connect to the Internet through Windows-based PCs or Macintosh computers. IRC clients have been developed for both platforms, offering the point-and-click ease-of-use characteristic of graphical user interfaces (GUIs). The major GUI clients receive ongoing attention from their developers, and excellent support is available for learners. The client of choice for many PC users using Windows operating systems is mIRC, a powerful, intuitive, and reliable application. Because PC users outnumber those on UNIX and Macintosh platforms, mIRC is probably the most widely used IRC client on the Internet today. Easy-to-use menus and buttons, customizable functions, and extensive user support contribute to the popularity of mIRC (see Figure 1). The most widely used IRC client for Macintosh computers is Ircle. A stable, full-featured IRC client, Ircle provides buttons, menus, and icons to facilitate common IRC functions. Ircle users may also use AppleScript to modify the client to their custom specifications. Good user support and innovative features place IRC interactions within easy reach even for beginning Ircle users.

IRCops, Chanops, and Users

The IRC system hierarchy of networks, servers, channels, and clients is reflected in an administrative hierarchy of people who oversee each level of the system. End users who direct their IRC client to connect to a network should be aware of the scope of authority and control exerted by IRC operators and channel operators. Newbies sometimes embarrass themselves and irritate others by inappropriately posing questions or filing complaints with the person they perceive to be in charge of a channel or server.

IRCops

IRC operators generally oversee the operation of an IRC server, maintain routing functions in relation to other servers on the network, modify server settings, and monitor general activity on the server. Sometimes the original server administrator fulfills the role of IRCop, and sometimes the administrator selects one or more experienced and qualified users to serve as IRCop. Servers typically have more than one operator, in order to ensure constant observation of activity on the server. In the event of a server failure or network fault, IRCops work to restore network connections. They also enforce the policies and procedures of the server they oversee. If a user violates policy or misbehaves in some way, the IRCop usually issues a warning. Users who are reprimanded by an IRCop are sometimes unaware of the power the operator has to control activity on the server. For example, an IRCop can issue a */kill* command that effectively bans the offending user from further access to the server and, in some cases, the entire network. Determining the identity of a server's IRCops is not always easy. When they are listed in the MOTD (message of the day) or active user lists, their "user mask" (nickname plus host name) is usually marked with an asterisk (**Stinkbug!skb220@rhl.net*). The command */stats o* may be used to identify active operators, and some IRC clients support the command */who -oper*. Many IRC users never have direct communication with an IRC operator unless their activity on the server violates accepted practice and attracts the operator's attention. IRC operators do not exert control over channel activities; they leave those functions to the channel operators.

Chanops

Each IRC channel (chat group) is initiated or overseen by a channel operator, or chanop. Channel operators exert management and control over the channel's topic, mode, and settings, and they regulate how many users and, specifically, which users are allowed to interact on the channel. If users misbehave, become obnoxious, or simply irritate the channel operator, most chanops do not hesitate to ban them from the channel. Any IRC user who creates a new channel with the */join #channelname* command automatically becomes the operator for that channel. Because of this, it is not uncommon for chanops to misbehave as well (Herring 1999, The rhetorical dynamics of gender harassment on-line). Chanop status is valid only for the duration of the current IRC session, and when chanops leave the channel, they ordinarily lose their operator status. However, if operators are registered as super-ops with an IRC channel service, they can effectively maintain control over a channel even during their absence. Many IRC channels have several operators active at any given time, but occasionally a channel may function with no operator. Channel operators are usually identified with an @ sign before their nickname (*@SuperTig*). Most IRC clients support the command */who -chops* as a means of identifying channel operators.

Chanops can remove users from a channel and ban them from future access. On password-protected channels, they can invite users to join and can issue them the key to enter. On moderated channels, chanops can give selected users a voice that allows them to post messages to the channel while other users can only receive messages. Channel operators can grant chanop status to other users, and they can remove chanop status from other operators. When a new channel is created, some basic channel modes and settings should immediately be set to establish guidelines for the activity allowed by users and operators on the channel.

Common User Commands

Table 2 contains a sampling of user commands commonly used across different IRC clients and servers. Users of text-based clients enter these commands manually, whereas users of GUI clients usually click on icons or dropdown menus to engage the function, and the client automatically generates the command. Some commands contain specific parameters or are qualified by "flags" that set the limits of the command output. Table 3 contains the most common commands used by channel operators.

IRC AND CONVERSATIONAL DYNAMICS

As with all online communication systems, IRC is more than a network of computers relaying electronic files among themselves. Fundamentally, IRC systems are composed of humans who use the computer network to exchange information or conversation with others. As a somewhat specialized online community, IRC has drawn those who are more technically proficient, whose computer skills enable them to easily perform tasks such as downloading and installing software from an FTP site; learning intuitively the features and functions of new software applications; using line commands, scripting, or hand coding to accomplish tasks; adapting to the specific styles and conventions of online communication forums; and maintaining sufficient safeguards to protect their personal privacy and system security.

Many individuals "meet" regularly on IRC channels, where, in much the same way as with instant messaging and Web chat, they develop close relationships and a true sense of community. On some channels, the basis for commonality is the agreed-upon topic (such as advanced applications of certain software), and participants willingly share techniques and resources in mutual support of one another. Other channels are predominantly social in nature, marked by spontaneous casual conversation. In both types of IRC communities, casual online acquaintances are the norm, but significant one-on-one relationships sometimes develop. There are reports of IRC users who decided to move their relationships offline and meet face to face, and some have become business partners or marriage partners (e.g., Hoff and Hoff 1999). Of course, the majority of IRC relationships are restricted to the online context, but they constitute legitimate relationships that fill meaningful social roles for many users. Friends made on IRC are not only "virtual" friends but also "real" friends.

Although there are some resemblances to other communication media, text-based chat technologies represent a new form of interaction.

Table 2: Basic User Commands

/join #channelname	Joins the user to a global channel on the network, unless the user is banned or the channel is restricted (invite-only, secret, etc.).
/join channel1, #channel2	Allows the user to simultaneously participate in both of the channels listed.
/mode MyNickname +i	Sets the mode of the user "MyNickname" to invisible, enhancing privacy and security.
/list	Produces a list of channels on the server; often used with various flags and parameters.
/set hold_mode on	Prevents a long list from scrolling beyond the monitor's limits.
/names	Shows a list of nicknames of users currently on the network (potentially a huge listing, so always use parameters).
/names #channelname	Shows a list of nicknames of users currently on the channel (also very large on some channels, so use parameters).
/who #channelname	Lists nicknames, usermasks, and other information about current users on a channel.
/whois NewName	Produces basic information from the server's database about the user "NewName."
/msg NewName	Sends a private message to the user NewName; messages to all users are entered without the */msg* command.
/dcc chat NewName	Requests direct client connection with the user "NewName"; if NewName accepts, a direct private chat will bypass the IRC server (may be more private, have less lag).
/nick othername	Changes a user's nickname to the one specified.
/ignore badguy	Blocks or ignores messages from user called "badguy."
/part or /leave	Signs a user off of a channel; may be followed by a parting comment.
/quit	Terminates connection to the network; may include a brief comment.

Table 3: Basic Channel Operator Commands

/join #NewChannel	Creates a new channel with the specified name.
/mode #NewChannel +o|l|m|v|t	Sets the channel modes to Operator (chanop status can be assigned or removed), Limit (limits the number of users allowed at one time), Moderated (all users receive, but only some can post messages), Voice (grants selected users the ability to post messages), and Topic (set by operators only); several other modes are available.
/mode #NewChannel	Reveals all the current mode settings for the channel.
/mode #NewChannel +o mybuddy	Gives the user "mybuddy" operator status.
/mode #NewChannel −o mybuddy	Removes chanop status from the user "mybuddy."
/mode #NewChannel +l 20	Limits the number of users on NewChannel to 20.
/mode #NewChannel −l	Removes the limit on number of users.
/mode #NewChannel +v angelbaby	Allows the user "angelbaby" to post messages to NewChannel.
/topic #NewChannel IRC clients	Changes channel topic to "IRC clients."
/kick #NewChannel satanson	Kicks the user "satanson" off the channel.
/invite mybuddy #NewChannel	Invites the user "mybuddy" to join NewChannel.

Linguistic Features of Chat Conversations

Because chat messages are composed before being displayed, the usual turn-taking mechanisms that provide for an orderly conversation (Grice 1975) break down. Chat messages appear in the temporal order in which the chat server receives them; several conversational turns may occur between a comment and its response. Because there are no mechanisms for the orderly exchange of the conversational floor—a linguistic term describing the social conventions that control who is expected to speak (or not) at any given point in time—threads of discussion tend to interleave in chat environments (Werry 1996). Although this has led many to speculate about the difficulties that can arise from these new threading structures (e.g., Farnham et al. 2000; Smith et al. 2002), reports of smaller group (i.e., less than about 15 people) discussions rarely identify this as a problem (e.g., McDaniel, Olson, and Magee 1996). Herring (1999, Interactional coherence in CMC), having analyzed this lack of interactional coherence related to threading structures, suggests that the popularity of chat in spite of this limitation may have to do with the new types of linguistic play enabled, such as the ability to participate in multiple "conversations" at once.

The linguistic structure of chat interaction tends to look somewhat like that of face-to-face interaction (Condon and Cech 1996), with some notable exceptions. Because the usual nonverbal behaviors are absent in the online context, a greater responsibility is placed on verbal messages for feedback, affect, and nuances of meaning. Typically, IRC users attempt to replace nonverbal messages through various means (Werry 1996), such as using acronyms like IMHO ("in my humble opinion") and LOL ("laughing out loud"), or by inserting affect cues <grin>, demonstrative punctuation (no!!!!!!!!!), or emoticons such as the smiley face :-) and its many variant forms. These abbreviations also serve as important linguistic markers to identify membership in a social in-group (Wenger 1998; Cherny 1999; Sassenberg 2002). Because of the reduced efficiency involved in typing, chat conversations typically omit unnecessary linguistic information, such as some grammatical structures and elaborations/repeats of ideas (Condon and Cech 1996).

Behavioral Features of Chat Conversations

Communication researchers study the social, relational, and communicative dynamics of online communication forums such as IRC. Overall, these studies indicate that computer-mediated communication (CMC) systems do support the development of meaningful relationships, effective decision-making groups, and a legitimate sense of community (Finholt, Sproull, and Kiesler 1990; Reid 1991; Walther 1996, 1997; Wood and Smith 2001). Nevertheless, research has also identified some important differences between face-to-face and online communication. For example, in face-to-face interactions, people normally communicate interpersonal liking through nonverbal cues such as eye contact, smiles, proximity, touch, open body positioning, and vocal expressiveness (Richmond and McCroskey 1999), but these are all re-created in new ways online (Walther 1996). The absence of nonverbal communication cues led some early researchers to judge online communication as incapable of conveying subtle relational messages and therefore as an unsatisfactory medium for meaningful interpersonal exchange (Kiesler, Siegel, and McGuire 1984). However, in the intervening years, online skills have improved and online communication norms have evolved, with the result that modern communicators routinely use IRC and other CMC systems to engage in effective and meaningful interaction of all types. Modern researchers generally accept that all of the social norms and cues necessary for meaningful interaction do arise in IRC—or any other CMC medium—but at a slower rate than in face-to-face conversations (Walther 1996).

THE DARK SIDE OF IRC: SECURITY AND LEGAL ISSUES

Hate and Harassment on IRC

The anonymous nature of online communication systems such as IRC may contribute to the use of aggressive or inflammatory verbal abuse in the form of harassment or hate speech. Most IRC interactions involve the use of nicknames only, and users rarely reveal their true identities. This anonymity may contribute to a perception of low accountability, with the result that some IRC users may verbally lash out against individuals or groups in ways that are offensive and illegal. For example, Herring (2002, 2003) documented instances of flagrant sexual harassment on IRC and posited that male-dominated online environments are often hostile to participants whom they perceive to be female.

For American citizens, First Amendment (free speech) privileges extend to IRC interactions, but so do criminal laws preventing hate speech, inciting violence, and stalking. U.S. federal laws expressly forbid cyberstalking and online harassment (Executive Order 13133, Unlawful Conduct Using the Internet), which occur when a user annoys, abuses, threatens, or repeatedly initiates unwanted communication with another. Responsible channel operators seek to eliminate such activity on IRC channels by banning the offending user and, if necessary, reporting the user to legal authorities. Occasionally, however, chanops themselves engage in unethical communication behaviors (Herring 1999, The rhetorical dynamics of gender harassment on-line). IRC communications are subject to surveillance by law enforcement authorities acting pursuant to lawful court orders. IRC service providers, including operators, are required by law to cooperate with law enforcement authorities to effectuate the surveillance. Of course, many IRC participants are not U.S. citizens and not constrained by American laws, pointing to the ethical and legal complexities of global communication networks.

Children and IRC

Although a significant percentage of overall Internet users are under the age of 18, the number of minors on IRC may be relatively smaller. In truth, IRC is not especially suited to the needs and concerns of children, who tend to hang out in other Web-based chat systems that maintain terms of service, restricting certain activities and topics of discussion. Offenders in these chat rooms can be quickly and effectively removed by administrators. IRC channels, on the other hand, are generally not restricted, and certainly not as well policed. It is not infrequent to encounter adult conversations and offensive language on IRCs that would be unsuitable for children. On moderated channels, chanops can always remove a user's "voice" and disable the offender's ability to contribute to further discourse, but such censorial functions are not characteristic of most IRC channels. IRC is perceived by many to be spontaneous, freewheeling, unrestricted, and unpredictable—a kind of "Wild West" communication context.

In carefully controlled and appropriate IRC channels, children may benefit from online conversation with other children from around the world, with teachers and classmates, and with extended family members or parents who are traveling. In fact, chat systems are a quite common component of many online, educational courses. Unsupervised, however, children on IRCs may encounter risks such as cyberstalking, possibly leading to physical stalking if the child reveals personal information; offensive and harmful conversations with unwholesome characters such as pedophiles; and exposure to sexual content, viruses, or other harmful material, if the child accepts a file transfer from an unknown IRC user. Numerous laws and regulations exist to protect minors on the Internet, and responsible IRC users should immediately report any suspicious activity involving a minor on IRC. Since 1997, the FBI has vigorously investigated and prosecuted online pedophiles and stalkers of children through its "Innocent Images" program. Agents go online and pose as children to attract the attention of these criminals. Once these criminals make their moves on what they think are vulnerable children, they are arrested and brought to justice. The program has already resulted in several hundred convictions.

Scripts and Viruses

Informed IRC users are aware of the many risks involved with file transfers, through both hard media and the Internet. When users install new software, download Web pages, or receive files from external sources through either networking or hard media such as disks or CDs, some degree of security risk is introduced. It is a rare occurrence, but even respected commercial software has been distributed with inadvertent flaws that damage systems. More common is the intentional or unintentional passing of a virus or harmful script from user to user through various Internet connections, including IRC. Responsible users minimize these risks by maintaining awareness of current security threats, practicing discretion when networking, and taking steps to keep applications and operating systems up to date.

Most viruses are in .exe or .ini files, but they can also be concealed in zipped files or embedded in completely unrelated file types such as .jpg or .gif files. When launched by an unsuspecting user, viruses can cause irreparable harm to individual computers and potentially spread throughout entire systems. Some viruses are not destructive but merely irritating, such as those with pop-up messages of a humorous or salacious nature. Others may disable or destroy hard drives, data files, operating systems, and peripheral components, or create havoc throughout entire networks.

People who share word-processing files, script files, graphics, or other file types on IRC may potentially be spreading viruses, Trojans, or worms. Trojans (or Trojan horses) are spread by users who transfer seemingly benign files containing harmful concealed code. Worms are viruses that propagate themselves and migrate from one application to another within a computer, and from one computer to another within a network.

Scripts represent another source of external control and increased security risk. Scripts are files containing macros (or mini-programs) that enable an application to combine or automate various functions. IRC users have created scripts for tasks such as completing nicknames from typed initials, automatically performing ping operations, generating automated "away" responses, and customizing the output of IRC interactions. Some early IRC users enhanced the function of their IRC clients by writing scripts that have subsequently been incorporated into more recent versions of the software. Within the IRC community, techniques of script-writing constitute a frequent topic of conversation, and the sharing of scripts among users is relatively common. A number of Web sites or FTP download sites serve as archives or clearinghouses for the open sharing of scripts and script paks (sets of coordinated scripts) for various IRC clients. When an IRC user downloads a script file from an archive or another user, however, there is always a risk that the file may contain concealed or deceptive code that may launch unexpected or harmful functions in the receiver's system.

Most IRC clients include options to limit or disable the automatic or unintentional running of scripts, just as the major Web browsers include settings to control scripting functions encountered on the World Wide Web. Because harmful functions can be inserted into otherwise legitimate scripts, cautious IRC users run scripts only after proofreading every line of the code. Safe practice also calls for the careful screening of IRC users before accepting from them any files of any type. Common practice states that files should never be accepted from an unknown person, and file transfers from known parties should always be scanned for viruses before being opened.

Mischief and Sabotage on IRC

Many people use IRC safely and never experience viruses, takeovers, or threats to their security. It is not uncommon, however, to encounter less serious offenses allegedly launched by mischievous youngsters known as "script kiddies." (For a more serious perspective on "script kiddies," see Gilboa 1996.) Anyone who has been on IRC very long has probably observed attempts by an aggressive user to take charge of a channel or disrupt the flow of messages on a channel or network. "Channel taking" may be accomplished if a user is granted chanop status or deceptively uses an operator's nickname, then "de-ops" the other operators and indiscriminately bans users, kicks them off the channel, or silences their voices by turning the channel into a moderated one. Sometimes malicious users simultaneously send multiple files to another user, known as "flooding." If practiced on a large scale, flooding can significantly increase lag on a channel or entire network. Most IRC clients include optional settings that limit flooding to that client.

A more serious form of sabotage exists in denial-of-service (DoS) attacks, harmful data packets that sneak through loopholes in an operating system's security and launch erroneous messages from or to the client. DoS attacks, sometimes called "nukes," are against the law and can cause the host to disconnect from the Internet, freeze, or crash entirely. IRC can be exploited to facilitate a DoS attack by sending scripts called "bots" to unsuspecting users. Bots use vulnerabilities in the operating system to initiate the attack simultaneously from multiple computers. Engaging in such destructive practices violates federal law, specifically the Computer Fraud and Abuse Act (18 U.S.C. § 1030), as well as many state statutes. As a result of these laws, even first-time offenders could get jail time and stiff fines.

Because internal security is especially critical to certain types of organizations, some companies or institutions have restricted the use of IRC and other Internet functions through the use of firewalls that prohibit any computer in their network from connecting to an IRC server. For any IRC user, whether institutional or private, the best defense against mischief and sabotage is to refuse to accept file transfers or DCC chat requests from unknown persons, to carefully peruse every line of script code before launching it, and to maintain updated security files for operating systems, IRC clients, and virus protection software.

THE FUTURE OF CHAT

Although IRC is no longer as popular as it once was, its legacy lives on in modern chat programs. IRC use may be declining relative to other technologies, but chat as originally defined by IRC remains as popular as ever. There are still many popular Web-based chat programs that are built using IRC protocols and a Web-based IRC client. For example, when ICQ—a popular instant messaging service—added chat services, network administrators ran their own IRC servers to support this interaction. Other services, like MSN Chat, have taken these ideas and interaction style and implemented them using proprietary network protocols, technically distinguishing them from IRC, although they work quite similarly from a user's perspective.

Although the Internet community has largely moved on from IRC, chat still remains a popular and evolving conversational medium. In both commercial services and the academic research community, new chat interfaces appear frequently (e.g., Churchill et al. 2000; Farnham et al. 2000; Erickson et al. 2002; Smith et al. 2002). In fact, there is an argument to be made that enormously popular instant messaging services—online services that facilitate primarily one-to-one, text-based conversations between Internet users who already know one another—have their foundations in chat and IRC. IRC may have dropped off the radar, but chat is still an exciting area with much potential for future development.

GLOSSARY

Ban: Status of a user forbidden by a chanop to enter a channel.

Channel: A virtual chat group in which users interact, discussing specific topics or engaging in general conversation.

Chanops: Channel operators; they monitor and maintain a channel by setting the parameters and inviting or pelling users.

Client: Software run by the local computer of an IRC participant, converting the user's actions into commands recognized by an IRC server.

Daemon (IRC daemon, or IRCD): Software run by a server connected to the Internet, accepting connection requests from clients and relaying messages among users.

Direct Client Connection (DCC): Connection established between two users that allows them to bypass the network for increased privacy and faster connection.

Flooding: Simultaneously sending many messages to a single user, thus "flooding" a channel or an entire network with unwanted messages, probably increasing lag.

Internet Relay Chat (IRC): Real-time, text-based communication medium that uses a network of servers to connect geographically separated users.

IRCops: IRC operators who monitor and maintain IRC servers; they generally have very little to do with the operation of channels.

Lag: A delay in the transmission of messages between users or between a user and a server.

MOTD (Message of the Day): An automated confirmation message containing certain information and practices relating to a channel, its activities, and its current participants.

Netsplit: Disruption in the connection between servers that results in the fracturing of the network into subdivided parts and in the disconnection of some users.

Newbie: A newcomer to IRC or other online contexts.

Nickname: An invented name that uniquely identifies the user on a network.

Scripts: Files containing code that enables an application to combine or automate various functions.

CROSS REFERENCES

See *Online Communities; The Internet Fundamentals*.

REFERENCES

Cherny, L. 1999. *Conversation and community: Chat in a virtual world*. Stanford, CA: CSLI Publications.

Churchill, E., J. Trevor, S. Bly, and L. Nelson. 2000. StickyChats: Remote conversations over digital documents. In *Proceedings of the 2000 Conference on Computer Supported Cooperative Work (CSCW)* (Vol. Video Program, pp. 350). Philadelphia: ACM Press.

Condon, S. L., and C. G. Cech. 1996. Functional comparisons of face-to-face and computer-mediated decisions making interactions. In *Computer-mediated communication: Linguistic, social, and cross-cultural perspectives*, edited by S. C. Herring, 65–80. Philadelphia: John Benjamins Publishing.

Erickson, T., C. Halverson, W. A. Kellogg, M. Laff, and T. Wolf. 2002. Social translucence: Designing social infrastructures that make collective activity visible. *Communications of the ACM* 45(4):40–4.

Farnham, S., H. R. Chesley, D. E. McGhee, R. Kawal, and J. Landau. 2000. Structured online interactions: Improving the decision-making of small discussion groups. In *Proceedings of the 2000 Conference on Computer Supported Cooperative Work (CSCW)*, 299–308. Philadelphia: ACM Press.

Finholt, T., L. Sproull, and S. Kiesler. 1990. Communication and performance in ad hoc task groups. In *Intellectual teamwork: Social and technological foundations of cooperative work*, edited by J. Galagher, R. E. Kraut, and C. Edigo, 291–325. Hillsdale, NJ: Erlbaum.

Gilboa, N. 1996. Elites, lamers, narcs and whores: Exploring the computer underground. In *Wired_women: Gender and new realities in cyberspace*, edited by L. Cherny and E. R. Weise, 98–113. Seattle: Seal Press.

Grice, H. P. 1975. Logic and conversation. In *Syntax and semantics*, vol. 3, edited by P. Cole and J. Mordan, 41–58. New York: Academic Press.

Herring, S. 1999. Interactional coherence in CMC. *Journal of Computer-Mediated Communication 4*(4). http://jcmc.indiana.edu/vol4/issue4/herring.html (accessed May 12, 2004).

Herring, S. C. 1999. The rhetorical dynamics of gender harassment on-line. *The Information Society* 15(3): 151–67.

Herring, S. C. 2002. Cyber violence: Recognizing and resisting abuse in online environments. *Asian Women* 14:187–212.

Herring, S. C. 2003. Gender and power in online communication. In *The handbook of language and gender*, edited by J. Holmes and M. Meyerhoff, 202–28. Oxford: Blackwell.

Hoff, M., and J. Hoff. 1999. Chatting on the Net. www.newircusers.com (accessed January 16, 2004).

Kiesler, S., J. Siegel, and T. W. McGuire. 1984. Social psychological aspects of computer-mediated communication. *American Psychologist* 39(10):1123–34.

McDaniel, S. E., G. M. Olson, and J. C. Magee. 1996. Identifying and analyzing multiple threads in computer-mediated and face-to-face conversations. In *Proceedings of the 1996 Conference on Computer Supported Cooperative Work (CSCW)*, 39–47. Boston: ACM Press.

Oikarinen, J. n.d. IRC history. www.irc.org/history_docs/jarkko.html (accessed October 27, 2005).

Reid, E. M. 1991. Electropolis: Communication and community on Internet relay chat. http://eserver.org/cyber/reid.txt (accessed May 12, 2004).

Richmond, V. P., and J. C. McCroskey. 1999. Nonverbal behavior in interpersonal relations. 4th ed. Boston: Allyn and Bacon.

Sassenberg, K. 2002. Common bond and common identity groups on the Internet: Attachment and normative behavior in on-topic and off-topic chats. *Group Dynamics: Theory, Research, and Practice* 6(1):27–37.

Smith, M., J. Cadiz, and B. Burkhalter. 2002. Conversation trees and threaded chats. In *Proceedings of the 2002 Conference on Computer Supported Cooperative Work (CSCW)*, 97–105. New Orleans: ACM Press.

Walther, J. B. 1996. Computer-mediated communication: Impersonal, interpersonal, and hyperpersonal interaction. *Communication Research* 23:3–43.

Walther, J. B. 1997. Group and interpersonal effects in international computer-mediated collaboration. *Human Communication Research* 23:342–69.

Wenger, E. 1998. *Communities of practice: Learning, meaning, and identity*. New York: Cambridge University Press.

Werry, C. C. 1996. Linguistic and interactional features of internet relay chat. In *Computer-mediated communication: Linguistic, social and cross-cultural perspectives*, edited by S. C. Herring, 47–63. Philadelphia: John Benjamins.

Wood, A. F., and M. J. Smith. 2001. Online communication: Linking technology, identity, and culture. Mahwah, NJ: Lawrence Erlbaum.

Online Communities

Lee Sproull and Manuel Arriaga, *New York University*

INTRODUCTION

The Internet was not invented as a social technology, but it has certainly become one. From the earliest days of the ARPAnet (network of communicating computers established in the late 1960s with U.S. government funding), people have shaped and used the technology for social purposes. Today, millions of people use the Net as a means of making and maintaining social connections with people who share a common experience, interest, or concern. Social connections are found on the Net in contexts ranging from small family e-mail exchanges to fantasy games with hundreds of thousands of players. This chapter focuses on a subset of Net-based social contexts, which in the 1990s came to be called "online communities." In these Net-based social contexts, large numbers of people who share a common experience, interest, or concern interact with one another primarily, if not exclusively, over the Net. Most members have no preexisting ties with one another, and most of them will never meet face to face. Online communities range in technical sophistication from Usenet discussion groups to complex multiplayer fantasy games supported by proprietary software. They range in purpose from entertainment to political dissent to developing free software. They range in accessibility from completely open to anyone with Net access to accessible only through paid subscription to completely hidden behind corporate firewalls.

This chapter describes how technical and social factors mutually interact to produce and sustain online communities. It also begins to offer a differentiated view of online communities. Online communities share some underlying attributes and processes, but they differ in member interests, goals, processes, and consequences for their members, sponsors, and society. A more differentiated view will make possible more productive theorizing, research, and design.

DEFINITION AND COMPONENTS

Definition

Communities in the offline world are defined as collectivities of people who share a common experience, interest, or conviction; who experience a positive regard for other members; and who contribute to member welfare and collective welfare (Bender 1978; Etzioni and Etzioni 1999; Knoke 1986; Putnam, 2000). Not all social collectivities in the offline world are communities: people may share a common experience or interest, such as shopping at the same grocery store or reading the same newspaper columnist, with no positive regard for others or commitment to the collective welfare of all who share that experience. Examples of communities in the offline world include neighborhood communities, religious communities, civic and social communities such as youth scouting or service clubs, and collections of like-minded enthusiasts such as fans of particular sports teams. Communities in the physical world can be described by structural attributes such as rules, roles, and resources that exist independent of any member (e.g., Lin 2001). Thus, one can talk about the size of a community, membership requirements and obligations, community resources, and amenities. Communities can also be described by observable member behaviors such as attendance, rule following, donation, and interaction. And they can be described by member psychological orientation to the community and its members, such as feelings of trust, alienation, identification, and commitment. In the physical world, structural, behavioral, and psychological attributes exist along a continuum, so one can find more or less well-structured communities with more or less active and committed members. In casual usage, the term *community* usually suggests positive feelings, prosocial behavior, and choice. (People rarely talk about a "prison community," even though its inmates interact and have experiences in common.) Analytically, however, the term is a neutral one. Communities and their members can do physical and economic damage to members, neighbors, and enemies, just as they may produce beneficial outcomes.

The definition of *online community* used in this chapter is also based on shared experience, interest, or conviction; positive regard for members; and members' voluntary contribution to member welfare and collective welfare. An *online community* is defined as a large collectivity of voluntary members whose primary goal is member and collective welfare, whose members share a common interest, experience, or conviction and positive regard for other members, and who interact with one another and contribute to the collectivity primarily over the Net. Online communities can have more or less structure and more- or less-committed members. They may yield positive or negative consequences for their members, sponsors, and society. It is difficult to tightly bound the concept of community, because all human interaction occurs in a continuum of social organization—from the dyad to the nation-state. Nevertheless, the definition of *electronic community* used in this chapter excludes some forms of organized online social interaction for reasons of focus and because they are deserving of consideration in their own right. Table 1 shows the attributes of organized online interaction that are emphasized or deemphasized in online communities. As shown in Table 1, our definitional focus excludes electronic work groups and teams, whose primary goal is economic, whose members are paid employees, and whose size is relatively small. It excludes ad hoc friendship groups and buddy lists, which are relatively small, with members who interact primarily in the offline world. These two exclusions highlight our focus on shared interest groups of large size with voluntary members who interact primarily on the Net. The definition also excludes nominal groups such as "all the people who use Google" or "all Netizens" (who neither share a common interest nor interact with one another) or "all the people who read a particular Web log" (who may share a common interest but do not interact with one another). This exclusion highlights our focus on social interaction around a common interest and positive regard for other participants. Others who have offered definitions of electronic communities include Figallo (1998), Kim (2000), Porter (2004), Powazek (2002), Preece (2000), Rheingold (2000), and Werry and Mowbray (2002).

Until the mid-1990s, almost no one used the term *online community*. Instead groups that today might be named "online communities" were named after the technology that supported them and were called "newsgroups," "listservs," "mailing lists," "BBSs," or "Free-nets." In some ways, online communities that are the focus of this chapter bear little resemblance to communities in the physical world. They own few tangible resources; they require no visible or tangible commitment from members (such as taxes, dues, attendance at meetings); and members may never see or meet one another face to face. Yet some online communities have resources that may be economically valuable: their domain name, the wisdom accumulated in their FAQs (frequently asked questions), the intellectual property created by their members. Fantasy game characters and properties have yielded nontrivial sums of money for their creators on eBay auctions. The members of one voluntary online community collected enough money in member donations to buy a new server to host the community (Boczkowski 1999). Nevertheless, calling any electronic site where people may gather an

Table 1: Descriptive Attributes Characterizing Online Social Collectivities

Type	Shared Interest	Size	Interaction among Members	Primarily Electronic	Voluntary Participation	Concern for Member/Collective Well-Being
Corporate electronic work groups	Strong	Small	Extensive	Sometimes	No (part of employment)	Economic well-being of collective
Buddy lists	Modest to strong	Small	Minimal to extensive	Sometimes	Yes	Member, but not collective
People who read a particular blog	Modest to strong	Small to large	Minimal	Yes	Yes	No
People who use Google	None	Large	None	Yes	Yes	None
Social network	Modest to large	Small to large	Minimal to modest	Often	Yes	Rarely
Discussion community	Yes	Large audience; smaller contribution core	Minimal for readers; extensive for posters	Yes	Yes	Varies by level of participation; significant for contribution core
Online collaborative work community	Yes	Large audience; smaller contribution core	Minimal for readers; extensive for contribution core	Yes	Yes	Varies by level of participation; significant for contribution core

Note: Online communities, denoted by shading, are a subset of online social collectivities.

"online community" does not make it one. As in the offline world, in common parlance the term carries positive connotations, and some who have used it are guilty merely of wishful thinking. This wishful thinking characterizes many of those who, in the late 1990s, aspired to create online communities for profit (e.g., Bressler and Grantham 2000; Hagel and Armstrong 1997).

Supporting Technologies

In addition to the packet-switching technology of networked communication, many online communities rely on message-based group communication applications to support member interaction. These applications generally support asynchronous or synchronous discussion and interaction. In asynchronous interaction, people do not have to be logged on at the same time because messages are saved for later reading. In synchronous discussion, people must be logged on at the same time because messages are not stored. Asynchronous discussion is often supported via mailing lists or bulletin board applications. Mailing lists, a push technology, send group messages to a person's e-mail inbox, where they intermingle with the person's other e-mail and are saved until the recipient logs on to read them. With bulletin boards, a pull technology, a person reads group messages organized by topic in a file exclusively devoted to that group. (Some people establish filters to move all mailing list messages into separate folders, thereby making distribution lists function somewhat more like bulletin boards.) Synchronous discussion may be supported via talk programs such as IRC (Internet relay chat), Instant Messenger, or text-based virtual reality (VR) environments. MUDs (multi-user dungeon, domain, or dimension) and MOOs (MUD object-oriented) began as text-based virtual reality games, a computer-based version of fantasy games such as Dungeons and Dragons. Today, some are still organized as fantasy games; others are organized for professional or social purposes. Their spatial metaphors and programmable objects and characters are the precursor of today's graphically based fantasy games. With the spread of the Web and graphical browsers in the late 1990s, many online communities, which previously would have used only text-based message applications, created Web sites to support more varied forms of interaction. Some include real-time chat for discussions that are scheduled and announced in advance. Some use special file formats to share image, sound, or video files. Online game communities are supported by more or less elaborate software that supports play in board games like chess or supports character creation and interaction in fantasy worlds. Most discussion among members on online community Web sites still occurs in message-based discussions, however. Even the fantasy games have discussion boards.

In the early years of the twenty-first century, technologies for preparing, publishing, and linking Web pages became easier to use and spread widely to support large social collectivities. The "blogosphere" consists of everyone who uses applications for preparing and publishing Web pages to publish a Web log (blog), which consists of an online journal with time-stamped entries displayed in reverse chronological order. The blogosphere is merely a very large nominal group, and not a community by our definition, but some bloggers who share a common interest in a topic may interact with one another indirectly through commenting on one another's blogs. Much of the "interaction" resembles online journalism or columns with linked letters to the editor, rather than the more interpersonal interaction found in message-based communities. (Nardi and colleagues [2004] identify five broad motivations that drive people to publish a blog, only one of which is related to community formation and maintenance.) However, some groups of blogs may be considered a community by our definition. These topical groups may crystallize in "Web blog rings" created by an application that places a banner at the bottom of related participant blogs; upon clicking on the banner, the reader is taken to another, randomly chosen blog that is a member of that "ring." Over time, blog-ring members may develop a psychological affiliation with the Web blog ring and interpersonal bonds with one another that go beyond merely posting and reading blog entries on a common topic. (Herring et al. [2004] report that fewer than 5 percent of blogs belong to a blog ring.)

Social networking Web sites allow their members to establish, develop, and maintain "social networks" through publishing and linking "profile" pages created by their members. These are structured Web pages in which members share information about themselves. The "social" nature of these sites essentially results from three features. First, the software allows users to add links to other people's profiles, thereby adding "friends" to one's network. Once in the same network, site members have easy access to one another's profiles through an automatically generated list of "friends" on their home page. Second, users are able both to exchange asynchronous messages among themselves and to "chat" synchronously online. The ability to broadcast a message (called "bulletins" on some of the sites) to all "friends" is also provided, as are "comments," which can be attached to a member's profile (thus becoming visible to all who visit that profile). Third, these sites typically support "groups," which members with a common interest or experience can join. This feature allows users to self-organize along lines other than those defined by their preexisting social networks and explore their "extended network" (the term used by one social networking site, MySpace, to characterize members who do *not* belong to a member's list of "friends") in yet another way. Social networking sites and applications are enormously popular (MySpace was the third most frequently visited Web site during July 2007). But like blogs, most social network sites do not exhibit all of the attributes enumerated in our definition of online community. Although creating a profile is an entirely voluntary act, the ability to join someone else's social network occurs only by invitation. Moreover, the concept of community welfare, a necessary attribute in our definition of online community, is rarely prominent in these sites. One sociologist commented that these sites are characterized by "voyeurism and exhibitionism . . . [like] hanging out at the mall or lounging on the quad . . . seeing and being seen" (Cassidy 2006).

A wiki is a software system that serves Web pages while providing site visitors the possibility to easily add, modify, or delete their contents. At its simplest, wikis merely generate HTML code that includes discrete links labeled "edit" interspersed along the page. If a user follows such a link, she will be presented with a form that allows her to edit the contents of the page that she was previously reading. The page is edited using a simple markup language; modern wiki implementations also provide a set of buttons through which the same functions (e.g., italicize text, create a hyperlink, etc.) can be accomplished without knowledge of that markup language. Either way, once a modification is done it is immediately reflected in the original page. The fundamental change introduced by the use of a wiki in comparison with traditional Web sites is that the authors and readers of a site are no longer two distinct groups: instead, active participant visitors can create and directly edit the content that attracts those same visitors to the site. Wikis are successfully used both by large online communities—the best-known example being Wikipedia (http://en.wikipedia.org), a collaborative effort to create an online encyclopedia; the English edition contained 1.9 million entries as of July 2007—as well as by work groups within organizations.

General Attributes and Processes

The Social Psychology of Text-Based Communication

Typically, online community members interact with one another while sitting alone at a computer keyboard. This solitary social behavior is characterized by fewer social context cues than are available in face-to-face gatherings. Weak social context cues mean that people who compose and send messages have few explicit reminders of the number of people who will read them. They have few reminders of their physical appearance, social status, or nonverbal reactions compared with face-to-face or telephone communication. Similarly, people who read messages or Web pages have relatively few reminders of the social attributes of people who create them in comparison with face-to-face gatherings. (In virtual reality communities, people can create entirely new personas. See Turkle [1995] for an exploration of multiple online identities.) Social context cues help to regulate communication in face-to-face and telephonic interaction. They provide feedback as to who is receiving communications and how those communications are being received and interpreted. People adjust the style and substance of their communications as a function of these cues. When those cues are attenuated, communication tends to be relatively frank and open (Kendall 2002; Reid 1999; Sproull and Kiesler 1991). Weak social context cues can lead to different effects, even within the same community. They can increase affiliation and commitment among members because objective differences among members are obscured while subjective similarities, based on members' common interest, are magnified (Galegher, Sproull, and Kiesler 1998; Mackenna and Bargh 1998; Sproull and Faraj 1995). Alternatively, they can increase disaffection and dropout because it may be more difficult to establish common ground or consensus and manage conflict (Carnevale and Probst 1997; Cramton 2001; Dibbell 1998; Herring 1994; Kollock and Smith 1996). Weak social context cues condition communication in many online communities. They allow for a potentially greater geographic and social diversity of participants than many physical communities do. At the same time, they offer few cues to that social diversity in interaction, except those revealed through language and linguistic cues (e.g., Herring 2001). Increasingly, Web-based community applications encourage members to upload profile files, which can display enduring personal information about members' identities and interests. Still, in 2007 most interaction among community members takes place via text messages in the absence of other individuating information.

Microcontributions

Many of the tools for electronic community participation are based on a relatively fine granularity of time and attention—the text message, the blog entry, the page edit. Although contributions can be any length, messages sent to asynchronous discussion communities typically range between ten and thirty lines, or one to two screens, of text. For example, Winzelberg (1997) reported a mean of 131 words; Galegher et al. (1998) reported a mean of eight to twenty lines of new text; Wasko and Faraj (2000) reported a mean of twenty-five to thirty lines of text; Sproull and Faraj (1995) reported a mean of twenty-two to forty-two lines of new text. The average blog entry, according to Herring et al. (2004), has a length of approximately 210 words. Wikipedia articles on average run to 415 words (Wikipedia: Size comparisons 2006). In asynchronous applications, people can read one or more messages or pages and post or send one or more messages/pages at their convenience. The message can be thought of as a microcontribution to the community. When people are online much of the day as a part of their work, voluntary microcontributions can be interspersed throughout the work day. For those who have Net access at home, participation can also be interspersed with other activities at home. Even in synchronous communities, some members report that they keep a community window open on their screen while they are doing other things. Every once in a while they "check in" on the community (Kendall 2002). Some people may devote hours a week to an online community, but they can do so in small units of time at their own convenience.

Voluntary communities based on microcontributions have relatively low barriers to entry. It is fairly easy to read enough microcontributions to know whether a particular community is relevant or appropriate. If so, that same reading readily demonstrates the appropriate form that a newcomer's own microcontributions should take. The production and posting of initial microcontributions takes relatively little effort. Then, if all goes well, the newcomer receives positive reinforcement in the form of (easy-to-produce) responding microcontributions from other community members. Whereas microcontributions create low barriers to entry, they may also create high barriers to commitment. It can be difficult to develop complex arguments or achieve nuanced understanding through microcontributions. Communities that are easy to join are often just as easy to leave (Butler 2001).

Aggregation Mechanisms and Management Processes

Although people can make ad hoc contributions to online communities at random, microcontributions must be aggregated and organized into larger units for efficiency and social effectiveness. Both technical and social mechanisms are used to organize the smallest unit of contribution into larger units that are useful to participants. Software for asynchronous discussion lets people indicate that their contribution is a response to a previous one. All contributions so designated can be aggregated by the software and displayed as "threads"—a seed message and all reactions to it. Forms of threads common from the earliest days of the Net include a question with replies and a proposal or statement with comments. Threads organize microcontributions so that everyone can see their constituent parts, making it easy for potential contributors and beneficiaries to see what has already been said. Software also allows readers to mark threads they have already read or to display only unread messages.

Asynchronous discussion communities may have tens or hundreds of threads active at the same time, necessitating a layer of organization above the self-organizing thread. In these cases, a human designer may suggest or impose a topic map or architecture to organize threads into more general topic categories. (In some older bulletin board systems, people would vote to create a new top-level topic, which would get its own separate bulletin board.) Web-based software can display these maps graphically so that users may click on a topic that interests them and see all threads related to that topic. The shared interest of a group usually suggests the type of topical map that may be created. For example, many communities centered on medical concern have topics for symptoms, medications and side effects, negotiating the health care system, and managing relationships with family and friends. Movie or television fan communities have topics for major and minor characters, actors who play those characters, past and future episodes. Communities that build software have categories for different types of code, bug reports, patches, and documentation.

Threads and topic maps may be insufficient to structure extremely large numbers of messages. Another form of microcontribution, the rating message, adds a quality dimension to message structuring. Some Web sites now give members the opportunity to rate the contribution of others' messages. Software then aggregates and displays these ratings in an overall quality index for contributions (e.g., Slashdot) or contributors (e.g., MotleyFool). Explicit ratings of contribution quality have been shown to increase economic trust within electronic markets like eBay (Kollock 1999). It is an open question whether they increase or inhibit emotional trust and cohesiveness within an electronic community setting, but at least some research suggests that they increase the average quality of messages and increase participant duration (Moon and Sproull 2006).

Software for synchronous interaction may organize contributions in channels or use a spatial metaphor to organize contributions in "rooms" (e.g., Schlager and Schank 1997). Online communities associated with a geographic locality may organize contributions around civic functions, like the garden club or public library (e.g., Sproull and Patterson 2004). As these communities increase in size, the organizers or members themselves construct new rooms, buildings, and territories to organize interaction. Some also offer rating and review functions to rate characters or contestants and properties.

In online software development communities, two technologies, in addition to mailing lists, support managing and aggregating contributions: revision control systems and a "diffing and patching" mechanism. Revision control systems allow developers to work independently on code in parallel and then automatically "merge" all the changes they have made, so that the result is a single, consolidated version of the code. Core developers and regular contributors will be granted "write-access," meaning that their account in the revision-control system allows them to introduce changes to the code (as opposed to only being able to download it). Those who lack write-access to the code repository download the latest version of the code, modify it, and then present the changes they introduced to one of the core developers for acceptance. They do so by running a program called "diff," which generates a small file describing the changes between two versions of one or more files. These small files are called "patches." The core developer who receives a "patch" can then use a second program (itself called "patch") to obtain the modified version of the code and determine whether it should be added to the code base.

Most wiki systems include several additional organizing features with the aim of addressing difficulties arising from disagreement over the site's contents and the risk of "wiki vandalism." First, each page on the wiki has an associated "talk page," where contributors can engage in a discussion of the changes they have introduced (or wish to introduce) on that particular page. Second, the system includes a "page history" function, through which participants can see a log of all changes introduced to a particular page. Most importantly, that same mechanism allows pages to be easily "reverted" to a previous state; it is through this mechanism that "edit wars"—in which groups with different views on an issue repeatedly try to modify the wiki's contents so that it reflects a particular group's perspective—take place. Third, and although it is often seen as being in contradiction with the democratic ideals of the wiki system, several platforms also allow the administrator(s) of the wiki to restrict the ability to introduce changes to certain pages. A well-known instance is that of Wikipedia and its several levels of protection: some pages can be edited by any visitor; others require an account on the Wikipedia Web site that is at least 4 days old but is otherwise unrestricted; and, finally, some other pages can be edited only by Wikipedia administrators.

Norms and Motivations

In addition to organizing mechanisms provided through software, norms of community behavior and motivations of community members serve to organize and influence member behavior. Some norms of community behavior, which were visible from the early days of the ARPAnet, prevail across many types of online communities. Most important is the norm of altruism. Online community members freely offer information, advice, and emotional support to one another with no expectation of direct reciprocity or financial reward. The fundamental dynamic supporting discussion communities is that someone asks a question or makes a proposal or statement and other people provide answers or comments. Utilitarian self-interest may be all that motivates the askers—a personal need for information. But pure self-interest does not explain the behavior of people who reply. By definition, volunteer members are not paid for their replies. Because they are unlikely to have a personal relationship with the person they help, neither friendship obligation nor the expectation of direct reciprocity is likely to compel their behavior. Indeed, an early influential paper (Thorn and Connolly 1987) predicted that computer-based information exchange systems that relied on volunteers would be doomed to failure. The authors argued that people who could give the best replies would have no incentive to participate because they would receive few benefits for doing so—it was unlikely that anyone could answer their questions; their time would be unrewarded. (In social dilemmas, helping in these situations is known as the "sucker's choice.") Over time, therefore, the quality of help would decline until people no longer even bothered to ask questions. The fallacy in this argument is the assumption that rewards to people who provide help must come in the same form as the help they give. Yet motivations for helping behavior can be quite complex. In studies of volunteers in the physical world, motivations include commitment to the cause or interest associated with the community, the desire to help others, benefits from displaying expertise, and the personal satisfaction and self-esteem derived from helping others (e.g., Clary et al. 1998; Omoto and Snyder 1995). Studies of electronic discussion communities document a similar combination of motivations for people who answer questions and otherwise support their online community (e.g., Butler et al. 2007; Kollock 1998; Lakhani and von Hippel 2003; Wasko and Faraj 2000). Self-expression and identity display are important motives in blogs and social networking sites.

A second extraordinarily important norm is peer review of content (Benkler 2002). In most volunteer online communities, there are no "authorities" to certify the accuracy of all content. Instead, it is expected that members themselves will comment on the quality, accuracy, completeness, and so on of one another's contributions. Similarly, peer review of behavior is also expected: it is normative for members to chastise or complain about inappropriate behavior and praise helpful behavior.

In virtual reality communities, the VR environment indexes participants' motives (Reid 1999). In VR game communities, the motives are tied to the rules of the game: amass property, kill enemies, design an award-winning room, and so on. In VR professional communities, the motives are tied to the profession: contribute to shared databases, review articles, participate in policy discussions. In VR social communities, the motives are tied to exploring social worlds. In collaborative work communities motives are tied, at least in part, to furthering the goals of the community such as building better software, distributing digital books, organizing volunteers, etc.

HISTORY OF ONLINE COMMUNITIES

Both the technical and social trajectories of electronic communities began with the design and early deployment of networked computing in the late 1960s and early 1970s. (See Table 2 for timeline.) Whereas computer networking was initially conceived as a way to share scarce computing resources located in one physical place with researchers at other places via remote access, it soon became a convenient way for people to gain access to people at remote sites as well as to remote computers (Licklider and Veza 1978; Sproull and Kiesler 1991). During the 1970s and 1980s, people created additional networks and wrote e-mail and bulletin board software, which represented technical innovations and improvements that made networked computing more useful for supporting human communication. During the 1990s, the technical innovations of the Web and the graphical browser supported the broad diffusion of electronic communication to millions of U.S. households and hundreds of millions of people worldwide. In the first years of the twenty-first century, easy personal publishing and page linking undergirded an explosive growth in social networking and blogging.

The social trajectory of electronic discussion communities had its beginnings in the same technical community that invented and refined the ARPAnet. By the mid-1970s, ARPA program officers and researchers around the country had begun using group e-mail to share results, discuss plans, and organize meetings. Some of these researchers also began using group e-mail for purposes unrelated to work: for example, to share opinions on cheap Chinese restaurants in Boston and Palo Alto, favorite science fiction books, inexpensive wine, and new movies. This research community invented both the technology (networking and group communication tools) and the new form of social organization (the voluntary electronic group). They appropriated technologies that were created for utilitarian purposes to create self-organizing forums for the voluntary discussion of common interests. The social trajectory of VR communities began in 1979–1980 with an effort to program a game that would be like the fantasy game Dungeons and Dragons that was played in the physical world. The first multi-user VR game was accessible on the ARPAnet in 1980.

By the twenty-fifth anniversary of the ARPAnet in 1994, electronic group communication had become a taken-for-granted process, and voluntary electronic discussion communities had become a taken-for-granted organizational form in universities, technical communities and scientific disciplines, and some corporations (e.g., Finholt and Sproull 1990; Kiesler and Sproull 1987; Orlikowski and Yates 1994; Walsh and Bayma 1996). Multiplayer games were also becoming popular on university campuses. Despite their growth, at this point both discussion groups and games were still in large measure the province of young, technically adept men. The final years of the twentieth century saw Net-based communication enter the mainstream of U.S. life because of a combination of technical and economic developments. The technical developments were the Web and the graphical browser, which made it much easier for ordinary people to find and access information and groups on the Net. The economic developments were the commercialization of the Net and AOL's business model. Once the Net began to be commercialized, corporations began to see potential economic value in electronic communities and so endeavored to support them

Table 2: Timeline for Community-Oriented Group Communication on the Net

Date	Name	Technical Developments	Social Developments
1965–1968	ARPA projects	Research on networking to share scarce computing resources	Networking research community forms across small number of labs
1969	ARPAnet	First four ARPA sites connected	
1972	RD	First ARPAnet e-mail management program	
1973			75 percent of ARPAnet traffic is e-mail
1975	MsgGroup	First ARPAnet mailing list	
1978	BBS	First bulletin board system	
1979	Usenet	Free software to share bulletin board discussions	
1979	MUD	First multiuser VR game	
1979	CompuServe	Began offering e-mail to customers	
1980	MUD	MUD first played over ARPAnet	
1981	Bitnet	Computer network for non-ARPAnet universities	University computer center directors band together to support this
1981	Sendmail	Free software to send mail across networks	
1984–1985	Delphi, Prodigy, AOL	Commercial information services founded that offered e-mail	
1985	Listserv	Free software to manage e-mail lists	
1986	IETF		Volunteers focused on technical operation and evolution of Internet
1988			>1000 public listservs
1990			>1000 Usenet groups; >4000 posts per day
1990	World Wide Web	Invented by Tim Berners-Lee	
1990	LambdaMOO	VR environment created at Xerox PARC	
1991	Linux	Free computer operating system	First message about Linux posted to Usenet group
1992	AOL	Connects to Internet	
1994	Netscape	Introduced graphical Web browser	
1994			>10,000 Usenet groups; >78,000 posts per day; estimated 3.8 million subscribers to commercial online services
1995	wiki	Software that allows for collaborative writing and editing of Web pages	
1999	blog	Term coined as contraction of "Web log," Web page journal with timestamped entries	
2000			34 million AOL subscribers; 44 million U.S. households online
2001			90,000 Usenet groups; 54,000 public Listserv groups
2001	Wikipedia		Anyone can create and edit an encyclopedia article on any topic
2002	Friendster	Social networking site founded	
2004			65 percent of U.S. citizens are online; 600 million people worldwide are online
July 2006			MySpace was most visited domain on the Internet; 1.3 million Wikipedia articles published; 97 million Americans use the Internet on an average day

IETF = Internet Engineering Task Force; MUD = multi-user dungeon, domain, or dimension; VR = virtual reality.

and, indeed, to "monetize" them (e.g., Hagel and Armstrong 1997). The commercial online game industry began to grow. AOL's business model emphasized e-mail and member discussion forums, in contrast with that of other commercial services that were still emphasizing access to databases. By 2000, AOL had 34 million members—more than all the other commercial services combined—many of them participating in electronic forums and communities of interest. That year, 44 million U.S. households were on the Net. (By 2004, nearly two-thirds of Americans were online [Fallows 2004].) Despite the enormous influx of people very different from the ARPAnet pioneers, four themes evident from the earliest days of the ARPAnet continued to characterize electronic communication at the beginning of the twenty-first century: access to people as much as to databases, group communication as well as dyadic communication, personal interest topics as well as utilitarian ones, and self-organizing voluntary electronic communities.

TYPES OF ONLINE COMMUNITIES

Until the early 1990s, most electronic communities used similar technology and their members had similar attributes. Highly educated, young, technically adept people congregated electronically with similar others who shared similar interests. These congregations were relatively homogeneous in structure, process, and membership. At the beginning of the twenty-first century, however, the diversity of Internet users and group goals and processes is so great that it is helpful to differentiate types of communities to understand their costs and benefits in more detail. This section categorizes and describes types of online communities based on the interests that members or sponsors have in common. (See Table 3 for examples.) It is neither an exhaustive nor a mutually exclusive characterization, but it does represent some prevalent types. Despite the differences across types of shared interest, all of these communities are characterized by any-time, any-place

Table 3: Examples of Online Communities

Consumer Communities	
www.audifans.com	Fans of the Audi marque
www.lugnet.com	Adult fans of Lego
www.Britney-Spears-portal.com	Fans of Britney Spears
http://Rec.arts.tv.soaps	Soap opera fans
(A)vocation Communities	
www.mastersrowing.org	For masters rowers and scullers
www.bikeforums.net	For the avid cyclist
www.Everquest.com	For EverQuest players
http://secondlife.com	Virtual reality world built and occupied by its inhabitants
www.chessclub.com	For chess fans
www.tappedin.sri.com	For K–12 teachers and teacher educators
www.LambdaMoo.info/	Virtual reality environment for social interaction
http://boogaj.typepad.com/knitting_blogs/	Knitting blogs Web ring
Place-Based Communities	
www.bev.net	Blacksburg Electronic Village
www.guerrillagardening.org	Volunteers who stealthily plant shrubs and flowers in London
http://web.mit.edu/knh/www/downloads/khampton01.pdf	Wired suburb of Toronto, Canada
www.backfence.com	"Do it yourself local news"
Condition Communities	
www.seniornet.org	For people over age 50
www.systers.org	For female computer scientists
www.deja.com/group/alt.support.depression	Usenet group for sufferers of depression
www.geocities.com/heartland/prairie/4727/bhnew.htm	Mailing list for people with hearing loss
www.deja.com/group/rec.soc.argentina	Mailing list for Argentinian expatriates

(continued)

Table 3: *(Continued)*

Concern Communities	
www.clearwisdom.net	For practitioners of Falun Gong
www.419legal.org	For Internet antifraud activitists
www.dailykos.com	Daily political news and commentary with a liberal perspective
www.moveon.org	For online political activists
www.deja.com/group/talk.guns	Usenet group for handgun advocates
www.deja.com/group/soc.religion.mormon	Usenet group for believers in Mormonism
Collaborative Work Communities	
http://vger.kernel.org/	Mailing list for developing the Linux kernel
www.wikipedia.com	Collaborative project to produce an online encyclopedia
www.ietf.org	For maintaining and improving the Internet
www.rhizome.org	For creating and discussing new media art
www.pgdp.net	For digitizing public domain books
www.OhmyNews.com	Online newspaper with contributions by "citizen reporters"

communication with relatively weak social context cues, aggregated microcontributions, and norms of interaction. The boundaries across types can be fuzzy; the descriptions indicate central tendencies within types.

Types by Member Interest

Consumer Communities: Brands and Fans

Consumer communities are composed of people who share a common interest in and are loyal to a particular brand, team, entertainer, or media property. Although people organized fan clubs prior to the Net, it was difficult to arrange fan club activities on a large scale and frequent basis. Online customer communities have a much broader reach. People voluntarily share their information and passion with thousands or hundreds of thousands of others who share their interests in a particular product, entertainer, or media property. AudiFans, for example, is composed of more than 1000 Audi enthusiasts who exchange information about parts suppliers and mechanics, post photos of their cars, and share the joys and sorrows of Audi ownership. The Britney Spears portal contains pictures, MP3 files, news, and forums where thousands of people comment (positively or negatively) on all things having to do with Britney. For most members of consumer communities, the shared interest may be an intense one, but it typically represents a fairly small and often short-lived portion of members' lives.

(A)vocation Communities

Experts and enthusiasts form and join voluntary (a)vocation communities to increase their pleasure and proficiency in their hobbies or work. Whereas a particular product may be a means to advancing a common interest in an (a)vocation community, the product is not the primary focus of attention, as it is in a consumer community. From bicycling to computer programming, dog training to quilting, karate to the Civil War, there are online communities for people who share these interests. "How-to" information prevails in (a)vocation community discussions; members who share their expertise are greatly appreciated. Network and Internet security are a topic for some (a)vocation communities. Usenet, for example, supports more than twenty-five groups on the topics of cracking, hacking, and network security where people discuss how to make or break secure systems. BikeForums, for example, has more than 3500 members who discuss and debate bicycle commuting, mountain biking, tandem biking, racing, training, and so on. The knitters web blog ring connects more than 900 authors of blogs about knitting. Tapped In is a professional VR community for K–12 educators whose 20,000 members, as of 2006, discuss curriculum, share lesson plans, and so on. The Internet Chess Club had more than 30,000 members in 2006 who play chess with other members, take lessons, play in tournaments, watch and discuss grandmaster competitions, and so on. EverQuest and Ultima are large online communities for people who delight in fantasy games. Second Life is a virtual world with more than 2 million inhabitants. The shared community interest in (a)vocation communities may represent a relatively enduring part of members' lives.

Place-Based Communities

These online communities are organized by and for people who live in a particular geographic locale. Their genesis in the early 1980s had a political agenda—to give residents a(n electronic) voice in the local political process (e.g., Schuler 1996; Schuler and Day 2004). More recent versions, such as Backfence, have had the broader goal of building social capital by increasing the density of electronic social connections among residents of physical communities (Hampton and Wellman 1999; Kavanaugh 2003; Sproull and Patterson 2004). In principle, the interest shared by place-based community members should last at least as long as people reside in the community. (Recent developments like MeetUp.com let people use the Internet to find others in their geographic area who share a common interest for the purpose of scheduling face-to-face meetings. These applications are not emphasized in this chapter because they focus primarily on arranging face-to-face meetings, not on sustaining broader electronic participation.)

Common Condition Communities

In these communities, people share the experience of, and interest in, a common condition. The condition may be based on a demographic characteristic such as race, age, or ethnic background; a medical or psychological condition such as arthritis or depression; or being an alumnus/a of a particular organization such as a college or branch of the military. People join condition communities to learn how others experience or are coping with their condition and to share their own experiences. Along with practical information and advice, a "you are not alone" sentiment prevails in many discussions. BeyondHearing, for example, has more than 1000 members who have a hearing loss or who have a loved one with a hearing loss. Topics range from cochlear implants to the best audiologists to funny stories about lip reading mistakes. Systers' membership is more than 2300 female computer scientists and engineers, as of 2006, who discuss female-friendly graduate schools and employers, how to manage male subordinates in the workplace, and so on. The shared community interest is often a long-term or lifetime one for members.

Concern Communities

In these communities, members share an interest in a common political, social, or ideological concern. Because members often wish to influence the state of affairs in the physical world, these communities usually have multifaceted ties to that world. They may announce and comment on real-world events and organize letter-writing campaigns, rallies, fund-raisers, and so forth. They may use click-and-donate applications to raise money or pledges of volunteer time. MoveOn, for example, began as an online petition drive to censure, but not impeach, U.S. President Bill Clinton and has grown to include many online advocacy groups that organize volunteer campaigns. The Howard Dean presidential candidacy used the Net for organizing in 2003–2004. More than 1000 members of alt.religion.mormon discuss and debate Mormon doctrine and practices. A number of blogs support concern communities, particular political concern communities (e.g., Dailykos supports Democratic and liberal/progressive policies and politicians). The shared interest underlying concern communities is likely to be a deep and abiding one for their members, although active participation may ebb and flow in concert with external events.

Collaborative Work Communities

Unlike other community types whose primary output is talk or self-expression, members of collaborative work communities use the Net to voluntarily produce real products, be they software, literary works, or other creations. Much open source software is produced in online voluntary communities today, despite the growing interest of the corporate sector (e.g., Raymond 1999). Indeed, much of the design and engineering of the Internet itself is accomplished by a voluntary community that conducts much of its business electronically, the Internet Engineering Task Force (n.d.). "Citizen journalists" contribute stories to an international online newspaper. Poets participate in writers' communities whose members thoroughly critique one another's work. A pragmatic writing community, Wikipedia, is creating a new encyclopedia. The community project has produced more than 1.7 million English language articles as of July 2007. The distributed proofreaders project has digitized, proofread, and posted more than 5000 public domain books. The shared interest of collaborative work communities is likely to be deeply involving for members, although it need not be as enduring as the shared interest in concern communities.

Types by Sponsor Interest

Only within the past 10 years have online communities been sponsored or organized by anyone other than members themselves (with a few exceptions such as The Well and geographically based bulletin board systems called Free-nets). Many recent third-party sponsors or organizers have been motivated by the profit potential of online communities, with revenue models based on either sales (of advertising, membership lists, products, etc.) or subscriptions. During the dot-com boom, third-party sponsors of some customer and demographic condition communities used sales-based revenue models. Profit-oriented community sites were created for, for example, L'eggs panty hose, Kraft food products, women (iVillage), Asian Americans (Asia Street), and African Americans (NetNoir). Some third-party-sponsored communities based on subscriptions experienced some years of economic health; arguably a substantial (but unknown) fraction of AOL's growth in the 1990s was a function of online community memberships. (In 2006 AOL abandoned its subscription-based model.) Within the game industry, subscription-based revenue models continue to be successful. Several multiplayer game communities have thousands or hundreds of thousands of members. Members of one game, EverQuest, report spending an average of more than 22 hours a week playing it (Yee 2001). At least one professional social networking site, LinkedIn, reports profitability based on subscription revenue. Other social networking sites, based on advertising revenues, do not disclose their financials. But one such site, MySpace, was purchased by News Corp. in 2005 for $580 million.

Some corporations have avoided revenue-based models and instead have supported online communities to build market share or increase customer satisfaction and loyalty. Sun Microsystems sponsors the Java Developer Connection, an (a)vocation community designed to support and expand the Java software developer community worldwide. The Lego Corporation supports several "adult-fans-of-Lego" sites, in addition to sponsoring its own site, to support loyal customers. Various software companies support voluntary technical discussion and support communities in the interest of increasing high-quality, inexpensive tech support. Harley-Davidson uses H.O.G., its online members-only group, to reinforce the brand loyalty of Harley owners worldwide. Whatever the motivation of corporate sponsors, if people do not experience enduring community membership benefits they will not participate, and the community will die.

In the not-for-profit sector, foundations and service organizations have sponsored communities for their target populations with the goal of improving their well-being. For example, the Markle Foundation sponsored the creation of Seniornet, a not-for-profit online community for people over age 50, which currently has 39,000 members. The National Science Foundation sponsored Tapped In, a not-for-profit online community for K–12 school teachers and teacher educators, which currently has more than 20,000 members.

CONSEQUENCES OF ONLINE COMMUNITIES

Positive Effects

Benefits to Members

Not surprisingly, most studies of online communities report that information benefits are important to their members (e.g., Baym 1999; Lakhani and von Hippel 2003; Wasko and Faraj 2000). What is noteworthy is the form that the information takes. It is not the disembodied, depersonalized information that can be found in databases or official documents, which are themselves easily accessible on the Web. Instead, it is often profoundly *personalized* information. Its form and content are personal—personal experiences and thoughts—whether they take the form of reflections published on blogs, profiles on social network sites, or posts on discussion sites. Likewise, its audience is personal. Questions or requests for comment do not look like database queries: They are framed for human understanding and response. (A discourse analysis of Usenet groups found that almost all questions included a specific reference to readers; the few that did not were much less likely to receive replies; Galegher et al. 1998.) Replies typically address the person or situation engendering the request and are based on the replier's own situation or experience. In consumer communities, personalized information can increase members' pleasure in using or experiencing the product or property. Personalized information can increase members' pleasure or competence in practicing their (a)vocation. It can also challenge one's assumptions and beliefs (e.g., Kendall 2002).

Members derive more than information benefits from online communities, however. Some also derive the social and emotional benefits that can come from interacting with other people: getting to know them, building relationships, making friends, having fun (e.g., Baym 1999; Butler et al. 2007; Cummings, Sproull, and Kiesler 2002; Kendall 2002; Quan y Hasse et al. 2002; Rheingold, 2000). Of course social benefits are the primary benefit of social networking sites. Occasionally these social benefits are strong enough that they lead some members to organize ancillary face-to-face group activities, such as parties, rallies, show and tell, reunions, or meetings at conferences or shows.

Members of medical and emotional condition communities may derive actual health benefits from their participation in addition to information and socio-emotional benefits. The evidentiary base for these benefits is small, but it comes from carefully designed studies that use either random assignment or statistical procedures to control for other factors that could influence health status. Reported benefits for active participants include shorter hospital stays (Gray et al. 2000), a decrease in pain and disability (Lorig et al. 2002), greater support seeking (Mickelson 1997), a decrease in social isolation (Galegher et al. 1998), and an increase in self-efficacy and psychological well-being (Cummings et al. 2002; Mackenna and Bargh 1998).

Membership benefits do not accrue equally to all members of online communities. Passive members—those who only read messages—may derive the least benefit. This observation is consonant with research on groups and communities in the offline world that finds that the most active participants derive the most benefit and satisfaction from their participation (e.g., Callero, Howard, and Piliavin 1987; Omoto and Snyder 1995). Most studies of online communities investigate only active participants because they use the e-mail addresses of posters to identify their research population; they have no way of identifying or systematically studying people who never post but only read. The few studies that have investigated passive members systematically find that they report mostly information benefits; their total level of benefits is lower than that for more active participants; and they are more likely to drop out (Butler et al. 2007; Cummings et al. 2002; Nonnecke and Preece 2000).

Among active participants, people who participate more extensively report having a greater sense of online community (Kavanaugh 2003; Quan y Hasse et al. 2002). More frequent seekers of information report receiving more helpful replies than less frequent seekers (Lakhani and von Hippel 2003). More frequent providers of information report greater social benefits, pleasure in helping others, and pleasure in advancing the cause of the community (Butler et al. 2007).

Benefits to Third Parties

Many attempts to directly "monetize" online communities through sales revenue from advertising or commerce have been relatively disappointing (Cothrel 2001; Figallo 1998; Sacharow 2000). Although the potential customer base could be quite large for brand or demographic communities, attracting and retaining customer/members is difficult. By contrast, subscription revenues—in the online game industry at least—have been relatively robust, with $2 billion in subscription revenue reported in 2005 (DFC Intelligence 2006).

In consumer communities and (a)vocation communities, substantial nonrevenue benefits may accrue to corporations through reinforcing customer brand loyalty, increasing customer satisfaction, and even generating input to new product development. Voluntary personal testimonials about a product or experience in the context of giving help can be quite persuasive, both to the person who asked for help or comment and to others reading the exchange. Motivational theories of attitude formation (e.g., Festinger, Schachter, and Back 1950) and information-processing theories of decision making (e.g., Nisbett and Ross 1980) both point to the influential nature of voluntary personal testimonials. The process can be so powerful that there have been unsubstantiated reports of paid shills masquerading as community members in consumer communities (Mayzlin 2001), a practice known as "astroturfing."

Much of the help offered in consumer communities and (a)vocational communities is personalized customer support—and potentially quite high-quality support at that. In the software industry, online communities have been recognized as the Best Technical Support Organization of the Year for 1997 and 1999 (Foster 1999). Information that solves customer problems or enhances their product experience is likely to increase customer satisfaction and loyalty. When it is provided by self-organized volunteers, the corporate cost is minimal and the benefits are substantial.

Some online communities offer potential product-development benefits. Most remarked are probably open source software communities that have generated product revenues for companies like Red Hat and product enhancements for companies like IBM and Sun Microsystems. Some game and hobby communities offer extensive product testing before widespread product release (e.g., Wallich 2001). Some actively propose, design, and discuss new product features (von Hippel and Krogh 2003; Jeppesen and Frederiksen 2006).

The strategic question for corporations today centers on what type of corporate involvement in online communities is likely to bring the greatest benefit. With few, but important, exceptions, direct corporate ownership and control of online communities is unlikely to be the answer. (This is not to say that corporations will not benefit from Web-based sales and customer support; e-commerce can be profitable even if online community revenue models are not likely to be.) Forging positive and productive relationships with independent online communities can be challenging, however. (See, for example, Moon and Sproull 2006.)

Benefits to Society

Rigorous empirical evidence is almost nonexistent for online community benefits to society. If members of communities formed around medical conditions achieve improved health status, the cost of their medical care to themselves and society could decrease. Alternatively, better informed members may seek out additional tests or treatments, thereby increasing the cost of their care. If members of targeted populations such as K–12 schoolteachers or senior citizens derive cognitive, social, and emotional benefits from participating in online communities, then the larger society may benefit as well. Data from Blacksburg Electronic Village suggests that participation in online community activities can increase offline civic involvement (Kavanaugh 2003). If members of online concern communities can more effectively mobilize, then the causes served by their advocacy are likely to benefit (e.g., Gurak 1997; Quan y Hasse et al. 2002). Note, however, that online communities can advocate for harmful causes just as easily as they can for helpful ones.

Negative Effects

Although anecdotes are widespread, systematic evidence on the negative consequences of online communities is sparse. Members can be harmed by erroneous, malicious, or destructive information. In social networking sites, lighthearted or unthinking profile information can later be used by potential employers as a reason not to hire someone. The norm of peer review of content in discussion communities acts as a damper on harm from erroneous or destructive information but cannot prevent it entirely. Assessments of the quality of information in online communities are difficult to produce; one study reported that the error rate in Wikipedia articles on scientific topics was essentially indistinguishable from that in the *Encyclopedia Britannica* (Giles 2005). Beyond information-based problems, individual members can be harmed by unhealthy, dangerous relationships that can form via online communities. Unscrupulous or criminal intent can be masked by an online persona that inspires trust and friendship within the community context. If a relationship moves away from community scrutiny and into private e-mail, it can lead to emotional harm, economic damage, or even physical danger. This is a particular concern when predators use online communities to identify and contact minors (e.g., Eichenwald 2006). In social networking sites such as MySpace, young people may be particularly vulnerable because of the disconnect between the perceived experience of "hanging out with friends" and the actuality of loose or nonexistent access controls that allow anyone to view profiles and contact their owners. Within VR communities, there have been a small number of widely publicized "attacks" that caused emotional harm to their members (Dibbell 1998; Schwartz 2001). A group itself can harm its members: cults can exist in cyberspace as well as in the offline world. One such, Pro-Ana, extols the joys and personal freedom of anorexia. Its members share tips on how to hide weight loss from family and friends, discuss the value of personal choice, and praise members' announcements of their weight loss.

Although participating in an online community may not be directly harmful to its members, involved members may withdraw from their relationships and responsibilities in the offline world. People who spend a great deal of time online must be spending less time doing something else. The research thus far has only examined the effects of aggregate number of hours spent online, not the effects of time spent specifically in online communities. One study found that the number of hours spent online was associated with a small decrease in social involvement and psychological well-being for a particular group of new users (Kraut et al. 1998), but that effect was erased with continued use (Kraut et al. 2002). Some studies have found the number of hours spent online to be associated with an expanded social circle in the physical world (Katz and Apsden 1997; Quan y Hasse et al. 2002; Kraut et al. 2002).

Just as members may be harmed by erroneous or malicious information, so too may be corporations. Corporate security weaknesses may be described and disseminated through cracker communities; network attacks may be organized in the same way. Companies may fear liability if advice promulgated in an online community leads to product failure or product-related damages. Customer complaints can be shared very rapidly with large numbers of people and can snowball into widespread mobilization. The Intel Corporation had to manage a wave of Internet protest, much of it organized through Usenet groups, as it learned about and took steps to correct a flaw in its Pentium processor in 1994. Ultimately, of course, fixing the error benefited Intel and its customers (Uzumeri and Snyder 1996). In a different case, members of a number of Internet groups mobilized to protest the introduction of a new household database product created by the Lotus Development Corporation, a protest that led to the withdrawal of the planned product (Culnan 1991). Online communities are not the only means of mobilizing discontent on the Net (e.g., Gurak 1997), but when they are characterized by member commitment, they can be particularly potent. In some countries, corporate desire to protect reputation or other assets or government desire for citizen control may collide with individuals' rights to freedom of expression (see Kranich 2004).

Intellectual-property infringement is another area of potential harm for corporations. Trademark infringement is widespread in many consumer communities. Copyright infringement can be particularly troublesome for media property companies. Fan community members create and discuss fan fiction—that is, new story lines or alternative plot endings for their favorite shows, movies, or characters. Corporations routinely issue cease-and-desist orders against these groups, fearing loss of copyright control (Jenkins 2002; Silberman 1996). As with mobilizing discontent, online communities are not the only mechanism on the Net for intellectual-property infringement. Unauthorized media file sharing represents a larger area of intellectual-property harm for media companies at the moment, but the social reinforcement that is generated when community members praise or critique one another's (arguably, intellectual-property infringing) creative work can be potent.

RESEARCH METHODS AND ISSUES

Much of the research on online communities is supported by two broad research traditions, which can be informally labeled as "insider studies" and "outsider studies." Participant observation studies began with Howard Rheingold's (2000) description of The Well, a Northern California online community begun in 1983. Examples of scholarly ethnographies include those of a soap opera discussion community (Baym 1999), a social MUD (Kendall 2002), a lesbian café (Correll 1995), an IRC arts community (Danet 2001), and an online game community (Steinkuehler 2006). In each case the writer/analyst was a member of the community for an extended period. The ethnography evokes the language, personalities, beliefs, interpretations, and daily lives of people inhabiting these worlds from the perspective of a member/researcher (Wilson and Peterson 2002).

"Outsider studies" typically extract records of online behavior or attitudes for study outside the community context. Linguists may extract text records for linguistic analysis of online talk (e.g., Herring 1996, 2001). Sociologists may analyze text records to understand norm development and strength or identity development (Forman, Ghose, and Wiesenfeld 2006; Sassenberg 2002; Moon 2004). Social psychologists may use questionnaires to survey community members about their social support systems in the online world and the offline world (e.g., Cummings et al. 2002; Mackenna and Bargh 1998). Sociologists and political scientists may use questionnaires to survey members about their social and civic activities and attitudes (Kavanaugh 1999; Wellman and Haythornthwaite 2002).

Online communities are appealing subjects for researchers. New or newly visible social phenomena are intrinsically interesting to the social scientist. Moreover, online access to one's subject of study offers beguiling efficiencies. Ethnographers can do ethnographic work without leaving the office. Survey researchers can administer questionnaires to multinational samples of respondents without buying a single postage stamp. Linguists have access to entire cultural corpora in digital form. The efficiencies are not problem-free, however. Ethnographers have a missing or incomplete picture of their community members' offline lives. Survey researchers often have no access to passive community members—ones who never post (e.g., Nonnecke and Preece 2000). Linguists do not see private or back-channel communication. Still, despite the drawbacks, the past 10 years have seen a substantial growth in social science research oriented toward understanding online communities.

Whether researchers use insider or outsider data-collection methods, they must confront issues of base rates and generalizability. Researchers typically study active communities and active members within those communities. It is easy to overlook the fact that many, if not most, online communities exist in name only, analogous to ghost towns in the physical world. For example, most open source projects hosted on SourceForge have no users; fewer than half of all Usenet groups are active; more than 60 percent of blogs have not been updated in more than 2 months (e.g., Henning 2003). Even within active communities, many members are free riders, and requests for interaction may not be reciprocated. For example, even though Wikipedia has more than 200,000 registered contributors, fewer than 3500 of them do 70 percent of the work. In some Usenet groups, 25 percent of questions go unanswered. In their designs and reports, researchers should acknowledge the likely base rates of the phenomena they are interested in and take care not to imply greater frequency or impact than the base rates warrant.

Whereas general principles of ethical research are widely shared within the academic social science community (and are governed by federal regulation), procedures for implementing those principles in research on online communities are under debate. Consider just the principles of informed consent and participant anonymity. If a person's words in an online community discussion are considered private, consent should be obtained before analyzing them. If they are considered public, consent should be obtained before quoting them (except for fair use). If a researcher plans a participant observation study, she or he should seek permission from community members before beginning the study. Because most communities are open, members who join after the study has begun do not have the same opportunity to give or revoke permission, however. When publishing results, the researcher must honor promises of anonymity by disguising participant identity. Yet powerful full-text search engines can use verbatim text, even with no identifier, to find the original (identified) source. Bruckman (2002) pointed out that norms in the humanities, in contrast with those in the social sciences, encourage attribution and reproduction. Several scholarly and professional associations are currently grappling with the ethics of online research (Frankel and Siang 1999; Kraut et al. 2003; Thomas 1996).

CONCLUSION

The Internet has been a home for self-organizing voluntary groups since its inception. As the Net grew, so did the pace of people and technology, mutually adapting to form and support new online communities of interest (e.g., Boczkowski 1999). Despite the large number of online communities and online community members today, the social form has been widespread for less than a decade. The nature of the Net means that experimentation and evolution into new variants of the social form can occur rapidly. The next 10 years should see more new community types, new ways of aggregating microcontributions, and new community processes.

The social form is also immature in terms of impact on members and on the offline world, but with a more differentiated view of community types, we should be able to better specify which types of online communities should or could have which kinds of impacts on which types of members. Nevertheless, people also live in the offline world. The biggest online community design payoffs may come from supporting online extensions of the places where people live, work, send their kids to school, recreate, vote, and worship (e.g., Hampton 2001). Television has had an enormous impact on family communication patterns, teen culture, political activity, and consumer behavior. Most of the decisions that led to those impacts were made by relatively small numbers of wealthy and influential individuals. In online communities, by contrast, everyone has the opportunity to shape the processes that will make a difference.

GLOSSARY

Dot-Com: Internet sites or businesses designed to make money during the late 1990s.

Internet Relay Chat (IRC): A program for simultaneous text communication among two or more users.

Listserv: A program for managing a distribution list of e-mail addresses.

MUD Object-Oriented (MOO): Text-based virtual reality environment in which users can program objects that have persistence.

Multi-User Dungeon/Domain/Dimension (MUD): A text-based virtual reality environment, initially used for fantasy games, now also used for social and professional purposes.

Seti@home: An activity organized over the Net in which people donate idle CPU cycles to process data looking for radio signals.

Usenet: A system of electronic bulletin boards.

Virtual Reality (VR): A text-based or graphics-based environment that evokes a self-contained world.

Wiki: A specific type of editable Web-based document collection.

CROSS REFERENCES

See *Internet Relay Chat (IRC)*; *The Internet Fundamentals*.

REFERENCES

Baym, N. 1999. *Tune in, log on: Soaps, fandom, and online community (new media cultures)*. Thousand Oaks, CA: Corwin Press.

Bender, T. 1978. *Community and social change in America*. Princeton, NJ: Rutgers University Press.

Benkler, Y. 2002. Coase's penguin, or, Linux and the nature of the firm. *The Yale Law Journal* 112:369–446.

Bidgoli, H. (Ed.). 2005. *The handbook of Internet security*. New York: Wiley.

Bidgoli, H. (Ed.). 2003. *The Internet encyclopedia*. New York: Wiley.

Boczkowski, P. J. 1999, Spring. Mutual shaping of users and technologies in a national virtual community. *Journal of Communication* 49:86–108.

Bressler, S. E., and C. E. Grantham. 2000. *Communities of commerce*. New York: McGraw-Hill.

Bruckman, A. 2002. Studying the amateur artist: A perspective on disguising data collected in human subjects research on the Internet. *Ethics and Information Technology* 4:217–31.

Butler, B. S. 2001. Membership size, communication activity, and sustainability: The internal dynamics of networked social structures. *Information Systems Research* 12(4):346–62.

Butler, B. S., S. Kiesler, R. E. Kraut, and L. Sproull. 2007. Community effort in online groups: Who does the work and why? In *Leadership at a distance*, edited by S. Weisband, Lawrence, KA: Erlbaum

Callero, P. L., J. A. Howard, and J. A. Piliavin. 1987. Helping behavior as a role behavior: Disclosing social structure and history on the analysis of prosocial action. *Social Psychology Quarterly* 50:247–56.

Carnevale, P. J., and T. M. Probst. 1997. Conflict on the Internet. In *Culture of the Internet*, edited by S. Kiesler, 233–55. Mahwah, NJ: Erlbaum.

Cassidy, J. 2006, May 15. Me media: How hanging out on the Internet became big business. *The New Yorker*, 50–9.

Castronova, E. 2001. *Virtual worlds: A first-hand account of market and society on the cyberian frontier*. http://papers.ssrn.com/abstract=294828 (accessed January 4, 2003).

Clary, E. G., M. Snyder, R. D. Ridge, J. Copeland, A. A. Stukas, J. Haugen, and P. Miene. 1998. Understanding and assessing the motivations of volunteers: A functional approach. *Journal of Personality and Social Psychology* 74:1516–30.

Correll, S. 1995. The ethnography of an electronic bar: The lesbian café. *Journal of Contemporary Ethnography* 24:270–98.

Cothrel, J. 2001. *Measuring the success of online communities*. www.participate.com/research/art-measuresuccess.asp (accessed October 27, 2002).

Cramton, C. 2001. The mutual knowledge problem and its consequences for dispersed collaboration. *Organization Science* 12:346–71.

Culnan, M. J. 1991. *The lessons of Lotus Marketplace: Implications for consumer privacy in the 1990s*. Presented at the First Conference on Computers, Freedom and Privacy. www.cpsr.org/conferences/cfp91/culnan.html (accessed October 27, 2002).

Cummings, J., L. Sproull, and S. Kiesler. 2002. Beyond hearing: Where real world and online support meet. *Group Dynamics: Theory, Research, and Practice* 6:78–88.

Danet, B. 2001. *Cyberpl@y: Communicating online*. Oxford, England: Berg. (Distributed in the United States by NYU Press.)

DFC Intelligence. 2006. www.dfcint.com/game_article/mar06article.html (accessed January 2, 2007).

Dibbell, J. 1998. *My tiny life: Crime and passion in a virtual world*. New York: Holt.

Eichenwald, K. 2006, August 21. From their own online world, pedophiles extend their reach. *The New York Times*, 1.

Etzioni, A., and O. Etzioni. 1999. Face-to-face and computer-mediated communities, a comparative analysis. *The Information Society* 15:241–8.

Fallows, D. 2004. *The Internet and daily life*. Washington, DC: Pew Internet and American Life Project.

Festinger, L., S. Schachter, and K. Back. 1950. *Social pressures in informal groups*. New York: Harper.

Figallo, C. 1998. *Hosting Web communities: Building relationships, increasing customer loyalty, and maintaining a competitive edge*. New York: Wiley.

Finholt, T., and L. Sproull. 1990. Electronic groups at work. *Organization Science* 1:41–64.

Forman, C., A. Ghose, and B. Wiesenfeld. 2006. A multilevel examination of the impact of social identities on economic transactions in electronic markets. Unpublished NYU Stern working paper.

Foster, E. 1999. Best technical support: It may not be the guy on the telephones any more. *InfoWorld*. www.infoworld.com/articles/op/xml/99/11/29/991129opfoster.xml (accessed July 7, 2007).

Frankel, M. S., and S. Siang. 1999. Ethical and legal aspects of human subjects research on the Internet: A report of a workshop. www.aaas.org/spp/dspp/sfrl/projects/intres/main.htm (accessed July 7, 2007).

Galegher, J., L. Sproull, and S. Kiesler. 1998. Legitimacy, authority, and community in electronic support groups. *Written Communication* 15:493–530.

Giles, J. 2005. Internet encyclopedias go head to head. *Nature*. www.nature.com/news/2005/051212/full/438900a.html (accessed July 7, 2007).

Gray, J. E., C. Safran, R. B. Davis, G. Pompilio-Wietzner, J. E. Stewart, L. Zacagnini, et al. 2000. Baby CareLink: Using the Internet and telemedicine to improve care for high-risk infants. *Pediatrics* 106:1318–24.

Gurak, L. J. 1997. *Persuasion and privacy in cyberspace: The online protests over Lotus Marketplace and the Clipper Chip*. New Haven, CT: Yale University Press.

Hagel, J., and A. G. Armstrong. 1997. *Net gain: Expanding markets through virtual communities*. Cambridge, MA: Harvard Business School Press.

Hampton, K. N. 2001. Living the wired life in the wired suburb. University of Toronto: Unpublished Ph.D. dissertation.

Hampton, K. N., and B. Wellman. 1999. Netville online and offline: Observing and surveying a wired suburb. *American Behavioral Scientist* 43:475–92.

Henning, J. 2003. The blogging iceberg—of 4.12 million hosted weblogs, most little seen, quickly abandoned. Perseus Development Corp. White Papers. www.perseus.com/blogsurvey/thebloggingiceberg.html (accessed July 7, 2007).

Herring, S. 1994. Politeness in computer culture: Why women thank and men flame. In *Cultural performances: Proceedings of the Third Berkeley Women and Language Conference*, edited by M. Bucholtz, A. C. Liang, L. A. Sutton, and C. Hines, 278–94. Berkeley: Berkeley Women and Language Group, University of California.

Herring, S. (Ed.). 1996. *Computer-mediated communication: Linguistic, social and cross-cultural perspectives*. Amsterdam: John Benjamins.

Herring, S. 2001. Computer-mediated discourse. In *Handbook of discourse analysis*, edited by D. Schriffin, D. Tannen, and H. E. Hamilton, 612–34. Oxford: Blackwell.

Herring, S. C., L. A. Scheidt, S. Bonus, and E. Wright. 2004. Bridging the gap: A genre analysis of weblogs. In *Proceedings of the 37th Hawaii International Conference on System Sciences (HICSS-37)*. Los Alamitos, CA: IEEE Computer Society Press. www.blogninja.com/DDGDD04.doc (accessed July 7, 2007).

Internet Engineering Task Force. (n.d.). A novice's guide to the Internet Engineering Task Force. www.ietf.org/tao.html (accessed September 22, 2002).

Jenkins, H. 2002, July. Treating viewers as criminals. *Technology Review*. http://www.technologyreview.com/Infotech/12903/

Jeppesen, L. B., and L. Frederiksen. 2006. Why do users contribute to firm-hosted user communities? The case of computer-controlled music instruments. *Organization Science* 17(1):45–63.

Katz, J. E., and P. Aspden. 1997. A nation of strangers? *Communications of the ACM* 40:81–6.

Kavanaugh, A. 2003. When everyone is wired. In *The wired homestead*, edited by J. Turow and A. Kavenaugh. Cambridge, MA: MIT Press.

Kendall, L. 2002. *Hanging out in the virtual pub: Masculinities and relationships online*. Berkeley: University of California Press.

Kiesler, S., and L. Sproull. 1987. *Computing and change on campus*. New York: Cambridge University Press.

Kim, A. J. 2000. *Community building on the Web: Secret strategies for successful online communities*. Berkeley, CA: Peachpit Press.

Knoke, D. 1986. Associations and interest groups. *Annual Review of Sociology* 12:1–21.

Kollock, P. 1998. The economics of on-line communication. In *Communities in cyberspace*, edited by M. A. Smith and P. Kollock. London: Routledge.

Kollock, P. 1999. The production of trust in online markets. *Advances in Group Processes* 16:99–123.

Kollock, P., and M. Smith. 1996. Managing the virtual commons: Cooperation and conflict in computer communities. In *Computer mediated communication: Linguistic, social, and cross-cultural perspectives*, edited by S. C. Herring, 226–42. Philadelphia: Benjamins.

Kranich, N. 2004. The information commons. www.fepproject.org/policyreports/infocommons.contentsexsum.html (accessed January 2, 2007).

Kraut, R., M. Patterson, V. Lundmark, S. Kiesler, T. Mukophadhyay, and W. Scherlis. 1998. Internet paradox: A social technology that reduces social involvement and psychological well-being? *American Psychologist* 53:1017–31.

Kraut, R., S. Kiesler, B. Boneva, J. Cummings, V. Helgeson, and A. Crawford. 2002. Internet paradox revisited. *Journal of Social Issues* 58:49–74.

Kraut, R. E., J. Olson, M. Manaji, A. Bruckman, J. Cohen, and M. Couper. 2003. Psychological research online: Opportunities and challenges. *American Psychologist* 59(2):105–17.

Lakhani, K. R., and E. von Hippel. 2003. How open source software works: Free user to user assistance. *Research Policy* 32(6):923–43.

Licklider, J. C. R., and A. Veza. 1978. Applications of information networks. *IEEE Proceedings* 66:1330–46.

Lin, N. 2001. *Social capital: A theory of social structure and action*. Cambridge, UK: Cambridge University Press.

Lorig, K. R., K. R. Lorca, D. D. Laurent, R. A. Deyo, M. E. Marnell, M. A. Minor, et al. 2002. Can a back pain e-mail discussion group improve health status and lower health care costs? *Archives of Internal Medicine* 162:792–6.

Mackenna, K. Y. A., and J. A. Bargh. 1998. Coming out in the age of the Internet: Identity "de-marginalization" from virtual group participation. *Journal of Personality and Social Psychology* 75:681–94.

Mayzlin, D. 2001. *Promotional chat on the Internet*. Unpublished manuscript, Yale University.

Mickelson, K. D. 1997. Seeking social support: Parents in electronic support groups. In *Culture of the Internet*, edited by S. Kiesler, 157–78. Mahwah, NJ: Erlbaum.

Moon, J. 2004. Identification processes in distributed electronic groups: A study of voluntary technical support groups on the Net. New York University: unpublished doctoral dissertation.

Moon, J., and L. Sproull, L. 2006. Managing an Internet-based volunteer workforce. Hong Kong University of Science and Technology unpublished paper.

Nardi, B. A., D. J. Schiano, M. Gumbrecht, and L. Swartz. Why we blog. *Communications of the ACM* 47(12): 41–6.

Nisbett, R., and L. Ross. 1980. *Human inference: Strategies and shortcomings of social judgment.* Englewood Cliffs, NJ: Prentice-Hall.

Nonnecke, B., and J. Preece. 2000. Lurker demographics: Counting the silent. In *Proceedings of Computer-human interaction 2000*, 73–80. New York: ACM Press.

Omoto, A., and M. Snyder. 1995. Sustained helping without obligation: Motivation, longevity of service, and perceived attitude change among AIDS volunteers. *Journal of Personality and Social Psychology* 68: 671–87.

Orlikowski, W., and J. Yates. 1994. Genre repertoire: The structuring of communicative practices in organizations. *Administrative Science Quarterly* 39:541–74.

Porter, C. E. 2004. A typology of virtual communities: A multi-disciplinary foundation for future research. *Journal of Computer-Mediated Communication* 10(3).

Powazek, D. 2002. *Design for community: The art of connecting real people in virtual places*. Indianapolis: New Riders.

Preece, J. 2000. *Online communities: Designing usability, supporting sociability.* New York: Wiley.

Putnam, R. 2000. *Bowling alone: The collapse and revival of American community*. New York: Simon & Schuster.

Quan y Hasse, A., B. Wellman, J. Witte, and K. Hampton. 2002. Capitalizing on the Internet: Social contact, civic engagement, and sense of community. In *The Internet in everyday life*, edited by B. Wellman and C. Haythornthwaite, 291–394. Oxford: Blackwell.

Raymond, E. 1999. *The cathedral & the bazaar: Musings on Linux and Open Source by an accidental revolutionary.* Cambridge, MA: O'Reilly.

Reid, E. 1999. Hierarchy and power: Social control in cyberspace. In *Communities in cyberspace*, edited by M. A. Smith and P. Kollock, 107–33. London: Routledge.

Rheingold, H. 2000. *The virtual community*. Revised ed. Cambridge, MA: MIT Press.

Sacharow, A. 2000. *Consumer-created content: Creating and valuing user-generated programming. Vision Report*. New York: Jupiter Media Metrix.

Sassenberg, K. 2002. Common bond and common identity groups on the Internet: Attachment and normative behavior in on-topic and off-topic chats. *Group Dynamics* 6:27–37.

Schlager, M. S., and P. Schank. 1997. TAPPED IN: A new on-line community concept for the next generation of Internet technology. In *Proceedings of the Second International Conference on Computer Support for Collaborative Learning*, edited by R. Hall, N. Miyake, and N. Enyedy, 231–40. Hillsdale, NJ: Erlbaum.

Schuler, D. 1996. *New community networks: Wired for change*. Reading, MA: Addison-Wesley.

Schuler, D., and P. Day (Eds.) 2004. *Shaping the network society: The future of the public sphere in cyberspace*. Cambridge, MA: MIT Press.

Schwartz, J. 2001, January 4. Virtual mayhem arouses real anger at hackers' attack. *New York Times*. www.nytimes.com/2001/01/04/technology/04HACK.html (accessed January 4, 2003).

Silberman, S. 1996. Paramount locks phasers on Trek fan sites. *Wired News*. www.wired.com/news/culture/0,1284,1076,00.html (accessed February 12, 2001).

Sproull, L., and S. Faraj. 1995. Atheism, sex and databases: The net as a social technology. In *Public access to the Internet*, edited by B. Kahin and J. Keller, 62–81. Cambridge, MA: MIT Press.

Sproull, L., and S. Kiesler. 1991. *Connections: New ways of working in the networked organization*. Cambridge, MA: MIT Press.

Sproull, L., and J. Patterson. 2004. Making information cities livable. *Communications of the ACM* 47(2):33–7.

Steinkuehler, C. A. 2006. Massively multiplayer online videogaming as participation in a discourse. *Mind, Culture, & Activity* 13(1):38–52.

Thomas, J. (Ed.). 1996. *The Information Society* 12 [Special issue].

Thorn, B. K., and T. Connolly. 1987. Discretionary data bases; a theory and some experimental findings. *Communication Research* 14:512–28.

Turkle, S. 1995. *Life on the screen: Identity in the age of the Internet*. New York: Simon & Schuster.

Uzumeri, M. V., and C. A. Snyder. 1996. Information technology and accelerated science: The case of the Pentium™ Flaw. *California Management Review* 38:44–63.

von Hippel, E., and V. Krogh 2003. Opensource software and the "private-collective" innovation model: Issues for organization science. *Organization Science* 14:209–23.

Wallich, P. 2001, September. Mindstorms: Not just a kid's toy. *IEEE Spectrum* 52–7.

Walsh, J. P., and T. Bayma. 1996. The virtual college: Computer-mediated communication and scientific work. *The Information Society* 12:343–63.

Wasko, M. M., and S. Faraj. 2000. "It is what one does": Why people participate and help others in electronic communities of practice. *Journal of Strategic Information Systems* 9:155–73.

Wellman, B., and C. Haythornthwaite (Eds.). 2002. *The Internet in everyday life*. Oxford. England: Blackwell.

Werry, C., and M. Mowbray. 2000. *Online communities: Commerce, community action, and the virtual university.* New York: Prentice Hall.

Wikipedia: Size comparisons. 2006, August 31. In *Wikipedia: The free encyclopedia*. http://en.wikipedia.org/wiki/Wikipedia:Size_comparisons (accessed August 31, 2006).

Wilson, S. M., and L. C. Peterson. 2002. The anthropology of online communities. *Annual Review of Anthropology* 31:449–67.

Winzelberg, A. 1997. The analysis of an electronic support group for individuals with eating disorders. *Computers in Human Behavior* 13:393–407.

Yee, N. 2001. *The Norrathian scrolls: A study of EverQuest*. www.nickyee.com/eqt/report.html (accessed July 7, 2007).

Mobile Commerce

Vijay Atluri, *Rutgers University*

INTRODUCTION

Mobile commerce is the buying and selling of goods and services or the exchange of information in the support of commercial activities through wireless handheld devices such as cellular telephones and personal digital assistants (PDAs). Mobile commerce enables users to access the Internet and conduct transactions with monetary value from anywhere, anytime. The success of mobile commerce relies on building on the established habits and practices of the consumers, and on the infrastructure, and then having additional benefits due to mobility. For instance, the added benefits may include instantaneous access and delivery, flexibility, convenience, personalization, location awareness, and better customer service. In addition, ease of use, convenience, and ensuring security and privacy should be salient features of mobile commerce.

The increase in the demand for applications dealing with moving objects can be seen in recent years. Furthermore, mobile phones and/or wireless PDAs have evolved into wireless terminals that are global positioning system (GPS)–enabled. In addition to wireless computing devices, tracking of other moving objects such as boats, trucks, automobiles, airplanes, and soldiers is also of growing interest. With the great demand on mobile devices, mobile commerce has become a gigantic market opportunity. The market for mobile business users is expected to increase from today's 77 million to over 109 million users by 2009. As many as 25 million wireless phone subscribers in North America could be using their mobile phones as mobile wallets by 2011, reports In-Stat (www.in-stat.com), a high-tech market research firm. The mobile customer base of the GSM (global system for mobile communications) family of technologies has grown to 1.85 billion users to make up more than 81 percent of the wireless mobile market worldwide, with total subscribers of code division multiple access (CDMA) at less than 300 million and a 13 percent market share (3G Americas 2006).

Worldwide, mobile commerce revenues are expected to exceed $88 billion by 2009 (Juniper Research Group 2004). According to the same Juniper Research Group report, it is expected that retailers will make up to $40 billion in sales from customers who will use mobile phones to spend cash on everything from cinema tickets to hourly car parking. According to a study by International Data Corporation (IDC) (www.idc.com), mobile entertainment will be worth $8 billion in Western Europe in 2008. The purchases consumers make will consist mainly of low-priced items, or what the industry calls "micropayments." It is also expected that RFID and infrared technologies will likely have a major influence on the future development of devices that allow for payments. The market for location-aware mobile applications such as mobile shopping, mobile advertising, mobile retailing, mobile entertainment, and mobile online banking is very promising. Figure 1 provides an overview of the essential mobile commerce components. We will review each of them in this chapter, with the exception of the standards and policies.

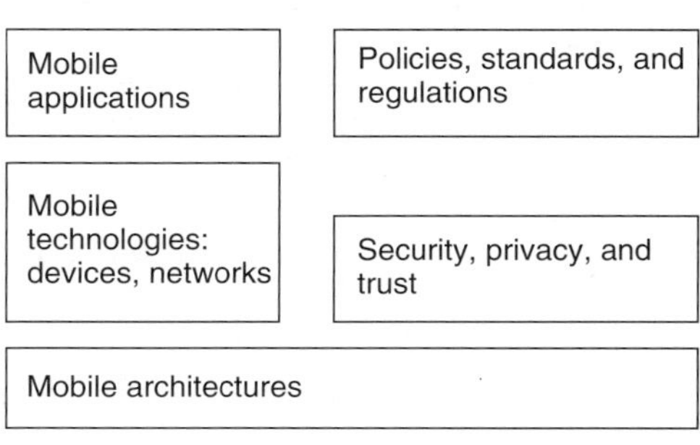

Figure 1: Mobile commerce: The big picture

MOBILE COMMERCE APPLICATIONS

As content delivery over wireless devices becomes faster, more secure, and scalable, it is believed that the mobile commerce market may exceed the traditional e-commerce. Mobile commerce applications can be categorized into the following classes: business-to-business (B2B), business-to-consumer (B2C), consumer-to-consumer (C2C), business-to-employee (B2E) (Lehmann and Lehner 2004), and government-to-citizen (G2C). Although security is not important in some information-service applications, it is of significant importance in certain transaction-oriented applications. For example, a cellular phone can be used as a personal trusted device (PTD). In such cases, mobile customers may use it to purchase goods and services that may typically include gas, soft drinks, and tickets to a football game, or to check their bank balances. In such scenarios, the mobile service calls for confidentiality, integrity, and identification and authentication requirements.

Many aspects of the mobile communications industry, including the importance of mobile communications and mobile applications, and the competitive landscape of the mobile phone market have been explored based on competing protocols or standards, airtime carriers, and handset providers (Kumar 2004). Table 1 summarizes different types of applications (not an exhaustive list) and their categories. We describe these applications in detail.

Mobile Financial Services: These services encompass: (1) mobile banking, through which customers access their bank accounts and pay their bills using handheld devices, and (2) mobile brokerage, through which customers obtain stock quotes that are displayed on their handheld devices and conduct trading using these devices. In both cases, the mobile customer uses his or her PTD to set up a secure session to the bank on his PTD.

Mobile Telecommunications Services: These include services provided by telecommunication companies, in which customers use their handheld devices for the purposes of service changes, bill payment, and account reviews.

Mobile Information Provisioning: These services include the delivery of financial and sports news and traffic updates to mobile customers. Other information-service provisioning applications include integrated information services, such as tourist services, traffic coordination, management, way-finding, weather reports and forecasts, stock quotes, traffic jams, travel itineraries and nearby restaurants, news updates, sports news, business and technology news, local town information, telephone directory, restaurant guide, dictionary service, and cooking recipes, among others.

Mobile Security Services: Many public-safety and security-related services can be provided through mobile devices, as one can track and pinpoint the location of the device. These safety-related services include: (1) tracking and locating stolen cars as well as automatically notifying the owner, (2) remotely controlling the car, for example, disabling the car engine, honking the horn, or starting the engine using a mobile device, (3) tracking of groups of vehicles and sending an alert when a vehicle crosses a predefined area, (4) alerting when a laptop moves beyond certain predefined areas, (5) tracking children, people with Alzheimer's disease or other mental disabilities, and pets, and automatic notification to the mobile users, (6) sending remote-control commands via phone or Web to let someone into the house, turn down the thermostat, or start an appliance, (7) enabling transmission of messages to individuals in emergency situations using a reverse 911 service, and (8) helping in dispatching 911, delivering real-time information on crime mapping, and providing access to federal and state databases and mug shots.

Mobile Remote Shopping: The mobile phone user browses in a wireless application protocol (WAP)–enabled shop, selects the desired goods, and pays for them with funds from his or her bank account or credit-card company. These include services or retail purchases as consumers are given the ability to place and pay for orders on-the-fly.

Mobile On-Site shopping: A mobile user may select the desired goods in a retail store and use his or her PTD to pay by logging on to the store's Bluetooth wireless LAN.

Mobile Ticketing: The user browses a WAP ticketer's site, selecting and paying for a ticket for a movie, a show, or a game. All ticket information is stored in the PTD's transaction database. At the venue, the user goes up to one of the wireless access nodes on the premises (similar to an ATM), calls up the ticket information from the PTD's database, and sends it via Bluetooth to this access node, which then prints out the user's ticket.

Mobile Advertising: This includes personalized, location-aware and context-sensitive advertising, as mobile devices are ideal for marketing channels for impulse buying (using short messaging service [SMS]–based or multimedia messaging service [MMS]–based technologies). For example, mobile users can be pushed information related to nearby hotels when they are not in their home location, nearby movies during evenings and weekends, nearby restaurants based on their preferences, etc.

Mobile Entertainment: This may include location-based games, character download, horoscope and fortune telling, karaoke information, hit songs, download ring tones, club event information, etc.

Table 1: Categories of mobile commerce applications

Category	Application
B2B	Advertising, location-based services (e.g., supply chain management)
B2C	Financial services, telecommunications services, information provisioning, security services, remote shopping, on-site shopping, ticketing, advertising, entertainment, location-based services
C2C	User-to-user applications, wireless videoconferencing,
B2E	Wireless videoconferencing, reporting, claim processing
G2C	Security services

Wireless Videoconferencing: Voice over IP (VoIP) and full-motion video communication over both WiFi and universal mobile telecommunications system (UMTS)–based networks to create videoconferences that can be billed.

Mobile User-to-User Applications: Share applications such as mobile games, pictures, cartoons, or personal files with friends and colleagues via a handset, user-to-user content provision, conversational applications (which provide means for bidirectional communication with real-time end-to-end information transfer) such as videoconferencing, groupware (collaborative work), messaging applications (which offer user-to-user or user-to-user group communication) such as messaging of photographs and video.

Location-Based Services: It has been estimated that worldwide revenues from location-based services would reach $9.9 billion by 2010 (Steinfield 2004). The demand for location-based services (LBSs) can be categorized into the following types (Rao and Minakakis 2003):

1. *Location and navigation service:* Maps, driving directions, directory and yellow-page listings, and business descriptions in a given geographical radius all constitute this service. These types of LBSs have become popular in Japan, while they are a more recent phenomenon in the United States. GPS capabilities may allow customers to find their way to their destinations and alert friends and colleagues to their whereabouts. If a person is relocated, they may use mobile LBSs to familiarize themselves with their new surroundings. Examples also include getting detailed maps and directions, real-time alerts on traffic conditions, and information about highway services such as gas, food, and lodgings. Although auto manufacturers are investing in making mobile platforms for cars, currently relatively inexpensive handheld devices are serving this purpose. These include devices such as golfing assistants mounted on golf carts that provide everything from course maps to teeing tips, fish finders that combine sonar and GPS capabilities to allow anglers to pinpoint the locations of schools of fish, and people locators, which enable parents to locate children in urban areas and shopping environments (Spagat 2002).
2. *Point-of-need information delivery:* This service is to request usable, personalized information delivered at the point of need, which includes information about new or interesting products and services, promotions, and targeting of customers based on more-advanced knowledge of customer profiles and preferences, automatic updates of travel reservations, etc. For example, a wireless shopping site can be designed to target users with content such as clothing items on sale, based on prior knowledge of their preferences and/or knowledge of their current location, such as proximity to a shopping mall (Venkatesh, Ramesh, and Massey 2003). To deliver such LBSs, service providers require access to customers' preference profiles either through a proprietary database or through an arrangement with an LBS provider, who matches customer profiles to vendor offerings. In order to implement such services, customization and personalization based on the location information, customer needs, and vendor offerings is required.
3. *Industrial and corporate applications:* This type of LBSs find their way into a number of applications, including tracking material through the supply chain and inventory, tracking physicians, patients, and equipment in the hospitals, etc. This relies on the deployment of RFID technologies, which is becoming inexpensive and will likely be used by a number of retail businesses, such as Wal-Mart.

BUSINESS MODELS IN THE M-COMMERCE ENVIRONMENT

A number of business models are being practiced by the vendors of mobile commerce. Notable ones among these include: (1) user-fee business model, (2) shopping business model, (3) marketing business model, (4) improved-efficiency business model, (5) advertising business model, and (6) revenue-sharing business model (Sadeh 2002). These are described briefly below.

User-Fee Business Model

Under this model, payment can be based on a subscription fee, or based on usage. This model is best suited for regularly updated content such as customized news and location-sensitive weather and traffic conditions. In reality, the content provider may rely on the mobile service provider to implement it and collect the appropriate fee. The obvious advantages of adopting a subscription-fee-based model over the user-fee model are that it is easier to collect the fees, and the income is relatively better predictable. However, the user-fee model would be more attractive to one-time or infrequent users.

Shopping Business Model

Under this model, the traditional Internet companies sell their goods and services through the new mobile medium to offer better services and convenience to reach their customers, and moreover to capture additional customers. Essentially, the traditional Internet companies seek a mobile presence. Payment is done with the mobile device, but typically involves a third party, such as a credit-card company or a bank.

Marketing Business Model

The traditional brick-and-mortar companies push the information about their products and services through the mobile channels directly to the mobile customers. However, the customers make their payments using traditional payment mechanisms without using their mobile devices.

Improved-Efficiency Business Model

Companies adopt mobile Internet to reduce their operating costs. Such services include mobile banking, mobile ticketing, etc. Whereas the shopping business models are those adopted by traditional Internet companies to expand their customer base, the improved efficiency business models offer mobile services to reduce their operating costs.

Advertising Business Model

This may typically involve gathering the profiles and preferences of mobile customers and targeting the advertising based on the location, time, and preferences. Typically, the advertiser passes on the information to the content provider, who would deliver the advertisements that are relevant to the user's queries. The advertiser pays for the content provider either as a flat fee, based on the traffic (number of ad impressions) or based on the performance (number of click-throughs or call-throughs).

Revenue-Sharing Business Model

Under this model, the mobile content owner uses the services of a mobile content provider. This is suitable in cases in which the content provided by a single owner is not sufficient to attract the attention of the mobile customer or is not valuable as standalone information. In such cases, the content provider combines the content from different owners and may enhance it with value-added information before delivering it to the mobile customer. For example, local weather reports, local traffic conditions, stock quotes and news updates can all be combined appropriately by the content provider. Typically, the content provider collects the payment and shares it with the content owners.

ENABLING TECHNOLOGIES

Mobile commerce has emerged as a result of the developments in several technologies. In this section, we review the advances in these different technologies that have propelled the growth of mobile commerce.

Mobile Devices

Mobile devices such as smart phones and personal digital assistants have reached new levels of usability, performance, and computing power. Increasingly, these devices are equipped with wireless-communications capabilities and location technologies. In order to exploit the m-commerce market potential, a number of industry initiatives have taken place to enable secure and reliable mobile commerce transactions. Handset manufacturers such as Nokia, Ericsson, Motorola, and Qualcomm are working with carriers such as AT&T Wireless and Sprint to develop WAP-enabled smart phones, transforming a mobile phone into a PTD. In addition, IBM and other companies are developing speech-recognition software to ensure security in mobile commerce transactions. Using Bluetooth technology, smart phones offer fax, e-mail, and phone capabilities all in one, paving the way for m-commerce to be accepted by an increasingly mobile workforce. The new generations of wireless networks such as UTMS provide much better speeds and always-on connectivity.

Wireless Networks

The enabling technologies for m-commerce include wide area wireless communication technologies, short-range wireless communication technologies such as WiFi and Bluetooth, and RFID technologies. In the following, we review their evolution over different generations—1G through 4G, of wide area wireless networking technologies, as well as short-range wireless technologies. Based on the technology use, the market growth in global GSM users has increased to 1.25 billion, global CDMA users to 202 million, global TDMA users to 120 million, and total 3G users to 130 million (www.cellular.co.za/stats/stats-main.htm). According to Pyramid Research (2004), WiFi users will surpass wireless wide area network users, and it is expected that by the year 2008 the number of WiFi users will reach 180 million, whereas that of 3G would be less than 100 million.

1G

The first generation of wireless technologies used analog transmission, which operates in the 800-MHz band and uses 30-KHz channels using frequency division multiple access (FDMA). It was introduced in North America in 1985 as advanced mobile phone service. Because of the limited bandwidth, this soon exhausts the available channels, thereby limiting the number of subscribers. Since digital signals can be compressed, enabling more effective use of the frequency spectrum, it was natural to use digital technology.

2G

The second-generation systems, which digitize not only the control link but also the voice signal, appeared in the early 1990s; they use time-division multiple access (TDMA) and CDMA. Unlike 1G, which primarily supports voice signals, 2G networks are capable of supporting voice, data, paging, and fax services. Moreover, they provide better quality and higher capacity at lower cost to consumers. GSM (global system for mobile communication) was the first commercially operated digital cellular system based on TDMA.

2.5G

One of the major enhancements of 2.5G over 2G is using the packet-switching technology. The general packet radio service (GPRS) is based on packet-switching technology, which sends packets of data over a radio wave (on the GSM network). It is a 2.5G mobile communications technology that enables mobile wireless service providers to offer their mobile subscribers packet-based data services. GPRS was standardized by the European Telecommunications Standards Institute (ETSI), but today is standardized by the Third Generation Partnership Program (3GPP).

With GPRS, a maximum speed of up to 171.2 kbps can be achieved, which is almost ten times faster than the current circuit-switched data services on GSM networks. But realistically they currently only have a maximum downstream speed of 50 kbps and upstream 10 to 28 kbps. Speeds will also depend on which GPRS version an operator uses, as well as how busy the network is at a particular time. In addition to achieving higher transmission speeds, unlike the users served by circuit-switching networks, GPRS users are "always connected."

GPRS data transmission technology is optimized for "bursty" communication services such as wireless Internet/intranet and multimedia services. It is also known as GSM-IP (Internet protocol) because it will connect users directly to Internet service providers. As a result, with GPRS, all Internet/intranet applications, such as Web browsing, chat, e-mail, telnet and FTP, multimedia services, and instant messaging, can be totally supported over the mobile network. GPRS therefore offers a smooth add-on to integrate into existing networks and supplements today's circuit-switched data and short message service. Future applications may have the ability to remotely access and control in-house appliances and machines. Voice calls can be made simultaneously over GSM-IP while a data connection is operating—depending on the phone class and type. Although users are always connected and always online, they may still be charged only for the amount of data that is transported.

3G

The 3G mobile phone technology enables the transmission of high-quality video images in the 2-GHz frequency band and realizes new mobile multimedia communications services. NTT DoCoMo was one of the first in the world to begin research and development on W-CDMA, a key foundation for 3G mobile phone technology. The universal mobile telecommunications system (UMTS) is a 3G mobile communications technology that provides wideband CDMA radio technology. With data rates up to 2 Mbps, UMTS provides increased capacity, increased data capability, and a far greater range of services. A variation of CDMA, called time division synchronous CDMA (TD-SCDMA) was proposed by the China Wireless Telecommunication Standards (CWTS) group, which uses the time division duplex (TDD) mode. The CDMA technology offers higher-throughput, real-time services, and end-to-end quality of service (QoS), and is capable of delivering pictures, graphics, customized infotainment, streaming video, video messaging to locational services, and other multimedia information as well as voice and data to mobile wireless subscribers. UMTS is standardized by the 3GPP. Another technology, EDGE/EGPRS, is implemented as a bolt-on enhancement to 2G and 2.5G GSM and GPRS networks, making it easier for existing GSM carriers to upgrade to it. EDGE/EGPRS is a superset to GPRS and can function on any network with GPRS deployed on it, provided the carrier implements the necessary upgrades. EDGE can carry data speeds up to 236.8 kbps in packet mode and will therefore meet the requirement of the International Telecommunications Union (ITU) for a 3G network, and has been accepted by the ITU as part of the IMT-2000 family of 3G standards. EDGE is generally classified as 2.75G network technology. Another technology, the evolution-data optimized (EvDO), can reach higher rates, up to 4.9 Mbps.

4G

The 4G mobile services are the advanced version of the 3G mobile communication services. The 4G mobile communication services provide broadband, large-capacity, high-speed data transmission, providing users with high-quality interactive multimedia services, including teleconferencing, color video images, 3D graphic animation games, and audio services. In addition, 4G networks are expected to offer global mobility, service portability, and scalability at lower cost. They are based on orthogonal frequency division multiplexing (OFDM), which is capable of having hundreds of parallel channels. The data-transmission rates are planned to be up to 20 Mbps. This technology allows seamless merging between different wireless standards, allowing one mobile device to move from indoor networks such as wireless LANs and Bluetooth, to cellular, to radio and TV broadcasting or to satellite communications. NewLogic claims that 4G digital IP-based high-speed cellular systems will account for 14 percent of total mobile wireless data revenues in 2007 and 50 million subscribers by the end of 2007; the 4G infrastructure sales could reach up to $5.3 billion during 2007 (NewLogic 2003).

Wireless LANs

Wireless LANs are also widely used for mobile commerce. IEEE 802.11 or WiFi (short for wireless fidelity) is a family of networking protocols, developed by the working group 11 of IEEE 802. WiFi is a trade term promulgated by the Wireless Ethernet Compatibility Alliance (WECA) and is used in place of 802.11b. Products certified as WiFi by WECA are interoperable with each other even if they are from different manufacturers. A user with a WiFi product can use any brand of access point with any other brand of client hardware that is built to the WiFi standard. WLANs are cheaper than wireless wide area network to install, maintain, and use, and are relatively mature technologies.

The 802.11 family currently includes three separate protocols, 802.11a, 802.11b, and 802.11g; 802.11b was the first widely accepted wireless networking standard, which was later followed by 802.11a and 802.11g (http://grouper.ieee.org/groups/802/11).

802.11b

802.11b has a range of about 50 m and a maximum throughput of 11 Mbps; 802.11 runs in the 2.4-GHz spectrum and uses carrier sense multiple access with collision avoidance (CSMA/CA) as its media access method. Extensions have been made to the 802.11b protocol to increase speeds to 22, 33, and 44 Mbps, but the extensions are proprietary and have not been endorsed by the IEEE.

802.11a

The 802.11a standard uses the 5-GHz band, and operates at a raw speed of 54 Mbps. It has not seen wide adoption because of the high adoption rate of 802.11b, and because of concerns about range: at 5 GHz, 802.11a cannot reach as far as 802.11b.

802.11g

In June 2003, a third standard for encoding was ratified—802.11g. This works in the 2.4-GHz band (like 802.11b), but operates at 54 Mbps raw, or about 24.7 Mbps net, throughput like 802.11a. It is fully backward-compatible with 11-Mbps 802.11b. It uses OFDM (orthogonal frequency division multiplexing) technology, and enables streaming media, video downloads, and a greater concentration of users without interference.

802.11n

In January 2004 IEEE announced that it would develop a new standard for local area wireless networks. The real speed would be 100 Mbps, and so up to 4 to 5 times faster than 802.11g, and perhaps 50 times faster than 802.11b; 802.11n offers a better operating distance than the above networks.

802.11i

This is an amendment to the 802.11 standard specifying security mechanisms for wireless networks. The draft standard was ratified on June 24, 2004, and supersedes the previous security specification, wired equivalent privacy (WEP), which was shown to have severe security weaknesses. WiFi protected access (WPA) had previously been introduced by the WiFi Alliance. It implemented a subset of 802.11i and makes use of the advanced encryption standard (AES) block cipher; WEP and WPA use only the RC4 stream cipher. In addition to improved encryption, it includes improvements in key management, user authentication through 802.1x, and data integrity of headers and contents using counter-mode/CBC-mac protocol (CCMP).

Bluetooth

Other wireless technologies include the short-range technologies such as Bluetooth, which can play an important role in applications such as mobile payments. It is an industrial specification for wireless personal area networks (PANs). Bluetooth provides a way to connect and exchange information between devices like personal digital assistants (PDAs), mobile phones, laptops, PCs, printers, and digital cameras via a secure, low-cost, globally available short-range radio frequency. Bluetooth lets these devices talk to each other when they come in range, as long as they are within 10 m of each other. Every device can be configured to constantly announce its presence to nearby devices in order to establish a connection. The protocol operates at 2.45 GHz and can reach speeds of 723.1 kbps. In order to avoid interfering with other protocols that use the 2.45-GHz band, the Bluetooth protocol divides the band into seventy-nine channels and changes channels up to 1600 times per second.

Bluetooth should not be compared to WiFi, which is a faster protocol requiring more expensive hardware that covers greater distances and uses the same frequency range. While Bluetooth is a cable replacement creating personal area networking between different devices, WiFi is a cable replacement for local area network access, which has a data rate of 2.1 Mbps.

One of the ways in which Bluetooth technology may become useful is in VoIP. Bluetooth may be used for communication between a cordless phone and a computer listening for VoIP and with an infrared peripheral component interconnect card acting as a base for the cordless phone. Cars can also install hands-free Bluetooth technology that allows users with Bluetooth-equipped cell phones to make use of some of the phone's features.

Radio-Frequency Identification

Another emerging wireless technology is radio-frequency identification (RFID). RFID is a method of remotely storing and retrieving data using devices called RFID tags. An RFID tag can either be attached to or incorporated into a product. RFID tags can be either active or passive. Passive RFID tags do not have their own power supply, but can respond to incoming radio-frequency signals. The range of passive tags can vary from 10 mm to 5 m. These tags cost less than $0.25. The aim to produce tags for less than $0.05 may make widespread RFID tagging commercially viable. Active RFID tags have a power source, have longer ranges, and contain larger memory than their passive counterparts. Active tags may have ranges in the order of tens of meters, and a battery life of up to several years.

There are four different kinds of tags commonly in use, their differences based on the level of their radio frequency: low-frequency tags (between 125 and 134 KHz), high-frequency tags (13.56 MHz), ultra-high-frequency (UHF) tags (868 to 956 MHz), and microwave tags (2.45 GHz). Low-frequency tags are primarily used for identification of subjects such as children and for animal identification and tracking, for antitheft systems, etc. High-frequency RFID tags can be used to track library books, pallets, airline baggage, and retail goods as well as for building access control. UHF tags can be typically used in pallet and container tracking, and truck and trailer tracking in shipping yards. Microwave tags can be used in long-range access control of vehicles. Some tollbooths use RFID tags for electronic toll collection (e.g., the EZ-Pass system).

Using RFID tags may have a number of advantages over bar-code technology. Unlike bar codes, which are the same for the same type of product, RFID codes are unique for each product. As a result, a product may be individually tracked as it moves from location to location, from manufacturers to wholesalers to retailers and finally to consumers. This may help companies to combat theft and other forms of product loss and can be used for point-of-sale automatic checkout, with the option of removing the tag at checkout. Moreover, cards embedded with RFID chips are widely used as electronic cash, for example, to pay fares in mass-transit systems and/or retails. EPCglobal is working on an international standard for the use of RFID and the electronic product code (EPC) to be used in tracking goods along the supply chain. It includes members from EAN International, Uniform Code Council, The Gillette Company, Procter & Gamble, Wal-Mart, Hewlett-Packard, Johnson & Johnson, and Auto-ID Labs. Futuristic uses include monitoring the expiration dates of the food in the refrigerator, etc. In summary, RFID technology can be used for collecting information from moving objects, and can also be used in applications such as supply chain management, advanced product tracking, inventory control, warehouse management, checking compliance regulations, recall, enhancement, accountability, and documentation.

However, RFID technology may raise a number of privacy concerns, as the tags affixed to products remain functional even after the products have been purchased and taken home, and can be read from a distance without the knowledge of the purchaser. This information can be potentially used for surveillance and other purposes that are not related to the supply chain inventory functions. Another privacy concern is due to RFID's support for anticollision, in which a reader enumerates all the tags responding to it without them interfering with each other. As a result, all but the last bit of each tag's serial number can be deduced by passively eavesdropping on the RFID reader. Juels, Rivest, and Szydlo (2003) have proposed a selective blocking approach using a blocker tag, as a way of protecting consumers from unwanted scanning of RFID tags attached to items they may be carrying or wearing. A blocker tag is a cheap passive RFID device that can simulate many ordinary RFID tags simultaneously and thus blocks RFID readers from reading the actual RFID tag. It can do so universally by simulating all possible RFID tags. Or a blocker tag can block selectively by simulating only selected subsets of ID codes, such as those by a particular manufacturer, or those in a designated privacy zone. Juels and Brainard (2004) extended the blocker tag approach to enforce flexible privacy policies in which partial or scrubbed data are revealed about private tags, in lieu of the all-or-nothing policy enforced by a blocker tag. Privacy-related guidelines proposed by EPCglobal include the requirement to give consumers clear notice of the presence of EPC and to inform them of the choice that they have to discard, disable, or remove EPC tags (www.epcglobalinc.org/public_policy/public_policy_guidelines.html).

Table 2 (partially from Umar [2004]) summarizes the bandwidth and range of different wireless technologies.

Other Technologies

Location Technologies

Although location technologies have been around for a number of years, they have evolved rapidly in recent years because of the increasing use of mobile applications. They can be broadly classified into outdoor and indoor technologies. Outdoor technologies include global positioning system (GPS), network-assisted GPS (A-GPS), time of arrival (TOA), uplink time of arrival (UL-TOA), enhanced observed time difference (E-OTD), and cell of origin (COO) (Andersson 2001). Indoor technologies include Active Badge system, developed by Olivetti Research Ltd. (ORL), PARC by Xerox, Shopping Assistant by AT&T Bell Laboratories, and Cyberguide by the Georgia Institute of Technology, among others. Although most mobile applications rely on outdoor technologies, indoor technologies have limited applications, such as the computerized visitor guides in museums. Wireless networks can provide approximate information about the location of a customer; this information exists as part of the routing information in the wireless network. GPS provides more accurate location but requires some add-in to the mobile device. This technology is typically used for driver assistance systems and in military applications such as guided missiles. For indoor applications, other technologies are used, such as the smart badge that was developed by Xerox Labs in the United Kingdom.

Application Protocols

The emerging technology behind m-commerce is the set of protocols called the WAP, which provide functionality similar to the traditional Internet protocols such as the TCP/IP, secure socket layer (SSL), hypertext transfer protocol (HTTP), and other application protocols. It is typical that the translation between the two sets of protocols is performed by some middleware at the mobile support station (MSS), which is part of the infrastructure of the wireless provider. (More details on WAP are provided in the next section.) The middleware services that connect the back-end services to the mobile devices provide translation between the different communications and applications protocols at both sides. WAP also includes a markup language based on extensible markup language (XML), called the wireless markup language (WML). IMode-enabled Web sites use cHTML, a subset of the familiar HTML 4.0 (Barnes 2003) that has been developed with the restrictions of the wireless infrastructure in mind, such as the limited bandwidth and high latencies of the networks, and small screens and limited functionality of the devices. Essentially, it removes certain features of conventional HTML, such as tables and frames. Mobile services equipped with WAP have been widely accepted, and the mobile devices equipped with Web-ready micro-browsers are much more common in Europe than in the United States. This growth is partly driven by the GPRS, WAP, Bluetooth technologies, and their use in mobile commerce applications.

Table 2: Bandwidth and range of different wireless technologies

	Data Rate	Range
Bluetooth	1 Mbps	10+ m
IEEE 802.11a	Up to 54 Mbps	<50 m
IEEE 802.11b	11 Mbps	100 m
IEEE 802.11g	Up to 54 Mbps	100 m
3G Cellular	Up to 2 Mbps	Cell sizes 5 to 10 km
RFID	Up to 2.45 Gbps	Up to tens of meters
Satellites	64 kbps	Thousands of miles

Semantic Web Technologies

M-commerce is benefiting from emerging technologies such as Web services, .NET technologies, and Ontologies. Several new technologies and standards are affecting the design of m-commerce applications. These include semantic Web technologies such as RDF, DAML, DAML-S, DAML+OIL, and OWL and service interaction technologies such as the universal description, discovery, and integration (UDDI) specifications. The .NET framework is the programming model for developing, deploying, and running Web services and applications. Web services are units of code that allow programs written in different programming languages and on different platforms to communicate and share data through standard Internet protocols such as XML, simple object access protocol (SOAP), Web Services Description Language (WSDL), and UDDI. They allow easy building of Web-based applications, including enterprise resource planning (ERP), customer relationship management (CRM), e-commerce, messaging and calendaring functionality, work-flow services, and the like.

Languages

Another driving force to mobile commerce is the standardization of programming language for mobile devices. Languages such as Java 2 Mobile Edition (J2ME) makes it possible to write powerful applications that can leverage and integrate the different capabilities of the device, including voice, telephony, security, communications, and location capabilities. These standards are geared for devices with small memory, and therefore are suitable for mobile devices.

ARCHITECTURAL COMPONENTS

A mobile communication network protocol should deliver similar functionalities provided by the different layers of the open system interconnection (OSI) model for enabling communication in the mobile Internet. Because destination nodes are mobile, traditional IP protocols are no longer applicable for the mobile communication environment. In the wired network, the convention is that the IP addresses are organized such that nodes in the same location have the same prefixes. This no longer holds, as the nodes themselves are moving and do not have a fixed location. To overcome this problem, it uses the concept of care-of-address, and employs tunneling. Essentially, under the mobile IP, each mobile node sends its location by sending its care-of-address to its home agent. The home agent then tunnels the packets destined for the mobile node by forwarding them to the care-of-address; they are then delivered to the mobile node. Several standards are in place today; however, they differ in the way in which they have adapted the standard transport and the network layer protocols of the TCP/IP. For example, the mobile IP is now part of the 3G standard; however, other standards such as the GPRS support only a simplified version of the mobile IP.

While the IP layers are responsible for routing and addressing, the TCP layers are responsible for the reliable delivery of the packets, assembling the packets in the right order, and finally handing them over to the target application. The TCP protocol is also responsible for congestion control to ensure graceful performance degradation. With respect to the mobile communication version of the TCP protocol, it has to address specific problems because connections are often lost and transmission errors are more common in the mobile communication environment; therefore, round-trip times are harder to predict.

In addition to adapting the TCP/IP to the mobile communication environment, the mobile Internet needs to take into consideration the limited power, memory, computing capacity, and screen size of mobile devices. Moreover, because of the unreliable network connections, even the most common protocols, such as the HTTP, do not work well. Furthermore, the Web languages responsible for displaying the Web content, such as HTML, are required to be modified.

WAP has been proposed as a standard to address these challenges. The WAP forum (www.wapforum.org) was originally founded in the summer of 1997 by Ericsson, Nokia, Motorola, and Unwired Planet for the purposes of defining an industry-wide specification for developing applications over wireless communications networks. Forum members represent over 90 percent of the global handset market, as well as leading infrastructure providers, software developers, and other organizations. The WAP Forum has now become part of the Open Mobile Alliance (OMA). The WAP forum with Open Mobile Architecture formed the OMA, which has several working groups; one of them is on mobile commerce. A comparison of the Internet and WAP technologies has been provided in Figure 2. WAP architecture, as published by the WAP Forum, is shown in Figure 3. More details of the WAP are discussed below.

WAP

WAP is the de facto standard for information services on wireless terminals. It is an intelligent messaging service for handheld mobile devices such as mobile phones. WAP is an application communication protocol, and is used

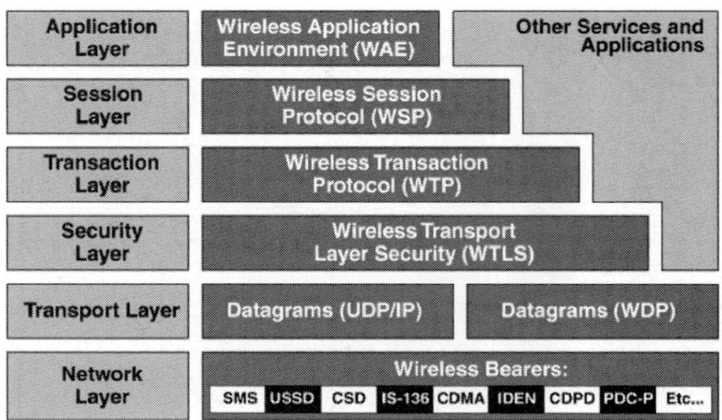

Figure 2: A Comparison of WAP and Internet technologies (*Source:* WAP Forum) (CDPD = cellular digital packet data; IDEN = integrated digital enhanced network; PDCP = packet data convergence protocol; UDP/IP = user datagram protocol/Internet protocol; USSD = unstructured supplementary service data; WDP = wireless datagram protocol)

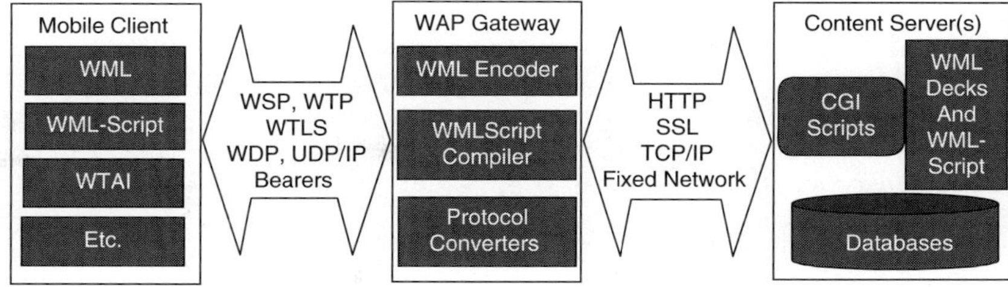

Figure 3: Architecture of the WAP gateway (*Source:* WAP Forum) (CGI = common gateway interface)

to access services and information. It is an application environment and a set of communication protocols for wireless devices designed to enable mobile users to have technology-independent access to the Internet and advanced telephony services. In particular, WAP specifications define a set of protocols in application, session, and transport layers of the communication protocol, as well as provide transactional and security services.

WAE

WAP also defines a wireless application environment (WAE) comprising of a micro-browser, scripting facilities, e-mail, Web-to-mobile-handset messaging, and mobile-to-telefax access. It allows digital content to be displayed on special WAP-enabled GSM mobile phones in a standard text format. It uses the wireless markup language WML (not HTML) to create Web applications for mobile devices so that they can be displayed in a WAP browser. As such, WAP is a protocol designed for micro-browsers. The WAP standard is based on Internet standards (HTML, XML, and TCP/IP). WML is defined as an XML application. It consists of a WML language specification, a WML script specification, and a wireless telephony application interface (WTAI) specification.

The functions of the different layers of the WAP are as follows: The WAP datagram protocol (WDP) is the transport layer that sends and receives messages via any available bearer network, including SMS, USSD, CSD, CDPD, IS-136 packet data, and GPRS. The wireless transport layer security (WTLS), an optional security layer, has encryption facilities that provide the secure transport service required by many applications, such as e-commerce. The WAP transaction protocol (WTP) layer provides transaction support, adding reliability to the datagram service provided by WDP. The WAP session protocol (WSP) layer provides a lightweight session layer to allow efficient exchange of data between applications. The HTTP interface serves to retrieve WAP content from the Internet requested by the mobile device. WML is based on XML. It is used to create pages that can be displayed in a WAP browser. The WML Script is a restricted Javascript language used by WML to run simple code on client machines. WML pages do not embed WML scripts, but only contain references to script URLs. Similar to the Java script, the WML scripts also need to be compiled into byte code on a server before they can run in a WAP browser. WAP uses a micro-browser to accommodate the small screens of the wireless devices. The micro-browser is a lightweight piece of software to display information written in WML and to interpret WML script.

SECURITY AND PRIVACY ISSUES

Similar to the traditional electronic commerce in the wired world, mobile commerce is also vulnerable to a range of security threats. However, since mobile commerce is a radio-frequency–operated system, it is easier to perpetrate some types of attacks compared to those in wired systems. The security requirements include: (1) confidentiality: requires the messages be kept secret from unauthorized recipients, (2) integrity: requires that messages are unaltered during the transit from the sender to the receiver, (3) authentication: requires ensuring that each party is who it claims to be, (4) nonrepudiation: guarantees that neither the sender nor the recipient can deny that the message exchange took place, and (5) replay attack prevention: ensures that any unauthorized resending of messages is detected and rejected. Several standards have been established in WAP to provide security at the application, transport, and management levels, which are described below.

WTLS

The basis of WAP security is in the wireless transport layer security (WTLS) protocol, which is analogous to the Internet's transport layer security (TLS) accomplished using the standard SSL protocol. WTLS is similar to the TLS, with a few differences. However, WAP 2.0 uses TLS instead of WTLS to overcome the WAP gap vulnerability (discussed next), and to provide end-to-end security at the transport level. It provides security services, including authentication and digital signatures, confidentiality by encrypting data, integrity by using hashing for detecting data modifications, and denial-of-service protection by TLS that detects and rejects data that have been replayed or not successfully verified. The WML script enables a user to digitally sign a message using the public key infrastructure (PKI).

Elliptic curve cryptography (ECC) is emerging as an attractive public key cryptosystem for mobile and wireless environments. Compared to traditional cryptosystems like RSA, ECC offers equivalent security with smaller key sizes, which results in faster computations, lower power consumption, and memory and bandwidth savings. As such, this is a more suitable choice for mobile devices, since mobile devices typically have limited CPU space power, and network connectivity. In fact, traditional signature schemes are viewed as impractical to implement in the wireless environment, as they require much more processing, memory, and storage resources, as compared with those with ECC. The keys for elliptic curve are typically on the order of six times smaller than equivalent keys in other signature schemes—for example, 164 bits versus 1024 bits. This creates great efficiencies in key storage, certificate size, memory usage, and digital-signature processing. ECC is fully supported by the WAP security standards and has been widely accepted by WAP device manufacturers.

The WAP identity module (WIM) is a tamper-resistant computer chip that resides in the WAP-enabled device—that is, mobile phones and PTDs. It is used to store the user's private key, the root public key of the PKI, etc. Mostly, WIMs are implemented using smart cards that typically have a CPU, some memory, and storage for data and programs. WML Script Crypto API (WMLSCrypt) is an application programming interface that allows access to basic security functions in the WML Script Crypto Library (WMLSCLib), such as key-pair generation, and encrypt and decrypt data, generate and verify digital signatures, store keys and other personal data, and control access to stored keys and data. WMLSCrypt also allows WAP applications to access and use the security objects and basic security services managed by other WAP security standards. WML script may optionally use a WIM Module to provide the crypto functionality. Wireless profiled TCP (WP-TCP) provides connection-oriented services. It is optimized for wireless environments and is fully interoperable with standard TCP implementations on the Internet.

Wireless Application PKI (WPKI)

WPKI is not an entirely new set of standards for PKI, but it is an optimized extension of traditional PKI for the wireless environment. It is concerned primarily with the policies that are used to manage mobile business and security environment by WTLS/TLS and WMLSCrypt in the wireless application environment. The WAP Forum provides the standards for WPKI. It requires the same components used in traditional PKI. However, the mobile device's applications and registration are implemented differently, and a new component referred to as the PKI portal is also required. The mobile device application in WPKI is implemented such that it runs in the WAP device. It relies on the WMLSCrypt application programming interface (API) for key services and cryptographic operations as well as including the traditional PKI functionalities. WPKI is an optimization of the traditional Internet Engineering Task Force (IETF) PKIX standards for the wireless environment. More specifically, it comprises optimized PKI protocols and certificate format as well as cryptographic algorithms and keys. As opposed to using the traditional basic encoding rules (BER) and distinguished encoding rules (DER) to handle PKI service requests, WPKI protocols are implemented using WML and WMLSCrypt. Similarly, the WPKI certificate format specification is a new certificate format for sever side certificates, which significantly reduces the size as compared with the standard X.509 certificate. Another significant reduction in the WPKI certificate can be attributed to ECC, with the savings in the size typically more than 100 bytes because of the smaller keys needed for ECC. WPKI has also limited the size of some of the data fields of the IETF PKIX certificate format. Since the WPKI certificate format is a subset of the PKIX certificate format, it is possible to maintain interoperability between standard PKIs.

The WAP Gap

One of the major security breaches in mobile commerce is due to the mobile network infrastructure used. When user information is transmitted from one mobile network to another, all the encrypted data need to be decrypted in order to send it to another network. When mobile devices make requests to Web pages of a network server, these requests originating from the WTSL protocol need to be translated at the originating WAP gateway. They are then encrypted, typically using SSL, and sent to the destination network. This is then processed by the HTTP in the destination network. During the translation process from one protocol to another, the data are required to be decrypted and then reencrypted. Because the data are in cleartext, they are vulnerable to attacks if an intruder can gain access to the mobile network. This vulnerability is commonly known as the WAP Gap. To alleviate this problem of WAP Gap, Juul (2002) proposes three alternative solutions: putting the WAP gateway inside the server, application layer, and mobile Internet.

Location Privacy

Identifying the location of a mobile customer is required because: (1) To function effectively, location-based services require information about the location of the communication device. As described in the section on "Mobile Commerce Applications," the location-based services present a major new market for the mobile industry. (2) In countries such as the United States, the European Union, and Japan, laws require that mobile telephones be able to provide location data with a fairly detailed accuracy for the purposes of emergency situations.

Unlike the Internet, location information has the potential to allow an adversary to physically locate a person, and therefore most wireless subscribers have legitimate concerns about their personal safety if such information should fall into the wrong hands. The 1996 Telecommunications Act included location information as customer proprietary network information (CPNI), along with time, date, and duration of a call and the number dialed. Because of the sensitive nature of location information, legal and regulatory approaches for controlling access to location information should be different from other CNPI. Specifically, consumers must be comfortable that they have control over who can obtain location information and when such information can be obtained in order form them to be willing to buy location-based services. Laws and rules of varying clarity, offering different degrees of protection, have been or are in the process of being enacted in the United States, the European Union, and Japan (Ackerman, Kempf, and Miki 2003).

Beresford and Stajano (2003, 2004) have proposed techniques that let users benefit from location-based applications, while preserving their location privacy. Mobile users, in general, do not permit the information to be shared among different location-based services. Primarily, the approach relies on hiding the true identity of a customer from the applications receiving the user's location, by frequently changing pseudonyms so that users avoid being identified by the locations they visit.

GLOSSARY

802.11b: (also referred to as **802.11 High Rate** or **WiFi**) Applies to wireless LANs and provides 11-Mbps transmission (with a fallback to 5.5-, 2-, and 1-Mbps depending on range and signal strength) in the 2.4-GHz band. 802.11b uses only DSSS (direct-sequence spread spectrum; DSSS is one of two types of spread spectrum radio). 802.11b was a 1999 IEEE ratification to the original 802.11 standard, allowing wireless functionality comparable to Ethernet.

3G: Third-generation wireless. Refers to developments in mobile communications. Increased bandwidth, from 128 Kbps while moving at high speeds to 2 Mbps for fixed stations, enables multimedia applications and advanced roaming features.

AP: Access point.

CCMP: Counter-mode/CBC-mac protocol. An IEEE 802.11i encryption algorithm. In the 802.11i standard, unlike WPA, key management and message integrity is handled by a single component CCMP built around AES.

CDMA: Code division multiple access. A digital method for simultaneously transmitting signals over a shared portion of the spectrum by encoding each distinct signal with a code chip. Terminals receive the aggregated signal from the tower, and use specific codes to unbundle the signals. CDMA devices are noted for their excellent connection quality and long battery life.

DSSS: Direct-sequence spread spectrum. DSSS is a transmission technology used in WLAN (wireless LAN) transmissions, in which a data signal at the sending station is combined with a higher-data-rate bit sequence, or chipping code, that divides the user data according to a spreading ratio. The chipping code is a redundant bit pattern for each bit that is transmitted, which increases the signal's resistance to interference. If one or more bits in the pattern are damaged during transmission, the original data can be recovered because of the redundancy of the transmission.

GPS: Global positioning system. Satellite-based radio positioning system capable of providing specific location information to suitably equipped users anywhere.

GPRS: General packet radio service. An enhancement to the GSM mobile communications system that supports data packets. GPRS enables continuous flows of IP data packets over the system for applications such as Web browsing and file transfer. GPRS differs from GSM's short messaging service (GSM-SMS), which is limited to messages of 160 bytes in length.

GSM: Global system for mobile communications. A digital cellular phone technology based on TDMA that is the predominant system in Europe, but is also used widely around the world. Developed in the 1980s, GSM was first deployed in seven European countries in 1992. Operating in the 900-MHz and 1.8-GHz bands in Europe and the 1.9-GHz PCS band in the United States, GSM defines the entire cellular system, not just the air interface.

UMTS: Universal mobile telecommunications system. The ITU standard for 3G wireless phone systems. UMTS, which is part of IMT-2000, provides service in the 2- GHz band and offers global roaming and personalized features. Designed as an evolutionary system for GSM network operators, which will marry the benefits of CDMA with the interoperability benefits of GSM, multimedia data rates up to 2 Mbps are expected. There are three branches of the UMTS standard: TD-SCDMA, UMTS TDD, and W-CDMA. CDMA2000 is not UMTS.

WAP: Wireless access protocol. A set of standards that allows Web access on mobile devices. WAP is supported by most wireless networks and operating systems. It supports HTML and XML but is designed for WML.

WiFi: Wireless fidelity. This is another name for IEEE 802.11b. It is a trade term promulgated by the Wireless Ethernet Compatibility Alliance (WECA). "WiFi" is used in place of 802.11b in the same way that "Ethernet" is used in place of IEEE 802.3. Products certified as WiFi by WECA are interoperable with each other even if they are from different manufacturers. A user with a WiFi product can use any brand of access point with any other brand of client hardware that is built to the WiFi standard.

WLA: Wireless LAN. A type of LAN that uses high-frequency radio waves rather than wires to communicate between nodes.

WML: Wireless markup language. A language developed to control the presentation of Web pages on mobile phones and PDAs in the same way that HTML does for PCs. Part of the wireless access protocol (WAP), WML is an open standard and is supported by most mobile phones.

XHTML: A reworking of HTML 4.0 designed to work as an application of XML. It allows anyone to create sets of markup tags for new purposes.

CROSS REFERENCES

See *Electronic Commerce*; *Electronic Data Interchange (EDI)*; *Electronic Payment Systems*; *The Internet Fundamentals*.

REFERENCES

3G Americas. 2006. *Users worldwide pick GSM ten to one*. www.mobiletechnews.com/info/2006/05/25/105926.html (accessed May 25, 2006).

Ackerman, L., J. Kempf, and T. Miki. 2003, November. Wireless location privacy: Law and policy in the U.S., EU and Japan. Internet Society. http://www.isoc.org/briefings/015/index.shtml.

Andersson. C. 2001. *GPRS and 3G wireless applications: The ultimate guide to maximizing mobile internet technologies*. New York: Wiley, 2001.

Barnes, S., and S. Huff. 2003. Rising sun: i-mode and the wireless Internet. Communications of the ACM, 46(11), pp. 78–84.

Beresford, A. R., and F. Stajano. 2003, January–March. Location privacy in pervasive computing. *Pervasive Computing*.

Beresford, A. R., and F. Stajano. 2004. Mix zones: User privacy in location-aware services. In *IEEE Workshop on Pervasive Computing and Communication Security (PerSec) 2004, a workshop in PerCom 2004*. pp. 127–131.

Juniper Research Group. 2004, August. Mobile commerce (m-commerce) & micropayment strategies. www.juniperresearch.com (accessed July 7, 2007).

Juels, A., R. L. Rivest, and M. Szydlo. 2003. The blocker tag: selective blocking of RFID tags for consumer privacy. In *Proceedings of the 10th ACM Conference on Computer and Communication Security*. pp. 103–111.

Juels, A., and J. Brainard. 2004. Soft blocking: Flexible blocker tags on the cheap. In *Workshop on Privacy in the Electronic Society (WPES)*, edited by S. De Capitani di Vimercati and P. Syverson. pp. 1–7.

Juul, N. C. 2002. Security issues in mobile commerce using WAP. In the *15th Bled Electronic Commerce Conference, e-Reality: Constructing the e-Economy, Bled, Slovenia, June 17–19*. pp. 444–462.

Kumar, S. 2004. Mobile communications: global trends in the 21st century. *International Journal of Mobile Communications (IJMC)* 2(1): pp. 67–86.

Lehmann, H., and F. Lehner. 2004. Is there a "killer application" in mobile technology? A tailored research approach. Working paper. Regensburg, Bavaria: University of Regensburg.

NewLogic Invests in 4G Mobile Technology. 2003, March 13. *Electronic News*.

Pyramid Research. 2004, April. Is WiFi wagging the 3G dog? http://www.umtsworld.com/articles/0406_global.pdf.

Rao, B., and L. Minakakis. 2003. Evolution of mobile location-based services. *Communications of the ACM* 46(12): pp. 61–65.

Sadeh, N. 2002. *M-commerce: Technologies, services and business models*. New York: Wiley Computer Publishing.

Spagat, E. 2002, September 11. Handheld homing devices: GPS hits household gadgets. *Wall Street Journal*.

Steinfield, C. 2004. The development of location based services in mobile commerce. In *Elife after the dot. com bust*, edited by B. Preissl, H. Bouwman, and C. Steinfield, 177–97. Berlin: Springer.

Umar, A. 2004. Mobile computing and wireless communications applications, networks, platforms, architectures, and security. NGE Solutions.

Venkatesh, V., V. Ramesh, and A. P. Massey. 2003. Understanding usability in mobile commerce. *Communications of the ACM* 46(12): pp. 53–56.

RESOURCES

The various resources include the Web pages of mobile technology vendors and conferences and journals in the area of mobile networks, mobile commerce, and electronic commerce. Examples include:

The ACM International Conference on Mobile Computing and Networking: www.sigmobile.org/mobicom

m-business—The International Conference on Mobile Business: www.mbussness2003.org

International Journal of Mobile Communications https://www.inderscience.com/browse/index.php?journalID=40

Wireless Communications & Mobile Computing: www.wileyeurope.com/WileyCDA/WileyTitle/productCd-WCM.html

Mobile Networks and Applications: www.kluweronline.com/issn/1383-469X

www.umtsworld.com

http://en.wikipedia.org/wiki/Main_Page

www.nttdocomo.com/

www.links2mobile.com/ListSubs.asp?cid=52&hd=Mobile+Commerce&ban=4

www.bus.iastate.edu/mennecke/server/Mcommerce.htm

http://cms.syr.edu/connecting/wireless/glossary.html

Online News

Bruce Garrison, *University of Miami,*
Marcus Messner, *Virginia Commonwealth University*

INTRODUCTION

Online news is flourishing, and its use is growing (Li 2006, Introduction; Greer and Mensing 2006). We are at the beginning of the online news era. About 100 million increasingly diverse persons in the United States read news online. Internationally, the growth of online newspapers is similar They are not only available in most nations and geographic locations throughout the world, their reach is also global (Chyi and Sylvie 2001). Research has shown that although online newspapers throughout the world are available to almost anyone with a computer and network access, they retain their local nature (Chyi and Sylvie 2001). Whereas the circulation of daily newspapers across the United States remains flat or in decline, Web sites that provide news content seem to be strong. The number of daily newspapers in the United States that are online grew about 13 percent from 2003 to 2004. Today, the number of newspapers online is almost equal to the number of newspapers that are being published (Journalism.org 2005). Newspaper Web sites, for example, grow at a yearly rate of about 11 percent in terms of visitors to their sites, with a total of nearly 40 million. One in four Internet users reads news online (Sharma 2005).

Online newspapers and online journalism in general have become a vital part of information available on the World Wide Web and the Internet. Growing numbers of people worldwide are reading news online. Since the mid-1990s, online magazines, wire services, newspapers, television stations, broadcast-cable networks, and subscription newsletters have matured to take advantage of their unique orientation and audiences. New technologies are introduced almost yearly that allow consumers new ways to obtain Web-based information. Wireless Internet technology that allows even greater access to online news and information is also growing rapidly. Airports, college campuses, business centers, downtown areas, and even entire communities are becoming wireless centers for laptop and notebook computer users and for personal digital assistant (PDA) handheld device users. Cellular telephone users have even greater wireless access for online news and information. It is common today for individuals to read Web-based news with browsers on their cell phones. New technologies that are in development—such as flat-screen portable tablets or improved handheld devices that also serve as telephones—are likely to become popular in the future as well.

Even with new wireless technologies for a variety of receiving devices, wired online services continue to grow in their availability and in use worldwide. News consumers are embracing these new communication tools. The new communication technologies have been viewed by news organizations as opportunities to extend their reach and contact with news consumers at international levels. The result is new forms and formats of news and information, such as news headlines and breaking story alerts delivery by e-mail and messaging services to subscribers that are at the cutting edge of communication today.

This chapter focuses on the changing nature and status of online news and journalism, including that practiced by newspapers, news magazines, and television news organizations. It provides an overview of the evolution of online news, including the developing use of Web logs and wikis. The chapter outlines the most significant economic models that have failed, have succeeded, or are currently being tested. Competition among online news media is also discussed. This chapter examines the impact of multimedia and convergence on their content and staffing. It also provides brief descriptions of leading American online news organizations. The primary service models for online news and a summary of online news market sizes and models conclude the discussion.

ORIGINS OF ONLINE NEWS

The news industry worldwide is diversifying. Today's news companies throughout the world own local and national newspapers; local television stations; cable television and radio networks; AM, FM, and satellite radio stations; general and specialized market magazines; subscription newsletter; professional sports teams; outdoor advertising companies; newsprint plants; Internet service providers; and a growing number of high-profile World Wide Web sites. These popular Web sites cover a lot of informational ground. They include news and information content, but also focus on activities such as entertainment and nightlife, business, tourism and travel, sports, and reference/research. News companies, particularly those that began as newspaper businesses several generations ago, have emerged as new enterprises in the multimedia world through expansion and contraction, redefinition, and restructuring. News companies have embraced this form of convergence and have moved fully into the digital age. They seek a unique role and function for their online news products (van der Wurff 2005).

The number of online news sites grew rapidly throughout the mid-1990s, paralleling the growth in popularity of the World Wide Web. But the origins of online news can be traced to the early 1980s. In 1983, the Knight-Ridder newspaper group and AT&T launched a revolutionary experiment to bring people news on demand through their computers or television sets. Development work on the videotext service, called "Viewtron," began in 1978, but took more than 5 years to debut. It remains noteworthy because it was a forerunner of today's online news media. Knight-Ridder Newspapers, which was bought by McClatchy Newspapers in early 2006, suspended the Viewtron operations on April 1, 1986, having fewer than 20,000 subscribers and having lost a staggering $50 million. A similar venture at the *Los Angeles Times.* called "Gateway," also closed operations in 1986, having only 3000 users. The failed ventures left journalists wondering whether there would ever be a market for news on demand via computers (Burgess 1993; Keefe 1996). Viewtron and its partners even adopted rapidly developing, but still new, desktop PCs to their service by aggressively marketing software for PCs in 1985–1986, but it was not enough. With the right timing, Viewtron or Gateway might have become an America Online or CompuServe, distinguishing itself with a strong component of news and information. Had the service existed only 5 years later, it would have been at the cutting edge of the then-new Web.

A handful of daily newspapers were available online through proprietary online services in the 1980s. These included eleven newspapers that did an experiment with CompuServe in 1982. A few other newspapers produced online sites in 1990, including *The Albuquerque Tribune*, the *Atlanta Journal and Constitution,* and the *Rocky Mountain News* in Denver. University of Florida Interactive Media Lab Director David Carlson has outlined this development with an online media timeline on the Web (http://iml.jou.ufl.edu/carlson/timeline.shtml).

The *Chicago Tribune* (www.chicagotribune.com) was the first newspaper to provide same-day editorial content to America Online in May 1992. Soon afterward, the *San Jose Mercury News* (www.bayarea.com/mld/mercurynews), also a pioneer in online news, was the first newspaper to put its entire contents online on AOL in 1993. At the time, when only 3 million Americans were online, the *Mercury News'* decision to put the newspaper's Mercury Center online was simply an experiment. Therefore, most observers regard the *San Jose Mercury News* to be the first online newspaper. It was not surprising that a San Jose newspaper would lead the way in online journalism. Given its location, it considers itself the newspaper of record for the famed Silicon Valley.

By the mid-1990s, as the Web expanded rapidly, broadcast news outlets were developing a significant presence on the Web. Broadcast and cable networks were among the earliest to put their news content on the Web, but local affiliates began to build Web sites with limited news content. The sites mostly served a promotional purpose by offering program listings, biographies and other information about air personalities, appearance schedules, and various forms of community service features.

Competitive amateur and professional sports have become a major drawing card for online news sites. Local and national news organizations have built a user base by providing information about local teams and major sports events while competition is underway. Local newspapers and television stations often offer running summaries and updated scores of events not always on television or radio. They enhance printed and broadcast coverage by offering statistics, schedules, archival content, and other information that, because of space or time limitations, cannot be published or broadcast. National news media often provide a similar service for professional teams and major college events.

There was also a growth of Web-based electronic magazines at about the same time. These topical online publications, often called "zines" or "e-zines," did not originate in printed form, but certainly were built upon the printed magazine tradition. They are often highly specialized and have been described as "independent publications characterized by idiosyncratic themes, low circulation, irregular frequency, ephemeral duration, and noncommercial orientation" (Rauch 2004, 153). Almost overnight, these energetic periodicals appeared all over the Web and received a large amount of popular media coverage and attention as the trend of the moment. The Web created opportunities for this new genre of specialized online news and information in the mid- and late 1990s and they have continued into the new century with a steady niche audience appeal. *Slate* (www.slate.com) and *Salon* (www.salon.com) are typical of successful zines. There are numerous zines on the Web today, and they attract an audience in the millions (Rauch 2004; Williams 2003).

CONVERGENCE AND THE CHANGING ONLINE NEWS WORLD

Convergence of mass media has arrived, and it is impacting online news. It is a slowly evolving process, but there is evidence of convergence in North America, Europe, Asia, and in other cutting-edge newsrooms around the world. Convergence has "amplified" the strategic importance of the Internet, wrote researchers Ju-Yong Ha, Steven J. Dick, and Seung Kwan Ryu (2003, 155). There is growing interest, they noted, in the merged content of television and other news and mass media, and it is expected to become more sophisticated in the years ahead.

An example of convergence at the regional level is the merger of newsrooms by Media General in Tampa, Florida. *The Tampa Tribune* (http://tampatrib.com), the morning daily newspaper serving Tampa Bay, and WFLA-TV (www.wfla.com) Channel 8, the NBC broadcast television affiliate, and Tampa Bay Online (www.tbo.com), the Web site serving both the newspaper and the television station, moved into a single facility in 2000 to share and work together in an early effort at convergence of newsrooms and technologies. The three news organizations share news resources, equipment, and staff. In fact, the large newsrooms, studios, work stations, and other facilities that are spread over several floors of the news center are anchored by a circular central news desk in the building's atrium. Journalists from each of the three news organizations staff the news desk and coordinate use of images, audio, video, wire content, local photographs, and news stories as well as other available content (Dupagne and Garrison, 2006; Singer 2004).

Convergence—the cooperation and sharing of resources of formerly separate news organizations as well as the delivery of news content through multiple means—is often viewed as an opportunity for the news media, and not as a process. Some view it as a threat to the news media because it is perceived to mean loss of newsroom jobs, more work for remaining journalists, more required skills, or a decline in the number of voices in a community. Yet others see it as the future of the news media and a chance for news to combine the best of its various media formats for consumers. They also feel that online news sites offer speed and depth to print or broadcast coverage (Kolodzy 2003; see also, Singer 2003, 2004; Deuze 2004; Dupagne and Garrison 2006).

The number of online users with high-speed connections is growing rapidly in the United States. A study by the Pew Internet & American Life Project released in 2006 said that Internet penetration increased from 58 percent of all adult Americans to 70 percent between 2002 and 2006. During the same period, home broadband penetration increased from 10 to 37 percent of adult Americans. A total of 74 million people access the Internet via broadband (Horrigan 2006). It is clear that American online users are entering the broadband age. The implications are clear. As more high-speed users are connected, more and more online news content can be accessed. This creates challenges for content providers to offer text, but also much more, such as audio, video, interactivity, and multimedia.

The best online newspapers have readily moved away from shovelware—the period when what they offered was little more than the reproduced published content of the traditional newspaper and the wire services—toward convergence. They seem to have matured past the point of scooping themselves when coverage of either the online or print edition carries a story that the other does not (Bressers and Bergen 2002; An Evolving Medium 1999; Fee 2002). Online newspapers have become standalone products (Greer and Mensing 2004), and online broadcast news sites have grown beyond their early promotional purposes (Chan-Olmsted and Park 2000). Not only do the best online newspapers today, such as *The New York Times*, offer much more than just the best content of the daily newspaper, they also offer an interactive Internet home for their established print edition readers as well as nonreader residents and visitors (Apcar 2006). They offer an interconnectedness that follows a many-to-many communication mode (Li 2006, Graphic use and interconnectedness). Many online newspapers also have developed online information *portals* for their communities (Miller 2001). They want to offer readers a wide range of interactive tools and technologies to experience news and information like it has never been provided before (The Impact of the Internet 2000).

Solving the reader puzzle is a high priority among online news media editors. The issue is not only what content to offer and, for online newspapers, whether and how to make it different from print editions, but also how much control to turn over to readers. With the Web, there is more content and less editorial decision making over what is published. This has been given to a degree to readers. "With that enhanced control, it appears online readers are particularly likely to pursue their own interests, and they are less likely to follow the cues of news editors and producers," noted media scholar David Tewksbury (2003, 694).

One of the most-publicized examples of national and international corporate media convergence was the America Online-Time Warner merger that was announced in early 2000. Some reports described it as a merger, but AOL stockholders actually owned 55 percent of the new company when the deal was completed. AOL obtained the immense resources of Time Warner, including Time Inc. and CNN, through the buyout involving $156 billion in AOL stock. This event set the stage for dozens of multimedia and convergence opportunities for the new corporation that now includes America Online's worldwide network access, its Internet services, and its proprietary Web content, Time Warner's CNN broadcast news networks, its widely circulated and respected magazines (e.g., *Time*, *Fortune*, *Sports Illustrated*, *Money*, *People*) and news services, its cable television and broadband customers, its music library, its film library and archives, and much more. It has been characterized by one media observer as a "new age, techno-cultural behemoth" (George 2000). The AOL-Time Warner marriage, however, has turned out to be less for its owners than had been hoped. Some observers have even characterized AOL as a burden for Time Warner and, recently, the company has been looking to sell off its America Online assets (Simon 2005).

Web portals provide much more than just news content. Many traditional news media have established portals for residents and visitors of their communities and regions. The *San Jose Mercury News* (www.bayarea.com/mld/mercurynews), for example, is the daily newspaper portal serving California's Silicon Valley. It serves the Bay Area with the equally suburban *Contra Costa Times* within a site called BayArea.com (www.bayarea.com). *The Boston Globe* has established a similar portal for New England with Boston.com (www.boston.com). Online newspaper and television portals provide a gateway to a series of sites and links about a region or metropolitan area. They are also often customizable so readers can select types of information displayed on the home page.

For the past half decade, news organizations have scrambled to keep up with competitors to establish a strong presence on the Web. In some studies, Internet use for reading and viewing news has been found to exceed traditional news media such as magazines and radio. One study found it approached the use levels of network and cable television (Internet Growing as News Medium 2002).

Online news media are working to define themselves. This has been difficult for news organizations, whether they are based in traditional news media or are independents and only on the Web. For online newspapers, the effort to determine the role and model in which to work has already gone through several iterations. There will be more to come. Just like radio and television before it, the newest technologies undergo a formation period. Online newspapers are experiencing an era of exploration and self-determination. Although there are no geographic boundaries for online newspapers, practically speaking, most people who access a local newspaper do it for local news. Online newspapers differ from most online news media in their intensely local nature, provided by the content they offer from their print editions (Singer 2001).

Online news media have matured with coverage of major breaking and ongoing stories, such as Operation Iraqi Freedom and the 2006 and 2004 election campaigns. The growth of blogging is one example. More traditional television, radio, newspaper, and magazine journalists use blogs as an extension of their reporting and as a means of presenting informed opinion expression. Furthermore, there are a wider number of innovative presentation formats for the breaking stories covered, for features, and for the opinions expressed (Palser 2003). Despite this view, some experts feel the news media have been stagnant and have not gone far enough. Experimentation and new online publications and formats continue to debut in a search for what works best for contemporary audiences (Reeves 2003). The University of Florida's new media expert David Carlson (2005) is typical of those who feel that online news media have incredible potential but do not yet live up to it. Carlson believes that "The problem with online newspapers is this: They are just like offline newspapers. That means they are not particularly interactive, they are barely customizable to individual preferences, they contain mostly outdated information, and they are hardly relevant to most readers' daily lives" (p. 68).

Formation of new media can trigger transformation of established media. New media may also have a destabilizing effect on old media, but old media also tend to embrace the new media (Samoriski 2002). For example, the development of television brought on change in movie news reels and, ultimately, their disappearance in theaters. However, it is also common for new media to complement and benefit existing outlets (Samoriski 2002). For example, print newspapers might advise readers to go online for more information not offered in the printed editions because of space limitations, or they can offer links to multimedia content—such as interviews with key newsmakers, photo galleries, video and audio of major events as they occurred—available on the newspaper's Web site.

Some authorities have offered views that another stage of online news change is in the near future. With the maturity of online advertising, with growing revenues, online news may experience a growth of stand-alone sites in the second half of this decade. Although first attempts at these failed, for the most part, some observers feel the time is right for these sites as well as the branded online editions of print news organizations and television networks to prosper (Dorror 2005).

Online newspapers require professional abilities and skills different from their print counterparts. While both forms require news judgment, speed, and other fundamental journalistic tools, online newspapers seek content producers with greater versatility to work in multimedia as well as computer network technologies (Dupagne and Garrison 2006). Old skills-based walls have been taken down in favor of individuals who can do it all—write, edit, compile, tell the story visually, and work with audio and video content. The changing staff needs have forced some online newspapers to recruit beyond their own newspaper newsrooms. News companies will continue to look for specialists in different skills areas such as print and television, but will also increasingly seek "multimedia superreporters," who cover the world with laptops, digital video and still cameras, and digital recorders (Gates 2002).

WEB LOGS AND WIKIS

Since the late 1990s, Web logs have developed into an influential, new online news format. Affordable and user-friendly software made it possible for anyone to maintain a Web log (Jensen 2003). A blogger can be an independent individual who is reporting from the field or who is commenting from his or her living room. It can also be someone who is affiliated with the traditional media in a newsroom, on assignment at a remote location, or who is commenting from home (Lascia 2002). Because of this unspecific definition of what a blogger may be, there is widespread debate among professionals and scholars whether bloggers should be considered journalists (Kramer 2004; Cooper 2005; Edmonds 2005; Lascia 2002; Blood 2003; Andrews 2003). Tensions between journalists and bloggers have been growing (Kramer 2004). Bloggers usually comment on the news of the day or bring attention to stories they feel were undercovered, rather than reporting their own news (Smolkin 2004). And the existence of bloggers combined with the lack of regard held for them by traditional news media managers suggests a "perilous future" for print media (Cooper 2005).

However, aside from the debate over professional standards, Web logs have had a great impact on online news. Web logs were instrumental in breaking the news about the Lewinsky/Clinton scandal in 1998, which led to the impeachment of President Bill Clinton, and the Trent Lott scandal in 2002, which led to the resignation of the U.S. Senate Majority Leader (Williams and Delli Carpini 2004). During the 2004 presidential campaign, Web logs became known to a more widespread audience. Howard Dean, who sought the Democratic Party presidential nomination, based part of his 2003–2004 campaign effort on blogs. Some bloggers discredited a CBS News report on President George W. Bush's National Guard service and others were invited by Republicans and Democrats to cover the national conventions (Perlmutter and McDaniel 2005). In the corporate world, Web logs have also had a great impact. For example, Web log attention caused lock producer Kryptonite to lose approximately $10 million because a posting in 2004 detailed how to open one of its bicycle lock products (Kirkpatrick, Roth, and Ryan 2005). Web logs also function as watchdogs over the traditional media. The resignations of CNN executive Eason Jordan and White House correspondent Jeff Gannon were instigated in early 2005 by the relentless reporting of bloggers (Kurtz 2005).

According to the search engine Technorati (2006), there were almost 38 million Web logs in the United States in spring 2006. But they are a truly global phenomenon. In China—the second largest Internet market in the world—Tsinghua University research estimated 37 million Web logs and about 60 million bloggers in 2006 (Reuters 2006). Some of the most prominent political Web logs are Instapundit (www.instapundit.com), DailyKos (www.dailykos.com), Power Line (http://powerlineblog.com), and Eschaton (http://atrios.blogspot.com). At the same time, the number of Web log readers worldwide is also steadily increasing. In 2005, 26 percent of Americans were very or somewhat familiar with Web logs (Cable News Network 2005). The number of Internet users who read Web logs increased from 17 percent in February 2004 to 27 percent in November 2004 (Rainie 2005). The credibility of Web logs is also increasing. Web-log users view Web logs as more credible than the traditional media (Johnson and Kaye 2004).

In recent years, another new information format developed parallel to Web logs—wikis. Although Web logs are generally written by a single person, wikis are a collective effort of a group of contributors. Individuals can add, edit, and delete content on these Web sites. The most prominent wiki is the online encyclopedia Wikipedia (www.wikipedia.org), which in the summer of 2007 had 1.9 million entries in English. The encyclopedia is also available in German, French, Japanese, Polish, Italian, Swedish, Dutch, Portuguese, and Spanish. Wikipedia has been called one of the greatest success stories of the Web (Dodson 2005), yet the Web site was at the center of a discussion about the reliability of information it offers in entries (Seigenthaler 2005). Besides Wikipedia, several other widely used wikis have developed. Wikinews (www.wikinews.org) and Wikimedia (www.wikimedia.org), for example, attempt to collaboratively gather news and conduct reporting and provide a collaborative collection of information resources, respectively (Weiss 2005).

ONLINE NEWS WRITING AND CONTENT

Online journalism has the opportunity to take the best features and characteristics of existing mass media and news media, eliminate most of the weaknesses, and place them into a new medium in which stories can be told in new ways using words, video, audio, and still photos together. To accomplish this, online news writing is evolving. It is, of course, quite different from newspaper, broadcast, or other news media writing. To be truly valuable to users, online news must take advantage of hypermedia and hypertext and their unique nonlinear nature. Writing for online news sites is often done in layers (e.g., headlines, summaries, leads, and other text), often called "chunking," and with an awareness of clicking and scrolling capabilities of browser software. Online storytelling should involve the wide variety of media forms available on the Web, not just basic text and images. This includes audio, video, and forms of reader-user interactivity such as chat rooms and instant opinion polls.

Another important part of writing for online newspapers is its style. Each publication develops its own style. Sometimes, it is personal, casual, and informal. Other approaches can be more formal. Often the style used is a function of the audience served (Rich 2007; Whittaker 2000; Wilber and Miller 2003). Although the Internet allows storing long articles easily, the compact style has not been abandoned. News writers still strive for brevity for many of their stories in order to display an entire story in one screen view without scrolling.

Online newspapers have a struggle similar to that of their print counterparts. Both are fighting for survival in a digital- and video-oriented world. With countless other online news sources coming from television, radio, and magazines, competition for online newspapers is intense. Add to the mix a new set of news providers—online services such as Google, Microsoft Network, America Online, and Yahoo!—and the job becomes much more difficult. If, as some AOL executives maintained, AOL is used by many of its customers for news and information instead of local online newspapers, the electronic editions of traditional newspapers and other news media have a long road ahead for success. As one critic wrote, online news consumers and journalists should "be afraid" of such ventures (Koerner 2001, 25).

The evolution of online newspapers has paralleled the development of other online news media (An Evolving Medium 1999; Strupp 1999). They are learning what works and what does not. Newspapers have offered electronic mail alert services for breaking and ongoing stories, severe weather bulletins, or even more routine notifications of new editions of their publications (Outing 2001; Langfield 2001). While interactive features, such as electronic mail used for news alert services and bulletins, have been successful, Web-based chat rooms have not been used as effectively (Perlman 1999; Pryor 2000). By the end of its first decade, online news has moved from a more passive and noninteractive model to more immediacy, content richness, and control given to users-readers (Bucy 2004).

Major U.S. natural and human-made tragedies, such as Hurricane Katrina during August 23–30, 2005, the terrorist attacks on September 11, 2001, and the student shootings at Columbine High School in Colorado on April 20, 1999, provided situations in which to use interactivity, but many online newspapers were criticized for failing to use them well (e.g., see Perlman 1999; Outing 2001). Other research has also shown less use of interactivity and hypertextuality than might be expected in online media and criticism that the medium of online newspapers remains immature (Oblak 2005; Salaverria 2005). At the very least, research has shown adoption of multimedia and interactivity in online newsrooms to be dependent on organizational structures and work practices, among other factors (Boczkowski 2004).

Newspaper sites have become quite popular during this learning period, but newspapers continue to learn how to use their Web edition to attract and serve readers and advertisers (Palser 2005; Pryor 2000). For example, the use of interactive features to enhance reader feedback seems to be growing in newspaper newsrooms (The Impact of the Internet 2000). Although there is growth in sophistication in developing news content, the same cannot be said about commercial endeavors that would support the news product. Electronic commerce and advertising opportunities remain a mystery to many in the industry. Online newspaper managers certainly have not learned everything necessary about turning the sites into profit centers for the company, but neither have other online news organizations at this point. The online news industry is so young that it has remained uncertain how its costs will be paid (McMillan 1998; Pryor 2000; Palser 2001, Pay-per-click; Chyi 2005).

SEARCHING FOR THE BEST ECONOMIC MODEL

It is a strange form of contradiction. On one hand, Internet users have been gradually convinced that they should buy music online. And services such as iTunes are earning revenues today after music lovers downloaded their favorites online for free. But pay for news online? Not yet. Although there are notable exceptions, such as *The Wall Street Journal* subscription fees and the premium content services subscriptions of *The New York Times* and CNN, most Internet news consumers love to read information online—at work, on the road, and at home—but they "loath to pay for it," as Katharine Seelye (2005, 17) wrote. In fact, *New York Times* Company Chairman and Publisher Arthur Sulzberger, Jr., effectively expressed the position of newspapers in the online age. He stated that "If we're going to define ourselves by our history, then we deserve to go out of business" (Gates 2002). "Newspapers cannot be defined by the second word—paper. They've got to be defined by the first—news. All of us have to become agnostic as to the method of distribution. We've got to be as powerful online, as powerful in television and broadcasting, as we are powerful in newsprint."

Newspapers, more than any other traditional news medium, raced to go online during the mid-1990s. In 1994 and 1995, they offered content for free. But some owners and managers felt they could charge for the content and switched to online subscriptions. This was short-lived, however, as the experiment failed when users found comparable information elsewhere on the Web (Grimes 2002). Owners and managers had expected to be part of a digital gold rush (Dibean and Garrison 2001), but the anticipated gold rush never came because the medium has not found a profitable economic model. To date, there simply has not been sufficient advertising volume and other revenue to support online news. News on the Web, some have observed, spreads very quickly, has a short shelf-life, and can be found for free if a user searches hard enough (Grimes 2002; see also Arampatzis 2004).

There are numerous business models for Web content, including the failed videotext model, the failed paid Internet model, the failed free Web model, the failed Internet/Web advertising "push" model, the present portals and personal portals models, and the evolving digital portals model (Picard 2000). Online news organizations are experimenting today with portal approaches. Within the various portal models, the subscription model may be the future despite previous failed efforts (Chyi 2005). Financial conditions often lead to such radical change, and the economic environment in late 2001 and 2002 following the September 11 terrorist attacks against the United States, combined with a recession, put pressure on sites to generate income. Online advertising was not producing sufficient revenue, and sites were forced to find a different economic model. Suddenly, the subscription model looked better and, as one publication in 2002 stated, "the free lunch is over" (Smith 2002, February; see also Smith 2002, April, and Trombly 2002). The collapse of free alternatives will lead consumers to accept the subscription or other fee-based models for operation of online news sites. Commercial sites with valued content have already found this to work. Arampatzis (2004) identified six basic subscription model variations currently in use:

1. Free content; advertising supported; paid subscription content and paid premium content.
2. Free content; advertising supported; ad-free access paid subscriptions.
3. Paid subscriptions; no or very limited free content; no advertising.
4. Paid subscriptions; no or very limited free content; advertising accepted.
5. Free content to in-market Internet users; paid subscriptions for out-of-market.
6. Regional content providers cooperate in charging scheme, everyone charges.

The Wall Street Journal and its online site, for example, had more than 768,000 worldwide subscribers in late 2005 (Christie and Edmonds 2006). "We already know that consumers will pay for highly valued, proprietary content that either makes or saves them money," *EContent* writer Steve Smith wrote (2002, February, 19). "For most other content brands, however, it gets more complicated. The fear of competition from free alternatives, the risks of severe traffic loss, and the overwhelming resistance among users has left the fee-based approach more of a pipe dream."

Despite this surge toward fee-based content, it is apparent that consumers have been conditioned to expect to find news online at no cost (Donatello 2002). Online users see the Web as an open frontier that is free to all, and they adamantly oppose paying even modest fees (Chyi 2005). Since 1997, some online newspapers ceased publication for lack of profitability. Some online newspapers have recently begun using registration schemes to begin orienting consumers toward paid subscriptions (Brown 2003).

Online news consumers are upscale and typically live in urban or metropolitan areas. The Pew Internet & American Life Project stated that "this information-elite . . . shapes how delivery of news and information will evolve online" (Horrigan 2006). A study of online newspaper consumers concluded there is an undeveloped newspaper market for paid access to local information and news. The study concluded that "substantial marketing efforts" were required to develop the consumer base. Consumers, the study stated, are (a) unwilling to pay for content because they are conditioned to finding it for free, (b) they do not see "incremental value" in online news, (c) newspapers are "strong enough to lure a core audience online, but not strong enough to make them pay," (d) the process of paying for content reinforces attitudes against paying for it, and (e) consumers are willing to register and provide personal information, but not to pay cash for access (Donatello 2002, 36; see also Ekstrand 2002).

Online news media, unlike their videotext forerunners, are popular. At the very least, newspapers, radio and television stations and networks, and news magazines sustain them to maintain their brand reputations in cyberspace. But until the industry can find a successful economic model for online news to make a profit, or at least sustain its operations, it will always be a promotional service in news organizations rather than a distinct editorial voice. For several years, news organizations have been searching to find the solution for a profitable Web site. According to one national analysis, about half of the newspapers participating in a survey reported slight profits, mostly from classified advertising, but they also earned some revenue from banner advertising, sponsorships, and Web-related services fees (Trombly 2002; Noack 1999; Scasny 2001; The Impact of the Internet 2000).

The financial models for online news media have not had enough time to test what works and what does not. In fact, one industry expert described the development of online business models as "short and wild" (Palser 2001, Pay-per-click, 82). In mid-2007, news organizations were still searching for a way to generate even further revenue from online subscriptions and end the "free ride" given to Internet readers (Seelye 2005). Still, at least a few of these experts feel it is not a bad idea if marketed prope rly (Palser 2001, Retooling online news, Pay-per-click) or, if news sites offer more value, paid access will succeed (Scasny 2001). It does not appear likely, in the minds of observers, that subscription revenues will overtake and replace advertising revenues in the near future. There are too many variables, such as sector served, markets, brands involved, and prices. Online news sites must explore content and merchandise offered. Sites may have to target highly specific audiences and meet their information needs, for instance, to succeed. Ultimately, the situation seems to involve redesigning content offered to create greater demand instead of simply getting customers accustomed to paying for something they used to get for free (Smith 2002, February).

THE COMPETITIVE DIMENSION

One of the main characteristics of online news media that make them different from more traditional news media is hypertext. In the early stages of online news, Fredin (1997) noted that in order for newspapers and other media to provide a news service online, "a computer-based interactive system requires a wide range of links or choices within stories" (p. 1). While the use of hyperlinking in online news stories has increased with the growth of the Internet (Tremayne 2004), most news organizations are only beginning to understand the uses of hypertext, linking, and integration of other media into their coverage of breaking news, features, and other information that can provide the depth and scope of coverage expected of newspapers and their online counterparts (Deuze 2003; Singer and Gonzalez-Velez 2003).

Multimedia news content distributed on the Web still has a lot of developing to do. Online audio and video quality is often a function of connection speed. Individuals connecting to an online news source with a modem or wireless device will often experience slide-show-like video and out-of-sync audio or worse (Palser 2000). Individuals with digital subscriber lines (DSL), cable modems, or faster connections still find difficulties with loading sound and video clips and getting them to play. The potential of high-speed Internet connections in enhancing online newspapers and their coverage, however, seems great no matter how it is seen today, especially for newspapers that have sister television and radio stations for shared content. When Web-based multimedia news works, it can be stunning in the same way that live television takes us to the scene of breaking stories. The recent emergence of podcasting, for instance, is a promising development in this direction (Potter 2006).

While daily newspapers almost universally have some presence on the Web, some small nondaily community newspapers do not. Research has shown that newspapers that are not online are typically not in competitive situations, nor are they owned by large media companies. If a smaller community-based newspaper goes online, it is usually because a corporate decision to do so was made elsewhere (Lowrey 2003).

Online news organizations are often restricted by their budgets and staff resources. Although these organizations may seek to use interactive and multimedia resources and to develop original content, the number of people available and their experience and skills levels, as well as the money available to pay the bills, often sets stark parameters in which the online edition operates (Arant and Anderson 2001; Fouhy 2000). In recent years, budgets of online newspapers and their staff sizes have been impacted by worsening economic conditions—increasing operational expenditures and decreasing revenues—that have led to numerous layoffs and curtailed services (Rieder 2001; Palser 2001, Retooling online news; Fouhy 2000). Survival became the focus of many online news sites as the new century began (Farhi 2000, Surviving in cyberspace). Some analysts have argued that such decisions were short-sighted and not in the future interests of online news (Rieder 2001; Palser 2001, Retooling online news). Cutbacks have led to greater dependence on automated Web-page production using software that builds HTML pages from news system databases, including those of the wire services.

Online managers use research about their audiences on a regular basis. It may not be conventional readership research in the same way newspapers or broadcast stations have conducted it over the years. Instead, Web-based news sites depend on traffic reports generated by software that monitors the Web site's server and visits to and from the site and its pages. Online news sites are also using information about Web-site users, such as how long they spend reading a site's pages, to help sell advertising and to target audiences more carefully (Nicholas and Huntington 2000).

TODAY'S LEADING U.S. ONLINE NEWS SITES

It is important to note that some of the most popular online news sites are operated by broadcasting and cable companies. This underlines the popularity of television as an entertainment and news source during the past four decades in the United States. Since the 1960s, the largest proportion of Americans has used television more than newspapers, magazines, or radio for daily news and information, and that brand success has carried over to the broadcast companies' presence on the World Wide Web.

Just as they have done in the print and broadcast world, a handful of online news sites have dominated the thus far short lifespan of online journalism. This has meant a combination of sites based on the nation's leading newspapers and television networks, as shown in Table 1. These top sites have typically been identified by their visitor traffic per day or other time period, but they are also distinguished by of their traditional content quality: CNN is the second-leading site overall, MSNBC is third, and Gannett Newspapers/*USA Today* and *The New York Times* offer the leading online-newspaper sites (Sharma 2005).

Table 1: Top 15 U.S. Online News Sites June 2007

	Visitors (in Millions)
All Global News	95.577
1. Yahoo! News	32.293
2. CNN Digital Network	28.321
3. MSNBC	27.434
4. AOL News	21.938
5. NYTimes.com	12.535
6. Gannett Newspapers	12.279
7. Tribune Newspapers	12.038
8. ABC News Digital Network	10.852
9. Google News	9.195
10. CBS News Digital Network	8.682
11. Hearst Newspapers Digital	8.624
12. USAToday.com	8.592
13. Fox News Digital Network	8.192
14. Washingtonpost.com	8.181
15. McClatchy Newspaper Network	7.708

Source: Nielsen/NetRatings (2007, June), Top news sites, www.cyberjournalist.net (accessed July 20, 2007).

The New York Times, MSNBC, and *USA Today* clearly are among the leaders in news brand identity (Van Wagener 2003).

The most popular online news site in the United States is the news aggregator Yahoo! News, which has no print or broadcast counterpart. Similar news sites among the most popular are AOL News and Google News. These news sites do not use editors or reporters and produce no original content. They manage information and help users to personalize their news selection (Palser 2004). Google, for instance, has an automated selection process based on its search engine's complex algorithms, by which wire stories are ranked, based on their position on 4500 other Web sites around the world (Schroeder and Kralemann 2005; Sreenivasan 2003; Loory 2005). This kind of news gathering without human intervention has been criticized as "robotic journalism" (Kurtz 2002; Loory 2005). "It does not seem likely that algorithm-driven technology can replace reporting, but it can do a lot of the work some editors now do," University of Missouri journalism professor Stuart Loory has stated (Loory 2005, 32). "Cost-conscious organizations could use it to make reductions that could greatly affect editorial decision-making."

Cable News Network (CNN)

The Atlanta-based Cable News Network, known worldwide as CNN, has become a dominant international and national news site (www.cnn.com) on the Internet. The television news network, which debuted in 1980, arrived early on the World Wide Web and established itself as one of the leading multimedia news sites in the world, just as its broadcast parent has become in the past decade. Taking advantage of its existing video and audio content and about 4000 news employees worldwide, the site combines content from the numerous television and radio services and networks with print sources to produce a news site that functions as a news portal for many users.

The site offers two editions. The U.S. edition is geared to cnn.com's largest audience. However, the site also offers an international edition (http://edition.cnn.com). The content on the two sites is similar in that both focus on breaking and daily news and events, weather, sports, business, politics, law, science/technology, space, health and medicine, travel, and education. The international sites are in English, but they offer readers connections to local languages. CNN offers video and a variety of interactive opportunities such as the CNN polls about current events and issues, viewer feedback, and e-mail newsletters and alerts about breaking news.

CNN's strongest attractions are its international and national coverage of news, but it also provides limited local market news through its affiliated network stations. The site has made the latest multimedia technologies, from live video streaming to audio packages, available to users. It also provides users access to searchable archives of news features and background information on the site. Like other major news sites, CNN's site is updated continuously throughout the day. *Time* and its well-established stable of international publications are available on the CNN site through a partnership with its corporate cousin.

Fox News Channel

Fox News Channel (www.foxnews.com) is a relative newcomer in television news in the United States as compared with the well-established ABC, CBS, NBC, and CNN networks, but it has come on strong in the past few years to become a popular site for online news users. The site features content related to the Fox News network news programs, the top news stories of the day, business news, sports, politics, weather, lifestyles and living, and opinion. Much of the content is generated by Fox News reporters, correspondents, and others in the Fox News Channel newsrooms around the world. The site also uses a large amount of Associated Press content.

The main sections of the site include TV Shows, which provide listings information about Fox News programs; Top Stories, which provides headlines and links to full stories about major news of the day; Politics, which focuses on international, national, and state political news from the world's capitals; Business, which offers headlines and stories on current business news and information from Standard and Poor's, financial and investment advice, and stock performance information and price quotes; and FoxLife, which concentrates on leisure activities such as movies and music, celebrities news, and other personal lifestyle news.

The Views section of the site offers opinion essays, commentaries, and columns from Fox News correspondents, news program hosts, and contributors from outside the newsroom. The Weather section provides local forecasts and conditions searches, AccuWeather dangerous weather alerts, and other almanac and historical information. The Fox News site also has a strong sports news and information presence that comes through integration with the Fox Sports Web site (www.foxsports.com). The Sports site is organized generally by sport and offers up-to-date partial and complete scores, sports programming listings, and headlines and stories of the current news cycle. Fox News provides an enhanced Web experience for its registered users.

Los Angeles Times

The *Los Angeles Times* is one of the world's leading newspapers, and a dominant news source for Southern California. Although it is internationally known, the newspaper seeks to serve its home region with its online presence. Nonetheless, in addition to its significant audience of Californians, it also has a national and international following, according to Richard Core (2002), editor of latimes.com. Core has responsibility for overseeing the editorial production of the site. Core says about half of the site's visitors come from the print edition's primary circulation area of Southern California; the other half is worldwide.

The site went on the Web in April 1995, but an earlier electronic edition, known as Times Link, was available in 1993 and 1994 on the proprietary Prodigy information system. The site has built a considerable amount of daily traffic. Core said there are about 1.7 million page views per day (the number of pages, not single advertisements, seen by users). The site offers news, sports, business, and entertainment news stories that originate from the newspaper. This is supplemented with wire service content and video from KTLA-TV, an affiliated Los Angeles television station. But the strength of the site is the newspaper's daily and weekend coverage. "We offer the whole package that you would get from a metropolitan newspaper," Core (2002) explains. *The Times'* entire print edition is not included on its Web site, however. This includes display advertising, tables in the Business section such as CD interest rates or Sports section results and statistics, syndicated content such as comics or advice columns. Almost all of the *Times'* news stories are posted, except in extremely rare cases. Some puzzles and some photographs are also not included, but the site producers plan to improve on this.

There is free content on the site. It includes Calendar Live! Web-only entertainment coverage, guides to Southern California, specially organized special reports, a searchable restaurant guide, searchable classifieds, and audio and video content. Original content also includes multimedia such as interviews with reporters on major local stories, documents to support reporting, and wire content. The site also presents affiliated television station video and audio clips and it offers graphics such as Flash presentations. A short-lived experiment that permitted readers to rewrite editorials—labeled by some observers as "Wikitorials"—was shut down in 2005, however, because the site was flooded with distasteful content (Mills 2005).

MSNBC

MSNBC is the combined effort of Microsoft Corporation in Redmond, Washington, and NBC News in New York. The joint product of the computer software giant and one of the major news networks in the United States created both a widely watched cable television network, MSNBC, and a leading online news site (www.msnbc.com). Much of its recent popularity with online news users was due to its coverage of the Olympics, the war in Afghanistan, and terrorism threats.

MSNBC is a leader in the creation of content solely for the Web. MSNBC content producers do not offer users as much repurposed content as newspaper sites do, for example. MSNBC.com uses the resources of NBC's network television and radio operation, its business-oriented channel CNBC, and NBC affiliate stations and news services. MSNBC on the Web provides content from the collection of news programs from NBC News, MSNBC TV, and CNBC and NBC Sports broadcasts. CNBC offers extensive business content to the site, including live stock-market coverage and frequent news updates that are included on the Web site. The site prepares coverage of major daily national and international stories, updates on breaking stories, and in-depth reports on issues.

The national award-winning site is searchable and keeps stories on the site for about a week. The site also offers Webcasts featuring hourly video news updates and extensive streaming video. The site has a reputation as a leader in breaking news and original journalism on the Internet. MSNBC.com also has developed a series of partnerships that generate site content as well. These include arrangements with *The Washington Post*, *Newsweek*, *The Wall Street Journal*, ZDNet, MSN Money Central, *The*

Sporting News, Expedia, E! Online, Pencil News, *FEED* magazine, *Science* magazine, BET.com, inc.com, Space.com, Inside.com, The Motley Fool, RedHerring.com, Internet Broadcasting Systems, and Pioneer Newspapers.

In addition, MSNBC.com programs interactive content for MSNBC TV and NBC News on WebTV Plus. The breadth and depth of coverage is combined with high levels of personalization. MSNBC.com content is also available through wireless services. The site permits a large degree of user customization. These features include the ability to design a personal front page to display predetermined categories of headlines and news, current stock quotes, and sports scores. Users can also find NBC local affiliate stations' local news content on a daily basis.

The New York Times

The New York Times is one of the world's preeminent newspapers. Its online edition, called New York Times On The Web (www.nytimes.com), debuted on January 20, 1996. The site truly serves the world. Its readers come from all over the globe. Editor Bernard Gwertzman (2002), who is in charge of the entire editorial operation online, determines the home page content each day. The site draws about one-quarter of its audience from outside the United States, another quarter of its audience from the New York metropolitan area, and the rest from other parts of the United States.

The site draws high audience numbers, partly because of its print edition content but also because of original content. The content of the site varies, but reflects the general news standards of the company, Gwertzman says. All of the newspaper's National Edition is offered on the online site, although the Web site pays, Gwertzman said, "a little more attention to entertainment." During the first 2 months of the war on terror in late 2001, for example, *The Times'* site carried a photographer's journal from Afghanistan narrated by photographer Vincent Laforet. The site relies on newspaper reporters and wire services for most of the online content, but content at any given moment is a function of the time of the day.

The Times requires online users to register at no cost and it uses the demographic information it obtains to understand its market and attract advertisers. However, some content, such as its leading columnists, is available only to users of the paid premium service. Readers can subscribe to free e-mail-based news alerts for major or breaking stories. These alerts were particularly valuable to readers in the aftermath of the attacks on the World Trade Center. Major stories are a way of life at the site. The site's producers displayed the stories that won the newspaper a record seven Pulitzer Prize medallions in 2002 for its coverage of the September 11 attacks, even though it is difficult to determine whether online coverage had any impact on the Pulitzers (Kramer 2002). The site has partnerships with the *Financial Times, Foreign Affairs,* the BBC, and the German news magazine *Der Spiegel*.

The Washington Post

The Washington Post (http://washingtonpost.com) has an international and national audience. Built on the reputation of the print brand of the national capitol's primary daily newspaper, the site has rapidly built a strong following since its debut in June 1996. Douglas Feaver (2002), executive editor, oversees content. He said the site does well providing online news and information to the Washington metropolitan area, including suburban Virginia and Maryland, as well as a large international market.

The Washington Post online has opted to present itself as a national and international online newspaper. The results have been impressive. Approximately 20 to 25 percent of the site's content is original. Feaver says about 60 to 75 percent of news content is original and about 33 percent of features are original to the site. Content is developed mostly by the newspaper's extensive staff, but it is also developed by online staff writers and Associated Press, Reuters, and Agence France-Presse wire services. Although about 240 persons are employed at washingtonpost.com, only five writers are devoted solely to developing online content. A number of other part-timers contribute news, features, business, health, and entertainment content. "We have the entire *Washington Post* and additional information that compose our content," Feaver (2002) stated. "This includes wire services, exclusive Internet stories, restaurant reviews, and audio."

USA Today

Gannett Corporation is one of the world's largest news businesses. It is the largest newspaper group in the United States, with ninety-five newspapers and a combined daily circulation of about 7.7 million. It also owns and operates twenty-two television stations. Its flagship newspaper is *USA Today,* which has a daily circulation of 2.3 million and is available in sixty countries worldwide. The company also publishes *USA Weekend,* a weekly magazine with a circulation of 24 million in almost 600 newspapers (Company Profile 2002). *USA Today* is internationally and nationally circulated five days per week and is one of the world's largest newspapers. Gannett is known for its corporate sharing, and this benefits all of its newspapers, broadcast stations, and online sites. The online edition has won national awards for its online journalism (Accolades 2002).

The Web edition is organized similarly to the newspaper, with main sections devoted to news, sports, money, and life. News includes daily coverage from the newspaper as well as columns, opinion pieces, U.S. Supreme Court decisions, health and science, and local city guides. One of the newspaper's widely recognized strengths is sports, and the online site mirrors that for Web readers. Baseball is one of the top attractions, drawing on Gannett's *Baseball Weekly,* but all other professional and amateur sports are also covered and updated regularly. The Money section offers business and financial world news as well as interactive opportunities to create and manage investment portfolios online. Small business tips are offered and consumers seeking information about automobiles find the site useful. The site's Life section reflects celebrities, television news and listings, movies and reviews, arts news, travel information, and a collection of columnists.

In addition to these sections, the site offers comprehensive and current weather information, a technology section, and a shopping section. Site visitors can take advantage of several interactive components of the site. These include "Talk Today," a chance for readers to chat online with experts and to subscribe to e-mail newsletters. Readers can subscribe to five different e-mail newsletters. These focus on the daily news briefing, daily technology report, weekly book publishing news, weekly automobile news and reviews, and weekly retail shopping deals and special offers.

The Wall Street Journal

The Wall Street Journal introduced its online edition in 1995. It has been designed to serve the business and financial communities in the United States and abroad, but it also focuses on general news, says managing editor Bill Grueskin (2002). Most of its content originates in the printed edition of the newspaper, but 2 to 3 percent, he says, is original. The original content, Grueskin described, is mostly additional feature content. From the printed *Journal,* the site uses news from its various editions. While much comes from the U.S. edition, it also depends heavily on its European, American, and Asian editions. The site's producers also place news from the Dow Jones news service and other wires on the site.

Subscriptions include access to the site's market news, research and charting, current and historical stock quotes, use of site personalization tools, e-mail and news alert services, access to the *Barron's* online edition, and access to the most recent thirty days of news archives. The online site is organized somewhat differently from the print edition. For example, Marketplace, the second section of the printed edition, does not appear as an online section. Instead, articles from that section appear online by subject. The staff of about eighty full-time reporters and editors put the next day's edition of the newspaper on the site at about midnight (ET) the evening before publication. The site provides audio and video multimedia content and interactivity such as discussions and reader feedback. The site can also be personalized for users to select priorities and preferences for content display. Its ultimate strength, in the view of editor Grueskin, is the exclusive online content.

ONLINE NEWS MARKETS AND SERVICE MODELS

News media often follow a market model on the World Wide Web that is based on geography, despite the fact that the Web and Internet have disposed of such limitations. This is often the case because the original print edition of a newspaper or television station is defined by a particular geographic orientation or signal limitation. There is much uncertainty about the economic and financial future of online news. At the least, the success or failure of online news depends on highly complex economics (Chyi and Sylvie 2001). Experts are unclear about whether online news, such as that from online newspapers, will become an economically viable business (Chan-Olmsted 2004; Chyi and Sylvie 2000). Some of this uncertainty and confusion is market-related. What market does an online news organization serve? There are four or five common levels of service: national/international (these may also be separated), regional, local, and specialized-niche (Chyi and Sylvie 1999; Dibean and Garrison 2001).

There are at least four models for online news functions. These include the twenty-four-hours-a-day continuous news model, the community bulletin board site model, the supplementary news site model, and the exclusive news site model. These models are neither distinct nor mutually exclusive, and two or more of them are generally found to exist within a single news site. In fact, many news sites at the national and international level in particular often use all four models at a given time. For example, if a weather threat or other natural disaster occurs, many online news sites update constantly, offer interactivity such as bulletin boards and other outlets for flow of personal information, offer supplementary coverage and information as it becomes available, and even create specialized sites devoted to coverage of that news story. This certainly happened in many communities in the United States and other nations following the terrorist attacks on September 11, 2001.

The Twenty-Four-Hours-a-Day Continuous News Model

Like the wire services and cable networks, online newspapers and broadcast television stations can be operated on an always-on-deadline or never-on-deadline circumstance (Smith 1999; Farhi 2000, The dotcom brain drain, Surviving in cyberspace). Some authorities argue that for an online news operation, especially traditional newspapers that have gone online, to survive in the new century, they must adopt a twenty-four-hours-a-day news radio or wire service approach. News organizations that offer constantly updated content must not only invest heavily in their Web sites, but must also provide both depth and ongoing effort to keep content current. They must be responsive to the peaks and valleys of their region (usually 10 A.M. to 5 P.M. local time) and update most intensely during the heaviest of traffic periods (Farhi 2000, The dotcom brain drain, Surviving in cyberspace). Some online news organizations take this approach only when major breaking news stories, such as the September 11 terrorist attacks, occur.

The Community Bulletin Board Site Model

Many online newspapers have done more than rehash their print copy. Some have opted for the community bulletin board site model. *The Boston Globe* (www.boston.com/globe), for example, was among the first major newspapers to design its online version to provide community information about events, featuring news about Boston's arts, weather, and commerce.

The Supplementary News Site Model

Some print and broadcast outlets also take advantage of the limitless space on the Web to add additional material to online news stories that appeared in their print and broadcast versions. Many local newspapers have followed this model, serving as local equivalents of CNN, taking advantage of online timeliness by reporting local breaking news stories which, if not covered online, would be reported on local radio or television before the newspapers (Heyboer 2000).

The Exclusive News Site Model

One model that print and broadcast news organizations have not adopted is the exclusive news site model. Exclusive news sites offer news not found in other forms, such as those other news media operated by the same news corporation or company. They are more common among zines, or electronic magazines, such as *Salon* and *Slate*. To date, however, few broadcasters, newspapers, or other news outlets have posted exclusives online, and this model remains more a conceptual model than one commonly used on the Web.

CONCLUSION

Online news is flourishing, and its use is growing. This is the beginning of the online news era. In the United States and internationally; growth of online news in recent years has been significant. Online news Web sites are not only available in most nations and geographic locations throughout the world, their reach is also global. Online news is available to almost anyone with a computer and network access worldwide, yet they retain their local nature. While the circulation of daily newspapers across the United States remains flat or in decline, Web sites that provide news content seem to be strong. Online journalism in general has become a vital part of information available on the World Wide Web and the Internet. Since the mid-1990s, online magazines, wire services, newspapers, television stations, broadcast-cable networks, and subscription newsletters have matured to take advantage of their unique orientation, the interactive tools of the Web, and audiences. New technologies are introduced almost yearly that allow consumers new ways to obtain Web-based information. News consumers are embracing these new communication devices. The new communication technologies have been viewed by news organizations as opportunities to extend their reach and contact with news consumers at international levels. The results are new forms and formats of news and information, such as news headlines and breaking story alerts delivery by e-mail and messaging services to subscribers that are at the cutting edge of communication today.

GLOSSARY

Alert: Notification about a breaking news event or story by an online news service, usually by e-mail.

Banner: Form of advertising that usually contains a graphic product image or message on a Web site. The size of the ad may vary, but often spreads horizontally across the top or other part of the page. Some banner ads, however, are designed in a vertical shape.

Brand: The recognizable name of a news company that has been given to a news product on the World Wide Web or other forms of communication on the Internet.

Convergence: Implementation of multimedia combining text, graphics, audio, and video in online news presentation as well as the combination of divergent media technologies to produce a new medium, form, or method of communicating with audiences.

Flash: Software that produces animation and video for Web pages and browsers. Content producers can quickly and easily prepare special effects through animation and other techniques, interactivity, sound, and video.

Headline: For an online news site, a brief sentence or short phrase summary of a news story, often with a brief abstract. These features are linked to longer stories and coverage elsewhere on the site.

Hypermedia: Links among any set of multimedia objects such as sound, animation, video, and virtual reality. Usually suggests higher levels of interactivity than in hypertext.

Hypertext: Organization of news and information into associations that a user can implement by clicking on the association with a mouse. The association is called a hypertext link.

Independent: An online news organization not grounded in traditional, branded news media, and only found on the World Wide Web or Internet.

Interactivity: For online news services, features such as e-mail feedback, instant opinion polls, chat rooms, and message boards that involve the site user in some form.

Market: The audience served by an online news organization. The grouping may be determined by founding or originating media markets, by geographic boundaries, specializations, or defined in other ways.

Online Journalism: News presentation on the World Wide Web or other Internet-based formats. This includes news offered by traditional news organizations (e.g., newspapers, television stations and networks, and magazines) as well as nontraditional sources such as Internet service providers (e.g., Yahoo! and America Online) and bulletin board services, Web "zines," and news groups.

Online News: Collection and presentation of current events information on the Web or other Internet-based formats, including traditional and nontraditional sources such as those discussed above under *Online Journalism.*

Package: The combination of audio, video, graphics, and hypertext components that create a news story on a Web site.

Portal: Entry points, or "doorways," to the Internet that often serve as home pages for users. These are offered by online newspapers, radio stations, and television stations and provide much more than just news content. These sites provide activity and entertainment listings, community calendars, government reference material, online interactive features, and multimedia content.

Producer: For an online news site, this is an individual who develops news content for a Web site. These individuals work with all forms of news media to prepare the coverage for a story.

Shovelware: Software that produces content of an online news site that is taken from the published content of a newspaper, television broadcast, and/or wire service.

Webcast: Live news broadcast or other video program distributed on the Web by an online news or media organization.

Web Edition: The online edition of a traditional printed newspaper. These editions often include breaking news as well as extra, and often extended, content not found in printed editions.

Web Log: (or **Blog**) Personal Web site that is prepared in dated log or diary format. It is an online journal that is regularly updated and has entries, called "posts," which are usually listed in reverse order. A blog is maintained by a blogger and the site is usually specialized and focuses on a single topic or subject area and offers information and observations from the author, contributors, or from other sites. Blogs create a community called the Blogosphere.

Wiki: A Web site that makes it possible for different users to add, edit, and delete content, with the purpose of building a collective Web site.

Zine: Independent publication on the Web that often offers idiosyncratic themes, irregular frequency of publication, ephemeral duration, and a noncommercial financial base.

CROSS REFERENCES

See *Digital Libraries; The Internet Fundamentals*.

REFERENCES

Accolades. 2002. *Accolades.* www.usatoday.com/a/adindex/omk/accolades.htm (accessed April 15, 2002).

Andrews, P. 2003. Is blogging journalism? *Nieman Reports* 57(3):63–4.

An evolving medium. 1999, April 26. *Online Newshour.* www.pbs.prg/newshour/bb/media/jan-june99/lasica_qa.html (accessed April 28, 1999).

Apcar, L. M. 2006, April 2. A letter to our readers. *NYTimes.com.* www.nytimes.com (accessed April 3, 2006).

Arampatzis, A. 2004. Online business models in Greece and the United Kingdom: A case of specialist versus generic and public versus privately owned online news media. *The International Journal on Media Management* 6(1&2):88–101.

Arant, D. M., and J. Q. Anderson. 2001. Newspaper online Editors support traditional standards. *Newspaper Research Journal* 22(4):57–69.

Blood, R. 2003. Weblogs and journalism: Do they connect? *Nieman Reports* 57(3):61–3.

Boczkowski, P. J. 2004. The processes of adopting multimedia and interactivity in three online newsrooms. *Journal of Communication* 54(2):197–213.

Bressers, B., and L. Bergen. 2002. Few university students reading newspapers online. *Newspaper Research Journal* 23(2/3):34.

Brown, D. 2003. Searching for online gold. *American Journalism Review* 25(5):58–9.

Bucy, E. P. 2004. Second generation net news: Interactivity and information accessibility in the online environment. *The International Journal on Media Management* 6(1&2):102–13.

Burgess, J. 1993, February 14. Firms face questions of technology's timing, cost. *The Washington Post*, H1.

Cable News Network. 2005. Poll: Most Americans unfamiliar with blogs. www.cnn.com/2005/TECH/internet/03/03/poll.blogs/index.html (accessed October 20, 2005).

Carlson, D. 2005. The news media's 30-year hibernation. *Nieman Reports* 59(3):61–71.

Chan-Olmsted, S. M. 2004. Traditional media and the Internet: The search for viable business models. *The International Journal on Media Management* 6(1&2):2–3.

Chan-Olmsted, S. M., and J. S. Park. 2000. From on-air to online world: Examining the content and structures of broadcast TV stations' web sites. *Journalism and Mass Communication Quarterly* 77(2):321–39.

Christie, R. H., and E. Edmonds. 2006, March 14. *Wall Street Journal* online launches home-page redesign to enhance ease of use. www.dj.com/Pressroom/PressReleases/Other/US/2006/0314_US_TheWallStreetJournalOnlineatWSJcom_3000.htm (accessed May 10, 2006).

Chyi, H. I. 2005. Willingness to pay for online news: An empirical study on the viability of the subscription model. *Journal of Media Economics* 18(2):131–42.

Chyi, H. I., and G. Sylvie. 1999, August. Opening the umbrella: An economic analysis of online newspaper geography. Presented to the Association for Education in Journalism and Mass Communication, New Orleans.

Chyi, H. I., and G. Sylvie. 2000. Online newspapers in the U.S.: Perceptions of markets, products, revenue, and competition. *Journal on Media Management* 2(11):69–77.

Chyi, H. I., and G. Sylvie. 2001. The medium is global, the content is not: The role of geography in online newspaper markets. *Journal of Media Economics* 14(4):213–48.

Company Profile. 2002. *Company Profile.* www.gannett.com/map/gan007.htm (accessed April 19, 2002).

Cooper, C. 2005, November 11. Perspective: All the news that's fit to blog. *CNET News.com.* http://news.com.com/All+the+news+thats+fit+to+blog/2010-1025_3-5946033.html (accessed November 16, 2005).

Core, R. 2002, May 2. Personal telephone interview with author.

Deuze, M. 2003. The web and its journalisms: Considering the consequences of different types of news media online. *New Media and Society* 5(2):203–30.

Deuze, M. 2004. What is multimedia journalism? *Journalism Studies* 5(2):139–52.

Dibean, W., and B. Garrison. 2001. How six online newspapers use Web technologies. *Newspaper Research Journal* 22(2):79–93.

Dodson, S. 2005, August 11. Online: Worldwide Wikimania: Free to use and free to edit, Wikipedia is growing fast. *The Guardian*, 23.

Donatello, M. 2002, May. What consumers tell us about paying for news online. *EContent* 25(5):36–40.

Dorror, J. 2005. Dotcom bloom: The Web seems poised to blossom with stand-alone news sites. *American Journalism Review* 27(3):37–41.

Dupagne, M., and B. Garrison. 2006. The meaning and influence of convergence: A qualitative case study of newsroom work at the Tampa News Center. *Journalism Studies* 7(2):237–55.

Ekstrand, V. S. 2002. Online news: User agreements and implications for readers. *Journalism & Mass Communication Quarterly* 79(3):602–18.

Edmonds, R. 2005, November 14. As blogs and citizen journalism grow, where's the news? *Poynter Online*. http://poynter.org/content/content_view.asp?id=91391 (accessed November 27, 2005).

Farhi, P. 2000. The dotcom brain drain. *America Journalism Review* 22(2):30.

Farhi, P. 2000. Surviving in cyberspace. *America Journalism Review* 22(7):22–7.

Feaver, D. 2002, April 10. Personal telephone interview with author.

Fee, F. 2002, March. New(s) players and new(s) values? A test of convergence in the newsroom. Paper presented to the Newspaper Division, Southeast Colloquium, Association for Education in Journalism and Mass Communication, Gulfport, Miss.

Fouhy, E. 2000. Which way will it go? *American Journalism Review 22*(4):18–9.

Fredin, E. S. 1997, September. Rethinking the news story for the Internet: Hyperstory prototypes and a model of the user. *Journalism & Mass Communication Monographs* 163:1–47.

Gates, D. 2002, May 1. The future of news: Newspapers in the digital age." *Online Journalism Review*. www.ojr.org/ojr/future/1020298748.php (accessed May 2, 2002).

George, W. 2000, January 11. The AOL/Time Warner merger: What it really means to the markets and Apple. *The Mac Observer*. www.macobserver.com/news/00/january/000111/aoltimewarner.shtml (accessed August 21, 2002).

Greer, J., and D. Mensing. 2004. U.S. news web sites better, but small papers still lag. *Newspaper Research Journal* 25(2):109.

Greer, J. and D. Mensing. 2006. The evolution of online newspapers: A longitudinal content analysis, 1997-2003. *Internet newspapers: The making of a mainstream medium*, edited by X. Li, 13–32. Mahwah, NJ: Lawrence Erlbaum.

Grimes, C. 2002, February 6. Premium payments may boost Web revenues. *Financial Times* (London), 3.

Grueskin, R. 2002, April 18. Personal telephone interview with author.

Gwertzman, B. 2002, April 10. Personal telephone interview with author.

Ha, J.-Y., S. J. Dick, and S. K. Ryu. 2003. Broadcast via the Internet: Technology, market, and the future. *Trends in Communication* 11(2):155–68.

Heyboer, K. 2000. Going live. *American Journalism Review* 22(1):38–43.

Horrigan, J. B. 2006. Online News. Pew Internet & American Life Project. www.pewinternet.org/pdfs/PIP_News.and.Broadband.pdf (accessed May 4, 2006).

The Impact of the Internet. 2000. *American Journalism Review* 22(2):4–5.

Internet growing as news medium, at times exceeding traditional media usage. 2002, January 7. Global News Wire and Business Wire *Financial Times*.

Jensen, M. 2003. A brief history of Weblogs. *Columbia Journalism Review* 42(3):22.

Johnson, T. J., and B. K. Kaye. 2004. Wag the blog: How reliance on traditional media and the Internet influence credibility perceptions of weblogs among blog users. *Journalism & Mass Communication Quarterly* 81(3):622–42.

Journalism.org. 2005. The state of the news media 2005: An annual report on American journalism. www.stateofthemedia.org/2005/narrative_newspapers_intro.asp?cat=1andmedia=2, (accessed May 8, 2006).

Keefe, R. 1996, October 13, New *Tribune* president arrives during time of transition. *St. Petersburg Times*, 1H.

Kirkpatrick, D., D. Roth, and O. Ryan. 2005. Why there's no escaping the blog. *Fortune* (Europe) 151(1):64–9.

Koerner, B. 2001. Click here for Britney! *The Washington Monthly* 33(7/8):25–30.

Kolodzy, J. 2003. Everything that rises: Media convergence is an opportunity, not a curse. *Columbia Journalism Review* 42(2):61.

Kramer, S. D. 2002, April 4. The elephant in the jury room: Maybe it's time to be as visionary as Joseph Pulitzer. *Online Journalism Review*. www.ojr.org/ojr/workplace/1018398261.phpm (accessed April 13, 2002).

Kramer, S. D. 2004, October 1. CBS scandal highlights tension between bloggers and news media. *Online Journalism Review*. www.ojr.org/ojr/workplace/1096589178.php (accessed November 10, 2004).

Kurtz, H. 2002, September 30. Robotic journalism: Google introduces human-less news. www.washingtonpost.com (accessed May 4, 2006).

Kurtz, H. 2005, February 13. In the blogosphere lightning strikes thrice. *The Washington Post*, D01.

Langfield, A. 2001, December 21. Net news lethargy: Most sites fail to make use of the medium's main strength—Speed. *Online Journalism Review*. http://ojr.usc.edu/content/story.cfm?request=676 (accessed January 2, 2002).

Lascia, J. D. 2002. Blogging as a form of journalism. *Online Journalism Review*. http://ojr.org/ojr/workplace/1017958873.php (accessed November 12, 2004).

Li, X. 2006. Introduction. In *Internet newspapers: The making of a mainstream medium*, edited by X. Li, 1–12. Mahwah, NJ: Lawrence Erlbaum.

Li, X. 2006. Graphic use and interconnectedness of Internet newspapers: A many-to-many communication model. In *Internet Newspapers: The Making of a Mainstream Medium*, edited by X. Li, 33–48. Mahwah, NJ: Lawrence Erlbaum.

Loory, S. 2005. Automated news gathering: Boon or bane to the future of journalism? *IPI Global Journalist* 11(2):32.

Lowrey, W. 2003. What influences small newspapers to decide to publish online news? *Newspaper Research Journal* 24(3):83–90.

McMillan, S. J. 1998, September. Who pays for content? *Journal of Computer Mediated Communication* 4(1). www.ascusc.org/jcmc/vol4/issue1/mcmillan.html (accessed December 6, 2001).

Miller, R. 2001, September 14. From niche site to news portal: How slashdot survived the attack. *Online Journalism Review*. http://ojr.usc.edu/content/story.cfm (accessed December 6, 2001).

Mills, E. 2005, June 20. L.A. Times shuts reader-editorial Web site. *CNET News.com*. http://news.com.com/L.A.+Times+shuts+reader-editorial+Web+site/2100-1023_3-5754202.html (accessed November 16, 2005).

Nicholas, D., and P. Huntington. 2000. Evaluating the use of newspaper Web sites' logs. *Journal on Media Management* 2(11):78–88.

Noack, D. 1999. Crossfire: Print vs. online newsrooms. *Editor & Publisher* February 14:38–41.

Oblak, T. 2005. The lack of interactivity and hypertextuality in online media. *Gazette* 67(1):87–106.

Outing, S. 2001, Fall. Crisis notes from the online media. *Poynter Report*. St. Petersburg, FL.: Poynter Institute for Media Studies, 48–49.

Palser, B. 2000. Not quite ready for prime time. *American Journalism Review* 22(6):84.

Palser, B. 2001. Retooling online news. *American Journalism Review* 23(2):70.

Palser, B. 2001. Pay-per-click. *American Journalism Review* 23(8):82.

Palser, B. 2003. Online advances. *American Journalism Review* 25(4):40–5.

Palser, B. 2004. The difference a year makes. *American Journalism Review* 26(1):58.

Palser, B. 2005. Bridging the gap. *American Journalism Review* 27(3):74.

Perlman, J. 1999, May 6. Print sites still wary of chatting it up. *Online Journalism Review.* www.ojr.org/ojr/business/1017968634.php (accessed April 12, 2002).

Perlmutter, D. D., and M. McDaniel. 2005. The ascent of blogging. *Nieman Reports* 59(3):60–4.

Picard, R. 2000. Changing business models of online content services: Their implications for multimedia and other content producers. *Journal on Media Management* 2(11):60–8.

Potter, D. 2006. iPod, you Pod, we all Pod. *American Journalism Review* 28(1):64.

Pryor, L. 2000, June 30. Some guidelines from one of online news' walking wounded. *Online Journalism Review.* http://ojr.usc.edu/content/story.cfm (accessed December 6, 2001).

Rainie, L. 2005. The state of blogging. *Pew Research Center.* www.pewinternet.org (accessed April, 27, 2004).

Rauch, J. 2004. Hands-on communication: Zine circulation rituals and the interactive limitations of Web self-publishing. *Popular Communication* 2(3): 153–69.

Reeves, J. 2003. The new online magazines: A hunger for voice. *Columbia Journalism Review* 42(3):25.

Reuters. 2006, May 6. China sees 60 million bloggers by year's end. *CNET News*. http://news.com.com/China+sees+60+million+bloggers+by+years+end/2100-1040_3-6069387.html?tag=nefd.top (accessed May 7, 2006).

Rich, C. 2007. *Writing and reporting news*, Belmont, CA: Thomson Wadsworth.

Rieder, R. 2001, March. At the crossroads. *American Journalism Review* 23(2):6.

Salaverria, R. 2005. An immature medium. *Gazette* 67(1):69–86.

Samoriski, J. 2002. *Issues in cyberspace: Communication, technology, law, and society on the Internet frontier*. Boston: Allyn and Bacon.

Scasny, R. 2001, November 23. Online news users have to pay: Change the product, give it more value and paid access will work. *Online Journalism Review* http://ojr.usc.edu/content/story.cfm?request=663 (accessed, December 6, 2001).

Schroeder, R., and M. Kralemann. 2005. Journalism ex machina—Google News Germany and its news selection processes. *Journalism Studies* 6(2):245–7.

Seelye, K. Q. 2005, March 16. Newspapers reconsider free ride: Publishers find it hard to keep giving away content online. *International Herald Tribune*, Finance, 17.

Seigenthaler, J. 2005, November 29. A false Wikipedia "biography." *USA Today* 11A.

Sharma, D. C. 2005, November 15. Study: Online newspapers flourish. *CNET News.com*. http://news.com.com/Study+Online+newspapers+flourish/2100-1025_3-5953393.html (accessed November 16, 2005).

Simon, E. 2005, November 30. Icahn threatens to sue Time Warner, board, Associated Press. *The Washington Post*. www.washingtonpost.com (accessed December 9, 2005).

Singer, J. 2001. The Metro Wide Web: Changes in newspapers' gatekeeping role online. *Journalism & Mass Communication Quarterly* 78(1):65–80.

Singer, J. 2003. Campaign contributions: Online newspaper coverage of election 2000. *Journalism & Mass Communication Quarterly* 80(1):39–56.

Singer, J. 2004. Strange bedfellows? The diffusion of convergence in four news organizations. *Journalism Studies* 5(1):3–18.

Singer, J., and M. Gonzalez-Velez. 2003. Envisioning the caucus community: Online newspaper editors conceptualize their political roles. *Political Communication* 20:433–52.

Smith, S. 2002, April. Content at your service. *EContent* 25(4):44–5.

Smith, S. 2002, February. The free lunch is over: Online content subscriptions on the rise. *EContent* 25(2):18–23.

Smith, T. 1999, April, 26. A new source of news. *Online Newshour*. www.pbs.org/newshour/bb/media/jan-june99/inews_4-26.html (accessed April 28, 1999).

Smolkin, R. 2004. The expanding blogosphere. *American Journalism Review* 26(3):38–43.

Sreenivasan, S. 2003. Google News. *Columbia Journalism Review* 42(1):11.

Strupp, J. 1999. Welcomed visitors. *Editor & Publisher* July 3:22–7.

Technorati. 2006. About Technorati. www.technorati.com (accessed May 4, 2006).

Tewksbury, D. 2003. What do Americans really want to know? Tracking the behavior of news readers on the Internet. *Journal of Communication* 53(4):694–710.

Tremayne, M. 2004. The Web of context: Applying network theory to the use of hyperlinks in journalism on the Web. *Journalism & Mass Communication Quarterly* 81(2):237–53.

Trombly, M. 2002. Looking for online dollars: News providers are finding ways to make their Web sites profitable. *Quill 90*(4):18–21.

van der Wurff, R. 2005. Impacts of the Internet on newspapers in Europe. *Gazette* 67(1):107–20.

Van Wagener, A. 2003, January 2. The best designed news sites. *Poynter Online*. www.poynter.org/column.asp?id=47andaid=14231 (accessed November 27, 2005).

Weiss, A. 2005, February 10. The unassociated press. *The New York Times*, G5.

Whittaker, J. 2000. *Producing for the Web*. London: Routledge.

Wilber, R., and Miller, R. 2003. *Modern media writing*. Belmont, CA: Thomson Wadsworth.

Williams, B. A., and M. X. Delli Carpini. 2004. Monica and Bill all the time and everywhere: The collapse of gatekeeping and agenda setting in the new media environment. *The American Behavioral Scientist* 47(9):1208–30.

Williams, J. 2003. The new online magazines: A hunger for voice. *Columbia Journalism Review* 42(3):25.

Travel and Tourism

Ulrike Gretzel, *Texas A&M University,* Youcheng Wang, *University of Central Florida,*
and Daniel R. Fesenmaier, *Temple University*

INTRODUCTION

The travel industry is the world's largest industry, exceeding $6.2 trillion in gross output (World Travel and Tourism Council [WTTC] 2005). Reports from the WTTC indicate that tourism employs over 221 million people worldwide, or approximately 8.3 percent of the global workforce. The emergence of travel as a significant economic activity began after World War II, as travel became widely accessible to the general population. As shown in Table 1, very few people traveled internationally in 1950 as measured by today's standards. Yet, from 1950 to 1970, international travel exploded, increasing by more than 550 percent. This growth in international travel continued through the 1980s and 1990s to reach over 763 million visitor arrivals in 2004, representing over $623 billion (U.S. dollars) in international tourism receipts. Since 1990, international travel has increased over 70 percent, and for a number of countries it has grown to be their largest commodity in international trade. Indeed, the travel industry now serves as one of the top three industries for almost every country worldwide (Goeldner and Ritchie 2002).

Table 1: World Tourism Growth

Year	International Tourism Arrivals (Millions)	International Tourist Receipts[a] (Billions US$)
1950	25	2
1960	69	7
1970	166	18
1980	286	105
1990	441	280
2000	681	496
2001	680	482
2002	700	482
2003	690	524
2004	763	623

[a]International transport receipts excluded.
Source: World Tourism Organization (2005).

Information technology has played a central role in the growth and development of the tourism industry. In the early years of mass global tourism (from the 1950s to the 1970s), the technology used was largely limited to computer systems that supported the internal functions of large operators in the transportation, hotel, and food service sectors. Also, a number of central reservation systems (CRSs) and global distribution systems (GDSs)—Sabre, Amadeus, Galileo, and Worldspan—were developed first by airlines and then by hotel companies to enable travel agencies (and other similar intermediaries) to directly access schedule and pricing information and to request reservations for clients. These intermediaries became the primary users of travel information systems, thus providing important links between travelers and industry players (World Tourism Organization Business Council [WTOBC] 1999).

During the late 1980s and early 1990s these systems and the information they contained emerged as important strategic tools and highly profitable ventures, enabling system operators such as American Airlines and Hilton Hotels to grow and successfully position themselves within the overall travel market. The work of Mayros and Werner (1982) and Wiseman (1985) describes this significant development in the travel and tourism industry. An important characteristic of the growth of these systems was the inclusion of detailed behavioral information about each customer. Armed with this information, existing systems were significantly enhanced (Poon 1993).

Even more important was the fact that these networks were proprietary and that the first movers in the market placed proprietary terminals with controlled content on the desks of travel suppliers and agents, thus creating high barriers to entry. As a consequence, the relationships of firms and organizations within the travel industry changed dramatically, placing emphasis on expanding strategic relationships in order to more fully exploit various business opportunities within the travel value chain.

The success of CRSs and GDSs paved the way for the Internet, enabling the travel and tourism industry to quickly exploit its many strengths. Indeed, in many ways the Internet is ideal for the travel and tourism industry. As a communication tool, it is simultaneously business- and consumer-oriented. The Internet is business-oriented because it enables businesses to communicate with potential visitors more easily and efficiently and allows them to better support and immediately respond to customer information needs through the provision of interactive travel brochures, virtual tours, and virtual travel communities. In addition, the Internet enables tourism-related enterprises to communicate with their partners more effectively in order to develop and design offers that meet the individual needs of potential visitors. The Internet is customer-oriented in that it empowers the user to easily access a wealth of information, enabling the traveler to almost "sample" the destination prior to an actual visit. Moreover, emerging ecommerce capabilities enable the traveler to make reservations, purchase tourism-related products, and share trip experiences with others.

Today, the Internet is one of the most important communication tools for travelers as well as travel and tourism enterprises. For example, studies by the Travel Industry Association of America (TIA; 2005) indicate that over one-third (37 percent) of American adults use the Internet to search for travel information and/or make reservations (see Table 2); for Americans who actually travel, this figure increases to 52 percent. Studies also show that the travel and tourism industry responded to the emergence of Internet-based technologies by adopting a number of new and innovative ways to communicate with consumers, as well as with other industry partners. As such, the travel and tourism industry is one of the most significant users of Internet technology as measured by the number of Web sites and Web pages and by online sales volume (Werthner and Klein 1999). Indeed, studies of online spending showed that in 2004 consumers spent $53 billion online for travel, which represents about one-third of all travel spending in that year. In contrast, online retail spending amounted to just 1.9 percent of all retail spending (European Travel Commission [ETC] 2005). In addition, travel sales amount to 43 percent of all online sales, making it the most important eCommerce category (eMarketer 2005). Further, surveys of American convention and visitor bureaus show that essentially every bureau maintains a Web site, with some offering more advanced e-commerce capabilities, and surveys of the Internet indicate that over 1 billion Web pages exist supporting the travel and tourism industry (Wang and Fesenmaier 2002).

This chapter presents an overview of many of the uses of the Internet and other network technology applications by travelers and the firms and organizations that compose the travel and tourism industry. The next section provides a brief synopsis of the structure of the industry and the role of network technologies, focusing on four major sectors: hotels, airlines, travel agents (and related intermediaries), and destination-marketing organizations (DMOs). It also discusses the newly emerging travel search engines, which could fundamentally change online distribution structures. Following this introduction, emerging marketing and management strategies are considered and various issues related to the development and use of Web sites and online management information systems are discussed. The subsequent section focuses on the role of network technologies from the travelers' perspective. A variety of consumer-related technologies are considered, including travel "brochure" Web sites, virtual tours, and mobile devices. As part of the discussion, changing patterns of use and their impact on the travel experience are considered. The last section of this chapter identifies five global technology-related trends affecting the future role of network technology applications in travel and tourism.

Table 2: Internet Use for Travel Planning: 1997–2005

Year	% of U.S. Adults	% of U.S. Travelers
1997	7	8
1998	18	21
1999	25	33
2000	30	40
2001	33	46
2002	31	45
2003	30	44
2004	30	44
2005	37	52

Source: TIA (2005).

THE TRAVEL AND TOURISM INDUSTRY

Structure of the Industry and the Role of Network Technologies

The travel and tourism industry is comprised of all organizations involved in the production and distribution of travel and tourism products. It can be viewed as an umbrella industry with a complex distribution chain (see Figure 1) containing a set of interrelated businesses, such as transportation companies, accommodation facilities, attractions, catering enterprises, tour operators, travel agents, and providers of recreation and leisure facilities, as well as a multitude of government agencies (Werthner and Klein 1999). In contrast to other industries, it is not a physical product but information that moves from suppliers to customers. To respond effectively to the dynamic character of the industry, this information must be able to flow smoothly among consumers,

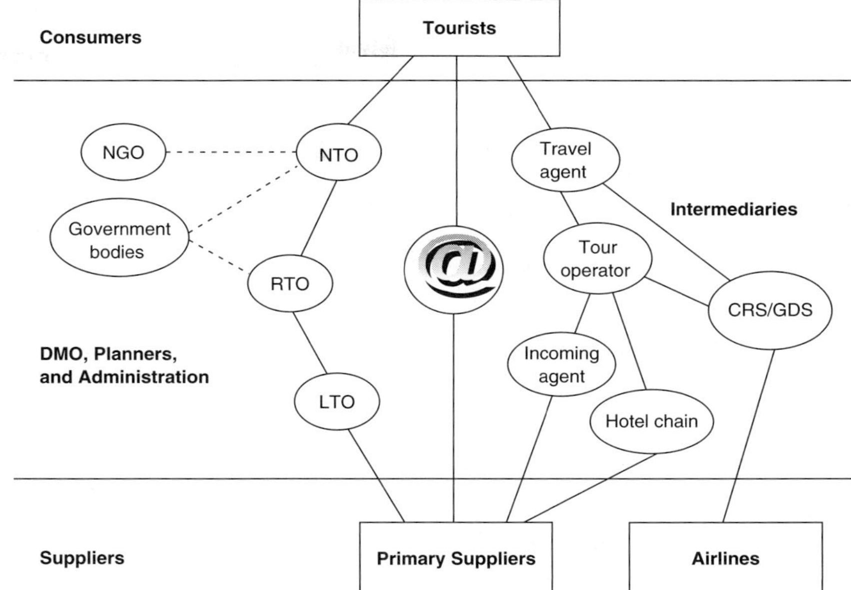

Figure 1: The travel and tourism industry value chain (adapted from Werthner and Klein 1999) (CRS = central reservation system; GDS = global distribution system; LTO = local tourism organization; NGO = nongovernmental organization; NTO = national tourism organization; RTO = regional tourism organization)

intermediaries, and each of the suppliers involved in serving customer needs. As a result, information technology (IT) has become an almost universal distribution platform for the tourism industry. IT reduces the cost of each transaction by minimizing print, coordination, communication, and distribution costs. It also allows short-notice changes, supports one-to-one interaction with the customer, and enables organizations to reach a broad audience (Poon 1993). Most communications and transactions are now supported by Web-based systems; however, the Internet has not been adopted equally by all tourism sectors. Certain sectors, such as airlines, have been aggressive adopters of technology, using it to help manage and streamline their operations and to gain strategic advantages (Buhalis 2004; McGuffie 1994). Especially the low-cost carriers have long received a majority of their bookings through their Web sites, helping them keep distribution and fulfillment costs below those of other airlines. Others, such as the hotel sector, have been less enthusiastic and have only recently begun to take advantage of many of the benefits that the technology can bring (Connolly and Olsen 1999). Many traditional travel agencies are also lagging behind other sectors in terms of technological adaptation, and it is increasingly evident that experienced consumers are often better informed than professional advisers. However, given the way in which IT is reshaping the structure of both commerce and society in general, its importance to the success of all types of tourism companies can only grow in the future. As a result, tourism companies have changed dramatically the way in which they conduct their business and are under pressure to invest further in new technology in order to maintain their competitive advantage.

Hotels

The hotel industry bases much of its distribution on direct contact with customers (Nyheim, McFadden, and Connolly 2004; WTOBC 1999). Historically, hotels have distributed information through print-based media, such as brochures, travel planners, and regional guides, and received reservations by mail, phone, and fax. Since the 1970s and 1980s, hotel rooms have been made more accessible for booking through GDSs and through direct access to hotels using CRSs. These connections were usually enabled by "switch" network providers (such as THISCO, WizCom, and Unirez) to link a hotel's reservation systems to a GDS. Such additional network "intermediaries" added considerable cost and complexity to these legacy distribution systems. In addition, such technologies have been inadequate, as customers have traditionally not had access to these systems and travel intermediaries have experienced difficulty and delay in finding and booking appropriate hotels, whereas hotels have experienced high clerical costs in attracting and processing bookings from customers. The high level of complexity and high administration/transaction costs of these systems kept many smaller hotel properties from participating in these distribution networks. The emergence of new information and communication technologies (i.e., Internet technologies) presents new opportunities to make these processes more accessible and more efficient.

Although the hotel sector overall, as compared to other industry sectors, has been slow to use the Internet (Connolly, Olsen, and Moore 1998), many hotel managers are becoming increasingly aware of the potential distribution, promotion, and interactive marketing advantages of the Internet. The Internet offers several advantages for hotels of all sizes. One of the advantages is increased effectiveness due to cost reduction and revenue growth. Another advantage is higher-quality customer relationships due to the possibility of personal contact services and dialogue with the customer (Morrison et al. 1999; Sterne 1999). For example, customers can answer questions about their personal preferences for rooms, and based on this information, customers receive services at the hotel that are adapted to their preferences. The decision to adopt technologies has become so important that many hospitality organizations have transformed their organizational structure to include functions and positions to oversee technology-related decisions (Nyheim et al. 2004). There are, however, many factors that may limit the use of new technology—particularly for smaller and/or independent accommodation properties, many of which have limited systems for managing inventory, pricing, and electronic distribution. Heading the list of potential barriers is the proprietary nature of customized technology solutions found throughout the hospitality industry, followed closely by closed IT architectures, lack of technology standards, limited technology skills, as well as unclear business cases or return on investment analyses associated with IT investment (Cline 2001).

Nevertheless, it is now generally agreed that Internet-related technologies are the single greatest force driving change in the hotel industry and will continue to have dramatic and sweeping implications on how hotels conduct business in the future. Hotels are expected to position themselves strongly on the Internet to take advantage of its distribution capabilities such as reach, content dissemination, feedback collection, interactivity, and one-to-one marketing. Further, current trends indicate that this greater involvement in IT by the hotel industry will increasingly encompass customer-centric approaches to capitalize on the cost structure and long-term potential of the Internet while at the same time differentiating products and building lasting value propositions.

Airlines

Air transportation systems worldwide are being dramatically affected by technological developments. Many of these developments focus on the use of Internet technology to improve the efficiency of operations (Sheldon 1997; Buhalis 2004). However, the early use of IT in the airline industry was characterized by asynchronous applications with low degrees of interactivity and integration (Jarach 2002). The first applications of computer technology to airline operations emerged in the 1950s when CRSs were designed. The primary function of computerized airline reservation systems was to simplify the process of booking flights by allowing travel agents to find relevant flight information and make reservations directly from their terminals without having to call airline reservations offices (Klein and Langenohl 1994; Buhalis 2003). Because of their many operational and cost-related advantages, CRSs became essential for the distribution of airline tickets through travel agencies.

Until the mid-1970s, airline computer reservation systems were used only for proprietary airline information, and the major airline companies all had their own CRSs (Sheldon 1997). Some of the CRSs were combined to become GDSs, which provided multiple carrier information and constituted important electronic distribution channels. The major GDSs include Galileo, Amadeus, Sabre, and Worldspan, and these are now available through the Internet. These airline reservation systems provide a number of functionalities to travel agencies, including flight schedules and availability, passenger information, fare quotes and rules, and ticketing. Most of the systems now also enable consumers to view schedules, fares, and fare rules and to book flights. In addition to developing reservation systems as the predominant distribution channel, many airlines have invested heavily in information systems to automate other areas of airline operations and management, which can be categorized into two sections: (1) systems for streamlining operations such as baggage and cargo handling, cabin automation, and safety control, and (2) decision-support systems to aid in decision-making related to flight scheduling and planning, crew scheduling and management, gate management, and departure control.

More recently, however, airlines have increasingly focused on consumer Web sites. The main attraction for carriers in adopting a Web site is the development of a radically new distribution channel that may encourage the use of new booking and sales processes. Thus, exploitation of the Internet at the customer interface has become a key catalyst in the transformation of the airline industry (McIvor, O'Reilly, and Ponsonby 2003). Another powerful application of new technology has been developed in the area of yield-management systems. These systems integrate sophisticated databases with complex mathematical modeling, thus allowing airlines to price tickets in real time based on changing availability and booking patterns. In an industry with a product as perishable as travel, yield management has been critical to effectively manage profitability. Airlines have pioneered and still lead the development of these yield-management information systems.

Travel Agencies/Online Intermediaries

Travel agencies are intermediaries that arrange travel plans and distribute travel information to individual travelers, with some agencies specializing in certain market segments or products. In addition, many travel agencies function as tour operators, designing their own package tours and selling them either directly to the traveler or through other agents. Travel agencies use information intensely and therefore need IT to process that information. In fact, information on travel products, destinations, schedules, fares, rates, and availability is their most important product and defines their existence. The more information a travel agency can access electronically, the more timely, accurate, and efficient services it can provide to its clients.

The most prevalent application of IT in travel agencies is the GDS terminal, which was first placed in travel agents' offices by major airlines to facilitate airline bookings in the 1970s (Sheldon 1997). GDS terminals are still the major information and booking tools used by travel agents for all types of travel products. However, the advent of the Internet has significantly changed the way travel and tourism products are distributed. Increasingly, consumers can access information online, and travel agents have been forced to adapt to this change. Travel agents have an ambivalent relationship with the Internet because it can be a threat in that it makes products available directly to the consumer and yet it also provides additional business opportunities. Many travel agencies offer services on the Internet, giving them a much broader geographic consumer base than if they operated in traditional ways. They can receive bookings from clients through the Internet and can even book passengers on flights without issuing paper tickets. Travel agents can also use the Internet as a research tool, and this might be particularly important in the future as some travel products become available only via the Internet. In addition, IT applications can be used by travel agencies to create value-added products or services through the online provision of their travel expertise in combination with the wider range of travel products and services available on the Internet. However, realizing that physical location is irrelevant in today's electronic marketplace, new types of travel agencies that exist only on the Internet, such as Expedia and Travelocity, are emerging and continue to raise the level of competition among travel agencies. Consequently, travel agencies that prosper on the Internet are those that offer specialist advice and services well beyond those available through simple booking agents.

Destination-Marketing Organizations

Destination-marketing organizations (DMOs) are typically not-for-profit, government-funded, small and medium-sized, information-intensive organizations that perform a wide range of activities to coordinate the diverse components of the tourism industry (Gartrell 1988). DMOs act as a liaison, collecting and providing information to both the consumer and the industry in order to facilitate tourism promotion and development of a specific area.

In general, DMOs have been slow to adopt IT in their operations and marketing activities (Wang and Fesenmaier 2006). It was not until the late 1980s that computer systems were adopted by the larger DMOs to enhance publications and information operations and, to a lesser extent, to support reservation services. During the late 1990s, as desktop computing technologies became more widely available, DMOs began to use IT more extensively. More and more DMO directors realized that Internet marketing was an inseparable, often critical part of their overall marketing endeavor (Yuan, Gretzel and Fesenmaier 2006). They have since developed a high level of interest in the Internet because the use of the Internet offers the potential to reach a large number of consumers at relatively low cost and provides information of greater depth and quality than traditional media. In other words, using Internet technology enables DMOs to promote their destinations' tourism products and services better, present associated organizations more equally, and collect customer information for effective customer relationship management (CRM). More importantly, the Internet allows them to improve business processes, conduct marketing research, provide customer service, and facilitate destination management and planning with less dependency on time and space. Indeed, the key to successful destination marketing efforts depends primarily on the representation and provision of timely and accurate information relevant to consumers' needs by using Internet technology (Wang and Fesenmaier 2006).

Despite this potential, DMOs have not been particularly quick in establishing a sophisticated Internet presence. Several factors have contributed to the current status of DMOs' Internet strategy. One factor is related to the complex structure and relationships of the various constituents DMOs represent. The travel and tourism industry has a very complex structure, with a large percentage of the organizations classified as small businesses (Gartrell 1988). Among the DMOs' constituents are government agencies, marketing organizations at different levels, suppliers, and distributors. Although each entity maintains critical relationships with other entities in order to deliver the desired products and services, the enormousness of this diverse industry as well as the different benefits these constituents are seeking make the job of DMOs complex and difficult.

The unique characteristics of the Internet and the capabilities required of DMOs for implementing effective Internet marketing have also been identified as important influences. Marketing is a creative and adaptive discipline that requires constant regeneration and transformation in accordance with changes in the environment (Brownlie et al. 1994; Cronin 1995). Thus, conventional marketing activities cannot be implemented on the Internet in their present form (Hoffman and Novak 1996). For Internet marketing strategies to be successful, DMOs have to be aware of the capabilities and characteristics of the Internet and need to start developing new marketing concepts and paradigms, because the Internet presents an environment for marketing activities that is fundamentally different from that of traditional media (Connolly and Sigala 2001). Despite these problems and challenges, DMOs have begun to recognize the opportunities that emerge from using the special features of the new medium, in particular the interactivity and multimedia capabilities it provides. As a result, the number of DMO Web sites is rising rapidly, offering online destination information with increasing quality and functionality. However, with the explosive growth of the Internet, destination information is available from many sources, including travelers themselves. In this extremely competitive environment DMOs have to constantly reevaluate their priorities in marketing activities to ensure their relevance. Thus, with the transparency of the Internet comes also a greater emphasis on measurement and reporting (Gretzel et al. 2005).

Travel Search Engines

Travel search engines (TSEs) constitute the latest addition to intermediaries in the tourism industry and, as in the case of CRSs, their emergence was technology-driven. Travel search engines allow consumers to conduct metasearches of several online travel booking sites. TSEs apply sophisticated search engine technology to search a network of proprietary databases, thus giving users a wider range of options and greater price transparency. TSEs are thought of as more consumer-friendly than other online booking Web sites because they crawl the Web sites of travel suppliers more frequently, consequently generating an even broader array of choices (Eyefortravel 2005, A strategic analysis). After a selection is made from the search results, TSEs send users directly to the supplier's Web site to complete the purchase. Thus, TSEs are moving up the value chain by offering travelers a one-stop search model, enriched content, and user-friendly interfaces.

Sidestep has emerged as the leading TSE, followed by Cheapflights. Other main players include Kayak, Yahoo! Farechase, Mobissimo, and Qixo (Eyefortravel 2005, The ultimate travel search engine). However, the TSE market is currently small and has not yet had a significant impact on the online tourism industry. As of mid-November 2004, the top six travel search engines held only a combined 0.42 percent share of all traffic to online travel sites. In contrast, Expedia, Travelocity, and Orbitz held a combined 16 percent share of online travel traffic for the same time period (EyeforTravel 2005, The ultimate travel search engine). However, TSEs have the possibility to directly impact existing revenue models in the online tourism industry because tourism suppliers consider TSEs a new marketing tool that drives traffic to their own Web sites (Eyefortravel 2005, The ultimate travel search engine). According to Hitwise (2005), the market share of visits to four of the major TSEs tripled from October 2004 to April 2005, whereas visits to the top five travel agency sites (Expedia, Travelocity, Orbitz, Yahoo! Travel, and CheapTickets) increased by only 11 percent. Hitwise also reports that visitors to top travel search engines are more likely to be older, with Mobissimo attracting the largest number of visitors over the age of 55 (25 percent of total visitors). It is expected that as Baby Boomers retire and have more leisure time, this price-conscious group will become a powerful driver of traffic to travel meta-search engines (Hitwise 2005).

Emerging Marketing and Management Strategies

The adoption of IT has transformed the way in which the tourism industry conducts business. With the assistance of new technology, especially the Internet, new opportunities have emerged for tourism organizations, which enable them to market their travel products and services and manage their daily business activities more effectively. In particular, innovative marketing and management strategies have evolved in the areas of Web development, Web advertising/promotion, e-commerce activities, customer relationship management, and the use of online destination management systems.

Web-Site Development

Hanson (2000) observed that there are three major stages in Web-site development: (I) publishing, (II) database retrieval, and (III) personalized interaction. Stage I sites provide the same information to all users. Though a stage I site can contain thousands of pages, pictures, sounds, and videos, it is limited in the dialogue it affords between the travel Web site and the user because it only broadcasts information from the Web site to the viewer. Modern Web tools make stage I travel Web sites easy and inexpensive to develop in that almost any document can be converted and moved online.

With experience and investment, the travel organization moves to stage II Web sites, which combine the publishing power of stage I with the ability to retrieve information in response to user requests. The responses are dynamically turned into Web pages or e-mail. Interactivity and dialogue have started, although this activity is limited to a series of "ask-respond" interactions. However, the ability to use Web sites as points of access to images, sounds, and databases is particularly valuable.

A stage III travel Web site dynamically creates a page catering to an individual customer. It moves beyond an "ask-respond" interaction into a dialogue and may anticipate user choices and suggest possible alternatives. A stage III travel Web site does more than just react to requests typed into forms or selected by clicking on an image. It requires the capabilities of stages I and II plus the customization of content and functions to the needs of a specific user.

DMOs use Web-based technologies in different ways and with varying intensity, owing to different backgrounds, financial resources, and marketing objectives (Yuan and Fesenmaier 2000). Some DMOs are at a preliminary stage of using Web technologies for marketing activities, and these Web sites are typically used only to broadcast information by providing brochure-like information. Others are more advanced and sophisticated in this regard, taking advantage of Web technologies to make business activities more effective and efficient, or even to reengineer whole business practices. More advanced DMO Web sites typically include more sophisticated capabilities, such as interactive queries and request forms, personalization, recommendation functions, streaming video, and interactive maps.

Web Advertising/Promotion

The Internet is an almost pure manifestation of marketing principles and practices (Inkpen 1998). It is a tourism marketer's dream because: (1) it enables travel companies of different sizes to compete on more equal terms, and (2) it allows a travel company to open up a direct and potentially personalized channel of communication with its customers. In other words, travel companies of all sizes are much more equal in their competition for consumers' attention on the Internet. Travel is the most important business on the Web in terms of the volume of advertising and promotion (eMarketer 1999). It is also most likely to generate revenues and achieve profits through its Web presence. However, in order to be successful in Web advertising/promotion, tourism organizations have realized that the Web is a medium that combines the elements of other media. Hoffman and Novak (1996) describe the new form of communication that the Internet provides as an "interactive multimedia many-to-many communication model," in which interactivity can be *with* the medium in addition to *through* the medium. Travel and tourism fit especially well with interactive media because they constitute an information-intensive industry in which transactions can be rather easily made online. The industry has therefore largely embraced new advertising techniques such as viral marketing, search-engine optimization, and cost-per-click advertising.

E-Commerce Activities

Before the onset of the Internet, electronic commerce was usually conducted over a proprietary network connecting a group of organizations such as airline companies, travel agents, and hotels through CRSs or GDSs. The nature of the transaction was purely business-to-business. Tourism businesses now use the Internet as a means of redefining their focus, creating new products, finding new distribution channels, and creating new markets. For example, the major airline sites now offer customer reservations, electronic tickets, seat selection, in-flight merchandise, and reward points; in addition, some of the airlines have enhanced their sites to offer lodging, transportation-package deals, and cruises through their alliance partners.

The use of the Internet in the travel and tourism industry has also been driven by the convergent forces of the shift of consumer behavior toward more intensive uses of online environments and the successful adaptation of marketing and sales strategies by the industry. For many consumers, online booking of travel is already the norm, and this can only be expected to strengthen in the immediate future. Travel is a product that online consumers want to purchase; indeed, according to Forrester Research (1999), it is the product that those who are online, but have not yet purchased online, want to purchase most. From the point of view of travel and tourism suppliers, however, there is some reticence from certain sectors of the industry, such as cruise lines, to compete directly with their traditional intermediaries by making the move to direct sales, whereas others, such as airlines, have embraced the new online channels with great enthusiasm.

From an industry perspective, increased e-commerce activities have led to greater disintermediation and more direct contact with consumers. Traditional intermediaries (e.g., wholesalers, incoming agents, tour operators, travel agents) built up a distribution system characterized by complexity and cost. The widespread growth of the Internet is creating a more complex but efficient information and distribution system in which distribution is handled through a variety of channels. This includes more direct distribution, where the supplier, regardless of location, sells directly over the Internet to the consumer. Disintermediation will drive more responsive product offerings from suppliers and a greater focus on customer loyalty and retention. Distribution continues to involve intermediaries who offer advice, aggregation, and value-added customer services, but pricing has become more transparent, and distribution cost is often paid by the travelers rather than just by the suppliers. Such a complex distribution environment emphasizes the importance of yield and channel management not only for major tourism companies but for suppliers of all sizes.

E-commerce solutions are gaining momentum and are expanding beyond reservations to include supply-chain management (e.g., procurement), internal business applications through intranets, and other business-to-business transactions as well as business-to-customer sales. It is certain that the Internet will continue to become faster, more reliable and secure, and also more feature-rich. In addition, it will become more mobile through portable devices such as personal digital assistants (PDAs) and cell phones that can communicate with ambient intelligent devices embedded in appliances and will increasingly be enabled by speech, thus truly giving customers anytime, anywhere access in a format conducive to their needs.

Customer Relationship Management

Customer relationship management (CRM) is a managerial philosophy that calls for the reconfiguration of the travel organization's activities around the customer. Successful CRM strategies evolve out of the ability to effectively capture exhaustive data about existing and potential customers, to profile them accurately, to identify their individual needs and idiosyncratic expectations, and to generate actionable customer knowledge that can be distributed for ad hoc use at the point of contact (Newell 2000). Further, the success of CRM initiatives is dependent on the ability to collect, store, and aggregate large amounts of customer information from various sources. One of the major driving forces of CRM using the Internet is the ability to target each individual interactively. With the Internet, individuals and travel marketers can interact, and this direct interaction creates customer value and sets the stage for relationship-building. Travel marketers continue to seek ways for compiling accurate databases of personal information such as sociodemographic, socioeconomic, geographic, and behavioral characteristics for potential customers. Such a database creates a wealth of relationship-marketing opportunities. Crucial to the establishment of such comprehensive customer databases is the ability to use software agents, without human intervention, to collect, categorize, and store large amounts of personal customer information in a cost-effective manner for later data mining. A second important issue is the ability to collect the desired information directly from the primary source rather than having to purchase it from secondary sources such as travel and tourism consultants. Nevertheless, many travel suppliers, notably airlines, have been slow in adopting or expanding CRM systems.

Online Destination Management Systems

The term *destination management system* (DMS) has come into use in recent years to describe the IT infrastructure of a DMO, and may be defined in a number of ways depending on the capabilities of the system. Increasingly, a DMS is regarded as having to support multiple functions. An integrated DMS supports not only the DMO's Web site, but also a wide range of other promotion, marketing, and sales applications (Sheldon 1997). These might include the design and production of printed materials, tourist information center services (for information and reservations), call-center services, kiosks, database marketing, project/event management, and marketing research. DMSs can greatly enhance a travel destination's Web presence by integrating information from various suppliers and intermediaries and are increasingly used as the informational and structural basis for regional Web portal sites. To date, only a minority of DMOs have invested in such integrated systems, and DMOs often have disparate technology platforms running a variety of applications. Investment in this area, however, is accelerating.

TRAVELERS AND THE INTERNET

Internet technologies have not only changed the structure of tourism and its related industries, but they have also had a profound impact on the way consumers search for tourism information, construct and share tourism experiences, and purchase tourism products and services. In contrast to many consumer goods and services, the consumption of tourism experiences involves often

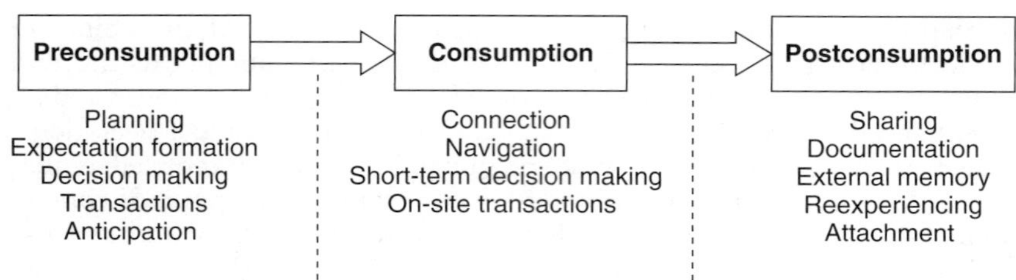

Figure 2: Communication and information needs in the three stages of tourism consumption

extensive preconsumption and postconsumption stages, in addition to the actual trip, which itself can spread over several weeks (Jeng and Fesenmaier 2002; Moutinho 1987). These stages of the tourism consumption process are typically information-intensive, and Internet technologies have come to play a significant role in supporting consumers throughout this multistage process. The specific ways in which the various technologies are used in the different stages depend on the particular communication and information needs they are expected to serve (see Figure 2). For instance, Internet technologies are used in the preconsumption phase to obtain information necessary for planning trips, formulate correct expectations, and evaluate, compare, and select alternatives, as well as to communicate with the providers of tourism products and services to prepare or execute transactions. In contrast, the functions served by technologies during the actual consumption of tourism experiences are more related to being connected and to obtaining detailed information relevant to a specific place and moment in time. During the postconsumption phase, Internet technologies are used in ways that allow sharing, documenting, storing, and reliving tourism experiences, as well as establishing close relationships with places, attractions, or product/service providers, as in the case of Frequent Flyer programs. For example, e-mail will typically be used in all stages, but mainly to obtain information or make reservations in the preconsumption phase, to stay connected with family and friends while traveling, and to share pictures and stories with members of one's travel party or other individuals after concluding a trip. Although all Internet technologies are probably used by travelers at some point or in some way, several applications have been identified as being of particular importance in the context of tourism experiences. The following provides an overview of these technologies, how they tend to be used, and the impact they have on consumers during the various stages of the tourism consumption process.

Preconsumption

It is in the initial phase of the tourism consumption process that most of the impacts related to Internet-based technologies are currently experienced. Consumers use the Internet and its diverse applications in this first stage of the tourism experience to gather information, formulate expectations, inform/support their decision making, and reserve or purchase the various components (transportation, accommodation, etc.) to be consumed during their trips.

Brochureware

Brochureware refers to Web sites or Web pages created by transferring the contents of printed tourism brochures directly to digital environments. Brochureware was one of the first Internet applications made available to tourism consumers, owing to the fact that tourism businesses quickly recognized the value of the Internet as a powerful publishing medium. Web sites designed as brochureware represent the simplest form of Web design and completely ignore the content presentation and communication possibilities the World Wide Web offers (Hanson 2000). Nevertheless, brochureware is the most common way in which tourism information is currently made available to consumers and, consequently, constitutes an integral part of tourism-related online experiences. Despite their obvious limitations, digitized tourism brochures on the Internet still support consumers in that they enable potential travelers to browse and evaluate tourism products without temporal or spatial limitations. Furthermore, even the very basic implementations of brochureware make use of hypertext and provide hyperlinks that allow consumers to move through online tourism information in ways that are typically not supported by printed brochures. Brochureware is expected to give way to more interactive forms of Web-site content presentation as more and more tourism businesses recognize the value of engaging consumers in experiential ways.

Virtual Tours

Virtual tours are tools that enable the potential consumers of tourism products to explore and immerse themselves within an interactive Web environment in order to gain the needed experiential information about a destination or tourism establishment (Cho and Fesenmaier 2001). The term *virtual tour* is widely used on the Web, and can range from a series of pictures or a slide show to streaming video and highly interactive virtual reality settings. The realism provided through virtual tours creates immersion, which, in turn, leads to immediate, direct, and real experiences that generate a strong sense of presence. As a result of this telepresence experienced through virtual tours, consumers are able to construct a more vivid picture of the tourism product and are therefore more likely to reach well-informed decisions. Thus, the significance of virtual tours in the context of tourism lies in providing consumers with an opportunity for "product trial" before the actual purchase. Tourism products are, in large part, experience-oriented intangible goods (Vogt and Fesenmaier 1998) that are typically consumed at a place far away from the point of purchase and often cannot be experienced without being consumed in their entirety. Consequently, product trial is usually not available to the potential consumers of tourism products. However, tourism bears many risks because its components are consumed in unfamiliar environments, constitute a significant expenditure for most consumers, and typically entail high involvement on the part of the consumer. Given the limited opportunity for prepurchase trial in the context of tourism, virtual tours, with their ability to represent tourism products and services in more realistic and dynamic ways than other promotional materials, play a crucial role in offering rich travel information.

Travel-Decision-Support Systems

The term *travel-decision-support systems* (TDSS) refers to information systems designed to simplify the travel-decision-making process and support consumers in the various steps involved in planning trips. Trip planning is a very complex process that consists of a number of decisions, which often condition each other (Dellaert, Ettema, and Lindh 1998; Jeng and Fesenmaier 2002; Woodside and MacDonald 1994). Also, each decision requires different kinds of information; thus, separate information-search activities are necessary. This increases the cost of the information-search process for the consumer and can often lead to information overload (Good et al. 1999; Hibbard 1997). The main function of a TDSS is to identify and present certain tourism products and services in accordance with consumer preferences, thus reducing the number of alternatives that the consumer would have to evaluate. The functionality of such systems ranges from more sophisticated search engines and intelligent-agent-supported information retrieval to true recommendation systems that enable the consumer to identify destinations or tourism products of interest (Vanhof and Molderez 1994). The use of a TDSS generally requires specifying preferences such as desired date of travel and preferred activities. In their most advanced form, these systems try to mimic face-to-face human interactions that could occur between a consumer and a travel agent. In such cases, the TDSS is typically referred to as a "travel counseling system" (Hruschka and Mazanec 1990). Current developments in the TDSS area focus on increasing the ability of such systems to capture consumer preferences and adapt information accordingly, as well as to learn from past interactions and support group decision-making (Delgado and Davidson 2002; Hwang and Fesenmaier 2001; Loban 1997; Mitsche 2001; Ricci and Werthner 2001). Consumers can take advantage of such systems and benefit from the customized information presented to them at various stages in the trip-planning process. However, the currently available TDSS versions are still more capable of supporting consumers with a clear understanding of what they desire than helping individuals with only a vague idea of what they are looking for. It is expected that these systems will play an increasingly important role in travel planning as they become more human-centric in design and truly adaptive with respect to the needs of consumers (Gretzel, Hwang, and Fesenmaier 2006).

E-Commerce Applications

E-commerce applications are technologies that support online transactions between the providers and consumers of tourism products and services. Online reservation and payment options were quickly adopted by many suppliers and consumers and led to the emergence of tourism as one of the most important e-commerce categories. It can be argued that the reasons for this rapid adoption of e-commerce in tourism lie in the particular fit between the characteristics of tourism products and the capabilities of e-commerce applications. The purchase of tourism-related products and services typically involves the movement of information rather than the physical delivery of goods and is often concluded using credit-card payments. Also, the complex and strictly hierarchical tourism distribution system of pre-Internet times led to enormous information asymmetries and little choice for consumers in terms of where or how to acquire tourism products. With the introduction of e-commerce, consumers were provided with a new means of buying that they were eager to adopt because it not only offered more choices through direct links to the many geographically dispersed industry players or new intermediaries such as online travel agencies, but also catered to consumers by providing new levels of convenience. E-tickets, for example, are a direct result of e-commerce initiatives and have tremendously simplified travel, especially business travel. Current developments in the area of e-commerce focus primarily on raising security and privacy standards to ensure safe and smooth transactions. In addition, efforts are being undertaken to make a wider range of tourism products available online. Destination management systems are becoming more widespread and promise more extensive e-commerce adoption, thus providing consumers with greater access to an increasing variety of tourism products and services.

Online Customer Support

Online customer support is a summary term for Internet technologies that allow consumers to contact the suppliers or distributors of tourism products if additional information or other forms of assistance are needed. Applications that provide consumers with the means to communicate more quickly and more easily in order to get support are especially important in the context of tourism. First, the special nature of tourism products and services (see Kotler, Bowen, and Makens 1999 for a detailed description) makes them more likely to require additional support. It is very difficult to describe the many experiential aspects of tourism accurately; thus, consumers often require further interpretation or more detailed explanations. Also, tourism products and services are usually purchased or at least reserved long before they are consumed, and many things can potentially happen during this extensive period of commitment between travel- and tourism-related businesses and consumers.

Second, geographical and cultural distances between travel and tourism suppliers and consumers render communication through traditional means very difficult. The Internet, on the other hand, provides consumers with fast, easy, and cost-effective ways of contacting the providers of travel and tourism-related goods and services.

Technologies of support include "Frequently Asked Questions" sections on Web sites, online request forms, bulletin boards, Internet phones, e-mail, real-time chat options, and instant-messaging applications. These technologies are currently used in very passive ways, which means consumers are required to initiate the contact. However, a growing number of tourism organizations are adopting more proactive approaches to online customer support. They provide consumers with active assistance either through automatic e-mail updates or by monitoring the behavior of Web-site visitors and offering real-time assistance through instant messaging or chat if they recognize search or click patterns that are typically associated with a need for help, such as seemingly uncoordinated click-streams. This innovative use of online customer-support technologies actively encourages consumers to communicate with customer representatives and has the potential to prevent confusion or misunderstandings instead of following the traditional model of solving problems after they have occurred. This trend is driven by a recognition that personal communication can be more effective in resolving complaints and building customer loyalty.

During Consumption

Internet technologies are used during the actual trip mainly for travelers to stay connected and to obtain en route information if, and only if, the need arises. The spread of Internet cafés at tourist destinations, the growing number of accommodation establishments offering (often high-speed) Internet connections, and the recent efforts of airlines to provide in-flight Internet access to travelers indicate that a substantial need for these kinds of information and communication links exists. En route Internet access means anywhere-and-anytime availability of tourism-related information for consumers. Therefore, many of the trip-planning and information-gathering tasks of travelers could shift from preconsumption to during consumption and make travel much more spontaneous if the Internet becomes more widely available to the traveling public.

Mobile technologies play an increasingly important role in tourism due to their ability to provide travelers with wireless and, thus, instantaneous and pervasive Internet access. Handheld devices such as personal digital assistants (PDAs) and cellular phones supported through a wireless application protocol (WAP), a global system for mobile communication (GSM), and short message service (SMS) allow travelers to take full advantage of the Internet while on the road. More ambitious developments of mobile technology go beyond simple access by providing real-time location-based services (Eriksson 2002; Oertel, Steinmüller, and Kuom 2002). Empowered by geographical information systems (GIS) and global positioning system technology (GPS) in combination with information available on the Internet, these advanced mobile applications identify the traveler's location in space and the spatial context of this position. This information is then used to generate personalized assistance in the form of location-specific and time-sensitive information. Many advancements related to mobile technologies are spurred by needs that directly arise from information and communication problems encountered during travel. Projects such as CRUMPET—creation of user-friendly mobile services personalized for tourism (Poslad et al. 2001; Schmidt-Belz, Makelainen, Nick, and Poslad 2002)—and the development of wireless-based tourism infrastructures (e.g., the ambient intelligence landscape described by the Information Society Technologies Advisory Group [ISTAG] [2001]), are two examples of the many efforts undertaken at the juncture of mobile technology and tourism, which represent developments with important implications for the future of the entire Internet.

Postconsumption

The postconsumption stage in the context of tourism involves treasuring souvenirs, remembering special moments, reliving an experience through photographs, sharing travel stories, and often developing a strong sense of attachment to a specific destination. Internet technologies play a significant role in these post-trip activities and have started to significantly influence memory practices as they relate to tourism.

Virtual communities are an example of Internet applications that provide consumers with support during the postconsumption phase. The term *virtual community* describes a group of people who are connected through computer-mediated communication technologies and share interests and feelings in cyberspace (Rheingold 1994). Virtual travel communities, then, are communities facilitated by computer-mediated communication that allow members to conduct various types of travel-related tasks, such as obtaining travel information, maintaining connections, finding travel companions, or simply having fun by telling each other interesting travel experiences and stories (Wang, Yu, and Fesenmaier 2002). Consumers can use these virtual travel communities to post photographs and stories/testimonials of their trip(s) on the community Web site, where they serve as information to other consumers. In addition to this purely functional aspect, virtual travel communities offer opportunities for members to fulfill hedonic, psychological, and social needs. A sense of belonging, fun, and self-identification are only a few of the benefits that can be derived from online community membership. In the context of tourism, the most important function virtual travel communities serve is the extension of travel/tourism-related experiences beyond the actual trip. Used as digital substitutes for traditional photo albums, the digital images uploaded onto community Web pages and discussion boards help recall aspects of trips and assist consumers in constructing memories of vacations. The travel stories and discussions that can be found in such communities mimic real-world storytelling activities typical of this last stage of the tourism consumption process.

Tourism experiences are an integral part of the collective memory of families and peer groups and, thus, require sharing. Consequently, consumer-generated media (CGM) have gained importance beyond the settings of virtual communities. In contrast to traditional conversations about the adventures, fun events, or other types of memorable moments of past trips, communication about travel experiences in blogs, virtual communities, other discussion forums, and personal Web pages takes place with an audience that has a very tailored interest in the topic and often resides outside the boundaries of one's usual social circle. Also, the information posted by consumers in the course of the postconsumption recollection of the travel experience serves as valid information for consumers in earlier stages, thus closing the loop of the tourism information cycle. The information provided by other consumers is especially valuable, as it represents personal accounts of probably alike consumers with actual product knowledge and no commercial interests. Thus, CGM can serve as a vehicle to control the quality of travel products and services through consumers' evaluation and ratings of a wide range of travel products and services. However, increasing numbers of advertisers and tourism businesses are discovering CGM as particularly suitable vehicles to communicate messages to and establish relationships with specific target markets. For instance, most major online travel agencies have started soliciting and featuring such content, moving it into the mainstream as an important customer service. This has also led to a new recognition, long observed in mainstream media but seldom in the tourism sector, of the delineation between editorial and commercial content. Importantly, it has focused greater attention on travel content (of any type) being authentic, real, and credible.

Impacts of Internet Technology on Travel Behavior

The Internet has had and will continue to have a tremendous impact on the way consumers search for, purchase, consume, and remember tourism experiences. However, the Internet is not the only channel through which consumers obtain information, communicate, or complete transactions. Rather, it is one of many options currently used by tourism consumers. Word of mouth, for instance, remains the most popular way of gaining access to firsthand knowledge about travel destinations and tourism experiences. Also, travel magazines and movies continue to be significant sources of inspiration. It seems that the concept of the "hybrid" consumer, who uses many media and technologies simultaneously (Wind, Mahajan, and Gunther 2002) is especially applicable to tourism. Thus, the Internet has not replaced traditional channels but has placed additional options in the hands of consumers. Nevertheless, many current technology developments aim at convergence and the creation of one channel that can satisfy all information search, transaction, and communication needs; therefore, this situation might change in the near future.

In general, the Internet and its many different applications have provided consumers with an incredible number of choices, opportunities for comparison shopping, and much more control over many processes related to the consumption of tourism experiences. The success of auction models such as Priceline.com, where consumers name prices rather than accepting the industry-imposed price, indicates that the market has shifted from a supplier- to a consumer-dominated market.

Tourism has always been characterized by many alternatives. Yet many consumers lacked the necessary information to take advantage of the variety of tourism offers available. The Internet has, to a large extent, closed this information gap. Internet consumers are much more informed, and this new level of information and knowledge among "new" consumers has opened up many choices. The larger extent and different, more experiential nature of information available to consumers has also led to more accurate expectation formation and more informed decision making, both of which are especially important for the consumers of information-intensive, intangible, and high-involvement tourism products and services. On the one hand, the ease with which information can be made available online has placed an abundance of information at the disposal of consumers. On the other hand, it causes situations of severe information overload and leads to many concerns about trust. The Internet facilitates information representation and distribution; however, it also makes it more difficult for consumers to identify false information. Many tourism businesses are very small and operate thousands of miles away from where their customers live. It is, thus, extremely difficult for consumers to verify their existence, not to speak of the nature and quality of their business practices. Consequently, the consumers of travel- and tourism-related products can be expected to continue relying on offline and online intermediaries as well as official Web portals such as destination marketing sites to obtain reliable and trustworthy information about tourism establishments.

The Internet has increased the speed with which information moves between tourism suppliers and consumers, and many consumers have started to expect instantaneous information and support with respect to all aspects of their trips. The Internet has influenced not only perceptions of speed but also the extent of personalization expected by the consumers of tourism information and products. These new expectations in terms of speed and personalization spurred by the Internet represent an enormous challenge for the tourism industry and leave many consumers disappointed with the level of service they receive.

One of the main advantages of the Internet is that it provides consumers with the opportunity for anytime-and-anywhere access to information. Many aspects of a trip that had to be planned well in advance can now be finalized while on the road. Internet technologies that provide consumers with such en route access to information have the potential to significantly transform trip planning and influence travel patterns. Recent trends indicate that travel is in the process of becoming more spontaneous and that many travelers choose to travel to destinations that they would not traditionally have considered because of the high risk. One can only speculate about the impact of this trend on tourism in the Internet era, as extensive planning is an integral part of the tourism consumption process and careful preparation is often essential to the success of a trip (and sometimes even crucial to the survival of the travel party).

The advent of the Internet has brought about many dystopian fears related to the future of tourism. Many predicted the end of travel per se and pictured tourism experiences as being confined to virtual-reality simulations. The future of tourism on the Internet from a utopian perspective of course looks much brighter. Such a perspective interprets Internet experiences as a substitute for travel and, thus, a great opportunity for individuals with disabilities or other constraints that limit them from traveling. Neither scenario has been realized so far. Internet technologies have discouraged some types of travel and encouraged others. The experiences presented on the Internet constitute far from real substitutes for actual travel, but they do provide invaluable information about accessibility and allow individuals with special needs to prepare more accurately for real-world trips. Consequently, when analyzing the influence of Internet technologies on consumer behavior in the context of tourism, one has to constantly remind oneself that the Internet is still in the process of becoming and that its impact on the consumers of travel and tourism products and services can be partly grasped but not yet fully understood.

TRAVEL AND TOURISM FUTURES

For the tourism industry, the Internet is clearly the biggest opportunity but simultaneously the biggest challenge. Looking to the future, of course, poses many questions; however, there are a number of general trends pointing in the direction of the future development of travel and tourism. In this section five technology-related trends will be considered: (1) the continuing speed and sophistication of information technology; (2) the continuing growth in the use and uses of information technology in tourism; (3) the changing forms of information technology as a medium for communication; (4) the emergence of a new tourism consumer; and (5) the emergence of experience as the foundation for defining tourism products. The following will identify and briefly discuss each trend, focusing attention on its impact on the tourism industry.

Trend # 1: The Continuing Speed and Sophistication of Information Technology

The personal computer celebrated its twenty-fifth birthday in 2006. In an article in *PC Magazine*, the personal computer (PC) was described as one of the most profound inventions in the history of mankind (Miller 2002). From its inception in 1981 the development of personal computer technology has been shown to follow Moore's law—that chip density, and therefore the speed of computers, will double every 18 months. Thus, computers and computer technology have grown from the very "primitive" Radio Shack TRS-80 and the IBM 4.7 MHz 64K RAM 8088 processor, an operating system called DOS, and software called VisiCalc and Wordstar to today's 3.8-GHz machines with up to 16 GB of RAM. Over the years, various competitors have infused the market with a variety of innovations focused on expanding the power of the machine and the ability of the system to address workplace needs and encouraging society to think/dream about what might be in the future (Miller 2002). As the systems grew more sophisticated and powerful and arguably more human-centric, the power of the network was recognized and spurred even greater innovation. In 1990, the World Wide Web was born, along with a new generation of innovators seeking to build an information infrastructure that could enable individuals to collaborate from distant locations. The outcome was Mosaic and a decade of unparalleled innovation and "build out" in information infrastructure. This new orientation also led to the development of a variety of computer-enabled devices, such as cell phones and personal digital assistants, which are now beginning to pervade human society (Norman 1999).

A number of scholars have recently reflected on the progress of computer technology and have concluded that there is much to be accomplished before computers/information technologies can truly enable society to benefit from their power. In *The Unfinished Revolution*, Dertouzos (2001, 6) argued that "the real utility of computers, and the true value of the Information Revolution, still lie ahead." He suggested that over the past twenty years society has evolved to "fit" around computers and that the productivity gains from computer technology have been "more hype than reality." Supporting this argument, Norman (1999) suggested that the real benefits will be realized only when computer technology becomes more human-centered—that is, when technology adapts to the needs and lifestyles of human beings. They argue that information appliances—computer systems that focus on specific tasks and are connected through the Internet or wireless technology—are the basis of human-centric and thus "invisible" computing. It appears that the focus of emerging technology is on empowering the individual within the framework of the human experience rather than defining human behavior around the needs of computer designers.

Examples of emerging technology that is beginning to be used in the travel and tourism industry include online mapping technology, RSS (really simple syndication) feeds, podcasting, travel recommendation systems, virtual reality, and travel guidance systems. A number of basic recommendation systems are available in a variety of travel-related Web sites including Ski-europe.com, Travelocity.com, and TIScover.com. Indeed, virtual reality and related technologies are evolving sufficiently to enable travelers to sample/experience the destinations prior to the actual trip. In addition, global positioning system (GPS)–supported travel guidance systems, which once were considered exotic, are actively marketed for automobiles. Further, tools to map locations, RSS feeds of travel news and podcasts of walking tours are now available on some DMO Web sites and are expected to be widely adopted within the next couple of years.

Trend # 2: Continuing Growth in the Use and Uses of Information Technology in Tourism

The number of Internet users continues to grow worldwide and as a result, the Internet's potential as a marketing medium has expanded greatly and continues to expand. As of March 2006 71.5 percent of American adults, or about 144 million people, used the Internet, up from 66 percent the previous year. Of these Internet users, 83.6 percent had had Internet access for 4 years or more, indicating that Internet users had also become more experienced (Pew Internet & American Life Project 2006). The worldwide Internet population was estimated at over 1 billion users in 2005 and is projected to reach 1.8 billion by 2010 (ClickZ.com 2005). The USC Annenberg School Center for the Digital Future (2005) reports that Internet use has been adopted across all segments of American society and that the Internet's importance as an information source is steadily increasing, with now 56 percent of adult Internet users considering it to be a very or extremely important source of information for them. The Digital Future Project survey further found that the number of hours spent online continues to grow, rising to an all-time high of on average 13.3 hours per week. More than two-thirds of home Internet users (70 percent) have high-speed Internet access (Pew Internet & American Life Project 2007, *Home Broadband Adoption*).

Looking for travel information is one of the Top 10 online activities of Internet users, with 73 percent of Internet users indicating that they have engaged in this activity (Pew Internet & American Life Project 2007, *Internet Activities*). TIA reports that online travel planners are more likely to be female, better educated, and married than those who do not plan and/or book travel online (TIA 2005). This most recent TIA study also shows that most (71 percent) of those planning trips online say they do at least half of their travel planning on the Internet. Further, the percentage of online travel planners who actually book or make travel reservations has increased significantly, to 82 percent of online travel planners or 64 percent of travelers with Internet access. Table 3 shows that airline tickets continue to be the travel product most frequently purchased online, followed by overnight accommodations and rental cars.

Table 3: Percent of Travel Products/Service Purchased Online in 2005 (among 64.8 Million U.S. Travelers Who Have Internet Access and Who Booked Travel Online)

Travel Products/Services	2004	2005
Airline ticket	55.6	55.6
Overnight lodging accommodations	46.3	49.4
Rental car or RV	27.3	26.2
Tickets—cultural event	16.0	20.7
Tickets—theme/amusement park	9.0	15.1
Travel package	9.4	13.6
Tickets—museum or festival	10.8	11.9
Tickets—spectator sporting event	7.6	11.1
Reservations for personal sports (like golf/skiing/water sports)	7.3	9.6
Tickets—tour or excursion	8.5	8.8
Cruise	5.7	7.1

Source: TIA (2005).

Trend # 3: Changing Forms of Information Technology as a Medium for Communication

Industry experts have increasingly questioned whether the Internet is different from other media and whether it needs to be addressed in new ways using new strategies (Godin 1999; Hoffman and Novak 1996; Zeff and Aronson 1999). The Internet is special in that both consumers and firms can interact with the medium, provide content to the medium, communicate one to one or one to many, and have more direct control over the way they communicate than using other media. When everyone can communicate with everyone else, not only the old communication models become obsolete but so do the communication channels that are based on them (Evans and Wurster 1999).

In contrast to traditional media, the Internet combines and integrates the following functional properties: (1) information representation; (2) collaboration; (3) communication; (4) interactivity; and (5) transactions. As a consequence, Internet communication can be much more holistic than communication through traditional media. The Internet can simultaneously integrate informational, educational, entertainment, and sales aspects; this flexibility makes the Internet rich and appealing but also very complex and difficult to deal with. Interactive media such as the Internet build the foundation for interactive marketing: "The essence of interactive marketing is the use of information *from* the customer rather than *about* the customer" (Day 1998, 47). It differs from traditional marketing because it is based on dialogue instead of one-way communication, and it deals with individual consumers instead of mass markets (Parsons, Zeisser, and Waitman 1998). Using these capabilities of the Internet may lead to deeper relationships with customers and greater personalization of goods and services. Travel and tourism fit especially well with this interactivity aspect of the Internet because they are an information-intensive and experience-based industry.

Network technologies enable travel and tourism organizations to blend together publishing, real-time communication, broadcast, and narrowcast (Hoffman, Novak, and Chatterjee 1995). It is a medium that attracts attention and creates a sense of community. It is a personal medium, an interactive medium, and a niche and a mass medium at the same time (Schwartz 1998). In contrast to traditional media, the trade-off between richness and reach is not applicable to the Web. Evans and Wurster (1999) define *richness* as the quality of the information presented (accuracy, bandwidth, currency, customization, interactivity, relevance, security). *Reach* refers to the number of people who participate in the sharing of that information. The trade-off between richness and reach leads to asymmetries of information. Thus, when DMOs are able to distribute and exchange rich information without constraint, "the channel choices for marketers, the inefficiencies of consumer search, the hierarchical structure of supply chains, the organizational pyramid, asymmetries of information, and the boundaries of the corporation itself will all be thrown into question" (Evans and Wurster 1999, 37).

Part of this trend will also be the development of mobile electronic devices and networks that will more effectively distribute complex travel content to travelers. Such applications will include GPS-enabled content, complex search capabilities; rich media, including video and mapping, plus real-time pricing and booking functionality. A series of network technology applications such as third-generation (3G) mobile networks and improved satellite coverage are now enabling the distribution of such rich content. With increasing usability and ever lower prices, it is expected that such technologies will be widely adopted and will increase consumers' expectations regarding the richness and relevance of information accessible to them.

Trend # 4: Emergence of a New Tourism Consumer

The Internet changes how people communicate and exchange information. The resulting abundance of information and ease of communication have led to profound changes in consumer attitudes and behavior. What makes new consumers "new" is that they are empowered by the Internet, which provides them with easy and cheap access to various information sources and extended communities (Windham and Orton 2000). New tourism consumers are well informed, are used to having many choices, expect speed, and use technologies to overcome the physical constraints of bodies and borders (Poon 1993). Lewis and Bridger (2000) describe the new consumer as being: (1) individualistic, (2) involved, (3) independent, and (4) informed. The Internet is a highly personalized medium, and new consumers expect marketers to address and cater to their complex personal preferences. Consequently, new tourism consumers are "in control" and have become important players in the process of creating and shaping brands.

New tourism consumers are also very independent in making consumption decisions but, at the same time, like to share stories about their travel experiences with members of different communities. Stories can convey emotional aspects of experiences and product/service qualities that are generally hard to express in writing and, consequently, are rarely included in traditional product descriptions. Storytelling is an important means of creating and maintaining communities (Muniz and O'Guinn 2000), and Internet technologies greatly facilitate this form of communication and community building among travelers through new technologies such as blogs and social networking applications. Importantly, the new scarcities of time and trust require new tourism consumers to rely heavily on word of mouth and the expert opinions of like-minded others. New travel-oriented communities are brand communities or communities of interest and are imagined, involve limited liability, and focus on a specific consumption practice (Muniz and O'Guinn 2000; Wang et al. 2002). Travelers in this networked world are expected to increasingly take advantage of (or contribute) to consumer-driven content—sharing their experiences or advice with others—across the Internet's global community. This will greatly empower consumers and will force travel product suppliers to strive for excellence. It will also challenge grand narratives constructed by the media and large travel companies and will give consumers an opportunity to construct knowledge about a destination or product offering from a great number of diverse sources. In addition, this trend will likely change host-guest interactions, as the new consumers increasingly seek contact with the locals through these new forms of networked communication.

At the same time, a wealth of information creates a poverty of attention (Lewis and Bridger 2000). New tourism consumers try to cope with this problem by scanning information depending on personal relevance and have become very capable of ignoring nonrelevant advertising. They are, therefore, much more active in their travel information search than old consumers, who were largely passive information recipients. Attention is increasingly reserved for marketers who have asked for permission and have established a long-term relationship with the consumer (Godin 1999). In return for his/her valuable attention, the new tourism consumer expects special benefits such as extremely personalized services. Attention peaks when these travelers reach a psychologically balanced state of mind, a so-called flow experience (Feather 2000). In order to reach flow, new tourism consumers are increasingly searching for personalized, emotional, and intriguing experiences through which they can learn about new travel and tourism products. Therefore, in the world of the new tourism consumer, the focus shifts from product attributes to consumption experiences.

Trend # 5: Emergence of Experience as the Foundation for Defining Tourism Products

It has long been recognized that travel is an experience and that tourism is a key part of the "experience industry" (Pine, Gilmore, and Pine 1999). However, the role of experience in consumption (including prepurchase, during purchase, and postpurchase) is only now being considered as one of the foundations for effective marketing. Research efforts have shown that the experiential aspects of products and services provide the starting point for effective marketing (O'Sullivan and Spangler 1998; Pine et al. 1999; Schmitt 1999). This research indicates that experiences are personal "events" that engage the individual in a meaningful way. As shown in Figure 3, the core element of travel experiences is the travel activity, whereas the tourism industry plays the part of an experience "facilitator"; importantly, the setting (social or personal) in which activities occur contributes substantially to the nature of the experience. It has been suggested that although the experiential aspects of travel are the foundation, the memories that are stored as a result of these experiences are the key to attracting new visitors as well as retaining current ones. Furthermore, it is suggested that stories—the mechanisms for communicating experiences through word of mouth or as "documentaries" of experiences (through articles, film, etc.) provide the path through which the tourism industry can build and extend markets.

Schmitt (1999) and others have argued that the new consumer evaluates products more on their experiential aspects than on "objective" features such as price and availability and that experiential marketing should focus on the experiential aspects that make the consumption

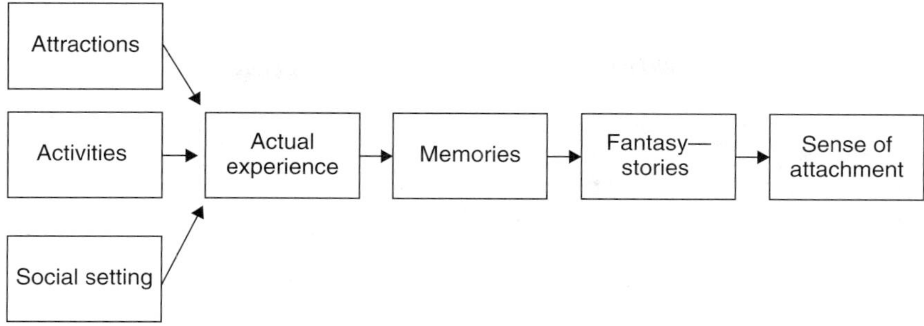

Figure 3: Sequence of travel experience

of the product most compelling—that is, the five senses. Effective experiential marketing is sensory and affective. It approaches consumption as a holistic experience and acknowledges that consumers can be either rational or emotional or both at the same time. Whereas traditional marketing is based on consumer behavior, product features, benefits, and quantifiable market segments, experiential marketing is driven by an understanding of consumer experiences and the need for personalization. New consumers require advertising that is entertaining, stimulating, and at the same time informative. Brands are no longer seen as mere identifiers but become themselves sources of experiences by evoking sensory, affective, creative, and lifestyle-related associations (Schmitt 1999). Thus, experiential marketing blurs the border between advertising, purchase, and use as it attempts to create a unique shopping experience and lets the new consumer anticipate what the consumption experience will be like.

CONCLUSION AND IMPLICATIONS FOR NETWORK TECHNOLOGY APPLICATIONS IN TOURISM

The Internet and emerging network technologies have had a profound impact on the tourism industry. The following briefly summarizes some expectations for the future role of these technologies in travel and tourism.

- Travel will continue to be one of the most popular online interests of consumers. This trend will increase in magnitude as travel providers create more effective means by which to communicate the nature of their offerings.
- The Internet and mobile communication devices are increasing the number of electronic connections between customers and the tourism industry. These new technologies will continue to provide an environment for creating relationships, allowing consumers to access information more efficiently, conducting transactions, and interacting electronically with businesses and suppliers. Examples of emerging technology in the travel industry include travel recommendation systems, travel guidance systems, and virtual reality.
- The changes in demographic profiles of Internet users over the past decade suggest that the evolving Internet and related systems will ultimately be adopted by the large majority of the traveling public and, therefore, the Internet will be considered the primary source for travel information.
- The demands of travelers, and in particular the purchase process(es) they use, will continue to evolve as consumers of travel products gain more experience and confidence in purchasing products over the Internet. Importantly, conversations among travelers (through travel clubs, virtual communities, etc.) will continue to grow and will increasingly be mediated through network technologies.
- Experience- and emotion-oriented communications will grow in importance as human-centric computing and emotionally intelligent interfaces are offered. These interfaces/systems will incorporate a variety of interpreted information, enabling the systems to recognize the information needs of the user within an emotional-psychological need context, in order to provide supportive interactions and suggestions.
- Blogging, podcasting, and social-networking technologies are expected to play an ever more important role in supporting travel-planning activities as well as the construction of memories and extended experiences in the postconsumption phase of travel. It is expected that there will be an increasing need to integrate such applications on tourism and travel Web sites.

As individuals become more mobile and also more reliant on network technologies, they will increasingly demand systems that can support their lifestyle during trips. Travelers will expect to be able to enjoy the same level of technology use on the road as they do at home. This means that systems have to become truly portable/wearable, wireless, global, integrated, and smart. Indeed, museums and hotel rooms provide ideal test-beds for networked applications such as ambient intelligence because of their limited range of user activities and their relatively small scale. Also, they can potentially serve as catalysts for the adoption of specific technologies, as they have the ability to expose applications to a significant number of potential users. Finally, increasing competition in the travel and tourism industry will force businesses to cooperate even more. Thus, the need for high-speed, reliable computer networking technology will not only be pushed by consumer needs but will also be driven by industry demands.

GLOSSARY

Blogging: The activity of writing entries to, adding content to, or maintaining a Web log (blog). A blog is an online publication with regular posts presented in reverse-chronological order.

Central Reservation System (CRS): A system that provides access to information about airline, hotel, or rental company inventories and is used for sales, marketing, and ticketing purposes. The elements of a CRS include a central processing unit, a central database, and a communications network that links information providers and users to the central information storage and processing system.

Consumer-Generated Media (CGM): Opinions, experiences, advice, or commentary related to products, companies, or destinations generated by consumers in the form of text, photos, and audio or video files and posted in product review sections on Web sites, blogs, virtual communities, discussion boards, etc.

Customer Relationship Management (CRM): A set of business principles with the aim of strengthening a tourism organization's relationships with its clients, optimizing customer service levels, and obtaining customer information that can be used for marketing purposes.

Destination-Management System (DMS): The information technology infrastructure used by destination marketing organizations to support a wide range of promotion, sales, and advertising efforts. Typical elements of such systems are technologies to design and produce printed materials, tourist information center services (including information and reservation systems), call-center services, kiosks, database marketing applications, project/event management software, and marketing research applications.

Destination Marketing Organization (DMO): An organization with responsibility for marketing a specific tourism destination to the travel trade and to individual travelers.

Distribution Channel: A set of interdependent organizations, such as tour operators or travel agents, involved in the process of making tourism products or services available to consumers.

En Route Information: Information obtained while traveling, as opposed to information collected before or after the trip; mainly used for navigational purposes or to support short-term decision making during the actual vacation.

Flow: A seamless, intrinsically enjoyable, self-reinforcing, and captivating psychological experience occurring when there is an optimal match between the challenge at hand and one's skills.

Global Distribution System (GDS): A system that links several central reservation systems, thus providing much more global coverage than individual computerized reservation systems.

Human-Centric Computing: The process of designing, developing, and implementing information technology that reflects the needs and lifestyles of its human users.

Intermediary: A third-party organization such as a travel agent, tour operator, incoming agent, hotel chain, or CRS/GDS provider that facilitates information transfer and/or transactions between the primary suppliers and consumers of tourism products and services.

Podcasting: A term used to refer to the technologies used for automatically distributing audio and video programs over the Internet.

Telepresence: A mental state in which a user feels physically present within a remote, computer-mediated environment.

Tourism Experience: The sum of sensory, cognitive, and emotional inputs derived from the activities pursued during a vacation.

Travel and Tourism Industry: The individuals and organizations that are involved in the production and distribution of travel and tourism-related products.

Travel Decision Support System (TDSS): An information system designed to simplify the travel decision-making process and support consumers in the various steps involved in planning trips.

Virtual Travel Community: A community facilitated by computer-mediated communication that allows its members to conduct various types of travel-related tasks, such as obtaining travel information, maintaining connections, finding travel companions, or simply having fun by telling each other interesting stories about travel experiences.

Virtual Tour: A tool that enables the potential consumers of tourism products to explore and immerse themselves within an interactive Web environment in order to gain the needed experiential information about a destination or tourism establishment.

Yield-Management System: Powerful computer system using advanced mathematical modeling and predictive algorithms that manage pricing and availability information for tourism companies including airlines, hotels, and attractions.

CROSS REFERENCES

See *Electronic Commerce; Electronic Payment Systems; Mobile Commerce; The Internet Fundamentals.*

REFERENCES

Brownlie, D., M. Saren, R. Whittinton, and R. Wensley. 1994. The new marketing myopia: Critical perspectives on theory and research in marketing—Introduction. *European Journal of Marketing* 28(3):6–12.

Buhalis, D. 2004. eAirlines: Strategic and tactical use of ICTs in the airline industry. *Information and Management* 41(7):805–25.

Cho, Y., and D. R. Fesenmaier. 2001. A new paradigm for tourism and electronic commerce: Experience marketing using the virtual tour. In *Tourism distribution channels: Practices, issues and transformations,* edited by E. Laws and D. Buhalis, 351–70. New York: CAB International.

ClickZ.com. 2005. Population explosion! www.clickz.com/stats/web_worldwide/print.php/151151 (accessed December 7, 2005).

Cline, R. 2001. The future of hospitality e-business: How the Internet has changed the hotel industry. *Lodging Hospitality* 57(7):24–30.

Connolly, D., and M. Olsen. 1999. *Hospitality technology in the new millennium: Findings of the IH&RA Think-Tanks on Technology.* Paris: International Hotel & Restaurant Association.

Connolly, D., M. Olsen, and R. G. Moore. 1998. The Internet as a distribution channel. *Cornell Hotel and Restaurant Administrative Quarterly* August:42–54.

Connolly, D., and M. Sigala. 2001. Major trends and IT issues facing the hospitality industry in the new economy: A review of the 5th Annual Pan-European Hospitality Technology Exhibition and Conference. *International Journal of Tourism Research* 3:325–7.

Cronin, M. J. 1995. *Doing business on the Internet*. New York: Van Nostrand Reinhold.

Day, G. S. 1998. Organizing for interactivity. *Journal of Interactive Marketing* 12(1):47–53.

Delgado, J., and R. Davidson. 2002. Knowledge bases and user profiling in travel and hospitality recommender systems. In *Information and Communication Technologies in Tourism 2002, Proceedings of the Annual Conference of the International Federation of Information Technology and Tourism,* edited by K. Wöber, A. J. Frew, and M. Hitz, 1–16. Vienna, Austria: Springer-Verlag.

Dellaert, B. G. C., D. F. Ettema, and C. Lindh. 1998. Multi-faceted tourist travel decisions: A constraints-based conceptual framework to describe tourists' sequential choices of travel components. *Tourism Management* 19(4):313–20.

Dertouzos, M. 2001. *The unfinished revolution*. New York: HarperCollins.

eMarketer. 1999. *eAdvertising Report Volume II*. www.emarketer.com (accessed December 23, 2002).

eMarketer. 2005. High-flying online travel segment gets down to business. www.emarketer.com (accessed March 9, 2005).

Eriksson, O. 2002. Location based destination information for the mobile tourist. In *Information and Communication Technologies in Tourism 2002, Proceedings of the Annual Conference of the International Federation of Information Technology and Tourism,* edited by K. Wöber, A. J. Frew, and M. Hitz, 255–64. Vienna, Austria: Springer-Verlag.

European Travel Commission. 2005. *New media review—Markets by country*. www.etcnewmedia.com (accessed December 5, 2005).

Evans, P., and T. S. Wurster. 1999. *Blown to bits.* Boston: Harvard Business School Press.

EyeforTravel. 2005. A strategic analysis of the travel search engine (TSE) market. www.eyefortravel.com/reports.asp (accessed September 2, 2005).

EyeforTravel. 2005. The ultimate travel search engine. www.eyefortravel.com/index.asp?news=45463 (accessed August 4, 2005).

Feather, F. 2000. *FutureConsumer.Com.* Toronto: Warwick.

Forrester Research. 1999. *Forrester Report: Dynamic trade voyage*. www.forrester.com/Voyage/PDF/0,2236,4823,00.pdf (accessed December 23, 2002).

Gartrell, R. 1988. *Destination marketing for convention and visitor bureaus*. Dubuque, IA: Kendall/Hunt.

Godin, S. 1999. *Permission marketing.* New York: Simon & Schuster.

Goeldner, C. R., and J. R. B. Ritchie. 2002. *Tourism: Principles, practices, philosophies*. 9th ed. New York: Wiley.

Good, N., J. B. Schafer, J. Konstan, A. Borchers, B. Sarwar, J. Herlocker, and J. Riedl. 1999. Combining collaborative filtering with personal agents for better recommendations. In *Proceedings of the Sixteenth National Conference on Artificial Intelligence and Eleventh Conference on Innovative Applications of Artificial Intelligence,* edited by J. Hendler, D. Subramanian, R. Uthurusamy, and B. Hayes-Roth, 439–46. Menlo Park, CA: AAAI Press.

Gretzel, U., D. R. Fesenmaier, and J. T. O'Leary. 2006. Searching for the future: Challenges facing destination marketing organizations. *Journal of Travel Research* 45(2):116–26.

Gretzel, U., Y.-H. Hwang, and D. R. Fesenmaier. 2006. A behavioral framework for destination recommendation systems design. In *Destination recommendation systems: Behavioral foundations and applications,* edited by D. R. Fesenmaier, H. Werthner, and K. Wöber. Cambridge, MA: CAB International.

Hanson, W. 2000. *Principles of Internet marketing.* Cincinnati: South-Western College.

Hibbard, J. 1997. Straight line to relevant data. *Information Week* 657:21–5.

Hitwise. 2005. Travel search engines rapid rise poses threat to travel agencies. www.hitwise.com/info/news/hitwiseHS2004/travel_search.html (accessed September 4, 2005).

Hoffman, D., and T. Novak. 1996, July. Marketing in hypermedia computer-mediated environments: Conceptual foundations. *Journal of Marketing* 60:50–68.

Hoffman, D., T. Novak, and P. Chatterjee. 1995. *Commercial scenarios for the Web: Opportunities and challenges*. www.ascusc.org/jcmc/vol1/issue3/hoffman.html (accessed December 20, 2002).

Hruschka, H., and J. Mazanec. 1990. Computer-assisted travel counseling. *Annals of Tourism Research* 17:208–27.

Hwang, Y.-H., and D. R. Fesenmaier. 2001. Collaborative filtering: Strategies for travel destination bundling. In *Information and Communication Technologies in Tourism 2001, Proceedings of the Annual Conference of the International Federation of Information Technology and Tourism,* edited by P. Sheldon, K. Wöber, and D. R. Fesenmaier, 167–75. Vienna, Austria: Springer-Verlag.

Information Society Technologies Advisory Group. 2001. *Scenarios for ambient intelligence in 2010*. ftp://ftp.cordis.lu/pub/ist/docs/istagscenarios2010.pdf (accessed December 20, 2002).

Inkpen, G. 1998. *Information technology for travel and tourism*. Singapore: Addison Wesley Longman.

Jarach, D. 2002. The digitalization of market relationships in the airline business: the impact and prospects of e-business. *Journal of Air Transportation Management* 8(2):115–20.

Jeng, J.-M., and D. R. Fesenmaier. 2002. Conceptualizing the travel decision-making hierarchy: A review of recent developments. *Tourism Analysis* 7(1):15–32.

Klein, S., and T. J. Langenohl. 1994. Co-ordination mechanisms and systems architectures in electronic market systems. In *Information and Communication Technologies in Tourism 1994, Proceedings of the Annual Conference of the International Federation of Information Technology and Tourism,* edited by W. Schertler, B. Schmid, A. M. Tjoa, and H. Werthner, 262–70. Vienna, Austria: Springer-Verlag.

Kotler, P., J. Bowen, and J. Makens. 1999. *Marketing for hospitality and tourism.* 2nd ed. Upper Saddle River, NJ: Prentice-Hall.

Lewis, D., and D. Bridger. 2000. *The soul of the new consumer.* London: Nicholas Brealey.

Loban, S. 1997. A framework for computer-assisted travel counseling, *Annals of Tourism Research* 24(4):813–31.

Mayros, V., and D. M. Werner. 1982. *Marketing information systems: Design and applications for marketers.* Radnor, PA: Chilton.

McGuffie, J. 1994. CRS development in the hotel sector. *EIU Travel and Tourism Analyst* 2:53–68.

McIvor, R., D. O'Reilly, and S. Ponsonby. 2003. The impact of Internet technologies on the airline industry: Current strategies and future developments. *Strategic Change* 12(1):31–47.

Miller, M. J. 2002, March 12. Living history—Retracing the evolution of the PC and *PC Magazine*. *PC Magazine* 137–59.

Mitsche, N. 2001. Personalized traveling counseling system: Providing decision support features for travelers. In *Information and Communication Technologies in Tourism 2001, Proceedings of the Annual Conference of the International Federation of Information Technology and Tourism,* edited by P. Sheldon, K. Wöber, and D. R. Fesenmaier, 160–6. Vienna, Austria: Springer-Verlag.

Morrison, A. M., S. Taylor, A. J. Morrison, and D. Morrison. 1999. Marketing small hotels on the World Wide Web. *Information Technology and Tourism* 2(2):35–44.

Moutinho, L. 1987. Consumer behavior in tourism. *European Journal of Marketing* 21:2–44.

Muniz, A. M., and T. C. O'Guinn. 2000, March. Brand community. *Journal of Consumer Research* 27:227–35.

Newell, F. 2000. *Loyalty.com.* New York: McGraw-Hill.

Norman, D. A. 1999. *The invisible computer: Why good products can fail, the personal computer is so complex and information appliances are the solution.* Cambridge, MA: MIT Press.

Nyheim, P., F. McFadden, and D. Connolly. 2004. *Technology strategies for the hospitality industry.* Upper Saddle River, NJ: Pearson Prentice Hall.

Oertel, B., K. Steinmüller, and M. Kuom. 2002. Mobile multimedia services for tourism. In *Information and Communication Technologies in Tourism 2002, Proceedings of the Annual Conference of the International Federation of Information Technology and Tourism,* edited by K. Wöber, A. J. Frew, and M. Hitz, 265–74. Vienna, Austria: Springer-Verlag.

O'Sullivan, E. L., and K. J. Spangler. 1998. *Experience marketing*. State College, PA: Venture.

Parsons, A., M. Zeisser, and R. Waitman. 1998. Organizing today for the digital marketing of tomorrow. *Journal of Interactive Marketing* 12(1):31–46.

Pew Internet & American Life Project. 2006, *February-March 2006 data set*. www.pewinternet.org/datasets.asp (accessed July 12, 2007).

Pew Internet & American Life Project. 2007. *Home broadband adoption 2007*. www.pewinternet.org/PPF/r/217/report_display.asp (accessed July 12, 2007).

Pew Internet & American Life Project. 2007. *Internet activities*. www.pewinternet.org/trends/Internet_Activities_6.15.07.htm (accessed July 12, 2007).

Pine, B. J., J. H. Gilmore, and B. J. Pine II. 1999. *The experience economy.* Boston: Harvard Business School Press.

Poon, A. 1993. *Tourism, technology and competitive strategies*. Wallingford, UK: CAB International.

Poslad, S., H. Laamanen, R. Malaka, A. Nick, P. Buckle, and A. Zipf. 2001. CRUMPET: Creation of user-friendly mobile services personalized for tourism. In *Proceedings of 3G 2001*. London: Institution of Electrical Engineers. www.eml.villa-bosch.de/english/homes/zipf/3g-crumpet2001.pdf (accessed December, 22, 2002).

Rheingold, H. 1994. A slice of life in my virtual community. In *Global networks: Computers and international communications,* edited by L. M. Harasim, 57–80. Cambridge, MA: MIT Press.

Ricci, F., and H. Werthner. 2001. Cased-based destination recommendations over an XML data repository. In *Information and Communication Technologies in Tourism 2001, Proceedings of the Annual Conference of the International Federation of Information Technology and Tourism,* edited by P. Sheldon, K. Wöber, and D. R. Fesenmaier, 150–9. Vienna, Austria: Springer-Verlag.

Schmidt-Belz, B., M. Makelainen, A. Nick, and S. Poslad. 2002. Intelligent brokering of tourism services for mobile users. In *Information and Communication Technologies in Tourism 2002, Proceedings of the Annual Conference of the International Federation of Information Technology and Tourism,* edited by K. Wöber, A. J. Frew, and M. Hitz, 265–74. Vienna, Austria: Springer-Verlag.

Schmitt, B. H. 1999. *Experiential marketing: How to get customers to sense, feel, think, act, and relate to your company and brands*. New York: Free Press.

Schwartz, E. I. 1998. *Webonomics: Nine essential principles for growing your business on the World Wide Web*. New York: Broadway Books.

Sheldon, P. J. 1997. *Tourism information technology*. Wallingford, UK: CAB International.

Sterne, J. 1999. *World Wide Web marketing*. New York: Wiley.

Travel Industry Association of America. 2005. *Travelers' use of the Internet.* Washington, DC: Travel Industry Association of America.

USC Annenberg School Center for the Digital Future. 2005. *Digital Future Project 2005*. www.digitalcenter.org (accessed December 8, 2005).

Vanhof, K., and I. Molderez. 1994. An advice system for travel agents. In *Information and Communication Technologies in Tourism 1994, Proceedings of the Annual Conference of the International Federation of Information Technology and Tourism,* edited by W. Schertler et al., 126–32. Vienna, Austria: Springer-Verlag.

Vogt, C. A., and D. R. Fesenmaier. 1998. Expanding the functional information search model. *Annals of Tourism Research* 25(3):551–78.

Wang, Y., and D. R. Fesenmaier. 2002. *Assessing Web marketing strategies: Approaches, issues, and implications: A report on the results of national survey of city and county tourism organizations in the United States of America*. Champaign, IL: National Laboratory for Tourism and eCommerce, University of Illinois.

Wang, Y., and D. R. Fesenmaier. 2006. Identifying the success factors of Web-based marketing strategy: An investigation of convention and visitors bureaus in the United States. *Journal of Travel Research* 44(3):239–49.

Wang, Y., Q. Yu, and D. R. Fesenmaier. 2002. Defining the virtual tourist community: Implications for tourism marketing. *Tourism Management* 23:407–17.

Werthner, H., and S. Klein. 1999. *Information technology and tourism—A challenging relationship*. Vienna, Austria: Springer-Verlag.

Wind, Y., R. Mahajan, and R. Gunther. 2002. *Convergence marketing*. Upper Saddle River, NJ: Prentice Hall.

Windham, L., and K. Orton. 2000. *The soul of the new consumer.* New York: Allworth Press.

Wiseman, C. 1985. *Strategy and computers: Information systems as competitive weapons*. Homewood, IL: Dow Jones–Irwin.

Woodside, A. G., and R. MacDonald. 1994. General system framework of customer choice processes of tourism services. In *Spoilt for choice. Decision making processes and preference change of tourists: Intertemporal and intercountry perspectives,* edited by V. Gasser and K. Weiermair, 30–59. Thaur, Austria: Kulturverlag.

World Tourism Organization. 2005. *Tourism highlights*. 2005 edition. www.world-tourism.org/facts/menu.html (accessed December 5, 2005).

World Tourism Organization Business Council. 1999, September. *Marketing tourism destinations online*. Madrid: Author.

World Travel and Tourism Council. 2005. *Sowing the seeds of growth—The 2005 travel & tourism economic research*. London: Author.

Yuan, Y., and D. R. Fesenmaier. 2000. Preparing for the new economy: The use of the Internet and intranet in American convention and visitor bureaus. *Information Technology and Tourism* 3(2):71–86.

Yuan, Y., U. Gretzel, and D. R. Fesenmaier. 2006. The role of information technology use in American convention and visitors bureaus. *Tourism Management* 27(2):326–41.

Zeff, R., and B. Aronson. 1999. *Advertising on the Internet*. 2nd ed. New York: Wiley.

Web-Based Training

Patrick J.Fahy, *Athabasca University, Canada*

INTRODUCTION

Web-based training (WBT) is learning at a distance using online training methods and delivery technologies. WBT is a subset of distance education, providing current content, adaptable and flexible access, and collaboration and interaction opportunities with other learners, tutors, and knowledge sources, potentially worldwide. Mobile learning (m-learning), the use of portable computing and communications devices, and pervasive computing, in which all aspects of a job or work environment are interconnected, are outgrowths of WBT (Leiner et al. 2002; Mobile learning 2004). WBT is grounded in the proven capacity of well-designed and well-moderated computer-mediated communications (CMC) to create and sustain effective collaborative and cooperative learning environments at a distance (Fulford and Zhang 1993; Rose 2004; Giguere, Formica, and Harding 2004).

Another key to WBT is the World Wide Web (www). The Web was at least occasionally available to 45 percent of the world's population in 2003 (OECD 2005), and in 2006 over a billion people were regarded as "Internet users" (Internet usage statistics 2006). The "digital divide" (between technology haves and have-nots) was even disappearing, according to some observers, early in the twenty-first century (Rupley 2005; Cheap tricks 2005).

The story of WBT is not without its ups and downs, however: the Web as a training tool has had both spectacular successes and disasters. While institutions such as the University of Phoenix, Concord Law School, the University of Monterey, and Canada's Athabasca University were successfully using online methods to offer courses throughout North and Latin America and Mexico, others (Columbia, Wharton School, Temple University, and NYU) were experiencing expensive failures with WBT (Higher Education Inc. 2005).

The theme of this chapter is that, as a training tool, the Web is potentially powerful, providing access to flexible, timely, relevant, and interpersonally satisfying collaborative training opportunities, including superior content learning and a sense of membership in an online community (Hiltz, Johnson, and Rabke 1980; Rovai and Barnum 2003; Fahy 2004; Conrad 2005). Wherever flexible training and professional development (PD) are central to organizations or nations, WBT can offer access to upgrading, training, retraining, and varied lifelong learning opportunities. Accompanying WBT's strengths, however, are potential challenges or outright shortcomings (Dede 1996; Barns' storming 2005).

Potential advantages of WBT include:

- WBT is available anyplace and anytime, reducing time and travel-subsistence costs, and increasing learner control (Kaye 1989; Wagner, 1994; Bates 1995; Harapniuk, Montgomerie, and Torgerson 1998; Rovai and Barnum 2003; Don't take my PC 2004).
- Skillful e-moderating and instructing strategies can produce an interpersonal experience equal, or even superior, to face-to-face learning, especially when traditional courses are crowded or instructors overworked (Walther 1996).
- Centrally stored materials can be continually and immediately revised and updated, ensuring accuracy and currency.
- Use of markup languages (HTML, XML, SGML), and other interoperability provisions that are part of the Web's history of openness, ensure cross-platform compatibility.

Challenges of WBT include:

- Training materials must be carefully designed, or redesigned, for Web delivery; a sometimes substantial initial investment may have to be made in equipment and training (including potentially costly content managements systems [CMSs] and learning management systems [LMSs]); and trainees and instructors may have to learn new technical (and teaching-learning) skills (Welsch 2002).
- Structure must be provided in the learning environment to prevent users from wasting time, or straying into misinformation (Warren et al. 1996). The concept of e-moderating, the use of online methods for assessing and responding to trainees' needs for guidance, feedback, motivation, and human contact, arises from the fact that users do not always or automatically use WBT technologies skillfully or willingly.
- Bandwidth and technical limitations may restrict or even prohibit access to some Web resources.
- Dropout rates may be a problem in WBT, if users' problems are not monitored and addressed.

In this chapter, the history, characteristics, potentials, and challenges of WBT will be reviewed. Included will be a discussion of some important underlying general training principles critical to the evolution of WBT, the Web's strengths and limitations for delivering learning opportunities, features (and limitations) of some of the technologies WBT draws upon, and future prospects of WBT.

FUNDAMENTAL TRAINING PRINCIPLES AND WBT

In the first half of the twentieth century, the pioneering work of researchers such as Thorndike (1971), Dewey (1938), Skinner (1971), and Keller (1968) led to the articulation of fundamental learning principles. (These individuals researched and wrote in the fields of psychology and education, but their theories have been incorporated into the design of effective teaching of all kinds, including WBT.)

Thorndike's three fundamental behavioral laws, now common in WBT, were among the first to be stated: (1) repetition strengthens new behaviors; (2) reward associated with a particular behavior increases the likelihood it will be repeated, while punishment or lack of reward diminishes the likelihood of recurrence; and (3) individuals often differ in their personal readiness to perform a new skill or behavior (Saettler 1990).

Dewey added that individual trainee differences were crucial in the success of training. He and Piaget (1952) both recognized the importance of each individual learner's personal background, and advocated that trainees' experiences and previous learning be considered carefully and accommodated as much as possible in any new training situation.

Skinner applied and extended behavioral principles, with the "teaching machines" movement of the 1950s and 1960s. In behavioral psychology, the trainer was "the manager of the contingencies of reinforcement" in the learning process. Besides describing the instructor's role in a new way, Skinner's work illustrated points vital to the subsequent development of technology-based training, including the value of "the program over the hardware," and the critical importance of the learning materials and the organization of the learning environment (Saettler 1990).

Keller's Individually Programmed Instruction (IPI) model applied Skinner's discoveries about the importance of instructional design. The IPI model (called the "Keller Plan") emphasized individual differences in instruction and evaluation, including principles, later core to WBT, such as self-pacing, mastery before advancement, high-quality materials, tutoring help, prompt feedback, and careful and frequent evaluation, including practice testing (Fox 2002). Experiments such as teaching Morse code to World War II recruits demonstrated convincingly that these principles could dramatically increase the efficiency of procedural and skill training.

Innovations such as IPI were impressive, but they encountered organizational resistance for several significant reasons that are relevant to WBT:

- As innovations, technology-based training models often make new demands on institutions, trainers, and trainees. In particular, technology-based training delivery increases the responsibility of trainees for their own learning, while limiting instructors' "platform" opportunities, serious flaws in the eyes of some trainers (and some trainees).
- Evaluations of technological innovations may initially yield "no significant difference" findings (www.nosignificantdifference.org); time may be needed to reveal their true value.
- Tepid managerial support may doom a technological innovation, especially if time and resources to prove its actual potential are in any way lacking.
- Individualized training models usually require more advance planning and preparation, while (at least initially) increasing workloads on instructors and administrators, and resource demands on programs, and while sometimes destabilizing programs during the adjustment phase.
- When granted responsibility for managing their own learning, some trainees may respond with demands for more individual treatment, including remedial and accelerated options. Overall, in individualized programs, including WBT, trainees expect their individual performance, needs, and preferences to be acknowledged and better met than in typical in face-to-face group training.

In the 1960s and 1970s, continued developments in instructional design, emerging consensus about "best practices" in adult learning, advances in cognitive and behavioral psychology, and new tools and approaches for the design and delivery of training converged to impact the emerging field of technology-based training and WBT. Other figures whose work influenced the evolution of technology-based training include Mager (1975), Suppes (1978), Glaser (1978), Gagne and Briggs (1979), Briggs and Wager (1981), and Dick and Carey (1978).

ASPECTS OF THE WEB AS A TRAINING TOOL

WBT's Payoffs and Demands

The Web emerged as a potentially powerful training tool, as training was transformed by new understandings of learning itself, and appreciation increased of the needs of trainees and training organizations (Biesenbach-Lucas 2004; Biuk-Aghai and Simoff 2004; Burbules and Callister 1998; Garrison, Anderson, and Archer 2000). Users responded to the Web's training potential differently, at least in part according to their appreciation of the importance of skill-training. Table 1 shows the range of possible engagement in training, from initial awareness to maintenance of a systematic training effort.

The potential of WBT to address critical training needs comes with costs, in the form of challenges to instructors and learners: different roles and responsibilities, changes in teaching methods and the learning environment, emphasis on individual differences, new financial and economic realities, and unprecedented security requirements.

Table 1: Employer Training Engagement Continuum

Stage 1	Stage 2	Stage 3	Stage 4	Stage 5
Gaining awareness of the general importance of skills	Recognizing and understanding the significance to their own organization	Making choices—to act or not to act?	Taking action—involving Sector Councils	Maintaining or increasing the training effort

Reprinted from Conference Board of Canada (2005, 3). Used with permission.

New Roles, Practices, Tools

Web-based training creates changes in the ways trainees interact with the trainer, the content, each other, and the learning system (Moore 1989). Because WBT allows shifting of place and pace of learning, roles change; the focus is on the trainees' skill development, and the tutor or trainer consequently becomes less the "sage on the stage" and more a "guide on the side" (Burge and Roberts 1993). Similarly, if permitted, equipped, and disposed to do so, trainees may assume more responsibility for their own learning, including accessing outside materials, communicating freely with the trainer, and collaborating with other trainees. Overall, successful WBT programs change trainees' experiences, providing greater individualization; making feasible self-pacing, on-demand review, acceleration, and practice testing; and providing ready linkages to a range of people and resources (Molinari 2004).

Because of the differences between online and traditional delivery, trainers in Web-based environments may find their duties and priorities changed. A study by the National Education Association (2000) of U.S. college instructors in a variety of institutions found that:

- Most reported WBT was more personally rewarding than traditional methods: distance methods were seen as giving trainees better access to information, better-quality materials, more help in mastering the subject matter, and more allowance for individual needs.
- Most instructors had at least some one-on-one contact with their Web-based learners, and those who had such contact reported higher levels of satisfaction.
- WBT required more instructor time, which, unfortunately, most training organizations did not formally recognize.
- Despite lack of organizational recognition of the greater time required, almost three-quarters of the survey respondents held positive feelings about distance teaching (14 percent reported negative feelings).

Materials and Instructional Activities

In traditional face-to-face teaching, instructional materials may be prepared at the last minute, or even simply dispensed with (trainees being required to take notes from the comments and chalkboard musings of the instructor). In WBT, materials preparation is a major stage in program development. Complete WBT materials are self-contained, including organizers and instructions, with guidance and feedback provided through embedded questions and other self-evaluation activities, and computer-mediated communications (CMC) with the instructor and other learners. Support and orientation are provided for the technologies used.

In well-designed and well-managed WBT, instructional activities and materials may use some or all of the following principles:

- Typically, a wider range of resources, some from outside the local environment (accessed via the Web)
- Experiential learning and simulations
- Collaboration replacing competition (Collins and Berge 1996).
- Problem- or case-based learning, increasing training's realism and authenticity (students are permitted, even urged, to refine questions and objectives themselves, without constant reliance on the trainer) (Berge 1995).
- Personal knowledge and experience valued and included in problem-solving activities (Newby et al. 2000).

Multimedia are sometimes used to enhance WBT experiences; the impact of multimedia ultimately depends on recognition of certain design principles that govern their impact (Mayer 2001). These principles underscore the importance of systematic design and monitoring of WBT. Failure to produce instructional materials based on sound learning principles results in, among other errors, the amateurish use of effects for their own sake (contemptuously called "dancing baloney" by Web professionals) (HIP 2000, 2000). Failure to monitor learners' responses results in greater transactional distance in the learning environment (Moore 1991), potentially leading to alienation and, in the worst cases, dropout (Frankola 2001).

New tools, such as blogs and podcasting, allow instructors and trainees to develop and "broadcast" (via Internet RSS feeds) audio programs on any subject, downloadable to portable devices (iPods) or PCs. These are examples of how technologies offer new possibilities for delivery of training, and, because of their ready availability, make sound instructional design in serious training programs even more important (Magid 2005, DIY).

"Best" Instructional Practices in WBT

Well-designed WBT incorporates specific strategies known to enhance learning. One training model recommends that trainers strive for a balance between interpersonal rapport and intellectual excitement, requiring the trainer to be interpersonally warm, open, reliable, and learner-centered, while also being clear and enthusiastic about the training content (Lowman 1994).

Another well-respected model suggests the following best instructional practices, applicable to WBT (Chickering and Gamson 1989):

- Encourage contacts between trainees and instructors.
- Develop reciprocity and cooperation among trainees.
- Use active learning techniques.
- Give proper and timely feedback.
- Emphasize time-on-task.
- Communicate high expectations.
- Respect diverse talents and ways of learning.

Bloom's (1984) classic description of the "alterable variables" of learning also provides guidance for Web-based developers and trainers. Research in mastery learning showed that the following principles, when emphasized, produced learning outcomes similar to what could be achieved under ideal training conditions (defined as one-to-one tutorials):

- Provide well-designed tutorial instruction.
- Give timely reinforcement.
- Give appropriate and sensitive corrective feedback.
- Provide cues and explanations, as needed.
- Encourage learner participation.
- Assure trainees make effective use of time on task.
- Help trainees improve reading and study skills, as required.

In general, adult education pedagogical principles of relevance, immediacy, learner control, autonomy, self-direction, self-pacing, and individualization are core to WBT practice (Kidd 1973; Knowles 1978; Cross 1981). One of the major differences between Web-based and more traditional forms of training is WBT's capacity for accommodating the individual expectations and preferences of trainees. This feature can be particularly valuable in meeting diagnosed "special" needs, or needs based on adult trainees' personal and situational variables. Personal variables include age, maturity, personal health, time availability (and management skills), motivation, previous learning, financial circumstances, and life and developmental stages. Situational variables include location (related to the location of any required site-based training), admission and training program requirements, availability of counseling and advisement services, and personal issues such as transportation, health, and child-care (Cross 1981).

WBT's capacity to accommodate differences effectively partially depends on the trainees' capacity and willingness to exercise independence, autonomy, and self-direction. Even if trainees are mature adults, the presence of the needed skills and confidence for self-directed learning cannot always be assumed. Trainees must be able and willing to exercise self-direction and independence in learning.

The needs analysis component of the design process is particularly critical, as problems can arise in WBT situations when there is a mismatch between the self-direction the learning system permits or requires and the expectations of the trainees. As previously noted, mismatches between teaching or training style and learning style can result in dissatisfaction with the learning experience, or worse (alienation, failure, dropout). Programs are more successful if aligned with the developmental stages of individual learners. Trainee readiness may range from nearly complete dependency to autonomous self-direction, requiring the trainer to function variously as an authority or coach, a motivator or guide, a facilitator or mentor, and, at the highest levels of self-direction, a consultant (Grow 1991). Failure to provide learning conditions compatible with trainees' expectations for support, interaction, or recognition may be one of the principal reasons for unacceptably high dropout rates in some WBT programs (Frankola 2001).

Economic Factors

The economics of WBT, though changing rapidly in the details, continue to directly impact training providers and consumers.

For Providers

Skills requirements continue to increase, motivating employers to retain proven employees with the potential to grow with the expectations of their jobs (see Figure 1).

While the economic argument for training is strong, costs of development of WBT can be considerable, and vary dramatically. Primarily text-based WBT, involving conversion of existing materials using one of the many available authoring tools, may be economically accomplished by a subject-matter expert (SME) possessing basic instructional design skills. On the other hand, development of 1 hour of computer-assisted learning (CAL) using high-level authoring languages might require up to 150 hours of design and programming (Szabo 1998). Financial considerations are primary in most WBT implementations: if an organization cannot afford the attendant costs (especially the often heavy initial investment in development), it may not be able to make the transition to WBT, even if the need is clear and the organization willing (Welsch 2002). Bates (2000) argues cogently that costs and accessibility are the two governing criteria in the successful adoption of technology; the same could reasonably be argued for WBT.

WBT must be promoted realistically, without overselling the possible benefits or impacts. Although WBT offers the potential for substantial increases in convenience and improvements in efficiency (including reduced training costs), it is important to acknowledge that results of WBT cannot be guaranteed to be better for all users. This is because of interactions among economic, technical, personal, organizational, and environmental factors. One of the paradoxes of the past decade's use of technology generally, including training applications, has been the persistent finding of "no significant difference" in training results, accompanied by the "productivity paradox," the failure of some industries to achieve economic benefits from technology implementations, while others made impressive performance gains (Fahy 1998). Nevertheless, when design converges advantageously with needs,

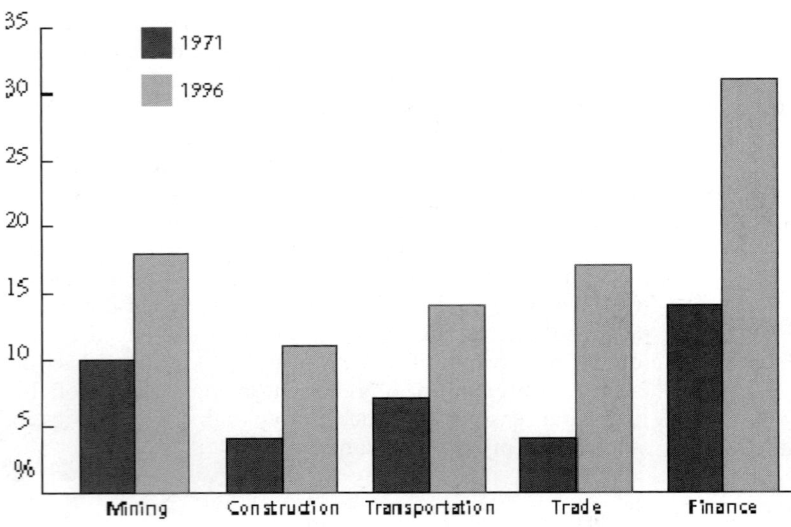

Figure 1: Skills requirements keep rising across all sectors—knowledge and management jobs as a share of total employment, 1971–1996 (*Source:* Human Resources and Skills Development Canada, 2002, p. 37. Reproduced with the permission of Her Majesty the Queen in Right of Canada 2006.)

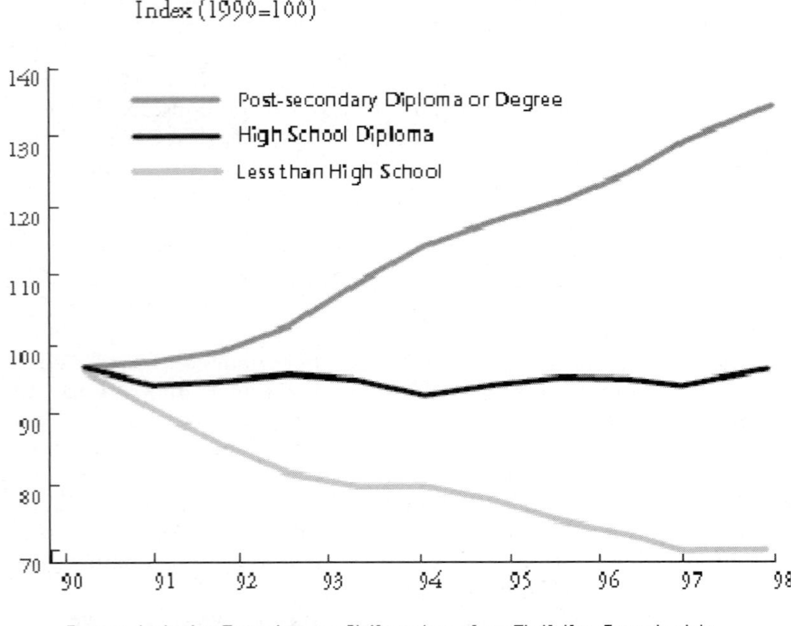

Figure 2: Employment growth by highest level of education (*Source:* Human Resources and Skills Development Canada, 2002, p. 7. Reproduced with the permission of Her Majesty the Queen in Right of Canada 2006.)

opportunities, and a willing corporate culture, WBT has proven both successful and cost-effective (Welsch 2002).

For Trainees

Just as employers have seen the value of trained and skilled employees increase, employees are also aware that their prospects are directly related to their skills, as shown in Figure 2.

As they have become increasingly aware of the need for personal skill training, employees have also come to expect that the workplace will provide timely, economical, high-quality, self-paced training, virtually anytime and anywhere (Vaas 2001). The keys to meeting these expectations are the cost and accessibility of the WBT technologies used (Bates 2000), and the relevance of WBT's interaction capabilities with respect to specific training applications (Fischer 1997; Inculcating culture 2006).

For trainees with "special" learning needs, WBT's interaction capabilities can provide important advantages. The mobility-handicapped, and those with learning disabilities, often find an environment with more learner controls, typical of WBT, helpful (Keller 1999). Two core features of WBT directly applicable to special-needs trainees include:

- Structure, including advance organizers; clearly stated objectives, schedules, and timelines; embedded comprehension checks; integrated media under learner control; multimodal presentations; user-accessible performance records and reports; and communication links with the trainer and other support resources.
- Flexibility—any place, any pace access.

Trainers working with special-needs audiences must have enhanced capabilities to monitor progress, including easy communications with other helpers and supports. Trainees without special needs can also benefit from features of WBT, as these can potentially increase satisfaction and lower stress in general by reducing potential conflicts between the demands of training and participants' careers and personal lives. WBT's emphasis on interaction may help address:

- Feelings of inadequacy at the sheer amount of material to be covered.
- Delays in receiving feedback or answers to questions.
- Keeping up with the variety of discussions and interaction often present in online (computer-mediated communications, or CMC) discussions.
- Adjusting to the absence of visual cues in group relations.
- Fatigue and health problems arising from reliance on unfamiliar technologies (eye strain or posture problems at the computer, for example).

Security Issues

System and Personal Security

Security is a critical element of Web-based systems in general, and of training systems in particular, especially wireless systems. By one estimate, malware of all kinds caused $55 billion in losses to Web users in 2003. Since 2003, damaging and hard-to-detect worms and Trojan horses have become the most common forms of malicious code. The threat is increasing: the virus-to-e-mail ratio was expected to go from 1 in 700 in 2000, to 1 in 2 by 2013; spyware has also become more prevalent and potentially damaging (Outbreak 2001; Airborne outbreak 2005).

In addition to protecting itself, a WBT training technology must also provide security for its users. Confirming and safeguarding the identities of trainees is a special problem in WBT, especially if they do not routinely meet face to face with instructors. Just as failure of a security system might expose a training organization to embarrassment, expensive down time, or even litigation, failure of an organization's screening and monitoring systems leading to a fraudulent registration, award of credit, or granting of a credential might be disastrous for its reputation. Biometric and other devices may make checking identities of trainees, supervising remote testing events, and blocking spyware (thus protecting the records and identities of participants) more practical and economical (Buderi 2005; Talbot 2006).

PRESENT AND FUTURE PROSPECTS OF WBT

While WBT has proven its potential value for training delivery, some barriers continue to restrict or slow its expansion and impact its uses in complex training environments. These barriers arise chiefly in relation to bandwidth availability, user access to and adoption of required technologies (especially for m-learning), and user activity (especially unproductive and addictive behavior). Major opportunities lie in mobile learning and pervasive computing.

Bandwidth and Access

Broadband

Today, most North American Internet users have broadband access, from home or work, though broadband is more accessible in many European and Asian countries than in North America (Free speech and witch hunts 2005; Internet usage statistics 2006). Comparisons can be complicated by the fact that technologies with the same name sometimes have different performance characteristics: ADSL (asymmetric digital subscriber line) in Korea, for example, delivers 20 Mbps, while in Japan the rate is 26 Mbps, and in Switzerland it can be as low as 500 to 700 Kbps (Broadband 2004).

One of the implications for WBT of the increasing ubiquity of broadband is the increasing availability and lower cost of the accompanying technologies, including broadband-based TV (IPTV), and voice over Internet protocol (VoIP; voice only, or voice plus video). IPTV competes with satellite and cable versions in functionality, at considerably lower cost (Telcom broadcasting 2005).

Voice over Internet Protocol

VoIP permits the use of computers for voice and limited video communications, either as two-way private conversations or in multipoint group (class) sessions. While broadband is helpful, voice-only users may require no more than dial-up access to the Web, plus a sound card, microphone, and speakers. For voice and video, VoIP typically provides a small video display, with a refresh rate governed by bandwidth. (IP video is currently not of full-motion quality; its jerkiness and grainy nature lead some users to switch it off completely, relying on audio alone.) The quality of IP audio is usually good to very good. VoIP services are cheap, and may even be free for small numbers of users. Technical advancements, the low cost of VoIP, and growing experience suggest that this technology has a bright future in WBT situations, offering immediate advantages for interaction and support (Miller 2004; Dvorak 2005, The coming death of cheap VoIP, 2005, Inside track).

Wireless Systems

The cost of installing short-range "fixed" wireless systems in buildings or campuses is less than the cost of wiring (or rewiring). Besides cost savings, wireless technologies install more quickly and are highly portable. Wi-Fi for small areas, and Wi-Max for areas up to 30 miles from the broadcast point, with transfer speeds of up to 15 Mbps, are available (Roush 2004; Hutson 2005; Fast tracked 2005; Why wait? 2005; Quain 2005). Wi-Max also offers a mobile capability, permitting reliable digital mobile TV transmission to handheld devices and PCs (Ellison 2005). The costs of other types of wireless technologies with wider coverage areas, such as cell phones and IM (instant messaging), are also dropping, and their reliability is increasing (Grimes 2003; Garfinkel 2004; Rupley 2004). All of these technologies have potential impacts on WBT, and some have already been tried successfully (www.wirelessdevnet.com).

Satellites provide a powerful, though more costly, alternative to ground-based data transmission for widespread, large-scale WBT systems. All the usual production costs apply to satellite-based delivery; costs may in fact be higher, since the greater potential audience warrants higher production values. In addition to the costs of developing and launching the satellite, the impact of equipment failure is significant, given the inconvenience of service calls.

Despite a downward trend in cost, wireless systems for WBT have some major disadvantages: even when transmission speeds are not slower than wired broadband (they often are), interference may lead to transmission errors, reducing effective speed (a problem exacerbated by the presence of other electronics); range depends on the site layout and configuration of the network (including building characteristics and materials); and wireless systems are more vulnerable to security threats.

Unproductive Internet Use and Addictive Behavior

Technology in general does not automatically increase productivity; in fact, there is evidence that it may even *decrease* productivity, especially in the short-term, while systems and people adjust to is presence (Fahy 1998; Dalal 2001). More serious problems arise from users' behavior, especially unauthorized use of technologies during work hours, and addiction. Both have implications for the productivity of WBT, especially where trainees are at a distance or are otherwise minimally supervised.

Huge amounts of time can be wasted online. In 2003, a study found that employees spent an average of 4.5 hours per week on the Internet at work for "personal reasons," leading 57 percent of employers to adopt policies defining legitimate Internet use (up from 33 percent in 2000) (Employees spend 2003). A more recent study found that half of employees surveyed spent from 1 to 5 hours online *daily* for personal reasons, most commonly reading the news, but also on travel, personal e-mail, shopping, and financial tasks (Punching out 2004). The problem is not new: some time ago, the U.S. Treasury Department noted that 40 percent of the inquiries it received came from workplaces, and e-Bay is one of the most often accessed Web sites from workplace locations. The problem is exacerbated by the fact that employees often do not perceive a problem with this use of their time and company resources: only one in ten employees in one survey felt using the Web for non-work reasons was unethical (Workers find 2001).

In addition to the potential for lost time (and drain on network resources) constituted by time spent online but off-task, some Web users become addicted to the technologies. For example, though only about one in four business e-mails actually requires immediate attention, one study found that substantial numbers of employees (34 percent) check their e-mail continually during the day, 42 percent check their business e-mail while on vacation, and 23 percent check it on weekends (E-mail addiction 2001), behavior that, if indicative of compulsive or addictive tendencies, requires WBT instructors' vigilance (Whittaker 2005; Breeding evil? 2005).

The above reinforces the point made previously that management of WBT requires attention to structure (to minimize intrusion of distractions) and dialogue (to discuss use of training time) (Moore 1991).

The Evolution of Media

Training media are changing as bandwidth improves, and as they do new technologies are presenting WBT designers with options and capabilities that were previously unavailable or uneconomical. Examples include the previously mentioned VoIP, and new portable presentation technologies, updated from the Web but used offline, and possessing high portability and vast storage capabilities.

Improvements in Storage and Portability of Information

For cheap, high-capacity storage, the CD has been replaced by the DVD. Blue-laser technology, though currently without a common standard, promises vastly greater storage (23 to 27 GB of storage currently demonstrated, with 50 GB promised), for both video and audio (Labriola 2004; Dvorak 2005, HD DVD).

Storage devices have also gotten much smaller, and capacities have soared: a terabyte (1000 GB, 35 to 100 hours of high-definition video) will soon reside on a device the size of a CD (Quain 2005, A new dimension). Conventional hard disks have also become smaller, while increasing in capacity (Miller 2004, Consumer electronics). Parallel developments in compression algorithms allow faster downloads and copying of popular formats such as MP-3 and MP-4, raising the effective storage capacities of existing devices (Murphy 2005; Make your own music 2004; MPEG-4 2005).

Practically speaking, there are few limitations to the capability of technology to store and deliver audio and, increasingly, video in highly portable forms for WBT. By downloading, users can take these materials with them, and use them when convenient, in an expanding variety of smaller and more portable hardware such as iPods, smart phones, and PDAs of various kinds.

M-learning developers see the implications of these technologies for video, but there are also impacts on stalwarts such as text and audio. E-books using e-paper can store up to 500 book-length documents on a portable device (Advanced materials 2005). Downloads are wireless. Portable devices also support podcasting, allowing anyone to produce and disseminate an audio only, or audio-plus-video, product, using only a PC, some (usually free) special software, and a microphone (with videocamera, if desired). With RSS (variously, real simple syndication, or rich site summary) software, Podcasts can be sent ("pushed") automatically to subscribers (Magid 2005, DIY, 2005, RSS). These technologies are outgrowths of the phenomenally popular blog (Web log), a method of making one's formerly personal thoughts and experiences available to others, relatively effortlessly. The ease with which these can be produced is even more incentive for good instructional design: poor designs will be all too common, as anyone potentially becomes a producer.

Standards, and Reusable Learning Objects (RLOs)

Training materials are increasingly designed to be reused ("repurposed"), through standards developed by organizations such as the Aviation Industry CBT Committee (AICC), the Instructional Management Systems (IMS) Global Learning Consortium, the Institute of Electrical and Electronics Engineers (IEEE), and the Advanced Distributed Learning (ADL) Initiative of the Department of Defense (developer of SCORM [the Shareable Courseware Object Reference Model]) (SCORM best practices guide 2005). WBT instructional materials developed under RLO standards are portable, for maximum present and future (re)use. Metadata tagging of RLOs attempts to ensure several outcomes relevant to potential WBT uses (Longmire 2000):

- Flexibility—material is designed for multiple contexts and easy adaptation for reuse.
- Ease of update, search, and content management—metadata tags provide sophisticated filtering and selecting capabilities.
- Customization—modular learning objects enable more rapid program development or revision.
- Interoperability—RLOs operate on a wide range of training hardware and operating systems.
- Competency-based training—competency-based approaches are promoted by RLOs; materials are tagged to competencies, rather than subjects, disciplines, or grade levels.

Evolution of the Internet: "New" Internets

Worldwide growth in commercial use of the public Web has resulted in ongoing efforts to replace it with a version reserved for research and academic use. In North America, Internet developments include Canada's CA*net 4, and the United States' Internet2.

CA*net 4 uses optical wavelengths to transmit data at a theoretical maximum shared rate of 40 Gbps. Termed the first such network in the world, by 2007 CA*net 4 will permit users "to establish and manage their own optical networks within a subset of the whole network" (RISQ 2005). Internet2 is a collaboration of 240 U.S. research and academic partners, including industry representatives, government (through the National Science Foundation), and international agencies (including Canada, through CA*net 2), to create an environment that "is not clogged with music, commercial entities and porn" (Rupley 2002). As with Canada's CA*net series of systems, research and education are the focus (Networking 2002). Both of these new Internets are capable of handling "torrents of data," without "the proliferation of closed architectures, the tendency for companies to protect their interests rather than invest in standards-based solutions, increased security and safety concerns across a wide range of sectors, and ongoing scalability challenges," weaknesses that plague the existing Internet (Talbot 2005).

Although these new versions of the Internet are not yet available for general WBT, they show what a renewed and more regulated Internet might be capable of providing to users, for purposes such as training and education. With the speed, security, applications, and overall stability these new systems promise, WBT would become even more attractive and sustainable (Next Internet 2005).

CONCLUSION

All indicators suggest that WBT will continue to expand, grow, and become central to more forms of future training worldwide. That prediction is safe, both because so much has already been invested in the Internet delivery infrastructure and because the Web has already proven to be so effective in reducing direct training costs, increasing access, and addressing serious skills deficiencies in an increasingly competitive and technological world (Kaven 2005). Satellite and cable TV took 35 years to be adopted by 50 percent of North Americans, VHS took 10 years, the Internet 9 years, and DVD 6 years; broadband will likely take still less (Lawrence 2005). The average global citizen appears to have little fear of new technologies; trainers, therefore, can be confident of this tool's continuing role and usefulness into the future.

But the evolution of the Web is required to ensure the future of WBT: computers are still too complex, those who support them admit, and their availability is still not sufficiently equably distributed (Behind the digital divide 2005; Pontin 2005). It may even turn out that the computer is the wrong device for some parts of the world to access information and interaction: by price, and direct impact on the gross domestic product, the London Business School argues that cell phones should be distributed to the world's 4 billion poorest people (Calling an end 2005). The infrastructure for that technology may already be in place: 80 percent of the world's population lives within range of a cell-phone network, but only 25 percent have a cell phone (Less is more 2005).

Simple availability or use of a technology are not necessarily the best measures of utility or impact, as the above descriptions of misuse of computer-based applications should make clear. Experience with traditional forms of training delivery have demonstrated that instructional design and conscientious monitoring, perhaps even more than the medium, makes training effective, and trainee support and overall relevance of the content make it appealing to users—lessons that have been available to WBT for some time (Dede 1991).

Although WBT cannot guarantee that future training will not be pedestrian or inefficient, its potential strengths may suggest how training of all kinds might be improved. The core elements of the Web as a training tool—ubiquity, accessibility, stability, redundancy, economy, and user-friendliness—are common to other successful teaching environments. For WBT to expand, developers, managers, trainers and trainees, and employers must see these aspects of the Web as potential assets for their training programs. If the inherent features of the Web are seen as important to training, continued growth and expansion of WBT will occur.

GLOSSARY

Asynchronous: "Different time" (and often different place, i.e., the trainees' workplace or home) training and interpersonal interactions, made possible by technologies that collect messages and make them available at the convenience of the reader. Examples include e-mail, CMC, and listservs.

Bandwidth: The capacity of a channel (e.g., a telephone line or a coaxial cable) to carry data. High bandwidth permits multimedia (audio, video, animation), while low bandwidth limits users to text or simple graphics, and may preclude VoIP and other new interactive tools.

Computer-Mediated Communications (CMC): Text-based, asynchronous communications, usually restricted by password to a designated group such as a class or training cohort, and moderated to ensure that the discussion stays on topic and is civil.

Content Management System (CMS): Software that permits the arrangement and presentation of training content through various fixed and m-learning devices.

Internet: The public network of linked computers accessible by anyone with a Web browser.

Intranet: A private computer network that may or may not also provide Web access, providing security and control not available on the public Internet by limiting access and controlling the content available to users.

Learning Management System (LMS): A tool for delivering, tracking, and reporting on the progress of trainees using m-learning systems, often in connection with a CMS.

Malware: Any form of malicious code intended to infect a computer or a network, including viruses, worms, and Trojan horse programs.

Markup Languages: Used for placing content on the Web; examples include HTML, XML, and SGML.

Metadata: The identifying material added to reusable learning objects (RLOs) to permit easy reuse or "repurposing."

Mobile Learning (M-Learning): Use of various portable communications devices to access information and training content.

Online: Training that provides synchronous or asynchronous (often Internet-based) interaction between the trainee and the trainer, the training content, and other trainees.

Pervasive Computing: Embedding information into the entire environment of an organization, through use of portable (including wearable) and desktop devices of all kinds.

(Reusable) Learning objects (RLOs): Materials modularized, packaged, and labeled (tagged) to encourage cataloguing, access, and reuse in multiple contexts.

Synchronous: Same time and (often) same place training or communication interactions—for example, face-to-face training.

Training: Instruction in procedural skills and knowledge primarily for practical purposes and relatively immediate application.

Voice (or Video) over Internet Protocol (VoIP): The capability of Internet-based programs to provide voice point-to-point or point-to-multipoint connections to anyone with a browser, a sound card, a microphone, and speakers; may also include limited video or graphics capabilities.

The Web: A synonym for the Internet (in the context of this paper).

Web-Based Training (WBT): Includes training-on-the-job (TOJ) and workplace training, formal on-campus technical training, and elements of training or professional development (PD), including some online components, with the Internet or an intranet as the access/delivery vehicle.

CROSS REFERENCES

See *Computer Conferencing and Distance Learning*; *The Internet Fundamentals*.

REFERENCES

Advanced materials on display. 2005. *Technology Review* 108(8):27.

Airborne outbreak. 2005. *Technology Review* 108(4):22.

Barns' storming. 2005. *The Economist* 374(8417):57.

Bates, A. W. 1995. *Technology, open learning and distance education.* New York: Routledge.

———. 2000. *Managing technological change.* San Francisco: Jossey-Bass.

Behind the digital divide. 2005, March 12. *The Economist* 374(8417):22–5.

Berge, Z. 1995. Computer-mediated communication and the online classroom in distance learning. *Computer-Mediated Communication Magazine* 2(4):6.

Biesenbach-Lucas, S. 2004. Asynchronous web discussions in teacher training courses: Promoting collaborative learning—or not? *Association for the Advancement of Computing in Education* 12(2). www.aace.org/pubs/aacej/temp/03lucas155-170.pdf (accessed October 8, 2004).

Biuk-Aghai, R. P., and S. J. Simoff. 2004. Patterns of virtual collaboration in online collaboration systems. In *Proceedings of the IASTED International Conference on Knowledge Sharing and Collaborative Engineering, St. Thomas, USVI, November 22–24,* 57–62. The International Association of Science and Technology for Development (IASTED), Calgary, Alberta, Canada.

Bloom, B. S. 1984. The 2 sigma problem: The search for methods of group instruction as effective as one-to-one tutoring. *Educational Researcher* June–July:4–16.

Breeding evil? 2005. *The Economist* 376(8438):9.

Briggs, L., and W. Wager. 1981. *Handbook of procedures for the design of instruction.* 2nd ed. Englewood Cliffs, NJ: Educational Technology.

Broadband. 2004. *PC Magazine* 23(13):17.

Buderi, R. 2005. Me, myself, and eye. *Technology Review* 108(2):64–69.

Burbules, N., and T. Callister. 1998. Universities in transition: The promise and the challenge of new technologies. http://lrs.ed.uiuc.edu/fft/higher-ed-8.html (accessed July 9, 2007).

Burge, E. J., and J. M. Roberts. 1993. *Classrooms with a difference: A practical guide to the use of conferencing technologies*. Toronto: University of Toronto (OISE), Distance Learning Office.

Calling an end to poverty. 2005, July 9. *The Economist* 376(8434):51–2.

Cheap Tricks. 2005. *The Economist* 377(8446):62.

Chickering, A., and Z. Gamson. 1989. Seven principles for good practice in undergraduate education. *AAHE Bulletin* March:3–7.

Collins, M., and Z. Berge. 1996. Facilitating interaction in computer-mediated online courses. http://jan.ucc.nau.edu/~mpc3/moderate/flcc.html (accessed June 6, 1999).

Conference Board of Canada. 2005. Changing employers' behaviour about training. Ottawa: Author. www.conferenceboard.ca/search.asp (accessed April 28, 2006).

Conrad, D. 2005. Building and maintaining community in cohort-based online learning. *Journal of Distance Education* 20(1):1–20.

Cross, P. 1981. *Adults as learners*. San Francisco: Jossey-Bass.

Dalal, S. 2001, October 26. Futzers draining production budgets. *The Edmonton Journal*, F-1, 8.

Dede, C. 1991. Emerging technologies: Impacts on distance learning. *Annals AAPSS* 514:146–58.

———. 1996. The evolution of distance education: Emerging technologies and distributed learning. *The American Journal of Distance Education* 10(2):4–36.

Dewey, J. 1938. *Experience and education*. New York: Macmillan.

Dick, W., and L. Carey. 1978. *The systematic design of instruction*. Dallas: Scott, Foresman.

Don't take my PC. 2004. *PC Magazine* 23(2):21.

Dvorak, J. C. 2005a, The coming death of cheap VoIP. *PC Magazine* 24(9):55.

———. 2005b, Inside track. *PC Magazine* 24(10):87.

———. 2005c, HD DVD, now what? *PC Magazine* 24(21):67.

Ellison, C. 2005. Unwired for speed. *PC Magazine* 24(10) 112–5.

E-mail addiction. 2001. *PC Magazine* 20(15):29.

Employees spend 4.5 hours weekly on Web. 2003, April 10. *The Edmonton Journal*, G-3.

Fahy, P. J. 1998. Reflections on the productivity paradox and distance education technology. *Journal of Distance Education* 13(2):66–73.

———. 2004. Web-based training. *The Internet Encyclopedia*, vol. 3, pp. 661–73. Hoboken, NJ: Wiley.

Fast tracked. 2005. *PC Magazine* 24(11):24.

Fischer, B. 1997. Instructor-led vs. interactive: Not an either/or proposition. *Corporate University Review* January/February:29–30.

Fox, E. A. 2002. Multimedia, hypertext and information access. Course notes, CS 4624, Virginia Polytechnic Institute and State University. http://ei.cs.vt.edu/~mm (accessed May 2002).

Frankola, K. 2001. Why online learners drop out. *Workforce*. www.workforce.com/archive/feature/22/26/22/index.php (accessed July 2002).

Free speech and witch hunts. 2005. *The Economist* 376(8439):35.

Fulford, C. P., and S. Zhang. 1993. Perception of interaction: The critical predictor in distance education. *The American Journal of Distance Education* 7(3):8–21.

Gagne, R., and L. Briggs. 1979. *Principles of instructional design*. 2nd ed. New York: Holt, Reinhart and Winston.

Garfinkel, S. 2004. *Technology Review* 107(7):92.

Garrison, R., T. Anderson, and W. Archer. 2000. Critical inquiry in a text-based environment: Computer conferencing in higher education. *Internet and Higher Education* 2(2):87–105.

Giguere, P. J., S. W. Formica, and W. M. Harding. 2004. Large-scale interaction strategies for web-based professional development. *The American Journal of Distance Education* 18(4):207–23.

Glaser, R. (Ed.). 1978. *Advances in instructional psychology*. Hillsdale, NJ: Lawrence Erlbaum.

Grimes, B. 2003. Instant messaging. *PC Magazine* 22(3):66.

Grow, G. 1991. Teaching learners to be self-directed. *Adult Education Quarterly* 41:125–49.

Harapniuk, D., T. C. Montgomerie, and C. Torgerson. 1998. Costs of developing and delivering a Web-based instruction course. In *Proceedings of WebNet 98—World Conference of the WWW, Internet, and Intranet*. Charlottesville: Association for the Advancement of Computing in Education. www.quasar.ualberta.ca/IT/research/nethowto/costs/costs.html (accessed July 2002).

Higher Education Inc. 2005. *The Economist* 376(8443):19–20.

Hiltz, S. R., K. Johnson, and A. M. Rabke. 1980. The process of communication in face-to-face verses computerized conferences: A controlled experiment using Bales' interaction process analysis. In *Proceedings of the Eighteenth Annual Meeting of the Association for Computational Linguistics, Philadelphia, USA, June 19–22*. http://acl.ldc.upenn/P/P80/P80-1020.pdf (accessed March 19, 2003).

HIP 2000. 2000, February 23. *The Edmonton Journal*, F1.

Human Resources and Skills Development Canada. 2002. *Knowledge matters: Skills and learning for Canadians*. Ottawa: Author. www.innovationstrategy.gc.ca (accessed July 12, 2007).

Hutson, S. 2005. Wireless devices catch bad code through the air and then infect supposedly secure computer systems. *Technology Review.com*. www.technologyreview.com/articles/05/05/issue/feature_emerging.asp?p=9 (accessed April 19, 2005).

Inculcating culture. 2006, January 21. *The Economist* 378(8461):11–2.

Internet usage statistics. 2006. Internet world stats. www.internetworldstats.com/stats.htm (accessed April 28, 2006).

Kaven, O. 2005. Will 2006 be Linux's year? *PC Magazine* 24(13):104.

Kaye, A. 1989. Computer mediated communication and distance education. In *Mindweave,* edited by R. Mason and A. Kaye, 3–21. Toronto: Pergamon Press.

Keller, F. S. 1968. Goodbye, teacher! *Journal of Applied Behavioral Analysis* 1(1):79–89.

Keller, V. 1999. *Adaptation and application of a transcript analysis tool to analyze a computer-mediated communication (CMC) distance education course transcript*. Unpublished master's thesis, Athabasca University, Athabasca, Alberta.

Kidd, J. R. 1973. *How adults learn.* Chicago: Follett.

Knowles, M. 1978. *The adult learner: A neglected species*. 2nd ed. Houston: Gulf.

Labriola, D. 2004. Blue lasers boost DVD capacity. *PC Magazine* 23(13):30.

Lawrence, S. 2005. Digital media make their mark. *Technology Review* 108(7):31.

Leiner, B., V. Cerf, D. Clark, R. Kahn, L. Kleinrock, D. C. Lynch, J. Postel, L. G. Roberts, and S. Wolf. 2002. *A brief history of the Internet*. www.isoc.org/internet/history/index.shtml (accessed May 2002).

Less is more. 2005, July 9. *The Economist* 376(8434):11.

Longmire, W. 2000, March. A primer on learning objects: Learning circuits. www.learningcircuits.com/mar2000/primer.html (accessed June 2001).

Lowman, J. 1994. What constitutes masterful teaching? In *Teaching and learning in the college classroom,* edited by K. Feldman and M. Paulsen, 213–25. Needham Heights, MA: Simon & Schuster.

Mager, R. 1975. *Preparing instructional objectives.* 2nd ed. Belmont, CA: Fearon.

Magid, L. 2005. DIY: Create your own Podcasts. *PC Magazine* 24(18):66–7.

———. 2005. RSS: The Web at your fingertips, *PC Magazine* 24(18):62–5.

Make your own music. 2004. *PC Magazine* 23(11):28.

Mayer, R. E. 2001. *Multimedia learning*. New York: Cambridge University Press.

Miller, M. J. 2004. The VoIP revolution. *PC Magazine* 23(7): 7.

———. 2004. Consumer electronics leads the way. *PC Magazine* 23(4):5.

Mobile learning. 2004. Mobile learning group. http://www3.telus.net/~kdeanna/mlearning (accessed April 28, 2006).

Molinari, D. L. 2004. The role of social comments in problem-solving groups in an online class. *The American Journal of Distance Education* 18(2):89–101.

Moore, M. G. 1989. Three types of interaction. *American Journal of Distance Education* 3(2):1–6.

———. 1991. Distance education theory. *The American Journal of Distance Education* 5(3):1–6.

MPEG-4, the container for digital media. 2005. www.apple.com/quicktime/technologies/mpeg4 (accessed March 31, 2006).

Murphy, D. 2005. Audio format glossary. *PC Magazine* 24(12):122.

National Education Association. 2000. A survey of traditional and distance learning higher education members. www.nea.org/he/abouthe/distance.html (accessed August 2000).

Networking. 2002, May 22. CA*net 4 coming down the pipe. *Networking* 6(5). www.thenode.org/networking/may2002/briefs.html#1 (accessed July 12, 2002).

Newby, T., D. Stepich, J. Lehman, and J. Russell. 2000. *Instructional technology for teaching and learning.* 2nd ed. Upper Saddle River, NJ: Merrill.

Next Internet. 2005. *PC Magazine* 24(18):20.

Outbreak. 2001. *PC Magazine* 20(21):30.

OECD. 2005. Key ICT indicators. www.oecd.org/document/23/0,2340,en_2825_495656_33987543_1_1_1_1,00.html (accessed April 22, 2005).

Piaget, J. 1952. *The origins of intelligence in children* (trans.). New York: International Universities Press.

Pontin, J. 2005. Mediating poverty. *Technology Review* 108(8):14.

Punching out: Workplace Web surfing. 2004. *PC Magazine* 23(11):25.

Quain, J. R. 2005. Beyond WiMAX. *PC Magazine* 24(10):23.

———. 2005. A new dimension in storage. *PC Magazine* 24(11):23

RISQ. 2005. Services. www.risq.qc.ca/services/canet/index.php?LANG=EN#premier (accessed December 21, 2005).

Rose, M. A. 2004. Comparing productive online dialog in two groups styles: Cooperative and collaborative. *The American Journal of Distance Education* 18(2):73–88.

Roush, W. 2004. Why WiMax? *Technology Review* 107(9):20–1.

Rovai, A. P. and K. T. Barnum. 2003. Online course effectiveness: An analysis of student interactions and perceptions of learning. *Journal of Distance Education* 18(1):57–73.

Rupley, S. 2002. I2, Near you. *PC Magazine* 21(4):21.

———. 2004. P2P problems. *PC Magazine* 23(4):19.

———. 2005. A computer for every kid. *PC Magazine* 24(19/20):23.

Saettler, P. 1990. *The evolution of American educational technology*. Englewood, CO: Libraries Unlimited.

SCORM best practices guide for content developers. 2005. Carnegie Mellon Learning Systems Architecture Lab. www.lsal.cmu.edu/lsal/expertise/projects/developersguide (accessed December 23, 2005).

Skinner, B. F. 1971. *Beyond freedom and dignity*. New York: Bantam Books.

Suppes, P. 1978. The role of global psychological models in instructional technology. In *Advances in instructional technology*, *1*, edited by R. Glaser, 229–59. Hillsdale, NJ: Lawrence Erlbaum.

Szabo, M. 1998. *Survey of educational technology research*. The Educational Technology Professional Development Project (ETPDP) Series. Edmonton, Alberta: Grant MacEwan Community College and Northern Alberta Institute of Technology.

Talbot, D. 2005. Next-generation networks. *Technology Review*. www.technologyreview.com/InfoTech-Search/wtr_15937,308,p1.html (accessed December 21, 2005).

———. 2006. Malware menace. *Technology Review* 109(1):22.

Telcom broadcasting: On its way. 2005. *PC Magazine* 24(19/20):23.

Thorndike, R. L. (Ed.). 1971. *Educational measurement*. Washington, DC: American Council on Education.

Vaas, L. 2001. The e-training of America. *PC Magazine* 20(22):ibiz1–ibiz4.

Wagner, E. 1994. In support of a functional definition of interaction. *American Journal of Distance Education* 8:6–29.

Walther, J. B. 1996. Computer-mediated communication: Impersonal, interpersonal and hyperpersonal interaction. *Communication Research* 20(1):3–43.

Warren, A., D. Brunner, P. Maier, and L. Barnett. 1996. *Technology in teaching and learning*. London: Kogan Page.

Welsch, E. 2002. Cautious steps ahead. *Online Learning* 6:20–4.

Whittaker, S. 2005, April 13. Growing number of workers don't know how to close office door. *The Edmonton Journal*, H5.

Why wait for WiMax? 2005. *The Economist* 376(8440):51.

Workers find online surfing too tempting. 2000, February 22. *The Edmonton Journal*, A-3.

RFID (Radio-Frequency Identification)

Stephen A. Weis, *Google*

INTRODUCTION

Radio-frequency identification (RFID) is a rapidly growing technology that has the potential to make great economic impacts on many industries. Although RFID is a relatively old technology, more recent advances in chip manufacturing technology are making RFID practical for new applications and settings, particularly tagging at the consumer-item level. These advances have the potential to revolutionize supply-chain management, inventory control, and logistics.

At its most basic, RFID systems consist of small transponders, or tags, attached to physical objects. RFID tags may soon become the most pervasive microchip in history. When wirelessly interrogated by RFID transceivers, or readers, tags respond with some identifying information that may be associated with arbitrary data records. Thus, RFID systems are one type of automatic identification system, similar to optical bar codes. There are many kinds of RFID systems used in different applications and settings. These systems have different power sources, operating frequencies, and functionalities. The properties and regulatory restrictions of a particular RFID system will determine its manufacturing costs, physical specifications, and performance. Some of the most familiar RFID applications are item-level tagging with electronic product codes, proximity cards for physical access control, and contact-less payment systems. Many more applications will become economical in the coming years.

RFID adoption yields many efficiency benefits, but it still faces several hurdles. Besides the typical implementation challenges faced in any information technology system and economic barriers, there are major concerns over security and privacy in RFID systems. Without proper protection, RFID systems could create new threats to both corporate security and personal privacy.

In this section, we present a brief history of RFID and automatic identification systems. I summarize several major applications of RFID. I also present a primer on basic RFID principles and discuss the taxonomy of various RFID systems. Then I address the technical, economic, security, and privacy challenges facing RFID adoption. Finally, I briefly discuss emerging technologies relevant to RFID.

RFID Origins

The origins of RFID technology lie in the nineteenth century, when luminaries of that era made great scientific advances in electromagnetism. Of particular relevance to RFID are Michael Faraday's discovery of electronic inductance, James Clerk Maxwell's formulation of equations describing electromagnetism, and Heinrich Rudolf Hertz's experiments validating Faraday and Maxwell's predictions. Their discoveries laid the foundation for modern radio communications.

Precursors to automatic radio-frequency identification systems were automatic object-detection systems. One of the earliest patents for such a system was a radio transmitter for object detection designed by John Logie Baird in 1926 (Baird 1928; Auto-ID Labs 2006). More well known is Robert Watson-Watt's 1935 patent for a "Radio Detection and Ranging" system, or RADAR. The passive communication technology often used in RFID was first presented in Henry Stockman's seminal paper "Communication by Means of Reflected Power" in 1948.

One of the first applications of a radio-frequency identification system was in "Identify Friend or Foe" (IFF) systems deployed by the British Royal Air Force during World War II (Royal Air Force 2006). IFF allowed radar operators and pilots to automatically distinguish friendly aircraft from enemies via RF signals. IFF systems helped prevent "friendly fire" incidents and aided in intercepting enemy aircraft. Advanced IFF systems are used today in aircraft and munitions, although much of the technology remains classified.

Electronic detection, as opposed to identification, has a long history of commercial use. By the mid- to late 1960s, electronic article surveillance (EAS) systems were commercially offered by several companies, including Checkpoint Systems and Sensormatic. These EAS systems typically consisted of a magnetic device embedded in a commercial product and would be deactivated or removed when an item was purchased. The presence of an activated tag passing through an entry portal would trigger an alarm. These types of systems are often used in libraries, music stores, and clothing stores. Unlike RFID, these types of EAS systems do not automatically identify a particular tag; they just detect its presence.

Auto-Identification and RFID

In terms of commercial applications, RFID systems may be considered an instance of a broader class of automatic identification (auto-ID) systems. Auto-ID systems essentially attach a name or identifier to a physical object by some means that may be automatically read. This identifier may be represented optically, electromagnetically, or even chemically.

Perhaps the most successful and well-known auto-ID system is the universal product code (UPC). The UPC is a one-dimensional, optical barcode encoding product and brand information. UPC labels can be found on most consumer products in the United States. Similar systems are deployed worldwide.

The Uniform Code Council (UCC), a standards body originally formed by members of the grocery manufacturing and food distribution industries, originally specified the UPC (Uniform Code Council 2006). A precursor body to the UCC first met in 1969 to discuss the need for an interindustry auto-ID system. By 1973, a one-dimensional (or linear) barcode design was chosen. In 1974, a supermarket in Ohio scanned the first UPC-labeled product: a package of Wrigley's gum.

Adoption of the UPC grew steadily throughout the following years, to the point at which UPC barcode scanners are found in a vast majority of large American retailers. Today, over 5 billion barcodes are scanned around the world each day. Shipping and transit companies, such as United Parcel Service, Federal Express, and the U.S. Postal Service, commonly use two-dimensional barcodes, which can carry more data in a smaller surface area.

Optical barcodes offer faster, more reliable, and more convenient inventory control and consumer check-out than checking out by hand. Several weaknesses of optical barcodes are that they require line-of-sight and may be smudged or obscured by packaging. In most circumstances, optical barcodes still require some human manipulation to align a barcode label with a reader. Supermarket shoppers have certainly experienced a checker struggling to scan an optical barcode.

Auto-ID systems that transmit data via RF signals (i.e., RFID) do not have the same performance limitations as optical systems. Data may be read without line-of-sight and without human or mechanical intervention. A key advantage in RF-based auto-ID systems is parallelism. Modern RFID systems may offer read rates of hundreds of items per second.

APPLICATIONS

Early commercial examples of RFID applications include automatic tracking of train cars, shipping containers, and automobiles. Railroad cars were originally labeled with optical bar code labels for tracking. These labels began to deteriorate and be obscured by dirt, causing reads to fail. As a solution, railroad companies began to tag railcars with RFID devices. By 1994, these devices were mandatory, and nearly every railcar in the United States was tagged.

RFID devices began to be used for automated toll collection in the late 1980s and early 1990s. Electronic toll systems have since been adopted around the world. Like railway and shipping applications, electronic toll systems may use sturdy, self-powered RFID devices. Automobiles, railcars, and shipping containers are all high-value items, with ample physical space that can accommodate more expensive and bulky RFID devices. These types of tags could offer much more functionality than simple identification. For example, shipping containers might have accelerometer sensors, tamper alarms, or satellite tracking integrated into an identification device.

As manufacturing costs dropped, RFID systems began to be used for lower-value items in industries other than transportation. An example is in animal identification of both pets and livestock. Glass-encapsulated RFID devices have been implanted in millions of pets throughout the United States. These tags allow lost animals to be identified and returned to their rightful owners. These tags have a very short read range. Livestock, particularly cattle, are often labeled with a RFID device that is clamped or pierced through their ear, attached to a collar, or swallowed. Unlike implanted pet tags, these RFID devices are rugged and able to be read from greater distances. Concerns over bovine spongiform encephalopathy (mad cow disease) have motivated proposals for universal tracking of livestock with these types of RFID systems. Like transport applications, animal tracking is still essentially a low-volume, high-value market that may justify relatively expensive RFID systems.

Other widespread applications of RFID systems include contact-less payment, access control, or stored-value systems. Since 1997, ExxonMobil gasoline stations have offered a system called Speedpass that allows customers to make purchases with an RFID fob, typically a keychain-sized form factor (ExxonMobil Speedpass 2006). In 2005, American Express launched a credit card enhanced with RFID that allows customers to make purchases without swiping a card (RFID Journal 2005).

RFID proximity cards or "prox cards" are commonly used for building access control at many companies and universities throughout the world. Similar systems have been used for ski-lift access control at ski resorts. Many subway and bus systems, for example in Singapore, use stored-value RFID proximity cards.

There are several applications that use RFID as an anticounterfeiting measure. In 2005, the Wynn Casino in Las Vegas first opened and deployed RFID-integrated gaming tables and gambling tokens. These "chips-in-chips" are designed to frustrate counterfeiting, prevent theft, detect fraud, and offer enhanced games or service. Besides stored-value tokens like casino chips or event tickets, there have also been proposals to tag currency (Juels and Pappas 2003). In 2005, a controversial proposal to attach tags carrying biometric identification data to U.S. passports began to be implemented.

These applications also exposed some shortcomings of RFID. For instance, some RFID technologies do not operate well in proximity to liquids or metals. Each technology has its own strengths and weaknesses, including variations in cost, size, power requirements, and environmental limits. There is no "one size fits all" RFID technology. The term *RFID technology* actually describes an entire array of technologies, which are each applicable to different types of applications. The section on "Principles" offers a detailed discussion of these various technologies.

RFID continues to lower the costs of tracking high-value items; however, an untapped and lucrative market lies in tracking cheap, everyday consumer goods. Companies like Proctor & Gamble, Coca-Cola, and Wal-Mart have hundreds of billions of products and components in their supply chains. Tracking and managing the flow of goods through these supply chains is a complex and expensive enterprise.

RFID technology may streamline these supply-chain processes and save billions of dollars, savings that ultimately may be passed on to consumers. Shipping pallets or, ideally, individual items may be tracked and traced from manufacturers, through transport, wholesale, and retail into the hands of the consumer at a point of sale. Products could even be tracked postconsumer as they are recycled, refurbished, or disposed of. What happens with respect to privacy while RFID-tagged items are in the hands of a consumer has been an issue of major contention and will be addressed in the section on "Security and Privacy."

Supply-chain management and inventory-control applications of this scale require an extremely low-cost tag to be economically viable. In settings like animal identification, proximity cards, electronic toll systems, or stored-value systems, RFID tags costing as much several U.S. dollars could be justified. However, items in consumer supply-chain management and inventory-control applications are much cheaper than in traditional settings. Ideally, RFID tags in these applications should be as simple and cheap as the traditional UPC optical bar code.

EPCglobal, an RFID standards body, has developed specifications for low-cost electronic product code (EPC) tags as a replacement for the ubiquitous UPC (EPCglobal 2006). In the past, the lack of an open standard was a barrier to RFID adoption. The EPC standard, and to some extent, the ISO-18000 standard (International Organization for Standardization 2004) will make it easier for users to integrate their RFID systems.

The potential for EPC may be huge. Globally, over 5 billion barcode transactions are conducted daily (Uniform Code Council 2006). Even minuscule savings per transaction could translate into a huge aggregate cost savings. The market has already begun to adopt low-cost RFID on a large scale. A single RFID IC manufacturer, Philips Semiconductor, has already shipped several billion RFID chips.

Organizations with large supply chains are the driving force behind RFID adoption. In 2003, Wal-Mart, the world's largest retailer, mandated that all suppliers attach RFID tags to shipping pallets by the end of 2006 (RFID Journal 2003, Wal-Mart). The U.S. Department of Defense (2006) issued a similar mandate for its own suppliers.

An illustrative example of an industry adopting RFID by way of mandate is the prescription drug industry, which must contend with a counterfeit drug market predicted to grow to $75 billion by 2010 (World Health Organization 2006). In response to the growing problem of counterfeit drugs, the Food and Drug Administration (FDA; 2004) recommended that all wholesale prescription drug shipments be labeled with RFID pedigrees. The goal of these pedigrees is to both attest to the authenticity of a drug shipment and detect simple theft in the supply chain.

Some consumer industries may be independently motivated to adopt RFID early. In 2003, razor manufacturer Gillette placed a single order of 500 million low-cost RFID tags from a manufacturer named Alien Technologies (RFID Journal 2003, Gillette). Gillette disposable razor blade cartridges are relatively expensive, costing $1 to $2 per blade or more.

Because these items are small and easily concealable and there is a constantly growing resale market, Gillette blades were one of the most frequently shoplifted consumer items. Somewhere between 15 and 20 percent of Gillette's blades are stolen (or "shrink") between manufacturer and the consumer point of sale. The high costs of "shrinkage" justified incorporating RFID tags into every razor blade package that Gillette sells.

The fashion industry has also been an early RFID adopter. Several fashion makers like Swatch watches, Ecco shoes, Prada, and Benetton (which will be discussed more in the section on "Challenges") have all tagged clothing with RFID labels. These tags are typically for retail inventory control, since retail clothing stores often face a high level of shrinkage, as well a lot of legitimate movement of inventory by customers trying on clothing.

RFID tags have also been used as a pedigree for high-fashion items or to enhance the consumer shopping experience. For example, Prada's retail store in New York City offers an RFID-enhanced dressing room that displays product information and suggests matching apparel.

Clothing is particularly suited for RFID, since it does not contain metals or liquids that interfere with some types of RFID systems. Retail stores also typically do not have sensitive electronics, like medical equipment, that some RFID operating frequencies may interfere with. Clothing's relatively high per-unit value also justifies the use of RFID tags, which can be removed and recycled at purchase time. The clothing industry was an early adopter of simple EAS systems in the 1960s for these very reasons. It will likely be a leader in RFID adoption as well.

The next step in RFID for clothing may be to integrate tags directly in the product at the time of manufacture, rather than manually attaching temporary tags. This greatly lowers RFID handling costs. Directly incorporating RFID into products or packaging will likely become commonplace once the proper technology becomes economical. A promising direction is to print RFID labels directly into paper products during manufacturing. This would greatly lower the handling and processing costs of integrating RFID with consumer products. We discuss printed circuits more in the section on "Future Technologies."

Before delving into a more detailed discussion of various RFID technologies and principles, we will summarize several of the present and envisioned future applications of RFID:

- Tracking and identification:
  - Large assets—e.g., railway cars and shipping containers
  - Livestock with rugged tags
  - Pets with implanted tags
  - Supply-chain management with EPC
  - Inventory control with EPC
  - Retail checkout with EPC
  - Recycling and waste disposal
- Payment and stored-value systems:
  - Electronic toll systems
  - Contact-less credit cards—e.g., American Express Blue card
  - Stored-valued systems—e.g., ExxonMobil Speedpass
  - Subway and bus passes
  - Casino tokens and concert tickets
- Access control:
  - Building access with proximity cards
  - Ski-lift passes
  - Concert tickets
  - Automobile ignition systems
- Anticounterfeiting:
  - Casino tokens—e.g., Wynn Casino Las Vegas
  - High-denomination currency notes
  - Luxury goods—e.g., Prada products
  - Prescription drugs

PRINCIPLES

This section discusses basics of RFID systems and offers taxonomy for the many various types of RFID systems. We briefly discuss two major RFID standards and how they relate to practice.

System Essentials

Discussion of RFID technology tends to focus only on tag devices. It is more accurate to view RFID as a complete system that includes not only tags, but also other important components. RFID systems are composed of at least three core components:

- RFID tags, or transponders, carry object-identifying data.
- RFID readers, or transceivers, read and write tag data.
- Databases associate arbitrary records with tag identifying data.

We illustrate the interaction of these components in Figure 1. In this figure, three tags are readable by one or both of two readers, A and B. For instance, tag 1 is readable only by A, while 2 is readable by both A and B, perhaps because of access-control restrictions. The readers then may connect to databases with records associated with particular tag identifiers. In this case, two databases each have their own record for tag 1.

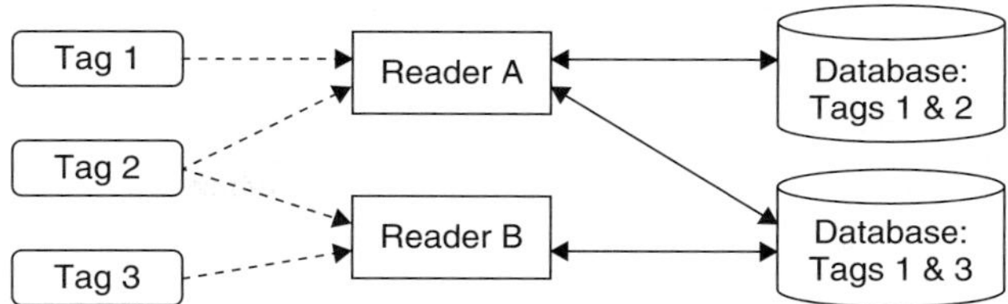

Figure 1: Illustration of RFID System Interaction

Tags

Tags are attached to all objects to be identified in an RFID system. A tag is typically composed of an antenna or coupling element and integrated circuitry. An important distinction that will be discussed later is a tag's power source. Often tags carry no on-board power source and must passively harvest all energy from an RF signal.

There are many types of tags that offer different functionalities, have different power sources, or operate at different radio frequencies. Each of these variables helps determine which applications a particular tag may be appropriate for and what the costs of a tag may be. These differences will be discussed further in the section on "Power Sources."

Modern tags tend to implement identification functionality on an integrated circuit (IC) that provides computation and storage. In the manufacturing process, this IC is attached or "strapped" to an antenna before being packaged in a form factor, like a glass capsule or foil inlay, that is integrated into a final product.

In practice, different vendors often perform each of these manufacturing steps. Other RFID designs may be "chipless" or have identifying information hardwired at fabrication time—that is, "write-once, read-many" tags. Newer technologies that allow RFID circuitry to be printed directly onto a product will be discussed in the section on "Emerging Technologies."

Readers

RFID readers communicate with tags through an RF channel to obtain identifying information. Depending on the type of tag, this communication may be a simple ping or may be a more complex multiround protocol. In environments with many tags, a reader may have to perform an anticollision protocol to ensure that communication conflicts do not occur. Anticollision protocols permit readers to rapidly communicate with many tags in serial order.

Readers often power what are called "passive tags" through their RF communication channel. These types of tags carry no on-board power and rely solely on a reader to operate. Since these tags are so limited, many subsequently rely on a reader to perform computation as well.

Readers come in many forms, operate on many different frequencies, and may offer a wide range of functionality. Readers may have their own processing power and internal storage, and may offer network connectivity. Readers might be a simple conduit to an external system, or could store all relevant data locally.

Currently, many applications rely on fixed reading devices. Early trials of EPC at a major supermarket chain integrated fixed readers into docking-bay entrances. These readers scan tags at the pallet level as shipments of products arrive. In the long term, readers may be integrated at a shelf level as a "smart shelf." Smart shelves would scan for tags at the item level and monitor when they are added and removed from a shelf.

RFID readers may also be integrated into handheld mobile devices. These mobile readers would allow someone to, for example, take inventory of a warehouse by walking through its aisles. The cellular phone manufacturer Nokia is already offering RFID-reading functionality in some of their cell phones (Nokia 2004). If EPC-type tags become highly successful, interesting and useful consumer applications might arise. If this occurs, RFID reading functionality might become a common feature on cellular phones, personal digital assistants (PDAs), or other handheld computing devices.

Databases

RFID databases associate tag-identifying data with arbitrary records. These records may contain product information, tracking logs, sales data, and expiration dates. Independent databases may be built throughout a supply chain by unrelated users, or they may be integrated in a centralized or federated database system.

Databases are assumed to have a secure connection to readers. Although there are scenarios in which readers may not be trusted, it is often useful to collapse the notions of reader and database into one entity. For example, if tags contain all relevant product information, there is no need to make a call to an off-site database.

One may imagine a federated system of back-end databases, perhaps in which each product manufacturer maintains its own product look-up service. In these settings, it may be useful to deploy an object naming service (ONS) to locate databases associated with some tag identification value. An ONS allows a reader to find a set of databases associated with a particular tag identification value. This is analogous to the Internet domain naming service (DNS) that returns addresses of name servers that can translate domain names to numerical IP addresses. ONS has not yet been adopted widely in practice.

Power Sources

As briefly mentioned above, tags may obtain their power in several different ways. The power source is an essential property of a tag, since it will determine a tag's potential read range, lifetime, cost, and kinds of functionalities it may offer. The power source will also be important in determining how a tag may be oriented and what physical forms it may take.

There are three main classes of tag power sources: active, semipassive, and passive. Active tags have their own source of power, such as a battery, and may initiate communication with a reader or other active tags. Because they contain their own power source, active tags typically have a much longer operating range than passive tags. Large-asset- and livestock-tracking applications often use active tags, since the items they are attached to (e.g. railcars, shipping containers, or cattle) are high in value and have physical space for a bulkier, rugged tag.

A key feature of active tags is that they are able to initiate their own communication with readers. Advanced active tags, or "smart dust," might even form ad hoc peer networks with each other. One useful application of active tags is in shipping containers, which can fall off ships over rough seas. These missing containers sometimes are not accounted for until well after the ship has docked. An active tag with an accelerometer sensor could detect when it was falling off a stack of containers and broadcast a log of its demise before it sank into the ocean. Active tags could also function as security alarms using the same functionality.

By contrast semipassive (or semiactive) tags have an internal battery, but are *not* able to initiate communications. This ensures that semipassive tags are active only when queried by a reader. Because semipassive tags do have an internal power source, they do offer a longer reader range than passive attacks, but at a higher cost.

An example application that often uses semipassive tags is electronic tollbooths. Semipassive tags are typically affixed to the inside of a car's windshield. When the car passes through a tollbooth, it will initiate a query to the semipassive tag and read an account identifier from the tag. The on-board battery lets the tag be read from a considerable distance. However, since the tag needs to broadcast only when queried, it can remain idle most of the time and save power. Semipassive tags are also often used in pallet-level tracking or for tracking components like automobile parts during manufacture.

Passive tags have neither their own power source nor the ability to initiate communication. Passive tags obtain energy by harvesting it from an incoming RF communication signal. At lower frequencies, this energy is typically harvested inductively, while at higher frequencies it is harvested through capacitance.

Passive tags have the shortest read range of all three powering types, and they are the cheapest to manufacture and the easiest to integrate into products. Batteries are relatively expensive and cannot easily be incorporated into some items, like paper packaging. For this reason, passive tags are the most common tags. EPC tags are passive. Lacking an internal power source dictates many properties of passive tags. First, they cannot operate without the presence of a reader, although passive tags could temporarily cache some energy in a capacitor. Because of their necessarily weak response signal, passive tags are often more sensitive to environmental noise or interference. Table 1 compares various properties of passive, semipassive, and active tags.

Operating Frequencies

Different RFID systems operate at a variety of radio frequencies. Each range of frequencies offers its own operating range, power requirements, and performance. Different ranges may be subject to different regulations or restrictions that limit what applications they can be used for.

The operating frequency determines which physical materials propagate RF signals. Metals and liquids typically present the biggest problem in practice. In particular, tags operating in the ultrahigh frequency (UHF) range do not function properly in close proximity to liquids or metal.

Table 1: Comparison of Passive, Semipassive, and Active Tags

Tag Type	Power Source	Communication	Max Range	Relative Cost	Example Applications
Passive	Harvesting RF energy	Response only	10 M	Least expensive	EPC Proximity cards
Semipassive	Battery	Response only	>100 M	More expensive	Electronic tolls Pallet tracking
Active	Battery	Respond or initiate	>100 M	Most expensive	Large-asset tracking Livestock tracking

Table 2: Common RFID Operating Frequencies

Frequency Range	Frequencies	Passive Read Distance
Low frequency (LF)	120–140 KHz	10–20 cm
High frequency (HF)	13.56 MHz	10–20 cm
Ultrahigh frequency (UHF)	868–928 MHz	3 m
Microwave	2.45 and 5.8 GHz	3 m
Ultrawide band (UWB)	3.1–10.6 GHz	10 m

Operating frequency is also important in determining the physical dimensions of an RFID tag. Different sizes and shapes of antennae will operate at different frequencies. The operating frequency also determines how tags physically interact with each other. For instance, stacking flat foil inlay tags on top of each other may cause interference and prevent tags from reading properly. Table 2 lists standard frequencies and their respective passive read distances.

Low Frequency

Low-frequency (LF) RFID tags typically operate in the 120-to-140-kHz range. Most commonly, LF tags are passively powered through induction. As a result, they typically have very short read ranges of 10 to 20 cm.

LF tags can be used in rugged environments and can operate in proximity to metal, liquids, or dirt. This makes them useful for applications like implantable pet identification tags or laundry-management tags. One disadvantage of LF tags is that they have a very low data read rate compared with other operating frequencies.

LF tags are often used in car-immobilization and access-control systems. In these systems, a car will start only if an LF tag, typically attached to the ignition key, is in proximity to the ignition. This takes advantage of LF's short read range and uses it as a security feature.

In 2006, LF passive tags may be purchased in bulk for $1 per tag or less. Two major manufacturers of LF tags are Texas Instruments and Phillips Semiconductor. The ISO 18000-2 standard offers specifications for LF RFID tags (International Organization for Standardization 2004).

High Frequency

High-frequency (HF) RFID tags operate at the 13.56-MHz frequency. HF tags are often packaged in a foil inlay or credit card form factor. This makes HF tags useful for building access control, contact-less credit cards, and ID badges. Again, the relatively short read range of HF is an advantage in these settings.

HF tags are also used in many asset-tracking applications. Libraries and bookstores often use HF foil inlays to track books. Some airports have started using HF RFID luggage tags for baggage-handling applications.

HF tags offer a higher data read rate than LF tags, but do not perform as well as LF tags in proximity to metals or liquids. HF tags do, however, offer better performance near metals or liquids than UHF tags do.

The HF frequency range lies on a heavily regulated part of the radio spectrum. Signals broadcast by readers must operate in a narrow frequency band. This presents a problem for environments with sensitive electronics, like medical equipment, that operate on similar frequencies. This makes HF tags inappropriate for environments like hospitals. In 2006, HF passive tags may be purchased in quantity for $0.50 or less per tag. Texas Instruments and Phillips both offer HF tag lines, although there are many smaller and specialized manufacturers or integrators in the HF space.

International Standards Organization (ISO) specifications for HF RFID tags are specified by the ISO 18000-3 standard (International Organization for Standardization 2004). Related specifications for HF contact-less smart cards and proximity cards appear in ISO standards 14443 and 15693 (International Organization for Standardization 2003).

Ultrahigh Frequency

Ultrahigh frequency (UHF) RFID tags operate in the 868-to-928-MHz range. European tags typically operate within the 868-to-870-MHz range, while the United States and Canada operate at 902 to 928 MHz.

UHF tags are most commonly used for item tracking and supply-chain-management applications. This is largely because they offer a longer read range and are cheaper to manufacture in bulk than LF or HF tags. The first-generation EPC tags operate at UHF.

A major disadvantage of UHF tags is that they experience interference in proximity to liquids or metals. Many applications like animal tracking, metal-container tracking, or even many access-control systems are not feasible with UHF tags. Some materials have been developed that may shield UHF tags from metal-related distortion, but these may be cost-prohibitive to use in practice. UHF readers may also interfere with sensitive electronics like medical equipment.

UHF tags are a relatively newer technology than LF or HF, and reader costs are typically higher than the lower-bandwidth LF readers. In 2006, UHF tags can be purchased in quantities for under $0.15 per passive tag. UHF tags costing as low $0.05 are likely to come to the market in coming years. Specifications for RFID tags operating at UHF frequencies are defined by both the ISO 18000-6 International Organization for Standardization 2004) standard and the EPCglobal standard (EPCglobal 2006).

Microwave

Microwave tags operate at either 2.45 or 5.8 GHz. This frequency range is sometimes referred to as super high frequency (SHF). Microwave RFID technology has come into use fairly recently and is rapidly developing. Microwave tags used in practice are typically semipassive or active, but may also come in passive form. Semipassive microwave tags are often used in fleet identification and electronic toll applications.

Microwave systems offer higher read rates than UHF and equivalent passive read ranges. Semipassive and active read ranges of microwave systems are often greater than their UHF counterparts. Some microwave active tags may be read from ranges of up to 30 m, which is less than comparable UHF tags. However, physical implementations of microwave RFID tags may be much smaller and more compact than lower-frequency RFID tags.

There are several downsides to microwave tags. One is that they consume comparatively more energy than their lower-frequency counterparts. Microwave tags are typically more expensive than UHF tags. Commercially available active tags cost as much as $25 per tag in 2006.

Another problem is that wireless 802.11b/g (WiFi) networks may interfere with microwave RFID systems. Devices implementing the upcoming ZigBee 802.15 wireless standard could also potentially conflict with microwave RFID devices as well. The ISO 18000-4 and the rejected ISO 18000-5 (International Organization for Standardization 2004) standards offer respective specifications for 2.45- and 5.8-GHz RFID tags.

Ultrawide Band

Ultrawide band (UWB) technology applied to RFID is fairly recent. Rather than sending a strong signal on a particular frequency, UWB uses low-power signals on a very broad range of frequencies. The signal on a particular frequency used by UWB is very weak, but in aggregate, communication is quite robust. In practice, some implementations of UWB operate from 3.1 to 10.6 GHz.

The advantages of UWB are that it has a very long line-of-sight read range, perhaps 200 m in some settings. UWB is also compatible with metal or liquids. Since the signal on a particular frequency is very weak, UWB does not interfere with sensitive equipment. Consequently, an early application was asset tracking in a hospital setting.

A disadvantage of current implementations of UWB is that it must be active or at least semipassive. However, since UWB tags broadcast very weak signals, they have relatively low power consumption. As of 2006, it is unclear whether the technology exists to create a passive UWB tag. (Multifrequency passive tags operating at HF, UHF, and microwave do exist in 2006. Although they do not operate as UWB tags, supporting multifrequency communications is possible in a passive setting.)

UWB RFID technology is still in its early phases and there are few commercial products available. Costs of $5 per tag in bulk are reasonable in the near future.

Functionality

The basic RFID functionality is identification. When queried by a reader, tags return some identifier that may be used to retrieve other data records. However, tags may offer various other functionalities useful in different applications. The underlying principles and technologies of these various types of tags are so closely related to strict RFID tags, that they often collectively referred to as "RFID." Although not strictly RFID, I discuss several major classes of RFID-related devices.

RFID-style tags are split into five broad classes: EAS, read-only EPC, EPC, sensor tags, and motes. These will be referred to as classes A through E. EPCglobal (2006) offers five similar classes of tag based on functionality dubbed class 0 through class 4. The EPCglobal classes closely align with ours, but differ somewhat. These five classes are summarized in Table 3.

Difficult technical and economic problems arise in class B and particularly class C devices. EAS tags are so limited in function that they are extremely simple and cheap to manufacture. By contrast, class D and E devices offer enough functionality to justify higher manufacturing

Table 3: Tag Functionality Classes

Class	Name	Memory	Power Source	Features
A	EAS	None	Passive	Article surveillance
B	Read-only EPC	Read-only	Passive	Identification only
C	EPC	Read/write	Passive	Data logging
D	Sensor tags	Read/write	Semipassive	Environmental sensors
E	Motes	Read/write	Active	Ad hoc networking

costs and can offer relatively ample resources. The challenge "sweet spot" lies in class B and class C devices, which are part of crucial systems, yet are still subject to tight resource and cost constraints.

Electronic Article Surveillance

Electronic article surveillance (EAS) tags are the most basic RFID-type tag and have been in commercial use for over 40 years. EAS tags do not contain unique identifying information, so technically are not RFID tags. They simply announce their presence to a reader. In other words, EAS tags broadcast a single bit of information—"Something is here."

In practice, EAS tags are almost always passive and are often attached to compact discs, clothing items, or books in retail locations. EAS tags could be active or semipassive, but the added cost of a power source would greatly outweigh adding unique identifying functionality. Because of their limited functionality, EAS tags are the simplest and cheapest to manufacture.

Read-Only EPC

Unlike EAS tags, EPC tags contain some identifying information. EPCglobal refers to these tags as class B tags. This information may be a product code or a unique identifier. Read-only EPC tags have a single identifier that is written once when a tag is manufactured. Thus, class B tags offer strict RFID functionality. Class B tags will likely be passively powered. Although they could be semipassive or active, again the cost of a battery would greatly outweigh the cost of rewritable memory.

As the name suggests, EPC tags are used in basic item-tracking applications. However, many other practical applications of tags, such as smart cards or proximity cards, are using tags with read-only memory that offer simple identification. Read-only EPC tags are fairly simple and may even be "chipless," and thus are relatively cheap.

Electronic Product Code

Class C refers to simple identification tags offering write-once, read-many or rewritable memory. Rather than having an identifier set at manufacture time, identifiers may be set by an end user. If an electronic product code (EPC) tag offers rewritable memory, its identifier may be changed many times. (Because of technical issues, "rewriteable" tags in practice typically can be written only some fixed number of times, perhaps several hundred.) Class C tags still offer strictly RFID functionality.

Class C EPC tags may be used as a logging device, or can emulate Class B read-only EPC tags. In practice, class B EPC tags may be passive, semipassive, or active. Strict RFID functionality includes class B tags. Supporting nonvolatile, writable memory adds complexity to class B tags. Consequently, they may be significantly more expensive than read-only EPC or EAS tags.

Sensor Tags

Sensor tags may contain on-board environmental sensors, and may log and store data without the aid of a reader. These types of tags will be referred to here as class D. Sensor tags offer more than strict RFID functionality, and are typically not thought of as RFID.

Many sensor tags may form a "sensor net" that monitors a physical area's environmental properties. This may include temperature changes, rapid acceleration, changes in orientation, vibrations, the presence of biological or chemical agents, light, sound, etc. Because they operate without a reader present, sensor tags must necessarily be semipassive or active. An on-board power source and sensor functionality comes at a much higher manufacturing cost.

Motes

Class E tags, or "smart dust" motes (Pister 2004), are able to initiate communication with peers or other devices, and form ad hoc networks. Motes are essentially general pervasive computing devices and are much more complex than simple EPC-style RFID. Because they are able to initiate their own communication, mote devices are necessarily active. Commercial motes are available from Crossbow Technology. Ongoing research into smart dust and motes is being conducted at the University of California, Berkeley, and at Intel.

Standards

The two most relevant RFID standards are the International Organization for Standardization's ISO/IEC 18000 standard (International Organization for Standardization 2004) and EPCglobal's standards (EPCglobal 2006). These standards are not competing, and it is conceivable that EPCglobal's standard could eventually be adopted into an ISO standard.

EPCglobal defines specifications for EPC-type tags operating in the UHF range. The ISO 18000 standard has six parts addressing different frequency ranges:

- Part 1—General standards
- Part 2—LF
- Part 3—HF
- Part 4—Microwave, 2.45 GHz
- Part 5—Microwave, 5.8 GHz (withdrawn)
- Part 6—UHF

Two other ISO standards, ISO/IEC 14443 and ISO/IEC 15693 (International Organization for Standardization 2004), are related to smart card and proximity card interfaces operating in the HF range.

CHALLENGES

Technical

RFID systems still face many technical challenges and obstacles to practical adoption. A major hurdle is simply getting RFID systems to work in real-world environments. Systems that work perfectly in a lab setting may encounter problems when faced with environmental noise, interference, or human elements.

As an example, in 2005, a major retail chain tested RFID pallet-level tracking in their shipping and receiving cargo bays. The retailer experienced difficulties in achieving near 100 percent read rates and had unanticipated, mundane technical issues. However, these issues will likely be ironed out as adoption becomes more commonplace.

Readers and tags have often experienced interference caused by other wireless systems or unknown sources. This type of interference was not systematic, and it usually resulted from environmental idiosyncrasies. Addressing these issues required trial and error and practical experience to recognize what was causing the problem. For example, simply repositioning or realigning readers would often address performance issues.

Software support for RFID is still in its early stages as well. Getting distributed back-end database lookups to work in practice is a complex task that is often glossed over in the RFID literature. In particular, key management and network connectivity issues are often underemphasized. Many vendors do currently offer RFID software solutions. However, in the coming years it is likely that the industry will consolidate onto several standardized software interfaces.

The point of this digression is to emphasize that, like most information technology systems, RFID systems still require practical expertise to install, configure, and manage. End users should expect to experience mundane technical complications that arise while implementing RFID. Despite marketing claims to the contrary, RFID is not a "magic bullet" that is simple to implement out of the box.

Economic

A key hurdle that still remains in RFID systems is simply cost. This is especially the case with EPC item-level tagging. A commonly cited price point at which item-level tagging is supposed to be economically viable is $0.05 per UHF tag.

As of 2006, the "5-cent tag" does not exist. Tag ICs alone (not including antennae or packaging), do cost as little as $0.08, although these are being sold as a loss leader. It will likely be a number of years until tags are available at the 5-cent level, and then only in huge quantities. However, this may be an artificial breakpoint. Many applications could very well benefit from more expensive tags.

A second cost issue is readers, especially UHF readers, which retail in 2006 for well over $1,000. At this price level, many firms may only afford a small number of readers in loading bays. "Smart shelves" that incorporate readers throughout a retail or warehouse environment would be prohibitively expensive for most applications.

As the market grows, RFID costs will drop and new applications will become economical, especially as more investment is made into back-end architectures. However, for the near future, the costs of many envisioned applications, particularly for EPC tags, are simply not justified.

Security and Privacy

Many concerns have been expressed over the security and privacy of RFID systems. Traditional applications, like large-asset tracking, were typically closed systems in which tags did not contain sensitive information. Tags on railway cars contained the same information painted on the side of the cars themselves. However, as more consumer applications are developed, security, and especially privacy, will become important issues.

Much work has recently focused on issues of RFID security and privacy. Gildas Avoine (2006) maintains a comprehensive bibliography of RFID security and privacy papers. Ari Juels (2006) offers a survey of RFID security and privacy issues. These references provide a more comprehensive analysis.

Eavesdropping

Perhaps the biggest security concerns in RFID systems are espionage and privacy threats. As organizations adopt and integrate RFID into their supply chain and inventory-control infrastructure, more and more sensitive data will be entrusted to RFID tags. As these tags inevitably end up in consumers' hands, they could leak sensitive data or be used for tracking individuals.

An attacker able to eavesdrop long range could possibly spy on a passive RFID system. Despite the fact that passive tags have a short operating range, the signal broadcast from the reader may be monitored from a long distance. This is because the reader signal actually carries the tag's power, and thus necessarily must be strong.

A consequence is that a reader communicating with a passive tag in, for instance, a UHF setting might be monitored from a range up to 100 to 1000 m. Although this only reveals one side of a communication protocol, some older protocols actually broadcast sensitive tag data over the forward channel. Newer specifications, like EPCglobal class-1 generation-2, take care to avoid this.

Although short-range eavesdropping requires nearby physical access, it can still be a threat in many settings. For example, a corporate spy could carry a monitoring device while a retail store conducts its daily inventory. Alternatively, a spy could simply place bugging devices that log protocol transmissions.

Espionage need not be passive. Attackers could actively query tags for their contents. Rather than waiting to eavesdrop on legitimate readers, active attackers could simply conduct tag read operations on their own. Active attackers may be easy to detect in a closed retail or warehouse environment, but may be difficult to detect in the open.

Both eavesdropping and active queries pose threats to individual privacy. RFID tags can be embedded in clothes, shoes, books, key cards, prescription bottles, and a slew of other products. Many of these tags will be embedded without the consumer ever realizing they are there. Without proper protection, a stranger could tell what drugs you are carrying, what books you are reading, perhaps even what brand of underwear you prefer.

Many privacy advocates are extremely concerned about RFID (Albrecht and McIntyre 2005). In 2003, Benetton, a clothing maker, announced plans to label clothing with RFID and was promptly boycotted by several groups (Krane 2003). This illustrates the potential of consumer backlash over privacy to impede RFID adoption.

Besides leaking sensitive data, individuals might be physically tracked by the tags they carry. Of course, cellular phones can already track individuals. Unlike a cell phone, which is only supposed to be able to be tracked by a cellular provider, RFID tags might be tracked by anyone (granted, within a relatively short read range). Readers will eventually be cheap to acquire and easy to conceal.

Clearly, tracking someone is trivial if an attacker is able to actively query unique identifying numbers from tags. Even if unique serial numbers are removed from tags, an individual might be tracked by the "constellation" of brands they carry. A unique fashion sense might let someone physically track you through an area by your set of favorite brands.

Many privacy countermeasures have been proposed that may efficiently mitigate many of these risks. We refer the reader to Juels' survey (2006) and Avoine's bibliography (2006) for more information.

Forgery

Rather than simply trying to glean data from legitimate tags, adversaries might try to imitate tags. This is a threat to RFID systems currently being used for access-control and payment systems. Although an adversary able to physically obtain a tag can almost always clone it, the real risk is someone being able to "skim" tags wirelessly for information that can be used to produce forgeries. For instance, if tags simply respond with a static identification number, skimming is trivial.

Forgery is obviously a major issue in RFID systems used specifically as an anticounterfeiting device. For example, the FDA (2004) proposed attaching RFID tags to prescription drug bottles as a pedigree. Someone able to produce forgeries could steal legitimate shipments and replace them with valid-looking decoys, or could simply sell counterfeit drugs with fake pedigree labels.

A cautionary example is the ExxonMobil Speedpass (2006), which uses an RFID keychain fob that allows customers to make purchase at ExxonMobil gas stations. A team of researchers from Johns Hopkins University and RSA Security broke the weak security in Speedpass and produced forgeries that could be used to make purchases at retail locations (Bono et al. 2005).

Fortunately, low-cost security countermeasures have been developed that allow readers to authenticate tags. For example, Juels and Weis (2005) offer a low-cost authentication protocol based on a hard learning problem that is efficient to implement in a tag. However, as of 2006, these protocols exist only on paper and are not available in any commercial products.

Denial of Service

Weaker attackers unable to conduct espionage or forgery attacks may still be able to sabotage RFID systems or conduct denial-of-service attacks. An adversary may simply jam communication channels and prevent readers from identifying tags. An attacker could also seed a physical space with "chaff" tags intended to confuse legitimate readers or poison databases. Locating and removing chaff tags might be very difficult in a warehouse environment, for instance.

Powerful electromagnetic signals could physically damage or destroy RF systems in a destructive denial-of-service attack. Fortunately, attempting these attacks from long range would require so much power that it would affect other electronic components and be easily detected.

Although these denial-of-service and sabotage attacks may seem to be simply nuisances, they could represent serious risks. This is especially true in defense or medical applications. For example, the U.S. Department of Defense is moving toward RFID-based logistics control. An attack against the RFID infrastructure could delay crucial shipments of war materiel or slow down troop deployments.

Viruses

In 2006, researchers demonstrated an RFID virus based on an system query language (SQL) injection attack (Rieback, Crispo, and Tanenbaum 2006). The virus payload was an SQL database query that would overwrite existing RFID identifiers in the database with the virus payload. When tags were updated from the infected database, the virus would be propagated.

This virus assumes that RFID contents are essentially "executed" without any validation. It also assumes that future reads from an infected system can overwrite tag contents, which is often not the case in practice. In fact, nothing about the virus was particular to RFID systems. Input from any source, whether a network connection, USB port, or keyboard, could spread viruses when insecurely executed without validation.

CONCLUSION AND FUTURE TECHNOLOGIES

Two promising technological developments especially relevant to RFID are printed circuits and organic components (Subramanian et al. 2006; University of California, Berkeley Organic Electronics Group 2006). These technologies have the potential to greatly lower manufacturing costs and to produce RFID tags built out of flexible plastic materials instead of silicon.

The long-term vision is that a large-scale packaging manufacturer could print RFID tags directly into paper or plastic as it is produced. Product makers would not use this RFID-enhanced packaging material as they normally would. One advantage in terms of privacy is that RFID tags would be attached only to product packaging, and not to the product itself.

This technology is still years away from being economical, and there are many hurdles to overcome. Currently, circuits printed by an inkjet printer have a very low resolution; circuit gates take much more surface area than traditionally fabricated circuits. Other technologies like gravure printing also produce relatively large circuit surface areas.

Regardless, much research is being focused on organic components for other purposes, like flexible displays. Developments in this area will benefit RFID, potentially opening the door to many inexpensive and interesting future applications.

GLOSSARY

Active Tag: A tag with its own battery that can initiate communications.

Auto-ID: Automatic identification. Auto-ID systems automatically identify physical objects through the use of optical, electromagnetic, or chemical means.

EAS: Electronic article surveillance. An RF device that announces its presence but contains no unique identifying data. EAS tags are frequently attached to books or compact discs.

EPC: Electronic product code. A low-cost RFID tag designed for consumer products as a replacement for the UPC.

HF: High frequency. ≥13.56 MHz.

IFF: Identify friend or foe. Advanced RFID systems used to automatically identify military aircraft.

LF: Low frequency. 120–140 KHz.

Linear Barcode: A one-dimensional, optical bar code used for auto-ID.

Passive Tag: A tag with no on-board power source that harvests its energy from a reader-provided RF signal.

Reader: An RFID transceiver, providing read and possibly write access to RFID tags.

RF: Radio frequency.

RFID: Radio-frequency identification. Describes a broad spectrum of devices and technologies, and is used to refer both to individual tags and overall systems.

Semipassive Tag: A tag with an on-board power source that is unable to initiate communications with a reader.

Skimming: An attack in which an adversary wirelessly reads data from a RFID tag, enabling forgery or cloning.

Tag: An RFID transponder, typically consisting of an RF coupling element and a microchip that carries identifying data. Tag functionality may range from simple identification to being able to form ad hoc networks.

UCC: Uniform Code Council. A standards committee originally formed by grocery manufacturers and food distributors that designed the UPC barcode.

UHF: Ultrahigh frequency. 868–928 MHz.

UPC: Universal product code. A one-dimensional, optical barcode found on many consumer products.

UWB: Ultrawide band. A weak communication signal is broadcast over a very wide band of frequencies—e.g., 3.1–10.6 GHz.

CROSS REFERENCES

See *Principles and Applications of Ad Hoc and Sensor Networks*; *Social Engineering*; *Worms and Viruses*.

REFERENCES

Albrecht, K., and L. McIntyre. 2005. *Spychips: How major corporations and government plan to track your every move with RFID*. Nashville: Nelson Current.

Auto-ID Labs. 2006. www.autoidlabs.org. (accessed March 11, 2006).

Avoine, G. 2006. *Security and privacy in RFID systems bibliography*. http://lasecwww.epfl.ch/~gavoine/rfid (accessed: March 11, 2006).

Baird, J. L. 1928. *Improvements in or relating to apparatus for transmitting views or images to a distance*. U.S. Patent #GB292,185.

Bono, S., M. Green, A. Stubblefield, A. Rubin, A. Juels, and M. Szydlo. 2005. *Analysis of the Texas Instruments DST RFID*. http://rfidanalysis.org (accessed March 9, 2006).

EPCglobal. 2006. www.epcglobalinc.org (accessed March 11, 2006).

ExxonMobil Speedpass. 2006. www.speedpass.com (accessed March 11, 2006).

Food and Drug Administration. 2004. *Combating counterfeit drugs*. Technical Report. U.S. Department of Health and Human Services. www.fda.gov/oc/initiatives/counterfeit/report02_04.html (accessed: March 11, 2006).

International Organization for Standardization (ISO). 2003. Identification cards—Contactless integrated circuit(s) cards—Vicinity cards. ISO/IEC 14443 and 15693.

———. 2004. RFID for item management. ISO/IEC 18000.

Juels, A. 2006. RFID security and privacy: A research survey. *IEEE Journal on Selected Areas of Cryptography* 21(2):381–94 .

Juels, A., and R. Pappu. 2003. Squealing euros: Privacy-protection in RFID-enabled banknotes. Financial cryptography. New York: Springer Lecture Notes in Computer Science, 2742:103–21.

Juels, A., and S. A. Weis. 2005. Authenticating pervasive devices with human protocols. In *Advances in Cryptology—Crypto '05*. New York: Springer Lecture Notes in Computer Science, 3621:293–308.

Krane, J. 2003. Benetton clothing to carry tiny tracking transmitters. Associated Press.

Nokia. 2004. Nokia Mobile RFID Kit. www.nokia.com/nokia/0, 55738,00.html. (accessed March 11, 2006).

Pister, K. 2004. Smart dust: Autonomous sensing and communications in a cubic millimeter. http://robotics.eecs.berkeley.edu/~pister/SmartDust (accessed: March 11, 2006).

RFID Journal. 2003. Gillette confirms RFID purchase. www.rfidjournal.com/article/articleview/258/1/1. (accessed: March 11, 2006).

———. 2003. Wal-Mart Expands RFID Mandate. www.rfidjournal.com/article/articleview/539/1/1 (accessed March 11, 2006).

———. 2005. AmEx adds RFID to blue credit cards. www.rfidjournal.com/article/articleview/1646/1/1 (accessed March 11, 2006).

Rieback, M. R., B. Crispo, and A. S. Tanenbaum. 2006. Is your cat infected with a computer virus? In *IEEE International Conference on Pervasive Computing and Communications*, 169–79. Los Alamitos, CA: IEEE Press.

Royal Air Force. 2006. Royal Air Force History. www.raf.mod.uk/history/line1940.html (accessed March 11, 2006).

Stockman, H. 1948. Communication by means of reflected power. In *Proceedings of the Institute of Radio Engineers, October*, 1196–204. Los Alamitos, CA: IEEE Press.

Subramanian, V., P. Chang, D. Huang, J. Lee, S. Molesa, D. Redinger, and S. Volkman. 2006. In *2006. Conference on VLSI Design*, 709–14. Los Alamitos, CA: IEEE Press.

Uniform Code Council. 2006. www.uc-council.org (accessed March 11, 2006).

University of California, Berkeley Organic Electronics Group. 2006. http://organics.eecs.berkeley.edu (accessed March 11, 2006).

U.S. Department of Defense. 2006. Radio frequency identification. www.acq.osd.mil/log/rfid/index.htm (accessed March 11, 2006).

World Health Organization. 2006. Counterfeit medicines. www.who.int/mediacentre/factsheets/fs275/en (accessed March 11, 2006).

Active Networking

Stephen F. Bush, *GE Global Research*

INTRODUCTION

The goal of active networking is to create communication networks that reposition static, low-level network operation into dynamic, differentiated, and adaptable behavior, often implemented by transferring low-level network operating code within the same packets that carry network traffic. This allows communication hardware to be more fully used given that its operation can be tailored to specific application requirements. This also enables a more flexible and survivable communication network. Active networking decouples the network protocol from its transport by allowing easy insertion of protocols on top of the transport layer. Active networking also minimizes requirements for global agreement; it does not require years of standards negotiation to introduce new protocols. Active networking enables on-the-fly experimentation given easy insertion of new protocols and network applications, thus enabling the rapid deployment of new services and applications. The mechanism for implementing an active network is to enable communication packets to carry network code as well as data. This code may be installed on the fly into low-level network devices as the packet flows through the network.

If one compares and contrasts the current Internet protocols and active and programmable networking shown in Figure 1, it should be noted that Internet protocols have become fossilized, in other words resistant to radical change, whereas an active network is built for change. The Internet protocols are becoming burdened with layer upon layer of complexity; for example, there are on the order of 4000 RFCs (Requests for Comment) describing Internet protocols and operation. In contrast, a goal of active networking is to reduce complexity by allowing a common framework for protocol insertion. The Internet protocol has an inability to customize quickly or efficiently because of a long standardization process, whereas the active network concept is to provide a framework for rapid and efficient customization. The Internet protocols are well known for their lack of common or operable security paradigms. In contrast, the Security Framework for Active Networks has received considerable attention in order to provide a secure framework from the start. Finally, the Internet protocols appear to be on a downward slope in terms of innovation; in other words, new standards tend to add smaller and smaller evolutionary changes. In contrast, active networking allows significant room for an upward trend in innovation.

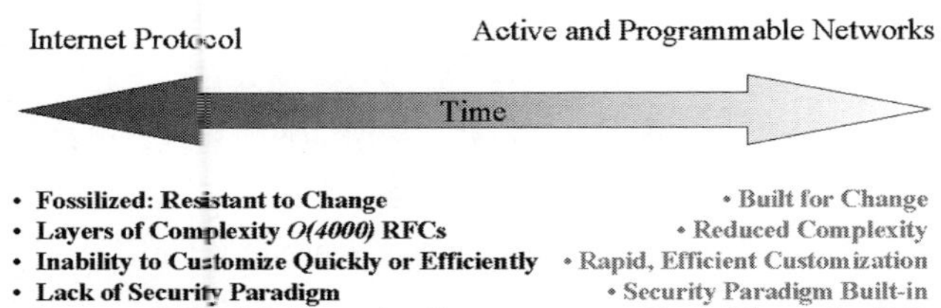

Figure 1: The contrast between current networks and active networks (RFC = Request for Comment)

Active networking paradigms are being used in wireless and ad hoc communications. A trend is the exploration of self-organization and emergent behavior among autonomous packets. The latest research in this area can be found in conferences listed in the Further Reading section at the end of this chapter and in a journal issue focused on active networks (Bush and Kalyanaraman 2006).

The active network model provides user-driven customization of the network infrastructure, allowing new services to be deployed at a faster pace than can be sustained by vendor-driven consensus or through standardization. The essential feature of active networks is the programmability of its infrastructure. New capabilities and services can be added to the networking infrastructure on demand. This creates a versatile network that can easily adapt to future application needs. The ability to program new services into the network will lead to a user-driven innovation process in which the availability of new services will be dependent on their acceptance in the marketplace. In short, active networking enables the rapid deployment of novel and innovative services and protocols into the network. For example, a videoconferencing application can inject a custom packet-filtering algorithm into the network that, in times of congestion, filters video packets and allows only audio packets to reach the receivers. Under severe congestion, the algorithm compresses audio packets to reduce network load and alleviate congestion. This enables the application to handle performance degradation due to network problems gracefully and in an application-specific manner.

In an active network, applications not only determine the protocol functions as necessary at the end points of communication, but also inject new protocols into the network. The concept of active networking evolved from discussions within the Department of Defense's Defense Advanced Research Projects Agency (DARPA) community regarding future directions in communication networks. The purpose of these discussions was to design networks that overcome problems and limitations of existing networks. Some of the problems identified were:

- Existing networks cannot support rapid development and deployment of new protocols and services. Designing a new protocol requires acceptance from a standardization committee and later implementation and support from vendors before applications can use the protocol. Experience has shown that this is usually a long and tedious process. For example, work on the design of the Internet Protocol version 6 (IPv6) was initially started in 1995 but the protocol has still not found widespread deployment.
- The existing Internet model allows limited security in the form of secure sockets, application data encryption and firewalls, but it is still difficult to create seamless, secure virtual private networks over the Internet.
- Network functionality is scattered across routers, switches, end systems, link-level hardware and applications, which prevents gathering of coherent state and makes network management extremely difficult.
- Mobile devices have to be treated as static devices because it is not currently possible to move a mobile state seamlessly across the network.
- It is not possible to deploy new services such as adaptive transcoding or in-network data-fusion, when and where you want them dynamically. In current networks, services are rigidly built into kernels of operating systems of end systems and network devices, preventing on-the-fly customization of these services by the applications

To overcome the above limitations, DARPA began working on a set of ideas collectively referred to as active networking. The principal tenet of active networking is to devise the network architecture so that new features and services can be programmed into the network. The idea of carrying computation into the network is a natural evolution from circuit switching and packet switching, in terms of increasingly greater computational role in the network, as shown in Figure 2.

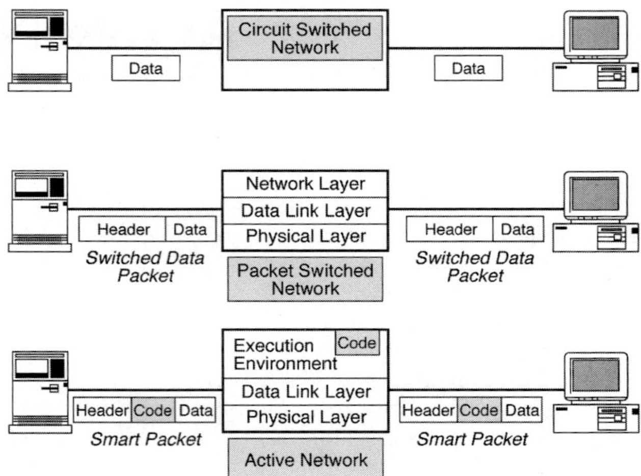

Figure 2: Active networks appear as a natural evolution of legacy networking

Research into active networking has provided the incentive to revisit what has traditionally been classified as distinct properties and characteristics of information transfer, such as protocol versus service; at a more fundamental level, this chapter considers the blending of computation and communication by means of descriptive complexity, discussed later. The specific active service examined in this chapter is network self-prediction enabled by an active application. Computation/communication is analyzed via Kolmogorov complexity. The result is a mechanism to understand and improve the performance of active networking.

Custom code is injected into the network in one of two ways, as shown in Figure 3. One approach is to download code to active nodes separately from data packets. The downloaded code carries computation required for some or all of the data packets flowing through the node. The code is invoked when the intended data packets reach the node. This is known as the discrete approach. The

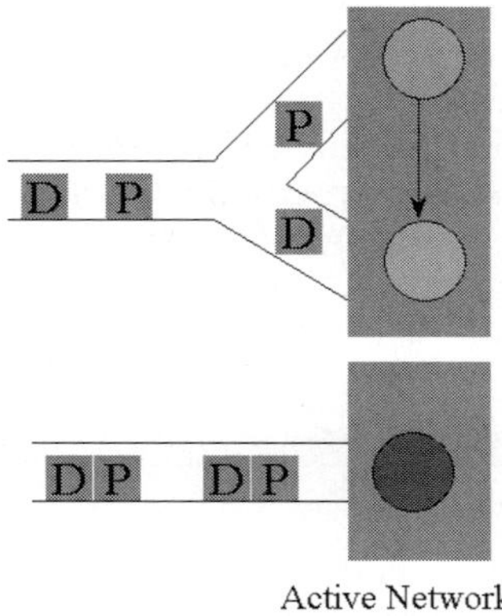

Figure 3: Integrated (upper portion of figure) versus discrete (lower portion of figure) active packets (P = program) (D = data)

other approach is the capsule or integrated approach. In this approach, packets carry both computation as well as data. As packets flow through intermediate network nodes, the custom code is installed at some or all the nodes in the network. These packets are called "capsules" or "SmartPackets." These are the basic unit of communication in an active network. Applications inject SmartPackets in the network and active nodes process the code inside the SmartPackets.

BACKGROUND

There is a general consensus that network architectures must be made programmable to enable application-specific customization of network resources and the rapid introduction of new services into the network. As a result, there are two schools of thought on the approach to be taken to make networks programmable. One effort is spearheaded by the OpenSig community, which argues that networks can be designed using a set of open programmable interfaces, opening access to network devices such as switches, routers, and hubs and thereby enabling third-party developers to devise custom solutions for their applications. The other approach is that of active networks, in which packets can contain custom code that executes in the execution environment provided by the nodes of the network. Thus, an active network is no longer node-centric but packet-centric; that is, the code in the active packets is executed at the intermediate network devices as the packet travels through the network. The result is that customized processing is accomplished as the packet is transmitted through the network. This enables experimentation and the rapid deployment of new services.

After the concept of active networking was initially conceived, researchers at the Massachusetts Institute of Technology developed a small proof-of-concept prototype using a Tcl (originally from "tool command language," but nonetheless conventionally rendered as "Tcl" rather than "TCL," and pronounced "tickle," a *scripting language*) shell to demonstrate the potential of the new idea. This sparked interest among researchers initially in the United States (primarily because of the DARPA effort) and later worldwide. This can be evidenced from the chapters submitted to the March 2000 issue of the *IEEE Communications Magazine* and the participation in the International Conference on Active Networks (IWAN). There were a considerable number of research efforts that attempted to develop complex and varied execution platforms to study different facets of the model. This led to a plethora of custom execution platforms on small-scale active networks. However, the prototypes were limited to testbeds in individual research laboratories, which did not bode well for the deployment of active networks on a global scale. Therefore, in 1998, researchers across the active networking community challenged themselves to develop plans to deploy active networks on a large scale. The principal hurdle toward this goal was the total lack of interoperability between the execution platforms. The community decided that while the richness in diversity is desirable, it was necessary to develop a scheme that enabled diverse active network prototypes to communicate with each other.

The solution was to define a skeleton framework for an active node that divided its functionality into layers and to define the scope and properties of each layer. This enabled researchers to collaborate in the design of an active network in which active nodes can host several different execution platforms and yet can be connected to each other to provide an active network backbone. The framework is defined in a working document called the "Architectural Framework for Active Networks" (Calvert 1998).

Active networking provides a programmable infrastructure using a well-defined structure for packets that contain general-purpose program code and a uniform standardized execution platform on the nodes of the network. The next sections give the reader an overview of the basic model of an active network. They describe basic components and introduce common terminology.

ACTIVE NETWORK FRAMEWORK

There had been a few pioneering efforts that predate the term *active networks;* most notably, SOFTNET was used as an active ad hoc network in the early 1980s from the Radio Communication Systems Lab, Royal Institute of Technology, Stockholm, Sweden, which allowed dynamic network programming within packets; however, rapid acceleration in the development of active networks did not occur until the mid-1990s, with the funding by DARPA. Some early examples of active network applications included active routers that provide soft-state storage and "best-effort" caching so that lost packets can be retransmitted by the nearest upstream router and nacks (negative acknowledgments) are fused on the way to the sender; the sender receives only one nack instead of one per receiver. The general concept of data fusion is shown in Figure 4, in which data are processed as they traverse the network, and such processing reduces the aggregate data size. This differs from current networks, in which all data are transferred to a central location before they are processed, potentially resulting in large amounts of redundant data transfer and unnecessary load on the network.

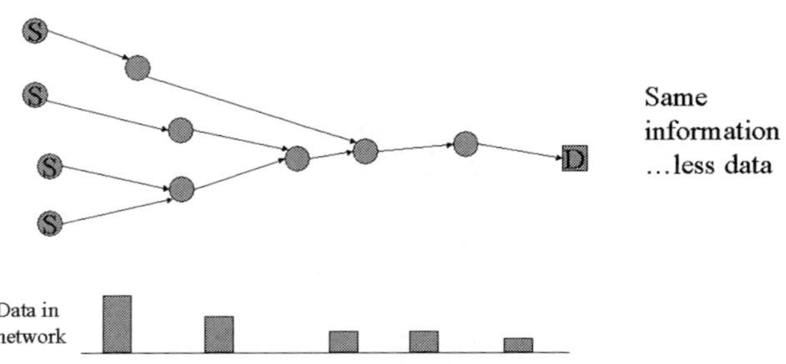

Figure 4: Data from many sources (S) are fused as they are processed along their route to the destination (D), resulting in reduced load

The reference model for active networks is comprised of a set of nodes, not all of which need be active, connected by a variety of technologies. Each active node runs a node operating system and one or more execution environments as shown in Figure 5. The node operating system (NodeOS) are responsible for allocating and scheduling node resources. Each execution environment implements a virtual machine capable of interpreting active packets arriving at the node. Several execution environments have been developed with different capabilities. For example, some may be completely general—that is, Turing complete—while others may allow only very limited execution. The set of programs running within execution environments across the network comprise an active application. This very general reference model allows for a wide variety of network service models, including those supporting a mixture of both active and nonactive traffic.

Some of the underlying assumptions are that the unit of multiplexing within the network is a packet. Another underlying assumption is that the primary function of the active network is communication and not computation. Computation may occur, but the primary benefit of such computation must be in support of communications. Assumptions regarding underlying technologies need to be minimized since the reference architecture should allow for active networking on top of any lower-layer technology. Another assumption, common to any large Internet architecture, is that administration of individual nodes may be under the control of an organization, but no organization controls all active nodes. Thus, the issue of trust among administrations will vary, and security is a primary issue.

The objectives of the architectural framework document are to specify the minimal amount of information needed to operate active components without overspecifying, or constraining, innovative solutions. Some of the objectives explicitly stated in the reference architecture document are to minimize the amount of global agreement required and to enable dynamic modification of those aspects that do not require global agreement within the network. In addition, the active network should be compatible with, and allow implementations of, current standard forwarding techniques. In other words, the active network should allow architectures with processing speeds at least as fast as today's architectures permit. Another objective is the ability to scale to very large global networks. Finally, network management, at all levels, must be supported.

The distinction is made between node and network architectural issues. Node issues deal with how packets are processed and how local node resources are used and managed. In contrast, network architecture deals with global matters such as addressing and end-to-end allocation of resources. The active network is comprised of three main components—namely, the node operating system, an execution environment, and active applications. The execution environment reveals a programming interface or virtual machine controlled by active packets entering the node. The execution environment has been compared to a UNIX shell program. Note that multiple execution environments may be present on a single active node.

The node operating system manages resources of the active node and mediates demands from the execution environments that it supports. These can include things such as transmission, computation, and storage. This allows the execution environments to focus on supporting the active packet programs without having to be directly concerned with limited resources on the node or negotiating with other execution environments on the same node for resources. It is noted that an identifier, which indicates the user making the request, may accompany execution environment requests for service. This information allows requests for resources to be granted within the limits of the quality of service for that particular user. The reference architecture uses the term *principal* to designate any entity whose actions can be authorized. The principal may be a user or another active network component, such as an execution environment.

Explicit mention is made of a distinguished management execution environment responsible for the critical operations local to the node such as configuration and policy control. Such management functions acting through the management execution environment require strict security. Figure 6 shows the architectural components in more detail.

General processing of packets occurs when packets arrive at an active node, as shown in Figure 7. Information in the header of the packet specifies both protocol processing and the type of execution environment capable of handling that packet. It is the execution environment that announces its ability to handle certain types of packets through the creation of a channel. Classification

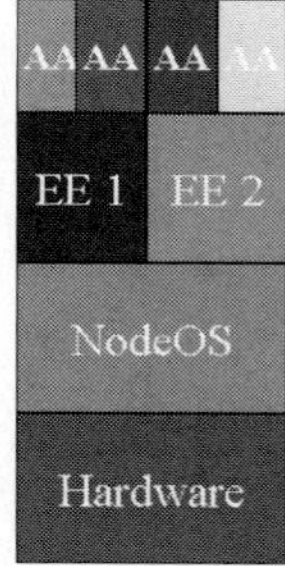

Figure 5: Active applications (AAs) reside on the execution environment (EE), which reside on the NodeOS

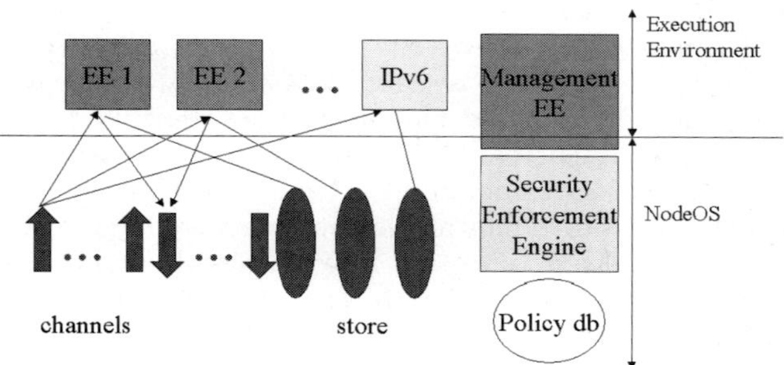

Figure 6: The interface between the NodeOS and execution environments shown in greater detail

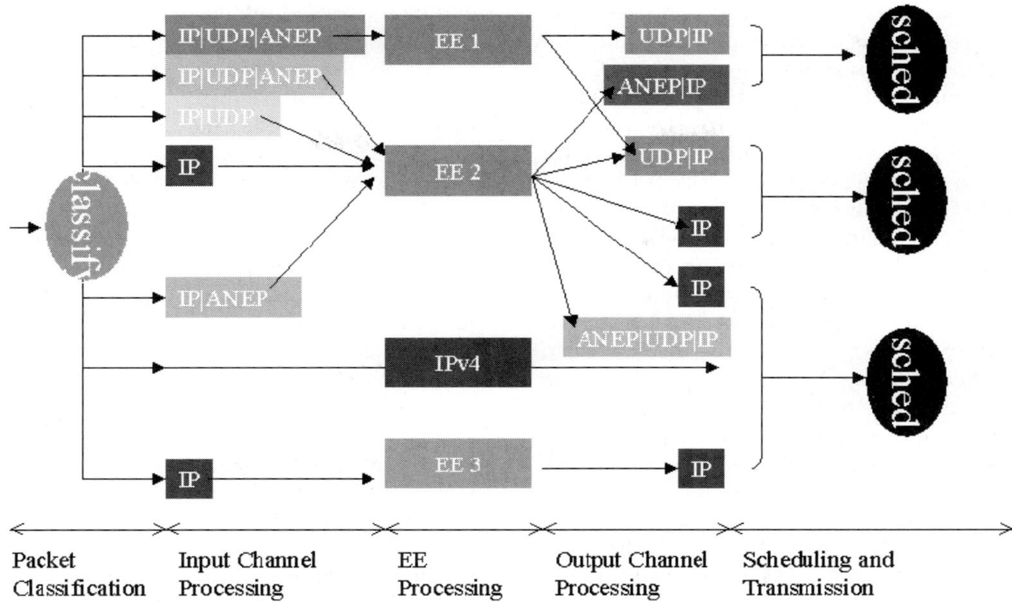

Figure 7: Classification of packets occurs in channels within the node operating system. Packets may flow through an EE for processing. (ANEP = active networking encapsulation protocol; UDP = user datagram protocol)

of the packet and subsequent determination of the type of execution environment suitable for that packet occurs within the channel. Packets entering the node that cannot be classified or that match no pattern suggesting a resident execution environment are dropped. Execution environments, after executing any active code within the packet, transmit resulting packets through output channels. The output channel can include the implementation of scheduling algorithms. It should be noted that there is not an assumed one-to-one correspondence between input and output packets. Input active packets may reside within the execution requirement without leaving the node. In addition, packets may be spontaneously generated from a node, without corresponding input packets. In other words, it depends on the active code remaining on the node from prior packets. Another possibility is that packets may be aggregated and sent as a combined packet; again, this is a function of the code within each of the active packets working together.

It is up to the node operating system to ensure that a misbehaving execution environment does not consume all the node's resources. Scheduling mechanisms in the active networking environment must be more sophisticated than in legacy systems. This is because computation time must be taken into account as well as transmission time. It is suggested that input channels be scheduled only with respect to computation, and output channels must be scheduled with respect to both computation and transmission. This divides bandwidth equally among the set of classes.

The active networking encapsulation protocol (ANEP) is used to embed active network packets over other media. It includes a header with a type-identifier field. Well-known type IDs are assigned to particular execution environments. It is the TypeID that allows the channel to route incoming active packets to the proper execution environment. Note that legacy packets—that is, those that do not contain an ANEP header—are also processed if the appropriate channels are set up. A common example is an execution environment that mimics IPv4 forwarding behavior. Another is an execution environment that provides enhanced TCP services, which may transparently change header bits. Note that the ANEP header also allows an indication of what the node should do with regard to error handling, for example, when an execution environment within a particular node cannot process the packet. The ANEP header would indicate whether the packet should be dropped or attempt to forward it via other means. In addition the ANEP header contains suggested security measures. It is likely to be impractical for every node in the network to authenticate every packet passing through it. However, it may be feasible for a packet to be authenticated once when it initially enters the network and afterward be verified node-to-node using shared keys between neighboring nodes. The ANEP header is thus a good location for holding a node-to-node credential.

An execution environment defines a programming interface for a virtual machine that can be controlled by sending the appropriate code instructions to it within active packets. The function of this machine is left open—that is, the architectural framework does not define it. It is the NodeOS that provides a basic set of capabilities that can be used by the execution environments to implement the virtual machine. A variety of EEs have been constructed and tested; some are universal machines—that is, they can be programmed to simulate other machines—all others offer more restricted programming interfaces that allow the user limited program capability. The reason for limited program capability is to maintain communication efficiency and keep the focus on enhancing transmission rather than on general programming.

An active application is comprised of code running within execution environments that provides an end-to-end service within the network. Thus, it is the active application that provides the customized services for end-user applications. The active network framework allows for both active code carried in packets along with the data or code that is installed within EEs using out-of-band techniques. The out-of-band loading of new code within EEs may happen during a separate signaling phase or on demand when a packet arrives. Great pains have been taken within the active network framework architecture to minimize constraints and to enable the composition of active applications. For example, it should be possible for users to access multiple active applications and combine them in flexible ways, for example, mobility and multicast even though these are separate active applications.

Deployment of new EEs requires that the application-programming interface to the EE be specified so that active applications can be built. In addition, the well-known ANEP packet types supported by the EE must be made public. The active network framework architecture does not specify a standard method for installing new execution environments on an active node. In addition, the active network framework architecture does not provide a standard for inter-EE communication. Such communication can occur by packet transfer between EEs on the same node or by shared memory, known as small state.

The typical high-speed networking router/switch accepts packets on an input port, parses and validates the packets on the input port card, looks up the destination address in a forwarding table, and then sends the packet through a switch fabric to the appropriate output ports as shown in Figure 8. It is the output port card that handles encapsulation for the link and queues and schedules the packet for transmission. An active device would require general-purpose processor cards to be incorporated into this mechanism so that active packet code can be executed as shown in the bottom portion of Figure 8. Ideally, packets entering the input port would also be entering the previously defined active network channel

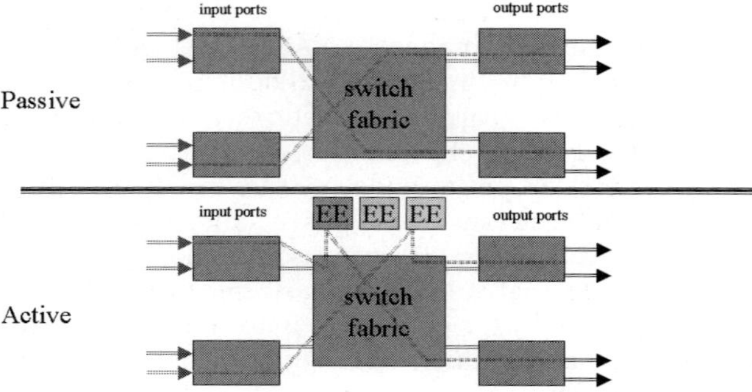

Figure 8: Active network hardware allows packets to be switched through a general-purpose processor before leaving the hardware

and be forwarded by the switch fabric to the appropriate execution environment residing on a separate processor card. This architecture will allow legacy packets to be cut through the switch fabric, bypassing the active network processor if desired. This approach is scalable because more processing cards and port cards can be added. It is recognized, however, that the NodeOS using this technique becomes a distributed operating system. Global state must be shared across multiple processing cards. This increases the complexity of the operating system, requiring additional synchronization and multiple access techniques. It is also noted that the execution environment in this architecture is physically separated from the output port cards. This limits direct access from the execution environment to the output queues. The alternative architecture divides the processing between input and output cards while leaving the switch fabric untouched. However, dividing the execution environment into separate input and output processing again causes distributed operating system problems, such as coordination between the input and output execution environment processing.

A significant concern is the potential waste of resources by erroneous or malicious active packets. Thus, mechanisms must be in place to drop packets using too much processing time. In addition, all scheduling algorithms must be work-conserving. This means that packets must be scheduled for execution in such a manner that the processor is not delayed. In general, it is very important to have a precise quantification of resources. The bit is assumed to be the universal quantitative measure of information transmission. Similarly, the byte is understood to be a measure of storage capacity. In addition, the time dimension should be added to provide a bound on the effect of storing a byte indefinitely. Quantifying computational requirements with respect to communications is an open issue and has been one of the key analytical challenges in active networks (Galtier et al. 2001). This topic is discussed further in the section on "Analysis of Active Networks." Techniques for quantifying computational resources have included removing loops from code destined to an execution environment. This allows the size of the packet to be proportional to the amount of processor time required to execute the packet. Another technique for quantifying computation involves the use of algorithmic information theory and Kolmogorov complexity. The intuition behind the use of this technique is to consider the descriptive complexity of code to be executed.

Another open issue concerns the division of labor between the execution environments and the NodeOS. Specifically, information placed in the NodeOS provides a common repository for all execution environments residing on the same node, whereas the same information placed within each execution environment on the same node would be redundant. However, placing all functionality in the NodeOS increases the complexity of the NodeOS.

Given that every node may not support every possible execution environment, a default routing mechanism should be in place for active packets, as illustrated in Figure 9. One possibility for making an active packet more ubiquitously executable is to place multiple versions of code within the packet, one for each possible

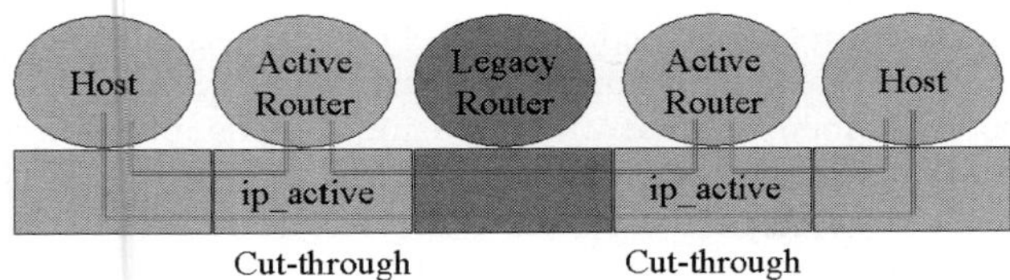

Figure 9: Active and current node interoperability may be achieved by enabling active nodes to mimic legacy nodes

execution environment. Because this could make packets prohibitively large, the active network framework document encourages the universal deployment of only a small number of execution environments.

ACTIVE NETWORK ARCHITECTURE

All nodes within the active network provide a common base functionality, which is defined by the node architecture. The node architecture deals with how packets are processed and how local resources are managed. The network architecture deals with global matters such as addressing, end-to-end allocation of resources, and so on; as such, it is tied to the interface presented by the network to the end-user. The node architecture is explicitly designed to allow for more than one such "network application programming interface (API)." Several factors motivate this approach. First, multiple APIs already exist, and given the early state of our understanding it seems desirable to let them "compete" side by side. Second, it supports the goal of fast-path processing for those packets that want a "plain old forwarding service." Third, this approach provides a built-in evolutionary path, not only for new and existing APIs, but also for backward-compatibility: IPv4 or IPv6 functionality can be regarded as simply another API.

The functionality of the active network node is divided between the execution environments (execution environments or just "environments") and the NodeOS. The general organization of these components was shown in Figure 5. Each execution environment exports an API or virtual machine that users can program or control by directing packets to it. Thus, an execution environment acts like the "shell" program in a general-purpose computing system, providing an interface through which end-to-end network services can be accessed. The architecture allows for multiple execution environments to be present on a single active node. However, development and deployment of an execution environment is considered a nontrivial exercise, and it is expected that the number of different execution environments supported at any one time will be relatively small. The NodeOS provides the basic functions on which execution environments build the abstractions presented to the user. As such, it manages the resources of the active node and mediates the demand for those resources, including transmission, computing, and storage. The NodeOS thus isolates execution environments from the details of resource management and from the effects of the behavior of other execution environments. The execution environments in turn hide from the NodeOS most of the details of interaction with the end user. To provide adequate support for quality of service, the NodeOS allows for allocation of resources at a finer level of granularity than just execution environments.

When an execution environment requests a service from the NodeOS, an identifier (and possibly a credential) accompanies the request for the principal on whose behalf the request is made. This principal may be the execution environment itself, or another party—a user—in whose behalf the execution environment is acting. The NodeOS presents this information to an enforcement engine, which verifies its authenticity and checks that the node's security policy database as shown in Figure 6 authorizes the principal to receive the requested service or perform the requested operation.

Execution Environment

An EE defines a virtual machine and "programming interface" that is available to users of the active network. Users control that virtual machine by sending the appropriate coded instructions to the EE in packets. Execution of these instructions will in general cause the state of the EE and the active node to be updated, and may cause the EE to transmit one or more packets, either immediately or at some later time. The function of the virtual machine provided by any EE is not defined by the architecture. The NodeOS provides a basic set of capabilities that can be used by EEs to implement a virtual machine. Thus, the EE defines most aspects of the network architecture.

EEs allow users some control over the way their packets are processed. If an EE implements a universal virtual machine—that is, one that can be programmed to simulate other machines—a user may provide a complete description of required packet processing. Other EEs may supply a more restricted form of programming, in which the user supplies a set of parameters and/or simple policy specifications. In any case, the "program" may be carried in-band with the packet itself, or installed out-of-band. Out-of-band programming may happen in advance of packet transmission or on demand, upon packet arrival; it may occur automatically (e.g., when instructions carried in a packet invoke a method not present at the node, but known to exist elsewhere) or under explicit user control.

An interesting feature of some EEs is that of SmallState, a named cache that enables SmartPackets to leave information at a node that can be retrieved later by other SmartPackets. SmallState thus becomes an interpacket communication (IPC) mechanism, providing a mechanism for packets to talk to each other and implement collaborative behavior in the network. The extent of the IPC depends on the control mechanisms defined by the EEs for their SmallState. In some EEs, like Magician, SmartPackets explicitly create, modify, and destroy SmallState. Access policies are defined for SmallStates at the time of creation. This includes defining access-control lists or access masks for accessing, reading, and writing SmallState.

Node Operating System

It has already been mentioned that the overall architecture of an active network is comprised of three layers of code: the node operating system at the lowest level, one or more EEs, and at the top level the active applications. It is assumed that the node operating system would handle multiplexing the node's internal communication memory and computational resources of packet flows that cross the node. EEs define the programming language in which the active packet's code is written. It is the active applications that provide the end users with their network services.

The following three high-level design goals are explicitly stated in the node operating system architecture document, namely, that the NodeOS interface primary role should be designed around supporting network packet flows—namely, packet processing, resource utilization, and admission control—done on a per-flow basis. It is also recognized that flows themselves can be defined at different granularities—for example, port-to-port flows, host-to-host flows, application flows, etc.; thus, there is no assumed single definition of a flow. It is also not assumed that all implementations of the NodeOS will export exactly the same set of features. Some implementations will have special capabilities that the EEs and their associated active applications may desire. Finally, whenever the NodeOS requires a mechanism that is not particular to active networks it should borrow from established operating system interfaces.

The abstractions defined for the NodeOS are important to understand. These consist of thread pools, memory pools, channels, files, and domains. The domain is the primary abstraction for accounting, admission control, and scheduling, as shown in Figure 10. Each domain contains the resources needed to support a packet flow.

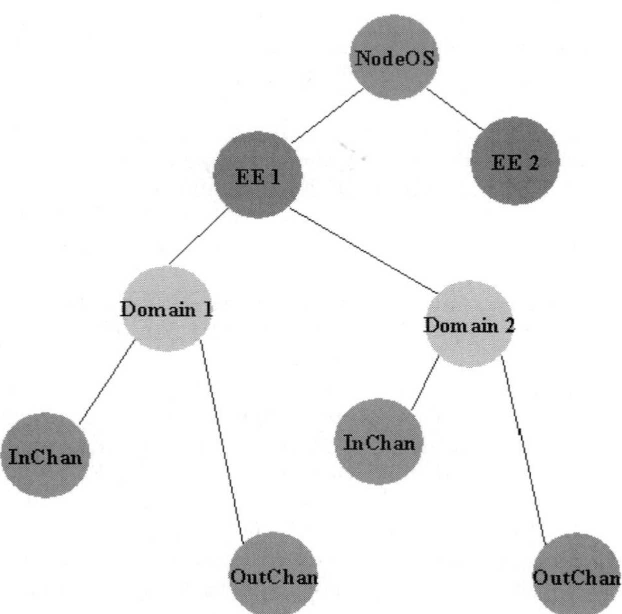

Figure 10: An example of domains to control resource usage in the active node

The domain typically contains a set of channels on which messages are received and sent, memory pools, and thread pools. Remember that the EE, using threads, processes active packets arriving on the input channel, and memory is allocated to that domain, and the packets are then transmitted on an output channel. Thus, a channel consumes not only network bandwidth but also CPU cycles and memory. Thus, intuitively, the domain encapsulates the resources used across both the NodeOS and the EE on behalf of a packet flow. Domains will be created in the context of existing domains, so they can be thought of as a hierarchy with the root domain corresponding to the NodeOS itself.

Note that a domain can create a subdomain in order to more finely encapsulate individual flows with resources. The thread pool is the primary abstraction of computation. Example parameters that are specified in creating a thread pool include the maximum number of threads, the scheduler to be used, the cycle rate at which the thread pool is allowed to consume the CPU, the maximum length of time a thread can execute, and a stack size for each thread, etc. Threads execute on an end-to-end basis—that is, the threads cut across the NodeOS up to the EE. This allows record keeping of resource usage for a flow.

The memory pool is the primary abstraction of memory. Such memory can implement packet buffers as well as hold an EE-specific state. Whenever memory or processing by the EE becomes excessive—that is, if the resources are overused—the NodeOS will warn the EE of the situation, and if the EE does not correct the situation the entire domain will be destroyed.

It is the domain that creates the channels discussed previously in the active network framework architecture, to send, receive, and forward packets. The distinction is made between anchored channels and cut-through channels, as illustrated in Figure 11. Anchored channels are used to send packets between the EE and the underlying communication substrate. Anchored channels are further characterized as either incoming or outgoing. Cut-through channels forward packets through the active node, without being intercepted and processed by an EE. Note that the EEs still allocate the cut-through channels.

When creating the channel, the domain must specify which arriving packets are to be delivered on this channel,

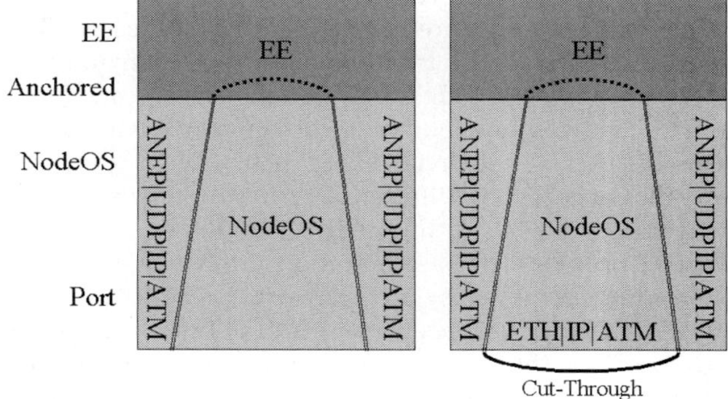

Figure 11: Anchored and cut-through channels through the node operating system (ATM = asynchronous transfer mode)

a buffer pool to hold the packets, and a function to handle the packets. The packets to be delivered are described by an address specification string and a demultiplexing key. When creating an out-channel, the domain must specify where the packets are to be delivered and how much link bandwidth the channel is allowed to consume.

It is possible that an EE wants to demultiplex multiple packet flows out of a single protocol. The demultiplex key specifies this information, and it consists of typical network components such as offset, length, value, and mask. This demultiplex key is compared to the payload of the packet, thus allowing precise pattern specification of which packets should be sent on which channels.

A suggested nomenclature for the formation of channels uses the protocol components separated by a slash. An example would be "IF.0/IP/UDP/ANEP," which specifies that packets tunnel through IP. Another example would be "IP/IF," which specifies outgoing IP packets. Cut-through channels would have a syntax using a pipe symbol to denote transition from incoming packet processing to outgoing packet processing. An example would be "IP/UDP| UDP/IP." In addition, packet addresses and port numbers may be used to further specify packet flows. Note that the cut-through channels allow the NodeOS to forward packets without the involvement of either an EE or an AA. In summary, channels and domains support a flow-centered model. The domain encapsulates the resources that are applied to a flow, while the channel specifies packets belonging to the flow and the functions that are applied to the flow.

Files are the abstraction for persistent storage and coarse-grained sharing of data. The files intuitively follow the common concept of a file in an operating system. The node architecture document goes to the point of specifying the actual names of individual function calls.

To provide for quality of service, the NodeOS has scheduling mechanisms that control access to the computation and transmission resources of the node. These mechanisms isolate, to some degree, one user's traffic from the effects of other users' traffic, so that each appears to have its own virtual machine and/or virtual link. When channels are created, the requesting EE specifies the desired treatment by the scheduler(s).

Such treatment may include:

- Reservation of a specific amount of bandwidth (transmission or processing) and isolation from other traffic
- Isolation from other channels' traffic and guarantee of a "fair share" of available bandwidth; the available bandwidth is divided more or less equally among all channels in this class.
- Best-effort—that is, no isolation from other traffic in this class.

The NodeOS may deny requests for channels with the first two types of service when resources are in high demand. Note that input channels are scheduled only with respect to computation, while output channels are scheduled with respect to both computation and transmission.

Active Networking Encapsulation Protocol

The ANEP defines a method by which active packets may be transmitted over different media. The ANEP implements the objectives within the active network framework document by supporting the coexistence of different EEs and the multiplexing of received active packets through the different channels. The active network encapsulation protocol defines a header. The primary reason for the header is to allow quick determination of the environment required to support execution of the active code within the packet—in other words, to identify whether the correct EE exists for the received packet. The header also provides some indication of the fault processing if the EE does not exist on the node. The header also has room for security information. The format of the ANEP packet, similar to most protocol packets, contains the version, flags, type ID, header length, packet length, options, the largest portion which is the payload, namely the active contents itself. In this description we focus on version 1 of ANEP, shown in Figure 12.

The type ID field indicates the environment required for execution of the active packet. The Active Networks Assigned Numbers Authority (ANANA), which is similar to the Internet Assigned Numbers Authority (IANA), maintain type IDs. TypeID zero is reserved for possible future network layer error messages. If a particular node does not recognize the type ID, the most significant bit of the flag field should be checked to decide how to handle the packet. If the most significant bit of the flag is 0, the node should try to forward the packet using the default routing mechanism, by checking information available in the options part of the header. If the most significant bit of the flags field is 1, the node should discard the packet. The ANEP header length field specifies the length of the ANEP header in 32-bit words. Finally the ANEP packet length field indicates the length of the entire packet in octets.

The options portion of the packet is in the form of type, length, and values (TLV). Values used are maintained by the assigned numbers authority, which also maintains the option type field. Other entities can use their own values if the most significant bit of the flags field, bit 0, is set. These options are meaningful only inside the indicated EE, so it is up to the type ID owner to specify these values. The option length field contains the length of the TLV in units of 32-bit words. This includes lengths of the flags, option type, option length, and option payload. There exist predefined options indicated as follows. The source identifier error option uniquely identifies the sender

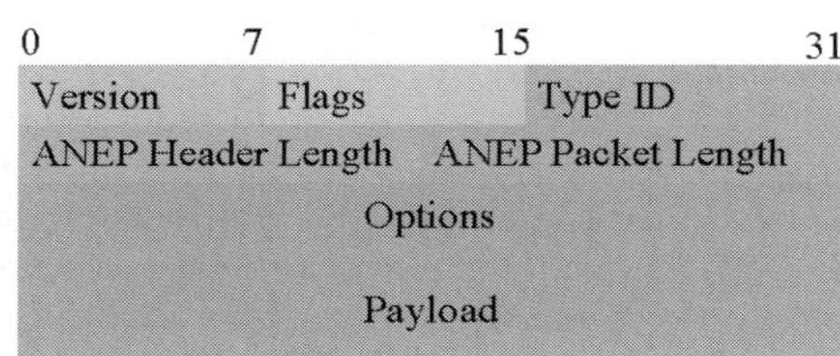

Figure 12: The active network encapsulation protocol packet structure

of the packet within the active network. It contains a 32-bit value, which identifies the addressing scheme in use, followed by the actual address. The scheme identifiers have been predefined as IPv4, IPv6, and 802.3. The destination identifier is an option that uniquely identifies the destination of the packet within the active network. This is the final destination, not an intermediate route. The format is the same as that for the source identifier option. Active nodes whose EE is not available might use this field. Another option is the integrity checksum. The value of this field is the 16-bit ones complement of the ones compliment of the entire ANEP packet, starting with the ANEP version field. Another option is the non-negotiated authentication. This option is used to provide one-way authentication. It assumes no prior negotiation between the packet originator and processing nodes. It has the 32-bit value that identifies the authentication scheme in use followed by the data. The following authentication mechanisms have been predefined SPKI and X.509. Additional values may be used by agreement of the assigned numbers authority.

End-to-End Considerations

Let us take a step back and consider the arguments opposed to active networking, then address them one by one. End-to-end arguments have suggested that functions placed at low levels of the system may be redundant or have little value when compared with the cost of providing them. Examples have been shown that include bit error recovery, security using encryption, message suppression, recovery from system crashes, and delivery acknowledgments. Essentially, the prescription is to move functionality upward within a system, that is, toward upper layers. It is said that the function in question can completely and correctly be implemented only with the knowledge and help of the application standing at the end points of the communication system. Therefore, attempting to provide that function within the communication system is not possible. This is known as the "end-to-end argument." Examples are given in which placing functionality within the network is either redundant, overly costly, or not useful. End-to-end arguments are often used as an Occam's razor when it to comes to choosing functions to be provided in the communication subsystem. It is interesting to note the use of Occam's razor in the above, since it is also used in determining the shortest packet code, described in section "Analysis of Active Networks" via Kolmogorov complexity. The principle states that "entities are not to be multiplied beyond necessity." In other words, *all things being equal, the simplest explanation is the best one.*

The following are key principles regarding the end-to-end arguments: Some services require the knowledge and help of the end system and thus cannot be implemented entirely within the network; if all applications do not make use of the service it should be implemented in such a way that only those applications using it have to pay for it; and finally, the amount of support for any given end-to-end service in the network is an engineering trade-off between the performance and the cost of implementing the service. Active networks actually support these principles, rather than violate them. Active networking requires that the interface to such functionality be carefully designed, the costs and benefits of each service be computed, and engineering trade-offs be carefully evaluated. In fact, some services can best be supported and enhanced using information that is available only from within the network. The network may have information that is not available to the application, and the timely use of that information can significantly enhance the service seen by the application. It is precisely these situations in which active networking shows significant gain and support of the end-to-end argument.

Note that the end-to-end argument was originally made with respect to a view of the network as a monolithic entity attempting to provide a single optimal quality of service to all users. Active networks actually increase the likelihood that services will be differentiated and useful to specific users. In fact, a market-driven approach will cause developers of active applications and users to be keenly aware of the costs involved and thus use and implement only what are necessary for particular applications. In effect, the active network is a framework for accelerating implementation of the end-to-end argument. As long as active networking provides cut-through capabilities to support at least services with current performance then active applications can be developed on a case-by-case basis.

A common mantra chanted by Internet developers is to keep the network simple, to avoid complexity. Although this is an admirable and useful goal, a significant challenge is that quantitative measures of simplicity and complexity are lacking. Thus, it is impossible to say definitively which architectures are simple and which architectures are complex. There is no way to prove that the Internet is simple and active networks are complex, except perhaps by using some ad hoc measure such as what "looks" or "feels" simple to a particular individual or small group with a particular common experience or background.

Security

Active packets contain code or references to code. The EE will extract code from the packet and execute the code on the node in which the packet resides. The result can be a modification of the state of the node, modification of a packet, or the transmission of packets. Legacy packets such as IPv4 or IPv6 may be forwarded before or they may receive services provided by the active network itself. Recall from the NodeOS framework that a domain may create a subdomain at any time. The principal assigned to a domain established at creation time governs activities of the domain. Note that the node begins operation with one or more domains assigned to EEs. Thus, an EE is permitted to start subdomains with more finely grained packet filters, as it desires. Therefore, the EE makes its own decisions as to whether the active code and a packet will run as part of the EE's domain or in some separate domain with the packet's principal privileges and separately allocated resources.

Consider what happens when an active packet arrives at a node. It is assigned by the node to an in-channel of the domain, either anchor or cut-through, and is processed. If the active packet processing occurs within the EE, then the active code has access to the EE's services and resources. The EE interface might pass the NodeOS interface through to the active code or might replace or augment that interface with its own services. It is possible that output packets may be created, in which case, resulting active packets are transmitted on an output channel. Remember that these output packets might have been forwarded in input packets, been modified in the packets, or been forwarded in newly created packets. It is also possible the processing of the packet's active code may result in changes to the state of the node or the EE.

The security paradigm within active networks uses abstractions, or models, comprised of actions taken by subjects upon objects. Each object must be authorized to take a specific action upon a specified object. Attributes of the subject, object, and an action can be compared to determine whether the action is authorized. If the authorization is valid, the operation may take place; if the authorization is invalid, operation is denied. The security policy is comprised of the valid authorizations.

The security policy is enforced by a particular component or subsystem. The policy specifies the subject and object attributes that must be compared and whether a valid match has occurred allowing the action to take place. The component must enforce the security policy to protect the resources for which it is responsible.

Subjects are the actors in the security model. The previously mentioned security policy determines what the subject is allowed to do. As a specific example, an active application is the subject when it requests that an EE run code. An EE is a subject when it requests a NodeOS to allocate a channel.

Objects are entities for which use must be authorized. Authorization is required in order to provide confidentiality and integrity and, for example, prevention of denial-of-service. The attributes associated with the particular object depend on the type of object to any entity, which provides access to that object. There are many types of objects within the active network, some of which include the NodeOS resources, such as thread pools, memory pools, channels, files, domains, etc. These object attributes would include file ownership and permissions and current resource pool usage. Other objects with the NodeOS may represent services such as reboot, control of an EE, and packet routing. These are obviously critical services and require strict authorization checks. EE objects include e-resources such as access to persistent state—that is, small state. Other objects include services, and these could include such things as rebooting the EE, stopping the EE, and controlling the active application. These are also critical services and should be available only after proper authorization. Finally, active applications are also objects. It is possible that an AA may be the object of another AA; in other words, one AA may perform an action upon another. This may include actions such as halting execution of the AA and sharing data among active applications.

Recall that actions are operations performed by subjects upon objects. Actions are dependent on the type of object and the resource provider; not all actions are relevant to all objects. The available actions should be defined within the API of each resource provider.

There are many entities within the active network whose assets need to be protected. These include the end user at the source and destination nodes, active nodes themselves, EEs, the active code within the active packets, and the domains within the active nodes. It is interesting to note that the active code—that is, the code within the active packet—stands as a proxy to the end user who launched the packet. Thus, it has the same security concerns that the end user would have. This may include things such as access to the domain in which it is executing and access to the sharable persistent state that it may create.

The types of attacks to be expected in an active network can be extrapolated from the attacks seen on traditional networks. These include: (1) unauthorized disclosure, which is countered by authorization and confidentiality services, (2) attacks resulting in deception, which are countered by integrity, authentication, and nonrepudiation security services, (3) destruction or denial of service, which are countered by authorization and integrity services, and (4) usurpation, to be countered by authorization, integrity, and confidentiality security services.

The security framework document concentrates on the enforcement of authorization policy to counter the previous threats. The sender of the active code, which has access to cryptographic operations in each node, controls confidentiality of the active packet payload.

Therefore, the major components of the active network that have resources requiring protection are the node itself, the EE, the sender of the packet that is being processed, and the active code that is executing in the node, as shown in Figure 13. The node is clearly interested in protecting itself; without survival of the node, nothing running on the node can be guaranteed to have integrity. The node needs to protect its resources from unauthorized usage threats to the node that can arise from EEs running on the node that may modify the node state or view sensitive node information. In addition, the sender of active packets who may maliciously send packets in such quantity as to exceed node resources potentially threatens the node. In addition, the node is susceptible to attack from active code within active packets, which may

This Column: Can See Threat From:

	Packet	Code	EE	Node
Sender		Yes	Yes	Yes
Code	Yes	Yes	Yes	Yes
EE	Yes	Yes	Yes	Yes
Node	Yes	Yes	Yes	

This Column: Can Be Protected From:

	Packet	Code	EE	Node
Sender	N/A	Yes	Not Really	Not Really
Code	Yes	Yes	Not Really	Not Really
EE	Yes	Yes	Yes	Not Really
Node	Yes	Yes	Yes and No	N/A

Figure 13: Active network components and their potential sources of threat (N/A = not applicable)

also consume resources or modify the node state or view sensitive node information, etc., while executing within the EE.

The EE must protect itself. Threats to the EE come from senders of packets and from active code running within it. The EE also sees possible threats from the node on which it resides. It is assumed that there is little defense that the EE can provide for itself from the node on which it resides; thus, before any EE is placed on the node, the administrator that distributes the EE must ensure that the node is secure.

The sender of the active packet is assumed to be interested in protecting the information, either active or passive, within the packet. Specifically, the sender is assumed to be concerned about the integrity and confidentiality of the information. The sender of the packet may perceive threats from other active code in the node, from the EE and from the node itself. Through cryptographic means, the sender protects the information from source to destination. Unfortunately, if the active packet must be decrypted in order to run on the node, for example, then the sender of the packet cannot protect it from the node or the EE. In this case, the sender must rely on the ability of the active code to avoid nodes and EEs that are not secure.

The active code is highly dependent on the packet in which it resides. This code may be able to create a state that can be shared with other active code or provide services to other active code. It is this code that wishes to protect itself, to protect a shared data and packet payload from unauthorized modification, or to protect its services from unauthorized use and to protect its resources against unauthorized consumption. The active code sees potential threats from other active packets, for other active code, from the EE, and from the node. It is conceded that the active code cannot protect itself against the EE and the node, which is executing. Thus, it must ensure that it does not forward itself to either unsecured nodes or unsecured EEs.

In the case of authorization, we need a language in which the authorization policy is expressed, a way of representing the principal being authorized, and mechanisms to ensure the authenticity of the claim to principal identities and the integrity of the packet. The language for the authorization policies may be simple access control lists. See the work done in Policy-Maker and Keynote (http://www.dmtf.org/education/academicalliance/pilz.pdf,KeyNote; http://www1.cs.columbia.edu/~angelos/keynote.html), which are two related efforts to offer sophisticated policy expression capabilities. The Seraphim active capabilities have full Turing expressibility.

It is recognized that conflicts may occur in the expression of the security policy. For example, the creator of an object, the sender of an object, and the node in which the object is stored may have conflicting security policies for the same object. Thus, there should be a uniform way in which access to these objects is controlled. Resolution of conflicts can occur by a predefined compositional logic, prioritization that is setting precedents among the policies, and having a configurable meta-policy. The node should have a final determination as to how composition of policies will be performed.

Hop-by-hop protection is needed to ensure the communication and signaling between neighboring active nodes. Always keep in mind that not all nodes will be active nodes; however, neighboring nodes must somehow be identified so that the keys can be shared to protect the Internet communication. End-to-end protection of packets requires cryptographic techniques, which can be divided into two types: asymmetric and symmetric. Asymmetric techniques require that only the originator be trusted. Only the entity holding the private key can verify the originator's identity associated with the key. However, if the packets change in a node, the digital signature will fail the next verification. Attempting to share the private key with the receiving node so that it can recompute the digital signature with the changed contents would cause the private key to be shared with many other nodes, defeating the privacy of the private key.

Symmetric techniques would solve the problem of allowing intermediate nodes to recompute the digital signature of the packet. However, installing keys to each node of a packets' path through the network would greatly broaden the trust model. This model depends strongly on the method of key distribution. It is possible that a symmetric key could be distributed by an active application. It should be noted that distribution of symmetric keys are expensive in terms of processing and latency and that it is important that the active packets requiring the key follow the precise path through which the keys have been distributed. If keys are distributed by an active application, this application must be secure. Also note that a symmetric key could be distributed at the NodeOS level by signing the key at the originating point and encrypting the signed key hop-by-hop for the neighboring node. This means that all nodes receiving the key can produce a packet that looks like it is coming from the originator. This key distribution technique allows the nodes to protect applications that are not secure, since this is done at the NodeOS level.

The active packet is divided into two areas: the area containing the code and an area that may vary. The digital signature covers the static area only, leaving the variable area unprotected. Symmetric techniques can cover either the static area, the variable area, or both.

Recall that a principal in the security architecture is an entity that can make a request subject to authorization. Examples of attributes of code can include the author or vendor, quality attributes like "virus-free" or "ISO-9000," or proof-carrying code. In order to trust such an attribute, it needs to be certified by some trusted authority. The cryptographic association in the form of a code credential is used to provide a binding between the code and its attributes. In fact, given the dynamic nature of an active network, the attributes are added to a packet as it traverses a network. References to the code could be placed within the variable portion of the packet. The packet structure must support lists of credentials and the separation of static and variable packet payload in both asymmetric and symmetric cryptographic authentication.

Responsibility for authentication of packets is placed in the NodeOS because these functions are of common use to all EEs, the NodeOS, which has resources of its own to protect, requires the functionality itself, and cut-through channels would be difficult to protect if the authentication support were in the EE.

Whenever active code executes on a node, there must be a component that is responsible for binding the security context to the execution of code such that the context is available to authorized management entities but not to the executing code. Enforcement includes intercepting requests for access to an object, extracting the security context, retrieving policy for the context, object, and request, evaluating the policy, and composing evaluation of separate policy components if necessary.

It is helpful to think about the security events involved as an active packet progresses through the network. First, the hop-by-hop key identifier is pulled out of the packet and used to retrieve the appropriate key, algorithms, etc. The hop-by-hop integrity is checked, and failure causes the packet to be dropped. Next, the packet is matched to a domain filter. Then, the list of credentials is extracted and retrieved, and credentials are verified. If any credential fails the verification process, the packet processing will continue, but using only those credentials that succeeded. Next, the NodeOS checks the authorization of the EE to be receiving this type of packet, then the NodeOS checks the authorization of the domain to be receiving this type of packet, then the NodeOS checks the packet's authenticated identity according to the authorization policy of the domain. At this point, the ANEP header and hop-by-hop integrity fields have been used and are no longer needed; thus, the packet is stripped of these components. The code is extracted from the packet or retrieved if necessary. The code could be within the packet, reside in the code cash, or stored within another node. It is assumed that the retrieval process for the code will have its own security protections. Next, all of the authenticated credentials are bound to the domain's execution in a security context. Finally, the domain can begin execution of the active packet code.

The code may attempt access to another active application's resources. This can be mediated by the EE. Packets sent by the domain are cryptographically protected by the NodeOS and packets transmitted by the NodeOS have hop-by-hop integrity applied. It is also possible that code may call for a new subdomain to be created. When creating a new subdomain, the active code must specify which packets are authorized for processing in the new domain.

An interesting problem with active networks resides around revocation not only of privileges, but also of active code. It must be possible to revoke code that has been previously distributed throughout the network. Revocation notices are sent in anticipation of or in response to suspicious activity within the network, and such notices are propagated using active mechanisms. It is possible for a node to be executing a revoked piece of code between the time the revocation is issued and the time the distribution reaches the node. Note that revocation notices are objects in their own right. The NodeOS affords the best opportunity to apply revocation notices.

It should be noted that active networks provide the capability for innovative new security paradigms. Although a traditional node cannot recover if it does not have all the security information necessary to authorize an incoming request, an active node could encapsulate an unauthorized packet with a protective wrapping to monitor its activities.

IMPLEMENTATIONS OF ACTIVE NETWORK COMPONENTS

Execution Environments

There are a number of EEs developed for active nodes to study various issues such as resource allocation, service composition, and security. This section discusses features of execution environments. A few popular EEs are listed in Table 1. Note that Caml is a strongly typed functional programming language from the meta language (ML) family of languages.

Researchers developed many different EEs that concentrated on particular facets of active networking mechanisms. This provides an opportunity to enumerate and classify properties that execution environments possess to make code transport and execution possible. This section discusses the following principal features of EEs:

- Code download
- Implementation platform and language

Table 1: Execution Environments

EE Name	Institution	VM Platform	Approach
ANTS	Massachusetts Institute of Technology (MIT)	Java	Capsule
CANeS	Georgia Tech	Unity	Capsule
Magician	University of Kansas	Java	Capsule
NetScript	Columbia University	Netscript	Discrete
Switchware	University of Pennsylvania	Caml	Hybrid
SmartPackets	BBN Technologies	Assembly code	Capsule

- Composition
- Security and authentication
- Resource allocation and monitoring
- Interpacket communication

The vision of active networks is that of a framework of networking components from which services are composed to provide users with a flexible, customizable networking infrastructure. Active networks will allow the composition of user-injected services with those that are preconfigured at the network nodes, enabling users to develop highly customized solutions in the network to handle their application data. The EE has to be able to provide modular service components for users to draw on as building blocks. Users will compose their own custom framework by using the "glue" provided by the EE in which their code will execute. The glue can be in the form of library modules, a scripting language, or an API.

The glue language itself can be a high-level language like Java, C++, or C, or it can be a scripting language like Perl or Tcl. In this case, developers do not have to go through a learning curve, and this enables them to reuse existing code and integrate it into the active network framework. The glue language can also be custom designed for active networks.

The advantage of a custom language is that the language can be designed keeping in the mind the unique requirements of active packets and the constraints that may be imposed on their functionality. For example, SwitchWare provides service components called switchlets that are resident at the nodes for users to customize node behavior. On the other hand, Magician provides components that implement various pieces of communication functionality.

SwitchWare and NetScript use a script-like programming language that accesses the heavyweight service components. On the other hand, Magician and ANTS allow the user to leverage a high-level language like Java to compose custom services from basic components.

Components should have a formal, well-defined interface that abstracts the inner workings, yet presents the user with a rich representation of its behavior. This is defined as introspection. Introspection enables a user to access an implementation state and work with abstractions to it. This increases reusability because the component can be reused in different protocol frameworks. The property of intercession enables a user to modify the behavior of an abstraction. The user can refine existing behavior or adjust the implementation strategy to improve performance. This is usually achieved through the mechanism of inheritance in object modeling. This enables users to customize previously developed active network components, tailoring them to the needs of the application without having to write new components from scratch.

Execution environments can provide explicit security mechanisms for the execution, authentication, and authorization of packets. Minimally, EEs have to execute packets within a sandboxed environment that is protected from unintentional and malicious incursions by other packets. In addition, EEs may implement trust mechanisms to authenticate various properties of the code contained in the packets, such as its ownership, creator, source, rights, and privileges.

ANTS: Active Network Toolkit

Written in Java, ANTS (Wetherall, Guttag, Tennenhouse 1999) primes the package delivery path within necessary protocol code during the initial delivery only, since the packets can use code without the overhead of transporting it. This is done using capsules, which carry both code and data. In the active network toolkit active messages are called "capsules." A unique type based on the message digest algorithm 5 (MD5) of the capsule code identifies capsules. When a capsule arrives at a node, a cache of protocol code is checked for the presence of the capsule code, which may already reside at the current node. If the code does not exist on the current node, a load request is made to the node from which the capsule originated. The originating node receives the load request and responds with the entire code. The current node then incorporates the code into its cache. Processing functions may update capsule fields and store application-defined information in the shared node cache of soft state.

ANTS provides a mechanism for protocol composition using the CodeGroup attribute of the ANTS capsule. Code belonging to the same protocol suite (or stack) shares the same CodeGroup attribute. Protocol modules are demand-loaded separately into the active node prior to capsule execution. A wrapper module (which is the main class for the protocol) puts together the protocol modules in the manner desired by the programmer. ANTS is written in Java; therefore, it supports modularity, inheritance, and encapsulation. The base implementation available from MIT does not support any security features beyond those provided by the Java virtual machine. Other groups, such as Trusted Information Systems Laboratory at Network Associates Inc., have modified the ANTS prototype to add security and authentication mechanisms.

CANEs

The Composable Active Network Elements (CANEs) (Bhattacharjee et al. 2002) execution environment was developed after the Architectural Framework Group and the NodeOS Working Group put together their specifications. Thus, the CANEs environment is a NodeOS specification-compliant EE that sits on top of the Bowman node operating system. CANEs uses a slot processing model that comprises two parts: a fixed part, also called the underlying program, that represents the common processing applied by an active node on every packet passing through the node, and an injected program implementing user-specified functionality. The injected program is bound to a specific slot, which when called causes the bound program to be executed. The underlying program provides basic services, such as forwarding, that can be chosen and that are well known and preinstalled on every active node. A set of injected programs is then selected to customize the underlying program. These injected programs can be available at the active node or they can be downloaded from a remote site. CANEs thus uses a discrete approach for downloading code.

Because CANEs is built on top of Bowman, which uses the NodeOS specification, Bowman handles resource allocation and security issues. Bowman also implements the IPC mechanism, called state-store, to exchange data between packets without sharing variables. CANEs programs are written in a custom language called CANEs User Interface (CUI). It comprises distinct computation and communication parts.

The computation part is a directed acyclic graph (DAG) in which the underlying program sits at the root of the graph and the injected programs are at the leaves. The arcs in the DAG identify the slot to which the child is bound. Multiple programs can be bound to the same slot. Binding of the injected programs to the slots is done when CANEs parses the computation part. The communication part of the CUI program identifies a routing schema for the user. The user may also specify a set of classifier rules that are used to select incoming packets upon which the flow acts.

Magician

Magician is a toolkit that provides a framework for creating SmartPackets as well as an environment for executing the SmartPackets. Magician is implemented in Java version 1.1. Version 1.1 was chosen primarily because it was the first version to support serialization. In Magician, the executing entity is a Java object whose state is preserved as it traverses the active network. Serialization preserves the state of an object so that it can be transported or saved, and re-created at a later time. Magician uses a model in which an active node is represented as a class hierarchy. Every protocol is derived from an abstract base protocol. Every active node provides some basic functionality in the form of certain default protocols—for example, routing. Users may prefer to use these default protocols if they do not wish to implement their own schemes. To foster privacy and safety, a unique state is created for each invocation of the protocol.

State that is common to all invocations of a protocol is inviolable and is accessible only to users that have appropriate authorization. Providing each user with a protected copy of the state enables the user to customize state if necessary. Users are permitted to install their own protocols. A user creates a new protocol from scratch by extending the base abstract protocol. When a SmartPacket carries over the protocol to the active node, a new branch is created for that protocol. Alternatively, the user extends an existing protocol class at the active node and customizes it to implement application-specific behavior as shown by the example of a user-defined routing algorithm in the figure. Thus, the user is able to inherit certain basic properties of the parent protocol and provide minor or major behavioral modifications to tailor it to the application's requirements. In this model, the active node is thus perceived as an object with behavior that can be modified dynamically. SmartPackets are treated as objects that carry custom protocols in the form of executable code, which when installed at the active nodes, modifies their behavior to suit application requirements.

The class hierarchy model for active nodes is advantageous in many respects. It provides the user with the ability to customize default functionality at the active nodes using the extension-by-inheritance philosophy. The inheritance model also provides default functionality for user SmartPackets that choose not to implement their own. That enables the active node to emulate behavior of traditional nodes to support transport of conventional packets. The unique state space provided to each invocation of a protocol corresponds to the instantiation of an object from its class definition. This affords privacy and safety to the SmartPacket executing in that state. It also provides an isolated, secure environment for the execution of user code so that the active node can monitor and regulate its activities. The class-model approach differs from the data flow composition model, wherein protocol functionality is activated only by data flow. In the class model, instead of data being transferred between protocol components, execution control is transferred between the protocol components. Protocol components have access to the user data and can choose to act on the data or perform other activities.

The class model also exhibits three of the five properties listed earlier, namely modularity, introspection, and intercession. Modularity is achieved by breaking down communication functionality into distinct protocol components. The functionality of the components is defined as a Java class. The property of introspection is satisfied when protocol components are designed as suitable abstractions and specified with well-defined interfaces that promote reuse. Using the principles of inheritance and aggregation, these components are brought together to form a composite that implements the functionality desired of a service to be injected in the network. This satisfies the intercession property.

NetScript

NetScript (da Silva, Florissi, and Yemini 1998) is a dataflow programming language in which computation consists of a collection of interconnected programs that process data streams flowing through them. The language supports the construction of packet processing programs, interconnecting these programs and allocating resources to them. NetScript programs communicate with each other through their input and output ports. The arrival of data at an input port triggers execution of sequential event-handling code inside the program.

NetScript is not a full-blown language, and it lacks traditional programming constructs like iteration control, functions, and data types. Therefore, the programs (called "boxes" in NetScript) themselves are written in languages such as C and Java. NetScript provides constructs for gluing together the protocol-processing boxes and thus is viewed more as a coordination language. Protocol composition is achieved by using the NetScript constructs to define and establish interconnection between the various boxes. Dynamic composition is achieved using the concept of box templates. A box template describes the input/output port signature and the internal topological structure of the dataflow program. The port signatures define the types of messages that the box accepts and generates. The topological structure describes the interconnections between the internal boxes. It is possible to create one or more instances of this box template on active engines across the network. Defining a composite box template that describes the protocol components and their interconnections creates a new protocol framework. The protocol components themselves can be box templates or they can be primitive programs. The framework thus constructed is deployed in the network by dispatching it to individual NetScript engines at the network nodes. When a NetScript engine receives a new box template, it creates a running instance of it by examining its port specification and internal topological structure. The engine then loads and instantiates each internal box, makes appropriate connections between box ports, and starts up the new instance to allow protocol messages to flow through it. The composition mechanism is rich enough to enable composition of layered protocols or the extension of protocol components with new features. However, the extension mechanism is not as rich as the extension mechanism of an inheritance model. It is not possible to override only a few properties of a box. The box must be used with its established properties or a new box defined with the unwanted properties replaced by the desired ones.

PLAN

Switchware (Alexander et al. 1998) provides protocol composition using a two-level architecture that consists of switchlets and user programs in active packets. Each switchlet provides services in the form of methods manipulating protocols implemented for that switchlet. The switchlets' services are implemented in a high-level language and are dynamically loaded at the network nodes. Active packets are user packets that invoke the services provided by the switchlets. The code in the active packets is written in a language called PLAN (Hicks et al. 1999) specifically designed for active networks.

PLAN is a stateless, strongly typed, functional-style lambda calculus system with pointer-safe access, which addresses safety and security concerns. PLAN programs also make statements about resource needs and bounds. A PLAN program is initially assigned resource units, which are depleted as it executes or it spawns new PLAN programs. Since resource units cannot increase, they eventually are exhausted, which guarantees program termination. PLAN packets contain fields to help manage the packet: evaluation destination, resource bound, and routing function. Although PLAN is implemented in Java, the programming language PLAN provides to the user is based on ML with some added primitives to express remote evaluation. PLAN programs can allow resident data to remain on a node after the program terminates.

Table 2 provides a snapshot of some of the prominent research efforts in each of the areas outlined above. This list is by no means exhaustive. There are other internal efforts at other institutions that have not received much attention. The rest of this section provides a high-level description of the projects listed in the table on the next page.

KU SmartPackets

KU SmartPackets can operate in both discrete and integrated mode; the packets are called "datagrams" and "management" packets, respectively. SmartPackets can leave information on active nodes after its execution environment expires. A time-to-live parameter for the cached information is assigned when the information is cached.

Spanner and Sprocket

Spanner and Sprocket are an active network assembly and high-level language, respectively. Sprocket is similar to C language. In addition, it has built-in functionality for querying Simple Network Management Protocol (SNMP) Management Information Base (MIB) object data. This would make it ideal for network management algorithm development.

Liquid Software

This EE gains speed in two ways. First, it uses Java to C translators in conjunction with C compilers, thus avoiding the need to interpret byte code at run time. Second, it uses compilers that execute quickly and can be run at the point of execution.

NODE OPERATING SYSTEMS

The vast difference in the increasing slopes between communication data rates and computational rates is pushed down to the level of the node operating system. Data rates have typically increased at twice the speed of computer processing power. For the time it takes processors to double their computing power, data rates will have increased by a factor of four. The result is that the active node operating system and its supporting hardware must be extremely intelligent regarding efficient packet processing. Thus, there has been a considerable amount of research on the development of active network node operating systems; space limitations do not allow a detailed discussion here. Instead, the goal of this section is to provide an introduction to a few active network operating systems and how they have approached the challenge of providing manageable and efficient interfaces between the active execution environments and the active node hardware. Much of this work has focused on developing paradigms, or abstractions, that facilitate development while maintaining efficiency via a tight coupling among the EE, the NodeOS, and ultimately, the hardware. Some operating systems have focused on simplicity, safety, and security, while others have chosen to focus on performance, and still others have focused on features and flexibility.

One may give the honor of being the first known active network to SoftNet (Zander and Forchheimer 1983, 1988), a programmable packet radio network developed in 1983. One might consider its Forth environment, called MFORTH (Zander 1984), a NodeOS/EE. Because SoftNet allowed packets carrying code to modify its behavior, it is consistent with the definition of an active network. However, a discussion of more recent node operating systems follows.

MIT (Tennenhouse et al. 1997) had constructed a prototype active network node infrastructure based on the ACTIVE IP option in IPv4, which enabled active packets (capsules) to be passed to a computational engine. Given that it was a prototype, Tcl was used. Most subsequent

Table 2: Research Areas

Research Area	**Project**	**Organization**
Network management	Robust Multi—Scalable Network Management (MIT)	MIT
	NESTOR—*NESTOR : NEtwork Self managemenT and ORganization* (Columbia)	Columbia University
	Active Virtual Network Management Protocol (GE)	GE Global Research
Security prototypes	Secure Active Network Prototype (NA)	Network Associates
	New Cryptographic Mechanisms (NA)	Network Associates
	Dynamic Interoperable Security Mechanisms (U of I)	University of Illinois
	Active Intrusion Detection and Response (NAI Labs and Boeing)	NAI Labs and Boeing
	PANDA: planning and negotiation of active network agent deployment (UCLA)	UCLA
Mobile and wireless applications	SpectrumWare (MIT)	MIT
	MAGIC-II: Adaptive Applications for Wireless Networks (U of K)	University of Kansas
	Proactive Infrastructure (UCLA)	University of California, Berkeley
Enhanced network services	Active Web Caching (UCLA)	UCLA
	Composable Active Network Elements (GA Tech)	Georgia Tech and University of Kentucky
	Active Network Applications (U of W & U of M)	University of Washington and University of Massachusetts
	Specialized Active Network Technologies for Distributed Simulation (SANDS) (U of M)	University of Washington
		University of Massachusetts
Quality of service	Critical Technologies for Universal Information Access	MIT
	Active Quality of Service	General Electric (GE Global Research)
Mobile code and safe languages	PLAN	University of Pennsylvania
	NetScript	Columbia University
	Liquid Software	University of Arizona

implementations were done in Java. At that time, there were concerns about deficiencies in the Java programming model regarding both security and resource consumption control as well as scheduling concerns, making resource constraint at the programming language level impossible.

The Extremely Reliable Operating System, EROS (Shapiro et al. 1997), recognized the fact that nodes are shared between users and that this unfortunately brings with it the fact that users have possibly conflicting or mutually adversarial desires. EROS began to wrestle with many of the active network operating system questions concerning resource control, security, and containment of faults, all while focusing on efficient network operation.

RCANE (Menage 1999) defines a resource-controlled framework for active network services. It is interoperable with PLAN (Pradhan and Chiueh 2000). RCANE supports resource reservations for network bandwidth, memory use, and computation, much like the NodeOS. The primary difference between RCANE and the NodeOS is NodeOS's flexible communication abstraction. RCANE allows only link-layer communication, while the NodeOS allows any supported protocol to be used.

As the active network framework began to crystallize, new active operating systems were developed with the active network framework in mind. Bowman (Merugu et al. 2000), which runs on top of Solaris, was the first NodeOS developed by the active network community. Bowman implements a subset of the NodeOS interface and does not provide resource controls. SuezOS (Kohler et al. 2000), Click (Kohler et al. 2000), and Router Plugins (Decasper et al. 1998) allow various degrees of extensibility. Each system enables configuration of safe extensions into the kernel that can extend router functionality.

Scout, Janos, and AMP

Janos (Peterson et al. 2001) is a NodeOS built in the Scout operating system. It encapsulates the flow of input/output data through the system in an explicit path abstraction. Scout is thus able to implement both the traditional and the active forwarding services using exactly the same mechanism. This makes it possible to integrate the NodeOS interface into a Scout-based router in a way that does not negatively impact the forwarding of nonactive packets.

The principal that creates a forwarding path must provide three pieces of information: (1) a sequence of modules that define how messages will be processed along the path; (2) a demultiplexing key, which identifies the packets that will be processed by the path; and (3) resource limits placed on the path, (e.g., how many packets can be buffered, the rate at which CPU cycles may be consumed, etc.). The NodeOS module is able to implement domain, channel, thread, and memory operations as simple wrappers around a Scout's path. More interestingly, a cut-through channel is simply implemented by a Scout forwarding path that does not pass through the NodeOS module, while in and out channels map onto a Scout path that includes the NodeOS module.

Active Network Node

The Active Network Node (ANN) (DeCasper 1999) seeks to balance the tension between the unprecedented network flexibility enabled by active networks and the efficiency of dedicated hardware that performs static processing, such as Application-Specific Integrated Circuits (ASICs). A single central CPU serving all ports is unable to keep up with link speed even for a small number of ports and relatively low bandwidth links (e.g., 10 Mbps). In ANN a general-purpose CPU and a Field Programmable Gate Array (FPGA) are used on every port of a switch backplane. This combination of CPU and FPGA is termed the "processing engine." The CPU takes care of the majority of active functions applied to a packet, while the FPGA implements performance-critical functions. Since both can be programmed on the fly, this approach seems to balance the tension between flexibility and speed.

As can be seen repeatedly in NodeOS architectures, there is an attempt at a tight coupling between the processing engine and the network. Also, as commonly occurs in active networks, the per-flow instance creation and management introduces a relatively high one-time overhead. Subsequent packets on the flow experience improved performance.

Active Network Hardware and Network Processors

Some researchers have suggested that at the level immediately below the active node operating system should lie network processors. The genesis of the network processor (NP) was driven by an increasing demand for high throughput combined with flexibility in packet routers. As a first step in the evolution to NPs, a switch fabric replaced the bus connecting network interface cards with the central control processor (CP). As demand for bandwidth grew, simple network interface cards were replaced by ASICs, which relieved the CP of many forwarding tasks. ASIC-based routers, however, were not flexible enough to meet the needs of the network equipment market. Hardware development cycles tended to be too slow to accommodate the demand for new features and protocol support. The next step led the NP, namely the use of Application-Specific Instruction-Set Processors (ASIPs). These processors can be programmed relatively easily and quickly according to protocol and deployment needs.

Network processors (Kind 2002) implement a balance between hardware and software that helps to meet the demand for performance and programmability that active networks require. The topic of network processors is a large subject area in its own right, and space limitations require that a brief introduction be presented here. Application-specific integrated circuits have clear advantages in terms of performance; the hardware functions do not provide sufficient flexibility. In contrast, packet forwarding based on General Purpose Processors (GPPs) provides high flexibility, but FPGAs can be reprogrammed at the gate level, combining features from ASICs and GPPs. Unfortunately, high-level programmability of FPGAs still is very limited. NPs are specifically designed for fast and flexible packet handling. Typically based on an embedded processor with application-specific instructions and coprocessor support, NPs can achieve even packet processing at network interface speeds of several gigabits per second.

NPs have simpler arithmetic and caching units than GPPs; their speed is achieved through parallel packet processing in multiple execution threads. In addition, common packet-handling functions, such as tree look-up, classification, metering, policing, checksum computation, interrupt and timer handling, bit manipulation, and packet scheduling, are frequently supported by coprocessors or specific functional hardware units. Moreover, NPs are often teamed with an embedded GPP for more complex tasks. APIs provide an abstract view of the resources of the network node on an NP. The APIs are dedicated to different data-plane, control-plane, and management-plane services of the NP and can be used for developing portable network applications. APIs allow network-wide services to be implemented simply and quickly.

Active packets are typically small because of maximum transmission unit (MTU) limitations and are likely to be based on a simple instruction set. Execution of the packet is inherently conservative in its memory usage and as such can be implemented on NPs with limited memory. Within the NP, a packet would not be required to execute on a GPP, thus reducing the delay between arrival and program execution as well as full and quick access to router state.

It has been suggested that active code need not be inserted in active packets, but rather packets contain a pointer to existing code. This approach is useful when the active code is large and will need to be executed repeatedly. From an NP point of view, there are two options for the installation of the active code component. If the component contains a performance-critical code segment with the purpose of extending forwarding code, it has to be linked dynamically into the existing forwarding code on the NP. This may be in the form of either interpreted byte code for a preinstalled virtual machine or native core processor code. NPs provide mechanisms to direct non-performance-critical packets to the control processor (e.g., using IP header options). Since active packets used for network management are generally less time-critical than user data, NPs can handle these intelligently.

NPs have been used to increase active network performance by just-in-time (JIT) compilation of active code. Although native NP code is extremely fast, Java byte code is convenient and flexible but slow. It has been shown that the Java byte code can be converted to NP code within the network, yielding performance gains. The time to compile the code (required only once) is on the order of the time it takes to interpret the code as Java does. Subsequent use of the same code would then be at the native NP speed. This can be coupled with code-caching techniques to further increase active network performance. For efficient JIT operation within the NP, the NP should have write access to the instruction memory and a sufficiently large instruction memory to hold the compiler and the JIT-compiled active code; currently not all NPs support these requirements.

ANALYSIS OF ACTIVE NETWORKS

Although there is a large body of results on architectural aspects of active networking, less research has been done on new forms of quantitative analyses of the unique aspects of active networking. One of these unique aspects is the tight integration between computation and communication networking.

Research at NIST (Carlinet et al. 2000; Galtier et al. 2000) has examined the computational aspect by seeking a uniform measure of CPU processing time for heterogeneous network architectures. The model consists of two parts: a node model and an application model. A semistochastic state-transition model represents CPU usage requirements of active applications. Active ping and multicast applications were shown to match analytical results. Three different scaling factors were proposed to transform a model accurate on one node into terms that prove accurate on another. Without this approach, crude techniques such as estimated time-to-live (TTL) values were assigned to each packet and then decreased at each hop or each time a packet created another packet. Another crude approach has been to enforce an arbitrary limit on the CPU time that a packet can use at each node. Using an arbitrary limit ensures only a worst upper bound, and may also allocate less CPU time than an application requires.

Ultimately, the essence and fundamental uniqueness of active networking is the flexibility introduced by a tight integration of code and data within, and in service of, the communication network. As illustrated in Figure 14, both code and data flow within, and change the operation of, the network. Developers and researchers of legacy networks, comprised of inflexible and statically defined processing, have focused on improving the flow of data based on Shannon's fundamental insights into entropy and the bit, as well as analyses in support of moving bits, such as queuing theory (shown along the left side of the figure). With the tighter integration of code and data in an active network, a broader view of information encompassing both code and data in the form of Kolmogorov complexity (shown along the right side of the figure) is required. In this form of analysis, there is a focus on code and data as a combined entity (Bush 2002). Active packets in the Kolmogorov complexity framework may vary from static data, as in legacy networks, to pure executable code; as code, the packets act as small executable models of information.

Kolmogorov complexity is a measure of the descriptive complexity contained in an object. It refers to the minimum length of a program such that a universal computer can generate a specific data sequence. A good introduction to Kolmogorov complexity is contained in Ming and Vitanyi (1993). Kolmogorov complexity is related to Shannon entropy in that the expected value of $K(x)$ for a random sequence is approximately the entropy of the source distribution for the process generating the sequence. However, Kolmogorov complexity differs from entropy in that it relates to the specific string being considered rather than the source distribution. A challenge in applying Kolmogorov complexity is that it is not computable. Any program that produces a given string is an upper bound on the Kolmogorov complexity for this

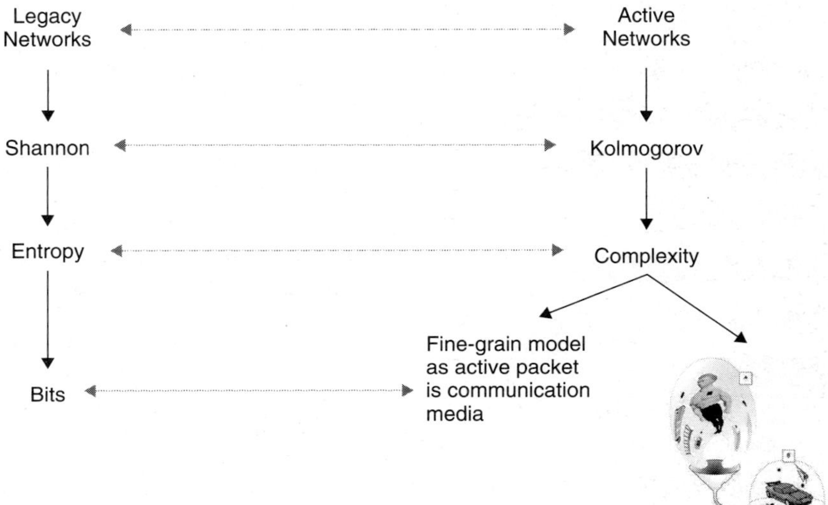

Figure 14: Legacy versus active information frameworks

string; however, one cannot compute the lower bound. Estimates have been shown to be useful in providing information assurance and intrusion detection.

Because the word *active* in *active networks* refers to the ability to dynamically move code and modify execution of components deep within the network, this typically leads to the challenge of determining the optimal proportion of an active application that should be implemented as code versus data. A method for obtaining the answer to this question comes from application of the minimum description length (MDL) (Gao, Li, and Vitanyi 2000; Wallace and Dowe 1999). Let D_x be a binary string representing x. Let H_x be a hypothesis or model, in algorithmic form, that attempts to explain how x is formed. H_x is a predictor of x. MDL states that the sum of the length of the shortest encoding of a hypothesis about the model generating the string and the length of the shortest encoding of the string encoded by the hypothesis will estimate the Kolmogorov complexity of string x (Eq. 1).

$$K(x) = K(H_x) + K(D_x|H_x) \tag{1}$$

Note that error in the hypothesis (or model) must be compensated within the encoding. A small hypothesis with a large amount of error does not yield the smallest encoding, nor does an excessively large hypothesis with little or with no error. A method for determining $K(x)$ can be viewed as separating randomness from nonrandomness in x by "squeezing out" nonrandomness, which is computable, and representing the nonrandomness algorithmically. The random part of the string—that is, the part remaining after all pattern has been removed—represents pure randomness, unpredictability, or simply error. Thus, the goal is to minimize $l(H_e) + l(D_x|H_e) + l(E)$, where $l(x)$ is the length of string x, H_e is the estimated hypothesis used to encode the string (D_x), and E is the error in the hypothesis. The more accurately the hypothesis describes string x and the shorter the hypothesis, the shorter the encoding of the string.

A series of active packets carrying the same information are measured as shown in Figure 15. Choosing an optimal proportion of code and data minimizes the packet length. The goal is to learn how to optimize the combination of communication and computation enabled by an active network. Clearly, if $K(x)$ is estimated to be high for the transfer of a piece of information, then the benefit of having code within an active packet is minimal. On the other hand, if the complexity estimate is low, then there is great potential benefit in including it in algorithmic form within the active packet. When this algorithmic information changes often and impacts low-level network devices, then active networking provides the best framework for implementing solutions (a specific example of separating nonrandomness from randomness, although not explicitly stated as such, can be found in predictive mobility management as discussed in Bush and Kulkarni [2001]). An active packet that has been reduced to the length of the best estimate of the Kolmogorov complexity of the information it transmits will be called the "minimum size active packet." When the minimum size active packet is executed to regenerate string x, the $D_x|H_e$ portion of the packet predicts x using static data (E) to correct for inaccuracy in the estimated hypothesis.

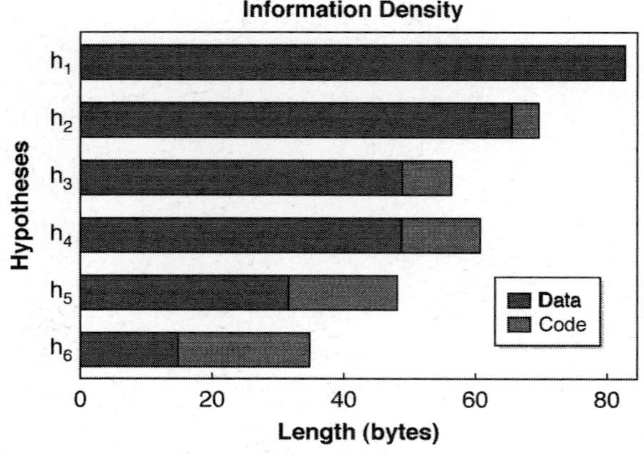

Figure 15: Trade-off between static data and algorithmic content and length as hypotheses vary for the same information

In general, a wide range of programs, or algorithmic descriptions, can generate a bit-string. Often, it is the case that the size of a program, or with regard to the definition above, the algorithmic description, can be traded off for speed. Thus, we need to be careful to distinguish the above definition of complexity from space and time complexity. From the standpoint of bandwidth, we desire small size—namely, the descriptive complexity, which must be approximately equal to, or smaller than, the static data. However, from the standpoint of processing speed, faster, but possibly larger, code would be desired.

Consider the definition of conditional complexity (Eq. 2). In this case, the descriptive complexity of x is conditioned upon y. One can think of this as meaning that executing program p with input y generates x.

$$K_\phi(x \mid y) = \begin{Bmatrix} \min\limits_{\phi(p,y)=x}(l(p)) \\ \infty, \textit{if there is no p such that } \phi(p,y) = x \end{Bmatrix} \tag{2}$$

Conditional complexity is important because an active packet can contain both code and data, the proportion of which may vary. Consider p as the code in an active packet, y as static data in the packet, and x as the final "piece" of information represented by the packet. The function f could be considered the network processing (NodeOS/EE) upon which an active packet is executed.

SELECTED APPLICATIONS

In order to consolidate the material in this chapter, this section examines two applications that take advantage of the unique capabilities of active networks. The first is a proactive network management system called Atropos (Bush and Goel 2005) that views active packets as small models rather than data. The second is a network capable of automatically evolving network services as needed, using the extreme flexibility of the active network.

The Atropos architecture is designed to use benefits of active networking: the ability to use fine-grained executable models in the network to enhance communication. A virtual message is an active packet that carries state information anticipated to exist in the future. A streptichron (from classical Greek meaning to "bend time") is a virtual message in the form of an active packet facilitating prediction by carrying information in algorithmic form affecting a node's notion of time. Fine-grained executable models, necessary to represent future behavior, carried by streptichrons are introduced in the form of active packets. The models are called "fine-grained" because they are intended to represent small portions in space and/or time. Executable code representing future behavior has the potential to be more compact than transmitting equivalent nonexecutable data in a piecemeal fashion. The justification for this can be found in the relationship among compression, prediction, and computation defined via Kolmogorov complexity as discussed in the previous section.

An Active Network Management System

Atropos provides a framework to accomplish fault prediction using a coupling of concepts from distributed simulation (Jefferson and Sowizral 1982) and active networking. Results collected from a single Atropos node for load prediction are shown in Figure 16. In today's management systems, a management information base (MIB) maintains current state values. In Atropos, load is predicted as real-time (called "Wallclock") advances. Thus, future as well as current values are available on the node. In Figure 16, the local virtual time (LVT) (future time), runs ahead of Wallclock time (current time). Predicted load values are refined until Wallclock reaches the LVT of a particular value. This data was collected using the simple network management protocol by polling an active execution environment that was enhanced with Atropos. Valleys occur between the sampled values in the surface plot shown in Figure 16 because no interpolation is attempted between samples.

A diagonal line on the LVT/Wallclock plane from the right corner to the left corner separates LVT in the past from LVT in the future; future LVT is toward the back of the graph, past LVT is in the front of the graph. Starting from the right-hand corner, examine slices of fixed Wallclock over LVT; this illustrates both the past values and the predicted value for that fixed Wallclock. As Wallclock progresses the system corrects for out-of-tolerance predictions. Thus, LVT values in the past relative to Wallclock are corrected. By examining a fixed LVT slice, the prediction accuracy can be determined from the graph. Consider a line defined by an LVT slice equal to a value of y LVT time units. Load values remain constant for all values of Wallclock equal to or greater than y time units. The final value, which remains invariant, is the actual value that occurred, while previous values were attempts to refine predictions.

Temporal Overlay

The goal of incorporating an optimistic parallel and discrete event simulation as part of network operation is to allow as much concurrent and parallel operation as possible within the network for projecting future events. Each node processes its portion of the simulation ahead of Wallclock time at the same time as other nodes. The Atropos framework enables an individual node to simulate its operation forward in time on multiple nodes. For simplicity, the simpler case of each node simulating its own future is presented. This can be logically viewed as a virtual overlay network running temporally ahead of the actual network. As shown in Figure 17, a virtual network modeling the actual network can be viewed as overlaying the actual network. The axis labeled "Space" represents the efficient use of large numbers of nodes, while the axis labeled "Time" represents the LVT of

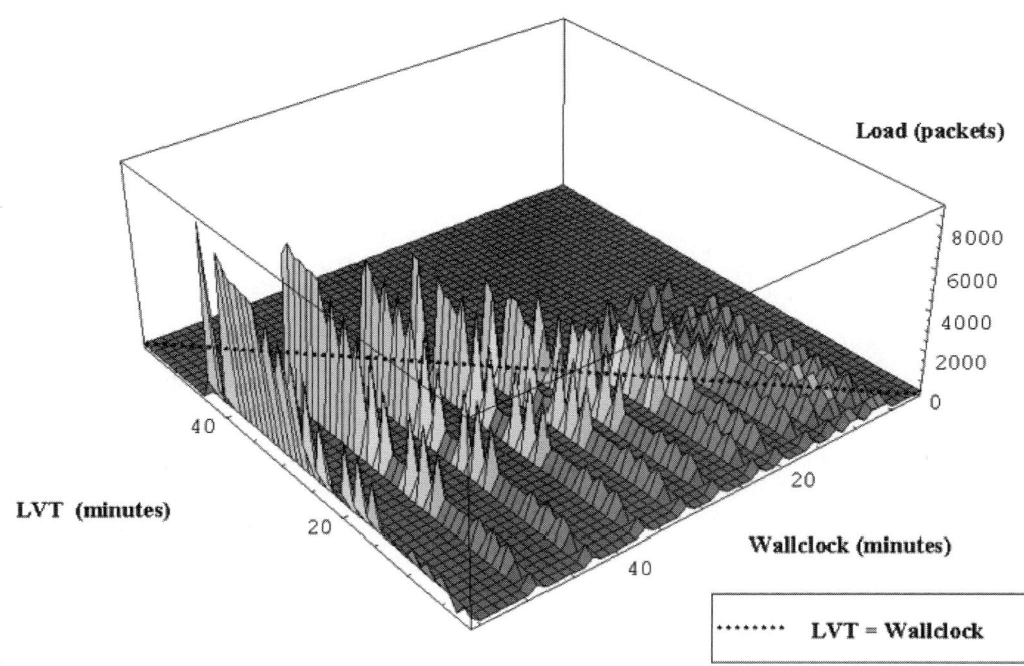

Figure 16: Load-prediction application results on a single node

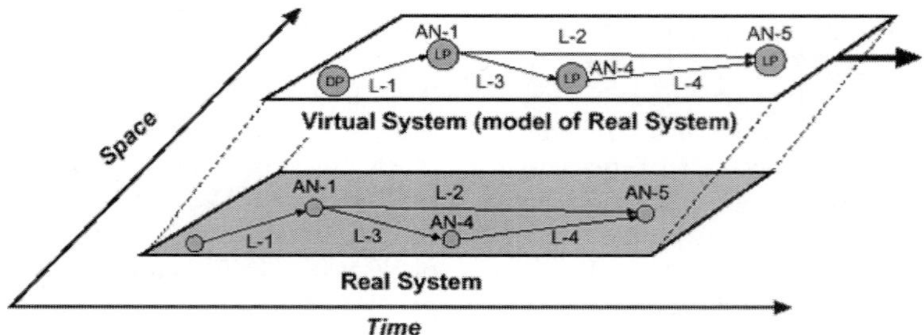

Figure 17: Temporal overlay (AN = active network node; L = logical process)

each node. The overlay shown above the actual system is sliding ahead of the actual system in time. A motivating factor for this approach is apparent when Atropos is viewed as a model-based predictive control technique in which the model resides inside the system to be controlled. The network environment is an inherently parallel one; using a technique that takes maximum advantage of parallelism enhances predictive capability.

The Magician (Kulkarni et al. 1998) execution environment is used in the implementation described in this work. Atropos messages are encapsulated inside Magician SmartPackets following the active network encapsulation protocol (Alexander et al. 1997) format. Several alternative active network architectures were considered before proceeding. At the time of our platform evaluation, Magician appeared to offer the most programming conveniences in terms of considering support for SmallState as resource control options that would ensure that active packets would not interfere among different users or applications as well as exceed per-node processing requirements. See Galtier (2001) and Bush and Goel (2005) for performance details.

Next, consider another active network application that takes advantage of the extreme flexibility provided by network code transported within packets. The active network differs from traditional architecture primarily in what it does not specify. In particular, it does not define how nodes work together to provide a network service; rather, it describes open programmable slots that must be instantiated to provide a particular network service. This is a new degree of freedom in network architectures speeding up network evolution.

A Self-Healing Communication Network

Fault-tolerant and self-healing systems should have the ability to self-compose solutions to faults. This should be an inherent part of system operation, rather than a structure imposed from "outside" the system. Genetic algorithms are on the path toward self-composing solutions; however, genetic algorithms as currently implemented require external control to manipulate the genetic material. In other words, the genetic algorithm itself must be programmed into the system. If the genetic algorithm code failed, then the self-healing capability would fail. Although this situation is not ideal, it is explored as a possible step toward a truly self-healing system.

Many active network components and services have been designed and implemented and are undergoing experimentation. The ABone (active network backbone) implements a relatively large scale (given the novelty of the technology) active network (*O(100)* [Big-O notation; on the order of 100] nodes). However, the fundamental science required to understand and take full advantage of active networking is lagging behind the ability to engineer and build such networks. In fact, the current Internet, whose protocols were built on the ill-defined goal of simplicity, is only slowly being understood. An outcry from the Internet community, with its carefully crafted, static protocol processing, with massive documentation (*O(4000)* Request for Comments) of passive (nonexecutable) packets is that the Internet is already "too" complex.

It is unlikely that an adaptive fault-tolerant system, no matter how resilient, would be accepted by industry or the community if it were considered "complex" in the colloquial sense. How can such systems, which require complexity to be adaptive, at the same time appear simple to understand and manage? Are active networks really more complex than the current Internet? Are adaptive applications built on active networks any more or less complex than the same applications built on the legacy Internet? Does a measure of complexity exist that would allow an objective comparison to be made? What are the benefits of an active network with respect to passive networks? Although these are extremely difficult questions to answer, this chapter attempts to lay the groundwork to answer them by proposing a complexity measure, Kolmogorov complexity, and proposing an adaptation mechanism, a genetic algorithm, based on an analogy with biological systems.

Descriptive complexity was applied to optimize the combined use of communication and computation within an active network to determine the optimal amount of code versus data. It was shown that if the Kolmogorov complexity of the information related to the prediction of the future state of the network is estimated to be high, then the ability to develop code, representing the nonrandom or algorithmic portion of that information, is low. This results in a low potential benefit for algorithmic coding of the information. The benefit of having code within an active packet would appear to be minimal in such cases.

Conversely, if the complexity estimate is low, then there is great potential benefit in representing information in

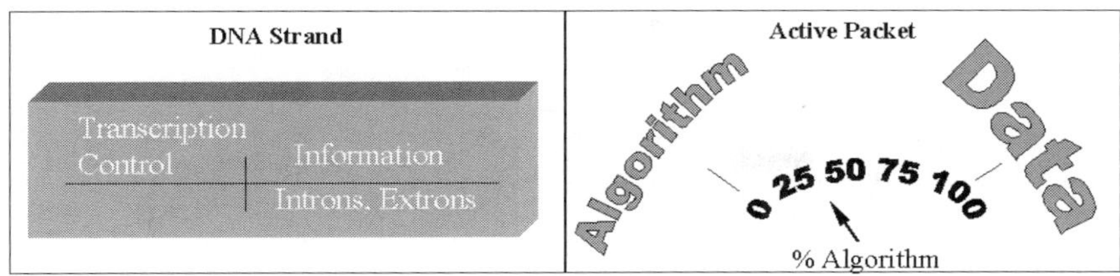

Figure 18: Active packet as DNA

algorithmic form within an active packet. It has been suggested (Bush 2002) that if the algorithmic portion of information changes often and impacts the operation of network devices, then active networking provides the best framework for implementing solutions. This is precisely the case in genetically programmed network services, a new class of services that are not predefined but that evolve themselves in response to the state of the network. In this chapter, we will restrict this class to the services that are programmatic solutions for perceived faults that occur in a network. Further research is required to generalize this class to include other types of network services.

Complexity and evolution are intimately linked. Kolmogorov complexity ($K(x)$) is the optimal compression of string x. This incomputable, yet fundamental, property of information has vast implications in a wide range of applications, including system management and optimization (Kulkarni and Bush 2000) and security (Bush and Evans 2001; Goel and Bush 2003). Active networks form an ideal environment in which to study the effects of trade-offs in algorithmic and static information representation, because an active packet is concerned with the efficient transport of both code and data. As noted in Figure 18, there is a striking similarity between an active packet and DNA. Both carry information having algorithmic and nonalgorithmic portions. The algorithmic portion of DNA has transcription-control elements as well as the codons (Bush 2003). The active packet has control code and may contain data as well. Kolmogorov complexity and genetic programming have complementary roles. Genetic programming has been used to estimate Kolmogorov complexity (Conte et al. 1997; De Falco et al. 2000). Genetic programming benefits from Kolmogorov complexity as a measure and means of controlling not only the complexity, but also the size and generality of the result. One of the most obvious uses for complexity in networking is programmatic compression. In this chapter, the foundation is developed for using complexity to enable the network to self-heal.

A criticism of this approach might be that a genetically engineered protocol stack will create a complex framework that will be difficult to understand and maintain. However, our approach is to compose the framework from simple components. Each of these components will be individually verifiable with respect to its properties and actions. As the components are arbitrarily composed to form a protocol stack, some protocol stacks may be generated that violate the principles of safety, consistency, and correctness. One way to approach this is to define a fitness function that verifies the suitability of the stack with respect to the properties desired.

Genetic Algorithm for Service Composition

The Magician Active network (Bush and Kulkarni 2001; Kulkarni et al. 1998) is used to test the feasibility of the genetically programmed network service concept. An active packet representing the nucleus (assuming network nodes are like eukaroytes—cells containing nuclei) is injected into all the network nodes. The nucleus contains a population of chromosomes—strings of functional units. Operation of genetic network programming begins with injecting basic building blocks, known as "functional units," into the network, as shown in Figure 19. Currently, this "genetic material" is flooded into each active node. However, the material will remain inactive in each active node until a fitness function is injected

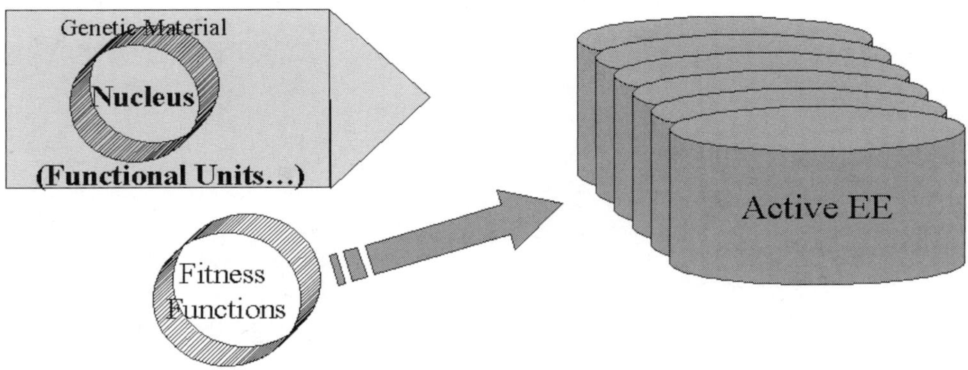

Figure 19: Injection of nucleus and functional units at start-up

into the network. Receipt of a fitness function will cause evolution to proceed. Table 3 is a flowchart of the steps involved.

Functional units are very small pieces of code blocks that perform simple, well-defined operations on an active packet. Examples of functional units are Delay, Split, Join, Clone, and Forward. There is also a Null functional unit whose use is explained later. Chromosomes are strings of functional units as shown in Figure 20. Once a chromosome is assembled, the codons can be translated into amino acids at the ribosome. In other words, the string of functional units will operate on active packets from other applications (or other functional units) that traverse the node. The chromosome is represented in the code in a form similar to a Lisp symbolic expression, for example: *((Null Join Split) (Delay Split Join Delay))*.

Mutation and recombination occur among a population of genes. Mutation is a probabilistic change of a functional unit to another functional unit. Recombination is the exchange of chromosome sections from two different chromosomes. In Figure 20, a close-up of a single node can be seen containing a very short chromosome strand. A single incoming traffic stream, as shown in Figure 21, entering the center node is split into multiple streams. A different chromosome processes each stream. Note that currently in our implementation, the full traffic stream is split along each chromosome. However, it is hypothesized that traffic sampling could be used to reduce the overhead in creating the multiple streams.

Fitness functions can be designed to measure quality of service (QoS) at different layers of the traditional protocol stack. In this particular case, fitness measures are shown at the transport, network, and link layers. As a particular example, jitter control might have a fitness function that minimized per frame variance at the link layer. The network layer uses its capabilities to maximize successful packet reception probability, in other words, perform the function of routing packets. The transport layer would have a fitness function that attempts to minimize end-to-end packet variance. The key is that each of these

Table 3: Adaptive In-Line Genetic Communication Network Programming Algorithm

1) Inject functional units.
   a. Propagate to all nodes.
2) Inject nucleus.
   a. Propagate to all nodes.
3) Inject fitness function.
   a. Propagate to all nodes.
   b. Choose three functional units to form three independent chromosomes.
4) Clone "normal" packet traffic through each chromosome while simultaneously performing step 5.
5) Begin operation.
   a. If mutation event is to occur:
      i. Generate a random change in one of the functional units to another available functional unit.
   b. If recombination event is to occur:
      i. Select a cross-over point and swap portions of best parent chromosomes.
   c. Otherwise, for each chromosome, select an available functional unit at random and append to each chromosome.
   d. Compute fitness.
      i. "Normal" packets flow through each chromosome.
      ii. Compute a fitness value based on monitoring desired chromosome objectives, such as latency or jitter.
      iii. Return fitness value to the nucleus.
   e. Assign fitness to each chromosome.
   f. Repeat from step 5a until a desired fitness threshold is reached.

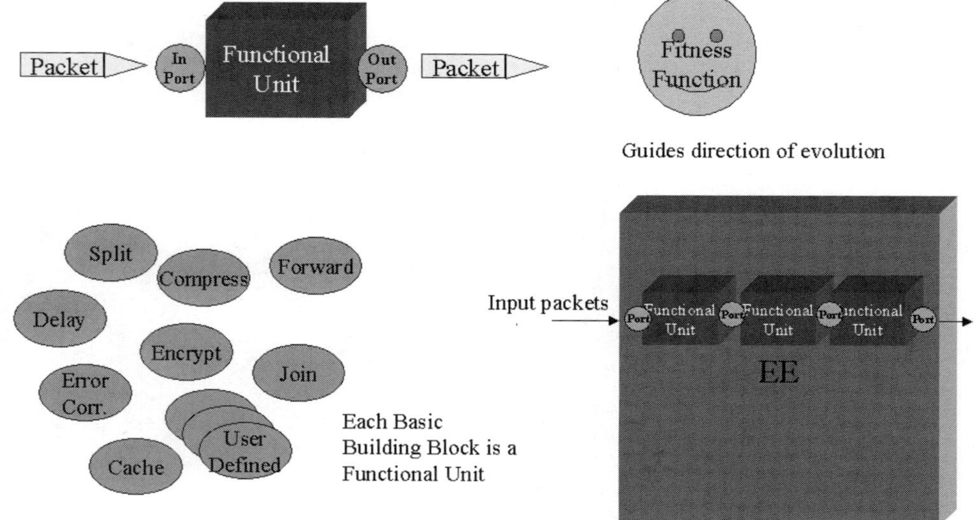

Figure 20: Architecture of a single node

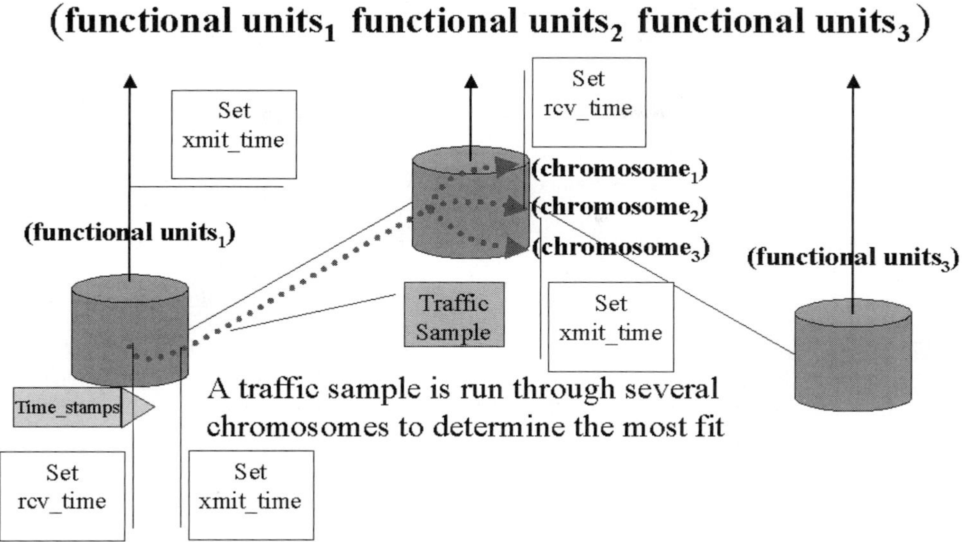

Figure 21: Breeding traffic streams

fitness functions must work together toward reaching the stated goal in a reasonable manner.

Recombination can occur both within a node and between two nodes. In addition, changing the route of a packet also effectively accomplishes a recombination because the packet processing will be dependent on the genetic material at each node traversed. A key component of the evolutionary process is the fitness function. Fitness functions are "user" defined and injected into the network to control the evolution of the genetic population. For example, in our initial tests, minimizing variance in transmission time was used as a simple fitness function. However, initial experiments quickly demonstrated that the design of the fitness function is the most critical element. It reminds one of the saying, "Be careful what you pray for . . . because you might get it." Often the fitness was achieved, but in ways that were unexpected and sometimes detrimental to the intended operation of the network. As a trivial example, slowing the traffic to a near halt can minimize the variance. Thus, a low-latency term had to be added to the jitter control fitness function.

Although a priori techniques have been developed for jitter control in legacy networks, jitter control forms a simple, easily measured and controlled application for the network genetic algorithm. The functional units injected into the network should allow the evolution of a variety of interesting solutions to reduce variance, including adding delays and forwarding along different paths, or perhaps ideas that have not been thought of yet. An adaptive jitter-control mechanism was developed on a fixed, wired active communication network. The genetic algorithm was implemented as an active application in the Magician Active network execution environment. The dominant contributors to packet-link transit-time variability are the fact that the active network is an overlay network that has unspecified lower-layer traffic and that packets are loaded and executed within a Java Virtual Machine residing in each node and are subject to Java garbage collection, which runs at unspecified times.

The fitness function on all nodes returns a greater fitness when link transfer-time variance on the destination node is minimized. As previously mentioned, the fitness function is itself an active packet that consists of an objective function. The function is highly general and can be comprised of any mathematical function of accessible metrics. Bush (2003) shows packet-link transit-time variance through three of the chromosomes on the destination node and shows packet-link transit-time variance with no jitter-control mechanism at the destination node. Initial observation of the graphs shows that, overall, the chromosomes significantly reduced packet transit-time variance by a factor of 100. Another observation of the experimental data is that the genetically programmed transit-time variance was initially worse than transit-time variance with no control mechanism. The reason for this is that the chromosomes begin operation with a random set of functional units and require time to converge to an optimal value.

ACKNOWLEDGMENT

The work discussed in this chapter has been funded by the Defense Advanced Research Projects Agency (DARPA) contract F30602-01-C-0182 and managed by the Air Force Research Laboratory (AFRL) Information Directorate, under the auspices of the Fault Tolerant Networks program. Our thanks go to Doug Maughan, the Active Networks Program Manager, and Scott Shyne, Air Force Rome Labs (AFRL), for their generous support.

GLOSSARY

Active Application (AA): The execution environment on an active network device supports an active application. The active application consists of active packets that support a particular application.

Autoanaplasis: Autoanaplasis is the self-adjusting characteristic of streptichrons used in Atropos. One of the virtues of the Atropos algorithm is the ability for the predictive system to adjust itself as it operates. This is accomplished in two ways. When real time reaches the time at which a predicted value had been cached, a comparison is made between the real value and the predicted value. If the values differ beyond a given tolerance, then the logical process rolls backward in time. Also, active packets, which implement virtual messages, adjust, or refine, their predicted values as they travel through the network.

Channel: An active network channel is a communications link upon which active packets are received. The channel determines the type of active packet and forwards the packet to the proper execution environment. Principals use anchored channels to send packets between the execution environment and the underlying communication substrate. Other channels are cut through, meaning that they forward packets through the active node—from an input device to an output device—without being intercepted and processed by an execution environment. Channels are in general full duplex, although a given principal might send or receive packets only on a particular channel.

Execution Environment (EE): The node operating system on an active device supports the execution environment. The execution environment receives active packets and executes any code associated with the active packet.

Node Operating System (NodeOS): The node operating system is the base level operating system for an active network device. The node operating system supports the execution environments.

Principal: The primary abstraction for accounting and security purposes is the principal. All resource allocation and security decisions are made on a per-principal basis. In other words, a principal is admitted to an active node once it has authenticated itself to the node, and it is allowed to request and use resources.

SmallState: SmallState is a named cache within an active network node's execution environment that allows active packets to store information. This allows packets to leave information behind for other packets to use.

CROSS REFERENCES

See *Computer Network Management; Distributed Intelligent Networks; Fault Tolerant Systems; Network Reliability and Fault Tolerance*.

REFERENCES

Alexander, D. S., W. A. Arbaugh, M. W. Hicks, P. Kakkar, A. D. Keromytis, J. T. Moore, C. A. Gunter, S. M. Nettles, and J. M. Smith. 1998. The SwitchWare active network architecture. *IEEE Network* 12(3):27–36.

Alexander, D. S., B. Braden, C. Gunter, A. Jackson, A. Keromytis, G. Minden, and D. Wetherall (Eds.). 1997. *Active network encapsulation protocol (ANEP)*. Request for Comments: draft. Active Networks Group. http://www.cis.upenn.edu/~switchware/ANEP/docs/ANEP.txt.

Bhattacharjee, S., C. Y. Calvert, S. Merugu, M. Sanders, and E. Zegura. 2002. CANEs: An execution environment for composable services. In *Proceedings of the 2002 DARPA Active Networks Conference and Exposition (DANCE 2002), San Francisco, CA, May 2002*, 255–272. Los Alamitos, CA: IEEE Press

Bush, S. F. 2002. Atropos: Complexity as a framework for prediction, optimization, and assurance. In *Proceedings of the 2002 DARPA Active Networks Conference and Exposition (DANCE 2002), May 29–30, 2002, San Francisco, California, USA*, 534–553. Los Alamitos, CA: IEEE Press.

Bush, S. F. 2003, November/December. Genetically induced communication network fault tolerance. *Complexity Journal* 9(2):Special Issue: Resilient and Adaptive Defense of Computing Networks. www.research.ge.com/~bushsf/pdfpapers/ComplexityJournal.pdf (accessed July 13, 2007).

Bush, S. F., and S. C. Evans. 2001. Kolmogorov complexity for information assurance. Technical Report 2001CRD148. 2001, Niskayuna, NY: General Electric Corporate Research and Development.

Bush, S. F., and S. Goel. 2005. An active model-based prototype for predictive network management. *IEEE Journal on Selected Areas in Communications* 23(10):2049–57.

Bush, S., and S. Kalyanaraman (Guest Eds.). 2006, March. *Journal of Network and Systems Management* 14(1):Special issue on Management of Active and Programmable Networks.

Bush, S. F., and A. B. Kulkarni. 2001. *Active networks and Atropos: A proactive management framework*. New York: Kluwer Academic/Plenum.

Calvert, K. 1998. Architectural framework for active networks (version 0.9). 1998. Active Networks Working Group. http://citeseer.ist.psu.edu/470576.html.

Carlinet, Y., V. Galtier, K. L. Mills, S. Leigh, and A. Rukhin. 2000. Calibrating an active network node. In *Proceedings of the 2nd Workshop on Active Middleware* Services, August 2000. IEEE.

Conte, M., G. Tautteur, I. De Falco, A. Della Cioppa, and E. Tarantino. 1997. Genetic programming estimates of Kolmogorov complexity. In *Genetic Algorithms: Proceedings of the Seventh International Conference, Michigan State University, East Lansing, MI, USA, 19–23 1997*, edited by T. Back, 743–50. San Mateo, CA: Morgan Kaufmann.

da Silva, S., D. Florissi, and Y. Yemini. 1998. Composing active services in NetScript. In *Proceedings of the DARPA Active Networks Workshop (Tucson, Arizona)*. DARPA Workshop. http://citeseer.ist.psu.edu/428846.html.

Decasper, D., Z. Dittia, G. Parulkar, and B. Plattner. 1998. Router plugins: A software architecture for next generation routers. *In Proceedings of the SIGCOMM Conference, Vancouver, BC, Canada, September 1998*, 229–40. ACM (Association for Computing Machinery).

Decasper, D. S., and B. Plattner, G. M. Parulkar, S. Choi, J. D. DeHart, and T. Wolf. 1999. A scalable high-performance active network node. *IEEE Network*, January/February 1999.

De Falco, T., A. Iazzetta, E. Tarantino, A. Della Cioppa, and G. Trautteur. 2000. A Kolmogorov complexity-based genetic programming tool for string compression. In *Proceedings of the Genetic and Evolutionary Computation Conference (GECCO-2000), Las Vegas, Nevada, USA, 10-12 2000*, Edited by D. Whitley, D. Goldberg, E. Cantu-Paz, L. Spector, I. Parmee, and H.-G. Beyer, 427–34. San Mateo, CA: Morgan Kaufmann.

Galtier, V., K. Mills, Y. Carlinet, S. Bush, and A. Kulkarni. 2001. Predicting resource demand in heterogeneous active networks. In *Milcom 2001, Mclean, VA, October 28–31*. IEEE.

Galtier, V., K. L. Mills, Y. Carlinet, S. Leigh, and A. Rukhin. 2000. *Expressing meaningful processing requirements among heterogeneous nodes in an active network*. Presented at the 2nd International Workshop on Software Performance—WOSP 2000. McLean, VA: IEEE.

Galtier, V., and K. L. Mills, Y. Carlinet, S. F. Bush, and A. B. Kulkarni. 2001. Prediction and controlling resource usage in a heterogeneous active network. Third Annual International Workshop on Active Middleware Services 2001, San Francisco, CA, August 6, 2001. *Artificial Intelligence* 121:1–29.

Gao, Q., M. Li, and P. M. Vitanyi. 2000. *Applying MDL to learning best model granularity*. arXiv: physics/0005062.

Goel, S., and S. F. Bush. 2003, November–December. Kolmogorov complexity estimates for detection of viruses in biologically inspired security systems: A comparison with traditional approaches. *Complexity Journal* 9(2):Special Issue: Resilient and Adaptive Defense of Computing Networks.

Hicks, M., P. Kakkar, J. T. Moore, C. A. Gunter, and S. Nettles. 1999. PLAN: A programming language for active networks. *ACM SIGPLAN Notices* 34(1):86–93.

Jefferson, D. R., and H. A. Sowizral. 1982. Fast concurrent simulation using the time warp mechanism, Part I: Local control. Technical Report TR-83–204. Santa Monica, CA: The Rand Corporation.

Kind, A. 2002. The role of network processors in active networks. In *Proceedings of the First International Workshop on Active Network Technologies and Applications (ANTA 2002), Tokyo, Japan, March 2002*. Tokyo: Institute of Electronics Information and Communications Engineers.

Kohler, E., R. Morris, B. Chen, J. Jannotti, and M. F. Kaashoek. 2000. The click modular router. *ACM Transactions in Computer Systems* 18(4):263–97.

Kulkarni, A. B., and S. F. Bush. 2000. Active network management, Kolmogorov complexity, and streptichrons. GE-CRD Class I Technical Report 2000CRD107. www.research.ge.com/~bushsf/ftn (accessed July 13, 2007).

Kulkarni, A. B. G. J. Minden, R. Hill, Y. Wijata, S. Sheth, H. Pindi, F. Wahhab, A. Gopinath, and A. Nagarajan. 1998. Implementation of a prototype active network. In *OPENARCH, '98*. San Francisco: IEEE OpenArch.

Menage, P. 1999. RCANE: A resource controlled framework for active network services. In *Proceedings of the 1st International Working Conference on Active Networks, July 1999*. New York: Springer Lecture Notes in Computer Science, 1653:25–36.

Merugu, S., S. Bhattacharjee, E. Zegura, and K. Calvert. 2000. Bowman: A node OS for active networks. Presented at the IEEE INFOCOM, Tel-Aviv, Israel, March 2000.

Ming, L., and P. M. Vitanyi,. 1993. *Introduction to Kolmogorov complexity and its applications*. New York: Springer-Verlag.

Peterson, L, Y. Gottlieb, M. Hibler, P. Tullmann, J. Lepreau, S. Schwab, H. Dandekar, A. Purtell, and J. Hartman. 2001. An OS interface for active routers. *IEEE Journal on Selected Areas in Communications* 19(3):473–87.

Pradhan, P., and T.-C. Chiueh. 2000. *Computation framework for an extensible network router: design, implementation and evaluation*. Stony Brook, NY: SUNY.

Shannon, C. E. 1948. A mathematical theory of communication. *Bell System Technical Journal* 27:379–423, 623–656.

Shapiro, J. S., S. J. Muir, J. M. Smith, and D. J. Farber. 1997, February 8. Operating system support for active networks, Department of Computer and Information Science, Technical Report MS-CIS-97-03. Philadelphia: University of Pennsylvania Department of Computer Information Science.

Tennenhouse, D. L., et al. 1997. A survey of active network research. *IEEE Communications* 35(1):80–86.

Wallace, C. S., and D. L. Dowe. 1999. Minimum message length and Kolmogorov complexity. *The Computer Journal* 42(4):270–83.

Wetherall, D., J. Guttag, and D. Tennenhouse. 1999. ANTS: Network services without the red tape. *Computer* 32(4):42–48.

Zander, J. 1984, April. MFORTH—Programmer's manual. Technical Report LiTH-ISY-I-0660. Linkvping, Sweden: Linkvping University.

Zander, J., and R. Forchheimer. 1983. SOFTNET—An approach to high-level packet communication. In the *2nd ARRL Amateur Radio Computer Networking Conference, San Francisco, CA*. San Francisco: Amateur Radio Relay League.

Zander, J., and R. Forchheimer. 1988. The SOFTNET project: A retrospect. In 8th European Conference on Electrotechnics, June 1988. Conference Proceedings on Area Communication. 343–5. http://ieeexplore.ieee.org/xpl/freeabs_all.jsp?arnumber=11172.

FURTHER READING

Proceedings of the 2002 DARPA Active Networks Conference and Exposition (DANCE 2002), 534–53. Los Alamitos, CA: IEEE Press.

Bush, S. F., and A. Kulkarni. 2001. *Active networks and active network management: A proactive management framework*. New York: Kluwer Academic/Plenum.

Conferences

International Working Conference on Active and Programmable Networks. http://www.iwan2005.net.

IEEE Open Architectures and Network programming (OpenArch).

International Workshop on Active Middleware Services (AMS).

Applications of Biological Concepts to Designs of Computer Networks and Network Applications

Tatsuya Suda, Tadashi Nakano, and Keita Fujii, *University of California, Irvine*

INTRODUCTION

Future computer networks will be autonomous, scalable, adaptive, and robust. They will be autonomous and operate with minimal human intervention. They will scale and support billions of nodes and users. They will adapt to diverse user demands as well as dynamically changing network conditions. They will be robust and survive against network failures and attacks and remain available to users.

Key features of future computer networks mentioned above—that is, autonomy, scalability, adaptability, and robustness—have already been achieved in biological systems. For example, scalability is observed in large-scale social insect colonies (e.g., ant colonies) that contain millions of entities (e.g., worker ants), yet exhibit highly sophisticated and coordinated behaviors (e.g., division of labor in foraging and nest building). Insect colonies also adapt to dynamically changing conditions (e.g., change in the amount of food in the ant colony) through local interaction of entities that adjust their behavior based on conditions (e.g., more ants go out of a colony and gather food when the food level in the colony becomes low). Based on the observation that biological systems exhibit key features that future computer networks require, an increasing number of researchers are currently investigating the feasibility of applying biological concepts and principles to computer networks design.

The idea of drawing inspiration from biological systems exists not only in computer networks, but also in general computing. In biologically inspired computing, biological concepts and principles have been applied and resulted in new and widely accepted computing paradigms. Such biologically inspired computing may be divided into two types: in silico computing, in which biological concepts and mechanisms are implemented on computers to perform computation, and in vitro computing, in which physical properties of biological materials are exploited to perform computation. In silico computing includes evolutionary computation (Mitchell 1998; Koza 1992), neural networks (Yao 1993), ant colony optimization (Dorigo, Di Caro, and Gambardella 1999), and amorphous computing (Abelson 2001). In vitro computing includes DNA computing (Adleman 1994) and cellular computing (Amos 2004). For an overview of biologically inspired computing, see, for instance, Castro and Von Zuben (2004).

This chapter is devoted to biologically inspired networking, applications of biological concepts to designs of computer networks. This chapter describes example biological systems and novel networking paradigm designs based on biological systems. The section on "Biologically Inspired Networking Paradigms" presents the key biological concepts and principles found in biological systems (e.g., nervous systems, immune systems, ant colonies, evolving systems, and cellular systems) and describes how inspiration is drawn from biological systems to create novel networking paradigms. It then provides examples of biologically inspired networking. The discussion section covers the current status and future directions of biologically inspired networking research.

BIOLOGICALLY INSPIRED NETWORKING PARADIGMS

This section presents new networking paradigms inspired by the observation of biological systems. The section consists of five subsections, each of which describes a different biological system: nervous systems, immune systems, ant colonies, evolving systems, and cellular systems. Each subsection first describes a biological system and highlights key biological principles and mechanisms, and then it describes how the key biological principles and mechanisms are applied to designs of computer networks.

Networking Paradigms Inspired by Nervous Systems

Nervous Systems

A nervous system is perhaps one of the most complex systems in nature. A human brain, for instance, involves billions of neurons, each interconnecting thousands of other neurons. Neurons running throughout a body, for instance, communicate to regulate and control various bodily functions.

A nervous system consists of the central nervous system (CNS) and the peripheral nervous system (PNS) (Figure 1). The CNS is composed of a brain and a spinal cord, and is responsible for processing information received from the PNS. The PNS is a network of neurons responsible for transmitting information between the CNS and the rest of a body (i.e., depicted as "Internal Environment" in Figure 1). The PNS is divided into the somatic nervous system and the autonomic nervous system. The somatic nervous system is responsible for controlling the body's muscle movements and also for receiving stimuli from the external environment—that is, external stimuli. The autonomic nervous system is responsible for managing the internal environment of an organism (e.g., heartbeat, blood pressure), and also for receiving internal stimuli.

The autonomic nervous system has a feature of maintaining internal equilibrium of a body of an organism, called "homeostasis," enabling the body of an organism to be highly robust against various environmental perturbations. The autonomic nervous system does so using negative feedback. For example, the autonomic nervous system of a homeothermal animal acts toward generating heat in response to low temperature (e.g., by causing shivering), while reducing heat production in response to high temperature (e.g., causing no shivering), and maintains body temperature at around 37°C. The autonomic nervous system regulates low-level details of body functions without requiring awareness or explicit control by an organism and maintains internal conditions within physiological ranges. By maintaining homeostasis, an organism can function more effectively. For instance, heterothermic animals tend to become sluggish at low temperatures, whereas homeothermal animals remain active.

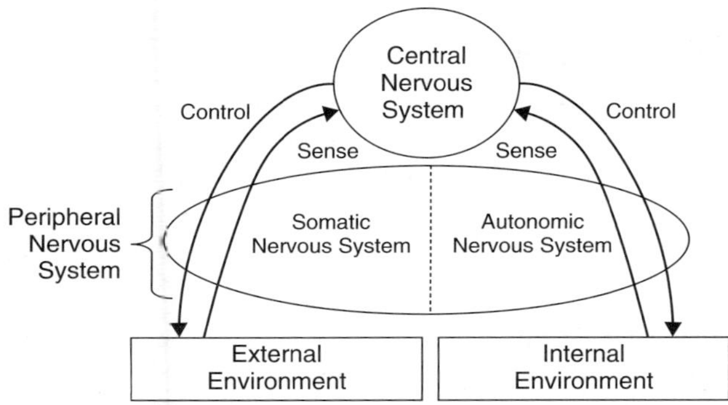

Figure 1: The architecture of a nervous system

Autonomic Computing and Networking

Inspired by the autonomic nervous system, autonomic computing research was initiated by IBM (Kephart and Chess 2003; White et al. 2004), and is currently being carried out at a number of research institutions and universities. See IBM's Web site (www.research.ibm.com/autonomic/research/projects.html) and published papers (Parashar and Hariri 2005; Hariri et al. 2006) for a list of autonomic computing research projects.

The main research challenge in autonomic computing is creating a computer system that self-configures, self-optimizes, self-heals, and self-protects in a manner the same as or similar to that of the autonomic nervous system. Analogous to autonomic nervous systems, an autonomic computing system is expected to operate without requiring external control and constant monitoring by human administrators. To fulfill those requirements, Parashar and Hariri (2005) proposed an architecture of autonomic computing based on the Ashby's (1960) model, a model that explains the ability of an organism to maintain equilibrium through a nervous system.

Ashby first assumed that certain parameters of an organism (e.g., blood pressure) are more critical and are more closely linked to the survivability of the organism; he called such parameters "essential variables." Ashby assumed that in order for an organism to survive, its essential variables must be kept within physiological ranges, and observed that many organisms undergo two types of disturbances: frequent and small impulses, and occasional and large stepwise changes. Based on this observation, Ashby proposed an architecture that consists of two key components: an environment and a reacting part, and contains two closed loops: one loop that reacts to frequent and small disturbances and another that reacts to occasional and large disturbances (Figure 2). The environment includes both types of environments described in Figure 1: the internal environment (or conditions) of an organism, and the external environment (or conditions) surrounding the organism. The reacting part represents a set of behaviors that the organism may trigger to maintain essential variables within physiological ranges. In the case of frequent and small disturbances, essential variables of an organism stay within physiological ranges, and an organism responds to the environmental disturbances by simply choosing an appropriate behavior from its existing behavior set. This response of an organism is called "primary feedback," and is one way of maintaining homeostasis (or equilibrium with the environment). In the case of occasional and

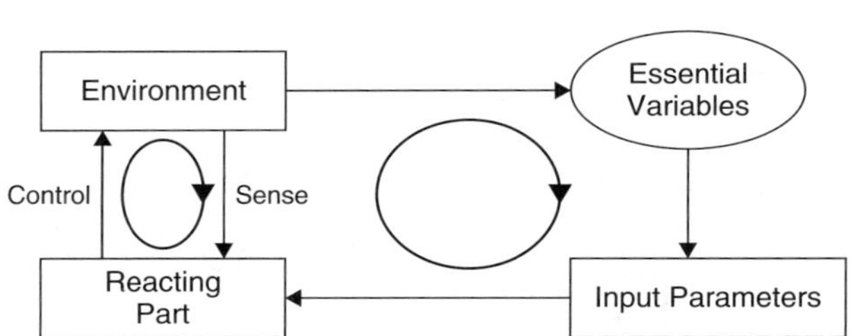

Figure 2: Ashby's model

large disturbances, its essential variables go out of physiological ranges, and an organism modifies the existing set of behaviors to adapt to the environmental disturbances. This is called "secondary feedback," and is another way of maintaining homeostasis. In Ashby's model, primary and secondary feedbacks are considered essential for an organism to maintain homeostasis.

Based on Ashby's model, Parashar and Hariri (2005) designed autonomic elements, which are the smallest functional units in an autonomic computing system (Figure 3). As in Ashby's model, an autonomic element contains two key components: an environment and a reacting part. The environment represents both internal and external factors impacting an autonomic element. The reacting part represents executable codes and data (or behaviors) of an autonomic element. Furthermore, inspired by Ashby's model, Parashar and Hariri introduced two types of control loops between an autonomic element and its environment: local loops and global loops, corresponding respectively to primary feedbacks and secondary feedbacks in Ashby's model. An autonomic element relies on a local loop to handle known situations based on local knowledge embedded in the autonomic element, and it relies on a global loop to handle unknown situations. For example, when a local system load exceeds a predetermined threshold value, an autonomic element invokes a local loop to apply the embedded local knowledge and control local resources to meet load-balancing requirements. On the other hand, when an autonomic element encounters unknown situations (e.g., when invoking a local loop fails to satisfy a requirement on load balancing), an autonomic element invokes a global loop to change existing behaviors; for instance, it invokes machine learning to introduce new knowledge.

The architecture shown in Figure 3 is an example of autonomic computing paradigms. Many other architectures for autonomic computing have also been proposed,

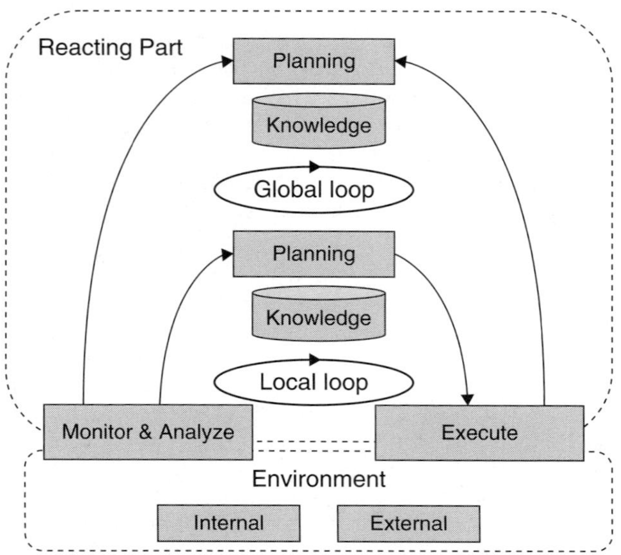

Figure 3: The architecture of autonomic elements

as listed on the IBM Web site (www.research.ibm.com/autonomic/research/projects.html). Although the idea of making computer systems fully autonomous and hiding all their complex and detailed operations from their human operators is still controversial, we believe that applying a nervous system model for computing system design has the potential to create efficient and stable computing systems.

Networking Paradigms Inspired by Immune Systems

Immune Systems

A natural immune system is a large-scale, complex, and adaptive system. It consists of multitudes of immune cells that interact through exchanging molecules within an organism. An immune system protects an organism against infections by pathogens such as bacteria, viruses, and parasites (Alberts et al. 2002). In vertebrates, there are two types of immune responses: innate immune responses and adaptive immune responses. Innate immune responses are the first line of defense and are carried out by particular types of immune cells. Innate immune responses are not specific to particular pathogens but can quickly respond by detecting molecules that are common to many pathogens and are absent in the organism. Adaptive immune responses are carried out by white blood cells, called "lymphocytes," such as T cells and B cells, and are more specific to particular pathogens. Adaptive immune responses are slower but provide the ability to learn new infections.

The adaptive immune responses learn to fight new infection through trial and error. For example, T cells are created with randomly generated receptors, and within an organ called the thymus, T cells are trained not to bind to self but only to non-self. In the training process, T cells are exposed to self-proteins (i.e., proteins synthesized within the body of an organism). The T cells that bind strongly to self-proteins induce apoptosis (i.e., programmed cell death) and die, while others that do not bind to self-proteins are allowed to migrate in a body to detect foreign objects.

The ability to learn to fight new infection is enhanced through an adaptive process called "affinity maturation." Affinity maturation is also achieved through trial and error. In affinity maturation, B cells with a higher affinity for a pathogen become activated with a higher probability, and clone themselves to proliferate. In order to increase affinity for pathogens, when B cells clone themselves, they mutate receptors at a high mutation rate (hypermutation), resulting in cloning of B cells with a slightly different affinity for pathogens. If the cloned B cells exhibit an even higher affinity than the parent B cell, the cloned B cells can be activated more easily and proliferate. Through the trial-and-error processes, an immune system achieves a high affinity for a particular pathogen. After a pathogen is eliminated, the lymphocytes with a high affinity for the particular pathogen become differentiated into long-lived memory lymphocytes that remain in the organism so that they can quickly respond if they encounter the same pathogen in the future.

Network Intrusion Detection

Natural immune systems, as described in the section "Immune Systems," and computer networks share a common goal of protecting themselves against attacks and intrusion, and various concepts and mechanisms from natural immune systems have been implemented for intrusion detection of computer networks. Existing research that applies concepts and mechanisms from artificial immune systems includes an intrusion-detection system for wired networks (Kephart 1994; Forrest, Hofmeyr, and Somayaji 1997) and for wireless sensor networks (Bokareva, Bulusu, and Jha 2005). (For an extensive survey and the comparison of various models proposed in the literature, see Aickelin, Greensmith, and Twycross [2004].) The following provides a brief introduction to an architecture for artificial immune systems (ARTIS) proposed by Hofmeyr and Forrest (2000).

Analogous to natural immune systems, the ARTIS performs classification of self and non-self in an intrusion detection sense. Namely, given an arbitrary string representing a network activity (e.g., a network connection), the ARTIS performs classification of legitimate and illegitimate activities. In order to classify legitimate and illegitimate activities, the ARTIS uses mechanisms from natural immune systems, as described in the section on "Immune Systems." For example, analogous to natural immune systems, which randomly generate receptors for pathogens, the ARTIS randomly generates detectors, each detector containing a randomly generated bit string, to recognize illegitimate activities. In the ARTIS, generated detectors are first exposed to the environment of self and non-self (i.e., legitimate and illegitimate network connections), represented as a set of bit strings (Figure 4). If a detector (i.e., a bit string of a detector) matches any bit string in the self-environment, the detector is eliminated. If it does not match or partially matches, it may become a mature detector and it is then released into the network to detect illegitimate activities.

A released matured detector is activated when similarity (e.g., Hamming distance) of the two bit strings representing the detector and a given network activity exceeds an activation threshold. An activated detector then performs a programmed action, such as notifying network administrators of possible illegitimate activities. When multiple detectors at a node are activated by the same non-self string, the detector with the closest match becomes a memory detector, analogous to affinity maturation of natural immune systems, in which lymphocytes with high affinity for pathogens become easily activated. In addition, the ARTIS relies on a mechanism called "memory-based detection" to remember past intrusion, inspired by the mechanism of natural immune systems to remember pathogens encountered in the past. In the ARTIS, memory detectors obtain a lower activation threshold than non-memory detectors so that they become activated easily in future responses. Memory detectors then clone themselves and spread to neighboring nodes.

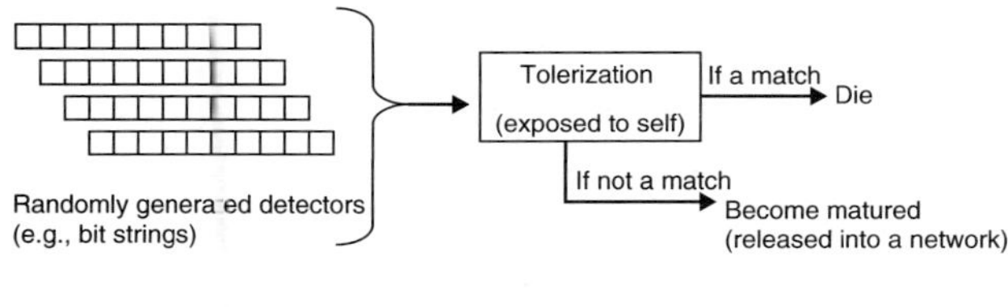

Figure 4: Generating detectors in ARTIS

The ARTIS and other artificial immune systems have successfully captured the essence of biological immune systems and achieved distributed intrusion detection for computer networks. Current artificial immune systems for computer networks are, however, simplistic and not fully autonomous, in the sense that human administrators need to make a decision about how to respond to detected illegitimate activities. One promising direction is to design more autonomous artificial immune systems that require minimal human intervention—for example, by incorporating necessary mechanisms of biological counterparts such as costimulation (a mechanism to reduce the chances of false-positive detection, thereby reducing human involvement) and other similar mechanisms (Hofmeyr and Forrest 2000).

Networking Paradigms Inspired by Ant Colonies

Ant Colonies

Social insects such as ants and bees form a large-scale and highly organized colony. Such an insect colony is decentralized, and there is no global coordination and communication among individual insects. In a large-scale insect colony, when individual insects with a set of very simple behavioral rules interact, intelligent group behaviors emerge from local interactions among individual insects. For example, an ant colony may contain millions of worker ants, yet through local interactions, it efficiently divides labor of nest repair, enlargement, and defense (Bourke and Franks 1995). Similarly, a bee colony that consists of thousands of honeybees coordinates through local interactions to efficiently collect nectar, pollen, and water (Seeley 1995).

The coordinated group behavior of social insects arising from local interactions, known as swarm intelligence, relies on two types of interactions among social insects: direct and indirect (Bonabeau, Dorigo, and Theraulaz 1999). Direct interactions are a straightforward mechanism, and allow insects to communicate through direct contact (e.g., by exchanging food and liquid). Indirect interactions are those in which some insects modify the environment and other nearby insects detect the environmental change and respond to it. This form of communication (i.e., indirect communication through the environment) is called "stigmergy," and is observed in many of their intelligent group activities, including food foraging, nest building, and cemetery building. For example, in finding food sources, ants indirectly interact with each other by depositing and following a chemical substance called a "pheromone." This simple mechanism of interactions leads to finding the shortest (or a shorter) path to a food source, as explained below. Consider a situation in which ants randomly forage and find two different paths to a food source; one path being shorter than the other. Ants that take the shorter path can travel between the nest and the food source more often than the ants taking the longer path; thus, more pheromones are accumulated on the shorter path. Since a higher concentration of pheromones attracts more ants, the shorter path is further reinforced by many more ants, eventually leading most of the ants to follow the shorter path. (See the next section for more details.)

Network Routing

Inspired by the foraging behavior of ants, Dorigo et al. (1999) proposed ACO (ant colony optimization) as a solution to optimization problems in networks such as shortest-path-finding problems. Several routing mechanisms based on ant foraging behavior have also been proposed for the Internet (Di Caro and Dorigo 1998) and for mobile ad hoc networks (Gunes, Sorges, and Bouazzi 2002; Roth and Wicker 2003; Wedde et al. 2005). In addition, several frameworks to implement and evaluate various ant-based algorithms have been proposed (Montresor 2001; Montresor, Meling, and Babaoglu 2002; Bean and Costa 2005). The following briefly describes AntNet, a well-known routing mechanism based on ant foraging behavior, and Anthill, an application development framework for peer-to-peer networks.

AntNet is a routing mechanism for IP (Internet protocol) datagram networks inspired by the foraging behavior of social ants (Di Caro and Dorigo 1998). The particular metaphor taken from the observation of ant colonies is stigmergy (indirect communication through the environment). In AntNet, there are two types of ants, forward and backward ants, which interact indirectly by modifying a routing table of a networked node. This is analogous to real ants indirectly interacting by modifying the environment through pheromones. Each node of AntNet periodically launches a forward ant toward a probabilistically selected destination node to discover the best path to the node. Forward ants are initially routed according to a probabilistic routing table at each node, i.e., forward ants decide which node to go to next based on the probability specified in the routing table of a node. While traveling toward a destination, a forward ant records the routing path it takes (i.e., a stack of nodes it visits) and the time it visits each node on the routing path. When a forward ant reaches a destination, it calculates the goodness of the path it just took (such as the total time required on the routing path to reach the destination node). It then creates a backward ant that carries information on the path and the path goodness. (The forward ant then dies.) A backward ant travels the path that the forward ant took in the opposite direction. While "backwarding" the path, a backward ant updates a routing table at each node, according to the goodness of the path, to lead more forward ants onto a better path (i.e., a path with better goodness value). This routing mechanism is analogous to ant forging behavior, in which ants deposit pheromones on paths; shorter paths attract more ants, eventually leading to the shortest path (Figure 5). The performance of AntNet is compared against six other existing routing mechanisms, and is verified to result in higher throughputs and smaller packet delays.

In order to ease the implementation and evaluation of peer-to-peer applications, an application development framework for peer-to-peer networks—Anthill—has been proposed (Montresor 2001; Montresor et al. 2002). In Anthill, a network application is constructed by a network of peers called "nests." A nest (i.e., a PC hosting Anthill) provides a storage space for documents and generates queries called "ants" (i.e., software agents) in response to a user's request for a document. Ants travel over a network of nests in search of a requested document. During the search, ants indirectly interact with other ants by modifying the information that each nest maintains. For example, ants may leave a pheromone containing information regarding other documents and nests in order to facilitate the search processes of other ants. Anthill also supports evolution that allows some ants to mutate and exhibit different behaviors, which increases the variation and robustness of ant-based algorithms. Anthill provides a set of run-time libraries for development and monitoring to ease the implementation and evaluation of peer-to-peer applications.

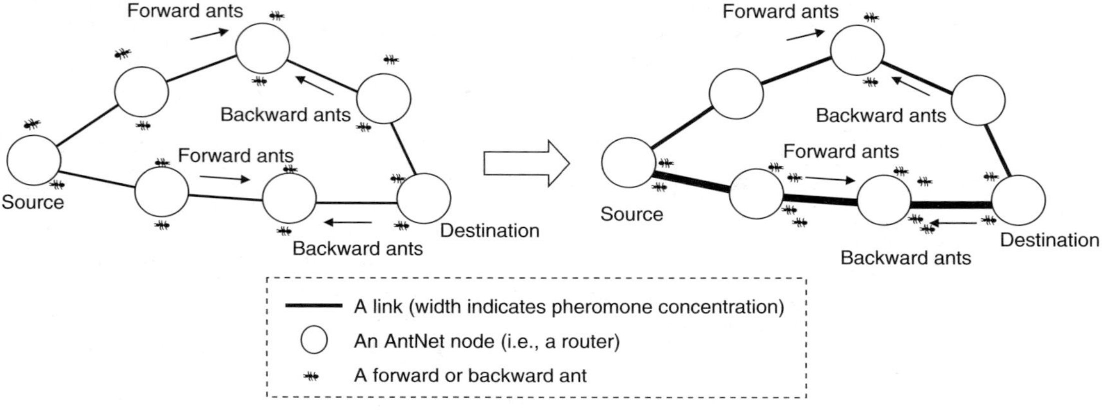

Figure 5: Shortest path finding in AntNet

Ant-based mechanisms such as the ones described in this subsection are known to be useful for solving various complex problems, including the traveling salesman problem (Dorigo 1992), unicast and multicast routing (Guoying, Zemin, and Zheng 2000), and the clustering problem (Handl, Knowles, and Dorigo 2003). However, ant-based mechanisms are a variation of distributed learning algorithms, and thus, they require some time to obtain history and derive the optimal solutions. One key research issue in applying ant foraging behaviors is how to improve efficiency of the mechanisms.

Networking Paradigms Inspired by Evolving Systems

Evolution through Natural Selection

Biological systems evolve to adapt to and survive in a dynamically changing environment. Evolution in biological systems occurs as a result of natural selection from diverse behavioral characteristics of individual biological entities.

In the biological world, food (or energy) serves as a natural selection mechanism. Biological entities naturally strive to gain energy by seeking and consuming food. Biological entities that successfully obtain energy may reproduce more and survive longer than those that are not successful in obtaining energy.

In the biological world, diversity is maintained through various mechanisms such as mutation and crossover of genetic information (i.e., genes). When a biological entity (asexually) replicates, an offspring entity probabilistically undergoes mutation that modifies its genetic information. When two biological entities (sexually) reproduce, an offspring entity inherits a part of genetic information from a parent and the remaining genetic information from the other parent. Mutation and crossover of genetic information may allow an offspring to acquire behavioral characteristics that are different from those of a parent or parents, resulting in diverse behavior characteristics of individual biological entities.

Through natural selection of diverse biological entities over generations, beneficial features are retained, while detrimental behaviors become dormant or extinct, and the biological systems evolve to adapt to and survive in a dynamically changing environment.

Middleware Framework

Inspired by biological evolution through natural selection, Suda, Itao, and Matsuo (2005) and Wang and Suda (2001) proposed the Bio-Networking Architecture as a middleware framework for the design and development of network applications. The Bio-Networking Architecture supports the design and development of a wide range of applications, including content distribution services (Wang and Suda 2001) and dynamic service composition (Itao et al. 2004). In addition, the various aspects of the Bio-Networking Architecture have been empirically examined (Suzuki and Suda 2005) and investigated through simulation (Nakano and Suda 2005). The following explains how biological evolution is incorporated into the Bio-Networking Architecture.

In the Bio-Networking Architecture, network applications are implemented by a group of distributed, autonomous entities called the "cyber-entities" (analogous to a bee colony consisting of multiple bees). Each cyber-entity implements a functional component related to its service. It also follows simple behavior rules (such as migration, replication, reproduction, death, and energy exchange) similar to biological entities.

In the Bio-Networking Architecture, useful application functionality emerges from the collaborative execution of services carried by cyber-entities, and useful system behaviors and characteristics (e.g., self-organization, adaptation, scalability, and survivability) arise through the interaction of individual cyber-entities following simple behavior rules.

Within a biological system, diversity of behaviors is necessary for the system to adapt and evolve to suit a wide variety of environmental conditions. In the Bio-Networking Architecture, multiple cyber-entities are created to implement the same service but with different behavior policies (e.g., one cyber-entity with a migration policy of moving toward a user, and another cyber-entity with a migration policy of moving toward a node with a less expensive resource cost) to ensure a sufficient degree of behavioral diversity. In addition, the Bio-Networking Architecture creates and retains behavioral diversity among cyber-entities through mutation and crossover. Mutation may occur in replication and reproduction of cyber-entities, and it randomly modifies the genetic information that encodes behavior rules of offspring cyber-entities. Crossover may occur in reproduction, in which two parent cyber-entities create an offspring cyber-entity with mixed genetic information. Figure 6 illustrates crossover and mutation in a reproduction process, where genetic information of a cyber-entity encodes its behavior (e.g., migration behavior) as a set of weights (i.e., a series of rectangles in Figure 6, where each rectangle represents a weight). As shown in Figure 6, crossover randomly takes a weight from either parent (parent A or B) to create a new set of weights, and then mutation randomly changes some weights. An offspring entity that acquires the resulting set of weights may behave differently from either of the parents.

Within a biological system, food (or energy) serves as a natural selection mechanism. Similar to a biological entity, each cyber-entity in the Bio-Networking Architecture stores and expends energy for living (Figure 7). Cyber-entities gain energy in exchange for performing

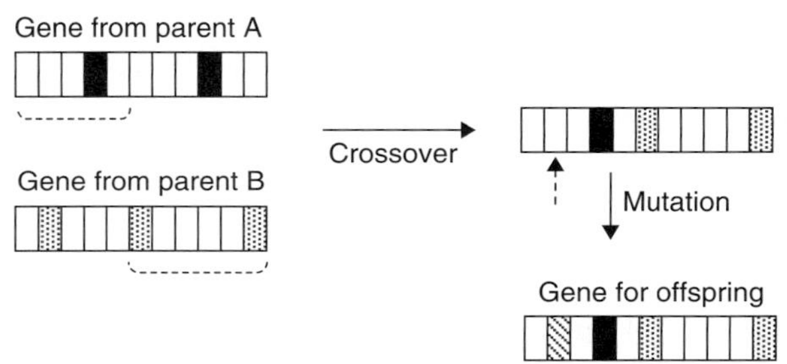

Figure 6: Crossover and mutation

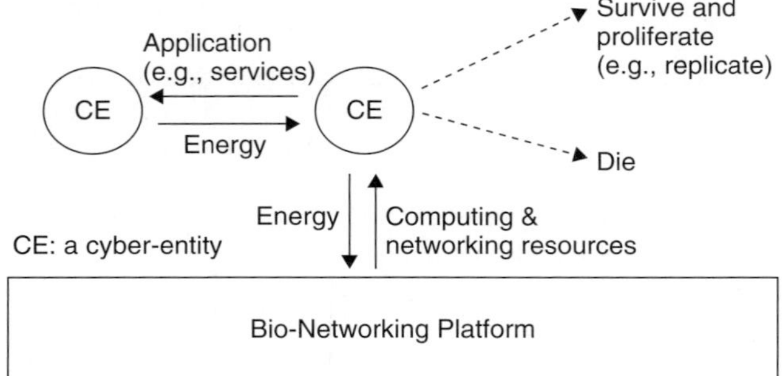

Figure 7: Energy acquisition and consumption as a natural-selection mechanism

a service for other cyber-entities, and they pay energy to use network and computing resources on the Bio-Networking Platform (i.e., an execution environment of cyber-entities). The abundance or scarcity of stored energy affects various behaviors of cyber-entities and contributes to the natural selection process in evolution. For example, an abundance of stored energy is an indication of high demand for the cyber-entity; thus, the cyber-entity may reproduce often. A scarcity of stored energy (an indication of lack of demand or ineffective behaviors) may eventually cause the cyber-entity to die out.

Reproduction and replication create a population of cyber-entities with diverse behaviors. Through natural selection, fitter cyber-entities accumulate energy and proliferate, while others exhaust energy and die. Cyber-entities are able to adapt in this manner to the environment as well as to environmental changes.

Biologically inspired evolution mechanisms designed for the Bio-Networking Architecture relies on random processes (i.e., mutation), and thus, it may require significant time to achieve desired application performance (e.g., low latency in content delivery). In addition, there is no guarantee that a network application achieves optimal performance. Evolution may not even improve but rather degrade performance because evolution has to go through a large number of generations, consuming network and computing resources. Because evolution takes time and requires resources, applying the concept of evolution may not be viable in implementing applications for highly dynamic networks and applications for limited computing and networking resources.

Networking Paradigms Inspired by Cellular Systems

Cellular Systems

A multicellular organism starts with a single cell (i.e., a fertilized egg) and successfully develops into complex structures, such as tissues and organs. In the developmental process of multicellular organisms, gene expression in a cell controls the following four essential cellular behaviors: proliferation, specialization, interactions, and movement. Cell proliferation produces cells through cell division. Cell specialization creates cells with different characteristics at different positions. Cell interactions allow cells to coordinate with nearby cells, for example, through the use of diffusive signal molecules. Cell movement rearranges the cells to form structured tissues and organs. In developmental processes, cells express a particular set of genes to trigger these four essential cellular behaviors to form a complex multicellular structure.

The development process of multicellular organisms typically progresses massively in parallel without central control (Alberts et al. 2002). For example, consider the development process of an embryo. Although all cells within a developing embryo contain identical genetic information, cells develop into different parts of an organism by expressing different sets of genes based on the internal and external environmental conditions of a cell. Different sets of genes are expressed in different cells of a developing embryo. Which set of genes to express in a cell depends on the environmental conditions (e.g., concentration gradients of signal molecules such as morphogens) of the cell and is not controlled by a central entity. Cells share the common set of genes, yet they are able to form a complex multicellular structure with precision.

Application Development Framework

Cellular systems have inspired networking paradigms. For example, cell-based programming is an application development framework that is inspired by the developmental process of multicellular organisms (George, Evans, and Marchette 2002). *Design patterns from biology* is a conceptual framework to design network applications inspired by the common cellular behaviors and processes such as interactions through the use of diffusive signal molecules (Babaoglu et al. 2005). Other examples include attempts to apply cellular signaling mechanisms to the design of autonomous and scalable communication systems (Krüger and Dressler 2004; Dressler 2005). The following introduces one of the above-mentioned networking paradigms—cell-based programming and its application to computer networks.

Cell-based programming is an application development framework based on developmental processes of multicellular organisms (George et al. 2002). Analogous to a multicellular organism, an application in the cell-based programming paradigm is created by a group of artificial cells. Every artificial cell of an application contains a set of identical behavior rules, corresponding to DNA of a biological counterpart. Each artificial cell follows a set of behavior rules (i.e., cell proliferation and specialization described above). For example, cells proliferate through cell division and become specialized when placed at different positions. Cells emit artificial signal molecules into the environment, and the emitted signal molecules diffuse according to the environmental conditions such as concentrations of signal molecules. Cells may die when environmental conditions change. Although all artificial cells contain an identical set of behavior rules, it is possible to form a complex structure by activating a different subset of the behavior rule set as reactions to different environmental conditions and by cascading cellular reactions (e.g., by making a local reaction lead to another interaction). This is analogous to a multicellular organism, in which constituting cells express different sets of genes and become specialized to form a multicellular structure.

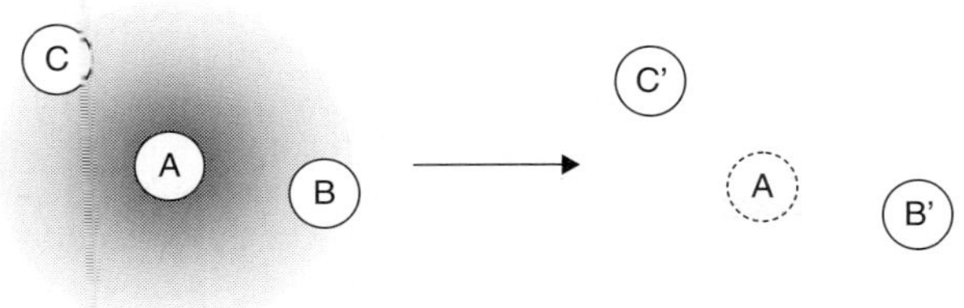

Figure 8: Interactions between artificial cells in cell-based programming

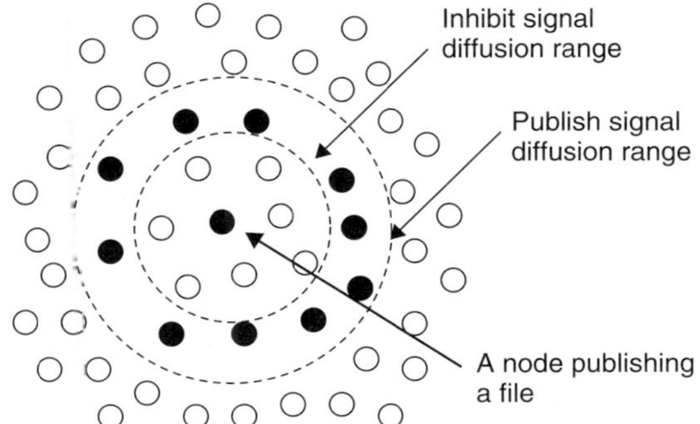

Figure 9: File distribution based on cell-based programming

Figure 8 illustrates local interactions among cells. Assume that artificial cell A that is diffusing signals dies. After artificial cell A dies, artificial cells B and C detect that the signal concentration around them decreases, alter their states, and become specialized into B' and C'.

Applications developed using cell-based programming are highly fault-tolerant and exhibit a self-healing property, since an assembled cellular structure in cell-based programming can recover from damage (e.g., loss of a group of cells) through cell division and coordination (e.g., signal diffusion) without using global knowledge and communications. It is important to note that a robust structure may be formed from unreliable and fragile cells following a simple set of behavior rules.

George et al. (2002) has applied the cell-based programming paradigm to the design of a peer-to-peer file-sharing service for mobile wireless networks. The goal of the application is to reliably distribute files over a network of unreliable nodes (e.g., unreliable cells). In the application, when a node publishes a file, it broadcasts two types of signals: replicate and inhibit (Figure 9). Replicate signals propagate over a larger area than inhibit signals. A node that receives replicate signals but does not receive inhibit signals (i.e., shaded nodes in Figure 9) makes a copy of the file, stores that copy, and further diffuses inhibit and replicate signals for the file it copied. In this manner, a certain distribution of files (e.g., a certain structure of cells) is created. Analogous to a robust biological cellular structure, the file distribution generated in this manner without central control and global knowledge is highly robust against node failures and exhibits a self-healing property.

As seen in cell-based programming, current approaches mimic only macroscopic cellular behaviors and may be too simplistic. Further study is necessary to analyze dynamic behaviors and complex properties of cells in biological systems, and to incorporate them into a design of computer networks. We believe that applying dynamic behaviors and complex properties of cells allows the emergence of robust structures with highly functional components in computer networks, as evident in biological systems.

CONCLUSION

Biological systems present fascinating features such as scalability and adaptability; thus, they have inspired new networking paradigms. Specific inspiration or model systems used in literature, as in this chapter, include autonomic nervous systems, immune systems, insect colonies (ant colonies), evolving systems, and cellular systems. The feasibility of applying biological concepts and mechanisms to computer networks has been extensively investigated through various simulation studies. Some of the simulation studies used data from real networks and confirmed the improved performance over existing approaches (see, for example, Di Caro and Dorigo 1998 and Hofmeyr and Forrest 2000). In addition, various bio-inspired experimental systems have been developed and are available for empirical investigation and application development (e.g., Montresor 2001 and Suzuki 2005).

Future work in biologically inspired networking includes exploring molecular and cell biology, and identifying new design principles applicable to computer networks. Some areas worth exploring in molecular and cell biology include signal transduction (e.g., biochemical reactions within a cell or across a cell membrane that results in cascading reactions, leading to various cellular processes), gene regulatory networks (e.g., networks of messenger RNA, which regulate DNA transcription or gene expression), oscillatory processes (e.g., cyclic behavior such as circadian clocks that enable a cell to adapt to a day-and-night cycle), and cell-cycle regulation (e.g., mechanisms to correct errors in cell cycles and to regulate metabolic activities). Such biological systems may be viewed as distributed information-processing systems, and some of the design principles found in such biological systems may be applicable to computer network designs.

Future work also includes establishment of a unified framework based on common mechanisms found across different biological systems. Such an abstracted framework may serve as a generic model and provide general design principles for computer networks. Some of the important design principles found in biological systems may include the following:

- *A large number of redundant components*. A biological system is composed of a large number of redundant components, as seen in all five biological systems described in this chapter. A nervous system may contain billions of neurons, and an ant colony may contain a million of ants. Because of the large number of redundant components, a biological system is robust in the event of failures and misbehaviors of a small number of components.

- *Local interactions and collective behavior*. Useful group properties and behaviors often emerge from local interaction of individuals with a simple set of behavioral rules. For example, although individual immune cells may sometimes erroneously identify foreign objects, an immune system (i.e., collection of interacting immune cells) as a whole reliably detects and eliminates foreign objects. This is a result of individual immune cells interacting and coordinating to minimize the impact of errors caused by individual immune cells. Similarly, although individual ants are not able to find the shortest path to a food source, a group of ants as a whole finds the shortest path as a result of individual ants interacting through pheromones.
- *Stochastic or probabilistic nature*. The stochastic nature of biological systems often contributes to exploring search space. For example, ants do not always follow the already-found shortest path; rather, they probabilistically choose different paths to seek possible shorter paths. The stochastic nature also contributes to increasing diversity, thereby improving adaptability to the environment. In genetic evolution, for example, mutation randomly alters genetic information, which may create fitter organisms, enabling a population of individuals to become more adapted to the environment.
- *Feedbacks*. Biological systems often use two types of feedbacks: negative feedback to reduce the effect of environmental noise, and positive feedback to amplify signals in the environment. For example, in homeostatic biological systems, negative feedbacks are used to maintain an organism's essential variables within physiological ranges, providing the organism with stability and robustness against environmental perturbations. In ant foraging, on the other hand, ants use positive feedbacks to amplify signals (i.e., pheromones) and to recruit more ants toward a particular path; that is, ants follow a path with higher pheromone concentrations, resulting in further enhancement of the pheromone concentration of the path.

In addition to identifying important design principles by analyzing various biological systems, it is also important to establish metrics to evaluate key system properties such as autonomy, scalability, adaptability, and robustness. Such evaluation metrics would help in evaluating and comparing computer networks modeled after various biological concepts and mechanisms.

GLOSSARY

Autonomic Nervous System: A part of peripheral nervous system that is responsible for managing the internal environment of an organism and receiving internal stimuli.

B Cells: Lymphocytes that produce antibodies.

Central Nervous System (CNS): A part of the nervous system that consists of the brain and the spinal cord.

Crossover: The process by which two chromosomes exchange some distal portion of their genes.

Hamming Distance: The number of positions for which the corresponding symbols are different.

Homeostasis: Internal equilibrium of a body of an organism.

Mutation: Change of gene caused by copying errors in the genetic material during cell division.

Peripheral nervous system (PNS): Nerves and neurons that reside or extend outside the central nervous system (CNS).

Somatic Nervous System: A part of peripheral nervous system that is responsible for controlling the body's muscle movements and receiving stimuli from the external environment.

Stigmergy: A method of communication in emergent systems in which the individual parts of the system communicate with one another by modifying their local environment.

Swarm Intelligence: An artificial intelligence technique based on collective behavior in which simple agents interacting locally with one another and with their environment lead to the emergence of global behavior.

T Cells: Lymphocytes with receptors responsible for recognizing antigens.

CROSS REFERENCES

See *Cellular Communications Channels; Intrusion Detection Systems; Molecular Communication: New Paradigm for Communication among Nano-scale Biological Machines*.

REFERENCES

Abelson, H., D. Allen, D. Coore, C. Hanson, E. Rauch, G. J. Sussman, and R. Weiss 2001. Amorphous computing. *Communications of the ACM* 43(5):74–82.

Adleman, L. M. 1994. Molecular computation of solutions to combinatorial problems. *Science* 226:1021–4.

Aickelin, U., J. Greensmith, and J. Twycross. 2004. Immune system approaches to intrusion detection—A review. *Proceedings of the 3rd International Conference on Artificial Immune Systems*. New York: Springer: Lecture Notes in Computer Science 3239:316–29.

Alberts, B., A. Johnson, J. Lewis, M. Raff, K. Roberts, and P. Walter. 2002. *Molecular biology of the cell*. New York: Garland Science.

Amos, M. 2004. *Cellular computing*. Cambridge, UK: Oxford University Press.

Ashby, W. R. 1960. *Design for a brain*. London: Chapman & Hall.

Babaoglu, O., G. Canright, A. Deutsch, G. Di Caro, F. Ducatelle, L. Gambardella, N. Ganguly, M. Jelasity, R. Montemanni, and A. Montresor. 2005. Design patterns from biology for distributed computing. In *Proceedings of the European Conference on Complex Systems*.

Bean, N., and A. Costa. 2005. An analytic modeling approach for network routing algorithms that use "ant-like" mobile agents. *International Journal of Computer and Telecommunications Networking* 49(2):234–68.

Bonabeau, E., M. Dorigo, and G. Theraulaz. 1999. *Swarm intelligence: From natural to artificial systems*. Cambridge, UK: Oxford University Press.

Bokareva, T., N. Bulusu, and S. Jha. 2005. SASHA: Toward a self-healing hybrid sensor network architecture.

In *Proceedings of the Second IEEE Workshop on Embedded Networked Sensors*.

Bourke, A. F. G., and N. R. Franks. 1995. *Social evolution in ants*. Princeton, NJ: Princeton University Press.

Castro, L. N., and F. J. Von Zuben 2004. *Recent developments in biologically inspired computing*. Hershey, PA: Idea Group.

Di Caro, G., and M. Dorigo. 1998. AntNet: Distributed stigmergetic control for communications networks. *Journal of Artificial Intelligence Research (JAIR)* 9:317–65.

Dorigo, M., G. Di Caro, and L. M. Gambardella. 1999. Ant algorithms for discrete optimization. *Artificial Life* 5(3):137–72.

Dorigo, M. 1992. Optimization, learning and natural algorithms. Ph.D. thesis, Politecnico di Milano, Italy.

Dressler F. 2005. Efficient and scalable communication in autonomous networking using bio-inspired mechanisms—An overview. *Informatica—An International Journal of Computing and Informatics* 29(2):183–8.

Forrest, S., S. Hofmeyr, and A. Somayaji. 1997. Computer immunology. *Communications of the ACM* 40(10): 88–96.

George, S., D. Evans, and S. Marchette. 2002. A biological programming model for self-healing. In *Proceedings of the 2003 ACM workshop on Survivable and Self-Regenerative Systems*, 72–81.

Gunes, M., U. Sorges, and I. Bouazzi. 2002. ARA: The ant-colony based routing algorithm for MANETs. In *Proceedings of the 2002 International Conference on Parallel Processing Workshops on Ad Hoc Networks*.

Guoying, L., L. Zemin, and Z. Zheng. 2000. Multicast routing based on ant algorithm for delay-bounded and load-balancing traffic, In *Proceedings of the 25th Annual IEEE Conference on Local Computer Networks*, 362–8.

Handl, J., J. Knowles, and M. Dorigo. 2003. On the performance of ant-based clustering. *Frontiers in Artificial Intelligence and Applications* 104:204–213.

Hariri, S., B. Khargharia, H. Chen, J. Yang, Y. Zhang, M. Parashar, and H. Liu. 2006. The autonomic computing paradigm. *Cluster Computing: The Journal of Networks, Software Tools, and Applications* 9(1):5–17.

Hofmeyr, S. A., and S. Forrest. 2000. Architecture for an artificial immune system. *Evolutionary Computation* 8(4):443–73.

Itao, T., S. Tanaka, T. Suda, and T. Aoyama. 2004. A framework for adaptive UbiComp applications based on the Jack-in-the-Net architecture. *Kluwer/ACM Wireless Network Journal* 10(3):287–99.

Kephart, J. O. 1994. A biologically inspired immune system for computers. In *Proceedings of the Fourth International Workshop on the Synthesis and Simulation of Living Systems*, 130–9.

Kephart, J. O., and D. M. Chess. 2003. The vision of autonomic computing. *IEEE Computer* 36(1):41–50.

Koza, J. R. 1992. *Genetic programming*. Cambridge, MA: MIT Press.

Krüger, B., and F. Dressler. 2004. Molecular processes as a basis for autonomous networking. In *Proceedings of the International IPSI-2004 Stockholm Conference: Symposium on Challenges in the Internet and Interdisciplinary Research*.

Mitchell, M. 1998. *An introduction to genetic algorithms*. Cambridge, MA: MIT Press.

Montresor, A. 2001. Anthill: A framework for the design and analysis of peer-to-peer systems. In *Proceedings of the 4th European Research Seminar on Advances in Distributed Systems*.

Montresor, A., H. Meling, and O. Babaoglu. 2002. Messor: Load-balancing through a swarm of autonomous agents. In *Proceedings of the 1st International Workshop on Agents and Peer-to-Peer Computing*.

Nakano, T., and T. Suda. 2005. Self-organizing network services with evolutionary adaptation. *IEEE Transactions on Neural Networks* 16(5; Special Issue on Adaptive Learning Systems in Communication Networks):1269–1278.

Parashar, M., and S. Hariri. 2005. *Autonomic computing: An overview*. Berlin: Springer Lecture Notes in Computer Science, 3566:247–59.

Roth, M., and S. Wicker. 2003. Termite: Emergent ad-hoc networking. In *Proceedings of the Second Mediterranean Workshop on Ad-Hoc Networks*.

Seeley, T. 1995. *The wisdom of the hive*. Cambridge, MA: Harvard University Press.

Suda, T., T. Itao, and M Matsuo. 2005. The Bio-Networking Architecture: The biologically inspired approach to the design of scalable, adaptive, and survivable/available network applications. In *The Internet as a large-scale complex system* (Santafe Institute Book Series), edited by K. Park, Cambridge, UK: Oxford University Press.

Suzuki, J., and T. Suda. 2005. A middleware platform for a biologically-inspired network architecture supporting autonomous and adaptive applications. *IEEE Journal on Selected Areas in Communications* 23(2; Special Issue on Intelligent Services and Applications in Next Generation Networks):249–60.

Wang, M., and T. Suda. 2001. The Bio-Networking Architecture: A biologically inspired approach to the design of scalable, adaptive, and survivable/available network applications. In *Proceedings of the 1st IEEE Symposium on Applications and the Internet*.

Wedde, H. F., M. Farooq, T. Pannenbaecker, B. Vogel, C. Mueller, J. Meth, and R. Jeruschkat, BeeAdHoc. 2005. An energy efficient routing algorithm for mobile ad hoc networks inspired by bee behavior. In *Proceedings of the 2005 Conference on Genetic and Evolutionary Computation*, 153–60.

White, S. R., J. E. Hanson, I. Whalley, D. M. Chess, and J. O. Kephart. 2004. An architectural approach to autonomic computing. In *Proceedings of the IEEE International Conference on Autonomic Computing (ICAC'04)*, 2–9.

Yao, X. 1993. A review of evolutionary artificial neural networks. *International Journal of Intelligent Systems* 8(4):539–67.

Nanotechnology for Communication Systems

Syed H. Murshid and Azhar M. Khayrattee, *Florida Institute of Technology*

INTRODUCTION

The prefix nano means 1/1,000,000,000 or simply a billionth. Nanotechnology deals with structures or devices that are 100 nm or less in size (the diameter of a human hair is roughly 50 μm and the smallest thing visible to the human eye is around 10 μm). Nanotechnology has applications in virtually all disciplines, including electronics and optics. It promises to revolutionize computers, communications, and interdisciplinary sciences. Every communication system has three basic building blocks: the signal source, communication media, and signal detector. A subset of components, such as signal modulators, filters, amplifiers, switches, routers, and encryption devices complement these basic blocks. Current state of the art in nanotechnology offers a wide range of devices that encompass most aspects of communications system. These devices are gradually transitioning out of the research environment and are slowly maturing into commercial products. The vertical-cavity surface-emitting laser (VCSEL) is an example of a commercially available nanoscale signal source that has replaced conventional laser diodes in many applications. Similarly, photonic crystals are finding a multitude of applications in optical communication media such as optical waveguides, planar waveguides, fibers, and filters. Quantum cryptography is an encryption scheme that is nearly impossible to crack. This technique generally relies on single-photon devices. Quantum dots are used to build devices such as single-photon sources and detectors. Quantum dots can also be used as sources and generators of entangled electron pairs. Carbon nanotubes exhibit remarkable electrical properties, with many applications in all the three basic communication blocks. Similarly, MEMS and NEMS (microelectromechanical and nanoelectromechanical systems) are used in a wide variety of nanoscale devices for switching and routing applications (www.allaboutmems.com/memsapplications.html). A host of chemical dendrimers, that include monomers and polymers, are increasingly used in optical amplifiers like erbium-doped fiber amplifier (EDFAs) to enhance efficiency. In addition, various nanodevices such as transistors, Mach-Zehnder modulators, and terahertz lasers are also available for communication-related applications. Silicon photonics and surface plasmons are both relatively new areas of focus in nanotechnology. Their applications to nanoscale communication are discussed in this chapter. Some devices presented in this chapter may fall outside the 100-nm range, but these devices are often referred to as nanodevices in the literature and there is a continuous effort to scale down these larger devices to the nanorange (Poole and Owens 2003; Ratner and Ratner 2002).

VERTICAL-CAVITY SURFACE-EMITTING LASER

A vertical-cavity surface-emitting laser (VCSEL) is one of the smallest commercially available laser sources.

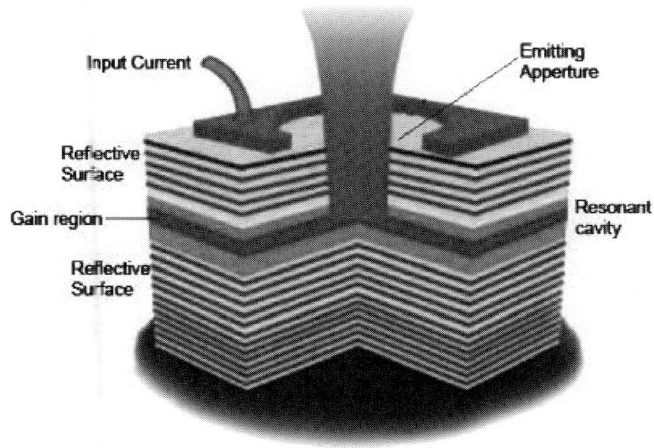

Figure 1: Typical VCSEL structure (adapted from www.atvoigt.de/modules/EZCMS/pictures/VCSEL.jpg)

Up to 20,000 VCSELs can be packed on a 3-in. wafer (ICielo Communications). A regular laser diode consists of multiple semiconductor layers and emits its infrared energy parallel to these layers. A VCSEL, on the other hand, emits its infrared energy perpendicular to these layers. As shown in Figure 1, the resonant cavity consists of two distributed Bragg reflector mirrors parallel to the wafer surface with an active region consisting of one or more quantum wells for generation of laser energy between them. The planar distributed Bragg reflector mirrors consist of layers with alternating high and low refractive indices. Typical VCSEL junction diodes have their upper and lower mirrors doped as p-type and n-type, respectively, while materials used for manufacture include gallium arsenide (GaAs), aluminum gallium arsenide (AlGaAs), and indium gallium arsenide nitride (InGaAsN). A VCSEL manufactured with GaAs/AlGaAs usually emits in the 850-nm wavelength range. To achieve different wavelengths, different materials are used. VCSELs have extremely short cavity lengths, usually only a few microns long, which allows single-frequency operation as well as some wavelength tunability. VCSELs can operate up to 10 Gbps. They have many advantages, including low power consumption, high transmission speeds, relatively low manufacturing cost, high reliability, and high efficiency. The room-temperature operation of VCSELs eliminates the use of extensive cooling systems. VCSELs have low manufacturing cost, as surface emission allows testing at the wafer level, before individual VCSELs are packaged. The circular and low divergence output beam of VCSELs eliminates the need for corrective optics. VCSELs are commercially available as single-mode and multimode devices, both of which can operate in the gigabit region (www.lightreading.com/document.asp?doc_id=2580&page_number=3; Verdeyen 1995). Surface plasmon-based VCSELs are actively being investigated as low-power and high-data-rate laser devices. Such VCSELs will be discussed in the later sections of this chapter.

PHOTONIC CRYSTALS

Photonic crystals are multidimensional periodic dielectric nanostructures that are designed to control and manipulate the propagation of electromagnetic waves. A major source of noise in lasing systems is spontaneous emission. Photonic crystals tend to inhibit spontaneous emission by eliminating certain electromagnetic modes; they do this by modifying the radiative field coupling. This significantly reduces the threshold current and noise in semiconductor lasers (Joannopoulos, Meade, and Winn 1995; Johnson and Joannopoulos 2002).

Optical Waveguides

Photonic crystals can also be used as optical waveguides. Conventional optical waveguides rely on total internal reflection and yield acceptable results only in cases in which the bending radius of the waveguide is larger than the wavelength of the light. This scenario is not practical if we want to scale down optical equipment to the nanoscale. In such situations, most of the light will be lost at the bend. Photonic crystal waveguides rely on photonic band gaps to propagate light. The crystal is fashioned in such a way that the light is allowed to propagate only along specific paths, as depicted by the arrow in Figure 2. This allows sharp bends with no light loss. On the whole, photonic crystal waveguides offer virtually no absorption and are perfect mirrors as compared with conventional waveguides (Fan et al. 2001; Johnson et al. 2000).

Filters

Photonic crystals can also be used to make filters. As previously mentioned, a photonic crystal can manipulate and control the propagation of electromagnetic waves, depending on its structure. The nanostructures

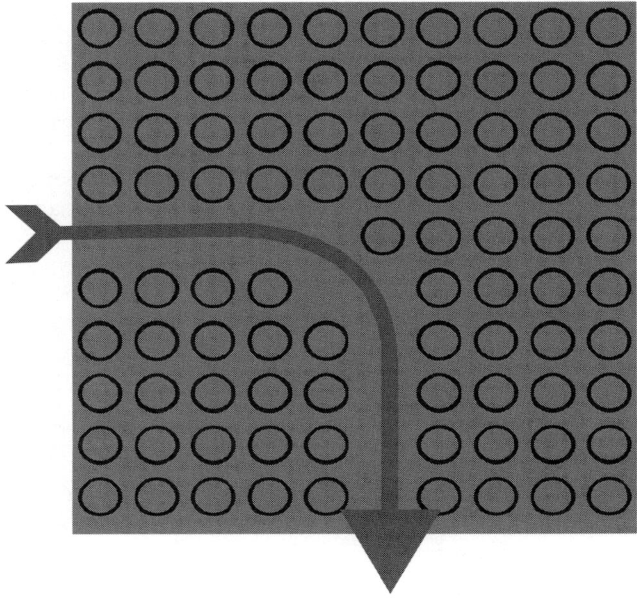

Figure 2: Photonic crystal optical waveguide

can be arranged in a fashion that allows only certain wavelengths to travel through the material, and filters out others. Such filters are more efficient, less bulky, and more accurate than conventional filters. Photonic crystal filters are important devices in nanoscale optical communication. Polarizing filters can also be made using the birefringence property of photonic crystals (Solli and Hickmann 2004).

Planar Antennas

Planar antenna substrate is another application of photonic crystals. The efficiency of a conventional planar antenna is approximately less than 50 percent because half of the energy of the propagating wave is absorbed by the semiconductor substrate. One way to overcome this problem is to design the substrate in such a fashion that it acts as a mirror reflecting back the energy of the electromagnetic wave toward the antenna surface. A photonic crystal can be used to make this type of reflecting surface, as illustrated in Figure 3. This modification renders planar antennas more efficient, along with the added benefit of size reduction. Planar antennas are very important in monolithic millimeter-wave integrated circuits (MMICs). MMICs are increasingly used in satellite systems, in which smaller circuits are needed. MMICs are also useful in systems for which the parasitic reactance, inherent in hybrid integrated circuits, degrades the circuit performance, especially in the upper microwave and millimeter-wave spectrum. Communication devices and systems such as phased-array antennas and high-frequency radars rely heavily on MMICs. The use of photonic crystals in these circuits greatly improves the overall efficiency of the system (Brown, McMahon, and Parker 1998; Brown, Parker, and Yablonovitch 1993).

Fibers

Photonic crystals can be used to make optical fibers. These fibers are also called "holey fibers," "hole-assisted fibers," or "microstructure fibers." Unlike other photonic crystal devices that derive their properties from periodic spatial arrangements, the photonic crystal fiber (PCF) owes its waveguide properties to an arrangement of tiny air holes that run through the entire length of the fiber, as illustrated in Figure 4. Different arrangements of air holes yield different properties. These fibers have relatively high numerical aperture (0.6 or 0.7) and offer single-mode guidance over a large range of wavelengths; they exhibit low sensitivity to bend losses, even for large mode areas. They can be manufactured to offer the possibility of a fundamental mode cut-off, allowing the design of single-polarization fibers and the suppression of Raman scattering. In short, photonic crystal fibers are used for many applications, including amplifiers, nonlinear devices (frequency combs, Raman conversion or pulse compression), and quantum optics (www.crystal-fibre.com/support/dictionary.shtm; www.rp-photonics.com/photonic_crystal_fibers.html; Bjarklev, Broeng, and Bjarklev 2003; Russell 2003).

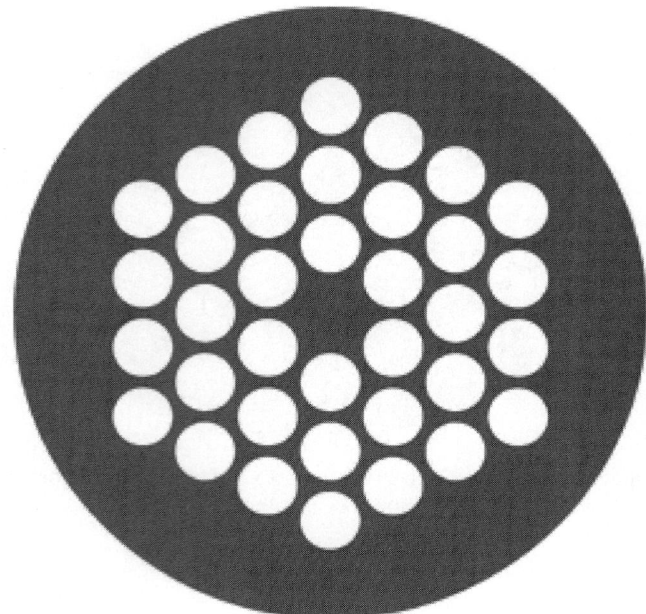

Figure 4: PCF fiber (notice air holes)

Photonic crystals are used to build a number of optical communication components, whose properties are far superior to traditional devices. These components can also be used to manufacture photonic integrated circuits—circuits using photons instead of electrons in semiconductor integrated circuits. The photon-only system is optimal for optical communications and will greatly boost transmission capabilities.

QUANTUM COMPUTING

Quantum computing uses certain quantum mechanical properties, such as superposition and entanglement, for computations. Unlike conventional computers that use binary bits, quantum computers use quantum bits (also known as qubits). Superposition occurs when a particle simultaneously possesses two or more values for a measurable quantity, such as energy. Quantum entanglement occurs when the quantum states of two particles have to

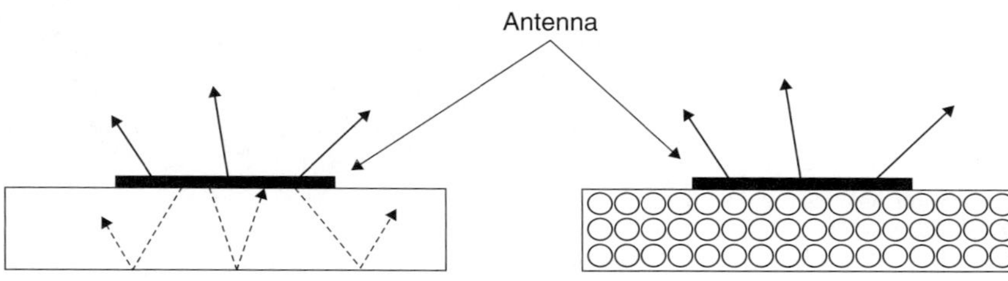

Figure 3: Radiation being absorbed by semiconductor substrate (left) and reflected by photonic crystal (right)

be described with reference to each other, even if they are spatially separated. A qubit differs from a binary bit in the sense that it is not binary but quaternary in nature. It can exist in the state 0 or 1 or simultaneously at both 0 and 1, with a probability for each state. The blend of states 0 and 1 is termed *superposition*. The details of the operation of a quantum computer are beyond the scope of this chapter. This paragraph serves as an introduction to discuss some communication systems based on quantum mechanics (www.cs.caltech.edu/~westside/quantum-intro.html; www.trnmag.com/Stories/2005/121905/HIW_Quantum_computing_121905.html).

Quantum Cryptography

Traditional cryptography relies on mathematical equations to encrypt information that restricts eavesdroppers from learning the contents of the message. Although the methods used nowadays are very reliable, there is always a probability that an eavesdropper can decrypt the message. Quantum cryptography promises to eliminate eavesdropping completely. It uses the physical properties of photons or electrons to encrypt the information. In order to decrypt the message, the eavesdropper has to measure the quantum carrier of information (usually the photon or the electron, though other entities are also used); however, doing so disturbs the system. This disturbance is recognized as a security breach, thus terminating the secure connection. This technology is reasonably mature, and many commercial products are available. ID Quantique and MagicQ are some commercial entities that provide various devices for quantum cryptography such as quantum key distributors, quantum random number generators, and quantum encryptors.

SINGLE-PHOTON DEVICES

Photons are often used as information carriers. Encoding information into these photons as qubits requires novel devices capable of emitting and detecting a single photon. A conventional optical communications network requires the signal to be above a certain threshold. In contrast, a qubit decoding system has to be able to detect each individual photon that has been transmitted, as each photon contains vital information. The same principle applies to the encoding process as well.

A single-photon source must possess some of the following basic properties, among others. It must be capable of generating the photons one by one, it must be efficient, it must allow polarization control, and it must allow photon generation on demand. Examples of such devices include single-photon light-emitting diodes (LEDs), quantum dots and some lasers with attenuators. On the other hand, a single-photon detector must have very high quantum efficiency, approaching 100 percent. Quantum efficiency of a detector can be defined as the ratio of the number of output quanta to the number of input quanta. It must have a low dark count rate, ensuring elimination of false count and afterpulsing. In addition, it must have a fast operating speed and must be able to resolve the amount of energy or the number of photons. Avalanche photodiodes, photomultiplier tubes, quantum dots, and superconducting single-photon detectors are just a few devices that can be used as photon counters. Upconversion (the process by which a low-energy photon is converted to a high-energy photon) is a popular method of counting photons.

QUANTUM DOTS

A quantum dot is a semiconductor crystal measuring between 2 nm and 10 nm in diameter. Simply stated, a quantum dot is a structure whose size has been reduced to the quantum scale in all three dimensions. Quantum dots can be differentiated with quantum wires which have their sizes reduced to the quantum scale in only two dimensions, and size reduction in quantum wells, is one dimension only. Discussed below are some nanoscale devices that can be modeled after the quantum dot.

Quantum-Dot Laser

The quantum-dot laser is a relatively new development in the field of nanoscale communications. It is based on quantum dots, which are densely packed in the active region of the device. The quantum dots are excited into a high-energy state and the transitions to the lower-energy states release energy in the form of photons. Exciting an array of quantum dots thus creates lasing. The major advantage of a quantum-dot laser over its semiconductor counterpart is its ability to maintain constant output despite temperature fluctuations. The structure of quantum dots causes electrons to show a discrete atomic-like energy spectrum. The energy difference between these discrete states is greater than the thermal energy available to the electrons because of the size of the quantum dot (Klimov 2003). Thus, the quantum-dot laser is temperature-insensitive. Fujitsu and the University of Tokyo have successfully developed a 10-Gbps quantum-dot laser operating at a wavelength of 1.3 μm. This laser is immune to variations in temperature between 20°C and 70°C (www.fujitsu.com/global/news/pr/archives/month/2006/20060420-01.html; www.fujitsu.com/global/news/pr/archives/month/2004/20040910-01.html; www.fujitsu.com/news/pr/archives/month/2004/20040910-01.html; Phillips et al. 1999).

Single-Photon Source

Quantum dots can also be used to manufacture single-photon sources. Such devices are necessary for quantum communication. Quantum dots can be excited to emit light of a unique wavelength. The wavelength of the emitted light depends on the dot size. NIST (National Institute of Standards and Technology) has used an infrared laser to excite a quantum dot, leading to serial emission of photons. However, this behavior is achievable only at extremely low temperatures, approaching absolute zero. Another single-photon LED based on the quantum dot was developed by Toshiba (Ward et al. 2005). The LED uses a single quantum dot to produce the photon. Because the quantum dot is a single quantum system, it can hold only one electron in a particular excited energy level. Whenever the electron relaxes to a lower energy level, it releases one photon. Thus, every time the quantum dot is excited, it releases one photon. Using voltage pulses, a stream of photons can be created. Typical materials used to manufacture the LED are gallium arsenide and indium arsenide. Indium arsenide is generally used for the quantum dot (Farahani et al. 2005; Ikushima et al. 2005; Shields et al. 2001).

Single-Photon Detector

Quantum dots have been successfully used as single-photon detectors. A quantum dot is encased in a resonant diode that has an insulating aluminum arsenide layer sandwiched between two conducting gallium arsenide layers. As a result the resonant diode is modified in a fashion that allows the diode to turn on when the quantum dot is excited by an incoming electron. In general, the diode is on when the two gallium arsenide layers have the correct voltage polarity. This device can find applications in quantum communication.

Another type of quantum-dot single-photon detector has been developed by Toshiba (Shields et al. 2001). The device is based on a transistor structure. The conducting channel of the transistor consists of a layer of closely spaced quantum dots. Since the separation of the quantum-dot layer and the conducting channel is on the order of a few nanometers, the resistance of the transistor is dependent on the change in the occupancy of a single quantum dot by a single electron. Hence, when photons are absorbed, a change in the resistance of the transistor channel occurs. This type of photon detector has many advantages over conventional photon detectors based on the avalanche process. The conventional photon detectors are relatively bulky, inefficient, expensive, require cooling systems and often require high voltages (Farahani et al. 2005; Ikushima et al. 2005; Ward et al. 2005).

Entangled Photon Pairs

Entangled photon pairs consist of photons that are inextricably linked. The state of each photon can be deduced by measuring the other, irrespective of the distance between the photons. Entanglement enables secure communication by detecting instances of eavesdropping. Consider the case of an encrypted connection. Encryption keys have to be exchanged between the two parties. If one of the keys is intercepted by an external agent, the properties of the entangled pair will change, and both parties should be able to detect it. As a result, entanglement leads to virtually unbreakable encryption. Such a quantum-dot device (developed by Toshiba and Cambridge University in 2005) is made from gallium arsenide and indium arsenide quantum dots. When excited by a laser pulse, this device produces two entangled photons. However, this behavior is currently limited to low temperatures.

CARBON NANOTUBES

Nanotubes are members of the fullerene structural family. A nanotube is basically a graphene sheet that has been rolled up into a cylindrical shape with at least one of the ends closed off by a semi-buckyball structure, as shown in

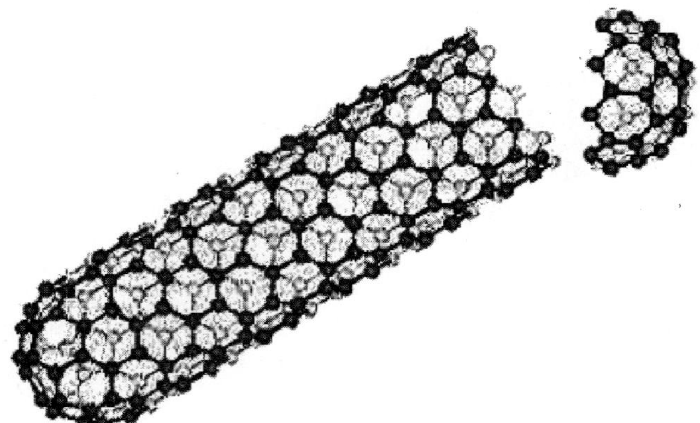

Figure 5: Carbon nanotube structure (adapted from www.nanomedicine.com/NMI/Figures/2.16.jpg)

Figure 5. (Buckyballs are strong, rigid natural molecules arranged in a series of interlocking hexagonal shapes, forming structures that resemble soccer balls). They are usually only a few nanometers in diameter, while the length can be up to a few centimeters. Nanotubes have high electrical conductivity (10^{-6} Ωm) and high thermal conductivity (1750–5899 W/mK). As electrical conductors, nanotubes can carry high current densities (10^7 to 10^9 A/cm^2). They are also inert and are not susceptive to corrosion by acids or alkalis (http://nanotechweb.org/articles/news/4/10/7/1; www.azonano.com/details.asp?ArticleID=980; Poole and Owens 2003; Ratner and Ratner 2002). Some applications of nanotubes in nanoscale communication are discussed briefly in the following sections.

Satellite Communication

Typical microwave amplifiers are based on thermionic emission sources, which tend to be bulky and heavy. Satellites are equipped with many such amplifiers, which add considerably to the weight, and hence it is expensive to launch a satellite. The thermionic emission source is also referred to as a hot cathode source. In essence, the hot cathode generates electrons that are modulated to produce electronic signals; these signals are processed to obtain the desired output. The efficiency of such systems is usually under 50 percent and decreases with increase in frequency. The thermionic emission source can be replaced by a nanotube device that acts as an electron source (de Jonge et al. 2005). The nanotube device is basically an array of equally sized and equally spaced nanotubes. When the nanotubes are exposed to an electric field, they release electrons from their tips. A radio-frequency wave is used to produce a high-frequency electron beam by exciting the nanotube array. The input signal is amplified by a process called "temporal modulation." Frequencies of up to 32 GHz have been achieved. This novel system is both compact and relatively light compared to the conventional microwave amplifiers. The system can be instantly turned on and off. The efficiency is much higher than the hot cathode system because the electrons are produced instantaneously at the nanotube source array (www.physorg.com/news8719.html).

Quantum Wires

Quantum wires, or nanowires, measure from one to a few nanometers in diameter, while the length is not restricted. Nanowires can be made out of metallic, semiconducting, or insulating materials. Molecular nanowires are made out of repeating molecular units. Nanowires tend to have relatively high resistance due to their narrow radii. Resistance-free propagation is possible only through relatively short distances, determined by the mean free path of carriers in the given material. However, carbon-nanotube–based nanowires have very low resistance. Nanowires are important components in nanoscale electronics and have many applications. For example, nanowires can be used to build transistors. A nanowire-based transistor has been developed by researchers at Harvard University (Xiang et al. 2006). Figure 6 illustrates the concept of nanowire-based transistors. These transistors can operate at least four times faster than their conventional silicon counterparts and can definitely boost computing and communication speeds of futuristic systems.

Actuators

Nanotube-based actuators are used to build optical switches. Current optical switches are generally electromechanical. These devices are prone to wear and tear and thus are not very reliable. Nanotube actuators do not have any sliding components and therefore need little maintenance and have much longer lifetimes. Figure 7 shows the difference between a mechanical actuator and a nanotube-based actuator. The switching operation of these actuators use nanotube coated regions that can be made to selectively contract and expand. The differential strain produces the bending action (Lu and Panchapakesan 2005; Fukuda et al. 2004).

MICROELECTROMECHANICAL SYSTEMS (MEMS) AND NANOELECTROMECHANICAL SYSTEMS (NEMS)

MEMS are micrometer-sized mechanical components. Typically, MEMS lie outside the definition of nanodevices, as they are beyond the 100-nm range. They are briefly introduced here for the sake of completion, as some literature refers to them as nanodevices. Smaller components within the nanometer scale are referred to as nanoelectromechanical systems (NEMS). MEMS are manufactured using techniques very similar to semiconductor fabrication, and have a good likelihood of shrinking down to NEMS. Surface micromachining, bulk micromachining, electro-discharge machining, and etching are just a few of the manufacturing techniques used. MEMS are also referred to as micromechanics, micromachines, or microsystem technology (MST). Silicon is generally used to manufacture MEMS, but metals and polymers are also used.

Optical Networks

MEMS devices can be used as switches to route light from one fiber to another. The conventional method used to

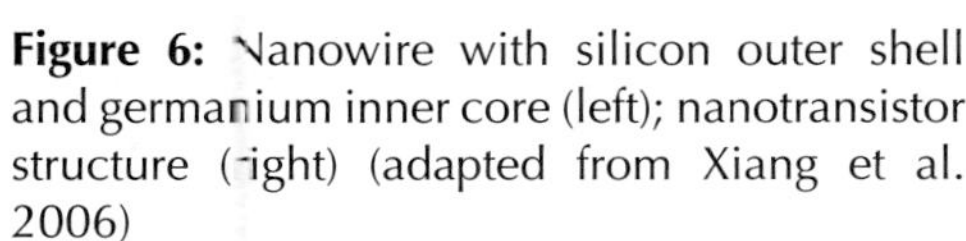

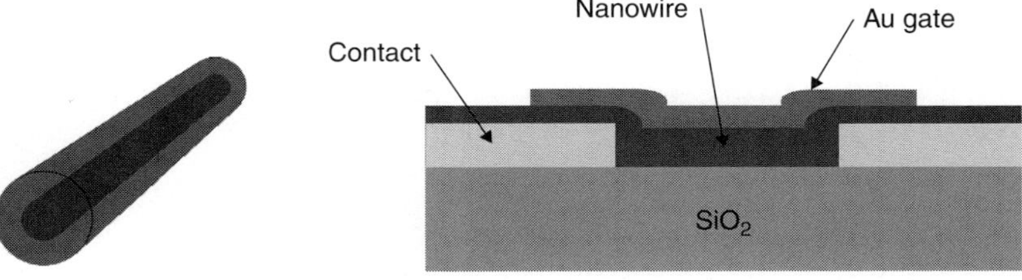

Figure 6: Nanowire with silicon outer shell and germanium inner core (left); nanotransistor structure (right) (adapted from Xiang et al. 2006)

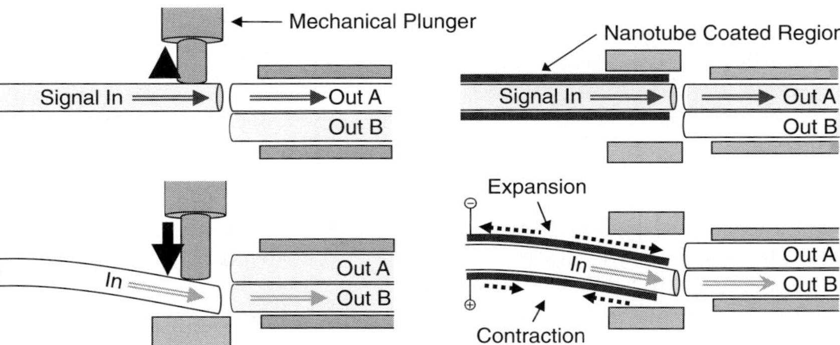

Figure 7: Mechanical switches and nanotube actuators (Dalton 2002)

route data to different fibers is to convert the light to an electrical signal using photodetectors, perform the routing, and convert it back to optical domain and transmit it to the destination fiber. Use of MEMS-based switches eliminates the need for the optical-to-electrical-to-optical conversion, which tends to be the biggest bottleneck in communication systems. The MEMS switches use an array of micromirrors to reroute photons to the desired fiber. The networks can thus be all optical, greatly boosting communication-system data rates. Active sources, tunable filters, variable optical attenuators, gain equalization, and dispersion compensation devices are other application of MEMS. The integration of these electronically controlled mechanical parts and mirrors is paving the way to a fairly new field in nanoscale applications called nano-electro-optical-mechanical systems, or NEOMS. NEOMS devices are expected to play a major role in the development of futuristic optical communications.

Resonators

Most electronic devices, including wireless communication devices, rely on resonators for frequency generation. The quartz crystal is a very popular material used for resonators. Despite being very reliable, crystal oscillators cannot be scaled down to nanometer scale. Electronic nanoscale communication devices require crystal oscillators for timing purposes, and if the quartz oscillator cannot be miniaturized, it would be impossible to develop such systems. MEMS can be used to manufacture resonators, thus allowing development of nanoscale resonators. There are many different types of MEMS resonators. One of these types—the dome resonator—is usually fabricated using a prestressed thin polysilicon film deposited over a sacrificial silicon dioxide layer. The resonant frequency of the film is a function of localized heating, which induces thermomechanical stress in the film. MEMS resonators can operate at hundreds of megahertz, whereas regular quartz crystals usually operate at around 30 MHz (www.mwrf.com/Articles/Index.cfm?Ad=1&ArticleID=5767).

Wireless Devices

Wireless communication is integrated in most mobile device, such as cell phones, personal digital assistants (PDAs), and laptops. Wireless communication uses many different schemes, such as time division multiple access (TDMA), code division multiple access (CDMA), third-generation (3G), global system for mobile [communications] (GSM), and Bluetooth. As technology progresses, novel wireless protocols will be developed. Because of politics or personal preferences, different organizations/countries use different wireless protocols. A mobile device moving from one region to another needs to be compatible with the wireless host protocol to stay connected to its base station, which is not always possible. Cell phones that are compatible with every wireless protocol currently in use are very expensive because the different radio-frequency (RF) components are expensive to integrate. Using RF-MEMS to replace conventional RF chips decreases price and size. Furthermore, the MEMS-based RF components are also more reliable and offer better performance. Some RF-MEMS devices and their advantages are as follows:

1. *RF MEMS Switch:* Usually has very low insertion loss and can operate in the gigahertz region. One type of RF MEMS switch (shunt on silicon) has an insertion loss of 0.4±0.1 dB at 90 GHz (Varadan 2003).
2. *RF MEMS Capacitor:* Has a high quality factor and great tunability (rendered possible by a movable MEMS structure). Capacitors can also be made using nanotubes, which greatly increases charge storage, since the nanotubes increase the effective surface areas. RF MEMS capacitors can operate up to 20 GHz (Varadan 2003).
3. *RF MEMS Inductor:* Has a high quality factor, high resonant frequency, up to 73 GHz, and is very compact in size (Varadan 2003).
4. *RF MEMS Filters:* Use of RF MEMS capacitors and RF MEMS inductors result in very compact high-quality filters.
5. *RF MEMS Phase Shifters:* Inexpensive to manufacture and more compact than the ferrite-based ones
6. *RF MEMS Transmission Lines:* Greatly reduce dielectric loss; any loss is due to the conductor material.

Reconfigurable Antennas

Reconfigurable antennas can switch the resonant frequency on the fly. To achieve such functionality, high-quality switches, variable capacitors, and inductors are needed. The conventional counterparts of these components cannot be used because they cannot be tuned automatically. However, the MEMS equivalent provides instantaneous tuning while maintaining a high quality. Reconfigurable antennas have many applications in wireless devices and satellites. Since nanoscale components are used, more functionality is added without compromising the size and weight.

NANOANTENNAS

Antennas basically focus and convert electromagnetic waves into an electric current. Radio waves and microwaves are the most common waves in the electromagnetic (EM) spectrum that are used for communication. The size of an antenna is related to the wavelength of the EM wave. Smaller EM waves allow smaller antennas. Using light as a carrier requires nanometer-sized antennas. Carbon nanotubes have been used successfully to convert light into an electric current. Such an antenna is on the nanometer scale and can be used for a multitude of applications. The fundamental function of an antenna is to focus the electromagnetic wave. An antenna that works with the frequency of light can also be used as a lens, since it focuses light. Researchers at University of Basel, Switzerland (Mühlschlegel et al. 2005) have successfully used gold strips to build an optical antenna. Contrary to conventional optical lenses, the nanoantenna has better optical resolution and can be integrated in nanoscale devices. Such nanoantennas can improve the performance of conventional LEDs, single-photon sources, and optical communication networks.

DENDRIMERS

A dendrimer is a human-made molecule with a three-dimensional highly branched tree-like structure. The word *dendrimer* comes from the Greek word *dendra*, which means tree. A dendrimer molecule has a central core from which all the branches emanate. Each branch is referred to as a monomer. Dendrimers have unique electronic, optical, opto-electronic, and magnetic properties. They are very useful in nanoscale communication devices, particularly optical devices. Dendrimers are currently used to manufacture polymer electro-optic modulators, optical waveguides, photo-switching devices, and LEDs (Otomo et al. 2000; Kim et al. 2001; Markham et al. 2002).

ERBIUM-DOPED FIBER AMPLIFIER

The erbium-doped fiber amplifier (EDFA) is an "all optical amplifier," and it is an extremely important component of the modern-day long haul fiber optic communication systems. It amplifies incoming optical signals without the need for optical-to-electrical conversion. EDFAs are made by doping low concentrations of erbium inside the core of the optical fiberglass substrate. They have low noise and polarization profiles with negligible interchannel cross talk and offer exceptionally high gain over short optical lengths. However, the efficiency of EDFAs tends to suffer because of collision broadening. Nanotechnology can play an important role in overcoming the problems associated with relaxation due to the collisions between erbium ions. This can be achieved by coating the erbium ions with a very thin layer of dendrimer that is approximately 8 to 17 Å in thickness. This dendrimer coating minimizes collision broadening to greatly increase the lifetime of the excited state of the erbium ions and leads to higher efficiencies.

NANO TRANSISTORS

Transistors are indispensable in digital electronics. VLSI circuits consist of millions of transistors, which are basically switches. The faster the switching speed, the faster is the computing speed of the system. The switching speed is a function of the length of the channel—the shorter the length, the lesser the distance traveled by the electrons and the faster the switching speed. Semiconductor technology is already operating in the 35-nm range. These devices require novel photolithography techniques, which can project structures of such small dimensions with minimal errors. A better technique to construct smaller transistors is to build them on the molecular scale. Literature review suggests that lately there has been a significant interest in the construction of nanotransistors using bacteria and DNA molecules.

Current semiconductor-based transistors are plagued by electronic-current–induced heating effects. Molecular transistors have extremely low power consumption; they significantly lower heating, as they work with only a few electrons; and their switching speed is drastically improved. Communication devices use transistors extensively. The bandwidth of most optical communication links is limited by the switching speed of transistors and there is a difference of four orders of magnitude between the optical and electronic frequencies. Nanotransistors can theoretically bridge this gap.

Ballistic Transistors

Ballistic transistor is a term applied to transistors that allow electrons to flow at very high speeds without colliding with atoms, thereby removing the resistance encountered in conventional transistors. Currently, the preferred material for fabricating ballistic transistors is graphene. Physicists in the United Kingdom and Russia have successfully used graphene sheets one atom thick to fabricate ballistic transistors (Novoselov et al. 2004). These transistors can operate at room temperature and allow electrons to flow without being scattered by atomic collisions. However, the current operating frequency of the device is low (Walters, Bourianoff, and Atwater 2005; Xiang et al. 2006).

Spintronic Transistors

A spintronic transistor uses the spin of an electron. According to quantum physics, an electron can exhibit only one of two states: either spin up or spin down. The spin of the electron is used to encode information. Unlike conventional transistors, the state of the spintronic transistor can be changed without the use of electric current. Consequently, power requirements are drastically reduced. In 2005, researchers at the University of Basel, Switzerland, developed a spintronic transistor using a single carbon nanotube by connecting two magnetic electrodes to alter the spin of the electrons (Babic, Iqbal, and Schönenberger 2003).

Quantum Interference Effect Transistors (QuIET)

Though still in the experimental stages, the quantum interference effect is a very promising technique to produce nanotransistors. The duality principle states that a particle can behave both as a particle and a wave. On the nanoscale level, these particles or waves interfere with each other. This process is called "quantum interference." A QuIET-based single molecule has been developed at the University of Arizona (Cardamone, Stafford, and Mazumdar 2005). The device consists of an organic ring molecule that has two electrodes attached at the meta positions, as illustrated in Figure 8. Such an arrangement produces quantum interference, which cuts the flow of current, turning off the transistor. The QuIET is switched off by the presence of quantum interference. Conversely, the device is switched on when quantum interference disappears. Such a state is called a "decoherence." At present, decoherence is produced by either bringing the tip of a scanning tunneling microscope close to the molecule or by attaching a donor molecule, in which case the

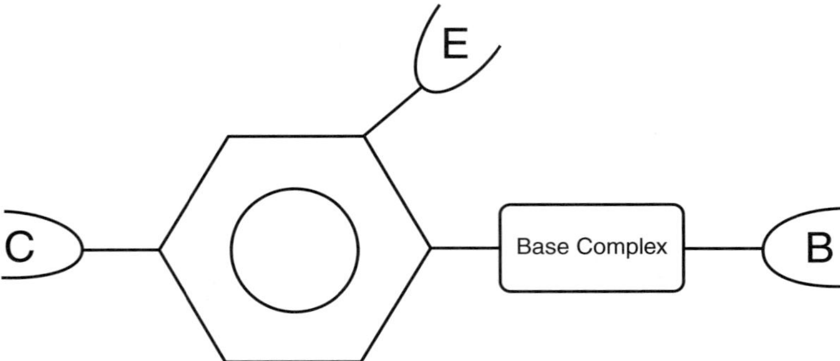

Figure 8: QuIET transistor with organic ring and donor molecule (adapted from Cardamone, Stafford, and Mazumdar 2005)

polarization of the donor molecule controls the decoherence. Such a molecular device is expected to shrink the size of communication components and is definitely a promising step toward molecular computing devices.

MACH-ZEHNDER MODULATORS

Modulation of optical or electrical signals is fundamental to conveying information across physical channels. A very popular optical modulator is the Mach-Zehnder modulator, which uses the Mach-Zehnder interferometer. A laser beam is split into two at a Y-junction (optical coupler) and then recombined at another junction. The output of such a system depends on the difference of the optical path length of the two split beams of light. Any relative difference can be used to produce a modulated output. The modulated output is a function of the interference between the two signals. Figure 9 illustrates a simple implementation of the Mach-Zehnder modulator. This modulator modifies the phase of one of the signals in order to modulate the output.

Typical materials used to manufacture small-scale Mach-Zehnder modulators include GaAs, AlGaAs, InP, InGaAsP, and other III-V materials. These materials have wide bandgap with higher carrier mobility and higher electron-photon interaction probability (Verdeyen 1995).

SILICON PHOTONICS

Silicon photonics is an evolving field that has gained significant momentum in the communications area and has the potential to fulfill many of the requirements necessary for faster and more reliable optical communication. Silicon already dominates the semiconductor industry because of its availability, good thermal and mechanical properties, and ease of manufacturing. Among other things, the speed of communication links is limited by the computation power, which is dependant on the semiconductor circuits. Transistor miniaturization is approaching the point of diminishing returns. Even if we could pack more transistors on a single chip, the delays due to coupling, signal latency, and signal cross talk will greatly hamper the operating frequency of the device. A potential solution to this problem is silicon photonics. Photonic integrated circuits are inherently immune to electrical signal cross talk and resistor-inductor delays. Using photonic circuits for computers will lead to the cherished goal of optical computing, while their applications to communication links can result in greatly enhanced operating speeds and reliability. Examples of components required for photonic integrated circuits, needed for communication, are briefly discussed below. Most of these components are already on the nanoscale (Ossicini, Pavesi, and Priolo 2004).

Silicon Waveguides

One of the most important components in silicon photonics is the waveguide. Silicon has desirable refractive index, good electro-optical properties, and low losses. However, the size needs to be comparable to a complementary metal oxide semiconductor (CMOS) device, to allow integration of a large number of components on a single chip. Silicon nitride–based waveguides (Bulla et al. 1999) and

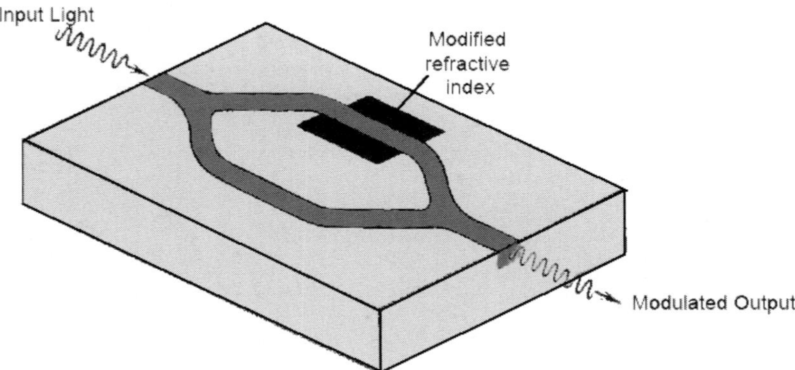

Figure 9: Simple Mach-Zehnder modulator

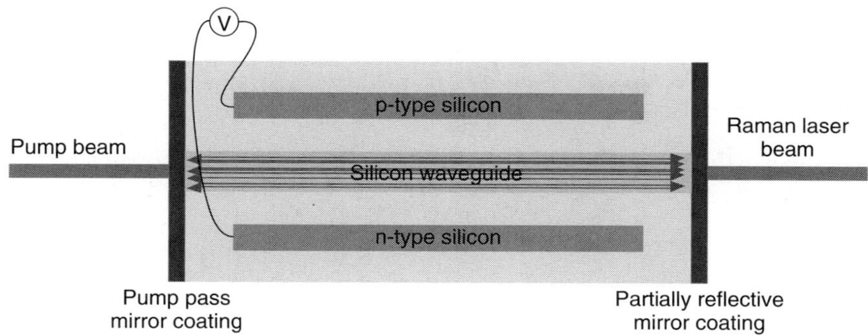

Figure 10: Raman laser developed by Intel

silicon oxynitride waveguides (Hilleringmann and Goser 1995) show losses lower than 0.5 dB cm^{-1} at 633 nm and bending radii of less than 200 μm. Silicon-on-insulator (SOI) is another popular combination of materials that is used as waveguides. Such waveguides have optical losses as low as 0.1 dB cm^{-1} at 1.55 μm (optical mode cross section, 0.2×4 μm^2) (Masini et al. 1999; www.intel.com/technology/silicon/sp/index.htm; Charlton, Roberts, and Parker 1997; Pavesi 2003; Salib et al. 2004).

Silicon Modulators

Silicon-based modulators are inexpensive to produce but until recently commercially available silicon modulators were limited to about 20 MHz. This speed was insufficient, given that most Ethernet adapters already work in the gigabit region. In 2004, Intel developed a silicon-based optical modulator that is similar to a transistor. The required phase shift for modulation is induced by an electrical charge. The device can operate at 1 GHz, and research suggests that the technology can be scaled up to operate at about 10 GHz. Additionally, there are indications that silicon photonics may also find application in microprocessors in addition to nanoscale communication.

Silicon Nanocrystals

Silicon nanocrystals have better optical properties than bulk silicon. When a nanocrystal is in the excited state, both the electrons and the holes are spatially confined and are at higher potential energy. The electron-hole pair combines to form an exciton that decays to release a photon. This property makes the silicon nanocrystal a good candidate to manufacture modulators, optical amplifiers, and light-emitting diodes. In 2005, researchers at California Institute of Technology successfully manufactured a transistor that emits light using bulk silicon and silicon nanocrystals ranging from 2 to 4 nm in size (Walters et al. 2005). The size of the nanocrystal determines the color of the emitted light. The device is called a "nanocrystal field-effect light-emitting device (FELED)," and it consumes very little power.

Silicon Lasers

Silicon nanocrystals can also be used to manufacture lasers. In 2005, Intel reported the development of one such laser (Rong et al. 2005). The Raman effect and the silicon crystalline structure are used to amplify the signal as it passes through the device. Though this device is still in a developmental stage, the applications are endless. Figure 10 illustrates this device (Claps et al. 2004; Pavesi, Gaponenko, and Dal Negro 2003).

TERAHERTZ LASERS

The 4- to 10-THz range, also known as the 30- to 75-μm very long wavelength infrared region, is currently not exploited because there are no devices that operate at these frequencies. A purely experimental chip-based laser operating at 4.4 THz has been developed by researchers from Italy and England (Kohler et al. 2002). It is a quantum cascade device made from a stack of around 1500 alternating layers of gallium arsenide and aluminum gallium arsenide totaling a thickness of 12 μm such that most of the individual layers are on the nanoscale. An electronic staircase is built and electrons bounce down the staircase releasing a photon at each step. However, currently this device operates only at very low temperatures. Research is being done to allow operation at higher temperatures. Such a device is expected to play an important role in futuristic communications because of its high operating frequency.

Surface Plasmons

Surface plasmons exist at the interface between a metal and a dielectric. Plasma oscillations are periodic oscillations of charge density in metals or plasmas. The particle (quasiparticle to be more precise), resulting from quantization of plasma oscillations is the plasmon. Surface plasmon resonance occurs when the surface plasmons are excited by light. The optical properties of metals are greatly influenced by plasmons. Light with frequency less than the plasma oscillations is reflected, whereas light with higher frequency is transmitted. Since plasmons can support frequencies up to hundreds of terahertz, they can be used to replace wires on computer chips. Because of their small wavelengths, they can also be used for nanolithography. Since plasmons interact with light, they can have numerous applications in optical communication. For example, in May 2006 a VCSEL based on surface plasmon resonance was developed by Matsushita Electric Industrial Co., Ltd. The main feature of this VCSEL is an array of silver nanoholes on a "surface plasmon mirror." Such a VCSEL has a high power output and can be used for high-speed and short-distance optical communication like optical interconnection and plastic fiber communication. In addition, in March of 2006 physicists in France and Denmark developed an optical waveguide based on surface plasmons. The waveguide allows light to pass through channels smaller than the wavelength of light without significant attenuation (Bozhevolnyi et al. 2006). Such surface-plasmon–based waveguides have tremendous potential applications in photonic circuits and optical communication. Lately, surface-plasmon–based nanophotonics is generating lots of interest among the research community, and it promises to play a key role in enabling high-density optical communications at the nanoscale (Bozhevolnyi et al. 2006).

CONCLUSION

Applying nanotechnology to communication devices can revolutionize communications and networking environments. Nanoscale devices can boost data rates and help tap the full potential of currently used communication media. If photons were used on computers as information carriers, there would be no need for any electrical-to-optical interface. Such development will also allow full utilization of the potential of optical fibers. For example, silicon photonics, photonic crystals, and MEMS can convert existing optical fiber communication links to an "all optical system" by eliminating the electrical-to-optical interface, which tends to be the biggest bottleneck in modern optical communication systems. Research in the field of silicon photonics and surface plasmons have brought the idea of optical computing closer to reality. Although optical computing and optical networks are ideal for high-speed communications, current transistor-based systems can still achieve higher speeds with the advent of practical nanotransistors. Ballistic transistors, spintronic transistors, and quantum interference effect transistors are expected to boost the operating frequency of transistors. Similarly, fruition of research in quantum computing and quantum cryptography promises to immunize networks from malicious activities such as eavesdropping. In short, nanotechnology can make the current networking environment faster, more efficient, and virtually impenetrable. The next logical step appears to be the development of intelligent, self-healing communications devices that can adapt to meet bandwidth and load requirements with little human intervention.

GLOSSARY

Dendrimer: Synthetic material with unique electrical, optical, and opto-electric properties.

Erbium-Doped Fiber Amplifier: Very compact and efficient amplifier.

Microelectromechanical System: Also known as MEMS. They have various applications in wireless communication.

Nanotube: Can be used for satellite communication, nanowires, and actuators.

Photonic Crystal: Multidimensional periodic dielectric nanostructures designed to control and manipulate the propagation of electromagnetic waves. Can be used to manufacture various optical components in communication devices.

Quantum Dot: Can be used for single-photon sources and detectors.

Silicon Photonics: Using silicon-based materials to develop optical components, such as waveguides, modulators, and lasers that can be used to manufacture photonic integrated circuits.

Surface Plasmons: Exist at the interface between a metal and a dielectric. They have application in VCSELs and optical waveguides.

Vertical Cavity Surface Emitting Laser: Emits its infrared energy perpendicular to semiconductor layers.

CROSS REFERENCES

See *Fiberoptic Filters and Multiplexers; Optical Transmitters, Receivers, and Noise.*

REFERENCES

Babic, B., M. Iqbal, and C. Schönenberger. 2003. Ambipolar field-effect transistor on as-grown single-wall carbon nanotubes. *Nanotechnology* 14(2):327–31.

Bjarklev, A., J. Broeng, and A. S. Bjarklev. 2003. *Photonic crystal fibres*. Boston: Kluwer.

Bozhevolnyi, S. I., V. S. Volkov, E. Devaux, J.-Y. Laluet, and T. W. Ebbesen. 2006. Channel plasmon subwavelength waveguide components including interferometers and ring resonators. *Nature* 440:508–11.

Brown, E. R., O. B. McMahon, and C. D. Parker. 1998. Photonic-crystal antenna substrates. *Lincoln Laboratory Journal* 11(2):159–74.

Brown, E. R., C. D. Parker, and E. Yablonovitch 1993, February. Radiation properties of a planar antenna on a photonic-crystal substrate. *Journal of the Optical Society of America B* 10:404–7.

Bulla, D. A. P., et al. 1999. Design and fabrication of SiO2/Si3N4 CVD optical waveguides. In *Proceedings of IMOC '99 Microwave and Optoelectronics Conference, 1999, SBMO/IEEE MTT-S APS and LEOS–IMOC '99 International, Rio de Janeiro Brazil*.

Cardamone, D. M., C. A. Stafford, and S. Mazumdar. 2005 *The quantum interference effect transistor*. Tucson, AZ: Department of Physics, University of Arizona.

Charlton, M. D. B., S. W. Roberts, and G. J. Parker. 1997. Guided mode analysis and fabrication of a 2-dimensional visible photonic band structure confined within a planar semiconductor waveguide. *Material Sciences and Engineering* B49:155.

Claps, R., V. Raghunathan, D. Dimitropoulos, and B. Jalali. 2004. Influence of nonlinear absorption on Raman amplification in silicon waveguides. *Optics Express* 12:2774–80.

Colace, L., G. Masini, G. Assanto, H. C. Luan, K. Wada, and L. C. Kimerling. 2000. Efficient high-speed near-infrared Ge photodectors integrated on Si substrates. *Applied Physics Letters* 76:1231.

de Jonge, N., M. Allioux, M. Doytcheva, J. T. Oostveen, K. B. K. Teo, and W. I. Milne. 2005. Low noise and stable emission from carbon nanotube electron sources. *Applied Physics Letters* 87:133118.

Dalton, L. 2002. Breaking the bandwidth bottleneck in telecommunications and information processing: New electro-optic materials. In *10th Foresight Conference on Molecular Nanotechnology. Bethesda, Maryland 20814*.

Fan, S., S. G. Johnson, J. D. Joannopoulos, C. Manolatou, and H. A. Haus. 2001. Waveguide branches in photonic crystals. *Journal of the Optical Society of America* B18(2):162–5.

Farahani, J. N., D. W. Pohl, H.-J. Eisler, and B. Hecht. 2005 Single quantum dot coupled to a scanning optical antenna: A tunable superemitter. *Physical Review Letters* 95:017402.

Fukuda, T., F. Arai, L. Dong, and Y. Imaizumi. 2004. Perspective of nanotube sensors and nanotube actuators. In *2004 4th IEEE Conference on Nanotechnology. IEEE, Nagoya University, Furo-Cho, Chikusa-ku, Nagoya 464–8603 Japan*.

Hilleringmann, U., and K. Goser. 1995. System integration of optical devices and analog CMOS amplifiers. *IEEE Transactions on Electronic Devices* 42:841.

Ikushima, K., T. Hasegawa, S. Komiyama, T. Ueda, and K. Hirakawa. 2005. Quantum-dot photon detectors and photon-counting terahertz imaging. In *30th International Conference on Infrared and Millimeter Waves and the 13th International Conference on Terahertz Electronics, Williamsburg USA September 2005*.

Joannopoulos, J. D., R. D. Meade, and J. N. Winn. 1995. *Photonic crystals: Molding the flow of light*. Princeton, NJ: Princeton University Press.

Johnson, S. G., and J. D. Joannopoulos. 2002. *Photonic crystals: The road from theory to practice*. Boston: Kluwer.

Johnson, S. G., P. R. Villeneuve, S. Fan, and J. D. Joannopoulos. 2000. Linear waveguides in photonic-crystal slabs. *Physics Reviews* B62:8212–2.

Kim, J.-M., J.-H. Son, H.-C. Yoon, J.-Y. Seo, S.-Y. Yoo, H. K. Shin, E.-M. Park, J.-K. Kim, and Y.-S. Kwon. 2001. Characteristics of dendrimer functionalized with azobenzene for the application to nano-level photo-switching device. In *Nanotechnology, 2001. IEEE-NANO 2001. Proceedings of the 2001 1st IEEE Conference on 28–30 Oct. 2001*, 185–8. Busan, Korea: Department of Electrical Eng. Dong-A University.

Klimov, V. I. 2003 Nanocrystal quantum dots: From fundamental photophysics to multicolor lasing. *Los Alamos Science* 28.

Kohler, R., A. Tredicucci, F. Beltram, H. E. Beere, E. H. Linfield, A. G. Davies, D. A. Ritchie, R. C. Iotti, and F. Rossi. 2002. Terahertz semiconductor-heterostructure lasers. *Nature* 417(6885):156.

Lu, S., and B. Panchapakesan. 2005. Optically driven nanotube actuators. *Nanotechnology* 16:2548–54

Markham, J. P. J., S.-C. Lo, N. H. Male, T. Anthopoulos, O. Salata, P. L. Burn, and I. D. W. Samuel. 2002. Efficient electrophosphorescent dendrimer LEDs. *15th Annual Meeting of the IEEE* 1:195–6.

Masini G., L. Colace, G. Assanto, K. Wada, and L. C. Kimerling. 1999. High responsivity near infrared Ge photodetectors integrated on Si. *Electronics Letters* 35:1467.

Mühlschlegel, P., H.-J. Eisler, O. J. F. Martin, B. Hecht, and D. W. Pohl. 2005. Resonant optical antennas. *Science* 308(5728):1607–9.

Novoselov, K. S., A. K. Geim, S. V. Morozov, S. V. Dubonos, Y. Zhang, and D. Jiang. 2004. *Room-temperature electric field effect and carrier-type inversion in graphene films*. http://arxiv.org/pdf/cond-mat/0410631.

Ossicini, S., L. Pavesi, and F. Priolo. 2004. *Light emitting silicon for microphotonics*. Berlin, Germany: Springer.

Otomo, A., S. Yokoyama, S. Otomo, T. Nakahama, and S. Mashiko. 2000. Single-mode random laser in weakly scattering dendrimer waveguides. In *Lasers and Electro-Optics Europe, 2000. Conference Digest. 2000 Conference on 10–15 Sept. 2000. Nice, France*.

Pavesi, L. 2003. Will silicon be the photonic material of the third millennium? *Journal of Physics: Condensed Matter* 15(26):R1169–96.

Pavesi, L., S. Gaponenko, and L. Dal Negro. 2003. *Towards the first silicon laser*. NATO Science Series II, vol. 93. Dordrecht, The Netherlands: Kluwer.

Phillips, J., D. Klotzkin, Qasaimeh, W. Zhou, and P. Bhattacharya. 1999. High-speed modulation of quantum-dot lasers. In *Nanostructures and Quantum Dots/WDM Components/VCSELs and Microcavities/RF Photonics for CATV and HFC Systems, 1999 Digest of the LEOS Summer Topical Meetings, San Diego, CA*.

Poole, C. P., Jr,. and F. J. Owens. 2003 *Introduction to nanotechnology*. New York: Wiley.

Ratner, M., and D. Ratner. 2002. *Nanotechnology*. Upper Saddle River, NJ: Prentice Hal.

Rong, H., R. Jones, A. Liu, and M. Paniccia. 2005. Silicon laser and amplifier based on stimulated Raman scattering. In *Proceedings CLEO 2005, May 21–26, Long Beach, CA, USA, Late Paper. Intel*.

Russell, P. St. J. 2003. Photonic crystal fibers. *Science* 299:358–62.

Salib, M., L. Liao, R. Jones, M. Morse, A. Liu, D. Samara-Rubio, A. Alduino, and M. Paniccia. 2004 *Silicon Photonics. Intel Technology Journal* 8(2):1535–864.

Shields A. J., M. P. O'Sullivan, I. Farrer, D. A. Ritchie, M. L. Leadbeater, N. K. Patel, R. A. Hogg, C. E. Norman, N. J. Curson, and M. Pepper. 2001. Single photon detection with a quantum dot transistor. *Japanese Journal of Applied Physics* 40:2058–64.

Solli, D. R., and J. M. Hickmann. 2004. Photonic crystal based polarization control devices. *Journal of Physics D: Applied Physics* 37(24):R263–8.

Varadan V. K. 2003. *RF MEMS and their applications*. New York: Wiley.

Verdeyen, J. 1995. *Laser electronics*. Upper Saddle River, NJ: Prentice Hall.

Walters, R. J., G. I. Bourianoff, and H. A. Atwater. 2005. Field-effect electroluminescence in silicon nanocrystals. *Nature Materials* 4(2):143–6.

Ward, M. B., O. Z. Karimov, D. C. Unitt, Z. Yuan, P. See, D. G. Gevaux, A. J. Shields, P. Atkinson, and D. A. Ritchie. 2005. Telecom wavelength quantum dot single photon source. *Quantum Electronics and Laser Science Conference* 1:132–46.

Xiang, J., W. Lu, Y. Hu, Y. Wu, H. Yan, and C. M. Lieber. 2006. Ge/Si nanowire heterostructures as high-performance field-effect transistors. *Nature* 441:489–93.

Yao, J. J. 2000. RF MEMS from a device perspective. *Journal of Micromechanics and Microengineering* 10:R9–38.

Molecular Communication: New Paradigm for Communication among Nanoscale Biological Machines

Michael Moore, Akihiro Enomoto, Tatsuya Suda, Tadashi Nakano, and Yutaka Okaie,
University of California, Irvine

INTRODUCTION

Biological nanomachines (or "nanomachines," for short) are nanoscale and microscale devices that either exist in the biological world or are artificially created from biological materials (i.e., molecules) and that perform simple functions such as sensing, logic, and actuation. Molecular communication is a new paradigm for communication between nanomachines over a short (nanoscale or microscale) range. It is the process of communication between nanomachines through encoding information onto molecules, rather than electrons or electromagnetic waves, and exchanging the molecules between nanomachines (Hiyama, Moritani, and Suda 2006). Using electrons or electromagnetic waves for communication is particularly limited at the nanoscale and microscale range because of power constraints and limitations in the size of communication components. Because nanomachines are too small and simple to communicate using electrons or electromagnetic waves, molecular communication provides a novel mechanism for nanomachines to communicate by propagating molecules that represent the information.

In biological systems, a nanomachine (such as a cell or a protein complex) is a basic building block of organisms, and nanomachines use various forms of molecular communication to transmit information to other nanomachines. For instance, cells communicate by releasing hormones into the bloodstream, exchanging Ca^{2+} ions through protein channels, or transferring DNA instructions. Some nanomachines in biological systems also have the ability to self-replicate (through, for instance, biological cell reproduction) and to self-assemble into organisms that coordinate through molecular communication. The nanomachines communicate with hormones to activate and synchronize the activity of replication and nanomachine organization. Existing research on artificially creating (or engineering) molecular communication is based on understanding the design of molecular communication in biological systems and on modifying the functionality of existing molecular communication in biological systems. Creating molecular communication, thus, represents an interdisciplinary research area that spans the areas of biology, nanotechnology, and computer science.

This chapter is organized in the following manner. The remainder of this section describes possible applications of molecular communication, the key components and phases of molecular communication, and key characteristics of molecular communication. Then we describe molecular communication that occurs in biological systems. We go on to discuss existing research in engineering molecular communication and to describe existing research to engineer a molecular communication network—that is, a system of communicating nanomachines.

Applications

Molecular communication integrates techniques from biology to interact with biological systems, from nanotechnology to perform nanoscale and microscale interactions, and from computer science to integrate into larger-scale information and communication processing. Molecular communication has significant potential, since it interacts directly with biological systems at nanoscales and microscales and may enable new applications through integrated nanomachines.

Molecular communication may impact how nanomachines interact with biological systems (Montemagno 2001). For instance, a biological system (e.g., the human body) is composed of a large number of cells (i.e., nanomachines). Each cell performs simple and specific operations such as uptake, processing, and release of molecules. Cells interact to perform various functions of the body (e.g., distributing molecules for metabolism and replication of cells). Molecular communication provides mechanisms to transport molecules between cells, and thus, it may help perform targeted delivery of drugs by providing mechanisms to transport drugs (information-encoded molecules) between drug repositories embedded in the human body (sender nanomachines) and specific cells in the human body (receiver nanomachines). Molecular communication also provides mechanisms for nanomachines to communicate, and thus, it may help drug repositories (sender nanomachines) to coordinate and control the amount and timing of drug release. Targeting delivery of drugs to specific cells in a human body and creating molecular communication for such applications involve understanding how molecules are transported within a biological system, how molecules are addressed to specific locations within a biological system (i.e., molecule-addressing mechanisms in a biological system), or even adding receptor molecules to a biological system to produce an addressing mechanism (Langer 2001; Peppas and Huang 2004; Allen and Cullis 2004). Molecular communication may eventually provide a mechanism to interact with the human body at the molecular level (Moritani, Hiyami, and Suda 2006, Molecular communication for health care applications).

Molecular communication may impact the size and the complexity of systems that nanomachines can form. Nanomachines (both naturally existing in biological systems and artificially created from biological materials with existing technology) are limited to performing simple functions (i.e., sensing, logic, and actuation). Nanomachines with simple functions may communicate with nearby nanomachines through molecular communication; thus, the nanomachines can self-organize into larger machines with more complex functions (Balzani, Venturi, and Credi 2003). For instance, nanomachines may communicate and coordinate through molecular communication to amplify a signal starting at the nano scale into a signal detectable at the human scale.

Molecular communication may impact what forms of information may be exchanged among nanomachines. It may also allow transmission of information that cannot be readily represented in a digital format, such as chemical composition of cells or emotion (represented as the chemical state of human brain and body). It may also transmit molecules storing energy or heat.

Overview of Molecular Communication

The generic molecular communication (Figure 1) consists of components functioning as information molecules (i.e., molecules such as proteins or ions) that represent the information to be transmitted (Smith 2000), sender nanomachines that release the information molecules, receiver nanomachines that detect information molecules, and the environment in which the information molecules propagate from the sender nanomachine to the receiver nanomachine (Suda et al. 2005; You et al. 2004). It may also include transport molecules (e.g., molecular motors) that transport information molecules, guide molecules (e.g., microtubule or actin filaments) that direct the movement of transport molecules, and interface molecules (e.g., vesicles) that allow any type of information molecule to be transported by a transport molecule (Moritani, Hiyami, and Suda 2006, Molecular communication among nanomachines using vesicles).

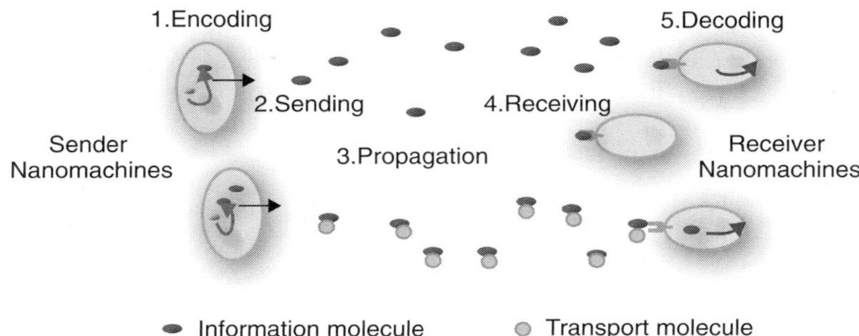

Figure 1: Phases of a molecular communication: (1) a sender nanomachine encodes information onto information molecules, (2) the sender nanomachine releases the information molecules into the environment, (3) the information molecules propagate in the environment by diffusion or with direction by binding to transport molecules, (4) a receiver nanomachine with appropriate receptors receives the information molecules, (5) a receiver chemically interacts with the information molecules and decodes information.

Components of molecular communication are made up of molecules, and must be designed with the thought in mind that molecular communication occurs in an aqueous or air environment, which generates a significant amount of noise. The noise in the environment comes from a number of factors. For instance, the environment contains energy and forces that constantly interact with the various molecular communication components. Such energy and forces include thermal energy, electrical fields, magnetic fields, and electromagnetic waves (e.g., light energy that is absorbed by molecules). The environment also contains molecules and nanomachines that do not participate in molecular communication, and these generate noise. Such molecules and nanomachines include solvent molecules (e.g., water molecules), solute molecules (e.g., energy molecules necessary to support the nanomachines), and other nanomachines (e.g., nanomachines to maintain chemical concentrations in the environment or act as structural components). The noise in the environment determines the degree of randomness in molecular communication (e.g., randomness in the movement of information molecules and randomness in the timing of, rate of, and energy for chemical reactions).

The components in molecular communication perform the following general phases of communication (Figure 1): encoding of information into an information molecule by the sender nanomachine, sending of the information molecule into the environment, propagation of the information molecule through the environment, receiving of the information molecule by the receiver nanomachine, and decoding of the information molecule into a chemical reaction at the receiver nanomachine.

Encoding

Encoding is the phase during which a sender nanomachine translates information into information molecules that the receiver nanomachine can detect. Information may be encoded onto the type of information molecules used. Information may also be encoded in various characteristics of information molecules such as the three-dimensional structure of the information molecule, in the specific molecules that compose the information molecules, or in the concentration of information molecules (the number of information molecules per unit volume of solvent molecules).

The amount of information that a sender encodes onto a single information molecule is limited by the molecular structure of a receiver nanomachine. A receiver nanomachine is capable of only a limited number of configurations; thus, when a receiver nanomachine receives an information molecule, the receiver nanomachine receives only the amount of information corresponding to the number of configurations possible in the receiver nanomachine (Schneider 1991). If a receiver nanomachine achieves only two configurations, the receiver nanomachine only understands one bit of information at a time.

A sender nanomachine may transmit information about which a receiver nanomachine does not have information. For instance, in biological systems, certain types of cells communicate through exchanging DNA molecules. An arbitrary DNA sequence is decoded at a receiving cell into proteins that introduce new functionality into a receiver cell. If a sender nanomachine in molecular communication can transmit arbitrary information molecules, it is possible to send new functionality to the receiver nanomachine.

Sending

Sending is the phase during which a sender nanomachine releases information molecules into the environment. A sender nanomachine may release information molecules by either unbinding the information molecules from the sender nanomachine (e.g., by budding vesicles from a biological cell if a sender nanomachine is a biological cell with endoplasmic reticulum), or by opening a gate that allows the information molecule to diffuse away (e.g., by opening a gap junction channel in the cell membrane of a sender nanomachine). A sender nanomachine may also catalyze a chemical reaction that produces transport molecules elsewhere.

Because of its size, a sender nanomachine contains a limited amount of energy and information molecules. This results in a limited communication capability that the single sender nanomachine alone can generate. Thus, the sender nanomachine of molecular communication generally relies on the environment for supplying (chemical) energy and information molecules. In addition, multiple sender nanomachines may release the same information molecules, resulting in a stronger signal in the environment.

Propagation

The sender and receiver nanomachines are at different locations in the environment, and propagation is the phase during which the information molecule moves from the sender nanomachine through the environment to the receiver nanomachine. The information molecule may diffuse passively through the environment without using chemical energy or may bind to a transport molecule (e.g., a molecular motor that generates motion [Barron, Gu, and Parillo 1998]) and actively propagate through the environment using energy.

In passive transport, information molecules randomly move according to forces in the environment. Large information molecules or high-viscosity environments result in slower diffusion through the environment. In active transport, a transport molecule carries information molecules through the environment, and it consumes chemical energy to reduce the randomness in its movement in the environment. By providing more control over the movement of information molecules, active transport may decrease the time necessary for information molecules to reach the receiver nanomachine and also increase the probability of information molecules successfully reaching the receiver nanomachine.

During propagation, an interface molecule may also be necessary to protect information molecules from noise in the environment. For instance, information molecules may be contained in a vesicle-based interface molecule and propagate through the environment (Moritani, Hiyami, and Suda 2006, Molecular communication among nanomachines using vesicles).

The vesicle prevents the information molecules from chemically reacting with other molecules outside the vesicle.

Receiving/Decoding

Receiving is the phase during which the receiver nanomachine captures information molecules being propagated in the environment. Decoding is the phase during which the receiver nanomachine, upon capturing information molecules, decodes the received molecules into a chemical reaction. One option for capturing information molecules is to use receptors that are capable of binding to a specific type of information molecule. Another option for capturing them is to use channels (e.g., gap-junction channels) that allow them to flow into a receiver nanomachine without using receptors. Chemical reactions for decoding at the receiver nanomachine may include producing new molecules, performing a simple task, or producing another signal (e.g., sending other information molecules).

Because of possible noise in the environment and also because of possible errors in receiving information molecules, molecular communication may not rely on sending a single information molecule. For instance, in biological systems, a sender nanomachine (e.g., a cell) and a receiver nanomachine (e.g., another cell) exchange a number of information molecules, and the receiver nanomachine has a number of receptors to detect the concentration of information molecules. There are also often a number of sender and receiver nanomachines that each has the capability of sending, detecting, and chemically reacting to information molecules.

Similar to computer networks, in which a layering architecture separates concerns of communication, molecular communication in biological systems may be viewed in terms of a layered architecture. At the lowest layer (the physical layer) in computer networks, information is encoded onto electrons and electromagnetic waves. In molecular communication, information is encoded onto information molecules (e.g., onto the types of the information molecules used, in various characteristics of information molecules, or onto the concentration of the information molecule). At the second layer (the data-link layer) in computer networks, information is transmitted reliably between neighboring computers through feedback (e.g., flow-control acknowledgment). In molecular communication, biological systems often use positive and negative feedback to reliably control the number of information molecules released. In biological systems, communication to a specific receiver is achieved through molecular-level addressing. For instance, a mechanism for addressing is through the type of information molecule and the type of receptor used (i.e., a sender nanomachine uses a certain type of information molecules to send to a receiver nanomachine, and the receiver nanomachine has receptors to chemically react to the type of information molecules that the sender nanomachine uses) or through the three-dimensional distribution of the information molecules (e.g., during organism development processes, sender nanomachines establish chemical concentrations around themselves, and nearby receiver nanomachines react to the detected chemical concentrations to form patterns of receiver nanomachines). Existing molecular communication research is primarily concerned with these lower two layers, and thus, this chapter discusses issues at these two lower layers.

Characteristics of Molecular Communication

A variety of molecular communication's characteristics result from using nanomachines as senders and as receivers, using molecules as an information carrier, and from the propagation of information molecules through an aqueous environment. First, the size of nanomachines contributes significantly to their limited functionality, including functionality available for communication. Second, the aqueous environment generates a significant amount of noise; thus, it is difficult for nanomachines to operate reliably in the environment and for humans to control individual nanomachines (Service 2001). Environment noise also causes the propagation of information molecules to be fundamentally stochastic and to have a relatively long communication delay. Third, since information is encoded onto molecules in molecular communication, the amount of information that a receiver nanomachine receives is limited by the number of possible configurations in the receiver nanomachine. In addition, a sender nanomachine may transmit information about which a receiver nanomachine does not have information. Thus, molecular communication may have characteristics of nonbinary encoding. Fourth, the biological molecules and materials used to create components for molecular communication cause that communication to exhibit characteristics of asynchronous communication, biocompatibility, and energy efficiency. Each of the unique characteristics of molecular communication is described below.

Stochastic

The stochastic behavior of molecular communication arises from environmental factors such as unpredictable movement of molecules in the environment, as well as from communication component factors such as nanomachines stochastically reacting to information molecules and nanomachines and information molecules degrading over time. Environmental factors and communication component factors inherently affect the design of molecular communication. For instance, in order to be robust to the environmental noise, the sender nanomachines increase the signal-to-noise ratio by releasing a large number of information molecules, and receiver nanomachines chemically react to information molecules only when a relatively large number of information molecules are present in the environment. Sending a large number of information molecules is highly redundant, so that degradation of a few information molecules during propagation does not impact communication. In addition, non-information molecules (noise-causing molecules) in the environment may not trigger chemical reaction at a receiver nanomachine as long as the noise from those molecules is significantly less than the signal from a large number of information molecules.

Delay

Molecules in the environment that do not participate in molecular communication cause information molecules to propagate slowly through the environment. In both passive and active transport, the speed of propagation is bounded at a relatively lower speed (i.e., micrometers per second in an aqueous environment) because of the large amount of interference with the molecules in the environment. In addition, because of the possibly large delay in the environment, information molecules may remain in the environment for a period of time and arrive at a receiver nanomachine after a widely varying amount of time (e.g., hours after release at the sender nanomachine).

The delay in an information molecule propagating from a sender to a receiver nanomachine determines various communication characteristics of molecular communication. If the information molecules stay in the environment for an extended length of time (e.g., DNA molecules can be chemically stable for months), a sender nanomachine must delay a new communication until the information molecules used in an old communication degrade in the environment to prevent the old communication from interfering with the new communication. "Thus, the frequency at which a sender nanomachine send information is limited by the length of time information molecules stay in the environment" before degrading.

Nonbinary Encoding

As explained in the section on "Overview of Molecular Communication," in molecular communication, information may be encoded onto the type of information molecules used. Information may also be encoded in various characteristics of information molecules such as the three-dimensional structure, chemical structure (e.g., protein), sequence information (e.g., DNA), or concentration (e.g., calcium concentration) of information molecules (Schneider 1991). A physical substance (i.e., the information molecule) propagates from a sender nanomachine to a receiver nanomachine, and the receiver nanomachine chemically reacts to incoming information molecules. Because information is encoded onto molecules in molecular communication, the amount of information that a sender encodes onto a single information molecule (or the amount of information that a receiver nanomachine receives) is limited by the number of possible configurations in the receiver nanomachine. In addition, a sender nanomachine may transmit information about which a receiver nanomachine does not have information. Thus, information molecules in molecular communication can encode information that is not readily represented by binary encoding.

Asynchronous Communication

Molecular communication in biological systems is asynchronous. Sender and receiver nanomachines in biological systems do not require a synchronizing signal. A sender nanomachine releases information molecules independently from other sender nanomachines and from receiver nanomachines, which react to the incoming information molecules on receiving the information molecules. For instance, the concentration of glucose (a metabolite consumed as energy by cells) is determined asynchronously by separate groups of cells that perform specific functions to maintain homeostasis (i.e., stable chemical concentrations). These groups of cells communicate through the concentration of the glucose and determine independently what chemical process to perform to produce or consume it without requiring a synchronization signal.

Biocompatibility

Sender and receiver nanomachines in molecular communication communicate through sending, receiving, and decoding (chemically reacting to) information molecules. Since molecular communication uses the same communication mechanisms as biological systems, nanomachines in molecular communication can directly communicate with various natural components in a biological system using encoding and decoding methods available to the biological system. Biocompatibility of molecular communication may enable applications such as inserting nanomachines into a biological system for medical applications that require biologically friendly nanomachines.

Energy Efficiency

Through the fine-tuning of natural evolution, molecular communication in biological systems has achieved a high degree of energy efficiency. For example, under some conditions, myosin (a type of a molecular motor) converts chemical energy (i.e., ATP) to mechanical work with 90 percent energy efficiency (Howard 2001; Yasuda et al. 1998). Energy efficiency may be useful to reduce the energy cost of using nanomachines for applications in which the human body is the energy source or for low-cost production of objects.

OBSERVATIONS OF MOLECULAR COMMUNICATION IN BIOLOGICAL SYSTEMS

Molecular communication is a common communication method in biological systems for transmission of information between biological nanomachines (Dixon 1990; Lee and Chang 2003). In biological systems, information molecules propagate through passive transport (using random movement of molecules caused by thermal energy) and through active transport (using transport molecules that consume energy to transport information molecules). This section describes some representative examples of nanomachines and molecular communication in biological systems.

Molecular communication in biological systems occurs at multiple scales. For instance, at the nanoscale, a protein complex may chemically react with another protein complex using a single type of information molecule. At the microscale level, a cell may communicate with other cells through one or more types of information molecules. At the system level, a group of cells (e.g., microbe/bacterial cells) form a group of sender nanomachines that communicate with another group of cells (a group of receiver nanomachines) (Zhou et al. 2005).

Biological Nanomachines in Biological Systems

There are a number of nanomachines found in biological systems. Cells and various molecules inside a cell (e.g., DNA, RNA, and proteins) are at nanoscale or microscale and perform simple functions (such as replication, movement, and metabolism) and are all examples of nanomachines in biological systems. Cells are the basic building blocks in biological systems (Alberts et al. 2002). They are capable of sending and receiving information molecules. For instance, in bacterial conjugation, a sender bacterium extends a pilus that attaches to a receiver bacterium and the sender bacterium transports DNA (i.e., a plasmid encoding a set of proteins) through the established pilus to the receiver bacterium. The plasmid may encode various useful proteins such as antibiotic resistance, allowing the receiver bacteria to acquire new functionality.

Many molecules inside a cell are nanomachines and interact with other molecules inside the cell. For instance, DNA inside a cell interacts with other molecules within the cell (Figure 2) to produce messenger RNA (mRNA) through a process called "transcription," and the mRNA produced interacts with tRNA to synthesize a chain of amino acids (a protein), through a process called "translation." In this example, DNA represents a sender nanomachine that generates (i.e., encodes) and sends mRNA, and tRNA represents a receiver nanomachine that receives mRNA and synthesizes (i.e., decodes) a protein.

Communication Processes in Biological Systems

Biological nanomachines in biological systems exhibit a wide variety of mechanisms for exchanging information at the nanoscale and the microscale, including mechanisms for intracellular transport (to transport molecules within a single cell) and for intercellular transport (to transport molecules between cells). Sender and receiver nanomachines exist in biological systems in a wide variety of forms at the nanoscale and the microscale. In intracellular transport, sender and receiver nanomachines are components within the cell, and information molecules are ions, peptides, mRNA, and other metabolites (i.e., consumable molecules in the environment or products of chemical reactions). For intercellular communication, the sender and receiver nanomachines are cells, and information molecules are ions, peptides, metabolites, or DNA.

For intracellular transport, information molecules are transported inside a biological cell. For instance, an inert vesicle that contains the neurotransmitter acetylcholine is transported to the end of a neuron for chemical reaction. For small molecules, passive diffusion is sufficient to randomly move the information molecules. However, for large molecules that do not diffuse well, the cell requires molecular motors (e.g., myosin, kinesin) to actively transport large molecules within the cell. A molecular motor is a protein or a protein complex that converts chemical energy (e.g., ATP hydrolysis) into mechanical work at the molecular scale (Figure 3). Inside a cell, molecular motors transport large information molecules or large vesicles (e.g., liposomes, cell organelles) that contain information molecules (Oiwa and Sakakibara 2005; Shima et al. 2006; Toba and Oiwa 2006). Molecular motors consume chemical energy (e.g., ATP) to transport the information molecules or the vesicles along the preestablished guide molecules (e.g., along a star-shaped topology that the guide molecules form inside a cell). A vesicle acts as an interface molecule that can store a variety of information molecules. It provides an inert container so that the information molecules inside the vesicle do not cause chemical reactions until they reach the receiver nanomachine. For instance, inside some neuron cells, molecular motors (e.g., kinesin and dynein) transport vesicles

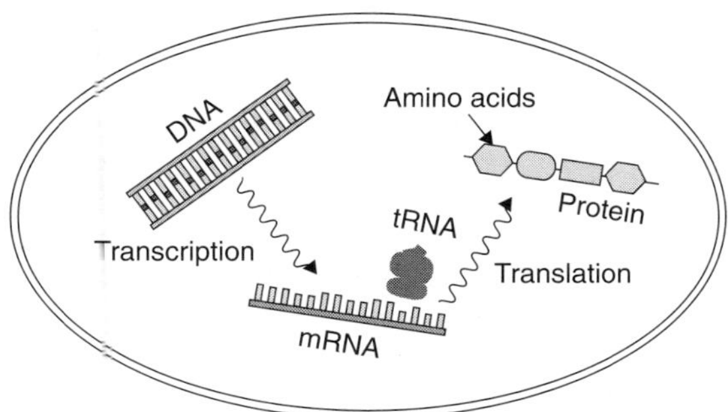

Figure 2: Biological nanomachines in a cell: DNA sequences are transcribed into mRNA sequences. mRNA sequences are translated into proteins using tRNA. DNA, mRNA, and proteins interact and regulate the transciption/translation of the cell. DNA represents a sender nanomachine that encodes information onto mRNA and sends mRNA, mRNA represents the information molecule, and tRNA represents a receiver nanomachine that receives mRNA and decodes the information into a sequence of amino acids (i.e., a protein). Through these regulatory processes, a cell controls its functions such as metabolism, growth, and repair. These information molecules are contained inside a lipid bilayer cell membrane.

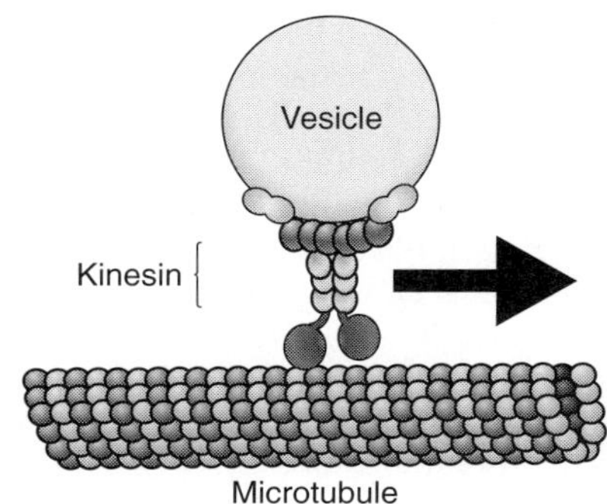

Figure 3: Transport of a vesicle by a molecular motor: A kinesin molecule is a type of molecular motor. The kinesin molecule consumes chemical energy (i.e., ATP) to mechanically walk in one direction along a microtubule inside a cell. The molecular motor can selectively bind to vesicles and thus transport a vesicle containing information molecules.

containing acetylcholine along cytoskeletal tracks in the axon of the neuron. The transported acetylcholine is released at the end of the axon and causes a response in the adjacent neuron with a receptor for acetylcholine (Alberts et al. 2002).

In the intercellular transport, biological cells use various mechanisms to transport information molecules (e.g., peptides or ions) among cells. For short-range communication (within a few cell lengths away) among cells, cells release information molecules (e.g., proteins and peptides) into the extracellular environment, and neighboring cells capture the information molecules with protein receptors (e.g., G-protein-linked receptors, enzyme-linked receptors, and ion-channel-linked receptors), thus resulting in the activation of a chemical reaction (e.g., increased metabolism or transcription of cellular proteins). Another type of short-range communication between cells is through physical contact using cell-cell junction channels such as gap-junction channels. Gap-junction channels allow connected cells to share small molecules such as Ca^{2+} (calcium ions), and therefore, enable coordinated actions among adjacent cells in response to extracellular signals (Alberts et al. 2002).

For long-range intercellular communication cells communicate through the environment by sensing and modifying molecules of the environment (Alberts et al. 2002; Devlin 2001; Mathews, van Holde, and Ahern 1999; Nelson and Cox 2000). One example of intercellular communication is the regulation of thyroxine. The overall process of thyroxine regulation represents a homeostatic system in which multiple cells communicate with each other through the concentration of a certain chemical substance in the environment. Thyroxine is a hormone that invokes the process to control the basal metabolic rate of cells. The process of regulating thyroxine concentration involves two glands—the pituitary and the thyroid. Cells in the pituitary gland called "thyrotropes" (Villalobos, Nunez, and Garcia-Sancho 2004) secrete thyroid-stimulating hormone (TSH). The secreted TSH propagates through the blood circulation system to cells throughout the body. Upon receiving TSH, the epithelial cells of the thyroid gland produce thyroxine. When the thyroxine concentration becomes too high, the pituitary gland decreases the secreted amount of TSH, and this, in turn, causes epithelial cells of the thyroid gland to produce less thyroxine. Through this interactive process between the pituitary gland and thyroid gland, the thyroxine concentration is stabilized in the human body.

Another example of the intercellular transport (i.e., cellular communication among multiple cells) is quorum sensing. Bacterial cells perform quorum sensing by releasing an autoinducer, acyl homoserine lactone (AHL), and detecting the concentration of AHL, to estimate the number of nearby bacteria. AHL released by bacteria diffuses through the environment. When the AHL concentration is sufficiently high in the environment, the bacteria interpret this as a large number of bacteria in the environment, and thus, the bacteria start transcribing DNA to perform group functions (e.g., enough bacteria to generate an infection, form a biofilm, or generate luminescence) (de Kievit and Iglewski 2000).

Yet another example of the intercellular transport (i.e., cellular communication among multiple cells) is the transmission of genetic information stored in DNA between cells. For instance, a bacterium transmits DNA to another bacterium through the process of conjugation. In the process of DNA transmission, two types of bacteria, a sender bacterium with an F-plasmid (i.e., a genetic sequence that enhances the transfer of genetic information) and a receiver bacterium without F-plasmid, transfer a DNA chromosome through a pilus (i.e., a projection from the sender bacterium to the receiver bacterium forming a bridge for transmitting DNA). Transfer of DNA between bacteria may allow the receiver bacterium to acquire DNA that produces some useful cellular functionality (e.g., protein production, antibiotic resistance). Bacteria also move through the environment (using molecular motors such as flagella or cilia), and thus, may transport DNA or other information molecules to other bacteria in the environment (Tamarin 1999; Berg, Tymoczko, and Stryer 2002). The receiver bacterium may also release pheromones that form a chemical gradient that guides a sender bacterium toward a receiver bacterium (i.e., the closer to the receiver, the higher the chemical concentration).

Passive Transport-Based Molecular Communications in Biological Systems

Examples of passive transport of information molecules in biological systems include diffusion of molecules among organisms or communication between adjacent cells through gap junctions, described in the section on "Biological Nanomachines in Biological Systems." Passive transport of information molecules provides a simple and robust method of propagating information in biological systems. It is simple, as it does not require a transport molecule that chemically reacts with energy molecules. It is robust, as it functions even if the environment drastically changes.

Some passive transport uses free diffusion and transmits in all available directions. This makes diffusion-based passive transport independent of the position of the receiving nanomachines in the environment, making it particularly suited to environments that are highly dynamic and unpredictable. Diffusion-based passive transport is also suited to situations in which infrastructure for communications is not feasible between a sender and a receiver. For instance, plants release pheromone molecules into the air to signal other plants without using any preestablished infrastructure (Lucas and Lee 2004). The sender plant communicates information regarding attacks from pathogens (e.g., bacteria that attack the plant), animals consuming the plant, and environmental conditions (e.g., availability of water). Upon receiving pheromone molecules from a sender plant, the receiver plant performs a corresponding behavior (such as producing chemicals to repel bacteria).

Some passive transport systems use impulses to achieve frequent and fast communication. As a result of the quick increase and decrease of the information molecule concentration in the environment, the information molecule concentration appears as a directed impulse that propagates away from the sender nanomachine. For instance, some epithelial (skin) cells produce impulses of calcium ions (Ca^{2+}) for intercellular communication. The endoplasmic reticulum (ER) in a cell gathers and stores calcium ions, and when the sender cell is stimulated (e.g., by a physical stimulus), it releases the stored calcium ions from the ER and the calcium diffuses to adjacent cells through cell-cell junction channels. The diffused calcium in turn stimulates the adjacent cells, causing a chain reaction of calcium stimulation. Shortly after being stimulated and releasing calcium, a cell pumps calcium within the cell back into the ER and suppresses further stimulation, thus creating a short impulse of calcium through the cell. Because the communication propagates in a short impulse of calcium concentration, the sender cell can communicate at a higher frequency. Neurons similarly produce ion impulses that propagate over the length of the neuron.

Active Transport-Based Molecular Communications in Biological Systems

Examples of active transport of information molecules in biological systems include motor-based transport of molecules within a biological cell in intracellular communication and transfer of DNA through bacteria conjugation described in the section on "Biological Nanomachines in Biological Systems." Active transport of information molecules provides a communication mechanism to transport large molecules to specific locations in a biological system. It is directional, because transport molecules move along guide molecules. Active transport can move large information molecules over relatively longer distances (up to meters in length) as compared with diffusion-based passive transport. Large information molecules and vesicles diffuse poorly in passive transport because of their size; on the other hand, active transport consumes chemical energy and generates sufficient force to directionally transport large information molecules (Bullock et al. 2005).

Active transport in biological systems provides a communication mechanism with a high degree of reliability even when the number of information molecules to transport is small. Because the transport of information molecules in active transport is directional, the probability of information molecules reaching the receiver nanomachine is higher than when using passive transport, and thus active transport requires fewer information molecules to perform communication.

Active transport requires significant communication infrastructure to produce and maintain the transport, guide, and interface molecules (e.g., molecular motors, microtubules filaments, and vesicles). Transport molecules must consume a regular supply of energy to overcome the chemical interactions between the information molecule and molecules in the environment.

Molecular Communication Networks in Biological Systems

Biological cells form into larger-scale organisms with a variety of functions. Thus, the biological system requires an entire network of molecular communications to coordinate among the many cells. The functionality of a network of molecular communication is necessary to coordinate self-organization of the cells during a developmental phase and also to coordinate cells in the complete organism.

In order for a single cell (e.g., an egg) to develop into a large-scale multicellular organism (e.g., a mouse), cells use molecular communication. For instance, cells in a developing embryo (Forgacs and Newman 2005) use molecular communication and develop into specific shapes and structures through the cellular morphogenesis process. During the cellular morphogenesis process, a single cell replicates into multiple cells that self-organize into different organs (e.g., a cell differentiates into a skin cell or a neuron) with specific shapes and locations in the organism (e.g., a group of cells forms the shape of a finger or the shape of a wrist). Cells in the developing embryo diffuse molecular signals for the purposes of establishing gradients in the environment, synchronizing cells, and identifying the role of each cell. Sender and receiver nanomachines (e.g., cells in the finger and wrist) also use molecular signals to control the relative position of cells (e.g., to grow the hand at the end of the wrist), the amount of growth (e.g., to determine the length of each finger), and the pattern of growth (e.g., to grow five fingers). A sender nanomachine (or a group of sender nanomachines) controls the number of information molecules produced (e.g., in order to create a high enough concentration of specific information molecules to cause cells to differentiate into a finger) and the timing of molecule release (e.g., releasing information molecules for a certain duration to determine the length of the finger).

Molecular communication also provides a mechanism for nanomachines to communicate and coordinate within a developed large-scale functional biological system. After a single cell develops into a multicellular organism, the cells in the multicellular organism use a network of molecular signals to control many complex signaling pathways. For instance, cells use glucose molecules as molecular signals to regulate various metabolic pathways. From the high-level architectural view, the metabolite molecules form a molecule interaction graph that consists of a set of nodes and edges. The nodes of the graph represent metabolites (i.e., information molecules) and the edges of the graph represent chemical pathways to convert one metabolite into another. Cells synthesize glucose molecules from the many different forms of chemical energy available to the cells (e.g., various metabolites) and the cells convert the glucose molecules into a large number of different molecules such as amino acids, sugars, and nucleotides (Broder et al. 200; Csete and Doyle 2004). The graph of the metabolites reveals that it is simple to add a new energy source, since it is necessary only to add a new edge from the energy source to the glucose molecule and the edges (i.e., chemical reactions) from the glucose molecule to the receiver nanomachines do not require changes. The network structure identified in the graph of metabolites may serve as a foundation for molecular communication system design.

ENGINEERING OF MOLECULAR COMMUNICATION

Observations of biological systems provide a starting point for understanding nanomachines, processes in passive and active transport in molecular communication, and how to organize molecular communication systems. It has now become possible to artificially engineer nanomachines and molecular communication between nanomachines to produce systems of nanomachines. One approach for engineering molecular communication is extending the existing molecular communication in biological systems described in the section on "Observations of Molecular Communication in Biological Systems." Accordingly, many engineered molecular communications use or modify components of molecular communication from biological systems.

Research in engineering molecular communication consists of engineering nanomachines (e.g., sender nanomachines, receiver nanomachines, information molecules) and engineering passive and active transport mechanisms for information molecules. Empirical research also exists to demonstrate the feasibility of, to observe the characteristics of, and to fine-tune engineered nanomachines and molecular communication. Research also exists to create both mathematical and simulation models from experimental observation. These models serve as a basis for predicting properties of larger-scale and complex engineered molecular communication that is experimentally difficult or costly to produce.

Nanomachines

Engineering nanomachines is necessary to introduce new communication functionality and communication signals to use for molecular communication. Sender and receiver nanomachines in engineered molecular communication need new communication functionality such as that to release specific information molecules (at a sender nanomachine), to control the rate of information molecule release (at a sender nanomachine), and to detect specific information molecules (at a receiver nanomachine). There are three classes of approaches for developing nanomachines: they are modifying existing biological nanomachines such as cells and bacteria (e.g., through genetic engineering), producing simplified cell-like structures using biological materials (e.g., through embedding proteins in a vesicle), or designing other chemical reactions that produce logic and communications.

Modified Biological Cells

One of the three classes of approaches to introduce new communication functionality and communication signals to use for molecular communication is to modify existing nanomachines in biological systems through genetic engineering of their DNA. For instance, a new DNA sequence may be added to a bacterium to add a new functionality. One technique to add a new DNA sequence into a bacterium is to synthesize a DNA sequence in the form of a plasmid (a segment of DNA) that encodes the desired functionality and to have the bacterium cell uptake the plasmid. Current DNA synthesis techniques can reliably produce arbitrary DNA sequences of up to approximately 10,000 base pairs (Baker et al. 2006). A DNA sequence of 10,000 base pairs is still sufficient to encode a large protein (plus nearby regulator sequences) and produce (e.g., proteins and logic components) useful functionality in a bacterial cell. With the advancement of the technology, it may become possible to artificially synthesize longer DNA sequences and, thus, to increase the ability to introduce new functionality into cells.

In the area of synthetic biology, researchers have demonstrated, through genetic engineering of DNA, creation of bacteria that are capable of performing a simple logic such as an oscillator (Elowitz and Leibler 2000). The bacterium has inserted DNA sequences that cause the bacterium to oscillate the concentration of three protein products (TetR, cI, LacI) over time. The DNA to be inserted into the bacterium was selected so that TetR blocked the promoter sequence of cI, cI blocked the promoter sequence of LacI, and LacI blocked the promoter sequence of TetR. Thus, at time t, TetR is active; cI is blocked; and LacI starts being produced. At time $t + 1$, LacI becomes active; TetR is blocked; and cI starts being produced. The oscillation cycle is dependent on the time for transcribing DNA and the time for the cI, LacI, or TetR to block a promoter sequence; the oscillation, therefore, is slow—on the order of tens of minutes.

Using cells (such as bacteria) as a sender nanomachine has several drawbacks. For instance, some applications may require inserting a DNA sequence into bacteria for new functionality in addition to the oscillator; however, selecting the new DNA sequence may be difficult, since using the molecules TetR, LacI, and cI or similar molecules will influence the activity of the bacteria to act as an oscillator. Another drawback results from cells controlling molecular communication by regulating DNA. Regulating DNA introduces significant processing delay (minutes to hours), since specific DNA sites must be regulated by information molecules (e.g., TetR, cI, or LacI), and the DNA must be transcribed (copied to mRNA) and translated (converted to a protein sequence) to perform chemical reactions for the production of information molecules (e.g., to produce proteins that lead to TetR, cI, or LacI). Also, the environment must be maintained at conditions in which biological cells will survive (e.g., at around 37°C), thus limiting the applicability for molecular communication.

Engineering Cells Using Biological Materials

One of the three classes of approaches to introduce new communication functionality and communication signals to use for molecular communication is to produce simplified cell-like structures using biological materials (e.g., through embedding of proteins in a vesicle). Simplification of biological systems (e.g., cells) may lead to components that are easier to engineer.

One example of the approach of simplification is to start with a lipid bilayer and then add functionality as necessary (Kikuchi, Ikeda, and Hashizume 2004). The lipid bilayer is similar to the membrane that encloses a cell. The lipid bilayer forms into a vesicle (a spherical lipid bilayer), and functional proteins (e.g., a receptor) are either embedded into the vesicle (Figure 4) or are

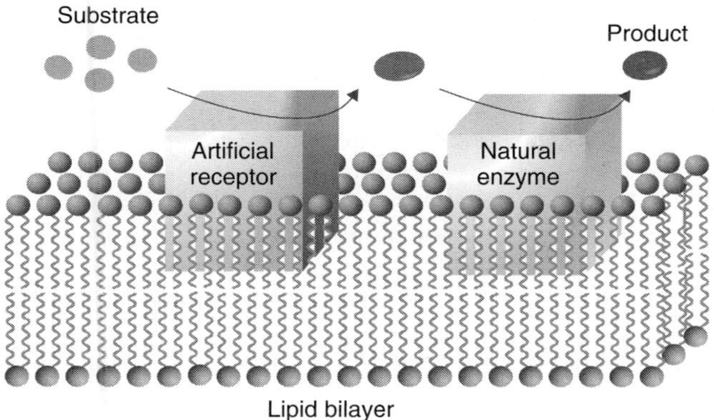

Figure 4: A functionality-embedded lipid bilayer: This is a highly simplified system of an artificial receptor and enzyme components inserted into a lipid bilayer (Kikuchi et al. 2004; Sasaki et al. 2006). An artificial receptor reacts to a substrate, which leads to the formation of a product.

captured inside the vesicle. Kikuchi et al. (2004) successfully embedded an active receptor and enzyme into a lipid bilayer, producing sender and receiver functionalities. By restricting the number of functionalities that are embedded in the vesicle, it is not necessary to consider the various complex processes (e.g., other metabolic pathways in the cell and processes to maintain the structure of the cell) occurring in a natural biological nanomachine. For instance, it is possible to select chemicals to cause the vesicles to form tubular projections to connect the vesicles without having the complete set of chemical processes from a normal cell (Akiyoshi et al. 2003; Nomura et al. 2005). Note that, on the other hand, the engineered vesicle is more dependent on a supply of metabolite molecules from outside the vesicle.

Engineering of Nanomachines Using Chemical Reactions

One of the three classes of approaches to engineer new nanomachines is to use other molecules, such as DNA sequences or other non-DNA molecules, rather than to use cells or cell-like structures. Nanomachines produced from other molecules are able to perform logic functions, form structures, or provide a method of encryption.

DNA sequences can be selected to produce useful logic and communication functionality in a nanomachine. Note that the DNA sequences exist freely in solution and are not contained inside a cell. For instance, a DNA sequence can act as a receiver of information molecules (e.g., proteins or other DNA sequences). The information molecule binds to the DNA sequence and/or changes the sequence of base pairs in the DNA. The chemical reactions using DNA sequences are highly specific, since only certain molecules (e.g., specific proteins or other DNA sequences) will recognize and react to a specific DNA sequence. The specificity of chemical reactions involving DNA sequences allows them to perform logic functions (e.g., when DNA sequences A and B are both present, DNA with structure C will form) (Benenson et al. 2004). Such DNA logic functions can select DNA sequences that represent solutions to NP-complete (nondeterministic polynomial time) problems in a massively parallel fashion (Adleman 1994; Winfree et al. 1998); however, scalability of searching for a specific DNA sequence for NP-complete problems is currently limited (Cox, Cohen, and Ellington 1999).

The specificity of chemical reactions involving DNA sequences also applies to forming three-dimensional structures. Nanomachines may require a three-dimensional shape to position molecules in an environment for a larger-scale molecular communication device. One approach to form three-dimensional structures is to bind single-stranded DNA sequences together (DNA naturally occurs in a double-stranded state, which is formed from two complementary single-stranded DNA sequences). A single-stranded DNA sequence contains exposed sequences that readily bind to a single-stranded DNA sequence that contains a complementary sequence. A single-stranded DNA sequence can also bind to itself and fold itself into a certain shape (e.g., to form a hairpin structure) if a part of a single-stranded DNA sequence is complementary to another part of its DNA sequence. If pieces of a single-stranded DNA sequence remain exposed after binding to a complementary sequence, other single-stranded DNA can subsequently bind to the exposed pieces of the single-stranded DNA. Thus, the single-stranded DNA can repeatedly bind to more single-stranded DNA to form larger structures (Sakamoto et al. 2000; Mao et al. 2000). Structures created by a single-stranded DNA sequence through binding may be complex and may provide a potential scaffold for precise binding of other single-stranded DNA sequences onto the scaffold.

The specificity of chemical reactions involving DNA sequences also applies to performing encryption of information into DNA sequences (Gehani et al. 2004). For instance, information may be encoded onto a sequence of DNA, and the information-encoded DNA sequence may bind another DNA sequence that represents an address tag for the information-encoded DNA sequence. The information-encoded DNA sequence with the address tag is then mixed into a large number of other random DNA sequences and can be retrieved only by using a DNA sequence that chemically binds to the tag. Security is important in communication, and since nanomachines may be too simple to perform complex security functions, approaches such as this may provide techniques for security in molecular communication.

In addition to using DNA sequences, non-DNA molecules (artificially designed molecules using chemistry techniques) may be used to introduce new communication functionality and communication signals for molecular communication. Artificially designed molecules have been identified with chemical characteristics that also receive information molecules and perform useful logic functions. If the artificially designed molecules are integrated to form a system of chemical reactions, more complex logic functions may be possible (Zauner and Conrad 2001); however, large-scale integration of artificially designed molecules remains to be experimentally demonstrated.

Passive Transport

Research in engineering molecular communication includes developing passive and active transport mechanisms for propagating information molecules through the environment. This section describes passive transport mechanisms. Later sections describe passive transport by which information molecules propagate using free diffusion through the environment and another type of passive transport by which information molecules propagate in a wave-like impulse.

Passive Transport Using Free Diffusion

The simplest method for propagating information molecules through the environment is passive transport of information molecules using free diffusion. Passive transport using free diffusion represents a broadcast communication to all receiver nanomachines in range; however, the concentration of information molecules released in the environment generally decreases as the distance from the sender increases (e.g., it is inversely proportional to the square or cube of the distance from the sender). The concentration of information molecules, thus, may be undetectable by receivers if they are distant from the sender.

In free diffusion–based passive transport, it is beneficial to have mechanisms for the sender nanomachine to address a specific receiver nanomachine (or a set of specific receiver nanomachines), since communication is inherently a broadcast with free diffusion. In free diffusion–based passive transport, a receiver nanomachine may have receptors that are specific and that respond only when a certain type of information molecule is present in a high enough concentration (Weiss and Knight 2000; Gerchman and Weiss 2004). Thus, the sender nanomachine may select the receiver nanomachine by sending the information molecules that cause a response at the receptors of the desired receiver nanomachine. The sender nanomachine may also set the concentration of information molecules (by adjusting the number of information molecules to transmit) so that only nearby receiver nanomachines with the specific receptor are capable of responding, and distant receivers do not respond. For instance, an engineered bacterium produces VAI (*Vibrio fischeri* autoinducer) information molecules, and the VAI information molecules diffuse through the environment and bind to VAI-specific receptors (i.e., a specific DNA sequence that binds VAI) in a receiver bacterium (Weiss and Knight 2000). The receiver bacterium decodes the VAI information molecule into the production of GFP (green fluorescent protein) (Haraguchi, Koujin, and Hiraoka 2000). The VAI-specific receptor thus acts as an address tag of the receiver bacterium. With a sufficiently high concentration of information molecules (VAI) received at a receiver bacterium, GFP is produced inside the receiver bacterium in large enough amounts for fluorescence to be visible under ultraviolet (UV) light (Figure 5). Note that this addressing is not dynamic, since the sender bacterium must have prior knowledge regarding which information molecules (e.g., VAI) are necessary to contact the receiver bacterium.

Passive Transport Using Impulse-Based Communication

In addition to the free diffusion–based passive transport, an alternative and more complex form of passive transport is possible. This form of passive transport uses additional (non-information) molecules in the environment. These additional molecules in the environment release/generate information molecules (in response to information molecules created by a sender nanomachine) and cause a wave-like impulse of information molecules that propagate through the environment. Examples of such passive transport using impulse-based communication are a BZ (Belousov-Zhabotinsky) reaction and calcium signaling inside a cell and between cells.

The first example of passive transport using impulse-based communication is to use a BZ reaction. A BZ reaction generates an impulse wave of chemical concentrations through nonequilibrium chemical reactions.

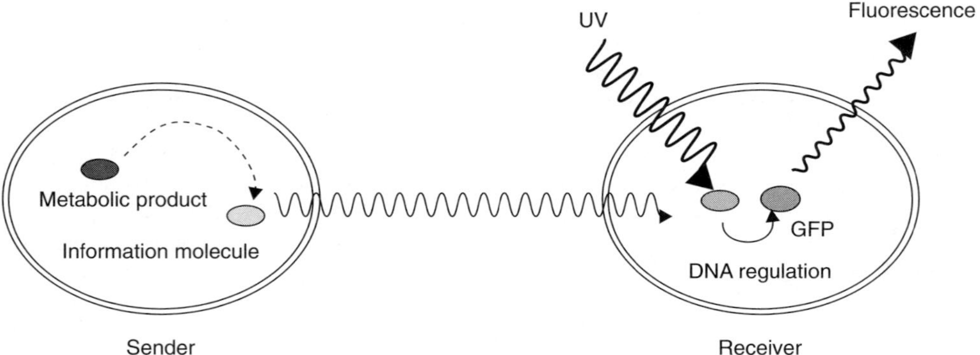

Figure 5: Addressing in passive transport using free diffusion. Chemical reactions in a sender bacterium convert a metabolic product into a steroid-like information molecule (e.g., VAI). The VAI molecules freely diffuse in the environment and reach a receiver bacterium. which contains a receptor specific to VAI. Upon arrival at the receiver bacterium, the VAI molecules bind to the receptor. With some probability, information molecules freely diffuse into a DNA regulation site inside a receiver bacterium and activate DNA, resulting in production of GFP (Weiss and Knight 2000). Receiver bacteria with GFP produce visible fluorescence under UV light. The DNA regulation site represents the address of the receiver bacterium, since other receiver bacteria without an appropriate DNA regulation site (e.g., a DNA sequence that binds to VAI) will not respond to the information molecule.

Figure 6: In a BZ reaction, the chemical concentration oscillates and generates a visible impulse wave of chemical reactions. This figure illustrates an impulse wave of chemical reactions in a BZ reaction originating from a single point and emanating in an expanding circular pattern. The actual information molecules from the origin point do not propagate with the wave, and only the impulse wave propagates.

A BZ reaction caused by a specific set of chemicals [e.g., $HBrO_2$, Br^-, ferriin (blue), and ferroin (red)] generates an impulse wave that spatially and temporally oscillates (Figure 6). The oscillation in a BZ reaction is caused by continuous reactions among the set of chemicals, and it may be modeled as a positive and negative feedback system.

In a BZ reaction, the chemical bromous acid ($HBrO_2$) (i.e., the information molecule) increases its concentration through an autocatalytic reaction. The increase in $HBrO_2$, in turn, promotes nearby ferroin (red) to convert to ferriin (blue) (Adamatzky 2004; Ichino et al. 2003). This positive feedback increases ferriin (blue) in the environment. When the concentration of ferriin (blue) becomes very high in the environment, ferriin (blue) starts to convert back to ferroin (red). When ferriin (blue) converts to ferroin (red), it produces bromide ion Br^-, which in turn suppresses the autocatalytic reaction to produce $HBrO_2$. This suppression of the autocatalytic reaction and natural decay of $HBrO_2$in the environment form a negative feedback and result in reduction of the concentration of $HBrO_2$ in the environment. This positive and negative feedback generates an impulse wave that propagates in the environment.

Through the positive and negative feedback described above, the BZ reaction continuously generates impulse waves that propagate in the environment. Note that in a BZ reaction the chemicals [e.g., $HBrO_2$, Br^-, ferriin (blue) and ferroin (red)] that generate an impulse wave do not actually propagate with the impulse wave, and only the impulse wave propagates.

Nanomachines may use a BZ reaction to perform logic functions in a manner similar to the logic in electrical computer components. For instance, an AND gate may result from two input BZ reaction waves colliding and producing an output wave through a chemical reaction of the two colliding input BZ reaction waves. Synchronization between the two input waves may be necessary to generate an output wave at a desired location, introducing a difficulty in design. However, implementing a logic gate using BZ reactions may lead to novel devices such as a detector for the distance to a wave source (Gorecki et al. 2005) or a detector for the direction to the wave source (Nagahara, Ichino, and Yoshikawa 2004).

The second example of passive transport using impulse-based communication is to use calcium signaling inside a biological cell (i.e., intracellular calcium signaling). Inside a cell, a calcium store (e.g., ER) has calcium channels (e.g., ryanodine receptor calcium channels). The calcium channels release calcium signals from the calcium store when calcium signals activate the calcium channels. Released calcium signals diffuse inside a cell and activate nearby calcium channels, which, in turn, release calcium signals from their calcium stores. The concentration of calcium inside a cell increases through this positive feedback. When the concentration of calcium becomes high, the cell uses various calcium pumps to remove calcium signals from the cell. This acts as a negative feedback. Similar to the BZ reaction, the positive and negative feedback produce a propagating impulse wave of calcium signals inside a cell. An impulse wave of calcium signals may be used to perform logic operations (Hentschel, Pencea, and Fine 2004). For instance, an AND gate may be composed of two calcium channels acting as inputs to and one calcium channel acting as an output from the AND gate (Figure 7). Each of these calcium channels is associated with a calcium store and releases calcium signals upon activation by calcium signals. In this AND gate, the output calcium channel releases calcium signals from the calcium store that it is associated with only when two input calcium channels are active, releasing calcium signals from their associated calcium stores.

Yet another example of passive transport using impulse-based communication is to use calcium signaling between biological cells (i.e., intercellular calcium signaling). Multiple cells are coupled through cell-cell channels called gap-junction channels. Gap-junction channels allow passage of small molecules between cells, and a calcium impulse wave generated inside a cell (as described in the previous paragraph) propagates through gap-junction channels to its adjacent cell. Similar to the AND gate design based on intracellular calcium signaling described in the previous paragraph, impulse waves of calcium signals between cells may be used to perform logic operations. For instance, cells may be placed on a glass surface to create a desired pattern of cells (Ostuni et al. 2000), and a logic gate may be designed in a manner similar to that described in the previous paragraph using impulse waves of calcium signals between cells (Figure 8) (Nakano et al. 2005). In addition, since it is possible to dynamically control and modify permeability and gating properties of gap-junction channels, it may be feasible to design a more complex logic gate using calcium impulse waves propagating through gap-junction channels between cells placed on a glass surface.

Using impulse waves of calcium signals inside a cell and between cells for performing logic operations may lead to the development of biocomputing devices that are highly compatible with biological systems. Note, however, that such devices may be slower to operate and more difficult to control than those developed using currently available electrical technology.

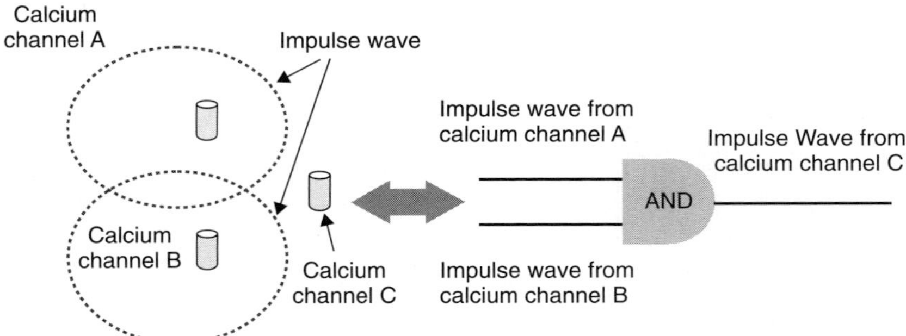

Figure 7: A design of an AND gate based on impulse-based passive transport using intracellular calcium signaling: The design shows an AND gate with two inputs (i.e., two impulse waves from calcium channels A and B) and an output (i.e., an impulse wave from calcium channel C). Each of the three calcium channels is associated with a calcium store and releases calcium signals when activated by calcium signals. When activated, calcium channels A and B generate input impulse waves that propagate in the environment (as indicated by the dotted circles). Calcium channel C generates an output impulse wave only when receiving impulse waves from both calcium channels A and B. The three calcium channels together, thus, perform as an AND gate.

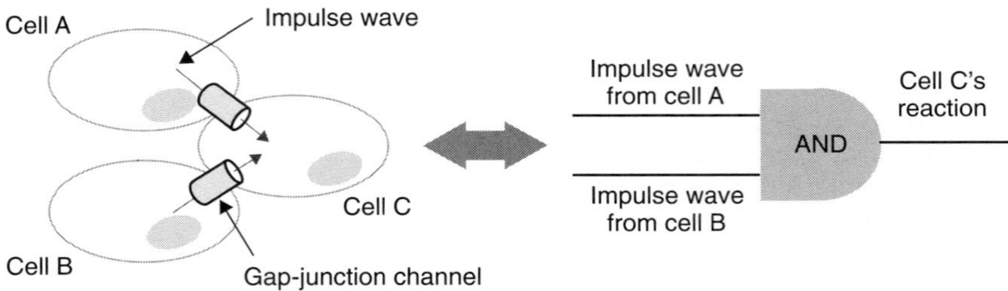

Figure 8: Design of an AND gate based on impulse-based passive transport using intercellular calcium signaling: The design shows patterned cells collectively acting as a logic gate with two inputs (i.e., two calcium impulse waves from cells A and B) and an output (i.e., a reaction of cell C). Cells A and B generate input calcium impulse waves that propagate through gap-junction channels to cell C. Cell C produces a reaction only when receiving calcium impulse waves from both cells A and B, and, thus, the patterned cells collectively perform as an AND gate.

Active Transport

In active transport, transport molecules propagate information molecules (or interface molecules containing information molecules) along the guide molecules. Active transport consumes energy, and thus, it provides a communication mechanism to transport large molecules (large information molecules or large interface molecules) to specific locations over relatively long distances (up to meters in length) (Ebeling and Schweitzer 2003). It is directional, because transport molecules move along guided molecules. Active transport, however, requires significant communication infrastructure to produce and maintain the transport, guide, and interface molecules (e.g., molecular motors, microtubules, and vesicles). For instance, transport molecules require a regular supply of chemical energy to transport information molecules or interface molecules.

Existing research in engineering active transport systems is experimental and focuses on examining various methods for controlling the propagation (e.g., direction of movement) of molecular motors and developing new methods of self-organizing a communication infrastructure. Determining the locations of molecular communication components (e.g., sender and receiver nanomachines, guide molecules) in a self-organizing manner, is particularly important in engineering active transport, since the location of molecular communication components may significantly impact the performance of molecular communication. On the other hand, in passive transport, a broadcast of information molecules reduces the need for precise location of molecular communication components.

The following subsections describe two types of active transport, active transport using molecular motors (borrowed from biology) and active transport using DNA walkers (using artificially designed chemical reactions).

Active Transport Using Biological Molecular Motors

One type of active transport is to use molecular motors to transport information molecules or interface molecules containing information molecules. Biological systems include a variety of molecular motors (e.g., kinesin, myosin, cilia, flagella, etc.). Existing research on engineering active transport, however, focuses on only a few types of molecular motors (i.e., kinesin, dynein). Three examples of active transport using molecular motors are molecular motors walking on filaments, filaments propagating on a patterned surface coated with molecular motors and biological cells moving through an aqueous solution using molecular motors.

In the first example, engineered active transport uses molecular motors, guide molecules (e.g., microtubule filaments) that self-organize into a network, and molecular motors (e.g., dynein, kinesin) that actively transport information molecules along the guide molecules (Suda et al. 2005; Moore et al. 2006). This first example uses components and processes similar to the active transport mechanisms in biological systems. In biological systems, a network of guide molecules (e.g., actin or microtubule filaments) is created within a cell in a self-organizing manner through dynamic instability (Figure 9) of guide molecules, and molecular motors (such as dynein and kinesin) transport information molecules to specific locations within the cell by walking along a network of guide molecules. Engineering of the self-organization of the filaments can produce simple patterns of filaments (e.g., a star-shaped pattern or a random mesh pattern) (Chakravarty, Howard, and Compton 2004; Enomoto et al. 2006; Hayashi et al. 2006). Through designing self-organization processes of creating filament patterns and through selectively transporting on the designed filament pattern, molecular motors may be guided to desired locations (e.g., desired receiver nanomachine or a desired set of receiver nanomachines). However, the patterns of filaments that are created through engineering self-organization of the filaments are currently simple and limited, since control over self-organization remains difficult.

In the second example of engineered active transport using molecular motors, the arrangement of microtubules and motors is inverted. A surface of a glass is coated with the molecular motor (e.g., kinesin), and the motors push the filaments along the surface. In this arrangement, transport molecules (i.e., the filament) load information molecules at a sender nanomachine and unload the information molecules at a receiver nanomachine (Hess et al. 2003; Hiyama et al. 2004). The direction of filament movement is guided by adding walls (e.g., deposited proteins) onto the glass surface through lithographic techniques.

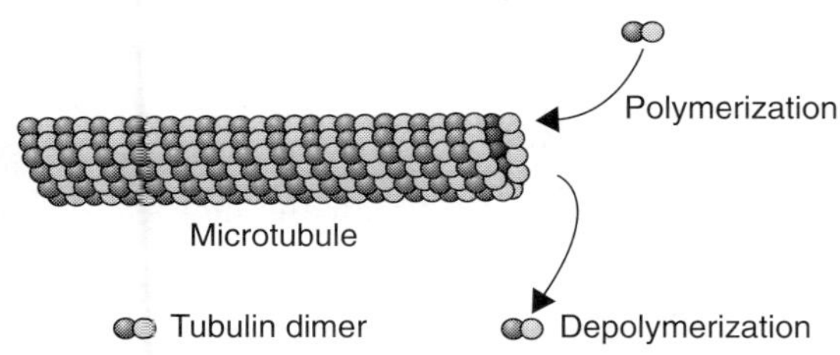

Figure 9: A microtubule and dynamic instability. A microtubule is a protein polymer consisting of tubulin dimers forming a hollow cylinder. A microtubule grows and shrinks through dynamic instability: the microtubule grows slowly by polymerizing tubulin dimers and stochastically shrinks by depolymerizing tubulin dimers. Tubulin dimers after depolymerization are still available in the environment for microtubule growth.

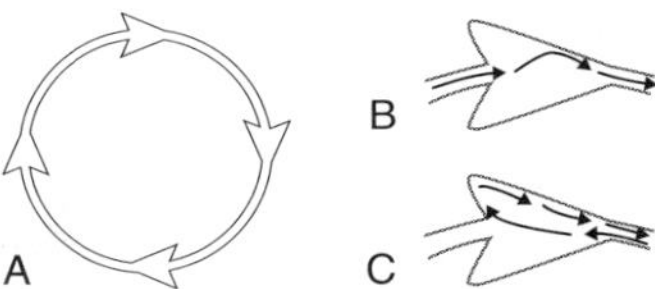

Figure 10: Rectifying the direction of a filament during active propagation on a patterned glass surface. Filaments move along a glass surface coated with molecular motors: (A) Patterned walls on the surface guide filament molecules. (B) When the filament moves in the direction of the arrow, movement direction is preserved. (C) When the filament moves against the direction of the arrow, the walls cause the filament to reverse its direction into the direction of the arrow.

Various patterns may be generated that gather filaments toward a receiver nanomachine. For instance, an arrow-shaped wall pattern acts a directional rectifier (Figure 10) to ensure that filaments propagate in a single direction (e.g., only clockwise) by rectifying filaments that are propagating opposite the arrowhead direction (Hiratsuka et al. 2001).

In the third example of engineered active transport using molecular motors, a transport molecule itself is a nanomachine using molecular motors to move itself toward a receiver nanomachine along chemical gradients in the environment. This third example uses components and processes similar to self-propulsion of single-cell organisms (e.g., a bacterium) through an aqueous solution. In biological systems, a bacterium (i.e., a transport nanomachine) uses cilia or flagella (molecular motors that generate propeller-like forces) to move itself along chemical gradients toward favorable conditions (e.g., food source, light) and away from unfavorable conditions (e.g., harmful chemicals, light). The receiver nanomachine may generate guide molecules (similar to a gradient of a food source or pheromone in the environment in the bacterium example) to indicate where the receiver nanomachine is and to influence the direction in which the transport nanomachine moves through the environment. The transport nanomachine does not require preestablished filament networks, since guide molecules emitted by a receiver nanomachine randomly diffuse to form the chemical gradient around the receiver nanomachine. For instance, the pseudopodia of a cell (projections from a cell) can form complex shapes such as a structure that links the entrance and exit of a maze (Nakagaki, Yamada, and Tóth 2000). The pseudopodia form the structure by growing toward a chemical gradient of food originating from both the entrance and the exit of the maze. Active transport using pseudopodia is robust, since the pseudopodia adapt to match the shape of the maze.

Active Transport Using DNA Walkers

Another type of active transport uses DNA walkers that actively transport information molecules. A DNA walker is an artificially designed DNA sequence that walks along a DNA track (Shin and Pierce 2004; Yin et al. 2004).

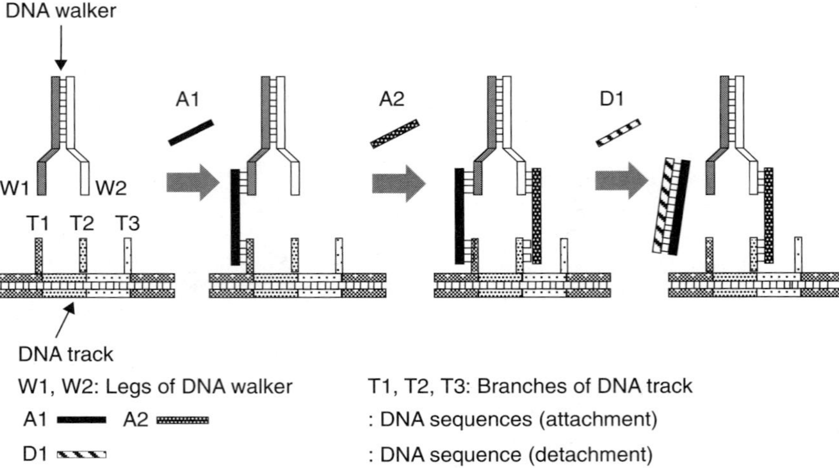

Figure 11: A DNA walker progressing along a DNA track from left to right. The DNA walker has two legs, W1 and W2 (i.e., the two single-stranded DNA sequences), and three branches, T1, T2, and T3 (i.e., the three single-stranded DNA sequences protruding from the DNA track). The DNA walker progresses by attaching to and detaching from the DNA track. First, DNA sequence A1 is partially complementary to both W1 and T1, and when A1 is introduced in the environment, A1 forms a bridge to bind W1 to T1. Second, DNA sequence A2 is partially complementary to both W2 and T2, and when A2 is introduced in the environment, A2 forms a bridge to bind W2 to T2. Third, DNA sequence D1 is perfectly complementary to A1, and when D1 is introduced in the environment, D1 detaches W1 from T1, freeing leg W1 from the DNA track. An additional walker step is possible by introducing a DNA sequence that can bridge from W1 to T3.

Figure 11 illustrates a DNA walker. In the example shown in Figure 11, the DNA walker has two single-stranded DNA sequences (i.e., W1, W2), called "legs," to walk along the DNA track. The DNA track has three branches of single-stranded DNA sequences (i.e., T1, T2, and T3) protruding from the DNA track. A series of DNA hybridization and dehybridization allows one leg of the DNA walker to bind to the next branch of the DNA track, while keeping the other leg bound to a branch, so that the DNA walker progresses without detaching from the DNA track. The DNA track is, thus, a guide molecule that determines the position of each step of the DNA walker. Similar to molecular motors, the DNA walker may transport a cargo (i.e., information molecules or interface molecules containing information molecules) along the DNA track. Alternatively, the DNA walker itself may represent information (e.g., a DNA sequence representing some information).

DNA walkers have several properties that are different from molecular motors described in the section on "Active Transport Using Biological Molecular Motors." Binding between DNA sequences is strong, and thus, active transport using DNA walkers is likely to be highly reliable and may require few information molecules to achieve communication. On the other hand, binding of protein molecular motors is weak, and molecular motors may stochastically unbind at any step of the walk; thus, a large number of molecular motors may be necessary to achieve successful communication. In addition, DNA walkers allow precise control over each step of movement. On the other hand, molecular motors walk stochastically; thus, it is difficult to precisely control the walking. Although existing research on DNA walkers has only demonstrated limited walking capability, continued research on DNA walkers may provide a scaffold for precise movement of DNA walkers on a grid of DNA tracks.

ENGINEERING OF MOLECULAR COMMUNICATION NETWORKS

As described in the section above on "Engineering of Molecular Communication," the existing research in molecular communication focuses on building components for molecular communication (e.g., nanomachines that have new communication functionality and communication signals, active and passive transport that transport information molecules or interface molecules containing information molecules). Such components, however, must work together to produce useful molecular communication (Drexler 1999; Zauner and Conrad 2001). An entire system of molecular communication (referred to as a "molecular communication network") will allow nanomachines to communicate not only through exchanging a low-level signal at the physical layer but also through exchanging information with higher-level meaning so that groups of nanomachines are able to perform complex and meaningful functions.

Existing research in creating an entire system of molecular communication (i.e., existing research toward creating a molecular communication network) includes research on providing a generic interface for interacting with a biological system, creating an addressing mechanism to enhance communications, and engineering simple molecular communication networks. In addition, research in asynchronous systems may provide mechanisms to handle properties of stochasticity and large propagation delay in molecular communication and provide methods to design a molecular communication network. Continued research into techniques in biology and nanotechnology, and computer science, may lead to some of the applications described in the section on "Applications."

Components for a Molecular Communication Network: Communication Interface

A communication interface provides a generic abstraction for communication that is reused by a variety of communication mechanisms. In molecular communication, a generic and abstract communication interface allows sender and receiver nanomachines to transport a variety of molecules using the same communication mechanism (Chen, Torchilin, and Langer 1996). Creating a generic and abstract communication interface is important in a molecular communication network, since, with such a communication interface, a communication component is designed without requiring details of other communication components.

One example of a generic and abstract communication interface is found in drug delivery. In drug delivery, varieties of drugs are encapsulated in nanoscale capsules and target some location in the human body (Figure 12). Targeting molecules embedded in the nanoscale capsule bind to a specific receptor embedded in the target location inside the human body. The location of the receptor molecule in the human body thus determines the eventual location of the nanoscale capsules. With this interface, drug targeting mechanisms do not rely on characteristics of the drug (i.e., the information molecule) being transported. Nanoscale capsules act as a generic and abstract communication interface. The interface molecules allow any type of information molecule to concentrate at the correct location, which reduces the amount of drug necessary for results, and thus reduces side effects from drugs reaching undesired locations. The nanoscale capsule also protects information molecules from environmental noise and prevents the information molecules from chemically reacting with molecules outside the interface during the propagation.

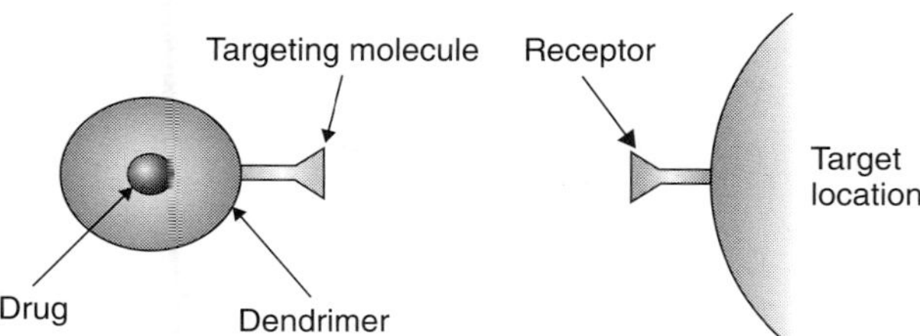

Figure 12: Drug delivery using a dendrimer communication interface (Sakthivel and Florence, n.d.). A dendrimer is a branched molecule with drugs embedded in the dendrimer. The dendrimer has targeting molecules on its surface. The receiver cell has a receptor that recognizes the targeting molecule and captures the dendrimer, and the drug is released at the target receiver cell. Alternatively, quorum-sensing mechanisms may apply at the target location to synchronize release of drugs at the target location (Weiss and Knight 2000).

Components for a Molecular Communication Network: Addressing Mechanism

One important feature in communication is the ability to send information to a specific receiver. In molecular communication, an addressing mechanism allows a sender nanomachine to specify the receiver nanomachine independent of the type of information molecules used. With a generic addressing mechanism, the sender nanomachine would have a generic abstraction for specifying receiver nanomachines. In diffusion-based communication in biological systems, a receiver nanomachine is addressed according to which information molecule is being used (see section on "Passive Transport-Based Molecular Communications in Biological Systems"). On the other hand, a molecular communication system using a generic addressing mechanism is more flexible and imposes fewer constraints on which information molecules are used in molecular communication.

One approach for a generic addressing mechanism is using DNA sequences (Hiyama et al. 2005). In the addressing mechanism investigated, the information molecule includes a single-stranded DNA with a sequence that specifies the address of a receiver nanomachine. The receiver nanomachine has an address DNA that is complementary to and thus binds to the single-stranded DNA on the information molecule. Using DNA sequences in addressing provides a method for generating a large number of addresses, since DNA sequences may be arbitrarily produced (with existing technology, DNA up to 10,000 base pairs in length) and binding of DNA sequence is understood (as evidenced by construction of various shapes from designed DNA sequences). Adding an addressing mechanism to molecular communication would allow the creation of more complex molecular communication networks.

Techniques to Create a Molecular Communication Network

Various approaches to create a molecular communication network have come from engineering simple molecular communication networks. Some approaches include: (1) creating standard techniques and standard communication components to develop a molecular communication network, (2) techniques to automatically predict chemical reactions and undesired chemical interactions among communication components, (3) techniques to modify the design of a communication network, and (4) techniques to position nanomachines and communication components.

Creating standard techniques and standard communication components to develop a molecular communication network may improve the ability to successfully design and create a molecular communication network. In computer engineering, new hardware components (e.g., an electric circuit) are integrated into a standardized catalog so that developers can quickly identify and use existing hardware components. In synthetic biology, it is envisioned that computing components that are made of biological materials are specified and cataloged in a manner similar to the circuit design used in engineering (Baker et al. 2006; MIT Registry 2007). Computing systems with several computing components (e.g., logic gates) made of biological materials have been demonstrated (Nitta and Suyama 2004). Having standard techniques and standard communication components may lead to ease in designing a molecular communication network, similar to standardization of protocols in electronic computer networks.

Techniques to automatically predict chemical reactions and undesired chemical interactions among communication components improve the ability to develop new molecular communication networks. In existing research, reengineered chemical pathways in bacteria produce antimalarial drugs (Martin et al. 2003; Ro et al. 2006); however, such procedures are manual, with a high degree of trial and error. Creating a computing system made of biological materials is complex, since computing components perform chemical reactions, and various computing components may interfere with each other, creating undesired chemical interactions among computing components. Existing techniques to automatically predict chemical reactions and undesired chemical interactions are limited. For instance, techniques from drug development, such as massively parallel assays, reduce the time to test for some undesired chemical interactions (i.e., drug side effects); however, such techniques do not provide conclusive results regarding potential drug interactions. Similar to creating a computing system from computing components made of biological materials, techniques to automatically predict chemical reactions and undesired chemical interactions among communication components are required to create an entire system of molecular communication (a molecular communication network) in which various components of molecular communication work together (e.g., nanomachines that have new communication functionality, active and passive transport molecules that transport information molecules, and interface molecules containing information molecules).

Techniques to modify the design of the communication network improve the ability to improve the design of existing molecular communication networks. Materials from biological systems may be modified and used in creating various components of molecular communication and a molecular communication network. Modifying such materials remains difficult. For instance, cells from biological systems remain difficult to modify, since the DNA and its interactions in biological systems are complex and not fully understood. (For instance, DNA code overlaps so that modification of one base pair in a DNA sequence can change the sequence of two proteins.) One possible approach for modifying and engineering the pathway of proteins is to apply genetic algorithms to select combinations of proteins that produce desired features; however, achieving the correct design through random processes in the genetic algorithm is time consuming. Another possible approach for producing desired functionality in a cell is to rewrite the DNA sequence of cells into a more human-readable format (Endy 2005). This technique improves the human-readability of DNA interactions by removing DNA that appears unnecessary and by expanding DNA sequences so that no code overlaps. However, DNA sequences are long (3 billion base pairs in a human), and existing techniques to read and write DNA still limit the ability to reengineer biological cells. Improving the ability to modify the DNA of biological cells will improve the ability to add new or remove existing communication functionality from components of molecular communication and from a molecular communication network.

Techniques to position nanomachines and communication components provide an additional technique to increase the functionality of a molecular communication network. If nanomachines are at precise locations on a glass surface, the nanomachines can perform addressing according to distance (by the passive transport using free diffusion, as discussed above). One scalable technique is to use masking techniques from computer circuit design to form cells into a complex pattern on a surface. In amorphous computing, different types of cells are spatially arranged on a surface to produce multiple logic gates (Abelson et al. 1999). In amorphous computing, a group of cells of the same type forms a single logic gate with the same functionality. Multiple groups of cells connect through molecular communication and form a circuit of connected logic gates. Lithography (or another photo techniques) is applied to produce a desired pattern of chemical receptors on a glass surface for placement of cells. Different types of cells recognize and bind to a specific type of chemical receptor on the surface, and thus form the desired pattern of cells (i.e., to form multiple logic gates) on a surface (Healy, Lom, and Hockberger 1994). Another technique to form cells into a complex pattern on a surface is to use a single type of biological cells that differentiates into a type of cell after the cell receives an external signal (e.g., light with a specific wavelength). As a step toward such a technique, existing research has demonstrated genetically modified cells that absorb light and change activity (i.e., produce GFP resulting in a photograph-like image) in response to the absorption of light. Extension of existing research may eventually lead to simple top-down engineering of complex cell patterns (rather than the bottom-up self-organizing creation of patterns in morphogenesis). These techniques produce patterns similar to patterns in electronic circuit design, and thus, techniques from electronic circuit design may extend to aid in producing a wide range of molecular communication devices. These techniques, however, may need to consider that cells may randomly migrate to different locations on a surface or may stochastically respond to external control signals.

Asynchronous Communication in a Molecular Communication Network

Concepts and techniques from asynchronous computing systems may provide guidelines for the design of an entire system of molecular communication (a molecular communication network) in which components of molecular communication work together. Asynchronous computing systems address timing and coordination issues that also appear in a molecular communication network.

Cellular automata, one type of asynchronous computing systems, provide a discrete-time model of the interactions occurring in spatially distributed components of a computing system, and it may apply to describing and understanding the interactions among various components of molecular communication (such as sender and receiver nanomachines). In cellular automata, autonomous "cells" are located on an N-dimensional grid. Note that a cell in cellular automata is not a biological cell and refers to a functional unit that performs simple logic action including a cell changing its state, a cell replicating into an empty adjacent cell (causing the adjacent cell to have the same state as the cell), or exchanging resources among neighboring cells. At discrete time intervals, each cell considers information from adjacent cells and follows predefined logic functions to decide what action it takes. Cellular automata may provide some intuition regarding pattern formation in the morphogenesis of biological systems (e.g., transmitting waves of information or modeling of limb formation). Cellular automata may also provide insights into the design of some simple logic that achieves given patterns. In applying cellular automata to design of a molecular communication network, however, it is necessary to consider the stochastic nature of various components of a molecular communication network: their stochastic nature may disrupt the ability of adjacent cells to transmit information molecules in a correct and timely manner.

Asynchronous computing systems require no synchronizing clocks (Davis and Nowick 1997). Developing a synchronizing clock for molecular communication is difficult, since the sender and receiver nanomachines need to integrate information from both information molecules and the synchronizing signal. In molecular communication, an asynchronous architecture may allow a sender nanomachine to transmit an information molecule to the receiver nanomachine and the receiver nanomachine to respond when it is ready for the next information molecule. This form of communication applying feedback from the receiver nanomachine to the sender nanomachine requires no synchronizing clocks. Molecular communication networks will likely benefit from asynchronous communication to address issues of probabilistic delays in molecular communication and biological systems.

CONCLUSION

Molecular communication first began as observations of molecular-based communication between biological entities (e.g., individual bacteria cells). Initial research of engineering molecular communication began as development of drugs and their delivery; however, early research in drug development and delivery only modified the activity of signal pathways that already existed in a receiver cell. Molecular communication, since then, has progressed to reengineering molecular communication pathways inside a receiver cell so that other, new drugs can modify the activity of the receiver cell. It has also progressed to consider molecular communication components that are not found in biological systems. The expansion of components available for molecular communication may find applicability in a number of biological systems or in harsh environments where biological components do not function well.

Molecular communication is still an emerging field. Existing research in molecular communication considers both the lowest layer of communication (namely, how information molecules are exchanged between a sender and a receiver nanomachine) and integration of multiple nanomachine devices. There is little research done to address higher-layer issues. The following research issues still need to be addressed: develop a feedback mechanism between sender and receiver nanomachines; route information molecules over a complicated topology of guide molecules (in case of active transport); and encode information onto information molecules in a generalized manner that receiver nanomachines understand and that creates a desired chemical reaction at the receiver nanomachine.

Although research in molecular communication is in its infancy and has only reproduced functionality already available either in biological systems or through other existing technologies (e.g., logic gates, light-sensitive surfaces, mechanisms to transport molecules using molecular motors), continuing research in molecular communication will lead to a molecular communication network in which various components of molecular communication work together to provide full communication functionality and enable new and novel applications that increase interaction with biological systems. Molecular communication also poses some concern about impacting ecological systems and introducing potentially harmful artificial systems (Check 2006). The field of molecular communication is progressing toward standardizing techniques for creating molecular communication components and may eventually lead to disciplined design of nanoscale communication systems that addresses concerns about safety and ecology.

GLOSSARY

ATP (Adenosine 5'-Triphosphate): Cells use ATP as an energy source in various biological cellular processes, including metabolic activities, motility, and cell division.

Axon: A distinctive part of a nerve cell or neuron that propagates electrical impulses. An axon is typically 1 μm in diameter, and it may extend from 1 mm to 1 m in length.

Cell: The basic functional and structural unit of all living organisms, from unicellular organisms such as bacteria to multicellular organisms such as plants and animals. Cells are classified as prokaryotic and eukaryotic. A eukaryotic cell contains a nucleus and is relatively large (1–100 μm). A eukaryotic cell contains organelles to perform a variety of functions such as a nucleus to store DNA molecules, mitochondria to produce ATP, chloroplasts to absorb light energy, and vacuoles for storage/structural support. A prokaryotic cell has a simple structure without a nucleus and is relatively small in size (1–10 μm).

DNA (Deoxyribonucleic Acid): A DNA molecule is a sequence of nucleic acids that stores genetic information of a living organism. A DNA molecule contains information necessary to construct various cellular components such as proteins. Specific proteins and molecules regulate the activity of segments of a DNA sequence.

Drug Delivery System: The goal of a drug delivery system is to deliver a controlled amount of pharmaceutical compounds to a target site of a body. Existing research in drug delivery systems includes design and development of drugs that are transported to a target site of a body and become activated only at the target site.

ER (Endoplasmic Reticulum): A cellular organelle found in all eukaryotic cells. ER has a membrane structure in which protein translation, folding, and transport occur.

Filament: A long chain of proteins found in a cell. Examples include microtubules and actin filaments.

Gap-Junction Channel: A cell-cell channel connecting two adjacent cells. Gap junction channels allow passage of small molecules (normally smaller than 1000 Da) between cells, enabling coordination and communication between cells.

GFP (Green Fluorescent Protein): A fluorescent protein produced by the jellyfish *Aequorea victoria*. GFP emits green fluorescence when exposed to blue light. In molecular and cell biology studies, GFP is often used as a marker protein for observing expression and dynamics of proteins of interest.

Liposome: A vesicle formed of a spherical lipid bilayer membrane.

Molecular Motor: A protein or protein complex that transforms chemical energy (i.e., ATP) into mechanical work at the molecular scale. The examples of molecular motors include myosins, kinesins, and dyneins.

Nanomachine: Nanomachines include naturally existing biological systems (e.g., cells), genetically altered biological systems, artificially synthesized devices, and hybrid biological-artificial systems, whose sizes are all measured in nanometers or micrometers.

Neuron: A nerve cell that plays a major role in transmitting electrical impulses within a nervous system.

Protein: An organic compound made of a linear chain of amino acids. Each protein or complex of proteins provides some functions such as regulating gene expression and sensing the environment.

Receptor: A protein complex located on a cell membrane or membranes of intracellular organelles such as the nucleus. Receptors react to molecules and activate signaling pathways that initiate cellular responses.

CROSS REFERENCES

See *Applications of Biological Concepts to Designs of Computer Networks and Network Applications; Cellular Communications Channels; Intrusion Detection Systems.*

REFERENCES

Abelson, H., D. Allen, D. Coore, C. Hanson, T. Knight, R. Nagpal, E. Rauch, G. Sussman and R. Weiss. 1999. Amorphous computing. White Paper. Cambridge, MA: MIT Artificial Intelligence Laboratory.

Adamatzky, A. 2004. Collision-based computing in Belousov–Zhabotinsky medium. *Chaos, Solitons and Fractals* 21:1259–64.

Adleman, L. M. 1994. Molecular computation of solutions to combinatorial problems. *Science* 266:1021–4.

Akiyoshi, K., A. Itaya, S. M. Nomura, N. Ono, and K. Yoshikawa. 2003. Induction of neuron-like tubes and liposome networks by cooperative effect of gangliosides and phospholipids. *Federation of European Biochemical Societies Letters* 534(1–3):33–8.

Alberts, B., A. Johnson, J. Lewis, M. Raff, K. Roberts, and P. Walter. 2002. *Molecular biology of the cell*. New York: Garland Science.

Allen, T. M., and P. R. Cullis. 2004. Drug delivery systems: Entering the mainstream. *Science* 303:1818–22.

Baker, D., G. Church, J. Collins, D. Endy, J. Jacobson, J. Keasling, P. Modrich, C. Smolke, and R. Weiss. 2006. Engineering life: Building a FAB for biology. *Scientific American* June:44–51.

Balzani, V., M. Venturi, and A. Credi. 2003. *Molecular devices and machines: A journey into the nanoworld*. Weinheim, Germany: Wiley-VCH.

Barron, J. T., L. Gu, and J. E. Parrillo. 1998. Malate-aspartate shuttle, cytoplasmic NADH redox potential, and energetics in vascular smooth muscle. *Journal of Molecular Cellular Cardiology* 30:1571–9.

Benenson, Y., B. Gil, U. Ben-Dor, R. Adar, and E. Shapiro. 2004. An autonomous molecular computer for logical control of gene expression. *Nature* 429:423–9.

Berg, J. M., J. L. Tymoczko, L. Stryer, and N. D. Clarke 2002. *Biochemistry*. 5th ed. New York: W. H. Freeman and Company.

Broder, A., R. Kumar, F. Maghoul, P. Raghavan, S. Rajagopalan, R. Stata, A. Tomkins, and J. Wiener. 2000. Graph structure in the Web. *Computer Networks* 33:309–20.

Bullock, T. H., M. V. L. Bennett, D. Johnston, R. Josephson, E. Marder, and R. D. Fields. 2005. The neuron doctrine: Redux. *Science* 310:791–3.

Chakravarty, A., L. Howard, and D. A. Compton. 2004. A mechanistic model for the organization of microtubule asters by motor and non-motor proteins in a mammalian mitotic extract. *Molecular Biology of the Cell* 15:2116–32.

Check, E. 2006. Synthetic biologists try to calm fears. *Nature* 441:388–9.

Chen, H., V. Torchilin, and R. Langer. 1996. Lectin-bearing polymerized liposomes as potential oral vaccine carriers. *Pharmaceutical Research* 13(9):1378–83.

Cox, J. C., D. S. Cohen, and A. D. Ellington. 1999. The complexities of DNA computation. *Trends in Biotechnology* 17:151–4.

Csete, M., and J. Doyle. 2004. Bow ties, metabolism and disease. *Trends in Biotechnology* 22(9):446–50.

Davis, A., and S. M. Nowick. 1997. An introduction to asynchronous circuit design. Technical Report UUCS-97-013. Salt Lake City: Computer Science Department, University of Utah.

de Kievit, T. R., and B. H. Iglewski. 2000. Bacterial quorum sensing in pathogenic relationships. *Infection and Immunity* 68(9):4839–49.

Devlin, T. M. 2001. *Textbook of biochemistry with clinical correlations*. 5th ed. New York: Wiley-Liss.

Dixon, R. A., and C. J. Lamb. 1990. Molecular communication in interactions between plants and microbial pathogens. *Annual Review of Plant Physiology and Plant Molecular Biology* 41:339–67.

Drexler, K. E. 1999. Building molecular machine systems. *Trends in Biotechnology* 17:5–7.

Ebeling, W., and F. Schweitzer. 2003. Self-organization, active Brownian dynamics, and biological applications. *Nova Acta Leopoldina NF* 88(332):169–88.

Elowitz, M. B., and S. Leibler. 2000. A synthetic oscillatory network of transcriptional regulators. *Nature* 403:335–8.

Endy, D. 2005. Foundations for engineering biology. *Nature* 438:449–53.

Enomoto. A., M. Moore, T. Nakano, R. Egashira, T. Suda, A. Kayasuga, H. Kojima, H. Sakakibara, and K. Oiwa. 2006. A molecular communication system using a network of cytoskeletal filaments. In *Technical Proceedings of the 2006 NSTI Nanotechnology Conference and Trade Show* 1:725–8.

Fiedler, S., S. Shirley, T. Schnelle, and G. Fuhr. 1998. Dielectrophoretic sorting of particles and cells in a microsystem. *Analytical Chemistry* 70:1909–15.

Forgacs, G., and S. A. Newman. 2005. *Biological physics of the developing embryo*. Cambridge, UK: Cambridge University Press.

Fu, A. Y., C. Spence, A. Scherer, F. H. Arnold, and S. R. Quake. 1999. A microfabricated fluorescence-activated cell sorter. *Nature Biotechnology* 17:1109–11.

Gehani, A., T. LaBean, and J. Reif. 2004. DNA-based cryptography. *Aspects of Molecular Computing—Essays Dedicated to Tom Head on the Occasion of His 70th Birthday* 2950:167–88.

Gerchman, Y., and R. Weiss. 2004. Teaching bacteria a new language. *Proceedings of the National Academy of Sciences* 101(8):2221–2.

Gorecki, J., J. N. Gorecka, K. Yoshikawa, Y. Igarashi, and H. Nagahara. 2005. Sensing the distance to a source of periodic oscillations in a nonlinear chemical medium with the output information coded in frequency of excitation pulses. *Physical Review* 72:Epub 046201.

Haraguchi, T., T. Koujin, and Y. Hiraoka. 2000. Application of GFP: Time-lapse multi-wavelength fluorescence imaging of living mammalian cells. *Acta Histochemica et Cytochemica* 33:169–75.

Hayashi, A., H. Asakawa, T. Haraguchi, and Y. Hiraoka. 2006. Reconstruction of the kinetochore during meiosis in fission yeast Schizosaccharomyces pombe. *Molecular Biology of the Cell* 17:5173–84.

Healy, K. E., B. Lom, and P. E. Hockberger. 1994. Spatial distribution of mammalian cells dictated by material surface chemistry. *Biotechnology & Bioengineering* 43:792–800.

Hentschel, H. G. E., C. S. Pencea, and A. Fine. 2004. Computing with calcium stores and diffusion. *Neurocomputing* 58–60:455–60.

Hess, H., C. M. Matzke, R. K. Doot, J. Clemmens, G. D. Bachand, B. C. Bunker, and V. Vogel. 2003. Molecular shuttles operating undercover: A new photolithographic approach for the fabrication of structured surfaces supporting directed motility. *Nano Letters* 3(12):1651–5.

Hiratsuka, Y., T. Tada, K. Oiwa, T. Kanayama, and T. Q. P. Uyeda. 2001. Controlling the direction of kinesin-driven microtubule movements along microlithographic tracks. *Biophysical Journal* 81:1555–61.

Hiyama, S., Y. Isogawa, T. Suda, Y. Moritani, and K. Suto. 2005. *A design of an autonomous molecule loading/transporting/unloading system using DNA hybridization and biomolecular linear motors in molecular communication.* Grenoble, France: European Nano Systems.

Hiyama, S., Y. Moritani, and T. Suda. 2006. Molecular communication. *Proceedings of the Transaction of Institute of Electronics Information and Communication Engineers (IEICEJ)* 89(2):162–6.

Howard, J. 2001. *Mechanics of motor proteins and the cytoskeleton*. Sunderland, MA: Sinauer.

Ichino, T., Y. Igarashi, I. N. Motoike, and K. Yoshikawa. 2003. Different operations on a single circuit: Field computation on an excitable chemical system. *Journal of Chemical Physics* 118(18):8185–90.

Kikuchi, J., A. Ikeda, and M. Hashizume. 2004. Biomimetic materials. *Encyclopedia of Biomaterials and Biomedical Engineering*. New York: Marcel Dekker.

Langer, R. 2001. Perspectives: Drug delivery—drugs on target. *Science* 293:58–9.

Lee, D. K., and C. Chang. 2003. Molecular communication between androgen receptor and general transcription machinery. *Journal of Steroid Biochemistry & Molecular Biology* 84:41–9.

Lucas, W. J., and J.-Y. Lee. 2004. Plasmodesmata as a supracellular control network in plants. *Nature Reviews Molecular Cell Biology* 5:712–26.

Mao, C., T. H. LaBean, J. H. Relf, and N. C. Seeman. 2000. Logical computation using algorithmic self-assembly of DNA triple-crossover molecules. *Nature* 407:493–96.

Martin, V. J. J., D. J. Pitera, S. T. Withers, J. D. Newman, and J. D. Keasling. 2003. Engineering a mevalonate pathway in Escherichia coli for production of terpenoids. *Nature Biotechnology* 21:796–802.

Mathews, C. K., K. E. van Holde, and K. G. Ahern. 1999. *Biochemistry*. 3rd ed. Upper Saddle River, NJ: Prentice Hall.

The MIT Registry of Standard Biological Parts. http://parts.mit.edu (accessed July 14, 2007).

Montemagno, C. D. 2001. Nanomachines: A roadmap for realizing the vision. *Biomedical Journal of Nanoparticle Research* 3(1):1–3.

Moore. M, A. Enomoto, T. Nakano, R. Egashira, T. Suda, A. Kayasuga, H. Kojima, H. Sakakibara, and K. Oiwa. 2006. A design of a molecular communication system for nanomachines using molecular motors. In *Proceedings of the Fourth Annual IEEE Conference on Pervasive Computing and Communications Workshops.* Washington, DC: IEEE Computer Society.

Moritani, Y., S. Hiyama, and T. Suda. 2006. Molecular communication among nanomachines using vesicles. In *NSTI Nanotechnology Conference and Trade Show*. Cambridge, MA: NSTI.

Moritani, Y., S. Hiyama, and T. Suda. 2006. Molecular communication for health care applications. In *Proceedings of the Fourth Annual IEEE International Conference on*

Pervasive Computing and Communications Workshops. Washington, DC: IEEE Computer Society.

Nagahara, H., T. Ichino, and K. Yoshikawa. 2004. Direction detector on an excitable field: Field computation with coincidence detection. *Physical Review* 70:Epub 036221.

Nakagaki, T., H. Yamada, and Á. Tóth. 2000. Maze-solving by an amoeboid organism. *Nature* 407:470.

Nakano, T., T. Suda, M. Moore, R. Egashira, A. Enomoto, and K. Arima. 2005. Molecular communication for nanomachines using intercellular calcium signaling. In Proceedings of the 5th IEEE Conference on Nanotechnology, Nagoya, Japan, July 11–15, 2005.

Nelson, D. L., and M. M. Cox. 2000 *Lehninger principles of biochemistry*. 3rd book and CD ed. New York: Freeman.

Nitta, N., and A. Suyama. 2004. Autonomous biomolecular computer modeled after retroviral replication. *DNA Computing, Lecture Notes in Computer Science* 2943:203–12.

Nomura, S. M., Y. Mizutani, K. Kurita, A. Watanabe, K. Akiyoshi. 2005. Changes in the morphology of cell-size liposomes in the presence of cholesterol: Formation of neuron-like tubes and liposome networks. *Biochimica Biophysica Acta* 1669(2):164–9.

Oiwa, K., and H. Sakakibara. 2005. Recent progress in dynein structure and mechanism. *Current Opinion in Cell Biology* 17:98–103.

Ostuni, E., R. Kane, C. S. Chen, D. E. Ingber, and G. M. Whitesides. 2000. Patterning mammalian cells using elastomeric membranes. *Langmuir* 16:7811–9.

Peppas, N. A., and Y. Huang. 2004. Nanoscale technology of mucoadhesive interactions. *Advanced Drug Delivery Reviews* 56:1675–87.

Ro, D. K., E. M. Paradise, M. Ouellet, K. J. Fisher, K. L. Newman, J. M. Ndungu, K. A. Ho, R. A. Eachus, T. S. Ham, J. Kirby, M. C. Y. Chang, S. T. Withers, Y. Shiba, R. Sarpong, and J. D. Keasling. 2006. Production of the antimalarial drug precursor artemisinic acid in engineered yeast. *Nature* 440:940–43.

Sakamoto, K., H. Gouzu, K. Komiya, D. Kiga, S. Yokoyama, T. Yokomori, and M. Hagiya. 2000. Molecular computation by DNA hairpin formation. *Science* 288:1223–6.

Sakthivel, T., and A. T. Florence. n.d. *Dendrimers & dendrons: Facets of pharmaceutical nanotechnology*. www.drugdeliverytech.com/cgi-bin/articles.cgi?idArticle=153 (accessed July 30, 2007).

Sasaki, Y., Y. Shioyama, W. Tian, S. Fan, and J. Kikuchi. 2006. Nano sensory device utilizing intermolecular communication on lipid membrane. In *Proceedings of the 4th Annual IEEE Conference on Pervasive Computing and Communications Workshops*, 543–8. Washington, DC: IEEE Computer Society.

Schneider, T. D. 1991. Theory of molecular machines. I, Channel capacity of molecular machines. *Journal of Theoretical Biology* 148:83–123.

Service, R. F. 2001. Nanocomputing: Optical lithography goes to extremes—and beyond. *Science* 293:785–786.

Shima, T., T. Kon, K. Imamula, R. Ohkura, and K. Sutoh. 2006. Two modes of microtubule sliding driven by cytoplasmic dynein. *Proceedings of the National Academy of Sciences* 103(47):17736–40.

Shin, J. S., and N. A. Pierce. 2004. A synthetic DNA walker for molecular transport. *Journal of the American Chemical Society* 126:10834–5.

Smith, J. M. 2000. The concept of information in biology. *Philosophy of Science* 67(2):177–94.

Suda, T., M. Moore, T. Nakano, R. Egashira, and A. Enomoto. 2005. Exploratory research on molecular communication between nanomachines. In *2005 Genetic and Evolutionary Computation Conference, Late-Breaking Papers*. New York: ACM Press.

Tamarin, R. H. 1999. *Principles of genetics*. New York: WCB/McGraw-Hill.

Toba, S., and K. Oiwa. 2006. Swing or embrace? New aspects of motility inspired by dynein structure in situ. *BIOforum Europe*. 10:14–6.

Villalobos, C., L. Nunez, and J. Garcia-Sancho. 2004. Anterior pituitary thyrotropes are multifunctional cells. *American Journal of Physiology Endocrinology Metabolism* 287:E1166–70.

Weiss, R., and T. F. Knight. 2000. Engineered communications for microbial robotics. DNA computing. In *6th International Meeting on DNA Based Computers, DNA 2000*. New York: Springer Lecture Notes in Computer Science, 2054.

Winfree, E., F. Liu, L. A. Wenzler, and N. C. Seeman. 1998. Design and self-assembly of two-dimensional DNA crystals. *Nature* 394:539–44.

Yasuda, R., H. Noji, K. Kinosita, and M. Yoshida. 1998. F1-ATPase is a highly efficient molecular motor that rotates with discrete 120° steps. *Cell* 93:1117–24.

Yin, P., H. Yan, X. G. Daniell, A. J. Turberfield, and J. H. Reif. 2004. A unidirectional DNA walker that moves autonomously along a track. *Communications of Angewandte Chemie International Edition* 43:4906–11.

You, L., R. S. Cox III, R. Weiss, and F. H. Arnold. 2004. Programmed population control by cell-cell communication and regulated killing. *Nature* 428:868–71.

Zauner, K. P., and M. Conrad. 2001. Molecular approach to informal computing. *Soft Computing* 5:39–44.

Zhou, T., L. Chen, and K. Aihara. 2005. Molecular communication through stochastic synchronization induced by extracellular fluctuations. *Physical Review Letters* 95:178103.

Reviewers List

Abaza, Mahmoud, Athabasca University, Canada
Abbas, Kaja, University of California, Irvine
Abdel Hamid, Ayman Adel, Arab Academy for Science, Technology, and Maritime Transport, Egypt
Abdeljabbar, Wael, Mission College
Abdel-Wahab, Hussein, Old Dominion University
Abdu, Hasina, The University of Michigan, Dearborn
Ablowitz, Mark J., University of Colorado, Boulder
Abolmaesumi, Purang, Queen's University, Canada
Adams, Chris, University of Colorado, Boulder
Agathoklis, Pan, University of Victoria, Canada
Agrawal, Gopal, Texas A&M University, Texarkana
Akkaya, Kemal, Southern Illinois University
Akl, Robert, University of North Texas
Albright, Richard, Goldey-Beacom College
Ali, Sanwar, Indiana University of Pennsylvania
Aliyazicioglu, Zekeriya, California State Polytechnic University, Pomona
Al-Jaroodi, Jameela, University of Bahrain, Kingdom of Bahrain
Allan, Robert J., Daresbury Laboratory, UK
Allen, James M., University of North Dakota
AlRegib, Ghassan, Georgia Institute of Technology
Al-Shaer, Ehab, DePaul University
Altay, Gökmen, Bahcesehir University, Turkey
Altintas, Ayhan, Bilkent University, Turkey
Amin, Mohammad, National University
Amjad Umar, Fordham University
Anderson, Anne H., Sun Microsystems, Inc.
André, Paulo Sérgio de Brito, Universidade de Aveiro, Portugal
Andreozzi, Sergio, Istituto Nazionale di Fisica Nucleare (INFN), Italy
Ankiewicz, Adrian, Australian National University, Australia
Antonio, Patricia San, University of Maryland, Baltimore County
Anwar, Zahid, Intel Corporation
Ardakani, Masoud, University of Alberta, Canada
Argles, David, University of Southampton, UK
Argüello, Francisco, University of Santiago de Compostela, Spain
Arifler, Dogu, Eastern Mediterranean University, North Cyprus
Astani, Marzie, Winona State University
Atai, Javid, University of Sydney, Australia
Atti, Venkatraman, Arizona State University
Avoine, Gildas, Massachusetts Institute of Technology
Awan, Asad, Purdue University
Azad, Abul K. M., Northern Illinois University

Baaren-Hopper, Joanna van, University of Connecticut
Babula, Eduard, Universidad Carlos III de Madrid, Spain
Babulak, Eduard, University of Pardubice, Czech Republic
Badia, Leonardo, Università degli Studi di Padova, Italy
Baehr, Craig, Texas Tech University
Baeza-Yates, Ricardo, Yahoo! Research, Spain
Baggag, Abdelkader, McGill University, Canada
Bakos, Jason D., University of South Carolina
Baldwin, Rusty O., Air Force Institute of Technology
Barnes, Frank, University of Colorado, Boulder
Barnes, Stuart J., University of East Anglia, UK
Barnhart, Billy S., Webster University and AT&T
Bartolacci, Michael R., Penn State University, Berks
Basu, Kalyan, University of Texas, Arlington
Baudoin, Geneviève, ESIEE, France
Baumgartner, Robert, Vienna University of Technology, Austria
Beavers, Gordon, University of Arkansas
Bedell, Paul, Independent Consultant
Bellardo, John M., California Polytechnic State University
Bellavista, Paolo, DEIS—Università degli Studi di Bologna, Italy
Ben Slimane, Slimane, The Royal Institute of Technlogy (KTH), Sweden
Benhaddou, Driss, University of Houston
Benkabou, Fatima Zohr, Université de Moncton, Canada
Bennette, Daniel, University of Maryland University College Europe
Benvenuto, Nevio, University of Padova, Italy
Berg, George, University at Albany, SUNY
Berkes, Jem E., University of Waterloo, Canada
Berlemann, Lars, Swisscom Innovations, Switzerland
Berman, David J., DBM Technology Consulting
Bernstein, Larry, Stevens Institute of Technology
Bertoss, Alan A., University of Bologna, Italy
Biagioni, Edoardo S., University of Hawaii, Mānoa
Bianc, Andrea, Politecnico di Torino, Italy
Binsted, Kim, University of Hawaii, Manoa
Birant, Derya, Dokuz Eylul University, Turkey
Birru, Dagnachew (Dan), Philips Research North America
Biswas, Abhijit, Jet Propulsion Laboratory, California Institute of Technology
Biswas, Anjan, Delaware State University
Bjerke, Bjorn A., Qualcomm, Inc.
Bocchino Jr., Robert L., University of Illinois
Bocquet, Wladimir, France Telecom R&D, Japan
Bode, Arndt, Technische Universität München, Germany
Bodnar, Bohdan L., Motorola, Inc.
Bohn, Jürgen, Wernher von Braun Center for Advanced Research, Brazil
Bollen, Johan, Los Alamos National Laboratory
Bolyard, John W., University of West Florida
Bonnel, Wanda, University of Kansas
Boppana, Rajendra V., University of Texas, San Antonio
Border, Charles, Rochester Institute of Technology
Boroson, Don M., MIT Lincoln Laboratory
Bose, Sanjay K., Nanyang Technological University, Singapore
Bostian, Charles W., Virginia Tech
Bouras, Christos, University of Patras, Greece
Brännström, Robert, Luleå University of Technology, Sweden
Braun, Mark J., Gustavus Adolphus College

Braun, Torsten, University of Bern, Switzerland
Brewster, Gregory, DePaul University
Briscoe, Bob, BT, UK
Broughton, S. Allen, Rose-Hulman Institute of Technology
Brown, Andrew, University of Southampton, UK
Brown, Eric Paul, Canyon College
Brown, Stuart M., New York University
Bryan, David A., College of William and Mary and SIPeerior Technologies, Inc.
Buchholz, Dale, DePaul University
Bucy, Erik P., Indiana University
Buhari, M. I. Seyed Mohamed, University Brunei Darussalam, Brunei
Burn, David R., Southern Illinois University, Carbondale
Burpee III, Howard A., Southern Maine Community College
Butler, Donald, University of Texas, Arlington
Byrd, Gregory T., North Carolina State University

Cabri, Danijela, University of California, Berkeley
Cai, Qingbo, Case Western Reserve University
Cai, Yu, Michigan Technological University
Caini, Carlo, Università di Bologna, Italy
Calabresi, Leonello, Univerity of Maryland, University College
Ćalić, Janko, University of Bristol, UK
Callahan, Dale, University of Alabama, Birmingham
Camarillo, Gonzalo, Ericsson
Can Vuran, Mehmet, Georgia Institute of Technology
Candan, K. Selcuk, Arizona State University
Cannistra, Robert M., Marist College
Cantrell, Cyrus D., The University of Texas, Dallas
Cao, Lei, The University of Mississippi
Cao, Xiaojun, Rochester Institute of Technology
Cardei, Ionut, Florida Atlantic University
Cardell-Oliver, Rachel, The University of Western Australia, Australia
Careglio, Davide, Universitat Politècnica de Catalunya, Spain
Carlson, David E., University of Florida
Carroll, Bill D., The University of Texas, Arlington
Castane, Laurent, Onera, France
Castillo, Carlos, Yahoo! Research, Spain
Cernocky, Jan "Honza," Brno University of Technology, Czech Republic
Chaffin, Dorothea S., Park University
Chambers, Robert, Lightspeed Systems
Champion, Jean-Luc, UN/CEFACT Forum, Belgium
Chan, Sammy, City University of Hong Kong, Hong Kong
Chan, Tom S., Southern New Hampshire University
Chandra, Vigs, Eastern Kentucky University
Chandrashekhara, K., University of Missouri, Rolla
Chaudet, Claude, GET/ENST, France
Che, Hao, University of Texas, Arlington
Chen, Chien-Chung, National Taiwan University, Taiwan
Chen, Jim Q., University of Maryland, University College
Chen, Ju-Ya, National Sun Yat-Sen University, Taiwan
Chen, Li-Wei, Vanu Inc.
Chen, Runhua, The University of Texas, Austin
Chen, Whai-En, National Chiao Tung University, Taiwan
Chen, Yu-Che, Northern Illinois University
Cheng, Tee Hiang, Nanyang Technological University, Singapore
Chepkevich, Richard A., "Sam," Hawaii Pacific University
Chess, David M., IBM Watson Research Center
Chiani, Marco, DEIS, University of Bologna, Italy
Chiao, J. C., The University of Texas, Arlington
Cho, Pak S., CeLight, Inc.
Choi, Byung K., Michigan Technological University
Choi, Young B., James Madison University
Choksy, Carol E. B., Indiana University, Bloomington
Christensen, Ken, University of South Florida
Chuah, Chen-Nee, University of California, Davis
Chuah, Teong-Chee, Multimedia University, Malaysia
Chudoba, Katherine M., Florida State University
Chung, Chia-Jung, California State University, Sacramento
Chung, Sam, University of Washington, Tacoma
Clarke, Roger, Xamax Consultancy Pty Ltd, Australia, and University of Hong Kong
Cohen, Daniel, George Mason University
Cohen, David J., University of Maryland, University College
Collings, Neil, University of Cambridge, UK
Collins, J. Stephanie, Southern New Hampshire University
Colonna, Danilo, ENEA C. R. Frascati, Italy
Comellas, Jaume, Universitat Politècnica de Catalunya, Spain
Connel, Mark, State University of New York, Cortland
Conti, Claudio, Research Center Enrico Fermi, Italy
Coopman, Ted M., University of Washington
Corazza, Giovanni E., University of Bologna, Italy
Cordeiro, Carlos, Philips Research North America
Craenen, B. G. W., Napier University, UK
Craig, Richard, San Jose State University
Crawford, George W., Penn State McKeesport
Crnkovic, Jakov, University at Albany (SUNY)
Cronin, Eric, University of Pennsylvania
Crowcroft, Jon, University of Cambridge, UK
Cui, Dongzhe, Bell Labs—Lucent Technologies
Cui, Yi, Vanderbilt University

Dai, Huaiyu, North Carolina State University
Dai, Yuan-Shun, Indiana University Purdue University Indianapolis
Daniels, Robert C., The University of Texas, Austin
Danielson, David R., Stanford University
Daoud, Moh, Las Positas College
Daskalopulu, Aspassia, University of Thessaly, Greece
David, John J., Wake Forest University
De Leenheer, Marc, Ghent University, Germany
Debbah, Merouane, Eurecom Institute, France
Debrunne, Christian H., Colorado School of Mines
DeJoie, Anthony, Telcordia Technologies
Dellacca, David, Indiana University-Purdue University Indianapolis (IUPUI)
Desai, Uday B., Indian Institute of Technology, India
Deters, Ralph, University of Saskatchewan, Canada
Develi, Ibrahim, Engineering Erciyes University, Turkey
Dhadwal, Harbans S., State University of New York, Stony Brook
Di Cecca, Angelo, Alcatel Alenia Space
Diaz, Michel, LAAS-CNRS, France
Dick, Steven J., Southern Illinois University, Carbondale
Dietrich, Sven, CERT
Ding, Hao, Norwegian University of Science and Technology, Norway
Ding, Qin, Pennsylvania State University, Harrisburg
Ding, Wei, The University of Houston, Clear Lake

Dor, Jean-Baptiste, France Telecom, France
Doran, K. Brewer, Salem State College
Dorsz, Jeff, Saddleback College
Downing, Rob, IP Infusion
Drábek, Vladimír, Brno University of Technology, Czech Republic
Dringus, Laurie P., Nova Southeastern University
Drummond, Lúcia Maria de A., Universidade Federal Fluminense, Brazil
Durbano, James P., EM Photonics, Inc.
Dyo, Vladimir, University College London, UK

Edd, Wesley M., Verizon Federal Network Systems / NASA Glenn Research Center
Eddie Rabinovitch, ECI Technology
Edirisinghe, Ruwini Kodikara, Monash University, Australia
Edwards, Paul N., University of Michigan, Ann Arbor
Efstathiou, Elias C., Athens University of Economics and Business, Greece
Egbert, Brian G., Sprint Nextel
Egedigwe, Eges, Eastfield College of Dallas County Community College System
Ehrensberger, Juergen, HEIG-VD, Switzerland
Ehrich, Thomas A., Golden Gate University
Ekbia, Hamid R., Indiana University
El Fatmi, Sihem Guemara, High School of Communications, Tunisia
Elin, Larry, Syracuse University
Elliot, Stephen John, Purdue University
Elmusrati, Mohammed Salem, University of Vaasa, Finland
Enck, William, The Pennsylvania State University
Erbacher, Robert F., Utah State University
Erenshteyn, Roman, Goldey-Beacom College
Erol, Ali, University of Nevada, Reno
Esmahi, Larbi, Athabasca University, Canada
Evans, Gary, Southern Methodist University
Ewert, Craig, University of Maryland University College (UMUC)

Faber, Brenton, Clarkson University
Falconer, David, Carleton University, Canada
Fallah, M. Hosein, Stevens Institute of Technology
Fan, Guangbin, Intel Research, China
Farahat, Nader, Polytechnic University of Puerto Rico
Farhang-Boroujeny, Behrouz, University of Utah
Farley, Toni, Arizona State University
Farren, Margaret, Dublin City University, Ireland
Faruque, Abdullah, Southern Polytechnic State University
Fazel, Khaled, Ericsson GmbH, Germany
Feiler, Michael, Merritt College
Feng, Jack, Bradley University
Fernandes, Stenio F. L., Federal Center for Education in Technology (CEFET), Brazil
Fernback, Jan, Temple University
Ferner, Clayton, University of North Carolina, Wilmington
Ficek, Zbigniew, The University of Queensland, Australia
Figg, William C., Dakota State University
Fitkov-Norris, Elena, Kingston University, UK
Fitzek, Frank H. P., Aalborg University, Denmark
Fitzgibbons, Patrick W., SUNY Institute of Technology
Fitzpatrick, John, University College Dublin, Ireland
Fleisc, Brett D., University of California, Riverside
Fleischmann, Kenneth R., Florida State University, and Drexel University
Fonseka, John P., University of Texas, Dallas
Ford, Davis, Zeno Consulting, Inc.
Ford, Steve, Northeastern State University
Foschini, Luca, DEIS—Università degli Studi di Bologna, Italy
Fowler, Thomas B., Mitretek Systems
Fox, Geoffrey, Indiana University
Fox, Louis, University of Washington
Frank, Michael P., FAMU-FSU College of Engineering
Frantti, Tapio, Technical Research Centre, Finland
Freed, Shirley Ann, Andrews University
Freelan, Joseph Curtis, University of Notre Dame
Fricke, Justus Ch., University of Kiel, Germany
Friesen, Norm, Simon Fraser University, Canada
Fritts, Jason E., Saint Louis University
Frolik, Jeff, University of Vermont
Fu, Xiang, Georgia Southwestern State University
Fukami, Cynthia V., University of Denver
Fuller, Dorothy P., Black Hills State University

Gallagher, Helen, Computer Clarity, Glenview, Illinois
Gao, Jie, State University of New York, Stony Brook
Gao, Liang, Huazhong University of Science and Technology, China
Garcia-Armada, Ana, University Carlos III de Madrid, Spain
Gauch, John M., The University of Kansas
Gavrilenko, Vladimir, Norfolk State University
Gebali, Fayez, University of Victoria, Canada
Gentzsch, Wolfgang, University of North Carolina, Chapel Hill
Ghafouri-Shiraz, H., University of Birmingham, UK
Giambene, Giovanni, University of Siena, Italy
Giangarra, Paul P., IBM
Glick, Madeleine, Intel Research Cambridge, UK
Glushko, Robert J., University of California, Berkeley
Goffe, William L., State University of New York, Oswego
Gong, Yili, Chinese Academy of Sciences, China
Gonzalez Benitez, Ruben A., Universidad Veracruzana, Mexico
Goodarzy, Hormoz, Cambridge College
Goodsell, David S., The Scripps Research Institute
Gordon, Jr., Horace C., University of South Florida
Govindavajhala, Sudhakar, Princeton University
Grandy, Holger, University of Augsburg, Germany
Graupner, Sven, Hewlett-Packard Laboratories, Palo Alto
Gray, Charles G., Oklahoma State University
Greaves, David, University of Cambridge, UK
Grimaud, Gilles, INRIA/CNRS/ University, France
Groth, Dennis P., Indiana University
Guan, Yong Liang, Nanyang Technological University, Singapore
Guenach, Mamoun, Department of Telecommunication and Information Processing
Gunther, Jake, Utah State University
Guo, Jinhua, University of Michigan, Dearborn
Guo, Li-Qiang, University of Limerick, Ireland
Guo, Yile, Nokia
Gurses, Eren, The Norwegian University of Science and Technology, Norway
Gurusamy, Mohan, National University of Singapore, Singapore

Haddadi, Hamed, University College London, UK
Hadidi, Rassule, University of Illinois, Springfield
Hadjicostis, Christoforos, University of Illinois, Urbana-Champaign
Haenggi, Martin, University of Notre Dame

Haghverdi, Esfandiar, Indiana University, Bloomington
Hague, Rob, Independent Consultant, UK
Hammell II, Robert J., Towson University
Hammer, Florian, Telecommunications Research Center Vienna (ftw.), Austria
Han, Youngnam, Information and Communications University, Korea
Hanchey, Cindy Meyer, Oklahoma Baptist University
Hansse, Øyvind, University of Tromsø, Norway
Haque, Saira N., Syracuse University
Härmä, Aki, Philips Research Laboratories
Harper, Christopher, Temple University
Harris, Jr., Frederick C., University of Nevada, Reno
Hartel, Pieter, University of Twente, The Netherlands
Hasan, Aamir, University of Texas, Austin
Hasan, Mohammad Masud, University of Texas, Dallas
Hasina Abdu, The University of Michigan, Dearborn
Havill, Jessen T., Denison University
Hawkin, Joseph, University of Alaska, Fairbanks
Hayden, Patrick, McGill University, Canada
Hayee, M. Imran, University of Minnesota, Duluth
He, Dan, University of Surrey, UK
Heckenberg, Norman, The University of Queensland, Australia
Heidari, Sam, Ikanos Communications, Inc.
Heijenk, Geert, Uniiversity of Twente, The Netherlands
Heim, Gregory R., Boston College
Heintzelman, Matthew Z., Saint John's University
Helfers, Eric C., University of Maryland, University College, and Johns Hopkins University
Helm, Pamela C., Radford University
Henkel, Werner, International University Bremen (IUB), Germany
Henry, Joel, University of Montana, Missoula
Hershey, John E., GE, Research
Hesselbach-Serra, Xavier, Universitat Politècnica de Catalunya, Spain
Hettak, Khelifa, Industry Canada, Canada
Higgs, Bryan J., Rivier College
Hiwasaki, Yusuke, NTT Corp., Japan
Hizlan, Murad, Cleveland State University
Ho, Chen-Shie, National Taiwan University, Taiwan
Hoag, John C., Ohio University
Hoffmeyer, Jim, Western Telecom Consultants, Inc.
Hogrefe, Dieter, Georg-August-Universitaet Goettingen, Germany
Hole, Kjell Jørgen, University of Bergen, Norway
Holzer, Richard, University of Passau, Germany
Hong, Edwin, University of Washington, Tacoma
Horan, Stephen, New Mexico State University
Horikis, Theodoros P., University of Colorado, Boulder
Hostetler, Michael, Park University
Howenstine, Erick, Northeastern Illinois University
Hu, Yuh-Jong, National Chengchi University, Taiwan
Huang, Chin-Tser, University of South Carolina
Huang, Freeman Yufei, Queen's University, Canada
Hudson, James M., Georgia Institute of Technology
Huemer, Mario, University of Erlangen-Nuremberg, Germany
Hunsinger, Jeremy, Virginia Polytechnic Institute and State University
Hurley, Stephen, Cardiff University, UK
Hussmann, Heinrich, University of Munich, Germany
Huston, Geoff, Asia Pacific Network Information Center (APNIC)

Ibrahim, Hassan, University of Maryland
Iftode, Liviu, Rutgers University
Ilk, H. Gokhan, Ankara University, Turkey
Ingram, Mary Ann, Georgia Institute of Technology
Ionescu, Dan, University of Ottawa, Canada
Iraqi, Youssef, Dhofar University, Oman
Ishaq, A. Faiz M., The University of Lahore, Pakistan
Iskander, Cyril-Daniel, The MathWorks Inc.
Islam, M. Saif, University of California, Davis
Iversen, Jakob Holden, University of Wisconsin, Oshkosh

Jablonski, Dan, John Hopkins University
Jackson, Henry L. "Jack," Austin Community College
Jacobs, Raymond A., Ashland University
Jajszczyk, Andrzej, AGH University of Science and Technology, Poland
Jank, Wolfgang, University of Maryland
Jayakar, Krishna, The Pennsylvania State University
Jenkins, David, University of Plymouth, UK
Jenq, Yih-Chyun, Portland State University
Ji, Ping, City University of New York
Jia, Weijia, City University of Hong Kong, Hong Kong
Jiang, Tao, University of Michigan, Dearborn
Jiang, Yuming, Norwegian University of Science and Technology, Norway
Jin, Hai, Huazhong University of Science and Technology, China
Joadat, Reza, Richmond University, UK
Johnson, J. T., Institute for Analytic Journalism
Johnson, Michael P., Carnegie Mellon Universitiy
Jones III, Creed, Seattle Pacific University
Jones, James G., University of North Texas
Jordan, Kurt, Calumet College of St. Joseph
Jun, Jaeyeon, Mazu Networks

Kabara, Joseph, University of Pittsburgh
Kan, Min-Yen, National University of Singapore, Singapore
Kandus, Gorazd, Jozef Stefan Institute, Slovenia
Kang, Jaewon, Rutgers University
Kang, Joonhyuk, Information & Communications University, Korea
Kapfhammer, Gregory M., Allegheny College
Karandikar, Abhay, Indian Institute of Technology, India
Karapetyan, Aram, Yerevan State University, Armenia
Karp, Tanja, Texas Tech University
Karush, Gerald, Southern New Hampshire University
Kato, Nei, Tohoku University, Japan
Katos, Vasilios, University of Portsmouth, UK
Katzy, Bernhard R., University Bw Munich (D) and Leiden University (NL), Germany
Kawanish, Tetsuya, National Institute of Information and Communications Technology, Japan
Kayssi, Ayman, American University of Beirut, Lebanon
Keenan, Susan M., University of Northern Colorado
Keliher, Liam, Mount Allison University, Canada
Kent, M. Allen, Montana State University
Kerrigan, John E., University of Medicine and Dentistry of New Jersey
Kesden, Gregory, Carnegie Mellon University
Keselman, Yakov, Microsoft Corporation
Kesidis, George, Pennsylvania State University
Keys, Anthony C., University of Wisconsin, Eau Claire

Khatri, Farzana I., MIT Lincoln Laboratory
Kholodovych, Vladyslav, University of Medicine & Dentistry of New Jersey
Khosla, Raj, Colorado State University
Khunboa, Chatchai, Khon Kaen University, Thailand
Kim, Jinoh, University of Minnesota
Kim, JongWon, Gwangju Institute of Science & Technology, Korea
Kim, Su Myeon, Samsung Advanced Institute of Technology
Kimmel, Howard, New Jersey Institute of Technology
Kivshar, Yuri, Australian National University, Australia
Kleist, Virginia Franke, West Virginia University
Knolle, Jonathan W., California State University, Chico
Kobtsev, Sergey, Novosibirsk State University, Russia
Kocyigit, Altan, Middle East Technical University, Turkey
Kodi, Avinash, University of Arizona
Kolias, Christos, University of Southern California
Kolumban, Geza, Budapest University of Technology and Economics, Hungary
Kong, Albert, The University of the West Indies, Trinidad & Tobago
Koppler, Alois, Kukla Electronics, Austria
Kornhauser, Alain L., Princeton University
Korpeoglu, Ibrahim, Bilkent University, Turkey
Koucheryavy, Yevgeni, Tampere University of Technology, Finland
Kretschmer, Tobias, London School of Economics, UK
Kriehn, Gregory R., California State University, Fresno
Krishnamurthy, Prashant, University of Pittsburgh
Krishnan, Iyengar N., Johns Hopkins University
Kritzinger, Pieter S., University of Cape Town, South Africa
Krotov, Vlad, University of Houston
Kruger, Anton, The University of Iowa
Kruger, Lennard G., Library of Congress
Kuhn, Marc, Institut für Kommunikationstechnik, Switzerland
Kumar, Aarti, Motorola Inc.
Kumar, Chiranjeev, Indian School of Mines University (ISM), India
Kumar, Santosh, University of Memphis
Kumar, Saurabh, University of Southern California
Kummerfeld, Sarah, Stanford University
Kumwilaisak, Wuttipong, King Mongkut's University of Technology, Thailand
Kurkovsky, Stan, Central Connecticut State University
Kurkowski, Stuart, Colorado School of Mines
Kursh, Steven R., Northeastern University
Kut, Alp, Dokuz Eylul University, Turkey
Kwok, Yu-Kwong Ricky, The University of Hong Kong, Hong Kong
Kwon, James Minseok, Rochester Institute of Technology
Kyperountas, Spyros, Motorola Labs
Kyprianou, Andreas, University of Cyprus, Cyprus

Lacity, Mary C., University of Missouri
Lagerstrom, Eric J. "Rick," Golden Gate University
Lamblin, Claude, France Telecom R&D, France
Land, Martin, Hadassah College, Israel
Landfeldt, Bjorn, University of Sydney, Australia
Langar, Rami, University of Waterloo, Canada
Langendoen, Koen, Delft University of Technology, The Netherlands
Larson, Robert E., University of Washington
Lassous, Isabelle Guerin, INRIA ARES/CITI, France
Law, K. L. Eddie, Ryerson University, Canada
Lawrence, Ramon, University of British Columbia Okanagan, Canada
Leangsuksun, Chokchai, Louisiana Tech University
LeBlanc, Cathie, Plymouth State University
Lee, Gyungho, University of Illinois, Chicago
Lee, Jung Woo, Stanford University
Lehman, Ann C., University of Illinois, Urbana-Champaign
Lehr, William, Massachusetts Institute of Technology
Leitgeb, Erich, Graz University of Technology, Austria
Leonardo Badia, IMT Lucca, taly
Li, Chih-Peng, National Sun Yat-Sen University, Taiwan
Li, Frank Y., University of Oslo, Norway
Li, Honglin, North Dakota State University
Li, Jun, University of Oregon
Li, Tongtong, Michigan State University
Li, Zexian, Nokia
Liang, Chuck C., Hofstra University
Liang, Jie, Simon Fraser University, Canada
Liebenau, Jonathan, London School of Economics, UK
Light, Jennifer S., Northwestern University
LiKamWa, Patrick, University of Central Florida
Lin, Bin, Northwestern University
Lin, Xiaojun, Purdue University
Lineman, Jeffrey P., Northwest Nazarene University
Liszka, Kathy J., The University of Akron
Liu, Boan, Tsinghua University, China
Liu, Chang, Northern Illinois University
Liu, Fenghai, Mintera Corporation
Liu, Huaping, Oregon State University
Liu, Xiang, Bell Labs, Lucent Technologies
Liu, Xiangqian, University of Louisville
Llewellyn, Mark, University of Central Florida
Lo, Shou-Chih, National Dong Hwa University, Taiwan
Lodwig, Sunita, University of South Florida
Löh, Hermann, CeTIM, Germany
Lorenz, Pascal, University of Haute Alsace, France
Losada, David E., University of Santiago de Compostela, Spain
Love, John, Australian National University, Australia
Lozano-Nieto, Albert, The Pennsylvania State University
Lu, Guo-Wei, The Chinese University of Hong Kong, Hong Kong
Lu, Yuanqiu, New Jersey Institute of Technology
Lugmayr, Artur R., Tampere University of Technology
Luo, Jun, Ecole Polytechnique Fédérale de Lausanne (EPFL), Switzerland

Ma, Maode, Nanyang Technological University, Singapore
Mabry, Edward A., University of Wisconsin, Milwaukee
Mache, Jens Mache, Lewis & Clark College, Oregon
Magistretti, Eugenio, DEIS—Università degli Studi di Bologna, Italy
Maguire, Paul, Dublin City University (DCU), Ireland
Mahanti, Anirban, University of Calgary, Canada
Mai, Bin, Northwestern State University, Louisiana
Mailaender, Laurence, Lucent Technologies, Bell Labs
Majumdar, Abhik, University of California, Berkeley
Makani, Joyline, Dalhousie University, Canada
Malkevitch, Joseph, York College (CUNY)
Mambretti, Joe, Northwestern University
Mandujano, Salvador, Intel Corporation
Mann, Catherine L., Brandeis University and Peterson Institute for International Economics
Mano, Chad D., University of Notre Dame
Mao, Shiwen, Auburn University

Mapp, Glenford, Middlesex University, UK
Markman, Kris M., Bridgewater State College
Marks, Gregory A., University of Michigan and Merit Network
Marsic, Ivan, Rutgers University
Marsteller, Matthew R., Carnegie Mellon University
Martel, Normand M., Medical Technology Research Corp.
Martin, Jim, Clemson University
Martin, Richard K., The Air Force Institute of Technology (AFIT)
Martins, Luis L., Georgia Institute of Technology
Mashburn, Ronald, West Texas A & M University
Mason, Sharon P., Rochester Institute of Technology
Mateti, Prabhaker, Wright State University
McConn, Charlotte Eudy, Penn State University
McFadden, Anna C., The University of Alabama
McFarland, Daniel J., Rowan University
McKeever, Susan, Dublin Institute of Technology, Ireland
Mehlenbacher, Brad, North Carilina State
Menif, Mourad, Ecole Supérieure des Communications (SupCom), Tunisia
Menth, Michael, University of Wuerzburg, Germany
Mertins, Alfred, University of Oldenburg, Germany
Metesh, Ed, Montana Tech
Miers, Judson, University of Kansas
Mihaila, George Andrei, IBM Research
Milenkovic, Aleksandar, The University of Alabama, Huntsville
Millard, Bruce R., Arizona State University
Miller, Holmes E., Muhlenberg College
Miller, Joseph B., University of Kentucky
Milosevic, Milos, Schlumberger Technology Corporation
Minoli, Daniel, Stevens Institute of Technology
Mirchandani, Vinod, The University of Sydney, Australia
Miscetti, Stefano, Laboratori Nazionali di Frascati dell' INFN, Italy
Mishra, Piyush, Michigan Technological University
Misra, Christopher, University of Massachusetts, Amherst
Mitchell, John, University College London, UK
Mitchell, Joseph N., Southwest Research Institute, San Antonio
Moerman, Ingrid, Ghent University, Belgium
Mohanty, Saraju P., University of North Texas
Moision, Bruce, Jet Propulsion Laboratory (JPL), California Institute of Technology
Mokhtar, Simohamed Lotfy, Ecole Militaire Polytechnique, Algeria
Monberg, John, University of Kansas
Montante, Robert, Bloomsburg University of Pennsylvania
Montpetit, Marie-Jose, Motorola Connected Home Solutions
Morgan, Brian M., Marshall University
Moser, Allen W., Everett Community College
Mostafa, Javed, Indiana University, Bloomington
Motlagh, Bahman S., University of Central Florida
Mucchi, Lorenzo, University of Florence, Italy
Mueller, Milton L., Syracuse University
Murata, Masayuki, Osaka University, Japan
Murphy, John, University College Dublin, Ireland
Murphy, Richard, Southwest Research Institute, San Antonio, Texas
Murray, Alan, Ohio State University

Naimi, Linda L., Purdue University
Nair, Suku, Southern Methodist Unversity
Natarajan, Preethi, University of Delaware
Nelson, David Allen, University of Central Oklahoma
Nesbary, Dale, Oakland University
Neufeld, Derrick J., The University of Western Ontario, Canada
Neuman, Clifford, University of Southern California
Ngom, Alioune, University of Windsor, Canada
Ni, Jun, University of Iowa
Niar, Smail, University of Valenciennes, France
Nickerson, Matthew, Southern Utah University
Nithiyanandam, N., Sri Venkateswara College of Engineering, India
Noble, Bradley L., Southern Illinois University, Edwardsville
Nohlberg, Marcus, University of Skövde, Sweden
Noll, John, Santa Clara University
Nolle, Daniel E., United States Treasury Department
Noonan, Liam, Tipperary Institute, Ireland
Nuaymi, Loutfi, ENST Bretagne, France

Okazaki, Shintaro, Autonomous University of Madrid, Spain
Olan, Michael J., Richard Stockton College
Oldham, Joseph D., Centre College
Ole Bernsen, Niels, University of Southern Denmark, Denmark
Oliver Jr., Walter E., Howard University
Olsen, Torodd, Telenor Research and Innovation
Ong, Hong, Oak Ridge National Laboratory (ORNL)
Ortiz, Therezita K., St Petersburg College
Östling, Per-Erik, Aalborg University, Denmark
Ostrowski, John W., California State University, Long Beach
Ozmen, Andy, University of Cambridge, UK

Pagli, Linda, Dipartimento di Informatica, Pisa, Italy
Pak Shing, Cho, CeLight, Inc.
Palazzo, Sergio, Università di Catania, Italy
Paliwal, Kuldip K., Griffith University, Australia
Panetta, Karen, Tufts University
Pang, Qixiang, The University of British Columbia, Canada
Pangburn, Michael S., University of Oregon
Pantos, George, National Technical University of Athens, Greece
Paolo, Bellavista, DEIS—Università degli Studi di Bologna, Italy
Paprzycki, Marcin, Polish Academy of Science, Poland
Paragas, Fernando, University of the Philippines, Philippines
Parks, Lance Michael, Cosumnes River College
Parlos, Alexander G., Texas A&M University
Parssian, Amir, Instituto de Empresa
Passarella, Andrea, University of Cambridge, UK
Patel, Nilesh, University of Michigan, Dearborn
Patel, Ram Bahadur, M. M. Engineering College, India
Patrick, Eric, Northwestern University
Pelish, Matthew D., University at Albany, SUNY
Pérez, Jorge, Kennesaw State University
Perkis, Andrew, The Norwegian University of Science and Technology, Norway
Perlot, Nicolas, German Aerospace Center (DLR), Germany
Peroni, Isidoro, Università degli Studi di Roma, Italy
Perrig, Adrian, Carnegie Mellon University
Phanse, Kaustubh S., Luleå University of Technology, Sweden
Phifer, Lisa, Core Competence Inc.
Phillips, W. Greg, Royal Military College of Canada, Canada
Piotrowski, Victor, University of Wisconsin, Superior
Place, Jerry P., University of Missouri, Kansas City

Podell, Harold J., Johns Hopkins University
Polajnar, Andrej, University of Maribor, Slovenia
Poland, Ron A., Clinton Community College
Polycarpou, Andreas H., University of Denver
Ponterio, Robert, SUNY College, Cortland
Pontes, Marlene, WiNGS Telecom, Brazil
Poole, Melissa J., University of Missouri, Columbia
Porter, J. David, Oregon State University
Porter, Jr., Lon A., Wabash College
Potkonjak, Miodrag, University of California, Los Angeles
Poutrina, Ekaterina, University of Rochester
Pratter, Frederick E., Eastern Oregon University
Preece, Alun, University of Aberdeen, UK
Preston, Jon A., Clayton State University
Pritsky, N. Todd, Hill Associates, Inc., and Champlain College
Prunier, James (Tom), Southwestern College
Pucella, Riccardo, Northeastern University
Puliafito, Antonio, Università di Messina, Italy

Qad, Ala, University of Nebraska, Lincoln

Ra, Ikyeun, University of Colorado, Denver and Health Sciences Center
Raatikainen, Pertti, VTT Telecommunications, Finland
Rachidi, Tajje-eddine, Al Akhawayn Univertsity, Morocco
Radu, Mihaela E., Rose-Hulman Institute of Technology
Raghuwanshi, Pravin M., DeVry University
Raja, M. Yasin Akhtar, University of North Carolina, Charlotte
Rajput, Saeed, Think-Sync, Inc.
Rakocevic, Veselin, City University, UK
Rao, Soma Venugopal, Indian Institute of Technology, India
Rapeli, Juha, University of Oulu, Finland
Rasmussen, Jeremy, Sypris Electronics, LLC
Raynal, Michel, Irisa Université de Rennes 1, France
Razaghi, Peyman, University of Toronto, Canada
Razavi, Mohsen, Massachusetts Institute of Technology
Razmov, Valentin, University of Washington
Recor, Jeff, CTG, Inc.
Redi, Jason K., BBN Technologies
Reed, Lisa J., University of Portland
Refai, Hakki H., The University of Oklahoma, Tulsa
Rehrl, Karl, Salzburg Research, Austria
Reichinger, Kurt, Vienna University of Technology, Austria
Reichl, Peter, Telecommunications Research Center Vienna (ftw.), Austria
Reiher, Peter, University of California, Los Angles
Reinschmidt, Kenneth F., Texas A&M University
Reiter, Joshua J., Johns Hopkins University
Ren, Jian, Michigan State University
Requicha, Aristides A. G., University of Southern California
Riabov, Vladimir V., Rivier College
Richard A. Stanley, Worcester Polytechnic Institute
Robila, Stefan A., Montclair State University
Rogers, David V., Communications Research Centre, Canada
Rollins, Sami, Mount Holyoke College
Romero, Alfonso E., University of Granada, Spain
Rose, Chris, Erudio College
Roset, Cesare, University of Rome "Tor Vergata," Italy
Rosu, Marcel C., IBM T. J. Watson Research Center
Rovati, Luigi, University of Modena and Reggio Emilia, Italy
Rupf, John A., Southern Polytechnic State University
Ryan, Kevin, Stevens Institute of Technology
Ryoo, Jungwoo, Pennsylvania State University, Altoona

Sabelli, Nora H., SRI International
Sachdev, D. K., SpaceTel Consultancy LLC and George Mason University
Saengudomlert, Poompat, Asian Institute of Technology, Thailand
Safaai Jazi, Ahmad, Vigina Tech
Salane, Douglas E., John Jay College of Criminal Justice
Saliba, Anthony, Charles Sturt University, Australia
Saligheh Rad, Hamidreza, Harvard University
Sampei, Seiichi, Osaka University, Japan
Sandy, Mary F., DePaul University
Sankar, Ravi, University of South Florida
Sarac, Kamil, University of Texas, Dallas
Satterlee, Brian, Liberty University
Savoie, Michael J., The University of Texas, Dallas
Schaumont, Patrick, Virginia Tech
Scheets, George, Oklahoma State University
Schlager, Mark, SRI International
Schmidt, Dieter S., University of Cincinnati
Schmitz, Corby, Loyola University Chicago
Schneider, Gerardo, University of Oslo, Norway
Schoute, Frits C., Delft University of Technology, The Netherlands
Schreiner, Wolfgang, Johannes Kepler University, Austria
Schubin, Mark, Technological Consultant
Schultz, E. Eugene, High Tower Software
Schwaig, Kathy S., Kennesaw State University
Schwarz, Thomas, S. J., Santa Clara University
Schwebel, Joseph P., University of St. Thomas
Scornavacc, Eusebio, Victoria University of Wellington, New Zealand
Seltzer, Wendy, Berkman Center for Internet & Society, Harvard Law
Selviah, David R., University College London, UK
Semrau, Penelope, California State University, Los Angeles
Servetti, Antonio, Politecnico di Torino, Italy
Sessions, Chad, Essex Corporation
Sethi, Adarshpal, University of Delaware
Shah, Dinesh S., Portland State University
Shah, Rahul, Intel Corporation
Shalunov, Stanislav, Internet2
Shamsi, Mehrdad, University of Toronto, Canada
Shand, Brian, University of Cambridge, UK
Shank, Patti, Learning Peaks LLC
Shao, Zili, The Hong Kong Polytechnic University, Hong Kong
Sharma, Vimal, Cardiff University, UK
Shay, William, University of Wisconsin, Green Bay
Shedletsky, Leonard J., University of Southern Maine
Shen, Dou, Hong Kong University of Science and Technology, Hong Kong
Shepard, Scott, University of Central Florida
Sherman, Richard C., Miami University
Shi, Qicai, Motorola Labs
Shimeall, Timothy J., Carnegie Mellon University
Shin, Dongwan, New Mexico Tech
Shokrani, Arash, Carlton University, Canada
Shrestha, Deepesh Man, Ajou University, South Korea
Shumba, Rose, Indiana University of Pennsylvania
Siekkinen, Matti, University of Oslo, Norvay

Simco, Greg, Nova Southeastern University
Simmons, Ken, Augusta Technical College
Simpson, Jr., Charles Robert (Robby), Georgia Institute of Technology
Singh, Manpreet, Cornell University and Google
Singh, Nirvikar, University of California, Santa Cruz
Singh, Vijay P., University of Kentucky
Sisalem, Dorgham, Tekelec Inc.
Sivrikaya, Fikret, Rensselaer Polytechnic Institute
Skoglund, Mikael, Royal Institute of Technology, Sweden
Slay, Jill, University of South Australia, Australia
Slimani, Yahya, Sciences of Tunis, Tunisia
Sloan, Joseph H., Webster University
Smith, Alan, BT Group
Smit, Anthony H., Purdue University
Smith II, Raife F., Southern University
Smith, Garry, University of Edinburgh, UK
Smith, Lloyd M., University of Wisconsin, Madison
Smith, Richard E., University of St. Thomas
Snow, Charles, George Mason University
Somasundaram, Siva, Stevens Institute of Technology
Song, Hongjun, University of Memphis
Song, Xiaoyu, Portland State University
Sopitkamol, Monchai, Kasetsart University, Thailand
Spegel, Marjan, J. Stefan Institute, Slovenia
Speidel, Joachim, University of Stuttgart, Germany
Spon, Kenneth, Federal Reserve Bank of Kansas City
Srinivasan, Bhaskar, Robert Bosch Corporation
Stachursk, Dale, University of Maryland, University College
Stackpole, Bill R., Rochester Institute of Technology
Stahl, Bernd Carsten, De Montfort University, UK
Stamp, Mark, San Jose State University
Stan, Sorin G., Philips Consumer Electronics, The Netherlands
Stastny, Richard, OeFEG Telekom, Austria
Stavrou, Angelos, Columbia University
Stavrou, Stavros, University of Surrey, UK
Steckler, Brian D., Naval Postgraduate School
Stefanov, Andrej, Polytechnic University
Stefanovic, Darko, University of New Mexico
Stern, Harold P. E., University of Alabama
Stevens, J. Richard, Southern Methodist University
Stiber, Michael, University of Washington, Bothell
Stiemerling, Oliver, ecambria systems GmbH, Germany
Stolfo, Salvatore J., Columbia University
Stork, Milan, University of West Bohemia, Czech Republic
Stout, Glenn Allan, Colorado Technical University
Striegel, Aaron, University of Notre Dame
Stylianos Drakatos, Florida International University
Sud, Seema, George Mason University
Suh, Changsu, Hanback Electronic, Republic of Korea
Sullivan, Richard J., Federal Reserve Bank of Kansas City
Sun, Chen, ATR Wave Engineering Laboratories, Japan
Sun, Hongxia, University of Calgary, Canada
Sun, Zhili, University of Surrey, UK
Sunda, S. Shyam, Penn State University
Sung, Dan Keun, Korea Advanced Institute of Science and Technology, Korea
Sur, Sayantan, The Ohio State University
Swedin, Eric G., Weber State University

Tabak, Leon, Cornell College
Tang, Zaiyong, Louisiana Tech University
Tangsangiumvisai, Nisachon, Chulalongkorn University, Thailand
Tarhuni, Naser G., Helsinki University of Technology, Finland
Tayahi, Moncef Benjamin, University of Nevada, Reno
Taylor, Nolan J., Indiana University, Indianapolis
Teitelbaum, Ben, Internet2 and BitTorrent
Tel, Gerard, University of Utrecht, The Netherlands
Temelkuran, Burak, Omniguide, Inc.
Terrell, Thomas F., University of South Florida
Tewari, Hitesh, Trinity College, Ireland
Teyeb, Oumer M., Aalborg University, Denmark
Thiruvathukal, George K., Loyola University, Chicago
Thomas, George, University of Louisiana, Lafayette
Thomas, Joseph R., University of Maryland
Thompson, Charles, Univeristy of Massachusetts, Lowell
Thompson, Dale R., University of Arkansas
Thompson, Steve C., University of California, San Diego
Thorne, Steven L., The Pennsylvania State University
Tirkel, Andrew, Monash University, Australia
Todd, Byron, Tallahassee Community College
Tomasin, Stefano, University of Padova, Italy
Tomažič, Sačo, University of Ljubljana, Slovenia
Tomlin, Chas, University of Southampton, UK
Toniatti, Tiziana, Siemens Networks
Toppin, Ian N., Clayton State University
Toumpis, Stavros, University of Cyprus, Cyprus
Trabelsi, Chokri, Lucent Technologies
Tran, Duc A., University of Dayton
Traynor, Patrick, Penn State University
Trigon, Niki, University of London, UK
Trostmann, Manfred F., University of Maryland, University College, Europe
Troxel, Ian, University of Florida
Tucker, Catherine, Massachusetts Institute of Technology
Turner, Stephen W., The University of Michigan, Flint
Tweedy, Edward, Rockingham Community College
Tyrer, Harry W., University of Missouri, Columbia

Ugur, Ahmet, Central Michigan University
Ugweje, Okechukwu, The University of Akron
Ulusoy, Özgür, Bilkent University, Turkey
Umar, Amjad, University of Pennsylvania
Uyar, Ahmet, At Mersin University, Mersin, Turkey

Valcourt, Scott A., University of New Hampshire
Van Camp, Julie C., California State University, Long Beach
Van den Boom, Henrie, Eindhoven University of Technology, The Netherlands
Van Engelen, Robert, Florida State University
Van Hook, Pamela, DeVry University
VanDeGrift, Tammy, University of Portland
Vanderster, Daniel C., University of Victoria, Canada
Vanelli-Coralli, Alessandro, University of Bologna, Italy
Varela, Martin, VTT Electronics, Finland
Vartiainen, Matti, Helsinki University of Technology, Finland
Vasconcelos, Wamberto Weber, University of Aberdeen, UK
Vaughan, Norman Vaughan, The University of Calgary, Canada

Venables, Phil, Independent Consultant
Verdurmen, E. J. M., Eindhoven University of Technology, The Netherlands
Verticale, Giacomo, Politecnico di Milano, Italy
Vidács, Attila, Budapest University of Technology and Economics, Hungary
Viehland, Dennis, Massey University, New Zealand
Villanti, Marco, DEIS—University of Bologna, Italy
Vishnevsky, Vladimir M., Russian Academy of Sciences, Russia
Viswanathan, Harish, Bell Labs, Alcatel-Lucent
Vivekanandan, Vijayanth, The University of British Columbia, Canada
Vogel, Christine, University of Texas, Austin
Vyavahare, Prakash, SGSITS, India

Wahl, Mark, University of Texas, Austin
Walden, Eric, Texas Tech University
Wall, Kevin W., Qwest Information Technologies, Inc.
Wallace, Layne, University of North Florida
Wan, Tat-Chee, Universiti Sains Malaysia, Malaysia
Wang, David C., Verizon Communications
Wang, Haomin, Dakota State University
Wang, Lan, University of Memphis
Wang, Minhua, State University of New York, Canton
Wang, Qian, Dublin Institute of Technology, Ireland
Wang, Suosheng, Indiana University
Wang, Yongge, University of North Carolina, Charlotte
Wang, Yu, University of North Carolina, Charlotte
Wang, Zhicheng, Clark Atlanta University
Warfield, Andrew, University of Cambridge, UK
Weatherspoon, Hakim, University of California, Berkeley
Webb, William, Ofcom, UK
Weinig, Shelly, Colombia University
Wellens, Matthias, RWTH Aachen University, Germany
Werstein, Paul, University of Otago, New Zealand
Whitaker, Roger, Cardiff University, UK
White, Curt M., DePaul University
White, Gregory B., The University of Texas, San Antonio
White, Stephanie, Long Island University
Wietfeld, Christian, University of Dortmund, Germany
Wijesekera, Duminda, George Mason University
Wilkerson, Trena Lashley, Baylor University
Wilkinson, Anthony Barry, University of North Carolina, Charlotte
Wilkinson, Timothy D., University of Cambridge, UK
Williams, Kevin, University of Cambridge, UK
Williamson, Carey, University of Calgary, Canada
Wilson, C. Diane, Central Missouri State University
Wing, William R., Oak Ridge National Labs
Witschnig, Harald, Philips Semiconductors, Austria
Wolff, Richard S., Montana State University
Wong, Yue-Ling, Wake Forest University
Wood, David, MITRE Corporation
Woolley, Sandra I., University of Birmingham, UK
Wu, Jingxian, Sonoma State University
Wu, Ke-Li, The Chinese University of Hong Kong, Hong Kong
Wu, Kui, University of Victoria, Canada
Wu, Ningning, University of Arkansas, Little Rock
Wu, Zhiqiang (John), Wright State University
Wulich, Dov, Ben-Gurion University, Israel
Wykle, Helen H., University of North Carolina, Asheville

Xiao, Yang, The University of Memphis
Xie, Shizhong, Tsinghua University, China
Xu, Kaixin, Scalable Network Technologies, Inc.
Xu, Xizhen, New Jersey Institute of Technology
Xue, Fei, University of California, Davis

Yagami, Raymond, University of Maryland
Yam, Scott S-H., Queen's University, Canada
Yamagiwa, Shinichi, INESC-ID/IST, Portugal
Yang, Cheer-Sun, West Chester University
Yang, Laurence T., St. Francis Xavier University, Canada
Yang, Lie-Liang, University of Southampton, UK
Yang, Shanchieh Jay, Rochester Institute of Technology
Yang, Xiuge, Ansoft Corporation
Yang, Y. R., Yale University
Yao, JingTao, University of Regina, Canada
Yao, Wenbing, Brunel University, UK
Yaprak, Ece, Wayne State University
Yedavalli, Kiran, University of Southern California
Yee, Wai Gen, Illinois Institute of Technology
Yi, Kwan, University of Kentucky
Yi, Yunjung, Honeywell Inc.
Yildiz, Melda N., William Paterson University
Yin, Lijun, State University of New York, Binghamton
Yin, Si, New Jersey Institute of Technology
Yoneki, Eiko, University of Cambridge, UK
Yoon, Jaewan, Old Dominion University
Youssef, Mahmoud, Rutgers University
Yu, Ming, State University of New York
Yu, William Emmanuel S., Ateneo de Manila University, Philippines
Yu, Chansu, Cleveland State University
Yuksel, Murat, Rensselaer Polytechnic Institute

Zaharov, Viktor, Polytechnic University of Puerto Rico
Zakhidov, Erkin, Uzbekistan Academy of Sciences, Uzbekistan
Zaki, Mohammed J., Rensselaer Polytechnic Institute
Zaman, Muhammad H., The University of Texas, Austin
Zawacki-Richter, Olaf, HfB—Business School of Finance & Management, Germany
Zehm, Brenda, Axia College of Western International University
Zekavat, Seyed Alireza (Reza), Michigan Technological University
Zeng, Qing-An, University of Cincinnati
Zerfos, Petros, Deutsche Telekom Laboratories, Germany
Zghal, Mourad, Sup'Com, Tunisie
Zhang, Chi, Florida International University
Zhang, Jinye, University of Victoria, Canada
Zhang, Liqiang, Indiana University, South Bend
Zhang, Zhao, Iowa State University
Zhao, Jiying, University of Ottawa, Canada
Zhao, Julie Yuhua, Miami University
Zho, Bo, University of Surrey, UK
Zhou, Luying, Institute for Infocomm Research, Singapore
Zhou, Zhaoxian, University of Southern Mississippi
Zhu Liu, AT&T Labs, Research
Zhu, Yifeng, University of Maine
Zimermann, Alfred E., Hawai'i Pacific University
Zou, Hanli, Broadcom Corporation
Zubairi, Junaid Ahmed, State University of New York, Fredonia
Zuo, Yongrong, Qualcomm Incorporated
Zuuring, Hans, University of Montana
Zvonar, Zoran, Analog Devices

Index